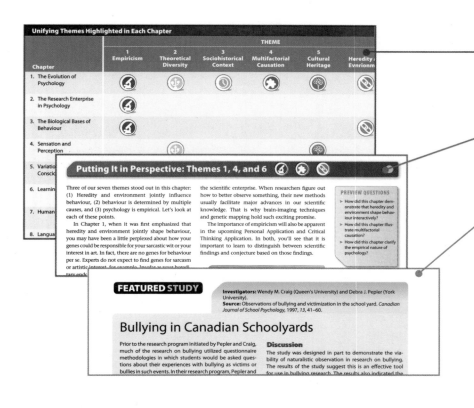

Unifying Themes Highlighted in Each Chapter

Chapter	Empirism	Theoretical Diversity	Sociohistorical Context	Multifactorial Causation	Cultural Heritage	Heredity & Evironm
1. The Evolution of Psychology						
2. The Research Enterprise in Psychology						
3. The Biological Bases of Behaviour						
4. Sensation and Perception						
5. Variation Conscio						
6. Learnin						
7. Human						
8. Langua						

Putting It in Perspective: Themes 1, 4, and 6

Three of our seven themes stood out in this chapter: (1) Heredity and environment jointly influence behaviour, (2) behaviour is determined by multiple causes, and (3) psychology is empirical. Let's look at each of these points.

In Chapter 1, when it was first emphasized that heredity and environment jointly shape behaviour, you may have been a little perplexed about how your genes could be responsible for your sarcastic wit or your interest in art. In fact, there are no genes for behaviour per se. Experts do not expect to find genes for sarcasm or artistic interest, for example. Insofar as your heredi tary endo

the scientific enterprise. When researchers figure out how to better observe something, their new methods usually facilitate major advances in our scientific knowledge. That is why brain-imaging techniques and genetic mapping hold such exciting promise.

The importance of empiricism will also be apparent in the upcoming Personal Application and Critical Thinking Application. In both, you'll see that it is important to learn to distinguish between scientific findings and conjecture based on those findings.

PREVIEW QUESTIONS
- How did this chapter demonstrate that heredity and environment shape behaviour interactively?
- How did this chapter illustrate multifactorial causation?
- How did this chapter clarify the empirical nature of psychology?

FEATURED STUDY

Investigators: Wendy M. Craig (Queen's University) and Debra J. Pepler (York University).
Source: Observations of bullying and victimization in the school yard. *Canadian Journal of School Psychology*, 1997, *13*, 41–60.

Bullying in Canadian Schoolyards

Prior to the research program initiated by Pepler and Craig, much of the research on bullying utilized questionnaire methodologies in which students would be asked questions about their experiences with bullying as victims or bullies in such events. In their research program, Pepler and

Discussion
The study was designed in part to demonstrate the viability of naturalistic observation in research on bullying. The results of the study suggest this is an effective tool for use in bullying research. The results also indicated the

● **Unifying themes** help you make sense of it all. In Chapter 1, the authors introduce seven themes that reappear as you move from chapter to chapter. Use these themes as a framework for organizing information as you learn.

● **Putting It in Perspective** sections at the end of each chapter put the chapter's contents into perspective by recalling the book's seven overarching themes—helping you think about important topics in new ways.

● **Featured Studies** found in every chapter give you an over-the-shoulder look at interesting, real-life research—showing you how psychologists conduct and report their research.

● **Personal Applications** in every chapter give you practical advice that will be helpful in improving your academic performance and your daily life.

● **Critical Thinking Applications** in every chapter offer specific, concrete ways to improve your thinking skills. You'll have opportunities to practice your newly learned skills on chapter material.

● **Web Links** appear throughout every chapter. This book is a rich resource for expanding your knowledge of psychology topics online. Carefully selected by Web expert Vincent Hevern (the Internet editor for the *Society for the Teaching of Psychology*) and author Doug McCann, the book's Web links help you clarify your understanding of psychology and learn about current research. Because Web addresses change frequently, we recommend that you access these links through the book Web site (accessible at **http://www.themesandvariations3ce.nelson.com)** where the URLs are periodically updated.

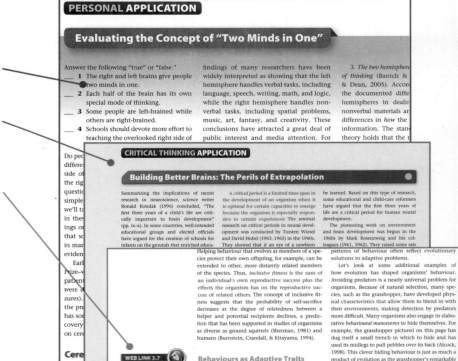

PERSONAL APPLICATION

Evaluating the Concept of "Two Minds in One"

Answer the following "true" or "false."

___ **1** The right and left brains give people two minds in one.
___ **2** Each half of the brain has its own special mode of thinking.
___ **3** Some people are left-brained while others are right-brained.
___ **4** Schools should devote more effort to teaching the overlooked right side of

Do peo differe side of the rig questio simple we'll ta in thes ings or that sc in mar eviden

Earl rize—w patien were a zures). the pre has so covery on cere

Cere and Proc

Using have special hemisp exten

findings of many researchers have been widely interpreted as showing that the left hemisphere handles verbal tasks, including language, speech, writing, math, and logic, while the right hemisphere handles nonverbal tasks, including spatial problems, music, art, fantasy, and creativity. These conclusions have attracted a great deal of public interest and media attention. For

3. *The two hemispher of thinking* (Banich & & Dean, 2005). Accord the documented diffe hemispheres in dealin nonverbal materials ar differences in *how* the information. The stan theory holds that the

CRITICAL THINKING APPLICATION

Building Better Brains: The Perils of Extrapolation

Summarizing the implications of recent research in neuroscience, science writer Ronald Kotulak (1996) concluded, "The first three years of a child's life are critically important to brain development" (pp. ix–x). In some countries, well-intended educational groups and elected officials have argued for the creation of schools for infants on the grounds that enriched educa-

A *critical period* is a limited time span in the development of an organism when it is optimal for certain capacities to emerge because the organism is especially responsive to certain experiences. The seminal research on critical periods in neural development was conducted by Torsten Wiesel and David Hubel (1963, 1965) in the 1960s. They showed that if an eye of a newborn

be learned. Based on this type of research, some educational and child-care reformers have argued that the first three years of life are a critical period for human neural development.

The pioneering work on environment and brain development was begun in the 1960s by Mark Rosenzweig and his colleagues (1961, 1962). They raised some rats

Helping behaviour that evolves as members of a species protect their own offspring, for example, can be extended to other, more distantly related members of the species. Thus, *inclusive fitness* is the sum of an individual's own reproductive success plus the effects the organism has on the reproductive success of related others. The concept of inclusive fitness suggests that the probability of self-sacrifice decreases as the degree of relatedness between a helper and potential recipients declines, a prediction that has been supported in studies of organisms as diverse as ground squirrels (Sherman, 1981) and humans (Burnstein, Crandall, & Kitayama, 1994).

Behaviours as Adaptive Traits

Scholarly analyses of evolution have focused primarily on the evolution of *physical characteristics* in the animal kingdom, but from the very beginning, Darwin recognized that natural selection was applicable to *behavioural traits* as well. Studying the evolution of behaviour is more difficult than studying the evolution of physical traits because behaviour is more transient—crucial behaviours by an organism may occur infrequently and may not last long. For example, female wood frogs are sexually receptive just one night per year. Additionally, although the fossil record *can* leave clues about past organisms' behaviour (such as its prey or

patterns of behaviour often reflect evolutionary solutions to adaptive problems.

Let's look at some additional examples of how evolution has shaped organisms' behaviour. Avoiding predators is a nearly universal problem for organisms. Because of natural selection, many species, such as the grasshopper, have developed physical characteristics that allow them to blend in with their environments, making detection by predators more difficult. Many organisms also engage in elaborative *behavioural manoeuvres* to hide themselves. For example, the grasshopper pictured on this page has dug itself a small trench in which to hide and has used its midlegs to pull pebbles over its back (Alcock, 1998). This clever hiding behaviour is just as much a product of evolution as the grasshopper's remarkable camouflage.

The "stotting" behaviour exhibited by Thomson's gazelles when they spot a cheetah is another example of a behavioural adaptation. The cheetah is a feared predator that elicits evasive actions in Thomson's gazelles. But as the gazelles start to flee, they often slow up briefly to *stot*—that is, they jump high into the air with all four legs held straight and their white rump fully displayed. Slowing up when fleeing may not sound adaptive, but research has revealed that gazelles stot to signal to the cheetah that they have spotted the predator, they are off and running, and they will be difficult to catch. Consistent with this interpretation, stotting increases the likelihood that

WEB LINK 3.7
Human Behavior and Evolution Society
The HBES is an interdisciplinary organization devoted to the exploration of human behaviour from the perspective of evolutionary theory. This site provides a particularly rich set of links to published and online materials and organizations dealing with the evolutionary perspective on behaviour.

THIRD CANADIAN EDITION

Psychology

THEMES & VARIATIONS

Wayne Weiten
University of Nevada, Las Vegas

Doug McCann
York University

With Critical Thinking Applications by

Diane F. Halpern
Claremont McKenna College

NELSON EDUCATION

NELSON / EDUCATION

Psychology: Themes and Variations, **Third Canadian Edition**

by Wayne Weiten and Doug McCann

Vice President, Editorial Higher Education:
Anne Williams

Executive Editor:
Lenore Taylor-Atkins

Marketing Manager:
Ann Byford

Managing Developmental Editor
Sandy Matos

Photo Researcher:
Jessie Coffey

Permissions Coordinator:
Jessie Coffey

Content Production Manager:
Claire Horsnell

Production Service:
MPS Limited, a Macmillan Company

Copy Editor:
Valerie Adams

Proofreader:
Maura Brown

Cold Reader:
June Trusty

Indexer:
Edwin Durbin

Senior Manufacturing Coordinator:
Joanne McNeil

Design Director:
Ken Phipps

Managing Designer:
Franca Amore

Interior Design:
David Murphy at Valid Design

Cover Design:
Martyn Schmoll

Cover Image:
© Corbis

Compositor:
MPS Limited, a Macmillan Company

Printer:
R.R. Donnelley

Library and Archives Canada Cataloguing in Publication

Weiten, Wayne, 1950-
   Psychology : themes and variations / Wayne Weiten, Doug McCann.—3rd Canadian ed.

Includes bibliographical references and index.

ISBN 978-0-17-650373-4

   1. Psychology—Textbooks.
I. McCann, Douglas, 1951- II. Title.

BF121.W44 2012   150
C2011-906810-9

ISBN-13: 978-0-17-650373-4
ISBN-10: 0-17-650373-0

For Nancy,
D. M.

Beth, this one is for you
W. W.

WAYNE WEITEN is a graduate of Bradley University and received his Ph.D. in social psychology from the University of Illinois, Chicago, in 1981. He currently teaches at the University of Nevada, Las Vegas. He has received distinguished teaching awards from Division Two of the American Psychological Association (APA) and from the College of DuPage, where he taught until 1991. He is a Fellow of Divisions 1 and 2 of the American Psychological Association. In 1991, he helped chair the APA National Conference on Enhancing the Quality of Undergraduate Education in Psychology and in 1996–1997 he served as President of the Society for the Teaching of Psychology. Wayne Weiten has conducted research on a wide range of topics, including educational measurement, jury decision making, attribution theory, stress, and cerebral specialization. His recent interests have included pressure as a form of stress and the technology of textbooks. He is also the co-author of *Psychology Applied to Modern Life* (Wadsworth, 2006) and the creator of an educational CD-ROM titled PsykTrek: *A Multimedia Introduction to Psychology*.

DOUG McCANN received his B.A. from the University of Waterloo and his M.A. and Ph.D. from the University of Western Ontario. Following completion of his Ph.D., he did a post-doctoral fellowship at Ohio State University. He has been a member of the Psychology Department at York University since 1983. At York he has taught at the graduate level in the Clinical, Developmental, and Social/Personality programs and at the undergraduate level his current teaching interests focus on Introductory Psychology, Social Psychology, and the Psychology of Depression. He has won a variety of teaching awards while at York University. His research interests focus on social cognition, the self, and information processing models of depression. Doug McCann's interests include mindfulness meditation, mawashi geri, and playing serious ball with his dog Tucker. He would be delighted to receive comments about this textbook—just email him at dmccann@yorku.ca.

Brief Contents

© Rebecca Atkins, York University

CHAPTER 1

The Evolution of Psychology

© tc397/iStockphoto.com

CHAPTER 2

The Research Enterprise in Psychology

© Rebecca Atkins, York University

The Biological Bases of Behaviour

© Colette R. Orfeo, Athabasca University

CHAPTER 4

Sensation and Perception

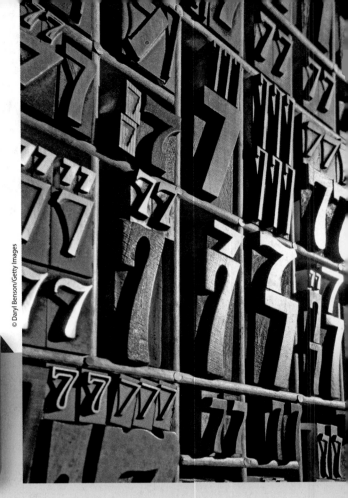
© Daryl Benson/Getty Images

CHAPTER 5

Variations in Consciousness

© Dave Brosha Photography

CHAPTER 6

Learning

© Debbie Steel, Trent University

CHAPTER 7

Human Memory

Courtesy of Debbie Steel

CHAPTER 8

Language and Thought

© Rebecca Atkins, York University

CHAPTER 9

Intelligence and Psychological Testing

Jim Arbogast/Digital Vision/Getty Images

CHAPTER 10

Motivation and Emotion

CHAPTER 11

Human Development across the Life Span

Tui De Roy/Minden Pictures/Getty Images

CHAPTER 12

Personality: Theory, Research, and Assessment

Courtesy of John Dalkin

CHAPTER 13

Stress, Coping, and Health

© Sandy Matos

CHAPTER 14

Psychological Disorders

Image Source/Getty Images

CHAPTER 15

Treatment of Psychological Disorders

Three Images/Lifesize/Getty Images

CHAPTER 16

Social Behaviour

Welcome to the third Canadian edition of *Psychology: Themes and Variations*. In the first and second Canadian editions published in 2006 and 2010, respectively, we decided to build on the considerable strengths of the U.S. text by increasing its relevance to a Canadian college and university audience. We added over 300 new references to Canadian research and the Canadian context in the first edition and 900 in the second, supplied relevant Canadian statistics, and highlighted issues of particular concern to Canadians, such as bilingualism, cultural diversity, First Nations peoples' issues, and the contribution of women to Canadian psychology and Canadian life. We also highlighted the narrative structure of psychology by telling students a little about the background and context of research and theory and of some of the scholars involved in this work.

Our revisions to the third Canadian edition are based on our own survey of the developing literature in psychology and on the extensive critical feedback we received from instructors and students across the country. We appreciated receiving all of your comments and suggestions regarding the second Canadian edition; you caught small grammatical and text errors and told us what was clear in the book and what wasn't. Thank you so much for your participation in this revision: You will see evidence of many of your comments in this new edition. Just as we invited many students to contribute to this edition by submitting photos to be used in the book, we invite you to send us your comments so you can impact future editions. We would greatly appreciate your feedback on this new edition, also. Please feel free to contact Doug McCann at dmccann@yorku.ca.

In this third Canadian edition, we not only updated the information already covered in the first and second editions, but also added a significant amount of new material, including over 1700 new references to research and theory in psychology from all over the world. This new work was integrated into the existing text sometimes as updates, and sometimes as entire new sections such as the addition of a focus on childhood psychopathology toward the middle of Chapter 14. We also highlighted emerging trends such as the increasing focus on neuroscience in most areas of psychology and the changing nature of the DSM. Rather than simply dropping this material in a focus box or new paragraph, we integrated it with the existing material to show both the strengths and limitations of these new approaches. While in the first two Canadian editions we intentionally highlighted research conducted by Canadian scientists, our focus in the third Canadian edition was to include the most significant new work overall in the field of psychology. Since so much dynamic research across a broad spectrum of study has been done in Canada, it is not surprising that much of this material involves Canadian scholars and researchers.

In this edition, we have added new Featured Studies executed by prominent researchers, and have supplied several revised introductory vignettes to provide an immediate and compelling Canadian context for the chapter's material. The topics of some of our vignettes introducing the chapters include high school students' reactions to bullying in their school in Nova Scotia, eccentric Canadian geniuses who display various types of high intelligence, and the use of CIA-funded brainwashing techniques in Canadian psychiatric institutions.

If we had to sum up in a single sentence what we hope will distinguish this text, that sentence would be this: We set out to create a *paradox* instead of a *compromise*. To elaborate, an introductory psychology text must satisfy two disparate audiences: instructors and students. Because of the tension between the divergent needs and preferences of these audiences, textbook authors usually indicate that they have attempted to strike a compromise between being theoretical versus practical, comprehensive versus comprehensible, research-oriented versus applied, rigorous versus accessible, and so forth. However, we believe that many of these dichotomies are false. As Kurt Lewin once remarked, "What could be more practical than a good theory?" Similarly, is rigorous really the opposite of accessible? Not in our teaching. We think that many of the disparate goals that we strive for in our textbooks only *seem* incompatible and that we may not need to make compromises as often as we assume.

In our estimation, a good introductory textbook is a paradox in that it integrates characteristics and goals that appear contradictory. With this in mind, we have endeavoured to write a book that is paradoxical in three ways. First, in surveying psychology's broad range of content, we have tried to show that its interests are characterized by both diversity *and* unity. Second, we have emphasized both research *and* application, and how they work in harmony. Finally, we have aspired to write a compelling book that is challenging to think about *and* easy to learn from. Let's take a closer look at these goals.

Goals

1. *To show both the unity and the diversity of psychology's subject matter.* Students entering an introductory psychology course are often unaware of the immense diversity of subjects studied by psychologists. We find this diversity to be part of psychology's charm, and throughout the book we highlight the enormous range of questions and issues addressed by psychology. Of course, psychology's diversity proves disconcerting for some students, who see little continuity between such disparate areas of research as physiology, motivation, cognition, and abnormal behaviour. Indeed, in this era of specialization, even some psychologists express concern about the fragmentation of the field. Since we believe that the subfields of psychology overlap considerably, we emphasize their common core, portraying psychology as an integrated whole.

2. *To illuminate the process of research and its intimate link to application.* For us, a research-oriented book is not one that bulges with summaries of many studies but one that enhances students' appreciation of the logic and excitement of empirical inquiry. We want students to appreciate the strengths of the empirical approach and to see scientific psychology as a creative effort to solve intriguing behavioural puzzles. For this reason, the text emphasizes not only *what* psychologists know (and don't know) but *how* they attempt to find out. The book examines behavioural processes in some detail, and encourages students to adopt the skeptical attitude of a scientist and to think critically about claims regarding behaviour. Throughout the book, we also share the practical implications of the work of psychologists, satisfying students' desire for concrete, personally useful information.

3. *To make the textbook challenging to think about and easy to learn from.* Perhaps most of all, we have sought to create a *book of ideas* rather than a compendium of studies. We consistently emphasize concepts and theories over facts, and focus on major issues and tough questions that cut across the subfields of psychology (e.g., the extent to which behaviour is governed by nature, nurture, and their interaction), as opposed to parochial debates (such as the merits of averaging versus adding in impression formation). Challenging students to think also means urging them to confront the complexity and ambiguity of psychological knowledge. Hence, the text doesn't skirt around grey areas, unresolved questions, and theoretical controversies. Instead, it encourages readers to contemplate open-ended questions, to examine their assumptions about behaviour, and

to apply psychological concepts to their own lives. Our goal is not simply to describe psychology but to stimulate students' intellectual growth.

Admittedly, these goals are ambitious. If you're skeptical, you have every right to be. Let us explain how we have tried to realize these objectives.

Special Features

The book contains a variety of unusual features, each contributing in its own way to the book's paradoxical nature. These special elements include unifying themes, Featured Studies, Personal Application sections, Critical Thinking Application sections, a didactic illustration program, Web Links and other Internet-related features, an integrated running glossary, Concept Checks, Preview Questions, interim Reviews of Key Points, and Practice Tests.

Unifying Themes

Chapter 1 introduces seven key ideas that serve as unifying themes throughout the text. The themes serve several purposes. First, they provide threads of continuity across chapters that help students see the connections among various areas of research in psychology. Second, as the themes evolve over the course of the book, they provide a forum for a relatively sophisticated discussion of enduring issues in psychology, thus helping to make this a "book of ideas." Third, the themes focus a spotlight on a number of basic insights about psychology and its subject matter that should leave lasting impressions on your students.

In selecting the themes, the question we asked ourselves (and other instructors) was "What do we really want students to remember five years from now?" The resulting themes are grouped into two sets.

THEMES RELATED TO PSYCHOLOGY AS A FIELD OF STUDY

Theme 1: Psychology is empirical. This theme is used to enhance the student's appreciation of psychology's scientific nature and to demonstrate the advantages of empiricism over uncritical common sense and speculation. We also use this theme to encourage the reader to adopt a scientist's skeptical attitude and to engage in more critical thinking about information of all kinds.

Theme 2: Psychology is theoretically diverse. Students are often confused by psychology's theoretical pluralism and view it as a weakness. We don't downplay or apologize for the field's theoretical diversity, because we believe that it is one of psychology's greatest strengths. Throughout the book, we provide concrete examples of how clashing theories have stimulated productive research, how converging on a question from several perspectives can yield increased understanding, and how competing theories are sometimes reconciled in the end.

Theme 3: Psychology evolves in a sociohistorical context. This theme emphasizes that psychology is embedded in the ebb and flow of everyday life. The text shows how the spirit of the times has often shaped psychology's evolution and how progress in psychology leaves its mark on our society.

THEMES RELATED TO PSYCHOLOGY'S SUBJECT MATTER

Theme 4: Behaviour is determined by multiple causes. Throughout the book, we emphasize, and repeatedly illustrate, that behavioural processes are complex and that multifactorial causation is the rule. This theme is used to discourage simplistic, single-cause thinking and to encourage more critical reasoning.

Theme 5: Behaviour is shaped by cultural heritage. This theme is intended to enhance students' appreciation of how cultural factors moderate psychological processes and how the viewpoint of one's own culture can distort one's interpretation of the behaviour of people from other cultures. The discussions that elaborate on this theme do not simply celebrate diversity. They strike a careful balance—one that accurately reflects the research in this area—highlighting both cultural variations *and* similarities in behaviour.

Theme 6: Heredity and environment jointly influence behaviour. Repeatedly discussing this theme permits us to air out the nature versus nurture issue in all of its complexity. Over a series of chapters, students gradually learn how biology shapes behaviour, how experience shapes behaviour, and how scientists estimate the relative importance of each. Along the way, students will gain an in-depth appreciation of what it means when we say that heredity and environment interact.

Theme 7: People's experience of the world is highly subjective. All of us tend to forget the extent to which people view the world through their own personal lenses. This theme is used to explain the principles that underlie the subjectivity of human experience, to clarify its implications, and to repeatedly remind the readers that their view of the world is not the only legitimate view.

After introducing all seven themes in Chapter 1, we discuss different sets of themes in each chapter as they are relevant to the subject matter. The connections between a chapter's content and the unifying themes are highlighted in a standard section near the end of the chapter, "Putting It in Perspective," in which we reflect on the "lessons to be learned" from the chapter. We have not tried to make every chapter illustrate a certain number of themes. Rather, the themes were allowed to emerge naturally, and we found that two to five surfaced in any given chapter. The chart on the next page shows which themes are highlighted in each chapter. Colour-coded icons at the beginning of each "Putting It in Perspective" section indicate the specific themes featured in each chapter.

Featured Studies

Each chapter includes a Featured Study that provides a relatively detailed but clear summary of a particular piece of research. Each Featured Study is presented in the conventional purpose–method–results–discussion format seen in journal articles, followed by a comment in which we discuss why the study is featured (to illustrate a specific method, raise ethical issues, and so forth). By showing research methods in action, we hope to improve students' understanding of how research is done while also giving them a painless introduction to the basic format of journal articles. Additionally, the Featured Studies show how complicated research can be, so students can better appreciate why scientists may disagree about the meaning of a study. The Featured Studies are fully incorporated into the flow of discourse in the text and are *not* presented as optional boxes.

In selecting the Featured Studies, we assembled a mixture of classic and recent studies that illustrate a wide variety of methods. To make them enticing, we tilted our selections in favour of those that students find interesting. So, readers will encounter explorations of the long-term effects of watching TV violence as children, the effects of fear on sexual attraction, bullying in Canadian schoolyards, the brain and mental time travel, and the relationship between depression and heart disease. This edition includes several new Featured Studies selected to reflect some of the groundbreaking work being conducted by Canadian psychologists, including studies of infant babbling and studies of suicide rates among First Nations youth.

Unifying Themes Highlighted in Each Chapter

Chapter	THEME						
	1 Empiricism	2 Theoretical Diversity	3 Sociohistorical Context	4 Multifactorial Causation	5 Cultural Heritage	6 Heredity and Environment	7 Subjectivity of Experience
1. The Evolution of Psychology	●	●	●	●	●	●	●
2. The Research Enterprise in Psychology	●						●
3. The Biological Bases of Behaviour	●					●	
4. Sensation and Perception		●			●		●
5. Variations in Consciousness		●	●	●	●		●
6. Learning			●	●		●	
7. Human Memory		●					●
8. Language and Thought	●				●	●	●
9. Intelligence and Psychological Testing			●	●	●	●	
10. Motivation and Emotion		●	●	●	●	●	
11. Human Development across the Life Span		●	●		●	●	
12. Personality: Theory, Research, and Assessment		●	●		●		
13. Stress, Coping, and Health				●			●
14. Psychological Disorders			●	●	●	●	
15. Treatment of Psychological Disorders		●			●		
16. Social Behaviour	●				●		●

Personal Applications

To reinforce the pragmatic implications of theory and research stressed throughout the text, each chapter closes with a Personal Application section that highlights the practical side of psychology. Each Personal Application devotes three to six pages of text (rather than the usual box) to a single issue that should be of special interest to many of your students. Although most of the Personal Application sections have a "how to" character, they continue to review studies and summarize data in much the same way as the main body of each chapter. Thus, they portray research and application not as incompatible polarities but as two sides of the same coin. Many of the Personal Applications—such as those on finding and reading journal articles, understanding art and illusion, and improving stress management—provide topical coverage unusual for an introductory text.

Critical Thinking Applications

A great deal of unusual coverage can also be found in the Critical Thinking Applications that follow the Personal Applications. Conceived by Diane Halpern (Claremont McKenna College), a leading authority on critical thinking, these applications are based on the assumption that critical thinking skills can be taught. They do not simply review research critically, as is typically the case in other introductory texts. Instead, they introduce and model a host of critical thinking *skills,* such as looking for contradictory evidence or alternative explanations; recognizing anecdotal evidence, circular reasoning, hindsight bias, reification, weak analogies, and false dichotomies; evaluating arguments systematically; and working with cumulative and conjunctive probabilities.

The specific skills discussed in the Critical Thinking Applications are listed in the accompanying table (p. xxvii), where they are organized into five categories using a taxonomy developed by Halpern (2004). In each chapter, some of these skills are applied to topics and issues related to the chapter's content. For instance, in the chapter that covers drug abuse (Chapter 5), the concept of alcoholism is used to highlight the immense power of definitions and to illustrate how circular reasoning can seem so seductive. Skills that are particularly important may surface in more than one chapter, so students see them applied in a variety of contexts. For example, in Chapter 7, students learn how hindsight bias can contaminate memory, and in Chapter 12 they see how hindsight can distort analyses of personality. Repeated practice across chapters should help students to spontaneously recognize the relevance of specific critical thinking skills when they encounter certain types of information. The skills approach taken to critical thinking and the content it has generated are unprecedented for an introductory psychology text.

A Didactic Illustration Program

When we outlined our plans for the third Canadian edition of the text, we wanted every aspect of the illustration program to have a genuine didactic purpose. We were intimately involved in planning every detail of the illustration program. We have endeavoured to create a program of figures, diagrams, photos, and tables that work hand in hand with the prose to strengthen and clarify the main points in the text. We significantly improved the illustrations that have a physiological focus which were created by the talented medical illustrators Fredric Harwin and Jeanne Koelling.

The most obvious results of this didactic approach to illustration are the seven summary spreads that combine tabular information, photos, diagrams, and sketches to provide well-organized overviews of key ideas in the areas of history, learning, senses, development, personality theory, psychopathology, and psychotherapy. But we hope you will also notice the subtleties of the illustration program. For instance, diagrams of important concepts (conditioning, synaptic transmission, experimental design, and so forth) are often repeated in several chapters (with variations) to highlight connections among research areas and to enhance students' mastery of key ideas. Numerous easy-to-understand graphs of research results underscore psychology's foundation in research, and photos and diagrams often bolster each other (e.g., see the treatment of classical conditioning in Chapter 6). Colour is used carefully as an organizational device, and visual schematics are used to simplify hard-to-visualize concepts (e.g., see Figure 9.15 on page 417, which explains reaction range for intelligence). All of these efforts were made in the service of one master: the desire to make this an inviting book that is easy to learn from.

Internet-Related Features

The Internet is rapidly altering the landscape of modern life, and students clearly need help dealing with the information explosion in cyberspace. To assist them, this text has three features. First, Web expert Vincent Hevern (Le Moyne College), the Internet editor for the Society for the Teaching of Psychology, has written a concise preface that explains the essentials of the Internet to the uninitiated. This preface, which follows the student preface, briefly explains URLs, domain names, hyperlinks, search engines, and so forth. Second, cognizant of the highly variable quality and frequently questionable validity of much of the information available on the Web, Dr. Hevern was asked to write an essay on how to critically evaluate websites and online resource materials. His highly informative essay is found in the back of the book in Appendix D.

Third, Dr. Hevern was asked to evaluate hundreds of psychology-related sites on the Web and come up with some recommended sites that appear to provide reasonably accurate, balanced, and empirically sound information. Short descriptions of these recommended websites (called Web Links) are dispersed throughout the chapters, adjacent to related topical coverage. In the third Canadian edition of Weiten's text, we supplemented and sometimes changed other recommended websites to reflect the Canadian context and research. Through the Web Links provided

Taxonomy of Skills Covered in the Critical Thinking Applications

Verbal Reasoning Skills

Understanding the way definitions shape how people think about issues	Chapter 5
Identifying the source of definitions	Chapter 5
Avoiding the nominal fallacy in working with definitions and labels	Chapter 5
Understanding the way language can influence thought	Chapter 8
Recognizing semantic slanting	Chapter 8
Recognizing name-calling and anticipatory name-calling	Chapter 8
Recognizing and avoiding reification	Chapter 9

Argument/Persuasion Analysis Skills

Understanding the elements of an argument	Chapter 10
Recognizing and avoiding common fallacies, such as irrelevant reasons, circular reasoning, slippery slope reasoning, weak analogies, and false dichotomies	Chapters 10 and 11
Evaluating arguments systematically	Chapter 10
Recognizing and avoiding appeals to ignorance	Chapter 9
Understanding how Pavlovian conditioning can be used to manipulate emotions	Chapter 6
Developing the ability to detect conditioning procedures used in the media	Chapter 6
Recognizing social influence strategies	Chapter 16
Judging the credibility of an information source	Chapter 16

Skills in Thinking as Hypothesis Testing

Looking for alternative explanations for findings and events	Chapters 1, 9, and 11
Looking for contradictory evidence	Chapters 1, 3, and 9
Recognizing the limitations of anecdotal evidence	Chapters 2 and 15
Understanding the need to seek disconfirming evidence	Chapter 7
Understanding the limitations of correlational evidence	Chapters 11 and 13
Understanding the limitations of statistical significance	Chapter 13
Recognizing situations in which placebo effects might occur	Chapter 15

Skills in Working with Likelihood and Uncertainty

Utilizing base rates in making predictions and evaluating probabilities	Chapter 13
Understanding cumulative probabilities	Chapter 14
Understanding conjunctive probabilities	Chapter 14
Understanding the limitations of the representativeness heuristic	Chapter 14
Understanding the limitations of the availability heuristic	Chapter 14
Recognizing situations in which regression toward the mean may occur	Chapter 15
Understanding the limits of extrapolation	Chapter 3

Decision-Making and Problem-Solving Skills

Using evidence-based decision making	Chapter 2
Recognizing the bias in hindsight analysis	Chapters 7 and 12
Seeking information to reduce uncertainty	Chapter 13
Making risk–benefit assessments	Chapter 13
Generating and evaluating alternative courses of action	Chapter 13
Recognizing overconfidence in human cognition	Chapter 7
Understanding the limitations and fallibility of human memory	Chapter 7
Understanding how contrast effects can influence judgments and decisions	Chapter 4
Recognizing when extreme comparitors are being used	Chapter 4

in this text, students will have access to fundamental and applied research and research groups in Canada and around the world. Insofar as students are interested in visiting these sites, we recommend that they do so through the *Psychology: Themes & Variations, Third Canadian Edition* CourseMate website: **http:// www.themesandvariations3Ce.nelson.com**. Links to all of the recommended websites are maintained there, by chapter, and the Nelson webmaster periodically updates the URLs.

Integrated Running Glossary

An introductory text should place great emphasis on acquainting students with psychology's technical language—not for the sake of jargon, but because a great many of the key terms are also cornerstone concepts (e.g., *independent variable*, *reliability*, and *cognitive dissonance*). This text handles terminology with a running glossary embedded in the prose itself. The terms are set off in **boldface italics**, and the definitions follow in **boldface roman type**. This approach retains the two advantages of a conventional running glossary: Vocabulary items are made salient, and their definitions are readily accessible. However, the approach does so without interrupting the flow of discourse, while eliminating redundancy between text matter and marginal entries.

Concept Checks

To help students assess their mastery of important ideas, Concept Checks are sprinkled throughout the book (two to four per chapter). In keeping with the goal of making this a book of ideas, the Concept Checks challenge students to apply ideas instead of testing rote memory. For example, in Chapter 6 the reader is asked to analyze realistic examples of conditioning and identify conditioned stimuli and responses, reinforcers, and schedules of reinforcement.

Many of the Concept Checks require the reader to put together ideas introduced in different sections of the chapter. For instance, in Chapter 2, students are asked to look for various types of deficiencies in hypothetical studies, and in Chapter 4, students are asked to identify parallels between vision and hearing. Some of the Concept Checks are quite challenging, but students find them engaging and they report that the answers (available in Appendix A) are often illuminating.

Preview Questions and Reviews of Key Points

To help students organize and remember important ideas, each chapter includes five to eight sets of Preview Questions and companion Reviews of Key Points. Generally speaking, the Preview Questions are found at the beginning of each major section in a chapter, in the margin, adjacent to a level-one heading; the Reviews of Key Points are found at the end of each major section, just before the next level-one heading. Of course, some exceptions to this rule-of-thumb had to be made to accommodate very long or very brief sections under level-one headings.

The Preview Questions are short, thought-provoking learning objectives that should help students focus on the key issues in each section. Each Review of Key Points is an interim summary that addresses the issues posed in the preceding Preview Questions. Interspersing these reviews throughout the chapters permits students to check their understanding of each section's main ideas immediately after finishing the section instead of waiting until the end of the chapter. This approach also allows students to work with more modest-sized chunks of information.

Another approach used in the Review of Key Points relates to its design. Psychology research does have relevance to our lives, sometimes in grand ways, for example biological discoveries, and sometimes in smaller ways. In an article published in the *Journal of Cognition*, psychologists tested how using unusual font style increased participants memory. Our memory for material can be enhanced when that material is presented in an unconventional font style. In the third Canadian edition we designed the Review of Key Points with this research in mind, using an unconventional type style, in Comic Sans font. We hope that using a different font style will assist in your retention of the information contained in the Review of Key Points feature.

Practice Tests

Each chapter ends with a multiple-choice Practice Test of 15 questions that should give students a realistic assessment of their mastery of that chapter and valuable practice taking the type of test that many of them will face in the classroom (if the instructor uses the Test Bank). This feature grew out of some research that Weiten conducted on students' use of textbook pedagogical devices (see Weiten, Guadagno, & Beck, 2006). This research indicated that students pay scant attention to some standard pedagogical devices. When Weiten grilled his students to gain a better understanding of this finding, it quickly became apparent that students are very pragmatic about pedagogy. Essentially, their refrain was "We want study aids that will help us pass the next test." These tests should be very realistic, as most of the items were taken from previous editions of the Test Bank (these items do not appear in the Test Bank for this edition).

The Practice Tests follow the Nelson Education Teaching Advantage (NETA) guidelines. You can read more about the NETA guidelines in the section called "Instructors Supplements" on page xxxv.

In addition to the special features just described, the text includes a variety of more conventional, "tried and true" features. Opening *outlines* preview each chapter, and a thorough *Recap* of key ideas appears at the end of each chapter, along with lists of *Key Terms* and *Key People* (important theorists and researchers). The back of the book contains a standard *alphabetical glossary*. We make frequent use of *italics for emphasis,* and we depend on *frequent headings* to maximize organizational clarity. The preface for students describes these pedagogical devices in more detail.

Content

The text is divided into 16 chapters, which follow a traditional ordering. The chapters are not grouped into sections or parts, primarily because such groupings can limit your options if you want to reorganize the order of topics. The chapters are written in a way that facilitates organizational flexibility, as we assume that some chapters might be omitted or presented in a different order.

The topical coverage in the text is relatively conventional, but there are some subtle departures from the norm. For instance, Chapter 1 presents a relatively "meaty" discussion of the evolution of ideas in psychology. This coverage of history lays the foundation for many of the crucial ideas emphasized in subsequent chapters. The historical perspective is also our way of reaching out to the students who find that psychology just isn't what they expected it to be. If we want students to contemplate the mysteries of behaviour, we must begin by clearing up the biggest mysteries of them all: "Where did these rats, statistics, synapses, and JNDs come from, what could they possibly have in common, and why doesn't this course bear any resemblance to what I anticipated?" We use history as a vehicle to explain how psychology evolved into its modern form and why misconceptions about its nature are so common.

We also devote an entire chapter (Chapter 2) to the scientific enterprise—not just the mechanics of research methods but the logic behind them. We believe that an appreciation of the nature of empirical evidence can contribute greatly to improving students' critical thinking skills. Ten years from now, many of the "facts" reported in this book will have changed, but an understanding of the methods of science will remain invaluable. An introductory psychology course, by itself, isn't going to make a student think like a scientist, but we can't think of a better place to start the process. Essential statistical concepts are introduced in Chapter 2, but no effort is made to teach actual calculations. For those who emphasize statistics, Appendix B expands on statistical concepts.

New and Updated in the Third Canadian Edition

The following list of specific chapter changes highlights some of the new key and updated topics and examples that have been included in the third Canadian edition.

Chapter 1: The Evolution of Psychology
NEW
- Section highlighting the historical links between the study of philosophy and physiology and the study of psychology.

UPDATED
- Introductory chapter vignette describing the Reena Virk case and links to leading Canadian research on bullying
- Material on the context and contributions of John Watson
- Updated Illustrated Overview of the Evolution of Psychology

Chapter 2: The Research Enterprise in Psychology
NEW
- Illustrated Overview of Key Research Methods in Psychology
- New section discussing the qualitative research methods
- New sections distinguishing within- and between-subjects designs
- New section on historical origins of Fisher's inferential statistics
- New section on statistics, covering topics such as distributions, variability and standard deviation, and percentiles
- New section on meta-analysis with examples
- New section on sampling bias in psychology and the undersampling of ethnic minorities and people from non-Western cultures
- New statistics on Canadians' use of the Internet

UPDATED
- Introductory vignette
- Section on field experiments
- Section on naturalistic observation
- Material on the placebo effect
- Material on implicit measures in psychology

Chapter 3: The Biological Bases of Behaviour
NEW
- Material on endorphins and the neurochemical bases of pain and pleasure
- Material on the excitatory and inhibitory effects of the corpus callosum
- Discussion on hemispheric specialization
- Section on the hormone oxytocin and its effects on reproduction, bonding and trust
- Section on epigenetics

UPDATED
- Introductory vignette
- Material on the role of GABA
- Discussion on the origins and use of EEG technology
- Material on H.M. and his role in the development of neuroscience
- Description of the role of the cerebellum and the hippocampus beyond their respective roles in motor functions and memory
- Material on hemispheric specialization

Chapter 4: Sensation and Perception
NEW
- Section on visual agnosia and prosopagnosia
- Section on the effects of colour on behaviour
- Material on inattentional blindness
- Material on the effects of motivational states on depth perception
- Material on 3-D movie perception
- Material on umami, a fifth basic taste
- Section on distinction between tasters and nontasters
- Comparative sensitivity to smells
- Material on the role of glia cells in pain perception
- The effects of context on pain perception

UPDATED
- Illustrated overview of sensation and perception
- The nature of saccades
- Facial perception
- Trichromatic theory
- Auditory perception and hearing loss
- Reconciling place and frequency theories of hearing
- Subliminal perception
- Human sensitivity to smells

Chapter 5: Variations in Consciousness
NEW
- Section on unconscious thought effects
- Featured study on the merits of unconscious thought
- Canadian statistics on sleep and sleeplessness
- Material on functions of sleep
- Material on sleep and the elderly
- Section on the effects of sleep deprivation and emotions
- Section on neurogenesis and sleep
- Section on sleep loss and health
- Section on REM sleep behaviour disorder
- Material on types of meditation and their effects on the brain and pain tolerance
- Canadian statistics on drug use
- Material on the use of hallucinogens in psychological research and Timothy Leary

UPDATED
- Introductory vignette
- Discussion on consciousness
- Material on circadian rhythms, travel, and physical health
- Material on the brain and sleep
- Material on insomnia and its treatment
- Material on sleep apnea
- Material on nightmares
- Discussion on narcotics and opiates
- Discussion of cannabis and its health risks
- Material on lucid dreaming

Chapter 6: Learning
NEW
- Canadian statistics on incidence of social phobia
- Material on the functional perspective on Pavlovian conditioning
- Section on conditioned fear and anxiety
- Section on evaluative conditioning of attitudes
- Material on the mysterious case of Little Albert and classical conditioning
- Discussion of Skinner and his development of the baby box
- Discussion of the renewal effect in operant conditioning
- Section on latent learning and cognitive maps
- Canadian statistics on kids and TV watching
- Discussion of media violence and desensitization and the brain
- Material on mirror neurons and the development of empathy

UPDATED

- Introductory vignette
- Material on superstitious behaviour
- Discussion of the renewal effect in classical conditioning
- Discussion of the effects of corporal punishment on children
- Discussion of the concept of preparedness
- Material on evolutionary perspectives on learning

Chapter 7: Human Memory
NEW

- Section on the "Seven Sins of Memory"
- Discussion on attention and the use of cell phones while driving
- Material on distinction between Ebbinghaus's and Bartlett's memory research
- Bartlett's approach to reconstructive memory
- Discussion of destination monitoring error in memory
- Discussion of the Deese-Roediger-McDermott paradigm in memory research
- Material concerning H.M.'s contribution to memory research
- Section on the testing effect in memory
- Information on the implications of recent work in neuroscience for the study of memory

UPDATED

- Introductory vignette
- Material on working memory capacity
- Flashbulb memories
- Hypnosis and memory
- Schemas and memory
- Eyewitness memory
- Discussion of reality and source monitoring
- Recovered memories
- Discussion of declarative and nondeclarative memory

Chapter 8: Language and Thought
NEW

- Section on behavioural economics
- Section on the effects of incubation in problem solving
- Section on uncertainty and decision making
- Section on deliberation and decision making
- Material on intelligence and decision making
- Section on myside bias in decision making
- Material on Ellen Bialystok's work on bilingualism and its effects

UPDATED

- Infants' acquisition of language
- Analogies in problem solving
- Culture, social orientation, and problem solving
- Consumers, number of product alternatives, and decision making

Chapter 9: Intelligence and Psychological Testing
NEW

- Section on the stability of IQ scores
- Section on cognitive abilities and IQ
- Section on savants
- Material on achievement and giftedness
- Discussion and data on the relations between IQ and longevity
- Discussion of the background of Sternberg's work on IQ
- New examples and data on the topic of creativity and mental illness

UPDATED

- Introductory vignette
- Section on debate about the structure of intelligence
- Material on the validity of IQ tests
- Discussion of terminology and intellectual disability
- Statistics on the heritability of IQ
- Material on stereotype threat
- Discussion of physiological indices of IQ
- Material relating personality and creativity with new examples
- Discussion of the relations between IQ and creativity
- Discussion on emotional efference
- Material on facial emotional expression by individuals who are blind
- Discussion of adaptive value of disgust

Chapter 10: Motivation and Emotion
NEW

- Canadian statistics on obesity
- Section on sensitivity to external cues and eating
- Canadian statistics on sexual behaviour of Canadian youth
- Material on emotive ratings for words
- Section on affective forecasting
- Material on wealth and subjective happiness
- Factors contributing to happiness

UPDATED

- Discussion on the brain and hunger
- Material on hormonal influences on eating
- Discussion on variables influencing food consumption
- Advertising and food consumption
- Obesity and mortality
- Human sexual response
- Gender differences in sexual behaviour
- Emotions in everyday life

Chapter 11: Human Development across the Life Span
NEW

- Section on the effects of maternal illness and exposure to toxins
- Section on fetal origins of disease
- Material on Vygotsky
- Discussion of the validity of Marcia's theory of identity status
- New statistics on marital satisfaction
- Statistics and discussion on aging and suicide in Canada
- Canadian statistics on the activity level of Canadian seniors
- Discussion on cognitive training for seniors
- Material on the gender gap in math

UPDATED

- Material on the effects of maternal drug use
- Discussion on cross-sectional and longitudinal designs
- Material on temperament
- Discussion on adjusting to marriage
- Discussion on Alzheimer's disease

Chapter 12: Personality: Theory, Research, and Assessment
NEW

- Introductory vignette
- Discussion of Anna Freud and her contribution to psychoanalysis
- Section on recent directions in research on the self
- Discussion of self-discrepancy theory
- Section on personality and neuroscience
- Section discussing new research and theory into the nature and implications of narcissism and the increase in narcissism in society
- Discussion of the concepts of individualism and collectivism and its impact on the development of personality
- Recent revisions to Maslow's pyramid theory of motivation

UPDATED

- Discussion of the Big Five personality traits
- Material personality and health
- Material on the role of sociocultural context on the development of Freud's theory of psychoanalysis
- Material on terror management theory

Chapter 13: Stress, Coping, and Health
NEW

- Statistics on commuting time for Canadians
- Distinctions drawn between primary and secondary appraisal in the coping process
- Statistics on Canadians feeling stress because of a time crunch
- Discussion of the functional role played by positive emotions and the connection between happiness and longevity
- Material on gender differences in reactivity to stress
- Statistics on gambling in Canada and on Internet addiction in youth
- The Dawson College tragedy and PTSD
- Canadian statistics on hypertension
- Canadian statistics on fitness and youth
- Psychology Foundation of Canada recommendations concerning how to combat stress

UPDATED

- Introductory vignette
- Material on work pressure and health problems
- Stress and psychological disorders
- Research on choking under pressure
- Coping and resilience
- Section on social support and health

Chapter 14: Psychological Disorders
NEW

- Section on disorders of childhood with a focus on autism
- Canadian statistics on incidence of psychological distress and suicide
- Canadian statistics on use of antianxiety and antidepressant medications
- Discussion of proposed changes to the DSM
- Material on categorical versus dimensional approaches to classifying psychological disorders
- Figure describing frequency of common phobias
- Section describing the contribution of hormonal factors to the onset of depression
- Section on the links between concussions and depression
- Canadian statistics on childhood psychological disorders

UPDATED

- Statistics on the prevalence of anxiety disorders and obsessive compulsive disorders
- Discussion of the links between perfectionism and depression
- John Nash and paranoid schizophrenia
- Discussion of the link between cannabis and psychopathology
- Material concerning the results of brain-imaging studies and neural correlates of schizophrenia
- Culture and psychopathology
- Personal Application on eating disorders

Chapter 15: Treatment of Psychological Disorders

NEW

- Section on couples therapy and family therapy
- Material on the Psy.D. degree in Canada
- Section addressing the nature and significance of the therapeutic alliance in therapy
- Section detailing mindfulness-based cognitive behaviour therapy for anxiety
- Figure relating suicide risk and time to treatment

UPDATED

- Introductory vignette
- Statistics on use of medication in treatment of psychopathology
- Description of core features of modern psychodynamic therapies
- Interventions related to positive psychology
- Relative effectiveness of insight therapies
- Description of exposure therapy
- Discussion of the effectiveness of drug therapies
- Culture and mental illness stigma

Chapter 16: Social Behaviour

NEW

- Section on the Internet and close relationships
- Discussion of John Bargh's research examining the behavioural effects of priming stereotypes
- Section on implicit attitudes, their measurement and application to the study of prejudice
- Description and implications for attitude formation of the mere exposure effect
- Material on social neuroscience presenting some of the most recent trends in theory and research relating the brain and social behaviour

UPDATED

- Personal Application: Understanding Prejudice
- Physical appearance and impressions
- Material on the social effects of attractiveness

Writing Style

In writing this text, we attempted a down-to-earth, conversational writing style; effective communication is always the paramount goal. Our intent is to talk *with* the reader rather than throw information *at* the reader. We were thrilled to receive unsolicited comments from students across the country on the first and second Canadian editions of *Psychology: Themes and Variations*. When one student commented that "I felt like I was talking to the authors" while she was reading the book, we knew we were on the right track. To clarify concepts and maintain student interest, we frequently provide concrete examples that students can relate to. As much as possible, we avoid using technical jargon when ordinary language will do.

Making learning easier depends, above all else, on clear, well-organized writing. For this reason, we've worked hard to ensure that chapters, sections, and paragraphs are organized in a logical manner, so that key ideas stand out in sharp relief against supportive information.

Psychology Photography Contest

For the third Canadian edition, we held a contest to find images that would be featured in the text. The theme of the contest was "7." Students were asked to submit photos where the number 7 was represented or to submit photos that fit one of the seven themes discussed throughout the textbook. The contest was open to all full-time and part-time psychology and photography students.

We received a number of entries and we would like to thank all the students who entered the contest for their creative take on the theme of "7." We would also like to thank the Nelson Education Ltd. marketing and sales teams that worked very hard to spread the word of the contest across all colleges and universities in Canada. Special thanks to Aurelio Zappia, site leader, for creating a stellar website for the photography contest and Eugene Lo, designer, for creating the poster that was distributed by Nelson Education sales representatives.

The winning photos of the contest can be found in a number of the chapter openers throughout this text. The winning photos were selected for their creativity and artistic impression, depiction of the "7" theme, style, originality, and psychological aspect. Congratulations to the following students for their winning photos:

Colette R. Orfeo, *Athabasca University*
Debbie Steel, *Trent University*
Rebecca Rosalie Andekas Atkins, *York University*

Student Supplements

Concept Charts for Study and Review

To help your students organize and assimilate the main ideas contained in the text, we have created a booklet of Concept Charts that is included with each new copy of the text. This booklet contains a two-page Concept Chart for each chapter that provides a detailed visual map of the key ideas found in the main body of that chapter. These colour-coded, hierarchically organized charts create snapshots of the chapters that should allow your students to quickly see the relationships among ideas and sections.

CourseMate

Psychology: Themes and Variations, Third Canadian Edition includes CourseMate, which helps you make the grade.

CourseMate includes:

- an interactive eBook, with highlighting, note taking and search capabilities
- interactive learning tools including:
  ○ Quizzes
  ○ Flashcards
  ○ Videos
  ○ Animations, Simulations, and PowerVisuals
  ○ and more!

Go to login.nelsonbrain.com to access these resources, and look for this icon in the chapters to find the interactive figures found in the text on CourseMate.

CengageNOW™

This online diagnostic tool identifies each student's unique needs with a pre-test that generates a personalized study plan for each chapter, helping students to focus on concepts they're having the most difficulty mastering. Students then take a post-test to measure their understanding of the material. An instructor gradebook is available to track and monitor student progress. A key component of the study plan is the inclusion of visually and pedagogically rich modules that begin with clearly stated learning objectives, followed by knowledge-building animations with audio to present key concepts. Modules also include discovery activities and self-check quizzes that confirm student understanding of the module material.

Study Guide (by Richard Stalling and Ronald Wasden, and adapted by Andrew Howell)

An exceptionally thorough *Study Guide* is available to help your students master the information in the text.

The review of key ideas for each chapter is made up of an engaging mixture of matching exercises, fill-in-the-blank items, free-response questions, and programmed learning. Each review is organized around learning objectives. The *Study Guide* also includes a review of key terms, a review of key people, and a self-test for each chapter in the text.

Aplia™

Aplia is a Cengage Learning online homework system dedicated to improving learning by increasing student effort and engagement. Aplia makes it easy for instructors to assign frequent online homework assignments. Aplia provides students with immediate detailed feedback to help them learn as they work through the questions and features interactive tutorials to fully engage them in learning course concepts. Automatic grading and powerful assessment tools give instructors real-time reporting of student progress, participation, and performance, and its easy-to-use course management features let instructors flexibly administer course announcements and materials online. With Aplia, students will show up to class fully engaged and prepared, and instructors will have more time to do what they do best . . . teach.

PsykTrek™ 3.0: A Multimedia Introduction to Psychology

PsykTrek 3.0 is a multimedia supplement that will provide students with new opportunities for active learning and reach out to "visual learners" with greatly increased efficacy. *PsykTrek* is intended to give students a second pathway to learning much of the content of introductory psychology. Although it does not cover all of the content of the introductory course, we think you will see that a great many key concepts and principles can be explicated *more effectively* in an interactive audio–visual medium than in a textbook.

PsykTrek 3.0 consists of four components. The main component is a set of 65 *Interactive Learning Modules* that present the core content of psychology in a whole new way. These tutorials include thousands of graphics, hundreds of photos, hundreds of animations, approximately four hours of narration, 35 carefully selected videos, and about 160 uniquely visual Concept Checks and quizzes. The *Simulations* allow students to explore complex psychological phenomena in depth. They are highly interactive, experiential demonstrations that will enhance student appreciation of research methods. New modules can be found in *PsykTrek 3.0*. A *Multimedia Glossary* allows students to look up over 800 psychological terms, access hundreds of pronunciations of obscure words, and pull up hundreds of related diagrams, photos, and videos. The *Video Selector* allows students to directly access the 35 video segments that are otherwise embedded in the Interactive Learning Modules.

The key strength of *PsykTrek* is its ability to give students new opportunities for active learning outside of the classroom. For example, students can run themselves through re-creations of classic experiments to see the complexities of data collection in action. Or they can play with visual illusions on-screen in ways that will make them doubt their own eyes. Or they can stack colour filters on-screen to demonstrate the nature of subtractive colour mixing. *PsykTrek* is intended to supplement and complement *Psychology: Themes and Variations*. For instance, after reading about operant conditioning in the text, a student could work through three interactive tutorials on operant principles, watch three videos (including historic footage of B. F. Skinner shaping a rat), and then try to shape Morphy, the virtual rat, in one of the simulations.

Instructor Supplements

The teaching/learning package that has been developed to supplement *Psychology: Themes and Variations* also includes many other useful tools. The development of all its parts was carefully coordinated so that they are mutually supported. Moreover, the materials have been created and written by highly experienced, top-flight professors we have worked hard to recruit.

Instructor's Resource Manual (coordinated by Randolph Smith and revised by C. Darren Piercey)

A talented roster of professors has contributed to the *Instructor's Resource Manual (IRM)* in their respective areas of expertise. The *IRM* was developed under the guidance of Randolph Smith, the editor of the journal *Teaching of Psychology*. It contains a wealth of detailed suggestions for lecture topics, class demonstrations, exercises, discussion questions, and suggested readings, organized around the content of each chapter in the text. The IRM also highlights the connections between the text coverage and *Psyk.Trek* content and features an expanded collection of masters for class handouts. Also included are the following sections:

- *Strategies for Effective Teaching,* by Joseph Lowman (University of North Carolina), discusses practical issues such as what to put in a course syllabus, how to handle the first class meeting, how to cope with large classes, and how to train and organize teaching assistants.

- *AV Media for Introductory Psychology,* by Russ Watson (College of DuPage), provides a comprehensive, up-to-date critical overview of educational films relevant to the introductory course.

- *The Use of Computers in Teaching Introductory Psychology,* by Susan J. Shapiro and Michael Shapiro (Indiana University–East), offers a thorough listing of computer materials germane to the introductory course and analyzes their strengths and weaknesses.

- *Integrating Writing into Introductory Psychology,* by Jane Jegerski (Elmhurst College), examines the writing-across-the-curriculum movement and provides suggestions and materials for specific writing assignments chapter by chapter.

- *Crossing Borders/Contrasting Behaviours: Using Cross-Cultural Comparisons to Enrich the Introductory Psychology Course,* by Bill Hill and Michael Reiner (Kennesaw State University), discusses the movement toward "internationalizing" the curriculum and provides suggestions for lectures, exercises, and assignments that can add a cross-cultural flavour to the introductory course.

- *Teaching Introductory Psychology with the World Wide Web,* by Michael R. Snyder (University of Alberta), discusses how to work Internet assignments into the introductory course and provides a guide to many psychology-related sites on the World Wide Web.

- *Using InfoTrac® in Introductory Psychology* by Randolph Smith discusses how to make effective use of the *InfoTrac* subscription that is made available to students with this text. *InfoTrac College Edition* is an online database of recent full-text articles from hundreds of scholarly and popular periodicals.

Nelson Education Teaching Advantage

The **Nelson Education Teaching Advantage (NETA) program** delivers research-based resources that promote student engagement and higher-order thinking and enable the success of Canadian students and educators.

NETA ASSESSMENT

Recognizing the importance of multiple-choice testing in today's classroom and in response to instructors' concerns, Nelson Education has created the NETA Assessment program. NETA Assessment is a research-based program that improves the quality of our test banks by ensuring our test banks measure not just recall (as is typical with test banks) but **_higher-level thinking_** skills as well.

The NETA Assessment program was created in partnership with David DiBattista, a 3M National Teaching

Fellow, professor of psychology at Brock University, and researcher in the area of multiple-choice testing.

All NETA test banks include David DiBattista's guide for instructors, *Multiple Choice Tests: Getting Beyond Remembering*. This guide has been designed to assist you in using Nelson test banks to achieve the desired outcomes in your course. Select the "NETA Assessment" button on the *Psychology: Themes and Variations Instructor's Resource DVD* for this valuable resource. At the same location you will find the *Psychology: Themes and Variations* test bank and computerized test bank (see "Instructor's Resource DVD" below for more information about the test bank.)

Test Bank, Volume I (by S. A. Hensch; adapted and revised by Lynne Honey)

The test bank that accompanies the text was adapted for Canadian readers by Lynne Honey of Grant MacEwan University. She has paid particular attention to ensuring that the questions reflect the material in the third Canadian edition while matching the outstanding U.S. original in the scope, effectiveness, and accuracy of test items. A careful effort has been made to ensure personal names used in the questions reflect Canada's ethnic diversity, underscoring the fact that psychology is for everyone. The questions are closely tied to chapter learning objectives and to the lists of key terms and key people found in both the text and the *CourseMate website*. The items follow Bloom's Taxonomy and are categorized as remember and higher order. All essay-type questions are accompanied by suggested answers. The Test Bank, volume I, can be found on the Instructor's Resource DVD.

Test Bank, Volume II (by S. A. Hensch; adapted and revised by Lynne Honey)

This alternative test bank allows instructors to draw from an entirely new set of questions, offering more varied test materials and ensuring that students are challenged by fresh items. Each chapter has 100 to 125 multiple-choice questions. The Test Bank, volume II, is available on a separate CD.

Computerized Test Items

Electronic versions of Volumes I and II of the *Test Bank* are available for a variety of computer configurations. The *ExamView* software is user-friendly and allows teachers to insert their own questions and to customize those provided. For additional testing questions please contact your Nelson Education sales representative.

INSTRUCTOR'S RESOURCE DVD (ISBN 978-0-17-1664771-1)

- Instructor's Manual
- NETA Assessment
  - *Multiple-Choice Testing: Getting Beyond Remembering*
  - ExamView® Computerized Test Bank volume I
  - Test Bank (.rtf files) volume I
- Microsoft® PowerPoint® (**adapted and revised by Dax Urbszat, University of Toronto**)
- Image Library includes jpegs of figures, tables, and some images from the textbook so that professors can incorporate them into their lecture slides or notes.
- DayOne slides. Talk to your Nelson sales representative about how these slides can help your students succeed in their higher education pursuits!

Wayne Weiten
Doug McCann

Acknowledgments for the Third Canadian Edition

Working on this third Canadian edition of *Psychology: Themes and Variations* has proven to be a pleasure. Wayne Weiten's text was a joy to work with, and his support and advice for the Canadian edition has been invaluable. Wayne and I were delighted by the reception the first two Canadian editions received and looked forward to revising the text for this edition. Creating a text such as this is a complicated challenge, and I am indebted to a group of dedicated professionals at Nelson Education Ltd. for all the assistance they provided. The editorial and production team for this second edition was almost entirely new, so I was thrilled with how seamlessly the team worked together.

Sandy Matos, managing developmental editor at Nelson, was a constant source of innovative ideas and guidance, and was invaluable to this project. Working with Sandy was a pleasure. Valerie Adams was a superb copy editor whose expertise was much appreciated. I would like to thank Lenore Taylor-Atkins, senior acquisitions editor; Ann Byford, marketing manager; and Jessie Coffey, permissions editor and photo researcher.

A host of psychologists deserve thanks for the contributions they made to this adaptation, including Vic Catano of Saint Mary's University for his work on the appendix on industrial and organizational psychology; Andrew Howell for his work on the *Study Guide*; David DiBattista for his expertise, dedication, and guidance in establishing a process for writing test questions that will challenge students and instructors; Lynne Honey for adapting both volumes of the Test Bank and the Practice Tests that appear after each chapter (your work on this revision has been excellent); Dax Urbszat for taking on the PowerPoint slides and accompanying Lecture Outlines; and Lisa Best for her work on the Self-Study Assessment Questions found in CengageNOW™.

I would also like to thank the many reviewers and chapter consultants who provided insightful and constructive critiques of various portions of the manuscript:

Michelle Eskritt, *Mount Saint Vincent University*
Rebecca Jubis, *York University*
Russell Kositis, *Redeemer College*
Jason Leeboe, *University of Manitoba*
David Lethbridge, *Okanagan College*
Stacy MacKinnon, *University of Prince Edward Island*
Colleen MacQuarrie, *University of Prince Edward Island*
C. Darren Piercey, *University of New Brunswick*
Cynthia Whissell, *Laurentian University*
Sandra Wright, *Sir Wilfred Grenfell College*

In working on the third Canadian edition, I was fortunate to be surrounded by a world-class group of colleagues who were more than willing to talk to me about issues in psychology and to give generously of their time and expertise. They include Gordon Flett, Chris Green, Alex Rutherford, Hiroshi Ono, Thomas Teo, Maxine Wintre, the late Ann-Marie Wall, Henny Westra, Frances Wilkinson, Janice Johnson, Laurence Harris, Doug Crawford, Regina Schuller, Myriam Mongrain, and Richard Lalonde. Two of these colleagues deserve special mention: Richard Lalonde was helpful as always in contributing ideas and enthusiasm for the teaching of introductory psychology, and Myriam Mongrain went far beyond the call of duty and provided me with exhaustive comments on the entire text, suggesting additions, deletions, and resources, and catching errors in the first edition. Myriam, you have improved the text.

I would also like to thank all of my graduate students, both for their encouragement for the work and their patience when it took a little longer than usual to arrange a meeting with me. Thanks too to Chris Cornell and Dave Grohl, both of whom helped with the background.

Thanks also to Harry who served as a research assistant on this project—your work made everything more interesting. Harry read the book from the perspective of a first-year university student who is taking a beginning course in psychology. His suggested changes appear throughout the book. Harry was well qualified for the task, not only is he an astute critic and grammarian, he is a first-year university student taking psychology for the first time this year at the University of Waterloo. Harry shared the *bunker* with me while we worked on the book. He tracked down material, provided needed comic relief and seemingly endless breaks, and produced perfect multiple tsuki te's whenever he thought I needed one to keep me on track.

I would also like to thank all of the Canadian researchers I contacted who made their ideas readily available to me. Thanks also to Norm Endler; his legendary aoristic red pen still affects my work.

During the time the book was in preparation, I was fortunate to have the support and enthusiasm of a small group who made the task easy and enjoyable. Thanks to Tuck for allowing me to try out language and ideas while we played serious ball. Tuck was particularly helpful with regard to the comparative psychology sections. Thanks to David for continuing to pull out all the stops in helping us all out; I hope the picture is enough. Thanks to Sensei Waith for his support and encouragement and to Dr. Zindel Segal of CAMH for introducing me to mindfulness meditation.

In the end, as always, it comes down to the ineffable Nancy. Thanks for getting it started, for sharing, and for keeping the motivation for research and writing going when it seemed to stop. Her enthusiasm for the project never wavered. She could even find a smile for all the Sundays I was at the office. I could always depend on her good counsel whenever a problem came up: her knowledge of pedagogy never fails to inspire.

Doug McCann

Welcome to your introductory psychology textbook. In most university and college courses, students spend more time with their textbooks than with their instructors, so it helps if students *like* their textbooks. Making textbooks likable, however, is a tricky proposition. By its very nature, a textbook must introduce students to many complicated concepts, ideas, and theories. If it doesn't, it isn't much of a textbook, and instructors won't use it. Nevertheless, in writing this book, we've tried to make it as likable as possible without compromising the academic content that your instructor demands. We've especially tried to keep in mind your need for a clear, well-organized presentation that makes the important material stand out and yet is interesting to read. Above all else, we hope you find this book challenging to think about and easy to learn from.

Before you plunge into your first chapter, let's look at the book's key features. Becoming familiar with how the book works will help you to get more out of it.

Key Features

You're about to embark on a journey into a new domain of ideas. Your text includes some important features that are intended to highlight certain aspects of psychology's landscape.

Changes to the Third Canadian Edition

Our goal in the third Canadian edition was to make the material in this book as up to date as possible while retaining the readability that our texts are known for. To this end, we have included over 1700 new references to research and theory in psychology from all over the world. Whenever possible, we have also provided a Canadian context for the work we presented in an attempt to have psychology relate to things you yourself may have experienced or thought about. We have improved the illustrations that are so central to the material covered in many of the chapters in the hope that they too will help make the material come alive for you. Throughout the text, we have included material reflecting the importance of neuroscience to contemporary psychology. Over the years, psychology has seen several significant trends emerge and an emphasis on neuroscience is one of the more recent ones. You will see this throughout the book. We have also tried to embrace a narrative style in telling you something about the important figures in psychology and the sociocultural context in which they worked.

We have added new content throughout the book that reflects issues of importance to all of us. For example, in Chapter 5, we have added a Featured Study examining the merits of unconscious thought and decision making. Maybe there is some value in taking a break from conscious deliberation—taking a break may be useful to us all. In Chapter 4 we explain how it's possible not to see something that is right in front of your face, a phenomenon referred to as inattentional blindness. In Chapter 6 we tell you about an eminent scientist's experiment in mechanizing the raising of children; he developed the *baby box*. In Chapter 7 we describe the *seven sins of memory,* seven ways that your memory system can lead you astray. In Chapter 15 we provide an elaborate discussion of new forms of therapy, such as mindfulness-based cognitive therapy, an approach to psychotherapy that is rooted both in classic cognitive theory and in the practice of meditation. It is one of the newest models of "talk therapy."

These are only a few examples. There is much more that is new in this edition than we have described here, and we hope you will enjoy your journey through the text. We would also really like to hear your comments, so please feel free to e-mail Doug McCann at dmccann@yorku.ca.

Unifying Themes

To help you make sense of a complex and diverse field of study, seven themes are introduced in Chapter 1 and reappear in a number of variations as we move from chapter to chapter. These unifying themes are meant to provoke thought about important issues and to highlight the connections between chapters. They are discussed at the end of each chapter in a section called "Putting It in Perspective."

Featured Studies

Every chapter includes a Featured Study, which is an in-depth look at an interesting piece of research. The Featured Studies are presented much as if they were journal articles. We hope they will enhance your understanding of how psychologists conduct and report their research.

Personal Applications

Toward the end of each chapter, you'll find a Personal Application section that shows how psychology is relevant to everyday life. Some of these sections provide concrete, practical advice that could be helpful to you in your educational endeavours, such as those on improving academic performance, improving everyday memory, and achieving self-control. So, you may want to jump ahead and read some of these Personal Applications early.

Critical Thinking Applications

Each Personal Application is followed by a two-page Critical Thinking Application that teaches and models basic critical thinking skills. We think you will find these sections refreshing and interesting. Like the Personal Applications, they are part of the text's basic content and should be read (unless you are told otherwise by your instructor). Although the "facts" of psychology will gradually change after you take this course (thanks to scientific progress), the critical thinking skills modelled in these sections should prove valuable for many years to come.

Web Links and Internet Essays

To help make this book a rich resource guide, we have included dozens of Web Links, which are recommended websites that can provide you with additional information on a wide variety of topics. Many of the recommended sites were selected by Professor Vincent Hevern, who sought out resources that are interesting and that provide accurate, empirically sound information. Others were researched specifically for their relevance to Canadian students. The Web Links are dispersed throughout the chapters, adjacent to related topical coverage.

While Web Links include the site URLs, we recommend that if you are interested in visiting these sites, you do so through the *Psychology: Themes & Variations* CourseMate at **http://www. themesandvariations3Ce.nelson.com**. Links to all of the recommended websites are maintained there and the Nelson webmaster periodically updates the URLs. By the way, if you are not particularly sophisticated about the Internet, it is strongly suggested that you read Professor Hevern's essay on Internet basics, which follows this preface. And even if you *are* sophisticated about the Internet, you can probably benefit from reading Appendix D, which discusses how to evaluate the quality and credibility of Web-based resources.

Learning Aids

This text contains a great deal of information. A number of learning aids have been incorporated into the book to help you digest it all.

An *outline* at the beginning of each chapter provides you with an overview of the topics covered in that chapter. Think of the outlines as road maps, and bear in mind that it's easier to reach a destination if you know where you're going.

Headings serve as road signs in your journey through each chapter. Different levels of headings are used to make it easy to see the organization of each chapter.

Preview Questions, found at the beginning of major sections, can help you focus on the key issues in the material you are about to read.

Reviews of Key Points, found at the end of major sections, are interim summaries that permit you to check your understanding of a section's main ideas immediately after finishing the section. The different font used in this box has been done so to impact memory.

Italics (without boldface) are used liberally throughout the text to emphasize crucial points.

An *integrated running glossary* provides an on-the-spot definition of each key term as it's introduced in the text. The *key terms* are identified with ***italicized boldface*** type (in blue) to alert you that these are important vocabulary items that are part of psychology's technical language. The definitions that follow these key terms are printed in **boldface** type (also in blue). The key terms, with page references, are also listed at the end of each chapter. Becoming familiar with psychology's terminology is an essential part of learning about the field. The integrated running glossary should make this learning process easier. In addition, an *alphabetical glossary* is provided in the back of the book. Most key terms are formally defined in the integrated running glossary only when they are first introduced. So if you run into a technical term a second time and can't remember its meaning, it may be easier to look it up in the alphabetical glossary than to try to find the definition where the term was originally introduced.

Concept Checks are sprinkled throughout the chapters to let you test your mastery of important ideas. Generally, they ask you to integrate or organize a number of key ideas, or to apply ideas to real-world situations. Although they're meant to be engaging and fun, they do check conceptual *understanding,* and some are challenging. But if you get stuck, don't worry; the answers (and explanations, where they're needed) are in the back of the book in Appendix A.

Illustrations in the text are important elements in your complete learning package. Some illustrations provide enlightening diagrams of complicated concepts; others furnish examples that help flesh out ideas or provide concise overviews of research results. Careful attention to the tables and figures in the book will help you understand the material discussed in the text.

A *Recap* at the end of each chapter provides a summary of the chapter's *key ideas,* a list of *key terms,* and a list of *key people* (important theorists and researchers). It's wise to read over these review materials to make sure you've digested the information in the chapter.

Each chapter ends with a 15-item *Practice Test* that should give you a realistic assessment of your mastery of that chapter and valuable practice in taking multiple-choice tests. Answers to these Practice Tests are included at the back of the book in Appendix A.

A Few Footnotes

Psychology textbooks customarily identify the studies, theoretical treatises, books, and articles that information comes from. These *citations* occur (1) when names are followed by a date in parentheses, as in "Smith (003) found that . . ." or (2) when names and dates are provided together within parentheses, as in "In one study (Smith, Miller, & Jones, 2001), the researchers attempted to . . . ." All of the cited publications are listed by author in the alphabetized *References* section at the back of the book. The citations and references are a necessary part of a book's scholarly and scientific foundation. Practically speaking, however, you'll probably want to glide right over them as you read. You definitely don't need to memorize the names and dates. The only names you may need to know are the handful listed in the Key People list in each chapter Recap (unless your instructor mentions a personal favourite that you should know).

Concept Charts for Study and Review

Your textbook should be accompanied by a booklet of Concept Charts that are designed to help you organize and master the main ideas contained in each chapter. Each Concept Chart provides a detailed visual map of the key ideas found in the main body of that chapter. Seeing how it all fits together should help you to better understand each chapter. You can use these charts to preview chapters, to get a handle on how key ideas fit together, to double-check your mastery of the chapters, and to memorize the crucial principles in chapters.

PsykTrek™ 3.0: A Multimedia Introduction to Psychology

PsykTrek 3.0, available in both CD-ROM and online format, is an enormously powerful learning tool that can enhance your understanding of many complex processes and theories, provide you with an alternative way to assimilate many crucial concepts, and add a little more fun to your journey through introductory psychology. *PsykTrek* has been designed to supplement and complement your textbook. We strongly encourage you to use it. The CD icons that you will see in many of the headings in the upcoming chapters refer to the content of *PsykTrek*.

An icon indicates that the textbook topic referred to in the heading is covered in the Interactive Learning Modules or Simulations found on *PsykTrek*. The relevant simulations (SIM1, SIM2, and so forth) and the relevant Interactive Learning Modules (1A, 1B, 1C, and so forth) are listed to the right of the icons.

A Word About the Study Guide

A *Study Guide* is available to accompany this text. It was written by two of Wayne Weiten's former professors, who introduced him to psychology years ago, and adapted for the Canadian edition by **Andrew Howell of Grant MacEwan College.** They have done a great job of organizing review materials to help you master the information in the book. You should seriously consider using it to help you study.

A Final Word

We are pleased to be a part of your first journey into the world of psychology, and sincerely hope that you'll find the book as thought-provoking and as easy to learn from as we've tried to make it. If you have any comments or advice on the book, please either e-mail Doug McCann at dmccann@yorku.ca or write to us in care of the publisher (Nelson Education Ltd., 1120 Birchmount Road, Toronto, Ontario, M1K 5G4). You can be sure that we'll pay careful attention to your feedback. Finally, we wish you good luck. We hope you enjoy your course and learn a great deal.

Wayne Weiten
Doug McCann

On the Web

▶ **CourseMate**
Go to this site to find online resources directly linked to your book, including more quizzes, a glossary, flash cards, videos, and more!

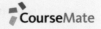

▶ **CengageNow**
Go to this site for the link to CengageNOW™, your one-stop study shop. Take a pre-test for this chapter and CengageNOW™ will generate a personalized study plan based on your test results! The study plan will identify the topics you need to review and direct you to online resources to help you master those topics. You can then take a post-test to help you determine the concepts you have mastered and what you still need to work on.

▶ **Aplia**
Aplia™ is an online interactive learning solution that helps you improve comprehension—and your grade—by integrating a variety of mediums and tools such as video, tutorials, practice tests, and an interactive e-book.

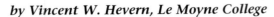

by Vincent W. Hevern, Le Moyne College

After dinner one night, Wayne Weiten, an author of this textbook, challenged me: Using no more than three pages, could I tell introductory psychology students the most important things they need to know about the Internet? Wait a minute, I thought, that's tough! I've been using the Net intensively for more than seven years in teaching and research with undergraduates, so I know there's an awful lot to talk about. But, after a couple of days I decided to accept his challenge. So, I'm going to share with you here what I believe to be the really important stuff about the Internet—information that should make your life as a student easier and, in the end, help you to learn even more about the fascinating world of psychology.

General Comments about the Internet

We now know that something of a fundamental change in the way people exchange ideas and information took place during the 1990s. For over 20 years, the Internet had been the tool of a relatively small group of lab scientists communicating mostly with each other. Suddenly, in the mid-1990s, the Net began to expand rapidly beyond the research laboratory. It first reached tens and then hundreds of millions of people as vast numbers of computers, large and small, were interconnected to form what is often called *cyberspace*. In the 21st century, learning to navigate the Internet will become as crucial as learning to read or to write—most of us will probably use the Net in some form at work or at home for the rest of our lives.

So, what are some basic notions necessary to understanding the Internet and how it works? Let me propose briefly eight crucial ideas.

1. *The goal of the Internet is communication—the rapid exchange of information—between people separated from each other.* Electronic mail (e-mail) and the World Wide Web (WWW, or just "the Web") are currently the two most important ways of communicating in cyberspace, even though the Net also uses other formats to do so.

2. *Every piece of information on the Net—every Web page, every graphic, every movie or sound, every e-mail box—has a unique, short, and structured address called a URL (or uniform resource locator).* The URL for this text's Student Resources is:

▶ **http://www.themesandvariations3Ce.nelson. com/student**

This example shows the three elements of a URL: (a) to the left of the double forward slashes (//) is the protocol that tells the Net how to transfer the information. Here it is *http:* which means "use hypertext transfer protocol"—the most frequent protocol on the Net; (b) to the right of the double slashes up to the first forward slash (/) is the *domain name* that indicates which computer on the Net from which to get the information. Here the name of the computer is "www.themesandvariations3Ce. nelson.com"; (c) finally, everything after the first forward slash is called the *pathway*, which indicates where the information is located within that particular computer. Here the pathway comprises the location "student."

3. *The foundation of the Web rests on hypertext links ("hyperlinks"), which are contained within documents (or "Web pages") displayed online.* A hyperlink is a highlighted word, phrase, or graphic image within an onscreen document that refers to some other document or Web page elsewhere. Part of every hyperlink on a computer screen includes the URL for the document that is hidden from view but stored within the computer displaying the document. Users can easily move from one document to another on-screen because of hypertext links and their URLs.

4. *Pay attention to the last element of the domain name (the "domain" itself), which indicates what type of organization sponsors the link.* Important domains are .ca (Canadian websites), .com (commercial businesses), .edu (U.S. colleges and universities), .gc and .gov (Canadian and U.S. federal governmental agencies), and .org (nonprofit organizations).

5. *The Internet is too large for any one individual to know all of the important resources that can be found there.* Users, even experienced ones, often need help to find what they're looking for. In the chapters ahead, you will find many recommended websites that we have carefully selected based on their quality and their suitability for undergraduates. In making these selections, we emphasize quality over quantity and strive to send you to excellent gateway sites that are rich in links to related sites. We hope these suggested Web links help you begin to explore the field of psychology on the Internet.

6. *URLs are relatively unstable.* Many websites are moved or changed each year, as new computer systems are installed to replace older ones. Thus, links or URLs that are good one day may be useless the next.

If you want to check out a recommended website, we suggest that you do so through the *Psychology: Themes and Variations*, third Canadian edition home page at the Nelson Education Ltd website (**http://www .themesandvariations3Ce.nelson.com**). Links to all of the recommended websites will be maintained there, and the Nelson webmaster will periodically update the URLs.

7. *The Web is a worldwide democracy on which anyone can post materials.* Hence, the quality of information found online varies tremendously. Some material is first-rate, up-to-date, and backed up by good research and professional judgment. But a great deal of information online is junk—based on poor or invalid research and filled with many errors. Frankly, some sites are downright wacky, and others are run by hucksters and hate-mongers. Thus, users need to learn to tell the difference between reputable and disreputable Web resources (see Appendix D in the back of the book).

8. *Knowledge has a monetary value.* Although the Internet started out as a noncommercial enterprise where almost everything was free, things have changed swiftly. Owners of knowledge (the holders of commercial "copyrights") usually expect to be paid for sharing what they own over the Net. Thus, many commercial businesses, such as the publishers of academic journals or books, either do not make journal articles available online or expect users to pay some type of fee for accessing their materials. Cognizant of this problem, the publisher of this text has entered into an agreement with a major online resource for magazine and journal articles and other types of information called InfoTrac. Your text may have come bundled with a subscription to InfoTrac, which provides easy access to full-text versions of thousands of periodicals. If you received an InfoTrac subscription with this book, it would be wise to take advantage of this valuable resource.

Some Suggestions for Action

In light of these ideas, how might you approach the Internet? What should you do to make the most of your time online? Let's review some general suggestions for exploring the Internet.

1. *Learn to navigate the Net before you get an assignment requiring you to do so.* If you've never used the Net before, start now to get a feel for it. Consider doing what lots of students do: Ask a friend who knows the Net to work with you directly so you can quickly get personal experience in cyberspace. What if you "hate" computers or they make you uncomfortable? Recent research has shown that students' fears of using computers tend to diminish once they get some practical experience in the course of a single semester.

2. *Learn how the software browser on your computer works.* The two most popular Web browser programs, Netscape Navigator and Microsoft Internet Explorer, are filled with many simple tricks and helpful shortcuts. Ask your friends or the computer consultants at school. Learning the tricks makes Net-based research much easier. (Hint: Find out what happens when you hold down the right-hand mouse button on a PC or the whole button on a Mac once you have the cursor on top of a hyperlink.)

3. *Get to know the different types of online help to find resources on the Web.* These resources currently fall into three general categories: (a) *General guides or directories* like Yahoo! (www.yahoo.ca) are similar to the Yellow Pages for telephones. You ask the online guide to show you what's listed in its directory under a category heading you supply. (b) *Search engines* such as Google (www.google.com or www.google.ca) or AllTheWeb (www.alltheweb.com), and *meta-search engines* such as those listed on York University's website (http://www.library.yorku.ca/ccm/Home/eResources/internetsearchtools.htm) are huge databases that generally collect the names and URLs of millions of pages on the Net, along with many lines of text from these pages. They can be searched by either key words or phrases and provide ranked listings of Web pages that contain the search target words or phrases. (c) *Expert subject guides* such as Russ Dewey's *PsychWeb* (http://www.psychwww.com) or Jeffrey Browndyke's *Neuropsychology Central* (http://www.neuropsychologycentral.com) provide links to online resources in more narrow or specific fields. Volunteer specialists who claim to be experts on the topic select the links.

4. *Check very carefully everything you type online* because even the slightest error in spelling a URL or an e-mail address will cause a failure to retrieve the Web page or to deliver the e-mail message. Remember that computers are stupid and will do exactly and only what you tell them to do. They don't read minds.

Using the Internet in Psychology

Here are five specific suggestions to help students of psychology when using the Net.

1. *Plan what to look for before going online.* Too many psychology students jump right to the Web when they're given a research task, before giving careful thought to what they're looking for. They easily get frustrated because the Web doesn't seem to have anything about the topic. It would be better (a) to think about the subject you are researching and what specifically you want to learn about that

topic, (b) to recall what you already know that relates to the topic, especially psychological concepts and vocabulary words associated with the topic, and (c) to devise a strategy for getting the information you desire. Consult your school's reference library staff or your teachers for suggestions.

2. *Do not rely on the Internet as your principal or only source of data or references in a research project* (especially if you want a good grade). The Net may be easy to use, but your teachers will expect you to cite journal articles, books, and other printed sources more than you cite Internet materials in research. Developing your library skills is essential.

3. *As noted before, don't expect to find many full-text journal articles or other copyrighted commercial materials online for free.* Consult your school's reference librarians about online access to such materials. You are more likely to uncover government reports, specialized technical materials from non-profit organizations, current news and opinion, and general sorts of information rather than findings of specific research studies (although, if the findings were recently in the news, you may find some news reports describing the research).

4. *Learn to recognize the characteristics of a good online resource site.* Good sites have webmasters or editors personally identified by name and affiliation. Such persons may be professionals or staff members at a reputable institution such as a hospital or university. These sites tend to provide a broad set of resources, are balanced and reasonably objective in their content, and avoid sensational or one-sided viewpoints. Reputable sites tend not to promote specific products or services for money—or, if they do, they acknowledge that there are other resources that people may want to consider. The challenge of evaluating the quality of online resources is such an important skill for students to master that we have included a much more detailed discussion of this matter in Appendix D.

5. *If you contact anyone online for help, be courteous.* Introduce yourself as you would if you were standing in a faculty member's office. Give your name, your school, and a full statement of what help you are asking for and what you've tried to do that hasn't worked. Don't demand that someone help you. Be sure you've done adequate research on your own before contacting an expert on the Web. And don't be surprised if your request for help is turned down by a webmaster or editor. Frankly, he or she has already done a lot of volunteer work by editing the site online.

I hope some of these ideas and suggestions help. The Internet offers an awesome array of learning resources related to psychology. Welcome to an exciting new world of discovery.

Psychology

THEMES & VARIATIONS

CHAPTER 1

The Evolution of Psychology

© Rebecca Atkins, York University

According to her mother, Suman, Reena Virk was a troubled 14-year-old girl who desperately wanted to fit in. Reena had a difficult time living in Victoria, British Columbia. She rebelled against parental authority and had been bullied frequently. Things were difficult but somehow she managed. On the night of November 14, 1997, things took a more serious turn. According to testimony at the original trial, Reena had wanted to be part of Kelly Ellard's group—Reena and Kelly were acquainted but were not friends. Reena was lured out the night of November 14 to be with members of the group (Carmichael, 2005). That night, she was swarmed by the group, which consisted of seven girls aged 14–16 and one male aged 16. She was beaten repeatedly and burned with cigarettes (Godfrey, 2005). She managed to escape from them but was dragged by two of the group members to a nearby waterway. Her body was found one week later by police divers a kilometre or so away from where she was beaten.

Two members of the group, Warren Glowatski and Kelly Ellard, were convicted of second-degree murder (Ten-Year Anniversary, 2007). After a series of trials, Ellard was sentenced on July 7, 2005, to life in prison with no chance of parole for seven years. Ellard appealed her conviction, and in September 2008, the British Columbia Court of Appeal granted her appeal for a fourth trial (Fong, 2008). In a later hearing, the Supreme Court upheld her conviction and she was denied a new trial. She is now serving her sentence (Armstrong & Makin, 2009; Reena Virk's Killer, 2010). Glowatski, now 26, was convicted in 1999 and was granted day parole in June 2007 (Tearful Killer, 2007). Reena Virk's parents supported his application for parole, visited him in prison, and attended his parole hearing (Tearful Killer, 2007). Unlike Ellard, Warren Glowatski has expressed remorse for his role in the assault and murder. After the parole hearing, Reena's mother said, "Today I think we see a young man who has taken responsibility for his actions and is trying to amend the wrong that he did" (Tearful Killer, 2007). Glowatski is now trying to put his life back together, going to school, and trying to find a job, although he admits that the transition back to society is difficult (Reena Virk's Killer, 2010). Reena Virk's parents have tried to move on and Manjit Virk, Reena's father, has written a very moving book about this daughter's short life (Virk, 2009).

The circumstances surrounding Reena's death received national attention in Canada. Canadians were outraged by the events. Reena's life and death, along with those of other high-profile bullying casualties such as Dawn-Marie Wesley of Mission, British Columbia, have focused society's attention on bullying and related violent acts. The circumstances surrounding Dawn-Marie's suicide were the subject of Lynn Glazier's 2004 documentary *It's a Girl's World*. The film was broadcast nationally in Canada and provoked considerable debate and reflection. What was particularly noteworthy to many Canadians was that in both of these cases, most of the perpetrators were young girls. Bullying by means of physical aggression had been thought to be the province of young males. These and other events made it clear that bullying could quickly escalate to physical harm and that while boys might be the more frequent physical aggressors, girls were not averse to employing physical violence in their attempts to intimidate others. In fact, bullying episodes involving girls are on the rise in Canada compared to those involving boys (Craig, 2009; Molcho, 2009). This narrowing of the gender gap is also reflected in the increased number of adult women charged in Canada with violent crime (Statistics Canada, 2008a). While the group members in the Virk case were brought to justice, countless bullying episodes go unreported, cases in which the victims, often very young children, suffer alone.

These and similar high-profile events motivate and energize researchers in psychology to attempt to document and understand such acts in the hope of reducing their occurrence. Surveys have indicated that this interest has increased due to evidence of a link between traditional bullying and electronic bullying (Raskauskas & Stolz, 2007) and evidence that bullying rates in Canada are exceptionally high compared to other countries (Javed, 2010). Canadian researchers are at the forefront of the research effort examining bullying. Some, such as Marlene Moretti of Simon Fraser University (e.g., Moretti, Jackson & Obsuth, in press; Greeves and Moretti, in press), Tracy Vaillancourt of McMaster University (Vaillancourt et al., in press), Debra Pepler of York University (Pepler, Craig, Jiang, & Connolly, 2008), and Wendy Craig of Queen's University (e.g., Pepler & Craig, in press), have made important contributions to the growing scientific literature on bullying. You will read more about their research and their advice for children and parents regarding bullying later in the text. We will summarize their findings and their suggestions regarding what to do about such episodes.

The Evolution of Psychology

In this chapter, as in all chapters, we include a Featured Study that gives you a look at interesting and relevant real-life research and shows you how psychologists conduct and report their research. The Featured Study in this chapter, on page 19, is by Craig and Pepler (1997) on bullying in a school-yard. More information on bullying and what to do about it can be found on the many websites that have been developed since Reena Virk's murder in 1997 (e.g., http://www.bullyfreealberta.ca, http://www.bullying.org). Researchers in this area have established PREVNet, a network of researchers and organizations dedicated to promoting healthy relationships and eradicating bullying (Craig & Pepler, 2007). If you are interested in this topic, you are encouraged to visit the PREVNet website.

One of the reasons that students and researchers are drawn to psychology is that it has much to offer in the analysis and possible prevention of such social problems. Psychologists seek to describe, explain, and predict the occurrence of such behaviour. By the rigorous application of scientific methods, psychologists can often offer possible explanations for this behaviour, as well as suggestions about what to do about it immediately in order to cope with it and prevent its occurrence in the future.

As you begin your course in introductory psychology and start reading this textbook, you may be wondering, "What is psychology?" Your initial answer to this question is likely to bear little resemblance to the picture of psychology that will emerge as you work your way through this book. Many students initially associate psychology with the study of psychological disorders or abnormal psychology. While abnormal psychology is an important component, psychology is about much more than that.

When we took our first courses in psychology, we were surprised to learn that psychology is about a great many things other than abnormal psychology. It's also about how people are able to perceive colour, how hunger is regulated by the brain, whether chimpanzees can use language to communicate, what causes bullying and aggression and how you can protect yourself, and a multitude of other topics. We are confident that you will come away from your study of this text with a new appreciation for the subject matter of psychology and what it can do for you. Psychology is practical, but it is more than that—it is a way of thinking.

We are all exposed to claims about psychological issues. You see reports in the newspapers and on television programs. In some cases, the sources are quite authoritative, such as CBC's *The Nature of Things* with David Suzuki. Sometimes the validity of the material is less clear. Many truisms about behaviour come to be widely believed even though they really are misconceptions or myths. These myths include such ideas as "people use only 10 percent of their brains," "most mentally ill people are violent," and "electroconvulsive (shock) therapy is a physically dangerous and brutal treatment" (Lillenfeld, Lynn, Ruscio, & Beyerstein, 2010). These are misconceptions, as you will learn in the upcoming chapters.

THE CANADIAN PRESS/Adrian Wyld

CP Photo

Modern psychology ranges widely in its investigations, looking at divergent topics such as work, sleep, stress, trauma, and brain function. It covers situations in which you work as a member of a group, such as an Olympic gold medal-winning hockey team, and situations in which individual motivation is key. As you progress through this book, you will see that the range and diversity of psychology's subject matter are enormous.

We hope that as a result of reading this text, you will be in a position to think critically about such matters and motivated to approach psychological issues in the same way that a psychologist would. As a science, psychology demands that researchers ask precise questions about such issues and that they test their ideas through systematic observation. Psychology provides a way of building knowledge that is relatively accurate and dependable. As you will see in this text, psychologists study an amazing variety of topics.

Mental illness; rats running in mazes; the physiology of hunger; the mysteries of love, creativity, and prejudice—what ties all of these subjects together in a single discipline? How did psychology come to be so diverse? Why is it so different from what most people expect? If psychology is a social science, why do psychologists study subjects such as brain chemistry and the physiological basis of vision? To answer these questions, we begin our introduction to psychology by retracing its development. By seeing how psychology grew and changed, you will discover why it has the shape it has today.

After our journey into psychology's past, we will examine a formal definition of psychology. We'll also look at psychology as it is today—a sprawling, multifaceted science and profession (Brock, 2006). To help keep psychology's diversity in perspective, the chapter concludes with a discussion of seven unifying themes that will serve as connecting threads in the chapters to come. Finally, in the chapter's Personal Application, we'll review research that gives insights on how to be an effective student, and in the Critical Thinking Application, we'll discuss how critical thinking skills can be enhanced.

From Speculation to Science: How Psychology Developed

Psychology's story is one of people groping toward a better understanding of themselves. As psychology has evolved, its focus, methods, and explanatory models have changed (Schachter, 1996). In this section, we'll look at how psychology has developed from philosophical speculations about the mind and early work in physiology into a modern science. A pictorial overview of the highlights of psychology's history can be found on pages 24–25.

Philosophy, Physiology, and Psychology

The term *psychology* comes from two Greek words, *psyche*, meaning the soul, and *logos*, referring to the study of a subject. These two Greek root words were first put together to define a topic of study in the 16th century, when *psyche* was used to refer to the soul, spirit, or mind, as distinguished from the body (Boring, 1966). Not until the early 18th century did the term *psychology* gain more than rare usage among scholars. By that time it had acquired its literal meaning, "the study of the mind."

Of course, people have always wondered about the mysteries of the mind and human behaviour. In that sense, psychology is as old as the human race. But it was only a little over a century ago that psychology emerged as a scientific discipline.

Scholars interested in the history of psychology often point to developments in philosophy and physiology as influencing the course of early psychology (Green & Groff, 2003; Pickren & Rutherford, 2010). Ancient Greek philosophers such as Socrates (469–399 B.C.E.), Plato (427–347 B.C.E.), and Aristotle (385–322 B.C.E.) considered and debated issues of relevance to psychology, including such subjects as the separation of mind and body and whether knowledge is inborn (nativism) or gained through experience (empiricism) (Hothersall, 1995). Many of their early ideas in one form or another are still with us today. Aristotle's theory of memory, for example, although proposed hundreds of years ago, is still foundational to many contemporary theories of memory (Hothersall, 1995). His conception of memory suggested that memories are the result of three principles of association; similarity, contrast, and contiguity. We will see related ideas when we consider the nature of memory in Chapter 7. The impact of philosophy on the development of ideas about mind, behaviour, and human nature continued as classic philosophy itself developed through the periods of Renaissance (e.g., René Descartes [1596–1650]), post-Renaissance (e.g., Thomas Hobbes [1588–1679] and John Locke [1632–1704]), and Associationism (e.g., David Hume [1711–1776] and John Stuart Mill [1806–1873]). Descartes famously argued for the dualism of mind and body (Goodwin, 1999), that the mind and body were

PREVIEW QUESTIONS

► What were Wundt's and Hall's key ideas and accomplishments?

► What were the chief tenets of structuralism and functionalism?

► What was the main idea underlying behaviourism?

separate and fundamentally different, with the mind (soul) being immaterial and the "province of God" (Pickren & Rutherford, 2010, p. 5). He also believed that processes and functions such as memory, perception, dreaming, and emotions were "properties" of the body, and thus open to being understood in naturalistic terms. Many see this as being one of his most important legacies to psychology, the idea that humans are part of nature and are understandable in those terms.

As ideas in philosophy concerning the nature of mind and behaviour continued to develop, other disciplines, such as the study of experimental physiology and medicine, left their own marks on the later development of psychology. Beginning with William Harvey's empirical demonstration in 1682 of the fact that blood circulation was a function of the operation of the heart, physiologists and physicians such as Robert Whyte (1714–1766), Franz Gall (1758–1828), Paul Broca (1824–1880), and Johannes Müller (1801–1858) showed that important insights could be gained into the workings of the body and brain through the application of systematic, empirical methods. One of Müller's students, Hermann von Helmholtz (1821–1894), began one of the first experimental examinations of human reaction time. He argued for the separation (Pickren & Rutherford, 2010) of sensation and perception as topics of study. We will discuss Helmholtz and his contribution to our understanding of sensation in Chapter 4.

Wilhelm Wundt
1832–1920

"Physiology informs us about those life phenomena that we perceive by our external senses. In psychology, the person looks upon himself as from within and tries to explain the interrelations of those processes that this internal observation discloses."

Although all of this work was important to the eventual form of psychology, many date the emergence of psychology as a distinct discipline to the work of Wilhelm Wundt (1832–1920).

A New Science Is Born: The Contributions of Wundt and Hall 1a

As just discussed, psychology's intellectual parents were the disciplines of philosophy and physiology. By the 1870s, a small number of scholars in both fields were actively exploring questions about the mind. How are bodily sensations turned into a mental awareness of the outside world? Are people's perceptions of the world accurate reflections of reality? How do mind and body interact? The philosophers and physiologists who were interested in the mind viewed such questions as fascinating issues within their respective fields. It was a German professor, Wilhelm Wundt, who eventually changed this view. Wundt mounted a campaign to make psychology an independent discipline rather than a stepchild of philosophy or physiology. Wundt's pioneering work had an enormous impact on the development of psychology (Wong, 2009).

The time and place were right for Wundt's appeal. German universities were in a healthy period of expansion, so resources were available for new disciplines. Furthermore, the intellectual climate favoured the scientific approach that Wundt advocated. Hence, his proposals were well received by the academic community. In 1879, Wundt succeeded in establishing the first formal laboratory for research in psychology at the University of Leipzig. In deference to this landmark event, historians have christened 1879 as psychology's "date of birth." Soon afterward, in 1881, Wundt established the first journal devoted to publishing research on psychology. All in all, Wundt's campaign was so successful that today he is widely characterized as the founder of psychology.

Wundt's conception of psychology was influential for decades. Borrowing from his training in physiology, Wundt (1874) declared that the new psychology should be a science modelled after fields such as physics and chemistry. What was the subject matter of the new science? According to Wundt, psychology's primary focus was consciousness—the awareness of immediate experience. Thus, psychology became the scientific study of conscious

The establishment of the first research laboratory in psychology by Wilhelm Wundt (far right) marked the birth of psychology as a modern science.

Archives of the History of American Psychology, The Center for the History of Psychology—University of Akron

experience. This orientation kept psychology focused on the mind and mental processes. But it demanded that the methods psychologists used to investigate the mind be as scientific as those of chemists and physicists.

Wundt was a tireless, dedicated scholar who generated an estimated 54 000 pages of books and articles in his career (Bringmann & Balk, 1992). Outstanding young scholars came to Leipzig to study under Wundt. Many of Wundt's students then fanned out across Germany and North America, establishing the research laboratories that formed the basis for the new, independent science of psychology. Indeed, it was in North America that Wundt's new science grew by leaps and bounds.

Between 1883 and 1893, some 24 new psychological research laboratories sprang up in the United States and Canada at the schools shown in Figure 1.1 (Benjamin, 2000). Many of the laboratories were started by Wundt's students or by his students' students.

G. Stanley Hall (1846–1924), who studied briefly with Wundt, was a particularly important contributor to the rapid growth of psychology in the United States. Toward the end of the 19th century, Hall reeled off a series of "firsts" for American psychology. To begin with, he established America's first research laboratory in psychology at Johns Hopkins University in 1883. Four years later, he launched America's first psychology journal. Furthermore, in 1892, he was the driving force behind the establishment of the American Psychological Association (APA) and

was elected its first president. Today, the APA is the world's largest organization devoted to the advancement of psychology, with over 154 000 members and affiliates. Hall never envisioned such a vast membership when he and 26 others set up their new organization. Two early psychologists from the University of Toronto, James Mark Baldwin and James Gibson Hume, were among those who attended meetings designed to establish the American Psychological Association (Green, 2004; Hoff, 1992). Psychology in Canada and some of the figures who were important in the establishment of it will be discussed later in this chapter.

Exactly why Americans took to psychology so quickly is hard to say. Perhaps it was because America's relatively young universities were more open to new disciplines than were the older, more tradition-bound universities in Europe. In any case, although psychology was born in Germany, it blossomed into adolescence in America. Like many adolescents, however, the young science was about to enter a period of turbulence and turmoil.

The Battle of the "Schools" Begins: Structuralism versus Functionalism

While reading about how psychology became a science, you might have imagined that psychologists became a unified group of scholars who busily added

WEB LINK 1.2

History of Psychology
This site, maintained by the Department of Psychology at Athabasca University, contains links to many articles and sites focusing on the history of psychology.

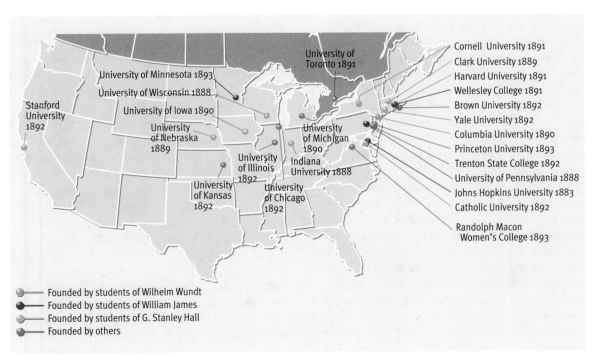

Founded by students of Wilhelm Wundt
Founded by students of William James
Founded by students of G. Stanley Hall
Founded by others

FIGURE 1.1

Early research laboratories in North America.

This map highlights the location and year of founding of the first 24 psychological research labs established in North American colleges and universities. As the colour coding shows, a great many of these labs were founded by the students of Wilhelm Wundt, G. Stanley Hall, and William James.

Source: Based on Garvey, 1929; Hilgard, 1987.

William James
1842–1910

"It is just this free water of consciousness that psychologists resolutely overlook."

WEB LINK 1.3

Mind and Body: René Descartes to William James
Designed originally to celebrate psychology's first century as an independent discipline, this online exhibition traces three historical themes: the mind–body problem posed in the 17th century by philosopher René Descartes, the rise of experimental psychology, and the beginnings of psychology in America.

new discoveries to an uncontested store of "facts." In reality, no science works that way. Competing schools of thought exist in most scientific disciplines. Sometimes the disagreements among these schools are sharp. Such diversity in thought is natural and often stimulates enlightening debate. In psychology, the first two major schools of thought, structuralism and functionalism, were entangled in the field's first great intellectual battle.

Structuralism emerged through the leadership of Edward Titchener, an Englishman who immigrated to the United States in 1892 and taught for decades at Cornell University. Although Titchener earned his degree in Wundt's Leipzig laboratory and expressed great admiration for Wundt's work, he brought his own version of Wundt's psychology to America (Hilgard, 1987; Thorne & Henley, 1997). *Structuralism* was based on the notion that the task of psychology is to analyze consciousness into its basic elements and investigate how these elements are related. Just as physicists were studying how matter is made up of basic particles, the structuralists wanted to identify and examine the fundamental components of conscious experience, such as sensations, feelings, and images.

Although the structuralists explored many questions, most of their work concerned sensation and perception in vision, hearing, and touch. To examine the contents of consciousness, the structuralists depended on the method of *introspection, the careful, systematic self-observation of one's own conscious experience.* As practised by the structuralists, introspection required training to make the subject—the person being studied—more objective and more aware. Once trained, subjects were typically exposed to auditory tones, optical illusions, and visual stimuli under carefully controlled and systematically varied conditions and were asked to analyze what they experienced. Limitations associated with the use of introspection were a factor that contributed to the demise of structuralism. If you depend solely on an individual's reflection to document a phenomenon, there is no independent objective evaluation of that claim.

The functionalists took a different view of psychology's task. *Functionalism was based on the belief that psychology should investigate the function or purpose of consciousness, rather than its structure.* The chief impetus for the emergence of functionalism was the work of William James (1842–1910), a brilliant American scholar (and brother of novelist Henry James). James's formal training was in medicine. However, he did not find medicine to be intellectually challenging, and he felt he was too sickly to pursue a medical practice (Ross, 1991). Hence, when

an opportunity arose in 1872, he joined the faculty of Harvard University to pursue a less arduous career in academia. Medicine's loss proved to be psychology's gain, as James quickly became an intellectual giant in the field. James's landmark book, *Principles of Psychology* (1890), became standard reading for generations of psychologists and is perhaps the most influential text in the history of psychology (Weiten & Wight, 1992).

James's thinking illustrates how psychology, like any field, is deeply embedded in a network of cultural and intellectual influences (Green, 2009). James had been impressed with Charles Darwin's concept of *natural selection* (1859, 1871). According to the principle of *natural selection,* heritable characteristics that provide a survival or reproductive advantage are more likely than alternative characteristics to be passed on to subsequent generations and thus come to be "selected" over time. This cornerstone notion of Darwin's evolutionary theory suggested that the typical characteristics of a species must serve some purpose. Applying this idea to humans, James (1890) noted that consciousness obviously is an important characteristic of our species. Hence, he contended that psychology should investigate the functions rather than the *structure* of consciousness.

James also argued that the structuralists' approach missed the real nature of conscious experience. Consciousness, he argued, consists of a continuous *flow* of thoughts. In analyzing consciousness into its "elements," the structuralists were looking at static points in that flow. James wanted to understand the flow itself, which he called the *stream of consciousness.*

Whereas structuralists naturally gravitated to the laboratory, functionalists were more interested in how people adapt their behaviour to the demands of the real world around them. This practical slant led the functionalists to introduce new subjects into psychology. Instead of focusing on sensation and perception, functionalists such as James McKeen Cattell and John Dewey began to investigate mental testing, patterns of development in children, the effectiveness of educational practices, and behavioural differences between the sexes. These new topics may have played a role in attracting the first women into the field of psychology, some of whom played critical roles in the developing science of psychology. Margaret Floy Washburn was the first woman in the United States to receive a Ph.D. in psychology. She was the author of the book *The Animal Mind* (1908), which served as a precursor to behaviourism, a theoretical approach discussed on page 7. Another pioneering female psychologist,

Leta Hollingworth, did important work on children's intelligence and was influential in debunking some of the theories current at the time that were proposed to explain why women were "inferior" to men. Mary Whiton Calkins, who studied with William James, went on to become the first woman to serve as president of the American Psychological Association. You can learn more about women in psychology by visiting the American Psychological Society's Web page for the Society for the Psychology of Women Heritage Site (http://www.psych.yorku.ca/femhop). The site is maintained by York University psychologist Alexandra Rutherford.

The impassioned advocates of structuralism and functionalism saw themselves as fighting for high stakes: the definition and future direction of the new science of psychology. Their war of ideas continued energetically for many years. Who won? Most historians give the edge to functionalism. Although both schools of thought gradually faded away, functionalism fostered the development of two descendants that have dominated modern psychology: behaviourism and applied psychology.

Watson Alters Psychology's Course as Behaviourism Makes Its Debut

The debate between structuralism and functionalism was only the prelude to other fundamental controversies in psychology. In the early 1900s, another major school of thought appeared that dramatically altered the course of psychology (Todd & Morris, 1994). Founded by John B. Watson (1878–1958), *behaviourism is a theoretical orientation based on the premise that scientific psychology should study only observable behaviour.* It is important to understand what a radical change this definition represents. Watson (1913, 1919) was proposing that psychologists abandon the study of consciousness altogether and focus exclusively on behaviours that they could observe directly. In essence, he was redefining what scientific psychology should be about.

Why did Watson argue for such a fundamental shift in direction? Because to him, the power of the scientific method rested on the idea of verifiability. In principle, scientific claims can always be verified (or disproved) by anyone who is able and willing to make the required observations. However, this power depends on studying things that can be observed objectively. Otherwise, the advantage of using the scientific approach—replacing vague speculation and personal opinion with reliable, exact

knowledge—is lost. For Watson, mental processes were not a proper subject for scientific study because they are ultimately private events. After all, no one can see or touch another's thoughts. Consequently, if psychology were to be a science, it would have to give up consciousness as its subject matter and become instead the *science of behaviour.*

Behaviour refers to any overt (observable) response or activity by an organism. Watson asserted that psychologists could study anything that people do or say—shopping, playing chess, eating, complimenting a friend—but they could not study scientifically the thoughts, wishes, and feelings that might accompany these observable behaviours.

Watson's radical reorientation of psychology did not end with his redefinition of its subject matter. He also staked out a rather extreme position on one of psychology's oldest and most fundamental questions: the issue of nature versus nurture. This age-old debate is concerned with whether behaviour is determined mainly by genetic inheritance ("nature") or by environment and experience ("nurture"). To oversimplify, the question is this: Is a great concert pianist or a master criminal born, or made? Watson argued that each is made, not born. In other words, he downplayed the importance of heredity, maintaining that behaviour is governed primarily by the environment. Indeed, he boldly claimed:

> Give me a dozen healthy infants, well-formed, and my own specified world to bring them up in and I'll guarantee to take any one at random and train him to become any type of specialist I might select—doctor, lawyer, artist, merchant-chief, and yes, even beggar-man and thief, regardless of his talents, penchants, tendencies, abilities, vocations and race of his ancestors. I am going beyond my facts and I admit it, but so have the advocates of the contrary and they have been doing it for many thousands of years. (Watson, 1924, p. 82)

For obvious reasons, Watson's tongue-in-cheek challenge was never put to a test. Although this widely cited quotation overstated and oversimplified Watson's views on the nature–nurture issue (Todd & Morris, 1992), his writings contributed to the strong environmental slant that became associated with behaviourism (Horowitz, 1992).

The behaviourists eventually came to view psychology's mission as an attempt to relate overt behaviours ("responses") to observable events in the environment ("stimuli"). A *stimulus* is any detectable input from the environment. Stimuli can range from light and sound waves to such complex inputs

WEB LINK 1.4

History and Philosophy of Psychology Web Resources
Professor Christopher Green of York University has assembled a wide range of Web-based materials relating to psychology's theoretical and historical past, including a collection of sites focused on specific individuals. Web pages devoted to key figures mentioned in this chapter (such as Mary Whiton Calkins, William James, B. F. Skinner, and Margaret Floy Washburn) can be accessed here. It contains lists of and links to hundreds of classic papers in psychology. It has been in operation since the late 1990s and to date has received over 10 million hits. If you need a classic important paper, you will likely find it here. It even includes a link to the floor plans and a description of the first experimental psychology laboratory established in Canada (in 1891 at the University of Toronto). Christopher Green has also written and produced a series of podcasts on the topic.

**John B. Watson
1878–1958**

"The time seems to have come when psychology must discard all references to consciousness."

as the words on this page, advertisements on TV, or sarcastic remarks by a friend. Because the behaviourists investigated stimulus–response relationships, the behavioural approach is often referred to as *stimulus–response (S–R) psychology*.

Although it met resistance and skepticism in some quarters, Watson's behavioural point of view gradually took hold (Samelson, 1981, 1994). Actually, psychology had already been edging away imperceptibly from the study of consciousness toward the study of behaviour for two decades before Watson made his case for behaviourism (Leahey, 1992). The gradual emergence of behaviourism was partly attributable to an important discovery made around the turn of the last century by Ivan Pavlov, a Russian physiologist. As you'll learn in Chapter 6, Pavlov (1906) showed that dogs could be trained to salivate in response to an auditory stimulus such as a tone. This deceptively simple demonstration provided insight into how stimulus–response bonds are formed. Such bonds were exactly what behaviourists wanted to investigate, so Pavlov's discovery paved the way for their work.

Behaviourism's stimulus–response approach contributed to the rise of animal research in psychology. Having deleted consciousness from their scope of concern, behaviourists no longer needed to study human subjects who could report on their mental processes. Many psychologists thought that animals would make better research subjects, anyway. One key reason was that experimental research is often more productive if experimenters can exert considerable *control* over their subjects. Otherwise, too many complicating factors enter into the picture and contaminate the experiment. Obviously, a researcher can exert much more control over a laboratory rat or pigeon than over a human subject, who arrives at a lab with years of uncontrolled experience and who will probably insist on going home at night. Thus, the discipline that had begun its life a few decades earlier as the study of the mind now found itself heavily involved in the study of simple responses made by laboratory animals.

Although Watson's views shaped the evolution of psychology for many decades, his ideas did not go unchallenged. In Germany, opposition came from an emerging school of thought called *Gestalt* psychology. The Gestalt theorists, who were primarily concerned with perception (we'll discuss their ideas in Chapter 4), argued that psychology should continue to study conscious experience rather than overt behaviour. Another alternative conception of psychology emerged from Austria, where an obscure

concept **check 1.1**

Understanding the Implications of Major Theories: Wundt, James, and Watson

Check your understanding of the implications of some of the major theories reviewed in this chapter by indicating who is likely to have made each of the statements quoted below. Choose from the following theorists: (a) Wilhelm Wundt, (b) William James, and (c) John B. Watson. You'll find the answers in Appendix A in the back of the book.

_____ 1. "Our conclusion is that we have no real evidence of the inheritance of traits. I would feel perfectly confident in the ultimately favourable outcome of careful upbringing of a healthy, well-formed baby born of a long line of crooks, murderers and thieves, and prostitutes."

_____ 2. "The book which I present to the public is an attempt to mark out a new domain of science.... The new discipline rests upon anatomical and physiological foundations.... The experimental treatment of psychological problems must be pronounced from every point of view to be in its first beginnings."

_____ 3. "Consciousness, then, does not appear to itself chopped up in bits. Such words as 'chain' or 'train' do not describe it fitly.... It is nothing jointed; it flows. A 'river' or 'stream' are the metaphors by which it is most naturally described."

physician named Sigmund Freud had been contemplating the mysteries of unconscious mental processes. (We'll look at Freud's ideas in the next section.)

Watson himself ended up watching the field's progress from the sidelines. Due to a heavily publicized divorce scandal in 1920, Watson was forced to resign from Johns Hopkins University (Buckley, 1994). Bitterly disappointed, he left academia at the age of 42, never to return. Psychology's loss proved to be the business world's gain, as Watson went on to become an innovative, successful advertising executive (Brewer, 1991; Coon, 1994). The advertising industry was just emerging as a national force in the 1920s and Watson quickly became one of its most prominent practitioners at the J. Walter Thompson agency. He pioneered fear appeals, testimonials, selling the "prestige" of products, and the promotion of style over substance—all of which remain basic principles in modern marketing (Buckley, 1982). Moreover, "through an enormous output of books, magazine articles, and radio broadcasts he was able to establish himself as the public spokesman for the profession of psychology and an expert on subjects ranging from child-rearing to economics. In effect, Watson became the first 'pop' psychologist" (Buckley, 1982, p. 217). So, ironically, Watson became the public face of the discipline that had banished him from its mainstream.

Freud Brings the Unconscious into the Picture

Sigmund Freud (1856–1939) was an Austrian physician who early in his career dreamed of achieving fame by making an important discovery. His determination was such that in medical school he dissected 400 male eels to prove for the first time that they had testes. His work with eels did not make him famous, but his subsequent work with people did. Indeed, his theories made him one of the most controversial intellectual figures of modern times.

Freud's approach to psychology (1900/1953) grew out of his efforts to treat mental disorders. In his medical practice, Freud treated people troubled by psychological problems such as irrational fears, obsessions, and anxieties with an innovative procedure he called *psychoanalysis* (described in detail in Chapter 15). Decades of experience probing into his patients' lives provided much of the inspiration for Freud's theory. He also gathered material by looking inward and examining his own anxieties, conflicts, and desires.

His work with patients and his own self-exploration persuaded Freud of the existence of what he called the *unconscious*. According to Freud, the *unconscious* contains thoughts, memories, and desires that are well below the surface of conscious awareness but that nonetheless exert great influence on behaviour. Freud based his concept of the unconscious on a variety of observations. For instance, he noticed that seemingly meaningless slips of the tongue (such as "I decided to take a summer school curse") often appeared to reveal a person's true feelings. He also noted that his patients' dreams often seemed to express important feelings they were unaware of. Knitting these and other observations together, Freud eventually concluded that psychological disturbances are largely caused by personal conflicts existing at an unconscious level. More generally, his *psychoanalytic theory* attempts to explain personality, motivation, and mental disorders by focusing on unconscious determinants of behaviour.

Sigmund Freud 1856–1939

"The unconscious is the true psychical reality; in its innermost nature it is as much unknown to us as the reality of the external world."

Courtesy of the Clark University Archives

A portrait taken at the famous Clark University psychology conference, September 1909. Pictured are (seated, left to right) Sigmund Freud, G. Stanley Hall, and Carl Jung, and (standing) three of Freud's students and associates: Abraham Brill, Ernest Jones, and Sandor Ferenczi.

Freud's concept of the unconscious was not entirely new (Lothane, 2006). However, it was a major departure from the prevailing belief that people are fully aware of the forces affecting their behaviour. In arguing that behaviour is governed by unconscious forces, Freud made the disconcerting suggestion that people are not masters of their own minds. Other aspects of Freud's theory also stirred up debate. For instance, he proposed that behaviour is greatly influenced by how people cope with their sexual urges. At a time when people were far less comfortable discussing sexual issues than they are today, even scientists were offended and scandalized by Freud's emphasis on sex. Small wonder, then, that Freud was soon engulfed in controversy.

In part because of its controversial nature, Freud's theory gained influence only very slowly, but where it did get noticed, it had considerable impact (Gitre, 2010). However, he gradually won acceptance within medicine, attracting prominent followers such as Carl Jung and Alfred Adler. Important public recognition from psychology came in 1909, when G. Stanley Hall invited Freud to give a series of lectures at Clark University in Massachusetts.

By 1920, psychoanalytic theory was widely known around the world, but it continued to meet with considerable resistance in psychology (Fancher, 2000). Why? The main reason was that it conflicted with the spirit of the times in psychology. Many psychologists were becoming uncomfortable with their earlier focus on conscious experience and were turning to the less murky subject of observable behaviour. If they felt that conscious experience was inaccessible to scientific observation, you can imagine how they felt about trying to study unconscious experience. Most psychologists contemptuously viewed psychoanalytic theory as unscientific speculation that would eventually fade away (Hornstein, 1992).

They turned out to be wrong. Psychoanalytic ideas steadily gained credence in the culture at large, influencing thought in medicine, the arts, and literature (Rieber, 1998). According to Hornstein (1992), by the 1940s, "Psychoanalysis was becoming so popular that it threatened to eclipse psychology entirely" (p. 258). Thus, the widespread popular acceptance of psychoanalytic theory essentially forced psychologists to apply their scientific methods to the topics Freud had studied: personality, motivation, and abnormal behaviour and therapy (Shedler, 2010). As they turned to these topics, many of them saw merit in some of Freud's notions (Rosenzweig, 1985). Although psychoanalytic theory continued to generate heated debate, it survived to become an influential theoretical perspective. Today, many psychoanalytic concepts have filtered into the mainstream of psychology (Pincus, 2006; Westen, Gabbard, & Ortigo, 2008).

Skinner Questions Free Will as Behaviourism Flourishes

While psychoanalytic thought was slowly gaining a foothold within psychology, a young psychologist at Harvard, B. F. Skinner (1904–1990), was emerging as a central figure in behaviourism and the history of psychology. Skinner had set out to be a writer but concluded that he had "nothing important to say" (1967, p. 395). However, he had many important things to say within psychology about behaviour. His impact on society was significant; in fact, he became arguably the most famous scientist of his time (Rutherford, 2009).

Although Skinner was influenced by Watson's methodological behaviourism and by Pavlov's work on conditioned reflexes, he eventually developed a system based on his own philosophy of *radical behaviourism* that represented a departure from earlier forms of behaviourism and neo-behaviourism (Rutherford, 2009).

Skinner did not deny the existence of internal, mental events but he redefined them as private events and did not think that they should be given special status when explaining behaviour. Skinner noted that these private events are much more difficult to

B. F. Skinner created considerable controversy when he asserted that free will is an illusion.

study and much of his own science of behaviour is based on public observable events. Although they could be studied scientifically, he believed that there was little need to do so.

According to Skinner, if the stimulus of food is followed by the response of eating, we can fully describe what is happening without making any guesses about whether the animal is experiencing hunger. Like Watson, Skinner also emphasized how environmental factors mould behaviour. Although he repeatedly acknowledged that an organism's behaviour is influenced by its biological endowment, he argued that psychology could understand and predict behaviour adequately without resorting to physiological explanations (Delprato & Midgley, 1992).

The fundamental principle of behaviour documented by Skinner is deceptively simple: Organisms tend to repeat responses that lead to positive outcomes, and they tend not to repeat responses that lead to neutral or negative outcomes. Despite its simplicity, this principle turns out to be quite powerful. Working primarily with laboratory rats and pigeons, Skinner showed that he could exert remarkable control over the behaviour of animals by manipulating the outcomes of their responses. He was even able to train animals to perform unnatural behaviours. For example, he once trained some pigeons to play ping-pong! Skinner's followers eventually showed that the principles uncovered in their animal research could be applied to complex human behaviours as well. Behavioural principles are now widely used in factories, schools, prisons, mental hospitals, and a variety of other settings (see Chapter 6).

Skinner's ideas had repercussions that went far beyond the debate among psychologists about what they should study. Skinner spelled out the full implications of his findings in his book *Beyond Freedom and Dignity* (1971). There, he asserted that all behaviour is fully governed by external stimuli. In other words, your behaviour is determined in predictable ways by lawful principles, just as the flight of an arrow is governed by the laws of physics. Thus, if you believe that your actions are the result of conscious decisions, you're wrong. According to Skinner, people are controlled by their environment, not by themselves. In short, Skinner arrived at the conclusion that *free will is an illusion*.

As you can readily imagine, such a disconcerting view of human nature was not universally acclaimed. Like Freud, Skinner was the target of harsh criticism. Much of this criticism stemmed from misinterpretations of his ideas that were disseminated in the popular press (Rutherford, 2000). For example, his analysis of free will was often misconstrued as an attack on the concept of a free society—which it was not—and he was often mistakenly condemned for advocating an undemocratic "scientific police state" (Dinsmoor, 1992).

There is no doubt that Skinner significantly impacted the developing field of psychology. But his influence went beyond academia. Some of his books topped the popular bestsellers' lists. According to Alexandra Rutherford, a Canadian psychologist specializing in the history of psychology (Rutherford, 2006), at the height of his influence, his was a household name. Coverage of Skinner appeared in magazines and newspapers, and on radio and television. He himself popularized some of his ideas by writing for mass consumer magazines. For example, he wrote an article on the topic of the "Baby in a Box" for the *Ladies' Home Journal* in 1947. His development of mechanical teaching machines was widely covered by the popular press (Rutherford, 2004). He also published a fictional account of the application of his principles of operant conditioning to produce a utopian society in his book *Walden Two* (1948a/2005) in 1948. Not everyone was pleased by his message. According to Rutherford, the public furor over his messages reached its greatest heights upon publication of his book *Beyond Freedom and Dignity* in 1971.

It seems clear that Skinner and his ideas influenced both academia and the general population to a degree matched by few psychologists. For many laypersons, for a time at least, Skinner was the face of psychology. Whatever the exact nature of the relationship between Skinner and the general public, it seems quite clear that it was not a simple one. As Rutherford (2003) points out, the influence was most likely a bi-directional one. As she notes, "Skinner was both a product of the American context and a challenger of some of its most prized ideals" (p. 20). This interrelationship and Skinner's impact will become clearer in Chapter 6.

Despite all the controversy, however, behaviourism flourished as the dominant school of thought in psychology during the 1950s and 1960s (Gilgen, 1982). And when 93 psychology department chairpersons were surveyed in 1990 about the field's most important contributors (Estes, Coston, & Fournet, 1990), Skinner was ranked at the top of the list (see Table 1.1).

The Humanists Revolt

By the 1950s, behaviourism and psychoanalytic theory had become the most influential schools of thought in psychology. However, many psychologists found these theoretical orientations unappealing. The principal charge hurled at both schools was that they were "dehumanizing." Psychoanalytic

**B. F. Skinner
1904–1990**
"I submit that what we call the behaviour of the human organism is no more free than its digestion."

The Evolution of Psychology

Rank	Individual	Rank Points
1	B. F. Skinner	508
2	Sigmund Freud	459
3	William James	372
4	Jean Piaget	237
5	G. Stanley Hall	216
6	Wilhelm Wundt	203
7	Carl Rogers	192
8	John B. Watson	188
9	Ivan Pavlov	152
10	E. L. Thorndike	124

TABLE 1.1

Important Figures in the History of Psychology

In a 1990 survey, 93 chairpersons of psychology departments ranked psychology's most important contributors (Estes, Coston, & Fournet, 1990, as cited in Korn et al., 1991). As you can see, B. F. Skinner edged out Sigmund Freud for the top ranking. Although these ratings of scholarly eminence are open to considerable debate, the data should give you some idea of the relative impact of various figures in the history of psychology.

Source: Adapted from Korn, J.H., Davis, R., & Davis, S.F. (1991). Historians' and chairpersons' judgments of eminence among psychologists. *American Psychologist, 46*, 789–792. Copyright © 1991 by the American Psychological Association. Adapted with permission.

theory was attacked for its belief that behaviour is dominated by primitive, sexual urges. Behaviourism was criticized for its preoccupation with the study of simple animal behaviour. Both theories were criticized because they suggested that people are not masters of their own destinies. Above all, many people argued, both schools of thought failed to recognize the unique qualities of *human* behaviour.

Beginning in the 1950s, the diverse opposition to behaviourism and psychoanalytic theory blended into a loose alliance that eventually became a new school of thought called "humanism" (Bühler & Allen, 1972). In psychology, *humanism* is a theoretical orientation that emphasizes the unique qualities of humans, especially their freedom and their potential for personal growth. Some of the key differences between the humanistic, psychoanalytic, and behavioural viewpoints are summarized in Table 1.2, which compares six influential contemporary theoretical perspectives in psychology.

Humanists take an *optimistic* view of human nature. They maintain that people are not pawns of either their animal heritage or environmental circumstances. Furthermore, they say, because humans are fundamentally different from other animals,

Perspective and Its Influential Period	Principal Contributors	Subject Matter	Basic Premise
Behavioural (1913–present)	John B. Watson, Ivan Pavlov, B. F. Skinner	Effects of environment on the overt behaviour of humans and animals	Only observable events (stimulus–response relationships) can be studied scientifically.
Psychoanalytic (1900–present)	Sigmund Freud, Carl Jung, Alfred Adler	Unconscious determinants of behaviour	Unconscious motives and experiences in early childhood govern personality and mental disorders.
Humanistic (1950s–present)	Carl Rogers, Abraham Maslow	Unique aspects of human experience	Humans are free, rational beings with the potential for personal growth, and they are fundamentally different from animals.
Cognitive (1950s–present)	Jean Piaget, Noam Chomsky, Herbert Simon	Thoughts; mental processes	Human behaviour cannot be fully understood without examining how people acquire, store, and process information.
Biological (1950s–present)	James Olds, Roger Sperry, David Hubel, Torsten Wiesel	Physiological basis of behaviour in humans and animals	An organism's functioning can be explained in terms of the bodily structures and biochemical processes that underlie behaviour.
Evolutionary (1980s–present)	David Buss, Martin Daly, Margo Wilson, Leda Cosmides, John Tooby	Evolutionary basis of behaviour in humans and animals	Behaviour patterns have evolved to solve adaptive problems; natural selection favours behaviours that enhance reproductive success.

TABLE 1.2

Overview of Six Contemporary Theoretical Perspectives in Psychology

concept check 1.2

Understanding the Implications of Major Theories: Freud, Skinner, and Rogers

Check your understanding of the implications of some of the major theories reviewed in this chapter by indicating who is likely to have made each of the statements quoted below. Choose from the following: (a) Sigmund Freud, (b) B. F. Skinner, and (c) Carl Rogers. You'll find the answers in Appendix A at the back of the book.

___B___ **1.** "In the traditional view, a person is free.... He can therefore be held responsible for what he does and justly punished if he offends. That view, together with its associated practices, must be re-examined when a scientific analysis reveals unsuspected controlling relations between behaviour and environment."

___A___ **2.** "He that has eyes to see and ears to hear may convince himself that no mortal can keep a secret. If the lips are silent, he chatters with his fingertips; betrayal oozes out of him at every pore. And thus the task of making conscious the most hidden recesses of the mind is one which it is quite possible to accomplish."

___C___ **3.** "I do not have a Pollyanna view of human nature.... Yet one of the most refreshing and invigorating parts of my experience is to work with [my clients] and to discover the strongly positive directional tendencies which exist in them, as in all of us, at the deepest levels."

research on animals has little relevance to the understanding of human behaviour. The most prominent architects of the humanistic movement have been Carl Rogers (1902–1987) and Abraham Maslow (1908–1970). Rogers (1951) argued that human behaviour is governed primarily by each individual's sense of self, or "self-concept"—which animals presumably lack. Both he and Maslow (1954) maintained that to fully understand people's behaviour, psychologists must take into account the fundamental human drive toward personal growth. They asserted that people have a basic need to continue to evolve as human beings and to fulfill their potential. In fact, the humanists argued that many psychological disturbances are the result of thwarting these uniquely human needs.

Fragmentation and dissent have reduced the influence of humanism in recent decades, although some advocates are predicting a renaissance for the humanistic movement (Taylor, 1999). To date, the humanists' greatest contribution to psychology has probably been their innovative treatments for psychological problems and disorders. More generally, the humanists have argued eloquently for a different picture of human nature than those implied by psychoanalysis and behaviourism (Wertz, 1998).

Psychology in Canada

While Wundt is credited with establishing the first experimental laboratory in psychology in Leipzig, Germany, in 1879, North American psychology was not far behind. G. Stanley Hall established the first experimental laboratory in psychology in 1883 at Johns Hopkins University in Baltimore, Maryland. The first experimental laboratory in the British Empire was established by James Mark Baldwin at the University of Toronto in 1891 (Green, 2004; Hoff, 1992). While this date marks the birth of experimental psychology in Canada, psychology began as an academic topic in Canadian universities before then. The first psychology course offered at a Canadian university was likely at Dalhousie in 1838 (Wright & Myers, 1982). According to Wright and Myers (1982), the teaching of psychology at universities in Canada became more common in the 1850s, beginning then at McGill University in Montreal and the University of Toronto. In many cases, however, these first courses in psychology were taught through philosophy departments (Green, 2004; Hoff, 1992; Kenwood, 1999; Pols, 2002). As elsewhere, psychology in Canada had its beginnings in philosophy (Hagman, 1999; Kenwood, 1999; Jung, 1999; Tolman, 1999). The first distinct academic department of psychology was established at McGill University in 1924, with the University of Toronto (in 1926), the University of Western Ontario (in 1931), and University of Manitoba (in 1936) not far behind (Wright & Myers, 1982). John Wallace Baird, who was born in Ontario in 1869, became the first Canadian psychologist to serve as the president of the American Psychological Association; he was elected in 1918 (Titchener, 1919).

The years have given evidence of many significant trends in Canadian psychology in terms of research (e.g., Pols, 2002), its administration (e.g., Wright, 1992a), and the role of women (see Storm & Gurevich, 2001). The Canadian Psychological Association (CPA) was formed in 1939 (see the special

Carl Rogers
1902–1987

"It seems to me that at bottom each person is asking, 'Who am I, really? How can I get in touch with this real self, underlying all my surface behaviour? How can I become myself?'"

issue of *Canadian Psychology* published in 1992 on the 50th anniversary of CPA's formation; Wright, 1992a, 1992b, 1992c). It was established to advance psychology as a science (Ferguson, 1993) and continues to play a vital role in psychology in Canada. The CPA has a current membership of 6313 (Canadian Psychological Association, 2008; for more information on the CPA, visit its website at http://www.cpa.ca).

While in the past, women have been underrepresented in psychology and science in general, recently things have begun to change (Ceci et al., 2009; Pettit, 2008; Wright, 1992c). Women now make up the majority of undergraduate and M.A. students at Canadian universities (German, 2007; Statistics Canada, 2008b). Recent data suggest that women are now in the majority in undergraduate programs in the social and behavioural sciences, in law (Statistics Canada, 2008b), and in graduate programs in psychology (Boatswain et al., 2001). In the last decade or so, the number of female university teachers across disciplines has increased by over 50 percent

(Statistics Canada, 2005d). According to a survey by Statistics Canada, in the 2002–2003 academic year, women made up about 30 percent of full-time professors (Statistics Canada, 2005d), and currently they make up 38.6 percent of new faculty appointments (German, 2007). The increasing number of women in psychology has been paralleled by an increased focus on related issues, such as guidelines for practice, counselling, and therapy with women (American Psychological Association, 2007; Church, Pettifor, & Malone, 2006).

Few psychologists have made a more important contribution to psychology in Canada than Brenda Milner of McGill University. She obtained her Ph.D. in psychology from McGill and has taught at the University of Montreal and at McGill. She has made crucial contributions to our understanding of memory and was one of the founders of neuropsychology in Canada. We discuss some of her contributions in Chapters 3 and 7. Three other women who have made significant contributions to psychology in Canada are profiled in Figure 1.2.

FIGURE 1.2

Women pioneers in Canadian psychology. These three female psychologists represent just some of the different forms of significant contributions that women have made to psychology in Canada.

Sources: Bretherton, I., & Main, M. (2000). Mary Dinsmore Salter Ainsworth (1913–1999). *American Psychologist*, 55, 1148–1149 [Ainsworth]; Wright, M. J. (1993). Women Groundbreakers in Canadian Psychology: World War II and its aftermath. *Canadian Psychology*, 33, 14–26 [Wright]; Simon Fraser University document retrieved March 15, 2005, from http://www.sfu.ca/~dkimura/dkhome .htm, and profiles retrieved March 15, 2005, from Science.ca, http://www .science.ca/scientists/scientistprofile .php?pID=10 and the Society for Academic Freedom and Scholarship, http://www .safs.ca/academic.html [Kimura].

Dan Grogan Photography

Image courtesy of Huron University College

Image courtesy of Dr. Doreen Kimura

Mary Salter Ainsworth

Mary Salter Ainsworth (1913–1999) was one of the most important figures in developmental psychology in the last century. Although born in Ohio, she moved to Toronto at the age of four and earned her Ph.D. from the University of Toronto. She lectured at the University of Toronto and then joined the Canadian Women's Army Corps, where she attained the rank of major. After the war, Ainsworth returned to teaching at the University of Toronto. She married another student of that university and went with him to London, England, while he completed his studies. There she worked with John Bowlby, who was interested in attachment. She later went on to a position at Johns Hopkins University and made important contributions to attachment theory and the study of developmental psychology. She retired in 1984 from the University of Virginia.

Mary Wright

Mary Wright was a professor of psychology at the University of Western Ontario, retiring in 1980. She was a developmental psychologist who made important contributions to educational psychology and developmental training at the University of Western Ontario, establishing a laboratory preschool there that now bears her name. Wright served during World War II in the Canadian Children's Service in charge of training childcare workers. She is a historian of academic psychology in Canada (Wright & Myers, 1982), she served as president of the Ontario Psychological Association (OPA: 1951–1952), and she was the first female president of the Canadian Psychological Association (CPA: 1968–1969). She has received numerous honorary degrees and awards, including two Distinguished Contribution Awards from the OPA and the CPA Gold Medal Award for Distinguished Lifetime Contribution to Canadian Psychology.

Doreen Kimura

Doreen Kimura is currently a visiting professor at Simon Fraser University. Before that, she was a professor of psychology at University of Western Ontario for 30 years. She received her undergraduate and graduate training at McGill University. Kimura has made significant and sustained contributions to the study of the brain, including neuromotor mechanisms in human communication and sex differences in cognition. She is also active in the area of promoting academic freedom; she was the founding president (1992–1993) of the Society for Academic Freedom and Scholarship and remains active in that organization. She is a fellow of the Royal Society of Canada and was honoured in 1985 by the Canadian Psychological Association with its Donald O. Hebb Award for Distinguished Contributions to Psychology as a Science.

Psychology Comes of Age as a Profession

The 1950s also saw psychology come of age as a profession. As you know, psychology is not all pure science. It has a highly practical side. Many psychologists provide a variety of professional services to the public. Their work falls within the domain of *applied psychology,* the branch of psychology concerned with everyday, practical problems.

This branch of psychology, so prominent today, was actually slow to develop (Benjamin et al., 2003). The first applied arm of psychology to emerge was *clinical psychology*. As practised today, *clinical psychology* is the branch of psychology concerned with the diagnosis and treatment of psychological problems and disorders. In the early days, however, the emphasis was almost exclusively on psychological testing, and few psychologists were involved in clinical work. Although the first psychological clinic was established as early as 1896, by 1937 only about one in five members of the American Psychological Association reported an interest in

clinical psychology (Goldenberg, 1983). Clinicians were a small minority in a field devoted primarily to research.

That picture was about to change with dramatic swiftness. The impetus was a world war (Pickren, 2007). During World War II (1939–1945), many academic psychologists were pressed into service as clinicians. They were needed to screen military recruits and to treat soldiers suffering from trauma. Many of these psychologists (often to their surprise) found the clinical work to be challenging and rewarding, and a substantial portion continued to do clinical work after the war. More significant, some 40 000 American veterans returned to seek post-war treatment in Veterans Administration (VA) hospitals for their psychological scars. With the demand for clinicians far greater than the supply, the VA stepped in to finance many new training programs in clinical psychology. These programs, emphasizing training in the treatment of psychological disorders as well as psychological testing, proved to be attractive. Within a few years, about half of the new Ph.D.s in psychology were specializing in clinical psychology and most went on to offer professional services to the public (Goldenberg, 1983). Thus, during the 1950s, the pre-war orphan of applied/professional psychology rapidly matured into a robust, powerful adult.

In the halls of academia, many traditional research psychologists were alarmed by the professionalization of the field. They argued that the energy and resources previously devoted to research would be diluted. Because of conflicting priorities, tensions between the research and professional arms of psychology have continued to grow. Although the American Psychological Association continues to work diligently to represent both the scientific and professional branches of psychology, recent decades have brought complaints from many researchers that the APA has come to be dominated by clinicians. In 1988, this rift stimulated some research psychologists to form a new organization (Cautin, 2009a, 2009b), the American Psychological Society (APS), to serve exclusively as an advocate for the science of psychology. In Canada, similar concerns regarding the direction of the Canadian Psychological Association led to the formation of the Canadian Society for Brain, Behaviour and Cognitive Science (CSBBCS: http://www.csbbcs.org) in the early 1990s.

Despite these conflicts, the professionalization of psychology has continued at a steady pace. In fact, the trend has spread into additional areas of psychology. Today, the broad umbrella of applied psychology covers a variety of professional specialties, including school psychology, industrial and organizational psychology, and counselling psychology. Whereas psychologists were once almost exclusively academics, the vast majority of today's psychologists devote some of their time to providing professional services.

In Canada, clinical psychologists are licensed and governed by the various provincial and territorial psychology colleges and boards of examiners. The websites of these organizations contain information about practice, standards, and relevant legislation. In some circumstances, these organizations may be responsible for disciplinary action toward a psychologist. For an example, visit the College of Psychologists of British Columbia's website at http://www.collegeofpsychologists.bc.ca for some details regarding practice in British Columbia.

Psychology Returns to Its Roots: Renewed Interest in Cognition and Physiology

While applied psychology has blossomed in recent decades, research has continued to evolve. Ironically, two of the relatively recent trends in research hark back more than a century to psychology's beginning, when psychologists were principally interested in consciousness and physiology. Today, psychologists are showing renewed interest in consciousness (now called *cognition*) and the physiological bases of behaviour.

Cognition refers to the mental processes involved in acquiring knowledge. In other words, cognition involves thinking or conscious experience. For many decades, the dominance of behaviourism discouraged investigation of "unobservable" mental processes, and most psychologists showed little interest in cognition (Mandler, 2002). During the 1950s and 1960s, however, research on cognition slowly began to change (Miller, 2003). The research of Swiss psychologist Jean Piaget (1954) focused increased

attention on the study of children's cognitive development, while the work of Noam Chomsky (1957) elicited new interest in the psychological underpinnings of language. Around the same time, Herbert Simon and his colleagues (Newell, Shaw, & Simon, 1958) began influential, groundbreaking research on problem solving that eventually led to a Nobel Prize for Simon (in 1978). These advances along with many others (e.g., Benjafeld, 2008; Kelly, 1955) sparked a surge of interest in cognitive processes.

Since then, cognitive theorists have argued that psychology must study internal mental events to fully understand behaviour (Gardner, 1985; Neisser, 1967). Advocates of the *cognitive perspective* point out that people's manipulations of mental images surely influence how they behave. Consequently, focusing exclusively on overt behaviour yields an incomplete picture of why individuals behave as they do. Equally important, psychologists investigating decision making, reasoning, and problem solving have shown that methods can be devised to study cognitive processes scientifically. Although the methods are different from those used in psychology's early days, modern research on the inner workings of the mind has put the psyche back in psychology. In fact, many observers maintain that the cognitive perspective has become the dominant perspective in contemporary psychology—and some interesting data support this assertion, as can be seen in Figure 1.3 (Robins, Gosling, & Craik, 1999).

The 1950s and 1960s also saw many discoveries that highlighted the interrelations among mind, body, and behaviour (Thompson & Zola, 2003). For example, Canadian psychologist James Olds (1956) demonstrated that electrical stimulation of the brain could evoke emotional responses such as pleasure and rage in animals. Other work, which eventually earned a Nobel Prize for Roger Sperry (in 1981), showed that the right and left halves of the brain are

---

FIGURE 1.3

The relative prominence of three major schools of thought in psychology.

To estimate the relative influence of various theoretical orientations in recent decades, Robins, Gosling, and Craik (1999) analyzed the subject matter of four prestigious general publications in psychology, measuring the percentage of articles relevant to each school of thought. Obviously, their approach is just one of many ways one might gauge the prominence of various theoretical orientations in psychology. Nonetheless, the data are thought-provoking. Their findings suggest that the cognitive perspective surpassed the behavioural perspective in influence sometime around 1970. As you can see, the psychoanalytic perspective has always had a modest impact on the mainstream of psychology.

Source: Adapted from Robins, R.W., Gosling, S.D., & Craik, K.H. (1999). An empirical analysis of trends in psychology. *American Psychologist, 54*, 117–128. Copyright © 1999 by the American Psychological Association. Reprinted by permission of the author.

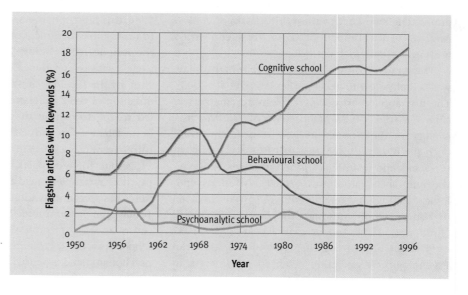

specialized to handle different types of mental tasks (Gazzaniga, Bogen, & Sperry, 1965). The 1960s also brought the publication of David Hubel and Torsten Wiesel's (1962, 1963) Nobel Prize–winning work on how visual signals are processed in the brain.

One important figure in this area was Donald Hebb (Jusczyk & Klein, 1980). He was a professor of psychology at McGill University in Montreal whose pioneering ideas are credited with highlighting the importance of physiological and neuropsychological perspectives and as having paved the way for the recent cognitive revolution in psychology (Klein, 1999). In fact, some have claimed recently that Hebb's early work provides the long-sought-after integrative approach for psychology (Posner & Rothbart, 2004).

Born in Nova Scotia, Hebb began his academic career as a school principal and part-time student in psychology at McGill University. He later went to work on his Ph.D. with Karl Lashley, a pioneer in physiological psychology at Harvard. After obtaining his Ph.D. and pursuing some important other educational experiences, he returned to Montreal and joined the faculty of the psychology department at McGill, where he became chair of the department in 1948 (Klein, 1999). His seminal book, *The Organization of Behavior: A Neuropsychological Theory*, appeared in 1949 and immediately attracted the interest of international scholars. According to Klein (1999), Hebb's book "made McGill University a North American mecca for scientists interested in brain mechanisms of behaviour … and steered contemporary psychology onto a more fruitful path" (p. 1).

Hebb's emphasis on the importance of the brain in behaviour provided an important counterweight to that time's dominance of the behaviourist models. He argued that the locus of behaviour should be sought in the brain. One of the pivotal concepts he introduced was the cell assembly. Hebb suggested that repeated stimulation leads to the development of cell assemblies. These cell assemblies resemble cognitive units that together or in concert with other cell assemblies facilitate behaviour. Recent research in neuroscience continues to provide support for these ideas (O'Neill, Senior, Allen, Huxter, & Csicsvari, 2007). Hebb's ideas suggested how neural networks might work and be organized. He proposed that the key to understanding this was activity at the neuronal level. According to many, his innovative ideas set the stage for contemporary developments in cognition and neuroscience and underscored the importance of the neuropsychological approach to understanding behaviour (Posner & Rothbart, 2004; Wikelgren, 1999).

McGill University Archives, PR000387

Donald Hebb's pioneering ideas highlighted the importance of physiological and neuropsychological perspectives.

In fact, interest in the neuroscience approach to psychology has increased dramatically in the past few years. The prominence of the neuroscience perspective (Marshall, 2009) has grown steadily since the 1950s (Spear, 2007). Whereas, in the past, interest in neuroscience was primarily restricted to those working in experimental and biological psychology, today many of the areas of psychology have taken a greater interest in a neuroscience perspective on issues of traditional interest to them. These include developmental, clinical, personality, and social psychology (Engelmann, 2006; Fliessback, Weber, Trautner, Dohmen, Sunde, Elger, & Falk, 2007; Harmon-Jones & Winkielman, 2007; Ito, Thompson, & Cacioppo, 2004; Nelson & Luciana, 2001).

As interest and work in the area of neuroscience has progressed, so too has concern for the how information concerning our brain and its connection to behaviour is used (Gazzaniga, 2005). This concern with ethics in neuroscience research (Gazzaniga, 2005) is referred to as *neuroethics*. In Chapter 3, we discuss the biological and neuropsychological approach to understanding behaviour. In subsequent chapters, we will highlight some of the recent developments in neuroscience that are relevant to the topics discussed in those particular chapters. For example, in Chapter 16, "Social Behaviour," we discuss the traditional social psychological research on topics such as prejudice and impression formation or person perception.

In Chapter 16, we also highlight some of the recent work done within a neuroscience framework that examines similar issues. We don't think there is any more important or rapidly developing perspective in psychology than the neuroscience approach. We will return to Hebb's ideas in later chapters and we will see his influence in various areas of psychology. His conception of the link between brain and behaviour, although over 50 years old, continues to influence contemporary thinking. His significance to the shape of contemporary psychology has been acknowledged internationally. His stature in Canadian psychology has been acknowledged by the Canadian Psychological Association, which named one of its most prestigious awards the "Donald O. Hebb Award for Distinguished Contributions to Psychology as a Science." The award is given annually to a Canadian psychologist who has made significant and sustained contributions to the science of psychology.

Discoveries in the 1950s and 1960s stimulated an increase in research on the biological bases of behaviour. Advocates of the biological perspective maintain that much of human and animal behaviour can be explained in terms of the bodily structures and biochemical processes that allow organisms to behave. In the 19th century, the young science of psychology had a heavy physiological emphasis. Thus, the recent interest in the biological bases of behaviour represents another return to psychology's heritage.

Although adherents of the cognitive and biological perspectives haven't done as much organized campaigning for their viewpoints as the proponents of the older, traditional schools of thought have, these newer perspectives have become important theoretical orientations in modern psychology (Spear, 2007). They are increasingly influential regarding what psychology should study and how. The cognitive and biological perspectives are compared to other contemporary theoretical perspectives in Table 1.2 (p. 12).

Psychology Broadens Its Horizons: Increased Interest in Cultural Diversity

Throughout psychology's history, most researchers have worked under the assumption that they were seeking to identify general principles of behaviour that would be applicable to all of humanity (Smith, Spillane, & Annus, 2006). In reality, however, psychology has largely been a Western (North American and European) enterprise with a remarkably provincial slant (Gergen et al., 1996; Norenzayan & Heine, 2005). The vast preponderance of psychology's research has been conducted in the United States by middle- and upper-class white psychologists who have used mostly middle- and upper-class white males as participants (Hall, 1997; Norenzayan & Heine, 2005). Traditionally, Western psychologists have paid scant attention to how well their theories and research might apply to non-Western cultures, to ethnic minorities in Western societies, or even to women as opposed to men.

Why has the focus of Western psychology been so narrow? A host of factors have probably contributed (Heine & Norenzayan, 2006; Markus & Hamedani, 2007; Segall, Lonner, & Berry, 1998). First, cross-cultural research is costly, difficult, and time-consuming. It has always been cheaper, easier, and more convenient for academic psychologists to study the middle-class white students enrolled in their schools. Second, some psychologists worry that cultural comparisons may inadvertently foster stereotypes of various cultural groups, many of which already have a long history of being victimized by prejudice. Third, *ethnocentrism*—the tendency to view one's own group as superior to others and as the standard for judging the worth of foreign ways—may have contributed to Western psychologists' lack of interest in other cultures.

Despite these considerations, Western psychologists in recent decades have begun to recognize that their neglect of cultural variables has diminished the value of their work, and they are devoting increased attention to culture as a determinant of behaviour. What brought about this shift? Some of the impetus probably came from the sociopolitical upheavals of the 1960s and 1970s (Bronstein & Quina, 1988). The civil rights movement, the women's movement, and the gay rights movement all raised doubts about whether psychology had dealt adequately with human diversity. Above all else, however, the new interest in culture appears attributable to two recent trends: (1) Advances in communication, travel, and international trade have "shrunk" the world and increased global interdependence, bringing more and more North Americans and Europeans into contact with people from non-Western cultures, and (2) the ethnic makeup of the Western world has become an increasingly diverse multicultural mosaic (Brislin, 2000; Hermans & Kempen, 1998; Mays et al., 1996).

FEATURED STUDY

Investigators: Wendy M. Craig (Queen's University) and Debra J. Pepler (York University).
Source: Observations of bullying and victimization in the school yard. *Canadian Journal of School Psychology,* 1997, *13,* 41–60.

Bullying in Canadian Schoolyards

Prior to the research program initiated by Pepler and Craig, much of the research on bullying utilized questionnaire methodologies in which students would be asked questions about their experiences with bullying as victims or bullies in such events. In their research program, Pepler and Craig employed a naturalistic method in which they videotaped elementary school children during the schoolday on the school playground. In this study, the authors look at the behaviour observed in bullying episodes.

Method

Participants. The participants in this study were 34 teacher-nominated aggressive and 31 teacher-nominated socially competent children who had been videotaped on the school playground during unstructured lunch and recess activities. These children (average age 9.9 years) were a subset of the entire original sample of videotaped children who had all participated in bullying episodes either as a victim or bully. In the study, target children wore microphones that could pick up their conversations.

Measures. Children were categorized as socially competent or aggressive as a result of ratings made by their teachers, which were then verified by ratings made by their classmates.

Procedure. The videotapes were viewed and content coded by two trained experimenters. The similarity of the raters' judgments was assessed and found to be satisfactory. The raters made many types of judgments that were divided into four broad categories: nature of the bullying, individual characteristics of bullies and victims, social interactional factors, and social ecology (e.g., location and covertness of the episode).

Results

This is a very large study with many significant and interesting results, only a few of which can be mentioned here. There were over 300 bullying episodes identified in the 48 hours of taping. Half of the episodes involved verbal aggression (50 percent); physical aggression (29 percent) and a combination of physical and verbal aggression (21 percent) accounted for the rest of the episodes. Boys were involved in bullying at a rate about double that of girls. Interestingly, those with aggressive reputations (being identified as an aggressive child) did not seem to be engaged in more bullying than those who were seen as socially competent. Bullying does not seem to take place in an isolated social setting: peers were involved to some extent (as aggressors, witnesses, etc.) 85 percent of the time.

Discussion

The study was designed in part to demonstrate the viability of naturalistic observation in research on bullying. The results of the study suggest this is an effective tool for use in bullying research. The results also indicated the degree to which bullying is a social phenomenon, with most episodes involving peers. According to the authors, this is critical information in attempts to develop anti-bullying programs in schools.

Comment

This study was selected not only because it is an excellent example of the use of a particular methodology—naturalistic observation—in psychological research, but also because it illustrates the fact that psychologists often do research on topics that affect people's everyday lives. While you will see many examples of basic theory-testing research throughout the text, psychologists also do research on issues that have direct application to our lives. Some research, of course, does both simultaneously.

While naturalistic observation as a research technique has many advantages (including allowing the researchers to document an important phenomenon outside of the constraints of the laboratory), it does not allow for clear causal statement regarding the phenomenon under investigation. In many cases, the use of naturalistic observation allows the researchers to observe behaviour that is uncontaminated by the intervention of the scientists. One question you might have about this study by Craig and Pepler is the effect that wearing a microphone might have had on the behaviour of the children. Craig and Pepler maintain that the children habituated readily to the microphones and that they did not affect the children's behaviour. You might want to think about whether or not it would affect your own behaviour under similar circumstances.

At the very beginning of the chapter we indicated that recent research in bullying has highlighted bullying by girls. This recent focus on girls and bullying is likely the result of several factors. While males overall have been found to be more involved in serious violence than females, the rate of violence involving females seems to be increasing at a faster rate than that for males (Moretti & Odgers, 2002). In addition, the term *bullying* in the past has been used primarily to refer to physical aggression. More recently, its meaning has been expanded to include relational and control-oriented bullying often associated with the interpersonal relationships of girls. Finally, recent high-profile cases of bullying involving girls have alerted researchers and the Canadian public to its dangers.

There is no question that Canada is becoming more diverse. A survey by Statistics Canada gives a snapshot of Canada's increasing diversity (Chard & Badets, 2004), and some of the results are shown in Figure 1.4. These data report on respondents' ethnic ancestry by generational status. (First-generational status refers to respondents born outside Canada; second-generational status includes respondents born in Canada with at least one parent born outside Canada; and third-generational status includes respondents born in Canada, both of whose parents were also born in Canada). The survey shows, among other things, increasing ethnic diversity in those with first-generational status. These trends and other factors led to a dramatic surge in research on cultural factors that began in the 1980s and continues today.

Today, more and more Western psychologists are broadening their horizons and incorporating cultural factors into their theories and research (Matsumoto & Yoo, 2006). These psychologists are striving to study previously underrepresented groups of subjects to test the generality of earlier findings and to catalogue both the differences and similarities among cultural groups. They are working to increase knowledge of how culture is transmitted through socialization practices and how culture colours one's view of the world. They are also seeking to learn how people cope with cultural change and to find ways to reduce misunderstandings and conflicts in intercultural interactions. In addition, they are trying to enhance understanding of how cultural groups are affected by prejudice, discrimination, and racism. In all of these efforts, they are striving to understand the unique experiences of culturally diverse people

from the point of view of those people. These efforts to ask new questions, study new groups, and apply new perspectives promise to enrich the discipline of psychology in the 21st century (Fowers & Davidov, 2006; Lehman, Chiu, & Schaller, 2004; Matsumoto, 2003; Sue, 2003).

Psychology Adapts: The Emergence of Evolutionary Psychology

Another development in psychology has been the emergence of evolutionary psychology, a theoretical perspective that is likely to be influential in the years to come. This renewed focus on evolutionary principles in psychology has its roots in earlier human and comparative research (Goetz et al., 2010; Premack, 2010). We previously mentioned the impact that Darwin's ideas had on William James and early functionalism. Evolutionary psychologists assert that the patterns of behaviour seen in a species are products of evolution in the same way that anatomical characteristics are. *Evolutionary psychology* examines behavioural processes in terms of their adaptive value for members of a species over the course of many generations. The basic premise of evolutionary psychology is that natural selection favours behaviours that enhance organisms' reproductive success—that is, passing on genes to the next generation. Thus, if a species is highly aggressive, evolutionary psychologists argue that it's because aggressiveness conveys a survival or reproductive advantage for members of that species, so genes that promote aggressiveness are more likely to be passed on to the next generation. Although evolutionary psychologists have a natural interest in animal behaviour, they have not been bashful about analyzing the evolutionary bases of human behaviour, personality, and development (e.g., Donnellan, Burt, Levendosky, & Klump, 2008; Finlay, 2007). As La Cerra and Kurzban (1995) put it, "The human mind was sculpted by natural selection, and it is this evolved organ that constitutes the subject matter of psychology" (p. 63).

Consider, for instance, evolutionary psychologists' analysis of differences between males and females in visual-spatial ability. On the average, males tend to perform slightly better than females on most visual-spatial tasks, including tasks involving mental rotation of images and navigation in space (Halpern, 2000; see Chapter 11). Canadian psychologist Irwin Silverman and his colleagues at

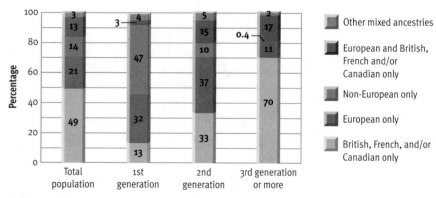

FIGURE 1.4

Ethnic ancestry by generational status.

Source: Adapted from Statistics Canada. Chard, J., & Badets, J. (2004). *Ethnic Identification in Canada: Data from the* Ethnic Diversity Survey. Paper presented at the Canadian Population Survey Annual Meetings, June 4, 2004. Retrieved March 15, 2005, from http://www.statcan.ca/english/freepub/89-593-XIE/89-593-XIE2003001.pdf.

York University maintain that these gender differences originated in human evolution as a result of the sex-based division of labour in ancient hunting-and-gathering societies (Silverman & Phillips, 1998; Silverman et al., 2000). According to this analysis, males' superiority in mental rotation and navigation developed because the chore of hunting was largely assigned to men over the course of human history, and these skills would have facilitated success on hunting trips and thus been favoured by natural selection. In contrast, women in ancient societies generally had responsibility for *gathering* food rather than hunting it. Hence, Silverman and Eals (1992) hypothesized that females ought to be superior to males on spatial skills that would have facilitated gathering, such as memory for locations, which is exactly what they found in a series of four studies. Thus, evolutionary psychologists explain gender differences in spatial ability—and many other aspects of human behaviour—in terms of how such abilities evolved to meet the adaptive pressures faced by our ancestors.

Looking at behavioural patterns in terms of their evolutionary significance is not an entirely new idea (Graziano, 1995). As noted earlier, William James and other functionalists were influenced by Darwin's concept of natural selection over a century ago. Until recently, however, applications of evolutionary concepts to *psychological* processes were piecemeal, half-hearted, and not particularly well received. The 1960s and 1970s brought major breakthroughs in the field of evolutionary biology (Hamilton, 1964; Trivers, 1971, 1972; Williams, 1966), but these advances had little immediate impact in psychology. The situation began to change in the 1980s. A growing cadre of evolutionary psychologists, led by David Buss (1985, 1988, 1989), McMaster University's Martin Daly and Margo Wilson (1985, 1988), and Leda Cosmides and John Tooby (Cosmides & Tooby, 1989; Tooby & Cosmides, 1989), published widely cited studies on a broad range of topics, including mating preferences, jealousy, aggression, sexual behaviour, language, decision making, personality, and development. In 1989–1990, Buss, Daly, Wilson, Cosmides, and Tooby gathered at the Center for Advanced Study in the Behavioral Sciences in Palo Alto, California, to sketch out an ambitious research agenda for evolutionary psychology (Buss, 1999). By the mid-1990s, it became clear that psychology was witnessing the birth of its first major, new theoretical perspective since the cognitive revolution in the 1950s and 1960s.

As with all prominent theoretical perspectives in psychology, evolutionary theory has its critics (Buller, 2009; Lickliter & Honeycutt, 2003; Plotkin, 2004; Richardson, 2007; Rose & Rose, 2000). They argue that many evolutionary hypotheses are untestable, that human behaviour is the result of learning and socialization, not evolution, and that evolutionary explanations are post hoc, speculative accounts for obvious behavioural phenomena (see the Critical Thinking Application for this chapter, p. 38). However, evolutionary psychologists have articulated persuasive rebuttals to these and other criticisms (Buss & Reeve, 2003; Confer et al., 2010; Conway & Schaller, 2002; Hagen, 2005), and the evolutionary perspective has become increasingly influential.

Psychology Moves in a Positive Direction: The Positive Psychology Movement

Shortly after Martin Seligman was elected president of the American Psychological Association in 1997, he experienced a profound insight that he characterized as an "epiphany." This pivotal insight came from an unusual source—Seligman's five-year-old daughter, Nikki. She scolded her over-achieving, task-oriented father for being "grumpy" far too often. Provoked by his daughter's criticism, Seligman suddenly realized that his approach to life *was* overly and unnecessarily negative. More important, he recognized that the same assessment could be made of the field of psychology—that it, too, was excessively and needlessly negative in its approach (Seligman, 2003; Seligman, Parks, & Steen, 2006; Seligman, Rashid, & Parks, 2006). This revelation inspired Seligman to launch a new initiative within psychology that came to be known as the *positive psychology movement.*

Seligman went on to argue convincingly that the field of psychology had historically devoted too much attention to pathology, weakness, damage, and ways to heal suffering. He acknowledged that this approach had yielded valuable insights and progress, but he argued that it also resulted in an unfortunate neglect of the forces that make life worth living. Seligman convened a series of informal meetings with influential psychologists and then more formal conferences to gradually outline the philosophy and goals of positive psychology. There is even a journal, *The Journal of Positive Psychology,* devoted to publishing work in this area. Other major architects of the positive psychology movement have included Mihaly Csikszentmihalyi (2000), Christopher Peterson (2000), and Barbara Fredrickson (2002).

Martin Seligman
Martin Seligman of the University of Pennsylvania is the founder of the *positive psychology movement* in psychology.

Like humanism before it, positive psychology seeks to shift the field's focus away from negative experiences (Gable & Haidt, 2005). As Seligman and Csikszentmihalyi (2000) put it, "The aim of positive psychology is to begin to catalyze a change in the focus of psychology from preoccupation with only repairing the worst things in life to also building positive qualities" (p. 5). Thus, *positive psychology* *uses theory and research to better understand the* *positive, adaptive, creative, and fulfilling aspects of* *human existence.*

The emerging field of positive psychology has three areas of interest (Seligman, 2003). The first is the study of *positive subjective experiences,* or positive emotions, such as happiness, love, gratitude, contentment, and hope. The second focus is on *positive individual traits*—that is, personal strengths and virtues. Theorists are working to identify, classify, and analyze the origins of human strengths and virtues, such as courage, perseverance, nurturance, tolerance, creativity, integrity, and kindness. The third area of interest is in *positive institutions and communities.* Here the focus is on how societies can foster civil discourse, strong families, healthy work environments, and supportive neighbourhood communities.

Although it has proven far less controversial than evolutionary psychology, positive psychology has its critics (La Torre, 2007, Richardson & Guignon, 2008; Sugarman, 2007). For example, Richard Lazarus (2003) has argued that dividing human experience into positive and negative domains is an oversimplification and that the line between them is not as clear and obvious as most have assumed. Lazarus expresses concern that positive psychology may be little more than "one of the many fads that come and go in our field" (p. 93). Only time will tell, as positive psychology is still in its infancy. It will be fascinating to see whether and how this new movement reshapes psychology's research priorities and theoretical interests in the years to come.

Our review of psychology's past has shown the field's evolution. We have seen psychology develop from philosophical speculation into a rigorous science committed to research. We have seen how a highly visible professional arm involved in mental health services emerged from this science. We have seen how psychology's focus on physiology is rooted in its 19th-century origins. We have seen how and why psychologists began conducting research on lower animals. We have seen how psychology has evolved from the study of mind and body to the study of behaviour. And we have seen how the investigation of mind and body has been welcomed back into the mainstream of modern psychology. We have seen how various theoretical schools have defined the scope and mission of psychology in different ways. We have seen how psychology's interests have expanded and become increasingly diverse. Above all else, we have seen that psychology is a growing, evolving intellectual enterprise.

Psychology's history is already rich, but its story has barely begun. The century or so that has elapsed since Wilhelm Wundt put psychology on a scientific footing is only an eye-blink of time in human history. What has been discovered during those years, and what remains unknown, is the subject of the rest of this book.

REVIEW OF KEY POINTS

▷ Stimulated by the demands of World War II, clinical psychology grew rapidly in the 1950s. Thus, psychology became a profession as well as a science. This movement toward professionalization eventually spread to other areas in psychology.

▷ During the 1950s and 1960s, advances in the study of cognition led to renewed interest in mental processes, as psychology returned to its roots. Advocates of the cognitive perspective argue that human behaviour cannot be fully understood without considering how people think.

▷ The 1950s and 1960s also saw advances in research on the physiological bases of behaviour. Advocates of the biological perspective assert that human and animal behaviour can be explained in terms of the bodily structures and biochemical processes that allow organisms to behave.

▷ In the 1980s, Western psychologists, who had previously been rather provincial, developed a greater interest in how cultural factors influence behaviour. This trend was sparked in large part by growing global interdependence and by increased cultural diversity in Western societies.

▷ The 1990s witnessed the emergence of a new theoretical perspective called *evolutionary psychology.* The central premises of this new school of thought are that patterns of behaviour are the product of evolutionary forces and that natural selection favours behaviours that enhance reproductive success. Around the beginning of the 21st century, the positive psychology movement became an influential force in psychology.

Psychology Today: Vigorous and Diversified

We began this chapter with an informal description of what psychology is about. Now that you have a feel for how psychology has developed, you can better appreciate a definition that does justice to the field's modern diversity: *Psychology* is the science that studies behaviour and the physiological and cognitive processes that underlie it, and it is the profession that applies the accumulated knowledge of this science to practical problems.

Psychology's vigorous presence in modern society is also demonstrated by the great variety of settings in which psychologists work. Psychologists were once found almost exclusively in the halls of academia. Today, however, colleges and universities are the primary work setting for less than one-third of North American psychologists. The remaining two-thirds work in hospitals, clinics, police departments, research institutes, government agencies, business and industry, schools, nursing homes, counselling centres, and private practice. Figure 1.5 shows the distribution of psychologists employed in various categories of settings.

Clearly, contemporary psychology is a multifaceted field, a fact that is especially apparent when we consider the many areas of specialization within psychology today. Let's look at the current areas of specialization in both the science and the profession of psychology.

Research Areas in Psychology

Although most psychologists receive broad training that provides them with knowledge about many areas of psychology, they usually specialize when it comes to doing research. Such specialization is necessary because the subject matter of psychology has become so vast over the years. Today it is virtually impossible for anyone to stay abreast of the new research in all specialties. Specialization is also necessary because specific skills and training are required to do research in some areas.

The seven major research areas in modern psychology are (1) developmental psychology, (2) social psychology, (3) experimental psychology, (4) physiological psychology, (5) cognitive psychology, (6) personality, and (7) psychometrics. Figure 1.6 describes these areas briefly and shows the percentage of research psychologists in the APA who identify each area as their primary interest. As you can see, social psychology and developmental psychology have become especially active areas of research.

Professional Specialties in Psychology

Applied psychology consists of four clearly identified areas of specialization: (1) clinical psychology, (2) counselling psychology, (3) educational and school psychology, and (4) industrial and organizational psychology. Descriptions of these specialties can be found in Figure 1.7, along with the percentage of professional psychologists in the APA who are working in each area. As the graphic indicates, clinical psychology is the most prominent and widely practised professional specialty in the field.

The data in Figures 1.6 and 1.7 are based on APA members' reports of their single, principal area of specialization. However, many psychologists work on both research and application. Some academic psychologists work as consultants, therapists, and counsellors on a part-time basis. Similarly, some applied psychologists conduct basic research on issues related to their specialty. For example, many clinical psychologists are involved in research on the nature and causes of abnormal behaviour.

PREVIEW QUESTIONS

► What evidence suggests that psychology is a vigorous, growing discipline?
► What are the main areas of research in psychology?
► What are the four professional specialties in psychology?
► How do clinical psychology and psychiatry differ?

WEB LINK 1.5

American Psychological Association (APA)
The APA website is a treasure trove of resources on psychology in all of its rich diversity. The section for the public includes electronic pamphlets on practical topics such as depression, aging, and anger. A wealth of information on career possibilities in the field is also available here.

WEB LINK 1.6

Canadian Psychological Association (CPA)
This website contains information about the CPA and what it does. In addition, it provides information about upcoming events and conferences, psychology Web links, links to the provincial and territorial psychological associations, careers in psychology, how to obtain the services of a psychologist, and much more.

Elementary and secondary schools
4.2%

Business and government
6.3%

Other
8.5%

Colleges and universities
28.0%

Private practice
33.6%

Hospitals and clinics
19.4%

FIGURE 1.5

Employment of psychologists by setting.
The work settings in which psychologists are employed have become very diverse. Survey data on the primary employment setting of APA members indicates that one-third are in private practice (compared to 12 percent in 1976) and only 28 percent work in colleges and universities (compared to 47 percent in 1976). These data may slightly underestimate the percentage of psychologists in academia, given the competition between the APA and the APS to represent research psychologists.

Source: Based on *2000 APA Directory Survey.*

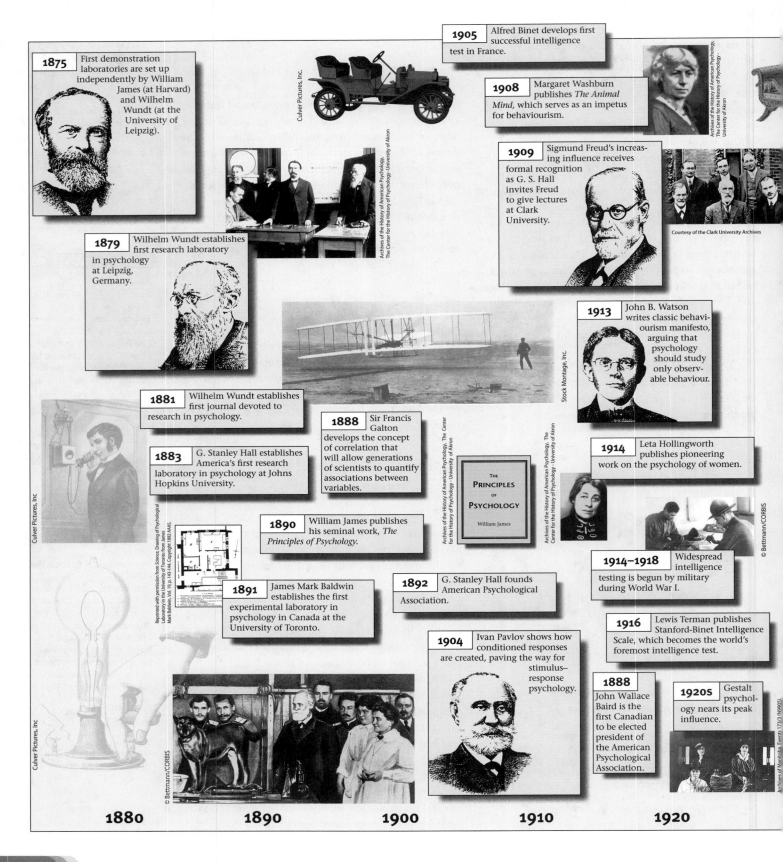

1875 First demonstration laboratories are set up independently by William James (at Harvard) and Wilhelm Wundt (at the University of Leipzig).

1879 Wilhelm Wundt establishes first research laboratory in psychology at Leipzig, Germany.

1881 Wilhelm Wundt establishes first journal devoted to research in psychology.

1883 G. Stanley Hall establishes America's first research laboratory in psychology at Johns Hopkins University.

1888 Sir Francis Galton develops the concept of correlation that will allow generations of scientists to quantify associations between variables.

1890 William James publishes his seminal work, *The Principles of Psychology.*

1891 James Mark Baldwin establishes the first experimental laboratory in psychology in Canada at the University of Toronto.

1892 G. Stanley Hall founds American Psychological Association.

1904 Ivan Pavlov shows how conditioned responses are created, paving the way for stimulus–response psychology.

1888 John Wallace Baird is the first Canadian to be elected president of the American Psychological Association.

1905 Alfred Binet develops first successful intelligence test in France.

1908 Margaret Washburn publishes *The Animal Mind,* which serves as an impetus for behaviourism.

1909 Sigmund Freud's increasing influence receives formal recognition as G. S. Hall invites Freud to give lectures at Clark University.

1913 John B. Watson writes classic behaviourism manifesto, arguing that psychology should study only observable behaviour.

1914 Leta Hollingworth publishes pioneering work on the psychology of women.

1914–1918 Widespread intelligence testing is begun by military during World War I.

1916 Lewis Terman publishes Stanford-Binet Intelligence Scale, which becomes the world's foremost intelligence test.

1920s Gestalt psychology nears its peak influence.

THE PRINCIPLES OF PSYCHOLOGY

William James

1880 **1890** **1900** **1910** **1920**

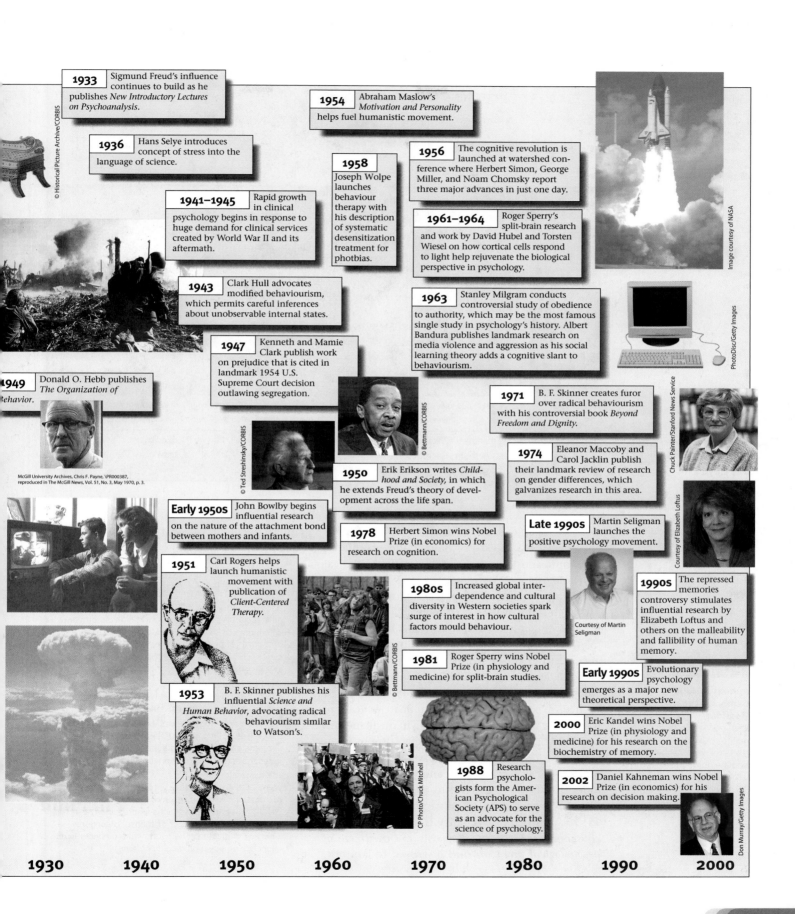

1933 Sigmund Freud's influence continues to build as he publishes *New Introductory Lectures on Psychoanalysis*.

© Historical Picture Archive/CORBIS

1936 Hans Selye introduces concept of stress into the language of science.

1941–1945 Rapid growth in clinical psychology begins in response to huge demand for clinical services created by World War II and its aftermath.

1943 Clark Hull advocates modified behaviourism, which permits careful inferences about unobservable internal states.

1947 Kenneth and Mamie Clark publish work on prejudice that is cited in landmark 1954 U.S. Supreme Court decision outlawing segregation.

1949 Donald O. Hebb publishes *The Organization of Behavior*.

McGill University Archives, Chris F. Payne, \PR000387, reproduced in The McGill News, Vol. 51, No. 3, May 1970, p. 3.

Early 1950s John Bowlby begins influential research on the nature of the attachment bond between mothers and infants.

1951 Carl Rogers helps launch humanistic movement with publication of *Client-Centered Therapy*.

1953 B. F. Skinner publishes his influential *Science and Human Behavior*, advocating radical behaviourism similar to Watson's.

1954 Abraham Maslow's *Motivation and Personality* helps fuel humanistic movement.

1958 Joseph Wolpe launches behaviour therapy with his description of systematic desensitization treatment for photbias.

1950 Erik Erikson writes *Childhood and Society*, in which he extends Freud's theory of development across the life span.

© Ted Streshinsky/CORBIS

© Bettmann/CORBIS

1956 The cognitive revolution is launched at watershed conference where Herbert Simon, George Miller, and Noam Chomsky report three major advances in just one day.

1961–1964 Roger Sperry's split-brain research and work by David Hubel and Torsten Wiesel on how cortical cells respond to light help rejuvenate the biological perspective in psychology.

1963 Stanley Milgram conducts controversial study of obedience to authority, which may be the most famous single study in psychology's history. Albert Bandura publishes landmark research on media violence and aggression as his social learning theory adds a cognitive slant to behaviourism.

Image courtesy of NASA

PhotoDisc/Getty Images

1971 B. F. Skinner creates furor over radical behaviourism with his controversial book *Beyond Freedom and Dignity*.

1974 Eleanor Maccoby and Carol Jacklin publish their landmark review of research on gender differences, which galvanizes research in this area.

1978 Herbert Simon wins Nobel Prize (in economics) for research on cognition.

1980s Increased global interdependence and cultural diversity in Western societies spark surge of interest in how cultural factors mould behaviour.

© Bettmann/CORBIS

1981 Roger Sperry wins Nobel Prize (in physiology and medicine) for split-brain studies.

1988 Research psychologists form the American Psychological Society (APS) to serve as an advocate for the science of psychology.

CP Photo/Chuck Mitchell

Chuck Painter/Stanford News Service

Courtesy of Elizabeth Loftus

Late 1990s Martin Seligman launches the positive psychology movement.

Courtesy of Martin Seligman

1990s The repressed memories controversy stimulates influential research by Elizabeth Loftus and others on the malleability and fallibility of human memory.

Early 1990s Evolutionary psychology emerges as a major new theoretical perspective.

2000 Eric Kandel wins Nobel Prize (in physiology and medicine) for his research on the biochemistry of memory.

2002 Daniel Kahneman wins Nobel Prize (in economics) for his research on decision making.

Don Murray/Getty Images

| 1930 | 1940 | 1950 | 1960 | 1970 | 1980 | 1990 | 2000 |

FIGURE 1.6

Major research areas in contemporary psychology.

Most research psychologists specialize in one of the seven broad areas described here. The figures in the pie chart reflect the percentage of academic and research psychologists belonging to APA who identify each area as their primary interest.

Source: Based on *2000 APA Directory Survey.*

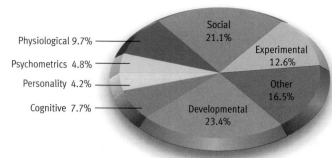

Physiological 9.7%
Psychometrics 4.8%
Personality 4.2%
Cognitive 7.7%
Social 21.1%
Experimental 12.6%
Other 16.5%
Developmental 23.4%

Area	Focus of research
Developmental psychology	Looks at human development across the life span. Developmental psychology once focused primarily on child development but today devotes a great deal of research to adolescence, adulthood, and old age.
Social psychology	Focuses on interpersonal behaviour and the role of social forces in governing behaviour. Typical topics include attitude formation, attitude change, prejudice, conformity, attraction, aggression, intimate relationships, and behaviour in groups.
Experimental psychology	Encompasses the traditional core of topics that psychology focused on heavily in its first half-century as a science: sensation, perception, learning, conditioning, motivation, and emotion. The name *experimental psychology* is somewhat misleading, as this is not the only area in which experiments are done. Psychologists working in all the areas listed here conduct experiments.
Physiological psychology	Examines the influence of genetic factors on behaviour and the role of the brain, nervous system, endocrine system, and bodily chemicals in the regulation of behaviour.
Cognitive psychology	Focuses on "higher" mental processes, such as memory, reasoning, information processing, language, problem solving, decision making, and creativity.
Personality	Is interested in describing and understanding individuals' consistency in behaviour, which represents their personality. This area of interest is also concerned with the factors that shape personality and with personality assessment.
Psychometrics	Is concerned with the measurement of behaviour and capacities, usually through the development of psychological tests. Psychometrics is involved with the design of tests to assess personality, intelligence, and a wide range of abilities. It is also concerned with the development of new techniques for statistical analysis.

WEB LINK 1.7

Marky Lloyd's Career Page
For those who think they might want to find a job or career in psychology or a related field, Marky Lloyd of Georgia Southern University has put together a fine set of resources to help in both planning and making choices.

WEB LINK 1.8

A Student's Guide to Careers in the Helping Professions
Written by Melissa J. Himeline of the University of North Carolina at Asheville, this online guide provides detailed career information for 15 of the most important helping professions that psychology majors often consider entering.

Some people are confused about the difference between clinical psychology and psychiatry. The confusion is understandable, as both clinical psychologists and psychiatrists are involved in analyzing and treating psychological disorders. Although some overlap exists between the two professions, the training and educational requirements for the two are quite different. Clinical psychologists go to graduate school to earn one of several doctoral degrees (Ph.D., Ed.D., or Psy.D.) in order to enjoy full status in their profession. Psychiatrists go to medical school for their postgraduate education, where they receive general training in medicine and earn an M.D. degree. They then specialize by completing residency training in psychiatry at a hospital. Clinical psychologists and psychiatrists also differ in the way they tend to approach the treatment of mental disorders, as we will see in Chapter 15. To summarize, **psychiatry** *is a branch of medicine concerned with the diagnosis and treatment of psychological problems and disorders.* In contrast, clinical psychology takes a nonmedical approach to such problems.

REVIEW OF KEY POINTS

▷ Contemporary psychology is a diversified science and profession that has grown rapidly in recent decades. The main work settings for contemporary psychologists are (1) private practice, (2) colleges and universities, and (3) hospitals and clinics.

▷ Major areas of research in modern psychology include developmental psychology, social psychology, experimental psychology, physiological psychology, cognitive psychology, personality, and psychometrics.

▷ Applied psychology encompasses four professional specialties: clinical psychology, counselling psychology, educational and school psychology, and industrial and organizational psychology.

▷ Although clinical psychology and psychiatry share some of the same interests, they are different professions with different types of training. Psychiatrists are physicians who specialize in the diagnosis and treatment of mental disorders, whereas clinical psychologists take a nonmedical approach to psychological problems.

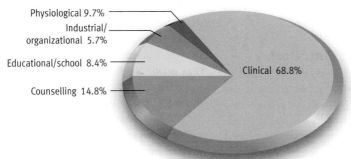

FIGURE 1.7

Principal professional specialties in contemporary psychology.
Most psychologists who deliver professional services to the public specialize in one of the four areas described here. The figures in the pie chart reflect the percentage of APA members delivering professional services who identify each area as their chief specialty.

Source: Based on *2000 APA Directory Survey.*

Specialty	Focus of professional practice
Clinical psychology	Clinical psychologists are concerned with the evaluation, diagnosis, and treatment of individuals with psychological disorders, as well as treatment of less severe behavioural and emotional problems. Principal activities include interviewing clients, psychological testing, and providing group or individual psychotherapy .
Counselling psychology	Counselling psychology overlaps with clinical psychology in that specialists in both areas engage in similar activities—interviewing, testing, and providing therapy. However, counselling psychologists usually work with a somewhat different clientele, providing assistance to people struggling with everyday problems of moderate severity. Thus, they often specialize in family, marital, or career counselling.
Educational and school psychology	Educational psychologists work to improve curriculum design, achievement testing, teacher training, and other aspects of the educational process. School psychologists usually work in elementary or secondary schools, where they test and counsel children having difficulties in school and aid parents and teachers in solving school-related problems.
Industrial and organizational psychology	Psychologists in this area perform a wide variety of tasks in the world of business and industry. These tasks include running human resources departments, working to improve staff morale and attitudes, striving to increase job satisfaction and productivity, examining organizational structures and procedures, and making recommendations for improvements.

Putting It in Perspective: Seven Key Themes

The enormous breadth and diversity of psychology make it a challenging subject for the beginning student. Even those in the field have trouble keeping up with all the developments and in forecasting what trends will emerge in the future (Barrett, 2009; Belsky & Pluess, 2009; Buss, 2009; Funder, 2009; Oakes, 2009). In this book we will try to help you make your way through the vast scientific literature that has grown up in psychology. In the pages ahead, you will be introduced to many areas of research and a multitude of ideas, concepts, and principles. Fortunately, ideas are not all created equal: Some are far more important than others. In this section, we will highlight seven fundamental themes that will reappear in a number of variations as we move from one area of psychology to another in this text. You have already met some of these key ideas in our review of psychology's past and present. Now we will isolate them and highlight their significance. In the remainder of the book, these ideas serve as organizing themes

to provide threads of continuity across chapters and to help you see the connections among the various areas of research in psychology.

In studying psychology, you are learning about both behaviour and the scientific discipline that investigates it. Accordingly, our seven themes come in two sets. The first set consists of statements highlighting crucial aspects of psychology as a way of thinking and as a field of study. The second set consists of broad generalizations about psychology's subject matter: behaviour and the cognitive and physiological processes that underlie it.

Themes Related to Psychology as a Field of Study

Looking at psychology as a field of study, we see three crucial ideas: (1) psychology is empirical, (2) psychology is theoretically diverse, and (3) psychology

PREVIEW QUESTIONS

▶ What is the purpose of the text's unifying themes?

▶ What are the first three themes that elucidate the nature of psychology?

▶ What are the remaining four themes that emphasize crucial insights about behaviour?

evolves in a sociohistorical context. Let's look at each of these ideas in more detail.

Theme 1: Psychology Is Empirical

Everyone tries to understand behaviour. Most of us have our own personal answers to questions such as why some people are hard workers, why some are overweight, and why others stay in demeaning relationships. If all of us are amateur psychologists, what makes scientific psychology different? The critical difference is that psychology is empirical. This aspect of psychology is fundamental, and virtually every page of this book reflects it.

What do we mean by empirical? Empiricism is the premise that knowledge should be acquired through observation. This premise is crucial to the scientific method that psychology embraced in the late 19th century. To say that psychology is empirical means that its conclusions are based on direct observation rather than on reasoning, speculation, traditional beliefs, or common sense. Psychologists are not content with having ideas that sound plausible. They conduct research to test their ideas. Is intelligence higher, on average, in some social classes than in others? Are men more aggressive than women? Psychologists find a way to make direct, objective, and precise observations to answer such questions. The empirical approach requires a certain attitude—a healthy brand of skepticism. Empiricism is a tough taskmaster. It demands data and documentation. Psychologists' commitment to empiricism means that they must learn to think critically about generalizations concerning behaviour.

Theme 2: Psychology Is Theoretically Diverse

Although psychology is based on observation, a string of unrelated observations would not be terribly enlightening. Psychologists do not set out to just collect isolated facts; they seek to explain and understand what they observe. To achieve these goals they must construct theories. A theory is a system of interrelated ideas used to explain a set of observations. In other words, a theory links apparently unrelated observations and tries to explain them. As an example, consider Sigmund Freud's observations about slips of the tongue, dreams, and psychological disturbances. On the surface, these observations appear unrelated. By devising the concept of the unconscious, Freud created a theory that links and explains these seemingly unrelated aspects of behaviour.

Our review of psychology's past should have made one thing abundantly clear: Psychology is marked by theoretical diversity. Why do we have so many competing points of view? One reason is that no single theory can adequately explain everything that is known about behaviour. Sometimes different theories focus on different aspects of behaviour—that is, different collections of observations. Sometimes there is simply more than one way to look at something. Is the glass half empty or half full?

Students are often troubled by psychology's many conflicting theories, which they view as a weakness. However, contemporary psychologists increasingly recognize that theoretical diversity is a strength rather than a weakness (Hilgard, 1987). As we proceed through this text, you will see how differing theoretical perspectives often provide a more complete understanding of behaviour than could be achieved by any one perspective alone.

Theme 3: Psychology Evolves in a Sociohistorical Context

Science is often seen as an "ivory tower" undertaking, isolated from the ebb and flow of everyday life. In reality, however, psychology and other sciences do not exist in a cultural vacuum. Dense interconnections exist between what happens in psychology and what happens in society at large (Altman, 1990; Braginsky, 1985; Danziger, 1990). Trends, issues, and values in society influence psychology's evolution. Similarly, progress in psychology affects trends, issues, and values in society. To put it briefly, psychology develops in a *sociohistorical* (social and historical) context.

Our review of psychology's past is filled with examples of how social trends have left their imprint on psychology. In the late 19th century, psychology's rapid growth as a laboratory science was due, in part, to its fascination with physics as the model discipline. Thus, the spirit of the times fostered a scientific approach rather than a philosophical approach to the investigation of the mind. Similarly, Freud's groundbreaking ideas emerged out of a specific sociohistorical context. Cultural values in Freud's era encouraged the suppression of sexuality. Hence, people tended to feel guilty about their sexual urges to a much greater extent than is common today. This situation clearly contributed to Freud's emphasis on unconscious sexual conflicts. As another example, consider the impact of World War II on the development of psychology as a profession. The rapid

Social trends and values have shaped the evolution of psychology and progress in psychology has left its mark on everyday life in our society. For example, standardized psychological tests are pervasive in our educational system, where they exert great influence over students' lives.

growth of professional psychology was largely due to the war-related surge in the demand for clinical services. Hence, World War II reshaped the landscape of psychology in a remarkably short time. Finally, in recent years, we have seen how growing global interdependence and increased cultural diversity have prompted psychologists to focus new attention on cultural factors as determinants of behaviour.

If we reverse our viewpoint, we can see that psychology has in turn left its mark on society. Consider, for instance, the pervasive role of mental testing in modern society. Your own career success may depend in part on how well you weave your way through a complex maze of intelligence and achievement tests made possible (to the regret of some) by research in psychology. As another example of psychology's impact on society, consider the influence that various theorists have had on parenting styles. Trends in child-rearing practices have been shaped by the ideas of John B. Watson, Sigmund Freud, B. F. Skinner, and Carl Rogers—not to mention a host of other psychologists yet to be discussed. In short, society and psychology influence each other in complex ways. In the chapters to come, we will frequently have occasion to notice this dynamic relationship.

Themes Related to Psychology's Subject Matter

Looking at psychology's subject matter, we see four additional crucial ideas: (4) behaviour is determined by multiple causes, (5) behaviour is shaped by cultural heritage, (6) heredity and environment jointly influence behaviour, and (7) people's experience of the world is highly subjective.

Theme 4: Behaviour Is Determined by Multiple Causes

As psychology has matured, it has provided more and more information about the forces that govern behaviour. This growing knowledge has led to a deeper appreciation of a simple but important fact: Behaviour is exceedingly complex, and most aspects of behaviour are determined by multiple causes.

Although the complexity of behaviour may seem self-evident, people usually think in terms of single causes. Thus, they offer explanations such as "Andrea flunked out of school because she is lazy." Or they assert that "teenage pregnancies are increasing because of all the sex in the media." Single-cause explanations are sometimes accurate as far as they go, but they usually are incomplete. In general, psychologists find that behaviour is governed by a complex network of interacting factors, an idea referred to as the *multifactorial causation of behaviour*.

As you proceed through this book, you will learn that complexity of causation is the rule rather than the exception. If we expect to understand behaviour, we usually have to take into account multiple determinants.

Theme 5: Behaviour Is Shaped by Cultural Heritage

Among the multiple determinants of human behaviour, cultural factors are particularly prominent. Just as psychology evolves in a sociohistorical context, so, too, do individuals. People's cultural backgrounds exert considerable influence over their behaviour. What is culture? It's the human-made part of the environment. More specifically, *culture* refers to the widely shared customs, beliefs, values, norms, institutions, and other products of a community that are transmitted socially across generations.

Culture is a broad construct, encompassing everything from a society's legal system to its assumptions about family roles, from its dietary habits to its political ideals, from its technology to its attitudes about time, from its modes of dress to its spiritual beliefs, and from its art and music to its unspoken rules about sexual liaisons. We tend to think of culture as belonging to entire societies or broad ethnic groups within societies—which it does—but the concept can also be applied to small groups (a tiny Aboriginal tribe in Australia, for example) and to non-ethnic groups (gay/homosexual culture, for instance).

Much of a person's cultural heritage is invisible (Brislin, 1993, 2000). Assumptions, ideals, attitudes, beliefs, and unspoken rules exist in people's minds and may not be readily apparent to outsiders. Moreover, because a cultural background is widely shared, members feel little need to discuss it with others and often take it for granted. For example, you probably don't spend much time thinking about the importance of living in rectangular rooms, trying to minimize body odour, limiting yourself to one spouse at a time, or using credit cards to obtain material goods and services. Although we generally fail to appreciate its influence, our cultural heritage has a pervasive impact on our thoughts, feelings, and behaviour.

Let's look at a couple of examples of this influence. In North America, when people are invited to dinner in someone's home, they generally show their appreciation of their host's cooking efforts by eating all of the food they are served. In India, this behaviour would be insulting to the host, as guests are expected to leave some food on their plates. The leftover food acknowledges the generosity of the host, implying that he or she provided so much food the guest could not eat it all (Moghaddam, Taylor, & Wright, 1993). Cultures also vary in their emphasis on punctuality. In North America, we expect people to show up for meetings on time; if someone is more than 10 to 15 minutes late, we begin to get upset. We generally strive to be on time, and many of us are quite proud of our precise and dependable punctuality. However, in many Asian and Latin American countries, social obligations that arise at the last minute are given just as much priority as scheduled commitments. Hence, people often show up for important meetings an hour or two late with little remorse, and they may be quite puzzled by the consternation of their Western visitors (Brislin, 2000).

These examples may seem trivial, but as you will see in upcoming chapters, culture can also influence crucial matters, such as educational success, mental health, and vulnerability to physical illnesses.

Although the influence of culture is everywhere, generalizations about cultural groups must always be tempered by the realization that great diversity also exists within any society or ethnic group. Researchers may be able to pinpoint genuinely useful insights about Ethiopian, Korean, or Ukrainian culture, for example, but it would be foolish to assume that all Ethiopians, Koreans, or Ukrainians exhibit identical behaviour. It is also important to realize that both differences and similarities in behaviour occur across cultures. As we will see repeatedly, psychological processes are characterized by both cultural variance and invariance. Caveats aside, if we hope to achieve a sound understanding of human

behaviour, we need to consider cultural determinants (Heine & Buchtel, 2009; Oyserman & Lee, 2008; Sue et al., 2009).

Theme 6: Heredity and Environment Jointly Influence Behaviour

Are individuals who they are—athletic or artistic, quick-tempered or calm, shy or outgoing, energetic or laid-back—because of their genetic inheritance or because of their upbringing? This question about the importance of nature versus nurture, or heredity versus environment, has been asked in one form or another since ancient times. Historically, the nature-versus-nurture question was framed as an all-or-none proposition. In other words, theorists argued that personal traits and abilities are governed either entirely by heredity or entirely by environment. John B. Watson, for instance, asserted that personality and ability depend almost exclusively on an individual's environment. In contrast, Sir Francis Galton, a pioneer in mental testing, maintained that personality and ability depend almost entirely on genetic inheritance.

Today, most psychologists agree that heredity and environment are both important. A century of research has shown that genetics and experience jointly influence an individual's intelligence, temperament, personality, and susceptibility to many psychological disorders (Grigorenko & Sternberg, 2003; Plomin, 2004, Rutter, 2006). If we ask whether individuals are born or made, psychology's answer is "Both." This does not mean that nature versus nurture is a dead issue. Lively debate about the relative influence of genetics and experience continues unabated. Furthermore, psychologists are actively seeking to understand the complex ways in which genetic inheritance and experience interact to mould behaviour.

Theme 7: People's Experience of the World Is Highly Subjective

Even elementary perception—for example, of sights and sounds—is not a passive process. People actively process incoming stimulation, selectively focusing on some aspects of that stimulation while ignoring others. Moreover, they impose organization on the stimuli that they pay attention to. These tendencies combine to make perception personalized and subjective.

The subjectivity of perception was demonstrated nicely in a classic study by Hastorf and Cantril (1954). They showed students at Princeton and Dartmouth universities a film of a recent football game between the two schools. The students were told to watch for rules infractions. Both groups saw the same film, but the Princeton students "saw" the Dartmouth players engage in twice as many infractions as the Dartmouth students "saw." The investigators concluded that the game "actually was many different games and that each version of the events that transpired was just as 'real' to a particular person as other versions were to other people" (Hastorf & Cantril, 1954). In this study, the subjects' perceptions were swayed by their motives. It shows how people sometimes see what they *want* to see.

Other studies reveal that people also tend to see what they expect to see. For example, Harold Kelley (1950) showed how perceptions of people are influenced by their reputation. Kelley told students that their class would be taken over by a new lecturer, whom they would be asked to evaluate later. Before the class, the students were given a short description of the incoming instructor, with one important variation. Half the students were led to expect a "warm" person, while the other half were led to expect a "cold" one (see Figure 1.8). All of the subjects were exposed to the same 20 minutes of lecture and interaction with the new instructor. However, the group of subjects who expected a warm person rated the instructor as more considerate, sociable, humorous, good-natured, informal, and humane than the subjects in the group who had expected a cold person.

Thus, it is clear that motives and expectations colour people's experiences. To some extent, individuals see what they want to see or what they expect

to see. This subjectivity in perception turns out to explain a variety of behavioural tendencies that would otherwise be perplexing (Pronin, Lin, & Ross, 2002; Pronin, Gilovich, & Ross, 2004).

Mr. Blank is a graduate student in the Department of Economics and Social Science here at MIT. He has had three semesters of teaching experience in psychology at another college. This is his first semester teaching Ec. 70. He is 26 years old, a veteran, and married. People who know him consider him to be a very warm person, industrious, critical, practical, and determined.

Yuri Arcurs/Shutterstock

FIGURE 1.8

Manipulating person perception.

Read the accompanying description of Mr. Blank carefully. If you were about to hear him give a lecture, would this description bias your perceptions of him? You probably think not, but when Kelley (1950) altered one adjective in this description (replacing the word *warm* with *cold*), the change had a dramatic impact on subjects' ratings of the guest lecturer.

Source: Description from Kelley, H. H. (1950). The warm–cold variable in first impressions of persons. *Journal of Personality, 8,* 431–439. Copyright © 1950 by the Ecological Society of America.

concept **check 1.3**

Understanding the Seven Key Themes

Check your understanding of the seven key themes introduced in the chapter by matching the vignettes with the themes they exemplify. You'll find the answers in Appendix A.

Themes

_____ **1.** Psychology is empirical.

_____ **2.** Psychology is theoretically diverse.

_____ **3.** Psychology evolves in a sociohistorical context.

_____ **4.** Behaviour is determined by multiple causes.

_____ **5.** Behaviour is shaped by cultural heritage.

_____ **6.** Heredity and environment jointly influence behaviour.

_____ **7.** People's experience of the world is highly subjective.

Vignettes

_____ **a.** Several or more theoretical models of emotion have contributed to our overall understanding of the dynamics of emotion.

_____ **b.** According to the stress-vulnerability model, some people are at greater risk for developing certain psychological disorders for genetic reasons. Whether these people actually develop the disorders depends on how much stress they experience in their work, families, or other areas of their lives.

_____ **c.** Physical health and illness seem to be influenced by a complex constellation of psychological, biological, and social system variables.

_____ **d.** One of the difficulties in investigating the effects of drugs on consciousness is that individuals tend to have different experiences with a given drug because of their different expectations.

The Evolution of Psychology

Human subjectivity is precisely what the scientific method is designed to counteract. In using the scientific approach, psychologists strive to make their observations as objective as possible. In some respects, overcoming subjectivity is what science is all about. Left to their own subjective experience, people might still believe that the earth is flat and that the sun revolves around it. Thus, psychologists are committed to the scientific approach because they believe it is the most reliable route to accurate knowledge.

Now that you have been introduced to the text's organizing themes, let's turn to an example of how psychological research can be applied to the challenges of everyday life. In our first Personal Application, we'll focus on a subject that should be highly relevant to you: how to be a successful student. In the Critical Thinking Application that follows it, we discuss the nature and importance of critical thinking skills.

REVIEW OF KEY POINTS

- As we examine psychology in all its many variations, we will emphasize seven key ideas as unifying themes. First, psychology is empirical because psychologists base their conclusions on observation through research rather than reasoning or common sense.

- Psychology is theoretically diverse, as there are many competing schools of thought in the field. This diversity has fuelled progress and is a strength rather than a weakness. Psychology also evolves in a sociohistorical context, as trends, issues, and values in society influence what goes on in psychology, and vice versa.

- Behaviour is determined by multiple causes, as most aspects of behaviour are influenced by complex networks of interacting factors. Although cultural heritage is often taken for granted, it has a pervasive impact on people's thoughts, feelings, and behaviour.

- Lively debate about the relative importance of nature versus nurture continues, but it is clear that heredity and environment jointly influence behaviour. People's experience of the world is highly subjective, as they sometimes see what they want to see or what they expect to see.

Improving Academic Performance

Answer the following "true" or "false."

___ 1 It's a good idea to study in as many different locations (your bedroom or kitchen, the library, lounges around school, and so forth) as possible.

___ 2 If you have a professor who delivers chaotic, hard-to-follow lectures, there is little point in attending class.

___ 3 Cramming the night before an exam is an effective method of study.

___ 4 In taking lecture notes, you should try to be a "human tape recorder" (that is, write down everything your professor says).

___ 5 You should never change your answers to multiple-choice questions, because your first hunch is your best hunch.

All of the above statements are false. If you answered them all correctly, you may have already acquired the kinds of skills and habits that facilitate academic success. If so, however, you are not typical. Today, many students enter college and university with poor study skills and habits—and it's not entirely their fault. The educational system generally provides minimal instruction on good study techniques. In this first Application, we will try to remedy this situation to some extent by reviewing some insights that psychology offers on how to improve academic performance. We will discuss how to promote better study habits, how to enhance reading efforts, how to get more out of lectures, and how to improve test-taking strategies. You may also want to jump ahead and read the Personal Application for Chapter 7, which focuses on how to improve everyday memory.

Developing Sound Study Habits

Effective study is crucial to success in college and university. Although you may run into a few classmates who boast about getting good grades without studying, you can be sure that if they perform well on exams, they do study. Students who claim otherwise simply want to be viewed as extremely bright rather than as studious.

Learning can be immensely gratifying, but studying usually involves hard work. The first step toward effective study habits is to face up to this reality. You don't have to feel guilty if you don't look forward to studying. Most students don't. Once you accept the premise that studying doesn't come naturally, it should be apparent that you need to set up an organized program to promote adequate study. According to Siebert (1995), such a program should include the following considerations:

1. Set up a schedule for studying. If you wait until the urge to study strikes you, you may still be waiting when the exam rolls around. Thus, it is important to allocate definite times to studying. Review your various time obligations (work, chores, and so on) and figure out in advance when you can study. When allotting certain times to studying, keep in mind that you need to be wide awake and alert. Be realistic about how long you can study at one time before you wear down from fatigue. Allow time for study breaks—they can revive sagging concentration.

It's important to write down your study schedule. A written schedule serves as a reminder and increases your commitment to following it. You should begin by setting up a general schedule for the quarter or semester, like the one in Figure 1.9. Then, at the beginning of each week, plan the specific assignments that you intend to work on during each study session. This approach to scheduling should help you avoid cramming for exams at the last minute. Cramming is an ineffective study strategy for most students (Underwood, 1961; Zechmeister & Nyberg, 1982). It will strain your memorization capabilities, it can tax your energy level, and it may stoke the fires of test anxiety.

FIGURE 1.9

One student's general activity schedule for a semester. Each week, the student fills in the specific assignments to work on during each study period.

Weekly Activity Schedule							
	Monday	**Tuesday**	**Wednesday**	**Thursday**	**Friday**	**Saturday**	**Sunday**
8 A.M.						Work	
9 A.M.	History	Study	History	Study	History	Work	
10 A.M.	Psychology	French	Psychology	French	Psychology	Work	
11 A.M.	Study	French	Study	French	Study	Work	
Noon	Math	Study	Math	Study	Math	Work	Study
1 P.M.							Study
2 P.M.	Study	English	Study	English	Study		Study
3 P.M.	Study	English	Study	English	Study		Study
4 P.M.							
5 P.M.							
6 P.M.	Work	Study	Study	Work			Study
7 P.M.	Work	Study	Study	Work			Study
8 P.M.	Work	Study	Study	Work			Study
9 P.M.	Work	Study	Study	Work			Study
10 P.M.	Work			Work			

cont...

In planning your weekly schedule, try to avoid the tendency to put off working on major tasks such as term papers and reports. Time-management experts such as Alan Lakein (1996) point out that many people tend to tackle simple, routine tasks first, saving larger tasks for later when they supposedly will have more time. This common tendency leads many individuals to repeatedly delay working on major assignments until it's too late to do a good job. A good way to avoid this trap is to break major assignments down into smaller component tasks that can be scheduled individually.

Research on the differences between successful and unsuccessful students suggests that successful students monitor and regulate their use of time more effectively (Allgood et al., 2000). You can assess other aspects of your time-management practices by responding to the questionnaire in Figure 1.10.

2. Find a place to study where you can concentrate. Where you study is also important. The key is to find a place where distractions are likely to be minimal. Most people cannot study effectively while the TV or stereo is on or while other people are talking. Don't depend on willpower to carry you through such distractions. It's much easier to plan ahead and avoid the distractions altogether. In fact, you would be wise to set up one or two specific places to be used solely for study (Hettich, 1998).

3. Reward your studying. One reason that it is so difficult to be motivated to study regularly is that the payoffs often lie in the distant future. The ultimate reward, a

degree, may be years away. Even short-term rewards, such as an A in the course, may be weeks or months away. To combat this problem, it helps to give yourself immediate, tangible rewards for studying, such as a snack, TV show, or phone call to a friend. Thus, you should set realistic study goals for yourself and then reward yourself when you meet them. The systematic manipulation of rewards involves harnessing the principles of *behaviour modification* described by B. F. Skinner and other behavioural psychologists. These principles are covered in the Chapter 6 Personal Application.

Improving Your Reading

Much of your study time is spent reading and absorbing information. These efforts must be active. Many students deceive themselves into thinking that they are studying by running a marker through a few sentences here and there in their textbook. If they do so without thoughtful selectivity, they are simply turning a textbook into a colouring book. Research suggests that highlighting selected textbook material is a useful strategy—if students are reasonably effective in identifying the main ideas in the

Some locations are far more conducive to successful studying than others.

Supri Suharjoto/Shutterstock

FIGURE 1.10

Assessing your time management. This brief questionnaire (from LeBoeuf, 1980) is designed to evaluate the quality of one's time management. It should allow you to get a rough handle on how well you manage your time.

How Well Do You Manage Your Time?

Listed below are ten statements that reflect generally accepted principles of good time management. Answer these items by circling the response most characteristic of how you perform. Please be honest. No one will know your answers except you.

1 Each day I set aside a small amount of time for planning and thinking about my responsibilities.
0. Almost never 1. Sometimes 2. Often 3. Almost always

2 I set specific, written goals and put deadlines on them.
0. Almost never 1. Sometimes 2. Often 3. Almost always

3 I make a daily "to do" list, arrange items in order of importance, and try to get the important items done as soon as possible.
0. Almost never 1. Sometimes 2. Often 3. Almost always

4 I am aware of the 80/20 rule and use it. (The 80/20 rule states that 80 percent of your effectiveness will generally come from achieving only 20 percent of your goals.)
0. Almost never 1. Sometimes 2. Often 3. Almost always

5 I keep a loose schedule to allow for crises and the unexpected.
0. Almost never 1. Sometimes 2. Often 3. Almost always

6 I delegate everything I can to others.
0. Almost never 1. Sometimes 2. Often 3. Almost always

7 I try to handle each piece of paper only once.
0. Almost never 1. Sometimes 2. Often 3. Almost always

8 I eat a light lunch so I don't get sleepy in the afternoon.
0. Almost never 1. Sometimes 2. Often 3. Almost always

9 I make an active effort to keep common interruptions (visitors, meetings, telephone calls) from continually disrupting my workday.
0. Almost never 1. Sometimes 2. Often 3. Almost always

10 I am able to say no to others' requests for my time that would prevent my completing important tasks.
0. Almost never 1. Sometimes 2. Often 3. Almost always

To get your score, give yourself	If you scored	
3 points for each "almost always"	0–15	Better give some thought to managing your time.
2 points for each "often"		
1 point for each "sometimes"	16–20	You're doing OK, but there's room for improvement.
0 points for each "almost never"	21–25	Very good.
Add up your points to get your total score.	26–30	You cheated!

Source: Reprinted with permissions from *Business Horizons.* Copyright © 1980 by the Board of Trustees of Indiana University, Kelley School of Business.

material and if they subsequently review the main ideas they have highlighted (Caverly, Orlando, & Mullen, 2000).

You can use a number of methods to actively attack your reading assignments. One of the more widely taught strategies is Robinson's (1970) SQ3R method. *SQ3R is a study system designed to promote effective reading, which includes five steps: survey, question, read, recite, and review.* "SQ3R" stands for the five steps in the procedure: survey, question, read, recite, and review.

Step 1: Survey. Before you plunge into the reading itself, glance over the topic headings in the chapter. If you know where the chapter is going, you can better appreciate and organize the information you are about to read.

Step 2: Question. Once you have an overview of your reading assignment, you should proceed through it one section at a time. Take a look at the heading of the first section and convert it into a question. Doing so is usually quite simple. If the heading is "Prenatal Risk Factors," your question should be "What are sources of risk during prenatal development?" If the heading is "Stereotyping," your question should be "What is stereotyping?" Asking these questions gets you actively involved in your reading and helps you identify the main ideas.

Step 3: Read. Only now, in the third step, are you ready to sink your teeth into the reading. Read only the specific section that you have decided to tackle. Read it with an eye toward answering the question you have just formulated. If necessary, reread the section until you can answer that question. Decide whether the segment addresses any other important questions and answer them as well.

Step 4: Recite. Now that you can answer the key question for the section, recite the answer out loud to yourself in your own words. Don't move on to the next section until you

understand the main ideas of the current section. You may want to write down these ideas for review later. When you have fully digested the first section, you may go on to the next. Repeat steps 2 through 4 with the next section. Once you have mastered the crucial points there, you can go on.

Step 5: Review. When you have read the entire chapter, refresh your memory by going back over the key points. Repeat your questions and try to answer them without consulting your book or notes. This review should fortify your retention of the main ideas. It should also help you to see how the main ideas are related.

The SQ3R method should probably be applied to many textbooks on a paragraph-by-paragraph basis. Obviously, doing so will require you to formulate some questions without the benefit of topic headings. If you don't have enough headings, you can simply reverse the order of steps 2 and 3. Read the paragraph first and then formulate a question that addresses the basic idea of the paragraph. Then work at answering the question in your own words. The point is that you can be flexible in your use of the SQ3R technique.

Using the SQ3R method does not automatically lead to improved mastery of textbook reading assignments. It won't be effective unless it is applied diligently and skillfully, and it tends to be more helpful to students with low to medium reading ability (Caverly, Orlando, & Mullen, 2000). Any strategy that facilitates active processing of text material, the identification of key ideas, and effective review of these ideas should enhance your reading.

Besides topic headings, your textbooks may contain various other learning aids you can use to improve your reading. If a book provides a chapter outline, chapter summary, learning objectives, or preview questions, don't ignore them. They can help you to recognize the important points in the chapter. Graphic organizers (such as the Concept Checks in this text) can enhance understanding of text material (Nist &

Holschuh, 2000). A lot of effort and thought goes into formulating these and other textbook learning aids. It is wise to take advantage of them.

Getting More Out of Lectures

Although lectures are sometimes boring and tedious, it is a simple fact that poor class attendance is associated with poor grades. For example, in one study, Lindgren (1969) found that absences from class were much more common among "unsuccessful" students (grade average C− or below) than among "successful" students (grade average B or above), as shown in Figure 1.11. Even when you have an instructor who delivers hard-to-follow lectures, it is still important to go to class. If nothing else, you can get a feel for how the instructor thinks, which can help you anticipate the content of exams and respond in the manner expected by your professor.

Fortunately, most lectures are reasonably coherent. Studies indicate that attentive note-taking is associated with enhanced learning and performance in university

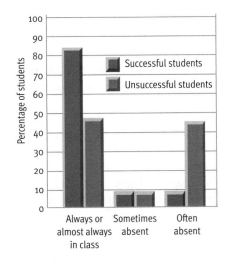

FIGURE 1.11

Attendance and grades.

When Lindgren (1969) compared the class attendance of successful students (B average or above) and unsuccessful students (C− average or below), he found a clear association between poor attendance and poor grades.

Source: Copyright © 1969 by Henry Clay Lindgren. Adapted by permission of H.C. Lindgren.

cont...

classes (Titsworth & Kiewra, 2004; Williams & Eggert, 2002). However, research also shows that many students' lecture notes are surprisingly incomplete, with the average student often recording less than 40 percent of the crucial ideas in a lecture (Armbruster, 2000). Thus, the key to getting more out of lectures is to stay motivated, stay attentive, and expend the effort to make your notes as complete as possible. Books on study skills (Longman & Atkinson, 2002; Sotiriou, 2002) offer a number of suggestions on how to take good-quality lecture notes, some of which are summarized here:

- Extracting information from lectures requires *active listening*. Focus your full attention on the speaker. Try to anticipate what's coming and search for deeper meanings.
- When course material is especially complex, it is a good idea to prepare for the lecture by *reading ahead* on the scheduled subject in your text. Then you have less brand-new information to digest.
- You are not supposed to be a human tape recorder. Insofar as possible, try to write down the lecturer's thoughts *in your own words*. Doing so forces you to organize the ideas in a way that makes sense to you. In taking notes, pay attention to clues about what is most important. These clues may range from subtle hints, such as an instructor repeating a point, to not-so-subtle hints, such as an instructor saying, "You'll run into this again."
- *Asking questions* during lectures can be helpful. Doing so keeps you actively involved in the lecture and allows you to clarify points that you may have misunderstood. Many students are more bashful about asking questions than they should be. They don't realize that most professors welcome questions.

Improving Test-Taking Strategies

Let's face it—some students are better than others at taking tests. *Testwiseness* is the ability to use the characteristics and format of a cognitive test to maximize one's score.

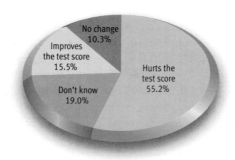

FIGURE 1.12

Beliefs about the effects of answer changing on tests.

Ludy Benjamin and his colleagues (1984) asked 58 college faculty whether changing answers on tests is a good idea. Like most students, the majority of the faculty felt that answer changing usually hurts a student's test score, even though the research evidence contradicts this belief (see Figure 1.13).

Students clearly vary in testwiseness, and such variations are reflected in performance on exams (Geiger, 1997; Rogers & Yang, 1996). Testwiseness is not a substitute for knowledge of the subject matter. However, skill in taking tests can help you to show what you know when it is critical to do so (Flippo, Becker, & Wark, 2000).

A number of myths exist about the best way to take tests. For instance, it is widely believed that students shouldn't go back and change their answers to multiple-choice questions. Benjamin, Cavell, and Shallenberger (1984) found this to be the dominant belief among university *faculty* as well as students (see Figure 1.12). However, the old adage that "your first hunch is your best hunch on tests" has been shown to be wrong. Empirical studies clearly and consistently indicate that, over the long run, changing answers pays off. Benjamin and his colleagues reviewed 20 studies on this issue; their findings are presented in Figure 1.13. As you can see, answer changes that go from a wrong answer to a right answer outnumber changes that go from a right answer to a wrong one by a sizable margin. The popular belief that answer changing is harmful is probably attributable to painful memories of right-to-wrong changes. In any case, you can see how it pays to be familiar with sound test-taking strategies.

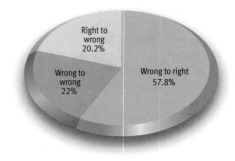

FIGURE 1.13

Actual effects of changing answers on multiple-choice tests.

When the data from all the relevant studies were combined by Benjamin et al. (1984), they indicated that answer changing on tests generally increased rather than reduced students' test scores. It is interesting to note the contrast between beliefs about answer changing (see Figure 1.12) and the actual results of this practice.

General Tips The principles of testwiseness were first described by Millman, Bishop, and Ebel (1965). Let's look at some of their general ideas:

- If efficient time use appears crucial, set up a mental schedule for progressing through the test. Make a mental note to check whether you're one-third finished when a third of your time is gone.
- Don't waste time pondering difficult-to-answer questions excessively. If you have no idea at all, just guess and go on. If you need to devote a good deal of time to the question, skip it and mark it so you can return to it later if time permits.
- Adopt the appropriate level of sophistication for the test. Don't read things into questions. Sometimes students make things more complex than they were intended to be. Often, simple-looking questions are just what they appear to be.
- If you complete all of the questions and still have some time remaining, review the test. Make sure that you have recorded your answers correctly. If you were unsure of some answers, go back and reconsider them.

Tips for Multiple-Choice Exams Sound test-taking strategies are especially important with multiple-choice (and true–false) questions. These types of questions often include clues that may help you converge on the correct answer (Mentzer, 1982; Weiten, 1984). You may be able to improve your performance on such tests by considering the following points (Flippo, 2000):

- As you read the stem of each multiple-choice question, anticipate the answer if you can, before looking at the options. If the answer you anticipated is among the options, it is likely to be the correct one.

- Always read each question completely. Continue reading even if you find your anticipated answer among the options. A more complete option may be farther down the list.

- Learn how to quickly eliminate options that are highly implausible. Many questions have only two plausible options, accompanied by "throwaway" options for filler. You should work at spotting these implausible options so that you can quickly discard them and narrow your task.

- Be alert to the fact that information relevant to one question is sometimes given away in another test item.

- On items that have "all of the above" as an option, if you know that just two of the options are correct, you should choose "all of the above." If you are confident that one of the options is incorrect, you should eliminate the "all of the above" option and choose from the remaining options.

- Options that represent broad, sweeping generalizations tend to be incorrect. You should be vigilant for words such as *always, never, necessarily, only, must, completely, totally,* and so forth that create these improbable assertions.

- In contrast, options that represent carefully qualified statements tend to be correct. Words such as *often, sometimes, perhaps, may,* and *generally* tend to show up in these well-qualified statements.

Tips for Essay Exams Little research has been done on testwiseness as it applies to essay exams. That's because there are relatively few clues to take advantage of in the essay format. Nonetheless, various books (Flippo, 2000; Pauk, 1990; Walter & Siebert, 1990) offer tips based on expert advice, including the following:

- Time is usually a crucial factor on essay tests. Therefore, you should begin by looking over the questions and making time allocations on the basis of (1) your knowledge, (2) the time required to answer each question, and (3) the points awarded for answering each question. It's usually a good idea to answer the questions that you know best first.

- Many students fail to appreciate the importance of good organization in their essay responses. If your instructor can't follow where you are going with your answers, you won't get many points. Test essays are often poorly organized because students feel pressured for time and plunge into answering questions without any planning. It will pay off in the long run if you spend a minute getting organized first. Also, many examiners appreciate it if you make your organization quite explicit by using headings or by numbering the points you're making.

- In many courses, you'll learn a great deal of jargon or technical terminology. Demonstrate your learning by using this technical vocabulary in your essay answers.

In summary, sound study skills and habits are crucial to academic success. Intelligence alone won't do the job (although it certainly helps). Good academic skills do not develop overnight. They are acquired gradually, so be patient with yourself. Fortunately, tasks such as reading textbooks, writing papers, and taking tests get easier with practice. Ultimately, we think you'll find that the rewards—knowledge, a sense of accomplishment, and progress toward a degree—are worth the effort.

REVIEW OF KEY POINTS

▶ To foster sound study habits, you should devise a written study schedule and reward yourself for following it. You should also try to find one or two specific places for studying that are relatively free of distractions.

▶ You should use active reading techniques to select the most important ideas from the material you read. SQ3R is one approach to active reading that can be helpful if it is used diligently.

▶ The key to good note-taking is to strive to make lecture notes as complete as possible. It's important to use active listening techniques and to record lecturers' ideas in your own words. It also helps if you read ahead to prepare for lectures and ask questions as needed.

▶ Being an effective student requires sound test-taking skills. In general, it's a good idea to devise a schedule for progressing through an exam, to adopt the appropriate level of sophistication, to avoid wasting time on troublesome questions, and to review your answers whenever time permits.

▶ On multiple-choice tests it is wise to anticipate answers, to read questions completely, and to quickly eliminate implausible options. Options that represent carefully qualified assertions are more likely to be correct than options that create sweeping generalizations.

▶ On essay tests, it is wise to start with questions you know, to emphasize good organization, and to use technical vocabulary when it is appropriate.

Developing Critical Thinking Skills: An Introduction

If you ask any group of professors, parents, employers, or politicians, "What is the most important outcome of an education?" the most popular answer is likely to be "the development of the ability to think critically." *Critical thinking* is the use of cognitive skills and strategies that increase the probability of a desirable outcome. Such outcomes would include good career choices, effective decisions in the workplace, wise investments, and so forth. In the long run, critical thinkers should have more desirable outcomes than people who are not skilled in critical thinking (Halpern, 1998, 2003). Critical thinking is purposeful, reasoned, goal-directed thinking that involves solving problems, formulating inferences, working with probabilities, and making carefully thought-out decisions. Here are some of the skills exhibited by critical thinkers:

- They understand and use the principles of scientific investigation. (How can the effectiveness of punishment as a disciplinary procedure be determined?)
- They apply the rules of formal and informal logic. (If most people disapprove of sex sites on the Internet, why are these sites so popular?)
- They carefully evaluate the quality of information. (Can I trust the claims made by this politician?)
- They analyze arguments for the soundness of the conclusions. (Does the rise in drug use mean that a stricter drug policy is needed?)

The topic of thinking has a long history in psychology, dating back to Wilhelm Wundt in the 19th century. Modern cognitive psychologists have found that a useful model of critical thinking has at least two components: (1) knowledge of the skills of critical thinking—the *cognitive component*, and (2) the attitude or disposition of a critical thinker—the *emotional or affective component*. Both are needed for effective critical thinking.

The Skills of Critical Thinking

Instruction in critical thinking is based on two assumptions: (1) a set of skills or strategies exists that students can learn to recognize and apply in appropriate contexts; (2) if the skills are applied appropriately, students will become more effective thinkers (Halpern, 2007). Critical thinking skills that would be useful in any context might include understanding how reasons and evidence support or refute conclusions; distinguishing among facts, opinions, and reasoned judgments; using principles of likelihood and uncertainty when thinking about probabilistic events; generating multiple solutions to problems and working systematically toward a desired goal; and understanding how causation is determined. This list provides some typical examples of what is meant by the term *critical thinking skills*. Because these skills are useful in a wide variety of contexts, they are sometimes called *transcontextual skills*.

The Attitude of a Critical Thinker

It is of little use to know the skills of critical thinking if you are unwilling to exert the hard mental work to use them or if you have a sloppy or careless attitude toward thinking. A critical thinker is willing to plan, flexible in thinking, persistent, able to admit mistakes and make corrections, and mindful of the thinking process. The use of the word *critical* represents the notion of a critique or evaluation of thinking processes and outcomes. It is not meant to be negative (as in a "critical person") but rather to convey that critical thinkers are vigilant about their thinking (Riggio & Halpern, 2006).

The Need to Teach Critical Thinking

Decades of research on instruction in critical thinking have shown that the skills and attitudes of critical thinking need to be deliberately and consciously taught, because they often do not develop by themselves with standard instruction in a content area (Nisbett, 1993). For this reason, each chapter in this text ends with a Critical Thinking Application. The material presented in each of these Critical Thinking Applications relates to the chapter topics, but the focus is on how to think about a particular issue, line of research, or controversy. Because the emphasis is on the thinking process, you may be asked to consider conflicting interpretations of data, judge the credibility of information sources, or generate your own testable hypotheses. The specific critical thinking skills highlighted in each lesson are summarized in a table so that they are easily identified. Some of the skills will show up in multiple chapters because the goal is to help you spontaneously select the appropriate critical thinking skills when you encounter new information. Repeated practice with selected skills across chapters should help you to develop this ability.

An Example

As explained in the main body of the chapter, *evolutionary psychology* is emerging as an influential school of thought. To show you how critical thinking skills can be applied to psychological issues, let's examine the evolutionary explanation of gender differences in spatial talents and then use some critical thinking strategies to evaluate this explanation.

On the average, males tend to perform slightly better than females on most visual-spatial tasks, especially tasks involving mental rotation of images and navigation in space (Halpern, 2000; Silverman & Choi, 2005; see Figure 1.14). Irwin Silverman and his colleagues maintain that these gender differences originated in human evolution as a result of the sex-based division of labour in ancient hunting-and-gathering societies (Silverman & Phillips, 1998; Silverman et al., 2000).

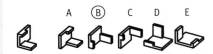

FIGURE 1.14

An example of a spatial task involving mental rotation.

Spatial reasoning tasks can be divided into a variety of subtypes. Studies indicate that males perform slightly better than females on most, but not all, spatial tasks. The tasks on which males are superior often involve mentally rotating objects, such as in the problem shown here. In this problem, the person has to figure out which object on the right (A through E) could be a rotation of the object at the left.

Source: Stafford, R. E. (1962). *Identical Blocks, Form AA.* University Park: Pennsylvania State University, Office of Student Affairs.

TABLE 1.3	Critical Thinking Skills Discussed in This Application
Skill	
Looking for alternative explanations for findings and events	In evaluating explanations, the critical thinker explores whether there are other explanations that could also account for the findings or events under scrutiny.
Looking for contradictory evidence	In evaluating the evidence presented on an issue, the critical thinker attempts to look for contradictory evidence that may have been left out of the debate.

According to this analysis, males' superiority in mental rotation and navigation developed because the chore of *hunting* was largely assigned to men over the course of human history, and these skills would have facilitated success on hunting trips (by helping men to traverse long distances, aim projectiles at prey, and so forth) and thus been favoured by natural selection. In contrast, women in ancient societies generally had responsibility for *gathering* food rather than hunting it. This was an efficient division of labour because women spent much of their adult lives pregnant, nursing, or caring for the young and, therefore, could not travel long distances. Hence, Silverman and Eals (1992) hypothesized that females ought to be superior to males on spatial skills that would have facilitated gathering, such as memory for locations, which is exactly what they found in a series of four studies. Thus, evolutionary psychologists explain gender differences in spatial ability—like other aspects of human behaviour—in terms of how such abilities evolved to meet the adaptive pressures faced by our ancestors.

How can you critically evaluate these claims? If your first thought was that you need more information, good for you, because you are already showing an aptitude for critical thinking. Some additional information about gender differences in cognitive abilities is presented in Chapter 11 of this text. You also need to develop the habit of asking good questions, such as "Are there alternative explanations for these results?

Are there contradictory data?" Let's briefly consider each of these questions.

Are there alternative explanations for gender differences in spatial skills? Well, there certainly are other explanations for males' superiority on most spatial tasks. For example, one could attribute this finding to the gender-typed activities that males are encouraged to engage in more than females, such as playing with building blocks, Lego sets, Lincoln Logs, and various types of construction sets, as well as a host of spatially oriented video games. These gender-typed activities appear to provide boys with more practice than girls on most types of spatial tasks (Voyer, Nolan, & Voyer, 2000), and experience with spatial activities appears to enhance spatial skills (Lizarraga & Ganuza, 2003). For example, one study conducted by researchers at the University of Toronto found that just ten hours of playing an action video game could produce substantial gains in spatial ability and significantly reduce gender differences in spatial attention and mental rotation ability (Feng, Spence, & Pratt, 2007). If we can explain gender differences in spatial abilities in terms of disparities in the everyday activities of contemporary males and females, we may have no need to appeal to natural selection.

Are there data that run counter to the evolutionary explanation for modern gender differences in spatial skills? Again, the answer is yes. Some scholars who have studied hunting-and-gathering societies suggest that women often travelled long distances to gather food and that women were often involved in hunting (Adler, 1993). In addition, women wove baskets and clothing and worked on other tasks that required spatial thinking (Halpern, 1997). Moreover—think about it—men on long hunting trips obviously needed to develop a good memory for locations or they might never have returned home. So, there is room for some argument about exactly what kinds of adaptive pressures males and females faced in ancient hunting-and-gathering societies.

Thus, you can see how considering alternative explanations and contradictory evidence weakens the evolutionary explanation of gender differences in spatial abilities. The questions we raised about alternative explanations and contradictory data are two generic critical thinking questions that can be asked in a wide variety of contexts. The answers to these questions do *not* prove that evolutionary psychologists are wrong in their explanation of gender differences in visual-spatial skills, but they do *weaken* the evolutionary explanation. In thinking critically about psychological issues, you will see that it makes more sense to talk about the *relative strength of an argument,* as opposed to whether an argument is right or wrong, because we will be dealing with complex issues that rarely lend themselves to being correct or incorrect.

REVIEW OF KEY POINTS

▷ Critical thinking is the use of cognitive skills and strategies that increase the probability of a desirable outcome. A critical thinker is flexible, vigilant, able to admit mistakes, and mindful of the thinking process.

▷ Evolutionary psychologists attribute gender differences in spatial abilities to the sex-based division of labour in hunting-and-gathering societies. However, alternative explanations have been offered for these differences, focusing on the gender-typed activities that modern males and females engage in. There also are contradictory data regarding the adaptive pressures faced by females and males in hunting-and-gathering societies.

Key Ideas

From Speculation to Science: How Psychology Developed

● Psychology's intellectual parents included classic philosophy and 19th-century philosophy and physiology, which shared an interest in the mysteries of the mind. Psychology was born as an independent discipline when Wilhelm Wundt established the first psychological research laboratory in 1879 at Leipzig, Germany. He argued that psychology should be the scientific study of consciousness.

● The structuralists believed that psychology should use introspection to analyze consciousness into its basic elements. Functionalists, such as William James, believed that psychology should focus on the purpose and adaptive functions of consciousness.

● Behaviourists, led by John B. Watson, argued that psychology should study only observable behaviour. Thus, they campaigned to redefine psychology as the science of behaviour. Emphasizing the importance of the environment over heredity, they began to explore stimulus–response relationships, often using laboratory animals as subjects.

● Sigmund Freud's psychoanalytic theory emphasized the unconscious determinants of behaviour and the importance of sexuality. Freud's ideas were controversial, and they met with resistance in academic psychology.

● Behaviourism continued as a powerful force in psychology, boosted greatly by B. F. Skinner's research. Skinner in his research emphasized observable behaviour, and he generated controversy by arguing that free will is an illusion.

● Finding both behaviourism and psychoanalysis unsatisfactory, advocates of a new theoretical orientation called *humanism* became influential in the 1950s. Humanism, led by Abraham Maslow and Carl Rogers, emphasized humans' freedom and potential for personal growth.

● The first experimental laboratory in Canada was established in 1891 at the University of Toronto by James Mark Baldwin. Rapid growth in Canadian psychology has been evident over the last century.

● Stimulated by the demands of World War II, clinical psychology grew rapidly in the 1950s. Thus, psychology became a profession as well as a science. This movement toward professionalization eventually spread to other areas in psychology.

● During the 1950s and 1960s, advances in the study of cognitive processes and the physiological bases of behaviour led to renewed interest in cognition and physiology, as psychology returned to its original roots.

● In the 1980s, Western psychologists, who had previously been rather provincial, developed a greater interest in how cultural factors influence thoughts, feelings, and behaviour. This trend was sparked in large part by growing global interdependence and by increased cultural diversity in Western societies.

● The 1990s witnessed the emergence of a new theoretical perspective called *evolutionary psychology.* The central premise of this school of thought is that patterns of behaviour are the product of evolutionary forces, just as anatomical characteristics are shaped by natural selection. The turn of the 21st century saw the emergence of the *positive psychology* movement.

Psychology Today: Vigorous and Diversified

● Contemporary psychology is a diversified science and profession that has grown rapidly in recent decades. Major areas of research in modern psychology include developmental psychology, social psychology, experimental psychology, physiological psychology, cognitive psychology, personality, and psychometrics.

● Applied psychology encompasses four professional specialties: clinical psychology, counselling psychology, educational and school psychology, and industrial and organizational psychology.

Putting It in Perspective: Seven Key Themes

● As we examine psychology in all its many variations, we will emphasize seven key ideas as unifying themes. Looking at psychology as a field of study, our three key themes are (1) psychology is empirical, (2) psychology is theoretically diverse, and (3) psychology evolves in a sociohistorical context.

● Looking at psychology's subject matter, the remaining four themes are (4) behaviour is determined by multiple causes, (5) behaviour is shaped by cultural heritage, (6) heredity and environment jointly influence behaviour, and (7) people's experience of the world is highly subjective.

PERSONAL APPLICATION • Improving Academic Performance

● To foster sound study habits, you should devise a written study schedule and reward yourself for following it. You should also try to find one or two specific places for studying that are relatively free of distractions.

● You should use active reading techniques to select the most important ideas from the material you read. SQ3R, one approach to active reading, breaks a reading assignment into manageable segments and requires that you understand each segment before you move on.

● Good note-taking can help you get more out of lectures. It's important to use active listening techniques and to record lecturers' ideas in your own words.

● Being an effective student also requires sound test-taking skills. In general, it's a good idea to devise a schedule for progressing through an exam, to adopt the appropriate level of sophistication, to avoid wasting time on troublesome questions, and to review your answers whenever time permits.

CRITICAL THINKING APPLICATION • Developing Critical Thinking Skills: An Introduction

● Critical thinking is the use of cognitive skills and strategies that increase the probability of a desirable outcome. Critical thinking is purposeful, reasoned thinking. A critical thinker is flexible, persistent, able to admit mistakes, and mindful of the thinking process.

● Evolutionary psychologists have attributed contemporary gender differences in spatial abilities to the sex-based division of labour in hunting-and-gathering societies. However, alternative explanations have been offered for these differences, focusing on the gender-typed activities that modern males and females engage in. There also are contradictory data regarding the adaptive pressures faced by females and males in hunting-and-gathering societies.

Key Terms

Applied psychology, 15
Behaviour, 7
Behaviourism, 7
Clinical psychology, 15
Cognition, 16
Critical thinking, 38
Culture, 29
Empiricism, 28
Ethnocentrism, 18
Evolutionary psychology, 20
Functionalism, 6
Humanism, 12
Introspection, 6
Natural selection, 6
Positive psychology, 22
Psychiatry, 26
Psychoanalytic theory, 9
Psychology, 23
SQ3R, 35
Stimulus, 7
Structuralism, 6
Testwiseness, 36
Theory, 28
Unconscious, 9

Key People

Sigmund Freud, 9
G. Stanley Hall, 24
Donald Hebb, 17
William James, 6
Brenda Milner, 14
Carl Rogers, 13
Martin Seligman, 21
B. F. Skinner, 11
John B. Watson, 7
Wilhelm Wundt, 4

1. For which of the following achievements is psychologist Wilhelm Wundt primarily known?
   A. the establishment of the first formal laboratory for research in psychology
   B. the distinction between mind and body as two separate entities
   C. the discovery of how signals are conducted along nerves in the body
   D. the development of the first formal program for training in psychotherapy

2. For which of the following reasons is G. Stanley Hall noteworthy in the history of psychology?
   A. He founded the psychology department at Harvard University.
   B. He was the key figure associated with the school of thought known as *structuralism*.
   C. He established the American Psychological Association and was its first president.
   D. He pioneered the use of research ethics boards for psychological research.

3. Which of the following approaches to psychology can be compared to examining a movie frame by frame rather than viewing it as a moving image?
   A. structuralism
   B. functionalism
   C. dualism
   D. humanism

4. A tennis coach insists that he can make any reasonably healthy individual into an internationally competitive tennis player. The coach's perspective echoes the statements of which of the following psychologists?
   A. Sigmund Freud
   B. John B. Watson
   C. Abraham Maslow
   D. William James

5. A young man forgets to pick up his mother at the airport. Which of the following approaches would suggest that his forgetfulness is an unconscious way of saying that he does not welcome her visit?
   A. psychoanalytic
   B. behavioural
   C. humanistic
   D. cognitive

6. Which of the following statements is one that Skinner's followers would agree with?
   A. Most behaviour is controlled by unconscious desires and conflicts.
   B. The goal of behaviour is self-actualization.
   C. Nature is more influential than nurture.
   D. Free will is an illusion.

7. Which of the following approaches holds the most optimistic view of human nature?
   A. humanism
   B. behaviourism
   C. psychoanalysis
   D. structuralism

8. Which of the following historical events created a demand for clinicians that was far greater than the supply?
   A. World War I
   B. the Great Depression
   C. World War II
   D. the Korean War

9. Which of the following psychologists would most likely undertake the study of the endocrine system and genetic mechanisms?
   A. a clinical psychologist
   B. a physiological psychologist
   C. a social psychologist
   D. an educational psychologist

10. Which of the following pairs holds similar viewpoints?
   A. psychoanalysis and humanism
   B. behaviourism and cognitive psychology
   C. structuralism and positive psychology
   D. functionalism and evolutionary psychology

11. Which of the following statements best fits the theoretical perspective of positive psychology?
   A. Humans have a great capacity for achievement and happiness. Research in psychology can help us understand and reach those positive states.
   B. The only way to understand a healthy, functioning human is to study humans who have serious disorders. Knowing what can go wrong allows us to define what is right.
   C. Research results are valuable only if they demonstrate statistically significant findings. Positive results are the only ones worth publishing.
   D. Psychology should be a progressive discipline, moving forward and "getting with the times." New trends and technologies will be necessary to fully understand human thinking and neuroanatomy.

12. If you wanted to become a psychiatrist, which of the following degrees would be required?
   A. Ph.D.
   B. Psy.D.
   C. Ed.D.
   D. M.D.

13. When students change answers on multiple-choice tests, which of the following types of change is most common?
   A. changing wrong answers to right ones
   B. changing right answers to wrong ones
   C. changing wrong answers to wrong ones
   D. changing once, then changing back to the original answer

14. Which of the following describes the development of critical thinking skills?
   A. They are innate abilities that are not significantly modified by experience.
   B. They usually develop spontaneously through learning about new topics.
   C. They usually develop spontaneously even without instruction or exposure to particular ideas or experiences.
   D. They need to be deliberately taught because often they do not develop without explicit practice and demonstration.

15. In which of the following areas of psychology did the well-known Canadian psychologist Donald Hebb conduct research?
   A. developmental psychology
   B. social psychology
   C. neuropsychology
   D. clinical psychology

See Appendix A for answers to this Practice Test.

On the Web

▶ **CourseMate**

Go to this site to find online resources directly linked to your book, including more quizzes, a glossary, flash cards, videos, and more!

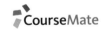

▶ **CengageNow**

Go to this site for the link to CengageNOW™, your one-stop study shop. Take a pre-test for this chapter and CengageNOW™ will generate a personalized study plan based on your test results! The study plan will identify the topics you need to review and direct you to online resources to help you master those topics. You can then take a post-test to help you determine the concepts you have mastered and what you still need to work on.

▶ **Aplia**

Aplia™ is an online interactive learning solution that helps you improve comprehension—and your grade—by integrating a variety of media and tools such as video, tutorials, practice tests, and an interactive e-book.

CHAPTER 2

The Research Enterprise in Psychology

© tc397/iStockphoto.com

We both remember well our first course in psychology. If you are now like we were then, one of the reasons you are taking this course is because you want to better understand why people behave in the ways that they do. You likely have many questions about human behaviour, yours and that of others, that you hope you can answer after you read this book. Where do these answers come from? In Chapter 1, you learned that psychology is a scientific enterprise in which formal research methods are employed in an attempt to answer such questions. Is it possible to provide answers to all of these questions? Some of the questions you have may concern intimate and personal emotions and feelings you have about yourself. Are psychologists able to scientifically examine emotions or to evaluate explanations of how and why they occur? You may be concerned about things happening around you, such as the level of violence in society, and you may be wondering if psychology has discovered anything about these issues that can be used to lessen their frequency. If so, how do psychologists evaluate the effectiveness of any interventions designed to help?

For example, consider the range of emotions experienced by those involved in a series of events that took place in Nova Scotia in 2007. One Grade 9 boy who was a student at Central Kings Rural High School in Cambridge, Nova Scotia, was bullied after he wore a pink polo shirt on the first day of high school. He was bullied, harassed, called gay, and threatened with physical aggression (Bullied Student, 2007). You can just imagine the range of emotions he experienced that day, starting with excitement at his first day in high school, but then turning to fear, embarrassment, and confusion. But the event and his emotional roller-coaster ride weren't over yet. Two Grade 12 students in the school, David Shepherd and Travis Price, decided to do something about the bullying. After school, they went to a nearby discount store and bought up all the pink shirts they could. They e-mailed their friends, who quickly got on board with the Grade 12 students' idea. When the bullied Grade 9 student came to school the next day, he was greeted by a sea of pink-clad students, some wearing pink shirts and some clad in pink from head to toe. According to David Shepherd, the Grade 9 student went from "looking right depressed to being as happy as can be." The events became known throughout the province and resulted in the province establishing an annual "Stand up against bullying day" (Nova Scotia Department of Education, 2007). The action of the two Grade 12 students was publicized and celebrated not just in Canada, but internationally (Fratangelo, 2007). This anti-bullying campaign started on the east coast of Canada has now spread all across Canada to the west coast (CTV News, 2010).

Why did the Grade 9 student feel the way he did? What motivated David Shepherd and Travis Price to do what they did? How did David Shepherd know that the Grade 9 student had gone from depressed to happy? While we will explore the psychology of emotions in Chapter 10 and aggression in Chapter 16, in this chapter, we will examine some of the research methods that have been used to scientifically explore not only bullying, but also our emotions and other seemingly "hidden" psychological events. Bullying is just one type of interpersonal aggression that psychologists have examined in their research.

Most of us are very concerned about the level of aggression in society, especially in the context of personal relationships. The media are frequently filled with reports of relationship abuse (Brown, 2005). For example, according to all reports, Tony Brookes had a long history of spousal abuse before he beat and tried to shoot his wife in the food court of a busy building in downtown Toronto on August 26, 2004. Fortunately, his gun jammed. After fleeing the scene, Brookes took a female McMaster University student hostage at gunpoint outside Union Station. At this point, no one knew whether his gun was operational or not. He was later shot and killed by Emergency Task Force sniper Gord Lusby (Diebel & Roy, 2005). What do we know about the nature of domestic and relationship violence and is there anything we can do about it? What do we know about the types of emotions that Officer Lusby and the many onlookers were feeling as the events took place?

Courtesy of Sandor Fizli

David Shepherd and Travis Price from Central Kings Rural High School in Nova Scotia decided to act when they heard about the bullying of a Grade 9 student for wearing pink on his first day of school. Here they are pictured wearing pink in support of that student. They convinced many of the other students in the school to wear pink, too.

Questions, questions, questions—we all have questions about behaviour. Perhaps the most basic question is: How can we investigate these and other questions? Although we will touch briefly on some of the research on emotions and relationship violence, this chapter is about the more basic question of how research in psychology is conducted. As you learned in Chapter 1, psychology is empirical. Psychologists use a variety of research methods in answering questions about human behaviour. Different types of questions may call for different types of research strategies. For example, if we were interested more in the "meaning" of a specific experience, we might adopt a *qualitative* research method. Qualitative researchers, rather than necessarily working with variables defined in advance by the researchers, often tend to let the meanings assigned to the experience emerge from the data they collect (Dunn, 2009; Kazdin, 1998; Willig, 2008; Willig & Stainton-Rogers, 2008). Their data often consist of words and narratives of experiences. One common use of this method is in research designed to examine the process of psychotherapy. For example, themes that emerge in psychotherapy can be identified by interviewing clients and studying videos or transcripts of psychotherapy sessions. These themes and the experiential processes (Goldman, Greenberg, & Pos, 2005) surrounding them can then be related to psychotherapy outcomes to determine, for example, what thematic experiences are related to successful therapy outcomes. This type of qualitative approach can be distinguished from *quantitative* methods, which are designed primarily to examine cause-and-effect relationships where variables may be defined ahead of time (Marchel & Owens, 2007) and where the data are numerical. "Quantitative research involves empirical observations of the world reported as numeric quantities. Qualitative researchers make empirical observations of the work and report these observations as narratives" (Marchel & Owens, 2007, p. 303). While both methods are used in psychology, quantitative methods are currently dominant and thus will be emphasized in this chapter. Of course, enterprising researchers may utilize both in their research. Part of the creativity involved in psychology is figuring out how to make systematic observations that will shed light on the puzzles and questions that concern them.

In this chapter, we will examine the scientific approach to the study of behaviour and then look at the specific research methods that psychologists use most frequently. We'll also see why psychologists use statistics in their research. After you learn how research is done, you'll also learn how *not* to do it. That is, we'll review some common flaws in doing research.

Finally, we will take a look at ethical issues in behavioural research. In the Personal Application, you'll learn how to find and read journal articles that report on research. In the chapter's Critical Thinking Application, we'll examine the nature and validity of anecdotal evidence. As we consider and learn about the research enterprise in psychology, we will highlight some attempts to answer some of our questions about research on emotions and relationship violence.

The Scientific Approach to Behaviour

PREVIEW QUESTIONS

► What are the goals of the scientific enterprise?

► What are the key steps required by a scientific investigation?

► What are the principal advantages of the scientific approach?

Goals of the Scientific Enterprise

Psychologists and other scientists share three sets of interrelated goals: measurement and description, understanding and prediction, and application and control.

1. *Measurement and description.* Science's commitment to observation requires that an investigator figure out a way to measure the phenomenon under study. For example, if you were interested in the effects of different situations on emotion, you would first have to develop some means of measuring emotions. Thus, the first goal of psychology is to develop measurement techniques that make it possible to describe behaviour clearly and precisely.

2. *Understanding and prediction.* A higher-level goal of science is understanding. Scientists believe that they understand events when they can explain the reasons for the occurrence of the events. To evaluate their understanding, scientists make and test predictions called *hypotheses*. A *hypothesis* is a tentative statement about the relationship between two or more variables. *Variables* are any measurable conditions, events, characteristics, or behaviours that are controlled or observed in a study. If we hypothesized that physiological arousal would affect emotions, as did the authors of our Featured Study, Dutton and Aron (see pages 47–48), the variables in our study would be physiological arousal and emotional state.

3. *Application and control.* Ultimately, many scientists hope that the information they gather will be of some practical value in helping to solve everyday problems. Once people understand a phenomenon, they often can exert more control over it. Today, the profession of psychology attempts to apply research findings to practical problems in schools, businesses, factories, and mental hospitals. For example, a clinical psychologist might use what we know about typical, everyday emotions to assist individuals suffering from emotional disorders. In the Featured Study, you will see how one group of researchers employed these concepts in their examination of emotions. A psychologist might use what he or she knows about the roots and nature of violence in relationships to design a treatment program with the objective of lowering the probability of such violence in the future. Of course, to be sure that such an intervention program works, the psychologist might design a scientific examination of the intervention's effectiveness.

How do theories help scientists to achieve their goals? As noted in Chapter 1, psychologists do not set out just to collect isolated facts about relationships between variables. To build toward a better understanding of behaviour, they construct theories. A *theory* is a system of interrelated ideas used to explain a set of observations. For example, using a handful of concepts, such as children's cognitive development, semantics, and parental interaction, Canada Research Chair Susan Graham at the University of Calgary attempted to explain some important characteristics of language development (e.g., Chamber, Graham, & Turner, 2008; Graham & Kilbreath, 2007). We will discuss language development in Chapter 11. For your interest, the Canada Research Chair program was developed by the federal government to highlight and support the research efforts of excellent researchers across Canada. For a complete list of Canada Research Chairs, go to http://www.chairs.gc.ca.

Thus, by integrating apparently unrelated facts and principles into a coherent whole, theories permit psychologists to make the leap from the *description* of behaviour to the *understanding* of behaviour. Moreover, the enhanced understanding afforded by theories guides future research by generating new predictions and suggesting new lines of inquiry (Higgins, 2004).

A scientific theory must be testable, as the cornerstone of science is its commitment to putting ideas to an empirical test. Most theories are too complex to be tested all at once. For example, it would be impossible to devise a single study that could test all of the many facets of evolutionary theory. Rather, in a typical study, investigators test one or two specific hypotheses derived from a theory. If their findings support the hypotheses, confidence in the theory that the hypotheses were derived from grows. If their findings fail to support the hypotheses, confidence in the theory diminishes, and the theory may be revised or discarded (see Figure 2.1). Thus, theory construction is a gradual, iterative process that is always subject to revision.

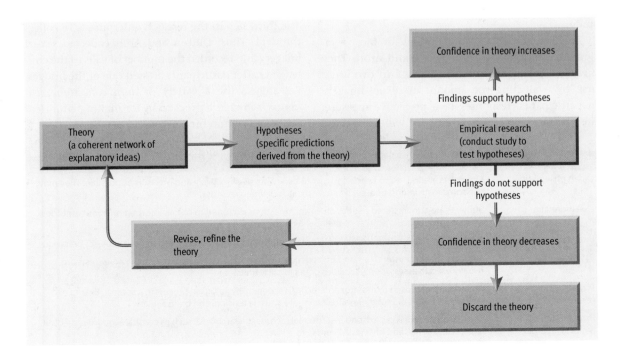

FIGURE 2.1

Theory construction.

A good theory will generate a host of testable hypotheses. In a typical study, only one or a few of these hypotheses can be evaluated. If the evidence supports the hypotheses, our confidence in the theory they were derived from generally grows. If the hypotheses are not supported, confidence in the theory decreases and revisions to the theory may be made to accommodate the new findings. If the hypotheses generated by a theory consistently fail to garner empirical support, the theory may be discarded altogether. Thus, theory construction and testing is a gradual process.

 Log on to CourseMate to access this interactive figure.

The Research Enterprise in Psychology

Steps in a Scientific Investigation

Curiosity about a question provides the point of departure for any kind of investigation, scientific or otherwise. Scientific investigations, however, are *systematic*. They follow an orderly pattern described below in steps 1 through 5. They are reflected in the Featured Study by University of British Columbia researchers Donald Dutton and Arthur Aron on the effects of fear arousal on sexual attraction (Dutton & Aron, 1974). You should read this Featured Study on pages 47–48 before continuing with this section.

Step 1: Formulate a Testable Hypothesis

The first step in a scientific investigation is to translate a theory or an intuitive idea into a testable hypothesis. Normally, hypotheses are expressed as predictions. In their research, Dutton and Aron predict that increased arousal would heighten the sexual attraction of their research participants to members of the opposite sex to whom they were just introduced. This hypothesis was based on previous work on emotions, such as that by Schachter (1964).

To be testable, scientific hypotheses must be formulated precisely, and the variables under study must be clearly defined. Researchers achieve these clear formulations by providing operational definitions of the relevant variables. An *operational definition describes the actions or operations that will be used to measure or control a variable.* Operational definitions—which may be quite different from the concepts' dictionary definitions—establish precisely what is meant by each variable in the context of a study.

To illustrate, let's examine some of the operational definitions used by Dutton and Aron. They measured sexual attraction in Study 1 in two ways: first, by evaluating the amount of sexual imagery in participants' responses to a projective measure, the *Thematic Apperception Test* (you will learn more about the nature of projective tests in Chapter 12); and second, by assessing the number of participants in various conditions who called the experimental confederate (i.e., the male or female they had just met after crossing the bridge) after the experiment had ended.

Step 2: Select the Research Method and Design the Study

The second step in a scientific investigation is to figure out how to put the hypothesis to an empirical test. The research method chosen depends to a large degree on the nature of the question under study. The various methods—experiments, case studies, surveys, naturalistic observation, and so forth—each have advantages and disadvantages. The researcher has to ponder the pros and cons and then select the strategy that appears to be the most appropriate and practical. In this case, Dutton and Aron decided that they would use an experiment. Once researchers have chosen a general method, they must make detailed plans for executing their study. Thus, Dutton and Aron had to decide what kind of experiment they would conduct, who their participants would be, how many participants they needed, and where they would get their participants. *Participants*, or *subjects*, are the persons or animals whose behaviour is systematically observed in a study. For their study, Dutton and Aron decided to use males crossing either a high (high-anxiety or high-arousal) or low (low-anxiety or low-arousal) bridge across the Capilano River in North Vancouver, British Columbia.

Step 3: Collect the Data

The third step in the research enterprise is to collect the data. Thus, Dutton and Aron collected sexual imagery and recorded the number of calls to the confederate after participants crossed one of the bridges. Researchers use a variety of *data collection techniques,* which are procedures for making empirical observations and measurements (see Table 2.1).

TABLE 2.1

Key Data Collection Techniques in Psychology

Technique	Description
Direct observation	Observers are trained to watch and record behaviour as objectively and precisely as possible. They may use some instrumentation, such as a stopwatch or video recorder.
Questionnaire	Subjects are administered a series of written questions designed to obtain information about attitudes, opinions, and specific aspects of their behaviour.
Interview	A face-to-face dialogue is conducted to obtain information about specific aspects of a subject's behaviour.
Psychological test	Subjects are administered a standardized measure to obtain a sample of their behaviour. Tests are usually used to assess mental abilities or personality traits.
Physiological recording	An instrument is used to monitor and record a specific physiological process in a subject. Examples include measures of blood pressure, heart rate, muscle tension, and brain activity.
Examination of archival records	The researcher analyzes existing institutional records (the archives), such as census, economic, medical, legal, educational, and business records.

FEATURED STUDY

Investigators: Donald G. Dutton and Arthur P. Aron (University of British Columbia)
Source: Donald G. Dutton and Arthur P. Aron, Some evidence for heightened sexual attraction under conditions of high anxiety, *Journal of Personality and Social Psychology*, 1974, *30*, 510–517.

Can Fear Increase Sexual Attraction?

In Chapter 10, you will learn more about various theories of emotion. One theory proposed by Schachter (1964) suggests that salient environmental cues can be used to provide emotional labels for physiological arousal. This suggests that you might relabel a naturally occurring emotion such as fear or anxiety as another emotion if cues relevant to that other emotion were highly salient. In previous work, Aron (1970) had proposed that even unambiguous emotions such as fear or anxiety can, under specific conditions, be relabelled as sexual attraction. The specific hypothesis being tested was that an attractive female would be seen as more attractive "by males who encounter her while they experience a strong emotion (fear) than by males not experiencing a strong emotion" (Dutton & Aron, 1974, p. 511).

Method

Participants. The participants were males between the ages of 18 and 35 who chose to cross alone either of two bridges spanning the Capilano River in North Vancouver. The "control" bridge was low, solid, and unlikely to arouse much fear or anxiety in the participants. The "experimental" fear-arousing bridge was a high suspension bridge with a "tendency to tilt, sway, and wobble, creating the impression that one is about to fall over the side" (p. 511).

Materials. Participants were asked to complete portions of the *Thematic Apperception Test* (TAT). The TAT is a projective test. We will discuss the nature of projective tests more fully in Chapter 12. Briefly, projective tests ask participants to respond to vague, ambiguous stimuli in ways that may reveal the participants' needs, feelings, and personality traits. In this case, the participants' responses to the TAT were scored to reveal the degree of sexual imagery in their responses. See Figure 12.19 (page 583) for an example of stimuli used in the TAT.

Design. There were two *independent* variables in the experiment. Participants were approached after they crossed either the high, fear-arousing bridge or the low, nonfear-arousing bridge (first independent variable). The participants were approached by either a male or female confederate (second independent variable). Whether they were approached by the male or female was randomly determined.

Procedure. After crossing the bridge, the males were met by a male or female confederate (someone working for the researchers, engaging in predetermined behaviours). The confederates individually approached a participant and asked him to fill out a short questionnaire. Included was a measure of sexual imagery taken from the TAT. Participants were then offered the confederate's phone number to call later in the day if they wanted more explanation about the study. It was assumed that if participants who were met by a female confederate called more after crossing the high than the low bridge, then they had been more attracted to the female confederate, mislabelling their fear as sexual attraction. The *dependent* variables in the study were the degree of sexual imagery in participants' responses to the TAT and the proportion of participants who crossed each bridge who called the confederate later.

Results

The results were just as the researchers had predicted. Participants who crossed the high bridge and who were met by the female confederate evidenced more sexual arousal in their TAT stories than did those who crossed the low bridge (average scores of 2.47 versus 1.41). In addition, a higher proportion of males who took the confederate's phone number called the female confederate back if they had crossed the high as compared to the low bridge. If the participants were met by a male confederate, not only were they less likely to call him later on, but whether they crossed the high or low bridge did not seem to affect callback rates.

Discussion

The results of the study suggest that naturally occurring emotions can be relabelled as other emotions if salient and relevant environmental cues are present. Results such as these provide support for theories such as Schachter's (1964), suggesting that arousal combines with cognitive

Pictured here is the "experimental" bridge mentioned in our Featured Study. It was used in the study to elicit fear arousal. Imagine what it would be like to cross that bridge on a windy day!

© Craig Balfour Evans/Alamy

labelling to produce distinct emotions. You will learn more about this and other perspectives on emotion in later chapters.

Comment

This study was featured because it addresses an interesting question using a reasonably straightforward experimental design. It was selected in particular because it employed a very naturalistic experimental procedure, using participants who were not recruited from undergraduate courses in psychology. The fact that some research is conducted in relatively artificial settings and employs only first-year psychology students are two criticisms sometimes made of research in psychology. A review by York University psychologist Maxine Wintre and her colleagues (Wintre, North, & Sugar, 2001) revealed that there has been no decrease in the use of undergraduate research participants despite the latter criticism. Wintre's paper also includes a review of the types of criticisms levelled at this practice.

In the case of the research conducted by Dutton and Aron, the researchers conducted three studies, only one of which was a traditional laboratory-based experiment (Study 3, which was not discussed here). The best research strategy might be to use a variety of research methods and settings so that you can take advantage of the strengths of each methodology. The study also illustrates the importance of collecting empirical data to answer psychological questions. We wonder how many of you would have predicted the findings before you read about the study. A well-conducted set of experiments can serve to increase our confidence in the validity and reliability of the findings.

Step 4: Analyze the Data and Draw Conclusions

The observations made in a study are usually converted into numbers, which constitute the raw data of the study. Researchers use *statistics* to analyze their data and to decide whether their hypotheses have been supported. Thus, statistics play an essential role in the scientific enterprise.

Step 5: Report the Findings

The publication of research results is a fundamental aspect of the scientific enterprise (Roberts, Brown, & Smith-Boydston, 2003). Scientific progress can be achieved only if researchers share their findings with one another and with the general public. Therefore, the final step in a scientific investigation is to write a concise summary of the study and its findings. Typically, researchers prepare a report that is delivered at a scientific meeting and submitted to a journal for publication. A *journal is a periodical that publishes technical and scholarly material, usually in a narrowly defined area of inquiry.* The study by Dutton and Aron was published in the *Journal of Personality and Social Psychology* in 1974. This journal is one of the most prestigious journals in that area of research.

The process of publishing scientific studies allows other experts to evaluate and critique new research findings. Sometimes this process of critical evaluation discloses flaws in a study. If the flaws are serious enough, the results may be discounted or discarded.

This evaluation process is a major strength of the scientific approach because it gradually weeds out erroneous findings.

Advantages of the Scientific Approach

Science is certainly not the only method that can be used to draw conclusions about behaviour. Everyone uses logic, casual observation, and good old-fashioned common sense. Because the scientific method often requires painstaking effort, it seems reasonable to ask what advantages make it worth the trouble.

Basically, the scientific approach offers two major advantages. The first is its clarity and precision. Commonsense notions about behaviour tend to be vague and ambiguous. Consider the old adage "Spare the rod and spoil the child." What exactly does this generalization about child-rearing amount to? How severely should children be punished if parents are not to "spare the rod"? How do we assess whether a child qualifies as "spoiled"? The scientific approach requires that people specify *exactly* what they are talking about when they formulate hypotheses. This clarity and precision enhances communication about important ideas.

The second and perhaps greatest advantage offered by the scientific approach is its relative intolerance of error. Scientists are trained to be skeptical. They subject their ideas to empirical tests. They also scrutinize one another's findings with a critical eye.

They demand objective data and thorough documentation before they accept ideas. When the findings of two studies conflict, the scientist tries to figure out why, usually by conducting additional research.

All of this is not to say that science has an exclusive copyright on truth. However, the scientific approach does tend to yield more accurate and dependable information than casual analyses and armchair speculation do. Knowledge of scientific data can thus provide a useful benchmark against which to judge claims and information from other kinds of sources.

Now that we have had an overview of how the scientific enterprise works, we can focus on how specific research methods are used. *Research methods* consist of various approaches to the observation, measurement, manipulation, and control of variables in empirical studies. In other words, they are general strategies for conducting studies. No single research method is ideal for all purposes and situations. Much of the ingenuity in research involves selecting and tailoring the method to the question at hand. The next two sections of this chapter discuss the two basic types of methods used in psychology:

experimental research methods and *descriptive/correlational research methods*.

REVIEW OF KEY POINTS

▷ The scientific approach assumes that there are laws of behaviour that can be discovered through empirical research. The goals of the science of psychology include (1) the measurement and description of behaviour, (2) the understanding and prediction of behaviour, and (3) the application of this knowledge to the task of controlling behaviour.

▷ By integrating apparently unrelated facts into a coherent whole, theories permit psychologists to make the leap from the description of behaviour to the understanding of behaviour. Confidence in a theory increases when hypotheses derived from it are supported by research.

▷ A scientific investigation follows a systematic pattern that includes five steps: (1) formulate a testable hypothesis, (2) select the research method and design the study, (3) collect the data, (4) analyze the data and draw conclusions, and (5) report the findings.

▷ Scientists use operational definitions to clarify what their variables mean. They depend on statistics to analyze their data. The two major advantages of the scientific approach are its clarity in communication and its relative intolerance of error.

Looking for Causes: Experimental Research

The *experiment* is a research method in which the investigator manipulates a variable under carefully controlled conditions and observes whether any changes occur in a second variable as a result. The experiment is a relatively powerful procedure that allows researchers to detect cause-and-effect relationships. Psychologists depend on this method more than any other.

Although its basic strategy is straightforward, in practice, the experiment is a fairly complicated technique. A well-designed experiment must take into account a number of factors that could affect the clarity of the results. To see how an experiment is designed, let's use Dutton and Aron's study as an example.

Independent and Dependent Variables   1b   PSYKTREK

The purpose of an experiment is to find out whether changes in one variable (let's call it *X*) cause changes in another variable (let's call it *Y*). To put it more

concisely, we want to find out *how X affects Y*. In this formulation, we refer to *X* as the *independent variable* and to *Y* as the *dependent variable*.

An *independent variable* is a condition or event that an experimenter varies in order to see its impact on another variable. The independent variable is the variable that the experimenter controls or manipulates. It is hypothesized to have some effect on the dependent variable, and the experiment is conducted to verify this effect. The *dependent variable* is the variable that is thought to be affected by manipulation of the independent variable. In psychology studies, the dependent variable is usually a measurement of some aspect of the participants' behaviour. The independent variable is called *independent* because it is *free* to be varied by the experimenter. The dependent variable is called *dependent* because it is thought to *depend* (at least in part) on manipulations of the independent variable.

In Dutton and Aron's experiment in the Featured Study (pages 47–48), one independent variable was the anxiety or arousal level of the participants. Participants crossing the high bridge were assumed

PREVIEW QUESTIONS

▷ What is the difference between an independent variable and a dependent variable?

▷ What is the purpose of experimental and control groups?

▷ What are extraneous variables and confounded variables?

▷ How can experiments vary in format?

▷ How did Dutton and Aron use the experimental method to evaluate the role of arousal in emotional experience?

▷ What are the strengths and weaknesses of experimental research?

WEB LINK 2.3

Research Methods and Statistics

There are many websites that offer resources and link for students interested in specific topic in research methods. One excellent site has been developed by the Department of Psychology at Alberta's Athabasca University. Here you can get information and access links for a wide range of topics in research methods.

and found to have higher levels of arousal than did those crossing the low bridge. After crossing the bridge, participants were asked to complete the TAT and were given the means to call the experimental confederate later as measures of sexual attraction. Participants' sexual imagery scores on the TAT and whether or not they called the confederate later were the dependent measures.

Experimental and Control Groups 1b

In an experiment, the investigator typically assembles two groups of subjects who are treated differently with regard to the independent variable. These two groups are referred to as the *experimental group* and the *control group*. *The experimental group* consists of the subjects who receive some special treatment in regard to the independent variable. The *control group* consists of similar subjects who do not receive the special treatment given to the experimental group.

Consider, for example, a study conducted by David Wolfe and his colleagues (Wolfe, Jaffe, & Crooks, 2006) at the University of Western Ontario. Wolfe was interested in the effects of treatment on dating abuse on the part of male and female teens who were at risk of abusive relationships based on their own history of maltreatment. All of the participants were teens who had suffered maltreatment and who were under a protection, supervision, or wardship order. Recent theories had linked previous maltreatment with aggression in one's own current relationships. Half of the participants were assigned to a psychoeducational treatment program (an 18-session intervention including skill-based and learning-based approaches), while the other half of the participants were those who received the existing standard Child Protection Services program consisting of social worker visits and basic shelter and care. In this case, those teens receiving the standard program, who did not receive the special intervention program, comprised the control group. The researchers found that the intervention was effective in reducing the frequency and severity of the teens' experience of abuse in relationships with others. For more information on relationship violence and its prevention, see the website developed by David Wolfe and his colleagues at http://youthrelationships.org and/or their recent research (Wolfe, 2007; Wolfe, Jaffe, & Crooks, 2006).

It is crucial that the experimental and control groups in a study be alike, except for the different treatment that they receive in regard to the independent variable. This stipulation brings us to the logic that underlies the experimental method. If the two groups are alike in all respects *except for the variation created by the manipulation of the independent variable,* any differences between the two groups on the dependent variable *must be due to the manipulation of the independent variable.* In this way, researchers isolate the effect of the independent variable on the dependent variable.

concept **check 2.1**

Recognizing Independent and Dependent Variables

Check your understanding of the experimental method by identifying the independent variable (IV) and dependent variable (DV) in the following investigations. Note that one study has two IVs and another has two DVs. You'll find the answers in Appendix A at the back of the book.

1. A researcher is interested in how heart rate and blood pressure are affected by viewing a violent film sequence as opposed to a nonviolent film sequence.

IV_____

DV_____

2. An organizational psychologist develops a new training program to improve clerks' courtesy toward customers in a large chain of retail stores. She conducts an experiment to see whether the training program leads to a reduction in the number of customer complaints.

IV_____

DV_____

3. A researcher wants to find out how stimulus complexity and stimulus contrast (light/dark variation) affect infants' attention to stimuli. He manipulates stimulus complexity and stimulus contrast and measures how long infants stare at various stimuli.

IV_____

DV_____

4. A social psychologist investigates the impact of group size on subjects' conformity in response to group pressure.

IV_____

DV_____

Extraneous Variables   1b

As we have seen, the logic of the experimental method rests on the assumption that the experimental and control groups are alike except for their treatment in regard to the independent variable. Any other differences between the two groups can cloud the situation and make it impossible to draw conclusions about how the independent variable affects the dependent variable.

In practical terms, of course, it is impossible to ensure that two groups of participants are exactly alike in *every* respect. The experimental and control groups have to be alike only on dimensions relevant to the dependent variable. Thus, Dutton and Aron did not need to worry about whether their two groups were similar in hair colour, height, or interest in music, as these variables were unlikely to influence the dependent variable of emotion.

Instead, experimenters concentrate on ensuring that the experimental and control groups are alike on a limited number of variables that could have a bearing on the results of the study. These variables are called extraneous, secondary, or nuisance variables. *Extraneous variables* are any variables other than the independent variable that seem likely to influence the dependent variable in a specific study.

In the Dutton and Aron study, one extraneous variable would have been the participants' personality or risk-taking propensity. Why? Because the males could choose to cross the high or low bridge themselves, different types of people may have decided to cross the high (perhaps sports enthusiasts or risk-takers) and the low (more cautious types) bridge, and participant personality might by itself affect the sexual attraction measures. For example, high risk-takers might have been more likely to call the female confederate than more cautious persons, regardless of which bridge they crossed. Here, personality and arousal would have been confounded. You might wish to take a moment to think about how you might redo the experiment in a way that would make this problem less of an issue in this case (you will see shortly how the experimenters decided to rid themselves of this potential confound). A *confounding of variables* occurs when two variables are linked together in a way that makes it difficult to sort out their specific effects. When an extraneous variable is confounded with an independent variable, a researcher cannot tell which is having what effect on the dependent variable.

Unanticipated confoundings of variables have wrecked innumerable experiments. That is why so much care, planning, and forethought must go into designing an experiment. One of the key qualities that separates a talented experimenter from a mediocre one is the ability to foresee troublesome extraneous variables and control them to avoid confoundings.

Experimenters use a variety of safeguards to control for extraneous variables. For instance, subjects are usually assigned to the experimental and control groups randomly. *Random assignment of subjects occurs when all subjects have an equal chance of being assigned to any group or condition in the study.* When experimenters distribute subjects into groups through some random procedure, they can be reasonably confident that the groups will be similar in most ways.

How did Dutton and Aron deal with the potential confounding of personality differences between those who crossed the high and low bridges and the intended variable of differences in arousal or anxiety? They conducted a second study employing a procedure very much like that used in Study 1 except that all the participants were males who crossed only the high bridge. To look at the effect of arousal on sexual attraction, the confederates approached one-half of the participants immediately after they crossed the high bridge and were then given the dependent measures, with the other half of the participants contacted about 10 minutes after they had crossed the bridge. The authors reasoned that the latter group would be less aroused than those who had just crossed the bridge—after all, they had 10 minutes to rest and calm down—so that any observed differences in sexual arousal and/or proportion of participants calling the confederate later on the phone would not likely be due to personality differences (because all had chosen to cross the same bridge) but to differences in arousal. In this follow-up study, only a female confederate was used. As illustrated in Table 2.2, those participants contacted immediately after crossing the bridge showed evidence of greater sexual attraction than did those contacted 10 minutes later. As you can see, there is a great deal of creativity and art to conducting an experiment well. You will encounter many other examples of this type of creativity as you read through the text.

	Participants Approached Immediately	Participants Approached after 10 Minutes
Sexual imagery	2.99	1.92
Proportion calling female confederate	65%	30%

TABLE 2.2

Results from Study Two of Dutton and Aron's (1974) Research on Fear and Emotion

Source: Dutton, D.G., & Aron, A.P. (1974). Some evidence for heightened sexual attraction under conditions of high anxiety. *Journal of Personality and Social Psychology, 30*, 510–517. Published by the American Psychological Association. Reprinted with permission.

Variations in Designing Experiments 1b

Some experiments are conducted with a simple design, with just one independent variable and one dependent variable. For example, the study conducted by Wolfe and his colleagues included just one independent variable: whether the teens were or were not receiving the specially designed intervention program. Actually, many variations are possible in conducting experiments. These variations warrant a brief mention.

First, it is sometimes advantageous to use only one group of subjects who serve as their own control group. The effects of the independent variable are evaluated by exposing this single group to two different conditions—an experimental condition and a control condition. For example, imagine that you wanted to study the effects of loud music on typing performance (see Figure 2.2). You could have a group of participants work on a typing task while loud music was played (experimental condition) and in the absence of music (control condition).

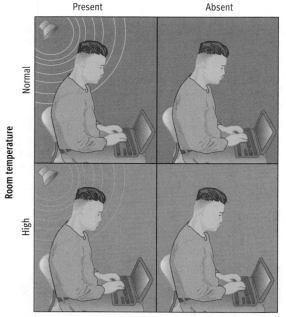

Distracting music

Present / Absent

Room temperature — Normal / High

FIGURE 2.2

Manipulation of two independent variables in an experiment.

As this example shows, when two independent variables are manipulated in a single experiment, the researcher has to compare four groups of subjects (or conditions) instead of the usual two. The main advantage of this procedure is that it allows an experimenter to see whether two variables interact.

This approach would ensure that the participants in the experimental and control conditions would be alike on any extraneous variables involving their personal characteristics, such as motivation or typing skill. After all, the same people would be studied in both conditions. When subjects serve as their own control group, the experiment is said to use a *within-subjects design* because comparisons are made within the same group of participants. In contrast, when two or more independent groups of subjects are exposed to a manipulation of an independent variable, the experiment is said to use a *between-subjects design* because comparisons are made between two different groups of participants. Although within-subjects designs are not used as frequently as between-subjects designs, they are advantageous for certain types of investigations (Curran & Bauer, 2011). They also require fewer participants and they ensure that the experimental and control groups are equivalent (Davis & Bremner, 2006).

Second, *it is possible to manipulate more than one independent variable in a single experiment.* Researchers often manipulate two or three independent variables to examine their joint effects on the dependent variable. Of course, after reading the Featured Study, you know that arousal wasn't the only independent variable manipulated by Dutton and Aron. Dutton and Aron included two independent variables in their study. Participants were chosen after crossing the high or low bridge (first independent variable) and were met on the other side by a male or female confederate (second independent variable). Their hypothesis was that arousal will heighten sexual attraction only if there are situation cues relevant to sexual attraction. In this case, assuming mostly heterosexual participants, arousal should increase sexual attraction primarily in the context of the female confederate. The main advantage of this approach is that it permits the experimenter to see whether two variables interact. An *interaction* means that the effect of one variable depends on the effect of another. In the case of Dutton and Aron's experiment, arousal affected sexual attraction only when the males were met on the other side of the bridge by the female confederate, just as their hypothesis predicted.

Third, it is also possible to use more than one dependent variable in a single study. Researchers frequently use a number of dependent variables to get a more complete picture of how experimental manipulations affect subjects' behaviour. This is precisely what Dutton and Aron did. They used both a questionnaire (i.e., the TAT) and a behavioural measure (i.e., calling the confederate) of sexual attraction.

Advantages and Disadvantages of Experimental Research

The experiment is a powerful research method. Its principal advantage is that it permits conclusions about cause-and-effect relationships between variables. Researchers are able to draw these conclusions about causation because the precise control available in the experiment allows them to isolate the relationship between the independent variable and the dependent variable, while neutralizing the effects of extraneous variables. No other research method can duplicate this strength of the experiment. This advantage is why psychologists usually prefer to use the experimental method whenever possible.

For all its power, however, the experiment has limitations. One problem is that experiments are often artificial. Because experiments require great control over proceedings, researchers must often construct simple, contrived situations to test their hypotheses experimentally. For example, to investigate decision making in juries, psychologists have conducted many experiments in which subjects read a brief summary of a trial and then record their individual "verdicts" of innocence or guilt. This approach allows the experimenter to manipulate a variable, such as the race of the defendant, to see whether it affects the participants' verdicts. However, critics have pointed out that having a participant read a short case summary and make an individual decision cannot really compare to the complexities of real trials (Weiten & Diamond, 1979). In actual court cases, jurors may spend weeks listening to confusing testimony while making subtle judgments about the credibility of witnesses. They then retire for hours of debate to arrive at a group verdict, which is quite different from rendering an individual decision. Many researchers have failed to do justice to this complex process in their laboratory experiments. When experiments are highly artificial, doubts arise about the applicability of findings to everyday behaviour outside the experimental laboratory. One way to address this limitation is to conduct a *field experiment*. Field experiments are research studies that use settings that are very much like real life; in fact, the research may occur in the context of everyday life and events. Our Featured Study in this chapter is an example of a field experiment. In conducting field experiments, the researcher may sacrifice some control over extraneous variables for greater *generalizability*. Some researchers believe that the results of field experiments are more generalizable or applicable to everyday life than are the typically more artificial lab experiments, and some have suggested that the use of field experimentation is on the rise (Shadish & Cooke, 2009). Not all researchers see the artificiality of the typical lab experiment as a serious limitation (Mook, 1983). The best strategy might be to use both approaches in your research program.

Another disadvantage is that the experimental method can't be used to explore some research questions. Psychologists are frequently interested in the effects of factors that cannot be manipulated as independent variables because of ethical concerns or practical realities. In some cases manipulations of variables are difficult or impossible. For example, you might want to know whether being brought up in an urban as opposed to a rural area affects people's values. An experiment would require you to randomly assign similar families to live in urban and rural areas, which obviously is impossible to do. To explore this question, you would have to use descriptive/correlational research methods, which we turn to next.

REVIEW OF KEY POINTS

▷ Experimental research involves the manipulation of an independent variable to determine its effect on a dependent variable. This research is usually done by comparing experimental and control groups, which must be alike in regard to important extraneous variables.

▷ Any differences between the groups in the dependent variable ought to be due to manipulation of the independent variable, as long as there are no confounds. Variables are said to be confounded when they vary together so that researchers cannot isolate the effect of the independent variable on the dependent variable.

▷ Experimental designs may vary. For example, sometimes an experimental group serves as its own control group. And many experiments have more than one independent variable or more than one dependent variable.

▷ Some of these variations were seen in the Featured Study, which examined the effects of level of fear or anxiety on sexual attraction.

▷ An experiment is a powerful research method that permits conclusions about cause-and-effect relationships between variables. However, the experimental method is often not usable for a specific problem, and many experiments tend to be artificial.

Looking for Links: Descriptive/Correlational Research

PREVIEW QUESTIONS

► How is naturalistic observation used to examine psychological phenomena?

► How can case studies be used to look for general principles of behaviour?

► Why do researchers use surveys?

► What are the strengths and weaknesses of descriptive/correlational research?

In some situations, psychologists cannot exert experimental control over the variables they want to study, for either ethical or practical reasons. For example, if you were interested in the effects of nutritious and non-nutritious maternal diets on the health of babies, you would never try to get some expectant mothers to follow poor nutritional habits. In such situations, investigators must rely on *descriptive/correlational research methods*. These methods include naturalistic observation, case studies, and surveys. What distinguishes these methods is that the researcher cannot manipulate the variables under study. This lack of control means that these methods cannot be used to demonstrate cause-and-effect relationships between variables. *Descriptive/correlational methods permit investigators to only describe patterns of behaviour and discover links or associations between variables.* That is not to suggest that associations are unimportant. You'll see in this section that information on associations between variables can be extremely valuable in our efforts to understand behaviour.

Naturalistic Observation

What determines whether drivers stop or continue when they see a yellow light? Are there ethnic differences in sociability? These are just a couple of examples of the kinds of questions that have been explored through naturalistic observation in recent studies. In *naturalistic observation* a researcher engages in careful observation of behaviour without intervening directly with the research subjects or participants. This type of research is called *naturalistic* because behaviour is allowed to unfold naturally (without interference) in its natural environment—that is, the setting in which it would normally occur. Of course, researchers have to make careful plans to ensure systematic, consistent observations (Angrosino, 2007). Let's look at two examples. One recent study concerned with accident prevention used a system of three video cameras to record drivers' reactions to yellow lights at an intersection (Elmitiny et al., 2010). The cameras and other equipment allowed the researchers to gather information on the vehicles' place in the flow of traffic, speed, and distance from the light and then relate these data to the drivers' on-the-fly decisions when the traffic light changed from green to yellow. The study provided some useful insights into the factors that lead people to inadvertently run red lights.

Another recent study (Ramirez-Esparza et al., 2009) examined ethnic differences in sociability using an innovative device called an *electronically activated recorder* (EAR). The EAR is an unobtrusive, portable audio recorder carried by participants that periodically records their conversations and other ambient sounds as they go about their normal daily activities (Mehl, 2007). Using this clever device, the researchers investigated an interesting paradox—stereotypes suggest that Mexicans are outgoing and sociable, but when asked, they rate themselves as less sociable than Americans. The study found, as usual, that Mexican participants rated themselves as less extraverted than American participants rated themselves. But the EAR data on their actual daily behaviour showed that they were *more* sociable than their American counterparts.

The major strength of naturalistic observation is that it allows researchers to study behaviour under conditions that are less artificial than in experiments. Another plus is that engaging in naturalistic observation can represent a good starting point when little is known about the behaviour under study. And, unlike case studies and surveys, naturalistic observation can be used to study animal behaviour. Many landmark studies of animal behaviour, such as Jane Goodall's (2000) work on the social and family life of chimpanzees, have depended on naturalistic observation. More recent examples of naturalistic observation with animals include studies of communication in Australian sea lions (Charrier, Pitcher, & Harcourt, in press), mating preferences in Eastern bluebirds (Liu et al., 2009), and tool use in wild spider monkeys (Lindshield & Rodrigues, 2009).

A major problem with naturalistic observation is that researchers often have trouble making their observations unobtrusively so they don't affect their participants' behaviour. *Reactivity occurs when a subject's behaviour is altered by the presence of an observer.* Even animals may exhibit reactivity if observational efforts are readily apparent (Iredale, Nevill, & Lutz, 2010). Another disadvantage is that it often is difficult to translate naturalistic observations into numerical data that permit precise statistical analyses.

Case Studies

What portion of people who commit suicide suffer from psychological disorders? Which disorders are most common among victims of suicide? In

Jane Goodall is known internationally for her pioneering work with chimpanzees in Gombe Stream National Park in Tanzania. Her study of the social interactions of the chimpanzees over the past five decades demonstrates the power of observational techniques in research.

health-care visits during the final month of their lives, do people who commit suicide communicate their intent to do so? A research team in Finland wanted to investigate the psychological characteristics of people who take their own lives (Henriksson et al., 1993; Isometsa et al., 1995). Other researchers had explored these questions, but the Finnish team planned a comprehensive, national study of unprecedented scope. Their initial sample consisted of all the known suicides in Finland for an entire year.

The research team decided that their question called for a case study approach. *A case study* is an in-depth investigation of an individual subject. When this method is applied to victims of suicide, the case studies are called *psychological autopsies*. A variety of data collection techniques can be used in case studies. In normal circumstances, when the participants are not deceased, typical techniques include interviewing the subjects, interviewing people who are very close to the subjects, direct observation of the subjects, examination of records, and psychological testing. In this study, the investigators conducted thorough interviews with the families of the suicide victims and with the health-care professionals who had treated them. The researchers also examined the suicide victims' medical, psychiatric, and social agency records, as well as relevant police investigations and forensic reports. Comprehensive case reports were then assembled for each person who committed suicide.

These case studies revealed that in 93 percent of the suicides, the victim suffered from a significant psychological disorder (Henriksson et al., 1993). The most common diagnoses, by a large margin, were depression and alcohol dependence. In 571 cases, victims had a health-care appointment during the last four weeks of their lives, but only 22 percent

of these people discussed the possibility of suicide during their final visit (Isometsa et al., 1995). Even more surprising, the sample included 100 people who saw a health professional on the same day they killed themselves, yet only 21 percent of these individuals raised the issue of suicide. The investigators concluded that mental illness is a contributing factor in virtually all completed suicides and that the vast majority of suicidal people do not spontaneously reveal their intentions to health-care professionals.

Clinical psychologists, who diagnose and treat psychological problems, routinely do case studies of their clients (see Figure 2.3). When clinicians

WEB LINK 2.5

PSYCLINE: Your Guide to Psychology and Social Science Journals on the Web
Relatively few journals actually post their articles online for free. But this searchable index to the online sites of more than 1900 psychology journals may lead you to recent tables of contents or abstracts or help you identify research resources on more unusual topics in psychology.

Case Study   Page 2

   Jennie is a 21-year-old single college student with no prior psychiatric history. She was admitted to a short-term psychiatric ward from a hospital emergency room with a chief complaint of "I think I was psychotic." For several months prior to her admission she reported a series of "strange experiences." These included religious experiences, increased anxiety, a conviction that other students were conspiring against her, visual distortions, auditory hallucinations, and grandiose delusions. During the week prior to admission, the symptoms gradually worsened, and eventually she became agitated and disorganized.

   A number of stressful events preceded this decompensation. A maternal aunt, a strong and central figure in her family, had died four months previously. As a college senior, she was struggling with decisions about her career choices following graduation. She was considering applying to graduate programs but was unable to decide which course of study she preferred. She was very much involved with her boyfriend, also a college senior. He, too, was struggling with anxiety about graduation, and it was not clear that their relationship would continue. The patient also reported feeling pressured and overextended.

   The patient's older sister had suffered two psychotic episodes. This sister had slowly deteriorated, particularly after

FIGURE 2.3

An example of a case study report.

As this example illustrates, case studies are particularly appropriate for clinical situations in which efforts are made to diagnose and treat psychological problems. Usually, one case study does not provide much basis for deriving general laws of behaviour. However, if you examine a series of case studies involving similar problems, you can look for threads of consistency that may yield general conclusions.

Source: Greenfield, D. (1985). *The psychotic patient: Medication and psychotherapy.* New York: The Free Press. Copyright © 1985 by David Greenfield. Reprinted by permission of the author.

assemble a case study for diagnostic purposes, they generally are *not* conducting empirical research. Case study *research* typically involves investigators analyzing a collection of case studies to look for patterns that permit general conclusions. For example, one recent study (Arcelus et al., 2009) evaluated the efficacy of a treatment called *interpersonal psychotherapy* (IPT) for people suffering from bulimia (an eating disorder marked by out-of-control overeating followed by self-induced vomiting, fasting, and excessive exercise). Careful case assessments were made of 59 bulimic patients before, during, and after the 16-session course of IPT treatment. The results demonstrated that interpersonal therapy can be an effective treatment for bulimic disorders.

Case studies are particularly well suited for investigating certain phenomena, such as psychological disorders and neuropsychological issues. For example, Brenda Milner of McGill University made important contributions to our knowledge about the importance of the temporal lobes of the brain in memory and the existence of multiple memory systems in the brain by using this method. She made extensive use of her case study of a patient known as H. M. in her early work (Milner, Corking, & Teuber, 1968). (We will discuss this and other work in neuropsychology and memory in Chapters 3 and 7.)

Case studies can also provide compelling, real-life illustrations that bolster a hypothesis or theory. However, the main problem with case studies is that they can be highly subjective. Information from several sources must be knit together in an impressionistic way. In this process, clinicians and researchers may focus selectively on information that fits with their expectations, which usually reflect their theoretical slant. Thus, it is relatively easy for investigators to see what they expect to see in case study research.

Surveys

One research method that many of us are frequently exposed to is the survey. In a *survey*, researchers use questionnaires or interviews to gather information about specific aspects of participants' behaviour. Large companies may survey the buying habits of specific segments of the buying public. Political parties often do extensive polling before they call an election or propose specific legislation. Surveys may also be used to gather information on important social issues that may have legal and public policy implications, such

as the study conducted by Memorial University researchers on the frequency of sexual harassment taking place in Canadian high schools (Walsh, Duffy, & Gallagher-Duffy, 2007). As such, surveys are often used to obtain information on aspects of behaviour that are difficult to observe directly. Surveys also make it relatively easy to collect data on attitudes and opinions from large samples of participants. As Fife-Schaw (2006b, p. 212) notes, "The humble questionnaire is probably the most common research tool in the social sciences."

The major problem with surveys is that they depend on self-report data. As we'll discuss later, intentional deception, wishful thinking, memory lapses, and poorly worded questions can distort participants' verbal reports about their behaviour (Krosnick, 1999). In addition, not all surveys are conducted with care. One problem discussed in more detail later in the chapter is that of sampling bias. A survey is characterized by sampling bias if the sample on which it is based is not representative of the population that it is intended to describe. Throughout this book we present statistics based on surveys conducted by Statistics Canada (Statistics Canada, 2010a). Statistics Canada goes to great lengths to conduct its surveys properly, and researchers can obtain a manual on how to properly conduct surveys (Statistics Canada, 2010b). You should critically evaluate the surveys you are exposed to. For example, some popular websites invite students to rate the teaching ability of their professors. But what do we know about the sample upon which the results are based? One of this book's authors, looking at his own ratings, was struck by the fact that fewer than 200 students rated him on the site, yet in the time period covered by the rating he has taught over 5000 students. Exactly who is doing the rating? Do only specific types of students do these ratings (e.g., males, A students, C students)? Are these students representative of the students in his classes? He'd like to think so—the ratings are very high! But before he made any important career decisions based on this data, he would need to know a great deal more about the sample characteristics.

Advantages and Disadvantages of Descriptive/Correlational Research

Descriptive/correlational research methods have advantages and disadvantages, which are compared to the strengths and weaknesses of experimental research in Figure 2.4. As a whole, the foremost advantage of these methods is that they give researchers a

Research method	Description	Example	Advantages	Disadvantages
Experiment 	Manipulation of an independent variable under carefully controlled conditions to see whether any changes occur in a dependent variable	Youngsters are randomly assigned to watch a violent or nonviolent film, and their aggression is measured in a laboratory situation	Precise control over variables; ability to draw conclusions about cause-and-effect relationships	Contrived situations often artificial; ethical concerns and practical realities preclude experiments on many important questions
Naturalistic observation 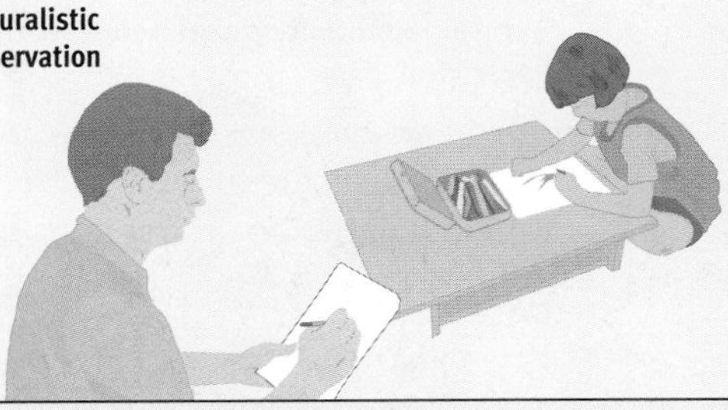	Careful, usually prolonged observation of behaviour without direct intervention	Youngsters' spontaneous acts of aggression during recreational activities are observed unobtrusively and recorded	Minimizes artificiality; can be good place to start when little is known about phenomena under study	Often difficult to remain unobtrusive; can't explain why certain patterns of behaviour were observed
Case studies 	In-depth investigation of a single participant using direct interview, direct observation, and other data collection techniques	Detailed case histories are worked up for youngsters referred to counselling because of excessive aggressive behaviour	Well-suited for study of certain phenomena; can provide compelling illustrations to support a theory	Subjectivity makes it easy to see what one expects to see based on one's theoretical slant; clinical samples often unrepresentative
Surveys 	Use of questionnaires or interviews to gather information about specific aspects of participants' behaviour	Youngsters are given questionnaire that describes hypothetical scenarios and are asked about the likelihood of aggressive behaviour	Can gather data on difficult-to-observe aspects of behaviour; relatively easy to collect data from large samples	Self-report data often unreliable, due to intentional deception, social desirability bias, response sets, memory lapses, and wishful thinking

FIGURE 2.4

Comparison of major research methods.

This chart pulls together a great deal of information on key research methods in psychology and gives a simple example of how each method might be applied in research on aggression. As you can see, the various research methods each have their strengths and weaknesses.

way to explore questions that could not be examined with experimental procedures. For example, after-the-fact analyses would be the only ethical way to investigate the possible link between poor maternal nutrition and birth defects in humans. In a similar vein, if researchers hope to learn how urban and rural upbringing relate to people's values, they have to depend on descriptive methods, since they can't control where subjects grow up. Thus, *descriptive/correlational research broadens the scope of phenomena that psychologists are able to study.*

Unfortunately, descriptive methods have one significant disadvantage: Investigators cannot control events to isolate cause and effect. *Consequently, correlational research cannot demonstrate conclusively that two variables are causally related.* In

Matching Research Methods to Questions

Check your understanding of the uses and strengths of various research methods by figuring out which method would be optimal for investigating the following questions about behavioural processes. Choose from the following methods: (a) experiment, (b) naturalistic observation, (c) case study, and (d) survey. Indicate your choice (by letter) next to each question. You'll find the answers in Appendix A in the back of the book.

_____ **1.** Are people's attitudes about nuclear disarmament related to their social class or education?

_____ **2.** Do people who suffer from anxiety disorders share similar early childhood experiences?

_____ **3.** Do troops of baboons display territoriality—that is, do they mark off an area as their own and defend it from intrusion by other baboons?

_____ **4.** Can the presence of food-related cues (delicious-looking desserts in advertisements, for example) cause an increase in the amount of food that people eat?

correlational studies assessing the relationship between two variables, you never know if the correlation between them is actually due to the relationship between each of them and some third variable you did not even measure. For example, if you took all of the students in your school and correlated their heights and weights, you would likely find a strong association. All you can conclude is that they are related to each other; you cannot draw any conclusions about which factor causes the other. In fact, they are both likely due to some other factor you did not consider, such as age or nutrition. These and related issues are discussed in the next section.

REVIEW OF KEY POINTS

▷ Psychologists rely on descriptive/correlational research when they are unable to manipulate the variables they want to study. Naturalistic observation involves careful, prolonged observation of behaviour in its natural setting without any intervention.

▷ Clinical research depends heavily on case studies, which involve in-depth investigations of individuals. In a survey, researchers interview participants or administer questionnaires to gather information on specific aspects of behaviour.

▷ Descriptive/correlational research methods allow psychologists to explore issues that might not be open to experimental investigation. However, these research methods cannot demonstrate cause-and-effect relationships.

Looking for Conclusions: Statistics and Research

PREVIEW QUESTIONS

▷ What are the three measures of central tendency?

▷ How do researchers measure variability?

▷ What is the difference between positive and negative correlations?

▷ How is correlation related to prediction and causation?

▷ What does *statistical significance* mean?

Whether researchers use experimental or correlational methods, they need some way to make sense of their data. *Statistics* is the use of mathematics to organize, summarize, and interpret numerical data. Statistical analyses permit researchers to draw conclusions based on their observations. Many students find statistics intimidating, but statistics are an integral part of modern life. Although you may not realize it, you are bombarded with statistics nearly every day. When you read about economists' projections for inflation, when you check a baseball player's batting average, when you see the popularity ratings of television shows, you are dealing with statistics.

Statistics are essential in order to understand and draw conclusions from research. This is true of most research, even in informal studies. In fact, it was a very

informal study conducted by R. A. Fisher that led to his insight about the importance of statistical probability in drawing conclusions in hypothesis testing in research (Nolen & Heinzen, 2011; Salsburg, 2001). Fisher (1935) is a significant figure in the development of statistics. One afternoon when pouring tea for a friend, Fisher added the tea to the cup before the milk. His friend, Dr. Muriel Bristol, declined the cup of tea, asserting that for a cup of tea to taste best the milk must be added first. Fisher thought this was nonsense, that it would taste no different whether the tea or the milk was added first. He told Dr. Bristol that he did not believe she could tell the difference between tea with the tea poured first and tea with the milk poured first. They devised an experiment in which he gave her several cups of tea, some with the milk added first and some with the tea added first. Fisher's hypothesis was, that "she could not tell the difference." Fisher reasoned that probability was important, for if she could not tell the difference she would likely guess right about 50 percent of the time. But what percentage of the time would she have to guess right to convince him that she could indeed tell the difference—51 percent accuracy, 55 percent, 60 percent . . .? This shows the use of *inferential* statistics in hypothesis testing, as discussed on page 64. For Fisher and psychologists who followed him, statistics and research were linked. You may be wondering if Dr. Bristol could tell the difference. In fact, she could tell the difference—so much so that Fisher found her accuracy uncanny.

In this section, we will examine a few basic statistical concepts that will help you understand the research discussed throughout this book. For the most part, we won't concern ourselves with the details of statistical *computations*. At this juncture, we will discuss only the purpose, logic, and value of the two basic types of statistics: descriptive statistics and inferential statistics. Statistics are a key element in understanding and evaluating research, and research on statistics is an active research area in its own right (e.g., Flora, 2008; Graham, 2009; McArdle, 2009; Trafimow & Rice, 2009).

Descriptive Statistics

Descriptive statistics are used to organize and summarize data. They provide an overview of numerical data. Key descriptive statistics include measures of central tendency, measures of variability, and the coefficient of correlation. Let's take a brief look at each of these.

Central Tendency

In summarizing numerical data, researchers often want to know what constitutes a typical or average score. To answer this question, they use three measures of central tendency: the median, the mean, and the mode. The *median* is the score that falls exactly in the centre of a distribution of scores. Half of the scores fall above the median and half fall below it. The *mean* is the arithmetic average of the scores in a distribution. It is obtained by adding up all the scores and dividing by the total number of scores. Finally, the *mode* is the most frequent score in a distribution.

In general, the mean is the most useful measure of central tendency because additional statistical manipulations can be performed on it that are not possible with the median or mode. However, the mean is sensitive to extreme scores in a distribution,

which can sometimes make the mean misleading. To illustrate, imagine that you're interviewing for a sales position at a company. Unbeknownst to you, the company's five salespeople earned the following incomes in the previous year: $20 000, $20 000, $25 000, $35 000, and $200 000. You ask how much the typical salesperson earns in a year. The sales director proudly announces that her five salespeople earned a *mean* income of $60 000 last year (the calculations are shown in Figure 2.5). However, before you order that expensive new sports car, you had better inquire about the *median* and *modal* income for the sales staff. In this case, one extreme score ($200 000) has inflated the mean, making it unrepresentative of the sales staff's earnings. In this instance, the median ($25 000) and the mode ($20 000) both provide better estimates of what you are likely to earn.

Lack of agreement between measures of central tendency usually occurs when a few extreme scores pull the mean away from the centre of the distribution, as shown in Figure 2.6. The curves plotted in Figure 2.6 are simply "smoothed-out" frequency polygons based on data from many subjects. A *frequency polygon* is a line figure used to present data from a frequency distribution. A *frequency distribution* is an orderly arrangement of scores indicating the frequency of each score or a group of scores. They show that when a distribution is symmetric, as in Figure 2.6(a), the measures of central tendency fall together, but this is not true in skewed or unbalanced distributions.

Figure 2.6(b) shows a *negatively skewed distribution*, in which most scores pile up at the high end of the scale (*negative skew* refers to the direction in which the curve's "tail" points). A *positively skewed distribution*, in which scores pile up at the low end

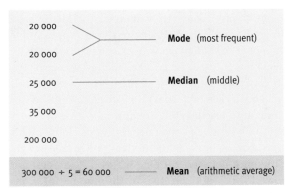

FIGURE 2.5

Measures of central tendency.
The three measures of central tendency usually converge, but that is not always the case, as these data illustrate. Which measure is most useful depends on the nature of the data. Generally, the mean is the best index of central tendency, but in this instance the median is more informative.

The Research Enterprise in Psychology

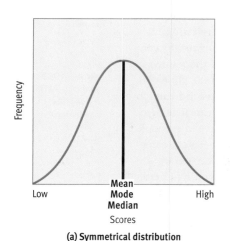

(a) Symmetrical distribution

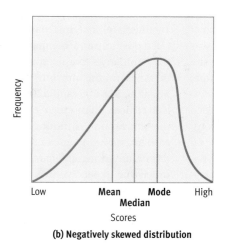

(b) Negatively skewed distribution

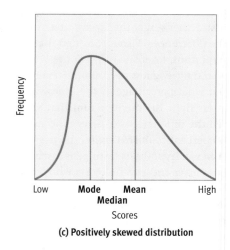

(c) Positively skewed distribution

FIGURE 2.6

Measures of central tendency in skewed distributions.
In a symmetrical distribution (a), the three measures of central tendency converge. However, in a negatively skewed distribution (b) or in a positively skewed distribution (c), the mean, median, and mode are pulled apart as shown here. Typically, in these situations, the median provides the best index of central tendency.

of the scale, is shown in Figure 2.6(c). In both types of skewed distributions, a few extreme scores at one end pull the mean, and to a lesser degree the median, away from the mode. In these situations, the mean may be misleading and the median usually provides the best index of central tendency.

1c

Variability

In describing a set of data, it is often useful to have some estimate of the variability among the scores. *Variability* refers to how much the scores in a data set vary from each other and from the mean. Just as there are several measures of central tendency, there are also different measures of variability. The simplest is referred to as the *range*. Calculating the range is easy; you simply subtract the lowest score in your sample from the highest score. For example, suppose the students in your class have the following ages: 7, 8, 9, 11, 3, 12, and 14. Then the range of ages in your class is 14 − 3 = 11 years. As any teacher will tell you, a class with that range in ages would be very difficult to teach. While giving you a sense of dispersion in your scores, the range is limited in its usefulness. For example, while it gives you an idea of the difference between extreme scores (i.e., highest and lowest), it is not sensitive to the number of scores that lie between these extremes (Dunn, 2009). In some circumstances this might be important. A far more useful measure of dispersion or variability is called the *standard deviation*.

The *standard deviation* is an index of the amount of variability in a set of data. It gives you a measure of how the scores in your sample cluster around

the average. When variability is great, the standard deviation will be relatively large. When variability is low, the standard deviation will be smaller. This relationship is apparent if you examine the two sets of data in Figure 2.7. The mean is the same for both sets of scores, but variability clearly is greater in set B than in set A. This greater variability yields a higher standard deviation for set B than for set A. Estimates of variability play a crucial role when researchers use statistics to decide whether the results of their studies support their hypotheses.

Speed (kilometres per hour)		
Set A **Perfection Boulevard**		**Set B** **Wild Street**
35		21
34		37
33		50
37		28
38		42
40		37
36		39
33		25
34		23
30		48
35	Mean	35
2.87	Standard deviation	10.39

FIGURE 2.7

Variability and the standard deviation.
Although these two sets of data produce the same mean, or average, an observer on Wild Street would see much more variability in the speeds of individual cars than an observer on Perfection Boulevard would. As you can see, the standard deviation for set B is higher than that for set A because of the greater variability in set B.

The standard deviation is also useful in understanding another important concept in psychology and statistics, the *normal curve or normal distribution*. The *normal distribution* is a symmetrical, bell-shaped curve that represents the pattern in which many human characteristics are dispersed in the population. A great many physical qualities (e.g., height, nose length, and running speed) and psychological traits (intelligence, spatial reasoning ability, introversion) are distributed in a manner that closely resembles this bell-shaped curve. When a trait is normally distributed, most scores fall near the centre of the distribution (the mean), and the number of scores gradually declines as one moves away from the centre in either direction. The normal distribution is *not* a law of nature. It's a mathematical function, or theoretical curve, that approximates the way nature seems to operate.

The normal distribution is the bedrock of the scoring system for most psychological tests, such as intelligence quotient (IQ) tests. As we discuss in Chapter 9, psychological tests are *relative measures*; they assess how people score on a trait in comparison to other people. The normal distribution gives us a precise way to measure how people stack up in comparison to each other. The scores under the normal curve are dispersed in a fixed pattern, with the standard deviation serving as the unit of measurement, as

shown in Figure 2.8. About 68 percent of the scores in the distribution fall within plus or minus 1 standard deviation of the mean, while 95 percent of the scores fall within plus or minus 2 standard deviations of the mean. Given this fixed pattern, if you know the mean and standard deviation of a normally distributed trait, you can tell where any score falls in the distribution for the trait.

Test scores such as those derived from IQ tests that place examinees in the normal distribution can always be converted to percentile scores, which are a little easier to interpret. A *percentile score* indicates the percentage of people who score at or below a particular score. For example, if you score at the 60th percentile on an IQ test, 60 percent of the people who take the test score the same or below you, while the remaining 40 percent score above you. There are tables available that permit us to convert any standard deviation placement in a normal distribution into a precise percentile score. Figure 2.8 gives some percentile conversions for the normal curve.

Of course, not all distributions are normal. As we saw in Figure 2.6, some distributions are skewed in one direction or the other. As an example, consider what would happen if your psychology exam was much too easy or much too hard. If the test was too easy, scores would be bunched up at the high end of the scale, as in Figure 2.6(b). If the test was too hard,

WEB LINK 2.6

HyperStat Online
For psychology researchers who find they've temporarily misplaced their statistics textbook, here's one written in hypertext by Professor David M. Lane of Rice University, and it's always available online for free. He also includes links to excellent resources involving statistics, the analysis of experimental data, and even some statistical humour.

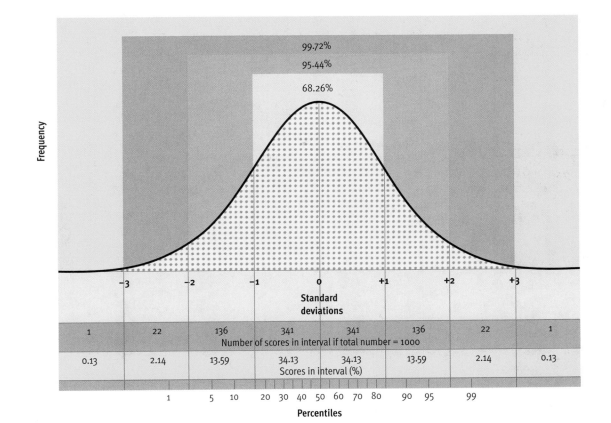

FIGURE 2.8

The normal distribution.
Many characteristics are distributed in a pattern represented by this bell-shaped curve (each dot represents a case). The horizontal axis shows how far above or below the mean a score is (measured in plus or minus standard deviations). The vertical axis shows the number of cases obtaining each score. In a normal distribution, most cases fall near the centre of the distribution, so that 68.26 percent of the cases fall within plus or minus 1 standard deviation of the mean. The number of cases gradually declines as one moves away from the mean in either direction, so that only 13.59 percent of the cases fall between 1 and 2 standard deviations above or below the mean, and even fewer cases (2.14 percent) fall between 2 and 3 standard deviations above or below the mean.

scores would be bunched up at the low end, as in Figure 2.6(c).

The next statistic we consider is the correlation coefficient. Correlational analyses can be very useful in answering a wide variety of research questions.

Correlation

A correlation exists when two variables are related to each other. Investigators often want to quantify the strength of an association between two variables, such as between class attendance and course grade, or between cigarette smoking and physical disease. In this effort, they depend extensively on a useful descriptive statistic: the correlation coefficient. *The correlation coefficient* is a numerical index of the degree of relationship between two variables. A correlation coefficient indicates (1) the direction (positive or negative) of the relationship and (2) how strongly the two variables are related.

Positive versus Negative Correlation. A *positive correlation* indicates that two variables co-vary in the *same* direction. This means that high scores on variable X are associated with high scores on variable Y and that low scores on variable X are associated with low scores on variable Y. For example, there is a positive correlation between high school grade point average (GPA) and subsequent university GPA. That is, people who do well in high school tend to do well in university, and those who perform poorly in high school tend to perform poorly in university (see Figure 2.9).

In contrast, a *negative* correlation indicates that two variables co-vary in the *opposite* direction. This means that people who score high on variable X tend to score low on variable Y, whereas those who score low on X tend to score high on Y. For example, in most university courses, there is a negative correlation between how frequently students are absent and how well they perform on exams. Students who have a high number of absences tend to get low exam scores, while students who have a low number of absences tend to earn higher exam scores (see Figure 2.9). The nature of positive and negative correlations is also discussed and illustrated through the use of scatterplots in Appendix B (see page A-7).

If a correlation is negative, a minus sign ($-$) is always placed in front of the coefficient. If a correlation is positive, a plus sign ($+$) may be placed in front of the coefficient, or the coefficient may be shown with no sign. Thus, if there's no sign, the correlation is positive.

Strength of the Correlation. Whereas the positive or negative sign indicates the direction of an association, the *size of the coefficient* indicates the *strength* of an association between two variables. The coefficient can vary between 0 and $+1.00$ (if positive) or between 0 and -1.00 (if negative). A coefficient near zero indicates no relationship between the variables; that is, high or low scores on variable X show no consistent relationship to high or low scores on variable Y. A coefficient of $+1.00$ or -1.00 indicates a perfect, one-to-one correspondence between the two variables. Most correlations fall between these extremes.

FIGURE 2.9
Positive and negative correlation.

Notice that the terms *positive* and *negative* refer to the direction of the relationship between two variables, not to its strength. Variables are positively correlated if they tend to increase and decrease together and are negatively correlated if one tends to increase when the other decreases.

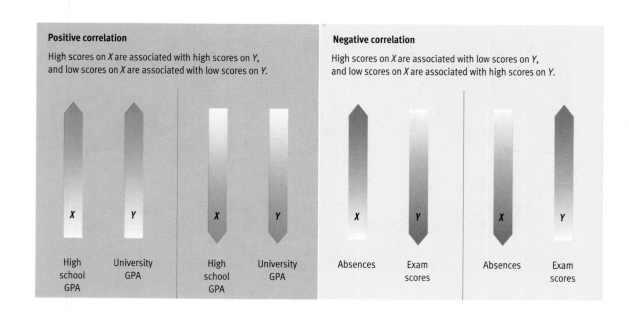

Positive correlation

High scores on X are associated with high scores on Y, and low scores on X are associated with low scores on Y.

Negative correlation

High scores on X are associated with low scores on Y, and low scores on X are associated with high scores on Y.

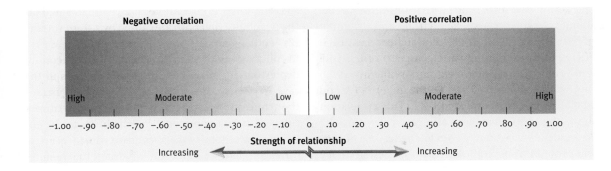

FIGURE 2.10

Interpreting correlation coefficients.

The magnitude of a correlation coefficient indicates the strength of the relationship between two variables. The sign (plus or minus) indicates whether the correlation is positive or negative. The closer the coefficient comes to +1.00 or −1.00, the stronger the relationship between the variables.

The closer the correlation to either −1.00 or +1.00, the stronger the relationship (see Figure 2.10). Thus, a correlation of 0.90 represents a stronger tendency for variables to be associated than a correlation of 0.40 does. Likewise, a correlation of −0.75 represents a stronger relationship than a correlation of −0.45. Keep in mind that the *strength* of a correlation depends only on the size of the coefficient. The positive or negative sign simply indicates the direction of the relationship. Therefore, a correlation of −0.60 reflects a stronger relationship than a correlation of +0.30.

Correlation and Prediction. You may recall that one of the key goals of scientific research is accurate prediction. A close link exists between the magnitude of a correlation and the power it gives scientists to make predictions. *As a correlation increases in strength (gets closer to either −1.00 or +1.00), the ability to predict one variable based on knowledge of the other variable increases.*

To illustrate, consider the various subtests of the *Graduate Record Exam* (GRE). The GRE is a standardized test developed by the Educational Testing Service (http://www.ets.org) that you may be asked to take if you apply for graduate study in psychology at most Canadian universities. Many psychology departments in Canada require students' scores on this test as part of the application package.

concept **check 2.3**

Understanding Correlation

Check your understanding of correlation by interpreting the meaning of the correlation in item 1 and by guessing the direction (positive or negative) of the correlations in item 2. You'll find the answers in Appendix A.

1. Researchers have found a substantial positive correlation between youngsters' self-esteem and their academic achievement (measured by grades in school). Check any acceptable conclusions based on this correlation.

_____ **a.** Low grades cause low self-esteem.

_____ **b.** There is an association between self-esteem and academic achievement.

_____ **c.** High self-esteem causes high academic achievement.

_____ **d.** High ability causes both high self-esteem and high academic achievement.

_____ **e.** Youngsters who score low in self-esteem tend to get low grades, and those who score high in self-esteem tend to get high grades.

2. Indicate whether you would expect the following correlations to be positive or negative.

_____ **f.** The correlation between age and visual acuity (among adults).

_____ **g.** The correlation between years of education and income.

_____ **h.** The correlation between shyness and the number of friends one has.

The GRE has several subtests that examine specific abilities such as verbal, analytical, and quantitative reasoning. (GRE, 2008). Researchers have been interested in examining various aspects of the GRE tests. For example, Sternberg and Williams (1997) showed that students' scores on the quantitative and analytical subtests correlated 0.47. This correlation shows that the two abilities as measured by the GRE are moderately positively correlated. Because of this, you should be able to predict with modest accuracy how well students do on one test from scores on the other. If the correlation was much higher, say 0.90, you would be able to predict one from the other with much higher accuracy. In contrast, if the correlation was 0.20, one test's prediction of the other would be much less meaningful.

Correlation and Causation. Although a high correlation allows us to predict one variable from another, it does not tell us whether a cause-and-effect relationship exists between the two variables. The problem is that variables can be highly correlated even though they are not causally related. For example, there is a substantial positive correlation between the size of young children's feet and the size of their vocabulary. That is, larger feet are associated with a larger vocabulary. Obviously, increases in foot size do not *cause* increases in vocabulary size. Nor do increases in vocabulary size cause increases in foot size. Instead, both are caused by a third variable: an increase in the children's age.

When we find that variables X and Y are correlated, we can safely conclude only that X and Y are related. We do not know *how* X and Y are related. We do not know whether X causes Y or Y causes X or whether both are caused by a third variable. For example, survey studies have found a positive correlation between smoking and the risk of experiencing a major depressive disorder (Breslau, Kilbey, & Andreski, 1991, 1993). Although it's clear that there is an association between smoking and depression, it's hard to tell what's causing what. The investigators acknowledge that they don't know whether smoking makes people more vulnerable to depression or whether depression increases the tendency to smoke. Moreover, they note that they can't rule out the possibility that both are caused by a third variable (Z). Perhaps anxiety and neuroticism increase the likelihood of both taking up smoking and becoming depressed. The plausible causal relationships in this case are diagrammed in Figure 2.11, which illustrates the "third variable problem" in interpreting correlations. This is a common problem in research, and you'll see this type of diagram again when we discuss other correlations. Thus, it is important to remember that *correlation is not equivalent to causation.*

Inferential Statistics

After researchers have summarized their data with descriptive statistics, they still need to decide whether their data support their hypotheses. *Inferential statistics* are used to interpret data and draw conclusions. Working with the laws of probability, researchers use inferential statistics to evaluate the possibility that their results might be due to the fluctuations of chance.

To illustrate this process, envision a hypothetical experiment. A computerized tutoring program (the independent variable) is designed to increase sixth graders' reading achievement (the dependent variable). Our hypothesis is that program participants (the experimental group) will score higher than nonparticipants (the control group) on a standardized reading test given near the end of the school year. Let's assume that we compare 60 subjects in each group. We obtain the following results, reported in terms of participants' grade-level scores for reading:

Control Group		Experimental Group
6.3	Mean	6.8
1.4	Standard deviation	2.4

We hypothesized that the training program would produce higher reading scores in the experimental group than in the control group. Sure enough, that is indeed the case. However, we have to ask ourselves a critical question: Is this observed difference between

FIGURE 2.11

Three possible causal relationships between correlated variables.

If variables X and Y are correlated, does X cause Y, does Y cause X, or does some hidden third variable, Z, account for the changes in both X and Y? As the relationship between smoking and depression illustrates, a correlation alone does not provide the answer. We will encounter this problem of interpreting the meaning of correlations frequently in this text.

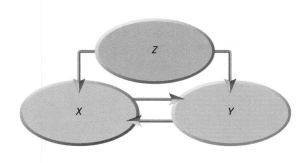

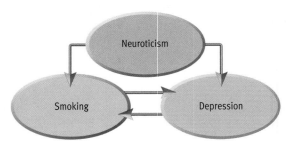

the two groups large enough to support our hypothesis? That is, do the higher scores in the experimental group reflect the effect of the training program? Or could a difference of this size have occurred by chance? If our results could easily have occurred by chance, they don't provide meaningful support for our hypothesis.

When statistical calculations indicate that research results are not likely to be due to chance, the results are said to be *statistically significant*. You will probably hear your psychology professor use this phrase quite frequently. In discussing research, it is routine to note that "statistically significant differences were found." In statistics, the word *significant* has a precise and special meaning. *Statistical significance* is said to exist when the probability that the observed findings are due to chance is very low. "Very low" is usually defined as fewer than 5 chances in 100, which is referred to as the 0.05 level of significance.

Notice that in this special usage, *significant* does not mean "important," or even "interesting." Statistically significant findings may or may not be theoretically significant or practically significant. They simply are research results that are unlikely to be due to chance.

You don't need to be concerned here with the details of how statistical significance is calculated. However, it is worth noting that a key consideration is the amount of variability in the data. That is why the standard deviation, which measures variability, is such an important statistic. When the necessary computations are made for our hypothetical experiment, the difference between the two groups does *not* turn out to be statistically significant. Thus, our results would not be adequate to demonstrate that our tutoring program leads to improved reading achievement. Psychologists have to do this kind of

statistical analysis as part of virtually every study. Thus, inferential statistics are an integral element in the research enterprise.

Statistics even provide you with a way of combining the results of several experiments that have examined the same issues. In *meta-analysis*, the results of findings obtained in several studies are integrated to allow for conclusions regarding the set of observed results. For example, you may be aware of several studies that have examined the effects of insight therapy for the treatment of depression. Through the use of meta-analysis, you can generate conclusions regarding the size of the therapeutic effects. Meta-analysis is discussed in the next section.

REVIEW OF KEY POINTS

▶ Psychologists use descriptive statistics to organize and summarize their numerical data. The mean, median, and mode are widely used measures of central tendency. The mean tends to be the most useful of these indexes, but it can be distorted by extreme scores. Variability is usually measured with the standard deviation, which increases as the variability in a data set grows.

▶ Correlations may be either positive (when two variables co-vary in the same direction) or negative (when two variables co-vary in the opposite direction). The closer a correlation is to either +1.00 or −1.00, the stronger the association is.

▶ As a correlation increases in strength, the ability to predict one variable based on knowledge of the other variable increases. However, a correlation is no assurance of causation. When variables are correlated, we do not know whether X causes Y, or Y causes X, or a third variable causes both.

▶ Hypothesis testing involves deciding whether observed findings support the researcher's hypothesis. Findings are statistically significant only when they are unlikely to be due to chance.

Looking for Flaws: Evaluating Research

Scientific research is a more reliable source of information than casual observation or popular belief. However, it would be wrong to conclude that all published research is free of errors. As we just saw, when researchers report statistically significant differences at the 0.05 level, there are 5 chances in 100 that the results really are a misleading by-product of chance fluctuation. This probability is pretty low, but it's not zero. Moreover, scientists' effort to minimize the probability of obtaining significant differences when none really exist increases the likelihood of the opposite mistake—failing to find significant differences when the groups really are different. Thus, even when research is conducted in a sound fashion,

there's still a small chance of erroneous conclusions. Above and beyond this problem, we need to recognize that scientists are fallible human beings who do not conduct flawless research. Their personal biases in designing and interpreting studies can also distort research results (MacCoun, 1998).

For these reasons, researchers are reluctant to settle scientific questions on the basis of just one empirical study. Instead, important questions usually generate a flurry of studies to see whether key findings will stand the test of replication. *Replication* is the repetition of a study to see whether the earlier results are duplicated. The replication process helps science identify and purge erroneous findings. Of course, the

PREVIEW QUESTIONS

▶ What is sampling bias?
▶ What are placebo effects, and how can you guard against them?
▶ What is the social desirability bias?
▶ What are response sets?
▶ What is experimenter bias, and how can you guard against it?

replication process sometimes leads to contradictory results. You'll see some examples in later chapters. Inconsistent findings on a research question can be frustrating and confusing for students. However, some inconsistency in results is to be expected, given science's commitment to replication. This raises the question of how students and research consumers can make sense of inconsistent results. One of the strengths of the empirical approach is that scientists work to reconcile or explain conflicting results. In their efforts to make sense of inconsistent research results, psychologists are increasingly depending on a technique called *meta-analysis,* which came into vogue in the 1980s (Cooper, 1990, 2010).

Meta-Analysis

A *meta-analysis* is the combination of the statistical results of many studies of the same question, yielding an estimate of the size and consistency of a variable's effects. In conducting a meta-analysis the researcher is analyzing the results of research studies that have already been conducted and analyzed (Dunn, 2009). In the meta-analysis, the results of these research studies are combined and then evaluated using a set of sophisticated statistical analytic techniques (Cooper & Hedges, 1994; Rosenthal, 1991; Smith & Glass, 1977). Rather than directly using research participants' responses as data, this analysis uses the results of many studies on a specific topic as the data for analysis. The results of a meta-analysis can give researchers details regarding the consistency and predictability of an experimental effect examined in many studies that may have used different types of participants and methods. Meta-analysis is a tool that allows researchers to test the generalizability of findings and the strength of a variable's effects across people, places, times, and variations in procedure in a relatively precise and objective way (Durlak, 2003; O'Sullivan, 2006).

In conducting meta-analyses, researchers have to be careful in selecting studies and in ensuring that their sample of studies is comprehensive. Meta-analyses have been conducted on many topics, including expectancy effects (Rosenthal & Rubin, 1978); gender differences (Eagly & Steffen, 1986), physical attractiveness (Feingold, 1992), and the effects of playing violent video games on aggression (Anderson et al., 2010). The study by Anderson and his colleagues, for example, was designed to assess the effects of violent video games on, among other things, the level of aggressive behaviour of those playing the games. The final set of studies they selected included results based on over 130 000 participants from both Western and Eastern cultures. Their meta-analysis allowed them to conclude that playing violent video games was "positively associated with aggressive behavior, aggressive cognition, and aggressive affect" (Anderson et al., 2010, p. 167; see also Ferguson & Kilburn, 2010; Bushman, Rothstein, & Anderson, 2010).

As you will see in upcoming chapters, scientific advances often emerge out of efforts to double-check perplexing findings or to explain contradictory research results. Thus, like all sources of information, scientific studies need to be examined with a critical eye. This section describes a number of common methodological problems that often spoil studies. Being aware of these pitfalls will make you more skilled in evaluating research.

Sampling Bias

A *sample* is the collection of subjects selected for observation in an empirical study. In contrast, the *population* is the much larger collection of animals or people (from which the sample is drawn) that researchers want to generalize about (see Figure 2.12). For example, when political pollsters attempt to predict elections, all of the voters in a jurisdiction represent the population, and the voters who are actually surveyed constitute the sample. If a researcher was interested in the ability of six-year-old

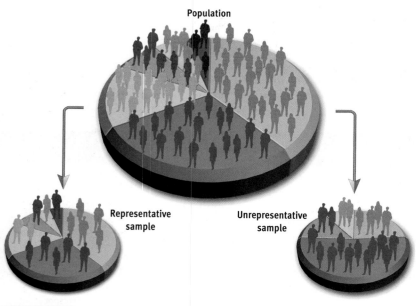

FIGURE 2.12

The relationship between the population and the sample.

The process of drawing inferences about a population based on a sample works only if the sample is reasonably representative of the population. A sample is representative if its demographic makeup is similar to that of the population, as shown on the left. If some groups in the population are overrepresented or underrepresented in the sample, as shown on the right, inferences about the population may be skewed or inaccurate.

children to form concepts, those six-year-olds actually studied would be the sample and all similar six-year-old children (perhaps those in modern, Western cultures) would be the population.

Empirical research always involves making statistical inferences about a population based on a sample. The strategy of observing a limited sample in order to generalize about a much larger population rests on the assumption that the sample is reasonably *representative* of the population. A sample is representative if its composition is similar to the composition of the population. *Sampling bias* exists when a sample is not representative of the population from which it was drawn. When a sample is not representative, generalizations about the population may be inaccurate. For instance, if a political pollster were to survey only people in posh shopping areas frequented by the wealthy, the pollster's generalizations about the voting public as a whole would be off the mark.

As we discussed in Chapter 1, North American psychologists have historically tended to undersample ethnic minorities and people from non-Western cultures. In fact, some critics have referred to the typical participant as being drawn almost entirely from WEIRD societies (Henrich, Heine, & Norenzayan, 2010). The letters in WEIRD refer to Western, Educated, Industrialized, Rich, and Democratic. This has led to a healthy debate about whether it is appropriate to generalize from these types of participants, and whether any conclusions drawn in studies employing WEIRD participants can be used to draw more general claims about "human nature" (e.g., Asttuti & Bloch, 2010; Baumard & Sperber, 2010; Chaio & Cheon, 2010; Danks & Rose, 2010; Fernald, 2010; Gachter, 2010). In one analysis of this problem, Jeffrey Arnett (2008) reviewed the sample composition of studies published in six major APA-owned journals in recent years. He found that 68 percent of the samples came from the United States and another 27 percent from Europe or English-speaking countries, with only 5 percent coming from the remainder of the world. He asserts that the focus on American subjects is extremely disproportionate given that the United States accounts for less than 5 percent of the world's population. Moreover, although the United States has become more culturally diverse, Arnett notes that the vast majority of American samples were predominantly European American, and that they have depended much too heavily on white middle- and upper-class college students (Guthrie, 1976). He argues that this excessive reliance on American samples and college students almost surely seems likely to distort findings in many research areas. In general, then, when you have concerns or doubts about the results of a study, the first thing to examine is the composition of the sample.

Placebo Effects

In pharmacology, a *placebo* is a substance that resembles a drug but has no actual pharmacological effect. In studies that assess the effectiveness of medications, placebos are given to some subjects to control for the effects of a treacherous extraneous variable: participants' expectations. Placebos are used because researchers know that participants' expectations can influence their feelings, reactions, and behaviour (Stewart-Williams, 2004). Thus, *placebo effects* occur when participants' expectations lead them to experience some change even though they receive empty, fake, or ineffectual treatment. In medicine, placebo effects are well documented (Benedetti, 2009). Many physicians tell of patients being "cured" by prescriptions of sugar pills. Placebo effects have also been seen in laboratory experiments on the effects of alcohol. In these studies, some of the participants are led to believe that they are drinking alcoholic beverages when in reality the drinks only appear to contain alcohol. Many of the subjects show effects of intoxication even though they haven't really consumed any alcohol (Assefi & Garry, 2003). If you know people who show signs of intoxication as soon as they start drinking, before their alcohol intake could take effect physiologically, you have seen placebo effects in action. Placebo effects are attributable to people's expectations (Colagiuri & Boakes, 2010). However, recent studies have demonstrated that mere expectations can have important physiological effects. For example, studies of placebos given to subjects to reduce pain suggest that the placebos actually alter activity in brain circuits that are known to suppress pain (Zubieta et al., 2005).

In the realm of research, the problem is that psychologists have found that participants' expectations can be powerful determinants of their perceptions and behaviour when they are under the microscope in an empirical study. For example, placebo effects have been seen in research on meditation. A number of studies have found that meditation can improve people's energy level, mental and physical health, and happiness (Alexander et al., 1990; Reibel et al., 2001; Walton et al., 2004). However, in many of the early studies of meditation, researchers assembled their experimental groups with volunteer subjects eager to learn meditation. Most of these subjects *wanted* and *expected* meditation to have beneficial effects. Their positive expectations may have coloured their subsequent ratings of their energy level, happiness, and so on. Better-designed studies have shown that meditation can be beneficial (see Chapter 5). However, placebo effects have probably

Before accepting the results of a survey poll, one should know something about how the poll was conducted. A polling could, for instance, contain sampling bias. Opinions collected solely from middle-class people but generalized to the voting public as a whole would be an example of such bias.

exaggerated these benefits in some studies (Canter, 2003; Caspi & Burleson, 2005; Shapiro, 1987).

Researchers should guard against placebo effects whenever subjects are likely to have expectations that a treatment will affect them in a certain way. The possible role of placebo effects can be assessed by including a fake version of the experimental treatment (a placebo condition) in a study.

Distortions in Self-Report Data

Research psychologists often work with *self-report data,* consisting of subjects' verbal accounts of their behaviour. This is the case whenever questionnaires, interviews, or personality inventories are used to measure variables. Self-report methods can be quite useful, taking advantage of the fact that people have a unique opportunity to observe themselves full-time (Baldwin, 2000). However, self-reports can be plagued by several kinds of distortion.

One of the most problematic of these distortions is the *social desirability bias,* which is a tendency to give socially approved answers to questions about oneself. Subjects who are influenced by this bias work overtime trying to create a favourable impression (Holtgraves, 2004). For example, many survey respondents will report that they voted in an election or gave to a charity when, in fact, it is possible to determine that they did not (Granberg & Holmberg, 1991). Respondents influenced by social desirability bias also tend to report that they are healthier, happier, and less prejudiced than other types of evidence would suggest.

In some areas of research, the possibility of participants engaging in socially desirable responding is particularly problematic; for example, in research on prejudice and stereotyping. Researchers in these areas

recently have developed a new set of measures that, according to the University of Western Ontario's Bertram Gawronski (Gawronski, LeBel, and Peters, 2007; Gawronski, LeBel, Banse, & Peters, 2009), don't depend on a participant's conscious introspection. These are referred to as *implicit measures* (Greenwald & Banaji, 1995) and they are assumed by many to be less open to biased responding (Dunham, Baron, & Banaji, 2006). These types of measures—for example, the *Implicit Association Test* (IAT: Nosek & Greenwald, 2009; Nosek, Greenwald, & Banaji, 2007)— have proven to be particularly popular in research in social psychology (e.g., Dijksterhuis & Aarts, 2009; Gawronski & Payne, 2010; Gawronski, LeBel, Peters, & Banse, 2009; Houwer & Teige-Mocigemba, 2009). Although originally developed by Tony Greenwald and his associates to measure attitudes and biases operating below the level of awareness, the IAT has proven to be useful in many other domains, including assessing implicit prejudice and as a predictor of relationship breakup (Lee Rogge, & Reis, 2010). We will discuss them more fully in Chapter 16.

Other problems can also produce distortions in self-report data (Krosnick, 1999; Schuman & Kalton, 1985). Respondents misunderstand questionnaire items surprisingly often, and the way questions are worded can shape subjects' responses (Schwarz, 1999). Memory errors can undermine the accuracy of verbal

Harvard psychologist Mahzarin Banaji, along with Anthony Greenwald of the University of Washington, developed the *Implicit Association Test* (IAT), one of the most widely used of the new implicit measures. This approach is often used in research on prejudice and research on self-concept. You can take (anonymously) an implicit test of your own unconscious levels of prejudice about age, gender, race, self-esteem and other things by visiting the IAT website at https://implicit.harvard.edu.

reports. Response sets are yet another problem. A *response set* is a tendency to respond to questions in a particular way that is unrelated to the content of the questions. For example, some people tend to agree with nearly everything on a questionnaire (Krosnick & Fabrigar, 1998).

Yet another source of concern is the halo effect (Nisbett & Wilson, 1977). The *halo effect* occurs when one's overall evaluation of a person, object, or institution spills over to influence more specific ratings. For example, a supervisor's global assessment of an employee's merit might sway specific ratings of the employee's dependability, initiative, communication, knowledge, and so forth. The crux of the problem is that a rater is unable to judge specific evaluative dimensions independently. Obviously, distortions like these can produce inaccurate results. Although researchers have devised ways to neutralize these problems—such as carefully pre-testing survey instruments—we should be cautious in drawing conclusions from self-report data (Schaeffer, 2000).

Experimenter Bias

As scientists, psychologists try to conduct their studies in an objective, unbiased way so that their own views will not influence the results. However, objectivity is a *goal* that scientists strive for, not an accomplished fact that can be taken for granted (MacCoun, 1998). In reality, most researchers have an emotional investment in the outcome of their research. Often they are testing hypotheses that they have developed themselves and that they would like to see supported by the data. It is understandable, then, that *experimenter bias* is a possible source of error in research.

Experimenter bias occurs when a researcher's expectations or preferences about the outcome of a study influence the results obtained. Experimenter bias can slip through to influence studies in many subtle ways. One problem is that researchers, like others, sometimes *see what they want to see*. For instance, when experimenters make apparently honest mistakes in recording subjects' responses, the mistakes tend to be heavily slanted in favour of supporting the hypothesis (O'Leary, Kent, & Kanowitz, 1975).

Research by Robert Rosenthal (1976) suggests that experimenter bias may lead researchers to unintentionally influence the behaviour of their subjects. In one study, Rosenthal and Fode (1963) recruited undergraduate psychology students to serve as the "experimenters." The students were told that they would be collecting data for a study of how participants rated the success of people portrayed in photographs. In

a pilot study, photos were selected that generated (on the average) neutral ratings on a scale extending from -10 (extreme failure) to $+10$ (extreme success). Rosenthal and Fode then manipulated the expectancies of their experimenters. Half of them were told that, based on pilot data, they would probably obtain average ratings of -5. The other half were led to expect average ratings of $+5$. The experimenters were forbidden to converse with their subjects except for reading some standardized instructions. Even though the photographs were exactly the same for both groups, the experimenters who *expected* positive ratings *obtained* significantly higher ratings than those who expected negative ratings.

How could the experimenters have swayed the participants' ratings? According to Rosenthal, the experimenters may have unintentionally influenced their subjects by sending subtle nonverbal signals as the experiment progressed. Without realizing it, they may have smiled, nodded, or sent other positive cues when participants made ratings that were in line with the experimenters' expectations. Thus, experimenter bias may influence both researchers' observations and their subjects' behaviour (Rosenthal, 1994, 2002).

The problems associated with experimenter bias can be neutralized by using a double-blind procedure. The *double-blind procedure* is a research strategy in which neither subjects nor experimenters know which subjects are in the experimental or control groups. It's not particularly unusual for participants to be "blind" about their treatment condition. However, the double-blind procedure keeps the experimenter in the dark as well. Of course, a member of the research team who isn't directly involved with subjects keeps track of who is in which group.

Robert Rosenthal

"Quite unconsciously, a psychologist interacts in subtle ways with the people he is studying so that he may get the response he expects to get."

REVIEW OF KEY POINTS

▷ Scientists often try to replicate research findings to double-check their validity. Although this process leads to some contradictory findings, science works toward reconciling and explaining inconsistent results.

▷ Sampling bias occurs when a sample is not representative of the population of interest. Placebo effects occur when participants' expectations cause them to change their behaviour in response to a fake treatment.

▷ Distortions in self-reports, such as response sets and the social desirability bias, are a source of concern whenever questionnaires and personality inventories are used to collect data. Experimenter bias occurs when researchers' expectations and desires distort their observations or unintentionally influence their subjects' behaviour.

RESEARCH METHOD	DESCRIPTION	EXAMPLE APPLIED TO RESEARCH ON AGGRESSION

EXPERIMENT

Manipulation of an independent variable under carefully controlled conditions to see whether any changes occur in a dependent variable.

Example: Schachter's (1959) study of whether increased anxiety leads to increased affiliation.

Hypothesis: Anxiety increases affiliation

Random assignment — Subjects randomly assigned to experimental and control groups

Manipulation of independent variable — Experimental group "Shocks will be very painful" (high anxiety) / Control group "Shocks will be mild and painless" (low anxiety)

Measurement of dependent variable — High-anxiety group indicated a desire to wait with others more than did low-anxiety group

© Cengage Learning 2013

Youngsters are randomly assigned to watch a violent or nonviolent film (manipulation of the independent variable), and some aspect of aggression (the dependent variable) is measured in a laboratory situation.

© T.M.O.Pictures/Alamy; (TV screen) © Andre Blais/Shutterstock

NATURALISTIC OBSERVATION

Careful, usually prolonged observation of behavior in its natural setting, without direct intervention.

Example: The Ramirez-Esparza et al. (2007) study comparing sociability in Mexican and American samples, using an electronically activated recorder (EAR).

Jack Hollingsworth/Photodisc/Getty Images

Youngsters' spontaneous acts of aggression during recreational activities on their playgound are recorded unobtrusively by a team of carefully trained observers.

© Laurence Mouton/Getty Images

CASE STUDIES

In-depth investigation of a single individual using direct interview, direct observation, review of records, interviews of those close to the person, and other data sources.

Example: The Isometsa et al. (1995) study of all known suicide cases in Finland for an entire year.

© Alain SHRODER/Getty Images

Detailed case histories are worked up for youngsters referred to counseling because of excessive aggressive behavior in school. The children are interviewed, as are their parents and teachers.

© Will & Deni McIntyre/CORBIS

SURVEYS

Use of questionnaires or interviews to gather information about specific aspects of participants' behavior, attitudes, and beliefs.

Example: The Stamatakis et al. (2009) study of sedentary behavior, which related hours per day devoted to TV viewing to social class and physical health.

© Gabe Palmer/Alamy

A large sample of youngsters are given a questionnaire describing hypothetical scenarios that might be expected to trigger aggressive behavior and are asked about how they think they would respond in the situations.

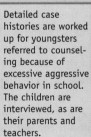

© David Grossman/Alamy

ADVANTAGES

DISADVANTAGES

Precise control over variables can eliminate alternative explanations for findings.

Researchers are able to draw conclusions about cause-and-effect relationships between variables.

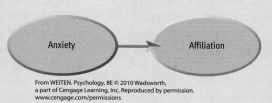

From WEITEN. Psychology, 8E © 2010 Wadsworth, a part of Cengage Learning, Inc. Reproduced by permission. www.cengage.com/permissions

Confounding of variables must be avoided.

Contrived laboratory situations are often artificial, making it risky to generalize findings to the real world.

Ethical concerns and practical realities preclude experiments on many important questions.

Artificiality that can be a problem in laboratory studies is minimized.

It can be good place to start when little is known about the phenomena under study.

Unlike other descriptive/correlational methods, it can be used to study animal as well as human behavior.

© Jens Schlueter/AFP/Getty Images

It can be difficult to remain unobtrusive; even animal behavior may be altererd by the observation process.

Researchers are unable to draw causal conclusions.

Observational data are often difficult to quantify for statistical analyses.

Case studies are well suited for study of psychological disorders and therapeutic practices.

Individual cases can provide compelling illustrations to support or undermine a theory.

Subjectivity makes it easy to see what one expects to see based on one's theoretical slant.

Researchers are unable to draw causal conclusions.

Clinical samples are often unrepresentative and suffer from sampling bias.

Data collection can be relatively easy, saving time and money.

Researchers can gather data on difficult-to-observe aspects of behavior.

Questionnaires are well suited for gathering data on attitudes, values, and beliefs from large samples.

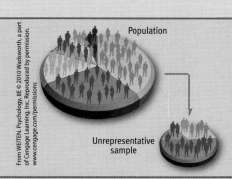

From WEITEN. Psychology, 8E © 2010 Wadsworth, a part of Cengage Learning, Inc. Reproduced by permission. www.cengage.com/permissions

Self-report data are often unreliable, due to intentional deception, social desirability bias, response sets, memory lapses, and poor wording of questions.

Researchers are unable to draw causal conclusions.

The Internet is revolutionizing many aspects of modern life. Some experts compare the emergence of the Web to the shift from speech to writing, the invention of the printing press, and the widespread distribution of electricity (Weiten, 2002). Use of the Internet by Canadians continues to increase, with higher rates of use associated with higher education, income, and urban dwelling. The highest rate of Internet use by Canadians is by those aged 16–24; 98 percent in that age group reported using the Internet in 2009, as compared to 66 percent of those aged 45 or older (Statistics Canada, 2010c). The Internet has profoundly changed how we obtain information, conduct business, socialize, and search for information (Dunn, 2009). Small wonder, then, that the Internet is gradually altering the ways in which psychological research is conducted.

Internet-mediated research refers to studies in which data collection is done using the Web. All of the different methods that we have discussed in this chapter can be used in Internet-mediated research. Mostly, investigators have conducted online experiments and distributed online surveys. An example of a Web experiment would be a study by Göritz (2006), which compared various cash lottery incentives to see which would yield the highest response rates in online studies. An example of a Web survey would be a study by Tower and Krasner (2006), in which over 1100 online participants responded to measures of marital closeness and depressive symptoms to explore the correlation between marital adjustment and depression. Although experiments and surveys have dominated Internet-mediated research, the Web has also afforded psychologists enlightening opportunities to engage in naturalistic observation of social interaction in online communities, such as chat rooms and newsgroups (Glaser & Kahn, 2005; McKenna & Bargh, 2000; McKenna & Seidman, 2005).

Why have researchers been drawn to the Web? Because the Internet offers some very enticing advantages in the data collection process. For example, studies conducted via the Internet can often obtain samples that are much larger and much more diverse than the samples that are typically used in laboratory research (Buchanan, 2000; Reips, 2007). If a researcher is interested in some special population, whether it is gamblers, steroid users, atheists, dentists, elderly marathon runners, or lesbians living in rural areas, creative recruitment via the Internet can yield sizable samples that would be difficult or impossible to obtain through traditional research procedures (Mathy et al., 2002; Skitka & Sargis, 2005). Moreover, once an online survey or experiment is set up, data can be collected effortlessly 24 hours a day, 7 days a week. Research assistants do not need to spend endless hours running subjects in a lab and participants' responses can be saved automatically into data files for statistical analyses. Thus, Internet-mediated research can reduce costs and save time (Göritz, 2007; Skitka & Sargis, 2006). Studies that might require six months or a year of data collection in the laboratory can sometimes be completed in a few weeks instead.

As you can see, Internet-mediated research offers many attractive benefits, but this approach also has some weaknesses that concern researchers (Birnbaum, 2004). One major concern is the potential for sampling bias. Although the population of Web users grows daily, not everyone has access to the Internet. Web users tend to be younger, brighter, and more affluent than non-users (Lenert & Skoczen, 2002). A related issue is that Web studies tend to have lower participation rates than conventional studies (Skitka & Sargis, 2005). In laboratory studies, although subjects can always elect to not participate, the vast majority generally tend to go along with whatever study they are assigned to. In most Web studies, broad invitations to participate are issued via e-mail or posted announcements, and only a small minority of potential subjects typically choose to volunteer their time. Researchers worry that their self-selected volunteers might be systematically different from the majority of people who, for one reason or another, chose not to participate. Sampling bias due to self-selection can also occur in lab research, but it appears to be a much more troublesome issue in Internet-mediated research. Web studies also tend to have higher dropout rates than laboratory studies, which increases another possible source of sampling bias (Birnbaum, 2004b).

Another issue in Internet-mediated research is that data are collected under far less controlled conditions than in traditional studies (Buchanan, 2007; Hewson, 2003). Laboratory studies are conducted under carefully controlled conditions that are held constant for all participants. Researchers routinely obsess over details such as room temperature, lighting, and the gender of the research assistant who interacts with subjects. In contrast, subjects in Web studies usually participate from home, where environmental conditions are uncontrolled and unknown. Some participants may be distracted by TV, some may sit around and discuss their data input with friends, some may provide data while intoxicated, and some may ignore crucial instructions. Similar problems can crop up in traditional approaches to research—for example, when subjects fill out paper-and-pencil surveys at home. But lack of control appears to be a more serious problem for Internet-mediated research than for conventional research.

So, given problems such as these, will Internet-mediated research turn out to be a temporary fad? Or will it become the wave of the future? It seems likely that Internet-mediated research will continue to grow. Although Web studies have created some new complexities related to sampling bias, they appear to have the *potential* to yield more diverse and representative samples than traditional approaches to research (Hewson, 2003). The control problem seems more worrisome, but when investigators have run identical studies over the Web and through traditional methods, the results have generally turned out to be highly similar (Birnbaum, 2004b; McGraw, Tew, & Williams, 2000). These findings suggest that the control issue may be less problematic than feared. And while some researchers have expressed concern about the greater anonymity of participants in Web studies, this increased anonymity actually may reduce the impact of social desirability bias (Hewson, 2007; Skitka & Sargis, 2006). In sum, it appears that the Internet will gradually alter the landscape of psychological research, just as it has altered the landscape of communication, shopping, politics, real estate, entertainment, and many other aspects of modern life.

Looking at Ethics: Do the Ends Justify the Means?

When we took our first course in psychology, as students we were required to participate in research studies as part of that course, as is often the case now. One of us showed up at the appointed time for a study on extrasensory perception (ESP). When he arrived, he was shown a black curtain and was told that behind the curtain a famous psychic was sitting who would telepathically transmit a set of numbers between 1 and 10; it was the research participant's job to identify the numbers on a series of trials. He was told that others would be taking part simultaneously and, to ensure privacy, everyone would be taken to different cubicles and would communicate via an intercom. Each time a trial began, he heard the others give their guesses first, with his guess coming last. He gave the study his all because he was very interested in psychology.

Once the experiment was over, he was told that (surprise!) the experiment was not about ESP but was an experiment in conformity. There were no other participants. What he heard were tape-recorded voices and the purpose was to see if the numbers guessed by the other "participants" would influence his own judgments. At that point he felt a number of emotions, ranging from relief to embarrassment.

Should researchers be allowed to play with your feelings in this way? Should they be permitted to deceive subjects in such a manner? Is this the cost that must be paid to advance scientific knowledge?

As these questions indicate, the research enterprise sometimes presents scientists with difficult ethical dilemmas. *These dilemmas reflect concern about the possibility for inflicting harm on participants.* In psychological research, the major ethical concerns centre on the use of deception and on guidelines for the participation of humans and animals in psychological research.

While ethical abuses are the exceptions, they can often be very serious. In the *Tuskegee Syphilis Study* carried out in the United States from 1932 to 1972, a group of Black men who had contracted syphilis were enrolled in the study but were never told that they had the disease and the doctors conducting the study never treated them for it. In a study often referred to as the "Monster Study" by some of the participants (Dvorak, 2003), normal-speaking orphan children were labelled stutterers and "belittled" every time they showed a speech imperfection, in order to test a theory about the psychological origins of stuttering (Goldfarb, 2006; Silverman, 1988). Or consider the secret CIA-funded experiments carried out at the Allan Memorial Institute in Montreal in the 1950s and 1960s. The abuses inflicted on the unsuspecting patients were horrifying, such as being left in drug-induced comas for days at a time. Patients were not informed about the nature of the research, and it was typically carried out without their consent. This set of experiments was thankfully exposed in

PREVIEW QUESTIONS

▶ What are the arguments against using deception in research?

▶ What are the ethical guidelines that researchers must adhere to, and where do they come from?

▶ Are there any special ethical guidelines for research with animals?

WEB LINK 2.7

The Troubling Legacy of the *Tuskegee Syphilis Study*
The enduring damage of unethical scientific and medical research—here seen in the infamous 1932–1972 *Tuskegee Syphilis Study* among 399 poor Black men in Alabama—is detailed in several government reports and a rare presidential apology to the victims.

the 1970s. This research is discussed more fully in Chapter 15.

Elaborate deception, such as that experienced by one of the authors in his first research experience in psychology, has been fairly common in psychological research since the 1960s, especially in the area of social psychology (Epley & Huff, 1998; Korn, 1997). Critics argue against the use of deception on several grounds (Baumrind, 1985; Kelman, 1982; Ortmann & Hertwig, 1997). First, they assert that deception is only a nice word for lying, which they see as inherently immoral. Second, they argue that by deceiving unsuspecting participants, psychologists may undermine many individuals' trust in others. Third, they point out that many deceptive studies produce distress for participants who were not forewarned about that possibility. Specifically, subjects may experience great stress during a study or be made to feel foolish when the true nature of a study is explained. Those who defend the use of deception in research maintain that many important issues could not be investigated if experimenters were not permitted to sometimes mislead participants (Bröder, 1998). While there may be no easy answers to questions concerning such matters as deception and the use of animals in psychological research, it is clear that psychologists and their professional associations are very serious about protecting the rights of clients and research participants. Of course, especially important are safeguards for research using children as participants (Boccia, Campbell, Goldman, & Skinner, 2009). In this section, we will review some of the ethical guidelines that oversee research in psychology in Canada.

Ethical Guidelines for Research in Psychology in Canada

In Chapter 1, we introduced you to the major organization for psychology in Canada, the Canadian Psychological Association (CPA). Like its more senior counterpart in the United States, the American Psychological Association, the CPA has spent a great deal of effort developing ethical guidelines to inform psychological research. Both organizations are continually evaluating and updating their ethical guidelines (e.g., Dozois, 2008; Koocher, 2007). Researchers are frequently presented with new issues as they explore topics of interest. For example, Canadian researchers (Flicker & Guta, 2008) have suggested that surveying high school students who need parental consent to participate in the research may introduce bias into the research, especially on topics such as substance use and sexuality (Rojas et al., 2008). Notably, the requirement of parental consent for minors, a guideline introduced to protect vulnerable participants, may introduce a self-selection bias in which a representative sample cannot be obtained; some parents will not be comfortable having their children respond to survey questions on such topics and this lack of participation may not be random. It may be tied to specific demographic characteristics. As we discussed earlier in this chapter, having a representative sample is important when you are interpreting and generalizing survey results. Ethical questions are often quite complex and the answers to such dilemmas aren't easy. While the CPA's statements on ethics are quite detailed (the interested reader is referred to the Canadian Code of Ethics for Psychologists: http://www.cpa.ca/aboutcpa/committees/ethics, and click on "Code of Ethics for Psychologists"), we will refer to the four principles underlying the CPA's ethical guidelines. The general principles and their relative ranking of importance are illustrated in Table 2.3.

Some of the background of the development of the Canadian Psychological Association's ethical guidelines is discussed in a paper by University of Manitoba psychologist John Adair (2001). Some of the similarities and differences between the CPA's and APA's codes of ethics have been considered by the University of Regina's Thomas Hadjistavropoulos and his colleagues (Hadjistavropoulos et al., 2002). A special issue of the journal *Canadian Psychology* (Volume 52, Issue 3) published in August 2011 was devoted to the topic of the code of ethics.

The CPA ethical principles deal with how people with whom the psychologist comes into contact should be treated. All such persons should be treated with dignity and the psychologist should ensure that their value is not dependent upon culture, race,

Key principles of the Canadian Psychological Association's *Code of Ethics for Psychologists* are presented here. These principles are designed to ensure the welfare of both human and animal participants:

- Principle I: Respect for the Dignity of Persons.
- Principle II: Responsible Caring.
- Principle III: Integrity in Relationships.
- Principle IV: Responsibility to Society.

TABLE 2.3

Ethics in Research

Source: Canadian Psychological Association (2000), *Code of Ethics for Psychologists* (3rd ed.). Retrieved September 20, 2008, from http://www.cpa.ca/aboutcpa/committees/ethics; click on "Code of Ethics for Psychologists."

nationality, or other such factors. Psychologists have a responsibility to protect the rights, privacy, personal liberty, and self-determination of others. Psychologists are also expected to be especially vigilant to provide safeguards to protect the vulnerable (e.g., children) and to ensure in all cases that freedom of consent is assured. Psychologists should take all available measures to ensure that their activities will benefit (or at least, do no harm to) those with whom they interact in a professional capacity. Psychologists should emphasize integrity in their relationships with their clients, students, and research participants. Finally, psychologists must recognize that psychology has a responsibility to society to increase knowledge and promote the welfare of all human beings.

The principles also have implications for psychologists who employ animals in their research. For example, every effort must be made to minimize the discomfort felt by such participants and to ensure that animals will not be used unless there is a strong expectation that the results will benefit both humans and animals. Additional guidelines regarding the treatment of animals have been developed by the Canadian Council on Animal Care (see http://www.ccac.ca). This national organization is responsible for setting guidelines for the care and use of animals in research.

In Canadian universities, great care is taken in the application of high ethical standards to research conducted by their members. Before students participate in university-sponsored research, that research must be approved at a variety of levels. Most psychology departments have their own research ethics boards or committees to approve research. It is also typical that the research has to be approved by a committee at the university level consisting of members from various academic departments and groups. Finally, most university research conducted in Canada is funded by the federal government, by the Social Sciences and Humanities Research Council, the National Sciences and Engineering Research Council, and/or the Canadian Institutes of Health Research. These three federal funding agencies, known collectively as the Tri-Council, have formulated their own set of ethical standards that must be adhered to for any research to be eligible for funding (see http://www.pre.ethics .gc.ca).

While many of these decisions are not easy, such as on the use of animals in research, psychologists hope that ethical guidelines such as those described here will promote responsible and ethical treatment of all clients and research participants.

Neal Miller
"Who are the cruel and inhumane ones, the behavioural scientists whose research on animals led to the cures of the anorexic girl and the vomiting child, or those leaders of the radical animal activists who are making an exciting career of trying to stop all such research and are misinforming people by repeatedly asserting that it is without any value?"

The use of rats and other animals in scientific research is now a major ethical issue. Researchers claim that experiments on animals often yield results and knowledge beneficial to humankind. Opponents maintain that humans have no right to subject animals to harm for research purposes. What is your view?

Two of our seven unifying themes have emerged strongly in this chapter. First, the entire chapter is a testimonial to the idea that psychology is empirical. Second, the discussion of methodological flaws in research provides numerous examples of how people's experience of the world can be highly subjective. Let's examine each of these points in more detail.

As explained in Chapter 1, the empirical approach entails testing ideas, basing conclusions on systematic observation, and relying on a healthy brand of skepticism. All of those features of the empirical approach have been apparent in our review of the research enterprise in psychology.

As you have seen, psychologists test their ideas by formulating clear hypotheses that involve predictions about relationships between variables. They then use a variety of research methods to collect data so they can see whether their predictions are supported. The data collection methods are designed to make researchers' observations systematic and precise. The entire venture is saturated with skepticism. Psychologists are impressed only by research results that are highly unlikely to have occurred by chance. In planning and executing their research, they are constantly on the lookout for methodological flaws. They publish their findings so that other experts can subject their methods and conclusions to critical scrutiny. Collectively, these procedures represent the essence of the empirical approach.

The subjectivity of personal experience became apparent in the discussion of methodological problems, especially placebo effects and experimenter bias. When subjects report beneficial effects from a fake treatment (the placebo), it's because they expected to see these effects. As pointed out in Chapter 1, psychologists and other scientists are not immune to the effects of subjective experience. Although they are trained to be objective, even scientists may see what they expect to see or what they want to see. This is one reason that the empirical approach emphasizes precise measurement and a skeptical attitude. The highly subjective nature of experience is exactly what the empirical approach attempts to neutralize.

The publication of empirical studies allows us to apply a critical eye to the research enterprise. However, you cannot critically analyze studies unless you know where and how to find them. In the upcoming Personal Application, we will discuss where studies are published, how to find studies on specific topics, and how to read research reports. In the subsequent Critical Thinking Application, we'll analyze the shortcomings of anecdotal evidence, which should help you to appreciate the value of empirical evidence.

REVIEW OF KEY POINTS

▶ Internet-mediated research has grown in recent years because it offers access to larger and more diverse samples and to specialized samples while reducing costs and saving time. However, Internet-mediated research raises its own concerns about sampling bias and uncontrolled conditions during data collection.

▶ Research sometimes raises complex ethical issues. Critics argue that it is unethical to deceive subjects and to expose animals to harmful treatments. Those who defend deception in research argue that many important issues could not be investigated without misleading subjects.

▶ Psychologists who defend animal research argue that it has brought major advances that are worth the costs. The CPA has formulated ethical principles to serve as guidelines for researchers who employ humans and animals in their research.

▶ Two of the book's unifying themes are apparent in this chapter's discussion of the research enterprise in psychology: Psychology is empirical, and people's experience of the world is highly subjective.

Finding and Reading Journal Articles

Answer the following "yes" or "no."

___ **1** I have read about scientific studies in newspapers and magazines and sometimes wondered, "How did they come to those conclusions?"

___ **2** When I go to the library, I often have difficulty figuring out how to find information based on research.

___ **3** I have tried to read scientific reports and found them to be too technical and difficult to understand.

If you responded "yes" to any of the above statements, you have struggled with the information explosion in the sciences. We live in a research-oriented society. The number of studies conducted in most sciences is growing at a dizzying pace. This expansion has been particularly spectacular in psychology. Moreover, psychological research increasingly commands attention from the popular press because it is often relevant to people's personal concerns.

This Personal Application is intended to help you cope with the information explosion in psychology. It assumes that there may come a time when you need to examine original psychological research. Perhaps it will be in your role as a student (working on a term paper, for instance), in another role (parent, teacher, nurse, administrator), or merely out of curiosity. In any case, this Personal Application explains the nature of technical journals and discusses how to find and read articles in them. You can learn more about how to use library resources in psychology from an excellent little book entitled *Library Use: A Handbook for Psychology* (Reed & Baxter, 1992, 2003).

The Nature of Technical Journals 1e

As you will recall from earlier in the chapter, a *journal* is a periodical that publishes technical and scholarly material, usually in a narrowly defined area of inquiry. Scholars in most fields—whether economics, chemistry, education, or psychology—publish the bulk of their work in these journals. Journal articles represent the core of intellectual activity in any academic discipline.

In general, journal articles are written for other professionals in the field. Hence, authors assume that their readers are other interested economists or chemists or psychologists. Because journal articles are written in the special language unique to a particular discipline, they are often difficult for nonprofessionals to understand. You will be learning a great deal of psychology's special language in this course, which will improve your ability to understand articles in psychology journals.

In psychology, most journal articles are reports that describe original empirical studies. These reports permit researchers to disseminate their findings to the scientific community. Another common type of article is the review article. *Review articles* summarize and reconcile the findings of a large number of studies on a specific issue. Some psychology journals also publish comments or critiques of previously published research, book reviews, theoretical treatises, and descriptions of methodological innovations.

Finding Journal Articles 1e

Reports of psychological research are commonly mentioned in newspapers and popular magazines. These summaries can be helpful to readers, but they often embrace the most sensational conclusions that might be drawn from the research. They also tend to include many oversimplifications and factual errors. Hence, if a study mentioned in the press is of interest to you, you may want to track down the original article to ensure that you get accurate information.

Most discussions of research in the popular press do not mention where you can find the original technical article. However, there is a way to find out. A computerized database called PsycINFO makes it possible to locate journal articles by specific researchers or scholarly work on specific topics. This huge online database, which is updated constantly, contains brief summaries, or *abstracts*, of journal articles, books, and chapters in edited books, reporting, reviewing, or theorizing about psychological research. Over 1800 journals are checked regularly to select items for inclusion. The abstracts are concise—about 75 to 175 words. They briefly describe the hypotheses, methods, results, and conclusions of the studies. Each abstract should allow you to determine whether an article is relevant to your interests. If it is, you should be able to find the article in your library (or to order it), because a complete bibliographic reference is provided.

Although news accounts of research rarely mention where a study was published, they often mention the name of the researcher. If you have this information, the easiest way to find a specific article is to search PsycINFO for materials published by that researcher. For example, let's say you read a news report that summarizes an interesting study on whether alcohol hangovers affect managerial effectiveness in the business world that was published by Siegfried Streufert in the mid-1990s. To track down the original article, you would search for journal articles authored by Streufert. Given that you know the approximate year of publication, you could select the PsycINFO option to narrow your search to materials published between 1990 and 1996. If you conducted this search, you would turn up the list of eight articles shown in Figure 2.13. The sixth item in the list appears to be the article you are interested in. Figure 2.14 shows what you would see if you clicked to obtain the abstract and citation for this article. As you can see, the source note shows that the original report was published in the October 1995 issue of *Alcoholism: Clinical and Experimental Research*. Armed with this information, you could obtain the article easily.

cont...

found 8 documents, (8 returned).
for Your Query : (streufert, siegfried):Author

1. **Effects of alcohol intoxication on risk taking, strategy, and error rate in visuomotor performance.**
By Streufert, Siegfried; Pogash, Rosanne M.; Roache, John D.; Gingrich, Dennis; et al
Journal of Applied Psychology. 1992 Aug Vol 77(4) 515-524
Abstract and Citation | Full PsycINFO Record | Full Text of Article

2. **Age and management team performance.**
By Streufert, Siegfried; Pogash, Rosanne; Piasecki, Mary; Post, Gerald M.
Psychology & Aging. 1990 Dec Vol 5(4) 551-559
Abstract and Citation | Full PsycINFO Record | Full Text of Article

3. **Authoring of complex learning environments: Design considerations for dynamic simulations.**
By Breuer, Klaus; Streufert, Siegfried
Journal of Structural Learning. 1996 Nov Vol 12(4) 315-321
Abstract and Citation | Full PsycINFO Record

4. **Effects of alprazolam on complex human functioning.**
By Streufert, Siegfried; Satish, Usha; Pogash, Rosanne; Gingrich, Dennis; et al
Journal of Applied Social Psychology. 1996 Nov Vol 26(21) 1912-1930
Abstract and Citation | Full PsycINFO Record

5. **Effects of caffeine deprivation on complex human functioning.**
By Streufert, Siegfried; Pogash, Rosanne; Miller, Jill; Gingrich, Dennis; et al
Psychopharmacology. 1995 Apr Vol 118(4) 377-384
Abstract and Citation | Full PsycINFO Record

6. **Alcohol hangover and managerial effectiveness.**
By Streufert, Siegfried; Pogash, Rosanne; Braig, Daniela; Gingrich, Dennis; et al
Alcoholism: Clinical & Experimental Research. 1995 Oct Vol 19(5) 1141-1146
Abstract and Citation | Full PsycINFO Record

7. **Alcohol and management performance.**
By Streufert, Siegfried; Pogash, Rosanne; Roache, John; Severs, Walter; et al
Journal of Studies on Alcohol. 1994 Mar Vol 55(2) 230-238
Abstract and Citation | Full PsycINFO Record

8. **Alcohol and complex functioning.**
By Streufert, Siegfried; Pogash, Rosanne M.; Gingrich, Dennis; Kantner, Anne; et al
Journal of Applied Social Psychology. 1993 Jun Vol 23(11) 847-866
Abstract and Citation | Full PsycINFO Record

FIGURE 2.13

Searching PsycINFO.

If you searched PsycINFO for journal articles authored by Siegfried Streufert during the period of 1990–1996, the database would return the eight titles shown here. For each article, you can click to see its abstract or its full PsycINFO record (the abstract plus subject descriptors and other details). In some cases (depending on the version of PsycINFO that your library has ordered) you can even click to see the *full text* of articles that appeared in journals published in recent years by the APA, the APA Educational Publishing Foundation, the CPA, and Hogrefe Publishing Group.

You can also search PsycINFO for research literature on particular topics, such as achievement motivation, aggressive behaviour, alcoholism, appetite disorders, or artistic ability. These computerized literature searches can be much more powerful, precise, and thorough than traditional, manual searches in a library. PsycINFO can sift through a couple of million articles in a matter of seconds to identify *all* the articles on a subject, such as alcoholism.

Obviously, there is no way you can match this efficiency stumbling around in the stacks at your library. Moreover, the computer allows you to pair up topics to swiftly narrow your search to exactly those issues that interest you.

The PsycINFO database can be accessed online at many libraries or via the Internet (see Web Link 2.2 on p. 48 for a description of PsycINFO Direct). The database is also available at some libraries that have the information stored on CD-ROM discs. This version of the database is updated monthly. The summaries contained in PsycINFO can also be found in a monthly print journal called *Psychological Abstracts,* but fewer and fewer libraries are subscribing to this traditional publication because it cannot match the swift and efficient search capabilities of PsycINFO.

Reading Journal Articles

Once you find the journal articles that you want to examine, you need to know how to decipher them. You can process the information in such articles more efficiently if you understand how they are organized. Depending on your needs and purpose, you may want to simply skim through some of the sections. Journal articles follow a fairly standard organization, which includes the following sections and features.

Abstract Most journals print a concise summary at the beginning of each article. This abstract allows readers scanning the journal to quickly decide whether articles are relevant to their interests.

Introduction The introduction presents an overview of the problem studied in the research. It mentions relevant theories and quickly reviews previous research that bears on the problem, usually citing shortcomings in previous research that necessitate the present study. This review of the current state of knowledge on the topic usually progresses to a specific and precise statement regarding the hypotheses under investigation.

Method The method section provides a thorough description of the research methods used in the study. Information is provided on the subjects used, the procedures followed, and the data collection techniques employed. This description is made detailed enough to permit another researcher to attempt to replicate the study.

Results The data obtained in the study are reported in the results section. This section

TITLE	Alcohol hangover and managerial effectiveness.
ABSTRACT	21 male managers who normally drank moderate amounts of alcohol participated in a placebo-controlled, double-blind, crossover experiment to determine whether alcohol-induced hangovers would influence managerial/professional task performance characteristics. Ss consumed either placebo or alcoholic drinks to attain a breath alcohol level of 0.10 during the evening before participation in Strategic Management Simulations. By the following morning, breath alcohol levels were measured at 0.00. Questionnaire responses indicated considerable hangover discomfort. Responses to semantic differential evaluative scales suggested that Ss evaluated their own managerial performance in the simulation setting as impaired. However, multiple measures of decision-making performance obtained in the simulation task did not show any deterioration of functioning. (PsycINFO Database Record © 2000 APA, all rights reserved)
AUTHOR	*Streufert, Siegfried;* Pogash, Rosanne; Braig, Daniela; Gingrich, Dennis; et al.
AFFILIATION	Pennsylvania State U, Coll of Medicine, Dept of Behavioral Science, Hershey, USA
SOURCE	Alcoholism: Clinical & Experimental Research. 1995 Oct Vol 19(5) 1141-1146

FIGURE 2.14

Example of a PsycINFO abstract.

This information is what you would see if you clicked to see the abstract of item 6 in the list shown in Figure 2.13. It is a typical abstract from the online PsycINFO database. Each abstract in PsycINFO provides a summary of a specific journal article, book, or chapter in an edited book, and complete bibliographical information. (It is also possible to combine topics in a PsycINFO search to pinpoint articles dealing with specific topics. For example, combining a search for articles on marijuana and articles on memory to yield a smaller subset of articles on marijuana and memory.)

often creates problems for novice readers because it includes complex statistical analyses, figures, tables, and graphs. This section does *not* include any inferences based on the data, as such conclusions are supposed to follow in the next section. Instead, it simply contains a concise summary of the raw data and the statistical analyses.

Discussion In the discussion section, you will find the conclusions drawn by the author(s). In contrast to the results section, which is a straightforward summary of empirical observations, the discussion section allows for interpretation and evaluation of the data. Implications for theory and factual knowledge in the discipline are discussed. Conclusions are usually qualified carefully, and any limitations in the study may be acknowledged. This section may also include suggestions for future research on the issue.

References At the end of each article, you will find a list of bibliographical references for any studies cited. This list permits you to examine firsthand other relevant studies mentioned in the article. The references list is often a rich source of leads about other articles that are germane to the topic that you are looking into.

For additional hints on reading journal articles, see the paper published by two psychologists writing at the University of Waterloo, Christian Jordan and Mark Zanna (1999).

REVIEW OF KEY POINTS

- Journals publish technical and scholarly material. Usually they are written for other professionals in a narrow area of inquiry. In psychology, most journal articles are reports of original research.

- PsycINFO is a computerized database that contains brief summaries of newly published journal articles, books, and chapters in edited books. Works on specific topics and publications by specific authors can be found by using the search mechanisms built into the database.

- Computerized literature searches can be much more powerful and precise than manual searches. The information contained in PsycINFO is also available in a monthly print journal called *Psychological Abstracts*.

- Journal articles are easier to understand if you are familiar with the standard format. Most articles include six elements: abstract, introduction, method, results, discussion, and references.

The Perils of Anecdotal Evidence: "I Have a Friend Who ..."

Anecdotes readily sway people because they often are concrete, vivid, and memorable.

© digitalskillet/iStockphoto.com

Here's a tough problem. Suppose you are the judge in a family law court. As you look over the cases that will come before you today, you see that one divorcing couple has managed to settle almost all of the important decisions with minimal conflict—such as who gets the house, who gets the car and the dog, and who pays which bills. However, there is one crucial issue left: Each parent wants custody of the children, and because they could not reach an agreement on their own, the case is now in your court. You will need the wisdom of the legendary King Solomon for this decision. How can you determine what is in the best interests of the children?

Child custody decisions have major consequences for all of the parties involved. As you review the case records, you see that both parents are loving and competent, so there are no obvious reasons for selecting one parent over the other as the primary caretaker. In considering various alternatives, you mull over the possibility of awarding *joint custody*, an arrangement in which the children spend half of their time with each parent, instead of the more usual arrangement where one parent has primary custody and the other has visitation rights. Joint custody seems to have some obvious benefits, but you are not sure how well these arrangements actually work. Will the children feel more attached to both parents if the parents share custody equally? Or will

the children feel hassled by always moving around, perhaps spending half of the week at one parent's home and half at the other parent's home? Can parents who are already feuding over child custody issues make these complicated arrangements work? Or is joint custody just too disruptive to everyone's life? You really don't know the answer to any of these vexing questions.

One of the lawyers involved in the case knows that you are thinking about the possibility of joint custody. She also understands that you want more information about how well joint custody tends to work before you render a decision. To help you make up your mind, she tells you about a divorced couple that has had a joint custody arrangement for many years and offers to have them appear in court to describe their experiences "first-hand." They and their children can answer any questions you might have about the pros and cons of joint custody. They should be in the best position to know how well joint custody works because they are living it. Sounds like a reasonable plan. What do you think?

Hopefully, you said, "No, No, No!" What's wrong with asking someone who's been there how well joint custody works? The crux of the problem is that the evidence a single family brings to the question of joint custody is *anecdotal evidence,* which consists of personal stories about specific incidents and experiences. Anecdotal evidence can be very seductive. For example, one study found that psychology majors' choices of future courses to enroll in were influenced more by a couple of students' brief anecdotes than by extensive statistics on many other students' ratings of the courses from the previous term (Borgida & Nisbett, 1977). The power of anecdotes was also apparent in a more recent study

that explored how to persuade people to take a personal health risk (for hepatitis B infection) more seriously. The researchers found that anecdotal accounts had more persuasive impact than sound factual and statistical evidence (de Wit, Das, & Vet, 2008). Anecdotes readily sway people because they often are concrete, vivid, and memorable. Indeed, people tend to be influenced by anecdotal information even when they are explicitly forewarned that the information is *not* representative (Hamill, Wilson, & Nisbett, 1980). Many politicians are keenly aware of the power of anecdotes and they frequently rely on a single vivid story rather than solid data to sway voters' views. However, anecdotal evidence is fundamentally flawed (Ruscio, 2002; Stanovich, 2004).

What, exactly, is wrong with anecdotal evidence? Let's use some of the concepts introduced in the main body of the chapter to analyze the shortcomings of anecdotal evidence. First, in the language of research designs, the anecdotal experiences of one family resemble a single *case study*. The story they tell about their experiences with joint custody may be quite interesting, but their experiences—good or bad—cannot be used to generalize to other couples. Why not? Because they are only one family, and they may be unusual in some way that affects how well they manage joint custody. To draw general conclusions based on the case study approach, you need a systematic series of case studies, so you can look for threads of consistency. A single family is a sample size of one, which surely is not large enough to derive broad principles that would apply to other families.

Second, anecdotal evidence is similar to *self-report data,* which can be distorted for a variety of reasons, such as people's tendency to give socially approved information about themselves (the *social desirability bias*). When researchers use tests and surveys to gather self-report data, they can take steps to reduce or assess the impact of distortions in their data, but there are no comparable safeguards with anecdotal evidence. Thus, the family that appears in your courtroom may be eager to make a good impression and unknowingly slant their story accordingly.

Anecdotes are often inaccurate and riddled with embellishments. We will see in Chapter 7 that memories of personal experiences are far more malleable and far less reliable than widely assumed (Roediger, Wheeler, & Rajaram, 1993). And, although it would not be an issue in this case, in other situations, *anecdotal evidence often consists of stories that people have heard about others' experiences.* Hearsay evidence is not accepted in courtrooms for good reason. As stories are passed on from one person to another, they often become increasingly distorted and inaccurate.

Can you think of any other reasons for being wary of anecdotal evidence? After reading the chapter, perhaps you thought about the possibility of *sampling bias.* Do you think that the lawyer will pick a couple at random from all those who have been awarded joint custody? It seems highly unlikely. If she wants you to award joint custody, she will find a couple for whom this arrangement worked very well, and if she wants you to award sole custody to her client, she will find a couple whose inability to make joint custody work had dire consequences for their children. One reason people love to work with anecdotal evidence is that it is so readily manipulated; they can usually find an anecdote or two to support their position, whether or not these anecdotes are representative of most people's experiences.

If the testimony of one family cannot be used in making this critical custody decision, what sort of evidence should you be looking for? One goal of effective critical thinking is to make decisions based on solid evidence. This process is called *evidence-based decision making.* In this case, you would need to consider the overall experiences of a large sample of families who have tried joint custody arrangements. In general, across many different families, did the children in joint custody develop well? Was there a disproportionately high rate of emotional problems or other signs of stress for the children or the parents? Was the percentage of families who returned to court at a later date to change their joint custody arrangements higher than for other types of custody arrangements? You can probably think of additional information that you would want to collect regarding the outcomes of various custody arrangements.

In examining research reports, many people recognize the need to evaluate the evidence by looking for the types of flaws described in the main body of the chapter (sampling bias, experimenter bias, and so forth). Curiously, though, many of the same people then fail to apply the same principles of good evidence to their personal decisions in everyday life. The tendency to rely on the anecdotal experiences of a small number of people is sometimes called the "*I have a friend who*" syndrome, because no matter what the topic is, it seems that someone will provide a personal story about a friend as evidence for his or her particular point of view. In short, when you hear people support their assertions with personal stories, a little skepticism is in order.

TABLE 2.4	**Critical Thinking Skills Discussed in This Application**
Skill	**Description**
Recognizing the limitations of anecdotal evidence	The critical thinker is wary of anecdotal evidence, which consists of personal stories used to support one's assertions.
	Anecdotal evidence tends to be unrepresentative, inaccurate, and unreliable.
Using evidence-based decision making	The critical thinker understands the need to seek sound evidence to guide decisions in everyday life.

Key Ideas

The Scientific Approach to Behaviour

● The scientific approach assumes that there are laws of behaviour that can be discovered through empirical research. The goals of the science of psychology include (1) the measurement and description of behaviour, (2) the understanding and prediction of behaviour, and (3) the application of this knowledge to the task of controlling behaviour.

● A scientific investigation follows a systematic pattern that includes five steps: (1) formulate a testable hypothesis, (2) select the research method and design the study, (3) collect the data, (4) analyze the data and draw conclusions, and (5) report the findings. The two major advantages of the scientific approach are its clarity in communication and its relative intolerance of error.

● By integrating apparently unrelated facts into a coherent whole, theories permit psychologists to make the leap from the description of behaviour to understanding behaviour.

Looking for Causes: Experimental Research

● Experimental research involves the manipulation of an independent variable to ascertain its effect on a dependent variable. This research is usually done by comparing experimental and control groups, which must be alike in regard to important extraneous variables.

● Experimental designs may vary. For example, sometimes an experimental group serves as its own control group. And many experiments have more than one independent variable or more than one dependent variable. Some of these variations were seen in the Featured Study, in which more than one independent variable was used.

● An experiment is a powerful research method that permits conclusions about cause-and-effect relationships between variables. However, the experimental method is often not usable for a specific problem, and many experiments tend to be artificial.

Looking for Links: Descriptive/Correlational Research

● Psychologists rely on descriptive/correlational research when they are unable to manipulate the variables they want to study. Key descriptive methods include naturalistic observation, case studies, and surveys.

● Descriptive/correlational research methods allow psychologists to explore issues that might not be open to experimental investigation. However, these research methods cannot demonstrate cause-and-effect relationships.

Looking for Conclusions: Statistics and Research

● Psychologists use descriptive statistics, such as measures of central tendency and variability, to organize and summarize their numerical data. The mean, median, and mode are widely used measures of central tendency. Variability is usually measured with the standard deviation.

● Correlations may be either positive (when two variables co-vary in the same direction) or negative (when two variables co-vary in opposite directions). The closer a correlation is to either +1.00 or −1.00, the stronger the association. Higher correlations yield greater predictability. However, a correlation is no assurance of causation.

● Hypothesis testing involves deciding whether observed findings support the researcher's hypothesis. Findings are statistically significant only when they are unlikely to be due to chance.

Looking for Flaws: Evaluating Research

● Scientists often try to replicate research findings to double-check their validity. Sampling bias occurs when a sample is not representative of the population of interest. Placebo effects occur when subjects' expectations cause them to change their behaviour in response to a fake treatment.

● Distortions in self-reports are a source of concern whenever questionnaires and personality inventories are used to collect data. Experimenter bias occurs when researchers' expectations and desires distort their observations or unintentionally influence their subjects' behaviour.

Looking at Ethics: Do the Ends Justify the Means?

● Research sometimes raises complex ethical issues. In psychology, the key questions concern the use of deception with human subjects and the use of harmful or painful manipulations with animal subjects. The CPA has formulated ethical principles to serve as guidelines for researchers.

Putting It in Perspective: Themes 1 and 7

● Two of the book's unifying themes are apparent in this chapter's discussion of the research enterprise in psychology: Psychology is empirical, and people's experience of the world can be highly subjective.

PERSONAL APPLICATION • Finding and Reading Journal Articles

● Journals publish technical and scholarly material. Usually they are written for other professionals in a narrow area of inquiry.

● PsycINFO is a computerized database that contains brief summaries of published journal articles, books, and chapters in edited books. Works on specific topics and publications by specific authors can be found by using the search mechanisms built into the database.

● Journal articles are easier to understand if one is familiar with the standard format. Most articles include six elements: abstract, introduction, method, results, discussion, and references.

CRITICAL THINKING APPLICATION • The Perils of Anecdotal Evidence: "I Have a Friend Who . . ."

● Anecdotal evidence consists of personal stories about specific incidents and experiences. Anecdotes often influence people because they tend to be concrete, vivid, and memorable.

● However, anecdotal evidence is usually based on the equivalent of a single case study, which is not an adequate sample, and there are no safeguards to reduce the distortion often found in self-report data. Many anecdotes are inaccurate, secondhand reports of others' experiences. Effective critical thinking depends on evidence-based decision making.

Key Terms

Anecdotal evidence, 80
Case study, 55
Confounding of variables, 51
Control group, 50
Correlation, 62
Correlation coefficient, 62
Data collection techniques, 46
Dependent variable, 49
Descriptive statistics, 59
Double-blind procedure, 69
Experiment, 49
Experimental group, 50
Experimenter bias, 69
Extraneous variables, 51
Frequency distribution, 59
Frequency polygon, 59
Hypothesis, 44
Independent variable, 49
Inferential statistics, 64
Internet-mediated research, 72
Journal, 48
Mean, 59
Median, 59
Meta-analysis, 66
Mode, 59
Naturalistic observation, 54
Negatively skewed distribution, 59
Normal distribution, 61

Operational definition, 46
Participants, 46
Percentile score, 61
Placebo effects, 67
Population, 66
Positively skewed distribution, 59
Random assignment, 51
Reactivity, 54
Replication, 65
Research methods, 49
Response set, 69
Sample, 66
Sampling bias, 67
Social desirability bias, 68
Standard deviation, 60
Statistical significance, 65
Statistics, 58
Subjects, 46
Survey, 56
Theory, 45
Variability, 60
Variables, 44

Key People

Arthur Aron, 46
Donald Dutton, 46
Neal Miller, 75
Robert Rosenthal, 69
David Wolfe, 50

1. Which of the following terms is defined as "a tentative prediction about the relationship between two variables"?
   A. confounding of variables
   B. operational definition
   C. theory
   D. hypothesis

2. Which of the following steps in the research process relates to the amount of control that researchers will exert over a study?
   A. They provide operational definitions of their variables.
   B. They decide if their study will be experimental or correlational.
   C. They use statistics to summarize their findings.
   D. They decide how many subjects should participate in their study.

3. A researcher found that clients who were randomly assigned to same-sex groups participated in group therapy sessions to a greater extent than clients who were randomly assigned to co-ed groups. Which of the following is the independent variable in this experiment?
   A. the amount of participation in the group therapy sessions
   B. whether or not the group was co-ed
   C. the clients' attitudes toward group therapy
   D. how much the clients' mental health improved

4. A researcher wants to see whether a protein-enriched diet will enhance the maze-running performance of rats. For the duration of the study, the researcher feeds one group of rats a high-protein diet; the other group continues to receive its regular diet. In this experiment, what is the term used to describe the maze-running performance of the rats?
   A. correlated variable
   B. control variable
   C. dependent variable
   D. independent variable

5. A research study examines the effect of a new teaching technique on students' achievement test scores. Which of the following student characteristics would be considered an important extraneous variable?
   A. hair colour
   B. athletic skills
   C. IQ scores
   D. sociability

6. When you have a cold, you rest in bed, take medication, and drink plenty of fluids. If you wanted to know which of those three actions led to the improvement of your symptoms, which of the following research problems would prevent you from knowing for sure?
   A. confounding of variables
   B. distorted self-report data
   C. sampling bias
   D. experimenter bias

7. A psychologist monitors a group of nursery school children, recording each instance of altruistic behaviour when it occurs. Which of the following research methods is the psychologist using?
   A. experimental method
   B. naturalistic observation
   C. case study
   D. survey method

8. Which of the following statements explains the main advantage of descriptive/correlational research?
   A. It allows investigators to isolate cause and effect.
   B. It permits researchers to study variables that would be impossible to manipulate.
   C. It can demonstrate conclusively that two variables are causally related.
   D. It is simpler to conduct because it does not require evaluation by a research ethics board.

9. Which of the following correlation coefficients indicates the strongest relationship between two variables?
   A. −0.85
   B. 0.19
   C. 0.58
   D. 1.94

10. When psychologists say that research results are statistically significant, which of the following explains what they mean?
    A. The results have important practical applications.
    B. The results have important implications for scientific theory.
    C. The results are unlikely to be due to the fluctuations of chance.
    D. The results will be reproduced consistently if the study is replicated.

11. When does sampling bias occur?
    A. when the data are analyzed using statistical software
    B. when the group of participants are not representative of the population

C. when two variables are confounded
D. when deception is used in order to conceal the effect of an independent variable

12. Which of the following strategies would allow researchers to avoid the problem of experimenter bias?
    A. Don't tell subjects about the hypothesis of the experiment.
    B. Tell subjects that there are no "right" or "wrong" answers.
    C. Don't tell experimenters which subjects are in the experimental and control groups.
    D. Have experimenters use only nonverbal signals when communicating with subjects.

13. Which of the following studies would be *most* likely to be influenced by a placebo effect?
    A. Participants' heart rates and brain activity are monitored as they do a series of activities including yoga, reading, and watching TV.
    B. One participant is asked to describe each of the physical sensations associated with doing a yoga pose for one minute.
    C. Participants are asked to track their moods and record all activities for a week.
    D. Participants learn yoga, and then are asked to report whether their moods improve as a result of doing yoga.

14. Which of the following statements summarizes the evidence regarding the relative risk of using deception in research?
    A. Many deceptive studies significantly distress subjects who are not told about the possibility of deception.
    B. Deceptive studies are enjoyable for most subjects, who report they didn't mind being misled.
    C. Deceptive research seriously undermines subjects' trust in other people.
    D. The use of deception in research leads to biased results because subjects are unsure about what to do during the study.

15. Which of the following best describes PsycINFO?
    A. It is a new journal that recently replaced *Psychological Abstracts*.
    B. It is a computerized database that contains information about studies not yet published.
    C. It is a reference book that explains the format and techniques for writing journal articles.
    D. It is a computerized database that contains abstracts of articles, chapters, and books reporting psychological research.

See Appendix A for answers to this Practice Test.

On the Web

▶ **CourseMate**

Go to this site to find online resources directly linked to your book, including more quizzes, a glossary, flash cards, videos, and more!

▶ **CengageNow**

Go to this site for the link to CengageNOW™, your one-stop study shop. Take a pre-test for this chapter and CengageNOW™ will generate a personalized study plan based on your test results! The study plan will identify the topics you need to review and direct you to online resources to help you master those topics. You can then take a post-test to help you determine the concepts you have mastered and what you still need to work on.

▶ **Aplia**

Aplia™ is an online interactive learning solution that helps you improve comprehension—and your grade—by integrating a variety of media and tools such as video, tutorials, practice tests, and an interactive e-book.

© Rebecca Atkins, York University

Most people seem to have an almost endless fascination with the human brain. And why not? It is assumed to be the basis of most of what differentiates us from other mammals—language, reasoning, consciousness, the self, and many other human qualities and characteristics. When it is working well, so are we. When it encounters difficulties, the problems can be both overwhelming and intriguing, and these problems generate many questions about the brain. Why do people with Alzheimer's disease forget central things about themselves and those they love, perhaps even being unable to recognize their own spouse or children? If someone suffers a stroke, why does language sometimes disappear, but not always? Why does the accompanying paralysis show up on the opposite side of the body relative to the side of the brain in which the stroke occurred? Why are athletes such as Eric Lindros, Bret Hart, Troy Aikman, Keith Primeau, and Steve Young forced to retire early after suffering concussions? Whereas athletes who sustained head injuries 20 years ago were simply told to "walk it off," today there is increased recognition that concussions may result in irreparable brain damage. The issue is of such a concern that professional athletes have begun to agree to donate their brains after they die to Boston University's Center for the Study of Traumatic Encephalopathy (Schwarz, 2008). The athletes making this commitment include professional football, soccer, hockey, and basketball players, along with professional wrestlers and Olympic athletes (The Brain Injury Association of Canada, 2009). They recognize that research into the brain, both damaged and normal, is essential in our attempt to understand the normal workings of the brain and the nature and effects of trauma. The study of the brain and its connections to behaviour is one of the focal topics in this chapter.

There are few more rapidly developing areas of research than biological approaches to psychology, especially neuropsychology, the study of the brain (Cacioppo et al., 2008; Poldrack & Wagner, 2008). The study of the brain is one of those areas of psychology where Canadian researchers have made pivotal discoveries (Hayman-Abello, Hayman-Abello, & Rourke, 2003). After reading this chapter, you will be familiar with the pioneering contributions of senior Canadian scholars such as Wilder Penfield, Donald Hebb, and Brenda Milner. Even before you read this chapter, however, you may have heard about the work of neuroscientists such as McMaster University's Sandra Witelson or Dalhousie University's John Connolly.

Sandra Witelson, who is well known for her research and for having one of the most extensive collections of preserved human brains, was given the opportunity to study one of the world's most famous brains—that of Albert Einstein. The tale of how Einstein's brain got to Witelson is fascinating in itself and has been the subject of numerous articles and Carolyn Abraham's (2002) book *Possessing Genius*. Einstein died in April 1955 from a ruptured aneurysm for which he had previously refused surgery. His brain was removed by Tom Harvey, a hospital pathologist, and injected with formalin to preserve it. Einstein's eyes were taken by his friend Henry Abrams, an ophthalmologist, who kept them in a safety deposit box. According to various conflicting sources, Harvey either "stole" the brain when he left his job at Princeton Hospital, or Einstein's son agreed that "it could be left to science, in the custody of Harvey" (Abraham, 2002). The latter would seem to be the case, because the brain remained in Harvey's possession.

Over the years, Harvey donated small pieces of the brain for analysis, although he was waiting for the right person who could conduct a scientific examination of the brain. Eventually, Harvey read about the scientific work of Sandra Witelson and offered her the brain. He drove across the border in 1996 with Einstein's brain in the trunk of his car and delivered it to her.

Witelson examined and measured the pieces of the brain and examined photos originally taken of the brain. She compared the results of her examination of Einstein's brain with other "control" brains she had in her laboratory. Witelson found that Einstein's brain seemed highly similar overall to most other brains; it was about the same size and weight (Witelson, Kigar, & Harvey, 1999). But there were a couple of important exceptions, including a wider parietal region (toward the top and back of the brain) and a distinct sylvian fissure (a fissure or groove separating the frontal lobe from the temporal lobe). Witelson speculated that these differences made sense in light of Einstein's intellect and approach to science: "Visuospatial cognition, mathematical thought, and imagery of movement are strongly dependent on this region. Einstein's exceptional intellect in these cognitive domains and his self-described mode of scientific thinking may be related to the atypical anatomy in his inferior parietal lobules" (Witelson et al., 1999, p. 2152).

One of the enduring mysteries in the study of the brain relates to localization of function—discovering which parts of the brain are associated with specific behaviours and functions. In this chapter, you will learn about the parts of the brain and their functions. We will also describe the wide range of techniques that neuroscientists have to assist them in their research. One traditional method was to examine the electrical activity of the brain through EEG recordings.

Dalhousie University's John Connolly used EEG to unravel the mystery surrounding one of the brains he became involved with. This brain was also remarkable, but it was remarkable in quite a different way. It belonged to a young man who had general aphasia and whose cognitive status could not be ascertained in traditional ways. While working at a bar, the 21-year-old man was stabbed in the head (more specifically, in the left temporal region) with a 30-cm knife. At the hospital, the staff needed to determine whether he would benefit from rehabilitation; it seemed that he was in a vegetative state and that recovery was unlikely. Rehabilitation seemed not to be warranted. But no one really knew his cognitive status, because he could not communicate in any way with others. The possibility existed that he was alert but trapped in an unresponsive body, a victim of locked-in syndrome. Connolly devised an innovative method (Connolly & D'Arcy, 2000) of assessing the patient's status by recording EEG responses to carefully selected stimuli that were presented to the patient (Connolly, Mate-Kole, & Joyce, 1999). As we will describe later in this chapter, the brain responds with measurable electrical activity when stimulated. On the basis of this assessment, Connolly and his colleagues were optimistic about the patient's chances for recovery. Rehabilitation was successfully reinstated and the patient experienced substantial recovery.

Locked-in syndrome was the subject of a book (Bauby, 1997) and movie, both entitled *The Diving Bell and the Butterfly*, the memoir of a French journalist who suffered a stroke. Jean-Dominique Bauby learned to communicate by blinking his left eye, the only part of his body he could control. He dictated his book by blinking to indicate specific letters of the alphabet, and it has been reported that it took him over 100 000 blinks to dictate his book. Locked-in syndrome has recently become a very active area of research in neuroscience (Chisholm & Gillett, 2005; Owen et al., 2006; Wang et al., 2004).

While much of the research you will read about in this chapter is not as dramatic as these three examples, it has the potential for unlocking some of the mysteries of the brain and improving the lives of individuals suffering from various types of disorders. The research discussed in this chapter will consider the countless ways in which biology is fundamental to the study of behaviour.

Communication in the Nervous System

PREVIEW QUESTIONS

▶ What are the key parts of the neuron, and what are their functions?

▶ What is an action potential?

▶ How does synaptic transmission take place?

▶ Which neurotransmitters regulate which aspects of behaviour?

Imagine that you are watching a scary movie. As the tension mounts, your palms sweat and your heart beats faster. You begin shovelling popcorn into your mouth, carelessly spilling some in your lap. If someone were to ask you what you are doing at this moment, you would probably say, "Nothing—just watching the movie." Yet some highly complex processes are occurring without your thinking about them. A stimulus (the light from the screen) is striking your eye. Almost instantaneously, your brain is interpreting the light stimulus and signals are flashing to other parts of your body, leading to a flurry of activity. Your sweat glands are releasing perspiration, your heartbeat is quickening, and muscular movements are enabling your hand to find the popcorn and, more or less successfully, lift it to your mouth.

Even in this simple example, you can see that behaviour depends on rapid information processing. Information travels almost instantaneously from your eye to your brain, from your brain to the muscles of your arm and hand, and from your palms back to your brain. In essence, your nervous system is a complex communication network in which signals are constantly being transmitted, received, and integrated. The nervous system handles information, just as the circulatory system handles blood. In this section, we take a close look at communication in the nervous system.

Nervous Tissue: The Basic Hardware 2a

Your nervous system is living tissue composed of cells. The cells in the nervous system fall into two major categories: *glia* and *neurons*. *Neurons* are individual cells in the nervous system that receive, integrate, and transmit information. They are the basic links that permit communication within the nervous system. The vast majority of them communicate only with other neurons. However, a small minority receive signals from outside the nervous system (from sensory organs) or carry messages from the nervous system to the muscles that move the body.

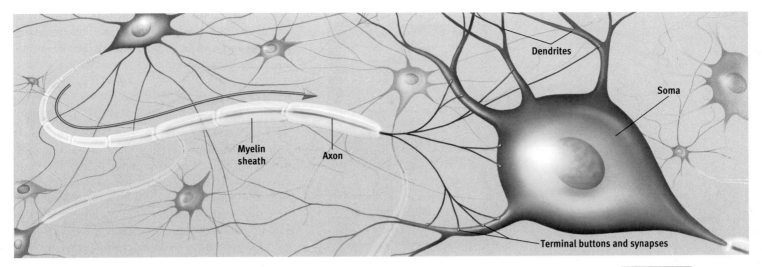

Dendrites

Soma

Myelin sheath

Axon

Terminal buttons and synapses

A highly simplified drawing of two "typical" neurons is shown in Figure 3.1. Actually, neurons come in such a tremendous variety of types and shapes that no single drawing can adequately represent them. Trying to draw the "typical" neuron is like trying to draw the "typical" tree. In spite of this diversity, the drawing in Figure 3.1 highlights some common features of neurons.

The *soma,* or *cell body,* contains the cell nucleus and much of the chemical machinery common to most cells (*soma* is Greek for *body*). The rest of the neuron is devoted exclusively to handling information. The neurons in Figure 3.1 have a number of branched, feeler-like structures called *dendritic trees* (*dendrite* is a Greek word for *tree*). Each individual branch is a *dendrite. Dendrites* are the parts of a neuron that are specialized to receive information. Most neurons receive information from many other cells—sometimes thousands of others—and so have extensive dendritic trees.

From the many dendrites, information flows into the cell body and then travels away from the soma along the *axon* (from the Greek for *axle*). The *axon* is a long, thin fibre that transmits signals away from the soma to other neurons or to muscles or glands. Axons may be quite long (sometimes over a metre), and they may branch off to communicate with a number of other cells.

In humans, many axons are wrapped in cells with a high concentration of a white, fatty substance called *myelin. The myelin sheath* is insulating material, derived from glial cells, that encases some axons. The myelin sheath speeds up the transmission of signals that move along axons (Zorumski, Isenberg, & Mennerick, 2009). If an axon's myelin sheath deteriorates, its signals may not be transmitted effectively. The loss of muscle control seen with the disease *multiple*

sclerosis is due to a degeneration of myelin sheaths (Joffee, 2009).

The axon ends in a cluster of *terminal buttons,* which are small knobs that secrete chemicals called *neurotransmitters.* These chemicals serve as messengers that may activate neighbouring neurons. The points at which neurons interconnect are called *synapses. A synapse* is a junction where information is transmitted from one neuron to another (*synapse* is from the Greek for *junction*). To summarize, information is received at the dendrites, is passed through the soma and along the axon, and is transmitted to the dendrites of other cells at meeting points called *synapses.*

Glia

Glia are cells found throughout the nervous system that provide various types of support for neurons. Glia (literally, *glue*) tend to be much smaller than neurons but they outnumber neurons by about ten to one, so glial cells appear to account for over 50 percent of the brain's volume. Among other things, glial cells supply nourishment to neurons, help remove neurons' waste products, and provide insulation around many axons. The myelin sheaths that encase some axons are derived from special types of glial cells. Glia also play a complicated role in orchestrating the development of the nervous system in the human embryo.

These functions, which have been known for many years, made glial cells the unsung heroes of the nervous system. Until recently, it was thought that the "glamorous" work in the nervous system—the transmission and integration of informational signals—was the exclusive province of the neurons. New research, however, suggests that glia may also send and receive chemical signals (Deitmer & Rose, 2010; Fields, 2004) and that they may be implicated in diseases such as amyotrophic lateral sclerosis

FIGURE 3.1

Structure of the neuron.

Neurons are the communication links of the nervous system. This diagram highlights the key parts of a neuron, including specialized receptor areas (dendrites), the cell body (soma), the axon fibre along which impulses are transmitted, and the terminal buttons, which release chemical messengers that carry signals to other neurons. Neurons vary considerably in size and shape and are usually densely interconnected.

 Log on to CourseMate to access this interactive figure.

The Biological Bases of Behaviour

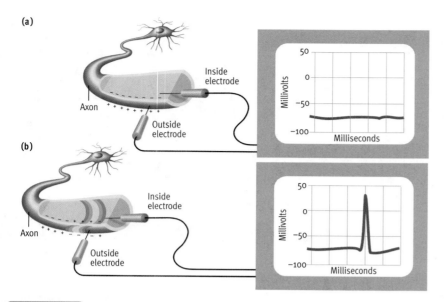

(a)

(b)

Inside electrode

Outside electrode

Axon

Inside electrode

Outside electrode

Axon

FIGURE 3.2

The neural impulse.

The electrochemical properties of the neuron allow it to transmit signals. The electric charge of a neuron can be measured with a pair of electrodes connected to an oscilloscope, as Hodgkin and Huxley (1952) showed with a squid axon. Because of its exceptionally thick axons, the squid has frequently been used by scientists studying the neural impulse. (a) At rest, the neuron's voltage hovers around 70 millivolts. (b) When a neuron is stimulated, a brief jump occurs in the neuron's voltage, resulting in a spike on the oscilloscope recording of the neuron's electrical activity. This change in voltage, called an *action potential*, travels along the axon like a spark travelling along a trail of gunpowder.

WEB LINK 3.1

Neuropsychology Central

This content-rich site, maintained by Dr. Ernest J. Bordini of Clinical Psychology Associates of North Central Florida, is dedicated to all aspects of human neuropsychology, from the perspectives of the experimental research laboratory to the applied clinical setting of the hospital and professional office.

(ALS) and Parkinson's disease (Lobsiger & Cleveland, 2007). Research findings also suggest that glial cells may play an important role in memory formation (Bains & Oliet, 2007) and that gradual deterioration of glial tissue might contribute to the emergence of Alzheimer's disease (Streit, 2005). Other research suggests that glial cells play a crucial role in the experience of chronic pain (Milligan & Watkins, 2009) and that impaired neural–glial communication might contribute to psychological disorders such as schizophrenia (Hashimoto, Shimizu, & Iyo, 2005) and mood disorders (Lee et al., 2007).

Although glial cells may contribute to information processing in the nervous system, the bulk of this crucial work is handled by the neurons. Thus, we need to examine the process of neural activity in more detail.

The Neural Impulse: Using Energy to Send Information

2a

What happens when a neuron is stimulated? What is the nature of the signal—the *neural impulse*—that moves through the neuron? These were the questions that Alan Hodgkin and Andrew Huxley set out to answer in their groundbreaking experiments with

axons removed from squid. They chose to work with squids because these mollusks have "giant" axons that are easier to work with—axons 100 times the size of those in humans.

The Neuron at Rest: A Tiny Battery

2a

Hodgkin and Huxley (1952) learned that the neural impulse is a complex electrochemical reaction. Both inside and outside the neuron are fluids containing electrically charged atoms and molecules called *ions.* The cell membrane is semipermeable, permitting movement of some ions. Positively charged sodium and potassium ions and negatively charged chloride ions flow back and forth across the cell membrane, but they do not cross at the same rate. The difference in flow rates leads to a slightly higher concentration of negatively charged ions inside the cell. The resulting voltage means that the neuron at rest is a tiny battery, a store of potential energy. *The resting potential of a neuron is its stable, negative charge when the cell is inactive.* As shown in Figure 3.2(a), this charge is about −70 millivolts, roughly one-twentieth of the voltage of a flashlight battery.

The Action Potential

2a

As long as the voltage of a neuron remains constant, the cell is quiet and no messages are being sent. When the neuron is stimulated, channels in its cell membrane open, briefly allowing positively charged sodium ions to rush in. For an instant, the neuron's charge is less negative, or even positive, creating an action potential (McCormick, 2008). *An action potential is a very brief shift in a neuron's electrical charge that travels along an axon.* The firing of an action potential is reflected in the voltage spike shown in Figure 3.2(b). Like a spark travelling along a trail of gunpowder, the voltage change races down the axon.

After the firing of an action potential, the channels in the cell membrane that opened to let in sodium close up. Some time is needed before they are ready to open again, and until that time, the neuron cannot fire. *The absolute refractory period is the minimum length of time after an action potential during which another action potential cannot begin.* This "downtime" isn't very long, only one or two milliseconds. It is followed by a brief *relative refractory period.* During the relative refractory period, the neuron can fire, but its threshold for firing is elevated, so more intense stimulation is required to initiate an action potential.

The All-or-None Law

The neural impulse is an all-or-none proposition, like firing a gun. You can't half-fire a gun. The same is true of the neuron's firing of action potentials. Either the neuron fires or it doesn't, and its action potentials are all the same size (Kandel, 2000). That is, weaker stimuli do not produce smaller action potentials.

Even though the action potential is an all-or-nothing event, neurons *can* convey information about the strength of a stimulus. They do so by varying the *rate* at which they fire action potentials. In general, a stronger stimulus will cause a cell to fire a more rapid volley of neural impulses than a weaker stimulus will. For example, a dim light might trigger five action potentials per second in a visual cell, whereas brighter lights might trigger 100 to 200 impulses per second (Burkhardt, 2010).

Various neurons transmit neural impulses at different speeds. For example, thicker axons transmit neural impulses more rapidly than thinner ones do. Although neural impulses do not travel as fast as electricity along a wire, they *are* very fast, moving at up to 100 metres per second, which is equivalent to more than 300 kilometres per hour. The entire, complicated process of neural transmission takes only a few thousandths of a second. In the time it has taken you to read this description of the neural impulse, billions of such impulses have been transmitted in your nervous system!

The Synapse: Where Neurons Meet

In the nervous system, the neural impulse functions as a signal. For that signal to have any meaning for the system as a whole, it must be transmitted from the neuron to other cells. As noted earlier, this transmission takes place at special junctions called *synapses,* which depend on *chemical* messengers.

Sending Signals: Chemicals as Couriers

A "typical" synapse is shown in Figure 3.3. The first thing that you should notice is that the two neurons don't actually touch. They are separated by the *synaptic cleft,* a microscopic gap between the terminal button of one neuron and the cell membrane of another neuron. Signals have to cross this gap to permit neurons to communicate. In this situation, the neuron that sends a signal across the gap is called the *presynaptic neuron* and the neuron that receives the signal is called the *postsynaptic neuron.*

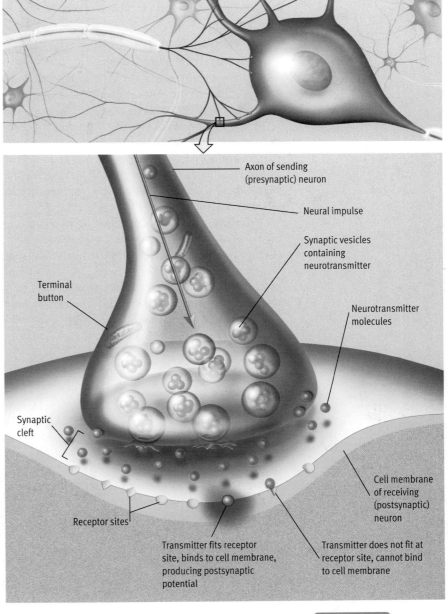

- Axon of sending (presynaptic) neuron
- Neural impulse
- Synaptic vesicles containing neurotransmitter
- Terminal button
- Neurotransmitter molecules
- Synaptic cleft
- Cell membrane of receiving (postsynaptic) neuron
- Receptor sites
- Transmitter fits receptor site, binds to cell membrane, producing postsynaptic potential
- Transmitter does not fit at receptor site, cannot bind to cell membrane

FIGURE 3.3

The synapse.

When a neural impulse reaches an axon's terminal buttons, it triggers the release of chemical messengers called *neurotransmitters.* The neurotransmitter molecules diffuse across the synaptic cleft and bind to receptor sites on the postsynaptic neuron. A specific neurotransmitter can bind only to receptor sites that its molecular structure will fit into, much like a key must fit a lock.

How do messages travel across the gaps between neurons? The arrival of an action potential at an axon's terminal buttons triggers the release of *neurotransmitters*—chemicals that transmit information from one neuron to another. Within the buttons, most of these chemicals are stored in small sacs, called *synaptic vesicles.* The neurotransmitters are released when a vesicle fuses with the membrane of the presynaptic cell and its contents spill into the synaptic cleft (Schwartz, 2008). After their release, neurotransmitters diffuse across the synaptic cleft to the membrane of the receiving cell. There they may bind with special molecules in the postsynaptic cell membrane at various *receptor sites.* These sites are specifically "tuned" to recognize and respond to some neurotransmitters but not to others.

Receiving Signals: Postsynaptic Potentials

When a neurotransmitter and a receptor molecule combine, reactions in the cell membrane cause a *postsynaptic potential (PSP)*, a voltage change at a receptor site on a postsynaptic cell membrane. Postsynaptic potentials do *not* follow the all-or-none law as action potentials do. Instead, postsynaptic potentials are *graded*. That is, they vary in size and they increase or decrease the *probability* of a neural impulse in the receiving cell in proportion to the amount of voltage change.

Two types of messages can be sent from cell to cell: excitatory and inhibitory. An *excitatory PSP* is a positive voltage shift that increases the likelihood that the postsynaptic neuron will fire action potentials. An *inhibitory PSP* is a negative voltage shift that decreases the likelihood that the postsynaptic neuron will fire action potentials. The direction of the voltage shift, and thus the nature of the PSP (excitatory

or inhibitory), depends on which receptor sites are activated in the postsynaptic neuron (Kandel, 2000).

The excitatory or inhibitory effects produced at a synapse last only a fraction of a second. Then neurotransmitters drift away from receptor sites or are inactivated by enzymes that metabolize (convert) them into inactive forms. Most are reabsorbed into the presynaptic neuron through *reuptake*, a process in which neurotransmitters are sponged up from the synaptic cleft by the presynaptic membrane. Reuptake allows synapses to recycle their materials. Reuptake and the other key processes in synaptic transmission are summarized in Figure 3.4.

Integrating Signals: Neural Networks

A neuron may receive a symphony of signals from *thousands* of other neurons. The same neuron may pass its messages along to thousands of neurons as well. Thus, a neuron must do a great deal more than simply relay messages it receives. It must *integrate* signals arriving at many synapses before it "decides"

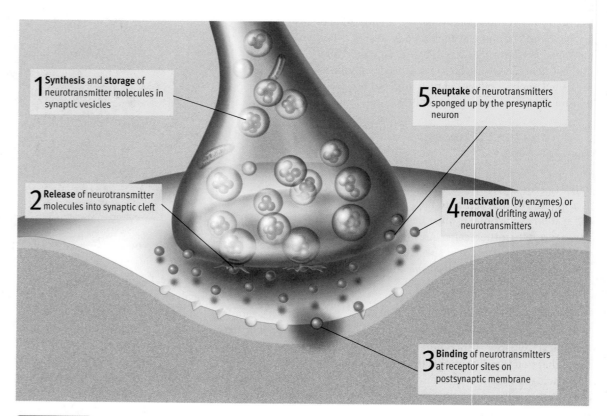

1 **Synthesis** and **storage** of neurotransmitter molecules in synaptic vesicles

5 **Reuptake** of neurotransmitters sponged up by the presynaptic neuron

2 **Release** of neurotransmitter molecules into synaptic cleft

4 **Inactivation** (by enzymes) or **removal** (drifting away) of neurotransmitters

3 **Binding** of neurotransmitters at receptor sites on postsynaptic membrane

FIGURE 3.4

Overview of synaptic transmission.

The main elements in synaptic transmission are summarized here, superimposed on a blowup of the synapse seen in Figure 3.3. The five key processes involved in communication at synapses are (1) synthesis and storage, (2) release, (3) binding, (4) inactivation or removal, and (5) reuptake of neurotransmitters. As you'll see in this chapter and the remainder of the book, the effects of many phenomena—such as pain, drug use, and some diseases—can be explained in terms of how they alter one or more of these processes (usually at synapses releasing a specific neurotransmitter).

whether to fire a neural impulse. If enough excitatory PSPs occur in a neuron, the electrical currents can add up, causing the cell's voltage to reach the threshold at which an action potential will be fired. However, if many inhibitory PSPs also occur, they will tend to cancel the effects of excitatory PSPs. Thus, the state of the neuron is a weighted balance between excitatory and inhibitory influences (Byrne, 2008).

As Rita Carter (1998) has pointed out in *Mapping the Mind,* "The firing of a single neuron is not enough to create the twitch of an eyelid in sleep, let alone a conscious impression. . . . Millions of neurons must fire in unison to produce the most trifling thought" (p. 19). Most neurons are interlinked in complex chains, pathways, circuits, and networks. Our perceptions, thoughts, and actions depend on *patterns* of neural activity in elaborate neural networks. These networks consist of interconnected neurons that frequently fire together or sequentially to perform certain functions (Song et al., 2005). The links in these networks are fluid, as new synaptic connections may be made while some old connections wither away (Hua & Smith, 2004).

Ironically, the *elimination of old synapses* appears to play a larger role in the sculpting of neural networks than the *creation of new synapses*. The nervous system normally forms more synapses than needed and then gradually eliminates the less-active synapses. For example, the number of synapses in the human visual cortex peaks at around age one and then declines, as diagrammed in Figure 3.5 (Huttenlocher, 1994). This elimination of old or less-active synapses is called *synaptic pruning*, and it is a key process in the formation of the neural networks that are crucial to communication in the nervous system (Tapia & Lichtman, 2008).

The linkage of neurons to form networks was the focus of the work of McGill University's Donald Hebb (to whom you were introduced in Chapter 1). Hebb's influential text *The Organization of Behavior* (Hebb, 1949) contained his analysis of the neural basis of behaviour and served to highlight his view that understanding the brain and its processes was fundamental to understanding behaviour. He realized that neurons do not act alone in influencing behaviour but that they are linked in complex networks or *cell assemblies*. One of his important contributions was the *Hebbian Learning Rule* specifying how these linkages might operate and come about. In his well-known neurophysiological

FIGURE 3.5

Synaptic pruning.

This graph summarizes data on the estimated number of synapses in the human visual cortex as a function of age (Huttenlocher, 1994). As you can see, the number of synapses in this area of the brain peaks around age one and then mostly declines over the course of the life span. This decline reflects the process of *synaptic pruning*, which involves the gradual elimination of less active synapses.

Source: Data based on Huttenlocher, P. R. (1994). Synaptogenesis in human cerebral cortex. In G. Dawson & K. W. Fischer (Eds.), *Human behavior and the developing brain.* New York: Guilford Press. Graphic adapted from Kolb, B., & Whishaw, I. Q. (2001). *An introduction to brain and behavior.* New York: Worth Publishers.

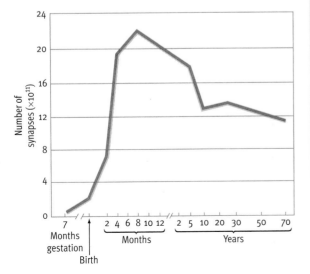

concept check 3.1

Understanding Nervous System Hardware Using Metaphors

A useful way to learn about the structures and functions of parts of the nervous system is through metaphors. Check your understanding of the basic components of the nervous system by matching the metaphorical descriptions below with the correct terms in the following list: (a) glia, (b) neuron, (c) soma, (d) dendrite, (e) axon, (f) myelin, (g) terminal button, (h) synapse. You'll find the answers in Appendix A.

____d____ **1.** Like a tree. Also, each branch is a telephone wire that carries incoming messages to you.

____f____ **2.** Like the insulation that covers electrical wires.

____b____ **3.** Like a silicon chip in a computer that receives and transmits information between input and output devices as well as between other chips.

____e____ **4.** Like an electrical cable that carries information.

____a____ **5.** Like the maintenance personnel who keep things clean and in working order so that the operations of the enterprise can proceed.

____g____ **6.** Like the nozzle at the end of a hose, from which water is squirted.

____h____ **7.** Like a railroad junction, where two trains may meet.

postulate, he said, "When an axon of cell A is near enough to excite a cell B and repeatedly or persistently takes part in firing it, some growth process or metabolic change takes place in one or both cells such that A's efficiency, as one of the cells firing B, is increased" (Hebb, 1949, p. 62). Thus, one neuron stimulating another neuron repeatedly produces changes in the synapse; learning has taken place. These ideas were foreshadowed by Hebb's earlier work on his master's thesis conducted in 1932 (Milner, 2003).

Although Hebb could not specify the exact character of the changes (Posner & Rothbart, 2004), he did speculate about their metabolic nature. His ideas are often referred to as the *Hebb Synapse* and continue to influence work today (Hinton, 2003; Milner, 2003; Sejnowski, 2003). Hebb's 1949 text set the stage for a focus on neurophysiology and has been listed as number four of the 100 most influential publications in cognitive science (Tees, 2003). Remarkably, over 50 years after its publication, it has been recently reissued (Hebb, 2002) and continues to serve as an important resource in neuroscience.

WEB LINK 3.2

Neurosciences on the Internet
Dr. Neil Busis has gathered what appears to be the largest collection of neuroscience links currently on the Web and provides a search engine to help visitors.

Neurotransmitters and Behaviour

2b

As we have seen, the nervous system relies on chemical couriers to communicate information between neurons. These *neurotransmitters* are fundamental to behaviour, playing a key role in everything from muscle movements to moods and mental health.

You might guess that the nervous system would require only two neurotransmitters—one for excitatory potentials and one for inhibitory potentials. In reality, there are nine well-established, classic (small-molecule) transmitters, about 40 additional neuropeptide chemicals that function, at least part-time, as neurotransmitters, and a handful of recently recognized "novel" neurotransmitters (Snyder, 2002; Zorumski et al., 2009).

Specific neurotransmitters work at specific kinds of synapses. You may recall that transmitters deliver their messages by binding to receptor sites on the postsynaptic membrane. However, a transmitter cannot bind to just any site. The binding process operates much like a lock and key, as was shown in Figure 3.3 (page 89). Just as a key has to fit a lock to work, a transmitter has to fit into a receptor site for binding to occur. Hence, specific transmitters can deliver signals only at certain locations on cell membranes. Such specialization reduces cross talk between densely packed neurons, making the nervous system's communication more precise (Deutch & Roth, 2008).

Why are there many neurotransmitters, each of which works only at certain synapses? This variety and specificity reduces cross talk between densely packed neurons, making the nervous system's communication more precise. Let's briefly review some of the most interesting findings about how neurotransmitters regulate behaviour, which are summarized in Table 3.1.

2b

Acetylcholine

The discovery that cells communicate by releasing chemicals was first made in connection with the transmitter *acetylcholine* (ACh). ACh has been found throughout the nervous system. It is the only transmitter between motor neurons and voluntary muscles. Every move you make—typing, walking, talking, breathing—depends on ACh released to your muscles by motor neurons (Kandel & Siegelbaum, 2000). ACh also appears to contribute to attention, arousal, and memory. An inadequate supply of ACh in certain areas of the brain is associated with the memory losses seen in Alzheimer's disease (Bourgeois, Seaman, & Servis, 2003). Although ACh depletion does *not* appear to be the crucial causal factor underlying Alzheimer's disease, the drug treatments currently available, which can slow the progress of the disease (slightly), work by amplifying ACh activity (Neugroschl et al., 2005).

TABLE 3.1

Common Neurotransmitters and Some of Their Functions

Neurotransmitter	Functions and Characteristics
Acetylcholine (ACh)	Activates motor neurons controlling skeletal muscles Contributes to the regulation of attention, arousal, and memory Some ACh receptors stimulated by nicotine
Dopamine (DA)	Contributes to control of voluntary movement, pleasurable emotions Decreased levels associated with Parkinson's disease Overactivity at DA synapses associated with schizophrenia Cocaine and amphetamines elevate activity at DA synapses
Norepinephrine (NE)	Contributes to modulation of mood and arousal Cocaine and amphetamines elevate activity at NE synapses
Serotonin	Involved in regulation of sleep and wakefulness, eating, aggression Abnormal levels may contribute to depression and obsessive-compulsive disorder Prozac and similar antidepressant drugs affect serotonin circuits
GABA	Serves as widely distributed inhibitory transmitter Valium and similar antianxiety drugs work at GABA synapses
Endorphins	Resemble opiate drugs in structure and effects Contribute to pain relief and perhaps to some pleasurable emotions

The activity of ACh (and other neurotransmitters) may be influenced by other chemicals in the brain. Although synaptic receptor sites are sensitive to specific neurotransmitters, sometimes they can be "fooled" by other chemical substances. For example, if you smoke tobacco, some of your ACh synapses will be stimulated by the nicotine that arrives in your brain. At these synapses, the nicotine acts like ACh itself. It binds to receptor sites for ACh, causing postsynaptic potentials (PSPs). In technical language, nicotine is an ACh agonist. An *agonist* is a chemical that mimics the action of a neurotransmitter.

Not all chemicals that fool synaptic receptors are agonists. Some chemicals bind to receptors but fail to produce a PSP (the key slides into the lock, but it doesn't work). In effect, they temporarily *block* the action of the natural transmitter by occupying its receptor sites, rendering them unusable. Thus, they act as antagonists. An *antagonist* is a chemical that opposes the action of a neurotransmitter. For example, the drug curare is an ACh antagonist. It blocks action at the same ACh synapses that are fooled by nicotine. As a result, muscles are unable to move. Some South American indigenous peoples use a form of curare on arrows. If they wound an animal, the curare blocks the synapses from nerve to muscle, paralyzing the animal.

Monoamines 2b  4d

The *monoamines* include three neurotransmitters: dopamine, norepinephrine, and serotonin. Neurons using these transmitters regulate many aspects of everyday behaviour. Dopamine (DA), for example, is used by neurons that control voluntary movements. The degeneration of such neurons in a specific area of the brain causes *Parkinsonism,* a disease marked by tremors, muscular rigidity, and reduced control over voluntary movements (DeLong, 2000). The drug that is used to treat Parkinsonism (L-dopa) is converted to dopamine in the brain to partially compensate for diminished dopamine activity.

Although other neurotransmitters are also involved, serotonin-releasing neurons appear to play a prominent role in the regulation of sleep and wakefulness (Jones, 2005) and eating behaviour (Klump & Culbert, 2007; Steiger et al., 2005). Considerable evidence also suggests that neural circuits using serotonin modulate aggressive behaviour in animals, and some preliminary evidence relates serotonin activity to aggression in humans (Carrillo et al., 2009; Wallner & Machatschke, 2009).

Former world heavyweight boxing champion Muhammad Ali and well-known Canadian actor Michael J. Fox are victims of Parkinson's disease. Parkinson's disease is caused by the decline in the synthesis of the neurotransmitter dopamine. The reduction in dopamine synthesis occurs because of the deterioration of a structure located in the midbrain. Fox's (2002) autobiography *Lucky Man: A Memoir* details the effects the disease has had on him and his family.

Abnormal levels of monoamines in the brain have been related to the development of certain psychological disorders. For example, people who suffer from depressive disorders appear to have lowered levels of activation at norepinephrine (NE) and serotonin synapses. Although other biochemical changes may also contribute to depression, abnormalities at NE and serotonin synapses seem to play a central role, as most antidepressant drugs exert their main effects at these synapses (Delgado & Moreno, 2006). Abnormalities in serotonin circuits has also been implicated as a factor in eating disorders (Halmi, 2008) and in obsessive-compulsive disorders (Hollander & Simeon, 2008).

In a similar fashion, the *dopamine hypothesis* asserts that abnormalities in activity at dopamine synapses play a crucial role in the development of *schizophrenia*. This severe mental illness is marked by irrational thought, hallucinations, poor contact with reality, and deterioration of routine adaptive behaviour. Afflicting roughly 1 percent of the population, schizophrenia requires hospitalization more often than any other psychological disorder (see Chapter 14). Studies suggest, albeit with many complications, that overactivity in dopamine circuits constitutes the neurochemical basis for schizophrenia (Javitt & Laruelle, 2006). Why? Primarily because the therapeutic drugs that tame schizophrenic symptoms are known to be DA antagonists that reduce the neurotransmitter's activity (Minzenberg, Yoon, & Carter, 2008).

Temporary alterations at monoamine synapses also appear to account for the powerful effects of amphetamines and cocaine. These stimulants seem

Solomon Snyder

"Brain research of the past decade, especially the study of neurotransmitters, has proceeded at a furious pace, achieving progress equal in scope to all the accomplishments of the preceding 50 years—and the pace of discovery continues to accelerate."

Candace Pert

"When human beings engage in various activities, it seems that neurojuices are released that are associated with either pain or pleasure."

to exert most of their effects by creating a storm of increased activity at dopamine and norepinephrine synapses (King & Ellinwood, 2005; Repetto & Gold, 2005). Interestingly, some theorists believe that the rewarding effects of most abused drugs depend on increased activity in a particular dopamine pathway (Koob, Everitt, & Robbins, 2008; see Chapter 5). Furthermore, dysregulation in this dopamine pathway appears to be the chief factor underlying drug craving and addiction (Nestler & Malenka, 2004).

GABA and Glutamate

Another group of transmitters consists of *amino acids*. Two of these, *gamma-aminobutyric acid* (GABA) and *glycine,* are notable in that they seem to produce only *inhibitory* postsynaptic potentials. Some transmitters, such as ACh and NE, are versatile. They can produce either excitatory or inhibitory PSPs, depending on the synaptic receptors they bind to. However, GABA and glycine appear to have inhibitory effects at virtually all synapses where either is present. GABA receptors are widely distributed in the brain and may be present at 40 percent of all synapses. GABA appears to be responsible for much of the inhibition in the central nervous system. Studies suggest that GABA is involved in the regulation of anxiety in humans and that disturbances in GABA circuits may contribute to some types of anxiety disorders (Garakani et al., 2009).

Glutamate is another amino acid neurotransmitter that is widely distributed in the brain. Whereas GABA has only inhibitory effects, glutamate always has excitatory effects. Glutamate is best known for its contribution to learning and memory (Baudry & Lynch, 2001; Lovinger, 2010). In recent decades, disturbances in glutamate circuits have been implicated as factors that might contribute to certain features of schizophrenic disorders that are not easily explained by the dopamine hypothesis (Javitt & Laruelle, 2006).

Endorphins

In 1970, after a horseback-riding accident, Candace Pert, a graduate student in neuroscience, lay in a hospital bed receiving frequent shots of morphine, a painkilling drug derived from the opium plant. This experience left her with a driving curiosity about how morphine works. A few years later, she and Solomon Snyder rocked the scientific

world by showing that *morphine exerts its effects by binding to specialized receptors in the brain* (Pert & Snyder, 1973).

This discovery raised a perplexing question: Why would the brain be equipped with receptors for morphine, a powerful, addictive opiate drug not normally found in the body? It occurred to Pert and others that the nervous system must have its own endogenous (internally produced), morphine-like substances. Investigators dubbed these as-yet undiscovered substances *endorphins*—internally produced chemicals that resemble opiates in structure and effects. A search for the body's natural opiate ensued. In short order, a number of endogenous, opiate-like substances were identified (Hughes et al., 1975). Subsequent studies revealed that endorphins and their receptors are widely distributed in the human body and that they clearly contribute to the modulation of pain (Apkarian et al., 2005; Basbaum & Jessell, 2000), as we will discuss in Chapter 4. Subsequent research has suggested that the endogenous opioids also contribute to the modulation of eating behaviour and the body's response to stress (Adam & Epel, 2007).

The discovery of endorphins has led to new theories and findings on the neurochemical bases of pain and pleasure. In addition to their painkilling effects, opiate drugs such as morphine and heroin produce highly pleasurable feelings of euphoria. This euphoric effect explains why heroin is so widely abused. Researchers suspect that the body's natural endorphins may also be capable of producing feelings of pleasure. This capacity might explain why joggers sometimes experience a "runner's high." The pain caused by a long run may trigger the release of endorphins, which neutralize some of the pain and create a feeling of exhilaration (Harte, Eifert, & Smith, 1995). The long-held suspicion that endorphins might underlie the "runner's high" experience was supported in a recent study that used brain-imaging technology to track endorphin release in the brain (Boecker et al., 2008). Ten joggers were administered brain scans just before and just after a two-hour endurance run. As hypothesized, the post-run brain scans showed a surge in the production of endorphins in selected areas of the participants' brains.

In this section, we have highlighted just a few of the more interesting connections between neurotransmitters and behaviour. Although scientists have learned a great deal about neurotransmitters and behaviour, much still remains to be discovered.

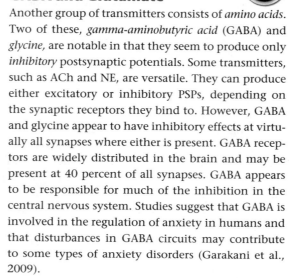

concept check 3.2

Linking Brain Chemistry to Behaviour

Check your understanding of relationships between brain chemistry and behaviour by indicating which neurotransmitters have been linked to the phenomena listed below. Choose your answers from the following list: (a) acetylcholine, (b) norepinephrine, (c) dopamine, (d) serotonin, (e) endorphins. Indicate your choice (by letter) in the spaces on the left. You'll find the answers in Appendix A.

_____ **1.** A transmitter involved in the regulation of sleep, eating, and aggression.

_____ **2.** The two monoamines that have been linked to depression.

_____ **3.** Chemicals that resemble opiate drugs in structure and that are involved in pain relief.

_____ **4.** A neurotransmitter for which abnormal levels have been implicated in schizophrenia.

_____ **5.** The only neurotransmitter between motor neurons and voluntary muscles.

REVIEW OF KEY POINTS

▷ Behaviour depends on complex information processing in the nervous system. Cells in the nervous system receive, integrate, and transmit information.

▷ Neurons are the basic communication links. They normally transmit a neural impulse along an axon to a synapse with another neuron. The neural impulse is a brief change in a neuron's electrical charge that moves along an axon. An action potential is an all-or-none event. Neurons convey information about the strength of a stimulus by variations in their rate of firing.

▷ Action potentials trigger the release of chemicals called *neurotransmitters* that diffuse across a synapse to communicate with other neurons. Transmitters bind with receptors in the postsynaptic cell membrane, causing excitatory or inhibitory PSPs.

▷ Whether the postsynaptic neuron fires a neural impulse depends on the balance of excitatory and inhibitory PSPs. Our thoughts and actions depend on patterns of activity in neural circuits and networks.

▷ The transmitter ACh plays a key role in muscular movement. Serotonin circuits may contribute to the regulation of sleep, eating, and aggression. Depression is associated with reduced activation at norepinephrine and serotonin synapses.

▷ Schizophrenia has been linked to overactivity at dopamine synapses. Cocaine and amphetamines appear to exert their main effects by altering activity at DA and NE synapses.

▷ GABA is an important amino acid transmitter whose inhibitory effects appear to regulate anxiety and sleep. Glutamate is another amino acid transmitter, which is best known for its role in memory. Endorphins, which resemble opiates, contribute to pain relief and may modulate eating and stress reactions

Organization of the Nervous System

Clearly, communication in the nervous system is fundamental to behaviour. So far we have looked at how individual cells communicate with one another. In this section, we examine the organization of the nervous system as a whole.

Experts estimate that there are roughly *100 billion* neurons in the human brain (Kandel, 2000). The multitudes of neurons in your nervous system have to work together to keep information flowing effectively. To see how the nervous system is organized to accomplish this end, we will divide it into parts. In many instances, the parts will be divided once again. Figure 3.6 presents an organizational chart that shows the relationships of all the parts of the nervous system.

The Peripheral Nervous System

2b **8c**

The first and most important division separates the *central nervous system* (the brain and spinal cord) from the *peripheral nervous system* (see Figure 3.7). The *peripheral nervous system* is made up of all those nerves that lie outside the brain and spinal cord. *Nerves* are bundles of neuron fibres (axons) that are routed together in the peripheral nervous system. This portion of the nervous system is just what it sounds like: the part that extends outside the central nervous system. The peripheral nervous system can be subdivided into the *somatic nervous system* and the *autonomic nervous system*.

PREVIEW QUESTIONS

▷ What are the subdivisions of the peripheral nervous system?

▷ What is the difference between afferent and efferent nerves?

▷ What does the autonomic nervous system regulate, and what are its subdivisions?

▷ What is the central nervous system made up of?

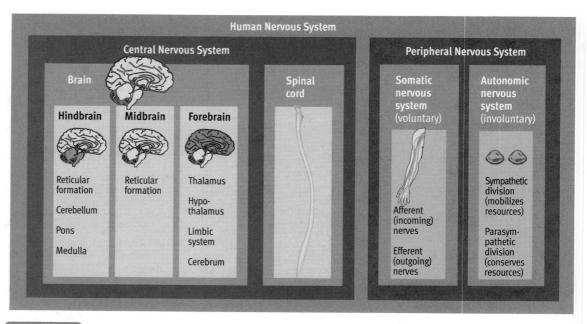

FIGURE 3.6

Organization of the human nervous system.

This overview of the human nervous system shows the relationships of its various parts and systems. The brain is traditionally divided into three regions: the hindbrain, the midbrain, and the forebrain. The reticular formation runs through both the midbrain and the hindbrain on its way up and down the brainstem. These and other parts of the brain are discussed in detail later in the chapter. The peripheral nervous system is made up of the somatic nervous system, which controls voluntary muscles and sensory receptors, and the autonomic nervous system, which controls the involuntary activities of smooth muscles, blood vessels, and glands.

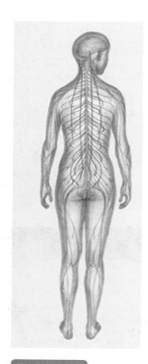

FIGURE 3.7

The central and peripheral nervous systems.

The central nervous system (CNS) consists of the brain and the spinal cord. The peripheral nervous system consists of the remaining nerves that fan out throughout the body. The peripheral nervous system is divided into the somatic nervous system, which is shown in blue, and the autonomic nervous system, which is shown in green.

The Somatic Nervous System

The *somatic nervous system* is made up of nerves that connect to voluntary skeletal muscles and to sensory receptors. These nerves are the cables that carry information from receptors in the skin, muscles, and joints to the central nervous system and that carry commands from the CNS to the muscles. These functions require two kinds of nerve fibres. *Afferent nerve fibres* are axons that carry information inward to the central nervous system from the periphery of the body. *Efferent nerve fibres* are axons that carry information outward from the central nervous system to the periphery of the body. Each body nerve contains many axons of each type. Thus, somatic nerves are "two-way streets" with incoming (afferent) and outgoing (efferent) lanes. The somatic nervous system lets you feel the world and move around in it.

The Autonomic Nervous System

The *autonomic nervous system (ANS)* is made up of nerves that connect to the heart, blood vessels, smooth muscles, and glands. As its name hints, the autonomic system is a separate (autonomous) system, although it is ultimately governed by the central nervous system. The autonomic nervous system controls automatic, involuntary, visceral functions that people don't normally think about, such as heart rate, digestion, and perspiration (Powley, 2008; see Figure 3.8).

The autonomic nervous system mediates much of the physiological arousal that occurs when people experience emotions. For example, imagine that you are walking home alone one night when a seedy-looking character falls in behind you and begins to follow you. If you feel threatened, your heart rate and breathing will speed up. Your blood pressure may surge, you may get goose bumps, and your palms may begin to sweat. These difficult-to-control reactions are aspects of autonomic arousal.

Walter Cannon (1932), one of the first psychologists to study this reaction, called it the *fight-or-flight response*. Cannon carefully monitored this response in cats—after confronting them with dogs. He concluded that organisms generally respond to threat by preparing physiologically for attacking (fight) or fleeing (flight) from the enemy. Unfortunately, as you will see in Chapter 13, this fight-or-flight response can backfire if stress leaves a person in a chronic state of autonomic arousal. According to McGill University's Hans Selye (1974), prolonged autonomic arousal can eventually contribute to the development of physical diseases.

The autonomic nervous system can be subdivided into two branches: the sympathetic division and the parasympathetic division (see Figure 3.8). The *sympathetic division* is the branch of the autonomic nervous system that mobilizes the body's resources for emergencies. It creates the fight-or-flight response. Activation of the sympathetic division slows digestive processes and drains blood from the periphery, lessening bleeding in the case of an injury. Key sympathetic nerves send signals to the adrenal glands, triggering the release of hormones that ready the body for exertion. In contrast, the *parasympathetic division* is the branch of the autonomic nervous system that generally conserves bodily resources. It activates processes that allow the body to save and store energy. For example, actions by parasympathetic nerves slow heart rate, reduce blood pressure, and promote digestion.

The Central Nervous System 2a

The central nervous system is the portion of the nervous system that lies within the skull and spinal column (see Figure 3.7 on page 96). Thus, the *central nervous system (CNS)* consists of the brain and the spinal cord. It is protected by enclosing sheaths called the *meninges* (hence, *meningitis*, the name for the disease in which the meninges become inflamed). In addition, the central nervous system is bathed in its own special nutritive "soup," the cerebrospinal fluid. *The cerebrospinal fluid (CSF)* nourishes the brain and provides a protective cushion for it. The hollow cavities in the brain that are filled with CSF are called *ventricles* (see Figure 3.9).

The Spinal Cord

The *spinal cord* connects the brain to the rest of the body through the peripheral nervous system. Although the spinal cord looks like a cable from which the somatic nerves branch, it is part of the central nervous system. Like the brain, it is enclosed by the meninges and bathed in CSF. In short, the spinal cord is an extension of the brain.

The spinal cord runs from the base of the brain to just below the level of the waist. It houses bundles of axons that carry the brain's commands to peripheral nerves and that relay sensations from the periphery

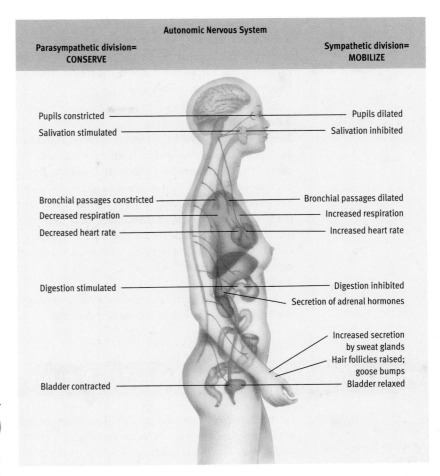

Autonomic Nervous System

Parasympathetic division= **CONSERVE**

Sympathetic division= **MOBILIZE**

Pupils constricted — Pupils dilated
Salivation stimulated — Salivation inhibited

Bronchial passages constricted — Bronchial passages dilated
Decreased respiration — Increased respiration
Decreased heart rate — Increased heart rate

Digestion stimulated — Digestion inhibited
Secretion of adrenal hormones

Increased secretion by sweat glands
Hair follicles raised; goose bumps
Bladder contracted — Bladder relaxed

FIGURE 3.8

The autonomic nervous system (ANS).

The ANS is composed of the nerves that connect to the heart, blood vessels, smooth muscles, and glands. The ANS is divided into the sympathetic division, which mobilizes bodily resources in times of need, and the parasympathetic division, which conserves bodily resources. Some of the key functions controlled by each division of the ANS are summarized in this diagram.

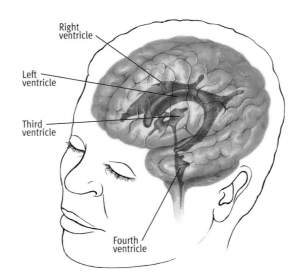

Right ventricle
Left ventricle
Third ventricle
Fourth ventricle

FIGURE 3.9

The ventricles of the brain.

Cerebrospinal fluid (CSF) circulates around the brain and the spinal cord. The hollow cavities in the brain filled with CSF are called *ventricles*. The four ventricles in the human brain are depicted here.

Source: Graphic adapted from Starr, C., & Taggart, R. (1998). *Biology: The unity and diversity of life.* Belmont, CA: Wadsworth. © 1998 Wadsworth Publishing. Reprinted by permission.

 Log on to CourseMate to access this interactive figure.

of the body to the brain. Many forms of paralysis result from spinal cord damage, a fact that underscores the critical role the spinal cord plays in transmitting signals from the brain to the motor neurons that move the body's muscles.

The Brain

The crowning glory of the central nervous system is, of course, the *brain.* Anatomically, the brain is the part of the central nervous system that fills the upper portion of the skull. Although it weighs only about 1.5 kilograms and could be held in one hand, the brain contains billions of interacting cells that integrate information from inside and outside the body, coordinate the body's actions, and enable human beings to talk, think, remember, plan, create, and dream.

Because of its central importance for behaviour, the brain is the subject of the next three sections of the chapter. We begin by looking at the remarkable methods that have enabled researchers to unlock some of the brain's secrets.

Looking Inside the Brain: Research Methods

Scientists who want to find out how parts of the brain are related to behaviour are faced with a formidable task. The geography, or *structure,* of the brain can be mapped out relatively easily by examining and dissecting brains removed from animals or from deceased humans who have donated their bodies to science. Mapping of brain *function,* however, requires a working brain. Thus, special research methods are needed to discover relationships between brain activity and behaviour.

Investigators who conduct research on the brain or other parts of the nervous system are called *neuroscientists.* Often, brain research involves collaboration by neuroscientists from several disciplines, including anatomy, physiology, biology, pharmacology, neurology, neurosurgery, psychiatry, and psychology. Neuroscientists use many specialized techniques to investigate connections between the brain and behaviour. Among the methods they have depended on most heavily are electrical recordings, lesioning, and electrical stimulation. In addition, brain-imaging techniques have enhanced neuroscientists' ability to observe brain structure and function.

Electrical Recordings   2c

The electrical activity of the brain can be recorded, much as Hodgkin and Huxley recorded the electrical activity of individual neurons (Kutas & Federmeier, 2011). Recordings of single cells in the brain have proven valuable, but scientists also need ways to record the simultaneous activity of many of the billions of neurons in the brain. While the existence of electrical activity in the brain was first identified in 1875, there was no way to access neurons without opening the skull (Rosler, 2005). Fortunately, in 1929 a German psychiatrist named Hans Berger invented a machine that could record broad patterns of brain electrical activity from intact skulls. The *electroencephalograph (EEG)* is a device that monitors the electrical activity of the brain over time by means of recording electrodes attached to the surface of the scalp (see Figure 3.10). An EEG electrode sums and amplifies electric potentials occurring in many thousands of brain cells. Berger's work laid the groundwork for many subsequent developments in experimental psychology and our understanding of many aspects of human behaviour, including information processing, sleep, consciousness, and the operation of the brain (Rosler, 2005).

Usually, many recording electrodes are attached (with paste) at various places on the skull. The resulting EEG recordings are translated into line tracings, commonly called *brain waves.* These brain-wave recordings provide a useful overview of the electrical activity in the brain. Different brain-wave patterns are associated with different states of mental activity (Martin, 1991; Westbrook, 2000), as shown in Figure 3.10. The EEG is often used in the

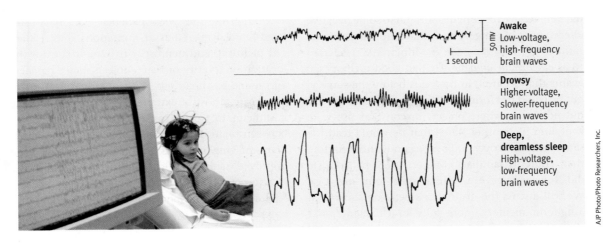

Awake
Low-voltage, high-frequency brain waves

1 second

Drowsy
Higher-voltage, slower-frequency brain waves

Deep, dreamless sleep
High-voltage, low-frequency brain waves

AJP Photo/Photo Researchers, Inc.

FIGURE 3.10

The electroencephalograph (EEG).
Recording electrodes attached to the surface of the scalp permit the EEG to record electrical activity in the cortex over time. The EEG provides output in the form of line tracings called *brain waves*. Brain waves vary in frequency (cycles per second) and amplitude (measured in voltage). Various states of consciousness are associated with different brain waves. Characteristic EEG patterns for alert wakefulness, drowsiness, and deep, dreamless sleep are shown here. The use of the EEG in research is discussed in more detail in Chapter 5.

Source: Brain wave graphic adapted from Hauri, P. (1982). *Current concepts: The sleep disorders.* Kalamazoo, MI: The Upjohn Company.

clinical diagnosis of brain damage and neurological disorders. In research applications, the EEG can be used to identify patterns of brain activity that occur when participants engage in specific behaviours or experience specific emotions. For example, in one study researchers used EEG recordings to investigate how meditation affects brain activity (Lagopoulos et al., 2009). Overall, EEG technology has contributed greatly to our understanding of brain–behaviour relationships (Rosler, 2005). For example, you'll see in Chapter 5 that the EEG has been particularly valuable to researchers exploring the neural basis of sleep. And as we discussed in the introduction to this chapter, psychologists such as John Connolly have used it to assess locked-in syndrome.

Lesioning 2c PSYKTREK

Brain tumours, strokes, head injuries, and other misfortunes often produce brain damage in people. Many major insights about brain–behaviour relationships have resulted from observations of behavioural changes in people who have suffered damage in specific brain areas. This type of research approach, as we discussed in Chapter 2, is referred to as the *case study method*. One of the most famous case studies of an individual suffering from specific brain damage was conducted by Brenda Milner. Milner was a Ph.D. student of Donald Hebb at McGill University and studied some of Wilder Penfield's patients. The patient she studied is referred to as "H. M." H. M. was to prove to be a very significant person in the

development of our knowledge of the brain and its connections to behaviour, in our understanding of the brain and memory. His brain has been referred to popularly as "the brain that changed everything" (Dittrich, 2010). When he died in 2008 at the age of 82, the wider community finally found out his full name, Henry Molaison. The researchers who worked with him in his over 55 years in science thought of him as much more than just a research participant. Over the years they became very close; he was more like a member of their families (Carey, 2008).

H. M. suffered from epilepsy as a child, a condition that was attributed by some to a childhood biking accident. As part of his treatment, H. M. had portions of his brain removed, including his medial temporal lobe, involving substantial portions of his hippocampus and amygdala. Although the surgery

McGill University Archives, PR000632

John Kennedy, *The Gazette* (Montreal)

Wilder Penfield and Brenda Milner, pioneers in neuroscience in Canada.

did help reduce his convulsions, it had some negative effects. After his surgery he suffered from a particular form of amnesia (Scoville & Milner, 1957) referred to as *anterograde amnesia*. He had good memory for events that occurred in the years before the surgery, but he could not form new long-term memories: "He did not know where objects in constant use were kept, and his mother stated that he would read the same magazines over and over again without finding their contents familiar" (Milner, 1965, p. 104). He did, however, have a normal short-term memory. We will discuss the distinctions between short- and long-term memory more fully in Chapter 7, but short-term memory is a limited-capacity memory store that can maintain unrehearsed information for about 20 seconds.

Milner's work with patients such as H. M. and her other research was pivotal in establishing the role of the medial structures of the temporal lobes in memory and the existence of multiple memory systems. From work with patients such as H. M., scientists were able to generate and examine many ideas about the connection between brain structures such as the hippocampus and memory and the existence of multiple memory systems. We will consider the idea of multiple memory systems in Chapter 7 and discuss further what was learned about memory from patients like H. M.

WEB LINK 3.3

The Visible Human Project
This site, established by the U.S. National Library of Medicine, provides a rich collection of online resources related to the highly detailed visual analysis of two human cadavers—a male and a female—that has been carried out over the last decade. This site is a good place to explore advanced techniques in the imaging of the human body, including the central nervous system.

Doing research with patients who have suffered brain damage has its limitations. Subjects are not plentiful, and neuroscientists can't control the location or severity of their subjects' brain damage. Furthermore, variations in the participants' histories create a host of extraneous variables that make it difficult to isolate cause-and-effect relationships between brain damage and behaviour. The modern brain-imaging methods that we will discuss have improved neuroscientists' ability to pinpoint the location of subjects' brain damage (Rorden, Karnath, & Bonilha, 2007), but this approach remains an inexact science.

To study the relationship between brain and behaviour more precisely, scientists sometimes observe what happens when specific brain structures in animals are purposely disabled. *Lesioning* involves destroying a piece of the brain. It is typically done by inserting an electrode into a brain structure and passing a high-frequency electric current through it to burn the tissue and disable the structure.

Lesioning requires researchers to get an electrode to a particular place buried deep inside the brain. They do so with a stereotaxic instrument, a device used to implant electrodes at precise locations in the brain. The use of this surgical device is described in Figure 3.11. Of course, appropriate anesthetics are used to minimize pain and discomfort for the animals. The lesioning of brain structures in animals has proven invaluable in neuroscientists' research on brain functioning.

Electrical Stimulation of the Brain

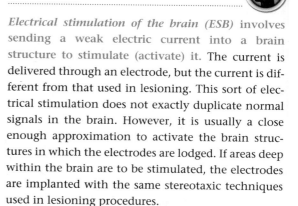

2c

Electrical stimulation of the brain (ESB) involves sending a weak electric current into a brain structure to stimulate (activate) it. The current is delivered through an electrode, but the current is different from that used in lesioning. This sort of electrical stimulation does not exactly duplicate normal signals in the brain. However, it is usually a close enough approximation to activate the brain structures in which the electrodes are lodged. If areas deep within the brain are to be stimulated, the electrodes are implanted with the same stereotaxic techniques used in lesioning procedures.

Most ESB research is conducted with animals. However, ESB is occasionally used on humans in the context of brain surgery required for medical purposes (see Moriarty et al., 2001, for an example). After a patient's skull is opened, the surgeons may stimulate areas to map the individual patient's brain (to some extent, each of us is unique), so that they

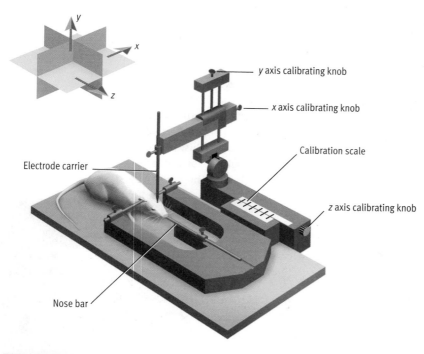

FIGURE 3.11

An anesthetized rat in a stereotaxic instrument.

This rat is undergoing brain surgery. After consulting a detailed map of the rat brain, researchers use the control knobs on the apparatus to position an electrode along the three axes (*x, y,* and *z*) shown in the upper-left corner. This precise positioning allows researchers to implant the electrode in an exact location in the rat's brain.

don't slice through critical areas. ESB research has led to advances in the understanding of many aspects of brain–behaviour relationships (Berman, 1991; Yudofsky, 1999).

Wilder Penfield was a gifted neurosurgeon and pioneer in neuroscience and the mapping of the functions of the brain (Penfield, 1977). One of his many accomplishments was the founding of the world-famous Montreal Neurological Institute and Hospital (http://www.mni.mcgill.ca). One of Penfield's specialties was the surgical treatment of epilepsy (Penfield & Jasper, 1954). During neurosurgery, the patient would remain conscious and alert. Working with more than 1000 such patients, Penfield was able to stimulate portions of the brain with a mild electrical probe. By carefully recording and categorizing his patients' responses and making reports of memories, sounds, and so on as a result of the stimulation, he was able to systematically map out many of the functions of the brain.

Transcranial Magnetic Stimulation

Transcranial magnetic stimulation (TMS) is a new technique that permits scientists to temporarily enhance or depress activity in a specific area of the brain. In TMS, a magnetic coil mounted on a small paddle is held over a specific area of a subject's head (see Figure 3.12). The coil creates a magnetic field that penetrates to a depth of 2 centimetres (Sack & Linden, 2003). By varying the timing and duration of the magnetic pulses, a researcher can either increase or decrease the excitability of neurons in the local tissue (George et al., 2007; Sandrini & Manenti, 2009). Thus far, researchers have primarily been interested in temporarily deactivating discrete areas of the brain to learn more about their functions. In essence, this technology allows scientists to create "virtual lesions" in human subjects for short periods of time, using a painless, noninvasive method (Siebner et al., 2009). Moreover, this approach circumvents the host of uncontrolled variables that plague the study of natural lesions in humans who have experienced brain damage (Rafal, 2001).

In using TMS to investigate brain function, researchers typically suppress activity in a discrete area of the brain and then put subjects to work on a specific type of perceptual or cognitive task to see if the virtual lesion interferes with performance of the task. For example, this approach has been used to explore whether specific areas of the brain are involved in visual–spatial processing (McKeefry, Burton, & Moreland, 2010), short-term memory (Silvantro & Cattaneo, 2010), and language (Manenti et al., 2010).

The chief limitation of TMS is that it cannot be used to study areas deep within the brain. Still, its potential as a research tool is enormous (Sparing, Hesse, & Fink, 2010). Moreover, scientists are studying whether it might have potential as a therapeutic treatment for eating disorders (Van den Eynde et al., 2010), anxiety disorders (Zwanger et al., 2009), depression (Fitzgerald, 2009), and schizophrenia (Matheson et al., 2010).

Brain-Imaging Procedures 2c

In recent decades, the invention of new brain-imaging devices has led to spectacular advances in science's ability to look into the brain (Cacioppo et al., 2008; Raichle, 2006). The *CT (computerized tomography) scan* is a computer-enhanced X-ray of brain structure. Multiple X-rays are shot from many angles, and the computer combines the readings to

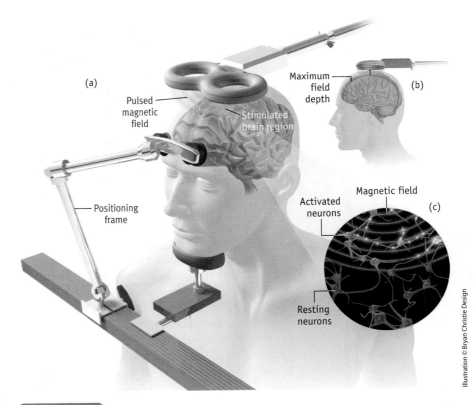

Illustration © Bryan Christie Design

FIGURE 3.12

Transcranial magnetic stimulation (TMS).

In TMS, (a) magnetic pulses are delivered to a localized area of the brain from a magnet mounted on a small paddle. (b) The magnetic field penetrates to a depth of only 2 centimetres. This technique can be used to either increase or decrease the excitability of the affected neurons. (c) The inset at the bottom right depicts neurons near the surface of the brain being temporarily activated by TMS.

(a) The patient's head is positioned in a large cylinder, as shown here.

(b) An X-ray beam and X-ray detector rotate around the patient's head, taking multiple X-rays of a horizontal slice of the patient's brain.

(c) A computer combines X-rays to create an image of a horizontal slice of the brain. This scan shows a tumour (in red) on the right.

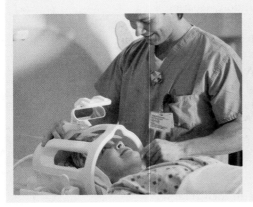

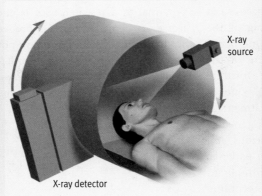

X-ray source

X-ray detector

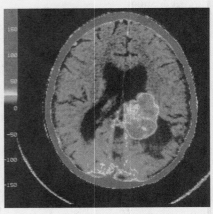

© Tim Pannell/Corbis

Dan McCoy—Rainbow/Science Faction/Getty Images

FIGURE 3.13

CT technology.

CT scans can be used in research to examine aspects of brain structure. They provide computer-enhanced X-rays of horizontal slices of the brain. (a) The patient's head is positioned in a large cylinder, as shown here. (b) An X-ray beam and X-ray detector rotate around the patient's head, taking multiple X-rays of a horizontal slice of the patient's brain. (c) A computer combines X-rays to create an image of a horizontal slice of the brain. This scan shows a tumour (in red) on the right.

create a vivid image of a horizontal slice of the brain (see Figure 3.13). The entire brain can be visualized by assembling a series of images representing successive slices of the brain. Of the new brain-imaging techniques, the CT scan is the least expensive, and it has been widely used in research. This research has uncovered an interesting association between schizophrenic disturbance and enlargement of the brain's ventricles (Shenton & Kubicki, 2009). Scientists are currently trying to determine whether this ventricular enlargement is a cause or consequence of schizophrenia (see Chapter 14).

In research on how brain and behaviour are related, *PET (positron emission tomography) scanning* is proving especially valuable (Staley & Krystal, 2009). Whereas CT scans can portray only brain *structure*, PET scans can examine brain *function*, mapping actual *activity* in the brain over time. In PET scans, radioactively tagged chemicals are introduced into the brain. They serve as markers of blood flow or metabolic activity in the brain, which can be monitored with X-rays. Thus, a PET scan can provide a colour-coded map indicating which areas of the brain become active when subjects clench a fist, sing, or contemplate the mysteries of the universe (see Figure 3.14). In this way, neuroscientists are using PET scans to better pinpoint the brain areas that handle various types of mental activities (Craik et al., 1999; Raichle, 1994). Because PET scans monitor chemical processes, they can

also be used to study the activity of specific neurotransmitters. For example, PET scans have helped researchers determine how cocaine affects activity in dopamine circuits in the human brain (Oswald et al., 2005). This chapter's Featured Study (see pages 103–104) involves the use of PET scans to determine the location of self-referent encoding in the brain.

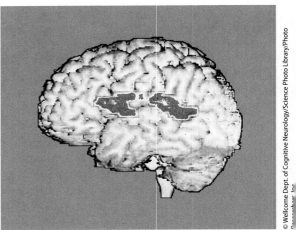

© Wellcome Dept. of Cognitive Neurology/Science Photo Library/Photo Researcher, Inc.

FIGURE 3.14

PET scans.

PET scans are used to map brain activity rather than brain structure. They provide colour-coded maps that show areas of high activity in the brain over time. The PET scan shown here pinpointed two areas of high activity (indicated by the red and green colours) when a research participant worked on a verbal short-term memory task.

FEATURED STUDY

Investigators: Fergus I. M. Craik (University of Toronto, Rotman Research Institute), Tara M. Moroz (University of Toronto), Morris Moscovitch (University of Toronto, Rotman Research Institute), Donald Struss (University of Toronto, Rotman Research Institute), Gordon Winocur (University of Toronto, Rotman Research Institute), Endel Tulving (Rotman Research Institute), and Shitij Kapur (Rotman Research Institute, Clarke Institute of Psychiatry)
Source: In search of the self: A positron emission tomography study. *Psychological Science*, 1999, *10*, 26–34.

Searching for the Self in the Brain

When facing an upcoming examination, students tend to look for specific study habits and test-taking strategies that might help them perform better on the exam. When we discuss memory in Chapter 7, we will look at many factors that have been found to enhance memory, including what has been referred to as *depth of processing*. According to a theory developed by University of Toronto researchers (Craik & Lockhart, 1972; Craik & Tulving, 1975), deeper and more elaborative encoding leads to better memory. *Encoding* refers to the process of forming a memory code, putting information into memory. The theory suggests that the more elaborative or rich the encoding, the better the memory is. For example, imagine you were given the following list of words to remember: *moderate, aoristic, perfectionist, moody*. One way to try to encode the information would be to focus on *structural* characteristics of the words, such as what font they are printed in, or on their *phonemic* characteristics, how they sound. Both of these are relatively shallow encoding strategies. As you might expect, a deeper encoding strategy in which you focus on the meaning of the words (*semantic encoding*) leads to enhanced memory. Research has found that an even better, deeper encoding strategy is *self-referent* encoding, in which you relate the to-be-remembered material to yourself (e.g., does the word "perfectionist" describe you?).

Previous PET scan research had shown that deep, semantic-type encoding is associated with the activation of the left prefrontal cortex and that this area is associated with the processing of meaning. While the self-task is an example of deeper, more elaborative semantic encoding, it differs from the other two semantic encoding tasks because it involves the self. One of the authors' objectives in this research was to determine what areas of the brain were activated when the processing task involved the self, when participants were encoding words with the task of determining if the trait words described them. They speculated that this latter task might involve activation of the right prefrontal cortex, which might be the area in the brain where the self is represented.

Method

Participants. Eight right-handed participants (four males and four females) were recruited for the study.

Procedure. Research participants were presented with eight lists of personality traits that they were asked to encode using four encoding tasks (two lists for each task): self-task—participants judged how well the word described them; other task—how well the word described a famous Canadian (Brian Mulroney, prime minister at the time); general task—how socially desirable the trait was; and a syllable task—how many syllables were in each word. While the first three tasks all involve some type of more elaborative encoding, the last clearly does not. However, only one task explicitly involves the self. Participants were also given a later test to examine their memory for the words. While participants were performing the encoding tasks, relative regional cerebral blood flow was measured (PET scan).

Results. The results indicated that the three semantic encoding tasks (i.e., self, general, and social desirability) were associated with better recognition memory for the trait words than was the less elaborative syllable task. The self-task words were associated with somewhat better memory than the other two semantic tasks. These results confirm what researchers in the area had found before: that deeper encoding leads to better memory. The self-related condition was also associated with the fastest recognition reaction time. The blood flow data were analyzed in two ways. The first analysis showed that all three semantic tasks were associated with increased left prefrontal activity as compared to the syllable task. All three tasks, then, involve some form of deeper, semantic-type encoding. The second, alternative PET scan analysis showed that only the self-condition was associated with increased right prefrontal activity.

Discussion

This study suggested some fascinating conclusions to the authors regarding the self and its representation in the brain. The self may in fact be represented in two ways. The first is a generalized *conceptual self* that is similar to the other context-free schemas that constitute our cognitive system. This is consistent with the similarity in left prefrontal activation produced by the three semantic tasks. The self also may be represented in a more specialized way, related to episodic memory retrieval. In Chapter 7, we discuss the distinctions between episodic and semantic memory in more detail.

Comment

This study was featured because it provides a relatively simple example of how brain-imaging technologies have yielded new insights about brain–behaviour relationships. Science depends on observation. Improvements in our ability to observe the brain have resulted in increased knowledge of how brain structure and function are related to psychological phenomena. This study by itself will not allow us to identify the location of the self in the brain, but it does give us some insight into how the brain functions in specific ways when the self is implicated. This is an issue of continuing interest. More recent fMRI research by Kelley, Macrae, Wyland, Caglar, Inati, and Heatherton (2002) has supported and extended this research by showing that processing related to the self is clearly dissociable from other types of semantic encoding such as that used in the current study. This work has been followed by more recent studies examining such things as whether there is a neurocognitive system underlying the sense of self-continuity that we all have (Magno & Allan, 2007), self-projection (Buckner & Carroll, 2006) and self-awareness (Uddin et al., 2007). These types of issues and questions can be answered only through more research. Thus, scientific inquiry is an endless process in which new knowledge stimulates new questions.

The *MRI (magnetic resonance imaging) scan* uses magnetic fields, radio waves, and computerized enhancement to map out brain structure. MRI scans provide much better images of brain structure than CT scans (Vythilingam et al., 2005), producing three-dimensional pictures of the brain that have remarkably high resolution [see Figure 3.15(a)]. MRI scans have provided useful insights about depressive disorders. For example, they were critical in determining that depression is associated with shrinkage of the hippocampus (Drevets, Gadde, & Krishnan, 2009). *Functional magnetic resonance imaging (fMRI)* is a new variation on MRI technology that monitors blood flow and oxygen consumption in the brain to identify areas of high activity (Mason, Krystal, & Sanacova, 2009). This technology is exciting because, like PET scans, it can map actual *activity* in the brain over time, but with vastly greater precision [see Figure 3.15(b)]. For example, using fMRI scans, researchers have identified patterns of brain activity associated with cocaine craving in cocaine addicts (Duncan et al., 2007), the contemplation of a loved one (Cheng et al., 2010), the visual recognition of shapes and textures (Stylianou-Korsnes et al., 2010), and the decision making required by risky gambles (Tom et al., 2007).

Research with fMRI scans has given neuroscientists a new appreciation of the complexity and interdependence of brain organization. The opportunity to look at ongoing brain function has revealed that even simple, routine mental operations depend on coordinated activation of several or more areas in the brain (Raichle, 2006). Both types of MRI technology have proven extremely valuable in behavioural research in the last decade.

fMRI imaging is proving useful even in assessing the state of locked-in patients' brains. Adrian Owen and his colleagues (Owen et al., 2006) asked their "locked-in" patient to imagine doing routine activities such as playing tennis or moving around her home. They were able to show that their patient's brain was indistinguishable on these tasks from those of healthy volunteers and concluded that they were able to demonstrate conscious awareness in the patient. By visiting Owen's

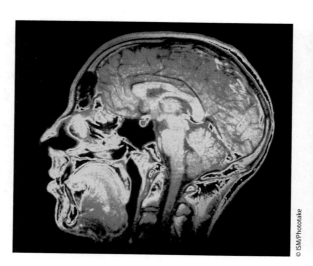
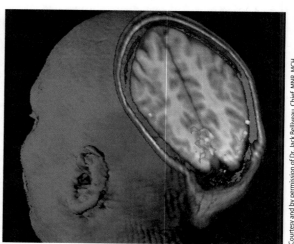

FIGURE 3.15

MRI scans.

(a) MRI scans can be used to produce remarkably high-resolution pictures of brain structure. A vertical view of a brain from the left side is shown here. (b) Like PET scans, functional MRIs can monitor chemical activity in the brain. This image shows regions of the brain that were activated by the visual stimulus of a flashing light.

website, http://www.mrc-cbu.cam.ac.uk/~adrian/Site/Homepage.html, you can read more details about this work and see some of the images that led to his conclusions.

The recent explosion of interest in neuroimaging has led to an exponential increase in research findings. There is so much research available now compared to just a few years ago that it can be difficult sometimes to make sense of it all. This is where the technique of meta-analysis we referred to in Chapter 2 might come in useful. In fact, some recent work has underscored the potential utility of meta-analysis in making sense of neuroimaging data (Kober & Wager, 2010). The advances in neuroimaging over the past few years have been very impressive—so impressive in fact that some are concerned about possible privacy issues (Olson, 2005). Will neuroimaging allow for such uses as an assessment of an individual's personality (Canli et al., 2002), decision making, or determination of whether or not someone is telling the truth (Spence, 2005; Yang, Raine, & Lencz, 2005)? These possibilities raise new ethical issues. As we suggested in Chapter 2, major organizations such as the Canadian and American Psychological Associations are continually updating their ethical guidelines to take into account recent developments in psychology. This is especially true in the area of neuroethics.

The Brain and Behaviour

Now that we have examined selected techniques of brain research, let's look at what researchers have discovered about the functions of various parts of the brain.

The brain can be divided into three major regions: the hindbrain, the midbrain, and the forebrain. The principal structures found in each of these regions are listed in the organizational chart of the nervous system in Figure 3.6 (page 96). You can see where these regions are located in the brain by looking at Figure 3.16. They can be found easily in relation to the *brainstem*. The brainstem looks like its name—it appears to be a stem from which the rest of the brain "flowers," like a head of cauliflower. At its lower end, it is contiguous with the spinal cord. At its higher end it lies deep within the brain.

We'll begin at the brain's lower end, where the spinal cord joins the brainstem. As we proceed upward, notice how the functions of brain structures go from the regulation of basic bodily processes to the control of "higher" mental processes.

The Hindbrain   2d

The *hindbrain* includes the cerebellum and two structures found in the lower part of the brainstem: the medulla and the pons. The *medulla*, which attaches to the spinal cord, is in charge of largely unconscious but vital functions, including circulating blood, breathing, maintaining muscle tone, and regulating reflexes such as sneezing, coughing, and salivating. The *pons* (literally "bridge") includes a bridge of fibres that connects the brainstem with the cerebellum. The pons also contains several clusters of cell bodies involved with sleep and arousal.

The *cerebellum* (literally "little brain") is a relatively large and deeply folded structure located adjacent to the back surface of the brainstem. The cerebellum is critical to the coordination of movement and to the sense of equilibrium, or physical balance (Mauk & Thach, 2008). Although the actual commands for muscular movements come from higher brain centres, the cerebellum plays a key role in organizing the sensory information that guides these movements. It is your cerebellum that allows you to hold your hand out to the side and then smoothly bring your finger to a stop on your nose. This is a useful roadside test for drunken driving because the cerebellum is one of the structures first depressed by alcohol. Damage to the cerebellum disrupts fine motor skills, such as those involved in writing, typing, or playing a musical instrument. Recent research has revealed

FIGURE 3.16

Structures and areas in the human brain.

(Top left) This photo of a human brain shows many of the structures discussed in this chapter. (Top right) The brain is divided into three major areas: the hindbrain, midbrain, and forebrain. These subdivisions actually make more sense for the brains of other animals than of humans. In humans, the forebrain has become so large that it makes the other two divisions look trivial. However, the hindbrain and midbrain aren't trivial; they control such vital functions as breathing, waking, and maintaining balance. (Bottom) This cross-section of the brain highlights key structures and some of their principal functions. As you read about the functions of a brain structure, such as the corpus callosum, you may find it helpful to refer back to this figure.

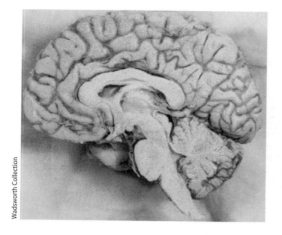

Wadsworth Collection

Forebrain

Midbrain

Hindbrain

Cerebrum
Responsible for sensing, thinking, learning, emotion, consciousness, and voluntary movement

Corpus callosum
Bridge of fibres passing information between the two cerebral hemispheres

Amygdala
Part of limbic system involved in emotion and aggression

Thalamus
Relay centre for cortex; handles incoming and outgoing signals

Hypothalamus
Responsible for regulating basic biological needs: hunger, thirst, temperature control

Cerebellum
Structure that coordinates fine muscle movement, balance

Pituitary gland
"Master" gland that regulates other endocrine glands

Reticular formation
Group of fibres that carry stimulation related to sleep and arousal through brainstem

Hippocampus
Part of limbic system involved in learning and memory

Pons
Involved in sleep and arousal

Medulla
Responsible for regulating largely unconscious functions such as breathing and circulation

Spinal cord
Responsible for transmitting information between brain and rest of body; handles simple reflexes

that the cerebellum contributes to the control of other functions besides motor skills. Brain circuits running from the cerebellum to the prefrontal cortex appear to be involved in surprisingly higher-order functions, including attention, planning, and visual perception (Dum & Strick, 2009).

The Midbrain 2d

The *midbrain* is the segment of the brainstem that lies between the hindbrain and the forebrain. The midbrain contains an area that is concerned with integrating sensory processes, such as vision and hearing (Stein, Wallace, & Stanford, 2000). An important system of dopamine-releasing neurons that projects into various higher brain centres originates in the midbrain. Among other things, this dopamine system is involved in the performance of voluntary movements. The decline in dopamine synthesis that causes Parkinson's disease is due to degeneration of a structure located in the midbrain (DeLong, 2000).

Running through both the hindbrain and the midbrain is the *reticular formation* (see Figure 3.16). Lying at the central core of the brainstem, the reticular formation contributes to the modulation of muscle reflexes, breathing, and pain perception (Saper, 2000). It is best known, however, for its role in the regulation of sleep and arousal. Activity in the ascending fibres of the reticular formation contributes to arousal (Coenen, 1998).

The Forebrain 2e 2f

The *forebrain* is the largest and most complex region of the brain, encompassing a variety of structures, including the thalamus, hypothalamus, limbic system, and cerebrum (see Figure 3.16 again). The thalamus, hypothalamus, and limbic system form the core of the forebrain. All three structures are located near the top of the brainstem. Above them is the *cerebrum*—the seat of complex thought. The wrinkled surface of the cerebrum is the *cerebral cortex*—the outer layer of the brain, which looks like a cauliflower.

The Thalamus: A Way Station 2e

The *thalamus* is a structure in the forebrain through which all sensory information (except smell) must pass to get to the cerebral cortex (Sherman, 2009). This way station is made up of clusters of cell bodies, or somas. Each cluster is concerned with relaying sensory information to a particular part of the cortex. However, it would be a mistake to characterize the

thalamus as nothing more than a passive relay station. The thalamus also appears to play an active role in integrating information from various senses.

The Hypothalamus: A Regulator of Biological Needs 2e

The *hypothalamus* is a structure found near the base of the forebrain that is involved in the regulation of basic biological needs. The hypothalamus lies beneath the thalamus (*hypo* means *under*, making the hypothalamus the area under the thalamus). Although no larger than a kidney bean, the hypothalamus contains various clusters of cells that have many key functions. One such function is to control the autonomic nervous system (Card, Swanson, & Moore, 2008). In addition, the hypothalamus serves as a vital link between the brain and the endocrine system (a network of hormone-producing glands, discussed later in this chapter).

The hypothalamus plays a major role in the regulation of basic biological drives related to survival, including the so-called "four Fs": fighting, fleeing, feeding, and mating. For example, when researchers lesion the lateral areas (the sides) of the hypothalamus, animals lose interest in eating. The animals must be fed intravenously or they starve, even in the presence of abundant food. In contrast, when electrical stimulation of the brain (ESB) is used to *activate* the lateral hypothalamus, animals eat constantly and gain weight rapidly (Grossman et al., 1978; Keesey & Powley, 1975). Does this mean that the lateral hypothalamus is the "hunger centre" in the brain? Not necessarily. The regulation of hunger turns out to be complex and multifaceted, as you'll see in Chapter 10. Nonetheless, the hypothalamus clearly contributes to the control of hunger and other basic biological processes, including thirst and temperature regulation (Kupfermann, Kandel, & Iversen, 2000).

The Limbic System: The Seat of Emotion 2e

The *limbic system* is a loosely connected network of structures located roughly along the border between the cerebral cortex and deeper subcortical areas (hence, the term *limbic*, which means *edge*). First described by Paul MacLean (1954), the limbic system is *not* a well-defined anatomical system with clear boundaries. Indeed, scientists disagree about which structures should be included in the limbic system (Van Hoesen, Morecraft, & Semendeferi, 1996). Broadly defined, the limbic system includes parts of the thalamus and hypothalamus, the hippocampus, the amygdala, and other structures. The limbic system is involved in the regulation of emotion, memory, and motivation and recently it has been linked to the tendency of some people to be optimistic in their approach to life (Schachter & Addis, 2007; Sharot et al., 2007). As we will learn later in Chapter 15, an optimistic bias or explanatory style has been shown to be related to good physical and psychological health.

The hippocampus and adjacent structures clearly play a role in memory processes (Shrager & Squire, 2009). Some theorists believe that the hippocampal region is responsible for the consolidation of memories for factual information (Dudai, 2004). Consolidation involves the conversion of information into a durable code. In this context it is important to note that the hippocampus is only one element in a complex system (see Chapter 7). Recent interest in the hippocampus, while continuing to point to its role in memory and related issues (Leuner & Gould, 2010), has also suggested that it plays a role in prediction and imagination. Results suggest that it is active when people imagine future events and that certain types of hippocampal damage lead to deficits in this predictive ability (Buckner, 2010). These are intriguing findings, especially when paired with what we know about the links between memory and imagining the future. We discuss this issue further in Chapter 7.

Similarly, there is ample evidence linking the limbic system to the experience of emotion, but the exact mechanisms of control are not yet well understood (Mega et al., 1997; Paradiso et al., 1997). For example, recent evidence suggests that the *amygdala* may play a central role in the learning of fear responses and the processing of other basic emotional responses (Phelps, 2006; LeDoux, Schiller, & Cain, 2009). Traditionally it was thought that the amygdala was mostly engaged in processing negativity or negative affect. More recent work by William Cunningham (Cunningham, Bavel, Johnsen, 2007), who began his career at the University of Toronto, and other researchers (Murray, 2007) calls this assumption into question. Their work suggests that the amygdala is active in processing both positive and negative stimuli. The limbic system is also one of the areas in the brain that appears to be rich in emotion-tinged "pleasure centres." This intriguing possibility first surfaced, quite by chance, in brain stimulation research with rats conducted by James Olds and Peter Milner (1954).

James Olds had come to McGill University to work with Donald Hebb as a postdoctoral fellow. He had earlier read Hebb's 1949 text and was influenced by Hebb's ideas. James Olds and Peter Milner (1954) accidentally discovered that a rat would press a lever repeatedly to send brief bursts of electrical stimulation to a specific spot in its brain where an electrode was implanted (see Figure 3.17). They thought that

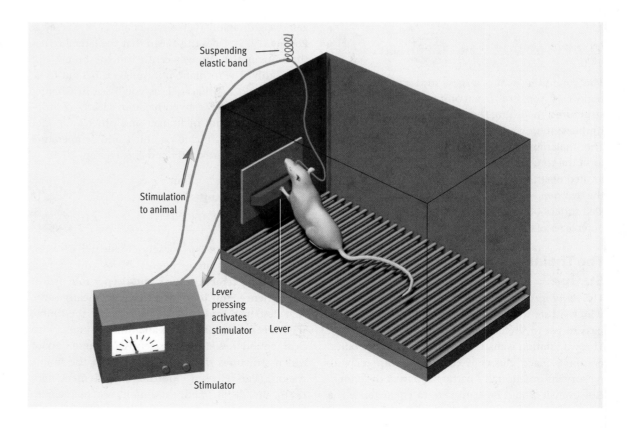

FIGURE 3.17

Electrical stimulation of the brain (ESB) of a rat.

Olds and Milner (1954) were using an apparatus like that depicted here when they discovered self-stimulation centres, or "pleasure centres," in the brain of a rat. In this setup, the rat's lever pressing earns brief electrical stimulation that is sent to a specific spot in the rat's brain where an electrode has been implanted.

Suspending elastic band

Stimulation to animal

Lever pressing activates stimulator

Lever

Stimulator

they had inserted the electrode in the rat's reticular formation. However, they learned later that the electrode had been bent during implantation and ended up elsewhere (probably in the hypothalamus). Much to their surprise, the rat kept coming back for more self-stimulation in this area. Subsequent studies showed that rats and monkeys would press a lever *thousands of times per hour,* until they sometimes collapsed from exhaustion, to stimulate certain brain sites. Although the experimenters obviously couldn't ask the animals about it, they *inferred* that the animals were experiencing some sort of pleasure.

There are self-stimulation centres located in the brain. Many of them have been found in the limbic system (Olds & Fobes, 1981). The heaviest concentration appears to be where the *medial forebrain bundle* (a bundle of axons) passes through the hypothalamus. The medial forebrain bundle is rich in dopamine-releasing neurons. The rewarding effects of ESB at self-stimulation sites may be largely mediated by the activation of these dopamine circuits (Koob et al., 2008). The rewarding, pleasurable effects of opiate and stimulant drugs (cocaine and amphetamines) also appear to depend in part on excitation of this dopamine system (Wise, 1999, 2002). Recent evidence suggests that the so-called "pleasure centres" in the brain may not be anatomical centres so much as neural circuits releasing dopamine.

The Cerebrum: The Seat of Complex Thought

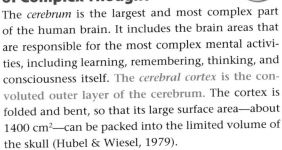
PSYKTREK 2f

The *cerebrum* is the largest and most complex part of the human brain. It includes the brain areas that are responsible for the most complex mental activities, including learning, remembering, thinking, and consciousness itself. The *cerebral cortex* is the convoluted outer layer of the cerebrum. The cortex is folded and bent, so that its large surface area—about 1400 cm²—can be packed into the limited volume of the skull (Hubel & Wiesel, 1979).

The cerebrum is divided into two halves called hemispheres. Hence, the *cerebral hemispheres* are the right and left halves of the cerebrum (see Figure 3.18). The hemispheres are separated in the centre of the brain by a longitudinal fissure that runs from the front to the back of the brain. This fissure descends to a thick band of fibres called the *corpus callosum* (also shown in Figure 3.18). The *corpus callosum is the structure that connects the two cerebral hemispheres.* We'll discuss the functional specialization of the cerebral hemispheres in the next section of this chapter. Each cerebral hemisphere is divided into four parts called *lobes.* To some extent, each of these lobes is dedicated to specific purposes. The location of these lobes can be seen in Figure 3.19.

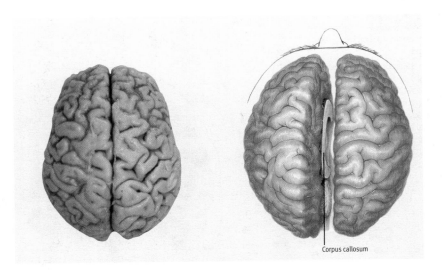
Corpus callosum

FIGURE 3.18

The cerebral hemispheres and the corpus callosum.

(Left) As this photo shows, the longitudinal fissure running down the middle of the brain (viewed from above) separates the left and right halves of the cerebral cortex. (Right) In this drawing, the cerebral hemispheres have been "pulled apart" to reveal the corpus callosum. This band of fibres is the communication bridge between the right and left halves of the human brain.

The *occipital lobe,* at the back of the head, includes the cortical area, where most visual signals are sent and visual processing is begun. This area is called the *primary visual cortex.* We will discuss how it is organized in Chapter 4.

The *parietal lobe* is forward of the occipital lobe. It includes the area that registers the sense of touch, called the *primary somatosensory cortex.* Various sections of this area receive signals from different regions of the body. When ESB is delivered in these parietal lobe areas, people report physical sensations—as if someone actually touched them on the arm or cheek, for example. The parietal lobe is also involved in integrating visual input and in monitoring the body's position in space. York University neuroscientist Doug Crawford has examined the role of the parietal cortex in enabling us to reach for and grasp objects with so much proficiency. He suggests that the parietal cortex mediates the visual control of reaching (Crawford, Medendorp, & Marotta, 2004).

The *temporal lobe* (meaning *near the temples*) lies below the parietal lobe. Near its top, the temporal lobe contains an area devoted to auditory processing, called the *primary auditory cortex.* As we will see in the next section, damage to an area in the temporal lobe on the left side of the brain can impair the comprehension of speech and language.

Continuing forward, we find the *frontal lobe,* the largest lobe in the human brain. It contains the principal areas that control the movement of muscles, called the *primary motor cortex.* ESB applied in these areas can cause actual muscle contractions. The

FIGURE 3.19

The cerebral cortex in humans.

The cerebral cortex is divided into right and left halves, called *cerebral hemispheres*. This diagram provides a view of the right hemisphere. Each cerebral hemisphere can be divided into four lobes (which are highlighted in the bottom inset): the occipital lobe, the parietal lobe, the temporal lobe, and the frontal lobe. Each lobe has areas that handle particular functions, such as visual processing. The functions of the prefrontal cortex are something of a mystery, but they appear to include working memory and relational reasoning.

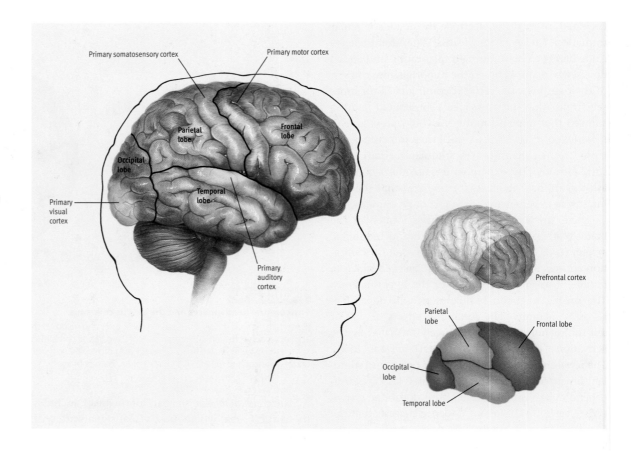

amount of motor cortex allocated to the control of a body part depends not on the part's size but on the diversity and precision of its movements. Thus, more of the cortex is given to parts we have fine control over, such as fingers, lips, and the tongue. Less of the cortex is devoted to larger parts that make crude movements, such as the thighs and shoulders (see Figure 3.20).

The portion of the frontal lobe to the front of the motor cortex, which is called the *prefrontal cortex* (see the inset in Figure 3.19), is something of a mystery. This area is disproportionately large in humans, accounting for about one-third of the cerebral cortex (Huey, Krueger, & Grafman, 2006). In light of this fact, it was once assumed to house the highest, most abstract intellectual functions. However, this view was eventually dismissed as an oversimplification. Still, recent studies suggest that the prefrontal cortex *does* contribute to an impressive variety of higher-order functions. These include working memory, which is a temporary buffer that processes current information (Sala & Courtney, 2007); reasoning about relationships between objects and events (Knowlton & Holyoak, 2009); and some types of decision making (Summerfield & Koechlin, 2009). Its contribution to working memory and reasoning out relationships has led some theorists to suggest that the prefrontal cortex houses some sort of "executive control system." This system is thought

to monitor, organize, integrate, and direct thought processes (Beer, Shimamura, & Knight, 2004; Kane & Engle, 2002). Much remains to be learned, however, as the prefrontal cortex constitutes a huge chunk of the brain with many subareas whose specific functions are still being worked out (Miller & Wallis, 2008).

The Plasticity of the Brain

It was once believed that significant changes in the anatomy and organization of the brain were limited to early periods of development in both humans and animals. However, according to University of Lethbridge behavioural neuroscientist Bryan Kolb (Kolb & Gibb, 2007), research has gradually demonstrated that the anatomical structure and functional organization of the brain are more "plastic" or malleable than widely assumed (Kolb, Gibb, & Robinson, 2003; Pascual-Leone, 2009). According to Kolb, *brain plasticity* refers to "the brain's ability to change structure and function" (Kolb & Whishaw, 1998, p. 85). He suggests that experience is an important stimulant of brain plasticity and that experience affects dendritic length, synapse formation, and altered metabolic activity.

Conclusions about brain plasticity in general are based on several lines of research. First, studies have shown that aspects of experience can sculpt features

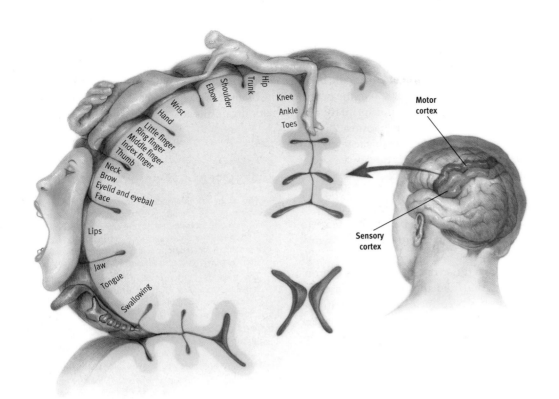

FIGURE 3.20

The primary motor cortex.
This diagram shows the amount of motor cortex devoted to the control of various muscles and limbs. The anatomical features in the drawing are distorted because their size is proportional to the amount of cortex devoted to their control. As you can see, more of the cortex is allocated to muscle groups that must make relatively precise movements.

Motor cortex

Sensory cortex

of brain structure. For example, neuroimaging studies have shown that an area in the somatosensory cortex that receives input from the fingers of the left hand is enlarged in string musicians who constantly use the left hand to finger the strings of their instruments (Elbert et al., 1995). In a similar vein, researchers find greater dendritic branching and synaptic density in rats raised in a stimulating, enriched environment, as opposed to a dull, barren environment (Rosenzweig & Bennet, 1996; see the Critical Thinking Application near the end of the chapter).

Second, research has shown that damage to incoming sensory pathways or the destruction of brain tissue can lead to neural reorganization. For example, when scientists amputated the third finger of an owl monkey, the part of its cortex that formerly responded to the third finger gradually became responsive to the second and fourth fingers (Kaas, 2000). And in blind people, areas in the occipital lobe that are normally dedicated to visual processing are "recruited" to help with verbal processing (Amedi et al., 2004). Neural reorganization has also been seen in response to brain damage as healthy neurons attempt to compensate for the loss of nearby neurons (Cao et al., 1994; Gilbert, 1993).

Third, *studies indicate that the adult brain can generate new neurons*. Until relatively recently, it was believed that *neurogenesis*—the formation of new neurons—did not occur in adult humans. It was thought that the brain formed all of its neurons by infancy at the latest. This doctrine was so strongly held that initial reports to the contrary were ignored or dismissed (Gross, 2000). However, research eventually demonstrated convincingly that adult humans can form new neurons in the olfactory bulb and the hippocampus (DiCicco-Bloo & Falluel-Morell, 2009). Furthermore, Elizabeth Gould and her colleagues (2002, 2004) have found that adult monkeys form *thousands* of new brain cells each day in the dentate gyrus of the hippocampus. These new neurons then migrate to areas in the cortex where they sprout axons and form new synapses with existing neurons, becoming fully integrated into the brain's communication networks. Neuroscientists are now scrambling to figure out the functional significance of neurogenesis. It does not appear to be a simple restorative process that compensates for the normal dying off of brain cells (Lledo, Alonso, & Grubb, 2006). But some theorists believe that neurogenesis might contribute to the natural repair processes that occur after brain damage (Kozorovitsky & Gould, 2007). Given the important role of the hippocampus in memory, it has been suggested that neurogenesis might contribute to learning, (Leuner, Gould, & Shors, 2006; see Chapter 7).

Recent research has continued to focus on ways to enhance the brain's natural plasticity and to examine ways to repair damaged brains. Perhaps due to our aging population and the association of increased age with various neurological difficulties and the numbers of people suffering from strokes and brain and spinal cord injuries, increased attention has been given to this work in the past few years. Research ranges from exploring the effects of increased exercise in protecting and enhancing brain functioning (Kramer & Erickson, 2007) to the potential benefits of the harvesting and transplantation of stem cells (Abbott, 2004; Gage, 2002; Kitner, 2002).

Stem cells are "unspecialized" cells that renew themselves through cell division and that can, under special circumstances, be "induced" to become cells suitable for other specialized purposes such as the beating cells of the heart (Stem Cell Basics, 2007) and neurons. It may be that such stem cells can be transplanted into diseased or damaged brains in order to relieve symptoms and dysfunction. While research into adult stem cells, in which the stem cells are harvested from adults (perhaps even from the patients themselves) continues, there has been increasing interest in the harvesting of embryonic stem cells from eggs that are fertilized in vitro. As you can imagine, this research is controversial and is rife with ethical and sociopolitical concerns (e.g., Condic, 2007; Shaky Arguments, 2007). There is little doubt that this work will continue at a rapid pace given the potential benefits and the progress that is being made in the area (Muller, Snyder, & Loring, 2006; Newborn Brain Cells, 2008). Work in Canada is guided by the Government of Canada's *Guidelines for Human Pluripotent Stem Cell Research* (*Updated Guidelines*, 2007).

In sum, research suggests that the brain is not "hard-wired" the way a computer is. It appears that the neural wiring of the brain is flexible and constantly evolving. That said, this plasticity is not unlimited. Rehabilitation efforts with people who have suffered severe brain damage clearly demonstrate that there are limits to the extent to which the brain can rewire

itself (Zillmer, Spiers, & Culbertson, 2008). And the evidence suggests that the brain's plasticity declines with age (Rains, 2002). Younger brains are more malleable than older brains. Still, the neural circuits of the brain show substantial plasticity, which certainly helps organisms adapt to their environments.

REVIEW OF KEY POINTS

▶ The brain has three major regions: the hindbrain, midbrain, and forebrain. Structures in the hindbrain include the medulla, pons, and cerebellum. These structures handle essential functions such as breathing, circulation, coordination of movement, and the rhythm of sleep and arousal.

▶ The midbrain contributes to the coordination of sensory processes. Deterioration of an area in the midbrain has been implicated as a factor in Parkinson's disease.

▶ The forebrain includes many structures that handle higher functions. The thalamus is primarily a relay station. The hypothalamus is involved in the regulation of basic biological drives such as hunger and sex.

▶ The limbic system is a network of loosely connected structures located along the border between the cortex and deeper subcortical areas. It includes the hippocampus, which appears to play a role in memory; the amygdala, which is involved in the regulation of emotion; and areas rich in self-stimulation sites.

▶ The cerebrum is the brain area implicated in most complex mental activities. The cortex is the cerebrum's convoluted outer layer, which is subdivided into four lobes.

▶ These lobes and their primary known functions are the occipital lobe (vision), the parietal lobe (touch), the temporal lobe (hearing), and the frontal lobe (movement of the body). The prefrontal cortex may contribute to working memory and relational reasoning. The structure and function of the brain appears to be more plastic than widely appreciated.

Right Brain/Left Brain: Cerebral Laterality

PREVIEW QUESTIONS

▶ How was the left hemisphere originally implicated in the control of language?

▶ How are sensory and motor information routed to the two hemispheres?

▶ What did split-brain research reveal about the right and left hemispheres of the brain?

▶ How do scientists study hemispheric specialization in normal subjects, and what have they learned?

As we noted previously, the cerebrum—the seat of complex thought—is divided into two separate hemispheres (see Figure 3.18 on page 109). Recent decades have seen an exciting flurry of research on the specialized abilities of the right and left cerebral hemispheres. Some theorists have gone so far as to suggest that we really have two brains in one!

Hints of this hemispheric specialization have been available for many years, based on cases in which one side of a person's brain has been damaged. The left hemisphere was implicated in the control of language as early as 1861, by Paul Broca, a

French surgeon. Broca was treating a patient who had been unable to speak for 30 years. After the patient died, Broca showed that the probable cause of his speech deficit was a localized lesion on the left side of the frontal lobe. Since then, many similar cases have shown that this area of the brain—known as *Broca's area*—plays an important role in the *production* of speech (see Figure 3.21). Another major language centre—*Wernicke's area*—was identified in the temporal lobe of the left hemisphere in 1874. Damage in Wernicke's area (also shown in Figure 3.21) usually leads to problems with the *comprehension* of language.

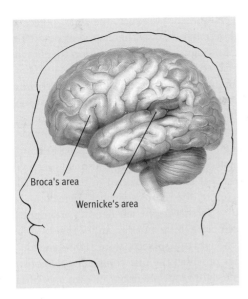

FIGURE 3.21

Language processing in the brain.
This view of the left hemisphere highlights the location of two centres for language processing in the brain: Broca's area, which is involved in speech production, and Wernicke's area, which is involved in language comprehension.

Evidence that the left hemisphere usually processes language led scientists to characterize it as the "dominant" hemisphere. Because thoughts are usually coded in terms of language, the left hemisphere was given the lion's share of credit for handling the "higher" mental processes, such as reasoning, remembering, planning, and problem solving. Meanwhile, the right hemisphere came to be viewed as the "nondominant," or "dumb," hemisphere, lacking any special functions or abilities.

This characterization of the left and right hemispheres as major and minor partners in the brain's work began to change in the 1960s. It all started with landmark research by Roger Sperry, Michael Gazzaniga, and their colleagues, who studied "split-brain" patients: individuals whose cerebral hemispheres had been surgically disconnected (Gazzaniga, 1970; Gazzaniga, Bogen, & Sperry, 1965; Levy, Trevarthen, & Sperry, 1972; Sperry, 1982). In 1981, Sperry received a Nobel Prize in physiology/medicine for this work.

Bisecting the Brain: Split-Brain Research

2f

In *split-brain surgery*, the bundle of fibres that connects the cerebral hemispheres (the corpus callosum) is cut to reduce the severity of epileptic seizures. It is a radical procedure that is chosen only in exceptional cases that have not responded to other forms of treatment. But the surgery provides scientists with an unusual opportunity to study people who have had their brain literally split in two (Lassonde & Quimet, 2010).

To appreciate the logic of split-brain research, you need to understand how sensory and motor information is routed to and from the two hemispheres. *Each hemisphere's primary connections are to the opposite side of the body.* Thus, the left hemisphere controls, and communicates with, the right hand, right arm, right leg, right eyebrow, and so on. In contrast, the right hemisphere controls, and communicates with, the left side of the body.

Vision and hearing are more complex. Both eyes deliver information to both hemispheres, but there still is a separation of input. Stimuli in the right half of the *visual field* are registered by receptors on the left side of each eye, which send signals to the left hemisphere. Stimuli in the left half of the visual field are transmitted by both eyes to the right hemisphere (see Figure 3.22). Auditory inputs to each ear also go to both hemispheres. However, connections to the opposite hemisphere are stronger or more immediate. That is, sounds presented exclusively to the right ear (through headphones) are registered in the left hemisphere first, while sounds presented to the left ear are registered more quickly in the right hemisphere.

For the most part, people don't notice this asymmetric, "crisscrossed" organization because the two hemispheres are in close communication with each other. Information received by one hemisphere is readily shared with the other via the corpus callosum. However, when the two hemispheres are surgically disconnected, the functional specialization of the brain becomes apparent.

In their classic study of split-brain patients, Gazzaniga, Bogen, and Sperry (1965) presented visual stimuli such as pictures, symbols, and words in a single visual field (the left or the right), so that the stimuli would be sent to only one hemisphere. The stimuli were projected onto a screen in front of the participants, who stared at a fixation point (a spot) in the centre of the screen (see Figure 3.23). The images were flashed to the right or the left of the fixation point for only a split second. Thus, the subjects did not have a chance to move their eyes, and the stimuli were glimpsed in only one visual field.

When pictures were flashed in the right visual field and thus sent to the left hemisphere, the split-brain subjects were able to name and describe the objects depicted (such as a cup or spoon). However, the subjects were *not* able to name and describe the same objects when they were flashed in the left visual field and sent to the right hemisphere. In a similar fashion, an object placed out of view in the right hand (communicating with the left hemisphere)

Roger Sperry
"Both the left and right hemispheres of the brain have been found to have their own specialized forms of intellect."

Michael Gazzaniga
"Nothing can possibly replace a singular memory of mine: that of the moment when I discovered that case W. J. could no longer verbally describe (from his left hemisphere) stimuli presented to his freshly disconnected right hemisphere."

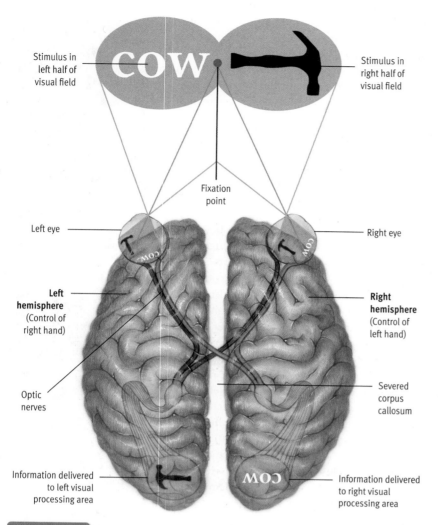

FIGURE 3.22

Visual input in the split brain.

If a participant stares at a fixation point, the point divides the subject's visual field into right and left halves. Input from the right visual field (a picture of a hammer in this example) strikes the left side of each eye and is transmitted to the left hemisphere. Input from the left visual field strikes the right side of each eye and is transmitted to the right hemisphere. Normally, the hemispheres share the information from the two halves of the visual field, but in split-brain patients, the corpus callosum is severed and the two hemispheres cannot communicate. Hence, the experimenter can present a visual stimulus to just one hemisphere at a time.

FIGURE 3.23

Experimental apparatus in split-brain research.

On the left is a special slide projector that can present images very briefly, before the subject's eyes can move and thus change the visual field. Images are projected on one side of the screen to present stimuli to just one hemisphere. The portion of the apparatus beneath the screen is constructed to prevent participants from seeing objects that they may be asked to handle with their right or left hand, another procedure that can be used to send information to just one hemisphere.

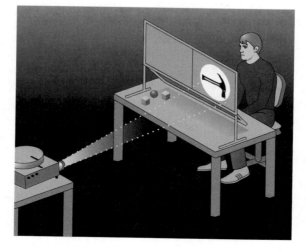

could be named. However, the same object placed in the left hand (right hemisphere) could not be. These findings supported the notion that language is housed in the left hemisphere.

Although the split-brain subjects' right hemisphere was not able to speak up for itself, further tests revealed that it *was* processing the information presented. If subjects were given an opportunity to *point out a picture* of an object they had held in their left hand, they were able to do so. They were also able to point out pictures that had been flashed to the left visual field. Furthermore, the right hemisphere (left hand) turned out to be *superior* to the left hemisphere (right hand) in assembling little puzzles and copying drawings, even though the subjects were right-handed. These findings provided the first compelling demonstration that the right hemisphere has its own special talents. Subsequent studies of additional split-brain patients showed the right hemisphere to be better than the left on a variety of visual–spatial tasks, including discriminating colours, arranging blocks, and recognizing faces.

In addition to its significance for our understanding of hemispheric specialization, research with split-brain subjects has opened a window for us into the function of the corpus callosum itself. But as in many areas of research on the brain, the final results are not in yet. Some research suggests that the corpus callosum plays an *excitatory* role in which it enables activation of both hemispheres by acting as a bridge between them (Lassonde & Quiment, 2010). Other findings suggest that it acts in an *inhibitory* role, preventing information from being transferred between the hemispheres. Given the recent advances in technology for examining the brain, it will likely not be long until we know which function it serves. Of course, the final answer might be that it does both (Lassonde & Quimet, 2010).

Hemispheric Specialization in the Intact Brain 2f

The problem with the split-brain operation, of course, is that it creates an abnormal situation. The vast majority of us remain "neurologically intact." Moreover, the surgery is done only with people who suffer from prolonged, severe cases of epilepsy. These people may have had somewhat atypical brain organization even before the operation. Furthermore, the number of split-brain patients has been quite small—only ten split-brain patients have been studied intensively (Gazzaniga, 2008). Thus, theorists couldn't help wondering whether it was safe to generalize broadly from the split-brain studies. For this reason, researchers developed methods that allowed them to study cerebral specialization in the intact brain.

Maryse Lassonde of the University of Montreal (Lassonde & Quimet, 2010) has been an active researcher in examining the effects of agenesis of the corpus callosum, a congenital malformation in which the corpus callosum is partially or completely absent. It has been referred to as a "natural model of the split brain" (Lassonde, Sauerwein, & Lepore, 2003). In some of her research, much like Sperry and his colleagues, she has recruited callosotomized (corpus callosum severed surgically) as well as acallosal (born without an intact corpus callosum) participants in order to examine the operation of the two hemispheres (De Guise et al., 1999). Overall, work with acallosal participants demonstrates that, while there is evidence for brain plasticity in these individuals, there are clear limits to that plasticity. While they don't typically show all of the deficits of split-brain participants, suggesting compensatory brain development, they clearly show some deficits similar to split-brain participants.

Along with her colleague Elaine De Guise, Lassonde has conducted similar research with children of different ages (6 to 16 years of age), all of whom have intact corpus callosums (De Guise & Lassonde, 2001). Younger children often show limitations in hemispheric communication because their callosum has not yet reached functional maturity.

In one study, De Guise and Lassonde (2001) presented four age groups of children (6–8, 9–11, 12–14, and 15–16) with a visuomotor task to learn on a computer. In a condition where the skills to be learned to successfully perform the task involved bihemispheric integration, only the older children (12 and above) tended to perform well. Only a mature corpus callosum allowed for sufficient integration of information between hemispheres. The authors suggest that findings such as these emphasize the "crucial role of the [corpus callosum] in transfer and integration of a procedural visuomotor skill" (p. 254). This doesn't mean that the younger children were not able to transfer information between hemispheres but that they showed deficits in learning a task that involved integration of information from both hemispheres.

Another method involves looking at *perceptual asymmetries*—left–right imbalances between the cerebral hemispheres in the speed of visual or auditory processing. As we just discussed, it is possible to present visual stimuli to just one visual field at a time. In normal individuals, the input sent to one hemisphere is quickly shared with the other. However, subtle differences in the "abilities" of the two hemispheres can be detected by precisely measuring how long it takes subjects to recognize different types of stimuli.

For instance, when *verbal* stimuli are presented to the right visual field (and thus sent to the *left hemisphere* first), they are identified more quickly and more accurately than when they are presented to the left visual field (and sent to the right hemisphere first). The faster reactions in the left hemisphere presumably occur because it can recognize verbal stimuli on its own, while the right hemisphere has to take extra time to "consult" the left hemisphere. In contrast, the *right hemisphere* is faster than the left on *visual–spatial* tasks, such as locating a dot or recognizing a face (Bradshaw, 1989; Bryden, 1982).

Researchers have also used a variety of other approaches to explore hemispheric specialization in normal people. For the most part, their findings have converged nicely with the results of the split-brain studies (Reuter-Lorenz & Miller, 1998). Overall, the findings suggest that the two hemispheres are specialized, with each handling certain types of cognitive tasks better than the other (Corballis, 2003; Gazzaniga, 2000; Springer & Deutsch, 1998). *The left hemisphere usually is better on tasks involving verbal processing, such as language, speech, reading, and writing. The right hemisphere exhibits superiority on many tasks involving nonverbal processing, such as most spatial, musical, and visual recognition tasks and tasks involving the perception of others' emotions.*

WEB LINK 3.6

Society for Neuroscience
The largest scientific association devoted solely to the study of the nervous system and its functioning has gathered a host of materials that will introduce visitors to the latest research on a full spectrum of brain-related topics.

concept **check 3.3**

Relating Disorders to the Nervous System

Imagine that you are working as a neuropsychologist at a clinic. You are involved in the diagnosis of the cases described below. You are asked to identify the probable cause(s) of the disorders in terms of nervous system malfunctions. Based on the information in this chapter, indicate the probable location of any brain damage or the probable disturbance of neurotransmitter activity. The answers can be found in the back of the book in Appendix A.

Case 1. Miriam is exhibiting language deficits. In particular, she does not seem to comprehend the meaning of words.

_____

_____

Case 2. Camille displays tremors and muscular rigidity and is diagnosed as having Parkinson's disease.

_____

_____

Case 3. Ricardo, a 28-year-old computer executive, has gradually seen his strength and motor coordination deteriorate badly. He is diagnosed as having multiple sclerosis.

_____

_____

Case 4. Wendy is highly irrational, has poor contact with reality, and reports hallucinations. She is given a diagnosis of schizophrenic disorder.

_____

_____

In recent years, research on hemispheric specialization has been increasingly conducted with modern brain-imaging technology, especially fMRI scans (Friston, 2003; Pizzagalli, Shackman, & Davidson, 2003). These scans can provide a more direct and precise view of hemispheric activation on various types of tasks than can the study of perceptual asymmetries. For the most part, this new approach has painted a picture that is consistent with previous findings but more nuanced and detailed. While imaging research has provided new insights into the workings of the brain, it is also clear that other techniques, such as manipulating response procedure in a dichotic listening task as used by University of New Brunswick researcher Daniel Voyer (Voyer, Bowes, & Soraggi, 2009) and his colleagues, are key tools in our attempt to understand laterality effects in the brain.

Hemispheric specialization is not unique to humans, as it has been observed in a variety of other species (Vallortigara & Rogers, 2005). Although comparisons are complicated, it appears that humans manifest more cerebral specialization than other animals. Theorists speculate that hemispheric specialization is adaptive in an evolutionary sense in that it increases the neural capacity of the brain (Hopkins & Cantalupo, 2008). Interestingly, when researchers have studied variations in the strength of hemispheric specialization among humans, they have found links between weak lateralization and certain negative outcomes. For instance, weak lateralization has been associated with lower IQ scores (Corballis, Hattie, & Fletcher, 2008) and with elevated vulnerability to schizophrenia (Spironelli, Angrilli, & Stegagno, 2008). However, much remains to be learned about these intriguing correlations.

Hemispheric specialization is a fascinating area of research that has broad implications, which we will discuss further in the Personal Application. For now, however, let's leave the brain and turn our attention to the endocrine system.

REVIEW OF KEY POINTS

▷ The cerebrum is divided into right and left hemispheres connected by the corpus callosum. Evidence that the left cerebral hemisphere usually processes language led scientists to view it as the dominant hemisphere.

▷ However, studies of split-brain patients revealed that the right and left halves of the brain each have unique talents, with the right hemisphere being specialized to handle visual-spatial functions.

▷ Studies of perceptual asymmetries in normal subjects also showed that the left hemisphere is better equipped to handle verbal processing, whereas the right hemisphere is more adept at nonverbal processing.

The Endocrine System: Another Way to Communicate

PREVIEW QUESTIONS

▷ What does the endocrine system consist of?

▷ What are hormones, and how do they resemble and differ from neurotransmitters?

▷ What is the master gland of the endocrine system?

▷ What are some aspects of behaviour regulated by hormones?

The major way the brain communicates with the rest of the body is through the nervous system. However, the body has a second communication system that is also important to behaviour. The *endocrine system* consists of glands that release hormones into the bloodstream; *hormones* help to control bodily functioning. In a way, hormones are like neurotransmitters in the nervous system. They are stored for subsequent release as chemical messengers, and once released, they diffuse through the bloodstream and bind to special receptors on target cells. In fact, some chemical substances do double duty, functioning as hormones when they're released in the endocrine system and as neurotransmitters in the nervous system (norepinephrine, for example). However, there are some important differences between hormones and neurotransmitters. Neural messages generally are transmitted short distances with lightning speed (measured in milliseconds) along very specific pathways, whereas hormonal messages often travel to distant cells at a much slower speed (measured in seconds and minutes) and tend to be less specific, as they can act on many target cells throughout the body.

As we will see, hormones have important effects on our body. They may even be the basis of some of the cognitive differences observed between males and females. According to Simon Fraser University neuroscientist Doreen Kimura, cognitive gender differences such as males' greater spatial ability and females' greater verbal fluency may be caused, in part, by the early effects of sex hormones on brain organization (Kimura, 1992, 2004). Hormonal differences may result in the fact that the "environment is acting on differently wired brains in boys and girls" (Kimura, 1992, p. 119). We will discuss some of the evidence for gender differences in cognitive abilities more fully in later chapters.

The major endocrine glands are shown in Figure 3.24. Some hormones are released in response to changing conditions in the body and act to regulate those conditions. For example, hormones released by the stomach and intestines help control digestion. Kidney hormones play a part in regulating blood pressure. And the pancreatic hormone (insulin) is essential for cells to use sugar from the blood. Hormone release tends to be *pulsatile*. That is, hormones tend to be released several times per day in brief bursts or pulses that last only a few minutes. The levels of many hormones increase and decrease in a rhythmic pattern throughout the day.

Much of the endocrine system is controlled by the nervous system through the *hypothalamus* (Gore, 2008). This structure at the base of the forebrain has intimate connections with the pea-sized *pituitary gland*. The *pituitary gland* releases a great variety of hormones that fan out around the body, stimulating actions in the other endocrine glands. In this sense, the pituitary is the "master gland" of the endocrine system, although the hypothalamus is the real power behind the throne.

The intermeshing of the nervous system and the endocrine system can be seen in the fight-or-flight response described earlier. In times of stress, the hypothalamus sends signals along two pathways—through the autonomic nervous system and through the pituitary gland—to the adrenal glands (Clow, 2001). In response, the adrenal glands secrete so-called "stress hormones" that radiate throughout the body, preparing it to cope with an emergency.

A topic of current research interest centres on the effects of *oxytocin*—a hormone released by the pituitary gland, which regulates reproductive behaviours. Oxytocin has long been known to trigger contractions when a woman gives birth and to stimulate the mammary glands to release milk for breastfeeding (Donaldson & Young, 2008). However, newer research suggests that this hormone has far-reaching effects on complex social behaviour.

For example, an extensive body of research indicates that oxytocin fosters adult–adult pair-bonding in many mammals (Lim & Young, 2006) and preliminary research suggests that similar effects may be found in humans (Bartz & Hollander, 2006; Donaldson & Young, 2008). In one study male participants worked on a task in which they tried to infer people's mental states from subtle social cues, thus measuring their empathy. Performance was enhanced when subjects inhaled an oxytocin spray prior to working on this "mind-reading" task (Domes et al., 2007). Another study found that oxytocin increased males' empathy levels in response to photos of emotional situations (Hurlemann et al., 2010).

Recent research also suggests that oxytocin may foster trust in humans. In one fascinating study, male students participated in an investment-bargaining simulation in which the "investors" could send a

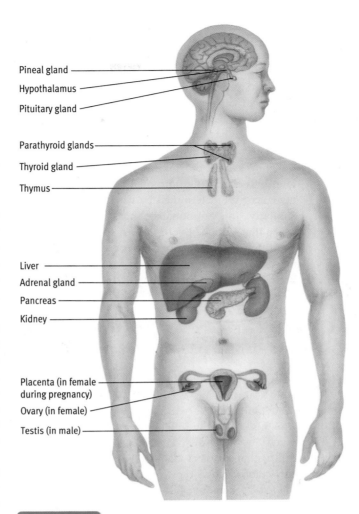

Pineal gland

Hypothalamus

Pituitary gland

Parathyroid glands

Thyroid gland

Thymus

Liver

Adrenal gland

Pancreas

Kidney

Placenta (in female during pregnancy)

Ovary (in female)

Testis (in male)

FIGURE 3.24

The endocrine system.

This graphic depicts most of the major endocrine glands. The endocrine glands release hormones into the bloodstream. These chemicals regulate a variety of physical functions and affect many aspects of behaviour.

portion of their financial stake to a "trustee," which tripled the money, but then they had to *hope* that the trustee would send a decent portion of the investment back to them (Kosfeld et al., 2005). Investors who inhaled an oxytocin spray before the simulation were far more trusting and sent more money to the trustees than control subjects. Other studies have also found a link between oxytocin and trusting behaviour (Morhenn et al., 2008; Zak, Kurzban, & Matzner, 2005).

Hormones also help to modulate human physiological development. For example, among the more interesting hormones released by the pituitary are the *gonadotropins,* which affect the *gonads,* or sexual glands. Prior to birth, these hormones direct the formation of the external sexual organs in the developing fetus (Gorski, 2000). Thus, your sexual identity as a male or female was shaped during prenatal development by the actions of hormones. At puberty, increased levels of sexual hormones are responsible for the emergence of secondary sexual characteristics, such as male facial hair and female breasts (Susman, Dorn, & Schiefelbein, 2003). The actions of other hormones are responsible for the spurt in physical growth that occurs around puberty (see Chapter 11).

These developmental effects of hormones illustrate how genetic programming has a hand in behaviour. Obviously, the hormonal actions that shaped your sex were determined by your genetic makeup. Similarly, the hormonal changes in early adolescence that launched your growth spurt and aroused your interest in sexuality were preprogrammed over a decade earlier by your genetic inheritance. Which brings us to the role of heredity in shaping behaviour.

REVIEW OF KEY POINTS

▷ The endocrine system consists of glands that secrete hormones, which are chemicals involved in the regulation of basic bodily processes. Hormone release tends to be pulsatile. The control centres for the endocrine system are the hypothalamus and the pituitary gland.

▷ Hormones regulate many aspects of behaviour, such as the fight-or-flight response, which occurs in response to stress. Hormones also regulate many aspects of physiological development, such as sexual differentiation.

▷ Recent research suggests additional effects of hormones. For example, oxytocin, a hormone regulating reproductive behaviours that is produced by the pituitary gland, has been found to have effects on complex social behaviour such as adult–adult pair bonding.

Heredity and Behaviour: Is It All in the Genes?

PREVIEW QUESTIONS

▷ What are the basic mechanisms of hereditary transmission?

▷ What is the difference between one's genotype and phenotype?

▷ How are family studies conducted, and what can they reveal?

▷ How are twin studies conducted, and what have they revealed about intelligence and personality?

▷ How do adoption studies assess the role of genetics and environment?

▷ What is genetic mapping, and how will it facilitate behavioural genetics research?

As you have learned throughout this chapter, your biological makeup is intimately related to your behaviour. That is why your genetic inheritance, which shapes your biological makeup, may have much to do with your behaviour. Most people realize that physical characteristics such as height, hair colour, blood type, and eye colour are largely shaped by heredity. But what about psychological characteristics, such as intelligence, moodiness, impulsiveness, and shyness? To what extent are people's behavioural qualities moulded by their genes? These questions are the central focus of *behavioural genetics*—an interdisciplinary field that studies the influence of genetic factors on behavioural traits.

As we saw in Chapter 1, questions about the relative importance of heredity versus environment are very old ones in psychology. However, research in behavioural genetics has grown by leaps and bounds since the 1970s, and this research has shed new light on the age-old nature-versus-nurture debate. Ironically, although behavioural geneticists have mainly sought to demonstrate the influence of heredity on behaviour, their recent work has also highlighted the importance of the environment, as we will see in this section.

Basic Principles of Genetics

Every cell in your body contains enduring messages from your mother and father. These messages are found on the *chromosomes* that lie within the nucleus of each cell.

Chromosomes and Genes

Chromosomes are strands of DNA (deoxyribonucleic acid) molecules that carry genetic information (see Figure 3.25). Every cell in humans, except the sex cells (sperm and eggs), contains 46 chromosomes. These chromosomes operate in 23 pairs, with one chromosome of each pair being contributed by each parent. Parents make this contribution when fertilization creates a *zygote*, a single cell formed by the union of a sperm and an egg. The sex cells that form a zygote each have 23 chromosomes; together they contribute the 46 chromosomes that appear in the zygote and in all of the body cells that develop from it. Each chromosome in turn contains thousands of biochemical messengers called *genes*. *Genes* are DNA segments that serve as the key functional units in hereditary transmission.

If all offspring are formed by a union of the parents' sex cells, why aren't family members identical clones? The reason is that a single pair of parents can produce an extraordinary variety of combinations of chromosomes. When sex cells form in each parent, it is a matter of chance as to which member of each chromosome pair ends up in the sperm or egg. Each parent's 23 chromosome pairs can be scrambled in over 8 million (2^{23}) different ways, yielding roughly 70 trillion (2^{46}) possible configurations when sperm and egg unite. Actually, this is a conservative estimate. It doesn't take into account complexities such as *mutations* (changes in the genetic code) or *crossing over* during sex-cell formation (an interchange of material between chromosomes). Thus, genetic transmission is a complicated process, and everything is a matter of probability. Except for identical twins, each person ends up with a unique genetic blueprint.

Like chromosomes, genes operate in pairs, with one gene of each pair coming from each parent. In the *homozygous condition*, the two genes in a specific pair are the same. In the *heterozygous condition*, the two genes in a specific pair are different (see Figure 3.26). In the simplest scenario, a single pair of genes determines a trait. Attached versus detached earlobes provide a nice example. When both parents contribute a gene for the same type of earlobe (the *homozygous* condition), the child will have an earlobe of that type. When the parents contribute genes for different types of earlobes (the *heterozygous* condition), one gene in the pair—called the *dominant gene*—overrides or masks the other, called the *recessive gene*. Thus, a *dominant gene* is one that is expressed when paired genes are different. A *recessive gene* is one that is masked when paired genes are different. In the case of earlobes, genes for detached earlobes are dominant over genes for attached earlobes.

Because genes operate in pairs, a child has a 50 percent probability of inheriting a specific gene in a particular gene pair from each parent. Hence, the *genetic relatedness* of parents and children is said to be 50 percent. The genetic relatedness of other types of relatives can be calculated in the same way; the results are shown in Figure 3.27. As you can see, genetic relatedness ranges from 100 percent for identical twins down to 6.25 percent for second cousins. The numbers in Figure 3.27 are purely theoretical, and for a variety of complicated reasons, they underestimate the actual genetic overlap among people. But the key to the concept of genetic relatedness is that members of a family share more of the same genes than nonmembers, and closer relatives share a larger proportion of genes than more distant relatives. These realities explain why family members tend to resemble one another and why this resemblance tends to be greater among closer relatives.

FIGURE 3.26

Homozygous and heterozygous genotypes.

Like chromosomes, genes operate in pairs, with one gene in each pair coming from each parent. When paired genes are the same, they are said to be *homozygous*. When paired genes are different, they are said to be *heterozygous*. Whether people have attached or detached earlobes is determined by a single pair of genes. In the heterozygous condition, genes for detached earlobes are dominant over genes for attached earlobes.

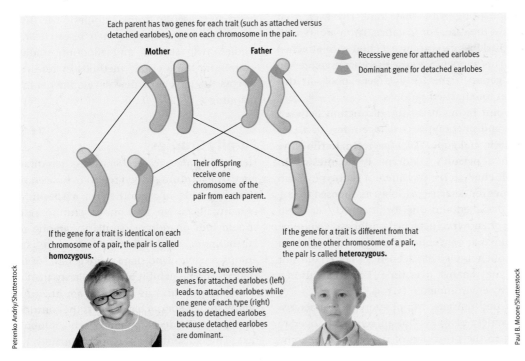

Each parent has two genes for each trait (such as attached versus detached earlobes), one on each chromosome in the pair.

Mother   Father

Recessive gene for attached earlobes

Dominant gene for detached earlobes

Their offspring receive one chromosome of the pair from each parent.

If the gene for a trait is identical on each chromosome of a pair, the pair is called **homozygous**.

If the gene for a trait is different from that gene on the other chromosome of a pair, the pair is called **heterozygous**.

In this case, two recessive genes for attached earlobes (left) leads to attached earlobes while one gene of each type (right) leads to detached earlobes because detached earlobes are dominant.

Petrenko Andriy/Shutterstock

Paul B. Moore/Shutterstock

Cell   Nucleus

Chromosomes

DNA

FIGURE 3.25

Genetic material.

This series of enlargements shows the main components of genetic material. (Top) In the nucleus of every cell are chromosomes, which carry the information needed to construct new human beings. (Centre) Chromosomes are thread-like strands of DNA that carry thousands of genes, the functional units of hereditary transmission. (Bottom) DNA is a double spiral chain of molecules that can copy itself to reproduce.

The Biological Bases of Behaviour

Relationship	Degree of relatedness	Genetic overlap
Identical twins		100%
Fraternal twins Brother or sister Parent or child	First-degree relatives	50%
Grandparent or grandchild Uncle, aunt, nephew, or niece Half-bother or half-sister	Second-degree relatives	25%
First cousin	Third-degree relatives	12.5%
Second cousin	Fourth-degree relatives	6.25%
Unrelated		0%

FIGURE 3.27

Genetic relatedness.

Research on the genetic bases of behaviour takes advantage of the different degrees of genetic relatedness between various types of relatives. If heredity influences a trait, relatives who share more genes should be more similar with regard to that trait than are more distant relatives, who share fewer genes. Comparisons involving various degrees of biological relationships will come up frequently in later chapters.

Genotype versus Phenotype

It might seem that two parents with the same manifest trait, such as detached earlobes, should always produce offspring with that trait. However, that isn't always the case. For instance, two parents with detached earlobes can produce a child with attached earlobes. This happens because there are unexpressed recessive genes in the family's gene pool—in this case, genes for attached earlobes.

This point brings us to the distinction between genotype and phenotype. *Genotype* refers to a person's genetic makeup. *Phenotype* refers to the ways in which a person's genotype is manifested in observable characteristics. Different genotypes (such as two genes for detached earlobes as opposed to one gene for detached and one for attached) can yield the same phenotype (detached earlobes). Genotype is determined at conception and is fixed forever. In contrast, phenotypic characteristics (hair colour, for instance) may change over time. They may also be modified by environmental factors.

Genotypes translate into phenotypic characteristics in a variety of ways. Not all gene pairs operate according to the principles of dominance. In some instances, when paired genes are different, they produce a blend, an "averaged-out" phenotype. In other cases, paired genes that are different strike another

type of compromise, and both characteristics show up phenotypically. In the case of type AB blood, for example, one gene is for type A and the other is for type B.

Polygenic Inheritance

Most human characteristics appear to be *polygenic traits*, or characteristics that are influenced by more than one pair of genes. For example, three to five gene pairs are thought to interactively determine skin colour. Complex physical abilities, such as motor coordination, may be influenced by tangled interactions among a great many pairs of genes. Most psychological characteristics that appear to be affected by heredity seem to involve complex polygenic inheritance (Plomin et al., 2001).

Investigating Hereditary Influence: Research Methods

7f

How do behavioural geneticists and other scientists disentangle the effects of genetics and experience to determine whether heredity affects behavioural traits? Researchers have designed special types of studies to assess the impact of heredity. Of course, with humans, they are limited to correlational rather than experimental methods, as they cannot manipulate genetic variables by assigning subjects to mate with each other (this approach, called *selective breeding*, is used in animal studies). The three most important methods in human research are family studies, twin studies, and adoption studies. After examining these classic methods of research, we'll discuss the impact of new developments in genetic mapping.

Family Studies

In *family studies*, researchers assess hereditary influence by examining blood relatives to see how much they resemble one another on a specific trait. If heredity affects the trait under scrutiny, researchers should find phenotypic similarity among relatives. Furthermore, they should find more similarity among relatives who share more genes. For instance, siblings should exhibit more similarity than cousins.

Illustrative of this method are the numerous family studies conducted to assess the contribution of heredity to the development of schizophrenic disorders. These disorders strike approximately 1 percent of the population, yet as Figure 3.28 reveals, 9 percent of the siblings of schizophrenic patients exhibit schizophrenia themselves (Gottesman, 1991). Thus, these first-degree relatives of schizophrenic patients show a risk for the disorder that is nine times higher than normal. This risk is greater than that observed for more distantly related, second-degree relatives, such as nieces and nephews (4 percent), who, in turn, are at greater risk than third-degree relatives, such as second cousins (2 percent). This pattern of results is consistent with the hypothesis that genetic inheritance influences the development of schizophrenic disorders (Kirov & Owen, 2009).

Family studies can indicate whether a trait runs in families. However, this correlation does not provide conclusive evidence that the trait is influenced by heredity. Why not? Because family members generally share not only genes but also similar environments. Furthermore, closer relatives are more likely to live together than more distant relatives. Thus, genetic similarity and environmental similarity *both* tend to be greater for closer relatives. Either of these confounded variables could be responsible when greater phenotypic similarity is found in closer relatives. Family studies can offer useful insights about the possible impact of heredity, but they cannot provide definitive evidence.

Twin Studies

7f PSYKTREK

Twin studies can yield better evidence about the possible role of genetic factors. In *twin studies,* researchers assess hereditary influence by comparing the resemblance of identical twins and fraternal twins with respect to a trait. The logic of twin studies hinges on the genetic relatedness of identical and fraternal twins (see Figure 3.29). *Identical (monozygotic) twins* emerge from one zygote that splits for unknown reasons. Thus, they have exactly the same genotype; their genetic relatedness is 100 percent. *Fraternal (dizygotic) twins* result when two eggs are fertilized simultaneously by different sperm cells, forming two separate zygotes. Fraternal twins are no more alike in genetic makeup than any two siblings born to a pair of parents at different times. Their genetic relatedness is only 50 percent.

Fraternal twins provide a useful comparison to identical twins because in both cases the twins usually grow up in the same home, at the same time, exposed to the same configuration of relatives, neighbours, peers, teachers, events, and so forth. Thus, both kinds of twins normally develop under equally similar environmental conditions. However, identical twins share more genetic kinship than fraternal twins. Consequently, if sets of identical twins tend to exhibit more similarity of a trait than sets of fraternal twins do, it is reasonable to infer that this

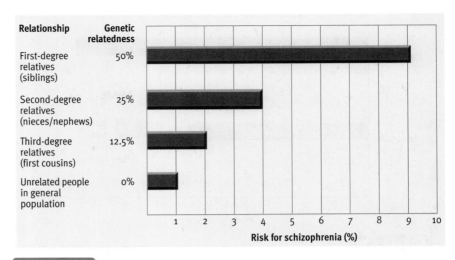

Family studies of risk for schizophrenic disorders.

First-degree relatives of schizophrenic patients have an elevated risk of developing a schizophrenic disorder (Gottesman, 1991). For instance, the risk for siblings of schizophrenic patients is about 9 percent instead of the baseline 1 percent for unrelated people. Second- and third-degree relatives have progressively smaller elevations in risk for this disorder. Although these patterns of risk do not prove that schizophrenia is partly inherited, they are consistent with this hypothesis.

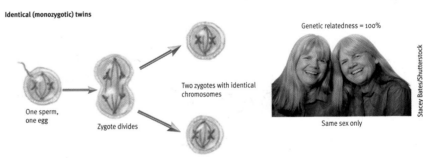

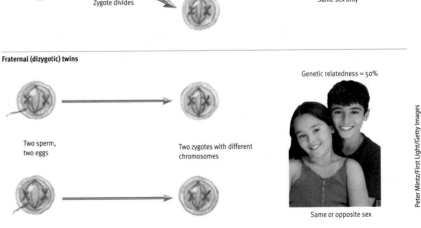

FIGURE 3.29

Identical versus fraternal twins.

Identical (monozygotic) twins emerge from one zygote that splits, so their genetic relatedness is 100 percent. Fraternal (dizygotic) twins emerge from two separate zygotes, so their genetic relatedness is only 50 percent.

Source: Adapted from Kalat, J. (1996). *Introduction to psychology,* 4th edition, © 1996 Belmont, CA: Wadsworth. Reprinted by permission.

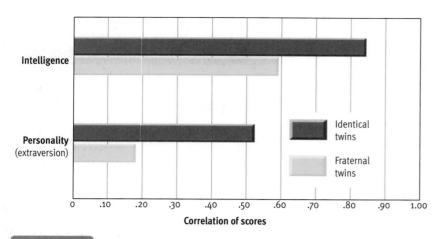

FIGURE 3.30

Twin studies of intelligence and personality.

Identical twins tend to be more similar than fraternal twins (as reflected in higher correlations) with regard to intelligence and specific personality traits, such as extraversion. These findings suggest that intelligence and personality are influenced by heredity. (Intelligence data from McGue et al., 1993; extraversion data based on Loehlin, 1992)

greater similarity is *probably* due to heredity rather than environment.

Twin studies have been conducted to assess the impact of heredity on a variety of traits. Some representative results are summarized in Figure 3.30. The higher correlations found for identical twins indicate that they tend to be more similar to each other than fraternal twins on measures of general intelligence (McGue et al., 1993) and measures of specific personality traits, such as extraversion (Plomin et al., 2008). These results support the notion that intelligence and personality are influenced to some degree by genetic makeup. However, the fact that identical twins are far from identical in intelligence and personality also shows that environment influences these characteristics.

Adoption Studies

7f

Adoption studies assess hereditary influence by examining the resemblance between adopted children and both their biological and their adoptive parents. Generally, adoptees are used as subjects in this type of study only if they were given up for adoption in early infancy and were raised without having contact with their biological parents. The logic underlying the adoption study approach is quite simple. If adopted children resemble their biological parents in a trait, even though they were not raised by them, genetic factors probably influence that trait. In contrast, if adopted children resemble their adoptive parents, even though they inherited no genes from them, environmental factors probably influence the trait.

In recent years, adoption studies have contributed to science's understanding of how genetics and the environment influence intelligence. The research shows modest similarity between adopted children and their biological parents, as indicated by an average correlation of 0.22 (Grigorenko, 2000). Interestingly, adopted children resemble their adoptive parents just as much (also an average correlation of about 0.20). These findings suggest that both heredity and environment have an influence on intelligence.

The Cutting Edge: Genetic Mapping

While behavioural geneticists have recently made great progress in documenting the influence of heredity on behaviour, *molecular geneticists*, who study the biochemical bases of genetic inheritance, have made even more spectacular advances in their efforts to unravel the genetic code. *Genetic mapping* is the process of determining the location and chemical sequence of specific genes on specific chromosomes. New methods of manipulating DNA are now allowing scientists to create detailed physical maps of the genetic material of chromosomes in plants, animals, and humans. The Human Genome Project, a huge international enterprise, has produced a working draft of the sequence of all 3 billion letters of DNA in the human genome, and the chromosomal location of almost all human genes has been identified (Collins et al., 2006; Kelsoe, 2004). Gene maps, by themselves, do not reveal which genes govern which traits. However, the compilation of a precise genetic atlas will fuel a quantum leap in the ability of scientists to pinpoint links between specific genes and specific traits and disorders.

Will genetic mapping permit researchers to discover the genetic basis for intelligence, extraversion, schizophrenia, musical ability, and other *behavioural* traits? Perhaps some day, but progress is likely to be painstakingly slow (Caspi & Moffitt, 2006; Plomin & McGuffin, 2003). Thus far, the major medical breakthroughs from genetic mapping have involved dichotomous traits (you either do or do not have the trait, such as muscular dystrophy) governed by a single gene pair. However, most behavioural traits do not involve a dichotomy, as everyone has varying amounts of intelligence, musical ability, and so forth. Moreover, virtually all behavioural traits appear to be *polygenic* and are shaped by many genes, rather than by a single gene. Because of these and many other complexities, scientists are not likely to find a single gene that controls intelligence, extraversion, or musical talent (Plomin, Kennedy, & Craig, 2006). The challenge will be to identify specific constellations of genes that each exerts modest influence over particular aspects of behaviour. What's exciting is that until recently, behavioural geneticists were largely limited to investigating *how much* heredity influences various traits. Genetic mapping will allow them to begin investigating *how* heredity influences specific aspects of behaviour (Plomin, 2004).

The Interplay of Heredity and Environment

We began this section by asking: Is it all in the genes? When it comes to behavioural traits, the answer clearly is no. According to Robert Plomin (1993, 2004), perhaps the leading behavioural genetics researcher in the last decade, what scientists find again and again is that heredity and experience jointly influence most aspects of behaviour. Moreover, their effects are interactive—genetics and experience play off each other (Gottesman & Hanson, 2005; Rutter & Silberg, 2002; Rutter, 2006, 2007).

For example, consider what researchers have learned about the development of schizophrenic disorders. Although the evidence indicates that genetic factors influence the development of schizophrenia, it does *not* appear that anyone directly inherits the disorder itself. Rather, what people appear to inherit is a certain degree of *vulnerability* to the disorder (McDonald & Murphy, 2003; Paris, 1999). Whether this vulnerability is ever converted into an actual disorder depends on each person's experiences in life. As we will discuss in Chapter 14, certain types of stressful experience seem to evoke the disorder in people who are more vulnerable to it. Thus, as Danielle Dick and Richard Rose (2002) put it in a major review of behavioural genetics research, "We inherit dispositions, not destinies."

In recent years, research in the emerging field of *epigenetics* has only served to further demonstrate that genetic and environmental factors are inextricably intertwined. *Epigenetics is the study of heritable changes in gene expression that do not involve modifications to the DNA sequence.* It turns out that specific genes' effects can be dampened or silenced by chemical events at the cellular level, leading to phenotypic alterations in traits, health, and behaviour (Tsankova et al., 2007). Moreover, these chemical events can be stimulated by environmental events, such as poor nurturance when offspring are young, exposure to stress, or peculiarities in diet (McGowan, Meaney, & Szyf, 2008). What has surprised scientists is that these *epigenetic marks* that influence gene expression can be passed on to successive generations (Masterpasqua, 2009). Theorists suspect that epigenetic changes may contribute to a

variety of psychological disorders, including schizophrenia (Zhang & Meaney, 2010). The finding that genes themselves are not exempt from environmental influence has a host of far-reaching implications. Among other things, it means that efforts to quantify the influence of heredity versus environment, informative though they may be, are ultimately artificial (Lickliter, 2009).

Robert Plomin

"The transformation of the social and behavioural sciences from environmentalism to biological determination is happening so fast that I find I more often have to say, 'Yes, genetic influences are substantial, but environmental influences are important, too.'"

REVIEW OF KEY POINTS

▷ The endocrine system consists of the glands that secrete hormones, which are chemicals involved in the regulation of basic bodily processes. The control centres for the endocrine system are the hypothalamus and the pituitary gland.

▷ Hormones regulate many aspects of behaviour, such as the fight-or-flight response, and many aspects of physiological development, such as sexual differentiation.

▷ The basic units of genetic transmission are genes housed on chromosomes. Genes operate in pairs and, when heterozygous, one may be dominant and one recessive. Genotypes are translated into phenotypes in many ways. Most behavioural qualities appear to involve polygenic inheritance.

▷ Researchers assess hereditary influence through a variety of methods, including family studies, twin studies, adoption studies, and genetic mapping. Family studies cannot provide conclusive evidence that a trait is influenced by heredity. Twin studies can provide much better evidence.

▷ Research indicates that most behavioural qualities are influenced jointly by heredity and environment, which play off of each other in complex interactions.

concept **check 3.4**

Recognizing Hereditary Influence

Check your understanding of the methods scientists use to explore hereditary influences on specific behavioural traits by filling in the blanks in the descriptive statements below. The answers can be found near the back of the book in Appendix A.

1. The findings from family studies indicate that heredity may influence a trait if _____ show more trait similarity than _____.

2. The findings from twin studies suggest that heredity influences a trait if _____ show more trait similarity than _____.

3. The findings from adoption studies suggest that heredity influences a trait if children adopted at a young age share more trait similarity with their _____ than their _____.

4. The findings from family studies, twin studies, and adoption studies suggest that heredity does not influence a trait when _____ is not related to _____.

The Biological Bases of Behaviour

The Evolutionary Bases of Behaviour

PREVIEW QUESTIONS

▶ What were Darwin's four key insights?

▶ Can adaptations linger in a population even if they are no longer adaptive?

▶ How do evolutionary theorists explain self-sacrifice?

▶ How can behaviours be adaptive?

Charles Darwin

"Can we doubt (remembering that many more individuals are born than can possibly survive) that individuals having any advantage, however slight, over others, would have the best chance of surviving and procreating their kind? . . . This preservation of favourable variations and the rejection of injurious variations, I call Natural Selection."

To round out our look at the biological bases of behaviour, we need to discuss how evolutionary forces have shaped many aspects of human and animal behaviour. *Evolutionary psychology* is a major new theoretical perspective in the field that analyzes behavioural processes in terms of their adaptive significance.

Darwin's Insights

Charles Darwin, the legendary British naturalist, was *not* the first person to describe the process of evolution. Well before Darwin's time, other biologists who had studied the earth's fossil record noted that various species appeared to have undergone gradual changes over the course of a great many generations. What Darwin (1859) contributed in his landmark book, *On the Origin of Species,* was a creative, new explanation for *how and why* evolutionary changes unfold over time. He identified *natural selection* as the mechanism that orchestrates the process of evolution (Dewsbury, 2009).

The mystery that Darwin set out to solve was complicated. He wanted to explain how the characteristics of a species might change over generations and why these changes tended to be surprisingly adaptive. In other words, he wanted to shed light on why organisms tend to have characteristics that serve them well in the context of their environments. For example, how did giraffes acquire their long necks that allow them to reach high into acacia trees to secure their main source of food? Darwin's explanation for the seemingly purposive nature of evolution centred on four crucial insights.

First, he noted that organisms vary in endless ways, such as size, speed, strength, aspects of appearance, visual abilities, hearing capacities, digestive processes, cell structure, and so forth. Second, he noted that some of these characteristics are heritable—that is, they are passed down from one generation to the next. Although genes and chromosomes had not yet been discovered, the concept of heredity was well established. In Darwin's theory, variations in hereditary traits provide the crude materials for evolution. Third, borrowing from the work of Thomas Malthus, he noted that organisms tend to produce offspring at a pace that outstrips the local availability of food supplies, living space, and other crucial resources. As a population increases and resources dwindle, the competition for precious resources intensifies.

Thus, it occurred to Darwin—and this was his grand insight—that variations in hereditary traits might affect organisms' ability to obtain the resources necessary for survival and reproduction. Fourth, building on this insight, Darwin argued that if a specific heritable trait contributes to an organism's survival or reproductive success, organisms with that trait should produce more offspring than those without the trait (or those with less of the trait), and the prevalence of that trait should gradually increase over generations—resulting in evolutionary change.

Although evolution is widely characterized as a matter of "survival of the fittest," Darwin recognized from the beginning that survival is important only insofar as it relates to reproductive success. Indeed, in evolutionary theory, *fitness* refers to the reproductive success (number of descendants) of an individual organism relative to the average reproductive success in the population. *Variations in reproductive success are what really fuel evolutionary change.* But survival is crucial because organisms typically need to mature and thrive before they can reproduce. So, Darwin theorized that there ought to be two ways in which traits might contribute to evolution: by providing either a survival advantage or a reproductive advantage. For example, a turtle's shell has great protective value that provides a survival advantage. In contrast, a firefly's emission of light is a courtship overture that provides a reproductive advantage.

To summarize, the principle of *natural selection* posits that heritable characteristics that provide a survival or reproductive advantage are more likely than alternative characteristics to be passed on to subsequent generations and thus come to be "selected" over time. Please note that the process of natural selection works on *populations* rather than *organisms.* Evolution occurs when the gene pool in a population changes gradually as a result of selection pressures.

Darwin's theory had at least two important, far-reaching implications (Buss, 2009). First, it suggested that the awe-inspiring diversity of life is the result of an unplanned, natural process rather than divine creation. Second, it implied that humans are not unique and that they share a common ancestry with other species. Although these implications would prove highly controversial, Darwin's theory eventually gained considerable acceptance because it provided a compelling explanation for how the characteristics of various species gradually changed over many generations and for the functional, adaptive direction of these changes.

Subsequent Refinements to Evolutionary Theory

Although Darwin's evolutionary theory quickly acquired many articulate advocates, it also remained controversial for decades. One legitimate objection was that the theory did not provide an adequate explanation for the details of the inheritance process. This shortcoming was gradually rectified first by the work of Gregor Mendel around 1900 and then by Theodore Dobzhansky in 1937.

Contemporary models of evolution recognize that natural selection operates on the gene pool of a population. The makeup of a gene pool is also shaped by genetic drift, mutations, and gene flow. *Genetic drift* consists of random fluctuation in gene frequencies over generations, as a result of chance alone. A *mutation* is a spontaneous, heritable change in a piece of DNA that occurs in an individual organism. Mutations are unpredictable errors in DNA replication. Although infrequent, mutations increase the variability in a gene pool and give natural selection new genetic material to work with. Most mutations are not beneficial, but the minority that prove adaptive are increasingly passed on to subsequent generations. *Gene flow* occurs when gene frequencies in a population shift because some individuals leave the population (emigration) and others enter it (immigration). Gene flow operates to keep neighbouring populations genetically similar. It can counterbalance gene pool differences between populations that have developed as a result of genetic drift, mutation, and natural selection. Conversely, when the gene flow between populations is minimal, the populations may evolve in divergent directions. This divergence can eventually contribute to the emergence of new species.

Adaptations are the key product of the process of evolution. An *adaptation* is an inherited characteristic that increased in a population (through natural selection) because it helped solve a problem of survival or reproduction during the time it emerged. Because of the gradual, incremental nature of evolution, adaptations sometimes linger in a population even though they no longer provide a survival or reproductive advantage. For example, as noted earlier, the physiological arousal associated with the fight-or-flight response that aided humans' survival in more primitive times appears to be more detrimental than adaptive today, as it leads to a variety of stress-related diseases (see Chapter 13). Similarly,

The fight-or-flight response discussed earlier in the chapter (see page 96) is an example of a behaviour that provides a survival advantage. Although traits that convey a survival advantage can contribute to evolution, it is variations in reproductive fitness that ultimately fuel evolutionary change.

humans show a taste preference for fatty substances that was adaptive in an era of hunting and gathering, when dietary fat was a scarce source of important calories. However, in our modern world, where dietary fat is typically available in abundance, this taste preference leads many people to consume too much fat, resulting in obesity, heart disease, and other health problems. Thus, the preference for fatty foods has become a liability for human survival (although its impact on reproductive success is more difficult to gauge). Organisms' environments often undergo changes so that adaptations that were once beneficial become obsolete. As you will see, evolutionary psychologists have found that many aspects of human nature reflect the adaptive demands faced by our ancient ancestors rather than contemporary demands. Of course, as natural selection continues to work, these formerly adaptive traits should gradually be eliminated, but the process is extremely slow.

In recent decades, theorists have broadened Darwin's original concept of reproductive fitness to better explain a variety of phenomena. For example, traditional evolutionary theory had difficulty explaining self-sacrifice. If organisms try to maximize their reproductive success, why does a blackbird risk death to signal the approach of a hawk to others in the flock? And why would a tribesman risk life and limb to race into a burning hut to save young children? In 1964, W. D. Hamilton proposed the theory of inclusive fitness to explain the paradox of self-sacrifice. According to Hamilton, an organism may contribute to passing on its genes by sacrificing itself to save others that share the same genes.

Helping behaviour that evolves as members of a species protect their own offspring, for example, can be extended to other, more distantly related members of the species. Thus, *inclusive fitness* is the sum of an individual's own reproductive success plus the effects the organism has on the reproductive success of related others. The concept of inclusive fitness suggests that the probability of self-sacrifice decreases as the degree of relatedness between a helper and potential recipients declines, a prediction that has been supported in studies of organisms as diverse as ground squirrels (Sherman, 1981) and humans (Burnstein, Crandall, & Kitayama, 1994).

Behaviours as Adaptive Traits

Scholarly analyses of evolution have focused primarily on the evolution of *physical characteristics* in the animal kingdom, but from the very beginning, Darwin recognized that natural selection was applicable to *behavioural traits* as well. Studying the evolution of behaviour is more difficult than studying the evolution of physical traits because behaviour is more transient—crucial behaviours by an organism may occur infrequently and may not last long. For example, female wood frogs are sexually receptive just one night per year. Additionally, although the fossil record *can* leave clues about past organisms' behaviour (such as its prey or nesting habits), it leaves much more detailed information about organisms' physical characteristics. Nonetheless, it is clear that a species' typical patterns of behaviour often reflect evolutionary solutions to adaptive problems.

Let's look at some additional examples of how evolution has shaped organisms' behaviour. Avoiding predators is a nearly universal problem for organisms. Because of natural selection, many species, such as the grasshopper, have developed physical characteristics that allow them to blend in with their environments, making detection by predators more difficult. Many organisms also engage in elaborative *behavioural manoeuvres* to hide themselves. For example, the grasshopper pictured on this page has dug itself a small trench in which to hide and has used its midlegs to pull pebbles over its back (Alcock, 1998). This clever hiding behaviour is just as much a product of evolution as the grasshopper's remarkable camouflage.

The "stotting" behaviour exhibited by Thomson's gazelles when they spot a cheetah is another example of a behavioural adaptation. The cheetah is a feared predator that elicits evasive actions in Thomson's gazelles. But as the gazelles start to flee, they often slow up briefly to *stot*—that is, they jump high into the air with all four legs held straight and their white rump fully displayed. Slowing up when fleeing may not sound adaptive, but research has revealed that gazelles stot to signal to the cheetah that they have spotted the predator, they are off and running, and they will be difficult to catch. Consistent with this interpretation, stotting increases the likelihood that a cheetah will abandon its pursuit of a gazelle (Caro, 1986). Thus, stotting is a behavioural adaptation in that it enhances the probability of survival by

WEB LINK 3.7

Human Behavior and Evolution Society
The HBES is an interdisciplinary organization devoted to the exploration of human behaviour from the perspective of evolutionary theory. This site provides a particularly rich set of links to published and online materials and organizations dealing with the evolutionary perspective on behaviour.

The behaviour that helps the grasshopper on the left hide from predators is a product of evolution, just like the physical characteristics that help it to blend in with its surroundings. As explained in the text, the stotting behaviour exhibited by Thomson's gazelles is adaptive in that it is intended to deter the pursuit of predators.

Courtesy of John Alcock

EcoPrint/Shutterstock

deterring pursuit and saves precious energy that may be needed to evade another predator.

Many behavioural adaptations are designed to improve organisms' chances of reproductive success. Consider, for instance, the wide variety of species in which females actively choose which male to mate with. In many such species, females demand material goods and services from males in return for copulation opportunities. For example, in one type of moth, males have to spend hours extracting sodium from mud puddles, which they then transfer to prospective mates, who use it to supply their larvae with an important nutritional element (Smedley & Eisner, 1996). In the black-tipped hangingfly, females insist on a nuptial gift of food before they mate. They reject suitors bringing unpalatable food, and they tie the length of subsequent copulation to the size of the nuptial gift (Thornhill, 1976).

Putting It in Perspective: Themes 1, 4, and 6

Three of our seven themes stood out in this chapter: (1) Heredity and environment jointly influence behaviour, (2) behaviour is determined by multiple causes, and (3) psychology is empirical. Let's look at each of these points.

In Chapter 1, when it was first emphasized that heredity and environment jointly shape behaviour, you may have been a little perplexed about how your genes could be responsible for your sarcastic wit or your interest in art. In fact, there are no genes for behaviour per se. Experts do not expect to find genes for sarcasm or artistic interest, for example. Insofar as your hereditary endowment plays a role in your behaviour, it does so *indirectly* by moulding the physiological machine that you work with. Thus, your genes influence your physiological makeup, which in turn influences your personality, temperament, intelligence, interests, and other traits. Bear in mind, however, that genetic factors do not operate in a vacuum. Genes exert their effects in an environmental context. The impact of genetic makeup depends on environment, and the impact of environment depends on genetic makeup.

The empirical nature of psychology was apparent in the numerous discussions of the specialized research methods used to study the physiological bases of behaviour. As you know, the empirical approach depends on precise observation. Throughout this chapter, you've seen how investigators have come up with innovative methods to observe and measure elusive phenomena such as electrical activity in the brain, neural impulses, brain function, cerebral specialization, and the impact of heredity on behaviour. The point is that empirical methods are the lifeblood of the scientific enterprise. When researchers figure out how to better observe something, their new methods usually facilitate major advances in our scientific knowledge. That is why brain-imaging techniques and genetic mapping hold such exciting promise.

The importance of empiricism will also be apparent in the upcoming Personal Application and Critical Thinking Application. In both, you'll see that it is important to learn to distinguish between scientific findings and conjecture based on those findings.

PREVIEW QUESTIONS

▶ How did this chapter demonstrate that heredity and environment shape behaviour interactively?

▶ How did this chapter illustrate multifactorial causation?

▶ How did this chapter clarify the empirical nature of psychology?

REVIEW OF KEY POINTS

▷ Darwin argued that if a heritable trait contributes to an organism's survival or reproductive success, organisms with that trait should produce more offspring than those without the trait and that the prevalence of that trait should gradually increase over generations—thanks to natural selection.

▷ Because of the gradual, incremental nature of evolution, adaptations sometimes linger in a population even though they no longer provide a survival or reproductive advantage. Hamilton proposed the theory of inclusive fitness to explain the paradox of self-sacrifice.

▷ Theorists have focused primarily on the evolution of *physical characteristics* in the animal kingdom, but from the very beginning, Darwin recognized that natural selection was applicable to *behavioural traits* as well.

▷ Three of the book's unifying themes stand out in this chapter. First, we saw how heredity interacts with experience to govern behaviour. Second, the discussions of biological factors underlying schizophrenia highlighted the multifactorial causation of behaviour. Third, we saw how innovations in research methods often lead to advances in knowledge, underscoring the empirical nature of psychology.

Evaluating the Concept of "Two Minds in One"

Answer the following "true" or "false."

___ **1** The right and left brains give people two minds in one.

___ **2** Each half of the brain has its own special mode of thinking.

___ **3** Some people are left-brained while others are right-brained.

___ **4** Schools should devote more effort to teaching the overlooked right side of the brain.

Do people have two minds in one that think differently? Do some people depend on one side of the brain more than the other? Is the right side of the brain neglected? These questions are too complex to resolve with a simple true or false, but in this Application, we'll take a closer look at the issues involved in these proposed applications of the findings on cerebral specialization. You'll learn that some of these ideas are plausible, but in many cases the hype has outstripped the evidence.

Earlier, we described Roger Sperry's Nobel Prize–winning research with split-brain patients whose right and left hemispheres were disconnected (to reduce epileptic seizures). The split-brain studies showed that the previously underrated right hemisphere has some special talents of its own. This discovery detonated an explosion of research on cerebral laterality.

Cerebral Specialization and Cognitive Processes

PSYKTREK 2f

Using a variety of methods, scientists have compiled mountains of data on the specialized abilities of the right and left hemispheres. These findings have led to extensive theorizing about how the right and left brains might be related to cognitive processes. Some of the more intriguing ideas include the following:

1. *The two hemispheres are specialized to process different types of cognitive tasks* (Corballis, 1991; Ornstein, 1977). The findings of many researchers have been widely interpreted as showing that the left hemisphere handles verbal tasks, including language, speech, writing, math, and logic, while the right hemisphere handles nonverbal tasks, including spatial problems, music, art, fantasy, and creativity. These conclusions have attracted a great deal of public interest and media attention. For example, Figure 3.31 shows a *Newsweek* artist's depiction of how the brain divides its work.

2. *Each hemisphere has its own independent stream of consciousness* (Bogen, 1985, 2000; Pucetti, 1981). For instance, Joseph Bogen has asserted, "Pending further evidence, I believe that each of us has two minds in one person" (Hooper & Teresi, 1986, p. 221). Supposedly, this duality of consciousness goes largely unnoticed because of the considerable overlap between the experiences of each independent mind. Ultimately, though, the apparent unity of consciousness is but an illusion.

3. *The two hemispheres have different modes of thinking* (Banich & Heller, 1998; Davis & Dean, 2005). According to this notion, the documented differences between the hemispheres in dealing with verbal and nonverbal materials are due to more basic differences in *how* the hemispheres process information. The standard version of this theory holds that the reason the left hemisphere handles verbal material well is that it is analytic, abstract, rational, logical, and linear. In contrast, the right hemisphere is thought to be better equipped to handle spatial and musical material because it is synthetic, concrete, nonrational, intuitive, and holistic. Robert Ornstein (1997) characterizes hemispheric differences in cognitive processing somewhat differently, asserting that the left hemisphere focuses on details while the right hemisphere responds to global patterns and the big picture.

4. *People vary in their reliance on one hemisphere as opposed to the other* (Bakan, 1971; Pinker, 2005). Allegedly, some people

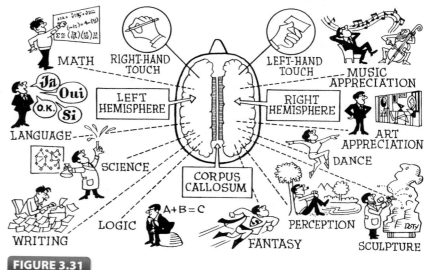

HOW THE BRAIN DIVIDES ITS WORK

FIGURE 3.31

Popular conceptions of hemispheric specialization.

As this *Newsweek* diagram illustrates, depictions of hemispheric specialization in the popular press have often been oversimplified.

Source: Cartoon courtesy of Roy Doty

are "left-brained." Their greater dependence on their left hemisphere supposedly makes them analytical, rational, and logical. Other people are "right-brained." Their greater use of their right hemisphere supposedly makes them intuitive, holistic, and irrational. Being right-brained or left-brained is thought to explain many personal characteristics, such as whether an individual likes to read, is good with maps, or enjoys music. This notion of "brainedness" has even been used to explain occupational choice. Supposedly, right-brained people are more likely to become artists or musicians, while left-brained people are more likely to become writers or scientists.

5. *Schools should place more emphasis on teaching the right side of the brain* (Kitchens, 1991; Prince, 1978). "A real reform of the educational system will not occur until individual teachers learn to understand the true duality of their students' minds," says Thomas Blakeslee (1980, p. 59). Those sympathetic to his view assert that schools overemphasize logical, analytical left-hemisphere thinking (required by English, math, and science) while short-changing intuitive, holistic right-hemisphere thinking (required by art and music). These educators have concluded that modern schools turn out an excess of left-brained graduates. They advocate curriculum reform to strengthen the right side of the brain in their students. This line of thinking has also spawned quite a collection of popular self-help books, such as *Whole-Brain Thinking* (Wonder, 1992), *Unleashing the Right Side of the Brain* (Williams & Stockmyer, 1987), and *Workout for the Balanced Brain* (Carter & Russell, 2001).

Complexities and Qualifications

The ideas just outlined are the source of considerable debate among psychologists and neuroscientists. These ideas are intriguing and have clearly captured the imagination of the general public. However, the research on cerebral specialization is complex, and doubts have been raised about many of these ideas (Efron, 1990; Springer & Deutsch, 1998). Let's examine each point.

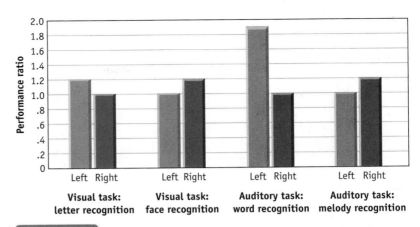

FIGURE 3.32

Relative superiority of one brain hemisphere over the other in studies of perceptual asymmetry.

These performance ratios from a study by Doreen Kimura (1973) show the degree to which one hemisphere was "superior" to the other on each type of task in one study of normal participants. For example, the right hemisphere was 20 percent better than the left hemisphere in quickly recognizing melodic patterns (ratio: 1.2 to 1). Most differences in the performance of the two hemispheres are quite small. (Data from Kimura, 1973)

1. There *is* ample evidence that the right and left hemispheres are specialized to handle different types of cognitive tasks, *but only to a degree* (Brown & Kosslyn, 1993; Corballis, 2003). While at the University of Western Ontario, Doreen Kimura (1973) compared the abilities of the right and left hemispheres to quickly recognize letters, words, faces, and melodies in a series of perceptual asymmetry studies, like those described earlier in the chapter. She found that the superiority of one hemisphere over the other was usually quite modest, as you can see in Figure 3.32, which shows superiority ratios for four cognitive tasks.

Furthermore, in normal individuals, the hemispheres don't work alone. As Hellige (1993a) notes, "In the intact brain, it is unlikely that either hemisphere is ever completely uninvolved in ongoing processing" (p. 23). Most tasks probably engage *both* hemispheres, albeit to different degrees (Beeman & Chiarello, 1998; Ornstein, 1997). For instance, imagine that you are asked the following question: "In what direction are you headed if you start north and make two right turns and a left turn?" In answering this question, you're confronted with a *spatial* task that should engage the right hemisphere. However, first you have to process the wording of the question, a *language* task that should engage the left hemisphere.

Furthermore, people differ in their patterns of cerebral specialization (Springer & Deutsch, 1998). Some people display little specialization—that is, their hemispheres seem to have equal abilities on various types of tasks. Others even reverse the usual specialization, so that verbal processing might be housed in the right hemisphere. These unusual patterns are especially common among left-handed people (Josse & Tzourio-Mazoyer, 2004). For example, when Rasmussen and Milner (1977) tested subjects for the localization of speech, they found bilateral representation in 15 percent of the left-handers. They found a reversal of the usual specialization (speech handled by the right hemisphere) in another 15 percent of the left-handed subjects (see Figure 3.33). Accomplished musicians may be another exception to the rule. Two recent studies have found that experienced musicians exhibit more bilateral cerebral organization than comparable nonmusicians (Gibson, Folley, & Park, 2009; Patson et al., 2007). This bilaterality may develop because musicians often have to use both hands independently to play their instruments. If this explanation is accurate, it would provide another example of how experience can shape brain organization. In any event, it is clear that the functional specialization of the cerebral hemispheres is not set in concrete.

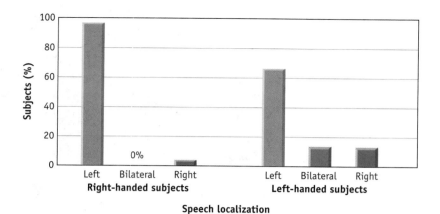

FIGURE 3.33

Handedness and patterns of speech localization.

Left-handed people tend to show more variety in cerebral specialization and more bilateral representation than right-handers. For example, speech processing is almost always localized in the left hemisphere of right-handed subjects. However, Rasmussen and Milner (1977) found the usual pattern of speech localization in only 70 percent of their left-handed subjects. (Data from Rasmussen & Milner, 1977)

2. The evidence for the idea that people have a separate stream of consciousness in each hemisphere is weak. There *are* clear signs of such duality among *split-brain patients* (Bogen, 1990; Mark, 1996). But this duality is probably a unique by-product of the radical procedure that they have undergone—the surgical disconnection of their hemispheres (Bradshaw, 1981). In fact, many theorists have been impressed by the degree to which even split-brain patients mostly experience *unity* of consciousness. There is little empirical basis for the idea that people have two independent streams of awareness neatly housed in the right and left halves of the brain.

3. Similarly, there is little direct evidence to support the notion that each hemisphere has its own mode of thinking, or *cognitive style* (Bradshaw, 1989; Corballis, 2007). This notion is plausible and there is some supportive evidence, but the evidence is inconsistent and more research is needed (Gordon, 1990; Reuter-Lorenz & Miller, 1998). One key problem with this idea is that aspects of cognitive style have proven difficult to define and measure (Brownell & Gardner, 1981). For instance, there is debate about the meaning of analytic versus synthetic thinking, or linear versus holistic thinking.

4. The evidence on the assertion that some people are left-brained while others are right-brained is inconclusive at best (Hellige, 1990). This notion has some plausibility—*if* it means only that some people consistently display more activation of one hemisphere than the other. However, researchers have yet to develop reliable measures of these possible "preferences" in cerebral activation. Hence, there are no convincing data linking brainedness to musical ability, occupational choice, or the like (Springer & Deutsch, 1998).

5. The idea that schools should be reformed to better exercise the right side of the brain represents intriguing but wild speculation. In neurologically intact people, it is impossible to teach just one hemisphere at a time (J. Levy, 1985). Many sound arguments exist for reforming schools to encourage more holistic, intuitive thinking, but these arguments have nothing to do with cerebral specialization.

In summary, the theories linking cerebral specialization to cognitive processes are highly speculative. There's nothing wrong with theoretical speculation. Unfortunately, the tentative, conjectural nature of these ideas about cerebral specialization has become lost in the popular book descriptions of research on the right and left hemispheres (Coren, 1992). Popular writers continue to churn out allegedly scientific books, applying brain lateralization concepts to a host of new topics on which there often is little or no real evidence. Thus, one can find books on how to have right-brain sex (Wells, 1991), develop right-brain social skills (Snyder, 1989), lose weight with a right-brain diet (Sommer, 1987), become better organized by relying on the right hemisphere (Silber, 2004), and maximize one's leadership effectiveness by shifting between right- and left-brain modes of leadership (Decosterd, 2008). Commenting on this popularization, Hooper and Teresi (1986) note, "A widespread cult of the right brain ensued, and the duplex house that Sperry built grew into the Kmart of brain science. Today our hairdresser lectures us about the 'Two Hemispheres of the Brain'. . ." (p. 223). Cerebral specialization is an important and intriguing area of research. However, it is unrealistic to expect that the hemispheric divisions in the brain will provide a biological explanation for every dichotomy or polarity in modes of thinking.

REVIEW OF KEY POINTS

▸ Split-brain research stimulated speculation about relationships between cerebral specialization and cognitive processes. Some theorists believe that each hemisphere has its own stream of consciousness and mode of thinking, which are applied to specific types of cognitive tasks.

▸ Some theorists also believe that people vary in their reliance on the right and left halves of the brain and that schools should work more to exercise the right half of the brain.

▸ The cerebral hemispheres *are* specialized for handling different cognitive tasks, but only to a degree, as most tasks engage both hemispheres. Moreover, people vary in their patterns of hemispheric specialization.

▸ Evidence for duality in consciousness divided along hemispheric lines is weak. Evidence on whether people vary in brainedness and whether the two hemispheres vary in cognitive style is inconclusive.

▸ There is no way to teach only one hemisphere of the brain, so a "right-brain curriculum" is pointless. Popular ideas about the right and left brain have gone far beyond the actual research findings.

Building Better Brains: The Perils of Extrapolation

Summarizing the implications of recent research in neuroscience, science writer Ronald Kotulak (1996) concluded, "The first three years of a child's life are critically important to brain development" (pp. ix–x). In some countries, well-intended educational groups and elected officials have argued for the creation of schools for infants on the grounds that enriched educational experiences during infancy will lead to enhanced neural development.

What are these practical, new discoveries about the brain that will permit parents and educators to optimize infants' brain development? Well, we will discuss the pertinent research momentarily, but it is not as new or as practical as suggested in many quarters. Unfortunately, as we saw in our discussion of research on hemispheric specialization, the hype in the media has greatly outstripped the realities of what scientists have learned in the laboratory (Chance, 2001).

This focus on the brain led many child-care advocates and educational reformers to use research in neuroscience as the rationale for the policies they sought to promote, as a host of books on "brain-based learning" were published (see Jensen, 2000; Sousa, 2000; Sprenger, 2001). The people advocating these ideas have good intentions, but the neuroscience rationale has been stretched to the breaking point. The result? An enlightening case study in the perils of overextrapolation.

The Key Findings on Neural Development

The education and child-care reformers who have used brain science as the basis for their campaigns have primarily cited two key findings: the discovery of critical periods in neural development and the demonstration that rats raised in "enriched environments" have more synapses than rats raised in "impoverished environments." Let's look at each of these findings.

A *critical period* is a limited time span in the development of an organism when it is optimal for certain capacities to emerge because the organism is especially responsive to certain experiences: The seminal research on critical periods in neural development was conducted by Torsten Wiesel and David Hubel (1963, 1965) in the 1960s. They showed that if an eye of a newborn kitten is sutured shut early in its development (typically the first four to six weeks), the kitten will become permanently blind in that eye, but if the eye is covered for the same amount of time at later ages (after four months) blindness does not result. Such studies show that certain types of visual input are necessary during a critical period of development or else neural pathways between the eye and brain will not form properly. Basically, what happens is that the inactive synapses from the closed eye are displaced by the active synapses from the open eye. Critical periods have been found for other aspects of neural development and in other species, but a great deal remains to

be learned. Based on this type of research, some educational and child-care reformers have argued that the first three years of life are a critical period for human neural development.

The pioneering work on environment and brain development was begun in the 1960s by Mark Rosenzweig and his colleagues (1961, 1962). They raised some rats in an impoverished environment (housed individually in small, barren cages) and other rats in an enriched environment (housed in groups of 10 to 12 in larger cages, with a variety of objects available for exploration), as shown in Figure 3.34. They found that the rats raised in the enriched environment performed better on problem-solving tasks than the impoverished rats and had slightly heavier brains and a thicker cerebral cortex in some areas of the brain. Subsequent research by William Greenough demonstrated that enriched environments resulted in heavier and thicker cortical areas by virtue of producing denser dendritic branching, more synaptic contacts,

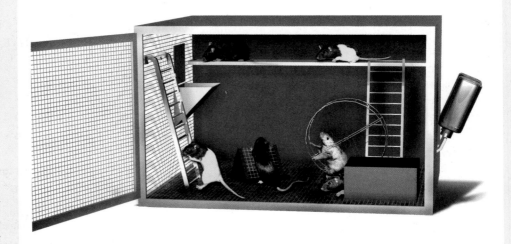

FIGURE 3.34

Enriched environments in the study of rats' neural development.

In the studies by Rosenzweig and colleagues (1961, 1962), rats raised in an impoverished environment were housed alone in small cages, whereas rats raised in enriched environments were housed in groups and were given playthings that were changed daily. Although the enriched conditions provided more stimulating environments than laboratory rats normally experience, they may not be any more stimulating than rats' natural habitats. Thus, the "enriched" condition may reveal more about the importance of normal stimulation than about the benefits of extra stimulation (Gopnik, Meltzoff, & Kuhl, 1999).

The Biological Bases of Behaviour

and richer neural networks (Greenough, 1975; Greenough & Volkmar, 1973). Based on this type of research, some child-care reformers have argued that human infants need to be brought up in enriched environments during the critical period before age three, to promote synapse formation and to optimize the development of their emerging neural circuits.

The findings on critical periods and the effects of enriched environments were genuine breakthroughs in neuroscience, but they certainly aren't *new* findings, as suggested by various political action groups. Moreover, one can raise many doubts about whether this research can serve as a meaningful guide for decisions about parenting practices, day-care programs, educational policies, and welfare reform (Thompson & Nelson, 2001). We discuss the research on critical periods in more detail in Chapter 11 on page 512.

The Risks of Overextrapolation

Extrapolation occurs when an effect is estimated by extending beyond some known values or conditions. Extrapolation is a normal process, but some extrapolations are conservative, plausible projections drawn from directly relevant data, whereas others are wild leaps of speculation based on loosely related data. The extrapolations made regarding the educational implications of critical periods and environmental effects on synapse formation are highly conjectural *overextrapolations*. The studies that highlighted the possible importance of early experience in animals have all used extreme conditions to make their comparisons, such as depriving an animal of all visual input or raising it in stark isolation. In light of the findings, it seems plausible to speculate that children probably need normal stimulation to experience normal brain development. However, great difficulty arises when these findings are extended to conclude that adding *more* stimulation to a normal environment will be beneficial to brain development (Shatz, 1992).

The ease with which people fall into the trap of overextrapolating has been particularly apparent in recent recommendations that infants should listen to classical music to enhance their brain development. These recommendations have been derived from two studies that showed that university students' performance on spatial reasoning tasks was enhanced slightly for about 10–15 minutes after listening to a brief Mozart recording (Rauscher, Shaw, & Ky, 1993, 1995). This peculiar finding, dubbed the "Mozart effect," has proven difficult to replicate, as shown in studies by researchers from the University of Toronto (Thompson, Schellenberg, & Husain, 2001) and others (Gray & Della Sala, 2007; McKelvie & Low, 2002; Steele, 2003). The pertinent point here is that there was no research on how classical music affects *infants*, no research relating classical music to *brain development*, and no research on anyone showing *lasting* effects. Nonetheless, many people were quick to extrapolate the shaky findings on the Mozart effect to infants' brain development. Ironically, there is much better evidence linking *musical training* to enhanced cognitive performance. Studies have found a thought-provoking association between measures of intelligence and the extent of individuals' exposure to music lessons (Schellenberg, 2004, 2005, 2006). Of course, if you think critically about this correlation, it might only mean that brighter youngsters are more likely to take music lessons (researchers are still working to sort it all out).

As discussed in Chapter 1, thinking critically about issues often involves asking questions such as: What is missing from this debate? Is there any contradictory evidence? In this case, there is some contradictory evidence that is worthy of consideration. The basis for advocating infant educational programs is the belief that the brain is malleable during the hypothesized critical period of birth to age three but not at later ages. However, Greenough's work on synaptic formation and other lines of research suggest that the brain remains somewhat malleable throughout life, responding to stimulation into old age (Thompson & Nelson, 2001). Thus, advocates for the aged could just as readily argue for new educational initiatives for the elderly to help them maximize their intellectual potential. Another problem is the implicit assumption that greater synaptic density is associated with greater intelligence. As noted earlier in the chapter, there is evidence that infant animals and humans begin life with an overabundance of synaptic connections and that learning involves selective *pruning* of inactive synapses (Huttenlocher, 2002; Rakic, Bourgeois, & Goldman-Rakic, 1994). Thus, in the realm of synapses, more may *not* be better.

In conclusion, there may be many valid reasons for increasing educational programs for infants, but research in neuroscience does not appear to provide a clear rationale for much in the way of specific infant care policies (Bruer, 2002). One problem in evaluating these proposals is that few people want to argue against high-quality child care or education. But modern societies need to allocate their limited resources to the programs that appear most likely to have beneficial effects, so even intuitively appealing ideas need to be subjected to critical scrutiny.

TABLE 3.2	Critical Thinking Skills Discussed in This Application	
Skill	**Description**	
Understanding the limits	The critical thinker appreciates that extrapolations are based on certain assumptions, vary in plausibility, and ultimately involve speculation.	
Looking for contradictory evidence	In evaluating the evidence presented on an issue, the critical thinker attempts to look for contradictory evidence that may have been left out of the debate.	

Key Ideas

Communication in the Nervous System

● Neurons are the basic communication links in the nervous system. They normally transmit a neural impulse (an electric current) along an axon to a synapse with another neuron. The neural impulse is a brief change in a neuron's electrical charge that moves along an axon. It is an all-or-none event.

● Action potentials trigger the release of chemicals called *neurotransmitters* that diffuse across a synapse to communicate with other neurons. Transmitters bind with receptors in the postsynaptic cell membrane, causing excitatory or inhibitory PSPs. Most neurons are linked in neural pathways, circuits, and networks.

● ACh plays a key role in muscular movement. Disturbances in the activity of the monoamine transmitters have been related to the development of depression and schizophrenia. GABA is a widely distributed inhibitory transmitter. Endorphins contribute to the relief of pain.

Organization of the Nervous System

● The nervous system can be divided into the central nervous system and the peripheral nervous system. The central nervous system consists of the brain and spinal cord.

● The peripheral nervous system can be subdivided into the somatic nervous system, which connects to muscles and sensory receptors, and the autonomic nervous system, which connects to blood vessels, smooth muscles, and glands.

Looking Inside the Brain: Research Methods

● The EEG can record broad patterns of electrical activity in the brain. Lesioning involves destroying a piece of the brain. Another technique is electrical stimulation of areas in the brain in order to activate them. In recent years, new brain-imaging procedures have been developed, including CT scans, PET scans, MRI scans, and fMRI scans.

The Brain and Behaviour

● The brain has three major regions: the hindbrain, midbrain, and forebrain. Structures in the hindbrain and midbrain handle essential functions. The thalamus is primarily a relay station. The hypothalamus is involved in the regulation of basic biological drives such as hunger and sex.

● The limbic system is involved in emotion, motivation, and memory. The cortex is the cerebrum's convoluted outer layer, which is subdivided into occipital, parietal, temporal, and frontal lobes. The brain's organization is somewhat malleable.

Right Brain/Left Brain: Cerebral Laterality

● The cerebrum is divided into right and left hemispheres connected by the corpus callosum. Studies of split-brain patients and perceptual asymmetries have revealed that the right and left halves of the brain each have unique talents.

The Endocrine System: Another Way to Communicate

● The endocrine system consists of the glands that secrete hormones, which are chemicals involved in the regulation of basic bodily processes. The control centres for the endocrine system are the hypothalamus and the pituitary gland.

Heredity and Behaviour: Is It All in the Genes?

● The basic units of genetic transmission are genes housed on chromosomes. Most behavioural qualities appear to involve polygenic inheritance. Researchers assess hereditary influence through a variety of methods, including family studies, twin studies, adoption studies, and genetic mapping.

The Evolutionary Bases of Behaviour

● Darwin argued that if a heritable trait contributes to an organism's survival or reproductive success, organisms with that trait should produce more offspring than those without the trait and the prevalence of that trait should gradually increase over generations—thanks to natural selection.

● Darwin recognized from the beginning that natural selection was applicable to behavioural traits as well as physical traits.

Putting It in Perspective: Themes 1, 4, and 6

● Three of the book's unifying themes stand out in this chapter. First, we saw how heredity interacts with experience to govern behaviour. Second, the discussions of biological factors underlying schizophrenia highlighted the multifactorial causation of behaviour. Third, we saw how innovations in research methods often lead to advances in knowledge, underscoring the empirical nature of psychology.

Personal Application • Evaluating the Concept of "Two Minds in One"

● The cerebral hemispheres are specialized for handling different cognitive tasks, but only to a degree, and people vary in their patterns of hemispheric specialization. Evidence on whether people vary in brainedness and whether the two hemispheres vary in cognitive style is inconclusive.

Critical Thinking Application • Building Better Brains: The Perils of Extrapolation

● Although some education and child-care reformers have used research in neuroscience as the basis for their campaigns, research has not demonstrated that birth to age three is a critical period for human neural development or that specific enrichment programs can enhance brain development. These assertions are highly conjectural overextrapolations from existing data.

Key Terms

Absolute refractory period, 88
Action potential, 88
Adaptation, 125
Adoption studies, 122
Afferent nerve fibres, 96
Agonist, 93
Antagonist, 93
Autonomic nervous system (ANS), 96
Axon, 87
Behavioural genetics, 118
Central nervous system (CNS), 97
Cerebral cortex, 109
Cerebral hemispheres, 109
Cerebrospinal fluid (CSF), 97
Chromosomes, 118
Corpus callosum, 109
Critical period, 131
Dendrites, 87
Dominant gene, 119
Efferent nerve fibres, 96
Electrical stimulation of the brain (ESB), 100
Electroencephalograph (EEG), 98
Endocrine system, 116
Endorphins, 94
Epigenetics, 123
Excitatory PSP, 90
Family studies, 120

Fitness, 124
Forebrain, 107
Fraternal (dizygotic) twins, 121
Genes, 118
Genetic mapping, 122
Genotype, 120
Glia, 87
Heterozygous condition, 119
Hindbrain, 105
Homozygous condition, 119
Hormones, 116
Hypothalamus, 107
Identical (monozygotic) twins, 121
Inclusive fitness, 126
Inhibitory PSP, 90
Lesioning, 100
Limbic system, 107
Midbrain, 107
Mutation, 125
Myelin sheath, 87
Natural selection, 124
Nerves, 95
Neurogenesis, 111
Neurons, 86
Neurotransmitters, 89
Oxytocin, 117
Parasympathetic division, 97
Perceptual asymmetries, 115
Peripheral nervous system, 95

Key People

1. A neural impulse is initiated when a neuron's charge momentarily becomes less negative. What is the name of this event?
   A. action potential
   B. resting potential
   C. impulse facilitation
   D. refractory period

2. How does a neuron convey information about a strong stimulus (like a bright light) compared to a weak stimulus (like a dim light)?
   A. It sends larger action potentials to other neurons.
   B. It has a higher rate of action potentials.
   C. It has excitatory rather than inhibitory action potentials.
   D. It communicates along the dendrite rather than at the synapse.

3. If you wanted to study the process of reuptake of neurotransmitters, which of the following locations would be the right place to look?
   A. the synapse
   B. the myelin sheath
   C. the receptor
   D. the soma

4. Which of the following pairs of neurotransmitters are known to both be associated with movement of the body?
   A. acetylcholine and dopamine
   B. serotonin and norepinephrine
   C. epinephrine and GABA
   D. epinephrine and norepinephrine

5. Jim barely avoided a head-on collision on a narrow road. His heart pounded, his hands shook, and he started to sweat as part of the body's fight-or-flight response. Which of the following parts of the nervous system controls this response?
   A. the empathetic division of the peripheral nervous system
   B. the parasympathetic division of the autonomic nervous system
   C. the somatic division of the peripheral nervous system
   D. the sympathetic division of the autonomic nervous system

6. Which of the following constitute the hindbrain?
   A. endocrine system and the limbic system
   B. reticular formation
   C. thalamus, hypothalamus, and cerebrum
   D. cerebellum, medulla, and pons

7. Neural impulses from the eyes ultimately reach the primary visual cortex. Before arriving at the primary visual cortex these neural impulses must first pass through which part of the brain?
   A. amygdala
   B. hypothalamus
   C. thalamus
   D. pons

8. Which lobe of the brain contains cortex devoted to basic auditory processing?
   A. frontal
   B. temporal
   C. parietal
   D. occipital

9. If a patient has profound difficulty in producing spoken language, then which of the following parts of the brain is likely damaged?
   A. the cerebellum
   B. Sperry's area
   C. Broca's area
   D. Wernicke's area

10. If you wanted a clear three-dimensional image of brain structure, which of the following recording methods would you use?
    A. electroencephalography (EEG)
    B. positron emission tomography (PET)
    C. computerized tomography (CT)
    D. magnetic resonance imaging (MRI)

11. Which of the following is related to the nervous system in the same way that hormones are related to the endocrine system?
    A. nerves
    B. synapses
    C. neurotransmitters
    D. action potentials

12. Jenny has brown hair and blue eyes, and is 175 cm tall. She is allergic to cats, and enjoys playing sports. Which of the following terms is used for this description of Jenny?
    A. genotype
    B. somatotype
    C. humanotype
    D. phenotype

13. Which of the following would provide evidence that a trait has a strong genetic influence?
    A. Identical twins are more likely than fraternal twins to both have the trait.
    B. Fraternal twins are more likely than other siblings to both have the trait.
    C. Male siblings are more likely than female siblings (who have no Y chromosome) to both have the trait.
    D. Adopted siblings are more likely than strangers to both have the trait.

14. Which of the following is the name for a spontaneous, heritable change, or error, in DNA replication?
    A. genetic drift
    B. gene flow
    C. adaptation
    D. mutation

15. Which of the following assertions about brain hemisphere specialization has the strongest empirical evidence?
    A. Each hemisphere is specialized for different types of cognitive tasks.
    B. A separate stream of consciousness occurs in each hemisphere.
    C. Each hemisphere has its own cognitive style.
    D. The dominance of one hemisphere over another determines whether people are right-brained, or left-brained.

See Appendix A for answers to this Practice Test.

On the Web

▶ **CourseMate**

Go to this site to find online resources directly linked to your book, including more quizzes, a glossary, flash cards, videos, and more!

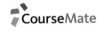

▶ **CengageNow**

Go to this site for the link to CengageNOW™, your one-stop study shop. Take a pre-test for this chapter and CengageNOW™ will generate a personalized study plan based on your test results! The study plan will identify the topics you need to review and direct you to online resources to help you master those topics. You can then take a post-test to help you determine the concepts you have mastered and what you still need to work on.

▶ **Aplia**

Aplia™ is an online interactive learning solution that helps you improve comprehension—and your grade—by integrating a variety of media and tools such as video, tutorials, practice tests, and an interactive e-book.

CHAPTER 4

Sensation and Perception

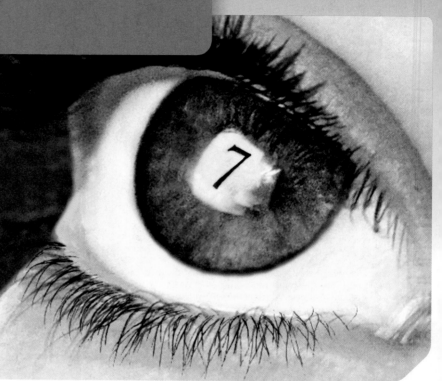

© Colette R. Orfeo, Athabasca University

While most students are probably aware of the fact that there is a Canadian astronaut program and that some of our astronauts have flown aboard the space shuttles into space, perhaps fewer know about the existence of the Canadian Space Agency and its role in coordinating Canadian involvement in space exploration and space-related research.

The Canadian Space Agency's mandate includes, among other things, the objective of promoting and facilitating space-related research. One of the first Canadian experiments carried out was research on the manufacturing of mirrors for use in space. If you can believe it, the experiment was designed by two Ottawa high school students. It was carried out in 1985 on the first flight of space shuttle *Atlantis*.

Canadian space psychology is a rapidly developing area of research and, according to the University of British Columbia's Peter Suedfeld (2003), includes examination of such matters as the effects of isolated and extreme environments and the nature and effects of multicultural interactions. Also important in understanding how astronauts will function in space is recent sensation/perception research. We all would agree that good hand–eye coordination is critical in space when using the Canadarm or docking with space stations. But the evidence suggests that astronauts in space experience a reduction in their hand–eye coordination. Canadian researchers are examining the reasons for this effect (Canadian Space Agency, n.d., c).

The space shuttle flights themselves have been the scene of some of these experiments. For example, in 1998, experiments designed by York University psychologist Ian Howard in collaboration with Massachusetts Institute of Technology's Charles Oman (Canadian Space Agency, n.d., c) examined the role of visual cues in spatial orientation. The research was directed at an important problem facing astronauts in space: While on earth, gravity provides important cues for people's judgment concerning the spatial orientation of their bodies (which way is up?), in space, astronauts can't depend on gravity as a cue—they lose sense of what is up and what is down. Among other problems, this can lead to disorientation, difficulty in task performance, and motion sickness. There may be discontinuity between sensory information derived from the vestibular system (organs in the inner ear) and visual cues. The research was designed, in part, to examine the role of vision in determining body position and sensory adaptation to microgravity. Some phases of the research were carried out using NASA's virtual environment generator, which was worn by the astronauts and which created a virtual visual environment (Canadian Space Agency, n.d., c). Interest in space-related research by sensation/perception psychologists has continued (e.g., Harris et al., 2010a;

Marc Garneau and Roberta Bondar were among the first Canadian astronauts to have joined one of NASA's space missions.

Sensation and Perception

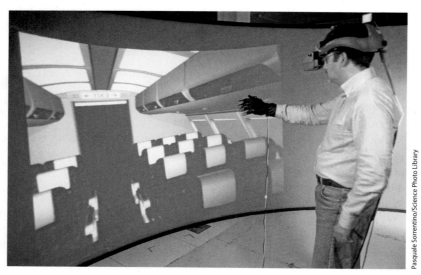

The Canadian Space Agency and NASA collaborated on an investigation of the role of visual cues in spatial orientation using the VEG (virtual environment generator) headgear.

Pasquale Sorrentino/Science Photo Library

3-D techniques were put to impressive use by James Cameron's 2009 Academy award–winning film *Avatar*. This film was the first movie in history to gross over US$2 billion.

Twentieth Century-Fox Film Corporation/The Kobal Collection/Art Resource, NY

Harris et al., 2010b), especially as travel to and length of stay in the International Space Station has increased.

Long before he was involved in space research, Ian Howard was known internationally as a pioneer in sensation/perception research, particularly in the area of binocular vision and human spatial orientation (Howard, 1974; Howard & Rogers, 1995; Howard & Templeton, 1966). Along with other colleagues such as Laurence Harris (Harris et al., 2010b), Howard has used rooms that tilt sideways and airplane flights that involve parabolic flight paths in order to experience normal, hypergravity, and microgravity environments. Ordinarily, people can rely on three types of cues to determine which way is up: visual,

gravity, and body direction. In space, astronauts are primarily dependent on visual cues and body orientation. Using the tilting-sideways room, they are able to isolate the three types of cues and have found that body orientation cannot help to establish the direction of up (Jenkin et al., 2003). This suggests that the astronaut is dependent on visual cues.

Sensation and perception are sometimes viewed only as topics in basic science, topics that may have little connection to our everyday lives. As you have learned from our brief discussion of space research and as you will learn in your study of this chapter, research in sensation and perception is very relevant to our experiences in our everyday life. After the success of James Cameron's 3-D blockbuster *Avatar*, interest in 3-D technology has paired vision scientists with film directors and producers (Flavelle, 2010). Among the issues currently being examined is the hypothesis that people differ in terms of how they perceive 3-D images (3-D FLIC, 2010).

Many people tend to use the terms *sensation* and *perception* interchangeably. For psychologists, however, they refer to related but distinct aspects of our contact with our environment. *Sensation* is the stimulation of sense organs. *Perception* is the selection, organization, and interpretation of sensory input. Sensation involves the absorption of energy, such as light or sound waves, by sensory organs, such as the ears and eyes. Perception involves organizing and translating sensory input into something meaningful, such as your best friend's face or other environmental stimuli (see Figure 4.1).

We'll begin our discussion of sensation and perception by examining some general concepts that are relevant to all of the senses. Next, we'll examine individual senses, in each case beginning with the sensory aspects and working our way through to the perceptual aspects. The chapter's Personal Application explores how principles of visual perception come into play in art and illusion. The Critical Thinking Application discusses how perceptual contrasts can be manipulated in persuasive efforts.

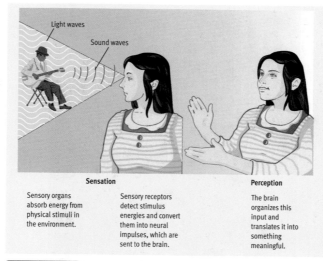

FIGURE 4.1

The distinction between sensation and perception.

Sensation involves the stimulation of sensory organs, whereas perception involves the interpretation of sensory input. The two processes merge at the point where sensory receptors convert physical energy into neural impulses.

Psychophysics: Basic Concepts and Issues

As you may recall from Chapter 1, the first experimental psychologists were interested mainly in sensation and perception. They called their area of interest *psychophysics*—the study of how physical stimuli are translated into psychological experience. A particularly important contributor to psychophysics was Gustav Fechner, who published a seminal work on the subject in 1860. Fechner was a German scientist working at the University of Leipzig, where Wilhelm Wundt later founded the first formal laboratory and journal devoted to psychological research. Even though these ideas were first generated over a century ago, interest in these fundamental issues continues today (Rouder & Morey, 2009).

Thresholds: Looking for Limits

Sensation begins with a *stimulus*, any detectable input from the environment. What counts as detectable, though, depends on who or what is doing the detecting. For instance, you might not be able to detect a weak odour that is readily apparent to your dog. Thus, Fechner wanted to know: For any given sense, what is the weakest detectable stimulus? For example, what is the minimum amount of light needed for a person to see that there is light?

Implicit in Fechner's question is a concept central to psychophysics: the threshold. *A threshold is a dividing point between energy levels that do and do not have a detectable effect.* For example, hardware stores sell a gadget with a photocell that automatically turns a lamp on when a room gets dark. The level of light intensity at which the gadget clicks on is its threshold.

An absolute threshold for a specific type of sensory input is the minimum amount of stimulation that an organism can detect. Absolute thresholds define the boundaries of an organism's sensory capabilities. Fechner and his contemporaries used a variety of methods to determine humans' absolute threshold for detecting light. They discovered that absolute thresholds are anything but absolute. When lights of varying intensity are flashed at a subject, there is no single stimulus intensity at which the subject jumps from no detection to completely accurate detection. Instead, as stimulus intensity increases, subjects' probability of responding to stimuli *gradually* increases, as shown in red in Figure 4.2. Thus, researchers had to arbitrarily define the absolute threshold as the stimulus intensity *detected 50 percent of the time.*

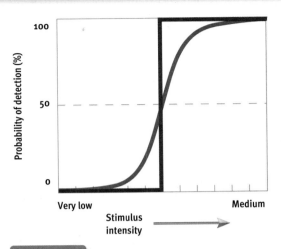

FIGURE 4.2

The absolute threshold.

If absolute thresholds were truly absolute, then the probability of detecting a stimulus at threshold intensity would jump from 0 to 100 percent, as graphed here in blue. In reality, the chances of detecting a stimulus increase gradually with stimulus intensity, as shown in red. Accordingly, an "absolute" threshold is defined as the intensity level at which the probability of detection is 50 percent.

Using this definition, investigators found that under ideal conditions, human abilities to detect weak stimuli were greater than previously thought. Some concrete examples of the absolute thresholds for various senses can be seen in Table 4.1. For example, on a clear, dark night, in the absence of other distracting lights, you could see the light of a candle burning 50 kilometres in the distance! Of course, we're talking about ideal conditions—you would have to go out to the middle of nowhere to find the darkness required to put this assertion to a suitable test.

TABLE 4.1

Examples of Absolute Thresholds

Sense	Absolute Threshold
Vision	A candle flame seen at 50 kilometres on a dark clear night
Hearing	The tick of a watch under quiet conditions at 6 metres
Taste	Five millilitres of sugar in 7.5 litres of water
Smell	One drop of perfume diffused into the entire volume of a six-room apartment
Touch	The wing of a fly falling on your cheek from a distance of 1 centimetre

Source: Galanter, E. (1962). Contemporary psychophysics. In R. Brown (Ed.), *New directions in psychology*. New York: Holt, Rinehart & Winston. © 1962 Eugene Galanter. Reprinted by permission.

PREVIEW QUESTIONS

▶ How is stimulus intensity related to absolute thresholds?

▶ What is a JND, and where does it fit in with Weber's and Fechner's laws?

▶ What is the central idea of signal-detection theory?

▶ What is the practical significance of subliminal perception?

▶ What is sensory adaptation?

Gustav Fechner

"The method of just noticeable differences consists in determining how much the weights have to differ so that they can just be discriminated."

Weighing the Differences: The JND

Fechner was also interested in people's sensitivity to differences between stimuli. *A just noticeable difference (JND) is the smallest difference in the amount of stimulation that a specific sense can detect.* JNDs are close cousins of absolute thresholds. In fact, an absolute threshold is simply the just noticeable difference from nothing (no stimulus input). JNDs vary by sense, and the smallest detectable difference is a fairly stable proportion of the size of the original stimulus.

This principle was first demonstrated by Fechner's brother-in-law, Ernst Weber, and came to be known as Weber's law. *Weber's law states that the size of a just noticeable difference is a constant proportion of the size of the initial stimulus.* This constant proportion is called the *Weber fraction*. Weber's law applies not only to weight perception but to all of the senses. However, different fractions apply to different types of sensory input. For example, the Weber fraction for lifting weights is approximately 1/30. That means that you should be just able to detect the difference between a 300-gram weight and a 310-gram weight (the JND for 300 grams is 10 grams). If you started with a 900-gram weight, however, you would not be able to tell the difference between it and a 910-gram weight. Why? Because the JND for 900 grams is 30 grams (1/30 of 900). In general, then, as stimuli increase in magnitude, the JND becomes larger.

Psychophysical Scaling

If one light has twice the energy of another, do you necessarily perceive it as being twice as bright? When asked to make this kind of judgment, you are being asked to *scale* the magnitude of sensory experiences. In his work on the scaling of sensory experiences, Fechner used the JND as his unit of measurement. His work yielded a principle that came to be known as *Fechner's law,* which states that the magnitude of a sensory experience is proportional to the number of JNDs that the stimulus causing the experience is above the absolute threshold.

An important ramification of Fechner's law is that constant increments in stimulus intensity produce smaller and smaller increases in the *perceived* magnitude of sensation. This principle is easy to illustrate. Imagine that you're in a dark room with a single lamp that has three bulbs of the same wattage. You turn a switch, and one bulb lights. After a dark room, the difference is striking. Turn again, and a second bulb comes on. The amount of light is doubled, but the room does not seem to be twice as bright. When you turn the third bulb on, it adds just as much light as the first or second, but you barely notice the difference. Thus, three equal increases in stimulus intensity (the amount of light) produce progressively smaller differences in the magnitude of sensation (perceived brightness).

What all this means is that perceptions can't be measured on absolute scales. In the domain of sensory experience, virtually everything is relative.

Signal-Detection Theory

The fact that perceptions can't be measured on absolute scales applies not only to sensory scaling but to sensory thresholds as well. *Signal-detection theory proposes that the detection of stimuli involves decision processes as well as sensory processes, which are both influenced by a variety of factors besides stimulus intensity* (Egan, 1975; Macmillan & Creelman, 2005).

Imagine that you are monitoring a radar screen, looking for signs of possible enemy aircraft. Your mission is to detect signals that represent approaching airplanes as quickly and as accurately as possible. In this situation, there are four possible outcomes, which are outlined in Figure 4.3: *hits* (detecting signals when they are present), *misses* (failing to detect signals when they are present), *false alarms* (detecting signals when they are not present), and *correct rejections* (not detecting signals when they are absent). Given these possibilities, signal-detection theory attempts to account for the influence of decision-making processes on stimulus detection. In detecting weak signals on the radar screen, you will often have to decide whether a faint signal represents

FIGURE 4.3

Possible outcomes in signal-detection theory.

This diagram shows the four outcomes that are possible in attempting to detect the presence of weak signals. The criterion you set for how confident you want to feel before reporting a signal will affect your responding. For example, if you require high confidence before reporting a signal, you will minimize false alarms but you'll be more likely to miss some signals.

an airplane or whether you're just imagining that it does. Your responses will depend in part on the *criterion* you set for how sure you must feel before you react. Setting this criterion involves higher mental processes rather than raw sensation and depends on your expectations and on the consequences of missing a signal or of reporting a false alarm.

According to signal-detection theory, your performance will also depend on the level of "noise" in the system (Kubovy, Epstein, & Gepshtein, 2003). Noise comes from all of the irrelevant stimuli in the environment and the neural activity they elicit. Noise is analogous to the background static on a radio station. The more noise in the system, the harder it will be for you to pick up a weak signal. The key point is that signal-detection theory replaces Fechner's sharp threshold with the concept of "detectability." Detectability is measured in terms of probability and depends on decision-making processes as well as sensory processes.

Perception without Awareness

The concepts of thresholds and detectability lie at the core of an interesting debate: Can sensory stimuli that fall beneath the threshold of awareness still influence behaviour? This issue centres on the concept of *subliminal perception*—the registration of sensory input without conscious awareness (*limen* is another term for *threshold*, so *subliminal* means below threshold). This question might be just another technical issue in the normally staid world of psychophysics, except that subliminal perception has become tied up in highly charged controversies relating to money, sex, religion, and rock music.

The controversy began in 1957 when an executive named James Vicary placed hidden messages such as "Eat popcorn" in a film showing at a theatre in New Jersey. The messages were superimposed on only a few frames of the film, so that they flashed by quickly and imperceptibly. Nonetheless, Vicary claimed in the press that popcorn sales increased by 58 percent, and a public outcry ensued (McConnell, Cutler, & McNeil, 1958). Since then, Wilson Bryan Key, a former advertising executive and academic, has written several books claiming that sexual words and drawings are embedded subliminally in magazine advertisements to elicit favourable unconscious reactions from consumers (Key, 1973, 1976, 1980).

One such advertisement discussed by Key is shown in Figure 4.4. If you look closely, you'll find the word "SEX" embedded in the ice cubes. Taking the sexual

Wilson Bryan Key/Mediaprobe, Inc.

FIGURE 4.4

Subliminal advertising: Is it all in the eye of the beholder?

If you look closely at the ice cubes in this ad, you will see the word "SEX" spelled out. Former advertising executive Wilson Bryan Key (1973) claims advertisers routinely place subliminal stimuli in their ads. Marketing companies maintain that people are merely reading things into their ads, much like you might see familiar forms in clouds. Although subliminal perception appears to be a genuine phenomenon, Thomas Creed (1987) has pinpointed a host of fallacies in Key's analysis, which he characterizes as pseudoscience.

manipulation theme a step further, entrepreneurs are now marketing music audiotapes containing subliminal messages that are supposed to help people seduce unsuspecting listeners. Subliminal self-help tapes intended to facilitate weight loss, sleep, memory, self-esteem, and the like have become a multimillion-dollar industry. Religious overtones were added to this controversy in the 1980s when subliminal messages encouraging devil worship were allegedly found in rock music played *backward* (Vokey & Read, 1985).

Can listening to *Led Zeppelin's "Stairway to Heaven"* promote satanic rituals? Can your sexual urges be manipulated by messages hidden under music? Can advertisers influence your product preferences with subliminal stimuli? Research on subliminal perception was sporadic in the 1960s and 1970s because scientists initially dismissed the entire idea as preposterous. However, empirical studies have begun to accumulate since the 1980s, and quite a number of these studies have found support for the existence of subliminal effects (Birgegard & Sohlberg, 2008; Dijkersterhuis, 2004).

Quite a number of studies have also found support for the existence of subliminal perception (De Houwer, 2001; Greenwald, 1992; Snodgrass, Bernat, & Shevrin, 2004). Using diverse methodological and conceptual approaches, researchers examining a variety of phenomena, such as unconscious semantic priming (Abrams, Klinger, & Greenwald, 2002), subliminal affective conditioning (Dijksterhuis, 2004), subliminal mere exposure effects (Monahan, Murphy, & Zajonc, 2000), subliminal visual priming (Haneda et al., 2003), and subliminal psychodynamic activation (Sohlberg & Birgegard, 2003), have found evidence that perception without awareness *can* take place.

For example, in one recent study, Karremans, Stroebe, and Claus (2006) set out to determine whether participants' inclination to consume a particular drink (Lipton Iced Tea) could be influenced without their awareness. Subjects were asked to work on a visual detection task that supposedly was designed to see whether people could perceive changes in visual stimuli. For half of the participants, subliminal presentations (at 23/1000 of a second) of the words "LIPTON ICE" were interspersed among these visual stimuli. Control subjects were given subliminal presentations of neutral words. After the visual detection task, subjects participated in a study of "consumer behaviour," and their inclination to drink Lipton Iced Tea was assessed with a variety of comparative ratings. As predicted, participants exposed subliminally to "LIPTON ICE" were significantly more interested in consuming Lipton Iced Tea, especially among those who indicated that they were thirsty (see Figure 4.5).

Other recent studies have also shown that subliminal stimuli can have important effects. For instance, Massar and Buunk (2009) subliminally exposed participants to drawings of attractive or unattractive bodies before having them read a jealousy-inducing scenario and rate how jealous they would feel in the situation. The participants exposed to the attractive body image reported significantly greater feelings of jealousy than those exposed to the unattractive body image. Another study found that subliminal exposures to one's national flag produced meaningful shifts in opinions on controversial political issues (Hassin et al., 2007). Yet another study in the realm of politics found that subliminal presentations of the word RATS had a negative impact on ratings of politicians (Weinberger & Westen, 2008). Thus, subliminal inputs can produce measurable, although small, effects in subjects who subsequently report that they did not consciously register the stimuli.

So, should we be worried about the threat of subliminal persuasion? The research to date suggests that there is little reason for concern. The effects of subliminal stimuli turn out to be nearly as subliminal as the stimuli themselves. Subliminal stimulation generally produces weak effects (De Houwer, Hendrickx, & Baeyens, 1997; Kihlstrom, Barnhardt, & Tataryn, 1992). These effects can be detected only by very precise measurement under carefully controlled laboratory conditions in which subjects are asked to focus their undivided attention on visual or auditory materials that contain the subliminal stimuli. Although these effects are theoretically interesting, they appear unlikely to have much practical importance (Merikle, 2000). More research on the manipulative potential of subliminal persuasion is needed, but so far there is no cause for alarm.

Sensory Adaptation

The process of sensory adaptation is yet another factor that influences registration of sensory input. *Sensory adaptation* is a gradual decline in sensitivity due to prolonged stimulation. For example, let's say you find that the garbage in your kitchen has started to smell. If you stay in the kitchen without removing the garbage, the stench will soon start to fade. In reality, the stimulus intensity of the odour is stable, but with continued exposure, your *sensitivity* to it decreases. Sensory adaptation is a pervasive aspect of everyday life. When you put on your clothes in the morning, you feel them initially, but the sensation quickly fades. Similarly, if you jump reluctantly into a pool of cold water, you'll probably find that the water temperature feels fine in a few moments after you *adapt* to it.

Sensory adaptation is an automatic, built-in process that keeps people tuned in to the *changes* rather than the *constants* in their sensory input. It allows people to ignore the obvious and focus

FIGURE 4.5

Results of Karremans et al. (2006) study of subliminal perception.

One measure of whether the subliminal presentation of "LIPTON ICE" affected participants' drink preferences was to ask them to choose between Lipton Iced Tea and another popular drink. As you can see, the experimental group subjects showed a decided preference for Lipton Iced Tea in comparison to the control group subjects, especially among subjects who indicated that they were thirsty.

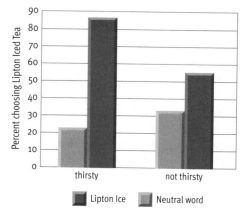

Source: Reprinted from *Journal of Experimental Social Psychology, 42 (6)*, Johan C. Karremans, Wolfgang Stroebe, and Jasper Claus, Beyond Vicary's fantasies: The impact of subliminal priming and brand choice, pp. 792–798. Copyright © 2006, with permission from Elsevier.

on changes in their environment that may signal threats to safety. Thus, as its name suggests, sensory adaptation probably is a behavioural adaptation that has been sculpted by natural selection (McBurney, 2010). Sensory adaptation also shows once again that there is no one-to-one correspondence between sensory input and sensory experience.

The general points we've reviewed so far begin to suggest the complexity of the relationships between the world outside and people's perceived experience of it. As we review each of the principal sensory systems in detail, we'll see repeatedly that people's experience of the world depends on both the physical stimuli they encounter and their active processing of stimulus inputs. We begin our exploration of the senses with vision—the sense that most people think of as nearly synonymous with a direct perception of reality. The case is actually quite different, as you'll see.

REVIEW OF KEY POINTS

▷ Psychophysicists use a variety of methods to relate sensory inputs to subjective perception. They have found that absolute thresholds are not really absolute.

▷ Weber's law states that the size of a just noticeable difference is a constant proportion of the size of the initial stimulus. Fechner's law asserts that larger and larger increases in stimulus intensity are required to produce just noticeable differences in the magnitude of sensation.

▷ According to signal-detection theory, the detection of sensory inputs is influenced by noise in the system and by decision-making strategies. Signal-detection theory replaces Fechner's sharp threshold with the concept of detectability and emphasizes that factors besides stimulus intensity influence detectability.

▷ In recent years, a host of researchers, using very different conceptual approaches, have demonstrated that perception can occur without awareness. However, research indicates that the effects of subliminal perception are relatively weak and of little or no practical concern.

▷ Prolonged stimulation may lead to sensory adaptation, which involves a reduction in sensitivity to constant stimulation.

Our Sense of Sight: The Visual System

"Seeing is believing." Good ideas are "bright," and a good explanation is "illuminating." This section is an "overview." Do you see the point? As these common expressions show, humans are visual animals. People rely heavily on their sense of sight, and they virtually equate it with what is trustworthy (seeing is believing). Although it is taken for granted, you'll see (there it is again) that the human visual system is amazingly complex. Furthermore, as in all sensory domains, what people "sense" and what they "perceive" may be quite different.

The Stimulus: Light   3a

For people to see, there must be light. *Light* is a form of electromagnetic radiation that travels as a wave, moving, naturally enough, at the speed of light. As Figure 4.6(a) shows, light waves vary in *amplitude* (height) and in *wavelength* (the distance between peaks). Amplitude affects mainly the perception of brightness, while wavelength affects mainly the perception of colour. The lights that humans normally see are mixtures of several wavelengths. Hence, light can also vary in its *purity* (how varied the mix is). Purity influences perception of the saturation, or richness, of colours. Saturation is difficult to describe,

but if you glance at Figure 4.7, you'll find it clearly illustrated. Of course, most objects do not emit light; they reflect it (the sun, lamps, and fireflies being some exceptions).

What most people call *light* includes only the wavelengths that humans can see. But as Figure 4.6(c) shows, the visible spectrum is only a slim portion of the total range of wavelengths. Vision is a filter that permits people to sense but a fraction of the real world. Other animals have different capabilities and so live in a quite different visual world. For example, many insects can see shorter wavelengths than humans can see, in the *ultraviolet* spectrum, whereas many fish and reptiles can see longer wavelengths, in the *infrared* spectrum. Although the sense of sight depends on light waves, for people to *see*, incoming visual input must be converted into neural impulses that are sent to the brain. Let's investigate how this transformation is accomplished.

The Eye: A Living Optical Instrument   3a

The eyes serve two main purposes: They channel light to the neural tissue that receives it, called the *retina*, and they house that tissue. The structure of

PREVIEW QUESTIONS

▷ What are the three properties of light?

▷ What do the lens and pupil contribute to visual functioning?

▷ What are the functions of rods and cones?

▷ How do visual receptive fields typically function?

▷ How are visual signals routed from the eye to the primary visual cortex?

▷ What are feature detectors?

WEB LINK 4.1

Vision Science: An Internet Resource for Research in Human and Animal Vision
Numerous online sites are devoted to the sense of sight and visual processes. Vision Science provides a convenient guide to the best of these sites, especially for online demonstrations and tutorials.

FIGURE 4.6

Light, the physical stimulus for vision.

(a) Light waves vary in amplitude and wavelength.
(b) Within the spectrum of visible light, amplitude (corresponding to physical intensity) affects mainly the experience of brightness. Wavelength affects mainly the experience of colour, and purity is the key determinant of saturation.
(c) If white light (such as sunlight) passes through a prism, the prism separates the light into its component wavelengths, creating a rainbow of colours. However, visible light is only the narrow band of wavelengths to which human eyes happen to be sensitive.

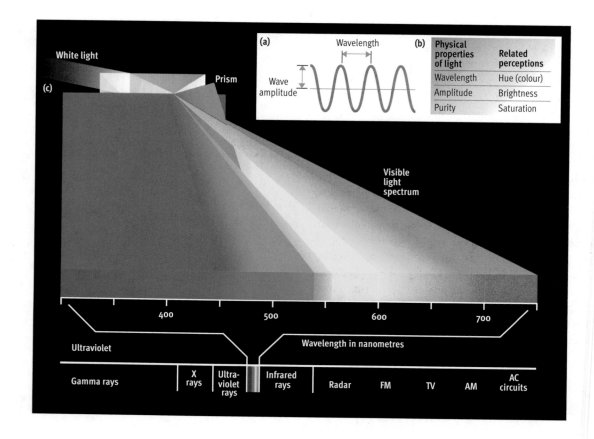

FIGURE 4.7

Saturation.

Variations in saturation are difficult to describe, but you can see examples for two colours here.

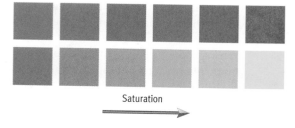

Saturation

the eye is shown in Figure 4.8. Each eye is a living optical instrument that creates an image of the visual world on the light-sensitive retina lining its inside back surface.

Light enters the eye through a transparent "window" at the front, the *cornea*. The cornea and the crystalline *lens*, located behind it, form an upside-down image of objects on the retina. It might seem disturbing that the image is upside down, but the brain knows the rule for relating positions on the retina to the corresponding positions in the world.

The lens is the transparent eye structure that focuses the light rays falling on the retina. The lens is made up of relatively soft tissue, capable of adjustments that facilitate a process called *accommodation*. Accommodation occurs when the curvature of the lens adjusts to alter visual focus. When you focus on a close object, the lens of your eye gets fatter (rounder) to give you a clear image. When you focus

on distant objects, the lens flattens out to give you a better image of the objects.

A number of common visual deficiencies are caused by focusing problems or by defects in the lens (Guyton, 1991). For example, in *nearsightedness, close objects are seen clearly but distant objects appear blurry* because the focus of light from distant objects falls a little short of the retina (see Figure 4.9). This focusing problem occurs when the cornea or lens bends the light too much, or when the eyeball is too long. In *farsightedness, distant objects are seen clearly but close objects appear blurry* because the focus of light from close objects falls behind the retina. This focusing problem typically occurs when the eyeball is too short.

The eye can make adjustments to alter the amount of light reaching the retina. The *iris* is the coloured ring of muscle surrounding the *pupil*, or black centre of the eye. The *pupil* is the opening in the centre of the iris that helps regulate the amount of light passing into the rear chamber of the eye. When the pupil constricts, it lets less light into the eye but it sharpens the image falling on the retina. When the pupil dilates (opens), it lets more light in but the image is less sharp. In bright light, the pupils constrict to take advantage of the sharpened image. But in dim light, the pupils dilate; image sharpness is

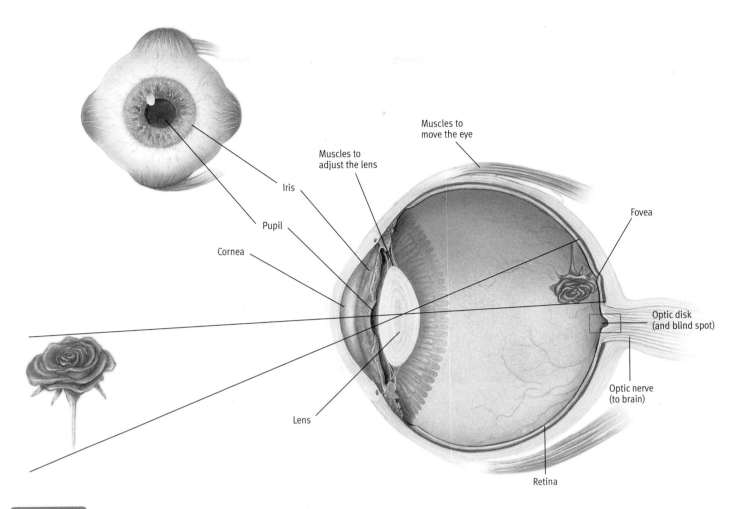

FIGURE 4.8

The human eye.

Light passes through the cornea, pupil, and lens and falls on the light-sensitive surface of the retina, where images of objects are reflected upside down. The lens adjusts its curvature to focus the images falling on the retina. The iris and pupil regulate the amount of light passing into the rear chamber of the eye.

 Log on to CourseMate to access this interactive figure.

sacrificed to allow more light to fall on the retina so that more remains visible.

The eye itself is constantly in motion, moving in ways that are typically imperceptible to us. When we are looking at something, our eyes are scanning the visual environment and making brief fixations at various parts of the stimuli. These eye movements are referred to as *saccades*. Saccades have been the subject of research interest for many years (e.g., M. R. Brown et al., 2004). These tiny movements are essential to good vision; if there is even a small reduction in these voluntary eye movements, our vision degrades (Martinez-Conde, 2006). In fact, if there were none of these eye movements, if you were able to stop these movements while looking at your sleeping dog for example, your visual system would adapt, and your dog, or any other static scene, would "simply fade from view" (Martinez-Conde &

Macknik, 2007, p. 56). This would be the ultimate disappearing act. Sensory adaptation is a characteristic of our sensory systems and was discussed on pages 142–143 of this chapter.

Not only are these eye movements necessary for our optimal visual experience, but there is even a suggestion that they may give away more than we intend. Based on research conducted by McGill's Zaid Hafed and James Clark (2002), it has been suggested that one form of saccade may give away your covert gaze even when you are looking somewhere else (Martinez-Conde & Macknik, 2007; see also Engbert & Kliegl, 2003). Thus, if someone were able to track your eye movements, they would be able to determine what really interests you, what is capturing your attention, even though you denied it and tried to avert your gaze and look elsewhere.

Nearsightedness

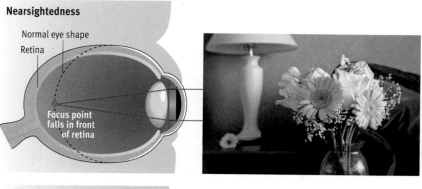

Normal eye shape
Retina

Focus point falls in front of retina

Farsightedness

Normal eye shape
Retina

Focus point falls behind retina

Courtesy of Joanne Woods

Courtesy of Joanne Woods

FIGURE 4.9

Nearsightedness and farsightedness.

These pictures simulate how a scene might look to nearsighted and farsighted people. Nearsightedness occurs because light from distant objects focuses in front of the retina. Farsightedness is due to the opposite situation—light from close objects focuses behind the retina.

Research on saccades has increased dramatically in the last few years. It has been used not only to measure gaze direction and attention, but also to assess the strength of visual distracters. It also has been used in special populations, such as people suffering from Huntington's disease and in the elderly (Van der Strigchel, 2010). In the latter case, it can be employed to detect deterioration in types of processes that are not easy to assess by other means. For example, research with the elderly (Campbell et al, 2009; Campbell et al., 2010) has used measures of saccades to suggest that declines with age in visual inhibitory activity are associated with processes in the frontal lobe of the brain (Niewenhuis et al., 2000). Visual inhibitory activity is important in many circumstances—"objects in the environment rarely occur in isolation and . . . successfully gazing to a stimulus of interest necessarily requires one to avoid looking at other distracting stimuli . . ." (Campbell et al., 2009, pp. 163). Just try to remember the last time you were to meet someone in a crowded mall, remember how difficult it was to keep from being distracted by all the lights, movement, store signs, and other people. The more we know about decline in such processes in the elderly, the better we may be able to design programs to enable them to compensate for this loss.

The *retina* is the neural tissue lining the inside back surface of the eye; it absorbs light, processes images, and sends visual information to the brain. You may be surprised to learn that the retina *processes* images. But it's a piece of the central nervous system that happens to be located in the eyeball. Much as the spinal cord is a complicated extension of the brain, the retina is the brain's envoy in the eye. Although the retina is only a paper-thin sheet of neural tissue, it contains a complex network of specialized cells arranged in layers (Rodieck, 1998), as shown in Figure 4.10.

The axons that run from the retina to the brain converge at the *optic disk,* a hole in the retina where the optic nerve fibres exit the eye. Because the optic disk is a *hole* in the retina, you cannot see the part of an image that falls on it. It is therefore known as the *blind spot.* You may not be aware that you have a blind spot in each eye, as each normally compensates for the blind spot of the other.

Visual Receptors: Rods and Cones 3b

PSYKTREK

The retina contains millions of receptor cells that are sensitive to light. Surprisingly, these receptors are located in the innermost layer of the retina. Hence, light must pass through several layers of cells before it gets to the receptors that actually detect it. Interestingly, only about 10 percent of the light arriving at the cornea reaches these receptors (Leibovic, 1990). The retina contains two types of receptors, *rods* and *cones*. Their names are based on their shapes, as rods are elongated and cones are stubbier. Rods outnumber cones by a huge margin, as humans have 100 million to 125 million rods, but only 5 million to 6.4 million cones (Frishman, 2001).

Cones are specialized visual receptors that play a key role in daylight vision and colour vision. The cones handle most of our daytime vision, because bright lights dazzle the rods. The special sensitivities of cones also allow them to play a major role in the perception of colour. However, cones do not respond well to dim light, which is why you don't see colour very well in low illumination. Nonetheless, cones provide better *visual acuity*—that is, sharpness and precise detail—than rods. Cones are concentrated most heavily in the centre of the retina and quickly fall off in density toward its periphery. The *fovea* is a tiny spot in the centre of the retina that contains only cones; visual acuity is greatest at this spot. When you want to see something sharply, you usually move your eyes to centre the object in the fovea.

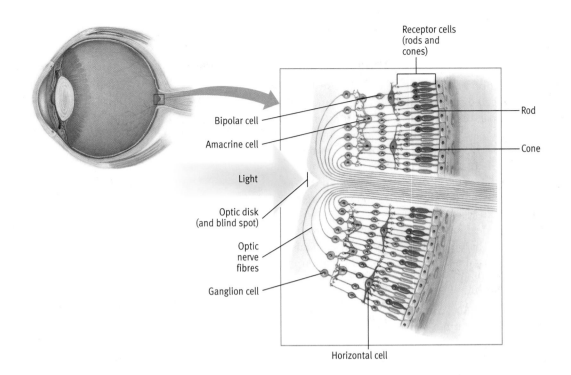

FIGURE 4.10

The retina.

The close-up shows the several layers of cells in the retina. The cells closest to the back of the eye (the rods and cones) are the receptor cells that actually detect light. The intervening layers of cells receive signals from the rods and cones and form circuits that begin the process of analyzing incoming information. The visual signals eventually converge into *ganglion cells*, whose axons form the optic fibres that make up the optic nerve. These optic fibres all head toward the "hole" in the retina where the optic nerve leaves the eye—the point known as the *optic disk* (which corresponds to the blind spot).

Rods are specialized visual receptors that play a key role in night vision and peripheral vision. Rods handle night vision because they are more sensitive than cones to dim light (Kefalov, 2010). They handle the lion's share of peripheral vision because they greatly outnumber cones in the periphery of the retina. The density of the rods is greatest just outside the fovea and gradually decreases toward the periphery of the retina. Because of the distribution of rods, when you want to see a faintly illuminated object in the dark, it's best to look slightly above or below the place where the object should be. Averting your gaze this way moves the image from the cone-filled fovea, which requires more light, to the rod-dominated area just outside the fovea, which requires less light. This trick of averted vision is well known to astronomers, who use it to study dim objects viewed through the eyepiece of a telescope.

Dark and Light Adaptation

3b PSYKTREK

You've probably noticed that when you enter a dark theatre on a bright day, you stumble around almost blindly. But within minutes, you can make your way around quite well in the dim light. This adjustment is called *dark adaptation*—the process in which the eyes become more sensitive to light in low illumination. Figure 4.11 maps out the course of this process. The declining absolute thresholds over time indicate that you require less and less light to see. Dark adaptation is virtually complete in about 30 minutes, with considerable progress occurring in

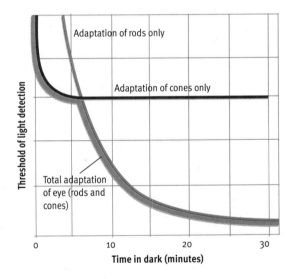

FIGURE 4.11

The process of dark adaptation.

The declining thresholds over time indicate that your visual sensitivity is improving, as less and less light is required to see. Visual sensitivity improves markedly during the first five to ten minutes after entering a dark room, as the eye's bright-light receptors (the cones) rapidly adapt to low light levels. However, the cones' adaptation, which is plotted in purple, soon reaches its limit, and further improvement comes from the rods' adaptation, which is plotted in red. The rods adapt more slowly than the cones, but they are capable of far greater visual sensitivity in low levels of light.

the first 10 minutes. The curve in Figure 4.11 that charts this progress consists of two segments because cones adapt more rapidly than rods (Reeves, 2010).

When you emerge from a dark theatre on a sunny day, you need to squint to ward off the overwhelming brightness, and the reverse of dark adaptation occurs. *Light adaptation* is the process whereby the eyes become less sensitive to light in high illumination. As with dark adaptation, light adaptation improves your visual acuity under the prevailing circumstances. Both types of adaptation are due in large part to chemical changes in the *rods* and *cones*, but neural changes in the receptors and elsewhere in the retina also contribute (Frumkes, 1990).

Information Processing in the Retina

3b

In processing visual input, the retina transforms a pattern of light falling onto it into a very different representation of the visual scene. Light striking the retina's receptors (rods and cones) triggers neural signals that pass into the intricate network of cells in the retina, which in turn send impulses along the *optic nerve*—a collection of axons that connect the eye with the brain (refer back to Figure 4.10). These axons, which depart from the eye through the optic disk, carry visual information, encoded as a stream of neural impulses, to the brain.

A great deal of complex information processing goes on in the retina itself before visual signals are sent to the brain. Ultimately, the information from over 100 million rods and cones converges to travel along "only" 1 million axons in the optic nerve (Slaughter, 1990). The collection of rod and cone receptors that funnel signals to a particular visual cell in the retina (or ultimately in the brain) make up that cell's *receptive field*. Thus, the *receptive field of a visual cell* is the retinal area that, when stimulated, affects the firing of that cell.

Receptive fields in the retina come in a variety of shapes and sizes. Particularly common are circular fields with a centre-surround arrangement (Levitt, 2010). In these receptive fields, light falling in the *centre* has the opposite effect of light falling in the *surrounding area* (see Figure 4.12). For example, the rate of firing of a visual cell might be *increased* by light in the *centre* of its receptive field and *decreased* by light in the *surrounding area*, as Figure 4.12 shows. Other visual cells may work in just the opposite way. Either way, when receptive fields are stimulated, retinal cells send signals both toward the brain and *laterally* (sideways) toward nearby visual cells. These lateral signals allow visual cells in the retina to have interactive effects on each other.

Lateral antagonism (also known as *lateral inhibition*) is the most basic of these interactive effects. *Lateral antagonism* occurs when neural activity in a cell opposes activity in surrounding cells. Lateral antagonism is responsible for the opposite effects that occur when light falls on the inner versus outer portions of centre-surround receptive fields. Lateral antagonism allows the retina to compare the light falling in a specific area against general lighting. This means that the visual system can compute the *relative* amount of light at a point instead of reacting to *absolute* levels of light. This attention to contrast is exactly what is needed, because most of the crucial information needed to recognize objects in a visual scene is contained in the pattern of contrasts (Tessier-Lavigne, 2000). If you look at Figure 4.13, you will experience a perplexing illusion attributable to lateral antagonism in the ganglion cells of the retina.

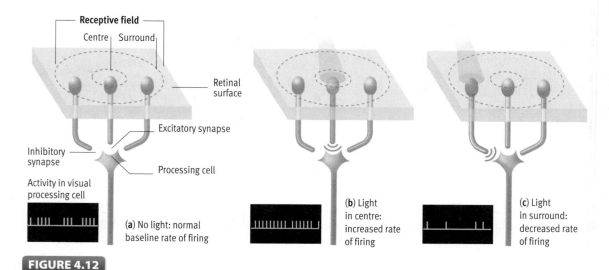

FIGURE 4.12

Receptive fields in the retina.

Visual cells' receptive fields—made up of rods and cones in the retina—are often circular with a centre-surround arrangement (a), so that light striking the centre of the field produces the opposite result of light striking the surround. In the receptive field depicted here, light in the centre produces excitatory effects (symbolized by green at the synapse) and increased firing in the visual cell (b), whereas light in the surround produces inhibitory effects (symbolized by red at the synapse) and decreased firing (c). Interestingly, no light in the receptive field and light in both centre and surround produce similar baseline rates of firing. This arrangement makes the visual cell particularly sensitive to *contrast*, which facilitates the extremely important task of recognizing the *edges* of objects.

FIGURE 4.13

The Hermann grid.

If you look at this grid, you will see dark spots at the intersections of the white bars, except in the intersection you're staring at directly. This illusion is due to lateral antagonism (see Concept Check 4.1).

Vision and the Brain 3c

Light falls on the eye, but you see with your brain. Although the retina does an unusual amount of information processing for a sensory organ, visual input is meaningless until it is processed in the brain.

Visual Pathways to the Brain 3c

How does visual information get to the brain? Axons leaving the back of each eye form the optic nerves, which travel to the *optic chiasm*—the point at which the optic nerves from the inside half of each eye cross over and then project to the opposite half of the brain. This arrangement ensures that signals from both eyes go to both hemispheres of the brain. Thus, as Figure 4.14 shows, axons from the left half of each retina carry signals to the left side of the brain, and axons from the right half of each retina carry information to the right side of the brain.

After reaching the optic chiasm, the optic nerve fibres diverge along two pathways. The main pathway projects into the thalamus, the brain's major relay station. Here, about 90 percent of the axons from the retinas synapse in the *lateral geniculate nucleus* (LGN). Visual signals are processed in the LGN and then distributed to areas in the occipital lobe that make up

concept **check 4.1**

Understanding Sensory Processes in the Retina

Check your understanding of sensory receptors in the retina by completing the following exercises. Consult Appendix A for the answers.

1. The receptors for vision are rods and cones in the retina. These two types of receptors have many important differences, which are compared systematically in the chart below. Fill in the missing information to finish the chart.

Dimension	Rods	Cones
Physical shape	_____	_____
Number in the retina	_____	_____
Area of the retina in which they are dominant receptor	_____	_____
Critical to colour vision	_____	_____
Critical to peripheral vision	_____	_____
Sensitivity to dim light	_____	_____
Speed of dark adaptation	_____	_____

2. The text notes that lateral antagonism in the retina is the probable cause of the illusory dark spots seen in the intersections of the Hermann grid (see Figure 4.13). Try to construct an explanation of how lateral antagonism might account for this phenomenon. This is no small challenge, so don't feel bad if you have to consult Appendix A for the answer. Hint: The centre-surround receptive fields shown in Figure 4.12 are crucial to the explanation. It will help if you draw a centre-surround receptive field at one of the intersections in the grid and another adjacent to it.

the *primary visual cortex* (see Figure 4.14). The second visual pathway leaving the optic chiasm branches off to an area in the midbrain called the *superior colliculus* before travelling through the thalamus and on to the occipital lobe. The principal function of the second pathway appears to be the coordination of visual input with other sensory input (Casanova et al., 2001; Stein & Meredith, 1993).

The main visual pathway is subdivided into two more specialized pathways called the *magnocellular* and *parvocellular* channels (based on the layers of the LGN they synapse in). These channels engage in *parallel processing*, which involves simultaneously extracting different kinds of information from the same input. For example, the parvocellular channel handles the perception of colour, while the magnocellular channel processes information regarding brightness (Wurtz & Kandel, 2000). Of course, this brief description hardly does justice to the immense complexity of visual processing in the brain.

Information Processing in the Visual Cortex 3c

Most visual input eventually arrives in the primary visual cortex, located in the occipital lobe. Explaining

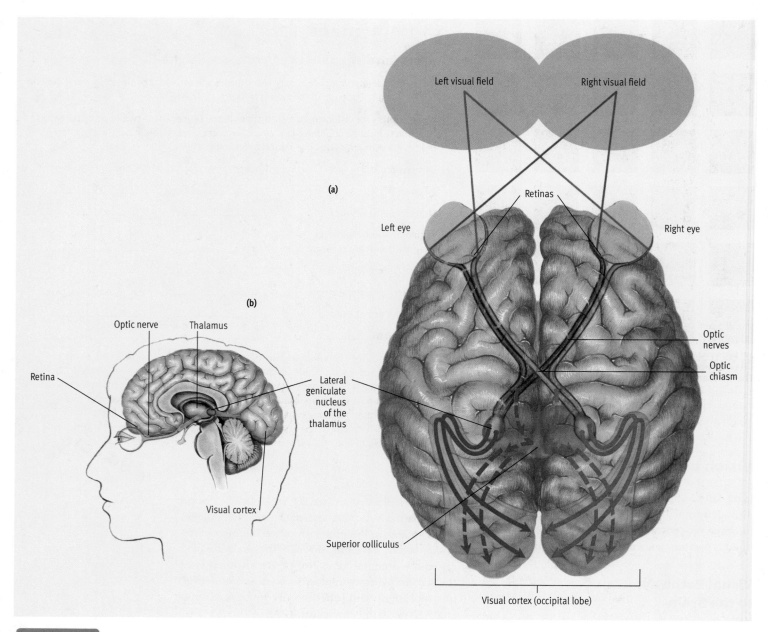

FIGURE 4.14

Visual pathways through the brain.

(a) Input from the right half of the visual field strikes the left side of each retina and is transmitted to the left hemisphere (shown in blue). Input from the left half of the visual field strikes the right side of each retina and is transmitted to the right hemisphere (shown in red). The nerve fibres from each eye meet at the optic chiasm, where fibres from the inside half of each retina cross over to the opposite side of the brain. After reaching the optic chiasm, the major visual pathway projects through the lateral geniculate nucleus in the thalamus and onto the primary visual cortex (shown with solid lines). A second pathway detours through the superior colliculus and then projects through the thalamus and onto the primary visual cortex (shown with dotted lines). (b) This inset shows a vertical view of how the optic pathways project through the thalamus and onto the visual cortex in the back of the brain (the two pathways mapped out in diagram (a) are virtually indistinguishable from this angle).

how the cortical cells in this area respond to light once posed a perplexing problem. Researchers investigating the question placed microelectrodes in the primary visual cortex of animals to record action potentials from individual cells. They would flash spots of light in the retinal receptive fields that the cells were thought to monitor, but there was rarely any response.

According to David Hubel and Torsten Wiesel (1962, 1963), they discovered the solution to this mystery quite by accident. One of the projector slides they used to present a spot to a cat had a crack in it. The spot elicited no response, but when they removed the slide, the crack moved through the cell's receptive field, and the cell fired like crazy in response to the moving dark line. It turns out that

FIGURE 4.15

Hubel and Wiesel's procedure for studying the activity of neurons in the visual cortex.

As the cat is shown various stimuli, a microelectrode records the firing of a neuron in the cat's visual cortex. The figure shows the electrical responses of a visual cell apparently "programmed" to respond to lines oriented vertically.

Time →

A vertical line elicits rapid firing in the cell.

A horizontal line elicits no response; the cell fires at its normal, baseline rate.

A line tilted away from vertical elicits moderate firing in the cell.

individual cells in the primary visual cortex don't really respond much to little spots—they are much more sensitive to lines, edges, and other more complicated stimuli. Armed with new slides, Hubel and Wiesel embarked on years of painstaking study of the visual cortex (see Figure 4.15). Their work eventually earned them a Nobel Prize in 1981.

Hubel, who was born in Windsor, Ontario, moved to Montreal with his family while he was a child. He went to university and medical school at McGill University. As we stated in Chapter 3, important work was being carried out in the 1940s and 1950s at the Montreal Neurological Institute by Wilder Penfield, Herbert Jasper, and others. Hubel's continued interest in the workings of the nervous system and the brain was influenced by the pioneering work of Penfield and his co-workers (Nobel Prize, n.d., a).

Hubel and Wiesel (1979, 1998, 2005) identified various types of specialized cells in the primary visual cortex that respond to different stimuli. For example, *simple cells* respond best to a line of the correct width, oriented at the correct angle, and located in the correct position in its receptive field. *Complex cells* also care about width and orientation, but they respond to any position in their receptive fields. Some complex cells are most responsive if a line sweeps across their receptive field—but only if it's moving in the "right" direction. The key point of all of this is that the cells in the visual cortex seem to be highly specialized. They have been characterized as *feature detectors,* neurons that respond selectively to very specific features of more complex stimuli. According to some theorists, most visual stimuli could ultimately be represented by combinations of lines such as those registered by these feature detectors (Maguire, Weisstein, & Klymenko, 1990).

After visual input is processed in the primary visual cortex, it is often routed to other cortical areas for additional processing. These signals travel through two streams: the *ventral stream*, which processes the details of *what* objects are out there (e.g., the perception of form and colour), and the *dorsal stream*, which processes *where* the objects are (e.g., the perception of motion and depth) (Connor et al., 2009; Pasternak et al. 2003). We consider these two streams more fully and the distinction between *vision for perception* and *vision for action* on pages 168–170).

As signals move farther along in the visual processing system, neurons become even more specialized or fussy about what turns them on, and the stimuli that activate them become more and more complex. For example, researchers have identified cells in the temporal lobe of monkeys and humans that are especially sensitive to pictures of faces (Kanwisher & Yovel, 2009). These neurons respond even to pictures that merely *suggest* the form of a face (Cox, Meyers, & Sinha, 2004). Interest in facial perception and the effect of context on that perception has increased in recent years (e.g., DeBruine et al., 2010; Righart & Gelder, 2008).

The discovery of neurons that respond to facial stimuli raises an obvious question: Why does the cortex have face detectors? Theorists are far from sure, but one line of thinking is that the ability to quickly recognize faces—such as those of friends or foes—probably has had adaptive significance over the course of evolution (Sugita, 2009). Thus, natural selection *may* have wired the brains of some species to quickly respond to faces. Consistent with this hypothesis, recent research has demonstrated that basic aspects of face perception are apparent in infants (McKone, Crookes, & Kanwisher, 2009).

© Ira Wyman/CORBIS Sygma

David Hubel

"One can now begin to grasp the significance of the great number of cells in the visual cortex. Each cell seems to have its own specific duties."

In any event, the discovery of the *what pathway* and the neurons inside it that respond specifically to faces has shed new light on visual disorders that have perplexed scientists for decades. For example, some people exhibit *visual agnosia*—an inability to recognize objects—even though their eyes function just fine (Behrmann, 2010). This perplexing condition now has a plausible explanation—it is probably due to damage somewhere along the visual pathway that handles object recognition. Consider also the condition of *prosopagnosia*, which is an inability to recognize familiar faces—including one's own face—even though other aspects of visual processing are largely unimpaired. Although much remains to be learned, this highly specific visual deficit may reflect damage to neural circuits that are sensitive to facial stimuli (Farah, 2006). Interestingly, a recent line of research suggests that people with acquired prosopagnosia compensate for it by developing heightened abilities to recognize voices (Hoover, Demonet, & Steeves, 2010).

Another dramatic finding in this area of research is that the neurons in the ventral stream pathway that are involved in perceiving faces can learn from experience (Gauthier & Curby, 2005; Palmeri & Gauthier, 2004). In one eye-opening study, participants were given extensive training in discriminating among similar artificial objects called "Greebles" (see Figure 4.16). After this training, neurons that are normally sensitive to faces were found to be almost as sensitive to Greebles as to faces (Gauthier et al., 1999). In other words, neurons that usually serve as face detectors were "retuned" to be responsive to other visual forms. Like many findings discussed in Chapter 3, these results demonstrate that the functional organization of the brain is somewhat "plastic," and that the brain can be rewired by experience.

Multiple Methods in Vision Research

As we discussed in Chapter 3, researchers interested in examining neurological functioning use a wide array of methods in their attempts to understand the operation of the brain. These include contemporary technologies such as functional magnetic resonance imaging (fMRI) as well as classic techniques such as observing the performance of individuals who have suffered specific types of brain damage. This is equally true of neuroscientists interested in vision. Throughout this chapter, you will read about research employing technologies such as fMRI or the use of microelectrodes, as in the research of Hubel and Wiesel. Vision researchers often complement this type of research by observations of the performance of individuals suffering from brain damage. For example, consider research on the *McCollough effect*.

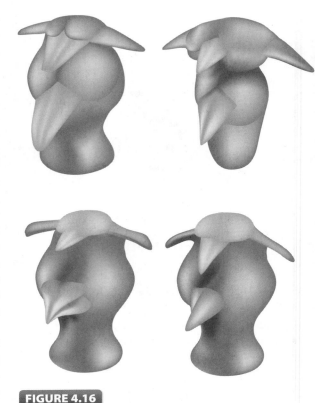

FIGURE 4.16

Distinguishing Greebles.

Gauthier et al. (1999) gave subjects seven hours of training in the recognition of novel stimuli called "Greebles," four of which are shown here. As the text explains, this training was conducted to explore whether neurons that normally respond to faces could be retuned by experience.

Source: From Gauthier, I., Tarr, M.J., Anderson, A.W., Skudlarski, P., and Gore, J.C. (1999). Activation of the middle fuisform 'face area' increases with expertise in recognizing novel objects. *Nature Neuroscience, 2*, 568–573 (Figure 1a, p. 569). Copyright © 1999, Nature Publishing Group. Reprinted by permission.

The McCollough effect is a well-known afterimage phenomenon that differs from other colour afterimage effects because it is contingent on both colour and pattern/form (i.e., line orientation). After alternating between the two circles on the top of Figure 4.17, if you were then asked to look at a circle like that at the bottom left of the figure, but one composed only of black and white lines, you would see an afterimage resembling the one illustrated in the bottom left of the figure. The colours you would see are complements of the colours in which the line pattern (vertical or horizontal) was presented in the top.

Several groups of Canadian researchers, including Peter Dodwell at Queen's University (Dodwell & Humphrey, 1990) and G. Keith Humphrey and his colleagues at the University of Western Ontario (Humphrey et al., 1999), have conducted research on the McCollough effect using a variety of contemporary and classic methods. For example, in addition to fMRI results, Humphrey and Goodale (1998) reviewed the results of experiments using individuals who suffered

The McCollough effect.

An illustration of typical induction and testing conditions for the McCollough effect. Subjects would alternately view the vertical red-and-black grating and the horizontal green-and-black grating for a few minutes. After such induction, black-and-white vertical gratings would appear green and horizontal gratings would appear pink (as in the simulated aftereffect shown in the lower left of the figure). Black-and-white oblique test gratings, as in the lower right of the figure, would not appear coloured.

Source: Reprinted from *Consciousness and Cognition, 7*(3), G. Keith Humphrey and Melvyn A. Goodale, Probing unconscious visual processing with the McCollough Effect, pp. 494–519. Copyright © 1998, with permission from Elsevier.

from *visual agnosia*. These patients had brain damage such that while they could perceive colour, they could not consciously perceive contour (line) orientation. Despite this deficit, they experienced the McCollough effect. This result, along with other available findings, suggests that the effect is mediated by the area of the brain known as *V1*, or the primary visual cortex, and that it does not depend on conscious form perception. The authors used these results to speculate on the nature of conscious visual experience.

Viewing the World in Colour

3d

So far, we've considered only how the visual system deals with light and dark. Let's journey now into the world of colour.

The Stimulus for Colour

3d

As noted earlier, the lights people see are mixtures of various wavelengths. Perceived colour is primarily a function of the dominant wavelength in these mixtures. In the visible spectrum, lights with the longest wavelengths appear red, whereas those with the shortest appear violet. Notice the word *appear*. Colour is a psychological interpretation. It's not a physical property of light itself.

Although wavelength wields the greatest influence, perception of colour depends on complex blends of all three properties of light. Wavelength is most closely related to hue, amplitude to brightness, and purity to saturation. These three dimensions of colour are illustrated in the *colour solid* shown in Figure 4.18.

As a colour solid demonstrates systematically, people can perceive many different colours. Indeed, experts estimate that humans can discriminate among millions of colours (Webster, 2010). Most of these diverse variations are the result of mixing a few basic colours. There are two kinds of colour mixture: subtractive and additive. *Subtractive colour mixing* works by removing some wavelengths of light, leaving less light than was originally there. You probably became familiar with subtractive mixing as a child when you mixed yellow and blue paints to make green. Paints yield subtractive mixing because

FIGURE 4.18

The colour solid.

The colour solid shows how colour varies along three perceptual dimensions: brightness (increasing from the bottom to the top of the solid), hue (changing around the solid's perimeter), and saturation (increasing toward the periphery of the solid).

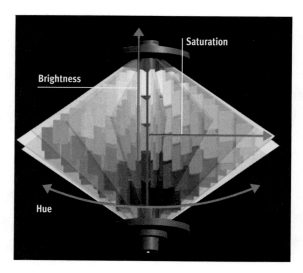
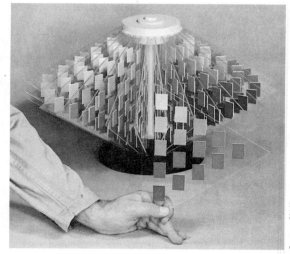

Courtesy of BASF

FIGURE 4.19

Additive versus subtractive colour mixing.

Lights mix additively because all of the wavelengths contained in each light reach the eye. If red, blue, and green lights are projected onto a white screen, they produce the colours shown on the left, with white at the intersection of all three lights. If paints of the same three colours were combined in the same way, the subtractive mixture would produce the colours shown on the right, with black at the intersection of all three colours.

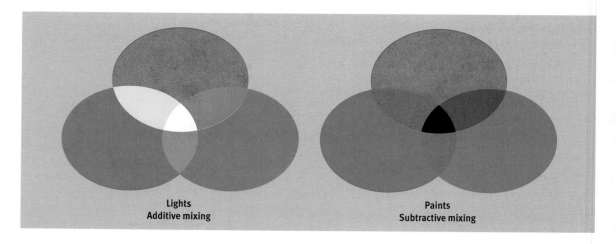

Lights
Additive mixing

Paints
Subtractive mixing

pigments *absorb* most wavelengths, selectively reflecting specific wavelengths that give rise to particular colours. Subtractive colour mixing can also be demonstrated by stacking colour filters. If you look through a sandwich of yellow and blue cellophane filters, they will block out certain wavelengths. The middle wavelengths that are left will look green.

Additive colour mixing works by superimposing lights, putting more light in the mixture than exists in any one light by itself. If you shine red, green, and blue spotlights on a white surface, you'll have an additive mixture. As Figure 4.19 shows, additive and subtractive mixtures of the same colours produce different results. Human processes of colour perception parallel additive colour mixing much more closely than subtractive mixing, as you'll see in the following discussion of theories of colour vision.

Trichromatic Theory of Colour Vision

3d PSYKTREK

The *trichromatic theory* of colour vision (*tri* for *three*, *chroma* for *colour*) was first stated by Thomas Young

and modified later by Hermann von Helmholtz (1852). The *trichromatic theory of colour vision* holds that the human eye has three types of receptors with differing sensitivities to different light wavelengths. Helmholtz theorized that the eye contains specialized receptors sensitive to the specific wavelengths associated with red, green, and blue. According to this model, people can see all of the colours of the rainbow because the eye does its own "colour mixing" by varying the ratio of neural activity among these three types of receptors.

The impetus for the trichromatic theory was the demonstration that a light of any colour can be matched by the additive mixture of three *primary colours*. Any three colours that are appropriately spaced out in the visible spectrum can serve as primary colours, although red, green, and blue are usually used. Does it sound implausible that three colours should be adequate for creating all other colours? If so, consider that this is exactly what happens on your colour TV screen and computer monitor (Stockman, 2010).

Most of the known facts about colour-blindness also meshed well with trichromatic theory. *Colour-blindness* encompasses a variety of deficiencies in the ability to distinguish among colours. Colour-blindness occurs much more frequently in males than in females. Actually, the term *colour-blindness* is somewhat misleading, since complete blindness to differences in colours is quite rare. Most people who are colour-blind are *dichromats*; that is, they make do with only two colour channels. There are three types of dichromats, and each type is insensitive to one of the primary colours—red, green, or blue—although the latter is rare (Reid & Usrey, 2008). The three deficiencies seen among dichromats support the notion that there are three channels for colour vision, as proposed by trichromatic theory.

Opponent Process Theory of Colour Vision

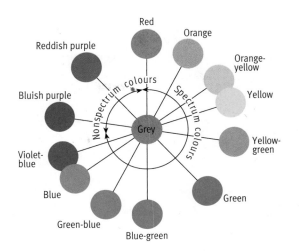

PSYKTREK 3d

Although trichromatic theory explained some facets of colour vision well, it ran aground in other areas. Consider complementary afterimages, for instance. *Complementary colours* are pairs of colours that produce grey tones when mixed together. The various pairs of complementary colours can be arranged in a *colour circle*, such as the one in Figure 4.20. If you stare at a strong colour and then look at a white background, you'll see an *afterimage*—a visual image that persists after a stimulus is removed. The colour of the afterimage will be the *complement* of the colour you originally stared at. Trichromatic theory cannot account for the appearance of complementary afterimages.

Here's another peculiarity to consider. If you ask people to describe colours but restrict them to using three names, they run into difficulty. For example, using only red, green, and blue, they simply don't feel comfortable describing yellow as "reddish green." However, if you let them have just one more name, they usually choose yellow; they can then describe any colour quite well (Gordon & Abramov, 2001). If colours are reduced to three channels, why are four colour names required to describe the full range of possible colours?

In an effort to answer questions such as these, Ewald Hering proposed the *opponent process theory* in 1878. The *opponent process theory of colour vision* holds that colour perception depends on receptors that make antagonistic responses to three pairs of colours. The three pairs of opponent colours posited by Hering were red versus green, yellow versus blue, and black versus white. The antagonistic processes in this theory provide plausible explanations for complementary afterimages and the need for four names

(red, green, blue, and yellow) to describe colours. Opponent process theory also explains some aspects of colour-blindness. For instance, it can explain why dichromats typically find it hard to distinguish either green from red or yellow from blue. Opponent process theory even seems to characterize the colour perception of people with other perceptual dysfunctions, for example, *grapheme-colour synesthesia*. In this rare condition, when individuals perceive a letter or digit, they concurrently and unintentionally experience the perception of an associated colour. Research by Nikolic, Lichti, and Singer (2007) demonstrated that these colour experiences are processed in "color opponent channels (red–green or blue–yellow)" (p. 481) in the same way that "real" colour perception is processed.

Reconciling Theories of Colour Vision

PSYKTREK 3d

Advocates of trichromatic theory and opponent process theory argued about the relative merits of their models for almost a century. Most researchers assumed that one theory must be wrong and the other must be right. In recent decades, however, it has become clear that *it takes both theories to explain colour vision*. Eventually, a physiological basis for both theories was found. Research that earned George Wald a Nobel Prize (Wald, 1964) demonstrated that *the eye has three types of cones*, with each type being most sensitive to a different band of wavelengths, as shown in Figure 4.21 (Gegenfurtner, 2010; Wald, 1964). The three types of cones represent the three different colour receptors predicted by trichromatic theory.

Researchers also discovered a biological basis for opponent processes. They found cells in the retina, the LGN, and the visual cortex *that respond in opposite ways to red versus green and blue versus yellow* (Purves, 2009; Zrenner et al., 1990). For example, there are ganglion cells in the retina that are excited by green and inhibited by red. Other ganglion cells in the

---

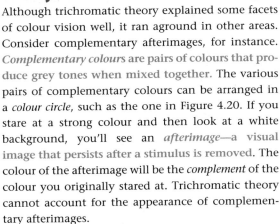

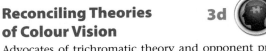

FIGURE 4.20

The colour circle and complementary colours.

Colours opposite each other on this colour circle are complements, or "opposites." Additively, mixing complementary colours produces grey. Opponent process principles help to explain this effect, as well as the other peculiarities of complementary colours noted in the text.

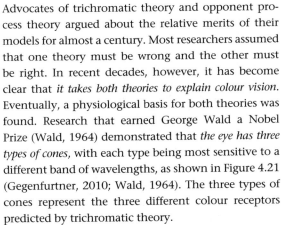

WEB LINK 4.2

The Joy of Visual Perception: A Web Book
This site shows the Internet at its best. Peter Kaiser of York University has crafted a comprehensive guide to human colour vision, supplying plenty of graphics and demonstrations to help visitors understand what laboratory research in psychology has learned about visual perception.

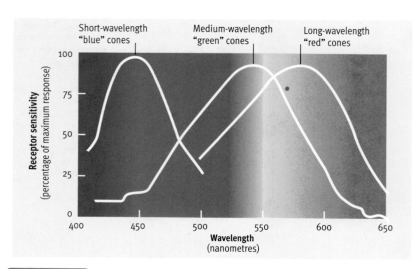

FIGURE 4.21

Three types of cones.

Research has identified three types of cones that show varied sensitivity to different wavelengths of light. As the graph shows, these three types of cones correspond only roughly to the red, green, and blue receptors predicted by trichromatic theory, so it is more accurate to refer to them as cones sensitive to short, medium, and long wavelengths.

Source: Wald, G., and Brown, P.K. (1965). Human Color vision and color blindness. *Symposium Cold Spring Harbor Laboratory of Quantitative Biology, 30,* 345–359 (p. 351). Copyright © 1965. Reprinted by permission of the author.

retina work in just the opposite way, as predicted in opponent process theory.

In summary, the perception of colour appears to involve sequential stages of information processing (Hurvich, 1981). The receptors that do the first stage of processing (the cones) seem to follow the principles outlined in trichromatic theory. In later stages of processing, at least some cells in the retina, the LGN, and the visual cortex seem to follow the principles

outlined in opponent process theory (see Figure 4.22). As you can see, vigorous theoretical debate about colour vision produced a solution that went beyond the contributions of either theory alone.

Effects of Colour on Behaviour

A newly emerging area of research concerns the effects that specific colours have on psychological functioning. Although there has long been an extensive popular literature on how colours affect behaviour, this literature has mostly been based on speculation rather than sound empirical research. Recently, however, Andrew Elliot and his colleagues (Elliot & Maier, 2007; Moller, Elliot, & Maier, 2009) have formulated a theory of how colour might influence behaviour and begun a series of carefully controlled experiments to test specific hypotheses. According to Elliot et al. (2007), colours can have automatic, unconscious effects on behaviour. They assert that these effects are probably rooted in two basic sources. First, people learn associations based on certain colours being paired repeatedly with certain experiences. For instance, red ink is usually used to mark students' errors and red lights and red signs are often used to warn of danger. Second, over the course of human evolution, certain colours may have had adaptive significance for survival or reproduction. For example, blood and fire, which often appear red, both can signal danger.

In their first study of the behavioural effects of colour, Elliot et al. (2007) theorized that red is associated with the danger of failure in achievement settings. Hence, they tested the hypothesis that

FIGURE 4.22

Reconciling theories of colour vision.

Contemporary explanations of colour vision include aspects of both the trichromatic and opponent process theories. As predicted by trichromatic theory, there are three types of receptors for colour—cones sensitive to short, medium, and long wavelengths. However, these cones are organized into receptive fields that excite or inhibit the firing of higher-level visual cells in the retina, thalamus, and cortex. As predicted by opponent process theory, some of these cells respond in antagonistic ways to blue versus yellow, red versus green, and black versus white.

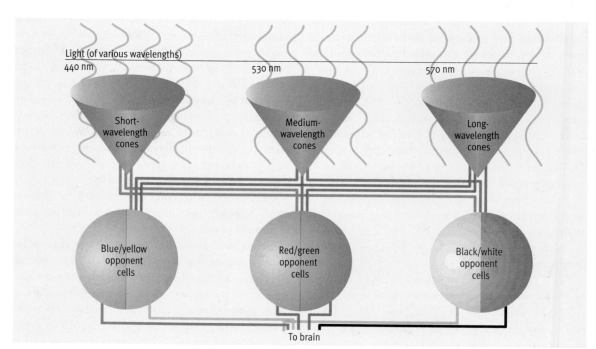

exposure to the colour red has a negative impact on performance in achievement situations. In one study, participants taking a subtest of an IQ test were exposed to a white, red, or green test booklet cover prior to taking the subtest. As hypothesized, subjects exposed to the red cover scored significantly lower on the test than those exposed to the green or white covers. Subsequent studies showed that the colour red undermines performance in achievement contexts by evoking avoidance tendencies that disrupt attention (Elliot et al., 2009; Maier, Elliot, & Lichtenfeld, 2008). Elliot (Elliot & Niesta, 2008; Elliot et al., 2010) has even found that the colour red affects ratings of attractiveness. In one of these studies (Elliot & Niesta 2008), participants were shown photos of a woman, dressed in either a red or blue blouse for different groups of participants. Participants made rating of the woman and it was found, among other things, that the red blouse led to significantly higher attractiveness, sexual desirability, and dating interest ratings than the blue blouse. Participants in the red condition also reported that they would be willing to spend more money on a date with the woman than those in the blue condition. In a more recent follow-up study, Elliot and his colleagues (2010) found that the colour red also fosters greater attraction when women evaluate men, although for somewhat different reasons.

In other contexts it has been found that our eyes seem to be able to follow red targets on a computer screen more quickly and easily than they can follow targets in other colours, such as green or yellow (Tchernikov & Fallah, 2010). According to vision researcher Maz Fallah, this may lead to "the perception that a red coloured object . . . appears to move faster than objects of other colours" (Yfile, 2010, p. 10). There is good news and bad news in this observation. It may mean that Olympic athletes who run in red-coloured uniforms, such as Canada's 100-metre-hurdle sensation Priscilla Lopes-Schliep, may look as if they are running even faster than they are in fact running. It also means, of course, that if you are driving a red Porsche, you may look to be travelling faster to the police officer following you than if you were driving a silver Porsche!

The study of sensation and perception is one of the oldest areas of scientific research in psychology. Yet this work shows that there are still fascinating areas of inquiry that remain unexplored. It just takes some creativity and insight to recognize them. The influence of colour on psychological functioning should be a fertile area of research in the future.

Perceiving Forms, Patterns, and Objects

 3c 3e

The drawing in Figure 4.23 is a poster for a circus act involving a trained seal. Take a good look at it. What do you see?

No doubt you see a seal balancing a ball on its nose and a trainer holding a fish and a whip. But suppose you had been told that the drawing is actually a poster for a costume ball. Would you have perceived it differently?

If you focus on the idea of a costume ball (stay with it a minute if you still see the seal and trainer), you will probably see a costumed man and woman in Figure 4.23. She's handing him a hat, and he has a sword in his right hand. This tricky little sketch was

While Canadian hurdler Priscilla Lopes-Schliep probably does not need the help, some athletes may benefit from wearing red uniforms, such as the ones worn by Canadian Olympic team members. Recent research suggests that red-coloured objects may appear to move faster than objects in other colours.

FIGURE 4.23

A poster for a trained seal act.

Or is it? The picture is an ambiguous figure, which can be interpreted as either of two scenes, as explained in the text.

Sensation and Perception

FIGURE 4.24

Another ambiguous figure.
What animal do you see here? As the text explains, two very different perceptions are possible. This ambiguous figure was devised around 1900 by Joseph Jastrow, a prominent psychologist at the turn of the 20th century (Block & Yuker, 1992).

made ambiguous quite intentionally. It's a *reversible figure*, a drawing that is compatible with two interpretations that can shift back and forth. Another classic reversible figure is shown in Figure 4.24. What do you see? A rabbit or a duck? It all depends on how you look at the drawing.

The key point is simply this: The same visual input can result in radically different perceptions. No one-to-one correspondence exists between sensory input and what you perceive. This is a principal reason that people's experience of the world is subjective. Perception involves much more than passively receiving signals from the outside world. It involves the interpretation of sensory input. To some extent, this interpretive process can be influenced by manipulating people's expectations. For example, information given to you about the drawing of the "circus act involving a trained seal" created a *perceptual set*—a readiness to perceive a stimulus in a particular way. A perceptual set creates a certain slant in how someone interprets sensory input.

Form perception also depends on the selection of sensory input—that is, what people focus their attention on (Chun & Wolfe, 2001). A visual scene may include many objects and forms. Some of them may capture viewers' attention while others may not. In fact, while much of what we have discussed so far is about what and how we see, sometimes it is even more interesting to consider what we fail to see and under what conditions we fail to see it. This fact has been demonstrated in dramatic fashion in studies of *inattentional blindness*, which involves the failure to see fully visible objects or events in a visual display (Bloom, 2010; Chabris & Simons, 2010; Memmert, Unkelbach, & Ganns, 2010). In what has become one of the most famous experiments in psychology in the past several years (Simons & Chabris, 1999), participants watched a video of a group of people in white shirts passing a basketball that was laid over another video of people in black shirts passing a basketball (the two videos were partially transparent). The observers were instructed to focus on one of the two teams and press a key whenever that team passed the ball. Thirty seconds into the task, a woman carrying an umbrella clearly walked through the scene for four seconds. You might guess that this bizarre development would be noticed by virtually all of the observers, but 44 percent of the participants failed to see the woman. Moreover, when someone in a gorilla suit strolled through the same scene, even more subjects (73 percent) missed the unexpected event.

This research program was conceived when Christopher Chabris (a graduate student) and Daniel Simons (a new professor) were talking about a recent legal case in which a police officer was mistakenly

apprehended (and beaten) by other police officers in a case of mistaken identity. The police officers who beat him left the severely injured officer alone on the ground and fled when they learned he was one of their own. The victim of the beating was suffering from facial wounds, a concussion, and some kidney damage. Another policeman, Officer Kenny Conley, who was near the spot where the beating took place, denied seeing the incident—it was assumed that Conley was covering up for the other officers who beat the victim. Conley denied seeing anything; in fact, when the events were described to him, he said that if that had happened, "I think I would have seen that" (Chabris & Simons, 2010, p. 3). The perpetrators of the assault were never charged with that crime. The only police officer who was charged was Kenny Conley. Conley was tried for perjury and convicted: The jury did not believe that he could not have seen the events, events that happened right in front of him. They assumed he must be covering up for the other officers. He had always claimed that he did not witness the events. Chablis and Simons wondered whether it was possible not to see something that was right in your line of vision. Ultimately the U.S. Supreme Court overturned Conley's conviction and he returned to the job as a police officer, but it took ten long years for this to happen.

Additional studies using other types of stimulus materials have demonstrated that people routinely overlook obvious forms that are unexpected

Officer Kenny Conley of the Boston Police Department was unable to identify the police officers who assaulted fellow police officer Michael Cox. Was Conley withholding evidence, or was he the victim of inattentional blindness?

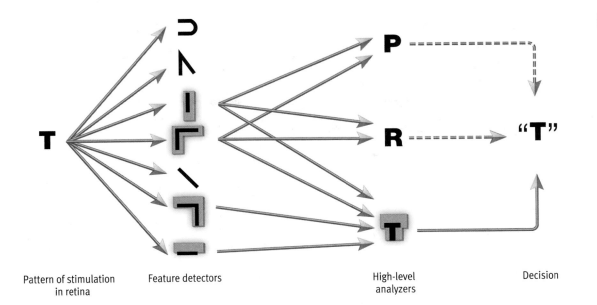

Pattern of stimulation in retina   Feature detectors   High-level analyzers   Decision

FIGURE 4.25

Feature analysis in form perception.

One vigorously debated theory of form perception is that the brain has cells that respond to specific aspects or features of stimuli, such as lines and angles. Neurons functioning as higher-level analyzers then respond to input from these "feature detectors." The more input each analyzer receives, the more active it becomes. Finally, other neurons weigh signals from these analyzers and make a "decision" about the stimulus. In this way, perception of a form is arrived at by assembling elements from the bottom up.

(Most et al., 2005). Inattentional blindness has been attributed to a perceptual set that leads people to focus most of their attention on a specific feature in a scene (such as the basketball passes) while neglecting other facets of the scene (Most et al., 2001). Consistent with this analysis, recent research has shown that the likelihood of inattentional blindness increases when people work on tasks that require a lot of attention or create a heavy perceptual load (Cartwright-Finch & Lavie, 2007). Inattentional blindness may account for many automobile accidents, as accident reports frequently include the statement "I looked right there, but never saw them" (Shermer, 2004). Although this can happen to an attentive and unimpaired driver, research shows that inattentional blindness increases when people talk on a cellphone or are even slightly intoxicated (Clifasefi, Takarangi, & Bergman, 2006; Strayer & Drews, 2007).

The idea that we see much less of the world than we think we do surprises many people, but an auditory parallel exists that people take for granted (Mack, 2003). Think of how often you have had someone clearly say something to you, but you did not hear a word of what was said because you were "not listening." Inattentional blindness is essentially the same thing in the visual domain.

An understanding of how people perceive forms and objects also requires knowledge of how people *organize* their visual inputs. Several influential approaches to this issue emphasize *feature analysis*.

Feature Analysis: Assembling Forms

3c PSYKTREK

The information received by your eyes would do you little good if you couldn't recognize objects

and forms—ranging from words on a page to mice in your cellar and friends in the distance. According to some theories, perceptions of form and pattern entail *feature analysis* (Lindsay & Norman, 1977; Maguire et al., 1990). *Feature analysis* is the process of detecting specific elements in visual input and assembling them into a more complex form. In other words, you start with the components of a form, such as lines, edges, and corners, and build them into perceptions of squares, triangles, stop signs, bicycles, ice cream cones, and telephones. An application of this model of form perception is diagrammed in Figure 4.25.

Feature analysis assumes that form perception involves *bottom-up processing*, a progression from individual elements to the whole (see Figure 4.26). The plausibility of this model was bolstered greatly when Hubel and Wiesel (1962) showed that cells in

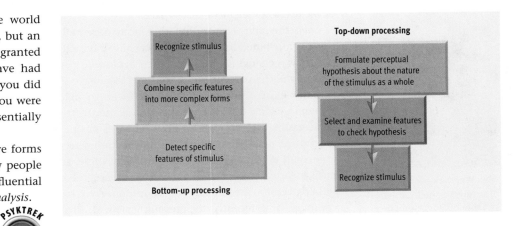

FIGURE 4.26

Bottom-up versus top-down processing.

As explained in these diagrams, bottom-up processing progresses from individual elements to whole elements, whereas top-down processing progresses from the whole to the individual elements.

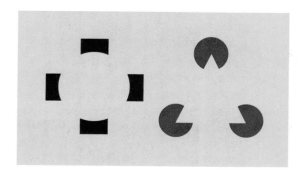

FIGURE 4.27

Subjective contours.

Our perception of the triangle on the right and the circle on the left results from subjective contours that are not really there. The effect is so powerful, the triangle and circle appear lighter than the background, which they are not. To demonstrate the illusory nature of these contours for yourself, cover the red circles that mark off the triangle. You'll see that the triangle disappears.

WEB LINK 4.3

Sensation and Perception Tutorials

John Krantz of Hanover College has assembled a collection of quality tutorials on sensation and perception. Topics covered include receptive fields, depth perception, Gestalt laws, and the use of perceptual principles in art.

Max Wertheimer

"The fundamental 'formula' of Gestalt theory might be expressed in this way: There are wholes, the behaviour of which is not determined by that of their individual elements."

the visual cortex operate as highly specialized feature detectors. Indeed, their findings strongly suggested that at least some aspects of form perception involve feature analysis.

Can feature analysis provide a complete account of how people perceive forms? Clearly not. A crucial problem for the theory is that form perception often does not involve bottom-up processing. In fact, there is ample evidence that perceptions of form frequently involve *top-down processing*, a progression from the whole to the elements (see Figure 4.27). For example, there is evidence that people can perceive a word before its individual letters, a phenomenon that has to reflect top-down processing (Johnston & McClelland, 1974). If readers depended exclusively on bottom-up processing, they would have to analyze the features of letters in words to recognize them and then assemble the letters into words. This would be a terribly time-consuming task and would slow down reading speed to a snail's pace.

Subjective contours are another phenomenon traditionally attributed to top-down processing, although that view is changing. The phenomenon of *subjective contours* is the perception of contours where none actually exist. Consider, for instance, the triangle shown in Figure 4.27. We see the contours of the triangle easily, even though no physical edges or lines are present. It is hard to envision how feature detectors could detect edges that are not really there, so most theorists have argued that bottom-up models of form perception are unlikely to account for subjective contours. Until recently, the prevailing view was that subjective contours depend on viewing stimulus configurations as wholes and then filling in the blanks (Rock, 1986). However, researchers have demonstrated that feature detectors *do* respond to the edges

in subjective contours (Peterhans & von der Heydt, 1991). At present, neural theories of subjective contours that emphasize bottom-up processing or both types of processing are under investigation, with promising results (Gunn et al., 2000; Lesher, 1995). In sum, it appears that both top-down and bottom-up processing have their niches in form perception.

Looking at the Whole Picture: Gestalt Principles

3e

Top-down processing is clearly at work in the principles of form perception described by the Gestalt psychologists. As mentioned in Chapter 1, *Gestalt psychology* was an influential school of thought that emerged out of Germany during the first half of the 20th century. (*Gestalt* is a German word for form or *shape*.) Gestalt psychologists repeatedly demonstrated that the whole can be greater than the sum of its parts. Although it is no longer an active theoretical orientation in psychology, it influenced the study of perception (Banks & Krajicek, 1991) and other areas of psychology (Asch, 1946).

A simple example of this principle is the *phi phenomenon*, first described by Max Wertheimer in 1912. The *phi phenomenon* is the illusion of movement created by presenting visual stimuli in rapid succession. You encounter examples of the phi phenomenon nearly every day. For example, movies and TV consist of separate still pictures projected rapidly one after the other. You see smooth motion, but in reality the "moving" objects merely take slightly different positions in successive frames. Viewed as a whole, a movie has a property (motion) that isn't evident in any of its parts (the individual frames). The Gestalt psychologists formulated a series of principles that describe how the visual system organizes a scene into discrete forms (Schirillo, 2010). Let's examine some of these principles.

Figure and Ground. Take a look at Figure 4.28. Do you see the figure as two silhouetted faces against a white background, or as a white vase against a black background? This reversible figure illustrates the Gestalt principle of *figure and ground*. Dividing visual displays into figure and ground is a fundamental way in which people organize visual perceptions (Baylis & Driver, 1995). The *figure* is the thing being looked at, and the *ground* is the background against which it stands. Figures seem to have more substance and shape, appear closer to the viewer, and seem to stand out in front of the ground. More often than not, your visual field may contain many

FIGURE 4.28

The principle of figure and ground.

Whether you see two faces or a vase depends on which part of this drawing you see as figure and which as background. Although this reversible drawing allows you to switch back and forth between two ways of organizing your perception, you can't perceive the drawing in both ways at once.

figures sharing a background. The following Gestalt principles relate to how these elements are grouped into higher-order figures (Palmer, 2003).

Proximity. Things that are close to one another seem to belong together. The black dots in the upper left panel of Figure 4.29(a) could be grouped into vertical columns or horizontal rows. However, people tend to perceive rows because of the effect of proximity (the dots are closer together horizontally).

Closure. People often group elements to create a sense of *closure*, or completeness. Thus, you may "complete" figures that actually have gaps in them. This principle is demonstrated in the upper right panel of Figure 4.29(b).

Similarity. People also tend to group stimuli that are similar. This principle is apparent in Figure 4.29(c), where viewers group elements of similar lightness into the number 2.

Simplicity. The Gestaltists' most general principle was the law of *Pragnanz*, which translates from German as *good form*. The idea is that people tend to group elements that combine to form a good figure. This principle is somewhat vague in that it's often difficult to spell out what makes a figure "good" (Biederman, Hilton, & Hummel, 1991). Some theorists maintain

that goodness is largely a matter of simplicity, asserting that people tend to organize forms in the simplest way possible [see Figure 4.29(d)]. But the concept of simplicity is also plagued by ambiguity (Donderi, 2006).

Continuity. The principle of continuity reflects people's tendency to follow in whatever direction they've been led. Thus, people tend to connect points that result in straight or gently curved lines that create "smooth" paths, as shown in Figure 4.29(e).

Formulating Perceptual Hypotheses

The Gestalt principles provide some indications of how people organize visual input. However, scientists are still one step away from understanding

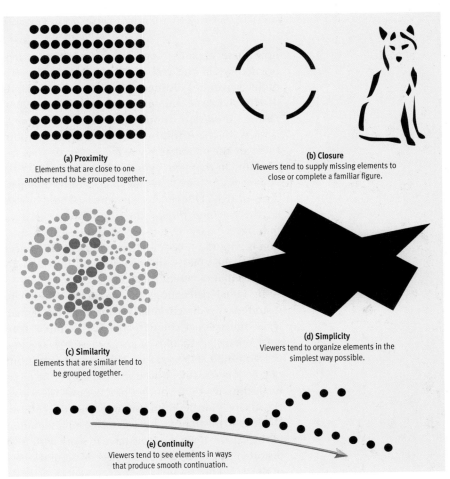

(a) Proximity
Elements that are close to one another tend to be grouped together.

(b) Closure
Viewers tend to supply missing elements to close or complete a familiar figure.

(c) Similarity
Elements that are similar tend to be grouped together.

(d) Simplicity
Viewers tend to organize elements in the simplest way possible.

(e) Continuity
Viewers tend to see elements in ways that produce smooth continuation.

FIGURE 4.29

Gestalt principles of perceptual organization.

Gestalt principles help explain some of the factors that influence form perception. (a) **Proximity**: These dots might well be organized in vertical columns rather than horizontal rows, but because of proximity (the dots are closer together horizontally), they tend to be perceived in rows. (b) **Closure**: Even though the figures are incomplete, you fill in the blanks and see a circle and a dog. (c) **Similarity**: Because of similarity of colour, you see dots organized into the number 2 instead of a random array. If you did not group similar elements, you wouldn't see the number 2 here. (d) **Simplicity**: You could view this as a complicated 11-sided figure, but given the preference for simplicity, you are more likely to see it as an overlapping rectangle and triangle. (e) **Continuity**: You tend to group these dots in a way that produces a smooth path rather than an abrupt shift in direction.

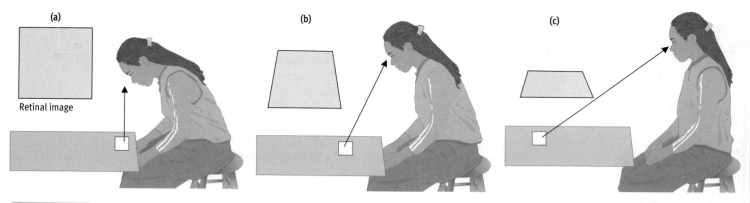

(a)   (b)   (c)

Retinal image

FIGURE 4.30

Distal and proximal stimuli.

Proximal stimuli are often distorted, shifting representations of distal stimuli in the real world. If you look directly down at a small, square piece of paper on a desk (a), the distal stimulus (the paper) and the proximal stimulus (the image projected on your retina) will both be square. But as you move the paper away on the desktop, as shown in (b) and (c), the square distal stimulus projects an increasingly trapezoidal image on your retina, making the proximal stimulus more and more distorted. Nevertheless, you continue to perceive a square.

how these organized perceptions result in a representation of the real world. Understanding the problem requires distinguishing between two kinds of stimuli: distal and proximal (Hochberg, 1988). *Distal stimuli* are stimuli that lie in the distance (that is, in the world outside the body). In vision, these are the objects that you're looking at. They are "distant" in that your eyes don't touch them. What your eyes do "touch" are the images formed by patterns of light falling on your retinas. These images are the *proximal stimuli*, the stimulus energies that impinge directly on sensory receptors. The distinction is important, because there are great differences between the objects you perceive and the stimulus energies that represent them.

In visual perception, the proximal stimuli are distorted, two-dimensional versions of their actual, three-dimensional counterparts. For example, consider the distal stimulus of a square such as the one in Figure 4.30. If the square is lying on a desk in front of you, it is actually projecting a trapezoid (the proximal stimulus) onto your retinas, because the top of the square is farther from your eyes than the bottom. Obviously, the trapezoid is a distorted representation of the square. If what people have to work with is so distorted a picture, how do they get an accurate view of the world out there?

One explanation is that people bridge the gap between distal and proximal stimuli by constantly making and testing *hypotheses* about what's out there in the real world (Gregory, 1973). Thus, a *perceptual hypothesis* is an inference about which distal stimuli could be responsible for the proximal stimuli sensed. In effect, people make educated guesses about what form could be responsible for a pattern of sensory stimulation. The square in Figure 4.30

may project a trapezoidal image on your retinas, but your perceptual system "guesses" correctly that it's a square—and that's what you see.

Let's look at another ambiguous drawing to further demonstrate the process of making a perceptual hypothesis. Figure 4.31 is a famous reversible figure, first published as a cartoon in a humour magazine. Perhaps you see a drawing of a young woman looking back over her right shoulder. Alternatively, you might see an old woman with her chin down on her chest. The ambiguity exists because there isn't enough information to force your perceptual system to accept only one of these hypotheses.

FIGURE 4.31

A famous reversible figure.

What do you see? Consult the text to learn what the two possible interpretations of this figure are.

Incidentally, studies show that people who are led to *expect* the young woman or the old woman generally see the one they expect (Leeper, 1935). This is another example of how perceptual sets influence what people see.

Psychologists have used a variety of reversible figures to study how people formulate perceptual hypotheses. Another example can be seen in Figure 4.32, which shows the *Necker cube*. The shaded surface can appear as either the front or the rear of the transparent cube. If you look at the cube for a while, your perception will alternate between these possibilities. People tend to experience a similar shift back and forth between two perceptions when they view the image in Figure 4.33.

The *context* in which something appears often guides people's perceptual hypotheses (Bravo, 2010). To illustrate, take a look at Figure 4.34. What do you see? You probably saw the words "THE CAT." But look again; the middle characters in both words are identical. You identified an "H" in the first word and an "A" in the second because of the surrounding letters, which created an expectation—another example of top-down processing in visual perception. The power of expectations explains why typographocal errors like those in this sentence often pass unoberved (Lachman, 1996).

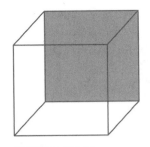

FIGURE 4.32

The Necker cube.
The tinted surface of this reversible figure can become either the front or the back of the cube.

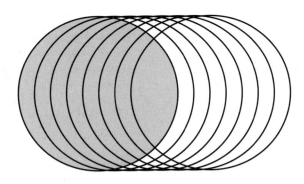

FIGURE 4.33

Another reversible figure.
The tinted surface of this reversible figure can become either the closer or farther end of the "tube." People's perceptions of this stimulus tend to dynamically go back and forth between these interpretations.

THE CHT

FIGURE 4.34

Context effects.
The context in which a stimulus is seen can affect your perceptual hypotheses.

REVIEW OF KEY POINTS

▷ Perceptions of colour (hue) are primarily a function of light wavelength, while amplitude affects brightness and purity affects saturation. There are two types of colour mixing: additive and subtractive. Human colour perception depends on processes that resemble additive colour mixing.

▷ The trichromatic theory holds that people have three types of receptors that are sensitive to wavelengths associated with red, green, and blue. The opponent process theory holds that colour perception depends on receptors that make antagonistic responses to red versus green, blue versus yellow, and black versus white. The evidence now suggests that both theories are necessary to account for colour vision.

▷ Reversible figures and perceptual sets demonstrate that the same visual input can result in very different perceptions. Form perception depends on both the selection and interpretation of sensory inputs. According to feature analysis theories, people detect specific elements in stimuli and build them into recognizable forms through bottom-up processing. However, form perception also involves top-down processing, which progresses from the whole to the elements.

▷ Gestalt psychology emphasized that the whole may be greater than the sum of its parts (features), as illustrated by the Gestalt principles of form perception, including figure–ground, proximity, similarity, continuity, closure, and simplicity. Other approaches to form perception emphasize that people develop perceptual hypotheses about the distal stimuli that could be responsible for the proximal stimuli that are sensed.

Perceiving Depth or Distance

3f

More often than not, forms and figures are objects in space. Spatial considerations add a third dimension to visual perception. *Depth perception* involves interpretation of visual cues that indicate how near or far away objects are. To make judgments of distance, people rely on quite a variety of clues, which can be classified into two types: binocular and monocular (Hochberg, 1988; Proffitt & Caudek, 2003).

Binocular Cues

3f

Because the eyes are set apart, each eye has a slightly different view of the world. *Binocular depth* cues are clues about distance based on the differing views of the two eyes. The new 3-D movies take advantage of this fact. Two cameras are used to record slightly different images of the same scene. The special polarized glasses that viewers wear separate the images for each eye. The brain then supplies the "depth" and you perceive a three-dimensional scene.

The principal binocular depth cue is *retinal disparity*, which refers to the fact that objects project images to slightly different locations on the right and left retinas, so the right and left eyes see slightly

PREVIEW QUESTIONS

▶ What are some binocular and monocular depth cues?

▶ Are there cultural differences in depth perception?

▶ What are perceptual constancies?

▶ What do optical illusions reveal about perceptual processes?

▶ What is the difference between vision for perception and vision for action?

different views of the object. The closer an object gets, the greater the disparity between the images seen by each eye. Thus, retinal disparity increases as objects come closer, providing information about distance. Another binocular cue is *convergence*, which involves sensing the eyes converging toward each other as they focus on closer objects.

Monocular Cues

Monocular depth cues are clues about distance based on the image in either eye alone. There are two kinds of monocular cues to depth. One kind is the result of active use of the eye in viewing the world. For example, if you cover one eye and move your head from side to side, closer objects appear to move more than distant objects. In a similar vein, you may notice when driving along a highway that nearby objects (such as fence posts along the road) appear to move by more rapidly than objects that are farther away (such as trees in the distance). Thus, you

get cues about depth from *motion parallax*, which involves images of objects at different distances moving across the retina at different rates. The study of motion parallax was one of the earliest areas of study in depth perception; it was first suggested as a depth cue over 300 years ago (Ono & Wade, 2005).

The other kind of monocular cues are *pictorial depth cues*—clues about distance that can be given in a flat picture. There are many pictorial cues to depth, which is why some paintings and photographs seem so realistic that you feel you can climb right into them. Six prominent pictorial depth cues are described and illustrated in Figure 4.35. *Linear perspective* is a depth cue reflecting the fact that lines converge in the distance. Because details are too small to see when they are far away, *texture gradients* can provide information about depth. If an object comes between you and another object, it must be closer to you, a cue called *interposition*. *Relative size* is a cue because closer objects appear larger. *Height in plane* reflects the fact that distant

FIGURE 4.35

Pictorial cues to depth.

Six pictorial depth cues are explained and illustrated here. Although one cue stands out in each photo, several pictorial cues are present in most visual scenes. Try looking at the *light-and-shadow* picture upside down. The change in shadowing reverses what you see.

objects appear higher in a picture. Finally, the familiar effects of shadowing make *light and shadow* useful in judging distance. Research also suggests that application of pictorial depth cues to pictures varies to some degree across cultures (Berry et al., 1992; Hudson, 1960).

Recent research has shown that estimates of distance can be skewed by people's motivational states. Studies suggest that people see desirable objects as closer to them than less desirable objects. For example, Balcetis and Dunning (2010) found that participants who are very thirsty estimate that a bottle of water sitting across a room is closer to them than participants who are not thirsty. In another study, subjects were asked to estimate the distance between them and a $100 bill that they had a chance to win or a $100 bill that they knew belonged to the experimenter. Once again, the more desirable object (the $100 bill that could be won) was perceived to be closer than the less desirable object. Thus, like other perceptual experiences, judgments of distance can be highly subjective.

Perceptual Constancies in Vision

When a person approaches you from a distance, his or her image on your retinas gradually changes in size. Do you perceive that the person is growing right before your eyes? Of course not. Your perceptual system constantly makes allowances for this variation in visual input. The task of the perceptual system is to provide an accurate rendition of distal stimuli based on distorted, ever-changing proximal stimuli. In doing so, it relies in part on perceptual constancies. A *perceptual constancy* is a tendency to experience a stable perception in the face of continually changing sensory input. Among other things, people tend to view objects as having a stable size, shape, brightness, hue, and texture (Goldstein, 2010).

The Power of Misleading Cues: Optical Illusions SIM3 3g

In general, perceptual constancies, depth cues, and principles of visual organization (such as the Gestalt laws) help people perceive the world accurately. Sometimes, however, perceptions are based on inappropriate assumptions, and *optical illusions* can result. An *optical illusion* involves an apparently inexplicable discrepancy between the appearance of a visual stimulus and its physical reality.

One famous optical illusion is the Müller-Lyer illusion, shown in Figure 4.36. The two vertical lines in this figure are equally long, but they certainly don't look that way. Why not? Several mechanisms probably play a role (Day, 1965; Gregory, 1978). The drawing on the left looks like the outside of a building, thrust toward the viewer, while the one on the right looks like an inside corner, thrust away (see Figure 4.37). The vertical line in the left-hand drawing therefore seems closer. If two lines cast equally long retinal images but one seems closer, the closer one is assumed to be shorter. Thus, the Müller-Lyer illusion may result from a combination of size constancy processes and misperception of depth. As we saw earlier with regard to the McCollough effect, visual illusions can be useful to probe the nature of visual systems and visual processing. Daniel Meegan of the University of Guelph and his colleagues (Meegan et al., 2004; Mendoza et al., 2006) have used the Müller-Lyer illusion to derive conclusions regarding the nature of visual representations underlying perception, motor control, and planning.

The geometric illusions shown in Figure 4.38 also demonstrate that visual stimuli can be highly deceptive. The *Ponzo illusion*, which is shown at the top left of this figure, appears to result from the same factors at work in the Müller-Lyer illusion (Coren & Girgus, 1978). The upper and lower horizontal lines are the same length, but the upper one appears to be longer. This illusion probably occurs because the converging lines convey linear perspective, a key depth cue suggesting that the upper line lies farther away. Figure 4.39 shows a drawing by Stanford University psychologist Roger Shepard (1990) that creates a similar illusion. The second monster appears much larger than the first, even though they are really identical in size.

Adelbert Ames designed a striking illusion that makes use of misperception of distance. It's called, appropriately enough, the *Ames room*. It's a specially contrived room built with a trapezoidal

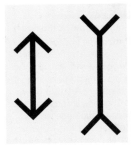

FIGURE 4.36

The Müller-Lyer illusion.
Go ahead, measure them: The two vertical lines are of equal length.

Log on to CourseMate to access this interactive figure.

FIGURE 4.37

Explaining the Müller-Lyer illusion.
The drawing on the left seems to be closer, since it looks like an outside corner, thrust toward you, whereas the drawing on the right looks like an inside corner thrust away from you. Given retinal images of the same length, you assume that the "closer" line is shorter.

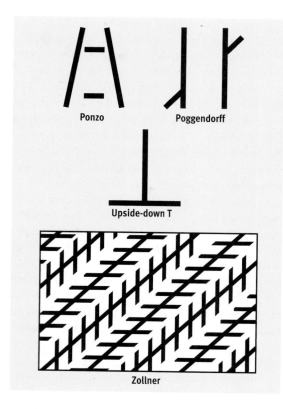

FIGURE 4.38

Four geometric illusions.

Ponzo: The horizontal lines are the same length. **Poggendorff:** The two diagonal segments lie on the same straight line. **Upside-down T:** The vertical and horizontal lines are the same length**. Zollner:** The long diagonals are all parallel (try covering up some of the short diagonal lines if you don't believe it).

Ponzo

Poggendorff

Upside-down T

Zollner

FIGURE 4.39

A monster of an illusion.

The principles underlying the Ponzo illusion also explain the striking illusion seen here, in which two identical monsters appear to be quite different in size.

Source: Shepard, R. N. (1990). *Mind sights*. New York: W.H. Freeman. Copyright © 1990 by Roger N. Shepard. Used by permission of Henry Holt & Co., LLC.

rear wall and a sloping floor and ceiling. When viewed from the correct point, as in the photo in Figure 4.40, it looks like an ordinary rectangular room. But in reality, the left corner is much taller and much farther from the viewer than the right corner, as the diagram in this figure shows. Hence, bizarre illusions unfold in the Ames room. People standing in the right corner appear to be giants, while those standing in the left corner appear to be midgets. Even more disconcerting, a person who walks across the room from right to left appears to

shrink before your eyes! The Ames room creates these misperceptions by toying with the perfectly reasonable assumption that the room is vertically and horizontally rectangular.

Impossible figures create another form of illusion. *Impossible figures* are objects that can be

concept **check 4.2**

Recognizing Pictorial Depth Cues

Painters routinely attempt to create the perception of depth on a flat canvas by using pictorial depth cues. Figure 4.35 on page 164 describes and illustrates six pictorial depth cues, most of which are apparent in Vincent van Gogh's colourful piece *Corridor in the Asylum* (1889) shown here. Check your understanding of depth perception by trying to spot the depth cues in the painting.

In the list below, check off the depth cues used by van Gogh. The answers can be found in the back of the book in Appendix A. You can learn more about how artists use the principles of visual perception in the Personal Application at the end of this chapter.

_____ **1.** Interposition	_____ **4.** Relative size
_____ **2.** Height in plane	_____ **5.** Light and shadow
_____ **3.** Texture gradient	_____ **6.** Linear perspective

Source: Image copyright © The Metropolitan Museum of Art / Art Resource, NY.

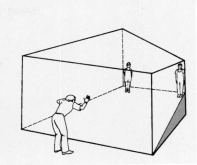

Wayne Weiten

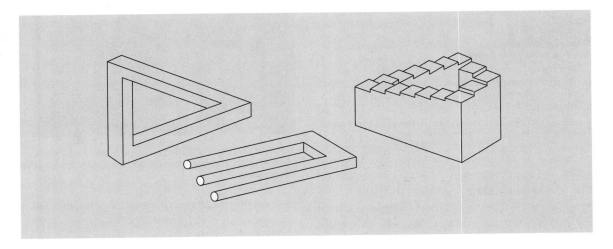

FIGURE 4.41

Three classic impossible figures.

The figures are impossible, yet they clearly exist—on the page. What makes them impossible is that they appear to be three-dimensional representations yet are drawn in a way that frustrates mental attempts to "assemble" their features into possible objects. It's difficult to see the drawings simply as lines lying in a plane—even though this perceptual hypothesis is the only one that resolves the contradiction.

WEB LINK 4.4

IllusionWorks

IllusionWorks bills itself as "the most comprehensive collection of optical and sensory illusions on the World Wide Web." At both "introductory" and "advanced" levels of explanation, this is an excellent resource for experiencing some of the strangest and most thought-provoking illusions ever created.

WEB LINK 4.5

The Moon Illusion Explained

Don McCready, professor emeritus at the University of Wisconsin (Whitewater), addresses the age-old puzzle of why the moon appears much larger at the horizon than overhead. He uses a helpful collection of illustrations in a comprehensive review of alternative theories.

represented in two-dimensional pictures but cannot exist in three-dimensional space. These figures may look fine at first glance, but a closer look reveals that they are geometrically inconsistent or impossible. Three widely studied impossible figures are shown in Figure 4.41, and a more recent impossible figure created by Roger Shepard (1990) can be seen in Figure 4.42. Notice that specific portions of these figures are reasonable, but they don't add up to a sensible whole (Macpherson, 2010). The parts don't interface properly. The initial illusion that the figures make sense is probably a result of bottom-up processing. You perceive specific features of the figure as acceptable but are baffled as they are built into a whole.

Obviously, illusions such as impossible figures and their real-life relative, the Ames room, involve a conspiracy of cues intended to deceive the viewer. Many visual illusions, however, occur quite naturally. A well-known example is the *moon illusion*. The full moon appears to be as much as 50 percent smaller when overhead than when looming on the horizon

(Ross & Plug, 2002; see the photo on page 168). As with many of the other illusions we have discussed, the moon illusion appears to be due mainly to size constancy effects coupled with the misperception of distance (Coren & Aks, 1990; Kaufman et al, 2007), although other factors may also play a role (Suzuki, 2007). The moon illusion shows that optical illusions are part of everyday life. Indeed, many people are virtually addicted to an optical illusion called television (an illusion of movement created by a series of still images presented in quick succession).

Cross-cultural studies have uncovered some interesting differences among cultural groups in their propensity to see certain illusions (Masuda, 2010). For example, Segall, Campbell, and Herskovits (1966) found that people from a variety of non-Western cultures are less susceptible to the Müller-Lyer illusion than Western samples. What could account for this difference? The most plausible explanation is that in the West, we live in a "carpentered world" dominated by straight lines, right angles, and rectangular rooms, buildings, and furniture. Thus, our experience

Sensation and Perception

FIGURE 4.42

Another impossible figure.

This impossible figure, drawn by Stanford University psychologist Roger Shepard (1990), seems even more perplexing than the classic impossible figure that it is based on (the one seen in the middle of Figure 4.41).

Source: Shepard, R. N. (1990). *Mind sights*. New York: W. H. Freeman. Copyright © 1990 by Roger N. Shepard. Used by permission of Henry Holt & Co., LLC.

A puzzling perceptual illusion common in everyday life is the moon illusion: The moon looks larger when at the horizon than when overhead.

prepares us to readily view the Müller-Lyer figures as inside and outside corners of buildings—inferences that help foster the illusion (Segall et al., 1990). In contrast, people in many non-Western cultures, such as the Zulu (see the photo on this page) who were tested by Segall and associates (1966), live in a less carpentered world, making them less prone to see the Müller-Lyer figures as building corners. Although there is some debate about the matter, cultural differences in illusion susceptibility suggest that people's perceptual inferences can be shaped by experience (Segall et al., 1990).

What do optical illusions reveal about visual perception? They drive home the point that people go through life formulating perceptual hypotheses about what lies out there in the real world. The fact that these are only hypotheses becomes especially striking when the hypotheses are wrong, as they are with illusions. Optical illusions also show how contextual factors such as depth cues shape perceptual hypotheses. Finally, like ambiguous figures, illusions clearly demonstrate that human perceptions are not simple reflections of objective reality. Once again, we see that perception of the world is subjective. These insights do not apply to visual perception only. We will encounter these lessons again as we examine other sensory systems, such as hearing.

Vision for Perception and Vision for Action

If you think about some of the theories and research discussed in this chapter and in Chapter 3 in the section on the brain, it should be apparent that there is a great deal of cross-fertilization between the two areas. Recent work by Mel Goodale (Goodale, 2010) and his colleagues at the University of Western

Unlike people in Western nations, the Zulus live in a culture where straight lines and right angles are scarce, if not entirely absent. Thus, they are not affected by such phenomena as the Müller-Lyer illusion nearly as much as people raised in environments that abound with rectangular structures.

Mel Goodale is internationally known for his work in the area of vision and neuroscience. He holds the Canada Research Chair in Visual Neuroscience in the departments of Psychology and Physiology at the University of Western Ontario. In 1999, he was awarded the D. O. Hebb Award by the Canadian Society for Brain, Behaviour, and Cognitive Science and was made a Fellow of the Royal Society of Canada in 2001.

Ontario (Goodale & Humphrey, 2001; Goodale & Milner, 1992, 2004; Milner & Goodale, 2008; Thaler & Goodale, 2010) is a good illustration of this point.

Goodale and Humphrey (2001) distinguish between two functions that vision serves. The first is to create an internal representation or model of the external world. This function is the subject of most of the research that we have discussed so far in this chapter. If you think about some of the things you might do as a result of being able to see the external world, it might give you a hint as to the nature of the second function that Goodale and Humphrey emphasized. The second function is not concerned with perceiving objects per se but with the related process of controlling your actions that are directed at those objects. Thus, if you are standing next to your best friend, one function of vision relates to creating an internal representation of that person and the second relates to guiding your actions in your attempt to, for example, pat him or her on the back as a means of congratulation. This second function, includes among other things, both avoiding obstacles and correcting for changes in location in the target you are reaching for (Chapman & Goodale, 2010). The first visual process is referred to as *vision for perception* and the second as *vision for action*. Goodale and his colleagues were led to this formulation by the work of previous researchers and

through observation of the deficits shown by individuals who suffered specific types of brain damage, such as that experienced by an individual referred to as "DF" (Goodale & Milner, 1992, 2004).

DF had suffered a tragic accident. She was young, well educated, and fluent in several languages. She was living at the time in Milan with her partner, Carlo. One day while taking a shower, she was overcome by carbon monoxide fumes—the water was heated by a propane heater. As a result of the carbon monoxide poisoning, she suffered brain damage. DF had difficulty with her vision, with seeing things and making sense out of them. Her visual problems were quite remarkable. She could see the surface detail of objects and their colour, but she could not use their form or contours to identify them. For example, although she could see grids of lines projected onto a screen, she could not tell whether they were vertical or horizontal: "[DF] has never regained a full and integrated experience of the visual world. The world she sees still lacks shape and form. [DF] is unable to identify objects on the basis of their form alone" (Goodale & Milner, 2004, p. 9). DF was unable to copy simple drawings but could draw them from memory (see Figure 4.43); these drawings show that her problems resulted from difficulties in perceptual organization, not in a "failure of the visual input to invoke the stored representation of the objects" (Goodale & Humphrey, 2001, p. 319). Her inability to recognize common objects is known as *agnosia*.

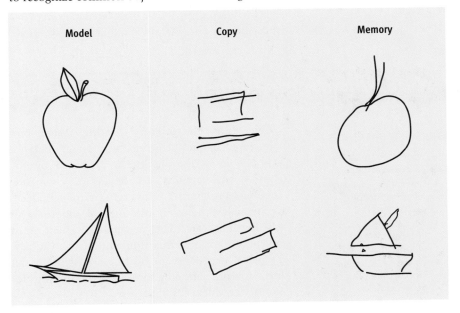

FIGURE 4.43

Samples of drawings made by DF.

The left column shows examples of line drawings that were shown to DF, the right column shows some of DF's drawings of the objects from memory, and the middle column shows examples of DF's copies of the line drawings shown in the left column.

Source: *Blackwell Handbook of Perception*, E. Bruce Goldstein, Glyn Humphreys, Margaret Shiffrar, and William Yost. Copyright © 2001 Blackwell Publishing Ltd. Reproduced with permission of Blackwell Publishing Ltd.

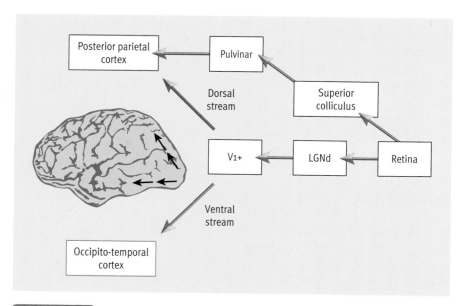

FIGURE 4.44

Schematic representation of the two streams of visual processing in the human cerebral cortex.
The retina sends projections to the dorsal part of the lateral geniculate nucleus in the thalamus, which projects in turn to the primary visual cortex (V1). Within the cerebral cortex, the ventral stream (red) arises from early visual areas (V1+) and projects to regions in the occipitotemporal cortex. The dorsal stream (blue) also arises from early visual areas but projects instead to the posterior parietal cortex. The posterior parietal cortex also receives visual input from the superior colliculus through the pulvinar, part of the thalamus.

Source: Reprinted from *Current Opinion in Neurobiology*, 14(2), Melvyn A. Goodale and David A. Westwood, An evolving view of duplex vision: Separate but interacting cortical pathways for perception and action, pp. 203–211. Copyright © 2004, with permission from Elsevier.

DF's neurological deficits were highly selective. For example, her motor abilities were intact. While testing DF one day, Goodale and Milner were struck by her ability to grasp a pencil they had placed in front of her, while she was not able to identify it. They wondered how she could perform all of the motor acts dependent on vision that enabled her to grasp the object, while still being unable to identify it. She had to be using some kind of vision. They went on to test DF's abilities systematically in the laboratory. Drawing on earlier work by Ungerleider and Mishkin (1982) and his own work (Goodale & Westwood, 2004) and that of others, Goodale suggested that these two types of vision follow different pathways in the brain. The two pathways (see Figure 4.44) are a *dorsal stream* for the visual control of action and a *ventral stream* for perception of the external world. Research examining this distinction and its connection to the brain is one of the most active research areas in vision (e.g., Crawford, Medendorp & Marotta, 2004; Wood & Goodale, 2010).

REVIEW OF KEY POINTS

▶ Binocular cues such as retinal disparity and convergence can contribute to depth perception. Depth perception depends primarily on monocular cues, including pictorial cues such as texture gradient, linear perspective, light and shadow, interposition, relative size, and height in plane. People from pictureless societies have some difficulty in applying pictorial depth cues to two-dimensional pictures.

▶ Optical illusions demonstrate that perceptual hypotheses can be inaccurate and that perceptions are not simple reflections of objective reality. Researchers have found some interesting cultural differences in susceptibility to the Müller-Lyer and Ponzo illusions.

▶ Vision for perception and vision for action are two types of visual systems. Each follows a different pathway in the brain.

Our Sense of Hearing: The Auditory System

PREVIEW QUESTIONS

▶ What are the three key properties of sound?

▶ How are these properties related to auditory perceptions?

▶ What are the key structures in the ear involved in the processing of sound?

▶ What were the central ideas of place theory and frequency theory?

▶ How were the two theories reconciled?

▶ What cues do people use to locate sounds in space?

Like vision, the auditory (hearing) system provides input about the world "out there," but not until incoming information is processed by the brain. A distal stimulus—a screech of tires, someone laughing, the hum of the refrigerator—produces a proximal stimulus in the form of sound waves reaching the ears. The perceptual system must somehow transform this stimulation into the psychological experience of hearing. We'll begin our discussion of hearing by looking at the stimulus for auditory experience: sound.

The Stimulus: Sound 3h

Sound waves are vibrations of molecules, which means that they must travel through some physical medium, such as air. They move at a fraction of the speed of light. Sound waves are usually generated by vibrating objects, such as a guitar string, a loudspeaker cone, or your vocal cords. However, sound waves can also be generated by forcing air past a chamber (as in a pipe organ), or by suddenly releasing a burst of air (as when you clap).

Like light waves, sound waves are characterized by their amplitude, their *wavelength*, and their *purity* (see Figure 4.45). The physical properties of amplitude, wavelength, and purity affect mainly the perceived (psychological) qualities of loudness, pitch, and timbre, respectively. However, the physical properties of sound interact in complex ways to produce perceptions of these sound qualities (Hirsh & Watson, 1996).

Human Hearing Capacities

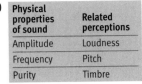

Wavelengths of sound are described in terms of their *frequency,* which is measured in cycles per second, or *hertz (Hz).* For the most part, higher frequencies are perceived as having higher pitch. That is, if you strike the key for high C on a piano, it will produce higher-frequency sound waves than the key for low C. Although the perception of pitch depends mainly on frequency, the amplitude of the sound waves also influences it.

Just as the visible spectrum is only a portion of the total spectrum of light, so, too, what people can hear is only a portion of the available range of sounds. Humans can hear sounds ranging from a low of 20 Hz up to a high of about 20 000 Hz. Sounds at either end of this range are harder to hear, and sensitivity to high-frequency tones declines as adults grow older (Dubno, 2010). Other organisms have different capabilities. Low-frequency sounds under 10 Hz are audible to homing pigeons, for example. At the other extreme, bats and porpoises can hear frequencies well above 20 000 Hz.

In general, the greater the amplitude of sound waves, the louder the sound perceived. Whereas frequency is measured in hertz, amplitude is measured in *decibels (dB).*

The relationship between decibels (which measure a physical property of sound) and loudness (a psychological quality) is very complex. A rough rule of thumb is that perceived loudness doubles about every 6–10 decibels (Florentine & Heinz, 2010). Very loud sounds can jeopardize the quality of your hearing. In work settings, chronic exposure to sounds above 85 decibels is considered risky and is strictly regulated (Eggermont, 2010). Even brief exposure to sounds over 120 decibels can be painful and can cause damage to your auditory system (Daniel, 2007).

In recent years there has been great concern about hearing loss in young people using personal listening devices who play their music too loudly (Morata, 2007). Portable music players can easily deliver over 100 decibels through headphones. One study found significant hearing impairment in 14 percent of the young people sampled (Peng, Tao, & Huang, 2001). Unfortunately, adolescents tend to not take the risk of hearing loss very seriously (Vogel et al., 2008). However, it is a serious problem that is likely to lead to a great deal of preventable hearing loss, given the increased popularity of portable music players (Daniel, 2007; Vogel et al., 2007).

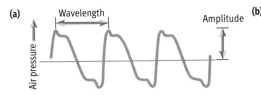

Physical properties of sound	Related perceptions
Amplitude	Loudness
Frequency	Pitch
Purity	Timbre

FIGURE 4.45

Sound, the physical stimulus for hearing.

(a) Like light, sound travels in waves—in this case, waves of air pressure. A smooth curve would represent a pure tone, such as that produced by a tuning fork. Most sounds, however, are complex. For example, the wave shown here is for middle C played on a piano. The sound wave for the same note played on a violin would have the same wavelength (or frequency) as this one, but the "wrinkles" in the wave would be different, corresponding to the differences in timbre between the two sounds. (b) The table shows the main relationships between objective aspects of sound and subjective perceptions.

As shown in Figure 4.46, the absolute thresholds for the weakest sounds people can hear differ for sounds of various frequencies. The human ear is most sensitive to sounds at frequencies near 2000 Hz. That is, these frequencies yield the lowest absolute thresholds. To summarize, amplitude is the principal determinant of loudness, but loudness ultimately depends on an interaction between amplitude and frequency.

People are also sensitive to variations in the purity of sounds. The purest sound is one that has only a single frequency of vibration, such as that produced by a tuning fork. Most everyday sounds are complex mixtures of many frequencies. The purity or complexity of a sound influences how *timbre* is perceived. To understand timbre, think of a note with precisely the same loudness and pitch played on a French horn and then on a violin. The difference you perceive in the sounds is a difference in timbre.

Sensory Processing in the Ear

Like your eyes, your ears channel energy to the neural tissue that receives it. Figure 4.47 shows that the human ear can be divided into three sections: the external ear, the middle ear, and the inner ear. Sound is conducted differently in each section. The external ear depends on the *vibration of air molecules.* The middle ear depends on the *vibration of movable bones.* And the inner ear depends on *waves in a fluid,* which are finally converted into a stream of neural signals sent to the brain (Hackney, 2010).

The *external ear* consists mainly of the *pinna,* a sound-collecting cone. When you cup your hand behind your ear to try to hear better, you are augmenting that cone. Many animals have large external ears that they can aim directly toward a sound source.

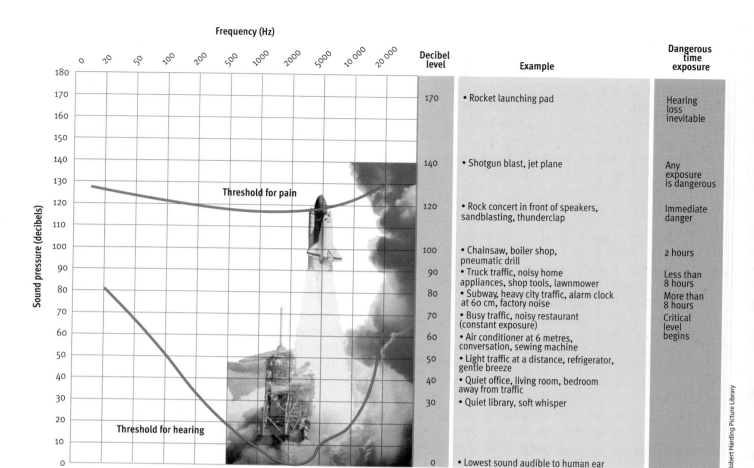

Frequency (Hz)

Decibel level	Example	Dangerous time exposure
170	• Rocket launching pad	Hearing loss inevitable
140	• Shotgun blast, jet plane	Any exposure is dangerous
120	• Rock concert in front of speakers, sandblasting, thunderclap	Immediate danger
100	• Chainsaw, boiler shop, pneumatic drill	2 hours
90	• Truck traffic, noisy home appliances, shop tools, lawnmower	Less than 8 hours
80	• Subway, heavy city traffic, alarm clock at 60 cm, factory noise	More than 8 hours
70	• Busy traffic, noisy restaurant (constant exposure)	Critical level begins
60	• Air conditioner at 6 metres, conversation, sewing machine	
50	• Light traffic at a distance, refrigerator, gentle breeze	
40	• Quiet office, living room, bedroom away from traffic	
30	• Quiet library, soft whisper	
0	• Lowest sound audible to human ear	

Threshold for pain

Threshold for hearing

Sound pressure (decibels)

Robert Harding Picture Library

FIGURE 4.46

Sound pressure and auditory experience.

The threshold for human hearing (graphed in green) is a function of both sound pressure (decibel level) and frequency. Human hearing is keenest for sounds at a frequency of about 2000 Hz; at other frequencies, higher decibel levels are needed to produce sounds people can detect. On the other hand, the human threshold for pain (graphed in red) is almost purely a function of decibel level. Some common sounds corresponding to various decibel levels are listed to the right of the graph, together with the amount of time at which exposure to higher levels becomes dangerous.

Source: Decibel level examples from Atkinson, R.L., Atkinson, R.C., Smith, E.F. and Hilgard, E.R. (1987). *Introduction to Psychology.* San Diego: Harcourt. Reprinted by permission of Wadsworth Publishing.

However, humans can adjust their aim only crudely, by turning their heads. Sound waves collected by the pinna are funnelled along the auditory canal toward the *eardrum,* a taut membrane that vibrates in response.

In the *middle ear,* the vibrations of the eardrum are transmitted inward by a mechanical chain made up of the three tiniest bones in your body (the hammer, anvil, and stirrup), known collectively as the *ossicles.* The ossicles form a three-stage lever system that converts relatively large movements with little force into smaller motions with greater force. The ossicles serve to amplify tiny changes in air pressure.

The *inner ear* consists largely of the *cochlea, a fluid-filled, coiled tunnel that contains the receptors for hearing.* The term *cochlea* comes from the Greek word for a spiral-shelled snail, which this chamber resembles (see Figure 4.48). Sound enters the cochlea through the *oval window,* which is vibrated by the ossicles. The ear's neural tissue, analogous to the retina in the eye, lies within the cochlea. This tissue sits on the basilar membrane that divides the cochlea into upper and lower chambers. *The basilar membrane,* which runs the length of the spiralled cochlea, holds the auditory receptors. The auditory receptors are called *hair cells* because of the tiny bundles of hairs that protrude from them. Waves in the fluid of the inner ear stimulate the hair cells. Like the rods and cones in the eye, the hair cells convert this physical stimulation into neural impulses that are sent to the brain (Hackett & Koss, 2009).

These signals are routed through the thalamus to the auditory cortex, which is located mostly in the temporal lobes of the brain. Studies demonstrate that the auditory cortex has specialized cells—similar to the feature detectors found in the visual cortex—that have special sensitivity to certain features of sound (Pickles, 1988). Evidence also suggests that the parallel processing of input seen in the visual system also occurs in the auditory pathways (Rouiller, 1997).

Auditory Perception: Theories of Hearing

Theories of hearing need to account for how sound waves are physiologically translated into the perceptions of pitch, loudness, and timbre. To date, most of the theorizing about hearing has focused on the perception of pitch, which is reasonably well understood. Researchers' understanding of loudness and timbre perception is primitive by comparison. Hence, we'll limit our coverage to theories of pitch perception.

Two theories have dominated the debate on pitch perception: *place theory* and *frequency theory*. You'll be able to follow the development of these theories more easily if you can imagine the spiralled cochlea unravelled, so that the basilar membrane becomes a long, thin sheet, lined with about 25 000 individual hair cells (see Figure 4.48).

Place Theory

Long ago, Hermann von Helmholtz (1863) proposed that specific sound frequencies vibrate specific portions of the basilar membrane, producing distinct pitches, just as plucking specific strings on a harp produces sounds of varied pitch. This model, called *place theory*, holds that perception of pitch corresponds to the vibration of different portions, or places, along the basilar membrane. Place theory assumes that hair cells at various locations respond independently and that different sets of hair cells are vibrated by different sound frequencies. The brain then detects the frequency of a tone according to which area along the basilar membrane is most active.

Frequency Theory

Other theorists in the 19th century proposed an alternative theory of pitch perception, called *frequency theory* (Rutherford, 1886). *Frequency theory* holds that perception of pitch corresponds to the rate, or frequency, at which the entire basilar membrane vibrates. This theory views the basilar membrane as more like a drumhead than a harp. According to frequency theory, the whole membrane vibrates in unison in response to sounds. However, a particular

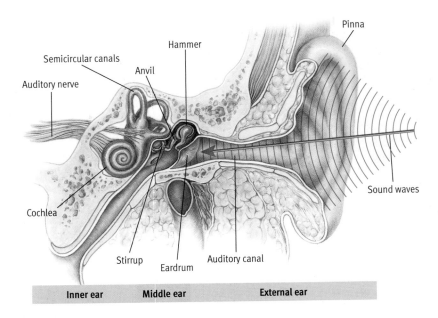

FIGURE 4.47

The human ear.
Converting sound pressure into information processed by the nervous system involves a complex relay of stimuli. Waves of air pressure create vibrations in the eardrum, which in turn cause oscillations in the tiny bones in the inner ear (the hammer, anvil, and stirrup). As they are relayed from one bone to the next, the oscillations are magnified and then transformed into pressure waves moving through a liquid medium in the cochlea. These waves cause the basilar membrane to oscillate, stimulating the hair cells that are the actual auditory receptors (see Figure 4.48).

Log on to CourseMate to access this interactive figure.

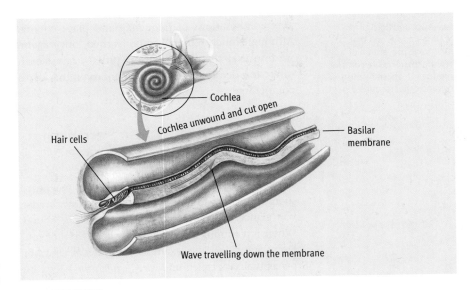

FIGURE 4.48

The basilar membrane.
This graphic shows how the cochlea might look if it were unwound and cut open to reveal the basilar membrane, which is covered with thousands of hair cells (the auditory receptors). Pressure waves in the fluid filling the cochlea cause oscillations to travel in waves down the basilar membrane, stimulating the hair cells to fire. Although the entire membrane vibrates, as predicted by frequency theory, the point along the membrane where the wave peaks depends on the frequency of the sound stimulus, as suggested by place theory.

Hermann von Helmholtz

"The psychic activities, by which we arrive at the judgment that a certain object of a certain character exists before us at a certain place, are generally not conscious activities but unconscious ones. . . . It may be permissible to designate the psychic acts of ordinary perception as unconscious inferences."

WEB LINK 4.6

Canadian Hearing Society

The Canadian Hearing Society's mission is to provide services that enhance the independence of deaf, deafened, and hard-of-hearing people, and that encourage prevention of hearing loss. The site contains information about hearing loss and other resources.

sound frequency, say 3000 Hz, causes the basilar membrane to vibrate at a corresponding rate of 3000 times per second. The brain detects the frequency of a tone by the rate at which the auditory nerve fibres fire.

Reconciling Place and Frequency Theories

The competition between these two theories is reminiscent of the dispute between the trichromatic and opponent process theories of colour vision. As with that argument, the debate between place and frequency theories generated roughly a century of research. Although both theories proved to have some flaws, *both turned out to be valid in part.*

Helmholtz's place theory was basically on the mark except for one detail: The hair cells along the basilar membrane are not independent. They vibrate together, as suggested by frequency theory. The actual pattern of vibration, described in Nobel Prize–winning research by Georg von Békésy (1947), is a travelling wave that moves along the basilar membrane. Place theory is correct, however, in that the wave peaks at a particular place, depending on the frequency of the sound wave.

The current thinking is that pitch perception depends both on place and frequency coding of vibrations along the basilar membrane (Moore, 2010; Yost, 2010). Low frequency tones appear to be translated into pitch through frequency coding. High-frequency pure tones appear to rely on place coding. And complex tones seem to depend on complex combinations of frequency and place coding. Although much remains to be learned, once again, we find that theories that were pitted against each other for decades are complementary rather than competing.

Auditory Localization: Perceiving Sources of Sound

You're driving down a street when suddenly you hear a siren wailing in the distance. As the wail grows louder, you glance around, cocking your ear to the sound. Where is it coming from? Behind you? In front of you? From one side? This example illustrates a common perceptual task called *auditory localization*—locating the source of a sound in space. The process of recognizing where a sound is coming from is analogous to recognizing depth or distance in vision. Both processes involve spatial aspects of sensory input. The fact that human ears are set *apart* contributes to auditory localization, just as the separation of the eyes contributes to depth perception.

Many features of sounds can contribute to auditory localization, but two cues are particularly important: the intensity (loudness) and the timing of sounds arriving at each ear (Yost, 2001). For example, a sound source to one side of the head produces a greater intensity at the ear nearer to the sound. This difference is due partly to the loss of sound intensity with distance. Another factor at work is the "shadow," or partial sound barrier, cast by the head itself (see Figure 4.49). The intensity difference between the two ears is greatest when the sound source is well to one side. The human perceptual system uses this difference as a clue in localizing sounds. Because the path to the farther ear is longer, a sound takes longer to reach that ear. This fact means that sounds can be localized by comparing the timing of their arrival at each ear. Such comparison of the timing of sounds is remarkably sensitive. People can detect timing differences as small as 1/100 000 of a second (Durlach & Colburn, 1978).

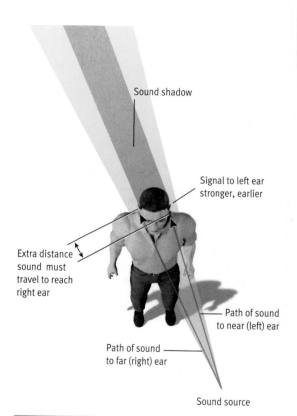

Sound shadow

Signal to left ear stronger, earlier

Extra distance sound must travel to reach right ear

Path of sound to near (left) ear

Path of sound to far (right) ear

Sound source

FIGURE 4.49

Cues in auditory localization.

A sound coming from the left reaches the left ear sooner than the right. When the sound reaches the right ear, it is also less intense because it has travelled a greater distance and because it is in the sound shadow produced by the listener's head. These cues are used to localize the sources of sound in space.

Music and Its Effects

Our auditory system provides us with one way to experience and relate to the world. In terms of our auditory experiences, music is something that most of us enjoy. Music is part of our culture and each seems to shape the other (Demorest et al, 2010). Music seems to be important to who we are as humans. In fact, Oliver Sacks, a renowned neurologist, argues that there is a special connection between music and the brain. Sacks suggests that the brains of musicians are identifiable and that they would be larger in areas such as the motor, auditory, and visuospatial areas of the cerebellum (Sacks, 2007) than the brains of nonmusicians.

According to McGill University neuropsychologist Daniel Levitin, a former professional musician, music is pivotal in human culture and was selected in as part of the natural selection process (Levitin, 2006; see Pinker, 1997, for an opposing view). Natural selection was discussed in Chapter 3. No matter the nature of its origins, we know that music is of clear significance to humans. It modulates our moods and can even be used therapeutically (Mongrain & Trambakoulos, 2007). Language and music seem to be related (Pinker, 1997), with links established between music training and some language abilities (Patel & Iversen, 2007).

Although we may disagree somewhat in terms of our musical preferences, music is important to most of us. Canadian researchers in the psychology of music (Ilie & Thompson, 2006; Thompson, Graham, & Russo, 2005) have been active in examining several features of this experience, such as processes of perceptual organization in the perception of tonality (Smith & Schmuckler, 2004) and the effects that music has on us. We often seek out musical experiences because they affect our mood, make us feel happier, or calm us down. It has even been suggested that music can enhance our spatial abilities—the so-called Mozart effect (Rauscher, Shaw, & Ky, 1993). While there is some disagreement on what produces this effect (Thompson, Schellenberg, & Husain, 2001), the fact that music influences us in many ways should not be a surprise.

But, what about all those years of practising the piano that you endured? Did they have any effect beyond improving your piano playing or causing conflict with your parents? A recent review of work in the area of brain plasticity by the University of Montreal's Isabelle Peretz and McGill's Robert Zatorre (Peretz & Zatorre, 2005) suggests that music training can induce functional and morphological changes in the brain. In addition, recent research by University of Toronto psychologist William Thompson (Thompson, 2009; Thompson & Quinto, in press) suggests that music training and lessons may facilitate your sensitivity to

human emotions reflected in speech prosody. *Speech prosody* refers to the musical aspects of speech, such as intonation (melody) and stress and timing (rhythm). This research is our Featured Study in this chapter (see page 176).

concept **check 4.3**

Comparing Vision and Hearing

Check your understanding of both vision and audition by comparing key aspects of sensation and perception in these senses. The dimensions of comparison are listed in the first column below. The second column lists the answers for the sense of vision. Fill in the answers for the sense of hearing in the third column. The answers can be found in Appendix A near the back of the book.

Dimension	Vision	Hearing
1. Stimulus	Light waves	
2. Elements of stimulus and related perceptions	Wavelength/hue Amplitude/brightness Purity/saturation	
3. Receptors	Rods and cones	
4. Location of receptors	Retina	
5. Main location of processing in brain	Occipital lobe/visual cortex	
6. Spatial aspect of perception	Depth perception	

REVIEW OF KEY POINTS

> Sound varies in terms of wavelength (frequency), amplitude, and purity. These properties affect mainly perceptions of pitch, loudness, and timbre, respectively. The human ear is most sensitive to sounds around 2000 Hz. Even brief exposure to sounds over 120 decibels can be painful and damaging.

> Sound is transmitted through the external ear via air conduction to the middle ear, where sound waves are translated into the vibration of tiny bones called *ossicles*. In the inner ear, fluid conduction vibrates hair cells along the basilar membrane in the cochlea. These hair cells are the receptors for hearing.

> Place theory proposed that pitch perception depends on where vibrations occur along the basilar membrane. Frequency theory countered with the idea that pitch perception depends on the rate at which the basilar membrane vibrates. Modern evidence suggests that these theories are complementary rather than incompatible.

> Auditory localization involves locating the source of a sound in space. People pinpoint where sounds have come from by comparing inter-ear differences in the intensity and timing of sounds.

> There is evidence to suggest that exposure to music does more than temporarily affect our moods. It may increase our ability to perform certain tasks and to correctly identify emotions in the speech of others.

Investigators: William Forde Thompson, E. Glenn Schellenberg, & Gabriela Husain (University of Toronto at Mississauga).

Source: Decoding speech prosody: Do music lessons help? *Emotion,* 2004, *4,* 46–64.

Decoding Speech Prosody: Do Music Lessons Help?

Thompson and his colleagues expected to find positive transfer from past music training to an individual's ability to decode or correctly identify emotions conveyed by prosody in speech. A connection between music and emotional experience has been documented in the past, as has a connection between emotion and speech prosody. *Speech prosody* refers to "the musical aspects of speech, including its *melody* (intonation) and its *rhythm* (stress and timing)" (p. 48). The researchers suggested that there are parallels between music and speech in terms of how emotions are expressed. Accordingly, they reasoned that musical training would enhance a person's ability to decode emotions from speech.

Method

Participants. Three studies were conducted. We will present the third study for illustrative purposes. In the study, 43 seven-year-old children, none of whom had any formal musical/arts training, were recruited. The experimenters arranged that 30 of the children were given one year of formal training in keyboard, drama, or singing at the Royal Conservatory of Music in Toronto. The remaining 13 children did not take part in this arts training.

Stimuli. The stimuli consisted of four neutral sentences (e.g., "The chairs are made of wood"), each spoken in four different ways to convey the emotions of happiness, fear, sadness, or anger. The sentences were presented to the children in English or an unfamiliar language, Tagalog, resulting in 16 sentences (four sentences times four emotions) for each language, for a total of 32 spoken sentences. Tagalog is a language spoken in the Philippines by about 25 percent of the population. In addition, musical analogues using musical tone sequences were prepared for each of the 32 spoken sentences. The construction of the musical analogues is quite fascinating, and interested students should read the journal article by Thompson and his colleagues to learn more about how this is accomplished.

Measures and Apparatus. The sentences and tone sequences were presented by a computer while the children listened through earphones. The children were asked to choose which of a pair of descriptions (e.g., happy or sad) applied to what they heard. For the tone sequences, the children were given an imagination task. They were asked to imagine that the tonal sequence was a sentence spoken by the computer and that they should decide if the computer sounded, for example, sad or happy.

Results

As you might expect, children's identification of emotions was better for spoken sentences than for tonal analogues, and better for English than for Tagalog sentences. What about the effects of training? First, for happy/sad sentences everyone did extremely well, so there were no differences in identification accuracy between participant groups. For the fearful/angry sentences, the music-training (only the keyboard group) and drama-training groups were better able to identify the correct emotions than was the no-training group.

Discussion

It is instructive to put the results of the third study together with the results of the other two studies Thompson and his colleagues conducted. The participants in the first two studies were university students who had no musical training or at least eight years of musical training. Once again, the results suggested that musical training enhanced participants' ability to decode emotions conveyed by speech prosody. In terms of the specific results of the third study, while the results for the keyboard group make sense, you might wonder why drama lessons facilitated this ability when the other music training, the singing lessons, did not. The authors report that the drama lessons taken by the children "focused specifically on training the speaking voice and the use of prosody" while the "singing lessons emphasize nonprosodic uses of the voice" (p. 58). Thus for the training to have an effect, it must incorporate the use of prosody. Why were there no training effects for happy/sad sentences? These distinctions were so easy that most of the children got most of them correct. This is referred to as a *ceiling effect*. Here, the identifications were so easy that the training had no additional room to positively affect performance.

Comment

The study of sensation and perception is one of the oldest areas of scientific research in psychology. Yet this study shows that there are still fascinating areas of inquiry that remain unexplored. It just takes some creativity and insight to recognize them. This research also illustrates the importance of using more than one way to examine an issue. The fact that very similar results were obtained with children and adult samples with varying lengths of training increases the authors' confidence in the results.

Our Chemical Senses: Taste and Smell

Psychologists have devoted most of their attention to the visual and auditory systems. Although less is known about the chemical senses, taste and smell also play a critical role in people's experience of the world. Let's take a brief look at what psychologists have learned about the *gustatory system*—the *sensory system for taste*—and its close cousin, the *olfactory system*—the sensory system for smell.

Taste: The Gustatory System

True wine lovers go through an elaborate series of steps when they are served a good bottle of wine. Typically, they begin by drinking a little water to cleanse their palate. Then they sniff the cork from the wine bottle, swirl a small amount of the wine around in a glass, and sniff the odour emerging from the glass. Finally, they take a sip of the wine, rolling it around in the mouth for a short time before swallowing it. At last they are ready to confer their approval or disapproval. Is all this activity really a meaningful way to put the wine to a sensitive test? Or is it just a harmless ritual passed on through tradition? You'll find out in this section.

The physical stimuli for the sense of taste are chemical substances that are soluble (dissolvable in water). The gustatory receptors are clusters of taste cells found in the *taste buds* that line the trenches around tiny bumps on the tongue (see Figure 4.50). When these cells absorb chemicals dissolved in saliva, they trigger neural impulses that are routed through the thalamus to the cortex. Interestingly, taste cells have a short life, spanning only about ten days, and they are constantly being replaced (Cowart, 2005). New cells are born at the edge of the taste bud and migrate inward to die at the centre.

It's generally agreed that there are four *primary tastes*: sweet, sour, bitter, and salty (Buck, 2000). However, scientists are suggesting we add a fifth primary taste called *umami*, which is a Japanese word for the savoury taste of glutamate found in foods like meats and cheeses (DuBois, 2010). The case of umami as a fifth basic taste has been strengthened by recent evidence that umami substances activate specific receptors on the tongue (De Lorenzo & Rosen, 2010). Sensitivity to the primary tastes is distributed somewhat unevenly across the tongue, but the variations in sensitivity are quite small and highly complicated (Bartoshuk, 1993b; see Figure 4.50). Perceptions of taste quality appear to depend on complex *patterns* of neural activity initiated by taste receptors (Erickson, Di Lorenzo, & Woodbury, 1994). Taste signals are routed through the thalamus and onto the *insular cortex* in

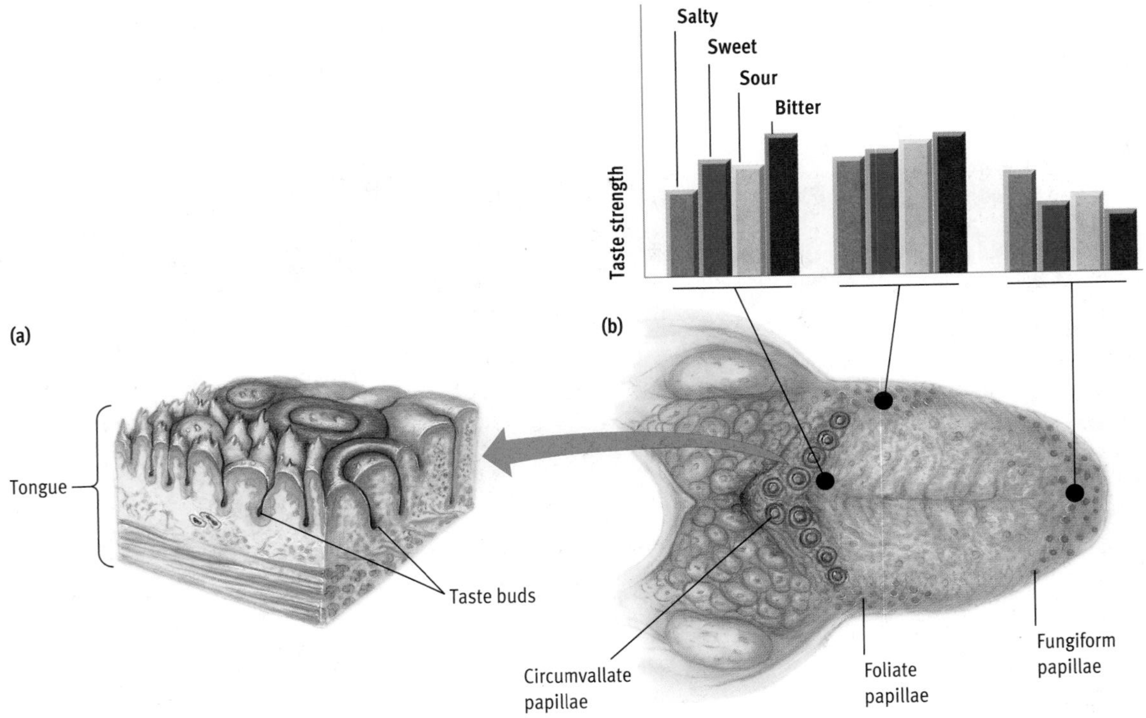

PREVIEW QUESTIONS

▶ Where are the receptors for taste?

▶ How many basic tastes are there?

▶ How do people vary in taste sensitivity?

▶ Where are the receptors for smell?

▶ Are there primary odours?

▶ How well do people perform when asked to name odours?

(a) Tongue — Taste buds

(b) Salty — Sweet — Sour — Bitter

Taste strength

Circumvallate papillae — Foliate papillae — Fungiform papillae

FIGURE 4.50

The tongue and taste.

(a) Taste buds line the trenches around tiny bumps on the tongue called *papillae*. There are three types of papillae, which are distributed on the tongue as shown in (b). The taste buds found in each type of papillae show slightly different sensitivities to the four basic tastes, as mapped out in the graph at the top. Thus, sensitivity to the primary tastes varies across the tongue, but these variations are small, and all four primary tastes can be detected wherever there are taste receptors. (Data adapted from Bartoshuk, 1993a).

 Log on to CourseMate to access this interactive figure.

Linda Bartoshuk

"Good and bad are so intimately associated with taste and smell that we have special words for the experiences (e.g., repugnant, foul). The immediacy of the pleasure makes it seem absolute and thus inborn. This turns out to be true for taste but not for smell."

the frontal lobe, where the initial cortical processing takes place (Di Lorenzo & Rosen, 2010).

Some basic taste preferences appear to be innate and to be automatically regulated by physiological mechanisms. In humans, for instance, newborn infants react positively to sweet tastes and negatively to strong concentrations of bitter or sour tastes (Cowart, 2005). To some extent, these innate taste preferences are flexible, changing to accommodate the body's nutritional needs (Scott, 1990).

Although some basic aspects of taste perception may be innate, taste preferences are largely learned and heavily influenced by social processes (Rozin, 1990). Most parents are aware of this fact and intentionally try—with varied success—to mould their children's taste preferences early in life (Patrick et al., 2005). This extensive social influence contributes greatly to the striking ethnic and cultural disparities found in taste preferences (Kittler & Sucher, 2008). Foods that are a source of disgust in Western cultures—such as worms, fish eyes, and blood—may be delicacies in other cultures (see Figure 4.51). Indeed, Rozin (1990) asserts that feces may be the only universal source of taste-related disgust in humans. To a large degree, variations in taste preferences depend on what one has been exposed to (Capaldi & VandenBos, 1991; Zellner, 1991). Exposure to various foods varies along ethnic lines because different cultures have different traditions in food preparation, different agricultural resources, different climates to work with, and so forth.

Research by Linda Bartoshuk and others reveals that people vary considerably in their sensitivity to certain tastes (Bartoshuk, 1993a). People characterized as *nontasters*, as determined by their insensitivity to PTC (phenythiocarbamide), or its close relative, PROP (propylthiouracil), tend to have about one-quarter as many taste buds per square centimetre as people at the other end of the spectrum, who are called *supertasters* (Miller & Reedy, 1990). Supertasters also have specialized taste receptors that are not found in nontasters (Bufe et al., 2005). In North America, roughly 25 percent of people are nontasters, another 25 percent are supertasters, and the remaining 50 percent fall between these extremes and are characterized as *medium tasters* (Di Lorenzo & Youngentob, 2003). Supertasters and nontasters respond similarly to many foods, but supertasters are much more sensitive to certain sweet and bitter substances (Prescott, 2010). These variations in sensitivity mean that when two people taste the same food they will not necessarily have the same sensory experience. In regard to taste, different people live in somewhat different sensory worlds (Breslin, 2010).

These differences in taste sensitivity influence people's eating habits in ways that can have important repercussions for their physical health. For example, supertasters, who experience taste with far greater intensity than average, are less likely to be fond of sweets (Yeomans et al., 2007) and tend to consume fewer high-fat foods, both of which are likely to reduce their risk for cardiovascular disease (Duffy, Lucchina, & Bartoshuk, 2004). Supertasters also tend to react more negatively to alcohol and smoking, which reduces their likelihood of developing drinking problems or nicotine addiction (Duffy, Peterson, & Bartoshuk, 2004; Snedecor et al., 2006). The main health disadvantage identified for supertasters thus far is that they respond more negatively to many vegetables, which seems to hold down

FIGURE 4.51

Culture and taste preferences.

Taste preferences are largely learned, and they vary dramatically from one society to the next, as these examples demonstrate.

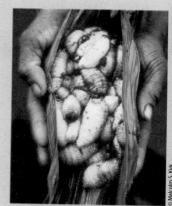

Grubs. For most North Americans, the thought of eating a worm would be totally unthinkable. For the Asmat of New Guinea, however, a favourite delicacy is the plump, white, 5-cm larva or beetle grub.

Fish eyes. For some Inuit children, raw fish eyes are like candy. Here you see a young girl using the Inuit's all-purpose knife to gouge out the eye of an already-filleted Arctic fish.

Blood. Several tribes in East Africa supplement their diet with fresh blood that is sometimes mixed with milk. They obtain the blood by puncturing a cow's jugular vein with a sharp arrow. The blood–milk drink provides a rich source of protein and iron.

their vegetable intake (Basson et al., 2005; Dinehart et al., 2006). Overall, however, supertasters tend to have better health habits than nontasters, thanks to their strong reactions to certain tastes (Duffy, 2004).

Women are somewhat more likely to be supertasters than men (Bartoshuk, Duffy, & Miller, 1994). Some psychologists speculate that the gender gap in this trait may have evolutionary significance. Over the course of evolution, women have generally been more involved than men in feeding children. Increased reactivity to sweet and bitter tastes would have been adaptive in that it would have made women more sensitive to the relatively scarce high-caloric foods (which often taste sweet) needed for survival and to the toxic substances (which often taste bitter) that hunters and gatherers needed to avoid.

So far, we've been discussing taste, but what we are really interested in is the *perception of flavour*. Flavour is a combination of taste, smell, and the tactile sensation of food in one's mouth (Smith & Margolskee, 2006). Odours make a surprisingly great contribution to the perception of flavour (Lawless, 2001). Although taste and smell are distinct sensory systems, they interact extensively. The ability to identify flavours declines noticeably when odour cues are absent. You might have noticed this interaction when you ate a favourite meal while enduring a severe head cold. The food probably tasted bland, because your stuffy nose impaired your sense of smell.

Now that we've explored the dynamics of taste, we can return to our question about the value of the wine-tasting ritual. This elaborate ritual is indeed an authentic way to put wine to a sensitive test. The aftereffects associated with sensory adaptation make it wise to cleanse one's palate before tasting the wine. Sniffing the cork and sniffing the wine in the glass are important because odour is a major determinant of flavour. Swirling the wine in the glass helps release the wine's odour. And rolling the wine around in your mouth is especially critical, because it distributes the wine over the full diversity of taste cells. It also forces the wine's odour up into the nasal passages. Thus, each action in this age-old ritual makes a meaningful contribution to the tasting.

Smell: The Olfactory System

Humans are usually characterized as being relatively insensitive to smell; often the only thing we can say about an odour is whether it is pleasant or not (Yeshurun & Sobel, 2010). In this regard humans are often compared unfavourably to dogs, which are renowned for their ability to track a faint odour over long distances. Are humans really inferior in the sensory domain of smell? Let's examine the facts.

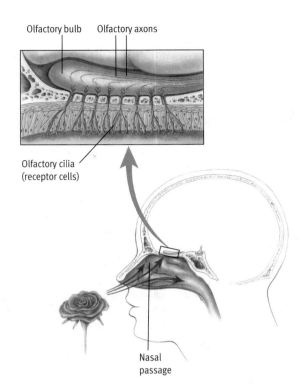

Olfactory bulb   Olfactory axons

Olfactory cilia (receptor cells)

Nasal passage

FIGURE 4.52

The olfactory system.
Odour molecules travel through the nasal passages and stimulate olfactory cilia. An enlargement of these hairlike olfactory receptors is shown in the inset. The olfactory nerves transmit neural impulses through the olfactory bulb to the brain.

In many ways, the sense of smell is much like the sense of taste. The physical stimuli are chemical substances—volatile ones that can evaporate and be carried in the air. These chemical stimuli are dissolved in fluid—specifically, the mucus in the nose. The receptors for smell are *olfactory cilia*, hairlike structures located in the upper portion of the nasal passages (see Figure 4.52). They resemble taste cells in that they have a short life (30–60 days) and are constantly being replaced (Buck, 2000). Olfactory receptors have axons that synapse with cells in the olfactory bulb and then are routed directly to various areas in the cortex (Scott, 2008). This arrangement is unique. *Smell is the only sensory system in which incoming information is not routed through the thalamus before it projects to the cortex.* Research by Linda Buck and Richard Axel (1991) has served to clarify some of the mechanisms involved in odour recognition. They have discovered a gene set consisting of 1000 different genes that affect the operation of our olfactory receptor cells. These olfactory receptor cells are highly specialized in that each has the ability to detect only a very limited number of odours. Axel and Buck were awarded the 2004 Nobel Prize in Physiology or Medicine for their work (Nobel Prize, n.d.).

Odours cannot be classified as neatly as tastes, since efforts to identify primary odours have proven unsatisfactory (Doty, 1991). Humans have about 350 different types of olfactory receptors (Buck, 2004). Most olfactory receptors respond to a wide range of odours. Specific odours trigger responses in different *combinations* of receptors (Doty, 2010). Like the other senses, the sense of smell shows sensory adaptation. The perceived strength of an odour usually fades to less than half its original strength within about four minutes (Cain, 1988).

Humans can distinguish among about 10 000 different odours (Axel, 1995). However, when people are asked to identify the sources of specific odours (such as smoke or soap), their performance is rather mediocre. For some unknown reason, people have a hard time attaching names to odours (Cowart & Rawson, 2001). Gender differences have been found in the ability to identify odours, as females tend to be somewhat more accurate than males on odour recognition tasks (de Wijk, Schab, & Cain, 1995).

The sense of smell is also involved as a mechanism of communication. *Pheromones* are chemical messages, typically imperceptible, that can be sent by one organism and received by another member of the same species. Although there is debate as to the definition of pheromones (American Psychological Association, 2002), as originally defined by Karlson & Luscher (1959), they were species-specific, composed of a single chemical, and had specific effects on the organisms that received them. In the literature they are often linked to sexual activity and physical attraction in many species (Kohl et al., 2003).

While the effects of pheromones are better established in insects than in humans (Doty, 2010), there are some intriguing results for humans. For example, McClintock has shown that the menstrual cycles of women living together tend to converge to the same time each month (McClintock, 1971) and that this convergence seemed to be a function of pheromones secreted from the women's underarms (Stern & McClintock, 1998). While the full implications of pheromones for human behaviour still remain to be determined, you will not be surprised to find out that some companies have begun to market

pheromone-based perfume additives (Benson, 2002) to increase such things as attraction. These claims have yet to be clearly scientifically documented.

So, then, how *do* human olfactory capacities compare to other species? We do have notably fewer olfactory receptors than many other animals (Wolfe et al., 2006). Our relative paucity of olfactory receptors probably reflects evolutionary trends that gradually allocated more and more of the brain to colour vision (Gilad et al., 2004). However, recent studies have found that humans and monkeys, when compared to other mammals, have a better sense of smell than previously thought (Laska, Seibt, & Weber, 2000; Sheperd, 2004). For example, one innovative study (Porter et al., 2007) that asked humans to get on their hands and knees to track the scent of chocolate oil that had been dribbled through a field, found that the subjects performed quite well and that their patterns of tracking mimicked those of dogs. Gordon Sheperd (2004) offers several possible explanations for our surprising olfactory capabilities, including the fact that "humans smell with bigger and better brains" (p. 0574).

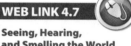

WEB LINK 4.7

Seeing, Hearing, and Smelling the World
Hosted by the Howard Hughes Medical Institute, this site provides a graphically attractive review of what scientific research has discovered about human sensory systems, with suggestions about where research will be moving in the future.

> ### REVIEW OF KEY POINTS
>
> ▸ The taste buds are sensitive to four basic tastes: sweet, sour, bitter, and salty. Sensitivity to these tastes is distributed unevenly across the tongue, but the variations are small.
>
> ▸ Taste preferences are largely learned and are heavily influenced by one's cultural background. The perception of flavour is influenced greatly by the odour of food.
>
> ▸ Like taste, smell is a chemical sense. Chemical stimuli activate receptors, called *olfactory cilia*, which line the nasal passages. Most of these receptors respond to more than one odour.
>
> ▸ Recent research has discovered a family of genes that seem to be responsible for olfaction.

Our Sense of Touch: Sensory Systems in the Skin

PREVIEW QUESTIONS

▸ How are tactile data routed to the brain?

▸ How are the two pathways for pain different?

▸ What does a useful theory of pain perception need to explain?

▸ How does the physiological evidence relate to gate-control theory?

If there is any sense that people trust almost as much as sight, it is the sense of touch. Yet, like all the senses, touch involves converting the sensation of physical stimuli into a psychological experience, and as such, it can be influenced by a variety of psychological factors (e.g., McCabe et al., 2008)—and it can be fooled.

The physical stimuli for touch are mechanical, thermal, and chemical energy that impinge on the skin. These stimuli can produce perceptions of tactile stimulation (the pressure of touch against the skin), warmth, cold, and pain. The human skin is saturated with at least six types of sensory receptors. To some

degree, these different types of receptors are specialized for different functions, such as the registration of pressure, heat, cold, and so forth. However, these distinctions are not as clear as researchers had originally expected (Sinclair, 1981).

Feeling Pressure

If you've been to a mosquito-infested picnic, you'll appreciate the need to quickly know where tactile stimulation is coming from. The sense of touch is set up to meet this need for tactile localization with admirable precision and efficiency. Cells in the nervous system that respond to touch are sensitive to specific patches of skin. These skin patches, which vary considerably in size, are the functional equivalents of *receptive fields* in vision. Like visual receptive fields, they often involve a centre-surround arrangement (see Figure 4.53). Thus, stimuli falling in the centre produce the opposite effect of stimuli falling in the surrounding area (Kandel & Jessell, 1991). If a stimulus is applied continuously to a specific spot on the skin, the perception of pressure gradually fades. Hence, sensory adaptation occurs in the perception of touch, as it does in other sensory systems.

The nerve fibres that carry incoming information about tactile stimulation are routed through the spinal cord to the brainstem. There, the fibres from each side of the body cross over, mostly to the opposite side of the brain. The tactile pathway then projects through the thalamus and onto the *somatosensory cortex* in the brain's parietal lobe. Some cells in the somatosensory cortex function like the *feature detectors* discovered in vision (Gardner & Kandel, 2000). They respond to specific features of touch, such as a movement across the skin in a particular direction.

Feeling Pain

As unpleasant as pain is, the sensation of pain is crucial to survival. Pain is a marvellous warning system. It tells people when they should stop shovelling snow, or it lets them know that they have a pinched nerve that requires treatment. However, chronic pain is a frustrating, demoralizing affliction that affects millions of people and is a major factor in lost productivity (Gatchel & Maddrey, 2004; Turk, 1994). For example, all you have to do is to talk with any of your friends who suffer recurrent migraines to get a sense of how pervasive the effects of this very painful condition can be. According to Statistics Canada (Gilmour & Wilkins, 2003), 8 percent of Canadians 12 years of age and older have had a clinical diagnosis of migraines. Although some advances have been made in this area (DaSilva et al., 2007), they do not come fast enough for those who suffer. Limitations due to pain are the most frequent type of activity limitation reported in the Canadian working-age population (Statistics Canada, 2001), and it has been estimated that chronic pain costs the Canadian economy more than $10 billion dollars annually because of medical expenses, lost income, and lost productivity (Jackson, 2007). Thus, there are pressing practical reasons for psychologists' keen interest in the perception of pain.

Pathways to the Brain

The receptors for pain are mostly free nerve endings in the skin. Pain messages are transmitted to the brain via two types of pathways that pass through different areas in the thalamus (Cholewiak & Cholewiak, 2010). One is a *fast pathway* that registers localized pain and relays it to the cortex in a fraction of a second. This is the system that hits you with sharp pain when you first cut your finger. The second system uses a *slow pathway* that lags a second or two behind the fast system. This pathway (which also carries information about temperature) conveys the less localized, longer-lasting, aching or burning pain that comes after the initial injury. The slow pathway depends on thin, unmyelinated neurons called *C fibres*, whereas the fast pathway is mediated by thicker, myelinated neurons called *A-delta fibres* (see Figure 4.54). Pain signals may be sent to many areas in the cortex, as well as to subcortical centres associated with emotion (such as the hypothalamus and amygdala), depending in part on the nature of the pain (Hung & Mantyh, 2001).

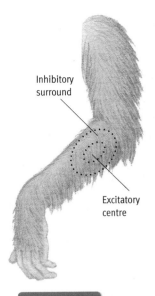

FIGURE 4.53

Receptive field for touch.

A receptive field for touch is an area on the skin surface that, when stimulated, affects the firing of a cell that responds to pressure on the skin. Shown here is a centre-surround receptive field for a cell in the thalamus of a monkey.

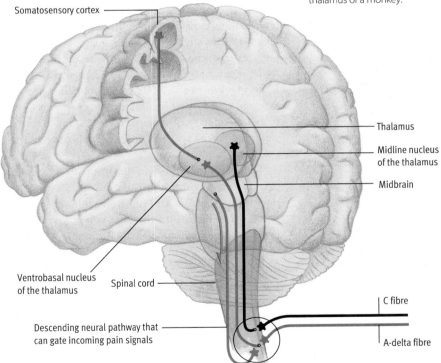

FIGURE 4.54

Pathways for pain signals.

Pain signals are sent inward from receptors to the brain along the two ascending pathways depicted here in red and black. The fast pathway, shown in red, and the slow pathway, shown in black, depend on different types of nerve fibres and are routed through different parts of the thalamus. The gate-control mechanism hypothesized by Melzack and Wall (1965) apparently depends on signals in a descending pathway (shown in green) that originates in an area of the midbrain.

Puzzles in Pain Perception

As with other perceptions, pain is not an automatic result of certain types of stimulation. The perception of pain can be influenced greatly by expectations, personality, mood, and other factors involving higher mental processes (Turk & Okifuji, 2003; Rollman, 1992; Stalling, 1992). The subjective nature of pain is illustrated by placebo effects. As we saw in Chapter 2, many people suffering from pain report relief when given a placebo—an inert "sugar pill" that is presented to them as if it were a painkilling drug (Benedetti, 2008; Stewart-Williams, 2004). Evidence regarding the subjective quality of pain has come from studies that have found ethnic and cultural differences in the pain associated with childbirth (Jordan, 1983) and the experience of chronic pain (Bates, Edwards, & Anderson, 1993). According to Melzack and Wall (1982), culture does not affect the process of pain perception so much as the willingness to tolerate certain types of pain, a conclusion echoed by Zatzick and Dimsdale (1990).

Several recent studies have also highlighted how contextual factors influence the experience of pain. For example, one recent study found that the experience of pain was reduced when female participants looked at a picture of their boyfriend or held their boyfriend's hand (Master et al., 2009). In a similar vein, another study found that looking at pleasant pictures reduced subjects' pain responses, while looking at unpleasant pictures led to stronger pain reactions (Roy et al., 2009). And a study by Gray and Wegner (2008) demonstrated that pain responses increase when participants believe that the pain was inflicted upon them intentionally, rather than accidentally.

The psychological element in pain perception becomes clear when something distracts your attention from pain and the hurting temporarily disappears. For example, imagine that you've just hit your thumb with a hammer and it's throbbing with pain. Suddenly, your child cries out that there's a fire in the laundry room. As you race to deal with this emergency, you forget all about the pain in your thumb. Of course, psychological factors also can work in the reverse. As pain researcher Joel Katz (Asmundson & Katz, 2009; Katz, Asmundson, McRae, & Halket, 2000) has shown, as the number of concerns and intrusive thoughts that patients experience about an upcoming surgery increases, so does the amount of pain medication they request after surgery, even if the amount of actual pain is controlled (Katz, Buis, & Cohen, 2008). Theories of pain clearly must include some explanation of such psychological effects on pain perception (Katz & Seltzer, 2009).

If being told about a fire leads to you forget about your painful thumb, then tissue damage that sends pain impulses on their way to the brain doesn't necessarily result in the experience of pain. Cognitive and emotional processes that unfold in higher brain centres can somehow block pain signals coming from peripheral receptors. Thus, any useful explanation of pain perception must be able to answer a critical question: How does the central nervous system block incoming pain signals?

In an influential effort to answer this question, McGill University psychologists Ronald Melzack and Patrick Wall (1965) devised the gate-control theory of pain. *Gate-control theory* holds that incoming pain sensations must pass through a "gate" in the spinal cord that can be closed, thus blocking ascending pain signals. The gate in this model is not an anatomical structure but a pattern of neural activity that inhibits incoming pain signals. Melzack and Wall suggested that this imaginary gate can be closed by signals from peripheral receptors or by signals from the brain. They theorized that the latter mechanism can help explain how factors such as attention and expectations can shut off pain signals. The measurement of pain is an important issue in this area and according to University of Regina psychologist Thomas Hadjistavropoulos, pain in certain populations (such as the very young and the elderly) with communication limitations can be particularly difficult to assess (Hadjistavropoulos, 2005).

Melzack has continued his research on pain and is well known for his development of the *McGill Pain Questionnaire*, which is one of the most important tools for research on pain (Melzack, 1975). Most recently, along with York University pain researcher Joel Katz, Melzack has examined the puzzle of phantom-limb pain, in which patients continue to "feel" the missing limb, including pain in the nonexistent limb (Melzack & Katz, 2004). Melzack's (2001) neuromatrix theory of pain suggests that pain is a multidimensional phenomenon, produced by many influences.

As a whole, research suggests that the concept of a gating mechanism for pain has merit (Craig & Rollman, 1999). However, relatively little support has been found for the neural circuitry originally hypothesized by Melzack and Wall in the 1960s. Other neural mechanisms, discovered after gate-control theory was proposed, appear to be responsible for blocking the perception of pain.

One of these discoveries was the identification of endorphins. As discussed in Chapter 3, *endorphins* are the body's own natural morphine-like

concept **check** 4.4

Comparing Taste, Smell, and Touch

Check your understanding of taste, smell, and touch by comparing these sensory systems on the dimensions listed in the first column below. A few answers are supplied; see whether you can fill in the rest. The answers can be found in Appendix A.

Dimension	Taste	Smell	Touch
1. Stimulus	_____	_____	_____
2. Receptors	_____	_____	_Many (at least 6) types_
3. Location of receptors	_____	_____	_____
4. Basic elements of perception	_sweet, sour, salty, bitter_	_____	_____

painkillers. Studies suggest that the endorphins play an important role in the modulation of pain (Pert, 2002). For example, placebo effects in the treatment of pain often (but not always) depend on the action of endorphins (Eippert et al., 2009; Price, Finniss, & Benedetti, 2008). Likewise, the analgesic effects that can be achieved through the ancient Chinese art of acupuncture appear to involve endorphins (Cabyoglu, Ergene, & Tan, 2006).

The other discovery involved the identification of a descending neural pathway that mediates the suppression of pain (Basbaum & Jessell, 2000). This pathway appears to originate in an area of the midbrain called the *periaqueductal gray (PAG)*. Neural activity in this pathway is probably initiated by endorphins acting on PAG neurons, which eventually trigger impulses sent down neural circuits that mostly release serotonin. These circuits synapse in the spinal cord, where they appear to release more endorphins, thus inhibiting the activity of neurons that would normally transmit incoming pain impulses to the brain (refer back to Figure 4.54 on page 181). The painkilling effects of morphine appear to be at least partly attributable to activity in this descending pathway, as cutting the fibres in this pathway reduces the analgesic effects of morphine (Jessell & Kelly, 1991). In contrast, activation of this pathway by electrical stimulation of the brain can produce an analgesic effect. Clearly, this pathway plays a central role in gating incoming pain signals.

Our understanding of the experience of pain continues to evolve. The newest discovery is that certain types of *glial cells* may contribute to the modulation of pain (Watkins, 2007). As noted in Chapter 3, only recently have neuroscientists realized that glial cells contribute to signal transmission in the nervous system (Fields, 2004). At least two types of glia in the spinal cord (astrocytes and microglia) appear to play an important role in *chronic pain* (Milligan & Watkins, 2009). These glia are activated by immune system responses to infection or by signals from neurons in pain pathways. Once activated, these glial cells appear to "egg on neurons in the pain pathway," thus amplifying the experience of chronic pain (Watkins & Maier, 2003; Watkins et al., 2007). That said, recent evidence suggests that in some circumstances glial cells may also serve protective functions that diminish or limit pain (Milligan & Watkins, 2009). The discovery that glia play multifaceted roles in the human pain system may eventually lead to the development of new drugs for treating chronic pain.

REVIEW OF KEY POINTS

▷ The skin houses many types of sensory receptors. They respond to pressure, temperature, and pain. Tactile localization depends on receptive fields similar to those seen for vision. Some cells in the somatosensory cortex appear to function like feature detectors.

▷ Pain signals are sent to the brain along two pathways that are characterized as fast and slow. The perception of pain is highly subjective and may be influenced by mood and distractions. Placebo effects in pain treatment and cultural variations in pain tolerance also highlight the subjective nature of pain perception.

▷ Gate-control theory holds that incoming pain signals can be blocked in the spinal cord. Endorphins and a descending neural pathway appear to be responsible for the suppression of pain by the central nervous system. Recent studies indicate that glial cells contribute to the modulation of chronic pain.

We have discussed the dynamics of sensation and perception in five sensory domains—vision, hearing, taste, smell, and touch. Since it is widely known that humans have five senses, that should wrap up our coverage, right? Wrong! People have still other sensory systems: the kinesthetic system (which monitors positions of the body) and the vestibular system (sense of balance).

The Kinesthetic System

The *kinesthetic system* monitors the positions of the various parts of the body. To some extent, you know where your limbs are because you commanded the muscles that put them there. Nonetheless, the kinesthetic system allows you to double-check these locations. Where are the receptors for your kinesthetic sense? Some reside in the joints, indicating how much they are bending. Others reside within the muscles, registering their tautness, or extension. Most kinesthetic stimulation is transmitted to the brain along the same pathway as tactile stimulation. However, the two types of information are kept separate (Vierck, 1978).

The Vestibular System

When you're jolting along in a bus, the world outside the bus window doesn't seem to jump about as your head bounces up and down. Yet a movie taken with a camera fastened to the bus would show a bouncing world. How are you and the camera different? Unlike the camera, you are equipped with a *vestibular system*, which responds to gravity and keeps you informed of your body's location in space. The vestibular system provides the sense of balance, or equilibrium, compensating for changes in the body's position.

The vestibular system shares space in the inner ear with the auditory system. The *semicircular canals* (consult Figure 4.47 on page 173 once again) make up the largest part of the vestibular system. They look like three inner tubes joined at the base. Any rotational motion of the head is uniquely represented by a combination of fluid flows in the semicircular canals (Kelly, 1991). These shifts in fluid are detected by hair cells similar to those found along the basilar membrane in the cochlea (Goldberg & Hudspeth, 2000). Your perceptual system integrates the vestibular input about your body's position with information from other senses. After all, you can see where you are and you know where you've instructed your muscles to take you.

This integration of sensory input raises a point that merits emphasis as we close our tour of the human sensory systems. Although we have discussed the various sensory domains separately, it's important to remember that all of the senses send signals to the same brain, where the information is pooled. We have already encountered examples of sensory integration. For example, it's at work when the sight and smell of food influence taste. *Sensory integration is the norm in perceptual experience.* For instance, when you sit around a campfire, you *see* it blazing, you *hear* it crackling, you *smell* it burning, and you feel the *touch* of its warmth. If you cook something over it, you may even *taste* it. Thus, perception involves building a unified model of the world out of integrated input from all of the senses.

Putting It in Perspective : Themes 2, 5, and 7

In this chapter, three of our unifying themes stand out in sharp relief. Let's discuss the value of theoretical diversity first. Contradictory theories about behaviour can be disconcerting and frustrating for theorists, researchers, teachers, and students alike. Yet this chapter provides two dramatic demonstrations of how theoretical diversity can lead to progress in the long run. For decades, the trichromatic and opponent process theories of colour vision and the place and frequency theories of pitch perception were viewed as fundamentally incompatible. As you know, in each case, the evidence eventually revealed that both theories were needed to fully explain the sensory processes that each sought to explain individually. If it hadn't been for these theoretical debates, current understanding of colour vision and pitch perception might be far more primitive, as the understanding of timbre still is.

Our coverage of sensation and perception should also have enhanced your appreciation of why human experience of the world is highly subjective. As ambiguous figures and optical illusions clearly show, there is no one-to-one correspondence between sensory input and perceived experience of the world. Perception is an active process in which people organize and interpret the information received by the senses. These interpretations are shaped by a host of factors, including the environmental context and perceptual sets. Small wonder, then, that people often perceive the same event in very different ways.

Finally, this chapter provided numerous examples of how cultural factors can shape behaviour—in an area of research where one might expect to find little cultural influence. Most people are not surprised to learn that there are cultural differences in attitudes, values, social behaviour, and development. But perception is widely viewed as a basic, universal process that should be invariant across cultures. In most respects it is, as the similarities among cultural groups in perception far outweigh the differences. Nonetheless, culture has been shown to have a variety of effects on our perceptual experiences (e.g. Goh et al., 2010; Goto et al., 2010; Jenkins et al., 2010). For example, in this chapter we discussed cultural variations in depth perception, susceptibility to illusions, taste preferences, and pain tolerance. Thus, even a fundamental, heavily physiological process such as perception can be modified to some degree by one's cultural background.

The following Personal Application demonstrates the subjectivity of perception once again. It focuses on how painters have learned to use the principles of visual perception to achieve a variety of artistic goals.

REVIEW OF KEY POINTS

▷ Sensory receptors in the skin respond to pressure, temperature, and pain. Tactile localization depends on receptive fields similar to those seen for vision. Some cells in the somatosensory cortex appear to function like feature detectors.

▷ Pain signals are sent to the brain along two pathways that are characterized as fast and slow. The perception of pain is highly subjective and may be influenced by mood, attention, and culture. Gate-control theory holds that incoming pain signals can be blocked in the spinal cord. Endorphins and a descending neural pathway appear responsible for the suppression of pain by the central nervous system.

▷ The kinesthetic system monitors the position of various body parts. Kinesthetic receptors, located in the joints and muscles, send signals to the brain along the same pathway as tactile stimulation. The sense of balance depends primarily on activity in the semicircular canals in the vestibular system.

▷ This chapter underscored three of our unifying themes: the value of theoretical diversity, the subjective nature of human experience, and the influence of culture on behaviour.

SENSE	STIMULUS	ELEMENTS OF THE STIMULUS

The Visual System: SIGHT

Light is electromagnetic radiation that travels in waves. Humans can register only a slim portion of the total range of wavelengths, from 400 to 700 nanometers.

Wave amplitude · Wavelength

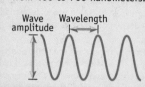

© hougaard malan/iStockphoto.com

Light waves vary in *amplitude, wavelength,* and *purity,* which influence perceptions as shown below.

Physical properties	Related perceptions
Wavelength	Hue (colour)
Amplitude	Brightness
Purity	Saturation

The Auditory System: HEARING

Andreas Gradin/Shutterstock

Sound waves are vibrations of molecules, which means that they must travel through some physical medium, such as air. Humans can hear wavelengths between 20 and 20 000 Hz.

Wavelength · Amplitude

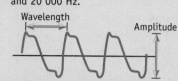

Sound waves vary in *amplitude, wavelength,* and *purity,* which influence perceptions, as shown below.

Physical properties	Related perceptions
Amplitude	Loudness
Frequency	Pitch
Purity	Timbre

The Gustatory System: TASTE

The stimuli for taste generally are chemical substances that are soluble (dissolvable in water). These stimuli are dissolved in the mouth's saliva.

AAGAMIA/Getty Images

It is generally, but not universally, agreed that there are four primary tastes: *sweet, sour, bitter,* and *salty.*

Many researchers have recently added *umami* to the list of primary tastes. *Umami* is a Japanese word for the savory taste of glutamates.

The Olfactory System: SMELL

Lindsey Parnaby/Getty Images

The stimuli are volatile chemical substances that can evaporate and be carried in the air. These chemical stimuli are dissolved in the mucus of the nose.

Efforts to identify primary odours have proven unsatisfactory. If primary odours exist, there must be a great many of them.

The Tactile System: TOUCH

The stimuli are mechanical, thermal, and chemical energy that impinge on the skin.

Yanik Chauvin/Shutterstock

Receptors in the skin can register *pressure, warmth, cold,* and *pain.*

NATURE AND LOCATION OF RECEPTORS

BRAIN PATHWAYS IN INITIAL PROCESSING

The *retina*, which is neural tissue lining the inside back surface of the eye, contains millions of receptor cells called *rods* and *cones*. Rods play a key role in night and peripheral vision; cones play a key role in daylight and colour vision.

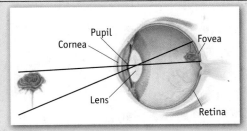

Cornea
Pupil
Fovea
Lens
Retina

Neural impulses are routed through the *LGN* in the *thalamus* and then distributed to the *primary visual cortex* at the back of the *occipital lobe*.

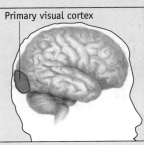

Primary visual cortex

The receptors for hearing are tiny *hair cells* that line the *basilar membrane* that runs the length of the *cochlea*, a fluid-filled, coiled tunnel in the inner ear.

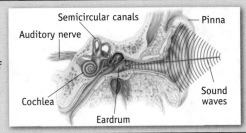

Semicircular canals
Auditory nerve
Pinna
Cochlea
Eardrum
Sound waves

Neural impulses are routed through the *thalamus* and then sent to the *primary auditory cortex*, which is mostly located in the *temporal lobe*.

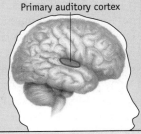

Primary auditory cortex

The gustatory receptors are clusters of *taste cells* found in the *taste buds* that line the trenches around tiny bumps in the tongue. Taste cells have a short life span (about 10 days) and are constantly being replaced.

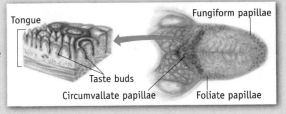

Tongue
Fungiform papillae
Taste buds
Circumvallate papillae
Foliate papillae

Neural impulses are routed through the *thalamus* and on to the *insular cortex* in the frontal lobe.

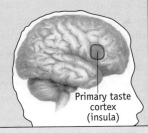

Primary taste cortex (insula)

The receptors for smell are *olfactory cilia*, hairlike structures in the upper portion of the nasal passages. Like taste cells, they have a short lifespan (about 30–60 days) and are constantly being replaced.

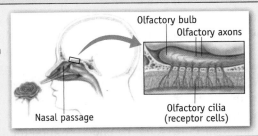

Olfactory bulb
Olfactory axons
Nasal passage
Olfactory cilia (receptor cells)

Neural impulses are routed through the *olfactory bulb* and then sent directly to the *olfactory cortex* in the *temporal lobe* and other cortical areas. Smell is the only sensory input not routed through the thalamus.

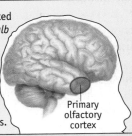

Primary olfactory cortex

The human skin is saturated with at least six types of sensory receptors. The four types shown here respond to pressure, whereas *free nerve endings* in the skin respond to pain, warmth, and cold.

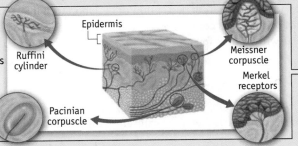

Epidermis
Ruffini cylinder
Meissner corpuscle
Merkel receptors
Pacinian corpuscle

Neural impulses are routed through the *brainstem* and *thalamus* and on to the *somatosensory cortex* in the *parietal lobe*.

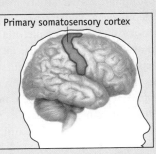

Primary somatosensory cortex

Appreciating Art and Illusion

Answer the following multiple-choice question: Artistic works such as paintings:

___ **a** render an accurate picture of reality.
___ **b** create an illusion of reality.
___ **c** provide an interpretation of reality.
___ **d** make us think about the nature of reality.
___ **e** all of the above.

The answer to this question is (e), "all of the above." Historically, artists have pursued many and varied purposes, including each of those listed in the question (Goldstein, 2001). To realize their goals, they have had to use a number of principles of perception—sometimes quite deliberately, and sometimes not. Let's use the example of painting to explore the role of perceptual principles in art and illusion.

The goal of most early painters was to produce a believable picture of reality. This goal immediately created a problem familiar to most of us who have attempted to draw realistic pictures: The real world is three-dimensional, but a canvas or a sheet of paper is flat. Paradoxically, then, painters who set out to re-create reality have to do so by creating an *illusion* of three-dimensional reality.

Prior to the Renaissance, efforts to create a convincing illusion of reality were relatively awkward by modern standards. Why? Because artists did not understand how to use the full range of depth cues. This is apparent in Figure 4.55, a religious scene painted around 1300. The painting clearly lacks a sense of depth. The people seem paper-thin. They have no real position in space.

Although earlier artists made some use of depth cues, Renaissance artists manipulated the full range of pictorial depth cues and really harnessed the crucial cue of linear perspective (Solso, 1994). Figure 4.56 dramatizes the resulting transition in art. It shows a scene depicted by Gentile and Giovanni Bellini, Italian Renaissance painters. It seems much more realistic and lifelike than

FIGURE 4.55

Master of the Arrest of Christ (detail, central part) by S. Francesco, Assisi, Italy (circa 1300).

Notice how the paucity of depth cues makes the painting seem flat and unrealistic.

Scala/Art Resource, New York

the painting in Figure 4.55. Notice how the buildings on the sides converge to make use of linear perspective. Additionally, distant objects are smaller than nearby ones, an application of relative size. This painting also uses height in plane, light and shadow, and interposition. By taking fuller advantage of pictorial depth cues, Renaissance artists enhanced the illusion of reality in paintings.

In the centuries since the Renaissance, painters have adopted a number of viewpoints about the portrayal of reality. For instance, the Impressionists of the 19th century did not want to re-create the photographic "reality" of a scene. They set out to interpret a viewer's fleeting perception or *impression* of reality. To accomplish this end, they worked with colour in unprecedented ways.

Consider, for instance, Claude Monet, a French Impressionist who began to work with separate daubs of pure, bright colours that blurred together to create an

alternating perceptual experience. If you view his paintings up close, you see only a shimmering mass of colour. When you step back, however, the adjacent colours begin to blend, and forms begin to take shape, as you can see in Figure 4.57. Monet achieved this duality through careful use of colour mixing and by working systematically with complementary colours.

Similar methods were used even more precisely and systematically by Georges Seurat, a French artist who used a technique called *pointillism*. Seurat carefully studied what scientists knew about the composition of colour in the 1880s, and then applied this knowledge in a calculated, laboratory-like manner. Indeed, critics in his era dubbed him the "little chemist." Seurat constructed his paintings out of tiny dots of pure, intense colours. He used additive colour mixing, a departure from the norm in painting, which usually depends on subtractive mixing of pigments. A famous result of Seurat's "scientific" approach to painting

FIGURE 4.56

Brera Predica di S. Marco Pinacoteca **by Gentile and Giovanni Bellini (circa 1480).**

In this painting, the Italian Renaissance artists use a number of depth cues—including linear perspective, relative size, height in plane, light and shadow, and interposition—to enhance the illusion of three-dimensional reality.

Source: Scala/Art Resource, New York.

was his renowned *Sunday Afternoon on the Island of La Grande Jatte* (see Figure 4.58). As the work of Seurat illustrates, modernist painters were moving away from attempts to re-create the world as it is literally seen.

If 19th-century painters liberated colour, their successors at the turn of the 20th century liberated form. This was particularly true of the Cubists. Cubism was begun in 1909 by Pablo Picasso, a Spanish artist who went on to experiment with other styles in his prolific career. The Cubists didn't try to *portray* reality so much as to *reassemble* it. They attempted to reduce everything to combinations of geometric forms (lines, circles, triangles, rectangles, and such) laid out in a flat space, lacking depth. In a sense, *they applied the theory of feature analysis to canvas*, as they built their figures out of simple features.

The resulting paintings were decidedly unrealistic, but the painters would leave realistic fragments that provided clues about the subject. Picasso liked to challenge his viewers to decipher the subject of his

FIGURE 4.57

Claude Monet's *Palazzo da Mula, Venice* **(1908).**

French Impressionist Monet often used complementary colours to achieve his visual effects.

Source: Monet, Claude, *Palazzo da Mula, Venice* (1908). Photo by Richard Carafelli, Chester Dale Collection, © Board of Trustees, National Gallery of Art.

Sensation and Perception

paintings. Take a look at the painting in Figure 4.59 and see whether you can figure out what Picasso was portraying.

The work in Figure 4.59 is entitled *Violin and Grapes*. Note how Gestalt principles of perceptual organization are at work to create these forms. Proximity and similarity serve to bring the grapes together in the bottom right corner. Closure accounts for your being able to see the essence of the violin.

Other Gestalt principles are the key to the effect achieved in the painting in Figure 4.60. This painting, by Marcel Duchamp, a French artist who blended Cubism and a style called Futurism, is entitled *Nude Descending a Staircase*. The effect clearly depends on the Gestalt principle of continuity.

The Surrealists toyed with reality in a different way. Influenced by Sigmund Freud's writings on the unconscious, the Surrealists explored the world of dreams and fantasy. Specific elements in their paintings are often depicted realistically, but the strange juxtaposition of elements yields a disconcerting irrationality reminiscent of dreams.

FIGURE 4.59

Violin and Grapes **by Pablo Picasso (1912).**

This painting makes use of the Gestalt principles of proximity, similarity, and closure.

Source: © Picasso Estate/SODRAC (2008). Pablo Picasso, *Violin and Grapes*. Ceret and Sorgues (spring-early fall 1912), oil on canvas, 20 × 24 inches (50.6 × 61 cm). Collection, The Museum of Modern Art, New York, Mrs. David M. Levy Bequest.

FIGURE 4.60

Marcel Duchamp's Nude Descending a Staircase, No. 2 (1912).

This painting uses the Gestalt principles of continuity and common fate.

Source: © Estate of Marcel Duchamp/SODRAC (2008). Duchamp, Marcel, 1912, *Nude Descending a Staircase*, No. 2, oil on canvas, 58 × 35 inches (145 × 87.5 cm). Philadelphia Museum of Art: Louise and Walter Arensburg Collection, #50-134–69.

FIGURE 4.61

Salvador Dali's *The Hallucinogenic Toreador* (1969–1970).

This surrealistic painting includes a reversible figure (the bullfighter is made up of Venus de Milo statues). Gestalt principles are crucial to the perception of the bull and the dalmatian near the bottom of the painting.

Source: © Salvador Dali Foundation Gala—Salvador Dali/SODRAC (2008). Dali, Salvador, *The Hallucinogenic Toreador* (1969–70), oil on canvas, 157 × 119 inches (398.7 × 302.3 cm). Collection of The Salvador Dali Museum, St. Petersburg, Florida.

A prominent example of this style is Salvador Dali's *The Hallucinogenic Toreador*, shown in Figure 4.61. Notice the reversible figure near the centre of the painting. The bullfighter is made up of Venus de Milo sculptures. Dali often used reversible figures to enhance the ambiguity of his bizarre visions.

Perhaps no one has been more creative in manipulating perceptual ambiguity than M. C. Escher, a modern Dutch artist. Escher's chief goal was to stimulate viewers to think about the nature of reality and the process of visual perception itself. Interestingly, Escher readily acknowledged his debt to psychology as a source of inspiration (Teuber, 1974). He followed the work of the Gestalt psychologists carefully and would even cite specific journal articles that served as the point of departure for his works. For example, *Waterfall*, a 1961 lithograph by Escher, is an impossible figure that appears to defy the law of gravity (see Figure 4.62). The puzzling problem here is that a level channel of water terminates in a waterfall that "falls" into the *same* channel two levels "below." This drawing is made up of two impossible triangles. In case you need help seeing them, the waterfall itself forms one side of each triangle.

The Necker cube, a reversible figure mentioned earlier, was the inspiration for Escher's 1958 lithograph *Belvedere*, shown in Figure 4.63. You have to look carefully to realize that this is another impossible figure. Note that the top storey runs at a

right angle from the first storey. Note also how the pillars are twisted around. The pillars that start on one side of the building end up supporting the second storey on the other side! Escher's debt to the Necker cube is manifested in several places. Notice, for instance, the drawing of a Necker cube on the floor next to the seated boy (on the lower left).

Like Escher, Victor Vasarely challenged viewers to think about the process of perception. A Hungarian artist, Vasarely pioneered an approach called _Kinetic Art_ because of his interest in creating illusions of motion. Like Georges Seurat, he went about his work with scientific precision. His paintings are based on optical illusions, as squares seem to advance and recede,

or spheres seem to inflate and deflate. For example, note how Vasarely used a variety of depth cues to convey the look of a sphere inflating in his painting _Vega-Tek_, shown in Figure 4.64.

While Escher and Vasarely challenged viewers to think about perception, Belgian artist René Magritte challenged people to think about the conventions of painting.

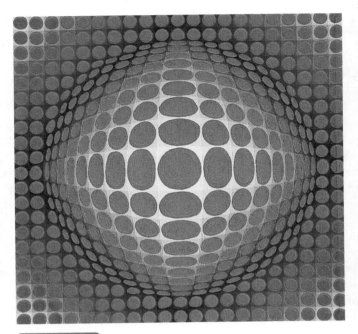

FIGURE 4.64

Victor Vasarely's *Vega-Tek* (1969).

In this painting, Vasarely manipulates a host of depth cues to create the image of a sphere inflating.

Source: Vasarely, Victor, *Vega-Tek*. Wool Aubusson tapestry. 1969. Copyright Art Resource, NY Private Collection. © Estate of Victor Vasarely / SODRAC 2011.

FIGURE 4.65

René Magritte's *Les Promenades d'Euclide* (1955).

Notice how the pair of nearly identical triangles look quite different in different contexts.

Source: © Estate of Rene Magritte/SODRAC (2008). Magritte, Rene, *Les Promenades d'Euclide*, The Minneapolis Institute of Arts, The William Hood Dunwoody Fund.

Many of his works depict paintings on an easel, with the "real" scene continuing unbroken at the edges. The painting in Figure 4.65 is such a picture within a picture. In addition, there are two identical triangles in the painting. One represents a road and the other a nearby tower. Notice how the identical triangles are perceived differently because of the variations in *context*.

Ultimately, Magritte's painting blurs the line between the real world and the illusory world created by the artist, suggesting that there is no line—that everything is an illusion. In this way, Magritte "framed" the ageless, unanswerable question: What is reality?

REVIEW OF KEY POINTS

▷ The principles of visual perception are often applied to artistic endeavours. Prior to the Renaissance, efforts to create a convincing illusion of three-dimensional reality were awkward because artists did not understand how to use depth cues. After the Renaissance, painters began to routinely use pictorial depth cues to make their scenes more lifelike.

▷ Nineteenth-century painters, such as the Impressionists, manipulated colour in creative, new ways. The Cubists were innovative in manipulating form, as they applied the theory of feature analysis to canvas. The Surrealists toyed with reality, exploring the world of fantasy and dreams.

▷ Modern artists such as Escher and Vasarely have tried to stimulate viewers to think about the process of perception. Among other things, Escher worked with the Necker cube and the impossible triangle.

Recognizing Contrast Effects: It's All Relative

You're sitting at home one night, when the phone rings. It's Simone, an acquaintance from school who needs help with a recreational program for youngsters that she runs for the local park district. She tries to persuade you to volunteer four hours of your time every Friday night throughout the school year to supervise the volleyball program. The thought of giving up your Friday nights and adding this sizable obligation to your already busy schedule makes you cringe with horror. You politely explain to Simone that you can't possibly afford to give up that much time and you won't be able to help her. She accepts your rebuff graciously, but the next night she calls again. This time she wants to know whether you would be willing to supervise volleyball every third Friday. You still feel like it's a big obligation that you really don't want to take on, but the new request seems much more reasonable than the original one. So, with a sigh of resignation, you agree to Simone's request.

What's wrong with this picture? Well, there's nothing wrong with volunteering your time for a good cause, but you just succumbed to a social influence strategy called *the door-in-the face technique*. The *door-in-the-face technique* involves making a large request that is likely to be turned down as a way to increase the chance that people will agree to a smaller request later (see Figure 4.66). The name for this strategy is derived from the expectation that the initial request will be quickly rejected (hence, the door is slammed in the requester's face). Although they may not be familiar with the strategy's name, many people use this manipulative tactic. For example, a husband who wants to coax his frugal wife into agreeing to buy a $25 000 sports car might begin by proposing that they purchase a $44 000 sports car. By the time the wife talks her husband out of the $44 000 car, the $25 000 price tag may look quite reasonable to her—which is what the husband wanted all along.

Research has demonstrated that the door-in-the-face technique is a highly effective persuasive strategy (Cialdini, 2001). One of the reasons it works so well is that it depends on a simple and pervasive perceptual principle. As noted in our discussion of psychophysical scaling (see page 140), in the domain of perceptual experience, *everything is relative*. This relativity means that people are easily swayed by *contrast effects*. For example, lighting a match or a small candle in a dark room will produce a burst of light that seems quite bright, but if you light the same match or candle in a well-lit room, you may not even detect the additional illumination. The relativity of perception is apparent in the painting by Josef Albers shown in Figure 4.67. The two Xs are exactly the same colour, but the X in the top half looks yellow, whereas the X in the bottom half looks brown. These varied perceptions occur because of contrast effects—the two Xs are contrasted against different background colours.

The same principles of relativity and contrast that operate when we are making judgments about the intensity or colour of visual stimuli also affect the way we make judgments in a wide variety of domains. For example, a 185-cm basketball player, who is really quite tall, can look downright small when surrounded by teammates who are all over 200 cm. And a salary of $30 000 per year for your first full-time job may seem like a princely sum, until a close friend gets an offer of $55 000 per year. The assertion that everything is relative raises the issue of relative to what? *Comparitors* are people, objects, events, and other standards used as a baseline for comparison in making judgments. It is fairly easy to manipulate many types of judgments by

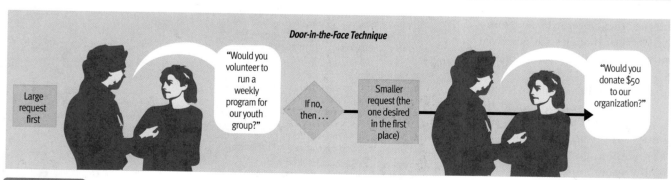

FIGURE 4.66

The door-in-the-face technique.

The door-in-the-face technique is a frequently used compliance strategy in which you begin with a large request and work down to the smaller request you are really after. It depends in part on contrast effects.

FIGURE 4.67

Contrast effects in visual perception.

This composition by Joseph Albers shows how one colour can be perceived differently when contrasted against different backgrounds. The top X looks yellow and the bottom X looks brown, but they're really the same colour.

Source: Albers, Joseph. *Interaction of Color.* Copyright © 1963 and reprinted by permission of the publisher, Yale University Press.

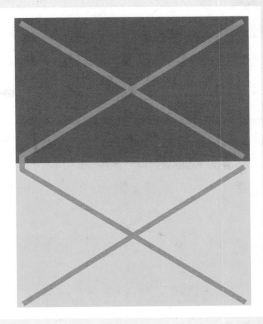

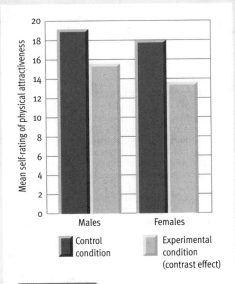

FIGURE 4.68

Contrast effects in judgments of physical attractiveness.

Participants rated their own physical attractiveness under two conditions. In the experimental condition, the ratings occurred after subjects were exposed to a series of photos depicting very attractive models. The resulting contrast effects led to lower self-ratings in this condition. (Data based on Thornton & Moore, 1993)

selecting *extreme* comparitors that may be unrepresentative.

The influence of extreme comparitors was demonstrated in a couple of interesting studies of judgments of physical attractiveness. In one study, undergraduate males were asked to rate the attractiveness of an average-looking female (who was described as a potential date for another male in the dorm) presented in a photo either just before or just after the participants watched a TV show dominated by strikingly beautiful women (Kenrick & Gutierres, 1980). The female was viewed as less attractive when the ratings were obtained just after the men had seen gorgeous women cavorting on TV as opposed to when they hadn't. In another investigation (Thornton & Moore, 1993), both male and female participants rated *themselves* as less attractive after being exposed to many pictures of extremely attractive models (see Figure 4.68). Thus, contrast effects can influence important social judgments that are likely to affect how people feel about themselves and others.

Anyone who understands how easily judgments can be manipulated by a careful choice of comparitors could influence your thinking. For example, a politician who is caught in some illegal or immoral act could sway public opinion by bringing to mind (perhaps subtly) the fact that many other politicians have committed acts that were much worse. When considered against a backdrop of more extreme comparitors, the politician's transgression will probably seem less offensive. A defence lawyer could use a similar strategy in an attempt to obtain a lighter sentence for a client by comparing the client's offence to much more serious crimes. And a realtor who wants to sell you an expensive house that will require huge mortgage payments will be quick to mention other homeowners who have taken on even larger mortgages.

In summary, critical thinking is facilitated by conscious awareness of the way comparitors can influence, and perhaps distort, a wide range of judgments. In particular, it pays to be vigilant about the possibility that others may manipulate contrast effects in their persuasive efforts. One way to reduce the influence of contrast effects is to consciously consider comparitors that are both worse and better than the event you are judging, as a way of balancing the effects of the two extremes.

TABLE 4.2	Critical Thinking Skills Discussed in This Application
Skill	**Description**
Understanding how contrast effects can influence judgments and decisions	The critical thinker appreciates how striking contrasts can be manipulated to influence many types of judgments.
Recognizing when extreme comparitors are being used	The critical thinker is on the lookout for extreme comparitors that distort judgments.

Key Ideas

Psychophysics: Basic Concepts and Issues

● Absolute thresholds are not really absolute. Fechner's law asserts that larger and larger increases in stimulus intensity are required to produce just noticeable differences in the magnitude of sensation.

● According to signal-detection theory, the detection of sensory inputs is influenced by noise in the system and by decision-making strategies. In recent years, it has become apparent that perception can occur without awareness. Prolonged stimulation may lead to sensory adaptation.

Our Sense of Sight: The Visual System

● Light varies in terms of wavelength, amplitude, and purity. Light enters the eye through the cornea and pupil and is focused on the retina by the lens. Rods and cones are the visual receptors found in the retina. Cones play a key role in daylight vision and colour perception, and rods are critical to night vision and peripheral vision. Dark and light adaptation both involve changes in the retina's sensitivity to light.

● The retina transforms light into neural impulses that are sent to the brain via the optic nerve. Receptive fields are areas in the retina that affect the firing of visual cells. Two visual pathways, which engage in parallel processing, send signals through the thalamus to the primary visual cortex. From there, visual signals are shuttled along pathways that have been characterized as the *what* and *where* pathways.

● Perceptions of colour (hue) are primarily a function of light wavelength, while amplitude affects brightness and purity affects saturation. Perceptions of many varied colours depend on processes that resemble additive colour mixing. The evidence now suggests that both the trichromatic and opponent process theories are necessary to account for colour vision.

● Form perception depends on the selection and interpretation of visual inputs. According to feature analysis theories, people detect specific elements in stimuli and build them into forms through bottom-up processing. However, evidence suggests that form perception also involves top-down processing.

● Gestalt psychology emphasized that the whole may be greater than the sum of its parts (features), as illustrated by Gestalt principles of form perception. Other approaches to form perception emphasize that people develop perceptual hypotheses about the distal stimuli that could be responsible for the proximal stimuli that are sensed.

● Depth perception depends primarily on monocular cues. Binocular cues such as retinal disparity and convergence can also contribute to depth perception.

● Perceptual constancies help viewers deal with the ever-shifting nature of proximal stimuli. Optical illusions demonstrate that perceptual hypotheses can be inaccurate and that perceptions are not simple reflections of objective reality.

Our Sense of Hearing: The Auditory System

● Sound varies in terms of wavelength (frequency), amplitude, and purity. These properties affect mainly perceptions of pitch, loudness, and timbre, respectively. Auditory signals are transmitted through the thalamus to the auditory cortex in the temporal lobe.

● Modern evidence suggests that place theory and frequency theory are complementary rather than incompatible explanations of pitch perception. People pinpoint the source of sounds by comparing inter-ear differences in the intensity and timing of sounds.

● Exposure to music has been found to affect our emotions. In addition, as revealed in the Featured Study, music training affects our ability to decode emotions in the speech of others.

Our Chemical Senses: Taste and Smell

● The taste buds are sensitive to four basic tastes: sweet, sour, bitter, and salty. Taste preferences are largely learned and are heavily influenced by one's cultural background. Supertasters are more sensitive to bitter and sweet tastes than others are.

● Like taste, smell is a chemical sense. Chemical stimuli activate olfactory receptors lining the nasal passages. Most of these receptors respond to more than one odour. Humans exhibit surprising difficulty attaching names to odours.

Our Sense of Touch: Sensory Systems in the Skin

● Sensory receptors in the skin respond to pressure, temperature, and pain. Pain signals are sent to the brain along two pathways characterized as fast and slow. The perception of pain is highly subjective and may be influenced by mood, attention, personality, and culture. Gate-control theory holds that incoming pain signals can be blocked in the spinal cord. Endorphins and a descending neural pathway appear responsible for the suppression of pain by the central nervous system.

Our Other Senses

● The kinesthetic system monitors the position of various body parts. The sense of balance depends on activity in the vestibular system.

Putting It in Perspective : Themes 2, 5, and 7

● This chapter underscored three of our unifying themes: the value of theoretical diversity, the subjective nature of human experience, and the influence of culture on behaviour.

PERSONAL APPLICATION • Appreciating Art and Illusion

● The principles of visual perception are often applied to artistic endeavours. Painters routinely use pictorial depth cues to make their scenes more lifelike. Colour mixing, feature analysis, Gestalt principles, reversible figures, and impossible figures have also been used in influential paintings.

CRITICAL THINKING APPLICATION • Recognizing Contrast Effects: It's All Relative

● The study of perception often highlights the relativity of experience. This relativity can be manipulated by arranging for contrast effects. Critical thinking is enhanced by an awareness of how comparitors can distort many judgments.

Key Terms

Absolute threshold, 139
Additive colour mixing, 154
Afterimage, 155
Auditory localization, 174
Basilar membrane, 172
Binocular depth cues, 163
Bottom-up processing, 159
Cochlea, 172
Colour-blindness, 155
Comparitors, 194
Complementary colours, 155
Cones, 146
Convergence, 164
Dark adaptation, 147
Depth perception, 163
Distal stimuli, 162
Door-in-the-face technique, 194
Farsightedness, 144
Feature analysis, 159
Feature detectors, 151
Fechner's law, 140
Fovea, 146
Frequency theory, 173
Gate-control theory, 182
Gustatory system, 177
Impossible figures, 166
Just noticeable difference (JND), 140
Kinesthetic system, 184
Lateral antagonism, 148
Lens, 144
Light adaptation, 147
Monocular depth cues, 164
Motion parallax, 164
Nearsightedness, 144
Olfactory system, 177
Opponent process theory, 155
Optic chiasm, 149
Optic disk, 146
Optical illusion, 165
Parallel processing, 149
Perception, 138

Perceptual constancy, 165
Perceptual hypothesis, 162
Perceptual set, 158
Phi phenomenon, 160
Pheromones, 180
Pictorial depth cues, 164
Place theory, 173
Prosopagnosia, 152
Proximal stimuli, 162
Psychophysics, 139
Pupil, 144
Receptive field of a visual cell, 148
Retina, 146
Retinal disparity, 163
Reversible figure, 158
Rods, 147
Saccades, 145
Sensation, 138
Sensory adaptation, 142
Signal-detection theory, 140
Subjective contours, 160
Subliminal perception, 141
Subtractive colour mixing, 153
Threshold, 139
Top-down processing, 160
Trichromatic theory, 154
Vestibular system, 184
Visual agnosia, 152
Weber's law, 140

Key People

Linda Bartoshuk, 178
Mel Goodale, 169
Gustav Fechner, 140
David Hubel, 151
Ronald Melzack, 182
Hermann von Helmholtz, 154, 174
Patrick Wall, 182
Max Wertheimer, 160
Torsten Wiesel, 150

1. Which of the following is the definition of the absolute threshold, for the purpose of psychophysical research?
   A. the stimulus intensity that can be detected 100 percent of the time
   B. the stimulus intensity that can be detected 50 percent of the time
   C. the minimum amount of difference in intensity needed to tell two stimuli apart
   D. a constant proportion of the size of the initial stimulus

2. For someone who is tone-deaf, musical notes must be very different in order to tell them apart. Thus, which of the following must be larger for a tone-deaf person compared to a person with normal auditory perception?
   A. the just-noticeable-difference
   B. the relative threshold
   C. the differential equation
   D. the Fechner fraction

3. In which of the following situations is sensory adaptation most beneficial?
   A. You need to concentrate, but there is noise coming from the next apartment.
   B. You're trying to read a sign that is very far away and you can't quite make out the words.
   C. You hear dogs barking, and you're trying to determine if your dog is one of them.
   D. You're trying to learn a new song, so you play it over and over again.

4. Which of the following statements concerning farsightedness is correct?
   A. Close objects are seen clearly.
   B. The focus of light from close objects falls behind the retina.
   C. The focus of light from distant objects falls a little short of the retina.
   D. It typically occurs when the lens bends the light too much.

5. What is the name for the collection of rod and cone receptors that funnel signals to a particular visual cell in the retina?
   A. fovea
   B. optic disk
   C. opponent process field
   D. receptive field

6. Which of the following characterizes (i) the visual pathway that travels through the dorsal stream to the parietal lobes and (ii); the visual pathway that travels through the ventral stream to the temporal lobes?
   A. (i) the what pathway; (ii) the where pathway
   B. (i) the where pathway; (ii) the what pathway
   C. (i) the opponent process pathway; (ii) the trichromatic pathway
   D. (i) the trichromatic pathway; (ii) the opponent process pathway

7. Which theory of colour vision predicts that the Canadian flag will have a green and black afterimage?
   A. subtractive colour mixing
   B. trichromatic theory
   C. additive colour mixing
   D. opponent process theory

8. Which of the following increases the likelihood that someone will experience inattentional blindness?
   A. genetic predisposition
   B. looking at a scene generally, rather than focusing on a specific feature
   C. slight alcohol intoxication
   D. working on a fairly simple task

9. An artist draws converging lines so that a set of train tracks appears to go off into the distance. What is the name for this monocular cue for depth perception?
   A. linear perspective
   B. texture gradient
   C. subjective contour
   D. interposition

10. Which of the following actions would you expect to produce the phi phenomenon?
    A. music training
    B. staring at a bright red colour and then closing your eyes
    C. rapidly scanning a sequence of pictures of your best friend water skiing
    D. listening to several rapidly played musical notes, each separated by a semitone

11. Which of the following types of perceptual cue is manipulated by 3-D movie technology but not by regular movies?
    A. linear perspective
    B. convergence
    C. motion parallax
    D. interposition

12. What is the role of the hair cells found on the basilar membrane of the ear?
    A. They filter out debris that would otherwise damage the ear and interfere with auditory perception.
    B. They convert physical sound stimulation into neural impulses.
    C. They vibrate and make a noise that is perceived by the ear drum.
    D. They cushion the cochlea and ossicles.

13. Which of the following is true of both taste and odour perception?
    A. There are four primary stimulus groups for both senses.
    B. Both systems are routed through the thalamus on the way to the cortex.
    C. The physical stimuli for both senses are soluble chemicals.
    D. Both senses rely on receptors that are hardy and have a long life span.

14. Which of the following would be most likely to cause problems with balance?
    A. poor visual acuity or blindness
    B. release of endorphins as a result of pain
    C. congenital deafness
    D. damage to the inner ear

15. Which of the following explains the success of the door-in-the-face technique, as well as reductions in self-esteem by people who view a lot of highly attractive models?
    A. contrast effects
    B. Gestalt principles
    C. perceptual set
    D. subliminal perception

See Appendix A for answers to this Practice Test.

On the Web

▶ **CourseMate**

Go to this site to find online resources directly linked to your book, including more quizzes, a glossary, flash cards, videos, and more!

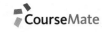

▶ **CengageNow**

Go to this site for the link to CengageNOW™, your one-stop study shop. Take a pre-test for this chapter and CengageNOW™ will generate a personalized study plan based on your test results! The study plan will identify the topics you need to review and direct you to online resources to help you master those topics. You can then take a post-test to help you determine the concepts you have mastered and what you still need to work on.

▶ **Aplia**

Aplia™ is an online interactive learning solution that helps you improve comprehension—and your grade—by integrating a variety of media and tools such as video, tutorials, practice tests, and an interactive e-book.

CHAPTER 5

Variations in Consciousness

© Daryl Benson/Getty Images

S leep and conversation seem to be interconnected. While only some people seem to talk *in* their sleep (referred to as *somniloquy*) it seems as if everyone likes to talk *about* their sleep. Or, to be more accurate, most people like to talk about their lack of sleep. To ask someone, anyone, how they slept last night seems to be an open invitation for complaint. According to Statistics Canada, many Canadians have cut down on the amount of sleep they get in order to squeeze more out of their days (Williams, 2001). We have all had experience with a lack of sleep, so we know that if we do not get enough sleep, the next day will be more difficult for us and, if we care to admit it, for those who are close to us. For those of us who are lucky enough to sleep well most of the time, sleep becomes part of our conversation and consciousness only after those occasional nights when we do not sleep well. For others, though, sleep, lack of sleep, and sleep disorders and disturbances can be much more significant. For these individuals, lack of sleep is not just an occasional inconvenience—it can alter one's life, or even end it.

One of us had first-hand experience with significant sleep disturbance in graduate school when we had a professor in a small seminar class who would periodically and very suddenly fall deeply asleep during class; one minute he would be awake and, the next, asleep. He wasn't bored; in fact, it seemed to happen most often when the discussion was just heating up. It wasn't just that he had had a bad night—it was that he suffered from a sleep disorder termed *narcolepsy*, a serious sleep disorder in which those who suffer from it often fall asleep uncontrollably during their everyday routine. According to pioneer sleep researcher William Dement, it is the only disorder that is known to be "due to a flaw in the primary sleep systems in the brain" (Dement, 1999, p. 508). Although it was initially disconcerting to us, once we learned the details, we were surprised to find out that it was a serious disorder and that it dramatically and negatively affected our professor's life in many ways, from his inability to drive a car to his professional and personal lives. For him, sleep and the lack thereof dominated his life. This seems a significant enough complication to be introduced by sleep-related disorders, but then consider for a moment the impact of sleep-related events on the life of Ken Parks.

Ken Parks always had difficulty with sleep and had a history of sleepwalking. One night in 1987, while asleep, he drove almost 40 kilometres to where his wife's parents lived. There, while still asleep, he

Ken Parks, pictured here, was acquitted of the murder of his mother-in-law partially based on a history of sleep-walking.

CP PHOTO/Globe & Mail—Erik Christensen

proceeded to assault them both and ultimately kill his mother-in-law. He had no trouble doing it; he was a large and athletic man at over 195 centimetres and 113 kilograms. Did he intend to do it? By all reports, he had a comfortable relationship with his in-laws. All he really remembered of that night was lying in bed alone watching *Saturday Night Live* and then later stumbling into a police station shouting, "Oh my god. I think I just killed two people" (Callwood, 1990, p. 7). Even more startling to some than the murder itself was the fact that he was ultimately acquitted of the crime. He was examined by experts and it was decided that the crime had most likely been committed while he was sleepwalking (Broughton et al., 1994). You can read about Ken Parks in a book by June Callwood (1990) entitled *The Sleepwalker*.

Of course, we all know that most of us do not have the kinds of experiences that Ken Parks had. But why do we sleep and what does it do for us, anyway? You may not know that sleep has many important functions for us in addition to allowing us to work more effectively and to be in a better mood the next day. In fact, without sleep animals die. Students who continually stay up late at night cramming often do less well than students who do not pull all-nighters (Thatcher, 2008). The amount of sleep you have before receiving a vaccination may affect the effectiveness of the shot (Spiegel, Sheridan, & Van Cauter, 2002). Sleep has been shown to play an important role in helping us remember things (Walker & Stickgold, 2006). Sleep deprivation has been linked to a variety of negative outcomes, including increasing the chances of experiencing a fatal car crash (Oliveira, 2008), and things such as immune regulation impairment and metabolic control (Walker & Stickgold, 2006).

Sleep deprivation also seems to be associated with irritability—at least in most of our personal experience. If you have a younger sibling at home, you are likely more than just a little familiar with this phenomenon. This effect was confirmed in recent research that found a connection between sleep deprivation and increased brain sensitivity to negative emotional stimuli (Yoo et al., 2006). These authors even suggested a possible link between sleep deprivation and psychopathology. And in teens, one of the age groups that seem to need the most sleep, sleep deprivation may put them at risk for a host of problems, including emotional difficulties, accidents, cognitive difficulties, and even psychopathology (Carpenter, 2001). In fact, some school districts in Canada and the United States have experimented with later start times for schools, especially for high schools (Carpenter, 2001; Rushowy, 2007; Wolfson et al., 2007), with positive effects being reported in terms of students' behaviour, grades, and overall emotional well-being. Sufficient sleep seems to be critical to well-being.

Recent reports by Statistics Canada give us a hint about some of the factors that seem to be associated with sleeplessness for Canadians. Men tend to get less sleep than women, and increases in stress and working full-time are associated with getting less sleep. Those with higher incomes sleep less, and married adults sleep less than unmarried adults. Finally, and this will not come as a surprise if you have any children of your own, Canadians with children get less sleep than those couples without children, and the more children you have, the less sleep you get (Hurst, 2008). Given that one in seven Canadians reports sleep difficulties (Statistics Canada, 2005h), it should come as no surprise that sleep research is an extremely active research area in the psychology of consciousness.

Sleep deprivation is an increasing problem in contemporary society. The negative effects of sleep deprivation are varied but are significant enough that some high schools in Canada start classes later so that students can get more sleep.

It may seem a little surprising that we are discussing the topic of sleep in a chapter devoted to consciousness: When we are sleeping, aren't we unconscious, don't our brains shut off and rest during sleep? As you will see later in the chapter, our brains are anything but inactive during sleep. But it is true that the topic of consciousness includes more than just the scientific examination of sleep, both in its typical and atypical forms. It also includes an examination of our typical everyday awareness of things that are going on around us and inside us, as well as altered states of consciousness such as mediation, hypnosis, and drug- and alcohol-induced conditions. Consciousness is quite dynamic, and we tend to drift in and out of specific states throughout the day. In this chapter, we will consider these various states of consciousness. But first, let's consider the nature of our consciousness in general.

The Nature of Consciousness

PREVIEW QUESTIONS

▶ What is consciousness?

▶ Can we always control what we think about?

▶ What is the difference between controlled and automatic processes?

Consciousness is the awareness of internal and external stimuli. As you read this sentence, it becomes part of your consciousness. But as you read the last sentence, you were probably not aware of the weight of the textbook in your hands until you got to this section of this sentence. We even seem to maintain some degree of awareness when we are asleep, and sometimes even when we are under anesthesia for surgery.

Your consciousness is continuously changing, a fact that led William James (1902) to describe this continuous flow as the *stream of consciousness.* Some of the thoughts entering your stream of consciousness are the result of intention: We seem to

be easily able to shift our attention to things of importance or interest in our environment. Many psychologists see attention as a fundamental concept in psychology and some have even suggested that attention and its basis in our neural networks may be a concept that, following along from earlier ideas proposed by Donald Hebb (whose work was discussed in Chapter 1), could serve as a unifying concept in psychology (Posner & Rothbart, 2007). We will consider the role of attention again in Chapter 7, "Human Memory." The topic of consciousness has long fascinated scholars in psychology and other disciplines (Ingram, 2005). Consciousness and its basis in neural cell assemblies was considered by Francis Crick, who won the Nobel Prize for his work examining DNA, to be one of the most important fundamental issues in all of science today (Crick, 1994). Investigators lament that while we know a great deal about the events occurring before and after the "big bang," we know surprisingly little about how consciousness, or subjective experience, arises from the functioning of the brain (Koch & Greenfield, 2007). The study of consciousness and the search for the neuronal correlates of consciousness (NCC) are part of an extremely active area of neuroscience research (Crick & Koch, 2003; Greenfield, 2008; Greenfield & Collins, 2005; Koch, 2004).

The interest of psychologists in the study of consciousness seems obvious: Psychologists are interested in understanding human behaviour and, after all, isn't our behaviour the result of conscious thought? While there is no question that conscious thoughts cause behaviour (Baumeister, Mascicampo, & Vohs, 2011), it appears that this not the whole story. Psychologists are also interested in unconscious influences on behaviour (Bargh & Morsella, 2008) and the suggestion that "almost every human behavior comes from a mixture of conscious and unconscious processing" (Baumeister et al., 2011, p. 331).

Variations in Awareness and Control

While attention and consciousness are clearly closely related, they are not identical, and as Koch and Tsuchiya (2006) have argued, you can have either one without the other. While some of what enters our consciousness seems intentional and designed to further specific goals or motivations—for example, your tendency to listen carefully to what your professor has to say in class, especially as the exam draws closer—other thoughts seem to just meander into our minds. Psychologists such as Michael Kane at the University of North Carolina at Greensboro and Jonathan Schooler at the University of British Columbia and others have explored the concept of the restless or wandering mind (Kane et al., 2006; Baars, 2010; McVay & Kane, 2010; Smallwood, 2010; Watkins, 2010). *Mind wandering* refers to people's experience of task-unrelated thoughts, thoughts that are not related to what they are intentionally trying to do at a given moment. Mind wandering is something we have all had experience with; it is estimated that people spend 15 to 50 percent of

their time mind wandering (Smallwood & Schooler, 2006). Smallwood and Schooler suggest that mind wandering might be less likely to occur if the task you are engaged in is one that requires significant cognitive resources, that mind wandering is associated with less accurate awareness of external information, and that there may even be a connection between mind wandering and creativity in some contexts.

Of course, we have already encountered the role of psychological processes of which we are unaware in this textbook. In Chapter 1, we discussed Freud's concept of the unconscious. (We will return to a discussion of the unconscious in Chapter 12.) The distinction between what we control about our mental processes and what just seems to happen is often referred to as the difference between *controlled and automatic processes* (Bargh, 1999; Schneider & Chein, 2003; Schneider & Shiffrin, 1977). In contrast to controlled processes—judgments or thoughts that we exert some control over, that we intend to occur—automatic processing and its effects happen without our intentional control or effort. While not everyone agrees about the value of this dichotomy (Keren & Schul, 2009; Sherman et al., 2008), it has served as an important explanatory concept in many domains (Bargh & Morsella, 2008). We referred to similar concepts in Chapter 2 when we introduced the notion of implicit processes on page 70. As an example, it has been shown that research participants who were asked to rate the likability of pictures of people's faces were affected by the pleasantness of odours to which they had been subliminally exposed (Li et al., 2007). That is, the same faces were rated as more or less likable depending on whether the participant had been exposed subliminally to a pleasant or unpleasant odour. Odour affected ratings without the participants being aware of either the odours or their effects. We will consider the nature of implicit processes and effects in more detail in Chapter 16.

The implications of automatic processing for our thinking and behaviour have been popularized by Malcolm Gladwell (2005) in his best-selling book *Blink*. Gladwell's use of the term *blink* refers to how quickly (in the blink of an eye) and effortlessly some of our judgments and choices seem to be made. Things sometimes just seem to happen. Gladwell's book is an excellent summary of some of the work in this area. Interestingly, Gladwell's interest in and exposure to psychology is long-standing: Gladwell's mother is a psychotherapist.

Unconscious Thought Effects

Take a minute and try to remember the last time you had an important decision to make. Perhaps it concerned which university to attend or which apartment to rent, or maybe you were evaluating and deciding upon a potential roommate. How did you go about making that decision? Most likely, you followed the advice of your family and friends—to gather information and then to think very carefully, in a conscious, rational, and controlled manner in the hope of arriving at the best, most accurate decision possible. While there is no doubt that this is good advice, that conscious, rational decision making (see the discussion on decision making in Chapter 8) can be effective, are there times when unconscious thought might also be useful?

According to the theory of unconscious thought proposed by Ap Dijksterhuis of the University of Amsterdam, under some circumstances the quality of decisions made under conditions when individuals do not have the opportunity to engage in conscious thought may sometimes be more accurate (Dijksterhuis, 2004; Dijksterhuis & Nordren, 2006; Strick, Dijksterhuis & van Baaren, 2010). Dijksterhuis suggests that if people are distracted or diverted from "conscious deliberation," some decisions may actually be enhanced (Dijksterhuis et al., in press), compared to conditions under which people have ample opportunity for conscious deliberation (see also Waroquier, Marchiori, Klein, & Cleeremans, 2010). According to the theory, attention is the key to distinguishing between conscious and unconscious thought processes. "Conscious thought is thought with attention; unconscious thought is thought without attention (or with attention directed elsewhere)" (Dijksterhuis & Nordgren, 2006, p. 96). Conscious thought is constrained by capacity limitations such that you often consider only a small subset of all the relevant information when making a decision or evaluation. The advantage of unconscious thought is that it does not have the same capacity constraints. Dijksterhuis examined the role of unconscious thought in a 2004 study (see the Featured Study in this chapter).

Consciousness and Brain Activity

4b

Consciousness does not arise from any distinct structure in the brain but rather from activity in distributed networks of neural pathways (Kinsbourne, 1997;

Singer, 2007). Scientists are increasingly using brain-imaging methods to explore the link between brain activity and levels of consciousness (Gawryluk et al., 2010; Wager, Hernandez, & Lindquist, 2009). But historically, the most commonly used indicator of variations in consciousness has been the EEG, which records activity from broad swaths of the cortex. The *electroencephalograph (EEG)* is a device that monitors the electrical activity of the brain over time by means of recording electrodes attached to the surface of the scalp. Ultimately, the EEG summarizes the rhythm of cortical activity in the brain in terms of line tracings called *brain waves*. These brain-wave tracings vary in *amplitude* (height) and *frequency* (cycles per second, abbreviated *cps*). You can see what brain waves look like if you glance ahead to Figure 5.4 on page 209. Human brain-wave activity is usually divided into four principal bands, based on the frequency of the brain waves. These bands, named after letters in the Greek alphabet, are *beta* (13–24 cps), *alpha* (8–12 cps), *theta* (4–7 cps), and *delta* (under 4 cps).

Different patterns of EEG activity are associated with different states of consciousness, as summarized in Table 5.1. For instance, when you are alertly engaged in problem solving, beta waves tend to dominate. When you are relaxed and resting, alpha waves increase. When you slip into deep, dreamless sleep, delta waves become more prevalent. Although these correlations are far from perfect, changes in EEG activity are closely related to variations in consciousness (Wallace & Fisher, 1999).

As we discussed in Chapter 2, measures of association such as correlations between mental states and brain waves don't allow you to make firm statements regarding causation. We do not know based on such measures whether changes in mental states cause brain wave changes or vice versa. Also, it could be that some third factor, such as signals coming from a subcortical structure of the brain, is causing both (see Figure 5.1).

TABLE 5.1

EEG Patterns Associated with States of Consciousness

EEG Pattern	Frequency (cps)	Typical States of Consciousness
Beta (β)	13–24	Normal waking thought, alert problem solving
Alpha (α)	8–12	Deep relaxation, blank mind, meditation
Theta (θ)	4–7	Light sleep
Delta (Δ)	Less than 4	Deep sleep

Investigator: Ap Dijksterhuis, University of Amsterdam
Source: Think different: The merits of unconscious thought in preference development and decision making, *Journal of Personality and Social Psychology*, *87*, 586–598.

Merits of Unconscious Thought

This study was designed to test the hypothesis that unconscious thought might be superior to conscious thought processes under certain conditions. This idea runs counter to most of the advice that we encounter in our educational and social settings. Here, careful, conscious deliberation is typically encouraged. Of course, as Dijksterhuis points out, not everyone agrees with this. For example, Freud suggested that "When making a decision of minor importance, I have always found it advantageous to consider all the pros and cons. In vital matters, however, such as the choice of a mate or a profession, the decision should come from the unconscious, from somewhere within ourselves" [Quoted in Malcolm Gladwell's *Blink* (2005)]. While Dijksterhuis is not talking about the same type of unconscious as was Freud, his view does share a focus on processes occurring outside conscious awareness. According to Dijksterhuis, conscious thought is constrained by capacity limitations; you can consider only so many pieces of information at one time in conscious deliberations. Accordingly, unconscious thought should be superior when making especially complex decisions. In this research, five studies were conducted to test this assumption. In some of the studies, conscious and unconscious thought were compared in terms of choices of which apartment to rent, and in others the tasks concerned potential roommates. The alternatives, apartments, or roommates were described by multiple attributes that consisted of both positive and negative characteristics. In each case, one alternative was made more desirable than the other. We describe in detail Study Two in order to illustrate the findings of this research.

Method

Participants. The participants in Study Two were all undergraduate students at the University of Amsterdam. There were 94 participants in total—80 females and 14 males. Some participants received course credit for their participation and some were paid a nominal fee.

Procedure and Materials. Participants were recruited for a decision-making study. Each participant was presented with 12 pieces of information about each of three roommates. They were asked to imagine sharing a room with the potential roommates. Each roommate was described by some positive (e.g., is neat, has fun friends) and some negative (e.g. is messy, has annoying friends) information items. One potential roommate (roommate A) was clearly the most attractive (eight positive, four negative items), one (roommate B) was of medium attractiveness (six positive and six negative items), and the third (roommate C) was clearly less attractive (four positive and eight negative descriptors). Participants were asked to choose a roommate from the set of three by indicating their attitude toward each of the choices on a 10-point scale ranging from 1 (extremely negative) to 9 (extremely positive). There was clearly only one best answer, roommate A. Before making their decision, participants were randomly assigned to one of three experimental conditions. In the immediate decision condition, participants were asked for their decision immediately. In the conscious thought condition, they were given four minutes to decide and they were instructed to think carefully about each of the roommates and their attitudes toward them. In the unconscious thought condition, the participants were given a demanding task to complete for four minutes that was designed to keep them from reflecting on their choice.

Results

In order to determine which participants made the best decisions, each participant's attitudes toward the least attractive roommate was subtracted from his or her attitude toward the most attractive roommate. This difference score would indicate how well participants in each condition differentiated the roommates in terms of their attitudes or preferences toward them. As expected, participants in the unconscious decision-making condition showed the greatest difference in attitude (M = 3.15; Sd = 1.92). Participants in the immediate decision condition showed the least differentiation (M = 2.08; Sd = 1.80), with the participants in the conscious decision-making group falling in between the other two (M = 2.72; Sd = 1.60). Analyses of variance indicated that these differences between the groups were significant, with participants in the unconscious group performing significantly better than the immediate, $F_{(1.88)} = 8.07$; $p < .01$, and the conscious decision-making group, $F_{(1.84)} = 4.60$; $p < .04$.

Discussion

The results of this study confirmed the author's hypothesis about the merits of unconscious thought. Participants who were not given the opportunity to consciously reflect on the qualities of potential roommates made more accurate evaluations than did those who were asked to make immediate ratings or those that had time to reflect and engage in conscious thought. According to the theory, this type of situation is ideal for showing the value of unconscious thought—it was a complex decision based on many pieces of information. The other four studies in the research replicated these findings, with ratings and decisions about potential apartments that participants were asked to choose between. The results also showed that those in the unconscious thought condition tended to make more polarized, integrated, and clearer representations in memory. Those in the unconscious thought condition also tended to make more global judgments, basing their judgments on more information, compared to those in the conscious condition, who tended to focus on only a few attributes. We return to a discussion of conscious and unconscious decision-making processes in Chapter 8.

Comment

This study was selected for its straightforward examination of an issue that is obviously relevant to students' lives. We are all continuously faced with important decisions

and the more we know about these decision-making processes, the better off we all will be. Do the results of this research mean that we should never reflect, never engage in conscious decision making? While these results do not allow for this strong conclusion, they do indicate that there are times when this conscious reflection may get in the way. At this point, there is much more that we need to know. Dijksterhuis himself notes that we still do not understand the "exact process" by which such unconscious thought leads to a decision or judgment (Dijksterhuis & Nordgren, 2006). He and other researchers are busy exploring the nature and limit of this process (Acker, 2008; Waroquier et al., 2010).

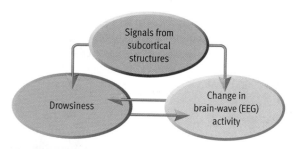

FIGURE 5.1

The correlation between mental states and electrical activity in the brain.

As discussed in Chapter 2, correlations alone do not establish causation. For example, there are strong correlations between drowsiness and a particular pattern of cortical activity, as reflected by EEG brain waves. But does drowsiness cause a change in cortical activity, or do changes in cortical activity cause drowsiness? Or does some third variable account for the changes in both?

Measures of brain-wave activity have provided investigators with a method for mapping out the mysterious state of consciousness called *sleep*. As we will see in the next two sections of the chapter, this state turns out to be far more complex and varied than you might expect.

REVIEW OF KEY POINTS

▶ William James emphasized that consciousness is a continually changing stream of mental activity. Consciousness varies along a continuum of levels of awareness.

▶ Our degree of intentional control over our cognitive processes varies. Controlled processes are those over which we have intentional control while automatic processes occur without our intention.

▶ Brain waves vary in amplitude and frequency (cps) and are divided into four bands: beta, alpha, theta, and delta. Variations in consciousness are related to variations in brain activity, as measured by the EEG.

Biological Rhythms and Sleep

PREVIEW QUESTIONS

▶ What are biological rhythms?

▶ How are circadian rhythms related to falling asleep?

▶ Which physiological structures control our biological clocks?

▶ How are circadian rhythms related to jet lag?

▶ How do rotating work shifts tend to affect sleep?

▶ What are the pros and cons of using melatonin as a sleep aid?

While sleep is the subject of serious scientific investigation today, this was not always the case. According to Canadian scholar Kenton Kroker in his seminal history of sleep research entitled *The Sleep of Others* (Kroker, 2007), sleep was initially considered only from people's individual experiences, not as the subject of serious biomedical investigation. Since sleep was thought of as the "absence of phenomena (of consciousness, of movement, of sensation) rather than the presence of anything at all" (Kroker, p. 5), it did not seem to demand or even warrant serious scientific scrutiny. But along with technological and conceptual advances came

a realization that sleep was more than just a passive activity, that important psychological events and processes might be taking place. While dreams had always been of general interest, the discovery of rapid eye movements (REM) and the realization by William Dement (Dement & Wolpert, 1958) of their significance for the study of sleep seemed to fuel scientific interest in sleep. Dement of Stanford University is credited with creating the first modern scientific laboratory dedicated to sleep and for transforming sleep research from the study of dreams to the study of the nature of sleep and clinically relevant sleep problems.

According to University of Ottawa psychologist Joseph De Koninck, the past three decades have increasingly demonstrated the critical impact that sleep has on many of the important processes and tasks that we engage in every day (De Koninck, 1997). This work has also indicated the important links between sleep quality and the body's natural rhythm. Canadian sleep research labs have played an important role in much of this research. For a list of some of the sleep centres across Canada, visit the website for the Canadian Sleep Society (http://www.css.to).

Variations in consciousness are shaped in part by biological rhythms. Rhythms pervade the world around us. The daily alternation of light and darkness, the annual pattern of the seasons, and the phases of the moon all reflect this rhythmic quality of repeating cycles. Humans, many other animals, and even plants display biological rhythms that are tied to these planetary rhythms (Foster, 2004). *Biological rhythms* are periodic fluctuations in physiological functioning. The existence of these rhythms means that organisms have internal "biological clocks" that somehow monitor the passage of time.

The Role of Circadian Rhythms

PSYKTREK

4a

Circadian rhythms are the 24-hour biological cycles found in humans and many other species. In humans, circadian rhythms are particularly influential in the regulation of sleep (Lavie, 2001). However, daily cycles also produce rhythmic variations in blood pressure, urine production, hormonal secretions, and other physical functions (see Figure 5.2), as well as alertness, short-term memory, and other aspects of cognitive performance (Refinetti, 2006; Van Dongen & Dinges, 2005). For instance, body temperature varies rhythmically in a daily cycle, usually peaking in the afternoon and reaching its low point in the depths of the night.

Research indicates that people generally fall asleep as their body temperature begins to drop and awaken as it begins to rise once again (Szymusiak, 2009). Researchers have concluded that circadian rhythms can leave individuals physiologically primed to fall asleep most easily at a particular time of day (Richardson, 1993). This optimal time varies from person to person, depending on their schedules. Finding your ideal bedtime may help promote better-quality sleep during the night (Akerstedt et al., 1997). People often characterize themselves as a "night person" or a "morning person." These preferences reflect individual variations in circadian rhythms (Minkel & Dinges, 2009).

To study biological clocks, researchers have monitored physiological processes while subjects are cut off from exposure to the cycle of day and night and all other external time cues. These studies have demonstrated that circadian rhythms generally persist even when external time cues are eliminated. However,

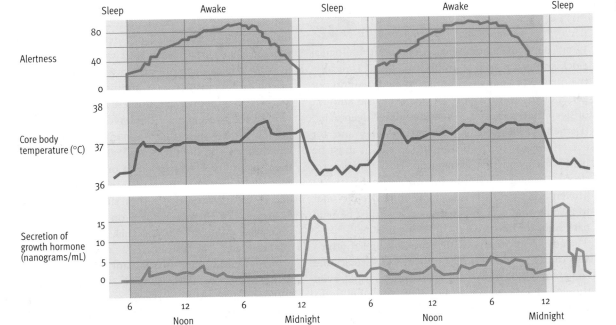

FIGURE 5.2

Examples of circadian rhythms.

These graphs show how alertness, core body temperature, and the secretion of growth hormone typically fluctuate in a 24-hour rhythm. Note how alertness tends to diminish with declining body temperature.

Source: "Circadian rhythms graph" from the book *WIDE AWAKE AT 3 AM* by Richard M. Coleman. Copyright © 1986 by Richard M. Coleman. Reprinted by permission of Henry Holt and Company, LLC.

when people are isolated in this way, their cycles run a little longer than normal, about 24.2 hours on the average (Czeisler et al., 2005). Investigators aren't sure why this drift toward a longer cycle occurs, but it is not apparent under normal circumstances because daily exposure to light *readjusts* people's biological clocks.

In fact, researchers have worked out many of the details regarding how the day–night cycle resets biological clocks. When exposed to light, some receptors in the retina send direct inputs to a small structure in the hypothalamus called the *suprachiasmatic nucleus (SCN)* (Weaver & Reppert, 2008). According to Simon Fraser University sleep researcher Ralph Mistlberger and his colleague Mary Harrington (Harrington & Mistlberger, 2000), the SCN sends signals to the nearby *pineal gland,* whose secretion of the hormone *melatonin* plays a key role in adjusting biological clocks (Norman, 2009).

Much of the research in this area has been focused on exploring the neural mechanisms linked with circadian rhythms (Mistlberger & Rusak, 2005; Rusak & Zucker, 1979). While research has implicated the role of this central circadian pacemaker, Dalhousie psychologist Benjamin Rusak suggests that mammalian circadian systems are more complex and that a more multifaceted structure might be a more appropriate model (Rusak, 1990). Circadian rhythms in humans actually appear to be regulated by *multiple* internal clocks, with a central pacemaker located in the SCN (Foster, 2004).

Ignoring Circadian Rhythms

4a

What happens when you ignore your biological clock and go to sleep at an unusual time? Typically, the quality of your sleep suffers. What if you do not get enough sleep? If you get less than the amount of sleep that you need, you accumulate "sleep debt" (Dement, 1999). Sleep debt accumulates and for everything to return to normal for you, it must be paid back by getting extra sleep. How much extra sleep? Dement offers the following advice: "Until proven otherwise, it is reasonable and certainly safer to assume that accumulated sleep loss must be paid back hour for hour" (Dement, 1999, p. 60).

Getting out of sync with your circadian rhythms also causes *jet lag*. When you fly across several time zones, your biological clock keeps time as usual, even though official clock time changes. You then go to sleep at the "wrong" time and are likely to experience difficulty falling asleep and poor-quality sleep. This inferior sleep, which can continue to occur for

several days, can make you feel fatigued, sluggish, and irritable during the daytime (Arendt, Stone, & Skene, 2005). Moreover, chronic jet lag appears to be associated with measurable deficits in cognitive performance (Cho et al., 2000). If your job entails significant transcontinental travel, that travel may have negative effects on your sleep and may also lead to increased stress-related problems such as heart disease and autoimmune disorders (Pinker, 2010).

People differ in how quickly they can reset their biological clocks to compensate for jet lag but a rough rule of thumb for jet lag is that the readjustment process takes about a day for each time zone crossed when you fly eastward, and about two-thirds of a day per time zone when you fly westward (Monk, 2006).

Changes in your normal schedule of three hours or more take several days to adjust (Valdez, Ramirez, & Garcia, 2003). In addition, the speed of readjustment depends on the direction travelled. Generally, readjustment is easier when you fly westward and lengthen your day than it is when you fly eastward and shorten your day (Arendt et al., 2005). This east–west disparity in jet lag is sizable enough to have an impact on the performance of sports teams. Studies have found that teams flying westward perform significantly better than teams flying eastward in professional baseball (Recht, Lew, & Schwartz, 1995; see Figure 5.3) and college football (Worthen & Wade, 1999).

Of course, you don't have to hop on a jet to get out of sync with your biological clock. For many of us, going to work means something other than the standard workday. Nearly one-third of Canadian workers (30 percent of males and 26 percent of females) surveyed in 2001 reported that they worked on some type of shift-work schedule (Statistics Canada, 2002c). For most, shift work does not represent a choice but rather a job requirement. Some of you as students may be working part-time as shift workers to support your studies. If you are a shift worker, then you know it can have important effects on you. Studies show that workers get less total sleep when they go on rotating shifts. When they do sleep, their quality of sleep is poor. In one survey, 30 percent of Canadian shift workers reported that they had trouble getting to sleep or staying asleep, and 62 percent of them cut down on sleep when they were busy (Williams, 2001). Lack of sleep or poor-quality sleep can also increase workers' accident proneness and their mental and physical health (Cruz, dell Rocco, & Hackworth, 2000; Waage et al., 2009). Canadian shift workers also report more stress and a lower sense of mastery or control (Statistics Canada, 2002c). Studies have also linked rotating shifts to a higher incidence of many physical diseases,

WEB LINK 5.2

NSF Center for Biological Timing
The role of biological rhythms in the functioning of living organisms has become an important focus of both medical and psychological research. This centre's online tutorial about biological timing, or "chronobiology," is a broad and well-illustrated introduction to this field.

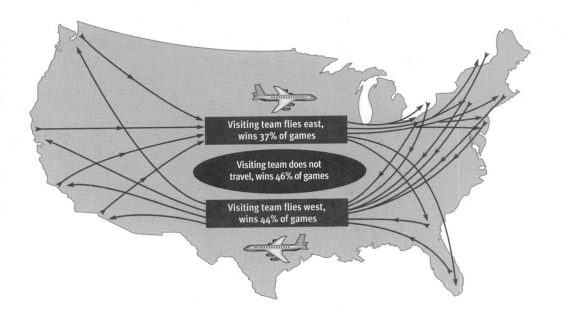

FIGURE 5.3

Effects of direction travelled on the performance of professional baseball teams.

To gain some insight into the determinants of jet lag, Recht, Lew, and Schwartz (1995) analyzed the performance of visiting teams in major league baseball over a three-year period. In baseball, visiting teams usually play three or four games in each destination city, so there are plenty of games in which the visiting team has not travelled the day before. These games, which served as a baseline for comparison, were won by the visiting team 46 percent of the time. Consistent with the observation that flying west creates less jet lag than flying east, visiting teams that flew westward the day (or night) before performed only slightly worse, winning 44 percent of the time. In contrast, visiting teams that flew eastward the day before won only 37 percent of their games, presumably because flying east and shortening one's day creates greater jet lag.

Source: Adapted from Kalat, J. W. (2001). *Biological psychology.* Belmont, CA: Wadsworth. Reprinted by permission.

including cancer, diabetes, ulcers, high blood pressure, and heart disease (Kriegsfeld & Nelson, 2009). University of British Columbia psychologist Stanley Coren (1996a) suggests that the sleep lost when the clock is set ahead in the spring shift to Daylight Saving Time is associated with an increase in traffic accidents during the week after the switch.

Melatonin and Circadian Rhythms

As scientists have come to appreciate the importance of circadian rhythms, they have begun to look for new ways to help people harness their daily rhythms. A promising line of research has focused on giving people small doses of the hormone melatonin, which appears to regulate the human biological clock. The evidence from a number of studies suggests that melatonin *can* reduce the effects of jet lag by helping travellers resynchronize their biological clocks, but the research results are inconsistent (Arendt & Skene, 2005; Monk, 2006). One reason for the inconsistent findings is that when melatonin is used to ameliorate jet lag, the timing of the dose is crucial; because calculating the optimal timing is rather complicated, it is easy to get it wrong (Arendt, 2009).

Researchers have also tried carefully timed exposure to bright light as a treatment to realign the circadian rhythms of rotating shift workers in industrial settings. Positive effects have been seen in some studies (Lowden, Akerstedt, & Wibom, 2004). This treatment can accelerate workers' adaptation to a new sleep–wake schedule, leading to improvements in sleep quality and alertness during work hours.

However, the effects of bright-light administration have been modest and somewhat inconsistent (Rogers & Dinges, 2002), and it isn't a realistic option in many work settings. Another strategy to help rotating shift workers involves carefully planning their rotation schedules to reduce the severity of their circadian disruption (Smith, Fogg, & Eastman, 2009). The negative effects of shift rotation can be reduced if workers move through progressively later starting times (instead of progressively earlier starting times) and if they have longer periods between shift changes (Kostreva, McNelis, & Clemens, 2002). Although enlightened scheduling practices can help, the unfortunate reality is that most people find rotating shift work very difficult (Arendt, 2010).

REVIEW OF KEY POINTS

▸ Biological rhythms are periodic fluctuations in physiological functioning, which indicate that most organisms have internal biological clocks. The cycle of sleep and wakefulness is influenced considerably by circadian rhythms, even when people are cut off from the cycle of light and darkness. Exposure to light resets biological clocks by affecting the activity of the suprachiasmatic nucleus and the pineal gland, which secretes the hormone melatonin.

▸ Ignoring your biological clock by going to sleep at an unusual time may have a negative effect on your sleep. Being out of sync with circadian rhythms is one reason for jet lag and for the unpleasant nature of rotating shift work. Melatonin may have value in efforts to alleviate the effects of jet lag. Bright-light administration and circadian-friendly rotation schedules can sometimes reduce the negative effects of rotating shift work.

PREVIEW QUESTIONS

▶ What happens when people fall asleep?

▶ How is REM sleep different from non-REM sleep?

▶ How do sleep stages evolve over the course of a night's sleep?

▶ How does age affect patterns of sleeping?

▶ Which aspects of sleep are influenced by culture?

▶ Which brain centres and neurotransmitters are involved in the modulation of sleep?

Sleep is a state that we have all had a great deal of experience with and it is characteristic of many organisms beyond humans. It won't surprise you to learn that scholars have speculated on its evolutionary significance. While theorists agree that it must be adaptive, there is debate as to how exactly it is adaptive. It may help us conserve energy (Siegel, 2009), or it may have served a function of reducing our exposure to predators because it is characterized by relative inactivity. It is also hypothesized that sleep might be adaptive because it helps animals restore bodily resources depleted by waking activities (Humber & Tononi, 2009). No matter what its specific adaptive significance, it is clearly important in our lives and worthy of scientific examination.

Although it is a familiar state of consciousness, sleep is widely misunderstood. Generally, people consider sleep to be a single, uniform state of physical and mental inactivity, during which the brain is "shut down" (Dement, 2003). In reality, sleepers experience quite a bit of physical and mental activity throughout the night. Scientists have learned a great deal about sleep since the landmark discovery of REM sleep in the 1950s.

The advances in psychology's understanding of sleep are the result of hard work by researchers who have spent countless nighttime hours watching other people sleep. This work is done in sleep laboratories, where volunteer subjects come to spend the night. Sleep labs have one or more "bedrooms" in which

the subjects retire, usually after being hooked up to a variety of physiological recording devices. In addition to an EEG, the other two crucial devices are an *electromyograph (EMG)*, which records muscular activity and tension, and an *electrooculograph (EOG)*, which records eye movements (Carskadon & Rechtschaffen, 2005; Collop, 2006). Typically, other instruments are also used to monitor heart rate, breathing, pulse rate, and body temperature. The researchers observe the sleeping subject through a window (or with a video camera) from an adjacent room, where they also monitor their elaborate physiological recording equipment (see the photo to the left). For most people, it takes just one night to adapt to the strange bedroom and the recording devices and return to their normal mode of sleeping (Carskadon & Dement, 1994, Pace-Schott, 2009; Rosenthal, 2006).

Cycling through the Stages of Sleep

4b

Not only does sleep occur in a context of daily rhythms, but subtler rhythms are evident within the experience of sleep itself. During sleep, people cycle through a series of five stages. Let's take a look at what researchers have learned about the changes that occur during each of these stages (Carskadon & Dement, 2005).

Stages 1–4

4b

Although it may take only a few minutes, the onset of sleep is gradual and there is no obvious transition point between wakefulness and sleep (Rechtschaffen, 1994). The length of time it takes people to fall asleep varies considerably. It depends on quite an array of factors, including how long it has been since the person has slept, where the person is in his or her circadian cycle, the amount of noise or light in the sleep environment, and the person's age, desire to fall asleep, boredom level, recent caffeine or drug intake, and stress level, among other things (Broughton, 1994). In any event, stage 1 is a brief transitional stage of light sleep that usually lasts only a few (1–7) minutes. Breathing and heart rate slow as muscle tension and body temperature decline. The alpha waves that probably dominated EEG activity just before falling asleep give way to lower-frequency EEG activity in which theta waves are prominent (see Figure 5.4). *Hypnic jerks*, those brief muscular contractions that

Researchers in a sleep laboratory can observe subjects while using elaborate equipment to record physiological changes during sleep. This kind of research has disclosed that sleep is a complex series of physical and mental states.

Ed Young/Science Photo Library

occur as people fall asleep, generally occur during stage 1 drowsiness (Broughton, 1994).

As the sleeper descends through stages 2, 3, and 4 of the cycle, respiration rate, heart rate, muscle tension, and body temperature continue to decline. During stage 2, which typically lasts about 10–25 minutes, brief bursts of higher-frequency brain waves, called *sleep spindles,* appear against a background of mixed EEG activity (refer again to Figure 5.4). Gradually, brain waves become higher in amplitude and slower in frequency, as the body moves into a deeper form of sleep, called *slow-wave sleep.* **Slow-wave sleep (SWS) consists of sleep stages 3 and 4, during which high-amplitude, low-frequency delta waves become prominent in EEG recordings.** Typically, individuals reach slow-wave sleep in about half an hour and stay there for roughly 30 minutes. Then the cycle reverses itself and the sleeper gradually moves back upward through the lighter stages. That's when things start to get especially interesting.

REM Sleep

When sleepers reach what should be stage 1 once again, they usually go into the fifth stage of sleep, which is most widely known as *REM sleep.* As we have seen, *REM* is an abbreviation for the *rapid eye movements* prominent during this stage of sleep. In a sleep lab, researchers use an electrooculograph to monitor these lateral (side-to-side) movements that occur beneath the sleeping person's closed eyelids. However, they can be seen with the naked eye if you closely watch someone in the REM stage of sleep (little ripples move back and forth across the person's closed eyelids).

REM sleep was discovered accidentally in the 1950s in Nathaniel Kleitman's lab at the University of Chicago (Aserinsky & Kleitman, 1953; Dement, 2005). After hooking sleep study participants to an apparatus designed to measure eye movements for the first time, the researchers noticed very rapid eye movements at some points during sleep. At first, they thought the rapid movements recorded by the machine were errors—due to using an old and possibly defective machine. Only when they decided to walk in and personally observe sleeping participants were they convinced the rapid eye movements were real. In retrospect, it is amazing that no one had discovered the rapid eye movements before. The term *REM sleep* was coined by grad student William Dement, who went on to become one of the world's foremost sleep researchers. The REM stage tends to be a "deep" stage of sleep in the conventional sense that people are relatively hard to awaken from it

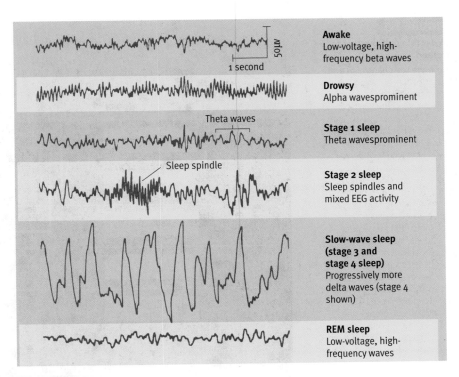

FIGURE 5.4

EEG patterns in sleep and wakefulness.

Characteristic brain waves vary, depending on one's state of consciousness. Generally, as people move from an awake state through deeper stages of sleep, their brain waves decrease in frequency (cycles per second) and increase in amplitude (height). However, brain waves during REM sleep resemble "wide-awake" brain waves.

Source: Adapted from Hauri, P. (1982). *Current concepts: The sleep disorders.* Kalamazoo, MI: The Upjohn Company. Reprinted by permission.

(although arousal thresholds vary during REM). The REM stage is also marked by irregular breathing and pulse rate. Muscle tone is extremely relaxed—so much so that bodily movements are minimal and the sleeper is virtually paralyzed. *Although REM is a relatively deep stage of sleep, EEG activity is dominated by high-frequency beta waves that resemble those observed when people are alert and awake* (see Figure 5.4 again).

REM sleep is not unique to humans. Nearly all mammals and birds exhibit REM sleep. The only known exceptions among warm-blooded vertebrates are dolphins and some whales (Morrison, 2003). Dolphins are particularly interesting, as they sleep while swimming, resting one hemisphere of the brain while the other hemisphere remains alert.

FIGURE 5.5

An overview of the cycle of sleep.

The white line charts how a typical, healthy, young adult moves through the various stages of sleep during the course of a night. This diagram also shows how dreams and rapid eye movements tend to coincide with REM sleep, whereas posture changes occur between REM periods (because the body is nearly paralyzed during REM sleep). Notice how the person cycles into REM four times, as descents into NREM sleep become shallower and REM periods become longer. Thus, slow-wave sleep is prominent early in the night, while REM sleep dominates the second half of a night's sleep. Although these patterns are typical, keep in mind that sleep patterns vary from one person to another and that they change with age.

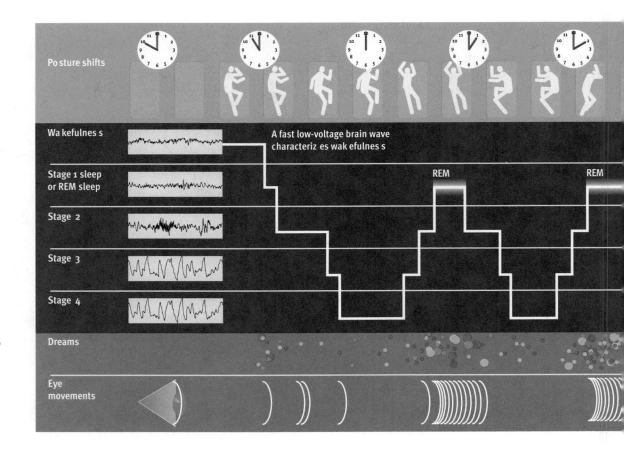

This paradox is probably related to the association between REM sleep and dreaming. As noted earlier, when subjects are awakened during various stages of sleep and asked whether they are dreaming, most dream reports come from the REM stage (Dement, 1978; McCarley, 1994). Although REM dreams may be more frequent, vivid, and memorable (Pace-Schott, 2005), there is evidence to suggest that mentation or dreaming does occur in non-REM sleep periods, too. Research by Tore Nielsen of the University of Montreal and his colleagues (Esposito, Nielsen, & Paquette, 2004; Nielsen, 2000; Nielsen & Zadra et al., 2003) has been exploring the similarities and differences between REM and non-REM dreaming. They have been interested in examining whether recall of dreams from both REM and non-REM sleep is explained better by assuming the existence of a single dream generator or two different dream generators.

Carlyle Smith, a psychology professor at Trent University, is a prominent sleep researcher who has been active in examining the relationships between brain functioning in sleep and memory (Smith, 1996, 2003). His research suggests that brain activity during sleep is central to consolidation of information acquired during the day. He also suggests that different stages of sleep may be implicated in

memory for different types of tasks or information. For example, stage 2 sleep may be important for consolidation of procedural motor-type tasks, while REM sleep may be important for complex logic-type tasks (Nader & Smith, 2003; Smith & Fazekas, 1997).

While sleep is important for learning, it may be that different types of sleep are important for different types of learning. This is an important consideration given that there are changes in sleep as we age. Smith's current research is examining the links between age, sleep, and memory (Trent University, 2005).

To summarize, *REM sleep* is a relatively deep stage of sleep marked by rapid eye movements; high-frequency, low-amplitude brain waves; and vivid dreaming. It is such a special stage of sleep that the other four stages are often characterized simply as *non-REM sleep*. *Non-REM (NREM) sleep* consists of sleep stages 1 through 4, which are marked by an absence of rapid eye movements, relatively little dreaming, and varied EEG activity.

Repeating the Cycle 4b

During the course of a night, people usually repeat the sleep cycle about four times. As the night wears

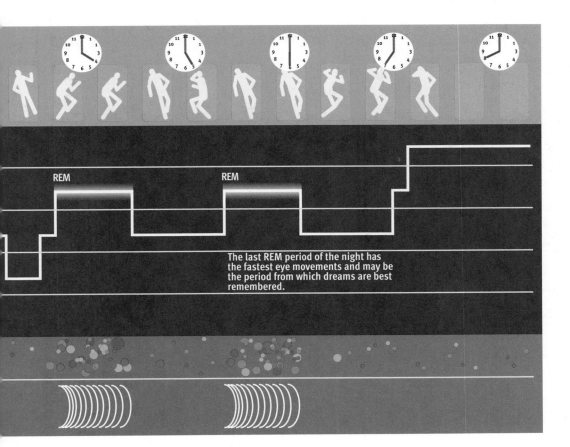

REM

REM

The last REM period of the night has the fastest eye movements and may be the period from which dreams are best remembered.

on, the cycle changes gradually. The first REM period is relatively short, lasting only a few minutes. Subsequent REM periods get progressively longer, peaking at around 40–60 minutes in length. Additionally, NREM intervals tend to get shorter, and descents into NREM stages usually become more shallow. These trends can be seen in Figure 5.5, which provides an overview of a typical night's sleep cycle. These trends mean that most slow-wave sleep occurs early in the sleep cycle and that REM sleep tends to pile up in the second half of the sleep cycle. Summing across the entire cycle, young adults typically spend about 15–20 percent of their sleep time in slow-wave sleep and another 20–25 percent in REM sleep (Rama, Cho, & Kushida, 2006). What we have described thus far is the big picture—the typical structure of sleep averaged over many people. However, recent research by Tucker, Dinges, and Van Dongen (2007) has shown that the "architecture" of sleep—how quickly one falls asleep, how long one sleeps, how one cycles through the various stage—does differ across people.

Age Trends in Sleep

 4b

Age alters the sleep cycle. What we have described so far is the typical pattern for young adults. Children,

however, display different patterns (Bootzin et al., 2001; Roffwarg, Muzio, & Dement, 1966). The sleep cycle of babies immediately after birth is quite simple: There are only two sleep types: REM and non-REM sleep (Dement, 1999). Newborns will sleep six to eight times in a 24-hour period, often exceeding a total of 16 hours of sleep. Fortunately for parents, during the first several months, much of this sleep begins to be consolidated into one particularly long nighttime sleep period (Huber & Tononi, 2009). Interestingly, infants spend much more of their sleep time in the REM stage than adults do. In the first few months, REM accounts for about 50 percent of babies' sleep, as compared to 20 percent of adults' sleep.

During the remainder of the first year, the REM portion of infants' sleep declines to roughly 30 percent (Ohayon et al., 2004). The REM portion of sleep continues to decrease gradually until it levels off at about 20 percent (see Figure 5.6). During adulthood, gradual age-related changes in sleep continue. Although the proportion of REM sleep remains fairly stable (Bliwise, 2005), the percentage of slow-wave sleep declines dramatically and the percentage of time spent in stage 1 increases slightly, with these trends stronger in men than in women (Bliwise, 2005). These shifts toward lighter sleep *may*

Courtesy of William Dement

William Dement
"Sleep deprivation is a major epidemic in our society. . . . Americans spend so much time and energy chasing the American dream, that they don't have much time left for actual dreaming."

FIGURE 5.6

Changes in sleep patterns over the life span.

Both the total amount of sleep per night and the portion of sleep that is REM sleep change with age. Sleep patterns change most dramatically during infancy, with total sleep time and amount of REM sleep declining sharply in the first two years of life. After a noticeable drop in the average amount of sleep in adolescence, sleep patterns remain relatively stable, although total sleep and slow-wave sleep continue to decline gradually with age.

Source: Adapted from an updated revision of a figure in Roffwarg, H.P., Muzio, J.N., and Dement, W.C. (1966). Ontogenetic development of human sleep-dream cycle. *Science, 152,* 604–609. Copyright © by the American Association for the Advancement of Science. Adapted and revised by permission of the authors.

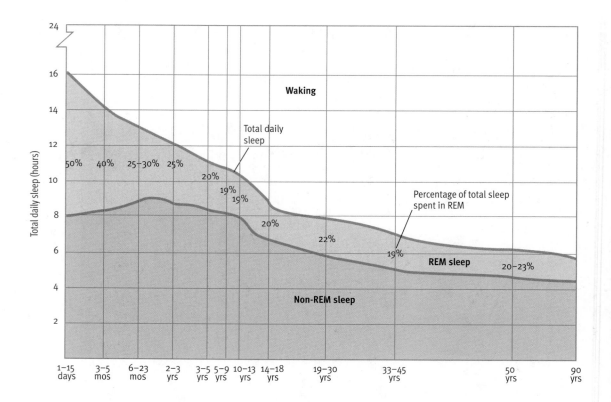

contribute to the increased frequency of nighttime awakening seen among the elderly. As Figure 5.6 shows, the average amount of total sleep time also declines with advancing age.

Until recently, it was assumed that this decline in sleep time was due to older people having more difficulty initiating sleep or remaining asleep. In other words, it was attributed to a decrease in their ability to sleep effectively. However, a recent, carefully controlled laboratory study that allowed for extended sleep opportunities found that older adults (aged 60–80) showed significantly less sleepiness during the day than younger adults (aged 18–30), even though the older group chose to sleep an average of 1.5 hours less per day (Klerman & Dijk, 2008). The authors conclude that the elderly *may* simply need less sleep than younger adults. Consistent with this line of thinking, another recent study yielded the surprising finding that older adults tolerate sleep deprivation with less impairment than younger adults (Duffy et al., 2009). Older people do have more difficulty adapting to circadian phase shifts, such as those produced by jet lag or rotating work shifts (Monk, 2005), but excessive daytime sleepiness does not increase with age (Young, 2004). The bottom line is that growing older, by itself, does not appear to lead to poor sleep if elderly people remain healthy (Vitiello, 2009). Although sleep complaints escalate with age, much of this escalation is due to increases in health problems that interfere with sleep.

Culture and Sleep

Although age clearly affects the nature and structure of sleep itself, the psychological and physiological experience of sleep does not appear to vary systematically across cultures. Cultural disparities in sleep are limited to more peripheral matters, such as sleeping arrangements and napping customs. For example, there are cultural differences in *co-sleeping*, the practice of children and parents sleeping together (McKenna, 1993). In modern Western societies, co-sleeping is actively discouraged. In contrast, co-sleeping is more widely accepted in the Japanese culture, which emphasizes interdependence and group harmony (Latz et al., 1999). Around the world as a whole, co-sleeping is normative (Ball, Hooker, & Kelly, 2000). Strong pressure against co-sleeping appears to be largely an urban, Western phenomenon.

Napping practices also vary along cultural lines. In many societies, shops close and activities are curtailed in the afternoon to permit people to enjoy a one- to two-hour midday nap. These "siesta cultures" are found mostly in tropical regions of the world (Webb & Dinges, 1989). There, this practice is adaptive in that it allows people to avoid working during the hottest part of the day.

The Neural Bases of Sleep

The rhythm of sleep and waking appears to be regulated by subcortical structures that lie deep within the brain. One brain structure that is important to sleep and wakefulness is the *reticular formation* in the core of the brainstem (Garcia-Rill, 2009; Steriade, 2005). The *ascending reticular activating system (ARAS)* consists of the afferent fibres running through the reticular formation that influence physiological arousal. As you can see in Figure 5.7, the ARAS projects diffusely into many areas of the cortex. When these ascending fibres are cut in the brainstem of a cat, the result is continuous sleep (Moruzzi, 1964). Electrical stimulation along the same pathways produces arousal and alertness.

Many other brain structures are also involved in the regulation of sleeping and waking (Marks, 2006). For example, activity in the *pons* and adjacent areas in the *midbrain* seems to be critical to the generation of REM sleep (Siegel, 2005). Recent research has focused on the importance of various areas in the *hypothalamus* for the regulation of sleep and wakefulness (Fuller & Lu, 2009). Specific areas in the medulla, thalamus, and basal forebrain have also been noted

in the control of sleep and a variety of neurotransmitters are involved (see Figure 5.7). Thus, the ebb and flow of sleep and waking is regulated through activity in a *constellation* of interacting brain centres (Pace-Schott, Hobson, & Stickgold, 2008).

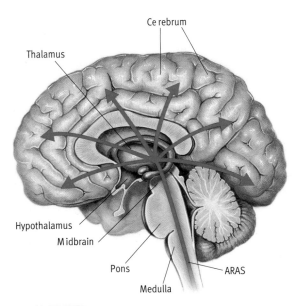

FIGURE 5.7

The ascending reticular activating system (ARAS).
A number of brain areas and structures interact to regulate sleep and waking, including all of those highlighted in this graphic. Particularly important is the ARAS (represented by the green arrows), which conveys neural stimulation to many areas of the cortex.

Labels in figure: Cerebrum, Thalamus, Hypothalamus, Midbrain, Pons, Medulla, ARAS

REVIEW OF KEY POINTS

▷ Research on sleep is typically done in laboratories, where volunteers come to spend the night. Participants are hooked up to an EEG, EOG, EMG, and instruments that monitor heart rate, respiration, pulse rate, and body temperature.

▷ When people fall asleep, they evolve through a series of stages in cycles of approximately 90 minutes. Slow-wave sleep consists of stages 3 and 4, during which delta waves are prominent. During the REM stage, sleepers experience rapid eye movements, brain waves that are characteristic of waking thought, and vivid dreaming. The sleep cycle tends to be repeated about four times a night, as REM sleep gradually becomes more predominant and NREM sleep dwindles.

▷ The REM portion of sleep declines during childhood, levelling off at around 20 percent. During adulthood, slow-wave sleep declines. Total sleep time decreases for most elderly people, although it increases for some. Culture appears to have little impact on the physiological experience of sleep, but it does influence napping patterns and sleeping arrangements, such as co-sleeping.

▷ The neural bases of sleep are complex. Arousal depends on activity in the ascending reticular activating system, but a constellation of brain structures and neurotransmitters contribute to regulation of the sleep and waking cycle.

Doing Without: Sleep Deprivation

Scientific research on sleep deprivation presents something of a paradox. On the one hand, research suggests that sleep deprivation is not as detrimental as one might expect. On the other hand, evidence suggests that sleep deprivation may be a major social problem, undermining efficiency at work and contributing to countless accidents. Many sleep experts warn that we should not ignore our own individual internal clocks, that doing so may put our physical and psychological health at risk.

Sleep Restriction

Research has mostly focused on *partial sleep deprivation*, or *sleep restriction*, which occurs when people make do with substantially less sleep than normal over a period of time. Many sleep experts believe that much of North American society chronically suffers from partial sleep deprivation (Walsh, Dement, & Dinges, 2005). It appears that more and more people are trying to squeeze additional waking

PREVIEW QUESTIONS

▶ What are the effects of sleep deprivation?

▶ What is known about the causes and prevalence of insomnia?

▶ What is the role of sedative drugs in the treatment of insomnia?

▶ What are the symptoms of narcolepsy? Sleep apnea? Nightmares? Night terrors? Somnambulism?

hours out of their days as they attempt to juggle work, family, household, and school responsibilities, leading William Dement to comment that most of us "no longer know what it feels like to be fully alert" (Toufexis, 1990, p. 79).

How serious are the effects of partial sleep deprivation? Studies suggest that the effects depend on the amount of sleep lost and on the nature of the task at hand (Bonnet, 2000). Negative effects are most likely when subjects are asked to work on long-lasting, difficult, or monotonous tasks, or when subjects are asked to restrict their sleep to less than five hours for many nights (Gillberg & Akerstedt, 1998). Interestingly, people often do not appreciate the degree to which sleep deprivation has a negative impact on their functioning (Pilcher & Walters, 1997). For example, Pilcher and Walters recruited university students to volunteer for 24 hours of sleep deprivation. Their performance on a series of cognitive tasks was later compared to another group of students who followed their normal sleep routine. While the sleep-deprived students performed more poorly on the cognitive tests, these students actually rated their effort, concentration, and performance higher than did the normal-routine students. Although the sleep-deprived students showed clear impairment on an objective measure of their cognitive performance, they felt their performance was fine. The implications of this are disturbing when you think about sleep-deprived drivers setting out on long trips, believing that they will be just fine. Unfortunately, research shows that sleep-deprived individuals are not particularly good at predicting if and when they will fall asleep (Kaplan, Itoi, & Dement, 2007). Thus, tired drivers often fail to pull off the road when they should.

In recent decades, a number of major disasters, such as the nuclear accidents at Three Mile Island and Chernobyl, the running aground of the *Exxon Valdez* in Alaska, and the *Challenger* space shuttle tragedy have been blamed in part on lapses in judgment and attention resulting from sleep deprivation (Doghramji, 2001). Experts such as Stanley Coren (1996a) have *estimated* that accidents attributed to drowsiness induced by sleep deprivation cost the U.S. economy over US$56 billion annually, lead to the loss of over 52 million work days each year, and result in over 24 000 deaths per year.

While most of the research on the effects of sleep deprivation has focused on performance and cognitive deficits, there has been increased interest in the effects of sleep deprivation on our emotions and their regulation (Watkins, 2009). These effects go beyond just the increase in irritability and that has been associated with too little sleep (Horn, 1985). Research

by Matthew Walker at the University of California and his colleagues suggests that sleep is important in our ability to regulate our emotional life during our waking hours (Walker & van der Helm, 2009). In one study, Walker had one group of participants stay awake for 35 hours before exposing them to a series of photos that varied from neutral to very negative (e.g., mutilated bodies). He assessed the activity level of specific parts of the brain through fMRI task scanning. He compared the responses of the sleep-deprived group to a similar group of participants who had normal sleep and found that the amygdalas of the sleep-deprived group were significantly more active in response to the negative photos. He also found that their amygdalas exhibited less connectivity to other structures in the brain associated with prefrontal control. In essence, there was more emotional reactivity and less control in response to negative stimuli in the parts of the brain implicated in emotional processing as a function of sleep deprivation. Walker described those in the sleep-deprived group as being turned from rational beings into "emotional jello." In understanding the results of the study he said that "It's almost as though, without sleep, the brain had reverted back to more primitive patterns of activity, in that it was unable to put emotional experiences into context and produced controlled, appropriate responses" (Anwar, 2007, p. 1). Not only are the results intriguing for what they tell us about the potential affective consequences of sleep deprivation but also because of what light they may shed on some types of psychopathology. As we will describe in Chapter 14, sleep disturbance is common in many forms of psychopathology (Harvey, 2008) and it has often been difficult to separate the effects of the sleep disturbance and the effects of the psychopathology itself on an individual's symptoms and behaviour. Walker sees this type of research as a first step toward gaining insight into the connection between psychopathology and sleep (Yoo et al., 2007).

Selective Deprivation

The unique quality of REM sleep led researchers to look into the effects of a special type of partial sleep deprivation—*selective deprivation*. In a number of laboratory studies, subjects were awakened over a period of nights whenever they began to go into the REM stage. These subjects usually got a decent amount of sleep in NREM stages, but they were selectively deprived of REM sleep.

What are the effects of REM deprivation? The evidence indicates that it has little impact on daytime functioning and task performance, but it *does* have some interesting effects on subjects' patterns of sleeping (Bonnet, 2005). As the nights go by in REM-deprivation studies, it becomes necessary to awaken the subjects more and more often to deprive them of their REM sleep, because they spontaneously shift into REM more and more frequently. In one study, researchers had to awaken a subject 64 times by the third night of REM deprivation, as shown in Figure 5.8 (Borbely, 1986). Furthermore, when a REM-deprivation experiment comes to an end and subjects are allowed to sleep without interruption, they experience a "rebound effect." That is, they spend extra time in REM periods for one to three nights to make up for their REM deprivation (Bonnet, 2005).

Similar results have been observed when subjects have been selectively deprived of slow-wave sleep (Klerman, 1993). As the nights go by, more awakenings are required to prevent slow-wave sleep, and after deprivation of SWS, people experience a rebound effect (Borbely & Achermann, 2005). What do theorists make of these spontaneous pursuits of REM and slow-wave sleep? They conclude that people must have specific needs for REM and slow-wave sleep—and rather strong needs at that.

Why do we need REM and slow-wave sleep? Some recent studies suggest that REM and slow-wave sleep contribute to firming up learning that takes place during the day. It has also been suggested that REM sleep and slow-wave sleep each promote different types of memory (Marshall & Born, 2007). The general effect of firming up learning that has taken place during the day is often referred to as *memory consolidation* (Gais & Born, 2004; Stickgold, 2001; Walker & Stickgold, 2006). Efforts to explore this hypothesis have led to some interesting findings in recent years. For example, in one study, participants were given training on a perceptual-motor task and then retested 12 hours later. Subjects who slept during the 12-hour interval showed substantial *improvement* in

performance that was not apparent in subjects who did not sleep (Walker et al., 2002).

A host of similar studies have shown that sleep seems to enhance subjects' memory of specific learning activities that occurred during the day (Walker, 2009; Walker & Stickgold, 2004, 2006). These studies also find that the length of time spent in REM and SWS correlates with subjects' increments in learning. Some studies suggest that sleep may foster creative insights the next morning related to the previous day's learning (Stickgold & Walker, 2004;

concept **check 5.1**

Comparing REM and NREM Sleep

A table here could have provided you with a systematic comparison of REM sleep and NREM sleep, but that would have deprived you of the opportunity to check your understanding of these sleep phases by creating your own table. Fill in each of the blanks below with a word or phrase highlighting the differences between REM and NREM sleep with regard to the various characteristics specified. You can find the answers near the back of the book in Appendix A.

Characteristic	REM Sleep	NREM Sleep
1. Type of EEG activity		
2. Eye movements		
3. Dreaming		
4. Depth (difficulty in awakening)		
5. Percentage of total sleep (in adults)		
6. Increases or decreases (as a percentage of sleep) during childhood		
7. Timing in sleep cycle (dominates early or late)		

FIGURE 5.8

The effects of REM deprivation on sleep.

This graph plots how often researchers had to awaken a subject over the course of three nights of REM deprivation. Notice how the awakenings rapidly became more frequent during the course of each night and from night to night. This pattern of awakenings illustrates how a REM-deprived subject tends to compensate by repeatedly slipping back into REM sleep.

Source: Adapted from Borbely, A. (1986). *Secrets of sleep* (English translation). New York: Basic Books. Copyright © 1986 by Basic Books. Reprinted by permission of Basic Books, a member of Perseus Books, LLC.

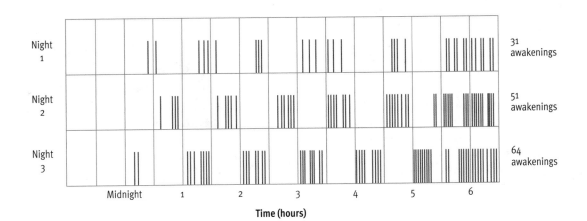

Wagner et al., 2004) and that if the memories can be reactivated during sleep, the representation of the memories in the brain will be enhanced (Rasch et al., 2007; Stickgold, 2007). The theoretical meaning of these findings is still being debated, but the most widely accepted explanations centre on how time spent in specific stages of sleep may stabilize or solidify memories formed during the day (Rasch & Born, 2009; Stickgold, 2005). The practical meaning of these results, however, should be rather obvious: Sound sleep habits should facilitate learning. In related research, investigators have found that REM sleep appears to foster the recently discovered process of *neurogenesis* (Guzman-Marin, 2008; Meerlo et al., 2009). As noted in Chapter 3, *neurogenesis refers to the formation of new neurons*. This finding meshes with the data linking REM sleep to memory consolidation, because independent lines of research suggest that neurogenesis contributes to learning (Leuner, Gould, & Shors, 2006). As we discuss in Chapter 7, the hippocampus is critical in the formation of memories. The research reviewed by Leuner et al. (2006) suggests that the adult hippocampus produces substantial numbers of new neurons (neurogenesis) and it is hypothesized that such adult neurogenesis facilitates learning and memory processes related to hippocampal functions. It is important to note that research suggesting a link between the process of adult neurogenesis and learning and memory is still limited but given the potential importance of this work, we can expect a great deal of research activity in this area in the future.

Sleep Loss and Health

In recent years, researchers have begun to investigate the notion that sleep deprivation might have serious health consequences. Accumulating evidence suggests that sleep loss can affect physiological processes in ways that may undermine physical health. For example, sleep restriction appears to trigger hormonal changes that increase hunger (Grandner, Patel, et al., 2010). Consistent with this finding, studies have found a link between short sleep duration and increased obesity, which is a risk factor for a number of health problems (Cappuccio et al., 2008; Watanabe, 2010). Researchers have also found that sleep loss leads to impaired immune system functioning (Motivala & Irwin, 2007) and increased inflammatory responses (Patel et al., 2009), which are likely to heighten vulnerability to a variety of diseases. Hence, it's not surprising that studies have uncovered links between short sleep duration and an increased risk for diabetes (Knutson & Van Cauter, 2008), hypertension (Gangwisch et al.,

2006), and cardiovascular disease (King et al., 2008; Sabanayagam & Shankar, 2010).

These findings have motivated researchers to explore the correlation between habitual sleep time and overall mortality. The results of this research have provided a bit of a surprise. As expected, people who consistently sleep less than seven hours exhibit an elevated mortality risk—but so do those who routinely sleep *more* than eight hours. In fact, mortality rates are especially high among those who sleep over 10 hours (see Chien et al., 2010; Grandner, Hale, et al., 2010). Researchers are now trying to figure out why long sleep duration is correlated with elevated mortality. It could be that prolonged sleep is a "marker" for other problems, such as depression or a sedentary lifestyle, that have negative effects on health (Patel et al., 2006). Bear in mind, also, that the studies linking typical sleep duration to mortality have depended on participants' *self-report estimates* of how long they normally sleep, which could be inaccurate. In any event, the relationship between sleep and health is an emerging area of research that probably will yield some very interesting findings in the years to come.

Problems in the Night: Sleep Disorders

Not everyone is able to consistently enjoy the luxury of a good night's sleep (Gradisar, Gardner, & Dohnt, 2011). According to the American Sleep Disorders

Heath Ledger, the Australian star of movies such as *Brokeback Mountain* and *The Dark Knight*, suffered from insomnia. Just before his untimely death in 2008 from a possible accidental overdose of, among other things, sleep medications, he reported that he had been sleeping less than two hours a night (Graham, 2008).

Association's *International Classification of Sleep Disorders: Diagnostic and Coding Manual*, there are 78 different types of sleep disorders (Dement, 1999). While we will not be able to discuss them all, in this section we will briefly discuss what is currently known about a variety of relatively common or well-known sleep disorders.

Insomnia

Insomnia is the most common sleep disorder. *Insomnia* refers to chronic problems in getting adequate sleep. It occurs in three basic patterns: (1) difficulty in falling asleep initially, (2) difficulty in remaining asleep, and (3) persistent early-morning awakening. Difficulty falling asleep is the most common problem among young people, whereas trouble staying asleep and early-morning awakenings are the most common syndromes among middle-aged and elderly people (Hublin & Partinen, 2002). Insomnia may sound like a minor problem to those who haven't struggled with it, but it can be a very unpleasant malady. Insomniacs have to endure the agony of watching their precious sleep time tick away as they toss and turn in restless frustration. Moreover, insomnia is associated with daytime fatigue, impaired functioning, an elevated risk for accidents, reduced productivity, absenteeism at work, depression, anxiety, substance abuse, hypertension, and increased health problems (Benca, 2001; Edinger & Means, 2005; Kyle, Morgan, & Espie, 2010; Vhontzas et al, 2009).

Prevalence. Estimates of the prevalence of insomnia vary considerably because surveys have to depend on respondents' highly subjective judgments of whether their sleep is adequate. Another complicating consideration is that nearly everyone suffers *occasional* sleep difficulties because of stress, disruptions of biological rhythms, or other temporary circumstances. Fortunately, these problems clear up spontaneously for most people. Caveats aside, the best estimates suggest that about 34–35 percent of adults report problems with insomnia and about half of these people (15–17 percent) suffer from severe or frequent insomnia (Zorick & Walsh, 2000). The prevalence of insomnia increases with age and is about 50 percent more common in women than in men (Partinen & Hublin, 2005).

Some people may suffer from "pseudo-insomnia," or *sleep state misperception,* which means that they just *think* they are getting an inadequate amount of sleep (Edinger & Krystal, 2003). When actually monitored in a sleep clinic, about 5 percent of insomniac patients show sound patterns of sleep (Hauri, 2000).

In one well-known case of exaggerated complaining, a British insomniac claimed that he hadn't slept in ten years! When invited to stay at a sleep clinic for observation, he seemed determined to prove his chronic sleeplessness. However, on the second night, he nodded off for 20 minutes. By the fourth night, he could barely keep his eyes open, and soon he was snoring blissfully for hours (Oswald & Adam, 1980). Misperceptions of sleep efficiency are not unique to pseudo-insomniacs. Many people underestimate how much sleep they get (Reynolds et al., 1991). The discrepancy between individuals' feelings about how much they sleep and objective reality shows once again that states of consciousness are highly subjective.

Causes. Insomnia has many causes (Hauri, 2002; Roehrs, Zorick, & Roth, 2000; Roth & Drake, 2004). In some cases, excessive anxiety and tension prevent relaxation and keep people awake. Insomnia is frequently a side effect of emotional problems, such as depression, or of significant stress, such as pressures at work. Understandably, health problems such as back pain, ulcers, and asthma can lead to insomnia. The use of certain drugs, especially such stimulants as cocaine and amphetamines, may also lead to problems in sleeping. All that said, recent research has suggested that the primary cause of insomnia may be that some people are predisposed to insomnia because they have a higher level of physiological arousal than the average person (Stepanksi, 2006). According to this *hyperarousal model* of insomnia, some people exhibit hormonal patterns that fuel arousal, elevated heart rate, high metabolic activation, increased body temperature, and EEG patterns associated with arousal (Bonnett & Arand, 2010). The chronic, heightened physiological activation presumably makes these people especially vulnerable to insomnia (Riemann et al., 2010).

Treatment. A large proportion of people suffering from insomnia do not pursue professional treatment (Sivertsen et al., 2006). Many of them probably depend on over-the-counter sleep aids, which have questionable value (Mahowald & Schenck, 2005). The most common approach in the medical treatment of insomnia is the prescription of two classes of drugs: *benzodiazepine sedatives* (such as Dalmane, Halcion, and Restoril), which were originally developed to relieve anxiety, and newer *nonbenzodiazepine sedatives* (such as Ambien, Sonata, and Lunesta), which were designed primarily for sleep problems (Mendelson, 2005). Both types of sedative medications are fairly effective in helping people fall asleep more quickly. They reduce nighttime awakenings and increase total sleep (Lee-Chiong & Sateia, 2006; Mendelson, 2005). Nonetheless, sedative drugs may be used to combat insomnia *too* frequently. Many sleep experts argue that in the past physicians prescribed sleeping pills far too readily. Nonetheless, about 5–15 percent of adults still use sleep medication with some regularity (Hublin & Partinen, 2002).

Sedatives can be a poor long-term solution for insomnia, for a number of reasons (Roehrs & Roth, 2000; Wesson et al., 2005). One problem is that sedatives have carryover effects that can make people drowsy and sluggish the next day and impair their functioning (Vermeeren, 2004). They can also cause an overdose in combination with alcohol or opiate drugs. Moreover, with continued use most sedatives gradually become less effective, so some people increase their dose to higher levels, creating a vicious circle of escalating dependency and daytime sluggishness (Lader, 2002; see Figure 5.9). Another problem is that when people abruptly discontinue their sleep medication, they can experience unpleasant withdrawal symptoms and increased insomnia (Lee-Chiong & Sateia, 2006). Fortunately, the newer generation of nonbenzodiazepine sedatives have reduced (but not eliminated) many of the problems associated with previous generations of sleeping pills (Sanger, 2004). In conclusion, sedatives need to be used cautiously and conservatively.

Treatment programs based in psychology have also been shown to be useful. Relaxation procedures and behavioural interventions can be helpful for many individuals (Morin, 2002, 2005; Stepanski, 2000). Recent studies suggest that behavioural treatments are just as effective as medication in the short term and that behavioural interventions

A large number of traffic accidents occur because drivers become drowsy or fall asleep at the wheel. Although the effects of sleep deprivation seem innocuous, sleep loss can be deadly.

produce more long-lasting benefits than drug therapies (Morin et al., 1999; M. T. Smith et al., 2002). Charles Morin and his colleagues at Laval University in Montreal have been actively involved in exploring the effects of psychological treatments such as cognitive-behavioural therapy (CBT) for insomnia (Morin, Bastien, & Savard, 2003). In a meta-analysis of clinical trials, they concluded that CBT can have real benefits for many individuals suffering from insomnia. They suggest that as many as 70–80 percent of individuals suffering from primary insomnia may benefit in some way from CBT-based treatment. They caution, however, that not all become good sleepers. Cognitive therapies generally emphasize recognizing and changing negative thoughts and maladaptive beliefs. Some additional insights about how to combat insomnia are presented in the Personal Application near the end of this chapter. Cognitive-behavioural therapy is discussed in greater detail in Chapter 15.

Other Sleep Problems

Although insomnia is the most common difficulty associated with sleep, people are plagued by many other types of sleep problems as well. Let's briefly look at the symptoms, causes, and prevalence of five additional sleep problems, as described by Kryger, Roth, and Dement (2005) and Hirshowitz, Seplowitz, Hafkin, and Sharafkhaneh (2009).

Narcolepsy is a disease marked by sudden and irresistible onsets of sleep during normal waking periods. It was first identified by a German psychiatrist named Carl Friedrich Otto Westphal in 1877 (Marschall, 2007). A person suffering from

FIGURE 5.9

The vicious circle of dependence on sleeping pills.

Because of the body's ability to develop tolerance to drugs, using sedatives routinely to "cure" insomnia can lead to a vicious circle of escalating dependency as larger and larger doses of the sedative are needed to produce the same effect.

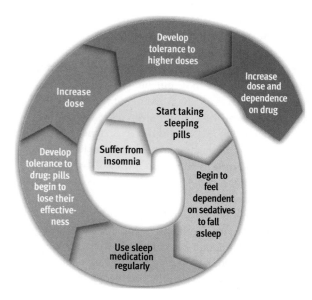

Develop tolerance to higher doses

Increase dose and dependence on drug

Increase dose

Start taking sleeping pills

Suffer from insomnia

Develop tolerance to drug: pills begin to lose their effectiveness

Begin to feel dependent on sedatives to fall asleep

Use sleep medication regularly

narcolepsy goes directly from wakefulness into REM sleep, usually for a short period of time (10–20 minutes). This is a potentially dangerous condition, since some victims fall asleep instantly, even while driving a car or operating machinery. Narcolepsy is relatively infrequent, as it is seen in only about 0.05 percent of the population (Partinen & Hublin, 2005). Its causes are not well understood, but some people appear to be genetically predisposed to the disease (Mignot, 2000). Stimulant drugs have been used to treat this condition, with modest success (Guilleminault & Fromherz, 2005). But as you will see in our upcoming discussion of drugs, stimulants carry many problems of their own.

Sleep apnea involves frequent, reflexive gasping for air that awakens a person and disrupts sleep. Some victims are awakened from their sleep hundreds of times a night. Apnea occurs when a person literally stops breathing for a minimum of ten seconds. It is usually defined by the presence of at least five such events per hour of sleep (Anselm et al., 2008). According to University of Ottawa researcher Anjali Anselm and her colleagues, heart failure is prevalent among people with some specific types of sleep apnea (Anselm et al., 2008). This disorder, which is usually accompanied by loud snoring, is seen in about 2 percent of women and about 4 percent of men between the ages of 30 and 60 (Bassiri & Guilleminault, 2000). As you might expect, sleep apnea can have a very disruptive effect on sleep, leading to excessive daytime sleepiness. Sleep apnea is a more serious disorder than widely appreciated because it increases vulnerability to hypertension, coronary disease, and stroke (Hahn, Olson, & Somers, 2006). In fact, one study found that severe apnea tripled individuals' mortality risk (Young et al., 2008). Apnea may be treated via lifestyle modifications (weight loss, reduced alcohol intake, improved sleep hygiene), drug therapy, special masks and oral devices that improve airflow, and upper airway and craniofacial surgery (Phillips & Kryger, 2005; Veasey, 2009).

Nightmares are anxiety-arousing dreams that lead to awakening, usually from REM sleep (see Figure 5.10). Typically, a person who awakens from a nightmare recalls a vivid dream and may have difficulty getting back to sleep. There is evidence that nightmares are associated with measures of an individual's well-being. Significant stress in one's life is associated with increased frequency and intensity of nightmares (Nielsen & Levin, 2009). Montreal psychologists and sleep researchers A. L. Zadra and D. C. Donderi (2000) found significant correlations between number of nightmares and measures of well-being; higher frequencies of nightmares were associated with increased scores on variables such as

neuroticism, trait anxiety, state anxiety, and depression. Levin and Nielsen (2009) suggest that one of the functions that normal dreams serve is a fear-extinction function, meaning that dreams provide us with a way to deal with and discard old fear-laden memories so that we can proceed in our waking lives ready for new events and experiences. Accordingly, nightmares, where our negative memories and fear take central stage, reflect a failure in "emotional regulation" that they suggest is critical in our ability to deal with our everyday experiences. Thus, nightmares not only negatively affect us during the night, but might also have negative effects on our ability to cope at other times too.

Although about 10 percent of adults have occasional nightmares, these frightening episodes are mainly a problem among children. Most youngsters have occasional nightmares, but *persistent* nightmares may reflect an emotional disturbance. If a child's nightmares are frequent and unpleasant, counselling may prove helpful. Otherwise, treatment is unnecessary, as most children outgrow the problem.

Night terrors (also called "sleep terrors") are abrupt awakenings from NREM sleep, accompanied by intense autonomic arousal and feelings of panic. Night terrors, which can produce remarkable accelerations of heart rate, usually occur during stage 4 sleep early in the night, as shown in Figure 5.10 (Nielsen & Zadra, 2000). Victims typically let out a piercing cry, bolt upright, and then stare into space. They do not usually recall a coherent dream, although they may remember a simple, frightening image. The panic normally fades quickly, and a return to sleep is fairly easy. Night terrors occur in adults, but they are especially common in children aged three to eight.

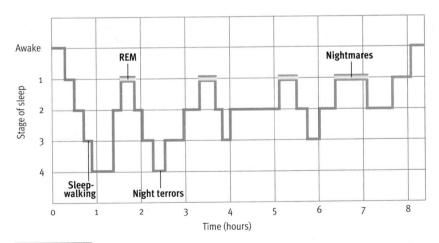

FIGURE 5.10

Sleep problems and the cycle of sleep.
Different sleep problems tend to occur at different points in the sleep cycle. Whereas sleepwalking and night terrors are associated with slow-wave sleep, nightmares are associated with the heightened dream activity of REM sleep.

Night terrors are not indicative of an emotional disturbance. Treatment may not be necessary, as night terrors are often a temporary problem.

Somnambulism, or sleepwalking, occurs when a person arises and wanders about while remaining asleep. Sleepwalking tends to occur during the first two hours of sleep, when individuals are in slow-wave sleep (see Figure 5.10). Episodes may last from 15 seconds to 30 minutes (Aldrich, 2000). Sleepwalkers may awaken during their journey, or they may return to bed without any recollection of their excursion. The causes of this unusual disorder are unknown, although it appears to have a genetic predisposition (Keefauver & Guilleminault, 1994). Sleepwalking does not appear to be a manifestation of underlying emotional or psychological problems (Mahowald, 1993). However, sleepwalkers are prone to accidents (Gunn & Gunn, 2006). In light of this reality, it is important to note that, contrary to popular myth, it is safe to awaken people (gently) from a sleepwalking episode—much safer than letting them wander about.

REM sleep behaviour disorder (RBD) is marked by potentially troublesome dream enactments during REM periods. People who exhibit this syndrome may talk, yell, gesture, flail about, or leap out of bed during their REM dreams. When questioned, many report that they were being chased or attacked in their dreams. Their dream enactments can get surprisingly violent and they often hurt themselves or their bed partners (Mahowald & Schenck, 2005). RBD occurs mostly in men who typically begin experiencing this problem in their 50s or 60s. As noted earlier, people in REM sleep normally are virtually paralyzed, which prevents dream enactments. The cause of RBD appears to be some sort of deterioration in the brainstem structures that are normally responsible for this immobilization during REM periods (Tippmann-Peikert et al., 2006). Treatment of this disorder can be difficult and RBD has been found to coexist with some of the other sleep disorders we have described (Mayo Clinic, 2011).

REVIEW OF KEY POINTS

▷ The effects of sleep deprivation depend on a variety of factors. Increased sleepiness can be a significant problem that appears to contribute to many transportation accidents and mishaps at work.

▷ Research on selective sleep deprivation suggests that people need REM sleep and slow-wave sleep. These stages of sleep may contribute to memory consolidation. Short sleep duration is associated with a variety of health problems. People who sleep seven to eight hours per day have lower mortality rates than individuals who are long or short sleepers. Many people are troubled by sleep disorders. Insomnia has a variety of causes. Sleeping pills generally are a poor solution. The optimal treatment for insomnia depends on identification of its apparent cause.

▷ Narcolepsy is a disease marked by sudden, irresistible onsets of sleep during normal waking periods. Sleep apnea involves frequent gasping for air, which occurs when people stop breathing. Night terrors are abrupt awakenings from NREM sleep accompanied by panic, whereas nightmares are anxiety-arousing dreams that typically awaken one from REM sleep. Somnambulism typically occurs during slow-wave sleep. REM sleep behavior disorder (RBD) is marked by potentially troublesome dream enactments during REM periods.

The World of Dreams

PREVIEW QUESTIONS

▷ What is a dream, and how are views on this question changing?

▷ What is known about the contents of people's dreams?

▷ Can external events affect the content of dreams?

▷ How does culture affect dream recall and dream content?

▷ How do the Freudian, cognitive, and activation-synthesis models view dreams?

For the most part, dreams are not taken very seriously in Western societies. Paradoxically, though, Robert Van de Castle (1994) points out that dreams have sometimes changed the world. For example, Van de Castle describes how René Descartes' philosophy of dualism, Frederick Banting's discovery of insulin, Elias Howe's refinement of the sewing machine, Mohandas Gandhi's strategy of nonviolent protest, and Lyndon Johnson's withdrawal from the 1968 U.S. presidential race were all inspired by dreams. He also explains how Mary Shelley's *Frankenstein* and Robert Louis Stevenson's *The Strange Case of Dr. Jekyll and Mr. Hyde* emerged out of their dream experiences. In his wide-ranging discussion, Van de Castle also relates how the Surrealist painter Salvador Dali characterized his works as "dream photographs," and how legendary filmmakers Ingmar Bergman, Orson Welles, and Federico Fellini all drew on their dreams in making their films. Thus, Van de Castle concludes that "dreams have had a dramatic influence on almost every important aspect of our culture and history" (p. 10).

What exactly is a dream? This question is more complex and controversial than you might guess (Pagel et al., 2001). The conventional view is that dreams are mental experiences during REM sleep that have a story-like quality, include vivid visual imagery, are often bizarre, and are regarded as perceptually real by the dreamer (Antrobus, 1993). However, theorists have begun to question virtually every aspect of this characterization. Decades of research on the contents of dreams, which we will discuss soon, have shown that dreams are not as bizarre as widely assumed (Cartwright, 1994). Recent years have seen renewed interest in the fact that dreams are not the exclusive property of REM sleep (Nir & Tononi, 2009). Moreover, studies that have focused on dream reports from non-REM stages of sleep have found that these dreams appear to be less vivid, visual, and story-like than REM dreams (Antrobus & Wamsley, 2009; McNamara et al., 2007). And research suggests that dreamers realize they are dreaming more often than previously thought and that mental processes during sleep are more similar to waking thought processes than is widely assumed (Kahan & LaBerge, 1994, 1996). Thus, the concept of dreaming is undergoing some revision in scientific circles.

The Contents of Dreams

What do people dream about? Overall, dreams are not as exciting as advertised. Perhaps dreams are seen as exotic because people are more likely to remember their more bizarre nighttime dramas (De Koninck, 2000). After analyzing the contents of more than 10 000 dreams, Calvin Hall (1966) concluded that most dreams are relatively mundane. They tend to unfold in familiar settings with a cast of characters dominated by family, friends, and colleagues. We *are* more tolerant of logical discrepancies and implausible scenarios in our dreams than our waking thought (Kahn, 2007), but in our dreams we generally move through coherent sensible, realistic virtual worlds (Nielsen & Stenstrom, 2005). The one nearly universal element of dreams is a coherent sense of self—we almost always experience dreams from a first-person perspective (Valli & Revonsuo, 2009).

Certain themes tend to be more common than others in dreams. In one large study, sleep researchers from the University of Montreal, Trent University, and the University of Alberta administered the *Typical Dreams Questionnaire* to over 1000 first-year Canadian university students. The dream themes and their frequency as reported by those students are shown in Figure 5.11.

Take a look at the results in Figure 5.11. Do the dreams of these students seem similar to yours? The most frequent types of dreams related to "being chased or pursued, but not physically injured" and "sexual experiences." In addition to the general frequency of different types of dreams, the researchers obtained several other interesting results. There were significant differences between males and females. Several dream types demonstrated gender differences, with the

affective tone of the dreams differentiating males and females. The dreams distinctly associated with males tended to be positive in nature, while those associated with females tended to be more negative, including dreams with themes related to phobias (snakes, spiders), performance anxiety (failure), and control (loss of control). There were also some differences in dream

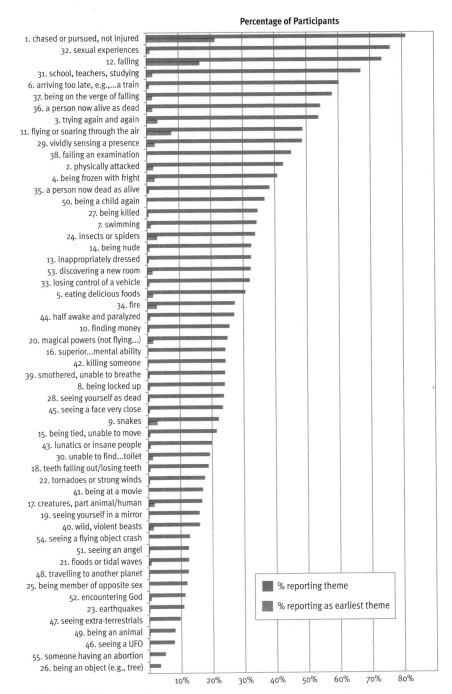

FIGURE 5.11

The typical dreams of Canadian university students.

This figure shows the percentage of participants reporting each of the 55 dream themes.

Source: Nielsen, T.A., Zadra, A., Simard, V., Saucier, S., Stenstrom, P., Smith, C., and Kuiken, D. (2003) The typical dreams of Canadian university students. *Dreaming, 13*(4), 216. Copyright © 2003 by the American Psychological Association. Reprinted by permission.

prevalence across student samples. For example, the theme of "being half awake and paralyzed" distinguished McGill students from the other samples, and the theme of "finding money" differentiated students from Alberta. Participants were also asked how many nightmares they recalled and, on average, they recalled almost one every two weeks! Overall, however, the study revealed substantial consistency of dream content over age, region, and gender.

Relatively little research has been done on developmental trends in dream reports, but the available data suggest that children's dreams are different from adults' dreams (Foulkes, 1982, 1999). For one thing, the rate of dream recall after REM awakenings is only 20–30 percent until ages 9–11, when the recall rate begins to approach adult levels (typically around 80 percent). Dream reports from children under age five consist mostly of static, bland images with no storyline.

Children aged five to eight report dream narratives, but they are not well developed and common adult themes of aggression and misfortune are notably infrequent. The contents of children's dreams don't become adult-like until around ages 11–13. These findings suggest that dreaming is a cognitive ability that develops gradually, like other cognitive abilities.

Links between Dreams and Waking Life

Although dreams seem to belong in a world of their own, what people dream about is affected by what is going on in their lives (Kramer, 1994). If you're struggling with financial problems, worried about an upcoming exam, or sexually attracted to a classmate, these themes may very well show up in your dreams. As Domhoff (2001) puts it, "dream content in general is continuous with waking conceptions and emotional preoccupations" (p. 13). Does stress show up in dreams? Does the stress of exams show up in the dreams of students? Answers to the effect of stress on stress-themed content seem to be mixed. In one study, University of Ottawa researchers found that students who were experiencing stress concerning upcoming exams did not necessarily have more exam-themed dreams (Delorme, Lortie-Lussier, & De Koninck, 2002). The relationship of daily stress to dreams may depend on a variety of factors, including the nature of the stressor. The authors note that not all stressors are the same, and that particular types of stressors such as imminent surgery might be more likely to affect dream content than impending exams. It seems that not all daytime events are equally likely to affect dream content. Freud noticed long ago that the contents of waking life often tended to spill into dreams; he labelled this spillover the *day residue*.

On occasion, the content of dreams can also be affected by stimuli experienced while one is dreaming (De Koninck, 2000). For example, William Dement sprayed water on one hand of sleeping subjects while they were in the REM stage (Dement & Wolpert, 1958). Subjects who weren't awakened by the water were awakened by the experimenter a short time later and asked what they had been dreaming about. Dement found that 42 percent of the subjects had incorporated the water into their dreams. They said that they had dreamt that they were in rainfalls, floods, baths, swimming pools, and the like. Some people report that they occasionally experience the same sort of phenomenon at home when the sound of their alarm clock fails to awaken them. The alarm is incorporated into their dream as a loud engine or a siren, for instance. As with day residue, the incorporation of external stimuli into dreams shows that people's dream world is not entirely separate from their real world.

Sometimes people may realize they are dreaming while still in the dream state. These are often referred to as "lucid dreams" (Gackenbach & Sheikh, 1991). In some of these dreams, the dreamer may be able to exert some control over the dream. According to members of the Dream and Nightmare Laboratory established at Montreal's Sacré-Coeur Hospital in 1991 (*Lucid Dreaming*, 2005), it has been suggested that lucid dreaming might be useful in the treatment of nightmares. To be useful, however, the therapist must be able to somehow control or influence the onset of the lucid dreams. Thus, one of the issues here is the induction of lucid dreaming for therapeutic use. Antonio Zadra, a University of Montreal psychologist and member of the Dream and Nightmare Laboratory, has done research on lucid dreaming induction (Zadra, Donderi, & Pihl, 1992). It may be easier to induce lucid dreaming in some individuals than in others.

Culture and Dreams

Striking cross-cultural variations occur in beliefs about the nature of dreams and the importance attributed to them. In modern Western society, people typically make a distinction between the "real" world they experience while awake and the "imaginary" world they experience while dreaming. Some people realize that events in the real world can affect their dreams, but few believe that events in their dreams hold any significance for their waking life. Although a small minority of individuals take their dreams seriously, in Western cultures, dreams

TABLE 5.2

Examples of Common Dream Interpretations among the Toraja of Indonesia

"Good" Dreams	Interpretation		"Bad" Dreams	Interpretation
Receive gold	Good rice harvest		Buffalo in the rice fields	Rats will eat rice harvest
Carry pig or buffalo meat	Good rice harvest		Naked	Get sick
Act "crazy"	Receive wealth		Enter burial cave	Die
Objects are thrown at dreamer	Rain will fall		Carried off by an ancestor	Die
Stand on mountaintop	Become a leader		Objects are stolen/lost/carried away	Lose those objects
Steal objects	Receive those objects/become wealthy		House burns or is destroyed	Lose wealth/become poor
Swim in ocean or river	Receive wealth			
Jump over or cross water	Become wise/clever			
Gored by a buffalo	Buy a buffalo			

Source: Adapted from Hollan, D. (1989). The personal use of dream beliefs in the Toraja Highlands. *Ethos, 17*, 166–186. Copyright © 1989 by the American Anthropological Association. Reproduced by permission. Not for further reproduction.

are largely written off as insignificant, meaningless meanderings of the unconscious (Tart, 1988).

In many non-Western cultures, however, dreams are viewed as important sources of information about oneself, about the future, or about the spiritual world (Kracke, 1991). Although no culture confuses dreams with waking reality, many view events in dreams as another type of reality that may be just as important as, or perhaps even more important than, events experienced while awake. Among the Inuit who live in the far north of Canada, *angakoks* or shamans often had the power to travel and visit hidden places that other people were unable to visit. They made these visits through their trances and dreams. Dreams clearly played an important part in the Inuit culture (Houston, 2008). And among Australian Aborigines, for example, "Dreaming is the focal point of traditional aboriginal existence and simultaneously determines their way of life, their culture, and their relationship to the physical and spiritual environment" (Dawson, 1993, p. 1). Dreams continue to play a large role in contemporary Canadian Aboriginal culture in, for example, works such as the *Rez Sisters* by Canadian Cree playwright, author, and musician Tomson Highway (1988).

In regard to dream content, both similarities and differences occur across cultures in the types of dreams that people report (Domhoff, 2005b; H. Hunt, 1989). Some basic dream themes appear to be nearly universal (falling, being pursued, having sex). However, the contents of dreams vary somewhat from one culture to another because people in different societies deal with different worlds while awake. For example, in a 1950 study of the Siriono, a hunting-and-gathering people of the Amazon who were almost always hungry and spent most of their time in a grim search for food, *half* of the reported dreams focused on hunting, gathering,

and eating food (D'Andrade, 1961). Shared systems for interpreting the contents of dreams also vary from one society to another. Table 5.2 lists a number of common dream interpretations among the Toraja of Indonesia (Hollan, 1989). Although some of these interpretations might be common in other societies (example: stand on a mountaintop = become a leader), some clearly are peculiar to Toraja society (example: buffalo in the rice fields = rats will eat the rice harvest).

Theories of Dreaming

Many theories have been proposed to explain why people dream. Sigmund Freud (1900), who analyzed clients' dreams in therapy, believed that the principal purpose of dreams is *wish fulfillment*. He thought that people fulfill ungratified needs from waking hours through wishful thinking in dreams. For example, someone who is sexually frustrated might have highly erotic dreams, while an unsuccessful person might dream about great accomplishments. Although these examples involve blatant wishful thinking, Freud asserted that the wish-fulfilling quality of many dreams may not be readily apparent because the true meaning of dreams may be disguised. Freud's influential theory sounded plausible when it was proposed over 100 years ago, but research has not provided much support for Freud's conception of dreaming (Fisher & Greenberg, 1996).

Other theorists, such as Rosalind Cartwright (1977; Cartwright & Lamberg, 1992), have proposed that dreams provide an opportunity to work through everyday problems. According to her *cognitive, problem-solving view*, there is considerable continuity between waking and sleeping thought. Proponents of this view believe that dreams allow people to engage in creative thinking about problems because dreams

Sigmund Freud
"[Dreams are] the royal road to the unconscious."

Three theories of dreaming.

Dreams can be explained in a variety of ways. Freud stressed the wish-fulfilling function of dreams. Cartwright emphasizes the problem-solving function of dreams. Hobson and McCarley assert that dreams are merely a by-product of periodic neural activation. All three theories are speculative and have their critics.

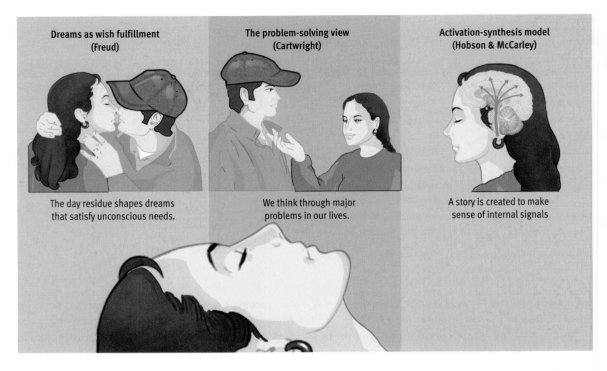

Dreams as wish fulfillment (Freud)

The day residue shapes dreams that satisfy unconscious needs.

The problem-solving view (Cartwright)

We think through major problems in our lives.

Activation-synthesis model (Hobson & McCarley)

A story is created to make sense of internal signals

Courtesy of Rosalind Cartwright

Rosalind Cartwright

"One function of dreams may be to restore our sense of competence. . . . It is also probable that in times of stress, dreams have more work to do in resolving our problems and are thus more salient and memorable."

Dr. Cartwright obtained her undergraduate and master's training at the University of Toronto. She is currently Chair of Psychology at Rush-Presbyterian-St. Luke's Medical Center in Chicago and serves on the Scientific and Professional Advisory Board of the False Memory Syndrome Foundation (http://www.fmsonline.org).

are not restrained by logic or realism. Consistent with this view, Cartwright (1991) has found that women going through divorce frequently dream about divorce-related problems. Cartwright's analysis is thought-provoking, but critics point out that just because people dream about problems from their waking life doesn't mean they are dreaming up solutions (Blagrove, 1992, 1996). Nonetheless, research showing that sleep can enhance learning (Walker & Stickgold, 2004) adds new credibility to the problem-solving view of dreams (Cartwright, 2004).

J. Allan Hobson and Robert McCarley argue that dreams are simply the byproduct of bursts of activity emanating from subcortical areas in the brain (Hobson, 2002; Hobson & McCarley, 1977; Hobson, Pace-Schott, & Stickgold, 2000). Their *activation-synthesis model* proposes that dreams are side effects of the neural activation that produces "wide-awake" brain waves during REM sleep. According to this model, neurons firing periodically in lower brain centres send random signals to the cortex (the seat of complex thought). The cortex supposedly synthesizes (constructs) a dream to make sense out of these signals. The activation-synthesis model does *not* assume that dreams are meaningless. As Hobson (1988) puts it, "Dreams are as meaningful as they can be under the adverse working conditions of the brain in REM sleep" (p. 214). In contrast to the theories of Freud and Cartwright, this theory obviously downplays the role of emotional factors as determinants of dreams. Like other theories of dreams, the activation-synthesis model has its share of critics. They point out that the model cannot accommodate

the fact that dreaming occurs outside of REM sleep and that the contents of dreams are considerably more meaningful than the model would predict (Domhoff, 2005a; Foulkes, 1996).

These approaches, summarized in Figure 5.12, are only three of a host of theories about the functions of dreams. All of these theories are based more on conjecture than solid evidence, and none of them has been tested adequately. In part, this is because the private, subjective nature of dreams makes it difficult to put the theories to an empirical test. Thus, the purpose of dreaming remains a mystery.

REVIEW OF KEY POINTS

▷ The conventional view is that dreams are mental experiences during REM sleep that have a story-like quality, include vivid imagery, are often bizarre, and are regarded as real by the dreamer, but theorists have begun to question many aspects of this view.

▷ Researchers have found modest differences between men and women in dream content that seem to reflect conventional gender roles. The content of one's dreams may be affected by what is going on in one's life and by external stimuli that are experienced during the dream.

▷ In many non-Western cultures, dreams are viewed as important sources of information. Cultures vary in beliefs about the nature of dreams, dream recall, dream content, and dream interpretation.

▷ Freud argued that the principal purpose of dreams is wish fulfillment. Cartwright has articulated a problem-solving view, whereas Hobson and McCarley assert that dreams are side effects of the neural activation seen during REM sleep. Ultimately, theories of dreaming remain largely untested.

Hypnosis: Altered Consciousness or Role Playing?

Hypnosis has a long and chequered history (Schmit, 2010). According to hypnosis researcher Nicholas Spanos of Carleton University, some believe that there are even events described in the Old and New Testaments that refer to hypnosis-like phenomena (Spanos & Chaves, 1991). In terms of more contemporary events, however, the recent history of hypnosis begins with a flamboyant 18th-century Austrian physician by the name of Franz Anton Mesmer. Working in Paris, Mesmer claimed to cure people of illnesses through an elaborate routine involving a "laying on of hands." Mesmer had some complicated theories about how he had harnessed "animal magnetism." However, we know today that he had simply stumbled onto the power of suggestion. It was rumoured that the French government offered him a princely amount of money to disclose how he effected his cures. He refused, probably because he didn't really know. Eventually he was dismissed as a charlatan and run out of town by the local authorities. Although officially discredited, Mesmer inspired followers—practitioners of "mesmerism"—who continued to ply their trade. To this day, our language preserves the memory of Franz Mesmer: When we are under the spell of an event or a story, we are "mesmerized."

Eventually, a Scottish physician, James Braid, became interested in the trancelike state that could be induced by the mesmerists. It was Braid who popularized the term *hypnotism* in 1843, borrowing it from the Greek word for *sleep*. Braid thought that hypnotism could be used to produce anesthesia for surgeries. However, just as hypnosis was catching on as a general anesthetic, more powerful and reliable chemical anesthetics were discovered, and interest in hypnotism dwindled.

Since then, hypnotism has led a curious dual existence. On the one hand, it has been the subject of numerous scientific studies. Furthermore, it has enjoyed considerable use as a clinical tool by physicians, dentists, and psychologists for over a century and has empirically supported value in the treatment of a variety of psychological and physical maladies (Lynn et al., 2000; Spiegel, Greenleaf, & Spiegel, 2000). On the other hand, however, an assortment of entertainers and quacks have continued in the less respectable tradition of mesmerism, using hypnotism for parlour tricks and chicanery. It is little wonder, then, that many myths about hypnosis have come to be widely accepted (see Figure 5.13). In this section, we'll work on clearing up some of the confusion surrounding hypnosis.

Hypnotic Induction and Susceptibility

Hypnosis is a systematic procedure that typically produces a heightened state of suggestibility. It may also lead to passive relaxation, narrowed attention, and enhanced fantasy. If only in popular films, virtually everyone has seen a *hypnotic induction* enacted with a swinging pendulum. Actually many techniques can be used for inducing hypnosis (Meyer, 1992). Usually, the hypnotist will suggest to the subject that he or she is relaxing. Repetitively and softly, subjects are told that they are getting tired, drowsy, or sleepy. Often, the hypnotist vividly describes bodily sensations that should be occurring. Subjects are told

PREVIEW QUESTIONS

► What is the history of hypnosis?

► What are some correlates of hypnotic susceptibility?

► What are some prominent hypnotic phenomena?

► What lines of evidence support the social-cognitive or role-playing theory of hypnosis?

► What is Hilgard's explanation for how hypnosis works?

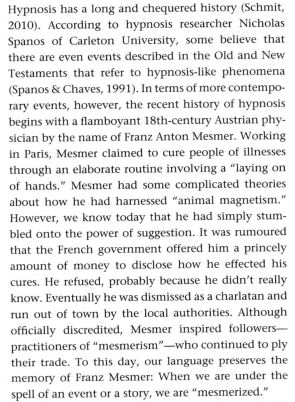

Hypnosis: Myth and Reality	
If you think . . .	**The reality is . . .**
Relaxation is an important feature of hypnosis.	It's not. Hypnosis has been induced during vigorous exercise.
It's mostly just compliance.	Many highly motivated subjects fail to experience hypnosis.
It's a matter of willful faking.	Physiological responses indicate that hypnotized subjects generally are not lying.
It has something to do with a sleeplike state.	It does not. Hypnotized subjects are fully awake.
Responding to hypnosis is like responding to a placebo.	Placebo responsiveness and hypnotizability are not correlated.
People who are hypnotized lose control of themselves.	Subjects are perfectly capable of saying no or terminating hypnosis.
Hypnosis can enable people to "relive" the past.	Age-regressed adults behave like adults play-acting as children.
When hypnotized, people can remember more accurately.	Hypnosis may actually muddle the distinction between memory and fantasy and may artificially inflate confidence.
Hypnotized people do not remember what happened during the session.	Posthypnotic amnesia does not occur spontaneously.
Hypnosis can enable people to perform otherwise impossible feats of strength, endurance, learning, and sensory acuity.	Performance following hypnotic suggestions for increased muscle strength, learning, and sensory acuity does not exceed what can be accomplished by motivated subjects outside hypnosis.

FIGURE 5.13

Misconceptions regarding hypnosis.

Mistaken ideas about the nature of hypnosis are common. Some widely believed myths about hypnosis are summarized here along with more accurate information on each point, based on an article by Michael Nash (2001), a prominent hypnosis researcher. Many of these myths and realities are discussed in more detail in the text.

Source: Adapted from Nash, M.R. (2001, July). The truth and the hype of hypnosis. *Scientific American, 285,* 36–43. Copyright © 2001 by Scientific American, Inc.

that their arms are going limp, their feet are getting warm, their eyelids are getting heavy. Gradually, most subjects succumb and become hypnotized.

People differ in how well they respond to hypnotic induction. Ernest and Josephine Hilgard have done extensive research on this variability in *hypnotic susceptibility*. Responsiveness to hypnosis is a stable, measurable trait. It can be estimated with the *Stanford Hypnotic Susceptibility Scale* (SHSS) or its derivative, the *Harvard Group Scale of Hypnotic Susceptibility* (Perry, Nadon, & Button, 1992). The distribution of scores on the SHSS is graphed in Figure 5.14. Not everyone can be hypnotized. About 10–20 percent of the population doesn't respond well at all. At the other end of the continuum, about 10–15 percent of people are exceptionally good hypnotic subjects (Hilgard, 1965). As Kihlstrom (2007, p. 446) notes, "the most dramatic phenomena of hypnosis—the ones that really count as reflecting alterations in consciousness—are generally observed in those 'hypnotic virtuosos' who comprise the upper 10 to 15% of the distribution of hypnotizability." People who are highly hypnotizable may even slip in and out of hypnotic-like states spontaneously without being aware of it (Spiegel, 2007).

What makes some people highly susceptible to hypnosis? Variations in hypnotic susceptibility were originally assumed to depend on differences in personality traits, but decades of research on the personality correlates of hypnotizability have turned up relatively little (Kihlstrom, 2007). According to Spiegel, Greenleaf, and Spiegel (2005), high hypnotizability is made up of three components: absorption, dissociation, and suggestibility. *Absorption* involves the capacity to reduce or block peripheral awareness and narrow the focus of one's attention. *Dissociation* involves the ability to separate aspects of perception, memory, or identity, from the mainstream of conscious awareness. *Suggestibility* involves the tendency to accept directions and information relatively uncritically.

Research has demonstrated that people who are responsive to suggestion under hypnosis are just as responsive to suggestion without being hypnotized (Braffman & Kirsch, 1999). In other words, their "hypnotic susceptibility" is not unique to hypnosis and is part of a broader trait that Kirsch and Braffman (2001) characterize as *imaginative suggestibility*. Kirsch and Braffman argue that future research should focus on measuring the determinants and repercussions of this broader trait. It remains to be seen whether this proposal will enhance our understanding of why some people are more responsive to hypnosis than others.

Hypnotic Phenomena

Many interesting effects can be produced through hypnosis. Some of the more prominent include:

1. *Anesthesia.* Under the influence of hypnosis, some participants can withstand treatments that would normally cause considerable pain (Patterson, 2004). As a result, some physicians and dentists have used hypnosis as a substitute for anesthetic drugs. Admittedly, drugs are far more reliable pain relievers, making hypnosis something of a scientific curiosity as a solo treatment for acute pain (Gibson & Heap, 1991). Nonetheless, hypnosis can be a surprisingly effective anesthetic in the treatment of both acute and chronic pain (Patterson & Jensen, 2003).

2. *Sensory distortions and hallucinations.* Hypnotized participants may be led to experience auditory or visual hallucinations (Spiegel, 2003a). They may hear sounds or see things that are not there, or fail to hear or see stimuli that are present. In one study, for instance, hypnotized participants were induced to "see" a cardboard box that blocked their view of a television (Spiegel et al., 1985). Subjects may also have their sensations distorted so that something sweet tastes sour or an unpleasant odour smells fragrant.

3. *Disinhibition.* Generally, it is difficult to get hypnotized participants to do things that they would normally consider unacceptable. Nonetheless,

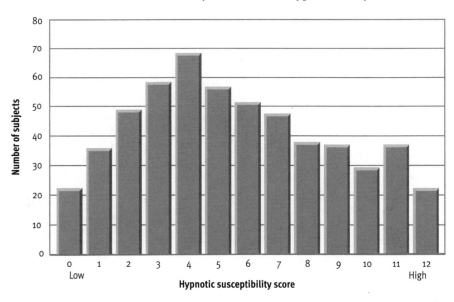

FIGURE 5.14

Variation in hypnotic susceptibility.

This graph shows the distribution of scores of more than 500 subjects on the *Stanford Hypnotic Susceptibility Scale*. As you can see, responsiveness to hypnotism varies widely, and many people are not very susceptible to hypnotic induction.

Source: Adapted from Hilgard, E. (1965). *Hypnotic susceptibility*. San Diego: Harcourt Brace Jovanovich. Copyright © 1965 by Ernest R. Hilgard. Reprinted by permission of Ernest R. Hilgard.

hypnosis *can* sometimes reduce inhibitions that would normally prevent subjects from acting in ways that they would see as socially undesirable. In experiments, hypnotized participants have been induced to throw what they believed to be nitric acid into the face of a research assistant. Similarly, stage hypnotists are sometimes successful in getting people to disrobe in public. One lay hypnotist even coaxed a man into robbing a bank (Deyoub, 1984). This disinhibition effect may occur simply because hypnotized people feel that they cannot be held responsible for their actions while they are hypnotized.

4. *Posthypnotic suggestions and amnesia.* Suggestions made during hypnosis may influence a subject's later behaviour (Barnier, 2002). The most common posthypnotic suggestion is the creation of posthypnotic amnesia. That is, participants are told that they will remember nothing that happened while they were hypnotized. Such subjects usually claim to remember nothing, as ordered. However, when pressed, many of these subjects acknowledge that they have not really forgotten the information (Kirsch & Lynn, 1998).

Theories of Hypnosis

Although a number of theories have been developed to explain hypnosis, it is still not well understood. One popular view is that hypnotic effects occur because participants are put into a special, altered state of consciousness, called a *hypnotic trance.* Although hypnotized subjects may feel as though they are in an altered state, their patterns of EEG activity cannot be distinguished from their EEG patterns in normal waking states (Dixon & Laurence, 1992; Orne & Dinges, 1989). The failure to find any special physiological changes associated with hypnosis has led some theorists to conclude that hypnosis is a normal state of consciousness that is simply characterized by dramatic role playing.

Social-Cognitive Theory of Hypnosis: Hypnosis as Role Playing

Theodore Barber (1979) and Carleton University's Nicholas Spanos (1986; Spanos & Coe, 1992) have been the leading advocates of the view that hypnosis produces a normal mental state in which suggestible people act out the role of a hypnotic subject and behave as they think hypnotized people are supposed to. According to this notion, hypnosis is not the result of a person being in a "trance" but rather results from normal everyday processes including an individual's expectations and attitudes. Thus, it is subjects' role expectations

that produce hypnotic effects, rather than a special trancelike state of consciousness.

Two lines of evidence support the role-playing view. First, many of the seemingly amazing effects of hypnosis have been duplicated by nonhypnotized participants or have been shown to be exaggerated (Kirsch, 1997; Kirsch, Mazzoni, & Montgomery, 2007). For example, much has been made of the fact that hypnotized subjects can be used as "human planks," but it turns out that nonhypnotized subjects can easily match this feat (Barber, 1986). In a similar vein, anecdotal reports that hypnosis can enhance memory have not stood up well to empirical testing. Although hypnosis may occasionally facilitate recall in some people, experimental studies have tended to find that hypnotized participants make more memory errors than nonhypnotized participants, even though they often feel more confident about their recollections (McConkey, 1992; Scoboria et al., 2002). These findings suggest that no special state of consciousness is required to explain hypnotic feats.

The second line of evidence involves demonstrations that hypnotized participants are often acting out a role. For example, Martin Orne (1951) regressed hypnotized subjects back to their sixth birthday and asked them to describe it. They responded with detailed descriptions that appeared to represent great feats of hypnosis-enhanced memory. However, instead of accepting this information at face value, Orne compared it with information that he had obtained from the subjects' parents. It turned out that many of the participants' memories were inaccurate and invented! Many other studies have also

Theodore Barber

"Thousands of books, movies, and professional articles have woven the concept of 'hypnotic trance' into the common knowledge. And yet there is almost no scientific support for it."

Ernest Hilgard

"Many psychologists argue that the hypnotic trance is a mirage. It would be unfortunate if this skeptical view were to gain such popularity that the benefits of hypnosis are denied to the numbers of those who could be helped."

Some feats performed under hypnosis can be performed equally well by nonhypnotized subjects. Here "The Amazing Kreskin" demonstrates that proper positioning is the only requirement for the famous human plank feat.

found that age-regressed subjects' recall of the distant past tends to be more fanciful than factual (Green, 1999; Perry, Kusel, & Perry, 1988). Thus, the role-playing explanation of hypnosis suggests that situational factors lead some subjects to act out a certain role in a highly cooperative manner (Lynn, Kirsch, & Hallquist, 2008; Wagstaff et al., 2010).

Hypnosis as an Altered State of Consciousness

Despite the doubts raised by role-playing explanations, many prominent theorists still maintain that hypnotic effects are attributable to a special, altered state of consciousness (Beahrs, 1983; Fromm, 1979, 1992; Hilgard, 1986; Spiegel, 1995, 2003b; Woody & Sadler, 2008). These theorists argue that it is doubtful that role playing can explain all hypnotic phenomena. For instance, they assert that even the most cooperative subjects are unlikely to endure surgery without a drug anesthetic just to please their physician and live up to their expected role. They also cite studies in which hypnotized participants have continued to display hypnotic responses when they thought they were alone and not being observed (Perugini et al., 1998). If hypnotized participants were merely acting, they would drop the act when alone.

The most impressive research undermining the role-playing view has come from recent brain-imaging studies, which suggest that hypnotized participants experience changes in brain activity that appear consistent with their reports of hypnosis-induced hallucinations (Spiegel, 2003b) or pain suppression (Hofbauer et al., 2001).

The most influential explanation of hypnosis as an altered state of awareness has been offered by Ernest Hilgard (1986, 1992). According to Hilgard, hypnosis creates a *dissociation* in consciousness. *Dissociation is a splitting off of mental processes into two separate, simultaneous streams of awareness.* In other words, Hilgard theorizes that hypnosis splits consciousness into two streams. One stream is in communication with the hypnotist and the external world, while the other is a difficult-to-detect "hidden observer." Hilgard believes that many hypnotic effects are a product of this divided consciousness. For instance, he suggests that a hypnotized subject might appear to be unresponsive to pain because the pain isn't registered in the portion of consciousness that communicates with other people.

One appealing aspect of Hilgard's theory is that *divided consciousness* is a common, normal experience. For example, people will often drive a car a great distance, responding to traffic signals and other cars, with no recollection of having consciously done so. In such cases, consciousness is clearly divided between driving and the person's thoughts about other matters. Interestingly, this common experience has long been known as *highway hypnosis*. In this condition, there is even an "amnesia" for the component of consciousness that drove the car, similar to posthypnotic amnesia. In summary, Hilgard presents hypnosis as a plausible variation in consciousness that has continuity with everyday experience (Bowers, 2002).

Meditation: Pure Consciousness or Relaxation?

PREVIEW QUESTIONS

▶ What is meditation and how is it practised?

▶ How does meditation affect physiological responding?

▶ What's the evidence on the long-term benefits of meditation?

Recent years have seen growing interest in the ancient discipline of meditation. *Meditation refers to a family of practices that train attention to heighten awareness and bring mental processes under greater voluntary control.* There are many approaches to meditation. In North America, the most widely practised approaches are those associated with yoga, Zen, and transcendental meditation (TM). All three of these approaches are rooted in Eastern religions (Hinduism, Buddhism, and Taoism). However, meditation has been practised throughout history as an element of all religious and spiritual traditions, including Judaism and Christianity (Walsh & Shapiro, 2006). Moreover, the practice of meditation can be largely divorced from religious beliefs. In fact, most North Americans who meditate have only vague ideas regarding its religious significance.

Of interest to psychology is the fact that meditation involves a deliberate effort to alter consciousness.

Approaches to meditation can be classified into two main styles that reflect how attention is directed: *focused attention* or *open monitoring* (Cahn & Polich, 2006; Manna et al., 2010). In focused attention approaches, attention is concentrated on a specific object, image, sound, or bodily sensation (such as breathing). The intent in narrowing attention is to clear the mind of its clutter. In open monitoring approaches, attention is directed to the contents of one's moment-to-moment experience in a nonjudgmental and nonreactive way. The intent in expanding attention is to become a detached observer of the flow of one's own sensations, thoughts, and feelings. Both approaches seek to achieve a "higher" form of consciousness than people normally experience.

The meditative disciplines that have received the most research attention are TM and mindfulness meditation. Mindfulness meditation is an open monitoring approach with roots in Zen Buddhism, whereas TM is primarily a focused attention approach with roots in Hinduism. As we discuss in Chapter 15, mindfulness meditation has been integrated with cognitive-behavioural therapy (CBT) to produce a particularly effective form of psychotherapy used in the treatment of many disorders, including depression (Segal, Williams et al., 2007) and anxiety and obsessive-compulsive disorders (Baxter et al., 1992; Hayes, 2004), among others.

Physiological Correlates

What happens when an experienced meditator goes into the meditative state? One intriguing finding is that alpha waves and theta waves become more prominent in EEG recordings (Cahn & Polich, 2006; Logopoulos et al., 2009). Many studies also find that subjects' heart rate, skin conductance, respiration rate, oxygen consumption, and carbon dioxide elimination decline (see Figure 5.15; Dillbeck & Orme-Johnson, 1987; Fenwick, 1987; Travis, 2001). Taken together, these changes suggest that meditation leads to a potentially beneficial physiological state characterized by suppression of bodily arousal. However some researchers have argued that a variety of systematic relaxation training procedures can produce similar results (Holmes, 1987; Shapiro, 1984). But mere relaxation hardly seems like an adequate explanation for the transcendent experiences reported by many meditators.

To shed new light on this lingering question, some researchers have begun to use new brain-imaging technologies in an effort to identify the neural circuits that are affected by meditation (Newberg et al., 2001). Among other things, Newberg and his colleagues found increased activity in the prefrontal cortex during meditation, which they suggested reflected the "active process" of meditation in which the individuals willfully and intentionally concentrate on their meditation (p. 120). In general, the results of research employing brain-imaging techniques such as PET and fMRI scans are extremely complicated, in part because different approaches to meditation appear to produce different patterns of change in brain activity, but the changes observed seem unlikely to be due to simple relaxation effects (Lutz, Dunne, & Davidson, 2007).

Long-Term Benefits

What about the long-term benefits that have been claimed for meditation? Research suggests that meditation may have some value in reducing the effects of stress (Grossman, 2004; Salmon et al, 2004). In particular, regular meditation is associated with lower levels of some "stress hormones" (Infante et al., 2001) and enhanced immune response (Davidson et al., 2003a). Research also suggests that meditation can improve mental health while reducing anxiety and drug abuse (Alexander et al., 1994). Other studies report that meditation may have beneficial effects on blood pressure (Barnes, Treiber, & Davis, 2001), self-esteem (Emavardhana & Tori, 1997), mood and one's sense of control (Easterlin & Cardena, 1999), happiness (W. P. Smith, Compton, & West, 1995), cardiovascular health (Walton et al., 2004), patterns of sleep (Pattanshetty et al., 2010), and overall physical health and well-being (Reibel et al., 2001). One recent study even reported that regular meditation led to increased creativity and intelligence in a sample of high school students (So & Orme-Johnson, 2001). Finally, although more difficult to measure, some theorists assert that meditation can enhance human potential by improving focus, heightening awareness, building emotional resilience, and fostering moral maturity (Walth & Shapiro, 2006).

At first glance, these results are profoundly impressive, but they need to be viewed with some caution. At least some of these effects may be just as attainable through systematic relaxation or other mental focusing procedures (Shapiro, 1984; J. C. Smith, 1975).

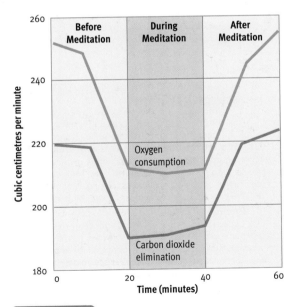

FIGURE 5.15

The suppression of physiological arousal during transcendental meditation.

The physiological changes shown in the graph are evidence of physical relaxation during the meditative state. However, critics argue that similar changes may also be produced by systematic relaxation procedures.

Source: Adapted from Wallace, R.K., and Benson, H. (1972, February). The physiology of meditation. *Scientific American, 226,* 85–90. Graphic redrawn from illustration on p. 86 by Lorelle A. Raboni. Copyright © 1972 by Scientific American, Inc.

Critics also wonder whether placebo effects, sampling bias, and other methodological problems may contribute to some of the reported benefits of meditation (Bishop, 2002; Canter, 2003; Caspi & Burleson, 2005). That said, the quality of meditation research appears to be improving and recent years have brought some eye-opening findings.

For example, a number of recent experiments have demonstrated that meditation can increase the tolerance of pain, which could have important implications for the management of a variety of health problems (Grant & Rainville, 2009; Grant et al., 2010; Zeidan et al., 2010). Grant and Rainville (2009) compared the pain sensitivity of 13 experienced Zen meditators and 13 comparable nonmeditators. Carefully controlled pain was administered by applying a heating plate to participants' calves. The meditators were able to handle considerably more pain than the nonmeditators. Moreover, a follow-up study suggested that the meditators' greater pain tolerance was associated with increased thickness in brain regions that register pain (Grant et al., 2010). In other words, it appeared that meditation experience had produced

enduring alterations in brain structure that were responsible for meditators' increased pain tolerance. Other recent studies have also reported evidence that suggests that meditation may have the potential to modify brain structure. For instance, Luders et al. (2009) examined experienced meditators and found that they had significantly more grey matter (than control subjects) in several regions of the brain. Clearly, a great deal of additional research is needed, but these are impressive, thought-provoking findings that would seem to undermine the idea that meditation is nothing more than relaxation.

Famed Miami Dolphin running back Ricky Williams used to turn to illegal drugs to relieve his stress and discomfort. These days he is an important advocate for and practitioner of meditation to relieve the stress and pain that accompanies his life as a professional athlete. He advocates the benefits of mediation for everyone and each week leads classes in the Miami area for anyone who wants to attend.

Ronald C. Modra/Sports Imagery/Getty Images

concept check 5.2

Relating EEG Activity to Variations in Consciousness

Early in the chapter we emphasized the intimate relationship between brain activity and variations in consciousness. Check your understanding of this relationship by indicating the kind of EEG activity (alpha, beta, theta, or delta) that would probably be dominant in each of the following situations. The answers are in Appendix A.

B	1.	You are playing a video game.
A	2.	You are deep in meditation.
T	3.	You have just fallen asleep.
D	4.	You are sleepwalking across the lawn.
B	5.	You are in the midst of a terrible nightmare.

REVIEW OF KEY POINTS

▷ Hypnosis has had a long and curious history since the era of mesmerism in the 18th century. Hypnotic susceptibility is a stable trait. It is only weakly correlated with personality, but highly hypnotizable people tend to score somewhat higher than others in absorption and imaginativeness. Hypnosis can produce anesthesia, sensory distortions, disinhibition, and posthypnotic amnesia.

▷ One approach to hypnosis, the social cognitive approach, views it as a normal state of consciousness in which subjects assume a hypnotic role. Another approach asserts that hypnosis leads to an altered state in which consciousness is split into two streams of awareness.

▷ *Meditation* refers to a family of practices that train attention to heighten awareness and bring mental processes under greater voluntary control. Evidence suggests that meditation leads to a potentially beneficial physiological state characterized by suppression of bodily arousal. However, some experts suggest that the benefits of meditation are not unique to meditation and are a product of any effective relaxation procedure.

Altering Consciousness with Drugs

Like hypnosis and meditation, drugs are commonly used in deliberate efforts to alter consciousness. In this section, we focus on the use of drugs for nonmedical purposes, commonly referred to as "drug abuse" or "recreational drug use." Drug abuse reaches into every corner of modern society. In spite of extraordinary efforts to reduce drug abuse, it seems reasonable to conclude that widespread recreational drug use is here to stay for the foreseeable future.

As with other controversial social problems, recreational drug use often inspires more rhetoric than reason. For instance, a former president of the American Medical Association made headlines when he declared that marijuana "makes a man of 35 sexually like a man of 70." In reality, the research findings do not support this assertion. This influential physician later retracted his statement, admitting that he had made it simply to campaign against marijuana use (Leavitt, 1995). Unfortunately, such scare tactics can backfire by undermining the credibility of drug education efforts.

Recreational drug use involves personal, moral, political, and legal issues that are not matters for science to resolve. However, the more knowledgeable you are about drugs, the more informed your decisions and opinions about them will be. Accordingly, this section describes the types of drugs that are most commonly used for recreational purposes and summarizes their effects on consciousness, behaviour, and health.

Principal Abused Drugs and Their Effects

 4c

The drugs that people use recreationally are *psychoactive*. *Psychoactive drugs* are chemical substances that modify mental, emotional, or behavioural functioning. Not all psychoactive drugs produce effects that lead to recreational use. Generally, people prefer drugs that elevate their mood or produce other pleasurable alterations in consciousness.

A 2004 survey on addictions, the *Canadian Addiction Survey* (CAS) by Health Canada and the Canadian Centre of Substance Abuse (CCSA), identified the prevalence and use of various drugs. For example, while 79 percent of those surveyed indicated that they drank alcohol over the past year, only 14 percent indicated they had used cannabis. Of those surveyed and who drank alcohol in the past year, 17 percent were considered to be high-risk drinkers. High-risk drinking is more characteristic of men than women: 8.9 percent of women and 25 percent of men were considered to be high-risk drinkers. As we know, of course, heavy drinking is not without it risks, both for the drinker and for those around him or her. This fact is highlighted in the survey by the finding that 32.7 percent of the respondents reported having been harmed in some way because of the drinking of someone else.

More recent research released by Health Canada (2010) supplements the 2004 data by indicating to us what has happened to Canadians' drug use from 2004 to 2009. While the reported use of cannabis by 15- to 24-year-olds in Canada decreased (37 percent to 26.3 percent) from 2004 to 2009, the use of cocaine or crack (1.2 percent), ecstasy (0.9 percent), speed (0.4 percent), and hallucinogens (0.7 percent) remained unchanged. Drug use by this age group, 15- to 24-year-olds, is significantly higher than for those over 25 years of age. Three-quarters of Canadian youth report using alcohol and the prevalence of frequent drinking in youth aged 15 to 24 is three times higher than that of Canadians over age 25.

Alcohol abuse continues to be a critical social concern, even reaching into arenas of major sporting events. A recent study by Darin Erikson at the University of Minnesota shows that 8 percent of fans leaving major sporting events are legally intoxicated (Erikson, 2011) and that this is especially true of younger (under 35) fans. Increased binge drinking among youth is also of concern. Binge drinking is typically defined as five or more drinks in a single session (Courtney & Polich, 2009). A recent survey of American underage drinkers revealed that 19 percent were binge drinkers, with the levels reaching 44 percent in university and college students (Wechsler et al., 1994). Research by the Centre for Addiction and Mental Health suggested that 32 percent of Canadian undergraduates drink at dangerous levels (Adlaf, Demers, & Gliksman, 2005). Given that binge drinking has been shown to have negative cognitive effects (e.g., frontal lobe and working memory deficits), physiological effects (specific neural deficits), and alcohol withdrawal effects (Courtney & Polich, 2009), this topic will likely remain of interest to investigators and policymakers alike.

The principal types of recreational drugs are described in Table 5.3. The table lists representative drugs in each of six categories. It also summarizes how the drugs are taken, their medical uses, their effects on consciousness, and their common side

PREVIEW QUESTIONS

▶ What are the principal categories of abused drugs, and what are their main effects?

▶ What kinds of factors influence drug experiences?

▶ Where do drugs exert their effects in the brain?

▶ What is the difference between physical and psychological dependence?

▶ What are the three ways in which abused drugs can harm health?

▶ What are the health risks associated with the use of marijuana and MDMA?

TABLE 5.3

Psychoactive Drugs: Methods of Ingestion, Medical Uses, and Effects

Drugs	Methods of Ingestion	Principal Medical Uses	Desired Effects	Potential Short-Term Side Effects
Narcotics (opiates) Morphine Heroin	Injected, smoked, oral	Pain relief	Euphoria, relaxation anxiety reduction, pain relief	Lethargy, drowsiness, nausea, impaired coordination, impaired mental functioning, constipation
Sedatives Barbiturates, (e.g., Seconal) Nonbarbiturates (e.g., Quaalude)	Oral, injected	Sleeping pill, anticonvulsant	Euphoria, relaxation, anxiety reduction, reduced inhibitions	Lethargy, drowsiness, severely impaired coordination, impaired mental functioning, emotional swings, dejection
Stimulants Amphetamines Cocaine	Oral, sniffed, injected, freebased, smoked	Treatment of hyperactivity and narcolepsy, local anesthetic (cocaine only)	Elation, excitement, increased alertness, increased energy, reduced fatigue	Increased blood pressure and heart rate, increased talkativeness, restlessness, irritability, insomnia, reduced appetite, increased sweating and urination, anxiety, paranoia, increased aggressiveness, panic
Hallucinogens LSD Mescaline Psilocybin	Oral	None	Increased sensory awareness, euphoria, altered perceptions, hallucinations, insightful experiences	Dilated pupils, nausea, emotional swings, paranoia, jumbled thought processes, impaired judgment, anxiety, panic reaction
Cannabis Marijuana Hashish THC	Smoked, oral	Treatment of glaucoma and chemotherapy-induced nausea and vomiting; other uses under study	Mild euphoria, relaxation, altered perceptions, enhanced awareness	Bloodshot eyes, elevated heart rate, dry mouth, reduced short-term memory, sluggish motor coordination, sluggish mental functioning, anxiety
Alcohol	Drinking	None	Mild euphoria, relaxation, anxiety reduction, reduced inhibitions	Severely impaired coordination, impaired mental functioning, increased urination, emotional swings, depression, quarrelsomeness, hangover

effects (based on Julien, Advokat, & Comaty, 2008; Levinthal, 2002; Lowinson et al., 2005). The six categories of psychoactive drugs that we will focus on are narcotics, sedatives, stimulants, hallucinogens, cannabis, and alcohol. We will also discuss one specific drug that is not listed in the table (because it does not fit into traditional drug categories) but that cannot be ignored in light of its escalating popularity: MDMA, better known as "ecstasy."

Narcotics, or *opiates*, are drugs derived from opium that are capable of relieving pain. The main drugs in this category are heroin and morphine, although less potent opiates such as codeine, Demerol, and methadone are also abused. The emerging problem in this category is a new drug called oxycodone (trade name: OxyContin). Its time-release format was supposed to make it an effective analgesic with less potential for abuse than the other opiates (Cicero, Inciardi, & Munoz, 2005). But people quickly learned that they could grind it up and gain a powerful high. This has led to a new epidemic of serious drug abuse, especially in rural areas (Tunnell, 2005). The opiate drugs can produce an overwhelming sense of euphoria or well-being. This euphoric effect has a relaxing "Who cares?" quality that makes the high an attractive escape from reality.

Common side effects include lethargy, nausea, and impaired mental and motor functioning.

Sedatives are sleep-inducing drugs that tend to decrease central nervous system (CNS) activation and behavioural activity. People abusing sedatives, or "downers," generally consume larger doses than are prescribed for medical purposes. The desired effect is a euphoria similar to that produced by drinking large amounts of alcohol. Feelings of tension or dejection are replaced by a relaxed, pleasant state of intoxication, accompanied by loosened inhibitions. Prominent side effects include drowsiness, unpredictable emotional swings, and severe impairments in motor coordination and mental functioning.

Stimulants are drugs that tend to increase central nervous system activation and behavioural activity. Stimulants range from mild, widely available drugs such as caffeine and nicotine, to stronger, carefully regulated ones such as cocaine. We will focus on cocaine and amphetamines. Cocaine is a natural substance that comes from the coca shrub. In contrast, amphetamines are synthesized in a pharmaceutical laboratory. Cocaine and amphetamines have fairly similar effects, except that cocaine produces a briefer high. Stimulants produce a euphoria very different from that created by narcotics or sedatives. They produce a buoyant, elated, energetic "I can conquer the world!" feeling accompanied by increased alertness. In recent years, cocaine and amphetamines have become available in much more potent (and dangerous) forms than before. "Freebasing" is a chemical treatment used to extract nearly pure cocaine from ordinary street cocaine. "Crack" is the most widely distributed by-product of this process, consisting of chips of pure cocaine that are usually smoked. Amphetamines are increasingly sold as a crystalline powder, called "crank," that can be snorted or injected intravenously. Drug dealers are also beginning to market a smokable form of methamphetamine called "ice" or "crystal meth." In Canada, 605 of the drug labs that were raided by the RCMP in 2005 were involved in the production of crystal meth (Dark Crystal, 2005). Side effects of stimulants vary with dosage and potency but may include restlessness, anxiety, paranoia, and insomnia.

Hallucinogens are a diverse group of drugs that have powerful effects on mental and emotional functioning, marked most prominently by distortions in sensory and perceptual experience. The principal hallucinogens are LSD (lysergic acid diethylamide), mescaline, and psilocybin. These drugs have similar effects, although they vary in potency. Hallucinogens produce euphoria, increased sensory awareness, and a distorted sense of time. In some users, they lead to profound, dreamlike, "mystical" feelings that are difficult to describe. The latter effect is why they have been used in religious ceremonies for centuries in some cultures and why they were adopted by members of the counterculture in the 1960s.

In the fall of 1960 a group of academics centred at Harvard University began a psychedelic research project focused on the use of LSD for personal growth and development. This group included Timothy Leary, a Harvard professor, personality, and clinical psychologist (e.g., Leary, 1957); Huston Smith, a professor of philosophy at the Massachusetts Institute of Technology; Richard Alpert, another Harvard psychology professor (who later changed his name to Ram Dass); and Dr. Andrew Weil, who is well known now as an advocate of holistic medicine (Greenfield, 2006; Higgs, 2006; Lattin, 2010). Leary, the best known of the group, began his experiences with psilocybin, popularizing it and LSD as routes to enlightenment to the counterculture in the 1960s and as a possible tool for use in psychotherapy. He declared that people should "turn on, tune in, and drop out." He was eventually dismissed by Harvard University and was labelled by U.S. President Nixon as the "most dangerous man in America" (Mansnerus,

1996). Interestingly, research on the potential uses of psychedelics has a Canadian connection, as it was used for such purposes both in Saskatchewan (Dyck, 2008) and Ontario (Rice & Harris, 1993). Because of poor outcomes and social pressure, among other issues, these programs were discontinued. Also playing a role in this diminished enthusiasm were the negative and highly disturbing effects that these drugs often had on users. While some users experienced "euphoria," at the other end of the emotional spectrum, hallucinogens also produced nightmarish feelings of anxiety and paranoia, commonly called a "bad trip." Other side effects include impaired judgment and jumbled thought processes.

Cannabis is the hemp plant from which marijuana, hashish, and THC are derived. Marijuana is a mixture of dried leaves, flowers, stems, and seeds taken from the plant. Hashish comes from the plant's resin. Smoking is the usual route of ingestion for both marijuana and hashish. THC, the active chemical ingredient in cannabis, can be synthesized for research purposes (for example, to give to animals, who can't very well smoke marijuana). When smoked, cannabis has an immediate impact that may last several hours. The desired effects of the drug are a mild, relaxed euphoria and enhanced sensory awareness. Unintended effects may include anxiety, sluggish mental functioning, and impaired memory.

Alcohol encompasses a variety of beverages containing ethyl alcohol, such as beers, wines, and distilled spirits. The concentration of ethyl alcohol varies from about 4 percent in most beers to 40 percent in 80-proof liquor—and occasionally more in higher-proof liquors. When people drink heavily, the central effect is a relaxed euphoria that temporarily boosts self-esteem, as problems seem to melt away and inhibitions diminish. Common side effects include severe impairment in mental and motor functioning, mood swings, and quarrelsomeness. Alcohol is the most widely used recreational drug in

Overindulging in alcohol is particularly widespread among university students.

WEB LINK 5.8

Web of Addictions

From the earliest days of the World Wide Web, this page at *The Well* has been regularly recognized as a primary source of accurate and responsible information about alcohol and other drugs.

Variations in Consciousness

our society. Because alcohol is legal, many people use it casually, without even thinking of it as a drug.

MDMA ("ecstasy") is a compound drug related to both amphetamines and hallucinogens, especially mescaline. MDMA was originally formulated in 1912 but was not widely used in North America until the 1990s, when it became popular in the context of raves and dance clubs. MDMA produces a short-lived high that typically lasts a few hours or more. Users report that they feel warm, friendly, euphoric, sensual, insightful, and empathetic, but alert and energetic. Problematic side effects include increased blood pressure, muscle tension, sweating, blurred vision, insomnia, and transient anxiety.

Factors Influencing Drug Effects

The drug effects summarized in Table 5.3 (see page 232) are the *typical* ones. Drug effects can vary from person to person and even for the same person in different situations. The frequency of use and quantity consumed often play a role. Phenomena such as "binge drinking" seem to be on the rise. At the Hospital for Sick Children in Toronto, for example, the number of young adolescents seen for excessive drinking tripled from 2000 to 2004 (Lawson, 2005). The impact of any drug depends in part on the user's age, mood, motivation, personality, previous experience with the drug, body weight, and physiology. The dose and potency of a drug, the method of administration, and the setting in which a drug is taken also influence its effects (Leavitt, 1995). Our theme of *multifactorial causation* clearly applies to the effects of drugs.

So, too, does our theme emphasizing the *subjectivity of experience*. Expectations are potentially powerful factors that can influence the user's perceptions of a drug's effects. You may recall from our discussion of placebo effects in Chapter 2 that some people who are misled to *think* that they are drinking alcohol actually show signs of intoxication (Wilson, 1982). If people *expect* a drug to make them feel giddy, serene, or profound, their expectation may contribute to the feelings they experience.

A drug's effects can also change as the person's body develops a tolerance for the chemical as a result of continued use. *Tolerance* refers to a progressive decrease in a person's responsiveness to a drug. Tolerance usually leads people to consume larger and larger doses of a drug to attain the effects they desire. Most drugs produce tolerance effects, but some do so more rapidly than others. For example, tolerance to alcohol usually builds slowly, while tolerance to heroin increases much more quickly. Table 5.4 indicates whether various categories of drugs tend to produce tolerance rapidly or gradually.

Mechanisms of Drug Action 4d

Most drugs have effects that reverberate throughout the body. However, psychoactive drugs work primarily by altering neurotransmitter activity in the brain. As we discussed in Chapter 3, neurotransmitters are chemicals that transmit information between neurons at junctions called *synapses*.

The actions of amphetamines and cocaine illustrate how drugs have selective, multiple effects on neurotransmitter activity (see Figure 5.16). Amphetamines exert their main effects on two of the monoamine neurotransmitters: norepinephrine (NE) and dopamine (DA). Indeed, the name *amphetamines* reflects the kinship between these drugs and the *monoamines*. Amphetamines mainly increase the

TABLE 5.4

Psychoactive Drugs: Tolerance, Dependence, Potential for Fatal Overdose, and Health Risks

Drugs	Tolerance	Risk of Physical Dependence	Risk of Psychological Dependence	Fatal Overdose Potential	Health Risks
Narcotics (opiates)	Rapid	High	High	High	Infectious diseases, accidents, immune suppression
Sedatives	Rapid	High	High	High	Accidents
Stimulants	Rapid	Moderate	High	Moderate to high	Sleep problems, malnutrition, nasal damage, hypertension, respiratory disease, stroke, liver disease, heart attack
Hallucinogens	Gradual	None	Very low	Very low	Accidents
Cannabis	Gradual	None	Low to moderate	Very low	Accidents, lung cancer, respiratory disease, pulmonary disease
Alcohol	Gradual	Moderate	Moderate	Low to high	Accidents, liver disease, malnutrition, brain damage, neurological disorders, heart disease, stroke, hypertension, ulcers, cancer, birth defects

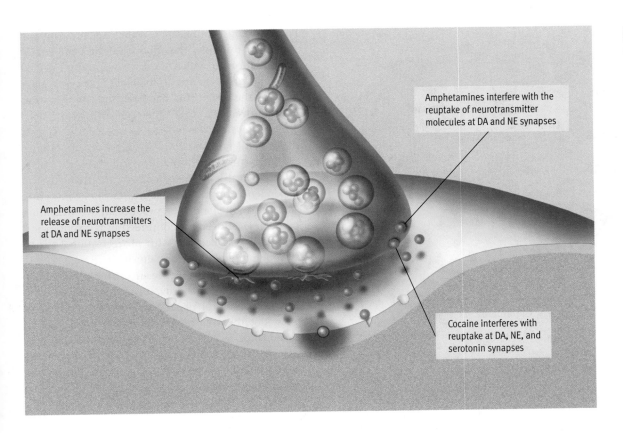

FIGURE 5.16

Stimulant drugs and neurotransmitter activity.

Like other psychoactive drugs, amphetamines and cocaine alter neurotransmitter activity at specific synapses. Amphetamines primarily increase the release of dopamine (DA) and norepinephrine (NE) and secondarily inhibit the reuptake of these neurotransmitters. Cocaine slows the reuptake process at DA, NE, and serotonin synapses. The psychological and behavioural effects of the drugs have largely been attributed to their impact on dopamine circuits.

Amphetamines interfere with the reuptake of neurotransmitter molecules at DA and NE synapses

Amphetamines increase the release of neurotransmitters at DA and NE synapses

Cocaine interferes with reuptake at DA, NE, and serotonin synapses

release of DA and NE by presynaptic neurons. They also interfere with the reuptake of DA and NE from synaptic clefts (Koob & Le Moal, 2006). These actions serve to increase the levels of dopamine and norepinephrine at the affected synapses. Cocaine shares some of these actions, which is why cocaine and amphetamines produce similar stimulant effects. Cocaine mainly blocks reuptake at DA, NE, and serotonin synapses. For both amphetamines and cocaine, elevated activity in certain *dopamine circuits* is believed to be crucial to the drugs' pleasurable, rewarding effects (Volkow et al., 2004).

The discovery of endorphins (the body's internally produced opiate-like chemicals) has led to new insights about the actions of opiate drugs (see Chapter 3). These drugs apparently bind to specific subtypes of endorphin receptors, and their actions at these receptor sites indirectly elevate activity in the dopamine pathways that modulate reward (Cami & Farre, 2003). In the 1990s, scientists discovered two types of receptors in the brain for THC, the active chemical ingredient in marijuana, which are called *cannabinoid receptors* (Stephens, 1999). Soon after, they found two internally produced chemicals similar to THC—christened *endocannabinoids*—that activate these receptors and thereby influence activity at GABA and glutamate synapses (Julien et al., 2008). It appears that THC from marijuana "hijacks" the brain's cannabinoid receptors (Piomelli, 2004),

eventually leading to increased release of endorphins and activation of the dopamine circuits associated with reward (Solinas et al., 2003, 2006).

Although specific drugs exert their initial effects in the brain on a wide variety of neurotransmitter systems, many theorists believe that virtually all abused drugs eventually increase activity in a particular neural pathway, called the *mesolimbic dopamine pathway* (Nestler & Malenka, 2004). This neural circuit, which runs from an area in the midbrain through the *nucleus accumbens* and on to the prefrontal cortex (see Figure 5.17), has been characterized as a "reward pathway" (Pierce & Kumaresan, 2006). Large and rapid increases in the release of dopamine along this pathway are thought to be the neural basis of the reinforcing effects of most abused drugs (Knapp & Kornetsky, 2009; Volkow, Fowler, & Wang, 2004).

Drug Dependence   4c

People can become either physically or psychologically dependent on a drug. Physical dependence is a common problem with narcotics, sedatives, alcohol, and stimulants. *Physical dependence* exists when a person must continue to take a drug to avoid withdrawal illness. The symptoms of withdrawal illness depend on the specific drug. Withdrawal from heroin, barbiturates, and alcohol can produce fever,

WEB LINK 5.9

National Institute on Alcohol Abuse and Alcoholism
Just two of the many research sources here are the entire collection of the bulletin *Alcohol Alert,* issued since 1988 on specific topics related to alcoholism, and the ETOH Database, a searchable repository of more than 100 000 records on alcoholism and alcohol abuse.

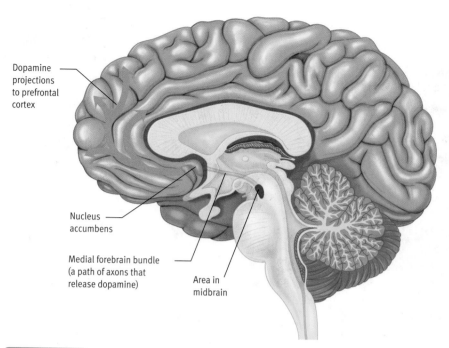

Dopamine
projections
to prefrontal
cortex

Nucleus
accumbens

Medial forebrain bundle
(a path of axons that
release dopamine)

Area in
midbrain

FIGURE 5.17

The "reward pathway" in the brain.

The neural circuits shown here in purple make up the *mesolimbic dopamine pathway*. Axons in this pathway run from an area in the midbrain through the medial forebrain bundle to the *nucleus accumbens* and on to the prefrontal cortex. Recreational drugs affect a variety of neurotransmitter systems, but theorists believe that heightened dopamine activity in this pathway—especially the portion running from the midbrain to the nucleus accumbens—is responsible for the reinforcing effects of most abused drugs.

Source: Adapted from Kalat, J.W. (2001). *Biological psychology*. Belmont, CA: Wadsworth. Reprinted by permission.

chills, tremors, convulsions, vomiting, cramps, diarrhea, and severe aches and pains. Withdrawal from stimulants can lead to a more subtle syndrome, marked by fatigue, apathy, irritability, depression, and feelings of disorientation.

McMaster University psychologist Shepard Siegel has found that some of the withdrawal symptoms experienced by addicts are conditioned responses that are elicited by stimuli that have been paired with the drug in the past (McDonald & Siegel, 2004; Siegel, 2002). According to McDonald and Siegel, "Cues accompanying the drug effect function as conditional stimuli (CSs), and the direct drug effect constitutes the unconditional stimulus (US)" (p. 3). This means when addicts are presented with cues typically associated with drug injections in the past, they may experience withdrawal symptoms. Thus, if an addict always injects in a particular room, entering the room itself may produce withdrawal symptoms. You will learn more about the process of classical conditioning and about conditioned responses in Chapter 6. In general, classical conditioning is a type of learning in which a stimulus has acquired the capacity to evoke a response that was originally evoked by another stimulus. According to Siegel (2002),

conditioning is implicated in dependency in many ways. For example, the situational cues present in the situation in which a drug is typically injected may contribute to the individual's increased tolerance of the drug. This has been termed the "situational specificity of tolerance" (Siegel, 1976).

Psychological dependence exists when a person must continue to take a drug to satisfy intense mental and emotional craving for the drug. Psychological dependence is more subtle than physical dependence, but the need it creates can be powerful. Cocaine, for instance, can produce an overwhelming psychological need for continued use. Psychological dependence is possible with all recreational drugs, although it seems rare for hallucinogens.

Both types of dependence are established gradually with repeated use of a drug. It was originally assumed that only physical dependence has a physiological basis, but theorists now believe that both types of dependence reflect alterations in synaptic transmission (Di Chiara, 1999; Self, 1997). Dysregulation in the mesolimbic dopamine pathway appears to be the chief factor underlying drug craving and addiction (Nestler & Malenka, 2004). Drugs vary in their potential for creating either physical or psychological dependence. Table 5.4 (page 234) provides estimates of the risk of each kind of dependence for the six categories of recreational drugs covered in our discussion.

Drugs and Health

In humans, recreational drug use can affect health in a variety of ways. The three principal ways are by triggering an overdose, by producing various types of physiological damage (direct effects), and by causing health-impairing behaviour (indirect effects).

Overdose

Any drug can be fatal if a person takes enough of it, but some drugs are much more dangerous than others. Table 5.4 shows estimates of the risk of accidentally consuming a lethal overdose of each listed drug. Drugs that are CNS depressants—sedatives, narcotics, and alcohol—carry the greatest risk of overdose. It's important to remember that these drugs are synergistic with each other, so many overdoses involve lethal *combinations* of CNS depressants. What happens when a person overdoses on these drugs? The respiratory system usually grinds to a halt, producing coma, brain damage, and death within a brief period.

Fatal overdoses with CNS stimulants usually involve a heart attack, stroke, or cortical seizure. Deaths due to overdoses of stimulant drugs used to be relatively infrequent, but cocaine overdoses have increased sharply as more people have experimented with freebasing, smoking crack, and other more dangerous modes of ingestion (Repetto & Gold, 2005).

Direct Effects

In some cases, drugs cause tissue damage directly. For example, snorting cocaine can damage nasal membranes. Cocaine can also alter cardiovascular functioning in ways that increase the risk of heart attack and stroke, and crack smoking is associated with a host of respiratory problems (Gold & Jacobs, 2005; Gourevitch & Arnsten, 2005). Long-term, excessive alcohol consumption is associated with an elevated risk for a wide range of serious health problems, including liver damage, ulcers, hypertension, stroke, heart disease, neurological disorders, and some types of cancer (Johnson & Ait-Daoud, 2005; Mack, Franklin, & Frances, 2003).

Indirect Effects

The negative effects of drugs on physical health are often indirect results of the drugs' impact on attitudes, intentions, and behaviour. For instance, people using stimulants tend not to eat or sleep properly. Sedatives increase the risk of accidental injuries because they severely impair motor coordination. People who abuse downers often trip down stairs, fall off stools, and suffer other mishaps. Tara MacDonald of Queen's University, in a series of studies, has found that alcohol can affect students' intentions to engage in risky sexual behaviour, including unprotected sex (Ebel-Lam, MacDonald, Zanna, & Fong, 2009; Klein, Geaghan, & MacDonald, 2007; MacDonald & Hynie, 2008; MacDonald, Fong, et al., 2000). For example, intoxicated students who were sexually aroused reported more favourable intentions toward having unprotected sex.

According to University of Waterloo researchers (G. MacDonald, Zanna, & Holmes, 2000), alcohol can also play a causal role in relationship conflict, a result that mirrors some of the harm results reported in the *Canadian Abuse Survey*. That survey also suggested that physical abuse was frequently associated with alcohol intoxication. Of course, not everyone who becomes intoxicated becomes violent. According to McGill psychologist Robert Pihl and his colleagues (Pihl, Assaad, & Hoaken, 2003), certain types of people are more at risk for intoxicated aggression than are other types of people (Assaad et al., 2006).

Many drugs impair driving ability, increasing the risk of automobile accidents. Alcohol, for instance, may contribute to roughly 40 percent of all automobile fatalities (Liu et al., 1997). Intravenous drug users risk contracting infectious diseases that can be spread by unsterilized needles. In recent years, acquired immune deficiency syndrome (AIDS) has been transmitted at an alarming rate through the population of intravenous drug users (Des Jarlais, Hagan, & Friedman, 2005).

The major health risks (other than overdose) of various recreational drugs are listed in the sixth column of Table 5.4. As you can see, alcohol appears to have the most diverse negative effects on physical health. The irony, of course, is that alcohol is the only recreational drug listed that is legal.

Controversies Concerning Marijuana

The possible health risks associated with marijuana use have generated considerable debate in recent years. The preponderance of evidence suggests that heavy use of marijuana *probably* increases the risk for respiratory and pulmonary disease, including lung cancer (Aldington et al., 2007; Tashkin et al., 2002). Although cannabis impairs driving less than alcohol intoxication, there's convincing evidence that marijuana increases the risk of automobile accidents if users drive while high (Richer & Bergeron, 2009). The combination of cannabis and alcohol may be particularly dangerous (Sewell, Poling, & Sofuoglu, 2009). People under the influence of marijuana alone tend to appreciate their impairment and try to compensate for being high (by driving more slowly, for instance), but alcohol suppresses these compensatory strategies and increases risk taking (Hall & Degenhardt, 2009). Finally, a rash of recent studies have reported an unexpected link between cannabis use and severe psychotic disorders, including schizophrenia (Barrigon et al., 2010; DiForti et al., 2007). Obviously, the vast majority of marijuana users do not develop psychoses, but it appears that cannabis may trigger psychotic illness in individuals who have a genetic vulnerability to such disorders (Degenhardt et al., 2009; D'Souza, 2007). These dangers are listed in Table 5.4. Some other widely publicized dangers are omitted because the findings on these other risks have been exaggerated or remain debatable. Here is a brief overview of the evidence on some of these debates:

- *Does marijuana reduce one's immune response?* Research with animals clearly demonstrates that cannabis can suppress various aspects of immune system response (Cabral & Pettit, 1998). However, infectious diseases do not appear to be more common among marijuana smokers than among nonsmokers. Thus, it is unclear whether marijuana increases susceptibility to infectious diseases in humans (Bredt et al., 2002; Hall & Degenhardt, 2009).

- *Does marijuana lead to impotence and sterility in men?* In animal research, cannabis temporarily decreases testosterone levels and sperm production (Brown & Dobs, 2002). Citing these findings, the popular media have frequently implied that marijuana is likely to make men sterile and impotent. However, research with humans has yielded weak, inconsistent, and reversible effects on testosterone and sperm levels (Brown & Dobs, 2002). At present, the evidence suggests that marijuana has little lasting impact on male smokers' fertility or sexual functioning (Grinspoon, Bakalar, & Russo, 2005).

- *Does marijuana have long-term negative effects on cognitive functioning?* Until relatively recently, studies had failed to find any durable cognitive deficits attributable to cannabis use. However, a flood of studies in the last decade using more elaborate and precise assessments of cognitive functioning *have* found an association between chronic, heavy marijuana use and measurable impairments in attention, learning, and memory that show up when users are not high (Hanson et al., 2010; Medina et al., 2007; Solowij et al., 2002). That said, the cognitive deficits that have been observed are modest and certainly not disabling. And some research suggests that the deficits may disappear after three to four weeks of marijuana abstinence (Hanson et al., 2010; Pope et al., 2001). Although more research is needed, the recent studies in this area provide some cause for concern.

New Findings Regarding Ecstasy

Like marijuana, ecstasy is viewed as a harmless drug in some quarters, but accumulating empirical evidence is beginning to alter that perception. Research on MDMA is in its infancy, so conclusions about its risks must be tentative. MDMA does not appear to be especially addictive, but psychological dependence clearly can become a problem for some people. MDMA has been implicated in cases of stroke and heart attack, seizures, heat stroke, and liver damage, but its exact contribution is hard to gauge, given all the other drugs that MDMA users typically consume and the fact that ecstasy often contains contaminants (Grob & Poland, 2005; Scholey et al., 2004). Heavy use of ecstasy appears to be associated with sleep disorders, depression, and elevated anxiety and hostility (Fisk, Montomery, & Murphy, 2009; Morgan, 2000). Moreover, studies of former MDMA users suggest that ecstasy may have subtle, long-term effects on cognitive functioning (Parrott, 2000). Quite a few studies have found memory deficits in former users (Hadjiefthyvoulou et al., 2010; Laws & Kokkalis, 2007). Other studies have found decreased performance on laboratory tasks requiring attention and learning (Murphy et al., 2009).

Thus, although a great deal of additional research is needed, the preliminary evidence suggests that MDMA may be more harmful than widely assumed. According to media reports (Sallot, 2005), Canada appears to be playing a major role in ecstasy production. While Canada used to be just a transit point for some of the ingredients, it appears that more labs are now being set up to produce it. In fact, the increased production in Canada has become a problem for the U.S. government, which has targeted this issue as an emerging threat (Sallot, 2005). Of particular concern recently has been the flood of ecstasy pills that are "laced" with crystal meth. This specific combination of drugs is seen to be particularly harmful and potentially life-threatening, especially if it is consumed along with alcohol (Battagello, 2008).

Putting It in Perspective: Themes 2, 3, 5, and 7

PREVIEW QUESTIONS

▶ How did this chapter show that psychology evolves in a sociohistorical context?

▶ How did this chapter illustrate the subjective nature of human experience?

▶ How did this chapter draw attention to the importance of cultural influences?

▶ How did this chapter highlight psychology's theoretical diversity?

This chapter highlights four of our unifying themes. First, we can see how psychology evolves in a sociohistorical context. Psychology began as the science of consciousness in the 19th century, but consciousness proved difficult to study empirically. Research on consciousness dwindled after John B. Watson and others redefined psychology as the science of behaviour. However, in the 1960s, people began to turn inward, showing a new interest in altering consciousness through drug use, meditation, hypnosis, and biofeedback. Psychologists responded to these social trends by beginning to study variations in consciousness in earnest. This renewed interest in consciousness shows how social forces can have an impact on psychology's evolution.

A second theme that predominates in this chapter is the idea that people's experience of the world is highly subjective. We encountered this theme at the start of the chapter when we mentioned the difficulty that people have describing their states of consciousness. The subjective nature of consciousness was apparent elsewhere in the chapter, as well. For instance, we found that the alterations of consciousness produced by drugs depend significantly on personal expectations.

Third, we saw once again how culture moulds some aspects of behaviour. Although the basic physiological process of sleep appears largely invariant from one society to another, culture influences certain aspects of sleep habits and has a dramatic impact on whether people remember their dreams and how they interpret and feel about their dreams.

Fourth, we learned once again that behaviour is governed by multifactor causation. For example, we discussed how the effects of jet lag, sleep deprivation, and psychoactive drugs depend on a number of interacting factors. Likewise, we saw that insomnia is rooted in a constellation of factors.

Finally, the chapter illustrates psychology's theoretical diversity. We discussed conflicting theories about dreams, hypnosis, and meditation. For the most part, we did not see these opposing theories converging toward reconciliation, as we did in the areas of sensation and perception. However, it's important to emphasize that rival theories do not always merge neatly into tidy models of behaviour. Many theoretical controversies go on indefinitely. This fact does not negate the value of theoretical diversity. While it's always nice to resolve a theoretical debate, the debate itself can advance knowledge by stimulating and guiding empirical research.

Indeed, our upcoming Personal Application demonstrates that theoretical debates need not be resolved in order to advance knowledge. Many theoretical controversies and enduring mysteries remain in the study of sleep and dreams. Nonetheless, researchers have accumulated a great deal of practical information on these topics, which we'll discuss in the next few pages.

REVIEW OF KEY POINTS

▷ The principal categories of abused drugs are narcotics, sedatives, stimulants, hallucinogens, cannabis, and alcohol. Although it's possible to describe the typical effects of various drugs, the actual effect on any individual depends on a host of factors, including subjective expectations and tolerance to the drug.

▷ Psychoactive drugs exert their main effects in the brain, where they alter neurotransmitter activity at synaptic sites in a variety of ways. For example, amphetamines increase the release of DA and NE, and like cocaine, they slow reuptake at DA and NE synapses. The mesolimbic dopamine pathway may mediate the reinforcing effects of most abused drugs.

▷ Recreational drug use can prove harmful to health by producing an overdose, by causing tissue damage, or by increasing health-impairing behaviour. The chances of accidentally consuming a lethal overdose are greatest for the CNS depressants and cocaine. Direct tissue damage occurs most frequently with alcohol and cocaine. The health risks of marijuana have generated debate. Preliminary evidence suggests that MDMA may be more dangerous than widely assumed.

▷ Four of our unifying themes were highlighted in this chapter. We saw that psychology evolves in a sociohistorical context, that experience is highly subjective, that culture influences many aspects of behaviour, and that psychology is characterized by extensive theoretical diversity.

Addressing Practical Questions about Sleep and Dreams

Indicate whether the following statements are "true" or "false."

____ **1.** Naps rarely have a refreshing effect.
____ **2.** Some people never dream.
____ **3.** When people cannot recall their dreams, it's because they are trying to repress them.
____ **4.** Only an expert in symbolism, such as a psychoanalytic therapist, can interpret the real meaning of dreams.

These assertions were all drawn from the *Sleep and Dreams Information Questionnaire* (Palladino & Carducci, 1984), which measures practical knowledge about sleep and dreams. Are they true or false? You'll see in this Application.

Common Questions about Sleep

How much sleep do people need? The average amount of daily sleep for young adults is 7.5 hours. However, there is considerable variability in how long people sleep. Based on a synthesis of data from many studies, Webb (1992b) estimates that sleep time is normally distributed as shown in Figure 5.18. Sleep needs vary some from person to person. That said, many sleep experts believe that most people would function more effectively if they increased their amount of sleep (Banks & Dinges, 2007). Bear in mind also, that research suggests that people who sleep seven to eight hours per night have the lowest mortality rates (Patel et al., 2004; Tamakoshi et al., 2004).

Can short naps be refreshing? Some naps are beneficial and some are not. The effectiveness of napping varies from person to person. Also, the benefits of any specific nap depend on the time of day and the amount of sleep one has had recently (Dinges, 1993). On the negative side, naps are not very *efficient* ways to sleep because you're often just getting into the deeper stages of sleep when your nap time is up. Naps tend to be more

beneficial when they are rich in slow-wave sleep or REM sleep (Mednick & Drummond, 2009). Another potential problem is that overly long naps or naps that occur too close to bedtime can disrupt nighttime sleep (Thorpy & Yager, 2001).

Nonetheless, many highly productive people (including Thomas Edison, Winston Churchill, and John F. Kennedy) have made effective use of naps. Naps can enhance subsequent alertness and task performance and reduce sleepiness (Ficca et al., 2010). Evidence also suggests that naps can improve learning and memory—even more so than loading up on caffeine (Mednick et al., 2008). In conclusion, naps can be refreshing for most people (so the first statement opening this Application is false), and they can pay off in the long run if they don't interfere with nighttime sleep.

How do alcohol and drugs affect sleep? Obviously, stimulants such as cocaine and amphetamines make it difficult to sleep. More surprising is the finding that most

of the CNS depressants that facilitate sleep (such as alcohol, analgesics, sedatives, and tranquilizers) actually disrupt the normal sleep cycle (Carskadon & Dement, 2005). The principal problem is that many drugs reduce the time spent in REM sleep and slow-wave sleep (Hyde, Roehrs, & Roth, 2006). Unfortunately, these are the sleep stages that appear to be most important to a refreshing night's sleep.

What is the significance of yawning and snoring? Yawning is a universal phenomenon seen in all cultural groups—not to mention other mammals, birds, fish, and reptiles (Baenninger, 1997). Contrary to popular belief, yawning *is not* a response to a buildup of carbon dioxide or a shortage of oxygen (Provine, 2005). However, as reputed, yawning *is* correlated with sleepiness and boredom (Provine, 2005). According to one theory, the principal function of yawning is to cool the brain (Gallup & Gallup, 2007). The most fascinating and perplexing facet of yawning is that

---

FIGURE 5.18

Variation in sleep needs.

Based on data from a variety of sources, Webb (1992b) estimates that average sleep length among young adults is distributed normally, as shown here. Although most young adults sleep an average of 6.5 to 8.5 hours per night, some people need less sleep and some people need more.

Source: Adapted from Webb, W.B. (1992). *Sleep, the gentle tyrant* (2nd ed.). Bolton, MA: Anker Publishing Co. Copyright © 1992 by Anker Publishing Co. Adapted by permission.

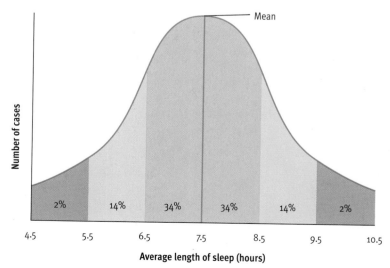

it is contagious—seeing others yawn creates a powerful urge to follow suit (Platek, Mohamed, & Gallup, 2005).

Snoring is a common phenomenon seen in roughly 30–40 percent of adults (Hoffstein, 2005). Snoring increases after age 35, occurs in men more than women, and is more frequent among people who are overweight (Kryger, 1993; Stoohs et al., 1998). Many factors, including colds, allergies, smoking, and some drugs, can contribute to snoring, mainly by forcing people to breathe through their mouths while sleeping. Some people who snore loudly disrupt their own sleep as well as that of their bed partners. It can be difficult to prevent snoring in some people, whereas others are able to reduce their snoring by simply losing weight or by sleeping on their side instead of their back (Lugaresi et al., 1994). Snoring may seem like a trivial problem, but it is associated with sleep apnea and cardiovascular disease, and it may have considerably more medical significance than most people realize (Dement & Vaughn, 1999; Olson & Park, 2006).

What can be done to avoid sleep problems? There are many ways to improve your chances of getting satisfactory sleep (see Figure 5.19). Most of them involve developing sensible daytime habits that won't interfere with sleep (see Foldvary-Schaefer, 2006; Maas, 1998; Stepanski & Wyatt, 2003; Thorpy & Yager, 2001; Zarcone, 2000). For example, if you've been having trouble sleeping at night, it's wise to avoid daytime naps so that you will be tired when bedtime arrives. Some people find that daytime exercise helps them fall asleep more readily at bedtime (King et al., 1997). Of course, the exercise should be part of a regular regimen that doesn't leave one sore or aching.

It's also a good idea to minimize consumption of stimulants such as caffeine or nicotine. Because coffee and cigarettes aren't prescription drugs, people don't appreciate how much the stimulants they contain can heighten physical arousal. Many foods (such as chocolate) and beverages (such as cola drinks) contain more caffeine than people realize. Also, bear in mind that ill-advised eating habits can interfere with sleep. Try to avoid going to bed hungry, uncomfortably stuffed, or soon after eating foods that disagree with you.

FIGURE 5.19

Suggestions for better sleep.

In his book *Power Sleep*, James Maas (1998) offers the following advice for people concerned about enhancing their sleep. Maas argues convincingly that good daytime habits can make all the difference in the world to the quality of one's sleep.

Source: From *POWER SLEEP* by James B. Maas and M. L. Wherry, copyright © 1998 by James B. Maas, Ph.D. Used by permission of Villard Books, a division of Random House, Inc.

1. Reduce stress as much as possible.
2. Exercise to stay fit.
3. Keep mentally stimulated during the day.
4. Eat a proper diet.
5. Stop smoking.
6. Reduce caffeine intake.
7. Avoid alcohol near bedtime.
8. Take a warm bath before bed.
9. Maintain a relaxing atmosphere in the bedroom.
10. Establish a bedtime ritual.
11. Have pleasurable sexual activity.
12. Clear your mind at bedtime.
13. Try some bedtime relaxation techniques.
14. Avoid trying too hard to get to sleep.
15. Learn to value sleep.

In addition to these prudent habits, two other preventive measures are worth mentioning. First, try to establish a reasonably regular bedtime. This habit will allow you to take advantage of your circadian rhythm, so you'll be trying to fall asleep when your body is primed to cooperate. Second, create a favourable environment for sleep. This advice belabours what should be obvious, but many people fail to heed it. Make sure you have a good bed that is comfortable for you. Take steps to ensure that your bedroom is quiet enough and that the humidity and temperature are to your liking.

What can be done about insomnia? First, don't panic if you run into a little trouble sleeping. An overreaction to sleep problems can begin a vicious circle of escalating problems, like that depicted in Figure 5.20. If you jump to the conclusion that you are becoming an insomniac, you may approach sleep with anxiety that will aggravate the problem. The harder you work at falling asleep, the less success you're likely to have. As noted earlier, temporary sleep problems are common and generally clear up on their own.

One sleep expert, Dianne Hales (1987), lists 101 suggestions for combating insomnia in her book *How to Sleep Like a Baby*. Many involve "boring yourself to sleep" by playing alphabet games, reciting poems, or listening to your clock. Another recommended strategy is to engage in some not-so-engaging activity. For instance, you might try reading your dullest textbook. It could turn out to be a superb sedative. Whatever you think about, try to avoid

People typically get very upset when they have difficulty falling asleep. Unfortunately, the emotional distress tends to make it even harder for people to get to sleep.

© Topham/The Image Works

cont...

FIGURE 5.20

The vicious circle of anxiety and sleep difficulty.
Anxiety about sleep difficulties leads to poorer sleep, which increases anxiety further, which in turn leads to even greater difficulties in sleeping.

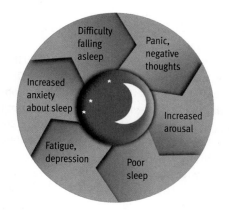

FIGURE 5.21

Thoughts and emotions associated with insomnia.
This graph depicts the percentage of insomniacs and control subjects reporting various pre-sleep feelings and thoughts. Insomniacs' tendency to ruminate about their problems contributes to their sleep difficulties.

Source: Data from Kales, A., and Kales, J.D. (1984). *Evaluation and treatment of insomnia*. New York: Oxford University Press. Copyright © 1984 by Oxford University Press. Reprinted by permission.

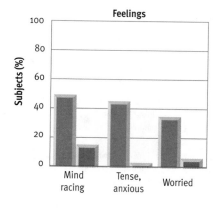 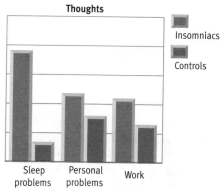

ruminating about the current stresses and problems in your life. Research has shown that the tendency to ruminate is one of the key factors contributing to insomnia (Kales et al., 1984), as the data in Figure 5.21 show.

Anything that relaxes you—whether it's music, meditation, prayer, or a warm bath—can aid you in falling asleep. Experts have also devised systematic relaxation procedures that can make these efforts more effective. You may want to learn about techniques such as *progressive relaxation* (Jacobson, 1938), *autogenic training* (Schultz & Luthe, 1959), or the *relaxation response* (Benson & Klipper, 1988). If you have to consult a professional for help, the good news is that there are a variety of nondrug interventions that have proven effective in the treatment of insomnia (Kierlin, 2008).

Common Questions about Dreams

Does everyone dream? Yes. Some people just don't *remember* their dreams. However, when these people are brought into a sleep lab and awakened from REM sleep, they report having been dreaming—much to their surprise (statement 2 at the start of this Application is false). Scientists have studied a small number of people who

have sustained brain damage in the area of the pons that has wiped out their REM sleep, but even these people report dreams (Klosch & Kraft, 2005).

Why don't some people remember their dreams? The evaporation of dreams appears to be quite normal. Most dreams are lost forever unless people wake up during or just after a dream. Even then, dream recall fades quickly (Nir & Tononi, 2009). Most of the time, people who *do* recall dreams upon waking are remembering either their *last* dream from their final REM period or a dream that awakened them earlier in the night. Hobson's (1989) educated guess is that people probably forget 95–99 percent of their dreams. This forgetting is natural and is not due to repression, so statement 3 is also false. People who never remember their dreams probably have a sleep pattern that puts too much time between their last REM/dream period and awakening, so even their last dream is forgotten.

Are dreams instantaneous? No. It has long been speculated that dreams flash through consciousness almost instantaneously. According to this notion, complicated plots that would require 20 minutes to think through in waking life could bolt through the dreaming mind in a second or two. However, modern research suggests that this isn't the case (LaBerge, 2007; Weinstein, Schwartz, & Arkin, 1991).

Do dreams require interpretation? Most theorists would say yes, but interpretation may not be as difficult as generally assumed. People have long believed that dreams are symbolic and that it is necessary to interpret the symbols to understand the meaning of dreams. We saw earlier in the chapter that Freud, for instance, believed that dreams have a hidden ("latent") content that represent their true meaning. Thus, a Freudian therapist might equate sexual intercourse with such dream events as walking into a tunnel or riding a horse.

Freudian theorists assert that dream interpretation is a complicated task requiring considerable knowledge of symbolism. However, many dream theorists argue that symbolism in dreams is less deceptive and mysterious than Freud thought (Faraday, 1974; Foulkes, 1985). Calvin Hall (1979) makes the point that dreams require some interpretation simply because they are more visual than verbal. That is, pictures need to be translated into ideas. According to Hall, dream symbolism is highly personal and the dreamer may be the person best equipped to decipher a dream (statement 4 is also false). Thus, it is not unreasonable for you to try to interpret your own dreams. Unfortunately, you'll never know whether you're "correct," because there is no definitive way to judge the validity of different dream interpretations.

Frank and Ernest

BOOKSTORE
NEW RELEASE "INTERPRET YOUR DREAMS"

I DON'T NEED IT --- I DREAM IN ENGLISH.

THAVES

What is lucid dreaming? Even though we discussed this topic earlier in this chapter it is of such interest to many people that a reminder about the nature of *lucid dreaming* is in order. Generally, when people dream, they aren't aware that they're dreaming. Occasionally, however, some people experience "lucid" dreams in which they recognize that they're dreaming (LaBerge, 2007). Typically, normal dreams become lucid when people question something strange in a dream and recognize that they must be dreaming. In *lucid dreams* people can think clearly about the circumstances of waking life and the fact that they are dreaming, yet they remain asleep in the midst of a vivid dream. Perhaps the most intriguing aspect of this dual consciousness is that people can often exert some control over the events unfolding in their lucid dreams (LaBerge, 1990).

Could a shocking dream be fatal? According to folklore, if you fall from a height in a dream, you'd better wake up on the plunge downward, for if you hit the bottom, the shock to your system will be so great that you will actually die in your sleep. Think about this one for a moment. *If* it were a genuine problem, who would have reported it? You can be sure that no one has ever testified to experiencing a fatal dream. This myth presumably exists because many people do awaken during the downward plunge, thinking that they've averted a close call. A study by Barrett (1988–1989) suggests that dreams of one's own death are relatively infrequent. However, people do have such dreams—and live to tell about them.

REVIEW OF KEY POINTS

▷ Naps can prove helpful, but alcohol and many other widely used drugs have a negative effect on sleep. Yawning appears to be associated with boredom and sleepiness but is not well understood. Snoring may have more medical significance than most people realize.

▷ People can do many things to avoid or reduce sleep problems. Individuals troubled by transient insomnia should avoid panic, pursue effective relaxation, and try distracting themselves so they don't work too hard at falling asleep.

▷ Everyone dreams, but some people don't remember their dreams. Freud asserted that dreams require interpretation, but modern theorists assert that this process may not be as complicated as Freud assumed. In lucid dreams, people consciously recognize that they are dreaming and exert some control over the events in their dreams.

Is Alcoholism a Disease? The Power of Definitions

Alcoholism is a major problem in most, perhaps all, societies. As we saw in the main body of the chapter, alcohol is a dangerous drug. Alcoholism destroys countless lives, tears families apart, and is associated with an elevated risk for a host of physical maladies (Johnson & Ait-Daoud, 2005). With the huge numbers of problem drinkers in our society, it seems likely that alcoholism has touched the lives of most of us.

In almost every discussion about alcoholism, someone will ask, "Is alcoholism a disease?" If alcoholism is a disease, it is a strange one, because the alcoholic is the most direct cause of his or her own sickness. If alcoholism is *not* a disease, then what else might it be? Over the course of history, alcoholism has been categorized under many labels, from a personal weakness to a crime, a sin, a mental disorder, and a physical illness (Meyer, 1996). Each of these definitions carries important personal, social, political, and economic implications.

Consider, for instance, the consequences of characterizing alcoholism as a disease. If that is the case, then alcoholics should be treated like diabetics, heart patients, or victims of other physical illnesses. That is, they should be viewed with sympathy and should be given appropriate medical and therapeutic interventions to foster recovery from their illness. These treatments should be covered by medical insurance and delivered by health-care professionals. Just as important, if alcoholism is defined as a disease, it should lose much of its stigma. After all, we don't blame people with diabetes or heart disease for their illnesses. Yes, alcoholics admittedly contribute to their own disease (by drinking too much), but so do many victims of diabetes and heart disease, who eat the wrong foods, fail to control their weight, and so forth (McLellan et al., 2000). And, as is the case with many physical illnesses, one can inherit a genetic vulnerability to

alcoholism (Lin & Anthenelli, 2005), so it is difficult to argue that alcoholism is caused solely by one's behaviour.

However, if alcoholism is defined as a personal failure or a moral weakness, alcoholics are less likely to be viewed with sympathy and compassion. They might be admonished to quit drinking, be put in prison, or be punished in some other way. These responses to their alcoholism would be administered primarily by the legal system rather than the health-care system, as medical interventions are not designed to remedy moral failings.

The key point here is that definitions lie at the centre of many complex debates, and they can have profound and far-reaching implications. People tend to think of definitions as insignificant, arbitrary, abstruse sets of words found buried in the obscurity of thick dictionaries compiled by ivory tower intellectuals. Well, much of this characterization may be accurate, but definitions are *not* insignificant. They are vested with enormous power to shape how people think about important issues. And an endless array of issues boil down to matters of definition. For example, the next time you hear people arguing over whether a particular movie is pornographic or whether spanking is child abuse, you'll find it helps to focus the debate on clarifying the definitions of the crucial concepts.

The Power to Make Definitions

So, how can we resolve the debate about whether alcoholism is a disease? Scientists generally try to resolve their debates by conducting research to achieve a better understanding of the phenomena under scrutiny. You may have noticed already that the assertion "We need more research

on this issue . . ." is a frequent refrain in this text. Is more research the answer in this case? For once, the answer is no. There is no conclusive way to determine whether alcoholism is a disease. It is not as though there is a "right" answer to this question that we can discover through more and better research.

The question of whether alcoholism is a disease is a *matter of definition:* Does alcoholism fit the currently accepted definition of what constitutes a disease? If you consult medical texts or dictionaries, you will find that *disease is typically defined as an impairment in the normal functioning of an organism that alters its vital functions.* Given that alcoholism clearly impairs people's normal functioning and disrupts a variety of vital functions (see Figure 5.22), it seems reasonable to characterize it as a disease, and this has been the dominant view since the middle of the 20th century (Maltzman, 1994; Meyer, 1996). Still, many critics express vigorous doubts about the wisdom of defining alcoholism as a disease (Peele, 2000). They often raise a question that comes up frequently in arguments about definitions: Who should have the power to make the definition? In this case, the power lies in the hands of the medical community, which seems sensible, given that disease is a medical concept. But some critics argue that the medical community has a strong bias in favour of defining conditions as diseases because this creates new markets and fuels economic growth for the health industry (Nikelly, 1994). Thus, debate about whether alcoholism is a disease seems likely to continue for the indefinite future.

To summarize, definitions generally do not emerge out of research. They are typically crafted by experts or authorities in a specific field who try to reach a consensus about how to best define a particular concept. Thus, in analyzing the validity of a

FIGURE 5.22

Physiological malfunctions associated with alcoholism.

This diagram amply demonstrates that alcoholism is associated with a diverse array of physiological maladies. In and of itself, however, this information does not settle the argument about whether alcoholism should be regarded as a disease. It all depends on one's definition of what constitutes a disease.

Source: Edlin, G., and Golanty, E. (1992). *Health and wellness: A holistic approach*, 4th ed., p. 286. Boston: Jones & Bartlett. Copyright © 1992 by Jones & Bartlett Publishers, Inc., Sudbury, MA. www.jbpub.com. Reprinted by permission.

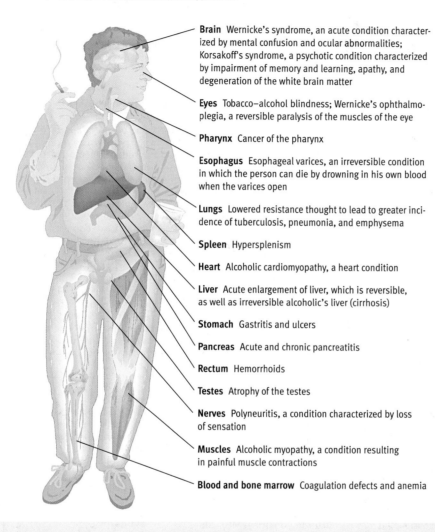

Brain Wernicke's syndrome, an acute condition characterized by mental confusion and ocular abnormalities; Korsakoff's syndrome, a psychotic condition characterized by impairment of memory and learning, apathy, and degeneration of the white brain matter

Eyes Tobacco–alcohol blindness; Wernicke's ophthalmoplegia, a reversible paralysis of the muscles of the eye

Pharynx Cancer of the pharynx

Esophagus Esophageal varices, an irreversible condition in which the person can die by drowning in his own blood when the varices open

Lungs Lowered resistance thought to lead to greater incidence of tuberculosis, pneumonia, and emphysema

Spleen Hypersplenism

Heart Alcoholic cardiomyopathy, a heart condition

Liver Acute enlargement of liver, which is reversible, as well as irreversible alcoholic's liver (cirrhosis)

Stomach Gastritis and ulcers

Pancreas Acute and chronic pancreatitis

Rectum Hemorrhoids

Testes Atrophy of the testes

Nerves Polyneuritis, a condition characterized by loss of sensation

Muscles Alcoholic myopathy, a condition resulting in painful muscle contractions

Blood and bone marrow Coagulation defects and anemia

TABLE 5.5

Critical Thinking Skills Discussed in This Application

Skill	Description	
Understanding the way definitions shape how people think about issues	The critical thinker appreciates the enormous power of definitions and the need to clarify definitions in efforts to resolve disagreements.	
Identifying the source of definitions	The critical thinker recognizes the need to determine who has the power to make specific definitions and to evaluate their credibility.	
Avoiding the nominal fallacy in working with definitions and labels	The critical thinker understands that labels do not have explanatory value.	

definition, you need to look not only at the definition itself but at where it came from. Who decided what the definition should be? Does the source of the definition seem legitimate and appropriate? Did the authorities who formulated the definition have any biases that should be considered?

Definitions, Labels, and Circular Reasoning

There is one additional point about definitions that is worth discussing. Perhaps because definitions are imbued with so much power, people have an interesting tendency to incorrectly use them as *explanations* for the phenomena they describe. This logical error, which equates *naming* something with *explaining* it, is sometime called the *nominal fallacy*. Names and labels that are used as explanations may sound reasonable at first glance, but definitions do not really have any explanatory value; they simply specify what certain terms mean. Consider an example. Let's say your friend, Frank, has a severe drinking problem. You are sitting around with some other friends discussing why Frank drinks so much. Rest assured, at least one of these friends will assert that "Frank drinks too much because he is an alcoholic." This is circular reasoning, which is just as useless as explaining that Frank is an alcoholic because he drinks too much. It tells us nothing about *why* Frank has a drinking problem.

The diagnostic labels that are used in the classification of mental disorders—labels such as schizophrenia, depression, autism, and obsessive-compulsive disorder—seem to invite this type of circular reasoning. For example, people often say things like "That person is delusional because she is schizophrenic," or "He is afraid of small, enclosed places because he is claustrophobic." These statements are just as logical as saying "She is a redhead because she has red hair." The logical fallacy of mistaking a label for an explanation will get us as far in our understanding as a dog gets in chasing its own tail.

Key Ideas

The Nature of Consciousness

● Consciousness is the continually changing stream of mental activity. There is some degree of awareness during sleep and sometimes even when patients are under anesthesia.

● Consciousness clearly is adaptive, but the question of exactly why it evolved is open to debate. Variations in consciousness are related to brain activity, as measured by the EEG.

Biological Rhythms and Sleep

● The cycle of sleep and wakefulness is influenced by circadian rhythms. Exposure to light resets biological clocks by affecting the activity of the suprachiasmatic nucleus and the pineal gland, which secretes melatonin.

● Being out of sync with circadian rhythms is one reason for jet lag and for the unpleasant nature of rotating shift work. Melatonin may have some value in treating jet lag and other sleep problems, but more research is needed.

The Sleep and Waking Cycle

● During a night's sleep, you evolve through a series of stages in cycles of approximately 90 minutes. During the REM stage, you experience rapid eye movements, brain waves characteristic of waking thought, and vivid dreaming. The sleep cycle tends to be repeated four times in a night, as REM sleep gradually becomes more predominant and NREM sleep dwindles.

● The REM portion of sleep declines during childhood, levelling off at around 20 percent. During adulthood, slow-wave sleep declines. Culture appears to have little impact on the physiological experience of sleep, but it does influence sleeping arrangements and napping patterns.

● People often underestimate the impact of sleep deprivation. Going without sleep appears to contribute to many transportation accidents and mishaps at work. Research on selective sleep deprivation suggests that people need REM sleep and slow-wave sleep.

● Many people are troubled by sleep disorders. Foremost among these disorders is insomnia, which has a variety of causes. Other common sleep problems include narcolepsy, sleep apnea, night terrors, nightmares, and somnambulism.

The World of Dreams

● The conventional view is that dreams are mental experiences during REM sleep that have a story-like quality, include vivid imagery, are often bizarre, and are regarded as real by the dreamer, but theorists have begun to question many aspects of this view.

● The content of one's dreams may be affected by one's age and gender, events in one's life, and external stimuli experienced during the dream. There are variations across cultures in dream recall, content, and interpretation.

● Freud argued that the purpose of dreams is wish fulfillment. Cartwright has articulated a problem-solving view, whereas Hobson and McCarley assert that dreams are side effects of the neural activation seen during REM sleep.

Hypnosis: Altered Consciousness or Role Playing?

● Hypnosis has a long and curious history. People vary greatly in their susceptibility to hypnosis. Among other things, hypnosis can produce anesthesia, sensory distortions, disinhibition, and posthypnotic amnesia.

● There are two major theoretical approaches to hypnosis that view it either as an altered state of consciousness or as a normal state of consciousness in which subjects assume a hypnotic role.

Meditation: Pure Consciousness or Relaxation?

● Evidence suggests that meditation leads to a potentially beneficial physiological state characterized by suppression of bodily arousal. However, the long-term benefits of meditation may not be unique to meditation and critics are worried about methodological flaws in meditation research.

Altering Consciousness with Drugs

● Recreational drug use involves an effort to alter consciousness with psychoactive drugs. Psychoactive drugs exert their main effects in the brain, where they alter neurotransmitter activity in a variety of ways. The mesolimbic dopamine pathway may mediate the reinforcing effects of most abused drugs.

● Drugs vary in their potential for psychological and physical dependence. Likewise, the dangers to health vary, depending on the drug. Recreational drug use can prove harmful to health by producing an overdose, by causing tissue damage, or by increasing health-impairing behaviour.

Putting It in Perspective: Themes 2, 3, 5, and 7

● Four of our unifying themes were highlighted in this chapter. We saw that psychology evolves in a sociohistorical context, that experience is highly subjective, that culture influences many aspects of behaviour, and that psychology is characterized by theoretical diversity.

PERSONAL APPLICATION • Addressing Practical Questions about Sleep and Dreams

● People's sleep needs vary, and the value of short naps depends on many factors. Sleep learning is possible, but only in primitive ways.

● People can do many things to avoid or reduce sleep problems. Mostly, it's a matter of developing good daytime habits that do not interfere with sleep. Individuals troubled by transient insomnia should avoid panic, pursue relaxation, and try distracting themselves.

● Everyone dreams, but some people cannot remember their dreams, probably because of the nature of their sleep cycle. In lucid dreams, people consciously recognize that they are dreaming and exert some control over the events in their dreams. Most theorists believe that dreams require some interpretation, but this may not be as complicated as once assumed.

CRITICAL THINKING APPLICATION • Is Alcoholism a Disease? The Power of Definitions

● Like many questions, the issue of whether alcoholism should be regarded as a disease is a matter of definition. In evaluating the validity of a definition, one should look not only at the definition but also at where it came from. People have a tendency to use definitions as explanations for the phenomena they describe, but doing so involves circular reasoning.

Key Terms

Alcohol, 233
Ascending reticular activating system (ARAS), 213
Biological rhythms, 205
Cannabis, 233
Circadian rhythms, 205
Dissociation, 228
Electroencephalograph (EEG), 202
Electromyograph (EMG), 208
Electrooculograph (EOG), 208
Hallucinogens, 233
Hypnosis, 225
Insomnia, 217
Lucid dreams, 222, 243
MDMA (ecstasy), 234
Meditation, 228
Mind wandering, 201
Narcolepsy, 218
Narcotics, 232
Neurogenesis, 216
Night terrors, 219
Nightmares, 219
Non-REM (NREM) sleep, 210

Opiates, 232
Physical dependence, 235
Psychoactive drugs, 231
Psychological dependence, 236
REM sleep, 210
REM sleep behaviour disorder, 220
Sedatives, 232
Sleep apnea, 219
Slow-wave sleep (SWS), 209
Somnambulism, 220
Stimulants, 232
Tolerance, 234

Key People

Theodore Barber, 227
Rosalind Cartwright, 224
William Dement, 211
Sigmund Freud, 223
Calvin Hall, 221
Ernest Hilgard, 227
J. Allan Hobson, 224
William James, 200
Shepard Siegel, 236
Nicholas Spanos, 225

1. If an EEG assessed your brain wave activity while you take this test, what type of brain wave activity would be most prominent?
   A. alpha
   B. beta
   C. delta
   D. theta

2. In terms of jet lag, flying in which direction leads to the greatest difficulty?
   A. northward
   B. southward
   C. eastward
   D. westward

3. During slow-wave sleep, which pattern of EEG activation is prominent?
   A. alpha
   B. beta
   C. delta
   D. theta

4. Which of the following statements describes what tends to happen to people as their sleep cycle evolves through the night?
   A. They spend more time in REM sleep and less time in NREM sleep.
   B. They spend more time in NREM sleep and less time in stage 3 sleep.
   C. They experience more sleep spindles later in the sleep cycle.
   D. They experience longer periods of delta- and theta-wave activity.

5. Which of the following individuals spends the most time in REM sleep?
   A. an infant
   B. a teenager
   C. a young adult
   D. an elderly adult

6. Tamara takes part in a three-day study in which she is wakened every time she goes into REM sleep. Which of the following is most likely to occur when she returns home and sleeps without interference?
   A. She will exhibit psychotic symptoms for a few nights.
   B. She will experience severe insomnia for about a week.
   C. She will spend extra time in REM sleep for a few nights.
   D. She will demonstrate a pattern of spontaneous waking consistent with the pattern in the study.

7. Which of the following events generally occurs during REM sleep?
   A. sleep apnea
   B. somnambulism
   C. night terrors
   D. nightmares

8. What would you expect to happen to an animal if the fibres of its ascending reticular activating system were severed?
   A. It would experience constant sleep.
   B. Each sleep cycle would be composed of REM sleep, with no other stages in between.
   C. It would be constantly alert and unable to sleep.
   D. It would persist in a permanent state of near sleep, characterized by alpha waves.

9. Which of the following statements is most consistent with the activation-synthesis theory of dreaming?
   A. Dreams are simply the by-product of bursts of activity in the brain.
   B. Dreams provide an outlet for energy invested in socially undesirable impulses.
   C. Dreams represent the brain's attempt to process information taken in during waking hours.
   D. Dreams are an attempt to restore a neurotransmitter balance within the brain.

10. "Highway hypnosis" is a common experience for drivers whose awareness is divided between the act of driving and a conscious train of thought. This phenomenon is consistent with which of the following ideas about hypnosis?
    A. It is an exercise in role playing.
    B. It is a dissociated state of consciousness.
    C. It is a goal-directed fantasy.
    D. It is not an altered state of consciousness.

11. Which of the following pairs includes both (i) stimulant and (ii) depressant?
    A. (i) cocaine; (ii) alcohol
    B. (i) mescaline; (ii) barbiturates
    C. (i) caffeine; (ii) amphetamines
    D. (i) alcohol; (ii) barbiturates

12. Amphetamines work by increasing the levels of which of the following substances?
    A. GABA and glycine
    B. melatonin and serotonin
    C. acetylcholine and endorphins
    D. norepinephrine and dopamine

13. Which of the following drugs would most likely result in a fatal overdose?
    A. LSD
    B. mescaline
    C. marijuana
    D. oxycodone

14. What is the long-term effect of CNS depressants on sleep patterns?
    A. They make it difficult to fall asleep.
    B. They reduce the overall need for sleep, which can be mistaken for insomnia.
    C. They reduce time spent in REM and slow-wave sleep, so sleep is not refreshing.
    D. They increase the likelihood of naps, so sleep occurs in multiple short phases rather than one long phase.

15. What feature characterizes a lucid dream?
    A. It is experienced in colour, whereas regular dreams are in shades of black and white.
    B. You know you are dreaming while experiencing the dream.
    C. You can plan to have the dream before you fall asleep.
    D. You are able to remember the dream in vivid detail even years after you've experienced the dream.

See Appendix A for the answers to this Practice Test.

On the Web

▶ **CourseMate**

Go to this site to find online resources directly linked to your book, including more quizzes, a glossary, flash cards, videos, and more!

▶ **CengageNow**

Go to this site for the link to CengageNOW™, your one-stop study shop. Take a pre-test for this chapter and CengageNOW™ will generate a personalized study plan based on your test results! The study plan will identify the topics you need to review and direct you to online resources to help you master those topics. You can then take a post-test to help you determine the concepts you have mastered and what you still need to work on.

▶ **Aplia**

Aplia™ is an online interactive learning solution that helps you improve comprehension—and your grade—by integrating a variety of media and tools such as video, tutorials, practice tests, and an interactive e-book.

CHAPTER 6

Learning

© Dave Brosha Photography

- In 1953 a Japanese researcher observed a young macaque (a type of monkey) on the island of Koshima washing a sweet potato in a stream before eating it. No one had ever seen a macaque do this before. Soon, other members of the monkey's troop were showing the same behaviour. Several generations later, macaques on Koshima still wash their potatoes before eating them (De Waal, 2001).
- In 2005 Wade Boggs was elected to baseball's Hall of Fame. Boggs was as renowned for his superstitions as he was for his great hitting. For 20 years, Boggs ate chicken every day of the year. Before games, he followed a strict set of rituals that included stepping on the bases in reverse order, running wind sprints at precisely 17 minutes past the hour, and tossing exactly three pebbles off the field. Every time he stepped up to hit during a game, he drew the Hebrew letter *chai* in the dirt with his bat. For Boggs, the slightest change in this routine was very upsetting (Gaddis, 1999; Vyse, 2000).
- Barn swallows in Minnesota built nests inside a Home Depot warehouse store, safe from the weather and from predators. So how do they get in and out to bring food to their chicks when the doors are closed? They flutter near the motion sensors that operate the doors until they open.
- A firefighter in Georgia routinely braves life-threatening situations to rescue people in distress. Yet the firefighter is paralyzed with fear whenever he sees someone dressed as a clown. He has been terrified of clowns ever since the third grade (Ryckeley, 2005).

What connects a superstitious ballplayer or a clown-phobic firefighter to potato-washing monkeys and door-opening swallows? What do all of these scenarios have in common? At first glance, very little. The answer is *learning*. To a psychologist, *learning is any relatively durable change in behaviour or knowledge that is due to experience.* Macaques aren't born with the habit of washing their sweet potatoes, nor do swallows begin life knowing how to operate motion sensors. Wade Boggs adopted his superstitious rituals because they seemed to be related to his success in hitting a baseball. The firefighter in Georgia wasn't born with a fear of clowns, since he only began to be frightened of them when he was in Grade 3. In short, all these behaviours are the product of experience—that is, they represent learning. When most people think of learning, they imagine someone reading a textbook, studying for an exam, or taking lessons to learn how to snowboard. Although these do involve learning, they represent only the tip of the iceberg in psychologists' eyes.

Perhaps we can illustrate some of the range of phenomena covered by what psychologists refer to as *learning* by telling you some things you may not know about hockey icon Wayne Gretzky. As a player, his talents were legendary. For example, on December 30, 1981, he put the puck into an empty net in a game against the Philadelphia Flyers, giving the Edmonton Oilers the victory. The goal he scored not only won the game for his team but also secured his place in hockey history because it was his 50th goal, a goal scored in his 39th game (50 Goals, n.d.). It broke the record of the Montreal Canadiens' Rocket Richard, who had first scored 50 goals in 50 games—a record no one expected to be broken. Breaking this record was unexpected by most, but not by Wayne's father, Walter, his greatest supporter. When Wayne phoned his father after the game, Walter gave his congratulations and remarked, "What took you so long?" (Gretzky & Reilly, 1990, p. 61)

Gretzky went on to win four Stanley Cups with Edmonton and then to revitalize hockey in Los Angeles as a member of the Los Angeles Kings. After his playing career was over, he became a part-owner of an NHL team, and as general manager guided Canada's men's hockey team to an Olympic gold medal in 2002, Canada's first in 50 years. He went on to be co-owner and coach of the Phoenix Coyotes of the National Hockey League.

Wayne Gretzky had many superstitions while playing hockey. He is well known for tucking in his jersey on only one side before each game. His superstitions also affected the way he put on his equipment for the game and what he ate just before the game.

AP Photos/Matt York

But, you may be wondering, what does Gretzky have to do with learning? The most obvious answer is to point to his skill as a player. While there is no doubt that he has great natural ability, he goes to great lengths to point out the importance of the practice and skill-acquisition training sessions conducted when he was young by his father. In addition, as a player, Gretzky was extremely superstitious: He ate the same food each day before a game; when on a scoring streak, he often would not cut his hair; he always tucked in only the right side of his hockey jersey; he would not let his stick touch other players' sticks or cross each other; and he put on his equipment exactly the same way each time he dressed for a game. You may even have superstitions of your own—perhaps a favourite pen to use when writing an exam or a lucky shirt to wear when flying in an airplane. One of us buys a new pencil each time he begins to write a new academic journal article. He started this when he was a graduate student and the first paper he wrote for a journal with a new pencil was published; he still does this even though now he never even uses a pencil to write—he writes on a computer. But still he buys the pencil!

Superstitions like these are often the result of obtaining a reward after engaging in some behaviour. Boston Bruins hockey legend Phil Esposito was known for always wearing a black turtleneck under his hockey jersey. It all began before one game when he put on a turtleneck because he was suffering from a cold. That night he scored a hat trick, and so wore a turtleneck under his uniform every game until he retired (Esposito's Turtleneck, n.d.). Athletes frequently believe that if they repeat the behaviour, such as wearing a black turtleneck or donning new soccer boots for each game, the good luck will continue, thus giving them an edge over the competition (Todd, 2003). As we will discuss later in the chapter, this is a prototypical example of what psychologists are referring to when they use the term *learning*—in this case, a type of learning known as *operant conditioning.*

Another Gretzky characteristic is also noteworthy in connection with a chapter on learning. Gretzky was afraid to fly (Gretzky & Reilly, 1990). He frequently rented limousines to take him to hockey games in other cities if it was possible to get there by car in time. When he had to fly, his teammates sometimes had to sit on him to keep him in his seat. Most often he depended on Garnet Edwards "Ace" Bailey, a teammate and hockey scout, to calm him down when he flew (Duhatschek, 2011). Such fears are termed *phobias.* Tragically, Bailey died when United Airlines Flight 175 crashed into the World Trade Center on September 11, 2001.

Phobias are irrational fears of specific objects or situations and are often the result of another learning process termed *classical conditioning.* Phobias are relatively common. According to data released by Health Canada (2002), the one-year prevalence rate for specific phobias (e.g., fear of flying, fear of heights) is 6.2–8 percent in Canadians 15–64 years of age, and the rate for social phobia is 6.7 percent.

Phobias can be treated, but sometimes they come to an abrupt but unplanned end on their own. Psychologist Elizabeth Dunn was an avid surfer, travelling all over the world to surf, even though she had a shark phobia. On March 23, 2006, her worst fears were realized when she was attacked and bitten by a shark while surfing in Hawaii. While it was a terrifying experience for her, it did have a positive consequence. She now feels "much safer," since she knows the statistical chances of any one person being bitten twice by a shark are ridiculously small (Fujimori, 2006). We will read more about Elizabeth Dunn's scientific research (e.g., Dunn, Buchtel, & Aknin, 2011) at the University of British Columbia in Chapter 16, and you will learn more about phobias and how they are more typically treated in Chapter 14.

Learning is a key topic in psychology. When you think about it, it would be hard to name a lasting change in behaviour that is *not* the result of experience. That's why learning is one of the most fundamental concepts in all of psychology. Learning shapes personal habits, such as nail-biting; personality traits, such as shyness; personal preferences, such as a distaste for formal clothes; and emotional responses, such as reactions to favourite songs. If all your learned responses could somehow be stripped away, little of your behaviour would be left. You wouldn't be able to talk, read a book, or cook yourself a hamburger. You'd be about as complex and interesting as a doorknob.

Elizabeth Dunn, a social psychologist from the University of British Columbia, has many varied research interests including affective forecasting, self-knowledge, and implicit social cognition. In addition, she has made significant contributions to the psychology of happiness.

As the examples in this section show, learning is not an exclusively human process. Learning is pervasive in the animal world as well, a fact that won't amaze anyone who's ever owned a dog or seen a trained seal in action. Another insight, however, is even more startling: *The principles that explain learned responses in animals explain much of human learning, too.* Thus, the same mechanisms that explain how barn swallows learn to operate an automated door can account for a professional athlete's bizarre superstitions. In fact, many of the most fascinating discoveries in the study of learning originated in studies of animals.

In this chapter, you'll see how fruitful the research into learning has been and how wide-ranging its applications are. We'll focus most of our attention on a specific kind of learning: conditioning. *Conditioning involves learning connections between events that occur in an organism's environment* (eating chicken and having success hitting a baseball is one example). In researching conditioning, psychologists study learning at a fundamental level. This strategy has paid off with insights that have laid the foundation for the study of more complex forms of learning, such as learning by observation (the kind of learning that may account for the Koshima macaques picking up one monkey's habit of washing her sweet potatoes). In the Personal Application, you'll see how you can harness the principles of conditioning to improve your self-control. The Critical Thinking Application shows how conditioning procedures can be used to manipulate emotions.

Classical Conditioning

Do you go weak in the knees at the thought of standing on the roof of a tall building? Does your heart race when you imagine encountering a harmless garter snake? If so, you can understand, at least to some degree, what it's like to have a phobia—an irrational fear of a specific object or situation. Mild phobias are commonplace (Eaton, Dryman, & Weissman, 1991). Over the years, students in our classes have described their phobic responses to a diverse array of stimuli, including bridges, elevators, tunnels, heights, dogs, cats, bugs, snakes, professors, doctors, strangers, thunderstorms, and germs. If you have a phobia, you may have wondered how you managed to acquire such a perplexing fear. Chances are, it was through classical conditioning (Antony & McCabe, 2003).

Classical conditioning is a type of learning in which a stimulus acquires the capacity to evoke a response that was originally evoked by another stimulus. The process was first described around 1900 by Ivan Pavlov, and it is sometimes called *Pavlovian conditioning* in tribute to him. The term *conditioning* comes from Pavlov's determination to discover the "conditions" that produce this kind of learning.

Pavlov's Demonstration: "Psychic Reflexes" 5a

Ivan Pavlov was a prominent Russian physiologist who did Nobel Prize–winning research on digestion. According to psychologist and historian Ray Fancher (1979), Pavlov was something of a "classic" himself—he was an absent-minded but brilliant professor obsessed with his research. He was absent-minded about many things, including money, sometimes forgetting to pick up his pay for months. He rarely carried money with him. One exception was on his first trip to New York, where he was mugged of $800—a great deal of money in those days. He might have been absent-minded about money, but he was very serious about his work. Legend has it that Pavlov once reprimanded an assistant who arrived late for an experiment because of trying to avoid street fighting in the midst of the Russian Revolution. The assistant defended his tardiness, saying, "But, Professor, there's a revolution going on, with shooting in the streets!" Pavlov supposedly replied, "What the hell difference does a revolution make when you've work to do in the laboratory? Next time there's a revolution, get up earlier!" Apparently, dodging bullets wasn't an adequate excuse for delaying the march of scientific progress (Fancher, 1979; Gantt, 1975).

Pavlov was one of those who was responsible for turning psychology from research focusing on subjective accounts of experience, *introspection*, to a more objective, rigorous, scientific approach. His work showed how stimuli in the external world controlled our actions and behaviour (Pickren & Rutherford, 2010). He de-emphasized the mind, and mentalistic accounts of behaviour, and showed how learning was under the influence of experience and that "associations could be built up in consciousness" (Pickren & Rutherford, 2010, p. 59).

Ivan Pavlov
"Next time there's a revolution, get up earlier!"

Time & Life Pictures/Getty Images

WEB LINK 6.1

Phobias

For more information on phobias and how to deal with them, check out this page of the Canadian Psychological Association's website.

Surrounded by his research staff, the great Russian physiologist Ivan Pavlov (white beard) demonstrates his famous classical conditioning experiment with dogs.

Pavlov was studying the role of saliva in the digestive processes of dogs when he stumbled onto what he called "psychic reflexes" (Pavlov, 1906). Like many great discoveries, Pavlov's was partly accidental, although he had the insight to recognize its significance. His subjects were dogs restrained in harnesses in an experimental chamber (see Figure 6.1). Their saliva was collected by means of a surgically implanted tube in the salivary gland. Pavlov would present meat powder to a dog and then collect the resulting saliva. As his research progressed, he noticed that dogs accustomed to the procedure would start salivating *before* the meat powder was presented.

For instance, they would salivate in response to a clicking sound made by the device that was used to present the meat powder.

Intrigued by this unexpected finding, Pavlov decided to investigate further. To clarify what was happening, he paired the presentation of the meat powder with various stimuli that would stand out in the laboratory situation. For instance, in some experiments, he used a simple auditory stimulus—the presentation of a tone. After the tone and the meat powder had been presented together a number of times, the tone was presented alone. What happened? The dogs responded by salivating to the sound of the tone alone.

What was so significant about a dog salivating when a tone was presented? The key is that the tone started out as a *neutral* stimulus. That is, it did not originally produce the response of salivation. However, Pavlov managed to change that by pairing the tone with a stimulus (meat powder) that did produce the salivation response. Through this process, the tone acquired the capacity to trigger the response of salivation. What Pavlov had demonstrated was how learned associations—which were viewed as the basic building blocks of the entire learning process—were formed by events in an

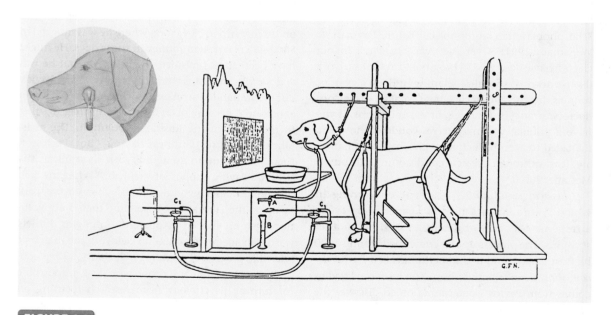

FIGURE 6.1

Classical conditioning apparatus.

An experimental arrangement similar to the one depicted here (taken from Yerkes & Morgulis, 1909) has typically been used in demonstrations of classical conditioning, although Pavlov's original setup (see inset) was quite a bit simpler. The dog is restrained in a harness. A tone is used as the conditioned stimulus (CS) and the presentation of meat powder is used as the unconditioned stimulus (UCS). The tube inserted into the dog's salivary gland allows precise measurement of its salivation response. The pen and rotating drum of paper on the left are used to maintain a continuous record of salivary flow. (Inset) The less elaborate setup that Pavlov originally used to collect saliva on each trial is shown here (Goodwin, 1991).

Sources: Adapted from Yerkes, R.M., and Morgulis, S. (1909). The Method of Pavlov in Animal Psychology, *Psychological Bulletin, 6*, 257–273. American Psychological Association. Inset: From Goodwin, C.J., Misportraying Pavlov's Apparatus, 1991. *American Journal of Psychology, 104* (1): 135–141. © 1991 by the Board of Trustees of the University of Illinois.

organism's environment. Based on this insight, he built a broad theory of learning that attempted to explain aspects of emotion, temperament, neuroses, and language (Windholz, 1997). His research and theory proved hugely influential around the world and remains so today (Boakers, 2003; Marks, 2004). Recently, for example, some scholars have extended this work by suggesting a "functional perspective" on Pavlovian conditioning. Impressed by the prevalence of examples of Pavlovian conditioning across species and response systems, psychologists such as Michael Domjan of the University of Texas (Domjan, 2005; Matthews et al., 2007) suggest that such conditioning must be evolutionarily adaptive, contributing to our reproductive fitness.

Terminology and Procedures 5a

A special vocabulary is associated with classical conditioning. It often looks intimidating to the uninitiated, but it's really not all that mysterious. The bond Pavlov noted between the meat powder and salivation was a natural, unlearned association. It did not have to be created through conditioning. It is therefore called an *unconditioned* association. Thus, the *unconditioned stimulus (UCS)* is a stimulus that evokes an unconditioned response without previous conditioning. The *unconditioned response (UCR)* is an unlearned reaction to an unconditioned stimulus that occurs without previous conditioning.

In contrast, the link between the tone and salivation was established through conditioning. It is therefore called a *conditioned* association. Thus, the *conditioned stimulus (CS)* is a previously neutral stimulus that has, through conditioning, acquired the capacity to evoke a conditioned response. The *conditioned response (CR)* is a learned reaction to a conditioned stimulus that occurs because of previous conditioning. Ironically, the names for the four key elements in classical conditioning (the UCS, UCR, CS, and CR) are the by-product of a poor translation of Pavlov's writing into English. Pavlov actually used the words condition*al* and uncondition*al* to refer to these concepts (Todes, 1997).

To avoid possible confusion, it is worth noting that the unconditioned response and conditioned response often consist of the same behaviour, although there may be subtle differences between them. In Pavlov's initial demonstration, the UCR and CR were both salivation. When evoked by the UCS (meat powder), salivation was an unconditioned response. When evoked by the CS (the tone), salivation was a conditioned response. The procedures

involved in classical conditioning are outlined in Figure 6.2.

Pavlov's "psychic reflex" came to be called the *conditioned reflex*. Classically conditioned responses have traditionally been characterized as reflexes and are said to be *elicited* (drawn forth) because most of them are relatively automatic or involuntary. However, research in recent decades has demonstrated that classical conditioning is involved in a

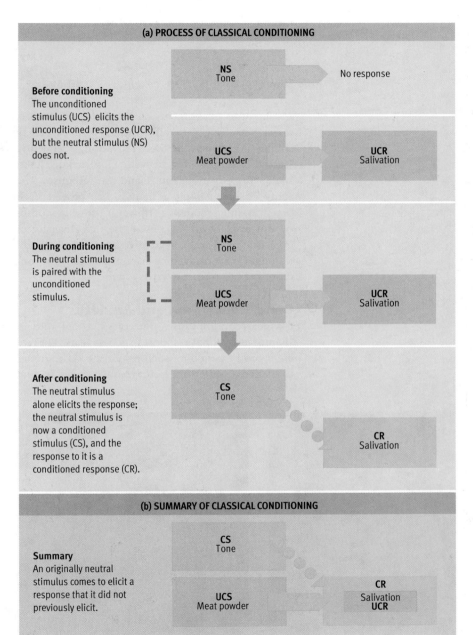

FIGURE 6.2

The sequence of events in classical conditioning.

(a) Moving downward, this series of three panels outlines the sequence of events in classical conditioning, using Pavlov's original demonstration as an example. **(b)** As we encounter other examples of classical conditioning throughout the book, we will see many diagrams like the one in this panel, which will provide snapshots of specific instances of classical conditioning.

wider range of human and animal behaviour than previously appreciated, including some types of non-reflexive responding (Allan, 1998). Finally, a *trial* in classical conditioning consists of any presentation of a stimulus or pair of stimuli. Psychologists are interested in how many trials are required to establish a particular conditioned bond. The number needed to form an association varies considerably. Although classical conditioning generally proceeds gradually, it *can* occur quite rapidly, sometimes in just one pairing of the CS and UCS.

Classical Conditioning in Everyday Life 5a

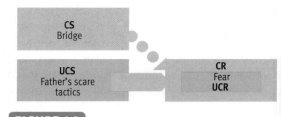

In laboratory experiments on classical conditioning, researchers have generally worked with extremely simple responses. Besides salivation, frequently studied favourites include eyelid closure, knee jerks, the flexing of various limbs, and fear responses. The study of such simple responses has proven both practical and productive. However, these responses do not even begin to convey the rich diversity of everyday behaviours regulated by classical conditioning. Let's look at some examples of classical conditioning taken from everyday life.

Conditioned Fear and Anxiety

Classical conditioning often plays a key role in shaping emotional responses such as fears. Phobias are a good example of such responses. Case studies of patients suffering from phobias suggest that

FIGURE 6.3

Classical conditioning of a fear response.
Many emotional responses that would otherwise be puzzling can be explained by classical conditioning. In the case of one woman's bridge phobia, the fear originally elicited by her father's scare tactics became a conditioned response to the stimulus of bridges.

many irrational fears can be traced back to experiences that involve classical conditioning (Antony & McCabe, 2003; Muris & Mercklebach, 2001). It's easy to imagine how such conditioning can occur outside of the lab. For example, one of our students troubled by a severe bridge phobia was able to pinpoint childhood conditioning experiences as the source of her phobia (see Figure 6.3). Whenever her family drove to visit her grandmother, they had to cross a rickety, old bridge in the countryside. Her father, in a misguided attempt at humour, would stop short of the bridge and carry on about the great danger. The young girl was terrified by her father's joke. Hence, the bridge became a conditioned stimulus eliciting great fear. The fear then spilled over to *all* bridges and 40 years later she was still troubled by this phobia. If we had a chance to talk to Wayne Gretzky, we might be able to determine what early event contributed to his fear of flying. Incidentally, he is certainly not the only professional athlete who suffers from this phobia—a real problem, of course, when flying is part of your job. Boxing great Muhammad Ali, fearless in the ring, sometimes wore a parachute when sitting in his seat in a plane. Pittsburgh Steeler great James Harrison maintains that he is not afraid of flying—rather, he is afraid of crashing. Toronto Maple Leaf Tyler Bozak has to endure some kidding by his teammates along with his fear of flying. Bozak maintains that flying is unnatural: "All that weight floating through the air. Just doesn't sound right" (McGran, 2010, p. A1). When the plane takes off, his teammates often shout "Just doesn't sound right" just to make sure he notices that the flight has started.

Everyday fear responses that are less severe than phobias may also be products of classical conditioning. For instance, if you cringe when you hear the sound of a dentist's drill, this response is a result of classical conditioning. In this case, pain has been paired with the sound of the drill, which became a CS eliciting your cringe. That is *not* to say that traumatic experiences associated with stimuli *automatically*

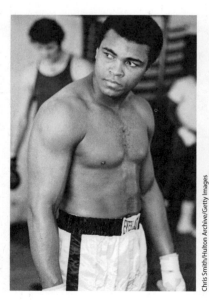

Many professional athletes have to deal with fear of one of the necessities of their occupation—flying. Legendary boxer Muhammad Ali and Pittsburgh Steeler James Harrison are two athletes with a fear of flying.

lead to conditioned fears or phobias. Whether fear conditioning takes place depends on many factors. Some people acquire conditioned fears less readily than others, probably because of differences in their genetic makeup (Hettema et al., 2003).

Of course, everyday conditioning effects are not restricted to negative emotions such as fear. You can likely come up with many examples of things that continue to make you smile, given their pairing with happy times you had as a child. Even now, a particular song that you haven't heard for years may elicit a positive emotion related to a specific activity you were engaged in when you first heard it.

Evaluative Conditioning of Attitudes

Pavlovian conditioning can also influence people's attitudes. In recent decades, researchers have shown great interest in a subtype of classical conditioning called *evaluative conditioning*. *Evaluative conditioning refers to changes in the liking of a stimulus that result from pairing that stimulus with other positive or negative stimuli*. In other words, evaluative conditioning involves the acquisition of likes and dislikes, or preferences, through classical conditioning. Typically, a neutral stimulus is paired with unconditioned stimuli that trigger positive reactions so that the neutral stimulus becomes a conditioned stimulus that elicits similar positive reactions. For example, in one recent study, pleasant music paired with two unknown brands of root beer had significant effects on participants' liking for the drinks (Redker & Gibson, 2009). Another study showed that pairing an attractive face gazing directly at the viewer with various peppermint brands swayed subjects' brand preferences (Strick, Holland, & Knippenberg, 2008). In another investigation, funny cartoons paired with two types of energy drinks increased participants' liking of the drinks (Strick et al., 2009).

Obviously, advertising campaigns routinely try to take advantage of evaluative conditioning (see the Personal Application for this chapter). Advertisers often pair their products with USs that elicit pleasant emotions (Till & Priluck, 2000). The most common strategy is to present a product in association with an attractive person or enjoyable surroundings (see Figure 6.4). Advertisers hope that these pairings will make their products conditioned stimuli that evoke good feelings. For example, automobile manufacturers like to show their sports-utility vehicles in beautiful outdoor scenes that evoke pleasant feelings and nostalgic thoughts of past vacations. Puppies and cute children are also popular stimuli used in advertisements designed to promote positive associations with their product. Politicians know this, too, and

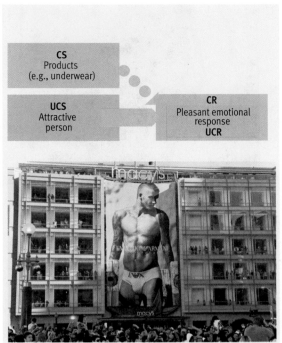

FIGURE 6.4

Classical conditioning in advertising.
Many advertisers attempt to make their products conditioned stimuli that elicit pleasant emotional responses by pairing their products with attractive or popular people or sexual imagery.

they often have pictures taken with popular people, perhaps in an attempt to boost their own popularity. This practice is great news for Olympic athletes who often have trouble making ends meet. Athletes such as Canadian Olympic medalists Alex Bilodeau and Joannie Rochette have obtained lucrative endorsement deals after their success at the 2010 Olympics. However, few can match American snowboarder and skateboarder Shaun White, who had US$8 million in endorsements and prize money before the 2010 Winter Games even began (Flavell, 2011).

A current source of debate is whether evaluative conditioning is a special (i.e., somewhat different) form of classical conditioning. Some studies suggest that attitudes can be shaped through evaluative conditioning without participants' conscious awareness (Olson & Fazio, 2001) and that evaluative conditioning is remarkably durable (Walther, Nagengast, & Trasselli, 2005). Other studies suggest that awareness is crucial to evaluative conditioning (Stahl, Unkelbach, & Corneille, 2009) and that it does not display exceptional durability (Lipp, Oughton, & LeLievre, 2003). Consensus on these issues does not appear to be on the horizon. Nonetheless, a great deal of empirical evidence attests to the fact that evaluative conditioning can shape people's attitudes (Hofmann et al., 2010).

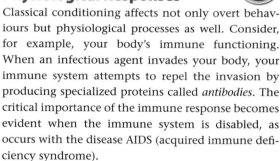

2010 Olympic gold medalist and professional skateboarder Shaun White has used his athletic success to develop many lucrative product endorsement deals.

Conditioning and Physiological Responses

PSYKTREK 5a

Classical conditioning affects not only overt behaviours but physiological processes as well. Consider, for example, your body's immune functioning. When an infectious agent invades your body, your immune system attempts to repel the invasion by producing specialized proteins called *antibodies*. The critical importance of the immune response becomes evident when the immune system is disabled, as occurs with the disease AIDS (acquired immune deficiency syndrome).

Research has revealed that the functioning of the immune system can be influenced by psychological factors, including conditioning (Ader, 2001, 2003). Robert Ader and Nicholas Cohen (1984, 1993) have shown that classical conditioning procedures can lead to *immunosuppression*—a decrease in the production of antibodies. In a typical study, animals are injected with a drug (the US) that *chemically* causes immunosuppression while they are simultaneously given an unusual-tasting liquid to drink (the CS). Days later, after the chemical immunosuppression has ended, some of the animals are re-exposed to the CS by giving them the unusual-tasting solution. Measurements of antibody production indicate that animals exposed to the CS show a reduced immune response (see Figure 6.5).

FIGURE 6.5

Classical conditioning of immunosuppression.

When a neutral stimulus is paired with a drug that chemically causes immunosuppression, it can become a CS that elicits immunosuppression on its own. Thus, even the immune response can be influenced by classical conditioning.

Immune resistance is only one example of the subtle physiological processes that can be influenced by classical conditioning. Studies suggest that classical conditioning can also elicit *allergic reactions* (MacQueen et al., 1989) and that classical conditioning contributes to the growth of *drug tolerance* and the experience of withdrawal symptoms when drug use is halted (McDonald & Siegel, 2004; Siegel, 2001). You may recall that we introduced you to the work of McMaster University's Shepard Siegel in Chapter 5. Siegel suggests that the events that occur during administration of a drug and the context of the drug use may come to serve as CSs for drug-related effects. In Chapter 5, we also discussed the concept of drug tolerance. Continued use of drugs may lead to increased drug tolerance, in which increasing amounts of the drug are needed to produce the same effect. Drug use leads the body to produce compensatory responses in an attempt to counteract or compensate for the effects of the drug on the body. The greater the compensatory response, the more of the drug that is needed to produce the same effect. The role of conditioning in producing drug tolerance is discussed more fully in the next section.

Studies have also demonstrated that classical conditioning can influence *sexual arousal* (Pfaus, Kippin, & Centeno, 2001). For example, research has shown that quail can be conditioned to become sexually aroused by a neutral, nonsexual stimulus—such as a red light—that has been paired with opportunities to copulate (Domjan, 1992, 1994). Conditioned stimuli can even elicit *increased sperm release* in male quail—a conditioned response that would convey an obvious evolutionary advantage (Domjan, Blesbois, & Williams, 1998). Researchers have also conditioned quail to develop fetishes for inanimate objects (Cetinkaya & Domjan, 2006; Koksal et al, 2004). This line of research bolsters the idea that stimuli routinely paired with human sexual interactions, such as seductive nightgowns, mood music, lit candles, and the like, probably become conditioned stimuli that elicit arousal (as you might guess, this hypothesis has been difficult to investigate with human subjects). Classical conditioning may also underlie the development of *fetishes* for inanimate objects. If quail can be conditioned to find a red light arousing, it seems likely that humans may be conditioned to be aroused by objects such as shoes, boots, leather, and undergarments that may be paired with events eliciting sexual arousal.

Conditioning and Drug Effects

As we discussed in Chapter 5, *drug tolerance* involves a gradual decline in responsiveness to a drug with repeated use, so that larger and larger doses are required to attain the user's customary effect. Most theories assert that drug tolerance is largely attributable to physiological changes in the user. However, research by Shepard Siegel (2005) demonstrates that classical conditioning also contributes to drug tolerance—sometimes in unexpected ways.

Stimuli that are consistently paired with the administration of drugs can acquire the capacity to elicit conditioned responses in both humans and laboratory animals. There is a special wrinkle, however, when drug administration serves as a US. In many instances, the conditioned responses are physiological reactions that are just the *opposite* of the normal effects of the drugs (Siegel et al., 2000). These opponent responses, which have been seen as the result of conditioning with narcotics, stimulants, and alcohol, are called *compensatory CRs* because they partially compensate for some drug effects. These compensatory CRs help to maintain homeostasis (internal balance) in physiological processes. They are adaptive in the short term, as they counterbalance some of the potentially dangerous effects of various drugs.

What role do these compensatory CRs play in drug tolerance? Most drug users have routines that lead to the consistent pairing of drug administration and certain stimuli, such as syringes, cocaine bottles, and specific settings and rituals. Even the drug administration process itself can become a CS associated with drug effects (Weise-Kelly & Siegel, 2001). According to Siegel (2005), these environmental cues eventually begin to elicit compensatory CRs that partially cancel out some of the anticipated effects of abused drugs. As these compensatory CRs strengthen, they neutralize more and more of a drug's pleasurable effects, producing a gradual decline in the user's responsiveness to the drug (in other words, tolerance).

Things can go awry, however, when drug users depart from their normal drug routines. If drugs are taken in new ways or in new settings, the usual compensatory CRs may not occur. With their counterbalancing effects eliminated, the drugs may have a much stronger impact than usual, thus increasing the risk of an overdose (Siegel, 2001). This model may explain why heroin addicts seem more prone to overdose when they shoot up in unfamiliar settings. Another problem is that when people try to quit drugs, exposure to drug-related cues—in the absence of actual drug administration—may trigger compensatory CRs that increase drug cravings and fuel drug addiction and relapse (McDonald & Siegel, 2004). Thus, complicated conditioning processes appear to play a role in drug tolerance, drug craving, and drug overdoses, which need to be factored into the treatment of drug addiction (Siegel & Ramos, 2002).

The contextual cues (in the park, by the swings) may themselves come to elicit (conditioned) compensatory responses that contribute to the development of tolerance for the drug. "When the drug is administered repeatedly in the context of the usual pre-drug cues, these cues elicit a CCR that attenuates the drug effect. As the drug is administered more and more often, and the CCR grows in strength, the attenuation of the drug effect becomes more pronounced" (Siegel, 2002, p. 4). In addition, when the drug user is in the company of the cues associated with drug use but is not administering the drug itself, withdrawal symptoms may be produced (McDonald & Siegel, 2004).

Basic Processes in Classical Conditioning 5b

Classical conditioning is often portrayed as a mechanical process that inevitably leads to a certain result. This view reflects the fact that most conditioned responses are reflexive and difficult to control—Pavlov's dogs would have been hard-pressed to withhold their salivation. Similarly, most people with phobias have great difficulty suppressing their fear. However, this vision of classical conditioning as an "irresistible force" is misleading because it fails to consider the many factors involved in classical conditioning (Kehoe & Macrae, 1998). In this section, we'll look at basic processes in classical conditioning to expand on the rich complexity of this form of learning.

Acquisition: Forming New Responses 5b

We have already discussed *acquisition* without attaching a formal name to the process. *Acquisition* refers to the initial stage of learning something. Pavlov theorized that the acquisition of a conditioned response depends on *stimulus contiguity*. Stimuli are contiguous if they occur together in time and space.

WEB LINK 6.2

Behaviour Analysis and Learning
A multitude of annotated links, all focusing on learning through conditioning, can be found at the excellent Centre for Psychology Resources site at Athabasca University in Alberta.

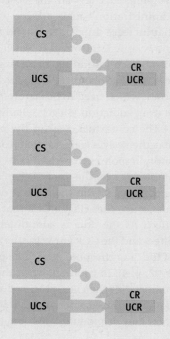
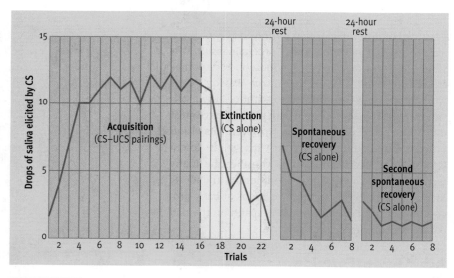

FIGURE 6.6

Acquisition, extinction, and spontaneous recovery.

During acquisition, the strength of the dog's conditioned response (measured by the amount of salivation) increases rapidly and then levels off near its maximum. During extinction, the CR declines erratically until it's extinguished. After a "rest" period in which the dog is not exposed to the CS, a spontaneous recovery occurs, and the CS once again elicits a (weakened) CR. Repeated presentations of the CS alone re-extinguish the CR, but after another "rest" interval, a weaker spontaneous recovery occurs.

Stimulus contiguity is important, but learning theorists now realize that contiguity alone doesn't automatically produce conditioning (Miller & Grace, 2003). People are bombarded daily by countless stimuli that could be perceived as being paired, yet only some of these pairings produce classical conditioning. Consider the woman who developed a conditioned emotional reaction to the smell of Beemans gum and cigarettes. There were, no doubt, other stimuli that shared contiguity with her boyfriend, Charlie. He smoked, so ashtrays were probably present, but she doesn't get weak in the knees at the sight of an ashtray.

If conditioning does not occur to all of the stimuli present in a situation, what determines its occurrence? Evidence suggests that stimuli that are novel, unusual, or especially intense have more potential to become CSs than routine stimuli, probably because they are more likely to stand out among other stimuli (Hearst, 1988).

Extinction: Weakening Conditioned Responses   5b

Fortunately, a newly formed stimulus–response bond does not necessarily last indefinitely. If it did, learning would be inflexible, and organisms would have difficulty adapting to new situations. Instead, the right circumstances produce *extinction,* the gradual weakening and disappearance of a conditioned response tendency.

What leads to extinction in classical conditioning? The consistent presentation of the conditioned stimulus *alone,* without the unconditioned stimulus. For example, when Pavlov consistently presented *only* the tone to a previously conditioned dog, the tone gradually lost its capacity to elicit the response of salivation. Such a sequence of events is depicted in the yellow portion of Figure 6.6, which graphs the amount of salivation by a dog over a series of conditioning trials. Note how the salivation response declines during extinction.

How long does it take to extinguish a conditioned response? That depends on many factors, but particularly the strength of the conditioned bond when extinction begins. Some conditioned responses extinguish quickly, while others are difficult to weaken.

Spontaneous Recovery: Resurrecting Responses

Some conditioned responses display the ultimate in tenacity by "reappearing from the dead" after having been extinguished. Learning theorists use the term *spontaneous recovery* to describe such a resurrection from the graveyard of conditioned associations.

Spontaneous recovery is the reappearance of an extinguished response after a period of nonexposure to the conditioned stimulus.

Pavlov (1927) observed this phenomenon in some of his pioneering studies. He fully extinguished a dog's CR of salivation to a tone and then returned the dog to its home cage for a "rest interval" (a period of nonexposure to the CS). On a subsequent day, when the dog was brought back to the experimental chamber for retesting, the tone was sounded and the salivation response reappeared. Although it had returned, the rejuvenated response was weak. The salivation was less than when the response was at its peak strength. If Pavlov consistently presented the CS by itself again, the response re-extinguished quickly. However, in some of the dogs, the response made still another spontaneous recovery (typically even weaker than the first) after they had spent another period in their cages (consult Figure 6.6 once again).

More recent studies have uncovered a related phenomenon called the *renewal effect*—if a response is extinguished in a different environment than it was acquired, the extinguished response will reappear if the animal is returned to the original environment where acquisition took place. This phenomenon, along with the evidence on spontaneous recovery, suggests that extinction somehow *suppresses* a conditioned response rather than *erasing* a learned association (Bouton, Todd, Vurbi, & Winterbauer, 2011). In other words, *extinction does not appear to lead to unlearning* (Bouton & Woods, 2009). The theoretical meaning of spontaneous recovery and the renewal effect is complex and the subject of some debate. However, their practical meaning is quite simple. Even if you manage to rid yourself of an unwanted conditioned response (such as cringing when you hear a dental drill), there is an excellent chance that it may make a surprise reappearance later. This reality may also help explain why people who manage to give up cigarettes, drugs, or poor eating habits for a while often relapse and return to their unhealthy habits (Bouton, 2000, 2002). The renewal effect is also one of the reasons why conditioned fears and phobias are difficult to extinguish permanently (Hermans et al., 2006).

Stimulus Generalization and the Mysterious Case of Little Albert

 5b

After conditioning has occurred, organisms often show a tendency to respond not only to the exact CS used but also to other, similar stimuli. For example,

Pavlov's dogs might have salivated in response to a different-sounding tone, or you might cringe at the sound of a jeweller's as well as a dentist's drill. These are examples of stimulus generalization. *Stimulus generalization* occurs when an organism that has learned a response to a specific stimulus responds in the same way to new stimuli that are similar to the original stimulus. Generalization is adaptive, given that organisms rarely encounter the exact same stimulus more than once (Thomas, 1992). Stimulus generalization is also commonplace. We have already discussed a real-life example: the woman who acquired a bridge phobia during her childhood because her father scared her whenever they went over a particular old bridge. The original CS for her fear was that specific bridge, but her fear was ultimately *generalized* to all bridges.

The likelihood and amount of generalization to a new stimulus depend on the similarity between the new stimulus and the original CS (Balsam, 1988). The basic law governing generalization is this: *The more similar new stimuli are to the original CS, the greater the generalization.* This principle can be quantified in graphs called *generalization gradients*, such as those shown in Figure 6.7. These generalization gradients map out how a dog conditioned to salivate to a tone of 1200 hertz might respond to other tones. As you can see, the strength of the generalization response declines as the similarity between the new stimuli and the original CS decreases.

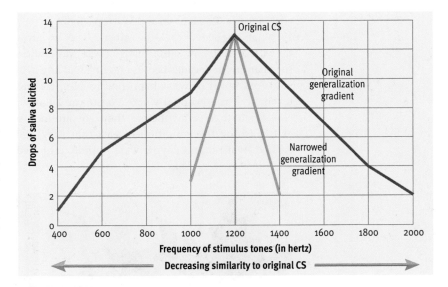

FIGURE 6.7

Generalization gradients.

In a study of stimulus generalization, an organism is typically conditioned to respond to a specific CS, such as a 1200-hertz tone, and then is tested with similar stimuli, such as other tones between 400 and 2000 hertz. Graphs of the organism's responding are called *generalization gradients*. The graphs normally show, as depicted here, that generalization declines as the similarity between the original CS and the new stimuli decreases. When an organism gradually learns to *discriminate* between a CS and similar stimuli, the generalization gradient tends to narrow around the original CS.

The process of generalization can have important implications. For example, it appears to contribute to the development of *panic disorder,* which involves recurrent, overwhelming anxiety attacks that occur suddenly and unexpectedly (see Chapter 14). Recent research suggests that panic patients have a tendency to overgeneralize—that is, to have broader generalization gradients than control subjects—when exposed to stimuli that trigger anxiety (Lissek et al., 2010). Thus, conditioned fear to a stimulus environment where panic occurs (say, a specific shopping mall) readily generalizes to similar stimulus situations (all shopping malls), fuelling the growth of patients' panic disorder.

John B. Watson, the founder of behaviourism (see Chapter 1), conducted an influential early study of generalization. Watson and a colleague, Rosalie Rayner, examined the generalization of conditioned fear in an 11-month-old boy, known in the annals of psychology as "Little Albert." Like many babies, Albert was initially unafraid of a live white rat. Then Watson and Rayner (1920) paired the presentation of the rat with a loud, startling sound (made by striking a steel gong with a hammer). Albert *did* show fear in response to the loud noise. After seven pairings of the rat and the gong, the rat was established as a CS eliciting a fear response. Five days later, Watson and Rayner exposed the youngster to other stimuli that resembled the rat in being white and furry. They found that Albert's fear response generalized to a variety of stimuli, including a rabbit, a dog, a fur coat, a Santa Claus mask, and Watson's hair.

What happened to Little Albert? Did he grow up with a phobia of Santa Claus? There was endless speculation for decades because no one had any idea who Albert was or what happened to him. He was taken from the hospital where Watson and Rayner conducted their study before they got around to extinguishing the conditioned fears that they had created. Watson and Rayner were roundly criticized

in later years for failing to ensure that Albert experienced no lasting ill effects. Their failure to do so clearly was remiss by today's much stricter code of research ethics, but normal for the time. Recently, after 90 years of mystery, a team of history sleuths managed to track down Little Albert's identity and explain why he vanished into thin air (Beck, Levinson, & Irons, 2009). While there is still some controversy (Beck, Levinson & Irons, 2010; Powell, 2010; Reese, 2010), information uncovered by Beck et al. (2009) suggests his real name was Douglas Merritte, the son of a wet nurse who worked near Watson's lab. Sadly, he had a very brief life, perishing at the age of six from acquired hydrocephalus. Little information is available on his short life, so we will never know whether he experienced any ill effects from his participation in one of psychology's most legendary studies.

Stimulus Discrimination

Stimulus discrimination is just the opposite of stimulus generalization. *Stimulus discrimination* occurs when an organism that has learned a response to a specific stimulus does not respond in the same way to new stimuli that are similar to the original stimulus. Like generalization, discrimination is adaptive in that an animal's survival may hinge on its being able to distinguish friend from foe, or edible from poisonous food (Thomas, 1992). Organisms can gradually learn to discriminate between an original CS and similar stimuli if they have adequate experience with both. For instance, let's say your pet dog runs around, excitedly wagging its tail, whenever it hears your car pull into the driveway. Initially it will probably respond to *all* cars that pull into the driveway (stimulus generalization). However, if there is anything distinctive about the sound of your car, your dog may gradually respond with excitement to only your car and not to other cars (stimulus discrimination).

The development of stimulus discrimination usually requires that the original CS (your car) continues to be paired with the UCS (your arrival) while similar stimuli (the other cars) not be paired with the UCS. As with generalization, a basic law governs discrimination: *The less similar new stimuli are to the original CS, the greater the likelihood (and ease) of discrimination.* Conversely, if a new stimulus is quite similar to the original CS, discrimination will be relatively difficult to learn. What happens to a generalization gradient when an organism learns a discrimination? The generalization gradient gradually narrows around the original CS, which means that the organism is generalizing to a smaller and smaller range of similar stimuli (consult Figure 6.7 again).

Little Albert was conditioned by Watson to fear a white rat. The conditioned fear then generalized to other objects.

Archives of the History of American Psychology, The Center for the History of Psychology—University of Akron

Higher-Order Conditioning

5b

Imagine that you were to conduct the following experiment. First, you condition a dog to salivate in response to the sound of a tone by pairing the tone with meat powder. Once the tone is firmly established as a CS, you pair the tone with a new stimulus—let's say a red light, for 15 trials. You then present the red light alone, without the tone. Will the dog salivate in response to the red light?

The answer is "yes." Even though the red light has never been paired with the meat powder, it will acquire the capacity to elicit salivation by virtue of being paired with the tone (see Figure 6.8). This is a demonstration of *higher-order conditioning,* in which a conditioned stimulus functions as if it were an unconditioned stimulus. Higher-order conditioning shows that classical conditioning does not depend on the presence of a genuine, natural UCS. An already established CS will do just fine. In higher-order conditioning, new conditioned responses are built on the foundation of already-established conditioned responses. For example, using Pavlov's original method, once conditioning has occurred and the tone reliably elicits the salivation, the tone itself can then be paired with another stimulus such as a light. After subsequent conditioning trials, the light itself then will serve to elicit the salivation. Many human conditioned responses are the product of higher-order conditioning (Rescorla, 1980). The phenomenon of higher-order conditioning greatly extends the reach of classical conditioning.

REVIEW OF KEY POINTS

▷ Learning is defined as a relatively durable change in behaviour or knowledge due to experience. Classical conditioning explains how a neutral stimulus can acquire the capacity to elicit a response originally elicited by another stimulus. This kind of conditioning was originally described by Ivan Pavlov, who conditioned dogs to salivate in response to the sound of a tone.

▷ In classical conditioning, the unconditioned stimulus (UCS) is a stimulus that elicits an unconditioned response without previous conditioning. The unconditioned response (UCR) is an unlearned reaction to an unconditioned stimulus that occurs without previous conditioning. The conditioned stimulus (CS) is a previously neutral stimulus that has acquired the capacity to elicit a conditioned response. The conditioned response (CR) is a learned reaction to a conditioned stimulus.

▷ Classically conditioned responses are said to be *elicited*. Many kinds of everyday responses are regulated through classical conditioning, including phobias, mild fears, and pleasant emotional responses. Even subtle physiological responses such as immune system functioning respond to classical conditioning. Sexual arousal can be influenced by Pavlovian conditioning, and this process may have adaptive significance.

▷ Stimulus contiguity plays a key role in the acquisition of new conditioned responses. A conditioned response may be weakened and extinguished entirely when the CS is no longer paired with the UCS. In some cases, spontaneous recovery occurs, and an extinguished response reappears after a period of nonexposure to the CS.

▷ Conditioning may generalize to additional stimuli that are similar to the original CS.

▷ The opposite of generalization is discrimination, which involves not responding to stimuli that resemble the original CS. When an organism learns a discrimination, the generalization gradient narrows around the original CS. Higher-order conditioning occurs when a CS functions as if it were a UCS.

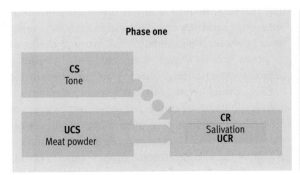
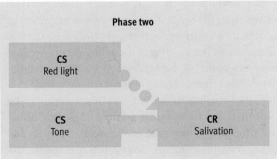

FIGURE 6.8

Higher-order conditioning.

Higher-order conditioning involves a two-phase process. In the first phase, a neutral stimulus (such as a tone) is paired with an unconditioned stimulus (such as meat powder) until it becomes a conditioned stimulus that elicits the response originally evoked by the UCS (such as salivation). In the second phase, another neutral stimulus (such as a red light) is paired with the previously established CS, so that it also acquires the capacity to elicit the response originally evoked by the UCS.

Recent Directions in Pavlovian Conditioning

Even though Pavlovian conditioning was first described more than a century ago, research into its origins and applications continues. For example, work reviewed by Fanselow and Poulos (2005) and others has been designed to examine the neuroscience of associative learning focusing on, for example, the role played by the amygdala and cerebellum in Pavlovian fear and eye-blink conditioning, respectively.

Others, such as Ap Dijksterhuis, have used subliminal conditioning to raise people's self-esteem level (Dijksterhuis, 2004). In one of a series of experiments, Dijksterhuis exposed participants to a number of trials in which they were presented with simple words. On some of the trials, the word presented was the word "I." For participants in the experimental condition, presentation of "I" was followed by subliminal (i.e., below level of awareness) presentation of a positive-trait term such as *wise*, or *healthy*, or *smart*. For the control participants, "I" was followed by subliminal presentation of neutral words such as *chair* or *bike*. When the participants' self-esteem was subsequently evaluated, the participants in the experimental condition had significantly higher implicit self-esteem. It is important to note, as pointed out by Dijksterhuis, that the conditioning effect on implicit self-esteem was produced "while bypassing consciousness altogether" (p. 352). We have no doubt that research on such conditioning will continue in the future. Research such as the effect of conditioning on self-esteem has clear implications for psychological disorders that are associated with self-esteem deficits, such as depression. In fact, a variety of classical conditioning phenomena have implications for understanding and treating psychological disorders (e.g., LaBar et al., 1998; LeDoux et al., 1990). These are discussed in detail in Chapters 14 and 15.

Operant Conditioning

PREVIEW QUESTIONS

▶ How did Thorndike's law of effect anticipate Skinner's findings?

▶ What are the key elements in operant conditioning?

▶ How do organisms acquire new responses through operant conditioning?

▶ What is resistance to extinction, and why does it matter?

▶ How does stimulus control fit into operant responding?

▶ How do primary and secondary reinforcers differ?

Even Pavlov recognized that classical conditioning is not the only form of conditioning. Classical conditioning best explains reflexive responding that is largely controlled by stimuli that *precede* the response. However, humans and other animals make a great many responses that don't fit this description. Consider the response that you are engaging in right now: studying. It is definitely not a reflex (life might be easier if it were). The stimuli that govern it (exams and grades) do not precede it. Instead, your studying is mainly influenced by stimulus events that *follow* the response—specifically, its *consequences*.

In the 1930s, this kind of learning was christened *operant conditioning* by B. F. Skinner. The term was derived from his belief that in this type of responding, an organism "operates" on the environment instead of simply reacting to stimuli. Learning occurs because responses come to be influenced by the outcomes that follow them. Thus, *operant conditioning* is a form of learning in which responses come to be controlled by their consequences. Learning theorists originally distinguished between classical and operant conditioning on the grounds that the former regulated reflexive, involuntary responses, whereas the latter governed voluntary responses. This distinction holds up much of the time, but it is not absolute. Research in recent decades has shown that classical conditioning sometimes contributes to the regulation of voluntary behaviour, that operant conditioning can influence involuntary, visceral responses, and that the two types of conditioning jointly and interactively govern some aspects of behaviour (Allan, 1998; Turkkan, 1989). Indeed, some theorists have argued that classical and operant conditioning should be viewed as just two different aspects of a single learning process (Donahoe & Vegas, 2004).

Thorndike's Law of Effect

Another name for operant conditioning is *instrumental learning*, a term introduced earlier by Edward L. Thorndike (1913). Thorndike wanted to emphasize that this kind of responding is often *instrumental* in obtaining some desired outcome. His pioneering work provided the foundation for many of the ideas proposed later by Skinner (Chance, 1999). Thorndike began studying animal learning around the turn of the last century. Setting out to determine whether animals could think, he conducted some classic studies of problem solving in cats. In these studies, a hungry cat was placed in a small cage or "puzzle box" with food available just outside. The cat could escape to obtain the food by performing a specific response, such as pulling a wire or depressing a lever (see Figure 6.9). After each escape, the cat was rewarded with a small amount of food and then returned to the cage for another trial. Thorndike monitored how long it took the cat to get out of the box over a series of trials. If the cat could think, Thorndike reasoned, there would be a sudden drop in the time required to escape when the cat recognized the solution to the problem.

Instead of a sudden drop, Thorndike observed a gradual, uneven decline in the time it took cats to escape from his puzzle boxes (see the graph in Figure 6.9). The decline in solution time showed that the cats *were learning*. But the gradual nature of this decline suggested that this learning did *not* depend on thinking and understanding. Instead, Thorndike attributed this learning to a principle he called the *law of effect*. According to the *law of effect*, if a response in the presence of a stimulus leads to satisfying effects, the association between the stimulus and the response is strengthened. Thorndike viewed instrumental learning as a mechanical process in which successful responses are gradually "stamped in" by their favourable effects. His law of effect became the cornerstone of Skinner's theory of operant conditioning, although Skinner used different terminology.

Skinner's Demonstration: It's All a Matter of Consequences

 5c

Like Pavlov, Skinner (1953, 1969, 1984) conducted some deceptively simple research that became enormously influential (Lattal, 1992). Ironically, he got off to an inauspicious start. His first book, *The Behavior of Organisms* (1938), sold only 80 copies in its first four years in print. Nonetheless, he went on to become, in the words of historian Albert Gilgen (1982), "without question the most famous American psychologist in the world" (p. 97). He was a very recognizable face to North Americans and wrote popular as well as scientific articles (Rutherford, 2005). He was an inveterate inventor, applying his scientific knowledge and ingenuity to many problems. One of his most (in)famous inventions was the so-called *Baby Box* (named a *Baby Tender*, or later the *Air Crib* by Skinner himself) (Rutherford, 2005). It was an enclosed temperature- and humidity-controlled crib that Skinner designed for his daughter Deborah after his wife asked him for some assistance in improving ways to bring up a baby. He had hoped to modernize child-rearing and to improve things for everyone—babies and parents included. His attempts to popularize this idea to the masses were less than successful. According to psychologist-historian Alexandra Rutherford (2005), when he wrote about the invention and its advantages in a popular magazine, the editors changed his title from "Baby care can be modernized" to "Baby in a Box—Introducing the Mechanical Baby Tender" (Rutherford, 2005). Of course, this title change did nothing to inspire an

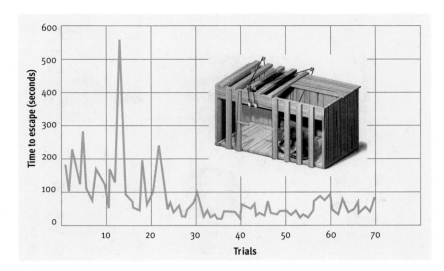

FIGURE 6.9

The learning curve of one of Thorndike's cats.

The inset shows one of Thorndike's puzzle boxes. The cat had to perform three separate acts to escape the box, including depressing the pedal on the right. The learning curve shows how the cat's escape time declined gradually over a number of trials.

enthusiastic response and there were many criticisms of the idea and even rumours and assertions that Skinner had used Deborah in his experiments (Slater, 2004) and that she grew up traumatized and psychotic (*Time*, 1971). Deborah Skinner herself denies these rumours and, based on her own experiences, expresses surprise that the "contraption" never really took off and became popular (Skinner, 2004).

Skinner even used his work on operant conditioning to help with the American war effort in World War II. In a government-funded secret project, he experimented with training pigeons by means of operant conditioning principles to be able to use their beaks to keep pecking in order to guide missiles to their target. As a demonstration, one group of pigeons was trained to simulate guiding missiles to specific targets on the New Jersey coast (Skinner, 1960). Ultimately, the American government focused on other priorities and the project was cancelled, leaving Skinner, in his own words, with a "loft full of useless

Skinner designed the Air Crib to assist in raising his daughter Deborah. He hoped to modernize the raising of children.

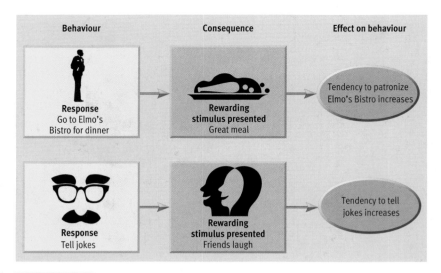

Behaviour | **Consequence** | **Effect on behaviour**

Response
Go to Elmo's
Bistro for dinner
→
Rewarding
stimulus presented
Great meal
→
Tendency to patronize
Elmo's Bistro increases

Response
Tell jokes
→
Rewarding
stimulus presented
Friends laugh
→
Tendency to tell
jokes increases

FIGURE 6.10

Reinforcement in operant conditioning.

According to Skinner, reinforcement occurs when a response is followed by rewarding conse-quences and the organism's tendency to make the response increases. The two examples dia-grammed here illustrate the basic premise of operant conditioning—that voluntary behaviour is controlled by its consequences. These examples involve positive reinforcement (for a comparison of positive and negative reinforcement, see Figure 6.15 on page 273).

Courtesy of B.F. Skinner

B. F. Skinner

"Operant conditioning shapes behaviour as a sculptor shapes a lump of clay."

equipment" and a group of trained pigeons with a peculiar "interest in a feature of the New Jersey coast" (Skinner, 1960, p. 34). In training his pigeons, Skinner made use of *reinforcement* principles. What is *reinforcement* and how does it work?

The fundamental principle of operant condi-tioning is uncommonly simple and was anticipated by Thorndike's law of effect. *Skinner demonstrated that organisms tend to repeat those responses that are followed by favourable consequences.* This fundamental principle is embodied in Skinner's concept of rein-forcement. *Reinforcement* occurs when an event fol-lowing a response increases an organism's tendency to make that response. In other words, a response is strengthened because it leads to rewarding conse-quences (see Figure 6.10).

The principle of reinforcement may be simple, but it is immensely powerful. Skinner and his fol-lowers have shown that much of everyday behav-iour is regulated by reinforcement. For example, you put money in a pop vending machine and you get a soft drink back as a result. Paradoxically, though, this principle emerged out of Skinner's research on the behaviour of rats and pigeons in exceptionally simple situations. Let's look at that research.

Terminology and Procedures

5c

Like Pavlov, Skinner created a prototype experimental procedure that has been repeated (with variations)

thousands of times. In his research, Skinner typically used pigeons or rats. They made ideal participants for his research where the focus was on observ-able behaviour. In the typical procedure, a rat or a pigeon is placed in an *operant chamber* that has come to be better known as a "Skinner box." An *operant chamber,* or *Skinner box,* is a small enclosure in which an animal can make a specific response that is recorded while the consequences of the response are systematically controlled. In the boxes designed for rats, the main response made available is pressing a small lever mounted on one side wall (see Figure 6.11). In the boxes made for pigeons, the designated response is pecking a small disk mounted on a side wall. Because operant responses tend to be voluntary, they are said to be *emitted* rather than *elicited. To emit* means to send forth.

The Skinner box permits the experimenter to control the reinforcement contingencies that are in effect for the animal. *Reinforcement contingencies* are the circumstances or rules that determine whether responses lead to the presentation of reinforcers. Typically, the experimenter manipulates whether positive consequences occur when the animal makes the designated response. The main positive conse-quence is usually delivery of a small bit of food into a food cup mounted in the chamber. Because the animals are deprived of food for a while prior to the experimental session, their hunger virtually ensures that the food serves as a reinforcer.

The key dependent variable in most research on operant conditioning is the subjects' *response rate* over time. An animal's rate of lever pressing or disk pecking in the Skinner box is monitored continu-ously by a device known as a cumulative recorder (see Figure 6.11). The *cumulative recorder* creates a graphic record of responding and reinforcement in a Skinner box as a function of time. The recorder works by means of a roll of paper that moves at a steady rate underneath a movable pen. When there is no responding, the pen stays still and draws a straight horizontal line, reflecting the passage of time. Whenever the designated response occurs, however, the pen moves upward a notch. The pen's movements produce a graphic summary of the ani-mal's responding over time. The pen also makes slash marks to record the delivery of each reinforcer.

The results of operant-conditioning studies are usually portrayed in graphs. In these graphs, the hor-izontal axis is used to mark the passage of time, while the vertical axis is used to plot the accumulation of responses, as shown in Figure 6.12. In interpreting these graphs, the key consideration is the *slope* of the line that represents the record of responding. *A rapid response rate produces a steep slope, whereas a*

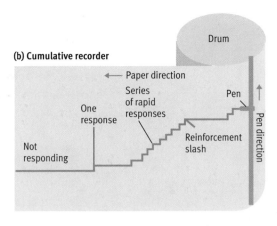

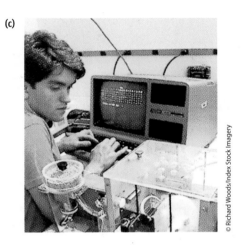

(b) Cumulative recorder

Paper direction

Drum

Series of rapid responses

Pen

One response

Not responding

Reinforcement slash

Pen direction

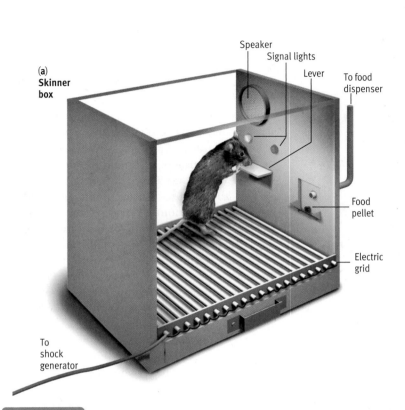

Speaker

Signal lights

Lever

To food dispenser

(a) Skinner box

Food pellet

Electric grid

To shock generator

(c)

© Richard Woods/Index Stock Imagery

FIGURE 6.11

Skinner box and cumulative recorder.

(a) This diagram highlights some of the key features of an operant chamber, or Skinner box. In this apparatus designed for rats, the response under study is lever pressing. Food pellets, which may serve as reinforcers, are delivered into the food cup on the right. The speaker and light permit manipulations of visual and auditory stimuli, and the electric grid gives the experimenter control over aversive consequences (shock) in the box. **(b)** A cumulative recorder connected to the box keeps a continuous record of responses and reinforcements. A small segment of a cumulative record is shown here. The entire process is automatic as the paper moves with the passage of time; each lever press moves the pen up a step, and each reinforcement is marked with a slash. **(c)** This photo shows the real thing—a rat being conditioned in a Skinner box. Note the food dispenser on the left, which was omitted from the diagram.

slow response rate produces a shallow slope. Because the response record is cumulative, the line never goes down. It can only go up as more responses are made or flatten out if the response rate slows to zero. The magnifications shown in Figure 6.12 show how slope and response rate are related.

Basic Processes in Operant Conditioning SIM4 5c

Although the principle of reinforcement is strikingly simple, many other processes involved in operant conditioning make this form of learning just as complex as classical conditioning. In fact,

some of the *same* processes are involved in both types of conditioning. In this section, we'll discuss how the processes of acquisition, extinction, generalization, and discrimination occur in operant conditioning.

Acquisition and Shaping SIM4 5c

As in classical conditioning, *acquisition* in operant conditioning refers to the initial stage of learning some new pattern of responding. However, the procedures used to establish a tendency to emit an operant response are different from those used to create the typical conditioned response. Operant responses are usually established through a gradual

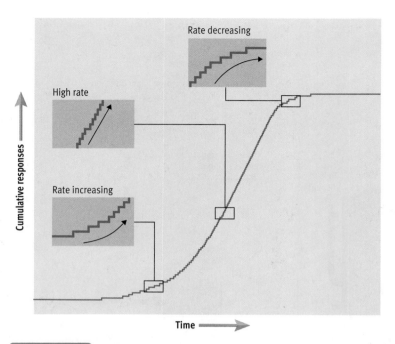

FIGURE 6.12

A graphic portrayal of operant responding.

The results of operant conditioning are often summarized in a graph of cumulative responses over time. The insets magnify small segments of the curve to show how an increasing response rate yields a progressively steeper slope (bottom); a high, steady response rate yields a steep, stable slope (middle); and a decreasing response rate yields a progressively flatter slope (top).

process called *shaping*, which consists of the reinforcement of closer and closer approximations of a desired response.

Shaping is necessary when an organism does not, on its own, emit the desired response. One of our colleagues used shaping to help her housetrain her new puppy. Because the dog, named Meisje, was small and quiet, our colleague had difficulty in determining when the puppy needed to go outside. She thought that she would train the puppy to ring a bell but, of course, puppies do not naturally ring bells. So she began to shape the puppy by rewarding him as he came progressively closer to the bell, finally reinforcing Meisje's behaviour only when he rang the bell with his nose. Of course, ultimately he was rewarded for bell ringing with a trip outside and a congratulatory "Good boy" on successful completion of his very important task. He now can communicate his needs to her easily. Our colleague reports a couple of other interesting effects. When she leaves town, she can readily find someone to dog-sit her puppy because no matter where he stays, she brings along the bell and he can let the caretaker know when he needs to go outside. Curiously, however, at home, she finds herself frequently getting up and running to the back door whenever she hears any bell—she suspects the puppy may be ringing the bell just to see her run to the back door.

Shaping was an important component of Skinner's research. For example, when a rat is first placed in a Skinner box, it may not press the lever at all. In this case, an experimenter begins shaping by releasing food pellets whenever the rat moves toward the lever. As this response becomes more frequent, the experimenter starts requiring a closer approximation of the desired response, possibly releasing food only when the rat actually touches the lever. As reinforcement increases the rat's tendency to touch the lever, the rat will spontaneously press the lever on occasion, finally providing the experimenter with an opportunity to reinforce the designated response. These reinforcements will gradually increase the rate of lever pressing.

The mechanism of shaping is the key to training animals to perform impressive tricks. When you go to a zoo, circus, or marine park and see bears riding bicycles, monkeys playing the piano, and whales leaping through hoops, you are witnessing the results of shaping. To demonstrate the power of shaping techniques, Skinner once trained some pigeons so that they appeared to play Ping-Pong. They would run about on opposite ends of a Ping-Pong table and peck the ball back and forth. Keller and Marian Breland, a couple of psychologists influenced by Skinner, went into the business of training animals for advertising and entertainment purposes. One of their better-known feats was shaping "Priscilla, the Fastidious Pig" to turn on a radio, eat at a kitchen table, put dirty clothes in a hamper, run a vacuum, and then "go shopping" with a shopping cart. Of course, Priscilla picked the sponsor's product off the shelf in her shopping expedition (Breland & Breland, 1961).

Extinction

SIM4   5c

In operant conditioning, *extinction* refers to the gradual weakening and disappearance of a response tendency because the response is no longer followed by a reinforcer. Extinction begins in operant conditioning whenever previously available reinforcement is stopped. In laboratory studies with rats, this usually means that the experimenter stops delivering food when the rat presses the lever. When the extinction process is begun, a brief surge often occurs in the rat's responding, followed by a gradual decline in response rate until it approaches zero.

A key issue in operant conditioning is how much *resistance to extinction* an organism will display when reinforcement is halted. *Resistance to extinction* occurs when an organism continues to make a response after delivery of the reinforcer has been terminated. The greater the resistance to

Shaping—an operant technique in which an organism is rewarded for closer and closer approximations of the desired response—is used in teaching both animals and humans. It is the main means of training animals to perform unnatural tricks. Breland and Breland's (1961) famous subject, "Priscilla, the Fastidious Pig," is shown in the middle.

extinction, the longer the responding will continue. Thus, if a researcher stops giving reinforcement for lever pressing and the response tapers off slowly, the response shows high resistance to extinction. However, if the response tapers off quickly, it shows relatively little resistance to extinction.

Resistance to extinction may sound like a matter of purely theoretical interest, but it's actually quite practical. People often want to strengthen a response in such a way that it will be relatively resistant to extinction. For instance, most parents want to see their child's studying response survive even if the child hits a rocky stretch when studying doesn't lead to reinforcement (good grades). In a similar fashion, a casino wants to see patrons continue to gamble, even if they encounter a lengthy losing streak. Thus, a high degree of resistance to extinction can be desirable in many situations. Resistance to extinction depends on a variety of factors. Chief among them is the *schedule of reinforcement* used during acquisition, a matter that we will discuss a little later in this chapter.

Finally, you may recall that in our discussion of extinction in classical conditioning on page 259 we discussed the concept of the *renewal effect*—if a response is extinguished in a different environment than it was acquired, the extinguished response will reappear if the animal is returned to the original environment where acquisition took place. The renewal effect is also true of extinction of a response acquired

as a result of operant conditioning (Bouton, Todd, & Vurbic, 2011). According to Bouton et al., (2011), this finding has clear implications for a variety of issues related to psychopathology and voluntary problematic behaviour such as substance abuse. For example, this might explain some of the difficulties faced by recovering addicts after their treatments in a drug treatment facility ends; treatments based solely on extinction practices might be specific to the extinction context. Renewal effects, whether based in classical or operant conditioning procedures, complicate clinical intervention (Martin, LaRow, & Malcolm, 2010; Stasiewicz, Brandon, & Bradizza, 2007).

Stimulus Control: Generalization and Discrimination

Operant responding is ultimately controlled by its consequences, as organisms learn response–outcome (R–O) associations (Colwill, 1993). However, stimuli that *precede* a response can also exert considerable influence over operant behaviour. When a response is consistently followed by a reinforcer in the presence of a particular stimulus, that stimulus comes to serve as a "signal," indicating that the response is likely to lead to a reinforcer. Once an organism learns the signal, it tends to respond accordingly (Honig & Alsop, 1992). For example, a pigeon's disk pecking may be reinforced only when a small light behind the disk is lit. When the light is out, pecking does not lead to the reward. Pigeons quickly learn to peck the disk only when it is lit. The light that signals the availability of reinforcement is called a *discriminative stimulus*. *Discriminative stimuli* are cues that influence operant behaviour by indicating the probable consequences (reinforcement or nonreinforcement) of a response.

Discriminative stimuli play a key role in the regulation of operant behaviour. For example, birds learn that hunting for worms is likely to be reinforced after a rain. Human social behaviour is also regulated extensively by discriminative stimuli. Consider the behaviour of asking someone for a date. Many people emit this response only cautiously, after receiving many signals (such as eye contact, smiles, encouraging conversational exchanges) that reinforcement (a favourable answer) is fairly likely.

Reactions to a discriminative stimulus are governed by the processes of *stimulus generalization* and *stimulus discrimination,* just like reactions to a CS in classical conditioning. For instance, envision a cat that comes running into the kitchen whenever it hears the sound of a can opener because that sound has become a discriminative stimulus signalling a good chance of its getting fed. If the cat also responded to the sound of a new kitchen appliance (say, a blender), this response would represent *generalization*—responding to a new stimulus as if it were the original. *Discrimination* would occur if the cat learned to respond only to the can opener and not to the blender.

As you have learned in this section, the processes of acquisition, extinction, generalization, and discrimination in operant conditioning parallel these same processes in classical conditioning. Table 6.1 compares these processes in the two kinds of conditioning.

Reinforcement: Consequences That Strengthen Responses 5e

Although it is convenient to equate reinforcement with reward and the experience of pleasure, strict behaviourists object to this practice. Why? Because the experience of pleasure is an unobservable event that takes place within an organism. As explained in Chapter 1, most behaviourists believe that scientific assertions must be limited to what can be observed.

In keeping with this orientation, Skinner said that reinforcement occurs whenever an outcome strengthens a response, as measured by an increase in the rate of responding. This definition avoids the issue of what the organism is feeling and focuses on observable events. Thus, the central process in reinforcement is the *strengthening of a response tendency.* To know whether an event is reinforcing, researchers must make it contingent on a response and observe whether the rate of this response increases after the supposed reinforcer has been presented.

Thus, reinforcement is defined *after the fact,* in terms of its *effect* on behaviour. Something that is clearly reinforcing for an organism at one time may not function as a reinforcer later (Catania, 1992). Food will reinforce lever pressing by a rat only if the rat is hungry. Similarly, something that serves as a reinforcer for one person may not function as a reinforcer for another person. For example, parental approval is a potent reinforcer for most children, but not all.

Operant theorists make a distinction between unlearned, or primary, reinforcers as opposed to

TABLE 6.1

Comparison of Basic Processes in Classical and Operant Conditioning

Process and Definition	Description in Classical Conditioning	Description in Operant Conditioning
Acquisition: The initial stage of learning	CS and UCS are paired, gradually resulting in CR.	Responding gradually increases because of reinforcement, possibly through shaping.
Extinction: The gradual weakening and disappearance of a conditioned response tendency	CS is presented alone until it no longer elicits CR.	Responding gradually slows and stops after reinforcement is terminated.
Stimulus generalization: An organism's responding to stimuli other than the original stimulus used in conditioning	CR is elicited by new stimulus that resembles original CS.	Responding increases in the presence of new stimulus that resembles discriminative stimulus.
Stimulus discrimination: An organism's response to stimuli that are similar to the original stimulus used in conditioning	CR is not elicited by new stimulus that resembles original CS.	Responding does not increase in the lack of presence of new stimulus that resembles the original discriminative stimulus.

conditioned, or secondary, reinforcers. *Primary reinforcers* are events that are inherently reinforcing because they satisfy biological needs. A given species has a limited number of primary reinforcers because they are closely tied to physiological needs. In humans, primary reinforcers include food, water, warmth, sex, and perhaps affection expressed through hugging and close bodily contact. *Secondary*, or *conditioned, reinforcers* are events that acquire reinforcing qualities by being associated with primary reinforcers. The events that function as secondary reinforcers vary among members of a species because they depend on learning. Examples of common secondary reinforcers in humans include money, good grades, attention, flattery, praise, and applause. Similarly, people *learn* to find stylish clothes, sports cars, fine jewellery, and exotic vacations reinforcing.

Reinforcement and Superstitious Behaviour

Reinforcement, of course, is key to the development of the kinds of superstitious behaviours exhibited by professional athletes (Todd, 2003) described in the introduction to this chapter on page 250. In the case of superstitious behaviours, the reinforcement is most likely accidental—for example, a hat trick when one just happens to be wearing a black turtleneck underneath one's hockey uniform. Skinner himself was fascinated by the development of superstitious behaviour and even designed an experiment in 1948 to chart its development in pigeons (Skinner, 1948b). Pigeons were placed in an experimental cage into which Skinner introduced a reinforcer (food), which according to Skinner had *"no reference whatsoever to the bird's behavior"* (p. 168). Skinner observed that the birds would tend to repeat whatever behaviour they had been engaged in when the food was presented, behaviour that was, in a sense, accidentally reinforced. Among the "superstitious" behaviours he engendered were a bird who turned counterclockwise about the cage, a bird who repeatedly thrust its head into one of the upper corners of the cage, and a third who developed an unusual "tossing" motion with its head, as if it was "placing its head beneath an invisible bar and lifting it repeatedly" (p. 168). It is not so far, perhaps, from head tossing to the tucking in of one's hockey jersey on only one side or the wearing of black turtlenecks. Skinner himself observed that the behaviour of his pigeons was no different from the behaviour of a bowler who twists and turns his or her body after releasing the ball. The bowler's behaviour, like the head tossing of the pigeon, has no real impact on the probability of receiving a reward, be it food or a strike. But, the behaviour continues. Skinner's theory that noncontingent reinforcement is the basis for superstitious behaviour held sway for many years, although some have argued that not all research consistently replicated his findings (Staddon & Simmelhag, 1971). Thus, noncontingent reinforcement clearly may not be as powerful or influential as Skinner originally believed.

That said, superstitious behaviour is extremely common and accidental reinforcements *may* sometimes contribute to these superstitions, along with various types of erroneous reasoning (Ono, 1987; Vyse, 1997). As we discussed at the beginning of this chapter, there are extensive anecdotal reports of athletes exhibiting superstitious responses, such as those displayed by baseball legend Wade Boggs, whom we discussed at the beginning of the chapter. Tiger Woods wears a red golf shirt on Sundays, traditionally the last day of a golf tournament, and basketball great Michael Jordan wore his University of Carolina college basketball shorts underneath his professional basketball uniform all through his career (Damisch, Stoberock, & Mussweiler, 2010). Numerous other athletes have reported wearing a special pair of socks, eating the same lunch, going through special rituals, and so on, to enhance their chances of success (Bleak & Frederick, 1998; Ciborowski, 1997; Gmelch, 1978). And these quirks are certainly not limited to athletes (Wargo, 2008). For example, many people compulsively need to "knock on wood" after mentioning their good fortune in some area. One recent study (Risen & Gilovich, 2008) showed that many people subscribe to the belief that it is bad luck to "tempt fate." In one part of the study, participants read about a student named Jon who had applied to prestigious Stanford University for graduate school. Jon's mother sent him a Stanford T-shirt before he had learned whether he had been accepted by Stanford. The subjects believed that Jon's prospects of acceptance would be higher if he did not tempt fate by wearing the T-shirt before getting accepted.

Contemporary research on superstitious behaviour tends to ascribe it to normal cognitive biases and errors that promote irrational reasoning (discussed in Chapter 8) rather than to the unpredictable vagaries of operant conditioning (Pronin et al., 2006; Wegner & Wheatley, 1999). Interestingly, a recent study found that superstitious beliefs can actually enhance performance (Damisch et al., 2010). Participants who were given a "lucky ball" sank more putts on a putting green than control subjects. And subjects who were allowed to hang onto a lucky charm performed better on memory and reasoning tasks than those who had to surrender their lucky charm. So, silly

Professional athletes such as Michael Jordan and Tiger Woods often display superstitious behaviour.

PREVIEW QUESTIONS

▶ What are the typical effects of various schedules of reinforcement?

▶ How do researchers study choice in operant behaviour, and what have they discovered?

▶ How do positive and negative reinforcement differ?

▶ How does two-process theory explain the persistence of avoidance behaviour?

▶ What is the difference between negative reinforcement and punishment?

▶ What are some side effects of punishment and some factors that influence its efficacy?

REVIEW OF KEY POINTS

▶ Operant conditioning involves largely voluntary responses that are governed by their consequences. Thorndike paved the way for Skinner's work by investigating instrumental conditioning and describing the law of effect.

▶ Skinner pioneered the study of operant conditioning, working mainly with rats and pigeons in Skinner boxes. He demonstrated that organisms tend to repeat those responses that are followed by reinforcers. Operant responses are said to be *emitted*.

▶ The key dependent variable in operant conditioning is the rate of response over time, which is tracked by a device called a *cumulative recorder*. When responding over time is shown graphically, steep slopes indicate rapid responding.

▶ New operant responses can be shaped by gradually reinforcing closer and closer approximations of the desired response. Shaping is the key to training animals to perform impressive tricks. In operant conditioning, extinction occurs when reinforcement for a response is terminated and the rate of that response declines. There are variations in resistance to extinction.

▶ Operant responses are regulated by discriminative stimuli that are cues for the likelihood of obtaining reinforcers. These stimuli are subject to the same processes of generalization and discrimination that occur in classical conditioning.

▶ The central process in reinforcement is the strengthening of a response. Primary reinforcers are unlearned; they are closely tied to the satisfaction of physiological needs. In contrast, secondary reinforcers acquire their reinforcing quality through conditioning.

though they may seem, superstitions may actually influence people's outcomes: "[T]he present findings suggest that it may have been the well-balanced combination of existing talent, hard training, and good-luck underwear that made Michael Jordan perform as well as he did" (Damisch et al., 2010, p. 1018).

Schedules of Reinforcement

5d

Organisms make innumerable responses that do not lead to favourable consequences. It would be nice if people were reinforced every time they took an exam, watched a movie, hit a golf shot, asked for a date, or made a sales call. However, in the real world, most responses are reinforced only some of the time. How does this fact affect the potency of reinforcers? To find out, operant psychologists have devoted an enormous amount of attention to how *intermittent schedules of reinforcement* influence operant behaviour (Ferster & Skinner, 1957; Skinner, 1938, 1953).

A *schedule of reinforcement* determines which occurrences of a specific response result in the presentation of a reinforcer. The simplest pattern is continuous reinforcement. *Continuous reinforcement* occurs when every instance of a designated response is reinforced. In the laboratory, experimenters often use continuous reinforcement to shape and establish a new response before moving on to more realistic schedules involving intermittent reinforcement. *Intermittent, or partial, reinforcement occurs when a designated response is reinforced only some of the time.*

Which do you suppose leads to longer-lasting effects—being reinforced every time you emit a response, or being reinforced only some of the time? Studies show that, given an equal number of reinforcements, *intermittent* reinforcement makes a response more resistant to extinction than continuous reinforcement does (Falls, 1998; Schwartz & Robbins, 1995). In other words, organisms continue responding longer after removal of reinforcers when a response has been reinforced only *some* of the time. In fact, schedules of reinforcement that provide only sporadic delivery of reinforcers can yield great resistance to extinction. This finding explains why behaviours that are reinforced only occasionally—such as youngsters' temper tantrums—can be very durable and difficult to eliminate.

Reinforcement schedules come in many varieties, but four particular types of intermittent schedules have attracted the most interest. These schedules are described here along with examples drawn from the laboratory and everyday life (see Figure 6.13 for additional examples).

Ratio schedules require the organism to make the designated response a certain number of times to gain each reinforcer. With a *fixed-ratio (FR) schedule*, the reinforcer is given after a fixed number of nonreinforced responses. *Examples:* (1) A rat is reinforced for every tenth lever press. (2) A salesperson receives a bonus for every fourth set of encyclopedias sold. With a *variable-ratio (VR) schedule*, the reinforcer is given after a variable number of nonreinforced responses. The number of nonreinforced responses varies around a predetermined average. *Examples:* (1) A rat is reinforced for every tenth lever press on the average. The exact number of responses required for reinforcement varies from one time to the next. (2) A slot machine in a casino pays off once every six tries on the average. The number of nonwinning responses between payoffs varies greatly from one time to the next.

Interval schedules require a time period to pass between the presentation of reinforcers. With a *fixed-interval (FI) schedule*, the reinforcer is given for the first response that occurs after a fixed time interval has elapsed. *Examples:* (1) A rat is reinforced for the first lever press after a two-minute interval has elapsed and then must wait two minutes before being able to earn the next reinforcement. (2) A man washing his clothes periodically checks to see whether each load is finished. The reward (clean clothes) is available only after a fixed time interval (corresponding to how long

FIGURE 6.13

Reinforcement schedules in everyday life.
Complex human behaviours are regulated by schedules of reinforcement. Piecework in factories is reinforced on a fixed-ratio schedule. Playing slot machines is based on variable-ratio reinforcement. Watching the clock at work is rewarded on a fixed-interval basis (the arrival of quitting time is the reinforcer). Surfers waiting for a big wave are rewarded on a variable-interval basis.

the washer takes to complete a cycle) has elapsed, and checking responses during the interval are not reinforced. With a *variable-interval (VI) schedule*, the reinforcer is given for the first response after a variable time interval has elapsed. The interval length varies around a predetermined average. *Examples:* (1) A rat is reinforced for the first lever press after a one-minute interval has elapsed, but the following intervals are three minutes, two minutes, four minutes, and so on—with an average length of two minutes. (2) A person repeatedly dials a busy phone number (getting through is the reinforcer).

More than 50 years of research has yielded an enormous volume of data on how these schedules of reinforcement are related to patterns of responding (Williams, 1988; Zeiler, 1977). Some of the more prominent findings are summarized in Figure 6.14, which depicts typical response patterns generated by each schedule. For example, with fixed-interval schedules, a pause in responding usually occurs after each reinforcer is delivered, and then responding gradually increases to a rapid rate at the end of the interval. This pattern of behaviour yields a "scalloped" response curve. In general, ratio schedules tend to produce more rapid responding than interval schedules. Why? Because faster responding leads to reinforcement sooner when a ratio schedule is in effect. Variable

Learning

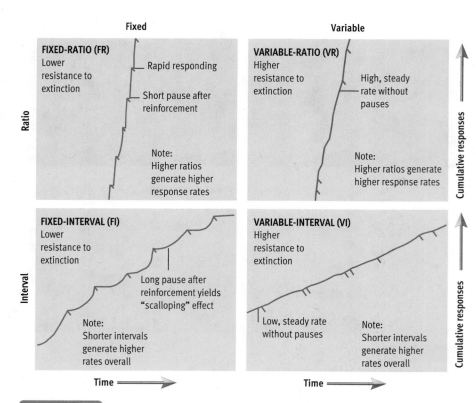

Fixed

FIXED-RATIO (FR)
Lower resistance to extinction

— Rapid responding

— Short pause after reinforcement

Note: Higher ratios generate higher response rates

Ratio

Variable

VARIABLE-RATIO (VR)
Higher resistance to extinction

— High, steady rate without pauses

Note: Higher ratios generate higher response rates

FIXED-INTERVAL (FI)
Lower resistance to extinction

Long pause after reinforcement yields "scalloping" effect

Note: Shorter intervals generate higher rates overall

Interval

VARIABLE-INTERVAL (VI)
Higher resistance to extinction

Low, steady rate without pauses

Note: Shorter intervals generate higher rates overall

Time ⟶

Time ⟶

Cumulative responses

Cumulative responses

FIGURE 6.14

Schedules of reinforcement and patterns of response.

Each type of reinforcement schedule tends to generate a characteristic pattern of responding. In general, ratio schedules tend to produce more rapid responding than interval schedules (note the steep slopes of the FR and VR curves). In comparison to fixed schedules, variable schedules tend to yield steadier responding (note the smoother lines for the VR and VI schedules on the right) and greater resistance to extinction.

concept **check 6.2**

Recognizing Schedules of Reinforcement

Check your understanding of schedules of reinforcement in operant conditioning by indicating the type of schedule that would be in effect in each of the examples below. In the spaces on the left, fill in CR for continuous reinforcement, FR for fixed-ratio, VR for variable-ratio, FI for fixed-interval, and VI for variable-interval. The answers can be found in Appendix A near the back of the book.

_____ **1.** Sarah is paid on a commission basis for selling computer systems. She gets a bonus for every third sale.

_____ **2.** Juan's parents let him earn some pocket money by doing yard work approximately once a week.

_____ **3.** Martha is fly-fishing. Think of each time that she casts her line as the response that may be rewarded.

_____ **4.** Jamal, who is in the fourth grade, gets a gold star from his teacher for every book he reads.

_____ **5.** Skip, a professional baseball player, signs an agreement that his salary increases will be renegotiated every third year.

schedules tend to generate steadier response rates and greater resistance to extinction than their fixed counterparts.

Most of the research on reinforcement schedules was conducted on rats and pigeons in Skinner boxes. However, the available evidence suggests that humans react to schedules of reinforcement in much the same way as animals (de Villers, 1977; Perone, Galizio, & Baron, 1988). For example, when animals are placed on ratio schedules, shifting to a higher ratio (that is, requiring more responses per reinforcement) tends to generate faster responding. Managers of factories that pay on a piecework basis (a fixed-ratio schedule) have seen the same reaction in humans. Shifting to a higher ratio (more pieces for the same pay) usually stimulates harder work and greater productivity (although workers often complain).

There are many other parallels between animals' and humans' reactions to different schedules of reinforcement. For instance, with rats and pigeons, variable-ratio schedules yield steady responding and great resistance to extinction. Similar effects are routinely observed among people who gamble. Most gambling is reinforced according to variable-ratio schedules, which tend to produce rapid, steady responding and great resistance to extinction— exactly what casino operators want.

Positive Reinforcement versus Negative Reinforcement 5e · 5f

PSYKTREK *PSYKTREK*

According to Skinner, reinforcement can take two forms, which he called *positive reinforcement* and *negative reinforcement. Positive reinforcement* occurs when a response is strengthened because it is followed by the presentation of a rewarding stimulus. Thus far, for purposes of simplicity, our examples of reinforcement have involved positive reinforcement. Good grades, tasty meals, paycheques, scholarships, promotions, nice clothes, nifty cars, attention, and flattery are all positive reinforcers.

In contrast, *negative reinforcement* occurs when a response is strengthened because it is followed by the removal of an aversive (unpleasant) stimulus. Don't let the word *negative* confuse you. Negative reinforcement *is* reinforcement. As with all reinforcement, it involves a favourable outcome that *strengthens* a response tendency. However, this strengthening takes place because a response leads to the *removal of an aversive stimulus* rather than the arrival of a pleasant stimulus (see Figure 6.15).

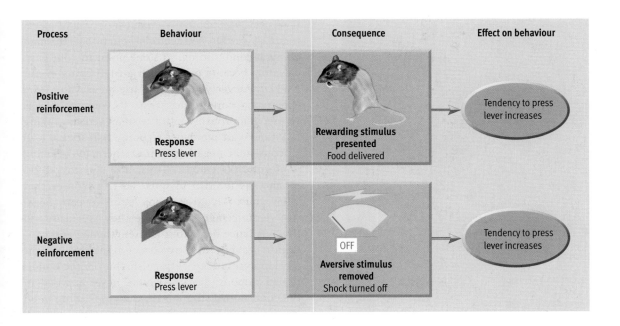

Process	Behaviour	Consequence	Effect on behaviour

Positive reinforcement

Response
Press lever

Rewarding stimulus presented
Food delivered

Tendency to press lever increases

Negative reinforcement

Response
Press lever

OFF

Aversive stimulus removed
Shock turned off

Tendency to press lever increases

FIGURE 6.15

Positive reinforcement versus negative reinforcement.

In positive reinforcement, a response leads to the presentation of a rewarding stimulus. In negative reinforcement, a response leads to the removal of an aversive stimulus. Both types of reinforcement involve favourable consequences and both have the same effect on behaviour: The organism's tendency to emit the reinforced response is strengthened.

In laboratory studies, negative reinforcement is usually accomplished as follows. While a rat is in a Skinner box, a moderate electric shock is delivered to the animal through the floor of the box. When the rat presses the lever, the shock is turned off for a period of time. Thus, lever pressing leads to removal of an aversive stimulus (shock). Although this sequence of events is different from those for positive reinforcement, it reliably strengthens the rat's lever-pressing response.

Everyday human behaviour is regulated extensively by negative reinforcement. Consider a handful of examples. You rush home in the winter to get out of the cold. You clean house to get rid of a disgusting mess. You give in to your child's begging to halt the whining. You take medication to get rid of pain or discomfort. You give in to a roommate or spouse to bring an unpleasant argument to an end.

Negative Reinforcement and Avoidance Behaviour

 5f

You have probably noticed that many people tend to avoid facing awkward situations, difficult challenges, and sticky personal problems. Consistent reliance on avoidance is not a very effective coping strategy. How do people learn to rely on such a strategy? In large part, it may be through negative reinforcement.

5f

Escape Learning

The roots of avoidance lie in escape learning. In *escape learning,* an organism acquires a response that decreases or ends some aversive stimulation. Psychologists often study escape learning in the laboratory with rats that are conditioned in a *shuttle box.* The shuttle box has two compartments connected by a doorway, which can be opened and closed by the experimenter, as depicted in Figure 6.16(a). In a typical study, an animal is placed in one compartment and an electric current in the floor of that chamber is turned on, with the doorway open. The animal learns to escape the shock by running to the other compartment. This escape response leads to the removal of an aversive stimulus (shock), so it is strengthened through negative reinforcement. If you were to leave a party where you were getting picked on by peers, you would be engaging in an escape response. Escape learning doesn't necessarily entail leaving the scene of the aversive stimulation. Any behaviour that decreases or ends aversive stimulation (e.g., turning on the air conditioner to get rid of stifling heat) represents escape learning.

 5f

Avoidance Learning

Escape learning often leads to avoidance learning. In *avoidance learning,* an organism acquires a response that prevents some aversive stimulation from occurring. In laboratory studies of avoidance learning, the experimenter simply gives the animal a signal that a shock is forthcoming. The typical signal is a light that goes on a few seconds prior to the shock. At first, the rat runs only when shocked (escape learning). Gradually, however, the animal learns to run to the safe compartment as soon as the

Learning

FIGURE 6.16

Escape and avoidance learning.

(a) Escape and avoidance learning are often studied with a shuttle box like that shown here. Warning signals, shock, and the animal's ability to flee from one compartment to another can be controlled by the experimenter.
(b) Avoidance begins because classical conditioning creates a conditioned fear that is elicited by the warning signal (panel 1). Avoidance continues because it is maintained by operant conditioning (panel 2). Specifically, the avoidance response is strengthened through negative reinforcement, since it leads to removal of the conditioned fear.

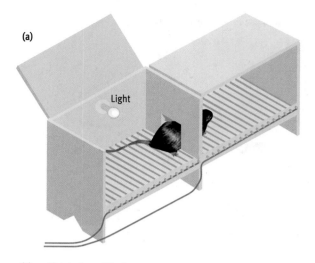

(a)

Light

(b) 1. Classical conditioning

CS Light		
UCS Shock		CR Fear UCR

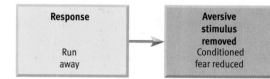

2. Operant conditioning
(negative reinforcement)

Response	Aversive stimulus removed
Run away	Conditioned fear reduced

light comes on, demonstrating avoidance learning. Similarly, if you were to quit going to parties because of your concern about being picked on, this would represent avoidance learning.

Avoidance learning presents an interesting example of how classical conditioning and operant conditioning can work together to regulate behaviour (Levis, 1989; Mowrer, 1947). In avoidance learning, the warning light that goes on before the shock becomes a CS (through classical conditioning), eliciting reflexive, conditioned fear in the animal. However, the response of fleeing to the other side of the box is operant behaviour. This response is strengthened through *negative reinforcement* because it reduces the animal's conditioned fear (see Figure 6.16). Thus, in avoidance learning, a fear response is acquired through classical conditioning and an avoidance response is maintained by operant conditioning.

The principles of avoidance learning shed some light on why phobias are so resistant to extinction

(Levis, 1989). Suppose you have a phobia of elevators. Chances are, you acquired your phobia through classical conditioning. At some point in your past, elevators became paired with a frightening event. Now whenever you need to use an elevator, you experience conditioned fear. If your phobia is severe, you probably take the stairs instead. Taking the stairs is an avoidance response that should lead to consistent negative reinforcement by relieving your conditioned fear. Thus, it's hard to get rid of phobias for two reasons. First, responses that allow you to avoid a phobic stimulus earn negative reinforcement each time they are made—so the avoidance behaviour is strengthened and continues. Second, these avoidance responses prevent any opportunity to extinguish the phobic conditioned response because you're never exposed to the conditioned stimulus (in this case, riding in an elevator).

Punishment: Consequences That Weaken Responses

5e

Reinforcement is defined in terms of its consequences. It *increases* an organism's tendency to make a certain response. Are there also consequences that *decrease* an organism's tendency to make a particular response? Yes. In Skinner's model of operant behaviour, such consequences are called *punishment*.

Punishment occurs when an event following a response weakens the tendency to make that response. In a Skinner box, the administration of punishment is very simple. When a rat presses the lever or a pigeon pecks the disk, it receives a brief shock. This procedure usually leads to a rapid decline in the animal's response rate (Dinsmoor, 1998). Punishment typically involves presentation of an aversive stimulus (for instance, spanking a child). However, punishment may also involve the removal of a rewarding stimulus (for instance, taking away a child's TV-watching privileges).

The concept of punishment in operant conditioning is confusing to many students on two counts. First, they often confuse it with negative reinforcement, which is entirely different. Negative reinforcement involves the *removal* of an aversive stimulus, thereby *strengthening* a response. Punishment, on the other hand, involves the *presentation* of an aversive stimulus, thereby *weakening* a response. Thus, punishment and negative reinforcement are opposite

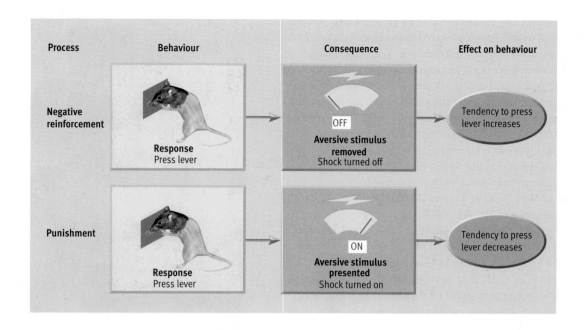

FIGURE 6.17

Comparison of negative reinforcement and punishment.

Although punishment can occur when a response leads to the removal of a rewarding stimulus (negative punishment), it more typically involves the presentation of an aversive stimulus (positive punishment). Students often confuse positive punishment with negative reinforcement because they associate both with aversive stimuli. However, as this diagram shows, punishment and negative reinforcement represent opposite procedures that have opposite effects on behaviour.

procedures that yield opposite effects on behaviour (see Figure 6.17).

The second source of confusion involves the tendency to equate punishment with *disciplinary procedures* used by parents, teachers, and other authority figures. In the operant model, punishment occurs any time that undesirable consequences weaken a response tendency. Defined in this way, the concept of punishment goes far beyond things like parents spanking children and teachers handing out detentions. For example, if you wear a new outfit and your classmates make fun of it, your behaviour will have been punished and your tendency to emit this response (wear the same clothing) will probably decline. Similarly, if you go to a restaurant and have a horrible meal, your response will have been punished, and your tendency to go to that restaurant will probably decline. Although punishment in operant conditioning encompasses far more than disciplinary acts, it is used frequently for disciplinary purposes. In light of this reality, it is worth looking at the research on punishment as a disciplinary measure.

Side Effects of Physical Punishment

About three-quarters of parents report that they sometimes spank their children (Straus & Stewart, 1999), but quite a bit of controversy exists about the wisdom of using physical punishment. Some parents use punishments such as spanking as a way of disciplining and socializing their children. Other parents disagree that such physical means

are appropriate. For example, Alisa Watkinson of Saskatchewan felt so strongly that physical punishment should not be used with children that she went to the Supreme Court of Canada to legally challenge its use (Supreme Court, 2004). The Supreme Court, in a vote of six to three, ruled to uphold Section 43 of the Canadian Criminal Code. The Court ruled that "reasonable corrective force" can be used, but only for children between the ages of 2 and 12. It further ruled that it was not acceptable to use objects in hitting the child, and that the child should not be hit about the head. How frequently are Canadian children spanked? It's often hard to obtain good data, but in a survey of Ontario adults (MacMillan et al., 1999), 20 percent reported they had never been slapped or spanked, 41 percent reported "rarely," 33 percent reported "sometimes," and 5.5 percent reported that they had often been slapped or spanked. Significant organizations such as the Canadian Paediatric Society and the Public Health Agency of Canada oppose the use of spanking and almost three dozen countries across the world, including Sweden, Finland, Norway, and Austria, have outlawed the practice (CBC, 2009).

Opponents of corporal punishment argue that it produces many unintended and undesirable side effects (Hyman, 1996; Lytton, 1997; Straus, 2000). These views were bolstered by a comprehensive review of the empirical research on the physical punishment of children conducted by Elizabeth Thompson Gershoff (2002). Summarizing the results of 88 studies, Gershoff concluded that physical punishment is associated with poor-quality parent–child relationships, elevated aggression, delinquency, and behavioural problems in youngsters, and is associated with an increased likelihood of children being abused. Moreover, she concluded that these effects can carry over into adulthood, as studies find increased aggression, criminal behaviour, mental health problems, and child abuse among adults who were physically punished as children. These conclusions about the negative effects of corporal punishment have been echoed in more recent studies (Aucoin, Frick, & Bodin, 2006; Lynch et al., 2006; Mulvaney & Mebert, 2007).

In the wake of Gershoff's (2002) stinging indictment of physical punishment, critics have raised some doubts about her conclusions, arguing for example that her review failed to distinguish between the effects of frequent, harsh, heavy-handed physical punishment and the effects of occasional, mild spankings, used as a backup when other disciplinary strategies fail (Baumrind, Larzelere, & Cowan, 2002). Critics also point out that the evidence linking spanking to negative effects is correlational, and correlation is no assurance of causation (Kazdin & Benjet, 2003). Perhaps spanking causes children to be more aggressive, but it is also plausible that aggressive children cause their parents to rely more on physical punishment (see Figure 6.18). Based on objections such as these, Baumrind et al. (2002) assert that the empirical evidence "does not justify a blanket injunction against mild to moderate disciplinary spanking" (p. 586).

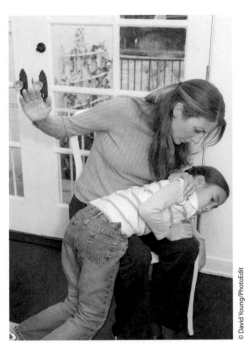

Although physical punishment is frequently administered to suppress aggressive behaviour, in the long run it actually is associated with an increase in aggressive behaviour.

Since then, however, evidence on the negative effects of corporal punishment has continued to pile up (Lynch et al., 2006; Mulvaney & Mebert, 2007). Many of these newer studies have statistically controlled for children's initial level of aggression and other confounding variables, which strengthens the case for a causal link between spanking and negative outcomes. For example, Straus and Paschall (2009) assessed how often children were spanked and their cognitive ability in a group aged two to four and another group aged five to nine. They retested the children's cognitive ability four years later and found that those who were spanked showed a disadvantage in IQ scores. Another study found that spanking at age one predicted increased aggressive behaviour at age two and lower cognitive ability scores at age three (Berlin et al., 2009). Yet another carefully controlled, large-scale study found that heavy use of physical punishment when children were age three was associated with higher levels of aggression at age five (Taylor et al., 2010). In light of findings such as these, an American Psychological Association task force recently concluded that parents should not use corporal punishment (Graham-Bermann, 2009).

Although many experts believe that punishment is overused in disciplinary efforts, it does have a role to play. The following guidelines summarize

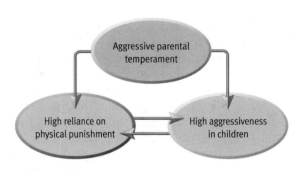

FIGURE 6.18

The correlation between physical punishment and aggressiveness.

As we have discussed before, a correlation does not establish causation. It seems plausible that extensive reliance on physical punishment causes children to be more aggressive, as many experts suspect. However, it is also possible that highly aggressive children cause their parents to depend heavily on physical punishment. Or perhaps parents with an aggressive, hostile temperament pass on genes for aggressiveness to their children, who then also prefer to rely on heavy use of physical punishment.

evidence on how to make punishment more effective while reducing its side effects.

1. *Apply punishment swiftly.* A delay in delivering punishment tends to undermine its impact (Abramowitz & O'Leary, 1990). When a mother says, "Wait until your father gets home . . .," she is making a fundamental mistake in the use of punishment. This problem with delayed punishment also explains the ineffectiveness of punishing a pet hours after it has misbehaved, when the owner finally returns home. For instance, it won't do any good to hit your dog with a newspaper while shoving its face in the feces it previously left on your carpet. This common punishment doesn't teach your dog to stop defecating on your carpet—it teaches the dog to keep its face out of its feces.

2. *Use punishment just severe enough to be effective.* The intensity of punishment is a two-edged sword. Severe punishments usually are more effective in weakening unwanted responses. However, they also increase the likelihood of undesirable side effects. Thus, it's best to use the least severe punishment that seems likely to have the necessary impact (Powell, Symbaluk, & MacDonald, 2002).

3. *Make punishment consistent.* If you want to eliminate a response, you should punish the response every time it occurs. When parents are inconsistent about punishing a particular behaviour, they create more confusion than learning (Acker & O'Leary, 1996).

4. *Explain the punishment.* When children are punished, the reason for their punishment should be explained as fully as possible, given the constraints of their age. Punishment combined with reasoning is more effective than either alone (Larzelere et al., 1996; Parke, 2002). The more that children understand why they were punished, the more effective the punishment tends to be.

5. *Use noncorporal punishments, such as withdrawal of privileges.* Given the concerns about physical punishment, many experts argue that noncorporal punishments are a more prudent means to achieve disciplinary goals. For example, Kazdin and Benjet (2003, p. 103) assert that "mild noncorporal punishments such as a brief time-out from reinforcement or short-term loss of privileges in the context of praise and rewards can accomplish the goals for which spanking is usually employed." Although more research is needed, physical punishment often may not be as effective as most people assume (Holden, 2002). Even a vigorous spanking isn't felt by a child an hour later. In contrast, withdrawing valued privileges can give children hours to contemplate the behaviour that got them into trouble.

REVIEW OF KEY POINTS

> Schedules of reinforcement influence patterns of operant responding. Continuous reinforcement occurs when every designated response is reinforced. Intermittent schedules of reinforcement include fixed-ratio, variable-ratio, fixed-interval, and variable-interval schedules.

> Intermittent schedules produce greater resistance to extinction than similar continuous schedules. Ratio schedules tend to yield higher rates of response than interval schedules. Shorter intervals and higher ratios are associated with faster responding.

> Responses can be strengthened either through the presentation of positive reinforcers or through the removal of negative reinforcers. Negative reinforcement regulates escape and avoidance learning. The two-process theory provides the best explanation of avoidance behaviour and may shed light on why phobias are so difficult to eliminate.

> Punishment involves unfavourable consequences that lead to a decline in response strength. Positive punishment involves the application of aversive consequences, and negative punishment involves the removal of a reward. Problems associated with the application of punishment as a disciplinary procedure include emotional side effects and increased aggressive behaviour. To be effective, punishment of children should be swift, consistent, explained, nonphysical, and just severe enough to have an impact.

concept check 6.3

Recognizing Outcomes in Operant Conditioning

Check your understanding of the various types of consequences that can occur in operant conditioning by indicating whether the examples below involve positive reinforcement (PR), negative reinforcement (NR), punishment (P), or extinction (E). The answers can be found in Appendix A.

_____ **1.** Antonio gets a speeding ticket and is fined.

_____ **2.** Diane's supervisor compliments her on her hard work.

_____ **3.** Audrey lets her dog out so she won't have to listen to its whimpering.

_____ **4.** Richard shoots up heroin to ward off tremors and chills associated with heroin withdrawal.

_____ **5.** Sharma constantly complains about minor aches and pains to obtain sympathy from colleagues at work. Three co-workers who share an office with her decide to ignore her complaints instead of responding with sympathy.

PREVIEW QUESTIONS

▶ What is *instinctive drift*?

▶ Why are conditioned taste aversions so easy to acquire?

▶ Why are some phobias much more common than others?

▶ To what degree are the laws of learning universal across species?

▶ How does the predictive value of a CS affect conditioning?

▶ Are responses that are followed by favourable consequences always strengthened?

As you learned in Chapter 1, science is constantly evolving and changing in response to new research and new thinking. Such change has certainly occurred in the study of conditioning. In this section, we will examine two major changes in thinking about conditioning. First, we'll consider the recent recognition that an organism's biological heritage can limit or channel conditioning. Second, we'll discuss the increased appreciation of the role of cognitive processes in conditioning.

Recognizing Biological Constraints on Conditioning

Learning theorists have traditionally assumed that the fundamental laws of conditioning have great generality—that they apply to a wide range of species. Although no one ever suggested that hamsters could learn physics, until the 1960s, most psychologists assumed that associations could be conditioned between any stimulus that an organism could register and any response that it could make. However, findings in recent decades have demonstrated that there are limits to the generality of conditioning principles—limits imposed by an organism's biological heritage.

Instinctive Drift: The Case of the Miserly Raccoons

One biological constraint on learning is *instinctive drift*. *Instinctive drift* occurs when an animal's innate response tendencies interfere with conditioning processes. Instinctive drift was first described by the Brelands, the operant psychologists who went into the business of training animals for commercial purposes (Breland & Breland, 1966). They have described many amusing examples of their "failures" to control behaviour through conditioning. For instance, they once were training some raccoons to deposit coins into a piggy bank. They were successful in shaping the raccoons to pick up a coin and put it into a small box, using food as the reinforcer. However, when they gave the raccoons a couple of coins, an unexpected problem arose: The raccoons wouldn't give the coins up! In spite of the reinforcers available for depositing the coins, they would sit and rub the coins together like so many little misers: "Now the raccoon really had problems. . . . Not only would he not let go of the coins, but he spent seconds, even minutes, rubbing them together (in a most miserly fashion)" (Breland & Breland, 1961, p. 682).

What had happened to disrupt the conditioning program? Apparently, associating the coins with food had brought out the raccoons' innate food-washing behaviour. Raccoons often rub things together to clean them. The Brelands report that they have run into this sort of instinct-related interference on many occasions with a wide variety of species.

Conditioned Taste Aversion: The "Sauce Béarnaise Syndrome"

A number of years ago, a prominent psychologist, Martin Seligman, dined out with his wife and enjoyed a steak with sauce béarnaise. About six hours afterward, he developed a wicked case of stomach flu and endured severe nausea. Subsequently, when he ordered sauce béarnaise, he was chagrined to discover that its aroma alone nearly made him throw up.

Seligman's experience was not unique. Many people develop aversions to food that has been followed by nausea from illness, alcohol intoxication, or food poisoning (Rosenblum, 2009). However, Seligman was puzzled by what he called his "sauce béarnaise syndrome" (Seligman & Hager, 1972). On the one hand, it appeared to be the straightforward result of classical conditioning. A neutral stimulus (the sauce) had been paired with an unconditioned stimulus (the flu), which caused an unconditioned response (the nausea). Hence, the béarnaise sauce became a conditioned stimulus eliciting nausea (see Figure 6.19).

On the other hand, Seligman recognized that his aversion to béarnaise sauce seemed to violate certain basic principles of conditioning. First, the lengthy delay of six hours between the CS (the sauce) and the UCS (the flu) should have prevented conditioning from occurring. In laboratory studies, a delay of more

FIGURE 6.19

Conditioned taste aversion.

Taste aversions can be established through classical conditioning, as in the "sauce béarnaise syndrome." However, as the text explains, taste aversions can be acquired in ways that seem to violate basic principles of classical conditioning.

than *30 seconds* between the CS and UCS makes it difficult to establish a conditioned response, yet this conditioning occurred in just one pairing. Second, why was it that *only* the béarnaise sauce became a CS eliciting nausea? Why not other stimuli that were present in the restaurant? Shouldn't plates, knives, tablecloths, or his wife, for example, also trigger Seligman's nausea?

The riddle of Seligman's sauce béarnaise syndrome was solved by John Garcia (1989) and his colleagues. They conducted a series of studies on *conditioned taste aversion* (Garcia, Clarke, & Hankins, 1973; Garcia & Koelling, 1966; Garcia & Rusiniak, 1980). In these studies, they manipulated the kinds of stimuli preceding the onset of nausea and other noxious experiences in rats, using radiation to artificially induce the nausea (see Figure 6.20). They found that when taste cues were followed by nausea, rats quickly acquired conditioned taste aversions. However, when taste cues were followed by other types of noxious stimuli (such as shock), rats did *not* develop conditioned taste aversions. Furthermore, visual and auditory stimuli followed by nausea also failed to produce conditioned aversions. In short, Garcia and his co-workers found that it was almost impossible to create certain associations, whereas taste–nausea associations (and odour–nausea associations) were almost impossible to prevent.

What is the theoretical significance of this unique readiness to make connections between taste and nausea? Garcia argues that it is a by-product of the evolutionary history of mammals. Animals that consume poisonous foods and survive must learn not to repeat their mistakes. Natural selection will favour organisms that quickly learn what *not* to eat. Thus, evolution may have biologically programmed some organisms to learn certain types of associations more easily than others. Interest in the antecedents of, processes involved in, and consequences of taste-aversion continue today (e.g., Vidal & Chamizo, 2009).

Preparedness and Phobias

According to Martin Seligman, evolution has also programmed organisms to acquire certain fears more readily than others because of a phenomenon he calls *preparedness*. *Preparedness* involves a species-specific predisposition to be conditioned in certain ways and not others. Seligman (1971) believes that preparedness can explain why certain phobias are vastly more common than others. People tend to develop phobias to snakes, spiders, heights, and darkness relatively easily. However, even after painful experiences with hammers, knives, hot stoves, and electrical outlets, phobic fears of these objects are infrequent. What characteristics do common phobic objects share? Most were once genuine threats to our ancestors. Consequently, a fear response to such objects has survival value for our species. According to Seligman, evolutionary forces gradually programmed humans to acquire conditioned fears of these objects easily and rapidly.

Lab simulations of phobic conditioning have provided some support for the concept of preparedness (Mineka & Öhman, 2002). For example, slides of phobic stimuli (snakes, spiders) for which we seem to show a preparedness and slides of neutral stimuli (flowers, mushrooms) or modern fear-relevant stimuli (guns, knives) have been paired with shock. Consistent with the concept of preparedness, physiological monitoring of the participants indicates that the prepared phobic stimuli tend to produce more rapid conditioning, stronger fear responses, and greater resistance to extinction. Arne Öhman and Susan Mineka (2001) have elaborated on the theory of preparedness, outlining the key elements of what they call an *evolved module for fear learning*. They assert that this evolved module is (1) preferentially activated by stimuli related to survival threats in evolutionary history, (2) automatically activated by these stimuli, (3) relatively resistant to conscious efforts to suppress the resulting fears, and (4) dependent on neural circuitry running through the amygdala.

Evolutionary Perspectives on Learning

Clearly, several lines of research suggest that there are species-specific biological constraints on

John Garcia

"Taste aversions do not fit comfortably within the present framework of classical or instrumental conditioning: These aversions selectively seek flavors to the exclusion of other stimuli. Interstimulus intervals are a thousandfold too long."

Courtesy of John Garcia

FIGURE 6.20

Garcia and Koelling's research on conditioned taste aversion.

In a landmark series of studies, Garcia and Koelling (1966) demonstrated that some stimulus–response associations are much easier to condition than others. Their apparatus is depicted here. Rats drink saccharin-flavoured water out of the tube on the right. When they make contact with the tube, they may trigger a bright light and buzzer, or a brief electric shock, or radiation exposure that will make them nauseated. This setup allowed Garcia and Koelling to pair various types of stimuli, as discussed in the text.

People tend to develop phobias very easily but to electrical outlets rarely, even though the latter are just as dangerous. Preparedness theory can explain this paradox.

learning. So, what is the current thinking on the idea that the laws of learning are *universal* across various species? The predominant view among learning theorists seems to be that the basic mechanisms of learning are *similar* across species but that these mechanisms have sometimes been modified in the course of evolution as species have adapted to the specialized demands of their environments (Shettleworth, 1998). According to this view, learning is a very general process because the biological bases of learning and the basic problems confronted by various organisms are much the same across species. For example, developing the ability to recognize stimuli that signal important events (such as lurking predators) is probably adaptive for virtually any organism. However, given that different organisms confront different adaptive problems to survive and reproduce, it makes sense that learning has evolved along somewhat different paths in different species (Hollis, 1997; Sherry, 1992).

Recognizing Cognitive Processes in Conditioning

Historically there has often been a tension between behaviourism and cognitive theory (Shanks, 2010). Pavlov, Skinner, and their followers traditionally viewed conditioning as a mechanical process in which stimulus–response associations are stamped in by experience. Learning theorists asserted that if creatures such as flatworms can be conditioned, conditioning can't depend on higher mental processes. Although this viewpoint did not go entirely unchallenged (e.g., Tolman, 1922, 1932, 1938), mainstream theories of conditioning did not allocate a major role to cognitive processes.

The first major "renegade" to chip away at the conventional view of learning was Edward C. Tolman (1932, 1938), an American psychologist who was something of a gadfly for the behaviourist movement in the 1930s and 1940s. Tolman came from an academic family; his brother was one of the physicists who worked on the Manhattan Project building the first atomic bomb. Tolman himself was a pacifist and this belief resulted in him losing his job at Northwestern University (Pickren & Rutherford, 2010). While his first degree was in theoretical chemistry, Tolman (1948) went on to study psychology at Harvard University and conduct studies at the University of California at Berkeley that suggested cognitive processes play a role in conditioning. But his ideas were ahead of their time, and mostly attracted rebuttals and criticism from the influential learning theorists of his era (Hilgard, 1987). In the long run, however, Tolman's ideas prevailed, as models of conditioning were eventually forced to incorporate cognitive factors. In recent decades, research findings have led theorists to shift toward more cognitive explanations of conditioning. Let's review some of these findings and the theories that highlighted the potential role of cognition.

Latent Learning and Cognitive Maps

Tolman and his colleagues conducted a series of studies that posed some difficult questions for the prevailing views of conditioning. In one landmark study (Tolman & Honzik, 1930), three groups of food-deprived rats learned to run a complex maze over a series of once-a-day trials. The rats in Group A received a food reward when they got to the end of the maze each day. Because of this reinforcement, their performance in running the maze gradually improved over the course of 17 days. The rats in Group B did not receive any food reward. Lacking reinforcement, this group showed only modest improvement in performance. Group C was the critical group; they did not get any reward for their first 10 trials in the maze, but they were rewarded from the 11th trial onward. The rats in this group showed little improvement in performance over the first 10 trials (just like Group B). But once reinforcement began on the 11th trial, they showed sharp improvement on subsequent trials. In fact, their performance was even a little better than that of the Group A rats who had been rewarded after every trial.

Tolman concluded that the rats in Group C had been learning about the maze all along, just as much as the rats in group A, but they had no motivation to demonstrate this learning until a reward was introduced. Tolman called this phenomenon *latent learning*—learning that is not apparent from behaviour when it first occurs. *Why did these findings present a challenge for the prevailing view of learning?* First, they suggested that learning can take place in the absence of reinforcement—at a time when learned responses were thought to be stamped in by reinforcement. Second, they suggested that the rats

Edward Tolman developed one of the first major cognitive theories of learning.

Archives of the History of American Psychology, The Center for the History of Psychology—University of Akron

concept **check 6.4**

Distinguishing between Classical Conditioning and Operant Conditioning

Check your understanding of the usual differences between classical conditioning and operant conditioning by indicating the type of conditioning process involved in each of the following examples. In the space on the left, place a C if the example involves classical conditioning, an O if it involves operant conditioning, or a B if it involves both. The answers can be found in Appendix A.

_____ **1.** Whenever Midori takes her dog out for a walk, she wears the same old blue windbreaker. Eventually, she notices that her dog becomes excited whenever she puts on this windbreaker.

_____ **2.** The Creatures are a successful rock band with three hit albums to their credit. They begin their world tour featuring many new, unreleased songs, all of which draw silence from their concert fans. The same fans cheer wildly when the Creatures play any of their old hits. Gradually, the band reduces the number of new songs it plays and starts playing more of the old standbys.

_____ **3.** When Cindy and Mel first fell in love, they listened constantly to the Creatures' hit song "Transatlantic Obsession." Although several years have passed, whenever they hear this song they experience a warm, romantic feeling.

_____ **4.** For nearly 20 years, Ralph has worked as a machinist in the same factory. His new supervisor is never satisfied with his work and criticizes him constantly. After a few weeks of heavy criticism, Ralph experiences anxiety whenever he arrives at work. He starts calling in sick more and more frequently to evade this anxiety.

who displayed latent learning had formed a *cognitive map* of the maze (a mental representation of the spatial layout) at a time when cognitive processes were thought to be irrelevant to understanding conditioning even in humans.

Signal Relations

The cognitive element in conditioning is especially prominent in research conducted by Robert Rescorla (1978, 1980; Rescorla & Wagner, 1972). Rescorla asserts that environmental stimuli serve as signals and that some stimuli are better, or more dependable, signals than others. Hence, he has manipulated *signal relations* in classical conditioning—that is, CS–UCS relations that influence whether a CS is a good signal. A "good" signal is one that allows accurate prediction of the UCS.

In essence, Rescorla manipulates the *predictive value* of a conditioned stimulus. How does he do so? He varies the proportion of trials in which the CS and UCS are paired. Consider the following example. A tone and shock are paired 20 times for one group of rats. Otherwise, these rats are never

Robert Rescorla

"Pavlovian conditioning is a sophisticated and sensible mechanism by which organisms represent the world.... I encourage students to think of animals as behaving like little statisticians.... They really are very finely attuned to small changes in the likelihood of events."

University of Pennsylvania

shocked. For these rats, the CS (tone) and UCS (shock) are paired in 100 percent of the experimental trials. Another group of rats also receive 20 pairings of the tone and shock. However, the rats in this group are also exposed to the shock on 20 other trials when the tone does *not* precede it. For this group, the CS and UCS are paired in only 50 percent of the trials. Which group would be more likely to expect a shock following the tone? The two groups of rats have had an equal number of CS–UCS pairings, but the CS is a better signal or predictor of shock for the 100 percent CS–UCS group than for the 50 percent CS–UCS group.

What did Rescorla find when he tested the two groups of rats for conditioned fear? He found that the CS elicits a much stronger response in the 100 percent CS–UCS group than in the 50 percent CS–UCS group. Given that the two groups have received an equal number of CS–UCS pairings, this difference must be due to the greater predictive power of the CS for the 100 percent group. Numerous studies of signal relations have shown that the predictive value of a CS is an influential factor governing classical conditioning (Rescorla, 1978). Through his work he introduced a cognitive element—predictions/expectations—into the models of learning.

Response–Outcome Relations and Reinforcement

Studies of response–outcome relations and reinforcement also highlight the role of cognitive processes in conditioning. Imagine that on the night before an important exam, you study hard while repeatedly playing a Rage Against the Machine song—for example, their cover of Bob Dylan's "Maggie's Farm." The next morning you earn an A on your exam. Does this result strengthen your tendency to play "Maggie's Farm" and other Rage songs before exams? Probably not. Chances are, you will recognize the logical relationship between the response of studying hard and the reinforcement of a good grade, and only the response of studying will be strengthened (Killeen, 1981).

Thus, reinforcement is *not* automatic when favourable consequences follow a response. People actively reason out the relationships between responses and the outcomes that follow. When a response is followed by a desirable outcome, the response is more likely to be strengthened if the person thinks that the response *caused* the outcome. You might guess that only humans would engage in this causal reasoning. However, evidence suggests that under the right circumstances, even pigeons can learn to recognize causal relationships between responses and outcomes (Killeen, 1981).

In sum, modern, reformulated models of conditioning view it as a matter of detecting the *contingencies* among environmental events (Matute & Miller, 1998). According to these theories, organisms actively try to figure out what leads to what (the contingencies) in the world around them. Stimuli are viewed as signals that help organisms minimize their aversive experiences and maximize their pleasant experiences. The new, cognitively oriented theories of conditioning are quite a departure from older theories that depicted conditioning as a mindless, mechanical process. We can also see this new emphasis on cognitive processes in our next subject, observational learning.

REVIEW OF KEY POINTS

▷ Recent decades have brought profound changes in our understanding of conditioning. Instinctive drift occurs when an animal's innate response tendencies interfere with conditioning. Conditioned taste aversions can be readily acquired even when there is a lengthy delay between the CS and UCS. Seligman's concept of preparedness may explain why certain phobias are far more common than others.

▷ The findings on instinctive drift, conditioned taste aversion, and preparedness have led to the recognition that there are species-specific biological constraints on conditioning. Some evolutionary psychologists argue that learning processes vary immensely across species because different species have to grapple with very different adaptive problems.

▷ Tolman emphasized the role of cognition in learning, and he added the concepts latent learning and cognitive maps to the study of learning.

▷ Rescorla's work on signal relations showed that the predictive value of a CS is an influential factor governing classical conditioning. When a response is followed by a desirable outcome, the response is more likely to be strengthened if it appears that the response caused the outcome. Studies of signal relations in classical conditioning and response-outcome relations in operant conditioning suggest that cognitive processes play a larger role in conditioning than originally believed.

Observational Learning

Can classical and operant conditioning account for all learning? Absolutely not. Consider how people learn a fairly basic skill such as driving a car. They do not hop naïvely into an automobile and start emitting random responses until one leads to favourable consequences. On the contrary, most people learning to drive know exactly where to place the key and how to get started. How are these responses acquired? Through *observation*. Most new drivers have years of experience observing others drive, and they put those observations to work. Learning through observation accounts for a great deal of learning in both animals and humans.

Observational learning occurs when an organism's responding is influenced by the observation of others, who are called *models*. This process has been investigated extensively by Albert Bandura (1977, 1986). Bandura's theory and research on observational learning is one of the pivotal contributions to the psychology of learning in the past few decades. Interestingly, Bandura, who was born in Alberta and did his undergraduate studies at the University of British Columbia, began his career in psychology almost by chance (Evans, 1989). He commuted to classes with friends who were early risers so he found himself with morning class periods to fill. One of the courses available was in psychology and the rest, as they say, is history. Bandura's insights on the mediating role of modelling or observational learning came from his analysis of the differences between animal and human learning. The literature on human conditioning suggested to him at the time that for humans "representation of the connection between action and consequence is an important determinant of whether or not a change will occur" (Evans, 1980, p. 161). While this might seem obvious to us now, it was not an insight that was compatible with the prevailing orientation of learning theory at the time.

Bandura does not see observational learning as entirely separate from classical and operant conditioning. Instead, he asserts that it greatly extends the reach of these conditioning processes. Whereas previous conditioning theorists emphasized the organism's direct experience, Bandura has demonstrated that both classical and operant conditioning can take place vicariously through observational learning.

Essentially, observational learning involves being conditioned indirectly by virtue of observing another's conditioning (see Figure 6.21). To illustrate, suppose you observe a friend behaving assertively with a car salesperson. You see your friend's assertive behaviour reinforced by the exceptionally good buy she gets on the car. Your own tendency to behave assertively with salespeople might well be strengthened as a result. Notice that the reinforcement is experienced by your friend, not you. The good buy should strengthen your friend's tendency to bargain assertively, but your tendency to do so may also be strengthened indirectly.

Basic Processes

Bandura has identified four key processes that are crucial in observational learning. The first two—attention and retention—highlight the importance of the type of cognition he was referring to in the quote on the right in this type of learning.

- *Attention.* To learn through observation, you must pay attention to another person's behaviour and its consequences.
- *Retention.* You may not have occasion to use an observed response for weeks, months, or even years. Hence, you must store in your memory a mental representation of what you have witnessed.
- *Reproduction.* Enacting a modelled response depends on your ability to reproduce the response by converting your stored mental images into overt behaviour. This may not be easy for some responses. For example, most people cannot execute a breathtaking windmill dunk after watching Steve Nash do it in a basketball game.

PREVIEW QUESTIONS

► How can conditioning occur indirectly?

► What are the key processes in observational learning?

► What does Bandura have to say about acquisition versus performance?

► What are some practical implications of observational learning?

Photo courtesy of Albert Bandura

Albert Bandura
"Most human behavior is learned by observation through modeling."

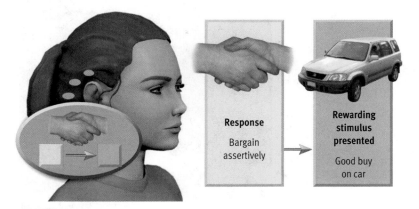

Response

Bargain assertively

Rewarding stimulus presented

Good buy on car

FIGURE 6.21

Observational learning.

In observational learning, an observer attends to and stores a mental representation of a model's behaviour (e.g., assertive bargaining) and its consequences (e.g., a good buy on a car). If the observer sees the modelled response lead to a favourable outcome, the observer's tendency to emit the modelled response will be strengthened.

- *Motivation.* Finally, you are unlikely to reproduce an observed response unless you are motivated to do so. Your motivation depends on whether you encounter a situation in which you believe that the response is likely to pay off for you.

Observational learning has proven especially valuable in explaining complex human behaviours, but animals can also learn through observation. A simple example is the thieving behaviour of the English titmouse, a small bird renowned for its early-morning raids on its human neighbours. The titmouse has learned how to open cardboard caps on bottles of milk delivered to the porches of many homes in England. Having opened the bottle, the titmouse skims the cream from the top of the milk. This clever learned behaviour has been passed down from one generation of titmouse to the next through observational learning.

Acquisition versus Performance

Bandura points out that people have many learned responses that they may or may not perform, depending on the situation. Thus, he distinguishes between the *acquisition* of a learned response and the *performance* of that response. He maintains that reinforcement affects which responses are actually performed more than which responses are acquired. People emit those responses that they think are likely to be reinforced. For instance, you may study hard for a course in which the professor gives fair exams, because you expect studying to lead to reinforcement in the form of a good grade. In contrast, you may hardly open the text for a course in which the professor gives arbitrary, unpredictable exams, because you do not expect studying to be reinforced. Your performance is different in the two situations because you think the reinforcement contingencies are different. Thus, like Skinner, Bandura asserts that reinforcement is a critical determinant of behaviour. However, Bandura maintains that reinforcement influences performance rather than learning per se.

Observational Learning and the Media Violence Controversy

It is the power of observational learning that makes television such an influential determinant of behaviour. We know that excessive TV watching can have important negative effects. For example, sitting in front of the screen, a computer screen or TV, for long periods is linked to obesity in Canadians (Shields & Tremblay, 2008). The Canadian Paediatric Society (Psychosocial Paediatrics Committee, 2003) concluded that Canadian children watch excessive amounts of TV and that such TV watching may have negative effects on academic performance and health.

Observational learning occurs in both humans and animals. For example, the English titmouse has learned how to break into containers to swipe cream from its human neighbours and this behaviour has been passed across generations through observational learning. In a similar vein, children acquire a diverse array of responses from role models.

They recommend that kids watch TV for no more than two hours per day. But we know that many Canadian children spend much more than two hours per day in front of a screen. Children spend an average of about 40 hours per week with various types of entertainment media, and more than half of that time is devoted to watching television, videotapes, and DVDs (Bushman & Anderson, 2001). A recent study of Montreal youth revealed that one-third spent more than 40 hours per week in front of a screen and that 10 percent spent more than 50 hours (CBC, 2008).

Children are very impressionable, and extensive evidence indicates that they pick up many responses from viewing models on TV (Huston et al., 1992). Social critics have expressed concern about the amount of violence on television ever since TV became popular in the 1950s. In the 1960s, Bandura and his colleagues conducted landmark research on the issue that remains widely cited and influential. Along with his colleague and first graduate student Richard Walters (later a professor at the University of Waterloo), Bandura was an early advocate of the application of learning principles to explain aggression in children (Bandura & Walters, 1959, 1963). Young children are especially impressionable, and extensive evidence indicates that they pick up many responses—including aggressive behaviours—from viewing models on TV (Huston & Wright, 1982; Liebert & Sprafkin, 1988).

Bandura conducted a series of classic experiments on aggression often referred to as the "Bobo doll" experiments (Bandura, 1965; Bandura, Ross, & Ross, 1961, 1963a). In these and other studies, Bandura showed that children would imitate aggressive behaviour directed toward a Bobo doll (a large, inflatable toy clown) by an adult model. Children who saw the model rewarded were more likely than children who saw the model punished for the aggression to aggress (i.e., performance) themselves toward the Bobo doll when left alone with it. However, all of the children behaved aggressively (i.e., acquisition) if they were offered a reward for imitating the model's behaviour. This early research by Bandura suggested a connection between children watching violence on television and their own aggressiveness. Because of the significance of Bandura's modelling research, the Bobo doll has achieved a type of stardom on its own. Bandura states that when he visits and lectures at other universities, the hosts often place Bobo dolls close to the stage and that people frequently bring him Bobo dolls to autograph (Evans, 1989).

More recently, Bandura examined the concepts of self-efficacy and human agency and their implications for society (Bandura, 2001a, 2001b). We will consider some of his work on self-efficacy and agency in Chapter 12. While Bandura's work on modelling was first initiated as "knowledge pursued for its own sake" (Foster, 2007), he found that it had implications for social issues such as the effects of watching violence on TV on kids' aggression. He has testified before the U.S. Congress on the issue and his work resulted in, among other things, new advertising standards in the United States.

The Bobo doll was employed in Bandura's well-known research on observational learning and aggression.

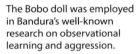
Photo courtesy of Albert Bandura

FEATURED STUDY

Investigators: L. Rowell Huesmann, Jessica Moise-Titus, C.-L. Podolski, & Leonard Eron (University of Michigan)
Source: Longitudinal relations between children's exposure to TV violence and their aggressive and violent behavior in young adulthood: 1977–1992. *Developmental Psychology*, 2003, *39*, 201–221.

The Long-Term Effects of Watching Violence on TV

As discussed in the text, research conducted by Bandura and his colleagues on modelling and aggression found that observing aggressive behaviour is associated with children's own increased aggressiveness. This research, along with the work of others, has implications for the controversy around the effects of violent TV programs on children's aggression; the suggestion is that watching violence on TV is related to increased aggression. Bandura and his colleagues wanted to determine if childhood exposure to violent TV programs would predict adult aggression 15 years later. In most of the early studies in this area, the aggression was measured immediately after the children had viewed the violent programming or model. In this Featured Study, the authors were interested in examining more long-term effects of children watching violent TV programs. The authors followed up a group of children who had been the subject of an earlier study begun in 1977 on TV-violence viewing and aggression (Huesmann & Eron, 1986; Huesmann, Lagerspetz, & Eron, 1984). The authors located most of the original participants to determine the relationship between TV-violence viewing habits as children and their level of aggression 15 years later when they were in their early to mid-twenties.

Method

Subjects. Of the original 1977 sample of 557 six- to ten-year old children, 329 were located and agreed to participate in this study 15 years later.

Procedure. In the 1977 study, a variety of types of information was collected concerning the children and their behaviour. This included their level of aggressiveness, TV-violence viewing habits, their tendency to identify with aggressive TV characters, and their judgments concerning how realistic the children thought various violent TV programs were. Twenty years later, the level of aggressive and antisocial behaviour of the now adult participants was assessed. Their level of aggressiveness was assessed by self-report, in which participants answered questions regarding their frequency of engaging in specific acts of aggression: *verbal* (e.g., calling people names), *indirect* (e.g., trying to get others to dislike a specific person), *mild physical* (e.g., responding to another person by shoving the person), and *severe* (responding to another person by beating that person). They were also asked about aggression toward a close friend, spouse, or significant other, and the frequency of committing a series of crimes and traffic violations. Participant aggressiveness was also assessed by other-report, in which a close friend, spouse, or significant other answered similar questions about the participant's aggressive behaviour. The authors also searched archival records to obtain records concerning criminal convictions.

Results

A composite aggression score was calculated for each participant by combining the information gathered about the participant's level of adult aggressiveness and anti-social behaviour from the various sources. This level of adult aggressiveness was then correlated with some of the measures concerning the children's characteristics and behaviour obtained 15 years earlier in the original 1977 study. The correlations demonstrated that adult levels of aggression were significantly correlated with childhood TV-violence viewing, the children's perceptions that TV violence reflects real life, and the tendency of the children to identify with same-sex aggressive TV characters. These results held both for males and females.

Discussion

The results revealed that children's TV-violence viewing habits, their identification with violent TV characters, and their tendency to view these violent TV programs as real-istic were related to their level of aggressiveness as adults. The results of the study supplement the work of Bandura and others by showing that childhood TV-violence viewing habits are related not just to levels of aggression at the time, but to levels of adult aggressiveness measured 15 years later (see Table 6.2). This relationship was true even when, in other statistical analyses, the authors controlled

TABLE 6.2

Correlations between Childhood TV Violence Measures and Adult Aggression 15 Years Later

Child TV Measures	Adult Composite Aggression	
	Men	**Women**
TV-violence viewing	0.21*	0.19*
Perceived realism of TV violence	0.22*	0.25†
Identification with aggressive female characters	0.15‡	0.23*
Identification with aggressive male characters	0.29†	0.22*

Note: For men, $n = 153$; for women, $n = 176$.
*$p < 0.01$
†$p < 0.001$
‡$p < 0.10$

Source: From L.R. Huesmann, J. Moise-Titus, C.-L. Podolski, and L. Eron. (2003). Longitudinal relations between children's exposure to TV violence and their aggressive and violent behavior in young adulthood: 1977–1992. *Developmental Psychology, 39*: 201–221. © American Psychological Association. Adapted with permission of the APA.

for the participants' level of aggression when they were children. The authors also found that the link between TV-violence viewing and adult aggression was especially true for boys who, as children, identified with the violent TV characters.

Comment

This study was included for several reasons. First, it provides an important supplement to the original research on modelling and aggression. One of the criticisms of the original work was that the effects would most likely disappear after a short period of time, that the link between viewing aggression and one's own aggressive behaviour was temporary. This research undermines that view—children's TV-violence viewing habits are related to their aggressiveness at least 15 years later. The study also illustrates one of the most important research designs used in research on human development: the longitudinal design. In a longitudinal design, participants are tested repeatedly over a period of time to examine developmental trends. Another design used in developmental research is the cross-sectional design, in which investigators compare participants, who differ in age, at a single point in time to determine developmental trends. These designs and their relative strengths and weaknesses are discussed in more detail in Chapter 11 on pages 498–499.

A review of the literature by University of Toronto psychologist Jonathan Freedman confirmed the link between viewing media violence and aggressiveness (Freedman, 2002). The causal connection between media violence and aggression and the limits of the effect are still being debated (Feshback & Tangney, 2008).

Subsequent research demonstrated that youngsters are exposed to an astonishing amount of violence when they watch TV. The *National Television Violence Study*, a large-scale study of the content of network and cable television shows conducted in 1994–1997, revealed that 61 percent of programs contained violence; 44 percent of the violent characters portrayed in the programs were enticing role models (i.e., the "good guys"); 75 percent of violent actions occurred without punishment or condemnation; and 51 percent of violent actions were "sanitized," as they featured no apparent pain (Anderson et al., 2003). It has been estimated that the typical child has vicariously witnessed 8000 murders and 100 000 other acts of violence on TV by the time that child finishes grade school (Huston et al., 1992).

Does this steady diet of media violence foster increased aggression? Decades of research since Bandura's pioneering work indicate that the answer is "yes" (Bushman & Huesmann, 2001). The short-term effects of media violence have been investigated in hundreds of experimental studies. These studies consistently demonstrate that exposure to TV and movie violence increases the likelihood of physical aggression, verbal aggression, aggressive thoughts, and aggressive emotions in both children and adults (Anderson et al., 2003).

A particular source of concern in recent research has been the finding that exposure to media violence appears to desensitize people to the effects of aggression in the real world (Strenzoik et al., 2010). Desensitization means that people show muted reactions to real violence. For example, in one study participants were randomly assigned to play violent or nonviolent video games for 20 minutes. Then their physiological reactions to video recordings of real-life aggression (prison fights, police confrontations, and such) were monitored. The subjects who had played violent video games for a mere 20 minutes showed smaller physiological reactions to the aggression than those who played nonviolent games (Carnagey, Anderson, & Bushman, 2007). A follow-up study suggested that the "numbing" effect of media violence makes people less sensitive to the suffering of others and less likely to help others in need (Bushman & Anderson, 2009). In this study, participants who had just played a violent or nonviolent video game overheard a staged fight (just outside the door of the lab) in which one person was injured. The aggressive actor clearly had left the scene, so there was no perceived danger to the participants. Researchers monitored how long it took subjects to come out into the hall to offer help to the groaning victim. Participants who had just played a violent video game took much longer to help (on average, 73 seconds) than those who had just played a nonviolent game (16 seconds). Thus, it appears that media violence can desensitize individuals to acts of aggression.

Recent neuroscience research by Maren Strenzoik and her colleagues (Strenziok et al., 2010) gives us some hints about how watching media violence may affect the functioning of a teenager's brain. Boys from 14–17 years of age were shown violent media clips while some of their physiological and brain functions were assessed. The results indicated that with continued violent video viewing, the participants showed clear physiological signs of desensitization

Type of learning	Procedure	Diagram	Result

Classical conditioning

Ivan Pavlov

A neutral stimulus (for example, a tone) is paired with an unconditioned stimulus (such as food) that elicits an unconditioned response (salivation).

The neutral stimulus becomes a conditioned stimulus that elicits the conditioned response (for example, a tone triggers salivation).

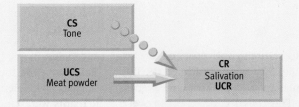

CS Tone

UCS Meat powder

CR Salivation **UCR**

Operant conditioning

B. F. Skinner

In a stimulus situation, a response is followed by favourable consequences (reinforcement) or unfavourable consequences (punishment).

If reinforced, the response is strengthened (emitted more frequently); if punished, the response is weakened (emitted less frequently).

Response Press lever

Rewarding or aversive stimulus presented or removed Food delivery or shock

Observational learning

Albert Bandura

An observer attends to a model's behaviour (for example, aggressive bargaining) and its consequences (for example, a good buy on a car).

The observer stores a mental representation of the modelled response; the observer's tendency to emit the response may be strengthened or weakened, depending on the consequences observed.

Response

Bargain assertively

Rewarding stimulus presented Good buy on car

Typical kinds of responses	Examples in animals	Examples in humans

Mostly (but not always) involuntary reflexes and visceral responses

Dogs learn to salivate to the sound of a tone that has been paired with meat powder.

© Bettmann/CORBIS

Political candidates draw on the power of classical conditioning when they associate with popular celebrities who elicit positive feelings among many voters.

THE CANADIAN PRESS/Tom Hanson

Mostly (but not always) voluntary, spontaneous responses

Trained animals perform remarkable feats because they have been reinforced for gradually learning closer and closer approximations of responses they do not normally emit.

© Gerald Davis by permission of Karen Davis

Casino patrons tend to exhibit high, steady rates of gambling, as most games of chance involve complex variable-ratio schedules of reinforcement.

Beth Perkins/Taxi/Getty Images

A young boy performs a response that he has acquired through observational learning.

© Frank Siteman/Index Stock Imagery, Inc.

Mostly voluntary responses, often consisting of novel and complex sequences

An English titmouse learns to break into milk bottles by observing the thievery of other titmice.

© J. Markham/Bruce Coleman, Inc.

and adaptation. For example, the parts of the brain concerned with emotional reactivity decreased in activation level and this was especially true for those boys who were more frequently exposed to violent media in their everyday lives. Skin conductance measures showed a similar desensitization and adaptation to the violent material. The authors suggest that "exposure to aggressive media results in a blunting of emotional responses, which in turn may prevent the connection of consequences of aggression with an appropriate emotional response, and therefore may increase the likelihood that aggression is seen as acceptable behavior" (Strenzoik et al., 2010, p. 11). In the same age group, the authors have also found that even imagining an aggressive encounter with a peer affects the brain's functioning. There are many reasons then for parents and the rest of us to be concerned about the viewing habits of our youth.

The real-world and long-term effects of media violence have been investigated through correlational research. The findings of these studies show that the more violence children watch on TV, the more aggressive the children tend to be at home and at school (Huesmann & Miller, 1994). Of course, critics point out that this correlation could reflect a variety of causal relationships. Perhaps high aggressiveness in children causes an increased interest in violent television shows. However, a handful of long-term studies, such as the Featured Study in this chapter (see pages 286–287), that have followed the same subjects since the 1960s and 1970s have clarified the causal relations underlying the link between media violence and elevated aggression. These studies show that the extent of youngsters' exposure to media violence in childhood predicts their aggressiveness in adolescence and early adulthood, but not vice versa (Huesmann, 1986; Huesmann et al., 2003). In other words, high exposure to media violence precedes, and presumably causes, high aggressiveness.

Although the empirical evidence linking media violence to aggression is clear, convincing, and unequivocal, the general public remains uncertain, perhaps even skeptical (Bushman & Anderson, 2001). One reason is that everyone knows individuals (perhaps themselves) who were raised on a robust diet of media violence but who do not appear to be particularly aggressive. If media violence is so horrible, why aren't we all axe murderers? The answer is that aggressive behaviour is influenced by a number of factors besides media violence, which has only a "modest" effect on people's aggressiveness. The problem, experts say, is that TV and movies reach millions upon millions of people, so even a small effect can have big repercussions (Bushman & Anderson, 2001). Suppose that 25 million people watch an extremely violent program. Even if only 1 in 100 viewers becomes a little more prone to aggression, this means that 250 000 people are a bit more likely to wreak havoc in someone's life.

In any event, the heated debate about media violence shows that observational learning plays an important role in regulating behaviour. It represents a third major type of learning that builds on the first two types—classical conditioning and operant conditioning. These three basic types of learning are summarized and compared in the pictorial table on pages 288–289.

Observational Learning and the Brain: Mirror Neurons

To date, a variety of explanations have been offered to account for observational learning and modelling that often depend on principles and processes related to learning theory. More recent research has suggested the relevance of a specific type of neuron—the mirror neuron—in imitation, observational learning, and other facets of social cognition (e.g., de Vignemont & Haggard, 2008; Keysers & Gazzola, 2006; Schilbach et al., 2008).

Research into the nature and role of mirror neurons began almost by accident. *Mirror neurons are neurons that are activated by performing an action or by seeing another monkey or person perform the same action.* A team of neuroscientists at the University of Parma in Italy led by Giacomo Rizzolatti was recording the activity of individual neurons in the brains of two macaque monkeys (Rizzolatti & Sinigaglia, 2008; Rizzolatti et al., 1996) as the monkeys performed a series of reaching and grasping movements with their hands. As the monkeys performed the actions, the researchers were able to record brain activity. In an important discovery, the researchers found that some of these same neurons also became activated when the animals observed one of the experimenters performing similar actions, at a point when the monkeys themselves were not engaged in the action. It was quite accidental; a member of the research team happened to reach out and pick up one of the objects the monkeys had been working with.

In interpreting the activity in these mirror neurons, Rizzolatti and his colleagues highlighted the view that "mirror neurons are neurons that internally represent an action" (1996, p. 137). Further research by Rizzolatti and others confirmed that similar mirror neurons exist in humans. In human subjects, it is difficult to record from individual neurons, but researchers have used fMRI scans to demonstrate that humans also have mirror neuron circuits, which have been found in both the frontal lobe and the parietal lobe (Iacoboni & Dapretto, 2006; Rizzolatti & Craighero, 2004). The operation of mirror neurons and related structures and processes of the brain may underlie imitation and observational learning (Society for Neuroscience, 2008). It has also been suggested that mirror neurons may underlie our ability to understand others, to understand what is going on in the minds of others, making "intersubjectivity" possible, thus setting the stage for our social behaviour (Iacoboni, 2009). They may be responsible for our ability to empathize with others. They are part of our evolution because they confer these advantages on us (Iacoboni, 2009). New thinking in the area suggests a parallel between impairment in their operation and some of the symptoms of autism; in the future they may provide a key to understanding this disorder (Rizzolatti, Fabbri-Destro, & Cattaneo, 2009). Research in the area is ongoing. The next time you wince in sympathy when Sidney

Crosby takes a brutal hit or smile when you see a group of people across the street laugh at what one of the group says, perhaps you are a witness to the effects of activity in your mirror neurons!

Neuroscientists are understandably very excited by the identification of mirror neurons and by a consideration of their possible effects (Keysers & Perrett, 2004; Ramachandran & Oberman, 2006; van der Gaag, Minderaa, & Keysers, 2007). Some have even suggested that the mirror neuron will be as important to psychology as the discovery of DNA has been for biology (Miller, 2005). We will have to wait to see if this prediction is realized. It is possible that, in the future, research on mirror neurons may even provide an explanation for why viewing TV violence produces increased aggression on the part of the viewer. But it seems clear that the accidental discovery of mirror neurons may have a dramatic impact on brain-behaviour research in the years to come.

Putting It in Perspective: Themes 3 and 6

Two of our seven unifying themes stand out in this chapter. First, you can see how nature and nurture interactively govern behaviour. Second, looking at psychology in its sociohistorical context, you can see how progress in psychology spills over to affect trends and values in society at large. Let's examine each of these points in more detail.

In regard to nature versus nurture, research on learning clearly demonstrates the enormous power of the environment in shaping behaviour. Pavlov's model of classical conditioning shows how experiences can account for everyday fears and other emotional responses. Skinner's model of operant conditioning shows how reinforcement and punishment can mould everything from a child's bedtime whimpering to an adult's restaurant preferences. Indeed, many learning theorists once believed that *all* aspects of behaviour could be explained in terms of environmental determinants. In recent decades, however, evidence on instinctive drift, conditioned taste aversion, and preparedness has shown that there are biological constraints on conditioning. Thus, even in explanations of learning—an area once dominated by nurture theories—we see once again that heredity and environment jointly influence behaviour.

The history of research on conditioning also shows how progress in psychology can seep into every corner of society. For example, the behaviourists' ideas about reinforcement and punishment have influenced patterns of discipline in our society. Research on operant conditioning has also affected management styles in

the business world, leading to an increased emphasis on positive reinforcement. In the educational arena, the concept of individualized, programmed learning is a spinoff from behavioural research. The fact that the principles of conditioning are routinely applied in homes, businesses, schools, and factories clearly shows that psychology is not an ivory tower endeavour.

In the upcoming Personal Application, you will see how you can apply the principles of conditioning to improve your self-control, as we discuss the techniques of behaviour modification.

PREVIEW QUESTIONS

► How did this chapter demonstrate that nature and nurture jointly influence behaviour?

► How did this chapter show that psychology evolves in a sociohistorical context?

REVIEW OF KEY POINTS

▷ In observational learning, an organism is conditioned vicariously by watching a model's conditioning. Both classical and operant conditioning can occur through observational learning, which depends on the processes of attention, retention, reproduction, and motivation.

▷ According to Bandura, reinforcement influences which of several already acquired responses one will perform more than it influences the acquisition of new responses.

▷ Observational learning can account for the influence of mass media (such as television) on behaviour. The principles of observational learning have also been used to explain why physical punishment increases aggressive behaviour.

▷ Two of our key themes were especially apparent in our coverage of learning and conditioning. One theme involves the interaction of heredity and environment in learning. The other involves the way progress in psychology affects society at large.

Achieving Self-Control through Behaviour Modification

Answer the following "yes" or "no."

___ **1** Do you have a hard time passing up food, even when you're not hungry?

___ **2** Do you wish you studied more often?

___ **3** Would you like to cut down on your smoking or drinking?

___ **4** Do you experience difficulty in getting yourself to exercise regularly?

___ **5** Do you wish you had more willpower?

If you answered "yes" to any of these questions, you have struggled with the challenge of self-control. This Personal Application discusses how you can use the techniques of behaviour modification to improve your self-control. If you stop to think about it, self-control—or rather a lack of it—underlies many of the personal problems that people struggle with in everyday life.

Behaviour modification is a systematic approach to changing behaviour through the application of the principles of conditioning. Advocates of behaviour modification assume that behaviour is a product of learning, conditioning, and environmental control. They further assume that *what is learned can be unlearned*. Thus, they set out to "recondition" people to produce more desirable patterns of behaviour.

The technology of behaviour modification has been applied with great success in schools, businesses, hospitals, factories, child-care facilities, prisons, and mental health centres (Kazdin, 1982, 2001; O'Donohue, 1998; Rachman, 1992). Moreover, behaviour modification techniques have proven particularly valuable in efforts to improve self-control. Our discussion will borrow liberally from an excellent book on self-modification by David Watson and Roland Tharp (2002). We will discuss five steps in the process of self-modification, which are outlined in Figure 6.22.

Specifying Your Target Behaviour

The first step in a self-modification program is to specify the target behaviour(s) that you want to change. Behaviour modification can be applied only to a clearly defined, overt response, yet many people have difficulty pinpointing the behaviour they hope to alter. They tend to describe their problems in terms of unobservable personality *traits* rather than overt *behaviours*. For example, asked what behaviour he would like to change, a man might say, "I'm too irritable." That may be true, but it is of little help in designing a self-modification program. To use a behavioural approach, vague statements about traits need to be translated into precise descriptions of specific target behaviours.

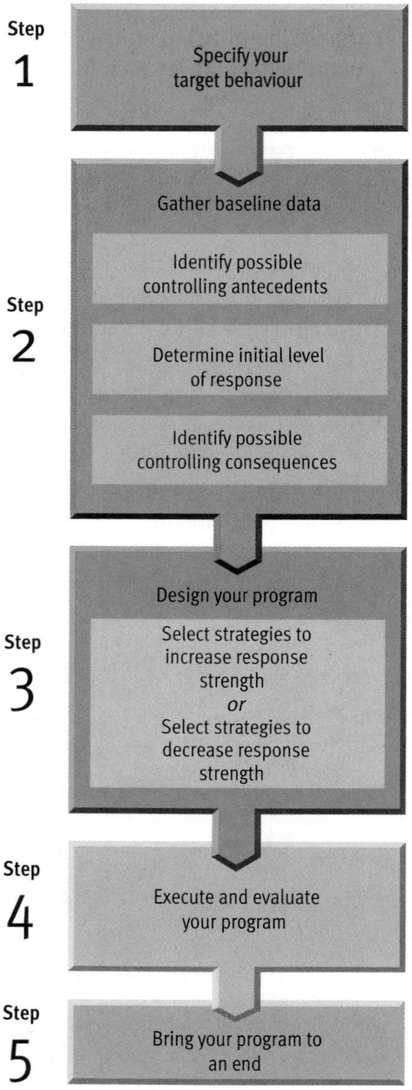

To identify target responses, you need to ponder past behaviour or closely observe future behaviour and list specific *examples* of responses that lead to the trait description. For instance, the man who regards himself as "too irritable" might identify two overly frequent responses, such as arguing with his wife and snapping at his children. These are specific behaviours for which he could design a self-modification program.

Gathering Baseline Data

The second step in behaviour modification is to gather baseline data. You need to systematically observe your target behaviour for a period of time (usually a week or two) before you work out the details of your program. In gathering your baseline data, you need to monitor three things.

First, you need to determine the initial response level of your target behaviour. After all, you can't tell whether your program is working effectively unless you have a baseline for comparison. In most cases, you would simply keep track of how often the target response occurs in a certain time interval. Thus, you might count the daily frequency of snapping at your children, smoking cigarettes, or biting your fingernails. If studying is your target behaviour, you will probably monitor hours of study. If you want to modify your eating, you will probably keep track of how many calories you consume. Whatever the unit of measurement, *it is crucial to gather accurate data*. You should keep permanent written records, and it is usually best to portray these records graphically (see Figure 6.23).

Step 1 Specify your target behaviour

Step 2 Gather baseline data
- Identify possible controlling antecedents
- Determine initial level of response
- Identify possible controlling consequences

Step 3 Design your program
- Select strategies to increase response strength
- *or*
- Select strategies to decrease response strength

Step 4 Execute and evaluate your program

Step 5 Bring your program to an end

FIGURE 6.22

Steps in a self-modification program.

This flow chart provides an overview of the five steps necessary to execute a self-modification program.

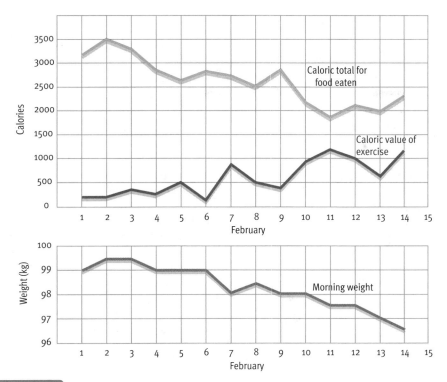

FIGURE 6.23

Example of record-keeping in a self-modification program.

Graphic records are ideal for tracking progress in behaviour modification efforts. The records shown here illustrate what people would be likely to track in a behaviour modification program for weight loss.

Second, you need to monitor the antecedents of your target behaviour. *Antecedents are events that typically precede the target response.* Often these events play a major role in evoking your target behaviour. For example, if your target is overeating, you might discover that the bulk of your overeating occurs late in the evening while you watch TV. If you can pinpoint this kind of antecedent–response connection, you may be able to design your program to circumvent or break the link.

Third, you need to monitor the typical consequences of your target behaviour. Try to identify the reinforcers that are maintaining an undesirable target behaviour or the unfavourable outcomes that are suppressing a desirable target behaviour. In trying to identify reinforcers, remember that avoidance behaviour is usually maintained by negative reinforcement. That is, the payoff for avoidance is usually the removal of something aversive, such as anxiety or a threat to self-esteem. You should also take into account the fact that a response may not be reinforced every time, as most behaviour is maintained by intermittent reinforcement.

Designing Your Program

Once you have selected a target behaviour and gathered adequate baseline data, it is time to plan your intervention program. Generally speaking, your program will be designed either to increase or to decrease the frequency of a target response.

Increasing Response Strength Efforts to increase the frequency of a target response depend largely on the use of positive reinforcement. In other words, you reward yourself for behaving properly. Although the basic strategy is quite simple, doing it skillfully involves a number of considerations.

Selecting a Reinforcer. To use positive reinforcement, you need to find a reward that will be effective for you. Reinforcement is subjective—what is reinforcing for one person may not be reinforcing for another. Figure 6.24 lists questions you can ask yourself to help you determine your personal reinforcers. Be sure to be realistic and choose a reinforcer that is really available to you.

You don't have to come up with spectacular new reinforcers that you've never experienced before. *You can use reinforcers that you are already getting.* However, you have to restructure the contingencies so that you get them only if you behave appropriately. For example, if you normally buy two CDs per week, you might make these purchases contingent on studying a certain number of hours during the week. Making yourself earn rewards that you used to take for granted is often a useful strategy in a self-modification program.

Overeating is just one of the many types of maladaptive behaviour that can be changed with a self-modification program.

FIGURE 6.24

Selecting a reinforcer.
Finding a good reinforcer to use in a behaviour modification program can require a lot of thought. The questions listed here can help people identify their personal reinforcers.

Source: Adapted from Watson, D. L., & Tharp, R. G. (1997). *Self-directed behavior: Self-modification for personal adjustment.* Belmont, CA: Wadsworth. Reprinted by permission.

1. What will be the rewards of achieving your goal?
2. What kind of praise do you like to receive, from yourself and others?
3. What kinds of things do you like to have?
4. What are your major interests?
5. What are your hobbies?
6. What people do you like to be with?
7. What do you like to do with those people?
8. What do you do for fun?
9. What do you do to relax?
10. What do you do to get away from it all?
11. What makes you feel good?
12. What would be a nice present to receive?
13. What kinds of things are important to you?
14. What would you buy if you had an extra $20? $50? $100?
15. On what do you spend your money each week?
16. What behaviours do you perform every day? (Don't overlook the obvious or commonplace.)
17. Are there any behaviours you usually perform instead of the target behaviour?
18. What would you hate to lose?
19. Of the things you do every day, which would you hate to give up?
20. What are your favourite daydreams and fantasies?

Arranging the Contingencies. Once you have chosen your reinforcer, you have to set up reinforcement contingencies. These contingencies will describe the exact behavioural goals that must be met and the reinforcement that may then be awarded. For example, in a program to increase exercise, you might make spending $50 on clothes (the reinforcer) contingent on having jogged 25 kilometres during the week (the target behaviour).

Try to set behavioural goals that are both challenging and realistic. You want your goals to be challenging so that they lead to improvement in your behaviour. However, setting unrealistically high goals—a common mistake in self-modification—often leads to unnecessary discouragement.

You also need to be concerned about doling out too much reinforcement. If

reinforcement is too easy to get, you may become *satiated*, and the reinforcer may lose its motivational power. For example, if you were to reward yourself with virtually all the CDs you wanted, this reinforcer would lose its incentive value.

One way to avoid the satiation problem is to put yourself on a token economy. A *token economy* is a system for doling out symbolic reinforcers that are exchanged later for a variety of genuine reinforcers. Thus, you might develop a point system for exercise behaviour, accumulating points that can be spent on CDs, movies, restaurant meals, and so forth (see Figure 6.25).

Decreasing Response Strength Let's turn now to the challenge of reducing the frequency of an undesirable response. You can go about this task in a number of ways. Your principal options include reinforcement, control of antecedents, and punishment.

Reinforcement. Reinforcers can be used in an indirect way to decrease the frequency of a response. This may sound paradoxical, since you have learned that reinforcement strengthens a response. The trick lies in how you define the target behaviour. For

Response earning tokens		
Response	Amount	Number of tokens
Jogging	1 km	4
Jogging	2 km	8
Jogging	4 km	16
Tennis	1 hour	4
Tennis	2 hours	8
Sit-ups	25	1
Sit-ups	50	2

Redemption value of tokens	
Reinforcer	Tokens required
Purchase one compact disc of your choice	30
Go to movie	50
Go to nice restaurant	100
Take special weekend trip	500

FIGURE 6.25

Example of a token economy.
This token economy was set up to strengthen three types of exercise behaviour (jogging, tennis, and sit-ups). The person can exchange the tokens earned for four types of reinforcers that require different numbers of tokens. A token economy allows for immediate reinforcement (you can award yourself tokens each time you exercise) and it can allow you to use a variety of reinforcers.

example, in the case of overeating, you might define your target behaviour as eating more than 1600 calories a day (an excess response that you want to decrease) or eating fewer than 1600 calories a day (a deficit response that you want to increase). You can choose the latter definition and reinforce yourself whenever you eat fewer than 1600 calories in a day. Thus, you can reinforce yourself for not emitting a response, or for emitting it less, and thereby decrease a response through reinforcement.

Control of Antecedents. A worthwhile strategy for decreasing the occurrence of an undesirable response may be to identify its antecedents and avoid exposure to them. This strategy is especially useful when you are trying to decrease the frequency of a consummatory response, such as smoking or eating. In the case of overeating, for instance, the easiest way to resist temptation is to avoid having to face it. Thus, you might stay away from enticing restaurants, minimize time spent in your kitchen, shop for groceries just after eating (when willpower is higher), and avoid purchasing favourite foods. Control of antecedents can also be helpful in a program to increase studying. The key often lies in *where* you study. You can reduce excessive socializing by studying somewhere devoid of people. Similarly, you can reduce loafing by studying someplace where there is no TV, stereo, or phone to distract you.

Punishment. The strategy of decreasing unwanted behaviour by punishing yourself for that behaviour is an obvious option that people tend to overuse. The biggest problem with punishment in a self-modification effort is that it is difficult to follow through and punish yourself. Nonetheless, there may be situations in which your manipulations of reinforcers need to be bolstered by the threat of punishment.

If you're going to use punishment, keep two guidelines in mind. First, do not use punishment alone. Use it in conjunction with positive reinforcement. If you set up a program in which you can earn only negative consequences, you probably won't stick to it. Second, use a relatively mild punishment so that you will actually be able to administer it to yourself. Nurnberger and

Zimmerman (1970) developed a creative method of self-punishment. They had subjects write out a cheque to an organization they hated (e.g., the campaign of a political candidate whom they despised). The cheque was held by a third party who mailed it if subjects failed to meet their behavioural goals. Such a punishment is relatively harmless, but it can serve as a strong source of motivation.

Executing and Evaluating Your Program

Once you have designed your program, the next step is to put it to work by enforcing the contingencies that you have carefully planned. During this period, you need to continue to accurately record the frequency of your target behaviour so you can evaluate your progress. The success of your program depends on your not "cheating." The most common form of cheating is to reward yourself when you have not actually earned it.

You can do two things to increase the likelihood that you will comply with your program. One is to make up a *behavioural contract*—a written agreement outlining a promise to adhere to the contingencies of a behaviour modification program. The formality of signing such a contract in front of friends or family seems to make many people take their program more seriously.

You can further reduce the likelihood of cheating by having someone other than you dole out the reinforcers and punishments.

Behaviour modification programs often require some fine-tuning, so don't be surprised if you need to make a few adjustments. Several flaws are especially common in designing self-modification programs. Among those that you should look out for are (1) depending on a weak reinforcer, (2) permitting lengthy delays between appropriate behaviour and delivery of reinforcers, and (3) trying to do too much too quickly by setting unrealistic goals. Often, a small revision or two can turn a failing program around and make it a success.

Ending Your Program

Generally, when you design your program, you should spell out the conditions under which you will bring it to an end. Doing so involves setting terminal goals such as reaching a certain weight, studying with a certain regularity, or going without cigarettes for a certain length of time. Often, it is a good idea to phase out your program by planning a gradual reduction in the frequency or potency of your reinforcement for appropriate behaviour.

If your program is successful, it may fade away without a conscious decision on your part. Often, new, improved patterns of behaviour become self-maintaining. Responses such as eating right, exercising regularly, and studying diligently may become habitual. Whether or not you end your program intentionally, you should always be prepared to reinstitute the program if you find yourself slipping back into your old patterns of behaviour.

REVIEW OF KEY POINTS

▷ In behaviour modification, the principles of learning are used to change behaviour directly. Behaviour modification techniques can be used to increase one's self-control. The first step in self-modification involves specifying the overt target behaviour to be increased or decreased.

▷ The second step involves gathering baseline data about the initial rate of the target response and identifying any typical antecedents and consequences associated with the behaviour.

▷ The third step is to design a program. If you are trying to increase the strength of a response, you'll depend on positive reinforcement. The reinforcement contingencies should spell out exactly what you have to do to earn your reinforcer. A number of strategies can be used to decrease the strength of a response, including reinforcement, control of antecedents, and punishment.

▷ The fourth step involves executing and evaluating your program. Self-modification programs often require some fine-tuning. The final step is to determine how and when you will phase out your program.

Manipulating Emotions: Pavlov and Persuasion

With all due respect to the great Ivan Pavlov, when we focus on his demonstration that dogs can be trained to slobber in response to a tone, it is easy to lose sight of the importance of classical conditioning. At first glance, most people do not see a relationship between Pavlov's slobbering dogs and anything that they are even remotely interested in. However, in the main body of the chapter, we saw that classical conditioning actually contributes to the regulation of many important aspects of behaviour, including fears, phobias, and other emotional reactions; immune function and other physiological processes; food preferences; and even sexual arousal. In this Application you will learn that classical conditioning is routinely used to manipulate emotions in persuasive efforts. If you watch TV, you have been subjected to Pavlovian techniques. An understanding of these techniques can help you recognize when your emotions are being manipulated by advertisers, politicians, and the media.

Perhaps the most interesting aspect of classically conditioned emotional responses is that people often are unaware of the origin of these responses, or even that they feel the way they do. Consistent with this observation, research by Jim Olson of the University of Western Ontario has shown that attitudes can be shaped through classical conditioning without participants' conscious awareness (Olson & Fazio, 2001; Walther, Nagengast, & Trasselli, 2005). The key to the process is simply to manipulate the automatic, subconscious associations that people make in response to various stimuli. Let's look at how this manipulation is done in advertising, business negotiations, and the world of politics.

Classical Conditioning in Advertising

The art of manipulating people's associations has been perfected by the advertising industry (Till & Priluck, 2000). Advertisers consistently endeavour to pair the products they are peddling with stimuli that seem likely to elicit positive emotional responses. An extensive variety of stimuli are used for this purpose. Products are paired with well-liked celebrity spokespersons (Wayne Gretzky is a popular choice, promoting a car company and a fast-food company); depictions of warm, loving families; beautiful pastoral scenery; cute, cuddly pets; enchanting, rosy-cheeked children; upbeat, pleasant music; opulent surroundings that reek of wealth; and, above all else, extremely attractive models—especially glamorous, alluring women (Reichert, 2003; Reichert & Lambiase, 2003). Advertisers also like to pair their products with exciting events, such as the Stanley Cup or Grey Cup, and cherished symbols, such as flags and the Olympic rings insignia.

Advertisers mostly seek to associate their products with stimuli that evoke pleasurable feelings of a general sort, but in some cases they try to create more specific associations. For example, cigarette brands sold mainly to men are frequently paired with tough-looking men in rugged settings to create an association between the cigarettes and masculinity. In contrast, cigarette brands that are mainly marketed to women are paired with images that evoke feelings of femininity. In a similar vein, manufacturers of designer jeans typically seek to forge associations between their products and things that are young, urban, and hip. Advertisers marketing expensive automobiles or platinum credit cards pair their products with symbols of affluence, luxury, and privilege, such as mansions, butlers, and dazzling jewellery.

Classical Conditioning in Business Negotiations

In the world of business interactions, two standard practices are designed to get customers to make an association between one's business and pleasurable feelings. The first is to take customers out to dinner at fine restaurants. The provision of delicious food and fine wine in a luxurious environment is a powerful unconditioned stimulus that reliably elicits pleasant feelings that are likely to be associated with one's host. The second practice is the strategy of entertaining customers at major events, such as concerts and hockey games. Over the last decade, many sports arenas have been largely rebuilt with vastly more "luxury skyboxes" to accommodate this business tactic. One of us has a friend who uses his Toronto Blue Jays season tickets solely for entertaining business clients. He maintains that the cost of the tickets is more than offset by the increased business this practice brings him. This practice pairs the host with both pleasant feelings and the excitement of a big event.

It is worth noting that these strategies take advantage of other processes besides classical conditioning. They also make use of the *reciprocity norm*—the social rule that one should pay back in kind what one receives from others (Cialdini, 2001). Thus, wining and dining clients creates a sense of obligation that they should reciprocate their hosts' generosity—presumably in their business dealings.

The practice of taking customers out to dinner at expensive, luxurious restaurants takes advantage of the process of classical conditioning.

Classical Conditioning in the World of Politics

Like advertisers, candidates running for election need to influence the attitudes of many people quickly, subtly, and effectively—and they depend on classical conditioning to help them do so. For example, have you noticed how politicians show up at an endless variety of pleasant public events (such as the opening of a new mall) that often have nothing to do with their public service? When a sports team wins some sort of championship, local politicians are drawn like flies to the subsequent celebrations. Past prime ministers have made a practice of calling the Grey Cup winners. It is noteworthy that they do this during the postgame celebrations when many Canadians are watching the festivities on TV, ensuring the prime minister maximum coverage. They want to pair themselves with these positive events, so that they are associated with pleasant emotions.

Election campaign ads use the same techniques as commercial ads. Candidates are paired with popular celebrities, wholesome families, pleasant music, and symbols of patriotism. Cognizant of the power of classical conditioning, politicians also exercise great care to ensure that they are not paired with people or events that might trigger negative feelings.

The ultimate political perversion of the principles of classical conditioning probably occurred in Nazi Germany. The Nazis used many propaganda techniques to create prejudice toward Jews and members of other targeted groups (such as Gypsies). One such strategy was the repeated pairing of disgusting, repulsive images with stereotypical pictures of Jews. For example, the Nazis would show alternating pictures of rats or roaches crawling over filthy garbage and stereotypical Jewish faces, so that the two images would become associated in the minds of the viewers. Thus, the German population was conditioned to have negative emotional reactions to Jews and to associate them with vermin subject to extermination. The Nazis reasoned that if people would not hesitate to exterminate rats and roaches, then why not human beings associated with these vermin?

Becoming More Aware of Classical Conditioning Processes

How effective are the efforts to manipulate people's emotions through Pavlovian conditioning? It's hard to say. In the real world, these strategies are always used in combination with other persuasive tactics, which creates multiple confounds that make it difficult to assess the impact of the Pavlovian techniques (Walther, Nagengast, & Trasselli, 2005). Laboratory research can eliminate these confounds, but surprisingly little research on these strategies has been published, and virtually all of it has dealt with advertising. The advertising studies suggest that classical conditioning can be effective and leave enduring imprints on consumers' attitudes (Grossman & Till, 1998; Stuart, Shimp, & Engle, 1991; Walther & Grigoriadis, 2003), but a great deal of additional research is needed. Given the monumental sums that advertisers spend using these techniques, it seems reasonable to speculate that individual companies have data on their specific practices to demonstrate their efficacy, but these data are not made available to the public.

What can you do to reduce the extent to which your emotions are manipulated through Pavlovian procedures? Well, you could turn off your radio and TV, close up your magazines, stop your newspaper, disconnect your modem, and withdraw into a media-resistant shell, but that hardly seems practical for most people. Realistically, the best defence is to make a conscious effort to become more aware of the pervasive attempts to condition your emotions and attitudes. Some research on persuasion suggests that *to be forewarned is to be forearmed* (Pfau et al., 1990). In other words, if you know how media sources try to manipulate you, you should be more resistant to their strategies.

THE CANADIAN PRESS/Tom Hansen

Political candidates are very savvy about the potential power of classical conditioning. For example, they like to be seen in public with popular celebrities who elicit positive feelings among many voters.

TABLE 6.3	Critical Thinking Skills Discussed in This Application	
Skill	**Description**
Understanding how Pavlovian conditioning can be used to manipulate emotions	The critical thinker understands how stimuli can be paired together to create automatic associations that people may not be aware of.
Developing the ability to detect conditioning procedures used in the media	The critical thinker can recognize Pavlovian conditioning tactics in commercial and political advertisements.

Key Ideas

Classical Conditioning

● Classical conditioning explains how a neutral stimulus can acquire the capacity to elicit a response originally evoked by another stimulus. This kind of conditioning was originally described by Ivan Pavlov.

● Many kinds of everyday responses are regulated through classical conditioning, including phobias, fears, and pleasant emotional responses. Even physiological responses, such as immune and sexual functioning, respond to classical conditioning.

● A conditioned response may be weakened and extinguished entirely when the CS is no longer paired with the UCS. In some cases, spontaneous recovery occurs, and an extinguished response reappears after a period of nonexposure to the CS.

● Conditioning may generalize to additional stimuli that are similar to the original CS. The opposite of generalization is discrimination, which involves not responding to stimuli that resemble the original CS. Higher-order conditioning occurs when a CS functions as if it were a UCS to establish new conditioning.

Operant Conditioning

● Operant conditioning involves largely voluntary responses that are governed by their consequences. Following the lead of E. L. Thorndike, B. F. Skinner investigated this form of conditioning, working mainly with rats and pigeons in Skinner boxes.

● The key dependent variable in operant conditioning is the rate of response over time. When this responding is shown graphically, steep slopes indicate rapid responding. New operant responses can be shaped by gradually reinforcing closer and closer approximations of the desired response. In operant conditioning, extinction occurs when reinforcement for a response is terminated and the rate of that response declines.

● Operant responses are regulated by discriminative stimuli that are cues for the likelihood of obtaining reinforcers. These stimuli are subject to the same processes of generalization and discrimination that occur in classical conditioning.

● Delayed reinforcement slows the process of conditioning. Primary reinforcers are unlearned; secondary reinforcers acquire their reinforcing quality through conditioning.

● Intermittent schedules of reinforcement produce greater resistance to extinction than similar continuous schedules. Ratio schedules tend to yield higher rates of response than interval schedules. Shorter intervals and higher ratios are associated with faster responding.

● Responses can be strengthened through either the presentation of positive reinforcers or the removal of negative reinforcers. Negative reinforcement regulates escape and avoidance learning. The two-process theory provides the best explanation of avoidance behaviour and may shed light on why phobias are so difficult to eliminate.

● Positive and negative punishments involve consequences that lead to a decline in response strength. Some of the problems associated with punishment as a disciplinary procedure are emotional side effects and increased aggressive behaviour.

Changing Directions in the Study of Conditioning

● The findings on instinctive drift, conditioned taste aversion, and preparedness have led to the recognition that there are species-specific biological constraints on conditioning. Some evolutionary psychologists argue that learning processes vary considerably across species.

● Studies of signal relations in classical conditioning and response–outcome relations in operant conditioning suggest that cognitive processes play a larger role in conditioning than originally believed.

Observational Learning

● In observational learning, an organism is conditioned by watching a model's conditioning. Both classical and operant conditioning can occur through observational learning, which depends on the processes of attention, retention, reproduction, and motivation.

● Observational learning can account for the influence of mass media (such as television) on behaviour. The principles of observational learning have also been used to explain why physical punishment increases aggressive behaviour.

Putting It in Perspective: Themes 3 and 6

● Two of our key themes were especially apparent in our coverage of learning and conditioning. One theme involves the interaction of heredity and environment in learning. The other involves the way progress in psychology affects society at large.

PERSONAL APPLICATION • Achieving Self-Control through Behaviour Modification

● The first step in self-modification is specifying the target behaviour to be increased or decreased. The second step is gathering baseline data.

● The third step is to design a program, using procedures such as reinforcement, control of antecedents, and punishment. The fourth step involves executing and evaluating your program. The final step is to determine how and when you will phase out your program.

CRITICAL THINKING APPLICATION • Manipulating Emotions: Pavlov and Persuasion

● Advertisers routinely pair their products with stimuli that seem likely to elicit positive emotions or other specific feelings. The practice of taking customers out to dinner or to major events also takes advantage of Pavlovian conditioning. Politicians also work to pair themselves with positive events. The best defence against these tactics is to become more aware of efforts to manipulate your emotions.

Key Terms

Acquisition, 257
Antecedents, 293
Avoidance learning, 273
Behaviour modification, 292
Behavioural contract, 295
Classical conditioning, 251
Conditioned reinforcers, 269
Conditioned response (CR), 253
Conditioned stimulus (CS), 253
Conditioning, 251
Continuous reinforcement, 270
Cumulative recorder, 264
Discriminative stimuli, 268
Elicit, 253
Emit, 264
Escape learning, 273
Evaluative conditioning, 255
Extinction, 258
Fixed-interval (FI) schedule, 271
Fixed-ratio (FR) schedule, 271
Higher-order conditioning, 261
Immunosuppression, 256
Instinctive drift, 278
Instrumental learning, 262
Intermittent reinforcement, 271
Latent learning, 281
Law of effect, 263
Learning, 249
Mirror neurons, 290
Negative reinforcement, 272
Observational learning, 283
Operant chamber, 264
Operant conditioning, 262

Partial reinforcement, 271
Pavlovian conditioning, 251
Phobias, 250
Positive reinforcement, 272
Preparedness, 279
Primary reinforcers, 269
Punishment, 274
Reinforcement, 264
Reinforcement contingencies, 264
Renewal effect, 259
Resistance to extinction, 266
Schedule of reinforcement, 270
Secondary reinforcers, 269
Shaping, 265
Skinner box, 264
Spontaneous recovery, 259
Stimulus discrimination, 260
Stimulus generalization, 259
Token economy, 294
Trial, 254
Unconditioned response (UCR), 253
Unconditioned stimulus (UCS), 253
Variable-interval (VI) schedule, 271
Variable-ratio (VR) schedule, 271

Key People

Albert Bandura, 283
John Garcia, 279
Ivan Pavlov, 251
Robert Rescorla, 281
Martin Seligman, 278
B. F. Skinner, 264
E. L. Thorndike, 262

1. Pavlov repeatedly paired the presentation of meat powder with a particular tone, and found that dogs learned to salivate when the tone was presented. In this experiment, which of the following terms describes the dogs' salivation in response to the tone?
   A. unconditioned stimulus
   B. unconditioned response
   C. conditioned stimulus
   D. conditioned response

2. Sam's wife always wears the same black nightgown whenever she is "in the mood" for sexual relations, and Sam becomes sexually aroused as soon as he sees his wife in that nightgown. The nightgown represents which of the following for Sam?
   A. an unconditioned stimulus
   B. an unconditioned response
   C. a conditioned stimulus
   D. a conditioned response

3. After ten-year-old Amir broke his brother's favourite toy, his parents took away one of Amir's favourite toys for a week. Which of the following consequences best describes the action taken by the parents?
   A. positive punishment
   B. negative punishment
   C. positive reinforcement
   D. negative reinforcement

4. Which of the following situations is an example of higher-order conditioning?
   A. Victoria salivates when she hears the sound of the ice-cream truck even though her mother rarely lets her buy ice cream.
   B. Daisy gets nervous whenever her teacher asks her to present in class because Daisy has repeatedly been embarrassed during class presentations.
   C. Wei expects good things to happen when both her best friend and her boyfriend are present.
   D. Tia was bullied by Andrea as a child. Andrea grew up to be a pilot. Tia gets angry when she sees airplanes.

5. Which of the following likely involves only classical conditioning?
   A. avoiding sunburn by putting on sunscreen
   B. being frustrated by a class in which you study hard but don't earn good grades
   C. sneezing when you see a cat that has previously triggered your allergies
   D. sleeping soundly after having a great workout at the gym

6. A pigeon in a Skinner box pecks a disk at a high, steady rate, and a graph portrays the pigeon's rate of responding over time. Which of the following describes the slope of the line in that graph?
   A. a steep, fairly straight line
   B. a shallow, fairly straight line
   C. a steep line that looks like a staircase
   D. a shallow line that looks like a staircase

7. Which of the following is always true about a primary reinforcer?
   A. It elicits an unconditioned response.
   B. It elicits a conditioned response.
   C. It is emitted very early in life, prior to pronounced socialization.
   D. It is the most effective reinforcer in operant conditioning situations.

8. A person plays a slot machine at a steady, rapid pace of responding. The pattern of responding is typical of which of the following kinds of reinforcement schedules?
   A. fixed-ratio
   B. variable-ratio
   C. fixed-interval
   D. variable-interval

9. Which of the following situations illustrates the effect of negative reinforcement?
   A. Alexei is willing to do dishes in order to go to a basketball game.
   B. Shaun will study only after his parents yell at him.
   C. Cody washes his father's car so that he won't lose driving privileges.
   D. Sandeep walks the dog so that his sister will stop nagging him.

10. Which of the following provides an explanation for why phobias are so resistant to extinction?
    A. two-process avoidance learning
    B. higher-order conditioning
    C. partial reinforcement extinction effect
    D. social learning theory

11. Nolan used to love tequila, but recently he drank too much of it and became very sick. His tendency to drink tequila has since declined dramatically. What does this sequence of events represent in operant terms?
    A. aversive conditioning
    B. negative reinforcement
    C. escape learning
    D. punishment

12. According to Rescorla, which of the following situations would result in the strongest conditioned response?
    A. The CS is presented with the UCS 20 times, and without the UCS 10 times.
    B. The CS is presented with the UCS 20 times, and without the UCS 20 times.
    C. The CS is presented with the UCS 20 times, and without the UCS 3 times.
    D. The CS is presented with the UCS 30 times, and without the UCS 20 times.

13. Which of the following theorists would be most likely to state that reinforcement affects the performance of a behaviour but not necessarily the acquisition of that behaviour?
    A. Tolman
    B. Skinner
    C. Rescorla
    D. Bandura

14. According to the recommendations about effective use of punishment, which of the following helps to explain why speeding tickets are not effective at reducing the behaviour of speeding?
    A. The fines are too expensive for first offences, so drivers are too angry to change the behaviour.
    B. Tickets are received infrequently, so speeding is not consistently punished.
    C. Speeding is not sufficiently voluntary to be affected by operant conditioning.
    D. Fines are examples of negative punishment, which is typically less effective than positive punishment.

15. Which of the following problems with behaviour modification can be solved by using a token economy?
    A. reinforcer satiation
    B. ineffective punishment contingencies
    C. inaccurate baseline data
    D. unrealistic goals

See Appendix A for answers to this Practice Test.

On the Web

▶ **CourseMate**

Go to this site to find online resources directly linked to your book, including more quizzes, a glossary, flash cards, videos, and more!

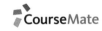

▶ **CengageNow**

Go to this site for the link to CengageNOW™, your one-stop study shop. Take a pre-test for this chapter and CengageNOW™ will generate a personalized study plan based on your test results! The study plan will identify the topics you need to review and direct you to online resources to help you master those topics. You can then take a post-test to help you determine the concepts you have mastered and what you still need to work on.

▶ **Aplia**

Aplia™ is an online interactive learning solution that helps you improve comprehension—and your grade—by integrating a variety of media and tools such as video, tutorials, practice tests, and an interactive e-book.

CHAPTER 7

Human Memory

© Debbie Steel, Trent University

Have you ever thought about the possibility of travelling through time? If you are like most people, you have likely imagined how useful it might be in some situations. Time travel would allow you to accomplish more—for example, to take those extra classes that you are so interested in, allowing you to complete your degree sooner than is ordinarily possible. The concept of time travel is fascinating and has been the subject of many books and movies. Can you remember any books you have read or movies you have seen in the past couple of years in which time travel plays an important role? Of course, there are many well-known novels, including Charles Dickens *A Christmas Carol* (1843), H. G. Wells *The Time Machine* (1895), Robert Heinlein's *All You Zombies* (1959), Kurt Vonnegut's *Slaughterhouse-Five* (1969), Douglas Adams's *The Restaurant at the End of the Universe* (1980), and Michael Crichton's *Timeline* (1999). By the way, there was another famous book published in 1999 that involved time travel. If you are like most others of your age (any age really, both of us are fans), you have probably read the book or seen the movie of the same name that was released in 2004. Do you remember the name of the book now? As a hint, we can tell you that the author was J. K. Rowling. *Harry Potter and the Prisoner of Azkaban* is the answer. That was too easy! Let's test your Harry Potter trivia knowledge again. Do you remember the name of the object that allowed Hermione to time travel? (If not, you can find the answer at the end of this section.) This might be more difficult—take a moment. If you can't answer right away, it might seem that you almost know, that the answer is, well, on the tip of your tongue. Memory is a fascinating topic and process. While you are trying to remember, reflect a little on how you might describe to someone else how you are able to remember such things or, perhaps, why you cannot. These processes, including remembering, forgetting, the tip-of-the-tongue phenomenon, and much more, constitute the subject matter of this chapter on human memory.

Our memory is something that helps define who we are and it is intimately tied to our ability to function effectively and efficiently in the immediate moment. In order to get to school on time, you have to remember where you left your room keys so you can lock the door before you leave. The importance of memory in our ability to orient ourselves in the present is clear. So, what does memory have to do with time travel?

Time travel itself, while clearly fascinating, isn't as rare as you might think; in fact, most of us can do it and if you think carefully about it, it shouldn't surprise you to know that such time travel is intimately linked with the nature of our cognition and memory systems (Ainslie, 2007; Schacter & Addis, 2007a, 2007b). It is the nature of our cognitive and memory processes that allows us all to travel through time (Roberts, 2002; Tulving, 1983, 1993, 2005; Tulving & Kim, 2007). We can go backwards to remember specific events that happened to us, such as attending a screening of *The Prisoner of Azkaban* and the people with whom we attended the movie. Other memories are not tied to us personally, but may relate more to general knowledge, such as what the word *prisoner* means or what kind of animal a *hippogriff* is.

These two kinds of memory—memory for general information and memory for personal events—were labelled *semantic* and *episodic* memory, respectively, by psychologist Endel Tulving (1972). Tulving's well-known patient referred to as K. C. gives a dramatic example of the distinction between these types of memories. K. C. suffered serious brain damage in 1981 after a motorcycle accident. But you might never realize it if you restricted yourself to asking him questions such as "Who wrote *The Time Machine*?" After the accident, K. C.'s semantic memory for facts was unimpaired. He was not distinguishable from anyone else and frequently outperformed "normal" undergraduates at the University of Toronto, where Tulving conducted his work, on various cognitive/perceptual tasks. What is impaired, however, is his episodic memory: No matter how hard he tries, he cannot remember anything that has ever happened *to him* (Tulving, 2001). He depends on a PDA to remind him to eat. K. C. admits that without the device "I would get hungry but wouldn't remember to eat. I wouldn't know what time to go for lunch" (Branswell & Hall, 2007, p. A6).

K. C. has been important in terms of our understanding of memory (Rosenbaum et al., 2005). Research with K. C. has contributed to, among other things, our knowledge about the distinction between semantic and episodic memory, the distinction between implicit and explicit memory, and new learning in amnesia (Rosenbaum et al., 2005). We will discuss in much more detail the notion of types of memory and the theories and work of Endel Tulving in this chapter. Tulving is an internationally recognized expert in the nature of memory. He was awarded the Donald O. Hebb award by the Canadian Psychological Association in 1983 and was also awarded, along with neuroscientist Brenda Milner of McGill University, the 2005 Gairdner Award. Interestingly, while not a criterion for the award, both researchers study memory.

Of course, we are not constrained to the past in our time travelling. Our cognitive systems also allow us to experience the present and to travel forward in time to plan and anticipate things in the future. Some of these characteristics are unique to humans. Can your dog anticipate you coming home from class, can he reflect on and remember what he did all day? William Roberts (2002) of the University of Western Ontario argues that animals are "stuck in time," as they have no episodic memory or ability to anticipate events far in the future (see Atance & Meltzoff, 2007; Bar, 2007; Bischof-Köhler & Bishchof, 2007; Buckner, 2007; Suddendorf & Corballis, 2007). It is episodic memory, of course, that affords humans the ability to "time travel" (Tulving, 1993). Memory is a fascinating topic relevant to our everyday lives. For most of us, memory is not a concern. For some, however, memory—or rather, lack of it—is a priority issue. In a Statistics Canada (2002b) survey that focused on Canadians with some type of disability, one out of seven reported a significant disability, and of those 15 and older, 12.3 percent reported significant memory impairment and confusion. While this problem increased with age, it was not entirely restricted to the elderly. There are, however, specific memory deficits associated with aging. We will deal more specifically with aging and issues such as Alzheimer's disease in Chapter 11.

In this chapter we focus on the nature of our memory systems. As the preceding discussion suggests, memory involves more than taking information in and storing it in some mental compartment. In fact, psychologists probing the workings of memory have had to grapple with three enduring questions:

1. How does information get *into* memory?
2. How is information *maintained* in memory?
3. How is information pulled *back out* of memory?

These three questions correspond to the three key processes involved in memory: *encoding* (getting information in), *storage* (maintaining it), and *retrieval* (getting it out).

Some theorists have drawn an analogy between these three processes and elements of information processing by computers. *Encoding* involves forming a memory code. For example, when you form a memory code for a word, you might emphasize how it looks, how it sounds, or what it means. Encoding usually requires attention. Encoding is analogous to entering data using a computer keyboard. *Storage* involves maintaining encoded information in memory over time. Storage is analogous to saving data in a file on your computer. Psychologists have focused much of their memory research on trying to identify just what factors help or hinder memory storage.

Information storage isn't enough to guarantee that you'll remember something. You need to be able to get information out of storage. *Retrieval* involves recovering information from memory stores. Retrieval is analogous to calling up a file and then displaying it on your computer monitor. Research issues concerned with retrieval include the study of how people search memory and why some retrieval strategies are more effective than others. The analogies for encoding and retrieval work pretty well, but the storage analogy is somewhat misleading. When information is stored on your computer hard drive, it remains unchanged indefinitely and you can retrieve an exact copy. As you will learn in this chapter, memory storage is a much more dynamic process. Our memories change over time and are rough reconstructions rather than exact copies of past events.

Most of this chapter is devoted to an examination of memory encoding, storage, and retrieval. As you'll see, these basic processes help explain the ultimate puzzle in the study of memory: why people forget. Just as memory involves more than storage, forgetting involves more than "losing" something from the memory store. Forgetting may be due to deficiencies in any of the three key processes in memory—encoding, storage, or retrieval. After our discussion of forgetting, we will take a brief look at the physiological bases of memory. Finally, we will discuss the theoretical controversy about whether there are separate memory systems for different types of information. The chapter's Personal Application provides some practical advice on how to improve your memory. The Critical Thinking Application discusses some reasons why memory is less reliable than people assume it to be.

We began this introductory section discussing the concept of time travel. It is of interest to psychologists not only because it seems to be tied up with our memory system, but also because it has been suggested that the ability to imagine oneself in the future gives us an adaptive advantage in terms of our flexibility in dealing with novel situations (Quoidbach, Wood, & Hanenne, 2009; Suddendorf & Corballis, 2007). It has also been found that specific types of future mental time travel may help increase our happiness and reduce our stress (Quoidbach et al., 2009). Oh yes, we almost *forgot*: Hermione used a *Time Turner* in order to be able to attend more classes than she had time for. The use of the *Time Turner* also allowed for the rescue of Sirius Black and Buckbeak (a hippogriff).

Have you ever been introduced to someone and then realized only 30 seconds into your interaction that you had already forgotten his or her name? More often than not, this familiar kind of forgetting results from a failure to form a memory code for the name. When you're introduced to people, you're often busy sizing them up and thinking about what you're going to say. With your attention diverted in this way, names go in one ear and out the other. Sometimes the information just doesn't seem important, so you devote very little or no attention to it. For example, can you remember the first name of either author of this book? While we are a little disappointed that you can't, we are not surprised. You don't remember them because they aren't encoded for storage into memory. This common problem illustrates that active encoding is a crucial process in memory. In this section, we discuss the role of attention in encoding, various types of encoding, and the ways to enrich this process.

The Role of Attention

You generally need to pay attention to information if you intend to remember it (Lachter, Forster, & Ruthruff, 2004; Mulligan, 1998). For example, if you sit through a class lecture but pay little attention to it, you're unlikely to remember much of what the professor had to say. *Attention* involves focusing awareness on a narrowed range of stimuli or events. Selective attention is critical to everyday functioning. If your attention were distributed equally among all stimulus inputs, life would be utter chaos. You need to screen out most of the potential stimulation around you in order to read a book, converse with a friend, or even carry on a coherent train of thought.

Attention is often likened to a *filter* that screens out most potential stimuli while allowing a select few to pass through into conscious awareness. However, a great deal of debate has been devoted to *where* the filter is located in the information-processing system. The key issue in this debate is whether stimuli are screened out *early*, during sensory input, or *late*, after the brain has processed the meaning or significance of the input (see Figure 7.1).

Evidence on the "cocktail party phenomenon" suggests the latter. For example, imagine a young woman named Tamara at a crowded party where many conversations are taking place. Tamara is paying attention to her conversation with a friend and filtering out the other conversations. However, if someone in another conversation mentions her name, Tamara may notice it, even though she has been ignoring that conversation. In experimental simulations of this situation, about 35 percent of participants report hearing their own name (Wood & Cowan, 1995). If selection is early, how can these people register input they've been blocking out? This cocktail party phenomenon suggests that attention involves *late* selection, based on the *meaning* of input.

Which view is supported by the weight of scientific evidence—early selection or late selection? Studies have found ample evidence for *both* as well as for intermediate selection (Cowan, 1988; Treisman 2009). These findings have led some theorists to conclude that the location of the attention filter may be flexible rather than fixed (Shiffrin, 1988). According to Lavie (2005, 2007), the location of our attention filter depends on the "cognitive load" of current information processing. When we are attending to

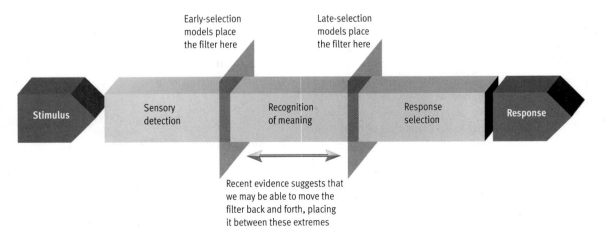

Early-selection models place the filter here

Late-selection models place the filter here

Stimulus — Sensory detection — Recognition of meaning — Response selection — Response

Recent evidence suggests that we may be able to move the filter back and forth, placing it between these extremes

FIGURE 7.1

Models of selective attention.

Early-selection models propose that input is filtered before meaning is processed. Late-selection models hold that filtering occurs after the processing of meaning. There is evidence to support early, late, and intermediate selection, suggesting that the location of the attentional filter may not be fixed.

complicated, high-load tasks that consume much of our attentional capacity, selection tends to occur early. However, when we are involved in simpler, low-load tasks, more attentional capacity is left over to process the meaning of distractions, allowing for later selection.

Wherever filtering occurs, it is clear that people have difficulty if they attempt to focus their attention on two or more inputs simultaneously. For example, if Tamara tried to continue her original conversation while also monitoring the other conversation in which she was mentioned, she would struggle in her efforts to attend to both conversations and would remember less of her original conversation. Studies by Fergus Craik indicate that when participants are forced to divide their attention between memory encoding and some other task, large reductions in memory performance are seen (Craik, 2001; Craik & Kester, 2000). He has also conducted important work with Ellen Bialystok on bilingualism (Craik & Bialystok, 2005) and has made important contributions to the literature on cognition and aging. We will consider work on bilingualism in Chapter 10 and Craik's contributions on aging in Chapter 11.

Moreover, the negative effects of divided attention are not limited to memory. Divided attention can have a negative impact on the performance of quite a variety of tasks, especially when the tasks are complex or unfamiliar (Pashler, Johnston, & Ruthruff, 2001). Although people tend to think that they can multitask with no deterioration in performance, research suggests that the human brain can effectively handle only one attention-consuming task at a time (Lien, Ruthruff, & Johnston, 2006). When people multitask, they really are switching their attention back and forth among tasks, rather than processing them simultaneously. That may be fine in many circumstances, but not in others.

Take, for example, the controversy about driving while talking on a cell phone. Carefully controlled research clearly demonstrates that cell-phone conversations undermine people's driving performance, even when hands-free phones are used (Horrey & Wickens, 2006; Kass, Cole, & Stanny, 2007). One study of a simulated driving task found that cell-phone conversations increased the chances of missing traffic signals and slowed down reactions to signals that were detected (Strayer & Johnston, 2001). Another study found that "the impairments associated with using a cell phone while driving can be as profound as those associated with driving while drunk" (Strayer, Drews, & Crouch, 2006).

A recent study shed some light on why cell-phone conversations are more distracting to drivers than conversations with passengers. The research showed that passengers adapt their conversation to the demands of the traffic and provide assistance to the driver (Drews, Pasupathi, & Strayer, 2008). In other words, when passengers see that traffic is heavy or that the driving task has become complicated, they reduce the rate and complexity of their communication and try to help the driver navigate through the situation. As distracting as cell-phone conversations are, recent research indicates that texting while driving is substantially more dangerous (Drews et al., 2009). Many provinces and territories have banned these practices while driving, yet many drivers continue to resist these prohibitions. Provincial and territorial governments have stepped in with legislation and fines for those who disobey. In Ontario, for example, you can be fined up to $500 for using a hand-held device while driving, and in British Columbia, the fine is accompanied by demerit points (CBC News, 2009). Other countries around the world, including the United States, Australia, Britain, Singapore, Brazil, and many others have similar legislation (CBC News, 2004).

Attention and deficits related to it may help us understand some of the cognitive difficulties faced by some elderly people. Lynn Hasher and her colleagues (Hasher & Zacks, 1974; Ikier, Yang, & Hasher, 2008; Yang, Hasher, & Wilson, 2007) suggest that while much of the information we want to remember is encoded as a result of *effortful processing*, some types of information may be acquired more *automatically*. In the first type of processing, you are picking up information because you are intentionally attempting to do so, such as when you are listening to your psychology professor's inspiring lectures. Other information, such as the frequency of word use (e.g., whether the word *bacon* or *pastrami* occurs more frequently in English), is picked up without your intending to do so (Hasher & Zacks, 1974). People are surprisingly accurate at answering questions about matters like word frequency without remembering how they acquired the knowledge. Under some circumstances, that type of information may be very important. The ability to answer questions based on each type of processing has been found to be a function of several factors, including circadian patterns and age (May, Hasher, & Foong, 2005).

Levels of Processing   SIM5   6a

Attention is critical to the encoding of memories. But not all attention is created equal. You can attend to things in different ways, focusing on different aspects of the stimulus input. According to some theorists, differences in *how* people attend to information are the main factors influencing how much they remember. Fergus Craik and Robert Lockhart (1972), both at the University of Toronto, proposed an important model in this area. In their formulation, they argue that different rates of forgetting occur because some methods of encoding create more durable memory codes than others.

Craik and Lockhart propose that incoming information can be processed at different levels. For instance, they maintain that in dealing with verbal information, people engage in three progressively deeper levels of processing: structural, phonemic, and semantic encoding (see Figure 7.2). *Structural encoding* is relatively shallow processing that emphasizes the physical structure of the stimulus. For example, if words are flashed on a screen, structural encoding registers such matters as how they were printed (capital letters, lowercase, and so on) or the length of the words (how many letters). Further analysis may result in *phonemic encoding,* which emphasizes what a word sounds like. Phonemic encoding involves naming or saying (perhaps silently) the words. Finally, *semantic encoding* emphasizes the meaning of verbal input; it involves thinking about the objects and actions the words represent. *Levels-of-processing theory* proposes that deeper levels of processing result in longer-lasting memory codes.

In one experimental test of levels-of-processing theory, Craik and Tulving (1975) compared the durability of structural, phonemic, and semantic encoding. They directed subjects' attention to particular aspects of briefly presented stimulus words by asking them questions about various characteristics of the words (see Figure 7.2). The questions were designed to engage the subjects in different levels of processing. The key hypothesis was that retention of the stimulus words would increase as subjects moved from structural to phonemic to semantic encoding. After responding to 60 words, the subjects received an unexpected test of their memory for the words. As predicted, the subjects' recall was low after structural encoding, notably better after phonemic encoding, and highest after semantic encoding (see Figure 7.3). While the theory is not without its critics, the hypothesis that deeper processing leads to enhanced memory has been replicated in many studies (Koriat & Melkman, 1987; Lockhart & Craik, 1990).

Enriching Encoding

6a

Structural, phonemic, and semantic encoding do not exhaust the options when it comes to forming

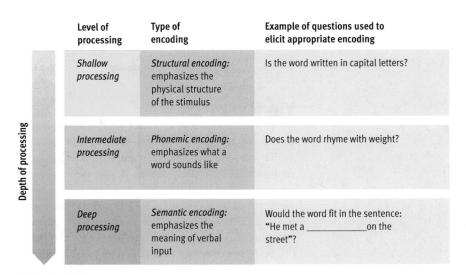

Level of processing	Type of encoding	Example of questions used to elicit appropriate encoding
Shallow processing	*Structural encoding:* emphasizes the physical structure of the stimulus	Is the word written in capital letters?
Intermediate processing	*Phonemic encoding:* emphasizes what a word sounds like	Does the word rhyme with *weight*?
Deep processing	*Semantic encoding:* emphasizes the meaning of verbal input	Would the word fit in the sentence: "He met a _____ on the street"?

Depth of processing

FIGURE 7.2

Levels-of-processing theory.

According to Craik (2002), Craik and Lockhart (1972), and Lockhart and Craik (1990), structural, phonemic, and semantic encoding—which can be elicited by questions such as those shown on the right—involve progressively deeper levels of processing, which should result in more durable memories.

memory codes. There are other dimensions to encoding, dimensions that can enrich the encoding process and thereby improve memory (Nairne, Pandeirada, & Thompson, 2008): elaboration, visual imagery, and self-referent coding.

Elaboration

Semantic encoding can often be enhanced through a process called *elaboration.* *Elaboration* is linking a stimulus to other information at the time of encoding. For example, let's say you read that phobias are often caused by classical conditioning, and you apply this idea to your own fear of spiders. In doing so, you are engaging in elaboration. The additional associations created by elaboration usually help people to remember information. Differences in elaboration can help explain why different approaches to semantic processing result in varied

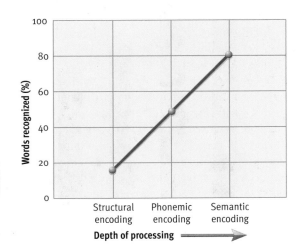

FIGURE 7.3

Retention at three levels of processing.

In accordance with levels-of-processing theory, Craik and Tulving (1975) found that structural, phonemic, and semantic encoding, which involve progressively deeper levels of processing, led to progressively better retention. (Data from Craik & Tulving, 1975)

amounts of retention (Craik & Tulving, 1975; Toyota & Kikuchi, 2004, 2005; Willoughby, Motz, & Wood, 1997).

Visual Imagery

6a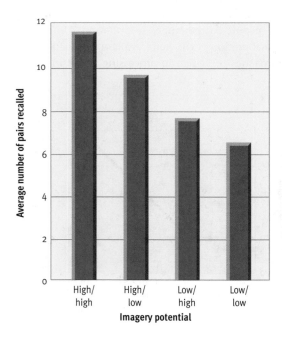

Imagery—the creation of visual images to represent the words to be remembered—can also be used to enrich encoding. Of course, some words are easier to create images for than others. If you were asked to remember the word *juggler,* you could readily form an image of someone juggling balls. However, if you were asked to remember the word *truth,* you would probably have more difficulty forming a suitable image. The difference is that *juggler* refers to a concrete object, whereas *truth* refers to an abstract concept. Allan Paivio (1969) points out that it is easier to form images of concrete objects than of abstract concepts. He believes that this ease of image formation affects memory.

The beneficial effect of imagery on memory was demonstrated in a study by Paivio, Smythe, and Yuille (1968). They asked subjects to learn a list of 16 pairs of words. They manipulated whether the words were concrete, high-imagery words, or abstract, low-imagery words. In terms of imagery potential, the list contained four types of pairings: high–high (*juggler–dress*), high–low (*letter–effort*), low–high (*duty–hotel*), and low–low (*quality–necessity*). Figure 7.4 shows the recall for each type of pairing. The impact of imagery is quite evident. The best recall was of high–high pairings, and the worst recall was of low–low pairings, showing that high-imagery words are easier to remember than low-imagery words. Similar results

were observed in another study that controlled for additional confounding factors (Paivio, Khan, & Begg, 2000).

According to Paivio (1986), imagery facilitates memory because it provides a second kind of memory code, and two codes are better than one. His *dual-coding theory* holds that memory is enhanced by forming semantic and visual codes, since either can lead to recall. Although some aspects of dual-coding theory have been questioned, it's clear that the use of mental imagery can enhance memory in many situations (Marschark, 1992; McCauley, Eskes, & Moscovitch, 1996).

Self-Referent Encoding

Making material *personally* meaningful can also enrich encoding. For example, if you ride a bus regularly, you've probably heard the driver call out the names of the stops day in and day out for months. Do you remember all of the stops? If you haven't made an effort to memorize them, probably not. But you could probably list those that you've used, or even the ones where your friends get on or off. People's recall of information tends to be slanted in favour of material that is personally relevant (Kahan & Johnson, 1992).

Self-referent encoding involves deciding how or whether information is personally relevant. This approach to encoding was compared to structural, phonemic, and semantic encoding in a study by Rogers, Kuiper, and Kirker (1977). Like Craik and Tulving (1975), these researchers manipulated

FIGURE 7.4

The effect of visual imagery on retention.

Participants given pairs of words to remember showed better recall for high-imagery pairings than for low-imagery pairings, demonstrating that visual imagery can enrich encoding. (Data from Paivio, Smythe, & Yuille, 1968)

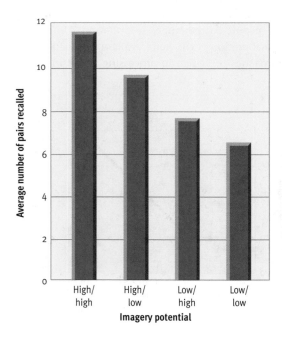

REVIEW OF KEY POINTS

▷ Three key processes contribute to memory: encoding, storage, and retrieval.

▷ Attention, which facilitates encoding, is inherently selective and has been compared to a filter. The cocktail party phenomenon suggests that input is screened late in mental processing. The empirical evidence indicates that people may have some flexibility in where they place their attention filter.

▷ According to levels-of-processing theory, the kinds of memory codes people create depend on which aspects of a stimulus are emphasized. Structural, phonemic, and semantic encoding emphasize the structure, sound, and meaning of words, respectively.

▷ Deeper processing results in better recall of information. Structural, phonemic, and semantic encoding represent progressively deeper levels of processing.

▷ Elaboration enriches encoding by linking a stimulus to other information, such as examples of an idea. The creation of visual images to represent words can enrich encoding. Visual imagery may help by creating two memory codes rather than just one. Encoding that emphasizes personal self-reference may be especially useful in facilitating retention.

encoding by asking their subjects certain kinds of questions. To induce self-referent encoding, subjects were asked to decide whether adjectives flashed on a screen applied to them personally. The results showed that self-referent encoding led to improved recall of the adjectives. Self-referent encoding appears to enhance recall by promoting additional elaboration and better organization of information (Symons & Johnson, 1997). Nick Kuiper (Kuiper & Rogers, 1979), now at the University of Western Ontario, has gone on to use the self-referent encoding to show that people who are depressed differ from nondepressed

people in the content of their self-concept or self-prototype. Depressed people have more negative content as part of their self-prototype (Kuiper & Derry, 1981). We will review some of the research findings with regard to self-concept and depression in Chapter 14.

The value of self-referent encoding demonstrates once again that encoding plays a critical role in memory. But encoding is only one of the three key processes in memory. We turn next to the process of storage, which for many people is virtually synonymous with memory.

Storage: Maintaining Information in Memory

In their efforts to understand memory storage, theorists have historically related it to the technologies of their age (Roediger, 1980). One of the earliest models used to explain memory storage was the wax tablet. Both Aristotle and Plato compared memory to a block of wax that differed in size and hardness for various individuals. Remembering, according to this analogy, was like stamping an impression into the wax. As long as the image remained in the wax, the memory would remain intact.

Modern theories of memory reflect the technological advances of the 20th century. For example, many theories formulated at the dawn of the computer age drew an analogy between information storage by computers and information storage in human memory (Atkinson & Shiffrin, 1968, 1971; Broadbent, 1958; Waugh & Norman, 1965). The main contribution of these *information-processing theories* was to subdivide memory into three separate memory stores (Estes, 1999; Pashler & Carrier, 1996). The names for these stores and their exact characteristics varied some from one theory to the next. For purposes of simplicity, we'll organize our discussion

around the model devised by Richard Atkinson and Richard Shiffrin, which proved to be the most influential of the information-processing theories. According to their model, incoming information passes through two temporary storage buffers—the sensory store and short-term store—before it is transferred into a long-term store (see Figure 7.5). Like the wax tablet before it, the information-processing model of memory is a metaphor; the three memory stores are not viewed as anatomical structures in the brain, but rather as functionally distinct types of memory.

Sensory Memory   6b

The *sensory memory* preserves information in its original sensory form for a brief time, usually only a fraction of a second. Sensory memory allows the sensation of a visual pattern, sound, or touch to linger for a brief moment after the sensory stimulation is over. In the case of vision, people really perceive an *afterimage* rather than the actual stimulus.

PREVIEW QUESTIONS

► What is sensory memory?
► What is the duration and capacity of the short-term store?
► What are the components of working memory?
► Is long-term storage permanent?
► Why have some theorists questioned the distinction between short-term and long-term memory?
► How is information organized and represented in memory?

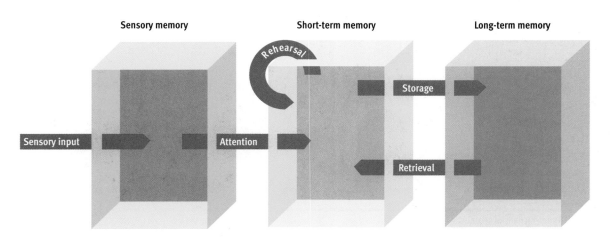

Sensory memory   **Short-term memory**   **Long-term memory**

Rehearsal

Sensory input   Attention   Storage   Retrieval

FIGURE 7.5

The Atkinson and Shiffrin model of memory storage.

Atkinson and Shiffrin (1971) proposed that memory is made up of three information stores. *Sensory memory* can hold a large amount of information just long enough (a fraction of a second) for a small portion of it to be selected for longer storage. *Short-term memory* has a limited capacity, and unless aided by rehearsal, its storage duration is brief. *Long-term memory* can store an apparently unlimited amount of information for indeterminate periods.

Because the image of the sparkler persists briefly in sensory memory, when the sparkler is moved fast enough, the blending of afterimages causes people to see a continuous stream of light instead of a succession of individual points.

You can demonstrate the existence of afterimages for yourself by rapidly moving a lighted sparkler or flashlight in circles in the dark. If you move a sparkler fast enough, you should see a complete circle even though the light source is only a single point (see the photo above). The sensory memory preserves the sensory image long enough for you to perceive a continuous circle rather than separate points of light.

The brief preservation of sensations in sensory memory gives you additional time to try to recognize stimuli. However, you'd better take advantage of sensory storage immediately, because it doesn't last long. This fact was demonstrated in a classic experiment by George Sperling (1960). His subjects saw three rows of letters flashed on a screen for just 1/20 of a second. A tone following the exposure signalled which row of letters the subject should report to the experimenter (see Figure 7.6). Subjects were fairly accurate when the signal occurred immediately. However, their accuracy steadily declined as the delay of the tone increased to one second. Why? Because the memory trace in the visual sensory store decays in about 1/4 of a second. Memory traces in the auditory sensory store also appear to last less than a second (Massaro & Loftus, 1996).

Short-Term Memory 6b

Short-term memory (STM) is a limited-capacity store that can maintain unrehearsed information for up to about 20 seconds. In contrast, information stored in long-term memory may last weeks, months, or years. However, there is a way that you can maintain information in your short-term store indefinitely. How? Primarily, by engaging in *rehearsal*—the process of repetitively verbalizing or thinking about the information. Cognitive psychologists often distinguish between *maintenance* rehearsal and more *elaborative* rehearsal or processing (e.g., Craik & Lockhart, 1972). In using maintenance rehearsal you are simply maintaining the information in consciousness, while

FIGURE 7.6

Sperling's (1960) study of sensory memory.

After the participants had fixated on the cross, the letters were flashed on the screen just long enough to create a visual afterimage. High, medium, and low tones signalled which row of letters to report. Because subjects had to rely on the afterimage to report the letters, Sperling was able to measure how rapidly the afterimage disappeared by varying the delay between the display and the signal to report.

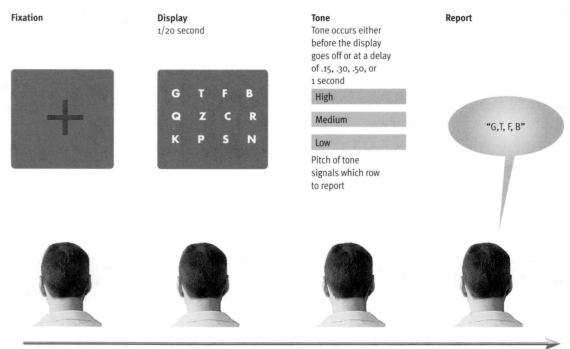

Time (fractions of seconds)

in more elaborative processing, you are increasing the probability that you will retain the information in the future (Brown & Craik, 2000) by, for example, focusing on the meaning of the words in the list you are trying to remember.

You surely have used the maintenance rehearsal process on many occasions. For instance, when you look up a phone number, you probably recite it over and over until you can dial it. Rehearsal keeps recycling the information through your short-term memory. In theory, this recycling could go on forever, but in reality something eventually distracts you and breaks the rehearsal loop.

Durability of Storage

6b

Without rehearsal, information in short-term memory is lost in less than 20 seconds (Wickens, 1999; Nairne, 2003). This rapid loss was demonstrated in a study by Peterson and Peterson (1959). They measured how long undergraduates could remember three consonants if they couldn't rehearse them. To prevent rehearsal, the Petersons required the students to count backward by threes from the time the consonants were presented until they saw a light that signalled the recall test (see Figure 7.7). Their results showed that subjects' recall accuracy was pretty dismal (about 10 percent) after only 15 seconds. Other approaches to the issue have suggested that the typical duration of STM storage may even be shorter (Baddeley, 1986). Theorists originally believed that the loss of information from short-term memory was due purely to time-related *decay* of memory traces,

but follow-up research showed that *interference* from competing material also contributes (Lewandowsky, Duncan, & Brown, 2004; Nairne, 2002).

Capacity of Storage

6b

Short-term memory is also limited in the number of items it can hold. The small capacity of STM was pointed out by George Miller (1956) in a famous paper called "The Magical Number Seven, Plus or Minus Two: Some Limits on Our Capacity for Processing Information." Miller noticed that people could recall only about seven items in tasks that required them to remember unfamiliar material. The common thread in these tasks, Miller argued, was that they required the use of STM. The limited capacity of STM constrains people's ability to perform tasks in which they need to mentally juggle various pieces of information (Baddeley & Hitch, 1974).

The capacity of short-term memory may even be less than widely assumed. Nelson Cowan (2005, 2010) cites evidence indicating that the capacity of STM might be even lower—*four* plus or minus *one*. The consensus on the capacity of STM seems to be moving toward this smaller estimate (Lustig et al., 2009). According to Cowan, the capacity of STM has historically been overestimated because researchers have often failed to take steps to prevent covert rehearsal or *chunking* by participants.

It has long been known that you can increase the capacity of your short-term memory by combining stimuli into larger, possibly higher-order units, called *chunks* (Simon, 1974). A *chunk* is a group

WEB LINK 7.1

The Magical Number Seven, Plus or Minus Two

In 1956, Princeton psychology professor George A. Miller published one of the most famous papers in the history of psychology: "The Magical Number Seven, Plus or Minus Two: Some Limits on Our Capacity for Processing Information." At this site, you'll find a copy of the original text, with tables, so that you can see why this is such an important research milestone in psychology.

Courtesy of George Miller

George Miller
"The Magical Number Seven, Plus or Minus Two."

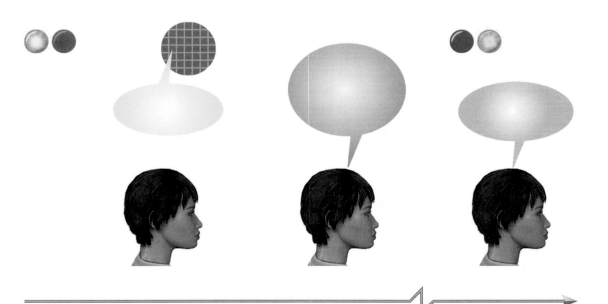

FIGURE 7.7

Peterson and Peterson's (1959) study of short-term memory.

After a warning light was flashed, the participants were given three consonants to remember. The researchers prevented rehearsal by giving the subjects a three-digit number at the same time and telling them to count backward by three from that number until given the signal to recall the letters. By varying the amount of time between stimulus presentation and recall, Peterson and Peterson (1959) were able to measure how quickly information is lost from short-term memory.

of familiar stimuli stored as a single unit. You can demonstrate the effect of chunking by asking someone to recall a sequence of 12 letters grouped in the following way:

NF - BCT - VC - BCIB - M

As you read the letters aloud, pause at the hyphens. Your subject will probably attempt to remember each letter separately because there are no obvious groups or chunks. But a string of 12 letters is too long for STM, so errors are likely. Now present the same string of letters to another person, but place the pauses in the following locations:

NFB - CTV - CBC - IBM

The letters now form four familiar chunks that should occupy only four slots in STM, resulting in successful recall (Bower & Springston, 1970).

To successfully chunk the letters I B M, a subject must first recognize these letters as a familiar unit. This familiarity has to be stored somewhere in long-term memory. Hence, in this case, information was transferred from long-term into short-term memory. This is not unusual. People routinely draw information out of their long-term memory banks to evaluate and understand information that they are working with in short-term memory.

Individuals who are experts in specific areas have been shown to process information related to that expertise differently than nonexperts. This was demonstrated by William Chase and 1978 Nobel Prize winner Herbert Simon, when they studied how expert and novice chess players remembered the positions of chess pieces on a chessboard after having a chance to look at the board for only a few seconds (Chase & Simon, 1973). If the pieces had been arranged in a meaningful way, in a way that might correspond to a real game, the expert was significantly better at remembering the positions of the pieces. However, if the pieces had been arranged in a random fashion, the expert was no better than the nonexperts. This effect is obtained in many areas other than chess, including music, medicine, bridge, and computer programming, among others (Ericsson & Lehmann, 1996). Chase and Simon (1973) suggested that the experts "chunked" the information differently and more effectively. But this advantage holds only when the chess pieces appear in meaningful and familiar patterns. In this case, the expert's advantage lies in the ability to "encode the position into larger perceptual chunks, each consisting of a familiar subconfiguration of pieces" (p. 80). Research continues into the effects of and processes responsible for the effects of expertise on memory (e.g., Hambrick & Oswald, 2005; Kellog et al., 2005; Rawson & Van Overschelde, 2008).

Short-Term Memory as "Working Memory" 6b

Research eventually uncovered a number of problems with the original model of short-term memory (Bower, 2000; Jonides et al., 2008). Among other things, studies showed that short-term memory is *not* limited to phonemic encoding as originally thought and that decay is *not* the only process responsible for the loss of information from STM. These and other findings suggested that short-term memory involves more than a simple rehearsal buffer, as originally envisioned. To make sense of such findings, Alan Baddeley (1986, 1989, 1992) proposed a more complex, modularized model of short-term memory that characterizes it as "working memory." According to Baddeley (2003), *working memory* is a limited capacity storage system that temporarily maintains and stores information by providing an interface between perception, memory, and action. Since its introduction, the concept of "working memory" has proven invaluable in our attempts to understand human behaviour and experience (e.g., O'Hare et al., 2008; Repovš & Bresjanac, 2006; Takeuchi et al., 2010). While the term was first used by Miller, Galanter, and Pribaum (1960), it is Baddeley's model that has been most influential.

Baddeley's model of working memory consists of four components (see Figure 7.8). The first component is the *phonological loop* that represented all of STM in earlier models. This component is at work when you use recitation to temporarily remember a

Working (short-term) memory

Maintenance rehearsal

Phonological rehearsal loop

Executive control system

Visuospatial sketchpad

Episodic buffer

FIGURE 7.8

Short-term memory as working memory.

This diagram depicts the revised model of the short-term store proposed by Alan Baddeley. According to Baddeley (2001), working memory includes four components: a phonological rehearsal loop, a visuospatial sketchpad, an executive control system, and an episodic buffer.

phone number. Baddeley (2003; Repovš & Baddeley, 2006) believes that the phonological loop evolved to facilitate the acquisition of language. The second component in working memory is a *visuospatial sketchpad* that permits people to temporarily hold and manipulate visual images. This element is at work when you try to mentally rearrange the furniture in your bedroom or map out a complicated route that you need to follow to travel somewhere. Researchers investigate this module of working memory by showing subjects visual sequences and spatial arrays, which they are asked to re-create.

The third component is a *central executive* system. It controls the deployment of attention, switching the focus of attention and dividing attention as needed (for example, dividing your attention between a message you are trying to text to your friend during a lecture and what your professor told the class about next week's exam, "What was that? Which chapters are on next week's exam?"). The central executive also coordinates the actions of the other modules. The fourth component is the *episodic buffer*, a temporary, limited-capacity store that allows the various components of working memory to integrate information and that serves as an interface between working memory and long-term memory. The two key characteristics that originally defined short-term memory—limited capacity and storage duration—are still present in the concept of working memory, but Baddeley's model accounts for evidence that STM handles a greater variety of functions than previously thought.

Baddeley's model of working memory has generated an enormous volume of research (Courtney, 2004; Theeuwes, Belopolsky, & Olivers, 2009). For example, one line of research has shown that people vary in how well they can juggle information in their working memory while fending off distractions (Engle, 2001). ***Working memory capacity (WMC) refers to one's ability to hold and manipulate information in conscious attention.*** WMC is a stable trait (Unsworth et al., 2005) that appears to be influenced to a considerable degree by heredity (Kremen et al., 2007). That said, WMC can be temporarily reduced by situational factors such as pressure to perform or excessive worry (Gimmig et al., 2006; Hayes, Hirsch, & Matthews, 2008).

Variations in WMC correlate positively with measures of high-level cognitive abilities, such as reading comprehension, complex reasoning, and even intelligence (Colflesh & Conway, 2007; Engle et al., 1999; Oberauer et al., 2007; Shelton et al., 2009, 2010). This finding has led some theorists to conclude that WMC plays a fundamental role in complex cognitive processes and intelligence (Lepine, Barrouillet, & Camos,

2005). Variations in WMC also appear to influence musical ability, as reading music while playing an instrument taxes working memory capacity (Meinz & Hambrick, 2010). Some theorists argue that increases in WMC tens of thousands of years ago were crucial to the evolution of complex cognitive processes and creativity in humans (Coolidge & Wynn, 2009). Their analyses, of course, are highly speculative, but they highlight the profound importance of working memory capacity (Balter, 2010).

Long-Term Memory 6b

Long-term memory (LTM) is an unlimited capacity store that can hold information over lengthy periods of time. Unlike sensory and short-term memory, which have very brief storage durations, LTM can store information indefinitely. In fact, one point of view is that all information stored in long-term memory is stored there *permanently*. According to this view, forgetting occurs only because people sometimes cannot *retrieve* needed information from LTM.

The notion that LTM storage may be permanent is certainly intriguing. A couple of interesting lines of research have seemed to provide compelling evidence of permanent storage. However, each line of research turns out to be less compelling than it appears at first glance. The first line of research consisted of some landmark studies conducted by neuroscientist Wilder Penfield in the 1960s (we referred to some of Penfield's work at the Montreal Neurological Institute in Chapter 3). He reported triggering long-lost memories through electrical stimulation of the brain (ESB) during brain surgeries (Penfield & Perot, 1963). When Penfield used ESB (see Chapter 3) to map brain function in patients undergoing surgery for epilepsy, he found that stimulation of the temporal lobe sometimes elicited vivid descriptions of events long past. Patients would describe events that apparently came from their childhood—such as "being in a lumberyard" or "watching Mom make a phone call"—as if they were there once again. Penfield and others inferred that these descriptions were exact playbacks of long-lost memories unearthed by electrical stimulation of the brain.

The second line of research centres on the phenomenon of *flashbulb memories,* which are unusually vivid and detailed recollections of momentous events. For instance, many people remember exactly where they were, what they were doing, and how they felt when they learned of the death of Princess Diana or Michael Jackson. Another example concerns the events surrounding the terrorist attacks

AP/Wide World Photos

Flashbulb memories are vivid and detailed recollections of momentous events. For example, many people will long remember exactly where they were and how they felt when they learned about the terrorist attacks on the World Trade Center.

loose reconstructions of events rather than exact replays of the past (Squire, 1987).

In a similar vein, subsequent research has undermined the notion that flashbulb memories represent an instance of permanent storage. Although flashbulb memories tend to be strong, vivid, and detailed, studies suggest that they are neither as accurate nor as special as once believed (Hirst et al., 2009; Lee & Brown, 2003; Neisser & Harsch, 1992; Schmolck, Buffalo, & Squire, 2000; Talarico & Rubin, 2003). Like other memories, they become less detailed and complete with time and are often inaccurate (Cubelli & Della Sala, 2008; Talarico & Rubin, 2009). Recent research suggests that it is not extraordinary accuracy or longevity that distinguishes flashbulb memories. Rather, what makes them special is that people subjectively feel that these memories are exceptionally vivid, people have exceptional confidence (albeit misplaced) in their accuracy, and there is more emotional intensity attached to them (Talarico & Rubin, 2003, 2007). So, perhaps flashbulb memories are "special," but not in the way originally envisioned. In sum, although the possibility cannot be ruled out completely, there is no convincing evidence that memories are stored away permanently and that forgetting is all a matter of retrieval failure (Payne & Blackwell, 1998; Schacter, 1996).

that took place in the United States on September 11, 2001; the events were traumatic for people all over the world. The vivid detail of people's memories of such events—especially those from decades ago—would seem to provide a striking example of permanent storage.

So, why don't these lines of evidence demonstrate that LTM storage is permanent? Let's look at each. Closer scrutiny eventually showed that the remarkable "memories" activated by ESB in Penfield's studies often included major distortions or factual impossibilities. For instance, the person who recalled being in a lumberyard had never actually been to one. The ESB-induced recollections of Penfield's subjects apparently were hallucinations, dreams, or

How Is Knowledge Represented and Organized in Memory?   6b

Over the years, memory researchers have wrestled endlessly with another major question relating to memory storage: How is knowledge represented and organized in memory? In other words, what forms do our mental representations of information take? Most theorists seem to agree that our mental

---

concept **check 7.1**

Comparing the Memory Stores

Check your understanding of the three memory stores by filling in the blanks in the table below. The answers can be found near the back of the book in Appendix A.

Feature	Sensory memory	Short-term memory	Long-term memory
Main encoding format	*copy of input*		*Largely semantic*
Storage capacity	*limited*		
Storage duration		*up to 20 seconds*	

representations probably take a variety of forms, depending on the nature of the material that needs to be tucked away in memory. Most of the theorizing to date has focused on how factual information may be represented in memory. In this section, we'll look at a small sample of the organizational structures that have been proposed for semantic information.

Clustering and Conceptual Hierarchies

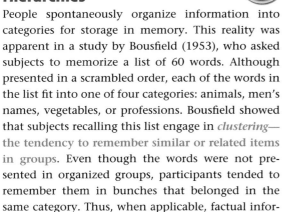

People spontaneously organize information into categories for storage in memory. This reality was apparent in a study by Bousfield (1953), who asked subjects to memorize a list of 60 words. Although presented in a scrambled order, each of the words in the list fit into one of four categories: animals, men's names, vegetables, or professions. Bousfield showed that subjects recalling this list engage in *clustering*— the tendency to remember similar or related items in groups. Even though the words were not presented in organized groups, participants tended to remember them in bunches that belonged in the same category. Thus, when applicable, factual information is routinely organized into simple categories.

Factual information is routinely represented in categories, and when possible, this information is organized into conceptual hierarchies. A *conceptual hierarchy* is a multilevel classification system based on common properties among items. A conceptual hierarchy that a person might construct for minerals can be found in Figure 7.9. According to Gordon Bower (1970), organizing information into a conceptual hierarchy can improve recall dramatically.

Schemas

Imagine that you've just visited your psychology professor 's office, which is shown in the photo above.

The professor's office is shown in this photo. Follow the instructions in the text to learn how Brewer and Treyens (1981) used it in a study of memory.

Take a brief look at the photo and then cover it up. Now pretend that you want to describe your professor's office to a friend. Write down what you saw in the picture of the office.

After you finish, compare your description with the picture. Chances are, your description will include elements—books or filing cabinets, for instance—that were *not* in the office. This common phenomenon demonstrates how *schemas* can influence memory.

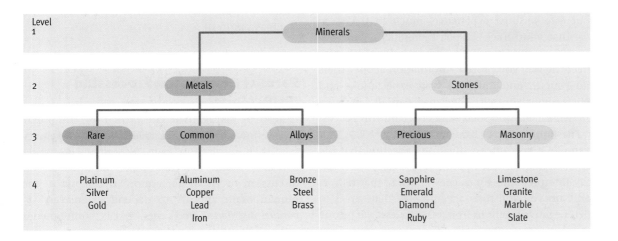

Level 1			Minerals			
2		Metals			Stones	
3	Rare	Common	Alloys	Precious		Masonry
4	Platinum Silver Gold	Aluminum Copper Lead Iron	Bronze Steel Brass	Sapphire Emerald Diamond Ruby		Limestone Granite Marble Slate

FIGURE 7.9

Conceptual hierarchies and long-term memory.

Some types of information can be organized into a multilevel hierarchy of concepts, like the one shown here, which was studied by Bower and others (1969). They found that subjects remember more information when they organize it into a conceptual hierarchy.

Source: Reprinted from *Cognitive Psychology*, 1(1), Gordon H. Bower, Organizational factors in memory, pp. 18–46. Copyright © 1970, with permission from Elsevier.

A *schema* is an organized cluster of knowledge about a particular object or event abstracted from previous experience with the object or event. For example, university students have schemas for what professors' offices are like. When Brewer and Treyens (1981) tested the recall of 30 subjects who had briefly visited the office shown in the photo on the previous page, most subjects recalled the desks and chairs, but few recalled the wine bottle or the picnic basket, which aren't part of a typical office schema. Moreover, nine subjects in the Brewer and Treyens study falsely recalled that the office contained books. Perhaps you made the same mistake.

These results and other studies (Tuckey & Brewer, 2003) suggest that *people are more likely to remember things that are consistent with their schemas than things that are not.* Although this principle seems applicable much of the time, the inverse is also true: *People sometimes exhibit better recall of things that violate their schema-based expectations* (Koriat, Goldsmith, & Pansky, 2000; Neuschatz et al., 2002). Information that really clashes with a schema may attract extra attention and deeper processing and thus become more memorable. For instance, if you saw a slot machine in a professor's office, you would probably remember it. In either case, it's apparent that information stored in memory is often organized around schemas (Brewer, 2000).

It is important to note that not only do we have schemas about physical settings like professors' offices, but we also have schemas about specific people, types of people, and social events. We will consider representations of specific others and types of persons in Chapter 16 when we discuss social psychology. Relational schemas are particularly important because, according to some, they may be related to a variety of disorders. Mark Baldwin of McGill University terms these representations of typical events surrounding interpersonal interactions as *relational schemas* (Baldwin, 1992). He suggests that these relational schemas represent *regularities* in your interpersonal experience, much in the same way that your office schema represents regularities in your exposure to offices. These relational schemas affect the way you process information about others and yourself and influence your expectations and beliefs about yourself. They may partially underlie low self-esteem and social anxiety (Baldwin, Baccus, & Fitzsimons, 2004; Baldwin & Main, 2001). For example, if you enter a situation expecting that the others in that context will dislike and reject you, you may interpret ambiguous cues in a way that reflects badly on you and then act in a way that serves to elicit negative reactions from others. Research by one

of the authors of this book (York University psychologist Doug McCann) suggests that this very cycle emerges for people with depression (McCann, 1990).

Semantic Networks

6b

Of course, not all information fits neatly into conceptual hierarchies or schemas. Much knowledge seems to be organized into less systematic frameworks, called *semantic networks* (Collins & Loftus, 1975). A *semantic network* consists of nodes representing concepts, joined together by pathways that link related concepts. A small semantic network is shown in Figure 7.10. The ovals are the nodes, and the words inside the ovals are the interlinked concepts. The lines connecting the nodes are the pathways. A more detailed figure would label the pathways to show how the concepts are related to one another. However, in this instance, the relationships should be fairly clear. The length of each pathway represents the degree of association between two concepts. Shorter pathways imply stronger associations.

Semantic networks have proven useful in explaining why thinking about one word (such as *butter*) can make a closely related word (such as *bread*) easier to remember (Meyer & Schvaneveldt, 1976). According to Collins and Loftus (1975), when people think about a word, their thoughts naturally go to related words. These theorists call this process *spreading activation* within a semantic network. They assume that activation spreads out along the pathways of the semantic network surrounding the word. They also theorize that the strength of this activation decreases as it travels outward, much as ripples decrease in size as they radiate outward from a rock tossed into a pond. Consider again the semantic network shown in Figure 7.10. If subjects see the word *red,* words that are closely linked to it (such as *orange*) should be easier to recall than words that have longer links (such as *sunrises*).

Connectionist Networks and Parallel Distributed Processing (PDP) Models

Instead of taking their cue from how computers process information, *connectionist models* of memory take their inspiration from how neural networks appear to handle information. As we noted in our discussion of visual perception in Chapter 4, the human brain appears to depend extensively on *parallel distributed processing*—that is, simultaneous

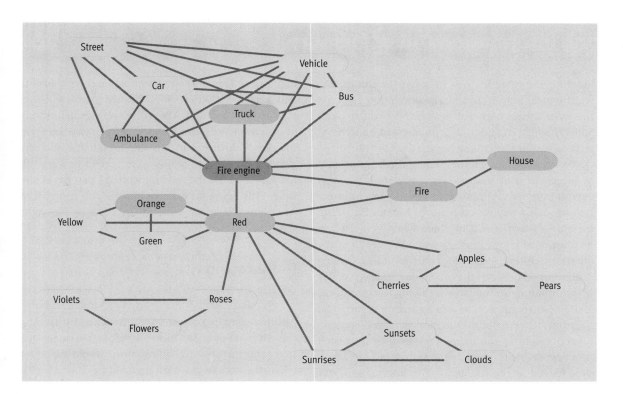

FIGURE 7.10

A semantic network.
Much of the organization of long-term memory depends on networks of associations among concepts. In this highly simplified depiction of a fragment of a semantic network, the shorter the line linking any two concepts, the stronger the association between them. The colouration of the concept boxes represents activation of the concepts. This is how the network might look just after a person hears the words *fire engine*.

Source: Adapted from Collins, A.M., and Loftus, E.F. (1975). A spreading activation theory of semantic processing. *Psychological Review, 82,* 407–428. Copyright © by the American Psychological Association. Adapted by permission of the authors.

processing of the same information that is spread across networks of neurons. Based on this insight and basic findings about how neurons operate, *connectionist*, or *parallel distributed processing (PDP)*, *models* assume that cognitive processes depend on patterns of activation in highly interconnected computational networks that resemble neural networks (McClelland, 2000; McClelland & Rogers, 2003; McClelland & Rumelhart, 1985; Smolensky, 1995).

A PDP system consists of a large network of interconnected computing units, or *nodes,* that operate much like neurons. These nodes may be inactive or they may send either excitatory or inhibitory signals to other units. Like an individual neuron, a specific node's level of activation reflects the weighted balance of excitatory and inhibitory inputs from many other units. Given this framework, *PDP models assert that specific memories correspond to particular patterns of activation in these networks* (McClelland, 1992). Connectionist networks bear some superficial resemblance to semantic networks, but there is a crucial difference. In semantic networks, specific nodes represent specific concepts or pieces of knowledge. In connectionist networks, a piece of knowledge is represented by a particular *pattern* of activation across an entire network. Thus, the information lies in the strengths of the *connections,* which is why the PDP approach is called *connectionism.*

REVIEW OF KEY POINTS

▷ Information-processing theories of memory assert that people have three kinds of memory stores: a sensory memory, a short-term memory, and a long-term memory. The sensory store preserves information in its original form, probably for only a fraction of a second.

▷ Short-term memory has a limited capacity of about seven chunks of information. However a more recent estimate puts the capacity at four items plus or minus one. STM can maintain unrehearsed information for up to about 20 seconds. Short-term memory is working memory, and it appears to involve more than a simple rehearsal loop. According to Baddeley, working memory also includes a visuospatial sketchpad, an executive control system, and an episodic buffer.

▷ Long-term memory is an unlimited capacity store that may hold information indefinitely. Penfield's ESB research and the existence of flashbulb memories suggest that LTM storage may be permanent, but the evidence is not convincing. Flashbulb memories are not as accurate as claimed. Some theorists have questioned the distinction between short-term and long-term memory.

▷ Information in long-term memory can be organized in simple clusters or multilevel classification systems called *conceptual hierarchies*. A schema is an organized cluster of knowledge about a particular object or sequence of events.

▷ Semantic networks consist of concepts joined by pathways. Research suggests that activation spreads along the paths of semantic networks to activate closely associated words. Parallel distributed processing models of memory assert that specific memories correspond to particular patterns of activation in connectionist networks.

Retrieval: Getting Information Out of Memory

PREVIEW QUESTIONS

▶ What does the tip-of-the-tongue phenomenon reveal about memory?

▶ Why does reinstating the context of an event aid in its recall?

▶ What is the misinformation effect?

▶ How can source-monitoring errors shed light on eyewitness suggestibility and inadvertent plagiarism?

▶ What is reality monitoring?

Entering information into long-term memory is a worthy goal, but an insufficient one if you can't get the information back out again when you need it. Some theorists maintain that understanding retrieval is the key to understanding human memory (Roediger, 2000). Understanding retrieval may also be important to success in your studies. When you study for your exams, you are attempting to encode the information in such a way that it is stored in your long-term memory so that it will be there when you need it. As most of us know, however, we don't get all of the questions correct. What does this indicate? Tulving distinguished between the *availability* and *accessibility* of information in memory (Tulving & Pearlstone, 1966). You might not be able to answer a particular question because the information is unavailable (no longer present in the memory system) or because it is not accessible (present in the system but not accessible to you at the moment). The information may not be accessible because the cues you are using in your attempt to answer the question are not effective.

Using Cues to Aid Retrieval

The *tip-of-the-tongue phenomenon*—the temporary inability to remember something you know, accompanied by a feeling that it's just out of reach—is a common experience that is typically triggered by a name that one can't quite recall. Most people experience this temporary frustration about once a week, although its occurrence increases with age (A. Brown, 1991; Burke & Shafto, 2004). It appears to be a universal experience found in widely diverse cultures (Brennen, Vikan, & Dybdal, 2007; Schwartz, 1999). Stronger tip-of-the-tongue experiences in which people feel like recall is particularly imminent are more likely to be resolved than weaker ones (B.L. Schwartz et al., 2000). The tip-of-the-tongue phenomenon clearly constitutes a failure in retrieval. Some of you may have had a tip-of-the-tongue experience when we asked you earlier what the name was of the object that allowed for time travel in the *Prisoner of Azkaban*. You knew it was the time . . . something. You could almost remember it but not quite. Providing yourself with a cue might have helped—for example, trying to remember the scene in which Hermione tells Harry about it, or perhaps trying to visualize what it looked like in the film.

Fortunately, memories can often be jogged with *retrieval cues*—stimuli that help gain access to

memories. This was apparent when Roger Brown and David McNeill (1966) studied the tip-of-the-tongue phenomenon. They gave subjects definitions of obscure words and asked them to come up with the words. Brown and McNeill found that subjects groping for obscure words were correct in guessing the first letter of the missing word 57 percent of the time. This figure far exceeds chance and shows that partial recollections are often headed in the right direction.

Reinstating the Context of an Event

Another principle of memory articulated by Tulving was the *encoding specificity principle*. He suggested that your memory for information would be better when the conditions during encoding and retrieval were similar (Tulving & Thomson, 1973). According to Tulving (1983, p. 223), cues used at retrieval will facilitate recall "if and only if the information about them and about their relation to the to-be-remembered words is stored at the same time" as the to-be-remembered information. Of course, this is more likely the more similar the encoding and retrieval conditions.

Let's test your memory: What did you have for breakfast two days ago? If you can't immediately answer, you might begin by imagining yourself sitting at the breakfast table. Trying to recall an event by putting yourself back into the context in which it occurred involves working with *context cues* to aid retrieval.

Context cues often facilitate the retrieval of information (S. Smith, 1988). Most people have experienced the effects of context cues on many occasions. For instance, when people return after a number of years to a place where they used to live, they typically are flooded with long-forgotten memories. Or consider how often you have gone from one room to another to get something (scissors, perhaps), only to discover that you can't remember what you were after. However, when you return to the first room (the original context), you suddenly recall what it was ("Of course, the scissors!"). These examples illustrate the potentially powerful effects of context cues on memory.

The technique of reinstating the context of an event has been used effectively in legal investigations to enhance eyewitness recall (Chandler & Fisher,

WEB LINK 7.3

Mind Tools—Tools for Improving Your Memory
The Mind Tools site details practical techniques to help people improve their cognitive efficiency in many areas. The page dedicated to memory functioning offers an excellent collection of suggestions for ways to enhance memory.

1996). The eyewitness may be encouraged to retrieve information about a crime by replaying the sequence of events. The value of reinstating the context of an event may account for how hypnosis *occasionally* stimulates eyewitness recall (Meyer, 1992). The hypnotist usually attempts to reinstate the context of the event by telling the witness to imagine being at the scene of the crime once again.

Although it is widely believed by the general public that hypnosis can help people remember things that they would not normally recall (Green, 2003), extensive research has failed to demonstrate that hypnosis can enhance retrieval (Mazzoni, Heap, & Scoboria, 2010). The notion that hypnotists can use age regression to recover long-lost memories by instructing subjects to go back in time and relive past events has been discredited (Mazzoni, Heap, & Scoboria, 2010). Quite to the contrary, research suggests that hypnosis often increases individuals' tendency to report *incorrect* information (Lynn, Neuschatz, & Fite, 2002; Mazzoni & Lynn, 2007). Moreover, popular beliefs about the supposed beneficial effects of hypnosis on memory often lead hypnotized subjects to feel overconfident about the accuracy of their recall (Scoboria et al., 2002). Concerns about the accuracy of hypnosis-aided recall have led courts to be extremely cautious about allowing hypnosis-aided recollections as admissible testimony.

This general principle extends beyond the effects of reinstating the context; it also seems to be true for *state-* and *mood-dependent* effects too. According to Fergus Craik (Brown & Craik, 2000) and others, the effect of matching the person's *internal* state of encoding at the retrieval phase is just a special case of the encoding specificity principle. For example, if you encoded information while intoxicated, your recall should be facilitated by attempting to retrieve the information while in a similar state (Brown & Craik, 2000). According to Eric Eich (Eich, 2007; Eich et al., in press; Schooler & Eich, 2000), similar effects are observed when considering the match or mismatch between the emotional state at encoding and retrieval of the individual attempting to retrieve the information (Eich & Metcalfe, 1989). Eich maintains that state-dependent memory effects are more readily observed for free-recall conditions than for recognition or cued-recall tests where retrieval cues are more abundant (Eich, 1980).

Reconstructing Memories and the Misinformation Effect

When you retrieve information from long-term memory, you're not able to pull up a "mental videotape" that provides an exact replay of the past. To some extent, your memories are sketchy reconstructions of the past that may be distorted and may include details that did not actually occur (Roediger, Wheeler, & Rajaram, 1993). The reconstructive nature of memory was first highlighted many years ago by Sir Frederic Bartlett, a prominent English psychologist at Cambridge University. Bartlett (1932) had his subjects read the tale "War of the Ghosts," which is reproduced in Figure 7.11. Subjects read the story twice and waited 15 minutes. Then they were asked to write down the tale as best they could recall it.

Note the difference here between the type of stimuli used by Bartlett and that used by another memory pioneer, Ebbinghaus, who earlier used nonsense syllables (consonant–vowel–consonant, for example, BAF, XOF) syllables as stimuli. We discuss Ebbinghaus's contribution on page 321. This change in stimulus type, to a more familiar and realistic type of stimulus, allowed Bartlett to examine social and cultural influences on memory. Although it is difficult to know for sure, Bartlett's radical change in approach to the study of memory may have been partially a result of the intellectual atmosphere he

WAR OF THE GHOSTS

One night two young men from Egulac went down to the river to hunt seals, and while they were there it became foggy and calm. Then they heard war cries, and they thought: "Maybe this is a war party." They escaped to the shore, and hid behind a log. Now canoes came up, and they heard the noise of paddles, and saw one canoe coming up to them. There were five men in the canoe, and they said:

"What do you think? We wish to take you along. We are going up the river to make war on the people."

One of the young men said: "I have no arrows."

"Arrows are in the canoe," they said.

"I will not go along. I might be killed. My relatives do not know where I have gone. But you," he said, turning to the other, "may go with them."

So one of the young men went, but the other returned home.

And the warriors went up the river to a town on the other side of Kalama. The people came down to the water, and they began to fight, and many were killed. But presently the young man heard one of the warriors say: "Quick, let us go home: that Indian has been hit." Now he thought: "Oh, they are ghosts." He did not feel sick, but they said he had been shot.

So the canoes went back to Egulac and the young man went ashore to his house, and made a fire. And he told everybody and said: "Behold I accompanied the ghosts, and we went to fight. Many of our fellows were killed, and many of those who attacked us were killed. They said I was hit, and I did not feel sick."

He told it all, and then he became quiet. When the sun rose he fell down. Something black came out of his mouth. His face became contorted. The people jumped up and cried.

He was dead.

FIGURE 7.11

A story used in a study of reconstructive memory by Bartlett (1932).

Subjects recalling the story tended to change details and to "remember" elements not in the original at all.

Source: Excerpt from Bartlett, F.C. (1932). *Remembering: A study in experimental and social psychology.* New York: Cambridge University Press, p. 65. Copyright © 1932.

encountered at Cambridge. Bartlett was at Cambridge University at a very intellectually stimulating time; philosophers Bertrand Russell and Alfred Whitehead and pivotal economist J. M. Keynes were among his colleagues. Bartlett also knew Norbert Weiner (profiled in Chapter 9 on pages 394–5), who influenced Bartlett's inventive choice of method in examining memory for the *War of the Ghosts* (Rosa, n.d.)

What did Bartlett find? As you might expect, subjects condensed the story, leaving out boring details. Of greater interest was Bartlett's discovery that subjects frequently *changed* the tale to some extent. The canoe became a boat or the two young men were hunting beavers instead of seals. Subjects often introduced entirely *new elements* and twists. For instance, in one case, the death at the end was attributed to fever and the character was described as "foaming at the mouth" (instead of "something black came out of his mouth"). Bartlett concluded that the distortions in recall occurred because subjects reconstructed the tale to fit with their established schemas. He thought that memory for events was more like a *reconstruction*. Information such as "The War of the Ghosts" story was assumed to be stored hierarchically, with the gist or general idea of the story stored at the highest level. This gist then influenced what was recalled and how it was remembered. Recall is often biased in the direction of higher-level schemas. Imagine, for example, that you and your friend witness someone who knocks the books out of another student's hands who was standing on a crowded bus. If you label the act at the time as the actor being *clumsy,* you will have a different recollection for the specific events that occurred than if your friend labelled him as *aggressive.* Even though you both witnessed the same event, your later recollection of the events, and even your evaluation of the actors (Higgins, Rholes, & Jones, 1977), will differ. Culture, recent experiences, personality differences, and familiarity are among the factors that will affect the gisting or labelling of events, and they affect which schemas are used in reconstructing the events (Higgins & King, 1980).

Bartlett was a significant figure in the development of modern schema-based models of memory. He stated that his experimental work on factors that influence recollection was motivated in part by differing memories about a lecture he gave in 1913. In discussing the talk later with a friend, they disagreed at to whether the weather on the afternoon of the lecture had been a "brilliant afternoon" or "pouring with rain" (Zangwill, 1972). Each was convinced that his recollection was accurate and that the other's was wrong. Bartlett was intrigued by this difference in memory for the event.

Bartlett had a major influence on memory research not only because of his theoretical and empirical contributions, but also because of his impact on generations of students and scholars. One of Bartlett's students was O. L. Zangwill, whose own student, Brenda Milner of McGill University, went on to have a major influence on the psychology of memory and neuroscience (Zandwill, 1972). We discussed her work in this chapter and in Chapter 1. Other scholars in the area of social memory and social cognition, including Tory Higgins of Columbia University, have identified Bartlett's work as significantly influential in their own (Higgins & King, 1980).

Modern schema theories also emphasize the reconstructive nature of memory (Hirt, McDonald, & Markman, 1998). These theories propose that part of what people recall about an event is the details of that particular event and part is a reconstruction of the event based on their schemas.

Research by Elizabeth Loftus (1979, 1992; Loftus & Bernstein, 2005) and others on the *misinformation effect* has shown that reconstructive distortions show up frequently in eyewitness testimony. The *misinformation effect* occurs when participants' recall of an event they witnessed is altered by introducing misleading post-event information. Studies of the misinformation effect include three stages. In the first stage, subjects view an event. In the second stage, they are exposed to information about this event, some of which is misleading. In the third stage, their recall of the original event is tested to see if the post-event misinformation altered their memory of the original event. For example, in one study, Loftus and Palmer (1974) showed subjects a videotape of an automobile accident. Subjects were then "grilled" as if they were providing eyewitness testimony, and biasing information was introduced. Some subjects were asked, "How fast were the cars going when they *hit* each other?" Other subjects were asked, "How fast were the cars going when they *smashed into* each other?" A week later, subjects' recall of the accident was tested and they were asked whether they remembered seeing any broken glass in the accident (there was none). Subjects who had earlier been asked about the cars *smashing into* each other were more likely to "recall" broken glass. Why would they add this detail to their reconstructions of the accident? Probably because broken glass is consistent with their schema for cars *smashing* together (see Figure 7.12).

The misinformation effect, which has been replicated in "countless studies," is a remarkably reliable phenomenon that "challenged prevailing views about the validity of memory" (Zaragoza, Belli, & Payment, 2007, p. 37). Indeed, the effect is difficult to escape, as even subjects who have been forewarned can be swayed by post-event misinformation (Loftus, 2005). Consider, for instance, a study by Chan, Thomas, and Bulevich, (2009). The investigators noted that in real-life situations, eyewitnesses are often immediately asked to systematically recall an event before there is much opportunity to introduce misinformation. In contrast, the typical misinformation experiment does not include a recall effort prior to the exposure to misinformation. Chan and colleagues reasoned that "immediate recall should enhance retention of the witnessed event, thereby rendering an eyewitness less susceptible to misinformation" (p. 66). Surprisingly, however, immediate recall not only failed to reduce the misinformation effect—it actually increased the impact of misinformation! This finding provides yet another dramatic demonstration of the pervasive power of misinformation and the reconstructive nature of memory.

One of us had the chance to see the power of this effect firsthand in 1978 when Elizabeth Loftus gave a public lecture at the University of Western Ontario. One of the most popular professors in the psychology department was deliberately delayed in arriving at the lecture by a colleague. Before he came, Loftus told us that she would attempt to influence his memory for a variation of her classic "smashed-versus-hit" car crash. Once he entered the room, we all watched the video of a car approaching an intersection. The car then turned right and proceeded down the street. She then *randomly* picked the popular professor out of the audience in order to ask him some innocuous questions about what he had seen. One of the questions concerned a stop sign that was located at the corner where the car turned. This was fine, except there was no stop sign in the video. Later in the lecture when she returned to him and asked about the stop sign, he responded exactly as did the participants in her original research. The effect unfolded right before our eyes—he definitely remembered seeing the stop sign. He could not figure out why so many of us were smiling when he talked about the stop sign he had seen that was located at the corner. When pressed, he maintained that he was 100 percent sure he had seen a stop sign. In the end, like all good experimenters, Loftus explained to him what the demonstration was all about, and the professor stated that he had no knowledge about the false memory—he just did not believe that his memory had been influenced!

Similar distortions routinely occur without any crafty manipulations. Recent research has demonstrated that the simple act of retelling a story can introduce inaccuracies into memory (Marsh, 2007). When people retell stories, they tend to make a number of "adjustments" that depend on their

Leading question asked during witness testimony

"About how fast were the cars going when they hit each other?"

"About how fast were the cars going when they smashed into each other?"

Possible schemas activated

Response of subjects asked one week later, "Did you see any broken glass?" (There was none.)

"Yes"—14%

"Yes"—32%

FIGURE 7.12

The misinformation effect.

In an experiment by Loftus and Palmer (1974), participants who were asked leading questions in which cars were described as *hitting* or *smashing* each other were prone to recall the same accident differently one week later, demonstrating the reconstructive nature of memory.

goals, their audience, and the social context. Think about it: People tell stories to entertain others, to inform others, to impress others, to gain sympathy from their friends, and so forth. Depending on one's goals, one may streamline a story, embellish the facts, exaggerate one's role, omit important situational considerations, and so forth. Not surprisingly, when participants in one study were asked to evaluate the accuracy of recent retellings, they admitted that 42 percent were "inaccurate" and that another one-third contained "distortions" (Marsh & Tversky, 2004). People may be aware that they're being a little loose with the facts. However, what's interesting is that their intentional distortions can reshape their subsequent recollections of the same events. Somehow, the "real" story and the storyteller's "spin" on it probably begin to blend imperceptibly. So, even routine retellings of events can contribute to the malleability of memory.

Source Monitoring and Reality Monitoring

The misinformation effect and similar memory distortions may be due, *in part*, to the unreliability of a retrieval process called *reality monitoring*, which has been studied by Marcia Johnson and her colleagues. *Reality monitoring* refers to the process of deciding whether memories are based on external sources (one's perceptions of actual events) or internal sources (one's thoughts and imaginations). People engage in reality monitoring when they reflect on whether something actually happened or they only thought about it happening. This dilemma may

Courtesy of Elizabeth Loftus

Elizabeth Loftus

"One reason most of us, as jurors, place so much faith in eyewitness testimony is that we are unaware of how many factors influence its accuracy."

Human Memory

sound like an odd problem that would arise only infrequently, but it isn't. People routinely ponder questions like "Did I pack the umbrella or only think about packing it?" "Did I take my morning pill or only intend to do so?" Studies indicate that people focus on several types of clues in making their reality-monitoring decisions (Johnson, 2006; Johnson, Kahan, & Raye, 1984; Kahan et al., 1999). When memories are rich in sensory information (you can recall the feel of shoving the umbrella into your suitcase) or contextual information (you can clearly see yourself in the hallway packing your umbrella), or when memories can be retrieved with little effort, one is more likely to infer that the event really happened. In contrast, one is more likely to infer that an event did *not* actually occur when memories of it lack sensory or contextual details or are difficult to retrieve. Age may influence reality monitoring, as older adults seem to be more vulnerable to reality monitoring errors than young adults (McDaniel et al., 2008).

Research on reality monitoring eventually led Marcia Johnson to explore a related process, which she called *source monitoring*. *Source monitoring involves making attributions about the origins of memories.* Johnson maintains that source monitoring is a crucial facet of memory retrieval that contributes to many of the mistakes that people make in reconstructing their experiences (Johnson, 1996, 2006; Mitchell & Johnson, 2000). According to Johnson, memories are not tagged with labels that specify their sources. Thus, when people pull up specific memory records, they have to make decisions *at the time of retrieval* about where the memories came from (e.g., "Did I read that in the *Vancouver Sun* or the *Peterborough Examiner*?"). Much of the time, these decisions are so easy and automatic, people make them without being consciously aware of the source-monitoring process. In other instances, however, they may consciously struggle to pinpoint the source of a memory. *A source-monitoring error occurs when a memory derived from one source is misattributed to another source.* For example, you might attribute your roommate's remark to your psychology professor, or something you heard from David Suzuki on *The Nature of Things* to your psychology textbook. Inaccurate memories that reflect source-monitoring errors may seem quite compelling. People often feel extremely confident about their authenticity even though the recollections really are inaccurate (Lampinen, Neuschatz, & Payne, 1999).

Source-monitoring errors appear to be commonplace and may shed light on many interesting memory phenomena. For instance, in studies of eye-witness suggestibility, some subjects have gone so far as to insist that they "remember" seeing something that was only verbally suggested to them. Most theories have a hard time explaining how people can have memories of events that they never actually saw or experienced. But this paradox doesn't seem all that perplexing when it's explained as a source-monitoring error (Lindsay et al., 2004).

Although the process of remembering the source of specific information has been the subject of a great deal of research, the opposite process—remembering who you have transmitted specific information to—has only recently become a focus of research. *Destination memory involves recalling to whom one has told what.* Gopie and MacLeod (2009) maintain that accurate destination memory is just as important as accurate source monitoring, although perhaps a bit more difficult. Indeed, in a recent experiment they found that memory for sources of information was notably better than destination memory (Gopie & MacLeod, 2009). They argue that destination memory is more fragile because when transmitting information people are self-focused on their message, leaving less attention capacity to devote to encoding whom one is talking with. This may help explain why your supervisor keeps telling you the same stories over and over again.

Marcia K. Johnson

"Our long-term goal is to develop ways of determining which aspects of mental experience create one's sense of a personal past and one's conviction (accurate or not) that memories, knowledge, beliefs, attitudes, and feelings are tied to reality in a veridical fashion."

REVIEW OF KEY POINTS

▷ The tip-of-the-tongue phenomenon shows that recall is often guided by partial information about a word. Reinstating the context of an event can facilitate recall. This factor may account for cases in which hypnosis appears to aid recall of previously forgotten information. However, hypnosis seems to increase people's tendency to report incorrect information.

▷ Memories are not exact replicas of past experiences. As Bartlett showed many years ago, memory is partially reconstructive. Research on the misinformation effect shows that information learned after an event can alter one's memory of it.

▷ Source monitoring is the process of making attributions about the origins of memories. Source-monitoring errors appear to be common and may explain why people sometimes "recall" something that was only suggested to them or something they only imagined. Reality monitoring involves deciding whether memories are based on perceptions of actual events or on just thinking about the events.

▷ Destination memory involves recalling to whom one has told what. It may be fragile because people are self-focused on their message when talking to others.

Forgetting: When Memory Lapses

Forgetting gets "bad press" that it may not deserve. People tend to view forgetting as a failure, weakness, or deficiency in cognitive processing. Although forgetting important information *can* be extremely frustrating, some memory theorists argue that forgetting is actually adaptive. How so? Imagine how cluttered your memory would be if you never forgot anything. According to Daniel Schacter (1999), we need to forget information that is no longer relevant, such as out-of-date phone numbers, discarded passwords, lines that were memorized for a play in Grade 10, and where you kept your important papers three apartments ago. Forgetting can reduce competition among memories that can cause confusion. In a recent exploration of this hypothesis, scientists used brain-imaging technology to track neural markers of cognitive effort in a series of tasks in which participants memorized pairs of words (Kuhl et al., 2007). They found that the forgetting of word pairs deemed "irrelevant" made it easier to remember the "relevant" word pairs and reduced the demands placed on crucial neural circuits. In a nutshell, they found that forgetting helped subjects remember the information they needed to remember.

Although forgetting may be adaptive in the long run, the fundamental question of memory research remains: Why do people forget information that they would like to remember? There isn't one simple answer to this question. Research has shown that forgetting can be caused by defects in encoding, storage, retrieval, or some combination of these processes.

How Quickly We Forget: Ebbinghaus's Forgetting Curve 6d

The first person to conduct scientific studies of forgetting was Hermann Ebbinghaus. He published a series of insightful memory studies way back in 1885. Ebbinghaus studied only one subject—himself. To give himself lots of new material to memorize, he invented *nonsense syllables*—consonant–vowel–consonant arrangements that do not correspond to words (such as BAF, XOF, VIR, and MEQ). He wanted to work with meaningless materials that would be uncontaminated by his previous learning.

Ebbinghaus was a remarkably dedicated researcher. For instance, in one study he went through over 14 000 practice repetitions, as he tirelessly memorized 420 lists of nonsense syllables (Slamecka, 1985).

He tested his memory of these lists after various time intervals. Figure 7.13 shows what he found. This diagram, called a *forgetting curve*, graphs retention and forgetting over time. Ebbinghaus's forgetting curve shows a precipitous drop in retention during the first few hours after the nonsense syllables were memorized. Thus, he concluded that most forgetting occurs very rapidly after learning something.

That's a depressing conclusion. What is the point of memorizing information if you're going to forget it all right away? Fortunately, subsequent research showed that Ebbinghaus's forgetting curve was unusually steep (Postman, 1985). Forgetting isn't usually quite as swift or as extensive as Ebbinghaus thought. One problem was that he was working with such meaningless material. When subjects memorize more meaningful material, such as prose or poetry, forgetting curves aren't nearly as steep. Studies of how well people recall their high school classmates suggest that forgetting curves for autobiographical information are much shallower (Bahrick, 2000). Also, different methods of measuring forgetting yield varied estimates of how quickly people forget. This variation underscores the importance of the methods used to measure forgetting, the matter we turn to next.

PREVIEW QUESTIONS

▶ What did Ebbinghaus discover about how quickly people forget?

▶ What are the three methods for measuring retention?

▶ What is the difference between the decay and interference explanations of forgetting?

▶ When are retrieval failures likely to occur?

▶ Why do some experts believe that recovered memories of childhood sexual abuse are mostly genuine, while other experts are skeptical?

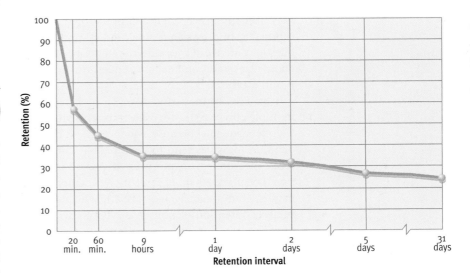

FIGURE 7.13

Ebbinghaus's forgetting curve for nonsense syllables.

From his experiments on himself, Ebbinghaus (1885) concluded that forgetting is extremely rapid immediately after the original learning and then levels off. Although this generalization remains true, subsequent research has shown that forgetting curves for nonsense syllables are unusually steep. (Data from Ebbinghaus, 1885)

Measures of Forgetting

Hermann Ebbinghaus

"Left to itself every mental content gradually loses its capacity for being revived.... Facts crammed at examination time soon vanish."

SIM5 **6** **6d**

To study forgetting empirically, psychologists need to be able to measure it precisely. Measures of forgetting inevitably measure retention as well. *Retention* refers to the proportion of material retained (remembered). In studies of forgetting, the results may be reported in terms of the amount forgotten or the amount retained. In these studies, the *retention interval* is the length of time between the presentation of materials to be remembered and the measurement of forgetting. The three principal methods used to measure forgetting are recall, recognition, and relearning (Lockhart, 1992).

Who is the current premier of Manitoba? What movie won the Academy Award for best picture last year? These questions involve recall measures of retention. A *recall* measure of retention requires subjects to reproduce information on their own without any cues. If you were to take a recall test on a list of 25 words you had memorized, you would simply be told to write down on a blank sheet of paper as many of the words as you could remember.

In contrast, in a recognition test you might be shown a list of 100 words and asked to choose the 25 words that you had memorized. A *recognition* measure of retention requires subjects to select previously learned information from an array of options. Subjects not only have cues to work with, they have the answers right in front of them. In educational testing, essay questions and fill-in-the-blank questions are recall measures of retention. Multiple-choice, true–false, and matching questions are recognition measures.

If you're like most students, you probably prefer multiple-choice tests over essay tests. This preference is understandable, because evidence shows that recognition measures tend to yield higher scores than recall measures of memory for the same information (Lockhart, 2000). This reality was demonstrated many decades ago by Luh (1922), who measured subjects' retention of nonsense syllables with both a recognition test and a recall test. As Figure 7.14 shows, subjects' performance on the recognition measure was far superior to their performance on the recall measure. There are two ways of looking at this disparity between recall and recognition tests. One view is that recognition tests are especially *sensitive* measures of retention. The other view is that recognition tests are excessively *easy* measures of retention.

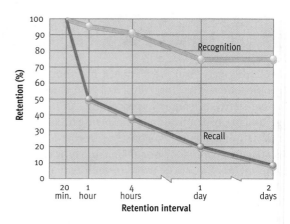

FIGURE 7.14

Recognition versus recall in the measurement of retention.

Luh (1922) had participants memorize lists of nonsense syllables and then measured their retention with either a recognition test or a recall test at various intervals up to two days. As you can see, the forgetting curve for the recall test was quite steep, whereas the recognition test yielded much higher estimates of subjects' retention. (Data from Luh, 1922)

Actually, there is no guarantee that a recognition test will be easier than a recall test. This tends to be the case, but the difficulty of a recognition test can vary greatly, depending on the number, similarity, and plausibility of the options provided as possible answers. To illustrate, see whether you know the answer to the following multiple-choice question:

The capital of Nunavut is
a. Umingmaktok
b. Rankin Inlet
c. Igloolik
d. Iqaluit

Many students who aren't from Nunavut find this a fairly difficult question. The answer is Iqaluit. Now take a look at the next question:

The capital of Nunavut is
a. London
b. New York
c. Tokyo
d. Iqaluit

Virtually anyone can answer this question because the incorrect options are readily dismissed. Although this illustration is a bit extreme, it shows that two recognition measures of the same information can be dramatically different in difficulty.

The third method of measuring forgetting is relearning. A *relearning* measure of retention requires a subject to memorize information a second time to determine how much time or how many practice trials are saved by having learned it before. Subjects' *savings scores* provide an estimate of their retention. Relearning measures can detect retention that is overlooked by recognition tests (Crowder & Greene, 2000).

Why We Forget 6d

Measuring forgetting is only the first step in the long journey toward explaining why forgetting occurs. In this section, we explore the possible causes of forgetting, looking at factors that may affect encoding, storage, and retrieval processes.

Ineffective Encoding 6d

A great deal of forgetting may only *appear* to be forgetting. The information in question may never have been inserted into memory in the first place. Since you can't really forget something you never learned, this phenomenon is sometimes called *pseudoforgetting*. People usually assume that they know what a penny looks like, but most have actually failed to encode this information. When presented with a picture of a real penny and some realistic fakes, however, most people have difficulty picking out the real penny. This is a good example of pseudoforgetting: Pseudoforgetting is usually due to *lack of attention*. Although we handle them every day, most of us do not really look at pennies closely.

Even when memory codes *are* formed for new information, subsequent forgetting may be the result of ineffective or inappropriate encoding (Brown & Craik, 2000). The research on levels of processing shows that some approaches to encoding lead to more forgetting than others (Craik & Tulving, 1975). For example, if you're distracted while you read your textbooks, you may be doing little more than saying the words to yourself. This is *phonemic encoding,* which is inferior to *semantic encoding* for retention of verbal material. When you can't remember the information that you've read, your forgetting may be due to ineffective encoding.

Decay 6d

Instead of focusing on encoding, decay theory attributes forgetting to the impermanence of memory *storage*. *Decay theory* proposes that forgetting occurs because memory traces fade with time. The implicit assumption is that decay occurs in the physiological mechanisms responsible for memories. According to decay theory, the mere passage of time produces forgetting. This notion meshes nicely with common-sense views of forgetting.

As we noted earlier, evidence suggests that decay does contribute to the loss of information from the sensory and short-term memory stores. However, the critical task for theories of forgetting is to explain the loss of information from long-term memory. Researchers have *not* been able to demonstrate that decay causes LTM forgetting (Slamecka, 1992).

If decay theory is correct, the principal cause of forgetting should be the passage of time. In studies of long-term memory, however, researchers have repeatedly found that time passage is not as influential as what happens during the time interval. Research has shown that forgetting depends not on the amount of time that has passed since learning but on the amount, complexity, and type of information that subjects have had to assimilate *during* the retention interval. The negative impact of competing information on retention is called *interference*.

Interference 6d

Interference theory proposes that people forget information because of competition from other material. Although demonstrations of decay in long-term memory have remained elusive, hundreds of studies have shown that interference influences forgetting (Anderson & Neely, 1996; Bjork, 1992; Bower, 2000). In many of these studies, researchers have controlled interference by varying the *similarity* between the original material given to subjects (the test material) and the material studied in the intervening period. Interference is assumed to be greatest when intervening material is most similar to the test material. Decreasing the similarity should reduce interference and cause less forgetting. This is exactly what McGeoch and McDonald (1931) found in an influential study. They had subjects memorize test material that consisted of a list of two-syllable adjectives. They varied the similarity of intervening learning by having subjects then memorize one of five lists. In order of decreasing similarity to the test material, they were synonyms of the test words, antonyms of the test words, unrelated adjectives, nonsense syllables, and numbers. Later, subjects' recall of the test material was measured. Figure 7.15 shows that as the similarity of the intervening material decreased, the amount of forgetting also decreased—because of reduced interference.

There are two kinds of interference: *retroactive* interference and *proactive* interference (Jacoby, Hessels, & Bopp, 2001). *Retroactive interference occurs when new information impairs the retention of previously learned information.* Retroactive interference occurs between the original learning and the retest on that learning, during the retention interval (see Figure 7.16). For example, the interference

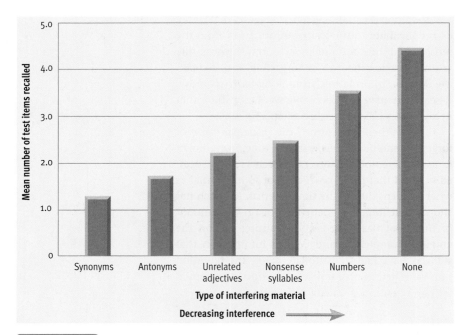

FIGURE 7.15

Effects of interference.

According to interference theory, more interference from competing information should produce more forgetting. McGeoch and McDonald (1931) controlled the amount of interference with a learning task by varying the similarity of an intervening task. The results were consistent with interference theory. The amount of interference is greatest at the left of the graph, as is the amount of forgetting. As interference decreases (moving to the right on the graph), retention improves. (Data from McGeoch & McDonald, 1931)

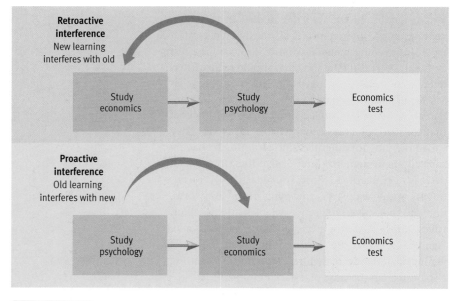

FIGURE 7.16

Retroactive and proactive interference.

Retroactive interference occurs when learning produces a "backward" effect, reducing recall of previously learned material. Proactive interference occurs when learning produces a "forward" effect, reducing recall of subsequently learned material. For example, if you were to prepare for an economics test and then study psychology, the interference from the psychology study would be retroactive interference. However, if you studied psychology first and then economics, the interference from the psychology study would be proactive interference.

manipulated by McGeoch and McDonald (1931) was retroactive interference. In contrast, *proactive interference* occurs when previously learned information interferes with the retention of new information. Proactive interference is rooted in learning that comes *before* exposure to the test material.

Retrieval Failure

People often remember things that they were unable to recall at an earlier time. This phenomenon may be obvious only during struggles with the tip-of-the-tongue phenomenon, but it happens frequently. In fact, a great deal of forgetting may be due to breakdowns in the process of retrieval.

Why does an effort to retrieve something fail on one occasion and succeed on another? That's a tough question. As we suggested earlier in our discussion of context- and state-dependent encoding, one theory is that retrieval failures may be more likely when a mismatch occurs between retrieval cues and the encoding of the information you're searching for. According to Tulving and Thomson (1973), a good retrieval cue is consistent with the original encoding of the information to be recalled. For example, if the sound of a word—its phonemic quality—was emphasized during encoding, an effective retrieval cue should emphasize the sound of the word. If the meaning of the word was emphasized during encoding, semantic cues should be best.

A general statement of the principle at work here was formulated by Tulving and Thomson. The *encoding specificity principle* states that the value of a retrieval cue depends on how well it corresponds to the memory code (Tulving & Thomson, 1973). This principle provides one explanation for the inconsistent success of retrieval efforts.

Another line of research also indicates that memory is influenced by the "fit" not just between the cues present during encoding and retrieval, but also by the degree of match between the type of *processing* engaged in at encoding and retrieval. *Transfer-appropriate processing* occurs when the initial processing of information is similar to the type of processing required by the subsequent measure of retention (Roediger, 2008). For example, Morris, Bransford, and Franks (1977) gave subjects a list of words and a task that required either semantic or phonemic processing. Retention was measured with recognition tests that emphasized either the meaning or the sound of the words. Semantic processing yielded higher retention when the testing emphasized semantic factors, while phonemic processing yielded higher retention when the testing emphasized phonemic factors. Thus, retrieval failures are more likely when there is a poor fit between the processing done during encoding and the processing invoked by the measure of retention (Roediger & Guynn, 1996).

Motivated Forgetting

6d

Many years ago, Sigmund Freud (1901) came up with an entirely different explanation for retrieval failures. As we noted in Chapter 1, Freud asserted that people often keep embarrassing, unpleasant, or painful memories buried in their unconscious. For example, a person who was deeply wounded by perceived slights at a childhood birthday party might suppress all recollection of that party. In his therapeutic work with patients, Freud recovered many such buried memories. He theorized that the memories were there all along, but their retrieval was blocked by unconscious avoidance tendencies.

The tendency to forget things one doesn't want to think about is called *motivated forgetting,* or to use Freud's terminology, *repression.* In Freudian theory, *repression* refers to keeping distressing thoughts and feelings buried in the unconscious (see Chapter 12). Although it is difficult to demonstrate the operation of repression in laboratory studies (Holmes, 1990), a number of experiments suggest that people don't remember anxiety-laden material as readily as emotionally neutral material, just as Freud proposed (Guenther, 1988; Reisner, 1998). Thus, when you forget unpleasant things such as a dental appointment, a promise to help a friend move, or a term paper deadline, motivated forgetting *may* be at work.

The Repressed Memories Controversy

SIM6

Although the concept of repression has been around for a century, interest in this phenomenon has surged in recent years, thanks to a spate of prominent reports involving the return of individuals' long-lost memories of sexual abuse and other traumas during childhood. The media have been flooded with reports of adults accusing their parents, teachers, and neighbours of horrific child abuse decades earlier, based on previously repressed memories of these travesties. For the most part, these parents, teachers, and neighbours have denied the allegations. Many of them have seemed genuinely baffled by the accusations, which have torn some previously happy families apart (Gudjonsson, 2001; McHugh et al., 2004). In an effort to make sense of the charges, some accused parents

have argued that their children's recollections are false memories created inadvertently by well-intentioned therapists through the power of suggestion.

The controversy surrounding recovered memories of abuse is complex and difficult to sort out. The crux of the problem is that child abuse usually takes place behind closed doors. In the absence of corroborative evidence, there is no way to reliably distinguish genuine recovered memories from false ones. A handful of recovered memory incidents have been substantiated by independent witnesses or belated admissions of guilt by the accused (Brewin, 2003, 2007; Bull, 1999; Shobe & Schooler, 2001). But in the vast majority of cases, the allegations of abuse have been vehemently denied, and independent corroboration has not been available. The issues surrounding maltreatment and memory are of great importance and have been the subject of a great deal of research (Goodman, Quas, & Ogle, 2009). What do psychologists and psychiatrists have to say about the authenticity of repressed memories? They are sharply divided on the issue.

Support for Recovered Memories

Many psychologists and psychiatrists, especially clinicians involved in the treatment of psychological disorders, largely accept recovered memories of abuse at face value (Banyard & Williams, 1999; Briere & Conte, 1993; Legault & Laurence, 2007; Skinner, 2001; Terr, 1994; Whitfield, 1995). They assert that sexual abuse in childhood is far more widespread than most people realize. For example, one large-scale Canadian survey (MacMillan et al., 1997), using a random sample of 9953 residents of Ontario, found that 12.8 percent of the females and 4.3 percent of the males reported that they had been victims of sexual abuse during childhood (see Figure 7.17).

Some psychologists and psychiatrists further assert that there is ample evidence that it is common for people to bury traumatic incidents in their unconscious (Del Monte, 2000; Karon & Widener, 1997; Wilsnack et al., 2002). For instance, in one widely cited study, L. M. Williams (1994) followed up on 129 female children who had been brought to a hospital emergency room for treatment of sexual abuse. When interviewed approximately 17 years later about a variety of things, including their history of sexual abuse, 38 percent of the women failed to report the original incident, which Williams largely attributed to amnesia for the incident. In a study of psychiatric patients hospitalized for post-traumatic or dissociative disorders (see Chapter 14), one-third of those who reported childhood sexual abuse said that they experienced complete amnesia for the abuse at some point in their lives (Chu et al., 1999). According to Freyd (1996, 2001; Freyd, DePrince, & Gleaves, 2007), sexual abuse by a parent evokes coping efforts that attempt to block awareness of the abuse because that awareness would interfere with normal attachment processes. The clinicians who accept the authenticity of recovered memories of abuse attribute the recent upsurge in recovered memories to therapists' and clients' increased sensitivity to an issue that people used to be reluctant to discuss.

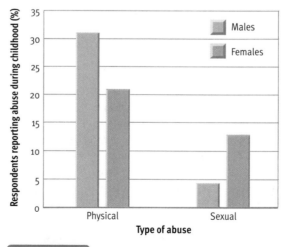

FIGURE 7.17

Estimates of the prevalence of childhood physical and sexual abuse.

In one of the better efforts to estimate the prevalence of child abuse, MacMillan and her colleagues (1997) questioned a random sample of almost 10 000 adults living in Ontario about whether they were abused during childhood. As you can see, males were more likely to have experienced physical abuse and females were more likely to have suffered from sexual abuse. The data support the assertion that millions of people have been victimized by childhood sexual abuse, which is far from rare. (Based on data from MacMillan et al., 1997)

Skepticism Regarding Recovered Memories

In contrast, many other psychologists, especially memory researchers, have expressed skepticism about the recent upsurge of recovered memories of abuse that began in the 1990s (Kihlstrom, 2004; Loftus, 1998, 2003; Lynn & Nash, 1994; McNally, 2003, 2007; Takarangi et al., 2008). They point out that the women in the Williams (1994) study may have failed to report their earlier sexual abuse for a variety of reasons besides amnesia, including embarrassment, poor rapport with the interviewer, normal forgetfulness, or a conscious preference not to revisit painful experiences from the past (Loftus, Garry, & Feldman, 1998; Pope & Hudson, 1998). Many memory researchers are also skeptical about retrospective self-reports of amnesia—such as those seen in the Chu et al. (1999) study—because self-assessments of personal memory are often distorted and because it is difficult to distinguish between a period when a memory was not *accessed* versus a period when a memory was not *available* due to repression (Belli et al., 1998; Schooler, 1999).

The skeptics do *not* say that people are lying about their previously repressed memories. Rather, they maintain that some suggestible people wrestling with emotional problems have been convinced by persuasive therapists that their emotional problems must be the result of abuse that occurred years before. Critics blame a minority of therapists who presumably have good intentions but who operate under the dubious assumption that virtually all psychological problems are attributable to childhood sexual abuse (Lindsay & Read, 1994; Spanos, 1994). Using hypnosis, dream interpretation, and leading questions, they supposedly prod and probe patients until they inadvertently create the memories of abuse that they are searching for (Lynn et al., 2003; Thayer & Lynn, 2006).

Psychologists who doubt the authenticity of repressed memories support their analysis by pointing to discredited cases of recovered memories (Brown, Goldstein, & Bjorklund, 2000). For example, with the help of a church counsellor, one woman recovered memories of how her minister father had repeatedly raped her, gotten her pregnant, and then aborted the pregnancy with a coat hanger; however, subsequent evidence revealed that the woman was still a virgin and that her father had had a vasectomy years before (Loftus, 1997; Testa, 1996). The skeptics also point to published case histories that clearly involved suggestive questioning and to cases in which patients have recanted recovered memories of sexual abuse after realizing that these memories were implanted by their therapists (Goldstein & Farmer, 1993; Loftus, 1994; Shobe & Schooler, 2001).

AP/Wide World Photos

Tom Rutherford (shown here with his wife, Joyce) received a US$1 million settlement in a suit against a church therapist and a Springfield, Missouri, church in a false memory case. Under the church counsellor's guidance, the Rutherfords' daughter, Beth, had "recalled" childhood memories of having been raped repeatedly by her minister father, had become pregnant, and had undergone a painful coat-hanger abortion. Her father lost his job and was ostracized. After he later revealed that he'd had a vasectomy when Beth was age four, and a physical exam revealed that at age 23 she was still a virgin, the memories were shown to be false.

Those who question the accuracy of repressed memories also point to findings on the misinformation effect, research on source-monitoring errors, and other studies that demonstrate the relative ease of creating "memories" of events that never happened (Laney & Loftus, 2005; Lindsay et al., 2004; Loftus & Cahill, 2007; Strange, Clifasefi, & Garry, 2007). For example, working with college students, Ira Hyman and his colleagues have managed to implant recollections of fairly substantial events (such as spilling a punch bowl at a wedding, being in a grocery store when the fire sprinkler system went off, being hospitalized for an earache) in about 25 percent of their subjects, just by asking them to elaborate on events supposedly reported by their parents (Hyman, Husband, & Billings, 1995; Hyman & Kleinknecht, 1999).

In a similar vein, building on earlier work by James Deese (1959), Roediger and McDermott (1995, 2000) have devised a simple laboratory paradigm involving the learning of word lists that is remarkably reliable in producing memory illusions. In this procedure, now known as the *Deese-Roediger-McDermott (DRM) paradigm,* a series of lists of 15 words are presented to participants. They are asked to recall the words immediately after each list is presented and are given a recognition measure of their retention at the end of the session. The trick is that each list consists of a set of words (such as *bed, rest, awake, tired*) that are strongly associated with another target word that is not on the list (in this case, *sleep*). When subjects *recall* the words on each list, they remember the nonpresented target word over 50 percent of the time, and when they are

given the final *recognition* test, they typically indicate that about 80 percent of the nonstudied target words were presented in the lists (see Figure 7.18). Using the DRM paradigm, false memories can be created reliably in normal, healthy participants in a matter of minutes, with no pressure or misleading information. Thus, this line of research provides a dramatic demonstration of how easy it is to get people to remember that they saw something they really didn't see (McDermott, 2007; Neuschatz et al., 2007).

Skepticism about the validity of recovered memories of abuse has also been fuelled by the following observations and research findings:

- Many repressed memories of abuse have been recovered under the influence of hypnosis. However, an extensive body of research indicates that hypnosis tends to increase memory distortions while paradoxically making people feel more confident about their recollections (Mazzoni, Heap, & Scorboria, 2010; Mazzoni & Lynn, 2007).
- Many repressed memories of abuse have been recovered through therapists' dream interpretations. But as you learned in Chapter 5, dream interpretation depends on highly subjective guesswork that cannot be verified. Moreover, research shows that bogus dream interpretations can lead

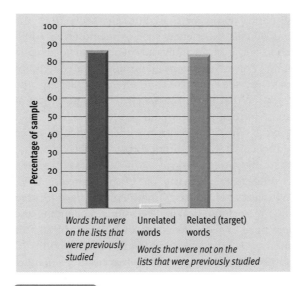

FIGURE 7.18

The prevalence of false memories observed by Roediger and McDermott (1995).

The graph shown here summarizes the recognition test results in Study 1 conducted by Roediger and McDermott (1995). Participants correctly identified words that had been on the lists that they had studied 86 percent of the time and misidentified unrelated words that had not been on the lists only 2 percent of the time, indicating that they were paying careful attention to the task. Nonetheless, they mistakenly reported that they "remembered" related target words that were *not* on the lists 84 percent of the time—a remarkably high prevalence of false memories. (Data from Roediger & McDermott, 1995)

normal subjects to believe that they actually experienced the events suggested in the dream analyses (Loftus, 2000; Loftus & Mazzoni, 1998).

- Some recovered memories have described incidents of abuse that occurred before the victim reached age three and even when the victim was still in the womb (Taylor, 2004). However, when adults are asked to recall their earliest memories, their oldest recollections typically don't go back before age two or three (Hayne, 2007; Morrison & Conway, 2010).

Rebuttals to the Skeptics

Of course, those who believe in recovered memories have mounted rebuttals to the numerous arguments raised by the skeptics. For example, Kluft (1999) argues that a recantation of a recovered memory of abuse does not prove that the memory was false. Gleaves (1994) points out that individuals with a history of sexual abuse often vacillate between denying and accepting that the abuse occurred. Harvey (1999) argues that in laboratory demonstrations it is easy to create false memories because they involve insignificant memory distortions that do not resemble the emotionally wrenching recollections of sexual abuse that have been recovered in therapy. Olio (1994) concludes, "The possibility of implanting entire multiple scenarios of horror that differ markedly from the individual's experience, such as memories of childhood abuse in an individual who does not have a trauma history, remains an unsubstantiated hypothesis" (p. 442). Moreover, even if one accepts the assertion that therapists *can* create false memories of abuse in their patients, some critics have noted that there is virtually no direct evidence on how often this occurs and no empirical basis for the claim that there has been an *epidemic* of such cases (Berliner & Briere, 1999; Leavitt, 2001; Pope & Brown, 1996; Wilsnack et al., 2002). Other rebuttals have focused on the sociopolitical repercussions of denying the existence of recovered memories, arguing that this position is intended to undermine the credibility of abused women and silence their accusations (Raitt & Zeedyk, 2003). Finally, many critics argue that contrived, artificial laboratory studies of memory and hypnosis may have limited relevance to the complexities of recovered memories in the real world (Brown, Scheflin, & Hammond, 1998; Gleaves et al., 2004; Pezdek & Lam, 2007).

Conclusions

So, what can we conclude about the emotionally charged recovered memories controversy? It seems pretty clear that therapists can unintentionally create false memories in their patients and that a significant portion of recovered memories of abuse are the product of suggestion (Follette & Davis, 2009; Ost, 2009). But it also seems likely that some cases of recovered memories are authentic (Brewin, 2007; Smith & Gleaves, 2007). It is difficult to estimate what proportion of recovered memories of abuse fall in each category. That said, recent evidence suggests that memories of abuse recovered through therapy are more likely to be false memories than those that are recovered spontaneously (McNally & Geraerts, 2009). People who report recovered memories of abuse seem to fall into two very different groups (Geraerts, Raymaekers, & Merckelbach, 2008). Some gradually recover memories of abuse with the assistance of suggestive therapeutic techniques, whereas others suddenly and unexpectedly recover memories of abuse when they encounter a relevant retrieval cue (such as returning to the scene of the abuse). A study that sought to corroborate reports of abuse from both groups found a much higher corroboration rate among those who recovered their memories spontaneously (37 percent) as opposed to those who recovered their memories in therapy (0 percent) (Geraerts et al., 2007).

Thus, the matter of recovered memories needs to be addressed with great caution. On the one hand, people should be extremely careful about accepting recovered memories of abuse in the absence of some corroboration. On the other hand, recovered memories of abuse cannot be summarily dismissed. It would be tragic if the repressed memories controversy made people overly skeptical about the all-too-real problem of childhood sexual abuse.

This controversy has helped inspire a great deal of research that has increased our understanding of just how fragile, fallible, malleable, and subjective human memory is. It's presumptuous to trust memory—whether recovered or not—to provide accurate recollections of the past. Moreover, the implicit dichotomy underlying the repressed memories debate—that some memories are true, whereas others are false—is misleading and oversimplified. Research demonstrates that all human memories are imperfect reconstructions of the past that are subject to many types of distortion.

Seven Sins of Memory: How Memory Goes Wrong

Our discussion of memory thus far has highlighted several important points. Memory is key to understanding who we are and what we do. For most of us in our everyday lives our memory serves us just fine. It enables us to get through the day without major mishap, to be where we are supposed to be at the right time, to get the things done we need to get done, to know the names of the people who are most important to us, and to remember when the next psychology test will be held. In fact, memory is typically so effective that we rarely think about it. When we do reflect on it, it is often because it has failed us—it has let us down. Memory doesn't fail us only because we simply forget; sometimes our memories for events are distorted and biased.

Do any of the following failures sound familiar? You don't remember where you left your keys. You show up to class on Monday sure that it was your psychology professor who told you this week's test was postponed when it was actually your sociology professor. You can't stop thinking about what your best friend said to you last night when you had a fight, and so on. We may forget things, our recollections may be distorted, or our memory for past events might haunt us like some unwelcome visitor we cannot get rid of. Memory failures strike us all. Former U.S. vice-presidential candidate Sarah Palin was taking no chances with memory failure when giving speeches and interviews during the 2008 U.S. presidential election campaign and afterwards: She wrote memory cues on her palms. One well-known picture for which she was mocked shows her palm with memory prompts for three key issues—energy, tax, and lifting American spirit (Christmas, 2010).

Daniel Schacter (2001) of Harvard University has collated and summarized the ways that memory fails us in what he refers to as the *seven sins of memory*. These seven sins are important not only because they affect us in our daily life, but also because knowing more about them gives us insight into how memory works and perhaps give us some insight into ways to help those with disorders such as Alzheimer's disease (Schacter & Dodson, 2001).

The first three memory sins, *transience, absentmindedness,* and *blocking,* according to Schacter, are sins of omission in which we cannot bring the memory to mind. *Transience* is the simple weakening of a memory over time. This is what we tend to think of most often when we think about memory failure. *Absentmindedness* refers to a memory failure that is often due to a failure to pay attention because we are perhaps preoccupied with other things. Examples might be losing your keys, misplacing your flash drive, or—like cellist Yo Yo Ma—leaving your $2.5 million cello in the trunk of a New York City taxi (it was later returned to him) (Murray, 2003). *Blocking* is an often temporary problem that occurs when we fail to retrieve an item of information such as someone's name when we meet them. Of course, this is similar to what we have referred to as the tip-of-the-tongue phenomenon (see page 316).

The next four sins, *misattribution, suggestibility, bias,* and *persistence,* are sins of commission. Sins of commission are memory problems where some type of memory is present, but the memory is either "incorrect or unwanted" (Schacter, 2001, p. 5). In *misattribution,* we assign a memory to the wrong source, as in the earlier example about whether the psychology professor or the sociology professor delayed the exam (see our discussion of source monitoring on page 320). In the sin of *suggestibility* our memory is distorted because of, for example, misleading questions (see the discussion of the misinformation effect on page 318). The sin of *bias* refers

U.S. vice-presidential candidate Sarah Palin was photographed several times with memory prompts written on her hands. If you look closely at her raised hand, you will see some of the memory cues.

Daniel Schacter of Harvard University is a memory researcher and neuroscientist. Among other things, he is well known for his cataloging of the seven sins of memory.

Human Memory

to inaccuracy due to the effect of our current knowledge on our reconstruction of the past. According to Schacter, we often edit or rewrite our previous experiences: "The result can be a skewed rendering of a specific incident, or even of an extended period in our lives, which says more about how we feel *now* than about what happened *then*" (Schacter, 2001, p. 5). For example, if currently you are having trouble with your romantic partner, your memory for past events in the relationship may be disproportionately negative (Murray, 2003). The final sin, *persistence,* involves unwanted memories or recollections that you cannot forget—memories that haunt you. While we all have experience with seemingly automatic, unwanted memories and thoughts, in the extreme they can be associated with depression and post-traumatic stress disorder (see Chapter 14).

While these memory sins or failures are clearly problematic and cause discomfort and embarrassment to us, does this mean that it is accurate to call our memory system a failed system? Not at all. As we suggested at the beginning of this section, most of the time, it serves us extremely well. Even though Shachter is well known for his analysis of memory sins, he comes to the same conclusion: "I suggest that the seven sins are by-products of otherwise adaptive features of memory, a price we pay for processes and functions that serve us well in many respects" (Schacter, 2001, p. 184). Each of the seven sins has an adaptive upside. For example, the forgetting that occurs over time (*transience)* allows us to reduce the accessibility of or to discard information that is no longer relevant, such as the date of your first test in psychology (so that you can concentrate on your next test!). The reality of the seven sins of memory doesn't mean that there aren't ways to improve it. You can read more about techniques to improve your memory in the Personal Application section at the end of this chapter (see page 340).

In Search of the Memory Trace: The Physiology of Memory

For decades, neuroscientists have ventured forth in search of the physiological basis for memory, often referred to as the "memory trace." On several occasions scientists have been excited by new leads, only to be led down blind alleys. For example, as we noted earlier, Montreal neurosurgeon Wilder Penfield's work with electrical stimulation of the brain during surgery suggested that the cortex houses exact tape recordings of past experiences (Penfield & Perot, 1963). At the time, scientists believed that this was a major advance. Ultimately, it was not.

Similarly, James McConnell rocked the world of science when he reported that he had chemically transferred a specific memory from one flatworm to another. McConnell (1962) created a conditioned reflex (contraction in response to light) in flatworms and then transferred RNA (a basic molecular constituent of all living cells) from trained worms to untrained worms. The untrained worms showed evidence of "remembering" the conditioned reflex. McConnell boldly speculated that in the future, chemists might be able to formulate pills containing

the information for Physics 201 or History 101! Unfortunately, the RNA transfer studies proved difficult to replicate (Rilling, 1996). Today, more than 30 years after McConnell's "breakthrough," we are still a long way from breaking the chemical code for memory.

Investigators continue to explore a variety of leads about the physiological bases for memory. In light of past failures, these lines of research should probably be viewed with guarded optimism. But we'll look at some of the more promising approaches.

The Neural Circuitry of Memory

One line of research suggests that memory formation results in *alterations in synaptic transmission* at specific sites. According to this view, specific memories depend on biochemical changes that occur at specific synapses. Like McConnell, Eric Kandel (2001) and his colleagues have studied conditioned reflexes in a simple organism—a sea slug. In research that earned a Nobel Prize for Kandel, they showed that reflex learning in the sea slug produces changes in the strength of specific synaptic connections by enhancing the availability and release of neurotransmitters at these synapses (Bailey & Kandel, 2009; Kennedy, Hawkins, & Kandel, 1992). Kandel believes that durable changes in synaptic transmission may be the neural building blocks of more complex memories as well.

Richard F. Thompson (1989, 1992, 2005) and his colleagues have shown that specific memories may depend on *localized neural circuits* in the brain. In other words, memories may create unique, reusable pathways in the brain along which signals flow. Thompson has traced the pathway that accounts for a rabbit's memory of a conditioned eye-blink response. The key link in this circuit is a microscopic spot in the *cerebellum*, a structure in the hindbrain (see Figure 7.19).

Evidence on *long-term potentiation* also supports the idea that memory traces consist of specific neural circuits. *Long-term potentiation (LTP)* is a long-lasting increase in neural excitability at synapses along a specific neural pathway. Researchers produce LTP artificially by sending a burst of high-frequency electrical stimulation along a neural pathway, but theorists suspect that natural events produce the same sort of potentiated neural circuit when a memory is formed (Abraham, 2006; Lynch, 2004; Sweatt, 2009). LTP appears to involve changes in both presynaptic (sending) and postsynaptic (receiving) neurons in neural circuits in the hippocampus (Bi & Poo, 2001). The evidence on LTP has inspired promising work

on the development of drugs that might enhance memory in humans (Lynch & Gall, 2006).

More recent research suggests that the process of *neurogenesis*—the formation of new neurons—may contribute to the sculpting of neural circuits that underlie memory. As we noted in Chapter 3, scientists have discovered that new brain cells are formed constantly in the *dentate gyrus* of the *hippocampus* (Gould, 2004; Leuner & Gould, 2010). Animal studies show that manipulations that suppress neurogenesis lead to memory impairments on many types of learning tasks, and conditions that increase neurogenesis are associated with enhanced learning on many tasks (Leuner, Gould, & Shors, 2006). According to Becker and Wojtowicz (2007), newly formed neurons are initially more excitable than mature neurons, so they may be more readily recruited into new neural circuits corresponding to memories. Moreover, neurogenesis provides the brain with a supply of neurons that vary in age and these variations may somehow allow the brain to "time-stamp" some memories. The theorizing about how neurogenesis contributes to memory encoding is highly speculative (Jessberger, Aimone, & Gage, 2009), but research on neurogenesis is an exciting new line of investigation.

The Anatomy of Memory

Cases of *organic amnesia*—extensive memory loss due to head injury—are another source of clues about the physiological bases of memory (Mayes, 1992). There are two basic types of amnesia: retrograde and anterograde (see Figure 7.20). *Retrograde amnesia* involves the loss of memories for events that occurred prior to the onset of amnesia. For example, a 25-year-old gymnast who sustains a head trauma might find the prior three years, or seven years, or her entire lifetime erased.

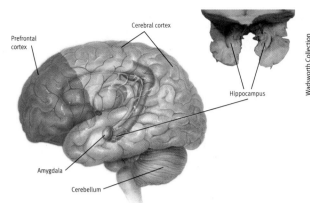

FIGURE 7.19

The anatomy of memory. All of the brain structures identified here have been implicated in efforts to discover the anatomical structures involved in memory. The hippocampus is the hub of the medial temporal lobe memory system, which is thought to play a critical role in the consolidation of long-term memories.

Wadsworth Collection

Prefrontal cortex

Cerebral cortex

Hippocampus

Amygdala

Cerebellum

Human Memory

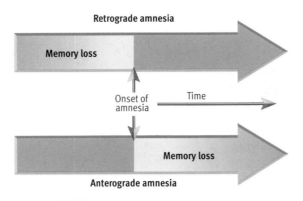

FIGURE 7.20

Retrograde versus anterograde amnesia.

In retrograde amnesia, memory for events that occurred prior to the onset of amnesia is lost. In anterograde amnesia, memory for events that occur subsequent to the onset of amnesia suffers.

Anterograde amnesia involves the loss of memories for events that occur after the onset of amnesia. For instance, after her accident, the injured gymnast might suffer impaired ability to remember people she meets, where she has parked her car, and so on.

The study of anterograde amnesia has proven to be an especially rich source of information about the brain and memory. One well-known case that we referred to in Chapters 1 and 3, that of a man referred to as H. M., has been followed by McGill's Brenda Milner and her colleagues since 1953 (Corkin, 1984; Milner, Corkin, & Teuber, 1968; Scoville & Milner, 1957). H. M. had a relatively normal childhood until, on his 16th birthday, he suffered his first of many grand mal seizures (Schaffhausen, 2007). By 1953 he was having as many as 11 epileptic seizures a week and he needed some type of intervention. He had surgery to relieve debilitating epileptic seizures in 1953. Unfortunately, the surgery inadvertently wiped out most of his ability to form long-term memories. H. M.'s short-term memory remained fine, but he had no recollection of anything that happened after 1953 (other than about the most recent 20–30 seconds of his life). He didn't recognize the doctors treating him and he couldn't remember routes to and from places. He could read a magazine story over and over, thinking he was reading it for the first time each time. He couldn't remember what he did the previous day, let alone what he had done decades earlier. He couldn't even recognize current photos of himself, despite having looked in the mirror every day, as aging had changed his appearance considerably. Although he could not form new long-term memories, H. M.'s intelligence remained intact. He could care for himself (around his own home), carry on complicated conversations, and solve crossword puzzles. H. M.'s misfortune provided a golden opportunity for memory researchers.

In the decades after his surgery, over 100 researchers have studied various aspects of his memory performance, leading to several major discoveries about the nature of memory (Maugh, 2008). As one scientist put it in commenting on H. M., "More was learned about memory by research with just one patient than was learned in the previous 100 years of research on memory" (Miller, 2009). After his death, H. M.'s brain was donated to a lab at the University of California, San Diego. It was subjected to extensive brain imaging and then one year after his death his brain was cut into thousands of thin slices for further study by scientists all over the world (Becker, 2009; Carey, 2009). The painstaking, methodical 53-hour dissection was broadcast live over the Web and watched by over 400 000 people. Named H. M. in order to protect his privacy while he was alive, his real name was Henry Molaison, and he was perhaps the most examined and important patient ever in neuroscience (LaFee, 2009).

H. M.'s memory losses were originally attributed to the removal of his *hippocampus* (see Figure 7.19), although theorists now understand that other nearby structures that were removed also contributed to H. M.'s dramatic memory deficits (Delis & Lucas, 1996). Based on decades of additional research, scientists now believe that the entire *hippocampal region* and the adjacent areas in the cortex are critical for many types of long-term memory (Zola & Squire, 2000). Many scientists now refer to this broader memory complex as the *medial temporal lobe memory system* (Shrager & Squire, 2009). Given its apparent role in long-term memory, it's interesting to note that the hippocampal region is one of the first areas of the brain to sustain significant damage in the course of Alzheimer's disease, which produces severe memory impairment in many people, typically after age 65 (Albert & Moss, 2002; see Chapter 11).

Do these findings mean that memories are stored in the hippocampal region and adjacent areas? Probably not. Many theorists believe that the hippocampal region plays a key role in the *consolidation* of memories (Alvarez & Squire, 1994; Gluck & Myers, 1997; Dudai, 2004). *Consolidation* is a hypothetical process involving the gradual conversion of information into durable memory codes stored in long-term memory. According to this view, memories are consolidated in the hippocampal region and then stored in diverse and widely distributed areas of the cortex (Eichenbaum, 2004; Markowitsch, 2000). This setup allows new memories to become independent of the hippocampal region and to gradually be integrated with other memories already stored in various areas of the cortex (Frankland & Bontempi, 2005). Interestingly, more recent research suggests that

Montreal Neurological Institute

Brenda Milner

"Some effects of temporal lobe lesions in man are hard to reconcile with any unitary-process theory of memory."

McGill researcher Brenda Milner was a co-winner of the 2005 Gairdner Award, along with Endel Tulving of the University of Toronto. The Gairdner Award is a prestigious international biomedical award.

WEB LINK 7.6

Alzheimer Society of Canada

The Alzheimer Society of Canada's site contains important information about Alzheimer's disease and links to resources across Canada.

much of the consolidation process may unfold while people sleep (Stickgold & Walker, 2005).

Neuroscientists continue to forge ahead in their efforts to identify the anatomical bases of memory. One recent advance has been the demonstration that the *amygdala seems to be critical to the formation of memories for learned fears* (Phelps, 2006; Schafe, Doyère, & LeDoux, 2005). This subcortical structure, which is a close neighbour of the hippocampus (see Figure 7.19), may also contribute to other emotional memories (Cahill & McGaugh, 1998; McGaugh, 2004). Researchers exploring the anatomy of memory have traditionally focused on the anatomical bases of *long-term memory*. However, recent years have brought progress in understanding the neural correlates of *working memory*. Various lines of research suggest that areas in the prefrontal cortex contribute to working memory (Runyan & Dash, 2005; E. Smith, 2000). Alan Baddeley (2003) suggests that the *central executive* component of working memory may be localized in the prefrontal cortex, whereas other components of working memory may be housed elsewhere. For example, the storage and rehearsal facets of the *phonological loop* are thought to be localized in several cortical areas in the left hemisphere, as shown in Figure 7.21. The *visuospatial sketchpad* is thought to depend on activity in several areas of the right hemisphere. These conclusions remain tentative, but even working memory depends on interactions among a constellation of neural structures.

As you can see, a variety of biochemical processes, neural circuits, and anatomical structures have been implicated as playing a role in memory. Looking for the physiological basis for memory is only slightly less daunting than looking for the physiological basis for thought itself.

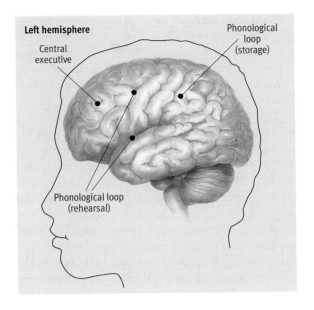

Left hemisphere

Central executive

Phonological loop (storage)

Phonological loop (rehearsal)

FIGURE 7.21

Anatomical bases of selected features of working memory.

Efforts to identify the brain areas that handle specific components of working memory are in their infancy (in comparison to the work on long-term memory), but some progress has been made. According to Baddeley (2003), the areas shown here in the left hemisphere are associated with the operation of the central executive and the phonological loop. The central executive is also represented in the right hemisphere (not shown), where four areas associated with the visuospatial sketchpad have been pinpointed. (Adapted from Baddeley, 2003)

REVIEW OF KEY POINTS

▷ Memory traces may reflect alterations in neurotransmitter release at specific locations. Manipulations of hormone levels and protein synthesis can affect memory.

▷ Thompson's research suggests that memory traces may consist of localized neural circuits. Memories may also depend on long-term potentiation, which is a durable increase in neural excitability at synapses along a specific neural pathway. Memory formation may also stimulate neural growth.

▷ In retrograde amnesia, a person loses memory for events prior to the amnesia. In anterograde amnesia, a person shows memory deficits for events subsequent to the onset of the amnesia. Studies of amnesia and other research suggest that the hippocampal complex is involved in the consolidation of memories.

Systems and Types of Memory

Some theorists believe that evidence on the physiology of memory is confusing because investigators are unwittingly probing into several distinct memory systems that have different physiological bases. A number of research findings inspired this view, foremost among them being the discovery of *implicit memory*. Let's look at this perplexing phenomenon.

Implicit versus Explicit Memory

As noted earlier, patients with anterograde amnesia often appear to have no ability to form long-term memories. If they're shown a list of words and subsequently given a test of retention, their performance is miserable. However, different findings emerge when "sneaky" techniques are used to measure their memory indirectly. For instance, they might be asked to work on a word recognition task that is not presented as a measure of retention. In this task, they are shown fragments of words (e.g., _ss_ss_ for *assassin*) and are asked to complete the fragments with the first appropriate word that comes to mind. The series of word fragments includes ones that correspond to words on a list they saw earlier. In this situation, the amnesiac

PREVIEW QUESTIONS

▶ What is the difference between implicit and explicit memory?

▶ How does this distinction relate to declarative versus procedural memory?

▶ Which type of memory is like an encyclopedia and which is like an autobiography?

▶ What is prospective memory?

subjects respond with words that were on the list just as frequently as normal subjects who also saw the initial list (Schacter, Chiu, & Ochsner, 1993). Thus, the amnesiacs *do* remember words from the list. However, when asked, they don't even remember having been shown the list.

The demonstration of long-term retention in amnesiacs who previously appeared to have no long-term memory shocked memory experts when it was first reported by Warrington and Weiskrantz (1970). However, this surprising finding has been replicated in many subsequent studies. This phenomenon has come to be known as *implicit memory*. *Implicit memory is apparent when retention is exhibited on a task that does not require intentional remembering*. Implicit memory is contrasted with *explicit memory*, *which involves intentional recollection of previous experiences*.

Is implicit memory peculiar to people suffering from amnesia? No. When normal subjects are exposed to material and their retention of it is measured indirectly, they, too, show implicit memory (Schacter, 1987, 1989). To draw a parallel with everyday life, implicit memory is simply incidental, unintentional remembering (Mandler, 1989). People frequently remember things that they didn't deliberately store in memory. For example, you might recall the colour of a jacket that your professor wore yesterday. Likewise, people remember things without deliberate retrieval efforts. For instance, you might be telling someone about a restaurant, which somehow reminds you of an unrelated story about a mutual friend.

Research has uncovered many interesting differences between implicit and explicit memory (May, Hasher, & Fong, 2005; Roediger, 1990; Tulving & Schacter, 1990). Explicit memory is conscious, is accessed directly, and can best be assessed with recall or recognition measures of retention. Implicit memory is unconscious, must be accessed indirectly, and can best be assessed with variations on relearning (savings) measures of retention. Implicit memory is largely unaffected by amnesia, age, the administration of certain drugs (such as alcohol), the length of the retention interval, and manipulations of interference. In contrast, explicit memory is affected very much by all of these factors.

Some theorists think these differences are found because implicit and explicit memory rely on *different cognitive processes* in encoding and retrieval (Graf & Gallie, 1992; Jacoby, 1988; Roediger, 1990). However, many other theorists argue that the differences exist because implicit and explicit memory are handled by *independent memory systems* (Schacter, 1992, 1994; Squire, 1994). These independent systems are referred to as *declarative* and *procedural memory*.

Declarative versus Procedural Memory   6c

Many theorists have suggested that people have separate memory systems for different kinds of information (see Figure 7.22). The most basic division of memory into distinct systems contrasts *declarative memory* with *nondeclarative* or *procedural memory* (Squire 2004, 2009; Winograd, 1975). *The declarative memory system* handles factual information. It contains recollections of words, definitions, names, dates, faces, events, concepts, and ideas. *The nondeclarative or procedural memory system* houses memory for actions, skills, operations, and conditioned responses. It contains *procedural* memories of how to execute such actions as riding a bike, typing, and tying one's shoes. To illustrate the distinction, if you know the rules of tennis (the number of games in a set, scoring, and such), this factual information is stored in declarative memory. If you remember how to hit a serve

Memory

- **Declarative memory system** (factual information, explicit memories)
  - **Semantic memory system** (general knowledge, stored undated) Example: John A. Macdonald
  - **Episodic memory system** (dated recollections of personal experiences) Example: First kiss
- **Nondeclarative/Procedural memory system** (actions, perceptual motor skills, conditioned reflexes, implicit memories) Example: Riding a bicycle

FIGURE 7.22

Theories of independent memory systems.

There is some evidence that different types of information are stored in separate memory systems, which may have distinct physiological bases. The diagram shown here, which blends the ideas of several theorists, is an adaptation of Larry Squire's (1987) scheme. Note that implicit and explicit memory are not memory systems. They are observed behavioural phenomena that appear to be handled by different hypothetical memory systems (the procedural and declarative memory systems), which cannot be observed directly.

Research suggests that memory for perceptual-motor skills, such as the skilled strokes that make Canadian Olympic gold medalist Daniel Nestor a tennis star, are stored in the procedural (nondeclarative) memory system. In contrast, memory for factual information, such as the rules of tennis or game strategies that have worked in the past, are thought to be stored in the declarative memory system.

and swing through a backhand, these perceptual-motor skills are stored in procedural memory. The nondeclarative system also includes the memory base for conditioned reactions based on previous learning, such as a person's tensing up in response to the sound of a dental drill.

Support for the distinction between declarative and nondeclarative memory comes from evidence that the two systems seem to operate somewhat differently (Squire, Knowlton, & Musen, 1993). For instance, the recall of factual information (declarative memory) generally depends on conscious, effortful processes, whereas memory for conditioned reflexes (nondeclarative memory) is largely automatic and memories for skills often require little effort and attention (Johnson, 2003). People execute perceptual-motor tasks such as playing the piano or typing with little conscious awareness of what they're doing. In fact, performance of such tasks sometimes deteriorates if people think too much about what they're doing. Another disparity is that the memory for skills (such as typing and bike riding) doesn't decline much over long retention intervals, while declarative memory appears more vulnerable to forgetting.

The notion that declarative and procedural memories are separate is supported by certain patterns of memory loss seen in amnesiacs. In many cases, declarative memory is severely impaired while procedural memory is left largely intact (Squire & Schrager, 2009). For example, H. M., the victim of amnesia discussed earlier, was able to learn and remember new motor skills, even though he couldn't remember what he looked like as he aged. The sparing of procedural memory in H. M. provided crucial evidence for the distinction between declarative and nondeclarative memory.

Researchers have made some progress toward identifying the neural bases of declarative versus nondeclarative memory. Declarative memory appears to be handled by the *medial temporal lobe* memory system and the far-flung areas of the cortex with which it communicates (Eichenbaum, 2003). Pinpointing the neural bases of nondeclarative memory has proven more difficult because it consists of more of a hodgepodge of memory functions. However, structures such as the cerebellum and amygdala appear to contribute (Delis & Lucas, 1996; Squire, 2004).

Semantic versus Episodic Memory

As we discussed at the beginning of the chapter, Endel Tulving (1986, 1993, 2002) has further subdivided declarative memory into episodic and semantic memory (see Figure 7.22). Both contain factual information, but episodic memory contains *personal facts* and semantic memory contains *general facts* (Mayes & Roberts, 2001; Tulving, 2001). The *episodic memory system* is made up of chronological, or temporally dated, recollections of personal experiences. Episodic memory is a record of things you've done, seen, and heard. It includes information about *when* you did these things, saw them, or heard them. It contains recollections about being in a school play, visiting the Parliament buildings in Ottawa, seeing Apocalyptica in concert, or going to see the long-awaited final episode of the *Harry Potter* film series.

While most of us frequently have trouble remembering specific events in our past and wish we had a better memory, what do you think it would be like to be able to remember almost everything that has ever happened to you and to have these memories unintentionally intrude on what you are trying to do now? This is the case for a woman named "AJ" who was born in 1965. Her episodic memory is so powerful that it "dominates" her waking life (Parker,

Endel Tulving

"Memory systems constitute the major subdivisions of the overall organization of the memory complex. . . . An operating component of a system consists of a neural substrate and its behavioral or cognitive correlates."

University of Toronto researcher Endel Tulving was co-winner of the 2005 Gairdner Award, along with Brenda Milner of McGill University.

Cahill, & McGaugh, 2006). According to her own account, it's a burden:

> *My memory has ruled my life. . . . There is no effort to it. . . . I want to know why I remember everything . . . . It's like a running movie that never stops. . . . I'll be talking to someone and seeing something else . . . . Like we're sitting here talking and I'm talking to you and in my head I'm thinking about something that happened to me in December 1982, it was a Friday, I started to work at G's (a store). . . . When I hear a date, I see it, the day, the month, the year. . . . I see it as I saw it that day. . . . it's a burden.* (Parker et al., 2006, p. 35)

AJ seems to be able to accurately remember almost everything that happened to her, especially since she was 14 years old. What a great thing to have this memory of her experiences, right? This superior autobiographical memory did not help her in school; she was a mediocre student. It also did not help her in her career; she has spent the past few years in a series of temporary jobs. She has suffered from several psychological disorders because of her unrelenting memory. Her autobiographical memory was so unique that the psychologists who did research on her memory gave it a new term: *hyperthymestic syndrome* (Parker et al., 2006). While she was known as "AJ" in the scientific community for years, because of the publication of her autobiography (Price, 2008), we now know that her real name is Jill Price.

While AJ's experiences are very unusual, for most of us our episodic memory is critical. Episodic memory is important to us in terms of keeping a record of our personal experiences. It is important to us in other ways too. For example, it affords us the opportunity for time travel (Tulving, 2002). In travelling through time, we use our episodic memories to simulate what might happen in the future, we "project ourselves into the future based on what we remember from the past" (Schacter & Addis, 2007c, p. 27).

The use of our memory systems to "re-experience" the past and to "pre-experience" the future brings us to our Featured Study by Donna Addis, Alana Wong, and Daniel Schacter (2007). Donna Addis graduated from the University of Toronto, where she worked with Morris Moscovitch. Donna Addis then did a postdoctoral fellowship at Harvard University. Daniel Schacter of Harvard University also obtained his Ph.D. at the University of Toronto, working under the supervision of Endel Tulving, whose work we have discussed throughout this chapter.

The *semantic memory system* contains general knowledge that is not tied to the time when the information was learned. Semantic memory contains information such as Christmas is December 25, dogs have four legs, and Saskatoon is located in Saskatchewan. You probably don't remember when you learned these facts. Information like this is usually stored undated. The distinction between episodic and semantic memory can be better appreciated by drawing an analogy to books: Episodic memory is like an autobiography, while semantic memory is like an encyclopedia.

Jill Price suffered from a memory disorder referred to as hyperthymestic syndrome which caused her to be haunted by her episodic memories.

Dan Tuffs/Getty Images

Courtesy of Donna Rose Addis

In the short span of time since Donna Rose Addis of Harvard University obtained her Ph.D. (2005), she has already made important contributions to our understanding of the neural bases of memory. Along with well-known neuroscientists Daniel Schacter and Alana Wong, both of Harvard University, she co-authored our Featured Study.

FEATURED STUDY

Investigators: Donna Addis, Alana Wong, and Daniel Schacter, all of Harvard University
Source: Remembering the past and imagining the future: Common and distinct neural substrates during event construction and elaboration. *Neuropsychologia,* 2007, *45,* 1363–1377.

The Neuroscience of Time Travel

Typically when we think about our episodic memory, we are focused on the past; it allows us to remember what has happened to us, it gives us a running record of our experiences. Many psychologists also suggest that our episodic memory gives us access to more than our past. In fact, they suggest that it is intimately linked with our ability to imagine the future, to simulate things that might happen to us in that future (Addis, Wong, & Schacter, 2008; Schacter & Addis, 2007d; Tulving, 2002). Some have even suggested that what we recollect about the past is useful only to the extent that it allows us to "anticipate" the future, to "pre-experience" that future (Schacter & Addis, 2007b). Based on the hypothesized linkage between re-experiencing the past, pre-experiencing the future, and the constructive nature of episodic memory, Schacter and Addis have proposed a *constructive episodic simulation* hypothesis. In this hypothesis, in part, they suggest that remembering the past and simulating the future should draw on similar kinds of information from episodic memory and utilize similar types of neural processes. In this study, the authors evaluate the degree of overlap in brain activation in these two activities.

Method

Participants. The participants consisted of 16 right-handed adults. They were healthy males (seven) and females (nine) between the ages of 18 and 33, without a history of neurological or psychological impairment. Two participants were eliminated because of data collection problems.

Procedure. While situated in an MRI machine, participants were presented with lists of concrete nouns (e.g., dress, star). In some of the randomly ordered trials, participants were asked to use a word as a cue to remember an event that had occurred to them during a specified time frame (e.g., last week, last year, during the last five years, or during the last 20 years) and on some trials, they were to use the word as a cue to imagine a future event that would occur within a specified time frame (e.g., next week, next year, during the next five years, or during the next 20 years). Once participants had an event in mind (the *construction* phase), they indicated this to the experimenters by pressing a button (which recorded how long they took on this task) and then they were asked to elaborate on the event by retrieving or generating as much detail as possible (the *elaboration* phase). Participants were also asked to make several ratings of their event. On other trials, the *control* trials, participants were asked, for example, to retrieve from memory two words that were semantically related to the cue word. Brain imaging took place both for the construction and elaboration phases.

Results

The principal findings from the brain imaging indicated that there was considerable overlap in the brain regions that were active in remembering the past and imagining the future, both in the construction and elaboration phases. For example, some medial temporal, parietal, and prefrontal regions showed increases in activity in remembering the past and imagining the future relative to the control conditions. Images relevant to the similarity in activity levels in two of these regions, the medial left prefrontal and parietal regions, are shown in Figure 7.23. Further, the authors noted that both remembering and imagining the future involved increased activity in the hippocampus, a brain structure that had previously been shown to be involved in constructive processing in memory. (We discussed the (re)constructive nature of memory on page 317.) As expected, the authors also found some specific differences in the activity of the brain in remembering the past and imagining the future. For example, while the left hippocampus was active in construction and elaboration both during remembering the past and imagining the future, the right hippocampus was active only during construction of future events.

Discussion

One of the most important outcomes of the study relates to the finding that activity in specific areas of the brain that had previously been associated with episodic

PAST AND FUTURE EVENT ELABORATION

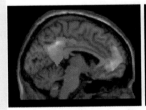 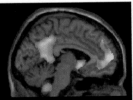

PAST EVENT > CONTROL   FUTURE EVENT > CONTROL

FIGURE 7.23

Past and future event elaboration.

Imaging results illustrating the striking commonalities in medial left prefrontal and parietal activity during the elaboration of **(a)** past and **(b)** future events (relative to the control tasks) at a threshold of $\rho < 0.001$, uncorrected (shown at $\rho < 0.005$, uncorrected).

Source: Reprinted from *Neuropsychologia, 45* (7), Donna Rose Addis, Alana T. Wong, Daniel L. Schacter, Remembering the past and imagining the future: Common and distinct neural substrates during event construction and elaboration, pp. 1363–1377. Copyright © 2007, with permission from Elsevier. Image courtesy of Donna Rose Addis.

remembering were also engaged by tasks that required participants to imagine specific events in the future. Thus, re-experiencing events and pre-experiencing events were similarly processed in the brain. This type of finding can be taken as support for the authors' *constructive episodic simulation* hypothesis. They suggest that the constructive nature of the episodic memory system is ideally suited for adaptive human behaviour and our ability to imagine events in the future. In this view, a constructive memory system does not retain an exact copy of the past and it has the ability to "draw on the elements and gist of the past, and extract, recombine and reassemble them into imaginary events that never occurred in that exact form" (Schacter & Addis, 2007c, p. 27).

Comment

As we suggested in Chapter 1, all areas of psychology are increasingly turning to neuroscience both as a source of experimental methods to test their ideas and as a source of new ideas to be used in understanding issues in their own particular areas of research. Cognitive psychologists and those interested in memory have long employed research on the brain in their work, as was illustrated throughout this chapter. They too are increasingly using modern techniques such as functional magnetic resonance imaging (fMRI) to evaluate their ideas. This Featured Study is an excellent illustration of this. As we discussed earlier, cognitive psychologists have speculated about the overlap between the processes involved in remembering and imagining the future. This Featured Study is one of a number of such studies that has used what we know about the brain and brain-imaging techniques to further examine this formulation.

Some studies suggest that episodic and semantic memory may have distinct neural bases (Schacter, Wagner, & Buckner, 2000; Tulving, 2002). For instance, some amnesiacs forget mostly personal facts, while their recall of general facts is largely unaffected (Szpunar & McDermott, 2009). Also consistent with this distinction is the case of patient K. C., to whom we referred earlier. K. C. retained much of his general knowledge of the world after suffering head trauma in an accident but was unable to remember any personally experienced events (Rosenbaum et al., 2005). However, debate continues about the neural substrates of episodic and semantic memory (Barba et al., 1998; Wiggs, Weisberg, & Martin, 1999).

Prospective versus Retrospective Memory

A 1984 paper with a clever title, "Remembering to Do Things: A Forgotten Topic" (Harris, 1984),

introduced yet another distinction between types of memory: *prospective memory* versus *retrospective memory* (see Figure 7.24). *Prospective memory involves remembering to perform actions in the future.* Examples of prospective memory tasks include remembering to walk the dog, to call someone, to grab the tickets for the big game, and to turn off your lawn sprinkler. In contrast, *retrospective memory involves remembering events from the past or previously learned information.* Retrospective memory is at work when you try to recall who won the Stanley Cup last year, when you reminisce about your high school days, or when you try to recall what your professor said in a lecture last week. Prospective memory has been a "forgotten" topic in that it has been the subject of relatively little study. But that has begun to change, as research on prospective memory has increased in recent years (McDaniel & Einstein, 2007).

Researchers interested in prospective memory argue that the topic merits far more study because it plays such a pervasive role in everyday life (Graf & Uttl, 2001). Think about it—a brief trip to attend class at school can be saturated with prospective memory tasks. You may need to remember to pack your notebook, take your umbrella, turn off your coffeemaker, and grab your car keys before you even get out the door. People seem to vary tremendously in their ability to successfully carry out prospective memory tasks (Searleman, 1996), and it is easy to forget these kinds of intentions (Einstein et al., 2003). Individuals who appear to be deficient in prospective memory are often characterized as "absent-minded."

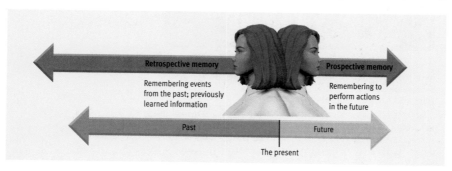

FIGURE 7.24

Retrospective versus prospective memory.

Most memory research has explored the dynamics of *retrospective memory*, which focuses on recollections from the past. However, *prospective memory*, which requires people to remember to perform actions in the future, also plays an important role in everyday life.

concept **check 7.3**

Recognizing Various Types of Memory

Check your understanding of the various types of memory discussed in this chapter by matching the definitions below with the following: (a) declarative memory, (b) episodic memory, (c) explicit memory, (d) implicit memory, (e) long-term memory, (f) procedural memory, (g) prospective memory, (h) retrospective memory, (i) semantic memory, (j) sensory memory, and (k) short-term memory. The answers can be found in Appendix A.

_____ **1.** Memory for factual information.

_____ **2.** An unlimited capacity store that can hold information over lengthy periods of time.

_____ **3.** The preservation of information in its original sensory form for a brief time, usually only a fraction of a second.

_____ **4.** Type of memory apparent when retention is exhibited on a task that does not require intentional remembering.

_____ **5.** Chronological, or temporally dated, recollections of personal experiences.

_____ **6.** The repository of memories for actions, skills, operations, and conditioned responses.

_____ **7.** General knowledge that is not tied to the time when the information was learned.

_____ **8.** Remembering to perform future actions.

_____ **9.** A limited-capacity store that can maintain unrehearsed information for about 20 seconds.

Putting It in Perspective: Themes 2, 4, and 7

One of our integrative themes—the idea that people's experience of the world is subjective—stood head and shoulders above the rest in this chapter. Let's briefly review how the study of memory has illuminated this idea.

First, our discussion of attention as inherently selective should have shed light on why people's experience of the world is subjective. To a great degree, what you see in the world around you depends on where you focus your attention. This is one of the main reasons that two people can be exposed to the "same" events and walk away with entirely different perceptions. Second, the reconstructive nature of memory should further explain people's tendency to view the world with a subjective slant. When you observe an event, you don't store an exact copy of the event in your memory. Instead, you store a rough, "bare bones" approximation of the event that may be reshaped as time goes by.

A second theme that was apparent in our discussion of memory is psychology's theoretical diversity. We saw illuminating theoretical debates about the nature of memory storage, the causes of forgetting, and the existence of multiple memory systems. Finally, the multifaceted nature of memory demonstrated once again that behaviour is governed by multiple causes. For instance, your memory of a specific event may be influenced by your attention to it, your

level of processing, your elaboration, your exposure to interference, how you search your memory store, how you reconstruct the event, and so forth. Given the multifaceted nature of memory, it should come as no surprise that there are many ways to improve memory. We discuss a variety of strategies in the Personal Application section.

REVIEW OF KEY POINTS

> Implicit memory involves unintentional remembering, whereas explicit memory involves intentional recall. Implicit memory is unconscious, must be accessed indirectly, and is largely unaffected by amnesia, age, drugs, and the length of the retention interval.

> Declarative memory is memory for facts, while procedural memory is memory for actions and skills. Theorists suspect that the declarative memory system handles explicit memory, whereas the procedural memory system handles implicit memory.

> Declarative memory can be subdivided into episodic memory for personal facts and semantic memory for general facts. Theorists have also distinguished between retrospective memory (remembering past events) and prospective memory (remembering to do things in the future).

> Our discussion of memory enhances our understanding of why people's experience of the world is highly subjective. Work in this area also shows that behaviour is governed by multiple causes and that psychology is characterized by theoretical diversity.

PREVIEW QUESTIONS

▸ How did this chapter demonstrate the subjectivity of experience?

▸ How did this chapter highlight psychology's theoretical diversity and multifactorial causation?

Improving Everyday Memory

Answer the following "true" or "false."

___ **1** Memory strategies were recently invented by psychologists.

___ **2** Imagery can be used to help remember concrete words only.

___ **3** Overlearning of information leads to poor retention.

___ **4** Outlining what you read is not likely to affect retention.

___ **5** Massing practice in one long study session is better than distributing practice across several shorter sessions.

Mnemonic devices are methods used to increase the recall of information. They have a long history, so the first statement is false. In fact, one of the mnemonic devices covered in this Application—the method of loci—was described in Greece as early as 86–82 B.C.E. (Yates, 1966). Actually, mnemonic devices were much more important in ancient times than they are today. In ancient Greece and Rome, for instance, paper and pencils were not readily available for people to write down things they needed to remember, so they had to depend heavily on mnemonic devices.

Are mnemonic devices the key to improving one's everyday memory? No. Mnemonic devices can clearly be helpful in some situations (Wilding & Valentine, 1996), but they are not a panacea. They can be difficult to use and difficult to apply to many everyday situations. Most books and training programs designed to improve memory probably overemphasize mnemonic techniques (Searleman & Herrmann, 1994). Although less exotic strategies such as increasing rehearsal, engaging in deeper processing, and organizing material are more crucial to everyday memory, we will discuss some popular mnemonics as we proceed through this Application. Along the way, you'll learn that all of our opening true–false statements are false.

Engage in Adequate Rehearsal

SIM5

Practice makes perfect, or so you've heard. In reality, practice is not likely to guarantee perfection, but it usually leads to improved retention. Studies show that retention improves with increased rehearsal (Weaver, 2010). This improvement presumably occurs because rehearsal helps to transfer information into long-term memory. Although the benefits of practice are well known, people have a curious tendency to overestimate their knowledge of a topic and how well they will perform on a subsequent memory test of this knowledge (Koriat & Bjork, 2005). That's why it is a good idea to informally test yourself on information that you think you have mastered before confronting a real test.

In addition to checking your mastery, recent research suggests that testing actually enhances retention, a phenomenon dubbed the *testing effect* (Karpicke & Roediger, 2008; Roediger & Karpicke, 2006). Studies have shown that taking a test on material increases performance on a subsequent test even more than studying for an equal amount of time. Interestingly, the testing effect is observed on both closed-book and open-book exams (Agarwal et al., 2008). And the favourable effects of testing are enhanced if participants are provided feedback on their test performance (Butler & Roediger, 2008). Moreover, recent studies have demonstrated that the laboratory findings on the testing effect replicate in real-world educational settings (Larsen, Butler, & Roediger, 2009; McDaniel et al., 2007). Unfortunately, given the recent nature of this discovery, relatively few students are aware of the value of testing (Karpicke, Butler, & Roediger, 2009).

Why is testing so beneficial? The key appears to be that testing forces students to engage in effortful retrieval of information, which promotes future retention (Roediger et al., 2010). Indeed, even *unsuccessful* retrieval efforts can enhance retention (Kornell, Hays, & Bjork, 2009). In any event, self-testing appears to be an excellent memory tool. (This suggests that it would be prudent to take the Practice Tests in this text and the additional tests available on the website for this book.)

It even pays to overlearn material (Driskell, Willis, & Copper, 1992). *Overlearning* refers to continued rehearsal of material after you first appear to have mastered it. In one study, after subjects had mastered a list of nouns (they recited the list without error), Krueger (1929) required them to continue rehearsing for 50 percent or 100 percent more trials. Measuring retention at intervals up to 28 days, Krueger found that greater overlearning was related to better recall of the list. Modern studies have also shown that overlearning can enhance performance on an exam that occurs within a week, although the evidence on its long-term benefits (months later) is inconsistent (Peladeau, Forget, & Gagne, 2003; Rohrer et al., 2005).

One other precaution is also worth mentioning. If you are memorizing some type of list, be aware of the serial-position effect, which is often observed when subjects are tested on their memory of lists (Murdock, 2001). The *serial-position* effect occurs when subjects show better recall for items at the beginning and end of a list than for items in the middle (see Figure 7.25). The reasons for the serial-position effect are complex and need not concern us, but its pragmatic implications are clear: If you need to learn a list, allocate extra practice trials to items in the middle of the list and check your memorization of those items very carefully.

Schedule Distributed Practice and Minimize Interference

Let's assume that you need to study nine hours for an exam. Should you cram all your studying into one nine-hour period (massed practice)? Or is it better to distribute your study among, say, three three-hour periods on successive days (distributed practice)? The evidence indicates that retention tends to be greater after distributed practice than after massed practice (Kornell et al., 2010; Roher & Taylor, 2006). Moreover, a recent review of over 300 experiments (Cepeda

FIGURE 7.25

The serial-position effect.

After learning a list of items to remember, people tend to recall more of the items from the beginning and the end of the list than from the middle, producing the characteristic U-shaped curve shown here. This phenomenon is called the *serial-position effect*.

Source: Adapted from Rundus, D. (1971). Analysis of rehearsal processes in free recall. *Journal of Experimental Psychology, 89,* 63–77. Copyright © 1971 by the American Psychological Association. Adapted by permission of the author.

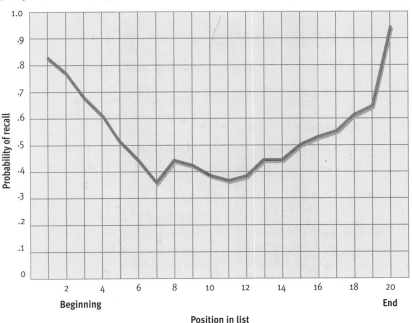

FIGURE 7.26

Effects of massed versus distributed practice on retention.

Children in the Underwood (1970) study showed better recall of information when practice sessions were distributed over time as opposed to being massed together in one session.

Source: Reprinted from *Journal of Verbal Learning and Verbal Behavior, 9*(5), Benton J. Underwood, A breakdown of the total-time law in free-recall learning, p. 95. Copyright © 1970, with permission from Elsevier.

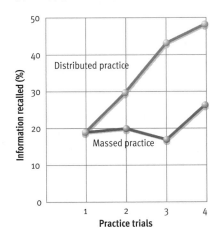

et al., 2006) showed that the longer the retention interval between studying and testing, the greater the advantage for massed practice (see Figure 7.26). The same review concluded that the longer the retention interval, the longer the optimal "break" between practice trials. When an upcoming test is more than two days away, the optimal interval between practice periods appears to be around 24 hours. The superiority of distributed practice over massed practice suggests that cramming is an ill-advised approach to studying for exams (Dempster, 1996).

Because interference is a major cause of forgetting, you'll probably want to think about how you can minimize it. This issue is especially important for students, because memorizing information for one course can interfere with the retention of information for another course. It may help to allocate study for specific courses to separate days. Thorndyke and Hayes-Roth (1979) found that similar material produced less interference when it was learned on different days. Thus, the day before an exam in a course,

you should study for that course only—if possible. If demands in other courses make that plan impossible, you should study the test material last.

Emphasize Deep Processing and Organize Information

Research on levels of processing suggests that how *often* you go over material is less critical than the *depth* of processing that you engage in (Craik & Tulving, 1975). Thus, if you expect to remember what you read, you have to wrestle fully with its meaning (Einstein & McDaniel, 2004). Many students could probably benefit if they spent less time on rote repetition and devoted more effort to actually paying attention to and analyzing the meaning of their reading assignments. In particular, it is useful to make material *personally* meaningful. When you read your textbooks, try to relate information to your own life and experience. For example, when you read about classical conditioning, try to think of responses that you display that are attributable to classical conditioning.

Retention tends to be greater when information is well organized (Einstein & McDaniel, 2004). Gordon Bower (1970) has shown that hierarchical organization is particularly helpful when it is applicable. Thus, it may be a good idea to *outline* reading assignments for school. Consistent with this reasoning, there is some empirical evidence that outlining material from textbooks can enhance retention of the material (McDaniel, Waddill, & Shakesby, 1996).

Enrich Encoding with Mnemonic Devices 6a

Many mnemonic devices—such as acrostics, acronyms, and narrative methods—are designed to make abstract material more meaningful. Other mnemonic devices depend on visual imagery. As you may recall, Allan Paivio (1986, 2007) believes that visual images create a second memory code and that two codes are better than one.

Acrostics and Acronyms *Acrostics* are phrases (or poems) in which the first letter of each word (or line) functions as a cue to help you recall information to be remembered (Herrmann, Raybeck, & Gruneberg, 2002). For instance, you may remember the order of musical notes with the saying "Every good boy does fine" (or "deserves favour"). A slight variation on acrostics is the *acronym*—a word formed out of the first letters of a series of words. Students memorizing the order of colours in the light spectrum often store the name "Roy G. Biv" to remember red, orange, yellow, green, blue, indigo, and violet. Notice that this acronym takes advantage of the principle of chunking.

Narrative Methods Another useful way to remember a list of words is to create a story that includes the words in the appropriate order. The narrative both increases the meaningfulness of the words and links them in a specific order (Bower, 2008). Examples of this technique can be seen in Figure 7.27. Bower and Clark (1969) found that this procedure greatly enhanced subjects' recall of lists of unrelated words (as shown in Figure 7.28).

Why—and how—would you use the narrative method? Let's assume that you always manage to forget to put one item in your gym bag on your way to the pool. Short of pasting a list on the inside of the bag, how can you remember everything you need? You could make up a story like the following that includes the items you need:

The wind and rain in COMBINATION nearly LOCKed out the rescue efforts. CAP, the flying ace, TOWELled the soap from his eyes, pulled his GOGGLES from his SUIT pocket, and COMBed the BRUSH for survivors.

Rhymes Another verbal mnemonic that people often rely on is rhyming. You've probably repeated, "I before E except after C. . . ." thousands of times. Perhaps you also remember the number of days in each month with the old standby, "Thirty days hath September. . . ." Rhyming something to remember it is an old and useful trick.

FIGURE 7.27

Narrative methods of remembering.

Bower and Clark (1969) presented participants with 12 lists of words. Subjects in the "narrative group" were asked to recall the words by constructing a story out of them (like the two stories shown here). Subjects in the control group were given no special instructions. Recoding the material in story form dramatically improved recall, as the graph clearly shows.

Source: Adapted from Bower, G.H., and Clark, M.C. (1969). Narrative stories as mediators of serial learning. *Psychonomic Science, 14*, 181–182. Copyright © 1969 by the Psychonomic Society.

Word lists	Stories
Bird Costume Mailbox Head River Nurse Theatre Wax Eyelid Furnace	A man dressed in a *Bird Costume* and wearing a *Mailbox* on his *Head* was seen leaping into the *River*. A *Nurse* ran out of a nearby *Theatre* and applied *Wax* to his *Eyelids*, but her efforts were in vain. He died and was tossed into the *Furnace*.
Rustler Penthouse Mountain Sloth Tavern Fuzz Gland Antler Pencil Vitamin	A *Rustler* lived in a *Penthouse* on top of a *Mountain*. His specialty was the three-toed *Sloth*. He would take his captive animals to a *Tavern* where he would remove *Fuzz* from their *Glands*. Unfortunately, all this exposure to sloth fuzz caused him to grow *Antlers*. So he gave up his profession and went to work in a *Pencil* factory. As a precaution he also took a lot of *Vitamin* E.

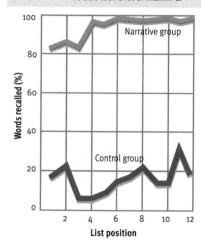

Enrich Encoding with Visual Mnemonics 6a

Memory can be enhanced by the use of visual imagery. As you may recall, Allan Paivio (1986) believes that visual images create a second memory code and that two codes are better than one for enhancing recall. Many popular mnemonic devices depend on visual imagery, including the link method, method of loci, and keyword method.

Link Method 6a

The *link method* involves forming a mental image of items to be remembered in a way that links them together. For instance, suppose you need to remember some items to pick up at the drugstore: a news magazine, shaving cream, film, and pens. To remember these items, you might visualize a public figure on the magazine cover shaving with a pen while being photographed. There is some evidence that the more bizarre you make your image, the more helpful it is likely to be (McDaniel & Einstein, 1986).

Method of Loci 6a

The *method of loci* involves taking an imaginary walk along a familiar path where images of items to be remembered are associated with certain locations. The first step is to commit to memory a series of loci, or places along a path. Usually these loci are specific locations in your home or neighbourhood. Then envision each thing you want to remember in one of these locations. Try to form distinctive, vivid images. When you need to remember the items, imagine yourself walking along the path. The various loci on your path should serve as cues for the retrieval of the images that you formed (see Figure 7.28). Evidence suggests that the method of loci can be effective in increasing retention (Cornoldi & De Beni, 1996; Moe & De Beni, 2004). Moreover, this method ensures that items are remembered in their *correct order* because the order is determined by the sequence of locations along the pathway. A recent study found that using loci along a pathway from home to work was more effective than a pathway through one's home (Massen et al., 2009).

Keyword Method

Visual images are also useful when you need to form an association between a pair of items, such as a person's name and face or a foreign word and its English translation. However, there is a potential problem that you may recall from our earlier discussion of visual imagery. It's difficult to generate images to

FIGURE 7.28

The method of loci.

In this example from Bower (1970), a person about to go shopping pairs items to remember with familiar places (loci) arranged in a natural sequence: (1) hot dogs/driveway; (2) cat food/garage interior; (3) tomatoes/front door; (4) bananas/coat closet shelf; (5) whiskey/kitchen sink. The shopper then uses imagery to associate the items on the shopping list with the loci, as shown in the drawing: (1) giant hot dog rolls down a driveway; (2) a cat noisily devours cat food in the garage; (3) ripe tomatoes are splattered on the front door; (4) bunches of bananas are hung from the closet shelf; (5) the contents of a bottle of whiskey gurgle down the kitchen sink. As the last panel shows, the shopper recalls the items by mentally touring the loci associated with them.

Source: From Bower, G.H. (1970). Analysis of a mnemonic device. *American Scientist, 58* (Sept–Oct), 496–499. Copyright © 1970 by Scientific Research Society. Reprinted by permission.

represent abstract words (Paivio, 1969). A way to avoid this problem is to use *the keyword method,* in which you associate a concrete word with an abstract word and generate an image to represent the concrete word.

A practical use of this method is to help you remember the names of people you meet (Morris, Jones, & Hampson, 1978). Just associate a concrete word with the name and then form an image of the associated word. The associated word, which is the *keyword,* should sound like the name that's being learned. For example, you might use *Garden* as a keyword for *Gordon.* And *debtor man* might be a good keyword for *Detterman,* if you form an image of Mr. Detterman dressed in ragged clothes. Research suggests that the keyword method can enhance the retention of foreign language and other types of educational material (Bellezza, 1996; Gruneberg, Sykes, & Gillett, 1994).

Levin and Levin (1990) trained students to apply the keyword method to unfamiliar terms in a plant classification system. They coupled this approach with the link method, which was used to group terms that belonged together in categories. The researchers found that these methods enhanced students' memory of the classification system (see Figure 7.29).

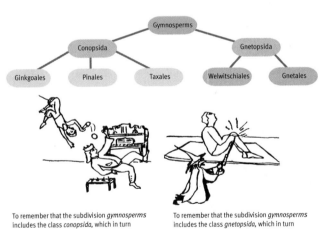

To remember that the subdivision *gymnosperms* includes the class *conopsida,* which in turn includes the three orders *ginkgoales, pinales,* and *taxales,* study the picture of the swinging gymnast with the ice cream cone in his hand. The ice cream is about to splat in the face of the king who is leaping from the bench of his royal piano after sitting on some tacks.

To remember that the subdivision *gymnosperms* includes the class *gnetopsida,* which in turn includes the two orders *welwitschiales* and *gnetales,* study the picture of the fallen gymnast holding his sore knee tops. He is being treated (or tricked!) by a witch doctor who is sticking a very long needle into his injured knee.

FIGURE 7.29

Combining the keyword and link methods to aid recall.

Levin and Levin (1990) set out to help students memorize a difficult plant classification system (a portion of the system is shown in the top part of the figure). They taught students to use a technique that essentially combines the keyword and link methods. Students were trained to generate keywords for the abstract terms in the hierarchy and to form images that linked the keywords that corresponded to portions of the classification system (two examples are shown in the bottom part of the figure). This creative use of visual imagery enhanced students' recall of the plant classification system.

Source: Adapted from Levin, M. E., & Levin, J. R. (1990). Scientific mnemonomics: Methods for maximizing more than memory. *American Educational Research Journal, 27* (2), 301–321. Copyright © 1990 by American Educational Research Association. Adapted by permission.

REVIEW OF KEY POINTS

▷ Mnemonic devices are methods used to increase the recall of information. Rehearsal, even when it involves over-learning, facilitates retention, although one should be wary of the serial-position effect. Distributed practice tends to be more efficient than massed practice.

▷ It is wise to plan study sessions so as to minimize interference and maximize deep processing. Evidence also suggests that organization enhances retention, so out-lining texts may be valuable.

▷ Meaningfulness can be enhanced through the use of verbal mnemonics such as acrostics, acronyms, and narrative methods. The link method, the method of loci, and the keyword method are mnemonic devices that depend on the value of visual imagery.

Understanding the Fallibility of Eyewitness Accounts

A number of years ago, the Wilmington, Delaware, area was plagued by a series of armed robberies committed by a perpetrator who was dubbed the "gentleman bandit" by the press because he was an unusually polite and well-groomed thief. The local media published a sketch of the gentleman bandit and eventually an alert resident turned in a suspect who resembled the sketch. Much to everyone's surprise, the accused thief was a Catholic priest named Father Bernard Pagano—who vigorously denied the charges. Unfortunately for Father Pagano, his denials and alibis were unconvincing and he was charged with the crimes. At the trial, *seven* eyewitnesses confidently identified Father Pagano as the gentleman bandit. The prosecution was well on its way to a conviction when there was a stunning turn of events—another man, Ronald Clouser, confessed to the police that he was the gentleman bandit. The authorities dropped the charges against Father Pagano and the relieved priest was able to return to his normal existence (Rodgers, 1982).

This bizarre tale of mistaken identity—which sounds like it was lifted from a movie script—raises some interesting questions about memory. How could seven people "remember" seeing Father Pagano commit armed robberies that he had nothing to do with? How could they mistake him for Ronald Clouser, when the two really didn't look very similar (see the photos below)? How could they be so confident when they were so wrong? Perhaps you're thinking that this is just one case and it must be unrepresentative (which would be sound critical thinking). Well, yes, it *is* a rather extreme example of eyewitness fallibility, but researchers have compiled mountains of evidence that eyewitness testimony is not nearly as reliable or as accurate as widely assumed (Cutler & Penrod, 1995; Kassin et al., 2001; Wells & Olson, 2003; see Schacter et al., 2008, for some methodological concerns). This finding is ironic in that people are most confident about their assertions

when they can say, "I saw it with my own eyes." Television news shows like to use the title *Eyewitness News* to create the impression that they chronicle events with great clarity and accuracy. And our legal system accords special status to eyewitness testimony because it is considered much more dependable than hearsay or circumstantial evidence. Canadian psychologists such as Daniel Yarmey of the University of Guelph, Rod Lindsay of Queen's University, Mark Howe of Lancaster University, and Regina Schuller of York University have been important contributors to the literature on false memories and the accuracy and role of eyewitness testimony and to the literature on psychology and the law more generally (Howe, Gagnon, & Thouas, 2008; Lindsay et al., 2007; Lindsay, Allen, Chan and Dahl, 2004; Schuller & Ogloff, 2001; Yarmey, 2003).

So, why are eyewitness accounts surprisingly inaccurate? Well, a host of factors and processes contribute to this inaccuracy. Let's briefly review some of the relevant processes that were introduced in the main body of the chapter; then we'll focus on two common errors in thinking that also contribute.

Can you think of any memory phenomena described in the chapter that seem likely to undermine eyewitness accuracy?

You could point to the fact that *memory is a reconstructive process*, and eyewitness recall is likely to be distorted by the schemas that people have for various events. A second consideration is that *witnesses sometimes make source-monitoring errors* and get confused about where they saw a face. For example, one rape victim mixed up her assailant with a guest on a TV show that she was watching when she was attacked. Fortunately, the falsely accused suspect had an airtight alibi, as he could demonstrate that he was on live television when the rape occurred (Schacter, 1996). Perhaps the most pervasive factor is the misinformation effect (Loftus, 1993a). *Witnesses' recall of events is routinely distorted by information introduced after the event* by police officers, lawyers, news reports, and so forth. In addition to these factors, eyewitness inaccuracy is fuelled by the *hindsight bias* and *overconfidence effects*.

The Contribution of Hindsight Bias

The *hindsight bias* is the tendency to mould our interpretation of the past to fit how events actually turned out. When you know the outcome of an event, this

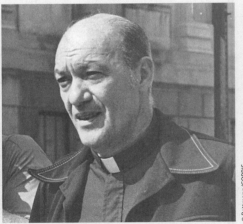

Although he doesn't look that much like the real "gentleman bandit," who is shown on the left, seven eyewitnesses identified Father Pagano (right) as the gentleman bandit, showing just how unreliable eyewitness accounts can be.

Although courts give special credence to eyewitness testimony, scientific evidence indicates that eyewitness accounts are less reliable than widely assumed.

knowledge slants your recall of how the event unfolded and what your thinking was at the time (Guilbault et al., 2004). With the luxury of hindsight, there is a curious tendency to say, "I knew it all along" when explaining events that objectively would have been difficult to foresee. With regard to eyewitnesses, their recollections may often be distorted by knowing that a particular person has been arrested and accused of the crime in question. For example, Wells and Bradfield (1998) had simulated eyewitnesses select a perpetrator from a photo lineup. The eyewitnesses' confidence in their identifications tended to be quite modest, which made sense given that the actual perpetrator was not even in the lineup. But when some subjects were told, "Good, you identified the actual suspect," they became highly confident about their identifications, which obviously were incorrect. In another study, participants read identical scenarios about a couple's first date that either had no ending or ended in a rape (described in one additional sentence). The subjects who received the rape ending reconstructed the story to be more consistent with their stereotypes of how rapes occur (Carli, 1999).

The Contribution of Overconfidence

Another flaw in thinking that contributes to inaccuracy in eyewitness accounts is people's tendency to be overconfident about

the reliability of their memory. When tested for their memory of general information, people tend to overestimate their accuracy (Lichtenstein, Fischhoff, & Phillips, 1982; Koriat & Bjork, 2005). In studies of eyewitness recall, participants also tend to be overconfident about their recollections. Although jurors tend to be more convinced by eyewitnesses who appear confident, the evidence indicates that there is only a modest correlation between eyewitness confidence and eyewitness accuracy (Shaw, McClure, & Dykstra, 2007).

Strategies to Reduce Overconfidence

Can you learn to make better judgments of the accuracy of your recall of everyday events? Yes, with effort you can get better at making accurate estimates of how likely you are to be correct in the recall of some fact or event. One reason that people tend to be overconfident is that if they can't think of any reasons that they might be wrong, they assume they must be right. Thus, overconfidence is fuelled by yet another common error in thinking—*the failure to seek disconfirming evidence*.

Thus, to make more accurate assessments of what you know and don't know, it helps to engage in a deliberate process of considering why you might be wrong. Here is an example. Based on your reading of Chapter 1, write down the schools of thought associated with the following major theorists: William James, John B. Watson, and Carl Rogers. After you provide your answers, rate your confidence that the

information you just provided is correct. Now, write three reasons that your answers might be wrong and three reasons that they might be correct. Most people will balk at this exercise, arguing that they cannot think of any reasons that they might be wrong, but after some resistance, they can come up with several. Such reasons might include "I was half asleep when I read that part of the chapter" or "I might be confusing Watson and James." Reasons that you think you're right could include "I distinctly recall discussing this with my friend" or "I really worked on those names in Chapter 1." After listing reasons that you might be right and reasons that you might be wrong, rate your confidence in your accuracy once again. Guess what? Most people are less confident after going through such an exercise than they were before (depending, of course, on the nature of the topic).

The new confidence ratings tend to be more realistic than the original ratings (Koriat, Lichtenstein, & Fischhoff, 1980). Why? Because this exercise forces you to think more deeply about your answers and to search your memory for related information. Most people stop searching their memory as soon as they generate an answer they believe to be correct. Thus, the process of considering reasons that you might be wrong about something—a process that people rarely engage in—is a useful critical thinking skill that can reduce overconfidence effects. Better assessment of what you know and don't know can be an important determinant of the quality of the decisions you make and the way you solve problems and reason from evidence.

TABLE 7.1	**Critical Thinking Skills Discussed in This Application**
Skill	**Description**
Understanding the limitations	The critical thinker appreciates that memory is reconstructive and that even eyewitness accounts may be distorted or inaccurate.
Recognizing the bias in hindsight analysis	The critical thinker understands that knowing the outcome of events biases our recall and interpretation of the events.
Recognizing overconfidence in human cognition	The critical thinker understands that people are frequently overconfident about the accuracy of their projections for the future and their recollections of the past.
Understanding the need to seek disconfirming evidence	The critical thinker understands the value of thinking about how or why one might be wrong about something.

Key Ideas

Encoding: Getting Information into Memory

● The multifaceted process of memory begins with encoding. Attention, which facilitates encoding, is inherently selective and has been compared to a filter.

● According to levels-of-processing theory, the kinds of memory codes people create depend on which aspects of a stimulus are emphasized; deeper processing (i.e., semantic encoding) results in better recall of information. Structural, phonemic, and semantic encoding represent progressively deeper and more effective levels of processing.

● Elaboration enriches encoding by linking a stimulus to other information. Visual imagery may work in much the same way, creating two memory codes rather than just one. Encoding that emphasizes personal self-reference may be especially useful in facilitating retention.

Storage: Maintaining Information in Memory

● Sensory memory preserves information in its original form for only a fraction of a second. Short-term memory has a limited capacity (traditionally it was thought that STM was capable of holding about seven chunks of information, but more recent research suggests four) and can maintain unrehearsed information for up to about 20 seconds. Short-term memory is working memory and appears to involve more than a simple rehearsal loop.

● Long-term memory is an unlimited capacity store that may hold information indefinitely. Certain lines of evidence suggest that LTM storage may be permanent, but the evidence is not convincing. Some theorists have raised doubts about whether short-term and long-term memory are really separate.

● Information in LTM can be organized in simple clusters, conceptual hierarchies, or semantic networks. A schema is an organized cluster of knowledge about a particular object or sequence of events. PDP models of memory assert that specific memories correspond to particular patterns of activation in connectionist networks.

Retrieval: Getting Information Out of Memory

● Reinstating the context of an event can facilitate recall. This factor may account for cases in which hypnosis appears to aid recall. Memories are not exact replicas of past experiences. Memory is partially reconstructive.

● Research on the misinformation effect shows that information learned after an event can alter one's memory of it. Source-monitoring and reality-monitoring errors may explain why people sometimes "recall" something that was only suggested to them or something they only imagined.

Forgetting: When Memory Lapses

● Ebbinghaus's early studies of nonsense syllables suggested that people forget very rapidly. Subsequent research showed that Ebbinghaus's forgetting curve was exceptionally steep. Forgetting can be measured by asking people to recall, recognize, or relearn information.

● Decay theory proposes that forgetting occurs spontaneously with the passage of time. It has proven difficult to show that decay occurs in long-term memory. Interference theory proposes that people forget information because of competition from other material.

● Repression involves the motivated forgetting of painful or unpleasant memories. Recent years have seen a surge of reports of repressed memories of sexual abuse in childhood. The authenticity of these recovered memories is the subject of controversy.

In Search of the Memory Trace: The Physiology of Memory

● Memory traces may reflect alterations in neurotransmitter release at specific locations. Memory traces may also consist of localized neural circuits that undergo long-term potentiation. The study of amnesia and other research has implicated the hippocampal region as a key player in memory processes. The hippocampal region may be responsible for the consolidation of memories, but its exact role remains the subject of debate.

Systems and Types of Memory

● Differences between implicit and explicit memory suggest that people may have several separate memory systems. Declarative memory is memory for facts, whereas nondeclarative or procedural memory is memory for actions and skills. Declarative memory can be subdivided into episodic memory for personal facts, and semantic memory for general facts. Theorists have also distinguished between retrospective and prospective memory.

Putting It in Perspective: Themes 2, 4, and 7

● Our discussion of attention and memory enhances understanding of why people's experience of the world is highly subjective. Work in this area also highlights the field's theoretical diversity and shows that behaviour is governed by multiple causes.

PERSONAL APPLICATION • Improving Everyday Memory

● Rehearsal, even when it involves overlearning, facilitates retention, although one should be wary of the serial-position effect. Distributed practice tends to be more efficient than massed practice. It is wise to plan study sessions so as to minimize interference. Processing during rehearsal should be deep.

● Meaningfulness can be enhanced with verbal mnemonics such as acrostics, acronyms, and narrative methods. The link method, the method of loci, and the keyword method are mnemonic devices that depend on visual imagery.

CRITICAL THINKING APPLICATION • Understanding the Fallibility of Eyewitness Accounts

● Research indicates that eyewitness memory is not nearly as reliable or as accurate as widely believed. Two common errors in thinking that contribute to this situation are the hindsight bias and overconfidence effects. The hindsight bias is the tendency to reshape one's interpretation of the past to fit with known outcomes.

Key Terms

Anterograde amnesia, 332
Attention, 303
Chunk, 309
Clustering, 313
Conceptual hierarchy, 313
Connectionist models, 315
Consolidation, 332
Decay theory, 323
Declarative memory system, 334
Destination memory, 320
Dual-coding theory, 306
Elaboration, 305
Encoding, 302
Encoding specificity principle, 324
Episodic memory system, 335
Explicit memory, 334
Flashbulb memories, 311
Forgetting curve, 321
Hindsight bias, 344
Implicit memory, 334
Interference theory, 323
Keyword method, 343
Levels-of-processing theory, 305
Link method, 342
Long-term memory (LTM), 311
Long-term potentiation (LTP), 331
Method of loci, 342
Misinformation effect, 318
Mnemonic devices, 340
Nondeclarative memory system, 334
Overlearning, 340
Parallel distributed processing (PDP) models, 315
Proactive interference, 324
Procedural memory system, 334
Prospective memory, 338
Reality monitoring, 319
Recall, 322
Recognition, 322
Rehearsal, 308

Relearning, 322
Repression, 325
Retention, 322
Retrieval, 302
Retroactive interference, 323
Retrograde amnesia, 331
Retrospective memory, 338
Schema, 314
Self-referent encoding, 306
Semantic memory system, 336
Semantic network, 314
Sensory memory, 307
Serial-position effect, 340
Short-term memory (STM), 308
Source monitoring, 320
Source-monitoring error, 320
Storage, 302
Tip-of-the-tongue phenomenon, 316
Transfer-appropriate processing, 324
Working memory, 310
Working memory capacity (WMC), 311

Key People

Richard Atkinson, 307
Alan Baddeley, 310
Frederic Bartlett, 317
William Chase, 310
Fergus Craik, 305
Hermann Ebbinghaus, 322
Marcia Johnson, 320
Robert Lockhart, 305
Elizabeth Loftus, 319
George Miller, 309
Brenda Milner, 332
Daniel Schacter, 329
Richard Shiffrin, 307
Herbert Simon, 310
George Sperling, 308
Endel Tulving, 335

1. The cocktail party effect provides evidence for which of the following models regarding attention?
   A. early selection model
   B. late selection model
   C. attentional capacity model
   D. cognitive load model

2. The word *big* is flashed on a screen. If you were trying to remember that word by thinking "large," "huge," or "tall," what type of encoding would you be using?
   A. semantic
   B. structural
   C. phonemic
   D. procedural

3. Miles listens to his mother go over a list of about 15 things that he needs to pack for an upcoming trip. According to George Miller, how many items from the list will Miles likely remember if he does not write them down as he hears them?
   A. fewer than five items
   B. about 10 to 12 items
   C. all the items
   D. five to nine items

4. When you hear the word *exam* you also think about words like *study, books* or even *panic*. Which of the following terms is illustrated by this example?
   A. spreading activation
   B. misinformation effect
   C. conceptual hierarchy
   D. proactive interference

5. Which of the following is the name for an organized cluster of knowledge about a particular object or event?
   A. a semantic network
   B. a conceptual hierarchy
   C. a schema
   D. a retrieval cue

6. Which of the following reflects the current evidence about the use of hypnosis for memory retrieval?
   A. It increases the likelihood that subjects will report incorrect information.
   B. It increases the quality of recall but does not increase the volume of recalled information.
   C. It decreases the likelihood that subjects will be confident in their memories.
   D. It decreases the quality of recall, but increases the overall volume of recalled information.

7. Roberto tells Rachel some gossip, but she stops him and reminds him that she told him this story about a week ago. Which of the following describes what had happened to Roberto's memory?
   A. He made a destination memory error.
   B. He made a reality-monitoring error.
   C. He made a source-monitoring error.
   D. He made a prospective memory error.

8. Which of the following statements is correct for decay theory?
   A. Information can never be permanently lost from long-term memory.
   B. Forgetting is simply a case of retrieval failure.
   C. The principal cause of forgetting should be the passage of time.
   D. Forgetting occurs due to overuse of the synapses associated with a memory.

9. Recently traded to a new football team, Bulldog McRae struggles to remember the plays for his new team because he mixes these up with the plays from his previous team. Which of the following phenomena is illustrated by Bulldog's problem?
   A. retroactive interference
   B. proactive interference
   C. transfer-inappropriate processing
   D. parallel distributed processing

10. If a patient is diagnosed with anterograde amnesia as a result of brain damage, which of the following processes will be most impaired?
    A. retrieval of past declarative memories
    B. consolidation of new declarative memories
    C. performance of motor skills that were learned years before the damage
    D. learning of new motor skills after the damage

11. How to brush your teeth is stored as which type of memory?
    A. declarative
    B. procedural
    C. structural
    D. episodic

12. Which of the following types of memory contains your knowledge that the sun rises in the east, that 2 + 2 = 4, and that birds fly?
    A. declarative
    B. procedural
    C. implicit
    D. episodic

13. Although Dorothy memorized her shopping list, when she got to the store, she forgot many of the items from the middle of the list. Which of the following describes what happened to Dorothy's memory?
    A. inappropriate encoding
    B. retrograde amnesia
    C. proactive interference
    D. the serial-position effect

14. Tessa is trying to memorize parts of the brain by associating each part with a room in her house. Which mnemonic method is Tessa using?
    A. the method of loci
    B. the link method
    C. the keyword method
    D. the method of narrative

15. Which of the following is the correct name for the tendency to mould one's interpretation of the past to fit the way events actually turned out?
    A. overconfidence effect
    B. selective amnesia
    C. retroactive interference
    D. hindsight bias

See Appendix A for answers to this Practice Test.

On the Web

▶ **CourseMate**

Go to this site to find online resources directly linked to your book, including more quizzes, a glossary, flash cards, videos, and more!

▶ **CengageNow**

Go to this site for the link to CengageNOW™, your one-stop study shop. Take a pre-test for this chapter and CengageNOW™ will generate a personalized study plan based on your test results! The study plan will identify the topics you need to review and direct you to online resources to help you master those topics. You can then take a post-test to help you determine the concepts you have mastered and what you still need to work on.

▶ **Aplia**

Aplia™ is an online interactive learning solution that helps you improve comprehension—and your grade—by integrating a variety of media and tools such as video, tutorials, practice tests, and interactive e-book.

Courtesy of Debbie Steel

CHAPTER 8

Language and Thought

On October 17, 1968, Prime Minister Pierre Elliott Trudeau introduced legislation, the Official Languages Bill, that he believed reflected the reality of the Canadian experience and that he hoped would promote Canadian unity in the context of its diversity. He suggested that both French and English should be official languages of Canada. This was essential, he argued, because both language groups were "strong enough in numbers and in material and intellectual resources to resist the forces of assimilation . . . this underlying reality of our country has not been adequately reflected in many of our public institutions" (Library and Archives Canada, 2002). The bill became law in July 1969. It manifested the recommendations of an earlier Royal Commission on Bilingualism and Biculturalism (1963) established by then–prime minister and Nobel Prize winner Lester B. Pearson (McCrae, 1998). On becoming officially bilingual, Canada joined a small set of countries around the world such as Finland, Sweden, Belgium, South Africa, and Afghanistan that have more than one official language. The themes begun in the Official Languages Bill were continued in the later Canadian Charter of Rights and Freedoms (1982) and then in the Official Languages Act (1988). The implications of the bill were far-reaching—socially, culturally, economically, politically, and educationally.

The opportunity to be educated in either or both of Canada's official languages is now well established. For example, many English-speaking students begin their primary school years not in English but in French immersion programs. Interestingly, French immersion began in Quebec in 1965 when a group of anglophone parents, concerned with the inadequate French language instruction their children were receiving, recommended a program of instruction that formed the basis for current immersion programs (Genesee, 1998). They had sociocultural and economic benefits in mind for their children and Canada.

The motivations underlying and challenges encountered in enrolling children in French immersion are varied and considerable—one of us knows this first-hand, having had children in immersion. While immersion programs will not make you completely bilingual—you are not living full-time in both languages—there are advantages to be derived from bilingualism and immersion education in a second language. Recent research by developmental psychologist Ellen Bialystok and others suggests that there may be additional cognitive benefits. These are discussed on pages 357–359.

In this chapter, we will look more closely at the potential cognitive benefits of bilingualism but before that we will consider the nature of language and language development in children in general. We will have to place the learning of two languages in the context of what we know about how children acquire language more generally.

Of course, bilingualism refers to more than just proficiency in English and French. Many students in Canada also have access to other heritage languages. After English and French, the languages most frequently spoken in Canada are Spanish, German, Italian, Hindi, Arabic, Chinese, Russian, and Hebrew (Office of Commissioner of Official Languages, 2004).

We will also consider the nature of cognition itself, a task we began in Chapter 7. Cognition and language are closely linked, as we will discuss later in the chapter. *Cognition* refers to the mental processes involved in acquiring knowledge. In other words, cognition involves thinking. As we discussed in Chapter 1, the study of cognition has seen peaks and valleys in psychology. When psychology first emerged, it focused on the mind and the research method of choice was *introspection*. But the limitations of that method and the rise of behaviourism, with its focus on observables (have you ever seen a thought?), led to the demise of cognition as a serious scientific topic. It was not until

Pierre Elliott Trudeau, prime minister of Canada (1968–1979 and 1980–1984), was a champion of bilingualism.

Penelope Breese/Getty Images

the 1950s that the study of cognition came back, an era often referred to as the "cognitive revolution" (Baars, 1986).

Besides memory, which we discussed in Chapter 7, cognitive psychologists investigate the complexities of language, inference, problem solving, decision making, and reasoning (e.g., Evans, 2008; Hayes, Heit, & Swendsen, 2010; Kruglanski & Orehek, 2007). We look at all of these topics in this chapter. Of course, this will not finish our consideration of cognition, since it overlaps with many other topics we will deal with later in the book, including developmental psychology (Chapter 11), clinical psychology (Chapter 14), and social psychology (Chapter 16).

Language: Turning Thoughts into Words

PREVIEW QUESTIONS

▶ What are the four key properties of language?

▶ How is language structured?

▶ How do children progress in their use of words and sentences?

▶ What types of mistakes do they tend to make?

▶ Does learning two languages at the same time affect language or cognitive development?

▶ What age is best for learning a second language?

Language obviously plays a fundamental role in human behaviour. Indeed, if you were to ask people, "What characteristic most distinguishes humans from other living creatures?" a great many would reply, "Language." In this section, we'll discuss the nature, structure, and development of language and related topics, such as bilingualism and whether animals can learn language.

What Is Language?

A *language* consists of symbols that convey meaning, plus rules for combining those symbols, that can be used to generate an infinite variety of messages. Language systems include a number of critical properties.

First, language is *symbolic*. People use spoken sounds and written words to represent objects, actions, events, and ideas. Symbols allow us to refer to objects that may be in another place and to events that happened at another time (e.g., a lamp broken at work yesterday). Language symbols are flexible in that a variety of somewhat different objects may be called by the same name (consider the diversity of lamps, for example).

Second, language is *semantic,* or meaningful. The symbols used in a language are arbitrary in that no built-in relationship exists between the look or sound of words and the objects they stand for. Take, for instance, the writing object that you may have in your hand right now. It's represented by the word *pen* in English, *stylo* in French, and *pluma* in Spanish. Although these words are arbitrary (others could have been chosen), they have *shared meanings* for people who speak English, French, and Spanish.

Third, language is *generative*. A limited number of symbols can be combined in an infinite variety of ways to *generate* an endless array of novel messages. Every day you create sentences that you have never spoken before. You also comprehend many sentences that you have never encountered before (like this one).

Fourth, language is *structured*. Although people can generate an infinite variety of sentences, these sentences must be structured in a limited number of ways. Rules govern the arrangement of words into phrases and sentences; some arrangements are acceptable and some are not. Let's take a closer look at the structural properties of language.

The Structure of Language

Human languages have a hierarchical structure (Ratner, Gleason, & Narasimhan, 1998). As Figure 8.1 shows, basic sounds are combined into units with meaning, which are combined into words. Words are combined into phrases, which are combined into sentences.

Phonemes

At the base of the language hierarchy are *phonemes, the smallest speech units in a language that can be distinguished perceptually.* Considering that an unabridged English dictionary contains more than 450 000 words, you might imagine that there must be a huge number of phonemes. In fact, linguists estimate that humans are capable of recognizing only about 100 such basic sounds. Moreover, no one language uses all of these phonemes. Different languages use different groups of about 20 to 80 phonemes.

For all its rich vocabulary, the English language is composed of about 40 phonemes, corresponding roughly to the 26 letters of the alphabet plus several variations (see Table 8.1). A letter in the alphabet can represent more than one phoneme if it has more than one pronunciation. For example, the letter *a* is pronounced differently in the words *father, had, call,* and *take.* Each of these pronunciations corresponds to a different phoneme. In addition, some phonemes are represented by combinations of letters, such as *ch* and *th.* Working with this handful of basic sounds, people can understand and generate all of the words in the English language—and invent new ones.

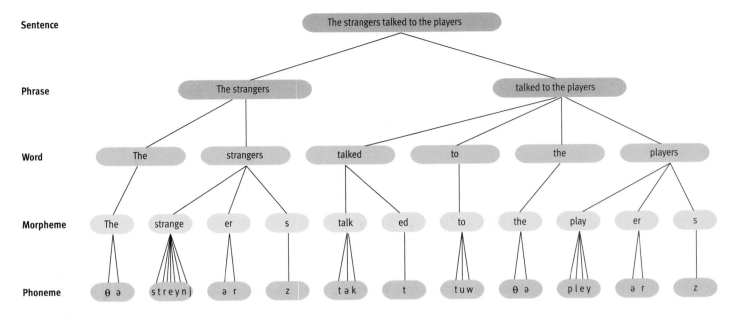

FIGURE 8.1

An analysis of a simple English sentence.

As this example shows, verbal language has a hierarchical structure. At the base of the hierarchy are the *phonemes,* which are units of vocal sound that do not, in themselves, have meaning. The smallest units of meaning in a language are *morphemes,* which include not only root words but also such meaning-carrying units as the past-tense suffix *ed* and the plural *s.* Complex rules of syntax govern how the words constructed from morphemes may be combined into phrases, and phrases into meaningful statements, or sentences.

Source: Clarke-Stewart, A., S. Friedman, S., and Koch, J. 1985. *Child development: A topical approach* (p. 417). Copyright © 1985. Reproduced with permission from John Wiley & Sons, Inc.

Morphemes and Semantics

Morphemes are the smallest units of meaning in a language. There are approximately 50 000 English morphemes, which include root words as well as prefixes and suffixes. Many words, such as *fire, guard,* and *friend,* consist of a single morpheme. Many others represent combinations of morphemes. For example, the word *unfriendly* consists of three morphemes: the root word *friend,* the prefix *un,* and the suffix *ly.* Each of the morphemes contributes to the meaning of the entire word. *Semantics* is the area of language concerned with understanding the meaning of words and word combinations. Learning about semantics entails learning about the infinite variety of objects and actions that words refer to. A word's meaning may consist of both its *denotation,* which is its dictionary definition, and its *connotation,* which includes its emotional overtones and secondary implications.

Syntax

Of course, most utterances consist of more than a single word. As we've already noted, people don't combine words randomly. *Syntax* is a system of rules that specify how words can be arranged into sentences. A simple rule of syntax is that a sentence must have both a *subject* and a *verb.* Thus, "The sound

annoyed me" is a sentence. However, "The sound" is not a sentence, because it lacks a verb.

Rules of syntax underlie all language use, even though you may not be aware of them. Thus, although they may not be able to verbalize the rule, virtually all English speakers know that an *article* (such as *the*) comes before the word it modifies. For example, you would never say *swimmer the* instead of *the swimmer.* How children learn the complicated rules of syntax is one of the major puzzles investigated by psychologists interested in language. Like

Consonants						Vowels			
/p/	p̲ill	/t/	t̲oe	/g/	g̲ill	/i/	b̲ee̲t	/i/	b̲i̲t
/b/	b̲ill	/d/	d̲oe	/ŋ/	ri̲n̲g	/e/	ba̲i̲t	/ɛ/	be̲t
/m/	m̲ill	/n/	n̲o	/h/	h̲ot	/u/	bo̲o̲t	/u/	fo̲o̲t
/f/	f̲ine	/s/	s̲ink	/ʔ/	u̲h̲-o̲h̲	/o/	bo̲a̲t	/ɔ/	ca̲u̲ght
/v/	v̲ine	/z/	z̲inc	/l/	l̲ow	/æ/	ba̲t	/a/	po̲t
/θ/	th̲igh	/č/	ch̲oke	/r/	r̲ow	/ʌ/	bu̲t	/ə/	s̲ofa
/ð/	th̲y	/ǰ/	j̲oke	/y/	y̲ou	/ar/	bi̲te	/au/	o̲u̲t
/š/	sh̲oe	/k/	k̲ill	/w/	w̲in	/ɔɪ/	bo̲y		
/ž/	trea̲s̲ure								

TABLE 8.1

Phonemic Symbols for the Sounds of English

Source: Hoff, E. (2001). *Language development.* Belmont, CA: Wadsworth. Reprinted by permission.

Language and Thought

other aspects of language development, children's acquisition of syntax seems to progress at an amazingly rapid pace. Let's look at how this remarkable development unfolds.

Milestones in Language Development

Learning to use language requires learning a number of skills that become important at various points in a child's development (Siegler, 1998). We'll examine this developmental sequence by looking first at how children learn to pronounce words, then at their use of single words, and finally at their ability to combine words to form sentences (see Table 8.2).

Moving toward Producing Words

Three-month-old infants display a surprising language-related talent: They can distinguish phonemes from all of the world's languages, including phonemes that they do not hear in their environment. In contrast, adults cannot readily discriminate phonemes that are not used in their native language. Actually, neither can one-year-old children, as this curious ability gradually disappears between four months and 12 months of age (Kuhl et al., 2008;

Werker & Tees, 1999). The exact mechanisms responsible for this transition are not understood, but it is clear that long before infants utter their first words, they are making remarkable progress in learning the sound structure of their native language (Mugitani et al., 2007). Progress toward recognizing whole words also occurs during the first year. Although they don't know what the words mean yet, by around eight months, infants begin to recognize and store common word forms (Swingley, 2008).

Janet Werker, a senior scientist at the University of British Columbia, has done pioneering work in the development of language in infants (Curtin, Byers-Heinlein, & Werker, 2011; Fais & Werker, in press; Gervain et al., 2011). She argues that human infants are well prepared to learn language and that babies have perceptual biases that facilitate and guide the "acquisition of phonology" (Werker, 2003). For example, even at two months, they show a tendency to selectively attend more to speech sounds than to complex nonspeech analogue sounds (Vouloumanos & Werker, 2004). Some of these perceptual biases that facilitate language acquisition may be derived from listening to speech *in utero*. In her recent work, Werker has turned to examining the acquisition of language by babies growing up in bilingual homes (Fennell, Byers-Heinlein, & Werker, 2007; Werker & Byers-Heinlein, 2008). Werker suggests that these perceptual sensitivities assist infants in separating their two languages even before they begin to speak them and that "we are as well equipped to learn two languages as we are one" (Werker & Byers-Heinlein, 2008, p. 149).

Werker argues that there are *optimal periods* for the different subsystems involved in language acquisition but that they are not as rigidly absolute as is

Age	General Characteristics
Months	
1–5	Reflexive communication: Vocalizes randomly, coos, laughs, cries, engages in vocal play, discriminates language from nonlanguage sounds
6–18	Babbling: Verbalizes in response to the speech of others; responses increasingly approximate human speech patterns
10–13	First words: Uses words, typically to refer to objects
12–18	One-word sentence stage: Vocabulary grows slowly; uses nouns primarily; overextensions begin
18–24	Vocabulary spurt: Fast mapping facilitates rapid acquisition of new words
Years	
2	Two-word sentence stage: Uses telegraphic speech; uses more pronouns and verbs
2.5	Three-word sentence stage: Modifies speech to take listener into account; overregularizations begin
3	Uses complete simple active sentence structure; uses sentences to tell stories that are understood by others; uses plurals
3.5	Expanded grammatical forms: Expresses concepts with words; uses four-word sentences
4	Uses five-word sentences
5	Well-developed and complex syntax: Uses more complex syntax; uses more complex forms to tell stories
6	Displays metalinguistic awareness

TABLE 8.2

Overview of Typical Language Development

Note: Children often show individual differences in the exact ages at which they display the various developmental achievements outlined here.

Janet Werker, Canada Research Chair in Psychology at the University of British Columbia, examines early processes involved in the acquisition of languages in infants. She was elected as a Fellow of the Royal Society of Canada in 2001.

Photo by Christine Dietrich, Photo courtesy of Janet Werker

sometimes thought (she prefers the term *optimal period* to terms such as *critical period* or *sensitive period* because the latter imply more invariance in the onset and offset of the periods; Werker & Tees, 2005). Thus, while very young infants can discriminate even phonemes not inherent in their language context, this facility disappears without exposure. As they develop through the first year of life, the language acquisition systems of the infant become tuned to the speech properties of their native language. Recently, Werker has developed a model of infant speech processing called PRIMIR (Processing Rich Information from Multidimensional Interactive Representations; Werker & Curtin, 2005).

During the first six months of life, a baby's vocalizations are dominated by crying, cooing, and laughter, which have limited value as a means of communication. Soon, infants are *babbling*, producing a wide variety of sounds that correspond to phonemes and, eventually, many repetitive consonant–vowel combinations, such as "lalalalalala." Babbling gradually becomes more complex and increasingly resembles the language spoken by parents and others in the child's environment (Hoff, 2005). Babbling lasts until around 18 months, continuing even after children utter their first words. According to Laura-Ann Petitto, babbling is considered to be one of the monumental milestones in language acquisition (Petitto et al., 2004). Interestingly, Petitto began her scientific work on language working with chimps. She lived with a chimpanzee while trying to teach it American Sign Language (ASL) (National Institute on Deafness, 2002).

While most agree that babbling is a universal stage in language acquisition, there is considerable

Laura-Ann Petitto is a University of Toronto psychologist who conducts research on various aspects of children's language acquisition.

Courtesy of Laura Petitto

disagreement about its origins. One view is that babbling is a motor achievement in which the babbling reflects the brain's maturation in controlling the motor operations needed to eventually produce speech—in essence, developing and practising the mechanics of speech. Here, the babbling is a by-product of the development of the brain and its control over motor operations. An alternative view is that it is a key linguistic achievement, a mechanism that affords the infant the opportunity to both discover and produce the "patterned structure of natural language" (Petitto et al., 2004, p. 44). Thus, babbling allows the infant to acquire the basics of language. Petitto and her colleagues have conducted a series of studies that support the latter interpretation.

Some of these studies were conducted in Montreal with normal and deaf babies. Petitto found that the deaf babies exhibited "manual babbling"—babbling with their hands in a manner similar to the verbal babbling of hearing babies (Petitto & Marentette, 1991). She also found that the deaf babies' first "signed words" were continuous with their babbling—much like a baby who verbally babbles "bababa" and whose first word is "baby" (Vihman, 1985). This study is the focus of our Featured Study.

Using Words

The first year of life is critical in the child's acquisition of language (Gervain & Mehler, 2010). At around 10 to 13 months of age, most children begin to utter sounds that correspond to words. Most infants' first words are similar in phonetic form and meaning—even in different languages (Waxman, 2002). The initial words resemble the syllables that infants most often babble spontaneously. For example, words such as *dada*, *mama*, and *papa* are names for parents in many languages because they consist of sounds that are easy to produce.

After children utter their first words, their vocabulary grows slowly for the next few months (Dapretto & Bjork, 2000). Toddlers typically can say between 3 and 50 words by 18 months. However, their *receptive vocabulary* is larger than their *productive vocabulary*. That is, they can comprehend more words spoken by others than they can actually produce to express themselves (Pan & Uccelli, 2009). Thus, toddlers can *understand* 50 words months before they can *say* 50 words. Toddlers' early words tend to refer most often to *objects* and secondarily to *social actions* (Camaioni, 2001). Children probably acquire nouns before verbs because the meanings of nouns, which often refer to distinct, concrete objects, tend to be easier to encode than the meanings of verbs, which often refer to more abstract relationships (Poulin-Dubois & Graham, 2007). However, this

Language and Thought

Investigators: Laura-Ann Petitto (McGill University) and Paula F. Marentette (McGill University)
Source: Babbling in the manual mode: Evidence for the ontogeny of language. *Science*, 1991, *251*, 1493–1496.

Babbling in the Manual Mode

The authors begin by reviewing the importance of babbling in the infant's language development and the prevailing view that babbling is a function of the continuing maturation of both the vocal tract and the neurophysiological mechanisms that are related to the mechanical production of speech. The authors support an alternative view, one that sees babbling as a function of the developing language capacity of the infant. Thus, babbling doesn't reflect so much the developing motor portions of the brain but rather reflects the maturation of the language capacity controlled by the brain. They note that it is difficult to test which view is the more correct one and offered an innovative solution: There are complex and sophisticated language forms that don't depend on speech, such as American Sign Language, a language form used by the deaf. Their hypothesis was "If babbling is due to the maturation of a language capacity and the articulatory mechanisms responsible for speech production, then it should be specific to speech. However, if babbling is due to the maturation of a brain-based language capacity and an expressive capacity capable of processing different types of signals, then it should occur in spoken and signed language modalities" (p. 1493).

Participants. The participants in this research consisted of five infants: two profoundly deaf infants of deaf parents acquiring American Sign Language as a first language, and three hearing infants acquiring spoken language.

Method. Each was tested and videotaped at 10, 12, and 14 months. All acoustic forms and sounds (for the hearing children) and manual activities (for the deaf children) were transcribed/videotaped and analyzed. To count as babbling, the same criteria were applied to the hearing and deaf children's utterances. For example, all utterances (vocal/hearing, manual/deaf) that were not words were examined for systematic organization. If this was found, further analysis was conducted to determine if the organization had phonetic and syllabic features common to spoken languages.

Results. The analysis of the babbling of the infants was clear. While all infants moved their arms and hands and gestured, only the deaf infants showed evidence of manual babbling. The results for manual babbling are shown in Figure 8.2. The manual babbling accounted for 32 percent to 71 percent of the manual activity of the deaf infants but accounted for only 4 percent to 15 percent of the hearing children's manual activity. The manual babbling of the

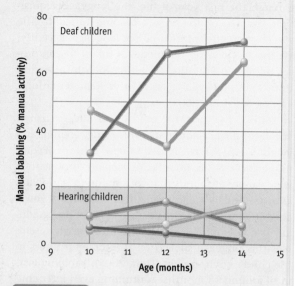

FIGURE 8.2

Manual babbling.

Manual babbling as a percentage of manual activity [manual babbling/(manual babbling + gesture)]. The required ratio is 20 percent (line) syllabic to total vocal utterances for children to be classed in the syllabic vocal babbling stage of language acquisition (7). The deaf children met and surpassed this ratio in their manual babbling, but the hearing children did not. Each line represents the manual babbling of one child in the study.

Source: From Petitto, L.A., and Marentette, P.F. (1991). Babbling in the manual mode: Evidence for the ontogeny of language. *Science 251*, 1493–1496. Copyright © 1991 AAAS. Reprinted with permission from AAAS.

deaf infants exhibited most of the other properties demonstrated by the hearing children in their babbling. For example, the deaf infants progressed through a similar set of babbling stages as was observed for hearing babies and at the same time course. As with hearing babies, the babbling of the deaf infants used only a subset of the possible phonetic units available in the language (American Sign Language). These are shown in Figure 8.3.

Discussion

The results of the study were quite convincing and clear. Deaf infants who are exposed to sign language babble like hearing babies, but they babble manually in their own

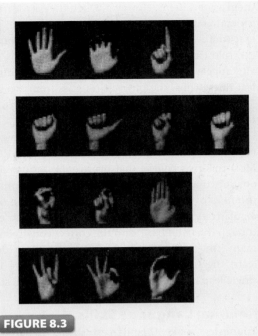

FIGURE 8.3

Handshape primes.

The 13 handshape primes produced by the deaf children in their manual babbling. The last handshape in the second row (handshape A4) does not occur in adult ASL; it is a possible but nonexistent phrase.

Source: From Petitto, L.A., and Marentette, P.F. (1991). Babbling in the manual mode: Evidence for the ontogeny of language. *Science 251*, 1493–1496. Copyright © 1991 AAAS. Reprinted with permission from AAAS.

language form. This suggests the conclusion that babbling is not simply a function of development of motor mechanisms but is instead tied to the developing language capacity of the infant.

Comment

This research was featured because it provides an interesting and convincing demonstration of one of the milestones of language development—babbling. It is a highly innovative study, using a novel procedure to test some of the ideas underlying the nature and meaning of babbling. It is a very significant study in the area and was published in the highly prestigious journal *Science*.

Petitto has also been examining what she refers to as an "island of tissue" in the brain that may trigger language development in children and the parts of the brain responsible for processing activities related to signed languages (Petitto, 1994) in the brain (American Psychological Association, 1998; Petitto et al., 2000). Petitto is now director of the Genes, Mind, and fNIRS Brain-Imaging Laboratory for Language, Bilingualism, and Child Development at the University of Toronto and is continuing her work on babbling and more recently on bilingualism. She is a major contributor to research on language development (Pettito, 209; Shalinky et al., 2009). You can learn more about her research program by visiting her website at http://www.utsc.utoronto.ca/~petitto.

---

generalization may not apply to all languages (Bates, Devescovi, & Wulfeck et al., 2001).

Most youngsters' vocabularies soon begin to grow at a dizzying pace, as a *vocabulary spurt* often begins at around 18–24 months (Bates & Carnevale, 1993; Camaioni, 2001; see Figure 8.4). By Grade 1, the average child has a vocabulary of approximately 10 000 words, which builds to an astonishing 40 000 words by Grade 5 (Anglin, 1993; see Figure 8.5). In building these impressive vocabularies, some two-year-olds learn as many as 20 new words every week. *Fast mapping* appears to be one factor underlying this rapid growth of vocabulary (Carey, 2010; Gershkoff-Stowe & Hahn, 2007). *Fast mapping* is the process by which children map a word onto an underlying concept after only one exposure. Thus, children often add words like *tank, board,* and *tape* to their vocabularies after their first encounter with objects that illustrate these concepts. The vocabulary spurt may be attributable to children's improved articulation skills, improved understanding of syntax, underlying cognitive development, or some combination of these factors (MacWhinney, 1998).

Of course, these efforts to learn new words are not flawless. Toddlers often make errors, such as

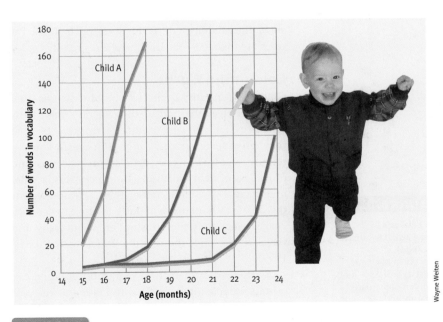

FIGURE 8.4

The vocabulary spurt.

Children typically acquire their first 10–15 words very slowly, but they soon go through a vocabulary spurt—a period during which they rapidly acquire many new words. The vocabulary spurt usually begins at around 18–24 months, but children vary, as these graphs of three toddlers' vocabulary growth show.

Source: Adapted from Goldfield, B. A., and Resnick, J. S. (1990). Early lexical acquisition: Rate, content, and the vocabulary spurt. *Journal of Child Language, 17,* 171–183. Copyright © 1990 by Cambridge University Press. Adapted by permission.

FIGURE 8.5

The growth of school children's vocabulary.

Vocabulary growth is rapid during the early years of grade school. Youngsters' estimated vocabulary doubles about every two years between Grade 1 and Grade 5.

Source: Anglin, J.M. (1993). Vocabulary development: A morphological analysis. *Child Development, 58*, Serial 238. Copyright © 1993 The Society for Research in Child Development. Reprinted by permission.

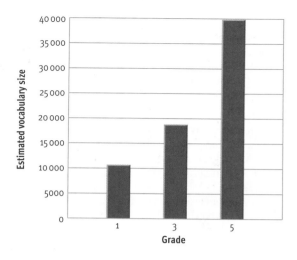

overextensions and underextensions (Harley, 2008). An *overextension* occurs when a child incorrectly uses a word to describe a wider set of objects or actions than it is meant to. For example, a child might use the word *ball* for anything round— oranges, apples, even the moon. Overextensions usually appear in children's speech between ages one and two-and-a-half. Specific overextensions typically last up to several months. Toddlers also tend to be guilty of *underextensions*, which occur when a child incorrectly uses a word to describe a narrower set of objects or actions than it is meant to. For example, a child might use the word *doll* to refer only to a single, favourite doll. Overextensions and underextensions show that toddlers are actively trying to learn the rules of language—albeit with mixed success.

Combining Words

Children typically begin to combine words into sentences near the end of their second year. Early sentences are characterized as *telegraphic* because they resemble telegrams. *Telegraphic speech* consists mainly of content words; articles, prepositions, and other less critical words are omitted. Thus, a child might say, "Give doll" rather than "Please give me the doll." Although not unique to the English language, telegraphic speech is not cross-culturally universal, as was once thought (de Villiers & de Villiers, 1999).

By the end of their third year, most children can express complex ideas such as the plural or the past tense. However, their efforts to learn the rules of language continue to generate revealing mistakes. *Overregularizations* occur when grammatical rules are incorrectly generalized to irregular cases where they do not apply. For example, children will say things like "The girl goed home" or "I hitted the ball." Typically, children initially use the correct noun, verb, or adjective forms, because they acquired

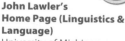

WEB LINK 8.1

John Lawler's Home Page (Linguistics & Language)
University of Michigan linguistics professor John Lawler has constructed a seemingly endless guide to Internet resources for the study of linguistics and language, a field allied with psychology. His home page is a gold mine of references and guides.

them as new items. However, when they are learning general grammatical rules (such as for plurals), they extend the rules to nouns that are exceptions to the rule (such as "foots"). Overregularizations usually appear after children begin to learn grammatical rules. Thus, the progression goes from "feet" to "foots" and back to "feet" when children have further mastered grammatical rules.

Cross-cultural research suggests that these overregularizations occur in all languages (Slobin, 1985). Most theorists believe that overregularizations demonstrate that children are working actively to master the *rules* of language (Marcus, 1996). Specific overregularizations often linger in a child's speech even though the child has heard the correct constructions many times (Maslen et al., 2004). Children don't learn the fine points of grammar and usage in a single leap but gradually acquire them in small steps.

Refining Language Skills

Youngsters make their largest strides in language development in their first four to five years. However, they continue to refine their language skills during their school-age years. They generate longer and more complicated sentences as they receive formal training in written language.

As their language skills develop, school-age children begin to appreciate ambiguities in language. They can, for instance, recognize two possible meanings in sentences such as "Visiting relatives can be bothersome." This interest in ambiguities indicates that they're developing *metalinguistic awareness—the ability to reflect on the use of language.* As metalinguistic awareness grows, children begin to "play" with language, coming up with puns and jokes. They begin to make more frequent and sophisticated use of metaphors, such as "We were packed in the room like sardines" (Gentner, 1988).

Between the ages of six and eight, most children begin to appreciate irony and sarcasm (Creusere, 1999). *Irony* involves conveying an implied meaning that is the opposite of a statement's literal meaning (on learning that he got a D on an exam, a student says, "Oh, that's just great"). *Sarcasm* is a variation on irony in which there is a caustic element directed at a particular person (commenting on a blunder by her husband, a woman says, "My husband, the genius").

Learning More Than One Language: Bilingualism

Given the complexities involved in acquiring one language, you may be wondering about the ramifications of being asked to learn *two* languages.

Bilingualism is the acquisition of two languages that use different speech sounds, vocabulary, and grammatical rules. Although not the norm in North America, bilingualism is quite common in Europe and many other regions, and nearly half of the world's population grows up bilingual (Hakuta, 1986; Snow, 1998). One assumption that some people have is that bilingualism hampers language development and has a negative impact on youngsters' educational progress. But does the empirical evidence support this assumption? Research on the topic of bilingualism is an extremely active area (Bialystok, 2010a, 2010b; Deuchar, 2008; Diamond, 2010); let's take a look at some of the recent research on bilingualism.

Does Learning Two Languages in Childhood Slow Down Language Development?

If youngsters are learning two languages simultaneously, does one language interfere with the other so that the acquisition of both is impeded? Given the far-reaching sociopolitical implications of this question, you might guess that many relevant studies have been conducted, but in reality there is only a modest body of research. Some studies *have* found that bilingual children have smaller vocabularies in each of their languages than monolingual children have in their one language (Umbel et al., 1992). But when their two overlapping vocabularies are added, their total vocabulary is similar or slightly superior to that of children learning a single language (Oller & Pearson, 2002).

Laura-Ann Petitto, whose research we looked at in our discussion of babbling, has studied children acquiring English and French and children acquiring French and the sign language "langues des signes Québécoise" (Petitto et al., 2001). She concluded that there was little evidence of language disadvantage. The bilingual children followed the normal pacing of language milestones, except in this case it was accomplished in *both* languages. Children seem to be adept at differentiating between the two languages before their first words appear (Petitto & Kovelman, 2003). Taken as a whole, the available evidence suggests that bilingual and monolingual children are largely similar in the course and rate of their language development (De Houwer, 1995; Nicoladis & Genesee, 1997). Thus, although more research is needed, so far there is little empirical support for the assumption that bilingualism has a negative effect on language development (Hoff, 2005). Moreover, recent research suggests that learning two languages can subsequently facilitate the acquisition of a third language. Comparisons of bilingual and monolingual subjects suggest that bilinguals are better language learners—that the experience of becoming bilingual can enhance the learning of another language (Kaushanskaya & Marian, 2009).

Does Bilingualism Affect Cognitive Processes and Skills?

Does knowing two languages make thinking more difficult, or could bilingualism enhance thought processes? While the evidence is somewhat mixed, depending on the variables measured and the exact nature of the subject populations that are compared, research suggests that bilingualism conveys some cognitive advantages that at least argue for the need for additional research on the topic. On some types of tasks, bilinguals may have a slight disadvantage in terms of raw language-processing *speed* (Taylor & Taylor, 1990). When middle-class bilingual subjects who are fluent in both languages are studied, they tend to score somewhat *higher* than monolingual subjects on measures of cognitive flexibility, analytical reasoning, selective attention, and metalinguistic awareness (Bialystok, 1999; Campbell & Sais, 1995; Lambert, 1990).

The issue of the potential cognitive benefits of bilingualism has been at the centre of Ellen Bialystok's recent research. Bialystok, of York University, has been examining the effects of bilingualism on children's cognition for many years. She suggests that there are some cognitive advantages to bilingualism for both children and adults. Her work has been guided by three hypotheses that have been supported by the results of research conducted in the past few years (Bialystok, 2007). First, since cognitive

The utility of bilingual education programs has been a hotly debated issue across Canada. Critics argue that bilingualism has a negative effect on children's language and cognitive development, but there is relatively little empirical support for this assertion. Recent research suggests that bilingualism may have some cognitive benefits.

executive processes are necessary to deal successfully with the use of two languages, she suggests that bilingual children should develop control over executive processes earlier than monolingual children. They are related, in part, to our ability to control attention. Second, that as adults, the enhanced executive control characteristic of bilinguals should afford them advantages in cognitive tasks implicating executive processing. Finally, since executive processes are one of the first cognitive abilities to decline with age, bilinguals, because of their "continued reliance" on executive processes for dealing with their two languages, should show delayed decline relative to monolingual adults.

Bialystok (2001) has found that bilingualism is associated with higher levels of controlled processing on tasks that require control of attention. That is, bilingual children demonstrate greater facility at tasks where there is some type of misleading/distracting information and where response choice is involved. This makes sense, given the tasks that typically confront a bilingual individual. According to Kroll (2008; Kroll, Bobb, & Wodniecka, 2006), the evidence suggests that even when bilinguals are reading, listening, or speaking in one language, both languages remain active. She further suggests that bilinguals not only are proficient at two languages, but that they also develop the cognitive control ability to "juggle" the two languages relatively easily. This is an important task because, as shown by Mark Howe and his colleagues at the University of British Columbia and the University of Manitoba (Howe, Gagnon, & Thouas, 2008), as bilinguals become more proficient in the second language, their conceptual stores for both languages overlap more and more. Cognitive skills related to this ability to "juggle" two languages may be partially responsible for the cognitive benefits of bilingualism documented in the work of Bialystok (e.g., Bialystok, 2007).

According to Bialystok, some of the executive processes implicated in these differences between bilingual and monolingual children are those involving selective attention, attentional inhibition to distracting/misleading information, and switching among competing alternatives. Bilingual children don't have an advantage on all tasks; they show an advantage on some aspects of metalinguistic awareness but not for phonemic awareness (Bialystok, Majumder, & Martin, 2003). Bilingual and monolingual children perform similarly on tasks involving representational processes, such as encoding problems in sufficient detail and gaining access to relevant information (Bialystok, 1991).

This research suggests that while bilingualism may not confer an advantage in all aspects of cognitive and linguistic processing, it is important to note that there are some documented advantages and few demonstrated disadvantages—even for children with some specific language impairments, as was found in a recent study by Johanne Paradis of the University of Alberta (Paradis et al., 2003), or those with more general below-average ability levels (Genesee, 2004). Another consideration is derived from the results of some of Bialystok's more recent work on bilingualism and aging, conducted with a team of psychologists at York University, Dalhousie University, and the University of Toronto (Bialystok et al., 2004). Here, Bialystok and her colleagues found that the advantage conferred by bilingualism on controlled processing persists into adulthood and old age, suggesting that bilingualism may help attenuate age-related losses in certain aspects of cognition (Bialystok & Craik, 2010; Craik & Bialystok, 2008, 2010). For example, one influential study focused on people suffering from *dementia* (severe impairment of memory and cognitive functioning). It found that bilingual patients experienced the onset of dementia four years later, on average, than comparable monolingual patients (Bialystok, Craik, & Freedman, 2007). Bialystok notes that one of the objectives of her research was to determine if bilingualism "would provide a defense against the decline of these executive processes that occurs with normal cognitive aging . . . the present results suggest that it does" (Bialystok et al., 2004, p. 301). In 2010, she was awarded a Killam Prize for her work; the $100 000 Killam prize is one of the most prestigious academic awards not only in Canada but also worldwide (Killam Trust, 2010).

Ellen Bialystok of York University was awarded a Killam Prize for her work on the effects of bilingualism on cognitive processes and abilities.

Given increasing globalization, interest and research about second language learning and its effects will likely only increase in the years to come. Research on the cognitive benefits of bilingualism, such as that conducted by Bialystok and her colleagues, will continue to be a focus of interest, as will research examining the neural functioning of bilinguals as compared to monolinguals. The results of these neuroscience investigations have proven to be intriguing. For example, Mechelli et al. (2004) found that bilingual individuals showed an increase in the density of grey matter in the left inferior parietal cortex as compared to monolingual individuals, and that the density increases with earlier ages of second language acquisition and with language proficiency. And some of the recent work from Laura-Ann Petitto's lab suggests that early bilingual experience may positively modify some of the language organization in the brain (Kovelman et al., 2008) and that bilinguals' brains may process language differently than the brains of monolinguals. Kovelman et al. (2008) conclude that this work suggests that early bilingual exposure has positive effects on the brain and that this type of evidence should be used to inform the judgments of "those who decide on educational settings for the nation's young bilinguals" (p. 1468).

Bilingualism and the processes of second language acquisition continue to be important research topics in Canada. One of the centres of research on this topic continues to be McGill University. McGill scholars, for example, were involved from the beginning in the development of French immersion in Canada. McGill psychologist Wallace Lambert worked closely with the parent group in St. Lambert that was concerned with the inadequate French language instruction their children were receiving, as mentioned at the beginning of the chapter. The

project also secured the support and encouragement of Wilder Penfield, the internationally known neuroscientist we discussed in Chapter 3.

You can find a fascinating account of the project in Lambert and Tucker's (1969) book *Bilingual Education in Canada*. Lambert was awarded the Donald O. Hebb Award by the Canadian Psychological Association in 1984. Lambert's work continues to be some of the most influential research in the social psychology of language in the world (Reynolds, 1991).

It is important to note that literacy and cognitive flexibility are not the only benefits to be derived from second language immersion. As Bialystok states, "The development of two languages in childhood turns out to be a profound event that ripples through the life of that individual" (Bialystok, 2001, p. 248). While there are many potential positive benefits to an educational experience in which the child is immersed in a second language, some cautions are also notable in certain circumstances, especially in the case of minority students. Research by Stephen Wright and his colleagues examining Inuit, white, and mixed-heritage children living in the Canadian sub-Arctic has shown that education of minority children exclusively in the majority language (i.e., English) may undermine both self-esteem and heritage language (i.e., Inuktitut) proficiency (Wright & Taylor, 1995; Wright, Taylor, & Macarthur, 2000). Exposure to the heritage language in an education setting can serve to reverse these effects.

What Factors Influence the Acquisition of a Second Language?

A great many bilingual individuals do not learn their two languages simultaneously. Rather, they learn their native language first and then learn a second language later. Do any key considerations influence the learning of a second language? Yes, the evidence clearly indicates that *age* is a significant correlate of how effectively people can acquire a second language—and younger is better (Johnson & Newport, 1989). For reasons that are not well understood, language learning unfolds more effectively when initiated prior to age seven, and younger continues to be better up through age 15. Older children and adults can certainly become proficient in a second language, but only a small minority become as proficient as native speakers are (Birdsong, 1999; Hakuta, Bialystok, & Wiley, 2003).

A second factor that influences the acquisition of a second language is *acculturation*—the degree to which a person is socially and psychologically integrated into a new culture. As you might guess, greater acculturation facilitates more rapid acquisition of the new culture's language (Schumann, 1978, 1993). This finding highlights the fact that language learning is more than a purely cognitive process. Language is a communication tool that is used in varied social contexts. Moreover, language lies at the very core of a nation's culture, which is probably why the debate about bilingualism has been so vigorous.

A third set of factors affecting second language learning relates to the learner's motivation and attitude toward the other group that uses the language to be learned. Wallace Lambert (1967) and his colleagues and students, including Robert Gardner of the University of Western Ontario, Donald Taylor of McGill, Richard Clément of the University of Ottawa, and Richard Lalonde of York University, have examined the role played by these factors in the learning of, among other things, both French and English (and even statistics) as a second language. In this research, begun in 1956 with Gardner's master's thesis, they found that second language learning—in this case, French—was associated both with language aptitude and what they termed *integrative motivation*, defined as a "willingness to be like valued members of the language community" (Gardner & Lambert, 1959).

Subsequent research suggests that second language learning depends on factors other than just an aptitude for language learning—social psychological factors such as a positive attitude toward the learning situation and an interest in the other language group (i.e., integrativeness) serve to promote the learner's motivation to acquire the second language and facilitate language acquisition (Clément, 1987; Gardner, 2000; Lalonde & Gardner, 1984, 1993; Lambert,

PREVIEW QUESTIONS

▶ What kind of progress has been made in teaching language to animals?

▶ What is the evolutionary significance of language?

▶ Do humans have an innate facility for learning language?

▶ Does language shape thought?

REVIEW OF KEY POINTS

▶ Languages are symbolic, semantic, generative, and structured. Human languages are structured hierarchically. At the bottom of the hierarchy are the basic sound units, called *phonemes*. At the next level are *morphemes*, the smallest units of meaning.

▶ The initial vocalizations by infants are similar across languages, but their babbling gradually begins to resemble the sounds from their surrounding language. Children typically utter their first words around their first birthday. Vocabulary growth is slow at first, but a vocabulary spurt often begins at around 18–24 months.

▶ Most children begin to combine words by the end of their second year. Their early sentences are telegraphic, in that they omit many nonessential words. Over the next several years, children gradually learn the complexities of syntax.

▶ Research does not support the assumption that bilingualism has a negative effect on language development or on cognitive development. The learning of a second language is facilitated by starting at a younger age and by acculturation.

1967). These "social psychological" factors that have been found to affect second language acquisition are particularly important considerations in Canada, given the history of French–English relations over the past few decades.

We turn next to another vigorous debate about language acquisition—the debate about whether animals can learn language.

Can Animals Develop Language?

Can other species besides humans develop language? Although this issue does not have the practical, sociopolitical repercussions of the debate about bilingualism, it has intrigued researchers for many decades and led to some fascinating research. Scientists have taught some language-like skills to a number of species, including dolphins (Herman, Kuczaj, & Holder, 1993), sea lions (Schusterman & Gisiner, 1988), and an African grey parrot (Pepperberg, 1993, 2002), but their greatest success has come with the chimpanzee, an intelligent primate widely regarded as humans' closest cousin.

In early studies, researchers tried to teach chimps to *speak* (Hayes & Hayes, 1951). However, investigators quickly concluded that chimps simply didn't have the appropriate vocal apparatus to acquire human speech.

Subsequently researchers tried training chimps to use a non-oral human language: American Sign Language (ASL). ASL is a complex language of hand gestures and facial expressions used by thousands of deaf people. The first effort of this sort with animals was begun by Allen and Beatrice Gardner (1967), who worked with a chimp named Washoe. The Gardners approached the task as if Washoe were a deaf child. They signed to her regularly, rewarded her imitations, and taught her complex signs by physically moving her hands through the required motions. In four years, Washoe acquired a sign vocabulary of roughly 160 words. She learned to combine these words into simple sentences, such as "Washoe sorry," "Gimme flower," and "More fruit."

Although these accomplishments were impressive, critics expressed doubts about whether Washoe and the other chimps that learned ASL had really acquired language skills. For example, Herbert Terrace (1986) argued that these chimps showed little evidence of mastering *rules* of language. According to Terrace, the chimps' sentences were the products of imitation and operant conditioning, rather than spontaneous generations based on linguistic rules.

In more recent years, Sue Savage-Rumbaugh and her colleagues have reported some striking advances with bonobo pygmy chimpanzees that have fuelled additional debate (Lyn & Savage-Rumbaugh, 2000; Savage-Rumbaugh, 1991; Savage-Rumbaugh, Rumbaugh, & Fields, 2006, 2009; Savage-Rumbaugh, Shanker, & Taylor, 1998). In this line of research, the bonobos have been trained to communicate with their caretakers by touching geometric symbols that represent words on a computer-monitored keyboard. Savage-Rumbaugh's star pupil has been a chimp named Kanzi, although many of his feats have been duplicated by his younger sister, Panbanisha. Kanzi has acquired hundreds of words and has used them in thousands of combinations. Many of these combinations were spontaneous and seemed to follow rules of language. For example, to specify whether he wanted to chase or be chased, Kanzi had to differentiate between symbol combinations in a way that appeared to involve the use of grammatical rules.

As the years went by, Kanzi's trainers noticed that he often seemed to understand the normal utterances that they exchanged with each other. Hence, they began to systematically evaluate his comprehension of spoken English. At age nine, they tested his understanding of 660 sentences that directed Kanzi to execute simple actions, such as "Put the collar in the water." To make sure that he really *understood* the sentences, they included many novel constructions in which the actions were not obvious given the objects involved, such as "Put the raisins in the shoe," or "Go get the balloon that's in the microwave." Kanzi correctly carried out 72 percent of the 660 requests. Moreover, he demonstrated remarkable understanding of sentence structure, as he could reliably distinguish the actions requested by "Pour the Coke in the lemonade," as opposed to "Pour the lemonade in the Coke."

How have the linguistics experts reacted to Kanzi's surprising progress in language development? Many remain skeptical. Wynne (2004) has raised questions about the scoring system used to determine whether Kanzi "understood" oral requests, arguing that it was extremely "generous." Wynne and other critics (Budiansky, 2004; Kako, 1999; Wallman, 1992) also question whether Kanzi's communications demonstrate all the basic properties of a language.

The newest evidence in the debate about whether language is unique to humans is a recent study of chimpanzees using brain-imaging technology. As you may recall from Chapter 3, *Broca's area* in humans is a small region in the left hemisphere of the brain that is crucial to language production (Figure 3.21 on page 113). Taglialatela and colleagues (2008) set out to determine if chimps have a comparable brain area in roughly the same location. Using PET scans

to map brain activity while chimps engaged in communication, they determined that chimps do have an analogous area in the left hemisphere. The investigators conclude that the neurological substrates underlying language may also be present in chimpanzees. So, what can we conclude? Overall, it seems reasonable to assert that the ability to use language—in a very basic, primitive way—may not be entirely unique to humans, as has been widely assumed.

However, make no mistake, there is no comparison between human linguistic abilities and those of apes or other animals. As remarkable as the language studies with apes are, they should make us marvel even more at the fluency, flexibility, and complexity of human language. A normal human toddler quickly surpasses even the most successfully trained chimps. In mastering language, children outstrip chimps the way jet airplanes outrace horse-drawn buggies. Why are humans so well suited for learning language? According to some theorists, this talent for language is a product of evolution. Let's look at their thinking.

Language in an Evolutionary Context

All human societies depend on complex language systems. Even primitive cultures employ languages that are just as complicated as those used in modern societies. The universal nature of language suggests that it is an innate human characteristic. Consistent with this view, Steven Pinker

Sue Savage-Rumbaugh

"What Kanzi tells us is that humans are not the only species that can acquire language if exposed to it at an early age."

Courtesy of Sue Savage-Rumbaugh, Georgia State University Language Research Center

Kanzi, a pygmy chimpanzee, has learned to communicate with his caretakers in surprisingly sophisticated ways via computer-controlled symbol boards, thus raising some doubt about whether language is unique to humans.

© Mike Nichols

Steven Pinker

"If human language is unique in the modern animal kingdom, as it appears to be, the implications for a Darwinian account of its evolution would be as follows: none. A language instinct unique to modern humans poses no more of a paradox than a trunk unique to modern elephants."

Noam Chomsky

"Even at low levels of intelligence, at pathological levels, we find a command of language that is totally unattainable by an ape."

argues that humans' special talent for language is a species-specific trait that is the product of natural selection (Pinker, 1994, 2004; Pinker & Jackendoff, 2005). Pinker, who was born in Montreal and obtained his undergraduate degree in psychology from McGill University, is one of the world's foremost authorities on language and language acquisition. According to Pinker, language is a valuable means of communication that has enormous adaptive value. As Pinker and Bloom (1992) point out, "There is an obvious advantage in being able to acquire information about the world second-hand . . . one can avoid having to duplicate the possibly time-consuming and dangerous trial-and-error process that won that knowledge" (p. 460).

Dunbar (1996) argues that language evolved as a device to build and maintain social coalitions in increasingly larger groups. Although the impetus for the evolution of language remains a matter of speculation and debate (Kirby, 2007), it does not take much imagination to envision how more effective communication among our ancient ancestors could have aided hunting, gathering, fighting, mating, and the avoidance of poisons, predators, and other dangers.

Although the adaptive value of language seems obvious, some scholars take issue with the assertion that human language is the product of evolution. For example, David Premack (1985) has expressed skepticism that small differences in language skill would influence reproductive fitness in primitive societies, where all one had to communicate about was the location of the closest mastodon herd. In an effort to refute this argument, Pinker and Bloom (1992) point out that very small adaptive disparities are sufficient to fuel evolutionary change. For example, they cite an estimate that a 1 percent difference in mortality rates among overlapping Neanderthal and human populations could have led to the extinction of Neanderthals in just 30 generations. They also note that a trait variation that produces on average just 1 percent more offspring than its alternative genetic expression would increase in prevalence from 0.1 percent to 99.9 percent of the population in 4000 generations. Four thousand generations may seem like an eternity, but in the context of evolution, it is a modest amount of time. More recently, Pinker (2003) has argued that it is likely that there are many genes for language and he suggests that new genes will be discovered that account for language disorders and individual variation in language. He suggests language may represent an adaptation for the "communication of knowledge and intentions" (Pinker & Jackendoff, 2005).

Whether or not evolution gets the credit, language acquisition in humans seems remarkably rapid. As you will see in the next section, this reality looms large in theories of language acquisition.

Theories of Language Acquisition

Since the 1950s, a great debate has raged about the key processes involved in language acquisition. As with arguments we have seen in other areas of psychology, this one centres on the *nature versus nurture* issue. The debate was stimulated by the influential behaviourist B. F. Skinner (1957), who argued that environmental factors govern language development. His provocative analysis brought a rejoinder from Noam Chomsky (1959), who emphasized biological determinism. Let's examine their views and subsequent theories that stake out a middle ground.

Behaviourist Theories

The behaviourist approach to language was first outlined by Skinner in his book *Verbal Behavior* (1957). He argued that children learn language the same way they learn everything else: through imitation, reinforcement, and other established principles of conditioning. According to Skinner, vocalizations that are not reinforced gradually decline in frequency. The remaining vocalizations are shaped with reinforcers until they are correct. Behaviourists assert that by controlling reinforcement, parents encourage their children to learn the correct meaning and pronunciation of words (Staats & Staats, 1963). For example, as children grow older, parents may insist on closer and closer approximations of the word *water* before supplying the requested drink.

Behavioural theorists also use the principles of imitation and reinforcement to explain how children learn syntax. According to the behaviourists' view, children learn how to construct sentences by imitating the sentences of adults and older children. If children's imitative statements are understood, parents are able to answer their questions or respond to their requests, thus reinforcing their verbal behaviour.

Nativist Theories

Skinner's explanation of language acquisition soon inspired a critique and rival explanation from Noam Chomsky (1959, 1965). Chomsky pointed out that there are an infinite number of sentences in a language. It's therefore unreasonable to expect that children learn language by imitation. For example, in English, we often add *ed* to the end of a verb to construct past tense. Children routinely overregularize this rule, producing incorrect verbs such as *goed, eated,* and *thinked*. Mistakes such as these are inconsistent with Skinner's emphasis on imitation, because most adult speakers don't use ungrammatical words like *goed*. Children can't imitate things they don't hear. According to Chomsky, children learn *the rules of language,* not specific verbal responses, as Skinner proposed.

An alternative theory favoured by Chomsky and others is that humans have an inborn or "native" propensity to develop language (Chomsky, 1975, 1986, 2006). In this sense, *native* is a variation on the word *nature* as it's used in the nature versus nurture debate. *Nativist theory* proposes that humans are equipped with a *language acquisition device (LAD)*—an innate mechanism or process that facilitates the learning of language. According to this view, humans learn language for the same reason that birds learn to fly—because they're biologically equipped for it. The exact nature of the LAD has not been spelled out in nativist theories. It presumably consists of brain structures and neural wiring that leave humans well prepared to discriminate among phonemes, to fast-map morphemes, to acquire rules of syntax, and so on.

Why does Chomsky believe that children have an innate capacity for learning language? One reason is that children seem to acquire language quickly and effortlessly. How could they develop so complex a skill in such a short time unless they have a built-in capacity for it? Another reason is that language development tends to unfold at roughly the same pace for most children, even though children obviously are reared in diverse home environments. This finding suggests that language development is determined by biological maturation more than personal experience. The nativists also cite evidence that the early course of language development is similar across very different cultures (Gleitman & Newport, 1996; Slobin, 1992). They interpret this to mean that children all over the world are guided by the same innate capabilities.

Interactionist Theories

Like Skinner, Chomsky has his critics (Bohannon & Bonvillian, 2009). They ask: What exactly is a language acquisition device? How does the LAD work? What are the neural mechanisms involved? They argue that the LAD concept is terribly vague. Other critics question whether the rapidity of early language development is as exceptional as nativists assume. They assert that it isn't fair to compare the rapid progress of toddlers, who are immersed in their native language, against the struggles of older students, who may devote only 10–15 hours per week to their foreign language course.

The problems apparent in Skinner's and Chomsky's explanations of language development have led some psychologists to outline *interactionist theories* of language acquisition. These theories assert that biology and experience *both* make important contributions to the development of language. Interactionist theories come in at least three flavours. *Cognitive theories* assert that language development is simply an important aspect of more general cognitive development—which depends on both maturation and experience (Meltzoff & Gopnik, 1989; Piaget, 1983). *Social communication theories* emphasize the functional value of interpersonal communication and the social context in which language evolves (Bohannon & Warren-Leubecker, 1989; Farrar, 1990). *Emergentist theories* argue that the neural circuits supporting language are not prewired but *emerge* gradually in response to language learning experiences (Bates, 1999; MacWhinney, 2001, 2004). These theories tend to assume that incremental changes in connectionist networks (see Chapter 7) underlie children's gradual acquisition of various language skills (Elman, 1999).

Like the nativists, interactionists believe that the human organism is biologically well equipped for learning language. They also agree that much of this learning involves the acquisition of rules. However, like the behaviourists, they believe that social exchanges with parents and others play a critical role in moulding language skills. Thus, interactionist theories maintain that a biological predisposition *and* a supportive environment both contribute to language development (see Figure 8.6).

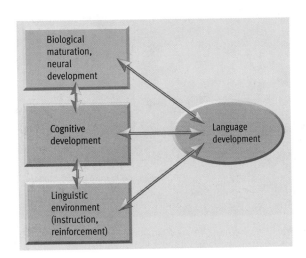

FIGURE 8.6

Interactionist theories of language acquisition.

The interactionist view is that nature and nurture are both important to language acquisition. Maturation is thought to drive language development directly and to influence it indirectly by fostering cognitive development. Meanwhile, verbal exchanges with parents and others are also thought to play a critical role in moulding language skills. The complex bi-directional relationships depicted here shed some light on why there is room for extensive debate about the crucial factors in language acquisition.

Culture, Language, and Thought

Another long-running controversy in the study of language concerns the relationships among culture, language, and thought (Fiedler, 2008). Obviously, people from different cultures generally speak different languages. But does your training in English lead you to think about certain things differently than someone who was raised to speak Chinese or French? In other words, does a cultural group's language determine their thoughts? Or does thought determine language?

Benjamin Lee Whorf (1956) has been the most prominent advocate of *linguistic relativity*, *the hypothesis that one's language determines the nature of one's thought*. Whorf speculated that different languages lead people to view the world differently. His classic example compared English and Inuit views of snow. He asserted that the English language has just one word for snow, whereas the Inuit language has many words that distinguish among falling snow, wet snow, and so on. Because of this language gap, Whorf argued that Inuit perceive snow differently than English-speaking people do. However, Whorf's conclusion about these perceptual differences was based on casual observation rather than systematic cross-cultural comparisons of perceptual processes. Moreover, critics subsequently noted that advocates of the linguistic relativity hypothesis had carelessly overestimated the number of Inuit words for snow, while conveniently ignoring the variety of English words that refer to snow, such as slush and blizzard (Martin, 1986; Pullum, 1991).

Nonetheless, Whorf's hypothesis has been the subject of spirited debate (Chiu, Leung, & Kwan, 2007; Gleitman & Papafragou, 2005). Many studies have focused on cross-cultural comparisons of how people perceive colours, because substantial variations exist among cultures in how colours are categorized with names. For example, some languages have a single colour name that includes both blue and green, whereas other languages view light blue and dark blue as fundamentally different colours (Davies, 1998). If a language doesn't distinguish between blue and green, do people who speak that language think about colours differently than people in other cultures do?

Early efforts to answer this question suggested that the colour categories in a language have relatively little influence on how people perceive and think about colours (Berlin & Kay, 1969; Rosch, 1973). However, some more recent studies have provided new evidence favouring the linguistic relativity hypothesis (Davidoff, 2001, 2004; Roberson et al., 2005). For example, studies of subjects who speak African languages that do not have a boundary between blue and green have found that language affects their colour perception, as they have more trouble making quick discriminations between blue and green colours than English-speaking subjects do (Ozgen, 2004).

Additional studies using a variety of methods have found that a culture's colour categories shape subjects' similarity judgments and groupings of colours (Pilling & Davies, 2004; Roberson, Davies, & Davidoff, 2000). These findings have led Ozgen (2004) to conclude that "it is just possible that what you see when you look at the rainbow depends on the language you speak" (p. 98). Moreover, the new support for linguistic relativity is not limited to the study of colour perception. Other studies have found

Does the language you speak determine how you think? Yes, said Benjamin Lee Whorf, who argued that the Inuit language, which has numerous words for snow, leads Inuit to perceive snow differently from English speakers. Whorf's hypothesis has been the subject of spirited debate.

© Wayne R. Bilenduke/Stone/Getty Images

REVIEW OF KEY POINTS

▷ Efforts to teach chimpanzees American Sign Language were impressive, but doubts were raised about whether the chimps learned rules of language. Sue Savage-Rumbaugh's work with Kanzi suggests that some animals are capable of some genuine language acquisition. Many theorists believe that humans' special talent for language is the product of natural selection.

▷ According to Skinner and other behaviourists, children acquire a language through imitation and reinforcement. Nativist theories assert that humans have an innate capacity to learn language rules. Today, theorists are moving toward interactionist perspectives, which emphasize the role of both biology and experience.

▷ The theory of linguistic relativity asserts that language determines thought, thus suggesting that people from different cultures may think about the world somewhat differently. The evidence supports only a weak version of the linguistic relativity hypothesis.

that language also has some impact on how people think about motion (Gennari et al., 2002), time (Boroditsky, 2001), and shapes (Roberson, Davidoff, & Shapiro, 2002).

So, what is the status of the linguistic relativity hypothesis? At present, the debate seems to centre on whether the new data are sufficient to support the original, "strong" version of the hypothesis—that a given language makes certain ways of thinking obligatory or impossible—or a "weaker" version of the hypothesis—that a language makes certain ways of thinking easier or more difficult. Either way, empirical support for the linguistic relativity hypothesis has increased dramatically in recent years.

Problem Solving: In Search of Solutions

Look at the two problems below. Can you solve them?

In the Thompson family, there are five brothers, and each brother has one sister. If you count Mrs. Thompson, how many females are there in the Thompson family?

Fifteen percent of the people in Halifax have unlisted telephone numbers. You select 200 names at random from the Halifax phone book. How many of these people can be expected to have unlisted phone numbers?

These problems, borrowed from Sternberg (1986, p. 214), are exceptionally simple, but many people fail to solve them. The answer to the first problem is *two:* The only females in the family are Mrs. Thompson and her one daughter, who is a sister to each of her brothers. The answer to the second problem is *none*—you won't find any people with *unlisted* phone numbers in the phone book.

Why do many people fail to solve these simple problems? You'll learn why in a moment, when we discuss barriers to effective problem solving. But first, let's examine a scheme for classifying problems into a few basic types.

Types of Problems SIM7 6d

Problem solving refers to active efforts to discover what must be done to achieve a goal that is not readily attainable. Obviously, if a goal is readily attainable, there isn't a problem. But in problem-solving situations, one must go beyond the information given to overcome obstacles and reach a goal. Jim Greeno (1978) has proposed that problems can be categorized into three basic classes:

1. *Problems of inducing structure* require people to discover the relationships among numbers, words, symbols, or ideas. The *series completion problems* and the *analogy problems* in Figure 8.7 are examples of problems of inducing structure.

2. *Problems of arrangement* require people to arrange the parts of a problem in a way that satisfies some criterion. The parts can usually be arranged in many ways, but only one or a few of the arrangements form a solution. The *string problem* and the *anagrams* in Figure 8.7 fit in this category. Arrangement problems are often solved with a burst of insight. *Insight is the sudden discovery of the correct solution following incorrect attempts based primarily on trial and error* (Mayer, 1995).

3. *Problems of transformation* require people to carry out a sequence of transformations in order to reach a specific goal. The *hobbits and orcs problem* and the *water jar problem* in Figure 8.7 are examples of transformation problems. Transformation problems can be challenging. Even though you know exactly what the goal is, it's often not obvious how the goal can be achieved.

Greeno's list is not an exhaustive scheme for classifying problems, but it provides a useful system for understanding some of the variety seen in everyday problems.

Barriers to Effective Problem Solving 6d

On the basis of their studies of problem solving, psychologists have identified a number of barriers that frequently impede subjects' efforts to arrive at solutions. Common obstacles to effective problem solving include a focus on irrelevant information, functional fixedness, mental set, and the imposition of unnecessary constraints.

Irrelevant Information

We began our discussion of problem solving with two simple problems that people routinely fail to solve (see above). The catch is that these problems contain *irrelevant information* that leads people astray. In the first problem, the number of brothers is irrelevant in determining the number of females

A. Analogy

What word completes the analogy?

Merchant : Sell : : Customer : _____

Lawyer : Client : : Doctor : _____

B. String problem

Two strings hang from the ceiling but are too far apart to allow a person to hold one and walk to the other. On the table are a book of matches, a screwdriver, and a few pieces of cotton. How could the strings be tied together?

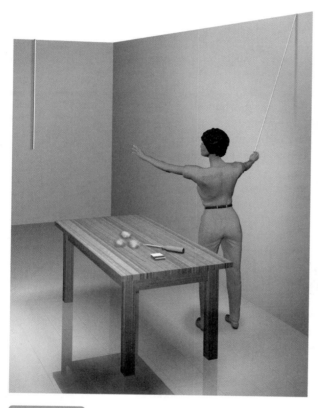

C. Hobbits and orcs problem

Three hobbits and three orcs arrive at a river bank, and they all wish to cross to the other side. Fortunately, there is a boat, but unfortunately, the boat can hold only two creatures at one time. Also, there is another problem. Orcs are vicious creatures, and whenever there are more orcs than hobbits on one side of the river, the orcs will immediately attack the hobbits and eat them up. Consequently, you should be certain that you never leave more orcs than hobbits on either river bank. How should the problem be solved? It must be added that the orcs, though vicious, can be trusted to bring the boat back! (From Matlin, 1989, p. 319)

D. Water jar problem

Suppose that you have a 21-cup jar, a 127-cup jar, and a 3-cup jar. Drawing and discarding as much water as you like, you need to measure out exactly 100 cups of water. How can this be done?

E. Anagram

Rearrange the letters in each row to make an English word.

RWAET
KEROJ

F. Series completion

What number or letter completes each series?

1 2 8 3 4 6 5 6 ____

A B M C D M ____

FIGURE 8.7

Six standard problems used in studies of problem solving.

Try solving the problems and identifying which class each belongs to before reading further. The problems can be classified as follows. The *analogy problems* and *series completion problems* are problems of inducing structure. The solutions for the analogy problems are *Buy* and *Patient*. The solutions for the series completion problems are 4 and *E*. The *string problem* and the *anagram problems* are problems of arrangement. To solve the string problem, attach the screwdriver to one string and set it swinging as a pendulum. Hold the other string and catch the swinging screwdriver. Then you need only untie the screwdriver and tie the strings together. The solutions for the anagram problems are *WATER* and *JOKER*. The *hobbits and orcs problem* and the *water jar problem* are problems of transformation. The solutions for these problems are outlined in Figures 8.8 and 8.9.

---

in the Thompson family. In the second problem, subjects tend to focus on the figures of 15 percent and 200 names. But this numerical information is irrelevant, since all the names came out of the phone book.

Sternberg (1986) points out that people often incorrectly assume that all of the numerical information in a problem is necessary to solve it. They therefore try to figure out how to use quantitative information before they even consider whether it's relevant. Focusing on irrelevant information can have adverse effects on reasoning and problem solving (Gaeth & Shanteau, 2000). Hence, effective problem solving requires that you attempt to figure out what information is relevant and what is irrelevant before proceeding.

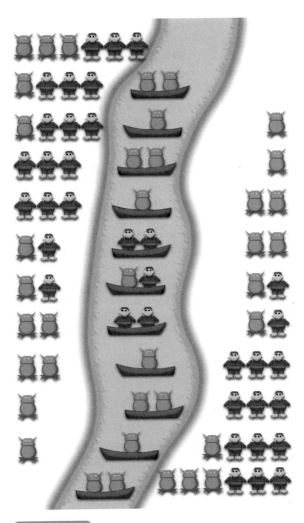

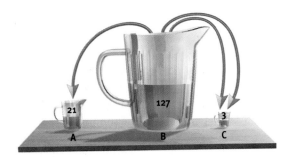

FIGURE 8.8

Solution to the hobbits and orcs problem.

This problem is difficult because it is necessary to temporarily work *away* from the goal.

FIGURE 8.9

The method for solving the water jar problem.

As explained in the text, the correct formula is B – A – 2C.

6d

Functional Fixedness

Another common barrier to successful problem solving, identified by Gestalt psychologists, is *functional fixedness*—the tendency to perceive an item only in terms of its most common use. Functional fixedness has been seen in the difficulties that people have with the string problem (Maier, 1931). Solving this problem requires finding a novel use for one of the objects: the screwdriver. Subjects tend to think of the screwdriver in terms of its usual functions—turning screws and perhaps prying things open. They have a hard time viewing the screwdriver as a weight. Their rigid way of thinking about the screwdriver illustrates functional fixedness (Dominowski & Bourne, 1994). Ironically, young children appear to be less vulnerable to functional fixedness than older children or adults because they have less knowledge about the conventional uses of various objects (Defeyter & German, 2003).

6d

Mental Set

Rigid thinking is also at work when a mental set interferes with effective problem solving. *A mental set exists when people persist in using problem-solving strategies that have worked in the past.* The effects of mental set were seen in a classic study by Gestalt psychologist Abraham Luchins (1942). He asked subjects to work a series of water jar problems, like the one introduced earlier. Six such problems are outlined in Figure 8.10, which shows the capacities of the three jars and the amounts of water to be measured out. Try solving these problems.

Were you able to develop a formula for solving these problems? The first four all require the same strategy, which was described in Figure 8.9. You have to fill jar B, draw off the amount that jar A holds once, and draw off the amount that jar C holds twice. Thus, the formula for your solution is B – A – 2C. Although there is an obvious and much simpler solution (A – C) for the fifth problem (see Figure 8.14 on page 370), Luchins found that most subjects stuck with the more cumbersome strategy that they had used in problems 1–4. Moreover, most subjects couldn't solve the sixth problem in the allotted time, because they kept trying to use their proven

	Capacity of empty jars			Desired amount of water
Problem	A	B	C	
1	14	163	25	99
2	18	43	10	5
3	9	42	6	21
4	20	59	4	31
5	23	49	3	20
6	28	76	3	25

FIGURE 8.10

Additional water jar problems.

Using jars A, B, and C, with the capacities indicated in each row, figure out how to measure out the desired amount of water specified on the far right. The solutions are shown in Figure 8.14. (Based on Luchins, 1942)

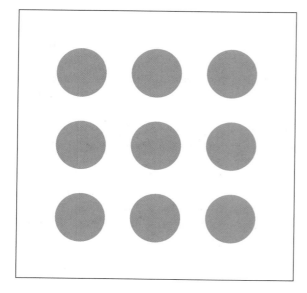

FIGURE 8.11

The nine-dot problem.

Without lifting your pencil from the paper, draw no more than four lines that will cross through all nine dots. For possible solutions, see Figure 8.15.

Source: Adams, J.L. (1980). *Conceptual blockbusting: A guide to better ideas.* New York: W.H. Freeman. Copyright © 1980 by James L. Adams. Reprinted by permission of W.H. Freeman & Co.

FIGURE 8.12

The matchstick problem.

Move two matches to form four equal squares. A solution can be found in Figure 8.16.

Source: Kendler, H.H. (1974). *Basic psychology.* Menlo Park, CA: Benjamin-Cummings. Copyright © 1974 The Benjamin-Cummings Publishing Co. Adapted by permission of Howard H. Kendler.

strategy, which does *not* work for this problem. The subjects' reliance on their "tried and true" strategy is an illustration of mental set in problem solving. This tendency to let one's thinking get into a rut is a common barrier to successful problem solving (Smith, 1995). Mental set may explain why having expertise in an area sometimes backfires and in fact hampers problem-solving efforts (Leighton & Sternberg, 2003).

Unnecessary Constraints

6d  PSYKTREK

Effective problem solving requires specifying all the constraints governing a problem *without assuming any constraints that don't exist.* An example of a problem in which people place an unnecessary constraint on the solution is shown in Figure 8.11 (Adams, 1980). Without lifting your pencil from the paper, try to draw four straight lines that will cross through all nine dots. Most people will not draw lines outside the imaginary boundary that surrounds the dots. Notice that this constraint is not part of the problem statement. It's imposed only by the problem solver. Correct solutions, two of which are shown in Figure 8.15 on page 370, extend outside the imaginary boundary. People often make assumptions that impose unnecessary constraints on problem-solving efforts. A recent model and analysis of insight by James MacGregor of the University of Victoria and his colleagues (MacGregor, Ormerod, and Chronicle, 2001) suggest that failure in such problems results from both constraint and from some type of drive or dynamic that "steers activity into the constraint" (Ormerod et al., 2002, p. 798).

In their classic treatise on problem solving, Allen Newell and Herbert Simon (1972) use a spatial metaphor to describe the process of problem solving. They use the term *problem space* to refer to the set of possible pathways to a solution considered by the problem solver. Thus, they see problem solving as a search in space. The problem solver's task is to find a solution path among the potential pathways that could lead from the problem's initial state to its goal state. The problem space metaphor highlights the fact that people must choose from among a variety of conceivable pathways or strategies in attempting to solve problems (Hunt, 1994). In this section, we'll examine some general strategies.

Using Algorithms and Heuristics

Trial and error is a common approach to solving problems. *Trial and error* involves trying possible solutions and discarding those that are in error until one works. Trial and error is often applied haphazardly, but people sometimes try to be systematic. An *algorithm* is a methodical, step-by-step procedure for trying all possible alternatives in searching for a solution to a problem. For instance, to solve the anagram IHCRA, you could write out all the possible arrangements of these letters until you eventually reached an answer (CHAIR). If an algorithm is available for a problem, it guarantees that one can eventually find a solution.

Algorithms can be effective when there are relatively few possible solutions to be tried out. However, algorithms do not exist for many problems, and they can become impractical when the problem space is large. Consider, for instance, the problem shown in Figure 8.12. The challenge is to move just two matches to create a pattern containing four equal squares. Sure, you could follow an algorithm in moving pairs of matches about. But you'd better allocate plenty of time to this effort, as there are over 60 000 possible rearrangements to check out (see Figure 8.16 on page 370 for the solution).

Because algorithms are inefficient, people often use shortcuts called *heuristics* in problem solving. A *heuristic* is a guiding principle or "rule of thumb" used in solving problems or making decisions. In solving problems, a heuristic allows you to discard some alternatives while pursuing selected alternatives that appear more likely to lead to a solution (Holyoak, 1995). Heuristics can be useful because they selectively narrow the problem space, but they don't guarantee success. Helpful heuristics in problem solving include forming subgoals, working backward, searching for analogies, and changing the representation of a problem.

Forming Subgoals

A useful strategy for many problems is to formulate *subgoals*, intermediate steps toward a solution. When you reach a subgoal, you've solved part of the problem. Some problems have fairly obvious subgoals, and research has shown that people take advantage of them. For instance, in analogy problems, the first subgoal usually is to figure out the possible relationship between the first two parts of the analogy. In a study by Simon and Reed (1976), subjects working on complex problems were given subgoals that weren't obvious. Providing subgoals helped the subjects solve the problems much more quickly.

The wisdom of formulating subgoals can be seen in the *tower of Hanoi problem*, depicted in Figure 8.13. The terminal goal for this problem is to move all three rings on peg A to peg C, while abiding by two restrictions: Only the top ring on a peg can be moved, and a larger ring must never be placed above a smaller ring. See whether you can solve the problem before continuing.

Dividing this problem into subgoals facilitates a solution (Kotovsky, Hayes, & Simon, 1985). If you think in terms of subgoals, your first task is to get ring 3 to the bottom of peg C. Breaking this task into sub-subgoals, subjects can figure out that they should move ring 1 to peg C, ring 2 to peg B, and ring 1 from peg C to peg B. These manoeuvres allow you to place ring 3 at the bottom of peg C, thus meeting your first subgoal. Your next subgoal—getting ring 2 over to peg C—can be accomplished in just two steps: Move ring 1 to peg A and ring 2 to peg C. It should then be obvious how to achieve your final subgoal—getting ring 1 over to peg C.

Working Backward

Try to work the *lily pond problem* described below:

> The water lilies on the surface of a small pond double in area every 24 hours. From the time the first water lily appears until the pond is completely covered takes 60 days. On what day is half of the pond covered with lilies?

If you're working on a problem that has a well-specified end point, you may find the solution more readily if you begin at the end and work backward. This strategy is the key to solving the lily pond problem (Davidson, 2003). If the entire pond is covered on the 60th day, and the area covered doubles every day, how much is covered on the 59th day?

FIGURE 8.13

The tower of Hanoi problem.
Your mission is to move the rings from peg A to peg C. You can move only the top ring on a peg and can't place a larger ring above a smaller one. The solution is explained in the text.

One-half of the pond will be covered, and that happens to be the exact point you were trying to reach. The lily pond problem is remarkably simple when you work backward. In contrast, if you move forward from the starting point, you wrestle with questions about the area of the pond and the size of the lilies, and you find the problem riddled with ambiguities.

Searching for Analogies

Searching for analogies is another of the major heuristics for solving problems (Holyoak, 2005). We reason by analogy constantly (Sternberg, 2009), and these efforts to identify analogies can facilitate innovative thinking (Gassmann & Zeschky, 2008). If you can spot an analogy between problems, you may be able to use the solution to a previous problem to solve a current one. Of course, using this strategy depends on recognizing the similarity between two problems, which may itself be a challenging problem. People often are unable to recognize that two problems are similar and that an analogy might lead to a solution (Kurtz & Lowenstein, 2007). One prominent reason that people have difficulty recognizing analogies between problems is that they tend to focus on superficial, surface features of problems rather than their underlying structure (Bassok, 2003). Nonetheless, analogies can be a powerful tool in efforts to solve problems. For example, one study of biologists' problem solving recorded during their lab meetings found that they threw out 3–15 analogies per hour (Dunbar & Blanchette, 2001). Another study of design engineers recorded during their product development meetings found that they came up with an average of 11 analogies per hour of deliberation (Christensen & Schunn, 2007).

Analogies can be a powerful tool in efforts to solve problems. Unfortunately, people often are unable to recognize that two problems are similar and that an analogy might lead to a solution

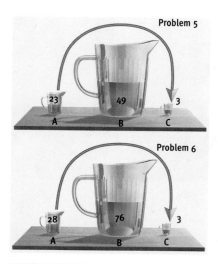

FIGURE 8.14

Solutions to the additional water jar problems.

The solution for problems 1–4 is the same (B – A – 2C) as the solution shown in Figure 8.10. This method will work for problem 5, but there also is a simpler solution (A – C), which is the only solution for problem 6. Many subjects exhibit a mental set on these problems, as they fail to notice the simpler solution for problem 5.

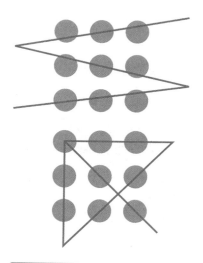

FIGURE 8.15

Two solutions to the nine-dot problem.

The key to solving the problem is to recognize that nothing in the problem statement forbids going outside the imaginary boundary surrounding the dots.

Source: Adams, J.L. (1980). *Conceptual blockbusting: A guide to better ideas.* New York: W.H. Freeman. Copyright © 1980 by James L. Adams. Reprinted by permission of W.H. Freeman & Co.

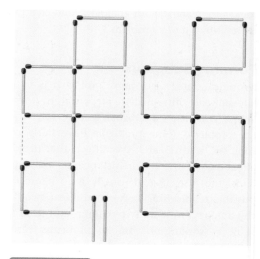

FIGURE 8.16

Solution to the matchstick problem.

The key to solving this problem is to "open up" the figure, something that many subjects are reluctant to do because they impose unnecessary constraints on the problem.

Source: Kendler, H.H. (1974). *Basic psychology.* Menlo Park, CA: Benjamin-Cummings. Copyright © 1974 The Benjamin-Cummings Publishing Co. Adapted by permission of Howard H. Kendler.

(Kurtz & Lowenstein, 2007). One reason that people have difficulty recognizing analogies between problems is that they often focus on surface features of problems rather than their underlying structure (Bassok, 2003). Try to make use of analogies to solve the following two problems:

> *A teacher had 23 pupils in his class. All but seven of them went on a museum trip and thus were away for the day. How many students remained in class that day?*

> *Susan gets in her car in Edmonton and drives toward Lethbridge, averaging 100 kilometres per hour. Twenty minutes later, Ellen gets in her car in Lethbridge and starts driving toward Edmonton, averaging 120 kilometres per hour. Both women take the same route, which extends a total of 440 kilometres between the two cities. Which car is nearer to Edmonton when they meet?*

These problems, adapted from Sternberg (1986, pp. 213 and 215), resemble the ones that opened our discussion of problem solving. Each has an obvious solution that's hidden in irrelevant quantitative information. If you recognized this similarity, you probably solved the problems easily. If not, take another look now that you know what the analogy is.

Neither problem requires any calculation whatsoever. The answer to the first problem is *seven*. As for the second problem, when the two cars meet they're in the same place. Obviously, they have to be the same distance from Edmonton.

Changing the Representation of the Problem

Whether you solve a problem often hinges on how you envision it—your *representation of the problem*. Many problems can be represented in a variety of ways, such as verbally, mathematically, or spatially. You might represent a problem with a list, a table, an equation, a graph, a matrix of facts or numbers, a hierarchical tree diagram, or a sequential flow chart (Halpern, 2003). Some studies have shown that diagrams can facilitate reasoning on some types of problems by making it easier to find crucial information and by making alternative possibilities more salient (Bauer & Johnson-Laird, 1993). There isn't one ideal way to represent problems. The best representation will depend on the nature of the problem. But when you fail to make progress with your initial representation, changing your representation is often a good strategy (Novick & Bassok, 2005). As an illustration, see whether you can solve the *bird and train problem* (adapted from Bransford & Stein, 1993, p. 11):

Two train stations are 50 kilometres apart. At 1 P.M. on Sunday, a train pulls out from each of the stations and the trains start toward each other. Just as the trains pull out from the stations, a bird flies into the air in front of the first train and flies ahead to the front of the second train. When the bird reaches the second train, it turns around and flies toward the first train. The bird continues in this way until the trains meet. Assume that both trains travel at the speed of 25 kilometres per hour and that the bird flies at a constant speed of 100 kilometres per hour. How many kilometres will the bird have flown when the trains meet?

This problem asks about the *distance* the bird will fly, so people tend to represent the problem spatially, as shown in Figure 8.17. Represented this way, the problem can be solved, but the steps are tedious and difficult. But consider another angle. The problem asks how far the bird will fly in the time it takes the trains to meet. Since we know how fast the bird flies, all we really need to know is how much *time* it takes

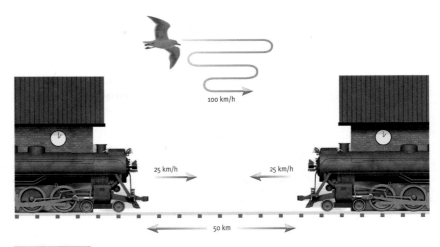

100 km/h

25 km/h   25 km/h

50 km

FIGURE 8.17

Representing the bird and train problem.

The typical inclination is to envision this problem spatially, as shown here. However, as the text explains, this representation makes the problem much more difficult than it really is.

for the trains to meet. Changing the representation of the problem from a question of *distance* to a question of *time* makes for an easier solution, as follows: The train stations are 50 kilometres apart. Since the trains are travelling toward each other at the same

WEB LINK 8.2

Critical Thinking Community
The many resources at the Critical Thinking Community website are directed primarily toward teachers at every level to help them develop their students' critical thinking skills. Visitors will find many online pamphlets on critical thinking and active learning.

concept check 8.2

Thinking about Problem Solving

Check your understanding of problem solving by answering some questions about the following problem. Begin by trying to solve the problem.

The candle problem. Using the objects shown—candles, a box of matches, string, and some tacks—figure out how you could mount a candle on a wall so that it could be used as a light.

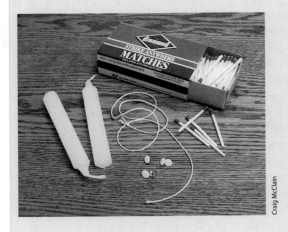

Craig McClain

Work on the problem for a while and then turn to page 372 to see the solution. After you've seen the solution, respond to the following questions. The answers are in Appendix A.

1. If it didn't occur to you that the matchbox could be converted from a container to a platform, this illustrates _____.

2. While working on the problem, if you thought to yourself, "How can I create a platform attached to the wall?" you used the heuristic of _____ _____.

3. If it occurred to you suddenly that the matchbox could be used as a platform, this realization would be an example of _____.

4. If you had a hunch that there might be some similarity between this problem and the string problem in Figure 8.7 on page 366 (the similarity is the novel use of an object), your hunch would illustrate the heuristic of _____.

5. In terms of Greeno's three types of problems, the candle problem is a(n) ____ problem.

Language and Thought

speed, they will meet midway and each will have travelled 25 kilometres. The trains are moving at 25 kilometres per hour. Hence, the time it takes them to meet 25 kilometres from each station is one hour. Since the bird flies at 100 kilometres per hour, it will fly 100 kilometres in the hour it takes the trains to meet.

Taking a Break: Incubation

When a problem is resistant to solution, there is much to be said for taking a break and not thinking about it for a while. After the break, you may find that you see the problem in a different light and new solutions may spring to mind. Obviously, there is no guarantee that a break will facilitate problem solving. But breaks pay off often enough that researchers have given the phenomenon a name: *incubation*. An *incubation effect* occurs when new solutions surface for a previously unsolved problem after a period of not consciously thinking about the problem. Depending on the nature of the problem, incubation periods may be measured in minutes, hours, or days. The likelihood of an incubation effect depends on a host of task-related factors, but on the whole, incubation does tend to enhance problem solving (Dodds, Ward, & Smith, in press; Sio & Ormerod, 2009). Research suggests that incubation effects can even occur during sleep (Cai et al., 2009; Stickgold & Walker, 2004). Some theorists believe that incubation effects occur because people continue to work on problems at an unconscious level after conscious effort has been suspended (Ellwood et al., 2009). However, a host of alternative explanations for incubation effects have also been proposed (Helie & Sun, 2010).

Culture, Cognitive Style, and Problem Solving

Do the varied experiences of people from different cultures lead to cross-cultural variations in problem solving? Yes, at least to some degree, as researchers have found cultural differences in the cognitive style that people exhibit in processing information and solving problems (Gutchess et al., 2010; Hedden, et al., 2008).

Back in the 1940s, Herman Witkin was intrigued by the observation that some airplane pilots would fly into a cloud bank upright but exit it upside down without realizing that they had turned over. Witkin's efforts to explain this aviation problem led to the discovery of an interesting dimension of cognitive style (Witkin, 1950; Witkin et al., 1962). *Field*

dependence–independence refers to individuals' tendency to rely primarily on external versus internal frames of reference when orienting themselves in space. People who are *field dependent* rely on external frames of reference and tend to accept the physical environment as a given instead of trying to analyze or restructure it. People who are *field independent* rely on internal frames of reference and tend to analyze and try to restructure the physical environment rather than accepting it as is. In solving problems, field-dependent people tend to focus on the total context of a problem instead of zeroing in on specific aspects or breaking it into component parts. In contrast, field-independent people are more likely to focus on specific features of a problem and to reorganize the component parts.

Research has shown that field dependence–independence is related to diverse aspects of cognitive, emotional, and social functioning (Witkin & Goodenough, 1981). Each style has its strengths and weaknesses, but studies have shown that field-independent subjects outperform field-dependent subjects on a variety of classic laboratory problems, including the string problem, matchstick problem, candle problem, and water jar problem (Witkin et al., 1962). Field-independent subjects' superiority on these types of problems has been attributed to their propensity to analyze and rearrange the elements of a problem and their ability to overcome the context in which problems are presented.

An extensive body of research suggests that some cultures encourage a field-dependent cognitive style, whereas others foster a field-independent style (Berry, 1990; Mishra, 2001). The educational practices in modern Western societies seem to nourish field independence. A field-independent style is also more likely to be predominant in nomadic societies that depend on hunting and gathering for subsistence and in societies that encourage personal autonomy. In contrast, a field-dependent style is found more in sedentary agricultural societies and in societies that stress conformity.

Richard Nisbett and his colleagues (2001; Nisbett & Miyamoto, 2005) have argued that people from East Asian cultures (such as China, Japan, and Korea) display a *holistic cognitive style* that focuses on context and relationships among elements in a field, whereas people from Western cultures (North America and Europe) exhibit an *analytic cognitive style* that focuses on objects and their properties rather than context. To put it simply, Easterners see wholes where Westerners see parts. Nisbett et al. (2001) trace Eastern societies' holistic style of thinking back to ancient Chinese philosophies, while they trace

The solution to the candle problem in Concept Check 8.2.

Craig McClain

Western societies' analytic style of thinking back to ancient Greek philosophies. Although these contrasting cognitive styles are rooted in ancient traditions, Nisbett and his colleagues argue that these styles continue to influence reasoning and problem solving in our contemporary world.

To demonstrate this influence, Masuda and Nisbett (2001) presented computer-animated scenes of fish and other underwater objects to Japanese and American participants and asked them to report what they had seen. The initial comments of American subjects typically referred to the focal fish, whereas the initial comments of Japanese subjects usually referred to background elements (see Figure 8.18). Furthermore, compared to the Americans, the Japanese participants made about 70 percent more statements about context or background and about twice as many statements about relationships between elements in the scenes. Other studies have shown that cultural variations in analytic versus holistic thinking influence subjects' patterns of logical reasoning, their vulnerability to hindsight bias (see Chapter 7), and their tolerance of contradictions (Nisbett, 2003; Nisbett et al., 2001). Research also suggests that people from Eastern cultures tend to be more field-dependent than their Western counterparts (Ji, Peng, & Nisbett, 2000), but Nisbett and his colleagues view field dependence–independence as just one facet of a broader preference for holistic versus analytic thinking. Based on these and many other findings, Nisbett et al. (2001) conclude that cultural disparities in cognitive style are substantial and that "literally different cognitive processes are often invoked by East Asians and Westerners dealing with the same problem" (p. 305).

These disparities in cognitive style seem to be rooted in variations in cultures' social orientation (Varnum et al., 2010). They appear to grow out of Western cultures' emphasis on the individual and independence as opposed to Eastern cultures' emphasis on the group and interdependence (see Chapters 12 and 16). Some theorists speculate that variations in cultural experiences may even lead to subtle cultural differences in neural structure, or how people's brains are "wired," but evidence on this hypothesis remains scant (Park & Huang, 2010).

Problems are not the only kind of cognitive challenge that people grapple with on a regular basis. Life also seems to constantly demand decisions. Accordingly, it is critical that psychologists examine cognition as it relates to real-world challenges (Kinstone, Smilek, & Eastwook, 2008). As you might expect, cognitive psychologists have shown great interest in the process of decision making (Weber & Johnson, 2009), which is our next subject.

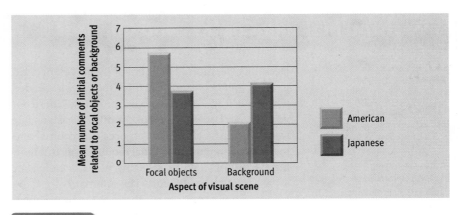

FIGURE 8.18

Cultural disparities in cognitive style.

In one of the studies conducted by Masuda and Nisbett (2001), the participants were asked to describe computer-animated visual scenes. As you can see, the initial comments made by American subjects referred more to focal objects in the scenes, whereas the initial comments made by Japanese subjects referred more to background elements in the scenes. These findings are consistent with the hypothesis that Easterners see wholes (a holistic cognitive style) where Westerners see parts (an analytic cognitive style). (Data from Masuda & Nisbett, 2001)

REVIEW OF KEY POINTS

▷ In studying problem solving, psychologists have differentiated among several types of problems. In problems that require inducing structure, the problem solver must discover the relationships among the parts of a problem. Transformation problems require that the problem solver carry out a sequence of transformations (moves) in order to reach a specific goal. Arrangement problems require the problem solver to arrange the parts in a way that satisfies a general goal.

▷ Common barriers to problem solving include functional fixedness, mental set, getting bogged down in irrelevant information, and placing unnecessary constraints on one's solutions. An algorithm is a procedure for trying all possible alternatives in searching for a solution to a problem.

▷ A variety of strategies, or heuristics, are used for solving problems. When people form subgoals, they try breaking the problem into several parts. Sometimes it is useful to start at the goal state and work backward toward the initial state. Other general strategies include searching for analogies between new problems and old problems, changing the representation of problems, and taking a break from working on the problem.

▷ Some cultures encourage a field-dependent cognitive style, whereas others foster more field independence. People who are field independent tend to analyze and restructure problems more than those who are field dependent. Research suggests that Eastern cultures exhibit a more holistic cognitive style, whereas Western cultures display a more analytic cognitive style.

PREVIEW QUESTIONS

▶ How do people make choices about preferences?

▶ What factors are important in risky decision making?

▶ What shortcuts do people use in judging probabilities?

▶ What do evolutionary psychologists have to say about error and bias in human decision making?

Herbert Simon

"The capacity of the human mind for formulating and solving complex problems is very small compared with the size of the problems whose solution is required for objectively rational behavior in the real world . . . ."

Carnegie-Mellon University

Decisions, decisions. Life is full of them. You decided to read this book today. Earlier today you decided when to get up, whether to eat breakfast, and if so, what to eat. Usually you make routine decisions like these with little effort. But on occasion you need to make important decisions that require more thought. Big decisions—such as selecting a car, a home, or a job—tend to be difficult. The alternatives usually have a number of attributes that need to be weighed. For example, in choosing which university to attend, you may want to compare climate, the number of scholarships available, whether the city in which it is located has any professional sports teams, whether there are multiple program options for majoring in psychology, and so on. Scientists study decision making and rationality because they are so essential to our fundamental values, nature, and well-being (Stanovich, 2009).

Decision making involves evaluating alternatives and making choices among them. Most people try to be systematic and rational in their decision making. However, the work that earned Herbert Simon the 1978 Nobel Prize in economics (Benjamin, 2003; Leahey, 2003; Pickren, 2003) showed that people don't always live up to these goals. Spurred by Simon's analysis, psychologists have devoted several decades to the study of how cognitive biases distort people's decision making. The results of this research have sometimes been disturbing, leading some theorists to conclude that "normal adult human subjects do a singularly bad job at the business of reasoning, even when they are calm, clearheaded, and under no pressure to perform quickly" (Stich, 1990, pp. 173–174). Researchers' focus on *biases and mistakes* in making decisions may seem a little peculiar, but as Kahneman (1991) has pointed out, the study of people's misguided decisions has illuminated the process of decision making, just as the study of illusions and forgetting has enhanced our understanding of visual perception and memory, respectively.

Making Choices about Preferences: Basic Strategies

Many decisions involve choices about *preferences*, which can be made using a variety of strategies (Goldstein & Hogarth, 1997). Barry Schwartz (2004) has argued that people in modern societies are overwhelmed by an overabundance of such choices about preferences. For example, Schwartz describes how a simple visit to a local supermarket can require a consumer to choose from 285 varieties of cookies, 61 types of suntan lotions, 150 varieties of lipsticks, and 175 kinds of salad dressings.

Although increased choice is most tangible in the realm of consumer goods, Schwartz (2004) argues that it also extends into more significant domains of life. Today, people tend to have unprecedented opportunities to make choices about how they will be educated, how and where they will work, how their intimate relationships will unfold, and even how they will look (due to advances in plastic surgery). Although enormous freedom of choice sounds attractive, Schwartz argues that the overabundance of choices in modern life has unexpected costs. He feels that people routinely make errors even when choosing among a handful of alternatives and that errors become much more likely when decisions become more complex. And he explains how having more alternatives increases the potential for rumination and post-decision regret. Ultimately, he argues, the malaise associated with choice overload undermines individuals' happiness and contributes to depression.

Consistent with this analysis, recent research has suggested that when consumers have too many choices (for a specific product), they are more likely to leave a store empty-handed (Jessup et al., 2009). Why? Studies suggest that when there are many choices available, people are more likely to struggle deciding which is the best option and so they defer their decision (White & Hoffrage, 2009). Researchers have also found that having to make a lot of decisions depletes mental resources and undermines subsequent self-control (Vohs et al., 2008). How many choices are too many? That depends on a host of factors, but it appears that people prefer more choices up to a point and then further increases in options lead to decreased satisfaction with the situation (Reutskaja & Hogarth, 2009).

It is hard to say whether choice overload is as detrimental to well-being as Schwartz believes, but it is clear that people wrestle with countless choices about preferences, and their reasoning about these decisions is often far from optimal. Let's look at some strategies that people use in making these types of decisions.

Imagine that your friend Boris has found two reasonably attractive apartments and is trying to decide between them. How should he go about selecting between his alternatives? If Boris wanted to

TABLE 8.3

Application of the Additive Model to Choosing an Apartment

| Attribute | Apartment | |
	A	B
Rent	+1	+2
Noise level	−2	+3
Distance to campus	+3	−1
Cleanliness	+2	+2
Total	**+4**	**+6**

use an *additive strategy,* he would list the attributes that influence his decision. Then he would rate the desirability of each apartment on each attribute. For example, let's say that Boris wants to consider four attributes: rent, noise level, distance to campus, and cleanliness. He might make ratings from −3 to +3, like those shown in Table 8.3, add up the ratings for each alternative, and select the one with the largest total. Given the ratings in Table 8.3, Boris should select apartment B. To make an additive strategy more useful, you can *weight* attributes differently, based on their importance (Shafir & LeBoeuf, 2004). For example, if Boris considers distance to campus to be twice as important as the other considerations, he could multiply his ratings of this attribute by 2. The distance rating would then be +6 for apartment A and −2 for apartment B, and apartment A would become the preferred choice.

People also make choices by gradually eliminating less attractive alternatives (Slovic, 1990; Tversky, 1972). This strategy is called *elimination by aspects* because it assumes that alternatives are eliminated by evaluating them on each attribute or aspect in turn. Whenever any alternative fails to satisfy some minimum criterion for an attribute, it is eliminated from further consideration. To illustrate, suppose Juanita is looking for a new car. She may begin by eliminating all cars that cost over $24 000. Then she may eliminate cars that don't average at least 10 litres per 100 km. By continuing to reject choices that don't satisfy some minimum criterion on selected attributes, she can gradually eliminate alternatives until only a single car remains. The final choice in elimination by aspects depends on the order in which attributes are evaluated. For example, if cost was the last attribute Juanita evaluated, she could have previously eliminated all cars that cost under $24 000. If she has only $24 000 to spend, her decision-making strategy would not have brought her very far. Thus, when using elimination by aspects, it's best to evaluate attributes in the order of their importance.

Both the additive and the elimination-by-aspects strategies have advantages, but which strategy do people actually tend to use? Research suggests that people adapt their approach to the demands of the task. When their choices are fairly simple, they use additive strategies, but as choices become very complex, they shift toward simpler strategies, such as elimination by aspects (Payne & Bettman, 2004).

Making Choices about Preferences: Quirks and Complexities

Beyond the basics we've been discussing, research has turned up a number of quirks and complexities that people exhibit in making decisions about preferences. Some of the more interesting findings include the following:

- Emotion influences decision making. When people decide between various options (let's say, two job opportunities), their evaluations of the options' specific attributes (such as salary, commute, and work hours) fluctuate more than most models of decision making anticipated (Shafir & LeBoeuf, 2004). Models of "rational" choice assumed that people know what they like and don't like and that these evaluations would be stable, but research suggests otherwise. One reason that these judgments tend to be unstable is that they are swayed by incidental emotional fluctuations (Lerner, Small, & Loewenstein, 2004).
- Another reason these evaluations tend to be inconsistent is that *comparative* evaluations of options tend to yield different results than *separate* evaluations (assessing an option on its own, in isolation) (Hsee, Zhang, & Chen, 2004). For example, when participants directly compare a job with an $80 000 salary at a firm where one's co-workers tend to earn $100 000 against a job with a $70 000 salary at a company where peers earn only $50 000, they rate the $80 000 job as more desirable. However, when two sets of subjects evaluate the same job options in isolation, the $70 000 job is rated as more desirable (LeBoeuf & Shafir, 2005). Thus, the dynamics and implications of comparative and separate evaluations can be quite different.
- If they can avoid it, people prefer to not have to grapple with uncertainty. Consider the perplexing findings reported by Gneezy, List, and Wu (2006). They found that people were willing to pay more for a $50 gift certificate to a bookstore than for a 50/50 opportunity get either a $50 or $100 gift certificate to the same store. It does not make

WEB LINK 8.3

Online Decision Research Center Experiments
Michael Birnbaum (California State University, Fullerton) presents a range of continuing and completed experiments conducted online that illustrate how people make decisions.

sense to value a known outcome more than an unknown outcome when the worst scenario for the unknown outcome ($50) is equal to the known outcome ($50) and the best scenario is clearly superior ($100). A number of explanations have been proposed for this *uncertainty effect*. Recent research by Simonsohn (2009) suggests that the best explanation is a simple one: People do not like uncertainty. Obviously, people's distaste for uncertainty can distort their decision making.

- Judgments about the quality of various alternatives, such as consumer products, can be swayed by extraneous factors such as brand familiarity and price. In one recent demonstration of this reality, participants tasted wines and rated their quality (Plassmann et al., 2008). In some cases, they thought they were tasting two different wines, but the same wine was presented at two very different prices (such as $10 and $90). As you might guess, the more "expensive" wine garnered higher ratings. Moreover, brain imaging (fMRI scans) during the wine tasting showed higher activity in a brain region thought to register the actual experienced pleasantness of stimuli when subjects consumed the more "expensive" wine. These findings suggest that people really do get what they pay for in terms of subjective pleasure. And they show that decisions about preferences can be distorted by considerations that should be irrelevant.

Another line of research has looked at whether decisions about preferences work out better when people engage in conscious deliberation or go with intuitive, unconscious feelings based on minimal deliberation. As you may recall, our Featured Study in Chapter 5

People often have to decide between alternative products, such as computers, cars, refrigerators, and so forth, that are not all that different. They often struggle with the abundant choices and delay making a decision. Extra deliberation does not necessarily lead to better decisions.

concerned the merits of unconscious thought (see page 203). In that research, Ap Dijksterhuis and his colleagues found that for some types of decisions, unconscious thought outperformed conscious deliberation. Dijksterhuis has conducted a great deal of research on this topic, attempting to identify those types of decisions that benefit from unconscious deliberation. He has found, for example, that when people are faced with complex choices, they tend to make better decisions if they don't devote careful attention to the matter (Dijksterhuis, Bos, Nordgren, & van Baaren, 2006). Dijksterhuis believes that deliberations are taking place—but outside of conscious awareness. Thus, like studies of subliminal perception (see Chapter 4) and studies showing that sleep can enhance memory and problem solving (see Chapter 5), this study suggests that unconscious mental processes are more influential than widely assumed. Critics note that it may be premature to broadly generalize these findings to diverse kinds of decision making in the real world (Haslam, 2007).

In the studies thus far, even the "complex" choices have involved relatively simple decisions about product preferences. It's quite a leap to assume that physicians, corporate managers, and government leaders, who confront choices of profound complexity and importance, would make better decisions if they avoided careful deliberation. Although other lines of research also suggest that intuition can sometimes be superior to logic and reflection (Gladwell, 2005; Myers, 2002), the boundary conditions of this phenomenon need to be determined (Payne et al., 2008).

Taking Chances: Factors Weighed in Risky Decisions

Suppose you have the chance to play a dice game in which you might win some money. You must decide whether it would be to your advantage to play. You're going to roll a fair die. If the number 6 appears, you win $5. If one of the other five numbers appears, you win nothing. It costs you $1 every time you play. Should you participate?

This problem calls for a type of decision making that is somewhat different from making choices about preferences. In selecting alternatives that reflect preferences, people generally weigh known outcomes (apartment A will require a long commute to campus, car B will use less gas, and so forth). In contrast, *risky decision making* involves making choices under conditions of uncertainty. Uncertainty exists when people don't know what will happen. At best, they know the probability that a particular event will occur.

One way to decide whether to play the dice game would be to figure out the *expected value* of participation in the game. To do so, you would need to calculate the average amount of money you could expect to win or lose each time you play. The value of a win is $4 ($5 minus the $1 entry fee). The value of a loss is −$1. To calculate expected value, you also need to know the probability of a win or loss. Since a die has six faces, the probability of a win is one out of six, and the probability of a loss is five out of six. Thus, on five out of every six trials, you lose $1. On one out of six, you win $4. The game is beginning to sound unattractive, isn't it? We can figure out the precise expected value as follows:

$$\text{Expected value} = (1/6 \times 4) + (5/6 \times -1)$$
$$= 4/6 + (-5/6)$$
$$= -1/6$$

The expected value of this game is −1/6 of a dollar, which means that you lose an average of about 17 cents per turn. Now that you know the expected value, surely you won't agree to play. Or will you?

If we want to understand why people make the decisions they do, the concept of expected value is not enough. People frequently behave in ways that are inconsistent with expected value (Slovic, Lichtenstein, & Fischhoff, 1988). Anytime the expected value is negative, a gambler should expect to lose money. Yet a great many people gamble at racetracks and casinos and buy lottery tickets. Although they realize that the odds are against them, they continue to gamble. Even people who don't gamble buy homeowner's insurance, which has a negative expected value. After all, when you buy insurance, your expectation (and hope!) is that you will lose money on the deal.

To explain decisions that violate expected value, some theories replace the objective value of an outcome with its *subjective utility* (Fischhoff, 1988). Subjective utility represents what an outcome is personally worth to an individual. For example, buying a few lottery tickets may allow you to dream about becoming wealthy. Buying insurance may give you a sense of security. Subjective utilities like these vary from one person to another. If we know an individual's subjective utilities, we can better understand that person's risky decision making.

Another way to improve our understanding of risky decision making is to consider individuals' estimates of the *subjective probability* of events (Shafer & Tversky, 1988). If people don't know actual probabilities, they must rely on their personal estimates of probabilities. These estimates can have interesting effects on the perceived utility of various outcomes.

Heuristics in Judging Probabilities

 7f

- What are your chances of passing your next psychology test if you study for only three hours?
- How likely is a major downturn in the stock market during the upcoming year?
- What are the odds of your getting into graduate school in the field of your choice?
- These questions ask you to make probability estimates. Amos Tversky and Daniel Kahneman (1974, 1982; Kahneman & Tversky, 2000) have conducted extensive research on the *heuristics,* or mental shortcuts, that people use in grappling with probabilities (Gigerenzer & Gaissmaier, 2011). This research on heuristics earned Kahneman the Nobel Prize in economics in 2002 (unfortunately, his collaborator, Amos Tversky, died in 1996).

Availability is one such heuristic. The *availability heuristic* involves basing the estimated probability of an event on the ease with which relevant instances come to mind. For example, you may

Daniel Kahneman was awarded the Noble Prize in Economics for his collaborative work with Amos Tversky on decision making. Kahneman is only the second noneconomist to win this prize. The other was John Nash, profiled in Chapter 14, who was a mathematician.

Daniel Kahneman

"The human mind suppresses uncertainty. We're not only convinced that we know more about our politics, our businesses, and our spouses than we really do, but also that what we don't know must be unimportant."

Amos Tversky

"People treat their own cases as if they were unique, rather than part of a huge lottery. You hear this silly argument that 'The odds don't apply to me.' Why should God, or whoever runs this lottery, give you special treatment?"

Language and Thought

estimate the divorce rate by recalling the number of divorces among your friends' parents. Recalling specific instances of an event is a reasonable strategy to use in estimating the event's probability. However, if instances occur frequently but you have difficulty retrieving them from memory, your estimate will be biased. For instance, it's easier to think of words that begin with a certain letter than words that contain that letter at some other position. Hence, people should tend to respond that there are more words starting with the letter *K* than words having a *K* in the third position. To test this hypothesis, Tversky and Kahneman (1973) selected five consonants (*K, L, N, R, V*) that occur more frequently in the third position of a word than in the first. Subjects were asked whether each of the letters appears more often in the first or third position. Most of the subjects erroneously believed that all five letters were much more frequent in the first than in the third position, confirming the hypothesis.

Representativeness is another guide in estimating probabilities identified by Kahneman and Tversky (1982). The *representativeness heuristic* involves basing the estimated probability of an event on how similar it is to the typical prototype of that event. To illustrate, imagine that you flip a coin six times and keep track of how often the result is heads (H) or tails (T). Which of the following sequences is more likely?

1. T T T T T T
2. H T T H T H

People generally believe that the second sequence is more likely. After all, coin tossing is a random affair, and the second sequence looks much more representative of a random process than the first. In reality, the probability of each exact *sequence* is precisely the same ($1/2 \times 1/2 \times 1/2 \times 1/2 \times 1/2 \times 1/2 = 1/64$). Let's look at another phenomenon in which the representativeness heuristic plays a key role.

The Tendency to Ignore Base Rates 7f

> *Steve is very shy and withdrawn, invariably helpful, but with little interest in people or in the world of reality. A meek and tidy soul, he has a need for order and structure and a passion for detail. Do you think Steve is a salesperson or a librarian? (Adapted from Tversky & Kahneman, 1974, p. 1124)*

Using the *representativeness heuristic,* subjects tend to guess that Steve is a librarian because he resembles

their prototype of a librarian (Tversky & Kahneman, 1982). In reality, this is not a very wise guess, because it *ignores the base rates* of librarians and salespeople in the population. Virtually everyone knows that salespeople outnumber librarians by a wide margin (roughly 75 to 1 in North America). This fact makes it much more likely that Steve is in sales. But in estimating probabilities, people often ignore information on base rates.

Although people do not *always* neglect base rate information, it is a persistent phenomenon (Birnbaum, 2004a; Koehler, 1996). Moreover, people are particularly bad about applying base rates to themselves. For instance, Weinstein (1984; Weinstein & Klein, 1995) has found that people underestimate the risks of their own health-impairing habits while viewing others' risks much more accurately. Thus, smokers are realistic in estimating the degree to which smoking increases someone else's risk of heart attack but underestimate the risk for themselves. Similarly, people starting new companies ignore the high failure rate for new businesses, and burglars underestimate the likelihood that they will end up in jail. Thus, in risky decision making, people often think that they can beat the odds. As Amos Tversky put it, "People treat their own cases as if they were unique, rather than part of a huge lottery. You hear this silly argument that 'The odds don't apply to me.' Why should God, or whoever runs this lottery, give you special treatment?" (McKean, 1985, p. 27).

The Conjunction Fallacy 7f

Imagine that you're going to meet a man who is an articulate, ambitious, power-hungry wheeler-dealer. Do you think it's more likely that he's a university professor or a university professor who's also a politician?

People tend to guess that the man is a "university professor who's also a politician" because the description fits with the typical prototype of politicians. But stop and think for a moment. The broader category of university professors completely includes the smaller subcategory of university professors who are politicians (see Figure 8.19). The probability of being in the subcategory cannot be higher than the probability of being in the broader category. It's a logical impossibility!

Tversky and Kahneman (1983) call this error the *conjunction fallacy*. The *conjunction fallacy* occurs when people estimate that the odds of two

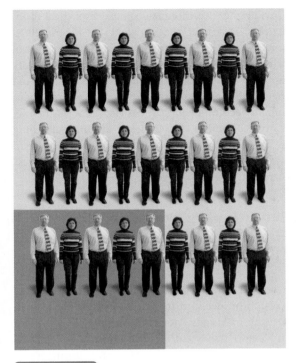

The conjunction fallacy.

People routinely fall victim to the conjunction fallacy, but as this diagram makes obvious, the probability of being in a subcategory (university professors who are also politicians) cannot be higher than the probability of being in the broader category (university professors). As this case illustrates, it often helps to represent a problem in a diagram.

uncertain events happening together are greater than the odds of either event happening alone. The conjunction fallacy has been observed in a number of studies and has generally been attributed to the powerful influence of the representativeness heuristic (Epstein, Donovan, & Denes-Raj, 1999), although some doubts have been raised about this interpretation (Fisk, 2004).

Behavioural Economics

After reading the title for this section, "Behavioural Economics," you may have wondered why we are discussing economics in a psychology textbook and what the two disciplines have to do with each other. There are separate departments for each discipline in most universities and, while some of you might be taking introductory courses in each subject, they might seem quite distinct. You would not be alone in thinking this way. Historically, they have followed different paths. As we described in Chapter 1, psychology has adopted the experimental methods of natural science. Economics, on the other hand, has focused on humans as "motivated by rational

concept check 8.3

Recognizing Heuristics in Decision Making

Check your understanding of heuristics in decision making by trying to identify the heuristics used in the following example. Each numbered element in the anecdote below illustrates a problem-solving heuristic. Write the relevant heuristic in the space on the left. You can find the answers in Appendix A.

_____ 1. Marsha can't decide on a major. She evaluates all of the majors available at her university on the attributes of how much she would enjoy them (likability), how challenging they are (difficulty), and how good the job opportunities are in the field (employability). She drops from consideration any major that she regards as "poor" on any of these three attributes.

_____ 2. When she considers history as a major, she thinks to herself, "Gee, I know four history graduates who are still looking for work," and concludes that the probability of getting a job using a history degree is very low.

_____ 3. She finds that every major gets a "poor" rating on at least one attribute, so she eliminates everything. Because this is unacceptable, she decides she has to switch to another strategy. Marsha finally focuses her consideration on five majors that received just one "poor" rating. She uses a four-point scale to rate each of these majors on each of the three attributes she values. She adds up the ratings and selects the major with the highest total as her leading candidate.

self-interest" and often employs mathematical models and the notion of revealed preferences (Hilton, 2008). While it is true that early economists included psychological variables in their analyses (Smith, 1759; but see Smith, 1784), most modern approaches have focused on the rationality of economic decision making, exploring theories such as *rational choice theory* (De Cremer, Zeelenberg, & Murnighan, 2006). More recently however, economics has been influenced by psychologists working in the area of decision making, and in current economics textbooks you will see references to behavioural economics (e.g., Samuelson & Nordhaus, 2005). *Behavioural economics is a field of study that examines the effects of humans' actual (not idealized) decision-making processes on economic decisions.*

As we suggested earlier, most people try to be systematic and rational in their decision making. This is a model followed traditionally by much of the work in economics; the emphasis is on rationality. Work in the psychology of decision making has served to introduce evidence that this assumption of rationality in decision making has clear limits. The work that earned Herbert Simon the 1978 Nobel Prize (Simon, 1991) in economics showed that people don't always live up to these goals of being systematic and rational. Before Simon's work,

Leda Cosmides and John Tooby

"The problems our cognitive devices are designed to solve do not reflect the problems our modern life experiences lead us to see as normal.... Instead, they are the ancient and seemingly esoteric problems that our hunter–gatherer ancestors encountered generation after generation over hominid evolution."

WEB LINK 8.4

Has Natural Selection Shaped How Humans Reason?

This link will take you to a recorded talk by Leda Cosmides and John Tooby (University of California, Santa Barbara) in which they discuss their evolutionary perspective on human decision making.

most traditional theories in economics assumed that people make rational choices to maximize their economic gains. Simon (1957) demonstrated that people have a limited ability to process and evaluate information on numerous facets of possible alternatives. Thus, Simon's *theory of bounded rationality* asserts that people tend to use simple strategies in decision making that focus on only a few facets of available options and often result in "irrational" decisions that are less than optimal.

Collaborative work by Kahneman and Tversky (Kahneman, 2003a, 2003b) on the nature and prevalence of biases in decision making, some of which we have just reviewed, had a significant impact on economic theory. In fact, their paper entitled "Prospect Theory" (Kahneman & Tversky, 1979), a model of decision making under uncertainty, is the most cited paper ever to appear in the major economics journal *Econimetrica* and it was the second most cited paper in all of economics between 1975 and 2000 (Wu, Zhang, & Gonzoles, 2004).

In their work, Kahneman and Tversky were able to document that humans in their decision making often departed from the "rationality" that dominated classical economic thought. They argued, for example, that how decision alternatives are *framed* dramatically affects our decisions. *Framing* refers to how decision issues are posed or how choices are structured. For instance, some oil companies charge gas station patrons more when they pay with a credit card. This fee clearly is a credit surcharge that results in a small financial loss. However, the oil companies never explicitly label it as a surcharge. Instead, they assert that they offer a discount for cash. Thus, they frame the decision as a choice between the normal price or an opportunity for a gain. They understand that it's easier for customers to forsake a gain than it is to absorb a loss. The concept of framing is further elaborated in the Personal Application on page 383.

Human thought is often biased—biased by processes such as a belief in the law of small numbers (discussed in the Personal Application near the end of this chapter), and by a tendency to rely on heuristics such as availability and representativeness. Since the pioneering work of Kahneman and Tversky, a vast literature has grown up at the interface of psychology and economics (e.g., Ariely, 2008; Camerer, Loewenstein, & Rabin, 2004; De Cremer, Zeelenberg, & Murnighan, 2006; Frey & Stutzer, 2007; Lewis, 2008; McKenzie, 2010), painting a more realistic picture of decision making. The term *behavioural economics* captures the orientation of this work as an attempt to increase the "explanatory power of economics by

providing it with more realistic psychological foundations" (Camerer, Loewenstein, & Rabin, 2004, p. 3). According to Kahneman, the starting point of behavioural economics is that "people are not fully rational." The work of Kahneman and Tversky and their colleagues has changed the way we think about human decision making. It has also changed the way many economists view decision making. According to Harvard professor Max Bazerman, Kahneman and Tversky started a "revolution in economics" (Lambert, 2006).

Evolutionary Analyses of Flaws in Human Decision Making

A central conclusion of the last three decades of research on decision making has been that human decision-making strategies are riddled with errors and biases that yield surprisingly irrational results (Goldstein & Hogarth, 1997; Shafir & LeBoeuf, 2002). Theorists have discovered that people have "mental limitations" and have concluded that people are not as bright and rational as they think they are.

So, we have quite a paradox: How can humans appear so dumb, when animals appear so bright? This paradox has led some evolutionary psychologists to reconsider the work on human decision making, and their take on the matter is quite interesting. First, they argue that traditional decision research has imposed an invalid and unrealistic standard of rationality, which assumes that people should be impeccable in applying the laws of deductive logic and statistical probability while objectively and precisely weighing multiple factors in arriving at decisions (Gigerenzer, 2000). Second, they argue that humans only *seem* irrational because cognitive psychologists have been asking the wrong questions and formulating problems in the wrong ways—ways that have nothing to do with the adaptive problems that the human mind has evolved to solve (Cosmides & Tooby, 1996).

According to Leda Cosmides and John Tooby (1994, 1996), the human mind consists of a large number of specialized cognitive mechanisms that have emerged over the course of evolution to solve specific adaptive problems, such as finding food, shelter, and mates and dealing with allies and enemies. Thus, human decision-making and problem-solving strategies have been tailored to handle real-world adaptive problems. Participants perform poorly in cognitive research, say Cosmides and Tooby, because it confronts them with contrived, artificial problems that do not involve natural categories and have no adaptive significance.

Thus, evolutionary theorists assert that many errors in human reasoning, such as neglect of base rates and the conjunction fallacy, should vanish if classic lab problems are reformulated in terms of raw frequencies rather than probabilities and base rates. Consistent with this analysis, evolutionary psychologists have shown that some errors in reasoning that are seen in lab studies disappear or are decreased when problems are presented in ways that resemble the type of input humans would have processed in ancestral times (Brase, Cosmides, & Tooby, 1998; Hertwig & Gigerenzer, 1999). So the debate continues (Keys & Schwartz, 2007; Shafir & LeBoeuf, 2002).

Fast and Frugal Heuristics

To further expand on the evolutionary point of view, Gerd Gigerenzer has argued that humans' reasoning largely depends on "fast and frugal heuristics" that are quite a bit simpler than the complicated mental processes studied in traditional cognitive research (Gigerenzer, 2000, 2004, 2008; Todd & Gigerenzer, 2000, 2007). According to Gigerenzer, organisms from toads to stockbrokers have to make fast decisions under demanding circumstances with limited information. In most instances, organisms (including humans) do not have the time, resources, or cognitive capacities to gather all of the relevant information, consider all of the possible options, calculate all of the probabilities and risks, and then make the statistically optimal decision. Instead, they use quick-and-dirty heuristics that are less than perfect but that work well enough most of the time to be adaptive in the real world.

To explore these fast and frugal heuristics, Gigerenzer and his colleagues have typically studied inferences from *memory*, which challenge participants to search some portion of their general knowledge, rather than inferences from *givens*, which challenge participants to draw logical conclusions from information provided by the experimenter. What has this research revealed? It has demonstrated that fast and frugal heuristics can be surprisingly effective. One heuristic that is often used in selecting between alternatives based on some quantitative dimension is the *recognition heuristic*, which works as follows: If one of two alternatives is recognized and the other is not, infer that the recognized alternative has the higher value. Consider the

following questions: Which city has more inhabitants: San Diego or San Antonio? Hamburg or Munich? In choosing between U.S. cities, American college students weighed a lifetime of facts useful for inferring population and made the correct choice 71 percent of the time; in choosing between German cities about which they knew very little, the same students depended on the recognition heuristic and chose correctly 73 percent of the time (Goldstein & Gigerenzer, 2002). Thus, the recognition heuristic allowed students to perform just as well with very limited knowledge as they did with extensive knowledge.

Gigerenzer and his colleagues have studied a variety of other quick, one-reason decision-making strategies and demonstrated that they can yield inferences that are just as accurate as much more elaborate and time-consuming strategies that carefully weigh many factors (Marewski, Gaissmaier, & Gigerenzerm 2010). And they have demonstrated that people actually use these fast and frugal heuristics in a diverse array of situations (Gigerenzer & Todd, 1999; Rieskamp & Hoffrage, 1999). Thus, the study of fast and frugal heuristics promises to be an intriguing new line of research in the study of human decision making.

How have traditional decision-making theorists responded to the challenge presented by Gigerenzer and other evolutionary theorists? They acknowledge that people often rely on fast and frugal heuristics, but they argue that this reality does not make decades of research on carefully reasoned approaches to decision making meaningless. Rather, they propose *dual-process theories*, positing that people depend on two very different modes or systems of thinking when making decisions (De Neys, 2006; Evans, 2007; Gilovich & Griffin, 2010; Kahneman, 2003; Stanovich & West, 2002). One system consists of quick, simple, effortless, automatic judgments, like Gigerenzer's fast and frugal heuristics, which traditional theorists prefer to characterize as "intuitive thinking." The second system consists of slower, more elaborate, effortful, controlled judgments, like those studied in traditional decision research. According to this view, the second system monitors and corrects the intuitive system as needed and takes over when complicated or important decisions loom. Thus, traditional theorists maintain that fast and frugal heuristics and reasoned, rule-governed decision strategies exist side by side and that both need to be studied to fully understand decision making.

Four of our unifying themes have been especially prominent in this chapter. The first is the continuing question about the relative influences of heredity and environment. The controversy about how children acquire language skills replays the nature versus nurture debate. The behaviourist theory, that children learn language through imitation and reinforcement, emphasizes the importance of the environment. The nativist theory, that children come equipped with an innate language acquisition device, argues for the importance of biology. The debate is far from settled, but the accumulating evidence suggests that language development depends on both nature and nurture, as more recent interactionist theories have proposed.

The second pertinent theme is the empirical nature of psychology. For many decades, psychologists paid little attention to cognitive processes, because most of them assumed that thinking is too private to be studied scientifically. During the 1950s and 1960s, however, psychologists began to devise creative new ways to measure mental processes. These innovations fuelled the cognitive revolution that put the *psyche* (the mind) back in psychology. Thus, once again, we see how empirical methods are the lifeblood of the scientific enterprise.

Third, the study of cognitive processes shows how there are both similarities and differences across cultures in behaviour. On the one hand, we saw that language development unfolds in much the same way in widely disparate cultures and that thought processes are largely invariant in spite of sharp differences in cultures' linguistic heritage. On the other hand, we learned that there are interesting cultural variations in cognitive style.

The fourth theme is the subjective nature of human experience. We have seen that decision making is a highly subjective process. For example, probabilities weighed in decisions that are objectively identical can subjectively seem very different. The subjectivity of decision processes will continue to be prominent in the upcoming Personal Application, which discusses some more common pitfalls in reasoning about decisions.

Understanding Pitfalls in Reasoning about Decisions

Consider the following scenario:

Laura is in a casino, watching people play roulette. The 38 slots in the roulette wheel include 18 black numbers, 18 red numbers, and 2 green numbers. Hence, on any one spin, the probability of red or black is slightly less than 50–50 (0.474, to be exact). Although Laura hasn't been betting, she has been following the pattern of results in the game very carefully. The ball has landed in red seven times in a row. Laura concludes that black is long overdue and she jumps into the game, betting heavily on black.

Has Laura made a good bet? Do you agree with Laura's reasoning? Or do you think that Laura misunderstands the laws of probability? You'll find out soon, as we discuss how people reason their way to decisions—and how their reasoning can go awry.

The pioneering work of Amos Tversky and Daniel Kahneman (1974, 1982) led to an explosion of research on risky decision making. In their efforts to identify the heuristics that people use in decision making, investigators stumbled onto quite a few misconceptions, oversights, and biases (Kahneman & Klein 2009). It turns out that people deviate in predictable ways from optimal decision strategies—with surprising regularity (Dawes, 2001; Gilovich, Griffin, & Kahneman, 2002). Moreover, it appears that no one is immune to these errors in thinking. In recent research, Stanovich and West (2008) examined the relationship between intelligence (estimated by SAT scores) and the ability to avoid a host of cognitive biases and flaws. For the most part they found that cognitive ability did not correlate with the ability to avoid irrational errors in thinking. In other words, extremely bright people are just as vulnerable to irrational thinking as everyone else. Fortunately, however, some research suggests that increased awareness of common shortcomings in reasoning about decisions can lead to fewer errors in thinking and improved decision making (Milkman, Chugh, & Bazerman, 2009;

Lilienfeld, Ammirati, & Landfield, 2009). With this goal in mind, let's look at some common pitfalls in decision making.

The Gambler's Fallacy 7f

As you may have guessed by now, Laura's reasoning in our opening scenario is flawed. A great many people tend to believe that Laura has made a good bet (Stanovich, 2003; Tversky & Kahneman, 1982). However, they're wrong. Laura's behaviour illustrates the *gambler's fallacy*—the belief that the odds of a chance event increase if the event hasn't occurred recently. People believe that the laws of probability should yield fair results and that a random process must be self-correcting (Burns & Corpus, 2004). These aren't bad assumptions in the long run. However, they don't apply to individual, independent events.

The roulette wheel does not remember its recent results and make adjustments for them. Each spin of the wheel is an independent event. The probability of black on each spin remains at 0.474, even if red comes up 100 times in a row! The gambler's fallacy reflects the pervasive influence of the *representativeness heuristic*. In betting on black, Laura is predicting that future results will be more representative of a random process. This logic can be used to estimate the probability of black across a *string of spins*. But it doesn't apply to a *specific spin* of the roulette wheel.

The Law of Small Numbers 7f

Envision a small urn filled with a mixture of red and green beads. You know that two-thirds of the beads are one colour and one-third are the other colour. However, you don't know whether red or green predominates. A blindfolded person reaches into the urn and comes up with three red beads and one green bead. These beads are put back

into the urn and a second person scoops up 14 red beads and 10 green beads. Both samplings suggest that red beads outnumber green beads in the urn. But which sample provides better evidence? (Adapted from McKean, 1985, p. 25)

Many subjects report that the first sampling is more convincing because of the greater preponderance of red over green. What are the actual odds that each sampling accurately reflects the dominant colour in the urn? The odds for the first sampling are four to one. These aren't bad odds, but the odds that the second sampling is accurate are much higher—16 to 1. Why? Because the second sample is substantially larger than the first. The likelihood of misleading results is much greater in a small sample than in a large one. For example, in flipping a fair coin, the odds of getting all heads in a sample of five coin flips dwarfs the odds of getting all heads in a sample of 100 coin flips.

Most people appreciate the value of a large sample as an abstract principle, but they don't fully understand that results based on small samples are more variable and more likely to be a fluke (Well, Pollatsek, & Boyce, 1990). Hence, they frequently assume that results based on small samples are representative of the population (Poulton, 1994). Tversky and Kahneman (1971) call this the *belief in the law of small numbers*. This misplaced faith in small numbers explains why people are often willing to draw general conclusions based on a few individual cases.

Overestimating the Improbable 7f

Various causes of death are paired up below. In each pairing, which is the more likely cause of death?

Asthma or tornadoes?

Accidental fall or firearms accident?

Tuberculosis or floods?

Suicide or murder?

Table 8.4 shows the actual mortality rates for each of the causes of death just listed. As you can see, the first choice in each pair is the more common cause of death. If you guessed wrong for several pairings, don't feel badly. Like many other people, you may be a victim of the tendency to *overestimate the improbable*. People tend to greatly overestimate the likelihood of dramatic, vivid—but infrequent—events that receive heavy media coverage. Thus, the number of fatalities due to tornadoes, firearms accidents, floods, and murders is usually overestimated (Slovic, Fischhoff, & Lichtenstein, 1982). Fatalities due to asthma and other common diseases, which receive less media coverage, tend to be underestimated. For instance, a majority of subjects estimate that tornadoes kill more people than asthma, even though asthma fatalities outnumber tornado fatalities by a ratio of 80 to 1. This tendency to exaggerate the improbable reflects the operation of the *availability heuristic* (Reber, 2004). Instances of floods, tornadoes, and such are readily available in memory because people are exposed to a great deal of publicity about such events.

Marc Serota/Reuters/Landov

The availability heuristic can be dramatized by juxtaposing the unrelated phenomena of floods and asthma. Many people are killed by floods, but far more die from asthma (see Table 8.4). However, since the news media report flood fatalities frequently and prominently, but rarely focus on deaths from asthma, people tend to assume that flood-related deaths are more common. Even in 2005, when Hurricane Katrina (whose devastation is shown in this photo) killed more than 1200 people, the death rate from floods was still below typical death rates for asthma.

Confirmation Bias and Belief Perseverance

Imagine a young physician examining a sick patient. The patient is complaining of a high fever and a sore throat. The physician must decide on a diagnosis from among a myriad of possible diseases. The physician thinks that it may be the flu. She asks the patient if he feels "achy all over." The answer is "yes." The physician asks if the symptoms began a few days ago. Again, the response is "yes." The physician concludes that the patient has the flu. (Adapted from Halpern, 1984, pp. 215–216)

Do you see any flaws in the physician's reasoning? Has she probed into the causes of the patient's malady effectively? No, she has asked about symptoms that would be consistent with her preliminary diagnosis, but she has not inquired about symptoms that could rule it out. Her questioning of the patient illustrates *confirmation bias*—the tendency to seek information that supports one's decisions and beliefs while ignoring disconfirming information (see Figure 8.20). This bias is common in medical diagnosis and other forms of decision making (Nickerson, 1998). There's nothing wrong with searching for confirming evidence to support one's decisions. However, people should also seek disconfirming evidence—which they often neglect to do.

A closely related problem is *myside bias*—the tendency to evaluate evidence in a manner slanted in favour of one's own opinions (Stanovich & West, 2007). For example, in one study (Stanovich & West, 2008) subjects read that "Ford Explorers are eight times more likely than a typical family car to kill occupants of another car in a crash." They were informed that the German government was considering banning Ford Explorers and asked whether they agreed with the ban. In another condition, similar subjects read that a specific German car was eight times more likely to kill occupants of other cars. They were told that the U.S. government was considering banning the car and asked whether they agreed with the ban. Although the situations were identical, American subjects were significantly more likely to support the ban of the German car than the ban of the Ford Explorer. Myside bias may also explain why people tend to believe that the candidates they support will prevail in elections. For instance, a study of American voters in the period leading up to the 2008 U.S. presidential election found that Democrats predicted that the Democratic candidate (Barack Obama) would win, whereas Republicans

TABLE 8.4

Actual U.S. Mortality Rates for Selected Causes of Death

Cause of Death	Rate	Cause of Death	Rate
Asthma	2 000	Tornadoes	25
Accidental falls	6 021	Firearms accidents	320
Tuberculosis	400	Floods	44
Suicide	11 300	Homicide	6 800

Note: Mortality rates are per 100 million people and are based on the *Statistical Abstract of the United States, 2001*.

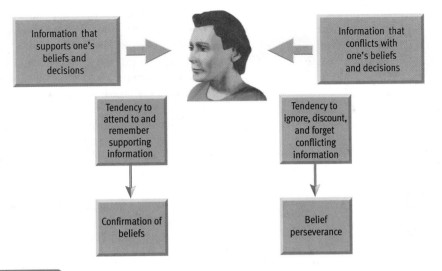

Confirmation bias and belief perseverance.
Confirmation bias exists when people seek out and react favourably to information that supports their beliefs. Belief perseverance is the tendency to cling to beliefs despite exposure to contradictory evidence.

considerably in their tendency to be over-confident (Stanovich, 1999), but overconfidence effects have been seen in perceptual judgments, predictions of sports results, and economic forecasts, among many other things (West & Stanovich, 1997). The overconfidence effect is seen even when people make probability predictions about themselves (Vallone et al., 1990). The overconfidence effect is also seen among experts in many walks of life (Fischhoff, 1988). Studies have shown that physicians, weather forecasters, military leaders, gamblers, investors, and scientists tend to be overconfident about their predictions. As Daniel Kahneman puts it, "The human mind suppresses uncertainty. We're not only convinced that we know more about our politics, our businesses, and our spouses than we really do, but also that what we don't know must be unimportant" (McKean, 1985, p. 27).

were much more likely to predict that the Republican candidate (John McCain) would win (Krizan, Miller, & Johar, 2010).

Confirmation bias contributes to another, related problem called *belief perseverance*—the tendency to hang on to beliefs in the face of contradictory evidence (Gorman, 1989). It is difficult to dislodge an idea after having embraced it. To investigate this phenomenon, researchers have given subjects evidence to establish a belief (e.g., high-risk takers make better firefighters) and later exposed the subjects to information discrediting the idea. These studies have shown that the disconfirming evidence tends to fall on deaf ears (Ross & Anderson, 1982). Thus, once people arrive at a decision, they are prone to accept supportive evidence at face value while subjecting contradictory evidence to tough, skeptical scrutiny.

The Overconfidence Effect 7f

Make high and low estimates for Canada's Department of National Defence's total spending budgeted for the year 2010. Choose estimates far enough apart to be 98 percent confident that the actual figure lies between them. In other words, you should feel that there is only a 2 percent chance that the correct figure is lower than your low estimate or higher than your high estimate. Write your estimates in the spaces provided, before reading further.

High estimate: _____
Low estimate: _____

When working on problems like this one, people reason their way to their best estimate and then create a confidence interval around it. For instance, let's say that you arrived at $8 billion as your best estimate of the defence budget. You would then expand a range around that estimate—say $6 billion to $10 billion—that you're sure will contain the correct figure. The answer in this case is $13 billion. If the answer falls outside your estimated range, you are not unusual. In making this type of estimate, people consistently tend to make their confidence intervals too narrow (Lichtenstein, Fischhoff, & Phillips, 1982; Soll & Klayman, 2004). For example, subjects' 98 percent confidence intervals should include the correct answer 98 percent of the time, but they actually do so only about 60 percent of the time.

The crux of the problem is that people tend to put too much faith in their estimates, beliefs, and decisions, even when they should know better, a principle called the *overconfidence effect*. People vary

The Effects of Framing 7f

Another consideration in making decisions involving risks is the framing of questions (Tversky & Kahneman, 1988, 1991). *Framing* refers to how decision issues are posed or how choices are structured. People often allow a decision to be shaped by the language or context in which it's presented, rather than explore it from different perspectives. Consider the following scenario, which is adapted from Kahneman and Tversky (1984, p. 343):

> *Imagine that a country is preparing for the outbreak of a dangerous disease, which is expected to kill 600 people. Two alternative programs to combat the disease have been proposed. Assume that the exact scientific estimates of the consequences of the programs are as follows:*

- *If Program A is adopted, 200 people will be saved.*
- *If Program B is adopted, there is a one-third probability that all 600 people will be saved and a two-thirds probability that no people will be saved.*

Kahneman and Tversky found that 72 percent of their subjects chose the "sure thing" (Program A) over the "risky gamble"

Language and Thought   **385**

(Program B). However, they obtained different results when the alternatives were reframed as follows:

- *If Program C is adopted, 400 people will die.*
- *If Program D is adopted, there is a one-third probability that nobody will die and a two-thirds probability that all 600 people will die.*

Although framed differently, Programs A and B represent exactly the same probability situation as Programs C and D (see Figure 8.21). In spite of this, 78 percent of the subjects chose Program D. Thus, subjects chose the sure thing when the decision was framed in terms of lives saved. They went with the risky gamble, however, when the decision was framed in terms of lives lost. Obviously, sound decision making should yield consistent decisions that are not altered dramatically by superficial changes in how options are presented, so framing effects once again highlight the foibles of human decision making.

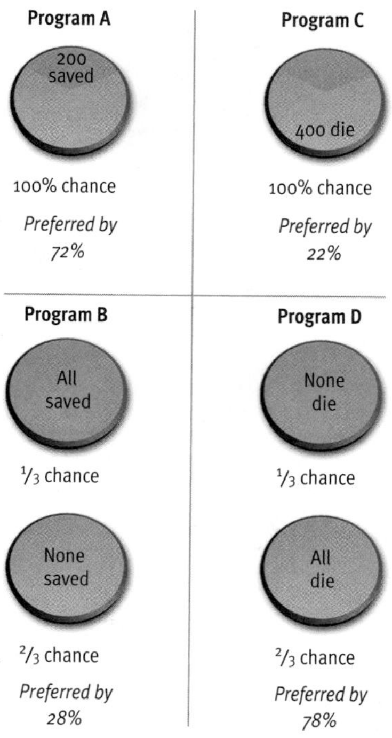

FIGURE 8.21

The framing of questions.

This chart shows that Programs A and C involve an identical probability situation, as do Programs B and D. When choices are framed in terms of possible gains, people prefer the safer plan. However, when choices are framed in terms of losses, people are more willing to take a gamble.

Loss Aversion

Another interesting phenomenon is *loss aversion*—in general, losses loom larger than gains of equal size (Kahneman & Tversky, 1979; Novemsky & Kahneman, 2005). Thus, most people expect that the negative impact of losing $1000 will be greater than the positive impact of winning $1000. Loss aversion can lead people to pass up excellent opportunities. For instance, subjects tend to decline a theoretical gamble in which they are given an 85 percent chance of doubling their life savings versus a 15 percent chance of losing their life savings, which mathematically is vastly more attractive than any bet one could place in a casino (Gilbert, 2006). Loss aversion can influence decisions in many areas of life, including choices of consumer goods, investments, business negotiations, and approaches to health care (Camerer, 2005; Klapper, Ebling, & Temme, 2005).

The problem with loss aversion, as Daniel Gilbert and his colleagues have shown, is that people generally overestimate the intensity and duration of the negative emotions they will experience after all sorts of losses, ranging from losing a job or romantic partner to botching an interview or watching one's team lose in a big game (Gilbert, Driver-Linn, & Wilson, 2002; Kermer et al., 2006) (see Chapter 10). Interestingly, people overestimate the emotional impact of losses because they do not appreciate how good most of us are at rationalizing, discounting, and distorting negative events in our lives.

REVIEW OF KEY POINTS

- The heuristics that people use in decision making can lead to various flaws in reasoning. For instance, the use of the representativeness heuristic contributes to the gambler's fallacy and faith in small numbers.
- The availability heuristic underlies the tendency to overestimate the improbable. People tend to cling to their beliefs in spite of contradictory evidence, in part because they exhibit confirmation bias—the tendency to seek only information that supports one's view.
- People generally fail to appreciate these shortcomings, which leads to the overconfidence effect. Evidence suggests that the more confident you feel about a prediction, the more likely it is that you are overconfident. In evaluating choices, it is wise to understand that decisions can be influenced by the language in which they are framed and by the fact that losses seem to loom larger than gains of the same size.

Shaping Thought with Language: "Only a Naïve Moron Would Believe That"

As explained in the chapter, the strong version of the *linguistic relativity hypothesis*—the idea that people's language determines how they think about things—has *not* been supported by research (Hunt & Agnoli, 1991). But research does show that carefully chosen words can exert subtle influence on people's feelings about various issues (Calvert, 1997; Johnson & Dowling-Guyer, 1996; Pohl, 2004; Weatherall, 1992). In everyday life, many people clearly recognize that language can tilt thought along certain lines. This possibility is the basis for some of the concerns that have been expressed about sexist language. Women who object to being called "girls," "chicks," and "babes" believe that these terms influence the way people think about and interact with women. In a similar vein, used car dealers that sell "pre-owned cars" and airlines that outline precautions for "water landings" are manipulating language to influence thought. Indeed, bureaucrats, politicians, advertisers, and big business have refined the art of shaping thought by tinkering with language, and to a lesser degree the same techniques are used by many people in everyday interactions. Let's look at two of these techniques: semantic slanting and name-calling.

Semantic Slanting

Semantic slanting refers to deliberately choosing words to create specific emotional responses. For example, consider the crafty word choices made in the incendiary debate about abortion (Halpern, 1996). The anti-abortion movement recognized that it is better to be *for* something than to be *against* something and then decided to characterize its stance as "pro-life" rather than "anti-choice." Likewise, the faction that favoured abortion rights did not like

Semantic slanting, which consists of carefully choosing words to create specific emotional reactions, has been used extensively by both sides in the debate about abortion.

Courtesy of Charles LeBlanc

the connotation of an "anti-life" or "pro-abortion" campaign, so they characterized their position as "pro-choice." The position advocated is exactly the same either way, but the label clearly influences how people respond. Thinking along similar lines, some "pro-life" advocates have asserted that the best way to win the debate about abortion is to frequently use the words *kill* and *baby* in the same sentence (Kahane, 1992). Obviously, these are words that push people's buttons and trigger powerful emotional responses.

In his fascinating book *Doublespeak*, William Lutz (1989) describes an endless series of examples of how government, business, and advertisers manipulate language to bias people's thoughts and feelings. For example, in the language of the military, an invasion is a "pre-emptive counterattack," bombing the enemy is providing "air

support," a retreat is a "backloading of augmentation personnel," civilians accidentally killed or wounded by military strikes are "collateral damage," and troops killed by their own troops are "friendly casualties." In the world of business, layoffs and firings become "headcount reductions," "workforce adjustments," or "career alternative enhancement programs," whereas bad debts become "nonperforming assets." And in the language of bureaucrats, hospital deaths become "negative patient care outcomes" and tax increases become "revenue enhancement initiatives," leading Lutz to quip that "Nothing in life is certain except negative patient care outcome and revenue enhancement." You can't really appreciate how absurd this process can become until you go shopping for "genuine imitation leather" or "real counterfeit diamonds."

Briefings on the status of military actions are renowned for their creative but unintelligible manipulation of language, which is often necessary to obscure the unpleasant realities of war.

Of course, you don't have to be a bureaucrat or military spokesperson to use semantic slanting. For example, if a friend of yours is annoyed at her 60-year-old professor for giving a tough exam and describes him as an "old geezer," she would be using semantic slanting. She would have communicated that the professor's age is a negative factor—one that is associated with a host of unflattering stereotypes about older people. And she would have implied that he gave an inappropriate exam because of his antiquated expectations or senile incompetence—all with a couple of well-chosen words. We are all the recipients of many such messages containing emotionally laden words and content. An important skill of critical thinking is to recognize when semantic slanting is being used to influence how you think so you can resist this subtle technique.

In becoming sensitive to semantic slanting, notice how the people around you and those whom you see on television and read about in the newspapers refer to people from other racial and ethnic groups. You can probably determine a politician's attitudes toward immigration, for example, by considering the words the politician uses when speaking about people from other countries. Are the students on your campus who come from other countries referred to as "international students" or "foreign students?" The term "international" seems to convey a more positive image, with associations of being cosmopolitan and worldly. On the other hand, the term "foreign" suggests someone who is strange. Clearly, it pays to be careful when selecting the words you use in your own communication.

Name-Calling

Another way that word choice influences thinking is in the way people tend to label and categorize others through the strategy of *name-calling*. People often attempt to neutralize or combat views they don't like by attributing such views to "radical feminists," "knee-jerk liberals," "right-wingers," "religious zealots," or "extremists." In everyday interactions, someone who inspires our wrath may be labelled as a "bitch," a "moron," or a "cheapskate." In these examples, the name-calling is not subtle and is easy to recognize. But name-calling can also be used with more cunning and finesse. Sometimes, there is an *implied threat* that if you make an unpopular decision or arrive at a conclusion that is not favoured, a negative label will be applied to you. For example, someone might say, "Only a naïve moron would believe that" to influence your attitude on an issue. This strategy of *anticipatory name-calling* makes it difficult for you to declare that you favour the negatively valued belief because it means that you make yourself look like a "naïve moron." Anticipatory name-calling can also invoke positive group memberships, such as asserting that "all good Canadians will agree . . ." or "people in the know think that . . .." Anticipatory name-calling is a shrewd tactic that can be effective in shaping people's thinking.

Regardless of your position on these issues, how would you respond to someone who says, "Only a knee-jerk liberal would support racial quotas or affirmative action programs that give unfair advantages to minorities." Or "Only a stupid bigot would oppose affirmative action programs that rectify the unfair discrimination that minorities face." Can you identify the anticipatory name-calling and the attempts at semantic slanting in each of these examples? More important, can you resist attempts like these to influence how you think about a host of complicated social issues?

TABLE 8.5	**Critical Thinking Skills Discussed in This Application**
Skill	**Description**
Understanding the way language can influence thought	The critical thinker appreciates that when you want to influence how people think, you should choose your words carefully.
Recognizing semantic slanting	The critical thinker is vigilant about how people deliberately choose certain words to elicit specific emotional responses.
Recognizing name-calling and anticipatory name-calling	The critical thinker is on the lookout for name-calling and the implied threats used in anticipatory name-calling.

Key Ideas

Language: Turning Thoughts into Words

● Languages are symbolic, semantic, generative, and structured. Human languages are structured hierarchically. At the bottom of the hierarchy are the basic sound units, called *phonemes*. At the next level are *morphemes*, the smallest units of meaning.

● Children typically utter their first words around their first birthday. Vocabulary growth is slow at first, but a vocabulary spurt often begins at around 18–24 months. Children begin to combine words by the end of the second year. Their early sentences are telegraphic, in that they omit many nonessential words. Over the next several years, children gradually learn the complexities of syntax.

● Research does not support the assumption that bilingualism has a negative effect on language development or on cognitive development. The learning of a second language is facilitated by starting at a younger age and by acculturation.

● Sue Savage-Rumbaugh's work with Kanzi suggests that some animals are capable of some genuine language acquisition. Many theorists believe that humans' special talent for language is the product of natural selection.

● According to Skinner and other behaviourists, children acquire a language through imitation and reinforcement. Nativist theories assert that humans have an innate capacity to learn language rules. Today, theorists are moving toward interactionist perspectives, which emphasize the role of both biology and experience. The evidence supports only a weak version of the linguistic relativity hypothesis.

Problem Solving: In Search of Solutions

● Psychologists have differentiated among several types of problems, including problems of inducing structure, problems of transformation, and problems of arrangement. Common barriers to problem solving include functional fixedness, mental set, getting bogged down in irrelevant information, and placing unnecessary constraints on one's solutions.

● A variety of strategies, or heuristics, are used for solving problems, including trial and error, forming subgoals, working backward, searching for analogies, and changing the representation of a problem.

● Some cultures encourage a field-dependent cognitive style, whereas others foster more field independence. People who are field independent tend to analyze and restructure problems more than those who are field dependent. Research suggests that Eastern cultures exhibit a more holistic cognitive style, whereas Western cultures display a more analytic cognitive style.

Decision Making: Choices and Chances

● Simon's theory of bounded rationality suggests that human decision strategies are simplistic and often yield irrational results. An additive decision model is used when people make decisions by rating the attributes of each alternative and selecting the alternative that has the highest sum of ratings.

● When elimination by aspects is used, people gradually eliminate alternatives if their attributes fail to satisfy some minimum criterion. To some extent, people adapt their decision-making strategy to the situation, moving toward simpler strategies when choices become complex.

● Models of how people make risky decisions focus on the expected value or subjective utility of various outcomes and the objective or subjective probability that these outcomes will occur.

● People use the representativeness and availability heuristics in estimating probabilities. These heuristics can lead people to ignore base rates and to fall for the conjunction fallacy.

● Evolutionary psychologists maintain that many errors and biases in human reasoning are greatly reduced when problems are presented in ways that resemble the type of input that humans would have processed in ancestral times.

Putting It in Perspective: Themes 1, 5, 6, and 7

● Four of our unifying themes surfaced in the chapter. Our discussion of language acquisition revealed once again that all aspects of behaviour are shaped by both nature and nurture. The recent progress in the study of cognitive processes showed how science depends on empirical methods. Research on decision making illustrated the importance of subjective perceptions. We also saw that cognitive processes are moderated—to a limited degree—by cultural factors.

PERSONAL APPLICATION • Understanding Pitfalls in Reasoning about Decisions

● The heuristics that people use in decision making lead to various flaws in reasoning. For instance, the use of the representativeness heuristic contributes to the gambler's fallacy and faith in small numbers. The availability heuristic underlies the tendency to overestimate the improbable.

● People tend to cling to their beliefs in spite of contradictory evidence, in part because they exhibit confirmation bias. People generally fail to appreciate these shortcomings, which leads to the overconfidence effect. In evaluating choices, it is wise to understand that decisions can be influenced by the language in which they are framed.

CRITICAL THINKING APPLICATION • Shaping Thought with Language: "Only a Naïve Moron Would Believe That"

● Language can exert a subtle influence over how people feel about various issues. *Semantic slanting* refers to the deliberate choice of words to create specific emotional responses, as has been apparent in the debate about abortion. In anticipatory name-calling, there is an implied threat that a negative label will apply to you if you express certain views.

Key Terms

Acculturation, 359
Algorithm, 368
Availability heuristic, 377
Behavioural economics, 379
Belief perseverance, 385
Bilingualism, 357
Cognition, 349
Confirmation bias, 384
Conjunction fallacy, 378
Decision making, 374
Fast mapping, 355
Field dependence–independence, 372
Framing, 380
Functional fixedness, 367
Gambler's fallacy, 383
Heuristic, 368
Incubation effect, 372
Insight, 365
Language, 350
Language acquisition device (LAD), 363
Linguistic relativity, 364
Mental set, 367
Metalinguistic awareness, 356
Morphemes, 351
Myside bias, 384
Overextension, 356

Overregularization, 356
Phonemes, 350
Problem solving, 365
Problem space, 368
Representativeness heuristic, 378
Risky decision making, 376
Semantics, 351
Syntax, 351
Telegraphic speech, 356
Theory of bounded rationality, 380
Trial and error, 368
Underextensions, 356

Key People

Benjamin Lee Whorf, 364
Ellen Bialystok, 358
Noam Chomsky, 362
Leda Cosmides, 380
Daniel Kahneman, 377
Wallace Lambert, 359
Laura-Ann Petitto, 353
Steven Pinker, 362
Sue Savage-Rumbaugh, 361
Herbert Simon, 374
B. F. Skinner, 362
John Tooby, 380
Amos Tversky, 377
Janet Werker, 352

1. Sophie refers to all four-legged animals as "doggie." Which of the following errors does Sophie make?
   A. underextension
   B. overextension
   C. overregularization
   D. underregularization

2. How many morphemes are there in the word "unchained"?
   A. two
   B. three
   C. six
   D. nine

3. Which of the following is the key reason why nonhuman primates cannot be taught to speak?
   A. They can learn the use of symbols, but they cannot learn language rules.
   B. Their short-term memory is insufficient for handling complex thoughts.
   C. They don't have brain regions that can handle production or comprehension of symbolic communication.
   D. Their throats and mouths are not appropriate for human-like vocalization.

4. Which of the following is consistent with the main proposition of Chomsky's theory of language learning?
   A. Children possess an innate language acquisition device.
   B. Children learn language (like other skills) through imitation, reinforcement, and shaping.
   C. Language is a complex cognitive skill that can be attained only if certain cognitive milestones are reached first.
   D. Language learning is necessary so that children's increasingly complex needs can be met.

5. One group of people has 100 different words for types of bicycles. A second group has only one word for bicycle. According to the linguistic relativity hypothesis, which of the following should be true?
   A. The first group should be faster than the second group at discriminating among types of bicycles.
   B. There should be no difference in discrimination ability between the two groups, but the first group should be more confident about its answers.
   C. The first group should also have better verbal skills, on average.
   D. The second group should have fewer words for most mechanical objects.

6. Which of the following describes how arrangement problems are often solved?
   A. by maximizing a mental set
   B. in small, incremental steps
   C. through fast mapping
   D. through a burst of insight

7. Micha wanted a small table for her bedroom, but didn't have any extra money to purchase one. She decided to create a "table" by stacking up her old textbooks next to her bed. Which barrier to effective problem solving did Micha overcome?
   A. mental set
   B. irrelevant information
   C. unnecessary constraints
   D. functional fixedness

8. Which of the following illustrates the use of a heuristic?
   A. writing out a step-by-step list of instructions
   B. applying a "rule of thumb" to solving a new problem
   C. systematically attempting all possible solutions to a problem
   D. choosing to abandon a problem because it is too difficult

9. Which of the following individuals would be likely to be fastest at solving the candle problem?
   A. someone who has a holistic cognitive style
   B. someone who is field-independent
   C. someone who was raised in a society that stresses conformity
   D. someone who was raised in a sedentary agricultural culture

10. You've gone to the store to select a new watch. Which of the following situations is likely to cause you to leave the store without making a choice?
    A. The range of prices was quite wide.
    B. The store didn't carry a specific brand of watch.
    C. There were too many different watches to choose from.
    D. There were too many people in the store.

11. In which of the following decision-making situations would people tend to use additive strategies?
    A. when decisions involve relatively few options
    B. when decisions involve many options
    C. when decisions involve familiar material and issues
    D. when decisions involve novel issues

12. Scott believes that there are more engineers in his city than there are psychologists, because he knows several engineers but doesn't know any psychologists. Which method of estimating probability does Scott use?
    A. the additive model
    B. the representativeness heuristic
    C. the availability heuristic
    D. the noncompensatory model

13. Which of the following is the main error associated with the "gambler's fallacy"?
    A. People don't realize that the probability of a win in a game of chance is impossible to calculate accurately.
    B. People assume that the base rate of wins is equal to the base rate of losses.
    C. People confuse the probability of a single event with the probability of a string of events.
    D. People are too emotionally involved with the problem, so they tend to use irrational heuristics.

14. You must choose between two treatment options for your sick dog so you start researching the treatments. One website tells you that Option A results in a death rate of 20 percent. Another website indicates that the same treatment results in an 80 percent survival rate. Which of the following terms is used to describe this difference in language use?
    A. loss aversion
    B. telegraphing
    C. linguistic relativity
    D. framing

15. The statement "Only a congenital pinhead would make that choice" represents which of the following uses of language?
    A. confirmation bias
    B. syntactic slanting
    C. anticipatory name-calling
    D. telegraphic speech

See Appendix A for answers to this Practice Test.

On the Web

▶ **CourseMate**

Go to this site to find online resources directly linked to your book, including more quizzes, a glossary, flash cards, videos, and more!

▶ **CengageNow**

Go to this site for the link to CengageNOW™, your one-stop study shop. Take a pre-test for this chapter and CengageNOW™ will generate a personalized study plan based on your test results! The study plan will identify the topics you need to review and direct you to online resources to help you master those topics. You can then take a post-test to help you determine the concepts you have mastered and what you still need to work on.

▶ **Aplia**

Aplia™ is an online interactive learning solution that helps you improve comprehension—and your grade—by integrating a variety of media and tools such as video, tutorials, practice tests, and an interactive e-book.

CHAPTER 9

Intelligence and Psychological Testing

© Rebecca Atkins, York University

As we suggested in Chapter 3, people seem to be endlessly fascinated with the brain. The research and theory we discussed in that chapter revealed the many important functions that the brain serves and the abilities it affords us. Among these, of course—and this may be part of the reason for our fascination—is the notion of intelligence. Being smart or highly intelligent is often seen as a guarantee of success. If this is true, and we will evaluate the validity of this idea later in the chapter, then it makes sense that we should try to determine our absolute or relative level of intelligence. As we are growing up, it seems as if we are always trying to answer questions such as "Am I smart?" or "Who is the smartest kid in the class?" Of course, these questions raise additional questions such as "What is intelligence?" and "How would you know if you were intelligent?" The last question is a difficult one to answer and it often leads us to look for markers of intelligence. Ken Jennings has reached an almost cult-like status because of his performance on the television game show *Jeopardy*; he is a person that many people often point to as being highly intelligent.

Jennings became the most successful contestant ever on *Jeopardy*, winning 75 straight games over almost two seasons, giving 2642 correct trivia answers and winning over US$2.5 million in the process (Jennings, 2006). What do *you* think "intelligence" is? Does having the ability to answer trivia questions very well mean that you are highly intelligent or a genius? If you said "yes," then you would find yourself in notable company. For example, Thomas Edison thought trivia was a way to assess intelligence and ability level and so he developed his own trivia intelligence test to give to prospective employees. But how do we know it is a valid test of intelligence? There was little scientific interest in Edison's test, but we do have one result that might help you decide about its status as a reliable and valid IQ test. On a visit to the United States in 1921, Albert Einstein took the test. His results were announced to the world by the *New York Times* in its headline: "Einstein sees Boston: Fails on Edison Test" (*New York Times*, 1921). Einstein did not know, for example, the speed of sound. He did not think it was important to remember such things since they are "readily available" in textbooks. Einstein's wife wasn't concerned about Einstein's performance, commenting that "while Edison was an inventor who dealt with practical things, her husband was a theorist who dealt with problems of space and of the universe" (*New York Times*, 1921, p. 15). Incidentally, Ken Jennings competed against an IBM computer known

Ken Jennings with Watson the computer on *Jeopardy*.

as Watson in 2011 and lost. Does that mean that the computer was more intelligent than Jennings?

No matter how dismal his performance on Edison's test, when many of us think of highly intelligent people we often apply the label "genius" to someone like Albert Einstein. Einstein made critical contributions to our understanding of the nature of the universe, some of which we are only now, decades later, able to evaluate and confirm (Holz, 2011). Closer to home, some of us might point to Gerhard Herzberg, a Canadian who won Canada's first Nobel Prize for Chemistry in 1971. Canadians have won the Nobel Prize for Chemistry six times. Herzberg's main contributions were to the field of atomic and molecular spectroscopy (Stoicheff, 2002). Incidentally, his son Paul is a psychologist.

While few of us would disagree that the term "genius" might properly be applied to an individual who wins a Nobel Prize, would it surprise you to know that some have also applied the term *genius*

Gerhard Herzberg won the Nobel Prize for Chemistry in 1971. He worked at the University of Saskatchewan and the National Research Council.

Intelligence and Psychological Testing

Canadian golfer Moe Norman was thought to possess the "perfect swing."

Courtesy of Sun Media/Toronto Sun

to another well-known Canadian—golfer Moe Norman? Many think of him as the greatest golf striker who ever lived and as a man possessing the "perfect swing." Norman was also a math prodigy and a high school dropout (Life and Times, n.d.). Interestingly, like Einstein, Norman was considered an eccentric. He was painfully shy and would hide in order to avoid trophy presentations after he won a tournament. He lived in rented rooms and kept his possessions in the trunk of his car (O'Connor, 1995). He never drank or smoked and claimed to have had only two dates in his life. Although eccentric, he showed a phenomenal gift for hitting a golf ball. "I don't know how anyone could hit the ball better than Moe Norman" (Trevino, 1995, p. xiii).

You may be wondering what success in academia has to do with athletic success. While one seems a natural fit with the topic of intelligence, the other seems to be out of place. What Herzberg and Norman have in common is exceptional ability, but each is demonstrating exceptional ability in quite different spheres. It may surprise you, but according to some recent theories of intelligence (e.g., Gardner, 1993), both sets of abilities may reflect different facets of high intelligence. The nature of intelligence is just one of the issues we will discuss in this chapter.

Variation in intelligence, especially assumed low intelligence, has had important personal consequences for many Canadians. Consider, for example, the story of Leilani Muir, who was sterilized in 1959 at the age of 14 in Alberta (Pringle, 1997). She had tested low on one IQ test and was considered a "mental defective." Before the operation, she was deceived and was told she was having surgery on her appendix. She was a resident of Alberta's Provincial Training School for Mental Defectives and was one of many who suffered a similar fate. Muir successfully sued the Alberta government in 1996. University of Alberta psychologist Douglas Wahlsten has written extensively about this case and related issues (Wahlsten, 1997a, 1999). Leilani's story is documented in the 1996 National Film Board production *The Sterilization of Leilani Muir*.

Many parents in our society seem to be especially concerned with the issue of variation in intelligence and in ensuring that their children have access to programs that frequently imply they are able to turn a child into a gifted child or a genius. Some believe that high intelligence is a direct pathway to success and high achievement. As we discuss in this chapter, the evidence suggests that it sometimes is associated with success, but not always.

Consider, for example, William James Sidis (1898–1944) and Norbert Wiener (1894–1964), who were both members of a group of gifted children who were allowed to enroll at Harvard University as children (Conway & Siegelman, 2005; Wallace, 1986). Sidis was reading by age two and had written a textbook on anatomy and one on grammar by age six. He was academically ready for Harvard by age nine, but was refused entry because the administrators thought that he was too young. Sidis was finally admitted to Harvard when he was 11, the youngest-ever undergraduate at Harvard, according to a 1909 *The New York Times* article. Wiener was equally talented. By eight, Wiener was doing algebra, geometry, and trigonometry in his head, and showed that he had a photographic memory. Wiener showed up for his first day of Harvard carrying one of his favourite books, Hibben's (1926) *The Problems of Philosophy*. He earned his Ph.D. from Harvard at about the same age that most individuals are just entering first-year university. Wiener's father, a professor at Harvard, was himself quite remarkable: He could speak 40 languages fluently (Conway & Siegelman, 2005).

While Norbert Wiener (Weiner, 1953) went on to great success in applied mathematics and to found the field of cybernetics, Sidis never capitalized on his potential. He often worked at menial jobs, some provided for him by Wiener, and became obsessed with trivia (Winner, 1996). Sidis was ridiculed in a 1937 article in *The New Yorker* magazine for his lack of success. He ended up suffering psychological problems and died at the age of 46. In this chapter, we will review some of the scientific work on this issue—the relationship of giftedness and success across the life span.

North American society has embraced psychological testing (Giordano, 2005). Each year in Canada alone, people take *millions* of intelligence and achievement tests. Scholarships, degrees, jobs, and self-concepts are on the line as Canadians attempt to hurdle a seemingly endless succession of tests. Because your life is so strongly affected by how you perform on psychological tests, it pays to be aware of their strengths and limitations. In this chapter we'll explore many questions about testing, including the following:

- How did psychological testing become so prevalent in modern society?
- How do psychologists judge the validity of their tests?
- What exactly do intelligence tests measure?
- Is intelligence inherited? If so, to what extent?
- How do psychological tests measure creativity?

We'll begin by introducing some basic concepts in psychological testing. Then we'll explore the history of intelligence tests, because they provided

Most children become familiar with standardized psychological tests— intelligence, achievement, and aptitude tests—in school settings.

Mike Flippo/Shutterstock.com

the model for subsequent psychological tests. Next we'll address practical questions about how intelligence tests work. After examining the nature-versus-nurture debate as it relates to intelligence, we'll explore some new directions in the study of intelligence. Along the way we will also discuss how racism has been implicated in the scientific debate about the nature of group differences in IQ and the primacy of genetics in explaining those group differences (Gould, 1996; Jensen, 1969). In the Personal Application, we'll discuss efforts to measure and understand another type of mental ability: creativity. In the Critical Thinking Application, we will critique some of the reasoning used in the vigorous debate about the roots of intelligence.

Key Concepts in Psychological Testing

A *psychological test* is a standardized measure of a sample of a person's behaviour. Psychological tests are measurement instruments. They're used to measure the *individual differences* that exist among people in abilities, aptitudes, interests, and aspects of personality.

Your responses to a psychological test represent a *sample* of your behaviour. The word *sample* should alert you to one of the key limitations of psychological tests: A particular behaviour sample may not be representative of your characteristic behaviour. Everyone has bad days. A stomachache, a fight with a friend, a problem with your car—all might affect your responses to a particular test on a particular day. Because of the limitations of the sampling process, test scores should always be interpreted *cautiously*.

Principal Types of Tests 7a

Psychological tests are used extensively in research, but most of them were developed to serve a practical

purpose outside of the laboratory. Most tests can be placed in one of two broad categories: mental ability tests and personality tests.

Mental Ability Tests 7a

Psychological testing originated with efforts to measure general mental ability. Today, tests of mental abilities remain the most common kind of psychological test. This broad class of tests includes three principal subcategories: intelligence tests, aptitude tests, and achievement tests.

Intelligence tests measure general mental ability. They're intended to assess intellectual potential rather than previous learning or accumulated knowledge. *Aptitude tests* are also designed to measure potential more than knowledge, but they break mental ability into separate components. Thus, *aptitude tests* assess specific types of mental abilities. For example, the *Differential Aptitude Tests* assess verbal reasoning, numerical ability, abstract

PREVIEW QUESTIONS

▶ Why is it wise to be cautious when interpreting test results?

▶ What are the two main categories of psychological tests?

▶ What makes a test standardized?

▶ What are test norms and percentile scores?

▶ What is reliability, and how can it be measured?

▶ What are the three types of test validity?

reasoning, perceptual speed and accuracy, mechanical reasoning, space relationships, spelling, and language usage. Like aptitude tests, *achievement tests* have a specific focus, but they're supposed to measure previous learning instead of potential. Thus, *achievement tests gauge a person's mastery and knowledge of various subjects* (such as reading, English, or history).

Personality Tests

7a

If you had to describe yourself in a few words, what words would you use? Are you introverted? Independent? Ambitious? Enterprising? Conventional? Assertive? Domineering? Words such as these refer to personality traits. These *traits* can be assessed systematically with personality tests, of which there are more than 500. *Personality tests measure various aspects of personality, including motives, interests, values, and attitudes.* Many psychologists prefer to call these tests personality *scales* because, unlike tests of mental abilities, the questions do not have right and wrong answers. We'll look at the various types of personality scales in Chapter 12.

Standardization and Norms   SIM8, 7a, 7b, 7c

Both personality scales and tests of mental abilities are *standardized* measures of behaviour. *Standardization refers to the uniform procedures used in the administration and scoring of a test.* All subjects get the same instructions, the same questions, and the same time limits so that their scores can be compared meaningfully. This means, for instance, that a person taking the *Differential Aptitude Tests* (DAT) in Madoc, Ontario, in 2011, another taking the DAT in Powell River, British Columbia, in 2012, and another taking it in 2014 in Bedford, Nova Scotia, all confront exactly the same test-taking task.

The standardization of a test's scoring system includes the development of test norms. *Test norms provide information about where a score on a psychological test ranks in relation to other scores on that test.* Why are test norms needed? Because in psychological testing, everything is relative. Psychological tests tell you how you score *relative to other people*. They tell you, for instance, that you are average in creativity or slightly above average in clerical ability. These interpretations are derived from the test norms that help you understand what your test score means.

Usually, test norms allow you to convert your "raw score" on a test into a *percentile*. A *percentile score* indicates the percentage of people who score at or below the score one has obtained. For example, imagine that you take a 40-item assertiveness scale and obtain a raw score of 26. In other words, you indicate a preference for the assertive option on 26 of the questions. Your score of 26 has little meaning until you consult the test norms and find out that it places you at the 82nd percentile. This normative information would indicate that you appear to be as assertive as or more assertive than 82 percent of the sample of people who provided the basis for the test norms.

The sample of people that the norms are based on is called a test's *standardization group*. Ideally, test norms are based on a large sample of people who were carefully selected to be representative of the broader population. For example, the American norms for most intelligence tests are based on samples of 2000–6000 people whose demographic characteristics closely match the overall demographics of the United States (Woodcock, 1994). Separate norms are developed for the use and interpretation of many intelligence tests, such as the WAIS-III in Canada ("WAIS" stands for **Wechsler Adult Intelligence Scale**) (Psychological Corporation, 2001). University of Calgary psychologist Donald Saklofske (Austin, Saklofske, & Mastoras, 2010) and his colleagues published Canadian norms for a general ability index for the WAIS-III (Longman, Saklofske, & Fung, 2007; Saklofske et al., 2005). Even though Canadian and American societies are similar in many ways, there are also many important differences in culture, language, and educational systems that might be important considerations when evaluating an individual's performance on a test. Thus, for many tests, the most appropriate comparison group is other Canadians of similar age and status. Although intelligence tests have been standardized pretty carefully, the representativeness of standardization groups for other types of tests varies considerably from one test to another.

Reliability   SIM8, 7d

Any kind of measuring device, whether it's a tire gauge, a stopwatch, or a psychological test, should be reasonably consistent. That is, repeated measurements should yield reasonably similar results. Psychologists call this quality *reliability*. Consistency in measurement is essential to accuracy in measurement.

Reliability refers to the measurement consistency of a test (or of other kinds of measurement techniques). Like most other types of measuring

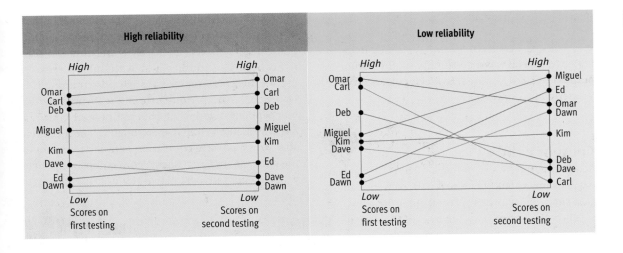

FIGURE 9.1

Test–retest reliability.

In each panel, subjects' scores on the first administration of an assertiveness test are represented on the left, and their scores on a second administration of the same test a few weeks later are shown on the right. If participants obtain similar scores on both administrations, as in the left panel, the test measures assertiveness consistently and has high test–retest reliability. If they get very different scores on the second administration, as in the right panel, the test has low reliability.

devices, psychological tests are not perfectly reliable. A test's reliability can be estimated in several ways (Hempel, 2005). One widely used approach is to check *test–retest reliability,* which is estimated by comparing subjects' scores on two administrations of a test. If we wanted to check the test–retest reliability of a newly developed test of assertiveness, we would ask a group of subjects to take the test on two occasions, probably a few weeks apart (see Figure 9.1). The underlying assumption is that assertiveness is a fairly stable aspect of personality that won't change in a matter of a few weeks. Thus, changes in participants' scores across the two administrations of the test would presumably reflect inconsistency in measurement.

Reliability estimates require the computation of correlation coefficients, which we introduced in Chapter 2 (see Figure 9.2 for a brief recapitulation). A *correlation coefficient* is a numerical index of the degree of relationship between two variables. In estimating test–retest reliability, the two variables that must be correlated are the two sets of scores from the two administrations of the test. If people get fairly similar scores on the two administrations of our hypothetical assertiveness test, this consistency yields a substantial positive correlation. The

magnitude of the correlation gives us a precise indication of the test's consistency. The closer the correlation comes to +1.00, the more reliable the test is.

There are no absolute guidelines about acceptable levels of reliability. According to Queens University researcher Cindy Fekken (Fekken, 2006), what's acceptable depends to some extent on the nature and purpose of the test. The reliability estimates for most psychological tests are above 0.70. Many exceed 0.90. The higher the reliability coefficient, the more consistent the test is. As reliability goes down, concern about measurement error increases.

Validity   SIM8, 7d

Even if a test is quite reliable, we still need to be concerned about its validity. *Validity* refers to the ability of a test to measure what it was designed to measure. If we develop a new test of assertiveness, we have to provide some evidence that it really measures assertiveness. Increasingly, the term *validity* is also used to refer to the accuracy or usefulness of the *inferences* or *decisions* based on a test (Moss, 1994). This broader conception of validity highlights the fact that a specific test might be valid for one purpose,

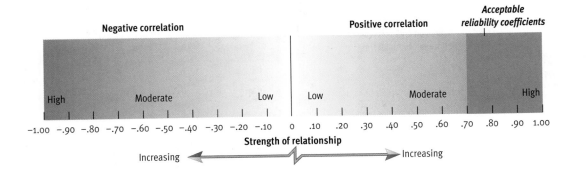

FIGURE 9.2

Correlation and reliability.

As explained in Chapter 2, a positive correlation means that two variables co-vary in the *same* direction; a negative correlation means that two variables co-vary in *opposite* directions. The closer the correlation coefficient gets to either −1.00 or +1.00, the stronger the relationship. At a minimum, reliability estimates for psychological tests must be moderately high positive correlations. Most reliability coefficients fall between 0.70 and 0.95.

such as placing students in school, and invalid for another purpose, such as making employment decisions for a particular occupation. Validity can be estimated in several ways, depending on the nature and purpose of a test (Golden, Sawicki, & Franzen, 1990; Wasserman & Bracken, 2003).

Content Validity

7b

Achievement tests and educational tests such as classroom exams should have adequate content validity. *Content validity* refers to the degree to which the content of a test is representative of the domain it's supposed to cover. Imagine a poorly prepared psychology exam that includes questions on material that was not covered in class or in assigned reading. The professor has compromised the content validity of the exam. Content validity is evaluated with logic more than with statistics.

Criterion-Related Validity

7b

Psychological tests are often used to make predictions about specific aspects of individuals' behaviour. They are used to predict performance in university, job capability, and suitability for training programs, as just a few examples. Criterion-related validity is a central concern in such cases. *Criterion-related validity* is estimated by correlating subjects' scores on a test with their scores on an independent criterion (another measure) of the trait assessed by

the test. For example, let's say you developed a test to measure aptitude for becoming an airplane pilot. You could check its validity by correlating subjects' scores on your aptitude test with subsequent ratings of their performance in their pilot training (see Figure 9.3). The performance ratings would be the independent criterion of pilot aptitude. If your test has reasonable validity, there ought to be a reasonably strong positive correlation between the test and the criterion measure. Such a correlation would help validate your test's predictive ability.

Construct Validity

SIM8, 7d

Many psychological tests attempt to measure abstract personal qualities, such as creativity, intelligence, extraversion, or independence. No obvious criterion measures exist for these abstract qualities, which are called *hypothetical constructs*. In measuring abstract qualities, psychologists are concerned about *construct validity*—the extent to which there is evidence that a test measures a particular hypothetical construct.

The process of demonstrating construct validity can be complicated. It depends on starting with a clear idea of the hypothetical construct to be measured (Clark & Watson, 2003; Jackson, 1968), and it usually requires a series of studies that examine the correlations between the test and various measures *related* to the trait in question. A thorough demonstration of construct validity requires looking at the

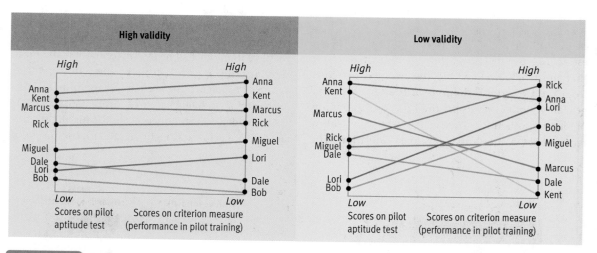

FIGURE 9.3

Criterion-related validity.

To evaluate the criterion-related validity of a pilot aptitude test, a psychologist would correlate subjects' test scores with a criterion measure of their aptitude, such as ratings of their performance in a pilot training program. The validity of the test is supported if the people who score high on the test also score high on the criterion measure (as shown in the left panel), yielding a substantial correlation between the two measures. If little or no relationship exists between the two sets of scores (as shown in the right panel), the data do not provide support for the validity of the test.

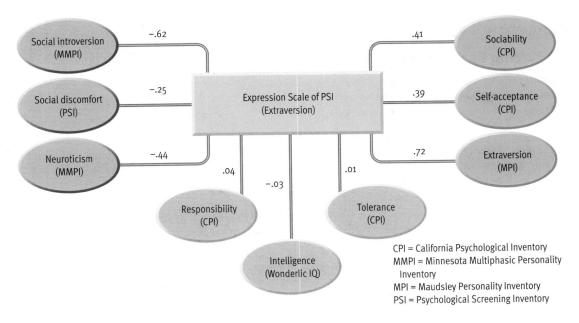

FIGURE 9.4

Construct validity.

Some of the evidence on the construct validity of the Expression Scale of the *Psychological Screening Inventory* is summarized here. This scale is supposed to measure the personality trait of *extraversion*. As you can see on the left side of this network of correlations, the scale correlates negatively with measures of social introversion, social discomfort, and neuroticism, just as one would expect if the scale is really tapping extraversion. On the right, you can see that the scale is correlated positively with measures of sociability and self-acceptance and another index of extraversion, as one would anticipate. At the bottom, you can see that the scale does not correlate with several traits that should be unrelated to extraversion. Thus, the network of correlations depicted here supports the idea that the Expression Scale measures the construct of extraversion.

relationship between a test and many other measures (Han, 2000). For example, some of the evidence on the construct validity of a measure of extraversion (the Expression Scale of the *Psychological Screening Inventory*) is summarized in Figure 9.4. This network of correlation coefficients shows that the Expression Scale correlates negatively, positively, or not at all with various measures, much as one would expect if the scale is really assessing extraversion. Ultimately, it's the overall pattern of correlations that provides convincing (or unconvincing) evidence of a test's construct validity.

The late Douglas Jackson of the University of Western Ontario was a well-known proponent of the importance of construct validity in test development (Jackson & Paunonen, 1980). The systematic application of construct validation principles to his test development work has resulted in his tests both of personality and of psychopathology being viewed as some of the best in their area of application. We will learn more about these types of tests in later chapters.

The complexities involved in demonstrating construct validity will be apparent in our upcoming discussion of intelligence testing. The ongoing debate about the construct validity of intelligence tests is one of the oldest debates in psychology. We'll look

first at the origins of intelligence tests; this historical review will help you appreciate the current controversies about intelligence testing.

REVIEW OF KEY POINTS

▷ Psychological tests are standardized measures of behaviour—usually mental abilities or aspects of personality. Test scores are interpreted by consulting test norms to find out what represents a high or low score.

▷ Standardization refers to the uniform procedures used in the administration and scoring of a test. Test scores are interpreted by consulting test norms to find out what represents a high or low score.

▷ As measuring devices, psychological tests should produce consistent results, a quality called *reliability*. Test-retest reliability is estimated by comparing subjects' scores on two administrations of a test. Reliability estimates should yield fairly high positive correlations.

▷ *Validity* refers to the degree to which there is evidence that a test measures what it was designed to measure. Content validity is crucial on classroom tests. Criterion-related validity is critical when tests are used to predict performance. Construct validity is critical when a test is designed to measure a hypothetical construct.

The Evolution of Intelligence Testing

The use of elaborate tests for selection purposes dates back to the Chinese imperial examinations that began over 1400 years ago, but the first modern psychological tests were invented only a little over a hundred years ago. Since then, reliance on psychological tests has grown gradually. In this section, we discuss the pioneers who launched psychological testing with their efforts to measure general intelligence.

Galton's Studies of Hereditary Genius

It all began with the work of a British scholar, Sir Francis Galton, in the later part of the 19th century (Galton, 1909). Galton studied family trees and found that success and eminence appeared consistently in some families over generations. For the most part, these families were much like Galton's: well-bred, upper-class families with access to superior schooling and social connections that pave the way to success. Yet Galton discounted the advantages of such an upbringing (Fancher, 2005). In his book *Hereditary Genius* (1869), Galton concluded that success runs in families because great intelligence is passed from generation to generation through genetic inheritance. Galton himself was an example—his half-cousin was Charles Darwin. According to York University's Ray Fancher (1979), while Galton and Darwin were never really close,

Darwin's evolutionary ideas did impact Galton's research and theories.

To better demonstrate that intelligence is governed by heredity, Galton needed an objective measure of intelligence. His approach to this problem was guided by the theoretical views of his day. Thus, he assumed that the contents of the mind are built out of elementary *sensations,* and he hypothesized that exceptionally bright people should exhibit exceptional sensory acuity. Working from this premise, he tried to assess innate mental ability by measuring simple sensory processes. Among other things, he measured sensitivity to high-pitched sounds, colour perception, and reaction time (the speed of one's response to a stimulus). His efforts met with little success. Research eventually showed that the sensory processes that he measured were largely unrelated to other criteria of mental ability that he was trying to predict, such as success in school or in professional life (Kaufman, 2000).

In pursuing this line of investigation, Galton coined the phrase *nature versus nurture* to refer to the heredity–environment issue (Fancher, 2009). Along the way, he also invented the concepts of *correlation* and *percentile test scores* (Roberts et al., 2005). Although Galton's mental tests were a failure, his work created an interest in the measurement of mental ability, setting the stage for a subsequent breakthrough by Alfred Binet, a prominent French psychologist.

Sir Francis Galton

"There is no escape from the conclusion that nature prevails enormously over nurture when the differences in nurture do not exceed what is commonly to be found among persons of the same rank of society and in the same country."

Wellcome Library, London

Binet's Breakthrough 7e

In 1904, a commission on education in France asked Alfred Binet to devise a test to identify mentally subnormal children. The commission was motivated by admirable goals: It wanted to single out youngsters in need of special training. It also wanted to avoid complete reliance on teachers' evaluations, which might often be subjective and biased.

In response to this need, Binet and a colleague, Theodore Simon, published the first useful test of general mental ability in 1905. They had the insight to load it with items that required abstract reasoning skills, rather than the sensory skills Galton had measured (Brody, 2000; Sternberg & Jarvin, 2003). Their scale was a success because it was inexpensive, easy to administer, objective, and capable of predicting children's performance in school fairly well (Siegler, 1992). Thanks to these qualities, its use spread across Europe and North America.

The Binet-Simon scale expressed a child's score in terms of "mental level" or "mental age." A child's *mental age* indicated that he or she displayed the mental ability typical of a child of that chronological (actual) age. Thus, a child with a mental age of six performed like the average six-year-old on the test. Binet realized that his scale was a somewhat crude initial effort at measuring mental ability. He revised it in 1908 and again in 1911. Unfortunately, his revising came to an abrupt end with his death in 1911. However, other psychologists continued to build on Binet's work.

Terman and the Stanford-Binet 7e

In the United States, Lewis Terman and his colleagues at Stanford University soon went to work on a major expansion and revision of Binet's test. Their work led to the 1916 publication of the *Stanford-Binet Intelligence Scale* (Terman, 1916). Although this revision was quite loyal to Binet's original conceptions, it incorporated a new scoring scheme based on the "intelligence quotient" suggested by William Stern (1914). An *intelligence quotient (IQ)* is a child's mental age divided by chronological age, multiplied by 100. As you can see, IQ scores originally involved actual quotients:

$$IQ = \frac{\text{Mental age}}{\text{Chronological age}} \times 100$$

The ratio of mental age to chronological age made it possible to compare children of different ages. In Binet's system, such comparisons were awkward. The IQ ratio placed all children (regardless of age) on the same scale, which was centred at 100 if their mental age corresponded to their chronological age (see Table 9.1 for examples of IQ calculations).

Terman made a strong case for the potential educational benefits of testing and became the key force behind American schools' widespread adoption of IQ tests (Chapman, 1988). As a result of his efforts, the Stanford-Binet quickly became the world's foremost intelligence test and the standard of comparison for virtually all intelligence tests that followed (White, 2000). Since its publication in 1916, the Stanford-Binet has been updated periodically but the modern version of the test remains loyal to the conception of intelligence originally put forth by Binet and Terman.

Wechsler's Innovations 7e

As chief psychologist at New York's massive Bellevue Hospital, David Wechsler was charged with overseeing the psychological assessment of thousands of adult patients. He found the Stanford-Binet somewhat unsatisfactory for this purpose. So, Wechsler set out to improve on the measurement of intelligence *in adults*. In 1939 he published the first high-quality IQ test designed specifically for adults, which came to be known as the *Wechsler Adult Intelligence Scale* (WAIS) (Wechsler, 1955, 1981). Ironically, Wechsler (1949, 1967, 1991, 2003) eventually devised downward extensions of his scale for children.

The Wechsler scales were characterized by at least two major innovations (Prifitera, 1994). First, Wechsler made his scales less dependent on subjects' verbal ability than the Stanford-Binet. He included many items that required nonverbal reasoning. To highlight the distinction between verbal and nonverbal ability, he formalized the computation of separate scores for verbal IQ, performance (nonverbal) IQ, and full-scale (total) IQ.

Alfred Binet

"The intelligence of anyone is susceptible of development. With practice, enthusiasm, and especially with method one can succeed in increasing one's attention, memory, judgment, and in becoming literally more intelligent than one was before."

Lewis Terman

"It is the method of tests that has brought psychology down from the clouds and made it useful to men; that has transformed the 'science of trivialities' into the 'science of human engineering.'"

David Wechsler

"The subtests [of the WAIS] are different measures of intelligence, not measures of different kinds of intelligence."

TABLE 9.1

Calculating the Intelligence Quotient

Measure	Child 1	Child 2	Child 3	Child 4
Mental age (MA)	6 years	6 years	9 years	12 years
Chronological age (CA)	6 years	9 years	12 years	9 years
$IQ = \frac{MA}{CA} \times 100$	$\frac{6}{6} \times 100 = 100$	$\frac{6}{9} \times 100 = 67$	$\frac{9}{12} \times 100 = 75$	$\frac{12}{9} \times 100 = 133$

© Paul Conklin/PhotoEdit

Second, Wechsler discarded the intelligence quotient in favour of a new scoring scheme based on the *normal distribution*. This scoring system has since been adopted by most other IQ tests, including the Stanford-Binet. Although the term *intelligence quotient* lingers on in our vocabulary, scores on intelligence tests are no longer based on an actual quotient. We'll take a close look at the modern scoring system for IQ tests a little later.

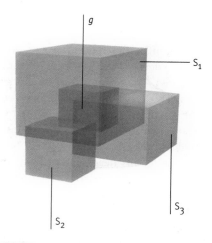

FIGURE 9.5

Spearman's *g*.

In his analysis of the structure of intellect, Charles Spearman found that *specific* mental talents (S1, S2, S3, and so on) were highly inter-correlated. Thus, he concluded that all cognitive abilities share a common core, which he labelled *g* for *general* mental ability.

The Debate about the Structure of Intelligence

The first half of the 20th century also witnessed a long-running debate about the structure of intellect. The debate was launched by Charles Spearman. He was a British psychologist who invented a complicated statistical procedure called *factor analysis*. In *factor analysis*, correlations among many variables are analyzed to identify closely related clusters of variables. If a number of variables correlate highly with one another, the assumption is that a single factor is influencing all of them. Factor analysis attempts to identify these hidden factors (Gorsuch, 1983).

Spearman (1904, 1927) used factor analysis to examine the correlations among tests of many specific mental abilities. He concluded that all cognitive abilities share an important core factor. He labelled this factor *g* for *general* mental ability. Spearman recognized that people also have "special" abilities (such as numerical reasoning or spatial ability). However, he thought that individuals' ability in these specific areas is largely determined by their general mental ability (see Figure 9.5).

Exploring Biological Correlates of Intelligence

A very different view of the structure of intellect was soon proposed by L. L. Thurstone. He was an American psychologist who developed the test that evolved into the *Scholastic Aptitude Test* (SAT; L. V. Jones, 2000). Using a somewhat different approach to factor analysis, Thurstone (1931, 1938, 1955) concluded that intelligence involves multiple abilities. Thurstone argued that Spearman and his followers placed far too much emphasis on *g*. In contrast, Thurstone carved intelligence into seven independent factors called *primary mental abilities:* word fluency, verbal comprehension, spatial ability, perceptual speed, numerical ability, inductive reasoning, and memory. Following in this tradition, J. P. Guilford (1959, 1985) upped the ante. Guilford's theory divided intelligence into 150 separate abilities and did away with *g* entirely (see Figure 9.6).

The debate about the structure of intelligence continued for many decades and in some respects the issue lingers in the background even today. Paradoxically, both views of the structure of intellect have remained influential. Armed with computers, modern researchers using enhanced approaches to factor analysis have shown again and again that batteries of cognitive tests are highly intercorrelated, as Spearman had suggested (Brody, 2005; Carroll, 1996; Gottfredson, 2009; Jensen, 1998). Today, researchers interested in the nature, determinants, and correlates of intelligence focus heavily on the Holy Grail of *g* in their quest to understand mental ability.

However, in the 1980s, the developers of IQ tests began moving in the opposite direction. Their motivation was to give clinicians, educators, and school systems more information (than a single, global score) that could better aid them in the diagnosis of learning disabilities and the evaluation of children's potential. For theoretical guidance they turned to a model of intelligence that proposed that *g* should be divided into *fluid intelligence* and *crystallized intelligence* (Carroll, 1993; Cattell, 1963; Horn, 1985). *Fluid intelligence* involves reasoning ability, memory capacity, and speed of information processing. *Crystallized intelligence* involves ability to apply acquired knowledge and skills in problem solving. This distinction between fluid and crystallized intelligence led to further efforts to break *g* into basic components. These models have broadly guided the most recent revisions of the Stanford-Binet (Roid & Tippin, 2009), the Wechsler scales (O'Donnell, 2009), and many other IQ tests (Kaufman, 2009). Contemporary IQ tests

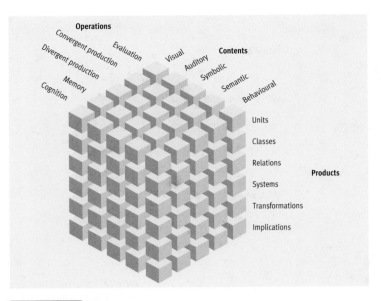

FIGURE 9.6

Guilford's model of mental abilities.

In contrast to Spearman (see Figure 9.5), J. P. Guilford concluded that intelligence is made up of many separate abilities. According to his analysis, we may have as many as 150 distinct mental abilities that can be characterized in terms of the operations, contents, and products of intellectual activity.

generally are based on a hierarchical model of intelligence, which subdivides *g* into 10–15 specific abilities. For example, the current version of the Stanford-Binet includes ten subtests.

Thus, we have a curious paradox. Researchers and theorists tend to be obsessed with Spearman's *g*. But clinicians and educators facing difficult diagnostic decisions, and the companies that develop tests for them, are more interested in the measurement of specific abilities in the tradition of Thurstone.

Basic Questions about Intelligence Testing

The nature of the questions found on IQ tests varies somewhat from test to test. These variations depend on whether the test is intended for children or adults (or both) and whether the test is designed for individuals or groups. Overall, the questions are fairly diverse in format. The Wechsler scales, with their numerous subtests, provide a representative example of the kinds of items that appear on most IQ tests. As you can see in Figure 9.7, the items in the Wechsler subtests require subjects to furnish information, recognize vocabulary, and demonstrate basic memory. Generally speaking, examinees are required to manipulate words, numbers, and images through abstract reasoning.

What Do Modern IQ Scores Mean?

7e

As we've discussed, scores on intelligence tests once represented a ratio of mental age to chronological age. However, this system has given way to one based on the normal distribution and the standard deviation (see Chapter 2). The *normal distribution* is a symmetric, bell-shaped curve that represents the pattern in which many characteristics are dispersed in the population. When a trait is normally distributed, most cases fall near the centre of the distribution (an average score) and the number of cases gradually declines as one moves away from the centre in either direction (see Figure 9.8).

Wechsler Adult Intelligence Scale (WAIS)		
Test	**Description**	**Example**
Verbal scale		
Information	Taps general range of information	On what continent is France?
Comprehension	Tests understanding of social conventions and ability to evaluate past experience	Why are children required to go to school?
Arithmetic	Tests arithmetic reasoning through verbal problems	How many hours will it take to drive 150 kilometres at 50 kilometres per hour?
Similarities	Asks in what way certain objects or concepts are similar; measures abstract thinking	How are a calculator and a typewriter alike?
Digit span	Tests attention and rote memory by orally presenting series of digits to be repeated forward or backward	Repeat the following numbers backward: 2 4 3 5 1 8 6
Vocabulary	Tests ability to define increasingly difficult words	What does audacity mean?
Performance scale		
Digit symbol	Tests speed of learning through timed coding tasks in which numbers must be associated with marks of various shapes	Shown: 1 2 3 4 ○ □ △ ⊙ Fill in: 1 4 3 2 ___ ___ ___ ___
Picture completion	Tests visual alertness and visual memory through presentation of an incompletely drawn figure; the missing part must be discovered and named	Tell me what is missing: 
Block design	Tests ability to perceive and analyze patterns by presenting designs that must be copied with blocks	Assemble blocks to match this design: 
Picture arrangement	Tests understanding of social situations through a series of comic-strip-type pictures that must be arranged in the right sequence to tell a story	Put the pictures in the right order:  1 2 3
Object assembly	Tests ability to deal with part/whole relationships by presenting puzzle pieces that must be assembled to form a complete object	Assemble the pieces into a complete object: 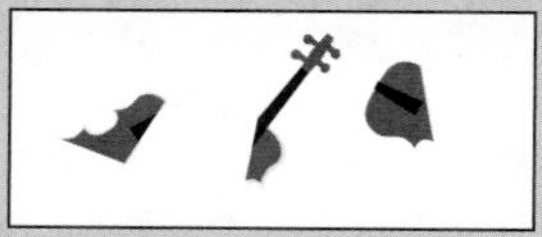

FIGURE 9.7

Subtests on the *Wechsler Adult Intelligence Scale* (WAIS).

The WAIS is divided into scales that yield separate verbal and performance (nonverbal) IQ scores. The verbal scale consists of six subtests and the performance scale is made up of five subtests. Examples of low-level (easy) test items that closely resemble those on the WAIS are shown above.

The normal distribution was first discovered by 18th-century astronomers. They found that their measurement errors were distributed in a predictable way that resembled a bell-shaped curve. Since then, research has shown that many human traits, ranging from height to running speed to spatial ability, also follow a normal distribution. Psychologists eventually recognized that intelligence scores also fall into a normal distribution. This insight permitted David Wechsler to devise a more sophisticated scoring system for his tests that has been adopted by virtually all subsequent IQ tests. In this system, raw scores are translated into *deviation IQ scores* that locate subjects precisely within the normal distribution, using the standard deviation as the unit of measurement.

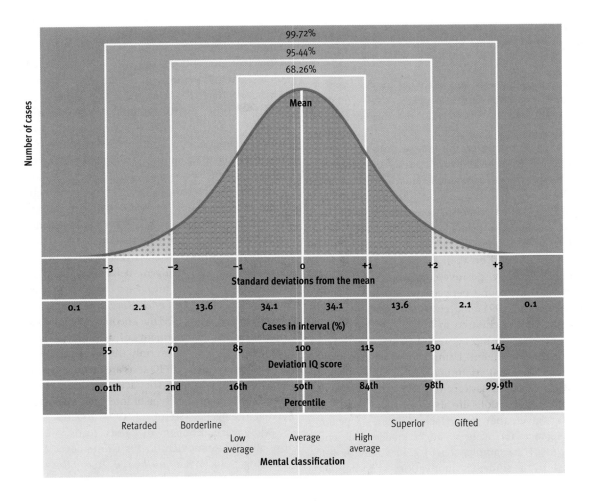

FIGURE 9.8

The normal distribution.
Many characteristics are distributed in a pattern represented by this bell-shaped curve. The horizontal axis shows how far above or below the mean a score is (measured in plus or minus standard deviations). The vertical axis is used to graph the number of cases obtaining each score. In a normal distribution, the cases are distributed in a fixed pattern. For instance, 68.26 percent of the cases fall between +1 and −1 standard deviation. Modern IQ scores indicate where a person's measured intelligence falls in the normal distribution. On most IQ tests, the mean is set at an IQ of 100 and the standard deviation at 15. Any deviation IQ score can be converted into a percentile score. The mental classifications at the bottom of the figure are descriptive labels that roughly correspond to ranges of IQ scores.

For most IQ tests, the mean of the distribution is set at 100 and the standard deviation (SD) is set at 15. These choices were made to provide continuity with the original IQ ratio (mental age to chronological age) that was centred at 100. In this system, which is depicted in Figure 9.8, a score of 115 means that a person scored exactly one SD (15 points) above the mean. A score of 85 means that a person scored one SD below the mean. A score of 100 means that a person showed average performance. You don't really need to know how to work with standard deviations to understand this system (but if you're interested, consult Appendix B). *The key point is that modern IQ scores indicate exactly where you fall in the normal distribution of intelligence.* Thus, a score of 120 does not indicate that you answered 120 questions correctly. Nor does it mean that you have 120 "units" of intelligence. A deviation IQ score places you at a specific point in the normal distribution of intelligence.

Deviation IQ scores can be converted into percentile scores (see Figure 9.8). In fact, a major advantage of this scoring system is that a specific score on a specific test always translates into exactly the same percentile score, regardless of the person's age group. The old system of IQ ratio scores lacked this consistency.

Do Intelligence Tests Have Adequate Reliability?

Do IQ tests produce consistent results when people are retested? Yes. Most IQ tests report commendable reliability estimates. The correlations generally range into the 0.90s (Kaufman, 2000). In comparison to most other types of psychological tests, IQ tests are exceptionally reliable. However, like other tests, they *sample* behaviour, and a specific testing may yield an unrepresentative score.

Variations in examinees' motivation to take an IQ test or in their anxiety about the test can sometimes produce misleading scores (Hopko et al., 2005; Zimmerman & Woo-Sam, 1984). The most common problem is that low motivation or high anxiety may drag a person's score down on a particular occasion. For example, a Grade 4 student who is made to feel that the test is really important may get jittery and be unable to concentrate. The same child might score much higher on a subsequent testing by another examiner who creates a more comfortable atmosphere. Although the reliability of IQ tests is excellent, caution is always in order in interpreting test scores.

Do Intelligence Tests Have Adequate Validity?

Do intelligence tests measure what they're supposed to measure? Yes, but this answer has to be qualified very carefully. IQ tests are valid measures of the kind of intelligence that's necessary to do well in academic work. But if the purpose is to assess intelligence in a broader sense, the validity of IQ tests is questionable.

As you may recall, intelligence tests were originally designed with a relatively limited purpose in mind: to predict school performance. This has continued to be the principal purpose of IQ testing. Efforts to document the validity of IQ tests have usually concentrated on their relationship to grades in school. Typically, positive correlations in the 0.40s and 0.50s are found between IQ scores and school grades (Kline, 1991). Moreover, a recent, huge study of over 70 000 children in England found an even stronger relationship between intelligence and educational achievement. Using composite measures of *g* and educational attainment, Deary and colleagues (2007) found correlations in the vicinity of 0.70.

These correlations are about as high as one could expect, given that many factors besides a person's intelligence are likely to affect grades and school progress. For example, school grades may be influenced by a student's motivation or personality, not to mention teachers' subjective biases. Indeed, a recent study reported that measures of students' *self-discipline* are surprisingly strong predictors of students' school performance (Duckworth & Seligman, 2005). Other studies suggest that students' subjective perceptions of their abilities influence their academic performance, even after controlling for actual IQ (Greven et al., 2009; Spinath et al., 2006). In other words, holding actual IQ constant, students who *think* they are talented tend to perform somewhat better than those with more negative views of their ability. Thus, given all the other factors likely to influence performance in school, IQ tests appear to be reasonably valid indexes of school-related intellectual ability, or academic intelligence.

But the abilities assessed by IQ tests are not as broad or general as widely assumed. When Robert Sternberg and his colleagues (1981) asked people to list examples of intelligent behaviour, they found that the examples fell into three categories: (1) *verbal intelligence*, (2) *practical intelligence*, and (3) *social intelligence* (see Figure 9.9). Thus, people generally recognize three basic components of intelligence. For the most part, IQ tests assess only the first of these three components. Although IQ tests are billed as measures of *general* mental ability, they actually focus somewhat narrowly on a specific type of intelligence: academic/verbal intelligence (Sternberg, 1998, 2003b).

Moreover, although the tests focus on *cognitive* abilities, Stanovich, in his Grawemeyer Award–winning book *What Intelligence Tests Miss* (2009), argues that they do not predict rational thinking and effective decision making in the real world nearly as well as one might expect. According to Stanovich, it

Verbal intelligence

Speaks clearly and articulately

Is verbally fluent

Is knowledgeable about a particular field

Reads with high comprehension

Practical intelligence

Sees all aspects of a problem

Sizes up situations well

Makes good decisions

Poses problems in an optimal way

Social intelligence

Accepts others for what they are

Has social conscience

Thinks before speaking and doing

Is sensitive to other people's needs and desires

FIGURE 9.9

Laypersons' conceptions of intelligence.

Robert Sternberg and his colleagues (1981) asked participants to list examples of behaviours characteristic of intelligence. The examples tended to sort into three groups that represent the three types of intelligence recognized by the average person: verbal intelligence, practical intelligence, and social intelligence. The three well-known individuals shown here are prototype examples of verbal intelligence (author J. K. Rowling), practical intelligence (scientist and broadcaster David Suzuki), and social intelligence (Craig Kielburger, founder of Free the Children).

Source: Adapted from Sternberg, R.J., Conway, B.E., Ketron, J.L., and Bernstein, M. (1981). People's conceptions of intelligence. *Journal of Personality and Social Psychology, 41*(1), 37–55. Copyright © 1981 by the American Psychological Association. Adapted by permission of the author.

Canada Research Chair in Education and University of Toronto Professor Keith Stanovich is a well-known researcher in psychology and education on the topics of reading and rationality.

is routine for people with high intelligence to make irrational, ill-advised decisions. He explains that this is not surprising because IQ tests do not assess the ability to think critically, weigh conflicting evidence, and engage in judicious reasoning. Interest in why intelligent people "may do dumb things" has increased in recent years. Researchers such as Maggie Toplak, who collaborates with Stanovich (Stanovich, West, & Toplak, in press; Toplak, West & Stanovich, in press), suggest not only that IQ tests don't adequately measure *rational quotient* (RQ), but that it may be possible to train people with specific types of low rational-thinking ability to improve their thinking. According to Toplak this research has potential implications not only for the average person, but also for special populations, such as pathological gamblers, people with attention deficit hyperactivity disorder (ADHD), and youth offenders (McLean, 2010).

Are Individuals' IQ Scores Stable over Time?

You may have heard of hopeful parents who have their two- or three-year-old preschoolers tested to see whether they're exceptionally bright. These parents would have been better off saving the money spent on preschool testing. IQ scores are relatively unstable during the preschool years and are not good predictors of scores in adolescence and adulthood. As children grow older, their IQ scores eventually stabilize (Brody, 1992; Hayslip, 1994). Around the ages of seven to ten, IQ tests become fairly accurate predictors of IQ at age 18. Studies that have followed participants into late adulthood have also found impressive stability. For instance, Deary et al. (2000) tracked down subjects who had been tested at age 11 and retested them 66 years later at age 77 and found a correlation of 0.63

between the two testings. Although IQ scores tend to stabilize by the age of nine, substantial changes are seen in a sizable minority of people (Weinert & Hany, 2003). In conclusion, IQ scores tend to be stable, but they are not set in concrete.

Do Intelligence Tests Predict Vocational Success?

Vocational success is a vague, value-laden concept that's difficult to quantify. Nonetheless, researchers have attacked this question by examining correlations between IQ scores and specific indicators of vocational success, such as income, the prestige of subjects' occupations, or ratings of subjects' job performance. The data relating IQ to occupational attainment are pretty clear. *People who score high on IQ tests are more likely than those who score low to end up in high-status jobs* (Gottfredson, 2003b; Herrnstein & Murray, 1994; Schmidt & Hunter, 2004). Because IQ tests measure school ability fairly well and because school performance is important in reaching certain occupations, this link between IQ scores and job status makes sense. Of course, the correlation between IQ and occupational attainment is moderate. For example, in a meta-analysis of many studies of the issue, Strenze (2007) found a correlation of 0.37 between IQ and occupational status. That figure means that there are plenty of exceptions to the general trend. Some people probably outperform brighter colleagues through bulldog determination and hard work. The relationship between IQ and income appears to be somewhat weaker. The meta-analysis by Strenze (2007) reported a correlation of 0.21 between IQ and income based on 31 studies. In one large-scale study of American baby boomers, the correlation between intelligence and income was 0.30 (Zagorsky, 2007). These findings suggest that intelligence fosters vocational success, but the strength of the relationship is modest.

There is far more debate about whether IQ scores are effective predictors of performance *within* a particular occupation. On the one hand, research suggests that (1) there is a substantial correlation (about 0.50) between IQ scores and job performance, (2) this correlation varies somewhat depending on the complexity of a job's requirements but does not disappear even for low-level jobs, (3) this association holds up even when workers have more experience at their jobs, and (4) measures of specific mental abilities and personality traits are much less predictive of job performance than measures of intelligence (Gottfredson, 2002; Ones, Viswesvaran, & Dilchert, 2005; Schmidt, 2002).

On the other hand, critics argue that a correlation of 0.50 provides only modest accuracy in prediction (accounting for about 25 percent of the variation in job performance) (Goldstein, Zedeck, & Goldstein, 2002; Sternberg & Hedlund, 2002). Concerns have also been raised that when IQ tests are used for job selection, they can have an adverse impact on employment opportunities for many minority groups that tend to score somewhat lower (on average) on such tests (Murphy, 2002; Outtz, 2002). In the final analysis, there is no question that intelligence is associated with vocational success, but there is room for argument about whether this association is strong enough to justify reliance on IQ testing in hiring employees.

Are IQ Tests Widely Used in Other Cultures?

In other Western cultures with European roots, the answer to this question is "yes." In most non-Western cultures, the answer is "very little." IQ testing has a long history and continues to be a major enterprise in many Western countries, such as Britain, France, Norway, and Australia, as well as the United States and Canada (Irvine & Berry, 1988). However, efforts to export IQ tests to non-Western societies have met with mixed results. The tests have been well received in some non-Western cultures, such as Japan, where the Binet-Simon scales were introduced as early as 1908 (Iwawaki & Vernon, 1988), but they have been met with indifference or resistance in other cultures, such as China and India (Chan & Vernon, 1988; Sinha, 1983).

According to well-known cross-cultural researcher John Berry of Queen's University, the bottom line is that Western IQ tests do not translate well into the language and cognitive frameworks of many non-Western cultures (Berry, 1994; Sternberg, 2004). Berry (1984) asserts that this approach assumes that the cultural life of the two cultures differs only in language and that the cognitive abilities characteristic of the two cultures differs only in level. Using an intelligence test with a cultural group other than the one for which it was originally designed can be problematic. The entire process of test administration, with its emphasis on rapid information processing, decisive responding, and the notion that ability can be quantified, is foreign to some cultures. Moreover, different cultures have different conceptions of what intelligence is and value different mental skills (Baral & Das, 2004; Sato et al., 2004; Sternberg, 2007).

REVIEW OF KEY POINTS

▷ In the modern scoring system, deviation IQ scores indicate where people fall in the normal distribution of intelligence for their age group. On most tests, the mean is set at 100 and the standard deviation is set at 15.

▷ IQ scores tend to stabilize around the ages of seven to nine, but meaningful changes are possible. IQ scores are associated with occupational attainment and income, but the correlations are modest. There is active debate about whether IQ scores predict performance within an occupation well enough to be used in hiring decisions.

▷ Intelligence testing is largely a Western enterprise and IQ tests are not widely used in most non-Western cultures. One reason is that different cultures have different conceptions of intelligence.

Extremes of Intelligence

What are the cutoff scores for extremes in intelligence that lead children to be designated as having intellectual disability or giftedness? On the low end, IQ scores roughly two standard deviations or more below the mean are regarded as subnormal. On the high end, children who score more than two or three standard deviations above the mean are regarded as gifted. However, designations of intellectual disability and giftedness should not be based exclusively on IQ test results. Let's look more closely at the concepts of intellectual disability and intellectual giftedness.

Intellectual Disability

The terminology used to refer to those who exhibit subnormal intelligence is undergoing a transition.

For decades, many authorities have expressed concerns about the term *retardation* because it is demeaning, stigmatizing, and powerful, in that people diagnosed with retardation seem to be totally defined by it (Bersani, 2007). These concerns finally led the American Association on Mental Retardation (AAMR) to change its name in 2006 to the American Association on Intellectual and Developmental Disabilities (AAIDD) (Schalock et al., 2007). The most recent edition of its classification manual, published in 2010, uses the term *intellectual disability* as a substitute for *mental retardation*. One can only hope that the new terminology will eventually reduce the stigma. Unfortunately, such attitude change in the general public is far from a certainty. Since 1919 the official term for subnormal intellectual functioning has been changed three times to make it less degrading (from *feebleminded* to *mentally deficient* to *mentally retarded*), but the stigma associated with intellectual disability remains strong (Detterman, 2010; King et al., 2009).

In any event, *intellectual disability* refers to subnormal general mental ability accompanied by deficiencies in adaptive skills, originating before age 18. Adaptive skills consist of everyday living skills in three broad domains. These domains are *conceptual skills* (examples: managing money, writing a letter), *social skills* (making friends, coping with others' demands), and *practical skills* (preparing meals, using transportation, shopping).

There are two noteworthy aspects to this definition. First, the IQ criterion of subnormality is arbitrary. In the 1992 release of its classification manual, the AAMR (as it was then known) set a flexible cutoff line, which was an IQ score of 70 to 75 or below. This cutoff line could be drawn elsewhere. Indeed, the AAMR made 70 the cutoff (with caveats) in its 2002 edition. These periodic changes in the scoring norms for IQ tests have had erratic effects on the percentage of children falling below the cutoffs (Flynn, 2000; Kanaya, Scullin, & Ceci, 2003). Five IQ points may not sound like much, but if the line is drawn exactly at 75 instead of 70, the number of people qualifying for special education programs doubles (King, Hodapp, & Dykens, 2005). Second, the requirement of deficits in everyday living skills is included because experts feel that high stakes decisions should not be based on a single test score (Lichten & Simon, 2007). This requirement acknowledges that "school learning" is not the only important kind of learning. Unfortunately, the methods available for measuring everyday living skills have tended to be vague, imprecise, and subjective, although efforts to improve these assessments are under way (Detterman, Gabriel, & Ruthsatz, 2000; Lichten & Simon, 2007).

Levels of Intellectual Disability

Historically, estimates of the prevalence of intellectual disability have varied between 1 percent and 3 percent. Recent evidence suggests that the prevalence of intellectual disability probably is closer to the 1 percent end of this range (Ursano, Kartheiser, & Barnhill, 2008). Intellectual disability has traditionally been classified into four levels characterized as mild, moderate, severe, or profound. Table 9.2 lists the IQ range for each level and the typical behavioural and educational characteristics of individuals at each level.

As Figure 9.10 shows, the vast majority of people diagnosed with intellectual disability fall in the *mild* category (King et al., 2009). Only about 15 percent of people diagnosed with intellectual disability exhibit the obvious mental deficiencies that most people envision when they think of intellectual disability. Many individuals with mild intellectual disability are not all that easily distinguished from the rest of the population. The mental deficiency of children in the mild disability category often is not noticed until they have been in school a few years. Outside of school, many are considered normal. Furthermore, as many as two-thirds of these children manage to shed the label of intellectual disability when they reach adulthood and leave the educational system (Popper et al., 2003). A significant portion of them become self-supporting and are integrated into the community. Some are even able to attend college and university (Getzel & Wehman, 2005).

Categories of Intellectual Disability

Note: As explained in the text, diagnoses of intellectual disability should not be made on the basis of IQ scores alone.

Category of Intellectual Disability	IQ Range	Education Possible	Life Adaptation Possible
Mild	51–70	Grade 6 (maximum) by late teens; special education helpful	Can be self-supporting in nearly normal fashion if environment is stable and supportive; may need help with stress
Moderate	36–50	Grade 2–4 by late teens; special education necessary	Can be semi-independent in sheltered environment; needs help with even mild stress
Severe	20–35	Limited speech, toilet habits, and so forth with systematic training	Can help contribute to self-support under total supervision
Profound	below 20	Little or no speech; not toilet-trained; relatively unresponsive to training	Requires total care

FIGURE 9.10

The prevalence and severity of intellectual disability.
The overall prevalence of intellectual disability is 2–3 percent of the general population. The vast majority (85 percent) of the intellectually disabled population fall into the mildly disabled category (IQ: 51–70). Only about 15 percent of the intellectually disabled population fall into the subcategories of moderate, severe, or profound intellectual disability.

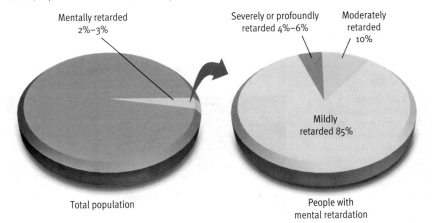

Mentally retarded 2%–3%

Severely or profoundly retarded 4%–6%

Moderately retarded 10%

Mildly retarded 85%

Total population

People with mental retardation

Origins

Many organic conditions can cause intellectual disability (Szymanski & Wilska, 2003). For example, *Down syndrome* is a condition marked by distinctive physical characteristics (such as slanted eyes, stubby limbs, and thin hair) that is associated with mild to severe intellectual disability. Most children exhibiting this syndrome carry an extra chromosome. Children with such distinctive physical characteristics are sometimes the victims of bullying. Activists such as Lauren Potter, a young woman with Down syndrome, hope that educating the general public will help eliminate this treatment. Interestingly, while Potter was not allowed to join her own high school cheerleading squad, she now plays a cheerleader on TV as the character Becky Jackson on the top-rated prime-time show *Glee* (see photo below).

The FRM 1 gene contributes to the development of *fragile X syndrome (FXS)*, a common cause of hereditary intellectual disability (Cornish, Sudhalter, & Turk, 2004). In FXS there is a mutation in the inherited gene. According to Kim Cornish, Canada Research Chair in Developmental Neuroscience and Education at McGill University, FXS is characterized by, among other things, an inhibitory control deficit. This deficit may lead to activation of neural connections irrelevant to the context or task facing the individual. *Phenylketonuria* is a metabolic disorder (due

to an inherited enzyme deficiency) that can lead to intellectual disability if it is not caught and treated in infancy. In *hydrocephaly,* an excessive accumulation of cerebrospinal fluid in the skull destroys brain tissue and causes retardation. Although about 1000 such organic syndromes are known to cause intellectual disability, with more being identified every year (Popper et al., 2003), diagnosticians are unable to pin down an organic cause for as many as 50 percent of cases (King et al., 2009).

The cases of unknown origin tend to involve milder forms of intellectual disability. A number of theories have attempted to identify the factors that underlie intellectual disability in the absence of a known organic pathology (Hodapp, 1994). Some theorists believe that subtle, difficult-to-detect physiological defects contribute to many of these cases. However, others believe the majority of cases are caused by a variety of unfavourable environmental factors. Consistent with this hypothesis, the vast majority of children with mild disability come from the lower socioeconomic classes (see Figure 9.11), where a number of factors—such as greater marital

Actress Lauren Potter (right) plays Becky Jackson, a student with Down syndrome who is a member of the Cheerios cheer squad, on the TV show *Glee*. Jane Lynch (left) plays the coach, Sue Sylvester. Potter, bullied as a child, has used her celebrity to advocate for the rights of children living with challenges.

Michael Yarish/© Fox/Courtesy Everett Collection

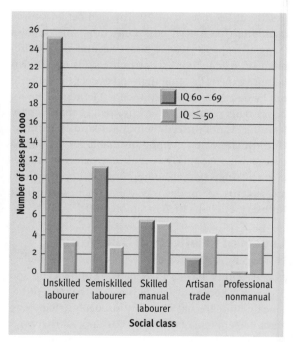

FIGURE 9.11

Social class and intellectual disability.

This graph charts the prevalence of mild intellectual disability (IQ 60 to 69) and more severe forms of intellectual disability (IQ below 50) in relation to social class. Severe forms are distributed pretty evenly across the social classes, a finding that is consistent with the notion that they are the product of biological aberrations that are equally likely to strike anyone. In contrast, the prevalence of mild intellectual disability is greatly elevated in the lower social classes, a finding that meshes with the notion that mild intellectual disability is largely a product of unfavourable environmental factors. (Data from Popper and Steingard, 1994)

instability and parental neglect, inadequate nutrition and medical care, and lower-quality schooling—may contribute to children's poor intellectual development (Popper et al., 2003).

Savants

Based on what we have learned so far, you might expect that someone who has below average IQ would not be expected to show any superior abilities or to show excellence in any intellectual or artistic domains. Consider then, the savant Kim Peek (Peek, 1996), who was the inspiration for Dustin Hoffman's character in the movie *Rain Man*. Kim walks with a "sidelong" gait, he is unable to manage the buttons on his clothes or to brush his teeth, or cope by himself with most of the ordinary demands of daily life (Treffert, 2010; Treffert & Christensen, 2006). He was born in 1951 with an enlarged head and with several brain abnormalities, including a malformed cerebellum, left hemisphere damage, and the complete absence of a corpus callosum (you will remember from Chapter 3 that this is the structure that connects the left and right brain). Given all of these issues, it might not surprise you to know that his tested IQ is below average. Kim was not diagnosed with autism, a disorder that is often linked to savants (we discuss autism in more detail in Chapter 14). Kim has shown evidence of amazing abilities. He memorized 9000 books and knows all the area codes and zip codes in the United States. He has memorized maps of most of the major cities in the United States and can provide "MapQuest-like travel directions with any major U.S. city or between any pair of them" (Treffert & Christensen, 2005, p. 50). He also has an appreciation of classical music. He cannot only identify and give biographical details about the composers of hundreds of compositions, but he can also enlighten on the "formal and tonal" aspects of the music. Other savants have shown equally amazing abilities in other domains including artistic pursuits (Sacks, 1990). One savant, Daniel Tammet, has become a best-selling author (Tammet, 2007, 2009), and is able to recite the first 22 514 digits of *pi*, a European record. Tammet has also written on ways the rest of us can use his experiences to improve our own cognitive performance (Lehrer, 2009).

There is still much that we do not know about savant syndrome, its characteristics, and its causes (Treffert, 2010). At the very least it should lead us to reconsider traditional notions of what intelligence is, for these conceptualizations do not help us explain individuals such as Kim Peek. Darold Treffert, a Wisconsin psychiatrist who researches savant syndrome, maintains a website on which he profiles

Courtesy of Dmadeo

UNITED ARTISTS/THE KOBAL COLLECTION

Dustin Hoffman (pictured on the left beside Tom Cruise) won an Academy Award for his portrayal of a savant in the 1988 film *Rain Man*. His portrayal was based partly on real-life savant Kim Peek (pictured above).

many of the best known the savants (http://www.wisconsinmedicalsociety.org/savant_syndrome).

Sadly, Kim Peek died in 2009 of a heart attack (*New York Times*, 2009). It is interesting to note that the notoriety Kim gained after the release of *Rain Man* changed his life in positive ways, enabling him to break out of his self-imposed social isolation. As he ventured into the public, he displayed a great sense of humour and a developing set of social skills:

> During a presentation Mr. Peek gave at Oxford University in England, after he fielded students' questions about the Lusitania *and about British monarchs, a young woman stood and asked him,* "Kim, are you happy?"
>
> "I'm happy just to look at you," Mr. Peek said. (*New York Times*, 2009, A30).

Giftedness

Like intellectual disability, giftedness is widely misunderstood. This misunderstanding is a result, in part, of television and movies inaccurately portraying gifted children as social misfits and "nerds."

Identifying Gifted Children

Definitions of giftedness vary considerably (Kaufman & Sternberg, 2010), and some curious discrepancies exist between ideals and practice in how gifted children are identified. The experts consistently assert that giftedness should not be equated with high intelligence and they recommend that schools not rely too heavily on IQ tests to select gifted children (Robinson & Clinkenbeard, 1998; Sternberg, 2005; von Károlyi & Winner, 2005). In practice, however, efforts to identify gifted children focus almost exclusively on IQ scores and rarely consider qualities such as creativity, leadership, or special talent (Newman, 2010). Most school districts consider children who fall in the upper 2–3 percent of the IQ distribution to be gifted. Thus, the minimum IQ score for gifted programs usually falls somewhere around 130. The types of school programs and services available to gifted students vary enormously from one school district to the next (Olszewski-Kubilius, 2003).

Personal Qualities of the Gifted

Gifted children have long been stereotyped as weak, sickly, socially inept "bookworms" who are often emotionally troubled. The empirical evidence *largely* contradicts this view. The best evidence comes from a major longitudinal study of gifted children begun by Lewis Terman in 1921 (Terman, 1925; Terman & Oden, 1959). Other investigators have continued to study this group through the present (Cronbach, 1992; Holahan & Sears, 1995; Lippa, Martin, & Friedman, 2000). This project represents psychology's longest-running study.

Terman's original subject pool consisted of around 1500 youngsters who had an average IQ of 150. In comparison to subjects with normal IQ scores, Terman's gifted children were found to be above average in height, weight, strength, physical health, emotional adjustment, mental health, and social

Ellen Winner

"Moderately gifted children are very different from profoundly gifted children.... Most gifted children do not grow into eminent adults."

Young Nirav Gathani made exam history in England when he became the youngest student to pass the General Certificate of Secondary Education at age seven. As amazing as this feat was, it is hard to say whether Nirav will go on to achieve eminence, which typically requires a combination of exceptional intelligence, motivation, and creativity.

maturity. As a group, Terman's subjects continued to exhibit better-than-average physical health, emotional stability, and social satisfaction throughout their adult years. A variety of other studies have also found that samples of high-IQ children are either average or above average in social and emotional development (Robinson, 2010).

However, some other lines of research raise some questions about this conclusion. For instance, Ellen Winner (1997, 1998) asserts that moderately gifted children (those with an IQ of 130–150) are very different from profoundly gifted children (those with an IQ above 180). She asserts that profoundly gifted children are often introverted and socially isolated. She also estimates that the incidence of interpersonal and emotional problems in this group is about twice as high as in other children. Another line of research, which is discussed in more detail in the Personal Application, has focused on samples of people who have displayed truly exceptional creative achievement. Contrary to the findings of the Terman study, investigators have found elevated rates of mental illness in these samples (Andreasen, 2005; Ludwig, 1998). Thus, the psychosocial adjustment of gifted individuals may depend in part on their level of giftedness.

Giftedness and Achievement in Life

Terman's gifted children grew up to be very successful by conventional standards. By midlife they had produced 92 books, 235 patents, and nearly 2200 scientific articles. Although Terman's gifted children accomplished a great deal, no one in the group achieved recognition for genius-level contributions. In retrospect, this finding may not be surprising. The concept of giftedness is applied to two very different groups. One consists of high-IQ children who are the cream of the crop in school. The other consists of eminent adults who make enduring contributions in their fields. According to Ellen Winner (2000), a sizable gap exists between these two groups. The accomplishments of the latter group involve a much higher level of giftedness.

Joseph Renzulli (1986, 1999, 2002) theorizes that this rarer form of giftedness depends on the intersection of three factors: high intelligence, high creativity, and high motivation (see Figure 9.12). He emphasizes that high intelligence alone does not usually foster genuine greatness. Thus, the vast majority of children selected for gifted school programs do not achieve eminence as adults or make genius-like contributions to society (Callahan, 2000; Richert, 1997; Winner, 2003).

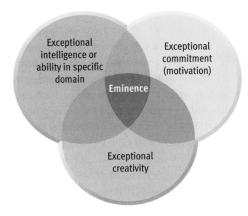

FIGURE 9.12

A three-ring conception of eminent giftedness.

According to Renzulli (1986), high intelligence is only one of three requirements for achieving eminence. He proposes that a combination of exceptional ability, creativity, and motivation leads some people to make enduring contributions in their fields.

Source: Adapted from Renzulli, J.S. (1986). The three-ring conception of giftedness: A developmental model for creative productivity. In R.J. Sternberg and J.E. Davidson (Eds.) *Conceptions of Giftedness* (pp. 53–92). New York: Cambridge University Press. Adapted by permission.

Judy Lupart, Canada Research Chair in Special Education at the University of Alberta, has done research on gifted education and the underrepresentation of female students in science. She has helped develop a mentoring program for girls in science and has won an award from the Women in Engineering Programs and Advocate Network for her work in this area.

Even in school itself, not all gifted children succeed. University of Alberta psychologist Judy Lupart and the University of Calgary's Michael Pyryt (1996) argue that specific subgroups of gifted children exist, including one they refer to as the "hidden gifted." These are gifted children who for a variety of reasons (e.g., learning disabled/gifted, cultural minority gifted, gifted females) may not be properly identified as gifted as they are underperforming academically. As a result, these hidden gifted students are not afforded the opportunities offered by educational programs designed to help gifted students meet their potential. These students often remain hidden because they underachieve in school—perhaps, in part, as a result of their attitudes toward school itself or because of the expectations of others. In their study, Lupart and Pyryt compared the expected performance of gifted students based on their IQ scores with their academic performance in school. In their sample, they found that 21 percent of their gifted students were underachieving in school.

In addition to her continuing research on giftedness (Lupart, 2004; Lupart, Pyryt, Watson, & Pierce, 2005), Lupart and her colleagues have gone on to examine the reasons for women's underrepresentation in science, and she has been involved in a mentoring program for girls called "SCIberMENTOR," in which girls are mentored in science and mathematics via computer by women in those fields (Lupart & Cannon, 2003).

Another hot issue in the study of giftedness concerns the degree to which extraordinary achievement depends on innate talent as opposed to

REVIEW OF KEY POINTS

▷ Intellectual disability refers to subnormal general mental ability accompanied by deficits in adaptive skills. IQ scores below 70 are usually diagnostic of intellectual disability. Such diagnoses should not be based solely on test results. Four levels of intellectual disability have been distinguished: mild, moderate, severe, and profound.

▷ About 1000 organic conditions can cause intellectual disability. But diagnosticians are unable to pinpoint a biological cause in 30–50 percent of cases. Research suggests that cases of unknown origin are mostly caused by unfavourable environmental factors, such as poverty, neglect, and poor nutrition.

▷ Savants are individuals who show extraordinary ability in one or more specific areas, such as memory or artistic or numerical ability, while demonstrating minimal capacity and performance in general intelligence tests and in most other tasks, including everyday skills. Savant syndrome may be the result of autism or dysfunctional brain development.

▷ Children who obtain IQ scores above 130 may be viewed as gifted. But cutoffs for accelerated programs vary, and schools rely too much on IQ scores. Research by Terman showed that gifted children tend to be socially mature and well adjusted. However, Winner has expressed some concerns about the adjustment of profoundly gifted individuals.

▷ Gifted youngsters typically become very successful. Most, however, do not make genius-level contributions because such achievements depend on a combination of high intelligence, creativity, and motivation. The drudge theory suggests that determination, hard work, and intensive training are the key to achieving eminence. But many theorists are reluctant to dismiss the importance of innate talent.

Intelligence and Psychological Testing

intensive training and hard work. In recent years, the emphasis has been on what Simonton (2001) calls the "drudge theory" of exceptional achievement. According to this view, eminence primarily or entirely depends on dogged determination; endless, tedious practice; and outstanding mentoring and training (Bloom, 1985; Dweck, 2008; Ericsson, Roring, & Nadagopal, 2007; Howe, 1999). This conclusion is based on studies of eminent scientists, artists, writers, musicians, and athletes, which show that they push themselves much harder and engage in far more deliberate practice than their less successful counterparts.

Although the evidence linking strenuous training and prodigious effort to world-class achievement is convincing, Winner (2000) points out that obsessive hard work and inborn ability may be confounded in retrospective analyses of eminent individuals. The youngsters who work the hardest may be those with the greatest innate talent, who are likely to find their efforts more rewarding than others. In other words, innate ability may be the key factor fostering the single-minded commitment that seems to be crucial to greatness. Simonton (1999b, 2005) has devised an elaborate theory of talent development that allocates a significant role to both innate ability and a host of supportive environmental factors.

In sum, recent research has clearly demonstrated that quality training, monumental effort, and perseverance are crucial factors in greatness, but many experts on giftedness maintain that extraordinary achievement also requires rare, innate talent.

Heredity and Environment as Determinants of Intelligence

PREVIEW QUESTIONS

▶ What types of evidence suggest that intelligence is inherited?

▶ What is heritability, and what are some limitations of heritability estimates?

▶ How has research demonstrated that environment influences IQ?

▶ How is the concept of reaction range used to explain the interaction of heredity and environment?

▶ How have Jensen and Herrnstein and Murray explained cultural disparities in average IQ scores?

▶ What are some alternative explanations for ethnic differences in average IQ scores?

Most early pioneers of intelligence testing maintained that intelligence is inherited (Cravens, 1992). Small wonder, then, that this view lingers on among many people. Gradually, however, it has become clear that both heredity and environment influence intelligence (Locurto, 1991; Plomin, 2003; Scarr, 1997). Does this mean that the nature versus nurture debate has been settled with respect to intelligence? Absolutely not. Theorists and researchers continue to argue vigorously about which of the two is more important, in part because the issue has such far-reaching sociopolitical implications.

Theorists who believe that intelligence is largely inherited downplay the value of special educational programs for underprivileged groups (Herrnstein & Murray, 1994; Kanazawa, 2006; Rushton & Jensen, 2005). They assert that a child's intelligence cannot be increased noticeably, because a child's genetic destiny cannot be altered. Other theorists take issue with this point, asserting that inherited characteristics are not necessarily unchangeable (Flynn, 2007; Sternberg, Grigorenko, & Kidd, 2005; Wahlsten, 1997b). The people in this camp tend to maintain that even more funds should be allocated for remedial education programs, improved schooling in lower-class neighbourhoods, and postsecondary financial aid for the underprivileged. Because the debate over the role of heredity in intelligence has direct relevance to important social issues and political decisions, we'll take a detailed look at this complex controversy.

Evidence for Hereditary Influence

Galton's observation that intelligence runs in families was quite accurate. However, *family studies* can determine only whether genetic influence on a trait is *plausible,* not whether it is certain (see Chapter 3). Family members share not just genes, but similar environments. If high intelligence (or low intelligence) appears in a family over several generations, this consistency could reflect the influence of either shared genes or shared environment. Because of this problem, researchers must turn to *twin studies* and *adoption studies* to obtain more definitive evidence on whether heredity affects intelligence.

Twin Studies

The best evidence regarding the role of genetic factors in intelligence comes from studies that compare identical and fraternal twins. The rationale for twin studies is that both identical and fraternal twins normally develop under similar environmental conditions. However, identical twins share more genetic kinship than fraternal twins. Hence, if pairs of identical twins are more similar in intelligence than pairs of fraternal twins, it's presumably because of their greater genetic similarity. (See Chapter 3 for a more detailed explanation of the logic underlying twin studies.)

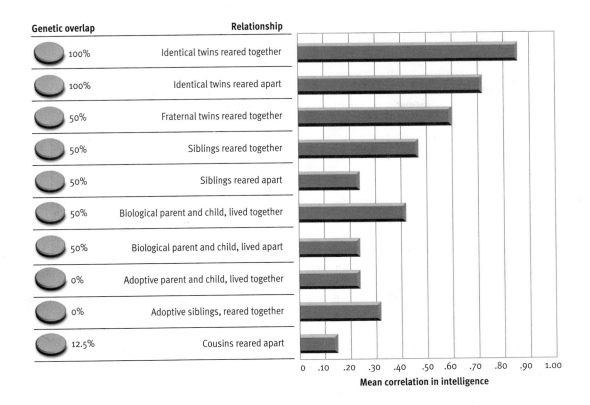

Genetic overlap	Relationship
100%	Identical twins reared together
100%	Identical twins reared apart
50%	Fraternal twins reared together
50%	Siblings reared together
50%	Siblings reared apart
50%	Biological parent and child, lived together
50%	Biological parent and child, lived apart
0%	Adoptive parent and child, lived together
0%	Adoptive siblings, reared together
12.5%	Cousins reared apart

Mean correlation in intelligence

FIGURE 9.13

Studies of IQ similarity.
The graph shows the mean correlations of IQ scores for people of various types of relationships, as obtained in studies of IQ similarity. Higher correlations indicate greater similarity. The results show that greater genetic similarity is associated with greater similarity in IQ, suggesting that intelligence is partly inherited (compare, for example, the correlations for identical and fraternal twins). However, the results also show that living together is associated with greater IQ similarity, suggesting that intelligence is partly governed by environment (compare, for example, the scores of siblings reared together and reared apart). (Data from McGue et al., 1993)

What are the findings of twin studies regarding intelligence? The data from over 100 studies of intellectual similarity for various kinds of kinship relations and child-rearing arrangements are summarized in Figure 9.13. This figure plots the average correlation observed for various types of relationships. As you can see, the average correlation reported for identical twins (0.86) is very high, indicating that identical twins tend to be quite similar in intelligence. The average correlation for fraternal twins (0.60) is significantly lower. This correlation indicates that fraternal twins also tend to be similar in intelligence, but noticeably less so than identical twins. These results support the notion that IQ is inherited to a considerable degree (Bouchard, 1998; Plomin & Spinath, 2004).

Of course, critics have tried to poke holes in this line of reasoning. They argue that identical twins are more alike in IQ because parents and others treat them more similarly than they treat fraternal twins. This environmental explanation of the findings has some merit. After all, identical twins are always the same sex, and gender influences how a child is raised. However, this explanation seems unlikely in light of the evidence on identical twins reared apart because of family breakups or adoption (Bouchard, 1997; Bouchard et al., 1990). *Although reared in different environments, these identical twins still display greater similarity in IQ (average correlation: 0.72) than fraternal twins reared together (average correlation: 0.60).*

Moreover, the gap in IQ similarity between identical twins reared apart and fraternal twins reared together appears to widen in middle and late adulthood, suggesting paradoxically that the influence of heredity increases with age (Pedersen et al., 1992).

Adoption Studies

Research on adopted children also provides evidence about the effects of heredity (and of environment, as we shall see). If adopted children resemble their biological parents in intelligence even though they were not reared by these parents, this finding supports the genetic hypothesis. The relevant studies indicate that there is indeed more than chance similarity between adopted children and their biological parents (Plomin et al., 2008; refer again to Figure 9.13).

Heritability Estimates

Various experts have sifted through mountains of correlational evidence to estimate the *heritability* of intelligence. A *heritability ratio* is an estimate of the proportion of trait variability in a population that is determined by variations in genetic inheritance. Heritability can be estimated for any trait. For example, the heritability of height is estimated to be around 90 percent and the heritability of weight is estimated to be around 85 percent (Bouchard, 2004).

Heritability can be estimated in a variety of ways that appear logically and mathematically defensible (Grigerenko, 2000; Loehlin, 1994). Given the variety of methods available and the strong views that experts bring to the IQ debate, it should come as no surprise that heritability estimates for intelligence vary considerably (see Figure 9.14).

At the high end, a few theorists, such as Arthur Jensen (1980, 1998), maintain that the heritability of IQ ranges as high as 80 percent (Bouchard, 2004). That is, they believe that only about 20 percent of the variation in intelligence is attributable to environmental factors. Estimates at the low end of the spectrum suggest that the heritability of intelligence is around 40 percent (Plomin, 2003), which means 60 percent would be attributable to environmental factors. In recent years, the consensus estimates of the experts tend to hover around 50 percent (Petrill, 2005; Plomin & Spinath, 2004).

However, it's important to understand that heritability estimates have certain limitations (Grigorenko, 2000; Johnson, et al., 2009; Reeve & Hakel, 2002). First, a heritability estimate is a *group statistic* based on studies of trait variability within a specific group. A heritability estimate cannot be applied meaningfully to *individuals*. In other words, even if the heritability of intelligence is 60 percent, this does not mean that each individual's intelligence is 60 percent inherited. Second, a specific trait's *heritability may vary from one group to another* depending on a variety of factors. For instance, in a group with a given gene pool, heritability will decrease if a shift occurs toward rearing youngsters in more diverse circumstances. Why? Because environmental variability will be increased.

Third, it is crucial to understand that "there really is no single fixed value that represents any true, constant value for the heritability of IQ or anything else" (Sternberg et al., 2005, p. 53). Heritability ratios are merely sample-specific estimates.

Evidence for Environmental Influence 7f

Heredity unquestionably influences intelligence, but a great deal of evidence indicates that upbringing also affects mental ability. In this section, we'll examine various approaches to research that show how life experiences shape intelligence.

Adoption Studies 7f

Research with adopted children provides useful evidence about the impact of experience as well as heredity (Dickens & Flynn, 2001; Locurto, 1990; Loehlin, Horn, & Willerman, 1997). Many of the correlations in Figure 9.13 reflect the influence of the environment. For example, adopted children show some resemblance to their adoptive parents in IQ. This similarity is usually attributed to the fact that their adoptive parents shape their environment. Adoption studies also indicate that siblings reared together are more similar in IQ than siblings reared apart. This is true even for identical twins, who have the same genetic endowment. Moreover, entirely unrelated children who are raised in the same home also show a significant resemblance in IQ. All of these findings indicate that environment influences intelligence.

Environmental Deprivation and Enrichment

If environment affects intelligence, children who are raised in substandard circumstances should experience a gradual decline in IQ as they grow older (since other children will be progressing more rapidly). This *cumulative deprivation hypothesis* was tested decades ago. Researchers studied children consigned to understaffed orphanages and children raised in the poverty and isolation of the back hills of Appalachia (Sherman & Key, 1932; Stoddard, 1943). Generally, investigators *did* find that environmental deprivation led to the predicted erosion in IQ scores.

Conversely, children who are removed from a deprived environment and placed in circumstances more conducive to learning should benefit from their environmental enrichment. Their IQ scores should gradually increase. This hypothesis has been

Heritability estimates for intelligence

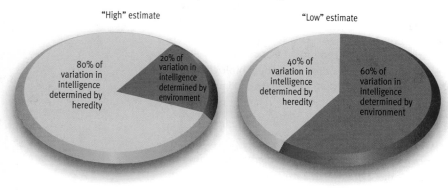

"High" estimate

80% of variation in intelligence determined by heredity

20% of variation in intelligence determined by environment

"Low" estimate

40% of variation in intelligence determined by heredity

60% of variation in intelligence determined by environment

FIGURE 9.14

The concept of heritability.

A heritability ratio is an estimate of the portion of variation in a trait determined by heredity—with the remainder presumably determined by environment—as these pie charts illustrate. Typical heritability estimates for intelligence range between a high of 80 percent and a low of 40 percent, although some estimates have fallen outside this range. Bear in mind that heritability ratios are *estimates* and have certain limitations that are discussed in the text.

tested by studying children who have been moved from disadvantaged homes or institutional settings into middle- and upper-class adoptive homes (Scarr & Weinberg, 1977, 1983; Schiff & Lewontin, 1986). A recent meta-analysis of relevant studies found that adopted children scored notably higher on IQ tests than siblings or peers "left behind" in institutions or disadvantaged homes (van IJzendoorn & Juffer, 2005). These gains are sometimes reduced if children suffer from severe, lengthy deprivation prior to their adoptive placement. But the overall trends clearly show that improved environments lead to increased IQ scores for most adoptees. These findings show that IQ scores are not unchangeable and that they are sensitive to environmental influences.

Generational Changes: The Flynn Effect

The most interesting, albeit perplexing, evidence showcasing the importance of the environment is the finding that performance on IQ tests has steadily increased over generations. This trend was not widely appreciated until recently because the tests are renormed periodically with new standardization groups, so that the mean IQ always remains at 100. However, in a study of the IQ tests used by the U.S. military, James Flynn noticed that the level of performance required to earn a score of 100 jumped upward every time the tests were renormed. Curious about this unexpected finding, he eventually gathered extensive data from 20 nations and demonstrated that IQ performance has been rising steadily all over the industrialized world since the 1930s (Flynn, 1987, 1994, 1998, 1999, 2003, 2007). Thus, the performance that today would earn you an average score of 100 would have earned you an IQ score of about 120 back in the 1930s (see Figure 9.15). Researchers who study intelligence are now scrambling to explain this trend, which has been dubbed the "Flynn effect." About the only thing they mostly agree on is that the Flynn effect has to be attributed to environmental factors, as the modern world's gene pool could not have changed overnight (in evolutionary terms, 70 years is more like a fraction of a second) (Dickens & Flynn, 2001; Neisser, 1998; Sternberg, Grigorenko, & Kidd, 2005).

The Interaction of Heredity and Environment 7f

Clearly, heredity and environment both influence intelligence to a significant degree. And their effects involve intricate, dynamic, reciprocal interactions

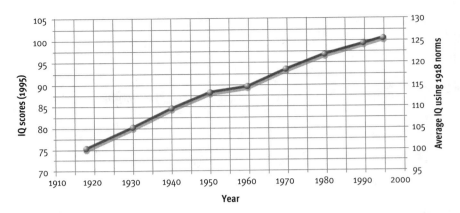

FIGURE 9.15

Generational increases in measured IQ.

IQ tests are renormed periodically so that the mean score remains at 100. However, research by James Flynn has demonstrated that performance on IQ tests around the world has been increasing throughout most of the last century. This graph traces the estimated increases in IQ in the United States from 1918 to 1995. In relation to the axis on the right, the graph shows how average IQ would have increased if IQ tests had continued to use 1918 norms. In relation to the axis on the left, the graph shows how much lower the average IQ score would have been in earlier years if 1995 norms had been used. The causes of the "Flynn effect" are unknown, but they have to involve environmental factors.

Source: Adapted from Flynn, J.R. (1998). IQ gains over time: Toward finding the causes. In U. Neisser (Ed.), *The rising curve: Long-term gains in IQ and related measure* (p. 37). Washington, DC: American Psychological Association. Copyright © 1998 by the American Psychological Association. Reprinted by permission of the author.

(Grigerenko, 2000; Johnson, 2010; Petrill, 2005). Genetic endowments influence the experiences that people are exposed to, and environments influence the degree to which genetic predispositions are realized. In fact, many theorists now assert that the question of whether heredity or environment is more important ought to take a back seat to the question of *how they interact* to govern IQ.

One influential model of this interaction was championed most prominently by Sandra Scarr (1991). The model posits that heredity may set certain limits on intelligence and that environmental factors determine where individuals fall within these limits (Bouchard, 1997; Weinberg, 1989). According to this idea, genetic makeup places an upper limit on a person's IQ that can't be exceeded even when environment is ideal. Heredity is also thought to place a lower limit on an individual's IQ, although extreme circumstances (for example, being locked in an attic until age ten) could drag a person's IQ beneath this boundary. Theorists use the term *reaction range* to refer to these genetically determined limits on IQ (or other traits).

According to the reaction-range model, children reared in high-quality environments that promote the development of intelligence should score near the top of their potential IQ range (see Figure 9.16). Children reared under less ideal circumstances should score lower in their reaction range. The concept of a reaction range can explain why high-IQ children sometimes come from poor environments. It can also

Sandra Scarr
"My research has been aimed at asking in what kind of environments genetic differences shine through and when do they remain hidden."

Intelligence and Psychological Testing

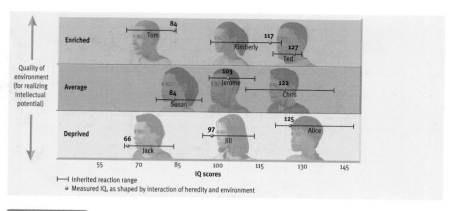

FIGURE 9.16

Reaction range.

The concept of reaction range posits that heredity sets limits on one's intellectual potential (represented by the horizontal bars), while the quality of one's environment influences where one scores within this range (represented by the dots on the bars). People raised in enriched environments should score near the top of their reaction range, whereas people raised in poor-quality environments should score near the bottom of their range. Genetic limits on IQ can be inferred only indirectly, so theorists aren't sure whether reaction ranges are narrow (like Ted's) or wide (like Chris's). The concept of reaction range can explain how two people with similar genetic potential can be quite different in intelligence (compare Tom and Jack) and how two people reared in environments of similar quality can score quite differently (compare Alice and Jack).

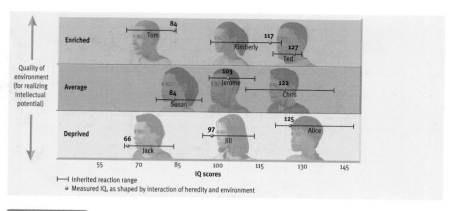

Arthur Jensen

"Despite more than half a century of repeated efforts by psychologists to improve the intelligence of children, particularly those in the lower quarter of the IQ distribution relative to those in the upper half of the distribution, strong evidence is still lacking as to whether or not it can be done."

explain why low-IQ children sometimes come from very good environments. Moreover, it can explain these apparent paradoxes without discounting the role that environment undeniably plays.

Scientists hope to achieve a more precise understanding of how heredity and environment interactively govern intelligence by identifying the specific genes that influence general mental ability. Advances in molecular genetics, including the mapping of the human genome, are allowing researchers to search for individual genes that are associated with measures of intelligence (Posthuma et al., 2005). However these studies have yielded minimal progress thus far (Johnson, 2010; Plomin, Kennedy, & Craig, 2006).

The problem with this new line of research is that intelligence may be influenced by hundreds of specific genes. Each gene may have a small effect that is extremely difficult to detect with current technologies (Petrill, 2005). In recent research, the *strongest* links found between genes and intelligence each were associated with less than one-half of 1 percent of the variation in intelligence (Plomin et al., 2006). Although researchers in this area hope to achieve breakthroughs as the technology of molecular genetics becomes more powerful, at this point the prospects for progress look rather bleak (Johnson, 2010).

Cultural Differences in IQ Scores

The age-old nature versus nurture debate lies at the core of the current controversy about ethnic differences in average IQ. Although the full range of IQ scores is seen in all ethnic groups, the average IQ for many of the larger minority groups in the United States (such as blacks, Native Americans, and Hispanics) is somewhat lower than the average for whites. The typical disparity is around 10 to 15 points, depending on the group tested and the IQ scale used (Hunt & Carlson, 2007; Loehlin, 2000; Nisbett, 2005; Rushton & Jensen, 2005). However, data from the standardization samples for the Stanford-Binet and Wechsler scales suggest that the gap between blacks and whites has shrunk by about 4–7 points since the 1970s (Dickens & Flynn, 2006). There is relatively little argument about the existence of these group differences, variously referred to as *racial*, *ethnic*, or *cultural differences in intelligence*. The controversy concerns *why* the differences are found. A vigorous debate continues as to whether cultural differences in intelligence are mainly attributable to the influence of heredity or of environment.

Heritability as an Explanation

In 1969, Arthur Jensen sparked a heated war of words by arguing that cultural differences in IQ are largely due to heredity. The cornerstone for Jensen's argument was his analysis suggesting that the heritability of intelligence is about 80 percent. Essentially, he asserted (1) that intelligence is largely genetic in origin and (2) that, therefore, genetic factors are "strongly implicated" as the cause of ethnic differences in intelligence. Jensen's article triggered outrage, bitter criticism, and even death threats, as well as a flurry of research that shed additional light on the determinants of intelligence.

Twenty-five years later, Richard Herrnstein and Charles Murray (1994) reignited the same controversy with the publication of their widely discussed book *The Bell Curve*. They argued that ethnic differences in average intelligence are substantial, not easily reduced by educational programs for the disadvantaged, and at least partly genetic in origin. The implicit message throughout *The Bell Curve* was that disadvantaged groups cannot avoid their fate because it's their genetic destiny. And as recently as 2010, based on an extensive review of statistical evidence, J. Phillipe Rushton and Arthur Jensen (2010) argued that genetic factors account for the bulk of the gap between races in average IQ.

Controversy seems to surround this issue. James Watson, a Nobel Prize winner in 1962 for his co-discovery of DNA, lost his position as chancellor of the Cold Spring Harbor Laboratory in New York because of his comments on race and IQ (Nisbett, 2007). Canadian psychologist

J. Phillipe Rushton (Rushton & Irwing, 2011) of the University of Western Ontario also created a great deal of controversy with his views concerning race and intelligence. Rushton (1994, 1995) argued from the nature perspective that the races could be ranked in terms of inherited intelligence, social behaviour, and physical attributes. He asserted that Asians are the most intelligent, most law-abiding, hardest working, and least sexually promiscuous, and have the largest brain size of the races. Blacks rank on the opposite ends of these dimensions, with whites in the middle. Rushton's views on racial hierarchies were condemned not only because of the social harm they might cause, but because his conclusions were based on bad science, sloppy reasoning, and inaccuracies. For example, one review of his 1995 book concluded "the low standards of scholarship evident in this book render it largely irrelevant for modern science" (*Race, Evolution and Behavior*, 1995, p. 129). Commenting on his work, Canadian psychologists Weizmann, Wiener, Wiesenthal, and Ziegler (1990) stated that "the collecting and cataloguing of *ad hoc* racial differences in behaviour says nothing about any evolutionary, genetic, or environmental origins and causes of such differences. It also betrays a naïve and outdated inductivist view of science" (p. 11).

"Our intellectual landscape has been disrupted by the equivalent of an earthquake." —MICHAEL NOVAK, NATIONAL REVIEW

THE BELL CURVE

Intelligence and Class Structure in American Life

The Controversial New York Times Bestseller

RICHARD J. HERRNSTEIN
CHARLES MURRAY

With a New Afterword by Charles Murray

In their 1994 bestseller, Herrnstein and Murray added fuel to the fire of the race–intelligence controversy.

concept check 9.2

Understanding Correlational Evidence on the Heredity–Environment Question

Check your understanding of how correlational findings relate to the nature versus nurture issue by indicating how you would interpret the meaning of each "piece" of evidence described below. The numbers inside the parentheses are the mean IQ correlations observed for the relationships described (based on McGue et al., 1993), which are shown in Figure 9.13 (p. 415). In the spaces on the left, enter the letter H if the findings suggest that intelligence is shaped by heredity, enter the letter E if the findings suggest that intelligence is shaped by the environment, and enter the letter B if the findings suggest that intelligence is shaped by both (or either) heredity and environment. The answers can be found in Appendix A.

_____ **1.** Identical twins reared apart are more similar (0.72) than fraternal twins reared together (0.60).

_____ **2.** Identical twins reared together are more similar (0.86) than identical twins reared apart (0.72).

_____ **3.** Siblings reared together are more similar (0.47) than siblings reared apart (0.24).

_____ **4.** Biological parents and the children they rear are more similar (0.42) than unrelated persons who are reared apart (no correlation if sampled randomly).

_____ **5.** Adopted children show similarity to their biological parents (0.24) and to their adoptive parents (0.24).

Rushton debated his views with David Suzuki on CBC television (*Rushton–Suzuki Debate*, 1989) in 1989. Although his job was protected by the principle of academic freedom, Rushton was investigated by the police and a provincial human rights board. David Peterson, then the premier of Ontario, said he would fire Rushton if he could, and the University of Western Ontario prohibited Rushton from using the undergraduate psychology participant pool for a period of time, cancelled some of his lectures, promised to monitor some of his future lectures, and apologized for any pain caused by his views (Helwig, 1989; Platiel & Strauss, 1989; Tenszen, 1989). Rushton has since continued his active research program on genetics and psychological variables (Rushton, 2008; Rushton & Jensen, 2010).

In addition to the specific criticisms of Rushton's work, heritability explanations for ethnic differences in IQ have, in general, a variety of flaws and weaknesses (Devlin et al., 2002; Horn, 2002; Myerson et al., 1998; Sternberg, 1995). For example, a heritability estimate applies only to the specific group on which the estimate is based. Heritability estimates for intelligence have been based on studies dominated almost entirely by white subjects (Brody, 1992). Hence, there is doubt about the validity of

WEB LINK 9.7

Human Intelligence
This website, developed by University of Toronto psychology professor Eyal Reingold, contains information on and links to many topics related to intelligence, including *The Bell Curve* and its critics.

WEB LINK 9.8

The Rushton–Suzuki Debate
Videos of J. Phillipe Rushton's debate with David Suzuki can be viewed at the archives of the CBC website.

FIGURE 9.17

Genetics and between-group differences on a trait.

Leon Kamin's analogy (see text) shows how between-group differences on a trait (the average height of corn plants) could be due to environment, even if the trait is largely inherited. The same reasoning presumably applies to ethnic-group differences in average intelligence.

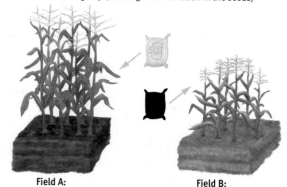

Individual variation in corn plant heights within each group (cause: genetic variation in the seeds)

Field A: More fertile soil

Field B: Less fertile soil

Differences in average corn plant height between groups (cause: the soils in which the plants were grown)

applying this estimate to other cultural groups (Grigorenko, 2000).

Moreover, even if one accepts the assumption that the heritability of IQ is very high, it does not follow logically that differences in *group averages* must be due largely to heredity. Leon Kamin has presented a compelling analogy that highlights the logical fallacy in this reasoning (see Figure 9.17):

> *We fill a white sack and a black sack with a mixture of different genetic varieties of corn seed. We make certain that the proportions of each variety of seed are identical in each sack. We then plant the seed from the white sack in fertile Field A, while that from the black sack is planted in barren Field B. We will observe that within Field A, as within Field B, there is considerable variation in the height of individual corn plants. This variation will be due largely to genetic factors (seed differences). We will also observe, however, that the average height of plants in Field A is greater than that in Field B. That difference will be entirely due to environmental factors (the soil). The same is true of IQs: differences in the average IQ of various human populations could be entirely due to environmental differences, even if within each population all variation were due to genetic differences!*
> (Eysenck & Kamin, 1981, p. 97)

This analogy shows that even if *within-group differences* in IQ are highly heritable, *between-groups differences* in average IQ could still be caused *entirely* by environmental factors (Block, 2002). For decades, critics of Jensen's thesis have relied on this analogy rather than actual data to make the point that between-groups differences in IQ do not necessarily reflect genetic differences. They depended on the analogy because no relevant data were available. However, the recent discovery of the Flynn effect has provided compelling new data that are directly

relevant (Dickens & Flynn, 2001; Flynn, 2003). Generational gains in IQ scores show that a between-groups disparity in average IQ (in this case the gap is between generations rather than ethnic groups) can be environmental in origin, even though intelligence is highly heritable.

The available evidence certainly does not allow us to rule out the possibility that ethnic and cultural disparities in average intelligence are partly genetic. And the hypothesis should not be dismissed without study simply because many people find it offensive or distasteful. However, there are several alternative explanations for the culture gap in intelligence that seem more plausible. Let's look at them.

Socioeconomic Disadvantage as an Explanation

Some theorists have approached the issue by trying to show that socioeconomic disadvantages are the main cause of ethnic differences in average IQ. Many social scientists argue that minority students' IQ scores are depressed because these children tend to grow up in deprived environments that create a disadvantage—both in school and on IQ tests. Obviously, living circumstances vary greatly within ethnic groups, but there is no question that, on the average, whites and minorities tend to be raised in very different circumstances. Most minority groups have endured a long history of economic discrimination and are greatly overrepresented in the lower social classes. A lower-class upbringing tends to carry a number of disadvantages that work against the development of a youngster's full intellectual potential (Bigelow, 2006; Evans, 2004; Lott, 2002; McLoyd, 1998; Noble, McCandliss, & Farah, 2007; Seifer, 2001).

In comparison to the middle and upper classes, lower-class children are more likely to come from large families and from single-parent homes, factors that may often limit the parental attention they receive. Lower-class children also tend to be exposed to fewer books, to have fewer learning supplies, to have less privacy for concentrated study, and to get less parental assistance in learning. Typically, they also have poorer role models for language development, experience less pressure to work hard on intellectual pursuits, and attend poorer-quality schools that are underfunded and understaffed. Many of these children grow up in crime-, drug-, and gang-infested neighbourhoods where it is far more important to develop street intelligence than school intelligence. Some theorists also argue that children in the lower classes are more likely to suffer from malnutrition or to be exposed to environmental toxins

(Brody, 1992). Either of these circumstances could interfere with youngsters' intellectual development (Bellinger & Adams, 2001; Grantham-McGregor, Ani, & Fernald, 2001).

In light of these disadvantages, it's not surprising that average IQ scores among children from lower social classes tend to run about 15 points below the average scores obtained by children from middle and upper class homes (Seifer, 2001; Williams & Ceci, 1997). This is the case even if race is factored out of the picture by studying whites exclusively. Admittedly, there is room for argument about the direction of the causal relationships underlying this association between social class and intelligence (Turkheimer, 1998). Nonetheless, given the over-representation of minorities in the lower classes, many researchers argue that ethnic differences in intelligence are really social class differences in disguise.

Stereotype Threat as an Explanation

Socioeconomic disadvantages probably are a major factor in various minority groups' poor performance on IQ and other standardized tests, but some theorists maintain that other factors and processes are also at work. For example, Claude Steele (1992, 1997), a social psychologist at Stanford University, has argued that derogatory stereotypes of stigmatized groups' intellectual capabilities create unique feelings of vulnerability in the educational arena. These feelings of *stereotype vulnerability* can undermine group members' performance on tests, as well as other measures of academic achievement. These feelings may also create *belonging uncertainty,* doubts in their mind about the quality of their social bonds and relationships in these situations (Walton & Cohen, 2007). All of these can contribute to poor performance in achievement situations.

Steele points out that demeaning stereotypes of stigmatized groups are widely disseminated, creating a subtle climate of prejudice, even in the absence of overt discrimination. He further notes that members of minority groups are keenly aware of any negative stereotypes that exist regarding their intellect. Hence, when a minority student does poorly on a test, he or she must confront a disturbing possibility: *that others will attribute the failure to racial inferiority.* Steele maintains that females face the same problem when they venture into academic domains where stereotypes suggest that they are inferior to males, such as mathematics, engineering, and the physical sciences. That is, *they worry about people blaming their failures on their sex.* According to Steele, minorities and women in male-dominated fields are in a no-win situation. When they do well and contradict stereotypes, people tend to view their success with suspicion, but when they do poorly, people readily view their failure as vindication of the stereotypes.

Steele maintains that stigmatized groups' apprehension about "confirming" people's negative stereotypes can contribute to academic underachievement in at least two ways. First, it can undermine their emotional investment in academic work. As Steele notes, "Doing well in school requires a belief that school achievement can be a promising basis of self-esteem, and that belief needs constant reaffirmation even for advantaged students" (1992, p. 72). When this belief is relentlessly undercut instead of frequently reaffirmed, students tend to "disidentify" with school and write off academic pursuits as a source of self-worth (Nussbaum & Steele, 2007). Their academic motivation declines and their performance suffers as a result. Second, standardized tests such as IQ tests may be especially anxiety-arousing for members of stigmatized groups because the importance attributed to the tests makes one's stereotype vulnerability particularly salient. This anxiety may impair students' test performance by temporarily disrupting their cognitive functioning.

Recent investigations into the processes implicated in stereotype threat and performance decline have suggested that several mechanisms are involved. First, the stress induced in these types of situations interferes with prefrontal brain processing. Stereotype threat also produces a tendency to actively monitor your performance in these situations and to inhibit or suppress negative thoughts and emotions. According to Schmader, Johns, and Forbes (2008), these three mechanisms combine to deplete executive resources that are necessary for successful task performance. In our Featured Study, we look at how Steele tested his original theory of stereotype threat.

The negative effects of stereotype threat have been replicated in numerous studies (Cadinu et al., 2005; Croizet et al., 2004; Shapiro & Neuberg, 2007). A recent meta-analysis of 39 stereotype threat experiments concluded that cognitive tests tend to underestimate the ability of negatively stereotyped students in real-world settings (Walton & Spencer, 2009). Recent research has also provided new insight into one way that stereotype threat impairs test performance (Schmader, 2010). The evidence suggests that reminders of negative stereotypes lead people to expend precious mental resources suppressing negative thoughts and monitoring themselves for signs of failure. These distractions hijack the very cognitive

Claude Steele

"I believe that in significant part the crisis in black Americans' education stems from the power of this vulnerability to undercut identification with schooling."

Investigators: Claude M. Steele (Stanford University) and Joshua Aronson (University of Texas, Austin)
Source: Stereotype threat and the intellectual test performance of African Americans. *Journal of Personality and Social Psychology*, 1995, *69*, 797–811.

Racial Stereotypes and Test Performance

In this article, Steele and Aronson report on a series of four studies that tested various aspects of Steele's theory about the ramifications of stereotype vulnerability. We will examine their first study in some detail and then discuss the remaining studies more briefly. The purpose of the first study was to test the hypothesis that raising the threat of stereotype vulnerability would have a negative impact on black students' performance on a mental ability test.

Method

Participants. The participants were 114 black and white undergraduates attending Stanford University who were recruited through campus advertisements. As expected, given Stanford's highly selective admissions, both groups of students were well above average in academic ability, as evidenced by their mean scores on the verbal subtest of the *Scholastic Aptitude Test* (SAT). The study compared black and white students with high and roughly equal ability and preparation (based on their SAT scores) to rule out cultural disadvantage as a factor.

Procedure. The participants were asked to take a challenging, 30-minute test of verbal ability comprising items from the verbal subtest of the *Graduate Record Exam* (GRE). In one condition, the issue of stereotype vulnerability was not made salient, as the test was presented to subjects as a device to permit the researchers to analyze participants' problem-solving strategies. In another condition, the spectre of stereotype vulnerability was raised, as the test was presented as an excellent index of one's general verbal ability. The principal dependent variable was subjects' performance on the verbal test.

Results

When the black students' stereotype vulnerability was not made salient, the performance of the black and white students did not differ, as you can see in Figure 9.18. However, when the same test was presented in a way that increased blacks' stereotype vulnerability, the black students scored significantly lower than their white counterparts (see Figure 9.18).

Discussion

Based on their initial study, the authors inferred that stereotype vulnerability does appear to impair minority group members' test performance. They went on to replicate their finding in a second study of 40 black and white female students. In a third study, they demonstrated that their manipulations of stereotype vulnerability were indeed activating thoughts about negative stereotypes, ability-related self-doubts, and performance apprehension

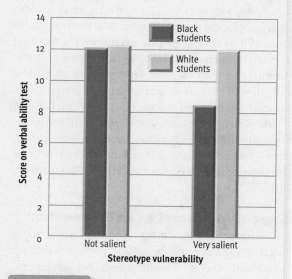

FIGURE 9.18

Stereotype vulnerability and test performance.
Steele and Aronson (1995) compared the performance of black and white students of equal ability on a 30-item verbal ability test constructed from difficult GRE questions. When the black students' stereotype vulnerability was not salient, their performance did not differ from that of the white students; but when the spectre of stereotype vulnerability was raised, the black students performed significantly worse than the white students.

Source: Adapted from Steele, C.M., and Aronson, J. (1995). Stereotype threat and the intellectual test performance of African Americans. *Journal of Personality and Social Psychology, 69*, 797–811. Copyright © 1995 by the American Psychological Association. Reprinted by permission of the author.

in their black participants. Their fourth study showed that stereotype vulnerability can be activated even when a test is not explicitly presented as an index of one's ability.

Comment

More evidence is clearly needed on the effects of stereotype vulnerability, but Steele's theory has been supported in a number of additional studies (Aronson et al., 1999; Croizet et al., 2004; Spencer, Steele, & Quinn, 1999). The concept of stereotype vulnerability has the potential to clear up some of the confusion surrounding the controversial issue of racial disparities in IQ scores. It seems likely that socioeconomic disadvantage makes a substantial contribution to cultural differences in average IQ, but various lines of evidence suggest that this factor cannot account for the culture gap by itself (Neisser et al., 1996). For years, many theorists have argued that test bias accounts for the rest of the culture gap, but as we will discuss soon, recent research suggests otherwise. Thus, Steele's groundbreaking research gives scientists

resource—working memory—that is critical to success on complex cognitive tests. This reduction in working memory capacity undermines test performance. Interest into ways to attenuate the effects of stereotype threat is ongoing, including the work of Kerry Kawakami (Kawakami et al., 2008). Experimental results obtained by researchers at the University of Arizona and the University of British Columbia suggest, among other things, that increased motivation and stereotype retraining may help reduce the effects observed as a result of stereotype threat (Forbes & Schmader, 2010). Clearly, there is little question that this is an important avenue for future experimental work.

Cultural Bias on IQ Tests as an Explanation

Some critics of IQ tests have argued that cultural differences in IQ scores are partly due to a cultural bias built into IQ tests. They argue that because IQ tests are constructed by white, middle-class psychologists, they naturally draw on experience and knowledge typical of white, middle-class lifestyles and use language and vocabulary that reflect the white, middle-class origins of their developers (Cohen, 2002; Helms, 1992, 2006; Hilliard, 1984). Fagan and Holland (2002, 2007) have collected data suggesting that the IQ gap between whites and blacks is due to cultural differences in knowledge due to disparities in *exposure to information.*

Most theorists acknowledge that IQ tests measure a combination of ability and knowledge (Ackerman

Courtesy of Kerry Kawakami

In her research, social psychologist Kerry Kawakami is interested in implicit prejudice and techniques that work to reduce prejudice and stereotyping.

REVIEW OF KEY POINTS

▸ The debate about the influence of heredity and environment on intelligence has important sociopolitical implications. Twin studies show that identical twins, even when raised apart, are more similar in IQ than fraternal twins, suggesting that intelligence is inherited. Adoption studies reveal that people resemble their parents in intelligence even when not raised by them. Estimates of the heritability of intelligence mostly range from 40 percent to 80 percent, but heritability ratios have certain limitations.

▸ Many lines of evidence, including adoption studies, studies of environmental deprivation and enrichment, home-environment studies, and research on the Flynn effect indicate that environment is also an important determinant of intelligence. The concept of reaction range posits that heredity places limits on one's intellectual potential while the environment determines where one falls within these limits.

▸ Arthur Jensen in the United States and J. Phillipe Rushton in Canada sparked great controversy by arguing that cultural differences in average IQ are largely due to heredity. Although Richard Herrnstein and Charles Murray, the authors of *The Bell Curve,* tried to sidestep the issue, their book ignited the same controversy.

▸ Genetic explanations for cultural differences in IQ have been challenged on a variety of grounds. Even if the heritability of IQ is great, group differences in average intelligence may not be due to heredity. Moreover, ethnicity varies with social class, so socioeconomic disadvantage may account for low IQ scores among minority students.

▸ Claude Steele has collected some thought-provoking data suggesting that stereotype vulnerability contributes to the culture gap in average IQ. Cultural bias on IQ tests may also contribute a little to ethnic differences in IQ, but it does not appear to be a crucial factor.

& Beier, 2005; Cianciolo & Sternberg, 2004). Test developers try to tilt the balance toward the assessment of ability as much as possible, but factual knowledge clearly has an impact on IQ scores. According to Fagan and Holland (2002, 2007), cultural disparities in IQ reflect differences in *knowledge* rather than differences in *ability*. That said, other approaches to this issue, which have focused on whether there are cultural disparities in the predictive validity of IQ tests, suggest that the cultural slant on IQ tests is modest. Many experts assert that the evidence indicates that cultural bias produces only weak and inconsistent effects on the IQ scores of minority examinees (Hunter & Schmidt, 2000; Reynolds, 2000; Reynolds & Ramsay, 2003). Thus, debate continues about the degree to which IQ tests may contain a cultural slant.

Taken as a whole, the various alternative explanations for cultural and ethnic disparities in average IQ provide serious challenges to genetic explanations, which appear weak at best—and suspiciously racist

at worst. Unfortunately, since the earliest days of IQ testing, some people have used IQ tests to further elitist goals. The current controversy about ethnic differences in IQ is just another replay of a record that has been heard before. For instance, beginning in 1913, Henry Goddard tested a great many immigrants to the United States at Ellis Island in New York. Goddard reported that the vast majority of Italian, Hungarian, and Jewish immigrants tested out as *feeble-minded* (Kamin, 1974). As you can see, claims about ethnic deficits in intelligence are nothing new—only the victims have changed.

The debate about ethnic differences in intelligence illustrates how IQ tests have often become entangled in thorny social conflicts. This is unfortunate, because it brings politics to the testing enterprise. Intelligence testing has many legitimate and valuable uses. However, the controversy associated with intelligence tests has undermined their value, leading to some of the new trends that we discuss in the next section.

New Directions in the Assessment and Study of Intelligence

PREVIEW QUESTIONS

▶ What evidence is there concerning brain correlates of intelligence and a link between IQ and mortality?

▶ What are the key features of Sternberg's theory of successful intelligence?

▶ What is Gardner's thesis about the nature of intelligence?

▶ What is *emotional intelligence*, and can it be measured?

Intelligence testing has been through a period of turmoil, and changes are on the horizon. In fact, many changes have occurred already. Let's discuss some of the major new trends and projections for the future.

Some researchers have begun to explore the relationship between brain size and intelligence (Lange et al., 2010). The early studies in this area used various measures of head size as an indicator of brain size. These studies generally found positive, but very small, correlations (average 0.15) between head size and IQ (Vernon et al., 2000), leading researchers to speculate that head size is probably a very crude index of brain size. This line of research might have languished, but the invention of sophisticated brain-imaging technologies gave it a huge shot in the arm. Since the 1990s, quite a few studies have examined the correlation between IQ scores and measures of brain volume based on MRI scans (see Chapter 3), yielding an average correlation of about 0.35 (Anderson, 2003; McDaniel, 2005; Rushton & Ankney, 2007). Thus, it appears that larger brains are somewhat predictive of greater intelligence.

Many investigators suspect that the association between brain size and intelligence may reflect the enlargement of particular areas in the brain, or growth in certain types of brain tissue, rather than a global increase in brain size. Hence, these researchers are exploring whether IQ correlates with the size of specific regions in the brain. Based on their review of

37 brain-imaging studies, Jung and Haier (2007) theorize that intelligence depends on interactions among a constellation of key areas in the brain, including the prefrontal cortex, Broca's and Wernicke's areas, the somatosensory association cortex, the visual association cortex, and the anterior cingulate. The evidence is complex and more data are needed, but researchers have found some intriguing correlations between the volume of these specific areas in the brain and measures of intelligence (Colom et al., 2009; Haier, 2009).

Other researchers have approached this question by analyzing the relationship between intelligence and measures of the amount of grey matter or white matter in individuals' brains (Lange et al., 2010). According to Luders et al. (2009), the amount of grey matter should index the density of neurons and their dendrites, which may be predictive of information processing capacity. In contrast, the amount of white matter should index the quantity of axons in the brain and their degree of myelinization, which may be predictive of the efficiency of neuronal communication. The findings thus far suggest that higher intelligence scores are correlated with increased volume of *both* grey matter and white matter, with the association being a little stronger for grey matter (Luders et al., 2009; Narr et al., 2007).

One obvious implication of these findings, eagerly embraced by those who tout the influence of heredity on intelligence, is that genetic inheritance gives some people larger brains than others and that larger brain size promotes greater intelligence (Rushton, 2003). However, as always, we must be cautious about interpreting correlational data. As discussed in Chapter 3, research has demonstrated that an enriched environment can produce denser neural networks and heavier brains in laboratory rats (Rosenzweig & Bennett, 1996). Hence, it is also possible that causation runs in the opposite direction—that developing greater intelligence promotes larger brain size, much like weightlifting can promote larger muscles.

Research on the biological correlates of intelligence has turned up another interesting finding that seems likely to occupy researchers for some time to come. IQ scores measured in childhood correlate with longevity decades later. For example, one study has followed a large cohort of people in Scotland who were given IQ tests in 1932 when they were 11 years old (Deary et al., 2004, 2009). People who scored one standard deviation (15 points) below average on the IQ test in 1932 were only 79 percent as likely as those who scored average or above to be alive in 1997. A handful of other studies have yielded the same conclusion: Smarter people live longer (Batty, Deary, & Gottfredson, 2007; Pearce et al., 2006, see Figure 9.19).

The evidence suggests that higher intelligence reduces a broad variety of health risks. For example, higher IQ is associated with decreased mortality from cardiovascular diseases, cancers, and external causes (injuries, poisoning, violence, etc.) (Leon et al., 2009). And a study linking adolescent IQ to health problems at age 40 found that higher IQ was associated with a decreased risk for chronic lung disease, heart problems, hypertension, diabetes, and arthritis/rheumatism (Der, Batty, & Deary, 2009).

Why is higher IQ linked to increased longevity? Researchers have offered a variety of explanations (Arden, Gottfredson, & Miller, 2009; Batterham, Christensen, & Mackinnon, 2009; Gottfredson & Deary, 2004). One possibility is that good genes could foster both higher intelligence and resilient health. A second possibility is that health self-care is a complicated lifelong mission, for which brighter people are better prepared. In other words, smarter people may be more likely to avoid health-impairing habits (such as smoking and overeating), be proactive about health (such as exercising and taking vitamins), and use medical care more effectively (such as knowing when to seek treatment). A third possibility is that intelligence fosters career success and higher social class decreases mortality. People in higher socioeconomic classes tend to have less stressful jobs with lower accident risks, reduced exposure to toxins and pathogens, better health insurance, and greater access to medical

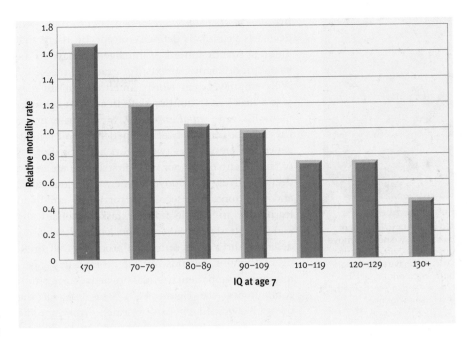

FIGURE 9.19

The relationship between childhood IQ and mortality.

In a recent study, Leon et al. (2009) examined the association between IQ measured at age seven and mortality through the age of 57 in a sample of over 11 000 people in the United Kingdom. The data in the graph are age-adjusted relative morality rates in comparison to the reference group of people scoring near average (90–109) in intelligence. Thus, in comparison to the reference group, people who scored 70–79 were 22 percent more likely to die by age 57, and people who scored over 130 were less than half as likely to die by age 57. As you can see, there is a clear trend. As IQ scores go up, mortality rates decline.

Source: From WEITEN. *Psychology*, 9E. © 2013 Wadsworth, a part of Cengage Learning, Inc. Reproduced by permission. www.cengage.com/permissions.

care. Thus, affluence could be the key factor linking intelligence to longevity. These explanations are not mutually exclusive. They might all contribute to the association between IQ and longevity.

Investigating Cognitive Processes in Intelligent Behaviour

As noted in Chapters 1 and 8, psychologists are increasingly taking a cognitive perspective in their efforts to study many topics. For over a century, the investigation of intelligence has been approached primarily from a *testing perspective*. This perspective emphasizes measuring the *amount* of intelligence people have and figuring out why some have more than others. In contrast, the *cognitive perspective* focuses on how people *use* their intelligence. The interest is in process rather than amount. In particular, cognitive psychologists focus on the information-processing strategies that underlie intelligence.

The application of the cognitive perspective to intelligence has been spearheaded by Robert Sternberg (1985, 1988b, 1991). His *triarchic theory of human intelligence* consists of three parts: the contextual, experiential, and componential subtheories. In

Robert Sternberg

"To understand intelligent behaviour, we need to move beyond the fairly restrictive tasks that have been used both in experimental laboratories and in psychometric tests of intelligence."

his *contextual subtheory*, Sternberg argues that intelligence is a culturally defined concept. He asserts that different manifestations of intelligent behaviour are valued in different contexts. For example, the verbal skills emphasized in North American culture may take a back seat to hunting skills in another culture.

In his *experiential subtheory*, Sternberg explores the relationships between experience and intelligence. He emphasizes two factors as the hallmarks of intelligent behaviour. The first is the ability to deal effectively with novelty—new tasks, demands, and situations. The second factor is the ability to learn how to handle familiar tasks automatically and effortlessly. Sternberg's *componential subtheory* describes three types of mental processes that intelligent thought depends on: metacomponents, performance components, and knowledge-acquisition components (see Figure 9.20). This part of the theory has guided extensive research on the specific thinking strategies that contribute to intelligent problem solving. Investigations of cognitive processes in intelligent behaviour have some interesting implications for intelligence testing. Cognitive research has shown that more-intelligent subjects spend more time figuring out how to best represent problems and planning how to solve them than less-intelligent subjects do. Because planning takes time, Sternberg (1985) argues that traditional IQ tests place too much emphasis on speed.

In more recent extensions of his theory, Sternberg (1999, 2003b, 2005a) has asserted that there are three aspects or facets of what he calls "successful intelligence": analytical intelligence, creative intelligence, and practical intelligence. *Analytical intelligence* involves abstract reasoning, evaluation, and judgment. It is the type of intelligence that is crucial to most schoolwork and that is assessed by conventional IQ tests. *Creative intelligence* involves the ability to generate new ideas and to be inventive in dealing with novel problems. *Practical intelligence* involves the ability to deal effectively with the kinds of problems that people encounter in everyday life, such as on the job or at home. A big part of practical intelligence involves learning what one needs to know to work efficiently in an environment that is not explicitly taught and that often is not even verbalized.

According to Sternberg, all three of the component processes underlying intelligence (metacomponents, performance components, and knowledge-acquisition components) contribute to each of the three facets of intelligence (analytical, creative, and practical intelligence). Sternberg and his colleagues have gathered data suggesting that all three facets of intelligence can be measured reliably and that they are relatively independent (uncorrelated). They have also shown that the assessment of all three aspects of intelligence can improve the prediction of intelligent behavior in the real world (Grigorenko & Sternberg, 2001; Henry, Sternberg, & Grigorenko, 2005; Sternberg et al., 1999, 2001). Recent findings suggest that measurements based on Sternberg's model can be used as supplements to traditional tests (such as the SAT) to enhance the prediction of academic achievement (Stemler et al., 2006; Sternberg et al., 2006). Some critics doubt that

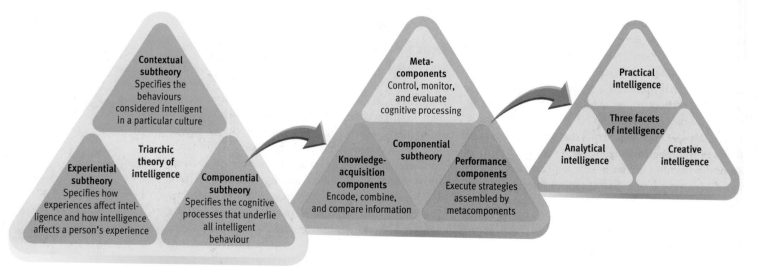

FIGURE 9.20

Sternberg's triarchic theory of intelligence.

Sternberg's model of intelligence consists of three parts: the contextual subtheory, the experiential subtheory, and the componential subtheory. Much of Sternberg's research has been devoted to the componential subtheory, as he has attempted to identify the cognitive processes that contribute to intelligence. He believes that these processes fall into three groups: metacomponents, performance components, and knowledge-acquisition components. All three component processes contribute to each of three aspects or types of intelligence: analytical intelligence, practical intelligence, and creative intelligence.

Sternberg's measures will facilitate better prediction of meaningful outcomes than traditional IQ tests (Gottfredson, 2003a). But that is an empirical question that should be resolved by future research. In any event, Sternberg certainly has been a strong voice arguing for a broader, expanded concept of intelligence, which is a theme that has been echoed by others.

Sternberg (2011) is one of the most important and prolific researchers in the area of intelligence. One of the reasons he became interested in the science of intelligence was because of his own experiences with IQ testing as a child. Sternberg performed so poorly on IQ tests as a child in elementary school that many of his teachers had very low expectations for his ability and future. In many ways he was saved by his Grade 4 teacher, Mrs. Alexa, who encouraged him in his work and who believed in his potential. He has since gone on to an incredibly successful career, authoring over 1000 publications on topics as varied as intelligence, love, creativity, and thinking styles (Indiana University, 2010). He dedicated his 1996 book, *Successful Intelligence,* to Mrs. Alexa.

Expanding the Concept of Intelligence

In recent years, a number of theorists besides Sternberg have concluded that the focus of traditional IQ tests is too narrow (Ceci, 1990; Greenspan & Driscoll, 1997). These theorists argue that to assess intelligence in a truly general sense, tests should sample from a wider range of tasks. The most prominent proponent of this view has been Howard Gardner (1983, 1993, 1998, 2004, 2006).

According to Gardner, IQ tests have generally emphasized verbal and mathematical skills to the exclusion of other important skills. He suggests the existence of a number of relatively autonomous *human intelligences*, which are listed in Table 9.3. To build his list of separate intelligences, Gardner reviewed the evidence on cognitive capacities in normal individuals, people suffering from brain damage, and special populations, such as prodigies and savants. He concluded that humans exhibit eight intelligences: logical–mathematical, linguistic, musical, spatial, bodily–kinesthetic, interpersonal, intrapersonal, and naturalist. Gardner (1999) has also suggested the possibility that other intelligences may be identified, including that of an existential intelligence, which he describes as the "intelligence of big questions" (Gardner, 2003, p. 7). But to date, according to Gardner, the evidence is most supportive of the eight listed in Table 9.3.

Some of the different facets described by Gardner certainly correspond with the different types of exceptional ability that we referred to in the beginning of the chapter in our discussion of Gerhard Herzberg and Moe Norman. These intelligences obviously include quite a variety of talents that are not assessed by conventional IQ tests. Gardner is investigating the extent to which these intelligences are largely independent, as his theory asserts. For the most part, he has found that people tend to display a mixture of strong, intermediate, and weak abilities, which is consistent with the idea that the various types of intelligence are independent.

Gardner's books have been very popular and his theory clearly resonates with many people (Shearer, 2004). His ideas have had an impact on educators around the world (Cuban, 2004; Kornhaber, 2004). He has done a superb job of synthesizing research from neuropsychology, developmental psychology, cognitive psychology, and other areas to arrive at fascinating speculations about the structure of human abilities. He has raised thought-provoking questions

TABLE 9.3

Gardner's Eight Intelligences

Source: Adapted from Gardner, H., & Hatch, T. (1989). Multiple intelligences go to school: Educational implications of the theory of multiple intelligences. *Educational Researcher, 18* (8), 4–10. American Educational Research Association. Additional information from Gardner, 1998.

Intelligence	End-States	Core Components
Logical–mathematical	Scientist Mathematician	Sensitivity to, and capacity to discern, logical or numerical patterns; ability to handle long chains of reasoning
Linguistic	Poet Journalist	Sensitivity to sounds, rhythms, and meanings of words; sensitivity to the different functions of language
Musical	Composer Violinist	Abilities to produce and appreciate rhythm, pitch, and timbre; appreciation of the forms of musical expressiveness
Spatial	Navigator Sculptor	Capacities to perceive the visual–spatial world accurately and to perform transformations on one's initial perceptions
Bodily–kinesthetic	Dancer Athlete	Abilities to control one's body movements and to handle objects skillfully
Interpersonal	Therapist Salesperson	Capacities to discern and respond appropriately to the moods, temperaments, motivations, and desires of other people
Intrapersonal	Person with detailed, accurate self-knowledge	Access to one's own feelings and the ability to discriminate among them and draw upon them to guide behaviour; knowledge of one's own strengths, weaknesses, desires, and intelligences
Naturalist	Biologist Naturalist	Abilities to recognize and categorize objects and processes in nature

about what abilities should be included under the rubric of intelligence (Eisner, 2004). However, he has his critics (Hunt, 2001; Klein, 1997; Morgan, 1996; Waterhouse, 2006). Some argue that his use of the term *intelligence* is so broad, encompassing virtually any valued human ability, that it makes the term almost meaningless. These critics wonder whether there is any advantage to relabelling talents such as musical ability and motor coordination as forms of intelligence. Critics also note that Gardner's theory has not generated much research on the predictive value of measuring individual differences in the eight intelligences he has described. This research would require the development of tests to measure the eight intelligences, but Gardner is not particularly interested in the matter of assessment and he loathes conventional testing. This reality makes it difficult to predict where Gardner's theory will lead, as research is crucial to the evolution of a theory.

Measuring Emotional Intelligence

In yet another highly publicized effort to expand the concept of intelligence, a variety of theorists have argued that the measurement of *emotional intelligence* can enhance the prediction of success at school, at work, and in interpersonal relationships (Mayer, Robert, & Barsade, 2008; Mayer, Salovey, &

Caruso, 2008). The concept of emotional intelligence was originally developed by Peter Salovey and John Mayer (1990). Their concept languished in relative obscurity until Daniel Goleman (1995) wrote a compelling book entitled *Emotional Intelligence*, which made the best-seller lists. Since then, empirical research on the measurement of emotional intelligence has increased dramatically.

Emotional intelligence consists of the ability to perceive and express emotion, assimilate emotion in thought, understand and reason with emotion, and regulate emotion. Emotional intelligence includes four essential components (Salovey, Mayer, & Caruso, 2002). First, people need to be able to accurately perceive emotions in themselves and others and have the ability to express their own emotions effectively. Second, people need to be aware of how their emotions shape their thinking, decision making, and coping with stress. Third, people need to be able to understand and analyze their emotions, which may often be complex and contradictory. Fourth, people need to be able to regulate their emotions so that they can dampen negative emotions and make effective use of positive emotions.

Several tests of emotional intelligence have already been developed. The test that has the strongest empirical foundation is the *Multifactor Emotional Intelligence Scale* (MEIS) devised by Mayer, Caruso, and Salovey (1999). More recently, James Parker of Trent University, along with his colleague Reuven Bar-On, developed a youth version of an emotional intelligence measure to assess children and adolescents (Bar-On & Parker, 2000a). Parker, a Canada Research Chair in Emotion and Health, is an active researcher in the area of emotional intelligence (Bar-On & Parker, 2000b; Keefer, Wood, & Parker, 2009; Parker et al., 2006). He has suggested that emotional intelligence may be particularly important in difficult transitional phases, such as moving from high school to university. When comparing first-year students who achieved university GPAs of 80 percent or better with students with GPAs of 59 percent or less, he found that emotional intelligence scores were good predictors of academic success (Parker et al., 2004). Parker's research certainly suggests the importance of emotional intelligence in, among other things, dealing with stressful events.

The concept of emotional intelligence has not been without its critics (e.g., Murphy, 2006). Skeptics have questioned whether sophistication about emotion should be viewed as a form of intelligence and they have noted that definitions of emotional intelligence vary and tend to be fuzzy (Matthews et al., 2006; Murphy & Sideman, 2006b). Critics also assert that claims about the practical utility of emotional

Howard Gardner

"It is high time that the view of intelligence be widened to incorporate a range of human computational capacities.... But where is it written that intelligence needs to be determined on the basis of tests?"

---

concept check 9.3

Recognizing Theories of Intelligence

Check your understanding of various theories on the nature of intelligence by matching the names of their originators with the brief descriptions of the theories' main themes that appear below. Choose from the following theorists: (a) Sir Francis Galton, (b) Howard Gardner, (c) Arthur Jensen, (d) Sandra Scarr, (e) Robert Sternberg, (f) Alfred Binet, and (g) David Wechsler. The answers are in Appendix A.

_____ **1.** This theorist posited eight human intelligences: logical-mathematical, linguistic, musical, spatial, bodily-kinesthetic, interpersonal, intrapersonal, and naturalist.

_____ **2.** On the basis of a study of eminence and success in families, this theorist concluded that intelligence is inherited.

_____ **3.** This theorist stated that the heritability of intelligence is about 80 percent and that IQ differences between ethnic groups are mainly due to genetics.

_____ **4.** This theorist stated that heredity sets certain limits on intelligence and that environmental factors determine where one falls within those limits.

_____ **5.** This person's theory of intelligence is divided into contextual, experiential, and componential subtheories and posits three facets of intelligence: analytical, practical, and creative intelligence.

intelligence in the business world have been exaggerated, and that a great deal of additional research will be needed to fully validate measures of emotional intelligence (Conte & Dean, 2006; Jordan, Ashton-James, & Ashkanasy, 2006). In spite of these concerns, the concept of emotional intelligence has been accepted with great enthusiasm in the realm of business management, and hundreds of consultants provide a plethora of intervention programs to enhance leadership, teamwork, and productivity (Schmit, 2006). Skeptics characterize these programs as little more than a fad in the business world, but many of these critics acknowledge that the concept may have some explanatory value if buttressed by more research (Hogan & Stokes, 2006; Murphy & Sideman, 2006a). Thus, the concept of emotional intelligence seems to have reached a crossroads. It will be interesting to see what unfolds over the next decade.

Putting It in Perspective: Themes 3, 5, and 6

As you probably noticed, three of our integrative themes surfaced in this chapter. Our discussions illustrated that cultural factors shape behaviour, that psychology evolves in a sociohistorical context, and that heredity and environment jointly influence behaviour.

Pervasive psychological testing is largely a Western phenomenon. The concept of general intelligence also has a special, Western flavour to it. Many non-Western cultures have very different ideas about the nature of intelligence. Within Western societies, the observed ethnic differences in average intelligence also illustrate the importance of cultural factors, as these disparities appear to be due in large part to cultural disadvantage and other culture-related considerations. Thus, we see once again that if we hope to achieve a sound understanding of behaviour, we need to appreciate the cultural contexts in which behaviour unfolds.

Human intelligence is shaped by a complex interaction of hereditary and environmental factors. We've drawn similar conclusions before in other chapters where we examined other aspects of behaviour. However, this chapter should have enhanced your appreciation of this idea in at least two ways. First, we examined more of the details of how scientists arrive at the conclusion that heredity and environment jointly shape behaviour. Second, we encountered dramatic illustrations of the immense importance attached to the nature versus nurture debate. For example, Arthur Jensen has been the target of savage criticism. After his controversial 1969 article, he was widely characterized as a racist. When he gave speeches, he was often greeted by protesters carrying signs, such as "Kill Jensen" and "Jensen Must Perish." J. Phillipe Rushton has had similar experiences in Canada. As you can see, the debate about the inheritance of intelligence inspires passionate feelings in many people. In part, this is because the debate has far-reaching social and political implications, which brings us to another prominent theme in the chapter.

There may be no other area in psychology where the connections between psychology and society at large are so obvious. Prevailing social attitudes have always exerted some influence on testing practices and the interpretation of test results. In the first half of the 20th century, a strong current of racial and class prejudice was apparent in North America and Britain. This prejudice supported the idea that IQ tests measured innate ability and that "undesirable" groups scored poorly because of their genetic inferiority. Although these beliefs did not go unchallenged within psychology, their widespread acceptance in the field reflected the social values of the time. It's ironic that IQ tests have sometimes been associated with social prejudice. When used properly, intelligence tests provide relatively objective measures of mental ability that are less prone to bias than the subjective judgments of teachers or employers.

Today, psychological tests serve many diverse purposes. In the upcoming Personal Application, we focus on creativity tests and on the nature of creative thinking and creative people.

PREVIEW QUESTIONS

▶ What did this chapter reveal about the importance of cultural factors and the nature-versus-nurture debate?

▶ How did this chapter illustrate the connections between psychology and the world at large?

REVIEW OF KEY POINTS

▷ Modern intelligence tests place a greater emphasis on the measurement of specific mental abilities and less emphasis on tapping Spearman's *g* than did their predecessors. The distinction between fluid and crystallized intelligence is the basis for the most recent revision of the Stanford-Binet IQ test.

▷ Research on intelligence increasingly uses a cognitive perspective, which emphasizes the need to understand how people use their intelligence. Many modern theorists, such as Robert Sternberg and Howard Gardner, argue that the concept of intelligence should be expanded to encompass a greater variety of skills. Researchers have made some progress in their efforts to measure emotional intelligence.

▷ Three of our integrative themes stood out in the chapter. Our discussions of intelligence showed how heredity and environment interact to shape behaviour, how psychology evolves in a sociohistorical context, and how one has to consider cultural contexts to fully understand behaviour.

Understanding Creativity

Answer the following "true" or "false."

___ **1** Creative ideas often come out of nowhere.

___ **2** Creativity usually occurs in a burst of insight.

___ **3** Creativity depends on inspiration far more than on perspiration.

Intelligence is not the only type of mental ability that psychologists have studied. They have devised tests to explore a variety of mental abilities. Among these, creativity is certainly one of the most interesting. People tend to view creativity as an essential trait for artists, musicians, and writers, but it is important in *many* walks of life. In this Application, we'll discuss psychologists' efforts to measure and understand creativity. As we progress, you'll learn that all of the statements above are false.

The Nature of Creativity

Creativity involves the generation of ideas that are original, novel, and useful. Creative thinking is fresh, innovative, and inventive (Baas, Carsten, & Nijstad, 2008). But novelty by itself is not enough. In addition to being unusual, creative thinking must be adaptive. It must be appropriate to the situation and problem.

Does Creativity Occur in a Burst of Insight?

It is widely believed that creativity usually involves sudden flashes of insight and great leaps of imagination. Robert Weisberg (1986) calls this belief the "Aha! myth." Undeniably, creative bursts of insight do occur (Feldman, 1988). However, the evidence suggests that major creative achievements generally are logical extensions of existing ideas, involving long, hard work and many small, faltering steps forward (Weisberg, 1993). Creative ideas do not come out of nowhere. Creative ideas come from a deep well of experience and training in a specific area, whether it's music, painting,

business, or science (Weisberg, 1999; 2006). As Snow (1986) puts it, "Creativity is not a light bulb in the mind, as most cartoons depict it. It is an accomplishment born of intensive study, long reflection, persistence, and interest" (p. 1033).

Does Creativity Depend on Divergent Thinking?

According to many theorists, the key to creativity lies in *divergent thinking*—thinking "that goes off in different directions," as J. P. Guilford (1959) put it. In his model of mental abilities (see Figure 9.6 on page 403), Guilford distinguished between convergent thinking and divergent thinking. In *convergent thinking*, one tries to narrow down a list of alternatives to converge on a single correct answer. For example, when you take a multiple-choice exam, you try to eliminate incorrect options until you hit on the correct response. Most training in school encourages convergent thinking. In *divergent thinking*, one tries to expand the range of alternatives by generating many possible solutions. Imagine that you work for an advertising agency. To come up with as many slogans as possible for a client's product, you must use divergent thinking. Some of your slogans may be clear losers, and eventually you will have to engage in convergent thinking to pick the best, but coming up with the range of new possibilities depends on divergent thinking.

Thirty years of research on divergent thinking has yielded mixed results. As a whole, the evidence suggests that divergent thinking contributes to creativity (Runco, 2004), but it clearly does not represent the essence of creativity, as originally proposed (Brown, 1989; Plucker & Renzulli, 1999; Weisberg, 2006). In retrospect, it was probably unrealistic to expect creativity to depend on a single cognitive skill. According to Sternberg (1988a), the cognitive processes that underlie creativity are multifaceted.

Measuring Creativity

SIM8

Although its nature may be elusive, creativity clearly is important in today's world. Creative masterpieces in the arts and literature enrich human existence. Creative insights in the sciences illuminate people's understanding of the world. Creative inventions fuel technological progress. Thus, it is understandable that psychologists have been interested in measuring creativity with psychological tests.

How Do Psychological Tests Measure Creativity?

SIM8

A diverse array of psychological tests has been devised to measure individuals' creativity (Plucker & Makel, 2010). Usually, the items on creativity tests assess divergent thinking by giving respondents a specific starting point and then requiring them to generate as many possibilities as they can in a short period of time. Typical items on a creativity test might include the following: (1) List as many uses as you can for a newspaper. (2) Think of as many fluids that burn as you can. (3) Imagine that people no longer need sleep and think of as many consequences as you can. Subjects' scores on these tests depend on the *number* of alternatives they generate and on the *originality* and *usefulness* of the alternatives.

One seminal test of creativity is the *Remote Associates Test* (RAT) developed by Sarnoff Mednick and Martha Mednick (1967). This test is based on the assumption that creative people see unusual relationships and make nonobvious connections between ideas. Items on the test require subjects to figure out the obscure links (the remote associations) among three words by coming up with a fourth word that is related to the three stimulus words. Examples of items similar to those found on the RAT are shown in Figure 9.21.

Instructions: For each set of three words, try to think of a fourth word that is related to all three words. For example, the words ROUGH, RESISTANCE, and BEER suggest the word DRAFT because of the phrases ROUGH DRAFT, DRAFT RESISTANCE, and DRAFT BEER.

1.	CHARMING	STUDENT	VALIANT
2.	FOOD	CATCHER	HOT
3.	HEARTED	FEET	BITTER
4.	DARK	SHOT	SUN
5.	CANADIAN	GOLF	SANDWICH
6.	TUG	GRAVY	SHOW
7.	ATTORNEY	SELF	SPENDING
8.	MAGIC	PITCH	POWER
9.	ARM	COAL	PEACH
10.	TYPE	GHOST	STORY

FIGURE 9.21

Remote associates as an index of creativity.

One groundbreaking creativity test is the *Remote Associates Test* (RAT) developed by Sarnoff Mednick and Martha Mednick (1967). The items shown here are similar to those on the RAT. See whether you can identify the remote associations between the three stimulus words by coming up with a fourth word that is related to all three. The answers can be found in Figure 9.22.

Source: Matlin, M.W. (1994) *Cognition* (3rd Ed.). Fort Worth, TX: Harcourt Brace. Reprinted by permission of the author.

How Well Do Tests Predict Creative Productivity?

In general, studies indicate that creativity tests are mediocre predictors of creative achievement in the real world (Hocevar & Bachelor, 1989; Plucker & Renzulli, 1999). Why? One reason is that these tests measure creativity in the abstract, as a *general trait*. However, the accumulation of evidence suggests that *creativity is specific to particular domains* (Amabile, 1996; Feist, 2004; Kaufman & Baer, 2002, 2004). Despite some rare exceptions, creative people usually excel in a single field, in which they typically have considerable training and expertise (Policastro & Gardner, 1999). A remarkably innovative physicist might have no potential to be a creative poet or an inventive advertising executive. Measuring this person's creativity outside of physics may be meaningless. Thus, creativity tests may have limited value because they measure creativity out of context.

Even if better tests of creativity were devised, predicting creative achievement would probably still prove difficult. Why? Because creative achievement depends on many factors besides creativity (Cropley, 2000). Creative productivity over the course of an individual's career will depend on his or her motivation, personality, and intelligence, as well as situational factors, including training, mentoring, and good fortune (Amabile, 2001; Feldman, 1999; Simonton, 1999a, 2004; Simonton & Damian, in press; Simonton & Floram, 2011).

Motivational factors may be particularly important. People who make creative breakthroughs tend to have a single-minded, "workaholic" commitment to their endeavours and show great perseverance in the face of obstacles and setbacks (Simonton, 1999a). Although their ideas are often attacked or dismissed, they do not give up easily. To underscore this point, Sternberg (2000a, 2001) asserts that creativity appears to be in large part a *decision*. By this he means that highly creative people often have to make a choice to defy conventional thinking.

Correlates of Creativity

What are creative people like? Are they brighter, or more open-minded, or less well adjusted than average? A great deal of research has been conducted on the correlates of creativity.

FIGURE 9.22

Answers to the remote associates items.

1.	PRINCE	6.	BOAT
2.	DOG	7.	DEFENCE
3.	COLD	8.	BLACK
4.	GLASSES	9.	PIT
5.	CLUB	10.	WRITER

Source: Matlin, M.W. (1994) *Cognition* (3rd Ed.). Fort Worth, TX: Harcourt Brace. Reprinted by permission of the author.

Is There a Creative Personality?

There is no single personality profile that accounts for creativity (Weisberg, 2006). However, investigators have found modest correlations between certain personality characteristics and creativity. Research suggests that highly creative people tend to be more independent, nonconforming, introverted, open to new experiences, self-confident, persistent, ambitious, dominant, and impulsive (Feist, 1998, 2010). At the core of this set of personality characteristics are the related traits of nonconformity and openness to new experiences. Creative people tend to think for themselves and are less easily influenced by the opinions of others than the average person is. The importance of openness to new experiences can be seen in a new line of research which suggests that living abroad enhances creativity.

Although living abroad has long been viewed as a rite of passage for creative artists and writers, no one thought to take an

Gertrude Stein was an American expatriate who lived for 40 years in Paris, primarily at 27 Rue De Fleurus. She was an important feminist, and her experimental writings helped launch modernism (Daniel, 2009). Her prodigious creativity flowered when she left the United States to live abroad in Paris and become part of the intellectual life there. She also facilitated the creativity and careers of many other Paris artists, including Picasso, Matisse, Renoir, and Hemmingway, at her famous Saturday night salons. Interestingly, she studied psychology at Harvard University and did research with William James. Her scientific publications appeared in important academic journals (e.g., Stein, 1898).

empirical look at the impact of living abroad until recently. In a series of studies, Maddux and Galinsky (2009) found that the amount of time spent living abroad correlated positively with measures of creativity.

Interestingly, time spent in tourist travel abroad did *not* predict creativity. The contrasting effects of living and travelling abroad seems to depend on acculturation. Maddux and Galinsky found that the degree to which people adapted to foreign cultures was responsible for the association between living abroad and creativity. A subsequent study found that multicultural learning experiences appear to foster flexibility in thinking, which could enhance creativity (Maddux, Adam, & Galinsky, 2010).

Are Creativity and Intelligence Related?
Are creative people exceptionally smart? Conceptually, creativity and intelligence represent different types of mental ability. Thus, it's not surprising that correlations between measures of creativity and measures of intelligence are generally weak (Sternberg & O'Hara, 1999). For example, a recent meta-analysis of many studies reported a correlation of only 0.17 (Kim, 2005). However, some findings suggest that the association between creativity and intelligence is somewhat stronger than that. When Silvia (2008) administered several intelligence scales and calculated estimates of g for subjects, this higher-order measure of intelligence correlated over 0.40 with creativity.

One widely cited model of the relationship between creativity and intelligence is the *threshold hypothesis* proposed decades ago by pioneering creativity researchers (Barron, 1963; Torrance, 1962). According to this theory, creative achievements require a minimum level of intelligence. Thus, most highly creative people are probably well above average in intelligence. An IQ of 120 has been proposed as the minimum threshold for creative achievement (Lubart, 2003). One assumption of this model is that the correlation between IQ and creativity should be weaker among people above this IQ threshold than for those below it. Recent research, however, has failed to support this assumption (Kim, Cramond, & VanTassel-Baska, 2010). At this point, all

FIGURE 9.23

Examples of people who achieved creative eminence and suffered from psychological disorders.
As these brief lists show, it is easy to compile rosters of great artists, scientists, composers, and writers who struggled with mental illness. However, while interesting, anecdotal evidence such as this cannot demonstrate that there is an association between creative eminence and mental disorder. [Based on information from Prentky (1980) and Rothenberg (1990).]

Artists	Scientists	Composers	Writers
Bosch	Copernicus	Beethoven	Blake
Durer	Descartes	Berlioz	Coleridge
Goya	Kepler	Chopin	Dostoyevsky
Kandinsky	Linnaeus	Handel	Hemingway
Raphael	Mendel	Saint-Saens	Kafka
Rembrandt	Newton	Schubert	Poe
van Gogh	Pascal	Tchaikovsky	Plath

Rembrandt
Rembrandt, Harmensz, van Rijn, *Self-Portrait with Beard*. Museu de Arte, Sao Paulo, Brazil.

Chopin
Delacroix, Eugene, *Portrait of Chopin*, Louvre, Paris

Copernicus
Pomerian, 16th cent. *Portrait of Nicolas Copernicus*. Museum, Torun, Poland.

one can conclude is that there appears to be a weak to modest association between IQ and creativity.

Is There a Connection between Creativity and Mental Illness?
There may be a connection between truly exceptional creativity and mental illness. The list of creative geniuses who have suffered from psychological disorders is endless (Prentky, 1989). Kafka, Hemingway, Rembrandt, van Gogh, Chopin, Tchaikovsky, Descartes, and Newton are but a few examples (see Figure 9.23). Of course, a statistical association cannot be demonstrated by citing a handful of examples.

In this case, however, some statistical data are available. And these data *do* suggest a correlation between creative genius and maladjustment—in particular, mood

disorders such as depression. When Nancy Andreasen studied 30 accomplished writers who had been invited as visiting faculty to the prestigious Iowa Writers' Workshop, she found that 80 percent of her sample had suffered a mood disorder at some point in their lives (Andreasen, 1987, 2005). In a similar study of 59 female writers from another writers' conference, Ludwig (1994) found that 56 percent had experienced depression. These figures are far above the base rate (roughly 15 percent) for mood disorders in the general population. Other studies have also found an association between creativity and mood disorders, as well as other kinds of psychological disorders (Nettle, 2001; Silvia & Kaufman, 2010). Perhaps the most ambitious examination of the issue has been Arnold Ludwig's (1995) analyses of the biographies of 1004 people who achieved

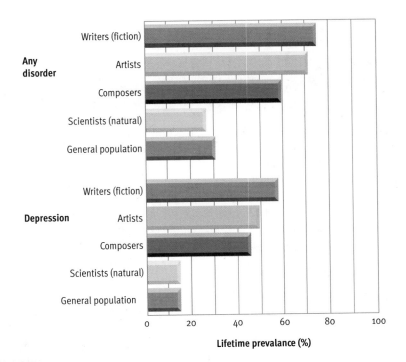

Estimated prevalence of psychological disorders among people who achieved creative eminence.
Ludwig (1995) studied biographies of 1004 people who had clearly achieved eminence in one of 18 fields and tried to determine whether each person suffered from any specific mental disorders in their lifetimes. The data summarized here show the prevalence rates for depression and for a mental disorder of any kind for four fields where creativity is often the key to achieving eminence. As you can see, the estimated prevalence of mental illness was extremely elevated among eminent writers, artists, and composers (but not natural scientists) in comparison to the general population, with depression accounting for much of this elevation.

Source: From WEITEN. *Psychology*, 7E. © 2007 Wadsworth, a part of Cengage Learning, Inc. Reproduced by permission. www.cengage.com/permissions.

eminence in 18 fields. He found greatly elevated rates of depression and other disorders among eminent writers, artists, and composers (see Figure 9.24). Recent studies suggest that mental illness may be especially elevated among poets (Kaufman, 2001, 2005).

Thus, accumulating empirical data tentatively suggest that a correlation may exist between major creative achievement and vulnerability to mood disorders and other forms of psychopathology (Carson, 2011). According to Andreasen (1996, 2005), creativity and maladjustment probably are *not* causally related. Instead, she speculates that certain personality traits and cognitive styles may both foster creativity and predispose people to psychological disorders. Another, more mundane possibility is that creative individuals' elevated pathology may simply reflect all the difficulty and frustration they experience as they struggle to get their ideas or works accepted in artistic fields that enjoy relatively little public support (Csikszentmihalyi, 1994, 1999).

REVIEW OF KEY POINTS

▷ Creativity involves the generation of original, novel, and useful ideas. Creativity does not usually involve sudden insight and it does not depend on unconscious thought processes. Divergent thinking contributes to creativity but does not represent its essence.

▷ Creativity tests are mediocre predictors of creative productivity in the real world. One problem is that creativity is specific to particular domains of expertise. Another problem is that creative achievement depends on a host of factors besides one's creativity.

▷ Creative people are more likely than others to exhibit certain personality traits, but the correlations between creativity and personality are weak. The association between creativity and intelligence is also modest, although creativity probably requires above-average intelligence. Recent evidence suggests that creative geniuses may exhibit heightened vulnerability to mood disorders.

The Intelligence Debate, Appeals to Ignorance, and Reification

A *fallacy* is a mistake or error in the process of reasoning. Cognitive scientists who study how people think have developed long lists of common errors that people make in their reasoning processes. One of these fallacies has a curious name, which is the *appeal to ignorance*. It involves misusing the general lack of knowledge or information on an issue (a lack of knowledge is a kind of ignorance) to support an argument. This fallacy often surfaces in the debate about the relative influence of heredity and environment on intelligence. Before we tackle the more difficult issue of how this fallacy shows up in the debate about intelligence, let's start with a simpler example.

The Appeal to Ignorance

Do ghosts exist? This is probably not the kind of question you expected to find in your psychology textbook, but it can clarify the appeal to ignorance. Those who assert that ghosts *do* exist will often support their conclusion by arguing that no one can prove that ghosts *do not* exist; therefore ghosts must exist. The lack of evidence or inability to show that ghosts do not exist is used to conclude the opposite. Conversely, those who assert that ghosts *do not* exist often rely on the same logic. They argue that no one can prove that ghosts exist; therefore, they must not exist. Can you see what is wrong with these appeals to ignorance? The lack of information on an issue cannot be used to support any conclusion—other than the conclusion that we are too ignorant to draw a conclusion.

One interesting aspect of the appeal to ignorance is that the same appeal can be used to support two conclusions that are diametrically opposed to each other. This paradox is a telltale clue that appeals to ignorance involve flawed reasoning. It is easy to see what is wrong with appeals to ignorance when the opposite arguments (ghosts exist—ghosts do not exist) are presented together and the lack of evidence

on the issue under discussion is obvious. However, when the same fallacy surfaces in more complex debates and the appeal to ignorance is not as blatant, the strategy can be more difficult to recognize. Let's look at how the appeal to ignorance has been used in the debate about intelligence.

As you saw in the main body of the chapter, the debate about the relative contributions of nature and nurture to intelligence is one of psychology's longest-running controversies. This complex and multifaceted debate is exceptionally bitter and acrimonious because it has far-reaching sociopolitical repercussions. In this debate, one argument that has frequently been made is that we have little or no evidence that intelligence can be increased by environmental (educational) interventions; therefore, intelligence must be mostly inherited. In other words, the argument runs: No one has demonstrated that intelligence is largely shaped by environment, so it must be largely inherited. This argument was part of Jensen's (1969) landmark treatise that greatly intensified the debate about intelligence, and it was one of the arguments made by Herrnstein and Murray (1994) in their controversial book *The Bell Curve*.

The argument refers to the fact that educational enrichment programs such as Head Start, which have been designed to enhance the cognitive development of underprivileged children, generally have not produced substantial, long-term gains in IQ (Neisser et al., 1996). The programs produce other benefits, including enduring improvements in school achievement, but short-term gains in IQ scores typically have faded by the middle grades (Barnett, 2004). These findings may have some implications for government policy in the educational arena. However, the way in which they have been applied to the nature–nurture debate regarding intelligence has resulted in an appeal to ignorance. In its simplest form, the absence of evidence showing that environmental changes can increase intelligence is used to support

the conclusion that intelligence is mostly determined by genetic inheritance. But the absence of evidence (ignorance) cannot be used to argue for or against a position.

By the way, if you have assimilated some of the critical thinking skills discussed in earlier chapters, you may be thinking, "Wait a minute. Aren't there alternative explanations for the failure of educational enrichment programs to increase IQ scores?" Yes, one could argue that the programs failed to yield improvements in IQ scores because they often were poorly executed, too brief, or underfunded (Ramey, 1999; Sigel, 2004). Moreover, Head Start programs were not really designed to increase IQ scores. They were designed to enhance deprived students' readiness for school (Schrag, Styfco, & Zigler, 2004). The inability of the enrichment programs to produce enduring increases in IQ does not necessarily imply that intelligence is unchangeable because it's largely a product of heredity.

You may also be wondering, "Aren't there contradictory data?" Once again, the answer is yes. Barnett (2004) argues that failures to find enduring gains in intelligence from Head Start programs can often be attributed to flaws and shortcomings in the research design of the studies. Furthermore, studies of some lesser-known educational enrichment programs attempted with smaller groups of children *have* yielded durable gains in IQ and other standardized test scores (Ramey & Ramey, 2004; Reynolds et al., 2001; Woodhead, 2004).

Reification

The dialogue on intelligence has also been marred by the tendency to engage in reification. *Reification* occurs when a hypothetical, abstract concept is given a name and then treated as though it were a concrete, tangible object. Some hypothetical constructs become so familiar and so taken for granted that we begin to think about them as if they were real. People often fall into this

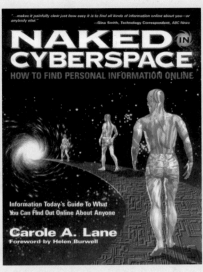

For the most part, educational enrichment programs for underprivileged children have not produced durable increases in participants' IQ scores. However, as the text explains, this finding does not provide logically sound support for the notion that intelligence is largely inherited.

trap with the Freudian personality concepts of id, ego, and superego (see Chapter 12). They begin to think of the *ego*, for instance, as a genuine entity that can be strengthened or controlled, when the ego is really nothing more than a hypothetical abstraction.

The concept of intelligence has also been reified in many quarters. Like the ego, intelligence is nothing more than a useful abstraction—a hypothetical construct that is estimated, rather arbitrarily, by a collection of paper-and-pencil measures called IQ tests. Yet people routinely act as if intelligence is a tangible commodity, fighting vitriolic battles over whether it can be measured precisely, whether it can be changed, and whether it can ensure job success. This reification clearly contributes to the tendency for people to attribute excessive importance to the concept of intelligence. It would be wise to remember that intelligence is no more real than the concept of "the environment" or "cyberspace."

Reification has also occurred in the debate about the *degree* to which intelligence is inherited. Arguments about the heritability coefficient for intelligence often imply that there is a single, true number lurking somewhere "out there," waiting to be discovered. In reality, heritability is a hypothetical construct that can be legitimately estimated in several ways that can lead to somewhat different results. Moreover, heritability ratios will vary from one population to the next, depending on the amount of genetic variability and the extent of environmental variability in the populations. No exactly accurate number that corresponds to "true heritability" awaits discovery (Hunt & Carlson, 2007; Sternberg et al., 2005). Thus, it is important to understand that

Reification occurs when we think of hypothetical constructs as if they were real. Like intelligence, the concept of cyberspace has been subject to reification. The fact that cyberspace is merely an abstraction becomes readily apparent when artists are asked to "draw" cyberspace for conference posters or book covers.

hypothetical constructs have great heuristic value in the study of complex phenomena such as human thought and behaviour, but they do not actually exist in the world—at least not in the same way that a table or a person exists.

TABLE 9.4	Critical Thinking Skills Discussed in This Application
Skill	**Description**
Recognizing and avoiding appeals to ignorance	The critical thinker understands that the lack of information on an issue cannot be used to support an argument.
Recognizing and avoiding reification	The critical thinker is vigilant about the tendency to treat hypothetical constructs as if they were concrete things.
Looking for alternative explanations for findings and events	In evaluating explanations, the critical thinker explores whether there are other explanations that could also account for the findings or events under scrutiny.
Looking for contradictory evidence	In evaluating the evidence presented on an issue, the critical thinker attempts to look for contradictory evidence that may have been left out of the debate.

Key Ideas

Key Concepts in Psychological Testing

● Psychological tests are standardized measures of behaviour—usually mental abilities or aspects of personality. Test scores are interpreted by consulting test norms to find out what represents a high or low score. Psychological tests should produce consistent results, a quality called *reliability*.

● *Validity* refers to the degree to which there is evidence that a test measures what it was designed to measure. Content validity is crucial on classroom tests. Criterion-related validity is critical when tests are used to predict performance. Construct validity is critical when a test is designed to measure a hypothetical construct.

The Evolution of Intelligence Testing

● The first crude efforts to devise intelligence tests were made by Sir Francis Galton, who wanted to show that intelligence is inherited. Modern intelligence testing began with the work of Alfred Binet, who devised a scale to measure a child's mental age.

● Lewis Terman revised the original Binet scale to produce the Stanford-Binet in 1916. It introduced the intelligence quotient and became the standard of comparison for subsequent tests. David Wechsler devised an improved measure of intelligence for adults and a new scoring system based on the normal distribution.

Basic Questions about Intelligence Testing

● In the modern scoring system, deviation IQ scores indicate where people fall in the normal distribution of intelligence for their age group. Although they are intended to measure potential for learning, IQ tests inevitably assess a blend of potential and knowledge.

● IQ tests are exceptionally reliable. They are reasonably valid measures of academic intelligence, but they do not tap social or practical intelligence.

● IQ scores are correlated with occupational attainment, but their ability to predict performance within occupations is the subject of debate. Intelligence testing is largely a Western enterprise; IQ tests are not widely used in most non-Western cultures.

Extremes of Intelligence

● IQ scores below 70–75 are usually diagnostic of intellectual disability but these diagnoses should not be based solely on test results. Four levels of intellectual disability have been distinguished. Most of the intellectually disabled population falls in the mild category. Although many biological conditions can cause intellectual disability, biological causes can be pinpointed in only about 25 percent of cases.

● Children who obtain IQ scores above 130 may be viewed as gifted, but cut-offs for accelerated programs vary. Research by Terman showed that gifted children tend to be socially mature and well adjusted, although Winner has raised concerns about the adjustment of profoundly gifted individuals. Extraordinary achievement seems to depend on intensive training and hard work, but innate talent may also contribute.

Heredity and Environment as Determinants of Intelligence

● Twin studies show that identical twins are more similar in IQ than fraternal twins, suggesting that intelligence is inherited, at least in part. Estimates of the heritability of intelligence mostly range from 50 percent to 70 percent, but heritability ratios have certain limitations.

● Many lines of evidence indicate that environment is also an important determinant of intelligence. Of particular interest is the recent discovery of generational increases in measured IQ. The concept of reaction range posits that heredity places limits on one's intellectual potential while the environment determines where one falls within these limits.

● Genetic explanations for cultural differences in IQ have been challenged on a variety of grounds. Even if the heritability of IQ is great, group differences in average intelligence may not be due to heredity. Moreover, ethnicity varies with social class, so socioeconomic disadvantage may account for low IQ scores among minority students. Stereotype vulnerability and cultural bias on IQ tests may also contribute to ethnic differences in average IQ.

New Directions in the Assessment and Study of Intelligence

● In contemporary testing, there is a greater emphasis on the measurement of specific mental abilities and less emphasis on tapping Spearman's *g*. The distinction between fluid and crystallized intelligence is the basis for the most recent revision of the Stanford-Binet IQ test.

● Biological indexes of intelligence are being explored; however, they seem to have little practical utility, although the inspection time measure appears to have potential. Research on intelligence increasingly takes a cognitive perspective, which emphasizes the need to understand how people use their intelligence. Many modern theorists, such as Robert Sternberg and Howard Gardner, argue that the concept of intelligence should be expanded to encompass a greater variety of skills.

Putting It in Perspective: Themes 3, 5, and 6

● Three of our integrative themes stood out in the chapter. Our discussions of intelligence showed how heredity and environment interact to shape behaviour, how psychology evolves in a sociohistorical context, and how one has to consider cultural contexts to fully understand behaviour.

PERSONAL APPLICATION • Understanding Creativity

● Creativity involves the generation of original, novel, and useful ideas. Creativity does not usually involve sudden insight, and it consists of more than divergent thinking. Creativity tests are mediocre predictors of creative productivity in the real world.

● Creativity is only weakly related to intelligence. The correlations are modest, but some personality traits are associated with creativity. Recent evidence suggests that creative geniuses may exhibit heightened vulnerability to psychological disorders, especially mood disorders.

CRITICAL THINKING APPLICATION • The Intelligence Debate, Appeals to Ignorance, and Reification

● The appeal to ignorance involves misusing the general lack of knowledge or information on an issue to support an argument. This fallacy has surfaced in the debate about intelligence, wherein it has been argued that because we have little or no evidence that intelligence can be increased by environmental interventions, intelligence must be mostly inherited.

● Reification occurs when a hypothetical construct is treated as though it were a tangible object. The concepts of intelligence and heritability have both been subject to reification.

Key Terms

Achievement tests, 396
Aptitude tests, 395
Construct validity, 398
Content validity, 398
Convergent thinking, 430
Correlation coefficient, 397
Creativity, 430
Criterion-related validity, 398
Crystallized intelligence, 403
Deviation IQ scores, 404
Divergent thinking, 430
Emotional intelligence, 428
Factor analysis, 402
Fluid intelligence, 403
Heritability ratio, 415
Intellectual disability, 409
Intelligence quotient (IQ), 401
Intelligence tests, 395
Mental age, 401
Normal distribution, 403

Percentile score, 396
Personality tests, 396
Psychological test, 395
Reaction range, 417
Reification, 434
Reliability, 396
Standardization, 396
Test norms, 396
Validity, 397

Key People

Alfred Binet, 401
Sir Francis Galton, 400
Howard Gardner, 428
Arthur Jensen, 418
Sandra Scarr, 417
Claude Steele, 421
Robert Sternberg, 406, 426
Lewis Terman, 401
David Wechsler, 401
Ellen Winner, 412

1. Which of the following tests does not belong with the others?
   A. aptitude tests
   B. personality tests
   C. intelligence tests
   D. achievement tests

2. You score at the 75th percentile on a standardized test. What does this mean?
   A. You passed the test.
   B. You scored higher than or equal to 75 percent of people who took the test.
   C. Your score was within one standard deviation of the mean for that sample.
   D. You answered at least 75 percent of the questions correctly.

3. Which of the following statements describes a test with good test–retest reliability?
   A. There are strong correlations among items on the test.
   B. The test accurately measures what it is intended to measure.
   C. The test can be used to predict performance on another task.
   D. The test yields similar scores if taken at two different times.

4. Which of the following statements is true regarding Francis Galton?
   A. He took the position that intelligence is largely determined by heredity.
   B. He advocated the development of special programs to tap the intellectual potential of the culturally disadvantaged.
   C. He developed tests that identified children who were likely to perform poorly in school.
   D. He took the position that intelligence is more a matter of environment than heredity.

5. Paul's IQ test score is 115. If the test is typical of modern intelligence tests, which of the following could be inferred about Paul?
   A. His IQ is exactly average.
   B. His IQ suggests that he may require assistance to do well in school.
   C. His IQ is an indication of genius.
   D. His IQ is one standard deviation above the mean.

6. IQ tests are good predictors of which of the following?
   A. social intelligence
   B. practical problem-solving intelligence
   C. school performance
   D. career success

7. Newton has been selected for a gifted children's program at school. Which of the following pieces of advice would be useful and accurate for Newton's parents?
   A. Pay attention to Newton's emotional stability, because those with high IQs tend to be maladjusted.
   B. Although he may go on to do great things, most gifted children do not make extraordinary contributions in adulthood.
   C. It would be a good idea to get Newton ready to deal with fame and unwanted attention.
   D. Learn to deal with the absence of social skills that is characteristic of gifted children, and especially among gifted boys.

8. Which of the following statements is true about intellectual disability?
   A. Most intellectually disabled people require a level of care that precludes a normal life.
   B. With special tutoring, an intellectually disabled person can attain average intelligence.
   C. The majority of intellectually disabled people fall into the mild category.
   D. Diagnoses of intellectual disability should be based exclusively on IQ scores.

9. Which of the following criteria is typically used to determine whether children are designated as gifted?
   A. They have IQ scores above 115.
   B. They score in the upper 2–3 percent of the IQ distribution.
   C. They consistently earn excellent grades in elementary school.
   D. They demonstrate high levels of leadership and creativity.

10. In which of the following pairs do you expect to find the greatest similarity in IQ?
    A. between identical twins
    B. between fraternal twins
    C. between nontwin siblings
    D. between parent and child

11. Which of the following findings provides evidence that upbringing affects one's mental ability?
    A. The correlation between IQ scores for fraternal twins is close to chance levels.
    B. Adopted children are no more similar to their biological parents than they are to their biological siblings in terms of IQ scores.
    C. Biological siblings reared together are more similar in IQ than are biological siblings reared apart.
    D. Twins reared apart are more similar in IQ than nontwins reared apart.

12. Just before an exam, Jenna's professor mentions that female students tend to perform poorly in that course. Jenna then did worse on that exam than she had on previous exams in the same course. This example is consistent with which of the following phenomena?
    A. the Flynn effect
    B. reaction range
    C. regression to the mean
    D. stereotype threat

13. Which of the following statements is consistent with both Sternberg's and Gardner's concepts of intelligence?
    A. Different people can be intelligent in different ways.
    B. There is a core form of intelligence that underlies skill in a variety of domains.
    C. Intelligence cannot be measured using standardized tests.
    D. People who have high scores on typical modern IQ tests are skilled in only a narrow range of abilities.

14. Which of the following processes takes place when someone tries to narrow down a list of alternatives to arrive at a single correct answer?
    A. convergent thinking
    B. reductionist thinking
    C. synaptic pruning
    D. narrow creativity

15. Nora is anticipating a blind date with Nick. When she hears that faculty in the art department consider Nick a true creative genius, she has second thoughts because she believes that creative genius is associated with mental illness. Does she have reason to be concerned?
    A. Yes. The stress of creative achievement often leads to schizophrenic symptoms.
    B. No. There is no connection between creativity and psychological disorders.
    C. Perhaps. There is a correlation between major creative achievement and vulnerability to mood disorders.
    D. Of course not. The stereotype of the mentally ill genius is merely a product of the availability heuristic.

See Appendix A for answers to this Practice Test.

On the Web

▶ **CourseMate**

Go to this site to find online resources directly linked to your book, including more quizzes, a glossary, flash cards, videos, and more!

▶ **CengageNow**

Go to this site for the link to CengageNOW™, your one-stop study shop. Take a pre-test for this chapter and CengageNOW™ will generate a personalized study plan based on your test results! The study plan will identify the topics you need to review and direct you to online resources to help you master those topics. You can then take a post-test to help you determine the concepts you have mastered and what you still need to work on.

▶ **Aplia**

Aplia™ is an online interactive learning solution that helps you improve comprehension—and your grade— by integrating a variety of media and tools such as video, tutorials, practice tests and interactive e-book.

CHAPTER 10

Motivation and Emotion

Jim Arbogast/Digital Vision/Getty Images

otivation and emotion are two important topics in psychology that are often discussed in the same chapter. While there are distinct literatures and theories in each of these areas, they are clearly linked. In the first part of the chapter, we discuss research and theory in the study of motivation. Motivation relates to the study of the processes involved in goal-directed behaviour. Our goal-directed behaviour, of course, is often associated with specific emotions. For example, think back to the goal you set for yourself on the first test in this course. You may have set a goal of getting an A on the first test and then studied hard to achieve it. Then think about your reaction when you found out your grade on that test. Your reaction would have been very different if you received an A than if you got a lower grade. Motivation and emotion, then, are often linked. Consider for a moment a different type of goal setting, setting a goal of winning an Olympic or Paralympic medal.

Chantal Petitclerc is one of Canada's finest athletes. Since losing the use of her legs in an accident at age 13, she has gone on to dominate women's wheelchair racing events. She holds many world, Commonwealth, and Paralympic records. At the 2008 Paralympic Games in Beijing, Petitclerc won five gold medals and set three world records (Hunter, 2008). She also won five gold medals at the 2004 Paralympic Games held in Athens, Greece. Also in 2004, Petitclerc was named both Canadian Female Athlete of the Year at the Canadian Sport Awards (Ewing, 2005) and Canadian of the Year (Gillis, 2004). In 2005, she was awarded the Laureus Prize as Paralympic Athlete of the Year. She became a Companion of the Order of Canada in 2009, and in 2010 she was inducted into the Canadian Sports Hall of fame.

Most of us can only begin to imagine the dedication and motivation that bring an athlete such as Chantal Petitclerc to these levels. When asked what drives her, she states, "No matter what you do or what your dreams are, you always do it to achieve a goal and also to see what your limits are and eventually to see you have no limits" (interview with Chantal Petitclerc, 1996). Whatever their individual reasons, Olympic athletes must be highly motivated to continue to prepare for and compete in their chosen sports. The Canadian Olympic committee appointed Dr. Kimberly Amirault as lead Olympic specialist for sport psychology for the 2010 Olympic Games (Dimanno, 2010). Among other things, sports psychologists are specialists in facilitating motivation. Dr. Amirault, who obtained her Ph.D. from the University of Calgary, has also consulted with professional teams in the NBA and NHL.

Paralympic wheelchair racer Chantal Petitclerc was just one of the highly motivated athletes who represented Canada in Beijing in 2008, winning five gold medals and setting three world records.

In this chapter, we will discuss the topic of motivation, looking at topics ranging from hunger motivation and eating to achievement motivation—the type of motivation that may have brought you to the study of psychology in the first place.

The other topic considered in this chapter is the study of emotion. Our lives are filled with emotions. Your reaction after obtaining your grade in the first test in this course would have been only one of many emotionally relevant experiences you had that day. In some cases, the explanation for our emotion is clear. Consider Perdita Felicien's reaction after the 2004 Olympic gold medal race in the

Sports psychologists such as Dr. David Cox, a clinical psychologist and a professor in the Department of Psychology at Simon Fraser University, consult with professional and Olympic athletes to enhance motivation and performance. Cox is shown here with Kelley Law, skip of the Richmond, BC, curling team that won a bronze medal in the 2002 Winter Olympics.

Motivation and Emotion

Olympic athletes such as Perdita Felicien experience the full range of emotions over the course of their athletic career. Felicien was expected to win the 100-metre hurdles in the 2004 Olympics, but was unable to finish because of a fall. She regained her form in 2005 and won a world championship medal in 2007, but was unable to compete in the 2008 Beijing Olympics due to a foot injury.

AP Photo/Julie Jacobson

© Tobias Schwartz/Reuters/Corbis

100-metre hurdles was over. Felicien was one of Canada's top medal hopes at the Olympics; she was expected to win, and why not? She was the reigning world champion. Unfortunately for her, the race did not end, or even begin, as it was expected to— she hit the first hurdle and fell. The race was won by American Joanna Hayes in a new Olympic record time. Felicien's reaction after the race was "This is my worst nightmare come true" (Athens, 2004). The look on her face after the fall tells you all you need to know about what she was feeling. As we will learn in this chapter, there is a close connection between what you are feeling and the expression on your face.

Felicien won her first comeback race in 2005 and was shown in media reports smiling broadly at the finish line. Just imagine how motivated she must

have been to come back after her Olympic experience. While the eliciting events and emotions experienced in her case seem quite obvious, it is not always so clear why we are feeling the way that we are or, indeed, what caused us to feel that way. In this chapter, we will discuss some of the theories and research examining our emotional experiences. You may be surprised at what some of the research tells us about our emotions. Think back to the Featured Study in Chapter 2 (see page 47) in which males crossed high or low bridges spanning the Capilano River in British Columbia. Did you expect that their emotions could have been so easily manipulated by the experimenters? In the last part of this chapter, we will learn more about what factors affect our subjective feeling states.

Motivational Theories and Concepts

PREVIEW QUESTIONS

▶ What is the distinction between drive, incentive, and evolutionary theories of motivation?

▶ How do evolutionary theories explain various motives?

Motives are the needs, wants, interests, and desires that propel people in certain directions. In short, *motivation* involves goal-directed behaviour. Motivation to achieve relevant goals can be an important determinant of adjustment. Street kids in research conducted by Donald Taylor of McGill University, for example, are often characterized by little motivation to reach *definable and coherent* goals (Taylor et al., 2004; Usborne, Lydon, & Taylor, 2009; Usborne & Taylor, in press). According to Taylor and his colleagues, street kids have rejected traditional

society and its standards and goals but have not replaced these goals with any long-term goals of their own. Without purpose, their lives become focused on the short-term and they become "aimless." Goals and our motivation to achieve them are often important characteristics of successful adjustment. Our goals can be the result both of intentional and automatic activation (Foster, Liberman, & Friedman, 2007). There are a number of theoretical approaches to motivation. Let's look at some of these theories and the concepts they employ.

Drive Theories

Many theories view motivational forces in terms of *drives*. The drive concept appears in a diverse array of theories that otherwise have little in common, such as psychoanalytic (Freud, 1915) and behaviourist formulations (Hull, 1943). This approach to understanding motivation was explored most fully by Clark Hull in the 1940s and 1950s (Madsen, 1968).

Drive theories apply the concept of *homeostasis*, a state of physiological equilibrium or stability, to behaviour. A *drive* is an internal state of tension that motivates an organism to engage in activities that should reduce this tension. These unpleasant states of tension are viewed as disruptions of the preferred equilibrium. For example, when your body temperature rises or drops noticeably, automatic responses occur (see Figure 10.1). According to drive theories, when individuals experience a drive, they're motivated to pursue actions that will lead to *drive reduction*. During a long class you may begin to feel hungry. The hunger motive has usually been conceptualized as a drive system—if you go without food for a while, you begin to experience some discomfort. This internal tension (the drive) motivates you to obtain food. Eating reduces the drive and restores physiological equilibrium.

Drive theories have been very influential, and the drive concept continues to be widely used in modern psychology. *However, drive theories cannot explain all motivation* (Berridge, 2004). Homeostasis appears irrelevant to some human motives, such as a "thirst for knowledge." Also, motivation may exist without drive arousal. You may stop for some ice cream after seeing an advertisement, even though you are not hungry. Because drive theories assume that people always try to reduce internal tension, they can't explain this behaviour very well. Incentive theories, which represent a different approach to motivation, can account for this behaviour more readily.

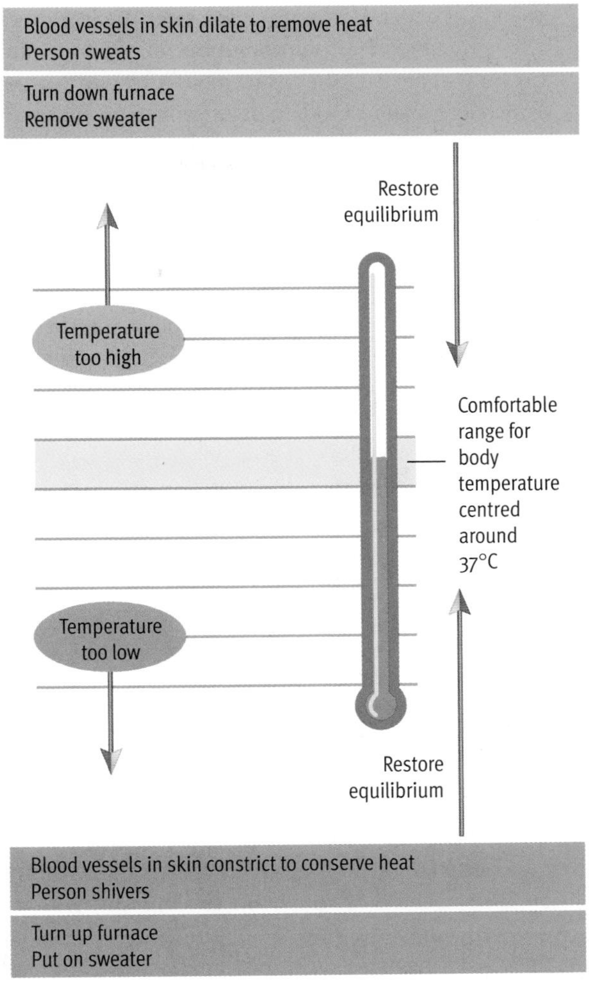

Incentive Theories

Incentive theories propose that external stimuli regulate motivational states (Bolles, 1975; McClelland, 1975; Skinner, 1953). An *incentive* is an external goal that has the capacity to motivate behaviour. Ice cream, a juicy steak, a monetary prize, approval from friends, an A on an exam, and a promotion at work are all incentives. Some of these incentives may reduce drives, but others may not.

Drive and incentive models of motivation are often contrasted as *push-versus-pull* theories. Drive theories emphasize how *internal* states of tension *push* people in certain directions. Incentive theories emphasize how *external* stimuli *pull* people in certain directions. According to drive theories, the source of motivation lies *within* the organism. According to incentive theories, the source of motivation lies *outside* the organism, in the environment. This means that incentive models don't operate according to the principle of homeostasis, which hinges on internal changes in the organism. Thus, in comparison to drive theories, incentive theories emphasize environmental factors and downplay the biological bases of human motivation.

As you're painfully aware, people can't always obtain the goals they desire, such as good grades or choice promotions. *Expectancy-value models* of motivation are incentive theories that take this reality into account (Atkinson & Birch, 1978). According to expectancy-value models, one's motivation to pursue a particular course of action will depend on two factors: (1) *expectancy* about one's chances of attaining the incentive and (2) the *value* of the desired incentive. Thus, your motivation to pursue a promotion at

FIGURE 10.1

Temperature regulation as an example of homeostasis.

The regulation of body temperature provides a simple example of how organisms often seek to maintain homeostasis, or a state of physiological equilibrium. When your temperature moves out of an acceptable range, automatic bodily reactions (such as sweating or shivering) occur that help restore equilibrium. Of course, these automatic reactions may not be sufficient by themselves, so you may have to take other action (such as turning a furnace up or down) to bring your body temperature back into its comfort zone.

Blood vessels in skin dilate to remove heat
Person sweats

Turn down furnace
Remove sweater

Restore equilibrium

Temperature too high

Comfortable range for body temperature centred around 37°C

Temperature too low

Restore equilibrium

Blood vessels in skin constrict to conserve heat
Person shivers

Turn up furnace
Put on sweater

work will depend on your estimate of the likelihood that you can snare the promotion (expectancy) and on how appealing the promotion is to you (value). Expectancy-value models have proven to be useful in understanding a range of human behaviours and motivations (e.g., Westaby, 2006).

Evolutionary Theories

Psychologists who take an evolutionary perspective assert that human motives and those of other species are the products of evolution, just as anatomical characteristics are (Durrant & Ellis, 2003). They argue that natural selection favours behaviours that maximize reproductive success—that is, passing on genes to the next generation. Thus, they explain motives such as affiliation, achievement, dominance, aggression, and sex drive in terms of their adaptive value. If dominance is a crucial motive for a species, they say, it's because dominance provides a reproductive or survival advantage.

Evolutionary analyses of motivation are based on the premise that motives can best be understood in terms of the adaptive problems they solved for our hunter–gatherer ancestors (Tooby & Cosmides, 2005). For example, the need for dominance is thought to be greater in men than women because it could facilitate males' reproductive success in a variety of ways, including (1) females may prefer mating with dominant males, (2) dominant males may poach females from subordinate males,

(3) dominant males may intimidate male rivals in competition for sexual access, and (4) dominant males may acquire more material resources, which may increase mating opportunities (Buss, 1999). David Buss (1995) points out that it is not by accident that achievement, power (dominance), and intimacy are among the most heavily studied social motives, as the satisfaction of each of these motives is likely to affect one's reproductive success. Consider also the *affiliation motive*, or need for belongingness. The adaptive benefits of affiliation for our ancient ancestors probably included help with rearing offspring, collaboration in hunting or defence, opportunities for sexual interaction, and so forth (Baumeister & Leary, 1995).

The Range and Diversity of Human Motives

Motivational theorists of all persuasions agree on one point: Humans display an enormous diversity of motives (Pittman & Zeigler, 2007). Most theories (evolutionary theories being a notable exception) distinguish between *biological motives* that originate in bodily needs, such as hunger, and *social motives* that originate in social experiences, such as the need for achievement.

People have a limited number of biological needs. According to K. B. Madsen (1968, 1973), most theories identify 10 to 15 such needs, some of which are listed on the left side of Figure 10.2. People all share the same biological motives, most of which are based on needs essential to survival, but their social motives vary, depending on their experiences. For example, we all need to eat, but not everyone acquires a need for orderliness. Although people have a limited number of biological motives, they can acquire an unlimited number of social motives through learning and socialization. Some examples of social motives—from an influential list compiled by Henry Murray (1938)—are shown on the right side of Figure 10.2. He theorized that most people have needs for achievement, autonomy, affiliation, dominance, exhibition, and order, among other things. Of course, the strength of these motives varies from person to person, depending on personal history.

Given the range and diversity of human motives, we can examine only a handful in depth. To a large degree, our choices reflect the motives psychologists have studied the most: hunger, sex, and achievement. After discussing these motivational systems, we will explore the elements of emotional experience and examine various theories of emotion.

Examples of Biological Motives in Humans	Examples of Social Motives in Humans
Hunger motive	Achievement motive (need to excel)
Thirst motive	Affiliation motive (need for social bonds)
Sex motive	Autonomy motive (need for independence)
Temperature motive (need for appropriate body temperature)	Nurturance motive (need to nourish and protect others)
Excretory motive (need to eliminate bodily wastes)	Dominance motive (need to influence or control others)
Sleep and rest motive	Exhibition motive (need to make an impression on others)
Activity motive (need for optimal level of stimulation and arousal)	Order motive (need for orderliness, tidiness, organization)
Aggression motive	Play motive (need for fun, relaxation, amusement)

FIGURE 10.2

The diversity of human motives.

People are motivated by a wide range of needs, which can be divided into two broad classes: biological motives and social motives. The list on the left (adapted from Madsen, 1973) shows some important biological motives in humans. The list on the right (adapted from Murray, 1938) provides examples of prominent social motives in humans. The distinction between biological and social motives is not absolute.

The Motivation of Hunger and Eating

Why do people eat? Because they're hungry. What makes them hungry? A lack of food. Any grade-school child can explain these basic facts. So hunger is a simple motivational system, right? Wrong! Hunger is deceptive. It only looks simple. Actually, it's a puzzling and complex motivational system. Despite extensive studies of hunger, scientists are still struggling to understand the factors that regulate eating behaviour. Let's examine a few of these factors.

Biological Factors in the Regulation of Hunger   2e 8a

You have probably had embarrassing occasions when your stomach growled loudly at an inopportune moment. Someone may have commented, "You must be starving!" Most people equate a rumbling stomach with hunger, and, in fact, the first scientific theories of hunger were based on this simple equation. In an elaborate 1912 study, Walter Cannon and A. L. Washburn verified what most people have noticed based on casual observation: There is an association between stomach contractions and the experience of hunger.

Based on this correlation, Cannon theorized that stomach contractions *cause* hunger. However, as we've seen before, correlation is no assurance of causation, and his theory was eventually discredited. Stomach contractions often accompany hunger, but they don't cause it. How do we know? Because later research showed that people continue to experience hunger even after their stomachs have been removed out of medical necessity (Wangensteen & Carlson, 1931). If hunger can occur without a stomach, then stomach contractions can't be the cause of hunger. This realization led to more elaborate theories of hunger that focus on a host of factors.

Brain Regulation   2e 8a

Research with lab animals eventually suggested that the experience of hunger is controlled in the brain—specifically, in the hypothalamus. As we have noted before, the *hypothalamus* is a tiny structure involved in the regulation of a variety of biological needs related to survival (see Figure 10.3). In the 1940s and 1950s, studies using brain lesioning techniques and electrical stimulation of the brain led to the conclusion that the *lateral hypothalamus (LH)* and the

ventromedial nucleus of the hypothalamus (VMH), were the brain's on–off switches for the control of hunger (Stellar, 1954). However, over the course of several decades, a variety of empirical findings undermined the dual-centres model of hunger (Valenstein, 1973; Winn, 1995). The current thinking is that the lateral and ventromedial areas of the hypothalamus are elements in the neural circuitry that regulates hunger. However, they are not the key elements, nor simple on–off centres (King, 2006; Meister, 2007). Today, scientists believe that two other areas of the hypothalamus—the *arcuate nucleus* and the *paraventricular nucleus*—play a larger role in the modulation of hunger (Scott, McDade, & Luckman, 2007). In recent years, the arcuate nucleus has been singled out as especially important (Becskei, Lutz, & Riediger, 2008). This area in the hypothalamus appears to

PREVIEW QUESTIONS

▶ Which physiological factors have been implicated in the regulation of hunger?

▶ How do fluctuations in blood glucose and hormones contribute to hunger?

▶ How is eating influenced by the availability of food, culture, and learned habits?

▶ What evidence is there regarding the prevalence and health significance of obesity?

▶ What have scientists learned about the causes of obesity?

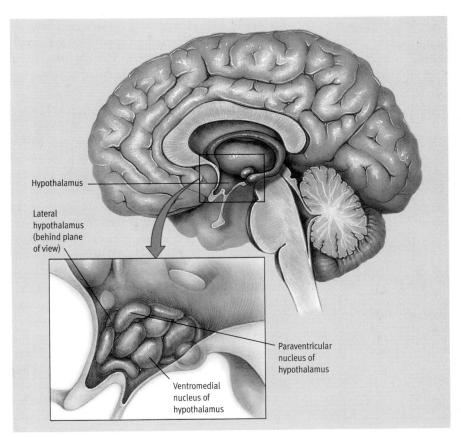

FIGURE 10.3

The hypothalamus.

This small structure at the base of the forebrain plays a role in regulating a variety of human biological needs, including hunger. The detailed blowup shows that the hypothalamus is made up of a variety of discrete areas. Scientists used to believe that the lateral and ventromedial areas were the brain's on–off centres for eating. However, more recent research suggests that the paraventricular nucleus may be more crucial to the regulation of hunger and that thinking in terms of neural circuits rather than anatomical centres makes more sense.

The rat in front has had its ventromedial hypothalamus lesioned, resulting in a dramatic increase in weight.

Judith Rodin

"People's metabolic machinery is constituted in such a way that the fatter they are, the fatter they are primed to become."

contain a group of neurons that are sensitive to incoming hunger signals and another group of neurons that respond to satiety signals.

Contemporary theories of hunger focus more on *neural circuits* that pass through areas of the hypothalamus rather than on *anatomical centres* in the brain. These circuits depend on a large variety of neurotransmitters and they appear to be much more complicated than anticipated. Evidence suggests that the neural circuits regulating hunger are massively and reciprocally interconnected with extensive parallel processing (Powley, 2009). This complex neural circuitry is sensitive to a diverse range of physiological processes.

Glucose and Digestive Regulation

8a PSYKTREK

Much of the food taken into the body is converted into *glucose*, which circulates in the blood. *Glucose is a simple sugar that is an important source of energy.* Actions that decrease blood glucose level can increase hunger. Actions that increase glucose level can make people feel satiated. Based on these findings, *glucostatic theory* proposed that fluctuations in blood glucose level are monitored in the brain where they influence the experience of hunger (Mayer, 1955, 1968). Like the dual-centres theory, the glucostatic theory of hunger gradually ran into many complications. Nonetheless, it appears that the arcuate nucleus of the hypothalamus is sensitive to glucostatic fluctuations that *contribute* to the modulation of eating (Woods & Stricker, 2008).

The digestive system also includes other mechanisms that influence hunger (Ritter, 2004). It turns out that Walter Cannon was not entirely wrong in hypothesizing that the stomach regulates hunger. After you have consumed food, cells in the stomach can send signals to the brain stem that inhibit further eating (Woods & Stricker, 2008). For example, the vagus nerve carries information about the stretching of the stomach walls that indicates when the stomach is full. Other nerves carry satiety messages

that depend on how rich in nutrients the contents of the stomach are.

Hormonal Regulation

8a PSYKTREK

A variety of hormones circulating in the bloodstream also appear to contribute to the regulation of hunger. *Insulin* is a hormone secreted by the pancreas. It must be present for cells to extract glucose from the blood. Indeed, an inadequate supply of insulin is what causes diabetes. The secretion of insulin is associated with increased hunger. And, in landmark research that blurred the distinction between biological and environmental determinants of hunger, Judith Rodin (1985) demonstrated that the mere sight and smell of enticing food can stimulate the secretion of insulin. Moreover, insulin levels appear to be sensitive to fluctuations in the body's fat stores (Seeley et al., 1996). These findings suggest that insulin secretions play a role in the fluctuation of hunger.

At least three other hormones play a key role in the short-term regulation of hunger. After going without food for a while, the stomach secretes *ghrelin*. This causes stomach contractions and promotes hunger (Cummings, 2006). In contrast, after food is consumed, the upper intestine releases a hormone called *CCK* that delivers satiety signals to the brain. This reduces hunger (Moran, 2004; Schwartz & Azzara, 2004).

Finally, the recent discovery of a previously undetected hormone, since christened *leptin*, has shed new light on the hormonal regulation of hunger as well as the regulation of numerous other bodily functions (Ahima & Osei, 2004). Leptin is produced by fat cells throughout the body and released into the bloodstream. Higher levels of fat generate higher levels of leptin (Schwartz et al., 1996). Leptin circulates through the bloodstream and ultimately provides the hypothalamus with information about the body's fat stores (Campfield, 2002). When leptin levels are high, the propensity to feel hungry diminishes.

The hormonal signals that influence hunger (the fluctuations of insulin, ghrelin, CCK, and leptin) all seem to converge in the hypothalamus. Most notably they converge in the arcuate and paraventricular nuclei of the hypothalamus (Kuo et al., 2007; Naslund & Hellstrom, 2007).

If all this sounds confusing, it is, and we haven't even mentioned *all* of the physiological processes involved in the regulation of hunger and eating. Frankly, researchers are still struggling to figure out exactly how all these processes work together, as hunger depends on complex interactions between neural circuits, neurotransmitter systems, digestive processes, and hormonal fluctuations (Berthoud & Morrison, 2008). These systems are far more decentralized and interconnected than originally thought (Powley, 2009).

Environmental Factors in the Regulation of Hunger

Hunger clearly is a biological need, but eating is not regulated by biological factors alone. Studies show that social and environmental factors govern eating to a considerable extent. Three key environmental factors are (1) the availability of food, (2) learned preferences and habits, and (3) stress.

Food Availability and Related Cues

Most of the research on the physiological regulation of hunger has been based on the assumption that hunger operates as a drive system in which homeostatic mechanisms are at work. However, some theorists emphasize the incentive value of food and argue that humans and other animals are often motivated to eat not by the need to compensate for energy deficits but by the anticipated pleasure of eating (Hetherington & Rolls, 1996; Ramsay et al., 1996). This perspective has been bolstered by evidence that the following variables exert significant influence over food consumption:

- *Palatability*. The better food tastes, the more of it people consume (de Castro, 2010). This principle is not limited to humans. The eating behaviour of rats and other animals is also influenced by palatability.
- *Quantity available*. A powerful determinant of the amount eaten is the amount available. People tend to consume what's put in front of them. The more people are served, the more they eat (Mrdjenovic & Levitsky, 2005; Rozin et al., 2003). For example, one study found that people consumed 45 percent more popcorn when it was served in larger containers (Wansink & Kim, 2005). Another study, in which participants unknowingly ate from soup bowls that imperceptibly refilled themselves, found that consumption soared 73 percent (Wansink, Painter, & North, 2005). Thus, the remarkably large and ever-expanding portions served in modern North American restaurants surely foster increased consumption (Geier, Rozin, & Doros, 2006).
- *Variety*. Humans and animals increase their consumption when a greater variety of foods is available (Raynor & Epstein, 2001; Temple et al., 2008). As you eat a specific food, its incentive value declines. This phenomenon is called *sensory-specific satiety* (Havermans, Siep, & Jansen, 2010). If only a few foods are available, the appeal of all of them can decline quickly. But if many foods are available, people can keep shifting to new foods and end up eating more overall. This principle explains why people are especially likely to overeat at buffets where many foods are available.
- *Presence of others*. On average, individuals eat 44 percent more when they eat with other people as opposed to eating alone. The more people present, the more people tend to eat (de Castro, 2010). When two people eat together, they tend to use each other as guides and eat similar amounts (Salvy et al., 2007). However, when women eat in the presence of an opposite-sex person they do not know well, they tend to reduce their intake (Young et al., 2009). When asked afterward, people seem oblivious to the fact that their eating is influenced by the presence of others (Vartanian, Herman, & Wansink, 2008).

Eating can also be triggered by exposure to environmental cues that have been associated with eating. You have no doubt had your hunger aroused by television commercials for delicious-looking food or by seductive odours coming from the kitchen. Consistent with this observation, studies by researchers such as Peter Herman and Janet Polivy of the University of Toronto and others have shown that hunger can be increased by exposure to pictures, written descriptions, and video depictions of attractive foods (Halford et al., 2004; Herman, Ostovich, & Polivy, 1999; Marcelino et al., 2001; Oakes & Slotterback, 2000). Studies have shown that exposure to soda and food advertisements incite hunger and lead to increased food intake (Harris, Bargh, & Brownell, 2009; Koordeman et al., 2010). Moreover, the foods consumed are not limited to those seen in the ads. And people tend to be unaware of how

According to incentive models of hunger, the availability and palatability of food are key factors regulating hunger. An abundance of diverse foods tends to lead to increased eating.

© Susan Van Etten/PhotoEdit

Motivation and Emotion

University of Toronto researchers Peter Herman and Janet Polivy are well known in the area of the psychology of eating. Their recent research has examined the effects of social cues on eating behaviour.

the ads influence their eating behaviour. Thus, it's clear that hunger and eating are governed in part by the incentive qualities of food. We consider more completely research on the effects of external cues on page 450 in the section entitled "Sensitivity to External Cues."

It is also clear that eating is often a social action. Herman, Polivy, and their colleagues have considered the effects of cues and of the presence of others on one's intake of food (Coelho, Polivy, & Herman, 2008; Herman, Roth, & Polivy, 2003). They suggest that social cues based on the behaviour of others are some of the most important determinants of food intake. They have integrated a variety of ideas about the effects of the presence of others on our eating in developing their inhibitory norm model of social influence on eating. They suggest that the presence of others generally inhibits eating. But, under certain specific conditions, eating may increase. In essence, they suggest that our eating is influenced by extant social norms determined by the behaviour of the others around us at the time. Thus, while it's clear that hunger and eating are governed in part by the availability of food and the presence of a variety of food-related cues, other social factors also play an important role. Given the continuing trend for adult Canadians to keep getting heavier (Statistics Canada, 2006), Herman and Polivy's view that more research is needed into the causes of overeating is very timely (Herman, van Strien, & Polivy, 2008).

Learned Preferences and Habits

8a

Are you fond of eating calves' brains? How about eels or snakes? Could we interest you in a grasshopper or some dog meat? Probably not, but these are delicacies in some regions of the world. Inuit in the Arctic like to eat maggots! You probably prefer chicken, apples, eggs, lettuce, potato chips, pizza, corn flakes,

or ice cream. These preferences are acquired through learning. People from different cultures display very different patterns of food consumption (Rozin, 2007). If you doubt this fact, just visit a grocery store in an ethnic neighbourhood (not your own, of course).

Humans do have some innate taste preferences of a general sort. For example, a preference for sweet tastes is present at birth (Mennella & Beauchamp, 1996), and humans' preference for high-fat foods appears to be at least partly genetic in origin (Schiffman et al., 1998). Evidence also suggests that an unlearned preference for salt emerges at around four months of age in humans (Birch & Fisher, 1996). Nonetheless, learning wields a great deal of influence over what people prefer to eat (Rozin, 2007). Taste preferences are partly a function of learned associations formed through classical conditioning (Appleton, Gentry, & Shephard, 2006). For example, youngsters can be conditioned to prefer flavours paired with high caloric intake or other pleasant events. Of course, as we learned in Chapter 6, taste aversions can also be acquired through conditioning when foods are followed by nausea (Schafe & Bernstein, 1996).

Conditioning also likely plays a role in our own experiences. When one of us goes to the Air Canada Centre to watch a Toronto Maple Leafs hockey game, he always heads first for the hot dog stand—that's what he thinks of first when he thinks of food at a hockey game. His 18-year-old son orders sushi. When the adult was growing up and attending hockey games, hot dogs were about all you could get to eat at a hockey game, so that is the type of food he associates with hockey games.

As you might expect based on our discussion of learning in Chapter 6, eating habits are also shaped by observational learning. To a large degree, food preferences are a matter of exposure (Cooke, 2007). People generally prefer familiar foods. But geographical, cultural, religious, and ethnic factors limit people's exposure to certain foods. Young children are more likely to taste an unfamiliar food if an adult tries it first. Repeated exposures to a new food usually lead to increased liking. However, as many parents have learned the hard way, forcing a child to eat a specific food can backfire (Benton, 2004).

Stress and Eating

You may behave like we sometimes do after an exceptionally stressful day and head straight for the refrigerator, a grocery store, or a restaurant—often in pursuit of something chocolate and sweet. If you do, it is not unusual. In fact, the stress associated with first-year university may account in part for the "freshman 15," the weight gain experienced by many first-year students. Studies have shown that

The fact that culture influences food preferences is evident in these photos, in which you can see delicacies such as grilled bat (left) and crocodile soup (right).

stress leads to increased eating in a substantial portion of people (Greeno & Wing, 1994; Laitinen, Ek, & Sovio, 2002). While there are several possible reasons for this connection between stress and eating, some people eat while stressed because they expect the enjoyable treats to make them feel better (Tice, Bratslavasky, & Baumeister, 2001). There is little evidence to support this belief (Thayer, 1996).

Eating and Weight: The Roots of Obesity

We just saw that hunger is regulated by a complex interaction of biological and psychological factors. The same kinds of complexities emerge when investigators explore the roots of *obesity, the condition of being overweight.* Obesity is increasingly recognized as a major health concern. Results from the *Canadian Community Health Survey* and the *National Population Health Survey* released by Statistics Canada (Statistics Canada, 2004a, 2005a) reveal the extent of the problem in Canada. In these surveys, definitions of *overweight* and *obese* are based on the *body mass index (BMI), which is an individual's weight (in kilograms) divided by height (in metres) squared.* A BMI over 30 is considered obese, while BMIs between 25 and 29.9 are considered overweight.

The surveys revealed a number of important findings. There is good news and bad news. The good news is that the overall rate of obesity in Canada from 2007 to 2009 was 10 percentage points lower than that in the United States, where one out of every five adults is obese (Le Petit & Berthelot, 2005; Statistics Canada, 2011). The bad news is that Canadians may be headed toward the same statistic, since obesity rates in Canada have doubled in the last two decades. See Figure 10.4, which shows obesity rates in both Canada and the United States. Data derived from the United States indicate that obesity lowers life expectancy considerably: 7.1 years for females and 5.8 years for males (Le Petit & Berthelot, 2005). While men were more likely to go from normal to overweight than women, women were more likely to go from overweight to obese. Since 1981, the prevalence of overweight and obese children has increased dramatically (Public Health Agency of Canada, n.d). Over one-third of Canadian children 2 to 11 years of age were considered overweight in 1998–1999, with about one-half of those considered obese (Statistics Canada, 2002a). Having obese parents increases the odds of obesity in children (Statistics Canada, 2003b), and it was found that once people are overweight, they are more likely than not to put on more weight (Statistics Canada, 2005a).

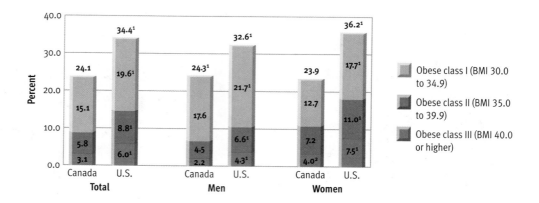

Obesity rates in North America.

Obesity rates have been increasing over the past few years. This figure reveals the obesity rates both in Canada and the United States. While obesity rates are increasing in both countries, they remain higher in the United States. Because the risk of adverse health effects increases at higher levels of body mass index (BMI), obesity is divided into three categories. In all three BMI categories, prevalence was significantly lower in Canada than in the United States. In the highest BMI category the prevalence was twice as high in the United States (6.0 percent) as in Canada (3.1 percent).

Notes:

[1]Significantly different from estimate for Canada ($p < 0.05$).

[2]Use with caution (coefficient of variation 16.6 percent to 33.3 percent).

Obesity class estimates do not sum to exact totals due to rounding.

Source: Statistics Canada, Adult obesity prevalence in Canada and the United States, *Health Fact Sheets*, 82-625-XIE2011001, No. 3, April 2011; http://www.statcan.gc.ca/bsolc/olc-cel/olc-cel?catno=82-625-XWE&lang=eng.

If obesity merely frustrated people's vanity, there would be little cause for concern. Unfortunately, obesity is a significant health problem that elevates one's mortality risk (Allison et al., 1999; Bender et al., 1999; Flegal et al., 2005; Fontaine et al., 2003; Ogden, 2010). Overweight people are more vulnerable than others to cardiovascular diseases, diabetes, hypertension, respiratory problems, gallbladder disease, stroke, arthritis, muscle and skeletal pain, and some types of cancer (Manson, Skerrett, & Willet, 2002; Pi-Sunyer, 2002). For example, Figure 10.5 shows how the prevalence of diabetes, hypertension, coronary disease, and musculoskeletal pain are elevated as BMI increases.

Evolutionary-oriented researchers have a plausible explanation for the dramatic increase in the prevalence of obesity (Pinel, Assanand, & Lehman 2000). They point out that over the course of history, most animals and humans have lived in environments in which there was fierce competition for limited, unreliable food resources and where starvation was a very real threat. Hence, warm-blooded, foraging animals evolved a propensity to consume more food than was immediately necessary when the opportunity presented itself, because food might not be available later. Excess calories were stored in the body (as fat) to prepare for future food shortages.

This approach to eating remains adaptive for most species of animals that continue to struggle with the ebb and flow of unpredictable food supplies. However, in today's modern, industrialized societies, the vast majority of humans live in environments that provide an abundant, reliable supply

Weight and the prevalence of various diseases.

This graph shows how obesity, as indexed by BMI, is related to the prevalence of four common types of illness. The prevalence of diabetes, heart disease, muscle pain, and hypertension all increase as BMI goes up. Clearly, obesity is a significant health risk. (Based on data in Brownell & Wadden, 2000)

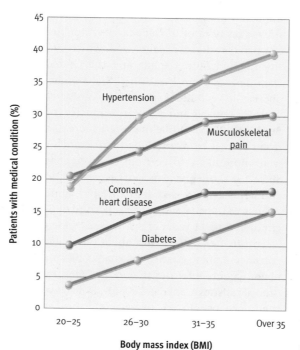

of tasty, high-calorie food. In these environments, humans' evolved tendency to overeat when food is plentiful leads most people down a pathway of chronic excessive food consumption. According to this line of thinking, most people in food-replete environments tend to overeat in relation to their physiological needs, but because of variations in genetics, metabolism, and other factors only some become overweight.

Cognizant of the health problems associated with obesity, many people attempt to lose weight. At any given time, about 21 percent of men and 39 percent of women are dieting (Hill, 2002). A recent Council of Ministers of Education in Canada survey of children revealed that about 12 percent of girls and 3–4 percent of boys in Grade 9 are actively dieting. The rate for Grade 7 boys is about the same as that for Grades 9 and 11 boys (4 percent), and the rate for Grade 7 girls is about 7 percent (Council of Ministers of Education, 2003). Although concerns have been raised that dieting carries its own risks, the evidence clearly indicates that weight loss efforts involving moderate changes in eating and exercise are more beneficial than harmful to people's health (Devlin, Yanovski, & Wilson, 2000).

While there are important reasons for obese individuals to consider weight reduction, recent research suggests that mortality rates among people who are *moderately overweight* (BMI 25–29.9) are *not* elevated in today's population (Flegal et al., 2005, 2007). One hypothesis to explain this surprising finding is that improvements in the treatment of cardiovascular diseases have neutralized much of the danger associated with being slightly overweight (Gibbs, 2005). These findings and other issues have led some critics (Campos, 2004; Oliver, 2005) to argue that the widely heralded obesity "epidemic/crisis" has been greatly exaggerated. Although the risks associated with moderate weight problems may be overrated, the fact remains that genuine obesity is a significant health problem. Hence, scientists have devoted a great deal of attention to the causes of obesity. Let's look at some of the factors they have identified.

Genetic Predisposition

You may know some people who can eat constantly without gaining weight. You may also know less-fortunate people who get chubby eating far less. Differences in physiological makeup must be the cause of this paradox. Research suggests that these differences have a genetic basis (Bouchard, 2002).

In one influential study, adults raised by adoptive parents were compared with their biological and adoptive parents in regard to body mass index

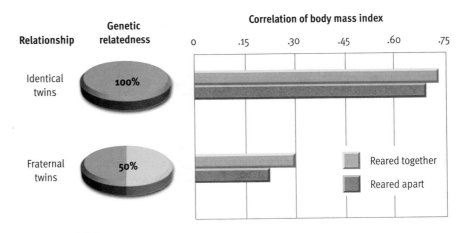

FIGURE 10.6

The heritability of weight.

These data from a twin study by Stunkard et al. (1990) reveal that identical twins are much more similar in body mass index than fraternal twins, suggesting that genetic factors account for much of the variation among people in the propensity to become overweight. (Data from Stunkard et al., 1990)

(Stunkard et al., 1986). The investigators found that the adoptees resembled their biological parents much more than their adoptive parents. In a subsequent *twin study*, Stunkard and colleagues (1990) found that identical twins reared apart were far more similar in BMI than fraternal twins reared together (see Figure 10.6). In another study of over 4000 twins, Allison and colleagues (1994) estimated that genetic factors account for 61 percent of the variation in weight among men, and 73 percent among women. Thus, it appears that some people inherit a genetic *vulnerability* to obesity (Cope, Fernandez, & Allison, 2004; Schwartz & Seeley, 1997).

Excessive Eating and Inadequate Exercise

The bottom line for overweight people is that their energy intake from food consumption chronically exceeds their energy expenditure from physical activities and resting metabolic processes. In other words, they eat too much in relation to their level of exercise (Wing & Polley, 2001). In modern North America, the tendency to overeat is easy to understand (Henderson & Brownell, 2004). Tasty, caloric, high-fat foods in ever-increasing portions are highly advertised and readily available nearly everywhere, not just in restaurants and grocery stores but in shopping malls, airports, gas stations, schools, and factories (Brownell, 2002). Nutritious foods can hardly compete with the convenience of highly caloric fast food. In recent decades, the size of grocery store packages, restaurant portions, and even dinnerware has increased steadily (Wansink, 2010). These bloated cues about what represents "normal" food consumption clearly fuel increased eating and escalating obesity. Kelly Brownell (2002) argues that modern societies have created a "toxic environment" for eating. This increasingly toxic eating environment has been paralleled by declining physical activity (Hill & Peters, 1998). Modern conveniences, such as cars and elevators, and changes in the world of work, such as the shift to more desk jobs, have conspired to make Canadian lifestyles more sedentary than ever before. On the most literal of levels, we physically move less and less. Inactivity seems to be more and more our chosen lifestyle.

Lower-income Canadians and those living in urban settings seem to be particularly vulnerable to inactivity (Statistics Canada, 2007a). Inadequate exercise is of special concern in children. The Public Health Agency of Canada reported that over half of Canadian children and youth between the ages of 5 and 17 are considered not active enough for "optimal growth and development" (Public Health Agency of Canada, n.d).

Sensitivity to External Cues

Stanley Schachter (1968) advanced the "externality hypothesis" that obese people are extrasensitive to external cues that affect hunger and are relatively insensitive to internal physiological signals, whereas the eating of normal-weight individuals is regulated by internal signals. According to this notion, overweight people respond readily to environmental cues, such as the availability and attractiveness of food, which often trigger unnecessary eating. In a series of studies, Schachter manipulated external cues such as how tasty food appeared, how obvious its availability was, and whether it appeared to be dinner time. All of these external cues were found to influence the eating behaviour of overweight individuals more than that of normal-weight subjects (Schachter, 1971).

Although Schachter's theory received extensive support, many studies also uncovered findings that were inconsistent with the theory (Petri & Govern, 2004). In an influential review of the evidence, Judith Rodin (1981) questioned key tenets of the theory. For example, she noted that the sight, smell, and sound of a grilling steak (external signals) can elicit insulin secretions (internal signals) that lead to increased hunger, thus blurring Schachter's key distinction between the internal and external determinants of hunger. She also highlighted findings showing that not all overweight people are hypersensitive to external cues, and that normal weight people are not necessarily insensitive to external food cues. Rodin's

critique had a dramatic impact as research on the influence of external cues declined and the externality hypothesis was widely viewed as discredited.

Recently, however, some theorists have begun to re-evaluate the dismissal of the externality hypothesis (Herman & Polivy, 2008; Stroebe, 2008). They acknowledge that Schachter's hypothesis was overstated and oversimplified. Decades of research have shown that obesity is a function of many factors and that obese people are not oblivious to physiological signals of hunger. But they argue that the central thesis of the externality hypothesis still has merit. After reviewing the evidence, Stroebe (2008) concludes that external cues do have a greater impact on the food intake of obese individuals than individuals of normal weight. To better understand how external cues relate to obesity, Herman and Polivy (2008) have introduced a distinction between *normative* as opposed to *sensory* external cues. Normative cues are indicators of socially appropriate food intake—what, when, and how much one should eat. Sensory cues are characteristics of the food itself, such as palatability, that make people more or less likely to consume it. *Herman and Polivy argue that it is sensory external cues that obese people are especially sensitive to.* Thus, the externality hypothesis is making a comeback. That said, its current advocates readily acknowledge that it is just one consideration among a constellation of factors that contribute to obesity.

The Concept of Set Point

People who lose weight on a diet have a rather strong (and depressing) tendency to gain back all of the weight they lose (Mann et al., 2007). The reverse is also true. People who have to work to gain weight often have trouble keeping it on. According to Richard Keesey (1995), these observations suggest that your body may have a *set point*, or a natural point of stability in body weight. *Set-point theory proposes that the body monitors fat-cell levels to keep them (and weight) fairly stable.* When fat stores slip below a crucial set point, the body supposedly begins to compensate for this change (Keesey, 1993). This compensation apparently leads to increased hunger and decreased metabolism.

Studies have raised some doubts about various details of set-point theory, leading John Pinel and his colleagues to propose an alternative called *settling-point theory* (Pinel, Assanand, & Lehman, 2000). *Settling-point theory proposes that weight tends to drift around the level at which the constellation of factors that determine food consumption and energy expenditure achieves an equilibrium.*

According to this view, weight tends to remain stable as long as there are no durable changes in any of the factors that influence it. Settling-point theory casts a much wider net than set-point theory, which attributes weight stability to very specific physiological processes. Another difference is that set-point theory asserts that an obese person's body will initiate processes that actively defend an excessive weight, whereas settling-point theory suggests that if an obese person makes long-term changes in eating or exercise, that person's settling point will drift downward without active resistance. Thus, settling-point theory is a little more encouraging to those who hope to lose weight.

Dietary Restraint

Some investigators have proposed that vacillations in *dietary restraint* contribute to obesity (Polivy & Herman, 1995; Wardle et al., 2000). According to this theory, chronic dieters are *restrained eaters*—people who consciously work overtime to control their eating impulses and who feel guilty when they fail. To lose weight, restrained eaters go hungry much of the time, but they are constantly thinking about food. However, when their cognitive control is disrupted, they become *disinhibited* and eat to excess (Lowe, 2002). The crux of the problem is that restrained eaters assume, "Either I am on a diet, or I am out of control." A variety of events, such as drinking alcohol or experiencing emotional distress, can disrupt restrained eaters' control (Federoff, Polivy, & Herman, 2003; Lattimore & Caswell, 2004). But for many, the most common source of disinhibition is simply the perception that they have cheated on their diet. "I've already blown it," they think to themselves after perhaps just one high-calorie appetizer, "so I might as well enjoy as much as I want." They then proceed to consume a large meal or to go on an eating binge for the remainder of the day. Restrained eaters even tend to prepare for planned diets by overeating (Urbszat, Herman, & Polivy, 2002). Paradoxically, then, dietary restraint is thought to lead to frequent overeating and thus contribute to obesity.

Dietary restraint also contributes to the tendency to overeat just before beginning a diet, as shown in a study conducted by University of Toronto researchers (Urbszat, Herman, & Polivy, 2002). Thus, it would appear that restrained eaters show a tendency to fall off the wagon before getting on—anticipation of food deprivation seems to act as another disinhibitor. Restrained eaters also seem to be particularly sensitive to the media's portrayal of idealized thin body types. York University psychologist Jennifer Mills

concept **check 10.1**

Understanding Factors in the Regulation of Hunger

Check your understanding of the effects of the various factors that influence hunger by indicating whether hunger would tend to increase or decrease in each of the situations described below. Indicate your choice by marking an I (increase), a D (decrease), or a ? (can't be determined without more information) next to each situation. You'll find the answers in Appendix A near the back of the book.

_____ 1. The ventromedial nucleus of a rat's brain is destroyed by lesioning.

_____ 2. The glucose level in Marlene's bloodstream decreases.

_____ 3. Norman just ate, but his roommate just brought home his favourite food—a pizza that smells great.

_____ 4. You're offered an exotic, strange-looking food from another culture and told that everyone in that culture loves it.

_____ 5. You are participating in an experiment on the effects of leptin and have just been given an injection of leptin.

_____ 6. Elton has been going crazy all day. It seems like everything's happening at once, and he feels totally stressed out. Finally, he's been able to break away for a few minutes so he can catch a bite to eat.

_____ 7. You have been on a successful diet, but you just broke down and ate some appetizers at a party.

(Mills et al., 2002) has shown that after viewing such idealized images, restrained eaters tended to report a thinner ideal body size than did unrestrained eaters and showed a tendency to report being thinner than they actually were. They also disinhibited their restraint to a greater extent, with the result that they ate more of the cookies that were placed in front of them.

Eating Disorders

We have just been considering some of the factors that affect eating behaviour, in particular, factors contributing to overeating. Of course, that is only one side of the problem that some people encounter in eating. While the topic of eating disorders will be considered more fully in Chapter 14, we want to introduce some of the concepts and issues here. According to Polivy and Herman (2002; Polivy et al., 2003), the late 1960s saw the increased prevalence of what was considered previously to be a very rare disorder: *anorexia nervosa*—a disorder in which (mostly) young women literally starve themselves, sometimes to death.

A related disorder, *bulimia nervosa*, in which (again, mostly) young women alternate between binge eating and purging, increased in profile in the 1970s. This disorder in particular became salient to Canadians when it was revealed that one of Canada's best female tennis players and athletes of the 1980s, Carling Bassett-Seguso, suffered from bulimia (Nunes, 2002). At 13, she was the best women's tennis player in Canada and at 14, the best under-18 player in the world. At 15, she joined the professional tour and was shown by another tour player how to vomit to maintain her weight. Her binging and purging contributed to an early end to her career.

A Health Canada study reveals the extent of the problem (Health Canada, 2002b). Eating disorders are more prevalent in women than men, affecting approximately 3 percent of Canadian women sometime in their lifetime. In Canada, since 1987, the rate of hospitalization for eating disorders has increased dramatically for young (under 15) and older (15–24 years) females alike (up 34 percent and 29 percent, respectively). As we will detail in Chapter 14, a variety of factors have been implicated in the occurrence of eating disorders, including biological, psychological, developmental, and social factors such as the overemphasis on idealized thin images (Polivy et al., 2003) and the pressure to be thin associated with various sports and professions. The impact of idealized thin images on an individual's body image is of particular importance for women (Grabe, Ward, & Hyde, 2008).

There are a variety of public and private treatment programs and support groups available in Canada. You can visit some of these through their websites, including the National Eating Disorder Information Centre (http://www.nedic.ca).

REVIEW OF KEY POINTS

▶ Drive theories apply a homeostatic model to motivation. They assume that organisms seek to reduce unpleasant states of tension called *drives*. In contrast, incentive theories emphasize how external goals energize behaviour.

▶ Evolutionary theorists explain motives in terms of their adaptive value. Madsen's list of biological needs and Murray's list of social needs illustrate that a diverse array of motives govern human behaviour.

▶ In the brain, the lateral and ventromedial areas of the hypothalamus were once viewed as on–off centres for the control of hunger. But that model proved to be an oversimplification. The arcuate and paraventricular areas and neural circuits may be more important.

▶ Fluctuations in blood glucose also seem to play a role in hunger. Hormonal regulation of hunger depends primarily on insulin, ghrelin, CCK, and leptin.

▶ Incentive-oriented models assert that eating is regulated by the availability and palatability of food. Learning processes, such as classical conditioning and observational learning, exert a great deal of influence over both what people eat and how much they eat. Cultural traditions also shape food preferences.

▶ Evidence indicates that there is a genetic predisposition to obesity. Weight problems occur when people eat too much in relation to their exercise level. Schachter theorized that obese people are extra sensitive to external cues that trigger eating. Although the externality hypothesis was oversimplified, obese individuals may be especially sensitive to sensory food cues. Research suggests that the body monitors fat stores to keep them fairly stable.

▶ Weight problems occur when people eat too much in relation to their exercise level. According to set-point theory, the body monitors fat stores to keep them fairly stable. Settling-point theory suggests that a multitude of factors contribute to weight stability. Vacillations in dietary restraint resulting in disinhibition may contribute to obesity in some people.

▶ Weight problems may also be manifested as eating disorders such as anorexia nervosa and bulimia nervosa. These disorders, which are more prevalent in women than in men, have a variety of causes.

Sexual Motivation and Behaviour

PREVIEW QUESTIONS

▶ What are the phases of the human sexual response?

▶ What has evolutionary-oriented research revealed about gender differences in sexual activity and mating preferences?

▶ How do erotic materials affect sexual behaviour?

How does sex resemble food? Sometimes it seems that people are obsessed with both. People joke and gossip about sex constantly. Magazines, novels, movies, and television shows are saturated with sexual activity and innuendo. The advertising industry uses sex to sell everything from mouthwash to designer jeans to automobiles. This intense interest in sex reflects the importance of sexual motivation.

Sex is clearly on people's minds. Children begin to experiment with sex as they enter their teens. Surveys

and reports by the Canadian Council of Ministers of Education (2003), the Public Health Agency of Canada (2003a, 2003b), and Statistics Canada (2005f) give us some insight into the sexual activities of Canadian teens and young adults. Approximately 28 percent of 15–17-year-olds report engaging in sexual intercourse, with the rate increasing to 80 percent for Canadians 20–24 years of age. In that age range, one-third of those who are sexually active report having more than one sexual partner in the previous year. Those who first have sexual intercourse by age 13 are more likely to have multiple sex partners than those who begin later. Girls with weak self-concepts at 13 are more likely than those with strong self-concepts to engage in sex early.

In this section, we will examine the physiology of the human sexual response, review evolutionary analyses of human sexual motivation, discuss some controversies surrounding pornography, and analyze the roots of sexual orientation.

The Human Sexual Response

Assuming people are motivated to engage in sexual activity, exactly what happens to them physically? This may sound like a simple question. But scientists really knew very little about the physiology of the human sexual response before William Masters and Virginia Johnson did groundbreaking research in the 1960s. Although our society seems obsessed with sex, until relatively recently (the 1980s) it did not encourage scientists to study sex. At first Masters and Johnson even had difficulty finding journals that were willing to publish their studies.

Masters and Johnson used physiological recording devices to monitor the bodily changes of volunteers engaging in sexual activities. They even equipped an artificial penile device with a camera to study physiological reactions inside the vagina. Their observations of, and interviews with, subjects yielded a detailed description of the human sexual response that eventually won them widespread acclaim.

Masters and Johnson (1966, 1970) divide the sexual response cycle into four stages: excitement, plateau, orgasm, and resolution. Figure 10.7 shows how the intensity of sexual arousal changes as women and men progress through these stages. Let's take a closer look at these phases in the human sexual response.

Excitement Phase

During the first phase of excitement, the level of physical arousal usually rises rapidly. In both sexes, muscle tension, respiration rate, heart rate, and blood pressure increase quickly. *Vasocongestion—engorgement of blood vessels—*produces penile erection and swollen testes in males. In females, vasocongestion leads to a swelling and hardening of the clitoris, expansion of the vaginal lips, and vaginal lubrication.

Plateau Phase

During the plateau phase, physiological arousal usually continues to build, but at a much slower pace.

In women, further vasocongestion produces a tightening of the vaginal entrance, as the clitoris withdraws under the clitoral hood. Many men secrete a bit of fluid at the tip of the penis. This is not ejaculate, but it may contain sperm. When foreplay is lengthy, fluctuation in arousal is normal for both sexes. This fluctuation is more apparent in men. Erections may increase and decrease noticeably. In women, this fluctuation may be reflected in changes in vaginal lubrication.

Orgasm Phase

Orgasm occurs when sexual arousal reaches its peak intensity. It discharges in a series of muscular contractions that pulsate through the pelvic area. Heart rate, respiration rate, and blood pressure increase sharply during this exceedingly pleasant spasmodic response. In males, orgasm is accompanied by ejaculation of the seminal fluid. The subjective experience of orgasm appears to be very similar for men and women.

However, there *are* some interesting gender differences in the orgasm phase of the sexual response

William Masters and Virginia Johnson

"The conviction has grown that the most effective treatment of sexual incompatibility involves the technique of working with both members of the family unit."

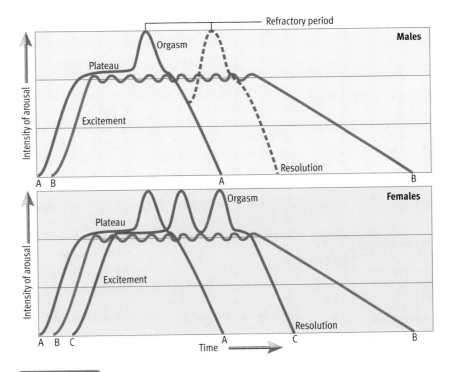

FIGURE 10.7

The human sexual response cycle.

There are similarities and differences between men and women in patterns of sexual arousal. Pattern A, which culminates in orgasm and resolution, is the ideal sequence for both sexes but not something one can count on. Pattern B, which involves sexual arousal without orgasm followed by a slow resolution, is seen in both sexes but is more common among women (see Figure 10.8). Pattern C, which involves multiple orgasms, is seen almost exclusively in women, as men go through a refractory period before they are capable of another orgasm.

Source: Based on Masters, W. H., and Johnson, V. E. (1966). *Human sexual response*. Boston: Little, Brown. Copyright © 1966 Little, Brown and Company.

Motivation and Emotion

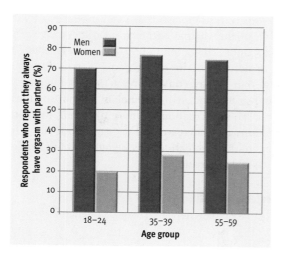

FIGURE 10.8

The gender gap in orgasm consistency.

In their sexual interactions, men seem to reach orgasm more reliably than women. The data shown here suggest that the gender gap in orgasmic consistency is pretty sizable. Both biological and sociocultural factors may contribute to this gender gap. (Data from Laumann et al., 1994)

cycle. On the one hand, women are more likely than men to be *multiorgasmic*. A woman is said to be multiorgasmic if she experiences more than one climax in a sexual encounter (pattern C in Figure 10.7). On the other hand, women are more likely than men to engage in intercourse without experiencing an orgasm. When respondents are asked whether they *always* have an orgasm with their partner, the gender gap in orgasmic consistency looks rather large. For example, among respondents aged 35–39, Laumann et al. (1994) found that 78 percent of men, but only 28 percent of women reported always having an orgasm. However, a recent, major survey of sexual behaviour approached the issue in a different way and found a smaller gender gap. Herbenick and colleagues (2010) asked respondents about many of the details of their *most recent sexual interaction* (what they did, how pleasurable it was, whether they had an orgasm, and so forth). Men were more likely to report having an orgasm, but the disparity was not as huge as when respondents were asked about always having an orgasm.

Whether this gender gap reflects attitudes and sexual practices versus physiological processes is open to debate. On the one hand, it's easy to argue that males' greater orgasmic consistency must be a product of evolution. It would have obvious adaptive significance for promoting men's reproductive fitness. On the other hand, gender differences in the socialization of guilt feelings about sex, as well as sexual scripts and practices that are less than optimal for women could play a part (Lott, 1987). Another consideration is that orgasm consistency seems to be influenced by relationship quality more in women than in men. Consistent with this analysis, one recent study found a correlation of 0.43 between the intensity of heterosexual

women's love for their partner and their ease in reaching orgasm (Ortigue, Grafton, & Bianchi-Demicheli, 2007).

Resolution Phase

During the resolution phase, the physiological changes produced by sexual arousal subside. If orgasm has not occurred, the reduction in sexual tension may be relatively slow and sometimes unpleasant. After orgasm, men experience a *refractory period,* a time following orgasm during which males are largely unresponsive to further stimulation. The length of the refractory period varies from a few minutes to a few hours and increases with age.

Evolutionary Analyses of Human Sexual Behaviour

As you have already seen in previous chapters, the relatively new evolutionary perspective in psychology has generated intriguing hypotheses related to a host of topics, including perception, learning, language, and problem solving. However, evolutionary theorists' analyses of sexual behaviour have drawn the most attention. Obviously, the task of explaining sexual behaviour is crucial to the evolutionary perspective, given its fundamental thesis that natural selection is fuelled by variations in reproductive success. The thinking in this area has been guided by Robert Trivers's (1972) *parental investment theory*, which maintains that a species' mating patterns depend on what each sex has to invest—in terms of time, energy, and survival risk—to produce and nurture offspring. According to Trivers, *the sex that makes the smaller investment will compete for mating opportunities with the sex that makes the larger investment, and the sex with the larger investment will tend to be more discriminating in selecting its partners.* Let's look at how this analysis applies to humans.

Like many mammalian species, human males are *required* to invest little in the production of offspring beyond the act of copulation, so their reproductive potential is maximized by mating with as many females as possible. The situation for females is quite different. Females have to invest nine months in pregnancy, and our female ancestors typically had to devote at least several additional years to nourishing offspring through breastfeeding. These realities place a ceiling on the number of offspring women can produce, regardless of how many males they mate with. Hence, females have little or no incentive for mating with many males. Instead,

WEB LINK 10.2

The Evolutionary Psychology FAQ
Maintained by Edward Hagen (Institute for Theoretical Biology, Humboldt University, Berlin), this site provides answers to a host of controversial questions on the subject of evolutionary psychology. Covered questions include: What is an adaptation? How can we identify psychological adaptations? Is evolutionary psychology sexist? If my genes made me do it, am I still responsible? Why do some people hate evolutionary psychology?

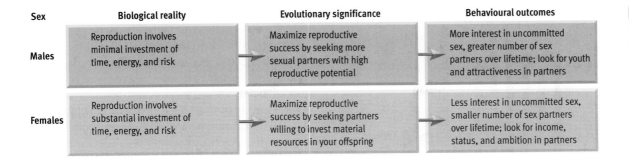

Sex	Biological reality	Evolutionary significance	Behavioural outcomes
Males	Reproduction involves minimal investment of time, energy, and risk	Maximize reproductive success by seeking more sexual partners with high reproductive potential	More interest in uncommitted sex, greater number of sex partners over lifetime; look for youth and attractiveness in partners
Females	Reproduction involves substantial investment of time, energy, and risk	Maximize reproductive success by seeking partners willing to invest material resources in your offspring	Less interest in uncommitted sex, smaller number of sex partners over lifetime; look for income, status, and ambition in partners

FIGURE 10.9

Parental investment theory and mating preferences.

Parental investment theory suggests that basic differences between males and females in parental investment have great adaptive significance and lead to gender differences in mating propensities and preferences, as outlined here.

females can optimize their reproductive potential by being selective in mating. Thus, in humans, males are thought to compete with other males for the relatively scarce and valuable "commodity" of reproductive opportunities.

Parental investment theory predicts that in comparison to women, men will show more interest in sexual activity, more desire for variety in sexual partners, and more willingness to engage in uncommitted sex (see Figure 10.9). In contrast, females are thought to be the conservative, discriminating sex that is highly selective in choosing partners. This selectivity supposedly entails seeking partners who have the greatest ability to contribute toward feeding and caring for offspring. Why? Because in the world of our ancient ancestors, males' greater strength and agility would have been crucial assets in the never-ending struggle to find food and shelter and defend one's territory. A female who chose a mate who was lazy or unreliable or who had no hunting, fighting, building, farming, or other useful economic skills would have suffered a substantial disadvantage in her efforts to raise her children and pass on her genes.

Gender Differences in Patterns of Sexual Activity

Consistent with evolutionary theory, males generally show a greater interest in sex than females do (Peplau, 2003). Men think about sex (see Figure 10.10) more often than women do (Laumann et al., 1994). They also initiate sex more often (Morokoff et al., 1997). Males have more frequent and varied sexual fantasies (Okami & Shackelford, 2001). Their subjective ratings of their sex drive tend to be higher than females' (Ostovich & Sabini, 2004). Men also tend to overestimate women's sexual interest in them (a cognitive bias not shared by women). This bias seems designed to ensure that males do not overlook sexual opportunities (Buss, 2001; Levesque, Nave, & Lowe, 2006). When heterosexual couples are asked about their sex lives, male partners are more likely than their female counterparts to report that they would like to have

sex more frequently. The findings of a recent study suggest that this disparity in sexual motivation only widens when people reach middle age (Lindau & Gavrilova, 2010). In the 55–64 age bracket, 62 percent of men, but only 38 percent of women report that they are still very interested in sex.

Men also are more motivated than women to pursue sex with a variety of partners (McBurney, Zapp, & Streeter, 2005). Buss and Schmitt (1993) found that college men indicate that they would ideally like to have 18 sex partners across their lives, whereas college women report that they would prefer only five partners. Similar findings were observed in a follow-up study (see Figure 10.11) that examined desire for sexual variety in over 16 000 subjects from ten major regions of the world (Schmitt et al., 2003). Males expressed a desire for more partners than

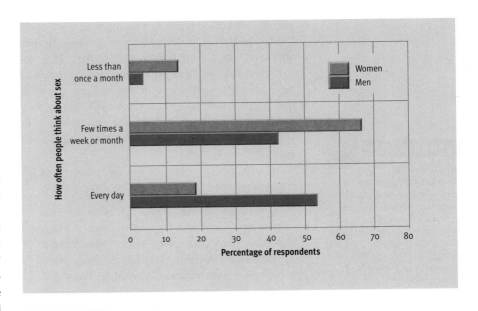

FIGURE 10.10

The gender gap in how much people think about sex.

This graph summarizes data on how often males and females think about sex, based on a large-scale survey by Laumann et al. (1994). As evolutionary theorists would predict, based on parental investment theory, males seem to manifest more interest in sexual activity than their female counterparts do. (Data from Laumann et al., 1994)

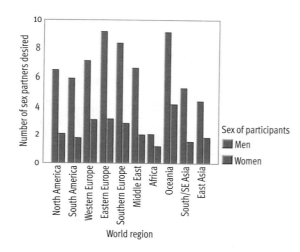

FIGURE 10.11

The gender gap in desire for a variety of sexual partners.
Schmitt et al. (2003) gathered cross-cultural data on gender disparities in the number of sex partners desired by people. Respondents were asked about how many sexual partners they ideally would like to have in the next 30 years. As evolutionary theorists would predict, males reported that they would like to have more sexual partners in all ten world regions examined.

Source: Schmitt, D.P., and 118 Members of the International Sexuality Description Project. (2003). Universal sex differences in the desire for sexual variety: Tests from 52 nations, 6 continents, and 13 islands. *Journal of Personality and Social Psychology, 85*, 85–104. Copyright © 2003 by the American Psychological Association. Reprinted by permission.

WEB LINK 10.3

Alice! Health Promotion Program
One of the longest-standing and most popular sources of frank information on the Internet has been *Alice!* from Columbia University's Health Education Program. Geared especially to the needs of undergraduate students, the site offers direct answers to questions about relationships, sexuality and sexual health, alcohol and drug consumption, emotional health, and general health.

females in all ten world regions. In most cases, the differences were substantial.

Clear gender disparities are also seen in regard to people's willingness to engage in casual or uncommitted sex. For example, in a compelling field study, Clark and Hatfield (1989) had average-looking men approach female (college-age) strangers and ask if they would go back to the man's apartment to have sex with him. None of the women agreed to this proposition. But when Clark and Hatfield had average-looking women approach males with the same proposition, 75 percent of the men eagerly agreed!

In a definitive review of the empirical evidence, Roy Baumeister and colleagues (2001a) conclude,

Across many different studies and measures, men have been shown to have more frequent and more intense sexual desires than women, as reflected in spontaneous thoughts about sex, frequency and variety of sexual fantasies, desired frequency of intercourse, desired number of partners, masturbation, liking for various sexual practices, willingness to forgo sex, and other measures. No contrary findings (indicating stronger sexual motivation among women) were found (p. 242).

That said, evidence suggests that the sexual disparities between males and females may be exaggerated a little by reliance on subjects' self-reports (Alexander & Fisher, 2003). Because of the "double standard" regarding sexuality, women worry more than men about being viewed as sexually permissive, which may lead them to underestimate or downplay their sexual motivation (Crawford & Popp, 2003).

Gender Differences in Mate Preferences

According to evolutionary theorists, if males had been left to their own devices over the course of history, they probably would have shown relatively little interest in long-term mating commitments, but females have generally demanded long-term commitments from males as part of consenting to sex (Buss, 1994a). As a result, long-term mating commitments are a normal part of the social landscape in human societies. However, parental investment theory suggests that there should be some glaring disparities between men and women in what they look for in a long-term mate (consult Figure 10.9 on page 455 again).

The adaptive problem for our male ancestors was to find a female with good reproductive potential who would be sexually faithful and effective in nurturing children. Given these needs, evolutionary theory predicts that men should place more emphasis than women on partner characteristics such as youthfulness (which allows for more reproductive years) and attractiveness (which is assumed to be correlated with health and fertility). In contrast, the adaptive problem for our female ancestors was to find a male who could provide material resources and protect his family and who was dependable and willing to invest his resources in his family. Given these needs, evolutionary theory predicts that women should place more emphasis than men on partner characteristics such as intelligence, ambition, income, and social status (which are associated with the ability to provide more material resources).

Evolutionary theorists are quick to point out that these differing priorities *do not reflect conscious strategies*. For the most part, people do not think about sex in terms of maximizing their reproductive potential. Instead, these different priorities are viewed as subconscious preferences that have been hard-wired into the human brain by evolutionary forces. In any event, if these evolutionary analyses of sexual motivation are on the mark, gender differences in mating preferences should be virtually universal and thus transcend culture.

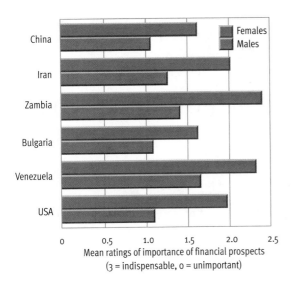

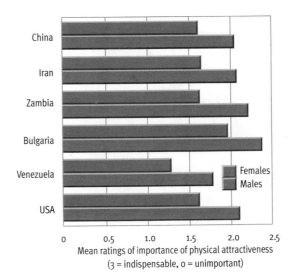

FIGURE 10.12

Gender and potential mates' financial prospects.

Consistent with evolutionary theory, Buss (1989) found that females place more emphasis on potential partners' financial prospects than males do. Moreover, he found that this trend transcends culture. The specific results for 6 of the 37 cultures studies by Buss are shown here. (Based on data from Buss, 1989).

FIGURE 10.13

Gender and potential mates' physical attractiveness.

Consistent with evolutionary theory, Buss (1989) found that all over the world, males place more emphasis on potential partners' good looks than females do. The specific results for 6 of the 37 cultures studies by Buss are shown here. (Based on data from Buss, 1989)

To test this hypothesis, David Buss (1989) and 50 scientists from around the world surveyed more than 10 000 people from 37 cultures about what they looked for in a mate. As predicted by parental investment theory, they found that women placed a higher value than men on potential partners' status, ambition, and financial prospects (see Figure 10.12). These priorities were not limited to industrialized or capitalist countries; they were apparent in Third World cultures, socialist countries, and all varieties of economic systems. In contrast, men around the world consistently showed more interest than women in potential partners' youthfulness and physical attractiveness (see Figure 10.13).

A host of studies, using diverse samples and a variety of research methods, have replicated the disparities between males and females in mating priorities and preferences (Neuberg, Kenrick, & Schaller, 2010; Shackelford, Schmitt, & Buss, 2005; Schmitt, 2005). Recent research also supports the notion that women pay more attention than men do to a potential partner's willingness to invest in children (Brase, 2006). The gender gap on this dimension occurs because men appear to be largely indifferent to females' potential for parental investment. Moreover, the same study showed that men who were perceived to be favourably disposed to investing in children were judged to be more attractive by women. That brings us to another fascinating study of women's perceptions of men's mating potential that will serve as our Featured Study for this chapter.

Investigators: J. R. Roney, K. N. Hanson, K. M. Durante, & D. Maestripieri
Source: Reading men's faces: Women's mate attractiveness judgments track men's testosterone and interest in infants. *Proceedings of the Royal Society of London B*, 2006, *273*, 2169–2175.

FEATURED STUDY

Can Women Judge Men's Mate Potential in Just One Glance?

According to evolutionary theories, human females can improve their reproductive fitness by seeking male partners who have access to material resources and who show a willingness to invest in children. And females can enhance their chances of passing on their genes by pursuing males who exhibit high masculinity, which is assumed to be a marker for genetic quality and reproductive potential. The present study looked at women's judgments of males' parental investment potential and masculinity, based on nothing more than a snapshot, and the impact of these judgments on women's ratings of males' mate potential. The investigators wanted to know whether women could draw meaningful inferences about males' masculinity and parental potential from facial cues.

Method

Stimulus targets and characteristics. The male stimulus persons were 39 students from the University of Chicago, with a mean age of 21. They were instructed to assume a neutral facial expression while their facial photos were shot from a standard distance. To operationalize their masculinity, saliva samples were taken to measure each stimulus person's testosterone level. To assess their parental investment potential, they each took a test that measured their interest in infants.

Participants and Procedure. The women who rated the men were 29 undergraduates from the University of California, Santa Barbara, with a mean age of 18. These women viewed the photos of the men in a standard order and were asked to rate each for "likes children," "masculine," "physically attractive," and "kind." After the first set of ratings, they were shown all of the photos again and asked to rate each male's mate potential for a short-term and for a long-term romantic relationship.

Results

The women's ratings of the male stimulus persons' masculinity correlated moderately well (0.34) with the males' actual testosterone levels. Likewise, the women's ratings of the degree to which the male stimulus persons liked children correlated (0.38) with the males' scores on the test of interest in infants. The data also showed that women's perceptions of masculinity and parental interest influenced their ratings of the male stimulus persons' mate potential. Higher ratings of masculinity fostered higher estimates of the males' short-term mate potential, whereas higher ratings of parental interest led to higher estimates of long-term mate potential.

Discussion

The authors conclude that "the present study provides the first direct evidence that women's attractiveness judgments specifically track both men's affinity for children and men's hormone concentrations" (p. 2173). They assert that their most interesting finding was the demonstration that women can draw meaningful inferences about males' parental interest based on a brief exposure to a single photograph.

Comment

A description of this study in the *Chicago Tribune* captured the essence of its remarkable findings: "Just from looking at a man's face, women can sense how much he likes children, gauge his testosterone level and decide whether he would be more suitable as a one-night stand or as a husband" (Gorner, 2006). Given the modest magnitude of the correlations observed that is a bit of an overstatement, but the study did provide fascinating new evidence that humans may subconsciously register subtle features of potential mates that are relevant to enhancing reproductive fitness, as predicted by evolutionary theory.

Criticism and Alternative Explanations

So, the findings on gender differences in sexual behaviour and mating priorities mesh nicely with predictions derived from evolutionary theory. But, evolutionary theory has its share of critics. Some skeptics argue that there are alternative explanations for the findings. For example, women's emphasis on males' material resources could be a by-product of cultural and economic forces rather than the result of biological imperatives (Eagly & Wood, 1999). Women may have learned to value males' economic clout because their own economic potential has historically been limited in virtually all cultures (Hrdy, 1997; Kasser & Sharma, 1999). In a similar vein, Roy Baumeister, has argued that the gender disparity in sexual motivation may be largely attributable to extensive cultural processes that serve to suppress female sexuality (Baumeister & Twenge, 2002). Evolutionary theorists counter these arguments by pointing out that the cultural and economic processes at work may themselves be products of evolution.

The Controversial Issue of Pornography

According to some social critics, we live in the golden age of pornography. As Strager (2003, p. 50) puts it, "Following the proliferation of video and the dawn of the Internet, never has so much pornography been available to so many so easily." One recent study of young adults found that 87 percent of men and 31 percent of women had viewed pornography (Carroll et al., 2008). The same study reported that 67 percent of males and 49 percent of females believed using porn was an "acceptable way to express one's sexuality." What effects do erotic photographs and films have on sexual desire? Laboratory studies show that erotic materials stimulate sexual desire in many people (Geer & Janssen, 2000). Generally speaking, men are more likely than women to report that they find erotic materials enjoyable and arousing (Gardos & Mosher, 1999; Koukounas & McCabe, 1997). However, this finding may partly reflect the fact that the vast majority of erotic materials are scripted to appeal to males and often portray women in degrading roles that elicit negative reactions from female viewers (Mosher & MacIan, 1994; Pearson & Pollack, 1997).

Historically, legal authorities have expressed great concern that pornography might incite sex crimes. The issue has been the subject of heated debate. However, efforts to find a link between the prevalence of erotica and sex crime rates have largely yielded negative results. Studies have not found correlations between greater availability of pornography and elevated rates of sex crimes (Diamond, 2009; Ferguson & Hartley, 2009). During the last 15–20 years the availability of Internet porn has grown exponentially, while rates of reported rapes have declined considerably in the United States (Ferguson & Hartley, 2009). Most male sex offenders admit to a history of using pornographic materials, but so do most males who are not sex offenders. The data show that sex offenders typically do not have earlier or more extensive exposure to pornography in childhood or adolescence than other people (Bauserman, 1996). Thus, pornography appears to play a minor role, if any, in fuelling sexual offences (Langevin & Curnoe, 2004).

Although erotic materials don't appear to incite overpowering sexual urges, they may alter *attitudes* in ways that eventually influence sexual behaviour. Zillmann and Bryant (1984) found that male and female undergraduates exposed to a large dose of pornography (three or six films per week for six weeks) developed more liberal attitudes about sexual practices. For example, they came to view premarital and extramarital sex as more acceptable. In a similar vein, Carroll et al. (2008) found a correlation between acceptance of pornography and more liberal attitudes about casual sex and a history of more sex partners in both young men and women. Hald and Malamuth (2008) examined young Danish adults' self-perceptions of how pornography use had affected the quality of their sex lives. Both sexes reported more positive effects on their sexual knowledge and attitudes than negative effects.

Nonetheless, research on *aggressive pornography* has raised some serious concerns about its effects. Aggressive pornography typically depicts violence against women. Many films show women who gradually give in to and enjoy rape and other sexually degrading acts after some initial resistance. Some studies indicate that this type of material increases male subjects' aggressive behaviour toward women, at least in the context of the research laboratory (Donnerstein & Malamuth, 1997; Hald, Malamuth, & Yeun, 2010; Vega & Malamuth, 2007). In the typical study, male subjects work on a laboratory task and are led to believe (falsely) that they are delivering electric shocks to other subjects. In this situation, their aggression toward females tends to be elevated after exposure to aggressive pornography. Exposure to aggressive pornography may also make sexual coercion seem less offensive and help perpetuate the myth that women enjoy being raped and ravaged (Allen et al., 1995). And these attitudes can influence actual behaviour. Research suggests that males who believe that "women who are raped asked for it" are more likely than others to commit sexual assault (Bohner, Siebler, & Schmelcher, 2006; Chiroro et al., 2004).

The effects of aggressive pornography are especially worrisome in light of evidence about rape. It is difficult to obtain accurate information about the prevalence of rape because only a minority of victims make reports to authorities (Fisher et al., 2003). Despite extensive rape prevention efforts, the incidence of rape appears to be unchanged (Rozee & Koss, 2001). Estimates suggest that as many as one-quarter of young women in North America may be victims of rape or attempted rape (Campbell & Wasco, 2005; Koss, 1993). In Canada, statistics indicate that sexual assaults are declining somewhat but that the numbers are still frightening; in 1999, there were approximately 24 000 sexual assaults reported to police in Canada (Statistics Canada, 1999a).

David Buss

"Evolutionary psychologists develop hypotheses about the psychological mechanisms that have evolved in humans to solve particular adaptive problems that humans have faced under ancestral conditions."

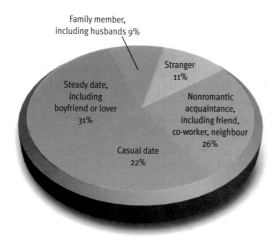

FIGURE 10.14

Rape victim–offender relationships.

Based on a national survey of 3187 U.S. college women, Mary Koss and her colleagues (1987) identified a sample of 468 women who indicated that they had been victims of rape and who provided information on their relationship to the offender. Contrary to the prevailing stereotype, only a small minority (11 percent) of these women were raped by a stranger. As you can see, many of the women were raped by men they were dating. (Based on data from Koss, Gidycz, & Wisniewski, 1987)

PREVIEW QUESTIONS

▶ Is sexual orientation an either–or distinction?

▶ How common is homosexuality?

▶ How have theorists explained the development of homosexuality?

Only a minority of reported rapes are committed by strangers (Rand, 2008; see Figure 10.14). Particularly common is *date rape,* which occurs when a woman is forced to have sex in the context of dating. Research suggests that victim–offender relationships are an important consideration (Ulman, et al., 2006) and that date rape is a serious problem on college campuses (Banyard et al., 2005). In one survey of students at 32 colleges and universities, one in seven women reported that they had been victimized by date rape or an attempted date rape (Koss, Gidycz, & Wisniewski, 1987). Moreover, one in 12 men admitted either to having forced a date into sex or to having tried to do so. However, *none* of these men identified himself as a rapist. Even more surprising, research has found that about half of women who report an experience that qualifies as rape do not label themselves as rape victims (McMullin & While, 2006). While acknowledging that statistics are difficult to obtain, the Public Health Agency of Canada found that between 16 percent and 35 percent of women surveyed reported at least one physical assault by a dating partner (Public Health Agency of Canada, n.d.). Although other factors are surely at work, many theorists, such as Neil Malamuth, who conducted much of his research at the University of Manitoba, believe that aggressive pornography has contributed to this failure to see sexual coercion for what it is (Kingston et al., 2009: Malamuth, Addison, & Koss, 2000).

REVIEW OF KEY POINTS

▷ The human sexual response cycle can be divided into four stages: excitement, plateau, orgasm, and resolution. The subjective experience of orgasm is fairly similar for both sexes. Intercourse leads to orgasm in women less consistently than in men. However, women are much more likely to be multiorgasmic.

▷ According to parental investment theory, males are thought to compete with other males for reproductive opportunities and females are assumed to be the discriminating sex that is selective in choosing partners. Consistent with evolutionary theory, males tend to think about and initiate sex more than females do and to have more sexual partners and more interest in casual sex than do females.

▷ Gender differences in mating preferences appear to largely transcend cultural boundaries. Males emphasize potential partners' youthfulness and attractiveness, whereas females emphasize potential partners' status and financial prospects. As our Featured Study showed, women also pay attention to males' willingness to invest in children and their masculinity, which is viewed as a marker for genetic quality.

▷ Research has considered the effects of erotic and aggressive pornography on sexual behaviour and attitudes, and their links to increased rape and sexual assault. Research conducted to date suggests links between viewing erotic material, especially aggressive pornography, and attitudes toward rape and sexual coercion.

The Mystery of Sexual Orientation

Sex must be a contentious topic, as the controversy swirling around evolutionary explanations of gender differences in sexuality is easily equalled by the controversy surrounding the determinants of *sexual orientation. Sexual orientation* refers to a person's preference for emotional and sexual relationships with individuals of the same sex, the other sex, or either sex. *Heterosexuals* seek emotional–sexual relationships with members of the other sex, *bisexuals* with members of either sex, and *homosexuals* with members of the same sex. In recent years, the terms *gay* and *straight* have become widely used to refer to homosexuals and heterosexuals, respectively. Although *gay* can refer to homosexuals of either sex, most homosexual women prefer to call themselves *lesbians.*

The controversy surrounding sexual orientation is particularly current in Canada. It was not so long ago (1965, in fact) that the Supreme Court of Canada upheld a lower court ruling that Everett Klippert be labelled a "dangerous offender" and imprisoned after he admitted to being gay and having sex with other

Singer Elton John married his partner of 11 years, David Furnish, after England's same-sex marriage law went into effect in December 2005.

16.5 percent of those same-sex couples were married (Statistics Canada, 2007b). One high-profile same-sex marriage in England was that of a Canadian, David Furnish, who married singer Elton John after England's same-sex marriage law went into effect in December 2005 (Elton John, 2005). Not everyone agrees on the factors affecting sexual orientation and, of course, not everyone supports this social trend. One index of this may be the higher rates of victimization reported by gays, lesbians, and bisexuals in Canada as compared to the rates reported by heterosexuals (Statistics Canada, 2008c).

People tend to view heterosexuality and homosexuality as an all-or-none distinction. However, in a large-scale survey of sexual behaviour, Alfred Kinsey and his colleagues (1948, 1953) discovered that many people who define themselves as heterosexuals have had homosexual experiences—and vice versa. Thus, Kinsey and others have concluded that it is more accurate to view heterosexuality and homosexuality as endpoints on a continuum (Haslam, 1997). Indeed, Kinsey devised a seven-point scale, shown in Figure 10.15, that can be used to characterize individuals' sexual orientation.

How common is homosexuality? No one knows for sure. Part of the problem is that this question is vastly more complex than it appears at first glance (LeVay, 1996; Savin-Williams, 2006). Given that sexual orientation is best represented as a continuum, where do you draw the lines between heterosexuality, bisexuality, and homosexuality? And how do you handle the distinction between overt behaviour and desire? Where, for instance, do you put a person who is married and has never engaged in homosexual behaviour but who reports homosexual fantasies and acknowledges being strongly drawn to members of the same sex?

males. He was finally released in 1971. In 1967, Pierre Elliott Trudeau, then the federal Justice minister, proposed an amendment to the Criminal Code that would relax the laws against homosexuality. It was passed in 1969 and began the process of the decriminalization of homosexuality (Same-Sex Rights, 2005). In 2005, the Liberal government of Paul Martin tabled legislation that would make it legal for same-sex couples to marry. The legislation was passed on June 28, 2005, and became law on July 20, 2005.

Figures from the most recent Canadian census indicate that the number of same-sex couples increased by over 30 percent between 2001 and 2006 and, reflecting the new 2005 legislation, that

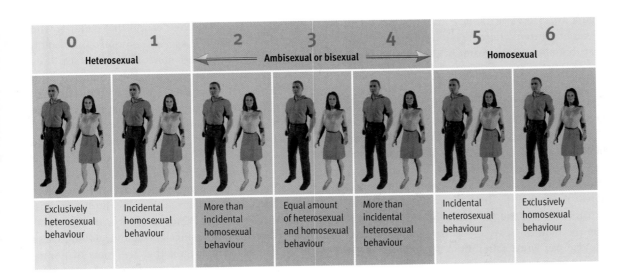

FIGURE 10.15

Homosexuality and heterosexuality as endpoints on a continuum.

Sex researchers view heterosexuality and homosexuality as falling on a continuum rather than making an all-or-none distinction. Kinsey and his associates (1948, 1953) created this seven-point scale (from 0 to 6) to describe people's sexual orientation. They used the term *ambisexual* to describe those who fall in the middle of the scale, but such people are commonly called *bisexual* today.

Motivation and Emotion

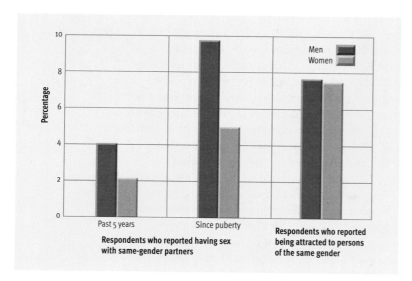

Both biological and environmental factors appear to contribute to homosexuality, although its precise developmental roots remain obscure.

FIGURE 10.16

How common is homosexuality?

The answer to this question is both complex and controversial. Michaels (1996) brought together data from two large-scale surveys to arrive at the estimates shown here. If you look at how many people have actually had a same-sex partner in the last five years, the figures are relatively low, but if you count those who have had a same-sex partner since puberty, the figures more than double. Still another way to look at it is to ask people whether they are attracted to people of the same sex (regardless of their actual behaviour). This approach suggests that about 8 percent of the population could be characterized as homosexual. (Data from Michaels, 1996)

WEB LINK 10.4

Queer Resources Directory (QRD)

In its mission statement, the *Queer Resources Directory* describes itself as "an electronic research library specifically dedicated to sexual minorities—groups that have traditionally been labeled as 'queer' and systematically discriminated against." Composed of more than 25 000 files and still growing, QRD offers a rich array of resources.

The other part of the problem is that many people have extremely prejudicial attitudes about homosexuality, which makes gays cautious and reluctant to give candid information about their sexuality (Herek, 2000, 2009). Small wonder then that estimates of the portion of the population that is homosexual vary pretty widely. A frequently cited estimate of the number of people who are gay is 10 percent, but some surveys suggest that this percentage may be an overestimate. Michaels (1996) has combined data from two of the better large-scale surveys in recent years to arrive at the estimates shown in Figure 10.16. As you can see, the numbers are open to varying interpretations, but as a whole they suggest that about 5–8 percent of the population could reasonably be characterized as homosexual.

Environmental Theories

Over the years, many environmental theories have been floated to explain the origins of homosexuality, but when tested empirically, these theories have garnered remarkably little support. For example, psychoanalytic and behavioural theorists, who usually agree on very little, both proposed environmental explanations for the development of homosexuality. The Freudian theorists argued that a male is likely to become gay when raised by a weak, detached, ineffectual father who is a poor heterosexual role model and by an overprotective, close-binding mother with whom the boy identifies. Behavioural theorists argued that homosexuality is a learned preference acquired when same-sex stimuli have been paired with sexual arousal, perhaps through chance seductions by adult homosexuals. Extensive research on homosexuals' upbringing and childhood experiences have failed to support either of these theories (Bell, Weinberg, & Hammersmith, 1981). Similarly, there is no evidence that parents' sexual orientation is linked to that of their children (Patterson, 2003). That is, homosexual parents are no more likely to produce homosexual offspring than heterosexual parents are.

However, efforts to research homosexuals' personal histories have yielded a number of interesting insights. Extremely feminine behaviour in young boys or masculine behaviour in young girls does predict the subsequent development of homosexuality (Bailey & Zucker, 1995; Bem, 2000). Recently, Rieger and colleagues (2008) asked homosexual and heterosexual adults to supply childhood home videos. Independent judges were asked to rate how gender nonconforming the young children were in the videos. The researchers found that children who would eventually identify as homosexual in adulthood were more gender nonconforming than those who identified as heterosexual. This finding held for both males and females. Consistent with this finding, most gay men and women report that they can trace their homosexual leanings back to their early childhood, even before they understood what sex was really about (Bailey, 2003). Most also report that because of negative parental and societal attitudes about homosexuality, they initially struggled to deny their sexual orientation. Hence, they felt that their homosexuality was not a matter of choice and not something that they could readily change (Breedlove, 1994). These findings obviously suggest that the roots of homosexuality are more biological than environmental.

Biological Theories

Despite indications that biology plays a greater role in homosexuality than environment, initial efforts to find a biological basis for homosexuality met with little success. We do know that there is evidence that gay males process some types of information differently than do heterosexual males and, according to neuroscientist Jennifer Steeves and her colleagues (Brewster, Mullin, Dobrin, & Steeves, 2010), differences in brain laterality may be implicated in this difference in processing. However, at this point, we do not know a great deal about the origin of these differences.

Most theorists originally assumed that hormonal differences between heterosexuals and homosexuals must underlie a person's sexual orientation (Doerr et al., 1976; Dorner, 1988). However, studies comparing circulating hormone levels in gays and straights found only small, inconsistent differences that could not be linked to sexual orientation in any convincing way (Bailey, 2003; Banks & Gartrell, 1995).

Thus, like environmental theorists, biological theorists were stymied for quite a while in their efforts to explain the roots of homosexuality. However, that picture changed in the 1990s when a pair of behavioural genetics studies reported findings suggesting that homosexuality has a hereditary basis. In the first study, conducted by Bailey and Pillard (1991), the subjects were gay men who had either a twin brother or an adopted brother. They found that 52 percent of the subjects' identical twins were gay, that 22 percent of their fraternal twins were gay, and that 11 percent of their adoptive brothers were gay. A companion study (Bailey et al., 1993) of lesbians yielded a similar pattern of results (see Figure 10.17). Given that identical twins share more genetic overlap than fraternal twins, who share more genes than unrelated adoptive siblings, these results suggest that there is a genetic predisposition to homosexuality (see Chapter 3 for an explanation of the logic underlying twin and adoption studies).

Many theorists suspect that the roots of homosexuality may lie in the organizing effects of prenatal hormones on neurological development (Byne, 2007; James, 2005). Several lines of research suggest that hormonal secretions during critical periods of prenatal development may shape sexual development, organize the brain in a lasting manner, and influence subsequent sexual orientation (Berenbaum & Snyder, 1995). For example, researchers have found elevated rates of homosexuality among women exposed to unusually high androgen levels during prenatal development (because their mothers had an adrenal disorder or were given a synthetic hormone to reduce the risk of miscarriage) (Breedlove, 1994; Meyer-Bahlburg et al., 1995). Several other independent lines of research suggest that atypical prenatal hormonal secretions may foster a predisposition to homosexuality (Mustanski, Chivers, & Bailey, 2002).

However, much remains to be learned about the roots of homosexuality. One complication is that the pathways to homosexuality may be somewhat different for males than for females. Females' sexuality appears to be characterized by more *plasticity* than males' sexuality (Baumeister, 2000, 2004). In other words, women's sexual behaviour may be more easily shaped and modified by sociocultural factors. For example, although sexual orientation is assumed to be a stable characteristic, research shows that lesbian and bisexual women often change their

Neuroscientist Jennifer Steeves has examined some of the ways in which gays and heterosexuals differ in terms of their processing of the coding of facial information.

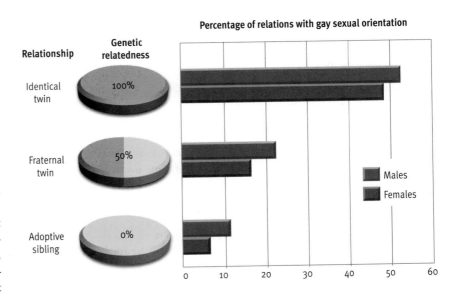

FIGURE 10.17

Genetics and sexual orientation.

If relatives who share more genetic relatedness show greater similarity on a trait than relatives who share less genetic overlap, this evidence suggests a genetic predisposition to the characteristic. Studies of both gay men and lesbian women have found a higher prevalence of homosexuality among their identical twins than among their fraternal twins, who, in turn, are more likely to be homosexual than their adoptive siblings. These findings suggest that genetic factors influence sexual orientation. (Data from Bailey & Pillard, 1991; Bailey et al., 1993)

sexual orientation over the course of their adult years (Diamond, 2003, 2007, 2008). And, in comparison to gay males, lesbians are less likely to trace their homosexuality back to their childhood and more likely to indicate that their attraction to the same sex emerged during adulthood (Tolman & Diamond, 2001). These findings suggest that sexual orientation may be more fluid and malleable in women than in men.

Once again, though, we can see that the nature versus nurture debate can have far-reaching social and political implications. Homosexuals have long been victims of extensive—and, in many instances, legal—discrimination. For example, until quite recently, gays could not legally formalize their unions in marriage in Canada. Other countries, such as the United States, have lagged behind in these areas. However, if research was to show that being gay is largely a matter of biological destiny, much like being female or short, many of the arguments against equal rights for gays would disintegrate.

Although many argue that discrimination against gays should be brought to an end either way, many individuals' opinions about gay rights may be swayed by the outcome of the nature–nurture debate on the roots of homosexuality.

REVIEW OF KEY POINTS

▷ Modern theorists view heterosexuality and homosexuality not as an all-or-none distinction but as endpoints on a continuum. Recent data on the prevalence of homosexuality suggest that 5–8 percent of the population may be gay. Although most gays can trace their homosexual leanings back to early childhood, research has not supported Freudian or behavioural theories of sexual orientation.

▷ Recent studies suggest that there is a genetic predisposition to homosexuality and that some subtle disparities in brain structure may be associated with homosexuality. Idiosyncrasies in prenatal hormonal secretions may also contribute to the development of homosexuality.

Achievement: In Search of Excellence

PREVIEW QUESTIONS

▶ What is the achievement motive, and how is it measured?

▶ How do those who score high in the need for achievement behave?

▶ What are some situational factors that can influence achievement strivings?

Courtesy of David C. McClelland

David McClelland
"People with a high need for achievement are not gamblers; they are challenged to win by personal effort, not by luck."

At the beginning of this chapter, we profiled some of Canada's Olympians. They have endured extraordinary hardships to achieve their goal. What motivates people to push themselves so hard? In all likelihood, it's a strong need for achievement. The *achievement motive is the need to master difficult challenges, to outperform others, and to meet high standards of excellence.* Above all else, the need for achievement involves the desire to excel, especially in competition with others.

David McClelland and his colleagues (McClelland, 1985; McClelland et al., 1953) have been studying the achievement motive for about 40 years. McClelland believes that achievement motivation is of the utmost importance.

McClelland sees the need for achievement as the spark that ignites economic growth, scientific progress, inspirational leadership, and masterpieces in the creative arts. It's difficult to argue with his assertion about the immense importance of achievement motivation. Consider how much poorer our culture would be if people such as Charles Darwin, Nelson Mandela, Thomas Edison, Alexander Graham Bell, Pablo Picasso, Marie Curie, Abraham Lincoln, Mother Teresa, Martin Luther King, and David Suzuki hadn't had a fire burning in their hearts.

Individual Differences in the Need for Achievement

PSYKTREK
8b

In May 2005, Steve Nash achieved what no Canadian before him had ever achieved: He was named the "Most Valuable Player" (MVP) in the National Basketball Association (NBA). Nash went on to win the award two years in a row. He was an undersized player (about 190 cm) in a sport often dominated by much taller players. He struggled to find a college willing to offer him a scholarship so he could refine his skill. He is only the sixth guard in NBA history to be designated MVP. In his first game after achieving this honour, he led his team to a dramatic playoff win over his former team, the Dallas Mavericks, while the crowd chanted "M–V–P" (Smith, 2005). While he is clearly a talented player, other factors were needed to bring him to the top. High among these was his desire to achieve.

The need for achievement is a fairly stable aspect of personality. Hence, research in this area has focused mostly on individual differences in achievement motivation. Subjects' need for achievement can be measured effectively with the *Thematic Apperception*

Canadian Steve Nash, who plays for the Phoenix Suns, was named the NBA's MVP for both the 2004 and in 2005 seasons. Early on, he was never considered to be a top player. He is known for his hard work and dedication to the game. But the contribution of his extremely high need for achievement should not be underestimated. He is known for having pushed himself in order to achieve his goals. In addition to his success on the court, Nash is also well known for his philanthropic work. He was named to the Order of Canada in 2007.

Test (C. P. Smith, 1992; Spangler, 1992). The *Thematic Apperception Test* (TAT) is a *projective test,* one that requires subjects to respond to vague, ambiguous stimuli in ways that may reveal personal motives and traits (see Chapter 12). The stimulus materials for the TAT are pictures of people in ambiguous scenes open to interpretation. Examples include a man working at a desk and a woman seated in a chair staring off into space. Subjects are asked to write or tell stories about what's happening in the scenes and what the characters are feeling. The themes of these stories are then scored to measure the strength of various needs. Figure 10.18 shows examples of stories dominated by the themes of achievement and affiliation (the need for social bonds and belongingness).

The research on individual differences in achievement motivation has yielded interesting findings on the characteristics of people who score high in the need for achievement. They tend to work harder and more persistently on tasks than people low in the need for achievement (M. Brown, 1974) and they handle negative feedback about task performance more effectively than others (Fodor & Carver, 2000). They also are more future-oriented than others and more likely to delay gratification in order to pursue long-term goals (Mischel, 1961; Raynor & Entin, 1982). As you might guess, given these characteristics, researchers often find a positive correlation between high need for achievement and educational attainment (Hustinx et al., 2009). In terms of careers, they typically go into competitive, entrepreneurial occupations that provide them with an opportunity to excel (Collins, Hanges, & Locke, 2004; Stewart & Roth, 2007). Apparently, their persistence and hard work often pay off. High achievement motivation correlates with measures of career success in business (Amyx & Alford, 2005; Winter, 2010).

Do people high in achievement need always tackle the biggest challenges available? Not necessarily. A curious finding has emerged in laboratory studies in which subjects have been asked to choose how difficult a task they want to work on. Subjects high in the need for achievement tend to select tasks of intermediate difficulty (McClelland & Koestner, 1992).

Affiliation arousal
George is an engineer who is working late. He is *worried that his wife will be annoyed* with him for neglecting her. She has been *objecting* that he cares more about his work than his wife and family. He seems *unable to satisfy* both his boss and his wife, but he *loves her* very much and will do his best to *finish up* fast and get home to her.

Achievement arousal
George is an engineer who *wants to win* a competition in which the man with the *most practicable drawing* will be awarded the contract to build a bridge. He is taking a moment to think *how happy he will be* if he wins. He has been *baffled by how to make such a long span strong,* but he remembers to *specify a new steel alloy* of great strength, submits his entry, but does not win, and is *very unhappy.*

FIGURE 10.18

Measuring motives with the *Thematic Apperception Test* (TAT).

Subjects taking the TAT tell or write stories about what is happening in a scene, such as this one showing a man at work. The two stories shown here illustrate strong affiliation motivation (the need to associate with others and maintain social bonds) and strong achievement motivation. The italicized parts of the stories are thematic ideas that would be identified by a TAT scorer.

Source: Stories reprinted by permission of Dr. David McClelland.

For instance, in one study, where subjects playing a ring-tossing game were allowed to stand as close to or as far away from the target peg as they wanted, high achievers tended to prefer a moderate degree of challenge (Atkinson & Litwin, 1960).

Situational Determinants of Achievement Behaviour

8b

Your achievement drive is not the only determinant of how hard you work. Situational factors can also influence achievement strivings. John Atkinson (1974, 1981, 1992) has elaborated extensively on McClelland's original theory of achievement motivation and has identified some important situational determinants of achievement behaviour. Atkinson theorizes that the tendency to pursue achievement in a particular situation depends on the following factors:

- The strength of one's *motivation* to *achieve success*. This is viewed as a stable aspect of personality.
- One's estimate of the *probability of success* for the task at hand. This varies from task to task.
- The *incentive value of success*. This depends on the tangible and intangible rewards for success on the specific task.

The last two variables are situational determinants of achievement behaviour (see Figure 10.19). That is, they vary from one situation to another. According to Atkinson, the pursuit of achievement increases as the probability and incentive value of success go up. Let's apply Atkinson's model to a simple example. According to his theory, your tendency to pursue a good grade in calculus should depend on your general motivation to achieve success, your estimate of the probability of getting a good grade in the class, and the value you place on getting a good grade in calculus. Thus, given a certain motivation to achieve success, you will pursue a good grade in calculus less vigorously if your professor gives impossible exams (thus lowering your expectancy of success) or if a good grade in calculus is not required for your major (lowering the incentive value of success).

The joint influence of these situational factors may explain why high achievers prefer tasks of intermediate difficulty. Atkinson notes that the probability of success and the incentive value of success on tasks are interdependent to some degree. As tasks get easier, success becomes less satisfying. As tasks get harder, success becomes more satisfying, but its likelihood obviously declines. When the probability and incentive value of success are weighed together, moderately challenging tasks seem to offer the best overall value in terms of maximizing one's sense of accomplishment.

According to Atkinson, a person's fear of failure must also be considered to understand achievement behaviour (Atkinson & Birch, 1978). He maintains that people vary in their *motivation to avoid failure*. This motive is considered to be a stable aspect of personality. Together with situational factors such as the probability of failure and the negative value placed on failure, it influences achievement strivings. Figure 10.19 diagrams all of the factors in Atkinson's model that are thought to govern achievement behaviour. Approach and avoidance are key concepts in Atkinson's approach to motivation. Atkinson's emphasis on distinguishing between approach and avoidance tendencies in the study of motivation has influenced more recent motivation theories, such

FIGURE 10.19

Determinants of achievement behaviour.

According to John Atkinson, a person's pursuit of achievement in a particular situation depends on several factors. Some of these factors, such as need for achievement or fear of failure, are relatively stable motives that are part of the person's personality. Many other factors, such as the likelihood and value of success or failure, vary from one situation to another, depending on the circumstances.

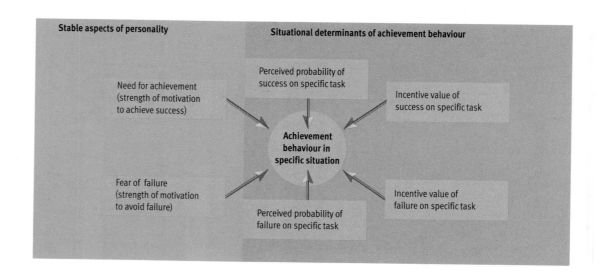

> Achievement, which was first investigated by David McClelland, involves the need to excel, especially in competition with others. The need for achievement is usually measured with a projective test called the TAT, which asks subjects to write stories about what is going on in ambiguous pictures.

> People who are relatively high in the need for achievement work harder and more persistently than others. They delay gratification well and pursue competitive careers. However, in choosing challenges they often select tasks of intermediate difficulty. The pursuit of achievement tends to increase when the probability of success and the incentive value of success are high. The joint influence of these factors may explain why people high in achievement need tend to prefer challenges of intermediate difficulty.

concept **check 10.2**

Understanding the Determinants of Achievement Behaviour

According to John Atkinson, one's pursuit of achievement in a particular situation depends on several factors. Check your understanding of these factors by identifying each of the following vignettes as an example of one of the following four determinants of achievement behaviour: (a) need for achievement, (b) perceived probability of success, (c) incentive value of success, (d) fear of failure. The answers can be found in Appendix A.

_____ **1.** Donna has just received a B in biology. Her reaction is typical of the way she responds to many situations involving achievement: "I didn't get an A, it's true, but at least I didn't flunk; that's what I was really worried about."

_____ **2.** Belinda is nervously awaiting the start of the finals of the 200-metre dash in the last meet of her high school career. "I've gotta win this race! This is the most important race of my life!"

_____ **3.** Corey grins as he considers the easy time he's going to have this semester. "This class is supposed to be a snap. I hear the professor gives an A to nearly everyone."

_____ **4.** Diana's just as hard-charging as ever. She's received the highest grade on every test throughout the semester, yet she's still up all night studying for the final. "I know I've got an A in the bag, but I want to be the best student Dr. McClelland's ever had!"

as the theory of uncertainty orientation, which was developed by Richard Sorrentino of the University of Western Ontario (Shuper et al., 2004; Sorrentino & Roney, 2000).

Fear is one of the most fundamental emotions. Thus, the relationship between achievement behaviour and *fear* of failure illustrates how motivation and emotion are often intertwined (Zurbriggen & Sturman, 2002). On the one hand, *emotion can cause motivation*. For example, *anger* about your work schedule may motivate you to look for a new job. *Jealousy* of an ex-girlfriend may motivate you to ask out her roommate. On the other hand, *motivation can cause emotion*. For example, your motivation to win a photography contest may lead to great *anxiety* during the judging and either great *joy* if you win

or great *gloom* if you don't. There may even be individual differences in the motivation to approach or avoid emotions (Maio & Esses, 2001). Thus, motivation and emotion are closely related, but that does not mean they're the same thing. We'll analyze the nature of emotion in the next section.

The Elements of Emotional Experience

Our emotions touch us in many different ways. Think of the emotions going through the minds of professional athletes when they execute a winning play. One of the reasons professional sports are so captivating to many of us is because they elicit such strong emotions both from fans and players. If you are a fan, win or lose, you are captivated by the spectacle on the field or in the area. While we do not often associate grief with professional sports, in one particular baseball game played on Thursday, May 19, 2011, the two were clearly linked. During that game some of the players on the Toronto Blue Jays baseball club unequivocally displayed their grief. Ricky Romero and J. P. Arencibia acknowledged their grief that day over the death of a young cancer victim, Ryley James Martin, two-and-a-half years old, whom

they had befriended two months earlier. They found out about his death just before game time. Before he threw his first pitch of the game, Romero stepped off the mound and traced Ryley's initials in the dirt. He continued to glance at the initials throughout the game. Arencibia hit a home run in the game and during the post-game interviews he held up a picture of Ryley and said, "This is the kid we played for tonight" (MacLeod, 2011). Incidentally, the Jays won the game "for the kid" 3–2 over the Tampa Bay Rays.

Emotions also colour your everyday experiences and judgments (Greifender, Bless, & Pham, 2011). For instance, you might experience *anger* when a professor treats you rudely, *dismay* when you learn that your car needs expensive repairs, *happiness* when you see that you aced your psychology exam,

PREVIEW QUESTIONS

> What is the cognitive component of emotion?

> How does a lie detector device work?

> What are the physiological and neural bases of emotions?

> What is the connection between emotion and body language?

> Are there cultural differences in how people recognize, describe, or express their emotions?

Blue Jay pitcher Ricky Romero publically acknowledged his grief over the death of a young fan, two-and-half-year-old Ryley James, when he died from cancer.

THE CANADIAN PRESS/Frank Gunn

and *sympathy* when one of your friends is currently in need of some assistance (Lishner, Batson, & Huss, 2011). It is also true that in some respects, emotions lie at the core of mental health. The two most common complaints that lead people to seek psychotherapy are *depression* and *anxiety*. Clearly, emotions play a pervasive role in everyone's lives.

But exactly what is an emotion? Everyone has plenty of personal experience with emotion, but it's an elusive concept to understand and define (Fontaine et al., 2007; Forgas, 2008; LeDoux, 1995). Emotion includes cognitive, physiological, and behavioural components, which are summarized in the following definition: *Emotion* involves (1) a subjective conscious experience (the cognitive component) accompanied by (2) bodily arousal (the physiological component) and by (3) characteristic overt expressions (the behavioural component). That's a pretty complex definition. Let's take a closer look at each of these three components of emotion.

The Cognitive Component: Subjective Feelings 8c

Emotions are pervasive in the human experience. It seems as if we constantly think about them by ourselves and discuss them with others. It should come as no surprise then that our language and words are filled with emotion. Hundreds of words in the English language refer to emotions (Averill, 1980). Analytical systems such as the ANEW program (Bradley & Lang, 1999) and the *Dictionary of Affect in Language* (DAL) (Whissell, 2008a), created by Laurentian University's Cynthia Whissell, have been developed to provide normative emotional ratings for the words we use. These systems allow researchers to examine a wide variety of features of human behaviour and experience (e.g., Whissell, 2006, 2008b).

Ironically, however, even given all this emotional content in our words, people often have difficulty describing their emotions to others (Zajonc, 1980).

Emotion is a highly personal, subjective experience. In studying the cognitive component of emotions, psychologists generally rely on subjects' verbal reports of what they're experiencing. Their reports indicate that emotions are potentially intense internal feelings that sometimes seem to have a life of their own. People can't click their emotions on and off like a bedroom light. If it were as simple as that, you could choose to be happy whenever you wanted. As Joseph LeDoux puts it, "Emotions are things that happen to us rather than things we will to occur" (1996, p. 19). Actually, some degree of emotional control is possible (Thayer, 1996; Wadlinger & Isaacowitz, 2011), but emotions tend to involve automatic reactions that are difficult to regulate (Ohman & Wiens, 2003). In some cases, these emotional reactions may occur at an unconscious level of processing, outside of one's awareness (Winkielman & Berridge, 2004).

People's cognitive appraisals of events in their lives are key determinants of the emotions they experience (Clore & Ortony, 2008; Ellsworth & Scherer, 2003; R. S. Lazarus, 1995). A specific event, such as giving a speech or singing in public (Sturm et al., 2008), may be highly threatening or embarrassing and thus anxiety-arousing for one person but a "ho-hum" routine matter for another. The conscious experience of emotion includes an *evaluative* aspect. People characterize their emotions as pleasant or unpleasant (Barrett et al, 2007; Neese & Ellsworth, 2009). Of course, individuals often experience "mixed emotions" that include both pleasant and unpleasant qualities (Cacioppo & Berntson, 1999). For example, an executive just given a promotion with challenging new responsibilities may experience both happiness and anxiety.

In recent years a curious finding has emerged regarding people's cognitive assessments of their emotions—we are not very good at anticipating our emotional responses to future setbacks and triumphs.

© Bob Daemmrich/The Image Works

Emotions involve automatic reactions that can be difficult to control.

Research on *affective forecasting*—efforts to predict one's emotional reactions to future events—demonstrates that people reliably mispredict their future feelings in response to good and bad events, such as getting a promotion at work, taking a long-awaited vacation, getting a poor grade in an important class, or being fired at work (Wilson & Gilbert, 2003, 2005). People tend to be reasonably accurate in anticipating whether events will generate positive or negative emotions, but they often are way off in predicting the initial intensity and duration of their emotional reactions.

For example, Dunn, Wilson, and Gilbert (2003) asked college students to predict what their overall level of happiness would be if a campus housing lottery assigned them to a desirable or undesirable dormitory. The students expected that their dormitory assignments would have a pretty dramatic effect on their well-being. But when their happiness was assessed a year later after actually being assigned to the good or bad dorms, it was clear that their happiness was not affected by their dorm assignments. In a similar vein, research shows that young professors overestimate the unhappiness they will feel five years after being turned down for tenure, college students overestimate how despondent they will be after the breakup of a romantic relationship, and job applicants overestimate how distressed they will feel after being rejected for a job (Gilbert et al., 1998).

Why are our predictions of our emotional reactions surprisingly inaccurate? A host of factors can contribute (Hoerger et al., 2009; Wilson & Gilbert, 2003). One consideration is that most of us do not fully appreciate how effective people tend to be in rationalizing, discounting, and overlooking failures and mistakes. People exhibit a host of cognitive biases that help them to insulate themselves from the emotional fallout of life's difficulties. However, people do not factor this peculiar "talent" into the picture when making predictions about their emotional reactions to setbacks. In any event, as you can see, emotions are not only hard to regulate—they are also hard to predict.

The Physiological Component: Diffuse and Multifaceted 8c

Emotional processes are closely tied to physiological processes, but the interconnections are enormously complex. The biological bases of emotions are diffuse, involving many areas in the brain and many neurotransmitter systems, as well as the autonomic nervous system and the endocrine system.

Autonomic Arousal

Imagine your reaction as your car spins out of control on an icy highway. Your fear is accompanied by a variety of physiological changes. Your heart rate and breathing accelerate. Your blood pressure surges, and your pupils dilate. The hairs on your skin stand erect, giving you "goose bumps," and you start to perspire. Although the physical reactions may not always be as obvious as in this scenario, *emotions are accompanied by visceral arousal* (Larsen et al., 2008). Surely you've experienced a "knot in your stomach" or a "lump in your throat"—thanks to anxiety.

Much of the discernible physiological arousal associated with emotion occurs through the actions of the *autonomic nervous system* (Janig, 2003), which regulates the activity of glands, smooth muscles, and blood vessels (see Figure 10.20). As you may recall from Chapter 3, the autonomic nervous system is responsible for the highly emotional *fight-or-flight*

FIGURE 10.20

Emotion and autonomic arousal.

The autonomic nervous system (ANS) is composed of the nerves that connect to the heart, blood vessels, smooth muscles, and glands (refer back to Figure 3.8 on page 97, for a more detailed view). The ANS is divided into the *sympathetic system*, which mobilizes bodily resources in response to stress, and the *parasympathetic system*, which conserves bodily resources. Emotions are frequently accompanied by sympathetic ANS activation, which leads to goose bumps, sweaty palms, and the other physical responses listed on the left side of the diagram.

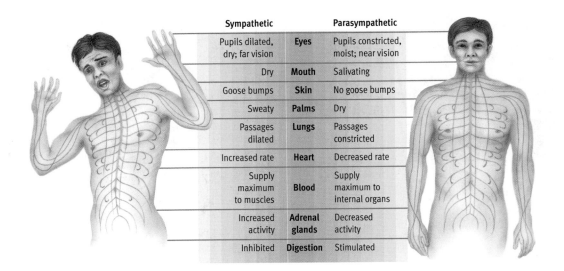

Sympathetic		Parasympathetic
Pupils dilated, dry; far vision	**Eyes**	Pupils constricted, moist; near vision
Dry	**Mouth**	Salivating
Goose bumps	**Skin**	No goose bumps
Sweaty	**Palms**	Dry
Passages dilated	**Lungs**	Passages constricted
Increased rate	**Heart**	Decreased rate
Supply maximum to muscles	**Blood**	Supply maximum to internal organs
Increased activity	**Adrenal glands**	Decreased activity
Inhibited	**Digestion**	Stimulated

response, which is largely modulated by the release of adrenal *hormones* that radiate throughout the body. Hormonal changes clearly play a crucial role in emotional responses to stress and may contribute to many other emotions as well (McEwen & Seeman, 2003).

One prominent part of emotional arousal is the *galvanic skin response (GSR),* an increase in the electrical conductivity of the skin that occurs when sweat glands increase their activity. GSR is a convenient and sensitive index of autonomic arousal that has been used as a measure of emotion in many laboratory studies.

The connection between emotion and autonomic arousal provides the basis for the *polygraph,* or *lie detector,* a device that records autonomic fluctuations while a subject is questioned. Scientific research into physiological markers of deception has a long history (e.g., Bunn, 2007; Gamer et al., 2008; Verschuere, Prati, & De Houwer, 2009; Verschuere et al., 2009). The polygraph was invented in 1915 by psychologist William Marston—who also dreamed up the comic book superhero Wonder Woman (Knight, 2004). A polygraph can't actually detect lies. It's really an emotion detector. It monitors key indicators of autonomic arousal, typically heart rate, blood pressure, respiration rate, and GSR. The assumption is that when subjects lie, they experience emotion (presumably anxiety) that produces noticeable changes in these physiological indicators (see Figure 10.21). The polygraph examiner asks a subject a number of nonthreatening questions to establish the subject's baseline on these autonomic indicators.

Then the examiner asks the critical questions (e.g., "Where were you on the night of the burglary?") and observes whether the subject's autonomic arousal changes.

The polygraph has been controversial since its invention (Grubin & Madsen, 2005). Polygraph advocates claim that lie detector tests are about 85–90 percent accurate and that the validity of polygraph testing has been demonstrated in empirical studies, but these claims clearly are not supported by the evidence (Branaman & Gallagher, 2005; Feidler, Schmid, & Stahl, 2002). Part of the problem is that people who are telling the truth may experience emotional arousal when they respond to incriminating questions. Thus, polygraph tests sometimes lead to accusations of lying against people who are innocent. Another problem is that some people can lie without experiencing anxiety or autonomic arousal. The crux of the problem, as Leonard Saxe (1994) notes, is that "there is no evidence of a unique physiological reaction to deceit" (p. 71). The polygraph *is* a potentially useful tool that can help police check out leads and alibis. However, polygraph results are not reliable enough to be submitted as evidence in most types of courtrooms.

Affective Neuroscience: Emotions and the Brain

The autonomic responses that accompany emotions are ultimately controlled in the brain. Psychologists and neuroscientists have had a longstanding interest

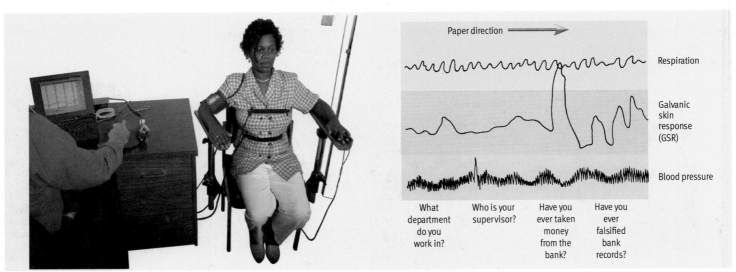

FIGURE 10.21

Emotion and the polygraph.

A lie detector device measures the autonomic arousal that most people experience when they tell a lie. After using nonthreatening questions to establish a baseline, a polygraph examiner looks for signs of arousal (such as the sharp change in GSR shown here) on incriminating questions. Unfortunately, the polygraph is not a very dependable index of whether people are lying.

in the nature of our emotional life and the role played by the brain in those experiences. Work at the intersection of emotion and neuroscience reached a critical point in the mid-1990s, resulting in the identification of a new subdiscipline in psychology—the study of *affective neuroscience* (Davidson & Sutton, 1995). The focus of research in this area was the examination of the neurobiology of emotions. While much work remains to be done, considerable insight into the neurobiology of our emotions has been acquired over the past few years (Davidson, 2004; Davidson, Jackson, & Kalin, 2000). Let's consider some of what this work has told us about the brain and our emotions.

The hypothalamus, amygdala, and adjacent structures in the *limbic system* have long been viewed as the seat of emotions (Izard & Saxton, 1988; MacLean, 1993). Although these structures do contribute to emotion, the limbic system is not a clearly defined anatomical system, and research has shown that a variety of brain structures that lie outside the limbic system play a crucial role in the regulation of emotion (Berridge, 2003).

Nonetheless, more recent evidence suggests that the amygdala (see Figure 10.22) plays a central role in the acquisition of conditioned fears (LeDoux & Phelps, 2008). According to Joseph LeDoux (1996, 2000), the amygdala lies at the core of a complex set of neural circuits that process emotion. He believes that sensory inputs capable of eliciting emotions arrive in the thalamus, which simultaneously routes the information along two separate pathways: a fast pathway to the nearby amygdala and a slower pathway to areas in the cortex (see Figure 10.22). The amygdala processes the information quickly, and if it detects a threat it almost instantly triggers neural activity that leads to the autonomic arousal and endocrine (hormonal) responses associated with emotion.

The processing in this pathway is extremely fast, so that emotions may be triggered even before the brain has had a chance to really "think" about the input. Meanwhile, the information shuttled along the other pathway is subjected to a more "leisurely" cognitive appraisal in the cortex. LeDoux believes that the rapid-response pathway evolved because it is a highly adaptive warning system that can "be the difference between life and death." Consistent with LeDoux's theory, evidence indicates that the amygdala can process emotion independent of cognitive awareness (Phelps, 2005). Research linking the amygdala to emotion has mainly focused on fear, but recent evidence suggests that the amygdala may play a role in positive emotions as well (Murray, 2007).

What other areas of the brain are involved in the modulation of emotion? The list is extensive and different emotions may be processed by different neural structures (Panksepp, 2008). Some of the more intriguing findings include the following:

- The *prefrontal cortex*, known for its role in planning and executive control, appears to contribute to efforts to voluntarily control emotional reactions (Davidson, Fox, & Kalin, 2007; Quirk, 2007). The prefrontal cortex also seems to modulate emotions associated with the pursuit of goals (Davidson et al., 2003b).
- The front portion of the *cingulate cortex* has been implicated in the processing of pain-related emotional distress (Berridge, 2003). This area also is activated when people wrestle with emotion-laden conflicts about choices (Miller & Cohen, 2001).
- As noted in Chapters 3 and 5, a neural circuit called the *mesolimbic dopamine pathway* plays a major role in the experience of pleasurable emotions associated with rewarding events (Berridge, 2003). In particular, this circuit is activated by cocaine and other abused drugs (Nestler & Malenka, 2004).

Joseph LeDoux

"In situations of danger, it is very useful to be able to respond quickly. The time saved by the amygdala in acting on the thalamic information, rather than waiting for the cortical input, may be the difference between life and death."

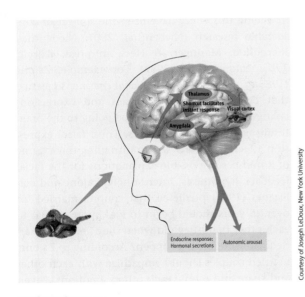

FIGURE 10.22

The amygdala and fear.

Emotions are controlled by a constellation of interacting brain systems, but the amygdala appears to play a particularly crucial role. According to LeDoux (1996), sensory inputs that can trigger fear (such as seeing a snake while out walking) arrive in the thalamus and then are routed along a fast pathway (shown in green) directly to the amygdala and along a slow pathway (shown in blue) that allows the cortex time to think about the situation. Activity in the fast pathway also elicits the autonomic arousal and hormonal responses that are part of the physiological component of emotion. (Adapted from LeDoux, 1994)

- As you may recall from Chapter 3 and Chapter 6, *mirror neurons* are neurons that are activated by performing an action or by seeing another monkey or person perform the same action. These recently discovered, specialized neurons appear to play a crucial role in the experience of the important emotion of empathy (Iacoboni, 2007, 2009).

Quite a variety of other brain structures have been linked to specific facets of emotion, including the hippocampus, the lateral hypothalamus, the septum, and the brainstem (Berridge, 2003). Thus, it is clear that emotion depends on activity in a *constellation of interacting brain centres.*

The Behavioural Component: Nonverbal Expressiveness 8c

At the behavioural level, people reveal their emotions through characteristic overt expressions such as smiles, frowns, furrowed brows, clenched fists, and slumped shoulders. In other words, *emotions are expressed in "body language," or nonverbal behaviour.*

Facial expressions reveal a variety of basic emotions (Lederman et al., 2007). In an extensive research project, Paul Ekman and Wallace Friesen asked subjects to identify what emotion a person was experiencing on the basis of facial cues in photographs. They have found that subjects are generally successful in identifying six fundamental emotions: happiness, sadness, anger, fear, surprise, and disgust (Ekman & Friesen, 1975, 1984). People can also identify a number of other emotions from facial expressions, such as contempt, embarrassment, shame, amusement, and sympathy, but less reliably than the basic six emotions (Keltner et al., 2003). Furthermore, the identification of emotions from facial expressions tends to occur quickly and automatically (Tracy & Robins, 2008).

Some theorists believe that muscular feedback from one's own facial expressions contributes to one's conscious experience of emotions (Izard, 1990; Tomkins, 1991). Proponents of the *facial feedback hypothesis* assert that facial muscles send signals to the brain and that these signals help the brain recognize the emotion that one is experiencing (see Figure 10.23). According to this view, smiles, frowns, and furrowed brows help create the subjective experience of various emotions. Consistent with this idea, studies show that if subjects are instructed to contract their facial muscles to mimic facial expressions associated with certain emotions, they tend to report that they actually experience these emotions to some degree (Kleinke, Peterson, & Rutledge, 1998; Levenson, 1992). The nature of the mechanisms producing this effect have been the subject of considerable research (Niedenthal, 2007; Niedenthal, Mermillod, Maringer, & Hess, in press; Zajonc, 1985; Zajonc et al., 1987). For example, Zajonc (1985) in his theory of *emotional efference* suggested that changes in facial muscles and expressions change the temperature of blood going to the brain resulting in distinct emotions. Thus, facial expression affects emotions. It's an intriguing theory, one of a number of possible explanations for the facial feedback hypothesis. Interestingly, Zajonc and colleagues (1987) predicted that couples married for over 25 years should begin to look more similar to each other than they did when they first were married. How might this happen? According to Zajonc, married couples should empathize with each other and share and mimic each others emotions. Given that they share emotions, "If the facial musculature plays a significant role in producing these emotional states and moods, then, with time, married partners should grow to resemble each other physically" (Zajonc et al., 1987, p. 344). This is precisely what he found!

The facial expressions that go with various emotions may be largely innate (Eibl-Ebesfeldt, 1975; Izard, 1994). For the most part, people who have been blind since birth smile and frown much like everyone else, even though they've never seen a

Our motions automatically express themselves nonverbally. Here, U.S. President Obama and his wife, First Lady Michelle Obama, watch as the car carrying Queen Elizabeth and Prince Philip pull up in front of the American ambassadorial residence in London, England, for a visit in May 2011. What do their faces tell you about the emotions they are experiencing at that moment?

AP Photo/Charles Dharapak

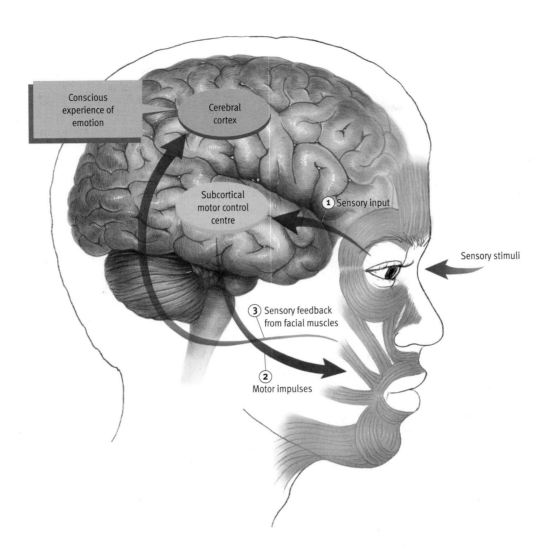

FIGURE 10.23

The facial feedback hypothesis.

According to the facial feedback hypothesis, inputs to subcortical centres automatically evoke facial expressions associated with certain emotions, and the facial muscles then feed signals to the cortex that help it to recognize the emotion that one is experiencing. According to this view, facial expressions help create the subjective experience of various emotions.

Source: Smith, R.E., (1993). *Psychology*, St. Paul, MN: West Publishing. Copyright © 1993 by West Publishing. Reprinted by permission of Wadsworth Publishing.

smile or frown (Galati, Scherer, & Ricci-Bitti, 1997). In an influential, recent study, David Matsumoto and Bob Willingham (2009) carefully photographed the facial expressions of congenitally blind judo athletes in the Paralympic Games and sighted judo athletes in the Olympic Games. The photos for comparison were taken just after the athletes had won or lost their crucial final matches (for gold, silver, or bronze medals). The analysis of thousands of photos of numerous athletes yielded clear results. The facial expressions of sighted and blind athletes were indistinguishable.

These findings strongly support the hypothesis that the facial expressions that go with emotions are wired into the human brain. The long-held suspicion that facial expressions of emotion might be biologically built in has also led to extensive cross-cultural research on the dynamics of emotion. Let's look at what investigators have learned about culture and the elements of emotional experience.

Canadian Olympian Alex Bilodeau expressed his emotions clearly when he was awarded a gold medal at the 2010 Olympics.

Culture and the Elements of Emotion

Are emotions innate reactions that are universal across cultures? Or are they socially learned reactions that are culturally variable? The voluminous research on this lingering question has not yielded a simple answer. Investigators have found both remarkable similarities and dramatic differences between cultures in the experience of emotion.

Cross-Cultural Similarities in Emotional Experience

After demonstrating that Western subjects could discern specific emotions from facial expressions, Ekman and Friesen (1975) took their facial-cue photographs on the road to other societies to see whether nonverbal expressions of emotion transcend cultural boundaries. Testing subjects in Argentina, Spain, Japan, and other countries, they found considerable cross-cultural agreement in the identification of happiness, sadness, anger, fear, surprise, and disgust based on facial expressions (see Figure 10.24). Still, Ekman and Friesen wondered whether this agreement might be the result of learning rather than biology, given that people in different cultures often share considerable exposure to Western mass media (magazines, newspapers, television, and so forth), which provide many visual depictions of people's emotional reactions. To rule out this possibility, they took their photos to a remote area in New Guinea and showed them to a group of indigenous people (the Fore) who had had virtually no contact with Western culture. Even the people from this preliterate culture did a fair job of identifying the emotions portrayed in the pictures (see the data in the bottom row of Figure 10.24). That is not to say that culture is *irrelevant* to the expression and perception of emotion. Research shows that subjects are somewhat more accurate in recognizing emotions expressed by people from their own culture than they are when asked to identify emotions expressed by a different cultural group (Elfenbein & Ambady, 2002, 2003).

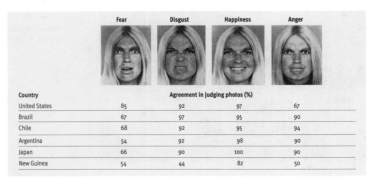

Country	Fear	Disgust	Happiness	Anger
	\multicolumn{4}{c}{Agreement in judging photos (%)}			
United States	85	92	97	67
Brazil	67	97	95	90
Chile	68	92	95	94
Argentina	54	92	98	90
Japan	66	90	100	90
New Guinea	54	44	82	50

FIGURE 10.24

Cross-cultural comparisons of people's ability to recognize emotions from facial expressions.

Ekman and Friesen (1975) found that people in highly disparate cultures showed fair agreement on the emotions portrayed in these photos. This consensus across cultures suggests that facial expressions of emotions may be universal and that they have a strong biological basis.

Source: Data from Ekman, R., and Friesen, W.V. (1975). *Unmasking the face.* Englewood Cliffs, NJ: Prentice-Hall. © 1975 by Paul Ekman.

Paul Ekman, Ph.D/Paul Ekman Group LLC.

Subsequent comparisons of many other societies have also shown considerable cross-cultural congruence in the judgment of facial expressions (Biehl et al., 1997; Ekman, 1992, 1993). Although some theorists disagree (J. A. Russell, 1994, 1995), there is reasonably convincing evidence that people in widely disparate cultures express their emotions and interpret those expressions in much the same way (Izard, 1994; Keltner et al., 2003; Matsumoto, 2001).

Cross-cultural similarities have also been found in the cognitive and physiological elements of emotional experience (Scherer & Wallbott, 1994). For example, in making cognitive appraisals of events that might elicit emotional reactions, people from different cultures generally think along the same lines (Matsumoto, Nezlek, & Koopmann, 2007; Mauro, Sato, & Tucker, 1992). That is, they evaluate situations along the same dimensions (pleasant versus unpleasant, expected versus unexpected, fair versus unfair, and so on). Understandably, then, the types of events that trigger specific emotions are fairly similar across cultures (Frijda, 1999; Matsumoto & Willingham, 2006). Around the globe, achievements lead to joy, injustices lead to anger, and risky situations lead to fear. Finally, as one might expect, the physiological arousal that accompanies emotion also appears to be largely invariant across cultures (Wallbott & Scherer, 1988). Thus, researchers have found a great deal of cross-cultural continuity and uniformity in the cognitive, physiological, and behavioural (expressive) elements of emotional experience.

Cross-Cultural Differences in Emotional Experience

The cross-cultural similarities in emotional experience are impressive, but researchers have also found many cultural disparities in how people think about, experience, regulate, and express their emotions (Matsumoto, Yoo, Nakagawa et al., 2008; Mesquita & Leu, 2007). For example, Japanese culture encourages the experience of *socially engaging emotions* (such as friendly feelings, sympathy, and guilt) more than North American culture and Japanese participants report experiencing these types of emotion more (Kitayama, Mesquita, & Karasawa, 2006). In contrast, North American culture encourages *socially disengaging emotions* (such as pride and anger) more than Japanese culture, and North American subjects report experiencing these kinds of emotion more.

Fascinating variations have also been observed in how cultures categorize emotions. Some basic categories of emotion that are universally understood in Western cultures appear to go unrecognized— or at least unnamed—in some non-Western cultures. James Russell (1991) has compiled numerous

Members of some eastern cultures, such as the Japanese victims of the 2011 tsunami, often exhibit a tendency not to display their grief and depression in public.

Canadian Olympic medalist Joannie Rochette did not hesitate to display her emotions over her mother's death during the 2010 Olympic Games.

examples of English words for emotions that have no equivalent in other languages. For example, Tahitians have no word that corresponds to *sadness*. Many non-Western groups, including the Yoruba of Nigeria, the Kaluli of New Guinea, and the Chinese, lack a word for *depression*. The concept of *anxiety* seems to go unrecognized among the Inuit, and the Quichua of Ecuador lack a word for *remorse*. However, a lack of words for emotional concepts does not necessarily mean that those emotions are not recognized in a culture. The Raramuri Indians in Mexico use one word to refer to both *guilt* and *shame,* but they differentiate between guilt and shame feelings in ways that are similar to cultures that have distinct words for these emotions (Breugelmans & Poortinga, 2006). These findings suggest that cultural disparities in naming emotions may not reflect differences in emotional processing.

Cultural disparities have also been found in regard to nonverbal expressions of emotion. Although the natural facial expressions associated with basic emotions appear to transcend culture, people can and do learn to control and modify these expressions. *Display rules* are norms that regulate the appropriate expression of emotions. They prescribe when, how, and to whom people can show various emotions. These norms vary from one culture to another (Ekman, 1992), as do attitudes about specific emotions (Eid & Diener, 2001). For instance, the Ifaluk

(a Pacific island culture) severely restrict expressions of happiness because they believe that this emotion often leads people to neglect their duties (Lutz, 1987). Japanese culture emphasizes the suppression of negative emotions in public. More so than in other cultures, the Japanese are socialized to mask emotions such as anger, sadness, and disgust with stoic facial expressions or polite smiling. Some of these cultural differences are evident in the ways that Canadian Olympian Joannie Rochette publically displayed her grief (DiManno, 2011a) over her mother's death, compared to how many of the survivors of the 2011 tsunami in Japan were unable to publically evidence their grief over relatives who were swept away by the tsunami (DiManno, 2011b).

Thus, nonverbal expressions of emotions vary somewhat across cultures because of culture-specific attitudes and display rules.

REVIEW OF KEY POINTS

▷ Emotion is made up of cognitive, physiological, and behavioural components. The cognitive component involves subjective feelings that have an evaluative aspect.

▷ The most readily apparent aspect of the physiological component of emotion is autonomic arousal. This arousal is the basis for the lie detector, which is really an emotion detector. Polygraphs are not all that accurate in assessing individuals' veracity. The amygdala appears to be the hub of an emotion-processing system in the brain.

▷ At the behavioural level, emotions are expressed through body language, with facial expressions being particularly prominent. Ekman and Friesen have found considerable cross-cultural agreement in the identification of emotions based on facial expressions.

▷ Cross-cultural similarities have also been found in the cognitive and physiological components of emotion. However, there are some striking cultural variations in how people categorize and display their emotions.

Motivation and Emotion

Theories of Emotion

PREVIEW QUESTIONS

▸ What are the differences between the James–Lange and Cannon–Bard theories of emotion?

▸ How did the two-factor theory of emotion try to reconcile these differences?

▸ How do evolutionary theorists explain emotions?

How do psychologists explain the experience of emotion? A variety of theories and conflicting models exist. Some have been vigorously debated for over a century. As we describe these theories, you'll recognize a familiar bone of contention. Like so many other types of theories, theories of emotion differ in their emphasis on the innate biological basis of emotion versus the social, environmental basis.

James–Lange Theory 8d

As we noted in Chapter 1, William James was a prominent early theorist who urged psychologists to explore the functions of consciousness. James (1884) developed a theory of emotion over 100 years ago that remains influential today. At about the same time, he and Carl Lange (1885) independently proposed that *the conscious experience of emotion results from one's perception of autonomic arousal.* Their theory stood common sense on its head. Everyday logic suggests that when you stumble onto a rattlesnake in the woods, the conscious experience of fear leads to visceral arousal (the fight-or-flight response).

The James–Lange theory of emotion asserts the opposite: that the perception of visceral arousal leads to the conscious experience of fear (see Figure 10.25). In other words, while you might assume that your pulse is racing because you're fearful, James and Lange argued that you're fearful because your pulse is racing.

The James–Lange theory emphasizes the physiological determinants of emotion. According to this view, *different patterns of autonomic activation lead to the experience of different emotions.* Hence, people supposedly distinguish emotions such as fear, joy, and anger on the basis of the exact configuration of physical reactions they experience.

Cannon–Bard Theory 8d

Walter Cannon (1927) found the James–Lange theory unconvincing. Cannon pointed out that physiological arousal may occur without the experience of emotion (if one exercises vigorously, for instance). He also argued that visceral changes are too slow to precede the conscious experience of emotion.

FIGURE 10.25

Theories of emotion.

Three influential theories of emotion are contrasted with one another and with the commonsense view. The James–Lange theory was the first to suggest that feelings of arousal cause emotion, rather than vice versa. Schachter (Schachter & Singer, 1962) built on this idea by adding a second factor—interpretation (appraisal and labelling) of arousal.

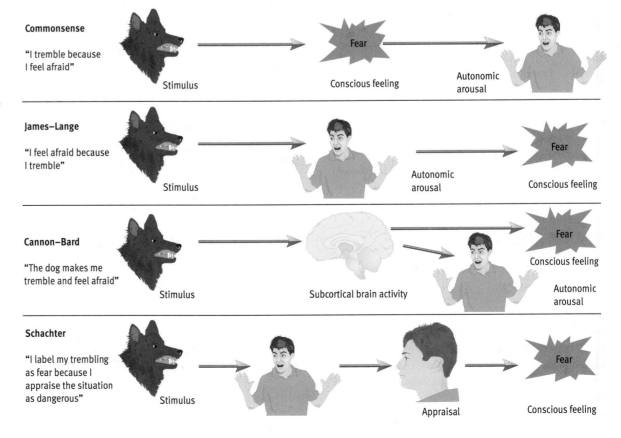

Finally, he argued that people experiencing very different emotions, such as fear, joy, and anger, exhibit almost identical patterns of autonomic arousal.

Thus, Cannon espoused a different explanation of emotion. Later, Philip Bard (1934) elaborated on it. The resulting Cannon–Bard theory argues that emotion occurs when the thalamus sends signals *simultaneously* to the cortex (creating the conscious experience of emotion) and to the autonomic nervous system (creating visceral arousal). The Cannon–Bard model is compared to the James–Lange model in Figure 10.25. Cannon and Bard were off the mark a bit in pinpointing the thalamus as the neural centre for emotion. However, many modern theorists agree with the Cannon–Bard view that emotions originate in subcortical brain structures (LeDoux, 1996; Panksepp, 1991; Rolls, 1990) and with the assertion that people do not discern their emotions from different patterns of autonomic activation (Frijda, 1999; Wagner, 1989).

Schachter's Two-Factor Theory 8d

In another influential analysis, Stanley Schachter asserted that people look at situational cues to differentiate among alternative emotions. According to Schachter (1964; Schachter & Singer, 1962, 1979), the experience of emotion depends on two factors: (1) autonomic arousal and (2) cognitive interpretation of that arousal. Schachter proposed that when you experience visceral arousal, you search your environment for an explanation (see Figure 10.25 again). If you're stuck in a traffic jam, you'll probably label your arousal as anger. If you're taking an important exam, you'll probably label it as anxiety. If you're celebrating your birthday, you'll probably label it as happiness.

You may recall that we used Schachter's theory in understanding the results of the Featured Study in Chapter 2 (see page 47). In the Dutton and Aron (1974) study, participants who crossed the high, arousal-producing bridge over the Capilano River in British Columbia and who were met by an attractive female confederate were found to be more sexually attracted to her than participants who were met by the same female confederate but after crossing a lower, solid, non-arousing bridge. In this case, arousal and salient cue (i.e., the female confederate) combined in influencing the emotional state of the participants.

Schachter agreed with the James–Lange view that emotion is inferred from arousal. However, he also agreed with the Cannon–Bard position that different emotions yield indistinguishable patterns of arousal. He reconciled these views by arguing that people look to external rather than internal cues to differentiate and label their specific emotions. In essence, Schachter suggested that people think along the following lines: "If I'm aroused and you're obnoxious, I must be angry."

Although the two-factor theory has received support, studies have revealed some limitations as well (Leventhal & Tomarken, 1986). Situations can't mould emotions in just any way at any time. And in searching to explain arousal, subjects don't limit themselves to the immediate situation (Sinclair et al., 1994). Thus, emotions are not as pliable as the two-factor theory initially suggested.

Evolutionary Theories of Emotion 8d

As the limitations of the two-factor theory were exposed, theorists began returning to ideas espoused by Charles Darwin over a century ago. Darwin (1872) believed that emotions developed because of their adaptive value. Fear, for instance, would help an organism avoid danger (Wise, 2011), and thus would aid in survival. Hence, Darwin viewed human emotions as a product of evolution. This premise serves as the foundation for several prominent theories of emotion developed independently by S. S. Tomkins (1980, 1991), Carroll Izard (1984, 1991), and Robert Plutchik (1984, 1993).

These *evolutionary theories* consider emotions to be largely innate reactions to certain stimuli. As such, emotions should be immediately recognizable under most conditions without much thought. After all, primitive animals that are incapable of complex thought seem to have little difficulty in recognizing their emotions. Evolutionary theorists believe that emotion evolved before thought. They assert that thought plays a relatively small role in emotion, although they admit that learning and cognition may have some influence on human emotions. Evolutionary theories generally assume that emotions originate in subcortical brain structures that evolved before the higher brain areas in the cortex associated with complex thought.

Evolutionary theories also assume that evolution has equipped humans with a small number of innate emotions with proven adaptive value. Hence, the principal question that many theories of emotion (e.g., Hutcherson & Gross, 2011), especially evolutionary theories, wrestle with is *What are the fundamental emotions?* Figure 10.26 summarizes the conclusions of the leading theorists in this area.

Stanley Schachter
"Cognitive factors play a major role in determining how a subject interprets his bodily feelings."

Silvan Tomkins	Carroll Izard	Robert Plutchik
Fear	Fear	Fear
Anger	Anger	Anger
Enjoyment	Joy	Joy
Disgust	Disgust	Disgust
Interest	Interest	Anticipation
Surprise	Surprise	Surprise
Contempt	Contempt	
Shame	Shame	
	Sadness	Sadness
Distress		
	Guilt	
		Acceptance

FIGURE 10.26

Primary emotions.

Evolutionary theories of emotion attempt to identify primary emotions. Three leading theorists—Silvan Tomkins, Carroll Izard, and Robert Plutchik—have compiled different lists of primary emotions, but this chart shows great overlap among the basic emotions identified by these theorists. (Based on Mandler, 1984)

As you can see, Tomkins, Izard, and Plutchik have not come up with identical lists, but there is considerable agreement. All three conclude that people exhibit eight to ten primary emotions. Moreover, five of these emotions appear on all three lists: fear, anger, joy, disgust, and surprise. The potential adaptive value of these basic emotions is key to the evolutionary argument. For example, consider *disgust*;

what adaptive value do you think it might have? According to Australian researcher Megan Oaten and her colleagues (Oaten, Stevenson, & Case, 2009), disgust serves an important function as a disease-avoidance mechanism.

Like all animals, humans are faced daily with potential contact with a variety of pathogens, including viruses and bacteria. According to Oaten, we have developed a variety of behaviours that enable us to avoid many pathogens and one key to avoiding disease is the emotion we label *disgust*. The "revulsion" and "nausea" that frequently accompany our disgust elicits avoidance behaviour. One of us remembers just like it happened yesterday (even though it happened 40 years ago) his disgust as a young boy at turning over a dead cat he found lying on the side of the road only to find it crawling with hundreds (it seemed like millions) of maggots. His disgust kicked in and he ran all the way home. In a careful and systematic review of studies conducted on the issue, Oaten concluded that the evidence supported the theory that disgust functions to enable us to avoid disease and infection. This analysis confirms the potential adaptive value of what is considered to be one of the basic human emotions.

concept **check** 10.3

Understanding Theories of Emotion

Check your understanding of theories of emotion by matching the theories we discussed with the statements below. Let's borrow William James's classic example: Assume that you just stumbled upon a bear in the woods. The first statement expresses the commonsense explanation of your fear. Each of the remaining statements expresses the essence of a different theory; indicate which theory in the spaces provided. The answers are provided in Appendix A.

1. You tremble because you're afraid.

   Common sense

2. You're afraid because you're trembling.

3. You're afraid because situational cues (the bear) suggest that's why you're trembling.

4. You're afraid because the bear has elicited an innate primary emotion.

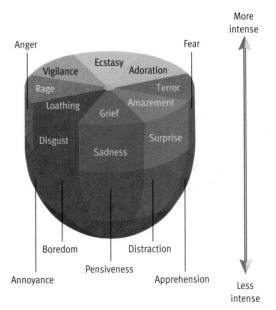

FIGURE 10.27

Emotional intensity in Plutchik's model.

According to Plutchik, diversity in human emotion is a product of variations in emotional intensity, as well as blendings of primary emotions. Each vertical slice in the diagram is a primary emotion that can be subdivided into emotional expressions of varied intensity, ranging from most intense (top) to least intense (bottom).

Source: Based on art in Plutchik, R. (1980). A language for emotions. *Psychology Today, 13* (9), 68–78. Reprinted with permission from *Psychology Today* magazine. Copyright © 1980 by Sussex Publishers.

Of course, people experience more than just eight to ten emotions. How do evolutionary theories account for this variety? They propose that the many emotions that people experience are produced by (1) blends of primary emotions and (2) variations in intensity. For example, Robert Plutchik (1980, 1993) has devised an elegant model of how primary emotions such as fear and surprise may blend into secondary emotions such as awe. Plutchik's model also posits that various emotions, such as apprehension, fear, and terror, involve one primary emotion experienced at different levels of intensity (see Figure 10.27).

Putting It in Perspective: Themes 2, 3, 4, 5, and 6

Five of our organizing themes were particularly prominent in this chapter: the influence of cultural contexts, the dense connections between psychology and society at large, psychology's theoretical diversity, the interplay of heredity and environment, and the multiple causes of behaviour.

Our discussion of motivation and emotion demonstrated once again that there are both similarities and differences across cultures in behaviour. The neural, biochemical, genetic, and hormonal processes underlying hunger and eating, for instance, are universal. But cultural factors influence what people prefer to eat, how much they eat, and whether they worry about dieting. In a similar vein, researchers have found a great deal of cross-cultural congruence in the cognitive, physiological, and expressive elements of emotional experience, but they have also found cultural variations in how people think about and express their emotions. Thus, as we have seen in previous chapters, psychological processes are characterized by both cultural variance and invariance.

Our discussion of the controversies surrounding evolutionary theory, aggressive pornography, and the determinants of sexual orientation show once again that psychology is not an ivory tower enterprise. It evolves in a sociohistorical context that helps to shape the debates in the field, and these debates often have far-reaching social and political ramifications for society at large. We ended the chapter with a discussion of various theories of emotion, which showed once again that psychology is characterized by great theoretical diversity.

Finally, we repeatedly saw that biological and environmental factors jointly govern behaviour. For example, we learned that eating behaviour, sexual desire, and the experience of emotion all depend on complicated interactions between biological and environmental determinants. Indeed, complicated interactions permeated the entire chapter, demonstrating that if we want to fully understand behaviour, we have to take multiple causes into account. In the upcoming Personal Application, we will continue our discussion of emotion, looking at recent research on the correlates of happiness. In the Critical Thinking Application that follows, we discuss how to carefully analyze the types of arguments that permeated this chapter.

PREVIEW QUESTIONS

▶ How did this chapter demonstrate the influence of cultural factors and the dense connections between psychology and society?

▶ How did this chapter illustrate psychology's theoretical diversity, the interplay of heredity and environment, and the multifactorial causation of behaviour?

REVIEW OF KEY POINTS

▷ The James–Lange theory asserts that emotion results from one's perception of autonomic arousal. The Cannon–Bard theory counters with the proposal that emotions originate in subcortical areas of the brain.

▷ According to Schachter's two-factor theory, people infer emotion from arousal and then label the emotion in accordance with their cognitive explanation for the arousal. Evolutionary theories of emotion maintain that emotions are innate reactions that require little cognitive interpretation.

▷ Our look at motivation and emotion showed once again that psychology is characterized by theoretical diversity, that biology and environment shape behaviour interactively, that behaviour is governed by multiple causes, that psychological processes are characterized by both cultural variance and invariance, and that psychology evolves in a sociohistorical context.

Exploring the Ingredients of Happiness

Indicate whether the following are "true" or "false."

___ **1** The empirical evidence indicates that most people are relatively unhappy.

___ **2** Although wealth doesn't *guarantee* happiness, wealthy people are much more likely to be happy than the rest of the population.

___ **3** People who have children are happier than people without children.

___ **4** Good health is an essential requirement for happiness.

___ **5** Good-looking people are happier than those who are unattractive.

All of the above statements are false. These assertions are all reasonable and widely believed hypotheses about the correlates of happiness, but they have not been supported by empirical research. Let's try another one related to the connection between money and happiness (Dunn, 2010; Dunn, Gilbert, & Wilson, 2011)—it should be easier. Imagine that a woman you know has some extra money to spend. Do you think she would be happier spending it on herself or happier if she spent the money on someone else? The answer would surprise many of us: People seem to be happier spending money on others than on themselves, according to the results of a recent study conducted by Elizabeth Dunn at the University of British Columbia (Dunn, Aknin, & Norton, 2008).

This raises the question: How well do we understand our own emotional reactions to situations and events? In general, we do not seem to be very good at predicting our own emotional reactions to either positive or negative events (Lench, 2009). As we discussed earlier in this chapter, research in the area of *affective forecasting* has shown that we are very inaccurate when trying to predict our emotional reactions to events in the future (Gilbert, 2006; Vasquez & Buehler, 2007). But our emotional reactions are critical to our overall sense of well-being, and envisioning the future may affect our happiness

(Quoidback, Wood, & Hansenne, 2009). Recent years have brought a surge of interest in the correlates of *subjective well-being*—individuals' personal perceptions of their overall happiness and life satisfaction.

The findings of these studies are quite interesting. As you have already seen from our true–false questions, many commonsense notions about happiness appear to be inaccurate. One of these inaccuracies is the apparently widespread assumption that most people are relatively unhappy. Writers, social scientists, and the general public seem to believe that people around the world are predominantly dissatisfied and unhappy, yet empirical surveys consistently find that the vast majority of respondents—even those who are poor or disabled—characterize themselves as fairly happy (Diener & Diener, 1996; Myers & Diener, 1995).

When people are asked to rate their happiness, only a small minority place themselves below the neutral point on the various scales used (see Figure 10.28). When the average subjective well-being of entire nations is computed, based on almost 1000 surveys, the means cluster toward the positive end of the scale, as shown in Figure 10.29 (Tov & Diener, 2007). That's not to say that everyone is equally happy. Researchers find substantial and thought-provoking disparities among people in subjective well-being and happiness (Kesebir & Diener, 2008), which we will analyze momentarily, but the overall picture seems rosier than anticipated. As Canadians we should know a great deal about happiness and subjective well-being. Worldwide surveys consistently put us at the top of these types of ratings. For example, according to the *Financial Post* (Badkar, 2011), of the top ten livable cities in the world, three are

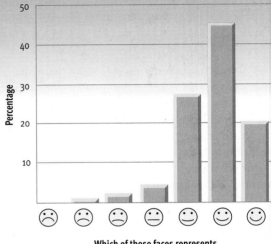

Which of these faces represents the way you feel about life as a whole?

FIGURE 10.28

Measuring happiness with a nonverbal scale.

Researchers have used a variety of methods to estimate the distribution of happiness. For example, in one study in the United States, respondents were asked to examine the seven facial expressions shown and select the one that "comes closest to expressing how you feel about your life as a whole." As you can see, the vast majority of participants chose happy faces. (Data adapted from Myers, 1992)

in Canada (with Calgary at number five, Toronto at number four, and Vancouver at number one). Even more to the point, a global well-being survey conducted by the Gallup organization determined that Canada was tied for second place in the world (Ray, 2011). What do we know about the factors that do and do not produce happiness and well-being?

Factors That Do Not Predict Happiness

Let us begin our discussion of individual differences in happiness by highlighting those things that turn out to be relatively unimportant determinants of subjective well-being. Quite a number of factors that you might expect to be influential appear to bear little or no relationship to general happiness.

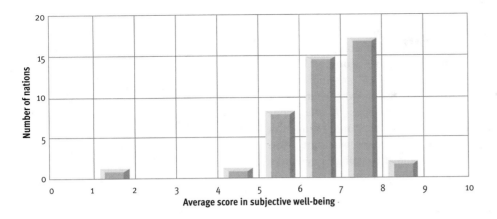

FIGURE 10.29

The subjective well-being of nations.

Veenhoven (1993) combined the results of almost 1000 surveys to calculate the average subjective well-being reported by representative samples from 43 nations. The mean happiness scores clearly pile up at the positive end of the distribution, with only two scores falling below the neutral point of 5. (Data adapted from Diener and Diener, 1996)

If beauty, wealth, fame, and success bring happiness, then actress Angelina Jolie should be as happy as they come, but her past struggles with depression demonstrate that the ingredients of happiness are more subjective and complex than one might guess.

Money

There *is* a positive correlation between income and subjective feelings of happiness, but in modern, affluent cultures the association is surprisingly weak (Diener & Seligman, 2004; Myers & Diener, 1995). For example, one study found a correlation of just 0.13 between income and happiness in the United States (Diener et al., 1993) and another investigation yielded an almost identical correlation of 0.12 (Johnson & Krueger, 2006). Admittedly, being very poor can make people unhappy. Yet it seems once people ascend above a certain level of income, additional wealth does not seem to foster greater happiness. One recent study in the United States estimated that once people exceed an income of around $75 000, little relationship is seen between wealth and subjective well-being (Kahneman & Deaton, 2010). The strength of the association between money and happiness also depends on how subjective well-being is assessed. The weak correlations we have discussed thus far are observed when participants are asked to make global evaluations of their life satisfaction. Higher correlations are observed if subjects are asked whether they experienced specific positive or negative emotions (enjoyment, happiness, worry, sadness) the previous day (Diener et al., 2010; Kahneman & Deaton, 2010).

Why isn't money a better predictor of happiness? One reason is that there seems to be a disconnect between actual income and how people feel about their financial situation. One study (Johnson & Krueger, 2006) suggests that the correlation between actual wealth and people's subjective perceptions of whether they have enough money to meet their needs is surprisingly modest (around 0.30). Another problem with money is that pervasive advertising and rising income fuel escalating material desires (Frey & Stutzer, 2002; Kasser et al., 2004). When these growing material desires outstrip what people can afford, dissatisfaction is likely (Solberg et al., 2002). Thus, complaints about not having enough money are routine even among people who are very affluent by objective standards. Interestingly, there is some evidence that people who place an especially strong emphasis on the pursuit of wealth and materialistic goals tend to be somewhat less happy than others (Kasser, 2002; Van Boven, 2005). Perhaps this is because they are so focused on financial success that they don't derive much satisfaction from their family life (Nickerson et al., 2003). Consistent with this view, one study (Kahneman et al., 2006) found that higher income was associated with working longer hours and allocating fewer hours to leisure pursuits. The results of another recent study suggested that wealthy people become jaded in a way that undermines their ability to savour positive experiences (Quoidbach et al., 2010).

Age

Age and happiness are consistently found to be unrelated. Age accounts for less than 1 percent of the variation in people's happiness (Inglehart, 1990; Myers & Diener, 1997). The key factors influencing subjective well-being may shift some as people grow older—work becomes less important, health more so—but people's average level of happiness tends to remain remarkably stable over the life span.

Parenthood

Children can be a tremendous source of joy and fulfillment, but they can also be a tremendous source of headaches and hassles. Compared to childless couples, parents worry more and experience more marital problems (Argyle, 1987). Apparently, the good and bad aspects of parenthood balance each other out, because the evidence indicates that people who have children are neither more nor less happy than people without children (Argyle, 2001).

Intelligence and Attractiveness

Intelligence and physical attractiveness are highly valued traits in modern society. Yet researchers have not found an association between either characteristic and happiness (Diener, Wolsic, & Fujita, 1995; Diener, Kesebir & Tov, 2009).

Moderately Good Predictors of Happiness

Research has identified three facets of life that appear to have a *moderate* association with subjective well-being: health, social activity, and religious belief.

Health

Good physical health would seem to be an essential requirement for happiness, but people adapt to health problems. Research reveals that individuals who develop serious, disabling health conditions aren't as unhappy as one might guess (Myers, 1992; Riis et al., 2005). Furthermore, Freedman (1978) argues that good health does not, by itself, produce happiness, because people tend to take good health for granted. Considerations such as these may help to explain why researchers find only a moderate positive correlation (average = 0.32) between health status and subjective well-being (Argyle, 1999). While health may promote happiness to a moderate degree, happiness may also foster better health, as recent research has found a positive correlation between happiness and longevity (Veenhoven, 2008).

Social Activity

Humans are social animals, and interpersonal relations *do* appear to contribute to people's happiness. Those who are satisfied with their social support and friendship networks and those who are socially active report above-average levels of happiness (Diener & Seligman, 2004; Myers, 1999). In addition, being kind to others serves to elevate our own level of happiness (Mongrain, Chin, & Shapiro, 2010).

And people who are exceptionally happy tend to report greater satisfaction with their social relationships than those who are average or low in subjective well-being (Diener & Seligman, 2002). One recent study that periodically recorded participants' daily conversations found that people who had more deep, substantive conversations were happier than those who mostly engaged in small talk (Mehl et al., 2010). This finding is not all that surprising, in that one would expect that people with richer social networks would have more deep conversations.

Religion

The link between religiosity and subjective well-being is modest, but a number of large-scale surveys suggest that people with heartfelt religious convictions are more likely to be happy than people who characterize themselves as nonreligious (Argyle, 1999; Myers, 2008). Researchers aren't sure how religious faith fosters happiness, but Myers (1992) offers some interesting conjectures. Among other things, he discusses how religion can give people a sense of purpose and meaning in their lives; help them accept their setbacks gracefully; connect them to a caring, supportive community; and comfort them by putting their ultimate mortality into perspective.

Strong Predictors of Happiness

The list of factors that turn out to have fairly strong associations with happiness is surprisingly short. The key ingredients of happiness appear to involve love and marriage, work, and genetics and personality.

Love and Marriage

Connecting to others is crucial to our own level of happiness (Brooks, 2011). Romantic relationships can be stressful, but people consistently rate being in love as one of the most critical ingredients of happiness (Myers, 1999). Furthermore, although people complain a lot about their marriages, the evidence indicates that marital status is a key correlate of happiness. Among both men and women, married people are happier than people who are single or divorced (Myers & Diener, 1995), and this relationship holds around the world in widely different cultures (Diener et al., 2000). And among married people, their level of marital satisfaction predicts their personal well-being (Proulx, Helms, & Buehler, 2007. However, the causal relationships underlying this correlation are unclear. It may be that happiness causes marital satisfaction more than marital satisfaction promotes happiness. Perhaps people who are happy tend to have better intimate relationships and more stable marriages, while people who are unhappy have more difficulty finding and keeping mates.

Work

Given the way people often complain about their jobs, one might not expect work to be a key source of happiness, but it is. Although less critical than love and marriage, job satisfaction has a substantial association with general happiness (Judge & Klinger, 2008; Warr, 1999). Studies also show that unemployment has strong negative effects on subjective well-being (Argyle, 1999; Lucas et al., 2004). It is difficult to sort out whether job satisfaction causes happiness or vice versa, but evidence suggests that causation flows both ways (Argyle, 1987, 2001).

Genetics and Personality

The best predictor of individuals' future happiness is their past happiness (Lucas & Diener, 2008). Some people seem destined to be happy and others unhappy, regardless of their triumphs or setbacks. The limited influence of life events was apparent in a stunning study that found only marginal differences in overall happiness between recent lottery winners and recent accident victims who became quadriplegics (Brickman, Coates, & Janoff-Bulman, 1978). Investigators were amazed that such extremely fortuitous and horrible events didn't have a dramatic impact on happiness.

Actually, several lines of evidence suggest that happiness does not depend on external circumstances—buying a nice house, getting promoted—as much as on internal factors, such as one's outlook on life (Lykken & Tellegen, 1996; Lyubomirsky, Sheldon, & Schkade, 2005). With this reality in mind, researchers have investigated whether there might be a hereditary basis for variations in happiness. These studies suggest that people's genetic predispositions account for a very substantial portion of the variance in happiness, perhaps as much as 50 percent (Lyubomirsky, Sheldon, & Schkade, 2005; Stubbe et al., 2005).

How can one's genes influence one's happiness? Presumably, by shaping one's temperament and personality, which are known to be heritable (Weiss, Bates, & Luciano, 2008). Hence, researchers have begun to look for links between personality and subjective well-being, and they have found some interesting correlations. For example, *extraversion* (sometimes referred to as *positive emotionality*) is one of the better predictors of happiness. People who are outgoing, upbeat, and sociable tend to be happier than others (Fleeson, Malanos, & Achille, 2002). Additional personality correlates of happiness include conscientiousness, agreeableness, self-esteem, and optimism (Lucas, 2008; Lyubomirsky, Tkach, & DiMatteo, 2006).

Conclusions about Subjective Well-Being

We must be cautious in drawing inferences about the causes of happiness, because the available data are correlational (see Figure 10.30). Nonetheless, the empirical evidence suggests that many popular beliefs about the sources of happiness are unfounded. The data also demonstrate that happiness is shaped by a complex constellation of variables. In spite of this complexity, however, a number of worthwhile insights about the ingredients of happiness can be gleaned from the recent flurry of research.

First, research on happiness demonstrates that the determinants of subjective well-being are precisely that: subjective. *Objective realities are not as important as subjective feelings.* In other words, your health, your wealth, and your job are not as influential as how you *feel* about your health, wealth, and job (Schwarz & Strack, 1999). These feelings are likely to be influenced by what your *expectations* were. Research suggests that bad outcomes feel worse when unexpected than when expected, and good outcomes feel better when unexpected than when expected (Shepperd & McNulty, 2002). Thus, the same objective event, such as a pay raise of $2000 annually, may generate positive feelings in someone who wasn't expecting a raise and negative feelings in someone expecting a much larger increase in salary.

Second, *when it comes to happiness, everything is relative* (Argyle, 1999; Hagerty, 2000). In other words, you evaluate what you have relative to what the people around you have. Generally, we compare ourselves with others who are similar to us. Thus, people who are wealthy assess what they have by comparing themselves with their wealthy friends and neighbours and their relative standing is crucial (Boyce, Brown, & Moore, 2010). This is one reason for the low correlation between wealth and happiness. You might have a lovely home, but if it sits next door to a neighbour's palatial mansion, it might be a source of more dissatisfaction than happiness.

Third, *research on subjective well-being indicates that people often adapt to their circumstances.* This adaptation effect is one reason that increases in income don't necessarily bring increases in happiness. Thus, *hedonic adaptation* occurs when the mental scale that people use to judge the pleasantness–unpleasantness of their experiences shifts so that their neutral point (or baseline for comparison) changes. Unfortunately, when people's experiences improve, hedonic adaptation may *sometimes* put them on a *hedonic treadmill*—their neutral point moves upward, so that the improvements yield no real benefits (Kahneman, 1999). However, when people have to grapple with major setbacks, hedonic adaptation probably helps protect their mental and physical health. For example, some people who are sent to prison and some people who develop debilitating diseases are not as unhappy as one might assume, because they adapt to their changed situations and evaluate events from a new perspective (Frederick & Loewenstein, 1999).

That's not to say that hedonic adaptation in the face of life's difficulties is inevitable or complete (Lucas, 2007). Evidence suggests that we adapt more slowly to negative events than to positive events (Larsen & Prizmic, 2008). Thus, even years later, people who suffer major setbacks, such as the death of a spouse or serious illness, often are not as happy as they were before the setback, but generally they are not nearly as unhappy as they or others would have predicted (Diener & Oishi, 2005). The downside to the concept of hedonic adaptation is that it suggests that there is nothing people can do to increase their happiness. Fortunately, more recent research on the upside of the hedonic treadmill is not as pessimistic as earlier research (Diener, Lucas, & Scollon, 2006). This research has shown that people vary considerably in the degree to which they experience hedonic adaptation and that enduring increases in individuals' set points for happiness can be achieved.

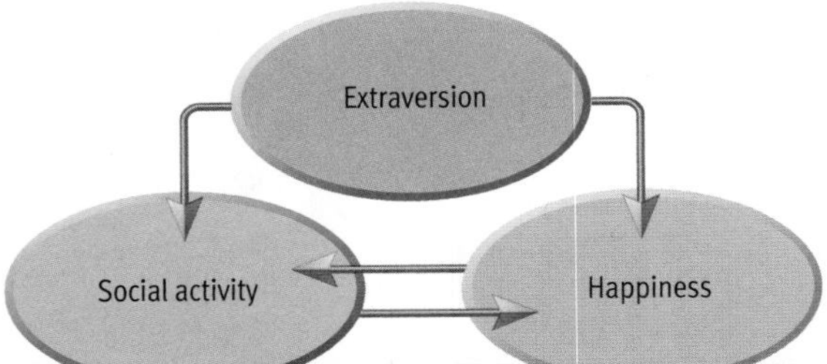

FIGURE 10.30

Possible causal relationships among the correlates of happiness.

Although we have considerable data on the correlates of happiness, it is difficult to untangle the possible causal relationships. For example, we know that a moderate positive correlation exists between social activity and happiness, but we can't say for sure whether high social activity causes happiness or whether happiness causes people to be more socially active. Moreover, in light of the research showing that a third variable—extraversion—correlates with both variables, we have to consider the possibility that extraversion causes both greater social activity and greater happiness.

REVIEW OF KEY POINTS

▸ Research on happiness reveals that many commonsense notions about the roots of happiness appear to be incorrect, including the notion that most people are unhappy. Factors such as income, age, parenthood, intelligence, and attractiveness are largely uncorrelated with subjective well-being.

▸ Physical health, good social relationships, and religious faith appear to have a modest impact on feelings of happiness. The only factors that are good predictors of happiness are love and marriage, work satisfaction, and genetics and personality.

▸ Research on happiness indicates that objective realities are not as important as subjective feelings and that subjective well-being is a relative concept. The evidence also indicates that people adapt to their circumstances and that the quest for happiness is almost never hopeless.

Motivation and Emotion

Analyzing Arguments: Making Sense Out of Controversy

Consider the following argument: "Dieting is harmful to your health because the tendency to be obese is largely inherited." What is your reaction to this reasoning? Do you find it convincing? We hope not, as this argument is seriously flawed. Can you see what's wrong? There is no relationship between the conclusion that "dieting is harmful to your health" and the reason given that "the tendency to be obese is largely inherited." The argument is initially seductive because you know from reading this chapter that obesity *is* largely inherited, so the reason provided represents a true statement. But the reason is unrelated to the conclusion advocated. This scenario may strike you as odd, but if you start listening carefully to discussions about controversial issues, you will probably notice that people often cite irrelevant considerations in support of their favoured conclusions.

This chapter was loaded with controversial issues that sincere, well-meaning people could argue about for weeks. Does the availability of pornography increase the prevalence of sex crimes? Are gender differences in mating preferences a product of evolution or of modern economic realities? Is there a biological basis for homosexuality? Unfortunately, arguments about issues such as these typically are unproductive in terms

of moving toward resolution or agreement because most people know little about the rules of argumentation. In this application, we will explore what makes arguments sound or unsound in the hope of improving your ability to analyze and think critically about arguments.

The Anatomy of an Argument

In everyday usage, the word *argument* is used to refer to a dispute or disagreement between two or more people, but in the technical language of rhetoric, an *argument* consists of one or more premises that are used to provide support for a conclusion. *Premises* are the reasons that are presented to persuade someone that a conclusion is true or probably true. *Assumptions* are premises for which no proof or evidence is offered. Assumptions are often left unstated. For example, suppose that your doctor tells you that you should exercise regularly because regular exercise is good for your heart. In this simple argument, the conclusion is "You should exercise regularly." The premise that leads to this conclusion is the idea that "exercise is good for your heart." An unstated assumption is that everyone wants a healthy heart.

In the language of argument analysis, premises are said to support (or not support) conclusions. A conclusion may be supported by one reason or by many reasons. One way to visualize these possibilities is to draw an analogy between the reasons that support a conclusion and the legs that support a table (Halpern, 1996, 2003). As shown in Figure 10.31, a tabletop (conclusion) could be supported by one strong leg (a single strong reason) or many thin legs (lots of weaker reasons). Of course, the reasons provided for a conclusion may fail to support the conclusion. Returning to our table analogy, the tabletop might not be supported because the legs are too thin (very weak reasons) or because the legs are not attached (irrelevant reasons).

Arguments can get pretty complicated, as they usually have more parts than just reasons and conclusions. In addition, there often are *counterarguments*, which are reasons that take support away from a conclusion. And sometimes the most important part of an argument is a part that is not there—reasons that have been omitted, either deliberately or not, that would lead to a different conclusion if they were supplied. Given all of the complex variations that are possible in arguments, it is impossible to give you simple rules for judging arguments,

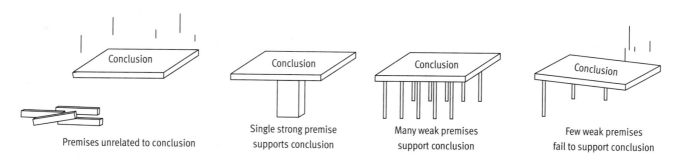

Premises unrelated to conclusion

Single strong premise supports conclusion

Many weak premises support conclusion

Few weak premises fail to support conclusion

FIGURE 10.31

An analogy for understanding the strength of arguments.

Halpern (1996) draws an analogy between the reasons that support a conclusion and the legs that support a table. She points out that a conclusion may be supported effectively by one strong premise or many weak premises. Of course, the reasons provided for a conclusion may also *fail* to provide adequate support.

Source: Halpern, D.F. (2003). *Thought and knowledge: An introduction to critical thinking.* Mahwah, NJ: Erlbaum. Copyright © 2003 Lawrence Erlbaum Associates. Reprinted by permission.

but we can highlight some common fallacies and then provide some criteria that you can apply in thinking critically about arguments.

Common Fallacies

As noted in previous chapters, cognitive scientists have compiled lengthy lists of fallacies that people frequently display in their reasoning. These fallacies often show up in arguments. In this section, we will describe five common fallacies. To illustrate each one, we will assume the role of someone arguing that pornographic material on the Internet (cyberporn) should be banned or heavily regulated.

Irrelevant Reasons

Reasons cannot provide support for an argument unless they are relevant to the conclusion. Arguments that depend on irrelevant reasons—either intentionally or inadvertently—are quite common. You already saw one example at the beginning of this Application. The Latin term for this fallacy is *non sequitur*, which literally translates to *it doesn't follow*. In other words, the conclusion does not follow from the premise. For example, in the debate about Internet pornography, you might hear the following non sequitur: "We need to regulate cyberporn because research has shown that most date rapes go unreported."

Circular Reasoning

In *circular reasoning* the premise and conclusion are simply restatements of each other. People vary their wording a little so it isn't obvious, but when you look closely, the conclusion is the premise. For example, in arguments about Internet pornography you might hear someone assert, "We need to control cyberporn because it currently is unregulated."

Slippery Slope

The concept of *slippery slope* argumentation takes its name from the notion that if you are on a slippery slope and you don't dig in your heels, you will slide and slide until you reach the bottom. A slippery slope argument typically asserts that if you allow X to happen, things will spin out of control and far worse events will follow. The trick is that there is no inherent connection between X and the events that are predicted to follow. For example, in the debate about medical marijuana, opponents have argued, "If you legalize medical marijuana, the next thing you know, cocaine and heroin will be legal." In the debate about cyberporn, a slippery slope argument might go, "If we don't ban cyberporn, the next thing you know, grade-school children will be watching smut all day long in their school libraries."

Weak Analogies

An *analogy* asserts that two concepts or events are similar in some way. Hence, you can draw conclusions about event B because of its similarity to event A. Analogies are useful in thinking about complex issues, but some analogies are weak or inappropriate because the similarity between A and B is superficial, minimal, or irrelevant to the issue at hand. For example, in the debate about Internet erotica, someone might argue, "Cyberporn is morally offensive, just like child molestation. We wouldn't tolerate child molestation, so we shouldn't permit cyberporn."

False Dichotomy

A *false dichotomy* creates an either–or choice between two outcomes: the outcome advocated and some obviously horrible outcome that any sensible person would want to avoid. These outcomes are presented as the only two possibilities, when in reality there could be other outcomes, including ones that lie somewhere between the extremes depicted in the false dichotomy. In the debate about Internet pornography, someone might argue, "We can ban cyberporn, or we can hasten the moral decay of modern society."

Evaluating the Strength of Arguments

In everyday life, you may frequently need to assess the strength of arguments made by friends, family, co-workers, politicians, media pundits, and so forth. You may also want to evaluate your own arguments when you write papers or speeches for school or prepare presentations for your work. The following questions can help you make systematic evaluations of arguments (adapted from Halpern, 1996, 2003):

- What is the conclusion?
- What are the premises provided to support the conclusion? Are the premises valid?
- Does the conclusion follow from the premises? Are there any fallacies in the chain of reasoning?
- What assumptions have been made? Are they valid assumptions? Should they be stated explicitly?
- What are the counterarguments? Do they weaken the argument?
- Is there anything that has been omitted from the argument?

TABLE 10.1 **Critical Thinking Skills Discussed in This Application**

Skill	Description
Understanding the elements of an argument	The critical thinker understands that an argument consists of premises and assumptions that are used to support a conclusion.
Recognizing and avoiding common fallacies, such as irrelevant reasons, circular reasoning, slippery slope reasoning, weak analogies, and false dichotomies.	The critical thinker is vigilant about conclusions based on unrelated premises, conclusions that are rewordings of premises, superficial analogies, and contrived dichotomies.
Evaluating arguments systematically	The critical thinker carefully assesses the validity of the premises, assumptions, and conclusions in an argument, and considers counterarguments and missing elements.

Key Ideas

Motivational Theories and Concepts

● Drive theories apply a homeostatic model to motivation. They assume that organisms seek to reduce unpleasant states of tension called *drives*. In contrast, incentive theories emphasize how external goals energize behaviour.

● Evolutionary theorists explain motives in terms of their adaptive value. Madsen's list of biological needs and Murray's list of social needs illustrate that a diverse array of motives govern human behaviour.

The Motivation of Hunger and Eating

● Eating is regulated by a complex interaction of biological and environmental factors. In the brain, the lateral, ventromedial, and paraventricular areas of the hypothalamus appear to be involved in the control of hunger, but their exact role is unclear.

● Fluctuations in blood glucose also seem to play a role in hunger. The stomach can send two types of satiety signals to the brain. Hormonal regulation of hunger depends primarily on ghrelin, CCK, insulin, and leptin secretions.

● Incentive-oriented models assert that eating is regulated by the availability and palatability of food. Learning processes, such as classical conditioning and observational learning, exert a great deal of influence over both what people eat and how much they eat. Cultural traditions also shape food preferences. Stress can stimulate eating.

● Evidence indicates that there is a genetic predisposition to obesity. According to set-point theory, the body monitors fat stores to keep them fairly stable. Settling-point theory suggests that a multitude of factors contribute to weight stability. Vacillations in dietary restraint resulting in disinhibition may contribute to obesity in some people.

Sexual Motivation and Behaviour

● The human sexual response cycle can be divided into four stages: excitement, plateau, orgasm, and resolution.

● Consistent with evolutionary theory, males tend to think about and initiate sex more than females and to have more sexual partners and more interest in casual sex than females. The Featured Study demonstrated that women can draw meaningful inferences about males' masculinity and parental interest based on a brief exposure to a single photograph.

● People respond to a variety of erotic materials, which may elevate sexual desire for only a few hours but may have an enduring impact on attitudes about sex. Aggressive pornography may make sexual coercion seem less offensive and may contribute to date rape.

● The determinants of sexual orientation are not well understood. Recent studies suggest that there may be a genetic predisposition to homosexuality and that idiosyncrasies in prenatal hormonal secretions may contribute, but much remains to be learned.

Achievement: In Search of Excellence

● David McClelland pioneered the use of the TAT to measure achievement motivation. People with a high need for achievement work harder and more persistently than others, although they often choose to tackle challenges of intermediate difficulty. The pursuit of achievement tends to increase when the probability of success and the incentive value of success are high.

The Elements of Emotional Experience

● Emotion is made up of cognitive, physiological, and behavioural components. The cognitive component involves subjective feelings that have an evaluative aspect. In the peripheral nervous system, the physiological component is dominated by autonomic arousal. In the brain, the amygdala seems to be the hub of the neural circuits that process emotion. At the behavioural level, emotions are expressed through body language, with facial expressions being particularly prominent.

● Ekman and Friesen have found considerable cross-cultural agreement in the identification of emotions based on facial expressions. Cross-cultural similarities have also been found in the cognitive and physiological components of emotion. However, there are cultural variations in how people categorize and display their emotions.

Theories of Emotion

● The James–Lange theory asserts that emotion results from one's perception of autonomic arousal. The Cannon–Bard theory counters with the proposal that emotions originate in subcortical areas of the brain. According to Schachter's two-factor theory, people infer emotion from arousal and then label the emotion in accordance with their cognitive explanation for the arousal. Evolutionary theories of emotion maintain that emotions are innate reactions that require little cognitive interpretation.

Putting It in Perspective: Themes 2, 3, 4, 5, and 6

● Our look at motivation and emotion showed once again that psychology is characterized by theoretical diversity, that biology and environment shape behaviour interactively, that behaviour is governed by multiple causes, that psychological processes are characterized by both cultural variance and invariance, and that psychology evolves in a sociohistorical context.

PERSONAL APPLICATION • Exploring the Ingredients of Happiness

● Factors such as income, age, parenthood, intelligence, and attractiveness are largely uncorrelated with subjective well-being. Physical health, good social relationships, and religious faith appear to have a modest impact on feelings of happiness. Strong predictors of happiness include love and marriage, work satisfaction, and genetics and personality.

● Research on happiness indicates that objective realities are not that important, that happiness is relative, that people adapt to their circumstances, and that the quest for happiness is almost never hopeless.

CRITICAL THINKING APPLICATION • Analyzing Arguments: Making Sense Out of Controversy

● An argument consists of one or more premises used to provide support for a conclusion. Arguments are often marred by fallacies in reasoning, such as irrelevant reasons, circular reasoning, slippery slope scenarios, weak analogies, and false dichotomies. Arguments can be evaluated more effectively by applying systematic criteria.

Key Terms

Achievement motive, 464
Affective forecasting, 469
Argument, 484
Assumptions, 484
Bisexuals, 460
Body mass index (BMI), 447
Display rules, 475
Drive, 441
Emotion, 468
Galvanic skin response (GSR), 470
Glucose, 444
Hedonic adaptation, 483
Heterosexuals, 460
Homeostasis, 441
Homosexuals, 460
Incentive, 441
Lie detector, 470
Motivation, 440
Obesity, 447
Orgasm, 453
Polygraph, 470
Premises, 484
Refractory period, 454

Set-point theory, 450
Settling-point theory, 450
Sexual orientation, 460
Subjective well-being, 480
Vasocongestion, 453

Key People

John Atkinson, 466
Philip Bard, 477
David Buss, 459
Walter Cannon, 476
Paul Ekman, 472
Wallace Friesen, 472
William James, 476
Virginia Johnson, 453
Carl Lange, 476
Joseph LeDoux, 471
William Masters, 453
David McClelland, 464
Henry Murray, 442
Judith Rodin, 444
Stanley Schachter, 477
A. L. Washburn, 443

1. Although Jackson had a huge breakfast and felt full when he arrived at work, he could not resist eating three of the doughnuts that a colleague brought to the morning staff meeting. Jackson's behaviour is NOT consistent with which of the following theories of motivation?
   A. incentive theories
   B. drive theories
   C. evolutionary theories
   D. Cannon–Bard theory

2. Sherry and Elaine eat roughly the same number of calories and burn approximately equal numbers of calories through exercise, yet Sherry has a significantly higher BMI than Elaine. Which of the following is a well-supported explanation for such a difference?
   A. Elaine is likely eating all her food at once, which is conducive to weight loss.
   B. Elaine is doing yoga, which is more effective than Sherry's jogging.
   C. Sherry has a common metabolic disorder that prevents her from losing weight.
   D. Sherry has a genetic predisposition toward a heavier body weight.

3. Restrained eaters can become disinhibited and overeat. Which of the following is the most common reason for disinhibition?
   A. They are emotionally unstable to begin with, and cannot maintain inhibition.
   B. They subconsciously fear becoming too thin.
   C. They drink alcohol in small quantities.
   D. They perceive they have already cheated on their diet.

4. Regarding progression through the stages of the sexual response cycle, which of the following situations would likely lead to a prolonged or unpleasant resolution phase?
   A. the absence of a plateau phase
   B. the absence of an orgasm phase
   C. a lengthy arousal phase
   D. a lengthy plateau phase

5. Which of the following would be predicted by parental investment theory?
   A. Men are more interested than women in uncommitted sex.
   B. Men typically have more sex partners in a lifetime than they would prefer.
   C. Women are only choosy when it comes to long-term relationships.
   D. Women have a lot to lose by committing to one relationship.

6. Which of the following statements describes Kinsey's view of sexual orientation?
   A. It depends on early classical conditioning experiences.
   B. It should be viewed as a continuum.
   C. It depends on normalities and abnormalities in the amygdala.
   D. It should be viewed as an either–or distinction.

7. Anika felt fear when she received an injection of epinephrine that caused her heart to beat faster, and other signs of autonomic arousal. This example is most compatible with which of the following theories of emotion?
   A. James–Lange theory
   B. Cannon–Bard theory
   C. Schachter's two-factor theory
   D. opponent-process theory

8. What is required of someone who is completing a projective test, like the TAT?
   A. making predictions about the future
   B. describing scenarios that would lead to happiness or contentment
   C. looking at ambiguous stimuli and generating impressions or stories
   D. proposing changes to an existing model in order to improve it

9. Which of the following describes how a polygraph (lie detector device) works?
   A. It monitors physiological indices of autonomic arousal.
   B. It directly assesses the truth of a person's statements.
   C. It monitors a person's facial expressions and brain waves.
   D. It compares a statement with the baseline probability that the statement is true.

10. According to Tomkins, Izzard, or Plutchik, which of the following is a primary emotion?
    A. frustration
    B. empathy
    C. suspicion
    D. disgust

11. Which of the following statements is best associated with the Cannon–Bard theory of emotion?
    A. The experience of emotion depends on autonomic arousal and on the cognitive interpretation of that arousal.
    B. Different patterns of autonomic activation lead to the experience of different emotions.
    C. Emotion occurs when the thalamus simultaneously sends signals to the cortex and the autonomic nervous system.
    D. Emotions develop because of their adaptive value.

12. Which of the following theories of emotion implies that people can change their emotions simply by changing the way they label their emotional arousal?
    A. James–Lange theory
    B. Cannon–Bard theory
    C. Schachter's two-factor theory
    D. opponent-process theory

13. Which of the following statements is consistent with evolutionary theories of emotion?
    A. Emotions change over the life span based on learning experiences.
    B. Emotions are reactions that help us to avoid danger and repeat beneficial actions.
    C. Emotional reactions to events will be identical among all individuals.
    D. Human emotions are the same as emotions in other species.

14. Which of the following factors is a strong predictor of happiness?
    A. having a career that you enjoy
    B. having children
    C. being physically attractive
    D. living in a collectivist culture

15. Consider this sales pitch: "We're the best dealership in town because the other dealerships just don't stack up against us." This statement is an example of which of the following concepts?
    A. false dichotomy
    B. semantic slanting
    C. circular reasoning
    D. slippery slope

See Appendix A for answers to this Practice Test.

On the Web

▶ **CourseMate**

Go to this site to find online resources directly linked to your book, including more quizzes, a glossary, flash cards, videos, and more!

▶ **CengageNow**

Go to this site for the link to CengageNOW™, your one-stop study shop. Take a pre-test for this chapter and CengageNOW™ will generate a personalized study plan based on your test results! The study plan will identify the topics you need to review and direct you to online resources to help you master those topics. You can then take a post-test to help you determine the concepts you have mastered and what you still need to work on.

▶ **Aplia**

Aplia™ is an online interactive learning solution that helps you improve comprehension—and your grade—by integrating a variety of media and tools such as video, tutorials, practice tests, and an interactive e-book.

Elena Schweitzer/Shutterstock.com

If you think about yourself now and compare yourself to how you looked and behaved ten years ago, and if you then add what has happened to you in the years in between, you would be able to generate a rather long list of the many ways in which you have changed and developed. But other things have remained the same. Your life provides an interesting illustration of the two themes that permeate the study of human development: *transition* and *continuity*. In investigating human development, psychologists study how people evolve through transitions over time. In looking at these transitions, developmental psychologists inevitably find continuity with the past.

As you grew older you undoubtedly were faced with new challenges. Some of the challenges you faced were likely quite difficult and you may have been able to talk about them with—and receive reassurance and support from—your parents or caregivers. While there are many things that you shared with your parents in conversation over the years, there is one thing that your parents should have told you, or talked to you about, before you found out on your own. No, we aren't referring to *that* talk but rather to another one. They should have confessed that, like most parents, they have talked and continue to talk about you all the time to all sorts of other people and that they have done so since the moment of your birth. That's why family, friends, and indeed even people you haven't met seem to know so much about you. If you are like our own children, you may not always appreciate this sharing. However, you may also have discovered that parents are not easily dissuaded from such activity.

Why do parents spend so much of their time talking about their children? This is likely a multidetermined behaviour, but a couple of the reasons are relevant to the issues discussed in this chapter. In part, this reflects the level of their engagement with you and their belief that a high level of engagement is important for your development. Their degree of involvement and parenting style affects many things, including your level of attachment. Attachment between a child and caregivers and its effects on later development are among the issues we will discuss in this chapter. You may recall in Chapter 1 that we introduced you to Mary Ainsworth, one of the major contributors to the scientific literature on attachment and related issues.

Another reason why your parents talk about you so much may be that they are continually amazed at the changes you have evidenced as you have grown and developed from a newborn to an infant, child, adolescent, young adult, and beyond. Cognitive and social–emotional development will also be a focus in this chapter. While children change dramatically in the way they think about themselves and the world, sometimes even very young children can show an amazing grasp of things. One of us had to pull his car over to the side of the road one day to catch his breath after his four-year-old son asked from the back seat, "Dad, what makes life possible?" Or consider another example, the definition recounted in a speech given in 1930 by famed Canadian artist Emily Carr when a young girl was asked about the process of creative art. When asked to describe how it's done, the young child responded, "I think, and then I draw a line round my think" (Carr, 1972, p. 8). Carr, herself a world-renowned artist, could not think of a better description of the creative process and she believed that children often grasp such things much more quickly and adequately than adults.

Even newborns and young infants have been found to show the most amazing abilities. Rather that being simply passive residents of their world, newborns and infants show evidence that very early they are on a journey of discovery and unfolding understanding concerning their world and those around them. For example, research by Kiley Hamlin of Yale University has shown that children as young as six months are able to use the behaviour they see adults enact toward others in their own evaluations of those adults (Hamlin, Wynn, & Bloom, 2007). Also, research conducted in Janet Werker's lab at the University of British Columbia by Whitney Weikum and her colleagues has shown that infants as young as four months can discriminate between speakers who are speaking English or French even when they can't hear the speakers' voices (Weikum et al., 2007). Would you have imagined that infants this young were capable of these things? On the other hand, young children frequently show the most amazing misunderstanding of even simple logic. What do we know about the young child's developing sense of the social and physical general world around her or him? Research in psychology has taken us some distance toward understanding this developing theory of the world and how it works and specific characteristics of children at different ages.

Much of a child's development is the result of relatively predetermined physiological changes. We will discuss some of these in this chapter—standing, crawling, walking, and so on. The physical challenges and accomplishments facing the typical developing child are enormous. Although important, physical changes are only part of the story we focus on in this chapter. Children and their development are also affected by cultural and social forces, forces that today may differ from those experienced by children in the past. Consider the experiences and

Human Development across the Life Span

Courtesy of Free the Children

© John Van Hasselt/CORBIS SYGMA

accomplishments of Craig Kielburger, who was born in Thornhill, Ontario, in 1982. Until the age of 12 he was just like most other Canadian children.

On April 19, 1995, all that changed (Kielburger, 1998). That morning, over breakfast, he was looking through the newspaper for some of his favourite comics to read while eating his cereal before heading off to school. He was stopped by a story on the front page detailing the murder of a child in India named Iqbal Masih. Iqbal had been given into slavery at the age of four in order to pay off a family debt of $16. Iqbal toiled for years as a child labourer before escaping and becoming a champion of children's rights while still a young teen. Iqbal had been threatened in an attempt to silence him and then was murdered. Craig decided to carry on Iqbal's work in crusading against child labour. He started that morning by requesting class time from his teacher in order to ask his classmates for volunteers to help. With a small group of volunteers, Craig started to work for children.

Later that year, he travelled to Asia by himself to investigate child labour conditions and to visit the grave of Iqbal. He was met by an adult mentor once he arrived. Since then, Free the Children (http://www.freethechildren.org) has grown to be an international organization dedicated to children's rights. Craig has met with and been endorsed by prime ministers, monarchs, Pope John Paul II, Mother Teresa, and international celebrities such as Oprah Winfrey. He believes that children are a critically important resource, that the developing child needs more than exposure to facts in school, that childhood is a critical time of formation, and that we should focus on "helping them to better understand themselves and the world around them, including their talents and what they have to offer. . . ." (Terry & Woonteiler, 2000).

It is not only children who are affected by changing social conditions. While it has been traditional for people like your parents to think of working to the age of 65 and then retiring, recently this idea has been challenged. While many adults look forward to retiring at 65, not all do. In previous chapters, we have described the pioneering work of McGill neuropsychologist Brenda Milner, who in 2011 at age 93, continues to teach and do research; if she had been forced to retire at 65 because of age, she said, it would have been terrible (Won, 2005). She must agree with Canadian humorist Stephen Leacock, who said, "But as to this retirement business, let me give you a word of advice. Have nothing to do with it" (Leacock, 1939, p. 175). By the way, Leacock also had amusing views on the nature and proper place of psychology; he referred to it as the "Black Art" (Leacock, 1939).

Life for many older Canadians may be different in the next few years compared to what would have happened just a few years ago. Mandatory retirement at age 65 has been retired itself in most of Canada. However, many provinces have provisions to allow mandatory retirement for jobs where physical ability is a must, such as firefighting and police work. Retirement is a complicated process and successful retirement requires planning ahead and systematic decision making and consultation (Adams & Rau, 2011; Feldman & Beehr, 2011; Schultz & Wang, 2011; Wang, Henkens, & van Solinge, 2011).

These types of social changes are also of interest to us in this chapter because the topic of development spans prenatal issues to adolescence, adulthood, and old age. As we see it, *development* is the sequence of age-related changes that occur as a person progresses from conception to death. It is a reasonably orderly, cumulative process that includes both the biological and behavioural changes that take place as people grow older. An infant's newfound ability to grasp objects, a child's gradual mastery of grammar, an adolescent's spurt in physical growth, a young adult's increasing commitment to a vocation, and an older adult's transition into the role of grandparent all represent development. These transitions are predictable changes that are related to age.

Traditionally, psychologists have been most interested in development during childhood. Our coverage reflects this emphasis. However, decades of research have clearly demonstrated that development is a lifelong process (Heckhausen, Wrosch, & Schulz, 2010). We'll divide the life span into four broad periods: (1) the prenatal period, between conception and birth, (2) childhood, (3) adolescence, and (4) adulthood. We'll examine aspects of development that are especially dynamic during each period. Let's begin by looking at events that occur before birth, during prenatal development.

Progress before Birth: Prenatal Development

Development begins with conception. Conception occurs when fertilization creates a *zygote*, a one-celled organism formed by the union of a sperm and an egg. All of the other cells in your body developed from this single cell. Each of your cells contains enduring messages from your parents carried on the *chromosomes* that lie within its nucleus. Each chromosome houses many *genes,* the functional units in hereditary transmission. Genes carry the details of your hereditary blueprints, which are revealed gradually throughout life (see Chapter 3 for more information on genetic transmission).

The *prenatal period* extends from conception to birth, usually encompassing nine months of pregnancy. A great deal of important development occurs before birth. In fact, development during the prenatal period is remarkably rapid. If you were an average-sized newborn and your physical growth had continued during the first year of your life at a prenatal pace, by your first birthday you would have weighed nearly 100 kilograms! Fortunately, you didn't grow at that rate—and no human does—because in the final weeks before birth, the frenzied pace of prenatal development tapers off dramatically. In this section, we'll examine the usual course of prenatal development and discuss how environmental events can leave their mark on development even before birth exposes the newborn to the outside world.

The Course of Prenatal Development 9a

The prenatal period is divided into three phases: (1) the germinal stage (the first two weeks), (2) the embryonic stage (two weeks to two months), and (3) the fetal stage (two months to birth). Some key developments in these phases are outlined here.

Germinal Stage

The *germinal stage* is the first phase of prenatal development, encompassing the first two weeks after conception. This brief stage begins when a zygote is created through fertilization. Within 36 hours, rapid cell division begins and the zygote becomes a microscopic mass of multiplying cells. This mass of cells slowly migrates along the mother's fallopian tube to the uterine cavity. On about the seventh day, the cell mass begins to implant itself in the uterine wall. This process takes about a week and is far from automatic. Many zygotes are rejected at this point. As many as one in five pregnancies end with the woman never being aware that conception has occurred (Simpson & Juaniaux, 2007).

During the implantation process, the placenta begins to form (Buster & Carson, 2002). The *placenta* is a structure that allows oxygen and nutrients to pass into the fetus from the mother's bloodstream, and bodily wastes to pass out to the mother. This critical exchange takes place across thin membranes that block the passage of blood cells, keeping the fetal and maternal bloodstreams separate.

Embryonic Stage

The *embryonic stage* is the second stage of prenatal development, lasting from two weeks until the end of the second month. During this stage, most of the vital organs and bodily systems begin to form in the developing organism, which is now called an *embryo*. Structures such as the heart, spine, and brain emerge gradually as cell division becomes more specialized. Although the embryo is typically only about 2.5 cm long at the end of this stage, it's already beginning to look human. Arms, legs, hands, feet, fingers, toes, eyes, and ears are already discernible.

The embryonic stage is a period of great vulnerability because virtually all of the basic physiological structures are being formed. If anything interferes with normal development during the embryonic phase, the effects can be devastating. Most miscarriages occur during this period (Simpson & Juaniaux, 2007). Most major structural birth defects are also due to problems that occur during the embryonic stage (Niebyl & Simpson, 2007).

Fetal Stage

The *fetal stage* is the third stage of prenatal development, lasting from two months through birth. Some

PREVIEW QUESTIONS

► What are the three stages of prenatal development and what happens in each stage?

► What are the effects of environmental factors on prenatal development?

Prenatal development is remarkably rapid. (Top left) This 30-day-old embryo is just 6 mm in length. (Bottom left) At 14 weeks, the fetus is approximately 5 cm long. Note the well-developed fingers. The fetus can already move its legs, feet, hands, and head and displays a variety of basic reflexes. (Right) After four months of prenatal development, facial features are beginning to emerge.

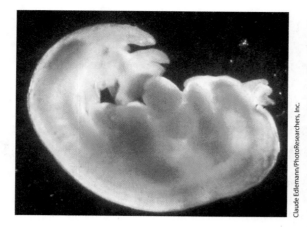

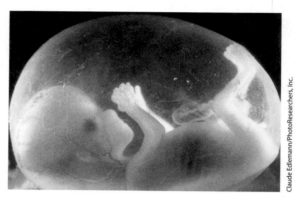

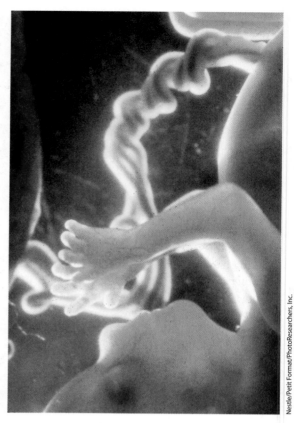

Claude Edelmann/PhotoResearchers, Inc.

Claude Edelmann/PhotoResearchers, Inc.

Nestle/Petit Format/PhotoResearchers, Inc.

highlights of fetal development are summarized in Figure 11.1. The first two months of the fetal stage bring rapid bodily growth, as muscles and bones begin to form (Moore & Persaud, 2008). The developing organism, now called a *fetus,* becomes capable of physical movements as skeletal structures harden. Organs formed in the embryonic stage continue to grow and gradually begin to function. Sex organs start to develop during the third month.

During the final three months of the prenatal period, brain cells multiply at a brisk pace. A layer of fat is deposited under the skin to provide insulation, and the respiratory and digestive systems mature. All of these changes ready the fetus for life outside the

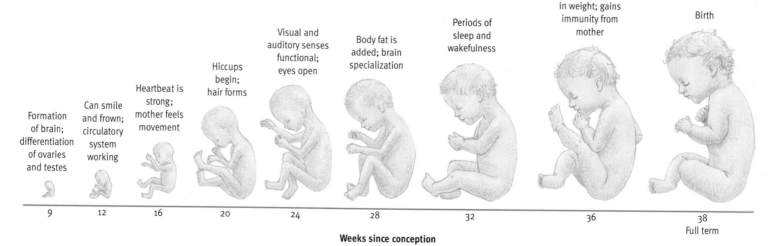

FIGURE 11.1

Overview of fetal development.

This chart outlines some of the highlights of development during the fetal stage.

cosy, supportive environment of its mother's womb. Sometime between 22 weeks and 26 weeks the fetus reaches the *age of viability*—the age at which a baby can survive in the event of a premature birth (Moore & Persaud, 2008). At 23 weeks the probability of survival is still slim (about 10–20 percent). It climbs rapidly over the next month, to around a 75 percent survival rate at 26 weeks (Iams & Romero, 2007). Unfortunately, a great many of the premature infants born near the threshold of viability go on to experience a wide range of developmental problems (Cunningham et al., 2010; Eichenwald & Stark, 2008).

Environmental Factors and Prenatal Development

Although the fetus develops in the protective buffer of the womb, events in the external environment can affect it indirectly through the mother. Because the developing organism and its mother are linked through the placenta, a mother's eating habits, drug use, and physical health, among other things, can affect prenatal development and have long-term health consequences (Hampton, 2004). *Teratogens* are any external agents, such as drugs or viruses, that can harm an embryo or fetus. Figure 11.2 shows the periods of prenatal development during which various structures are most vulnerable to damage.

Maternal Drug Use

A major source of concern about fetal and infant well-being is the mother's consumption of drugs, including such widely used substances as tobacco and alcohol as well as prescription and recreational drugs. Unfortunately, most drugs consumed by a pregnant woman can pass through the membranes of the placenta.

Virtually all "recreational" drugs (see Chapter 5) can be harmful, with sedatives, narcotics, and cocaine being particularly dangerous. Babies of heroin users are born addicted to narcotics and have an increased risk of early death due to prematurity, birth defects, respiratory difficulties, and problems associated with their addiction (Finnegan & Kandall, 2005). Prenatal exposure to cocaine is associated with increased risk of birth complications (Sokol et al., 2007) and a variety of cognitive deficits that are apparent in childhood (Singer et al., 2002, 2004). Peter Fried of Carleton University has conducted a research program examining the effects of prenatal exposure to marijuana and other substances (Fried & Smith, 2001; Porath & Fried, 2005). He has found that such exposure is associated with a variety of physical and cognitive effects. In a recent review of the available literature, he

suggested that although the data is limited, it seems that prenatal marijuana exposure may be linked to disturbances in executive functioning associated with the prefrontal part of the brain at age three. These functions have been implicated in disturbances in attention/impulsivity and problem-solving domains.

Problems can also be caused by a great variety of drugs prescribed for legitimate medical reasons, and even some over-the-counter drugs (Nieby & Simpson, 2007). The impact of drugs on the embryo or fetus varies greatly depending on the drug, the dose, and the phase of prenatal development.

Alcohol consumption during pregnancy also carries risks (Lebel et al., 2010). It has long been clear that heavy drinking by a mother can be hazardous to a fetus. *Fetal alcohol syndrome* is a collection of congenital (inborn) problems associated with excessive alcohol use during pregnancy. Typical problems include microcephaly (a small head), heart defects, irritability, hyperactivity, and delayed mental and motor development (Hannigan & Armant, 2000; Pellegrino & Pellegrino, 2008). Fetal alcohol syndrome is the most common known cause of

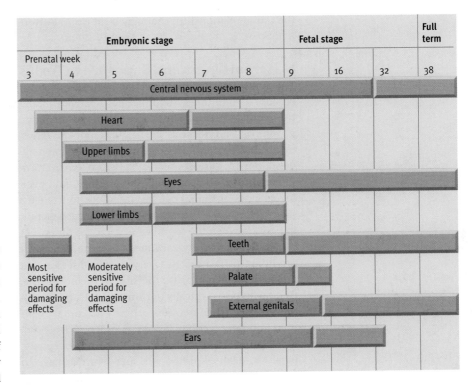

FIGURE 11.2

Periods of vulnerability in prenatal development.

Generally, structures are most susceptible to damage when they are undergoing rapid development. The red regions of the bars indicate the most sensitive periods for various organs and structures, while the purple regions indicate periods of continued, but lessened, vulnerability. As a whole, sensitivity is greatest in the embryonic stage, but some structures remain vulnerable throughout prenatal development.

Source: Adapted from Moore, K.L., & Persaud, T.V.N. (1998). *Before we are born: Essentials of embryology and birth defects.* Philadelphia: W.B. Saunders. Copyright © 1998 Elsevier Science (USA). All rights reserved. Reprinted by permission.

intellectual disability (Niccols, 2007), and it is related to an increased incidence of difficulties in school, depression, suicide, drug problems, and criminal behaviour in adolescence and adulthood (Kelly, Day, & Streissguth, 2000; Streissguth et al., 2004).

Furthermore, many children fall short of the criteria for fetal alcohol syndrome but still show serious impairments attributable to their mothers' drinking during pregnancy (Willford, Leech, & Day, 2006). A long-running study of pregnant women's drinking found that higher alcohol intake was associated with an elevated risk for deficits in IQ, motor skills, and attention span, and with increased impulsive, antisocial, and delinquent behaviour (Streissguth, 2007). Clearly, even moderate drinking during pregnancy can have enduring and substantial negative effects.

Tobacco use during pregnancy is also hazardous to prenatal development (Centers for Disease Control, 2011). Smoking appears to increase a mother's risk for miscarriage, stillbirth, and prematurity, and newborns' risk for sudden infant death syndrome (Shea & Steiner, 2008). Prenatal exposure to tobacco is also associated with slower than average cognitive development, attention deficits, hyperactivity, and conduct problems, although it is difficult to tease out the causal relationships that may be at work (Button, Maughan, & McGuffin, 2007; Knopik, 2009).

Maternal Illness and Exposure to Toxins

The fetus is largely defenceless against infections because its immune system matures relatively late in the prenatal period. The placenta screens out quite a number of infectious agents, but not all. Thus, many maternal illnesses can interfere with prenatal development. Diseases such as rubella (German measles), syphilis, cholera, smallpox, mumps, and even severe cases of the flu can be hazardous to the fetus (Bernstein, 2007). The nature of any damage depends, in part, on when the mother contracts the illness.

Genital herpes and acquired immune deficiency syndrome (AIDS) are two very deadly diseases that pregnant women can also transmit to their offspring. Genital herpes is typically transmitted during the birth process itself when newborns come into contact with their mothers' genital lesions (Gosden, Nicolaides, & Whitting, 1994). Herpes can cause microcephaly, paralysis, deafness, blindness, and brain damage in infants and is fatal for many newborns (Ismail, 1993). The HIV virus that causes AIDS can also be transmitted by pregnant women to their offspring. The transmission of AIDS may occur prenatally through the placenta, during delivery, or through breastfeeding. Up through the mid-1990s, about 20–30 percent of HIV-positive pregnant women passed the virus on to their babies. However, improved antiretroviral drugs (given to the mother) and more cautious obstetrical care have reduced this figure to about 2 percent in the United States (Cotter & Potter, 2006).

Research also suggests that babies in the womb are exposed to a surprising variety of *environmental toxins* that can have an impact on the fetus (Houlihan et al., 2005). For example, prenatal exposure to air pollution has been linked to impairments in cognitive development at age five (Edwards et al., 2010). In a similar vein, exposure to the chemicals used in flame-retardant materials correlates with slower mental and physical development up through age six (Herbstman et al., 2010).

Many of the prenatal dangers that we have discussed are preventable if pregnant women receive adequate care and guidance from health professionals. Good-quality medical care that begins early in pregnancy is associated with reduced prematurity and higher survival rates for infants (Malloy, Kao, & Lee, 1992). Canada ranks 16th in the prevention of infant mortality (see Figure 11.3).

Maternal Nutrition and Emotions

Guidelines are available from Health Canada regarding eating habits designed to promote healthy maternal nutrition and for material weight gain during pregnancy (Health Canada, 2002a). Too much or too little weight gain during gestation is associated with a variety of birth complications, and guidelines for maternal weight gain are based on pre-pregnancy body mass index. Health Canada suggests that if expectant mothers follow *Canada's Food Guide* (available at http://www.hc-sc.gc.ca/fn-an/food-guide-aliment/index_e.html) and maintain a relatively active lifestyle, they should encounter few difficulties regarding weight and nutrition.

The developing fetus needs a variety of essential nutrients. Thus, it's not surprising that severe maternal malnutrition increases the risk of birth complications and neurological defects for the newborn (Coutts, 2000; Fifer, Monk, & Grose-Fifer, 2001). The effects of severe malnutrition are a major problem in underdeveloped nations where food shortages are common. The impact of moderate malnutrition, which is more common in modern societies, is more difficult to gauge, in part because maternal malnutrition is often confounded with other risk factors associated with poverty, such as drug abuse and limited access to health care (Guerrini, Thomson, & Gurling, 2007). Still, even when pregnant women have ample access to food, it is important to consume a balanced diet that includes crucial vitamins and minerals. For example, a diet rich in folic acid can reduce the likelihood of a variety of birth defects (Reynolds, 2002).

Recent studies also suggest that maternal emotions can have an impact on prenatal development. For example, anxiety and depression in pregnant women are associated with an increased prevalence of various behavioural problems in their offspring (Bergner, Monk, & Werner, 2008). Moreover, research suggests that prospective mothers' emotional reactions to stressful events can disrupt the delicate hormonal balance that fosters healthy prenatal development (Douglas, 2010).

Fetal Origins of Disease

Research on prenatal development has generally focused on its connection to the risk for birth defects and adverse outcomes that are apparent during early childhood. Recently, however, researchers have begun to explore the links between prenatal factors and *adults'* physical and mental health. Recent evidence suggests that events during prenatal development can "program" the fetal brain in ways that influence one's vulnerability to various types of illness decades later. For example, prenatal malnutrition has been linked to vulnerability to schizophrenia, which usually emerges in late adolescence or early adulthood (Brown & Susser, 2008). Low birth weight, which is a marker for a variety of prenatal disruptions, has been found to be associated with an increased risk of heart disease many decades later in adulthood (Roseboom, de Rooij, & Painter, 2006). Studies have also linked aspects of prenatal development to adults' risk for depression and other mood disorders (Bale et al., 2010), obesity (Huang, Lee, & Lu, 2007), diabetes (Whincup et al., 2008), and some types of cancer (Ahlgren et al., 2007). These findings on the fetal origins of disease are provoking a dramatic reassessment of the factors that influence health and illness.

Science has a long way to go before it uncovers all of the factors that shape development before birth. Nonetheless, it's clear that critical developments unfold quickly during the prenatal period. In the next section, you'll learn that development continues at a fast pace during the early years of childhood. Of course, attention to maternal factors affecting the child's health continues long after birth. For example, maternal nutrition continues to affect the newborn during the breastfeeding period. Health Canada recommends that exclusive breastfeeding be maintained up to six months, at which point the infant can be introduced to nutrient-rich, solid foods. It is recommended that breastfeeding continue up to at least two years (Health Canada, 2004b).

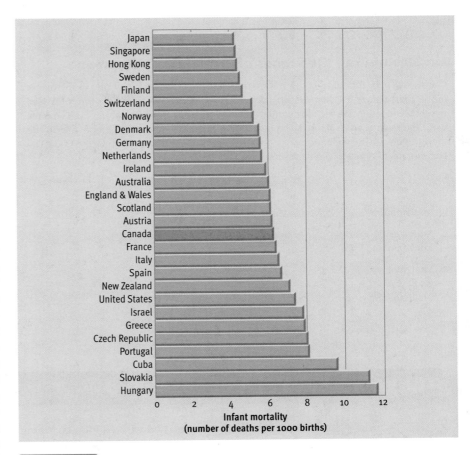

FIGURE 11.3

Cross-cultural comparisons of infant mortality.

Infant mortality is the death rate per 1000 births during the first year of life. Canada ranks 16th in the prevention of infant mortality.

Source: Adapted from Berk, L.E. (2002). *Infants, children, and adolescents.* Boston: Allyn & Bacon.

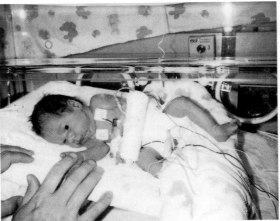

Premature births and infant deaths are much more common than most people realize. Shown here is Wayne Weiten's son, born prematurely in September 1992, receiving postnatal treatment in a hospital intensive care unit. Although prematurity is associated with a variety of developmental problems, T. J., like a great many premature infants, has matured into a robust, healthy teenager.

The Wondrous Years of Childhood

A certain magic is associated with childhood. Young children have an extraordinary ability to captivate adults' attention, especially their parents'. Legions of parents apologize repeatedly to friends and strangers alike as they talk on and on about the cute things their kids do. Most wondrous of all are the rapid and momentous developmental changes of the childhood years. Helpless infants become curious toddlers almost overnight. Before parents can catch their breath, these toddlers show impressive problem-solving skills (Keen, 2011) and develop into schoolchildren engaged in spirited play with young friends. Then, suddenly, they're insecure adolescents, worrying about dates, part-time jobs, cars, and university. The whirlwind transitions of childhood often seem miraculous.

Miraculous they are, but they should not be taken for granted. Developmental research not only allows us to map developmental trends and processes but also affords us the opportunity to provide supports for that development whenever possible. For example, one of the objectives of the well-known *Early Years Report*, produced under government mandate by Margaret Norrie McCain (New Brunswick's former lieutenant-governor) and McMaster University's Fred Mustard, was to review what we know about neuroscience and early child development and to make recommendations about how we can provide conditions in the home and in school settings that promote success for Canadian children (McCain & Mustard, 1999).

While the transformations that occur in childhood *seem* magical, they actually reflect an orderly, predictable (Kagan, 2011), gradual progression. In this section you'll see what psychologists have learned about this progression. We'll examine various aspects of development that are especially dynamic during childhood. (Language development is omitted from this section because we covered it in Chapter 8.) Let's begin by looking at motor development.

Exploring the World: Motor Development

One of the earliest topics studied by developmental psychologists was motor development. *Motor development* refers to the progression of muscular coordination required for physical activities. Basic motor skills include grasping and reaching for objects, manipulating objects, sitting up, crawling, walking, and running.

Basic Principles

A number of principles are apparent in motor development (Adolph & Berger, 2005). One is the *cephalocaudal trend*—the head-to-foot direction of motor development. Children tend to gain control over the upper part of their bodies before the lower part. You've seen this trend in action if you've seen an infant learn to crawl. Infants gradually shift from using their arms for propelling themselves to using their legs. The *proximodistal trend* is the centre-outward direction of motor development. Children gain control over their torso before their extremities. Thus, infants initially reach for things by twisting their entire body, but gradually they learn to extend just their arms.

Early motor development depends in part on physical growth, which is not only rapid during infancy but apparently more uneven than previously appreciated. Infants typically grow to roughly triple their birth weight during the first year, while height increases by about 45 percent (Needlman, 2004).

Early progress in motor skills has traditionally been attributed almost entirely to the process of maturation (Adolph & Berger, 2011). *Maturation is development that reflects the gradual unfolding of one's genetic blueprint.* It is a product of genetically programmed physical changes that come with age— as opposed to experience and learning. However, recent research that has taken a closer look at the *process* of motor development suggests that infants are active agents rather than passive organisms waiting for their brain and limbs to mature (Thelen, 1995; Thelen & Smith, 1994). According to the new view, the driving force behind motor development is infants' ongoing exploration of their world and their need to master specific tasks (such as grasping a larger toy or looking out a window). Progress in motor development is attributed to infants' experimentation and their learning and remembering of the consequences of their activities. Although modern researchers acknowledge that maturation facilitates motor development, they argue that its contribution has been oversimplified and overestimated.

Understanding Developmental Norms

Parents often pay close attention to early motor development, comparing their child's progress with developmental norms. *Developmental norms indicate the median age at which individuals display various behaviours and abilities.* Developmental norms are useful benchmarks as long as parents don't expect their children to progress exactly at the pace specified in the norms. Some parents become unnecessarily alarmed when their children fall behind developmental norms, but variations from the typical age of accomplishment are entirely normal. What these parents overlook is that developmental norms are group *averages*. Variations from the average are entirely normal. This normal variation stands out in Figure 11.4, which indicates the age at which 25 percent, 50 percent, and 90 percent of youngsters can demonstrate various motor skills. As Figure 11.4 shows, a substantial portion of children often don't achieve a particular milestone until long after the average time cited in norms.

Cultural Variations and Their Significance

Cross-cultural research has highlighted the dynamic interplay between experience and maturation in motor development. Relatively rapid motor development has been observed in some cultures that provide special practice in basic motor skills (Adooph, Karasik, & Tamis-Lemonda, 2010). For example, the Kipsigis people of Kenya begin active efforts to train their infants to sit up, stand, and walk soon after birth. Thanks to this training, Kipsigis children achieve these developmental milestones (but not others) about a month earlier than babies in North America (Super, 1976). In contrast, relatively slow motor development has been found in some cultures that discourage motor exploration. For example, among the Ache, a nomadic people living in the rain forests of Paraguay, safety concerns dictate that children under three rarely venture more than a metre from their mothers, who carry them virtually everywhere. As a result of these constraints, Ache children are delayed in acquiring a variety of motor skills and typically begin walking about a year later than other children (Kaplan & Dove, 1987).

Cultural variations in the emergence of basic motor skills demonstrate that environmental factors can accelerate or slow down early motor development. Nonetheless, the similarities across cultures in the sequence and timing of early motor development outweigh the differences. This fact suggests that *early* motor development depends to a considerable extent on maturation. *Later* motor development is another matter, however. As children in any culture grow older, they acquire more specialized motor skills, some of which may be unique to their culture. Maturation becomes less influential and experience becomes more critical. Obviously, maturation by itself will never lead to the development of ballet or football skills, for example, without exposure to appropriate training.

Easy and Difficult Babies: Differences in Temperament

Infants show considerable variability in temperament. *Temperament refers to characteristic mood, activity level, and emotional reactivity.* From the very beginning, some babies seem animated and cheerful while others seem sluggish and ornery. Infants show consistent differences in emotional tone, tempo of activity, and sensitivity to environmental stimuli very early in life (Martin & Fox, 2006).

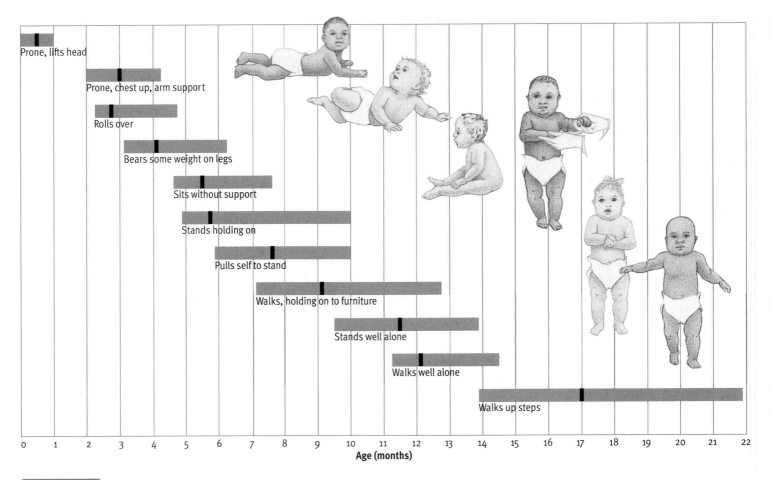

FIGURE 11.4

Landmarks in motor development.

The left edge, interior mark, and right edge of each bar indicate the age at which 25 percent, 50 percent, and 90 percent of infants have mastered each motor skill shown. Developmental norms typically report only the median age of mastery (the interior mark), which can be misleading in light of the variability in age of mastery apparent in this chart.

Tribes across the world use a variety of methods to foster rapid development of motor abilities in their children. The Kung San of the Kalahari, Botswana, teach their young to dance quite early, using poles to develop the kinesthetic sense of balance.

Alexander Thomas and Stella Chess have conducted a major *longitudinal* study of the development of temperament (Thomas & Chess, 1977, 1989; Thomas, Chess, & Birch, 1970). In a *longitudinal design*, investigators observe one group of participants repeatedly over a period of time. This approach to the study of development is often contrasted with the cross-sectional approach (the logic of both approaches is diagrammed in Figure 11.5). In a *cross-sectional design*, investigators compare groups of participants of differing age at a single point in time. For example, in a cross-sectional study, an investigator tracing the growth of children's vocabulary might compare 50 six-year-olds, 50 eight-year-olds, and 50 ten-year-olds. In contrast, an investigator using the longitudinal method would assemble one group of 50 six-year-olds and measure their vocabulary at age six, again at age eight, and once more at age ten.

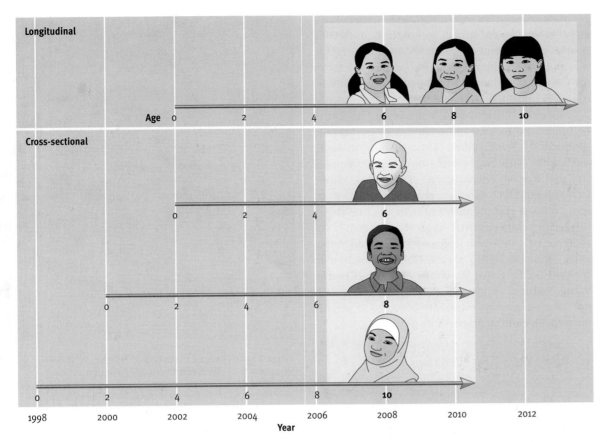

FIGURE 11.5

Longitudinal versus cross-sectional research.

In a longitudinal study of development between ages six and ten, the same children would be observed at six, again at eight, and again at ten. In a cross-sectional study of the same age span, a group of six-year-olds, a group of eight-year-olds, and a group of ten-year-olds would be compared simultaneously. Note that data collection could be completed immediately in the cross-sectional study, whereas the longitudinal study would require four years to complete.

Source: From WEITEN. *Psychology*, 8E. © 2010 Wadsworth, a part of Cengage Learning, Inc. Reproduced by permission. www.cengage.com/permissions.

Each method has its advantages and disadvantages. Cross-sectional studies can be completed more quickly, easily, and cheaply than longitudinal studies, which often extend over many years. However, in cross-sectional studies, changes that appear to reflect development may really be cohort effects (Hartmann, Pelzel, & Abbott, 2011). *Cohort effects* occur when differences between age groups are due to the groups growing up in different time periods. For example, if you used the cross-sectional method to examine gender roles in groups aged 20, 40, and 60 years, you would be comparing people who grew up before, during, and after the women's movement, which would probably lead to major differences as a result of historical context rather than development. Thus, *longitudinal designs tend to be more sensitive to developmental changes* (Magnusson & Stattin, 1998). Unfortunately, longitudinal designs have weaknesses too. When a longitudinal study takes years to complete, participants often drop out because they move away or lose interest. The changing composition of the sample may produce misleading developmental trends.

Thomas and Chess found that "temperamental individuality is well established by the time the infant is two to three months old" (Thomas & Chess, 1977, p. 153). They identified three basic styles of temperament that were apparent in most of the children. About 40 percent of the youngsters were *easy children* who tended to be happy, regular in sleeping and eating, adaptable, and not readily upset. Another 15 percent were *slow-to-warm-up children* who tended to be less cheery, less regular in their sleeping and eating, and slower in adapting to change. These children were wary of new experiences, and their emotional reactivity was moderate. *Difficult children* constituted 10 percent of the group. They tended to be glum, erratic in sleeping and eating, resistant to change, and relatively irritable. The remaining 35 percent of the children showed mixtures of these three temperaments.

According to Chess and Thomas (1996), a child's temperament at three months was a fair predictor of the child's temperament at age ten. Infants categorized as "difficult" developed more emotional problems requiring counselling than other children did. Although basic changes in temperament were seen in some children, temperament was generally stable over time.

One prominent example of contemporary research on temperament is the work of Jerome Kagan and his colleagues, who have relied on direct observations of children in their studies of temperament (Kagan & Snidman, 1991; Kagan, Snidman, & Arcus, 1992). They have found that about 15–20 percent of infants display an *inhibited temperament* characterized by shyness, timidity, and wariness of unfamiliar people, objects, and events. In contrast, about 25–30 percent of infants exhibit an *uninhibited temperament*. These children are less restrained, approaching unfamiliar people, objects, and events with little trepidation. An inhibited temperament appears to be a risk factor for anxiety disorders in adolescence and adulthood (Coles, Schofield, & Pietrefesa, 2006; Kagan, 2008).

Individual differences in temperament appear to be influenced to a considerable degree by heredity (Rothbart & Bates, 2008). Although temperament tends to be fairly stable over time, theorists emphasize that it is *not* unchangeable (Thompson, Winer, & Goodvin, 2011). Interestingly, there appear to be some modest cultural differences in the prevalence of specific temperamental styles (Kagan, 2010). For example, an inhibited temperament is seen somewhat more frequently among Chinese children in comparison to North American children (Chen & Wang, 2010; Chen, Wang, & DeSouza, 2006). It is not clear whether this disparity is rooted in genetic differences, cultural practices, or both.

Courtesy of Valerie Kuhlmeier

Valerie Kuhlmeier is a Canada Research Chair in Cognitive Development in the Department of Psychology at Queen's University. She does research on infants' cognitive abilities and inferences about the mental states of other humans. You can learn more about her research by visiting her Infant Cognition Group website at http://www.infantcognitiongroup.com/ResearchTeam/DrValerieKuhlmeier/tabid/63/Default.aspx.

REVIEW OF KEY POINTS

▷ Motor development follows cephalocaudal (head-to-foot) and proximodistal (centre-outward) trends and depends in part on physical growth, which appears to be more uneven than previously appreciated.

▷ Early motor development depends on both maturation and learning. Developmental norms for motor skills and other types of development are only group averages, and parents should not be alarmed if their children's progress does not match these norms exactly. Cultural variations in the pacing of motor development demonstrate the importance of learning.

▷ Cross-sectional and longitudinal studies are both well suited to developmental research. Cross-sectional studies are quicker, easier, and less expensive to conduct. Longitudinal studies are more sensitive to developmental changes.

▷ Temperamental differences among children are apparent during the first few months of life. Thomas and Chess found that most infants could be classified as easy, slow-to-warm-up, or difficult children. These differences in temperament are fairly stable and probably have a genetic basis.

PREVIEW QUESTIONS

▷ What are the three patterns of attachment seen in infants?

▷ What kinds of cultural variations have been observed in attachment patterns?

▷ What is the evolutionary significance of attachment patterns?

▷ What do stage theories have in common?

▷ How did Erikson explain personality development?

▷ What are the strengths and weaknesses of Erikson's theory?

Early Emotional Development: Attachment

 9b

Infants are continually being presented with novel information about their social and non-social world. According to research by Canada Research Chair in Cognitive Development Valerie Kuhlmeier (Dunfield, O'Connell, Kuhlmeier, & Kelley, 2011; Newman, Keil, Kulmeier, & Wynn, 2010), very early on they are able to differentiate these two aspects of their world (Kuhlmeier, Bloom & Wynn, 2004). What do we know about their developing emotional attachment to members of their social world, to some of those individuals with whom they share a special relationship? Do mothers and infants forge lasting emotional bonds in the first few hours after birth? Do early emotional bonds affect later development? These are just some of the questions investigated by psychologists interested in attachment.

Attachment refers to the close, emotional bonds of affection that develop between infants and their caregivers. Researchers have shown a keen interest in how infant–mother attachments are formed early in life. While infants eventually form attachments to various significant others including fathers and grandparents, older siblings, and others (Cassidy, 2008), the first important attachment is usually with the mother, because in most cultures she is the principal caregiver, especially in the early years of life (Lamb & Lewis, 2011).

Contrary to popular belief, infants' attachment to their mothers is not instantaneous but by six to eight months of age, they show a preference for her and protest when separated from her (Lamb, Ketterlinus, & Fracasso, 1992). This is the first manifestation of *separation anxiety*—emotional distress seen in many infants when they are separated from people with whom they have formed an attachment.

Even if fed by a wire surrogate mother, Harlow's infant monkeys cuddled up with a terry cloth surrogate that provided contact comfort. When threatened by a frightening toy, the monkeys sought security from their terry cloth mothers.

Separation anxiety, which may occur with fathers and other familiar caregivers as well as with mothers, typically peaks at around 14 to 18 months and then begins to decline.

Theories of Attachment

Initially, behaviourists argued that this special attachment between infant and mother develops because mothers are associated with the powerful, reinforcing event of being fed. Thus, the mother becomes a conditioned reinforcer. Many mothers would likely argue that there is more to this attachment than simple reinforcement. This view was supported by Harry Harlow's famous studies of attachment in infant rhesus monkeys (Harlow, 1958, 1959).

Harlow removed monkeys from their mothers at birth and raised them in the laboratory with two types of artificial "substitute mothers." One type of artificial mother was made of terry cloth and could provide contact comfort. The other type of artificial mother was made of wire. Half of the monkeys were fed from a bottle attached to a wire mother and the other half were fed by a cloth mother. The young monkeys' attachment to their substitute mothers was tested by introducing a frightening stimulus, such as a strange toy. If reinforcement through feeding were the key to attachment, the frightened monkeys should have scampered off to the mother that had fed them. This was not the case. The young monkeys

scrambled for their cloth mothers, even if they were *not* fed by them.

Harlow's work made a simple reinforcement explanation of attachment unrealistic for animals, let alone for more complex human beings. Attention then turned to an alternative explanation of attachment proposed by John Bowlby (1969, 1973, 1980). Bowlby was impressed by the importance of contact comfort to Harlow's monkeys and by the apparently unlearned nature of this preference. Influenced by evolutionary theories, Bowlby argued that there must be a biological basis for attachment. According to his view, infants are biologically programmed to emit behaviour (smiling, cooing, clinging, and so on) that triggers an affectionate, protective response from adults.

Bowlby also asserted that adults are programmed by evolutionary forces to be captivated by this behaviour and to respond with warmth, love, and protection. Obviously, these characteristics would be adaptive in terms of promoting children's survival. Attachment theory has had an evolutionary slant from its very beginning, long before evolutionary theory became influential in psychology. While John Bowlby (1969, 1973, 1980) analyzed attachment in terms of its *survival value* for infants, contemporary evolutionary theorists emphasize how attachment contributes to parents' and children's *reproductive fitness* (Belsky, Steinberg, & Draper, 1991; Chisholm, 1996; Simpson, 1999). For example, contemporary theorists point out that if parents expect to pass their genes on to future generations, they need to raise their offspring to reproductive age and help them develop the social maturity required for successful mating. Parent–child attachments make crucial contributions to these outcomes by fostering social and emotional development in children (Kobak, 1999).

Bowlby's theory has guided most of the research on attachment over the last several decades, including Mary Ainsworth's influential work on patterns of attachment, which we discuss next.

Patterns of Attachment

Research by Mary Ainsworth and her colleagues (Ainsworth, 1979; Ainsworth et al., 1978) suggests that attachment emerges out of a complex interplay between infant and mother. (You may recall that Mary Ainsworth was one of the three women pioneers in Canadian psychology profiled in Chapter 1.) Ainsworth used a method called the *strange situation procedure,* in which infants are exposed to a series of eight separation and reunion episodes to assess the quality of their attachment. The three-minute episodes in this carefully orchestrated laboratory procedure involve events such as a stranger entering a room where an infant is playing with

Mary Salter Ainsworth
"Where familial security is lacking, the individual is handicapped by the lack of what might be called a secure base from which to work."

FIGURE 11.6

Overview of the attachment process.

The unfolding of attachment depends on the interaction between a mother (or other caregiver) and an infant. Research by Mary Ainsworth and others suggests that attachment relationships fall into three categories—secure, avoidant, and anxious-ambivalent—that depend on how sensitive and responsive caregivers are to their children's needs. The feedback loops shown in the diagram reflect the fact that babies are not passive bystanders in the attachment drama; their reactions to caregivers can affect the caregivers' behaviour.

Source: WEBER, ANN L.; HARVEY, JOHN H., *PERSPECTIVES ON CLOSE RELATIONSHIPS*, 1st Edition, © 1994, p. 114. Reprinted by permission of Pearson Education, Inc., Upper Saddle River, NJ.

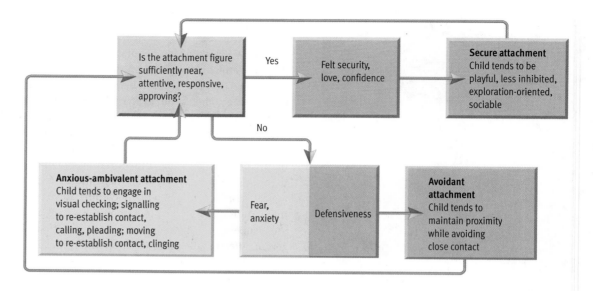

a parent nearby, followed by the parent leaving, returning, leaving, and returning again. The child's reactions (distress, comfort) to the parent's departures and returns are carefully monitored to gauge attachment quality.

Infant–mother attachments vary in quality. Ainsworth and her colleagues (1978) found that these attachments follow three patterns (see Figure 11.6). Fortunately, most infants develop a *secure attachment*. They play and explore comfortably with their mother present, become visibly upset when she leaves, and are quickly calmed by her return. However, some children display a pattern called *anxious-ambivalent attachment*. They appear anxious even when their mother is near and protest excessively when she leaves, but they are not particularly comforted when she returns. Children in the third category seek little contact with their mother and often are not distressed when she leaves, a condition labelled *avoidant attachment*. Years later, other researchers added a fourth category called *disorganized-disoriented* attachment (Main & Solomon, 1986, 1990). These children appear confused about whether they should approach or avoid their mother and are especially insecure (Lyons-Ruth & Jacobvitz, 2008).

Maternal behaviours appear to have considerable influence on the type of attachment that emerges between an infant and mother (Ainsworth et al., 1978; Posada et al., 2007). Mothers who are sensitive and responsive to their children's needs are more likely to promote secure attachments than mothers who are relatively insensitive or inconsistent in their responding (Nievar & Becker, 2008; van den Boom, 1994). However, infants also have an important role to play as this process unfolds. They are active participants who influence the process with their crying,

smiling, fussing, and babbling, and difficult infants slow the process of attachment (van IJzendoorn & Bakermans-Kranenburg, 2004). Thus, the type of attachment that emerges between an infant and mother may depend on the nature of the infant's temperament as well as the mother's sensitivity (Kagan & Fox, 2006).

Evidence suggests that the quality of the attachment relationship can have important consequences for children's subsequent development. Based on their attachment experiences, children develop *internal working models* of the dynamics of close relationships that influence their future interactions with a wide range of people (Bretherton & Munholland, 2008; Johnson, Dweck, & Chen, 2007). Infants with a relatively secure attachment *tend* to become resilient, competent toddlers with high self-esteem (Ranson & Urichuk, 2006; Thompson, 2008). In their preschool

Infant–mother attachments vary in strength and quality and these variations in attachment relationships may have long-lasting repercussions. In this picture, Doug McCann's son Harry is seen interacting with his mother.

years, they display more persistence, curiosity, self-reliance, and leadership and have better peer relations (Weinfield et al., 2008). In middle childhood, they exhibit more positive moods, healthier strategies for coping with stress, and fewer problems with hostility and aggression (Fearon et al., 2010; Kerns et al., 2007). Studies have also found a relationship between secure attachment and more advanced cognitive development during childhood and adolescence (Ranson & Urichuk, 2006).

The repercussions of attachment patterns in infancy appear to reach even into adulthood (Cassidy & Shaver, 1999; Mikulincer & Shaver, 2007; Sadikaj, Moskowitz, & Zuroff, 2011). In Chapter 16, we'll discuss thought-provoking evidence that infant attachment patterns set the tone for people's romantic relationships in adulthood, not to mention their gender roles, religious beliefs, and patterns of self-disclosure (Feeney, 2008; Kirkpatrick, 2005; Mikulincer & Shaver, 2007; Shaver & Mikulincer, 2009).

Culture and Attachment

Separation anxiety emerges in children at about six to eight months and peaks at about 14 to 18 months in cultures around the world (Grossmann & Grossmann, 1990). These findings, which have been replicated in quite a variety of non-Western cultures, suggest that attachment is a universal feature of human development. However, studies have found some modest cultural variations in the proportion of infants who fall into the three attachment categories described by Ainsworth. Working mostly with white, middle-class subjects in the United States, researchers have found that 67 percent of infants display a secure attachment, 21 percent an avoidant attachment, and 12 percent an anxious-ambivalent attachment (the fourth attachment pattern mentioned earlier is not included here because it has been tracked in only a minority of cross-cultural studies) (van IJzendoorn & Sagi-Schwartz, 2008). Studies in Japan and Germany have yielded somewhat different estimates of the prevalence of various types of attachment, as shown in Figure 11.7. That said, the differences are small and secure attachment appears to be the predominant type of attachment around the world.

Becoming Unique: Personality Development

9c

How do individuals develop their unique constellations of personality traits over time? Many theories have addressed this question. The first major theory of personality development was put together by

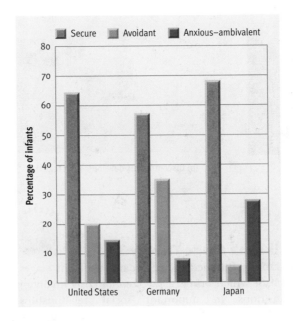

FIGURE 11.7

Cultural variations in attachment patterns.

This graph shows the distribution of the three original attachment patterns found in specific studies in Germany, Japan, and the United States. As you can see, secure attachment is the most common pattern in all three societies, as it is around the world. However, there are some modest cultural differences in the prevalence of each pattern of attachment, which are probably attributable to cultural variations in child-rearing practices. (Data from van IJzendoorn & Kroonenberg, 1988)

Sigmund Freud back around 1900. As we'll discuss in Chapter 12, he claimed that the basic foundation of an individual's personality is firmly laid down by age five. Half a century later, Erik Erikson (1963) proposed a sweeping revision of Freud's theory that has proven influential. Like Freud, Erikson concluded that events in early childhood leave a permanent stamp on adult personality. However, unlike Freud, Erikson theorized that personality continues to evolve over the entire life span.

Building on Freud's earlier work, Erikson devised a stage theory of personality development. As you'll see in reading this chapter, many theories describe development in terms of stages. A *stage* is a developmental period during which characteristic patterns of behaviour are exhibited and certain capacities become established. Stage theories assume that (1) individuals must progress through specified stages in a particular order because each stage builds on the previous stage, (2) progress through these stages is strongly related to age, and (3) development is marked by major discontinuities that usher in dramatic transitions in behaviour (see Figure 11.8).

© Ted Streshinsky/CORBIS

Erik Erikson

"Human personality in principle develops according to steps predetermined in the growing person's readiness to be driven toward, to be aware of, and to interact with a widening social radius."

WEB LINK 11.3

Erik Erikson Tutorial Homepage

This site includes a summary of Erikson's eight stages of development, biographical details, some controversies regarding his theories, and links to other online sources.

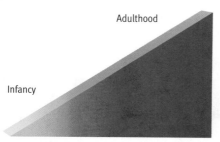

(a) Continuous development

(b) Discontinuous development (stages)

FIGURE 11.8

Stage theories of development.

Some theories view development as a relatively continuous process, albeit not as smooth and perfectly linear as depicted on the left. In contrast, stage theories assume that development is marked by major discontinuities (as shown on the right) that bring fundamental, qualitative changes in capabilities or characteristic behaviour.

Erikson's Stage Theory

Erikson partitioned the life span into eight stages, each of which brings a *psychosocial crisis* involving transitions in important social relationships. According to Erikson, personality is shaped by how individuals deal with these psychosocial crises. Each crisis involves a struggle between two opposing tendencies, such as trust versus mistrust or initiative versus guilt, both of which are experienced by the person. Erikson described the stages in terms of these antagonistic tendencies, which represent personality traits that people display in varying degrees over the remainder of their lives. Although the names for Erikson's stages suggest either–or outcomes, he viewed each stage as a tug of war that determined the subsequent *balance* between opposing polarities in personality. All eight stages in Erikson's theory are charted in Figure 11.9. We describe the first four childhood stages here and discuss the remaining

PSYKTREK
9c

stages in the upcoming sections on adolescence and adulthood.

Trust versus Mistrust. Erikson's first stage encompasses the first year of life, when an infant has to depend completely on adults to take care of its basic needs for such necessities as food, a warm blanket, and changed diapers. If an infant's basic biological needs are adequately met by his or her caregivers and sound attachments are formed, the child should develop an optimistic, trusting attitude toward the world. However, if the infant's basic needs are taken care of poorly, a more distrusting, pessimistic personality may result.

Autonomy versus Shame and Doubt. Erikson's second stage unfolds during the second and third years of life, when parents begin toilet training and other efforts to regulate the child's behaviour. The child must begin to take some personal responsibility for feeding, dressing, and bathing. If all goes well, he or she acquires a sense of self-sufficiency. But, if parents are never satisfied with the child's efforts and there are constant parent–child conflicts, the child may develop a sense of personal shame and self-doubt.

Initiative versus Guilt. In Erikson's third stage, lasting roughly from ages three to six, children experiment and take initiatives that may sometimes conflict with their parents' rules. Overcontrolling parents may begin to instill feelings of guilt, and self-esteem may suffer. Parents need to support their children's emerging independence while maintaining appropriate controls. In the ideal situation, children will

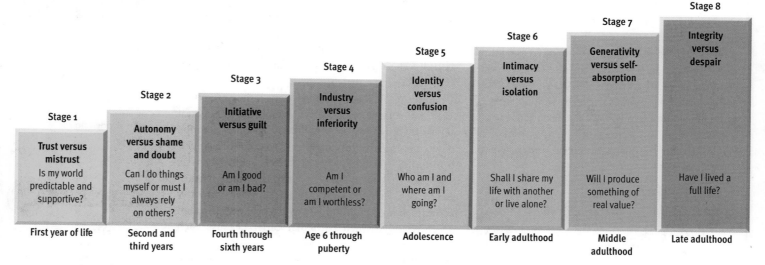

FIGURE 11.9

Erikson's stage theory.

Erikson's theory of personality development posits that people evolve through eight stages over the life span. Each stage is marked by a *psychosocial crisis* that involves confronting a fundamental question, such as "Who am I and where am I going?" The stages are described in terms of alternative traits that are potential outcomes from the crises. Development is enhanced when a crisis is resolved in favour of the healthier alternative (which is listed first for each stage).

retain their sense of initiative while learning to respect the rights and privileges of other family members.

Industry versus Inferiority. In the fourth stage (age six through puberty), the challenge of learning to function socially is extended beyond the family to the broader social realm of the neighbourhood and school. Children who are able to function effectively in this less nurturant social sphere where productivity is highly valued should learn to value achievement and to take pride in accomplishment, resulting in a sense of competence.

Evaluating Erikson's Theory

The strength of Erikson's theory is that it accounts for both continuity and transition in personality development. It accounts for transition by showing how new challenges in social relationships stimulate personality development throughout life. It accounts for continuity by drawing connections between early childhood experiences and aspects of adult personality. One measure of a theory's value is how much research it generates, and Erikson's theory continues to guide a fair amount of research (Thomas, 2005).

On the negative side of the ledger, Erikson's theory has depended heavily on illustrative case studies, which are open to varied interpretations (Thomas, 2005). Another weakness is that the theory provides an "idealized" description of "typical" developmental patterns. Thus, it's not well suited for explaining the enormous personality differences that exist among people. Inadequate explanation of individual differences is a common problem with stage

© Tom Stewart/CORBIS

According to Erik Erikson, school-age children face the challenge of learning how to function in social situations outside of their family, especially with peers and at school. If they succeed, they will develop a sense of competence; if they fail, they may feel inferior.

theories of development. This shortcoming surfaces again in the next section, where we'll examine Jean Piaget's stage theory of cognitive development.

The Growth of Thought: Cognitive Development 9d

Cognitive development refers to transitions in youngsters' patterns of thinking, including reasoning, remembering, and problem solving. The investigation of cognitive development was dominated in most of the second half of the 20th century by the theory of Jean Piaget (Kessen, 1996) and there is no doubt that questions related to cognitive development continue to predominate in developmental psychology (e.g., Klahr & Chen, 2011). Much of our discussion of cognitive development is devoted to Piaget's theory and the research it generated, although we'll also delve into other approaches to cognitive development.

Overview of Piaget's Stage Theory 9d

Jean Piaget (1929, 1952, 1970, 1983) was an interdisciplinary scholar whose own cognitive development was exceptionally rapid. In his early 20s, after he had earned a doctorate in natural science and published a novel, Piaget's interest turned to psychology. He met Theodore Simon, who had collaborated with Alfred Binet in devising the first useful intelligence tests (see Chapter 9). Working in Simon's Paris laboratory, Piaget administered intelligence tests to many children to develop better test norms. In doing this testing, Piaget became intrigued by the reasoning underlying

PREVIEW QUESTIONS

- What are Piaget's four major stages of cognitive development?
- What are the chief developments in each stage?
- What are the strengths and weaknesses of Piaget's theory?
- Why do some theorists believe that infants have innate cognitive abilities?
- How does children's understanding of mental states progress?
- What are Kohlberg's stages of moral development?
- What are the strengths and weaknesses of Kohlberg's theory?

REVIEW OF KEY POINTS

- Infants' attachments to their caregivers develop gradually. Separation anxiety usually appears around six to eight months of age. Research shows that attachment emerges out of an interplay between infant and mother. Infant-mother attachments fall into three categories: secure, anxious-ambivalent, and avoidant. A secure attachment fosters self-esteem, persistence, curiosity, and self-reliance, among other desirable traits.

- Bonding during the first few hours after birth does not appear to be crucial to secure attachment. Cultural variations in child-rearing can affect the patterns of attachment seen in a society.

- A stage is a developmental period during which characteristic patterns of behaviour are exhibited. Stage theories assume that individuals must progress through a series of specified stages in a particular order and that development is marked by major discontinuities.

- Erik Erikson's theory of personality development proposes that individuals evolve through eight stages over the life span. In each stage, the person wrestles with two opposing tendencies evoked by that stage's psychosocial crisis.

Jean Piaget

"It is virtually impossible to draw a clear line between innate and acquired behaviour patterns."

the children's *wrong* answers. He decided that measuring children's intelligence was less interesting than studying how children *use* their intelligence. In 1921, he moved to Geneva, where he spent the rest of his life studying cognitive development. Many of his ideas were based on insights gleaned from careful observations of his own three children during their infancy.

Like Erikson's theory, Piaget's model is a *stage theory* of development. Piaget proposed that youngsters progress through four major stages of cognitive development, which are characterized by fundamentally different thought processes: (1) the *sensorimotor period* (birth to age two), (2) the *preoperational period* (ages two to seven), (3) the *concrete operational period* (ages 7 to 11), and (4) the *formal operational period* (age 11 onward). Figure 11.10 provides an overview of each of these periods. Piaget regarded his age norms as approximations and acknowledged that transitional ages may vary, but he was convinced that all children progress through the stages of cognitive development in the same order.

Noting that children actively explore the world around them, Piaget asserted that interaction with the environment and maturation gradually alter the way children think. According to Piaget, children progress in their thinking through the complementary processes of assimilation and accommodation. *Assimilation* involves interpreting new experiences in terms of existing mental structures without changing them. In contrast, *accommodation* involves changing existing mental structures to explain new experiences. Accommodation and assimilation often occur interactively. For instance, a child who

has learned to call four-legged pets "puppies" may apply this scheme the first time she encounters a cat (assimilation), but she will eventually discover that puppies and cats are different types of animals and make adjustments to her mental schemes (accommodation). With the companion processes of assimilation and accommodation in mind, let's turn now to the four stages in Piaget's theory.

Sensorimotor Period. One of Piaget's foremost contributions was to greatly enhance our understanding of mental development in the earliest months of life. The first stage in his theory is the *sensorimotor period,* which lasts from birth to about age two. Piaget called this stage *sensorimotor* because infants are developing the ability to coordinate their sensory input with their motor actions.

The major development during the sensorimotor stage is the gradual appearance of symbolic thought. At the beginning of this stage, a child's behaviour is dominated by innate reflexes. But by the end of the stage, the child can use mental symbols to represent objects (e.g., a mental image of a favourite toy). The key to this transition is the acquisition of the concept of object permanence.

Object permanence develops when a child recognizes that objects continue to exist even when they are no longer visible. Although you surely take the permanence of objects for granted, infants aren't aware of this permanence at first. If you show a four-month-old an eye-catching toy and then cover the toy with a pillow, the child will not attempt to search for the toy. Piaget inferred from this observation that the child does not understand that the toy continues to exist under the pillow. The notion of object permanence does not dawn on children overnight. The first signs of this insight usually appear between four and eight months of age, when children will often pursue an object that is *partially* covered in their presence. Progress is gradual, and Piaget believed that children typically don't master the concept of object permanence until they're about 18 months old.

Preoperational Period. During the *preoperational period,* which extends roughly from age two to age seven, children gradually improve in their use of mental images. Although progress in symbolic thought continues, Piaget emphasized the *shortcomings* in preoperational thought.

Consider a simple problem that Piaget presented to youngsters. He would take two identical beakers and fill each with the same amount of water. After a child had agreed that the two beakers contained the same amount of water, he would pour the water from one of the beakers into a much taller and thinner

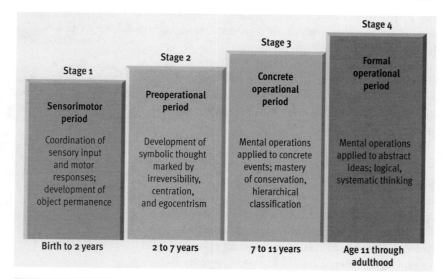

FIGURE 11.10

Piaget's stage theory.

Piaget's theory of cognitive development identifies four stages marked by fundamentally different modes of thinking through which youngsters evolve. The approximate age norms and some key characteristics of thought at each stage are summarized here.

Stage 1

Sensorimotor period

Coordination of sensory input and motor responses; development of object permanence

Birth to 2 years

Stage 2

Preoperational period

Development of symbolic thought marked by irreversibility, centration, and egocentrism

2 to 7 years

Stage 3

Concrete operational period

Mental operations applied to concrete events; mastery of conservation, hierarchical classification

7 to 11 years

Stage 4

Formal operational period

Mental operations applied to abstract ideas; logical, systematic thinking

Age 11 through adulthood

beaker (see Figure 11.11). He would then ask the child whether the two differently shaped beakers still contained the same amount of water. Confronted with a problem like this, children in the preoperational period generally said no. They typically focused on the higher water line in the taller beaker and insisted that there was more water in the slender beaker. They had not yet mastered the principle of conservation. *Conservation* is Piaget's term for the awareness that physical quantities remain constant in spite of changes in their shape or appearance.

Why are preoperational children unable to solve conservation problems? According to Piaget, their inability to understand conservation is due to some basic flaws in preoperational thinking. These flaws include centration, irreversibility, and egocentrism.

Centration is the tendency to focus on just one feature of a problem, neglecting other important aspects. When working on the conservation problem with water, preoperational children tend to concentrate on the height of the water while ignoring the width. They have difficulty focusing on several aspects of a problem at once.

Irreversibility is the inability to envision reversing an action. Preoperational children can't mentally "undo" something. For instance, in grappling with the conservation of water, they don't think about what would happen if the water was poured back from the tall beaker into the original beaker.

Egocentrism in thinking is characterized by a limited ability to share another person's viewpoint. Indeed, Piaget felt that preoperational children fail to appreciate that there are points of view other than their own. For instance, if you ask a preoperational girl whether her sister has a sister, she'll probably say no if they are the only two girls in the family. She's unable to view sisterhood from her sister's perspective (this also shows irreversibility).

A notable feature of egocentrism is *animism*— the belief that all things are living, just like oneself. Thus, youngsters attribute lifelike, human qualities to inanimate objects, asking questions such as "When does the ocean stop to rest?" or "Why does the wind get so mad?"

As you can see, Piaget emphasized the weaknesses apparent in preoperational thought. Indeed, that is why he called this stage *pre*operational. The ability to perform *operations*—internal transformations, manipulations, and reorganizations of mental structures—emerges in the next stage.

Concrete Operational Period. The development of mental operations marks the beginning of the *concrete operational period*, which usually lasts from about age 7 to age 11. Piaget called this stage *concrete* opera-

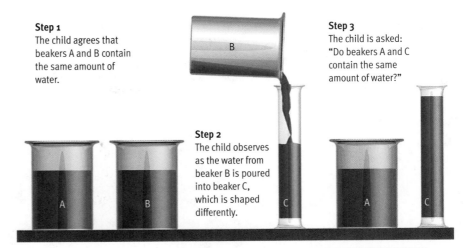

Step 1
The child agrees that beakers A and B contain the same amount of water.

Step 2
The child observes as the water from beaker B is poured into beaker C, which is shaped differently.

Step 3
The child is asked: "Do beakers A and C contain the same amount of water?"

FIGURE 11.11

Piaget's conservation task.
After watching the transformation shown, a preoperational child will usually answer that the taller beaker contains more water. In contrast, the child in the concrete operational period tends to respond correctly, recognizing that the amount of water in beaker C remains the same as the amount in beaker A.

tions because children can perform operations only on images of tangible objects and actual events.

Among the operations that children master during this stage are reversibility and decentration. *Reversibility* permits a child to mentally undo an action. *Decentration* allows the child to focus on more than one feature of a problem simultaneously. The newfound ability to coordinate several aspects of a problem helps the child appreciate that there are several ways to look at things. This ability in turn leads to a *decline in egocentrism* and *gradual mastery of conservation* as it applies to liquid, mass, number, volume, area, and length (see Figure 11.12).

As children master concrete operations, they develop a variety of new problem-solving capacities. Let's examine another problem studied by Piaget. Give a preoperational child seven carnations and three daisies. Tell the child the names for the two types of flowers and ask the child to sort them into carnations and daisies. That should be no problem. Now ask the child whether there are more carnations or more daisies. Most children will correctly respond that there are more carnations. Now ask the child whether there are more carnations or more flowers. At this point, most preoperational children will stumble and respond incorrectly that there are more carnations than flowers. Generally, preoperational children can't handle *hierarchical classification* problems that require them to focus simultaneously on two levels of classification. However, the child who has advanced to the concrete operational stage is not limited by centration and can work successfully with hierarchical classification problems.

Formal Operational Period. The final stage in Piaget's theory is the *formal operational period*, which typically begins around 11 years of age. In this stage, children begin to apply their operations to *abstract* concepts in addition to concrete objects. Indeed, during this stage, youngsters come to *enjoy* the heady

Human Development across the Life Span

FIGURE 11.12

The gradual mastery of conservation.

Children master conservation during the concrete operational period, but their mastery is gradual. As outlined here, children usually master the conservation of number at age six or seven, but they may not understand the conservation of area until age eight or nine.

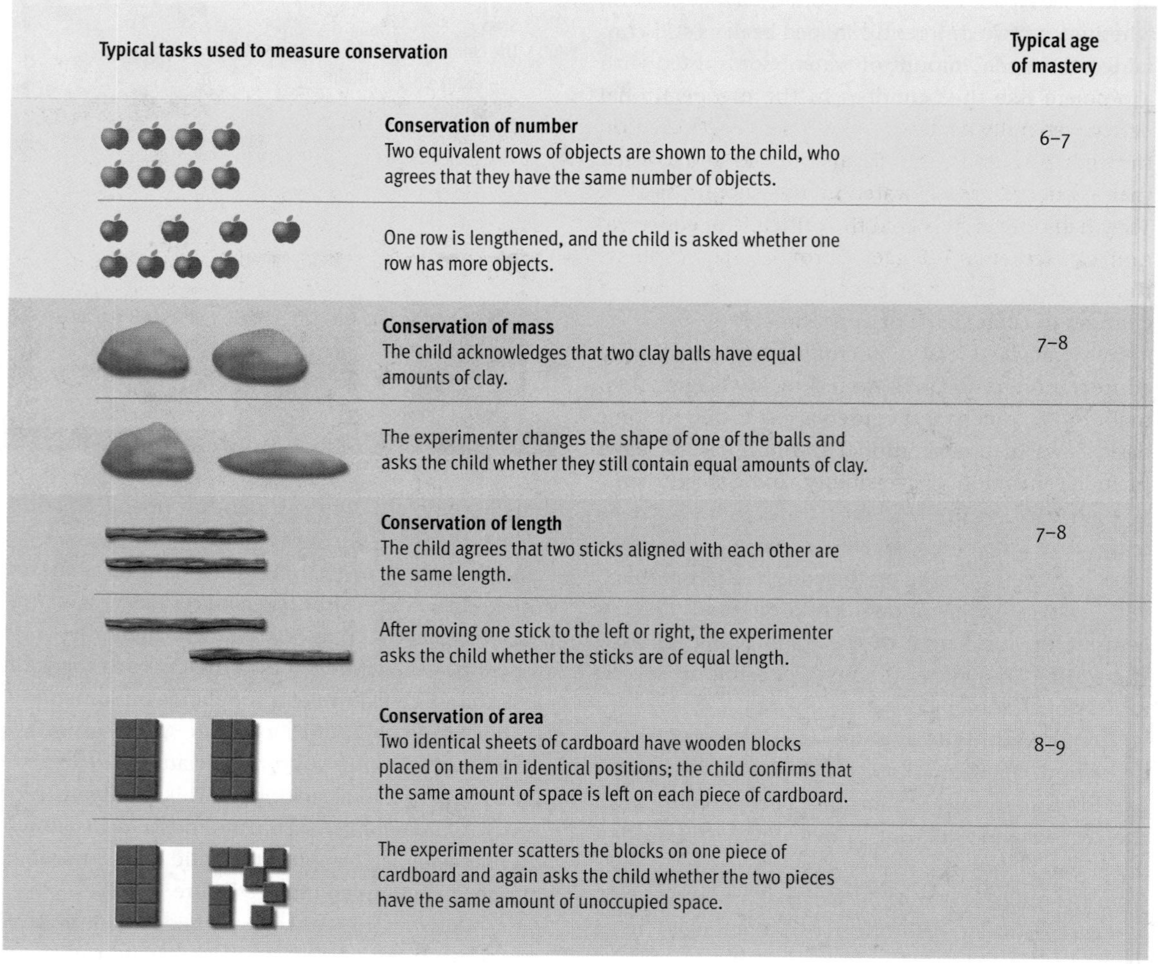

Typical tasks used to measure conservation	Typical age of mastery
Conservation of number Two equivalent rows of objects are shown to the child, who agrees that they have the same number of objects. One row is lengthened, and the child is asked whether one row has more objects.	6–7
Conservation of mass The child acknowledges that two clay balls have equal amounts of clay. The experimenter changes the shape of one of the balls and asks the child whether they still contain equal amounts of clay.	7–8
Conservation of length The child agrees that two sticks aligned with each other are the same length. After moving one stick to the left or right, the experimenter asks the child whether the sticks are of equal length.	7–8
Conservation of area Two identical sheets of cardboard have wooden blocks placed on them in identical positions; the child confirms that the same amount of space is left on each piece of cardboard. The experimenter scatters the blocks on one piece of cardboard and again asks the child whether the two pieces have the same amount of unoccupied space.	8–9

contemplation of abstract concepts. Many adolescents spend hours mulling over hypothetical possibilities related to abstractions such as justice, love, and free will.

According to Piaget, youngsters graduate to relatively adult modes of thinking in the formal operations stage. He did *not* mean to suggest that no further cognitive development occurs once children reach this stage. However, he believed that after children achieve formal operations, further developments in thinking are changes in *degree* rather than fundamental changes in the *nature* of thinking.

Adolescents in the formal operational period become more *systematic* in their problem-solving efforts. Children in earlier developmental stages tend to attack problems quickly, with a trial-and-error approach. In contrast, children who have achieved formal operations are more likely to think things through. They envision possible courses of action and try to use logic to reason out the likely consequences of each possible solution before they act. Thus, thought processes in the formal operational period can be characterized as abstract, systematic, logical, and reflective.

Evaluating Piaget's Theory

Jean Piaget made a landmark contribution to psychology's understanding of children in general and their cognitive development in particular (Beilin, 1992). He founded the field of cognitive development and fostered a new view of children that saw them as active agents constructing their own worlds (Fischer & Hencke, 1996). Above all else, he sought answers to new questions. Piaget's theory guided an enormous volume of productive research that continues through today (Brainerd, 1996; Feldman, 2003). This research has supported many of Piaget's central propositions (Flavell, 1996).

In such a far-reaching theory, however, there are bound to be some weak or controversial spots. For example, Piaget's theory views infant development as a relatively discontinuous process composed, as we have seen, of a series of discrete stages. A great deal of research has been conducted to examine this discontinuity assumption. While acknowledging that more research evidence is necessary, some developmental psychologists, such as Memorial University's Mary Courage and Lakehead University's Mark Howe (Courage & Howe,

2002), suggest that there is evidence suggestive of continuity at the end of the second year, a point at which it is assumed that discontinuity would be in evidence. These are difficult issues to examine empirically, but there does not seem to be any slowdown in researchers' attempts to learn more about Piaget's ideas about cognitive development. Let's briefly examine some other criticisms of Piaget's theory:

1. In many areas, Piaget appears to have underestimated young children's cognitive development (Lutz & Sternberg, 1999). For example, researchers have found evidence that children begin to develop object permanence much earlier than Piaget thought (Birney & Sternberg, 2011; Wang, Baillargeon, & Paterson, 2005).

2. Piaget's model suffers from problems that plague most stage theories. Like Erikson, Piaget had little to say about individual differences in development (Siegler, 1994). Also, people often simultaneously display patterns of thinking that are characteristic of several stages. This "mixing" of stages calls into question the value of organizing development in terms of stages (Bjorklund, 2005; Krojgaard, 2005).

3. Piaget believed that his theory described universal processes that should lead children everywhere to progress through uniform stages of thinking at roughly the same ages. Subsequent research has shown that the *sequence* of stages is largely invariant, but the *timetable* that children follow in passing through these stages varies considerably across cultures (Dasen, 1994; Rogoff, 2003). It seems fair to say today that Piaget underestimated the importance of the environment while focusing too heavily on the role of maturation (Birney et al., 2005; Maratsos, 2007).

As with any theory, Piaget's is not flawless. However, without Piaget's theory to guide research, many crucial questions about children's development might not have been confronted until decades later (if at all). By some measures, the direct influence of Piaget's theories themselves may be declining (Bjorklund, 1997), but ironically, even many of the new directions in the study of cognitive development grew out of efforts to test, revise, or discredit Piaget's theory (Flavell, 1996). Let's look at some of these new directions.

Neo-Piagetian Theories

There is no doubt that Piaget was one of the most influential developmental psychologists in the history of psychology. Many years after his death, his ideas continue to influence research. One group of scholars, known as neo-Piagetians, have extended some of his ideas, integrating them with current perspectives on the nature of information processing. As you may recall, we first introduced the perspective known as information

concept check 11.2

Recognizing Piaget's Stages

Check your understanding of Piaget's theory by indicating the stage of cognitive development illustrated by each of the examples below. For each scenario, fill in the letter for the appropriate stage in the space on the left. The answers are in Appendix A.

    A. Sensorimotor period   C. Preoperational period
    B. Concrete operational period   D. Formal operational period

_____ 1. Upon seeing a glass lying on its side, Sammy says, "Look, the glass is tired. It's taking a nap."

_____ 2. Maria is told that a farmer has nine cows and six horses. The teacher asks, "Does the farmer have more cows or more animals?" Maria answers, "More animals."

_____ 3. Alice is playing in the living room with a small red ball. The ball rolls under the sofa. She stares for a moment at the place where the ball vanished and then turns her attention to a toy truck sitting in front of her.

processing in Chapters 7 and 8. Two Canadian psychologists, Juan Pascual-Leone and Robbie Case, have been particularly influential in this area.

Pascual-Leone of York University introduced the term *neo-Piagetian* to the literature in 1969 (Pascual-Leone & Smith, 1969). When he went to study with Piaget as a Ph.D. student, Pascual-Leone was already a physician and neuropsychiatrist (Cardellini & Pascual-Leone, 2004), and this training allowed him to view some of Piaget's formulations in a novel way. Pascual-Leone analyzed the typical performances of children of different ages in the data collected by Piaget and suggested that one feature that changed was the complexity of the tasks, or the number of essential aspects, elements, and relationships that children must consider simultaneously to perform adequately at each age-appropriate task. By structurally analyzing the tasks, Pascual-Leone found that the complexity that children could deal with varied positively across age (Leone & Johnson, 2005).

This led Pascual-Leone to reinterpret Piaget's developmental stages and to implicate information-processing concepts in understanding cognitive development. One of his developments was the concept of M-capacity, a concept that predates but overlaps with a concept we discussed in Chapter 7, that of working memory. He suggests that an increase in information-processing capacity is one of the attributes that forms the basis of cognitive development. Progressive mental tasks increase the mental demand imposed on the child, and children are successful only if they possess the required mental power (Agostino, Johnson, & Pascual-Leone, 2010; Arsalidou, Pascual-Leone, & Johnson, 2010; Pascual-Leone, 2000). M-capacity relates to the maximum number of mental concepts that an individual can keep in mind at one time. Gifted students have been found to have a higher M-capacity than their mainstream peers (Johnson, Im-Boulter, & Pascual-Leone, 2003).

Robbie Case, working at the Ontario Institute for Studies in Education at the University of Toronto, developed a complementary neo-Piagetian view of cognitive development that, while based on Piaget's ideas, served to modify and extend them. He is best known for his *Staircase* model of development and the concept of central processing structures (Case, 1991a, 1998). Case suggests that one of the fundamental issues in developmental psychology is whether development can be conceptualized in terms of the development of one rather general intellectual attribute or factor, *or* a set of more discrete aspects (i.e., a more modular approach). Piaget is considered a proponent of the former. Case's view, building on the work of Piaget and other neo-Piagetians such as Pascual-Leone, is that there are four major stages of cognitive development but that each stage is assumed to have its own distinct structure and cognitive operation (Case, 1991b). He argues that, while cognitive development proceeds in line with Piaget's stage view of progression, there is a distinct set of cognitive skills involved that may show uneven development—children may show higher levels of development in some domains than others. Case acknowledges the important role played by culture in cognitive development and that age-related increases in central processing working memory capacity form an important basis of cognitive development.

Vygotsky's Sociocultural Theory

In recent decades, as the limitations and weaknesses of Piaget's ideas have become more apparent, some developmental researchers have looked elsewhere for theoretical guidance. Ironically, the theory that has recently inspired the greatest interest—Lev Vygotsky's *sociocultural theory*—dates back to around the same time that Piaget began formulating his theory in the 1920s and 1930s. Vygotsky was a prominent Russian psychologist whose research ended prematurely in 1934 when he died of tuberculosis at the age of 37. Western scientists had little exposure to his ideas until the 1960s, and it was only in 1986 that a complete version of his principal book, *Thought and Language* (Vygotsky, 1934), was published in English. Working in a perilous political climate in the post-Revolution Soviet Union, Vygotsky had to devise a theory that would not be incompatible with the Marxist social philosophy that ruled communist thinking (Thomas, 2005). Given the constraints placed on his theorizing, one might expect that 70 years later his ideas would not resonate with contemporary psychologists in capitalist societies. Yet the reality is just the opposite. His theory has become very influential (Daniels, 2005; Feldman, 2003).

Vygotsky's and Piaget's perspectives on cognitive development have much in common, but they also differ in several important respects (DeVries, 2000; Matusov & Hayes, 2000; Rowe & Wertsch, 2002). First, in Piaget's theory, cognitive development is primarily fuelled by individual children's active exploration of the world around them. The child is viewed as the agent of change. In contrast, Vygotsky places enormous emphasis on how children's cognitive development is fuelled by social interactions with parents, teachers, and older children who can provide invaluable guidance. Second, Piaget viewed cognitive development as a universal process that should unfold in largely the same way across widely disparate cultures. Vygotsky, on the other hand, asserted that culture exerts great influence over how cognitive growth unfolds (Wertsch & Tulviste, 2005). For example, the cognitive skills acquired in literate cultures that rely on schools for training will differ from those skills acquired in tribal societies with no formal schooling. Third, Piaget viewed children's gradual mastery of language as just another aspect of cognitive development, whereas Vygotsky argued that language acquisition plays a crucial, central role in fostering cognitive development (Kozulin, 2005).

According to Vygotsky, children acquire most of their culture's cognitive skills and problem-solving strategies through collaborative dialogues with more experienced members of their society. He saw cognitive development as more like an *apprenticeship* than a journey of individual discovery. His emphasis on the social origins of cognitive development is apparent in his theoretical concepts, such as the *zone of proximal development* and *scaffolding*.

RIA NOVOSTI/SCIENCE PHOTO LIBRARY

Lev Vygotsky was a Russian developmental psychologist who highlighted, among other things, the contribution of the social context, culture, and social interaction to the cognitive development of children.

The *zone of proximal development (ZPD)* is the gap between what a learner can accomplish alone and what he or she can achieve with guidance from more skilled partners. For example, a child trying to learn how to use his or her first iPod may become confused about how to use iTunes to load music onto the device. The child may quickly become frustrated and decide to give up. However, the same child may progress much further with a judicious hint here or there from an older sibling who has used an iPod for years. The ZPD for a task is the area in which new cognitive growth is likely and the area that should be the focus of instructional efforts. These efforts are more likely to be helpful when an instructor practises *scaffolding*: Scaffolding facilitates learning (Plumert & Nichols-Whitehead, 1996). *Scaffolding* occurs when the assistance provided to a child is adjusted as learning progresses. Typically, less and less help is provided as a child's competence on a task increases.

Vygotsky's emphasis on the primacy of language is reflected in his discussion of *private speech*. Preschool children talk aloud to themselves a lot as they go about their activities. Piaget viewed this speech as egocentric and insignificant. Vygotsky argued that children use this private speech to plan their strategies, regulate their actions, and accomplish their goals. They first begin by using the speech of others to help regulate their behaviour and then move to a phase where they use self-speech to accomplish the same end. As children grow older, this private speech is internalized and becomes the normal verbal dialogue that people have with themselves as they go about their business. Thus, language increasingly serves as the *foundation* for youngsters' cognitive processes.

Vygotsky's sociocultural theory is guiding a great deal of contemporary research on cognitive development (Feldman, 2003). This research has provided empirical support for many of Vygotsky's ideas (Rogoff, 1998; Winsler, 2003). Like Piaget's theory, Vygotsky's perspective promises to enrich our understanding of how children's thinking develops and matures (Veer, 2007).

Are Some Cognitive Abilities Innate?

The frequent finding that Piaget underestimated infants' cognitive abilities has led to a rash of research suggesting that infants have a surprising grasp of many complex concepts. The new findings have been made possible by some innovative research methods that permit investigators to draw inferences about the abilities of very young children. Many studies have made use of the *habituation–dishabituation paradigm*. *Habituation* is a gradual reduction in the strength of a response when a stimulus event is presented repeatedly. If you show infants the same event over and over (such as an object dropping onto a platform), they habituate to it—their heart and respiration rates decline and they spend less time looking at the stimulus. *Dishabituation* occurs if a new stimulus elicits an increase in the strength of a habituated response. Patterns of dishabituation can give researchers insights into what types of events infants can tell apart, which events surprise or interest them, and which events violate their expectations.

Working mostly with the habituation–dishabituation paradigm, researchers have discovered that infants understand basic properties of objects and some of the rules that govern them (Baillargeon, 2002, 2004). At three to four months of age, infants understand that objects are distinct entities with boundaries, that objects move in continuous paths, that one solid object cannot pass through another, that an object cannot pass through an opening that is smaller than the object, and that objects on slopes roll down rather than up (Baillargeon, 2008; Spelke & Newport, 1998). Infants also understand that liquids are different from objects. For example, five-month-old infants expect that liquids will change shape as they move and that they can be penetrated by solid objects (Hespos, Ferry, & Rips, 2009).

In this line of research, perhaps the most stunning discovery has been the finding that *infants seem to be able to add and subtract small numbers* (Lipton & Spelke, 2004; Wood & Spelke, 2005). If five-month-old infants are shown a sequence of events in which one object is added to another behind a screen, they expect to see two objects when the screen is removed,

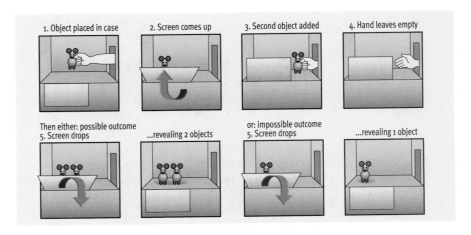

FIGURE 11.13

The procedure used to test infants' understanding of numbers.

To see if five-month-old infants have some appreciation of addition and subtraction, Wynn (1992, 1996) showed them sequences of events like those depicted here. If children express surprise (primarily assessed by time spent looking) when the screen drops and they see only one object, this result suggests that they understand that 1 + 1 = 2. Wynn and others have found that infants seem to have some primitive grasp of simple addition and subtraction.

Source: Adapted from Wynn, K. (1992). Addition and subtraction by human infants. *Nature, 358,* 749–750. Copyright © 1992 Macmillan Magazines, Ltd. Reprinted with permission.

and they exhibit surprise when their expectation is violated (see Figure 11.13). According to research conducted by Yale University's Karen Wynn (Wynn, 2008; Yamaguchi, Kuhlmeier, Wynn, & VanMarel, 2009), this expectation suggests that they understand that $1 + 1 = 2$ (Wynn, 1992, 1996). Similar manipulations suggest that infants also understand that $2 - 1 = 1$, that $2 + 1 = 3$, and that $3 - 1 = 2$ (Hauser & Carey, 1998; Wynn, 1998). Wynn, who received her undergraduate degree from McGill University, has shown in her more recent work that nine-month-old infants even have some understanding that $5 + 5 = 10$ and that $10 - 5 = 5$ (McCrink & Wynn, 2004).

Again and again in recent years, research has shown that infants appear to understand surprisingly complex concepts that they have had virtually no opportunity to learn about. These findings have led some theorists to conclude that certain basic cognitive abilities are biologically built into humans' neural architecture (Spelke & Kinzler, 2007). The theorists who have reached this conclusion tend to fall into two camps: nativists and evolutionary theorists. The *nativists* simply assert that humans are prewired to readily understand certain concepts without making any assumptions about *why* humans are prewired in these ways (Spelke, 1994; Spelke & Newport, 1998). Their principal interest is to sort out the complex matter of what is prewired and what isn't. *Evolutionary theorists* agree with the nativists that humans are prewired for certain cognitive abilities, but they are keenly interested in *why*. As you might expect, they maintain that this wiring is a product of natural selection, and they strive to understand its adaptive significance (Hauser & Carey, 1998; Wynn, 1998).

Critical Periods in Development

Some psychologists have argued that there are *critical or sensitive periods* for the development of some of our abilities and characteristics (Anderson, 2006; Lenneberg, 1967). Although the idea first surfaced many years ago and was made popular in the 1930s and 1940s by Konrad Lorenz in his formulation of animal imprinting (Lorenz, 1981), the issue of critical periods for development is still of concern today. A special issue of the journal *Developmental Psychobiology* edited by McMaster's Daphne Maurer (2005) was devoted to the topic. The idea is that there are age ranges or time periods that are optimal or essential for the development of particular abilities or characteristics. In our Chapter 3 Critical Thinking Application, Building Better Brains (page 131), we defined *critical period* as a *limited time span in the development of an organism when it is optimal for certain capacities to emerge because the organism is especially responsive to certain experiences.* The term *critical period* is traditionally used to suggest that if the ability or knowledge is not acquired at that point, it will not be possible to acquire it later.

The term *sensitive period* suggests an optimal period for acquisition but one that does not obviate acquisition at a later point. For example, Clancy and Finlay (2001) have argued that there are sensitive periods for language learning in which the plasticity in the brain facilitates the learning of language. This does not mean, however, that language cannot be learned later. Similar arguments have been made for the acquisition of other abilities such as musical ability (Trainor, 2005). Some educational systems, for example, Maria Montessori's model of education (Lillard, 2005; Montessori, 1973), have incorporated the notion of sensitive periods as foundational (Toronto Montessori Institute, n.d.). Research by Angeline Lillard of the University of Virginia has provided support for this approach (Lillard & Else-Quest, 2006).

We sometimes hear about cases in which children have suffered significant abuse and deprivation early in their lives. What do we know about the effects of early deprivation? In a recent longitudinal study examining the effects of early deprivation, Jana Kreppner and colleagues (Kreppner et al., 2007) followed up a group of adopted Romanian and British children. One hundred and forty-four of the Romanian children initially had been brought up in harsh Romanian state institutions that existed prior to the overthrow of the Ceauşescu regime in Romania in 1989. In these orphanages, they were exposed to early deprivation, neglect, or abuse up to the age of 43 months. In these institutions, the Romanian children "were confined to cribs or cots with high sides, had no toys, had very little interaction with staff or other children, and experienced impersonal feeding of gruel through propped-up bottles with large teats and group washing by means of hosing down with cold water" (Kreppner et al., 2007, p. 932). The British children had not been exposed to such conditions.

The children's adjustment was assessed at age six and at age 11. The results revealed the importance of what the authors referred to as a six-*month threshold*. If the institutional deprivation of the Romanian children lasted less than six months, there seemed to be little residual impairment compared to the British children. For children who suffered deprivation for longer than six months, there was a significant increase in impairment as the deprivation lengthened. The negative impact of early deprivation is consistent with the conclusions of Kim MacLean of St. Francis Xavier University, who reviewed studies of Romanian children who had been adopted in Canada (MacLean, 2003). Kreppner and her colleagues suggest that their findings provide support for the possibility of a sensitive period for development.

While there seems to be suggestive evidence for critical/sensitive periods in some areas, there is a great deal more to be done before we can generate a firm list of critical periods for human development (Johnson, 2005a). The issues are complex, as are the psychological and physiological processes involved. In many areas, such as with visual development, there are multiple periods for multiple components such as acuity, direction of motion, and face processing (Johnson, 2005a; Lewis & Maurer, 2005).

The same seems to be true for language processing (Thomas & Johnson, 2008; Werker & Tees, 2005). Researchers in the area even disagree on the terms to be used, some preferring the terms *sensitive* or *optimal period* (e.g., Werker & Tees, 2005) and some the term *critical period*. These are important issues with educational and clinical implications and the current view is that new technologies such as brain-imaging techniques will allow us greater insight in the future into the nature of critical or sensitive periods and the mechanisms that underlie them (Johnson, 2005b).

Theory of Mind. One of the most exciting and active areas of research over the past few years has been the work examining children's developing *theory of mind* (Legerstee, Haley, & Bornstein, in press; Mar, Tackett, & Moore, 2010). Research on theory of mind examines the development of children's understanding about the mind and mental states, and how children conceive of another person's thought processes, knowledge, beliefs, and feelings (Flavell, 2004; Johnson, 2005b; Legerstee, 2005). While cognitive and neurological approaches are often taken in this work, the concept of theory of mind also provides a bridge to classic ideas in developmental psychology. For example, Acadia University's Douglas Symons has discussed Vygotsky's notion of internalization as one mechanism important to the development of a child's theory of mind.

Imagine that you are witnessing the following scene. An experimenter shows a five-year-old child a candy box and asks her what she thinks it contains. She answers, "Candy." The child is then allowed to look inside the box and discovers that it really contains crayons. Then the experimenter asks the girl what another child who has *not* seen the contents of the box will think it contains. "Candy," she replies, showing her understanding of the planned deception. Now imagine the same experiment with a three-year-old. Events unfold in the same way until the experimenter asks what another child will think the candy box contains. The three-year-old typically will say, "Crayons," thinking that the other child will

know what he knows about the hidden contents of the box. More perplexing yet, if questioned further, the three-year-old will probably insist that he originally thought and said that there were crayons in the candy box (Flavell, 1999). Why does the three-year-old respond in this way? What does this tell us about the child's theory of mind? According to classic research in this area, most children under the age of four do not yet appreciate that people can hold *false beliefs* that do not accurately reflect reality (Wellman, 2002). The *false belief* method (Symons, Kristin-Lee, & Collins, 2006) is just one of several research paradigms that researchers have used to explore children's developing ideas about the mind.

Children's understanding of the mind seems to turn a corner between ages three and four, so that four-year-olds typically begin to grasp the fact that people may hold false beliefs (Wellman & Gelman, 1998). After age four, youngsters' reasoning about mental states continues to improve. For example, four-year-olds are relatively poor at introspection; they struggle when asked to reconstruct their recent thoughts about something, but their capacity for introspection gradually increases over the next several years (Flavell, 1999). An understanding of the concept of false belief is often seen as the developmental achievement that marks the child's progression to a more mature theory of mind.

Christopher Lalonde of the University of Victoria and the University of British Columbia's Michael Chandler suggest that there are further developments that mark this progression. For example, children initially develop a *copy* view of the mind in which they assume that the mind operates like a recording device that may produce accurate or inaccurate representations. A more mature theory of mind, referred to as the *interpretive theory of mind*, arrives near the beginning of the school years. In this view of mind, the children understand that minds "creatively construct and uniquely interpret reality" (Lalonde & Chandler, 2002, p. 192). An understanding of false belief is considered a necessary but not sufficient condition for this more mature theory of mind.

Researchers have mapped out some milestones in the development of children's understanding of mental states (Harris, 2006; Wellman, 2002). Around age two, children begin to distinguish between mental states and overt behaviour. The first mental states they understand are *desires* and *emotions*. By age three, children are talking about others' *beliefs* and *thoughts*, as well as their desires. It is not until about age four, however, that children consistently make the connection between mental states and behaviour. That is, they begin to understand how people's beliefs, thoughts, and desires motivate and

Lawrence Kohlberg

"Children are almost as likely to reject moral reasoning beneath their level as to fail to assimilate reasoning too far above their level."

direct their behaviour. Thus, they can appreciate that Harry *wants* to get a new watch, which would make him very *happy*, that he *believes* that it will be available at the mall, and that these mental states will *motivate* Harry to ask his dad to take him to the watch store. Of course, this developing theory of mind is essential if children are to competently enter their social world, where understanding others is critical.

Children's understanding of the mind seems to turn a corner between ages three and four, so that they gradually begin to grasp the fact that people may hold *false* beliefs (Amsterlaw & Wellman, 2006; Flynn, 2006). Interestingly, this transition in cognitive sophistication appears to occur around the same age in a variety of cultures (Callaghan et al., 2005). After age four, youngsters' reasoning about mental states continues to improve.

The Development of Moral Reasoning 9e

In Europe, a woman was near death from cancer. One drug might save her, a form of radium that a druggist in the same town had recently discovered. The druggist was charging $2000, ten times what the drug cost him to make. The sick woman's husband, Heinz, went to everyone he knew to borrow the money, but he could get together only about half of what it cost. He told the druggist that his wife was dying and asked him to sell it cheaper or let him pay later. But the druggist said, "No." The husband got desperate and broke into the man's store to steal the drug for his wife. Should the husband have done that? Why? (Kohlberg, 1969, p. 379)

What's your answer to Heinz's dilemma? Would you have answered the same way three years ago? When you were in Grade 5? Can you guess what you might have said at age six?

By presenting similar dilemmas to subjects and studying their responses, Lawrence Kohlberg (1976, 1984; Colby & Kohlberg, 1987) devised a model of how moral reasoning develops. What is morality? That's a complicated question that philosophers have debated for centuries. For our purposes, it will suffice to say that *morality* involves the ability to discern right from wrong and to behave accordingly.

Kohlberg's Stage Theory 9e

Kohlberg's model is the most influential of a number of competing theories that attempt to explain how youngsters develop a sense of right and wrong. His work was derived from much earlier work by Jean Piaget (1932), who theorized that moral development is determined by cognitive development. By this he meant that the way individuals think out moral issues depends on their level of cognitive development. This assumption provided the springboard for Kohlberg's research.

Kohlberg's theory focuses on moral *reasoning* rather than overt *behaviour*. This point is best illustrated by describing Kohlberg's method of investigation. He presented his subjects with thorny moral questions such as Heinz's dilemma. He then asked them what the actor in the dilemma should do and, more important, why. It was the *why* that interested Kohlberg. He examined the nature and progression of subjects' moral reasoning.

The result of this work is the stage theory of moral reasoning outlined in Figure 11.14. Kohlberg found that individuals progress through a series of three levels of moral development, each of which can be broken into two sublevels, yielding a total of six stages. Each stage represents a different approach to thinking about right and wrong.

Younger children at the *preconventional level* think in terms of external authority. Acts are wrong

FIGURE 11.14

Kohlberg's stage theory.

Kohlberg's model posits three levels of moral reasoning, each of which can be divided into two stages. This chart summarizes some of the key facets in how individuals think about right and wrong at each stage.

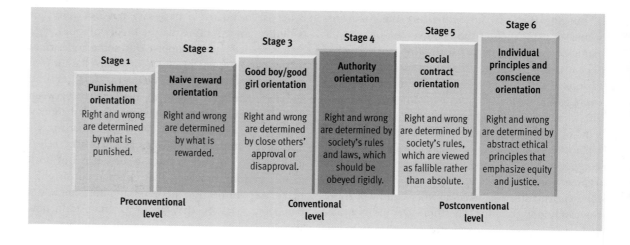

Stage 1	Stage 2	Stage 3	Stage 4	Stage 5	Stage 6
Punishment orientation	**Naive reward orientation**	**Good boy/good girl orientation**	**Authority orientation**	**Social contract orientation**	**Individual principles and conscience orientation**
Right and wrong are determined by what is punished.	Right and wrong are determined by what is rewarded.	Right and wrong are determined by close others' approval or disapproval.	Right and wrong are determined by society's rules and laws, which should be obeyed rigidly.	Right and wrong are determined by society's rules, which are viewed as fallible rather than absolute.	Right and wrong are determined by abstract ethical principles that emphasize equity and justice.
Preconventional level		Conventional level		Postconventional level	

because they are punished or right because they lead to positive consequences. Older children who have reached the *conventional level* of moral reasoning see rules as necessary for maintaining social order. They therefore accept these rules as their own. They "internalize" these rules not to avoid punishment but to be virtuous and win approval from others. Moral thinking at this stage is relatively inflexible. Rules are viewed as absolute guidelines that should be enforced rigidly.

During adolescence, some youngsters move on to the *postconventional level*, which involves working out a personal code of ethics. Acceptance of rules is less rigid, and moral thinking shows some flexibility. Subjects at the postconventional level allow for the possibility that someone might not comply with some of society's rules if they conflict with personal ethics. For example, subjects at this level might applaud a newspaper reporter who goes to jail rather than reveal a source of information who was promised anonymity.

Evaluating Kohlberg's Theory

How has Kohlberg's theory fared in research? The central ideas have received reasonable support. Progress in moral reasoning is indeed closely tied to cognitive development (Walker, 1988). Studies also show that youngsters generally do progress through Kohlberg's stages of moral reasoning in the order that he proposed (Walker & Taylor, 1991). Furthermore, relationships between age and level of moral reasoning are in the predicted directions (Rest, 1986; Walker, 1989). Representative age trends are shown in Figure 11.15. As children get older, stage 1 and stage 2 reasoning declines, while stage 3 and stage 4 reasoning increases. However, there is great variation in the age at which individuals reach specific stages. In addition, very few people reach stage 6, which raises doubts about its validity (Lapsley, 2006). Although these findings support the utility of Kohlberg's model, like all influential theorists, he has his critics. They have raised the following issues:

1. It's not unusual to find that a person shows signs of several adjacent levels of moral reasoning at a particular point in development (Walker & Taylor, 1991). As we noted in the critique of Piaget, this mixing of stages is a problem for virtually all stage theories.

2. Evidence is mounting that Kohlberg's dilemmas may not be valid indicators of moral development in some cultures (Nucci, 2002). Some critics believe that the value judgments built into Kohlberg's theory reflect a liberal, individualistic ideology characteristic of modern Western nations that is much more culture-specific than Kohlberg appreciated (Miller, 2006).

3. A consensus is building that Kohlberg's theory led to a constricted focus on reasoning about interpersonal conflicts while ignoring many other important aspects of moral development (Walker, 2007). Thus, contemporary researchers are increasingly turning their attention to other dimensions of moral development, including the development of empathy (Eisenberg, Spinrad, & Sadovsky, 2006), the emergence of conscience (Grusec, 2006), the development of prosocial (helping, sharing) behaviour (Carlo, 2006), and the significance of moral emotions (such as shame and guilt) (Tangney, Stuewig, & Mashek, 2007).

4. Other critics have argued that Kohlberg's theory was based primarily on male participants' responses and is biased against the equally principled moral reasoning of females. Carol Gilligan, who was initially a research assistant for Kohlberg, published her criticisms in her well-known 1982 book, *In a Different Voice: Psychological Theory and Women's Development*. She argues that males and females are socialized differently, a difference that promotes a focus on individualism reflected in what she terms a morality of justice in males and a focus on relationships reflected in a morality of care in females. In Kohlberg's system, these are equated with stage 4 and stage 3 reasoning, respectively. She suggests that these two orientations are equally principled but that Kohlberg's system is biased in favour of males.

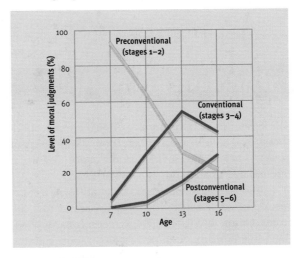

FIGURE 11.15

Age and moral reasoning.

The percentages of different types of moral judgments made by subjects at various ages are graphed here (based on Kohlberg, 1963, 1969). As predicted, preconventional reasoning declines as children mature, conventional reasoning increases during middle childhood, and postconventional reasoning begins to emerge during adolescence. But at each age, children display a mixture of various levels of moral reasoning.

Source: Adapted from Kohlberg, L.J. (1963). The development of children's orientations toward a moral order. 1: Sequence in the development of moral thought. *Vita Humana, 6*, 11–33. Copyright © 1963 by S. Karger AG. Reprinted by permission.

Analyzing Moral Reasoning

Check your understanding of Kohlberg's theory of moral development by analyzing hypothetical responses to the following moral dilemma:

A biologist has conducted numerous studies demonstrating that simple organisms such as worms and paramecia can learn through conditioning. It occurs to her that perhaps she could condition fertilized human ova, to provide a dramatic demonstration that abortions destroy adaptable, living human organisms. This possibility appeals to her, as she is ardently opposed to abortion. However, there is no way to conduct the necessary research on human ova without sacrificing the lives of potential human beings. She desperately wants to conduct the research, but obviously, the sacrifice of human ova is fundamentally incompatible with her belief in the sanctity of human life. What should she do? Why? [Submitted by a student (age 13) to Professor Barbara Banas at Monroe Community College.]

In the spaces on the left of each numbered response, indicate the level of moral reasoning shown, choosing from the following: (a) preconventional level, (b) conventional level, or (c) postconventional level. The answers are in Appendix A.

_____ **1.** She should do the research. Although it's wrong to kill, there's a greater good that can be realized through the research.

_____ **2.** She shouldn't do the research because people will think that she's a hypocrite and condemn her.

_____ **3.** She should do the research because she may become rich and famous as a result.

REVIEW OF KEY POINTS

▷ Like other stage theories, Erikson's theory of personality development proposes that individuals evolve through a series of stages over the life span. In each of the eight stages, the person wrestles with two opposing tendencies evoked by that stage's psychosocial crisis.

▷ According to Piaget's theory of cognitive development, the key advance during the sensorimotor period is the child's gradual recognition of the permanence of objects. The preoperational period is marked by certain deficiencies in thinking—notably, centration, irreversibility, and egocentrism. During the concrete operations period, children develop the ability to perform operations on mental representations. The stage of formal operations ushers in more abstract, systematic, and logical thought. Piaget may have underestimated some aspects of children's cognitive development and the impact of environmental factors.

▷ Vygotsky's sociocultural theory maintains that children's cognitive development is fuelled by social interactions with parents and others and that culture influences how cognitive growth unfolds. Recent research has shown that infants appear to understand surprisingly complex concepts that they have had virtually no opportunity to learn about, suggesting that basic cognitive abilities are built into humans' neural architecture. Children's theory of mind progresses gradually as they learn about desires, emotions, beliefs, and then false beliefs.

▷ According to Kohlberg, moral reasoning progresses through six stages that are related to age and determined by cognitive development. Age-related progress in moral reasoning has been found in research, although a great deal of overlap occurs between adjacent stages, and Kohlberg's theory is more culture-specific than he realized.

The Transition of Adolescence

▷ When do children reach pubescence and puberty?

▷ What changes do these landmarks bring?

▷ How do early attachment relationships appear to be related to the timing of sexual maturation?

▷ Does the empirical evidence support the notion that adolescence is a time of great turmoil?

▷ What is the chief challenge of adolescence, according to Erikson?

▷ What are Marcia's four identity statuses?

Adolescence is a transitional period between childhood and adulthood. Its age boundaries are not exact, but in our society, adolescence begins at around age 13 and ends at about age 22.

Although most societies have at least a brief period of adolescence, it is *not* universal across cultures (Larson & Wilson, 2004; Schlegel & Barry, 1991; Whiting, Burbank, & Ratner, 1986). In some cultures, young people move directly from childhood to adulthood. In our society, rapid technological progress has made lengthy education, and therefore prolonged economic dependence, the norm. Adolescence is a critical time for the development of important physical and psychological attributes, even a sense of identity (Meeus et al., 2010). The teenage years are a busy time according to Statistics Canada, with Canadian teens putting in long hours and experiencing increased stress (Marshall, 2007). These years provide opportunities to explore the adolescents' developing physical body, independence, sense of self, and romantic relationships (Connolly & Johnson, 1996). Let's begin our discussion of adolescent development with its most visible aspect—the physical changes that transform the body of a child into that of an adult.

Physiological Changes

Recall for a moment your junior high school days. Didn't it seem that your body grew so fast about this time that your clothes just couldn't "keep up"? This phase of rapid growth in height and weight is called the *adolescent growth spurt*. Brought on by hormonal changes, it typically starts at about 11 years of age in girls and about two years later in boys (Archibald, Graber, & Brooks-Dunn, 2003; Malina, 1990).

The timing of sexual maturation can have important implications for adolescents. Youngsters who mature unusually early or unusually late often feel uneasy about this transition.

Kris Timken/Blend Images/Jupiter Images

Scientists are not sure what triggers the hormonal changes that underlie the adolescent growth spurt, but recent evidence suggests that rising levels of *leptin,* the recently discovered hormone that reflects the body's fat cell storage (see Chapter 10), may provide the crucial signals (Spear, 2000).

The term *pubescence* is used to describe the two-year span preceding puberty, during which the changes leading to physical and sexual maturity take place. In addition to growing taller and heavier during pubescence, children begin to develop the physical features that characterize adults of their respective sexes. These features are termed *secondary sex characteristics*—physical features that distinguish one sex from the other but that are not essential for reproduction. For example, males go through a voice change, develop facial hair, and experience greater skeletal and muscle growth in the upper torso, leading to broader shoulders (see Figure 11.16). Females experience breast growth and a widening of the pelvic bones plus increased fat deposits in this area, resulting in wider hips (Susman & Rogol, 2004).

Note, however, that the capacity to reproduce is not attained in pubescence. This comes later. *Puberty* is the stage during which sexual functions reach maturity, which marks the beginning of adolescence. It is during puberty that the *primary sex characteristics*—the structures necessary for reproduction—develop fully. In the male, these include the testes, penis, and related internal structures. In the female, they include the ovaries, vagina, uterus, and other internal structures.

In females, the onset of puberty is typically signalled by *menarche*—the first occurrence of menstruation, which reflects the culmination of a series of hormonal changes (Dorn et al., 1999). North American girls typically reach menarche at about age 12½, with further sexual maturation continuing until approximately 16 (Susman, Dorn, & Schiefelbein, 2003). Most North American boys begin to produce sperm by age 14, with complete sexual maturation occurring around 18 (Archibald, Graber, & Brooks-Gunn, 2003). Interestingly, there have been *generational* changes in the timing of puberty. Today's adolescents begin puberty at a younger age, and

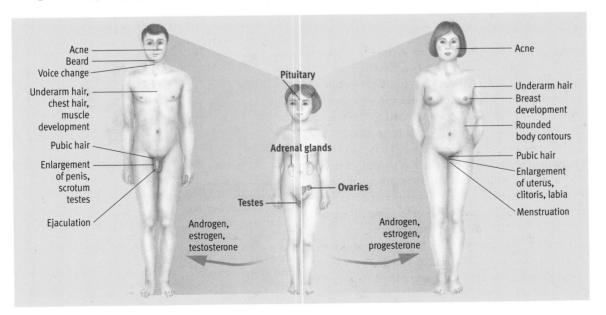

FIGURE 11.16

Physical development at puberty.

Hormonal changes during puberty lead not only to a growth spurt but also to the development of secondary sex characteristics. The pituitary gland sends signals to the adrenal glands and gonads (ovaries and testes), which secrete hormones responsible for various physical changes that differentiate males and females.

complete it more rapidly, than did their counterparts in earlier generations (Anderson, Dallal, & Must, 2003; Fredriks et al., 2000). This trend apparently reflects improvements in nutrition and medical care (Brooks-Gunn, 1991). The timing of puberty varies from one adolescent to the next over a range of about five years (10–15 for girls, 11–16 for boys). Much of this variability is governed by hereditary differences (Kaprio et al., 1995), but other factors also are influential, including the quality of a person's family relationships during early childhood (Ellis et al., 1999).

Although the determinants of the timing of puberty remain open to debate, more is known about the *consequences* of variation in the onset of puberty. Generally, *girls who mature early and boys who mature late seem to have more emotional difficulties with the transition to adolescence* (Susman et al., 2003). However, in both males and females, early maturation is associated with greater use of alcohol and drugs, more high-risk behaviour, and more trouble with the law (Lynne et al., 2007; Steinberg & Morris, 2001). Among females, early maturation is also correlated with poorer school performance, earlier experience of intercourse, more unwanted pregnancies, and greater risk for eating problems and disorders and a variety of psychological disorders (Archibald et al., 2003). Thus, we might speculate that early maturation often thrusts both sexes (but especially females) toward the adult world too soon.

Neural Development: The Teen Brain

If these physical changes were not enough, recent research has also suggested that there is a surprising amount of change going on in the adolescent's brain that may impact his or her behaviour and sense of self. Changes in the brain during the teen years has come under increased scientific scrutiny in the past few years (e.g., Tamnes et al., 2010). Scientists used to think that brain growth and change were primarily restricted to development in the womb and through the first 18 months of life. Some have referred to the teenage brain as a "work in progress" (Teen Brain, 2008).

The development of MRI scans, which can provide really clear images of the brain, has permitted neuroscientists to conduct entirely new investigations of whether there are age-related changes in brain structure. These studies have uncovered some interesting developmental trends during adolescence.

One set of changes relates to the grey and white matter in the brain. If you slice a brain from top to bottom and look at a cross-section of it, some of the brain matter will appear white and some grey.

Although we are oversimplifying the distinction a little, the white matter facilitates communication and linkages between regions of the brain; white matter development is important for a "smooth flow of information" through the brain (Paus, 2005).

The grey matter, on the other hand, is referred to as the "thinking" part of the brain, consisting of "neurons and their branch-like extensions" (Teen Brain, 2008). The growth of white matter seems to increase steadily in most areas of the brain from childhood to a point after puberty, at which point it slows. For example, Jay Giedd and his colleagues (Giedd et al., 1999) found a 12.4 percent increase in white matter from ages 4 to 22. This means that *neurons are becoming more myelinated* (see Chapter 3), which presumably leads to enhanced conductivity and connectivity in the brain. In contrast, grey matter decreases in volume (Toga, Thompson, & Sowell, 2006). This finding is thought to reflect the process of *synaptic pruning*—the elimination of less-active synapses—which plays a key role in the formation of neural networks.

Perhaps the most interesting discovery about the adolescent brain has been that increased myelinization and synaptic pruning are most pronounced in the *prefrontal cortex* (see Figure 11.17; Keating, 2004). Thus, *the prefrontal cortex appears to be the last area of the brain to fully mature,* and this maturation may not be complete until one's mid-20s (Gogtay et al., 2004). Much has been made of this finding, because the prefrontal cortex has been characterized as an "executive control centre" that is crucial to high-level cognitive functions, such as planning, organization, emotional regulation, and response inhibition (Nelson et al., 2002). Theorists have suggested that the immaturity of the prefrontal cortex may explain why risky behaviour (such as reckless driving, experimentation with drugs, dangerous stunts, binge drinking, unprotected sex, and so forth) peaks during adolescence (Compas, 2004; Dahl, 2003).

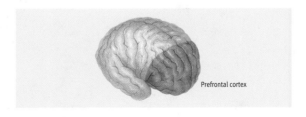

Prefrontal cortex

FIGURE 11.17

The prefrontal cortex.

Recent research suggests that neural development continues throughout adolescence. Moreover, the chief site for much of this development is the prefrontal cortex, which appears to be the last area of the brain to mature fully. This discovery may have fascinating implications for understanding the adolescent brain, as the prefrontal cortex appears to play a key role in emotional regulation and self-control.

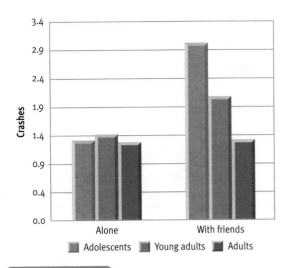

FIGURE 11.18

Peer influence on risk-taking.

Gardner and Steinberg (2005) had adolescents, young adults, and adults play a video game involving simulated driving in which participants had to make quick decisions about crash risks. The dependent variable, which indexed subjects' risk-taking, was the number of crashes experienced. Some participants played the video game alone, whereas others played in the presence of peers. The data showed that the presence of peers increased risk-taking by young adults moderately and by adolescents considerably, but adults' risk-taking was unaffected. These findings suggest that susceptibility to peer influence may increase risky behaviour among adolescents and young adults.

Source: Steinberg, L. (2007). Risk taking in adolescence: New perspectives from brain and behavioral science. *Current Directions in Psychological Science, 16*, 55–59. Copyright © 2007, Association for Psychological Science. Reprinted by permission of Blackwell Publishing.

That said, Kuhn (2006, p. 59) notes that media pundits have gotten carried away, blaming the immaturity of the adolescent prefrontal cortex for "just about everything about teens that adults have found perplexing." Other factors also contribute to risky behaviour during adolescence, one of which is susceptibility to peer influence (Steinberg, 2007). Adolescents spend a great deal of time with their peers. One elegant laboratory study found that the presence of peers more than doubled the number of risks taken by teenagers in a video game involving in-the-moment decisions about crash risks (Gardner & Steinberg, 2005). In contrast, older adults' risk-taking was not elevated by the presence of peers (see Figure 11.18).

Time of Turmoil?

Back around the turn of the last century, G. Stanley Hall (1904), one of psychology's great pioneers (see Chapter 1), proposed that the adolescent years are characterized by convulsive instability and disturbing inner turmoil. Hall attributed this turmoil to adolescents' erratic physical changes and resultant confusion about self-image. While there is continuity with other life stages (Mikami, 2010), there is no doubt

that adolescence is a time of change and transition. What do we know about this period? The picture is uneven. Results from the *National Longitudinal Survey of Children and Youth* (Statistics Canada, 1999c) reveal that most 12- and 13-year-olds are relatively happy with their lives. Some 93 percent say they are happy with the way things are, and 95 percent suggest that their future looks good. In the same survey, however, many participants reported that they have engaged in dysfunctional behaviours in the last year, including theft (31 percent), threatening others (41 percent), and fights (55 percent for males and 27 percent for females). For most, however, the absolute frequency was low. For example, only 10 percent of those who reported engaging in theft did so more than three times in the previous year. While most of the 12- and 13-year-olds surveyed reported being happy, it was also found that about 7 percent reported contemplating suicide, with the rate for boys about double that for girls.

Statistics on adolescent depression and suicide would seem to support the idea that adolescence is a time marked by turmoil and disturbance for some. We know that adolescence is a period of increased risk for a variety of problems (Frisco, Houle, & Martin, 2010; Rawana, Morgan, Ngyyen, & Craig, 2010). According to Constance Hammen at the University of California at Los Angeles, a prominent researcher in depression, depression rates in adolescents can be as high as 20 percent. But the depressions are short-lived for most (Teenage Depression, 2005). A much smaller percentage of adolescents go on to experience recurring depressive episodes, and this group has a distinctive pattern of poor and conflict-ridden social relationships. Having a mother who suffered from psychopathology was also found to be a risk factor (Espejo et al., 2006; Herr, Hammen, & Brennan, in press). As we discuss in Chapter 14, depression is a risk factor for suicide.

In the United States, suicide is the third leading cause of death among adolescents (Goldston et al., 2008). It is the second leading cause of death for Canadians between the ages of 10 and 24 (Canadian Mental Health Foundation, 2006). Suicide rates among teens have increased alarmingly over the past few decades. The Canadian Task Force on Preventive Health Care (2003) reported a fourfold increase in suicides for 15- to 19-year-old males and a threefold increase for females in that age group from 1960 to 1991; this was the greatest increase of any age group. It is important to note, however, that even with this increase, the rates for this age group, according to data from Statistics Canada (Langlois & Morrison, 2002), are lower than for older age groups (see Figure 11.19(a)). As is evident in Figure 11.19(b),

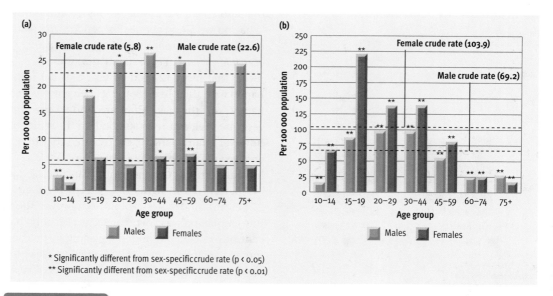

FIGURE 11.19

Adolescent suicide.

(a) The suicide rate for Canadian adolescents (15–19) has increased dramatically since 1960. Nonetheless, suicide rates for this age group remain lower than suicide rates for older age groups. (b) While teen males are more likely to commit suicide, hospitalization rates for attempted suicide are higher for adolescent females.

Source: Langlois, S., and Morrison, P. (2002). Suicide deaths and suicide attempts. *Health Reports, 13*(2), 9–23. Statistics Canada, Catalogue 82-003, http://www.statcan.ca/english/studies/82-003/feature/hrar2002013002s0a01.pdf. Chart 2, p. 13, and Chart 4, p. 15. Adapted from the Statistics Canada publication, *Health Reports*, Catalogue 82-003, *13*(2), January 2002.

attempted suicides are much higher for Canadian females than males, especially for adolescent girls.

Recent analyses of suicide rates have found that ethnic and racial groups differ both in suicide rates and their precipitants (Goldston et al., 2008). First Nations Canadians are especially vulnerable. The Canadian Task Force on Preventive Health Care (2003) reports that the suicide rates in this segment of Canadian society are twice the sex-specific rates and three times the age-specific rates reported for the general Canadian population. The particularly high suicide rate among teens is of special concern and recently it has been getting much-needed publicity. For example, Tom Jackson, a noted Canadian musician, actor, recipient of the National Aboriginal Achievement Award, and Officer of the Order of Canada, used his celebrity and musical talents to create and initiate the Dreamcatcher Tour in an attempt to highlight the issue of youth suicide in Aboriginal communities.

Canadian psychologists Michael Chandler and Christopher Lalonde have been conducting research in this area for many years (Chandler, 2000; Chandler & Lalonde, 2004, 2008; Lalonde, 2005, 2006). They suggest that the increased rate of suicide among First Nations Canadians is specific to certain contexts, rather than being true across that population. In some communities, the rate is as high as 800 times the national average, while in other communities, suicide is virtually unknown. Chandler and Lalonde

believe that *cultural continuity factors* differentiate the settings where suicide rates are high, and argue that a sense of personal and cultural continuity is necessary, especially in times of change, to serve as a critical foundation for personal and cultural identity. While acknowledging the inevitability and importance of change, Chandler and Lalonde argue that a sense of personal continuity or personal persistence is fundamental to psychological health.

Christopher Lalonde from the University of Victoria has been recognized for his important work on culture, identity, and suicide in First Nations Communities in Canada.

Investigators: Michael Chandler (University of British Columbia) and Christopher Lalonde (University of Victoria)
Source: Cultural continuity as a hedge against suicide in Canada's First Nations. *Transcultural Psychiatry*, 1998, *35*, 191–219.

Youth Suicide in Canada's First Nations

Chandler and Lalonde began with the disturbing observation that the suicide rate among Canada's First Nations youth is among the highest in any culturally identifiable group in the *world*. They also note, however, that there is incredible variation across Aboriginal communities (or bands) in the local suicide rate, ranging from many times the national average to zero. Their interest was in explicating the factors that might differentiate contexts where high and low youth suicide rates are in evidence.

They used their earlier research on non-Native youth as a starting point. Chandler and Lalonde assert that all of us have a need for belief in self-continuity or self-preservation and that this is a fundamental aspect of healthy self-concept. Adolescence is a time of change, and challenges are presented to this sense of self-continuity. The results of their earlier work suggest a distinction between those adolescents who are and are not actively suicidal. For the healthy youth, they found that "with exceptionless regularity, all of these young subjects were committed to the necessary importance of, and found some conceptual means of succeeding at, the task of weaving a continuous thread through the various episodes of their own and others' lives" (p. 196). Suicidal youth were typically those who "distinguished themselves by utterly failing in their efforts to find any personally persuasive means of warranting their own self-continuity in time" (pp. 196–197). Of course, culture is another source of continuity.

Chandler and Lalonde applied this reasoning to the variation in suicide rates found among First Nations bands in British Columbia. They then developed measures of *cultural continuity* that could be used to differentiate the bands. The extent to which a band provides markers for cultural continuity should facilitate an individual's process of searching for personal continuity, thereby reducing suicide rates.

Method

Procedure. All identifiable acts of suicide in the province are recorded by the Office of the Chief Coroner of British

Columbia. These records also include demographic information, which permitted a suicide to be categorized as Native or non-Native. Population statistics to allow for the calculation of suicide rates were obtained from federal and provincial government databases. A set of markers of cultural continuity was developed and used to categorize each First Nations community. The markers included:

- *Land claims* (whether the band was actively pursuing claims to traditional lands)
- *Self-government* (whether the band was establishing rights in law to relative independence and self-government)
- *Education services* (whether the band had secured some independence in education by having the majority of students attend a band school)
- *Police and fire services* (whether the band had substantial control over these services)
- *Health services* (whether the band had control over the provision of these services)
- *Cultural facilities* (number of communal facilities located in the community)

A summary cultural factors score counted the number of these markers present and assigned a score to the band of 0 to 6.

Results

The results revealed that the cultural markers did differentiate between the suicide rates of bands that did and did not show evidence of the markers. The differences were greatest for self-government, land claims, and education. When all the cultural factors were summed and related to suicide rates, the analysis revealed a strong linear relationship between suicide rates and cultural factors, with lower suicide rates in bands whose cultural practices worked to help preserve and restore Native culture (see Figure 11.20).

FIGURE 11.20

British Columbia youth suicide rates by the number of cultural factors present in the community.

Source: Reproduced from M.J. Chandler and C. Lalonde, Cultural continuity as a hedge against suicide in Canada's First Nations, *Transcultural Psychiatry* 213: 213. © SAGE, 1998, by permission of Sage Publications Ltd.

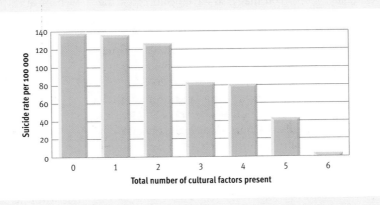

Discussion

The investigators concluded that the risk of suicide in First Nations youth is strongly connected to their developing sense of self-continuity in a period of personal and cultural change. They argue that the extent to which a community has mechanisms in place that preserve cultural continuity positively affects personal identity, which reflects itself in a reduced suicide rate for youth in that community. Adolescent youth are in a period of transition and change, which if combined with the challenges facing First Nations communities, serves to undermine their sense of personal continuity and ability to inhibit self-destructive thoughts and actions.

Comment

We featured this study for several reasons. First, it relates to some of the formulations presented in this chapter that highlight the importance of self-identity issues, especially in the period of adolescence. Second, it illustrates the interplay between basic research and its potential application to society. What began as a program of research by Chandler and Lalonde on the nature of self and identity in development has been shown to be relevant to an important social issue. Finally, the study serves to illustrate the range of methods and data that can be used to examine psychological theories. In this study, archival data were used to test and substantiate the authors' hypotheses about important concepts in human development. It is also important to note that this is a correlational study, which does not allow us any basis for causal statements.

WEB LINK 11.5

Youth Suicide
The Canadian Mental Health Association maintains a useful website devoted to youth suicide. Some of the warning signs listed include sudden changes in behaviour, apathy, change in eating patterns, unusual preoccupation with death, signs of depression and moodiness, previous suicide attempts, and a recent attempt at, or death by, suicide of a friend or family member.

WEB LINK 11.6

Teen Relationships Project
More information on bullying and its prevention can be obtained from this useful website.

WEB LINK 11.7

Gender and Aggression Project
Find out more about gender and bullying at this site maintained at Simon Fraser University.

Chandler and Lalonde feel that two important sets of circumstances may combine to cause the high suicide levels among First Nations teens. One is the set of changes that most adolescents experience. The other arises "whenever one's culture, out of which the particulars of one's identity are necessarily composed, is also thrown into serious disarray. In either case, the grounds upon which a sense of self is ordinarily made to rest are cut away, life is made cheap, and the prospect of one's own death becomes a matter of indifference" (Chandler & Lalonde, 1998, p. 193). The Featured Study for this chapter links suicide rates of First Nations youth to contexts in which cultural continuity has or has not been emphasized.

In recent years, the highly publicized problem of adolescent violence has led many people to conclude that adolescence is indeed a time of turmoil. The tragic 1999 shootings at Columbine High School in Littleton, Colorado, and W. R. Myers High School in Taber, Alberta, are examples. In both cases, the shooters were often described as alienated loners who were frequently bullied (Aronson, 2000; Faircairn, 2004; O'Malley, 1999). You may also have heard about the 2005 case of an alleged massacre plot in a high school in Saint John, New Brunswick, planned for the anniversary of the Columbine tragedy. The boys arrested were all Air Cadets, and police found pipe-bomb materials at their homes (High School Attack, 2005).

In Chapter 1, we introduced you to some of the Canadian research on bullying in schools (Craig & Pepler, 1997; Pepler & Craig, 1995; Pepler et al., 1993). Bullying is a reality in our schools and often involves more than one individual participating in the bullying episode (Pepler et al., 1993). Interpersonal conflict and bullying continue in the teenage years. While both male and female adolescents are involved in bullying and other crimes, more teenage girls have been charged with violent crimes than ever before (Aggressive Girls, n.d.). In fact, between 1986 and 2005, the rate of adolescent girls charged with violent crimes more than doubled.

What do we know about the origins of these behaviour patterns? Debra Pepler and her colleagues conducted a longitudinal study over seven years of preadolescent and adolescent boys and girls (Pepler et al., 2008) and found that those most at risk for continued bullying during teen years were characterized by troubled relationships with their parents and friends. While the origins of the problem are complex, based on the work of Pepler and her colleagues, we know that bullying is not just an individual problem, it is a relationship problem. One current focus in this area by scholars such as Marlene Moretti of Simon Fraser University is the increasing involvement of girls in interpersonal violence (Moretti, Odgers, & Jackson, 2004; Odger, Moretti, & Reppucci, 2010). For more information on bullying in Canada and what to do about it, visit the PREVNet website at http://prevnet.ca.

Marlene Moretti of Simon Fraser University is Senior Research Chair of the Canadian Institutes for Health Research and the Institute of Gender and Health. She is well known for her research on the developmental factors related to psychological health and well-being in adolescence.

Returning to our original question, does the weight of evidence support the idea that adolescence is usually a period of turmoil and turbulence? Overall, recent consensus of the experts has been that adolescence is *not* an exceptionally difficult period (Petersen et al., 1993; Steinberg & Levine, 1997). However, in a recent reanalysis of the evidence, Jerry Arnett (1999) has argued convincingly that "not all adolescents experience storm and stress, but storm and stress is more likely during adolescence than at other ages" (p. 317). Arnett is quick to emphasize that turmoil in adolescence is far from universal, but he maintains that, on average, adolescence is somewhat more stressful than other developmental periods.

Although turbulence and turmoil are not *universal* features of adolescence, challenging adaptations *do* have to be made during this period. In particular, most adolescents struggle to some extent in their effort to achieve a sound sense of identity.

The Search for Identity   9c

Erik Erikson was especially interested in personality development during adolescence, which is the fifth of the eight major life stages he described. According to Erikson (1968), the premier challenge of adolescence is the struggle to form a clear sense of identity. This struggle involves working out a stable concept of oneself as a unique individual and embracing an ideology or system of values that provides a sense of direction. In Erikson's view, adolescents grapple with questions such as "Who am I, and where am I going in life?"

Erikson recognized that the process of identity formation often extends beyond adolescence, as his own life illustrates (Coles, 1970; Roazen, 1976). During adolescence, Erikson began to resist family pressures to study medicine. Instead, he wandered about Europe until he was 25, trying to "find himself" as an artist. His interest in psychoanalysis was sparked by an introduction to Sigmund Freud's youngest daughter, Anna, a pioneer of child psychoanalysis. After his psychoanalytic training, he moved to the United States. When he became a naturalized citizen in 1939, he changed his surname from Homburger to Erikson. Clearly, Erikson was struggling with the question of "Who am I?" well into adulthood. Small wonder, then, that he focused a great deal of attention on identity formation.

Although the struggle for a sense of identity can be a lifelong process, it does tend to be especially intense during adolescence. Adolescents deal with identity formation in a variety of ways. According to Simon Fraser University's James Marcia (1966, 1980, 1994), the presence or absence of a sense of

<table>
<tr><td colspan="2" rowspan="2"></td><td colspan="2" align="center">Crisis</td></tr>
<tr><td align="center">Present</td><td align="center">Absent</td></tr>
<tr><td rowspan="2">Commitment</td><td>Present</td><td>Identity achievement (successful achievement of a sense of identity)</td><td>Identity foreclosure (unquestioning adoption of parental or societal values)</td></tr>
<tr><td>Absent</td><td>Identity moratorium (active struggling for a sense of identity)</td><td>Identity diffusion (absence of struggle for identity, with no obvious concern about it)</td></tr>
</table>

FIGURE 11.21

Marcia's four identity statuses.

According to Canadian psychologist James Marcia (1980), the occurrence of identity crisis and exploration and the development of personal commitments can combine into four possible identity statuses, as shown in this diagram. The progressively darker shades of blue signify progressively more mature identity statuses.

Source: Adapted from Marcia, J.E. (1980). Identity in adolescence. In J. Adelson (Ed.), *Handbook of adolescent psychology* (pp. 159–210). New York: John Wiley. Copyright © 1980 by John Wiley. Adapted by permission.

commitment (to life goals and values) and a sense of crisis (active questioning and exploration) can combine to produce four different *identity statuses* (see Figure 11.21). These are not stages that people pass through, but orientations that may occur at a particular time. In order of increasing maturity, Marcia's four identity statuses are as follows. *Identity diffusion* is a state of rudderless apathy, with no commitment to an ideology. *Identity foreclosure* is a premature commitment to visions, values, and roles—typically those prescribed by one's parents. Foreclosure is associated with conformity and not being very open to new experiences (Kroger, 2003). An *identity moratorium* involves delaying commitment for a while to experiment with alternative ideologies and careers. *Identity achievement* involves arriving at a sense of self and direction after some consideration of alternative possibilities. Identity achievement is associated with higher self-esteem, conscientiousness, security, achievement motivation, and capacity for intimacy (Kroger, 2003).

There is a long-running debate about whether Marcia's identity statuses should be viewed as stages that people pass through, or stable individual dispositions. A recent large-scale, longitudinal study found evidence to support both positions (Meeus et al., 2010). On the one hand, 63 percent of the sample showed the same identity status in all five annual assessments. That finding suggests that identity status is a relatively stable trait. On the other hand, the transitions that were seen in the remainder of the sample were mostly "progressive" shifts to a more mature status. This finding provides some support for the notion that identity statuses represent stages that individuals move through. Consistent with a stage view, the data also revealed

WEB LINK 11.8

Adolescent Health and Mental Health
This site on issues related to adolescence is edited by Michael Fenichel, a prominent psychologist interested in using the Internet to distribute quality professional information to the public.

that people tend to reach identity achievement at later ages than originally envisioned by Marcia. By late adolescence, only 22–26 percent of the sample had reached identity achievement. Thus, the struggle for a sense of identity routinely extends into young adulthood.

Emerging Adulthood as a New Developmental Stage

The finding that the search for identity routinely extends into adulthood is one of many considerations that have led Jeffrey Arnett to make the radical claim that we ought to recognize the existence of a new developmental stage in modern societies, which he has christened *emerging adulthood*. According to Arnett (2000, 2004, 2006), the years between age 18 and 25 (roughly) have become a distinct, new transitional stage of life. He attributes the rise of this new developmental period to a variety of demographic trends, such as more people delaying marriage and parenthood until their late 20s or early 30s, lengthier participation in higher education, increased barriers to financial independence, and so forth. "What is different today," he says, "is that experiencing the period from the late teens through the mid-20s as a time of exploration and instability is now the norm" (Arnett, 2006, p. 4).

Arnett (2000, 2006) maintains that emerging adulthood is characterized by a number of prominent features. A central feature is the subjective feeling that one is in between adolescence and adulthood. When 18- to 25-year-olds are asked, "Do you feel like you have reached adulthood?" the modal response is "Yes and no" (see Figure 11.22). They don't feel like adolescents, but most don't see themselves as adults either. Another feature of emerging adulthood is that it is an age of possibilities. It tends to be a time of great optimism about one's personal future. A third aspect of emerging adulthood is that it is a self-focused time of life. People in this period tend to be unfettered by duties, commitments, and social obligations, which gives them unusual autonomy and freedom to explore new options.

Finally, Arnett has found that, to a surprising degree, emerging adulthood is a period of identity formation. Although the search for identity has traditionally been viewed as an adolescent phenomenon, Arnett's research indicates that identity formation continues to be a crucial issue for most young adults. Arnett's provocative new theory has already inspired a good deal of research on the dynamics and

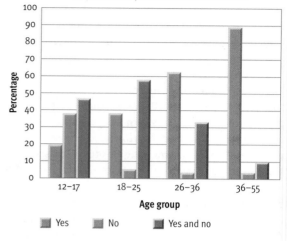

FIGURE 11.22

Emerging adulthood as a phase in between adolescence and adulthood.

Arnett (2006) characterizes emerging adulthood as an "age of feeling in-between." This characterization comes from a study (2001) in which he asked participants of various ages "Do you feel like you have reached adulthood?" As you can see in the data shown here, the dominant response in the 18–25 age group was an ambivalent "Yes and no," but it shifted to predominantly "Yes" in the 26–35 age group.

Source: Arnett, J.J. (2006). Emerging adulthood: Understanding the new way of coming of age. In J.J. Arnett and J.L. Tanner (Eds.), *Emerging adults in America: Coming of age in the 21st century.* Washington, DC: American Psychological Association (p. 11).

developmental significance of emerging adulthood (Aquilino, 2006; Côté, 2006; Labouvie-Vief, 2006; Tanner, 2006). This research needs to determine whether emerging adulthood really represents a new stage of development or a historical curiosity associated with recent decades.

REVIEW OF KEY POINTS

▷ The growth spurt at puberty is a prominent event involving the development of reproductive maturity and secondary sex characteristics.

▷ Adolescent suicide rates have climbed dramatically in recent decades, and attempted suicides have increased even more. Although school shootings remain rare, there is an association between adolescence and the prevalence of violent crime. Most theorists do not view adolescence as a time of turmoil, but Arnett argues that adolescence is slightly more stressful than other periods of life.

▷ According to Erikson, the key challenge of adolescence is to make some progress toward a sense of identity. Marcia identified four patterns of identity formation: identity diffusion, identity foreclosure, identity moratorium, and identity achievement.

The concept of development was once associated almost exclusively with childhood and adolescence, but today it is widely appreciated that development is a lifelong journey.

Interestingly, patterns of development during the adult years are becoming increasingly diverse. The boundaries between young, middle, and late adulthood are becoming blurred as more and more people have children later than one is "supposed" to, retire earlier or later than one is "supposed" to (Statistics Canada, 2009), and so on. In the upcoming pages we'll look at some of the major developmental transitions in adult life. As we do, you should bear in mind that in adulthood there are many divergent pathways and timetables.

Personality Development 9c

In recent years, research on adult personality development has been dominated by one key question: How stable is personality over the life span? We'll look at this issue and Erikson's view of adulthood in our discussion of personality development in the adult years.

The Question of Stability

After tracking subjects through adulthood, many researchers have been impressed by the amount of change observed (Helson, Jones, & Kwan, 2002; Whitbourne, et al., 2002). Roger Gould (1975) studied two samples of men and women and concluded that "the evolution of a personality continues through the fifth decade of life." In contrast, many other researchers have been struck by the stability and durability they have found in personality. The general conclusion that emerged from several longitudinal studies using objective assessments of personality traits was that personality tends to be quite stable over periods of 20 to 40 years (Block, 1981; Caspi & Herbener, 1990; Costa & McCrae, 1994, 1997).

How can these contradictory conclusions be reconciled (Kogan, 1990)? It appears that *both* conclusions are accurate. They just reflect different ways of looking at the data (Bertrand & Lachman, 2003). Recall from Chapter 9 that psychological test scores are *relative* measures. They show how one scores *relative to other people*. Raw scores are converted into *percentile scores* that indicate the precise degree to which one is above or below average on a particular trait. The data indicate that these percentile scores tend to be remarkably stable over lengthy spans of time. People's relative standing doesn't tend to change much (Kandler et al., 2010; Roberts, Wood, & Caspi, 2008).

However, if we examine participants' raw scores, we can see meaningful developmental trends. For example, adults' mean raw scores on extraversion, neuroticism, and openness to experience tend to decline moderately with increasing age, while measures of agreeableness and conscientiousness tend to increase (Bertrand & Lachman, 2003; Caspi, Roberts, & Shiner, 2005). Recent research with a nationally representative sample found that self-esteem tends to increase slowly from early adulthood through middle-age, peaking at about age 60 (Orth, Trzesniewski, & Robins, 2010). After age 60, self-esteem tends to gradually decline. Women and men tend to show similar trajectories, although women score slightly lower in self-esteem across most of the life span. In sum, it appears that personality in adulthood is characterized by *both* stability and change.

Erikson's View of Adulthood 9c

Insofar as personality changes during the adult years, Erik Erikson's (1963) theory offers some clues about the nature of changes people can expect. In his eight-stage model of development over the life span, Erikson divided adulthood into three stages. In the *early adulthood* stage, called *intimacy versus isolation*, the key concern is whether one can develop the capacity to share intimacy with others. Successful resolution of the challenges in this stage should promote empathy and openness. In *middle adulthood,* the psychosocial crisis pits *generativity versus self-absorption*. The key challenge is to acquire a genuine concern for the welfare of future generations, which results in providing unselfish guidance to younger people and concern with one's legacy.

During the *late adulthood* stage, called *integrity versus despair*, the challenge is to avoid the tendency to dwell on the mistakes of the past and on one's imminent death. People need to find meaning and satisfaction in their lives, rather than wallow in bitterness and resentment. Empirical research on the adult stages in Erikson's theory has been sparse, but generally supportive of the theory. For example, researchers have found that generativity increases between young adulthood and middle age, as Erikson's theory predicts (de St. Aubin, McAdams, & Kim, 2004; Stewart, Ostrove, & Helson, 2001).

Transitions in Family Life

Many of the important transitions in adulthood involve changes in family responsibilities and

PREVIEW QUESTIONS

► How stable is personality over the life span?

► How did Erikson describe adult development?

► How does marital satisfaction tend to evolve over the life span?

► How difficult are the transitions to parenthood and the empty nest?

► What kinds of physical changes occur in middle and late adulthood?

► What is dementia, and what is its chief cause in old age?

► How well do intelligence and memory hold up in middle and late adulthood?

relationships. Predictable patterns of development can be seen in families, just as they can in individuals (Carter & McGoldrick, 1988, 1999). The *family life cycle* is a sequence of stages that families tend to progress through. However, in contemporary North American society, shifting social trends are altering the traditional family life cycle. In the eyes of most people, the typical North American family consists of a husband and wife who have never been married to anyone else, rearing two or more children, with the man serving as the principal breadwinner and the woman filling the homemaker role (Coontz, 2000; McGraw & Walker, 2004). This configuration was never as dominant as widely assumed, and today it is estimated that only a small minority of North American families match this idealized image. The increasing prevalence of people remaining single, cohabitating, getting divorced, being single parents, having stepfamilies, voluntarily remaining childless, or having children out of wedlock, and of wives and mothers working has made the traditional nuclear family a deceptive mirage that does not reflect the diversity of family life.

Diversity aside, everyone emerges from a family, and most people go on to form their own family. However, the transitional period during which young adults are "between families" until they form a new family is being prolonged by more and more individuals. According to recent Canadian statistics, the percentage of young adults since the 1970s who are postponing marriage until their late 20s or early 30s has risen dramatically (Wu, 1998; see Figure 11.23). However, if viewed in the context of a longer time period, this upswing represents a return to marriage ages typical of the 1920s. There have also been changes in the structure of committed relationships, with a decline in number of marriages in the 1990s in Canada (Statistics Canada, 2004e). According to an analysis provided by the Canadian Department of Justice (Wichmann, 2005), common-law relationships have increased, going from 5.6 percent in 1981 to 13.8 percent in 2001. The trend toward increasing numbers of common-law relationships is particularly strong in Quebec.

Remaining single is a much more acceptable option today than it was a few decades ago (DeFrain & Olson, 1999). In 2001, there were over 1 million single mature adults and only about one-half of them expected to marry (Statistics Canada, 2005c). The adults who expected not to marry were found to have less conventional views about the importance of love, family, children, and marriage. Nonetheless, most adults—about 90 percent of Canadians—eventually marry. Recent data also indicate that, once married, fewer Canadians are getting divorced (a decline of 27.1 percent since the all-time peak in 1997), and when they do divorce, they are doing so at later ages. However, repeat divorces (people divorcing who have been divorced before) are accounting for an increasing percentage of all divorces in Canada (Statistics Canada, 2005e).

Adjusting to Marriage

Most new couples are pretty happy, but 8–14 percent of newlyweds score in the distressed range on measures of marital satisfaction, with the most commonly reported problems being difficulties balancing work and marriage and financial concerns (Schramm et al., 2005). You might guess that partners who cohabit prior to getting married ought to have an easier transition and greater marital success. However, until recently research demonstrated otherwise. Studies found an association between premarital cohabitation and increased divorce rates (Bumpass & Lu, 2000; Cohan & Kleinbaum, 2002; Teachman, 2003). Theorists speculated that people inclined to cohabit were less traditional, more individualistic, with a weaker commitment to the institution of marriage. However, in recent years the findings on the effects of cohabitation have become less consistent (de Vaus, Qu, & Weston, 2005; Liefbroer & Dourleijn, 2006). One reason may be that cohabitation prior to marriage has gradually become the norm rather than the exception. In the 1970s only about 10 percent of couples lived together before marriage, but by the 1990s that figure had risen to 60 percent (Tach & Halpern-Meekin, 2009). The findings of a recent, large-scale study in Australia that looked at trends over decades (from 1945 to 2000) suggest that the impact of cohabitation may be changing (Hewitt & de Vaus, 2009).

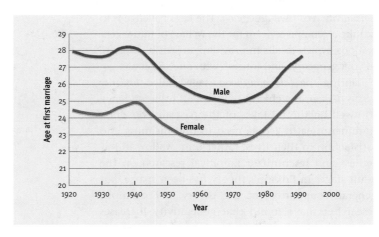

FIGURE 11.23

Median age at first marriage.

The median age at which people in Canada marry for the first time has been creeping up for both males and females since the mid-1970s. This trend indicates that more people are postponing marriage. But, if viewed in historical context since the 1920s, this change reflects a return to previous levels.

Source: Zheng Wu. (1998). Recent trends in marriage. *Policy Options*, September 4. Reprinted by permission of the Institute for Research on Public Policy.

Cohabitants had higher rates of marital dissolution up through 1988, but then the trend started to gradually reverse itself, with cohabitants showing lower rates of divorce. More data are needed, but changes in the composition of the population of people who cohabit may be altering the effect of cohabitation on marital stability.

One major source of conflict in many new marriages is the negotiation of marital roles in relation to career commitments. More and more women are aspiring to demanding careers. However, research shows that husbands' careers continue to take priority over their wives' career ambitions (Cha, 2010; Haas, 1999). Moreover, many husbands maintain traditional role expectations about housework, child care, and decision making. Men's contribution to housework has increased noticeably in recent decades: The 2006 Canadian *Census* showed that, from 1996 to 2006, men increased their contribution to housework and to the care of elderly parents and children. However, studies indicate that wives are still doing the bulk of the household chores all over the world, even when they work outside the home (Greenstein, 2009; Sayer, 2005). Nonetheless, most wives do not view their division of labour as unfair (Braun et al., 2008) because most women don't expect a 50–50 split (Coltrane, 2001).

Adjusting to Parenthood

Although an increasing number of people are choosing to remain childless, the vast majority of married couples continue to have children, and they rate the birth experience and resulting parenthood as a highly positive experience (Demo, 1992). A recent survey of Canadian women who recently gave birth indicated that the majority of them found the experience itself to be "very positive" (Statistics Canada, 2007b). Nonetheless, the arrival of the first child represents a *major* transition (Senior, 2010), and the disruption of old routines can be extremely stressful (Carter, 1999). Dual roles for the mother also increase the level of stress and the tendency to experience marital dissatisfaction. More Canadian women than ever are returning to the workplace after having children (Statistics Canada, 2007d). A review of decades of research on parenthood and marital satisfaction found that (1) parents exhibit lower marital satisfaction than comparable nonparents, (2) mothers of infants report the steepest decline in marital satisfaction, and (3) the more children couples have, the lower their marital satisfaction tends to be (Twenge, Campbell, & Foster, 2003). Consistent with these trends, a recent longitudinal study found that the transition to parenthood was associated with a sudden deterioration in relationship quality

(Doss et al., 2009). The decline in marital satisfaction tended to be small to medium in size. Ironically, the more satisfied couples were prior to birth of their first child, the more their marital satisfaction declined.

Crisis during the transition to first parenthood is far from universal, however (Cox et al., 1999). Couples who have high levels of affection and commitment prior to the first child's birth are likely to maintain a stable level of satisfaction after the birth (Shapiro, Gottman, & Carrère, 2000), and personal characteristics such as attachment levels can moderate the experiences of new parents (Rholes et al., 2011). The key to making this transition less stressful may be to have *realistic expectations* about parental responsibilities (Belsky & Kelly, 1994). Studies find that stress is greatest in new parents who have overestimated the benefits and underestimated the costs of their new role.

As children grow up, parental influence over them tends to decline, and the early years of parenting—that once seemed so difficult—are often recalled with fondness. When youngsters reach adolescence and seek to establish their own identities, gradual realignments occur in parent–child relationships. On the one hand, parent–adolescent relations generally are not as bitter or contentious as widely assumed (Laursen, Coy, & Collins, 1998). On the other hand, adolescents do spend less time in family activities (Larson et al., 1996) and their closeness to their parents declines while conflicts become more frequent (Smetana, Campione-Barr, & Metzger, 2006). The conflicts tend to involve everyday matters (chores and appearance) more than substantive issues (sex and drugs) (Barber, 1994). When conflicts occur, they seem to have more adverse effects on the parents than the children (Steinberg & Steinberg, 1994). Ironically, although research has shown that adolescence is not as turbulent or difficult for youngsters as once believed, their parents *are* stressed out (Steinberg, 2001).

Although children can be unparalleled sources of joy and satisfaction, the transition to parenthood can be extremely stressful, especially for mothers.

Human Development across the Life Span

Adjusting to the Empty Nest

When parents do manage to get all of their children launched into the adult world, they find themselves faced with an "empty nest." This period was formerly thought to be a difficult transition for many parents, especially mothers who were familiar with only the maternal role. In recent decades, however, more women have experience with other roles outside the home. Hence, recent evidence suggests that most parents adjust effectively to the empty nest transition (Umberson et al., 2005). For example, one recent study that followed a group of women for 18 years reported that the transition to an empty nest was associated with a clear increase in wives' marital satisfaction (Gorchoff, John, & Helson, 2008). The improvement in marital satisfaction appeared to be due primarily to an increase in the women's enjoyment of their time with their husbands. There is some evidence, however, that parents may experience problems if their children *return* to the once-empty nest (Blacker, 1999; Dennerstein, Dudley, & Guthrie, 2002).

Recent statistics indicate that this is an increasing issue for families. The likelihood of Canadian men and women returning to live in their parents' home after moving out has more than tripled since the 1950s (Beaupre, Turcotte, & Milan, 2006). These young adults are also taking longer to make key life transitions (e.g., entering the labour market, having children) than ever before (Statistics Canada, 2007e). These returning adult children are referred to as *boomerang children*. It will be interesting in the coming years to determine whether this pattern continues and, if so, what its effects will be on relationships with their parents and their own personal growth.

Aging and Physiological Changes

Our Canadian population is getting older. The life expectancies for Canadian women and men have increased in recent years. Lifestyle choices, genetics, and even personality seem to play a role in determining who will live past their mid-80s (Abraham, 2010; Friedman & Martin, 2011). For the first time in 2004, the combined expectancy for both sexes surpassed 80 years, with women expected to live about five years longer than men (Statistics Canada, 2006b). The aging of the Canadian population has raised concerns with regard to health care, the quality and availability of retirement living, and the possibility that suicides among seniors may rise. Marnin Heisel, a suicide expert at the University of Western Ontario (Heisel et al., 2010), has found that the baby boomers who will swell our ranks of seniors tend to have higher suicide rates (Canadian Institutes of Health Research, 2009) compared to other generations at the same age (Rakobowchuk, 2011). The Calgary Centre for Suicide Prevention, for example, notes that in 2003, 172 Canadian seniors between the ages of 75 and 89 took their own lives. The number for this age group increased to 221 in 2007 (Rakobowchuk, 2011). According to Heisel, these numbers can be expected to increase in the next few years.

With increasing age comes increasing attention to the physical changes associated with age. People obviously experience many physical changes as they progress through adulthood. In both sexes, hair tends to thin out and become grey, and many males confront receding hairlines and baldness. To the dismay of many, the proportion of body fat tends to increase with age, while the amount of muscle tissue decreases. Overall, weight tends to increase in most adults through the mid-50s, when a gradual decline may begin. These changes have little functional significance, but in our youth-oriented society, they often have an impact on self-concept, leading many people to view themselves as unattractive (Aldwin & Gilmer, 2004).

Curiously though, when elderly people are asked how old they feel, they mostly report feeling quite a bit younger than they actually are. For instance, in a study of people over the age of 70, on average the subjects reported that they felt 13 years younger than their chronological age (Kleinspehn-Ammerlahn, Kotter-Gruhn, & Smith, 2008). Obviously, there is some wishful thinking at work here, but it appears to be beneficial. Evidence suggests that feeling younger than one's real age is associated with better health and cognitive functioning and reduced mortality risk (Kotter-Gruhn et al., 2009).

In the sensory domain, the key developmental changes occur in vision and hearing. The proportion of people with 20/20 visual acuity declines with age, while farsightedness and difficulty seeing in low illumination become more common (Schieber, 2006). Sensitivity to colour and contrast also decline (Fozard & Gordon-Salant, 2001). Hearing sensitivity begins declining gradually in early adulthood but usually isn't noticeable until after age 50. Hearing loss tends to be greater in men than in women, and for high-frequency sounds more than low-frequency sounds (Yost, 2000). Even mild hearing loss can undermine speech perception. Such loss puts an added burden on cognitive processing (Wingfield, Tun, & McCoy, 2005).

Age-related changes also occur in hormonal functioning during adulthood. Among women, these changes lead to *menopause*. This ending of menstrual periods, accompanied by a loss of fertility, typically occurs at around age 50 (Grady, 2006). Most women experience at least some unpleasant symptoms (such as hot flashes, headaches, night sweats, and mood changes), but the amount of discomfort varies considerably (Grady, 2006; Williams et al., 2007). Menopause is also accompanied by an elevated vulnerability to depression (Deecher et al., 2008). Not long ago, menopause was thought to be almost universally accompanied by severe emotional strain. However, it is now clear that most women experience relatively modest psychological distress (George, 2002; Walter, 2000).

Aging and Neural Changes

The amount of brain tissue and brain weight decline gradually in late adulthood, mostly after age 60 (Victoroff, 2005). These trends appear to reflect both a decrease in the number of active neurons in some areas of the brain and shrinkage of still-active neurons, with neuron loss perhaps being less important than once believed (Albert & Killiany, 2001). Although this gradual loss of brain tissue sounds alarming, it is a normal part of the aging process. Its functional significance is the subject of some debate, but it doesn't appear to be a key factor in any of the age-related dementias. A *dementia* is an abnormal condition marked by multiple cognitive deficits that include memory impairment.

Dementia can be caused by quite a variety of diseases, such as Alzheimer's disease, Parkinson's disease, Huntington's disease, and AIDS, to name just a few (Caine & Lyness, 2000). Because many of these diseases are more prevalent in older adults, dementia is seen in about 15–20 percent of people over age 75 (Wise, Gray, & Seltzer, 1999). However, it is important to emphasize that dementia and "senility" are not part of the normal aging process. As Cavanaugh (1993) notes, "The term *senility* has no valid medical or psychological meaning, and its continued use simply perpetuates the myth that drastic mental decline is a product of normal aging" (p. 85).

Alzheimer's disease accounts for roughly 70 percent of all cases of dementia (Albert, 2008). The estimated prevalence of Alzheimer's disease is 1 percent for ages 65–74, 8 percent for ages 80–85, and 20 percent for those over 90 (Hybels & Blazer, 2005). Alzheimer's disease is accompanied by major structural deterioration in the brain. Alzheimer's patients exhibit profound and widespread loss of neurons and brain tissue and the accumulation of characteristic neural abnormalities known as *neuritic plaques* and *neurofibrillary tangles* (Haroutunian & Davis, 2003). In the early stages of the disease, this damage is largely centred in the hippocampal region, which is known to play a crucial role in many facets of memory, but as the disease advances it spreads throughout much of the brain (Bourgeois, Seaman, & Servis, 2008). Problems may appear in situations dependent on selective attention. Research by York University's

Susan Murtha and her colleagues (Levinoff et al., 2002) suggests that in the early stages of Alzheimer's, patients show deficits in one particular facet of selective attention—that of inhibition. You may recall our discussion of selective attention in Chapter 7.

Alzheimer's disease is a vicious affliction that can strike during middle age but usually emerges after age 65. The beginnings of Alzheimer's disease are so subtle they are often recognized only after the disease has progressed for a year or two. The hallmark early symptom is the forgetting of newly learned information after surprisingly brief periods of time (Albert & Killiany, 2001; Storandt, 2008). Impairments of working memory, attention, and executive function (planning, staying on task) are also quite common (Storandt, 2008). Eventually, patients fail to recognize familiar people, become completely disoriented, and are unable to care for themselves. The course of the disease is one of steady deterioration. Alzheimer's disease typically progresses over a period of eight to ten years before ending in death (Albert, 2008). The catastrophic effects of the onset of Alzheimer's, in this case in a 50-year-old woman, are dramatically illustrated in the novel *Still Alice* by neuroscientist Lisa Genova (2011). The novel details the early onset of Alzheimer's for Alice Howard, a renowned professor of neuroscience at Harvard University.

Studies continue to be conducted in attempts to document the range of memory deficits found in Alzheimer's patients. Research by Jill Rich and her colleagues (Rich et al., 2002), for example, has determined that language-based semantic judgments are especially impaired when a memory task is presented to patients with Alzheimer's in unstructured formats, as compared to relatively structured, supportive contexts. This suggests that Rich's sample of Alzheimer's patients were showing difficulties in the retrieval stage of memory. Results such as these emphasize the importance of supportive and structured environments for patients suffering from Alzheimer's. As the disease continues, many patients become restless and experience hallucinations, delusions, and paranoid thoughts. Eventually, victims become completely disoriented and are unable to care for themselves. There are some encouraging leads for treatments that might slow the progression of this horrific disease, but a cure does not appear to be on the horizon.

The causes that launch this debilitating neural meltdown are not well understood. Genetic factors clearly contribute (McQueen & Blacker, 2008), but their exact role remains unclear (Bertram & Tanzi, 2008). Recent evidence also implicates chronic inflammation as a contributing factor (Heneka et al., 2010). Some "protective" factors that diminish vulnerability to Alzheimer's disease have been identified (Hertzog et al., 2009). For example, risk is reduced among those who engage in regular exercise (Radak et al., 2010) and those with lower cardiovascular risk factors, such as high blood pressure and high cholesterol (Qui, Xu, & Fratiglioni, 2010). Decreased vulnerability to Alzheimer's disease is also associated with frequent participation in stimulating cognitive activities (Karp et al., 2009) and maintenance of active social engagement with friends and family (Krueger et al., 2009).

Aging and Cognitive Changes

The evidence indicates that general intelligence is fairly stable throughout most of adulthood, with a small decline in *average* test scores often seen after age 60 (Schaie, 1990, 1994, 1996, 2005). However, this seemingly simple assertion masks many complexities and needs to be qualified carefully (Verhaegen, 2011). First, group averages can be deceptive in that mean scores can be dragged down by a small minority of people who show a decline. For example, when Schaie (1990) calculated the percentage of people who maintain stable performance on various abilities (see Figure 11.24), he found that about 80 percent showed no decline by age 60 and that about two-thirds were still stable through age 81.

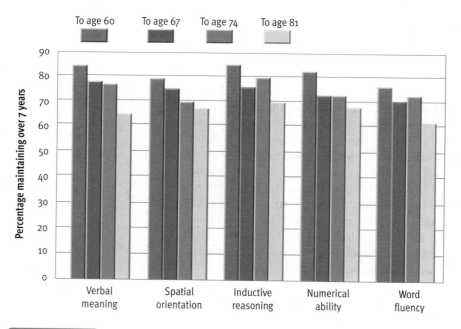

FIGURE 11.24

Age and the stability of primary mental abilities.

In his longitudinal study of cognitive performance begun in 1956, Schaie (1983, 1993) has repeatedly assessed the five basic mental abilities listed along the bottom of this chart. The data graphed here show the percentage of subjects who maintained stable levels of performance on each ability through various ages up to age 81. As you can see, even through the age of 81, the majority of subjects show no significant decline on most abilities.

Source: Adapted from Rollins, B.C., and Feldman, H. (1970). Marital satisfaction over the family cycle. *Journal of Marriage and Family, 32,* 20–28. Copyright © 1975 by the National Council on Family Relations. Reprinted by permission.

Second, even when age-related decreases in intellectual performance are found, they tend to be small in all but a few individuals (Salthouse, 1991). Third, some forms of intelligence are more vulnerable to aging than others. As we noted in Chapter 9, many theorists distinguish between *fluid intelligence,* which refers to basic information-processing skills, and *crystallized intelligence,* which refers to the application of accumulated knowledge. Research suggests that fluid intelligence is much more likely to decline with age, whereas crystallized intelligence tends to remain stable (Baltes, Staudinger, & Lindenberger, 1999; Horn & Hofer, 1992).

What about memory? Numerous studies report decreases in older adults' memory capabilities (Hoyer & Verhaeghen, 2006). Most researchers maintain that the memory losses associated with normal aging tend to be moderate and are *not* experienced by everyone (Dixon & Cohen, 2003; Shimamura et al., 1995). However, Salthouse (2003, 2004) takes a much more pessimistic view, arguing that age-related decreases in memory are substantial in magnitude, that they begin in early adulthood, and that they affect everyone. One reason for these varied conclusions may be that a variety of different types of memory can be assessed (see Chapter 7 for a review of various systems of memory). The most reliable decrements are usually seen in *episodic memory* and *working memory,* with less consistent losses observed on tasks involving *procedural memory* and *semantic memory* (Backman, Small, & Wahlin, 2001; Dixon & Cohen, 2003).

Another important component of memory that is relevant to aging is the concept of meta-memory, or the level of the senior's awareness of the nature of his or her own memory functioning. Angela Troyer of Toronto's Baycrest Centre for Geriatric Care and Jill Rich of York University (Troyer & Rich, 2002) developed a new questionnaire, known as the *Multifactorial Memory Questionnaire,* designed to assess the dimensions of satisfaction with one's memory ability, perception of everyday memory ability, and the use of everyday memory strategies and aids. This should prove to be a valuable tool in assessing memory functioning in seniors in the future.

In the cognitive domain, aging does seem to take its toll on *speed* first. Many studies indicate that speed in learning, solving problems, and processing information tends to decline with age (Salthouse, 1996). The evidence suggests that the erosion of processing speed may be a gradual, lengthy trend beginning in middle adulthood (Verhaeghen & Salthouse, 1997). The general nature of this trend (across differing tasks) suggests that it may be the result of age-related changes in neurological functioning (Salthouse, 2000), although doubts have been raised

Hazel McCallion, at age 90, is Mississauga's longest serving mayor. She was first elected in 1978 and has been re-elected continuously ever since. Her most recent victory, which she said was her last campaign, was in 2010.

about this conclusion (Bashore, Ridderinkhof, & van der Molen, 1997). Although mental speed declines with age, problem-solving ability remains largely unimpaired if older people are given adequate time to compensate for their reduced speed.

It should be emphasized that many people remain capable of great intellectual accomplishments well into their later years (Simonton, 1990, 1997). This fact was verified in a study of scholarly, scientific, and artistic productivity that examined lifelong patterns of work among 738 men who lived at least through the age of 79. Dennis (1966) found that the 40s decade was the most productive in most professions. However, productivity was remarkably stable through the 60s and even the 70s in many areas.

A hot issue in recent years has been whether high levels of mental activity in late adulthood can delay the typical age-related declines in cognitive functioning (Hertzog, Kramer, Wilson, & Lindenberger, 2009; King & Suzman, 2009). This possibility is sometimes referred to as the "use it or lose it" hypothesis. Several lines of evidence seem to provide support for this notion. For example, people who continue to work further into old age, especially people who remain in mentally demanding jobs, tend to show smaller decrements in cognitive abilities than their age-mates (Bosma et al., 2002; Schooler, 2007). Other studies suggest that bilingualism (Bialystok & Craik, 2010) and continuing to engage in intellectually challenging activities in late adulthood serves to buffer against cognitive declines (Kliegel, Zimprich, & Rott, 2004; Yaffe et al., 2009). You may recall that we reviewed Bialystok's research on bilingualism in Chapter 8. According to Bialystok, it is not that bilingualism prevents you from getting disorders such as Alzheimer's disease, but that bilinguals who suffer

from Alzheimer's are "able to continue functioning at a higher level. They could cope with the disease for longer" (Dreifus, 2011).

With regard to the effect of activity level, one recent study of 488 people between the ages of 75 and 85 found that participation in leisure activities (such as reading, writing, working crossword puzzles, and playing board games) was associated with a reduced decline in memory functioning (Hall et al., 2009). The effects of continued intellectual activity may be one reason for the increased use of the Internet by Canadian seniors. A recent Statistics Canada survey found that the highest growth rates in terms of age and Internet use are among Canadian seniors. From 2000 to 2007, there was little growth in the rate of Internet use by 15- to 24-year-olds in Canada. The rate of Internet use by seniors was *four* times higher for Canadian seniors in 2007 than it was in 2000 (Vennhof & Timusk, 2009). Seniors tend to use the Internet for various activities, including e-mail, surfing, obtaining weather reports, and travel information/travel arrangements.

With findings such as these in mind, some scientists have developed elaborate and challenging cognitive training programs for elderly people that are intended to slow their cognitive decline. Studies of these interventions have yielded promising results (Ball, Edwards, & Ross, 2007; Mahncke et al., 2006; Willis et al., 2006). For example, one recent study had subjects over the age of 65 spend one hour a day, five days a week, for 8 weeks on a computerized training program (Smith et al., 2009). Subsequent tests showed that the training enhanced

Contrary to widespread stereotypes, many people remain active and productive in their 70s, 80s, and even beyond. Pictured here is Wayne Weiten's Auntie Mildred, at age 99, having a little fun at a child's birthday party held at a rock-climbing facility. Now 102, Mildred still composes poetry and you can't pull her away from her personal computer.

Human Development across the Life Span

Stage of development	Infancy (birth–2)	
Physical and sensorimotor development	 Rapid brain growth; 75% of adult brain weight is attained by age 2. 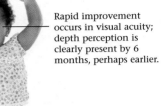 Rapid improvement occurs in visual acuity; depth perception is clearly present by 6 months, perhaps earlier. Ability to localize sounds is apparent at birth; ability to recognize parent's voice occurs within first week. © Jose Manuel Gelphi Diaz/iStockphoto.com Landmarks in motor development: Infants sit without support around 6 months, walk around 12–14 months, run freely around 2 years.	

Major stage theories	Piaget	Sensorimotor	
	Kohlberg	Premoral	
	Erikson	Trust vs. mistrust	Autonomy vs. shame
	Freud (see Chapter 12)	Oral	Anal

Cognitive development	 Object permanence gradually develops. Infant shows orienting response (pupils dilate, head turns) and attention to new stimulus, habituation (reduced orienting response) to repeated stimulus. Babbling increasingly resembles spoken language. First word is used around age 1; vocabulary spurt begins around 18 months; frequent overextensions (words applied too broadly) occur.

Social and personality development	Temperamental individuality is established by 2–3 months; infants tend to be easy, difficult, or slow to warm up. © George Shelley/CORBIS Attachment to caregiver(s) is usually evident around 6–8 months; secure attachment facilitates exploration. "Stranger anxiety" often appears around 6–8 months; separation anxiety peaks around 14–18 months.

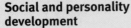
Information compiled by Barbara Hansen Lemme, College of DuPage

Early childhood
(2–6)

Visual acuity reaches 20/20.

Connections among neurons continue to increase in density.

Bladder and bowel control is established.

Hand preference is usually solidified by 3–4 years; coordination improves; children learn to dress themselves.

© Simone van den Berg/iStockphoto.com

Middle childhood
(6–12)

In girls, growth spurt begins around age 11, bringing dramatic increases in height and weight.

Level of pituitary activity and sex hormones increases.

In girls, puberty begins around age 12; menstruation starts.

Girls' secondary sex characteristics (such as breast development and widening hips) begin to emerge.

Amos Morgan/Photodisc/Getty Images

Preoperational	Concrete operational
Preconventional	Conventional
Initiative vs. guilt	Industry vs. inferiority
Phallic	Latency

Thought is marked by egocentrism (limited ability to view world from another's perspective).

Thought is marked by centration (inability to focus on more than one aspect of a problem at a time) and irreversibility (inability to mentally undo an action).

Telegraphic speech (omitting nonessential words) appears at 2–3 years; syntax is well developed by age 5; vocabulary increases dramatically.

Short-term memory capacity increases from two items at age 2 to five items around age 6–7; attention span improves.

Conservation (understanding that physical qualities can remain constant in spite of transformations in shape) is gradually mastered.

Child develops decentration (ability to focus on more than one feature of a problem at a time) and reversibility (ability to mentally undo an action).

Metalinguistic awareness (ability to reflect on use of language) leads to play with language, use of puns, riddles, metaphors.

Long-term memory improves with increasing use of encoding strategies of rehearsal and organization.

Child realizes that gender does not change and begins to learn gender roles and form gender identity; social behaviour is influenced by observational learning, resulting in imitation.

Child progresses from parallel (side-by-side, noninteractive) play to cooperative play.

Social world is extended beyond family; first friendships are formed.

Banana Stock/Jupiterimages

Child experiences great increase in social skills, improved understanding of others' feelings; social world is dominated by same-sex peer relationships.

Role-taking skills emerge; fantasy is basis for thoughts about vocations and jobs.

Altruism tends to increase, aggression tends to decrease; aggression tends to become verbal rather than physical, hostile more than instrumental.

Adolescence
(12–20)

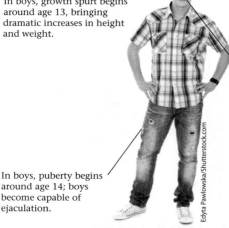

In boys, growth spurt begins around age 13, bringing dramatic increases in height and weight.

Level of pituitary activity and hormones increases.

Boys' secondary sex characteristics (such as voice change and growth of facial hair) begin to emerge.

In boys, puberty begins around age 14; boys become capable of ejaculation.

Young adulthood
(20–40)

Reaction time and muscular strength peak in early to mid-20s.

External signs of aging begin to show in 30s; skin loses elasticity; hair is thinner, more likely to be grey.

Maximum functioning of all body systems, including senses, attained; slow decline begins in 20s.

Lowered metabolic rate contributes to increased body fat relative to muscle; gain in weight is common.

Formal operational	
	Postconventional (if attained)
Identity vs. confusion	Intimacy vs. isolation
Genital	

Deductive reasoning improves; problem solving becomes more systematic, with alternative possibilities considered before solution is selected.

Thought becomes more abstract and reflective; individual develops ability to mentally manipulate abstract concepts as well as concrete objects.

Individual engages in idealistic contemplation of hypotheticals, "what could be."

Long-term memory continues to improve as elaboration is added to encoding strategies.

Intellectual abilities and speed of information processing are stable.

Greater emphasis is on application, rather than acquisition, of knowledge.

There is some evidence of a trend toward dialectical thought (ideas stimulate opposing ideas), leading to more contemplation of contradictions, pros and cons.

Person experiences increased interactions with opposite-sex peers; dating begins.

Attention is devoted to identity formation, questions such as "Who am I?" and "What do I want out of life?"

Realistic considerations about abilities and training requirements become more influential in thoughts about vocations and jobs.

Energies are focused on intimate relationships, learning to live with marriage partner, starting a family, managing a home.

Trial period is given for occupational choices, followed by stabilization of vocational commitment; emphasis is on self-reliance, becoming one's own person.

For many, close relationship develops with mentor (older person who serves as role model, adviser, and teacher).

Middle adulthood
(40–65)

Changes occur in vision: increased farsightedness and difficulty recovering from glare; slower dark adaptation.

The amount of brain tissue declines, but significance of this neural loss is unclear.

In women, meno-pause occurs around age 50; in both sexes, sexual activity declines, although capacity for arousal changes only slightly.

Sensitivity to high-frequency sounds decreases, especially in males after age 55.

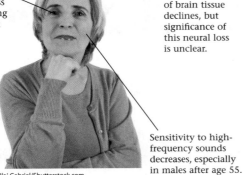

Blaj Gabriel/Shutterstock.com

Late adulthood
(65 and older)

Height decreases slightly because of changes in vertebral column; decline in weight also common.

Sensitivity of vision, hearing, and taste noticeably decreases.

Chronic diseases, especially heart disease, cancer, and stroke, increase.

Rate of aging is highly individualized.

Carme Balcells/Shutterstock.com

Generativity vs. self-absorption

There is some evidence for a trend toward improved judgment or "wisdom" based on accumulation of life experiences.

Effectiveness of retrieval from long-term memory begins slow decline, usually not noticeable until after age 55.

Individual experiences gradual decline in speed of learning, problem solving, and information processing.

In spite of decreased speed in cognitive processes, intellectual productivity and problem-solving skills usually remain stable.

Integrity vs. despair

Individual experiences gradual decline in cognitive speed and effectiveness of working memory.

Intellectual productivity depends on factors such as health and lifestyle; many people in 60s and 70s remain quite productive.

Decision making tends to become more cautious.

Fluid intelligence often declines, but crystallized intelligence remains stable or increases.

Midlife transition around age 40 leads to reflection, increased awareness of mortality and passage of time, but usually is not a personal crisis.

"Sandwich generation" is caught between needs of aging parents and children reaching adulthood.

Career development peaks; there is some tendency to shift energy from career concerns to family concerns.

Image Source/Jupiterimages

Steve Mason/Photodisc/Getty Images

Physical changes associated with aging require adjustments that affect life satisfaction.

Marital satisfaction often increases, but eventually death of spouse presents coping challenge.

Living arrangements are a significant determinant of satisfaction, as 60%–90% of time is spent at home.

many aspects of memory performance. That said, the improvement was not dramatic—just 4 percent. Another intriguing study found that a memory training program led to measureable changes in the brain. Fourteen hours of training produced an increase in the density of dopamine receptors in two critical areas of the brain (McNab et al., 2009). These findings are intriguing, but the evidence on memory training in the elderly is a mixed bag and there are skeptics (Papp, Walsh, & Snyder, 2009; Salthouse, 2006). It remains to be seen whether modest training effects can really diminish the negative effects of aging on cognitive functioning, or delay the onset of Alzheimer's disease.

Putting It in Perspective: Themes 2, 3, 4, 5, and 6

PREVIEW QUESTIONS

▶ How did this chapter illustrate the interplay of heredity and environment?

▶ What other unifying themes surfaced in this chapter?

Many of our seven integrative themes surfaced to some degree in our coverage of human development. We saw theoretical diversity in the discussions of attachment, cognitive development, and personality development. We saw that psychology evolves in a sociohistorical context, investigating complex, real-world issues. We encountered multifactorial causation of behaviour in the development of temperament and attachment, among other things. We saw cultural invariance and cultural diversity in our examination of attachment, motor development, cognitive development, and moral development.

But above all else, we saw how heredity and environment jointly mould behaviour. We've encountered the dual influence of heredity and environment before, but this theme is rich in complexity, and each chapter draws out different aspects and implications. Our discussion of development amplified the point that genetics and experience work *interactively* to shape behaviour. In the language of science, an interaction means that the effects of one variable depend on the effects of another. In other words, heredity and environment do not operate independently. Children with "difficult" temperaments will elicit different reactions from different parents, depending on the parents' personalities and expectations. Likewise, a particular pair of parents will affect children in different ways, depending on the inborn characteristics of the children. An interplay, or feedback loop, exists between biological and environmental factors. For instance, a temperamentally difficult child may elicit negative reactions from parents, which serve to make the child more difficult, which evokes more negative reactions. If this child develops into an ornery 11-year-old, which do we blame—genetics or experience? Clearly, this outcome is due to the reciprocal effects of both.

All aspects of development are shaped jointly by heredity and experience. We often estimate their relative weight or influence, as if we could cleanly divide behaviour into genetic and environmental components. Although we can't really carve up behaviour that neatly, such comparisons can be of great theoretical interest, as you'll see in our upcoming Personal Application, which discusses the nature and origins of gender differences in behaviour.

REVIEW OF KEY POINTS

▶ During adulthood, personality is marked by both stability and change. Adults who move successfully through the three stages of adulthood posited by Erikson should develop intimacy, generativity, and integrity.

▶ Many landmarks in adult development involve transitions in family relationships. Premarital cohabitation used to be predictive of an increased likelihood of marital dissolution later, but the situation seems to be changing. Difficulty adjusting to marriage is more likely when spouses have different role expectations, especially about housework. The transition to parenthood can be stressful, but realistic expectations can help. For most parents, the empty nest transition no longer appears to be as difficult as it once was.

▶ During adulthood, age-related physiological transitions include changes in appearance, sensory losses (especially in vision and hearing), and hormonal changes. Curiously, though, elderly people tend to feel younger than they are. Most women experience at least some unpleasant symptoms during menopause, but it is not as problematic as widely suggested.

▶ The prevalence of dementia increases as people age. Alzheimer's has a subtle onset marked by chronic forgetting of newly learned information, followed by a progressive deterioration over eight to ten years. The causes of this debilitating disease are not well understood, although genetic factors and chronic inflammation appear to contribute.

▶ In the cognitive domain, general intelligence is fairly stable, with a small decline in average test scores seen after the age of 60. Fluid intelligence is more likely to decline, whereas crystallized intelligence often remains stable. Many studies have found decreases in older adults' memory capabilities. Mental speed declines in late adulthood, but many people remain productive well into old age. Some studies suggest that high levels of mental activity in late adulthood can delay the typical age-related declines in cognitive functioning.

▶ Many of our seven integrative themes stood out in this chapter. But above all else, our discussion of development showed how heredity and environment interactively shape behaviour.

Understanding Gender Differences

Answer the following "true" or "false."

___ **1** Females are more socially oriented than males.

___ **2** Males outperform females on most spatial tasks.

___ **3** Females are more irrational than males.

___ **4** Males are less sensitive to nonverbal cues than females.

___ **5** Females are more emotional than males.

Are there genuine behavioural differences between the sexes similar to those mentioned above? If so, why do these differences exist? How do they develop? These are the complex and controversial questions that we'll explore in this Personal Application.

Before proceeding further, we need to clarify how some key terms are used, as terminology in this area of research has been evolving and remains a source of confusion. *Sex* usually refers to the biologically based categories of female and male. In contrast, *gender* usually refers to culturally constructed distinctions between femininity and masculinity. Individuals are born female or male. However, they become feminine or masculine through complex developmental processes that take years to unfold.

The statements at the beginning of this Application reflect popular gender stereotypes in our society. *Gender stereotypes* are widely held beliefs about females' and males' abilities, personality traits, and social behaviour. Table 11.1 lists some characteristics that are part of the masculine and feminine stereotypes in North American society. The table shows something you may have already noticed on your own: The male stereotype is much more flattering, suggesting that men have virtually cornered the market on competence and rationality. After all, everyone knows that females are more dependent, emotional, irrational, submissive, and talkative than males. Right? Or is that not the case? Let's look at the research.

How Do the Sexes Differ in Behaviour?

Gender differences are actual disparities between the sexes in typical behaviour or average ability. Mountains of research, literally thousands of studies, exist on gender differences. What does this research show? Are the stereotypes of males and females accurate? Well, the findings are a mixed bag. The research indicates that genuine behavioural differences *do* exist between the sexes and that people's stereotypes are not entirely inaccurate (Eagly, 1995; Halpern, 2000). But the differences are fewer in number, smaller in size, and far more complex than stereotypes suggest. As you'll see, only two of the differences mentioned in our opening true–false questions (the even-numbered items) have been largely supported by the research.

Cognitive Abilities In the cognitive domain, it appears that there are three genuine—albeit rather small—gender differences. First, on the average, females tend to exhibit slightly better *verbal skills* than males (Halpern et al., 2007). In particular, females seem stronger on tasks that require rapid access to semantic information in long-term memory and tasks that require the production or comprehension of complex prose (Halpern, 2004). Second, starting during high school, males show a slight advantage on tests of *mathematical ability*. When all students are compared, males' advantage is quite small (Hyde, 2005a). Indeed, in a recent review of research, Hyde and Mertz (2009) concluded that the gender gap in math has disappeared in the general population in the United States. Around the world, though, small to modest gender

TABLE 11.1

Elements of Traditional Gender Stereotypes

Masculine	Feminine
Active	Aware of others' feelings
Adventurous	Considerate
Aggressive	Creative
Ambitious	Cries easily
Competitive	Devotes self to others
Dominant	Emotional
Independent	Enjoys art and music
Leadership qualities	Excitable in a crisis
Likes math and science	Expresses tender feelings
Makes decisions easily	Feelings hurt
Mechanical aptitude	Gentle
Not easily influenced	Home-oriented
Outspoken	Kind
Persistent	Likes children
Self-confident	Neat
Skilled in business	Needs approval
Stands up under pressure	Tactful
Takes a stand	Understanding

Source: Ruble, T. L., Sex stereotypes: Issues of change in the 70s, *Sex Roles 9* (1983): 387–402. With kind permission from Springer Science+Business Media B.V.

disparities are still seen in some countries, especially those that do not endorse equal opportunities for men and women (Else-Quest, Hyde, & Linn, 2010). Also, at the high end of the ability distribution, a gender gap is still found. About three to four times as many males as females manifest exceptional math skills (Wai et al., 2010). Third, starting in the grade-school years, males tend to score higher than females on most measures of *visual-spatial ability* (Halpern et al., 2007). The size of these gender differences varies, depending on the exact nature of the spatial task. Males appear to be strongest on tasks that require mental rotations or tracking the movement of objects through three-dimensional space (Halpern, 2004). One study uncovered a gender gap in mental rotation that was apparent in infants that were only five months old (Moore & Johnson, 2008).

Personality and Social Behaviour

In regard to personality, recent research suggests that there are some modest gender differences on certain key personality traits. A study of personality across 55 cultures found that females tend to score somewhat higher than males on measures of *extraversion, agreeableness, conscientiousness,* and *neuroticism* (Schmitt et al., 2008). As for social behaviour, research findings support the existence of some additional gender differences (e.g., Guidice, 2011). First, studies indicate that males tend to be much more *physically aggressive* than females (Archer, 2005). This disparity shows up early in childhood. Its continuation into adulthood is supported by the fact that men account for a grossly disproportionate number of the violent crimes in our society (Kenrick, Trost, & Sundie, 2004). The findings on *verbal aggression* are more complex, as females appear to exhibit more relational aggression (snide remarks and so forth) (Archer, 2005). Second, there are gender differences in *nonverbal communication and interpersonal sensitivity*. The evidence indicates that females are more sensitive than males to subtle nonverbal cues (Hall, Carter, & Horgan, 2000; Hampson, van Anders, & Mullin, 2006) and that they pay more attention to interpersonal information (Hall & Mast, 2008). Third, males are more sexually active than females in a variety of ways, and they have more permissive attitudes about casual, premarital, and extramarital sex (Baumeister et al., 2001b; Hyde, 2005a; see Chapter 10).

Some Qualifications

Although research has identified some genuine gender differences in behaviour, bear in mind that these are group differences that indicate nothing about individuals. Essentially, research results compare the "average man" with the "average woman." However, you are—and every individual is—unique. The average female and male are ultimately figments of our imagination. Furthermore, the genuine group differences noted are relatively small (Hyde, 2005a, 2007). Figure 11.25 shows how scores on a trait, perhaps verbal ability, might be distributed for men and women.

Although the group averages are detectably different, you can see the great variability within each group (sex) and the huge overlap between the two group distributions.

Biological Origins of Gender Differences

What accounts for the development of various gender differences? To what degree are they the product of learning or of biology? This question is yet another manifestation of the nature versus nurture issue. Investigations of the biological origins of gender differences have centred on the evolutionary bases of behaviour, hormones, and brain organization.

Evolutionary Explanations Evolutionary analyses usually begin by arguing that gender differences in behaviour are largely the same across divergent cultures because cultural invariance suggests that biological factors are at work. Although research has turned up some fascinating exceptions, the better-documented gender differences in cognitive abilities, aggression, and sexual behaviour *are* found in virtually all cultures (Beller & Gafni, 1996; Kenrick et al., 2004). Evolutionary psychologists go on to argue that these universal gender differences reflect different natural selection pressures operating on males and females over the course of human history (Archer, 1996; Buss & Kenrick, 1998; Geary, 2007). For example, as we discussed in Chapter 10, males supposedly are more sexually active and permissive because they invest less than females in the process of procreation and can maximize their reproductive success by seeking many sexual partners (Buss, 1996; Schmitt, 2005; Webster, 2009).

The gender gap in aggression is also explained in terms of reproductive fitness. Because females are more selective about mating than males, males have to engage in more competition for sexual partners than females do. Greater aggressiveness is thought to be adaptive for males in this competition for sexual access because it should foster social dominance over other males and facilitate the acquisition of the material resources emphasized by females when they evaluate potential partners (Campbell, 2005; Cummins, 2005).

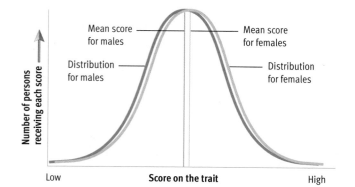

FIGURE 11.25

The nature of gender differences.

Gender differences are group differences that indicate little about individuals because of the overlap between the groups. For a given trait, one sex may score higher on the average, but far more variation occurs within each sex than between the sexes.

Source: Adapted from Schaie, K.W. (1990). Intellectual development in adulthood. In J.E. Birren and K.W. Schaie (Eds.), *Handbook of the psychology of aging* (pp. 291–309). San Diego: Academic Press. Copyright © 1990 Elsevier Science (USA), reproduced with permission from the publisher.

Evolutionary theorists assert that gender differences in spatial ability reflect the division of labour in ancestral hunting-and-gathering societies in which males typically handled the hunting and females the gathering. Males' superiority on most spatial tasks has been attributed to the adaptive demands of hunting (Newcombe, 2007; Silverman & Choi, 2005; see Chapter 1).

Evolutionary analyses of gender differences are interesting, but controversial. On the one hand, it seems eminently plausible that evolutionary forces could have led to some divergence between males and females in typical behaviour. On the other hand, evolutionary hypotheses are highly speculative and difficult to test empirically (Eagly & Wood, 1999; Halpern, 2000). The crucial problem for some critics is that evolutionary analyses are so "flexible" that they can be used to explain almost anything. For example, if the situation regarding spatial ability were reversed—if females scored higher than males—evolutionary theorists might attribute females' superiority to the adaptive demands of gathering food, weaving baskets, and making clothes—and it would be difficult to prove otherwise (Cornell, 1997).

The Role of Hormones Disparities between males and females in hormone levels may contribute to gender differences in behaviour (Hampson & Moffat, 2004; Hines, 2010). Hormones play a key role in sexual differentiation during prenatal development. The high level of androgens (the principal class of male hormones) in males and the low level of androgens in females lead to the differentiation of male and female genital organs. The critical role of prenatal hormones becomes apparent when something interferes with normal prenatal

hormonal secretions. About a half-dozen endocrine disorders can cause overproduction or underproduction of specific gonadal hormones during prenatal development. Scientists have also studied children born to mothers who were given an androgen-like drug to prevent miscarriage. The general trend in this research is that females exposed prenatally to abnormally high levels of androgens exhibit more male-typical behaviour than other females do, and that males exposed prenatally to abnormally low levels of androgens exhibit more female-typical behaviour than other males (Hines, 2004).

These findings suggest that prenatal hormones contribute to the shaping of gender differences in humans. But there are some problems with this evidence (Basow, 1992; Fausto-Sterling, 1992; Jordan-Young, 2010). First, the evidence is much stronger for females than for males. Second, it's always dangerous to draw conclusions about the general population based on small samples of people who have abnormal conditions. However, a recent study that approached the issue in a new way circumvented both of these problems. In this study, the level of testosterone (a critical androgen) in mothers' amniotic fluid was assessed and correlated with a later measure of their children's sex-typical play. Fetal testosterone levels were positively correlated with male-typical play in both boys and girls (Auyeung et al., 2009). These findings are important in that they are based on "normal" subjects from the general population and because they show similar trends for both males and females. Looking at the evidence as a whole, it does seem likely that hormones contribute to gender differences in behaviour. However, a great deal remains to be learned.

Differences in Brain Organization

Many theorists believe that gender differences in behaviour are rooted in male–female disparities in brain structure and organization (Cahill, 2006). For example, some theorists have tried to link gender differences to the specialization of the cerebral hemispheres in the brain (see Figure 11.26). As you may recall from Chapter 3, in most people, the left hemisphere is more actively involved in verbal processing, whereas the right hemisphere is more active in

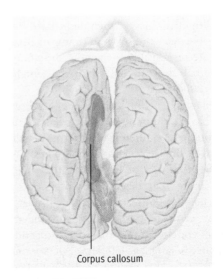

Corpus callosum

FIGURE 11.26

The cerebral hemispheres and the corpus callosum.

In this drawing, the cerebral hemispheres have been "pulled apart" to reveal the corpus callosum, the band of fibres that connects the right and left halves of the brain. Research has shown that the right and left hemispheres are specialized to handle different types of cognitive tasks (see Chapter 3), leading some theorists to speculate that patterns of hemispheric specialization might contribute to gender differences in visual and spatial abilities.

visual–spatial processing (Gazzaniga, Ivry, & Mangun, 2009). After these findings surfaced, theorists began to wonder whether this division of labour in the brain might be related to gender differences in verbal and spatial skills. Consequently, they began looking for sex-related disparities in brain organization.

Some thought-provoking findings *have* been reported. For instance, some studies have found that *males tend to exhibit more cerebral specialization than females* (Boles, 2005; Voyer, 1996). In other words, males tend to depend more heavily than females do on the left hemisphere in verbal processing and more heavily on the right hemisphere in spatial processing. Differences between males and females have also been found in the size of the corpus callosum, the band of fibres that connects the two hemispheres of the brain. Some studies suggest that *females tend to have a larger corpus callosum* (Bigler et al., 1997; Gur & Gur, 2007; Resnick, 2006), which might allow for better interhemispheric transfer of information, which, in turn, might underlie the less lateralized organization of females' brains (Innocenti, 1994). Thus, some theorists have concluded that differences between the sexes in brain organization are responsible for gender differences in verbal and spatial ability (Clements et al., 2006).

This idea is intriguing, but psychologists have a long way to go before they can explain gender differences in terms of right brain/left brain specialization. Studies have not been consistent in finding that males have more specialized brain organization than females (Kaiser et al, 2009). In fact, a recent meta-analysis of 26 neuroimaging studies concluded that there was no gender disparity in language lateralization (Sommer et al., 2008). Also, serious doubts have been raised about the finding that females have a larger corpus callosum (Fine, 2010; Halpern et al., 2007). Moreover, even if these findings were replicated consistently, no one is really sure just how they would account for the observed gender differences in cognitive abilities (Fine, 2010).

In summary, researchers have made some intriguing progress in their efforts to document the biological roots of gender differences in behaviour. However, the idea that "anatomy is destiny" has proven difficult to demonstrate. Many theorists remain convinced that gender differences are largely shaped by experience. Let's examine their evidence.

Environmental Origins of Gender Differences

Socialization is the acquisition of the norms and behaviours expected of people in a particular society. In all cultures, the socialization process includes efforts to train children about gender roles. *Gender roles are expectations about what is appropriate behaviour for each sex.* Although gender roles are in a period of transition in modern Western society, there are still many disparities in how males and females are brought up. Investigators have identified three key processes involved in the development of gender roles: operant conditioning, observational learning, and self-socialization. First we'll examine these processes. Then we'll look at the principal sources of gender-role socialization: families, schools, and the media.

Operant Conditioning In part, gender roles are shaped by the power of reward and punishment—the key processes in operant conditioning (see Chapter 6). Parents, teachers, peers, and others often reinforce (usually with tacit approval) "gender-appropriate" behaviour and respond negatively to "gender-inappropriate" behaviour (Bussey & Bandura, 1999; Matlin, 2008). If you're a man, you might recall getting hurt as a young boy and being told that "big boys don't cry." If you succeeded in inhibiting your crying, you may have earned an approving smile or even something tangible like an ice cream cone. The reinforcement probably strengthened your tendency to "act like a man" and suppress emotional displays. If you're a woman, chances are your crying wasn't discouraged as gender-inappropriate. Studies suggest that fathers encourage and reward gender-appropriate behaviour in their youngsters more than mothers do and that boys experience more pressure to behave in gender-appropriate

Gender-role socialization begins very early as parents provide their infants with "gender-appropriate" clothing, toys, and hairstyles.

ways than girls do (Levy, Taylor, & Gelman, 1995).

Observational Learning *Observational learning* (see Chapter 6) by children can lead to the imitation of adults' gender-appropriate behaviour. Children imitate both males and females, but most children tend to imitate same-sex role models more than opposite-sex role models (Bussey & Bandura, 2004). Thus, imitation often leads young girls to play with dolls, dollhouses, and toy stoves. Young boys are more likely to tinker with toy trucks, miniature gas stations, or tool kits.

Self-Socialization Children themselves are active agents in their own gender-role socialization. Several *cognitive theories* of gender-role development emphasize self-socialization (Bem, 1985; Cross & Markus, 1993; Martin & Ruble, 2004). Self-socialization entails three steps. First, children learn to classify themselves as male or female and to recognize their sex as a permanent quality (around ages five to seven). Second, this self-categorization motivates them to value those characteristics and behaviours associated with their sex. Third,

Who is the teacher most likely to call on? Some studies say that teachers may favour the boy and call on him before the girl, especially in math, science, and technology classes.

they strive to bring their behaviour in line with what is considered gender-appropriate in their culture. In other words, children get involved in their own socialization, working diligently to discover the rules that are supposed to govern their behaviour.

Sources of Gender-Role Socialization

There are three main sources of influence in gender-role socialization: families, schools, and the media. Of course, we are now in an era of transition in gender roles, so the generalizations that follow may say more about how you were socialized than about how children will be socialized in the future.

Families. A great deal of gender-role socialization takes place in the home (Berenbaum, Martin, & Ruble, 2008; Pomerantz, Ng, & Wang, 2004). Fathers engage in more "roughhousing" play with their sons than with their daughters, even in infancy (McBride-Chang & Jacklin, 1993). As children grow, boys and girls are encouraged to play with different types of toys (Freeman, 2007; Wood, Desmarais, & Gugula, 2002). Generally, boys have less leeway to play with "feminine" toys than girls do with "masculine" toys. When children are old enough to help with household chores, the assignments tend to depend on sex (Cunningham, 2001). For example, girls wash dishes and boys mow the lawn. And parents are more likely to explain scientific concepts to boys than to girls (Crowley et al., 2001).

Schools. Schools and teachers clearly contribute to the socialization of gender roles (Berenbaum et al., 2008). The books that children use in learning to read can influence their ideas about what is suitable behaviour for males and females (Diekman & Murnen, 2004). Traditionally, males have more likely been portrayed as clever, heroic, and adventurous in these books, while females have more likely been shown doing domestic chores. Preschool and grade-school teachers frequently reward sex-appropriate behaviour in their pupils (Fagot et al., 1985; Ruble & Martin, 1998). Interestingly, teachers tend to pay greater attention to males, helping them, praising them, and scolding them more than females (Sadker & Sadker, 1994). Schools may play a key role in the gender gap in outstanding math performance, as Hyde and Mertz (2009) note that girls traditionally have been much less likely than boys to be encouraged to enroll in advanced math, chemistry, and physics courses.

Media. Television and other mass media are another source of gender-role socialization (Bussey & Bandura, 2004). Although some improvement has been made in recent years, television shows have traditionally depicted men and women in highly stereotypic ways (Galambos, 2004; Signorielli, 2001). Women are often portrayed as submissive, passive, and emotional. Men are more likely to be portrayed as independent, assertive, and competent. Even commercials contribute to the socialization of gender roles (Furnham & Mak, 1999; Lippa, 2005). Recent research found an association between children's exposure to gender stereotyping in the media and their beliefs about gender roles (Oppliger, 2007).

Conclusion

As you can see, the findings on gender and behaviour are complex and confusing. Nonetheless, the evidence does permit one very general conclusion—a conclusion that you have seen before and will see again. Taken as a whole, the research in this area suggests that biological factors and environmental factors both contribute to gender differences in behaviour—as they do to all other aspects of development.

REVIEW OF KEY POINTS

▸ Gender differences in behaviour are fewer in number than gender stereotypes suggest. In the cognitive domain, research reviews suggest that there are genuine gender differences in verbal ability, mathematical ability, and spatial ability. In regard to social behaviour, differences have been found in aggression, nonverbal communication, and sexual behaviour. But most gender differences in behaviour are very small in magnitude.

▸ Evolutionary theorists maintain that gender differences transcend culture because males and females have confronted different adaptive demands over the course of human history. Extensive evidence suggests that prenatal hormones contribute to human gender differences, but the research is marred by interpretive problems. Research linking gender differences to cerebral specialization is intriguing, but much remains to be learned.

▸ A vast research literature shows that gender differences are shaped by socialization processes. Operant conditioning, observational learning, and self-socialization contribute to the development of gender differences. Families, schools, and the media are among the main sources of gender-role socialization.

Are Fathers Essential to Children's Well-Being?

Are fathers essential for children to experience normal, healthy development? This question is currently the subject of heated debate. While much of this research has been conducted in the United States, it is an important issue for Canadians, too, given recent findings on the number of female-headed single-parent families in Canada. According to the 2001 *Census*, of the 8.4 million families in Canada, 15.7 percent were single-parent families, with 81 percent of those lone parents being female (Vanier Institute of the Family, 2005).

In recent years, a number of social scientists have mounted a thought-provoking argument that father absence is the chief factor underlying a host of modern social ills. For example, David Blankenhorn (1995) argues that "fatherlessness is the most harmful demographic trend of this generation. It is the leading cause of declining child well-being in our society" (p. 1). Expressing a similar view, David Popenoe (1996) maintains that "today's fatherlessness has led to social turmoil-damaged children, unhappy children, aimless children, children who strike back with pathological behavior and violence" (p. 192).

The Basic Argument

What is the evidence for the proposition that fathers are essential to healthy development? Over the last 40 years, the proportion of children growing up without a father in the home has more than doubled (see Figure 11.27). During the same time, we have seen dramatic increases in teenage pregnancy, juvenile delinquency, violent crime, drug abuse, eating disorders, teen suicide, and family dysfunction. Moreover, mountains of studies have demonstrated an association between father absence and an elevated risk for these problems.

Summarizing this evidence, Popenoe (1996) asserts that "fatherless children have a risk factor two to three times that of fathered children for a wide range of negative outcomes, including dropping out of

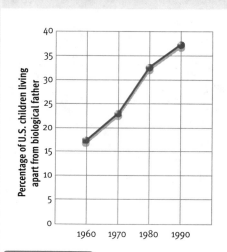

FIGURE 11.27

Increasing father absence in the United States.
Since 1960, the percentage of U.S. children who live in a home without their biological father has risen steadily and probably exceeds 40 percent today. (Data from Hernandez, 1993)

high school, giving birth as a teenager, and becoming a juvenile delinquent" (p. 192), which leads him to infer that "fathers have a unique and irreplaceable role to play in child development" (p. 197). Working from this premise, Popenoe concludes, "If present trends continue, our society could be on the verge of committing social suicide" (p. 192). Echoing this dire conclusion, Blankenhorn (1995) comments that "to tolerate the trend of fatherlessness is to accept the inevitability of continued societal recession" (p. 222).

You might be thinking, "What's all the fuss about?" Surely, proclaiming the importance of fatherhood ought to be no more controversial than advocacy for motherhood or apple pie. But the assertion that a father is essential to a child's well-being has some interesting sociopolitical implications. It suggests that heterosexual marriage is the only appropriate context in which to raise children and that other family configurations are fundamentally deficient. Based on this line of reasoning, some people have argued for new laws that would make it more difficult to obtain a divorce and other policies and programs that would favour

traditional families over families headed by single mothers, cohabiting parents, and gay and lesbian parents (Silverstein & Auerbach, 1999). Indeed, the belief that children need both a mother and a father has surfaced in some of the legal wrangling over same-sex marriage that has taken place in the United States. Thus, the question about the importance of fathers is creating a great deal of controversy, because it is really a question about alternatives to traditional family structure.

Evaluating the Argument

In light of the far-reaching implications of the view that fathers are essential to normal development, it makes sense to subject this view to critical scrutiny. How could you use critical thinking skills to evaluate this argument? At least three previously discussed ideas seem germane.

First, it is important to recognize that the position that fathers are essential for healthy development rests on a foundation of correlational evidence, and as we have seen repeatedly, *correlation is no assurance of causation*. Yes, there has been an increase in fatherlessness that has been paralleled by increases in teenage pregnancy, drug abuse, eating disorders, and other disturbing social problems. But think of all the other changes that have occurred over the last five decades, such as the decline of organized religion, the growth of mass media, dramatic shifts in sexual mores, and so forth. Increased fatherlessness has co-varied with a host of other cultural trends. Hence, it is highly speculative to infer that father absence is the chief cause of most modern social maladies.

Second, it always pays to think about whether there are specific, *alternative explanations* for findings that you might have doubts about. What other factors might account for the association between father absence and children's maladjustment? Think for a moment: What is the most frequent cause of father absence? Obviously, it is divorce. Divorces tend to be highly stressful events that disrupt children's entire

Digital Vision/Getty Images

Are fathers crucial to children's well-being? This seemingly simple question has sparked heated debate.

lives. Although the evidence suggests that a majority of children seem to survive divorce without lasting detrimental effects, it is clear that divorce elevates youngsters' risk for a wide range of negative developmental outcomes (Amato, 2006; Amato & Dorius, 2010; Hetherington, 1999, 2003). Given that father absence and divorce are inextricably intertwined, it is possible that the negative effects of divorce account for much of the association between father absence and social problems.

Are there any other alternative explanations for the correlation between fatherlessness and social maladies? Yes, critics point out that the prevalence of father absence co-varies with socioeconomic status. Father absence is much more common in low-income families (Anderson, Kohler, & Letiecq, 2002). Thus, the effects of father absence are entangled to some extent with the many powerful, malignant effects of poverty, which might account for much of the correlation between fatherlessness and negative outcomes (McLoyd, 1998).

A third possible strategy in thinking critically about the effects of father absence would be to ask *if there is contradictory evidence*. Once again, the answer is yes. Biblarz and Stacey (2010) reviewed studies comparing pairs of heterosexual parents against pairs of lesbian parents. If fathers are essential, the adjustment of children raised by heterosexual parents should be superior to that of children raised by lesbian parents. But the studies found negligible differences between these parental configurations.

A fourth strategy would be to look for some of the *fallacies in reasoning* introduced in Chapter 10 (irrelevant reasons, circular reasoning, slippery slope, weak analogies,

and false dichotomy). A couple of the quotes from Popenoe and Blankenhorn were chosen to give you an opportunity to detect two of these fallacies in a new context. Take a look at the quotes once again and see whether you can spot the fallacies.

Popenoe's assertion that "if present trends continue, our society could be on the verge of social suicide" is an example of *slippery slope argumentation*, which involves predictions that if one allows X to happen, things will spin out of control and catastrophic events will follow. "Social suicide" is a little vague, but it sounds as if Popenoe is predicting that father absence will lead to the destruction of modern society. The other fallacy that you might have spotted was the *false dichotomy* apparent in Blankenhorn's assertion that "to tolerate the trend of fatherlessness is to accept the inevitability of continued societal recession." A false dichotomy creates an either–or choice between the position one wants to advocate (in this case, new social policies to reduce father absence) and some obviously horrible outcome that any sensible person would want to avoid (social decay), while ignoring other possible outcomes that might lie between these extremes.

In summary, we can find a number of flaws and weaknesses in the argument that fathers are *essential* to normal development. However, our critical evaluation of this argument *does not mean that fathers are unimportant*. Many types of evidence suggest that fathers generally make significant contributions to their children's development (Phares, 1996; Rohner & Veneziano, 2001). We could argue with merit that fathers

typically provide a substantial advantage for children that fatherless children do not have. But there is a crucial distinction between arguing that fathers *promote* normal, healthy development and arguing that fathers are *necessary* for normal, healthy development. If fathers are *necessary*, children who grow up without them could not achieve the same level of well-being as those who have fathers, yet it is clear that a great many children from single-parent homes turn out just fine.

Fathers surely are important, and it seems likely that father absence *contributes* to a variety of social maladies. So, why do Blankenhorn (1995) and Popenoe (1996) argue for the much stronger conclusion—that fathers are *essential*? They appear to prefer the stronger conclusion because it raises much more serious questions about the viability of nontraditional family forms. Thus, they seem to want to advance a *political agenda* that champions traditional family values. They are certainly entitled to do so, but when research findings are used to advance a political agenda—whether conservative or liberal—a special caution alert should go off in your head. When a political agenda is at stake, it pays to scrutinize arguments with extra care, because research findings are more likely to be presented in a slanted fashion. The field of psychology deals with a host of complex questions that have profound implications for a wide range of social issues. The skills and habits of critical thinking can help you find your way through the maze of reasons and evidence that hold up the many sides of these complicated issues.

TABLE 11.2	Critical Thinking Skills Discussed in This Application
Skill	**Description**
Understanding the limitations of correlational evidence	The critical thinker understands that a correlation between two variables does not demonstrate that there is a causal link between the variables.
Looking for alternative explanations for findings and events	In evaluating explanations, the critical thinker explores whether there are other explanations that could also account for the findings or events under scrutiny.
Recognizing and avoiding common fallacies, such as irrelevant reasons, circular reasoning, slippery slope reasoning, weak analogies, and false dichotomies	The critical thinker is vigilant about conclusions based on unrelated premises, conclusions that are rewordings of premises, unwarranted predictions that things will spin out of control, superficial analogies, and contrived dichotomies.

Human Development across the Life Span

Key Ideas

Progress before Birth: Prenatal Development

● Prenatal development proceeds through the germinal, embryonic, and fetal stages as the zygote is differentiated into a human organism. During this period, development may be affected by maternal malnutrition, maternal drug use, and some maternal illnesses.

The Wondrous Years of Childhood

● Motor development follows cephalocaudal and proximodistal trends. Early motor development depends on both maturation and learning. Developmental norms for motor skills and other types of development only reflect typical performance.

● Temperamental differences among children are apparent during the first few months of life. These differences are fairly stable and may have far-reaching effects. Research shows that attachment emerges out of an interplay between infant and mother.

● Infant–mother attachments fall into three categories: secure, anxious-ambivalent, and avoidant. Cultural variations in child-rearing can affect the patterns of attachment seen in a society.

● Erik Erikson's theory of personality development proposes that individuals evolve through eight stages over the life span. In each stage, the person wrestles with changes (crises) in social relationships.

● According to Piaget's theory of cognitive development, the key advance during the sensorimotor period is the child's gradual recognition of the permanence of objects. The preoperational period is marked by certain deficiencies in thinking—notably, centration, irreversibility, and egocentrism.

● During the concrete operations period, children develop the ability to perform operations on mental representations, making them capable of conservation and hierarchical classification. The stage of formal operations ushers in more abstract, systematic, and logical thought.

● Recent research has shown that infants appear to understand surprisingly complex concepts that they have had virtually no opportunity to learn about, leading some theorists to conclude that basic cognitive abilities are innate. Children's understanding of the mind seems to turn a corner between ages three and four.

● According to Kohlberg, moral reasoning progresses through three levels that are related to age and determined by cognitive development. Age-related progress in moral reasoning has been found in research, although a great deal of overlap occurs between adjacent stages.

The Transition of Adolescence

● The growth spurt at puberty is a prominent event involving the development of reproductive maturity and secondary sex characteristics.

● Recent decades have brought a surge in attempted suicide by adolescents and there is an association between adolescence and the prevalence of violent crime. Evidence suggests that adolescence may be slightly more stressful than other periods of life. According to Erikson, the key challenge of adolescence is to make some progress toward a sense of identity. Marcia identified four patterns of identity formation.

The Expanse of Adulthood

● During adulthood, personality is marked by both stability and change. Many landmarks in adult development involve transitions in family relationships, including adjusting to marriage, parenthood, and the empty nest.

● During adulthood, age-related physical transitions include changes in appearance, sensory losses, and hormonal changes. Drastic mental decline is not a part of the normal aging process. However, 15–20 percent of adults over age 75 suffer from some form of dementia. In late adulthood, mental speed declines and working memory suffers, but many people remain productive well into old age.

Putting It in Perspective: Themes 2, 3, 4, 5, and 6

● Many of our seven integrative themes stood out in this chapter. But above all else, our discussion of development showed how heredity and environment interactively shape behaviour.

PERSONAL APPLICATION • Understanding Gender Differences

● Gender differences in behaviour are fewer in number and smaller in magnitude than gender stereotypes suggest. Research reviews suggest that there are genuine (albeit small) gender differences in verbal ability, mathematical ability, spatial ability, aggression, nonverbal communication, risk-taking, sexual behaviour, and several personality traits.

● Evolutionary theorists believe that gender differences reflect the influence of natural selection. Some research does link gender differences in humans to hormones and brain organization, but the research is marred by interpretive problems. Operant conditioning, observational learning, and self-socialization contribute to the development of gender differences.

CRITICAL THINKING APPLICATION • Are Fathers Essential to Children's Well-Being?

● Some social scientists have argued that father absence is the chief cause of a host of social problems and that fathers are essential for normal, healthy development. Critics have argued that there are alternative explanations for the association between father absence and negative developmental outcomes.

Key Terms

Accommodation, 506
Age of viability, 493
Animism, 507
Assimilation, 506
Attachment, 500
Centration, 507
Cephalocaudal trend, 496
Cognitive development, 505
Cohort effects, 499
Conservation, 507
Cross-sectional design, 498
Crystallized intelligence, 530
Dementia, 529
Development, 490
Developmental norms, 497
Dishabituation, 511
Egocentrism, 507
Embryonic stage, 491
Family life cycle, 526
Fetal alcohol syndrome, 493
Fetal stage, 491
Fluid intelligence, 530
Gender, 537
Gender differences, 537
Gender roles, 540
Gender stereotypes, 537
Germinal stage, 491
Habituation, 511
Irreversibility, 507
Longitudinal design, 498
Maturation, 497
Menarche, 517
Motor development, 496
Object permanence, 506
Placenta, 491

Prenatal period, 491
Primary sex characteristics, 517
Proximodistal trend, 497
Puberty, 517
Pubescence, 517
Scaffolding, 511
Secondary sex characteristics, 517
Separation anxiety, 500
Sex, 537
Socialization, 540
Stage, 503
Strange situation procedure, 501
Temperament, 497
Teratogens, 493
Zone of proximal development (ZPD), 511
Zygote, 491

Key People

Mary Salter Ainsworth, 501
Jeffrey Arnett, 524
Jay Belsky, 501
John Bowlby, 501
Robbie Case, 510
Michael Chandler, 520
Stella Chess, 498
Erik Erikson, 503
Lawrence Kohlberg, 514
Valerie Kuhlmeier, 500
Christopher Lalonde, 520
James Marcia, 523
Marlene Moretti, 522
Juan Pascual-Leone, 509
Jean Piaget, 505
Alexander Thomas, 498
Lev Vygotsky, 510

1. During which of the following stages of prenatal development is a developing organism most vulnerable to injury?
   A. zygotic stage
   B. germinal stage
   C. fetal stage
   D. embryonic stage

2. In which direction does the cephalocaudal trend in children's motor development occur?
   A. head-to-foot direction
   B. centre-outward direction
   C. foot-to-head direction
   D. body-to-appendages direction

3. Which of the following outcomes would be expected for children raised among the Ache of Paraguay, where children are carried everywhere?
   A. They will have an insecure attachment style.
   B. They will reach motor milestones, like walking, later in childhood.
   C. They will demonstrate earlier attainment of cognitive milestones.
   D. They will be delayed in social and emotional development associated with self-confidence.

4. Which of the following is the name for the type of study in which the development of the same subjects is monitored over a period of time?
   A. cross-sectional study
   B. life history study
   C. longitudinal study
   D. sequential study

5. Which of the following strongly predicts the quality of infant–caregiver attachment?
   A. the quality of bonding in the first few hours of life
   B. the infant's temperament
   C. the interaction between the infant's temperament and the caregiver's responsiveness
   D. the infant's response to the "strange situation"

6. During the second year of life, toddlers begin to take some personal responsibility for feeding, dressing, and bathing themselves. According to Erikson, which of the following characteristics is indicated by the child's attempt to establish these functions?
   A. sense of superiority
   B. sense of industry
   C. sense of generativity
   D. sense of autonomy

7. David watches you pour water from a short, wide glass into a tall, narrow one. Then he says there is now more water than before. Which of Piaget's stages is David in?
   A. sensorimotor
   B. preoperational
   C. concrete operational
   D. formal operational

8. Which of the following abilities develops after the age of approximately four months?
   A. object permanence
   B. habituation
   C. awareness that $1 + 1 = 2$
   D. awareness of the effects of gravity and momentum

9. Camilla's primary reason for not drawing with crayons on the living room wall is to avoid the punishment that would follow from this behaviour. Which of the following words would Kohlberg have used to describe Camilla's level of moral development?
   A. conventional
   B. postconventional
   C. preconventional
   D. unconventional

10. The key findings of the Featured Study on adolescent suicide risk in First Nations communities illustrate the importance of which of the following developmental stages?
    A. Erikson's trust versus mistrust stage
    B. Marcia's identity crisis
    C. Kohlberg's postconventional level of morality
    D. Piaget's formal operational stage

11. Which of the following patterns of physical maturity is predicted to lead to the greatest emotional difficulty for adolescents?
    A. developing early, for a girl
    B. developing early, for either sex
    C. developing late, for a girl
    D. developing late, for either sex

12. Sixteen-year-old Foster wants to spend a few years experimenting with different lifestyles and careers before settling on who and what he wants to be. Foster's behaviour illustrates which of the following forms of the identity status?
    A. identity moratorium
    B. identity foreclosure
    C. identity achievement
    D. identity diffusion

13. Which of the following adult transitions is typically associated with an increase in life satisfaction?
    A. having children
    B. getting a divorce
    C. living with adolescents
    D. the "empty nest" stage

14. If your 65-year-old neighbour asks how to stay "mentally young" after retirement, which of the following pieces of advice should you provide?
    A. Get lots of sleep.
    B. Eat a high-protein diet.
    C. Play with puzzles.
    D. Listen to music.

15. Which of the following patterns characterizes the relationship between prenatal hormone exposure and play behaviour in childhood?
    A. Children exposed to relatively high amounts of testosterone in utero demonstrated later development of normal play behaviour.
    B. Children exposed to relatively high amounts of testosterone in utero demonstrated more male-typical play behaviour.
    C. Children exposed to relatively high amounts of cortisol demonstrated more aggressive play behaviour.
    D. Children exposed to relatively high amounts of cortisol demonstrated more female-typical play behaviour.

See Appendix A for answers to this Practice Test.

On the Web

▶ **CourseMate**

Go to this site to find online resources directly linked to your book, including more quizzes, a glossary, flash cards, videos, and more!

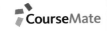

▶ **CengageNow**

Go to this site for the link to CengageNOW™, your one-stop study shop. Take a pre-test for this chapter and CengageNOW™ will generate a personalized study plan based on your test results! The study plan will identify the topics you need to review and direct you to online resources to help you master those topics. You can then take a post-test to help you determine the concepts you have mastered and what you still need to work on.

▶ **Aplia**

Aplia™ is an online interactive learning solution that helps you improve comprehension—and your grade—by integrating a variety of media and tools such as video, tutorials, practice tests, and an interactive e-book.

CHAPTER 12

Personality: Theory, Research, and Assessment

Tui De Roy/Minden Pictures/Getty Images

Have you ever been asked to provide a reference for a friend of yours who is looking for a job, to describe what your friend is like? Or, have you ever been asked to describe yourself, what you are like, perhaps in an interview or on a social networking site? After you have finished describing the basics—such as age, physical appearance, and gender—what do you say next? If you are like most of us, you then begin to describe someone's personality. Perhaps you would use terms such as "dependable," "ambitious," "mature," and "independent." In Chapter 16, we will talk more about how you derive impressions of yourself and the personality of others. For now, we will focus on the nature of *personality,* what it is, how we assess it, and what personality testing is typically used for. The scientific study of personality is one of the oldest topics in psychology. But interest in the nature of personality clearly exceeds the bounds of and predates the science of psychology. The ancient Greeks and Romans had their own view of character types and the causes of individual differences. In their theatre, actors used masks to signify different personalities and emotions (McDonald & Walton, 2007).

As you will see in the coming pages, there have been many conceptualizations of the nature of personality. While we will provide a more formal definition later, at this point it is sufficient to state that the study of personality focuses primarily on describing and understanding our individual differences. It seems as if everyone has a theory of what "kinds" of people there are in the world. Given the pet preferences of your textbook authors, apparently there are two types of people in the world—cat lovers and dog lovers. Or according to filmmaker Woody Allen, "There are two types of people in this world: the good and the bad. The good sleep better, but the bad seem to enjoy the waking hours much more."

One of the reasons we are all so interested in personality is that it is used as a way of predicting what someone will do—to predict their behaviour. Personality has been linked to various processes and outcomes important to us all. These include, among other things, happiness, physical and psychological health; marital, peer, and family relationships; personal identity; and criminal behaviour (Ozer & Benet-Martinez, 2006). Personality testing seems ubiquitous in North America. Among other things, personality tests are used in personnel selection and decisions. You may remember from our discussion in Chapter 1 that psychologists were pressed into service in World War II to use testing to assist in the selection and assignment of military personnel.

Personality testing is even part of the NASA selection and training program for astronauts (NASA, 2008). Astronaut candidates undergo a rigorous selection and training program lasting two years. In addition to personality evaluation, there are physical, intellectual, academic, and citizenship criteria. So far, nine Canadians have flown in space—eight astronauts, and one civilian. The civilian, Cirque du Soleil founder Guy Laliberte, paid $35 million to be launched into space on board a Russian rocket in 2009 (CBC, 2010). A series of research studies have been conducted examining personality and other characteristics that should be considered when selecting astronaut candidates (Endler, 2004; McFadden, Helmreich, Rose, & Fogg, 1994; Musson, Sandal, & Helmreich, 2004; Sekiguchi, Umikura, Sone, & Kume, 1994; Suefeld, 2003; Suefeld & Steel, 2000). According to Bishop and Primeau (2002), for example, the desired or favourable characteristics of astronauts include high levels of task focus, positive interpersonal orientation and achievement motivation, and low levels of hostility, aggressiveness, and competitiveness. In his analysis of research in this area, Gordon Flett, a prominent personality psychologist and Canada Research Chair, stated that the personality dimensions examined thus far are a useful beginning, but that "further developments can be obtained by including a focus on other personality measures (such as coping factors) . . ." (Flett, 2007, p. 22).

Psychologists have approached the study of personality from a variety of perspectives. Traditionally, the study of personality has been dominated by "grand theories" that attempt to explain a great

Eight Canadian astronauts have been launched into space. The eight are Marc Garneu, Steve MacLean, Julie Payette, Dave Williams, Roberta Bondar, Chris Hadfield, Robert Thirsk, and Bjarni Tryggvanson.

many facets of behaviour. Our discussion will reflect this emphasis. We'll devote most of our time to the sweeping theories of Freud, Skinner, Rogers, and several others. In recent decades, however, the study of personality has shifted toward narrower research programs that examine specific issues related to personality. This trend is reflected in our review of biological, cultural, and other contemporary approaches to personality in the last several sections of the chapter. In the Personal Application, we'll examine how psychological tests are used to measure aspects of personality. The Critical Thinking Application will explore how hindsight bias can taint people's analyses of personality.

The Nature of Personality

PREVIEW QUESTIONS

▶ What are the essential features of the concept of personality?

▶ What are personality traits?

▶ How many personality traits are necessary to describe personality adequately?

Personality is a complex hypothetical construct that has been defined in a variety of ways. Let's take a closer look at the concepts of personality and personality traits.

Defining Personality: Consistency and Distinctiveness

What does it mean to say that someone has an optimistic personality? This assertion indicates that the person has a fairly consistent tendency to behave in a cheerful, hopeful, enthusiastic way, looking at the bright side of things, across a wide variety of situations. Although no one is entirely consistent in behaviour, this quality of consistency across situations lies at the core of the concept of personality.

Distinctiveness is also central to the concept of personality. Personality is used to explain why not everyone acts the same way in similar situations. If you were stuck in an elevator with three people, each might react differently. One might crack jokes to relieve the tension. Another might make ominous predictions that "we'll never get out of here." The third might calmly think about how to escape. These varied reactions to the same situation occur because each person has a different personality. Each person has traits that are seen in other people, but each individual has his or her own distinctive *set* of personality traits.

In summary, the concept of personality is used to explain (1) the stability in a person's behaviour over time and across situations (consistency) and (2) the behavioural differences among people reacting to the same situation (distinctiveness). We can combine these ideas into the following definition: *Personality refers to an individual's unique constellation of consistent behavioural traits.* Let's look more closely at the concept of *traits*.

Personality Traits: Dispositions and Dimensions

Everyone makes remarks like "Jan is very conscientious." Or you might assert that "Bill is too timid to succeed in that job." These descriptive statements refer to personality traits. A *personality trait* is a durable disposition to behave in a particular way in a variety of situations. Adjectives such as *honest, dependable, moody, impulsive, suspicious, anxious, excitable, domineering,* and *friendly* describe dispositions that represent personality traits.

Most approaches to personality assume that some traits are more basic than others. According to this notion, a small number of fundamental traits determine other, more superficial traits. For example, a person's tendency to be impulsive, restless, irritable, boisterous, and impatient might all be derived from a more basic tendency to be excitable.

A number of psychologists have taken on the challenge of identifying the basic traits that form the core of personality. For example, Raymond Cattell (1950, 1966, 1990) used the statistical procedure of factor analysis to reduce a huge list of personality traits compiled by Gordon Allport (1937) to just 16 basic dimensions of personality. As you may recall from Chapter 9, in *factor analysis,* correlations among many variables are analyzed to identify closely related clusters of variables. If the measurements of a number of variables (in this case, personality traits) correlate highly with one another, the assumption is that a single factor is influencing all of them. Factor analysis is used to identify these hidden factors. In factor analyses of personality traits, these hidden factors are viewed as very basic, higher-order traits that determine less basic, more specific traits. Based on his factor analytic work, Cattell concluded that an individual's personality can be described completely by measuring just 16 traits. The 16 crucial traits are listed in Figure 12.21 (page 587) in the Personal Application, where we discuss a personality test that Cattell designed to assess these traits.

The Five-Factor Model of Personality Traits

In more recent years, Robert McCrae and Paul Costa (1987, 1997, 2003, 2008, 2008a) have used factor analysis to arrive at an even simpler, five-factor model of personality (see Figure 12.1). McCrae and Costa maintain that most personality traits are derived from just five higher-order traits that have come to be known as the "Big Five": extraversion, neuroticism, openness to experience, agreeableness, and conscientiousness. Let's take a closer look at these traits:

1. *Extraversion.* People who score high in extraversion are characterized as outgoing, sociable, upbeat, friendly, assertive, and gregarious. Referred to as *positive emotionality* in some trait models, extraversion has been studied extensively in research for many decades (Watson & Clark, 1997). Extraverts tend to be happier than others (Fleeson, Malanos, & Achille, 2002). They also have a more positive outlook on life and are motivated to pursue social contact, intimacy, and interdependence (Wilt & Revelle, 2009).

2. *Neuroticism.* People who score high in neuroticism tend to be anxious, hostile, self-conscious, insecure, and vulnerable. Like extraversion, this trait has been the subject of thousands of studies. Those who score high in neuroticism tend to overreact more in response to stress than others (Mroczek & Almeida, 2004). They also tend to exhibit more impulsiveness and emotional instability than others (Widiger, 2009).

3. *Openness to experience.* Openness is associated with curiosity, flexibility, vivid fantasy, imaginativeness, artistic sensitivity, and unconventional attitudes. People who are high in openness tend to be tolerant of ambiguity and have less need for closure on issues than others (McCrae & Sutin, 2009). McCrae (1996) maintains that its importance has been underestimated. Citing evidence that openness fosters liberalism, he argues that this trait is the key determinant of people's political attitudes and ideology. For example, evidence suggests that people high in openness tend to exhibit less prejudice against minorities than others (Flynn, 2005).

4. *Agreeableness.* Those who score high in agreeableness tend to be sympathetic, trusting, cooperative, modest, and straightforward. People who score at the opposite end of this personality dimension are

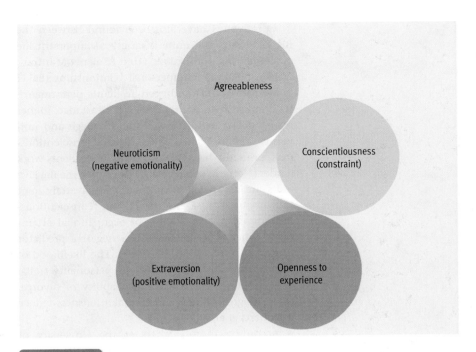

FIGURE 12.1

The five-factor model of personality.

Trait models attempt to analyze personality into its basic dimensions. McCrae and Costa (1985, 1987, 1997) maintain that personality can be described adequately with the five higher-order traits identified here, which are widely referred to as the "Big Five."

characterized as suspicious, antagonistic, and aggressive. Agreeableness is associated with constructive approaches to conflict resolution, making agreeable people less quarrelsome than others (Jensen-Campbell & Graziano, 2001). Agreeableness is also correlated with empathy and helping behaviour (Graziano & Tobin, 2009).

5. *Conscientiousness.* Conscientious people tend to be diligent, disciplined, well-organized, punctual, and dependable. Referred to as *constraint* in some trait models, conscientiousness is associated with strong self-discipline and the ability to regulate oneself effectively (Roberts et al., 2009). Studies have also shown that conscientiousness fosters diligence and dependability in the workplace (Lund et al., 2007) and that it is related to impression management (Meston, Heiman, Trapnell, & Paulus, 1998).

Research such as that conducted by Sampo Paunonen of the University of Western Ontario shows that Big Five traits are predictive of specific aspects of behaviour, as one would expect (Paunonen, 2003). For example, extraversion correlates positively with popularity and with dating a greater variety of people. Conscientiousness correlates with greater honesty, higher job performance ratings, and relatively low alcohol consumption. Openness to experience is associated with playing a musical instrument, whereas agreeableness correlates with honesty.

Correlations have also been found between the Big Five traits and quite a variety of important life outcomes (Ashton, 2007; Ozer & Benet-Martinez, 2006), including interpersonal relationships (Baker & McNulty, 2011) and even academic performance (O'Connor & Paunonen, 2007). For instance, higher grades (GPA) in high school and college and university are associated with higher conscientiousness, primarily because conscientious students work harder (Noftle & Robins, 2007). Several of the Big Five traits are associated with occupational attainment (career success). Extraversion and conscientiousness are positive predictors of occupational attainment, whereas neuroticism is a negative predictor (Roberts, Caspi, & Moffitt, 2003). The likelihood of divorce can also be predicted by personality traits, as neuroticism elevates the probability of divorce, whereas agreeableness and conscientiousness reduce it (Roberts et al., 2007).

According to researchers at the University of Calgary and the University of Waterloo, the Big Five have been found to be related to feelings of subjective well-being (Heller, Komar, & Lee, 2007; Steel, Schmidt, & Shultz, 2008). Two of the Big Five traits are related to health and mortality over the course of the life span. Neuroticism is associated with an elevated prevalence of virtually all major mental disorders, not to mention a host of physical illnesses (Lahey, 2009; Widiger, 2009). Conscientiousness, though, is correlated with the experience of less illness and with reduced mortality (Friedman & Martin, 2011; Kern & Friedman, 2008; Martin, Friedman, & Schwartz, 2007). In other words, conscientious people live longer than others. It is not hard to figure out why, as conscientiousness is inversely related to just about every health-impairing behaviour you can think of—such as excessive eating, smoking, drug use, lack of exercise, and various risky practices (Roberts et al., 2009). Recently, it has been found that the there are interesting relationships between the Big Five and socioeconomic status. For example, the probability of being strongly conscientious rises dramatically as social class goes up. The prevalence of high scores on openness and extraversion also increase, although more gradually, as socioeconomic level rises. In contrast, strong agreeableness and neuroticism are less prevalent in the upper classes. At present, the causal relations that might underlie these correlations are unclear.

Like Cattell, McCrae and Costa maintain that personality can be described adequately by measuring the basic traits that they've identified. Their bold claim has been supported in many studies by other researchers, and the five-factor model has become the dominant conception of personality structure in contemporary psychology (John, Naumann, & Soto, 2008; McCrae, 2005). These five traits have been characterized as the "latitude and longitude" along which personality should be mapped (Ozer & Reise, 1994, p. 361). However, some theorists have been critical of the model. Some critics of the five-factor model maintain that more than five traits are necessary to account for most of the variation seen in human personality (Boyle, 2008). For example, Brock University's Michael Ashton and his colleagues have argued that honesty–humility ought to be recognized as a fundamental sixth factor in personality (Ashton, Lee, & Goldberg, 2004; Lee & Ashton, 2008). And other theorists have argued that there are some important traits—such as being manipulative, frugal, conservative, humorous, and egotistical—that do not fit into the five-factor model (Paunonen & Jackson, 2000). Ironically, other theorists have argued for an even simpler three-factor theory of personality (De Radd et al., 2010).

The debate about how many dimensions are necessary to describe personality is likely to continue for many years to come. As you'll see throughout the chapter, the study of personality is an area in psychology that has a long history of "duelling theories." We'll divide these diverse personality theories into four broad groups that share certain assumptions, emphases, and interests: (1) psychodynamic perspectives, (2) behavioural perspectives, (3) humanistic perspectives, and (4) biological perspectives. We'll begin our discussion of personality theories by examining the life and work of Sigmund Freud.

REVIEW OF KEY POINTS

▸ The concept of personality explains the consistency in people's behaviour over time and across situations while also explaining their distinctiveness. Factor analysis can be used to identify higher-order traits from which specific traits are derived. There is considerable debate as to how many trait dimensions are necessary to account for the variation in personality.

▸ Nonetheless, the five-factor model has become the dominant conception of personality structure. The Big Five personality traits are extraversion, neuroticism, openness to experience, agreeableness, and conscientiousness. Recent research suggests that the Big Five traits are differentially correlated with social class. The Big Five traits are predictive of important life outcomes, such as grades, career success, and divorce. Neuroticism is associated with poorer health and elevated mortality, whereas the opposite relationships are seen for the trait of conscientiousness

Psychodynamic Perspectives

Psychodynamic theories include all of the diverse theories descended from the work of Sigmund Freud, which focus on unconscious mental forces. Freud inspired many brilliant scholars to follow in his intellectual footsteps. Some of these followers simply refined and updated Freud's theory. Others veered off in new directions and established independent, albeit related, schools of thought. Today, the psychodynamic umbrella covers a large collection of loosely related theories that we can only sample from in this text. In this chapter, we'll examine the ideas of Sigmund Freud in some detail. Then we'll take a briefer look at the psychodynamic theories of Carl Jung and Alfred Adler.

Freud's Psychoanalytic Theory 10a

Born in 1856 in what is now the Czech Republic, Sigmund Freud grew up in a middle-class Jewish home in Vienna, Austria. The country of his youth was to have an important impact on his future work since his case studies formed the basis of his future theory of psychoanalysis. His case studies were based upon his Viennese patients (Flett, 2007). He showed an early interest in intellectual pursuits and became an intense, hard-working young man, driven to achieve fame. He experienced his share of inner turmoil and engaged in regular self-analysis for over 40 years. Freud lived in the Victorian era, which was marked by sexual repression. His life was also affected by World War I, which devastated Europe, and by the growing anti-Semitism of the times. We'll see that the sexual repression and aggressive hostilities that Freud witnessed left their mark on his view of human nature.

Although trained initially as a medical doctor, Freud specialized in neurology and took an interest in psychiatric cases when he began his medical practice in Vienna toward the end of the 19th century. Like other neurologists in his era, he often treated people troubled by nervous problems such as irrational fears, obsessions, and anxieties. Eventually he devoted himself to the treatment of mental disorders using an innovative procedure he had developed, called *psychoanalysis*, that required lengthy verbal interactions with patients during which Freud probed deeply into their lives. Before beginning his psychiatric practice, he studied with and received scientific and research training with Ernst Brucke. According to Flett (2007), it was this training that led him to hope to establish psychoanalysis as a science. As we will discuss later,

this led to some controversy, as the method departed from critical scientific tenets such as *objectivity* and the *testability* of the theory (Storr, 1988).

Freud's (1901, 1924, 1940) psychoanalytic theory grew out of his decades of interactions with his clients in psychoanalysis. Psychoanalytic theory attempts to explain personality, motivation, and psychological disorders by focusing on the influence of early childhood experiences, on unconscious motives and conflicts, and on the methods people use to cope with their sexual and aggressive urges.

Most of Freud's contemporaries were uncomfortable with his theory for at least three reasons. First, in arguing that people's behaviour is governed by unconscious factors of which they are unaware, Freud made the disconcerting suggestion that individuals are not masters of their own minds. Second, in claiming that adult personalities are shaped by childhood experiences and other factors beyond one's control, he suggested that people are not masters of their own destinies. Third, by emphasizing the great importance of how people cope with their sexual urges, he offended those who held the conservative, Victorian values of his time.

Thus, Freud endured a great deal of criticism, condemnation, and outright ridicule, even after his work began to attract more favourable attention. Consider the following recollection from one of Freud's friends: "In those days when one mentioned Freud's name everyone would begin to laugh, as if someone had told a joke. Freud was the queer fellow who wrote a book about dreams. . . . He was the man who saw sex in everything. It was considered bad taste to bring up Freud's name in the presence of ladies" (Donn, 1988, p. 57). Let's examine the ideas that generated so much controversy.

Structure of Personality 10a

Freud divided personality structure into three components: the id, the ego, and the superego (see Figure 12.2). He saw a person's behaviour as the outcome of interactions among these three components.

The *id* is the primitive, instinctive component of personality that operates according to the pleasure principle. Freud referred to the id as the reservoir of psychic energy. By this he meant that the id houses the raw biological urges (to eat, sleep, defecate, copulate, and so on) that energize human behaviour. The id operates according to the *pleasure principle*, which demands immediate gratification of its urges. The

Sigmund Freud

"No one who, like me, conjures up the most evil of those half-tamed demons that inhabit the human beast, and seeks to wrestle with them, can expect to come through the struggle unscathed."

PREVIEW QUESTIONS

► How did Freud view the structure of personality?

► Why did Freud think sex and aggression were such important motives?

► How do defence mechanisms work?

► How did Freud explain the development of personality?

► How was Jung's view of the unconscious different from Freud's?

► How did Adler explain inferiority feelings?

► What are the strengths and weaknesses of the psychodynamic approach?

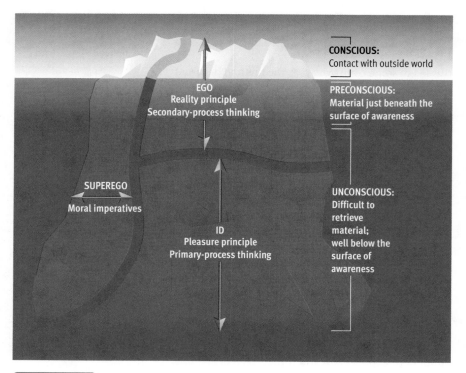

CONSCIOUS:
Contact with outside world

EGO
Reality principle
Secondary-process thinking

PRECONSCIOUS:
Material just beneath the surface of awareness

SUPEREGO
Moral imperatives

UNCONSCIOUS:
Difficult to retrieve material; well below the surface of awareness

ID
Pleasure principle
Primary-process thinking

FIGURE 12.2

Freud's model of personality structure.

Freud theorized that people have three levels of awareness: the conscious, the preconscious, and the unconscious. The enormous size of the unconscious is often dramatized by comparing it to the portion of an iceberg that lies beneath the water's surface. Freud also divided personality structure into three components—id, ego, and superego—which operate according to different principles and exhibit different modes of thinking. In Freud's model, the id is entirely unconscious, but the ego and superego operate at all three levels of awareness.

id engages in *primary-process thinking,* which is primitive, illogical, irrational, and fantasy-oriented.

The *ego* is the decision-making component of personality that operates according to the reality principle. The ego mediates between the id, with its forceful desires for immediate satisfaction, and the external social world, with its expectations and norms regarding suitable behaviour. The ego considers social realities—society's norms, etiquette, rules, and customs—in deciding how to behave. The ego is guided by the *reality principle,* which seeks to delay gratification of the id's urges until appropriate outlets and situations can be found. In short, to stay out of trouble, the ego often works to tame the unbridled desires of the id.

In the long run, the ego wants to maximize gratification, just as the id does. However, the ego engages in *secondary-process thinking,* which is relatively rational, realistic, and oriented toward problem solving. Thus, the ego strives to avoid negative consequences from society and its representatives (e.g., punishment by parents or teachers) by behaving "properly." It also attempts to achieve long-range goals that sometimes require putting off gratification.

While the ego concerns itself with practical realities, the *superego* is the moral component of personality that incorporates social standards about what represents right and wrong. Throughout their lives, but especially during childhood, people receive training about what constitutes good and bad behaviour. Many social norms regarding morality are eventually internalized. The superego emerges out of the ego at around three to five years of age. In some people, the superego can become irrationally demanding in its striving for moral perfection. Such people are plagued by excessive feelings of guilt. According to Freud, the id, ego, and superego are distributed differently across three levels of awareness, which we'll describe next.

10a PSYKTREK

Levels of Awareness

Perhaps Freud's most enduring insight was his recognition of how unconscious forces can influence behaviour. He inferred the existence of the unconscious from a variety of observations that he made with his patients. For example, he noticed that "slips of the tongue" often revealed a person's true feelings. He also realized that his patients' dreams often expressed hidden desires. Most important, through psychoanalysis, he often helped patients to discover feelings and conflicts of which they had previously been unaware.

Freud contrasted the unconscious with the conscious and preconscious, creating three levels of awareness. The *conscious* consists of whatever one is aware of at a particular point in time. For example, at this moment your conscious may include the train of thought in this text and a dim awareness in the back of your mind that your eyes are getting tired and you're beginning to get hungry. The *preconscious* contains material just beneath the surface of awareness that can easily be retrieved. Examples might include your middle name, what you had for supper last night, or an argument you had with a friend yesterday. The *unconscious* contains thoughts, memories, and desires that are well below the surface of conscious awareness but that nonetheless exert great influence on behaviour. Examples of material that might be found in your unconscious include a forgotten trauma from childhood, hidden feelings of hostility toward a parent, and repressed sexual desires.

Freud's conception of the mind is often compared to an iceberg that has most of its mass hidden beneath the water's surface (see Figure 12.2). He believed that the unconscious (the mass below the surface) is much larger than the conscious or preconscious. As you can see in Figure 12.2, he proposed that the ego and superego operate at all three levels of awareness. In contrast, the id is entirely unconscious, expressing its urges at a conscious level through the ego. Of course, the id's desires for immediate satisfaction often trigger internal conflicts with the ego and superego. These conflicts play a key role in Freud's theory.

Conflict and the Tyranny of Sex and Aggression

10a

Freud assumed that behaviour is the outcome of an ongoing series of internal conflicts. He saw internal battles between the id, ego, and superego as routine. Why? Because the id wants to gratify its urges immediately, but the norms of civilized society frequently dictate otherwise. For example, your id might feel an urge to clobber a co-worker who constantly irritates you. However, society frowns on such behaviour, so your ego would try to hold this urge in check. Hence, you would find yourself in conflict. You may be experiencing conflict at this very moment. In Freudian terms, your id may be secretly urging you to abandon reading this chapter so that you can fix a snack and watch some television. Your ego may be weighing this appealing option against your society-induced need to excel in school.

Freud believed that people's lives are dominated by conflict. He asserted that individuals careen from one conflict to another. The following scenario provides a concrete illustration of how the three components of personality interact to create constant conflicts:

> *Imagine lurching across your bed to shut off your alarm clock as it rings obnoxiously. It's 7 A.M. and time to get up for your history class. However, your id (operating according to the pleasure principle) urges you to return to the immediate gratification*

Freud's psychoanalytic theory was based on decades of clinical work. He treated a great many patients in the consulting room pictured here. The room contains numerous artifacts from other cultures—and the original psychoanalytic couch.

of additional sleep. Your ego (operating according to the reality principle) points out that you really must go to class since you haven't been able to decipher the textbook on your own. Your id (in its typical unrealistic fashion) smugly assures you that you will get the A grade that you need and suggests lying back to dream about how impressed your roommates will be. Just as you're relaxing, your superego jumps into the fray. It tries to make you feel guilty about all the money your parents paid in tuition for the class that you're about to skip. You haven't even gotten out of bed yet, but there's already a pitched battle in your psyche.

Let's say your ego wins the battle. You pull yourself out of bed and head for class. On the way, you pass a doughnut shop and your id clamours for cinnamon rolls. Your ego reminds you that you're supposed to be on a diet. Your id wins this time. After you've attended your history lecture, your ego reminds you that you need to do some library research for a paper in philosophy. However, your id insists on returning to your apartment to watch some sitcom reruns. As you re-enter your apartment, you're overwhelmed by how messy it is. It's your roommates' mess, and your id suggests that you tell them off. As you're about to lash out, however, your ego convinces you that diplomacy will be more effective. Three sitcoms later you find that you're in a debate with yourself about whether to go to the gym to work out or to the student union to play pool. It's only mid-afternoon—and already you've been through a series of internal conflicts.

Freud believed that conflicts centring on sexual and aggressive impulses are especially likely to have far-reaching consequences. Why did he emphasize sex and aggression? Two reasons were prominent in his thinking. First, he thought that sex and aggression are subject to more complex and ambiguous social controls than other basic motives. The norms governing sexual and aggressive behaviour are subtle, and people often get inconsistent messages about what's appropriate. Thus, Freud believed that these two drives are the source of much confusion.

Second, he noted that the sexual and aggressive drives are thwarted more regularly than other basic biological urges. Think about it: If you get hungry or thirsty, you can simply head for a nearby vending machine or a drinking fountain. But if a department store clerk infuriates you, you aren't likely to reach across the counter and slug him or her. Likewise, when you see a person who inspires lustful urges, you don't normally walk up and propose a tryst in a nearby broom closet. There's nothing comparable

WEB LINK 12.2

Sigmund Freud Museum
This online museum offers a detailed chronology of Freud's life and an explanation of the most important concepts of psychoanalysis.

Personality: Theory, Research, and Assessment

to vending machines or drinking fountains for the satisfaction of sexual and aggressive urges. Freud ascribed great importance to these needs because social norms dictate that they be routinely frustrated.

Anxiety and Defence Mechanisms

10a

Most internal conflicts are trivial and are quickly resolved one way or the other. Occasionally, however, a conflict will linger for days, months, or even years, creating internal tension. More often than not, such prolonged and troublesome conflicts involve sexual and aggressive impulses that society wants to tame. These conflicts are often played out entirely in the unconscious. Although you may not be aware of these unconscious battles, they can produce *anxiety*

FIGURE 12.3

Freud's model of personality dynamics.

According to Freud, unconscious conflicts among the id, ego, and superego sometimes lead to anxiety. This discomfort may lead to the use of defence mechanisms, which may temporarily relieve anxiety.

TABLE 12.1

Defence Mechanisms, with Examples

Note: See Table 13.2 on page 611 for additional examples of defence mechanisms.

Defence Mechanism	Definition	Example
Repression	Keeping distressing thoughts and feelings buried in the unconscious	A traumatized soldier has no recollection of the details of a close brush with death.
Projection	Attributing one's own thoughts, feelings, or motives to another	A woman who dislikes her boss thinks she likes her boss but feels that the boss doesn't like her.
Displacement	Diverting emotional feelings (usually anger) from their original source to a substitute target	After parental scolding, a young girl takes her anger out on her little brother.
Reaction formation	Behaving in a way that is exactly the opposite of one's true feelings	A parent who unconsciously resents a child spoils the child with outlandish gifts.
Regression	A reversion to immature patterns of behaviour	An adult has a temper tantrum when he doesn't get his way.
Rationalization	Creating false but plausible excuses to justify unacceptable behaviour	A student watches TV instead of studying, saying that "additional study wouldn't do any good anyway."
Identification	Bolstering self-esteem by forming an imaginary or real alliance with some person or group	An insecure young man joins a fraternity to boost his self-esteem.
Sublimation	Occurs when unconscious, unacceptable impulses are channelled into socially acceptable, perhaps even admirable, behaviours	A young man's longing for initimacy is channelled into his creative artwork.

that slips to the surface of conscious awareness. The anxiety can be attributed to your ego worrying about (1) the id getting out of control and doing something terrible that leads to severe negative consequences or (2) the superego getting out of control and making you feel guilty about a real or imagined transgression.

The arousal of anxiety is a crucial event in Freud's theory of personality functioning (see Figure 12.3). Anxiety is distressing, so people try to rid themselves of this unpleasant emotion any way they can. This effort to ward off anxiety often involves the use of defence mechanisms. *Defence mechanisms are largely unconscious reactions that protect a person from unpleasant emotions such as anxiety and guilt* (see Table 12.1). Typically, they're mental manoeuvres that work through self-deception. Consider *rationalization,* which is creating false but plausible excuses to justify unacceptable behaviour. For example, after cheating someone in a business transaction, you might reduce your guilt by rationalizing that "everyone does it."

According to Delroy Paulhus from the University of British Columbia and his colleagues, repression is "the flagship in the psychoanalytic fleet of defense mechanisms" (Paulhus, Fridhandler, & Hayes, 1997); repression is the most basic and widely used defence mechanism. *Repression is keeping distressing thoughts and feelings buried in the unconscious.* People tend to repress desires that make them feel guilty, conflicts that make them anxious, and memories that are painful. Repression has been called "motivated forgetting." If you forget a dental appointment or the name of someone you don't like, repression may be at work.

Self-deception can also be seen in projection and displacement. *Projection is attributing one's own thoughts, feelings, or motives to another.* Usually, the thoughts one projects onto others are thoughts that would make one feel guilty. For example, if lusting for a co-worker makes you feel guilty, you might attribute any latent sexual tension between the two of you to the other person's desire to seduce you. *Displacement is diverting emotional feelings (usually anger) from their original source to a substitute target.* If your boss gives you a hard time at work and you come home and slam the door, kick the dog, and scream at your spouse, you're displacing your anger onto irrelevant targets. Unfortunately, social constraints often force people to hold back their anger, and they end up lashing out at the people they love most.

Other prominent defence mechanisms include reaction formation, regression, and identification. *Reaction formation is behaving in a way that's exactly the opposite of one's true feelings.* Guilt about sexual desires often leads to reaction formation. For example, Freud theorized that many males who ridicule homosexuals are defending against their own latent homosexual impulses. The telltale sign of reaction formation is the exaggerated quality of the opposite behaviour. *Regression* is a reversion to immature patterns of behaviour. When anxious about their self-worth, some adults respond with childish boasting and bragging (as opposed to subtle efforts to impress others). For example, a fired executive having difficulty finding a new job might start making ridiculous statements about his incomparable talents and achievements. Such bragging is regressive when it's marked by massive exaggerations that virtually anyone can see through. *Identification* is bolstering self-esteem by forming an imaginary or real alliance with some person or group. Youngsters often shore up precarious feelings of self-worth by identifying with rock stars, movie stars, or famous athletes. Adults may join exclusive country clubs or civic organizations as a means of identification.

Finally, Freud described the defence of *sublimation,* which occurs when unconscious, unacceptable impulses are channelled into socially acceptable, perhaps even admirable, behaviours. For example, intense aggressive impulses might be rechannelled by taking up boxing or football. Freud believed that many creative endeavours, such as painting, poetry, and sculpture, were sublimations of sexual urges. For instance, he argued that Leonardo da Vinci's painting of Madonna figures was a sublimation of his longing for intimacy with his mother (Freud, 1910). By definition, sublimation is regarded as a relatively healthy defence mechanism.

Freud's work on defence mechanisms was important both to the development of psychoanalysis and its legacy since it is one aspect of his theory that endures and has contemporary currency (Erdelyi, 2001). Freud's daughter, Anna Freud, is well known for her contributions to the study of defence mechanisms (Freud, 1936) and as the founder of the child psychoanalytic movement (Flett, 2007).

Anna Freud, Sigmund Freud's youngest daughter, carried on and extended her father's work in psychoanalytic psychology. She made significant contributions to the development of child psychoanalysis and our understanding of defence mechanisms.

concept **check 12.1**

Identifying Defence Mechanisms

Check your understanding of defence mechanisms by identifying specific defences in the story below. Each example of a defence mechanism is underlined, with a number next to it. Write in the defence at work in each case in the numbered spaces after the story. The answers are in Appendix A.

My girlfriend recently broke up with me after we had dated seriously for several years. At first, I cried a great deal and <u>locked myself in my room, where I pouted endlessly.</u> *(1.) I was sure that my former girlfriend felt as miserable as I did.* <u>I told several friends that she was probably lonely and depressed.</u> *(2.) Later, I decided that I hated her.* <u>I was happy about the breakup and talked about how much I was going to enjoy my newfound freedom.</u> *(3.) I went to parties and socialized a great deal and just forgot about her.* <u>It's funny—at one point I couldn't even remember her phone number!</u> *(4.) Then I started pining for her again. But eventually I began to look at the situation more objectively. I realized that she had many faults and that* <u>we were bound to break up sooner or later, so I was better off without her.</u> *(5.)*

1. _____   4. _____

2. _____   5. _____

3. _____

Personality: Theory, Research, and Assessment

Development: Psychosexual Stages

Freud believed that "the child is father to the man." In fact, he made the rather startling assertion that the basic foundation of an individual's personality has been laid down by the tender age of five. To shed light on these crucial early years, Freud formulated a stage theory of development. He emphasized how young children deal with their immature but powerful sexual urges (he used the term *sexual* in a general way to refer to many urges for physical pleasure). According to Freud, these sexual urges shift in focus as children progress from one stage of development to another. Indeed, the names for the stages (oral, anal, genital, and so on) are based on where children are focusing their erotic energy during that period. Thus, *psychosexual stages* are developmental periods with a characteristic sexual focus that leave their mark on adult personality.

Freud theorized that each psychosexual stage has its own unique developmental challenges or tasks (see Table 12.2). The way these challenges are handled supposedly shapes personality. The process of fixation plays an important role in this process. *Fixation* is a failure to move forward from one stage to another as expected. Essentially, the child's development stalls for a while. Fixation can be caused by excessive gratification of needs at a particular stage or by excessive frustration of those needs. Either way, fixations left over from childhood affect adult personality. Generally, fixation leads to an overemphasis on the psychosexual needs prominent during the fixated stage. Freud described a series of five psychosexual stages. Let's examine some of the highlights in this sequence.

Oral Stage This stage encompasses the first year of life. During this period, the main source of erotic stimulation is the mouth (in biting, sucking, chewing, and so on). In Freud's view, the handling of the child's feeding experiences is crucial to subsequent development. He attributed considerable importance to the manner in which the child is weaned from the breast or the bottle. According to Freud, fixation at the oral stage could form the basis for obsessive eating or smoking later in life (among many other things).

Anal Stage In their second year, children get their erotic pleasure from their bowel movements, through either the expulsion or retention of feces. The crucial event at this time is toilet training, which represents society's first systematic effort to regulate the child's biological urges. Severely punitive toilet training leads to a variety of possible outcomes. For example, excessive punishment might produce a latent feeling of hostility toward the "trainer," usually the mother. This hostility might generalize to women as a class. Another possibility is that heavy reliance on punitive measures could lead to an association between genital concerns and the anxiety that the punishment arouses. This genital anxiety derived from severe toilet training could evolve into anxiety about sexual activities later in life.

Phallic Stage Around age four, the genitals become the focus for the child's erotic energy, largely through self-stimulation. During this pivotal stage, the Oedipal complex emerges. That is, little boys develop an erotically tinged preference for their mother. They also feel hostility toward their father, whom they view as a competitor for Mom's affection. Similarly, little girls develop a special attachment to their father. Around the same time, they learn that little boys have very different genitals, and supposedly they develop penis envy. According to Freud, young girls feel hostile toward their mother because they blame her for their anatomical "deficiency."

TABLE 12.2

Freud's Stages of Psychosexual Development

Stage	Approximate Ages	Erotic Focus	Key Tasks and Experiences
Oral	0–1	Mouth (sucking, biting)	Weaning (from breast or bottle)
Anal	2–3	Anus (expelling or retaining feces)	Toilet training
Phallic	4–5	Genitals (masturbating)	Identifying with adult role models; coping with Oedipal crisis
Latency	6–12	None (sexually repressed)	Expanding social contacts
Genital	Puberty onward	Genitals (being sexually intimate)	Establishing intimate relationships; contributing to society through working

According to Freud, early childhood experiences such as toilet training (a parental attempt to regulate a child's biological urges) can influence an individual's personality, with consequences lasting throughout adulthood.

To summarize, in the *Oedipal complex*, children manifest erotically tinged desires for their opposite-sex parent, accompanied by feelings of hostility toward their same-sex parent. The name for this syndrome was taken from a tragic myth from ancient Greece. In this story, Oedipus was separated from his parents at birth. Not knowing the identity of his real parents, when he grew up he inadvertently killed his father and married his mother. The complex in girls is sometimes referred to as the *Electra complex* but this was not endorsed by Freud himself (Corsini, 1999).

According to Freud, the way parents and children deal with the sexual and aggressive conflicts inherent in the Oedipal complex is of paramount importance. The child has to resolve the Oedipal dilemma by purging the sexual longings for the opposite-sex parent and by crushing the hostility felt toward the same-sex parent. In Freud's view, healthy psychosexual development hinges on the resolution of the Oedipal conflict. Why? Because continued hostility toward the same-sex parent may prevent the child from identifying adequately with that parent. Freudian theory predicts that without such identification, sex typing, conscience, and many other aspects of the child's development won't progress as they should.

Latency and Genital Stages From around age six through puberty, the child's sexuality is largely suppressed—it becomes latent. Important events during this *latency* stage centre on expanding social contacts beyond the immediate family. With puberty, the child progresses into the genital stage. Sexual urges reappear and focus on the genitals once again. At this point, sexual energy is normally channelled toward peers of the other sex, rather than toward oneself, as in the phallic stage.

In arguing that the early years shape personality, Freud did not mean that personality development comes to an abrupt halt in middle childhood. However, he did believe that the foundation for adult personality has been solidly entrenched by this time. He maintained that future developments are rooted in early, formative experiences and that significant conflicts in later years are replays of crises from childhood.

In fact, Freud believed that unconscious sexual conflicts rooted in childhood experiences cause most personality disturbances. His steadfast belief in the psychosexual origins of psychological disorders eventually led to bitter theoretical disputes with two of his most brilliant colleagues: Carl Jung and Alfred Adler. Jung and Adler both argued that Freud overemphasized sexuality. Freud rejected their ideas, and the other two theorists felt compelled to go their own way, developing their own theories of personality.

Jung's Analytical Psychology

Carl Jung was born to middle-class Swiss parents in 1875. The son of a Protestant pastor, he was a deeply introverted, lonely child, but an excellent student. Jung had earned his medical degree and was an established young psychiatrist in Zurich when he began to write to Freud in 1906. When the two men had their first meeting, they were so taken by each other's insights that they talked nonstop for 13 hours! They exchanged 359 letters before their friendship and theoretical alliance were torn apart. Their relationship was ruptured irreparably in 1913 by a variety of theoretical disagreements.

Jung called his new approach *analytical psychology* to differentiate it from Freud's psychoanalytic theory. Jung's analytical psychology eventually attracted many followers. Perhaps because of his conflicts with Freud, Jung claimed to deplore the way schools of thought often become dogmatic, discouraging new ideas. Although many theorists came to characterize themselves as "Jungians," Jung himself often remarked, "I am not a Jungian" and said, "I do not want anybody to be a Jungian. I want people above all to be themselves" (van der Post, 1975).

Carl Jung

"I am not a Jungian . . . I do not want anybody to be a Jungian. I want people above all to be themselves."

WEB LINK 12.3

C. G. Jung, Analytical Psychology, & Culture

Synchronicity, archetypes, collective unconscious, introversion, extraversion— these and many other important concepts arising from analytical psychology and Jung's tremendously influential theorizing are examined at this comprehensive site.

Like Freud, Jung (1921, 1933) emphasized the unconscious determinants of personality. However, he proposed that the unconscious consists of two layers. The first layer, called the *personal unconscious*, is essentially the same as Freud's version of the unconscious. The *personal unconscious* houses material that is not within one's conscious awareness because it has been repressed or forgotten. In addition, Jung theorized the existence of a deeper layer he called the *collective unconscious*. The *collective unconscious* is a storehouse of latent memory traces inherited from people's ancestral past. According to Jung, each person shares the collective unconscious with the entire human race (see Figure 12.4). It contains the "whole spiritual heritage of mankind's evolution, born anew in the brain structure of every individual" (Jung, quoted in Campbell, 1971, p. 45).

Jung called these ancestral memories *archetypes*. They are not memories of actual, personal experiences. Instead, *archetypes* are emotionally charged images and thought forms that have universal meaning. These archetypal images and ideas show up frequently in dreams and are often manifested in a culture's use of symbols in art, literature, and religion. According to Jung, symbols from very different cultures often show striking similarities because they emerge from archetypes that are shared by the whole human race. For instance, Jung found numerous cultures in which the *mandala*, or "magic circle," has served as a symbol of the unified wholeness of the self (see Figure 12.4). Jung felt that an understanding of archetypal symbols helped him make sense of his patients' dreams. This was of great concern to him, as he thought that dreams contain important messages from the unconscious. Like Freud, he depended extensively on dream analysis in his treatment of patients.

Jung's unusual ideas about the collective unconscious had little impact on the mainstream of thinking in psychology. Their influence was felt more in other fields, such as anthropology, philosophy, art, and religious studies. However, many of Jung's other ideas *have* been incorporated into the mainstream of psychology. For instance, Jung was the first to describe the introverted (inner-directed) and extraverted (outer-directed) personality types. *Introverts* tend to be preoccupied with the internal world of their own thoughts, feelings, and experiences. Like Jung himself, they generally are contemplative and aloof. In contrast, *extraverts* tend to be interested in the external world of people and things. They're more likely to be outgoing, talkative, and friendly, instead of reclusive.

Adler's Individual Psychology

Like Freud, Alfred Adler grew up in Vienna in a middle-class Jewish home. He was a sickly child who struggled to overcome rickets and an almost fatal case of pneumonia. At home, he was overshadowed by an exceptionally bright and successful older brother. Nonetheless, he went on to earn his medical degree, and he practised ophthalmology and general medicine before his interest turned to psychiatry. He was a charter member of Freud's inner circle—the Vienna Psychoanalytic Society. However, he soon began to develop his own theory of personality, perhaps because he didn't want to be dominated once again by an "older brother" (Freud). His theorizing was denounced by Freud in 1911, and Adler was forced to resign from the Psychoanalytic Society. He took 9 of its 23 members with him to form his own organization. Adler's new approach to personality was called *individual psychology*.

Like Jung, Adler (1917, 1927) argued that Freud had gone overboard in centring his theory on sexual conflicts. According to Adler, the foremost source of human motivation is a striving for superiority. In his view, this striving does not necessarily translate into

Mandalas from various cultures

Russia

Navajo Indians

Tibet

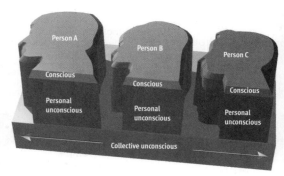

FIGURE 12.4

Jung's vision of the collective unconscious.

Much like Freud, Jung theorized that each person has conscious and unconscious levels of awareness. However, he also proposed that the entire human race shares a collective unconscious, which exists in the deepest reaches of everyone's awareness. He saw the collective unconscious as a storehouse of hidden ancestral memories, called *archetypes*. Jung believed that important cultural symbols emerge from these universal archetypes. Thus, he argued that remarkable resemblances among symbols from disparate cultures (such as the mandalas shown here) are evidence of the existence of the collective unconscious.

Source: Images from C.G. Jung, *Bild Und Wort*, © Walter-Verlag AG, Olten, Switzerland, 1977.

the pursuit of dominance or high status. Adler saw *striving for superiority* as a universal drive to adapt, improve oneself, and master life's challenges. He noted that young children understandably feel weak and helpless in comparison with more competent older children and adults. These early inferiority feelings supposedly motivate them to acquire new skills and develop new talents. Thus, Adler maintained that striving for superiority is the prime goal of life, rather than physical gratification (as suggested by Freud).

Adler asserted that everyone has to work to overcome some feelings of inferiority—a process he called compensation. *Compensation* involves efforts to overcome imagined or real inferiorities by developing one's abilities. Adler believed that compensation is entirely normal. However, in some people, inferiority feelings can become excessive, resulting in what is widely known today as an *inferiority complex*— exaggerated feelings of weakness and inadequacy. Adler thought that either parental pampering or parental neglect could cause an inferiority complex. Thus, he agreed with Freud on the importance of

Alfred Adler
"The goal of the human soul is conquest, perfection, security, superiority."

Adler's theory has been used to analyze the tragic life of the legendary actress Marilyn Monroe (Ansbacher, 1970). During her childhood, Monroe suffered from parental neglect that left her with acute feelings of inferiority. Her inferiority feelings led her to overcompensate by flaunting her beauty, marrying celebrities (Joe DiMaggio and Arthur Miller), keeping film crews waiting for hours, and seeking the adoration of her fans.

early childhood experiences, although he focused on different aspects of parent–child relationships.

Adler explained personality disturbances by noting that excessive inferiority feelings can pervert the normal process of striving for superiority. He asserted that some people engage in *overcompensation* to conceal, even from themselves, their feelings of inferiority. Instead of working to master life's challenges, people with an inferiority complex work to achieve status, gain power over others, and acquire the trappings of success (fancy clothes, impressive cars, or whatever looks important to them). They tend to flaunt their success in an effort to cover up their underlying inferiority complex. However, the problem is that such people engage in unconscious self-deception, worrying more about *appearances* than *reality*.

Adler's theory stressed the social context of personality development (Hoffman, 1994). For instance, it was Adler who first focused attention on the possible importance of *birth order* as a factor governing personality. He noted that first-borns, second children, and later-born children enter varied home environments and are treated differently by parents and that these experiences are likely to affect their personality. For example, he hypothesized that only children are often spoiled by excessive attention from parents and that first-borns are often problem children because they become upset when they're "dethroned" by a second child. Adler's theory stimulated hundreds of studies on the effects of birth order, but these studies generally failed to support his hypotheses and did not uncover any reliable correlations between birth order and personality (Ernst & Angst, 1983; J. R. Harris, 2000).

Frank Sulloway (1995, 1996), however, has argued persuasively that birth order does have an impact on personality. Sulloway's reformulated hypotheses focus on how the Big Five traits are shaped by competition among siblings as they struggle to find a "niche" in their family environments. For example, he hypothesizes that first-borns should be more conscientious but less agreeable and open to experience than later-borns. In light of these personality patterns, he further speculates that first-borns tend to be conventional and achievement-oriented, whereas later-borns tend to be liberal and rebellious. To evaluate his hypotheses, Sulloway reexamined decades of research on birth order. After eliminating many studies that failed to control for important confounding variables, such as social class and family size, he concluded that the results of the remaining, well-controlled studies provided impressive evidence in favour of his hypotheses. Some subsequent research has provided additional support

Personality: Theory, Research, and Assessment

Paul Trapnell is a personality psychologist at the University of Winnipeg. He conducts research on, among other things, the Big Five personality traits.

for Sulloway's analyses, such as that conducted by Paul Trapnell from the University of Winnipeg and his colleagues (Paulhus, Trapnell, & Chen, 1999), but other studies have not (Freese, Powell, & Steelman, 1999; J. R. Harris, 2000; Skinner, 2003). More studies will be needed, as research on birth order is enjoying a bit of a renaissance.

Evaluating Psychodynamic Perspectives

The psychodynamic approach has provided a number of far-reaching, truly "grand" theories of personality. These theories yielded some bold new insights when they were first presented. Although one might argue about exact details of interpretation, research has demonstrated that (1) unconscious forces can influence behaviour, (2) internal conflict often plays a key role in generating psychological distress, (3) early childhood experiences can have powerful influences on adult personality, and (4) people do use defence mechanisms to reduce their experience of unpleasant emotions (Bornstein, 2003; Porcerelli et al., 2010; Solms, 2004; Westen, Gabbard, & Ortigo, 2008).

In addition to being praised, psychodynamic formulations have also been criticized on several grounds, including the following (Eysenck, 1990b; Fine, 1990; Macmillan, 1991; Torrey, 1992):

1. *Poor testability.* Scientific investigations require testable hypotheses. Psychodynamic ideas have often been too vague and conjectural to permit a clear scientific test. For instance, how would you prove or disprove the assertion that the id is entirely unconscious?

2. *Inadequate evidence.* The empirical evidence on psychodynamic theories has often been characterized as "inadequate." Psychodynamic theories depend too heavily on clinical case studies in which it's much too easy for clinicians to see what they expect to see. Re-examinations of Freud's own clinical work suggest that he frequently distorted his patients' case histories to make them mesh with his theory (Esterson, 2001; Powell & Boer, 1995). Insofar as researchers have accumulated evidence on psychodynamic theories, the evidence has provided only modest support for many of the central hypotheses (Fisher & Greenberg, 1985, 1996; Westen & Gabbard, & Ortiga, 2008; Wolitzky, 2006).

3. *Sexism.* Many critics have argued that psychodynamic theories are characterized by a sexist bias against women. Freud believed that females'

Courtesy of Paul Trapnell

penis envy made them feel inferior to males. He also thought that females tended to develop weaker superegos and to be more prone to neurosis than males. The sex bias in modern psychodynamic theories has been reduced considerably. Nonetheless, the psychodynamic approach has generally provided a rather male-centred point of view (Lerman, 1986; Person, 1990).

4. *Unrepresentative samples.* Freud's theories were based on an exceptionally narrow sample of upper-class, neurotic, sexually repressed Viennese women. They were not even remotely representative of Western European culture, let alone other cultures.

It's easy to ridicule Freud for concepts such as penis envy, and it's easy to point to Freudian ideas that have turned out to be wrong. However, you have to remember that Freud, Jung, and Adler began to fashion their theories over a century ago. It's not entirely fair to compare these theories to other models that are only a decade or two old. That's like asking the Wright brothers to race a space shuttle. Freud and his colleagues deserve great credit for breaking new ground with their speculations about psychodynamics. In psychology as a whole, no other school of thought has been as influential, with the exception of behaviourism, which we turn to next.

Behavioural Perspectives

Behaviourism is a theoretical orientation based on the premise that scientific psychology should study only observable behaviour. As we saw in Chapter 1, behaviourism has been a major school of thought in psychology since 1913, when John B. Watson began campaigning for the behavioural point of view. Research in the behavioural tradition has focused largely on learning. For many decades behaviourists devoted relatively little attention to the study of personality. However, their interest in personality began to pick up after John Dollard and Neal Miller (1950) attempted to translate selected Freudian ideas into behavioural terminology. Dollard and Miller showed that behavioural concepts could provide enlightening insights about the complicated subject of personality.

In this section, we'll examine three behavioural views of personality, as we discuss the ideas of B. F. Skinner, Albert Bandura, and Walter Mischel. For the most part, you'll see that behaviourists explain personality the same way they explain everything else—in terms of learning.

Skinner's Ideas Applied to Personality

 10b

As we noted in Chapters 1 and 6, modern behaviourism's most prominent theorist has been B. F. Skinner, an American psychologist who lived from 1904 to 1990. Originally, Skinner had hoped to become a writer and he even sought out reviews of his work from famous authors, such as poet Robert Frost. Sadly for Skinner, he did not succeed as a writer. He then decided on a career in psychology (Skinner, 1980). After earning his doctorate in 1931, Skinner spent

most of his career at Harvard University. There he achieved renown for his research on the principles of learning, which were mostly discovered through the study of rats and pigeons. Skinner's (1953, 1957) concepts of operant conditioning were never meant to be a theory of personality. However, his ideas have affected thinking in all areas of psychology and have been applied to the explanation of personality. Here we'll examine Skinner's views as they relate to personality structure and development.

Personality Structure: A View from the Outside

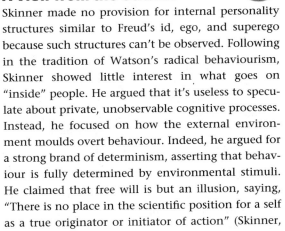 **10b**

Skinner made no provision for internal personality structures similar to Freud's id, ego, and superego because such structures can't be observed. Following in the tradition of Watson's radical behaviourism, Skinner showed little interest in what goes on "inside" people. He argued that it's useless to speculate about private, unobservable cognitive processes. Instead, he focused on how the external environment moulds overt behaviour. Indeed, he argued for a strong brand of determinism, asserting that behaviour is fully determined by environmental stimuli. He claimed that free will is but an illusion, saying, "There is no place in the scientific position for a self as a true originator or initiator of action" (Skinner, 1974, p. 225).

How can Skinner's theory explain the consistency that can be seen in individuals' behaviour? According to his view, people show some consistent patterns of behaviour because they have some stable response tendencies that they have acquired through experience. These response tendencies may change in the future, as a result of new experiences, but they're enduring enough to create a certain degree of

PREVIEW QUESTIONS

- ► How can Skinner's theory explain personality and its development?
- ► How did Bandura revise the behavioural approach to personality?
- ► What is self-efficacy, and how does it affect behaviour?
- ► How did Mischel question the concept of personality?
- ► What are the strengths and weaknesses of the behavioural approach?

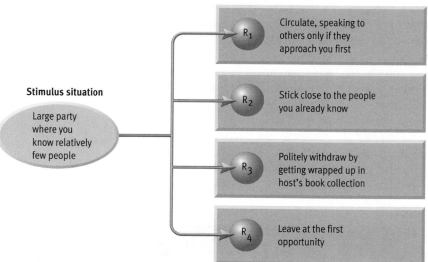

Operant response tendencies

Stimulus situation

Large party where you know relatively few people

R₁ — Circulate, speaking to others only if they approach you first

R₂ — Stick close to the people you already know

R₃ — Politely withdraw by getting wrapped up in host's book collection

R₄ — Leave at the first opportunity

FIGURE 12.5

A behavioural view of personality.

Staunch behaviourists devote little attention to the structure of personality because it is unobservable, but they implicitly view personality as an individual's collection of response tendencies. A possible hierarchy of response tendencies for a particular person in a specific stimulus situation (a large party) is shown here.

consistency in a person's behaviour. Implicitly, then, Skinner viewed an individual's personality as a collection of response tendencies that are tied to various stimulus situations. A specific situation may be associated with a number of response tendencies that vary in strength, depending on past conditioning (see Figure 12.5).

Personality Development as a Product of Conditioning

PSYKTREK
10b

Skinner's theory accounts for personality development by explaining how various response tendencies are acquired through learning (Bolling, Terry, & Kohlenberg, 2006). He believed that most human responses are shaped by the type of conditioning that he described: operant conditioning. As we discussed in Chapter 6, Skinner maintained that environmental consequences—reinforcement, punishment, and extinction—determine people's patterns of responding. On the one hand, when responses are followed by favourable consequences (reinforcement), they are strengthened. For example, if your joking at a party pays off with favourable attention, your tendency to joke at parties will increase (see Figure 12.6). On the other hand, when responses lead to negative consequences (punishment), they are weakened. Thus, if your impulsive decisions always backfire, your tendency to be impulsive will decline.

Because response tendencies are constantly being strengthened or weakened by new experiences, Skinner's theory views personality development as a continuous, lifelong journey. Unlike Freud and many other theorists, Skinner saw no reason to break the developmental process into stages. Nor did he attribute special importance to early childhood experiences.

Skinner believed that conditioning in humans operates much the same as in the rats and pigeons that he studied in his laboratory. Hence, he assumed that conditioning strengthens and weakens response tendencies "mechanically"—that is, without the person's conscious participation. Thus, Skinner was able to explain consistencies in behaviour (personality)

Hill Street Studios/Blend Images/Getty Images

Stimulus context
Party

Telling jokes → Laughter, attention, compliments

Response | **Reinforcer**

FIGURE 12.6

Personality development and operant conditioning.

According to Skinner, people's characteristic response tendencies are shaped by reinforcers and other consequences that follow behaviour. Thus, if your joking leads to attention and compliments, your tendency to be witty and humorous will be strengthened.

without being concerned about individuals' cognitive processes.

Skinner held to his radical position right to the end of his life. If anything, he stepped up his attacks on nonbehavioural theories once he knew that he was dying of terminal leukemia in 1990, giving his last speech on the topic eight days before he died (Flett, 2007). Skinner's ideas continue to be highly influential, but his mechanical, deterministic, noncognitive view of personality has not gone unchallenged by other behaviourists. In recent decades, several theorists have developed somewhat different behavioural models with a more cognitive emphasis.

Bandura's Social Cognitive Theory 10b

Albert Bandura is a modern theorist who has helped reshape the theoretical landscape of behaviourism. As you may recall, in Chapter 6, we highlighted some of Bandura's other contributions to learning theory, notably his groundbreaking research with Waterloo University's Richard Walters on modelling and aggression. Bandura, who was born in Alberta and earned his doctorate in psychology at the University of Iowa, has spent his entire academic career at Stanford University, where he has conducted influential research on behaviour therapy and the determinants of aggression.

Cognitive Processes and Reciprocal Determinism 10b

Bandura is one of several theorists who have added a cognitive flavour to behaviourism since the 1960s. Bandura (1977), Walter Mischel (1973), and Julian Rotter (1982) take issue with Skinner's "pure" behaviourism. They point out that humans obviously are conscious, thinking, feeling beings. Moreover, these theorists argue that in neglecting cognitive processes, Skinner ignored the most distinctive and important feature of human behaviour. Bandura and like-minded theorists originally called their modified brand of behaviourism *social learning theory*. Today, Bandura refers to his model as *social cognitive theory*. Bandura's impact has been such that he is considered by many to be the greatest living psychologist, ranking just behind luminaries such as Piaget, Freud, and Skinner in terms of his overall historical influence (Haggbloom et al., 2002).

Bandura (1982, 1986) agrees with the fundamental thrust of behaviourism in that he believes that personality is largely shaped through learning. However, he contends that conditioning is not a mechanical process in which people are passive participants. Instead, he maintains that "people are self-organizing, proactive, self-reflecting, and self-regulating, not just reactive organisms shaped and shepherded by external events" (Bandura, 1999a, p. 154). Thus, people routinely attempt to influence their lives and their outcomes (Bandura, 2008). Bandura (2001a, 2006) also emphasizes the important role of forward-directed planning, noting that "people set goals for themselves, anticipate the likely consequences of prospective actions, and select and create courses of action likely to produce desired outcomes and avoid detrimental ones" (Bandura, 2001a, p. 7).

Comparing his theory to Skinner's highly deterministic view, Bandura advocates a position called *reciprocal determinism*. According to this notion, the environment does determine behaviour (as Skinner would argue). However, behaviour also determines the environment (in other words, people can act to alter their environment). Moreover, personal factors (cognitive structures such as beliefs and expectancies) determine and are determined by both behaviour and the environment (see Figure 12.7). Thus, *reciprocal determinism is the idea that internal mental events, external environmental events, and overt behaviour all influence one another.* According to Bandura, humans are neither masters of their own destiny nor hapless victims buffeted about by the environment. To some extent, people shape their environments.

Observational Learning 10b

Bandura's foremost theoretical contribution has been his description of observational learning,

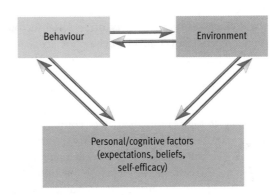

FIGURE 12.7

Bandura's reciprocal determinism.

Bandura rejects Skinner's highly deterministic view that behaviour is governed by the environment and that freedom is an illusion. Bandura argues that internal mental events, external environmental contingencies, and overt behaviour all influence one another.

B. F. Skinner

"The practice of looking inside the organism for an explanation of behavior has tended to obscure the variables which are immediately available for a scientific analysis. These variables lie outside the organism, in its environmental history.... The objection to inner states is not that they do not exist, but that they are not relevant."

Albert Bandura

"Most human behaviour is learned by observation through modeling."

WEB LINK 12.4

Television & Violence—Media and Communications Studies Site

Albert Bandura's early studies on the effect of television watching on the development of aggression spawned a wide spectrum of research about media influences on personality and behaviour. This page at Daniel Chandler's well-known site gathers important research and reflections on the issue.

which we introduced in Chapter 6. *Observational learning* occurs when an organism's responding is influenced by the observation of others, who are called *models*. According to Bandura, both classical and operant conditioning can occur vicariously when one person observes another's conditioning. For example, watching your sister get cheated by someone giving her a bad cheque for her old stereo could strengthen your tendency to be suspicious of others. Although your sister would be the one actually experiencing the negative consequences, they might also influence you—through observational learning.

Bandura maintains that people's characteristic patterns of behaviour are shaped by the models that they're exposed to. He isn't referring to the fashion models who dominate the mass media—although they do qualify. In observational learning, a *model* is a person whose behaviour is observed by another. At one time or another, everyone serves as a model for others. Bandura's key point is that many response tendencies are the product of imitation.

As research has accumulated, it has become apparent that some models are more influential than others (Bandura, 1986). Both children and adults tend to imitate people they like or respect more than people they don't. People are also especially prone to imitate the behaviour of people whom they consider attractive or powerful (such as rock stars). In addition, imitation is more likely when people see similarity between models and themselves. Thus, children tend to imitate same-sex role models somewhat more than opposite-sex models. Finally, people are more likely to copy a model if they observe that the model's behaviour leads to positive outcomes.

Self-Efficacy

Bandura discusses how a variety of personal factors (aspects of personality) govern behaviour. In recent years, the factor he has emphasized most is self-efficacy (Bandura, 1990, 1993, 1995). *Self-efficacy* refers to one's belief about one's ability to perform behaviours that should lead to expected outcomes. When self-efficacy is high, individuals feel confident that they can execute the responses necessary to earn reinforcers. When self-efficacy is low, individuals worry that the necessary responses may be beyond their abilities. Perceptions of self-efficacy are subjective and specific to certain kinds of tasks. For instance, you might feel extremely confident about your ability to handle difficult social situations but doubtful about your ability to handle academic challenges.

Perceptions of self-efficacy can influence which challenges people tackle and how well they perform.

Studies have found that feelings of greater self-efficacy are associated with greater success in giving up smoking (Schnoll et al., 2011), greater adherence to an exercise regimen (Ayotte, Margrett, & Hicks-Patrick, 2010), better outcomes in substance abuse treatment (Bandura, 1999b), more success in coping with medical rehabilitation (Waldrop et al., 2001), reduced disability from problems with chronic pain (Hadjistavropoulos et al., 2007), greater persistence and effort in academic pursuits (Zimmerman, 1995), higher levels of academic performance (Weiser & Riggio, 2010), reduced vulnerability to anxiety and depression in childhood (Muris, 2002), less jealousy in romantic relationships (Hu, Zhang, & Li, 2005), enhanced performance in athletic competition (Kane et al., 1996), greater receptiveness to technological training (Christoph, Schoenfeld, & Tansky, 1998), greater success in searching for a new job (Saks, 2006), higher work-related performance (Stajkovic & Luthans, 1998), reduced vulnerability to post-traumatic stress disorder in the face of severe stress (Hirschel & Schulenberg, 2009), and reduced strain from occupational stress (Grau, Salanova, & Peiro, 2001), among many other things.

Mischel and the Person–Situation Controversy

Walter Mischel was born in Vienna, not far from Freud's home. His family immigrated to the United States in 1939, when he was nine. After earning his doctorate in psychology, he spent many years on the faculty at Stanford, as a colleague of Bandura's. He has since moved to Columbia University. Like Bandura, Mischel (1973, 1984) is an advocate of social learning theory. Mischel's chief contribution to personality theory has been to focus attention on the extent to which situational factors govern behaviour (Eigsti et al., 2006).

According to Mischel, people make responses that they think will lead to reinforcement in the situation at hand. For example, if you believe that hard work in your job will pay off by leading to raises and promotions, you'll probably be diligent and industrious. But if you think that hard work in your job is unlikely to be rewarded, you may behave in a lazy and irresponsible manner. Thus, Mischel's version of social learning theory predicts that people will often behave differently in different situations. Mischel (1968, 1973) reviewed decades of research and concluded that, indeed, people exhibit far less consistency across situations than had been widely assumed. For example, studies show that a person who is honest in one situation may be dishonest in another.

Mischel's provocative ideas struck at the heart of the concept of personality, which assumes that people are reasonably consistent in their behaviour. His theories sparked a robust debate about the relative importance of the *person* as opposed to the *situation* in determining behaviour. This debate has led to a growing recognition that *both* the person and the situation are important determinants of behaviour (Funder, 2001; Roberts & Pomerantz, 2004). As William Fleeson (2004) puts it, "The person–situation debate is coming to an end because both sides of the debate have turned out to be right" (p. 83). Fleeson reconciles the two opposing views by arguing that each prevails at a different level of analysis. When small chunks of behaviour are examined on a moment-to-moment basis, situational factors dominate and most individuals' behaviour tends to be highly variable. However, when larger chunks of typical behaviour over time are examined, people tend to be reasonably consistent and personality traits prove to be more influential.

Norman Endler of York University was a well-known advocate of an interactional approach to personality. Along with his colleague David Magnusson, Endler argued that personality traits interact with situational factors to produce behaviour (Endler & Magnusson, 1976). So, in order to accurately predict how someone will behave, you not only need to know something about that person's standing on relevant personality traits, but

you also need information about the nature of the situational context he or she is facing. Neither factor alone will allow you to accurately predict an individual's behaviour.

Evaluating Behavioural Perspectives

Behavioural theories are firmly rooted in extensive empirical research rather than clinical intuition. Skinner's ideas have shed light on how environmental consequences and conditioning mould people's characteristic behaviour. Bandura's social cognitive theory has expanded the horizons of behaviourism and increased its relevance to the study of personality. Mischel deserves credit for increasing psychology's awareness of how situational factors shape behaviour. Of course, each theoretical approach has its weaknesses and shortcomings, and the behavioural approach is no exception. Major lines of criticism include the following (Liebert & Liebert, 1998; Pervin & John, 2001):

1. *Dehumanizing nature of radical behaviourism.* Skinner and other radical behaviourists have been criticized heavily for denying the existence of free

Walter Mischel

"It seems remarkable how each of us generally manages to reconcile his seemingly diverse behavior into one self-consistent whole."

University photographer Joe Pinerio, Columbia University

REVIEW OF KEY POINTS

▷ Behavioural theories explain how personality is shaped through learning. Skinner had little interest in unobservable cognitive processes and embraced a strong determinism.

▷ Skinner's followers view personality as a collection of response tendencies tied to specific stimulus situations. They assume that personality development is a lifelong process in which response tendencies are shaped and reshaped by learning, especially operant conditioning.

▷ Social cognitive theory focuses on how cognitive factors such as expectancies regulate learned behaviour. Bandura's concept of observational learning accounts for the acquisition of responses from models. High self-efficacy has been related to successful health regimens, academic success, and athletic performance, among other things.

▷ Mischel has questioned the degree to which people display cross-situational consistency in behaviour. Mischel's arguments have increased psychologists' awareness of the situational determinants of behaviour. According to Fleeson, situational factors dominate small chunks of behaviour, whereas personality traits shape larger chunks of behaviour.

▷ Behavioural approaches to personality are based on rigorous research. They have provided ample insights into how environmental factors and learning mould personalities. Radical behaviourism's dehumanizing view of human nature has been criticized, but more contemporary social cognitive theories have been knocked for diluting the behavioural approach.

will and the importance of cognitive processes. The critics argue that the radical behaviourist viewpoint strips human behaviour of its most uniquely human elements and that it therefore cannot provide an accurate model of human functioning.

2. *Dilution of the behavioural approach.* The behaviourists used to be criticized because they neglected

cognitive processes. The rise of social cognitive theory blunted this criticism. However, social cognitive theory undermines the foundation on which behaviourism was built—the idea that psychologists should study only observable behaviour. Thus, some critics complain that behavioural theories aren't very behavioural anymore.

Humanistic Perspectives

PREVIEW QUESTIONS

▶ What led to the emergence of humanism, and what are its central assumptions?

▶ How did Rogers explain the development of the self and defensive behaviour?

▶ How did Maslow organize motives?

▶ What was Maslow's view of the healthy personality?

▶ What are the strengths and weaknesses of the humanistic approach?

Humanistic theory emerged in the 1950s as something of a backlash against the behavioural and psychodynamic theories that we have just discussed (Cassel, 2000; DeCarvalho, 1991). The principal charge hurled at these two models was that they are dehumanizing. Freudian theory was criticized for its belief that behaviour is dominated by primitive, animalistic drives. Behaviourism was criticized for its preoccupation with animal research and for its mechanistic, fragmented view of personality. Critics argued that both schools of thought are too deterministic and that both fail to recognize the unique qualities of human behaviour.

Many of these critics blended into a loose alliance that came to be known as *humanism,* because of its exclusive focus on human behaviour. *Humanism* is a theoretical orientation that emphasizes the unique qualities of humans, especially their freedom and their potential for personal growth. Humanistic psychologists don't believe that animal research can reveal anything of any significance about the human condition. In contrast to most psychodynamic and behavioural theorists, humanistic theorists take an optimistic view of human nature. They assume that (1) people can rise above their primitive animal heritage and control their biological urges, and (2) people are largely conscious and rational beings who are not dominated by unconscious, irrational needs and conflicts.

Humanistic theorists also maintain that a person's subjective view of the world is more important than objective reality (Wong, 2006). According to this notion, if you think that you're homely or bright or sociable, this belief will influence your behaviour more than the realities of how homely, bright, or sociable you actually are. Therefore, the humanists embrace the *phenomenological approach,* which assumes that one has to appreciate individuals' personal, subjective experiences to truly understand their behaviour.

Rogers's Person-Centred Theory

10c

Carl Rogers (1951, 1961, 1980) was one of the founders of the human potential movement. This movement emphasizes self-realization through sensitivity training, encounter groups, and other exercises intended to foster personal growth. Rogers grew up in a religious, upper-middle-class home in the suburbs of Chicago. He was a bright student, but he had to rebel against his parents' wishes in order to pursue his graduate study in psychology. While he was working at the University of Chicago in the 1940s, Rogers devised a major new approach to psychotherapy. Like Freud, Rogers based his personality theory on his extensive therapeutic interactions with many clients. Because of its emphasis on a person's subjective point of view, Rogers's approach is called a *person-centred theory.*

10c

The Self

Rogers viewed personality structure in terms of just one construct. He called this construct the *self,* although it's more widely known today as the *self-concept.* A *self-concept* is a collection of beliefs about one's own nature, unique qualities, and typical behaviour. Your self-concept is your own mental picture of yourself. It's a collection of self-perceptions. For example, a self-concept might include beliefs such as "I'm easygoing" or "I'm sly and crafty" or "I'm pretty" or "I'm hard-working." According to Rogers, individuals are aware of their self-concept. It's not buried in their unconscious.

Rogers stressed the subjective nature of the self-concept. Your self-concept may not be entirely consistent with your experiences. Most people tend to distort their experiences to some extent to promote a relatively favourable self-concept. For example, you

Self-concept | Actual experience

Congruence
Self-concept meshes well with actual experience (some incongruence is probably unavoidable)

Self-concept | Actual experience

Incongruence
Self-concept does not mesh well with actual experience

FIGURE 12.8

Rogers's view of personality structure.

In Rogers's model, the self-concept is the only important structural construct. However, Rogers acknowledged that one's self-concept may not be consistent with the realities of one's actual experience—a condition called *incongruence*.

may believe that you're quite bright, but your grade transcript might suggest otherwise. Rogers called the gap between self-concept and reality *incongruence*. *Incongruence* is the degree of disparity between one's self-concept and one's actual experience. In contrast, if a person's self-concept is reasonably accurate, it's said to be congruent with reality (see Figure 12.8). Everyone experiences some incongruence. The crucial issue is how much. As we'll see, Rogers maintained that too much incongruence undermines one's psychological well-being.

Development of the Self

In terms of personality development, Rogers was concerned with how childhood experiences promote congruence or incongruence between one's self-concept and one's experience. According to Rogers, people have a strong need for affection, love, and acceptance from others. Early in life, parents provide most of this affection. Rogers maintained that some parents make their affection *conditional*. That is, it

depends on the child's behaving well and living up to expectations. When parental love seems conditional, children often block out of their self-concept those experiences that make them feel unworthy of love. They do so because they're worried about parental acceptance, which appears precarious.

At the other end of the spectrum, some parents make their affection *unconditional*. Their children have less need to block out unworthy experiences because they've been assured that they're worthy of affection, no matter what they do. Hence, Rogers believed that unconditional love from parents fosters congruence and that conditional love fosters incongruence. He further theorized that if individuals grow up believing that affection from others is highly conditional, they will go on to distort more and more of their experiences in order to feel worthy of acceptance from a wider and wider array of people (see Figure 12.9).

Anxiety and Defence

According to Rogers, experiences that threaten people's personal views of themselves are the principal cause of troublesome anxiety. The more inaccurate your self-concept, the more likely you are to have experiences that clash with your self-perceptions. Thus, people with highly incongruent self-concepts are especially likely to be plagued by recurrent anxiety (see Figure 12.9).

To ward off this anxiety, individuals often behave defensively in an effort to reinterpret their experience so that it appears consistent with their self-concept. Thus, they ignore, deny, and twist reality to protect and perpetuate their self-concept. Consider a young woman who, like most people, considers herself a "nice person." Let's suppose that in reality she is rather conceited and selfish. She gets feedback from both boyfriends and girlfriends that she is a "self-centred, snotty brat." How might she react in order to protect her self-concept? She might ignore or block out those occasions when she behaves selfishly. She might attribute her girlfriends' negative

Carl Rogers

"I have little sympathy with the rather prevalent concept that man is basically irrational, and that his impulses, if not controlled, will lead to destruction of others and self. Man's behavior is exquisitely rational, moving with subtle and ordered complexity toward the goals his organism is endeavoring to achieve."

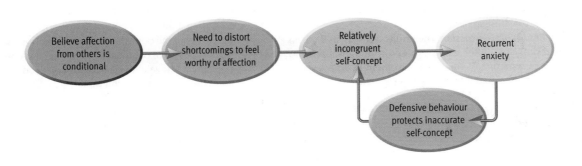

Believe affection from others is conditional → Need to distort shortcomings to feel worthy of affection → Relatively incongruent self-concept → Recurrent anxiety → Defensive behaviour protects inaccurate self-concept

FIGURE 12.9

Rogers's view of personality development and dynamics.

Rogers's theory of development posits that conditional love leads to a need to distort experiences, which fosters an incongruent self-concept. Incongruence makes one prone to recurrent anxiety, which triggers defensive behaviour, which fuels more incongruence.

Investigators: Mark W. Baldwin (McGill University), Suzanne Carrell (University of Waterloo), and David Lopez (University of Waterloo)
Source: Priming relationship schemas: My advisor and the Pope are watching me from the back of my mind. *Journal of Experimental Social Psychology, 26,* 1990, 435–454.

The Pope Is Watching You: Effects on Self-Concept

Self-theorists such as Carl Rogers and others have suggested that one factor that influences how an individual construes or judges himself or herself is what the individual believes others think about him or her. As Baldwin points out, this process of reflected appraisal has long been assumed by scholars interested in the self to be one of the most important factors affecting an individual's self-construal or concept. Especially important are signs from others suggesting that they approve or disapprove of you and your actions.

Baldwin wanted to determine the effects of activating cognitive structures that represent well-learned interaction patterns—for example, patterns reflecting your relationship with your parents or others with whom you have a significant relationship. In these two studies, the specific significant others employed were academic advisors for graduate students (Study 1) and the pope for Catholic girls (Study 2). What makes the studies really interesting is that cognitive structures representing these two sets of significant others were activated or primed subliminally, or without the research participants' awareness. In Study 1, Baldwin examined the effects of priming their advisor on how good graduate students thought their research ideas were, and in Study 2, he examined the effects of priming the pope on Catholic girls' views of themselves after they had read a sexual prose passage.

Study 1

Method. In this preliminary test of his ideas, Baldwin had 16 graduate students first think about and note three of their current research ideas. They were to rate one of the ideas after each of three types of slides had been presented to them. Then the students were given a task during which they were subliminally presented with four presentations each of a blank slide and then in randomized order the disapproving (i.e., scowling) face of their research supervisor or an approving (i.e., smiling) face of another Ph.D. in psychology they were acquainted with. After each type of slide had been presented and before the next type of slide was presented, they rated the quality and importance of one of their research ideas.

Results and Discussion. The results were just as Baldwin had predicted. After being exposed to the disapproving face of someone of significance to them in an academic context, the graduate students rated their ideas lower than after they had been exposed to an approving face. It is important to keep in mind that these effects on rating one's research ideas were obtained after the faces had

been presented without participants being aware of them. While the results confirmed the authors' hypothesis, the study was considered to be preliminary and it had some limitations. It had a very small sample size and there were some inadequacies with the method. But, given the generally supportive findings, the authors decided to do another study in which they were able to have a larger sample size and to clean up some of the problems encountered in Study 1.

Follow Up Study

A second study with the same general objective was then conducted. In this study, Baldwin and his colleagues wanted to determine the effects on participants' judgments of themselves. They wondered what the effect would be of having Catholic girls read a prose passage containing sexual content and then having them rate themselves after being subliminally exposed either to a scowling, disapproving face of the pope or a scowling face of someone with whom they had no contact. In fact, the unknown scowling face was the same face used in Study 1. In this case, however, the Study 1 scowling face was not someone who was significant to the participants.

Method. Forty-six female undergraduate students at the University of Waterloo participated in the study. All of the participants were Catholic. The participants first filled out some questionnaires and then read a prose passage that portrayed a permissive attitude toward sexuality. Participants then were exposed to subliminal presentations of a blank slide, a disapproving picture of Pope John Paul II, or the disapproving picture of the face used in Study 1. Participants then completed some questionnaires assessing their views about themselves in the areas of morality, competency, and anxiety. Participants also indicated the degree to which they were practising or nonpractising Catholics. For the pope to be a significant other, the authors reasoned that the participants must be practising Catholics.

Results and Discussion. Once again, the results supported the authors' hypothesis. Catholic girls rated themselves lower (see Table 12.3) after being exposed to the disapproving face of the pope than they did when exposed to the disapproving face of an unknown other. This effect of the pope on self-evaluations was observed only for practising Catholics for whom the pope serves as a truly significant other. Thus, it's not just the disapproving face that affected participants' self-ratings, but disapproval coming from someone with whom one has a personally significant relationship. The authors conclude that the results "are consistent with the hypothesis that a person's momentary sense of self can be shaped by cognitive structures representing significant interpersonal information" (p. 449). The study also shows that one need not even be aware of this influence on one's self-relevant judgments.

TABLE 12.3

Overall Self-Ratings* by High- and Low-Practising Catholics

Stimulus	Low Practising	High Practising
Control (blank)	6.93	7.11
Pope	6.70	6.00
Unknown other	6.64	7.77

*In making their self-ratings, participants were presented with a series of adjective pairs, for example, *dishonest/honest*. Participants were asked to rate themselves in the context of each pair on a scale of 1 to 9. Higher numbers indicate agreement with the more positive member of the pair.

Source: Adapted from Baldwin et al., 1990.

Comment

This study was featured because it took a creative approach to exploring an interesting phenomenon in a way that implicated processes occurring below the level of our conscious awareness. While scholars such as Rogers had speculated and collected data on the critical effects of our perceptions of others' views of us on our judgments and evaluation of ourselves, it had rarely been examined in the context of a subliminal activation of those relationships. Given the important impact of the significant others examined in this research, we can see just how critical the views of our parents can be in laying the groundwork for a child's sense of self. Rogers's views and work on the self helped to make the self an important topic of research and theory in personality psychology. The self was another one of the early casualties of the rise of behaviourism in which speculation of processes of consciousness and self-reflection was viewed as being irrelevant. Baldwin has continued his work on the self and self-esteem and has developed a series of computer games that are designed to raise self-esteem (Baccus, Baldwin, & Packer, 2004). You can play the games and learn more about them by visiting his website at http://www.selfesteemgames.mcgill.ca.

comments to their jealousy of her good looks. Perhaps she would blame her boyfriends' negative remarks on their disappointment because she won't get more serious with them. As you can see, people will sometimes go to great lengths to defend their self-concept.

Recent Directions in Research on the Self

Rogers's work emphasized the importance of the self and has influenced contemporary psychology in terms of its views of the centrality of the self for understanding personality (McCann & Sato, 2000), and the implications of incongruence in the self system for dysfunctional emotions (Higgins, 1987). For example, Tory Higgins of Columbia University has extended Rogers's ideas about self and congruence/incongruence in developing his influential theory of *self-discrepancy* (Higgins, 1987, 1999). According to Higgins, discrepancy between the *actual self* (our beliefs about the kind of person we think we are) and two standards we hold for the self (the *ought self* and the *ideal self*) can lead to emotional discomfort and even psychopathology if the discrepancy is extreme enough.

The *ideal self* refers to our beliefs about the kind of person we wish to be (e.g., a top student)—our hopes, goals, and aspirations for ourselves. The *ought self* refers to our beliefs about the kind of person we have a duty or obligation to be (e.g., a faithful spouse). According to Higgins, discrepancy between the actual and ought selves leads to agitation and, in extreme

cases, anxiety. And discrepancies between the actual and ideal selves lead to dejection and, in extreme cases, depression. Research has revealed impressive support for his theory (e.g., McCann & Sato, 2000). Higgins has subsequently extended his work in developing his theory of self-regulation and motivation and his conceptualizations of promotion and prevention focus (Appelt & Higgins, 2010; Higgins et al., 2010).

Another area of influence on research on the self impacted by the work of Rogers and others (Cooley, 1902; Mead, 1934) is a concern with the importance of others for one's view of the self (Baldwin, 1992, 2001; Baldwin & Sinclair, 1996; Baldwin et al., 2003). Our Featured Study in this chapter is one of Mark Baldwin's initial demonstrations of the relevance of others for our own views of self. In his research, Baldwin and his colleagues attempt to determine the effects of priming or activating a cognitive structure representing participants' relationship with a significant other on their self-relevant judgments. One of the interesting aspects of the study is that the cognitive structures relevant to the significant other are primed subliminally.

Maslow's Theory of Self-Actualization

10c

Abraham Maslow, who grew up in Brooklyn, New York, described his childhood as "unhappy, lonely, [and] isolated." To follow through on his interest in psychology, he had to resist parental pressures to go into law. Maslow spent much of his career at Brandeis University, where he created an influential theory of motivation and provided crucial leadership for the fledgling humanistic movement. Like Rogers, Maslow (1968, 1970) argued that psychology should take an optimistic view of human nature instead of dwelling on the causes of disorders. "To oversimplify the matter somewhat," he said, "it's as if Freud supplied to us the sick half of psychology and we must now fill it out with the healthy half" (1968, p. 5). Maslow's key contributions were his analysis of how motives are organized hierarchically and his description of the healthy personality.

Hierarchy of Needs

10c

Maslow proposed that human motives are organized into a *hierarchy of needs*—a systematic arrangement of needs, according to priority, in which basic needs must be met before less basic needs are aroused. This hierarchical arrangement is usually portrayed as a pyramid (see Figure 12.10). The needs toward the bottom of the pyramid, such as physiological or security needs, are the most basic. Higher levels in the pyramid consist of progressively less basic needs. When a person manages to satisfy a level of needs reasonably well (complete satisfaction is not necessary), *this satisfaction activates needs at the next level*.

Like Rogers, Maslow argued that humans have an innate drive toward personal growth—that is, evolution toward a higher state of being. Thus, he described the needs in the uppermost reaches of his hierarchy as *growth needs*. These include the needs for knowledge, understanding, order, and aesthetic beauty. Foremost among them is the *need for self-actualization, which is the need to fulfill one's potential; it is the highest need in Maslow's motivational hierarchy.* Maslow summarized this concept with a simple statement: "What a man can be, he must be." According to Maslow, people will be frustrated if they are unable to fully utilize their talents or pursue their true interests. For example, if you have great musical talent but must work as an accountant, or if you have scholarly interests but must work as a salesclerk, your need for self-actualization will be thwarted. Maslow's pyramid has penetrated popular culture to a remarkable degree. For example, Peterson and Park (2010) note that a Google search located over 766 000 images of Maslow's pyramid on the Internet—a figure that topped the number of images for the *Mona Lisa* and *The Last Supper*!

Recently, almost 70 years after Maslow first proposed his influential pyramid of needs, theorists have proposed a major renovation. Working from an evolutionary perspective, Kenrick and colleagues (2010) argue for a reworking of the upper levels of Maslow's hierarchy. They acknowledge that decades of research and theory provide support for the priority of the first four levels of needs. But they contend that the higher needs in the pyramid are not that fundamental and that they are really pursued in the service of esteem needs—that people seek knowledge, beauty, and self-actualization to impress others. After grouping Maslow's higher needs with

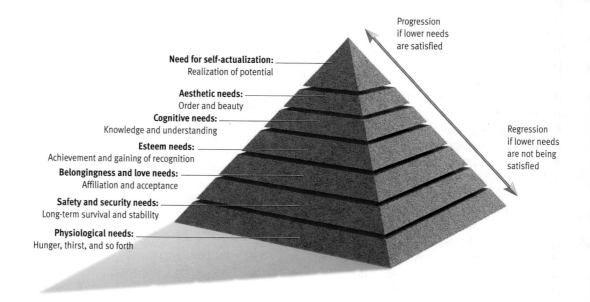

Progression if lower needs are satisfied

Regression if lower needs are not being satisfied

Need for self-actualization:
Realization of potential

Aesthetic needs:
Order and beauty

Cognitive needs:
Knowledge and understanding

Esteem needs:
Achievement and gaining of recognition

Belongingness and love needs:
Affiliation and acceptance

Safety and security needs:
Long-term survival and stability

Physiological needs:
Hunger, thirst, and so forth

the esteem needs, Kenrick et al. (2010) fill in the upper levels of their revised hierarchy with needs related to reproductive fitness—that is, passing on one's genes. Specifically, they propose that the top three needs in the pyramid should be the need to find a mate, the need to retain a mate, and the need to successfully parent offspring (see Figure 12.11).

It's hard to say whether this sweeping revision of Maslow's pyramid will gain traction. Most commentaries thus far acknowledge that Kenrick and his colleagues have compiled some compelling arguments in favour of their renovated pyramid. However, such a radical transformation of an iconic theoretical model is bound to invite second-guessing. For example, critics have argued that the revised hierarchy is no longer uniquely human (Kesebir, Graham, & Oishi, 2010), that it is premature to dismiss the need for self-actualization (Peterson & Park, 2010), and that parenting might not be all that fundamental of a human need (Lyubomirsky & Boehm, 2010). At a minimum, the proposed revision promises to revitalize research on Maslow's hierarchy of needs.

The Healthy Personality

Because of his interest in self-actualization, Maslow set out to discover the nature of the healthy personality. He tried to identify people of exceptional mental health so that he could investigate their characteristics. In one case, he used psychological tests and interviews to sort out the healthiest 1 percent of a sizable population of college students. He also studied admired historical figures (such as Thomas Jefferson and William James) and personal acquaintances characterized by superior adjustment. Over a period of years, he accumulated his case histories and gradually sketched, in broad strokes, a picture of ideal psychological health.

According to Maslow, *self-actualizing persons are people with exceptionally healthy personalities, marked by continued personal growth.* Maslow identified various traits characteristic of self-actualizing people. Many of these traits are listed in Figure 12.12. In brief, Maslow found that self-actualizers are accurately tuned in to reality and that they're at peace with themselves. He found that they're open and spontaneous and that they retain a fresh appreciation of the world around them. Socially, they're sensitive to others' needs and enjoy rewarding interpersonal relations. However, they're not dependent on others for approval or uncomfortable with solitude. They thrive on their work, and they enjoy their sense of humour. Maslow also noted

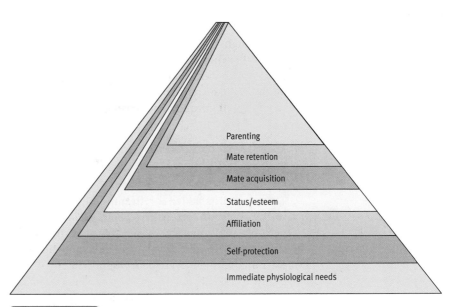

FIGURE 12.11

An updated hierarchy of fundamental human motives.

This figure integrates ideas from life-history development with Maslow's classic hierarchy. This scheme adds reproductive goals, in the order they are likely to first appear developmentally. The model also depicts the later developing goal systems as overlapping with, rather than completely replacing, earlier developing systems. Once a goal system has developed, its activation will be triggered whenever relevant environmental cues are salient.

Source: Kenrick, D. T., Griskevicius, V., Neuberg, S., & Schaller, M. (2010). Renovating the Pyramid of Needs: Contemporary Extensions Built Upon Ancient Foundations. *Perspectives on Psychological Science, 5*, 292–314. Copyright © 2010, Association for Psychological Science.

Characteristics of self-actualizing people	
• Clear, efficient perception of reality and comfortable relations with it	• Mystical and peak experiences
• Spontaneity, simplicity, and naturalness	• Feelings of kinship and identification with the human race
• Problem centring (having something outside themselves they "must" do as a mission)	• Strong friendships, but limited in number
• Detachment and need for privacy	• Democratic character structure
• Autonomy, independence of culture and environment	• Ethical discrimination between good and evil
• Continued freshness of appreciation	• Philosophical, unhostile sense of humour
	• Balance between polarities in personality

Abraham Maslow

"It is as if Freud supplied to us the sick half of psychology and we must now fill it out with the healthy half."

FIGURE 12.12

Maslow's view of the healthy personality.

Humanistic theorists emphasize psychological health instead of maladjustment. Maslow's description of characteristics of self-actualizing people evokes a picture of the healthy personality.

Source: Adapted from Potkay, C.R., and Allen, B.P. (1986). *Personality: Theory, research and application.* Pacific Grove, CA: Brooks/Cole. Copyright © 1986 by C. R. Potkay and B. P. Allen. Adapted by permission of the author.

that they have "peak experiences" (profound emotional highs) more often than others. Finally, he found that they strike a nice balance between many polarities in personality. For instance, they can be both childlike and mature, both rational and intuitive, both conforming and rebellious.

Evaluating Humanistic Perspectives

The humanists added a refreshing new perspective to the study of personality. Their argument that a person's subjective views may be more important than objective reality has proven compelling. As we noted earlier, even behavioural theorists have begun to take into account subjective personal factors such as beliefs and expectancies. The humanistic approach also deserves some of the credit for making the self-concept an important construct in psychology. Today, theorists of many persuasions use the self-concept in their analyses of personality. Finally, one could argue that the humanists' optimistic, growth- and health-oriented approach laid the foundation for the emergence of the positive psychology movement that is increasingly influential in contemporary psychology (Sheldon & Kasser, 2001; Taylor, 2001).

Of course, there's a negative side to the balance sheet as well. Critics have identified some weaknesses in the humanistic approach to personality, including the following (Burger, 2004):

1. *Poor testability*. Like psychodynamic theorists, the humanists have been criticized for generating hypotheses that are difficult to put to a scientific

REVIEW OF KEY POINTS

▷ Humanistic theories are phenomenological and take an optimistic view of people's conscious, rational ability to chart their own courses of action. Rogers focused on the self-concept as the critical aspect of personality. Incongruence is the degree of disparity between one's self-concept and actual experience.

▷ Rogers maintained that unconditional love fosters congruence, whereas conditional love fosters incongruence. Incongruence makes one vulnerable to recurrent anxiety, which tends to trigger defensive behaviour that protects one's inaccurate self-concept.

▷ Maslow theorized that needs are organized hierarchically and that psychological health depends on fulfilling one's need for self-actualization, which is the need to realize one's human potential. His work led to the description of self-actualizing persons as *idealized examples of psychological health*. Recently, theorists have proposed a major revision of Malsow's pyramid of needs in which the higher growth needs are replaced by motives related to reproductive fitness.

▷ Humanistic theories deserve credit for highlighting the importance of subjective views of oneself and for confronting the question of what makes for a healthy personality. Humanistic theories lack a firm base of research, are difficult to put to an empirical test, and may be overly optimistic about human nature.

concept check 12.2

Recognizing Key Concepts in Personality Theories

Check your understanding of psychodynamic, behavioural, and humanistic personality theories by identifying key concepts from these theories in the scenarios below. The answers can be found in Appendix A.

1. Thirteen-year-old Sarah watches a TV show in which the leading female character manipulates her boyfriend by acting helpless and purposely losing a tennis match against him. The female lead repeatedly expresses her slogan, "Never let them [men] know you can take care of yourself." Sarah becomes more passive and less competitive around boys her own age.

   Concept: _____

2. Yolanda has a secure, enjoyable, reasonably well-paid job as a tenured English professor at a community college. Her friends are dumbfounded when she announces that she's going to resign and give it all up to try writing a novel. She tries to explain, "I need a new challenge, a new mountain to climb. I've had this lid on my writing talents for years, and I've got to break free. It's something I have to try. I won't be happy until I do."

   Concept: _____

3. Vladimir, who is four years old, seems to be emotionally distant from and inattentive to his father. He complains whenever he's left with his Dad. In contrast, he often cuddles up in bed with his mother and tries very hard to please her by behaving properly.

   Concept: _____

test. Humanistic concepts such as personal growth and self-actualization are difficult to define and measure.

2. *Unrealistic view of human nature.* Critics also charge that the humanists have been unrealistic in their assumptions about human nature and their descriptions of the healthy personality. For instance, Maslow's self-actualizing people sound nearly perfect. In reality, Maslow had a hard time finding such people. When he searched among the living, the results were so disappointing that he turned to the study of historical figures. Thus, humanistic portraits of psychological health are perhaps a bit too optimistic.

3. *Inadequate evidence.* For the most part, humanistic psychologists haven't been particularly research-oriented. Although Rogers and Maslow both conducted and encouraged empirical research, many of their followers have been scornful of efforts to quantify human experience to test hypotheses. Much more research is needed to catch up with the theorizing in the humanistic camp. This is precisely the opposite of the situation that we'll encounter in the next section, which examines biological approaches to personality.

Biological Perspectives

Eysenck's Theory 10d

Hans Eysenck was born in Germany but fled to London, England, during the era of Nazi rule. He went on to become one of Britain's most prominent psychologists. Eysenck (1967, 1982, 1990a) views personality structure as a hierarchy of traits, in which many superficial traits are derived from a smaller number of more basic traits, which are derived from a handful of fundamental higher-order traits, as shown in Figure 12.13. His studies suggest that all aspects of personality emerge from just three higher-order traits: extraversion, neuroticism, and psychoticism. You have already learned about the first two of these traits, which are key elements in the Big Five. Extraversion involves being sociable, assertive, active, and lively. Neuroticism involves being anxious, tense, moody, and low in self-esteem. Psychoticism involves being egocentric, impulsive, cold, and antisocial. Each of these traits is represented in the theory as a bipolar dimension, with the endpoints for each dimension as follows: extraversion–introversion, stability–neuroticism (instability), and psychoticism–self-control.

According to Eysenck, "Personality is determined to a large extent by a person's genes" (1967, p. 20). How is heredity linked to personality in Eysenck's model? In part, through conditioning concepts borrowed from behavioural theory. Eysenck theorizes that some people can be conditioned more readily than others because of differences in their physiological functioning. These variations in "conditionability" are assumed to influence the personality traits that people acquire through conditioning processes.

Eysenck has shown a special interest in explaining variations in extraversion–introversion, the trait dimension first described years earlier by Carl Jung. He has proposed that introverts tend to have higher levels of physiological arousal, or perhaps higher "arousability," which makes them more easily conditioned than extraverts. According to Eysenck, people who condition easily acquire more conditioned

PREVIEW QUESTIONS

▶ How did Eysenck explain variations in extraversion–introversion?

▶ To what degree is personality heritable?

▶ Do family environments have much impact on personality?

▶ What do evolutionary theorists have to say about personality?

▶ What are the strengths and weaknesses of the biological approach?

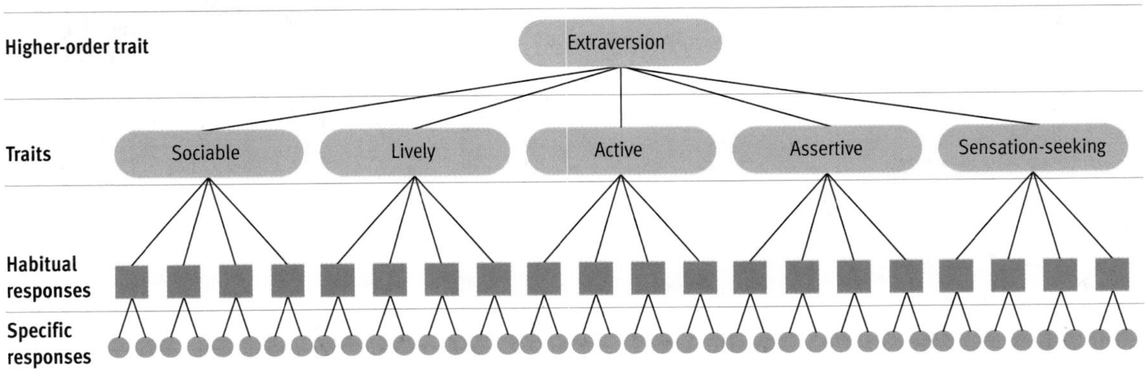

Higher-order trait				Extraversion					
Traits		Sociable		Lively		Active		Assertive	Sensation-seeking
Habitual responses									
Specific responses									

FIGURE 12.13

Eysenck's model of personality structure.

Eysenck described personality structure as a hierarchy of traits. In this scheme, a few higher-order traits, such as extraversion, determine a host of lower-order traits, which determine a person's habitual responses.

Source: Eysenck, H.J. (1976). The *biological basis of personality.* Springfield, IL: Charles C. Thomas. Reprinted by permission of the publisher.

inhibitions than others. These inhibitions make them more bashful, tentative, and uneasy in social situations. This social discomfort leads them to turn inward. Hence, they become introverted.

Behavioural Genetics and Personality   10d

Recent research in behavioural genetics (McCrae et al., 2010) has provided impressive support for the idea that many personality traits are largely inherited (Livesley, Jang, & Vernon, 2003; Rowe & van den Oord, 2005). A great deal of work in this area by researchers such as Philip Vernon, a professor at the University of Western Ontario, who has examined the heritability of the Big Five (Jang, Livesley, & Vernon, 1996; Livesley, Jang, & Vernon, 2002; Vernon et al., 2008). For instance, Figure 12.14 shows the mean correlations observed for identical and fraternal twins in studies of the Big Five personality traits. Higher correlations are indicative of greater similarity on a trait. On all five traits, identical twins have been found to be much more similar than fraternal twins (Plomin et al., 2008). Based on these and many other data, Loehlin (1992) and others conclude that genetic factors exert considerable influence over personality (see Chapter 3 for an explanation of the logic of twin studies).

Some skeptics wonder whether identical twins might exhibit more trait similarity than fraternal twins because they're treated more alike. In other words, they wonder whether environmental factors (rather than heredity) could be responsible for identical twins' greater personality resemblance. This nagging question can be answered only by studying identical twins reared apart, which is why the twin study at the University of Minnesota has been so important. The Minnesota study (Tellegen et al., 1988) was the first to administer the same personality test to identical and fraternal twins reared apart, as well as together. Most of the twins reared apart were separated quite early in life (median age of 2.5 months) and remained separated for a long time (median period of almost 34 years).

The results revealed that identical twins reared apart were substantially more similar in personality than fraternal twins reared together. The heritability estimates (see Chapter 9) for the traits examined ranged from 40 percent to 58 percent. Overall, five decades of research on the determinants of the Big Five traits suggest that the heritability of each trait is in the vicinity of 50 percent (Kreuger & Johnson, 2008). The investigators concluded that their results support the hypothesis that genetic blueprints shape the contours of personality.

Another large-scale twin study of the Big Five traits, conducted in Germany and Poland, yielded

Hans Eysenck

"Personality is determined to a large extent by a person's genes."

FIGURE 12.14

Twin studies of personality.
Loehlin (1992) has summarized the results of twin studies that have examined the Big Five personality traits. The N under each trait indicates the number of twin studies that have examined that trait. The chart plots the average correlations obtained for identical and fraternal twins in these studies. As you can see, identical twins have shown greater resemblance in personality than fraternal twins have, suggesting that personality is partly inherited. (Based on data from Loehlin, 1992)

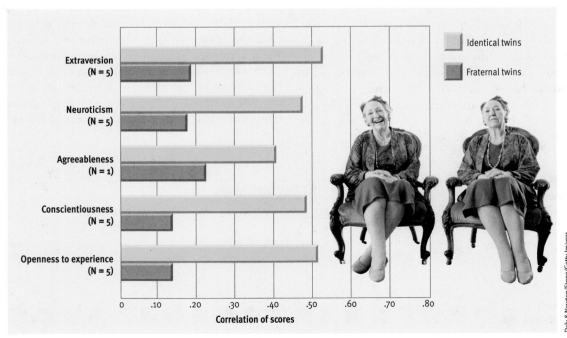

similar conclusions (Riemann, Angleitner, & Strelau, 1997). The heritability estimates based on the data from this study are in the same range as the estimates from the Minnesota study (see Figure 12.15). Moreover, a unique feature of this study was that it obtained peer ratings of subjects' personality traits, as well as the usual measures based on participants' responses to personality tests, and these independent ratings yielded roughly similar estimates of heritability. Thus, behavioural genetics research suggests that personality is shaped to a considerable degree by hereditary factors.

Research on the heritability of personality has inadvertently turned up an interesting finding that was apparent in the Riemann, Angleitner, & Strelau (1997) study. As you can see in Figure 12.15, shared family environment appears to have remarkably little impact on personality. This unexpected finding has been observed quite consistently in behavioural genetics research (Beer, Arnold, & Loehlin, 1998; Rowe & van den Oord, 2005). It is surprising in that social scientists have long assumed that the family environment shared by children growing up together led to some personality resemblance among them. This finding has led researchers to explore how children's subjective environments vary *within* families. But scientists continue to be perplexed by the minimal impact of shared family environment.

There has been considerable excitement—and controversy—about recent reports linking specific genes to specific personality traits. As we noted in Chapter 3, *genetic mapping* techniques are beginning to permit investigators to look for associations between specific genes and aspects of behaviour. A number of studies have found a link between a gene for a particular type of dopamine receptor and measures of extraversion, novelty seeking, and impulsivity, but many failures to replicate this association have also been reported (Canli, 2008; Munafo et al., 2008). In a similar vein, a variety of studies have reported a link between a serotonin transporter gene and measures of neuroticism, but many attempts at replication have failed (Canli, 2008; Sen, Burmeister, & Ghosh, 2004). Overall, the evidence suggests that both of these links are genuine, but difficult to replicate consistently because the correlations are very weak (Canli, 2008; Ebstein, 2006). Hence, subtle differences between studies in sampling or the specific personality tests used can lead to inconsistent findings. The ultimate problem, as we saw in genetic mapping studies of intelligence (see Chapter 9), is that specific personality traits may be influenced by

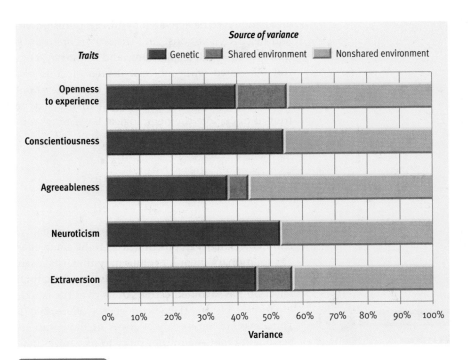

FIGURE 12.15

Heritability and environmental variance for the Big Five traits.

Based on the twin study data of Riemann, Angleitner, & Strelau (1997), Plomin and Caspi (1999) estimated the heritability of each of the Big Five traits. The data also allowed them to estimate the amount of variance on each trait attributable to shared environment and nonshared environment. As you can see, the heritability estimates hovered in the vicinity of 40 percent, with two exceeding 50 percent. As in other studies, the influence of shared family environment was very modest.

Source: Adapted from Plomin, R., and Caspi, A. (1999). Behavioral genetics and personality. In L.A. Pervin and O.P. John (Eds.), *Handbook of personality: Theory and research*. New York: Guilford Press.

hundreds of genes, each of which may have a very small effect that is difficult to detect (Kreuger & Johnson, 2008).

The Neuroscience of Personality

In recent years neuroscientists have begun to explore the relationships between specific personality traits and aspects of brain structure and function (e.g., Read et al., 2010). The thinking is that the behavioural regularities that reflect personality traits may have their roots in individual differences in the brain (DeYoung & Gray, 2009). Thus far, research and theory have focused primarily on the Big Five traits. For example, a recent study used MRI technology to look for associations between the Big Five traits and variations in the relative size of specific areas of the brain (DeYoung et al., 2010). The study uncovered some interesting findings. For example, participants' extraversion correlated with the volume of brain regions known to process reward. Variations in neuroticism correlated with the volume of brain areas known to be activated by threat, punishment, and negative emotions. And the size of brain areas thought to regulate planning and voluntary control correlated with subjects' degree of conscientiousness. This line of research is brand new, but the promising initial results suggest that it may be fruitful to explore the neurological bases of personality traits.

The Evolutionary Approach to Personality

In the realm of biological perspectives on personality, another recent development has been the emergence of evolutionary theory. Evolutionary theorists assert that personality has a biological basis because natural selection has favoured certain traits over the course of human history (Figueredo et al., 2005, 2009). Thus, evolutionary analyses focus on how various personality traits—and the ability to recognize these traits in others—may have contributed to reproductive fitness in ancestral human populations.

For example, David Buss (1991, 1995, 1997) has argued that the Big Five personality traits stand out as important dimensions of personality because those traits have had significant adaptive implications. Buss points out that humans historically have depended heavily on groups, which afford protection from predators or enemies, opportunities for sharing food, and a diverse array of other benefits. In the context of these group interactions, people have had to make difficult but crucial judgments about the characteristics of others, asking such questions as: Who will make a good member of my coalition? Whom can I depend on when in need? Who will share their resources? Thus, Buss (1995) argues, "those individuals able to accurately discern and act upon these individual differences likely enjoyed a considerable reproductive advantage" (p. 22).

According to Buss, the Big Five traits emerge as fundamental dimensions of personality because humans have evolved special sensitivity to variations in the ability to bond with others (extraversion), the willingness to cooperate and collaborate (agreeableness), the tendency to be reliable and ethical (conscientiousness), the capacity to be an innovative problem solver (openness to experience), and the ability to handle stress (low neuroticism). In a nutshell, Buss argues that the Big Five reflect the most salient features of others' adaptive behaviour over the course of evolutionary history.

Daniel Nettle (2006) takes this line of thinking one step further, asserting that the traits themselves (as opposed to the ability to recognize them in others) are products of evolution that were adaptive in ancestral environments. For example, he discusses how extraversion could have promoted mating success, how neuroticism could have fuelled competitiveness and avoidance of dangers, how agreeableness could have fostered the effective building of coalitions, and so forth. Nettle also discusses how each of the Big Five traits may have had adaptive costs (extraversion, for example, is associated with risky behaviour) as well as benefits. Thus, he argues that evolutionary analyses of personality need to weigh the *tradeoffs* between the adaptive advantages and disadvantages of the Big Five traits.

Evaluating Biological Perspectives

Researchers have compiled convincing evidence that biological factors exert considerable influence over personality. Nonetheless, we must take note

Courtesy of David. M. Buss

David Buss
"In sum, the five factors of personality, in this account, represent important dimensions of the social terrain that humans were selected to attend to and act upon."

REVIEW OF KEY POINTS

▸ Contemporary biological theories stress the genetic origins of personality. Eysenck views personality structure as a hierarchy of traits. He believes that heredity influences individual differences in physiological functioning that affect how easily people acquire conditioned inhibitions.

▸ Twin studies of the Big Five personality traits find that identical twins are more similar in personality than fraternal twins, thus suggesting that personality is partly inherited. Estimates for the heritability of personality hover in the vicinity of 50 percent. Recent research in behavioural genetics has suggested that shared family environment has surprisingly little impact on personality, although a variety of theorists have been critical of this conclusion.

▸ Neuroscientists have found some interesting correlations between Big Five traits and the size of certain brain regions.

▸ According to Buss, the ability to recognize and judge others' status on the Big Five traits may have contributed to reproductive fitness. Nettle argues that the Big Five traits themselves (rather than the ability to recognize them) are products of evolution that were adaptive in ancestral times.

▸ Researchers have compiled convincing evidence that genetic factors exert considerable influence over personality. However, the biological approach has been criticized because of methodological problems with heritability ratios and because the effort to carve personality into genetic and environmental components is ultimately artificial.

of some weaknesses in biological approaches to personality:

1. David Funder (2001, p. 207) makes the observation that behavioural genetics researchers exhibit something of an "obsession with establishing the exact magnitude of heritability coefficients." As we discussed in Chapter 9, heritability ratios are ballpark estimates that will vary depending on sampling procedures and other considerations. There is no one magic number awaiting discovery, so the inordinate focus on heritability does seem ill-advised.

2. The results of efforts to carve behaviour into genetic and environmental components are ultimately artificial. The effects of nature and nurture are twisted together in complicated interactions that can't be separated cleanly (Plomin, 2004; Rutter, 2007). For example, a genetically influenced trait, such as a young child's surly, sour temperament, might evoke a particular style of parenting. In essence then, the child's genes have moulded his or her environment. Thus, genetic and environmental influences on personality are not entirely independent because the environmental circumstances that people are exposed to may be shaped in part by their genes.

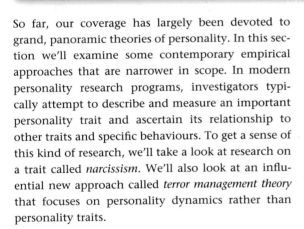

concept **check 12.3**

Understanding the Implications of Major Theories: Who Said This?

Check your understanding of the implications of the personality theories we've discussed by indicating which theorist is likely to have made the statements below. The answers are in Appendix A.

Choose from the following theorists:

Alfred Adler

Albert Bandura

Hans Eysenck

Sigmund Freud

Abraham Maslow

Walter Mischel

Quotes

1. "If you deliberately plan to be less than you are capable of being, then I warn you that you'll be deeply unhappy for the rest of your life."

2. "I feel that the major, most fundamental dimensions of personality are likely to be those on which [there is] strong genetic determination of individual differences."

3. "People are in general not candid over sexual matters . . . they wear a heavy overcoat woven of a tissue of lies, as though the weather were bad in the world of sexuality."

Contemporary Empirical Approaches to Personality

So far, our coverage has largely been devoted to grand, panoramic theories of personality. In this section we'll examine some contemporary empirical approaches that are narrower in scope. In modern personality research programs, investigators typically attempt to describe and measure an important personality trait and ascertain its relationship to other traits and specific behaviours. To get a sense of this kind of research, we'll take a look at research on a trait called *narcissism*. We'll also look at an influential new approach called *terror management theory* that focuses on personality dynamics rather than personality traits.

Renewed Interest in Narcissism

Narcissism is a personality trait marked by an inflated sense of importance, a need for attention and admiration, a sense of entitlement, and a tendency to exploit others. The term is drawn from the Greek myth of Narcissus, which is about an attractive young man's search for love. In the mythical tale he eventually sees his reflection in water and

falls in love with his own image and gazes at it until he dies, thus illustrating the perils of excessive self-love. The concept of narcissism was originally popularized over a century ago by pioneering sex researcher Havelock Ellis (1898) and by Sigmund Freud (1914).

The syndrome of narcissism was not widely discussed outside of psychoanalytic circles until 1980 when the American Psychiatric Association published a massive revision of its diagnostic system that describes various psychological disorders (see Chapter 14). The revised diagnostic system included a new condition called *narcissistic personality disorder* (NPD). Among other things, the key symptoms of this new disorder included (1) a grandiose sense of importance, (2) constant need for attention, (3) difficulty dealing with criticism, and (4) a sense of entitlement. NPD is viewed as an extreme, pathological manifestation of narcissism that is seen in only a small number (3–5 percent) of people.

The formal description of NPD inspired some researchers to start investigating lesser, nonpathological manifestations of narcissim in the general

PREVIEW QUESTIONS

► What is narcissism and what are its correlates and consequences?

► What are the chief concepts and hypotheses of terror management theory and how do reminders of death influence people's behaviour?

THEORIST AND ORIENTATION	SOURCE OF DATA AND OBSERVATIONS	KEY ASSUMPTIONS

A psychodynamic view

Sigmund Freud

Case studies from clinical practice of psychoanalysis

AP Photo

Past events in childhood determine our adult personality.

Our behaviour is dominated by unconscious, irrational wishes, needs, and conflicts.

Personality development progresses through stages.

A behavioural view

B. F. Skinner

Laboratory experiments, primarily with animals

© Richard Wood/Index Stock Imagery

Behaviour is determined by the environment, although this view was softened by Bandura's concept of reciprocal determinism.

Nuture (learning and experience) is more influential than nature (heredity and biological factors).

Situational factors exert great influence over behaviour.

A humanistic view

Carl Rogers

Case studies from clinical practice of client-centred therapy

© Zigy Kaluzny/Stone/Getty Images

People are free to chart their own courses of action; they are not hapless victims governed by the environment.

People are largely conscious, rational beings who are not driven by unconscious needs.

A person's subjective view of the world is more important than objective reality.

A biological view

Hans Eysenck

Twin, family, and adoption studies of heritability; factor analysis studies of personality structure

Daly & Newton/Stone/Getty Images

Behaviour is largely determined by the evolutionary adaptations, the wiring of the brains, and heredity.

Nature (heredity and biological factors) is more influential than nurture (learning and experience).

MODEL OF PERSONALITY STRUCTURE

Three interacting components (id, ego, superego) operating at three levels of consciousness

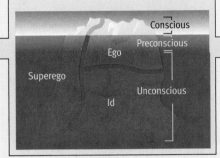

Collections of response tendencies tied to specific stimulus situations

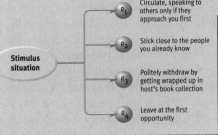

Self-concept, which may or may not mesh well with actual experience

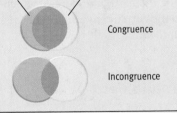

Hierarchy of traits, with specific traits derived from more fundamental, general traits

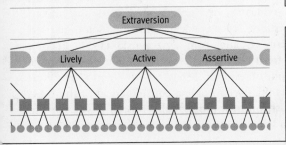

VIEW OF PERSONALITY DEVELOPMENT

Emphasis on fixation or progress through psychosexual stages; experiences in early childhood (such as toilet training) can leave lasting mark on adult personality.

Personality evolves gradually over the life span (not in stages); responses (such as extraverted joking) followed by reinforcement (such as appreciative laughter) become more frequent

Children who receive unconditional love have less need to be defensive; they develop more accurate, congruent self-concepts; conditional love fosters incongruence.

Emphasis on unfolding of genetic blueprint with maturation; inherited predispositions interact with learning experiences.

ROOTS OF DISORDERS

Unconscious fixations and unresolved conflicts from childhood, usually centring on sex and aggression

Maladaptive behaviour due to faulty learning; the "symptom" is the problem, not a sign of underlying disease.

Incongruence between self and actual experience (inaccurate self-concept); overdependence on others for approval and sense of worth

Genetic vulnerability activated in part by environmental factors

population. This research led to the development of scales intended to assess narcissism as a normal personality trait. Of these scales, the *Narcissistic Personality* Inventory (NPI) (Raskin & Hall, 1979, 1981; Raskin & Terry, 1988) has become the most widely used measure of narcissism. The NPI has been used in hundreds of studies.

These studies have painted an interesting portrait of those who score high in narcissism (Rhodewalt & Peterson, 2009). Narcissists have highly positive, but easily threatened self-concepts. Above all else, their behaviour is driven by a need to maintain their fragile self-esteem. They are far more interested in making themselves look powerful and successful than they are in forging lasting bonds with others (Campbell & Foster, 2007). They display a craving for approval and admiration that resembles an addiction (Baumeister & Vohs, 2001). Hence, they proactively work overtime to impress people with self-aggrandizing descriptions of their accomplishments. As you might guess, in this era of social networking via the Internet, those who are high in narcissism tend to post relatively blatant self-promotional content on *Facebook* and similar websites (Buffardi & Campbell, 2008; Mehdizadeh, 2010). Research has also shown that narcissists tend to be more impulsive than others (Vazire & Funder, 2006) and that they are prone to unprovoked aggression (Reidy, Foster, & Zeichner, 2010).

The social consequences of narcissism are interesting (Back, Schmukle, & Egloff, 2010; Paulhus, 1998). When they first meet people, narcissists are often perceived as charming, self-assured, humorous, and perhaps even charismatic. Thus, initially, they tend to be well-liked. With repeated exposure, however, their constant need for attention, brazen boasting, and sense of entitlement tend to wear thin. Eventually, they tend to be viewed as arrogant, self-centred, and unlikeable.

Based on a variety of social trends, Jean Twenge and colleagues (2008) suspected that narcissism might be increasing in recent generations (Dingfelder, 2011). To test this hypothesis they gathered data from 85 studies dating back to the 1980s in which American college students had been given the NPI. Their analysis revealed that NPI scores have been rising, going from a mean of about 15.5 in the 1980s to almost 17.5 in 2005–2006. This finding was replicated in a recent study that extended the trend through 2009 (Twenge & Foster, 2010). Figure 12.16 presents the narcissism results for students at the University of California–Davis. As you can see from

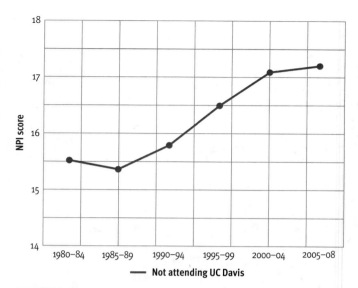

FIGURE 12.16

Mean *Narcissistic Personality Inventory* (NPI) scores across five time periods for students attending University of California (UC) Davis.

Note: Capped vertical bars denote +1 SE.

Source: Twengel J. M., & Foster, J. D. (2010). Birth cohort increases in narcissistic personality traits among American college students, 1982–2009. *Social Psychological and Personality Science, 1*(1), 99–106. Copyright © 2010, Social and Personality Psychology Consortium.

the figure, narcissism scores show a clear increase from 1980 to 2008. This increase in narcissism was not restricted to the University of California–Davis; Twenge and Foster's study showed that this increase was mirrored in a nationwide American sample.

In a discussion of the possible ramifications of this trend, Twenge and Campbell (2009) have argued that rising narcissism has fuelled an obsessive concern about being physically attractive in young people, leading to unhealthy dieting, overuse of cosmetic surgery, and steroid-fuelled body building. They also assert that narcissists' "me-first" attitude has led to increased materialism and overconsumption of the earth's resources, which have contributed to the current environmental crisis and economic meltdown.

Terror Management Theory

Terror management theory emerged as an influential perspective in the 1990s. Although the theory borrows from Freudian and evolutionary formulations, it provides its own unique analysis of the human condition. Developed by Sheldon Solomon, Jeff Greenberg, and Tom Pyszczynski (1991, 2004b), this fresh perspective is currently generating a huge volume of research. *Terror management theory* concerns the psychological consequences of the "juxtaposition of a biologically rooted desire for life with the awareness of the inevitability of death"

(Pyszczynski et al., 2004, p. 436). According to the theory, this juxtaposition has the potential to lead to a paralyzing terror. The theory, which emerged as an influential perspective in the 1990s , describes how humans have attempted to solve the problem posed by such an "existential terror" (e.g., Goldenberg & Arndt, 2008; Pyszczynski, Rothschild, & Abdollah, 2008; Routledge et al., 2010; Wakimoto, 2011) and has implications for a variety of topics, including self-esteem. In fact, one of the chief goals of terror management theory is to explain why people need self-esteem. Unlike other animals, humans have evolved complex cognitive abilities that permit self-awareness and contemplation of the future. These cognitive capacities make humans keenly aware that life can be snuffed out at any time. The collision between humans' self-preservation instinct and their awareness of the inevitability of death creates the potential for experiencing anxiety, alarm, and terror when people think about their mortality (see Figure 12.17).

How do humans deal with this potential for terror? According to terror management theory, "What saves us is culture. Cultures provide ways to view the world—worldviews—that 'solve' the existential crisis engendered by the awareness of death" (Pyszczynski, Solomon, & Greenberg, 2003, p. 16). Cultural worldviews diminish anxiety by providing answers to universal questions such as: Why am I here? What is the meaning of life? Cultures create stories, traditions, and institutions that give their members a sense of being part of an enduring legacy. Thus, faith in a cultural worldview can give people a sense of order, meaning, and context that can soothe their fear of death.

Where does self-esteem fit into the picture? Self-esteem is viewed as a sense of personal worth that depends on one's confidence in the validity of one's cultural worldview and the belief that one is living up to the standards prescribed by that worldview. Hence, self-esteem buffers people from the profound anxiety associated with the awareness that they are transient animals destined to die. In other words, self-esteem serves a *terror management* function (refer to Figure 12.17).

The notion that self-esteem functions as an *anxiety buffer* has been supported by numerous studies (Pyszczynski et al., 2004; Schmeichel et al., 2009). In many of these experiments, researchers have manipulated what they call *mortality salience—the degree to which subjects' mortality is prominent in their minds*. Typically, mortality salience is temporarily increased by asking participants to briefly think about their own future death. Consistent with the anxiety buffer hypothesis, reminding people of their mortality leads subjects to engage in a variety of behaviours that are likely to bolster their self-esteem, thus reducing anxiety.

Increasing mortality salience also leads people to work harder at defending their cultural worldview (Arndt & Vess, 2008; Burke, Martens, & Faucher, 2010). For instance, after briefly pondering their mortality, research participants (1) hand out harsher penalties to moral transgressors, (2) respond more negatively to people who criticize their country, and (3) show more respect for cultural icons, such as a flag. This need to defend one's cultural worldview may even fuel prejudice and aggression (Greenberg et al., 2009). Reminding subjects of their mortality leads to (1) more negative evaluations of people from different religious or ethnic backgrounds, (2) more stereotypic thinking about minorities, and (3) more aggressive behaviour toward people with opposing political views.

Terror management theory yields novel hypotheses regarding many phenomena. For instance, Solomon, Greenberg, and Pyszczynski (2004a) explain excessive materialism in terms of the anxiety-buffering function of self-esteem. Specifically, they argue that "conspicuous possession and consumption are thinly veiled efforts to assert that one is special and therefore more than just an animal fated to die and decay" (p. 134).

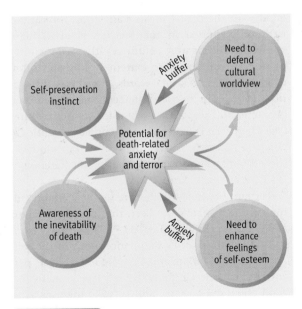

FIGURE 12.17

Overview of terror management theory.

This graphic maps out the relationships among the key concepts proposed by terror management theory. The theory asserts that humans' unique awareness of the inevitability of death fosters a need to defend one's cultural worldview and one's self-esteem, which serve to protect one from mortality-related anxiety.

At first glance, a theory that explains everything from prejudice to compulsive shopping in terms of death anxiety may seem highly implausible. After all, most people do not appear to walk around all day obsessing about the possibility of their death. The architects of terror management theory are well aware of this reality. They explain that the defensive reactions uncovered in their research generally occur when death anxiety surfaces on the fringes of conscious awareness and that these reactions are automatic and subconscious (Pyszczynski, Greenberg, & Solomon, 1999). Although the theory may seem a little far-fetched, the predictions of terror management theory have been supported in hundreds of experiments (Burke, Martens, & Faucher, 2010).

Culture and Personality

PREVIEW QUESTIONS

▶ Does the five-factor model have any relevance in non-Western cultures?

▶ How do conceptions of self vary across cultures?

▶ How does an interdependent view of self relate to self-enhancement?

Photo and Campus Services, University of Michigan

Courtesy of Sinobu Kitayama

Hazel Markus and Shinobu Kitayama

"Most of what psychologists currently know about human nature is based on one particular view—the so-called Western view of the individual as an independent, self-contained, autonomous entity."

Are there connections between culture and personality? In recent years, psychology's new interest in cultural factors has led to a renaissance of culture–personality research (e.g., Allik et al., 2010; Church, 2010; Heine, Buchtel, & Norenzayan, 2008; Klimstra et al., 2011). This research has sought to determine whether Western personality constructs are relevant to other cultures and whether cultural differences can be seen in the prevalence of specific personality traits. As with cross-cultural research in other areas of psychology, these studies have found evidence of both continuity and variability across cultures.

For the most part, continuity has been apparent in cross-cultural comparisons of the trait structure of personality. When English-language personality scales have been translated and administered in other cultures, the predicted dimensions of personality have emerged from the factor analyses (Chui, Kim, & Wan, 2008; Paunonen & Ashton, 1998). For example, when scales that tap the Big Five personality traits have been administered and subjected to factor analysis in other cultures, the usual five traits have typically emerged (Katigbak et al., 2002; McCrae & Costa, 2008b). Thus, research tentatively suggests that the basic dimensions of personality structure may be universal.

On the other hand, some cross-cultural variability is seen when researchers compare the average trait scores of samples from various cultural groups. For example, in a study comparing 51 cultures, McCrae and colleagues (2005b) found that Brazilians scored relatively high in neuroticism, Australians in extraversion, Germans in openness to experience, Czechs in agreeableness, and Malaysians in conscientiousness, to give but a handful of examples. These findings should be viewed as very preliminary, as more data are needed from larger and more carefully selected samples. Nonetheless, the findings suggest that there may be genuine cultural differences on some personality traits. That said, the cultural disparities in average trait scores that were observed were quite modest in size.

The availability of the data from the McCrae et al. (2005b) study allowed Terracciano et al. (2005) to revisit the concept of *national character*—the idea that various cultures have widely recognized prototype personalities. Terracciano and his colleagues asked subjects from many cultures to describe the *typical* member of *their* culture on rating forms guided by the five-factor model. Generally, subjects displayed substantial agreement on these ratings of what was typical for their culture. The averaged ratings, which served as the measures of each culture's national character, were then correlated with the actual mean trait scores for various cultures compiled in the McCrae et al. (2005b) study. The results were definitive—the vast majority of the correlations were extremely low and often even negative. In other words, there was little or no relationship between perceptions of national character and actual trait scores for various cultures (see Figure 12.18). People's beliefs about national character, which often fuel cultural prejudices, turned out to be profoundly inaccurate stereotypes (McCrae & Terracciano, 2006).

Perhaps the most interesting recent work on culture and personality has been that of Hazel Markus and Shinobu Kitayama (1991, 1994, 2003), comparing American and Asian conceptions of the self. According to Markus and Kitayama, American parents teach their children to be self-reliant, to feel good about themselves, and to view themselves as special individuals. Children are encouraged to excel in competitive endeavours and to strive to stand out from the crowd. They are told that "the squeaky wheel gets the grease" and that "you have to stand

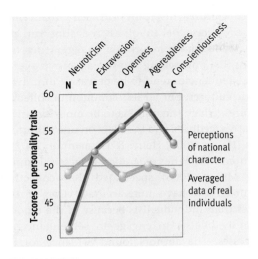

FIGURE 12.18

An example of inaccurate perceptions of national character.

Terracciano et al. (2005) found that perceptions of national character (the prototype or typical personality for a particular culture) are largely inaccurate. The data shown here for one culture—Canadians—illustrates this inaccuracy. Mean scores on the Big Five traits for a sample of real individuals from Canada are graphed here in orange. Averaged perceptions of national character for Canadians are graphed in purple. The discrepancy between perception and reality is obvious. Terracciano et al. found similar disparities between views of national character and actual trait scores for a majority of the cultures they studied. (Adapted from McCrae & Terracciano, 2006)

up for yourself." Thus, Markus and Kitayama argue that American culture fosters an *independent* view of the self. American youngsters learn to define themselves in terms of their personal attributes, abilities, accomplishments, and possessions. Their unique strengths and achievements become the basis for their sense of self-worth. Hence, they are prone to emphasize their uniqueness.

Most North Americans take this individualistic mentality for granted. Indeed, Markus and Kitayama maintain that "most of what psychologists currently know about human nature is based on one particular view—the so-called Western view of the individual as an independent, self-contained, autonomous entity" (1991, p. 224). However, they marshal convincing evidence that this view is not universal. They argue that in Asian cultures such as Japan and China, socialization practices foster a more interdependent view of the self, which emphasizes the fundamental connectedness of people to each other (see Figure 12.19). In these cultures, parents teach their children that they can rely on family and friends, that they should be modest about their personal accomplishments so they don't diminish others' achievements, and

that they should view themselves as part of a larger social matrix. Children are encouraged to fit in with others and to avoid standing out from the crowd. A popular adage in Japan reminds children that "the nail that stands out gets pounded down." Hence, Markus and Kitayama assert that Asian youngsters typically learn to define themselves in terms of the groups they belong to. Their harmonious relationships with others and their pride in group achievements become the basis for their sense of self-worth. Because their self-esteem does not hinge so much on personal strengths, they are less likely to emphasize their uniqueness. Consistent with this analysis, Markus and Kitayama report that Asian subjects tend to view themselves as more similar to their peers than American subjects do.

Personality has often been studied in relation to the cultural syndromes of *individualism versus collectivism,* which represent different value systems and worldviews (Triandis & Suh, 2002). *Individualism* involves putting personal goals ahead of group goals and defining one's identity in terms of personal attributes rather than group memberships. In contrast, *collectivism* involves putting group goals ahead of personal goals and defining one's identity in terms of the groups one belongs to (such as one's family, tribe, work group, social class, caste, and so on).

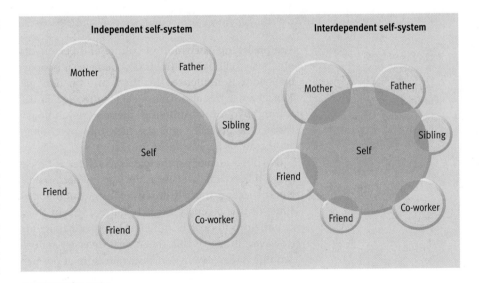

FIGURE 12.19

Culture and conceptions of self.

According to Markus and Kitayama (1991), Western cultures foster an independent view of the self as a unique individual who is separate from others, as diagrammed on the left. In contrast, Asian cultures encourage an interdependent view of the self as part of an interconnected social matrix, as diagrammed on the right. The interdependent view leads people to define themselves in terms of their social relationships (e.g., as someone's daughter, employee, colleague, or neighbour).

Source: Adapted from Markus, H.R., and Kitayama, S. (1991). Culture and the self: Implications for cognition, emotion, and motivation. *Psychological Review, 98,* 224–253. Copyright © 1991 by the American Psychological Association. Adapted by permission of the author.

Keren Su/Stone/Getty Images

Culture can shape personality. Children in Asian cultures, for example, grow up with a value system that allows them to view themselves as interconnected parts of larger social units. Hence, they tend to avoid positioning themselves so that they stand out from others.

These discrepant worldviews have a variety of implications for personality. For example, research has shown that individualism and collectivism foster cultural disparities in self-enhancement. *Self-enhancement* involves focusing on positive feedback from others, exaggerating one's strengths, and seeing oneself as above average. These tendencies tend to be pervasive in individualistic cultures, but far less common in collectivist cultures, where the norm is to be more sensitive to negative feedback and to reflect on one's shortcomings (Heine, 2003; Heine & Hamamura, 2007). In an interesting series of studies, Balacetis, Dunning, and Miller (2008) speculated that collectivists might tend to have more accurate views of themselves than individualists because of the tendency of individualists to engage in self-enhancement processes. The authors found evidence for their assumption. For example, individualists overestimated their generosity in redistributing a reward and their willingness to avoid being rude to someone. In contrast, collectivists were more accurate in making predictions of their actual behaviour in these contexts. The authors concluded that that collectivism may promote greater self-insight than individualism, as least when people contemplate whether they will engage in positive, socially desirable behaviours.

Putting It in Perspective: Themes 2, 3, and 5

PREVIEW QUESTIONS

▶ How did the chapter illustrate psychology's theoretical diversity?

▶ How did the chapter show that psychology evolves in a sociohistorical context?

The preceding discussion of culture and personality obviously highlighted the text's theme that people's behaviour is influenced by their cultural heritage. This chapter has also been ideally suited for embellishing two other unifying themes: psychology's theoretical diversity and the idea that psychology evolves in a sociohistorical context.

No other area of psychology is characterized by as much theoretical diversity as the study of personality, where there are literally dozens of insightful theories. Some of this diversity exists because different theories attempt to explain different facets of behaviour. However, much of this theoretical diversity reflects genuine disagreements on basic questions about personality. These disagreements are apparent on pages 578–579, which present an illustrated comparative overview of the ideas of Freud, Skinner, Rogers, and Eysenck, as representatives of the psychodynamic, behavioural, humanistic, and biological approaches to personality.

The study of personality also highlights the sociohistorical context in which psychology evolves.

Personality theories have left many marks on modern culture; we can mention only a handful as illustrations. The theories of Freud, Adler, and Skinner have had an enormous impact on child-rearing practices. The ideas of Freud and Jung have found their way into literature (influencing the portrayal of fictional characters) and the visual arts. For example, Freud's theory helped inspire surrealism's interest in the world of dreams (see Figure 4.61, Salvador Dali's *The Hallucinogenic Toreador*, on page 191). Social learning theory has become embroiled in the public policy debate about whether media violence should be controlled because of its effects on viewers' aggressive behaviour. Maslow's hierarchy of needs and Skinner's affirmation of the value of positive reinforcement have influenced approaches to management in the world of business and industry.

Sociohistorical forces also leave their imprint on psychology. This chapter provided many examples of how personal experiences, prevailing attitudes, and historical events have contributed to the evolution of ideas in psychology. For example, Freud's pessimistic view of human nature and his emphasis on the dark forces of aggression were shaped to some extent by his exposure to the hostilities of World War I and prevailing anti-Semitic sentiments. Freud's emphasis on sexuality was surely influenced by the Victorian climate of sexual repression that existed in his youth. Adler's views also reflected the social context in which he grew up. His interest in inferiority feelings and compensation appear to have sprung from his own sickly childhood and the difficulties he had to overcome. Likewise, it's reasonable to speculate that Jung's childhood loneliness and introversion may have sparked his interest in the introversion–extraversion dimension of personality. In a similar vein, we saw that both Rogers and Maslow had to resist parental pressures in order to pursue their career interests. Their emphasis on the need to achieve personal fulfillment may have originated in these experiences.

Progress in the study of personality has also been influenced by developments in other areas of psychology. For instance, the enterprise of psychological testing originally emerged out of efforts to measure general intelligence. Eventually, however, the principles of psychological testing were applied to the challenge of measuring personality. In the upcoming Personal Application we discuss the logic and limitations of personality tests.

REVIEW OF KEY POINTS

> Narcissism is a trait marked by an inflated sense of self, need for attention, and a sense of entitlement. People who score high in narcissism work overtime trying to impress others with self-aggrandizing tales of their accomplishments, all to protect their fragile self-esteem. They often are well-liked at first, but eventually seen as arrogant and self-centered. Research suggests that levels of narcissism have been increasing in recent generations.

> Terror management theory proposes that self-esteem and faith in a cultural worldview shield people from the profound anxiety associated with their mortality. Manipulations of mortality salience lead to harsh treatment for moral transgressions, elevated respect for cultural icons, and increased prejudice.

> Some studies suggest that the basic trait structure of personality may be much the same across cultures. However, some critics have voiced doubts about this conclusion.

> Markus and Kitayama assert that Western culture fosters an independent conception of self, whereas Asian cultures foster an interdependent view of the self. These different views of the self lead to cultural disparities in the tendency to engage in self-enhancement.

> The study of personality illustrates how psychology is characterized by great theoretical diversity. The study of personality also demonstrates how ideas in psychology are shaped by sociohistorical forces and how cultural factors influence psychological processes.

Understanding Personality Assessment

Answer the following "true" or "false."

___ **1** Responses to personality tests are subject to unconscious distortion.

___ **2** The results of personality tests are often misunderstood.

___ **3** Personality test scores should be interpreted with caution.

___ **4** Personality tests serve many important functions.

If you answered "true" to all four questions, you earned a perfect score. Yes, personality tests are subject to distortion. Admittedly, test results are often misunderstood, and they should be interpreted cautiously. In spite of these problems, however, psychological tests can be quite useful.

Everyone engages in efforts to size up his or her own personality as well as that of others. When you think to yourself that "Mary Ann is shrewd and poised," or when you remark to a friend that "Carlos is timid and submissive," you're making personality assessments. In a sense, then, personality assessment is an ongoing part of daily life. Given the popular interest in personality assessment, it's not surprising that psychologists have devised formal measures of personality.

Personality tests can be helpful in (1) making clinical diagnoses of psychological disorders, (2) vocational counselling, (3) personnel selection in business and industry, and (4) measuring specific personality traits for research purposes. Personality tests can be divided into two broad categories: *self-report inventories and projective tests*. In this Personal Application, we'll discuss some representative tests from both categories and discuss their strengths and weaknesses.

Self-Report Inventories 7a

Self-report inventories are personality tests that ask individuals to answer a series of questions about their characteristic behaviour. The logic underlying this approach is simple: Who knows you better? Who has known you longer? Who has more access to your private feelings? We'll look at three examples of self-report scales: the *Minnesota Multiphasic Personality Inventory* (MMPI), the *16 Personality Factor* (16PF) *Questionnaire*, and the *NEO Personality Inventory*.

The MMPI The most widely used self-report inventory is the *Minnesota Multiphasic Personality Inventory* (MMPI) (Butcher, 2005, 2006). The MMPI was originally designed to aid clinicians in the diagnosis of psychological disorders. It measures ten personality traits that, when manifested to an extreme degree, are thought to be symptoms of disorders. Examples include traits such as paranoia, depression, and hysteria.

Are the MMPI clinical scales valid? That is, do they measure what they were designed to measure? Originally, it was assumed that the ten clinical subscales would provide direct indexes of specific types of disorders. In other words, a high score on the depression scale would be indicative of depression, a high score on the paranoia scale would be indicative of a paranoid disorder, and so forth. However, research revealed that the relationships between MMPI scores and various types of mental illness are much more complex than originally anticipated. People with most types of disorders show elevated scores on *several* MMPI subscales. This means that certain score *profiles* are indicative of specific disorders (see Figure 12.20). Thus, the interpretation of the MMPI is quite complicated, perhaps overly complicated according to some critics (Helmes, 2008). Nonetheless, the MMPI can be a helpful diagnostic tool for the clinician. The fact that the inventory has been translated into more than 115 languages is a testimonial to its usefulness (Adams & Culbertson, 2005).

The 16PF and NEO Personality Inventory 7a

Raymond Cattell (1957, 1965) set out to identify and measure the *basic dimensions* of the *normal* personality. He started with a previously compiled list of 4504 personality traits. This massive list was reduced to 171 traits by weeding out terms that were virtually synonyms. Cattell then used factor analysis to identify clusters of closely related traits and the factors underlying them. Eventually, he reduced the list of 171 traits to 16 *source traits*. The *16 Personality Factor* (16PF) *Questionnaire* (Cattell, Eber, & Tatsuoka, 1970; Cattell, 2004) is a 187-item scale that assesses these 16 basic dimensions of personality, which are listed in Figure 12.21. The current (fifth) edition of this test continues to enjoy widespread use (Cattell & Mead, 2008).

As we noted in the main body of the chapter, some theorists believe that only five trait dimensions are required to provide a full description of personality. This view has led to the creation of a relatively new test—the *NEO Personality Inventory*. Developed by Paul Costa and Robert McCrae (1985, 1992), the NEO inventory is designed to measure the Big Five traits: neuroticism, extraversion, openness to experience, agreeableness, and conscientiousness. The NEO inventory is widely used in research and clinical work, and updated revisions of the scale have been released (Costa & McCrae, 2008; McCrae & Costa, 2004, 2007). An example of an NEO profile (averaged from many respondents) was shown in our discussion of culture and personality (see Figure 12.18 on page 583).

Strengths and Weaknesses of Self-Report Inventories To appreciate the strengths of self-report inventories, consider how else you might inquire about an individual's personality. For instance, if you want to know how assertive someone is, why not just ask the person? Why administer an

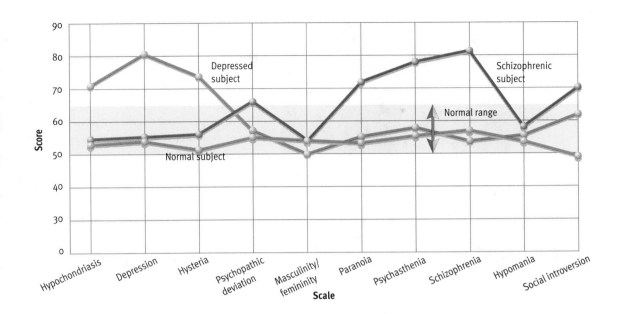

FIGURE 12.20

MMPI profiles.

Scores on the ten clinical scales of the MMPI are often plotted as shown here to create a profile for a client. The normal range for scores on each subscale is 50 to 65. People with disorders frequently exhibit elevated scores on several clinical scales rather than just one.

elaborate 50-item personality inventory that measures assertiveness? The advantage of the personality inventory is that it can provide a more objective and more precise estimate of the person's assertiveness, one that is better grounded in extensive comparative data based on information provided by many other respondents.

Of course, self-report inventories are only as accurate as the information that respondents provide. They are susceptible to several sources of error (Ben-Porath, 2003; Kline, 1995; Paulhus, 1991), including the following:

1. *Deliberate deception.* Some self-report inventories include many questions whose purpose is easy to figure out. This problem makes it possible for some respondents to intentionally fake particular personality traits (Rees & Metcalfe, 2003). Some studies suggest that deliberate faking is a serious problem when personality scales are used to evaluate job applicants (Birkeland et al., 2006), but other studies suggest that the problem is not all that significant (Hogan, Barrett, & Hogan, 2007).

2. *Social desirability bias.* Without realizing it, some people consistently respond to questions in ways that make them look good. The social desirability bias isn't a matter of deception so much as wishful thinking.

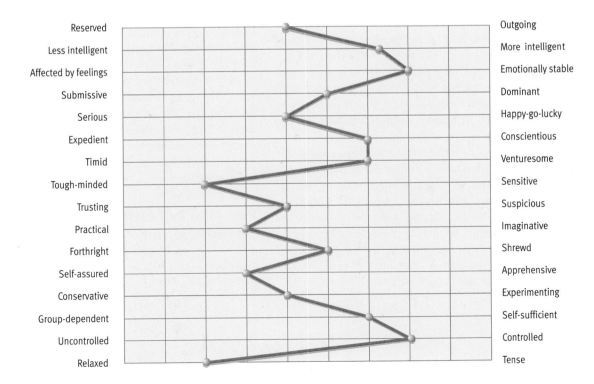

FIGURE 12.21

The Sixteen Personality Factor (16PF) Questionnaire.

Unlike the MMPI, Cattell's 16PF is designed to assess normal aspects of personality. The pairs of traits listed across from each other in the figure define the 16 factors measured by this self-report inventory. The profile shown is the average profile seen among a group of airline pilots who took the test.

Source: Cattell, R.B. (1973, July). Personality pinned down. *Psychology Today*, 40-46. Reprinted by permission of *Psychology Today* magazine. Copyright © 1973 Sussex Publishers, Inc.

3. *Response sets.* A response set is a systematic tendency to respond to test items in a particular way that is unrelated to the content of the items. For instance, some people, called *yea-sayers*, tend to agree with virtually every statement on a test. Other people, called *nay-sayers*, tend to disagree with nearly every statement.

Test developers have devised a number of strategies to reduce the impact of deliberate deception, social desirability bias, and response sets (Berry, Wetter, & Baer, 1995; Lanyon & Goodstein, 1997). For instance, it's possible to insert a "lie scale" into a test to assess the likelihood that a respondent is engaging in deception. The best way to reduce the impact of social desirability bias is to identify items that are sensitive to this bias and drop them from the test. Problems with response sets can be reduced by systematically varying the way in which test items are worded. Although self-report inventories have some weaknesses, carefully constructed personality scales remain "an indispensable tool for applied psychologists" (Hogan, 2005, p. 331).

Projective Tests   7a

Projective tests, which all take a rather indirect approach to the assessment of personality, are used extensively in clinical work. *Projective tests ask participants to respond to vague, ambiguous stimuli in ways that may reveal the subjects' needs, feelings, and personality traits.* The Rorschach test (Rorschach, 1921), for instance, consists of a series of ten inkblots. Respondents are asked to describe what they see in the blots. In the *Thematic Apperception Test* (TAT) (Murray, 1943), a series of pictures of simple scenes is presented to individuals who are asked to tell stories about what is happening in the scenes and what the characters are feeling. For instance, one TAT card shows a young boy contemplating a violin resting on a table in front of him (see Figure 12.22 for another example).

The Projective Hypothesis   7a

The "projective hypothesis" is that ambiguous materials can serve as a blank screen onto which people project their characteristic concerns, conflicts, and desires (Frank, 1939). Thus, a competitive person who is shown the TAT card of the boy at the table with the violin might concoct a story about how the boy is contemplating an upcoming musical competition at which he hopes to excel. The same card shown to a person high in impulsiveness might elicit a story about how the boy is planning to sneak out the door to go dirt-bike riding with friends.

The scoring and interpretation of projective tests is very complicated. Rorschach responses may be analyzed in terms of content, originality, the feature of the inkblot that determined the response, and the amount of the inkblot used, among other criteria. In fact, six different systems exist for scoring the Rorschach (Adams & Culbertson, 2005). TAT stories are examined in terms of heroes, needs, themes, and outcomes.

Strengths and Weaknesses of Projective Tests Proponents of projective tests assert that the tests have two unique strengths. First, they are not transparent to respondents. That is, the subject doesn't know how the test provides information to the tester. Hence, it may be difficult for people to engage in intentional deception (Groth-Marnat, 1997). Second, the indirect approach used in these tests may make them especially sensitive to unconscious, latent features of personality.

Unfortunately, the scientific evidence on projective measures is unimpressive (Garb, Florio, & Grove, 1998; Hunsley, Lee, & Wood, 2003). In a thorough review of the relevant research, Lilienfeld, Wood, and Garb (2000) conclude that projective tests tend to be plagued by inconsistent scoring, low reliability, inadequate test norms, cultural bias, and poor validity estimates. They also assert that, contrary to advocates' claims, projective tests are susceptible to some types of intentional deception (primarily, faking poor mental health). Based on their analysis, Lilienfeld and his colleagues argue that projective tests should be referred to as projective "techniques" or "instruments" rather than tests because "most of these techniques as used in daily clinical practice do not fulfill the traditional criteria for psychological tests" (p. 29). In spite of these problems, projective tests continue to be used by many clinicians. Although the questionable scientific status of these techniques is a very real problem, their continued popularity suggests that they yield subjective information that many clinicians find useful (Viglione & Rivera, 2003).

Personality Testing on the Internet

The Internet has had a considerable impact on the process of personality assessment.

Self-report inventories are increasingly being administered over the Internet by researchers, clinicians, and companies (Naglieri et al., 2004). Most of the widely used personality scales are available in an online format. The advantages of online testing are substantial (Buchanan, 2007). Tests can be completed quickly, with reduced labour costs, and the data flow directly into interpretive software. Online testing also allows test administrators to collect additional data that would not be available from a traditional paper-and-pencil test. For instance, they can track answer-changing and how long respondents ponder specific questions. Online testing also allows clinicians to deliver assessment services to rural clients who do not have access to local psychologists (Barak & Buchanan, 2004). Given all these advantages, Buchanan (2007, p. 450) notes that "it is easy to imagine a future where virtually all testing is conducted online."

Are there any disadvantages to online personality assessment? Well, there are issues that merit concern, but they appear to be manageable. The item content of some tests is closely guarded, so security is an issue for some tests (Naglieri et al., 2004). And when personality tests are used for hiring purposes, verifying the identity of the respondent is important. The chief theoretical issue is whether tests delivered online yield results that are equivalent to what is found when the same tests are administered in a paper-and-pencil format. For the most part, research suggests that online tests are equivalent to their offline counterparts, but this issue should be checked empirically whenever a specific test is migrated to an online format (Buchanan, 2007; Epstein & Klinkenberg, 2001). Overall, though, the future of online personality testing appears very bright. That said, consumers should remember that the Internet is utterly unregulated, so one can find an abundance of pop psychology tests online that have no scientific or empirical basis (Naglieri et al., 2004).

REVIEW OF KEY POINTS

▷ Self-report inventories ask subjects to describe themselves. The MMPI is a widely used inventory that measures pathological aspects of personality. The 16PF assesses 16 dimensions of the normal personality. The NEO personality inventory measures the Big Five personality traits. Self-report inventories are vulnerable to certain sources of error, including deception, the social desirability bias, and response sets.

▷ Projective tests assume that subjects' responses to ambiguous stimuli reveal something about their personality. In the Rorschach test, respondents describe what they see in ten inkblots, whereas subjects formulate stories about simple scenes when they take the TAT. While the projective hypothesis seems plausible, projective tests' reliability and validity are disturbingly low.

▷ Self-report inventories are increasingly being administered over the Internet. The advantages of online testing are substantial, although there are concerns about security and test equivalence.

Hindsight in Everyday Analyses of Personality

Consider the case of two close sisters who grew up together: Lorena and Christina. Lorena grew into a frugal adult who is careful about spending her money, shops only when there are sales, and saves every penny she can. In contrast, Christina became an extravagant spender who lives to shop and never saves any money. How do the sisters explain their striking personality differences? Lorena attributes her thrifty habits to the fact that her family was so poor when she was a child that she learned the value of being careful with money. Christina attributes her extravagant spending to the fact that her family was so poor that she learned to really enjoy any money that she might have. Now, it is possible that two sisters could react to essentially the same circumstances quite differently, but the more likely explanation is that both sisters have been influenced by the *hindsight bias*—the tendency to mould one's interpretation of the past to fit how events actually turned out. We saw how hindsight can distort memory in Chapter 7. Here, we will see how hindsight tends to make everyone feel as if they are personality experts and how it creates interpretive problems even for scientific theories of personality.

The Prevalence of Hindsight Bias

Hindsight bias is ubiquitous, which means that it occurs in many different settings, with all sorts of people. Most of the time, people are not aware of the way their explanations are skewed by the fact that the outcome is already known. The experimental literature on hindsight bias offers a rich array of findings on how the knowledge of an outcome biases the way people think about its causes (Hawkins & Hastie, 1990). For example, when university students were told the results of hypothetical experiments, each group of students could "explain" why the studies turned out the way they did, even though different groups were given opposite

results to explain (Slovic & Fischhoff, 1977). The students believed that the results of the studies were obvious when they were told what the experimenter found, but when they were given only the information that was available before the outcome was known, it was not obvious at all. This bias is also called the "I knew it all along" effect because that is the typical refrain of people when they have the luxury of hindsight. Indeed, after the fact, people often act as if events that would have been difficult to predict had in fact been virtually inevitable. Looking back at the disintegration of the Soviet Union and the end of the Cold War, for instance, many people today act as though these events were bound to happen, but in reality these landmark events were predicted by almost no one.

Hindsight bias shows up in many contexts. For example, when a couple announces that they are splitting up, many people in their social circle will typically claim they "saw it coming." When a football team loses in a huge upset, you will hear many fans claim, "I knew they were overrated and vulnerable." When public officials make a difficult decision that leads to a disastrous outcome—such as the FBI's 1993 attack on the Branch Davidian compound in Waco, Texas—many of the pundits in the press are quick to criticize, often asserting that only incompetent fools could have failed to foresee the catastrophe. Interestingly, people are not much kinder to themselves when they make ill-fated decisions. When individuals make tough calls that lead to negative results—such as buying a car that turns out to be a lemon, or investing in a stock that plummets—they often say things like, "Why did I ignore the obvious warning signs?" or "How could I be such an idiot?"

Hindsight and Personality

Hindsight bias appears to be pervasive in everyday analyses of personality. Think about it: If you attempt to explain why you

are so suspicious, why your mother is so domineering, or why your best friend is so insecure, the starting point in each case will be the personality outcome. It would probably be impossible to reconstruct the past without being swayed by your knowledge of these outcomes. Thus, hindsight makes everybody an expert on personality, as we can all come up with plausible explanations for the personality traits of people we know well. Perhaps this is why Judith Harris (1998) ignited a firestorm of protest when she wrote a widely read book arguing that parents have relatively little effect on their children's personalities beyond the genetic material that they supply.

In her book *The Nurture Assumption*, Harris summarizes behavioural genetics research and other evidence suggesting that family environment has surprisingly little impact on children's personality (see pages 574–575). As we discussed in the main body of the chapter, there is room for plenty of debate on this complex issue (Kagan, 1998; Tavris, 1998), but our chief interest here is that Harris made a cogent, compelling argument in her book, which attracted extensive coverage in the press— coverage that generated an avalanche of commentary from angry parents who argued that parents *do* matter. For example, *Newsweek* magazine received 350 letters, mostly from parents who provided examples of how they thought they influenced their children's personalities. However, parents' retrospective analyses of their children's personality development have to be treated with great skepticism, as they are likely to be distorted by hindsight bias (not to mention the selective recall frequently seen in anecdotal reports).

Unfortunately, hindsight bias is so prevalent it also presents a problem for scientific theories of personality. For example, the spectre of hindsight bias has been raised in many critiques of psychoanalytic theory (Torrey, 1992). Freudian theory was originally built mainly on a foundation of case studies of patients in therapy. Obviously, Freudian therapists who knew what their patients' adult personalities were like probably went looking for the types of childhood experiences hypothesized by Freud (oral fixations, punitive toilet training, Oedipal conflicts, and so forth) in their efforts to explain their patients' personalities.

Another problem with hindsight bias is that once researchers know an outcome, more often than not they can fashion some plausible explanation for it. For instance, Torrey (1992) describes a study inspired by Freudian theory that examined breast-size preferences among men. The original hypothesis was that men who scored higher in dependence—thought to be a sign of oral fixation—would manifest a stronger preference for women with large breasts. When the actual results of the study showed just the opposite—that dependence was associated with a preference for smaller breasts—the finding was attributed to reaction formation on the part of the men. Instead of failing to support Freudian theory, the unexpected findings were simply reinterpreted in a way that was consistent with Freudian theory.

Hindsight bias also presents thorny problems for evolutionary theorists, who generally work backward from known outcomes to reason out how adaptive pressures in humans' ancestral past may have led to those outcomes (Cornell, 1997). Consider, for instance, evolutionary theorists' assertion that the Big Five traits are found to be fundamental dimensions of personality around the world because those specific traits have had major adaptive implications over the course of human history (Buss, 1995; MacDonald, 1998). Their explanation makes sense, but what would have happened if some other traits had shown up in the Big Five? Would the evolutionary view have been weakened if dominance, or paranoia, or high sensation seeking had turned up in the Big Five? Probably not. With the luxury of hindsight, evolutionary theorists surely could have constructed plausible explanations for how these traits promoted reproductive success in the distant past. Thus, hindsight bias is a fundamental feature of human cognition, and the scientific enterprise is not immune to this problem.

Other Implications of "20/20 Hindsight"

Our discussion of hindsight has focused on its implications for thinking about personality, but there is ample evidence that hindsight can bias thinking in all sorts of domains. For example, consider the practice of obtaining second opinions on medical diagnoses. The doctor providing the second opinion usually is aware of the first physician's diagnosis, which creates a hindsight bias (Arkes et al., 1981). Second opinions would probably be more valuable if the doctors rendering them were not aware of previous diagnoses. Hindsight also has the potential to distort legal decisions in cases involving allegations of negligence. Jurors' natural tendency to think, "How could they have failed to foresee this problem," may exaggerate the appearance of negligence (LaBine & LaBine, 1996).

Hindsight bias is very powerful. The next time you hear of an unfortunate outcome to a decision made by a public official, carefully examine the way in which news reporters describe the decision. You will probably find that they believe that the disastrous outcome should have been obvious, because they can clearly see what went wrong after the fact. Similarly, if you find yourself thinking, "Only a fool would have failed to anticipate this disaster" or "I would have foreseen this problem," take a deep breath and try to review the decision *using only information that was known at the time the decision was being made*. Sometimes good decisions, based on the best available information, can have terrible outcomes. Unfortunately, the clarity of "20/20 hindsight" makes it difficult for people to learn from their own and others' mistakes.

TABLE 12.4	Critical Thinking Skill Discussed in This Application
Skill	**Description**
Recognizing the bias in hindsight analysis	The critical thinker understands that knowing the outcome of events biases our recall and interpretation of the events.

Key Ideas

The Nature of Personality

● The concept of personality explains the consistency in people's behaviour over time and situations, while also explaining their distinctiveness. There is considerable debate as to how many trait dimensions are necessary to account for the variation in personality, but the Big Five model has become the dominant conception of personality structure.

Psychodynamic Perspectives

● Freud's psychoanalytic theory emphasizes the importance of the unconscious. Freud described personality structure in terms of three components—the id, ego, and superego—which are routinely involved in an ongoing series of internal conflicts.

● Freud theorized that conflicts centring on sex and aggression are especially likely to lead to anxiety. According to Freud, anxiety and other unpleasant emotions such as guilt are often warded off with defence mechanisms.

● Freud described a series of five stages of development: oral, anal, phallic, latency, and genital. Certain experiences during these stages can have lasting effects on adult personality.

● Jung's most innovative and controversial concept was the collective unconscious. Adler's individual psychology emphasizes how people strive for superiority to compensate for their feelings of inferiority.

● Overall, psychodynamic theories have produced many groundbreaking insights about the unconscious, the role of internal conflict, and the importance of early childhood experiences in personality development. However, psychodynamic theories have been criticized for their poor testability, their inadequate base of empirical evidence, and their male-centred views.

Behavioural Perspectives

● Behavioural theories view personality as a collection of response tendencies tied to specific stimulus situations. They assume that personality development is a lifelong process in which response tendencies are shaped and reshaped by learning, especially operant conditioning.

● Social cognitive theory focuses on how cognitive factors such as expectancies and self-efficacy regulate learned behaviour. Bandura's concept of observational learning accounts for the acquisition of responses from models. Mischel has questioned the degree to which people display cross-situational consistency in behaviour.

● Behavioural approaches to personality are based on rigorous research. They have provided ample insights into how environmental factors and learning mould personalities. The behaviourists have been criticized for their overdependence on animal research, their fragmented analysis of personality, and radical behaviourism's dehumanizing view of human nature.

Humanistic Perspectives

● Humanistic theories are phenomenological and take an optimistic view of human potential. Rogers focused on the self-concept as the critical aspect of personality. Maslow theorized that psychological health depends on fulfilling one's need for self-actualization.

● Humanistic theories deserve credit for highlighting the importance of subjective views of oneself and for helping to lay the foundation for positive psychology. Humanistic theories lack a firm base of research, are difficult to put to an empirical test, and may be overly optimistic about human nature.

Biological Perspectives

● Contemporary biological theories stress the genetic origins of personality. Eysenck suggests that heredity influences individual differences in physiological functioning that affect how easily people acquire conditioned responses. Research on the personality resemblance of twins provides impressive evidence that genetic factors shape personality.

● One of the most recent directions of personality research examines associations between the brain and personality. To date most of this work has focused on the Big Five. This line of research is brand new, but the promising initial results suggest that it may be fruitful to explore the neurological bases of personality traits. Evolutionary theorists argue that the major dimensions of personality reflect humans' adaptive landscape. The biological approach has demonstrated that personality is partly heritable, but it has been criticized for its narrow focus on heritability and because it offers no systematic model of how physiology shapes personality.

A Contemporary Empirical Approach to Personality

● Narcissism is a trait marked by an inflated sense of self, need for attention, and a sense of entitlement. People who score high in narcissism work overtime trying to impress others with self-aggrandizing tales of their accomplishments, all to protect their fragile self-esteem. They often are well-liked at first, but

eventually are seen as arrogant and self-centred. Research suggests that levels of narcissism have been increasing in recent generations.

● Terror management theory describes the psychological implications of our realization that our death is inevitable. According to the theory, rather than being paralyzed with terror, our cultures provide us with worldviews that solve this existential problem. Self-esteem serves a terror management function as an anxiety buffer.

Culture and Personality

● Some studies suggest that the basic trait structure of personality may be much the same across cultures. However, notable differences have been found when researchers have compared cultural groups' conceptions of self.

Putting It in Perspective: Themes 2, 3, and 5

● The study of personality illustrates how psychology is characterized by great theoretical diversity. It also demonstrates how ideas in psychology are shaped by sociohistorical forces and how cultural factors influence psychological processes.

PERSONAL APPLICATION • Understanding Personality Assessment

● Personality assessment is useful in clinical diagnosis, counselling, personnel selection, and research. Self-report measures ask subjects to describe themselves. Self-report inventories are vulnerable to certain sources of error, including deception, the social desirability bias, and response sets.

● Projective tests assume that subjects' responses to ambiguous stimuli reveal something about their personality. While the projective hypothesis seems plausible, projective tests' reliability and validity are disturbingly low.

CRITICAL THINKING APPLICATION • Hindsight in Everyday Analyses of Personality

● Hindsight bias often leads people to assert that "I knew it all along" in discussing outcomes that they did not actually predict. Thanks to hindsight, people can almost always come up with plausible-sounding explanations for known personality traits.

Key Terms

Archetypes, 558
Behaviourism, 561
Collective unconscious, 558
Collectivism, 583
Compensation, 559
Conscious, 552
Defence mechanisms, 554
Displacement, 554
Ego, 552
Extraverts, 558
Factor analysis, 548
Fixation, 556
Hierarchy of needs, 570
Hindsight bias, 590
Humanism, 566
Id, 551
Identification, 555
Incongruence, 567
Individualism, 583
Introverts, 558
Model, 564
Mortality salience, 581
Narcissism, 577
Need for self-actualization, 570
Observational learning, 564
Oedipal complex, 557
Personal unconscious, 558
Personality, 548
Personality trait, 548
Phenomenological approach, 566
Pleasure principle, 551
Preconscious, 552
Projection, 554
Projective tests, 588
Psychodynamic theories, 551

Psychosexual stages, 556
Rationalization, 554
Reaction formation, 554
Reality principle, 551
Reciprocal determinism, 563
Regression, 555
Repression, 554
Self-actualizing persons, 571
Self-concept, 566
Self-efficacy, 564
Self-enhancement, 584
Self-report inventories, 586
Striving for superiority, 559
Sublimation, 555
Superego, 552
Terror management theory, 580
Unconscious, 552

Key People

Alfred Adler, 559
Albert Bandura, 563
David Buss, 576
Norman Endler, 565
Hans Eysenck, 574
Sigmund Freud, 551
Carl Jung, 557
Shinobu Kitayama, 582
Hazel Markus, 582
Abraham Maslow, 571
Walter Mischel, 565
Daniel Nettle, 576
Delroy Paulhus, 554
Carl Rogers, 567
B. F. Skinner, 563
Frank Sulloway, 559
Paul Trapnell, 560

1. Harvey has devoted his life to the search for physical pleasure and immediate gratification of his needs. According to Freud, which of the following dominates Harvey's actions?
   - A. ego
   - B. superego
   - C. id
   - D. transference

2. Furious at her boss for what she considers unjust criticism, Tyra takes out her anger on her subordinates. Which of the following is the name for her defence mechanism?
   - A. displacement
   - B. reaction formation
   - C. identification
   - D. replacement

3. According to Freud, which of the following is the source of most personality disturbances?
   - A. the failure of parents to reinforce healthy behaviour
   - B. a poor self-concept resulting from excessive parental demands
   - C. unconscious and unresolved sexual conflicts rooted in childhood experiences
   - D. the exposure of children to unhealthy role models

4. According to Alfred Adler, which of the following is the prime motivating force in a person's life?
   - A. physical gratification
   - B. existential anxiety
   - C. striving for superiority
   - D. need for power

5. Why did Skinner not describe personality development in terms of stages, the way that other theorists did?
   - A. He saw personality as being fairly fixed early in life, with little ongoing change.
   - B. He felt that development was a gradual ongoing process, rather than a series of discrete steps.
   - C. He described personality in terms of categories that were consistent across time.
   - D. He felt that stages were just labels, rather than useful constructs for research.

6. Irving, always a good student, is confident he will do well in his psychology course. According to Bandura's social cognitive theory, which of the following statements describes the nature of Irving's confidence?
   - A. He has strong feelings of self-efficacy.
   - B. He has a sense of superiority.
   - C. He has strong feelings of self-esteem.
   - D. He has strong defence mechanisms.

7. Which of the following approaches to personality is the least deterministic?
   - A. humanistic approach
   - B. psychoanalytic approach
   - C. Skinner's approach
   - D. behavioural approach

8. According to Carl Rogers, which of the following conditions fosters a congruent self-concept?
   - A. conditional love
   - B. appropriate role models
   - C. immediate need gratification
   - D. unconditional love

9. According to Maslow, which of the following series shows the correct hierarchical order of human needs?
   - A. physiological, belongingness, aesthetic, cognitive
   - B. belongingness, physiological, cognitive, aesthetic
   - C. physiological, belongingness, cognitive, aesthetic
   - D. physiological, cognitive, belongingness, aesthetic

10. Strong correlations in personalities among one of the following pairs provides significant support for the theory that personality is heavily influenced by genetics. Which pair is it?
    - A. identical twins reared apart
    - B. identical twins reared together
    - C. fraternal twins reared apart
    - D. fraternal twins reared together

11. If you know that the heritability estimate for a trait is 70 percent, what does that tell you about the role of genes for that trait?
    - A. The role of genes is strong, because you can predict 70 percent of a person's behaviour based on the behaviour of his or her parents.
    - B. The role of genes is strong, because you can explain 70 percent of the variance in a group based on genetic predisposition.
    - C. The role of genes is relatively weak, because the estimate is similar to chance.
    - D. The role of genes is weak, because 30 percent of the trait is unexplained.

12. According to terror management theory, which of the following explains the role of self-esteem?
    - A. It enables us to forget we are mortal.
    - B. It acts as a buffer against anxiety.
    - C. It causes anxiety because of its links to peer evaluation.
    - D. It is a mild delusional state that is a consequence of overcoming fear.

13. Which of the following clichés would seem most "correct" to an individual who was raised in a collectivist culture with interdependent values?
    - A. The squeaky wheel gets the grease.
    - B. Don't cover your light with a basket.
    - C. The early bird gets the worm.
    - D. The nail that sticks out gets pounded down.

14. Self-report inventories are vulnerable to intentional deception. Which of the following is a method used in test construction to reduce the impact of this problem?
    - A. adding a "lie scale" to the test to identify deceivers
    - B. removing questions that people are likely to lie on
    - C. wording the questions in a deceptive manner, as a counterstrategy
    - D. asking questions that tap into unconscious reactions, rather than conscious reactions

15. In *The Nurture Assumption*, Judith Harris presents evidence concerning the effects of family environment on children's personalities. Which of the following summarizes her argument?
    - A. The effect is mostly positive.
    - B. The effect is mostly negative.
    - C. The effect is surprisingly small.
    - D. The effect is particularly powerful.

See Appendix A for answers to this Practice Test.

On the Web

▶ **CourseMate**

Go to this site to find online resources directly linked to your book, including more quizzes, a glossary, flash cards, videos, and more!

▶ **CengageNow**

Go to this site for the link to CengageNOW™, your one-stop study shop. Take a pre-test for this chapter and CengageNOW™ will generate a personalized study plan based on your test results! The study plan will identify the topics you need to review and direct you to online resources to help you master those topics. You can then take a post-test to help you determine the concepts you have mastered and what you still need to work on.

▶ **Aplia**

Aplia™ is an online interactive learning solution that helps you improve comprehension—and your grade—by integrating a variety of media and tools such as video, tutorials, practice tests, and an interactive e-book.

CHAPTER 13

Stress, Coping, and Health

Courtesy of John Dalkin

Many circumstances can create stress. It comes in all sorts of packages: big and small, pretty and ugly, simple and complex. Students invariably experience stress at specific points throughout the academic year. Parents of students experience stress. No matter what they told you about how much they were looking forward to turning your bedroom at home into a new office, they were experiencing stress as you prepared to move away to university.

Sometimes stress is the result of everyday, relatively routine events, such as commuting or receiving an unexpected bill in the mail. Sometimes the package bringing your stress might be extraordinary. We know that new immigrants to Canada are particularly vulnerable to stress as they adapt to a new country, culture, and perhaps a new language (Levitt, Dane & Levitt, 2005; Sher & Vilens, 2010; Statistics Canada, 2011). Sometimes the events may involve personal danger. For example, imagine what was running through the mind of Deb Freele of London, Ontario, in 2010. She was attacked and bitten by a grizzly bear in Yellowstone National Park inside her tent. When the bear first began to bite her, she screamed as she felt her bones breaking. This enraged the bear and he increased his attacks. When she was able to calm herself down, she played dead and went limp. The bear then left her alone. She even had the presence of mind to apply her own tourniquets to stop the bleeding. Not everyone attacked by the bear that day survived (CBC News, 2010).

Or, consider how you might have reacted if you had been a passenger on the Canadian-based ecotourist ship *Explorer*. In November 2007, the ship was sailing in the waters off Antarctica when it hit a submerged object, rolled over, and began to sink (Passengers Head Home, 2007), stranding the 154 passengers and crew in a very inhospitable and dangerous environment. Fortunately, there were enough lifeboats for all, and help did arrive in time to save everyone. In interviews with the media, passengers talked about their worries and the stress they felt as they floated in the frigid Antarctic waters for six hours until they were rescued. Of course, not all circumstances that cause stress are like this one—just going to the dentist can be stressful for many people.

Do you think your reactions to stress differ depending on whether it is a relatively routine event or something out of the ordinary? We will answer this and many other questions you might

When the ecotourist ship *Explorer* sank in the Antarctic, the 154 passengers and crew had to retreat to the lifeboats and wait six hours until help arrived. While there are often individual differences in what people find stressful, no doubt all of the passengers and crew were stressed as a result of this incident.

Michael Nolan/SplashdownDirect.com

have about stress in this chapter. We'll discuss the nature of stress, how people cope with stress, and the potential effects of stress. Stress is more than just an academic topic—it's something we are all experts in, something with which we all have abundant experience, and something that can be difficult to handle and to treat (DeCicco, 2002). A recent survey by Statistics Canada revealed that one-fifth to one-quarter of Canadian adults report that most of their days are either quite stressful or extremely stressful (Gandhi, 2006), with Quebec adults reporting the highest levels of stress (26 percent) and those in Newfoundland reporting the lowest levels (15.2 percent). Stress seems to be a part of our everyday life.

Consider your own experiences at school this year: At this point in the academic year, all of you who were new to college or university in September are now veterans. Only a moment's reflection will tell you how much you have changed, how much you have experienced in a few short months, including the euphoria of becoming a university or college student, of being immersed in a new intellectual and social environment. You have also probably experienced the tension most students go through as they prepare for their first midterms or the "all-nighter" experience to get a paper in on time.

But shouldn't you be used to academic stress? One of us remembers a conversation he had with

Stress, Coping, and Health

a Grade 2 girl who was lined up for class, waiting for the bell, when all of her classmates were still playing in the schoolyard. She looked nervous and distressed. When asked why she was lining up so early, she replied that she had "way too much work to do" and that it was "stressing" her out. Although you have had previous experience with academic stress, university or college may provide additional and more varied stress-provoking situations. Generally, these settings offer a less structured environment than your high school environment, and one in which you may not have the immediacy of a supportive family. One Ipsos-Reid poll of Canadian university students revealed that while many students experience stress in university, 40 percent reported experiencing *high* stress at exam time (McKenzie, 2005).

Canadian universities and colleges have come to realize the importance of stress reduction for their students. Many now schedule *stress-buster* events to coincide with exam periods. A quick scan of university websites confirmed that this practice is common, including events such as free massages, guided meditation, professional advice on coping with stress, break dancing, carnival games, free video games, martial arts training, and sports competitions. The University of Alberta has interactive software on its website called "Students and Stress: How to Get Your Degree without Losing Your Mind" that provides stress

Students attending university or college experience stress firsthand during exam periods.

self-assessment tools and education regarding stress management (http://www.ualberta.ca/dept/health/web_docs/healthinfo/stressso.htm). The University of Prince Edward Island's website has a particularly good section on study and stress-reduction hints for students (http://studentservices.upei.ca/healthcentre/stress).

Our examination of the relationship between stress and physical illness will lead us into a broader discussion of the psychology of health. The way people in health professions think about physical illness has changed considerably in the past 30 years. The traditional view of physical illness as a purely biological phenomenon has given way to a biopsychosocial model of illness (Friedman & Adler, 2007; Suls, Luger, & Davidson, 2010). The *biopsychosocial model* holds that physical illness is caused by a complex interaction of biological, psychological, and sociocultural factors. This model does not suggest that biological factors are unimportant. It simply asserts that these factors operate in a psychosocial context that is also influential.

What has led to this shift in thinking? In part, it's a result of changing patterns of illness. Prior to the 20th century, the principal threats to health were *contagious diseases* caused by infectious agents—diseases such as smallpox, typhoid fever, diphtheria, yellow fever, malaria, cholera, tuberculosis, and polio. Today, none of these diseases is among the leading killers in North America. They were tamed by improvements in nutrition, public hygiene, sanitation, and medical treatment (Grob, 1983).

Unfortunately, the void left by contagious diseases has been filled all too quickly by *chronic diseases* that develop gradually, such as heart disease, cancer, and stroke (see Figure 13.1). Psychosocial factors, such as stress and lifestyle, play a large role in the development of these chronic diseases. The growing recognition that psychological factors influence physical health eventually led to the emergence of a new specialty in psychology, called *health psychology* (Friedman & Adler, 2007; Leventhal et al., 2008). *Health psychology* is concerned with how psychosocial factors relate to the promotion and maintenance of health and with the causation, prevention, and treatment of illness. In the second half of this chapter, we'll explore this new domain of psychology. In the Personal Application, we'll focus on strategies for enhancing stress management, and in the Critical Thinking Application we'll discuss strategies for improving health-related decision making.

Laurence Gough/Shutterstock.com

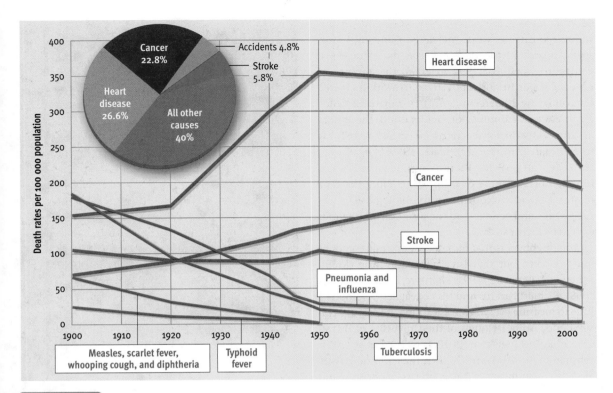

FIGURE 13.1

Changing patterns of illness.

Historical trends in the death rates for various diseases reveal that contagious diseases (shown in blue) have declined as a threat to health. However, the death rates for stress-related chronic diseases (shown in red) have remained quite high. The pie chart (inset) shows the results of these trends: Three chronic diseases (heart disease, cancer, and stroke) account for about 55 percent of all deaths. Although these chronic diseases remain the chief threat to health in modern societies, it is interesting to note that deaths due to heart disease have declined considerably since the 1980s. Many experts attribute much of this decline to improved health habits (Brannon & Feist, 2007), which demonstrates the important link between behaviour and health. [Based on data from *National Vital Statistics Reports*, 2008, *56*(10)]

The Nature of Stress

The word *stress* has been used in different ways by different theorists. We'll define *stress* as any circumstances that threaten or are perceived to threaten one's well-being and that thereby tax one's coping abilities. The threat may be to immediate physical safety, long-range security, self-esteem, reputation, peace of mind, or many other things that one values. Stress is a complex concept, so let's explore it a little further.

Stress as an Everyday Event

The word *stress* tends to spark images of overwhelming, traumatic crises. People may think of tornadoes, hurricanes, floods, and earthquakes. Undeniably, major disasters such as the tsunami that hit Japan in March 2011 and the subsequent

problems with the Fukushima nuclear power plant and the devastation caused by Hurricane Katrina in Louisiana in 2005 were extremely stressful events (*Managing Traumatic Stress*, 2005). Studies conducted in the aftermath of natural disasters typically find elevated rates of psychological problems and physical illness in the communities affected by these disasters (Stevens, Raphael, & Dobson, 2007; van Griensven et al., 2007; Weisler, Barbee, & Townsend, 2007). For example, 15 months after Hurricane Katrina devastated the New Orleans area, a survey of residents uncovered dramatic increases in physical and mental health problems (Kim et al., 2008). However, these unusual events are only a small part of what constitutes stress. Many everyday events, such as waiting in line, having car trouble, shopping for gifts, misplacing your cell phone, and even commuting are stressful. In fact, concerns about the effects of

PREVIEW QUESTIONS
▶ What is stress?
▶ How objective are our appraisals of stress?

commuting increase as the time we spend in our cars simply getting to work increases. Canadians now spend nearly 12 full days per year on average just getting to work. For 1992 to 2005, the amount of time we spent in our cars getting to work increased on average by 20 percent (Statistics Canada, 2006).

Of course, a number of factors affect the nature of any individual's reactions to stress. According to Anisman (Anisman & Merali, 1999; Magalhes et al., 2010), an individual's response to a stressor is a function of a number of factors, including the type of stressor and its controllability, biological factors such as age and gender, and the individual's previous experience with stress.

You might guess that minor stresses would produce minor effects, but that isn't necessarily true (Kohn, Lafrenier, & Gurevich, 1991; McIntyre, Korn, & Matuso, 2008). Richard Lazarus and his colleagues developed a scale to measure everyday hassles. One of Lazarus's collaborators, Anita Delongis of the University of British Columbia (Delongis et al., 2010; Lee-Flynn, et al., 2011; Lehman et al., 2011), has shown that routine hassles may have significant harmful effects on mental and physical health (Delongis, Folkman, & Lazarus, 1988). Other investigators, working with different types of samples and different measures of hassles, have also found that everyday hassles are predictive of impaired mental and physical health (Pettit et al., 2010; Sher, 2003). Why would minor hassles be so troublesome? The answer isn't entirely clear yet. It may be because of the *cumulative* nature of stress (Seta, Seta, & McElroy, 2002). Stress adds up. Routine stresses at home, at school, and at work might be fairly benign individually. Yet collectively they could create great strain.

Appraisal: Stress Lies in the Eye of the Beholder

The experience of feeling stressed depends on what events one notices and how one chooses to appraise or interpret them (Monroe & Slavich, 2007; Semmer, McGrath, & Beehr, 2005). Events that are stressful for one person may be routine for another (Steptoe, 2007). For example, many people find flying in an airplane somewhat stressful, but frequent fliers may not be bothered at all. Some people enjoy the excitement of going out on a date with someone new; others find the uncertainty terrifying.

In discussing appraisals of stress, Lazarus and Folkman (1984) distinguish between primary and secondary appraisal. *Primary appraisal* is an initial evaluation of whether an event is (1) irrelevant to you, (2) relevant but not threatening or (3) stressful.

Courtesy of Anita Delongis

Anita Delongis is a health psychologist on faculty at the University of British Columbia. Her research focuses on stress, coping, and the role of social support.

When you view an event as stressful, you are likely to make a *secondary appraisal*, which is an evaluation of your coping resources and options for dealing with the stress. Thus, your primary appraisal would determine whether you saw an upcoming psychology exam as stressful. Your secondary appraisal would determine how stressful the exam appeared, in light of your assessment of your ability to deal with the event.

Often, people aren't very objective in their appraisals of potentially stressful events. A study of hospitalized patients awaiting surgery showed only a slight correlation between the objective seriousness of a person's upcoming surgery and the amount of fear experienced by the patients (Janis, 1958). Clearly, some people are more prone than others to feeling threatened by life's difficulties. A number of studies have shown that anxious, neurotic people report more stress than others (Cooper & Bright, 2001; Espejo et al., 2011), as do people who are relatively unhappy (Cacioppo et al., 2008). Thus, stress lies in the eye (actually, the mind) of the beholder. People's appraisals of stressful events are highly subjective. Questionnaires such as the *Stress Appraisal Measure* developed by the University of Toronto's Edward Peacock and Trent University's Paul Wong can be used to assess individual differences in such appraisals (Peacock & Wong, 1990).

Courtesy of Richard S. Lazarus

Richard Lazarus

"We developed the Hassle Scale because we think scales that measure major events miss the point. The constant, minor irritants may be much more important than the large, landmark changes."

An enormous variety of events can be stressful for one person or another. To achieve a better understanding of stress, theorists have tried to analyze the nature of stressful events and divide them into subtypes. One sensible distinction involves differentiating between *acute stressors and chronic stressors* (Dougall & Baum, 2001; Stowell, 2008). *Acute stressors* are threatening events that have a relatively short duration and a clear endpoint. Examples would include having an encounter with a belligerent drunk, dealing with the challenge of a major exam, or having your home threatened by severe flooding. *Chronic stressors* are threatening events that have a relatively long duration and no readily apparent time limit. Examples would include persistent financial strains produced by huge credit card debts, ongoing pressures from a hostile boss at work, or the demands of caring for a sick family member over a period of years.

None of the proposed schemes for classifying stressful events has turned out to be altogether satisfactory. Classifying stressful events into nonintersecting categories is virtually impossible. Although this problem presents conceptual headaches for researchers, it need not prevent us from describing four major types of stress: frustration, conflict, change, and pressure. As you read about each of them, you'll surely recognize some familiar adversaries.

Frustration 11f

As psychologists use the term, *frustration* occurs in any situation in which the pursuit of some goal is thwarted. In essence, you experience frustration when you want something and you can't have it. Everyone has to deal with frustration virtually every day. Such things as traffic jams, difficult daily commutes, and annoying drivers are routine sources of frustration that can elicit anger and aggression (Hennessy & Wiesenthal, 1999, 2004; Rasmussen, Knapp, & Garner, 2000; Wickens & Wiesenthal, 2005). Fortunately, most frustrations are brief and insignificant.

Of course, some frustrations can be sources of significant stress. Failures and losses are two common kinds of frustration that are often highly stressful. Everyone fails in at least some of his or her endeavours. Losses can be especially frustrating because people are deprived of something that they're accustomed to having. Think back to how

you felt the last time you lost your cell phone—how frustrating was that?

Conflict 11f

Like frustration, conflict is an unavoidable feature of everyday life. The perplexing question "Should I or shouldn't I?" comes up countless times in everyone's life. *Conflict* occurs when two or more incompatible motivations or behavioural impulses compete for expression. As we discussed in Chapter 12, Sigmund Freud proposed over a century ago that internal conflicts generate considerable psychological distress.

Conflicts come in three types, which were originally described by Kurt Lewin (1935) and investigated extensively by Neal Miller (1944, 1959). These three basic types of conflict—approach–approach, avoidance–avoidance, and approach–avoidance—are diagrammed in Figure 13.2.

In an *approach–approach conflict*, a choice must be made between two attractive goals. The problem, of course, is that you can choose just one of the two goals. For example: You have a free afternoon, so should you play tennis or racquetball?

Among the three kinds of conflict, the approach–approach type tends to be the least stressful. People

PREVIEW QUESTIONS

▶ What is frustration?
▶ What are the three types of conflict?
▶ Which types of conflict are especially stressful?
▶ What evidence led to the conclusion that life changes are stressful?
▶ What is pressure?

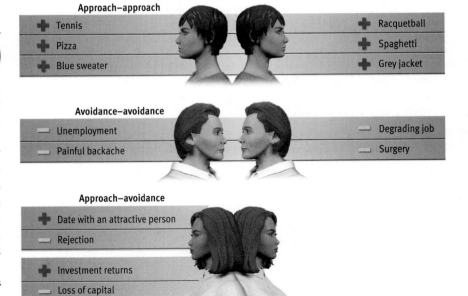

FIGURE 13.2

Types of conflict.

Psychologists have identified three basic types of conflict. In approach–approach and avoidance–avoidance conflicts, a person is torn between two goals. In an approach–avoidance conflict, there is only one goal under consideration, but it has both positive and negative aspects.

don't usually stagger out of restaurants exhausted by the stress of choosing which of several appealing entrées to eat. Approach–approach conflicts typically have a reasonably happy ending, whichever way you decide to go. Nonetheless, approach–approach conflicts over important issues may sometimes be troublesome. If you're torn between two appealing majors at university or two attractive boyfriends, you may find the decision-making process quite stressful, since whichever alternative is not chosen represents a loss of sorts.

In an *avoidance–avoidance conflict,* a choice must be made between two unattractive goals. Forced to choose between two repelling alternatives, you are, as they say, "caught between a rock and a hard place." For example, should you continue to collect unemployment cheques or should you take that degrading job at the car wash? Obviously, avoidance–avoidance conflicts are most unpleasant and highly stressful.

In an *approach–avoidance conflict,* a choice must be made about whether to pursue a single goal that has both attractive and unattractive aspects. For instance, imagine that you're offered a career promotion that will mean a large increase in pay, but you'll have to move to a city where you don't want to live. Approach–avoidance conflicts are common and can be quite stressful. Any time you have to take a risk to pursue some desirable outcome, you're likely to find yourself in an approach–avoidance conflict. Should you risk rejection by asking out a person that you are attracted to? Should you risk your savings by investing in a new business that could fail?

Approach–avoidance conflicts often produce *vacillation.* That is, you go back and forth, beset by indecision. You decide to go ahead, then you decide not to, and then you decide again to go ahead. Humans are not unique in this respect. Many years ago, Neal Miller (1944) observed the same vacillation in his groundbreaking research with rats. He created approach–avoidance conflicts in hungry rats by alternately feeding and shocking them at one end of a runway apparatus. Eventually, these rats tended to hover near the centre of the runway, alternately approaching and retreating from the goal box at the end of the runway.

Change 11f

It has been proposed that life changes, such as a change in marital status, divorce, for example, represent a key type of stress. *Life changes* are any noticeable alterations in one's living circumstances that require readjustment. The importance of life changes was first demonstrated by Thomas Holmes, Richard Rahe, and their colleagues in the 1960s (Holmes & Rahe, 1967; Rahe & Arthur, 1978). Theorizing that stress might make people more vulnerable to illness, they interviewed thousands of tuberculosis patients to find out what kinds of events had preceded the onset of their disease. Surprisingly, the most frequently cited events were not uniformly negative. There were plenty of aversive events, as expected, but there were also many seemingly positive events, such as getting married, having a baby, or getting promoted.

Why would positive events, such as moving to a nicer home, produce stress? According to Holmes and Rahe, it's because they produce *change.* In their view, changes in personal relationships, changes at work, changes in finances, and so forth can be stressful even when the changes are welcomed.

Based on this analysis, Holmes and Rahe (1967) developed the *Social Readjustment Rating Scale* (SRRS) to measure life change as a form of stress. The scale assigns numerical values to 43 major life events. These values are supposed to reflect the magnitude of the readjustment required by each change (see Table 13.1). In using the scale, respondents are asked to indicate how often they experienced any of these 43 events during a certain time period (typically, the past year). The numbers associated with each event checked are then added. This total is an index of the amount of change-related stress the person has recently experienced.

---

concept **check 13.1**

Identifying Types of Conflict

Check your understanding of the three basic types of conflict by identifying the type experienced in each of the following examples. The answers are in Appendix A.

Examples

_____ **1.** John can't decide whether to take a demeaning job in a car wash or to go on welfare.

_____ **2.** Desirée wants to apply to a highly selective law school, but she hates to risk the possibility of rejection.

_____ **3.** Vanessa has been shopping for a new car and is torn between a nifty little sports car and a classy sedan, both of which she really likes.

Types of Conflict

a. approach–approach
b. avoidance–avoidance
c. approach–avoidance

Life Event	Mean Value
Death of a spouse	100
Divorce	73
Marital separation	65
Jail term	63
Death of a close family member	63
Personal injury or illness	53
Marriage	50
Fired at work	47
Marital reconciliation	45
Retirement	45
Change in health of family member	44
Pregnancy	40
Sex difficulties	39
Gain of a new family member	39
Business readjustment	39
Change in financial state	38
Death of a close friend	37
Change to a different line of work	36
Change in number of arguments with spouse	35
Mortgage or loan for major purchase (home, etc.)	31
Foreclosure of mortgage or loan	30
Change in responsibilities at work	29
Son or daughter leaving home	29
Trouble with in-laws	29
Outstanding personal achievement	28
Spouse begins or stops work	26
Begin or end school	26
Change in living conditions	25
Revision of personal habits	24
Trouble with boss	23
Change in work hours or conditions	20
Change in residence	20
Change in school	20
Change in recreation	19
Change in church activities	19
Change in social activities	18
Mortgage or loan for lesser purchase (car, TV, etc.)	17
Change in sleeping habits	16
Change in number of family get-togethers	15
Change in eating habits	15
Vacation	13
Christmas	12
Minor violations of the law	11

TABLE 13.1

Social Readjustment Rating Scale

Source: Adapted from Holmes, T.H., & Rahe, R. (1967). The Social Readjustment Rating Scale. *Journal of Psychosomatic Research, 11*, 213–218. Copyright © 1967 by Elsevier Science Publishing Co. Reprinted by permission.

The SRRS and similar scales based on it have been used in thousands of studies by researchers all over the world (Dohrenwend, 2006). Overall, these studies have shown that people with higher scores on the SRRS tend to be more vulnerable to many kinds of physical illness and to many types of psychological problems as well (Derogatis & Coons, 1993; Scully, Tosi, & Banning, 2000; Surtees & Wainwright, 2007). These results have attracted a great deal of attention, and the SRRS has been reprinted in many popular newspapers and magazines. The attendant publicity has led to the widespread conclusion that life change is inherently stressful.

More recently, however, experts have criticized this research, citing problems with the methods used and raising questions about the meaning of the findings (Dohrenwend, 2006; Monroe, 2008; Wethington, 2007). At this point, it's a key interpretive issue that concerns us. Many critics have argued that the SRRS does not measure *change* exclusively. The main problem is that the list of life changes on the SRRS is dominated by events that are clearly negative or undesirable (death of a spouse, being fired from a job, and so on). These negative events probably generate great stress. Although there are some positive events on the scale, it turns out that negative life events cause most of the stress tapped by the SRRS (McLean & Link, 1994; Turner & Wheaton, 1995). Thus, it has become apparent that the SRRS assesses a wide range of stressful experiences, not just life change. At present, there's little reason to believe that change is inherently or inevitably stressful. Undoubtedly, some life changes may be quite challenging, but others may be quite benign.

Pressure 11f

At one time or another, most people have remarked that they're "under pressure." What does this mean? Sometimes the pressure comes from a mismatch between what we have to or want to do and the time available. In one survey, over half of the Canadians surveyed said they did not have enough time to both work and spend adequate time with their families. In addition, the survey found that the number of people who were identified as being severely time-stressed had increased between 1992 and 1998 (Statistics Canada, 1999b). This trend just seems to continue. According to the 2010 *Canadian Index of Wellbeing* (Brooker & Hyman, 2010), the number of Canadian adults who reported experiencing high levels of "time crunch" increased 16 percent from 1992 to 2005. People are working harder and longer at their jobs, with one recent survey of North Americans finding that one-third of workers surveyed indicated

Stress, Coping, and Health

that they had either fallen asleep at work or become extremely drowsy on the job (Nebenzahl 2010).

Of course, time pressure is only one type of pressure we face in our daily lives. More generally, *pressure* involves expectations or demands that one behave in a certain way. You are under pressure to *perform* when you're expected to execute tasks and responsibilities quickly, efficiently, and successfully. For example, salespeople are usually under pressure to move merchandise. Professors at research institutions are often under pressure to publish in prestigious journals. Stand-up comedians are under intense pressure to make people laugh. Pressures to *conform* to others' expectations are also common in our lives. People in the business world are expected to dress in certain ways. Suburban homeowners are expected to keep their lawns well manicured. Teenagers are expected to adhere to their parents' values and rules.

Although widely discussed by the general public, the concept of pressure has received scant attention from researchers. However, Weiten (1988b, 1998) has devised a scale to measure pressure as a form of life stress. It assesses self-imposed pressure, pressure from work and school, and pressure from family relationships, peer relationships, and intimate relationships. In research with this scale, a strong relationship has been found between pressure and a variety of psychological symptoms and problems. In fact, pressure has turned out to be more strongly related to measures of mental health than the SRRS and other established

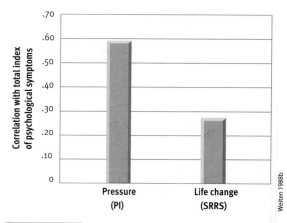

Weiten 1988b

FIGURE 13.3

Pressure and psychological symptoms.

A comparison of pressure and life change as sources of stress suggests that pressure may be more strongly related to mental health than change is. In one study, Weiten (1988b) found a correlation of 0.59 between scores on the *Pressure Inventory* (PI) and symptoms of psychological distress. In the same sample, the correlation between SRRS scores and psychological symptoms was only 0.28.

measures of stress are (see Figure 13.3). Moreover, a recent 15-year study of over 12 000 nurses found that increased pressure at work was related to an increased risk for heart disease (Vaananen, 2010). Participants who reported that their pressure at work was much too high were almost 50 percent more likely to develop heart disease than subjects who experienced normal levels of pressure.

concept **check 13.2**

Recognizing Sources of Stress

Check your understanding of the major sources of stress by indicating which type or types of stress are at work in each of the examples below. Bear in mind that the four basic types of stress are not mutually exclusive. There's some potential for overlap, so a specific experience might include both change and pressure, for instance. The answers are in Appendix A.

Examples

_____ **1.** Marie is late for an appointment but is stuck in line at the bank.

_____ **2.** Tamika decides that she won't be satisfied unless she gets straight As this year.

_____ **3.** José has just graduated from business school and has taken an exciting new job.

_____ **4.** Morris has just been fired from his job and needs to find another.

Types of stress

a. frustration
b. conflict

c. change
d. pressure

REVIEW OF KEY POINTS

▷ Stress involves circumstances and experiences that are perceived as threatening. Stress is a common, everyday event, and even seemingly minor stressors or hassles can be problematic. To a large degree, stress is subjective and lies in the eye of the beholder.

▷ Major types of stress include frustration, conflict, change, and pressure. Frustration occurs when an obstacle prevents one from attaining some goal.

▷ There are three principal types of conflict: approach–approach, avoidance–avoidance, and approach–avoidance. The third type is especially stressful. Vacillation is a common response to approach–avoidance conflict.

▷ A large number of studies using the SRRS suggest that change is stressful. Although this may be true, it is now clear that the SRRS is a measure of general stress rather than just change-related stress. Two kinds of pressure (to perform and to conform) also appear to be stressful.

Responding to Stress

People's response to stress is complex and multidimensional. You're driving home in heavy traffic and thinking about overdue papers, tuition increases, and parental pressures. Let's look at some of the reactions that were mentioned. When you groan in reaction to the traffic report, you're experiencing an *emotional response* to stress, in this case annoyance and anger. When your pulse quickens and your stomach knots up, you're exhibiting *physiological responses* to stress. When you shout insults at another driver, your verbal aggression is a *behavioural response* to the stress at hand. Thus, we can analyze a person's reactions to stress at three levels: (1) emotional responses, (2) physiological responses, and (3) behavioural responses. Figure 13.4 diagrams these three levels of response. It provides an overview of the stress process.

Emotional Responses 11g

When people are under stress, they often react emotionally. Studies that have tracked stress and mood on a daily basis have found intimate relationships between the two (Affleck et al., 1994; van Eck, Nicolson, & Berkhof, 1998).

Emotions Commonly Elicited 11g

No simple one-to-one connections have been found between certain types of stressful events and particular emotions. It may seem that our emotions go through phases during and after a stressful event. In

On May 16, 2011, fire swept through the town of Slave Lake, Alberta, forcing the evacuation of 7000 residents. With 40 percent of the town destroyed, returning residents had to deal with the trauma of losing all they owned. It may take considerable time to repair both the physical and the psychological damage caused by the fire.

commenting on people's reactions to the 2011 forest fire that destroyed much of the town of Slave Lake, Alberta, Alain Brunet, who was then chair of the Canadian Psychological Association Traumatic Stress Section, stated that it may only be after the threat is gone that we observe people's emotional reactions due to stress. At that point, "people start to think about what has happened. They start to count all the losses and that's when they typically break down" (Beilski, 2011, p. L1). What does research tell us about our emotional reactions after a stressful event?

Researchers *have* begun to uncover some strong links between *specific cognitive reactions to stress* (appraisals) and specific emotions (Smith & Lazarus, 1993). For example, self-blame tends to lead to guilt, helplessness to sadness, and so

PREVIEW QUESTIONS

► What are the roles of positive emotions and emotional arousal in response to stress?

► What are some of our physiological and behavioural responses to stress?

► Is there any adaptive value in giving up, aggression, and self-indulgence as coping responses?

► How do defence mechanisms work, and what is the nature of constructive coping?

Potentially stressful objective events
A major exam, a big date, trouble with one's boss, or a financial setback, which may lead to frustration, conflict, change, or pressure

Subjective cognitive appraisal
Personalized perceptions of threat, which are influenced by familiarity with the event, its controllability, its predictability, and so on

Emotional response
Annoyance, anger, anxiety, fear, dejection, grief

Physiological response
Autonomic arousal, hormonal fluctuations, neurochemical changes, and so on

Behavioural response
Coping efforts, such as lashing out at others, blaming oneself, seeking help, solving problems, and releasing emotions

FIGURE 13.4

Overview of the stress process.

A potentially stressful event, such as a major exam, elicits a subjective appraisal of how threatening the event is. If the event is viewed with alarm, the stress may trigger emotional, physiological, and behavioural reactions, as people's response to stress is multidimensional.

forth. Although many emotions can be evoked by stressful events, some are certainly more likely than others. Common emotional responses to stress include (a) annoyance, anger, and rage, (b) apprehension, anxiety, and fear, and (c) dejection, sadness, and grief (Lazarus, 1993; Woolfolk & Richardson, 1978).

Although investigators have tended to focus heavily on the connection between stress and negative emotions, research shows that positive emotions also occur during periods of stress (Finan, Zautra, & Wershba, 2011; Folkman, 2008). Although this finding seems counterintuitive, researchers have found that people experience a diverse array of pleasant emotions even while enduring dire circumstances. Consider, for example, a study that examined subjects' emotional functioning early in 2001 and again in the weeks following the 9/11 terrorist attacks in the United States (Fredrickson et al., 2003). Like most U.S. citizens, the participants reported many negative emotions in the aftermath of 9/11, including anger, sadness, and fear. However, within this "dense cloud of anguish," positive emotions also emerged. For example, people felt gratitude for the safety of their loved ones; many took stock and counted their blessings; and quite a few reported renewed love for their friends and family. Fredrickson et al. (2003) also found that the

frequency of pleasant emotions correlated positively with a measure of subjects' resilience, whereas the frequency of unpleasant emotions correlated negatively with resilience. Thus, contrary to common sense, positive emotions do *not* vanish during times of severe stress. Moreover, these positive emotions appear to play a key role in helping people bounce back from the difficulties associated with stress (Tugade & Fredrickson, 2004). How do positive emotions promote resilience in the face of stress? Barbara Fredrickson's (2001, 2005, 2006) *broaden-and-build theory of positive emotions* can shed light on this question. First, positive emotions alter people's mindsets, broadening their scope of attention, and increasing their creativity and flexibility in problem solving. Second, positive emotions can undo the lingering effects of negative emotions, and thus short-circuit the potentially damaging physiological responses to stress that we will discuss soon. Third, positive emotions can promote rewarding social interactions that help to build valuable social support, enhanced coping strategies, and other enduring personal resources.

Consistent with Fredrickson's model, recent research suggests that positive emotions widen people's scope of attention (Fredrickson & Branigan, 2005), promote healthy coping responses (Folkman, 2008), initiate upward spirals in emotional well-being (Burns et al., 2008), and facilitate flourishing mental health (Fredrickson & Losada, 2005). Studies have also found an association between positive emotion and lower levels of stress hormones (Steptoe et al., 2007) and reduced mortality in some populations (Pressman & Cohen, 2005).

One particularly interesting finding has been that a positive emotional style is associated with an enhanced immune response (Cohen & Pressman, 2006). Positive emotions also appear to be protective against heart disease (Davidson, Mostofsky, & Whang, 2010). These effects probably contribute to the recently discovered association between the tendency to report positive emotions and longevity (Ong, 2010; Xu & Roberts, 2010). Yes, people who experience a high level of positive emotions appear to live longer than others! One recent study exploring this association looked at photos of major league baseball players taken from the *Baseball Register* for 1952. The intensity of the players' smiles was used as a crude index of their tendency to experience positive emotions, which was then related to how long they lived. As you can see in Figure 13.5, players exhibiting full smiles (sometimes referred to as Duchenne smiles, which involve contraction of both zygomatic and orbicularis oculi muscles) showed longer life expectancy than did players with no smile or partial smiles. Thus, it appears that the benefits of

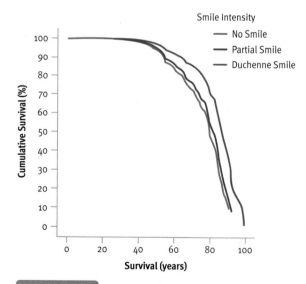

FIGURE 13.5

Percentage of Major League Baseball players surviving to a given age as a function of their smile intensity in photographs.

Each curve represents the probability as predicted by a particular behaviour: no smile, partial smile, or full smile. Greater smile intensity predicted greater longevity (Abel & Kruger, 2010).

Source: Abel, E.L. & Kruger, M.L. (2010). Smile intensity in photographs predicts longevity. *Psychological Science, February 26,* 542–544. Copyright © 2010, Association for Psychological Science.

Research has shown that smile intensity is linked to longevity in Major League Baseball players. This suggests that Toronto Blue Jays player and MLB 2010 home run king Jose Bautista pictured here should live a long and happy life.

positive emotions may be more diverse and more far-reaching than widely appreciated.

Effects of Emotional Arousal

11g

Emotional responses are a natural and normal part of life. Even unpleasant emotions serve important purposes. Like physical pain, painful emotions can serve as warnings that one needs to take action. However, strong emotional arousal can also interfere with efforts to cope with stress. For example, there is evidence that high emotional arousal can interfere with attention and memory retrieval and can impair

judgment and decision making (Janis, 1993; Lupien & Maheu, 2007; Mandler, 1993).

Although emotional arousal may hurt coping efforts, that isn't *necessarily* the case. The inverted-U hypothesis predicts that task performance should improve with increased emotional arousal—up to a point, after which further increases in arousal become disruptive and performance deteriorates (Anderson, 1990; Mandler, 1993). This idea is referred to as the *inverted-U hypothesis* because when performance is plotted as a function of arousal, the resulting graphs approximate an upside-down U (see Figure 13.6). In these graphs, the level of arousal at which performance peaks is characterized as the *optimal level of arousal* for a task.

This optimal level of arousal appears to depend in part on the complexity of the task at hand. The conventional wisdom is that *as a task becomes more complex, the optimal level of arousal (for peak performance) tends to decrease.* This relationship is depicted in Figure 13.6. As you can see, a fairly high level of arousal should be optimal on simple tasks (such as driving eight hours to help a friend in a crisis). However, performance should peak at a lower level of arousal on complex tasks (such as making a major decision in which you have to weigh many factors). Doubts have been raised about the validity of the inverted-U hypothesis (Hancock & Ganey, 2003). However, it does provide a plausible model of how emotional arousal could have either beneficial or disruptive effects on coping, depending on the nature of the stressful demands.

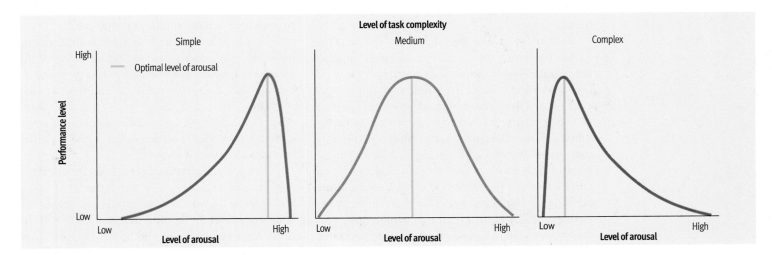

FIGURE 13.6

Emotional arousal and performance.

Graphs of the relationship between emotional arousal and task performance tend to resemble an inverted U, as increased arousal is associated with improved performance up to a point, after which higher arousal leads to poorer performance. The optimal level of arousal for a task depends on the complexity of the task. On complex tasks, a relatively low level of arousal tends to be optimal. On simple tasks, however, performance may peak at a much higher level of arousal.

Stress, Coping, and Health

As we just discussed, stress frequently elicits strong emotional responses. Now we'll look at the important physiological changes that often accompany these responses.

The Fight-or-Flight Response

Walter Cannon (1932) was one of the first theorists to describe the fight-or-flight response. The *fight-or-flight response* is a physiological reaction to threat in which the autonomic nervous system mobilizes the organism for attacking (fight) or fleeing (flight) an enemy. As you may recall from Chapter 3, the *autonomic nervous system (ANS)* controls blood vessels, smooth muscles, and glands. The fight-or-flight response is mediated by the *sympathetic division* of the ANS (McCarty, 2007). In one experiment, Cannon studied the fight-or-flight response in cats by confronting them with dogs. Among other things, he noticed an immediate acceleration in their breathing and heart rate and a reduction in their digestive processes.

The physiological arousal associated with the fight-or-flight response is also seen in humans. In a sense, this automatic reaction is a "leftover" from humanity's evolutionary past. It's clearly an adaptive response in the animal kingdom, where the threat of predators often requires a swift response of fighting or fleeing. But in our modern world, the fight-or-flight response may be less adaptive for human functioning than it was thousands of generations ago (Nesse, Bhatnagar, & Young, 2007). Most human stresses can't be handled simply through fight or flight.

Shelley Taylor and her colleagues (2000; 2006; Taylor & Master, 2011) have questioned whether the fight-or-flight model applies equally well to both males and females. They note that in most species, females have more responsibility for the care of young offspring than males do. Using an evolutionary perspective, they argue that this disparity may make fighting and fleeing less adaptive for females, as both responses may endanger offspring and thus reduce the likelihood of an animal passing on its genes. Taylor and her colleagues (Taylor, 2006; Taylor et al., 2000) maintain that evolutionary processes have fostered more of a "tend and befriend" response in females. According to this analysis, in reacting to stress, females allocate more effort to the care of offspring and to seeking help and support. More research is needed to evaluate this provocative analysis.

The General Adaptation Syndrome   11g   PSYKTREK

The concept of stress was identified and named by Hans Selye (1936, 1956, 1982). Selye was born in Vienna but came to Canada and began his professional career at McGill University in Montreal. He was also a professor and director of the Institute of Experimental Medicine and Surgery at the University of Montreal. Beginning in the 1930s, Selye exposed laboratory animals to a diverse array of both physical and psychological stressors (heat, cold, pain, mild shock, restraint, and so on). The patterns of physiological arousal seen in the animals were largely the same, regardless of the type of stress (Sapolsky, 1998). Thus, Selye concluded that stress reactions are *nonspecific*. In other words, he maintained that the reactions do not vary according to the specific type of stress encountered. Initially, Selye wasn't sure what to call this nonspecific response to a variety of noxious agents. In the 1940s, he decided to call it *stress,* and the word has been part of our vocabulary ever since (Russell, 2007).

Selye (1956, 1974) formulated an influential theory of stress reactions called the *general adaptation syndrome*. The *general adaptation syndrome* is a model of the body's stress response, consisting of three stages: alarm, resistance, and exhaustion. In the first stage of the general adaptation syndrome, an *alarm reaction* occurs when an organism first recognizes the existence of a threat. Physiological arousal occurs as the body musters its resources to combat the challenge. Selye's alarm reaction is essentially the fight-or-flight response originally described by Cannon.

However, Selye took his investigation of stress a few steps further by exposing laboratory animals to *prolonged* stress, similar to the chronic stress often endured by humans. As stress continues, the organism may progress to the second phase of the general adaptation syndrome, the *stage of resistance.* During this phase, physiological changes stabilize as coping efforts get under way. Typically, physiological arousal continues to be higher than normal, although it may level off somewhat as the organism becomes accustomed to the threat.

If the stress continues over a substantial period of time, the organism may enter the third stage, the *stage of exhaustion.* According to Selye, the body's resources for fighting stress are limited. If the stress can't be overcome, the body's resources may be depleted. Eventually, he thought the organism would experience hormonal exhaustion, although we now know that the crux of the problem is that chronic overactivation of the stress response can have damaging physiological effects on a variety of organ systems (Sapolsky, 2007). These harmful physiological effects can lead to what Selye called "diseases of adaptation."

In addition to being an internationally renowned scientist, Selye was a remarkable and accomplished person in other ways. He was fluent in eight languages and could converse in a total of 14 (Rosch, n.d.). Even though he is credited with introducing the term *stress*, Selye later said that perhaps the term *strain* would have been more appropriate. His work was known beyond the world of science, and the famous Spanish surrealist artist Salvador Dali created a painting for him to commemorate the Second International Symposium on the Management of Stress held in 1979. Selye was awarded the Companion of the Order of Canada in 1968, and in 1997, Hungary issued a Hans Selye stamp. In 1999, Canada Post also issued a Hans Selye stamp.

Brain–Body Pathways

11g

Even in cases of moderate stress, you may notice that your heart has started beating faster, you've begun to breathe harder, and you're perspiring more than usual. How does all this (and much more) happen?

It appears that there are two major pathways along which the brain sends signals to the endocrine system in response to stress (Dallman, Bhatnagar, & Viau, 2007; Felker & Hubbard, 1998; Tsigos, Kyrou, & Chrousos, 2005). As we noted in Chapter 3, the *endocrine system* consists of glands located at various sites in the body that secrete chemicals called *hormones*. The *hypothalamus* is the brain structure that appears to initiate action along these two pathways.

The first pathway (see Figure 13.7) is routed through the autonomic nervous system. In response to stress, your hypothalamus activates the sympathetic division of the ANS. A key part of this activation involves stimulating the central part of the adrenal glands (the adrenal medulla) to release large amounts of *catecholamines* into the bloodstream. These hormones radiate throughout your body, producing the physiological changes seen in the fight-or-flight response. The net result of catecholamine elevation is that your body is mobilized for action (Lundberg, 2007). Heart rate and blood flow increase, and more blood is pumped to your brain and muscles. Respiration and oxygen consumption speed up, which facilitates alertness. Digestive processes are inhibited to conserve your energy. The pupils of your eyes dilate, increasing visual sensitivity.

John Olson/Time Life Pictures/Getty Images

Hans Selye
"There are two main types of human beings: 'racehorses,' who thrive on stress and are only happy with a vigorous, fast-paced lifestyle, and 'turtles,' who in order to be happy require peace, quiet, and a generally tranquil environment."

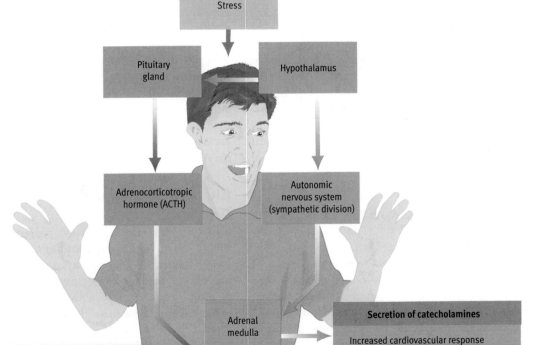

FIGURE 13.7

Brain–body pathways in stress.

In times of stress, the brain sends signals along two pathways. The pathway through the autonomic nervous system controls the release of catecholamine hormones that help mobilize the body for action. The pathway through the pituitary gland and the endocrine system controls the release of corticosteroid hormones that increase energy and ward off tissue inflammation.

Log on to CourseMate to access this interactive figure.

The second pathway involves more direct communication between the brain and the endocrine system (see Figure 13.7). The hypothalamus sends signals to the so-called *master gland* of the endocrine system, the pituitary. In turn, the pituitary secretes a hormone (ACTH) (Anisman & Merali, 1999) that stimulates the outer part of the adrenal glands (the adrenal cortex) to release another important set of hormones—*corticosteroids*. These hormones stimulate the release of chemicals that help increase your energy and help inhibit tissue inflammation in case of injury (Miller, Chen, & Zhou, 2007; Munck, 2007).

Recent research suggests that there may be sex differences in reactivity along both of these brain–body pathways. Evidence suggests that females' stress responses tend to be milder than males' stress reactions, at least from puberty through menopause (Kajantie & Phillips, 2006; Kudielka & Kirschbaum, 2005). The fact that this gender gap is found only between puberty and menopause suggests that females' higher levels of the hormone estrogen may play a key role in toning down women's physiological reactivity to stress. Some theorists speculate that this gender disparity in stress reactivity may contribute to the higher prevalence of cardiovascular disorders and certain other diseases in men (Kajantie, 2008).

An important new finding in research on stress and the brain is that stress can interfere with neurogenesis (McEwan, 2009; Mirescu & Gould, 2006). As you may recall from Chapter 3, scientists have recently discovered that the adult brain is capable of *neurogenesis*—the formation of new neurons, primarily in key areas in the hypothalamus. Neurogenesis appears to enhance learning and memory (see Chapter 7), and in Chapter 14 we will discuss evidence that suppressed neurogenesis may be a key cause of depression (Dranovsky & Hen, 2006). Thus, the capacity of stress to hinder neurogenesis may have important ramifications, which are currently the subject of intense research (Tanapat & Gould, 2007).

Behavioural Responses 11g PSYKTREK

Although people respond to stress at several levels, it's clear that *behaviour* is the crucial dimension of their reactions. Most behavioural responses to stress involve coping. *Coping* refers to active efforts to master, reduce, or tolerate the demands created by stress. Notice that this definition is neutral as to whether coping efforts are healthful or maladaptive. The popular use of the term often implies that coping is inherently healthful. When people say that someone "coped with her problems," the implication is that she handled them effectively.

In reality, however, coping responses may be adaptive or maladaptive (Folkman & Moskowitz, 2004; Kleinke, 2007). For example, if you were flunking a history course at midterm, you might cope with this stress by (1) increasing your study efforts, (2) seeking help from a tutor, (3) blaming your professor, or (4) giving up on the class without really trying. Clearly, the first two of these coping responses would be more adaptive than the last two. Thus, they may help or they may hurt, but coping tactics are the key determinant of whether stress leads to distress (Carver, 2007).

People cope with stress in many ways, but most individuals exhibit certain styles of coping that are fairly consistent across situations (Carver & Scheier, 1994; Heszen-Niejodek, 1997). York University's Norman S. Endler developed a model of coping based on the formulation that coping is a key aspect of personality, and that, as such, it is a stable, dispositional attribute (Endler, 1997). Along with Trent University's James Parker (whom we profiled in Chapter 9 for his work in emotional intelligence), Endler developed a measure designed to assess stable individual differences in coping (Endler & Parker, 1990). The *Coping Inventory for Stressful Situations* (CISS) measures three stable coping dimensions: task-oriented coping, emotion-oriented coping, and avoidance-oriented coping. We discussed Endler's views on the interactional nature of personality in Chapter 12. He was influenced in deciding to enter a career in psychology after taking Donald Hebb's course in psychology at McGill University.

Given the immense variety in coping strategies, we can highlight only a few of the more common patterns. In this section, we'll focus most of our attention on styles of coping that tend to be less than ideal. We'll discuss a variety of more healthful coping strategies in the Personal Application on stress management.

Giving Up and Blaming Oneself 11g PSYKTREK

When confronted with stress, people sometimes simply give up and withdraw from the battle. Some people routinely respond to stress with fatalism and resignation, passively accepting setbacks that might be dealt with effectively. This syndrome is referred to as *learned helplessness* (Seligman, 1974, 1992). *Learned helplessness* is passive behaviour produced by exposure to unavoidable aversive events. Learned helplessness seems to occur when individuals come to believe that events are beyond their control. As you might guess, giving up is not a highly regarded method of coping. Carver and his colleagues (Carver,

Scheier, & Weintraub, 1989; Carver et al., 1993) have studied this coping strategy, which they refer to as *behavioural disengagement,* and found that it is associated with increased rather than decreased distress. Furthermore, many studies suggest that learned helplessness can contribute to depression (Isaacowitz & Seligman, 2007).

Blaming oneself is another common response when people are confronted by stressful difficulties. The tendency to become highly self-critical in response to stress has been noted by a number of influential theorists. The late Albert Ellis (1973, 1987) called this phenomenon "catastrophic thinking." According to Ellis, catastrophic thinking causes, aggravates, and perpetuates emotional reactions to stress that are often problematic (see the Personal Application for this chapter). In a similar vein, Aaron Beck (1976, 1987) argues that negative self-talk can contribute to the development of depressive disorders (see Chapter 15). Although there is something to be said for recognizing one's weaknesses and taking responsibility for one's failures, Ellis and Beck agreed that excessive self-blame can be very unhealthy.

Striking Out at Others

People often respond to stressful events by striking out at others with aggressive behaviour. *Aggression is any behaviour that is intended to hurt someone, either physically or verbally.* Many years ago, a team of psychologists (Dollard et al., 1939) proposed the *frustration–aggression hypothesis,* which held that aggression is always caused by frustration. Decades of research have supported this idea of a causal link between frustration and aggression (Berkowitz, 1989). However, this research has also shown that there isn't an inevitable, one-to-one correspondence between frustration and aggression.

As we discussed in Chapter 12, this diversion of anger to a substitute target was noticed long ago by Sigmund Freud, who called it *displacement.* Unfortunately, research suggests that when people are provoked, displaced aggression is a common response (Hoobler & Brass, 2006; Marcus-Newhall et al., 2000).

Freud theorized that behaving aggressively could get pent-up emotion out of one's system and thus be adaptive. He coined the term *catharsis* to refer to this release of emotional tension. The Freudian notion that it's a good idea to vent anger has become widely disseminated and accepted in modern society. Books, magazines, and self-appointed experts routinely advise that it's healthy to "blow off steam." Doing so supposedly releases and reduces anger. However,

experimental research generally has *not* supported the catharsis hypothesis. Indeed, *most studies find just the opposite: Behaving in an aggressive manner tends to fuel more anger and aggression* (Bushman, 2002; Lohr et al., 2007).

Indulging Oneself

Stress sometimes leads to reduced impulse control, or *self-indulgence* (Tice, Bratslavsky, & Baumeister, 2001). When troubled by stress, many people engage in excessive consumption—unwise patterns of eating, drinking, smoking, using drugs, spending money, gambling, and so forth. It makes sense that when things are going poorly in one area of their lives, people may try to compensate by pursuing substitute forms of satisfaction. When this happens, self-indulgent responses tend to be relatively easy to execute and highly pleasurable. Thus, it's not surprising that studies have linked stress to increases in eating (O'Connor & Conner, 2011), smoking (McClernon & Gilbert, 2007), gambling (Wood & Griffiths, 2007), and consumption of alcohol and drugs (Grunberg, Berger, & Hamilton, 2011).

A recent study of gambling by Canadian adolescents conducted by members of McGill's renowned International Centre for Youth Gambling found that stress related to negative life events was associated with youth problem gambling (Bergevin et al., 2006). The results also indicated that problem gamblers used more maladaptive coping styles as compared to nongamblers in dealing with their stress. Severe gamblers were found to use less task-oriented coping and more avoidance-oriented coping strategies. Task-oriented coping is a more constructive form of coping than the tendency to avoid dealing with the stress-eliciting issue. We discuss constructive coping on page 611. According to the University of Calgary's David Hodgins (Hodgins, Stea, & Grant, 2011), problem gambling increasingly is viewed as a serious issue in Canada and across the world.

According to a study by Statistics Canada (2003d), problem gambling is increasingly becoming a problem in Canada. In that 2003 study, 1.2 million adult Canadians were identified as problem gamblers or as being at risk of becoming problem gamblers. In 2009, the net revenue from government-run lotteries, lottery terminals, casinos, and slot machines not in casinos was $13.75 billion (Statistics Canada, 2010). This figure doesn't even count all the other forms gambling can take. A 2005 nationwide survey of Canadian gambling problems found that the highest levels of problem gambling were in Manitoba and Saskatchewan, with Quebec and New Brunswick

Albert Ellis

"People largely disturb themselves by thinking in a self-defeating, illogical, and unrealistic manner."

Courtesy of Albert Ellis

WEB LINK 13.3

ProblemGambling.ca
Centre for Addiction and Mental Health

Youth Problem Gambling
McGill University: International Centre for Youth Gambling

reporting the lowest levels (Cox et al., 2005). According to data collected by the Centre for Addiction and Mental Health in Toronto, there are gender differences in problem gambling, with the rate of problem gambling for Canadian males being double that of females (*Facts about Adult Gambling*, 2008). While problem gambling undoubtedly has many causes, including the increasing accessibility of legal gambling venues in Canada, it seems clear that one important contributing factor is life stress and how people cope with their stress.

A relatively new manifestation of maladaptive coping with stress that has attracted much attention recently is the tendency to immerse oneself in the online world of the Internet. Kimberly Young (1996, 1998) has described a syndrome called *Internet addiction*, which consists of spending an inordinate amount of time on the Internet and inability to control online use. People who exhibit this syndrome tend to feel anxious, depressed, or empty when they are not online (Kandell, 1998). Their Internet use is so excessive, it begins to interfere with their functioning at work, at school, or at home, which leads them to start concealing the extent of their dependence on the Internet. Estimates of the prevalence of Internet addiction, which range from 1.5 percent to 8.2 percent of the population, vary considerably because the criteria of this new syndrome are still evolving (Weinstein & Lejoyeux, 2010). That said, it is clear that the syndrome is not rare. A recent study of Connecticut teens by Yale University's Timothy Liu concluded that one in 25 students showed evidence of what he defined as problematic Internet

Experts disagree about whether excessive Internet use should be characterized as an addiction, but the inability to control online activity appears to be an increasingly common syndrome that illustrates the coping strategy of indulging oneself.

use (Lui et al., 2011). There is, of course, active debate about the wisdom of characterizing excessive Internet surfing as an *addiction* (Czincz & Hechanova, 2009; Pies, 2009). Yet it's clear that this new coping strategy is creating very real problems for at least a portion of Internet users (Morahan-Martin, 2007).

Defensive Coping 10a   11g

Many people exhibit consistent styles of defensive coping in response to stress (Vaillant, 1994). We noted in Chapter 12 that Sigmund Freud originally developed the concept of the *defence mechanism*. Although rooted in the psychoanalytic tradition, this concept has gained widespread acceptance from psychologists of most persuasions (Cramer, 2000). Building on Freud's initial insights, modern psychologists have broadened the scope of the concept and added to Freud's list of defence mechanisms.

Defence mechanisms are largely unconscious reactions that protect a person from unpleasant emotions such as anxiety and guilt. Many specific defence mechanisms have been identified. For example, Laughlin (1979) lists 49 different defences. We also described seven common defence mechanisms in our discussion of Freud's theory in Chapter 12. Table 13.2 introduces another five defences that people use with some regularity. Although widely discussed in the popular press, defence mechanisms are often misunderstood. To clear up some of the misconceptions, we'll use a question/answer format to elaborate on the nature of defence mechanisms.

What exactly do defence mechanisms defend against? Above all else, defence mechanisms shield the individual from the emotional discomfort that's so often elicited by stress. Their main purpose is to ward off unwelcome emotions or to reduce their intensity. Foremost among the emotions guarded against is *anxiety*. Defences are also used to suppress dangerous feelings of *anger* so that they don't explode into acts of aggression. *Guilt* and *dejection* are two other emotions that people often try to evade through defensive manoeuvres.

How do they work? Through *self-deception*. Defence mechanisms accomplish their goals by distorting reality so that it doesn't appear so threatening (Aldwin, 2007). For example, suppose you're not doing well in school and you're in danger of flunking out. Initially you might use *denial* to block awareness of the possibility that you could flunk. This defence might temporarily fend off feelings of anxiety. If it becomes difficult to deny the obvious, you could resort to *fantasy*. You might daydream about how you'll salvage adequate grades by getting spectacular

Rob Melnychuk/PhotoDisc/Getty Images

TABLE 13.2

Additional Defence Mechanisms

Source: Adapted from Carson, R.C., Butcher, J.N., and Coleman, J.C. (1988). *Abnormal psychology and modern life.* Glenview, IL: Scott, Foresman and Company. Adapted by permission of the publisher.

Mechanism	Description	Example
Denial of reality	Protecting oneself from unpleasant reality by refusing to perceive or face it	A smoker concludes that the evidence linking cigarette use to health problems is scientifically worthless.
Fantasy	Gratifying frustrated desires by imaginary achievements	A socially inept and inhibited young man imagines himself chosen by a group of women to provide them with sexual satisfaction.
Intellectualization (isolation)	Cutting off emotion from hurtful situations or separating incompatible attitudes so that they appear unrelated	A prisoner on death row awaiting execution resists appeal on his behalf and coldly insists that the letter of the law be followed.
Undoing	Atoning for or trying to magically dispel unacceptable desires or acts	A teenager who feels guilty about masturbation ritually touches door knobs a prescribed number of times following each occurrence of the act.
Overcompensation	Covering up felt weakness by emphasizing some desirable characteristics, or making up for frustration in one area by overgratification in another	A dangerously overweight woman goes on eating binges when she feels neglected by her husband.

scores on the upcoming final exams, when the objective fact is that you're hopelessly behind in your studies. Thus, defence mechanisms work their magic by bending reality in self-serving ways. Defence mechanisms may operate at varying levels of awareness, although they're largely unconscious (Cramer, 2001; Erdelyi, 2001).

Are they healthy? This is a much more complicated question. More often than not, the answer is "no." Generally, defensive coping is less than optimal for a number of reasons. First, defensive coping is an avoidance strategy, and avoidance rarely provides a genuine solution to problems (Holahan et al., 2005).

Although defensive behaviour tends to be relatively unhealthful, Shelley Taylor and Jonathon Brown (1988, 1994) have reviewed several lines of evidence suggesting that "positive illusions" may be adaptive for mental health and well-being (Taylor et al., 2003). First, they note that "normal" people tend to have overly favourable self-images. In contrast, depressed subjects exhibit less favourable—but more realistic—self-concepts. Second, normal subjects overestimate the degree to which they control chance events. In comparison, depressed subjects are less prone to this illusion of control. Third, normal individuals are more likely than depressed subjects to display unrealistic optimism in making projections about the future. A variety of studies have provided support for the hypothesis that positive illusions can promote well-being (Segerstrom & Roach, 2008; Taylor, 2011; Taylor et al., 2003).

The findings on whether positive illusions are healthy are contradictory and controversial (Asendorpf & Ostendorf, 1998; Colvin, Block, & Funder, 1995), so it is hard to make sweeping generalizations about the adaptive value of self-deception. Roy Baumeister (1989) theorizes that it's all a matter of degree and that there is an "optimal margin of illusion." According to Baumeister, extreme distortions of reality are maladaptive, but small illusions are often beneficial.

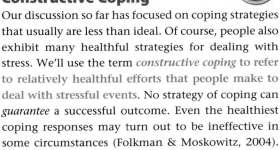

Constructive Coping

Our discussion so far has focused on coping strategies that usually are less than ideal. Of course, people also exhibit many healthful strategies for dealing with stress. We'll use the term *constructive coping* to refer to relatively healthful efforts that people make to deal with stressful events. No strategy of coping can *guarantee* a successful outcome. Even the healthiest coping responses may turn out to be ineffective in some circumstances (Folkman & Moskowitz, 2004). Thus, the concept of constructive coping is simply meant to connote a healthful, positive approach, without promising success.

What makes certain coping strategies constructive? Frankly, it's a grey area in which psychologists' opinions vary to some extent. Nonetheless, a consensus about the nature of constructive coping has emerged from the sizable literature on stress management. Key themes in this literature include the following:

1. Constructive coping involves confronting problems directly. It is task-relevant and action-oriented. It entails a conscious effort to rationally evaluate your options so that you can try to solve your problems.

2. Constructive coping is based on reasonably realistic appraisals of your stress and coping resources. A little self-deception may sometimes be adaptive, but excessive self-deception and highly unrealistic negative thinking are not.

3. Constructive coping involves learning to recognize, and in some cases regulate, potentially disruptive emotional reactions to stress.

Courtesy of Shelley Taylor

Shelley Taylor

"Rather than perceiving themselves, the world, and the future accurately, most people regard themselves, their circumstances, and the future as considerably more positive than is objectively likely.... These illusions are not merely characteristic of human thought; they appear actually to be adaptive, promoting rather than undermining good mental health."

These principles provide a rather general and abstract picture of constructive coping. We'll look at patterns of constructive coping in more detail in the Personal Application, which discusses various stress management strategies that people can use.

concept **check** 13.3

Identifying More Defence Mechanisms

In the last chapter, you checked your understanding of several defence mechanisms by identifying instances of them in a story. In this chapter, you've learned about five additional defence mechanisms that are sometimes used as ways of coping with stress. Check your understanding of these defence mechanisms by identifying them in the story below. Each example of a defence mechanism is underlined, with a number next to it. Write the name of the defence mechanism exemplified in each case in the numbered spaces after the story. The answers are in Appendix A.

The guys at work have been trying to break it to me gently that they think my job's on the line because I've missed work too many days this year. I don't know how they came up with that idea; <u>I've got nothing to worry about.</u> (1.) Besides, every day I missed, <u>I always did a lot of cleaning up and other chores around the house here.</u> (2.) One of these days, <u>the boss will finally recognize how really valuable I am to the company, and I'll be getting a big promotion.</u> (3.) Anyway, since the guys have been dropping these hints about my not missing any more days, <u>I've been trying really hard to make a good impression by saying "Hi" to everyone I see, especially the boss, and telling jokes.</u> (4.) You know, <u>it's really pretty interesting to observe how all these relationships unfold between guys who work together and the people who manage them.</u> (5.)

1. _____
2. _____
3. _____
4. _____
5. _____

REVIEW OF KEY POINTS

▶ Stress often triggers emotional reactions. These reactions typically include anger, fear, and sadness. In times of stress, emotions are not uniformly negative and positive emotions may foster resilience. Emotional arousal may interfere with coping. According to the inverted-U hypothesis, task performance improves with increased arousal up to a point and then declines. The optimal level of arousal on a task depends on the complexity of the task.

▶ Physiological arousal in response to stress was originally called the *fight-or-flight response* by Cannon. This automatic response has limited adaptive value in our modern world. Selye's general adaptation syndrome describes three stages in physiological reactions to stress: alarm, resistance, and exhaustion. Diseases of adaptation may appear during the stage of exhaustion.

▶ There are two major pathways along which the brain sends signals to the endocrine system in response to stress. The first pathway releases a class of hormones called *catecholamines*. The second pathway releases a class of hormones called *corticosteroids*.

▶ The behavioural response to stress takes the form of coping. Some relatively unhealthy coping responses include giving up, blaming oneself, and striking out at others with acts of aggression. Self-indulgence is another coping pattern that tends to be of limited value.

▶ Defensive coping is quite common. Defence mechanisms protect against emotional distress through self-deception. Several lines of evidence suggest that positive illusions may be healthful, but there is some debate about the matter. It is probably a matter of degree. Relatively healthful coping tactics are called *constructive coping*.

The Effects of Stress on Psychological Functioning

PREVIEW QUESTIONS

▶ Can stress interfere with task performance?

▶ What is burnout, and what are its causes?

▶ What is post-traumatic stress disorder (PTSD), and how common is it?

▶ What kinds of experiences cause PTSD?

▶ What other psychological problems and mental disorders are stress-related?

People struggle with many stresses every day. Most stresses come and go without leaving any enduring imprint. However, when stress is severe or when many stressful demands pile up, one's psychological functioning may be affected.

Research on the effects of stress has focused mainly on negative outcomes, so our coverage is slanted in that direction. However, it's important to emphasize that stress is not inherently bad. You would probably suffocate from boredom if you lived a stress-free existence. Stress makes life challenging and interesting. Along the way, though, stress can be harrowing, sometimes leading to impairments in performance, to burnout, and to other problems.

Impaired Task Performance

Frequently, stress takes its toll on the ability to perform effectively on a task at hand. For instance, Roy Baumeister's work shows how pressure can interfere with performance. Baumeister's (1984) theory assumes that pressure to perform often makes people self-conscious and that this elevated self-consciousness disrupts their attention. He found support for his theory in a series of laboratory experiments in which he manipulated the pressure to perform well on a simple perceptual-motor task and found that many people tend to "choke" under pressure (Butler & Baumeister, 1998; Wallace, Baumeister, & Vohs, 2005). His theory has also received some support in studies of the past performance of professional sports teams (Baumeister, 1995; Baumeister & Steinhilber, 1984). Pressure-induced performance decrements have also been found in studies of mathematical problem-solving and simple sports tasks (Beilock, 2010, 2008; Beilock & Gonso, 2008).

Other research suggests that Baumeister is on the right track in looking to *attention* to explain how stress impairs task performance. According to Beilock (2010), choking under pressure tends to occur when worries about performance distract attention from the task at hand and use up one's limited working memory capacity. Consistent with this analysis, a recent study found that chronic stress (preparing for difficult and hugely important medical board exams) undermined participants' performance on a task requiring attention shifts (Liston, McEwen, & Casey, 2009). Moreover, using fMRI scans, the investigators were able to pinpoint diminished activity in the prefrontal cortex as the underlying basis for subjects' impaired attentional control. Fortunately, these effects were short-lived. One month after the medical board exams, when participants' stress levels were back to normal, their attention was unimpaired.

Even though we have all had the experience of choking, especially on those all too important final exams, all is not lost. There is some evidence that our nervousness and stress in such a situation can be overcome by writing about our fears just before the exam. A study by Beilock and her colleagues showed that students, especially those who are typically test-anxious, could improve their grades through this simple technique. According to Beilock, "its as though the writing exercise helps them unload their angst so that they can focus all their attention on the test" (Taylor, 2011).

Burnout

Burnout is an overused buzzword that means different things to different people. Nonetheless, a few researchers, including Acadia University's Michael Leiter, have described burnout in a systematic way that has facilitated scientific study of the syndrome (Maslach & Leiter, 1997; Maslach & Leiter, 2007). *Burnout involves physical and emotional exhaustion, cynicism, and a lowered sense of self-efficacy that can be brought on gradually by chronic work-related stress.* Exhaustion, which is central to burnout, includes chronic fatigue, weakness, and low energy. Cynicism is manifested in highly negative attitudes toward oneself, one's work, and life in general. Reduced self-efficacy involves declining feelings of competence at work, which give way to feelings of hopelessness and helplessness.

Burnout causes problems for both employers and employees. As you might expect, burnout is associated with increased absenteeism and reduced productivity at work, as well as increased vulnerability to a variety of health problems (Maslach & Leiter, 2000). Recent studies by Statistics Canada (2006c, 2007f) found that Canadians with high-stress jobs were much more likely to take disability days off work, to report lower work activity because of the

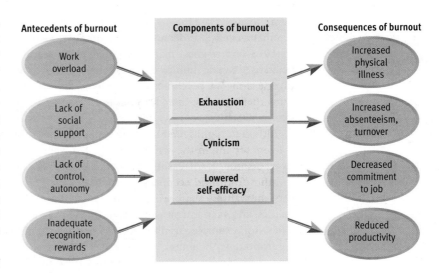

Antecedents of burnout — Work overload; Lack of social support; Lack of control, autonomy; Inadequate recognition, rewards

Components of burnout — Exhaustion; Cynicism; Lowered self-efficacy

Consequences of burnout — Increased physical illness; Increased absenteeism, turnover; Decreased commitment to job; Reduced productivity

FIGURE 13.8

The antecedents, components, and consequences of burnout.
Christina Maslach and Michael Leiter developed a systematic model of burnout that specifies the antecedents, components, and consequences of burnout. The antecedents on the left in the diagram are the stressful features of the work environment that cause burnout. The burnout syndrome itself consists of the three components shown in the centre of the diagram. Some of the unfortunate results of burnout are listed on the right. (Based on Leiter & Maslach, 2001)

stress, to report health-related work problems, and to experience stress-related depressive episodes.

What causes burnout? Factors in the workplace that appear to promote burnout include work overload, struggling with interpersonal conflicts at work, lack of control over work responsibilities and outcomes, and inadequate recognition for one's work (Leiter & Maslach, 2001; Maslach & Leiter, 2005; see Figure 13.8). One study by Statistics Canada (2003c) revealed a set of factors reported by Canadian workers that served as sources of workplace stress. One-third of respondents cited too many demands or work hours as the major source of stress. Other important sources of workplace stress included fear of job loss (13 percent), poor interpersonal relationships at work (15 percent), and risk of injury (13 percent). The latter source was most commonly reported by workers on rotating shifts (you may recall that we discussed some of the difficulties faced by shift workers in Chapter 5). Burnout is a potential problem in a wide variety of occupations (Lee & Ashforth, 1996). Decades of research have shown that burnout is found all over the world in a wide variety of cultures (Schaufeli, Leiter, & Maslach, 2009).

Post-Traumatic Stress Disorder

Extremely stressful, traumatic incidents can leave a lasting imprint on victims' psychological functioning. *Post-traumatic stress disorder (PTSD) involves enduring psychological disturbance attributed to the experience of a major traumatic event.* Researchers

WEB LINK 13.4

Canadian Mental Health Association
This CMHA site offers numerous resources devoted to psychological disorders. Included is information on PTSD, its signs, origins, and treatment.

WEB LINK 13.5

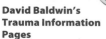

Disaster Psychiatry
In light of the traumatic terrorist attacks on 9/11 and their aftermath, the importance of first-rate information about how to respond to disasters is obvious. This site, maintained by the American Psychiatric Association, provides many valuable insights and links related to professional assistance at times of major emergencies.

WEB LINK 13.6

David Baldwin's Trauma Information Pages
This site has long been recognized as the premier repository for Web-based and other resources relating to emotional trauma, traumatic stress, and post-traumatic stress disorder. Psychologist David Baldwin has assembled more than 1000 links to information about these issues.

began to appreciate the frequency and severity of post-traumatic stress disorder after the Vietnam War ended in 1975 and a great many psychologically scarred veterans returned home. These veterans displayed a diverse array of psychological problems and symptoms that in many cases lingered much longer than expected (Schlenger et al., 1992).

Although highlighted in the context of American soldiers serving in the Vietnam War, post-traumatic stress disorder is increasingly associated with people in other front-line occupations, such as police officers, firefighters, ambulance attendants and paramedics, and even transit workers. In Canada's largest cities, for example, transit workers are frequently confronted with abuse and this has been associated with an increasing frequency of diagnosed cases of PTSD. In Toronto, for instance, the rate of driver PTSD doubled from 2006 to 2008 (Bruser, 2008). Concerns have also been noted regarding the increasing rates of PTSD in Canada's law enforcement agencies, including municipal and provincial police and the RCMP. Accurate statistics can sometimes be difficult to find since, according to Cheryl Regehr of the University of Toronto, many law enforcement officers feel that there is still a stigma associated with acknowledging such problems (Mason, 2008; Regehr & Bober, 2005).

PTSD is not restricted to individuals who work in these types of occupations. It can happen to anyone who suffers trauma; it has been associated with other types of events including rape, assault, witnessing a death, and so on. Unfortunately, traumatic events such as these appear to be much more common than widely assumed. A survey conducted by Murray Stein and his colleagues (Stein et al, 1997b), including University of Manitoba researcher Andrea Hazen, assessed the frequency of experience of various traumatic events (see Figure 13.9).

The effects on participants and witnesses in dramatic events can be long-lasting. You may remember hearing or reading about the shooting of students at Montreal's Dawson College in September 2006. Kimveer Gill entered the school and began shooting students, killing one student and injuring 19 others. The students and staff at the college had more than their physical wounds to deal with. Even though significant medical and psychological resources were devoted to the college, a follow-up study indicated that even 18 months after the incident, the students and staff at the college were 1.5 times more likely than average to be suicidal, 8 percent of them showed signs of significant residual stress, and they had double the expected rate of serious psychological disorders including PTSD and depression (Pereaux, L., 2010; Project Dawson, 2010). This was Montreal's third school shooting, after the horrific events at École Polytechnique in 1989 and the shootings at Concordia University in 1992.

Psychological Problems and Disorders

On the basis of clinical impressions, psychologists have long suspected that chronic stress might contribute to many types of psychological problems and mental disorders. Since the late 1960s, advances in the measurement of stress have allowed researchers to verify these suspicions in empirical studies. When

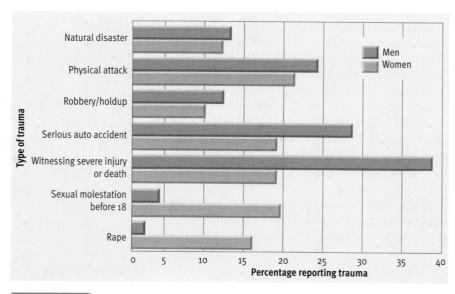

Research suggests that the victims of Kimveer Gill's shooting rampage at Montreal's Dawson College are still suffering the psychological effects of the trauma years after the September 13, 2006, tragedy.

FIGURE 13.9

The prevalence of traumatic events.
We tend to think that traumatic events are relatively unusual and infrequent, but research by Stein et al. (1997b) suggests otherwise. They interviewed over 1000 people in Winnipeg, and found that 74.2 percent of the women and 81.3 percent of the men reported experiencing at least one highly traumatic event. The percentage of respondents reporting specific types of traumatic events are summarized in this graph. (Based on data from Stein et al., 1997b)

it comes to common psychological problems, studies indicate that stress may contribute to poor academic performance (Akgun & Ciarrochi, 2003), insomnia and other sleep disturbances (Bernert et al., 2007; Kim & Dimsdale, 2007), sexual difficulties (Bodenmann et al., 2006), alcohol abuse (Sayette, 2007), and drug abuse (Grunberg, Berger, & Hamilton, 2011).

Above and beyond these everyday problems, research reveals that stress often contributes to the onset of full-fledged psychological disorders. In addition to PTSD, such disorders include depression (Monroe & Reid, 2009), schizophrenia (Walker, Mittal, & Tessner, 2008), and anxiety disorders (Beidel & Stipelman, 2007). We'll discuss these relationships between stress and mental disorders in detail in Chapter 14. Of course, stress is only one of many factors that may contribute to psychological disorders. Nonetheless, it's sobering to realize that stress can have a dramatic impact on one's mental health.

Positive Effects

The effects of stress are not entirely negative. Recent years have brought increased interest in the positive aspects of the stress process, including favourable outcomes that follow in the wake of stress (Folkman & Moskowitz, 2000). To some extent, the new focus on the possible benefits of stress reflects a new emphasis on "positive psychology." As we noted in Chapter 10, some theorists have argued that the field of psychology has historically devoted too much attention to pathology and suffering (Seligman & Csikszentmihalyi, 2000). The advocates of positive psychology argue for increased research on well-being, hope, courage, perseverance, tolerance, and other human strengths and virtues (Seligman, 2003). One of these strengths is *resilience* in the face of stress. *Resilience* refers to successful adaptation to significant stress and trauma, as evidenced by a lack of serious negative outcomes. Resilience used to be viewed as highly unusual, perhaps even rare. However, George Bonanno (2005) and his colleagues (Bonanno et al., 2002, 2005), have studied the long-term effects of serious traumatic events, such as bereavement and exposure to combat and terrorism. They have found that resilience is seen in as many as 35 percent to 55 percent of people. Admittedly, a great many people do experience lasting ill effects from traumatic stress, but resilience may not be the rare exception it was once believed to be. Recent work has even applied the idea of enhancing resilience to the military context (Cornum, Matthews, & Seligman, 2011).

Recent research on resilience suggests that stress can promote personal growth or self-improvement

Major disasters such as the 1998 ice storm in central and eastern Canada are among the types of calamitous events that can lead to post-traumatic stress disorder.

(Calhoun & Tedeschi, 2006, 2008). For example, studies of people grappling with major health problems show that the majority of respondents report that they derived benefits from their adversity (Tennen & Affleck, 1999). Stressful events sometimes force people to develop new skills, re-evaluate priorities, learn new insights, and acquire new strengths. In other words, the adaptation process initiated by stress may lead to personal changes that are changes for the better. Confronting and conquering a stressful challenge may lead to improvements in specific coping abilities and reduced reactivity to future stressful events (Bower, Moskowitz, & Epel, 2009). Thus, researchers have begun to explore the growth potential of stressful events (Helgeson, Reynolds, & Tomich, 2006; Park & Fenster, 2004).

REVIEW OF KEY POINTS

▷ Several lines of research, including Baumeister's work on choking under pressure, suggest that stress can interfere with task performance. Burnout involves exhaustion, cynicism, and lowered self-efficacy as a result of chronic work-related stress.

▷ Post-traumatic stress disorder is evidenced by psychological disturbances that surface in the aftermath of a major stressful event. PTSD appears to be fairly common and can be caused by a diverse array of traumatic experiences, ranging from auto accidents to natural disasters.

▷ Stress can contribute to a host of common problems, such as poor academic performance, insomnia, and sexual difficulties. Stress has also been related to the development of various psychological disorders, including depression, schizophrenia, anxiety disorders, and eating disorders. Research on the effects of stress traditionally has concentrated on negative outcomes, but positive effects may also occur and are currently the focus of some research.

The Effects of Stress on Physical Health

PREVIEW QUESTIONS

▶ What is the Type A personality, and how is hostility related to heart disease?

▶ Can stress trigger emotional reactions that cause heart attacks?

▶ How is depression related to heart disease?

▶ How does stress affect immune function and vulnerability to the common cold?

▶ How strong is the association between stress and illness?

The effects of stress are not limited to mental health. Stress can also have an impact on one's physical health. For example, a recent report on the social determinants of health in Canada identified stress as one of the mediators of the link between poverty, poor living conditions, and health problems (Mikkonen & Raphael, 2010). The authors of the report concluded that "continuous stress weakens the resistance to diseases and disrupts the functioning of the hormonal and metabolic systems" (p. 10). Data collected by Statistics Canada (2004c) found that adults who had suffered high stress in 1994–1995 had a higher probability of developing a number of illnesses by 2000–2001. Some of the chronic conditions implicated were arthritis, emphysema, ulcers, back problems, heart disease in males, and asthma and migraines in females.

The idea that stress can contribute to physical ailments is not entirely new. Evidence that stress can cause physical illness began to accumulate back in the 1930s. By the 1950s, the concept of *psychosomatic diseases* was widely accepted. *Psychosomatic diseases* were genuine physical ailments that were thought to be caused in part by stress and other psychological factors. The classic psychosomatic illnesses were high blood pressure, peptic ulcers, asthma, skin disorders such as eczema and hives, and migraine and tension headaches (Kaplan, 1989; Rogers, Fricchione, & Reich, 1999). Note, however, these diseases were not regarded as *imagined* physical ailments. The term *psychosomatic* has often been misused to refer to physical ailments that are "all in one's head," but that is an entirely different syndrome. Rather, psychosomatic diseases were viewed as *authentic* organic maladies that were heavily stress-related.

Since the 1970s, the concept of psychosomatic disease has gradually fallen into disuse because research has shown that stress can contribute to the development of a diverse array of other diseases previously believed to be purely physiological in origin (Dimsdale et al., 2005; Dougall & Baum, 2001). As a result, it has become apparent that there is nothing unique about psychosomatic diseases that requires a special category. Modern evidence continues to demonstrate that the classic psychosomatic diseases are influenced by stress, but as you will see, so are a host of other diseases (Levenson et al., 1999). In this section, we'll look at the evidence on the apparent link between stress and physical illness, beginning with heart disease.

Type A Personality, Hostility, and Heart Disease

Heart disease is one of the leading causes of death in North America. In Canada, by 1997, heart disease was second (a very close second) only to cancer (Statistics Canada, n.d.). *Coronary heart disease* involves a reduction in blood flow in the coronary arteries, which supply the heart with blood. This type of heart disease accounts for about 90 percent of heart-related deaths.

Atherosclerosis is the principal cause of coronary heart disease. This condition is characterized by a gradual narrowing of the coronary arteries (Chrousos & Kaltsas, 2007). Established risk factors for atherosclerosis include older age, smoking, lack of exercise, high cholesterol levels, and high blood pressure (Bekkouche et al., 2011). Recently, attention has shifted to the possibility that inflammation may contribute to atherosclerosis and elevated coronary risk (Miller & Blackwell, 2006). Evidence is mounting that inflammation plays a key role in the initiation and progression of atherosclerosis. It also may play a role in the acute complications that trigger heart attacks (Nabi et al., 2008).

Research on the relationship between *psychological* factors and heart attacks began in the 1960s and 1970s. A pair of cardiologists, Meyer Friedman and Ray Rosenman (1974), discovered an apparent connection between coronary risk and a syndrome they called the *Type A personality,* which involves self-imposed stress and intense reactions to stress (Shaw & Dimsdale, 2007). The *Type A personality* includes three elements: (1) a strong competitive orientation, (2) impatience and time urgency, and (3) anger and hostility. Type As are ambitious, hard-driving perfectionists who are exceedingly time-conscious. They routinely try to do several things at once. They fidget over the briefest delays. Often they are highly competitive, achievement-oriented workaholics who drive themselves with many deadlines. They are easily irritated and are quick to anger. In contrast, the *Type B personality* is marked by relatively relaxed, patient, easygoing, amicable behaviour. Type Bs are less hurried, less competitive, and less easily angered than Type As.

The characteristics associated with a Type A personality have been used as one explanation for results consistent with Stewart McCann's *precocity–longevity hypothesis* (McCann, 2001, 2003). McCann, who is at Cape Breton University, has analyzed the careers of politicians, actors, and scientists in support of his hypothesis. The precocity–longevity hypothesis suggests that factors associated with early peaks and success in an individual's career achievement may be the very factors that set the conditions for the early death of those who have this early success. He found, for example, in an analysis of 1672 U.S. state governors who served between the years of 1789 and 1978, that those who were elected at younger ages also died earlier. The same is true of Nobel Prize winners and those who win Academy Awards at younger ages.

One explanation offered by McCann (2001, 2003) for this connection between age of success and age at death refers to the Type A behaviour pattern. While Type As, because of their orientation toward work and stress, may experience early career success, these very characteristics have been hypothesized to lead to stress-related health problems such as heart attacks, leading to premature death. Work continues on the precocity–longevity hypothesis in an attempt to provide evidence for this and other possible explanations.

Decades of research uncovered a tantalizingly modest correlation between Type A behaviour and increased coronary risk. More often than not, studies found an association between Type A personality and an elevated incidence of heart disease, but the findings were not as strong or as consistent as expected (Baker, Suchday, & Krantz, 2007; Myrtek, 2007). Recently, researchers have found an even stronger link between personality and coronary risk by focusing on a specific component of the Type A personality—*anger and hostility* (Chida & Steptoe, 2009; Powell & Williams, 2007). For example, in one study of almost 13 000 men and women who had no prior history of heart disease (Williams et al., 2000), investigators found an elevated incidence of heart attacks among participants who exhibited an angry temperament. The participants, who were followed for a median period of 4.5 years, were classified as being low (37.1 percent), moderate (55.2 percent), or high (7.7 percent) in anger. Among participants with normal blood pressure, the high-anger subjects experienced almost three times as many coronary events as the low-anger subjects (see Figure 13.10). Thus, anger/hostility appears to be the key toxic element in the Type A syndrome.

Emotional Reactions, Depression, and Heart Disease

Although work on personality risk factors has dominated research on how psychological functioning contributes to heart disease, recent studies suggest that emotional reactions may also be critical. *One line of research has supported the hypothesis that transient mental stress and the resulting emotions that people experience can tax the heart* (Bekkouche et al., 2011; Dimsdale, 2008). Based on anecdotal evidence,

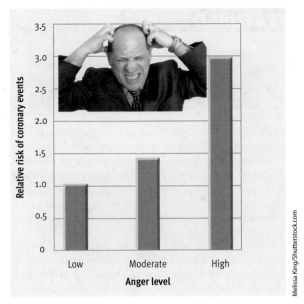

FIGURE 13.10

Anger and coronary risk.

Working with a large sample of healthy men and women who were followed for a median of 4.5 years, Williams et al. (2000) found an association between anger and the likelihood of a coronary event. Among subjects who manifested normal blood pressure at the beginning of the study, a moderate anger level was associated with a 36 percent increase in coronary attacks and a high level of anger nearly tripled participants' risk for coronary disease. (Based on data in Williams et al., 2000)

Melissa King/Shutterstock.com

cardiologists and laypersons have long voiced suspicions that strong emotional reactions might trigger heart attacks in individuals with coronary disease, but it has been difficult to document this connection. However, advances in cardiac monitoring have facilitated investigation of the issue.

As suspected, laboratory experiments with cardiology patients have shown that brief periods of mental stress can trigger acute symptoms of heart disease (Baker, Suchday, & Krantz, 2007). Overall, the evidence suggests that mental stress can elicit cardiac symptoms in about 30–70 percent of patients with stable coronary disease (Kop, Gottdiener, & Krantz, 2001). Outbursts of anger may be particularly dangerous (Lambert et al., 2009). A recent study also demonstrated that mental stress can trigger temporary increases in the *inflammation* that is thought to contribute to cardiovascular risk (Kop et al., 2008).

Another line of research has recently implicated depression as a risk factor for heart disease (Goldston & Baillie, 2008), especially for Canadian women as compared to Canadian men (Gilmour, 2008). *Depressive disorders,* which are characterized by persistent feelings of sadness and despair, are a fairly common form of mental illness (see Chapter 14). Elevated rates of depression have been found among patients suffering from heart disease, but most experts used to explain this correlation by asserting that being diagnosed with heart disease makes people depressed. Recent evidence, however, suggests that the causal relations may be just the opposite—*that the emotional dysfunction of depression may cause heart disease* (Frasure-Smith & Lesperance, 2005; Thomas, Kalaria, & O'Brien, 2004). This issue brings us to our Featured Study for this chapter, which examines the relationship between depression and cardiac health.

Investigators: B. W. J. H. Penninx, A. T. F. Beekman, A. Honig, D. J. H. Deeg, R. A. Schoevers, J. T. M. van Eijk, & W. van Tilburg
Source: Depression and cardiac mortality: Results from a community-based longitudinal survey. *Archives of General Psychiatry*, 2001, *58*, 221–227.

Is Depression a Risk Factor for Heart Disease?

In the 1990s, investigators began to suspect that depression might increase vulnerability to heart disease. A correlation between depression and coronary risk was reported in several studies, but given the profound importance of this issue, additional studies have been needed to replicate the finding in different types of samples and to get a more precise reading on the *degree* to which depression elevates coronary risk. Also, previous studies yielded conflicting results about whether depression elevates cardiac risk for healthy individuals or only among people who already have heart disease. Thus, the present study examined the impact of depression on cardiac mortality in people with and without pre-existing coronary disease.

Method

Participants. The sample was made up of 2847 men and women between the ages of 55 and 85 who were participating in an ongoing study of aging based in Amsterdam. The subjects were a randomly selected sample of community-dwelling older persons drawn from 11 municipalities in the Netherlands. The mean age of the participants was 70.5, and 52 percent were female.

Procedure and measures. The study used a longitudinal design (see Chapter 11), which entailed following the participants' health and mortality over a period of four years. Subjects were carefully screened for the existence of cardiac disease at the beginning of the study. Depressed subjects were identified through a two-step process. First, all the participants completed a widely used 20-item self-report measure of depression. Those who scored above a standard cutoff on this scale were evaluated four weeks later with a diagnostic interview. Those who met the criteria for a diagnosis of depressive disorder (based on the interview) were categorized as suffering from *major depression*. The remaining subjects who had scored above the cutoff on the screening scale, but did not meet the criteria for a full-fledged depressive disorder, were categorized as suffering from *minor depression*. The key dependent variable at the end of the study was the cardiac mortality rate among the subjects, which was based on tracking death certificates in the 11 municipalities where the participants resided.

Results

At the beginning of the study, 450 of the 2847 participants were found to have cardiac disease. Among these subjects, the cardiac mortality rate was elevated for those who had exhibited either minor or major depression. The rates of cardiac mortality calculated as mortality rate per 1000 person-years were 47.1, 72.4, and 126.8 for the no-depression, minor depression, and major depression groups, respectively. While the overall mortality rates were lower, similar trends were observed among the remaining 2397 subjects who were free of cardiac disease when the study was initiated. Here, the rates of cardiac mortality for the no-depression, minor depression, and major depression groups were 7.7, 16.2, and 22.3, respectively. The risk trends for both groups remained largely the same even after statistical adjustments were made to control for confounding variables, such as age, sex, weight, and smoking history.

Discussion

The increased cardiac mortality rate associated with depression was fairly similar in both subjects with and without pre-existing cardiac disease. For both groups, major depression roughly *tripled* subjects' risk of cardiac death. The findings for subjects without pre-existing cardiac disease were especially important. Given that these subjects' depressive disorders preceded their cardiac disease, one cannot argue that their heart disease caused their depression. It is far more likely that depression somehow contributed to the emergence of cardiac disease in these subjects.

Comment

This study is representative of a rich research tradition in health psychology in which various psychological factors (depression in this case) are examined in relation to health outcomes. These studies are crucial to our understanding of the determinants of wellness and disease. They illustrate the importance of correlational research, since predictors of disease generally cannot be studied using the experimental method.

A more recent study of almost 20 000 people who were initially free of heart disease reported similar results (Surtees et al., 2008). Participants who suffered from depression were 2.7 times more likely to die of heart disease during the follow-up period than people who were not depressed. Overall, studies have found that depression roughly doubles one's chances of developing heart disease (Herbst et al., 2007; Lett et al., 2004).

Stress, Other Diseases, and Immune Functioning

The development of questionnaires to measure life stress has allowed researchers to look for correlations between stress and a variety of diseases. These researchers have uncovered many connections between stress and illness. For example, researchers have found an association between life stress and the course of rheumatoid arthritis (Davis et al., 2008). Other studies have connected stress to the development of back pain (Lampe et al., 1998), diabetes (Landel-Graham, Yount, & Rudnicki, 2003), herpes (Padgett & Sheridan, 2000), and flare-ups of irritable bowel syndrome (Blanchard & Keefer, 2003). There are also links between stress and high blood pressure. Recent data collected by Health Canada and the Public Health Agency of Canada (Statistics Canada, 2010a) revealed that nearly 20 percent of the adult Canadian population suffers from hypertension, with the prevalence increasing sharply with age. Between the ages of 60 and 80, 53 percent of Canadian adults have high blood pressure

These are just a handful of representative examples of studies relating stress to physical diseases. Table 13.3 provides a longer list of health problems that have been linked to stress. Many of these stress–illness connections are based on tentative or inconsistent findings, but the sheer length and diversity of the list are remarkable. Why should stress increase the risk for so many kinds of illness? A partial answer may lie in immune functioning.

The apparent link between stress and many types of illness raises the possibility that stress may undermine immune functioning. The *immune response* is the body's defensive reaction to invasion by bacteria, viral agents, or other foreign substances. The immune response works to protect the body from many forms of disease. Immune reactions are multifaceted, but they depend heavily on actions initiated by specialized white blood cells, called *lymphocytes*.

Many studies indicate that experimentally induced stress can impair immune functioning *in animals* (Ader, 2001; Rose, 2007). That is, stressors such as crowding, shock, food restriction, and restraint reduce various aspects of immune reactivity in laboratory animals (Prolo & Chiapelli, 2007).

Studies by Janice Kiecolt-Glaser and her colleagues have also related stress to suppressed immune activity *in humans* (Kiecolt-Glaser & Glaser, 1995). In one study, medical students provided researchers with blood samples so that their immune response could be assessed (Kiecolt-Glaser et al., 1984). The students provided the baseline sample a month

TABLE 13.3

Health Problems That May Be Linked to Stress

Health Problem	Representative Evidence
AIDS	Ironson et al. (1994)
Appendicitis	Creed (1989)
Asthma	Sriram & Silverman (1998)
Cancer	Holland & Lewis (1993)
Chronic back pain	Lampe et al. (1998)
Common cold	Cohen (2005)
Complications of pregnancy	Dunkel-Schetter et al. (2001)
Coronary heart disease	Orth-Gomer et al. (2000)
Diabetes	Riazi & Bradley (2000)
Epileptic seizures	Kelly & Schramke (2000)
Hemophilia	Buxton et al. (1981)
Herpes virus	Padgett & Sheridan (2000)
Hypertension	Pickering et al. (1996)
Hyperthyroidism	Yang, Liu, & Zang (2000)
Inflammatory bowel disease	Searle & Bennett (2001)
Migraine headaches	Ramadan (2000)
Multiple sclerosis	Mitsonis et al. (2006)
Periodontal disease	Marcenes & Sheiham (1992)
Premenstrual distress	Wu-Holt & Boutte (1994)
Rheumatoid arthritis	Huyser & Parker (1998)
Skin disorders	Arnold (2000)
Stroke	Harmsen et al. (1990)
Ulcers	Murison (2001)
Vaginal infections	Williams & Deffenbacher (1983)

before final exams and contributed the "high-stress" sample on the first day of their finals. The subjects also responded to the SRRS as a measure of recent stress. Reduced levels of immune activity were found during the extremely stressful finals week. Reduced immune activity was also correlated with higher scores on the SRRS.

Recent research by Canadian psychologists has added to the evidence linking stress with immune functioning. For example, an analysis by Suzanne Segerstrom and the University of British Columbia's Gregory Miller found that acute (lasting a few minutes) and chronic or more long-term stressors have different effects on the body's immune system (Segerstrom & Miller, 2004), and a team of researchers in Ottawa found that the lengthy anticipatory phase before some protracted events, such as Ph.D. oral defence that has been scheduled far in advance, produces distinct neuroendocrine and immune alterations (Lacey et al., 2000).

Research has mainly focused on the link between stress and immune suppression. However, recent studies have shown that there are other important connections between immune function and vulnerability to illness. When the immune system responds to infection or injury it may release proinflammatory cytokines. Cytokines are proteins that "orchestrate a number of the immune activities that play a role in killing the pathogen and repairing damaged tissue" (Kemeny, 2007, p. 94). But exposure to long-term stress can sometimes foster persistent overproduction of proinflammatory cytokines. This can promote chronic inflammation (Christian et al., 2009; Robles, Glaser, & Kiecolt-Glaser, 2005).

Scientists have only begun to fully appreciate the potential ramifications of this chronic inflammation in recent years. As we noted earlier, inflammation has recently been recognized as a major factor in the development of heart disease. But that's not all. Research has also shown that chronic inflammation contributes to a diverse array of diseases. These diseases include arthritis, osteoporosis, respiratory diseases, diabetes, Alzheimer's disease, and some types of cancer (Feuerstein et al., 2007). Thus, chronic inflammation resulting from immune system dysregulation may be another key mechanism underlying the association between stress and wide variety of diseases.

Sizing Up the Link between Stress and Illness

A wealth of evidence shows that stress is related to physical health, and converging lines of evidence suggest that stress contributes to the *causation* of illness (Cohen, Janicki-Deverts, & Miller, 2007; Pedersen, Bobnjerg, & Zachariae, 2011). But we have to put this intriguing finding into perspective. Virtually all of the relevant research is correlational, so it can't demonstrate *conclusively* that stress causes illness (T. W. Smith & Gallo, 2001). Subjects' elevated levels of stress and illness could both be due to a third variable, perhaps some aspect of personality (see Figure 13.11). For instance, some evidence suggests that neuroticism may make people overly prone to interpret events as stressful and overly prone to interpret unpleasant sensations as symptoms of illness, thus inflating the correlation between stress and illness (Espejo et al., 2011).

In spite of methodological problems favouring inflated correlations, the research in this area consistently indicates that the *strength* of the relationship between stress and health is *modest*. The correlations typically fall in the 0.20s and 0.30s (Cohen, Kessler, & Gordon, 1995). Clearly, stress is not an irresistible

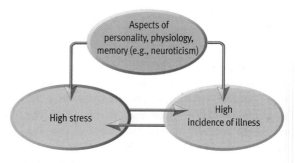

FIGURE 13.11

The stress–illness correlation.

One or more aspects of personality, physiology, or memory could play the role of a postulated third variable in the relationship between high stress and high incidence of illness. For example, neuroticism may lead some subjects to view more events as stressful and to remember more illness, thus inflating the apparent correlation between stress and illness.

force that produces inevitable effects on health. Actually, this fact should come as no surprise, as stress is but one factor operating in a complex network of biopsychosocial determinants of health. Other key factors include one's genetic endowment, exposure to infectious agents and environmental toxins, nutrition, exercise, alcohol and drug use, smoking, use of medical care, and cooperation with medical advice. Furthermore, some people handle stress better than others, which is the matter we turn to next.

REVIEW OF KEY POINTS

▸ The Type A personality has been implicated as a contributing cause of coronary heart disease. But the evidence has been equivocal. Recent research suggests that hostility may be the most toxic element of the Type A syndrome.

▸ Transient, stress-induced emotional reactions can elicit cardiac symptoms. Although depression can be a result of heart disease, research also suggests that depression can increase one's risk for cardiovascular disease. Our Featured Study found that depression was a predictor of increased cardiac mortality among initially healthy individuals.

▸ Stress appears to play a role in a host of diseases, perhaps because it can temporarily suppress the effectiveness of the immune system. Exposure to long-term stress can also promote chronic inflammation. Although there's little doubt that stress can contribute to the development of physical illness, the link between stress and illness is modest. Stress is only one factor in a complex network of biopsychosocial variables that shape health.

Factors Moderating the Impact of Stress

Some people seem to be able to withstand the ravages of stress better than others (Holahan & Moos, 1994). Why? Because a number of *moderator variables* can lessen the impact of stress on physical and mental health. We'll look at three key moderator variables—social support, optimism, and conscientiousness—to shed light on individual differences in how well people tolerate stress.

Social Support

Friends may be good for your health! This startling conclusion emerges from studies on social support as a moderator of stress. *Social support* refers to various types of aid and emotional sustenance provided by members of one's social networks. Many studies have found positive correlations between high social support and greater immune functioning (Uchino, Uno, & Holt-Lunstad, 1999). In contrast, the opposite of social support—loneliness and social isolation—was found to predict reduced immune responding in one study of college students (Pressman et al., 2005). In recent decades, a vast number of studies have found evidence that social support is favourably related to physical health (Taylor, 2007; Uchino & Birmingham, 2011).

The favourable effects of social support are strong enough to have an impact on participants' mortality! A recent meta-analysis of the results of 148 studies reported that solid social support increased people's odds of survival by roughly 50 percent (Holt-Lunstad, Smith, & Layton, 2010). The strength of social support's impact on mortality was surprising. To put this finding into perspective, the researchers compared the effect size of social support on mortality to other established risk factors. They note that the negative effect of inadequate social support is greater than the negative effects of being obese, not exercising, drinking excessively, and smoking (up to 15 cigarettes per day).

Recent research suggests that there are cultural disparities in the type of social support that people prefer. Studies have found that Asians are reluctant to seek support from others and that they assert that social support is not all that helpful to them (Kim et al., 2006; Taylor et al., 2004). In an effort to shed light on this puzzling observation, Shelley Taylor and colleagues (2007) discovered that Asians can benefit from social support, but they prefer a different kind of support than Americans. Taylor et al. (2007)

distinguish between *explicit social support* (overt emotional solace and instrumental aid from others) and *implicit social support* (the comfort that comes from knowing that one has access to close others who will be supportive). Research has shown that Americans generally prefer and pursue explicit social support. In contrast, Asians do not feel comfortable seeking explicit social support because they worry about the strain it will place on their friends and family (Kim, Sherman, & Taylor, 2008). But Asians do benefit from the implicit support that results when they spend time with close others (without discussing their problems) and when they remind themselves that they belong to valued social groups that would be supportive if needed.

Having connections with your community also seems to provide health benefits. A recent study (Shields, 2008) found that Canadians who perceive a strong sense of connection to their community were more likely to report having both good physical and mental health. Over two-thirds of those who felt they had a strong sense of community belonging reported good physical health and over 80 percent of those with a strong sense of community belonging reported good mental health. This study adds to the growing evidence that social relationships and bonds can be good for your health. The effect of some types of social support has also been found to be a function of culture, with individuals from cultures emphasizing community and interdependence benefiting more from emotional social support than those from cultures where independence is emphasized (Uchida et al., 2008).

Optimism and Conscientiousness

Defining *optimism* as a general tendency to expect good outcomes, Michael Scheier and Charles Carver (1985) found a correlation between optimism and relatively good physical health (Rasmussen, Scheier, & Greenhouse, 2009). Another study found optimism to be associated with more effective immune functioning (Segerstrom et al., 2007; Sergerstrom & Sephton, 2010). Research suggests that optimists cope with stress in more adaptive ways than pessimists (Aspinwall, Richter, & Hoffman, 2001; Carver & Scheier, 1999). Optimists are more likely to engage in action-oriented, problem-focused coping. They are more willing than pessimists to seek social support, and they are more likely to emphasize the

PREVIEW QUESTIONS
► How does social support influence people's health?
► How is optimism related to health?
► How is conscientiousness related to health?

positive in their appraisals of stressful events. In comparison, pessimists are more likely to deal with stress by giving up or engaging in denial.

Optimism versus pessimism is not the only dimension of personality that has been examined as a possible moderator of physical health (Kern & Friedman, 2008). Howard Friedman and his colleagues have found evidence that *conscientiousness,* one of the Big Five personality traits discussed in Chapter 12, may have an impact on physical health (Friedman et al., 1993; Martin, Friedman, & Schwartz, 2007). They have related personality measures to longevity in the gifted individuals first studied by Lewis Terman (see Chapter 9), who have been followed closely by researchers since 1921. Data were available on six personality traits, which were measured when the subjects were children. The one trait that predicted greater longevity was conscientiousness.

Why does conscientiousness promote longevity? According to Friedman (2007), several considerations may contribute. For example, conscientious people may tend to gravitate to healthy environments and they may show less reactivity to stress. But the key consideration appears to be that conscientiousness

fosters better health habits. People who are high in conscientiousness are less likely than others to exhibit unhealthy habits, such as excessive drinking, drug abuse, dangerous driving, smoking, overeating, and risky sexual practices (Bogg & Roberts, 2004; Roberts, Walton, & Bogg, 2005).

Individual differences among people in social support, optimism, and conscientiousness explain why stress doesn't have the same impact on everyone. Differences in lifestyle may play an even larger role in determining health. We'll examine some critical aspects of lifestyle in the next section.

REVIEW OF KEY POINTS

▷ There are individual differences in how much stress people can tolerate without experiencing ill effects. Social support is a key moderator of the relationship between stress and both physical and mental health.

▷ Optimism may lead to more effective coping with stress, whereas pessimism has been related to passive coping and poor health practices. A recent study of Terman's sample of gifted children suggests that conscientiousness is associated with greater longevity.

Health-Impairing Behaviour

PREVIEW QUESTIONS

▶ Why does smoking increase mortality?

▶ What are the health benefits of exercise?

▶ What are some misconceptions about HIV transmission?

▶ How do health-impairing habits get started?

On average, the life expectancy for Canadians is increasing. The life expectancy for women increased from 81.2 in 1995 to 83 in 2007. The life expectancy for males in the same time period increased from 75.4 to 78.3 (Statistics Canada, 2010b). While most Canadians are living longer lives, some people seem determined to dig an early grave for themselves. They do precisely those things that are bad for their health. For example, some people drink heavily even though they know that they're damaging their liver. Others eat all the wrong foods even though they know that they're increasing their risk of a second heart attack. Behaviour that's downright self-destructive is surprisingly common. In this section, we'll discuss how health is affected by smoking, nutrition, exercise, and drug use, and we'll look at behavioural factors in AIDS. We'll also discuss why people develop health-impairing lifestyles.

Smoking

The smoking of tobacco is widespread in our culture, but the percentage of people who smoke has declined noticeably since the mid-1980s (see Figure 13.12). Nonetheless, in Canada, as of 2004,

about 20 percent of adult men and 17 percent of adult women continue to smoke regularly (Health Canada, 2004a).

According to the Surgeon General of the United States, smokers ingest more than 7000 chemicals in each puff on a cigarette (Associated Press, 2010). The chemicals rapidly spread throughout the body causing widespread cellular damage. It is the leading cause of premature death in North America (Curry, Mermelstein, & Sporer, 2009). The evidence clearly shows that smokers face a much greater risk of premature death than nonsmokers. For example, the average smoker has an estimated life expectancy *13–14 years shorter* than that of a similar nonsmoker (Schmitz & DeLaune, 2005). The overall risk is positively correlated with the number of cigarettes smoked and their tar and nicotine content. Cigar smoking, which has increased dramatically in recent years, elevates health risks almost as much as cigarette smoking (Baker et al., 2000).

Why are mortality rates higher for smokers? Smoking increases the likelihood of developing a surprisingly large range of diseases (Thun, Apicella, & Henley, 2000; Woloshin, Schwartz, & Welch, 2002). Lung cancer and heart disease kill the largest number of smokers. However, smokers also have an elevated

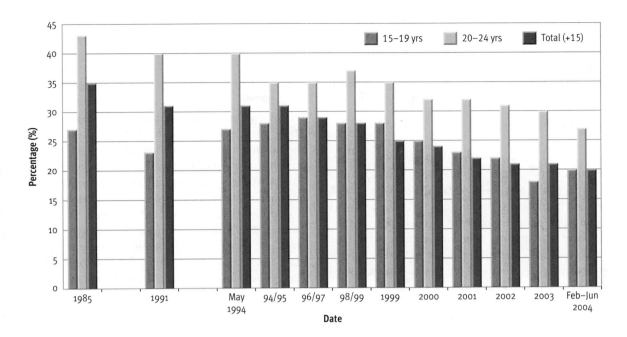

FIGURE 13.12

The prevalence of smoking in Canada.

This graph shows how the percentage of Canadian adults who smoke has declined steadily since the mid-1980s. The figure also illustrates the relatively high incidence of smoking in the 20- to 24-year-old group.

Source: Health Canada (2004a). *Canadian Tobacco Use Monitoring Survey (CTUMS).* (Statistics Canada conducted this survey for Health Canada.) Retrieved June 22, 2005, from http://www.hc-sc.gc.ca/hl-vs/ tobac-tabac/research-recherche/ stat/ ctums-esutc/index_e.html. (Data adapted from CTUMS).

risk for oral, bladder, and kidney cancer, as well as cancers of the larynx, esophagus, and pancreas; for arteriosclerosis, hypertension, stroke, and other cardiovascular diseases; and for bronchitis, emphysema, and other pulmonary diseases. Most smokers know about the risks associated with tobacco use, but they tend to underestimate the actual risks as applied to themselves (Ayanian & Cleary, 1999).

The dangers of smoking are not limited to smokers themselves. Family members and co-workers who spend a lot of time around smokers are exposed to *second-hand smoke* or *environmental tobacco smoke,* which can increase their risk for a variety of illnesses, including lung cancer (Vineis, 2005), heart disease (Venn & Britton, 2007), and breast cancer in women (Lash & Aschengrau, 1999). Young children with asthma are particularly vulnerable to the effects of second-hand smoke (Stoddard & Miller, 1995). By 2008, the data concerning the effects of second-hand smoke were convincing enough to lead some governments in Canada, including those in Ontario, Nova Scotia, and British Columbia, to ban smoking in cars carrying children. The first such ban in Canada passed by a municipality was approved by Wolfville, Nova Scotia, on November 18, 2007 (N.S. Town Bans, 2007).

Studies show that if people can give up smoking, their health risks decline reasonably quickly (Samet, 1992; Williams et al., 2002; see Figure 13.13). Evidence suggests that most smokers would like to quit but are reluctant to give up a major source of pleasure, and they worry about craving cigarettes, gaining weight, becoming anxious and irritable,

and feeling less able to cope with stress (Grunberg, Faraday, & Rahman, 2001).

Unfortunately, it's difficult to give up cigarettes. People who enroll in formal smoking cessation programs often aren't any more successful than people who try to quit on their own (Cohen et al., 1989; Swan, Hudmon, & Kroyan, 2003). Long-term success

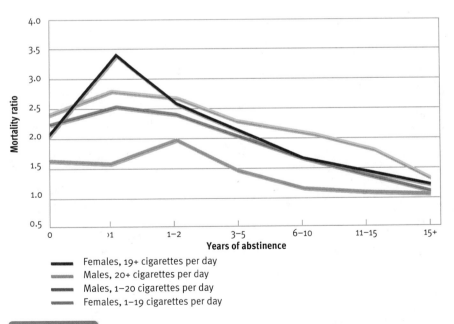

Females, 19+ cigarettes per day
Males, 20+ cigarettes per day
Males, 1–20 cigarettes per day
Females, 1–19 cigarettes per day

FIGURE 13.13

Quitting smoking and health risk.

Research suggests that various types of health risks associated with smoking decline gradually after people give up tobacco. The data shown here, from the U.S. Surgeon General's (1990) report on smoking, illustrate the overall effects on mortality rates. (Based on data from U.S. Department of Health and Human Services, 1990)

rates are in the vicinity of only 25 percent, and some studies report even lower figures. Evidence suggests that the readiness to give up smoking builds gradually as people cycle through periods of abstinence and relapse (Prochaska, 1994; Prochaska et al., 2004).

Lack of Exercise

Considerable evidence links the lack of exercise and increases in sedentary activities, such as watching TV, to poor health and obesity (Statistics Canada, 2008d). Research indicates that regular exercise is associated with increased longevity. For example, a study of over 15 000 men found that those who rated high in fitness had a 70 percent reduction in mortality compared to those who rated low (Kokkinos et al., 2007). Exercise provides similar benefits for women (Mora et al., 2007). A meta-analysis of 33 studies with over 100 000 male and female participants yielded similar conclusions (Kodama et al., 2009). Unfortunately, physical fitness and activity levels appear to be declining in North America. For example, only about one-third of American adults get an adequate amount of regular exercise (Carlson et al., 2010). The fitness levels of Canadian children and youth declined dramatically from 1981 to 2009, and among youth ages 15 to 19, when we should be most active, the proportion of Canadian youth whose waist circumference has increased enough

WEB LINK 13.7

Exercise and Sport Psychology
For anyone wondering about how psychological science deals with sports and athletics, this site, maintained by Division 47 of the American Psychological Association, is an excellent starting point, especially for those looking for career information.

to put them at a health risk has more than tripled (Statistics Canada, 2010c). This decline in fitness is accompanied by a sharp decline in the percentage of Canadian children who participate in regular, organized sports (Statistics Canada, 2008). Kids in Canada spend only 14 minutes on average after school engaged in physical activity (Picard, 2011). There are important reasons why we, as a society, should attempt to reverse these trends.

Why would exercise help people live longer? For one thing, an appropriate exercise program can enhance cardiovascular fitness and thereby reduce susceptibility to deadly cardiovascular problems (Zoeller, 2007). Second, fitness may indirectly reduce one's risk for a variety of obesity-related health problems, such as diabetes and respiratory difficulties (Corsica & Perri, 2003). Third, recent studies suggest that exercise can help to diminish chronic inflammation, which is thought to contribute to quite a variety of diseases (Flynn, McFarlin, & Markofski, 2007). Fourth, exercise can serve as a buffer that reduces the potentially damaging physical effects of stress (Plante, Caputo, & Chizmar, 2000). This buffering effect may occur because people rated high in fitness show less physiological reactivity to stress than those who are less fit (Forcier et al., 2006).

Exercise was one of the most frequently mentioned stress busters when we surveyed Canadian university websites, although the rate of physical inactivity remains high in Canada (see Figure 13.14). Data collected recently suggest that this trend is continuing, with a smaller percentage of Canadian children participating in organized sports activities today as compared to 1992 (Statistics Canada, 2008e). Given its status as a risk factor for many health problems including heart disease and stroke, these figures reflecting physical inactivity are a concern for all of us.

If these payoffs aren't enough to get people hustling to the gym, recent studies have turned up a new, unexpected benefit of exercise—it can facilitate the generation of new brain cells (Cotman, Berchtold, & Christie, 2007; Pereira et al., 2007). As noted earlier in the chapter (see p. 608), *neurogenesis* appears to be an important process that can be suppressed by stress. The finding that this neurodevelopmental process can be promoted by simple exercise may turn out to have profound implications.

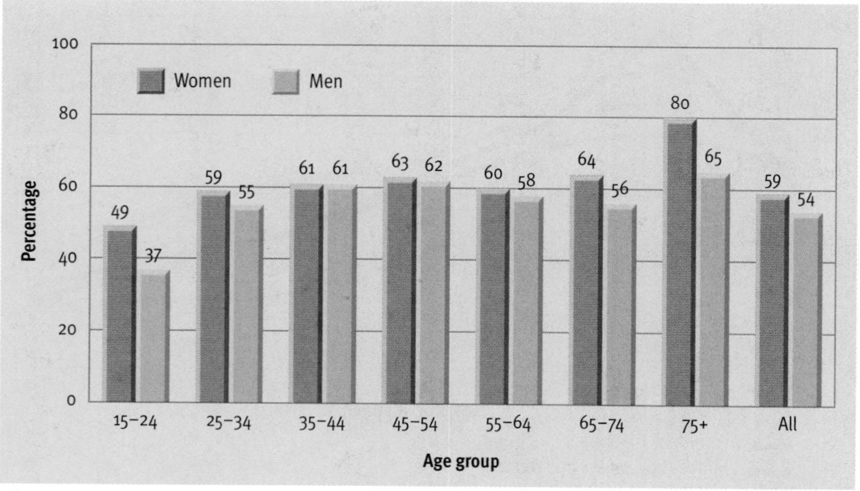

FIGURE 13.14

Physical inactivity in Canada.
Physical inactivity is associated with many health problems. The rates of inactivity remain high in Canada across age groups. This table shows the proportion of adults who are physically inactive by age and gender.

Source: Public Health Agency of Canada. (2004). *The changing face of heart disease and stroke in Canada, 2000.* Retrieved June 21, 2005, from http://www.phac-aspc.gc.ca/ccdpc-cpcmc/cvd-mcv/publications/pdf/card2ke.pdf. Adapted from Statistics Canada, *National Population Health Survey, 1996–1997.*

Alcohol and Drug Use   4c

Although there is some thought-provoking evidence that *moderate* drinking may offer some protection against cardiovascular disease (Brien et al., 2011;

Ronksley et al., 2011), heavy consumption of alcohol clearly increases one's risk for a host of diseases (Johnson & Ait-Daoud, 2005). Recreational drug use is another common health-impairing habit. The risks associated with the use of various drugs were discussed in detail in Chapter 5. Unlike smoking, poor eating habits, and inactivity, drugs can kill directly and immediately when they are taken in an overdose or when they impair the user enough to cause an accident. In the long run, various recreational drugs may also elevate one's risk for infectious diseases; respiratory, pulmonary, and cardiovascular diseases; liver disease; gastrointestinal problems; cancer; neurological disorders; and pregnancy complications (see Chapter 5). Ironically, the greatest physical damage in the population as a whole is caused by alcohol, the one recreational drug that's legal.

Behaviour and AIDS

At present, some of the most problematic links between behaviour and health may be those related to AIDS. June 2011 marks an important anniversary in the fight against AIDS. June 5, 2011, was the 30th anniversary of the date on which the first AIDS patients were reported in North America (CBC News, 2011). In 30 years, considerable progress had been made in terms of our understanding of AIDS. *AIDS* stands for *acquired immune deficiency syndrome, a disorder in which the immune system is gradually weakened and eventually disabled by the human immunodeficiency virus (HIV)*. Being infected with the HIV virus is *not* equivalent to having AIDS. AIDS is the final stage of the HIV infection process, typically manifested about ten years after the original infection (Carey & Vanable, 2003; Treisman, 1999). AIDS inflicts its harm indirectly by opening the door to other diseases because, with the onset of the syndrome, one is left virtually defenceless against a host of opportunistic infectious agents. The symptoms of AIDS vary widely, depending on the specific constellation of diseases that one develops (Cunningham & Selwyn, 2005). Unfortunately, the worldwide prevalence of this deadly disease continues to increase at an alarming rate, especially in certain underdeveloped regions of Africa (UNAIDS, 2006).

Prior to 1996–1997, the average length of survival for people after the onset of the AIDS syndrome was about 18 to 24 months. Encouraging advances in the treatment of AIDS with drug regimens referred to as *highly active antiretroviral therapy (HAART)* hold out promise for *substantially* longer survival (Anthony & Bell, 2008; Hammer et al., 2006). But these drugs have been rushed into service, and their long-term

Timothy Ray Brown of San Francisco, California, pictured here with his dog, is reported to be the first person in the world cured of AIDS.

AP Photo/Eric Risberg

efficacy is yet to be determined. Medical experts are concerned that the general public has gotten the impression that these treatments have transformed AIDS from a fatal disease to a manageable one, which may be a premature conclusion. HIV strains are evolving, and many have developed resistance to the currently available antiretroviral drugs. Moreover, some patients do not respond well to the new drugs, and many patients who are responsive have difficulty sticking to drug regimens that often have adverse side effects (Beusterien et al., 2008; Hammer et al., 2006). But still there is hope for advances in the treatment and cure of this disease. A San Francisco man, Timothy Ray Brown, is the first person in the world apparently cured of AIDS (CBC News, 2011).

Transmission

HIV is transmitted through person-to-person contact involving the exchange of bodily fluids, primarily semen and blood. The two principal modes of transmission in North America have been sexual contact and the sharing of needles by intravenous (IV) drug users. In North America, sexual transmission has occurred primarily among gay and bisexual men, but heterosexual transmission has increased (Centers for Disease Control, 2011) in recent years. In the world as a whole, infection through heterosexual relations has been much more common from the beginning (see Figure 13.15). In heterosexual relations, male-to-female transmission is estimated to be about eight times more likely than female-to-male transmission (Ickovics, Thayaparan, & Ethier, 2001). The virus can be found in the tears and saliva of infected individuals, but the concentrations are low and there is no evidence that the infection can be spread through casual contact. Even most forms of noncasual contact, including kissing, hugging, and

FIGURE 13.15

HIV transmission worldwide.

In North America, most HIV transmission thus far has occurred among gay men or intravenous drug users, perhaps leading to misconceptions about the ease of transmission via heterosexual relations. In the world as a whole, heterosexual relations are the predominant mode of transmission, as these data show.

Source: Mann, J., Tarantola, D.J.M., and Netter, T.W. (1992). *A global report: AIDS in the world.* New York: Oxford University Press. Reprinted by permission.

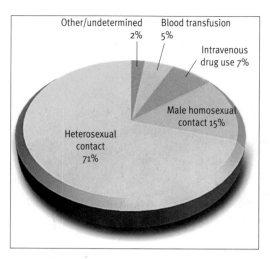

Other/undetermined 2%
Blood transfusion 5%
Intravenous drug use 7%
Male homosexual contact 15%
Heterosexual contact 71%

sharing food with infected individuals, appear to be safe (Kalichman, 1995).

One problem related to transmission is that many young heterosexuals who are sexually active with a variety of partners foolishly downplay their risk for HIV. They greatly underestimate the probability that their sexual partners previously may have used IV drugs or had unprotected sex with an infected individual. Also, many young people inaccurately believe that prospective sexual partners

who carry the HIV virus will exhibit telltale signs of illness. In reality, many HIV carriers do not know themselves that they are HIV-positive. In one study that screened over 5000 men for HIV, 77 percent of those who tested HIV-positive were previously unaware of their infection (MacKellar et al., 2005). Many myths about AIDS persist in spite of extensive efforts to educate the public about this complex and controversial disease. Figure 13.16 contains a short quiz to test your knowledge of the facts about AIDS.

Prevention

The behavioural changes that minimize the risk of developing AIDS are fairly straightforward, although making the changes is often much easier said than done (Coates & Collins, 1998). In all groups, the more sexual partners that a person has, the higher the risk that the person will be exposed to the virus. So, people can reduce their risk by having sexual contacts with fewer partners and by using condoms to control the exchange of semen.

Research by Canadian psychologists has examined some of the factors contributing to the tendency not to use condoms and to engage in risky sexual behaviours. Carolyn Hafer of Brock University and her colleagues have found links between an individual's *belief in a just world*, a relatively stable dispositional characteristic, and condom use (Hafer, Bogaert, & McMullen, 2001). Tara MacDonald of Queen's University has found links between intention to engage in risky sexual behaviour and specific conditions of alcohol use, and between such intention and negative mood combined with low self-esteem (Hynie, MacDonald, & Marques, 2006; MacDonald & Martineau, 2002; MacDonald, Fong et al., 2000). One would like to believe that, given all we know about the spread of AIDS and other sexually transmitted diseases, engaging in risky sexual behaviour would be in general decline. However, taken together, these findings do not bode well for efforts to slow the spread of AIDS.

How Does Health-Impairing Behaviour Develop?

It may seem puzzling that people behave in self-destructive ways. How does this happen? Several factors are involved. First, many health-impairing habits creep up on people slowly. For instance, drug use may grow imperceptibly over years, or exercise habits may decline ever so gradually. Second, many health-impairing habits involve activities that are

---

AIDS Risk Knowledge Test

Answer the following "true" or "false."

T F **1.** The AIDS virus cannot be spread through kissing.
T F **2.** A person can get the AIDS virus by sharing kitchens and bathrooms with someone who has AIDS.
T F **3.** Men can give the AIDS virus to women.
T F **4.** The AIDS virus attacks the body's ability to fight off diseases.
T F **5.** You can get the AIDS virus by someone sneezing, like a cold or the flu.
T F **6.** You can get AIDS by touching a person with AIDS.
T F **7.** Women can give the AIDS virus to men.
T F **8.** A person who got the AIDS virus from shooting up drugs cannot give the virus to someone by having sex.
T F **9.** A pregnant woman can give the AIDS virus to her unborn baby.
T F **10.** Most types of birth control also protect against getting the AIDS virus.
T F **11.** Condoms make intercourse completely safe.
T F **12.** Oral sex is safe if partners "do not swallow."
T F **13.** A person must have many different sexual partners to be at risk for AIDS.
T F **14.** It is more important to take precautions against AIDS in large cities than in small cities.
T F **15.** A positive result on the AIDS virus antibody test often occurs for people who do not even have the virus.
T F **16.** Only receptive (passive) anal intercourse transmits the AIDS virus.
T F **17.** Donating blood carries no AIDS risk for the donor.
T F **18.** Most people who have the AIDS virus look quite ill.

Answers: 1. T 2. F 3. T 4. T 5. F 6. F 7. T 8. F 9. T 10. F 11. F 12. F 13. F 14. F 15. F 16. F 17. T 18. F

FIGURE 13.16

An AIDS knowledge quiz.

Because misconceptions about AIDS abound, it may be wise to take this brief quiz to test your knowledge of AIDS. The answers are shown at the bottom of this figure.

Source: Adapted from Kalichman, S.C. (1995). *Understanding AIDS: A guide for mental health professionals.* Washington, DC: American Psychological Association. Reprinted by permission of the author.

quite pleasant at the time. Actions such as eating favourite foods, smoking cigarettes, or getting "high" are potent reinforcing events. Third, the risks associated with most health-impairing habits are chronic diseases such as cancer that usually lie 10, 20, or 30 years down the road. It's relatively easy to ignore risks that lie in the distant future.

Finally, people have a curious tendency to underestimate the risks that accompany their own health-impairing behaviours while viewing the risks associated with others' self-destructive behaviours much more accurately (Weinstein, 2003; Weinstein & Klein, 1996). Many people are well aware of the dangers associated with certain habits, but when it's time to apply this information to themselves, they often discount it. They figure, for instance, that smoking will lead to cancer or a heart attack in *someone else*.

So far, we've seen that physical health may be affected by stress and by aspects of lifestyle. Next, we'll look at the importance of how people react to physical symptoms, health problems, and health-care efforts.

REVIEW OF KEY POINTS

▷ People frequently display health-impairing lifestyles. Smokers have much higher mortality rates than nonsmokers because they are more vulnerable to a host of diseases. Health risks decline reasonably quickly for people who give up smoking, but quitting is difficult and relapse rates are high.

▷ Poor nutritional habits have been linked to heart disease, hypertension, and cancer, among other things. Lack of exercise elevates one's risk for cardiovascular diseases. Alcohol and drug use carry the immediate risk of overdose and elevate the long-term risk of many diseases.

▷ Aspects of behaviour influence one's risk of AIDS, which is transmitted through person-to-person contact involving the exchange of bodily fluids, primarily semen and blood. Misconceptions about AIDS are common, and the people who hold these misconceptions tend to fall into polarized camps, either overestimating or underestimating their risk of infection.

▷ Health-impairing habits tend to develop gradually and often involve pleasant activities. The risks may be easy to ignore because they lie in the distant future and because people tend to underestimate risks that apply to them personally.

Reactions to Illness

Some people respond to physical symptoms and illnesses by ignoring warning signs of developing diseases, while others engage in active coping efforts to conquer their diseases. Let's examine the decision to seek medical treatment, communication with health providers, and compliance with medical advice.

Deciding to Seek Treatment

Have you ever experienced nausea, diarrhea, stiffness, headaches, cramps, chest pains, or sinus problems? Of course you have; we all experience some of these problems periodically. However, whether we view these sensations as *symptoms* is a matter of individual interpretation. When two people experience the same unpleasant sensations, one may shrug them off as a nuisance while the other may rush to a physician (Martin & Leventhal, 2004). Studies suggest that people who have relatively high levels of anxiety and neuroticism tend to report more symptoms of illness than others do (Feldman et al., 1999; Leventhal et al., 1996). Those who are extremely attentive to bodily sensations and health concerns also report more symptoms than the average person (Barsky, 1988).

There are a couple of roadblocks to seeking treatment for medical problems. The first relates to the wait times for ER and specialist care in Canada. After seeing your family physician, you may be referred to a specialist. Unfortunately, waiting for a consultation with a specialist can add substantially to the overall wait time in Canada for medical care (Statistics Canada, 2010). Governments across Canada are committed to reducing these wait times (e.g., Ontario Ministry of Health, 2011). The second roadblock relates to how individuals appraise and react to health concerns. Variations in the perceived seriousness and disruptiveness of symptoms help explain some of the differences among people in their readiness to seek medical treatment (Cameron, Leventhal, & Leventhal, 1993). It has also been found that income level, gender, and whether you live in a city or rural area in Canada affect the frequency of seeing a physician. In Canada, city-dwelling women with higher incomes are more likely to visit a physician or a specialist (Statistics Canada, 2007g).

The biggest problem in regard to treatment-seeking is the tendency of many people to delay needed professional consultation. Delays can be critical because early diagnosis and quick intervention may facilitate more effective treatment of many health problems (Petrie & Pennebaker, 2004). Unfortunately, procrastination is the norm even when people are faced with a medical emergency, such as a heart attack.

PREVIEW QUESTIONS

▶ What is the biggest problem related to people's decisions to seek medical treatment?

▶ What are some barriers to effective communication between patients and their health providers?

▶ What can patients do to improve communication?

▶ How much of a problem is nonadherence to medical advice?

▶ What are the causes of nonadherence?

M. Robin DiMatteo

"A person will not carry out a health behaviour if significant barriers stand in the way, or if the steps interfere with favourite or necessary activities."

Courtesy of Steve Walag, University of California, Riverside

Why do people dawdle in the midst of a crisis? M. Robin DiMatteo (1991), a leading expert on patient behaviour, mentions a number of reasons, noting that people delay because they often (1) misinterpret and downplay the significance of their symptoms, (2) fret about looking silly if the problem turns out to be nothing, (3) worry about "bothering" their physician, (4) are reluctant to disrupt their plans (to go out to dinner, see a movie, and so forth), and (5) waste time on trivial matters (such as taking a shower, gathering personal items, or packing clothes) before going to a hospital emergency room.

Communicating with Health Providers

A large portion of medical patients depart their doctors' offices not understanding what they have been told and what they are supposed to do (DiMatteo, 1991; Johnson & Carlson, 2004). This reality is most unfortunate because good communication is a crucial requirement for sound medical decisions, informed choices about treatment, and appropriate follow-through by patients (Buckman, 2002; Haskard et al., 2008).

There are many barriers to effective provider–patient communication (Beisecker, 1990; DiMatteo, 1997; Marteau & Weinman, 2004). Economic realities dictate that medical visits are generally quite brief, allowing little time for discussion. Many providers use too much medical jargon and overestimate their patients' understanding of technical terms. Patients who are upset and worried about an illness may simply forget to report some symptoms or to ask questions they meant to ask.

Communication between health-care providers and patients tends to be far from optimal, for a variety of reasons.

Dana Hursey/Jupiterimages

Other patients are evasive about their real concerns because they fear a serious diagnosis. Many patients are reluctant to challenge doctors' authority and are too passive in their interactions with providers.

What can you do to improve your communication with health-care providers? The key is to not be a passive consumer of medical services (Ferguson, 1993; Kane, 1991). Arrive at a medical visit on time, with your questions and concerns prepared in advance. Try to be accurate and candid in replying to your doctor's questions. If you don't understand something the doctor says, don't be embarrassed about asking for clarification. If you have doubts about the suitability or feasibility of your doctor's recommendations, don't be afraid to voice them.

Adhering to Medical Advice

Many patients fail to adhere to the instructions they receive from physicians and other health-care professionals. The evidence suggests that nonadherence to medical advice may occur 30 percent to 60 percent of the time (DiMatteo, 1994). Nonadherence takes many forms. Patients may fail to begin a treatment regimen, stop the regimen early, reduce or increase the levels of treatment that were prescribed, or be inconsistent and unreliable in following treatment procedures (Dunbar-Jacob & Schlenk, 2001).

This point is not intended to suggest that you should passively accept all professional advice from medical personnel. However, when you have doubts about a prescribed treatment, you should speak up and ask questions. Passive resistance can backfire. For instance, if a physician sees no improvement in a patient who falsely insists that he has been taking his medicine, the physician may abandon an accurate diagnosis in favour of an inaccurate one. The inaccurate diagnosis could then lead to inappropriate treatments that might be harmful to the patient.

Why don't people comply with the advice that they've sought out from highly regarded health-care professionals? Physicians tend to attribute noncompliance to patients' personality traits, but research indicates that other factors are more important. In many cases, patients simply forget about the requirements of their treatment regimen (Dunbar-Jacob & Schlenk, 2001). Three other considerations are also especially prominent (DiMatteo & Friedman, 1982; Evans & Haynes, 1990; Ley, 1997):

1. Frequently, noncompliance is a result of the patient's failure to understand the instructions as given. Highly trained professionals often forget that what seems obvious and simple to them may be obscure and complicated to many of their patients.

2. Another key factor is how aversive or difficult the instructions are. If the prescribed regimen is unpleasant, compliance will tend to decrease. And the more that following instructions interferes with routine behaviour, the less probable it is that the patient will cooperate successfully.

3. If a patient has a negative attitude toward a physician, the probability of noncompliance will increase. When patients are unhappy with their interactions with a doctor, they're more likely to ignore the medical advice provided.

In response to the noncompliance problem, some health psychologists are exploring ways to increase patients' adherence to medical advice. Interventions have included simplifying instructions, providing more rationale for instructions, reducing the complexity of treatment regimens, helping patients with emotional distress that undermines adherence, and training patients in the use of behaviour modification strategies. All of these interventions can improve adherence. Their effects, though, tend to be modest (Christensen & Johnson, 2002; Roter et al., 1998).

Putting It in Perspective: Themes 4 and 7

Which of our themes were prominent in this chapter? As you probably noticed, our discussion of stress and health illustrated multifactorial causation and the subjectivity of experience. As we noted in Chapter 1, people tend to think simplistically, in terms of single causes. In recent years, the highly publicized research linking stress to health has led many people to point automatically to stress as an explanation for illness. In reality, stress has only a modest impact on physical health. Stress can increase the risk for illness, but health is governed by a dense network of factors. Important factors include inherited vulnerabilities, physiological reactivity, exposure to infectious agents, health-impairing habits, reactions to symptoms, treatment-seeking behaviour, compliance with medical advice, personality, and social support. In other words, stress is but one actor on a crowded stage. This should be apparent in Figure 13.17, which shows the multitude of biopsychosocial factors that jointly influence physical health. It illustrates multifactorial causation in all of its complexity.

The subjectivity of experience was demonstrated by the frequently repeated point that stress lies in the eye of the beholder. The same job promotion may be stressful for one person and invigorating for another. One person's pressure is another's challenge. When it comes to stress, objective reality is not nearly as important as subjective perceptions. More than anything else, the impact of stressful events seems to depend on how people view them. The critical importance of individual stress appraisals will continue to be apparent in the Personal Application on coping and stress management. Many stress management strategies depend on altering one's appraisals of events.

REVIEW OF KEY POINTS

▷ Ignoring physical symptoms may result in the delay of medical treatment. There are many barriers to effective communication between patients and health-care providers.

▷ Noncompliance with medical advice is a major problem. The likelihood of nonadherence is greater when instructions are difficult to understand, when recommendations are difficult to follow, and when patients are unhappy with a doctor.

▷ Two of our integrative themes were prominent in this chapter. First, we saw that behaviour and health are influenced by multiple causes. Second, we saw that experience is highly subjective, as stress lies in the eye of the beholder.

PREVIEW QUESTIONS

▶ How did this chapter illustrate multifactorial causation?

▶ How did this chapter highlight the subjectivity of human experience?

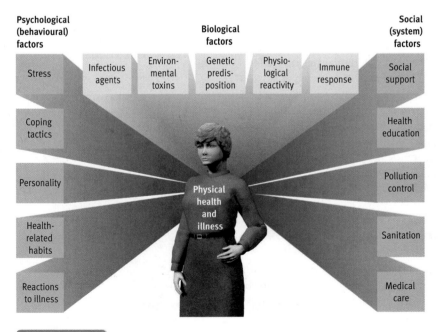

FIGURE 13.17

Biopsychosocial factors in health.

Physical health can be influenced by a remarkably diverse set of variables, including biological, psychological, and social factors. The many factors that affect health provide an excellent example of multifactorial causation.

Improving Coping and Stress Management

Answer the following "true" or "false."

___ **1** The key to managing stress is to avoid or circumvent it.

___ **2** It's best to suppress emotional reactions to stress.

___ **3** Laughing at one's problems is immature.

Courses and books on stress management have multiplied at a furious pace in the last couple of decades. They summarize experts' advice on how to cope with stress more effectively. How do these experts feel about the three statements above? As you'll see in this Application, most would agree that all three are false.

The key to managing stress does *not* lie in avoiding it. Stress is an inevitable element in the fabric of modern life. As Hans Selye noted, "Contrary to public opinion, we must not—and indeed cannot—avoid stress" (1973, p. 693). Thus, most stress management programs encourage people to confront stress rather than sidestep it. This requires training people to engage in action-oriented, rational, reality-based *constructive coping*. Fortunately, research suggests that stress management training can be beneficial in reducing the potential negative effects of stress (Evers et al., 2006; Storch et al., 2007).

As we noted earlier, some coping tactics are more healthful than others. In this Application, we'll examine a variety of constructive coping tactics, beginning with Albert Ellis's ideas about changing one's appraisals of stressful events.

Reappraisal: Ellis's Rational Thinking

Albert Ellis (1913–2007) was a prominent theorist who believed that people can short-circuit their emotional reactions to stress by altering their appraisals of stressful events (Ellis, 1977, 1985, 1996, 2001). Ellis's insights about stress appraisal are the foundation for a widely used system of therapy that he devised. *Rational-emotive therapy* is an approach that focuses on altering clients' patterns of irrational thinking to reduce maladaptive emotions and behaviour.

Ellis maintained that *you feel the way you think*. He argued that problematic emotional reactions are caused by negative self-talk, which he called *catastrophic thinking*. *Catastrophic thinking* involves unrealistically negative appraisals of stress that exaggerate the magnitude of one's problems. Ellis used a simple A–B–C sequence to explain his ideas (see Figure 13.18):

- **A: Activating event.** The A in Ellis's system stands for the activating event that produces the stress. The activating event may be any potentially stressful occurrence. Examples might include an automobile accident, the cancellation of a date, a delay while waiting in line at the bank, or a failure to get a promotion you were expecting.

- **B: Belief system.** B stands for your belief about the event, or your appraisal of the stress. According to Ellis, people often view minor setbacks as disasters. So, they engage in catastrophic thinking: "How awful this is. I can't stand it! Things never turn out right for me. I'll never get promoted."

- **C: Consequence.** C stands for the consequences of your negative thinking. When your appraisals of stressful events are overly negative, the consequence tends to be emotional distress. Thus, people feel angry, anxious, panic-stricken, or dejected.

Ellis asserted that most people don't understand the importance of phase B in this three-stage sequence. They unwittingly

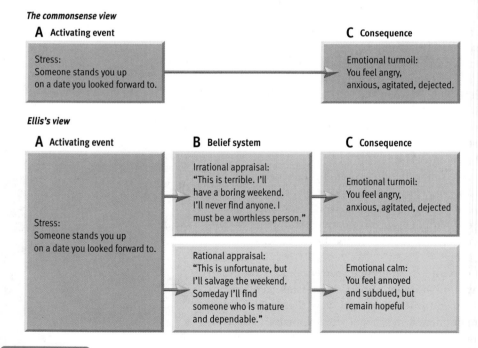

FIGURE 13.18

Albert Ellis's A–B–C model of emotional reactions.

Although most people attribute their negative emotional reactions directly to negative events that they experience, Ellis argues that events themselves do *not* cause emotional distress—rather, distress is caused by the way people *think* about negative events. According to Ellis, the key to managing stress is to change one's appraisal of stressful events.

believe that the activating event (A) causes the consequent emotional turmoil (C). However, Ellis maintained that A does *not* cause C. It only appears to do so. Instead, Ellis asserted, B causes C. One's emotional distress is actually caused by one's catastrophic thinking.

According to Ellis, it's commonplace for people to turn inconvenience into disaster and to make mountains out of molehills. Ellis theorized that unrealistic appraisals of stress are derived from irrational assumptions that people hold. He maintained that if you scrutinize your catastrophic thinking, you'll find that your reasoning is based on a logically indefensible premise, such as "I must have approval from everyone" or "I must perform well in all endeavours." These faulty assumptions, which people often unconsciously hold, generate catastrophic thinking and emotional turmoil.

How can you reduce your unrealistic appraisals of stress? Ellis asserted that you must learn (1) how to detect catastrophic thinking and (2) how to dispute the irrational assumptions that cause it. Detection involves acquiring the ability to spot unrealistic pessimism and wild exaggeration in your thinking. Disputing your irrational assumptions requires subjecting your reasoning process to scrutiny. Try to root out the assumptions from which you derive your conclusions. Once the underlying premises are unearthed, their irrationality may be obvious.

Using Humour as a Stress Reducer

A number of years ago, the Chicago area experienced its worst flooding in about a century. Thousands of people saw their homes wrecked when two rivers spilled over the banks. As the waters receded, the flood victims returning to their homes were subjected to the inevitable TV interviews. A remarkable number of victims, surrounded by the ruins of their homes, *joked* about their misfortune. When the going gets tough, it may pay to laugh about it. In a study of coping styles, McCrae (1984) found that 40 percent of his subjects used humour to deal with stress.

Empirical evidence showing that humour moderates the impact of stress has been accumulating over the last 25 years (M. H. Abel, 1998; Lefcourt, 2001, 2005), although Rod Martin at the University of Western Ontario has argued that the research to date has some inadequacies and that the area needs more theory-based, rigorous research (Martin, 2001, 2007). Martin and his colleagues have developed the *Humour Styles Questionnaire* that is designed to assess individual differences in humour use. He suggests it may be used to assess types of humour that might be connected to well-being (Martin et al., 2003). University of Waterloo psychologist Herbert Lefcourt and his colleagues (1995) argue that high-humour people may benefit from not taking themselves as seriously as low-humour people. As the authors put it, "If persons do not regard themselves too seriously and do not have an inflated sense of self-importance, then defeats, embarrassments, and even tragedies should have less pervasive emotional consequences for them" (p. 375).

Releasing Pent-Up Emotions

As we discussed in the main body of the chapter, stress often leads to emotional arousal. When this happens, there's merit in the commonsense notion that you should try to release the emotions welling up inside. Why? Because the physiological arousal that accompanies emotions can become problematic. For example, research suggests that people who inhibit the expression of anger and other emotions are somewhat more likely than other people to have elevated blood pressure (Jorgensen et al., 1996). Moreover, research suggests that efforts to actively suppress emotions result in increased stress and autonomic arousal (Butler et al., 2003; Gross, 2001) and, ultimately, the experience of more negative emotions and fewer positive emotions (John & Gross, 2007).

Although there's no guarantee of it, you can sometimes reduce your physiological arousal by *expressing* your emotions. Evidence is accumulating that writing or talking about life's difficulties can be valuable in

dealing with stress (Lyubomirsky, Sousa, & Dickerhoof, 2006; Smyth & Pennebaker, 1999). For example, in one study of university students, half the subjects were asked to write three essays about their difficulties in adjusting to university. The other half wrote three essays about superficial topics. The subjects who wrote about their personal problems enjoyed better health in the following months than the other subjects did (Pennebaker, Colder, & Sharp, 1990). Subsequent similar studies have replicated this finding (Francis & Pennebaker, 1992; Greenberg, Wortman, & Stone, 1996) and shown that emotional disclosure is associated with better immune functioning (Smyth & Pennebaker, 2001). So, if you can find a good listener, you may be able to discharge problematic emotions by letting your secret fears, misgivings, and suspicions spill out in a candid conversation.

Managing Hostility and Forgiving Others

Scientists have compiled quite a bit of evidence that hostility is related to increased risk for heart attacks and other types of illness (R. B. Williams, 2001). In light of this reality, many experts assert that people should strive to learn how to manage their feelings of hostility more effectively (Williams & Williams, 2001). The goal of hostility management is not merely to suppress the overt expression of hostility that may continue to seethe beneath the surface, but to actually reduce the frequency and intensity of one's hostile feelings.

We tend to experience hostility and other negative emotions when we feel "wronged"—that is, when we believe that the actions of another person were harmful, immoral, or unjust. When we feel wronged, our natural inclination is either to seek revenge or to avoid further contact with the offender (McCullough, 2001). *Forgiving* someone involves counteracting these natural tendencies and releasing the person from further liability for his or her transgression. Research suggests that forgiving is associated with better adjustment and well-being (McCullough & Witvliet, 2002; Thoresen, Harris, & Luskin, 1999;

Worthington & Scherer, 2004). For example, in one study of divorced or permanently separated women reported by McCullough (2001), the extent to which the women had forgiven their former husbands was positively related to several measures of well-being and inversely related to measures of anxiety and depression. Research also shows that vengefulness is correlated with more rumination and negative emotion and with lower life satisfaction (McCullough et al., 2001). Taken together, these findings suggest that it may be healthful for people to learn to forgive others more readily.

Learning to Relax

Relaxation is a valuable stress management technique that can soothe emotional turmoil and reduce problematic physiological arousal (McGuigan & Lehrer, 2007; Smith, 2007). The value of relaxation became apparent to Herbert Benson (1975; Benson & Klipper, 1988) as a result of his research on meditation. Benson, a Harvard Medical School cardiologist, believes that relaxation is the key to the beneficial effects of meditation. According to Benson, the elaborate religious rituals and beliefs associated with meditation are irrelevant to its effects. After "demystifying" meditation, Benson set out to devise a simple, nonreligious procedure that could provide similar benefits. He calls his procedure the *relaxation response*. Although there are several other worthwhile approaches to relaxation training, we'll examine Benson's procedure, as its simplicity makes it especially useful. From his study of a variety of relaxation techniques, Benson concluded that four factors promote effective relaxation:

1. *A quiet environment*. It's easiest to induce the relaxation response in a distraction-free environment. After you become experienced with the relaxation response, you may be able to practise it in a crowded subway. Initially, however, you should practise it in a quiet, calm place.
2. *A mental device*. To shift attention inward and keep it there, you need to focus your attention on a constant stimulus, such as a sound or word recited repetitively.

1. Sit quietly in a comfortable position.

2. Close your eyes.

3. Deeply relax all your muscles, beginning at your feet and progressing up to your face. Keep them relaxed.

4. Breathe through your nose. Become aware of your breathing. As you breathe out, say the word "one" silently to yourself. For example, breathe in . . . out, "one"; in . . . out, "one"; and so forth. Breathe easily and naturally.

5. Continue for 10 to 20 minutes. You may open your eyes to check the time, but do not use an alarm. When you finish, sit quietly for several minutes, at first with your eyes closed and later with your eyes opened. Do not stand up for a few minutes.

6. Do not worry about whether you are successful in achieving a deep level of relaxation. Maintain a passive attitude and permit relaxation to occur at its own pace. When distracting thoughts occur, try to ignore them by not dwelling on them, and return to repeating "one." With practice, the response should come with little effort. Practise the technique once or twice daily but not within two hours after any meal, since digestive processes seem to interfere with the elicitation of the relaxation response.

FIGURE 13.19

Benson's relaxation procedure.

Herbert Benson's relaxation procedure is described here. According to Benson, his simple relaxation response can yield benefits similar to meditation. To experience these benefits, you should practise the procedure daily.

Source: COPYRIGHT © 1975 BY WILLIAM MORROW & COMPANY, INC. Reprinted by permission of HarperCollins Publishers.

3. *A passive attitude*. It's important not to get upset when your attention strays to distracting thoughts. You must realize that such distractions are inevitable. Whenever your mind wanders from your attentional focus, calmly redirect attention to your mental device.
4. *A comfortable position*. Reasonable body comfort is essential to avoid a major source of potential distraction. Simply sitting up straight generally works well. Lying down is too conducive to sleep.

Benson's simple relaxation procedure is described in Figure 13.19. For full benefit, it should be practised daily.

Minimizing Physiological Vulnerability

Your body is intimately involved in your response to stress. The wear and tear of stress can be injurious to your health. To combat this potential problem, it helps to keep your body in relatively sound shape. Hence, it's a good idea to engage in at least a moderate amount of exercise. The potential benefits of regular exercise are substantial. Fortunately, evidence indicates that you don't have to be a dedicated athlete to benefit from exercise. Even a moderate amount of exercise—such as taking a brisk, half-hour walk each day—can reduce your risk of disease (Richardson et al., 2004; see Figure 13.20). Successful participation in an exercise program can also lead to improvements in your mood and ability to deal with stress (Hays, 1999; Plante, 1999b).

Embarking on an exercise program is difficult for many people. Exercise is time-consuming. Moreover, if you're out of shape, your initial attempts may be discouraging. People who do not get enough exercise cite lack of time, lack of convenience, and lack of enjoyment as their reasons (Jackicic & Gallagher, 2002). To circumvent these

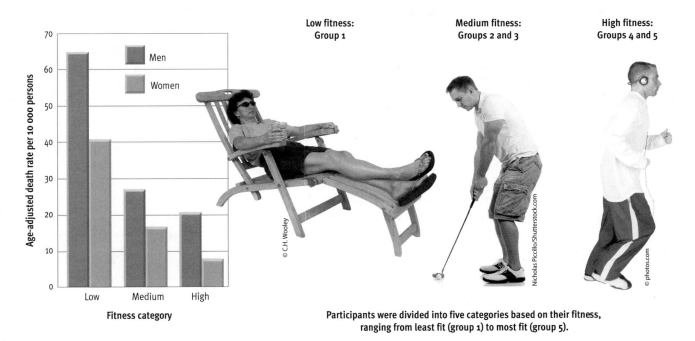

Low fitness:
Group 1

Medium fitness:
Groups 2 and 3

High fitness:
Groups 4 and 5

Participants were divided into five categories based on their fitness, ranging from least fit (group 1) to most fit (group 5).

FIGURE 13.20

Physical fitness and mortality.

Blair and colleagues (1989) studied death rates among men and women who exhibited low, medium, or high fitness. As you can see, fitness was associated with lower mortality rates in both sexes.

Source: Adapted from Blair, S.N., Kohl, W.H., Paffenbarger, R.S., Clark, D.G., Cooper, K.H., & Gibbons, L.W. (1989). Physical fitness and all-cause mortality. *Journal of the American Medical Association, 262*, 2395–2401. Copyright © 1989 American Medical Association. Reprinted by permission.

problems, it's wise to heed the following advice (Greenberg, 2002; Jackicic & Gallagher, 2002; Phillips, Kiernan, & King, 2001):

1. Select an activity that you find enjoyable.
2. Increase your participation gradually.
3. Exercise regularly without overdoing it.
4. Reinforce yourself for your efforts.

Good sleep habits can also help in the effort to minimize physiological vulnerability to stress. As we discussed in Chapter 5, sleep loss can undermine immune system responding (Motivala & Irwin, 2007) and fuel inflammatory responses (Patel et al., 2009). Evidence also suggests that poor sleep quality is associated with poor health (Benham, 2010) and that sleep loss can elevate mortality (Chien et al., 2010). Thus, sound sleep patterns can contribute to stress management. People need to get a sufficient amount of sleep and they should strive for consistency in their patterns of sleeping (Barber et al., 2010). Canadians are not doing very well in this regard and according to survey data collected by Statistics Canada (2008), some of the factors contributing to

our lack of sleep are commuting, job status, and having children at home.

Summary

In this Personal Application we have discussed various aspects of stress and how it negatively affects us. We end this section by summarizing our recommendations and adding in the top ten defences against the ravages of stress summarized by the Psychology Foundation of Canada (n.d.):

1. Aim to get seven to nine hours of sleep each night.
2. Prioritize so that you do not feel overwhelmed.
3. If you regularly commute long periods of time to work and back, try to reduce your stress levels on the road (e.g., listening to favourite CDs, carpooling)
4. Take care of your physical well-being.
5. Utilize all of your vacation time.
6. If you get sick, stay home.
7. Plan ahead.
8. Set firm boundaries between your work and your nonwork time.
9. Write down three things you are thankful for each day, even if you find it hard.
10. Create a strong support system.

REVIEW OF KEY POINTS

▶ Action-oriented, realistic, constructive coping can be helpful in managing the stress of daily life. Ellis emphasized the importance of reappraising stressful events to detect and dispute catastrophic thinking. According to Ellis, emotional distress is often due to irrational assumptions that underlie one's thinking.

▶ Humour may be useful in efforts to redefine stressful situations. In some cases, it may pay to release pent-up emotions. Talking it out may help drain off negative emotions and foster better health. Stress can also be reduced by learning to manage one's hostile feelings more effectively and by learning to be more forgiving toward others.

▶ Relaxation techniques, such as Benson's relaxation response, can reduce the wear and tear of stress. Physical vulnerability may also be reduced by following a regular exercise regimen.

Thinking Rationally about Health Statistics and Decisions

With so many conflicting claims about the best ways to prevent or treat diseases, how can anyone ever decide what to do? It seems that every day, a report in the media claims that yesterday's health news was wrong.

The inconsistency of health news is only part of the problem. We are also overwhelmed by health-related statistics. As mathematics pundit John Allen Paulos (1995, p. 133) puts it, "Health statistics may be bad for our mental health. Inundated by too many of them, we tend to ignore them completely, to accept them blithely, to disbelieve them close-mindedly, or simply to misinterpret their significance."

Making personal decisions about health-related issues may not be easy. Even medical personnel often struggle to make sense out of health statistics (Gigerenzer at al., 2007). Yet it's particularly important to try to think rationally and systematically about such issues. In this Application, we'll discuss a few insights that can help you to think critically about statistics on health risks. Then we'll briefly outline a systematic approach to thinking through health decisions.

Evaluating Statistics on Health Risks

News reports seem to suggest that there are links between some type of physical illness and virtually everything people do, touch, and consume. For example, media have reported that coffee consumption is related to hypertension, that sleep loss is related to mortality, and that a high-fat diet is related to heart disease. It's enough to send even the most subdued person into a panic. Fortunately, your evaluation of data on health risks can become more sophisticated by considering the following.

Correlation Is No Assurance of Causation It is not easy to conduct experiments on health risks, so the vast majority of studies linking lifestyle and demographic

factors to diseases are correlational studies. Hence, it pays to remember that there may not be a causal link between two variables that happen to be correlated. So, when you hear that a factor is related to some disease, try to dig a little deeper and find out why scientists think this factor is associated with the disease. The suspected causal factor may be something very different from what was measured.

Statistical Significance Is Not Equivalent to Practical Significance Reports on health statistics often emphasize that the investigators uncovered "statistically significant" findings. As explained in Chapter 2, statistically significant findings are findings that are not likely to be due to chance fluctuations. Statistical significance is a useful concept, but it can sometimes be misleading (Matthey, 1998). Medical studies are often based on rather large samples because they tend to yield more reliable conclusions than small samples. However, when a large sample is used, weak relationships and small differences between groups can turn out to be statistically significant, and these small differences may not have much practical importance. For example, in one study of sodium (salt) intake and cardiovascular disease, which used a sample of over 14 000 participants, He et al. (1999) found a statistically significant association between high sodium intake and the prevalence of hypertension among normal-weight subjects. However, this statistically significant difference was not particularly large. The prevalence of hypertension among subjects with the lowest sodium intake was 19.1 percent compared to 21.8 percent for subjects with the highest sodium intake—not exactly a difference worthy of panic.

Base Rates Should Be Considered in Evaluating Probabilities In evaluating whether a possible risk factor is associated with some disease, people often fail to consider the base rates of these events. If

the base rate of a disease is relatively low, a small increase can sound quite large if it's reported as a percentage. For example, in the He et al. (1999) study, the prevalence of diabetes among subjects with the lowest sodium intake was 2.1 percent compared to 3.8 percent for subjects with the highest sodium intake. Based on this small but statistically significant difference, one could say (the investigators did not) that high sodium intake was associated with an 81 percent increase ($[3.8 - 2.1] \div 2.1$) in the prevalence of diabetes. This would be technically accurate, but an exaggerated way of portraying the results. Base rates should also be considered when evaluating claims made about the value of medications and other medical treatments. If the base rate of a disease is low, a very modest decrease reported as a percentage can foster exaggerated perceptions of treatment benefits. For instance, Gigerenzer at al. (2007) describe an advertisement for Lipitor (a drug intended to lower cholesterol levels) that claimed that Lipitor reduced the risk of stroke by 48 percent. Although this was technically accurate, in absolute terms the protective benefits of Lipitor were actually rather modest. After four years, 1.5 percent of those taking Lipitor had a stroke versus 2.8 percent of those taking the placebo.

Thinking Systematically about Health Decisions

Health decisions are oriented toward the future, which means that there are always uncertainties. And they usually involve weighing potential risks and benefits. None of these variables is unique to health decisions—uncertainty, risks, and benefits play prominent roles in economic and political decisions as well as in personal decisions. Let's apply some basic principles of quantitative reasoning to a treatment decision involving whether to prescribe Ritalin for a boy who has been diagnosed with attention deficit disorder (ADD). Keep in mind that the general principles applied in this example can be used for a wide variety of decisions.

Seek Information to Reduce Uncertainty

Gather information and check it carefully for accuracy, completeness, and the presence or absence of conflicting information. For example, is the diagnosis of ADD correct? *Look for conflicting information* that does not fit with this diagnosis. For example, if the child can sit and read for a long period of time, maybe the problem is an undetected hearing loss that makes him appear to be hyperactive in some situations, or perhaps he is just a very active child who prefers physical activity to the sedentary. This is an important first step that is often omitted.

As you consider the additional information, begin *quantifying the degree of uncertainty* or its "flip side," your degree of confidence that the diagnosis is correct. A specific value is usually not possible, but a general approximation along a dimension ranging from "highly confident" to "not at all confident" is useful in helping you think about the next step. If you decide that you are not confident about the diagnosis, you may be trying to solve the wrong problem.

Make Risk–Benefit Assessments

What are the risks and benefits of Ritalin? How likely is this child to benefit from Ritalin, and just how much improvement can be expected? If the child is eight years old and unable to read and is miserable in school and at home, any treatment that could reduce his problems deserves serious consideration. As in the first step, the quantification is at an approximate level. A child who is two years behind in school and has no friends is, in a roughly quantifiable sense, worse off than one who is only six months behind in school and has at least one or two friends. How likely and how severe are the risks associated with Ritalin? If there is evidence that children do not grow as well when they are on Ritalin, for example, can they be taken off Ritalin over the summer months so they can catch up?

List Alternative Courses of Action

What are the alternatives to Ritalin? How well do they work? What are the risks associated with the alternatives, including the risk of falling further behind in school? *Consider the pros and cons of each alternative.* A special diet that sometimes works might be a good first step, along with the decision to start drug therapy if the child does not show improvement over some time period. What are the relative success rates for different types of treatment for children like the one being considered? To answer these questions, you will need to use probability estimates in your decision making.

As you can see from this example, many parts of the problem are quantified (confidence in the diagnosis, likelihood of improvement, probability of negative outcomes, and so forth). Precise probability values were not used because often the actual numbers are not known. Some of the values that are quantified reflect value judgments, others reflect likelihoods, and others assess the degree of uncertainty. The decision will have a different outcome depending on the particular child in question, the expected degree of success for alternative modes of treatment, and the associated risks for each. It is important to avoid the (understandable) tendency to give up and do nothing or to just do what the experts say to do, because every course of action has associated risks. It is also important to remember that doing nothing is also a decision, and it may not be the best one.

The decision-making process is not complete even after a decision is made. New decisions are needed as the future unfolds. When new information and new alternatives become available, the decision needs to be reviewed. Decision makers need to adopt deliberate strategies that require them to look for and seriously consider information that conflicts with any decision that was previously made, to avoid the tendency to notice and act only on information that confirms what you already believe to be true.

If you are thinking that the quantification of many unknowns in decision making is a lot of work, you are right. But, it is work worth doing. Whenever there are important decisions to be made about health, the ability to think with numbers will help you to reach a better decision. And yes, that assertion is a virtual certainty.

TABLE 13.4 **Critical Thinking Skills Discussed in This Application**

Skill	Description
Understanding the limitations of correlational evidence	The critical thinker understands that a correlation between two variables does not demonstrate that there is a causal link between the variables.
Understanding the limitations of statistical significance	The critical thinker understands that weak relationships can be statistically significant when large samples are used in research.
Utilizing base rates in making predictions and evaluating probabilities.	The critical thinker appreciates that the initial proportion of some group or event needs to be considered in weighing probabilities
Seeking information to reduce uncertainty	The critical thinker understands that gathering more information can often decrease uncertainty, and reduced uncertainty can facilitate better decisions.
Making risk–benefit assessments	The critical thinker is aware that most decisions have risks and benefits that need to be weighed carefully.
Generating and evaluating alternative courses of action	In problem solving and decision making, the critical thinker knows the value of generating as many alternatives as possible and assessing their advantages and disadvantages.

Key Ideas

The Nature of Stress

● Stress is a common, everyday event, and even seemingly minor stressors or hassles can be problematic. To a large degree, stress lies in the eye of the beholder, as appraisals of stress are highly subjective.

Major Types of Stress

● Major types of stress include frustration, conflict, change, and pressure. Frustration occurs when an obstacle prevents one from attaining some goal. There are three principal types of conflict: approach–approach, avoidance–avoidance, and approach–avoidance.

● A large number of studies with the SRRS suggest that change is stressful. Although this may be true, it is now clear that the SRRS is a measure of general stress rather than just change-related stress. Two kinds of pressure (to perform and to conform) also appear to be stressful.

Responding to Stress

● Emotional reactions to stress typically include anger, fear, and sadness, although positive emotions may also occur. Emotional arousal may interfere with coping. The optimal level of arousal on a task depends on the complexity of the task.

● Physiological arousal in response to stress was originally called the fight-or-flight response by Cannon. Selye's general adaptation syndrome describes three stages in physiological reactions to stress: alarm, resistance, and exhaustion.

● There are two major pathways along which the brain sends signals to the endocrine system in response to stress. Actions along these paths release two sets of hormones (catecholamines and corticosteroids) into the bloodstream.

● Some coping responses are less than optimal. Among these are giving up, blaming oneself, and striking out at others with acts of aggression. Indulging oneself is another coping pattern that tends to be of limited value. Defence mechanisms protect against emotional distress through self-deception. Small positive illusions about oneself may sometimes be adaptive.

The Effects of Stress on Psychological Functioning

● Common negative effects of stress in terms of psychological functioning include impaired task performance, burnout, post-traumatic stress disorder, and a variety of other psychological problems and disorders. Stress may also have positive effects, stimulating personal growth and the acquisition of new strengths.

The Effects of Stress on Physical Health

● The Type A personality has been implicated as a contributing cause of coronary heart disease, but hostility may be the toxic element of the Type A syndrome. Transient emotional reactions to stressful events and depression have also been identified as cardiovascular risk factors.

● Stress may play a role in a host of diseases because it can temporarily suppress the effectiveness of the immune system. The Featured Study examined the relationship between depression and cardiac health. Although there's little doubt that stress can contribute to the development of physical illness, the link between stress and illness is modest.

Factors Moderating the Impact of Stress

● Social support is a key moderator of the relationship between stress and illness and it is associated with better mental and physical health. Optimism and conscientiousness may lead to more effective coping with stress.

Health-Impairing Behaviour

● People display many forms of health-impairing behaviour. Smokers have much higher mortality rates than nonsmokers because they are more vulnerable to a host of diseases.

● Aspects of behaviour also influence one's risk of AIDS. Misconceptions about AIDS are common, and the people who hold these misconceptions tend

to fall into polarized camps, either overestimating or underestimating their risk of infection. Health-impairing habits tend to develop gradually and often involve pleasant activities.

Reactions to Illness

● Ignoring physical symptoms may result in the delay of needed medical treatment. There are many barriers to effective communication between patients and health-care providers. Noncompliance with medical advice is a major problem.

Putting It in Perspective: Themes 4 and 7

● Two of our integrative themes were prominent in this chapter. First, we saw that behaviour and health are influenced by multiple causes. Second, we saw that experience is highly subjective, as stress lies in the eye of the beholder.

PERSONAL APPLICATION • Improving Coping and Stress Management

● Action-oriented, realistic, constructive coping can be helpful in managing the stress of daily life. Ellis emphasized the importance of reappraising stressful events to detect and dispute catastrophic thinking. Humour may be useful in efforts to redefine stressful situations.

● In some cases, it may pay to release pent-up emotions by expressing them. Managing hostility and forgiving others' transgressions can also reduce stress. Relaxation techniques, such as Benson's relaxation response, can be helpful in stress management. Regular exercise can help to make one less vulnerable to the ravages of stress.

CRITICAL THINKING APPLICATION • Thinking Rationally about Health Statistics and Decisions

● Evaluations of statistics on health risks can be enhanced by remembering that correlation is no assurance of causation, statistical significance is not equivalent to practical significance, and base rates need to be considered in assessing probabilities. In trying to think systematically about health decisions, one should seek information to reduce uncertainty, make risk–benefit assessments, and consider alternative courses of action.

Key Terms

Acquired immune deficiency
    syndrome (AIDS), 625
Acute stressors, 599
Aggression, 609
Approach–approach conflict, 599
Approach–avoidance conflict, 600
Avoidance–avoidance conflict, 600
Biopsychosocial model, 596
Burnout, 613
Catastrophic thinking, 630
Catharsis, 609
Chronic stressors, 599
Conflict, 599
Constructive coping, 611
Coping, 608
Defence mechanisms, 610
Fight-or-flight response, 606
Frustration, 599
General adaptation syndrome, 606
Health psychology, 596
Immune response, 619
Internet addiction, 610
Learned helplessness, 608
Life changes, 600
Optimism, 621
Post-traumatic stress disorder
    (PTSD), 613
Pressure, 602

Primary appraisal, 598
Psychosomatic diseases, 616
Rational-emotive therapy, 630
Resilience, 615
Secondary appraisal, 598
Social support, 621
Stress, 597
Type A personality, 616
Type B personality, 616

Key People

Roy Baumeister, 612
Walter Cannon, 606
Anita Delongis, 598
M. Robin DiMatteo, 628
Albert Ellis, 609, 630
Norman S. Endler, 608
Meyer Friedman, 616
Thomas Holmes, 600
Janice Kiecolt-Glaser, 619
Richard Lazarus, 598
Michael Leiter, 613
Christina Maslach, 613
Neal Miller, 599
James Parker, 608
Richard Rahe, 600
Hans Selye, 607
Shelley Taylor, 606, 611
Wayne Weiten, 602

1. On the day before a major psychology exam Janine experiences total panic, even though she is thoroughly prepared and she aced the previous two psychology exams. Which of the following is indicated by her experience of panic?
   A. High arousal is best for complex tasks.
   B. Janine has misinterpreted her physiological reactions to stress.
   C. The appraisal of stress is highly subjective.
   D. Her adrenal cortex is malfunctioning.

2. Which of the following series represents the four principal sources of stress?
   A. frustration, conflict, pressure, and anxiety
   B. frustration, anger, pressure, and change
   C. anger, anxiety, depression, and annoyance
   D. frustration, conflict, pressure, and change

3. Your boss tells you that a complicated report you have not yet written must be on her desk by the afternoon. Which of the following conditions might you experience?
   A. burnout
   B. pressure
   C. a double bind
   D. catharsis

4. You want very badly to ask someone for a date, but you are afraid to risk rejection. Which of the following conditions are you experiencing?
   A. approach–avoidance conflict
   B. avoidance–avoidance conflict
   C. frustration
   D. self-imposed pressure

5. Under which of the following conditions is a high level of arousal likely to be best for the performance of a task?
   A. when the task is complex
   B. when the task is simple
   C. when there is no audience
   D. when there is an audience

6. Which of the following terms corresponds to the alarm stage of Hans Selye's general adaptation syndrome?
   A. the fight-or-flight response
   B. constructive coping
   C. catharsis
   D. secondary appraisal

7. The brain sends signals to the endocrine system along two major pathways. Which of the following parts of the brain is responsible for *initiating* action along those pathways?
   A. hypothalamus
   B. thalamus
   C. corpus callosum
   D. medulla

8. You have been doing poorly in your psychology class and you are in danger of failing. According to Freud, which of the following behaviours qualifies as a defence mechanism in response to this situation?
   A. You seek the aid of a tutor and spend a lot of time trying to catch up.
   B. You decide to withdraw from the class and take it another time, in order to increase the likelihood of success in the future.
   C. You don't change anything, because you're convinced that everything will work out just fine.
   D. You consult with the instructor to see what you can do to pass the class.

9. Which of the following refers to the condition of physical and emotional exhaustion, cynicism, and low self-efficacy that is attributable to chronic work-related stress?
   A. learned helplessness
   B. burnout
   C. fallout
   D. post-traumatic stress disorder

10. Which of the following traits seems to be most strongly related to increased risk of heart disease?
    A. Type B personality
    B. perfectionism
    C. competitiveness
    D. hostility

11. Often students develop colds and other minor ailments during final exams. Which of the following is likely the cause of this situation?
    A. Stress is associated with the release of corticosteroid hormones.
    B. Stress is associated with the release of catecholamine hormones.
    C. Burnout causes colds.
    D. Stress can suppress immune functioning.

12. Research that compares optimists and pessimists shows that optimists are more likely to do which of the following?
    A. take their time in confronting problems
    B. identify the negatives before they identify the positives
    C. engage in action-oriented, problem-focused coping
    D. blame others for their personal problems

13. Which of the following sexual behaviours is associated with the *greatest* risk of contracting the HIV virus?
    A. sexual contact with an infected man
    B. sexual contact with an infected woman
    C. contact with the saliva or tears of an infected person
    D. sharing food or beverages with an infected person

14. Which of the following series represents the three phases in Albert Ellis's explanation of emotional reactions?
    A. alarm, resistance, exhaustion
    B. id, ego, superego
    C. activating event, belief system, consequence
    D. antecedent conditions, behaviour, consequence

15. Which of the following statements is accurate and useful in evaluating health statistics?
    A. Statistical significance is equivalent to practical significance.
    B. Correlation is a reliable indicator of causation.
    C. Base rates are needed to assess probabilities.
    D. Gut reaction is nearly always the correct decision.

See Appendix A for answers to this Practice Test.

On the Web

▸ **CourseMate**

Go to this site to find online resources directly linked to your book, including more quizzes, a glossary, flash cards, videos, and more!

▸ **CengageNow**

Go to this site for the link to CengageNOW™, your one-stop study shop. Take a pre-test for this chapter and CengageNOW™ will generate a personalized study plan based on your test results! The study plan will identify the topics you need to review and direct you to online resources to help you master those topics. You can then take a post-test to help you determine the concepts you have mastered and what you still need to work on.

▸ **Aplia**

Aplia™ is an online interactive learning solution that helps you improve comprehension—and your grade—by integrating a variety of media and tools such as video, tutorials, practice tests, and an interactive e-book.

CHAPTER 14

Psychological Disorders

© Sandy Matos

The topic of psychological disorders draws many students to an introductory psychology course. Your interest in this topic may stem from your desire to understand the nature, prevalence, and cause of psychological disorders so that you can be better prepared to assist those in need. This is indeed a worthy aspiration and one that we are ourselves familiar with; it's one of the things that motivated us, too, in our early studies in psychology. You may also have been led to the topic because you are already too familiar with the costs that such disorders can exact on the afflicted and their families. We hope that this chapter on psychological disorders and Chapter 15, which deals with the treatment of psychological disorders, will contribute to your understanding of these important social and personal issues.

Given the rates of occurrence for the various disorders that we will discuss in this chapter, the chances are very good that you know someone, perhaps someone very close to you, who suffers from some type of psychological disturbance. According to a new survey conducted by the Centre for Addiction and Mental Health, symptoms of psychological distress continue to afflict millions of Canadians. In Ontario alone, one in seven adults, representing 1 400 000 adults, reports elevated distress (CAMH, 2011). In 2010, 17 000 Canadians were admitted to hospital for suicide and self-injury attempts (Picard, 2011). The results of the survey also revealed that the use of anti-anxiety and antidepressant medications has increased significantly in the past decade (CAMH, 2011). It has been estimated that mental illness costs Canada $33 billion annually (CBC News, 2009). Of course, we are not alone in this situation. Japan, for example, has one of the highest suicide rates in the world—over double the rate in Canada (Fushimi, Sugawara, & Shimizu, 2006; Statistics Canada, 2010), and suicide and depression are estimated to cost the Japanese economy $33.6 billion annually. Of course, beyond all of the statistics, views on etiology, and varieties of treatment, are the very human stories and the real suffering that result from psychological disorders.

One very notable story had its beginnings in the mid-1990s, and it has not yet been resolved for the people involved. By all accounts, Canadian Forces General Roméo Dallaire was at the apex of a long and distinguished career when he was given what all thought was a golden opportunity to put his considerable skills and experience to work for the good of others. As it turned out, however, he was being sent to do an impossible job—with inadequate resources and funding and virtually no support from his superiors.

Dallaire had been given the command of the United Nations Assistance Mission for Rwanda. Things were desperate in Rwanda at the time; genocide was being committed and in the end, approximately 800 000 Tutsis were slaughtered, many by machete, by their Hutu neighbours in Rwanda in just 100 days. As he has written in his book *Shake Hands with the Devil: The Failure of Humanity in Rwanda* (Dallaire, 2003), which was made into a feature film in 2007 and discussed in the award-winning documentary *Shake Hands with the Devil: The Journey of Roméo Dallaire*, Dallaire was restrained by the UN from intervening in the slaughter. In addition, he was unable to motivate anyone else in the international community to come to the Tutsis' aid. In fact, he believes he could have prevented the slaughter because of some advance information he had obtained. Dallaire had to stand by and do little but watch during the genocide.

The human toll included not only the murdered Tutsis and UN peacekeepers from Belgium, but also Dallaire himself. After his return to Canada, he began a much-publicized descent into psychological disturbance and suicide attempts, and at one point, was arrested in Ottawa after being found drunk under a park bench. The stress derived from what he saw and his inability to do anything about it led to his diagnosis and treatment for post-traumatic stress disorder (PTSD), which we discussed in Chapter 13 and will examine further in this chapter.

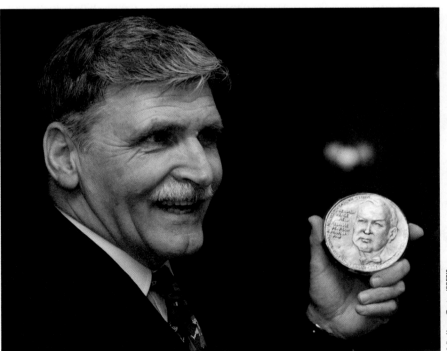

Retired General Roméo Dallaire was awarded the Pearson Peace Medal in 2005. He suffers from PTSD.

Psychological Disorders

The number of Canadian Forces veterans being given pensions because of PTSD has increased astronomically over the last decade (Freeze, 2005). In 2004, over 1100 PTSD pensions were awarded. According to a survey of Canadian Forces personnel, the one-year prevalence of PTSD is 2.8 percent, with a lifetime prevalence of 7.2 percent (National Defence, 2003). Even though Canadian Forces personnel are well prepared for military duty and combat, it may be impossible to prepare them for some of the things they are exposed to in the course of their duties. Recent research with Canadian military personnel serving in combat and peacekeeping operations found that witnessing atrocities was associated with an increased prevalence of a variety of psychological disorders and recognition by those military personnel involved that they required mental health care and support (Sareen et al., 2007).

Of course, you don't have to be a member of the military to suffer from a psychological disorder. Percy Paul was born in Patunack, a small Dene community in northern Saskatchewan. He started school early and very soon showed incredible promise in mathematics. He ended up studying at various universities, including Princeton. For the past few years, his real academic interest has been in the secrets of the universe (Chan, Paul, & Verlinde, 2000). Although his academic degrees are in math, his potential to make contributions to physics and the study of string theory has excited many academics in the field. String theory attempts to integrate Einstein's general theory of relativity and quantum mechanics in what might be the long-elusive, unified field theory, which many hope will end up to be the theory that explains everything in the universe (Greene, 1999, 2003). Paul was also

recruited by the Canadian government to work for the Financial Transactions Reports Analysis Centre of Canada, using his mathematical and computer skills to track down money laundering by terrorist groups.

Paul also suffers from bipolar disorder, in which his moods cycle from being very depressed and suicidal to the heights of mania. He finds the mania addictive, because when in this state, he has enormous energy and confidence in his ability and work. This disorder has disrupted both his personal and professional life, but Paul continues his studies in physics and on string theory at the University of Saskatchewan while battling the disorder's effects. Paul is profiled in the National Film Board 2007 documentary *Flight from Darkness*.

We discuss bipolar disorder on page 658.

In addition to having to deal with his disorder, Paul must also deal with the stigma that is so often attached to mental illness, the significance of which should not be underestimated. For example, the potential stigma associated with the label *manic-depressive* led some people who knew noted Canadian psychologist Norman Endler to advise him not to tell anyone about his depression. In fact, even his physician advised him to get a psychiatrist out of town so that he would not be *exposed* (Endler, 1982). In 2007, the Canadian government established the Mental Health Commission of Canada to develop a strategy to deal with mental disorders in Canada, to establish a national knowledge exchange network on mental health issues, and to combat the stigma that is often attached to those who suffer from psychological disorders (Curry, 2007).

What is the basis for judging behaviour as normal versus abnormal? One year, one of us (we won't tell you which one) decided to dress completely in exactly the same colour for every class he taught that year. Where would we place that behaviour on the continuum from normal to abnormal? Are people who have psychological disorders dangerous? Are they violent? How common are such disorders? Can they be cured? Have mental disorders always been stigmatized? These are just a few of the questions that we will address in this chapter as we discuss psychological disorders and their complex causes.

Before we begin to discuss psychological disorders, we should let you know that Dallaire received the Order of Canada in 2002 and in 2005 was given the Pearson Peace Medal recognizing his achievements in international service and understanding. He was made a Grand Officer of the National Order of Quebec in 2005, and received the Aegis Award for Genocide Prevention from the Aegis Trust (United Kingdom). Dallaire was appointed to the Canadian Senate in 2005 (visit his website at http://www.romeodallaire.com) and serves as a member of the United Nations Secretary-General's Advisory Committee on Genocide Prevention.

Courtesy of Alta Nova Pictures

Percy Paul is a gifted mathematician, born in Saskatchewan. He has also suffered from bipolar disorder for several years. His condition has interfered with his personal life and his ability to solve some of the questions he has posed about the nature of the universe through his work on string theory.

Misconceptions about abnormal behaviour are common, so we need to clear up some preliminary issues before we describe the various types of disorders. In this section, we will discuss (1) the medical model of abnormal behaviour, (2) the criteria of abnormal behaviour, (3) stereotypes regarding psychological disorders, (4) the classification of psychological disorders, and (5) how common such disorders are.

The Medical Model Applied to Abnormal Behaviour

The *medical model* proposes that it is useful to think of abnormal behaviour as a disease. This point of view is the basis for many of the terms used to refer to abnormal behaviour, including mental *illness,* psychological *disorder,* and psycho*pathology* (*pathology* refers to manifestations of disease). The medical model gradually became the dominant way of thinking about abnormal behaviour during the 18th and 19th centuries, and its influence remains strong today.

The medical model clearly represented progress over earlier models of abnormal behaviour. Prior to the 18th century, most conceptions of abnormal behaviour were based on superstition. People who behaved strangely were thought to be possessed by demons, to be witches in league with the devil, or to be victims of God's punishment. Their disorders were "treated" with chants, rituals, exorcisms, and such. If the people's behaviour was seen as threatening, they were candidates for chains, dungeons, torture, and death (see Figure 14.1).

The rise of the medical model brought improvements in the treatment of those who exhibited abnormal behaviour. As victims of an illness, they were viewed with more sympathy and less hatred and fear. Although living conditions in early asylums were typically deplorable, gradual progress was made toward more humane care of the mentally ill. It took time, but ineffectual approaches to treatment eventually gave way to scientific investigation of the causes and cures of psychological disorders.

However, in recent decades, some critics have suggested that the medical model may have outlived its usefulness (Boyle, 2007; Kiesler, 1999). Some critics are troubled because medical diagnoses of abnormal behaviour pin potentially derogatory labels on people (Hinshaw, 2007; Overton & Medina, 2008). Being labelled as psychotic, schizophrenic, or

mentally ill carries a social stigma that can be difficult to shake. Those characterized as mentally ill are viewed as erratic, dangerous, incompetent, and inferior (Corrigan & Larson, 2008). This is precisely why Norman Endler's friends counselled him against seeking psychiatric treatment in his local community in case others found out. These stereotypes promote distancing, disdain, prejudice, and rejection. Even after a full recovery, someone who has been labelled mentally ill may have difficulty finding a place to live, getting a job, or making friends (Thornicroft, 2006). The stigma of mental illness is not impossible to shed, but it undoubtedly creates additional difficulties for people who already have more than their share of problems (Hinshaw, 2007).

Culver Pictures, Inc.

FIGURE 14.1

Historical conceptions of mental illness.

In the Middle Ages, people who behaved strangely were sometimes thought to be in league with the devil. The top drawing depicts some of the cruel methods used to extract confessions from suspected witches and warlocks. Some psychological disorders were also thought to be caused by demonic possession. The bottom illustration depicts an exorcism.

Source (Bottom): *St. Catherine of Siena Exorcising a Possessed Woman,* c. 1500–1510. Girolamo Di Benvenuto. Denver Art Museum Collection, Gift of Samuel H. Kress Foundation Collection, 1967.171 © 2001 Denver Art Museum.

Courtesy of Thomas Szasz

Thomas Szasz

"Minds can be 'sick' only in the sense that jokes are 'sick' or economies are 'sick.'"

Unfortunately, the stigma associated with psychological disorders appears to be deep-rooted and not easily reduced. In recent decades, research has increasingly demonstrated that many psychological disorders are at least partly attributable to genetic and biological factors, making them appear more similar to physical illnesses, which carry far less stigma (Pescosolido, 2010; Schnittker, 2008). You would think that these trends would lead to a reduction in the stigma associated with mental illness, but research suggests that the stigmatization of mental disorders has remained stable or perhaps even increased (Hinshaw & Stier, 2008; Schnittker, 2008).

A particularly vocal critic of the medical model has been Thomas Szasz (1974, 1990). He asserts that "strictly speaking, disease or illness can affect only the body; hence there can be no mental illness. . . . Minds can be 'sick' only in the sense that jokes are 'sick' or economies are 'sick'" (1974, p. 267). He further argues that abnormal behaviour usually involves a deviation from social norms rather than an illness. He contends that such deviations are "problems in living" rather than medical problems. According to Szasz, the medical model's disease analogy converts moral and social questions about what is acceptable behaviour into medical questions.

The criticism of the medical model has some merit. It is important to recognize the social roots and ramifications of the medical model. However, the bottom line is that the medical model continues to dominate thinking about psychological disorders. Medical concepts such as *diagnosis, etiology,* and *prognosis* have proven valuable in the treatment and study of abnormality. *Diagnosis* involves distinguishing one illness from another. *Etiology* refers to the apparent causation and developmental history of an illness. A *prognosis* is a forecast about the probable course of an illness. These medically based concepts have widely shared meanings that permit clinicians, researchers, and the public to communicate more effectively in their discussions of abnormal behaviour.

Criteria of Abnormal Behaviour

If your next-door neighbour scrubs his front porch twice every day and spends virtually all of his time cleaning and recleaning his house, is he normal? If your sister-in-law goes to one physician after another seeking treatment for ailments that appear to be imaginary, is she psychologically healthy? How are we to judge what's normal and what's abnormal? More important, who's to do the judging?

These are complex questions. In making diagnoses, clinicians rely on a variety of criteria, the foremost of which are the following:

1. *Deviance.* As Szasz has pointed out, people are often said to have a disorder because their behaviour deviates from what their society considers acceptable. What constitutes normality varies somewhat from one culture to another, but all cultures have such norms. When people violate these standards and expectations, they may be labelled mentally ill. For example, *transvestic fetishism* is a sexual disorder in which a man achieves sexual arousal by dressing in women's clothing. This behaviour is regarded as disordered because a man who wears a dress, brassiere, and nylons is deviating from our culture's norms.

2. *Maladaptive behaviour.* In many cases, people are judged to have a psychological disorder because their everyday adaptive behaviour is impaired. This is the key criterion in the diagnosis of substance-use (drug) disorders. In and of itself, alcohol and drug use is not terribly unusual or deviant. However, when the use of cocaine, for instance, begins to interfere with a person's social or occupational functioning, a substance-use disorder exists. In such cases, it is the maladaptive quality of the behaviour that makes it disordered.

3. *Personal distress.* Frequently, the diagnosis of a psychological disorder is based on an individual's

MaxFX/Shutterstock.com

This man clearly exhibits a certain type of deviance, but does that mean that he has a psychological disorder? The criteria of mental illness are more subjective and complicated than most people realize, and to some extent, judgments of mental health represent value judgments.

report of great personal distress. This is usually the criterion met by people who are troubled by depression or anxiety disorders. Depressed people, for instance, may or may not exhibit deviant or maladaptive behaviour. Such people are usually labelled as having a disorder when they describe their subjective pain and suffering to friends, relatives, and mental health professionals.

Although two or three criteria may apply in a particular case, people are often viewed as disordered when only one criterion is met. As you may have already noticed, diagnoses of psychological disorders involve *value judgments* about what represents normal or abnormal behaviour (Widiger & Sankis, 2000). The criteria of mental illness are not nearly as value-free as the criteria of physical illness. In evaluating physical diseases, people can usually agree that a malfunctioning heart or kidney is pathological, regardless of their personal values. However, judgments about mental illness reflect prevailing cultural values, social trends, and political forces, as well as scientific knowledge (Kutchins & Kirk, 1997; Mechanic, 1999).

Antonyms such as *normal* versus *abnormal* and *mental health* versus *mental illness* imply that people can be divided neatly into two distinct groups: those who are normal and those who are not. In reality, it is often difficult to draw a line that clearly separates normality from abnormality. On occasion, everybody acts in deviant ways, everyone displays some maladaptive behaviour, and everyone experiences personal distress. People are judged to have psychological disorders only when their behaviour becomes *extremely* deviant, maladaptive, or distressing. Thus, normality and abnormality exist on a continuum. It's a matter of degree, not an either–or proposition (see Figure 14.2).

Stereotypes of Psychological Disorders

We've seen that mental illnesses are not diseases in a strict sense and that judgments of mental health are not value-free. However, still other myths about abnormal behaviour need to be exposed as such. Let's examine three stereotypes about psychological disorders that are largely inaccurate:

1. *Psychological disorders are incurable.* Admittedly, there are mentally ill people for whom treatment is largely a failure. However, they are greatly outnumbered by people who do get better, either spontaneously or through formal treatment (Lambert & Ogles, 2004). The vast majority of people who are diagnosed as mentally ill eventually improve and lead normal, productive lives. Even the most severe psychological disorders can be treated successfully.

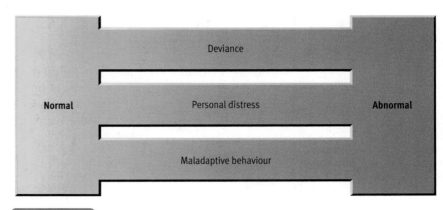

FIGURE 14.2

Normality and abnormality as a continuum.

There isn't a sharp boundary between normal and abnormal behaviour. Behaviour is normal or abnormal in degree, depending on the extent to which one's behaviour is deviant, personally distressing, or maladaptive.

2. *People with psychological disorders are often violent and dangerous.* Only a modest association has been found between mental illness and violence-prone tendencies (Monahan, 1997; Tardiff, 1999). This stereotype exists because incidents of violence involving the mentally ill tend to command media attention. A report released by the Public Health Agency of Canada (1996) on mental illness and violence concluded that the strongest predictor of violence was past violence and that there was no *consistent* evidence that psychological disorders uncomplicated by substance abuse are a significant risk factor for violence, once you control for past history of violence.

3. *People with psychological disorders behave in bizarre ways and are very different from normal people.* This is true only in a small minority of cases, usually involving relatively severe disorders. As noted earlier, the line between normal and abnormal behaviour can be difficult to draw. At first glance, people with psychological disorders usually are indistinguishable from those without disorders. A classic study by David Rosenhan (1973) showed that even mental health professionals may have difficulty distinguishing normality from abnormality. To study diagnostic accuracy, Rosenhan arranged for a number of normal people to seek admission to mental hospitals. These "pseudopatients" arrived at the hospitals complaining of one false symptom—hearing voices. Except for this single symptom, they acted as they normally would and gave accurate information when interviewed about their personal histories. *All* of the pseudopatients were admitted, and the average length of their hospitalization was 19 days!

As you might imagine, Rosenhan's study evoked quite a controversy about our diagnostic system for mental illness. Let's take a look at how this diagnostic system has evolved.

David Rosenhan
"How many people, one wonders, are sane but not recognized as such in our psychiatric institutions?"

Psychodiagnosis: The Classification of Disorders

Obviously, we cannot lump all psychological disorders together without giving up all hope of understanding them better. A sound system for classifying psychological disorders can facilitate empirical research and enhance communication among scientists and clinicians (First, 2008; Zimmerman & Spitzer, 2009). Hence, a great deal of effort has been invested in devising an elaborate system for this purpose—the American Psychiatric Association's *Diagnostic and Statistical Manual of Mental Disorders* (DSM) (see Figure 14.3). The current, fourth edition,

FIGURE 14.3

Overview of the DSM diagnostic system.

Published by the American Psychiatric Association, the *Diagnostic and Statistical Manual of Mental Disorders* is the formal classification system used in the diagnosis of psychological disorders. It is a *multiaxial* system, which means that information is recorded on the five axes described here. (Based on American Psychiatric Association, 1994, 2000)

Source: Adapted with permission from the *Diagnostic and Statistical Manual of Mental Disorders*, 4th ed. (*DSM-TR*). Copyright © 2000 American Psychiatric Association.

Axis I
Clinical Syndromes

1. **Disorders usually first diagnosed in infancy, childhood, or adolescence**
   This category includes disorders that arise before adolescence, such as attention deficit disorders, autism, enuresis, and stuttering.

2. **Organic mental disorders**
   These disorders are temporary or permanent dysfunctions of brain tissue caused by diseases or chemicals. Examples are delirium, dementia, and amnesia.

3. **Substance-related disorders**
   This category refers to the maladaptive use of drugs and alcohol. This category requires an abnormal pattern of use, as with alcohol abuse and cocaine dependence.

4. **Schizophrenia and other psychotic disorders**
   The schizophrenias are characterized by psychotic symptoms (for example, grossly disorganized behaviour, delusions, and hallucinations) and by over six months of behavioural deterioration. This category also includes delusional disorder and schizoaffective disorder.

5. **Mood disorders**
   The cardinal feature is emotional disturbance. These disorders include major depression, bipolar disorder, dysthymic disorder, and cyclothymic disorder.

6. **Anxiety disorders**
   These disorders are characterized by physiological signs of anxiety (for example, palpitations) and subjective feelings of tension, apprehension, or fear. Anxiety may be acute and focused (panic disorder) or continual and diffuse (generalized anxiety disorder).

7. **Somatoform disorders**
   These disorders are dominated by somatic symptoms that resemble physical illnesses. These symptoms cannot be fully accounted for by organic damage. This category includes somatization and conversion disorders and hypochondriasis.

8. **Dissociative disorders**
   These disorders all feature a sudden, temporary alteration or dysfunction of memory, consciousness, and identity, as in dissociative amnesia and dissociative identity disorder.

9. **Sexual and gender-identity disorders**
   There are three basic types of disorders in this category: gender identity disorders (discomfort with identity as male or female), paraphilias (preference for unusual acts to achieve sexual arousal), and sexual dysfunctions (impairments in sexual functioning).

10. **Eating disorders**
    Eating disorders are severe disturbances in eating behaviour characterized by preoccupation with weight concerns and unhealthy efforts to control weight. Examples include anorexia nervosa and bulimia nervosa.

Axis II
Personality Disorders or Mental Retardation

Personality disorders are long-standing patterns of extreme, inflexible personality traits that are deviant or maladaptive and lead to impaired functioning or subjective distress. *Mental retardation* refers to subnormal general mental ability accompanied by deficiencies in adaptive skills, originating before age 18.

Axis III
General Medical Conditions

Physical disorders or conditions are recorded on this axis. Examples include diabetes, arthritis, and hemophilia.

Axis IV
Psychosocial and Environmental Problems

Axis IV is for reporting psychosocial and environmental problems that may affect the diagnosis, treatment, and prognosis of mental disorders (Axes I and II). A psychosocial or environmental problem may be a negative life event, an environmental difficulty or deficiency, a familial or other interpersonal stress, an inadequacy of social support or personal resources, or another problem that describes the context in which a person's difficulties have developed.

Axis V
Global Assessment of Functioning (GAF) Scale

Code	Symptoms
100	Superior functioning in a wide range of activities
90	Absent or minimal symptoms, good functioning in all areas
80	Symptoms transient and expectable reactions to psychosocial stressors
70	Some mild symptoms or some difficulty in social, occupational, or school functioning, but generally functioning pretty well
60	Moderate symptoms or difficulty in social, occupational, or school functioning
50	Serious symptoms or impairment in social, occupational, or school functioning
40	Some impairment in reality testing or communication or major impairment in family relations, judgment, thinking, or mood
30	Behaviour considerably influenced by delusions or hallucinations, serious impairment in communication or judgment, or inability to function in almost all areas
20	Some danger of hurting self or others, occasional failure to maintain minimal personal hygiene, or gross impairment in communication
10	Persistent danger of severely hurting self or others
1	

referred to as DSM-IV, was released in 1994, and revised slightly in 2000.

The DSM-III employs a multiaxial system of classification, which asks for judgments about individuals on five separate dimensions, or "axes." Figure 14.3 provides an overview of the five axes. The diagnoses of disorders are made on Axes I and II. Clinicians record most types of disorders on Axis I. They use Axis II to list long-running personality disorders or intellectual disability (still known as *mental retardation* in the DSM). People may receive diagnoses on both Axes I and II.

The remaining axes are used to record supplemental information. A patient's physical disorders are listed on Axis III (General Medical Conditions). On Axis IV (Psychosocial and Environmental Problems), the clinician makes notations regarding the types of stress experienced by the individual in the previous year. On Axis V (Global Assessment of Functioning), estimates are made of the individual's current level of adaptive functioning (in social and occupational behaviour, viewed as a whole) and of the individual's highest level of functioning in the previous year. Figure 14.4 shows an example of a multiaxial evaluation. Most theorists agree that the multiaxial system is a step in the right direction because it recognizes the importance of information besides a traditional diagnostic label.

Work is currently underway to formulate the next edition of the diagnostic system (e.g., Andrews et al., 2009; Helzer et al., 2008; Regier et al., 2009), which will be identified as DSM-5 (instead of DSM-V), to facilitate incremental updates (such as DSM-5.1). It is tentatively scheduled for publication in 2013. Clinical researchers are collecting data, holding conferences, and formulating arguments about whether various syndromes should be added, eliminated, redefined, or renamed. Should complicated grief reactions become a standard diagnostic option (Lichtenthal, Cruess, & Prigerson, 2004)? Should the diagnostic system use the term drug *dependence* or drug *addiction* (O'Brien, Volkow, & Li, 2006)? Should pathological gambling be lumped with impulse-control disorders or addictive disorders (Petry, 2010)? Should night eating syndrome (regular eating binges after awakening from sleep) be recognized as a disorder (Stunkard et al., 2009)? Should Internet addiction be added to the official list of disorders (Pies, 2009)? Vigorous debates about issues such as these will occupy clinical researchers in the upcoming years.

By far, the biggest issue is whether to reduce the system's commitment to a categorical approach. In recent years, many critics of the DSM system have questioned the fundamental axiom that the diagnostic system is built on—the assumption that people can reliably be placed in discontinuous (non-overlapping) diagnostic categories (Helzer et al., 2008; Widiger & Trull, 2007). These critics note that there is enormous overlap among various disorders in symptoms, making the boundaries between diagnoses much fuzzier than would be ideal. They also point out that people often qualify for more than one diagnosis, a condition called *comorbidity—the coexistence of two or more disorders.* Widespread comorbidity raises the possibility that specific diagnoses may not reflect distinct disorders, but merely variations on the same underlying disorder (Lilienfeld & Landfield, 2008). Because of problems such as these, some theorists have argued that the current *categorical approach* to diagnosis should be replaced by a *dimensional approach.* A dimensional approach would describe individuals' pathology in terms of how they score on a limited number of continuous dimensions, such as the degree to which they exhibit anxiety, depression, agitation, hypochondria, paranoia, and so forth (Kraemer, 2008; Widiger, Livesley, & Clark, 2009). The practical logistics of shifting to a dimensional approach to psychological disorders are formidable. Agreement would have to be reached about what dimensions to assess and how to measure them. At this juncture, it appears that DSM-5 will retain a categorical approach, but it looks like there will be significant movement toward supplementing it with a dimensional approach to at least some disorders (Regier et al., 2009).

The Prevalence of Psychological Disorders

How common are psychological disorders? What percentage of the population is afflicted with mental

---

**A DSM multiaxial evaluation
(49-year-old male patient)**

Axis I	Major depressive disorder Cocaine abuse
Axis II	Borderline personality disorder (provisional, rule out dependent personality disorder)
Axis III	Hypertension
Axis IV	Psychosocial stressors: recent divorce, permitted to see his children only infrequently, job is in jeopardy
Axis V	Current global assessment of functioning (GAF): 46

FIGURE 14.4

Example of a multiaxial evaluation.
A multiaxial evaluation for a depressed man with a cocaine problem might look like this.

illness? Is it 10 percent? Perhaps 25 percent? Could the figure range as high as 40 percent or 50 percent?

Such estimates fall in the domain of *epidemiology*—**the study of the distribution of mental or physical disorders in a population.** The 1980s and 1990s brought major advances in psychiatric epidemiology, as a host of large-scale investigations provided a huge, new database on the distribution of mental disorders (Wang et al., 2008). In epidemiology, ***prevalence* refers to the percentage of a population that exhibits a disorder during a specified time period.** In the case of mental disorders, the most interesting data are the estimates of *lifetime prevalence,* the percentage of people who endure a specific disorder at any time in their lives.

Studies published in the 1980s and early 1990s found psychological disorders in roughly *one-third* of the population (Regier & Kaelber, 1995; Robins, Locke, & Regier, 1991). Subsequent research suggested that about 44 percent of the adult population will struggle with some sort of psychological disorder at some point in their lives (Kessler & Zhao, 1999; Regier & Burke, 2000). The most recent large-scale epidemiological study estimated the lifetime risk of a psychiatric disorder to be 51 percent (Kessler et al., 2005a). Obviously, all these figures are *estimates* that depend to some extent on the sampling methods and assessment techniques used (Wakefield, 1999b). The progressively higher estimates in recent years have begun to generate some controversy in the field. Some experts believe that recent estimates are implausibly high and that they may trivialize psychiatric diagnoses (Wakefield & Spitzer, 2002). The debate centres on where to draw the line between normal difficulties in functioning and full-fledged mental illness—that is, when symptoms qualify as a disease (Regier, Narrow, & Rae, 2004).

In any event, whether one goes with conservative or liberal estimates, the prevalence of psychological disorders is quite a bit higher than most people assume. Across all of North America, the most common types of psychological disorders are (1) substance (alcohol and drugs) use disorders, (2) anxiety disorders, and (3) mood disorders.

Data from Statistics Canada (2003a) and the Public Health Agency of Canada (2002) give us a snapshot of the prevalence and costs of psychological disorders in Canada. Figure 14.5 presents the reported rates of selected disorders for 2001–2002 in Canada (Statistics Canada, 2003a). Overall, one in ten Canadians over 15 years of age reported symptoms consistent with one of the categories of disorder listed. As you can see in Figure 14.5, while the overall rates for males and females are about equal (9.7 percent and 11.1 percent), there is gender variation across categories of disorder. Most (68 percent) of the people who reported symptoms consistent with one of these disorders *did not* seek assistance!

WEB LINK 14.2

National Alliance on Mental Illness (NAMI)
NAMI describes itself as "a grassroots, self-help support and advocacy organization of families and friends of people with serious mental illness, and those persons themselves." Its online site provides extensive and current information about schizophrenia, bipolar disorder, and other severe disorders.

	Total		Males		Females	
	Number	%	Number	%	Number	%
Major depression	1 120 000	4.5	420 000	3.4	700 000	5.5
Mania disorder	190 000	0.8	90 000	0.7	100 000	0.8
Any mood disorder	**1 210 000**	**4.9**	**460 000**	**3.8**	**750 000**	**5.9**
Panic disorder	400 000	1.6	130 000	1.1	270 000	2.1
Agoraphobia	180 000	0.7	40 000	0.4	140 000	1.1
Social anxiety disorder (social phobia)	750 000	3.0	310 000	2.6	430 000	3.4
Any anxiety	**1 180 000**	4.7	**440 000**	3.6	**740 000**	5.8
Alcohol dependence	640 000	2.6	470 000	3.8	170 000	1.3
Illicit drugs dependence	170 000	0.7	120 000	1.0	50 000	0.4
Substance dependence	**740 000**	**3.0**	**540 000**	**4.4**	**200 000**	**1.6**
Total – Any measured disorder or substance dependence	**2 600 000**	**10.4**	**1 190 000**	**9.7**	**1 410 000**	**11.1**

FIGURE 14.5

Reported one-year prevalence of psychological disorders.

This figure presents the estimated percentage of people who have suffered from one of a selected set of psychological disorders in the year preceding the survey. The estimates represent people surveyed with symptoms consistent with each type of disorder. The survey targeted Canadians 15 years and older and excluded members of the Canadian Forces, First Nations people living on reserves, and people confined to health-care institutions.

Source: Statistics Canada, Canadian community health survey: Mental health and well-being. *The Daily*, September 3, 2003, http://www.statcan.ca/Daily/English/030903/d030903a.htm.

REVIEW OF KEY POINTS

- The medical model assumes that it is useful to view abnormal behaviour as a disease. This view has been criticized on the grounds that it turns questions about deviance into medical questions. Nonetheless, the medical model has proven useful, although one should remember that it is only an analogy.
- Three criteria are used in deciding whether people suffer from psychological disorders: deviance, personal distress, and maladaptive behaviour. Often it is difficult to clearly draw a line between normality and abnormality. Contrary to popular stereotypes, people with psychological disorders are not particularly bizarre or dangerous, and even the most severe disorders are treatable.
- Research by David Rosenhan showed that pseudopatients were routinely admitted to mental hospitals, which were unable to detect the patients' normalcy. His study showed that the distinction between normality and abnormality is not clear-cut.
- DSM is the official psychodiagnostic classification system. This system asks for information about patients on five axes, or dimensions. The current version is DSM-IV. Work is underway on DSM-5, which may supplement the current categorical approach with a dimensional approach. It is difficult to obtain good data on the prevalence of psychological disorders. Nonetheless, it is clear that they are more common than widely believed.

The costs of these disorders for the individuals and their families are enormous. In addition, the costs to the health system are also substantial. The report produced by the Public Health Agency of Canada (2002) estimates that the 1993 costs of all psychological disorders were $7.331 billion. In 1999, 1.5 million hospital-days were due to admissions for anxiety disorders, major depression, bipolar disorders, schizophrenia, personality disorders, eating disorders, and suicidal behaviour. Hospital admissions for eating disorders increased by 34 percent between 1987 and 1999 for young women under the age of 15. Eating disorders are discussed in the Personal Application for this chapter, on pages 687–689.

In this chapter, we cannot discuss in detail all of the disorders listed in the DSM-IV. Some of the disorders we have discussed in previous chapters (e.g., see Chapter 5 for a discussion of substance abuse). However, we will introduce you to many of the major categories of disorder to give you an overview of the many forms that psychological disorder can take.

In discussing each set of disorders, we will begin with brief descriptions of the specific syndromes or subtypes that fall into a category. Then we'll focus on the *etiology* of the disorders in that category. Although many paths can lead to specific disorders, some are more common than others. We'll highlight some of the common paths to enhance your understanding of the roots of abnormal behaviour.

Anxiety Disorders   SIM9

Everyone experiences anxiety from time to time. It is a natural and common reaction to many of life's difficulties. For some people, however, anxiety becomes a chronic problem. These people experience high levels of anxiety with disturbing regularity. *Anxiety disorders are a class of disorders marked by feelings of excessive apprehension and anxiety.* We will look at five principal types of anxiety disorders: generalized anxiety disorder, phobic disorder, panic disorder and agoraphobia, obsessive-compulsive disorder, and post-traumatic stress disorder. These disorders are not mutually exclusive, as many people who develop one anxiety syndrome often suffer from another at some point in their lives (Merikangas & Kalaydjian, 2009). Studies suggest that anxiety disorders are quite common. They occur in roughly 19 percent of the population (Dew, Bromet, & Switzer, 2000; Regier & Burke, 2000).

Generalized Anxiety Disorder   11a

A *generalized anxiety disorder* is marked by a chronic, high level of anxiety that is not tied to any specific threat. This anxiety is sometimes called *free-floating anxiety* because it is nonspecific. People with this disorder worry constantly about yesterday's mistakes and tomorrow's problems. In particular, they worry about minor matters related to family, finances, work, and personal illness (Sanderson & Barlow, 1990). They hope that their worrying will help to ward off negative events (Beidel & Stipelman, 2007), but they nonetheless worry about how much

they worry (Barlow et al., 2003). They often dread decisions and brood over them endlessly. Their anxiety is commonly accompanied by physical symptoms such as trembling, muscle tension, diarrhea, dizziness, faintness, sweating, and heart palpitations. Generalized anxiety disorder tends to have a gradual onset and is seen more frequently in females than males (Rowa & Antony, 2008).

Phobic Disorder   11a

In a phobic disorder, an individual's troublesome anxiety has a specific focus. *A phobic disorder is marked by a persistent and irrational fear of an object or situation that presents no realistic danger.* Although mild phobias are extremely common, people are said to have a phobic disorder only when their fears seriously interfere with their everyday behaviour. Phobic reactions tend to be accompanied by physical symptoms of anxiety, such as trembling and palpitations (Rapee & Barlow, 2001).

People can develop phobic responses to virtually anything—even to things you take for granted, such as driving. Ryerson University's Dr. Martin Antony, an expert on anxiety disorders, panic disorders, and phobias (Antony & Rowa, 2008; Antony & Stein, 2008), estimates that 1–5 percent of Canadians suffer significant anxiety related to their driving fears (Pooley, 2004), but that those suffering from these disorders are by and large very good drivers.

While people can develop phobic responses to almost anything, certain types of phobias are more common than others. Particularly common are

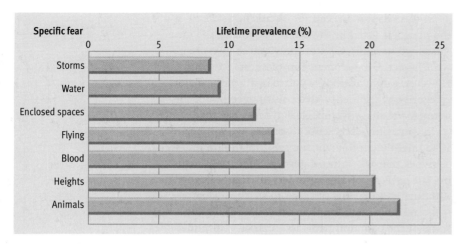

FIGURE 14.6

Common phobic fears.

This graph shows the lifetime prevalence of the most common types of phobic fears reported by participants in a study by Curtis et al. (1998). As you can see, a substantial number of people struggle with a variety of specific phobias. Bear in mind that only a portion of these people qualify for a diagnosis of phobic disorder, which is merited only if individuals' phobias seriously impair their everyday functioning.

Source: From WEITEN. *Psychology*, 9E. © 2013 Wadsworth, a part of Cengage Learning, Inc. Reproduced by permission. www.cengage.com/permissions.

acrophobia (fear of heights), claustrophobia (fear of small, enclosed places), brontophobia (fear of storms), hydrophobia (fear of water), and various animal and insect phobias (McCabe & Antony, 2008; see Figure 14.6). People troubled by phobias typically realize that their fears are irrational, but they still are unable to calm themselves when confronted by a phobic object. Among many of them, even *imagining* a phobic object or situation can trigger great anxiety (Thorpe & Salkovskis, 1995).

Panic Disorder and Agoraphobia

11a

A *panic disorder* is characterized by recurrent attacks of overwhelming anxiety that usually occur suddenly and unexpectedly. These paralyzing panic attacks are accompanied by physical symptoms of anxiety. After a number of panic attacks, victims often become apprehensive, wondering when their next panic will occur. Their concern about exhibiting panic in public may escalate to the point where they are afraid to leave home. This creates a condition called *agoraphobia,* which is a common complication of panic disorders.

Several studies have examined the rate of panic attacks in Canadian university students. Questionnaire studies suggest that as many as 34 percent of undergraduates suffer from this disorder (Norton et al., 1985). Many of these students, however, are likely suffering from *nonclinical* panic, which differs from a diagnosable panic attack. Research by University of

Manitoba psychologist Brian Cox suggests that this doesn't mean the problems for the nonclinical group are insignificant. While there are qualitative differences, many symptoms are shared by the two groups, differing only in quantity. Cox suggests that nonclinical and clinical levels of panic attacks may exist on a continuum (Cox, Endler, & Swinson, 1991).

Agoraphobia is a fear of going out to public places (its literal meaning is "fear of the marketplace or open places"). Because of this fear, some people become prisoners confined to their homes, although many will venture out if accompanied by a trusted companion (Hollander & Simeon, 2008). As its name suggests, agoraphobia has traditionally been viewed as a phobic disorder. However, more recent evidence suggests that agoraphobia is mainly a complication of panic disorder. About two-thirds of people who suffer from panic disorder are female (Taylor, Cox, & Asmundson, 2009). The onset of panic disorder typically occurs during late adolescence or early adulthood (McClure-Tone & Pine, 2009).

Obsessive-Compulsive Disorder

11a

Obsessions are *thoughts* that repeatedly intrude on one's consciousness in a distressing way. Compulsions are *actions* that one feels forced to carry out. Thus, an *obsessive-compulsive disorder* (OCD) is marked by persistent, uncontrollable intrusions of unwanted thoughts (obsessions) and urges to engage in senseless rituals (compulsions). Canadian comedian and TV personality Howie Mandel suffers from OCD (Mandel, 2009). A veteran of TV, movies, and stand-up comedy, Mandel hosted a popular TV game show, *Deal or No Deal,* and when he greeted new contestants, rather than shaking hands, he uses a "knuckle bump" in which he merely touches knuckles with them. It is his way of dealing with one of his obsessions, contamination and germs (mysophobia). While Mandel admits that he has had to shake hands once in a while, he wants to avoid what sometimes follows a handshaking episode. According to Mandel, "I have shaken hands and had a good evening, but I just don't want to trigger whatever I trigger. I would be in the bathroom for hours, and I'll scald [my hands] and I'll come out and then I can't think of anything else. I'll keep thinking I've got something to get off of my hands" (Hampson, 2007, p. R3). As Mandel explains it in his 2009 autobiography, *Here's the Deal: Don't Touch Me,* "it's not just that I'm scared of germs," he says. There's nothing wrong with shaking hands with someone and then washing your hands. But "there

Well-known Canadian comedian and TV personality Howie Mandel is very public about his OCD. He is a spokesperson for the Anxiety Disorders Association of America's "Treat it, don't repeat it: Break free from OCD" ad campaign, which is designed to raise awareness about the nature and treatment of various anxiety disorders. Visit the association's website at http://www.adaa.org to learn more about OCD.

is something wrong with being totally consumed that you didn't get everything off your hand, that there's things crawling, so you wash it again, and you're so consumed that you wash it again, and you wash it again and you wash it again and you wash it again," Mandel says. "When you can't get past that, that's obsessive-compulsive disorder. It's not that you're afraid of germs, it's that you obsess about that thought and have to do things like hand washing to relieve the worry. I always have intrusive thoughts and rituals."

Mandel's obsession with germs is also the reason why he has shaved his head, he says. "For my germ phobia, it kind of helps me. It feels cleaner. . . ." (Mandel Uses Knuckle Knock, 2006). When he enters a hotel room, he typically orders 26 clean towels so that he can lay a path across the room to walk on. He also constructed a special *sterile house* on his property, a place that he can escape alone to when he feels the need (Packer, 2007). He carries rubber gloves with him for times when he must touch things that cause him problems. Mandel is very forthcoming about his OCD and hopes that by publicizing his own issues,

he will make it easier for others who suffer from similar concerns. It is interesting to see how he has made accommodations to his obsessions that allow him to continue successfully in his profession.

Obsessions sometimes centre on inflicting harm on others, personal failures, suicide, or sexual acts. People troubled by obsessions may feel that they have lost control of their mind. Compulsions usually involve stereotyped rituals that temporarily relieve anxiety. Common examples include constant hand-washing, repetitive cleaning of things that are already clean, and endless rechecking of locks, faucets, and such (Pato, Eisen, & Phillips, 2003). Specific types of obsessions tend to be associated with specific types of compulsions. For example, obsessions about contamination tend to be paired with cleaning compulsions and obsessions about symmetry tend to be paired with ordering and arranging compulsions (Hollander & Simeon, 2008).

Many of us can be compulsive at times. Indeed, a recent study found that 17 percent of a sample of people without a mental disorder reported a significant obsession or compulsion (Fullana et al., 2009). However, full-fledged obsessive-compulsive disorders occur in roughly 2–3 percent of the population (Zohar, Fostick, & Juven). The prevalence of obsessive-compulsive disorder seems to be increasing, but this trend may simply reflect changes in clinicians' diagnostic tendencies (Stein et al., 1997a). Most cases of OCD emerge before the age of 35 (Kessler et al., 2005b; Otto et al., 1999).

While OCD is often seen as a unitary disorder, recent research by Laura Summerfeldt of Trent University, Martin Antony, and their colleagues suggests that it may be a heterogeneous disorder (Antony, Purdon, & Summerfeldt, 2006; Summerfeldt, 2004; Summerfeldt et al, 1999). They factor-analyzed the symptom structure of 203 Canadians diagnosed with OCD and found that four factors seemed to underlie the symptoms: obsessions and checking, symmetry and order, cleanliness and washing, and hoarding. They conclude that "Our findings add to the growing body of evidence for the multidimensionality of OCD, but suggest that a comprehensive model of symptom structure has yet to be identified" (Summerfeldt et al, 1999, p. 309).

Post-Traumatic Stress Disorder (PTSD)

Although we began this chapter with a discussion of PTSD suffered by members of the military, PTSD is not restricted to this context. PTSD is often elicited by any of a variety of traumatic events, including a

WEB LINK 14.3

Anxiety Disorders Association of Canada
This website is an excellent starting point to learn more about the various types of anxiety disorders, how they are treated, and where to get help for such disorders in Canada. The association is dedicated to promoting the prevention, treatment, and management of anxiety disorders and to improving the lives of people who suffer from them.

Natural disasters such as Hurricane Katrina result in enormous economic and personal devastation. The impact is both physical and psychological, and increased levels of PTSD are commonly found among the survivors.

rape or assault, a severe automobile accident, a natural disaster, or the witnessing of someone's death (Charuvastra & Cloitre, 2008; Koren, Arnon, & Klein, 1999; Stein et al., 1997b; Vernberg et al., 1996). In some instances, PTSD does not surface until many months or years after a person's exposure to severe stress (Holen, 2000) and is tied to memory for the events (Rubin, Bernsten, & Bohni, 2008; Rubin, Boals, & Berntsen, 2008). In 2005, the residents of New Orleans suffered one of the most devastating natural disasters that residents of the United States had ever experienced: Hurricane Katrina. Thousands of deaths and billions of dollars in property damage resulted from this hurricane. Mental health professionals were brought in to help with the effects of the disaster. They found that by seven months after the hurricane, almost one-half of the residents of New Orleans were estimated to be suffering from various mood and anxiety disorders, including a staggering 30 percent who were suffering from PTSD (Galea et al., 2007). It is difficult for the rest of us to imagine the continuing personal and economic cost of such a disaster.

Unfortunately, traumatic experiences appear to be much more common than widely assumed. Research suggests that 7–8 percent of people have suffered from PTSD at some point in their lives, with prevalence being higher among women (10 percent) than men (5 percent) (Flood, Davidson,

& Beckham, 2008; Resick, Monson, & Rizvi, 2008). Currently, there is great concern about the number of military returnees from wars overseas who will develop PTSD (DeAngelis, 2008; Ramchand et al., 2010; Sundin et al., 2010). Common symptoms of PTSD include re-experiencing the traumatic event in the form of nightmares and flashbacks, emotional numbing, alienation, problems in social relationships, an increased sense of vulnerability, and elevated levels of arousal, anxiety, anger, and guilt (McClure-Tone & Pine, 2009).

Research suggests that a variety of factors are predictors of individuals' risk for PTSD (McNally, 2009; Keane, Marshall, & Taft, 2006; Norris et al., 2001). As you might expect, increased vulnerability is associated with greater personal injuries and losses, greater intensity of exposure to the traumatic event, and more exposure to the grotesque aftermath of the event. Often overlooked are the reactions of children to such disasters, including mental health concerns (Becker-Blease, Turner, & Finkelhor, 2010). In general, one key predictor of vulnerability that emerged in a recent review of the relevant research is the *intensity of one's reaction at the time of the traumatic event* (Ozer et al., 2003). Individuals who have especially intense emotional reactions during or immediately after the traumatic event go on to show elevated vulnerability to PTSD. Vulnerability seems to be greatest among people whose reactions are so intense that they report dissociative experiences (a sense that things are not real, that time is stretching out, that one is watching oneself in a movie).

The frequency and severity of post-traumatic symptoms usually decline gradually over time, but recovery tends to be gradual and in many cases, the symptoms never completely disappear. Many years after his experiences in Rwanda, General Roméo Dallaire is still suffering the aftereffects of what he saw and heard about during his time in Rwanda.

Etiology of Anxiety Disorders

 11a

Like most psychological disorders, anxiety disorders develop out of complicated interactions among a variety of biological and psychological factors.

Biological Factors

 11a

In studies that assess the impact of heredity on psychological disorders, investigators look at *concordance rates*. A *concordance rate* indicates the percentage of twin pairs or other pairs of relatives who exhibit the same disorder. If relatives who share more genetic similarity show higher concordance rates than relatives who share less genetic overlap, this finding supports the genetic hypothesis. The results of both *twin studies* (see Figure 14.7) and *family studies* (see Chapter 3 for discussions of both methods) suggest that there is a moderate genetic predisposition to anxiety disorders (Fyer, 2009). These findings are consistent with the idea that inherited differences in temperament might make some people more vulnerable than others to anxiety disorders. As we discussed in Chapter 11, Jerome Kagan and his colleagues (1992) have found that about 15–20 percent of infants display an *inhibited temperament*. Such a temperament is characterized by shyness, timidity, and wariness, and appears to have a strong genetic basis. Research suggests that this temperament is a risk factor for the development of anxiety disorders (Coles, Schofield, & Pietrefesa, 2006).

Another line of research suggests that *anxiety sensitivity* may make people vulnerable to anxiety disorders (McWilliams et al., 2007; Reiss, 1991; Schmidt, Zvolensky, & Maner, 2006). According to this notion, some people are highly sensitive to the internal physiological symptoms of anxiety and are prone to overreact with fear when they experience these symptoms. Anxiety sensitivity may fuel an inflationary spiral in which anxiety breeds more anxiety, which eventually spins out of control in the

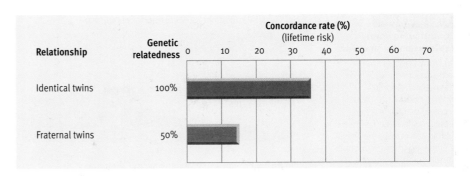

Relationship	Genetic relatedness	Concordance rate (%) (lifetime risk)

FIGURE 14.7

Twin studies of anxiety disorders.
The concordance rate for anxiety disorders in identical twins is higher than that for fraternal twins, who share less genetic overlap. These results suggest that there is a genetic predisposition to anxiety disorders. (Data based on Noyes et al., 1987; Slater & Shields, 1969; Torgersen, 1979, 1983)

form of an anxiety disorder. Cox and his colleagues suggest that some aspects of anxiety sensitivity may serve as vulnerabilities for both panic disorder and depression (Cox et al., 2001).

Recent evidence suggests that a link may exist between anxiety disorders and neurochemical activity in the brain. As you learned in Chapter 3, *neurotransmitters* are chemicals that carry signals from one neuron to another. Therapeutic drugs (such as Valium) that reduce excessive anxiety appear to alter neurotransmitter activity at GABA synapses. This finding and other lines of evidence suggest that disturbances in the neural circuits using GABA may play a role in some types of anxiety disorders (Rowa & Antony, 2009). Abnormalities in neural circuits using serotonin have recently been implicated in panic and obsessive-compulsive disorders (Pato et al., 2008; Stein & Hugo, 2004). Thus, scientists are beginning to unravel the neurochemical bases for anxiety disorders.

Conditioning and Learning

 11a

Many anxiety responses may be *acquired through classical conditioning and maintained through operant conditioning* (see Chapter 6). Imagine, for example, a young child who is buried briefly in the snow by a small avalanche, and who now, as an adult, is afraid of snow. According to Mowrer (1947), an originally neutral stimulus (the snow) may be paired with a frightening event (the avalanche) so that it becomes a conditioned stimulus eliciting anxiety (see Figure 14.8(a)).

Once a fear is acquired through classical conditioning, the person may start avoiding the anxiety-producing stimulus. The avoidance response is negatively reinforced because it is followed by a reduction in anxiety. This process involves operant

Psychological Disorders

FIGURE 14.8

Conditioning as an explanation for phobias.

(a) Many phobias appear to be acquired through classical conditioning when a neutral stimulus is paired with an anxiety-arousing stimulus. **(b)** Once acquired, a phobia may be maintained through operant conditioning. Avoidance of the phobic stimulus reduces anxiety, resulting in negative reinforcement.

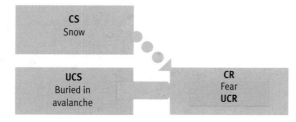

(a) Classical conditioning: Acquisition of phobic fear

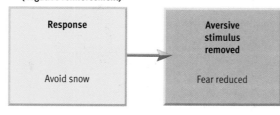

CS
Snow

UCS		CR
Buried in avalanche		Fear
		UCR

(b) Operant conditioning: Maintenance of phobic fear (negative reinforcement)

Response		Aversive stimulus removed
Avoid snow		Fear reduced

WEB LINK 14.4

National Institut of Mental Health
A wealth of information on psychological disorders is available in this part of the National Institute of Mental Health's massive site. Visitors will find detailed online booklets on generalized anxiety disorder, obsessive-compulsive disorder, panic disorder, depression, bipolar disorder, and other psychological disorders. Brief fact sheets, dense technical reports, and many other resources can also be found here.

conditioning (see Figure 14.8(b)). Thus, separate conditioning processes may create and then sustain specific anxiety responses (Levis, 1989). Consistent with this view, studies find that a substantial portion of people suffering from phobias can identify a traumatic conditioning experience that probably contributed to their anxiety disorder (McCabe & Antony, 2008; Mineka & Zinbarg, 2006).

The tendency to develop phobias of certain types of objects and situations may be explained by Martin Seligman's (1971) concept of *preparedness*. He suggests that people are biologically prepared by their evolutionary history to acquire some fears much more easily than others. His theory would explain why people develop phobias of ancient sources of threat (such as snakes and spiders) much more readily than modern sources of threat (such as electrical outlets or hot irons). As we noted in Chapter 6, Arne Öhman and Susan Mineka (2001) have updated the notion of preparedness, which they call an *evolved module for fear learning*. They maintain that this evolved module is automatically activated by stimuli related to survival threats in evolutionary history and relatively resistant to intentional efforts to suppress the resulting fears. Consistent with this view, phobic stimuli associated with evolutionary threats tend to produce more rapid conditioning of fears and stronger fear responses (Mineka & Öhman, 2002).

Critics note a number of problems with conditioning models of phobias (Rachman, 1990). For instance, many people with phobias cannot recall or identify a traumatic conditioning experience that led to their phobia. Conversely, many people endure extremely traumatic experiences that should create a phobia but do not (Coelho & Purkis, 2009). Moreover, phobic fears can be acquired indirectly, by observing another's fear response to a specific stimulus or by absorbing fear-inducing information (imagine a parent harping on how dangerous lightning is) (Coelho & Purkis, 2009). Thus, the development of phobias may depend on synergistic interactions among a variety of learning processes.

Cognitive Factors

Cognitive theorists maintain that certain styles of thinking make some people particularly vulnerable to anxiety disorders (Craske & Waters, 2005). According to these theorists, some people are more likely to suffer from problems with anxiety because they tend to (a) misinterpret harmless situations as threatening, (b) focus excessive attention on perceived threats, and (c) selectively recall information that seems threatening (Beck, 1997; McNally, 1994, 1996). In one intriguing test of the cognitive view, anxious and nonanxious subjects were asked to read 32 sentences that could be interpreted in either a threatening or a nonthreatening manner (Eysenck et al., 1991). For instance, one such sentence was "The doctor examined little Emma's growth," which could mean that the doctor checked either her height or the growth of a tumour. As Figure 14.9 shows, the anxious participants interpreted the sentences in a threatening way more often than the nonanxious participants did. Thus, consistent with our theme that human experience is highly subjective, the cognitive view holds that some people are prone to anxiety disorders because they see threat

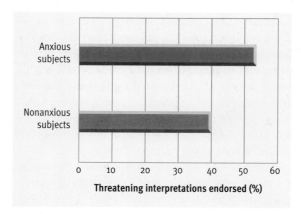

FIGURE 14.9

Cognitive factors in anxiety disorders.

Eysenck and his colleagues (1991) compared how subjects with anxiety problems and nonanxious subjects tended to interpret sentences that could be viewed as threatening or nonthreatening. Consistent with cognitive models of anxiety disorders, anxious subjects were more likely to interpret the sentences in a threatening light.

in every corner of their lives (Aikins & Craske, 2001; Riskind, 2005; Williams et al., 1997).

Stress

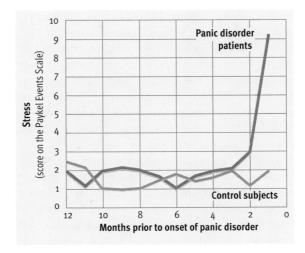

Finally, studies have supported the long-held suspicion that anxiety disorders are stress-related (Beidel & Stipelman, 2007: Sandin et al., 2004). For instance, Faravelli and Pallanti (1989) found that patients with panic disorder had experienced a dramatic increase

in stress in the month prior to the onset of their disorder (see Figure 14.10). In another study, Brown et al. (1998) found an association between stress and the development of social phobia. Thus, there is reason to believe that high stress often helps to precipitate the onset of anxiety disorders.

FIGURE 14.10

Stress and panic disorder.

Faravelli and Pallanti (1989) assessed the amount of stress experienced during the 12 months before the onset of panic disorder in a group of 64 patients with this disorder and in a control group drawn from hospital employees and their friends. As you can see, there was a dramatic increase in stress in the month prior to the onset of the patients' panic disorders. These data suggest that stress may contribute to the development of panic disorders.

Source: Adapted from C. Faravelli and S. Pallanti (1989). Recent life events and panic disorder. *American Journal of Psychiatry, 146* (May): 622-626. Reprinted with permission from the *American Journal of Psychiatry,* (Copyright © 1989). American Psychiatric Association.

REVIEW OF KEY POINTS

▷ The anxiety disorders include generalized anxiety disorder, phobic disorder, panic disorder, obsessive-compulsive disorder, and post-traumatic stress disorder. Many people who develop one anxiety disorder also suffer from another.

▷ Twin studies suggest that there is a weak genetic predisposition to anxiety disorders. These disorders may be more likely in people who are especially sensitive to the physiological symptoms of anxiety. Abnormalities in neurotransmitter activity at GABA synapses or serotonin synapses may also play a role in anxiety disorders.

▷ Many anxiety responses, especially phobias, may be caused by classical conditioning and maintained by operant conditioning. Parents who model anxiety may promote these disorders through observational learning.

▷ Cognitive theorists maintain that certain styles of thinking—especially a tendency to overinterpret harmless situations as threatening—make some people more vulnerable to anxiety disorders. Stress may also predispose people to anxiety disorders.

Dissociative Disorders

Dissociative disorders are probably the most controversial set of disorders in the diagnostic system. They spark heated debate among normally subdued researchers and clinicians (Simeon & Loewenstein, 2009). *Dissociative disorders* are a class of disorders in which people lose contact with portions of their consciousness or memory, resulting in disruptions in their sense of identity. We'll describe three dissociative syndromes: dissociative amnesia, dissociative fugue, and dissociative identity disorder. All of these appear to be relatively uncommon, although good data on the prevalence of these disorders are scarce (Kihlstrom, 2005).

Dissociative Amnesia and Fugue

Dissociative amnesia and fugue are overlapping disorders characterized by serious memory deficits.

Dissociative amnesia is a sudden loss of memory for important personal information that is too extensive to be due to normal forgetting. Memory losses may occur for a single traumatic event (such as an automobile accident or home fire) or for an extended period of time surrounding the event. Cases of amnesia have been observed after people have experienced disasters, accidents, combat stress, physical abuse, and rape, or after they have witnessed the violent death of a parent, among other things (Arrigo & Pezdek, 1997; Cardeña & Gleaves, 2007). In *dissociative fugue,* people lose their memory for their entire lives along with their sense of personal identity. These people forget their names, their families, where they live, and where they work. Despite this wholesale forgetting, they remember matters unrelated to their identity. They may, for example, remember how to drive a car or how to do math.

PREVIEW QUESTIONS

▷ What are the principal types of dissociative disorders, and what are their chief symptoms?

▷ What is the etiology of dissociative identity disorder?

Dissociative Identity Disorder

Dissociative identity disorder (DID) involves the coexistence in one person of two or more largely complete, and usually very different, personalities. The name for this disorder used to be *multiple personality disorder,* which still enjoys informal use. In dissociative identity disorder, the divergences in behaviour go far beyond those that people normally display in adapting to different roles in life. People with "multiple personalities" feel that they have more than one identity. Each personality has his or her own name, memories, traits, and physical mannerisms. Although rare, this "Dr. Jekyll and Mr. Hyde" syndrome is frequently portrayed in novels, television shows, and movies, such as the *Three Faces of Eve,* a 1957 film starring Joanne Woodward. In popular media portrayals, the syndrome is often mistakenly called *schizophrenia.* As you will see later, schizophrenic disorders are entirely different.

In dissociative identity disorder, the various personalities are often unaware of each other (Eich et al., 1997). In other words, the experiences of a specific personality are recalled only by that personality and not by the others. The alternate personalities commonly display traits that are quite foreign to the original personality. For instance, a shy, inhibited person might develop a flamboyant, extraverted alternate personality. Transitions between identities often occur suddenly. The disparities between identities can be bizarre, as different personalities may assert that they are different in age, race, gender, and sexual orientation (Kluft, 1996). Dissociative identity disorder rarely occurs in isolation. Most DID patients also have a history of anxiety or mood or personality disorders (Ross, 1999). Dissociative identity disorder is seen more in women than men (Simeon & Loewenstein, 2009).

Starting in the 1970s, there was a dramatic increase in the diagnosis of multiple-personality disorder (Kihlstrom, 2001). Only 79 well-documented cases had accumulated up through 1970, but by the late 1990s, about 40 000 cases were estimated to have been reported (Lilienfeld & Lynn, 2003). Some theorists believe that these disorders used to be underdiagnosed—that is, they often went undetected (Maldonado & Spiegel, 2008). However, other theorists argue that a handful of clinicians have begun overdiagnosing the condition and that some clinicians even *encourage and contribute* to the emergence of DID (McHugh, 1995; Powell & Gee, 1999). Consistent with this view, a survey of all the psychiatrists in Switzerland found that 90 percent of them had never seen a case of dissociative identity disorder, whereas three of the psychiatrists had each seen more than 20 DID patients (Modestin, 1992). The data from this study suggest that six psychiatrists (out of 655 surveyed) accounted for two-thirds of the dissociative identity disorder diagnoses in Switzerland.

Etiology of Dissociative Disorders

Psychogenic amnesia and fugue are usually attributed to excessive stress. However, relatively little is known about why this extreme reaction to stress occurs in a tiny minority of people but not in the vast majority who are subjected to similar stress. Some theorists speculate that certain personality traits—fantasy proneness and a tendency to become intensely absorbed in personal experiences—may make some people more susceptible to dissociative disorders, but adequate evidence is lacking on this line of thought (Kihlstrom, Glisky, & Angiulo, 1994).

The causes of dissociative identity disorders are particularly obscure. Some skeptical theorists, such as Carleton University psychologist Nicholas Spanos (1994, 1996) and others (Lilienfeld et al., 1999), believe that people with multiple personalities are engaging in intentional role-playing to use mental illness as a face-saving excuse for their personal failings. Spanos also argues that a small minority of therapists help create multiple personalities in their patients by subtly encouraging the emergence of alternate personalities. According to Spanos, dissociative identity disorder is a creation of modern North American culture, much as demonic possession was a creation of early Christianity. To bolster his argument, he discusses how multiple-personality patients' symptom presentations seem to have been influenced by popular media. For example, the typical patient with dissociative identity disorder used to report having two or three personalities, but since the publication of *Sybil* (Schreiber, 1973) and other books describing patients with many personalities, the average number of alternate personalities has climbed to about 15. In a similar vein, there has been a dramatic upsurge in the number of dissociative patients reporting that they were victims of ritual satanic abuse during childhood that dates back to the publication of *Michelle Remembers* (Smith & Pazder, 1980), a book about a multiple-personality patient who purportedly was tortured by a satanic cult.

Despite these concerns, some clinicians are convinced that DID is an authentic disorder (Gleaves, May, & Cardeña, 2007; van der Hart & Nijenhuis, 2009). They argue that there is no incentive for either patients or therapists to manufacture cases of multiple personalities, which are often greeted with skepticism and outright hostility. They maintain that most cases of dissociative identity disorder are rooted in severe emotional trauma that occurred during childhood (Maldonado & Spiegel, 2008). A substantial majority of people with dissociative identity disorder report a childhood history of rejection from parents and physical and sexual abuse (Foote et al., 2006; van der Hart & Nijenhuis, 2009). However, this abuse typically has not been independently verified (Lilienfeld & Lynn, 2003). Moreover, this link would not be unique to DID, as a history of child abuse elevates the likelihood of *many* disorders, especially among females (MacMillan et al., 2001). In the final analysis, very little is known about the causes of dissociative identity disorder, which remains a controversial diagnosis (Barry-Walsh, 2005). In one survey of American psychiatrists, only one-quarter of the respondents indicated that they felt there was solid evidence for the scientific validity of the DID diagnosis (Pope et al., 1999). Consistent with this finding, a more recent study found that scientific interest in DID has dwindled since the mid-1990s (Pope et al., 2006).

REVIEW OF KEY POINTS

> Dissociative amnesia involves sudden memory loss that is too extensive to be due to normal forgetting. In dissociative fugue, people also lose their sense of identity. Dissociative identity disorder is marked by the coexistence of two or more very different personalities. Since the 1970s, there has been a dramatic and controversial increase in the diagnosis of dissociative identity disorder.

> Some theorists believe that people with dissociative identity disorder are engaging in intentional role-playing to use an exotic mental illness as a face-saving excuse for their personal failings. These disorders may be rooted in emotional trauma that occurred during childhood.

Mood Disorders   SIM9

What do Kurt Cobain, Vincent van Gogh, Sting, Chris Cornell, Jean-Claude van Damme, Gwyneth Paltrow, Keanu Reeves, Ben Stiller, Axl Rose, Francis Ford Coppola, Marilyn Monroe, Margaret Trudeau, Winston Churchill, Leo Tolstoy, Jim Carrey, Margot Kidder, Sarah McLachlan, Percy Paul, and Canadian Olympic figure skater Elizabeth Manley have in common? Yes, they all achieved great prominence, albeit in different ways at different times. But, more pertinent to our interest, they all suffered from severe mood disorders.

PREVIEW QUESTIONS

> What are the principal mood disorders, and what are their chief symptoms?

> Which biological factors have been implicated in mood disorders?

> How do cognitive processes contribute to depressive disorders?

> How do social skills and stress contribute to depressive disorders?

Soundgarden front man Chris Cornell and actor/karate champion Jean-Claude van Damme are two of the many celebrities who have made public their struggles with depression. Many celebrities hope to use their disclosure of mental illness to highlight the disorder and to fight the stigma associated with mental illness.

FIGURE 14.11

Episodic patterns in mood disorders.

Time-limited episodes of emotional disturbance come and go unpredictably in mood disorders. People with unipolar disorders suffer from bouts of depression only, whereas people with bipolar disorders experience both manic and depressive episodes. The time between episodes of disturbance varies greatly with the individual and the type of disorder.

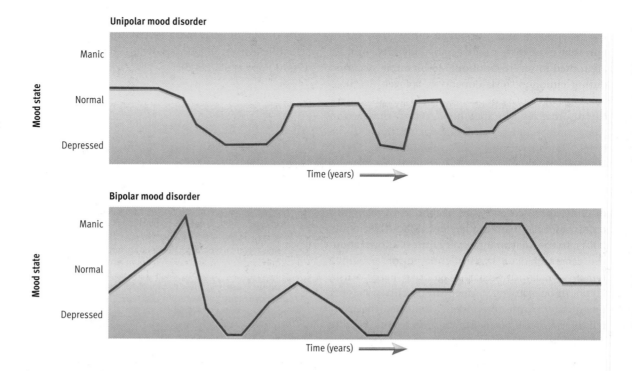

Although mood disorders can be terribly debilitating, people with mood disorders may still achieve greatness, because such disorders tend to be *episodic*. In other words, mood disturbances often come and go, interspersed among periods of normality. These episodes of disturbance can vary greatly in length, but they typically last 3–12 months (Akiskal, 2000).

Of course, everybody has ups and downs in terms of mood. Life would be dull indeed if people's emotional tone were constant. Everyone experiences depression occasionally. Likewise, everyone has days that he or she sails through on an emotional high. Such emotional fluctuations are natural, but some people are subject to extreme and sustained distortions of mood. We know that prolonged episodes of mood disorders can interfere with an individual's personal and professional life. In a recent survey, 80 percent of Canadian workers who suffered from depression reported that it interfered with their ability to work (Statistics Canada, 2007h). Friends and family typically are quite concerned when they witness prolonged periods of sadness or depression in their loved ones. They may try to help by suggesting that the depressed individuals say positive things to themselves—to use positive thinking. If only things were that simple. In fact, positive self-statements may even be harmful to some types of people in some circumstances (Wood, Perunovic, & Lee, 2009).

What are mood disorders and what do we know about their causes? *Mood disorders* are a class of disorders marked by emotional disturbances of varied kinds that may spill over to disrupt physical, perceptual, social, and thought processes. There are two basic types of mood disorders: unipolar and bipolar (see Figure 14.11). People with *unipolar disorder* experience emotional extremes at just one end of the mood continuum, as they are troubled only by *depression*. People with *bipolar disorder* are vulnerable to emotional extremes at both ends of the mood continuum, going through periods of both *depression* and *mania* (excitement and elation).

Major Depressive Disorder 11b

The line between normal dejection and unhappiness and abnormal depression can be difficult to draw (Akiskal, 2009). Ultimately, it requires a subjective judgment. Crucial considerations in this judgment include the duration of the depression and its disruptive effects. When a depression significantly impairs everyday adaptive behaviour for more than a few weeks, there is reason for concern.

In *major depressive disorder*, people show persistent feelings of sadness and despair and a loss of interest in previous sources of pleasure. Negative emotions form the heart of the depressive syndrome, but many other symptoms may also appear. The most common symptoms of major depression are summarized and compared with the symptoms of mania in Table 14.1. A central feature of depression is *anhedonia*—a diminished ability to experience pleasure. Depressed people lack the energy or motivation to tackle the tasks of living, to the point where they often have trouble getting out of bed (Craighead et al., 2008). Hence, they often give up activities that they used to find enjoyable. For example, a depressed person might quit going bowling or might give up a favourite hobby such as photography. Alterations in appetite and sleep patterns are common. People with depression often lack energy. They tend to move sluggishly and talk slowly. Anxiety, irritability, and brooding are commonly observed. Self-esteem tends to sink as the depressed person begins to feel worthless. Depression plunges people into feelings of hopelessness, dejection, and boundless guilt. To make matters worse, people who suffer from depression often exhibit other disorders as well. Coexisting anxiety disorders and substance-use disorders are particularly frequent (Boland & Keller, 2009).

The onset of depression can occur at any point in the life span but a substantial majority of cases emerge before age 40 (Hammen, 2003). Depression occurs in children as well as adolescents and adults (Gruenberg & Goldstein, 2003). The vast majority (75–95 percent) of people who suffer from depression experience more than one episode over the course of their lifetime (Joska & Stein, 2008), the average number of depressive episodes is five to six. The average length of these episodes is six months (Akisakal, 2009). In one longitudinal study, after recovery from one's first episode of depression, the cumulative probability of recurrence was 25 percent after one year, 42 percent after two years, and 60 percent after five years (Solomon et al., 2000).

Recent evidence suggests that an earlier age of onset is associated with more episodes of depression, more severe symptoms, and greater impairment of social and occupational functioning (Zisook et al., 2007). Although depression tends to be episodic, some people suffer from chronic major depression that may persist for years (Klein, 2010). Chronic major depression is associated with a particularly severe impairment of functioning. People with chronic depression tend to have a relatively early onset and high rates of comorbidity (additional disorders).

The severity of depressive disorders varies considerably. When people display relatively mild symptoms of depression, they're given a diagnosis of *dysthymic disorder*, which consists of chronic depression that is insufficient in severity to justify diagnosis of a major depressive episode.

Characteristics	Manic Episode	Depressive Episode
Emotional	Elated, euphoric, very sociable, impatient at any hindrance	Gloomy, hopeless, socially withdrawn, irritable
Cognitive	Characterized by racing thoughts, flight of ideas, desire for action, and impulsive behaviour; talkative, self-confident; experiencing delusions of grandeur	Characterized by slowness of thought processes, obsessive worrying, inability to make decisions, negative self-image, self-blame, and delusions of guilt and disease
Motor	Hyperactive, tireless, requiring less sleep than usual, showing increased sex drive and fluctuating appetite	Less active, tired, experiencing difficulty in sleeping, showing decreased sex drive and decreased appetite

TABLE 14.1

Comparisons of Common Symptoms in Manic and Depressive Episodes

Source: Sarason, I. G., and Sarason, B. G. (1987). *Abnormal psychology: The problem of maladaptive behavior*. Upper Saddle River, NJ: Prentice-Hall. © 1987 Prentice-Hall.

How common is depressive disorder in Canada? Very common. Recent estimates suggest that up to 10 percent of Canadians will experience a major depressive episode sometime in their lives, with about 1 percent suffering from bipolar disorder (Health Canada, 2002b; Patten & Juby, 2008). Other North American estimates put the lifetime prevalence rate of depression even higher, at 13–14 percent (Kessler et al., 1994).

Researchers also find that the prevalence of depression is about twice as high in women as it is in men (Nolen-Hoeksema & Hilt, 2009). The many possible explanations for this gender gap are the subject of considerable debate. Simon Fraser University psychologist Marlene Moretti suggests that women tend to adopt a self-regulatory style that is relational in nature (Moretti, Rein, & Wiebe, 1998). They are sensitive to discrepancies involving

Actor Jim Carrey and singer/songwriter Sarah McLachlan are two well-known Canadians who have struggled with mood disorders.

Susan Nolen-Hoeksema

"By adolescence, girls appear to me more likely than boys to respond to stress and distress with rumination—focusing inward on feelings of distress and personal concerns rather than taking action to relieve their distress."

their beliefs about themselves and the ideals they perceive that others hold for them. Moretti found that discrepancies were related to elevated levels of dysphoria. The same was not true for the males in her study. Such self-discrepancies are important because other research has found that self-discrepancies can contribute to an individual's negative self-evaluation and suicidal ideation (Cornette et al., 2008). Others, such as University of Western Ontario researchers Gillian Kirsch and Nick Kuiper (2002), have linked gender differences in depression to differences in self-schema. A small portion of the gender disparity may be the result of women's elevated vulnerability to depression at certain points in their reproductive life cycle (Nolen-Hoeksema & Hilt, 2009). Obviously, only women have to worry about the phenomena of postpartum and postmenopausal depression.

Susan Nolen-Hoeksema (2001) argues that women experience more depression than men because they are far more likely to be victims of sexual abuse and somewhat more likely to endure poverty, harassment, and role constraints. In other words, she attributes the higher prevalence of depression among women to their experience of greater stress and adversity. Nolen-Hoeksema also believes that women have a greater tendency than men to *ruminate* about setbacks and problems. Evidence suggests that this tendency to dwell on one's difficulties elevates vulnerability to depression, as we will soon discuss.

Bipolar Disorder 11b

Bipolar disorder (formerly known as *manic-depressive disorder*) is characterized by the experience of one or more manic episodes as well as periods of depression. One manic episode is sufficient to qualify for this diagnosis. The symptoms seen in manic periods generally are the opposite of those seen in depression (see Table 14.1 for a comparison). Canadian psychologist Norman Endler, whom we mentioned at the beginning of this chapter, suffered from bipolar disorder (Endler, 1982). In a manic episode, a person's mood becomes elevated to the point of euphoria. As was the case with Percy Paul, self-esteem often skyrockets as the person bubbles over with optimism, energy, and extravagant plans. He or she becomes hyperactive and may go for days without sleep. The individual talks rapidly and shifts topics wildly, as his or her mind races at breakneck speed. Judgment is often impaired. Some people in manic periods gamble

impulsively, spend money frantically, or become sexually reckless. Like depressive disorders, bipolar disorders vary considerably in severity. People are given a diagnosis of *cyclothymic disorder* when they exhibit chronic but relatively mild symptoms of bipolar disturbance.

You may be thinking that the euphoria in manic episodes sounds appealing. If so, you are not entirely wrong. In their milder forms, manic states can seem attractive. The increases in energy, self-esteem, and optimism can be deceptively seductive; Percy Paul even called his manic states *addictive*. Because of the increase in energy, many bipolar patients report temporary surges of productivity and creativity (Goodwin & Jamison, 2007).

Although manic episodes may have some positive aspects, these periods often have a paradoxical negative undercurrent of irritability and depression (Goodwin & Jamison, 2007). Moreover, mild manic episodes usually escalate to higher levels that become scary and disturbing. Impaired judgment leads many victims to do things that they greatly regret later, as you'll see in the following case history:

> Robert, a dentist, awoke one morning with the idea that he was the most gifted dental surgeon in the area. He decided that he should try to provide services to as many people as possible, so that more people could benefit from his talents. So, he decided to remodel his two-chair dental office, installing 20 booths so that he could simultaneously attend to 20 patients. That same day, he drew up plans for this arrangement, telephoned a number of remodellers, and invited bids for the work. Later that day, impatient to get rolling on his remodelling, he rolled up his sleeves, got himself a sledgehammer, and began to knock down the walls in his office. Annoyed when that didn't go so well, he smashed his dental tools, washbasins, and X-ray equipment.
>
> Later, Robert's wife became concerned about his behaviour and summoned two of her adult daughters for assistance. The daughters responded quickly, arriving at the family home with their husbands. In the ensuing discussion, Robert—after bragging about his sexual prowess—made advances toward his daughters. He had to be subdued by their husbands. (Adapted from Kleinmuntz, 1980, p. 309)

Although not rare, bipolar disorders are much less common than unipolar disorders. Bipolar disorder affects about 1 percent of the North American population (Merikangas & Pato, 2009). Unlike unipolar depressive disorder, bipolar disorder is seen equally often in males and females (Rihmer & Angst, 2009).

"Those? Oh, just a few souvenirs from my bipolar-disorder days."

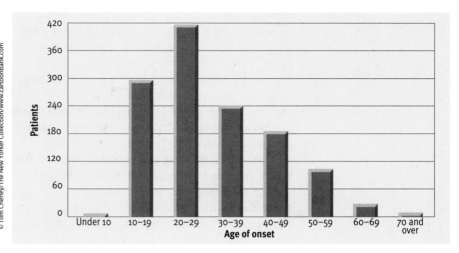

FIGURE 14.12

Age of onset for bipolar mood disorder.

The onset of bipolar disorder typically occurs in adolescence or early adulthood. The data graphed here, which were combined from ten studies, show the distribution of age of onset for 1304 bipolar patients. As you can see, bipolar disorder emerges most frequently during the 20s decade.

Source: Goodwin, F. K., and Jamison, K. R. (1990). *Manic-depressive illness* (p. 132). New York: Oxford University Press. Copyright © 1990 Oxford University Press, Inc. Reprinted by permission.

As Figure 14.12 shows, the onset of bipolar disorder is age-related. The typical age of onset is in the late teens. The mood swings in bipolar disorder can be patterned in many ways. Manic episodes typically last about four months (Angst, 2009). Episodes of depression tend to run somewhat longer and most bipolar patients end up spending more time in depressed states than manic states (Bauer, 2008).

Diversity in Mood Disorders

In the preceding discussion, we presented the differences between the two main types of mood disorders: major depressive disorder and bipolar disorder. Mood disorders are similar to most other major psychological disorders in terms of their heterogeneity in onset, presentation, etiology, and course. Within each of these two categories of disorder, however, the nature of the symptoms and course of the illness may differ somewhat from person to person.

The distinction between major depressive disorder and bipolar disorder does not exhaust the forms that mood disorders may take. The DSM system allows for "specifiers" that may accompany the mood disorder diagnosis. These specifiers contribute additional information that may be of use in understanding and treating the disorder. Two well-known examples of these subcategories of mood disorder are *seasonal affective disorder (SAD)*, a type of depression that follows a seasonal pattern, and *postpartum depression*, a type of depression that sometimes occurs after childbirth. In the former, the specifier relates to the seasonal pattern of the disorder and in the latter,

the specifier relates to an onset of the disorder postpartum, within four weeks of childbirth.

For some individuals who experience either bipolar or major depressive disorder, their symptoms may show a regular relationship with the seasons of the year (Rosenthal et al., 1984), the most common form being winter depression (Lewy, 1993). As you might expect, this type of mood disorder has in general been found to be more common in countries such as Canada, where there is less sunlight in the winter months. How common is this type of depression in Canada? One Canadian study found that 11 percent of the surveyed individuals who had depression evidenced the SAD subtype (Levitt et al., 2000), with an overall estimated prevalence in the population of almost 3 percent of Canadians. The rates are even higher among the Inuit in the Canadian Arctic (Haggarty et al., 2002). There are suggestions that the onset of SAD is related to melatonin production and circadian rhythms (Goodwin & Jamison, 1990; Wirtz-Justice, 1998). One form of treatment for SAD is phototherapy, in which individuals suffering from SAD are exposed systematically to therapeutic light (Lee et al., 1997). According to Toru Sato (1997), the beneficial effects of phototherapy can be achieved with light exposure for a couple of hours a day with a minimum of side effects.

The symptoms of postpartum depression, which can include both depression and mania, occur at a time of life when most women expect to be happiest and most excited—after their children are born

(Beck & Driscoll, 2006). Research on the prevalence of postpartum depression reveals a range of prevalence estimates but suggests that it occurs in about 10–20 percent of women who have given birth (Gaschler, 2008; Ross et al., 2005; Stewart et al., 2008).

Several variables affect the frequency of postpartum depression. For example, immigrant women in Canada appear to have an even higher rate of postpartum depression than do Canadian-born women. This higher risk for immigrant women may reflect increased stress related to their relocation, lack of social support, and unfamiliarity with the Canadian health-care system (Stewart et al., 2008). High-profile Canadian women such as Maureen McTeer and Margaret Trudeau, both wives of former Canadian prime ministers, have made their experiences with postpartum depression public (Galloway, 2006; McTeer, 2003) in an attempt to improve education about the disorder and increase funding for research into it.

Vancouver clinical psychologist Valerie Whiffen (Whiffen, 2004, 2006) has been very active in research and theory related to this issue (Whiffen, 1992). She has shown that the depressive symptoms of new mothers suffering depression are very similar to the symptoms of the depression experienced by other women and that the temperament of the baby plays a role in the depression experienced by the new mother (Whiffen & Gotlib, 1989, 1993). Research has pointed to factors such as previous episodes of depression, stress, and adjustment problems as risk factors for postpartum depression. There is even some suggestion emerging from recent work with animal models that impairments in GABA receptors may contribute to postpartum depression (Maguire & Mody, 2008; Nemeroff, 2008).

No matter what the eliciting factors or onset characteristics of the depression are, it can be a debilitating disorder that negatively impacts an individual's personal and professional life, as we saw in the case of Percy Paul. As is too often the case, as it was for Paul, depression can be associated with suicide and suicide attempts. In the next section, we consider mood disorders and suicide.

Mood Disorders and Suicide

A tragic, heartbreaking problem associated with mood disorders is suicide. Official statistics underscore the nature and degree of this type of tragedy. According to the World Health Organization, more people around the world die from suicide than are killed in all of the armed conflicts that plague the world. It is one of the three leading causes of death of people between the ages of 15 and 34 (World Health Organization, 2007). In Canada, the overall suicide rate has remained fairly constant over the past 50 years. In 2002, there were 3648 reported suicides in Canada (World Health Organization, 2007).

Suicide rates differ across various groupings, including gender, age, and rural/urban residence. In Canada, there are also differences in the rates of immigrant and native-born Canadians, with the rate of suicide among immigrants averaging about half that of native-born Canadians (Malenfant, 2004). But official statistics may underestimate the scope of the problem since many suicides are disguised as accidents, either by the suicidal person or by the survivors who try to cover up afterward. Moreover, experts estimate that suicide attempts may outnumber completed suicides by a ratio of as much as ten to one (Sudak, 2009).

Anyone can commit suicide, but some groups are at higher risk than others (Carroll-Ghosh, Victor, & Bourgeois, 2003). Overall, the evidence suggests that women *attempt* suicide three times more often than men. But men are more likely to actually kill themselves in an attempt, so they *complete* four times as many suicides as women. In regard to age, completed suicides peak in the over-75 age bracket. In Canada in 2002, there were 799 suicides by women and 2849 by men (World Health Organization, 2007).

With the luxury of hindsight, it is recognized that about 90 percent of the people who complete suicide suffer from some type of psychological disorder, although in some cases, this disorder may not be readily apparent beforehand (Melvin et al., 2008). As you might expect, suicide rates are highest for people with mood disorders, who account for about 60 percent of completed suicides (Mann & Currier, 2006). Both bipolar disorder and depression are associated with dramatic elevations in suicide rates. Studies suggest that the lifetime risk of completed suicide is about 15–20 percent in people with bipolar disorder and about 10 percent in those who have grappled with depression (Sudak, 2009), but some experts believe that these estimates are overly high (Joiner et al., 2009). Smaller elevations in suicide rates are seen among people who suffer from schizophrenia, alcoholism, and substance abuse (Mann & Currier, 2006). Unfortunately, there is no foolproof way to prevent suicidal people from taking their own lives, but we have compiled some useful tips in Figure 14.13.

1. *Take suicidal talk seriously.* When people talk about suicide in vague generalities, it's easy to dismiss it as "idle talk" and let it go. However, people who talk about suicide are a high-risk group and their veiled threats should not be ignored. The first step in suicide prevention is to directly ask such people if they're contemplating suicide.

2. *Provide empathy and social support.* It is important to show the suicidal person that you care. People often contemplate suicide because they see the world around them as indifferent and uncaring. Hence, you must demonstrate to the suicidal person that you are genuinely concerned. Suicide threats are often a last-ditch cry for help. It is therefore imperative that you offer to help.

3. *Identify and clarify the crucial problem.* The suicidal person is often terribly confused and feels lost in a sea of frustration and problems. It is a good idea to try to help sort through this confusion. Encourage the person to try to identify the crucial problem. Once it is isolated, the crucial problem may not seem quite so overwhelming.

4. *Do not promise to keep someone's suicidal ideation secret.* If you really feel like someone's life is in danger, don't agree to keep their suicidal plans secret to preserve your friendship.

5. *In an acute crisis, do not leave a suicidal person alone.* Stay with the person until additional help is available. Try to remove any guns, drugs, sharp objects and so forth that might provide an available means to commit suicide.

6. *Encourage professional consultation.* Most mental health professionals have some experience in dealing with suicidal crises. Many cities have suicide prevention centres with 24-hour hotlines. These centres are staffed with people who have been specially trained to deal with suicidal problems. It is important to try to get a suicidal person to seek professional assistance.

FIGURE 14.13

Preventing suicide.

As Sudak notes, "It is not possible to prevent all suicides or to totally and absolutely protect a given patient from suicide. What is possible is to reduce the likelihood of suicide" (2005, p. 2449). So the advice summarized here may prove useful if you ever have to help someone through a suicidal crisis. (Based on American Association of Suicidology, 2007; American Foundation for Suicide Prevention, 2007; Fremouw, de Perczel, & Ellis, 1990; Rosenthal, 1988; Shneidman, Farberow, & Litman, 1994).

Etiology of Mood Disorders 11b

Quite a bit is known about the etiology of mood disorders, although the puzzle certainly hasn't been assembled completely. There appear to be a number of routes into these disorders, involving intricate interactions between psychological and biological factors.

Genetic Vulnerability 11b

Twin studies suggest that genetic factors are involved in mood disorders (Lohoff & Berrettini, 2009; Kelsoe, 2009). Concordance rates average around 65 percent for identical twins but only 14 percent for fraternal twins, who share less genetic similarity (see Figure 14.14). Thus, evidence suggests that heredity can create a *predisposition* to mood disorders. Environmental factors probably determine whether this predisposition is converted into an actual disorder. The influence of genetic factors appears to be stronger for bipolar disorders than for unipolar disorders (Kieseppa et al., 2004). Some promising results have been reported in *genetic mapping* studies that have attempted to pinpoint the specific genes that shape vulnerability to mood disorders (Levinson, 2009). However, results have been disturbingly inconsistent and scientists do *not* appear to be on the verge of unravelling the genetic code for mood disorders, which probably depend on subtle variations in constellations of many genes (Bearden, Jasinka, & Friemer, 2009; Kendler, 2005a, 2005b).

Biological and Neurochemical Factors 11b

Heredity may influence susceptibility to mood disorders by creating a predisposition toward certain types of neurochemical abnormalities in the brain. Correlations have been found between mood disorders and abnormal levels of two neurotransmitters in the brain: norepinephrine and serotonin (Duman, Polan, & Schatzberg, 2008), although other neurotransmitter disturbances may also contribute

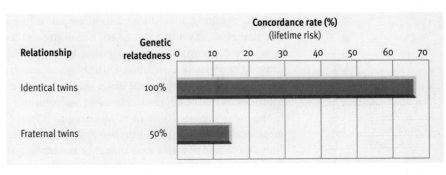

FIGURE 14.14

Twin studies of mood disorders.

The concordance rate for mood disorders in identical twins is much higher than that for fraternal twins, who share less genetic overlap. These results suggest that there must be a genetic predisposition to mood disorders. (Data from Gershon, Berrettini, & Goldin, 1989)

(Dunlop, Garlow, & Nemeroff, 2009). The details remain elusive, but it seems clear that a neurochemical basis exists for at least some mood disorders (Johnson et al., 2009).

A variety of drug therapies are fairly effective in the treatment of severe mood disorders. Most of these drugs are known to affect the availability (in the brain) of the neurotransmitters that have been related to mood disorders (Bhagwager & Heninger, 2009). Since this effect is unlikely to be a coincidence, it bolsters the plausibility of the idea that neurochemical changes produce mood disturbances. That said, after 40 years of enormous research effort, the neurochemical bases of mood disorders remain more mysterious than scientists would like (Delgado & Moreno, 2006).

Cognitive neuroscience approaches to depression that focus on the brain and depression are some of the most active areas of research into the causes and treatment of this disorder (Atchley & Ilardi, 2007; Ilardi et al., 2007; Levin et al., 2007). Studies have found some interesting correlations between mood disorders and a variety of structural abnormalities in the brain (Flores et al., 2004). Perhaps the best documented correlation is the association between depression and *reduced hippocampal volume* (Davidson, Pizzagalli, & Nitschke, 2009; Videbech, 2006). The *hippocampus*, which is known to play a major role in memory consolidation (see Chapter 7), tends to be about 8–10 percent smaller in depressed subjects than in normal subjects (Videbech, 2006; Videbech & Ravnkilde, 2004). A fascinating new theory of the biological bases of depression may be able to account for this finding. The springboard for this theory is the recent discovery that the human brain continues to generate new neurons in adulthood, especially in the hippocampal formation (Gage, 2002; see Chapters 3, 7, 11). This process is called *neurogenesis*. Jacobs (2004) has theorized that depression occurs when major life stress causes neurochemical reactions that suppress neurogenesis, resulting in reduced hippocampal volume (Duman et al., 2008; Jacobs, 2004). According to this view, the suppression of neurogenesis is the central cause of depression. Consistent with this view, Jacobs maintains that antidepressant drugs that elevate serotonin levels relieve depression because serotonin promotes neurogenesis (Duman & Monteggia, 2006). A great deal of additional research will be required to fully test this innovative new model of the biological bases of depressive disorders (Lilienfeld, 2007).

Hormonal Factors

In recent years researchers have begun to focus on how hormonal changes may contribute to the emergence of depression. As we discussed in Chapter 13, in times of stress the brain sends signals along two pathways. One of these runs from the hypothalamus to the pituitary gland to the adrenal cortex, which releases corticosteroid hormones (refer back to Figure 13.7 on page 607). This pathway is often referred to as the *hypothalamic-pituitary-adrenocortical (HPA) axis*. Evidence suggests that overactivity along the HPA axis in response to stress may often play a role in the development of depression (Goodwin, 2009). Consistent with this hypothesis, depressed patients tend to show elevated levels of cortisol, a key stress hormone produced by HPA activity (Thase, 2009). Some theorists believe that these hormonal changes eventually have an impact in the brain, where they may be the trigger for the suppression of neurogenesis that we just discussed (Duman et al., 2008).

Dispositional Factors

In the past few years, interest in the role of various personality factors in eliciting and maintaining depression has increased. Perfectionism or the setting of excessively high standards has been a characteristic long associated with depression (Beck, 1976). Research by the University of British Columbia's Paul Hewitt and his colleague, Canada Research Chair Gordon Flett (e.g., Hewitt et al., 2008), has explored the relationship of trait perfectionism to various aspects of depression. They have developed a multidimensional perfectionism scale that assesses three aspects of perfectionism (Hewitt & Flett, 1991): *self-oriented perfectionism*, or the tendency to set high standards for oneself; *other-oriented perfectionism*, which refers to setting high standards for others; and *socially prescribed perfectionism*, which is the tendency to perceive that others are setting high standards for oneself. In an active program of research, Hewitt and Flett have found links between perfectionism and eating disorders (Hewitt & Flett, 1991), symptoms of depression (Hewitt et al., 1998), and problematic interpersonal relationships (Flett & Hewitt, 2002) and other health problems, including postpartum depression. Flett suggests that new mothers who respond to problems associated with their perfectionism by covering it up might be most at risk. He suggests that for some of these new mothers, while everything seems perfect on the surface, "… in fact, it's just quite the opposite, that they're feeling quite badly but they're pretty good at covering it up" (Rettner, 2010). Perfectionism can affect you in many ways. Dr. Flett describes an interesting incident related to perfectionism. In an interview with the British Broadcasting Corporation (BBC, 2004), Flett developed a list of perfectionist traits in a list entitled the "Top Ten Signs Your a Perfectionist." Included in the list were (1) "You can't stop thinking about a mistake you made," (5) "You won't ask for help if asking can be perceived as a flaw or weakness," and (10) "You noticed the error in the title of this list." Of course, all of you reading this book noticed the error in the title, right? When the list was reproduced internationally in other newspapers the copy editors corrected the error, assuming it was unintentional. So, they changed "Your" to "You're." When perfectionist readers went through the list, they could not find an error. Dr. Flett (personal communication, June 18, 2011) commented that he had "people from around the world emailing me and wanting to know why I was driving them crazy because there was no error. . . . Of course, copyeditors are very high in perfectionism."

Two other personality-based models of depression, those proposed by Aaron Beck (1983) and Sidney Blatt (1995), suggest that specific personality variables serve as vulnerability factors for depression. According to Beck, two personality styles, sociotropy and autonomy, are related to depression. Sociotropic individuals are especially invested in interpersonal relationships; they are overconcerned with avoiding interpersonal problems and emphasize pleasing others. Autonomous individuals, on the other hand, are primarily oriented toward their own independence and achievement (Sato & McCann, 2002). Research on these personality factors has been conducted by Dennis Pusch and Keith Dobson and their colleagues in Calgary (Pusch et al., 1998). David Clark of the University of New Brunswick collaborated with Beck and other researchers in developing a widely used scale to assess these personality dimensions (Clark et al., 1995). Clark (1998) also edited a special issue of the *Canadian Journal of Behavioural Science* on the topic of Canadian research and theory in depression.

Blatt (1974, 1995) distinguishes between the introjective personality orientation, which involves excessive self-criticism, and the anaclitic orientation involving overdependence on others. Using instruments designed to assess both dependency and self-criticism, McGill University's David Zuroff and York University's Myriam Mongrain have examined some of the facets of these dispositional variables and their relationship to depression (Zuroff & Mongrain, 1987). Both Beck's and Blatt's formulations are consistent with a congruency model that suggests that the personality variables operate as vulnerabilities in response to stressors related to that specific disposition. For example, an individual who is high in dependency should suffer depressive symptoms only if he or she experiences difficulties in relationship or interpersonal domains and not if difficulties are experienced in achievement situations. Zuroff and Mongrain (1987) conducted one of the early tests of this type of congruency hypothesis. More recently, Mongrain has conducted a programmatic line of research examining, among other things, relationship issues and rejection in dependent and self-critical individuals (Mongrain, Lubbers, & Struthers, 2004; Mongrain & Trambakoulos, 2007; Mongrain et al., 1998; Schulte, Mongrain, & Flora, 2008).

Cognitive Factors

11b

A variety of theories emphasize how cognitive factors contribute to depressive disorders (Bieling & Grant, 2008; Christensen, Carney, & Segal, 2006; Haeffel et al., 2008). Perhaps the most influential of these theories is that proposed by Aaron Beck (1976, 1987, 2008). Since we will discuss his approach and its implications for therapy more fully in Chapter 15, we will introduce only a couple of concepts from his theory here. According to Beck, depressed individuals are characterized by a *negative cognitive triad*, which reflects their tendency to have negative views of themselves, their world, and their future. He suggests that dysfunctional schemas underlie many of the symptoms associated with depression. You may recall our discussion of schemas in Chapter 7. One of the effects of the depressive's negative schemas is the tendency to selectively attend to negative information about the self. Research by Zindel Segal at the Clarke Institute of Psychiatry in Toronto (Rector, Segal, & Gemar, 1998; Segal, 1988) and Scott McCabe at the University of Waterloo (McCabe, Gotlib, & Martin, 2000; McCabe & Toman, 2000) has served to evaluate and largely confirm these aspects of Beck's cognitive theory.

Another important cognitive theory is Martin Seligman's *learned helplessness model* of depression and its most recent descendant, *hopelessness theory*. Based largely on animal research, Seligman (1974) proposed that depression is caused by *learned helplessness*—passive "giving up" behaviour produced by exposure to unavoidable aversive events (such as uncontrollable shock in the laboratory). He then reformulated the theory, focusing on more cognitive features such as how people explain their negative experiences (Abramson, Seligman, & Teasdale, 1978). According to Seligman (1990), people who exhibit a *pessimistic explanatory style* are especially vulnerable to depression. These people tend to attribute their setbacks to their personal flaws instead of situational factors, and they tend to draw global, far-reaching conclusions about their personal inadequacies based on these setbacks.

According to *hopelessness theory* (Abramson, Alloy, & Metalsky, 1995), which builds on these insights, a pessimistic explanatory style is just one of several or more factors—along with high stress, low self-esteem, and so forth—that may contribute to hopelessness, and thus depression. Although hopelessness theory casts a wider net than the learned helplessness model, it continues to emphasize the importance of people's *cognitive reactions* to the events in their lives.

In accord with this line of thinking, Susan Nolen-Hoeksema (1991, 2000) has highlighted the importance of rumination and has found that depressed people who *ruminate* about their depression remain depressed longer than those who try to distract themselves. People who respond to depression with rumination repetitively focus their attention on their depressing feelings. They think constantly about how sad, lethargic, and unmotivated they are. Excessive rumination tends to foster and amplify episodes of depression by increasing negative thinking, impairing problem solving, and undermining social support (Nolen-Hoeksema, Wisco, & Lyubomirsky, 2008). As we noted earlier, Nolen-Hoeksema believes that women have a greater tendency to ruminate than men and that this disparity may be a major reason why depression is more prevalent in women. Moreover, the effects of rumination are not limited to aggravating depressive disorders. Rumination is also associated with increased anxiety, binge eating, and binge drinking (Nolen-Hoeksema et al., 2008).

In sum, cognitive models of depression maintain that negative thinking is what leads to depression

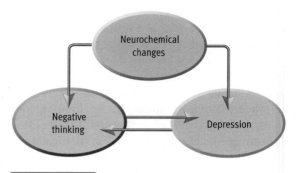

FIGURE 14.15

Interpreting the correlation between negative thinking and depression.

Cognitive theories of depression assume that consistent patterns of negative thinking cause depression. Although these theories are highly plausible, depression could cause negative thoughts, or both could be caused by a third factor, such as neurochemical changes in the brain.

in many people. The principal problem with cognitive theories is their difficulty in separating cause from effect (Feliciano & Arean, 2007). Does negative thinking cause depression? Or does depression cause negative thinking (see Figure 14.15)? A *clear* demonstration of a causal link between negative thinking and depression is not possible because it would require manipulating people's cognitive style (which is not easy to change) in sufficient degree to produce full-fledged depressive disorders (which would not be ethical). However, the research reported in our Featured Study provided impressive evidence consistent with a causal link between negative thinking and vulnerability to depression.

FEATURED STUDY

Investigators: Lauren B. Alloy (Temple University), Lyn Y. Abramson (University of Wisconsin), Wayne G. Whitehouse (Temple University), Michael E. Hogan (University of Wisconsin), Nancy A. Tashman (University of Maryland), Dena L. Steinberg (New York State Psychiatric Institute), Donna T. Rose (Counseling Associates of Madison), and Patricia Donovan (University of Wisconsin).
Source: Depressogenic cognitive styles: Predictive validity, information processing and personality characteristics, and developmental origins. *Behavior Research and Therapy*, 1999, *37*, 503–531.

Does Negative Thinking *Cause* Depression?

This article describes a series of studies conducted at Temple University and at the University of Wisconsin, collectively referred to as the *Temple–Wisconsin Cognitive Vulnerability to Depression Project*. Although the article provides a preliminary report on many facets of the project, we will focus on the study intended to test the hypothesis that a negative cognitive style is predictive of elevated vulnerability to depression.

Method

Participants. Over 5000 first-year students at the two universities responded to two measures of negative

thinking. Students who scored in the highest quartile on both measures were characterized as having a *high risk* for depression and those who scored in the lowest quartile on both measures were characterized as having a *low risk* for depression. Randomly selected subsets of these two groups were invited for additional screening to eliminate anyone who was currently depressed or suffering from any other major psychological disorder. The final sample consisted of 173 students in the high-risk group and 176 students in the low-risk group.

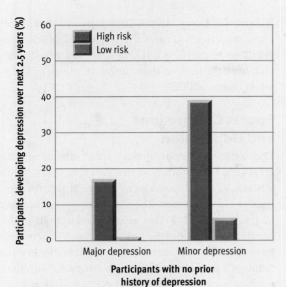

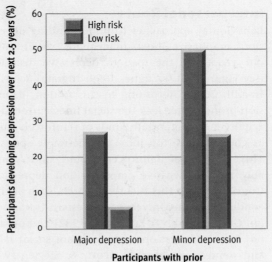

FIGURE 14.16

Negative thinking and prediction of depression.

Alloy and colleagues (1999) measured the cognitive style of first-year university students and characterized them as high risk or low risk for depression. This graph shows the percentage of these students who experienced major or minor episodes of depression over the next 2.5 years. As you can see, the high-risk students who exhibited a negative thinking style proved to be much more vulnerable to depression. (Data from Alloy et al., 1999)

Follow-up assessments. Self-report measures and structured interviews were used to evaluate the mental health of the participants every six weeks for the first two years and then every 16 weeks for an additional three years. The assessments were conducted by interviewers who did not know the subjects' risk group status. The report presented here summarizes the follow-up data for the first 2.5 years of the study.

Results

The data for students who had no prior history of depression showed dramatic differences between the high-risk and low-risk groups in vulnerability to depression. During the relatively brief 2.5-year period, a major depressive disorder emerged in 17 percent of the high-risk students in comparison to only 1 percent of the low-risk students. The high-risk subjects also displayed a much greater incidence of minor depressive episodes, as you can see in the left panel of Figure 14.16. The right panel of Figure 14.16 shows the comparisons for participants who had a prior history of depression (but were not depressed or suffering from any other disorder at the beginning of the study). The data show that high-risk subjects were more vulnerable to a recurrence of both major and minor depression during the 2.5-year follow-up.

Discussion

The high-risk participants, who exhibited a negative cognitive style, were consistently found to have an elevated likelihood of developing depressive disorders. Hence, the authors conclude that their results provide strong support for the cognitive vulnerability hypothesis, which asserts that negative thinking makes people more vulnerable to depression.

Comment

Previous studies of the correlation between negative thinking and depression used *retrospective designs,* which look backward in time from known outcomes. For example, investigators might compare depressed subjects versus nondepressed subjects on some measure of negative thinking. What makes the design retrospective is that the researchers already know which people experienced the outcome of depression. Retrospective designs can yield useful information, but they don't provide much insight about causation. Why? Because if you find an association between depression and negative thinking you can't determine whether the negative thinking preceded the depression or the depression preceded the negative thinking.

This study used a *prospective design,* which moves forward in time, testing hypotheses about future outcomes. Prospective studies are much more difficult and time-consuming to conduct, but they can provide more insight about causation because they can show that one event (in this instance, the development of a negative cognitive style) preceded another (the occurrence of depression). The data are still correlational, so they cannot definitively establish a causal link, but they provide much stronger evidence in favour of causation than retrospective data. Thus, the research by Alloy and her colleagues provides the best evidence to date in support of the hypothesis that negative thinking contributes to the causation of depressive disorders.

Interpersonal Roots

Behavioural approaches to understanding depression emphasize how inadequate social skills put people on the road to depressive disorders (see Figure 14.17; Coyne, 1999; Ingram, Scott, & Hamill, 2009). According to this notion, depression-prone people lack the social finesse needed to acquire many important kinds of reinforcers, such as good friends, top jobs, and desirable spouses. This paucity of reinforcers could understandably lead to negative emotions and depression. Consistent with this theory, research, such as that conducted at the University of Western Ontario by Ian Gotlib (Gotlib & Robinson, 1982) and others, has found associations between poor social skills and depression (Ingram, Scott, & Siegle, 1999; Joiner & Timmons, 2009).

Another interpersonal factor is that depressed people tend to be depressing (Joiner & Katz, 1999). Individuals suffering from depression often are irritable and pessimistic. They complain a lot and aren't particularly enjoyable companions. As a consequence, depressed people tend to court rejection from those around them (Joiner & Metalsky, 1995; Joiner & Timmons, 2009). Depressed people have fewer sources of social support than nondepressed people. Low social support can increase vulnerability to depression (Lakey & Cronin, 2008). Research suggests that lack of social support may make a larger contribution to depression in women than in men (Kendler, Myers, & Prescott, 2005).

Social rejection and lack of support may in turn aggravate and deepen a person's depression (Potthoff, Holahan, & Joiner, 1995). To compound these problems, evidence indicates that depressed people may gravitate to partners who view them unfavourably and hence reinforce their negative views of themselves (Joiner, 2002).

Sports Concussions and Depression

The topic of concussions in sport has received a great deal of attention in the past few years. While athletes in some sports were always at risk for head trauma, in years past they were often encouraged just to get back in the game. Recent high-profile concussions and deaths linked to these concussions have changed that attitude. For example, hockey star Sidney Crosby of the Pittsburgh Penguins suffered a concussion in the 2010–2011 NHL season and did not play for the last half of the season (Mirtle, 2011) or the beginning of the next season. NFL defensive back Andre Waters suffered severe head trauma and retired after 12 seasons playing football. After his retirement, Waters evidenced cognitive deficits as a result of his concussions, became depressed, and committed suicide (Farrey, 2007). The forensic pathologist who examined Waters's brain stated that "the condition of Waters's brain tissue was what would be expected in an 85-year-old man" (Farrey, 2007). Depression is a common feature of post-concussion syndrome. This is of clear concern not only to professional athletes but to ordinary people as well. As many as 30 000 Canadians suffer concussions each year (Ogilvie, 2011), and many more are likely not reported.

Research examining the links between concussions and mental health issues such as depression are still in their infancy. We do know, however, that depression rates in head trauma patients are many times higher than in the general population and that depression can be long-lasting (Deb, Lyons, & Koutzoukis, 1998; Jorge et al., 1993; Kreutzer, Seel, & Gourley, 2001). Research by Dr. Charles Tator in Toronto and by Jen-Kai Chen, Alain Ptito, and their colleagues (Chen et al., 2007; Chen et al., 2008; Ptito, Chen, & Johnstone, 2007) at the Montreal Neurological Institute is playing a key role in uncovering the nature of the connection between head trauma and depression. For example, in one study Chen and his colleagues (Chen et al., 2008) examined fMRI scans of a healthy control group and of athletes suffering from concussions with no depression, or with mild or moderate depression symptoms.

The results of the brain scans showed that athletes who had suffered from concussions and

FIGURE 14.17

Interpersonal factors in depression.

Behavioural theories about the etiology of depression emphasize how inadequate social skills may contribute to the development of the disorder through several mechanisms, as diagrammed here.

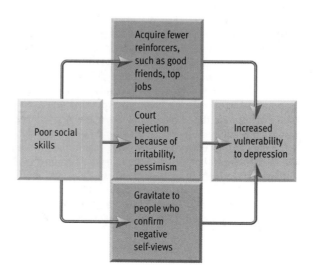

Many pro athletes who have suffered concussions, such as CFL great Matt Dunigan, have agreed to donate their brains to research on the physical and mental health consequences of head trauma.

depression, as compared to the other participants, showed "reduced activation in the dorsolateral prefrontal cortex and striatum and attenuated deactivation in medial frontal and temporal regions" (Chen et al., 2008, p. 81). The results also indicated that depression levels correlated with the level of neural response in areas typically associated with depression, along with grey matter loss in those areas. Although more studies of this kind are necessary before definitive conclusions are possible, the authors did suggest that the depression experienced by some of these athletes could be the result of the head trauma they suffered. Research on this topic will continue as many pro athletes, such as former CFL quarterback Matt Dunigan, who suffered a career-ending concussion, have decided to donate their brains to concussion research centres, such as the one run by Dr. Charles Tator (Brady, 2011) and his concussion awareness group ThinkFirst in Toronto, or Boston University's Center for the Study of Traumatic Encephalopathy.

Precipitating Stress

11b PSYKTREK

Mood disorders sometimes appear mysteriously in people who are leading benign, nonstressful lives.

For this reason, experts used to believe that mood disorders are not influenced much by stress. However, advances in the measurement of personal stress have altered this picture. The evidence available today suggests the existence of a moderately strong link between stress and the onset of mood disorders (Hammen, 2005; Monroe, Slavich, & Georgiades, 2009). Stress also appears to affect how people with mood disorders respond to treatment and whether they experience a relapse of their disorder (Monroe & Hadjiyannakis, 2002).

Of course, many people endure great stress without getting depressed (Monroe & Reid, 2009). The impact of stress varies, in part, because people vary in their degree of *vulnerability* to mood disorders (Lewinsohn, Joiner, & Rohde, 2001). Similar interactions between stress and vulnerability probably influence the development of many kinds of disorders, including those that are next on our agenda—the schizophrenic disorders.

WEB LINK 14.5

Dr. Ivan's Depression Central
Some might suggest that a better title for psychiatrist Ivan Goldberg's site would be "Everything You Ever Wanted to Know about Depression." He offers a wide variety of resources regarding mood disorders.

REVIEW OF KEY POINTS

> The principal mood disorders are depressive disorder, dysthymic disorder, bipolar disorder, and cyclothymic disorder. Mood disorders are episodic.

> Major depressive disorder is marked by profound sadness, slowed thought processes, low self-esteem, and loss of interest in previous sources of pleasure. Unipolar depression is more common than bipolar disorder, and it appears to be increasing in prevalence.

> Bipolar disorder is marked by the experience of both depressed and manic episodes. Manic episodes are characterized by inflated self-esteem, high energy, grandiose plans, and racing thoughts.

> Evidence indicates that people vary in their genetic vulnerability to mood disorders. These disorders are accompanied by changes in neurochemical activity in the brain. Abnormalities at norepinephrine and serotonin synapses appear particularly critical.

> Reduced hippocampal volume and suppressed neurogenesis are also associated with depression. Hormonal changes resulting from overactivity along the HPA axis may contribute to depression.

> Cognitive models posit that negative thinking contributes to depression. A pessimistic explanatory style has been implicated, as has a tendency to ruminate about one's problems. Our Featured Study reported impressive evidence in support of the cognitive vulnerability hypothesis of depression.

> Interpersonal inadequacies may contribute to depressive disorders. Poor social skills may lead to a paucity of life's reinforcers and frequent rejection. The development of mood disorders is affected by personal stress and also has been associated with head trauma.

PREVIEW QUESTIONS

▶ What are the general symptoms of schizophrenia?

▶ What are the four subtypes of schizophrenic disorders, and what are their chief symptoms?

▶ What is known about the course and outcome of schizophrenia?

▶ Which biological factors have been implicated in schizophrenic disorders?

▶ What is the neurodevelopmental hypothesis of schizophrenia?

▶ How do family dynamics and stress contribute to schizophrenic disorders?

Literally, *schizophrenia* means "split mind." However, when Eugen Bleuler coined the term in 1911, he was referring to the fragmentation of thought processes seen in the disorder—not to a "split personality." Unfortunately, writers in the popular media often assume that the split-mind notion, and thus schizophrenia, refers to the rare syndrome in which a person manifests two or more personalities. As you have already learned, this syndrome is actually called *dissociative identity disorder* or *multiple-personality disorder*. Schizophrenia is a much more common, and altogether different, type of disorder.

Schizophrenic disorders are a class of disorders marked by delusions, hallucinations, disorganized speech, and deterioration of adaptive behaviour. People with schizophrenic disorders often display some of the same symptoms seen in people with severe mood disorders; however, disturbed *thought* lies at the core of schizophrenic disorders, whereas disturbed *emotion* lies at the core of mood disorders. In fact, scholars such as Canadian schizophrenia expert Walter Heinrichs (Heinrichs, Ammari et al., 2008; Heinrichs, Goldberg et al., 2008) characterize schizophrenia as a biobehavioural disorder that is manifested first and foremost in cognition. Heinrichs suggests that cognitive assessment techniques are one of the best ways to examine the causes of schizophrenia and that impaired cognition is a primary feature of schizophrenia (Heinrichs, 2005).

A cognitive analysis of schizophrenia and review of the effectiveness of cognitive behavioural therapy for schizophrenia by Aaron Beck and the University of Toronto's Neil Rector echoes the emphasis that Heinrichs and others place on cognition in schizophrenia (Beck & Rector, 2004; Rector & Beck, 2001). You will recall that Beck is one of the originators of the cognitive approach to depression discussed earlier in this chapter. We will describe the cognitive-behavioural approach to therapy more fully in Chapter 15.

How common is schizophrenia? Prevalence estimates suggest that about 1 percent of the population may suffer from schizophrenic disorders (Lauriello, Bustillo, & Keith, 2005; Public Health Agency of Canada, 2006) although a recent meta-analysis concluded that the prevalence might be a little lower than that (McGrath, 2007). That may not sound like much, but it means that in North America alone, there may be several million people troubled by schizophrenic disturbances. Moreover, schizophrenia is an extremely costly illness for society,

because it is a severe, debilitating illness that tends to have an early onset and often requires lengthy hospital care (Samnaliev & Clark, 2008). Because of these considerations, the financial impact of schizophrenia is estimated to exceed the costs of all types of cancers combined (Buchanan & Carpenter, 2005).

While schizophrenia has a relatively low frequency compared to many of the other forms of psychopathology that we will discuss in this section, it does have a relatively high visibility both because of the severity of the illness and because of the way it has been portrayed in the media. An excellent example is the book *A Beautiful Mind* (Nasar, 1998) and director Ron Howard's (2002) film of the same name based on the book. The book and film describe the life of John Nash who suffered from paranoid schizophrenia. Nash is noteworthy, of course, because he won the 1994 Nobel Prize in Economics, despite his illness. Nash was vocal in speaking out against the stigma associated with mental illness and the factors that maintain them. It is also interesting to get a sense of how one comes to be nominated for a Nobel Prize (perhaps you have some aspirations in this regard). Creativity and innovative thinking appear to be the key, more important that the quantity of papers one produces. You might imagine that Nobel Prize winners have to publish hundreds of papers. Nash's formal publications number only 15 papers! Five of these are on game theory, for which he won his Nobel Prize, and ten are pure mathematics (Kuhn & Nasar, 2002).

General Symptoms   11c

There are a number of distinct schizophrenic syndromes, but they share some general characteristics that we will examine before looking at the subtypes. Many of these characteristics are apparent in the following case history (adapted from Sheehan, 1982, pp. 104–105).

Sylvia was first given a diagnosis of schizophrenia at age 15. She has been in and out of many types of psychiatric facilities since then. She has never been able to hold a job for any length of time. During severe flare-ups of her disorder, her personal hygiene deteriorates. She rarely washes, she wears clothes that neither fit nor match, she smears makeup on heavily but randomly, and she slops food all over herself. Sylvia occasionally hears voices talking to her. She tends to be argumentative, aggressive,

John Shearer/WireImage/Getty Images

Frank Micelotta/ImageDirect/Getty Images

In the movie *A Beautiful Mind*, Nobel Prize–winning mathematician John Nash is played by Russell Crowe.

and emotionally volatile. Over the years, she has been involved in innumerable fights with fellow patients, psychiatric staff members, and strangers. Her thoughts can be highly irrational, as is apparent from the following quote, which was recorded while she was a patient in a psychiatric facility called Creedmoor:

"Mick Jagger wants to marry me. If I have Mick Jagger, I don't have to covet Geraldo Rivera. Mick Jagger is St. Nicholas and the Maharishi is Santa Claus. I want to form a gospel rock group called the Thorn Oil, but Geraldo wants me to be the music critic on Eyewitness News, *so what can I do? Got to listen to my boyfriend. Teddy Kennedy cured me of my ugliness. I'm pregnant with the son of God. I'm going to marry David Berkowitz and get it over with. Creedmoor is the headquarters of the American Nazi Party. They're eating the patients here. Archie Bunker wants me to play his niece on his TV show. I work for Epic Records. I'm Joan of Arc. I'm Florence Nightingale. The door between the ward and the porch is the dividing line between New York and California. Divorce isn't a piece of paper, it's a feeling. Forget about Zip Codes. I need shock treatments. The body is run by electricity. My wiring is all faulty."*

Sylvia's case clearly shows that schizophrenic thinking can be bizarre and that schizophrenia can

be a severe and debilitating disorder. Although no single symptom is inevitably present, the following symptoms are commonly seen in schizophrenia (Lewis, Escalona, & Keith, 2009; Liddle, 2009).

Delusions and Irrational Thought

PSYKTREK

11c

Disturbed, irrational thought processes are the central feature of schizophrenic disorders (Barch, 2003; Heinrichs, 2005). Various kinds of delusions are common. *Delusions* are false beliefs that are maintained even though they clearly are out of touch with reality. For example, one patient's delusion that he is a tiger (with a deformed body) persisted for more than 15 years (Kulick, Pope, & Keck, 1990). More typically, affected persons believe that their private thoughts are being broadcast to other people, that thoughts are being injected into their minds against their will, or that their thoughts are being controlled by some external force (Maher, 2001). In *delusions of grandeur*, people maintain that they are famous or important. Sylvia expressed an endless array of grandiose delusions, such as thinking that Mick Jagger wanted to marry her, that she had dictated the *Hobbit* stories to J. R. R. Tolkien, and that she was going to win the Nobel Prize for medicine.

Another characteristic of schizophrenia is that the person's train of thought deteriorates. Thinking becomes chaotic rather than logical and linear. There is a "loosening of associations," as people shift topics in disjointed ways. The quotation from Sylvia illustrates this symptom dramatically.

Deterioration of Adaptive Behaviour

Schizophrenia usually involves a noticeable deterioration in the quality of the person's routine functioning in work, social relationships, and personal care. Friends will often make remarks such as "Hal just isn't himself anymore." This deterioration is readily apparent in Sylvia's inability to get along with others or to function in the work world. It's also apparent in her neglect of personal hygiene.

Hallucinations

A variety of perceptual distortions may occur with schizophrenia, the most common being auditory hallucinations. *Hallucinations are sensory perceptions that occur in the absence of a real, external stimulus or are gross distortions of perceptual input.* People with schizophrenia frequently report that they hear voices of nonexistent or absent people talking to them. Sylvia, for instance, said she heard messages from Paul McCartney. These voices often provide an insulting, running commentary on the person's behaviour ("You're an idiot for shaking his hand"). They may be argumentative ("You don't need a bath"), and they may issue commands ("Prepare your home for visitors from outer space").

Disturbed Emotions

WEB LINK 14.6

Doctor's Guide: Schizophrenia
Produced by a communications and medical education consulting company, the *Doctor's Guide* site is updated frequently to provide a current overview of the state of research on schizophrenic disorders. A more detailed set of resources for physicians parallels this site, which is intended primarily for patients and their families.

Normal emotional tone can be disrupted in schizophrenia in a variety of ways. Although it may not be an accurate indicator of their underlying emotional experience (Kring, 1999), some victims show little emotional responsiveness, a symptom referred to as "blunted or flat affect." Others show inappropriate emotional responses that don't jibe with the situation or with what they are saying. For instance, a person with schizophrenia might cry over a silly cartoon and then laugh about a news story describing a child's tragic death. People with schizophrenia may also become emotionally volatile. This pattern was displayed by Sylvia, who often overreacted emotionally in erratic, unpredictable ways.

Subtypes, Course, and Outcome

Four subtypes of schizophrenic disorders are recognized, including a category for people who don't fit neatly into any of the first three categories. The major symptoms of each subtype are as follows (Lewis et al., 2009; Minzenberg, Yoon, & Carter, 2008).

Paranoid Type

As its name implies, *paranoid schizophrenia* is dominated by delusions of persecution, along with delusions of grandeur. In this common form of schizophrenia, people come to believe that they have many enemies who want to harass and oppress them. They may become suspicious of friends and relatives or they may attribute the persecution to mysterious, unknown persons. They are convinced that they are being watched and manipulated in malicious ways. To make sense of this persecution, they often develop delusions of grandeur. They believe that they must be enormously important people, frequently seeing themselves as great inventors or as famous religious or political leaders.

Catatonic Type

Catatonic schizophrenia is marked by striking motor disturbances, ranging from muscular rigidity to random motor activity. Some patients go into an extreme form of withdrawal known as a *catatonic stupor*. They may remain virtually motionless and seem oblivious to the environment around them for long periods of time. Others go into a state of catatonic excitement. They become hyperactive and incoherent. Some alternate between these dramatic extremes. The catatonic subtype is not particularly common, and its prevalence seems to be declining.

Disorganized Type

In *disorganized schizophrenia*, a particularly severe deterioration of adaptive behaviour is seen. Prominent symptoms include emotional indifference, frequent incoherence, and virtually complete social withdrawal. Aimless babbling and giggling are common. Delusions often centre on bodily functions ("My brain is melting out my ears").

Undifferentiated Type

People who have schizophrenia but who cannot be placed into any of the three previous categories are said to have *undifferentiated schizophrenia, which is marked by idiosyncratic mixtures of schizophrenic symptoms.* The undifferentiated subtype is fairly common.

Positive versus Negative Symptoms

Many theorists have raised doubts about the value of dividing schizophrenic disorders into the four subtypes just described (Sanislow & Carson, 2001). Critics note that the catatonic subtype is disappearing and that undifferentiated cases aren't so much a subtype as a hodgepodge of "leftovers." Critics also point out that there aren't meaningful differences between the subtypes in etiology, prognosis, or response to treatment. The absence of such differences casts doubt on the value of the current classification scheme.

Because of such problems, Nancy Andreasen (1990) and others (Carpenter, 1992; McGlashan & Fenton, 1992) have proposed an alternative approach to subtyping. This new scheme divides schizophrenic disorders into just two categories, based on the predominance of negative versus positive symptoms. *Negative symptoms* involve behavioural deficits, such as flattened emotions, social withdrawal, apathy, impaired attention, and poverty of speech. *Positive symptoms* involve behavioural excesses or peculiarities, such as hallucinations, delusions, bizarre behaviour, and wild flights of ideas.

Theorists advocating this scheme hoped to find consistent differences between the two subtypes in etiology, prognosis, and response to treatment, and some progress along these lines *has* been made. For example, a predominance of positive symptoms is associated with better adjustment prior to the onset of schizophrenia and greater responsiveness to treatment (Combs & Mueser, 2007; Galderisi et al., 2002). However, the assumption that patients can be placed into discrete categories based on this scheme now seems untenable. Most patients exhibit both types of symptoms and vary only in the *degree* to which positive or negative symptoms dominate (Andreasen, 2009). It seems fair to say that the distinction between positive and negative symptoms has enhanced our understanding of schizophrenia. However, it has not yet yielded a classification scheme that can replace the traditional subtypes of schizophrenia.

Course and Outcome

Schizophrenic disorders usually emerge during adolescence or early adulthood, with 75 percent of cases manifesting by the age of 30 (Perkins, Miller-Anderson, & Lieberman, 2006). Those who develop schizophrenia usually have a long history of peculiar behaviour, along with cognitive and social deficits, although most do not manifest a full-fledged psychological disorder during childhood (Walker et al., 2004). The emergence of schizophrenia may be sudden, but usually is insidious and gradual. Once it clearly emerges, the course of schizophrenia is variable, but people with schizophrenia tend to fall into three broad groups. Some, presumably those with milder disorders, are treated successfully and enjoy a full recovery. Others experience a partial recovery so that they can return to independent living for a time. However, they experience regular relapses over the remainder of their lives. Finally, a third group endures chronic illness marked by relentless deterioration and extensive hospitalization. Estimates of the percentage of patients falling into each category vary.

Overall, the preponderance of studies have suggested that only about 20 percent of individuals suffering from schizophrenia enjoy a full recovery (Perkins, Miller-Anderson, & Lieberman, 2006; Robinson et al., 2004). However, to some extent, this low recovery rate may reflect the poor to mediocre quality of mental health care available for severe disorders in many countries (see Chapter 15). When comprehensive, well-coordinated, quality care is initiated promptly, higher recovery rates in the vicinity of 50 percent have been found (Hopper et al., 2007; Liberman & Kopelowicz, 2005). Although schizophrenia is often viewed as a disorder marked by relentless deterioration, it is clear that a decent portion of patients experience a reasonable degree of recovery (Jablensky, 2009). Thus, the outlook for schizophrenia may not need to be as pervasively negative as it has been.

Etiology of Schizophrenia

You can probably identify, at least to some extent, with people who suffer from mood disorders, somatoform disorders, and anxiety disorders. You can probably imagine events that could unfold that might leave you struggling with depression, grappling with anxiety, or worrying about your physical health. But what could account for Sylvia's thinking that she was Joan of Arc or that she had dictated the *Hobbit* stories to Tolkien? As mystifying as these delusions may seem, you'll see that the etiology of schizophrenic disorders is not all that different from the etiology of other psychological disorders. We'll begin our discussion by examining the matter of genetic vulnerability.

Nancy Andreasen
"Schizophrenia disfigures the emotional and cognitive faculties of its victims, and sometimes nearly destroys them."

Courtesy of Nancy Andreasen

Genetic Vulnerability 11c

Evidence is plentiful that hereditary factors play a role in the development of schizophrenic disorders (Glatt, 2008; Kirov & Owen, 2009). For instance, in twin studies, concordance rates average around 48 percent for identical twins, in comparison to about 17 percent for fraternal twins (Gottesman, 1991, 2001). Studies also indicate that a child born to two schizophrenic parents has about a 46 percent probability of developing a schizophrenic disorder (as compared to the probability in the general population of about 1 percent).

These and other findings that demonstrate the genetic roots of schizophrenia are summarized in Figure 14.18. Overall, the picture is similar to that seen for mood disorders. Several converging lines of evidence indicate that some people inherit a poly-genically transmitted *vulnerability* to schizophrenia (Cornblatt et al., 2009). Although some theorists suspect that genetic factors may account for as much as 80 percent of the variability in susceptibility to schizophrenia (Pogue, Geile, & Yrkley, 2010), genetic mapping studies have made only very modest progress in identifying the specific genes at work (Gunter, 2009; Walker & Tessner, 2008).

Neurochemical Factors 11c

Like mood disorders, schizophrenic disorders appear to be accompanied by changes in the activity of one or more neurotransmitters in the brain (Patel, Pinals, & Breier, 2008). Excess *dopamine* activity has

been implicated as a possible cause of schizophrenia, as discussed in Figure 14.19 (Abi-Dargham et al., 1998). This hypothesis makes sense because most of the drugs that are useful in the treatment of schizophrenia are known to dampen dopamine activity in the brain (Javitt & Laruelle, 2006). However, the evidence linking schizophrenia to high dopamine levels is riddled with inconsistencies, complexities, and interpretive problems (Bobo et al., 2008). In recent years, the dopamine hypothesis has become more nuanced and complex. Researchers believe that dysregulation occurs in dopamine circuits and that the nature of this dysregulation may vary in different regions of the brain (Howes & Kapur, 2009). Scientists are also investigating whether dysfunctions in neural circuits using glutamate play a role in schizophrenia (Downar & Kapur, 2008).

Recent research has suggested that marijuana use during adolescence may help to precipitate schizophrenia in young people who have a genetic vulnerability to the disorder (Compton, Goulding, & Walker, 2007; McGrath et al., 2010). This unexpected finding has generated considerable debate about whether and how cannabis might contribute to the emergence of schizophrenia (Castle, 2008; DeLisi, 2008). Some critics have suggested that it could be that schizophrenia leads to cannabis use rather than vice versa. In other words, emerging psychotic symptoms may prompt young people to turn to marijuana to self-medicate. However, a recent, carefully controlled, long-term study in Germany found no evidence in support of the self-medication explanation (Kuepper et al., 2011). After controlling for age, sex, social class, use of other drugs, occurrence of childhood trauma, and the presence of other disorders, the study found that marijuana use roughly doubled the risk of psychotic disturbance. The current thinking is that the key chemical ingredient in marijuana (THC) may increase neurotransmitter activity in dopamine circuits in certain areas of the brain (Di Forti et al., 2007; Kuepper et al., 2010). The data on this issue are still preliminary. More research will be needed to fully understand the association between marijuana use and schizophrenia.

Structural Abnormalities in the Brain 11c

For decades, studies have suggested that individuals with schizophrenia exhibit a variety of deficits in attention, perception, and information processing (Belger & Barch, 2009; Harvey, 2010). Impairments in working (short-term) memory are especially prominent (Silver et al., 2003). These cognitive deficits suggest that schizophrenic disorders may be caused by neurological defects (Perry & Braff, 1994). Until recent decades, this

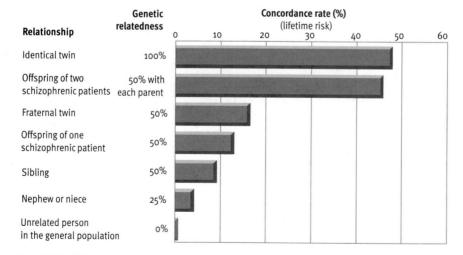

FIGURE 14.18

Genetic vulnerability to schizophrenic disorders.

Relatives of schizophrenic patients have an elevated risk for schizophrenia. This risk is greater among closer relatives. Although environment also plays a role in the etiology of schizophrenia, the concordance rates shown here suggest that there must be a genetic vulnerability to the disorder. These concordance estimates are based on pooled data from 40 studies conducted between 1920 and 1987. (Data from Gottesman, 1991)

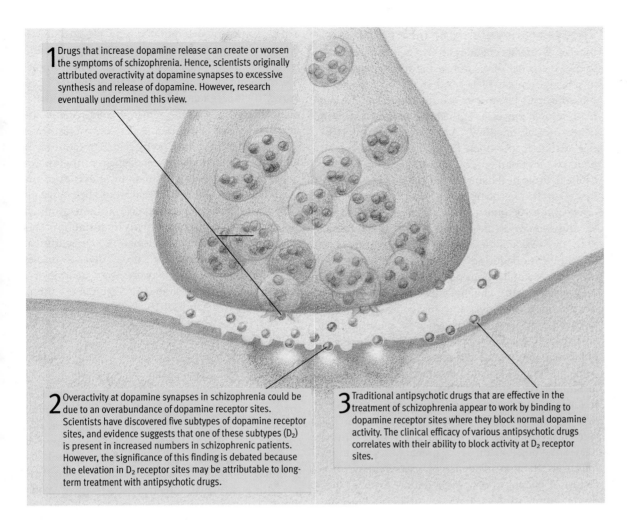

1 Drugs that increase dopamine release can create or worsen the symptoms of schizophrenia. Hence, scientists originally attributed overactivity at dopamine synapses to excessive synthesis and release of dopamine. However, research eventually undermined this view.

2 Overactivity at dopamine synapses in schizophrenia could be due to an overabundance of dopamine receptor sites. Scientists have discovered five subtypes of dopamine receptor sites, and evidence suggests that one of these subtypes (D_2) is present in increased numbers in schizophrenic patients. However, the significance of this finding is debated because the elevation in D_2 receptor sites may be attributable to long-term treatment with antipsychotic drugs.

3 Traditional antipsychotic drugs that are effective in the treatment of schizophrenia appear to work by binding to dopamine receptor sites where they block normal dopamine activity. The clinical efficacy of various antipsychotic drugs correlates with their ability to block activity at D_2 receptor sites.

FIGURE 14.19

The dopamine hypothesis as an explanation for schizophrenia.

Decades of research have implicated overactivity at dopamine synapses as a key cause of schizophrenic disorders. However, the evidence on the exact mechanisms underlying this overactivity, which is summarized in this graphic, is complex and open to debate. Recent hypotheses about the neurochemical bases of schizophrenia go beyond the simple assumption that dopamine activity is increased. For example, one theory posits that schizophrenia may be accompanied by decreased dopamine activity in one area of the brain (the prefrontal cortex) and increased activity or dysregulation in other areas of the brain (Egan & Hyde, 2000). Moreover, abnormalities in other neurotransmitter systems may also contribute to schizophrenia.

theory was based more on speculation than on actual research. Now, however, advances in brain-imaging technology have yielded mountains of intriguing data. The most reliable finding is that CT scans and MRI scans (see Chapter 3) suggest an association between enlarged brain ventricles (the hollow, fluid-filled cavities in the brain depicted in Figure 14.20) and schizophrenic disturbance (Belger & Dichter, 2006; Shenton & Kubicki, 2009). Enlarged ventricles are assumed to reflect the degeneration of nearby brain tissue. The significance of enlarged ventricles is hotly debated, however. This structural deterioration (or failure to develop) could be a *consequence* of schizophrenia, or it could be a contributing *cause* of the illness.

Brain-imaging studies have also uncovered other structural abnormalities including reductions in both grey matter and white matter in specific brain regions (Bobo et al., 2008; Karlsgodt, Sun, & Cannon, 2010). These reductions seem to reflect losses of synaptic density and myelinization (see Chapter 3). These findings suggest that schizophrenia is caused by disruptions in the brain's neural connectivity, which impairs the normal communication among neural circuits (Karlsgodt, Sun, & Cannon, 2010).

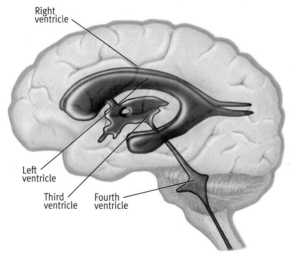

FIGURE 14.20

Schizophrenia and the ventricles of the brain.

Cerebrospinal fluid (CSF) circulates around the brain and spinal cord. The hollow cavities in the brain filled with CSF are called *ventricles*. The four ventricles in the human brain are depicted here. Recent studies with CT scans and MRI scans suggest that there is an association between enlarged ventricles in the brain and the occurrence of schizophrenic disturbance.

Source: Graphic adapted from Starr, C., and Taggart, R. (1998). *Biology: The unity and diversity of life*. Belmont, CA: Wadsworth. © 1998 Wadsworth Publishing. Reprinted by permission.

The Neurodevelopmental Hypothesis

In recent years, several new lines of evidence have led to the emergence of the *neurodevelopmental hypothesis* of schizophrenia, which posits that schizophrenia is caused in part by various disruptions in the normal maturational processes of the brain before or at birth (Fatemi & Folsom, 2009). According to this hypothesis, insults to the brain during sensitive phases of prenatal development or during birth can cause subtle neurological damage that elevates individuals' vulnerability to schizophrenia years later in adolescence and early adulthood (see Figure 14.21). What are the sources of these early insults to the brain? Thus far, research has focused on viral infections or malnutrition during prenatal development and obstetrical complications during the birth process.

The evidence on viral infections has been building since Sarnoff Mednick and his colleagues (1988) discovered an elevated incidence of schizophrenia among individuals who were in their second trimester of prenatal development during a 1957 influenza epidemic in Finland. Several subsequent studies in other locations have also found a link between exposure to influenza and other infections during prenatal development and increased prevalence of schizophrenia (Brown & Derkits, 2010). Another study, which investigated the possible impact of prenatal malnutrition, found an elevated incidence of schizophrenia in a cohort of people who were prenatally exposed to a severe famine in 1944–1945 due to a Nazi blockade of food deliveries in the Netherlands during World War II (Susser et al., 1996). A recent study looked at a new source of disruption during prenatal development: severe maternal stress. The study found an elevated prevalence of schizophrenia among the offspring of women who suffered severe stress during their pregnancy (Khashan et al., 2008). Other research has shown that schizophrenic patients are more likely than control subjects to have a history of obstetrical complications (Kelly et al., 2004; Murray & Bramon, 2005). Finally, research suggests that minor physical anomalies (slight anatomical defects of the head, hands, feet, and face) that would be consistent with prenatal neurological damage are more common among people with schizophrenia than among others (McNeil, Canton-Graae, & Ismail, 2000; Schiffman et al., 2002). Collectively, these diverse studies argue for a relationship between early neurological trauma and a predisposition to schizophrenia (King, St-Hilaire, & Heidkamp, 2010).

Expressed Emotion

Studies of expressed emotion have primarily focused on how this element of family dynamics influences the *course* of schizophrenic illness, after the onset of the disorder (Leff & Vaughn, 1985). *Expressed emotion (EE) is the degree to which a relative of a schizophrenic patient displays highly critical or emotionally overinvolved attitudes toward the patient.* Audiotaped interviews of relatives' communication are carefully evaluated for critical comments, resentment toward the patient, and excessive emotional involvement (overprotective, overconcerned attitudes) (Hooley, 2004).

Studies show that a family's expressed emotion is a good predictor of the course of a schizophrenic patient's illness (Hooley, 2007). After release from a hospital, people with schizophrenia who return to a family high in expressed emotion show relapse rates about three times that of patients who return to a family low in expressed emotion (see Figure 14.22; Hooley, 2009). Part of the problem for patients returning to homes high in expressed emotion is that their families are probably more sources of stress than of social support (Cutting & Docherty, 2000).

Precipitating Stress

Most theories of schizophrenia assume that stress plays a key role in triggering schizophrenic disorders (Walker & Tessner, 2008). According to this notion, various biological and psychological factors influence individuals' *vulnerability* to schizophrenia. High stress may then serve to precipitate a schizophrenic disorder in someone who is vulnerable (McGlashan

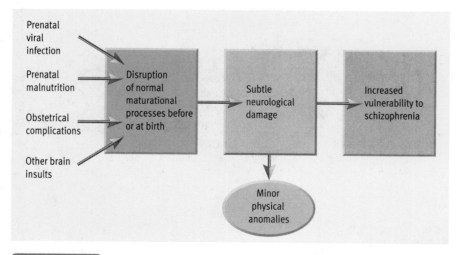

FIGURE 14.21

The neurodevelopmental hypothesis of schizophrenia.

Recent findings have suggested that insults to the brain sustained during prenatal development or at birth may disrupt crucial maturational processes in the brain, resulting in subtle neurological damage that gradually becomes apparent as youngsters develop. This neurological damage is believed to increase both vulnerability to schizophrenia and the incidence of minor physical anomalies (slight anatomical defects of the head, face, hands, and feet).

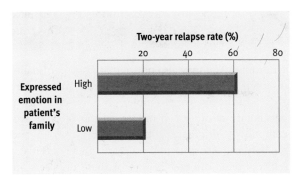

FIGURE 14.22

Expressed emotion and relapse rates in schizophrenia.
Schizophrenic patients who return to a home that is high in expressed emotion have higher relapse rates than those who return to a home low in expressed emotion. Thus, unhealthy family dynamics can influence the course of schizophrenia. (Data adapted from Leff & Vaughn, 1981)

& Hoffman, 2000). Research indicates that high stress can also trigger relapses in patients who have made progress toward recovery (Walker, Mittal, & Tessner, 2008). Patients who show strong emotional reactions to events seem to be particularly likely to have their symptoms exacerbated by stress (Docherty et al., 2009).

Schizophrenia is the last of the major Axis I diagnostic categories that we will consider. We'll complete our overview of various types of abnormal behaviour with a brief look at the personality disorders. These disorders are recorded on Axis II in the DSM classification system.

REVIEW OF KEY POINTS

▷ Schizophrenic disorders are characterized by deterioration of adaptive behaviour, irrational thought, delusions, hallucinations, and disturbed mood.

▷ Schizophrenic disorders are classified as paranoid, catatonic, disorganized, or undifferentiated. A new classification scheme based on the predominance of positive versus negative symptoms is under study. Schizophrenic disorders usually emerge during adolescence or young adulthood.

▷ Research has linked schizophrenia to a genetic vulnerability and changes in neurotransmitter activity at dopamine synapses. Structural abnormalities in the brain, such as enlarged ventricles, are associated with schizophrenia, but their significance is unclear.

▷ The neurodevelopmental hypothesis of schizophrenia asserts that schizophrenia is attributable to disruptions in the normal maturational processes of the brain before or at birth that are caused by prenatal viral infections, obstetrical complications, and other insults to the brain. Patients who come from homes high in expressed emotion have elevated relapse rates. This suggests that unhealthy family dynamics play a role in schizophrenia. High stress may also contribute to the onset of schizophrenia.

concept **check 14.1**

Distinguishing Schizophrenic and Mood Disorders

Check your understanding of the nature of schizophrenic and mood disorders by making preliminary diagnoses for the cases described below. Read each case summary and write your tentative diagnosis in the space provided. The answers are in Appendix A.

1. Max hasn't slept in four days. He's determined to write a great novel before his class reunion, which is a few months away. He expounds eloquently on his novel to anyone who will listen, talking at such a rapid pace that no one can get a word in edgewise. He feels like he's wired with energy and is supremely confident about the novel, even though he's written only 10 to 20 pages. Last week, he charged $8000 worth of new computer software, which is supposed to help him write his book.

Preliminary diagnosis: _____

2. Eduardo maintains that he invented the atomic bomb, even though he was born after its invention. He says he invented it to punish homosexuals, Nazis, and short people. It's short people that he's really afraid of. He's sure that all of the short people on TV are talking about him. He thinks that short people are conspiring to make him look like a Conservative. Eduardo frequently gets into arguments with people and is emotionally volatile. His grooming is poor, but he says it's okay because he's the Defence minister.

Preliminary diagnosis: _____

3. Margaret has hardly gotten out of bed for weeks, although she's troubled by insomnia. She doesn't feel like eating and has absolutely no energy. She feels dejected, discouraged, spiritless, and apathetic. Friends stop by to try to cheer her up, but she tells them not to waste their time on "pond scum."

Preliminary diagnosis: _____

Psychological Disorders

Personality Disorders

PREVIEW QUESTIONS

► What are the three clusters of personality disorders and what are the major diagnostic challenges with them?

► What are the symptoms of antisocial personality disorder and what is its etiology?

We have seen repeatedly that it is often difficult to draw that imaginary line between healthy and disordered behaviour. This is especially true in the case of personality disorders, which are relatively mild disturbances in comparison to most of the Axis I disorders. *Personality disorders* are a class of disorders marked by extreme, inflexible personality traits that cause subjective distress or impaired social and occupational functioning. Essentially, people with these disorders display certain personality traits to an excessive degree and in rigid ways that undermine their adjustment. Personality disorders usually emerge during late childhood or adolescence and often continue throughout adulthood.

DSM-IV lists ten personality disorders. Estimated prevalence rates for each of these disorders tend to fall in the range of 1–2 percent (Guzzetta & de Girolamo, 2009). These disorders are described briefly in Table 14.2. If you examine this table, you will find a diverse collection of maladaptive personality syndromes. You may also notice that some personality disorders essentially are mild versions of more severe Axis I disorders. For example, obsessive-compulsive personality disorder is a milder version of obsessive-compulsive disorder. Likewise, the schizoid and schizotypal personality disorders are milder cousins of schizophrenic disorders. Some of these disorders are more common in men and some in women, as the figures in the far right column of the table indicate.

The ten personality disorders are grouped into three related clusters, as shown in Table 14.2. The three disorders in the *anxious/fearful* cluster are marked by maladaptive efforts to control anxiety and fear about social rejection. People with the three disorders in the *odd/eccentric* cluster are distrustful, socially aloof, and unable to connect with others emotionally. The four personality disorders in the *dramatic/impulsive* cluster have less in common with each other than those grouped in the first two clusters. The histrionic and narcissistic personalities share

TABLE 14.2

Personality Disorders

Source: Estimated gender ratios from Millon (1981).

Cluster	Disorder	Description	% Male/ % Female
Anxious/fearful	Avoidant personality disorder	Excessively sensitive to potential rejection, humiliation, or shame; socially withdrawn in spite of desire for acceptance from others	50/50
	Dependent personality disorder	Excessively lacking in self-reliance and self-esteem; passively allowing others to make all decisions; constantly subordinating own needs to others' needs	31/69
	Obsessive-compulsive personality disorder	Preoccupied with organization, rules, schedules, lists, trivial details; extremely conventional, serious, and formal; unable to express warm emotions	50/50
Odd/eccentric	Schizoid personality disorder	Defective in capacity for forming social relationships; showing absence of warm, tender feelings for others	78/22
	Schizotypal personality disorder	Showing social deficits and oddities of thinking, perception, and communication that resemble schizophrenia	55/45
	Paranoid personality disorder	Showing pervasive and unwarranted suspiciousness and mistrust of people; overly sensitive; prone to jealousy	55/45
Dramatic/ impulsive	Histrionic personality disorder	Overly dramatic; tending to exaggerated expressions of emotion; egocentric, seeking attention	15/85
	Narcissistic personality disorder	Grandiosely self-important; preoccupied with success fantasies; expecting special treatment; lacking interpersonal empathy	70/30
	Borderline personality disorder	Unstable in self-image, mood, and interpersonal relationships; impulsive and unpredictable	38/62
	Antisocial personality disorder	Chronically violating the rights of others; failing to accept social norms, to form attachments to others, or to sustain consistent work behaviour; exploitive and reckless	82/18

a flair for overdramatizing everything. Impulsiveness is the common ground shared by the borderline and antisocial personality disorders. Affective dysregulation is characteristic of borderline personalities (Suvak et al., 2011) in particular.

Diagnostic Problems

Many critics have argued that the personality disorders overlap too much with Axis I disorders and with each other (Clark, 2007). The extent of this problem was documented in a study by Leslie Morey (1988). Morey reviewed the cases of 291 patients who had received a specific personality disorder diagnosis to see how many could have met the criteria for any of the other personality disorders. Morey found massive overlap among the diagnoses. For example, among patients with a diagnosis of histrionic personality disorder, 56 percent also qualified for a borderline disorder, 54 percent for a narcissistic disorder, 32 percent for an avoidant disorder, and 30 percent for a dependent disorder. Clearly, there are fundamental problems with Axis II as a classification system (Tyrer et al, 2007; Widiger, 2007). The overlap among the personality disorders makes it extremely difficult to achieve reliable diagnoses. Doubts have also been raised about the decision to place personality disorders on a separate axis, as there does not appear to be any fundamental distinction between personality disorders and Axis I disorders (Krueger, 2005).

In light of these problems, a variety of theorists have questioned the wisdom of the current *categorical approach* to describing personality disorders, which assumes (incorrectly, they argue) that people can reliably be placed in discontinuous (nonoverlapping) diagnostic categories (Verheul, 2005; Widiger & Trull, 2007). Support for a shift to a *dimensional approach* to diagnosis in DSM-5 is particularly strong for the personality disorders (Widiger, Livesley, & Clark, 2009; Widiger & Mullins-Sweatt, 2010).

The difficulties involved in the diagnosis of personality disorders have clearly hindered research on their etiology and prognosis. The only personality disorder that has a long history of extensive research is the antisocial personality disorder, which we examine next.

Antisocial Personality Disorder

The antisocial personality disorder has a misleading name. The *antisocial* designation does *not* mean that people with this disorder shun social interaction. In fact, rather than shrinking from social interaction, many are sociable, friendly, and superficially charming; in fact, they often make good first impressions on others (Lilienfeld & Arkowitz, 2007). People with this disorder are *antisocial* in that they choose to *reject widely accepted social norms* regarding moral principles and behaviour.

Description

People with antisocial personalities chronically violate the rights of others. They often use their social charm to cultivate others' liking or loyalty for purposes of exploitation. The *antisocial personality disorder* is marked by impulsive, callous, manipulative, aggressive, and irresponsible behaviour that reflects a failure to accept social norms. Since they haven't accepted the social norms they violate, people with antisocial personalities rarely feel guilty about their transgressions. Essentially, they lack an adequate conscience and an empathy for others (Hare, 1993; Kiehl & Buckholtz, 2010). Antisocial personality disorder occurs much more frequently among males than females. The reasons for this gender difference are not clear. Studies suggest that it is a moderately common disorder, seen in roughly 3–6 percent of males and about 1 percent of females (Widiger & Mullins, 2003).

Many people with antisocial personalities become involved in illegal activities. Moreover, according to University of British Columbia psychologist Robert Hare, antisocial personalities tend to begin their criminal careers at an early age, to commit offences at a relatively high rate, and to be versatile offenders who become involved in many types of criminal activity (Hare, 2006). However, many people with antisocial personalities keep their exploitive, amoral behaviour channelled within the boundaries of the law. Such people may even enjoy high status in our society. In other words, the concept of the antisocial personality disorder can apply to cutthroat business executives, scheming politicians, unprincipled lawyers, and money-hungry evangelists, as well as to con artists, drug dealers, thugs, burglars, and petty thieves.

Robert Hare is one of the world's leading experts on *psychopathy*, a term that is often used interchangeably with the term *antisocial personality disorder*. His influential book *Without Conscience: The Disturbing World of the Psychopaths Among Us* (Hare, 1999) is an important resource for scholars and laypersons alike. Hare (1991) developed an important assessment device for psychopathy, the *Psychopathy Checklist–Revised* (PCL–R). For many, this measure is the "single, most important advancement to date toward what will hopefully become our ultimate understanding of psychopathy" (Wormith, 2000, p. 134). Recent research by a team of psychologists from Queen's University and the Mental Health Centre at Penetanguishene (Skilling et al., 2002) supports the validity of the PCL–R.

Axis I category

Anxiety disorders

Edvard Munch's *The Scream* expresses overwhelming feelings of anxiety.

Mood disorders

Vincent van Gogh's *Portrait of Dr. Gachet* captures the profound dejection experienced in depressive disorders.

Schizophrenic disorders

The perceptual distortions seen in schizophrenia probably contributed to the bizarre imagery apparent in this portrait of a cat painted by Louis Wain.

Subtypes

Generalized anxiety disorder: Chronic, high level of anxiety not tied to any specific threat

Phobic disorder: Persistent, irrational fear of object or situation that presents no real danger

Panic disorder: Recurrent attacks of overwhelming anxiety that occur suddenly and unexpectedly

Obsessive-compulsive disorder: Persistent, uncontrollable intrusions of unwanted thoughts and urges to engage in senseless rituals

Major depressive disorder: Two or more major depressive episodes marked by feelings of sadness, worthlessness, despair

Bipolar disorder: One or more manic episodes marked by inflated self-esteem, grandiosity, and elevated mood and energy, usually accompanied by major depressive episodes

Paranoid schizophrenia: Delusions of persecution and delusions of grandeur; frequent auditory hallucinations

Catatonic schizophrenia: Motor disturbances ranging from immobility to excessive, purposeless activity

Disorganized schizophrenia: Flat or inappropriate emotions; disorganized speech and adaptive behaviour

Undifferentiated schizophrenia: Idiosyncratic mixtures of schizophrenic symptoms that cannot be placed into above three categories

Prevalence/well-known victim

Prevalence — 19%

The famous industrialist Howard Hughes suffered from obsessive-compulsive disorder.

Prevalence — 15%

Actor Jim Carrey has suffered from depression.

Prevalence — 1%

John Nash, the Nobel Prize–winning mathematician whose story was told in the film *A Beautiful Mind*, has struggled with schizophrenia.

Etiology: Biological factors

Genetic vulnerability: Twin studies and other evidence suggest a mild genetic predisposition to anxiety disorders.

Anxiety sensitivity: Oversensitivity to physical symptoms of anxiety may lead to overreactions to feelings of anxiety, so anxiety breeds more anxiety.

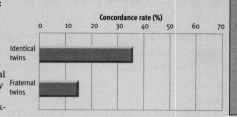

Concordance rate (%)

Neurochemical bases: Disturbances in neural circuits releasing GABA may contribute to some disorders; abnormalities at serotonin synapses have been implicated in panic and obsessive-compulsive disorders.

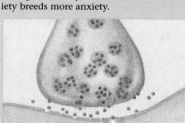

Genetic vulnerability: Twin studies and other evidence suggest a genetic predisposition to mood disorders.

Sleep disturbances: Disruption of biological rhythms and sleep patterns may lead to neurochemical changes that contribute to mood disorders.

Concordance rate (%)

Neurochemical bases: Disturbances in neural circuits releasing norepinephrine may contribute to some mood disorders; abnormalties at serotonin synapses have also been implicated as a factor in depression.

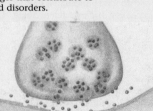

Genetic vulnerability: Twin studies and other evidence suggest a genetic predispositon to schizophrenic disorders.

Concordance rate (%)

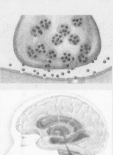

Neurochemical bases: Overactivity in neural circuits releasing dopamine is associated with schizophrenia; but abnormalities in other neurotransmitter systems may also contribute.

Structural abnormalities in brain: Enlarged brain ventricles are associated with schizophrenia, but they may be an effect rather than a cause of the disorder.

Etiology: Psychological factors

Learning: Many anxiety responses may be acquired through classical conditioning or observational learning; phobic responses may be maintained by operant reinforcement.

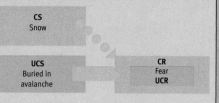

CS — Snow
UCS — Buried in avalanche
CR — Fear / UCR

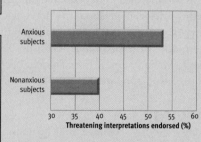

Threatening interpretations endorsed (%)

Stress: High stress may help to precipitate the onset of anxiety disorders.

Cognition: People who misinterpret harmless situations as threatening and who focus excessive attention on perceived threats are more vulnerable to anxiety disorders.

Interpersonal roots: Behavioural theories emphasize how inadequate social skills can result in a paucity of reinforcers and other effects that make people vulnerable to depression.

Stress: High stress can act as a precipitating factor that triggers depression or bipolar disorder.

Cognition: Negative thinking can contribute to the development of depression; rumination may extend and amplify depression.

Poor social skills → Acquire fewer reinforcers, such as good friends, top jobs / Court rejection because of irritability, pessimism / Gravitate to people who confirm negative self-views → Increased vulnerability to depression

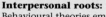

Negative thinking ⇄ Depression

Expressed emotion: A family's expressed emotion is a good predictor of the course of a schizophrenic patient's illness.

Stress: High stress can precipitate schizophrenic disorder in people who are vulnerable to schizophrenia.

Two-year relapse rate (%)

Expressed emotion in patient's family — High / Low

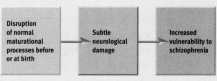

Disruption of normal maturational processes before or at birth → Subtle neurological damage → Increased vulnerability to schizophrenia

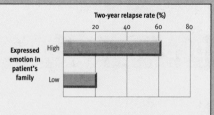

The neurodevelopmental hypothesis: Insults to the brain sustained during prenatal development or at birth may disrupt maturational processes in the brain, resulting in elevated vulnerability to schizophrenia.

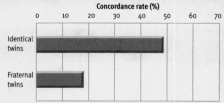

People with antisocial personalities exhibit quite a variety of maladaptive traits (Hare, 2006; Hare & Neumann, 2008; Patrick, 2007)). Among other things, they rarely experience genuine affection for others. However, they may be skilled at faking affection so they can exploit people. Sexually, they are predatory and promiscuous. Such individuals also tend to be irresponsible and impulsive. They can tolerate little frustration, and they pursue immediate gratification. These characteristics make them unreliable employees, unfaithful spouses, inattentive parents, and undependable friends. Many people with antisocial personalities have a chequered history of divorce, child abuse, and job instability. Paul Bernardo, who was convicted for the 1991 murders of Leslie Mahaffy and Kristen French, has the classic features of someone with antisocial personality disorder.

Etiology

Many theorists believe that biological factors contribute to the development of antisocial personality disorders. Various lines of evidence suggest a genetic predisposition toward these disorders (Moffitt, 2005; Waldman & Rhee, 2006). A review of twin studies found an average concordance rate of 67 percent for identical twins in comparison to 31 percent for fraternal twins (Black, 2001). The findings are consistent with a fairly strong genetic vulnerability to the disorder. Many observers have noted that people with antisocial personalities lack the inhibitions that most of us have about violating moral standards. Their lack of inhibitions prompted Hans Eysenck to theorize that such people might inherit relatively sluggish autonomic nervous systems, leading to slow acquisition of inhibitions through classical conditioning. The notion that antisocial personalities exhibit underarousal has received some support (Raine, 1997), but the findings have been inconsistent (Blackburn, 2006). Part of the problem in this area of research may be that arousal can be quantified in a great many different ways.

Efforts to relate psychological factors to antisocial behaviour have emphasized inadequate socialization in dysfunctional family systems (Farrington, 2006; Sutker & Allain, 2001). It's easy to envision how antisocial traits could be fostered in homes where parents make haphazard or half-hearted efforts to socialize their children to be respectful, truthful, responsible, unselfish, and so forth. Consistent with this idea, studies find that individuals with antisocial personalities tend to come from homes where discipline is erratic or ineffective, and homes where they experience physical abuse and neglect (Luntz & Widom, 1994; Widom, 1997). Such people are also more likely to emerge from homes where one or both parents exhibit antisocial traits (Black, 2001). These parents presumably model exploitive, amoral behaviour, which their children acquire through observational learning.

REVIEW OF KEY POINTS

▷ Personality disorders are marked by extreme personality traits that cause distress and impaired functioning. There are ten personality disorders allocated to Axis II in DSM-IV.

▷ Personality disorders can be grouped into three clusters: anxious-fearful, odd-eccentric, and dramatic-impulsive. Specific personality disorders are poorly defined and there is excessive overlap among them, creating diagnostic problems. Some theorists believe that these problems could be reduced by replacing the current categorical approach with a dimensional approach.

▷ The antisocial personality disorder involves manipulative, impulsive, exploitive, aggressive behaviour. Research on the etiology of this disorder has implicated genetic vulnerability, autonomic reactivity, inadequate socialization, and observational learning.

Disorders of Childhood

PREVIEW QUESTIONS

▷ What types of disorders are specifically associated with childhood?

▷ What are the three main deficits associated with autistic disorder?

▷ What is early intensive behavioural intervention designed to do, and how does it work?

If you think back to your own early years or our discussions in Chapter 11 of development across the life span, it is clear that for most of us, childhood is a time of growth, curiosity, exploration, friendships, and gradual maturity. We play, we run, we make friends, and we explore our limits, and our physical and social environments. Sure, there are obstacles along the way—sometimes our parents don't understand us, sometimes we cry, fight, and throw tantrums, and sometimes we are confused and sad. But those problems seem mostly transient against the backdrop of all the other adventures we have. However, not all children have these experiences. For some, the sadness lasts longer and seems deeper; for some the confusion never clears up. Just like adults and teens, children suffer from psychological illness. According to the Canadian Mental Health Association (2011), roughly 20 percent of the children and youth in Canada will suffer from such illnesses. Many will go undiagnosed and untreated. In the province of Ontario alone, these statistics translate into more than 560 000 children and youths

(Province of Ontario, 2010). Interest in infant and childhood disorders (Egger & Ede, 2011; Tronick & Beeghly, 2011) recently has become of increasing concern to professionals and laypersons alike.

Children suffer, much like adults, from too much stress, depression, PTSD, obsessive-compulsive disorder, and most of the other categories of disorders we have discussed so far in this chapter. In addition, however, there are a series of disorders that have traditionally been thought of as being specific to childhood and youth. These include disorders such as attention-deficit/hyperactivity disorder (ADHD), separation anxiety disorder, and pervasive developmental disorders including autistic disorder (or autism). We will concentrate in this section on a brief discussion of autism. *Autism* (or *autistic disorder*) refers to a developmental disorder characterized by social and emotional deficits, along with repetitive and stereotypic behaviours, interests, and activities.

Autism

Donald Gray Tripplett was the first person diagnosed with autism (Donovan & Zucker, 2010). He was the first subject of a series of case studies presented by Dr. Leo Kanner in a 1943 journal article (Kanner, 1943). Donald T (as he was referred to in the article) began life relatively normally but soon exhibited curious habits and obsessions. For example, he seemed to be obsessed with and developed a "mania" for spinning blocks and other objects, and when someone tried to interrupt his activities, he would throw a "tantrum." Soon thereafter, he exhibited an oddly detached orientation. He developed an "abstraction of the mind which made him perfectly oblivious, to everything about him . . . to get his attention almost requires one to break down a mental barrier between his inner consciousness and the outside world" (Kanner, 1943, p. 218). Kanner referred to this latter characteristic as *autistic aloneness*. Donald was exhibiting many of the symptoms that are classically associated with autism. Later work would extend Kanner's ideas on autism to consider autism as a *spectrum* of disorders including *Asperger's disorder* (Bernier & Gerdts, 2010).

While autism is relatively rare (Szatmari, 2003), it has been the subject of a great deal of publicity because of court cases in Canada dealing with the reluctance of some governments to fund its treatment (Parliament of Canada, 2006). In terms of the DSM categorization system, autism is placed in a category termed *pervasive developmental disorders* (PDD) (Olley & Gutentag, 1999). In the DSM-IV, three subtypes of autism are identified—autistic disorder, Asperger's disorder, and pervasive developmental disorders

not otherwise specified (PDD-NOS) (Boucher, 2009; Szatmari, 2000). While clearly multidetermined, genetic and neurobiological causes, among others, have been implicated in the disorder (Boucher, 2009; Cook, 2001; Tsai & Ghaziuddin, 1992).

Children suffering from autism exhibit three types of deficits—impairment in social interaction, impairment in communication, and repetitive, stereotyped behaviours/interests/activities (Bernier & Gerdts, 2010; Boucher, 2009; Oller & Oller, 2010; Zager, 1999). Children with autism show significant impairment in social interaction with others; this is the *autistic aloneness* Kanner (1973) referred to.

Autistic children really don't develop relationships with others that are typical of children their age, and they show inappropriate reactions to others, tending not to make eye contact or smile when expected. They may turn their backs on playmates and sometimes seem not to see or be aware of others (Volkmar & Weisner, 2009). They rarely initiate contact with others and may appear to be in a world of their own. While there are many questions regarding the origins of this deficit, it has been suggested that part of the problem may lie with a very limited *theory of mind* (Sigman, 1994; see our discussion of theory of mind in Chapter 11, page 513). As you will recall from Chapter 11, theory of mind deals with people's understanding of other people—their perspectives, intentions, affect, and so on.

In children with autism, development and use of language to communicate with others shows deficits from the very beginning stages of language development. This obviously impacts their social play. Many never really acquire socially useful speech patterns at all during their lifetimes, but the frequency of this specific problem seems to have decreased in recent years (Bernier & Gerdts, 2010). Children with this disorder often exhibit a pattern referred to as *echolia*, in which they mimic what they have heard from others and repeat back sentences others have just communicated to them. In some cases, they mimic what they have heard some time later (i.e., delayed echolia) (Bernier & Gerdts, 2010). Finally, as we saw with the description of Donald's interest in spinning blocks, children suffering from autistic disorder show obsessive-compulsive behaviour, engaging in ritualistic acts such as seemingly endless rocking and spinning, and being comfortable only with order and familiarity (Boucher, 2009; Haugaard, 2008). They may also show *higher-order repetitive behaviour* in which, for example, they have a special interest in specific topics, video games, or characters on TV (Bernier & Gerdts, 2010).

Treatment options for children suffering from autism are individualized, difficult, and labour-intensive. It is recommended that they receive early

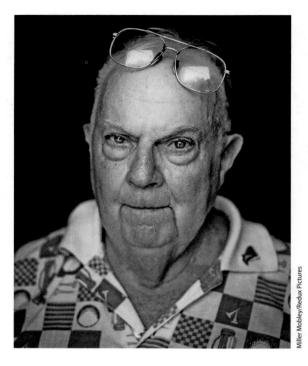

Donald Triplett, 78, who still lives in Forest, Mississippi, where he was born was the first child diagnosed with autism.

as Peter Szatmari, Susan Bryson (Szatmari & Reitzel, 2004; Szatmari, Bryson et al., 2003), and the members of York University's Autism Alliance Research Group (e.g., Bebko et al., 2006; Tamiji & Crawford, 2010) are making important contributions to understanding the nature of autism.

Finally, you may be interested in what happened to autism's first child (Donvan & Zucker, 2010), Donald Triplett. He continues to live (alone) in the house in which he was raised. Donald sticks to a few rooms of the house and follows his established routines. Surprisingly, and very mysteriously, he leaves town once a month and disappears. What does he do? Where does he go? Donald loves to travel. He travels all over the world by himself. This might seem quite surprising to you, that he would break free from his familiar surroundings to engage in this type of activity. But, of course, there are routines attached to his travel. For example, each trip lasts six days at most, and he tries to get photographs of scenes and buildings that he has already seen in pictures. He then places all the pictures in well-organized albums. He makes his own travel arrangements when travelling in the United States, and uses the same travel agent each time when he travels overseas.

Over the years, Donald has developed hobbies; he is an avid golfer and he loves to drive his Cadillac. He is comfortable living in the town of his birth. The small town he lives in protects and nurtures him, and his many friends warn strangers who come looking for Donald, "the celebrity," that "If what you are doing hurts Don, I know where to find you" (Donovan & Zucker, 2010).

and extensive intervention. Such interventions can be extremely expensive. For example, early intensive behavioural intervention (EIBI) can cost almost $60 000 per year. The treatment is recommended to be 40 hours per week, seven days a week, and 52 weeks a year (Parliament of Canada, 2006). EIBI (Ben-Itzchak & Zachor, 2007) refers to a group of interventions based on early work by Lovaas (1987) in which, generally, each individual skill is broken down into small steps, with each successful acquisition being reinforced. Canadian researchers such

Miller Mobley/Redux Pictures

Psychological Disorders and the Law

PREVIEW QUESTIONS

▶ What is the insanity defence?

▶ How often is it used?

Hamilton, Ontario, psychologist Lori Triano-Antidormi and her husband, Tony, a social worker, are mental health professionals. They had had a great deal of exposure to the nature of mental illness in the course of their educational experiences, but they were unprepared for the horrific intrusion that mental illness would make into their personal lives in 1997. A neighbour, Lucia Piovesan, became convinced that Lori and Tony's son, Zachary, was the soul of her own deceased son who was searching for some type of release. Piovesan tried to grant her son release by stabbing two-year-old Zachary to death in March 1997 (Could Zach's Death, 1999). When she was arrested, Piovesan was carrying a picture of her own son, Enrico, who had died six years before.

Zachary's parents had been concerned about Piovesan's obvious distress for some time but were unable to accomplish anything through the criminal

justice system (Adams, Pitre, & Smith, 2001). Later at trial, Piovesan was found to be *not criminally responsible* for the murder because of mental illness (Davison et al., 2008). She suffered from paranoid schizophrenia and had been refusing to take her medication for some time before the murder.

What does it mean to be *not criminally responsible on account of mental disorder*? How is it judged? We entrust our protection to various levels of government in our society. Societies use laws to enforce their norms regarding appropriate behaviour. Tragically, those agencies of Canadian society given this trust failed Zachary and his parents. The law in our society has something to say about many issues related to psychological disorder and abnormal behaviour. In this section, we examine the role of the legal system with regard to psychological disorder.

Insanity

When many people refer to individuals suffering from psychological disorder, they often use the term *insane* and refer to *insanity laws* or the *insanity defence*. In Canada, the proper term is not insanity. In Canadian law an individual can be judged "not criminally responsible on account of mental disorder." Neither it nor the older term, insanity, is a diagnosis. "Not criminally responsible on account of mental disorder" is an important legal concept, because criminal acts must be intentional. The law reasons that people who are "out of their mind" may not be able to appreciate the significance of what they're doing. This type of defence is used in criminal trials by defendants who admit that they committed the crime but claim that they lacked intent.

No simple relationship exists between specific diagnoses of mental disorders and court findings of insanity or not criminally responsible on account of mental disorder. Most people with diagnosed psychological disorders would *not* qualify as insane. The people most likely to qualify are those troubled by severe disturbances that display delusional behaviour. The courts apply various rules in making judgments about a defendant's mental state, depending on the jurisdiction (Simon & Shuman, 2008). According to one widely used rule, called the *M'Naghten rule*, insanity exists when a mental disorder makes a person unable to distinguish right from wrong. The M'Naghten rule originated in England when a delusional man attempted to kill the prime minister and shot one of the prime minister's assistants instead. This rule has served as the basis of insanity laws in many countries, including Canada. (As you can imagine, evaluating insanity as defined in the M'Naghten rule can be difficult for judges and jurors, not to mention the psychologists and psychiatrists who are called into court as expert witnesses.) According to York University professor Regina Schuller (e.g., Schuller, Kazoleas, & Kawakami, 2009; Klippenstine, Schuller, & Wall, 2007) and Simon Fraser University's James Ogloff, the "growth in clinical psychology over the first half of the twentieth century resulted in an increased demand from the legal system for clinical evaluations and diagnoses of mental disorders" (Schuller & Ogloff, 2001, p. 6).

Over the years since the establishment of the M'Naghten rule, changes have been made to how psychological disorders are used in court. In Canada, the designation of being found not guilty by reason of insanity (NGRI) was changed in 1991 to the term "not criminally responsible on account of mental disorder" (NCRMD) (Ogloff & Whittemore, 2001).

Psychologist Regina Schuller is an expert on the interface of psychology and Canadian law. Her research interests include cases involving violence against women.

Courtesy of Regina Schuller

According to Simon Fraser University psychologists Jocelyn Lymburner and Ronald Roesch (1999), the use and success of this defence are rarer than most Canadians assume. They suggest that it is rarely successful, and typically is used only in cases of the most severely disordered defendants.

According to a team of scholars from Carleton University (Pozzulo, Bennell, & Forth, 2006), issues of fitness, insanity, and automatism are relevant to the two cornerstones of English–Canadian law—*actus reus* (a wrongful deed) and *mens rea* (criminal intent). Mental health professionals may play an important role at several stages of a trial. Defendants may be found *unfit to stand trial* if they are judged unable to conduct a defence at any point in the legal proceedings because of a psychological disorder such as schizophrenia. This may be due to their inability to understand the proceedings or possible consequences, or an inability to communicate with their lawyers. If fitness is restored, a defendant may stand trial.

If found fit to stand trial, psychological issues may arise in terms of the not criminally responsible defence. If it is found that the defendant was unable to appreciate the quality of the act and the fact that it was wrong, the defendant may be found not criminally responsible on account of mental disorder. If found NCRMD, the defendant may be absolutely discharged, given a conditional discharge, or ordered to a psychiatric facility (Pozzulo, Bennell, & Forth, 2006).

A final issue relevant to our discussion is that of *automatism*. Here the idea is that you should not be held responsible if you had no control over your behaviour. The conditions that have been recognized in Canadian courts include having sustained physical blows, carbon monoxide poisoning, sleepwalking, and others. In Chapter 5, we referred to the successful sleepwalking defence used in the 1988 Ontario case of Ken Parks, who drove 23 kilometres and killed his mother-in-law. While a defendant may be sent to a psychiatric institution if he or she is judged NCRMD, a "successful (noninsane) automatism verdict means that the defendant is not guilty and is then released without conditions" (Pozzulo, Bennell, & Forth, 2006, p. 281).

Postscript: While alive, Zachary had a passion for music. After his death, his short life was honoured by the creation of a project designed to promote music to children: CDs of Zachary's favourite musician, the Canadian singer Raffi, were distributed to children's hospitals across Canada for children to enjoy (Famely, 2004).

Culture and Pathology

The legal rules governing mental disorders and involuntary commitment obviously are culture-specific. And we noted earlier that judgments of normality and abnormality are influenced by cultural norms and values. Stigmas about mental illness and its effects on such things as willingness to admit to and seek treatment for mental illness also vary by culture (Fung et al., 2007; Gim, Atkinson, & Kim, 1991; Yang, 2007). For example, Asian North Americans seem particularly unwilling to take their concerns to therapists, with this level affected by factors such as the client's level of acculturation and the ethnicity of the therapist (Gim, Atkinson, & Whiteley, 1990). Asian Canadians have been found to have one of the lowest levels of accessing mental health services of all minority groups in Canada (Chen, Kazanjian, Wong, & Goldner, 2010). In light of these realities, would it be reasonable to infer that psychological disorders are culturally variable phenomena? Social scientists are sharply divided on the answer to this question. Some embrace a *relativistic view* of psychological disorders, whereas others subscribe to a *universalistic or pancultural view* (Tanaka-Matsumi, 2001). Theorists who embrace the *relativistic view* argue that the criteria of mental illness vary greatly across cultures and that there are no universal standards of normality and abnormality. According to the relativists, the DSM diagnostic system reflects an ethnocentric, Western, white, urban, middle- and upper-class cultural orientation that has limited relevance in other cultural contexts. In contrast, those who subscribe to the *pancultural view* argue that the criteria of mental illness are much the same around the world and that basic standards of normality and abnormality are universal across cultures. Theorists who accept the pancultural view of psychopathology typically maintain that Western diagnostic concepts have validity and utility in other cultural contexts.

The debate about culture and pathology basically boils down to two specific issues: (1) Are the psychological disorders seen in Western societies found throughout the world? (2) Are the symptom patterns of mental disorders invariant across cultures? Let's briefly examine the evidence on these questions and then reconsider the relativistic and pancultural views of psychological disorders.

Are Equivalent Disorders Found around the World?

Most investigators agree that the principal categories of serious psychological disturbance—schizophrenia, depression, and bipolar illness—are identifiable in all cultures (Tsai et al., 2001). Most behaviours that are regarded as clearly abnormal in Western culture are also viewed as abnormal in other cultures. People who are delusional, hallucinatory, disoriented, or incoherent are thought to be disturbed in all societies, although there are cultural disparities in exactly what is considered delusional or hallucinatory.

Cultural variations are more apparent in the recognition of less severe forms of psychological disturbance (Mezzich, Lewis-Fernandez, & Ruiperez, 2003). Additional research is needed, but relatively mild types of pathology that do not disrupt behaviour in obvious ways appear to go unrecognized in many societies. Thus, syndromes such as generalized anxiety disorder, hypochondria, and narcissistic personality disorder, which are firmly established as diagnostic entities in the DSM, are viewed in some cultures as "run of the mill" difficulties and peculiarities rather than as full-fledged disorders.

Finally, researchers have discovered a small number of *culture-bound disorders* that further illustrate the diversity of abnormal behaviour around the world (Lewis-Fernandez, Buarnaccia, & Ruiz, 2009; Tseng, 2009). *Culture-bound disorders* are abnormal syndromes found only in a few cultural groups. For example, *koro,* an obsessive fear that one's penis will withdraw into one's abdomen, is seen only among Chinese males in Malaya and several other regions of southern Asia. *Windigo,* which involves an intense craving for human flesh and fear that one will turn into a cannibal, is seen only among Algonquin cultures, and *pibloktoq* is a type of Arctic hysteria associated with the Inuit. And until fairly recently, the eating disorder *anorexia nervosa,* discussed in this chapter's Personal Application, was largely seen only in affluent Western cultures (Russell, 2009).

Are Symptom Patterns Culturally Invariant?

Do the major types of psychological disorders manifest themselves in the same way around the world? It depends to some extent on the disorder. The more a disorder has a strong biological component, the more it tends to be expressed in similar ways across varied cultures (Marsella & Yamada, 2007). Thus, the constellations of symptoms associated with schizophrenia and bipolar illness are largely the same across widely disparate societies (Draguns, 1980, 1990). However, even in severe, heavily biological disorders, cultural variations in symptom patterns are also seen (Mezzich, Lewis-Fernandez, & Ruiperez, 2003). For example, delusions are a common symptom of schizophrenia in all cultures, but the specific delusions that people report are tied to their cultural heritage (Brislin, 1993). In technologically advanced societies, schizophrenic patients report that thoughts are being inserted into their minds through transmissions from electric lines, satellites, or microwave ovens. Victims of schizophrenia in less technological societies experience the same phenomenon but blame sorcerers or demons. The influence of culture on symptom patterns is illustrated by recent reports of a new delusion in modern societies—patients are erroneously insisting that they are the stars of reality TV shows (DeAngelis, 2009).

Of the major disorders, symptom patterns are probably most variable for depression. For example, profound feelings of guilt and self-deprecation lie at the core of depression in Western cultures but are far less central to depression in many other societies. In non-Western cultures, depression tends to be expressed in terms of somatic symptoms, such as complaints of fatigue, headaches, and backaches, more than psychological symptoms, such as dejection and low self-esteem (Tsai et al., 2001; Young, 1997). These differences presumably occur because people learn to express symptoms of psychological distress in ways that are acceptable in their culture.

So, what can we conclude about the validity of the relativistic versus pancultural views of psychological disorders? Both views appear to have some merit. As we have seen in other areas of research, psychopathology is characterized by both cultural variance and invariance. Investigators have identified some universal standards of normality and abnormality and found considerable similarity across cultures in the syndromes that are regarded as pathological and in their patterns of symptoms. However, researchers have also discovered many cultural variations in the recognition, definition, and symptoms of various psychological disorders.

Putting It in Perspective: Themes 3, 4, 5, and 6

Our examination of abnormal behaviour and its roots has highlighted four of our organizing themes: multifactorial causation, the interplay of heredity and environment, the sociohistorical context in which psychology evolves, and the influence of culture on psychological phenomena.

We can safely say that every disorder described in this chapter has multiple causes. The development of mental disorders involves an interplay among a variety of psychological, biological, and social factors. We also saw that most psychological disorders depend on an interaction of genetics and experience. This interaction shows up most clearly in the *stress-vulnerability models* for mood disorders and schizophrenic disorders (see Figure 14.23). *Vulnerability* to these disorders seems to depend primarily on heredity, whereas stress is largely a function of environment. According to stress-vulnerability theories, disorders emerge when high vulnerability intersects with high stress. A high biological vulnerability may not be converted into a disorder if a person's stress is low. Similarly, high stress may not lead to a disorder if vulnerability is low. Thus, the impact of heredity depends on the environment, and the effect of environment depends on heredity.

PREVIEW QUESTIONS

▶ How did this chapter illustrate multifactorial causation?

▶ How did this chapter highlight the interaction of heredity and environment?

▶ How did this chapter show that psychology evolves in a sociohistorical context?

▶ How did this chapter illustrate the importance of cultural factors?

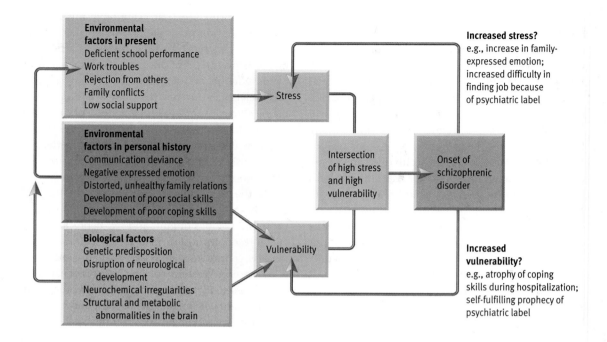

FIGURE 14.23

The stress-vulnerability model of schizophrenia.

Multifactorial causation is readily apparent in current theories about the etiology of schizophrenic disorders. A variety of biological factors and personal history factors influence one's vulnerability to the disorder, which interacts with the amount of stress one experiences. Schizophrenic disorders appear to result from an intersection of high stress and high vulnerability.

Environmental factors in present
Deficient school performance
Work troubles
Rejection from others
Family conflicts
Low social support

Environmental factors in personal history
Communication deviance
Negative expressed emotion
Distorted, unhealthy family relations
Development of poor social skills
Development of poor coping skills

Biological factors
Genetic predisposition
Disruption of neurological development
Neurochemical irregularities
Structural and metabolic abnormalities in the brain

Stress

Vulnerability

Intersection of high stress and high vulnerability

Onset of schizophrenic disorder

Increased stress?
e.g., increase in family-expressed emotion; increased difficulty in finding job because of psychiatric label

Increased vulnerability?
e.g., atrophy of coping skills during hospitalization; self-fulfilling prophecy of psychiatric label

This chapter also demonstrated that psychology evolves in a sociohistorical context. We saw that modern conceptions of normality and abnormality are largely shaped by empirical research, but social trends, economic necessities, and political realities also play a role. Finally, our discussion of psychological disorders showed once again that psychological phenomena are shaped to some degree by cultural parameters. Although some standards of normality and abnormality transcend cultural boundaries, cultural norms influence many aspects of psychopathology. Indeed, the influence of culture will be apparent in our upcoming Personal Application on eating disorders. These disorders are largely a creation of modern, affluent, Western culture.

REVIEW OF KEY POINTS

▷ Some psychological disorders are specific to childhood, such as autism, which is a pervasive developmental disorder. Children suffering from autism exhibit social and emotional deficits along with repetitive, ritualistic actions and interests.

▷ Insanity is a legal concept applied to people who cannot be held responsible for their actions because of mental illness. While the term *insanity* is used in some other countries, in Canada, the correct terminology is *not criminally responsible on account of mental disorder*. The insanity defence is used less frequently and less successfully than widely believed.

▷ The principal categories of psychological disturbance are identifiable in all cultures. But milder disorders may go unrecognized in some societies, and culture-bound disorders further illustrate the diversity of abnormal behaviour around the world. The symptoms associated with specific disorders are largely the same across different cultures, but cultural variations are seen in the details of how these symptoms are expressed.

▷ This chapter highlighted four of the text's unifying themes, showing that behaviour is governed by multiple causes, that heredity and environment jointly influence mental disorders, that psychology evolves in a sociohistorical context, and that pathology is characterized by both cultural variance and invariance.

Understanding Eating Disorders

Answer the following "true" or "false."

___ **1** Although they have attracted attention only in recent years, eating disorders have a long history and have always been fairly common.

___ **2** People with anorexia nervosa are much more likely to recognize that their eating behaviour is pathological than are people suffering from bulimia nervosa.

___ **3** The prevalence of eating disorders is twice as high in women as it is in men.

___ **4** The binge-and-purge syndrome seen in bulimia nervosa is not common in anorexia nervosa.

All of the above statements are false, as you will see in this Personal Application. The psychological disorders that we discussed in the main body of the chapter have largely been recognized for centuries and most of them are found in one form or another in all cultures and societies. Eating disorders present a sharp contrast to this picture; they have been recognized only in recent decades and they have largely been confined to affluent, Westernized cultures (G. F. M. Russell, 1995; Szmukler & Patton, 1995). In spite of these fascinating differences, eating disorders have much in common with traditional forms of pathology.

Description

Although most people don't seem to take eating disorders as seriously as other types of psychological disorders, you will see that they are dangerous and debilitating (Thompson, Roehrig, & Kinder, 2007). No other psychological disorder is associated with a greater elevation in mortality (Striegel-Moore & Bulik, 2007). *Eating disorders* are severe disturbances in eating behaviour characterized by preoccupation with weight and unhealthy efforts to control weight. In DSM-IV, two sometimes overlapping syndromes are recognized: *anorexia nervosa* and *bulimia nervosa*. A third syndrome, called *binge-eating disorder*, is described in the appendix of DSM-IV as a potential new disorder, pending further study. We will devote our attention in this Application to the two established eating disorders, but we will briefly outline the symptoms of this new disorder, as well.

Anorexia Nervosa

Anorexia nervosa involves intense fear of gaining weight, disturbed body image, refusal to maintain normal weight, and dangerous measures to lose weight. Two subtypes have been observed (Herzog & Delinsky, 2001). In *restricting type anorexia nervosa*, people drastically reduce their intake of food, sometimes literally starving themselves. In *binge-eating/purging type anorexia nervosa*, individuals attempt to lose weight by forcing themselves to vomit after meals, by misusing laxatives and diuretics, and by engaging in excessive exercise.

Both types suffer from disturbed body image. No matter how frail and emaciated they become, they insist that they are too fat. Their morbid fear of obesity means that they are never satisfied with their weight. If they gain half a kilogram, they panic. The only thing that makes them happy is to lose more weight. The frequent result is a relentless decline in body weight; people entering treatment for anorexia nervosa are typically 25–30 percent below their normal weight (Hsu, 1990). Because of their disturbed body image, people suffering from anorexia generally do *not* appreciate the maladaptive quality of their behaviour and rarely seek treatment on their own. They are typically coaxed or coerced into treatment by friends or family members who are alarmed by their appearance.

Anorexia nervosa eventually leads to a cascade of medical problems, including *amenorrhea* (a loss of menstrual cycles in women), gastrointestinal problems, low blood pressure, *osteoporosis* (a loss of bone density), and metabolic disturbances that can lead to cardiac arrest or circulatory collapse (Halmi, 2008; Russell, 2009). Anorexia is a very serious illness that leads to death in 5–10 percent of patients (Steinhausen, 2002).

Eating disorders have become common and have been seen in many prominent women, such as Lindsay Lohan and Mary Kate Olsen.

Psychological Disorders

Bulimia Nervosa

Bulimia nervosa involves habitually engaging in out-of-control overeating followed by unhealthy compensatory efforts, such as self-induced vomiting, fasting, abuse of laxatives and diuretics, and excessive exercise. The eating binges are usually carried out in secret and are followed by intense guilt and concern about gaining weight. These feelings motivate ill-advised strategies to undo the effects of overeating. However, vomiting prevents the absorption of only about half of recently consumed food, and laxatives and diuretics have negligible impact on caloric intake, so people suffering from bulimia nervosa typically maintain a reasonably normal weight (Fairburn, Cooper, & Murphy, 2009). Medical problems associated with bulimia nervosa include cardiac arrhythmias, dental problems, metabolic deficiencies, and gastrointestinal problems (Halmi, 2002, 2008). Bulimia often coexists with other psychological disturbances, including depression, anxiety disorders, and substance abuse (Hudson et al., 2007).

Obviously, bulimia nervosa shares many features with anorexia nervosa, such as a morbid fear of becoming obese, preoccupation with food, and rigid, maladaptive approaches to controlling weight that are grounded in naïve all-or-none thinking. The close relationship between the disorders is demonstrated by the fact that many patients who initially develop one syndrome cross over to display the other syndrome (Tozzi et al., 2005). However, the two syndromes also differ in crucial ways. First and foremost, bulimia is a much less life-threatening condition. Second, although their appearance is usually more "normal" than that seen in anorexia, people with bulimia are much more likely to recognize that their eating behaviour is pathological and are more likely to cooperate with treatment (Guarda et al., 2007). Nonetheless, like anorexia, bulimia is associated with elevated mortality rates (Crow et al., 2009).

Binge-Eating Disorder

A surprising number of people who exhibit disordered eating do not fit neatly into the anorexia or bulimia categories, which is why a third category has been proposed. *Binge-eating disorder* involves distress-inducing eating binges that are not accompanied by the purging, fasting, and excessive exercise seen in bulimia. Obviously, this syndrome resembles bulimia, but it is a less severe disorder. Still, this disorder creates great distress, as these people tend to be disgusted by their bodies and distraught about their overeating. People with binge-eating disorder are frequently overweight. Their excessive eating is often triggered by stress (Gluck, 2006). Research suggests that this comparatively mild syndrome may be more common than anorexia or bulimia (Hudson et al., 2007). Given the research that has been compiled since DSM-IV was released in 1994, it appears likely that binge-eating disorder will be recognized as an independent disorder in the forthcoming DSM-V (Striegel-Moore & Franko, 2008).

History and Prevalence

Historians have been able to track down descriptions of anorexia nervosa that date back centuries, so the disorder is *not* entirely new, but anorexia nervosa did not become a common affliction until the middle part of the 20th century (Vandereycken, 2002). Although binging and purging have a long history in some cultures, they were not part of pathological efforts to control weight, and bulimia nervosa appears to be a new syndrome that emerged gradually in the middle of the 20th century and was first recognized in the 1970s (Steiger & Bruce, 2009; Vandereycken, 2002).

Both disorders are a product of modern, affluent, Western culture, where food is generally plentiful and the desirability of being thin is widely endorsed. Until recently, these disorders were not seen outside of Western cultures (Hoek, 2002). However, in recent years, advances in communication have exported Western culture to far-flung corners of the globe, and eating disorders have started showing up in many non-Western societies, especially affluent Asian countries (Becker & Fay, 2006; Lee & Katzman, 2002).

There is a huge gender gap in the likelihood of developing eating disorders. About 90–95 percent of individuals with eating disorders are female (Hoek, 2002). This staggering discrepancy appears to be a result of cultural pressures rather than biological factors (Smolak & Murnen, 2001). Western standards of attractiveness emphasize slenderness more for females than for males, and women generally experience greater pressure to be physically attractive than men do (Strahan et al., 2008). Eating disorders mostly afflict *young* women. The typical age of onset for anorexia is 14 to 18 and for bulimia it is 15 to 21 (see Figure 14.24).

How common are eating disorders in Western societies? Studies of young women suggest that about 1 percent develop anorexia nervosa and about 2–3 percent develop bulimia nervosa (Anderson & Yager, 2005). However, prevalence rates appear to be trending higher in more recent studies (Thompson, Roehrig, & Kinder, 2007). In some respects, these figures may only scratch the surface of the problem. Evidence suggests that as many as 20 percent of female college students may struggle with transient bulimic symptoms (Anderson & Yager, 2005). And recent community surveys suggest that there may be more undiagnosed eating disorders among men than generally appreciated (Hudson et al., 2007).

Etiology of Eating Disorders

Like other types of psychological disorders, eating disorders are caused by multiple determinants that work interactively. Let's take a brief look at some of the factors that contribute to the development of anorexia nervosa and bulimia nervosa.

Genetic Vulnerability The evidence is not nearly as strong or complete as it is for many other types of psychopathology (such as anxiety, mood, and schizophrenic disorders), but some people may inherit a genetic vulnerability to eating disorder (Thornton, Mazzeo, & Bulik, 2011). Studies show that relatives of patients with eating disorders have elevated rates of anorexia nervosa and bulimia nervosa (Bulik, 2004). And twin studies suggest that a genetic predisposition may be at work (Steiger, Bruce, & Israel, 2003).

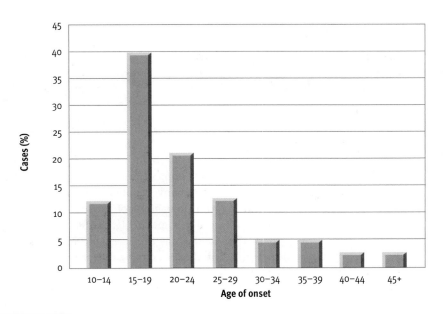

FIGURE 14.24

Age of onset for anorexia nervosa.

Eating disorders tend to emerge during adolescence, as these data for anorexia nervosa show. This graph shows how age of onset was distributed in a sample of 166 female patients in Minnesota. As you can see, over half of the patients experienced the onset of their illness before the age of 20, with vulnerability clearly peaking between the ages of 15 and 19.

Source: Adapted from Lucas, A. R., Beard, C. M., O'Fallon, W. M., and Kurland, L. T. (1991). 50-year trends in the incidence of anorexia nervosa in Rochester, Minn.: A population-based study. *American Journal of Psychiatry, 148,* 917–922. Reprinted with permission from the *American Journal of Psychiatry,* (Copyright © 1991). American Psychiatric Association.

Personality Factors Certain personality traits may increase vulnerability to eating disorders. There are innumerable exceptions, but victims of anorexia nervosa tend to be obsessive, rigid, and emotionally restrained, whereas victims of bulimia nervosa tend to be impulsive, overly sensitive, and low in self-esteem (Wonderlich, 2002). Recent research also suggests that perfectionism is a risk factor for anorexia (Sherry & Hall, 2009; Steiger & Bruce, 2009).

Cultural Values The contribution of cultural values to the increased prevalence of eating disorders can hardly be overestimated (Anderson-Fye & Becker, 2004; Stice, 2001; Striegel-Moore & Bulik, 2007). In Western society, young women are socialized to believe that they must be attractive, and to be attractive they must be as thin as the actresses and fashion models that dominate the media (Lavine, Sweeney, & Wagner, 1999). Thanks to this cultural milieu, many young women are dissatisfied with their weight because the societal ideals promoted by the media are unattainable for most of them (Thompson & Stice, 2001). Unfortunately, in a small portion of these women, the pressure to be thin, in combination with genetic vulnerability, family pathology, and other factors, leads to unhealthful efforts to control weight.

The Role of the Family Quite a number of theorists emphasize how family dynamics can contribute to the development of anorexia nervosa and bulimia nervosa in young women (Haworth-Hoeppner, 2000). Some theorists suggest that parents who are overly involved in their children's lives turn the normal adolescent push for independence into an unhealthy struggle (Minuchin,

Rosman, & Baker, 1978). Needing to assert their autonomy, some adolescent girls seek extreme control over their body, leading to pathological patterns of eating (Bruch, 1978). Other theorists maintain that some mothers contribute to eating disorders simply by endorsing society's message that "you can never be too thin" and by modelling unhealthy dieting behaviours of their own (Pike & Rodin, 1991).

Cognitive Factors Many theorists emphasize the role of disturbed thinking in the etiology of eating disorders (Williamson et al., 2001). For example, anorexic patients' typical belief that they are fat when they actually are wasting away is a dramatic illustration of how thinking goes awry. Patients with eating disorders display rigid, all-or-none thinking and many maladaptive beliefs, such as "I must be thin to be accepted," "If I am not in complete control, I will lose all control," "If I gain one kilogram, I'll go on to gain an enormous amount of weight." Additional research is needed to determine whether distorted thinking is a *cause* or merely a *symptom* of eating disorders.

REVIEW OF KEY POINTS

▷ The principal eating disorders are anorexia nervosa and bulimia nervosa. Both disorders reflect a morbid fear of gaining weight. Anorexia and bulimia both lead to a cascade of medical problems. Both disorders appear to be largely a product of modern, affluent, Westernized culture.

▷ Females account for 90–95 percent of eating disorders. The typical age of onset is roughly 15 to 20. There appears to be a genetic vulnerability to eating disorders. Cultural pressures on young women to be thin clearly help to foster eating disorders. Unhealthy family dynamics, certain personality traits, and disturbed thinking can also contribute to the development of eating disorders.

Working with Probabilities in Thinking about Mental Illness

As you read about the various types of psychological disorders, did you think to yourself that you or someone you know was being described? On the one hand, there is no reason to be alarmed. The tendency to see yourself and your friends in descriptions of pathology is a common one, sometimes called the *medical student's disease* because beginning medical students often erroneously believe that they or their friends have whatever diseases they are currently learning about. Consider the statistics in Figure 14.25, which outlines the lifetime prevalence of psychological disorders in the United States. According to the figure, the likelihood of anyone having at least one DSM disorder is estimated to be about 44 percent.

This estimate strikes most people as surprisingly high. Why is this so? One reason is that when people think about psychological

disorders they tend to think of severe disorders, such as bipolar disorder or schizophrenia, which are relatively infrequent, rather than "run of the mill" disturbances, such as anxiety and depressive disorders, which are much more common. When it comes to mental illness, people tend to think of patients in straitjackets or of obviously psychotic homeless people who do not reflect the broad and diverse population of people who suffer from psychological disorders. In other words, their *prototypes* or "best examples" of mental illness consist of severe disorders that are infrequent, so they underestimate the prevalence of mental disorders. This distortion illustrates the influence of the *representativeness heuristic,* in which the estimated probability of an event is based on how similar the event is to the typical prototype of that event (see Chapter 8).

Do you still find it hard to believe that the overall prevalence of psychological disorders is about 44 percent? Another reason this number seems surprisingly high is that many people do not understand that the probability of having *at least one* disorder is much higher than the probability of having the most prevalent disorder by itself. For example, the probability of having a substance-use disorder, the single most common type of disorder, is approximately 24 percent, but the probability of having a substance-use disorder *or* an anxiety disorder *or* a mood disorder *or* a schizophrenic disorder jumps to 44 percent. These "or" relationships represent *cumulative probabilities.*

Yet another consideration that makes the prevalence figures seem high is that many people confuse different types of *prevalence rates.* The 44 percent estimate is for *lifetime prevalence,* which means it is the probability of having *any* disorder *at least once* at any time in one's lifetime. The lifetime prevalence rate is another example of "or" relationships. It is a value that takes into account the probability of having a psychological disorder in childhood *or* adolescence *or* adulthood *or* old age. *Point prevalence rates,* which estimate the percentage of people manifesting various disorders *at a particular point in time,* are much lower because many psychological disorders last only a few months to a few years.

What about "and" relationships—that is, relationships in which we want to know the probability of someone having condition A *and* condition B? For example, given the lifetime prevalence estimates (from Figure 14.25) for each category of disorder, which are shown here in parentheses, what is the probability of someone having a substance-use disorder (24 percent prevalence) *and* an anxiety disorder (19 percent) *and* a mood disorder (15 percent) *and* a schizophrenic disorder (1 percent) during his or her lifetime? Such "and" relationships represent *conjunctive probabilities.* Stop and think: What must be true about the probability of having all four types of disorders? Will this probability be less than 24 percent, between

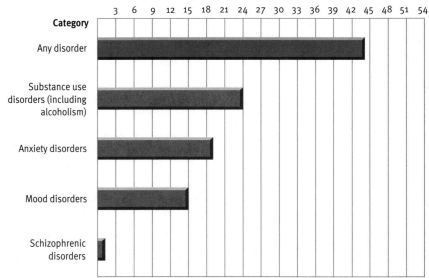

Portion of population meeting criteria for disorder (%)

FIGURE 14.25

Lifetime prevalence of psychological disorders.

The estimated percentage of people who have, at any time in their life, suffered from one of four types of psychological disorders or from a disorder of any kind (top bar) is shown here. Prevalence estimates vary somewhat from one study to the next, depending on the exact methods used in sampling and assessment. The estimates shown here are based on pooling data from Wave 1 and 2 of the *Epidemiological Catchment Area Studies* and the *National Comorbidity Study,* as summarized by Regier and Burke (2000) and Dew, Bromet, and Switzer (2000). These studies, which collectively evaluated over 28 000 subjects, provide the best data to date on the prevalence of mental illness in the United States.

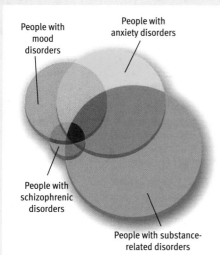

FIGURE 14.26

Conjunctive probabilities.

The probability of someone having all four disorders depicted here cannot be greater than the probability of the least common condition by itself, which is 1 percent for schizophrenia. The intersection of all four disorders (shown in black) has to be a subset of schizophrenic disorders and is probably well under 1 percent. Efforts to think about probabilities can sometimes be facilitated by creating diagrams that show the relationships and overlap among various events.

People with mood disorders

People with anxiety disorders

People with schizophrenic disorders

People with substance-related disorders

24 percent and 44 percent, or over 44 percent? You may be surprised to learn that this figure is probably well under 1 percent. You can't have all four disorders unless you have the least frequent disorder (schizophrenia), which has a prevalence of 1 percent, so the answer *must* be 1 percent or less. Moreover, of all of the people with schizophrenia, only a tiny subset of them are likely to have all three of the other disorders, so the answer is probably well under 1 percent (see Figure 14.26). If this type of question strikes you as contrived, think again. Epidemiologists have devoted an enormous amount of research to the estimation of *comorbidity*—the coexistence of two or more disorders—because it greatly complicates treatment issues.

These are two examples of using statistical probabilities as a critical thinking tool. Let's apply this type of thinking to another problem dealing with physical health. Here is a problem used in a study by Tversky and Kahneman (1983, p. 308) that many physicians got wrong:

A health survey was conducted in a sample of adult males in British Columbia, of all ages and occupations. Please give your best estimate of the following values:

What percentage of the men surveyed have had one or more heart attacks? _____

What percentage of the men surveyed both are over 55 years old and have had one or more heart attacks? _____

Fill in the blanks above with your best guesses. Of course, you probably have only a very general idea about the prevalence of heart attacks, but go ahead and fill in the blanks anyway.

The actual values are not as important in this example as the relative values are. Over 65 percent of the physicians who participated in the experiment by Tversky and Kahneman gave a higher percentage value for the second question than for the first. What is wrong with their answers? The second question is asking about the conjunctive probability of two events. Hopefully, you see why this figure *must* be less than the probability of either one of these events occurring alone. Of all of the men in the survey who had had a heart attack, only some of them are also over 55, so the second number must be smaller than the first. As we saw in Chapter 8, this common error in thinking is called the *conjunction fallacy*. The *conjunction fallacy occurs when people estimate that the odds of two uncertain events happening together are greater than the odds of either event happening alone.*

Why did so many physicians get this problem wrong? They were vulnerable to the conjunction fallacy because they were influenced by the *representativeness heuristic*, or the power of prototypes. When physicians think "heart attack," they tend to envision a man over the age of 55. Hence, the second scenario fit so well with their prototype of a heart attack victim, they carelessly overestimated its probability.

Let's consider some additional examples of erroneous reasoning about probabilities involving how people think about psychological disorders. Toward the beginning of the chapter, we discussed the fact that many people tend to stereotypically assume that mentally ill people are likely to be violent. Other research suggests that people tend to wildly overestimate (37-fold in one study) how often the insanity defence is used in criminal trials (Silver, Cirincion, & Steadman., 1994). These examples reflect the influence of the *availability heuristic, in which the estimated probability of an event is based on the ease with which relevant instances come to mind.* Because of the availability heuristic, people tend to overestimate the probability of dramatic events that receive heavy media coverage, even when these events are rare, because examples of the events are easy to retrieve from memory. Violent acts by former psychiatric patients tend to get lots of attention in the press. And because of the *hindsight bias*, journalists tend to question why authorities couldn't foresee and prevent the violence (see the Critical Thinking Application for Chapter 12), so the mental illness angle tends to be emphasized. In a similar vein, press coverage is usually intense when a defendant in a murder trial mounts a not criminally responsible defence.

In sum, the various types of statistics that come up in thinking about psychological disorders demonstrate that we are constantly working with probabilities, even though we may not realize it. Critical thinking requires a good understanding of the laws of probability because there are very few certainties in life.

TABLE 14.3 Critical Thinking Skills Discussed in This Application

Skill	Description
Understanding the limitations of the representativeness heuristic	The critical thinker understands that focusing on prototypes can lead to inaccurate probability estimates.
Understanding cumulative probabilities	The critical thinker understands that the probability of at least one of several events occurring is additive, and increases with time and the number of events.
Understanding conjunctive probabilities	The critical thinker appreciates that the probability of two uncertain events happening together is less than the probability of either event happening alone.
Understanding the limitations of the availability heuristic	The critical thinker understands that the ease with which examples come to mind may not be an accurate guide to the probability of an event.

Key Ideas

Abnormal Behaviour: Myths, Realities, and Controversies

● The medical model assumes that it is useful to view abnormal behaviour as a disease. This view has been criticized on the grounds that it turns ethical questions about deviance into medical questions.

● Three criteria are used in deciding whether people suffer from psychological disorders: deviance, personal distress, and maladaptive behaviour. People with psychological disorders are not particularly bizarre or dangerous, and even the most severe disorders are potentially curable.

● DSM-IV is the official psychodiagnostic classification system. This system asks for information about patients on five axes, or dimensions. Psychological disorders are more common than widely believed.

Anxiety Disorders

● The anxiety disorders include generalized anxiety disorder, phobic disorder, panic disorder, obsessive-compulsive disorder, and post-traumatic stress disorder. Heredity, oversensitivity to the physiological symptoms of anxiety, and abnormalities in GABA or serotonin activity may contribute to these disorders.

● Many anxiety responses, especially phobias, may be caused by classical conditioning and maintained by operant conditioning. Cognitive theorists maintain that a tendency to overinterpret harmless situations as threatening may make some people vulnerable to anxiety disorders. Stress may also trigger anxiety disorders.

Dissociative Disorders

● Dissociative disorders include dissociative amnesia and fugue and dissociative identity disorder. These disorders are uncommon and their causes are not well understood.

Mood Disorders

● The principal mood disorders are major depressive disorder and bipolar disorder. Mood disorders are episodic. Depression is more common in females than males.

● Evidence indicates that people vary in their genetic vulnerability to mood disorders. These disorders are accompanied by changes in neurochemical activity in the brain. Cognitive models posit that negative thinking contributes to depression. Depression is often rooted in interpersonal inadequacies and stress.

Schizophrenic Disorders

● Schizophrenic disorders are characterized by deterioration of adaptive behaviour, delusions, hallucinations, and disturbed mood. Research has linked schizophrenia to genetic vulnerability, changes in neurotransmitter activity, and structural abnormalities in the brain.

● The neurodevelopmental hypothesis asserts that schizophrenia is attributable to disruptions in the normal maturational processes of the brain before or at birth that are caused by prenatal viral infections, obstetrical complications, and other insults to the brain. Precipitating stress and unhealthful family dynamics, including high expressed emotion, may also modulate the course of schizophrenia.

Personality Disorders

● Ten personality disorders are allocated to Axis II in DSM. Personality disorders can be grouped into three clusters: anxious/fearful, odd/eccentric, and dramatic/impulsive.

● The antisocial personality disorder involves manipulative, impulsive, exploitive, and aggressive behaviour. Research on the etiology of this disorder has implicated genetic vulnerability, autonomic reactivity, inadequate socialization, and observational learning.

Disorders of Childhood

● Some psychological disorders are specific to childhood. One of these disorders is autism, which is a pervasive developmental disorder. Children suffering from autism are characterized by social deficits, emotional deficits, and an interest in ritualistic and repetitive actions and behaviours.

Psychological Disorders and the Law

● Insanity is a legal concept applied to people who cannot be held responsible for their actions because of mental illness.

Culture and Pathology

● The principal categories of psychological disturbance are identifiable in all cultures. But milder disorders may go unrecognized in some societies. The symptoms associated with specific disorders are largely the same across different cultures, but some variability is seen.

Putting It in Perspective: Themes 3, 4, 5, and 6

● This chapter highlighted four of our unifying themes, showing that behaviour is governed by multiple causes, that heredity and environment jointly influence mental disorders, that psychology evolves in a sociohistorical context, and that pathology is characterized by both cultural variance and invariance.

PERSONAL APPLICATION • Understanding Eating Disorders

● The principal eating disorders are anorexia nervosa and bulimia nervosa. Both disorders reflect a morbid fear of gaining weight and both appear to be largely a product of modern, affluent, Westernized culture. Females account for 90–95 percent of eating disorders.

● There appears to be a genetic vulnerability to eating disorders. Cultural pressures on young women to be thin clearly help foster eating disorders. Unhealthful family dynamics and disturbed thinking can also contribute.

CRITICAL THINKING APPLICATION • Working with Probabilities in Thinking about Mental Illness

● Probability estimates can be distorted by the representativeness heuristic and the availability heuristic. Cumulative probabilities are additive, whereas conjunctive probabilities are always less than the likelihood of any one of the events happening alone.

Key Terms

Key People

1. Which of the following statements is consistent with Thomas Szasz's perspective on mental illness?
   A. It causes behaviour that is statistically unusual.
   B. It is defined by behaviour that deviates from social norms.
   C. It is a disease of the mind.
   D. It is associated with biological imbalance or damage.

2. Sue is plagued by dread, worry, and anxiety, but she still fulfills her daily responsibilities. Which of the following statements about Sue's behaviour is true?
   A. Because she has a high level of adaptive functioning, her behaviour is considered normal.
   B. Because most people experience worry and anxiety at some time, her experience is normal.
   C. Because she feels great personal distress, she could be diagnosed with a mental disorder.
   D. Because she cannot continue to fulfill her daily responsibilities for much longer, she could be diagnosed with a mental disorder.

3. Gina has a phobia of snakes, even though she has never been harmed by a snake. She has repeatedly gotten electric shocks from her toaster, and yet she has no fear of her toaster. Which of the following perspectives on anxiety disorders can explain Gina's patterns of fear?
   A. classical conditioning   C. observational learning
   B. operant conditioning   D. preparedness

4. Which of the following disorders is characterized by the coexistence of two or more distinct personalities within the same person?
   A. dissociative amnesia   C. dissociative fugue
   B. dissociative schizophrenia D. dissociative identity disorder

5. Which of the following is a symptom of bipolar disorder, but not of other mood disorders?
   A. mania   C. dysthymia
   B. depression   D. anhedonia

6. Which of the following statements describes a concordance rate?
   A. It is the percentage of relatives who exhibit the same disorder.
   B. It is the percentage of those with the same disorder who are receiving treatment.
   C. It is the prevalence of a particular disorder in the general population.
   D. It is the rate of cure for a particular disorder.

7. One of the features of Eric's depression is a tendency to constantly think about a particular negative event or to focus on his own sadness. What is the term for this way of thinking?
   A. pessimism   C. learned helplessness
   B. hedonic attribution   D. rumination

8. Consider the case of Mary who believes that while she sleeps at night, space creatures invade her uterus, where they multiply until they are ready to take over the world. According to Mary, she was chosen for this task because she is the only one with the power to help the space creatures succeed. Which of the following types of schizophrenia would Mary most likely be diagnosed with?
   A. paranoid   C. disorganized
   B. catatonic   D. undifferentiated

9. It has been suggested that the various subtypes of schizophrenia could be divided into just two categories. What distinguishes those two categories?
   A. favourable or unfavourable prognosis
   B. mild or severe impairment
   C. presence or absence of mood symptoms
   D. negative or positive symptoms

10. Based on evidence from drug treatments, which of the following neurotransmitters is theorized to contribute to the symptoms of schizophrenia?
    A. norepinephrine   C. acetylcholine
    B. serotonin   D. dopamine

11. Which of the following statements represents the main problem with the current classification scheme for personality disorders?
    A. It falsely implies that nearly everyone has at least one personality disorder.
    B. The criteria for diagnosis are so detailed and specific that even extremely disturbed people fail to meet them.
    C. The categories often overlap, making diagnosis unreliable.
    D. It contains too few categories to be useful.

12. Which of the following descriptions applies to an individual diagnosed with antisocial personality disorder?
    A. withdrawal from social interaction due to an intense fear of rejection or criticism
    B. withdrawal from social interaction due to a lack of interest in interpersonal intimacy
    C. emotionally cold, suspicious of everyone, and overly concerned about being slighted by others
    D. callous, impulsive, and manipulative

13. Which of the following describes an individual who is found "not criminally responsible on account of mental disorder"?
    A. The person is incapable to stand trial because he or she cannot understand the legal process.
    B. The person appears to be a danger to himself or herself or others.
    C. The person could not tell the difference between right and wrong at the time of the crime.
    D. The person is innocent of the crime.

14. Those who embrace a relativistic view of psychological disorders would agree with which of the following statements?
    A. The criteria of mental illness vary considerably across cultures.
    B. There are universal standards of normality and abnormality.
    C. Western diagnostic concepts have validity and utility in other cultural contexts.
    D. The DSM diagnostic criteria should be interpreted differently depending on the severity of the symptoms.

15. Which of the following symptoms is common in people with anorexia nervosa, but not common in those with bulimia?
    A. excessive exercise   C. anxiety about weight gain
    B. intentional vomiting   D. amenorrhea

See Appendix A for answers to this Practice Test.

On the Web

▶ **CourseMate**

Go to this site to find online resources directly linked to your book, including more quizzes, a glossary, flash cards, videos, and more!

▶ **CengageNow**

Go to this site for the link to CengageNOW™, your one-stop study shop. Take a pre-test for this chapter and CengageNOW™ will generate a personalized study plan based on your test results! The study plan will identify the topics you need to review and direct you to online resources to help you master those topics. You can then take a post-test to help you determine the concepts you have mastered and what you still need to work on.

▶ **Aplia**

Aplia™ is an online interactive learning solution that helps you improve comprehension—and your grade— by integrating a variety of media and tools such as video, tutorials, practice tests, and an interactive e-book.

CHAPTER 15

Treatment of Psychological Disorders

Image Source/Getty Images

What do you imagine when you hear the term *psychotherapy*? Unless you've had some personal exposure to therapy, your conception of it has likely been shaped by depictions you've seen on TV or in the movies. Perhaps when you think of therapy, you imagine TV mobster Tony Soprano talking to his therapist, Dr. Jennifer Melfi, about problems he's having with his mother. Or you may think of a group of people sitting around discussing their problems with one another and a therapist. Or perhaps you think of yourself lying on a couch, with a therapist sitting beside you listening to your dreams. As you will see in this chapter, some of these images are to some degree accurate, but they don't exhaust the range of treatment contexts. Contemporary treatments of psychological disorders are varied and reflect a distinct set of theories about human functioning. We have touched on many of these theories in the preceding chapters.

The last 50 years has seen significant advances in the development and scientific evaluation of treatments for psychological disorders. The range of treatment approaches is vast (Hersen & Gross, 2008), ranging from those focusing on emotion, thought, and/or relationships, to biomedical treatments that rely on medication or physical treatments, some of which are designed to change specific aspects of the operation of the brain. This work is continually evolving, allowing clients and their therapists access to the most recent advances in psychology.

Over the years, however, the history of treatment for psychological disorders also has had its controversial side. As ideas regarding the nature of psychological disorders have changed, so have approaches to treatment. Not all of these approaches have turned out to be positive. For example, if you were suffering from a psychological disorder in Canada in the 1960s, one therapist you might have been referred to was Dr. D. Ewen Cameron. He was the founder and director of the Allan Memorial Institute in Montreal and was a well-known and influential figure in the treatment of psychological disorders. During the late 1950s and early 1960s, Cameron was engaged in CIA-funded research allegedly designed to examine brainwashing and thought-control techniques. In Cameron's facility, patients were exposed to experimental techniques that included extended drug-induced periods of sleep (sometimes for weeks at a time), massive electroconvulsive (shock) therapy regimens, sensory deprivation, hours upon hours of tape-recorded messages, psychic driving, and LSD treatment. According to the patients themselves, most of this treatment was done without their knowledge or consent. Cameron's objective was to *depattern* the patients and to rid them of old behaviour patterns and replace them with new ones. Cameron's work on this project and the toll it exacted on his patients is detailed in Anne Collins's 1988 compelling book *In the Sleep Room: The Story of the CIA Brainwashing Experiments in Canada*. Years later, many of the Canadian participants sued (Moore, 2007), and Canadian Justice minister Kim Campbell finally agreed to establish a compensation fund in 1992.

The use of LSD in psychotherapy has other, more legitimate connections to Canada (Mills, 2010). Reports of *d-lysergic acid diethylamide* (LSD) began appearing in the scientific literature in the 1940s, and its potential for psychiatric treatment was explored in a series of government-supported studies conducted by Dr. Humphrey Osmond and his colleagues at the Weyburn Mental Hospital in Saskatchewan in the 1950s and 1960s (Dyck, 2005, 2008). In addition to his work on the project, Dr. Osmond is notable for a couple of other things (Lattin, 2010). He coined the term *psychedelic* to describe the experience users have after taking mescaline, psilocybin, or LSD. He is also responsible for giving the famous writer Aldous Huxley his first experience with hallucinogens, immortalized by Huxley (1954) in his book *The Doors of Perception*. Despite some initial optimism, concern about methodological inadequacies and sociocultural concerns contributed to the end of the project. LSD was also used in treatment in the Social Therapy Unit at Ontario's maximum-security psychiatric institution, the Oak Ridge Division of the Penetanguishene Mental Health Centre. It was used as part of a very innovative treatment program for psychopaths designed by Dr. Elliot Barker in the mid-1960s (Rice & Harris, 1993; Weisman, 1995). Ultimately, the

McGill University Archives, PR019175

McCord Museum II-144/631

Dr. D. Ewen Cameron served as director of the Allan Memorial Institute when CIA-funded brainwashing research was conducted there in the late 1950s and early 1960s.

Treatment of Psychological Disorders

program was considered a failure and some former patients sued, claiming coercion and lack of full consent. As we discussed in Chapter 2, ethical practices have changed over the years to maximize protection of the research participants (Koocher, 2007). Many of the current safeguards were not in place 50 years ago.

In this chapter, we'll take a down-to-earth look at *psychotherapy*, using the term in its broadest sense, to refer to all the diverse approaches used in the treatment of mental disorders and psychological problems. We'll start by discussing some general questions about the provision of treatment. After considering these issues, we'll examine the goals, techniques, and effectiveness of some of the more widely used approaches to therapy and discuss recent trends and issues in treatment. Some of the therapies we consider are not without their controversial aspects (Barlow, 2010; Castonguay et al., 2010; Dimidjian & Hollon, 2010), and we will review some of these too. In the Personal Application, we'll look at practical questions related to finding and choosing a therapist and getting the most out of therapy. And in the Critical Thinking Application, we'll address problems involved in determining whether therapy actually helps.

The Elements of the Treatment Process

PREVIEW QUESTIONS

▶ What are the three major approaches to the treatment of psychological disorders?

▶ What professions are involved in the treatment of psychological disorders?

Sigmund Freud is widely credited with launching modern psychotherapy and with calling into question the view that we are logical, rational beings (Breger, 2009). Ironically, the landmark case that inspired Freud involved a patient who actually was treated by one of his colleagues, Josef Breuer (Breger, 2009). Around 1880, Breuer began to treat a young woman referred to as Anna O (which was a pseudonym—her real name was Bertha Pappenheim). Anna exhibited a variety of physical maladies, including headaches, coughing, and a loss of feeling in and movement of her right arm. Much to his surprise, Breuer discovered that Anna's physical symptoms cleared up when he encouraged her to talk about emotionally charged experiences from her past.

When Breuer and Freud discussed the case, they speculated that talking things through had enabled Anna to drain off bottled-up emotions that had caused her symptoms. Breuer found the intense emotional exchange in this treatment not to his liking, so he didn't follow through on his discovery. However, Freud applied Breuer's insight to other patients, and his successes led him to develop a systematic treatment procedure, which he called *psychoanalysis*. Anna O called her treatment "the talking cure." However, as you'll see, psychotherapy isn't always curative, and many modern treatments place little emphasis on talking.

Freud's breakthrough ushered in a century of progress for psychotherapy. Psychoanalysis spawned many offspring, as Freud's followers developed their own systems of treatment. Since then, approaches to treatment have steadily grown more numerous, more diverse, and more effective. Today, people can choose from a bewildering array of therapies.

The case of Anna O, whose real name was Bertha Pappenheim, provided the inspiration for Sigmund Freud's invention of psychoanalysis.

Mary Evans Picture Library/Sigmund Freud Copyrights

Treatments: How Many Types Are There?

In their efforts to help people, psychotherapists use many treatment methods. These include discussion, advice, emotional support, persuasion, conditioning procedures, relaxation training, role-playing, drug therapy, biofeedback, and group therapy. No one knows exactly how many distinct types of psychotherapy there are. One expert (Kazdin, 1994) estimates that there may be over 400 approaches to treatment. Fortunately, we can impose some order on this chaos. As varied as therapists' procedures are, approaches to treatment can be classified into three major categories:

1. *Insight therapies.* Insight therapy is "talk therapy" in the tradition of Freud's psychoanalysis. In insight therapies, clients engage in complex verbal interactions with their therapists. The goal in these discussions is to pursue increased insight regarding the nature of the client's difficulties and to sort through possible solutions. Insight therapy can be conducted with an individual or with a group. Broadly speaking, family therapy and marital therapy fall in this category.

2. *Behaviour therapies.* Behaviour therapies are based on the principles of learning, which were introduced in Chapter 6. Instead of emphasizing personal insights, behaviour therapists make direct efforts to alter problematic responses (phobias, for instance) and maladaptive habits (such as drug use). Behaviour therapists work on changing clients' overt behaviours. They use different procedures for different kinds of problems. Most of their procedures

involve classical conditioning, operant conditioning, or observational learning.

3. *Biomedical therapies.* Biomedical approaches to therapy involve interventions into a person's biological functioning. The most widely used procedures are drug therapy and electroconvulsive (shock) therapy. In recent decades, drug therapy has become one of the most dominant modes for treating psychological disorders. One large-scale survey found that 57 percent of mental health patients were treated with medication only, up from 44 percent just nine years earlier (Olfson & Marcus, 2010). As the name bio*medical* therapies suggests, these treatments have traditionally been provided only by physicians with a medical degree (usually psychiatrists). This situation may change, however, as psychologists have begun to campaign for prescription privileges (Gutierrez & Silk, 1998; Sammons et al., 2000). They have made some progress toward this goal in some jurisdictions—notably, psychologists have obtained prescription authority in two U.S. states (New Mexico and Louisiana) and have made legislative progress toward this goal in other states. In Canada, similar efforts are underway to allow prescription privileges for psychologists (Lavoie & Fleet, 2002).

Clients: Who Seeks Therapy?

According to a poll commissioned by the Canadian Mental Health Association (2005), Canadians are as concerned about their mental health as they are about their physical health, and over 90 percent report that they make a conscious effort to take care of their mental health on a regular basis. While Canadians seem to have good intentions regarding their mental health, they seem to be less sure what to do about it. The poll also revealed that fewer people were committed to improving their mental health than their physical health over the subsequent six months. If improvements are not forthcoming or if people suffer from unexpected difficulties, they may seek professional assistance.

In the *therapeutic triad* (therapists, treatments, clients), the greatest diversity of all is seen among the clients. People bring to therapy the full range of human problems: anxiety, depression, unsatisfactory interpersonal relationships, troublesome habits, poor self-control, low self-esteem, marital conflicts, self-doubt, a sense of emptiness, and feelings of personal stagnation. The two most common presenting problems are excessive anxiety and depression (Narrow et al., 1993).

Interestingly, people often delay for many years before finally seeking treatment for their psychological problems (Kessler, Olfson, & Berglund, 1998). One recent large-scale study (Wang, Berglund et al., 2005) found that the median delay in seeking treatment was six years for bipolar disorder and for drug dependence, eight years for depression, nine years for generalized anxiety disorder, and ten years for panic disorder!

A client in treatment does *not* necessarily have an identifiable psychological disorder. Some people seek professional help for everyday problems (career decisions, for instance) or vague feelings of discontent (Strupp, 1996). One surprising finding in recent research has been that only about half of the people who use mental health services in a given year meet the criteria for a full-fledged mental disorder (Kessler et al., 2005b).

People vary considerably in their willingness to seek psychotherapy. One of the biggest roadblocks is the stigma surrounding mental health treatment. You may recall from the beginning of Chapter 14 how some people, including his physician, advised psychologist Norman Endler not to seek psychological treatment in his hometown in case others found out. Unfortunately, many people equate seeking therapy with admitting personal weakness. Of course, nothing could be further from the truth. It appears that many people who need therapy don't receive it (Kessler et al., 2005b).

Therapists: Who Provides Professional Treatment?

People troubled by personal problems often solicit help from their friends, relatives, clergy, and primary care physicians. In fact, primary care physicians are extremely important in terms of most Canadians' access to mental health resources. According to recent research from Statistics Canada, for many Canadians, physicians are the main source of mental health care and information (Palin, Goldner, Koehoorn, & Hertzman, 2011). These sources of assistance may provide excellent advice, but their counsel does not qualify as therapy. Psychotherapy refers to *professional* treatment by someone with special training. However, a common source of confusion about psychotherapy is the variety of "helping professions" available to offer assistance (Murstein & Fontaine, 1993). Psychology and psychiatry are the principal professions involved in the provision of psychotherapy. However, therapy is increasingly provided by clinical social workers, psychiatric nurses, counsellors, and marriage and family therapists. Let's look at the various mental health professions.

National Library of Medicine

Sigmund Freud
"The news that reaches your consciousness is incomplete and often not to be relied on."

WEB LINK 15.1

Canadian Mental Health Association
It's important to know when to seek help, and the Canadian Mental Health Association website contains information concerning psychological disorders and how to seek assistance.

Psychologists

Two types of psychologists may provide therapy. *Clinical psychologists* and *counselling psychologists* specialize in the diagnosis and treatment of psychological disorders and everyday behavioural problems. Clinical psychologists' training emphasizes the treatment of full-fledged disorders. Counselling psychologists' training is slanted toward the treatment of everyday adjustment problems. In practice, however, there is quite a bit of overlap between clinical and counselling psychologists in training, skills, and the clientele that they serve.

Traditionally psychologists had to earn a doctoral degree (Ph.D., Psy.D., or Ed.D.) to practise. A doctorate in psychology requires about five to seven years of training beyond a bachelor's degree. More recently, some of the provinces and territories have changed their regulations, allowing that a psychologist may have either a Ph.D. or an M.A. (an M.A. degree typically takes two years). In some jurisdictions, those with Ph.D.s are referred to as *psychologists* and those with M.A.s as *psychological associates* (Hunsley & Johnson, 2000). A relatively new degree, a Psy.D., is offered in a limited number of graduate programs in Canada, including one at Memorial University in Newfoundland and Labrador. Psy.D. programs differ from Ph.D. programs in several ways, including a greater emphasis on the scientist–practitioner model in Ph.D. programs. For example, Memorial University's description of its Psy.D. program states that "the emphasis is on developing strong and knowledgeable professionals who understand and are educated consumers of research but may not necessarily produce original research as a primary part of their career path." The process of gaining admission to a graduate program in clinical psychology is highly competitive (about as difficult as getting into medical school). Psychologists receive most of their training in universities or independent professional schools. They then serve a one-year internship in a clinical setting, such as a hospital, often followed by one or two years of postdoctoral fellowship training. Currently, there are approximately 18 000 registered psychologists in Canada (Dobson, 2002).

In providing therapy, psychologists use either insight or behavioural approaches. In comparison to psychiatrists, they are more likely to use behavioural techniques and less likely to use psychoanalytic methods. Clinical and counselling psychologists do psychological testing as well as psychotherapy, and many also conduct research.

For some individuals needing professional assistance for psychological disorders, their choice of a health practitioner is limited by the fact that treatment by psychologists is not part of the government medical insurance funding system. According to Keith Dobson, former president of the Canadian Psychological Association, the current lack of inclusion in the health-care funding system is attributable to several factors, including the relatively recent establishment of the CPA, the pressures by governments to limit health-care funding, divisions within psychology itself, and limited pressure from the profession of psychology (Dobson, 2002).

Psychiatrists

Psychiatrists are physicians who specialize in the diagnosis and treatment of psychological disorders. Many psychiatrists also treat everyday behavioural problems. However, in comparison to psychologists, psychiatrists devote more time to relatively severe disorders (schizophrenia, mood disorders) and less time to everyday marital, family, job, and school problems.

People seeking help for psychological difficulties who access the medical system often begin with their family physician. A team of researchers from the University of British Columbia and the University of Manitoba recently surveyed the use of medical professionals in Manitoba by those seeking medical assistance for psychological difficulties (Watson et al., 2005). They found that 92 percent of those seeking assistance saw at least one family physician, 42 percent relied on their family physician and did not see a psychiatrist, 47 percent saw both, and a little over 2 percent relied exclusively on a psychiatrist.

Psychiatrists have an M.D. degree. Their graduate training requires four years of course work in medical school and a four-year apprenticeship in a residency at a hospital. Their psychotherapy training occurs during their residency, since the required course work in medical school is essentially the same for everyone, whether they are going into surgery, pediatrics, or psychiatry.

In their provision of therapy, psychiatrists increasingly emphasize drug therapies (Olfson et al., 2002), which the other, nonmedical helping professions cannot provide. In comparison to psychologists, psychiatrists are more likely to use psychoanalysis and less likely to use group therapies or behaviour therapies. That said, contemporary psychiatrists primarily depend on medication as their principal mode of treatment. Indeed, in one recent study of over 14 000 visits to psychiatrists, only 29 percent of the visits involved the provision of some therapy other than the prescription and management of medications (Mojtabai & Olfson, 2008). Less than a decade earlier, that figure was 44 percent of visits, so

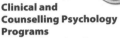

WEB LINK 15.2

Clinical and Counselling Psychology Programs
A list of clinical and counselling psychology programs accredited by the Canadian Psychological Association can be obtained from the CPA website.

WEB LINK 15.3

Online Dictionary of Mental Health
This thematically arranged "dictionary" comprises diverse links related to many forms of psychotherapy, the treatment of psychological disorders, and general mental health issues.

psychiatrists clearly are abandoning talk therapies in favour of drug treatments.

Other Mental Health Professionals

Several other mental health professions also provide psychotherapy services, and some of these professions are growing rapidly. In hospitals and other institutions, *clinical social workers* and *psychiatric nurses* often work as part of a treatment team with a psychologist or psychiatrist. Psychiatric nurses, who may have a bachelor's or master's degree in their field, play a large role in hospital inpatient treatment. Clinical social workers generally have a master's degree and typically work with patients and their families to ease the patient's integration back into the community. Although social workers and psychiatric nurses have traditionally worked in institutional settings, they increasingly provide a wide range of therapeutic services as independent practitioners.

Many kinds of *counsellors* also provide therapeutic services. Counsellors are usually found working in schools, colleges, and assorted human service agencies (youth centres, geriatric centres, family-planning centres, and so forth). Counsellors typically have a master's degree. They often specialize in particular types of problems, such as vocational counselling, marital counselling, rehabilitation counselling, and drug counselling.

Although there are clear differences among the helping professions in education and training, their roles in the treatment process overlap considerably. In this chapter, we will refer to psychologists or psychiatrists as needed, but otherwise we'll use the terms *clinician, therapist,* and *provider* to refer to mental health professionals of all kinds, regardless of their professional degrees.

Now that we have discussed the basic elements in psychotherapy, we can examine specific approaches to treatment in terms of their goals, procedures, and effectiveness. We'll begin with a few representative insight therapies.

> **REVIEW OF KEY POINTS**
>
> - Approaches to treatment are diverse, but they can be grouped into three categories: insight therapies, behaviour therapies, and biomedical therapies.
> - Clients bring a wide variety of problems to therapy and do not necessarily have a disorder. People vary in their willingness to seek treatment, and many people who need therapy do not receive it.
> - Therapists come from a variety of professional backgrounds. Clinical and counselling psychologists, psychiatrists, clinical social workers, psychiatric nurses, and counsellors are the principal providers of therapeutic services.
> - Each of these professions shows different preferences for approaches to treatment. Psychologists typically practise insight or behaviour therapy. Psychiatrists rely more heavily on drug therapies.

Insight Therapies

There are many schools of thought about how to do insight therapy. Therapists with various theoretical orientations use different methods to pursue different kinds of insights. However, what these varied approaches have in common is that *insight therapies* involve verbal interactions intended to enhance clients' self-knowledge and thus promote healthful changes in personality and behaviour.

Although there may be hundreds of insight therapies, the leading eight or ten approaches appear to account for the lion's share of treatment. In this section, we'll delve into psychoanalysis, related psychodynamic approaches, client-centred therapy, and positive psychology therapies. We'll also discuss how insight therapy can be done with groups as well as individuals.

Psychoanalysis 11d

After the case of Anna O, Sigmund Freud worked as a psychotherapist for almost 50 years in Vienna. Through a painstaking process of trial and error, he developed innovative techniques for the treatment of psychological disorders and distress. His system of *psychoanalysis* came to dominate psychiatry for many decades. Although the dominance of psychoanalysis has eroded in recent years, a diverse collection of psychoanalytic approaches to therapy continues to evolve and to remain influential today (Gabbard, 2005; Luborsky, O'Reilly-Landry, & Arlow, 2011; Ursano, Sonnenberg, & Lazar, 2008).

PREVIEW QUESTIONS

▶ What are the goals and techniques of psychoanalysis?

▶ What are the goals and techniques of client-centred therapy?

▶ What are the goals and techniques of therapies inspired by positive psychology?

▶ How is group therapy conducted?

▶ What is the evidence on the efficacy of insight therapy?

FIGURE 15.1

Freud's view of the roots of disorders.
According to Freud, unconscious conflicts among the id, ego, and superego sometimes lead to anxiety. This discomfort may lead to pathological reliance on defensive behaviour.

Psychoanalysis is an insight therapy that emphasizes the recovery of unconscious conflicts, motives, and defences through techniques such as free association and transference. To appreciate the logic of psychoanalysis, we have to look at Freud's thinking about the roots of mental disorders. Freud mostly treated anxiety-dominated disturbances, such as phobic, panic, obsessive-compulsive, and conversion disorders, which were then called *neuroses.*

Freud believed that neurotic problems are caused by unconscious conflicts left over from early childhood. As explained in Chapter 12, he thought that these inner conflicts involve battles among the id, ego, and superego, usually over sexual and aggressive impulses. He theorized that people depend on defence mechanisms to avoid confronting these conflicts, which remain hidden in the depths of the unconscious (see Figure 15.1). However, he noted that defensive manoeuvres often lead to self-defeating behaviour. Furthermore, he asserted that defences tend to be only partially successful in alleviating anxiety, guilt, and other distressing emotions. With this model in mind, let's take a look at the therapeutic procedures used in psychoanalysis.

Probing the Unconscious

Given Freud's assumptions, we can see that the logic of psychoanalysis is quite simple. The analyst attempts to probe the murky depths of the unconscious to discover the unresolved conflicts causing the client's neurotic behaviour. In a sense, the analyst functions as a "psychological detective." In this effort to explore the unconscious, the therapist relies on two techniques: free association and dream analysis.

In *free association,* clients spontaneously express their thoughts and feelings exactly as they occur, with as little censorship as possible. In free associating, clients expound on anything that comes to mind, regardless of how trivial, silly, or embarrassing it might be. Gradually, most clients begin to let everything pour out without conscious censorship.

The analyst studies these free associations for clues about what is going on in the client's unconscious.

In *dream analysis,* the therapist interprets the symbolic meaning of the client's dreams. Freud saw dreams as the "royal road to the unconscious," the most direct means of access to patients' innermost conflicts, wishes, and impulses. Clients are encouraged and trained to remember their dreams, which they describe in therapy. The therapist then analyzes the symbolism in these dreams to interpret their meaning.

To better illustrate these matters, let's look at an actual case treated through psychoanalysis (adapted from Greenson, 1967, pp. 40–41). Mr. N was troubled by an unsatisfactory marriage. He claimed to love his wife, but he preferred sexual relations with prostitutes. Mr. N reported that his parents also endured lifelong marital difficulties. His childhood conflicts about their relationship appeared to be related to his problems. Both dream analysis and free association can be seen in the following description of a session in Mr. N's treatment:

> Mr. N reported a fragment of a dream. All that he could remember is that he was waiting for a red traffic light to change when he felt that someone had bumped into him from behind. . . . The associations led to Mr. N's love of cars, especially sports cars. He loved the sensation, in particular, of whizzing by those fat, old expensive cars. . . . His father always hinted that he had been a great athlete, but he never substantiated it. . . . Mr. N doubted whether his father could really perform. His father would flirt with a waitress in a café or make sexual remarks about women passing by, but he seemed to be showing off. If he were really sexual, he wouldn't resort to that.

As is characteristic of free association, Mr. N's train of thought meandered about with little direction. Nonetheless, clues about his unconscious conflicts are apparent. What did Mr. N's therapist extract from this session? The therapist saw sexual overtones in the dream fragment, where Mr. N was bumped from behind. The therapist also inferred that Mr. N had a competitive orientation toward his father, based on the free association about whizzing by fat, old expensive cars. As you can see, analysts must *interpret* their clients' dreams and free associations. This is a critical process throughout psychoanalysis.

Interpretation

Interpretation refers to the therapist's attempts to explain the inner significance of the client's thoughts, feelings, memories, and behaviours. Contrary to popular belief, analysts do not interpret

In psychoanalysis, the therapist encourages the client to reveal thoughts, feelings, dreams, and memories, which can then be interpreted in relation to the client's current problems.

everything, and they generally don't try to dazzle clients with startling revelations. Instead, analysts move forward inch by inch, offering interpretations that should be just out of the client's own reach. Mr. N's therapist eventually offered the following interpretations to his client:

> I said to Mr. N near the end of the hour that I felt he was struggling with his feelings about his father's sexual life.
>
> He seemed to be saying that his father was sexually not a very potent man. . . . He also recalls that he once found a packet of condoms under his father's pillow when he was an adolescent and he thought, "My father must be going to prostitutes." I then intervened and pointed out that the condoms under his father's pillow seemed to indicate more obviously that his father used the condoms with his mother, who slept in the same bed. However, Mr. N wanted to believe his wish-fulfilling fantasy: Mother doesn't want sex with father and father is not very potent. The patient was silent and the hour ended.

As you may have already guessed, the therapist concluded that Mr. N's difficulties were rooted in an Oedipal complex (see Chapter 12). The man had unresolved sexual feelings toward his mother and hostile feelings about his father. These unconscious conflicts, rooted in Mr. N's childhood, were distorting his intimate relationships as an adult.

Resistance

11d

How would you expect Mr. N to respond to the therapist's suggestion that he was in competition with his father for the sexual attention of his mother? Obviously, most clients would have great difficulty

accepting such an interpretation. Freud fully expected clients to display some resistance to therapeutic efforts. *Resistance refers to largely unconscious defensive manoeuvres intended to hinder the progress of therapy.* Why would clients try to resist the helping process? Because they don't want to face up to the painful, disturbing conflicts that they have buried in their unconscious. Although they have sought help, they are reluctant to confront their real problems.

Resistance can take many forms. Clients may show up late for their sessions, may merely pretend to engage in free association, or may express hostility toward their therapist. For instance, Mr. N's therapist noted that after the session just described, "The next day he [Mr. N] began by telling me that he was furious with me . . . ." Analysts use a variety of strategies to deal with their clients' resistance. Often, a key consideration is the handling of transference, which we consider next.

Transference

11d

Transference occurs when clients unconsciously start relating to their therapist in ways that mimic critical relationships in their lives. Thus, a client might start relating to a therapist as though the therapist were an overprotective mother, a rejecting brother, or a passive spouse. In a sense, the client *transfers* conflicting feelings about important people onto the therapist. For instance, in his treatment, Mr. N transferred some of the competitive hostility that he felt toward his father onto his analyst.

Psychoanalysts often encourage transference so that clients can re-enact relationships with crucial people in the context of therapy. These re-enactments can help bring repressed feelings and conflicts to the surface, allowing the client to work through them. The therapist's handling of transference is complicated and difficult, because transference may arouse confusing, highly charged emotions in the client.

Undergoing psychoanalysis is not easy. It can be a slow, painful process of self-examination that routinely requires three to five years of hard work. It tends to be a lengthy process because patients need time to work through their problems and genuinely accept unnerving revelations (Williams, 2005). Ultimately, if resistance and transference can be handled effectively, the therapist's interpretations should lead the client to profound insights. For instance, Mr. N eventually admitted, "The old boy is probably right, it does tickle me to imagine that my mother preferred me and I could beat out my father. Later, I wondered whether this had something

Carl Rogers

"To my mind, empathy is in itself a healing agent."

to do with my own screwed-up sex life with my wife." According to Freud, once clients recognize the unconscious sources of conflicts, they can resolve these conflicts and discard their neurotic defences. While difficult, evidence does suggest that psychodynamic therapy can be effective in many cases. In fact, in a review of work examining the efficacy of psychodynamic psychotherapy, Jonathan Schedler (2010) went so far as to suggest that other forms of therapy "might be effective in part because the more skilled practitioners utilize techniques that have long been central to psychodynamic theory and practice" (p. 98).

Modern Psychodynamic Therapies

Although still available, classical psychoanalysis as done by Freud is not widely practised anymore (Kay & Kay, 2008). Freud's psychoanalytic method was geared to a particular kind of clientele that he was seeing in Vienna many years ago. As his followers fanned out across Europe and North America, many found it necessary to adapt psychoanalysis to different cultures, changing times, and new kinds of patients (Karasu, 2005). Thus, many variations on Freud's original approach to psychoanalysis have developed over the years. These descendants of psychoanalysis are collectively known as *psychodynamic approaches* to therapy.

Some of these adaptations, such as those made by Carl Jung (1917) and Alfred Adler (1927), were sweeping revisions based on fundamental differences in theory. Other variations, such as those devised by Melanie Klein (1948) and Heinz Kohut (1971), made substantial changes in theory while retaining certain central ideas. Still other revisions (Alexander, 1954; Stekel, 1950) simply involved efforts to modernize and streamline psychoanalytic techniques.

Hence, today we have a rich diversity of psychodynamic approaches to therapy (Magnavita, 2008). Recent reviews of these treatments suggest that interpretation, resistance, and transference continue to play key roles in therapeutic effects (Hoglend et al., 2008; Luborsky & Barrett, 2006). Other central features of modern psychodynamic therapies include (1) a focus on emotional experience, (2) exploration of efforts to avoid distressing thoughts and feelings, (3) identification of recurring patterns in patients' life experiences, (4) discussion of past experience, especially events in early childhood, (5) analysis of interpersonal relationships, (6) a focus on the therapeutic relationship itself, and (7) exploration of dreams and other aspects of fantasy life (Shedler, 2010). Recent research suggests that psychodynamic approaches can be helpful in the

treatment of a diverse array of disorders (Gibbons, Crits-Christoph, & Hearon, 2008; Leichsenring & Rabung, 2008; Shedler, 2010).

Client-Centred Therapy

11d

You may have heard of people going into therapy to "find themselves" or to "get in touch with their real feelings." These now-popular phrases emerged out of the human potential movement, which was stimulated in part by the work of Carl Rogers (1951, 1986). Using a humanistic perspective, Rogers devised client-centred therapy (also known as *person-centred therapy*) in the 1940s and 1950s. Rogers had an enormous impact on psychology, both in terms of our understanding of people and the nature of the self, and on psychotherapy. For example, in a recent poll conducted by *Psychotherapy Networker*, therapists were asked, "Over the past 25 years, which figures have most influenced your practice?" (*Psychotherapy Networker*, 2007). Rogers was nominated number one (Aaron Beck, whose work on cognitive behavioural therapy we discuss on page 713 was number two).

Client-centred therapy is an insight therapy that emphasizes providing a supportive emotional climate for clients, who play a major role in determining the pace and direction of their therapy. You may wonder why the troubled, untrained client is put in charge of the pace and direction of the therapy. Rogers (1961, pp. 11–12) provides a compelling justification:

> It is the client who knows what hurts, what directions to go, what problems are crucial, what experiences have been deeply buried. It began to occur to me that unless I had a need to demonstrate my own cleverness and learning, I would do better to rely upon the client for the direction of movement in the process.

Rogers's theory about the principal causes of neurotic anxieties is quite different from the Freudian explanation. As discussed in Chapter 12, Rogers maintains that most personal distress is due to inconsistency, or "incongruence," between a person's self-concept and reality (see Figure 15.2). According to his theory, incongruence makes people feel threatened by realistic feedback about themselves from others. For example, if you inaccurately viewed yourself as a hard-working, dependable person, you would feel threatened by contradictory feedback from friends or co-workers. According to Rogers, anxiety about such feedback often leads to reliance on defence mechanisms, to distortions of reality, and to stifled

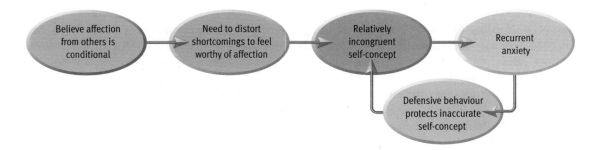

FIGURE 15.2

Rogers's view of the roots of disorders.

Rogers's theory posits that anxiety and self-defeating behaviour are rooted in an incongruent self-concept that makes one prone to recurrent anxiety, which triggers defensive behaviour, which fuels more incongruence.

personal growth. Excessive incongruence is thought to be rooted in clients' overdependence on others for approval and acceptance.

Given Rogers's theory, client-centred therapists seek insights that are quite different from the repressed conflicts that psychoanalysts go after. Client-centred therapists help clients to realize that they do not have to worry constantly about pleasing others and winning acceptance. They encourage clients to respect their own feelings and values. They help people restructure their self-concept to correspond better to reality. Ultimately, they try to foster self-acceptance and personal growth.

Therapeutic Alliance: The Importance of Therapy Climate

Almost all therapeutic orientations now emphasize the importance of the relationship between the therapist and the client in promoting successful outcomes in therapy. Freud early on recognized the significance of this feature of therapy, but his concern was very specific to psychoanalysis. For example, consider Freud's formulation of *transference*, which occurs when *clients unconsciously start relating to their therapist in ways that mimic critical relationships in their past.* For Freud, the nature of the transference relationship was important content to be used in understanding the patient's problems and their resolution.

The importance of the therapeutic alliance, more broadly considered as the nature of the bond between therapist and client (Safran & Muran, 2000), is central to most other contemporary therapeutic orientations (e.g., Sullivan, 1953). Special attention was given to the climate of therapy in client-centred therapy as developed by Rogers.

What do we mean by therapeutic alliance? According to Bordin (1979) in his influential analysis, the therapeutic alliance consists of the emotional bond between therapist and client, along with agreement on goals for the therapy and agreement on therapeutic tasks. Bordin asserted that the nature of the therapeutic alliance was critical to the success of the therapy. The notion of the alliance has spread widely

across most mainstream therapy orientations (Safran & Muran, 2000). Its importance to success in therapy has been the subject of a great deal of research (Crits-Christoph et al., 2011; Pos, Greenberg, & Warwar, 2009; Webb et al., 2011) and its relationship to positive therapy outcomes has been confirmed in numerous empirical studies (e.g., Horvath & Symonds, 1991; Martin, Garske, & Davis, 2000). For example, Alberta Pos and her colleagues concluded in their research on therapeutic alliance and experiential therapy outcome that in successful therapy "Alliances strengthen across therapy, became more significantly associated with emotional processing as therapy progressed . . . and contributed significantly to a core experiential therapy process that did directly predict improvement" (Pos et al., 2009, p. 1064). Research has also explored the nature of variables that inhibit the formation of successful alliances (Lysaker et al., 2011). Recently, a task force (Steering Committee, 2002) of the American Psychological Association's Psychotherapy Division recommended that therapists make the establishment and cultivation of a successful therapeutic relationship a primary focus in therapy and that this be a core topic in training programs (Crits-Christoph et al., 2011).

If, according to Rogers, the *process* of therapy is not as important as the emotional *climate* in which the therapy takes place, what does the therapist do to contribute to a positive climate? He believes that it is critical for the therapist to provide a warm, supportive, accepting climate. This creates a safe environment in which clients can confront their shortcomings without feeling threatened. The lack of threat should reduce clients' defensive tendencies and thus help them to open up. To create this atmosphere of emotional support, client-centred therapists must provide three conditions:

1. *Genuineness.* The therapist must be genuine with the client, communicating honestly and spontaneously. The therapist should not be phony or defensive.

2. *Unconditional positive regard.* The therapist must also show complete, nonjudgmental acceptance of

Treatment of Psychological Disorders

the client as a person. The therapist should provide warmth and caring for the client, with no strings attached. This does not mean that the therapist must approve of everything that the client says or does. A therapist can disapprove of a particular behaviour while continuing to value the client as a human being.

3. *Empathy.* Finally, the therapist must provide accurate empathy for the client. This means that the therapist must understand the client's world from the client's point of view. Furthermore, the therapist must be articulate enough to communicate this understanding to the client.

Rogers firmly believed that a supportive emotional climate is the critical force promoting healthy changes in therapy. However, some client-centred therapists, such as Laura Rice and Les Greenberg, have begun to place more emphasis on the therapeutic process (Rice & Greenberg, 1992).

Therapeutic Process

11d

In client-centred therapy, the client and therapist work together as equals. The therapist provides relatively little guidance and keeps interpretation and advice to a minimum (Raskin, Rogers, & Witty, 2011). So, just what does the client-centred therapist do, besides creating a supportive climate? Primarily, the therapist provides feedback to help clients sort out their feelings. The therapist's key task is *clarification.* Client-centred therapists try to function like human mirrors, reflecting statements back to their clients, but with enhanced clarity. They help clients become more aware of their true feelings by highlighting themes that may be obscure in the clients' rambling discourse.

By working with clients to clarify their feelings, client-centred therapists hope to gradually build toward more far-reaching insights. In particular, they try to help clients better understand their interpersonal relationships and become more comfortable with their genuine selves. Obviously, these are ambitious goals.

Influential Canadian psychologist Les Greenberg and his colleagues have developed *emotion-focused couples therapy* (Greenberg & Johnson, 1988; Johnson & Greenberg, 1995). Greenberg initially developed individual emotion-focused therapy (Goldman, Greenberg, & Pos, 2005) to be "the practice of therapy informed by an understanding of the role of emotion in psychotherapeutic change" (Greenberg, 2011, p. 3). He felt that *cognitive-behavioural therapy,* which dominated therapy at the time, while useful

in helping people cope, missed out on dealing with the people's core problems (McLean, 2010). *Emotion-focused couples therapy* takes this focus on emotions to the treatment of dysfunctional relationships.

One of the assumptions *of emotion-focused couples therapy* is that the relationship is not providing for the attachment needs of the relationship partners. In the process of therapy, the nature of the relationship issues and underlying emotions are first identified. The partners are then afforded an opportunity to identify and acknowledge their needs and are encouraged to express these needs and to arrive at solutions to the problems. Acknowledging and working with the underlying emotions are central to this approach. This type of emotion-focused therapy has its roots in earlier client-centred work by Carl Rogers and Fritz Perls and is considered important to any integrative approach to psychotherapy (L. S. Greenberg, 2002, 2008).

Emotion-focused therapy has been effectively applied in a wide variety of contexts, including University of Windsor psychologist Sandra Paivio's work with child abuse victims (Paivio, Holowaty, & Hall, 2004). Research has attested to the effectiveness of process-experiential approaches. For example, an evaluation study by Jeanne Watson and her colleagues at the University of Toronto demonstrated that process-experiential therapy was as effective as cognitive-behavioural therapy and that, additionally, process-experiential therapy resulted in a significant decrease in clients' reports of interpersonal problems (Watson et al., 2003).

Client-centred therapy resembles psychoanalysis in that both seek to achieve a major reconstruction of a client's personality. We'll see more limited and specific goals in cognitive therapy, which we will discuss soon.

Therapies Inspired by Positive Psychology

The growth of the positive psychology movement has begun to inspire new approaches to insight therapy (Duckworth, Steen, & Seligman, 2005; Peterson & Park, 2009). As noted in Chapters 1 and 10, positive psychology uses theory and research to better understand the positive, adaptive, creative, and fulfilling aspects of human existence. The advocates of positive psychology maintain that the field has historically focused far too heavily on pathology, weakness, and suffering (and how to heal these conditions) rather than health and resilience (Seligman, 2003; Seligman & Csikszentmihalyi, 2000). They argue for increased research on contentment, well-being, human strengths, and positive emotions.

This philosophical approach has led to new therapeutic interventions. For example, *well-being therapy*, developed by Giovanni Fava and colleagues (Fava, 1999; Ruini & Fava, 2004), seeks to enhance clients' self-acceptance, purpose in life, autonomy, and personal growth. It has been used successfully in the treatment of mood disorders and anxiety disorders (Fava et al., 2005).

Another new approach is *positive psychotherapy*, developed by Martin Seligman and colleagues (Rashid & Anjum, 2008; Seligman, Rashid, & Parks, 2006). So far, positive psychotherapy has been used mainly in the treatment of depression. Positive psychotherapy attempts to get clients to recognize their strengths, appreciate their blessings, savour positive experiences, forgive those who have wronged them, and find meaning in their lives. Preliminary research suggests that positive psychotherapy can be an effective treatment for depression. For example, in one study, positive psychotherapy was compared to *treatment as usual* (whatever the therapist would normally do) and *treatment as usual with medication*. The data shown in Figure 15.3 compare mean depression scores at the end of the study for participants in these three conditions (Seligman, Rashid, & Parks, 2006). As you can see, the lowest depression scores were observed in the group that received positive psychotherapy. Developments in this area continue at an exciting pace.

Recent work by Canadian psychologist Myriam Mongrain and her colleague Leah Shapira, for example, has examined the effectiveness of online interventions designed to increase either participants'

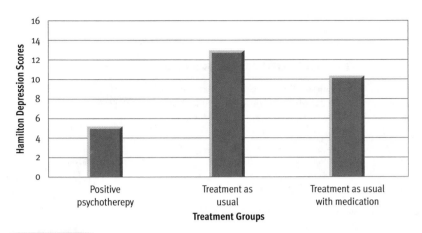

FIGURE 15.3

Positive psychotherapy for depression.

In a study of the efficacy of positive psychotherapy, it was compared to treatment as usual (clinicians delivered whatever treatment they deemed appropriate) and to treatment as usual combined with antidepressant medication. At the end of 12 weeks of treatment, symptoms of depression were measured with the widely used *Hamilton Rating Scale for Depression*. The mean depression scores for each group are graphed here. As you can see, the positive psychotherapy group showed less depression than the other two treatment groups, suggesting that positive psychotherapy can be an effective intervention for depression.

Source: Adapted from Seligman, M. E. P., Rashid, T., and Parks, A. C. (2006). Positive psychotherapy. *American Psychologist, 61*, 774–788. Figure 2, p. 784. Copyright © 2006 by the American Psychological Association.

self-compassion or optimism. The researchers were interested in the effects of these interventions on participants' depression and happiness scores. The interventions were deceptively simple in design. In the optimism intervention, for example, participants were asked to post online letters to themselves in which they wrote about visualizing "a future where current issues were resolved and gave themselves advice on how to get there" (Shapira & Mongrain, 2010, p. 378). Prior to the interventions,

Clinical psychologist Myriam Mongrain from York University is interested in the role played by individual differences as vulnerabilities for psychopathology. Her recent work has addressed, among other things, some of the implications of positive psychology interventions for individuals suffering from depression.

Client-centred therapists emphasize the importance of a supportive emotional climate in therapy. They also work to clarify, rather than interpret, the feelings expressed by their patients.

Treatment of Psychological Disorders

participants were assessed for their vulnerability to depression. Both the self-compassion and the optimism interventions were related to increases in happiness and decreases in depression scores, effects that were observed to last for several months. The results also suggested that individuals with particular types of vulnerabilities to depression might differentially benefit most from either the self-compassion or optimism interventions. Innovative interventions such as these, spurred by the positive psychology movement, are in their infancy, but the early findings seem promising and it will be interesting to see what the future holds.

Group Therapy

Although it dates back to the early part of the 20th century, group therapy came of age during World War II and its aftermath in the 1950s (Rosenbaum, Lakin, & Roback, 1992). During this period, the expanding demand for therapeutic services forced clinicians to use group techniques (Burlingame & Baldwin, 2011). *Group therapy* is the simultaneous treatment of several clients in a group. Most major insight therapies have been adapted for use with groups. In fact, the ideas underlying Rogers's client-centred therapy spawned the much-publicized encounter group movement. Although group therapy can be conducted in a variety of ways (Hopper, Kaklauskas, & Greene, 2008), we can provide a general overview of the process as it usually unfolds with

outpatient populations (see Spitz, 2009; Stone, 2008; Vinogradov, Cox, & Yalom, 2003).

Participants' Roles

A therapy group typically consists of 4 to 15 people, with 8 participants regarded as an ideal number (Cox et al., 2008). The therapist usually screens the participants, excluding people who seem likely to be disruptive. Some theorists maintain that judicious selection of participants is crucial to effective group treatment (Schlapobersky & Pines, 2009). There is some debate about whether it is best for the group to be homogeneous—made up of people who are similar in age, sex, and psychological problem. Practical necessities usually dictate that groups are at least somewhat diversified.

In group therapy, participants essentially function as therapists for one another (Stone, 2008). Group members describe their problems, trade viewpoints, share experiences, and discuss coping strategies. Most important, they provide acceptance and emotional support for each other. In this supportive atmosphere, group members work at peeling away the social masks that cover their insecurities. Once their problems are exposed, members work at correcting them. As members come to value one another's opinions, they work hard to display healthy changes to win the group's approval.

In group treatment, the therapist's responsibilities include selecting participants, setting goals for the group, initiating and maintaining the therapeutic process, and protecting clients from harm (Cox et al., 2008). The therapist often plays a relatively subtle role in group therapy, staying in the background and focusing mainly on promoting group cohesiveness (although this strategy will vary depending on the nature of the group). The therapist models supportive behaviours for the participants and tries to promote a healthy climate. He or she always retains a special status, but the therapist and clients are usually on a much more equal footing in group therapy than in individual therapy. The leader in group therapy expresses emotions, shares feelings, and copes with challenges from group members (Burlingame & McClendon, 2008).

Advantages of the Group Experience

Group therapies obviously save time and money, which can be critical in understaffed mental hospitals and other institutional settings (Cox et al.,

Group treatments have proven particularly helpful when members share similar problems, such as alcoholism, overeating, or having been sexually abused as a child.

2008). Therapists in private practice usually charge less for group than individual therapy, making therapy affordable for more people. However, group therapy is *not* just a less costly substitute for individual therapy. For many types of patients and problems, group therapy can be just as effective as individual treatment (Stone, 2008). Moreover, group therapy has unique strengths of its own. For example, in group therapy, participants often come to realize that their misery is not unique. They are reassured to learn that many other people have similar or even worse problems. Another advantage is that group therapy provides an opportunity for participants to work on their social skills in a safe environment. Yet another advantage is that certain types of problems and clients respond especially well to the social support that group therapy can provide.

Couples and Family Therapy

Like group therapy, marital and family therapy rose to prominence after World War II. As their names suggest, these interventions are defined in terms of who is being treated. *Couples* or *marital therapy* involves the treatment of both partners in a committed, intimate relationship, in which the main focus is on relationship issues. Couples therapy

is not limited to married couples. It is frequently provided to cohabiting couples, including gay couples. *Family therapy* involves the treatment of a family unit as a whole, in which the main focus is on family dynamics and communication. Family therapy often emerges out of efforts to treat children or adolescents with individual therapy. A child's therapist, for instance, might come to the realization that treatment is likely to fail because the child returns to a home environment that contributes to the child's problems, and thus propose a broader family intervention.

As with other forms of insight therapy, there are different schools of thought about how to conduct couples and family therapy (Fergus & Reid, 2002; Goldenberg, Goldenberg, & Pelavin, 2011). Some of these diverse systems are extensions of influential approaches to individual therapy, including psychodynamic, humanistic, and behavioural treatments. Other approaches are based on innovative models of families as complex systems and explicit rejection of individual models of treatment (Fergus & Reid, 2002). Although the various approaches to couples and family therapy differ in terminology and their theoretical models of relationship and family dysfunction, they tend to share common goals. First, they seek to understand the entrenched patterns of interaction that produce distress. In this endeavour they view individuals as parts of a family ecosystem and

Treatment of Psychological Disorders

they assume that people behave as they do because of their role in the system (Lebow, 2008). Second, they seek to help couples and families improve their communication and move toward healthier patterns of interaction.

What kinds of problems bring partners in for couples therapy? The full range of relationship problems, including constant arguments without resolution, resentment about power imbalances, perceptions of emotional withdrawal, the discovery or disclosure of affairs, sexual difficulties, the threat of relationship dissolution, concern about how relationship issues are affecting one's children (Spitz & Spitz, 2009), and the impact of health problems experienced by one or both of the partners (Fergus & Gray, 2009). Marital therapists attempt to help partners to clarify their needs and desires in the relationship, appreciate their mutual contribution to problems, enhance their communication patterns, increase role flexibility and tolerance of differences, work out their balance of power, and learn to deal with conflict more constructively (Ritvo, Melnick, & Glick, 2008).

What are some of the indications for family therapy? Family therapy is likely to be helpful when a youngster's psychological difficulties appear to be rooted in family pathology, when families are buffeted by severe stress such as a serious illness or a major transition, when blended families experience adjustment problems, when sibling conflicts spin out of control, and when someone tries to sabotage another family member's individual therapy (Bloch & Harari, 2009; Spitz & Spitz, 2009). Family therapists attempt to help family members recognize how their patterns of interaction contribute to family distress, to achieve more effective communication, to help them rethink inflexible roles and coalitions, to wrestle with power issues in the family system, and when relevant, to help them better understand children's psychiatric problems (Ritvo, Glick, & Berman, 2008).

How Effective Are Insight Therapies?

Whether insight therapies are conducted on a group or an individual basis, clients usually invest considerable time, effort, and money. Are these insight therapies worth the investment? Let's examine the evidence on their effectiveness.

Evaluating the effectiveness of any approach to treatment is a complex challenge (Crits-Christoph & Gibbons, 2009; Kendall, Holmbeck, & Verduin,

2004). For one thing, psychological disorders (like many physical illnesses) sometimes run their course and clear up on their own. A *spontaneous remission is a recovery from a disorder that occurs without formal treatment.* So, if a client experiences a recovery after treatment, one cannot automatically assume that the recovery was due to the treatment (see the Critical Thinking Application in this chapter).

Evaluating the effectiveness of treatment is especially complicated for insight therapies (Aveline, Strauss, & Stiles, 2005). If you were to undergo insight therapy, how would you judge its efficacy? By how you felt? By looking at your behaviour? By asking your therapist? By consulting your friends and family? What would you be looking for? Various schools of thought pursue entirely different goals. And clients' ratings of their progress are likely to be slanted toward a favourable evaluation because they

REVIEW OF KEY POINTS

▷ Insight therapies involve verbal interactions intended to enhance self-knowledge. Freudian approaches to therapy assume that neuroses originate from unresolved conflicts lurking in the unconscious. Therefore, free association and dream analysis are used in psychoanalysis to explore the unconscious.

▷ When an analyst's probing hits sensitive areas, resistance can be expected. The transference relationship may be used to overcome this resistance so that the client can handle interpretations that lead to insight. Classical psychoanalysis is not widely practised anymore, but Freud's legacy lives on in a rich diversity of modern psychodynamic therapies.

▷ Rogers's client-centred therapy assumes that neurotic anxieties are derived from incongruence between a person's self-concept and reality. Accordingly, the client-centred therapist tries to provide a supportive climate in which clients can restructure their self-concept. The process of client-centred therapy emphasizes clarification of the client's feelings and self-acceptance.

▷ The growth of the positive psychology movement has begun to inspire new approaches to insight therapy, such as well-being therapy. Positive psychotherapy attempts to get clients to recognize their strengths, appreciate their blessings, savour positive experiences, and find meaning in their lives.

▷ Most theoretical approaches to insight therapy have been adapted for use with groups. Participants in group therapy essentially act as therapists for one another, exchanging insights and emotional support. Group therapy has unique advantages in comparison to individual therapy.

▷ Evaluating the effectiveness of any approach to therapy is complex and difficult. Nonetheless, the weight of modern evidence suggests that insight therapies are superior to no treatment or to placebo treatment. Studies generally find the greatest improvement early in treatment.

want to justify their effort, their heartache, their expense, and their time. Even evaluations by professional therapists can be highly subjective (Luborsky et al., 1999). Moreover, people enter therapy with diverse problems of varied severity, creating huge confounds in efforts to assess the effectiveness of therapeutic interventions.

Despite these difficulties, thousands of outcome studies have been conducted to evaluate the effectiveness of insight therapy. These studies have examined a broad range of clinical problems and have used diverse methods to assess therapeutic outcomes, including scores on psychological tests and ratings by family members, as well as therapists' and clients' ratings. These studies consistently indicate that insight therapy *is* superior to no treatment or to placebo treatment and that the effects of therapy are reasonably durable (Lambert, 2011; Lambert & Archer, 2006; Torres & Saunders, 2009). And when insight therapies are compared head-to-head against drug therapies, they usually show roughly equal efficacy (Arkowitz & Lilienfeld, 2007; Pinquart, Duberstein, & Lyness, 2006).

Studies generally find the greatest improvement early in treatment (the first 13–18 weekly sessions), with further gains gradually diminishing in size over time (Lambert, Bergin, & Garfield, 2004). Overall, about 50 percent of patients show a clinically meaningful recovery within about 20 sessions, and another 25 percent of patients achieve this goal after about 45 sessions (Lambert & Ogles, 2004; see

Figure 15.4). Of course, these broad generalizations mask considerable variability in outcome, but the general trends are encouraging.

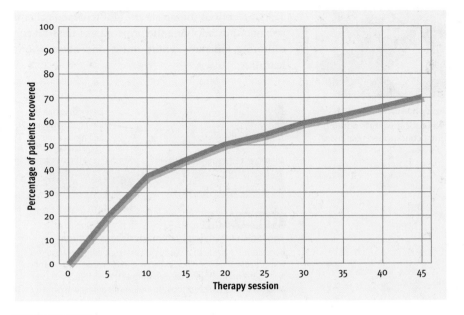

FIGURE 15.4

Recovery as a function of number of therapy sessions.

Based on a national sample of over 6000 patients, Lambert, Hansen, and Finch (2001) mapped out the relationship between recovery and the duration of treatment. These data show that about half of the patients had experienced a clinically significant recovery after 20 weekly sessions of therapy. After 45 sessions of therapy, about 70 percent had recovered.

Source: Adapted from Lambert, M. J., Hansen, N. B., and Finch, A. E. (2001). Patient-focused research: Using patient outcome data to enhance treatment effects. *Journal of Consulting and Clinical Psychology, 69,* 159–172. Copyright © 2001 by the American Psychological Association.

Behaviour Therapies

Behaviour therapy is different from insight therapy in that behaviour therapists make no attempt to help clients achieve grand insights about themselves. Why not? Because behaviour therapists believe that such insights aren't necessary to produce constructive change. For example, consider a client troubled by uncontrolled gambling. The behaviour therapist doesn't care whether this behaviour is rooted in unconscious conflicts or parental rejection. What the client needs is to get rid of the maladaptive behaviour. Consequently, the therapist simply designs a program to eliminate the uncontrolled gambling.

The crux of the difference between insight therapy and behaviour therapy is this: Insight therapists treat pathological symptoms as signs of an underlying problem, whereas behaviour therapists think that the symptoms *are* the problem. Thus, *behaviour therapies* involve the application of learning principles

to direct efforts to change clients' maladaptive behaviours.

Behaviourism has been an influential school of thought in psychology since the 1920s. Nevertheless, behaviourists devoted little attention to clinical issues until the 1950s, when behaviour therapy emerged out of three independent lines of research fostered by B. F. Skinner and his colleagues (Skinner, Solomon, & Lindsley, 1953) in the United States; by Hans Eysenck (1959) and his colleagues in Britain; and by Joseph Wolpe (1958) and his colleagues in South Africa (Wilson, 2011). Since then, there has been an explosion of interest in behavioural approaches to psychotherapy.

Behaviour therapies are based on certain assumptions (Stanley & Beidel, 2009). *First, it is assumed that behaviour is a product of learning.* No matter how self-defeating or pathological a client's behaviour might

PREVIEW QUESTIONS

▶ What assumptions are behaviour therapies based on?

▶ How do behaviour therapists treat phobias?

▶ How does aversion therapy work?

▶ What are the goals and techniques of social skills training?

▶ What are the techniques of cognitive-behavioural therapy?

▶ What is the evidence on the efficacy of behaviour therapy?

Joseph Wolpe
"Neurotic anxiety is nothing but a conditioned response."

be, the behaviourist believes that it is the result of past learning and conditioning. *Second, it is assumed that what has been learned can be unlearned.* The same learning principles that explain how the maladaptive behaviour was acquired can be used to get rid of it. Thus, behaviour therapists attempt to change clients' behaviour by applying the principles of classical conditioning, operant conditioning, and observational learning.

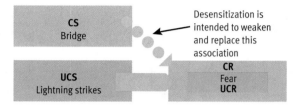

FIGURE 15.5

The logic underlying systematic desensitization.

Behaviourists argue that many phobic responses are acquired through classical conditioning, as in the example diagrammed here. Systematic desensitization targets the conditioned associations between phobic stimuli and fear responses.

An Anxiety Hierarchy for Systematic Desensitization	
Degree of fear	
5	I'm standing on the balcony of the top floor of an apartment tower.
10	I'm standing on a stepladder in the kitchen to change a light bulb.
15	I'm walking on a ridge. The edge is hidden by shrubs and treetops.
20	I'm sitting on the slope of a mountain, looking out over the horizon.
25	I'm crossing a bridge 2 metres above a creek. The bridge consists of a 45-cm-wide board with a handrail on one side.
30	I'm riding a ski lift 2.5 metres above the ground.
35	I'm crossing a shallow, wide creek on a 45-cm-wide board, 1 metre above water level.
40	I'm climbing a ladder outside the house to reach a second-storey window.
45	I'm pulling myself up a 30-degree wet, slippery slope on a steel cable.
50	I'm scrambling up a rock, 2.5 metres high.
55	I'm walking 3 metres on a resilient, 45-cm-wide board, which spans a 2.5-metre-deep gulch.
60	I'm walking on a wide plateau, 60 cm from the edge of a cliff.
65	I'm skiing an intermediate hill. The snow is packed.
70	I'm walking over a railway trestle.
75	I'm walking on the side of an embankment. The path slopes to the outside.
80	I'm riding a chair lift 5 metres above the ground.
85	I'm walking up a long, steep slope.
90	I'm walking up (or down) a 15-degree slope on a 1-metre-wide trail. On one side of the trail the terrain drops down sharply; on the other side is a steep upward slope.
95	I'm walking on a 1-metre-wide ridge. The slopes on both sides are long and more than 25 degrees steep.
100	I'm walking on a 1-metre-wide ridge. The trail slopes on one side. The drop on either side of the trail is more than 25 degrees.

FIGURE 15.6

Example of an anxiety hierarchy.

Systematic desensitization requires the construction of an anxiety hierarchy like the one shown here, which was developed for a woman who had a fear of heights but wanted to go hiking in the mountains.

Source: Rudestam, K. E. (1980). *Methods of self-change: An ABC primer.* Belmont, CA: Wadsworth. Copyright © 1980 by Wadsworth Publishing.

Systematic Desensitization — 11e

Devised by Joseph Wolpe (1958), systematic desensitization revolutionized psychotherapy by giving therapists their first useful alternative to traditional "talk therapy" (Fishman, Rego, & Muller, 2011). *Systematic desensitization* is a behaviour therapy used to reduce phobic clients' anxiety responses through counterconditioning. The treatment assumes that most anxiety responses are acquired through classical conditioning (as we discussed in Chapter 14). According to this model, a harmless stimulus (e.g., a bridge) may be paired with a fear-arousing event (lightning striking the bridge), so that it becomes a conditioned stimulus eliciting anxiety. The goal of systematic desensitization is to weaken the association between the conditioned stimulus (the bridge) and the conditioned response of anxiety (see Figure 15.5). Systematic desensitization involves three steps.

First, the therapist helps the client build an anxiety hierarchy. The hierarchy is a list of anxiety-arousing stimuli related to the specific source of anxiety, such as flying, academic tests, or snakes. The client ranks the stimuli from the least anxiety-arousing to the most anxiety-arousing. This ordered list of stimuli is the *anxiety hierarchy.* An example of an anxiety hierarchy for one woman's fear of heights is shown in Figure 15.6.

The second step involves training the client in deep muscle relaxation. This second phase may begin during early sessions while the therapist and client are still constructing the anxiety hierarchy. Various therapists use different relaxation training procedures. Whatever procedures are used, the client must learn to engage in deep, thorough relaxation on command from the therapist.

In the third step, the client tries to work through the hierarchy, learning to remain relaxed while imagining each stimulus. Starting with the least anxiety-arousing stimulus, the client imagines the situation as vividly as possible while relaxing. If the client experiences strong anxiety, he or she drops the imaginary scene and concentrates on relaxation. The client keeps repeating this process until he or she can imagine a scene with little or no anxiety. Once a particular scene is conquered, the client moves on to the next stimulus situation in the anxiety hierarchy. Gradually, over a number of therapy sessions, the client progresses through the hierarchy, unlearning troublesome anxiety responses. As clients conquer *imagined* phobic stimuli, they may be encouraged to confront the *real* stimuli.

Systematic desensitization is a behavioural treatment for phobias. Early studies of the procedure's efficacy often used people who had snake phobias as research subjects because people with snake phobias were relatively easy to find. This research showed that systematic desensitization is generally an effective treatment.

concept **check 15.2**

Understanding Therapists' Goals

Check your understanding of therapists' goals by matching various therapies with the appropriate description. The answers are in Appendix A.

Principal Therapeutic Goals

_____ **1.** Elimination of maladaptive behaviours or symptoms

_____ **2.** Acceptance of genuine self, personal growth

_____ **3.** Recovery of unconscious conflicts, character reconstruction

_____ **4.** Detection and reduction of negative thinking

Therapy

a. Psychoanalysis

b. Client-centred therapy

c. Cognitive therapy

d. Behaviour therapy

According to Wolpe (1958, 1990), the principle at work in systematic desensitization is simple. Anxiety and relaxation are incompatible responses. The trick is to recondition people so that the conditioned stimulus elicits relaxation instead of anxiety. This is *counterconditioning*—an attempt to reverse the process of classical conditioning by associating the crucial stimulus with a new conditioned response.

Although Wolpe's explanation of how systematic desensitization works has been questioned, the technique's effectiveness in eliminating specific anxieties has been well documented (Spiegler & Guevremont, 2010). That said, interventions emphasizing direct exposures to anxiety-arousing situations have become behaviour therapists' treatment of choice for phobic and other anxiety disorders (Rachman, 2009). In *exposure therapies,* clients are confronted with situations that they fear so that they learn that these situations are really harmless. The exposures take place in a controlled setting and often involve a very gradual progression from less-feared to more-feared stimuli. These real-life exposures to anxiety-arousing situations usually prove harmless and individuals' anxiety responses decline. In recent decades, some therapists have resorted to highly realistic virtual-reality presentations of feared situations via computer-generated imagery (Meyerbroker & Emmelkamp, 2010; Reger et al., 2011). Exposure therapies are versatile in that they can be used with the full range of anxiety disorders, including obsessive-compulsive disorder, post-traumatic stress disorder, and panic disorder.

Effective exposure treatments for phobias can even be completed in a single session! One-session treatment (OST) of phobias, pioneered by Lars-Göran Öst (1997), involves an intensive three-hour intervention that depends primarily on gradually increased exposures to specific phobic objects and situations. A person with a spider phobia, for instance, would be asked to approach a small spider in a series of steps. Once anxiety subsides at a particular distance, the person comes closer and waits again until anxiety diminishes. When the person manages to endure a close encounter with the small spider, the therapist may move on to a larger or more intimidating spider. OST has proven effective with a variety of specific phobias, including snakes, spiders, cats, dogs, darkness, thunderstorms, heights, and elevators (Ollendick et al., 2009; Öst, 1997; Öst et al., 2001).

Aversion Therapy 11e

Aversion therapy is far and away the most controversial of the behaviour therapies. It's not something that you would sign up for unless you were pretty desperate. Psychologists usually suggest it only as a

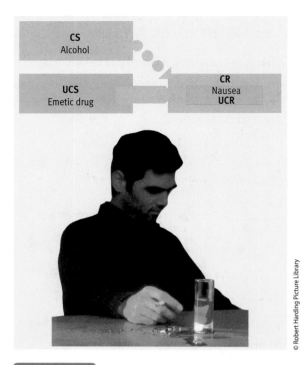

CS
Alcohol

UCS
Emetic drug

CR
Nausea
UCR

© Robert Harding Picture Library

FIGURE 15.7

Aversion therapy.

Aversion therapy uses classical conditioning to create an aversion to a stimulus that has elicited problematic behaviour. For example, in the treatment of drinking problems, alcohol may be paired with a nausea-inducing drug to create an aversion to drinking.

treatment of last resort, after other interventions have failed. What's so terrible about aversion therapy? The client has to endure decidedly unpleasant stimuli, such as shocks or drug-induced nausea.

Aversion therapy is a behaviour therapy in which an aversive stimulus is paired with a stimulus that elicits an undesirable response. For example, alcoholics have had an *emetic drug* (one that causes nausea and vomiting) paired with their favourite drinks during therapy sessions (Landabaso et al., 1999). By pairing the drug with alcohol, the therapist hopes to create a conditioned aversion to alcohol (see Figure 15.7).

Aversion therapy takes advantage of the automatic nature of responses produced through classical conditioning. Admittedly, alcoholics treated with aversion therapy know that they won't be given an emetic outside of their therapy sessions. However, their reflex response to the stimulus of alcohol may be changed so that they respond to it with nausea and distaste (remember the "sauce béarnaise syndrome" described in Chapter 6?). Obviously, this response should make it much easier to resist the urge to drink.

Aversion therapy is not a widely used technique, and when it is used, it is usually only one element in a larger treatment program. Troublesome behaviours

treated successfully with aversion therapy have included drug and alcohol abuse, sexual deviance, gambling, shoplifting, stuttering, cigarette smoking, and overeating (Bordnick et al., 2004; Emmelkamp, 1994; Grossman & Ruiz, 2004; Maletzky, 2002).

Social Skills Training

Many psychological problems grow out of interpersonal difficulties. Behaviour therapists point out that people are not born with social finesse—they acquire social skills through learning. Unfortunately, some people have not learned how to be friendly, how to make conversation, how to express anger appropriately, and so forth. Social ineptitude can contribute to anxiety, feelings of inferiority, and various kinds of disorders. In light of these findings, therapists are increasingly using social skills training in efforts to improve clients' social abilities. This approach to therapy has yielded promising results in the treatment of social anxiety (Bogels & Voncken, 2008), autism (Cappadocia & Weiss, 2010), attention deficit disorder (Monastra, 2008), and schizophrenia (Kurtz & Mueser, 2008).

Social skills training is a behaviour therapy designed to improve interpersonal skills that emphasizes modelling, behavioural rehearsal, and shaping. This type of behaviour therapy can be conducted with individual clients or in groups. Social skills training depends on the principles of operant conditioning and observational learning. With *modelling,* the client is encouraged to watch socially skilled friends and colleagues in order to acquire appropriate responses (eye contact, active listening, and so on) through observation. In *behavioural rehearsal,* the client tries to practise social techniques in structured role-playing exercises. The therapist provides corrective feedback and uses approval to reinforce progress. Eventually, of course, clients try their newly acquired skills in real-world interactions. Usually, they are given specific homework assignments. *Shaping* is used in that clients are gradually asked to handle more complicated and delicate social situations. For example, a nonassertive client may begin by working on making requests of friends. Only much later will he or she be asked to tackle standing up to the boss at work.

Cognitive-Behavioural Treatments

In Chapter 14, we learned that cognitive factors play a key role in the development of many anxiety and mood disorders. Citing the importance of such findings, behaviour therapists in the 1970s started to focus more attention on their clients' cognitions (Hollon & Digiuseppe, 2011). *Cognitive-behavioural treatments* use varied combinations of verbal interventions and behaviour modification techniques to help clients change maladaptive patterns of thinking. Some of these treatments, such as Albert Ellis's (1973) rational-emotive behaviour therapy and Aaron Beck's (1976) cognitive therapy, emerged out of an insight therapy tradition, whereas other treatments, such as the systems developed by Donald Meichenbaum (1977) and Michael Mahoney (1974), emerged from the behavioural tradition.

Here we will focus on Beck's cognitive therapy (Newman & Beck, 2009) as an example of a cognitive-behavioural treatment (see Chapter 13 for a discussion of some of Ellis's ideas). We also discuss some of the innovations introduced by Donald Meichenbaum, along with one of the most recent additions to cognitive-behavioural treatments, *mindfulness-based cognitive therapy* (Segal, Williams, & Teasdale, 2002).

Cognitive therapy uses specific strategies to correct habitual thinking errors that underlie various types of disorders. In recent years, cognitive therapy has been applied fruitfully to a wide range of disorders (Beck & Weishaar, 2011; Hollon, Stewart, & Strunk, 2006), but it was originally devised as a treatment for depression. According to cognitive therapists, depression is caused by "errors" in thinking (see Figure 15.8). They assert that depression-prone people tend to (1) blame their setbacks on personal inadequacies without considering circumstantial explanations, (2) focus selectively on negative events while ignoring positive events, (3) make unduly pessimistic projections about the future, and (4) draw negative conclusions about their worth as a person based on insignificant events. For instance, imagine that you got a low grade on a minor quiz in a class. If you made the kinds of errors in thinking just described, you might blame the grade on your woeful stupidity, dismiss comments from a classmate that it was an unfair test, gloomily predict that you will surely flunk the course, and conclude that you are not genuine college material.

The goal of cognitive therapy is to change clients' negative thoughts and appraisals, and maladaptive beliefs (Kellogg & Young, 2008; Moscovitch et al., 2011). To begin, clients are taught to detect their automatic negative thoughts. These are self-defeating statements that people are prone to make when analyzing problems. Examples might include "I'm just not smart enough," "No one really likes me," or "It's all my fault." Clients are then trained to subject these automatic thoughts to reality testing. The therapist helps them to see how unrealistically negative the thoughts are.

Cognitive therapy uses a variety of behavioural techniques, such as modelling, systematic monitoring of one's behaviour, and behavioural rehearsal (Beck & Weishaar, 2011; Wright, Beck, & Thase, 2003). Cognitive therapists often give their clients "homework assignments" that focus on changing the clients' overt behaviours. Clients may be instructed to engage in overt responses on their own, outside of the clinician's office. For example, one shy, insecure young man in cognitive therapy was told to go to a singles bar and engage three different women in conversation for up to five minutes each (Rush, 1984). He was instructed to record his thoughts before and after each of the conversations. This assignment elicited various maladaptive patterns of thought that gave the young man and his therapist plenty to work on in subsequent sessions.

Along with Ellis and Beck, University of Waterloo psychologist Donald Meichenbaum (2007) is considered to be one of the important innovators of cognitive-behavioural therapy. Meichenbaum has applied his techniques in cognitive therapy to a wide variety of issues, including post-traumatic stress disorder (Meichenbaum, 1994), and has been consulted in the aftermath of traumatic events, including the Oklahoma City bombing, the Columbine school shooting, and the 9/11 attacks (Yalom, 2002).

In one of his innovations, referred to as *self-instructional training* (Meichenbaum, 1977), clients are taught to develop and use verbal statements that help them to cope with difficult contexts. As we discussed in Chapter 13, having readily available coping strategies is critical in dealing with stress. Self-instructional training can help clients

WEB LINK 15.4

Association for Behavioral and Cognitive Therapies
The website for this professional organization has a variety of resources that are relevant to the general public. The most valuable of these resources are the fact sheets on cognitive-behavioural treatments for over 40 common problems and disorders. These fact sheets explain how cognitive-behavioural interventions can be used in the treatment of alcohol abuse, autism, chronic fatigue, eating disorders, insomnia, phobias, schizophrenia, shyness, and a host of other conditions.

Courtesy of Aaron T. Beck

Aaron Beck

"Most people are barely aware of the automatic thoughts which precede unpleasant feelings or automatic inhibitions."

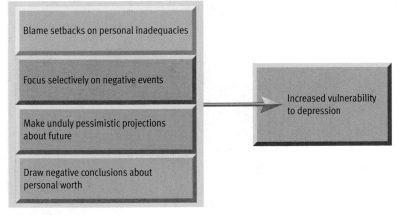

Negative thinking

Blame setbacks on personal inadequacies

Focus selectively on negative events

Make unduly pessimistic projections about future

Draw negative conclusions about personal worth

Increased vulnerability to depression

FIGURE 15.8

Beck's view of the roots of disorders.

Beck's theory initially focused on the causes of depression, although it was gradually broadened to explain other disorders. According to Beck, depression is caused by the types of negative thinking shown here.

Courtesy of Donald Meichenbaum

University of Waterloo psychologist Donald Meichenbaum is well known for his role in the development of cognitive-behavioural therapy techniques.

deal with current stressors and may serve to inoculate them against future stress. Interestingly, when discussing his self-instructional training method (Yalom, 2002), Meichenbaum sometimes refers to it as his "New York therapy." He grew up in New York City watching all kinds of people talk to themselves on the street. His mother once pointed out the similarity between his observation of people talking to themselves in New York and his therapy and asked him, "For this you get paid?" Recently, he developed a set of risk assessment items and guidelines for practice in evaluating suicidal patients (Meichenbaum, 2005). In 1989, Meichenbaum received the Canadian Psychological Association Award for Distinguished Contributions to Psychology as a Profession.

One of the most recent developments in cognitive-behavioural treatment was pioneered by Zindel Segal and his colleagues (Segal, Williams, & Teasdale, 2002). Segal is director of the Cognitive Behaviour Therapy Unit at the Centre for Addiction and Mental Health in Toronto. This therapy integrates key ideas drawn from cognitive therapy and from mindfulness meditation (Kabat-Zinn, 1995). In this approach, traditional cognitive-behavioural techniques, such as those just discussed are combined, with meditation-based techniques to heighten

awareness of dysfunctional changes in mind and body that can be targeted by the cognitive-behavioural techniques.

Mindfulness emphasizes both attention regulation and an open, accepting approach to experience (Chambers, Lo, & Allen, 2008; Fruzetti & Erikson, 2010). In mindfulness, full attention is given to the present-moment experience and that experience is "employed equanimously, in that whatever arises is acknowledged and examined without judgment, elaboration, or reaction" (Chambers, Lo, & Allen, 2008, p. 322). Mindfulness-based therapy is designed to prevent relapse in individuals who have previously but who do not currently suffer from depression (Crane et al., 2008). In therapy, individuals are taught to focus on troubling thoughts or emotions and to accept them without judging or elaborating on them. This allows the patient to observe and experience them without automatically reacting. According to Segal, this "helps you to step back from automatic reactions built into emotions for evolutionary reasons" (McIlroy, 2008, A4). Enabling vulnerable individuals to extricate themselves from negative automatic thoughts is a goal of this technique. The mindfulness approach has since been applied to clients with currently active depression (Kenny & Williams, 2007).

This approach to cognitive therapy has already been employed in a number of studies evaluating its effectiveness. The results are impressive (Crane et al., 2008; Segal, Williams, & Teasdale, 2002), with studies finding that previously depressed individuals who received mindfulness training evidenced reduced rates of relapse (Teasdale et al., 2000) and show significantly decreased dysfunctional recollection of past events (William, Teasdale, Segal, & Soulsby, 2000). In other research, mindfulness and mindfulness-based cognitive-behavioural therapy (MBCT) has been found to be associated with less worry, the generation of more specific future goals, and beliefs about self-efficacy for people with a history of suicidalilty, and distinct neural modes of self-reference, (Burg & Michalak, 2011; Crane et al., 2011; Evan & Segerstrom, 2010; Farb et al., 2007).

Clinicians have also taken the approaches developed initially in the treatment of depression to the treatment of other disorders (e.g., Breslin, Zack, & McMain, 2002: Garland, Gaylord, Boettiger, & Howard, 2010; Orsillo & Roemer, 2010). Orsillo and Roemer (2010), for example, have developed a mindfulness-based therapeutic approach to anxiety. They suggest that mindfulness practices are not only an important therapeutic tool, but that the skills people acquire will help them live the lives

Zindel Segal has been instrumental in the development of mindfulness-based cognitive therapy. This approach to cognitive therapy is based on mindfulness mediation and is directed at preventing relapse into depression. Segal is well known for his earlier research into and treatment of depression.

Courtesy of Zindel Segal

they want to live. These skills include (1) *increased awareness*—being able to notice where our attention is along with the ability to bring it back into focus, and expanding our awareness so that we will be able to capture the fullness of our experience; (2) *present moment*—being able to bring the mind back to the present moment whenever we begin to think of past difficulties and worries; (3) *self-compassion*—the ability to have compassion for yourself and your experiences; and (4) *accepting things as they are*—when we accept and respond to things as they are, we can avoid the dysfunctional reactivity that occurs when we contrast them to the way we want things to be.

Mindfulness-based practices are an exciting new tool that therapists can use in treating their clients. No doubt work in this area will continue and this approach to cognitive therapy will see increasing use with individuals who have suffered from recurrent depression and other disorders.

How Effective Are Behaviour Therapies?

Behaviour therapists have historically placed more emphasis on the importance of measuring therapeutic outcomes than insight therapists have. Hence, there is ample evidence attesting to the effectiveness of behaviour therapy (Jacob & Pelham, 2005; Stanley & Beidel, 2009). Of course, behaviour therapies are not well suited to the treatment of some types of problems (vague feelings of discontent, for instance). Furthermore, it's misleading to make global statements about the effectiveness of behaviour therapies, because they include many types of procedures designed for very different purposes. For example, the value of systematic desensitization for phobias has no bearing on the value of aversion therapy for sexual deviance.

For our purposes, it is sufficient to note that there is favourable evidence on the efficacy of most of the widely used behavioural interventions (Zinbarg & Griffith, 2008). Behaviour therapies can make important contributions to the treatment of phobias, obsessive-compulsive disorders, sexual dysfunction, schizophrenia, drug-related problems, eating disorders, psychosomatic disorders, hyperactivity, autism, and intellectual disability (Berkowitz, 2003; Emmelkamp, 2004; Hollon & Dimidjian, 2009; Wilson, 2011). Next we consider biomedical therapies. To some extent, the three major approaches to treatment have different strengths. Let's see where the strengths of the biomedical therapies lie.

concept **check 15.3**

Understanding the Types of Behaviour Therapy

Check your understanding of the varieties of behaviour therapy discussed in the text by matching the therapies with the appropriate description. Choose from the following: (a) systematic desensitization, (b) social skills training, and (c) aversion therapy. The answers are in Appendix A.

_____ **1.** Anxiety is reduced by conditioning the client to respond positively to stimuli that previously aroused anxiety.

_____ **2.** Unwanted behaviours are eliminated by conditioning the client to have an unpleasant response to stimuli that previously triggered the behaviour.

_____ **3.** Behavioural techniques are used to teach the client new behaviours aimed at enhancing the quality of their interactions with others.

WEB LINK 15.5

The Beck Institute for Cognitive Therapy and Research
This site offers a diverse array of materials relating to Aaron Beck's cognitive therapy. Resources include newsletters, a referral system, a bookstore, recommended readings for clients, and questions and answers about cognitive therapy.

REVIEW OF KEY POINTS

▷ Behaviour therapies use the principles of learning in direct efforts to change specific aspects of behaviour. Wolpe's systematic desensitization, a treatment for phobias, involves the construction of an anxiety hierarchy, relaxation training, and step-by-step movement through the hierarchy, pairing relaxation with each phobic stimulus.

▷ In aversion therapy, a stimulus associated with an unwanted response is paired with an unpleasant stimulus in an effort to eliminate the maladaptive response. Social skills training can improve clients' interpersonal skills through shaping, modelling, and behavioural rehearsal.

▷ Cognitive-behavioural treatments concentrate on changing the way clients think about events in their lives. Cognitive therapists re-educate clients to detect and challenge automatic negative thoughts that cause depression and anxiety. Cognitive therapy also depends on modelling, behavioural rehearsal, and homework assignments. Recent developments in cognitive therapy include mindfulness-based cognitive therapy, which integrates cognitive approaches to therapy with mindfulness meditation.

▷ Behaviour therapists have historically placed more emphasis on the importance of measuring therapeutic outcomes than insight therapists have. There is ample evidence that behaviour therapies are effective in the treatment of a wide variety of disorders.

PREVIEW QUESTIONS

► What are the principal types of psychiatric drugs, and what disorders are they used for?

► How effective are psychiatric drugs, and what are their disadvantages?

► What is ECT, and what is it used for?

► How effective is ECT, and what are the risks?

In the 1950s, a French surgeon looking for a drug that would reduce patients' autonomic response to surgical stress noticed that chlorpromazine produced a mild sedation. Based on this observation, Delay and Deniker (1952) decided to give chlorpromazine to hospitalized schizophrenic patients. They wanted to see whether the drug would have calming effects. Their experiment was a dramatic success. Chlorpromazine became the first effective antipsychotic drug (Bentall, 2009), and a revolution in psychiatry was begun. Hundreds of thousands of severely disturbed patients who had appeared doomed to spend the remainder of their lives in mental hospitals were gradually sent home, thanks to the therapeutic effects of antipsychotic drugs. Today, biomedical therapies such as drug treatment lie at the core of psychiatric practice.

Biomedical therapies are physiological interventions intended to reduce symptoms associated with psychological disorders. These therapies assume that psychological disorders are caused, at least in part, by biological malfunctions. As we discussed in the previous chapter, this assumption clearly has merit for many disorders, especially the more severe ones.

When laypersons hear the phrase *biomedical therapies*, many of them think of psychosurgery and lobotomies, the type of treatment portrayed in the classic film *One Flew Over the Cuckoo's Nest*, starring Jack Nicholson. While psychosurgery was performed thousands of times up to the middle of the 20th century, in the 1950s, it went into decline as a treatment and was replaced by the recently developed pharmacological treatments (Ackerknecht, 1968; Alexander & Selesnick, 1966; Millon, 2004), some of which we discuss in this section.

While a form of psychosurgery, *trephening*, was used by the Greeks and Romans and throughout the medieval period, modern use dates from 1888, when Swiss psychiatrist Gottleib Burckhardt removed portions of the cortex of six psychotic patients as a treatment for hallucinations (Millon, 2004). In the 1930s, Antonio Egas Moniz, a Portuguese psychiatrist, developed the *prefrontal leucotomy*, for which he was awarded the Nobel Prize in 1949. This type of treatment was modified and popularized by the American psychiatrist Walter Freeman in the 1940s.

Over 20 000 patients in North America received this treatment. The first lobotomies in Ontario were performed in 1944 by Dr. K. G. McKenzie, who did 19 such surgeries that year at the Toronto Psychiatric Hospital. Between 1944 and 1967, over 1000 lobotomies were

done in Ontario. After 1967, the frequency declined, with only 17 performed between 1968 and 1974. The last lobotomies were performed by Dr. Kenneth Livingstone at the Clarke Institute of Psychiatry in 1981. He performed three that year (Simmons, 1987). According to Simmons's archival research, the reasons particular lobotomies were performed were not even always treatment-related: "In some cases, psychosurgery was administered to ease staffing problems, for experimental purposes, or simply out of sheer curiosity. Often the consent of the patients or relatives was not obtained" (p. 537). The procedure has largely been abandoned except in a modified form (*cingulotomy*) in extreme situations, such as the treatment-refractory obsessive-compulsive disorders (Dougherty et al., 2002).

In this section, we will discuss two current biomedical approaches to psychotherapy: drug therapy and electroconvulsive (shock) therapy.

Treatment with Drugs   11e

Psychopharmacotherapy is the treatment of mental disorders with medication. We will refer to this kind of treatment more simply as *drug therapy*. The four main categories of therapeutic drugs for psychological problems are: (1) antianxiety drugs, (2) antipsychotic drugs, and (3) antidepressant drugs, and (4) mood-stabilizing drugs.

Antianxiety Drugs   11e

Most of us know someone who pops pills to relieve anxiety. The drugs involved in this common coping strategy are *antianxiety drugs,* which relieve tension, apprehension, and nervousness. The most popular of these drugs are Valium and Xanax. These are the trade names (the proprietary names that pharmaceutical companies use in marketing drugs) for diazepam and alprazolam, respectively.

Valium, Xanax, and other drugs in the *benzodiazepine* family are often called *tranquillizers*. These drugs exert their effects almost immediately, and they can be fairly effective in alleviating feelings of anxiety (Dubovsky, 2009). However, their effects are measured in hours, so their impact is relatively short-lived. Antianxiety drugs are routinely prescribed for people with anxiety disorders, but they are also given to millions of people who simply suffer from chronic nervous tension.

Side Effects	Patients Experiencing Side Effects (%)	
	Xanax	Valium
Drowsiness	36.0	49.4
Light-headedness	18.6	24.0
Dry mouth	14.9	13.0
Depression	11.9	17.0
Nausea, vomiting	9.3	10.0
Constipation	9.3	11.3
Insomnia	9.0	6.7
Confusion	9.3	14.1
Diarrhea	8.5	10.5
Tachycardia, palpitations	8.1	7.2
Nasal congestion	8.1	7.2
Blurred vision	7.0	9.1

TABLE 15.1

Side Effects of Xanax and Valium

Source: Evans, R. L. (1981). New drug evaluations: Alprazolam. *Drug Intelligence and Clinical Pharmacy, 15,* 633–637. Copyright © 1981 by Harvey Whitney Books Company. Reprinted by permission.

All of the drugs used to treat psychological problems have potentially troublesome side effects that show up in some patients but not others. The antianxiety drugs are no exception. The most common side effects of Valium and Xanax are listed in Table 15.1. Some of these side effects—such as drowsiness, depression, nausea, and confusion—present serious problems for some patients. These drugs also have potential for abuse, drug dependence, and overdose, although these risks have probably been exaggerated in the press (Martinez, Maragnell & Martinez, 2008). Another drawback is that patients who have been on antianxiety drugs for a while often experience withdrawal symptoms when their drug treatment is stopped (Edwards et al., 2008).

Antipsychotic Drugs

Antipsychotic drugs are used primarily in the treatment of schizophrenia. They are also given to people with severe mood disorders who become delusional. The trade names (with the generic names in parentheses) of some classic drugs in this category are Thorazine (chlorpromazine), Mellaril (thioridazine), and Haldol (haloperidol). *Antipsychotic drugs* are *used to gradually reduce psychotic symptoms, including hyperactivity, mental confusion, hallucinations, and delusions.* The traditional antipsychotics appear to decrease activity at dopamine synapses, although the exact relationship between their neurochemical effects and their clinical effects remains obscure (Miyamoto et al., 2008).

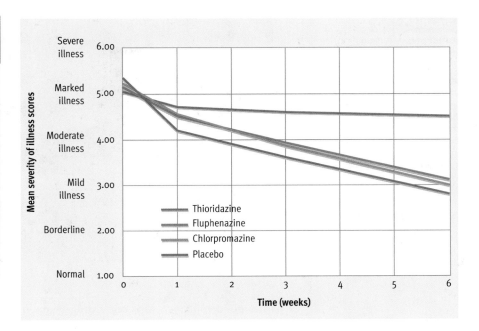

FIGURE 15.9

The time course of antipsychotic drug effects.

Antipsychotic drugs reduce psychotic symptoms gradually, over a span of weeks, as graphed here. In contrast, patients given placebo medication show little improvement.

Source: Cole, J. O., Goldberg, S. C., and Davis, J. M. (1966). Drugs in the treatment of psychosis. In P. Solomon (Ed.), *Psychiatric drugs.* New York: Grune & Stratton. From data in the *NIMH PSC Collective Study I.* Reprinted by permission of J.M. Davis.

Studies suggest that antipsychotics reduce psychotic symptoms in about 70 percent of patients, albeit in varied degrees (Kane, Stroup, & Marder, 2009). When antipsychotic drugs are effective, they work their magic gradually, as shown in Figure 15.9. Patients usually begin to respond within one to three weeks, but considerable variability in responsiveness is seen (Emsley, Rabinowitz, & Medori, 2006). Further improvement may occur for several months. Many schizophrenic patients are placed on antipsychotics indefinitely, because these drugs can reduce the likelihood of a relapse into an active schizophrenic episode (van Kammen, Hurford, & Marder, 2009).

Antipsychotic drugs undeniably make a huge contribution to the treatment of severe mental disorders, but they are not without problems. They have many unpleasant side effects (Dolder, 2008; Neunch & Hamer, 2010). Drowsiness, constipation, and a dry mouth are common. The drugs may also produce effects that resemble the symptoms of Parkinson's disease, including muscle tremors, muscular rigidity, and impaired motor coordination. After being released from a hospital, many schizophrenic patients, supposedly placed on antipsychotics indefinitely, discontinue their drug regimen because of the disagreeable side effects. Unfortunately, after patients stop taking antipsychotic medication, about 70 percent relapse within a year (van Kammen et al., 2009). One recent study found that even brief periods

WEB LINK 15.6

Treatments for Anxiety Disorders
The Anxiety Treatment and Research Centre at St. Joseph's Healthcare in Hamilton, Ontario, which is associated with McMaster University, is a well-known treatment centre for anxiety disorders. Its website contains updated information on the signs, symptoms, and treatment modes for various forms of anxiety disorder.

WEB LINK 15.7

Psych Central
The work of psychiatrist John Grohol, Psych Central is a superb source for learning about all aspects of mental health, including psychological disorders and treatment, professional issues, and information for mental health-care consumers. Almost 2000 annotated listings to information sources are offered here.

FIGURE 15.10

Antidepressant drugs' mechanisms of action.

The three types of antidepressant drugs all increase activity at serotonin synapses, which is probably the principal basis for their therapeutic effects. However, they increase serotonin activity in different ways, with different spillover effects (Marangell et al., 1999). Tricyclics and MAO inhibitors have effects at a much greater variety of synapses, which presumably explains why they have more side effects. The more recently developed SSRIs are much more specific in targeting serotonin synapses.

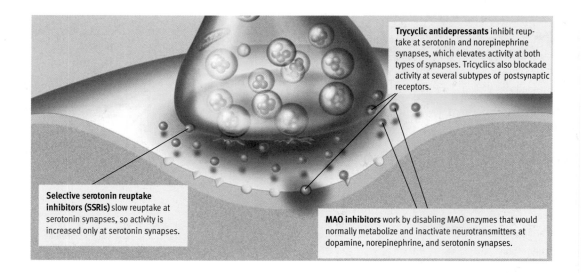

Trycyclic antidepressants inhibit reuptake at serotonin and norepinephrine synapses, which elevates activity at both types of synapses. Tricyclics also blockade activity at several subtypes of postsynaptic receptors.

Selective serotonin reuptake inhibitors (SSRIs) slow reuptake at serotonin synapses, so activity is increased only at serotonin synapses.

MAO inhibitors work by disabling MAO enzymes that would normally metabolize and inactivate neurotransmitters at dopamine, norepinephrine, and serotonin synapses.

of partial noncompliance with one's drug regimen increased the risk of relapse (Subotnik et al., 2011).

In addition to their nuisance side effects, antipsychotics may cause a more severe and lasting problem called *tardive dyskinesia,* which is seen in about 20–30 percent of patients who receive long-term treatment with traditional antipsychotics (Kane et al., 2009). *Tardive dyskinesia is a neurological disorder marked by involuntary writhing and tic-like movements of the mouth, tongue, face, hands, or feet.* Once this debilitating syndrome emerges, there is no cure, although spontaneous remission sometimes occurs after the discontinuation of antipsychotic medication.

Psychiatrists are currently enthusiastic about a newer class of antipsychotic agents called *atypical antipsychotic drugs,* such as clozapine, olanzapine, and quetiapine (Marder, Hurford, & van Kammen, 2009). These drugs appear to be roughly similar to the first-generation antipsychotics in therapeutic effectiveness, but they offer some advantages over the older drugs (Meltzer & Bobo, 2009). For instance, they can help some treatment-resistant patients who do not respond to traditional antipsychotics. And the second-generation antipsychotics produce fewer unpleasant side effects and carry less risk for tardive dyskinesia. Of course, like all powerful drugs, they carry some risks. This drug class appears to increase patients' vulnerability to diabetes and cardiovascular problems.

Antidepressant Drugs

11e

As their name suggests, *antidepressant drugs* gradually elevate mood and help bring people out of depression. Reliance on antidepressants has increased dramatically in the last 10 to 15 years, as antidepressants have become the most frequently prescribed class of medication in North America (Olfson & Marcus, 2009). Prior to 1987, there were two principal classes of antidepressants: *tricyclics* (such as Elavil) and *MAO inhibitors* (such as Nardil). These two sets of drugs affect neurochemical activity in different ways (see Figure 15.10) and tend to work with different patients. Overall, they are beneficial for about two-thirds of depressed patients (Gitlin, 2009), The tricyclics have fewer problems with side effects and complications than the MAO inhibitors (Potter et al., 2006).

Today, psychiatrists are more likely to prescribe a newer class of antidepressants, called *selective serotonin reuptake inhibitors (SSRIs),* which slow the reuptake process at serotonin synapses. The drugs in this class, which include Prozac (fluoxetine), Paxil (paroxetine), and Zoloft (sertraline), seem to yield therapeutic gains similar to the tricyclics in the treatment of depression (Boland & Keller, 2008) while producing fewer unpleasant or dangerous side effects (Kelsey, 2005). SSRIs have also proven valuable in the treatment of obsessive-compulsive disorders, panic disorders, and other anxiety disorders (Mathew, Hoffman, & Charney, 2009; Ravindran & Stein, 2009). However, there is some doubt about how effective the SSRIs (and other antidepressants) are in relieving episodes of depression among patients suffering from bipolar disorder (Berman et al., 2009).

Like antipsychotic drugs, the various types of antidepressants exert their effects gradually over a period of weeks, but about 60 percent of patients' improvement tends to occur in the first two weeks (Gitlin, 2009). A recent analysis that looked carefully at the severity of patients' depression when medication was initiated found that people with serious depression benefit the most from antidepressants (Fournier et al., 2010). This analysis focused on six studies that measured patients' initial level of depression precisely and included patients with the full range of symptom severity (many drug trials exclude patients with mild illness). The most provocative aspect of the findings was that antidepressants provided a relatively modest benefit for patients with mild to moderate depression.

A major concern in recent years has been evidence from a number of studies that SSRIs may increase the risk for suicide, primarily among adolescents and young adults (Healy & Whitaker, 2003; Holden, 2004). The challenge of collecting definitive data on this issue is much more daunting than one might guess, in part because suicide rates are already elevated among people who exhibit the disorders for which SSRIs are prescribed (Berman, 2009). Some researchers have collected data that suggest that suicide rates have *declined* slightly because of widespread prescription of SSRIs (Baldessarini et al., 2007; Isacsson et al., 2009), while others have found no association between SSRIs and suicide (Lapiere, 2003; Simon et al., 2006).

Overall, however, when antidepressants are compared to placebo treatment, the data suggest that antidepressants lead to a slight elevation in the risk of suicidal behaviour, from roughly 2 percent to 4 percent (Bridge et al., 2007; Dubicka, Hadley, & Roberts, 2006; Hammad, Laughren, & Racoosin, 2006). The increased suicide risk appears to be a problem mainly among a small minority of children and adolescents in the first month after starting antidepressants, especially during the first nine days (Jick, Kaye, & Jick, 2004). Thus, patients starting on SSRIs should be carefully monitored by their physicians and families (Culpepper et al., 2004).

Regulatory warnings from the U.S. Food and Drug Administration have led to a decline in the prescription of SSRIs among adolescents (Nemeroff et al., 2007). This trend has prompted concern that increases in suicide may occur among untreated individuals (Dudley et al., 2008). This concern seems legitimate in that suicide risk clearly peaks in the month prior to people beginning treatment for depression, whether that treatment involves SSRIs or psychotherapy (see Figure 15.11; Simon & Savarino, 2007). This pattern

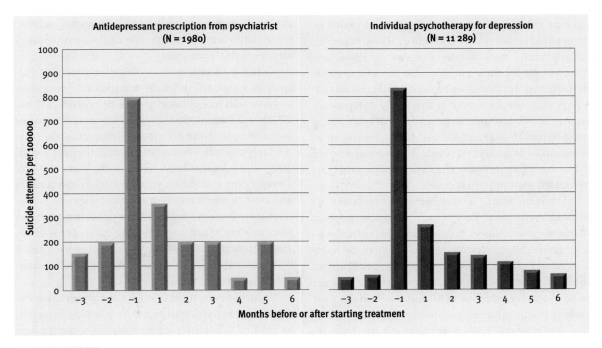

FIGURE 15.11

Probability of a suicide attempt in relation to the initiation of treatment.

Examining medical records for thousands of patients, Simon and Savarino (2007) were able to gather information on the likelihood of a suicide attempt in the months before and after commencing treatment for depression. They compared patients who were put on an antidepressant medication against those who started in some form of insight or behavioural therapy. The data shown here, for young patients under the age of 25, indicate that suicide risk is highest in the month prior to treatment and next highest in the month after treatment is begun for both groups. These findings suggest that elevated suicide rates are not unique to starting on antidepressants and that getting treatment (whether it is medication or psychotherapy) reduces the risk of suicide.

Source: From Simon, G. E., and Savarino, J., Suicide attempts among patients starting depression treatment with medications or psychotherapy. *American Journal of Psychiatry*, July 2007, *164*: 1029–1034. Adapted with permission from the American Journal of Psychiatry (Copyright © 2007). American Psychiatric Association.

Treatment of Psychological Disorders

presumably occurs because the escalating agony of depression finally prompts people to seek treatment, but it also suggests that getting treatment with drugs or therapy reduces suicidal risk. In the final analysis, this is a complex issue, but the one thing experts seem to agree on is that adolescents starting on SSRIs should be monitored closely.

The newest class of antidepressants consists of medications that inhibit reuptake at both serotonin and norepinephrine synapses, referred to as SNRIs. The first two drugs in this category are venlafaxine (Effexor) and duloxetine (Celexa). These drugs appear to produce slightly stronger antidepressant effects than the SSRIs (Thase & Denko, 2008). However, targeting two neurotransmitter systems also leads to a broader range of side effects, including troublesome elevations in blood pressure (Thase & Sloan, 2006).

Mood Stabilizers

Mood stabilizers are drugs used to control mood swings in patients with bipolar mood disorders. For many years, lithium was the only effective drug in this category. Lithium has proven valuable in preventing *future* episodes of both mania and depression in patients with bipolar illness (Post & Altshuler, 2009). Lithium can also be used in efforts to bring patients with bipolar illness out of *current* manic or depressive episodes (Keck & McElroy, 2006). However, antipsychotics and antidepressants are more frequently used for these purposes. On the negative side of the ledger, lithium does have some dangerous side effects if its use isn't managed skillfully (Jefferson & Greist, 2009). Lithium levels in the patient's blood must be monitored carefully, because high concentrations can be toxic and even fatal. Kidney and thyroid gland complications are the other major problems associated with lithium therapy.

In recent years, a number of alternatives to lithium have been developed. The most popular of these newer mood stabilizers is an anticonvulsant agent called *valproate,* which has become more widely used than lithium in the treatment of bipolar disorders (Thase & Denko, 2008). Valproate appears to be roughly as effective as lithium in efforts to treat current manic episodes and to prevent future affective disturbances, with fewer side effects (Muzina, Kemp, & Calabrese, 2008). In some cases, a combination of valproate and lithium may be used in treatment (Post & Altshuler, 2009).

How Effective Are Drug Therapies?

Drug therapies can produce clear therapeutic gains for many kinds of patients. What's especially impressive is that they can be effective with disorders that otherwise defy therapeutic endeavours. Nonetheless,

drug therapies are controversial. Critics of drug therapy have raised a number of issues (Bentall, 2009; Breggin, 2008; Healy, 2004; Kirsch, 2010; Whitaker, 2002). First, some critics argue that drug therapies are not as effective as advertised and that they often produce superficial, short-lived curative effects. For example, Valium does not really solve problems with anxiety; it merely provides temporary relief from an unpleasant symptom. Moreover, relapse rates are substantial when drug regimens are discontinued. Second, critics charge that many drugs are overprescribed and many patients overmedicated. According to these critics, a number of physicians routinely hand out prescriptions without giving adequate consideration to more complicated and difficult interventions. Consistent with this line of criticism, a recent study of office visits to psychiatrists found that they increasingly prescribe two and even three medications to patients, even though relatively little is known about the interactive effects of psychiatric drugs (Mojtabai & Olfson, 2010).

Third, some critics charge that the damaging side effects of therapeutic drugs are underestimated by psychiatrists and that these side effects are often worse than the illnesses that the drugs are supposed to cure. Citing problems such as tardive dyskinesia, lithium toxicity, and addiction to antianxiety agents, these critics argue that the risks of therapeutic drugs aren't worth the benefits.

Critics maintain that the negative effects of psychiatric drugs are not fully appreciated because of possible selective publication practices (Turner et al., 2008) and suggest that the pharmaceutical industry has managed to gain undue influence over the research enterprise as it relates to drug testing (Angell, 2000, 2004; Healy, 2004; Insel, 2010; Weber, 2006). Today, many researchers who investigate the benefits and risks of medications and write treatment guidelines have lucrative financial arrangements with the pharmaceutical industry (Bentall, 2009; Lurie et al., 2006; Pachter et al., 2007). Their studies are funded by drug companies, and they often receive substantial consulting fees.

Unfortunately, these financial ties appear to undermine the objectivity required in scientific research, as studies funded by drug companies are far less likely to report unfavourable results than nonprofit-funded studies (Bekelman, Li, & Gross, 2003; Perlis et al., 2005; Rennie & Luft, 2000). Consistent with this finding, when specific antipsychotic drugs are pitted against each other in clinical trials, the sponsoring company's drug is reported to be superior to the other drugs in 90 percent of studies (Heres et al., 2006). Industry-financed drug trials also tend to be much too brief to detect the long-term risks associated with new drugs (Vandenbroucke & Psaty, 2008). Additionally, when unfavourable results emerge, the data are often withheld from publication (Antonuccio, Danton, & McClanahan, 2003; Rising, Bacchetti, & Bero, 2008; Turner et al., 2008). Also, research designs are often slanted in a multitude of ways so as to exaggerate the positive effects and minimize the negative effects of the drugs under scrutiny (Carpenter, 2002; Chopra, 2003; Moncrieff, 2001). The conflicts of interest that appear to be pervasive in contemporary drug research raise grave concerns that require attention from researchers, universities, and government agencies.

Electroconvulsive Therapy (ECT)

In the 1930s, a Hungarian psychiatrist named Ladislas von Meduna speculated that epilepsy and schizophrenia could not coexist in the same body. On the basis of this observation, which turned out to be inaccurate, von Meduna theorized that it might be useful to induce epileptic-like seizures in schizophrenic patients. Initially, a drug was used to trigger these seizures. However, by 1938 a pair of Italian psychiatrists (Cerletti & Bini, 1938) demonstrated that it was safer to elicit the seizures with electric shock. Thus, modern electroconvulsive therapy was born.

Electroconvulsive therapy (ECT) is a biomedical treatment in which electric shock is used to produce a cortical seizure accompanied by convulsions. In ECT, electrodes are attached to the skull over the temporal lobes of the brain. A light anesthesia is induced, and the patient is given a variety of drugs to minimize the likelihood of complications. An electric current is then applied either to the right side or to both sides of the brain for about a second. Unilateral shock delivered to the right hemisphere is the preferred method of treatment today (Sackeim et al., 2009). The current triggers a brief (about 30 seconds) convulsive seizure. The patient normally awakens in an hour or two and manifests some confusion, disorientation, and nausea, which usually clear up in a matter of hours. People typically receive between 6 and 20 treatments over a period of a month or so (Fink, 2009).

The clinical use of ECT peaked in the 1940s and 1950s, before effective drug therapies were widely available. ECT has long been controversial, and its use did decline in the 1960s and 1970s. Only about 8 percent of psychiatrists administer ECT (Hermann et al., 1998), but it cannot be considered a rare form of treatment. Some critics argue that ECT is overused because it's a lucrative procedure that boosts psychiatrists' income while consuming relatively little of

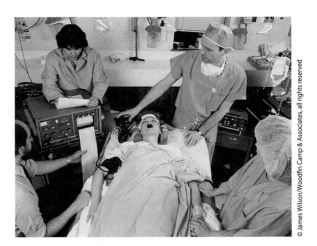

This patient is being prepared for electroconvulsive therapy (ECT). In ECT, an electric shock is used to elicit a brief cortical seizure. The shock is delivered through electrodes attached to the patient's skull.

their time in comparison to insight therapy (Frank, 1990). Conversely, some ECT advocates argue that ECT is underutilized because the public harbours many misconceptions about its effects and risks (McDonald et al., 2004). ECT is used in the treatment of a variety of disorders. In recent decades, however, it has primarily been recommended for the treatment of depression.

Controversy about ECT has been fuelled by patients' reports that the treatment is painful, dehumanizing, and terrifying. Substantial improvements in the administration of ECT have made it less disagreeable than it once was (Bernstein et al., 1998). Nonetheless, some patients continue to report that they find the treatment extremely aversive (Johnstone, 1999). Two personal reports by Canadians, one on each side of the controversy, are interesting places to begin your consideration of the use of ECT. One, written by Wendy Funk (1998), addresses concerns she has over her treatment. The other, by Canadian psychologist Norman Endler (1982), whom we profiled in Chapter 14, is based on his own ECT treatment and is supportive of its use.

Effectiveness of ECT

The evidence on the therapeutic efficacy of ECT is open to varied interpretations. Proponents of ECT maintain that it is a remarkably effective treatment for major depression (Fink, 2009; Prudic, 2009). Moreover, they note that many patients who do not benefit from antidepressant medication improve in response to ECT (Nobler & Sackeim, 2006). However, opponents of ECT argue that the available studies are flawed and inconclusive and that ECT is probably no more effective than a placebo (Breggin, 1991; Friedberg, 1983). Overall, there does seem to be enough favourable evidence to justify *conservative* use of ECT in treating severe mood disorders in patients who have not responded to medication (Metzger, 1999; Rudorfer & Goodwin, 1993).

Treatment of Psychological Disorders

Unfortunately, relapse rates after ECT are distressingly high. For example in one well-controlled study, 64 percent of patients relapsed within six months and the median time to relapse was only 8.6 weeks (Prudic et al., 2004). These relapse rates, however, can be reduced by giving ECT patients antidepressant drugs (Sackeim et al., 2001, 2009).

Risks Associated with ECT

Even ECT proponents acknowledge that memory losses, impaired attention, and other cognitive deficits are common short-term side effects of electroconvulsive therapy (Rowney & Lisanby, 2008; Sackeim et al., 2007). However, ECT proponents assert that these deficits are mild and usually disappear within a month or two (Glass, 2001). An American Psychiatric Association (2001) task force concluded that there is no objective evidence that ECT causes structural damage in the brain or that it has any lasting negative effects on the ability to learn and remember information. In contrast, ECT critics maintain that ECT-induced cognitive deficits are often significant and sometimes permanent (Breggin, 1991; Rose et al., 2003), although their evidence seems to be largely anecdotal. Given the doubts that have been raised about the efficacy and risks of ECT, it appears that this treatment will remain controversial for some time to come.

New Brain Stimulation Techniques

Given the side effects and risks associated with ECT and drug treatments, scientists are always on the lookout for new methods of treating psychological disorders that might exhibit greater efficacy or fewer complications. Some innovative, new approaches to treatment involving stimulation of the brain are being explored with promising results, although they remain highly experimental at this time.

One new approach is transcranial magnetic stimulation, which was discussed in Chapter 3 as a method for studying brain function. *Transcranial magnetic stimulation* (TMS) is a new technique that permits scientists to temporarily enhance or depress activity in a specific area of the brain. In TMS, a magnetic coil mounted on a small paddle is held over specific areas of the head to increase or decrease activity in discrete regions of the cortex (Nahas et al., 2007). Neuroscientists are experimenting with

concept **check** 15.4

Understanding Biomedical Therapies

Check your understanding of biomedical therapies by matching each treatment with its chief use. The answers are in Appendix A.

Treatment

_____ **1.** Antianxiety drugs

_____ **2.** Antipsychotic drugs

_____ **3.** Antidepressant drugs

_____ **4.** Mood stabilizers

_____ **5.** Electroconvulsive therapy (ECT)

Chief Purpose

a. To reduce psychotic symptoms

b. To bring a major depression to an end

c. To suppress tension, nervousness, and apprehension

d. To prevent future episodes of mania or depression in bipolar disorders

TMS mostly as a treatment for depression. So far, treatments delivered to the right and left prefrontal cortex show promise in reducing depressive symptoms (Jamicak et al., 2010; O'Reardon et al., 2007). TMS generally is well tolerated, with minimal side effects. But a great deal of additional research will be necessary before the therapeutic value of TMS can be determined.

The other new approach to treatment is deep brain stimulation. In *deep brain stimulation* (DBS), a thin electrode is surgically implanted in the brain and connected to an implanted pulse generator so that various electrical currents can be delivered to brain tissue adjacent to the electrode (George, 2003; see Figure 15.12). DBS has proven to be valuable in the treatment of the motor disturbances associated with Parkinson's disease, tardive dyskinesia, and some seizure disorders (Halpern et al., 2007). Researchers are currently exploring whether DBS may have value in the treatment of depression or obsessive-compulsive disorder (Denys et al., 2010; Sartorius et al., 2010). Obviously, this highly invasive procedure requiring brain surgery will never be a frontline therapy for mental disorders, but scientists hope that it may valuable for highly treatment-resistant patients who do not benefit from conventional therapies (Kuehn, 2007).

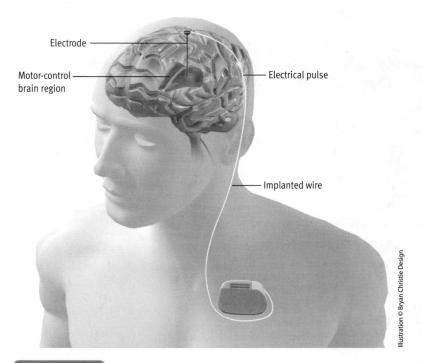

FIGURE 15.12

Deep brain stimulation.

Deep brain stimulation requires a surgical procedure in which a thin electrode (about the width of a human hair) is inserted into deep areas of the brain. The electrode is connected to a pulse generator implanted under the skin of the chest. The placement of the electrode and the type of current generated depend on what condition is being treated. The electrode shown here was implanted in a motor area of the brain to treat the tremors associated with Parkinson's disease. Researchers are experimenting with other electrode placements in efforts to treat depression and obsessive-compulsive disorder.

Current Trends and Issues in Treatment

As we saw in our discussion of insight, behavioural, and drug therapy, recent decades have brought many changes in the world of mental health care. In this section, we'll discuss two trends that are not tied to a specific mode of treatment. Specifically, we'll look at the trend toward blending various approaches to therapy and efforts to respond more effectively to increasing cultural diversity in Western societies.

Blending Approaches to Treatment

In this chapter, we have reviewed many approaches to treatment. While some research is intended to compare the effectiveness of competing orientations or to determine what therapy works best with what specific client type (e.g., Elkin et al., 1989; Fournier et al., 2008), other clinicians work with the assumption that there is no rule that a client must be treated with just one approach. Often, a clinician will use several techniques in working with a client (e.g., Hunt, et al., 2007). For example, a depressed person might receive cognitive therapy (an insight therapy), social skills training (a behaviour therapy), and antidepressant medication (a biomedical therapy). Multiple approaches are particularly likely when a treatment team provides therapy. Studies suggest that combining approaches to treatment has merit (Glass, 2004; Riba & Miller, 2003; Szigethy & Friedman, 2009), as you will see in our Featured Study for this chapter.

PREVIEW QUESTIONS

► What have researchers found when they have combined insight therapy and drug therapy?

► What is eclecticism in therapy?

► Why is therapy underutilized by some ethnic groups?

Therapy/founder

Roots of Disorders

Psychoanalysis

National Library of Medicine

Developed by Sigmund Freud in Vienna, from the 1890s through the 1930s

Intrapsychic conflict (among id, ego, and superego) → Anxiety → Reliance on defence mechanisms

Unconscious conflicts resulting from fixations in earlier development cause anxiety, which leads to defensive behaviour. The repressed conflicts typically centre on sex and aggression.

Client-centred therapy

Courtesy of the Center for Studies of the Person

Created by Carl Rogers at the University of Chicago during the 1940s and 1950s

Need to distort shortcomings to feel worthy of affection → Relatively incongruent self-concept → Recurrent anxiety

Defensive behaviour protects inaccurate self-concept

Overdependence on acceptance from others fosters incongruence, which leads to anxiety and defensive behaviour and thwarts personal growth.

Cognitive therapy

Courtesy of Aaron T. Beck

Devised by Aaron Beck at the University of Pennsylvania in the 1960s and 1970s

Blame setbacks on personal inadequacies

Focus selectively on negative events

Make unduly pessimistic projections about future

Draw negative conclusions about personal worth

→ Increased vulnerability to depression

Pervasive negative thinking about events related to self fosters anxiety and depression.

Behaviour therapy

Courtesy of Dr. Joseph Wolpe

Launched primarily by South African Joseph Wolpe's description of systematic desensitization in 1958

CS Bridge

UCS Lightning strikes

CR Fear **UCR**

Maladaptive patterns of behaviour are acquired through learning. For example, many phobias are thought to be created through classical conditioning and maintained by operant conditioning.

Biomedical therapy

Many researchers contributed; key breakthroughs in drug treatment made around 1950 by John Cade in Australia, Henri Laborit in France, and Jean Delay and Pierre Deniker, also in France

Overactivity at DA synapses may be caused by excessive release of DA or overabundance of DA receptor sites.

Most disorders are attributed to genetic predisposition and physiological malfunctions, such as abnormal neurotransmitter activity. For example, schizophrenia appears to be associated with overactivity at dopamine synapses.

Therapeutic Goals

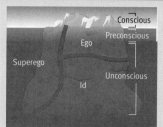

Insights regarding unconscious conflicts and motives; resolution of conflicts; personality reconstruction

Increased congruence between self-concept and experience; acceptance of genuine self; self-determination and personal growth

Reduction of negative thinking; substitution of more realistic thinking

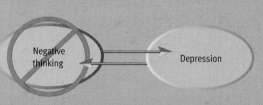

Elimination of maladaptive symptoms; acquisition of more adaptive responses

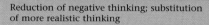
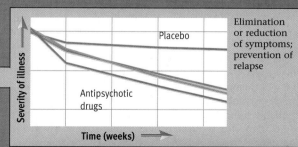

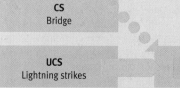

Elimination or reduction of symptoms; prevention of relapse

Therapeutic Techniques

Bruce Ayres/Stone/Getty Images

Free association, dream analysis, interpretation, transference

Zigy Kaluzny/Stone/Getty Images

Genuineness, empathy, unconditional positive regard, clarification, reflecting back to client

Rachael Epstein/PhotoEdit

Thought stopping, recording of automatic thoughts, refuting of negative thinking, homework assignments

iofoto/Shutterstock.com

Classical and operant conditioning, systematic desensitization, aversive conditioning, social skills training, reinforcement, shaping, punishment, extinction, biofeedback

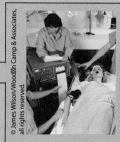

Antianxiety, antidepressant, and antipsychotic drugs; lithium; electroconvulsive therapy

Photodisc/Getty Images

FEATURED STUDY

Investigators: Charles F. Reynolds III, Ellen Frank, James F. Perel, Stanley D. Imber, Cleon Cornes, Mark D. Miller, Sati Mazumdar, Patricia R. Houck, Mary Amanda Dew, Jacqueline A. Stack, Bruce G. Pollock, and David J. Kupfer (University of Pittsburgh Medical Center)

Source: Nortriptyline and interpersonal psychotherapy as maintenance therapies for recurrent major depression: A randomized controlled trial in patients older than 59 years. *Journal of the American Medical Association,* 1999, *281,* 39–45.

Combining Insight Therapy and Medication

Depression is common in older people and contributes to physical health problems, chronic disability, and increased mortality among the elderly. Geriatric depression is also a highly recurrent problem. After successful treatment of depression, elderly patients tend to relapse more quickly and more frequently than younger clients. The purpose of this study was to determine whether a combination of insight therapy and antidepressant medication could reduce the recurrence of depression in an elderly population.

Method

Participants. The participants were 107 elderly patients diagnosed with recurrent, unipolar, major depression. The minimum age of the patients was 60 and the mean age at the beginning of the study was 67.6. The subjects had all been successfully treated for a recent episode of depression and had remained stable for four months.

Treatments. The medication employed in the study was nortriptyline, a tricyclic antidepressant that appears to be relatively effective and well tolerated in elderly populations. The insight therapy was interpersonal psychotherapy (IPT), an approach to therapy that emphasizes the social roots of depression and focuses on how improved social relationships can protect against depression (Klerman & Weissman, 1993). Clients learn how social isolation and unsatisfying interpersonal relationships can provoke depression and how confidants and supportive interactions can decrease vulnerability to depression.

Design. The subjects were randomly assigned to one of four maintenance treatment conditions: (1) monthly interpersonal therapy and medication, (2) medication alone, (3) monthly interpersonal therapy and placebo medication, and (4) placebo medication alone. A double-blind procedure was employed, so the clinicians who provided the treatments did not know which subjects were getting genuine medication as opposed to placebo pills. Patients remained in maintenance treatment for three years or until a recurrence of a major depressive episode.

Results

The relapse rates for the four treatment conditions are shown in Figure 15.13. The relapse rate for the combination of interpersonal therapy and medication was significantly less than that for either medication alone or interpersonal therapy alone (with placebo medication). The prophylactic value of the combined therapy proved most valuable to patients over 70 years of age and during the first year of the study, during which most relapses occurred.

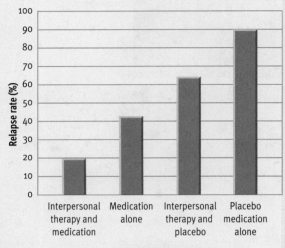

FIGURE 15.13

Relapse rates in the Reynolds et al. (1999) study.

Following up over a period of three years, Reynolds et al. (1999) compared the preventive value of (1) monthly interpersonal therapy and medication, (2) medication alone, (3) monthly interpersonal therapy and placebo medication, and (4) placebo medication alone in a sample of elderly patients prone to recurrent depression. The combined treatment of insight therapy and medication yielded the lowest relapse rates and thus proved superior to either insight therapy or drug therapy alone. (Data from Reynolds et al., 1999)

Discussion

The authors conclude that "the continuation of combined medication and psychotherapy may represent the best long-term treatment strategy for preserving recovery in elderly patients with recurrent major depression" (p. 44). They speculate that the combined treatment may be "best-suited for dealing with both the biological and psychosocial substrates of old-age depression" (p. 45). However, they acknowledge the need for further research and recommend additional studies with newer antidepressant drugs (the SSRIs) that are increasingly popular.

Comment

This study was featured because it illustrated how to conduct a well-controlled experimental evaluation of the efficacy of therapeutic interventions. It also highlighted the value of combining approaches to treatment, which is a laudable trend in the treatment of psychological disorders. The fact that the study was published in the highly prestigious *Journal of the American Medical Association* also demonstrates how prominent and important research on therapeutic efficacy has become.

The value of multiple approaches to treatment may explain why a significant trend seems to have crept into the field of psychotherapy: a movement away from strong loyalty to individual schools of thought and a corresponding move toward integrating various approaches to therapy (Norcross & Goldfried, 1992; D. A. Smith, 1999). Most clinicians used to depend exclusively on one system of therapy while rejecting the utility of all others. This era of fragmentation may be drawing to a close. One recent survey of psychologists' theoretical orientations found that 36 percent of respondents describe themselves as *eclectic* in approach (Norcross, Hedges, & Castle, 2002).

Eclecticism in the practice of therapy involves drawing ideas from two or more systems of therapy instead of committing to just one system. Therapists can be eclectic in a number of ways (Feixas & Botella, 2004; Goin, 2005; Norcross & Beutler, 2011). Two common approaches are theoretical integration and technical eclecticism. In *theoretical integration,* two or more systems of therapy are combined or blended to take advantage of the strengths of each. Paul Wachtel's (1977, 1991) efforts to blend psychodynamic and behavioural therapies are a prominent example. *Technical eclecticism* involves borrowing ideas, insights, and techniques from a variety of sources while tailoring one's intervention strategy to the unique needs of each client. Advocates of technical eclecticism, such as Arnold Lazarus (1989, 1992, 1995), maintain that therapists should ask themselves, "What is the best approach for this specific client, problem, and situation?" and then adjust their strategy accordingly.

Increasing Multicultural Sensitivity in Treatment

Modern psychotherapy emerged during the second half of the 19th century in Europe and North America, spawned in part by a cultural milieu that viewed the self as an independent, reflective, rational being, capable of self-improvement (Cushman, 1992). Psychological disorders were assumed to have natural causes like physical diseases and to be amenable to medical treatments derived from scientific research. But the individualized, medicalized institution of modern psychotherapy reflects Western cultural values that are far from universal (Sue & Sue, 1999). In many nonindustrialized societies, psychological disorders are attributed to supernatural forces (possession, witchcraft, angry gods, and so forth), and victims seek help from priests, shamans, and folk healers, rather than doctors (Wittkower & Warnes,

1984). Thus, efforts to export Western psychotherapies to non-Western cultures have met with mixed success. Indeed, some even argue that the highly culture-bound origins of modern therapies have raised questions about their applicability to ethnic minorities *within* Western culture (Miranda et al., 2005).

Research on how cultural factors influence the process and outcome of psychotherapy has burgeoned in recent years (Kirmayer, 2007), motivated in part by the need to improve mental health services for ethnic minority groups (Lee & Ramirez, 2000; Worthington, Soth-McNett, & Moreno, 2007). The data are ambiguous for a couple of ethnic groups, but studies suggest that North American minority groups generally underutilize therapeutic services (Bender et al., 2007; Folsom et al., 2007; Sue et al., 2009). Why? A variety of barriers appear to contribute to this problem, including the following (Snowden & Yamada, 2005; U.S. Department of Health and Human Services, 1999; Zane et al., 2004):

1. *Cultural barriers.* In times of psychological distress, some cultural groups are reluctant to turn to formal, professional sources of assistance. Given their socialization, they prefer to rely on informal assistance from family members, the clergy, respected elders, herbalists, acupuncturists, and so forth, who share their cultural heritage. Many members of minority groups have a history of frustrating interactions with bureaucracies and are distrustful of large, intimidating, foreign institutions, such as hospitals and community mental health centres (Pierce, 1992). We know, for example, that Asian Canadians, especially Chinese Canadians, are much less likely to use and access mental health services (Chen, Kazanjian, Wong, & Goldner, 2010; Tiwari & Wang, 2008). These groups are much more likely to shelter those family members who suffer from mental illness and to use family resources instead (Li & Browne, 2000; Naidoo, 1992; Peters, 1988). When they do see a professional, Asian Canadians are more likely to emphasize and report somatic or physical symptoms than emotional symptoms. Once again, this may be because of stigmas against admitting *psychological* illness in these communities (Lee, Lei, & Sue, 2001; Ryder et al., 2008). If you can make the illness *physical*, that is much more acceptable. In many cases, those suffering from psychological disorders are hidden from view because of these stigmas.

2. *Language barriers.* Effective communication is crucial to the provision of psychotherapy, yet most hospitals and mental health agencies are not adequately staffed with therapists who speak the languages used by minority groups in their service areas. The resulting communication problems make

Treatment of Psychological Disorders

WEB LINK 15.9

Aboriginal Mental Health Research Team
This McGill University–based group brings together community members (e.g., the Nunavik Regional Board of Health and Social Services, the Cree Board of Health and Social Services, the Native Friendship Centre of Montreal, the Native Women's Shelter of Montreal, and the Aboriginal Healing Foundation) in partnership with mental health professionals to implement Aboriginal concerns in the mental health system.

it awkward and difficult for many minority group members to explain their problems and to obtain the type of help that they need.

3. *Institutional barriers.* When all is said and done, Stanley Sue and Nolan Zane (1987) argue that the "single most important explanation for the problems in service delivery involves the inability of therapists to provide culturally responsive forms of treatment" (p. 37). The vast majority of therapists have been trained almost exclusively in the treatment of white, middle-class clients and are not familiar with the cultural backgrounds and unique characteristics of various ethnic groups. This culture gap often leads to misunderstandings, ill-advised treatment strategies, and reduced rapport. Unfortunately, there is a grievous shortage of ethnic therapists to meet the needs of various ethnic groups (Mays & Albee, 1992).

Issues concerning diversity are of clear relevance to the Canadian context. Canada is a true multicultural society in which diversity is highlighted and championed. In fact, approximately one in six people in Canada is an immigrant, born outside Canada (Government of Canada, 2006). To get a sense of the extent of diversity in Canada, all you have to do is to look around you in your classroom at the diversity represented by your peers. Nowhere is this diversity more evident than in Toronto. Maxine Wintre and her colleagues recently surveyed 1071 first-year undergraduates in Toronto concerning diversity issues and found that they represented 94 countries of origin, 69 languages spoken at home, and personal identifications with an amazing 203 cultural or ethnic groups (Wintre et al., 2000). When immigrant groups come to Canada, they are frequently met by a host of misconceptions and stereotypes such as those chronicled by the University of Toronto's Morton Beiser in his book on the "boat people's" first ten years in Canada (Beiser, 1999).

To treat their clients appropriately and effectively, clinicians need to be sensitive to diverse cultural conventions and sensitivities. This may be especially important with First Nations peoples. We saw in previous chapters that the suicide rate in some Aboriginal communities is extremely high, and these high suicide rates are accompanied by high rates of psychological disorders. In a study of First Nations, Métis, and Inuit peoples of Canada, McGill University's Laurence Kirmayer and his colleagues found elevated levels of many disorders and problems, including substance abuse, depression, violence, and suicide (Kirmayer, Brass, & Tait, 2000). The authors note that indigenous healing practices, often called *pan-Amerindian* healing movements, are increasingly visible and popular in Aboriginal

treatment centres. They also note that therapy settings that fail to take into account indigenous experience are not effective: "In most urban areas, mental health services have not adapted well to the needs of Aboriginal clients and this is reflected in low rates of use" (Kirmayer, Brass, & Tait, 2000, p. 612).

What can be done to improve mental health services for minority groups? Researchers in this area have offered a variety of suggestions (Hong, Garcia, & Soriano, 2000; Miranda et al., 2005; Pedersen, 1994; Yamamoto et al., 1993). Discussions of possible solutions usually begin with the need to recruit and train more ethnic minority therapists. Studies show that ethnic minorities are more likely to go to mental health facilities that are staffed by a higher proportion of people who share their ethnic background (Snowden & Hu, 1996; Sue, Zane, & Young, 1994). Individual therapists have been urged to work harder at building a vigorous *therapeutic alliance* (a strong supportive bond) with their ethnic minority clients. A strong therapeutic alliance is associated with better therapeutic outcomes regardless of ethnicity, but some studies suggest that it is especially crucial for minority clients (Bender et al., 2007; Comas-Diaz, 2006).

Finally, most authorities urge further investigation of how traditional approaches to therapy can be modified and tailored to be more compatible with specific cultural groups' attitudes, values, norms, and traditions (Hwang, 2006). A recent review of 76 studies that examined the effects of culturally adapted interventions found clear evidence that this tailoring process tends to yield positive effects

---

REVIEW OF KEY POINTS

▷ Combinations of insight, behavioural, and biomedical therapies are often used fruitfully in the treatment of psychological disorders. For example, our Featured Study showed how the tandem of interpersonal therapy and antidepressant medication could be valuable in preventing additional depressive episodes in an elderly population. Many modern therapists are eclectic, using specific ideas, techniques, and strategies gleaned from a number of theoretical approaches.

▷ The highly culture-bound origins of Western therapies have raised doubts about their applicability to other cultures and even to ethnic groups in Western society. Because of cultural, language, and access barriers, therapeutic services are underutilized by ethnic minorities in Canada.

▷ More culturally responsive approaches to treatment will require more minority therapists, special training for therapists, and additional investigation of how traditional therapies can be tailored to be more compatible with specific ethnic groups' cultural heritage.

(Griner & Smith, 2006). The benefits are particularly prominent when a treatment is tailored to a single, specific cultural group rather than a mixture of several or more cultural groups.

According to the University of Calgary's Meyen Hertzsprung and Keith Dobson, past president of the Canadian Psychological Association, while there are a host of arguments for incorporating diversity issues into clinical psychology training in Canada, the process has been slow and difficult. In a survey examining the extent of diversity training in clinical programs in Canada, Hertzsprung and Dobson (2000) conclude that while clear progress has been made, much more needs to be done in this area: "Indeed, there is a need for further *indigenous* research on diversity issues in Canada, which has a unique history, population composition, and cultural base" (p. 190).

Institutional Treatment in Transition

Traditionally, much of the treatment of mental illness has been carried out in institutional settings, primarily in mental hospitals. A *mental hospital* is a medical institution specializing in providing inpatient care for psychological disorders. In the United States, a national network of state-funded mental hospitals started to emerge in the 1840s through the efforts of Dorothea Dix and other reformers (see Figure 15.14). Prior to these reforms, the mentally ill who were poor were housed in jails and poorhouses or were left to wander the countryside. Dorothea Dix also played an important role in the treatment of those suffering from psychological disorders in Canada (Goldman, 1990).

Sable Island, a remote island 300 kilometres offshore from Halifax, once was a place where some Nova Scotians sent their relatives—often without their consent—who suffered from psychological disorders. Dorothea Dix often spent her summers in Halifax, where she heard about what were referred to at the time as the "banished lunatics," so she set sail for Sable Island to see things for herself (Goldman, 1990). At the time, Nova Scotia was the only Canadian province without a major psychiatric hospital. Dix advocated for a psychiatric hospital before the Nova Scotia legislature and even selected the Sable Island site. It opened on December 26, 1857.

Dix was not a woman to leave things unattended to—after noticing the inadequate life-saving resources available on Sable Island to rescue the victims of shipwrecks, she also raised money and purchased lifeboats for the island. Dix was also credited with helping to establish the psychiatric hospital in St. John's, Newfoundland, employing there, as elsewhere, her formidable skills in persuasion and fundraising.

Today, mental hospitals continue to play an important role in the delivery of mental health services. However, since World War II, institutional care for mental illness has undergone a series of major transitions—and the dust hasn't settled yet. Let's look at how institutional care has evolved in recent decades.

Disenchantment with Mental Hospitals

By the 1950s, it had become apparent that public mental hospitals were not fulfilling their goals very well (Mechanic, 1980; Menninger, 2005). Experts began to realize that hospitalization often *contributed* to the development of pathology instead of curing it.

What were the causes of these unexpected negative effects? Part of the problem was that the facilities were usually underfunded (Hogan & Morrison, 2008), which meant that the facilities were overcrowded and understaffed. Hospital personnel were undertrained

PREVIEW QUESTIONS

▶ What led to the community mental health movement?

▶ What is deinstitutionalization, and what problems has it been blamed for?

▶ Is increased homelessness a mental health problem or an economic problem?

Culver Pictures, Inc.

FIGURE 15.14

Dorothea Dix and the advent of mental hospitals in North America.

During the 19th century, Dorothea Dix (inset) campaigned tirelessly to obtain funds for building mental hospitals in the United States and in some parts of Canada. Many of these hospitals were extremely large facilities. Although public mental hospitals improved the care of the mentally ill, they had a variety of shortcomings, which eventually prompted the deinstitutionalization movement.

Source: Inset: photo by Ken Smith/LLR Collection. Main Painting: Culver Pictures, Inc.

and overworked, making them hard-pressed to deliver minimal custodial care. Despite gallant efforts at treatment, the demoralizing conditions made most public mental hospitals decidedly nontherapeutic (Scull, 1990). These problems were aggravated by the fact that mental hospitals served large geographic regions, resulting in the fact that many patients were uprooted from their communities and isolated from their social support networks.

Disenchantment with the public mental hospital system inspired the *community mental health movement* that emerged in the 1960s (Duckworth & Borus, 1999; Huey, Ford et al., 2009). The community mental health movement emphasizes (1) local, community-based care, (2) reduced dependence on hospitalization, and (3) the prevention of psychological disorders. Thus, in the 1960s much of the responsibility for the treatment of psychological disorders was turned over to community mental health centres, which supplement mental hospitals with decentralized and more accessible services.

Deinstitutionalization

Mental hospitals continue to care for many people troubled by chronic mental illness, but their role in patient care has diminished. Since the 1960s, a policy of deinstitutionalization has been followed in Canada, the United States, and most other Western countries (Fakhoury & Priebe, 2002). *Deinstitutionalization refers to transferring the treatment of mental illness from inpatient institutions to community-based facilities that emphasize outpatient care.* This shift in responsibility was made possible by two developments: (1) the emergence of effective drug therapies for severe disorders and (2) the deployment of community mental health centres to coordinate local care (Goff & Gudeman, 1999).

The exodus of patients from mental hospitals has been dramatic. In the United States, the average inpatient population in state and county mental hospitals dropped from a peak of nearly 550 000 in the mid-1950s to around 70 000 in the late 1990s. Similar trends have been observed in Canada. In their analysis of 40 years of deinstitutionalization in Canada, Patricia Sealy and Paul Whitehead of the University of Western Ontario note that deinstitutionalization is not just an event that took place in the 1960s—it has been continuous for the past four decades (Sealy & Whitehead, 2004). The number of beds in psychiatric hospitals per 100 000 population fell from four to one between 1964 and 1981, with Alberta and Quebec leading in the closings (Sealy & Whitehead, 2004).

These trends, however, do not mean that hospitalization for mental illness has become a thing of the past. A great many people are still hospitalized, but there's been a shift toward placing them in local general hospitals for brief periods instead of distant psychiatric hospitals for long periods (Hogan & Morrison, 2008). When people are admitted to psychiatric hospitals or specialized units, they tend to stay for shorter periods of time. In Canada, the length of stay in psychiatric hospitals and in psychiatric units in general hospitals has decreased dramatically since 1985. In keeping with the philosophy of deinstitutionalization, these local facilities try to get patients stabilized and back into the community as swiftly as possible.

How has deinstitutionalization worked out? It gets mixed reviews. On the positive side, many people have benefited by avoiding or shortening disruptive and unnecessary hospitalization. Ample evidence suggests that alternatives to hospitalization can be both as effective as and less costly than inpatient care (McGrew et al., 1999; Reinharz, Lesage, & Contandriopoulos, 2000). Moreover, follow-up studies of discharged patients reveal that a substantial majority prefer the greater freedom provided by community-based treatment (Leff, Trieman, & Gooch, 1996).

Nonetheless, some unanticipated problems have arisen (Elpers, 2000; Munk-Jorgensen, 1999; Talbott, 2004). Many patients suffering from chronic psychological disorders had nowhere to go when they were released. They had no families, friends, or homes to return to. Many had no work skills and were poorly prepared to live on their own. These people were supposed to be absorbed by "halfway houses," sheltered workshops, and other types of intermediate care facilities. Unfortunately, many communities were never able to fund and build the planned facilities (Hogan & Morrison, 2008; Lamb, 1998). Thus, deinstitutionalization left two major problems in its wake: a "revolving door" population of people who flow in and out of psychiatric facilities, and a sizable population of homeless mentally ill people.

Mental Illness, the Revolving Door, and Homelessness

Although the proportion of hospital days attributable to mental illness has dwindled, admission rates for psychiatric hospitalization have actually climbed. What has happened? Deinstitutionalization and drug therapy have created a revolving door through which many mentally ill people pass again and again (Geller, 1992; Langdon et al., 2001).

Most of the people caught in the mental health system's revolving door suffer from chronic, severe disorders that frequently require hospitalization (Haywood et al., 1995). They respond well to drug therapies in the hospital, but once they're stabilized through drug therapy, they no longer qualify for expensive hospital treatment according to the new standards created by deinstitutionalization. Thus, they're sent back out the door, into communities that often aren't prepared to provide adequate outpatient care. Because they lack appropriate care and support, their condition deteriorates and they soon require readmission to a hospital, where the cycle begins once again. Over two-thirds of all psychiatric inpatient admissions involve rehospitalizing a former patient. In addition, many end up in prisons. Over 500 000 mentally ill American men and women are currently serving time in jails and prisons. This phenomenon was detailed in a PBS documentary entitled *The New Asylums* (Navasky & O'Connor, 2005).

Deinstitutionalization has also been blamed for the growing population of homeless people. Studies have consistently found elevated rates of mental illness among the homeless. Taken as a whole, the evidence suggests that roughly one-third of the homeless suffer from severe mental illness (schizophrenic and mood disorders), that another one-third or more are struggling with alcohol and drug problems, that many qualify for multiple diagnoses,

and that the prevalence of mental illness among the homeless may be increasing (Bassuk et al., 1998; Folsom et al., 2005; North et al., 2004).

Ultimately, it's clear that our society is not providing adequate care for a sizable segment of the mentally ill population (Appelbaum, 2002; Elpers, 2000; Gittelman, 2005; Torrey, 1996). That's not a new development. Inadequate care for mental illness has always been the norm. Societies always struggle with the problem of what to do with the mentally ill and how to pay for their care (Duckworth & Borus, 1999). Ours is no different. Unfortunately, in recent years the situation has deteriorated rather than improved. Although overall health-care spending has been increasing steadily in recent years, funding for mental health care has diminished dramatically across North America (Geller, 2009). The number of beds in general hospitals dedicated to psychiatric care has declined precipitously since the late 1990s (Liptzin, Gottlieb, & Summergrad, 2007). Today, provinces in Canada and U.S. states have a shortage of psychiatric beds, resulting in waiting lists for admission, overcrowding, and increasingly brief hospitalizations (Geller, 2009).

Putting It in Perspective: Themes 2 and 5

In our discussion of psychotherapy, one of our unifying themes—the value of theoretical diversity—was particularly prominent, and one other theme—the importance of culture—surfaced briefly. Let's discuss the latter theme first. The approaches to treatment described in this chapter are products of modern, white, middle-class, Western culture. Some of these therapies have proven useful in some other cultures, but many have turned out to be irrelevant or counterproductive when used with different cultural groups, including ethnic minorities in Western society. Thus, we have seen once again that cultural factors influence psychological processes and that Western psychology cannot assume that its theories and practices have universal applicability.

As for theoretical diversity, its value can be illustrated with a rhetorical question: Can you imagine what the state of modern psychotherapy would be if everyone in psychology and psychiatry had simply accepted Freud's theories about the nature and treatment of psychological disorders? If not for theoretical diversity, psychotherapy might still be in the dark ages. Psychoanalysis can be a useful method of therapy, but it would be a tragic state of affairs if it were the *only* treatment available. Multitudes of people have benefited from alternative approaches to treatment that emerged out of tensions between psychoanalytic theory and other theoretical perspectives. People have diverse problems, rooted in varied origins, that call

for the pursuit of different therapeutic goals. Thus, it's fortunate that people can choose from a diverse array of approaches to treatment. The graphic overview on pages 724–725 summarizes and compares the approaches that we've discussed in this chapter. This illustrated overview shows that each of the major approaches to treatment has its own vision of the nature of human discontent and the ideal remedy.

Of course, diversity can be confusing. The range and variety of available treatments in modern psychotherapy leave many people puzzled about their options. So, in our Personal Application, we'll sort through the practical issues involved in selecting a therapist.

PREVIEW QUESTIONS

► How did this chapter illustrate the importance of cultural factors?

► How did this chapter illustrate the value of theoretical diversity?

REVIEW OF KEY POINTS

▷ Disenchantment with the negative effects of psychiatric hospitals led to the advent of more localized community mental health centres and a policy of deinstitutionalization. Long-term hospitalization for mental disorders is largely a thing of the past.

▷ Unfortunately, deinstitutionalization has left some unanticipated problems in its wake, including the revolving door problem and increased homelessness, although some theorists argue that homelessness is primarily an economic problem.

▷ Our discussion of psychotherapy highlighted the value of theoretical diversity. Conflicting theoretical orientations have generated varied approaches to treatment. Our coverage of therapy also showed once again that cultural factors shape psychological processes.

Looking for a Therapist

Answer the following "true" or "false."

___ **1** Psychotherapy is an art as well as a science.

___ **2** Psychotherapy can be harmful or damaging to a client.

___ **3** Psychotherapy does not have to be expensive.

___ **4** The type of professional degree that a therapist holds is relatively unimportant.

All of these statements are true. Do any of them surprise you? If so, you're in good company. Many people know relatively little about the practicalities of selecting a therapist.

The task of finding an appropriate therapist is complex. Should you see a psychologist or a psychiatrist? Should you opt for individual therapy or group therapy? Should you see a client-centred therapist or a behaviour therapist? The unfortunate part of this situation is that people seeking psychotherapy often feel overwhelmed by personal problems. The last thing they need is to be confronted by yet another complex problem.

Nonetheless, the importance of finding a good therapist cannot be overestimated. Treatment can sometimes have harmful rather than helpful effects. We have already discussed how drug therapies and ECT can sometimes be damaging, but problems are not limited to these interventions. Talking about your problems with a therapist may sound pretty harmless, but studies indicate that insight therapies can also backfire (Lambert & Ogles, 2004; Lilienfeld, 2007). Although a great many talented therapists are available, psychotherapy, like any other profession, has incompetent practitioners as well. Therefore, you should shop for a skilled therapist, just as you would for a good lawyer or a good mechanic.

In this Application, we'll go over some information that should be helpful if you ever have to look for a therapist for yourself or for a friend or family member (based on Beutler, Bongar, & Shurkin, 1998; Bruckner-Gordon, Gangi, & Wallman, 1988; Ehrenberg & Ehrenberg, 1994; Pittman, 1994).

Where Do You Find Therapeutic Services?

Psychotherapy can be found in a variety of settings. Contrary to general belief, most therapists are not in private practice. Many work in institutional settings such as community mental health centres, hospitals, and human service agencies. The principal sources of therapeutic services are described in Table 15.2. The exact configuration of therapeutic services available will vary from one community to another. To find out what your community has to offer, it is a good idea to consult your friends, your local phone book, or your local community mental health centre.

Is the Therapist's Profession or Sex Important?

Psychotherapists may be trained in psychology, psychiatry, social work, counselling, psychiatric nursing, or marriage and family therapy. Researchers have *not* found any reliable association between therapists' professional background and therapeutic efficacy (Beutler et al., 2004), probably because many talented therapists can be found in all of these professions. Thus, the kind of degree that a therapist holds doesn't need to be a crucial consideration in your selection process. At the present time, it is true that psychiatrists are the only type of therapist who can prescribe drugs. However, other types of therapists can refer you to a psychiatrist if they think that drug therapy would be helpful.

Whether a therapist's sex is important depends on your attitude (Nadelson, Notman, & McCarthy, 2005). If *you* feel that

TABLE 15.2

Principal Sources of Therapeutic Services

Source	Comments
Private practitioners	Self-employed therapists are listed in the Yellow Pages under their professional category, such as psychologists or psychiatrists. Private practitioners tend to be relatively expensive, but they also tend to be highly experienced therapists.
Community mental health centres	Community mental health centres have salaried psychologists, psychiatrists, mental health and social workers on staff. The centres provide a variety of services and often have staff available on weekends and at night to deal with emergencies.
Hospitals	Several kinds of hospitals provide therapeutic services. There are both public and private mental hospitals that specialize in the care of people with psychological disorders. Many general hospitals have a psychiatric ward, and those that do not usually have psychiatrists and psychologists on staff and on call. Although hospitals tend to concentrate on inpatient treatment, many provide outpatient therapy as well.
Human service agencies	Various social service agencies employ therapists to provide short-term counselling. Depending on your community, you may find agencies that deal with family problems, juvenile problems, drug problems, and so forth.
Schools and workplaces	Most high schools, colleges, and universities have counselling centres where students can get help with personal problems. Similarly, some large businesses offer in-house counselling to their employees.

we mentioned earlier, provincial health-care programs often cover the services of a psychiatrist, but the services of psychologists in private practice are not universally covered.

Is the Therapist's Theoretical Approach Important?

Logically, you might expect that the diverse approaches to therapy vary in effectiveness. For the most part, this is *not* what researchers find, however. After reviewing many studies of therapeutic efficacy, Jerome Frank (1961) and Lester Luborsky and his colleagues (Luborsky, Singer, & Luborsky, 1975) both quote the dodo bird who has just judged a race in *Alice in Wonderland*: "*Everybody* has won, and *all* must have prizes." Improvement rates for various theoretical orientations are fairly similar according to most studies (Lambert, Bergin, & Garfield, 2004; Luborsky et al., 2002; Wampold, 2001; see Figure 15.15).

However, these findings are a little misleading, as the estimates of overall effectiveness have been averaged across many types of patients and many types of problems. Most experts seem to think that *for certain types of problems, some approaches to therapy are more effective than others* (Beutler, 2002; Crits-Christoph, 1997; Norcross, 1995). For example, Martin Seligman (1995) asserts that panic disorders respond best to cognitive therapy, that specific phobias are most amenable to treatment with systematic desensitization, and that obsessive-compulsive disorders are best treated with behaviour therapy or medication. So, for a specific type of problem, a therapist's theoretical approach *may* make a difference.

It is also important to point out that the finding that different approaches to therapy are roughly equal in overall efficacy does not mean that all *therapists* are created equal. Some therapists unquestionably are more effective than others. However, these variations in effectiveness appear to depend on individual therapists' personal skills rather than on their theoretical orientation (Beutler et al., 2004). Good, bad, and mediocre therapists are found within each school of thought. Indeed, the tremendous variation among individual therapists, in

Finding the right therapist is no easy task. You need to take into account the therapist's training and orientation, fees charged, and personality. An initial visit should give you a good idea of what a particular therapist is like.

the therapist's sex is important, then for you it is. The therapeutic relationship must be characterized by trust and rapport. Feeling uncomfortable with a therapist of one sex or the other could inhibit the therapeutic process. Hence, you should feel free to look for a male or female therapist if you prefer to do so. This point is probably most relevant to female clients whose troubles may be related to the extensive sexism in our society (A. G. Kaplan, 1985). It is entirely reasonable for women to seek a therapist with a feminist perspective if that would make them feel more comfortable.

Speaking of sex, you should be aware that sexual exploitation is an occasional problem in the context of therapy. Studies indicate that a small minority of therapists take advantage of their clients sexually (Pope, Keith-Spiegel, & Tabachnick, 1986). These incidents almost always involve a male therapist making advances to a female client. The available evidence indicates that these sexual liaisons are usually very harmful to clients (Gabbard, 1994; Williams, 1992). There are absolutely no situations in which therapist–client sexual relations are an ethical therapeutic practice. If a therapist makes sexual advances, a client should terminate treatment.

Is Treatment Always Expensive?

Psychotherapy does not have to be prohibitively expensive. Private practitioners tend to be the most expensive, charging between $75 and $200 per (50-minute) hour. These fees may seem high, but they are in line with those of similar professionals, such as dentists and lawyers. Community mental health centres and social service agencies are usually supported by tax dollars. And as

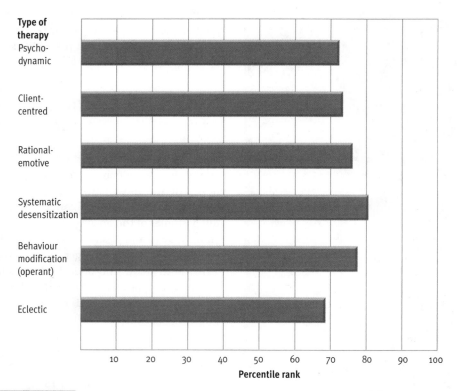

Type of therapy									

Psycho-dynamic

Client-centred

Rational-emotive

Systematic desensitization

Behaviour modification (operant)

Eclectic

10 20 30 40 50 60 70 80 90 100
Percentile rank

FIGURE 15.15

Estimates of the effectiveness of various approaches to psychotherapy.

Smith and Glass (1977) reviewed nearly 400 studies in which clients who were treated with a specific type of therapy were compared with a control group made up of individuals with similar problems who went untreated. The bars indicate the percentile rank (on outcome measures) attained by the average client treated with each type of therapy when compared to control subjects. The higher the percentile, the more effective the therapy was. As you can see, the various approaches were fairly similar in their overall effectiveness.

Source: Adapted from Smith, M.L., and Glass, G.V. (1977). Meta-analysis of psychotherapy outcome series. *American Psychologist, 32*, 752–760. Copyright © 1977 by the American Psychological Association. Adapted by permission of the author.

Therapy is both a science and an art. It is scientific in that practitioners are guided in their work by a huge body of empirical research. It is an art in that therapists often have to be creative in adapting their treatment procedures to individual patients and their idiosyncrasies.

skills, may be one of the main reasons why it is hard to find efficacy differences between theoretical approaches to therapy (Staines, 2008).

The key point is that effective therapy requires skill and creativity. Arnold Lazarus, who devised multimodal therapy, emphasizes that therapists "straddle the fence between science and art." Therapy is scientific in that interventions are based on extensive theory and empirical research (Forsyth & Strong, 1986). Ultimately, though, each client is a unique human being, and the therapist has to creatively fashion a treatment program that will help that individual (Goodheart, 2006).

What Should You Look for in a Prospective Therapist?

Some clients are timid about asking prospective therapists questions about their training, approach, fees, and so forth. However, these are reasonable questions, and the vast majority of therapists will be most accommodating in providing answers. Usually, you can ask your preliminary questions over the phone. If things seem promising, you may decide to make an appointment for an interview (for which you will probably have to pay). In this interview, the therapist will gather more information to determine the likelihood of helping you, given his or her training and approach to treatment. At the same time, you should be making a similar judgment about whether you believe the therapist can help you with your problems.

What should you look for? First, you should look for personal warmth and sincere concern. Try to judge whether you will be able to talk to this person in a candid, nondefensive way. Second, look for empathy and understanding. Is the person capable of appreciating your point of view? Third, look for self-confidence. Self-assured therapists will communicate a sense of competence without trying to intimidate you with jargon or boasting needlessly about what they can do for you. When all is said and done, you should *like* your therapist. Otherwise, it will be difficult to establish the needed rapport.

Given the very real possibility that poor progress may be due to resistance, you should not be too quick to leave therapy when dissatisfied. However, it *is* possible that your therapist isn't sufficiently skilled or that the two of you are incompatible. So, after careful and deliberate consideration, you should feel free to terminate your therapy.

What Should You Expect from Therapy?

It is important to have realistic expectations about therapy, or you may be unnecessarily disappointed. Some people expect miracles. They expect to turn their lives around quickly with little effort. Others expect their therapist to run their lives for them. These are unrealistic expectations.

Therapy is usually a slow process. Your problems are not likely to melt away quickly. Moreover, therapy is hard work, and your therapist is only a facilitator. Ultimately, *you* have to confront the challenge of changing your behaviour, your feelings, or your personality. This process may not be pleasant. You may have to face up to some painful truths about yourself. As Ehrenberg and Ehrenberg (1986) point out, "Psychotherapy takes time, effort, and courage."

REVIEW OF KEY POINTS

▷ Therapeutic services are available in many settings, and such services need not be expensive. Both excellent and mediocre therapists can be found in all of the mental health professions. So, therapists' personal skills are more important than their professional degrees.

▷ The various theoretical approaches to therapy appear to be fairly similar in overall effectiveness. However, for certain types of problems, some approaches are probably more effective than others, and all therapists are not created equal.

▷ In selecting a therapist, warmth, empathy, confidence, and likeability are desirable traits, and it is reasonable to insist on a therapist of one sex or the other. If progress is slow, your own resistance may be the problem.

From Crisis to Wellness—But Was It the Therapy?

It often happens this way. Problems seem to go from bad to worse—the trigger could be severe pressures at work, an acrimonious fight with your spouse, or a child's unruly behaviour spiralling out of control. At some point, you recognize that it might be prudent to seek professional assistance from a therapist, but where do you turn?

If you are like most people, you will probably hesitate before actively seeking professional help. People hesitate because therapy carries a stigma, because the task of finding a therapist is daunting, and because they hope that their psychological problems will clear up on their own—which *does* happen with some regularity. When people finally decide to pursue mental health care, it is often because they feel like they have reached rock bottom in terms of their functioning and they have no choice. Motivated by their crisis, they enter into treatment, looking for a ray of hope. Will therapy help them to feel better?

It may surprise you to learn that the answer *generally* would be "yes," even if professional treatment itself were utterly worthless and totally ineffectual. There are two major reasons that people entering therapy are likely to get better, regardless of whether their treatment is effective. You can probably guess one of these reasons, which has been mentioned repeatedly in the chapter: the power of the *placebo*. *Placebo effects* occur when people's expectations lead them to experience some change even though they receive a fake treatment (like being given a sugar pill instead of a real drug). Clients generally enter therapy with expectations that it will have positive effects, and as we have emphasized throughout this text, *people have a remarkable tendency to see what they expect to see.* Because of this factor, studies of the efficacy of medical drugs always include a placebo condition in which subjects are given fake medication (see Chapter 2). Researchers are often quite surprised by just how much the placebo subjects improve (Fisher & Greenberg, 1997; Walsh et al., 2002). Placebo effects can be very powerful and should be taken into consideration whenever efforts are made to evaluate the efficacy of some approach to treatment.

The other factor at work is the main focus in this Application. It is an interesting statistical phenomenon that we have not discussed previously: *regression toward the mean*. *Regression toward the mean* occurs when people who score extremely high or low on some trait are measured a second time and their new scores fall closer to the mean (average). Regression effects work in both directions: On the second measurement, high scorers tend to fall back toward the mean and low scorers tend to creep upward toward the mean. For example, let's say we wanted to evaluate the effectiveness of a one-day coaching program intended to improve performance on a new high school math test. We reason that coaching is most likely to help students who have performed poorly on the test, so we recruit a sample of participants who have previously scored in the bottom 20 percent on the test. Thanks to regression toward the mean, most of these students will score higher if they take that test a second time, so our coaching program may *look* effective even if it has no value.

By the way, if we set out to see whether our coaching program could increase the performance of high scorers, regression effects would be working *against* us. If we recruited a sample of students who had scored in the upper 20 percent on the math test, there would be a tendency for their scores to move downward when tested a second time, which could cancel out most or all of the beneficial effects of the coaching program. The processes underlying regression toward the mean are complex matters of probability, but they can be approximated by a simple principle: If you are near the bottom, there's almost nowhere to go but up, and if you are near the top, there's almost nowhere to go but down.

What does all of this have to do with the effects of professional treatment for psychological problems and disorders? Well, chance variations in the ups and downs of life occur for all of us. But recall that most people enter psychotherapy during a time of severe crisis, when they are at a really low point in their lives. If you measure the mental health of a group of people entering therapy, they will mostly get relatively low scores. If you measure their mental health again a few months later, chances are that most of them will score higher—with or without therapy—because of regression toward the mean. This is not a matter of idle speculation. Studies of untreated subjects demonstrate that poor scores on measures of mental health regress toward the mean when participants are assessed a second time (Flett, Vredenburg, & Krames, 1995; L. M. Hsu, 1995).

Does the fact that most people will get better even without therapy mean that there is no sound evidence that psychotherapy works? No, regression effects, along with placebo effects, do create major headaches for researchers evaluating the efficacy of various therapies, but these problems *can* be circumvented. Control groups, random assignment, placebo conditions,

Placebo effects and regression toward the mean are two prominent factors that make it difficult to evaluate the efficacy of various approaches to therapy.

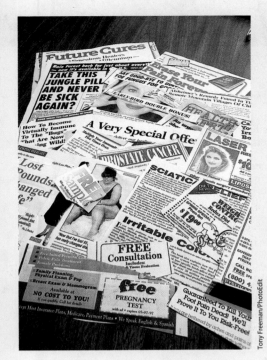

In North American society, we are frequently exposed to claims of programs that will improve our wellness. Rigorous and systematic scientific research is the only way to verify these claims.

Tony Freeman/PhotoEdit

and statistical adjustments can be used to control for regression and placebo effects, as well as for other threats to validity. As discussed in the main body of the chapter, researchers have accumulated rigorous evidence that most approaches to therapy have demonstrated efficacy. However, our discussion of placebo and regression effects shows you some of the factors that make this type of research far more complicated and challenging than might be anticipated.

Recognizing how regression toward the mean can occur in a variety of contexts is an important critical thinking skill, so let's look at some additional examples. Think about an outstanding young pro baseball player who has a fabulous first season and is named "Rookie of the Year." What sort of performance would you predict for this athlete for the next year? Before you make your prediction, think about regression toward the mean. Statistically speaking, our Rookie of the Year is likely to perform well above average the next year, but not as well as he did in his first year. If you are a sports fan, you may recognize this pattern as the "sophomore slump." Many sports columnists have written about the sophomore slump, which they typically blame on the athlete's personality or motivation ("He got lazy," "He got cocky," "The money and fame went to his head," and so forth). A simple appeal to regression toward the mean could explain this sort of outcome, with no need to denigrate the personality or motivation of the athlete. Of course, sometimes the Rookie of the Year performs even better during his second year. Thus, our baseball example can be used to emphasize an important point: Regression toward the mean is not an inevitability. It is a statistical tendency that predicts what will happen far more often than not, but it is merely a matter of probability—which means it is a much more reliable principle when applied to groups (say, the top ten rookies in a specific year) rather than to individuals.

Let's return to the world of therapy for one last thought about the significance of both regression and placebo effects. Over the years, a host of quacks, charlatans, con artists, herbalists, and faith healers have marketed and sold an endless array of worthless treatments for both psychological problems and physical maladies. In many instances, people who have been treated with these phony therapies have expressed satisfaction or even praise and gratitude. For instance, you may have heard someone sincerely rave about some herbal remedy or psychic advice that you were pretty sure was really worthless. If so, you were probably puzzled by their glowing testimonials. Well, you now have two highly plausible explanations for why people can honestly believe that they have derived great benefit from harebrained, bogus treatments: placebo effects and regression effects. The people who provide testimonials for worthless treatments may have experienced *genuine* improvements in their conditions, but those improvements were probably the results of placebo effects and regression toward the mean. Placebo and regression effects add to the many reasons that you should always be skeptical about anecdotal evidence. And they help explain why charlatans can be so successful and why unsound, ineffective treatments can have sincere proponents.

TABLE 15.3	Critical Thinking Skills Discussed in This Application
Skill	**Description**
Recognizing situations in which placebo effects might occur	The critical thinker understands that if people have expectations that a treatment will produce a certain effect, they may experience that effect even if the treatment was fake or ineffectual.
Recognizing situations in which regression toward the mean may occur	The critical thinker understands that when people are selected for their extremely high or low scores on some trait, their subsequent scores will probably fall closer to the mean.
Recognizing the limitations of anecdotal evidence	The critical thinker is wary of anecdotal evidence, which consists of personal stories used to support one's assertions. Anecdotal evidence tends to be unrepresentative, inaccurate, and unreliable.

Key Ideas

The Elements of the Treatment Process

● Approaches to treatment are diverse, but they can be grouped into three categories: insight therapies, behaviour therapies, and biomedical therapies.

● Therapists come from a variety of professional backgrounds. Clinical and counselling psychologists, psychiatrists, clinical social workers, psychiatric nurses, counsellors, and marriage and family therapists are key providers of therapeutic services.

Insight Therapies

● Insight therapies involve verbal interactions intended to enhance self-knowledge. In psychoanalysis, free association and dream analysis are used to explore the unconscious. When an analyst's probing hits sensitive areas, resistance can be expected.

● The transference relationship may be used to overcome this resistance so that the client can handle interpretations that lead to insight. Classical psychoanalysis is not widely practised anymore, but Freud's legacy lives on in a rich diversity of modern psychodynamic therapies.

● The client-centred therapist tries to provide a supportive climate in which clients can restructure their self-concept. The process of therapy emphasizes clarification of the client's feelings and self-acceptance.

● Most theoretical approaches to insight therapy have been adapted for use with groups. Evaluating the effectiveness of any approach to treatment is complex and difficult. Nonetheless, the weight of the evidence suggests that insight therapies are superior to no treatment or placebo treatment. Studies suggest that common factors make a significant contribution to the benefits of various therapies.

Behaviour Therapies

● Behaviour therapies use the principles of learning in direct efforts to change specific aspects of behaviour. Wolpe's systematic desensitization is a counter-conditioning treatment for phobias. In aversion therapy, a stimulus associated with an unwanted response is paired with an unpleasant stimulus in an effort to eliminate the maladaptive response.

● Social skills training can improve clients' interpersonal skills through shaping, modelling, and behavioural rehearsal. There is ample evidence that behaviour therapies are effective in the treatment of a wide variety of disorders.

● Beck's cognitive therapy concentrates on changing the way clients think about events in their lives. Cognitive therapists re-educate clients to detect and challenge automatic negative thoughts that cause depression and anxiety. Recently this approach has been coupled with ideas drawn from mindfulness meditation, which is referred to as behavioural.

Biomedical Therapies

● Biomedical therapies are physiological interventions for psychological problems. Antianxiety drugs are used to relieve excessive apprehension. Antipsychotic drugs are used primarily in the treatment of schizophrenia. Antidepressants are used to bring people out of episodes of depression. Bipolar mood disorders are treated with lithium and other mood stabilizers.

● Drug therapies can be quite effective, but they have their drawbacks. All of the drugs produce problematic side effects. The adverse effects of psychiatric drugs may be underestimated because pharmaceutical research is not as impartial as it should be.

● Electroconvulsive therapy (ECT) is used to trigger a cortical seizure that is believed to have therapeutic value for mood disorders, especially depression. There is contradictory evidence about the effectiveness and risks of ECT.

Current Trends and Issues in Treatment

● Combinations of insight, behavioural, and biomedical therapies are often used fruitfully in the treatment of psychological disorders. Many modern therapists are eclectic, using specific ideas, techniques, and strategies gleaned from a number of theoretical approaches.

● Because of cultural, language, and access barriers, therapeutic services are underutilized by ethnic minorities. However, the crux of the problem is the failure of institutions to provide culturally sensitive and responsive forms of treatment for ethnic minorities.

Institutional Treatment in Transition

● Disenchantment with the negative effects of mental hospitals led to the advent of more localized community mental health centres and a policy of deinstitutionalization. Long-term hospitalization for mental disorders is largely a thing of the past.

● Unfortunately, deinstitutionalization has left some unanticipated problems in its wake, such as the revolving door problem and increased homelessness. However, many theorists believe that homelessness is primarily an economic problem.

Putting It in Perspective: Themes 2 and 5

● Our discussion of psychotherapy highlighted the value of theoretical diversity. Conflicting theoretical orientations have generated varied approaches to treatment. Our coverage of therapy also showed once again that cultural factors shape psychological processes.

PERSONAL APPLICATION • Looking for a Therapist

● Therapeutic services are available in many settings, and such services need not be expensive. Excellent therapists and mediocre therapists can be found in all of the mental health professions, using the full range of therapeutic approaches.

● In selecting a therapist, warmth, empathy, confidence, and likability are desirable traits, and it is reasonable to insist on a therapist of one sex or the other. If progress is slow, your own resistance may be the problem.

CRITICAL THINKING APPLICATION • From Crisis to Wellness—But Was It the Therapy?

● People entering therapy are likely to get better even if their treatment is ineffective because of placebo effects and regression toward the mean. Regression toward the mean occurs when people selected for their extremely high or low scores on some trait are measured a second time and their new scores fall closer to the mean. Regression and placebo effects may also help explain why people can often be deceived by phony, ineffectual treatments.

Key Terms

Antianxiety drugs, 716
Antidepressant drugs, 718
Antipsychotic drugs, 717
Aversion therapy, 712
Behaviour therapies, 709
Biomedical therapies, 716
Client-centred therapy, 702
Cognitive-behavioural
  treatments, 713
Cognitive therapy, 713
Couples therapy, 707
Deep brain stimulation (DBS), 723
Deinstitutionalization, 730
Dream analysis, 700
Eclecticism, 727
Electroconvulsive therapy
  (ECT), 721
Exposure therapies, 711
Family therapy, 707
Free association, 700
Group therapy, 706
Insight therapies, 699
Interpretation, 700
Marital therapy, 707
Mental hospital, 729

Mood stabilizers, 720
Placebo effects, 736
Psychiatrists, 698
Psychoanalysis, 700
Psychopharmacotherapy, 716
Regression toward the mean, 736
Resistance, 701
Social skills training, 712
Spontaneous remission, 708
Systematic desensitization, 710
Tardive dyskinesia, 718
Transcranial magnetic stimulation
  (TMS), 722
Transference, 701

Key People

Aaron Beck, 713
Dorothea Dix, 729
Keith Dobson, 729
Hans Eysenck, 709
Sigmund Freud, 697
Les Greenberg, 704
Donald Meichenbaum, 714
Carl Rogers, 702
Zindel Segal, 714
Joseph Wolpe, 710

1. Which of the following describes the goal of behaviour therapy?
   A. to identify the client's unconscious early childhood conflicts that are the source of symptoms
   B. to change the client's thought patterns so that negative emotions can be controlled
   C. to alter the frequency of the client's specific problematic responses by using conditioning techniques
   D. to alter the client's brain chemistry by prescribing specific drugs

2. Which of the following psychotherapeutic professionals is most likely to use a biomedical treatment approach?
   A. clinical psychologist
   B. psychological associate
   C. counselling psychologist
   D. psychiatrist

3. According to Freudian theory, Suzanne behaves seductively toward her therapist because she has an unconscious sexual attraction to her father. Which of the following terms would Freud use to describe Suzanne's behaviour?
   A. resistance
   B. transference
   C. misinterpretation
   D. sublimation

4. Which of the following actions is the key task of the client-centred therapist?
   A. interpret the client's thoughts, feelings, memories, and behaviours
   B. clarify the client's feelings
   C. confront the client's irrational thoughts
   D. modify the client's problematic behaviours

5. A client says he is a failure as a man because his girlfriend left him. The therapist openly challenges him, insisting that he justify his statement with evidence. Which of the following types of therapy is probably being used?
   A. psychodynamic therapy
   B. client-centred therapy
   C. behaviour therapy
   D. cognitive therapy

6. Which of the following statements best represents the findings of effectiveness studies for insight therapy?
   A. Insight therapy is better than no treatment or a placebo treatment.
   B. Individual insight therapy is effective, but group therapy is not.
   C. Group therapy is effective, but individual insight therapy is not.
   D. No treatment or a placebo treatment is better than insight therapy.

7. Systematic desensitization is particularly effective in the treatment of which of the following anxiety disorders?
   A. generalized anxiety disorder
   B. panic disorder
   C. obsessive-compulsive disorder
   D. specific phobia

8. Following her therapist's advice, Linda practises active listening skills in structured role-playing exercises, and then later practises these skills with family members, friends and, finally, her boss. Which of the following approaches is Linda engaged in?
   A. systematic desensitization
   B. biofeedback
   C. a token economy procedure
   D. social skills training

9. Which of the following statements explains why many schizophrenic patients stop taking their antipsychotic medication after they are released from hospital?
   A. Their mental impairment causes them to forget.
   B. The medication causes unpleasant side effects.
   C. Most schizophrenics don't believe they are ill.
   D. The medications are not covered by health insurance plans.

10. Which of the following categories of disorders are often successfully treated with selective serotonin reuptake inhibitors (SSRIs)?
    A. depressive and anxiety disorders
    B. schizophrenia and other psychotic disorders
    C. bipolar disorder and cyclothymia
    D. autism and dissociative disorders

11. Which of the following biomedical therapies is *least* invasive?
    A. deep-brain stimulation
    B. electroconvulsive therapy
    C. transcranial magnetic stimulation
    D. prefrontal leucotomy

12. Which of the following describes the emphasis of the community mental health movement?
    A. segregation of the mentally ill from the general population
    B. increased dependence on long-term inpatient care
    C. local care and the prevention of psychological disorders
    D. focus on, and advocacy for, empirically validated treatments

13. People with mental disorders are frequently released and then readmitted to mental hospitals. Which of the following is an accurate explanation of this 'revolving door' phenomenon?
    A. There are few spaces for long-term inpatient care, so stable patients are released but then deteriorate again due to lack of outpatient care.
    B. Mental-health professionals have a poor record of accurately diagnosing disorders, so patients are not properly treated the first time around.
    C. Mental disorders are never truly cured, but the symptoms of one disorder may be treated only to lead to the emergence of another cluster of symptoms.
    D. Because all mental health treatment is voluntary, patients often sign themselves out before they are ready and then require further treatment.

14. If you were looking for a therapist, which of the following should you focus on to improve the likelihood that therapy will be successful?
    A. Does the therapist have a Ph.D.?
    B. Does the therapist have training in cognitive-behavioural therapy?
    C. Does the therapist have the ability to prescribe medication?
    D. Does the therapist make you feel comfortable?

15. Which of the following statements about bowling scores illustrates the term regression toward the mean?
    A. You get an average bowling score in one game and a superb score in the next game.
    B. You get an average bowling score in one game and a very low score in the next game.
    C. You get an average bowling score in one game and another average score in the next game.
    D. You get a terrible bowling score in one game and an average score in the next game.

See Appendix A for answers to this Practice Test.

On the Web

▶ **CourseMate**

Go to this site to find online resources directly linked to your book, including more quizzes, a glossary, flash cards, videos, and more!

▶ **CengageNow**

Go to this site for the link to CengageNOW™, your one-stop study shop. Take a pre-test for this chapter and CengageNOW™ will generate a personalized study plan based on your test results! The study plan will identify the topics you need to review and direct you to online resources to help you master those topics. You can then take a post-test to help you determine the concepts you have mastered and what you still need to work on.

▶ **Aplia**

Aplia™ is an online interactive learning solution that helps you improve comprehension—and your grade— by integrating a variety of media and tools such as video, tutorials, practice tests, and an interactive e-book.

CHAPTER 16

Social Behaviour

Three Images/Lifesize/Getty Images

NEL

The Canadian Charter of Rights and Freedoms (1982) establishes equality before and under the law and equal protection and benefits of the law. It acts as a standard for the treatment of persons in Canada. This is of critical importance when considering racism, stereotyping, and prejudice, which exist at all levels within Canada. Consider the complaint brought against a Quebec firm early in the 21st century.

The Centre Maraîcher Eugène Guinois Jr. is located outside of Montreal and is one of Canada's largest commercial vegetable farms, comprising about 530 hectares. At the centre of the complaint were allegations made by four black farm workers that the working conditions at the farm included segregation, racism, and neglect. They alleged that there were two cafeterias—one for the whites and one for the black workers. The blacks' cafeteria was unheated and lacked running water, proper toilets, and refrigeration facilities (Patriquin, 2005). The black farm workers stated that they were the victims of verbal and physical abuse and racist graffiti. During harvest time, black farm workers were bussed in from Longueuil, and they were referred to as the "workers from Longueuil." One full-time black employee, Celissa Michel, reported that when he tried to heat his food in the whites' cafeteria, he was pushed out. Another black worker who tried to sit at the picnic tables near the cafeteria was told by the owner's wife that those tables were only for *Quebecers*. Michel commented on the experience, "It's frustrating and it hurts, but I had to stay there and just take it" (Patriquin, 2005, p. A9).

The circumstances considered by the Human Rights Tribunal in Quebec seemed more the stuff of fiction, or events that might have transpired in the southern United States in the early to middle part of the last century—not in Canada and surely not now. The presiding judge, Michèle Pauzé, felt compelled to contextualize her decision with the following: "The events you are going to read happened here, in Quebec, during the years 2000 and 2001" (Patriquin, 2005, p. A1). The courts awarded compensation to some of the victims in this case.

While it may not be consistent with Canadians' views of themselves or their country, stereotyping, prejudice, and discrimination can be found here, as in other countries. In a poll conducted by Ipsos-Reid in March 2005, one in six Canadians reported that they had been victims of racism (One in Six People, 2005). While the rate of reported hate crimes in Canada is relatively low, race and ethnicity, religion, and sexual orientation emerge as the most common causes of reported hate crimes (Statistics Canada, 2010). Blacks are the most common target of racially oriented hate crimes, while in hate crimes targeting members of specific religions, Jews are the most frequent victims (Statistics Canada, 2008f). A recent study by a University of Toronto criminologist on racial profiling found that black motorists and pedestrians in Kingston, Ontario, were four times more likely to be stopped than were whites (Appleby, 2005).

Racism is an important issue in Canada. Historically, we can see this in the marginalization of Asian immigrants. This was reflected in the treatment of the Chinese immigrants who helped build the Canadian Pacific Railway and the internment and loss of rights and property of Japanese Canadians during World War II. Aboriginal peoples have often been the targets of racism and stereotyping, and the effects of the residential school policy are still being felt.

Canada is a country of diversity and, according to University of Western Ontario psychologists Victoria Esses and Bob Gardner (Esses & Gardner, 1996), the ethnic composition of Canada is changing, with an increase in the proportion of visible minorities. By 2017, it is projected that 20 percent of Canadians will be members of a visible minority (Statistics Canada, 2005b). The increase in visible minorities is fuelled by immigration, with about 70 percent of

Celissa Michel was one of the workers who brought a human rights complaint against a Quebec farm.

Courtesy of John Morstad

Saba Safdar of the University of Guelph conducts research in the area of cross-cultural psychology.

those identifying themselves as members of a visible minority in 2001 having been born outside of Canada.

Members of visible minorities are often the targets of racism and, according to research by the University of Guelph's Saba Safdar, they have specific stressors that are tied to their status (Safdar & Lay, 2003). In addition, emigrating from another country may challenge immigrants to weigh traditional values against the new values they find. Social psychologists such as York University's Richard Lalonde have studied the effects of cultural identity and family cultural influence on relationship partner choice (Lalonde et al., 2004).

How are we to make sense of stereotyping, prejudice, and discrimination (Lalonde, Jones, & Stroink, 2008)? What factors lead to such negative attitudes toward others? How do these attitudes affect our behaviour? Is there anything we can do to change such negative outcomes? These are just some of the issues we will be concerned with in this chapter, in which we examine social psychology. *Social psychology* is the branch of psychology concerned with the way individuals' thoughts, feelings, and behaviours are influenced by others. Our coverage of social psychology will focus on seven broad topics:

1. *Person perception.* How do we formulate our ideas about what others are like? To what extent do people's expectations colour their impressions of others?

2. *Attribution processes.* Whenever we observe the behaviour of others or reflect on our own behaviour, we often make attributions about that behaviour; we try to determine the causes of the behaviour. How do people use attributions to explain social behaviour?

3. *Interpersonal attraction.* What factors affect our attraction to other people? Why do we want to have relationships with some people and not others? What role do things such as similarity play in our attraction toward specific people?

4. *Attitudes.* How are attitudes formed? What leads to attitude change? How do attitudes affect people's behaviour?

5. *Conformity and obedience.* What factors influence conformity? Can people be coaxed into doing things that contradict their values?

6. *Behaviour in groups.* We all belong to various groups. Do people behave differently when they are in groups as opposed to when they are alone? Why do people in groups often think alike?

7. *Social neuroscience.* What structures and processes of the brain are associated with social phenomena such as prejudice and stereotyping?

Social psychologists study how people are affected by the actual, imagined, or implied presence of others. Their interest is not limited to individuals' interactions with others, as people can engage in social behaviour even when they're alone. For instance, if you were driving by yourself on a deserted highway and tossed your trash out of your car window, your littering would be a social action. It would defy social norms, reflect your socialization and attitudes, and have repercussions (albeit small) for other people in your society. Social psychologists often study individual behaviour in a social context. This interest in understanding individual behaviour should be readily apparent in our first section, on person perception.

Person Perception: Forming Impressions of Others

PREVIEW QUESTIONS

▶ How do aspects of physical appearance sway impressions of others?

▶ What are social schemas and stereotypes?

▶ How do illusory correlations and other phenomena illustrate subjectivity in person perception?

▶ How do evolutionary psychologists explain biases in person perception?

Can you remember the first meeting of your introductory psychology class? What impression did your professor make on you that day? Did your instructor appear to be confident? Easygoing? Pompous? Open-minded? Cynical? Friendly? Were your first impressions supported or undermined by subsequent observations? Our impressions of others are affected by a variety of factors including physical appearance. Take a moment to look at the man pictured on page 743. What do you think he is like? What does he do? What are his interests?

No matter whether you are correct or not, you probably found it easy to generate some idea of what he is like. We seem to be almost automatically drawn to trying to figure others out, to getting an impression of them. It might not surprise you to know that he currently works with computer software, developing software for video/film production. He just looks like a computer person, right? It might surprise you to know, however, that he was a musician and songwriter, and a pioneer in the use of computers in the Canadian music scene in the 1970s and 80s. His acquaintances include Andy Warhol, Brian Ferry, Boy George, Robert Fripp, and British billionaire Richard Branson. He worked with well-known bands such as the Spoons, Joy Division, Roxy Music, and the Eurythmics, to name just a few. Does this additional information change what kind of person you think he is? We are often faced with the task of updating impressions we have formed of people as

Our impressions of others are affected by physical appearance. What do you think this man is like?

we get to know them better. Some of the information we obtain about people plays a special role in our impressions.

While we often gather many pieces of information about another person, our final impressions can often be dramatically affected by just one piece of information. In some of the classic research into impression formation, Solomon Asch (1946) demonstrated the importance that what he called *central traits* can have on the impressions we form of others. When you interact with people, you're constantly engaged in *person perception,* the process of forming impressions of others. People show considerable ingenuity in piecing together clues about others' characteristics. However, impressions are often inaccurate because of the many biases and fallacies that occur in person perception. In this section, we consider some of the factors that influence, and often distort, people's perceptions of others.

Effects of Physical Appearance SIM10

"You shouldn't judge a book by its cover." "Beauty is only skin deep." People know better than to let physical attractiveness determine their perceptions of others' personal qualities. Or do they? Studies have shown that judgments of others' personality are often swayed by their appearance, especially their physical attractiveness. One recent study by researchers at the University of British Columbia showed that good-looking people command more of our attention than

less attractive individuals do (Lorenzo, Biesanz, & Human, 2010). People tend to ascribe desirable personality characteristics to those who are good-looking. Attractive people tend to be seen as more sociable, friendly, poised, warm, and well adjusted than those who are less attractive (Macrae & Quadflieg, 2010; van Leeuwen, Matthijs, & Macrae, 2004). In reality, research findings suggest that little correlation exists between attractiveness and personality traits (Feingold, 1992). Why do we inaccurately assume that a connection exists between good looks and personality? One reason is that extremely attractive people are vastly overrepresented in the entertainment media, where they are mostly portrayed in a highly favourable light (Smith, McIntosh, & Bazzini, 1999). Another reason is that our perceptions are swayed by our desire to bond with attractive people (Lemay, Clark, & Greenberg, 2010).

Karen Dion of the University of Toronto (Dion, Berscheid, & Walster, 1972), in a study conducted with University of Toronto undergraduates, found that not only were the attractive targets ascribed all those positive characteristics, but they were also expected to have better lives, to be better spouses, and to be more successful in their chosen careers. In another study, Dion (1973) showed that linking the *beautiful* with the *good* starts early. In that study, three- to six-and-a-half-year-old children were shown pictures of attractive and unattractive kids, and were asked to make a series of judgments. As you can see in Table 16.1, the attractive kids were viewed more positively on a variety of dimensions. For example: Unattractive kids are scarier and hit you without a good reason, while attractive kids won't hit you back even if you hit them first.

You might guess that physical attractiveness would influence perceptions of competence less than

TABLE 16.1

Frequency of Assignment of Behavioural Descriptions to Attractive versus Unattractive Children

* The items marked with an asterisk reflect significant differences.

Source: Adapted from Dion, K. (1973). Young children's stereotyping of facial attractiveness. *Journal of Personality and Social Psychology, 9,* 187. Copyright © 1972 by the American Psychological Association. Adapted with permission.

Behavioural item	Attractiveness of Child Chosen	
	Unattractive	Attractive
1. Fights a lot	37	24
2. Hits without a good reason	42	19*
3. Says angry things	37	24
4. Scares you	42	18*
5. Might hurt you	40	21*
6. Very friendly to other children	16	45*
7. Helps children when they're hurt or sad	28	33
8. Doesn't like fighting or shouting	18	43*
9. Doesn't hit, even if someone else hits first	21	40*

perceptions of personality, but the data suggest otherwise. A recent review of the relevant research found that people have a surprisingly strong tendency to view good-looking individuals as more competent than less attractive individuals (Langlois et al., 2000). This bias literally pays off for good-looking people, as they tend to secure better jobs and earn higher salaries than less attractive individuals (Collins & Zebrowitz, 1995; Engemann & Owyang, 2005; Senior et al., 2008). For example, a study of lawyers whose law school class photos were evaluated by independent raters found that physical attractiveness boosted their actual income by 10–12 percent (Engemann & Owyang, 2005). Another study (Judge, Hurst, & Simon, 2009) compared the impact of brains versus beauty on income. As one would expect (and hope) intelligence was more strongly related to earnings (correlation = 0.50) than good looks. But the correlation of 0.24 between attractiveness and income was not trivial.

Observers are also quick to draw inferences about people based on how they move, talk, and gesture—that is, their style of nonverbal expressiveness. Moreover, these inferences tend to be fairly accurate (Ambady & Rosenthal, 1993; Borkenau et al., 2004). For example, based on a mere ten seconds of videotape, participants can guess strangers' sexual orientation (heterosexual or homosexual) with decent accuracy (Ambady, Hallahan, & Conner, 1999). Based on similar "thin slices" of behaviour, observers can make accurate judgments of individuals' racial prejudice, social status, and intelligence (Ambady & Weisbuch, 2010). Even static photographs can provide telling cues about personality. One recent study found that participants were able to make meaningful inferences about stimulus persons' extraversion, openness to experience, agreeableness, and self-esteem based on simple photographs (Naumann et al., 2009).

Good looks, however, seem to have relatively little impact on perceptions of honesty and integrity (Eagly et al., 1991), but people do tend to view those with *baby-faced features*—such as large eyes, smooth skin, and a rounded chin—as more honest and trustworthy (Zebrowitz, Voinescu, & Collins, 1996). Baby-faced individuals are also seen as relatively warm, submissive, helpless, and naïve (Zebrowitz, 1996), although evidence suggests that there is no association between baby-faced features and these traits (Zebrowitz, Collins, & Dutta, 1998).

Cognitive Schemas

Even though every individual is unique, people tend to categorize one another. Such labels reflect the use

In general, people have a bias toward viewing good-looking men and women as bright, competent, and talented. However, people sometimes downplay the talent of successful women who happen to be attractive, attributing their success to their good looks instead of to their competence.

of cognitive schemas in person perception. As we discussed in Chapter 7, *schemas* are cognitive structures that guide information processing. Individuals use schemas to organize the world around them—including their social world. *Social schemas* are organized clusters of ideas about categories of social events and people. People have social schemas for events such as dates, picnics, committee meetings, and family reunions, as well as for certain categories of people, such as "dumb jocks," "social climbers," "frat rats," and "wimps" (see Figure 16.1). Individuals depend on social schemas because the schemas help them to efficiently process and store the wealth of information that they take in about others in their interactions. Hence, people routinely place one another in categories, and these categories influence the process of person perception (Fiske & Taylor, 2008).

Stereotypes

Some of the schemas that individuals apply to people are unique products of their personal experiences, while other schemas may be part of their shared cultural background. *Stereotypes* are special types of schemas that fall into the latter category. *Stereotypes* are widely held beliefs that people have certain characteristics because of their membership in a particular group.

The most common stereotypes in our society are those based on sex, age, and membership in ethnic or occupational groups. People who subscribe to traditional *gender stereotypes* tend to assume that women are emotional, submissive, illogical, and passive, while men are unemotional, dominant, logical, and aggressive. *Age stereotypes* suggest that elderly people are slow, feeble, rigid, forgetful, and asexual. Notions that Jews are mercenary, Germans are methodical, and Italians are passionate are examples of common *ethnic stereotypes*. *Occupational stereotypes* suggest that lawyers are manipulative, accountants are conforming, artists are moody, and so forth.

Stereotyping is a cognitive process that is frequently automatic and that saves on the time and effort required to get a handle on people individually (Devine & Monteith, 1999; Fiske & Russell, 2010). Stereotypes save energy by simplifying our social world. However, this conservation of energy often comes at some cost in terms of accuracy (Stangor, 2009). Stereotypes frequently are broad overgeneralizations that ignore the diversity within social groups and foster inaccurate perceptions of people (Hilton & von Hippel, 1996). Obviously, not all males, Jews, and lawyers behave alike. Most people who subscribe to stereotypes realize that not all members of a group are identical. For instance, they may admit that some men aren't competitive, some Jews aren't mercenary, and some lawyers aren't manipulative. However, they may still tend to assume that males, Jews, and lawyers are *more likely* than others to have these characteristics. Even if stereotypes mean only that people think in terms of slanted *probabilities,* their expectations may lead them to misperceive individuals with whom they interact. As we've noted in previous chapters, perception is subjective, and people often see what they expect to see.

Our perception of others is also subject to self-fulfilling prophecy. This was clearly demonstrated in a classic study by Mark Zanna and his colleagues (Word, Zanna, & Cooper 1974). Zanna, a professor of psychology at the University of Waterloo, received the CPA's Donald O. Hebb Award in 1993, and a $100 000 Killam Prize in 2011). The research had two studies. In the first study, researchers had white undergraduate males interview either a black or white job applicant. The applicant was, in fact, an experimental accomplice or confederate. It was

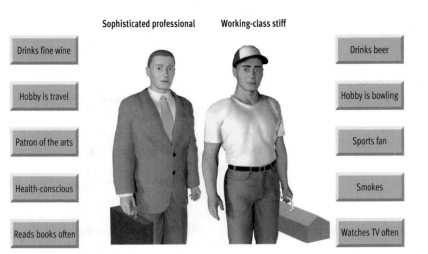

Sophisticated professional **Working-class stiff**

Drinks fine wine

Hobby is travel

Patron of the arts

Health-conscious

Reads books often

Drinks beer

Hobby is bowling

Sports fan

Smokes

Watches TV often

FIGURE 16.1

Examples of social schemas.

Everyone has social schemas for various "types" of people, such as sophisticated professionals or working-class stiffs. Social schemas are clusters of beliefs that guide information processing.

found that when the job applicant was black, the interviewers tended to sit farther away, end the interview more quickly, and make more speech errors (e.g., stuttering, stammering). Clearly, then, the white interviewers changed how they acted depending on the race of the interviewee. In interviewing a white accomplice, they adopted what was referred to as an *immediate* style (i.e., sitting closer, more eye contact), but when they interviewed a black accomplice they used a *nonimmediate style* (i.e., sitting farther away, making more speech errors, looking away).

In the second study, Word, Zanna, and Cooper attempted to find out how it would feel to have someone behave toward you in a nonimmediate style. In the study, white experimental accomplices interviewed other white students while adopting either the immediate or nonimmediate style. Students who had been interviewed in the nonimmediate style seemed more anxious and did not perform as well in the interview.

The study was designed to show the operation of self-fulfilling prophecy. If you hold strong beliefs about the characteristics of another group, you may behave in such a way so as to bring about these characteristics. If you believe, for example, that all professors do is read books, the next time you sit next to a professor on a bus, you might just ask about the books he or she has read. If the professor is like most people, he or she can report back to you on the latest book of fiction he or she has read. If things go like this, then you may leave the situation believing that, yes indeed, professors only read books. However, because of your stereotypes, you

Social Behaviour

may have failed to find out how much the professor likes the same music as you and that you share a favourite band—Soundgarden. You would also fail to learn that the professor was in the audience in Toronto—just like you were on July 2, 2011—for Soundgarden's first concert tour together in 14 years.

When we think about the effects of stereotypes, we often focus on the effects our stereotypes have on *others* and how self-fulfilling prophecy processes might serve to confirm those stereotypes. But, of course, our stereotypes also affect us; they influence our conceptualizations of our social environment. But the influence of our stereotypes on us doesn't end there; they can also directly affect our own behaviour. For example, consider the results of some innovative research by Yale University's John Bargh (Bargh, Chen, & Barrows, 1996). In his research, Bargh utilized prevailing stereotypes of the elderly to influence students' behaviour. As we mentioned at the beginning of this section, those stereotypes include such descriptions as slow, feeble and so on.

In his research, Bargh activated or *primed* stereotypes of the elderly in a group of university students by having the students, as part of a laboratory experiment, complete several scrambled sentence tasks in which participants were presented with 30 sets of words and were asked to write down a grammatically correct sentence using some of the words from each set. The sets of words in the critical experimental condition (i.e., the elderly prime condition) included words associated with the elderly, words such as *worried, Florida, lonely, grey, wrinkle, cautious, forgetful, retired, old, ancient,* and so on. In the control condition (neutral prime condition), the words included in the task were unrelated to stereotypes of the elderly, words such as *thirsty, clean,* and *private.* Once the students had completed the word tasks, they were thanked, debriefed, and shown where to find the elevator down the hall. The students thought the experiment was over, but it was not. Unknown to them, the experimenter timed how long it took the students to walk down the hall to the elevator, 9.75 metres away. The effects of the priming or stereotype activation on behaviour happened automatically, without the participants' awareness, and they were very dramatic (see Figure 16.2). In this experiment and a direct replication (Bargh et al., 1996, experiments 2a and 2b), students in the *elderly prime condition* had significantly slower walking times to the elevator than students in the *neutral prime condition.* Why did this happen?

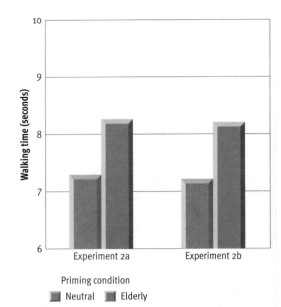

FIGURE 16.2

Average walking time.

Mean time (in seconds) to walk down the hallway after the conclusion of the experiment, by stereotype priming condition, separately, for participants in Experiment 2a and 2b.

Source: Bargh, J.A., Chen, M., & Burrows, L. (1996). Automaticity of social behavior: Direct effects of Trait construct and stereotype activation on action. *Journal of Personality and Social Psychology, 71,* 237. Copyright © 1996, American Psychological Association.

Being exposed to the elderly-related words served to activate or prime schemas/stereotypes associated with the elderly much in the same way as Mark Baldwin used pictures of the Pope to prime self-evaluation in Chapter 12's Featured Study (page 568). In each case, the primed schemas/stereotypes affected participants' self-evaluations or behaviour without them being aware of it. According to Bargh (Bargh & Morsella, 2008), when schemas are made active by priming, they can automatically and unconsciously affect behaviour (e.g., walking) and higher mental processes such as self-evaluation and judgment. In this case, once stereotypes of the elderly were activated, the participants enacted behaviour in line with the stereotypes, walking slowly just like the elderly. Similar effects have been found in other related studies. For example, students who had their *professor* schemas activated or primed did better on trivia tests than did control participants, whereas priming or activating participants' *soccer hooligan* stereotypes actually reduced trivia scores (Dijksterhuis & van Knippenberg, 1998)!

Subjectivity and Bias in Person Perception

Stereotypes and other schemas create biases in person perception that frequently lead to confirmation of people's expectations about others. According to University of Western Ontario social psychologist James Olson (Olson, Goffin, & Haynes, 2007), if someone's behaviour is ambiguous, people are likely to interpret what they see in a way that's consistent with their expectations (Olson, Roese, & Zanna, 1996). So, after dealing with a pushy female customer, a salesman who holds traditional gender stereotypes might characterize the woman as "emotional." In contrast, he might characterize a male who exhibits the same pushy behaviour as "aggressive."

People not only see what they expect to see, but also tend to overestimate how often they see it (Johnson & Mullen, 1994; Shavitt et al., 1999). *Illusory correlation* occurs when people estimate that they have encountered more confirmations of an association between social traits than they have actually seen. People also tend to underestimate the number of disconfirmations that they have encountered, as illustrated by statements like "I've never met an honest lawyer."

Memory processes can contribute to confirmatory biases in person perception in a variety of ways. Often, individuals selectively recall facts that fit with their schemas and stereotypes (Fiske, 1998; Quinn, Macrae, & Bodenhausen, 2003). Evidence for such a tendency was found in a study by Cohen (1981). In this experiment, participants watched a videotape of a woman, described as either a waitress or a librarian, who engaged in a variety of activities, including listening to classical music, drinking beer, and watching TV. When asked to recall what the woman did during the filmed sequence, participants tended to remember activities consistent with their stereotypes of waitresses and librarians. For instance, subjects who thought the woman was a waitress tended to recall her drinking beer, while subjects who thought she was a librarian tended to recall her listening to classical music.

An Evolutionary Perspective on Bias in Person Perception

Why is the process of person perception riddled with bias? Evolutionary psychologists like Simon Fraser University's Dennis Krebs argue that some of the biases seen in social perception were adaptive in humans' ancestral environment (Krebs & Denton, 1997). For example, they argue that person perception is swayed by physical attractiveness because attractiveness was associated with reproductive potential in women and with health, vigour, and the accumulation of material resources in men.

What about the human tendency to automatically categorize others? Evolutionary theorists attribute this behaviour to our distant ancestors' need to quickly separate friend from foe. They assert that humans are programmed by evolution to immediately classify people as members of an *ingroup*—a group that one belongs to and identifies with, or as members of an *outgroup*—a group that one does not belong to or identify with. This crucial categorization is thought to structure subsequent perceptions. As Krebs and Denton (1997) put it, "It is as though the act of classifying others as ingroup or outgroup members activates two quite different brain circuits" (p. 27). Ingroup members tend to be viewed in a favourable light, whereas outgroup members tend to be viewed in terms of various negative stereotypes. According to Krebs and Denton, these negative stereotypes ("They are inferior; they are all alike; they will exploit us") move outgroups out of our domain of empathy, so we feel justified in not liking them or in discriminating against them.

Evolutionary psychologists, then, ascribe much of the bias in person perception to cognitive mechanisms that have been shaped by natural selection. Their speculation is thought-provoking. However, empirical work is needed to test their hypotheses.

REVIEW OF KEY POINTS

▷ People's perceptions of others can be distorted by a variety of factors, including physical appearance. People tend to attribute desirable characteristics, such as intelligence, competence, warmth, and friendliness, to those who are good-looking.

▷ Baby-faced people are viewed as honest. Perceptions of people are also influenced by their style of nonverbal expressiveness. People use social schemas to categorize others into types. Stereotypes are widely held social schemas that lead people to expect that others will have certain characteristics because of their membership in a specific group.

▷ Gender, age, ethnic, and occupational stereotypes are common. In interacting with others, stereotypes may lead people to see what they expect to see and to overestimate how often they see it.

▷ Evolutionary psychologists argue that some of the biases in person perception were adaptive in humans' ancestral past. The human tendency to automatically categorize others may reflect the primitive need to quickly separate friend from foe.

It's Friday evening and you're sitting around at home feeling bored. You call a few friends to see whether they'd like to go out. They all say that they'd love to go, but they have other commitments and can't. Their commitments sound vague, and you feel that their reasons for not going out with you are rather flimsy. How do you explain these rejections? Do your friends really have commitments? Are they worn out by school and work? When they said that they'd love to go, were they being sincere? Or do they find you boring? Could they be right? Are you boring? These questions illustrate a process that people engage in routinely: the explanation of behaviour (Struthers, Dupuis, & Eaton, 2005). *Attributions* play a key role in these explanatory efforts. Hence, they have significant effects on social relations.

Just as there is often bias in our perception of others, there may be bias in our search for explanations of behaviour. Imagine being questioned by your parents after fighting with your brother. What would your answer be if you were asked who started the fight? Some attributional theorists suggest that our search for explanations often ends with an explanation that puts our own actions in the best possible light. Wilfrid Laurier University researcher Anne Wilson (Peetz, Wilson, & Strahan, 2009) and her colleagues found that siblings, even when questioned by strangers, tended to blame each other, especially when the incidents were more serious (Wilson et al., 2004).

What are attributions? *Attributions* are inferences that people draw about the causes of events, others' behaviour, and their own behaviour. If you conclude that a friend turned down your invitation because she's overworked, you have made an attribution about the cause of her behaviour (and, implicitly, have rejected other possible explanations). If you conclude that you're stuck at home with nothing to do because you failed to plan ahead, you've made an attribution about the cause of an event (being stuck at home). If you conclude that you failed to plan ahead because you're a procrastinator, you've made an attribution about the cause of your own behaviour. People make attributions mainly because they have a strong need to understand their experiences. They want to make sense out of their own behaviour, others' actions, and the events in their lives. In this section, we'll take a look at some of the patterns seen when people make attributions.

Internal versus External Attributions 12a

Fritz Heider (1958) was the first to describe how people make attributions. He asserted that people tend to locate the cause of behaviour either *within a person*, attributing it to personal factors, or *outside a person*, attributing it to environmental factors.

Elaborating on Heider's insight, various theorists have agreed that explanations of behaviour and events can be categorized as internal or external attributions (Jones & Davis, 1965; Kelley, 1967; Weiner, 1974). *Internal attributions* ascribe the causes of behaviour to personal dispositions, traits, abilities, and feelings. *External attributions* ascribe the causes of behaviour to situational demands and environmental constraints. For example, if a friend's business fails, you might attribute it to his or her lack of business acumen (an internal, personal factor) or to negative trends in the nation's economic climate (an external, situational explanation). Parents who find out that their teenage son has just banged up the car may blame it on his carelessness (a personal disposition) or on slippery road conditions (a situational factor).

Internal and external attributions can have a tremendous impact on everyday interpersonal interactions. Blaming a friend's business failure on poor business acumen as opposed to a poor economy will have a great impact on how you view your friend. Likewise, if parents attribute their son's automobile accident to slippery road conditions, they're likely to deal with the event very differently than if they attribute it to his carelessness.

Attributions for Success and Failure 12a

Some psychologists have sought to discover additional dimensions of attributional thinking besides the internal–external dimension. After studying the attributions that people make in explaining success and failure, Bernard Weiner (1980, 1986, 1994, 2004) concluded that people often focus on the *stability* of the causes underlying behaviour. According to Weiner, the stable–unstable dimension in attribution cuts across the internal–external dimension, creating four types of attributions for success and failure, as shown in Figure 16.3.

Let's apply Weiner's model to a concrete event. Imagine that you're contemplating why you failed to get a job that you wanted. You might attribute your setback to internal factors that are stable (lack of ability) or unstable (inadequate effort to put together an eye-catching résumé). Or you might attribute your setback to external factors that are stable (too much outstanding competition) or unstable (bad luck). If you got the job, your explanations for your success would fall into the same four categories: internal–stable (your excellent ability), internal–unstable (your hard work to assemble a superb résumé), external–stable (lack of top-flight competition), and external–unstable (good luck).

Bias in Attribution 12a

Attributions are only inferences. Your attributions may not be the correct explanations for events. Paradoxical as it may seem, people often arrive at inaccurate explanations even when they contemplate the causes of *their own behaviour*. Attributions ultimately represent *guesswork* about the causes of events, and these guesses tend to be slanted in certain directions. Let's look at the principal biases seen in attribution.

Actor–Observer Bias 12a

Your view of your own behaviour can be quite different from the view of someone else observing you. When an actor and an observer draw inferences about the causes of the actor's behaviour, they often make different attributions. A common form of bias seen in observers is the *fundamental attribution error*, which refers to observers' bias in favour of internal attributions in explaining others' behaviour. Of course, in many instances, an internal attribution may not be an "error." However, observers have a curious tendency to overestimate the likelihood that an actor's behaviour reflects personal qualities rather than situational factors (Krull, 2001). Why? One reason is that situational pressures may not be readily apparent to an observer. As Gilbert and Malone (1995) put it, "When one tries to point to a situation, one often stabs empty air" (p. 25).

According to Bertram Gawronski (Brochu, Gawronski, & Esses, 2011; Gawronski & Bodenhausen, 2011) of the University of Western Ontario, it is not that people assume that situational factors have little impact on behaviour (Gawronski, 2004). Rather, it's that attributing others' behaviour

FIGURE 16.3

Weiner's model of attributions for success and failure.

Weiner's model assumes that people's explanations for success and failure emphasize internal versus external causes and stable versus unstable causes. Examples of causal factors that fit into each of the four cells in Weiner's model are shown in the diagram.

Source: Weiner, B., Friese, I., Kukla, A., Reed, L., and Rosenbaum, R. M. (1972) Perceiving the causes of success and failure. In E. E. Jones, D. E. Kanouse, H. H. Kelley, R. E. Nisbett, S. Valins, and B. Weiner (Eds.), *Perceiving the causes of behavior*. Morristown, NJ: General Learning Press. Used by permission of Bernard Weiner.

to their dispositions is a relatively effortless, almost automatic process, whereas explaining people's behaviour in terms of situational factors requires more thought and effort (see Figure 16.4; Krull & Erickson, 1995). Another factor favouring internal attributions is that many people feel that few situations are so coercive that they negate all freedom of choice (Forsyth, 2004).

To illustrate the gap that often exists between actors' and observers' attributions, imagine that you're visiting your bank and you fly into a rage over a mistake made on your account. Observers who witness your rage are likely to make an internal attribution and infer that you are surly, temperamental, and quarrelsome. They may be right, but if asked, you'd probably attribute your rage to the frustrating situation. Perhaps you're normally a calm, easygoing person, but today you've been in line for 20 minutes, you just straightened out a similar error by the same bank last week, and you're being treated rudely by the teller. Observers are often unaware of historical and situational considerations such as these, so they tend to make internal attributions for another's behaviour (Gilbert, 1998).

In contrast, the circumstances that have influenced an actor's behaviour tend to be more salient to the actor. Hence, actors are more likely than observers to locate the cause of their behaviour in the situation. In general, then, *actors favour external attributions for their behaviour, whereas observers are more likely to explain the same behaviour with internal attributions* (Jones & Nisbett, 1971; Krueger, Ham, & Linford, 1996).

Fritz Heider

"Often the momentary situation which, at least in part, determines the behavior of a person is disregarded and the behavior is taken as a manifestation of personal characteristics."

University of Kansas

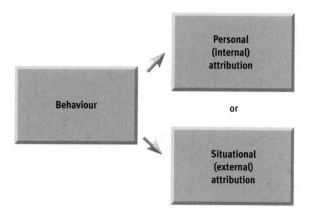

Traditional model of attribution

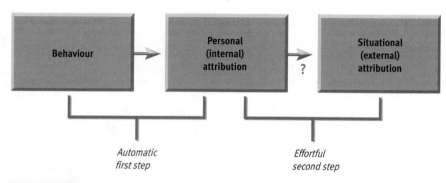

Alternative two-step model of attribution

Automatic first step

Effortful second step

FIGURE 16.4

An alternative view of the fundamental attribution error.

According to Gilbert (1989) and others, the nature of attribution processes favours the *fundamental attribution error*. Traditional models of attribution assume that internal and external attributions are an either–or proposition requiring equal amounts of effort. In contrast, Gilbert posits that people tend to automatically make internal attributions with little effort, and then they *may* expend additional effort to adjust for the influence of situational factors, which can lead to an external attribution. Thus, external attributions for others' behaviour require more thought and effort, which makes them less frequent than personal attributions.

Source: Gilbert, D.T. (1989). Thinking lightly about others: Automatic components of the social inference process. In J.S. Uleman & J.A. Bargh (Eds.), *Unintended thought limits of awareness, intention, and control.* New York: Guilford Press.

Defensive Attribution

PSYKTREK

12a

In attempting to explain the calamities and setbacks that befall other people, an observer's tendency to make internal attributions may become even stronger than normal. *Defensive attribution* is a tendency to blame victims for their misfortune, so that one feels less likely to be victimized in a similar way. Let's say that a friend gets mugged and severely beaten. You may attribute the mugging to your friend's carelessness or stupidity ("He should have known better than to be in that neighbourhood at that time") rather than to bad luck. Why? Because if you attribute your friend's misfortune to bad luck, you have to face the ugly reality that it could just as easily happen to you. To avoid disturbing thoughts such as these, people

often attribute mishaps to victims' negligence (Herzog, 2008; Idisis, Ben-David, & Ben-Nachum, 2007).

Hindsight bias probably contributes to this tendency, but blaming victims also helps people maintain their belief that they live in a just world, where they're unlikely to experience similar troubles (Lerner & Goldberg, 1999). Thus, people who strongly endorse the notion that the world is just are especially likely to engage in victim derogation (van den Bos & Maas, 2009). The *belief in a just world* theory was developed by University of Waterloo social psychologist Melvin Lerner (1980). He suggested that evidence telling us that the world is not a just place is threatening and that we feel compelled to restore the belief that it *is* a just world. One way in which we can restore this belief is to see victims as deserving their consequences. Carolyn Hafer of Brock University recently reviewed research on this theory and suggests that, while the results have been largely supportive, there are some inadequacies that should be addressed (Hafer & Begue, 2005).

The bias toward making defensive attributions can have unfortunate consequences. Blaming victims for their setbacks causes them to be seen in a negative light. Thus, undesirable traits are unfairly attributed to them. This could lead one to assume that burglary victims must be careless, that people who get fired must be incompetent, that poor people must be lazy, that rape victims must be loose ("She probably asked for it"), and so on. As you can see, defensive attribution can lead to unwarranted derogation of victims of misfortune.

Culture and Attributional Tendencies

Do the patterns of attribution observed in subjects from Western societies transcend culture? More research is needed, but the preliminary evidence suggests not. Some interesting cultural disparities have emerged in research on attribution processes.

According to Harry Triandis (1989, 1994, 2001; Triandis, Ang, & Van Dyne, 2008)), cultural differences in *individualism* versus *collectivism* influence attributional tendencies as well as other aspects of social behaviour (Morling & Lamoreaux, 2008). *Individualism* involves putting personal goals ahead of group goals and defining one's identity in terms of personal attributes rather than group memberships. In contrast, *collectivism* involves putting group goals ahead of personal goals and defining one's identity in terms of the groups one belongs to (such as one's family, tribe, work group, social class, caste, and so on). In comparison to

concept check 16.1

Analyzing Attributions

Check your understanding of attribution processes by analyzing possible explanations for an athletic team's success. Imagine that the women's track team at your school has just won a provincial championship that qualifies it for the national tournament. Around the campus, you hear people attribute the team's success to a variety of factors. Examine the attributions shown below and place each of them in one of the cells of Weiner's model of attribution (just record the letter inside the cell). The answers are in Appendix A.

	Unstable cause (temporary)	Stable cause (permanent)
Internal cause		
External cause		

a. "They won only because the best two athletes on Ottawa's team were out with injuries—talk about good fortune!"

b. "They won because they have some of the best talent in the country."

c. "Anybody could win in this province; the competition is far below average in comparison to the rest of the country."

d. "They won because they put in a great deal of last-minute effort and practice, and they were incredibly fired up for the regional tourney after last year's near miss."

WEB LINK 16.2

Social Cognition Paper Archive and Information Center
Eliot R. Smith at Indiana University maintains a popular site that includes information about papers (abstracts, mostly), people, and links to the wider social psychological research community.

individualistic cultures, collectivist cultures place a higher priority on shared values and resources, cooperation, mutual interdependence, and concern for how one's actions will affect other group members. Child-rearing patterns in collectivist cultures emphasize the importance of obedience, reliability, and proper behaviour, whereas individualistic cultures emphasize the development of independence, self-esteem, and self-reliance. Generally speaking, North American and Western European cultures tend to be individualistic, whereas Asian, African, and Latin American cultures tend to be collectivistic (Hofstede, 1980, 1983, 2001). Canada ranks fourth in individualism (tied with the Netherlands), behind the United States, Australia, and Great Britain (see Figure 16.5).

How does individualism versus collectivism relate to patterns of attribution? The evidence suggests that collectivist cultures may promote different biases than individualistic cultures (Masuda et al., 2008). For example, people from collectivist societies appear to be less prone to the *fundamental attribution error* than those from individualistic societies (Choi, Nisbett, & Norenzayan, 1999; Triandis, 2001). In contrast, collectivists, who value interdependence and obedience, are more likely to assume that one's behaviour reflects adherence to group norms.

There are also cultural differences in *self-serving attributional biases*. The *self-serving bias* is the

A common example of defensive attribution is the tendency to blame the homeless for their plight.

tendency to attribute one's successes to personal factors and one's failures to situational factors. According to Stanford University's Dale Miller and University of Waterloo's Mike Ross, the self-serving bias in attribution comes into play when people attempt to explain success and failure (Miller & Ross, 1975). This bias may either strengthen or weaken

salamanderman/Shutterstock.com

Hofstede's rankings of national cultures' individualism

Individualistic cultures	Intermediate cultures	Collectivist cultures
1. United States	19. Israel	37. Hong Kong
2. Australia	20. Spain	38. Chile
3. Great Britain	21. India	40. Singapore
4. Canada	22. Argentina	40. Thailand
4. Netherlands	23. Japan	40. West Africa region
6. New Zealand	24. Iran	42. El Salvador
7. Italy	25. Jamaica	43. South Korea
8. Belgium	26. Arab region	44. Taiwan
9. Denmark	27. Brazil	45. Peru
10. France	28. Turkey	46. Costa Rica
11. Sweden	29. Uruguay	47. Indonesia
12. Ireland	30. Greece	47. Pakistan
13. Norway	31. Philippines	49. Colombia
14. Switzerland	32. Mexico	50. Venezuela
15. West Germany	34. East Africa region	51. Panama
16. South Africa	34. Portugal	52. Ecuador
17. Finland	34. Yugoslavia	53. Guatemala
18. Austria	36. Malaysia	

FIGURE 16.5

Individualism versus collectivism around the world.

Hofstede (1980, 1983, 2001) used survey data from over 100 000 employees of a large, multinational corporation to estimate the emphasis on individualism versus collectivism in 50 nations and three regions. His large, diverse international sample remains unequalled to date. In the figure, cultures are ranked in terms of how strongly they embraced the values of individualism. As you can see, Hofstede's estimates suggest that North American and Western European nations tend to be relatively individualistic, whereas more collectivism is found in Asian, African, and Latin American countries.

Source: Adapted from Hofstede, G. (2001). *Culture's consequences* (2nd ed., p. 215). Thousand Oaks, CA: Sage. Copyright © 2001 Sage Publications. Adapted by permission of Dr. Geert Hofstede.

one's normal attributional tendencies, depending on whether one is trying to explain positive or negative outcomes (Mezulis et al., 2004; Shepperd, Malone, & Sweeney, 2008). Although the *self-serving bias* has been documented in a variety of cultures (Fletcher & Ward, 1988), it may be particularly prevalent in individualistic, Western societies, where an emphasis on competition and high self-esteem motivates people to try to impress others, as well as themselves (Mezulis et al., 2004). In contrast, Japanese subjects exhibit a *self-effacing bias* in explaining success (Akimoto & Sanbonmatsu, 1999; Markus & Kitayama, 1991), as they tend to attribute their successes to help they receive from others or to the ease of the task, while downplaying the importance of their ability. When they fail, Japanese subjects tend to be more self-critical than subjects from individualistic cultures, according to research conducted by the University of British Columbia's Steve Heine (Heine & Renshaw, 2002). Japanese subjects are more likely to accept responsibility for their failures and to use their setbacks as an impetus for self-improvement (Heine et al., 2001). A great deal of additional research is needed before any broad conclusions can be drawn, but collectivism may put a different spin on attributional bias (Heine & Ruby, 2010).

concept check 16.2

Recognizing Bias in Social Cognition

Check your understanding of bias in social cognition by identifying various types of errors that are common in person perception and attribution. Imagine that you're a nonvoting student member of a committee that is hiring a new political science professor at your university. As you listen to the committee's discussion, you hear examples of (a) the illusory correlation effect, (b) stereotyping, (c) the fundamental attribution error, and (d) defensive attribution. Indicate which of these is at work in the excerpts from committee members' deliberations below. The answers are in Appendix A.

_____ **1.** "I absolutely won't consider the fellow who arrived 30 minutes late for his interview. Anybody who can't make a job interview on time is either irresponsible or hopelessly disorganized. I don't care what he says about the airline messing up his reservations."

_____ **2.** "You know, I was very, very impressed with the young female applicant, and I would love to hire her, but every time we add a young woman to the faculty in liberal arts, she gets pregnant within the first year." The committee chairperson, who has heard this line from this professor before replies, "You always say that, so I finally did a systematic check of what's happened in the past. Of the last 14 women hired in liberal arts, only one has become pregnant within a year."

_____ **3.** "The first one I want to rule out is the guy who's been practising law for the last ten years. Although he has an excellent background in political science, I just don't trust lawyers. They're all ambitious, power-hungry, manipulative cutthroats. He'll be a divisive force in the department."

_____ **4.** "I say we forget about the two candidates who lost their faculty slots in the massive financial crisis at Western Polytechnic last year. I know it sounds cruel, but they brought it on themselves with their fiscal irresponsibility over at Western. Thank goodness we'll never let anything like that happen around here. As far as I'm concerned, if these guys couldn't see that crisis coming, they must be pretty dense."

Close Relationships: Liking and Loving

"I just don't know what she sees in him. She could do so much better for herself. I suppose he's a nice guy, but they're just not right for each other." You've probably heard similar remarks on many occasions. These comments illustrate people's interest in analyzing the dynamics of attraction. *Interpersonal attraction* refers to positive feelings toward another. Social psychologists use this term broadly to encompass a variety of experiences, including liking, friendship, admiration, lust, and love. In this section, we'll analyze key factors that influence attraction and examine some theoretical perspectives on the mystery of love.

Key Factors in Attraction

Many factors influence who is attracted to whom. Here we'll discuss factors that promote the development of liking, friendship, and love. Although these are different types of attraction, the interpersonal dynamics at work in each are largely similar.

Physical Attractiveness

Although people often say that "beauty is only skin deep," the empirical evidence suggests that most people don't really believe that homily (Fitness, Fletcher, & Overall, 2003). The importance of physical attractiveness was demonstrated in a study of college students in which unacquainted men and women were sent off on a "get-acquainted" date (Sprecher & Duck, 1994). The investigators were mainly interested in how communication might affect the process of attraction, but to put this factor into context, they also measured subjects' perceptions of their date's physical attractiveness and similarity to themselves. They found that the quality of

communication during the date did have some effect on females' interest in friendship, but the key determinant of romantic attraction for both sexes was the physical attractiveness of the other person.

Consistent with this finding, research has shown that, as one might expect, attractive people of both sexes enjoy greater mating success than their less-attractive peers (Rhodes, Simmons, & Peters, 2005).

Although people prefer physically attractive partners in romantic relationships, they may consider their own level of attractiveness in pursuing dates. What people want in a partner may be different from what they are willing to settle for (Regan, 1998). The *matching hypothesis* proposes that males and females of approximately equal physical attractiveness are likely to select each other as partners.

PREVIEW QUESTIONS

▷ To what extent are good looks and similarity important in interpersonal attraction?

▷ How do theorists distinguish among different types of love?

▷ How are attachment patterns related to intimate relationships?

▷ How does culture influence patterns of mating?

▷ How have mating strategies been shaped by evolution?

© Alamy Images

According to the matching hypothesis, males and females who are similar in physical attractiveness are likely to be drawn together. This type of matching may also influence the formation of friendships.

Elaine Hatfield

"Passionate love is like any other form of excitement. By its very nature, excitement involves a continuous interplay between elation and despair, thrills and terror."

The matching hypothesis is supported by evidence that married couples tend to be very similar in level of physical attractiveness (Regan, 1998, 2008). Not surprisingly, research suggests that attractive people expect to date more attractive individuals and unattractive people expect to date less attractive partners (Montoya, 2008). One recent study relevant to the matching hypothesis examined requests to get acquainted at the HOTorNOT.com website, where members routinely rate each others' level of physical attractiveness (Lee et al., 2008). As one would expect, the attractive members were more selective in agreeing to get acquainted with others than were the less attractive members. The study also looked at whether less attractive persons deluded themselves into thinking that their prospective partners were more attractive than others perceived them to be. The results did not support this "rationalization" hypothesis. Instead, the data suggested that less attractive people place less weight on physical attractiveness than those who are good-looking.

Similarity Effects

Is it true that "birds of a feather flock together," or do "opposites attract"? Research provides far more support for the former than the latter (Surra et al., 2006). Married and dating couples tend to be similar in age, race, religion, social class, personality, education, intelligence, physical attractiveness, and attitudes (Kalmijn, 1998; Watson et al., 2004). The similarity principle operates in both friendships and romantic relationships,

regardless of sexual orientation (Fehr, 2008; Morry, 2007, 2009; Peplau & Fingerhut, 2007). In a longitudinal study of best friends, researchers found that similarity among friends in 1983 actually predicted their closeness in 2002—19 years later (Ledbetter, Griffin, & Sparks).

Perspectives on the Mystery of Love

Love has proven to be an elusive subject of study. It's difficult to define, difficult to measure, and frequently difficult to understand. Nonetheless, psychologists have begun to make some progress in their study of love (Reis & Aron, 2008). Let's look at their theories and research.

Passionate and Companionate Love

12b

Two early pioneers in research on love were Elaine Hatfield (formerly Walster) and Ellen Berscheid (Berscheid, 1988, 2006; Berscheid & Walster, 1978; Hatfield & Rapson, 1993). They have proposed that romantic relationships are characterized by two kinds of love: passionate love and companionate love. *Passionate love* is a complete absorption in another that includes tender sexual feelings and the agony and ecstasy of intense emotion. *Companionate love* is warm, trusting, tolerant affection for another whose life is deeply intertwined with one's own. Passionate and companionate love *may* coexist, but they don't necessarily go hand in hand. Research suggests that, as a general rule, companionate love is more strongly related to relationship satisfaction than passionate love (Fehr, 2001).

The distinction between passionate and companionate love has been further refined by Robert Sternberg (1988a, 2006), who suggests that love has three facets rather than just two. He subdivides companionate love into intimacy and commitment. *Intimacy* refers to warmth, closeness, and sharing in a relationship. *Commitment* is an intent to maintain a relationship in spite of the difficulties and costs that may arise. Sternberg has mapped out the probable relationships between the passage of time and the three components of love, as shown in Figure 16.6. Like Hatfield and Berscheid, he suspects that passion reaches its zenith in the early phases of love and then erodes. He believes that intimacy and commitment increase with time, although at different rates.

Research suggests that passionate love is a powerful motivational force that produces profound

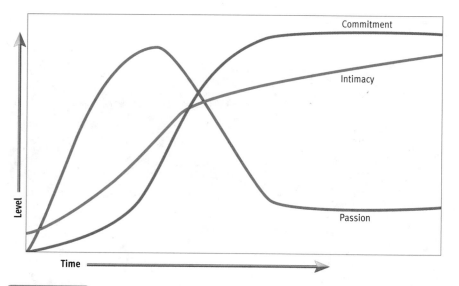

FIGURE 16.6

Sternberg's view of love over time.

In his theory of love, Robert Sternberg (1988a) hypothesizes that the various elements of love progress in different ways over the course of time. According to Sternberg, passion peaks early in a relationship, whereas intimacy and commitment typically continue to build gradually. (Graphs adapted from Trotter, 1986).

Source: Trotter, R.J. (1986). The three faces of love. *Psychology Today*, 46–54.

changes in people's thinking, emotion, and behaviour (Reis & Aron, 2008). Interestingly, brain-imaging research indicates that when people think about someone they are passionately in love with, these thoughts light up the dopamine circuits in the brain that are known to be activated by cocaine and other addictive drugs (Aron, Fisher, & Mashek, 2005). Perhaps this explains why passionate love sometimes resembles an addiction.

Love as Attachment

12b PSYKTREK

In another groundbreaking analysis of love, Cindy Hazan and Phillip Shaver (1987) have looked not at the components of love but at similarities between love and *attachment relationships* in infancy. We noted in Chapter 11 that infant–caretaker bonding, or attachment, emerges in the first year of life. Early attachments vary in quality, and infants tend to fall into one of three groups, which depend in part on parents' caregiving styles (Ainsworth et al., 1978). Most infants develop a *secure attachment*. However, some are very anxious when separated from their caretaker, a syndrome called *anxious-ambivalent attachment*. A third group of infants, characterized by *avoidant attachment,* never bond very well with their caretaker (see Figure 16.7).

According to Hazan and Shaver, romantic love is an attachment process, and people's intimate relationships in adulthood follow the same form as their attachments in infancy. According to their theory, a person who had an anxious-ambivalent attachment in infancy will tend to have romantic relationships marked by anxiety and ambivalence in adulthood. In other words, people relive their early bonding with their parents in their adult romantic relationships.

Hazan and Shaver's (1987) initial survey study provided striking support for their theory. They found that adults' love relationships could be sorted into groups that paralleled the three patterns of attachment seen in infants. *Secure adults* (56 percent of the subjects) found it relatively easy to get close to others, described their love relationships as trusting, rarely worried about being abandoned, and reported the fewest divorces. *Anxious-ambivalent adults* (20 percent of the subjects) reported a pre-occupation with love accompanied by expectations of rejection and described their love relationships as volatile and marked by jealousy. *Avoidant adults* (24 percent of the subjects) found it difficult to get close to others and described their love relationships as lacking intimacy and trust. Research eventually showed that attachment patterns are reasonably stable over time (Fraley, 2002; Mikulincer & Shaver, 2007). Thus, individuals' infant attachment experiences shape their intimate relationships in adulthood.

After years of research on adult attachment, many theorists now believe that attachment is best conceptualized in terms of where people fall on two continuous dimensions: attachment anxiety and attachment avoidance (Fraley & Shaver, 2000; Mikulincer, 2006). *Attachment anxiety* reflects how much people worry that their partners will not be available when needed. This vigilance about abandonment stems, in part, from their doubts about their lovability. *Attachment avoidance* reflects the degree to which people feel uncomfortable with closeness and intimacy and therefore tend to maintain emotional distance from their partners.

Although this new approach was intended to restructure thinking about attachment in terms of continuous dimensions, it is also compatible with the original emphasis on attachment style subtypes. But it yields one additional subtype, as people who score high or low on the two dimensions can be divided into four attachment styles. As explained in Figure 16.8, this scheme yields a *secure* subtype, a *preoccupied* subtype that is essentially equivalent to the original anxious-ambivalent subtype, and two variations on avoidant attachment: *avoidant-dismissing* and *avoidant-fearful*. Currently, some researchers measure attachment in terms of the original three subtypes of attachment style, whereas others measure attachment in terms of the two dimensions that can generate four subtypes.

Ellen Berscheid
"The emotion of romantic love seems to be distressingly fragile. As a 16th-century sage poignantly observed, 'The history of a love affair is the drama of its fight against time.'"

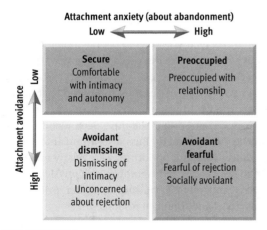

Attachment anxiety (about abandonment)
Low ⟷ High

	Low		High
Attachment avoidance Low	**Secure** Comfortable with intimacy and autonomy		**Preoccupied** Preoccupied with relationship
High	**Avoidant dismissing** Dismissing of intimacy Unconcerned about rejection		**Avoidant fearful** Fearful of rejection Socially avoidant

FIGURE 16.7

Attachment styles and their underlying dimensions.

Attachment styles can be viewed in terms of where people fall along two continuous dimensions that range from low to high: attachment avoidance and attachment anxiety (about abandonment). This system yields four attachment styles, which are described in the four cells shown here. (Adapted from Brennan, Clark, & Shaver, 1998; Fraley & Shaver, 2000)

Source: Adapted from Fraley, R.C., & Shaver, P.R. (2000). Adult romantic attachment: Theoretical developments, emerging controversies, and unanswered questions. *Review of General Psychology, 4,* 132–154.

Social Behaviour

FIGURE 16.8

Infant attachment and romantic relationships.

According to Hazan and Shaver (1987), people's romantic relationships in adulthood are similar in form to their attachment patterns in infancy, which are determined in part by parental caregiving styles. The theorized relationships between parental styles, attachment patterns, and intimate relationships are outlined here. (Data for parental caregiving styles and adult attachment styles based on Hazan and Shaver, 1986, 1987; infant attachment patterns adapted from Shaffer, 1985)

Parents' caregiving style	Infant attachment	Adult attachment style
Warm–responsive She/he was generally warm and responsive; she/he was good at knowing when to be supportive and when to let me operate on my own; our relationship was almost always comfortable, and I have no major reservations or complaints about it.	**Secure attachment** An infant–caregiver bond in which the child welcomes contact with a close companion and uses this person as a secure base from which to explore the environment	**Secure** I find it relatively easy to get close to others and am comfortable depending on them and having them depend on me. I don't often worry about being abandoned or about someone getting too close to me.
Cold–rejecting She/he was fairly cold and distant, or rejecting, not very responsive; I wasn't her/his highest priority, her/his concerns were often elsewhere; it's possible that she/he would just as soon not have had me.	**Avoidant attachment** An insecure infant–caregiver bond, characterized by little separation protest and a tendency of the child to avoid or ignore the caregiver	**Avoidant** I am somewhat uncomfortable being close to others; I find it difficult to trust them, difficult to allow myself to depend on them. I am nervous when anyone gets too close, and often love partners who want me to be more intimate than I feel comfortable being.
Ambivalent–inconsistent She/he was noticeably inconsistent in her/his reactions to me, sometimes warm and sometimes not; she/he had her/his own agenda, which sometimes got in the way of her/his receptiveness and responsiveness to my needs; she/he definitely loved me but didn't always show it in the best way.	**Anxious–ambivalent attachment** An insecure infant–caregiver bond, characterized by strong separation protest and a tendency of the child to resist contact initiated by the caregiver, particularly after a separation	**Anxious–ambivalent** I find that others are reluctant to get as close as I would like. I often worry that my partner doesn't really love me or won't want to stay with me. I want to merge completely with another person, and this desire sometimes scares people away.

Research on the correlates of adult attachment styles has grown exponentially since the mid-1990s. Consistent with the original theory, research has shown that securely attached individuals have more committed, satisfying, interdependent, well-adjusted, and longer-lasting relationships compared to people with anxious-ambivalent or avoidant attachment styles (Feeney, 2008). Moreover, studies have shown that people with different attachment styles are predisposed to think, feel, and behave differently in their relationships (Mikulincer & Shaver, 2008). For example, anxious-ambivalent people tend to report more intense emotional highs and lows in their romantic relationships. They also report having more conflicts with their partners, that these conflicts are especially stressful, and that these conflicts often have a negative impact on how they feel about their relationship (Campbell et al., 2005). In a similar vein, attachment anxiety promotes *excessive reassurance seeking*—the tendency to persistently ask for assurances from partners that one is worthy of love (Shaver, Schachner, & Mikulincer, 2005).

Culture and Close Relationships

Relatively little cross-cultural research has been conducted on the dynamics of close relationships. The limited evidence suggests both similarities and differences between cultures in romantic relationships (Hendrick & Hendrick, 2000; Schmitt, 2005). Psychologists such as the University of Toronto's Karen and Ken Dion suggest that cultures vary considerably in terms of how they understand and conceptualize love and relationships (Dion & Dion, 1996). They suggest that some of this variability is attributable to differences in societal and psychological differences in individualism and collectivism.

For the most part, similarities have been seen when research has focused on what people look for in prospective mates. As we discussed in Chapter 10, David Buss (1989, 1994a) has collected data on mate preferences in 37 divergent cultures and found that people all over the world value mutual attraction, kindness, intelligence, emotional stability, dependability, and good health in a mate. Buss also found that gender differences in mating priorities were nearly universal, with males placing more emphasis on physical attractiveness and females putting a higher priority on social status and financial resources.

Cultures vary, however, in their emphasis on love—especially passionate love—as a prerequisite for marriage. Love as the basis for marriage is an 18th-century invention of Western culture (Stone, 1977). As Hatfield and Rapson (1993) note, "Marriage-for-love represents an ultimate expression of individualism" (p. 2). In contrast, marriages arranged by families and other go-betweens remain common in cultures high in collectivism, including India, Japan, and China (Hatfield, Rapson, & Martel, 2007). This practice is declining in some societies as a result of Westernization, but in collectivist societies people contemplating marriage still tend to think in terms of "What will my parents and other people say?" rather than "What does my heart say?" (Triandis, 1994).

Studies show that attitudes about love in collectivist societies reflect these cultural priorities. For example, in comparison to Western participants, subjects from Eastern countries report that romantic love is less important for marriage (Levine et al., 1995; Medora et al., 2002). While mixed marriages are on the rise in Canada according to Statistics Canada (Statistics Canada, 2010b), sometimes the clash of cultural values can have tragic consequences. For example, Rajinder Singh Atwal of New Westminster, British Columbia, was convicted of second-degree murder in the July 2003 stabbing death of his 17-year-old-daughter, Amandeep, because she was in a relationship with Todd McIsaac, a boy of a different cultural group and religion. Atwal received an automatic life sentence, with no chance of parole for 16 years (Sikh Philosophy Network, 2005).

The Internet and Close Relationships

In recent years, the Internet has dramatically expanded opportunities for people to meet and develop close relationships through social networking services (such as *Facebook*), online dating services, e-mail, chat rooms, and news groups. Some critics worry that this trend will undermine face-to-face interactions. For example, recent research by Statistics Canada reveals that heavy Internet users spend more time alone during the day than do non–Internet users (Statistics Canada, 2009). In addition, there are concerns that many people will be lured into dangerous situations by unscrupulous people. But research to date generally paints a positive picture of the Internet's impact on people's connections with one another (Whitty, 2008). For example, the Internet offers a wealth of opportunities to interact for those who suffer from physical infirmities or social anxieties (McKenna & Bargh, 2000).

One recent survey, conducted by People Media, a company that operates online communities, reported that 49 percent of American adults indicated that they knew someone who had found a date online. According to a research survey (Madden & Lenhart, 2006), among those who used online dating sites, a majority (52 percent) reported "mostly positive" experiences, although a considerable portion (29 percent) had "mostly negative" experiences. The relevance of the Internet to interpersonal attraction is not limited to dating. Many people join various

© DPA/The Image Works

Marriages based on romantic love are the norm in Western cultures, whereas arranged marriages prevail in collectivist cultures.

types of social networking sites in the hopes of making new friends and their hopes are often realized (Fehr, 2008; McKenna, 2008).

Critics are concerned that Internet relationships are superficial. Research suggests, however, that virtual relationships are just as intimate as face-to-face ones and are sometimes even closer (Bargh, McKenna, & Fitzsimons, 2002). Moreover, many virtual relationships evolve into face-to-face interactions (Boase & Wellman, 2006). Researchers find that romantic relationships that begin on the Internet seem to be just as stable over two years as traditional relationships (McKenna, Green, & Gleason, 2002).

The power of similarity effects provides the foundation for some of the Internet's most successful online dating sites. Prior to 2000, Internet dating sites were basically just electronic variations on personal advertisements that had been around for decades—with the addition of sophisticated search capabilities. But in 2000, eHarmony.com launched the first matching website, followed by Perfectmatch.com in 2002. These sites claim to use a "scientific approach" to matching people based on compatibility. Members fill out lengthy questionnaires about their attitudes, values, interests, and so forth, and then matching algorithms are used to identify people who exhibit promising similarity. The commercial success of eHarmony.com has led many other online dating sites to add matching services. These sites have not published their matching formulas, so it is hard to say just how scientific they are, but many of the sites employ legitimate research experts as consultants (Sprecher et al., 2008). Hence, it seems likely that many of them use matching algorithms that are grounded in empirical

WEB LINK 16.3

Y? The National Forum on People's Differences
Did you ever want to ask a sensitive question of someone who was different from you—another race or religion or sexual orientation—but were too embarrassed or shy? In a cyberforum with clear rules for courteous and respectful dialogue, newspaper writer and editor Philip J. Milano allows visitors to share differences openly and frankly and to learn about topics that are frequently kept quiet.

Social Behaviour

research on interpersonal attraction. Of course, as you have already learned in this chapter, similarity is just one of many factors that play a role in the dynamics of attraction. Still, it is interesting to note that the growth of the Internet has brought psychological science into play in the domain of close relationships.

An Evolutionary Perspective on Attraction

Evolutionary psychologists have a great deal to say about heterosexual attraction. For example, they assert that physical appearance is an influential determinant of attraction because certain aspects of good looks can be indicators of sound health, good genes, and high fertility, all of which can contribute to reproductive potential (Gallup & Frederick, 2010).

Consistent with this analysis, research has found that some standards of attractiveness are more consistent across cultures than previously believed (Cunningham, Druen, & Barbee, 1997). For example, *facial symmetry* seems to be a key element of attractiveness in highly diverse cultures (Cunningham et al., 1995; Fink & Penton-Voak, 2002). Facial symmetry is thought to be valued because a host of environmental insults and developmental abnormalities are associated with physical asymmetries, which may serve as markers of relatively poor genes or health (Fink et al., 2006). Another facet of appearance that may transcend culture is *women's waist-to-hip ratio* (Singh et al., 2010). Around the world, men seem to prefer women with a waist-to-hip ratio around 0.70–0.80, which roughly corresponds to an "hourglass figure." This appears to be a meaningful correlate of females' reproductive potential (Gallup & Frederick, 2010), as it signals that a woman is healthy, young, and not pregnant.

The most thoroughly documented findings on the evolutionary bases of heterosexual attraction are the findings on gender differences in humans' mating preferences (Neubert, Kenrick, & Schaller, 2010). Consistent with the notion that humans are programmed by evolution to behave in ways that enhance their reproductive fitness, evidence indicates that men generally are more interested than women in seeking youthfulness and physical attractiveness in their mates because these traits should be associated with greater reproductive potential (see Chapter 10). On the other hand, research shows that women place a greater premium on prospective mates' ambition, social status, and financial potential because these traits should be associated with the ability to invest material resources in children.

There are some qualifications to these trends, but even these caveats make evolutionary sense. For example, when women are asked what they prefer in a *short-term partner* (for casual sex), they value physical attractiveness just as much as men (Li & Kenrick, 2006). And very attractive women, aware of their own high mate value, want it all—they want prospective male partners to exhibit excellent economic potential *and* physical attractiveness (Buss & Shackelford, 2008).

Women's menstrual cycles also influence their mating preferences. When women are in mid-cycle approaching ovulation—that is, when they are most fertile—their preferences shift to favour men who exhibit masculine facial and bodily features, attractiveness, and dominance (Gangestad, Thornhill, & Garver-Apgar, 2005; Gangestad et al., 2007; Little et al., 2007). Men seem to recognize this shift, as they rate masculine males as more threatening when their partners are in the fertile portion of their menstrual cycle (Burriss & Little, 2006). Interestingly, although ovulation is far from obvious in human females, strippers earn more tip money per night when they are in their most fertile period (Miller, Tybur, & Jordan, 2007). Researchers aren't sure whether male patrons are "detecting" the strippers' heightened fertility, or whether the ovulating lap dancers come on to the customers more because they are more sexually motivated.

REVIEW OF KEY POINTS

▷ People tend to like and love others who are physically attractive. The matching hypothesis asserts that people who are similar in physical attractiveness are more likely to be drawn together than those who are not.

▷ Research suggests that similarity causes attraction, although attitude alignment may also be at work.

▷ Berscheid and Hatfield have distinguished between passionate and companionate love. Sternberg builds on their distinction by dividing companionate love into intimacy and commitment.

▷ Hazan and Shaver's theory suggests that love relationships in adulthood mimic attachment patterns in infancy. People tend to be secure, avoidant, or anxious-ambivalent in their romantic relationships. Those who are secure tend to have more committed, satisfying relationships.

▷ The characteristics that people seek in prospective mates are much the same around the world. The gender differences in mating preferences seen in Western societies also appear to transcend culture. However, cultures vary considerably in their emphasis on passionate love as a prerequisite for marriage.

▷ According to evolutionary psychologists, certain aspects of good looks influence attraction because they are indicators of reproductive fitness. Consistent with evolutionary theory, men tend to seek youthfulness and attractiveness in their mates, whereas women emphasize prospective mates' financial potential and willingness to invest material resources in children.

Attitudes: Making Social Judgments

Social psychology's interest in attitudes has a much longer history than its interest in attraction. Indeed, in its early days, social psychology was defined as the *study of attitudes*. In this section, we'll discuss the nature of attitudes, efforts to change attitudes through persuasion, and theories of attitude change.

What are attitudes? *Attitudes* are positive or negative evaluations of objects of thought. "Objects of thought" may include social issues (capital punishment or gun control, for example), groups (liberals, farmers), institutions (the Lutheran church, the Supreme Court), consumer products (yogurt, computers), and people (the prime minister, your next-door neighbour).

Components and Dimensions of Attitudes

Social psychologists have traditionally viewed attitudes as being made up of three components: a cognitive component, an affective component, and a behavioural component. However, it gradually became apparent that many attitudes do not include all three components (Fazio & Olson, 2003), so it is more accurate to say that *attitudes may include up to three types of components* (Banaji & Heiphetz, 2010). The *cognitive component* of an attitude is made up of the beliefs that people hold about the object of an attitude. The *affective component* of an attitude consists of the *emotional feelings*

stimulated by an object of thought. The *behavioural component* of an attitude consists of *predispositions to act* in certain ways toward an attitude object. Figure 16.9 provides concrete examples of how someone's attitude about gun control might be divided into its components.

According to the University of Western Ontario's Jim Olson and the University of Waterloo's Mark Zanna, attitudes vary along several crucial dimensions, including their *strength, accessibility,* and *ambivalence* (Olson & Zanna, 1993). Definitions of *attitude strength* differ, but they generally view strong attitudes as ones that are firmly held (resistant to change) and durable over time, and that have a powerful impact on behaviour (Krosnick & Petty, 1995). The *accessibility* of an attitude refers to how often one thinks about it and how quickly it comes to mind. Highly accessible attitudes are quickly and readily available (Fazio, 1995). Attitude accessibility is correlated with attitude strength, as highly accessible attitudes *tend* to be strong, but the concepts are distinct and there is no one-to-one correspondence.

Ambivalent attitudes are conflicted evaluations that include both positive and negative feelings about an object of thought (Thompson, Zanna, & Griffin, 1995). Like attitude strength, attitude ambivalence has been measured in different ways (Priester & Petty, 2001). Generally speaking, ambivalence increases as the ratio of positive to negative evaluations gets closer to being equal. When ambivalence

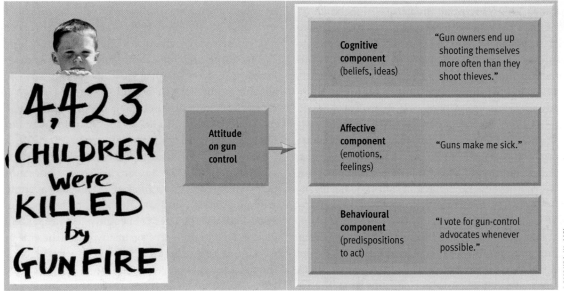

FIGURE 16.9

The possible components of attitudes.

Attitudes may include cognitive, affective, and behavioural components, as illustrated here for a hypothetical person's attitude about gun control.

© 2002 Wide World Photos

is high, an attitude tends to be less predictive of behaviour and more pliable in the face of persuasion (Fabrigar & Wegener, 2010).

Attitudes and Behaviour

In the early 1930s, when prejudice against Asians was common in North America, Richard LaPiere journeyed across the United States with a Chinese couple. He was more than a little surprised when they weren't turned away from any of the restaurants they visited in their travels—184 restaurants in all. About six months after his trip, LaPiere surveyed the same restaurants and asked whether they would serve Chinese customers. Roughly half of the restaurants replied to the survey, and over 90 percent of them indicated that they would not seat Chinese patrons. Thus, LaPiere (1934) found that people who voice prejudicial attitudes may not behave in discriminatory ways. Since then, theorists have often asked: Why don't attitudes predict behaviour better?

Admittedly, LaPiere's study had a fundamental flaw that you may already have detected. The person who seated LaPiere and his Chinese friends may not have been the same person who responded to the mail survey sent later. Nonetheless, numerous follow-up studies, using more sophisticated methods, have shown that attitudes are mediocre predictors of people's behaviour (Ajzen & Fishbein, 2005; McGuire, 1985). That's not to say that attitudes are irrelevant or meaningless. Wallace and his colleagues (2005) reviewed 797 attitude–behaviour studies and found that the average correlation between attitudes and behaviour was 0.41. That figure is high enough to justify Eagly's (1992) conclusion that researchers have identified "many conditions under which attitudes are substantial predictors of behaviour" (p. 697). But on the whole, social psychologists have been surprised by how often a favourable attitude toward a candidate or product does not translate into a vote or a purchase.

Why aren't attitude–behaviour relationships more consistent? One consideration is that until recently researchers failed to take variations in *attitude strength, accessibility, and ambivalence* into account (Fabrigar & Wegener, 2010). Accumulating evidence indicates that these factors influence the connection between attitudes and behaviour, but they have generally been left uncontrolled in decades of research on attitudes (Cooke & Sheeran, 2004; Olson & Maio, 2003). Research suggests that strong attitudes that are highly accessible and have been stable over time tend to be more predictive of behaviour (Glasman & Albarracin, 2006). Another consideration is that

attitudes are often measured in a *general, global* way that isn't likely to predict *specific* behaviours (Bohner & Schwarz, 2001). Although you may express favourable feelings about protecting the environment (a very general, abstract concept), you may not be willing to give $100 to the David Suzuki Foundation (a very specific action).

Inconsistent relationships between attitudes and behaviour are also seen because behaviour depends on situational constraints—especially your subjective perceptions of how people expect you to behave (Ajzen & Fishbein, 2000, 2005). The review of research cited earlier (Wallace et al., 2005), which found that attitudes correlate 0.41 with behaviour on average, also noted that when social pressures are high, this correlation diminishes to 0.30. Thus, attitudes interact with situational constraints to shape people's behaviour. Although you may be strongly opposed to marijuana use, you may not say anything when friends start passing a joint around at a party because you don't want to turn the party into an argument. However, in another situation governed by different norms, such as a class discussion, you may speak out forcefully against marijuana use.

Implicit Attitudes: Looking beneath the Surface

In recent years, theorists have begun to make a distinction between explicit and implicit attitudes (Bohner & Dickel, 2011). *Explicit attitudes are attitudes that we hold consciously and can readily describe.* For the most part, these overt attitudes are what social psychologists have always studied until fairly recently. *Implicit attitudes are covert attitudes that are expressed in subtle automatic responses over which we have little conscious control.* It was only in the mid-1990s that social psychologists started digging beneath the surface to explore the meaning and importance of implicit attitudes. People can have implicit attitudes about virtually anything. But implicit attitudes were discovered in research on prejudice and their role in various types of prejudice continues to be the main focus of current inquiry.

Why are implicit attitudes a central issue in the study of prejudice? Because in modern societies most people have been taught that prejudicial attitudes are inappropriate and something to be ashamed of. Today, the vast majority of people reject racial prejudice, as well as prejudice against women, the elderly, gays, and those who are disabled or mentally ill. At the same time, however, people grow up in a culture where negative stereotypes about these groups are widely disseminated. Although most of us want to be unbiased, research has shown that these negative ideas can seep into our subconscious mind and contaminate our reactions to others. Thus, many people express explicit attitudes that condemn prejudice, but unknowingly harbour implicit attitudes that reflect subtle forms of prejudice (Devine & Sharp, 2009; Dovidio & Gaertner, 2008).

How are implicit attitudes measured? A number of techniques have been developed, but the most widely used is the *Implicit Association Test* (IAT) (Greenwald & Banaji, 1995; Greenwald, McGhee, & Schwartz, 1998). This computer-administered test measures how quickly people associate carefully chosen pairs of concepts. Let's consider how the IAT would be used to assess implicit prejudice against blacks. A series of words and pictures are presented onscreen and subjects are urged to respond to these stimuli as quickly and accurately as possible. In the first series of trials respondents are instructed to press a specific key with their left hand if the stimulus is a black person or a positive word and to press another key with their right hand if the stimulus is a white person or a negative word (see Figure 16.10). In the second series of trials, the instructions are changed and participants are told to press the left-hand key if the stimulus is a black person or a negative word and to press the right-hand key if the stimulus is a white person or positive word. The various types of stimuli are presented in quick succession and the computer records precise reaction times. Research shows that reaction times are quicker when liked faces are paired with positive words and disliked faces with negative words. So, if respondents have negative implicit attitudes about black people, the second series of trials will yield shorter average reaction times. And if this is so, the size of the difference between average reaction times in the two series provides an index of the strength of participants' implicit racism.

Since 1998, millions of people have responded to a Web-based version of the IAT (Nosek, Banaji, & Greenwald, 2002; Nosek, Greenwald, & Banaji, 2007). Although surveys of people's explicit attitudes suggest that prejudice has declined considerably, the IAT results show that over 80 percent of respondents, both young and old, show negative implicit attitudes about the elderly. And about three-quarters of white respondents exhibit implicit prejudice against blacks. The findings also indicate that implicit prejudice against gays, the disabled, and the obese is common.

Do IAT scores based on tiny differences in reaction times predict prejudicial behaviour in the real world? Yes, IAT scores are predictive of subtle, but potentially important differences in behaviour (Greenwald et al., 2009). For instance, white participants' degree of implicit racial prejudice predicts how far they

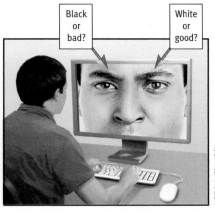

FIGURE 16.10

Measuring implicit attitudes.

The IAT assesses implicit prejudice against blacks by tracking how quickly subjects respond to images of black and white people paired with positive or negative words. If participants are prejudiced against black people, they will react more quickly to the pairings in the condition on the right. The IAT has been used to measure implicit attitudes toward a variety of groups.

Source: From WEITEN. *Psychology*, 9E. © 2013 Wadsworth, a part of Cengage Learning, Inc. Reproduced by permission. www.cengage.com/permissions.

choose to sit from a black partner with whom they expect to work on a task (Amodio & Devine, 2006). Higher implicit racism scores in white subjects are also associated with decreased smiling, reduced eye contact, shorter speaking time, and more speech hesitations in interracial interactions (Devos, 2008).

These are subtle, but potentially important differences in behaviour, which demonstrate that implicit attitudes can have far-reaching consequences. Although research on implicit attitudes has been dominated by work on various types of prejudice, the IAT method has also been used to gain insights about people's unconscious feelings about smoking (Huijding et al., 2005), drinking (Houben & Wiers, 2008), consumer products (Friese, Wanke, & Plessner, 2006), and their romantic partners (Banse, 2007). Thus, implicit attitudes can be relevant in a wide variety of situations.

Trying to Change Attitudes: Factors in Persuasion

The fact that attitudes aren't always good predictors of a person's behaviour doesn't stop others from trying to change those attitudes. Indeed, every day you're bombarded by efforts to alter your attitudes (Loken, 2006). Everyone from your parents to advertisers is trying to change your attitudes.

"Doesn't it ever let up?" you wonder. When it comes to persuasion, the answer is "no." As Anthony Pratkanis and Elliot Aronson (2000) put it, we live in the "age of propaganda." Social psychologists have been very active in examining factors that affect whether persuasion attempts work or not (Petty &

Social Behaviour

FIGURE 16.11

Overview of the persuasion process.

The process of persuasion essentially boils down to *who* (the source) communicates *what* (the message) *by what means* (the channel) *to whom* (the receiver). Thus, there are four sets of variables that influence the process of persuasion: source, message, channel, and receiver factors. The diagram lists some of the more important factors in each category (including some that are not discussed in the text due to space limitations). (Adapted from Lippa, 1994)

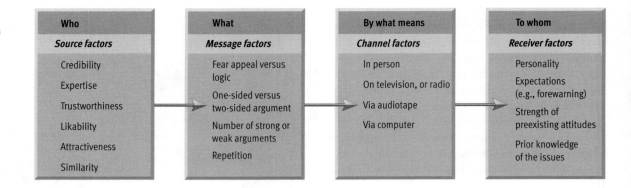

Brinol, 2008). Let's examine some of the factors that determine whether persuasion works.

The process of persuasion includes four basic elements: source, receiver, message, and channel (see Figure 16.11). The *source* is the person who sends a communication, and the *receiver* is the person to whom the message is sent. So, if you watch a political news conference on TV, the politician is the source, and you and millions of other viewers are the receivers. The *message* is the information transmitted by the source, and the *channel* is the medium through which the message is sent. Although the research on communication channels is interesting, we'll confine our discussion to source, message, and receiver variables, which are most applicable to persuasion.

Source Factors

Occasional exceptions to the general rule are seen, but persuasion tends to be more successful when the source has high *credibility* (Albarracin & Vargas, 2010). What gives a person credibility? Either expertise or trustworthiness. *Expertise* tends to be more influential when arguments are ambiguous (Chaiken & Maheswaran, 1994). People try to convey their expertise by mentioning their degrees, their training, and their experience or by showing an impressive grasp of the issue at hand.

Expertise is a plus, but *trustworthiness* can be even more important. Many people tend to accept messages from trustworthy sources with little scrutiny (Priester & Petty, 1995, 2003). If you were told that your province needs to reduce corporate taxes to stimulate its economy, would you be more likely to believe it from the president of a huge corporation in your province or from an economics professor in another province? Probably the latter. Trustworthiness is undermined when a source, such as the corporation president, appears to have something to gain. In contrast, trustworthiness is enhanced when people appear to argue against their own interests (Hunt, Smith, & Kernan, 1985). This effect

explains why salespeople often make remarks like, "Frankly, my snowblower isn't the best. They have a better brand down the street. Of course, you'll have to spend quite a bit more. . . ."

Likability also increases the effectiveness of a persuasive source (Johnson, Maio, & Smith-McLallen, 2005), and some of the factors at work in attraction therefore have an impact on persuasion. Thus, the favourable effect of *physical attractiveness* on likability can make persuasion more effective (Shavitt et al., 1994). We also respond better to sources who share *similarity* with us in ways that are relevant to the issue at hand (Mackie, Worth, & Asuncion, 1990).

The importance of source variables can be seen in advertising. Many companies spend a fortune to obtain an ideal spokesperson. Right now one of the most sought-after spokespersons in Canada is Sidney Crosby. Crosby is billed as one of the superstars of the NHL. Companies quickly abandon spokespersons when their likability declines. If Crosby doesn't continue to fulfill people's expectations for him, he will be dropped as advertisers look for the next superstar.

Message Factors

If you were going to give a speech to a local community group advocating a reduction in taxes on corporations, you'd probably wrestle with a number of questions about how to structure your message. Should you look at both sides of the issue, or should you present just your side? Should you use all of the arguments at your disposal, or should you concentrate on the stronger arguments? Should you deliver a low-key, logical speech? Or should you try to strike fear into the hearts of your listeners? These questions are concerned with message factors in persuasion.

Let's assume that you're aware that there are two sides to the taxation issue. On the one hand, you're convinced that lower corporate taxes will bring new companies to your city and stimulate economic growth. On the other hand, you realize that reduced tax revenues may hurt the quality of education and roads in your province, although you think the

Sidney Crosby, who plays for the Pittsburgh Penguins, is considered to be an NHL superstar and is highly sought after by advertisers. His very positive image is seen to be a real asset for their products.

Claudio Bresciani/SCANPIX/Kod 10090

benefits will outweigh the costs. Should you present a *one-sided argument* that ignores the possible problems for education and road quality? Or should you present a *two-sided argument* that acknowledges concern about education and road quality and then downplays the probable magnitude of these problems? The optimal strategy depends on a variety of considerations but, overall, two-sided arguments tend to be more effective (Petty & Wegener, 1998). Just mentioning that there are two sides to an issue can increase your credibility with an audience.

In presenting your side, should you use every argument you can think of, or should you focus on the stronger points? One study suggests that it is wise to concentrate on your strong arguments (Friedrich et al., 1996). The investigators exposed students to a variety of weak and strong arguments advocating a new senior comprehensive exam at their school. They found that adding strong arguments paid off, but adding weak arguments hurt

rather than helped (see Figure 16.12). It appears that weak arguments may actually raise doubts rather than add to your case.

Persuasive messages frequently attempt to arouse fear. Opponents of nuclear power scare us with visions of meltdowns. Anti-smoking campaigns emphasize the threat of cancer, and deodorant ads highlight the risk of embarrassment. You could follow their lead and argue that if corporate taxes aren't reduced, your province will be headed toward economic ruin and massive unemployment. *Do appeals to fear work?* Yes—if they are indeed successful in arousing fear. Research reveals that many messages intended to induce fear fail to do so. However, studies involving a wide range of issues (nuclear policy, auto safety, dental hygiene, and so on) have shown that messages that are effective in arousing fear tend to increase persuasion (Block & Keller, 1997; Witte & Allen, 2000). Fear appeals are most likely to work when your listeners view the dire consequences that you describe as exceedingly unpleasant, fairly probable if they don't take your advice, and avoidable if they do (Das, de Wit, & Stroebe, 2003).

Frequent repetition of a message also seems to be an effective strategy. The *truth effect* or *validity effect* refers to the finding that simply repeating a statement causes it to be perceived as more valid or true. It doesn't matter whether the statement is true, false, or clearly just an opinion (Boehm, 1994; Dechene et al., 2010; Weaver et al., 2007). If you repeat something often enough, some people come to believe it (Dechene et al., 2010; Weaver et al., 2007). Repetition works for both weak and strong arguments, but it is most effective when receivers are not motivated

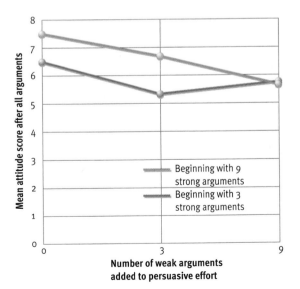

Number of weak arguments added to persuasive effort

Mean attitude score after all arguments

Beginning with 9 strong arguments
Beginning with 3 strong arguments

FIGURE 16.12

The effect of adding weak arguments to one's case.

Friedrich et al. (1996) exposed students to various arguments in favour of requiring a new comprehensive exam for seniors at their school. This graph shows the effects of adding zero, three, or nine weak arguments to three or nine strong arguments. As you can see, in this instance, adding weak arguments generally had a negative effect on overall persuasion. (Data from Friedrich et al., 1996)

Source: adapted from Friedrich, J., Fetherstonhaugh, D., Casey, S., & Gallagher, D. (1996). Argument integration and attitude change; Suppression effects in the integration of one-sided arguments that vary in persuasiveness. *Personality and Social Psychology Bulletin, 22*, 179–191.

Social Behaviour

FIGURE 16.13

The mere exposure effect.

In seminal research on the mere exposure effect, Robert Zajonc (1968) manipulated how often participants were exposed to various unfamiliar, neutral stimuli. As the data show here, he found that increased exposures led to increased liking. The mere exposure effect may shed light on why repetition is an effective strategy in persuasion.

Source: From WEITEN. *Psychology*, 9E. © 2013 Wadsworth, a part of Cengage Learning, Inc. Reproduced by permission. www.cengage.com/permissions.

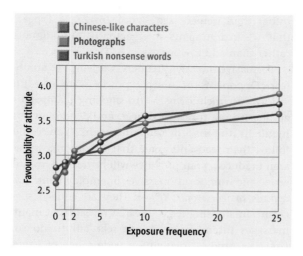

to pay close attention (Moons, Mackie, & Garcia-Marques, 2009).

The truth effect may depend in part on the mere exposure effect first described by prominent social psychologist Robert Zajonc (APS Observer, 2009). The *mere exposure effect* is the finding that repeated exposures to a stimulus promotes greater liking of the stimulus. In a groundbreaking study (Zajonc, 1968), participants were exposed to unfamiliar Turkish words 0, 1, 2, 5, 10, or 25 times. Subsequently, the subjects were asked to rate the degree to which they thought the words referred to something good or bad. The more subjects had been exposed to a specific word, the more favourably they rated it. Zajonc observed remarkably similar findings when participants rated the favourability of selected Chinese pictographs (the symbols used in Chinese writing) and when they rated the likability of people shown in yearbook photos (see Figure 16.13).

The mere exposure effect has been replicated with many types of stimuli including sounds, nonsense syllables, meaningful words, line drawings, photographs, and various types of objects (Albarracin & Vargas, 2010; Bornstein, 1989). The mere exposure effect may explain why companies such as Coca-Cola and McDonald's continue to spend enormous amounts of money on advertising when nearly everyone is already very familiar with their products. Mere exposure is a subtle process that appears to sway people's attitudes unconsciously and it may explain why repetition of a message can enhance persuasion.

Receiver Factors

What about the receiver of the persuasive message? Are some people easier to persuade than others? Undoubtedly, but researchers have not found any personality traits that are reliably associated with susceptibility to persuasion (Petty & Wegener, 1998). Other factors, such as the forewarning a receiver gets

about a persuasive effort and the receiver's initial position on an issue, generally seem to be more influential than the receiver's personality.

An old saying suggests that "to be forewarned is to be forearmed." The value of *forewarning* applies to targets of persuasive efforts (Janssen, Fennis, & Pruyn, 2010; Wood & Quinn, 2003). When you shop for a new TV, you *expect* salespeople to work at persuading you, and to some extent this forewarning reduces the impact of their arguments. Considerations that stimulate counterarguing in the receiver tend to increase resistance to persuasion.

Furthermore, studies show that *stronger attitudes are more resistant to change* (Eagly & Chaiken, 1998; Miller & Peterson, 2004). Strong attitudes may be tougher to alter because they tend to be embedded in networks of beliefs and values that might also require change (Erber, Hodges, & Wilson, 1995). Finally, *resistance can promote resistance*. That is, when people successfully resist persuasive efforts to change specific attitudes, they often become more certain about those attitudes (Tormala & Petty, 2002, 2004).

Our review of source, message, and receiver variables has shown that attempting to change attitudes through persuasion involves a complex interplay of factors—and we haven't even looked beneath the surface yet. How do people acquire attitudes in the first place? What dynamic processes within people produce attitude change? We turn to these theoretical issues next.

Theories of Attitude Formation and Change   12c

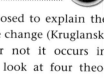

Many theories have been proposed to explain the mechanisms at work in attitude change (Kruglanski & Stroebe, 2005), whether or not it occurs in response to persuasion. We'll look at four theoretical perspectives: learning theory, dissonance theory, self-perception theory, and the elaboration likelihood model.

Learning Theory   12c

We've seen repeatedly that *learning theory* can help explain a wide range of phenomena, from conditioned fears to the acquisition of sex roles to the development of personality traits. Now we can add attitude formation and change to our list. Attitudes may be learned from parents, peers, the media, cultural traditions, and other social influences (Banaji & Heiphetz, 2010).

The affective, or emotional, component in an attitude can be created through classical conditioning, just as other emotional responses can (Olson & Fazio, 2001, 2002; Walther & Langer, 2008). As we discussed in Chapter 6, *evaluative conditioning* consists of efforts to transfer the emotion attached to a UCS to a new CS (Kruglanski & Stroebe, 2005; Schimmack & Crites, 2005). Advertisers routinely try to take advantage of classical conditioning by pairing their products with stimuli that elicit pleasant emotional responses, such as extremely attractive models, highly likable spokespersons, and cherished events, such as the Olympics (Grossman & Till, 1998; Till & Priluck, 2000). This conditioning process is diagrammed in Figure 16.14. It can occur without awareness and seems to be exceptionally resistant to extinction (Albarracin & Vargas, 2010).

Operant conditioning may come into play when you openly express an attitude, such as "I believe that husbands should do more housework." Some people may endorse your view, while others may jump down your throat. Agreement from other people generally functions as a reinforcer, strengthening your tendency to express a specific attitude (Bohner & Schwarz, 2001). Disagreement often functions as a form of punishment, which may gradually weaken your commitment to your viewpoint.

FIGURE 16.14

Classical conditioning of attitudes in advertising.

Advertisers routinely pair their products with likable celebrities in the hope that their products will come to elicit pleasant emotional responses. See the Critical Thinking Application in Chapter 6 (page 296) for a more in-depth discussion of this practice.

---

concept check 16.3

Understanding Attitudes and Persuasion

Check your understanding of the possible components of attitudes and the elements of persuasion by analyzing hypothetical political strategies. Imagine you're working on a political campaign and you're invited to join the candidate's inner circle in strategy sessions, as staff members prepare the candidate for upcoming campaign stops. During the meetings, you hear various strategies discussed. For each strategy below, indicate which component of voters' attitudes (cognitive, affective, or behavioural) is being targeted for change, and indicate which element in persuasion (source, message, or receiver factors) is being manipulated. The answers are in Appendix A.

1. "You need to convince this crowd that your program for regulating nursing homes is sound. Whatever you do, don't acknowledge the two weaknesses in the program that we've been playing down. I don't care if you're asked point-blank. Just slide by the question and keep harping on the program's advantages."

2. "You haven't been smiling enough lately, especially when the TV cameras are rolling. Remember, you can have the best ideas in the world, but if you don't seem likable, you're not gonna get elected. By the way, I think I've lined up some photo opportunities that should help us create an image of sincerity and compassion."

3. "This crowd is already behind you. You don't have to alter their opinions on any issue. Get right to work convincing them to contribute to the campaign. I want them lining up to give money."

Leon Festinger

"Cognitive dissonance is a motivating state of affairs. Just as hunger impels a person to eat, so does dissonance impact a person to change his opinions or his behavior."

Another person's attitudes may rub off on you through *observational learning* (Banaji & Heiphetz, 2010; Oskamp, 1991). If you hear your uncle say, "Conservatives are nothing but puppets of big business" and your mother heartily agrees, your exposure to your uncle's attitude and your mother's reinforcement of your uncle may influence your attitude toward the Conservative Party. Studies show that parents and their children tend to have similar political attitudes (Sears, 1975) and that college students living in residence halls tend to show some convergence in attitudes (Cullum & Harton, 2007). Observational learning presumably accounts for much of this similarity. The opinions of teachers, coaches, co-workers, talk-show hosts, rock stars, and so forth are also likely to sway people's attitudes through observational learning.

Dissonance Theory

Leon Festinger's *dissonance theory* assumes that inconsistency among attitudes propels people in the direction of attitude change. Dissonance theory had a profound impact on the directions taken by researchers in social psychology (Aronson, 2010). It burst into prominence in 1959 when Festinger and J. Merrill Carlsmith published a famous study of counterattitudinal behaviour. Let's look at their findings and at how dissonance theory explains them.

Festinger and Carlsmith (1959) had male college students come to a laboratory, where they worked on excruciatingly dull tasks such as turning pegs repeatedly. When a subject's hour was over, the experimenter confided that some participants' motivation was being manipulated by telling them that the task was interesting and enjoyable before they started it. Then, after a moment's hesitation, the experimenter asked if the subject could help him out of a jam. His usual helper was delayed and he needed someone to testify to the next "subject" (really an accomplice) that the experimental task was interesting. He offered to pay the subject if he would tell the person in the adjoining waiting room that the task was enjoyable and involving.

This entire scenario was enacted to coax participants into doing something that was inconsistent with their true feelings—that is, to engage in *counterattitudinal behaviour*. Some participants received a token payment of $1 for their effort, while others received a more substantial payment of $20 (an amount equivalent to about $80–$90 today, in light of inflation). Later, a second experimenter inquired about the subjects' true feelings regarding the dull experimental task. Figure 16.15 summarizes the design of the Festinger and Carlsmith study.

Who do you think rated the task more favourably—the subjects who were paid $1 or those who were paid $20? Both common sense and learning theory would predict that the subjects who received the greater reward ($20) should come to like the task more. In reality, however, the subjects who were paid $1 exhibited more favourable attitude change—just as Festinger and Carlsmith had predicted. Why? Dissonance theory provides an explanation.

According to Festinger (1957), *cognitive dissonance* exists when related cognitions are inconsistent—that is, when they contradict each other. Cognitive dissonance is thought to create an unpleasant state of tension that motivates people to reduce their dissonance—usually by altering their cognitions. In the study by Festinger and Carlsmith, the subjects' contradictory cognitions were "The task is boring" and "I told someone the task was enjoyable." The subjects who were paid $20 for lying had an obvious reason for behaving inconsistently with their true

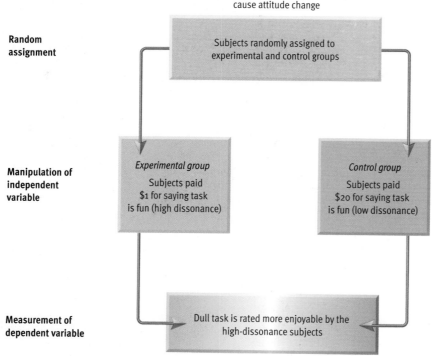

Hypothesis:
High dissonance about counterattitudinal behaviour will cause attitude change

Random assignment

Subjects randomly assigned to experimental and control groups

Manipulation of independent variable

Experimental group
Subjects paid $1 for saying task is fun (high dissonance)

Control group
Subjects paid $20 for saying task is fun (low dissonance)

Measurement of dependent variable

Dull task is rated more enjoyable by the high-dissonance subjects

Conclusion:
Dissonance about counterattitudinal behaviour does cause attitude change

FIGURE 16.15

Design of the Festinger and Carlsmith (1959) study.
The sequence of events in this landmark study of counterattitudinal behaviour and attitude change is outlined here. The diagram omits a third condition (no dissonance), in which subjects were not induced to lie. The results in the nondissonance condition were similar to those found in the low-dissonance condition.

attitudes, so these subjects experienced little dissonance. In contrast, the subjects paid $1 had no readily apparent justification for their lie and experienced high dissonance. To reduce it, they tended to persuade themselves that the task was more enjoyable than they had originally thought. Thus, dissonance theory sheds light on why people sometimes come to believe their own lies.

Cognitive dissonance is also at work when people turn attitudinal somersaults to justify efforts that haven't panned out, a syndrome called *effort justification.* Aronson and Mills (1959) studied effort justification by putting college women through a "severe initiation" before they could qualify to participate in what promised to be an interesting discussion of sexuality. In the initiation, the women had to read obscene passages out loud to a male experimenter. After all that, the highly touted discussion of sexuality turned out to be a boring, taped lecture on reproduction in lower animals. Subjects in the severe initiation condition experienced highly dissonant cognitions ("I went through a lot to get here" and "This discussion is terrible"). How did they reduce their dissonance? Apparently, by changing their attitude about the discussion, since they rated it more favourably than subjects in two control conditions. Effort justification may be at work in many facets of everyday life. For example, people who wait in line for an hour or more to get into an exclusive restaurant often praise the restaurant afterward even if they have been served a mediocre meal.

Dissonance theory has been tested in hundreds of studies with mixed, but largely favourable, results. The dynamics of dissonance appear to underlie many important types of attitude changes (Draycott & Dabbs, 1998; Hosseini, 1997; Keller & Block, 1999). Research has supported Festinger's claim that dissonance involves genuine psychological discomfort and even physiological arousal (Croyle & Cooper, 1983; Devine et al., 1999).

Dissonance theory is not without its critics. Daryl Bem (1967), for example, suggested that the effects typically attributed to dissonance were instead the result of what he referred to as *self-perception processes.* According to Bem's *self-perception theory,* people often *infer* their attitudes from their behaviour. Thus, Bem argued that in the study by Festinger and Carlsmith (1959), the subjects paid $1 probably thought to themselves, "A dollar isn't enough money to get me to lie, so I must have found the task enjoyable." Bem originally believed that most findings explained by dissonance were really due to self-perception. However, studies eventually showed that self-perception is at work primarily when subjects do not have well-defined attitudes regarding the issue at hand (Olson & Roese, 1995). Although self-perception theory did not

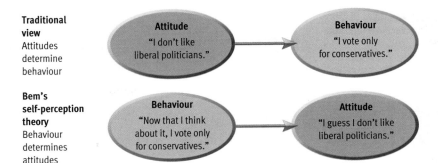

FIGURE 16.16

Bem's self-perception theory.

The traditional view is that attitudes determine behaviour. However, Bem stood conventional logic on its head when he proposed that behaviour often determines (or causes people to draw inferences about) their attitudes. Subsequent research on attribution has shown that sometimes people *do* infer their attitudes from their behaviour.

replace dissonance theory, Bem's work demonstrated that attitudes are sometimes inferred from one's own behaviour (Olson & Stone, 2005) (see Figure 16.16).

REVIEW OF KEY POINTS

▷ Attitudes may be made up of cognitive, affective, and behavioural components. Attitudes and behaviour aren't as consistent as one might assume, in part because attitude strength varies and in part because attitudes only create predispositions to behave in certain ways.

▷ Explicit attitudes are attitudes that we hold consciously and can readily describe. Implicit attitudes are covert attitudes that are expressed in subtle automatic responses. Implicit attitudes are measured by testing how quickly people associate carefully chosen pairs of concepts. Research with the IAT suggests that people harbour covert prejudices, which do affect overt behaviour.

▷ A source of persuasion who is credible, expert, trustworthy, likable, and physically attractive tends to be relatively effective in stimulating attitude change.

▷ Although there are some situational limitations, two-sided arguments and fear arousal are effective elements in persuasive messages. Repetition is helpful, but adding weak arguments to one's case may hurt more than help.

▷ Persuasion is undermined when a receiver is forewarned, when the sender advocates a position that is incompatible with the receiver's existing attitudes, or when strong attitudes are targeted.

▷ Attitudes may be shaped through classical conditioning, operant conditioning, and observational learning. Festinger's dissonance theory asserts that inconsistent attitudes cause tension and that people alter their attitudes to reduce cognitive dissonance.

▷ Dissonance theory has been used to explain attitude change following counterattitudinal behaviour and efforts that haven't panned out. Some of these results can be explained by self-perception theory, which posits that people may infer their attitudes from their behaviour.

▷ The elaboration likelihood model of persuasion (outlined on the next page) holds that the central route to persuasion tends to yield longer-lasting attitude change than the peripheral route.

FIGURE 16.17

The elaboration likelihood model.

According to the elaboration likelihood model (Petty & Cacioppo, 1986), the central route to persuasion leads to more elaboration of message content and more enduring attitude change than the peripheral route to persuasion.

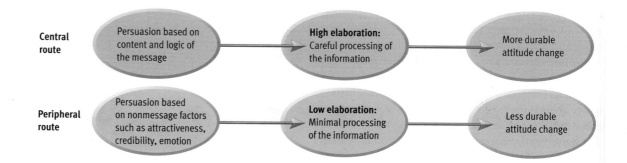

Elaboration Likelihood Model

12c  PSYKTREK

The *elaboration likelihood model* of attitude change, originally proposed by Richard Petty and John Cacioppo (1986), asserts that there are two basic "routes" to persuasion (Petty & Brinol, 2008; Petty & Wegener, 1999). The *central route* is taken when people carefully ponder the content and logic of persuasive messages. The *peripheral route* is taken when persuasion depends on nonmessage factors, such as the attractiveness and credibility of the source, or on conditioned emotional responses (see Figure 16.17). For example, a politician who campaigns by delivering carefully researched speeches that thoughtfully analyze complex issues is following the central route to persuasion. In contrast,

a politician who depends on marching bands, flag-waving, celebrity endorsements, and emotional slogans is following the peripheral route.

Both routes can lead to persuasion. However, according to the elaboration likelihood model, the durability of attitude change depends on the extent to which people elaborate on (think about) the contents of persuasive communications. Studies suggest that the central route to persuasion leads to more enduring attitude change than the peripheral route (Petty & Wegener, 1998). Research also suggests that attitudes changed through central processes predict behaviour better than attitudes changed through peripheral processes (Kruglanski & Stroebe, 2005; Petty, Petty, & Brinol, 2010).

Conformity and Obedience: Yielding to Others

PREVIEW QUESTIONS

▶ How did Asch study conformity, and what did he learn?

▶ How did Milgram study obedience, and what did he learn?

▶ Why were Milgram's findings so controversial?

▶ How well do North American findings on conformity and obedience generalize to other cultures?

Social influence can take many forms. Sometimes we change our behaviour as a result of adopting a new social role. *Social roles* are widely shared expectations about how people in certain positions are supposed to behave. This was shown dramatically by psychologist Philip Zimbardo in his famous Stanford prison simulation experiment conducted in 1971 (Zimbardo, 2007). He recruited average male undergraduates to take part in a simulation of a prison setting. Students were randomly assigned to play the role of a prisoner or a guard. The participants had a rough idea of what it meant to act like a guard or a prisoner and they were gradually *consumed* by their roles (Haney & Zimbardo, 1998). Thus, as the simulation progressed, guards and prisoners appeared to get caught up in playing their roles, with the guards becoming increasingly aggressive.

The guards quickly devised a variety of sometimes cruel strategies to maintain total control over their prisoners. Meals, blankets, and bathroom privileges were selectively denied to some prisoners to achieve

control. The prisoners were taunted, humiliated, called demeaning names, and they were forced to beg for opportunities to go to the bathroom. Pointless, petty rules were strictly enforced. Difficult prisoners were punished with hard labour (doing pushups and jumping jacks, cleaning toilets with their bare hands). The guards harassed the prisoners by waking them up in the middle of the night to assemble and count off. The guards also creatively turned a 60 cm × 60 cm closet into a "hole" for solitary confinement of rebellious prisoners. There was some variation among the guards; however, collectively they became mean, malicious, and abusive in fulfilling their responsibilities. How did the prisoners react? A few showed signs of emotional disturbance and had to be released early. But they mostly became listless, apathetic, and demoralized. Eventually, the simulation had to be stopped for the safety of all concerned. The study was designed to run two weeks. Zimbardo, though, decided that he needed to end it prematurely after just six days, because he was concerned about the rapidly escalating abuse and degradation of the prisoners. The subjects were then debriefed, offered counselling, and sent home.

The results of the Stanford prison simulation were eye-opening, to say the least. Within a short time, subjects with no obvious character flaws became tyrannical, sadistic, brutal guards. If this transformation can occur so swiftly in a make-believe prison, one can only imagine how the much stronger situational forces in real prisons readily promote abusive behaviour. Similar processes have been invoked in attempts to understand the behaviour of American military personnel in their treatment of Iraqi prisoners at Abu Ghraib. In a similar setting, atrocities (including the murder of a 16-year-old Somali boy) were carried out by members of the Canadian Airborne Regiment while they were on a peacekeeping mission in Somalia in 1993 (Cheney, 2004). While role-playing may explain such behaviour in part (Haney & Zimbardo, 1998), what sometimes also happens in these situations is that once people begin behaving in a certain way, others become caught up in the pressure to conform.

Of course, this is not the only form social influence can take. For example, we all have had experiences when we've had to decide between doing what we believe is right or just going along with the crowd or with someone perceived to be in authority. These situations are very difficult, and most people find themselves sometimes going with the crowd or obeying the authority figure even though they know it isn't right. What are the factors that influence our decisions in such contexts? In this section, we'll analyze the dynamics of social influence at work in conformity and obedience.

Conformity 12e

If you keep a well-manicured lawn, are you exhibiting conformity? If you are maintaining your lawn because you are afraid of being ostracized by your neighbours (Williams, 2007), what additional factors affect how willing you are to conform to their behaviour? According to social psychologists, it depends on whether your behaviour is the result of group pressure. *Conformity* occurs when people yield to real or imagined social pressure. For example, if you maintain a well-groomed lawn only to avoid complaints from your neighbours, you're conforming to social pressure. However, if you maintain a nice lawn because you genuinely prefer a nice lawn, that's *not* conformity.

In the 1950s, Solomon Asch (1951, 1955, 1956) devised a clever procedure that reduced ambiguity

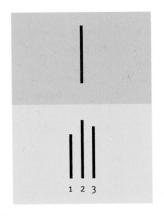

WEB LINK 16.4

The Stanford Prison Experiment
View slides of Philip Zimbardo's experiment and learn how it parallels more recent examples of conformity, such as the Abu Ghraib abuse scandal.

FIGURE 16.18

Stimuli used in Asch's conformity studies.

In groups of seven, subjects were asked to match a standard line (top) with one of three other lines displayed on another card (bottom). The task was easy—until the six experiment accomplices started responding with obviously incorrect answers, creating a situation in which Asch evaluated the seventh subject's conformity.

Source: Adapted from Asch, S. (1955). Opinion and social pressure. *Scientific American, 193* (5), 31–35. Based on illustrations by Sara Love. Copyright © 1955 by Scientific American, Inc. All rights reserved.

about whether subjects were conforming, allowing him to investigate the variables that govern conformity. Let's re-create one of Asch's (1955) classic experiments, which have become the most widely replicated studies in the history of social psychology (Markus, Kitayama, & Heiman, 1996). The subjects are male undergraduates recruited for a study of visual perception. A group of seven subjects is shown a large card with a vertical line on it and the subjects are then asked to indicate which of three lines on a second card matches the original "standard line" in length (see Figure 16.18). All seven subjects are given a turn at the task, and they announce their choice to the group. The subject in the sixth chair doesn't know it, but everyone else in the group is an accomplice of the experimenter, and they're about to make him wonder whether he has taken leave of his senses.

The accomplices give accurate responses on the first two trials. On the third trial, line 2 clearly is the correct response, but the first five "subjects" all say that line 3 matches the standard line. The genuine subject is bewildered and can't believe his ears. Over the course of the next 15 trials, the accomplices all give the same incorrect response on 11 of them. How does the real subject respond? The line judgments are easy and unambiguous. So, if the participant consistently agrees with the accomplices, he isn't making honest mistakes—he's conforming.

Averaging across all 50 participants, Asch (1955) found that the young men conformed on 37 percent of the trials. The subjects varied considerably in their tendency to conform, however. Of the 50 participants, 13 never caved in to the group, while 14 conformed on more than half of the trials. One could argue that the results show that people confronting a unanimous majority generally tend to *resist* the pressure to conform (Hodges & Geyer, 2006). However, given how clear and easy the line judgments were, most social scientists viewed the findings as a dramatic demonstration of humans' propensity to conform (Levine, 1999).

In subsequent studies, Asch (1956) found that *group size* and *group unanimity* are key determinants of conformity. To examine the impact of group size, Asch repeated his procedure with groups that included from 1 to 15 accomplices. Little conformity was seen when a subject was pitted against just one person, but conformity increased rapidly as group size went from two to four, and then levelled off (see Figure 16.19). Thus, Asch reasoned that as groups grow larger, conformity increases—up to a point, a conclusion that has been echoed by other researchers (Cialdini & Trost, 1998).

However, group size made little difference if just one accomplice "broke" with the others, wrecking their unanimous agreement. The presence of another dissenter lowered conformity to about one-quarter of its peak, even when the dissenter made *inaccurate* judgments that happened to conflict with the majority view. Apparently, the subjects just needed to hear someone else question the accuracy of the group's perplexing responses. The importance of unanimity in fostering conformity has been replicated in subsequent research (Hogg, 2010).

Why do people conform? Two key processes appear to contribute (Hogg, 2010). *Normative influence* operates when people conform to social norms for fear of negative social consequences. In other words, people often conform or comply because they are afraid of being criticized or rejected. People are also likely to conform when they are uncertain how to behave (Cialdini, 2008; Sherif, 1936). *Informational influence* operates when people look to others for guidance about how to behave in ambiguous situations. Thus, if you're at a nice restaurant and don't know which fork to use, you may watch others to see what they're doing. In situations like this, using others as a source of information about appropriate behaviour is a sensible strategy. Ultimately, informational influence is all about being right, whereas normative influence is all about being liked.

Obedience 12e

Obedience is a form of compliance that occurs when people follow direct commands, usually from someone in a position of authority. To a surprising extent, when an authority figure says, "Jump!" many people simply ask, "How high?" For most people, willingness to obey someone in authority is the rule, not the exception.

Milgram's Studies

Stanley Milgram wanted to study this tendency to obey authority figures. Like many other people after World War II, he was troubled by how readily the citizens of Germany had followed the orders of dictator Adolf Hitler, even when the orders required morally repugnant actions, such as the slaughter of millions of Jews. Milgram, who had worked with Solomon Asch, set out to design a standard laboratory procedure for the study of obedience, much like Asch's procedure for studying conformity. The clever experiment that Milgram devised became one of the most famous and controversial studies in the annals of psychology (Benjamin & Simpson, 2009; Blass, 2009). It has been hailed as a "monumental contribution" to science and condemned as "dangerous, dehumanizing, and unethical research" (Ross, 1988). Decades after the research was conducted, it still generates spirited debate (Berkowitz, 1999; Lutsky, 1995). Because of its importance, it's our Featured Study for this chapter.

Solomon Asch

"That we have found the tendency to conformity in our society so strong that reasonably intelligent and well-meaning young people are willing to call white black is a matter of concern."

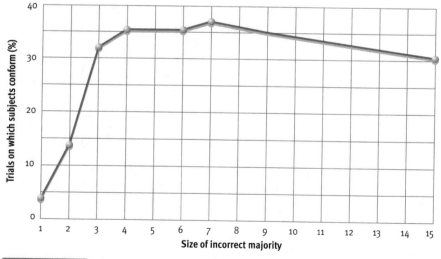

FIGURE 16.19

Conformity and group size.

This graph shows the percentage of trials on which participants conformed as a function of group size in Asch's research. Asch found that conformity became more frequent as group size increased up to about four, and then conformity levelled off. (Data from Asch, 1955)

Investigator: Stanley Milgram (Yale University)
Source: Behavioral study of obedience. *Journal of Abnormal and Social Psychology*, 1963, *67*, 371–378.

"I Was Just Following Orders"

"I was just following orders." That was the essence of Adolf Eichmann's defence when he was tried for his war crimes, which included masterminding the Nazis' attempted extermination of European Jews. Milgram wanted to determine the extent to which people are willing to follow authorities' orders. In particular, he wanted to identify the factors that lead people to follow commands that violate their ethics, such as commands to harm an innocent stranger.

Method

The participants were a diverse collection of 40 men from the local community, recruited through advertisements to participate in a study at Yale University. When a subject arrived at the lab, he met the experimenter and another subject, a likable 47-year-old accountant, who was actually an accomplice of the experimenter. The "subjects" were told that the study would concern the effects of punishment on learning. They drew slips of paper from a hat to get their assignments, but the drawing was fixed so that the real subject always became the "teacher" and the accomplice the "learner."

The participant then watched as the learner was strapped into an electrified chair through which a shock could be delivered to the learner whenever he made a mistake on the task (left photo in Figure 16.20). The "teacher" subject was told that the shocks would be painful but "would not cause tissue damage," and he was then taken to an adjoining room that housed the shock generator that he would control in his role as the teacher. This elaborate apparatus (right photo in Figure 16.20) had 30 switches designed to administer shocks varying from 15 to 450 volts, with labels ranging from "Slight shock" to "Danger: Severe shock" and "XXX." Although the apparatus looked and sounded realistic, it was a fake, and the learner was never shocked.

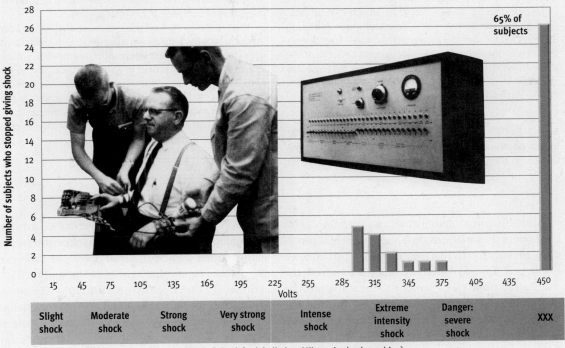

| Slight shock | Moderate shock | Strong shock | Very strong shock | Intense shock | Extreme intensity shock | Danger: severe shock | XXX |

Level of shock (as labelled on Milgram's shock machine)

FIGURE 16.20

Milgram's experiment on obedience.

The photo on the left shows the "learner" being connected to the shock generator during one of Milgram's experimental sessions. The photo on the right shows the fake shock generator used in the study. The surprising results of the Milgram (1963) study are summarized in the bar graph. Although "teacher" subjects frequently protested, the vast majority (65 percent) delivered the entire series of shocks to the "learner" subject.

Source (both photos): From the film *Obedience*, copyright © 1968 by Stanley Milgram, copyright renewed 1993 by Alexandra Milgram, and distributed by Penn State Media Sales.

As the "learning experiment" proceeded, the accomplice made many mistakes that necessitated shocks from the teacher, who was instructed to increase the shock level after each wrong answer. At "300 volts," the learner began to pound on the wall between the two rooms in protest and soon stopped responding to the teacher's questions. At this point, participants ordinarily turned to the experimenter for guidance. The experimenter, a 31-year-old male in a grey lab coat, firmly indicated that no response was the same as a wrong answer and that the teacher should continue to give stronger and stronger shocks to the now silent learner. If the participant expressed unwillingness to continue, the experimenter responded sternly with one of four prearranged prods, such as, "It is absolutely essential that you continue."

When a participant refused to obey the experimenter, the session came to an end. The dependent variable was the maximum shock the participant was willing to administer before refusing to cooperate. After each session, the true purpose of the study was explained to the subject, who was reassured that the shock was fake and the learner was unharmed.

Results

No participant stopped cooperating before the learner reached the point of pounding on the wall, but five quit at that point. As the graph in Figure 16.20 shows, only 14 out of 40 subjects defied the experimenter before the full series of shocks was completed. Thus, 26 of the 40 subjects (65 percent) administered all 30 levels of shock. Although they tended to obey the experimenter, many participants voiced and displayed considerable distress about harming the learner. The horrified subjects groaned, bit their lips, stuttered, trembled, and broke into a sweat, but they continued administering the shocks.

Discussion

Based on these results, Milgram concluded that obedience to authority is even more common than he or others had anticipated. Before the study was conducted, Milgram had described it to 40 psychiatrists and had asked them to predict how much shock subjects would be willing to administer to their innocent victims. Most of the psychiatrists had predicted that less than 1 percent of the subjects would continue to the end of the series of shocks!

In interpreting his results, Milgram argued that strong pressure from an authority figure can make decent people do indecent things to others. Applying this insight to Nazi war crimes and other travesties, Milgram asserted that some sinister actions may not be due to the actors' evil character as much as to situational pressures that can lead normal people to engage in acts of treachery and violence. Thus, he arrived at the disturbing conclusion that given the right circumstances, anyone might obey orders to inflict harm on innocent strangers.

Comments

In itself, obedience is not necessarily bad or wrong. Social groups of any size depend on obedience to function smoothly. Life would be chaotic if orders from police, parents, physicians, bosses, generals, and government officials were routinely ignored. However, Milgram's study suggests that many people are overly willing to submit to the orders of someone in command.

If you're like most people, you're probably confident that you wouldn't follow an experimenter's demands to inflict harm on a helpless victim. But the empirical findings indicate that you're probably wrong. After many replications, the results are deplorable, but clear: Most people can be coerced into engaging in actions that violate their morals and values. This finding is disheartening, but it sharpens our understanding of moral atrocities, such as the Nazi persecutions of Jews.

After his initial demonstration, Milgram (1974) tried about 20 variations on his experimental procedure, looking for factors that influence participants' obedience. In one variation, Milgram moved the study away from Yale's campus to see if the prestige of the university was contributing to the subjects' obedience. When the study was run in a seedy office building by the "Research Associates of Bridgeport," only a small decrease in obedience was observed (48 percent of the subjects gave all of the shocks). Even when the learner was in the same room with the subjects, 40 percent of the participants administered the full series of shocks. As a whole, Milgram was surprised at how high subjects' obedience remained as he changed various aspects of his experiment.

That said, there were some situational manipulations that reduced obedience appreciably. For example, if the authority figure was called away and the orders were given by an ordinary person (supposedly another participant), full obedience dropped to 20 percent. In another version of the study, Milgram borrowed a trick from Asch's conformity experiments and set up teams of three teachers that included two more accomplices. When they drew lots, the real subject was always selected to run the shock apparatus in consultation with the other two "teachers." When both accomplices accepted the experimenter's orders to continue shocking the learner, the pressure increased obedience a bit. However, if an accomplice defied the experimenter and supported the subject's objections, obedience declined dramatically (only 10 percent of the subjects gave all the shocks), just as conformity had dropped rapidly when dissent surfaced in Asch's conformity studies. These findings are interesting in that they provide further support for Milgram's thesis that situational factors exert great influence over behaviour. If the situational pressures favouring obedience are decreased, obedience declines, as one would expect.

The Ensuing Controversy

Milgram's study evoked a controversy that continues to the present. According to Murray Goddard of the University of New Brunswick (Goddard, 2009), some of the hesitation to accept Milgram's findings may have resulted from the fact that they were counter to human intuition. Other critics have argued that Milgram's results can't be generalized to apply to the real world (Baumrind, 1964; Orne & Holland, 1968). They maintain that the participants went along only because they knew it was an experiment and "everything must be okay." And some have argued that subjects who agree to participate in a scientific study *expect to obey* orders from an experimenter. Milgram (1964, 1968) replied by arguing that if subjects had thought, "everything must be okay," they wouldn't have experienced the enormous distress that they clearly showed.

As for the idea that research participants expect to follow an experimenter's commands, Milgram pointed out that so do real-world soldiers and bureaucrats who are accused of villainous acts performed in obedience to authority. "I reject Baumrind's argument that the observed obedience doesn't count because it occurred where it is appropriate," said Milgram (1964). "That is precisely why it *does* count." Overall, the evidence supports the generalizability of Milgram's results, which were consistently replicated for many years, in diverse settings, with a variety of subjects and procedural variations (Blass, 1999; Miller, 1986).

Critics also questioned the ethics of Milgram's procedure (Baumrind, 1964; Kelman, 1967). They noted that without prior consent, subjects were exposed to extensive deception that could undermine their trust in people and to severe stress that could leave emotional scars. Moreover, most participants also had to confront the disturbing fact that they caved in to the experimenter's commands to inflict harm on an innocent victim.

Milgram's defenders argued that the brief distress experienced by his subjects was a small price to pay for the insights that emerged from his obedience studies. Looking back, however, many psychologists seem to share the critics' concerns about the ethical implications of Milgram's work (Miller, 2004). His procedure is questionable by contemporary standards of research ethics, and no replications of his obedience study have been conducted in the United States from the mid-1970s (Blass, 1991) until recently (Elms, 2009), when Jerry Burger (2009) crafted a very cautious, *partial* replication that incorporated a variety of additional safeguards to protect the welfare of the participants.

Burger (2009) wanted to see whether Milgram's findings would hold up 45 years later. After all, the world has changed in countless ways since Milgram's original research in the early 1960s. To accommodate modern ethical standards, Burger had to change some features of the Milgram procedure. Among other things, he screened participants with great care, excluding those who seemed likely to experience excessive stress, emphasized repeatedly that participants could withdraw from the study without penalty at any time, and provided instant debriefing after each participant completed the procedure. Most importantly, he enacted Milgram's scenario only up through the level of 150 volts. Burger chose 150 volts as the maximum because in Milgram's series of studies the vast majority of subjects who went past this point went on to administer all the levels of shock. So, the amount of obedience seen through this level would permit a good estimate of the percentage of participants who would exhibit full obedience. Interestingly, in spite of the extra precautions, Burger's study yielded obedience rates that were only slightly lower than those observed by Milgram 45 years earlier. Given Burger's repeated assurances that participants could withdraw from the study (which one would expect to reduce obedience), it seems likely that people today are just as prone to obedience as they were in the 1960s.

Cultural Variations in Conformity and Obedience   12e

Stanley Milgram

"The essence of obedience is that a person comes to view himself as the instrument for carrying out another person's wishes, and he therefore no longer regards himself as responsible for his actions."

Are conformity and obedience unique to American or Western culture? By no means. Conformity and obedience experiments have been repeated in many countries including Canada, where they have yielded results roughly similar to those seen in the United States. Thus, the phenomena of conformity and obedience seem to transcend culture.

The replications of Milgram's obedience study have largely been limited to industrialized nations similar to the United States. Comparisons of the results of these studies must be made with caution because the composition of the samples and the experimental procedures have varied somewhat. But many of the studies have reported even

Social Behaviour

higher obedience rates than those seen in Milgram's American samples. For example, obedience rates of over 80 percent have been reported for samples from Italy, Germany, Austria, Spain, and the Netherlands (P. B. Smith & Bond, 1994). So, the surprisingly high level of obedience observed by Milgram does not appear to be peculiar to the United States.

The Asch experiment has been repeated in a more diverse range of societies than the Milgram experiment. Like many other cultural differences in social behaviour, variations in conformity appear subject to cultural influences (Murray, Trudeau, & Schaller, 2011), including being related to the degree of *individualism versus collectivism* seen in a society. Various theorists have argued that collectivistic cultures, which emphasize respect for group norms, cooperation, and harmony, probably encourage more conformity than individualistic cultures (Schwartz, 1990) and have a more positive view of conformity (Kim & Markus, 1999). As Matsumoto (1994, p. 162) puts it, "To conform in American culture is to be weak or deficient somehow. But this is not true in other cultures. Many cultures foster more collective, group-oriented values, and concepts of conformity, obedience, and compliance enjoy much higher status." Consistent with this analysis, studies *have* found higher levels of conformity in collectivistic cultures than in individualistic cultures (Bond & Smith, 1996; Smith, 2001).

REVIEW OF KEY POINTS

▷ The Stanford prison simulation, in which normal, healthy students were randomly assigned to be prisoners or guards, demonstrated that social roles and other situational pressures can exert tremendous influence over social behaviour. Zimbardo showed that situational forces can lead normal people to exhibit surprisingly callous, abusive behaviour.

▷ Conformity involves yielding to social pressure. Asch found that subjects often conform to the group, even when the group reports inaccurate judgments on a simple line-judging task. Conformity becomes more likely as group size increases, up to a group size of four, and then levels off. If a small group isn't unanimous, conformity declines rapidly.

▷ In Milgram's landmark study of obedience to authority, adult men drawn from the community showed a remarkable tendency, in spite of their misgivings, to follow orders to shock an innocent stranger. Milgram concluded that situational pressures can make decent people do indecent things. A recent partial replication by Burger showed that Milgram's findings are still relevant today.

▷ Critics asserted that Milgram's results were not generalizable to the real world and that his methods were unethical. The generalizability of Milgram's findings has stood the test of time, but his work also helped to stimulate stricter ethical standards for research.

▷ The Asch and Milgram experiments have been replicated in many cultures. These replications have uncovered modest cultural variations in the propensity to conform or to obey an authority figure.

Behaviour in Groups: Joining with Others   12e

PREVIEW QUESTIONS

▷ What is the bystander effect?

▷ What processes contribute to reduced individual productivity in larger groups?

▷ What is group polarization?

▷ What are the antecedent conditions and symptoms of groupthink?

In most modern societies, groups are a part of our everyday lives. Individuals who join groups have their own individual goals and orientations and for the group to function effectively, individuals are often faced with decisions about how much to contribute to the group itself (Goldstone, Roberts, & Gureckis, 2008; Kameda, Tsukasaki, Hastie, & Berg, 2011). Given their ubiquitous nature, it is no surprise that social psychologists have devoted considerable resources to studying groups as well as individuals, but exactly what is a group? Are all of the divorced fathers living in Saskatoon a group? Are three strangers moving skyward in an elevator a group? What if the elevator gets stuck? How about four students from your psychology class who study together regularly? A jury deciding a trial? The Vancouver Canucks? The Canadian Parliament? Some of these collections of people are groups and others aren't. Let's examine the concept of a group to find out which of these collections qualify.

In social psychologists' eyes, a *group* consists of *two or more individuals who interact and are interdependent*. The divorced fathers in Saskatoon aren't likely to qualify on either count. Strangers sharing an elevator might interact briefly, but they're not interdependent. However, if the elevator got stuck and they had to deal with an emergency together, they could suddenly become a group. Your psychology classmates who study together are a group, as they interact and depend on each other to achieve shared goals. So do the members of a jury, a sports team such as the Vancouver Canucks, and a large organization such as the Canadian Parliament. Historically, most groups have interacted on a face-to-face basis, but advances in telecommunications are changing that reality. In the era of the Internet, people can interact, become interdependent, and develop a group identity, without ever meeting in person (Bargh & McKenna, 2004; O'Leary & Cummings, 2007). Indeed, Hackman and Katz (2010) assert that the nature of groups is evolving due to advances in technology. They note that traditionally groups tended to be intact and stable with clear boundaries, whereas membership in modern groups is often continuously changing. Traditional groups usually have a designated leader, whereas modern groups often are self-managing with shared leadership. Similarly, traditional groups tended to be created in a top–down fashion, whereas modern groups often coalesce on their own to explore shared interests. It will be interesting to see whether these shifts have an impact on how groups function.

Groups vary in many ways. Obviously, a study group, the Vancouver Canucks, and Parliament are very different in terms of size, purpose, formality, longevity, similarity of members, and diversity of activities. Can anything meaningful be said about groups if they're so diverse? Yes. In spite of their immense variability, groups share certain features that affect their functioning. Among other things, most groups have *roles* that allocate special responsibilities to some members, *norms* about suitable behaviour, a *communication structure* that reflects who talks to whom, and a *power structure* that determines which members wield the most influence (Forsyth, 2006).

So, when people join together in a group, they create a social organism with unique characteristics and dynamics that can take on a life of its own. One of social psychology's enduring insights is that in a given situation you may behave quite differently when you're in a group than when you're alone. To illustrate this point, let's look at some interesting research on helping behaviour.

Behaviour Alone and in Groups: The Case of the Bystander Effect

Imagine that while waiting for the subway at the Yonge–Bloor station in downtown Toronto, you lose your balance and find yourself lying on the tracks with a train speeding toward you. Would you be better off if there were lots of people on the subway platform? It certainly makes sense since, after all, there's "safety in numbers." Logically, as group size increases, the probability of having a "good Samaritan" on the scene increases. Or does it?

Kaur-Hayer Harbajan, a 58-year-old mother, found herself facing a situation exactly like that on September 15, 2003 (Freed, 2003). As she was waiting for the subway train, she lost her balance and fell onto the tracks. She could see the train fast approaching her. Fortunately for her, 22-year-old Petru George Ciorau jumped down, and, seeing that he could not get her back onto the platform in time,

carried her across the tracks and squeezed them both against the tunnel wall as the train arrived. Mrs. Harbajan was lucky, because some classic research in social psychology tells us that the more people there are around, the less likely it is that help will be forthcoming. Ciorau was stunned by the inaction of others. He said, "I was wondering why most people wouldn't do that. If that's my mom down there and some people are watching I would want someone to jump in" (Freed, 2003, p. B5).

We've seen before that human behaviour isn't necessarily logical. When it comes to helping behaviour, many studies have uncovered an apparent paradox called the *bystander effect*: People are less likely to provide needed help when they are in groups than when they are alone. Evidence that your probability of getting help *declines* as group size increases was first described by John Darley and Bibb Latané (1968), who were conducting research on the determinants of helping behaviour. In the Darley and Latané study, students in individual cubicles connected by an intercom participated in discussion groups of three sizes. (The separate cubicles allowed the researchers to examine each individual's behaviour in a group context, a technique that minimizes confounded variables in individual–group comparisons.) Early in the discussion, a student who was an experimental accomplice hesitantly mentioned that he was prone to seizures. Later in the discussion, the same accomplice feigned a severe seizure and cried out for help. Although a majority of subjects sought assistance for the student, the tendency to seek help *declined* with increasing group size.

Similar trends have been seen in many other experiments, in some of which over 6000 subjects have had opportunities to respond to apparent emergencies, including fires, asthma attacks, faintings, crashes, and flat tires, as well as less-pressing needs to answer a door or to pick up objects dropped by a stranger (Latané & Nida, 1981). Many of the experiments have been highly realistic studies conducted in subways, stores, and shopping malls, and many have compared individuals against groups in face-to-face interaction. Pooling the results of this research, Latané and Nida (1981) estimated that subjects who were alone provided help 75 percent of the time, whereas subjects in the presence of others provided help only 53 percent of the time. They concluded that the only significant limiting condition on the bystander effect is that it is less likely to occur when the need for help is unambiguous. For example, the bystander effect is less likely to occur when someone is in obvious physical danger (Fischer et al., 2006). It is also less likely if the bystanders are friends rather than strangers (Levine & Crowther, 2008).

WEB LINK 16.5

The Psychology of Cyberspace
As the Internet continues to develop into an ever more important part of our lives, a number of social scientists have begun to examine human behaviour in the computer-mediated environment of cyberspace. This site, created by John Suler of Rider University, presents a major overview of the research being carried out in this new field.

What accounts for the bystander effect? A number of factors may be at work. Bystander effects are most likely in ambiguous situations because people look around to see whether others think there's an emergency. If everyone hesitates, their inaction suggests that there's no real need for help. The *diffusion of responsibility* that occurs in a group is also important. If you're by yourself when you encounter someone in need of help, the responsibility to provide help rests squarely on your shoulders. However, if other people are present, the responsibility is divided among you, and you may all say to yourselves, "Someone else will help." A reduced sense of responsibility may contribute to other aspects of behaviour in groups, as we'll see in the next section.

Interestingly, recent research has called into question some of the details of the incident that served to motivate the development of work on the *bystander effect* (Brock, 2008; Manning, Levine, & Collins, 2007, 2008). According to reports, in 1964 in New York City, Kitty Genovese was murdered while 38 witnesses failed to come to her aid (Latané & Darley, 1970). Newspaper reports at the time stated that "For more than half an hour thirty-eight respectable, law-abiding citizens in Queens watched a killer stalk and stab a woman . . . . Not one person telephoned the police during the assault . . . ." (McShane, 2007). People at the time were horrified, and this example of bystander apathy paved the way for the development of the bystander effect (Manning, Levine, & Collins, 2007). A careful analysis of the transcripts of the murder trial of Winston Mosley, Genovese's murderer, casts doubt on the "evidence for the presence of 38 witnesses, or that witnesses observed the murder, or that witnesses remained inactive" (Manning, Levine, & Collins, 2008. p. 555). Nonetheless, research evidence for the existence of the effect is well established.

Group Productivity and Social Loafing

Have you ever driven through a road construction project—at a snail's pace, of course—and become irritated because so many workers seem to be just standing around? Maybe the irony of the posted sign "Your tax dollars at work" made you imagine that they were all dawdling. And then again, perhaps not. Individuals' productivity often *does* decline in larger groups (Karau & Williams, 1993). This fact is unfortunate, as many important tasks can be accomplished only in groups. Group productivity is crucial to committees, sports teams, firefighting crews, sororities, study groups, symphonies, and work teams of all

kinds, from the morning crew in a little diner to the board of directors of a major company.

Two factors appear to contribute to reduced individual productivity in larger groups. One factor is *reduced efficiency* resulting from the *loss of coordination* among workers' efforts. As you put more people on a yearbook staff, for instance, you'll probably create more and more duplication of effort and increase how often group members end up working at cross-purposes.

The second factor contributing to low productivity in groups involves *effort* rather than efficiency. *Social loafing* is a reduction in effort by individuals when they work in groups as compared to when they work by themselves. To investigate social loafing, Latané and his colleagues (Latané, Williams, & Harkins, 1979) measured the sound output produced by subjects who were asked to cheer or clap as loud as they could. So that they couldn't see or hear other group members, the subjects were told that the study concerned the importance of sensory feedback and were asked to don blindfolds and put on headphones through which loud noise was played. This manoeuvre permitted a simple deception: Subjects were *led to believe* that they were either working alone or in a group of two or six, when in fact they were working alone and *individual* output was actually being measured.

When participants *thought* that they were working in larger groups, their individual output declined. Since lack of coordination could not affect individual output, the subjects' decreased sound production had to be due to reduced effort. Latané and his colleagues also had the same subjects clap and shout in genuine groups of two and six and found an additional decrease in production that was attributed to loss of coordination. Figure 16.21 shows how social loafing and loss of coordination combined to reduce productivity as group size increased.

The social-loafing effect has been replicated in numerous studies in which subjects have worked on a variety of tasks, including cheering, pumping air, swimming in a relay race, solving mazes, evaluating editorials, and brainstorming for new ideas (Karau & Williams, 1995; Levine & Moreland, 1998). Social loafing and the bystander effect appear to share a common cause: diffusion of responsibility in groups (Comer, 1995; Latané, 1981). As group size increases, the responsibility for getting a job done is divided among more people, and many group members ease up because their individual contribution is less recognizable. Thus, social loafing occurs in situations where individuals can "hide in the crowd" (Karau & Williams, 1993).

Social loafing is *not* inevitable. For example, people with high achievement motivation are less likely to

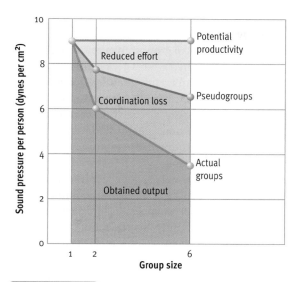

FIGURE 16.21

The effect of loss of coordination and social loafing on group productivity.

The amount of sound produced per person declined noticeably when people worked in actual groups of two or six (orange line). This decrease in productivity reflects both loss of coordination and social loafing. Sound per person also declined when subjects merely thought they were working in groups of two or six (purple line). This smaller decrease in productivity is due to social loafing.

Source: Adapted from Latané, B., Williams, K., and Harkins, S. (1979). Many hands make light the work: The causes and consequences of social loafing. *Journal of Personality and Social Psychology, 37*, 822–832. Copyright © 1979 by the American Psychological Association. Adapted by permission of the author.

exhibit social loafing than others (Hart et al., 2004). People who score high on the personality traits of agreeableness and conscientiousness also are less prone to social loafing (Klehe & Anderson, 2007). Social loafing is also less likely when individuals' personal contributions to productivity are readily identifiable (Hoigaard & Ingvaldsen, 2006), and when group norms encourage productivity and personal involvement (Hoigaard, Säfvenbom, & Tonnessen, 2006). And social loafing is reduced when people work in smaller and more cohesive groups (Liden et al., 2004). Cultural factors may also influence the likelihood of social loafing. Studies with subjects from Japan, China, and Taiwan suggest that social loafing may be less prevalent in collectivistic cultures, which place a high priority on meeting group goals and contributing to one's ingroups (Karau & Williams, 1995; Smith, 2001).

Decision Making in Groups

Productivity is not the only issue that commonly concerns groups. When people join together in groups, they often have to make decisions about what the group will do and how it will use its resources. Whether it's your study group deciding

what type of pizza to order, a jury deciding on a verdict, or Parliament deciding on whether to pass a bill, groups make decisions. There is good evidence that decision making in groups may sometimes display or accentuate important biases when compared to individual decision making. These biases may be reflected in a variety of decision-making contexts, such as the common chore of making predictions regarding completion of one of the group's tasks. For example, research by Wilfrid Laurier University's Roger Buehler and his colleagues has shown that the tendency of individuals to make optimistic predictions regarding how long it will take to complete a task is accentuated as a result of group discussion (Buehler, Messervey, & Griffin, 2005).

Evaluating decision making is often more complicated than evaluating productivity. In many cases, the "right" decision may not be readily apparent. Who can say whether your study group ordered the right pizza or whether Parliament passed the right bills? Nonetheless, social psychologists have discovered some interesting tendencies in group decision making. We'll take a brief look at *group polarization* and *groupthink*.

Group Polarization

Who leans toward more cautious decisions: individuals or groups? Common sense suggests that groups will work out compromises that cancel out members' extreme views. Hence, the collective wisdom of the group should yield relatively conservative choices. Is common sense correct? To investigate this question, Stoner (1961) asked individual subjects to give their recommendations on tough decisions and then asked the same subjects to engage in group discussion to arrive at joint recommendations. When Stoner compared individuals' average recommendation against their group decision generated through discussion, he found that groups arrived at *riskier* decisions than individuals did. Stoner's finding was replicated in other studies (e.g., Pruitt, 1971), and the phenomenon acquired the name *risky shift*.

However, investigators eventually determined that groups can shift either way, toward risk or caution, depending on which way the group is leaning to begin with (Friedkin, 1999; Myers & Lamm, 1976). A shift toward a more extreme position, an effect called *polarization,* is often the result of group discussion (Tindale, Kameda, & Hinsz, 2003; Von Swol, 2009). Thus, *group polarization* occurs when group discussion strengthens a group's dominant point of view and produces a shift toward a more extreme decision in that direction (see Figure 16.22). Group polarization does *not* involve widening the gap between factions in a group, as its name might

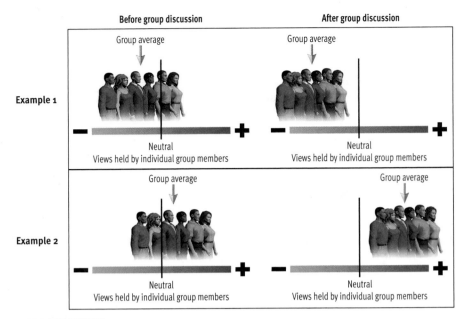

Before group discussion

Group average

Example 1

Neutral
Views held by individual group members

After group discussion

Group average

Neutral
Views held by individual group members

Group average

Example 2

Neutral
Views held by individual group members

Group average

Neutral
Views held by individual group members

FIGURE 16.22

Group polarization.

Two examples of group polarization are diagrammed here. In the first example (top), a group starts out mildly opposed to an idea, but after discussion, sentiment against the idea is stronger. In the second example (bottom), a group starts out with a favourable disposition toward an idea, and this disposition is strengthened by group discussion.

suggest. In fact, group polarization can contribute to consensus in a group, as we'll see in our upcoming discussion of groupthink.

Why does group polarization occur? One reason is that group discussion often exposes group members to persuasive arguments that they had not thought about previously (Stasser, 1991). Another reason is that when people discover that their views are shared by others, they tend to express even stronger views because they want to be liked by their ingroups (Hogg, Turner, & Davidson, 1990).

Groupthink

In contrast to group polarization, which is a normal process in group dynamics, groupthink is more like a "disease" that can infect decision making in groups. *Groupthink* occurs when members of a cohesive group emphasize concurrence at the expense of critical thinking in arriving at a decision. As you might imagine, groupthink doesn't produce very effective decision making. Indeed, groupthink can lead to major blunders that may look incomprehensible after the fact. Irving Janis (1972) first described groupthink in his effort to explain how former U.S. President John F. Kennedy and his advisors could have miscalculated so badly in deciding to invade Cuba at the Bay of Pigs in 1961. The attempted invasion failed miserably and, in retrospect, seemed remarkably ill-conceived.

Applying his many years of research and theory on group dynamics to the Bay of Pigs fiasco, Janis developed a model of groupthink that is summarized in Figure 16.23. When groups get caught up in groupthink, members suspend their critical judgment and the group starts censoring dissent as the pressure to conform increases. Soon, everyone begins to think alike. Moreover, some members serve as "mind guards" and try to shield the group from information that contradicts the group's view.

If the group's view is challenged from outside, victims of groupthink tend to think in simplistic "us versus them" terms. Members begin to overestimate the ingroup's unanimity, and they begin to view the outgroup as the enemy. Groupthink also promotes

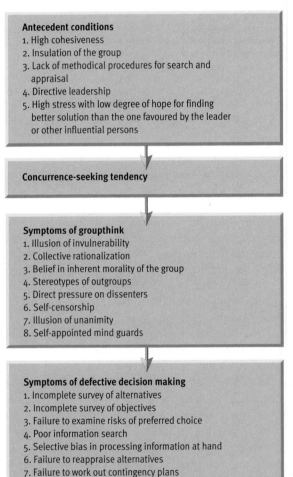

Antecedent conditions
1. High cohesiveness
2. Insulation of the group
3. Lack of methodical procedures for search and appraisal
4. Directive leadership
5. High stress with low degree of hope for finding better solution than the one favoured by the leader or other influential persons

Concurrence-seeking tendency

Symptoms of groupthink
1. Illusion of invulnerability
2. Collective rationalization
3. Belief in inherent morality of the group
4. Stereotypes of outgroups
5. Direct pressure on dissenters
6. Self-censorship
7. Illusion of unanimity
8. Self-appointed mind guards

Symptoms of defective decision making
1. Incomplete survey of alternatives
2. Incomplete survey of objectives
3. Failure to examine risks of preferred choice
4. Poor information search
5. Selective bias in processing information at hand
6. Failure to reappraise alternatives
7. Failure to work out contingency plans

FIGURE 16.23

Overview of Janis's model of groupthink.

The antecedent conditions, symptoms, and resultant effects of groupthink postulated by Janis (1972) are outlined here. His model of groupthink has been very influential, but practical difficulties have limited research on the theory.

incomplete gathering of information. Like individuals, groups often display a confirmation bias, as they tend to seek and focus on information that supports their initial views (Schulz-Hardt et al., 2000).

Recent research has uncovered another factor that may contribute to groupthink—individual members often fail to share information that is unique to them (Postmes, Spears, & Cihangir, 2001). Sound decision making depends on group members combining their information effectively (Winquist & Larson, 1998). However, when groups discuss issues, they have an interesting tendency to focus mainly on the information that the members already share as opposed to encouraging offers of information unique to individual members (Stasser, Vaughn, & Stewart, 2000). Additional research is needed to determine why groups are mediocre at pooling members' information.

What causes groupthink? According to Janis, a key precondition is high group cohesiveness. *Group cohesiveness* refers to the strength of the liking relationships linking group members to each other and to the group itself. Members of cohesive groups are close-knit, are committed, have "team spirit," and are very loyal to the group. Cohesiveness itself isn't bad. It can facilitate group productivity (Mullen & Copper, 1994) and help groups achieve great things. But Janis maintains that the danger of groupthink is greater when groups are highly cohesive. Groupthink is also more likely when a group works in relative isolation, when the group's power structure is dominated by a strong, directive leader, and when the group is under stress to make a major decision (see Figure 16.23). Under these conditions, group

discussions can easily lead to group polarization, strengthening the group's dominant view.

A relatively small number of experiments have been conducted to test Janis's theory, because the antecedent conditions thought to foster groupthink—such as high decision stress, strong group cohesiveness, and dominating leadership—are difficult to create effectively in laboratory settings (Aldag & Fuller, 1993). The evidence on groupthink consists mostly of retrospective case studies of major decision-making fiascos (Eaton, 2001). So, Janis's model of groupthink should probably be characterized as an innovative, sophisticated, intuitively appealing theory that needs to be subjected to much more empirical study (Esser, 1998).

WEB LINK 16.6

Group Dynamics
Donelson Forsyth of the University of Richmond maintains this excellent site devoted to the dynamics of group interaction. Topics of interest include group structure, group cohesiveness, influence in groups, conflict in groups, and the history of research on groups. The site also houses a rich set of links to organizations that study groups.

Social Neuroscience

A Neuroscience Perspective on Social Psychology

As we suggested in Chapter 1, one of the most popular orientations in psychology today is that of neuroscience. This approach emphasizes research examining the relationship of the brain, its structures and processes, to human social behaviour (Cacioppo & Berntson, 2005; Easton & Emery, 2005; Harmon-Jones & Winkielman, 2007). *Social neuroscience* is an approach to research and theory in social psychology that "integrates models of neuroscience and social psychology to study the mechanisms of social behavior" (Amodio, 2008, p. 1). Its emergence as a distinct orientation is dated from a conference held in 2001 at the University of California, Los Angeles

(Coleman, 2006), although its beginnings had roots much earlier (Cacioppo, 1994; Lieberman, 2010). Since that time it has rapidly gained in importance in the social psychological literature (Decety & Keenan, 2006; Lieberman, 2007, 2010; Willingham & Dunn, 2003). While psychologists in many areas of psychology have adopted a neuroscience approach in examining human behaviour for several years, social neuroscience differs from other areas of psychology in that it examines humans in their *social context*, not as isolated "units of analysis" (Cacioppo et al., 2007). Social neuroscientists employ the tools developed in neuroscience, primarily positron emission tomography (PET), functional magnetic resonance imaging (fMRI), event-related potentials (ERPs), the study of lesions, and transcranial magnetic stimulation (TMS)

PREVIEW QUESTIONS

► What is social neuroscience?

► How does this approach differ from traditional social psychology?

► What social psychological phenomena have social neuroscientists examined?

in examining the "mental mechanisms that create, frame, regulate, and respond to our experience of the social world" (Lieberman, 2010, p. 143). We discussed in detail these neuroscience methods in Chapter 3.

Topics in Social Neuroscience

The methods and theory of social neuroscience have been applied to a broad array of topics in social psychology, including understanding and controlling oneself, understanding others, and social psychological phenomena that occur at the interface of self and others (Lieberman, 2007). Some of the specific topics examined include theory of mind, aggression, attributions, social cognition, self and self-judgment, the social psychology of mental health, cognitive dissonance, and attitude change (Cacioppo et al., 2008; Harmon-Jones & Sigelman, 2001; Harmon-Jones et al., 2011; Libby, 2008; Lieberman et al., 2001; Mar, 2011; Mitchell, Macrae, & Banaji, 2004; Rilling, & Sanfey, 2011; Schmitz, Kawahara-Baccus, & Johnson, 2004). It has even proven possible to examine the some of the neuro-correlates of political attitudes using MRI scans as was shown recently by Ryota Kanai and his colleagues (Kanai, Feilden, Firth, & Rees, 2011). Incidentally, one of the co-authors of Kanai's paper was Colin Firth, who won the best actor Oscar at the 2011 Academy Awards for his portrayal of King George VI in the movie *The King's Speech* (2010).

Currently, one of the most researched topics is the neuroscience of ethnic relations (Amodio, 2008), including topics related to prejudice and stereotyping (Ronquillo et al., 2007). Let's consider one example of this work to illustrate the social neuroscience approach.

As we will discuss in the Personal Application, Understanding Prejudice, on page 782, social psychologists have been interested for some time in examining both explicit and implicit social judgments and evaluations. Explicit judgments and evaluations involve conscious and controlled thought, while implicit evaluation occurs automatically, without intention, and typically without the individual making the judgment even being aware of the process (Greenwald & Banaji, 1995). Among other things, explicit evaluations typically take more time to unfold than do implicit judgments.

William Cunningham, who was a faculty member at the University of Toronto, and his colleagues used the characteristics of implicit and explicit evaluations to explore the role of the amygdala in people's responses to white and black faces (Cunningham et al., 2004). Previous neuroscience research had often implicated the amygdala in fear responses (LaBar et al., 1998), and other social psychological research had shown that whites frequently show more negative evaluations of blacks than of whites. During the fMRI, white participants were presented with various stimuli, including neutral-expression black and white faces. The stimuli were presented briefly (30 milliseconds) or for a longer duration (525 milliseconds). Cunningham used the shorter presentation time to assess automatic responses to the stimuli, and the longer presentation times to assess controlled, conscious evaluations of the stimuli.

Cunningham expected that his white participants would show greater activation in the amygdala when presented with black faces, most notably under brief presentation times, when automatic responses were being assessed, and this is just what the result of his experiments revealed. In addition, Cunningham found that this heightened activation of the amygdala was especially true for participants that he had previously identified as being more racially biased. This and other similar research suggests that "implicit associations to a social group may result in automatic emotional response when encountering members of that group" (Cunningham et al., 2004, p. 811). Findings of greater amygdala response to black faces using fMRI methods is common in the literature (e.g., Lieberman et al., 2005; Ronquillo et al., 2007). Other parallel research in the area has employed ERP techniques (e.g., Ito & Urland, 2003). At this point, it is unclear whether these effects reflect negative evaluations of black faces or are the result of greater "perceptual" expertise on the part of white participants for the faces of ingroup (i.e., white) members (Lieberman, 2010). Considerable research effort currently is being devoted to these and other questions in the neuropsychology of stereotypes and prejudice (e.g., Krendl et al., 2006).

While the social neuroscience approach has clear limitations (Amodio, 2008; Willingham & Dunn, 2003), we believe it will increasingly contribute to our understanding of human behaviour in a social context and that the range of the phenomena to which it is applied will continue to expand Cunningham, Arbuckle, Jahn, Mower, & Abduljalil, 2010; Cunningham, Johnsen, & Waggoner, in press). As neuroscientists continue to explore ways of integrating models of neuroscience with models of social psychology, we expect the literature to offer more, and more refined, explanations that contribute to our understanding of ourselves and others.

REVIEW OF KEY POINTS

▷ Social neuroscience is a recently developed approach to examining our social behaviour.

▷ Social neuroscience integrates models drawn from both neuroscience and social psychology in examining a wide variety of social behaviour, including automatic judgments of ingroup and outgroup members.

Our discussion of social psychology has provided a final embellishment of three of our seven unifying themes. One of these is the value of psychology's commitment to empiricism—that is, its reliance on systematic observation through research to arrive at conclusions. The second theme that stands out is the importance of cultural factors in shaping behaviour, and the third is the extent to which people's experience of the world is highly subjective. Let's consider the virtues of empiricism first.

It's easy to question the need to do scientific research on social behaviour, because studies in social psychology often seem to verify common sense. While most people wouldn't presume to devise their own theory of colour vision, question the significance of REM sleep, or quibble about the principal causes of schizophrenia, everyone has beliefs about the nature of love, how to persuade others, and people's willingness to help in times of need. So, when studies demonstrate that credibility enhances persuasion, or that good looks facilitate attraction, it's tempting to conclude that social psychologists go to great lengths to document the obvious, and some critics say, "Why bother?"

You saw why in this chapter. Research in social psychology has repeatedly shown that the predictions of logic and common sense are often wrong. Consider just a few examples. Even psychiatric experts failed to predict the remarkable obedience to authority uncovered in Milgram's research. The bystander effect in helping behaviour violates mathematical logic. Dissonance research has shown that after a severe initiation, the bigger the letdown, the more favourable people's feelings are. These principles defy common sense. Thus, research on social behaviour provides dramatic illustrations of why psychologists put their faith in empiricism.

Our coverage of social psychology also demonstrated once again that, cross-culturally, behaviour is characterized by both variance and invariance. Thus, we saw substantial cultural differences in patterns of attribution, the role of love in mating relationships, attitudes about conformity, the tendency to obey authority figures, and the likelihood of social loafing. Although basic social phenomena such as stereotyping, attraction, obedience, and conformity probably occur all over the world, cross-cultural studies of social behaviour show that research findings based on North American samples may not generalize precisely to other cultures.

Research in social psychology is also uniquely well suited for making the point that people's view of the world is highly personal and subjective. In this chapter, we saw how physical appearance can colour perception of a person's ability or personality, how social schemas can lead people to see what they expect to see in their interactions with others, how pressure to conform can make people begin to doubt their senses, and how groupthink can lead group members down a perilous path of shared illusions.

The subjectivity of social perception will surface once again in our Application features for this chapter. The Personal Application focuses on prejudice, a practical problem that social psychologists have shown great interest in, whereas the Critical Thinking Application examines aspects of social influence.

PREVIEW QUESTIONS

► How did this chapter illustrate the value of empiricism?

► How did this chapter highlight the importance of cultural factors?

► How did this chapter demonstrate that human experience is highly subjective?

REVIEW OF KEY POINTS

▷ People who help someone in need when they are alone are less likely to provide help when a group is present. This phenomenon, called the *bystander effect*, occurs primarily because a group creates diffusion of responsibility.

▷ Individuals' productivity often declines in larger groups because of loss of coordination and because of social loafing. Social loafing seems to be due mostly to diffusion of responsibility and may be less prevalent in collectivist cultures.

▷ Group polarization occurs when discussion leads a group to shift toward a more extreme decision in the direction the group was already leaning. In groupthink, a cohesive group suspends critical judgment in a misguided effort to promote agreement in decision making.

▷ Social psychology illustrates the value of empiricism because research in this area often proves that common sense is wrong. Cross-cultural research on social behaviour illustrates that findings based on Western samples may not generalize precisely to other cultures. Additionally, several lines of research on social perception demonstrate that people's experience of the world is highly subjective.

Understanding Prejudice

Answer the following "true" or "false."

___ **1** Prejudice and discrimination amount to the same thing.

___ **2** Stereotypes are always negative or unflattering.

___ **3** Ethnic and racial groups are the only widespread targets of prejudice in modern society.

___ **4** People see members of their own ingroup as being more alike than the members of outgroups.

Prejudice is a major social problem. It harms victims' self-concepts, suppresses human potential, creates tension and strife between groups (Dion, 2003; Inzlicht & Kang, 2010; Major & Townsend, 2010; Ong, Fuller-Rowell, & Burrow, 2009), and even instigates wars. The first step toward reducing prejudice is to understand its roots. Hence, in this Application, we'll try to achieve a better understanding of why prejudice is so common. Along the way, you'll learn the answers to the true–false questions above.

Prejudice and discrimination are closely related concepts, and the terms have become nearly interchangeable in popular use. Social scientists, however, prefer to define their terms precisely, so let's clarify which is which. *Prejudice* **is a negative attitude held toward members of a group.** Like many other attitudes, prejudice can include three components (see Figure 16.24): beliefs ("Indians are mostly alcoholics"), emotions ("I despise Jews"), and behavioural dispositions ("I wouldn't hire a Mexican"). Racial prejudice receives the lion's share of publicity, but prejudice is *not* limited to ethnic groups. Women, homosexuals, the aged, the handicapped, and the mentally ill are also targets of widespread prejudice. Thus, many people hold prejudicial attitudes toward one group or another, and many have been victims of prejudice.

Prejudice may lead to *discrimination,* **which involves behaving differently, usually unfairly, toward the members of a group.** Prejudice and discrimination tend to go hand in hand, but as LaPiere's (1934) pioneering study of discrimination in restaurant seating showed, attitudes and behaviour do not necessarily correspond (see Figure 16.25). In our discussion, we'll concentrate primarily on the attitude of prejudice. Let's begin by looking at processes in person perception that promote prejudice.

Stereotyping and Subjectivity in Person Perception 12d

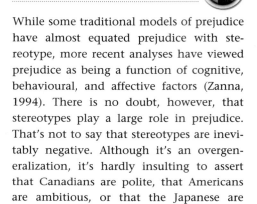

While some traditional models of prejudice have almost equated prejudice with stereotype, more recent analyses have viewed prejudice as being a function of cognitive, behavioural, and affective factors (Zanna, 1994). There is no doubt, however, that stereotypes play a large role in prejudice. That's not to say that stereotypes are inevitably negative. Although it's an overgeneralization, it's hardly insulting to assert that Canadians are polite, that Americans are ambitious, or that the Japanese are industrious. Unfortunately, many people do subscribe to derogatory stereotypes of various ethnic groups.

Although studies suggest that negative racial stereotypes have diminished over the last 50 years, they're not a thing of the past (Zarate, 2009). According to a variety of investigators, such as York University's Kerry Kawakami and her colleagues, modern racism has merely become more subtle (Dovidio, Gaertner, & Kawakami, 2010). Many people carefully avoid overt expressions of prejudicial attitudes but covertly continue to harbour negative views of racial minorities. These people endorse racial equality as an abstract principle but often oppose concrete programs intended to promote equality, on the grounds that discrimination is no longer a problem (Wright & Taylor, 2003). Recent studies suggest that modern sexism has become subtle in much the same way as racism (Swim & Hyers, 2009).

Research indicates that stereotypes are so pervasive and insidious they are often

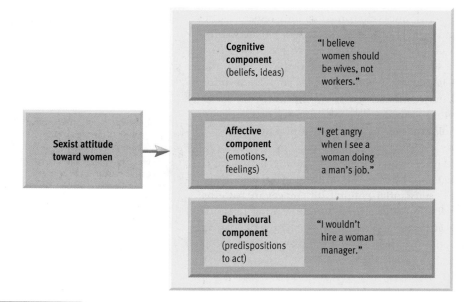

FIGURE 16.24

The three potential components of prejudice as an attitude.

Attitudes can consist of up to three components. The tri-component model of attitudes, applied to prejudice against women, would view sexism as negative beliefs about women (cognitive component) that lead to a feeling of dislike (affective component), which in turn leads to a readiness to discriminate against women (behavioural component).

Prejudice

	Absent	Present
Discrimination Absent	No relevant behaviours	A restaurant owner who is bigoted against gays treats them fairly because he needs their business.
Discrimination Present	An executive with favourable attitudes toward blacks doesn't hire them because he would get in trouble with his boss.	A professor who is hostile toward women grades his female students unfairly.

FIGURE 16.25

Relationship between prejudice and discrimination.

As these examples show, prejudice can exist without discrimination and discrimination without prejudice. In the green cells, there is a disparity between attitude and behaviour.

activated automatically (Bargh, 1999; Bodenhausen, Todd, & Richardson, 2009; Devine & Shapr, 2009), even in people who truly renounce prejudice. Thus, a man who rejects prejudice against homosexuals may still feel uncomfortable sitting next to a gay male on a bus, even though he regards his reaction as inappropriate.

Unfortunately, stereotypes are highly resistant to change. When people encounter members of a group that they view with prejudice who deviate from the stereotype of that group, they often discount this evidence. Stereotypes also persist because the *subjectivity* of person perception makes it likely that people will see what they expect to see when they actually come into contact with groups that they view with prejudice (Fiske & Russell, 2010). For example, Duncan (1976) had white subjects watch and evaluate interaction on a TV monitor that was supposedly live (actually it was a videotape) and varied the race of a person who gets into an argument and gives another person a slight shove. The shove was coded as "violent behaviour" by 73 percent of the subjects when the actor was black but by only 13 percent of the subjects when the actor was white. As we've noted before, people's perceptions are highly subjective. Because of stereotypes, even "violence" may lie in the eye of the beholder.

Biases in Attribution 12d

Attribution processes can also help perpetuate stereotypes and prejudice. Research taking its cue from Weiner's (1980) model

of attribution has shown that people often make *biased attributions for success and failure*. For example, men and women don't get equal credit for their successes (Swim & Sanna, 1996). Observers often discount a woman's success by attributing it to good luck, sheer effort, or the ease of the task (except on traditional feminine tasks). In comparison, a man's success is more likely to be attributed to his outstanding ability (see Figure 16.26). For example, one recent study found that when a man and woman collaborate on a stereotypically "male" task, both male and female observers downplay the woman's contribution (Heilman & Haynes, 2005). These biased patterns of attribution help sustain the stereotype that men are more competent than women.

Recall that the *fundamental attribution error* is a bias toward explaining events by pointing to the personal characteristics of the actors as causes (internal attributions). Research suggests that people are particularly likely to make this error when evaluating targets of prejudice (Hewstone, 1990). Thus, when people take note of ethnic neighbourhoods dominated by crime and poverty, the personal qualities of the residents are blamed for these problems, while other explanations emphasizing situational factors (job discrimination, poor police service, and so on) are downplayed or ignored. The old saying "They should be able to pull themselves up by their bootstraps" is a blanket dismissal of how situational factors may make it especially difficult for minorities to achieve upward mobility.

Forming and Preserving Prejudicial Attitudes 12d

If prejudice is an attitude, where does it come from? Many prejudices appear to be handed down as a legacy from parents (Killen, Richardson, & Kelly, 2010). Research by McGill University's Frances Aboud shows that prejudicial attitudes can be found in children as young as ages four or five (Aboud & Amato, 2001). This transmission of prejudice across generations presumably depends to some extent on *observational learning*. For example, if a young boy hears his father ridicule homosexuals, the boy's exposure to his father's attitude is likely to affect his own attitude about gays. If the young boy then goes to school and makes disparaging remarks about gays that are reinforced by

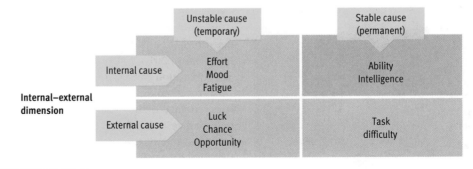

Stability dimension

	Unstable cause (temporary)	Stable cause (permanent)
Internal–external dimension Internal cause	Effort Mood Fatigue	Ability Intelligence
Internal–external dimension External cause	Luck Chance Opportunity	Task difficulty

FIGURE 16.26

Bias in the attributions used to explain success and failure by men and women.

Attributions about the two sexes often differ. For example, men's successes tend to be attributed to their ability and intelligence (blue cell), whereas women's successes tend to be attributed to hard work, good luck, or low task difficulty (green cells). These attributional biases help to perpetuate the belief that men are more competent than women.

Social Behaviour

approval from peers, his prejudice will be strengthened through *operant conditioning*. Of course, prejudicial attitudes are not acquired only through direct experience. Stereotypic portrayals of various groups in the media can also foster prejudicial attitudes (Mastro, Behm-Morawitz, Kopacz, 2008; Mutz & Goldman, 2010).

Explicit and Implicit Prejudice   12d

Another characteristic of modern prejudice or racism that serves to make it intractable is that it has moved underground, often below the level of awareness of people harbouring the prejudice. We all make social inferences and judgments when we meet others. While some of these judgments are intentional, many of them are not. We make many spontaneous judgments and inferences about others without awareness, intention, or effort (Uleman, Saribay, & Gonzalez, 2007).

In some cases, people may not even be aware that they are carrying around this prejudice—this is often referred to as *implicit prejudice* (Dovidio, Kawakami, & Gaertner, 2002). Implicit prejudice refers to negative associations to an outgroup that are activated automatically, without control or intention. If the racism is hidden, it may be even more difficult to change. But even here there is some hope. Research by University of Guelph psychologist Leanne Son Hing has shown that inducing feelings of hypocrisy (being reminded that you are not behaving in a manner that is consistent with your attitudes) in people high in implicit racism may serve to induce them to behave in a nondiscriminatory manner (Son Hing, Li, & Zanna, 2002).

Leanne Son Hing is a social psychologist at the University of Guelph. She conducts research in social cognition.

Competition between Groups

One of the oldest and simplest explanations for prejudice is that competition between groups can fuel animosity. If two groups compete for scarce resources, such as good jobs and affordable housing, one group's gain is the other's loss. *Realistic group conflict theory* asserts that intergroup hostility and prejudice are a natural outgrowth of fierce competition between groups.

A classic study at Robbers' Cave State Park in Oklahoma provided support for this theory many years ago (Sherif et al., 1961). The subjects were 11-year-old white boys attending a three-week summer camp at the park. They did not know that the camp counsellors were actually researchers (their parents knew). The boys were randomly assigned to one of two groups. During the first week, the boys got to know the other members of their own group through typical camp activities. They subsequently developed group identities. They called themselves the "Rattlers" and the "Eagles." In the second week, the Rattlers and Eagles were put into a series of competitive situations, such as a football game, a treasure hunt, and a tug of war, with trophies and other prizes at stake. As predicted by realistic group conflict theory, hostile feelings quickly erupted between the two groups. Food fights broke out in the mess hall, cabins were ransacked, and group flags were burned.

If competition between groups of innocent children pursuing trivial prizes can foster hostility, you can imagine what is likely to happen when adults from very different backgrounds battle for genuinely important resources. Research by the University of Western Ontario's Vicky Esses and her colleagues has shown that conflict over scarce resources can fuel prejudice and discrimination (Esses, Jackson, & Bennett-AbuAyyash, 2010). Even the mere *perception* of competition can breed prejudice.

If competition can fuel prejudice, perhaps contact highlighting cooperation can help reduce it (Amir, 1969). This reasoning is behind one of the most successful educational approaches to reducing prejudice—Elliot Aronson's *jigsaw classroom* technique (Aronson, 2000, 2010; Aronson & Bridgeman, 1979; Aronson et al., 1977). In this approach to education, students are divided into small groups in the classroom. The lesson for the day is broken down into small components and each student in the group is assigned the responsibility to learn/research his or her component. Then, each student reports back to the group the results of his or her work. In this way, the only way the group can complete the assignment is for the group members to learn from each group member. Each student is necessary and all have equal status in terms of the group's task. "Just as in a jigsaw puzzle, each piece—each student's part—is essential for the completion and full understanding of the final product" (Jigsaw Classroom, 2011). The highly successful technique emphasizes, among other things, interaction, cooperation, and equal status for all. Students who participated in these classrooms did better in school, and the classrooms and schools became less subject to racial tensions. After overseeing years of research, Aronson commented, "Over the years, as we continued to implement the jigsaw technique, the findings remained the same ... the schools that adopted this approach became more truly integrated" (Aronson, 2010, p. 206).

Dividing the World into Ingroups and Outgroups   12d

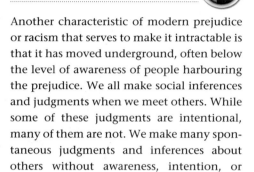

As noted in the main body of the chapter, when people join together in groups, they sometimes divide the social world into "us versus them," or *ingroups versus outgroups* (Taylor & Moghaddam, 1994; Lalonde & Gardner, 1989). This distinction has a profound impact on how we perceive, evaluate, and remember people (Dovidio & Gaertner, 2010). These social dichotomies can promote *ethnocentrism*—a tendency to view one's own group as superior to others and as the standard for judging the worth of foreign ways.

As you might anticipate, people tend to evaluate outgroup members less favourably than ingroup members (Krueger, 1996; Reynolds, Turner, & Haslam, 2000). One reason is that when people derogate an outgroup, they tend to feel superior as a result, and this feeling helps to affirm their self-worth (Fein & Spencer, 1997). The more strongly one identifies with an ingroup, the more one tends to note outgroup membership, and the more one tends to be prejudiced toward competing outgroups (Blascovich et al., 1997; Perreault & Bourhis, 1999).

Courtesy of Leanne S. Son Hing

People also tend to think simplistically about outgroups. They tend to see diversity among the members of their ingroup but to overestimate the homogeneity of the outgroup (Boldry, Gaertner, & Quinn, 2007; Ostrom & Sedikides, 1992). At a simple, concrete level, the essence of this process is captured by the statement "They all look alike." The illusion of homogeneity in the outgroup makes it easier to sustain stereotypic beliefs about its members (Ryan, Park, Judd, 1996). This point disposes of our last unanswered question from the list that opened the Application. Just in case you missed one of the answers, the statements were all false.

Threats to Social Identity

According to the *social identity perspective*, self-esteem depends on both one's *personal* identity and one's *social* identity (Abrams & Hogg, 2010; Turner et al., 1987). *Social identity* refers to the pride individuals derive from their membership in various groups, such as ethnic groups, religious denominations, occupational groups, neighbourhoods, country clubs, and so forth. The theory further proposes that self-esteem can be undermined by either threats to personal identity (you didn't get called for that job interview) or social identity (your football team loses a big game). Threats to both personal and social identity may motivate efforts to restore self-esteem. However, threats to social identity are more likely to provoke responses that foster prejudice and discrimination.

When social identity is threatened, individuals may react in two key ways to bolster it. One common response is to show *ingroup favouritism*. An example is tapping an ingroup member for a job opening or rating the performance of an ingroup member higher than that of an outgroup member (Capozza & Brown, 2000). A second common reaction is to engage in *outgroup derogation*—in other words, to "trash" outgroups that are perceived as threatening. Outgroup derogation is more likely when people identify especially strongly with the threatened ingroup (Levin et al, 2003; Schmitt & Maes, 2002). When people derogate an outgroup, they tend to feel superior as a result, and this feeling helps affirm their self-worth (Fein & Spencer, 1997). These unfortunate reactions are *not* inevitable.

But threats to social identity represent yet another dynamic process that can foster prejudice (Turner & Reynolds, 2001).

Remedial and Affirmative Action by the Disadvantaged

One issue that has surprisingly received only limited attention to date is analysis of factors that affect the tendency and ability of those disadvantaged by prejudice and discrimination to take affirmative actions that would benefit their group (Weiss & Lalonde, 2001). Under what conditions will the disadvantaged take action to redress their situation? What factors affect the tendency to engage in action?

An important line of research initiated by Mindi Foster of Wilfrid Laurier University has begun to redress this situation. She has shown, among other things, that social identity bases of discrimination and how the discrimination is perceived have implications for the tendency of the disadvantaged to take affirmative action (Foster, 1999, 2001). For example, she has found that if the discrimination is believed to be global and pervasive that action is more likely, and that women whose social identity is based on social experiences (e.g., feeling unsafe or being paid less than men) are more likely to endorse collective action against discrimination than women whose social identity is based on stereotypes (e.g., women as nurturing and emotional; Foster, 1999).

In a more recent line of research, Foster (2009a, 2009b) has examined the effects, over time, of perceiving that the discrimination you are experiencing is pervasive and not just an isolated, time-limited effect. She has convincingly demonstrated that the effects of

Courtesy of Mindi Foster

Wilfrid Laurier social psychologist Mindi Foster has examined the factors that affect the tendency of disadvantaged individuals to take action against discrimination and prejudice.

such perceived pervasive discrimination on action and coping are dynamic over time and that "perceiving discrimination to be isolated appears to ultimately promote an acceptance of the status quo, but recognizing the pervasiveness of discrimination can have motivational qualities over time" (Foster, 2009a, p. 179).

We look forward to seeing additional findings in the future from this line of investigation. We can never know too much about how to fight back against discrimination and prejudice and the types of factors that facilitate or inhibit such action.

Our discussion has shown that many processes conspire to create and maintain personal prejudices against a diverse array of outgroups. Most of the factors at work reflect normal, routine processes in social behaviour. So, it is understandable that most people—whether privileged or underprivileged, minority members or majority members—probably harbour some prejudicial attitudes. Our analysis of the causes of prejudice may have permitted you to identify prejudices of your own or their sources. Perhaps it's wishful thinking on our part, but an enhanced awareness of your personal prejudices may help you become a little more tolerant of the endless diversity seen in human behaviour. If so, that alone would mean that our efforts in writing this book have been amply rewarded.

REVIEW OF KEY POINTS

▷ Prejudice is supported by selectivity and memory biases in person perception and stereotyping. Stereotypes are highly resistant to change.

▷ Attributional biases, such as the tendency to assume that others' behaviour reflects their dispositions, can contribute to prejudice. The tendency to attribute others' failures to personal factors and the tendency to derogate victims can also foster prejudice.

▷ Negative attitudes about groups are often acquired through observational learning and strengthened through operant conditioning. The tendency to favour one's ingroups promotes ethnocentrism. The propensity to see outgroups as homogeneous serves to strengthen prejudice.

▷ People tend to be biased in favour of their ingroups. The propensity to see outgroups as homogeneous serves to strengthen prejudice. Threats to social identity can lead to ingroup favouritism and outgroup derogation. A variety of conditions affect the tendency of the disadvantaged groups to attempt remedial action.

Whom Can You Trust? Analyzing Credibility and Social Influence Tactics

You can run, but you can't hide. This statement aptly sums up the situation that exists when it comes to persuasion and social influence. There is no way to successfully evade the constant, pervasive, omnipresent efforts of others to shape your attitudes and behaviour. In this Application, we will discuss two topics that can enhance your resistance to manipulation. First, we will outline some ideas that can be useful in evaluating the credibility of a persuasive source. Second, we will describe some widely used social influence strategies that it pays to know about.

Evaluating Credibility

The salesperson at your local health food store swears that a specific herb combination improves memory and helps people stay healthy. A popular singer touts a psychic hotline, where the operators can "really help" with the important questions in life. Speakers at a "historical society" meeting claim that the Holocaust never happened. These are just a few real-life examples of how people are always attempting to persuade the public to believe something. In these examples, the "something" people are expected to believe runs counter to the conventional or scientific view, but who is to say who is right? After all, people are entitled to their own opinions, aren't they?

Yes, people *are* entitled to their own opinions, but that does not mean that all opinions are equally valid. Some opinions are just plain wrong, and others are highly dubious. Every person is not equally believable. In deciding what to believe, it is important to carefully examine the evidence presented and the logic of the argument that supports the conclusion (see the Critical Thinking Application in Chapter 10, page 484). In deciding what to believe, you also need to decide *whom* to believe, a task that requires assessing the *credibility* of the source of the information. Let's look at some questions that can provide guidance in this decision-making process.

Does the source have a vested interest in the issue at hand? If the source is likely to benefit in some way from convincing you of something, you need to take a skeptical attitude. In the examples just mentioned, it is easy to see how the salesclerk and the popular singer will benefit if you buy the products they are selling, but what about the so-called historical society? How would members benefit by convincing large numbers of people that the Holocaust never happened? Like the salesclerk and the singer, they are also selling something—in this case, a particular view of history that they hope will influence future events in certain ways. Someone does *not* have to have a financial gain at stake to have a vested interest in an issue. Of course, the fact that these sources have a vested interest does not necessarily mean that the information they are providing is false or that their arguments are invalid. But a source's credibility needs to be evaluated with extra caution when the person or group has something to gain.

What are the source's credentials? Does the person have any special training, an advanced degree, or any other basis for claiming special knowledge about the topic? The usual training for a salesclerk or a singer does not include how to assess research results in medical journals or claims of psychic powers. The Holocaust deniers are more difficult to evaluate. Some of them have studied history and written books on the topic, but the books are mostly self-published and few of these "experts" hold positions at reputable universities where scholars are subject to peer evaluation. That's *not* to say that legitimate credentials ensure a source's credibility. A number of popular diets that are widely regarded by nutritional experts as worthless, if not hazardous (Drewnowski, 1995; Dwyer, 1995), were created and marketed by genuine physicians. Of course, these physicians have a *vested interest* in the diets, as they have made millions of dollars from them.

Is the information grossly inconsistent with the conventional view on the issue? Just being different from the mainstream view certainly does not make a conclusion wrong. But claims that vary radically from most other information on a subject should raise a red flag that leads to careful scrutiny. Bear in mind that charlatans and hucksters are often successful because they typically try to persuade people to believe things that they want to believe. Wouldn't it be great if we could effortlessly enhance our memory, foretell the future, eat all we want and still lose weight, and earn hundreds of dollars per hour working at home? And wouldn't it be nice if the Holocaust had never happened? It pays to be wary of wishful thinking.

What was the method of analysis used in reaching the conclusion? The purveyors of miracle cures and psychic advice inevitably rely on anecdotal evidence. But you have already learned about the perils and unreliability of anecdotal evidence (see Chapter 2). One method frequently used by charlatans is to undermine the credibility of conventional information by focusing on trivial inconsistencies. This is one of the many strategies used by the people who argue that the Holocaust never occurred. They question the credibility of thousands of historical documents, photographs, and artifacts, and the testimony of countless people, by highlighting small inconsistencies among historical records relating to trivial matters, such as the number of people transported to a concentration camp in a specific week, or the number of bodies that could be disposed of in a single day (Shermer, 1997). Some inconsistencies are exactly what one should expect based on piecing together multiple accounts from sources working with different portions of incomplete information. But the strategy of focusing on trivial inconsistencies is a standard method for raising doubts about credible information. For example, this strategy was employed brilliantly by the defence lawyers in the O. J. Simpson murder trial.

Recognizing Social Influence Strategies

It pays to understand social influence strategies because advertisers, salespeople, and fundraisers—not to mention our friends and neighbours—frequently rely on them to manipulate our behaviour. Let's look at four basic strategies: the foot-in-the-door technique, misuse of the reciprocity norm, the lowball technique, and feigned scarcity.

Door-to-door salespeople have long recognized the importance of gaining a *little* cooperation from sales targets (getting a "foot in the door") before hitting them with the real sales pitch. The *foot-in-the-door technique* involves getting people to agree to a small request to increase the chances that they will agree to a larger request later. This technique is widely used in all walks of life. For example, groups seeking donations often ask people to simply sign a petition first.

In an early study of the foot-in-the-door technique (Freedman & Fraser, 1966), the large request involved asking homemakers whether a team of six men doing consumer research could come into their home to classify *all* of their household products. Only 22 percent of the control subjects agreed to this outlandish request. However, when the same request was made three days after a small request (to answer a few questions about soap preferences), 53 percent of the participants agreed to the large request. Why does the foot-in-the-door technique work? According to Burger (1999), quite a variety of processes contribute to its effectiveness, including people's tendency to try to behave consistently (with their initial response) and their reluctance to renege on their sense of commitment to the person who made the initial request.

Most of us have been socialized to believe in the *reciprocity norm*—the rule that we should pay back in kind what we receive from others. Robert Cialdini (2008) has written extensively about how the reciprocity norm is used in social influence efforts. For example, groups seeking donations routinely send address labels, key rings, and other small gifts with their pleas. Salespeople using the reciprocity principle distribute free samples to prospective customers. When they return a few days later, most of the customers feel obligated to buy some of their products. The reciprocity rule is meant to promote fair exchanges in social interactions. However, when people manipulate the reciprocity norm, they usually give something of minimal value in the hopes of getting far more in return (Howard, 1995).

The lowball technique is even more deceptive. The name for this technique derives from a common practice in automobile sales, in which a customer is offered a terrific bargain on a car. The bargain price gets the customer to commit to buying the car. Soon after this commitment is made, however, the dealer starts revealing some hidden costs. Typically, the customer learns that options assumed to be included in the original price are actually going to cost extra. Once they have committed to buying a car, most customers are unlikely to cancel the deal. Thus, the *lowball technique* involves getting someone to commit to an attractive proposition before its hidden costs are revealed.

Car dealers aren't the only ones who use this technique. For instance, a friend might ask whether you want to spend a week with him at his charming backwoods cabin. After you accept this seemingly generous proposition, he may add, "Of course there's some work for us to do. We need to repair the pier, paint the exterior, and. . . ." Lowballing is a surprisingly effective strategy (Cialdini & Griskevicius, 2010).

Many years ago, Jack Brehm (1966) demonstrated that telling people they can't have something only makes them want it more. This phenomenon helps explain why companies often try to create the impression that their products are in scarce supply. Scarcity threatens your freedom to choose a product, thus creating an increased desire for the scarce commodity. Advertisers frequently feign scarcity to drive up the demand for products. Thus, we constantly see ads that scream "limited supply available," "for a limited time only," "while they last," and "time is running out." Like genuine scarcity, feigned scarcity *can* enhance the desirability of a commodity (Cialdini & Griskevicius, 2010).

TABLE 16.2 **Critical Thinking Skills Discussed in This Application**

Skill	Description
Judging the credibility of an information source	The critical thinker understands that credibility and bias are central to determining the quality of information and looks at factors such as vested interests, credentials, and appropriate expertise.
Recognizing social influence strategies	The critical thinker is aware of manipulative tactics such as the foot-in-the-door and lowball techniques, misuse of the reciprocity norm, and feigned scarcity.

Key Ideas

Person Perception: Forming Impressions of Others
● People tend to attribute desirable characteristics to those who are good-looking. Perceptions of people are also influenced by their style of nonverbal expressiveness.
● Stereotypes are widely held social schemas that lead people to expect that others will have certain characteristics because of their membership in a specific group. In interacting with others, stereotypes may lead people to see what they expect to see and to overestimate how often they see it.

Attribution Processes: Explaining Behaviour
● Internal attributions ascribe behaviour to personal traits, whereas external attributions locate the cause of behaviour in the environment. Weiner's model proposes that attributions for success and failure should be analyzed in terms of the stability of causes, as well as along the internal–external dimension.
● Observers favour internal attributions to explain another's behaviour (the fundamental attribution error), while actors favour external attributions to explain their own behaviour. Cultures vary in their emphasis on individualism as opposed to collectivism, and these differences appear to influence attributional tendencies.

Close Relationships: Liking and Loving
● People tend to like and love others who are similar and who are physically attractive. Berscheid and Hatfield have distinguished between passionate and companionate love. Sternberg builds on their distinction by dividing companionate love into intimacy and commitment. Hazan and Shaver's theory suggests that love relationships in adulthood mimic attachment patterns in infancy.
● The characteristics that people seek in prospective mates are much the same around the world. However, cultures vary considerably in their emphasis on passionate love as a prerequisite for marriage.
● According to evolutionary psychologists, certain aspects of good looks influence attraction because they are indicators of reproductive fitness. Consistent with evolutionary theory, gender differences in mating preferences appear to transcend culture.

Attitudes: Making Social Judgments
● Attitudes may be made up of cognitive, affective, and behavioural components. Attitudes vary in strength, accessibility, and ambivalence. Attitudes and behaviour aren't as consistent as one might assume.
● A source of persuasion who is credible, expert, trustworthy, likable, and physically attractive tends to be relatively effective. Two-sided arguments and fear arousal are effective elements in persuasive messages.
● Attitudes may be shaped through classical conditioning, operant conditioning, and observational learning. Festinger's dissonance theory asserts that inconsistent attitudes cause tension and that people alter their attitudes to reduce cognitive dissonance.
● Self-perception theory posits that people may infer their attitudes from their behaviour. The elaboration likelihood model of persuasion holds that the central route to persuasion tends to yield longer-lasting attitude change than the peripheral route.

Conformity and Obedience: Yielding to Others
● Asch found that conformity becomes more likely as group size increases, up to a group size of four, and then levels off. If a small group isn't unanimous, conformity declines rapidly.
● In Milgram's study of obedience, subjects showed a remarkable tendency to follow orders to give electric shocks to an innocent stranger. The generalizability of Milgram's findings has stood the test of time, but his work also helped to stimulate stricter ethical standards for research.
● The Asch and Milgram experiments have been replicated in many cultures. These replications have uncovered modest cultural variations in the propensity to conform or to obey an authority figure.

Behaviour in Groups: Joining with Others
● The bystander effect occurs primarily because a group creates diffusion of responsibility. Individuals' productivity often declines in larger groups because of loss of coordination and because of social loafing.
● Group polarization occurs when discussion leads a group to shift toward a more extreme decision in the direction the group was already leaning. In groupthink, a cohesive group suspends critical judgment in a misguided effort to promote agreement in decision making.

Social Neuroscience
● Social neuroscience is a new orientation to examining individuals in a social context. It focuses on examining neural processes that underlie social phenomena such as attribution, impression formation, attitudes, and prejudice.

Putting It in Perspective: Themes 1, 5, and 7
● Our study of social psychology illustrated the value of empiricism, the cultural limits of research based on North American samples, and the subjectivity of perception.

PERSONAL APPLICATION • Understanding Prejudice
● Prejudice is supported by selectivity and memory biases in person perception and stereotyping. Attributional biases, such as the tendency to assume that others' behaviour reflects their dispositions, can contribute to prejudice.
● The tendency to attribute others' failures to personal factors and the tendency to derogate victims can also foster prejudice. The tendency to favour one's ingroups promotes ethnocentrism. The propensity to see outgroups as homogeneous serves to strengthen prejudice.

CRITICAL THINKING APPLICATION • Whom Can You Trust? Analyzing Credibility and Social Influence Tactics
● Useful criteria in judging credibility include whether a source has vested interests or appropriate credentials. One should also consider the method of analysis used in reaching conclusions and why information might not coincide with conventional wisdom.
● To resist manipulative efforts, it helps to be aware of social influence tactics, such as the foot-in-the-door technique, misuse of the reciprocity norm, the lowball technique, and feigned scarcity.

Key Terms

Attitudes, 759
Attributions, 748
Bystander effect, 775
Channel, 762
Cognitive dissonance, 766
Collectivism, 750
Commitment, 754
Companionate love, 754
Conformity, 769
Defensive attribution, 750
Discrimination, 782
Ethnocentrism, 784
Explicit attitudes, 760
External attributions, 748
Foot-in-the-door technique, 787
Fundamental attribution error, 749
Group, 774
Group cohesiveness, 779
Group polarization, 777
Groupthink, 778
Illusory correlation, 747
Implicit attitudes, 760
Individualism, 750
Informational influence, 770
Ingroup, 747
Internal attributions, 748
Interpersonal attraction, 753
Intimacy, 754
Lowball technique, 787
Matching hypothesis, 753
Mere exposure effect, 764
Message, 762
Normative influence, 770
Obedience, 770
Outgroup, 747

Passionate love, 754
Person perception, 743
Prejudice, 782
Receiver, 762
Reciprocity norm, 787
Self-serving bias, 751
Social loafing, 776
Social neuroscience, 779
Social psychology, 742
Social roles, 768
Social schemas, 744
Source, 762
Stereotypes, 745

Key People

Solomon Asch, 770
John Bargh, 746
Daryl Bem, 767
Ellen Berscheid, 755
Roger Buehler, 777
David Buss, 756
John Cacioppo, 768
J. Merrill Carlsmith, 766
William Cunningham, 780
Leon Festinger, 766
Elaine Hatfield, 754
Cindy Hazan, 755
Fritz Heider, 748
Irving Janis, 778
Stanley Milgram, 770, 773
Richard Petty, 768
Phillip Shaver, 755
Bernard Weiner, 748
Mark Zanna, 745
Robert Zajonc, 764
Philip Zimbardo, 768

1. When making judgments about a stranger, people are most likely to perceive which of the following people as honest or trustworthy?
   A. someone with a masculine face
   B. someone with baby-faced features
   C. someone who looks very familiar
   D. someone who is highly attractive

2. Illusory correlations influence the beliefs we hold. If you hold the belief that short men have a tendency to be insecure, which of the following will you tend to do?
   A. overestimate the frequency of insecurity among short men
   B. underestimate the frequency of insecurity in the population
   C. underestimate the frequency of insecurity among short men
   D. overestimate the frequency of insecurity in the population

3. Bob explains his failing grade on a term paper by saying that he really didn't work very hard. According to Weiner's model, Bob's explanation of his failure is an example of what kind of attribution?
   A. internal–stable
   B. internal–unstable
   C. external–stable
   D. external–unstable

4. The fundamental attribution error refers to which of the following tendencies?
   A. Observers tend to favour external attributions in explaining the behaviour of others.
   B. Observers tend to favour internal attributions in explaining the behaviour of others.
   C. Actors tend to favour external attributions in explaining the behaviour of others.
   D. Actors tend to favour situational attributions in explaining the behaviour of others.

5. Which of the following is often associated with the belief in a "just world"?
   A. prosocial acts like volunteer work
   B. blaming the victim of misfortune
   C. strong egalitarian beliefs
   D. poor self-esteem and self-efficacy

6. Which of the following statements corresponds to the view of Hazan and Shaver (1987) regarding relationship experiences in infancy and adulthood?
   A. Romantic relationships in adulthood follow the same form as attachment relationships in infancy.
   B. Those who had ambivalent attachments in infancy are unlikely to fall in love as adults.
   C. Those who had avoidant attachments in infancy often overcompensate by becoming excessively intimate in their adult love relationships.
   D. Those who had secure attachments in infancy are typically unsatisfied with the quality of their adult relationships.

7. In terms of love and marriage, which of the following aspects has the greatest cross-cultural similarities?
   A. the necessity of marriage in long-term relationships
   B. the overall value of romantic love
   C. passionate love as a prerequisite for marriage
   D. the traits that are valued in potential mates

8. According to cognitive dissonance theory, after people engage in counterattitudinal behaviour, which of the following will they do?
   A. convince themselves they really didn't perform the behaviour
   B. change their attitude to make it more consistent with their behaviour
   C. change their attitude to make it less consistent with their behaviour
   D. doubt whether they did perform the behaviour

9. In the context of attitude change and persuasion, which of the following would be considered a source factor?
   A. seeing a message on a billboard
   B. having a pre-existing opinion about the topic
   C. hearing the message from a trusted friend
   D. getting a message that has strong logic

10. Which of the following statements is consistent with the elaboration likelihood model of attitude change?
    A. The peripheral route results in more enduring attitude change.
    B. The central route results in more enduring attitude change.
    C. Only the central route to persuasion can be effective.
    D. Only the peripheral route to persuasion can be effective.

11. The results of Milgram's famous "shock" study (1963) suggest which of the following?
    A. In the real world, most people will refuse to follow orders to inflict harm on a stranger.
    B. Many people will obey an authority figure even if innocent people get hurt.
    C. Most people are willing to give obviously wrong answers when ordered to do so.
    D. Most people stick to their own judgment, even when group members unanimously disagree.

12. According to Latané (1981), social loafing is due to which of the following?
    A. social norms that stress the importance of positive interactions among group members
    B. duplication of effort among group members
    C. diffusion of responsibility in groups
    D. bias toward making internal attributions about the behaviour of others

13. Which of the following describes groupthink among members of a cohesive group?
    A. Members are initially unanimous about an issue.
    B. Members stress the importance of caution during group decision making.
    C. Members emphasize agreement at the expense of critical thinking.
    D. Members shift toward a less extreme position after group discussion.

14. Discrimination refers to which of the following?
    A. negative attitude toward members of a group
    B. unfair behaviour toward members of a group
    C. prejudice (either positive or negative) toward members of a group
    D. categorization of a particular group based on physical characteristics

15. Which of the following is an example of the foot-in-the-door technique?
    A. A teacher warns his students that if their homework isn't done by Monday, all students will have to stay after class.
    B. Door-to-door salespeople take a cute puppy with them, so that people will be friendlier.
    C. A car salesperson lets you test-drive an expensive new sports car. When you say you can't afford it, he then shows you the less expensive models.
    D. A politician gets you to sign a petition for a cause you believe in, and then a week later comes back to ask if you'll vote for him.

See Appendix A for answers to this Practice Test.

On the Web

▶ **CourseMate**

Go to this site to find online resources directly linked to your book, including more quizzes, a glossary, flash cards, videos, and more!

▶ **CengageNow**

Go to this site for the link to CengageNOW™, your one-stop study shop. Take a pre-test for this chapter and CengageNOW™ will generate a personalized study plan based on your test results! The study plan will identify the topics you need to review and direct you to online resources to help you master those topics. You can then take a post-test to help you determine the concepts you have mastered and what you still need to work on.

▶ **Aplia**

Aplia™ is an online interactive learning solution that helps you improve comprehension—and your grade—by integrating a variety of media and tools such as video, tutorials, practice tests, and an interactive e-book.

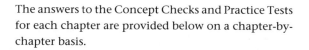
The answers to the Concept Checks and Practice Tests for each chapter are provided below on a chapter-by-chapter basis.

Chapter 1

Concept Check 1.1

1. c. John B. Watson (1930, p. 103), dismissing the importance of genetic inheritance while arguing that traits are shaped entirely by experience.

2. a. Wilhelm Wundt (1874/1904, p. v), campaigning for a new, independent science of psychology.

3. b. William James (1890), commenting negatively on the structuralists' efforts to break consciousness into its elements and his view of consciousness as a continuously flowing stream.

Concept Check 1.2

1. b. B. F. Skinner (1971, p. 17), explaining why he believed that freedom is an illusion.

2. a. Sigmund Freud (1905, pp. 77–78), arguing that it is possible to probe into the unconscious depths of the mind.

3. c. Carl Rogers (1961, p. 27), commenting on others' assertion that he had an overly optimistic (Pollyannaish) view of human potential and discussing humans' basic drive toward personal growth.

Concept Check 1.3

a. 2. Psychology is theoretically diverse.

b. 6. Heredity and environment jointly influence behaviour.

c. 4. Behaviour is determined by multiple causes.

d. 7. Our experience of the world is highly subjective.

Practice Test

1. A	p. 4	6. D	p. 11	11. A	p. 21
2. C	p. 5	7. A	p. 12	12. D	p. 26
3. A	p. 6	8. C	p. 15	13. A	p. 36
4. B	p. 7	9. B	p. 16	14. D	p. 38
5. A	p. 9	10. D	p. 20	15. C	p. 19

Chapter 2

Concept Check 2.1

1. IV: Film violence (present versus absent)

   DV: Heart rate and blood pressure (there are two DVs)

2. IV: Courtesy training (training versus no training)

   DV: Number of customer complaints

3. IV: Stimulus complexity (high versus low) and stimulus contrast (high versus low) (there are two IVs)

   DV: Length of time spent staring at the stimuli

4. IV: Group size (large versus small)

   DV: Conformity

Concept Check 2.2

1. d. Survey. You would distribute a survey to obtain information on subjects' social class, education, and attitudes about nuclear disarmament.

2. c. Case study. Using a case study approach, you could interview people with anxiety disorders, interview their parents, and examine their school records to look for similarities in childhood experiences. As a second choice, you might have people with anxiety disorders fill out a survey about their childhood experiences.

3. b. Naturalistic observation. To answer this question properly, you would want to observe baboons in their natural environment, without interference.

4. a. Experiment. To demonstrate a causal relationship, you would have to conduct an experiment. You would manipulate the presence or absence of food-related cues in controlled circumstances where subjects had an opportunity to eat some food, and monitor the amount eaten.

Concept Check 2.3

1. b. and e. The other three conclusions all equate correlation with causation.

2. a. Negative. As age increases, more people tend to have visual problems and acuity tends to decrease.

   b. Positive. Studies show that highly educated people tend to earn higher incomes and that people with less education tend to earn lower incomes.

   c. Negative. As shyness increases, the size of one's friendship network should decrease. However, research suggests that this inverse association may be weaker than widely believed.

Practice Test

1. D	p. 46	6. A	p. 51	11. B	p. 6
2. B	p. 46	7. B	p. 54	12. C	p. 69
3. B	p. 49	8. B	p. 56	13. D	p. 67
4. C	p. 49	9. A	p. 63	14. B	p. 74
5. C	p. 51	10. C	p. 65	15. D	p. 77

Chapter 3

Concept Check 3.1

1. d. dendrite

2. f. myelin

3. b. neuron

4. e. axon

5. a. glia

6. g. terminal button

7. h. synapse

Concept Check 3.2

1. d. serotonin

2. b. and d. serotonin and norepinephrine

3. e. endorphins

4. c. dopamine

5. a. acetylcholine

Concept Check 3.3

1. Left hemisphere damage, probably to Wernicke's area

2. Deficit in dopamine synthesis in an area of the midbrain

3. Degeneration of myelin sheaths surrounding axons

4. Disturbance in dopamine activity, possibly associated with enlarged ventricles in the brain

Note: Neuropsychological assessment is not as simple as this introductory exercise may suggest. There are many possible causes of most disorders, and we have discussed only a handful of leading causes for each.

Concept Check 3.4

1. Closer relatives; more distant relatives

2. Identical twins; fraternal twins

3. Biological parents; adoptive parents

4. Genetic overlap or closeness; trait similarity

Practice Test

1. A	p. 88	6. D	p. 105	11. C	p. 116
2. B	p. 89	7. C	p. 107	12. D	p. 120
3. A	p. 90	8. B	p. 109	13. A	p. 121
4. A	p. 92	9. C	p. 112	14. D	p. 118
5. D	p. 97	10. D	p. 104	15. A	p. 128

Chapter 4

Concept Check 4.1

1.

Dimension	Rods	Cones
Physical shape	Elongated	Stubby
Number in the retina	125 million	6.4 million
Area of the retina in which they are dominant receptor	Periphery	Centre/fovea
Critical to colour vision	No	Yes
Critical to peripheral vision	Yes	No
Sensitivity to dim light	Strong	Weak
Speed of dark adaptation	Slow	Rapid

2. Consider the responses of two ganglion cells in the retina whose firing is affected by light falling in centre-surround receptive fields, like those drawn onto the grid in the lower right corner. An identical amount of light falls in the centre of each receptive field. However, more light is falling in the surround of the receptive field on the left. Hence, the cell for this receptive field responds at a lower level than its neighbour because of greater inhibition by the surround (thanks to lateral antagonism). This reduced responding translates into the dark spots that you see. Why don't you see a dark spot at the intersection you are staring at? Because when you stare directly at a point, the image falls on the fovea, where receptive fields are much smaller, like the one drawn in the lower left corner. This receptive field does not produce a reduced response because an equal amount of light is falling in the centre and the surround.

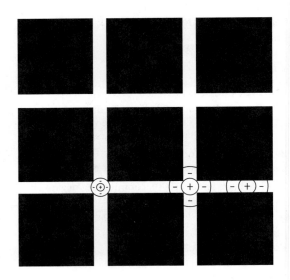

Concept Check 4.2

___✓___ 1. Interposition. The arches in front cut off part of the corridor behind them.

___✓___ 2. Height in plane. The back of the corridor is higher on the horizontal plane than the front of the corridor is.

___✓___ 3. Texture gradient. The more distant portions of the hallway are painted in less detail than the closer portions are.

___✓___ 4. Relative size. The arches in the distance are smaller than those in the foreground.

___✓___ 5. Light and shadow. Light shining in from the crossing corridor (it's coming from the left) contrasts with shadow elsewhere.

___✓___ 6. Linear perspective. The lines of the corridor converge in the distance.

Concept Check 4.3

Dimension	Vision	Hearing
1. Stimulus	Light waves	Sound waves
2. Elements of stimulus and related perceptions	Wavelength/hue Amplitude/brightness Purity/saturation	Frequency/pitch Amplitude/loudness Purity/timbre
3. Receptors	Rods and cones	Hair cells
4. Location of receptors	Retina	Basilar membrane
5. Main location of processing in brain	Occipital lobe, visual cortex	Temporal lobe, auditory cortex
6. Spatial aspect of perception	Depth perception	Auditory localization

Concept Check 4.4

Dimension	Taste	Smell	Touch
1. Stimulus	Soluble chemicals in saliva	Volatile chemicals in air	<u>Mechanical, thermal, and chemical energy due to external contact</u>
2. Receptors	Clusters of taste cells	<u>Olfactory cilia (hairlike structures)</u>	Many (at least 6) types
3. Location of receptors	<u>Taste buds on tongue</u>	Upper area of nasal passages	Skin
4. Basic elements of perception	Sweet, sour, salty, bitter	<u>No satisfactory classification scheme</u>	<u>Pressure, hot, cold, pain</u>

Practice Test

1.	B	p. 139	6.	B	p. 149	11.	B	p. 164
2.	A	p. 140	7.	D	p. 155	12.	B	p. 172
3.	A	p. 142	8.	C	p. 159	13.	C	p. 179
4.	B	p. 144	9.	A	p. 164	14.	D	p. 184
5.	D	p. 148	10.	C	p. 160	15.	A	p. 194

Chapter 5

Concept Check 5.1

Characteristic	REM sleep	NREM sleep
1. Type of EEG activity	"Wide awake" brain waves, mostly beta	Varied, lots of delta waves
2. Eye movements	Rapid, lateral	Slow or absent
3. Dreaming	Frequent, vivid	Less frequent
4. Depth (difficulty in awakening)	Varied, generally difficult to awaken	Varied, generally easier to awaken
5. Percentage of total sleep (in adults)	About 20%	About 80%
6. Increases or decreases (as percentage of sleep) during childhood	Percentage decreases	Percentage increases
7. Timing in sleep (dominates early or late)	Dominates late in cycle	Dominates early in cycle

Concept Check 5.2

1. Beta. Video games require alert information processing, which is associated with beta waves.

2. Alpha. Meditation involves relaxation, which is associated with alpha waves, and studies show increased alpha in meditators.

3. Theta. In stage 1 sleep, theta waves tend to be prevalent.

4. Delta. Sleepwalking usually occurs in deep NREM sleep, which is dominated by delta activity.

5. Beta. Nightmares are dreams, so you're probably in REM sleep, which paradoxically produces "wide awake" beta waves.

Practice Test

1.	B	p. 202	6.	C	p. 215	11.	A	p. 232
2.	C	p. 206	7.	D	p. 219	12.	D	p. 234
3.	C	p. 209	8.	A	p. 213	13.	D	p. 232
4.	A	p. 209	9.	A	p. 224	14.	C	p. 237
5.	A	p. 211	10.	B	p. 228	15.	B	p. 243

Chapter 6

Concept Check 6.1

1. CS: Fire in fireplace
   UCS: Pain from burn   CR/UCR: Fear

2. CS: Brake lights in rain
   UCS: Car accident   CR/UCR: Tensing up

3. CS: Sight of cat
   UCS: Cat dander   CR/UCR: Wheezing

Concept Check 6.2

1. FR. Each sale is a response and every third response earns reinforcement.

2. VI. A varied amount of time elapses before the response of doing yard work can earn reinforcement.

3. VR. Reinforcement occurs after a varied number of unreinforced casts (time is irrelevant; the more casts Martha makes, the more reinforcers she will receive).

4. CR. The designated response (reading a book) is reinforced (with a gold star) every time.

5. FI. A fixed time interval (three years) has to elapse before Skip can earn a salary increase (the reinforcer).

Concept Check 6.3

1. Punishment.

2. Positive reinforcement.

3. Negative reinforcement (for Audrey); the dog is positively reinforced for its whining.

4. Negative reinforcement.

5. Extinction. When Sharma's co-workers start to ignore her complaints, they are trying to extinguish the behaviour (which had been positively reinforced when it won sympathy).

Concept Check 6.4

1. Classical conditioning. Midori's blue windbreaker is a CS eliciting excitement in her dog.

2. Operant conditioning. Playing new songs leads to negative consequences (punishment), which weaken the tendency to play new songs. Playing old songs leads to positive reinforcement, which gradually strengthens the tendency to play old songs.

3. Classical conditioning. The song was paired with the passion of new love so that it became a CS eliciting emotional, romantic feelings.

4. Both. Ralph's workplace is paired with criticism so that his workplace becomes a CS eliciting anxiety. Calling in sick is operant behaviour that is strengthened through negative reinforcement (because it reduces anxiety).

Practice Test

1. D	p. 253	6. A	p. 265	11. D	p. 274
2. C	p. 253	7. A	p. 269	12. C	p. 281
3. B	p. 274	8. B	p. 271	13. D	p. 284
4. D	p. 261	9. D	p. 272	14. B	p. 274
5. C	p. 256	10. A	p. 274	15. A	p. 294

Chapter 7

Concept Check 7.1

Feature	Sensory memory	Short-term memory	Long-term memory
Main encoding format	Copy of input	Largely phonemic	Largely semantic
Storage capacity	Limited	Small (7 ± 2 chunks)	No known limit
Storage duration	About 1/4 second	Up to 20 seconds	Minutes to years

Concept Check 7.2

1. Ineffective encoding due to lack of attention

2. Retrieval failure due to motivated forgetting

3. Proactive interference (previous learning of Joe Cocker's name interferes with new learning)

4. Retroactive interference (new learning of sociology interferes with older learning of history)

Concept Check 7.3

1. a. declarative memory

2. e. long-term memory

3. j. sensory memory

4. d. implicit memory

5. b. episodic memory

6. f. procedural memory

7. i. semantic memory

8. g. prospective memory

9. k. short-term memory

Practice Test

1. B	p. 303	6. A	p. 317	11. B	p. 334
2. A	p. 305	7. C	p. 320	12. A	p. 334
3. D	p. 309	8. C	p. 323	13. D	p. 240
4. A	p. 314	9. B	p. 324	14. A	p. 340
5. C	p. 314	10. B	p. 332	15. D	p. 344

Chapter 8

Concept Check 8.1

1. 1. One-word utterance in which the word is over-extended to refer to a similar object.

2. 4. Words are combined into a sentence, but the rule for past tense is overregularized.

3. 3. Telegraphic sentence.

4. 5. Words are combined into a sentence, and past tense is used correctly.

5. 2. One-word utterance without overextension.

6. 6. "Longer" sentence with metaphor.

Concept Check 8.2

1. Functional fixedness

2. Forming subgoals

3. Insight

4. Searching for analogies

5. Arrangement problem

Concept Check 8.3

1. Elimination by aspects

2. Availability heuristic

3. Shift to additive strategy

Practice Test

1. B	p. 356	6. D	p. 365	11. A	p. 375
2. B	p. 351	7. D	p. 367	12. C	p. 377
3. D	p. 360	8. B	p. 368	13. C	p. 383
4. A	p. 363	9. B	p. 372	14. D	p. 385
5. A	p. 364	10. C	p. 374	15. C	p. 388

Chapter 9

Concept Check 9.1

1. Test–retest reliability

2. Criterion-related validity

3. Content validity

Concept Check 9.2

1. H. Given that the identical twins were reared apart, their greater similarity in comparison to fraternals reared together can be due only to heredity. This comparison is probably the most important piece of evidence supporting the genetic determination of IQ.

2. E. We tend to associate identical twins with evidence supporting heredity, but in this comparison, genetic similarity is held constant since both sets of twins are identical. The only logical explanation for the greater similarity in identicals reared together is the effect of their being reared together (environment).

3. E. This comparison is similar to the previous one. Genetic similarity is held constant and a shared environment produces greater similarity than being reared apart.

4. B. This is nothing more than a quantification of Galton's original observation that intelligence runs in families. Since families share both genes and environment, either or both could be responsible for the observed correlation.

5. B. The similarity of adopted children to their biological parents can be due only to shared genes, and the similarity of adopted children to their adoptive parents can only be due only to shared environment, so these correlations show the influence of both heredity and environment.

Concept Check 9.3

1. b. Gardner

2. a. Galton

3. c. Jensen

4. d. Scarr

5. e. Sternberg

Practice Test

1. D	p. 396	6. C	p. 407	11. C	p. 415
2. B	p. 396	7. B	p. 412	12. D	p. 421
3. D	p. 396	8. C	p. 409	13. A	p. 427
4. A	p. 400	9. B	p. 412	14. A	p. 430
5. D	p. 403	10. A	p. 415	15. C	p. 432

Chapter 10

Concept Check 10.1

1. I. Early studies indicated that lesioning the ventromedial nucleus of the hypothalamus leads to overeating (although it is an oversimplification to characterize the VMH as the brain's "stop-eating" centre).

2. I. According to Mayer, hunger increases when the amount of glucose in the blood decreases.

3. I or ?. Food cues generally trigger hunger and eating, but reactions vary among individuals.

4. D. Food preferences are mostly learned, and we tend to like what we are accustomed to eating. Most people will not be eager to eat a strange-looking food.

5. D. When leptin levels are increased, hunger tends to decrease.

6. I. Reactions vary, but stress generally tends to increased eating.

7. I. Research on dietary restraint suggests that when people feel that they have cheated on their diet, they tend to become disinhibited and eat to excess.

Concept Check 10.2

1. d. fear of failure

2. c. incentive value of success

3. b. perceived probability of success

4. a. need for achievement

Concept Check 10.3

2. James–Lange theory

3. Schachter's two-factor theory

4. Evolutionary theories

Practice Test

1. B	p. 441	6. B	p. 461	11. C	p. 476
2. D	p. 449	7. A	p. 476	12. C	p. 477
3. D	p. 451	8. C	p. 465	13. B	p. 477
4. B	p. 454	9. A	p. 470	14. A	p. 482
5. A	p. 454	10. D	p. 478	15. C	p. 485

Chapter 11

Concept Check 11.1

Event	Stage	Organism	Time span
1. Uterine implantation	Germinal	Zygote	0–2 weeks
2. Muscle and bone begin to form	Fetal	Fetus	2 months to birth
3. Vital organs and body systems begin to form	Embryonic	Embryo	2 weeks to 2 months

Concept Check 11.2

1. b. Animism is characteristic of the preoperational period.

2. c. Mastery of hierarchical classification occurs during the concrete operational period.

3. a. Lack of object permanence is characteristic of the sensorimotor period.

Concept Check 11.3

1. c. Commitment to personal ethics is characteristic of postconventional reasoning.

2. b. Concern about approval of others is characteristic of conventional reasoning.

3. a. Emphasis on positive or negative consequences is characteristic of preconventional reasoning.

Practice Test

1. D	p. 491	6. D	p. 504	11. A	p. 518
2. A	p. 496	7. B	p. 507	12. A	p. 523
3. B	p. 497	8. A	p. 545	13. D	p. 528
4. C	p. 498	9. C	p. 506	14. C	p. 531
5. C	p. 502	10. B	p. 523	15. B	p. 539

Chapter 12

Concept Check 12.1

1. Regression

2. Projection

3. Reaction formation

4. Repression

5. Rationalization

Concept Check 12.2

1. Bandura's observational learning. Sarah imitates a role model from television.

2. Maslow's need for self-actualization. Yolanda is striving to realize her fullest potential.

3. Freud's Oedipal complex. Vladimir shows preference for his opposite-sex parent and emotional distance from his same-sex parent.

Concept Check 12.3

1. Maslow (1970, p. 36), commenting on the need for self-actualization.

2. Eysenck (1977, pp. 407–408), commenting on the biological roots of personality.

3. Freud (in Malcolm, 1981), commenting on the repression of sexuality.

Practice Test

1. C	p. 551	6. A	p. 564	11. B	p. 574
2. A	p. 554	7. A	p. 566	12. B	p. 581
3. C	p. 557	8. D	p. 567	13. D	p. 583
4. C	p. 559	9. B	p. 570	14. A	p. 588
5. B	p. 561	10. A	p. 574	15. C	p. 590

Chapter 13

Concept Check 13.1

1. b. a choice between two unattractive options

2. c. weighing the positive and negative aspects of a single goal

3. a. a choice between two attractive options

Concept Check 13.2

1. a. frustration due to delay

2. d. pressure to perform

3. c. change associated with leaving school and taking a new job

4. a. frustration due to loss of job

   c. change in life circumstances

   d. pressure to perform (in quickly obtaining new job)

Concept Check 13.3

1. denial of reality

2. undoing

3. fantasy

4. overcompensation

5. intellectualization

Practice Test

1.	C	p. 608	6.	A	p. 606	11.	D	p. 619
2.	D	p. 699	7.	A	p. 607	12.	C	p. 621
3.	B	p. 601	8.	C	p. 610	13.	A	p. 625
4.	A	p. 600	9.	B	p. 613	14.	C	p. 630
5.	B	p. 605	10.	D	p. 616	15.	C	p. 634

Chapter 14

Concept Check 14.1

1. Bipolar disorder, manic episode (key symptoms: extravagant plans, hyperactivity, reckless spending)

2. Paranoid schizophrenia (key symptoms: delusions of persecution and grandeur, along with deterioration of adaptive behaviour)

3. Major depression (key symptoms: feelings of despair, low self-esteem, lack of energy)

Practice Test

1.	B	p. 642	6.	A	p. 661	11.	C	p. 677
2.	C	p. 642	7.	D	p. 664	12.	D	p. 677
3.	D	p. 652	8.	A	p. 670	13.	C	p. 683
4.	D	p. 654	9.	D	p. 671	14.	A	p. 684
5.	A	p. 656	10.	D	p. 672	15.	D	p. 687

Chapter 15

Concept Check 15.1

1. c   2. a   3. b

Concept Check 15.2

1. d   2. b   3. a   4. c

Concept Check 15.3

1. a. systematic desensitization

2. c. aversion therapy

3. b. social skills training

Concept Check 15.4

1. c   2. a   3. b   4. d   5. b

Practice Test

1.	C	p. 709	6.	A	p. 709	11.	C	p. 722
2.	D	p. 698	7.	D	p. 710	12.	C	p. 730
3.	B	p. 701	8.	D	p. 712	13.	A	p. 730
4.	B	p. 702	9.	B	p. 717	14.	D	p. 734
5.	D	p. 713	10.	A	p. 718	15.	D	p. 736

Chapter 16

Concept Check 16.1

	Unstable	Stable
Internal	d	b
External	a	c

Concept Check 16.2

1. c. Fundamental attribution error (assuming that arriving late reflects personal qualities)

2. a. Illusory correlation effect (overestimating how often one has seen confirmations of the assertion that young female professors get pregnant soon after being hired)

3. b. Stereotyping (assuming that all lawyers have these negative traits)

4. d. Defensive attribution (derogating the victims of misfortune to minimize the apparent likelihood of a similar mishap)

Concept Check 16.3

1. *Target:* Cognitive component of attitudes (beliefs about program for regulating nursing homes)

   Persuasion: Message factor (advice to use one-sided instead of two-sided arguments)

2. *Target:* Affective component of attitudes (feelings about candidate)

   Persuasion: Source factor (advice on smiling more and appearing sincere and compassionate)

3. *Target:* Behavioural component of attitudes (making contributions)

   Persuasion: Receiver factor (considering audience's initial position regarding the candidate)

Concept Check 16.4

1. False   2. True   3. False   4. True   5. False

Practice Test

1.	B	p. 744	6.	A	p. 755	11.	B	p. 772
2.	A	p. 747	7.	D	p. 756	12.	C	p. 776
3.	B	p. 749	8.	B	p. 766	13.	C	p. 778
4.	A	p. 749	9.	C	p. 762	14.	B	p. 782
5.	B	p. 750	10.	B	p. 768	15.	D	p. 787

Empiricism depends on observation; precise observation depends on measurement; and measurement requires numbers. Thus, scientists routinely analyze numerical data to arrive at their conclusions. Over 3000 empirical studies are cited in this text, and all but a few of the simplest ones required a statistical analysis. *Statistics* is the use of mathematics to organize, summarize, and interpret numerical data. We discussed statistics briefly in Chapter 2, but in this appendix we take a closer look.

To illustrate statistics in action, imagine a group of students who want to test a hypothesis that has generated quite an argument in their psychology class. The hypothesis is that university students who watch a great deal of television aren't as bright as those who watch TV infrequently. For the fun of it, the class decides to conduct a correlational study of itself, collecting survey and psychological test data. All of the classmates agree to respond to a short survey on their TV viewing habits.

Because everyone at that school has had to take the *Scholastic Aptitude Test* (SAT), the class decides to use scores on the SAT verbal subtest as an index of how bright students are. The SAT is one of a set of tests that high school students in the United States take before applying to college or university. Universities frequently use test scores like these, along with the students' high school grades and other relevant information, when considering admitting students to university. In this class, all of the students agree to allow the records office at the university to furnish their SAT scores to the professor, who replaces each student's name with a subject number (to protect students' right to privacy). Let's see how they could use statistics to analyze the data collected in their pilot study (a small, preliminary investigation).

Graphing Data 1c

After collecting the data, the next step is to organize the data to get a quick overview of our numerical results. Let's assume that there are 20 students in the class, and when they estimate how many hours they spend per day watching TV, the results are as follows:

3	2	0	3	1
3	4	0	5	1
2	3	4	5	2
4	5	3	4	6

One of the simpler things that they can do to organize data is to create a *frequency distribution—an orderly arrangement of scores indicating the frequency of each score or group of scores*. Figure B.1(a) shows a frequency distribution for the data on TV viewing. The column on the left lists the possible scores (estimated hours of TV viewing) in order, and the column on the right lists the number of subjects or participants with each score. Graphs can provide an even better overview of the data. One approach is to portray the data in a *histogram*, which is a bar graph that presents data from a frequency distribution. Such a histogram, summarizing our TV viewing data, is presented in Figure B.1(b).

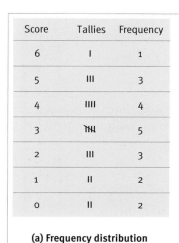

Score	Tallies	Frequency
6	I	1
5	III	3
4	IIII	4
3	THI	5
2	III	3
1	II	2
0	II	2

(a) Frequency distribution

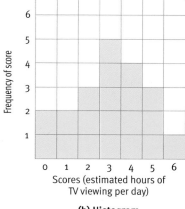

(b) Histogram

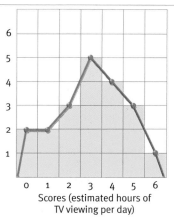

(c) Conversion of histogram into frequency polygon

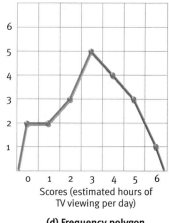

(d) Frequency polygon

FIGURE B.1

Graphing data.

(a) The raw data are tallied into a frequency distribution. **(b)** The same data are portrayed in a bar graph called a *histogram*. **(c)** A frequency polygon is plotted over the histogram. **(d)** The resultant frequency polygon is shown by itself.

Another widely used method of portraying data graphically is the *frequency polygon*—a line figure used to present data from a frequency distribution. Figures B.1(c) and B.1(d) show how the TV viewing data can be converted from a histogram to a frequency polygon. In both the bar graph and the line figure, the horizontal axis lists the possible scores and the vertical axis is used to indicate the frequency of each score. This use of the axes is nearly universal for frequency polygons, although sometimes it is reversed in histograms (the vertical axis lists possible scores, so the bars become horizontal).

The graphs improve on the jumbled collection of scores that they started with, but *descriptive statistics, which are used to organize and summarize data,* provide some additional advantages. Let's see what the three measures of central tendency tell us about the data.

Measuring Central Tendency

1c

In examining a set of data, it's routine to ask, "What is a typical score in the distribution?" For instance, in this case, we might compare the average amount of TV watching in the sample to national estimates, to determine whether the subjects appear to be representative of the population. The three measures of central tendency—the median, the mean, and the mode—give us indications regarding the typical score in a data set. As explained in Chapter 2, the *median is the score that falls in the centre of a distribution, the mean is the arithmetic average of the scores, and the mode is the score that occurs most frequently.*

All three measures of central tendency are calculated for the TV viewing data in Figure B.2. As you can see, in this set of data, the mean, median, and mode all turn out to be the same score, which is 3. Although our example in Chapter 2 emphasized that the mean, median, and mode can yield different estimates of central tendency, the correspondence among them seen in the TV viewing data is quite common.

Lack of agreement usually occurs when a few extreme scores pull the mean away from the centre of the distribution. When a distribution is symmetric, the measures of central tendency fall together, but this is not true in skewed or unbalanced distributions.

In a *negatively skewed distribution,* most scores pile up at the high end of the scale (*negative skew* refers to the direction in which the curve's "tail" points). In a *positively skewed distribution,* scores pile up at the low end of the scale. In both types

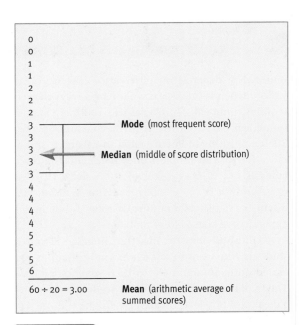

Mode (most frequent score)

Median (middle of score distribution)

60 ÷ 20 = 3.00   **Mean** (arithmetic average of summed scores)

FIGURE B.2

Measures of central tendency.
Although the mean, median, and mode sometimes yield different results, they usually converge, as in the case of the TV viewing data.

of skewed distributions, a few extreme scores at one end pull the mean, and to a lesser degree the median, away from the mode. In these situations, the mean may be misleading and the median usually provides the best index of central tendency.

In any case, the measures of central tendency for the TV viewing data are reassuring, since they all agree and they fall reasonably close to national estimates regarding how much young adults watch TV (Nielsen Media Research, 1998). Given the small size of the student group, this agreement with national norms doesn't *prove* that the sample is representative of the population, but at least there's no obvious reason to believe that it is unrepresentative.

Measuring Variability

1c

Of course, the subjects in the sample did not report identical TV viewing habits. Virtually all data sets are characterized by some variability. *Variability refers to how much the scores tend to vary or depart from the mean score.* For example, the distribution of golf scores for a mediocre, erratic golfer would be characterized by high variability, while scores for an equally mediocre but consistent golfer would show less variability.

The *standard deviation is an index of the amount of variability in a set of data.* It reflects the dispersion of scores in a distribution. This principle is portrayed graphically in Figure B.3, where the two distributions of golf scores have the same mean but

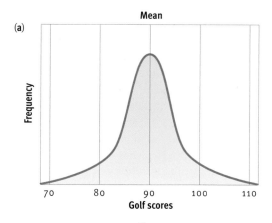

(a)

Mean

Golf scores

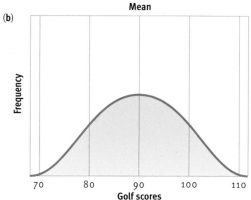

(b)

Mean

Golf scores

The standard deviation and dispersion of data.
Although both of these distributions of golf scores have the same mean, their standard deviations will be different. In **(a)** the scores are bunched together and there is less variability than in **(b)**, yielding a lower standard deviation for the data in distribution **(a)**.

the upper one has less variability because the scores are "bunched up" in the centre (for the consistent golfer). The distribution in Figure B.3(b) is characterized by more variability, as the erratic golfer's scores are more spread out. This distribution will yield a higher standard deviation than the distribution in Figure B.3(a).

The formula for calculating the standard deviation is shown in Figure B.4, where d stands for each score's deviation from the mean and Σ stands for summation. A step-by-step application of this formula to our TV viewing data, shown in Figure B.4, reveals that the standard deviation for our TV viewing data is 1.64. The standard deviation has a variety of uses. One of these uses will surface in the next section, where we discuss the normal distribution.

The Normal Distribution 1c

The hypothesis in the study was that brighter students watch less TV than relatively dull students. To test this hypothesis, the students decided to correlate

TV viewing with SAT scores. But to make effective use of the SAT data, they need to understand what SAT scores mean, which brings us to the normal distribution.

The *normal distribution* is a symmetrical, bell-shaped curve that represents the pattern in which many human characteristics are dispersed in the population. A great many physical qualities (e.g., height, nose length, and running speed) and psychological traits (intelligence, spatial reasoning ability, introversion) are distributed in a manner that closely resembles this bell-shaped curve. When a trait is normally distributed, most scores fall near the centre of the distribution (the mean), and the number of scores gradually declines as one moves away from the centre in either direction. The normal distribution is *not* a law of nature. It's a mathematical function, or

TV viewing score (X)	Deviation from mean (d)	Deviation squared (d²)
0	−3	9
0	−3	9
1	−2	4
1	−2	4
2	−1	1
2	−1	1
2	−1	1
3	0	0
3	0	0
3	0	0
3	0	0
3	0	0
4	+1	1
4	+1	1
4	+1	1
4	+1	1
5	+2	4
5	+2	4
5	+2	4
6	+3	9

$N = 20$

$\Sigma X = 60$ $\Sigma d^2 = 54$

$$\text{Mean} = \frac{\Sigma X}{N} = \frac{60}{20} = 3.0$$

$$\text{Standard deviation} = \sqrt{\frac{\Sigma d^2}{N}} = \sqrt{\frac{54}{20}}$$

$$= \sqrt{2.70} = 1.64$$

Steps in calculating the standard deviation.
(1) Add the scores (ΣX) and divide by the number of scores (N) to calculate the mean (which comes out to 3.0 in this case). **(2)** Calculate each score's deviation from the mean by subtracting the mean from each score (the results are shown in the second column). **(3)** Square these deviations from the mean and total the results to obtain (Σd^2), as shown in the third column. **(4)** Insert the numbers for N and Σd^2 into the formula for the standard deviation and compute the results.

theoretical curve, that approximates the way nature seems to operate.

The normal distribution is the bedrock of the scoring system for most psychological tests, including the SAT. As we discuss in Chapter 9, psychological tests are *relative measures*; they assess how people score on a trait in comparison to other people. The normal distribution gives us a precise way to measure how people stack up in comparison to each other.

Although you may not have realized it, you probably have taken many tests in which the scoring system is based on the normal distribution, such as IQ tests. On the SAT, for instance, raw scores (the number of items correct on each subtest) are converted into standard scores that indicate where a student falls in the normal distribution for the trait measured. In this conversion, the mean is set arbitrarily at 500 and the standard deviation at 100, as shown in Figure B.5. Therefore, a score of 400 on the SAT verbal subtest means that the student scored one standard deviation below the mean, while an SAT score of 600 indicates that the student scored one standard deviation above the mean. Thus, SAT scores tell us how many standard deviations above or below the mean a specific student's score was. This system also provides the metric for IQ scales and many other types of psychological tests (see Chapter 9).

Test scores that place examinees in the normal distribution can always be converted to percentile scores, which are a little easier to interpret. *A percentile score* indicates the percentage of people who score at or below a particular score. For example, if you score at the 60th percentile on an IQ test, 60 percent of the people who take the test score the same or below you, while the remaining 40 percent score above you. There are tables available that permit us to convert any standard deviation placement in a normal distribution into a precise percentile score.

Of course, not all distributions are normal. Some distributions are skewed in one direction or the other. As an example, consider what would happen if a classroom exam was much too easy or much too hard. If the test was too easy, scores would be bunched up at the high end of the scale. If the test was too hard, scores would be bunched up at the low end.

Measuring Correlation 1d

To determine whether TV viewing is related to SAT scores, the students have to compute a *correlation coefficient*—a numerical index of the degree of relationship between two variables. As discussed in Chapter 2, a *positive* correlation means that two variables—say X and Y—co-vary in the *same* direction. This means that high scores on variable X are associated with high scores on variable Y and that low scores on X are associated with low scores on Y.

A *negative* correlation indicates that two variables co-vary in the *opposite* direction. This means that people who score high on variable X tend to score low on variable Y, whereas those who score low on X tend to score high on Y. In their study, the psychology students hypothesized that as TV viewing increases, SAT scores will decrease, so they should expect a negative correlation between TV viewing and SAT scores.

The *magnitude* of a correlation coefficient indicates the *strength* of the association between two variables. This coefficient can vary between 0 and ±1.00. The coefficient is usually represented by the letter r (e.g., r = 0.45). A coefficient near 0 tells us that there is no relationship between two variables. A coefficient of +1.00 or −1.00 indicates that there is a perfect, one-to-one correspondence between two variables. A perfect correlation is found only rarely when working with real data. The closer the coefficient is to either −1.00 or +1.00, the stronger the relationship is.

The direction and strength of correlations can be illustrated graphically in scatter diagrams (see Figure B.6). *A scatter diagram* is a graph in which paired X and Y scores for each subject are plotted as single points. Figure B.6 shows scatter diagrams for positive correlations in the upper half and for negative correlations in the bottom half. A perfect positive correlation and a perfect negative correlation are shown

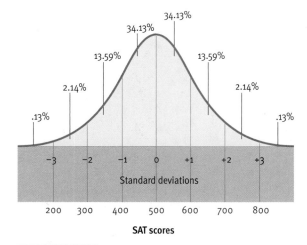

FIGURE B.5

The normal distribution and SAT scores.

The normal distribution is the basis for the scoring system on many standardized tests. For example, on the SAT, the mean is set at 500 and the standard deviation at 100. Hence, an SAT score tells you how many standard deviations above or below the mean a student scored. For example, a score of 700 means that person scored 2 standard deviations above the mean.

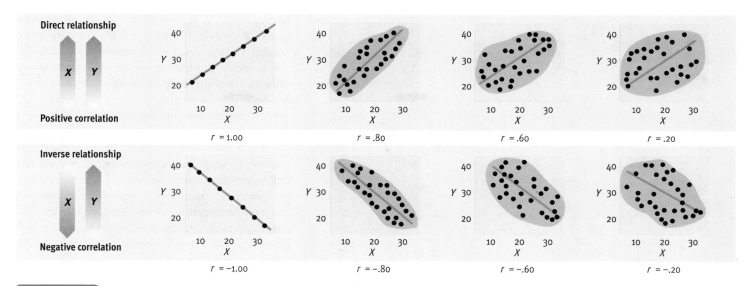

Scatter diagrams of positive and negative correlations.

Scatter diagrams plot paired *X* and *Y* scores as single points. Score plots slanted in the opposite direction result from positive (top row) as opposed to negative (bottom row) correlations. Moving across both rows (to the right), you can see that progressively weaker correlations result in more and more scattered plots of data points.

on the far left. When a correlation is perfect, the data points in the scatter diagram fall exactly in a straight line. However, positive and negative correlations yield lines slanted in the opposite direction because the lines map out opposite types of associations. Moving to the right in Figure B.6, you can see what happens when the magnitude of a correlation decreases. The data points scatter farther and farther from the straight line that would represent a perfect relationship.

What about the data relating TV viewing to SAT scores? Figure B.7 shows a scatter diagram of these

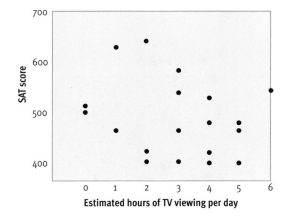

FIGURE B.7

Scatter diagram of the correlation between TV viewing and SAT scores.

The hypothetical data relating TV viewing to SAT scores are plotted in this scatter diagram. Compare it to the scatter diagrams shown in Figure B.6 and see whether you can estimate the correlation between TV viewing and SAT scores in the students' data (see the text for the answer).

data. Having just learned about scatter diagrams, perhaps you can estimate the magnitude of the correlation between TV viewing and SAT scores. The scatter diagram of our data looks a lot like the one shown in the bottom right corner of Figure B.6, suggesting that the correlation will be in the vicinity of −0.20.

The formula for computing the most widely used measure of correlation—the Pearson product–moment correlation—is shown in Figure B.8, along with the calculations for the data on TV viewing and SAT scores. The data yield a correlation of $r = -0.24$. This coefficient of correlation reveals that there is a weak inverse association between TV viewing and performance on the SAT. Among the sample of participants, as TV viewing increases, SAT scores decrease, but the trend isn't very strong. We can get a better idea of how strong this correlation is by examining its predictive power.

Correlation and Prediction

1d

As the magnitude of a correlation increases (gets closer to either −1.00 or +1.00), our ability to predict one variable based on knowledge of the other variable steadily increases. This relationship between the magnitude of a correlation and predictability can be quantified precisely. All we have to do is square the correlation coefficient (multiply it by itself) and this gives us the *coefficient of determination*, the percentage of variation in one variable that can be predicted based on the other variable. Thus, a

Subject number	TV viewing score (X)	X²	SAT score (Y)	Y²	XY
1	0	0	500	250 000	0
2	0	0	515	265 225	0
3	1	1	450	202 500	450
4	1	1	650	422 500	650
5	2	4	400	160 000	800
6	2	4	675	455 625	1350
7	2	4	425	180 625	850
8	3	9	400	160 000	1200
9	3	9	450	202 500	1350
10	3	9	500	250 000	1500
11	3	9	550	302 500	1650
12	3	9	600	360 000	1800
13	4	16	400	160 000	1600
14	4	16	425	180 625	1700
15	4	16	475	225 625	1900
16	4	16	525	275 625	2100
17	5	25	400	160 000	2000
18	5	25	450	202 500	2250
19	5	25	475	225 625	2375
20	6	36	550	302 500	3300
$N = 20$	$\Sigma X = 60$	$\Sigma X^2 = 234$	$\Sigma Y = 9815$	$\Sigma Y^2 = 4\,943\,975$	$\Sigma XY = 28\,825$

Formula for Pearson product–moment correlation coefficient

$$r = \frac{N\,\Sigma XY - (\Sigma X)(\Sigma Y)}{\sqrt{[(N)\,\Sigma X^2 - (\Sigma X)^2][(N)\,\Sigma Y^2 - (\Sigma Y)^2]}}$$

$$= \frac{(20)(28\,825) - (60)(9815)}{\sqrt{[(20)(234) - (60)^2][(20)(4\,943\,975) - (9815)^2]}}$$

$$= \frac{-12\,400}{\sqrt{[1080][2\,545\,275]}}$$

$$= -.237$$

FIGURE B.8

Computing a correlation coefficient.

The calculations required to compute the Pearson product–moment coefficient of correlation are shown here. The formula looks intimidating, but it's just a matter of filling in the figures taken from the sums of the columns shown above the formula.

correlation of 0.70 yields a coefficient of determination of 0.49 ($0.70 \times 0.70 = 0.49$), indicating that variable X can account for 49 percent of the variation in variable Y. Figure B.9 shows how the coefficient of determination goes up as the magnitude of a correlation increases.

Unfortunately, a correlation of 0.24 doesn't give us much predictive power. The students can account for only a little over 6 percent of the variation in variable Y. So, if they tried to predict individuals' SAT scores based on how much TV those individuals watched, their predictions wouldn't be very accurate. Although a low correlation doesn't have much practical, predictive utility, it may still have theoretical value. Just knowing that there is a relationship between two variables can be theoretically interesting. However, we haven't yet addressed the question of whether the observed correlation is strong enough to support the hypothesis that there is a relationship between TV viewing and SAT scores. To make this judgment, we have to turn to *inferential statistics* and the process of hypothesis testing.

Hypothesis Testing

Inferential statistics go beyond the mere description of data. *Inferential statistics are used to interpret data and draw conclusions.* They permit researchers to decide whether their data support their hypotheses.

In Chapter 2, we showed how inferential statistics can be used to evaluate the results of an experiment; the same process can be applied to correlational data. In the study of TV viewing, the students hypothesized that they would find an inverse relationship between the amount of TV watched and SAT scores.

FIGURE B.9

Correlation and the coefficient of determination.

The coefficient of determination is an index of a correlation's predictive power. As you can see, whether positive or negative, stronger correlations yield greater predictive power.

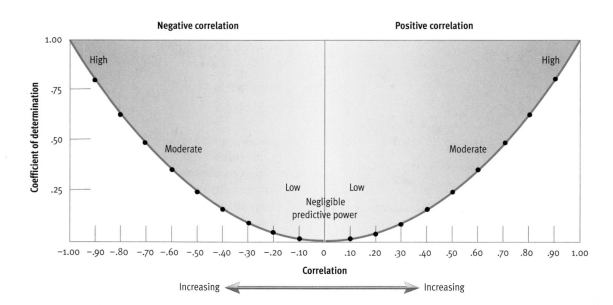

Sure enough, that's what they found. However, a critical question remains: Is this observed correlation large enough to support the hypothesis, or might a correlation of this size have occurred by chance?

We have to ask a similar question nearly every time we conduct a study. Why? Because we are working with only a sample. In research, we observe a limited *sample* (in this case, 20 participants) to draw conclusions about a much larger *population* (students in general). In any study, there's always a possibility that if we drew a different sample from the population, the results might be different. Perhaps our results are unique to our sample and not generalizable to the larger population. If we were able to collect data on the entire population, we would not have to wrestle with this problem, but our dependence on a sample necessitates the use of inferential statistics to precisely evaluate the likelihood that our results are due to chance factors in sampling. Thus, inferential statistics are the key to making the inferential leap from the sample to the population (see Figure B.10).

Although it may seem backward, in hypothesis testing, we formally test the *null hypothesis*. As applied to correlational data, the *null hypothesis* is the assumption that there is no true relationship between the variables observed. In the students' study, the null hypothesis is that there is no genuine association between TV viewing and SAT scores. They want to determine whether their results will permit them to *reject* the null hypothesis and thus conclude that their *research hypothesis* (that there *is* a relationship between the variables) has been supported.

In such cases, why do researchers directly test the null hypothesis instead of the research hypothesis? Because our probability calculations depend on assumptions tied to the null hypothesis. Specifically, we compute the probability of obtaining the results that we have observed if the null hypothesis is indeed true. The calculation of this probability hinges on a number of factors. A key factor is the amount of variability in the data, which is why the standard deviation is an important statistic.

Statistical Significance

When we reject the null hypothesis, we conclude that we have found *statistically significant* results. *Statistical significance* is said to exist when the probability that the observed findings are due to chance is very low, usually fewer than five chances in 100. This means that if the null hypothesis is correct and we conduct our study 100 times, drawing a new sample from the population each time, we will get results such as those observed only five times out of 100. If our calculations allow us to reject the null hypothesis, we conclude that our results support our research hypothesis. Thus, statistically significant results typically are findings that *support* a research hypothesis.

The requirement that there be fewer than five chances in 100 that research results are due to chance is the *minimum* requirement for statistical significance. When this requirement is met, we say the results are significant at the 0.05 level. If researchers calculate that there is less than one chance in 100 that their results are due to chance factors in sampling, the results are significant at the 0.01 level. If there is less than a one in 1000 chance that findings are attributable to sampling error, the results are significant at the 0.001 level. Thus, there are several *levels* of significance that you may see cited in scientific articles.

Because we are dealing only in matters of probability, there is always the possibility that our decision to accept or reject the null hypothesis is wrong. The various significance levels indicate the probability of erroneously rejecting the null hypothesis (and inaccurately accepting the research hypothesis). At the 0.05 level of significance, there are five chances in 100 that we have made a mistake when we conclude that our results support our hypothesis, and at the 0.01 level of significance, the chance of an erroneous conclusion is one in 100. Although researchers hold

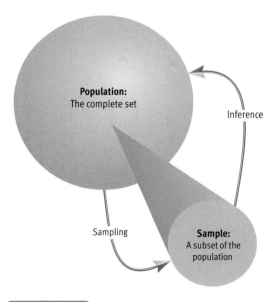

FIGURE B.10

The relationship between the population and the sample.

In research, we are usually interested in a broad population, but we can observe only a small sample from the population. After making observations of our sample, we draw inferences about the population, based on the sample. This inferential process works well as long as the sample is reasonably representative of the population.

the probability of this type of error quite low, the probability is never zero. This is one of the reasons that competently executed studies of the same question can yield contradictory findings. The differences may be due to chance variations in sampling that can't be prevented.

What do we find when we evaluate the data linking TV viewing to students' SAT scores? The calculations indicate that, given the sample size and the variability in the data, the probability of obtaining a correlation of −0.24 by chance is greater than 20 percent. That's not a high probability, but it's *not* low enough to reject the null hypothesis. Thus, the findings are not strong enough to allow us to conclude that the students have supported their hypothesis.

Statistics and Empiricism

In summary, conclusions based on empirical research are a matter of probability, and there's always a possibility that the conclusions are wrong. However, two major strengths of the empirical approach are its precision and its intolerance of error. Scientists can give you precise estimates of the likelihood that their conclusions are wrong, and because they're intolerant of error, they hold this probability extremely low. It's their reliance on statistics that allows them to accomplish these goals.

Key Terms

Coefficient of determination, A-11
Correlation coefficient, A-10
Descriptive statistics, A-8
Frequency distribution, A-7
Frequency polygon, A-8
Histogram, A-7
Inferential statistics, A-12
Mean, A-8
Median, A-8
Mode, A-8
Negatively skewed distribution, A-8
Normal distribution, A-9
Null hypothesis, A-13
Percentile score, A-10
Positively skewed distribution, A-8
Scatter diagram, A-10
Standard deviation, A-8
Statistical significance, A-13
Statistics, A-7
Variability, A-8

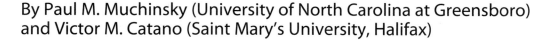

By Paul M. Muchinsky (University of North Carolina at Greensboro) and Victor M. Catano (Saint Mary's University, Halifax)

Throughout this book, we have seen many examples of how psychology has been applied to practical problems in a wide variety of settings. But we have yet to discuss in earnest one setting that has received a great deal of attention from the earliest beginnings of psychology—the work setting. *Industrial and organizational (I/O) psychology is the branch of psychology concerned with the application of psychological principles in the workplace.* The Canadian Society for Industrial and Organizational Psychology (CSIOP) is the major professional organization for I/O psychologists (http://psychology.uwo.ca/csiop). The number of I/O psychologists has more than doubled in recent years, and it appears that this growth will continue. I/O psychologists are mostly found in four work settings: industry, universities, government, and consulting firms (see Figure C.1).

People devote an enormous part of their lives to occupational activities, so I/O psychology is devoted to understanding one of the major domains of human behaviour. In broad terms, I/O psychology is concerned with behaviour in work situations. There are two sides of I/O psychology: science and practice. On the one hand, I/O psychology is a productive, fascinating area of scientific inquiry, concerned with advancing knowledge about behaviour in the workplace. In this respect, I/O psychology is an academic discipline that seeks to test hypotheses, gather data, and make generalizations about work-related behaviour.

On the other hand, I/O psychology is a profession concerned with the application of knowledge to solve real problems in the world of work. I/O psychologists strive to help organizations hire better employees, reduce absenteeism, improve communication at work, increase job satisfaction, and solve countless other problems. Accordingly, the education of I/O psychologists is founded on the *scientist-practitioner model,* which trains them in both scientific inquiry and practical applications.

I/O psychology was originally called *industrial psychology.* During its early years (roughly the first half of the 20th century), the field focused primarily on recruiting and selecting employees, training, evaluating job performance, and the nature of effective leadership in the workplace. In the 1950s and 1960s, psychologists in this area became more concerned with the organizational context in which work occurs. This shift in emphasis was also fuelled by changes in the economy, which gradually moved from a predominantly manufacturing base to more of a service economy. Because of these trends, the field's name was officially changed to industrial/organizational psychology in 1970. This name change is not merely cosmetic, as it captures the essence of the field. The topics of interest to contemporary I/O psychology generally fall into the traditional domain of *industrial psychology* or the more recently emerging domain of *organizational psychology.* Our coverage will reflect this reality, as we begin by discussing topics in industrial psychology and then turn to topics in organizational psychology.

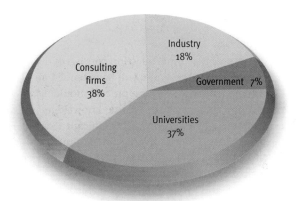

FIGURE C.1

Principal work settings of industrial/organizational psychologists.

I/O psychologists are mainly found in the four work settings identified here. As the pie chart shows, about three-quarters of I/O psychologists work either at universities or at consulting firms. (Based on Society for Industrial and Organizational Psychology 2001 member database)

Source: Muchinsky, P.M. (2003). *Psychology applied to work.* Belmont, CA: Wadsworth. Reprinted by permission.

Industrial Psychology

Industrial psychology focuses on topics associated with personnel matters. It is concerned with picking the right people for the right jobs and cultivating a productive work force (Hough & Oswald, 2000). We will discuss five topics of interest in the field of industrial psychology: recruitment, selection, employment discrimination, training, and performance appraisal.

Recruitment

Recruitment is the process of attracting people to apply for a job. Organizations can select from only those candidates who apply for their positions. If few people apply for a job, the odds of finding a strong candidate are lower than if many candidates apply. With the growing acceptability of conducting business via the Internet, organizations are now developing websites to attract job applicants. Online recruiting is the fastest-growing medium for attracting job applicants and is particularly popular for candidates in their 20s and 30s (Catano et al., 2005; Graham, 2000).

There is a relationship between the recruitment of job applicants and broad-based economic conditions. When the economy is stagnating or contracting, jobs are generally scarce and typically there will be many applicants for each opening. In contrast, when the economy is growing, competition among employers for qualified job applicants can be intense. Rynes (1993) noted that most of the emphasis on personnel decisions from an I/O psychology perspective centres on how employers can make better decisions in assessing applicants. However, as Rynes observed, the process can be viewed from the opposite perspective—that is, the extent to which applicants consider the company to be a desirable employer. Specifically, what impressions of the company are generated by the company's recruitment and assessment practices? Applicant reactions to assessment procedures are often vivid and highly emotional, as the following examples from Rynes (1993, p. 242) illustrate:

A married graduate student with a 3.9 grade point average reported that the first three questions in a company's psychological assessment procedure involved inquiries about her personal relationship with her husband and children. Although the company asked her what she thought of the procedure before she left, she lied because she was afraid that telling the truth would eliminate her from future consideration. Because of dual-career constraints, she continued to pursue an offer, but noted that if she got one, her first on-the-job priority would be to try to get the assessor fired.

The first interview question asked of a female student was, "We're a pretty macho organization. . . . Does that bother you?" Unfortunately it did, and she simply wrote the company out of her future interviewing plans.

These examples show that job applicants are not merely passive recipients of personnel selection procedures. Rather, applicants react to what they are asked to do or say to get a job. Sometimes a negative experience results in withdrawal from the application process. Companies and applicants should realize that the recruitment process is *mutual*—both parties are engaged in assessing the degree of fit with each other. L. Harris (2000) asserts that it might be wise for organizations to explain to rejected candidates why they were denied employment in a way that reduces negative feelings and damage to self-esteem rather than to provide explanations that are designed to protect the companies from potential litigation.

Selection

The process of personnel selection consists of deciding which of the job applicants will be extended an offer of employment. The selection process should be based on careful consideration of the knowledge, skills, and abilities possessed by each applicant (Sackett & Lievens, 2008). The goal is to get a good match or fit between the work demands of the job and the personal attributes of the applicant.

Schmitt and Chan (1998) identified five major changes in modern society that have affected the ways in which personnel selection decisions are made in many organizations. The first is the *speed of technological change*. With computer-based technology, work today is often conducted in ways that people couldn't even imagine 25 years ago. This rapid rate of change compels companies to hire workers who can adapt to ever-evolving work conditions. Emphasis is thus placed on a person's willingness and capacity to learn new job skills on a continuous basis.

Ryan McVay/Photodisc/Getty Images

The interviewing of prospective employees needs to be handled with finesse, as the recruitment process works both ways—prospective employers can appraise the candidates, and the candidates can determine whether they are interested in working for the organization. Companies sometimes lose talented prospects because of inappropriate interviewing techniques.

Second is the growing reliance on the *use of teams to accomplish work*. More and more work tasks require coordinated efforts by teams of employees as opposed to individual workers and their supervisors. Traditionally, however, personnel selection methods have been geared toward the selection of individuals based on their achievements. Today, organizations increasingly need to select employees who can fit well into the team concept.

The third factor consists of *changes in communication technology*. Faxes, e-mail, and hand-held electronic devices permit workers to communicate with others instantaneously around the world. It is no longer necessary to meet face to face or even communicate by telephone. These new, impersonal methods of communication have implications for classic organizational issues, such as the bond between coworkers, worker morale, and employee commitment. The fourth change is that *most large corporations are now global.* Many employees now work outside of Canada. The products of many Canadian companies are sold and serviced throughout the world. Hence, companies need to select employees who are adaptable and open to cultures other than their own.

Finally, the Canadian economy is continuing its long-running *transition from a manufacturing orientation to a service orientation.* Organizations that provide services must strive to hire employees who are likely to be sensitive to the customers' needs and adept at satisfying them. This objective has increased the emphasis on applicants' interpersonal skills.

These trends are likely to lead companies in the 21st century to select employees with somewhat different qualities than the companies sought in the past. If jobs are constantly changing, organizations will probably increase their emphasis on hiring candidates with high intelligence. Teaching them the specific knowledge or skills required on the job can be left to post-hiring training. If jobs are increasingly service-oriented, companies will want to hire people who are conscientious and interpersonally flexible. However, as Behling (1998) has noted, these skills are most appropriate when new employees will have to do a lot of problem solving, will have a lot of autonomy, will learn skills on the job that are more important than those brought to the job, and will need to adapt rapidly.

Of course, many jobs in modern society do not fit this description. In some jobs, it is still critical to pursue a match between the specific skills that applicants already have and specific job requirements. Thus, in a rapidly changing work environment, the desired match is more between the *person* and the *organization,* whereas in a stable work environment, the desired match is more between the *person* and the *job.*

I/O psychologists use a diverse array of personnel selection tools, including personality and intelligence tests, performance tests (e.g., a typing test), interviews, tests of physical ability, letters of recommendation, and drug tests. These techniques are all designed to gauge candidates' suitability for employment. I/O psychologists strive to devise selection methods that are accurate predictors of future job performance, legally defensible, appropriate for the job, and cost-efficient. Obviously, selection decisions can have profound effects on job candidates' lives. These decisions can also be critical to the success of organizations. Catano et al. (2005) provide more information on these selection tools and techniques.

Employment Discrimination

The tasks of employee recruitment and selection are intimately intertwined with the sometimes-controversial issue of employment discrimination. Understanding this topic necessitates an awareness of the cultural and social changes taking place in Canada. Until the 1970s, most immigrants to Canada were from the United States and Western Europe and reflected the culture and values of the English and French settlers. Today's immigrants are from various nations, cultures, races, and religions. However, over the course of history, some groups have been treated less equitably than others.

The injustice of discrimination became a prominent concern in the 1970s. Up until that time it was acceptable, for example, to pay a woman less money than a man even though they had equal job responsibilities, capabilities, and seniority. In response to changing values and mounting political pressures, the federal Parliament and the provincial and territorial legislatures have passed human rights legislation that prohibits discrimination in many areas of life, including the world of work. While there is variation among the different pieces of legislation, all Canadian jurisdictions prohibit discrimination on the basis of race or colour, religion or creed, age, sex, marital status, and physical/mental handicap or disability. In addition, the federal employment equity legislation is intended to promote the entry into the workplace and the retention of people from designated groups, including women, visible minorities, Aboriginal peoples, and people with disabilities.

These legislative efforts have had a dramatic impact on the field of industrial psychology, making it accountable to many new legal standards. In addition to ensuring that their employee recruitment and selection methods represent sound science and sound business practice, contemporary I/O psychologists must strive to ensure that their practices are legally sound.

Training

Organizations select employees on the basis of their predicted likelihood of succeeding on the job. Although some employees are expected to perform their jobs well immediately, the vast majority of employees are given some time to grow into their jobs. This growth process is expedited by formal organizational training processes. Training is designed to help new employees acquire the skills, rules, concepts, and attitudes that result in improved job performance.

Training is important because the knowledge and skill demands of work are continually escalating. Martocchio and Baldwin (1997) expressed this perspective clearly: "In an age of technological innovation in which robots, telecommunications, artificial intelligence, software, and lasers perform routine tasks, worker skills soon become obsolete. Put bluntly, today's jobs require new and different skills at all levels of an organization" (p. 6). One major reason for the increased emphasis on training is the growing reliance on computers in the conduct of work. Computer-assisted manufacturing and computer-assisted design are two major technological innovations in production. Manufacturing employees are now often expected to have some competence in computer-based operations. The acquisition of such skills often depends on post-hire training programs.

In 2000, Canadian business and labour leaders identified "skills shortages" among their top ten concerns (Sangster & Wortsman, 2001). Competition for Skills workers is becoming fierce. In addition, many people seeking to enter the work force lack essential skills needed for success. Human Resources and Skills Development Canada (HRSDC) initiated an essential skills development and literacy program in 2003 to ensure that Canadians have the right skills for changing work and life demands. Essential skills are those that make it possible to learn all other skills and enable people to participate fully in the workplace. These include reading text, document use, numeracy, writing, oral communication, working with others, thinking skills, computer use, and continuous learning.

The HRSDC website (http://www.hrsdc.gc.ca) provides access to over 200 occupational profiles, together with the most important skills and the level of each skill needed for the occupation. The profiles are also used to determine occupational training needs and priorities. In partnership with both private-sector and public-sector organizations, HRSDC provides many skills development and training programs designed to enhance both the essential and advanced skills of both young and older workers.

Pressures are growing in all areas of work to operate more efficiently and to enhance the overall quality of goods and services. Such changes require enhanced organizational performance in increasingly competitive markets. Training, therefore, is a process to improve the fit between job demands and employee attributes. Training needs to occur in virtually all organizations on a continuous basis. Thus, it might be advisable to think of your college or university years as "learning through education" and of your working years as "learning through training."

Obviously, training programs vary in their effectiveness. Successful training initiatives depend on four main considerations. First, the organization must value training, encourage employees to participate in training, and then design work so the training can be used back on the job. Second, there must be a clear understanding about what kind of training needs to occur, how it will benefit the organization, and which employees should receive the training. Third, there should be an approximate match between training methods and training needs. Some training methods are more geared to technical skill enhancement, while others are more suited for enhancing interpersonal skills. Fourth, there must be clear support systems in place to ensure that what is learned in training generalizes back to the job. The extent to which training actually improves job performance is the ultimate test of training effectiveness.

Performance Appraisal

With or without the input of I/O psychologists, employees continually have their job performance evaluated. Informal appraisals may be made from haphazard observations, memory, hearsay, or intuition. I/O psychologists endeavour to design performance appraisal methods that are formal, rational, systematic, accurate, fair, and useful to all concerned.

Performance appraisals serve many purposes for both employers and employees, as outlined in Figure C.2. Murphy and Cleveland (1995) maintain that effective performance appraisals can help organizations in several ways. First, they can enhance the quality of organizational decisions, ranging from pay raises to promotions to discharge. The purpose of the human resource function in an organization is to maximize the contributions of employees to the goals of the organization, and assessments of employee job performance can play a major role in accomplishing that function.

Second, performance appraisals can improve the quality of individual decisions, ranging from career choices to the development of future strengths. Accurate performance feedback is an important component of effective training and provides critical input for realistic self-assessments by employees. Performance feedback is also a key factor in promoting high levels of motivation in the work force.

Third, performance appraisals can affect employees' views of, and attachment to, their organization. A fair and effective appraisal system can help build employee morale and satisfaction. In contrast, employees who believe that an organization's performance appraisals are irrational or unfair are unlikely to develop a strong commitment to that organization.

Finally, formal performance appraisals provide a legally defensible basis for personnel decisions, which cannot be capricious. Organizations must have reasonable explanations for why some employees are promoted, discharged, or receive differential pay raises compared to others.

Performance appraisal often requires evaluation of many aspects of job performance. At the lower level of complexity, jobs typically require employees to show up for work on time, cooperate with co-workers, and so forth. At higher levels of complexity, jobs may require the demonstration of technical expertise or leadership capability. I/O psychologists assist in deciding which aspects of job performance should be appraised and in designing the appraisal methods. They also try to find ways to deal with the fact that many employees don't like to be appraised and some supervisors don't like to evaluate their colleagues. The challenge for I/O psychologists is to help foster an atmosphere within the organization that recognizes the legitimate need for all parties to provide honest and accurate performance appraisals.

Organizational Psychology

Organizational psychology is the branch of I/O psychology concerned with how the collective social context of the work environment affects workers' behaviour and attitudes. We will examine five topics that are important in contemporary organizational psychology: organizational culture, work teams, the psychological contract between employers and their employees, work motivation, and leadership.

Organizational Culture

The concept of *culture* has long been used to describe the customs, values, and norms of *societies,* but I/O psychologists have also found the concept useful in the description of *organizations.* An *organizational culture* consists of the language, values, attitudes, beliefs, and customs shared by the employees of a company. An organization's culture gives it its unique "flavour" or "personality." Several definitions of organizational

Employer and employee reasons for conducting appraisals

Employer perspective

1. Despite imperfect measurement, individual differences in performance make a difference.
2. Documentation of performance appraisal and feedback may be needed for legal defence.
3. Appraisal provides a rational basis for constructing a bonus or merit system.
4. Appraisal dimensions and standards can operationalize strategic goals and clarify performance expectations.
5. Providing individual feedback is part of a performance management process.
6. Despite the traditional individual focus, appraisal criteria can include teamwork and teams can be the focus of appraisal.

Employee perspective

1. Performance feedback is needed and desired.
2. Improvement in performance requires assessment.
3. Fairness requires that differences in performance levels across workers be measured and have an impact on outcomes.
4. Assessment and recognition of performance levels can motivate improved performance.

FIGURE C.2

Employer and employee perspectives on performance appraisals.

I/O psychologists often play an important role in designing performance appraisal systems. Although sometimes awkward for the people involved, performance appraisals serve many important purposes for both employers and employees. Some of the reasons that both organizations and workers desire fair and accurate appraisals are outlined here.

Source: Cardy, R.L. (1998). Performance appraisal in a quality context: A new look at an old problem. In J.W. Smither (Ed.), *Performance appraisal.* San Francisco: Jossey-Bass. Reprinted by permission.

culture have been proposed, but the most succinct was offered by Deal and Kennedy (1982): "The way we do things around here."

Furnham and Gunter (1993) proposed three features of organizational culture. First, an organization's culture can often be traced to its founders. These people often possess dynamic personalities, strong values, and a clear vision of what the organization should look like. They play a big role in the initial hiring of employees, and their ideas and values are readily transmitted to new employees. Second, culture often develops out of an organization's experience with the external environment. Every organization must establish its own identity in its industry and in the marketplace where it operates. As it struggles to do so, it may find that some values and practices are more effective than others. Third, an organizational culture develops from the need to maintain effective working relationships among employees. Depending on the nature of the organization's business and the characteristics of the people it hires, different expectations and values develop.

Deeply ingrained within organizational culture are communication processes, for it is through communication that culture is transmitted. Interactions with long-time organizational members ensure that new recruits are acculturated. New employees learn the language and appropriate behaviour of the group, hear its stories and legends, and observe the organization's rites and rituals. The culture of an organization can best be understood by analyzing its tangible and visible rites, including rites of passage (hiring and basic training), degradation (dismissal), conflict reduction (grievance committees), and integration (office holiday parties). New members must determine how to dress appropriately, how to arrange their workspace, and how much latitude they have in being on time for appointments and in meeting deadlines.

Culture may also be communicated through other channels, such as in-house memos, official policies, statements of corporate philosophy, and any other means of expressing values. Schein (1996) asserted that understanding the culture of an organization is critical to making sense of the behaviour observed in the organization. A description of behaviour divorced from the cultural context in which it occurs is of limited value.

Schneider (1996) emphasizes that it is the people who populate the organization who most define its culture. That is, employees are not actors who fill predetermined roles in an established culture, but rather their personalities, values, and interests make the organization what it is. Schneider (1987) proposed what he calls the *attraction–selection–attrition (ASA) cycle*. In this cycle, people with similar personalities and values are recruited by (*attraction*) and hired into certain organizations (*selection*); those who don't fit into the pattern of shared values eventually leave the organization (*attrition*). The ASA cycle is assumed to unfold gradually over time. It is often difficult to bring about a change in organizational culture because that would necessitate altering underlying values and beliefs that may be deeply entrenched. It is not surprising that many mergers between organizations with different cultures, such as Molson and Coors, encounter problems in their early stages. In any event, a full understanding of an organization requires some appreciation of its culture.

Work Teams

Historically, I/O psychologists have focused their attention on *individuals*—finding the right person for a job, training the person, and subsequently monitoring the individual's performance. However, recent years have seen an upsurge of interest in *work groups* (Ilgen et al., 2005; van Knippenberg & Shippers, 2007).

Teams are bounded social units that work within a larger social system—the organization. They are dynamic systems, both complex and adaptive (McGrath, Arrow, & Berdahl, 2000). A team has identifiable members (i.e., members and nonmembers know who is a member and who is not) and an identifiable task or set of tasks to perform. The team's work requires that members interact by exchanging information, sharing resources, and coordinating activities, so there is always some degree of interdependence among the members of a team. Organizations tend to give teams more decision authority than comparable employees working individually. The team members often must decide among themselves who will do what, where, when, and how.

What underlies the new emphasis on teams? Three factors are critical. The first is the burgeoning amount of information and knowledge available. Huge amounts of information from multiple sources often have to be absorbed to respond to complex business issues. Because no one person can have technical expertise in all areas of knowledge, a team approach, representing a pooling of mental resources, becomes more tenable.

Second, the working population is becoming better educated and trained. When the traditional organizational structures of 100 years ago were created, the work force was relatively uneducated. The members of the traditional working class were monitored by members of "management," who often possessed much more education or training than their subordinates. However, the workers of today are more highly qualified and better able to serve in the types of leadership roles called for in work teams. As an employee who now works in a production team in

The organizational culture of a company can have an enormous influence on employee productivity and satisfaction. This reality must have weighed heavily on company executives as they managed the merger of Molson Inc. with Adolph Coors Company. Mergers also have implications for the organizations' clients and consumers—including, in the case of the Molson–Coors merger, these two famous Canadians.

a manufacturing organization stated, "I'm no longer expected to check my brain at the front gate when I enter the factory."

The third factor is the rate of change in work activities and responsibilities. For many years, workers tended to have well-defined job responsibilities that rarely changed. In the current work world, there are pressures to make new products, modify services, alter processes to improve quality, and in general be in a continual state of transformation. Work teams are thought to be more adaptable to these ever-changing conditions of work.

The evolution of teams and teamwork has compelled I/O psychology to address a host of new issues (Ilgen, 1999). Some of what we have learned about individuals in the workplace generalizes to teams, but other issues are more specific to teams. However, teams are *not* universally superior to individuals for conducting work across all relevant performance indices. Teams do not necessarily produce better decisions than some individuals do. In fact, research in the area has shifted from examinations of what predicts team effectiveness to examinations of why some groups seem to be more effective than others (Ilgen et al., 2005). There is nothing magical about transforming individuals into work teams. Teams are merely one means of performing work.

I/O psychologists are concerned with the structure of teams, including their size, roles filled by various members, and the planned length of their existence. Issues relating to team processes include how older team members socialize new members, how diversity or differences between group members affect the group's product, as well as matters of team communication, conflict, cohesion, and trust (Jackson, Joshi, & Erhardt, 2003; van Knippenberg & Shippers, 2007). Some teams have members that have never met face to face. They interact only electronically and belong to "virtual teams." Some of what I/O psychologists have learned regarding the selection, training, and appraisal of individuals also applies to teams, but some aspects of team functioning require new concepts, insights, and research.

The Psychological Contract between Employers and Employees

Rousseau (1995) noted that employers and their employees enter into a *psychological contract*. It is not a formal written contract between the two parties but an implied relationship based on perceptions of mutual contributions and reciprocal obligations. Employees have beliefs about the organization's obligations to them as well as their obligations to the organization. Thus, employees may believe that the organization has agreed to provide job security and promotion opportunities in exchange for hard work and loyalty from the employee. The psychological contract is oriented toward the future. Without the promise of future exchange, neither party has incentive to contribute anything to the other, and the relationship may not endure.

The psychological contract is composed of a belief that some form of a promise has been made and that the terms and conditions of the contract have been accepted by both parties. However, this belief does not necessarily mean that both parties share a common understanding of all contract terms. The psychological contract is revised throughout the employee's tenure in the organization. The longer the relationship endures and the two parties interact, the broader the array of contributions that might be included in the contract.

Rousseau and Parks (1993) found that employment itself is perceived as a promise (the implied contract of continued future employment) and that an employee's performance is perceived as a contribution (a way of paying for the promise). Robinson, Kraatz, and Rousseau (1994) examined how psychological contracts change over time. They found that during the first two years of employment, employees came to perceive that they owed less to their employer while the employers in turn owed them more.

There is an element of power in all contracts. Unequal power is most common in employment relationships. Power inequities affect the perceived voluntariness of the exchange relationship, dividing the two parties into contract makers (relatively powerful) and contract takers (relatively powerless). As contract takers, employees cannot easily exit the employment relationship. This situation may result in a perceived loss of control in the relationship, which is likely to intensify feelings of mistreatment and injustice when violations are perceived. Because the employer is the more powerful party, the terms of the contract can be dictated to the less powerful employee, who must either accept them or exit the relationship.

The psychological contract is violated when one party in a relationship perceives the other as failing to fulfill promised obligations. The failure of one party to meet its obligations to another can be expected to undermine their mutual relationship. Violations by an employer may affect not only what an employee feels he or she is owed by the employer but also what an employee feels obligated to offer in return. Violation of a psychological contract undermines the very factors (such as trust) that led to the emergence of a relationship. If the employer reneges on an implied promise, the employer's integrity is questioned. A violation signals that the employer's original motives to build and maintain a mutually beneficial relationship have changed or were false from the beginning. The psychological contract binds the employee and the employer—a form of guarantee that if each does his or her part, then the relationship will be mutually beneficial. Thus, violations weaken this bond.

In recent decades, the changing nature of the psychological contract between employers and employees has required employees to assume greater responsibility for their own career development. Organizations are now far less likely to offer the implicit promise to provide career-advancing opportunities. Consider the following message found posted on the bulletin board of a plant experiencing widespread layoffs (as reported by Hall & Mirvis, 1995, p. 326):

> We can't promise you how long we'll be in business.
> We can't promise you that we won't be bought by another company.
> We can't promise that there'll be room for promotion.
> We can't promise that your job will exist until you reach retirement age.
> We can't promise that the money will be available for your pension.
> We can't expect your undying loyalty and we aren't sure we want it.

Based on a multinational study, Rousseau and Schalk (2000) concluded that the psychological contract as a promise-based exchange is widely generalizable to a variety of societies. Given the rise of global business, it is likely that the nature of cultural differences in the psychological contract will continue to evolve. For example, people from Asian cultures generally prefer to first establish a relationship between parties and then carry out business transactions. In contrast, people from Western cultures generally prefer to create a relationship through repeated business transactions. In the future, it is likely that both styles will manifest themselves in new and varied forms.

Work Motivation

Have you ever observed a person who appears driven to perform well or succeed? Perhaps you would describe yourself in that way. Such people may or may not have more ability than others, but it appears that they are willing to work harder or expend more effort than their peers. Psychologists refer to this attribute or trait as *ambition* or *motivation*. Motivation is not directly observable; it must be inferred from patterns of behaviour.

According to Pinder (1998; Latham & Pinder, 2005), *work motivation* refers to the set of forces that initiate work-related behaviour and determine its direction, intensity, and duration. As we discussed in Chapter 10, motivation is often the result of both internal and external factors. According to Latham and Pinder (2005), this is also true of work motivation; it is a function of the interaction between characteristics of the individual and characteristics of the environment.

There are three noteworthy components to Pinder's definition (Pinder, 1998). First, *direction* addresses the choice of activities that people make in expending effort. That is, people may choose to work diligently at some tasks and not at others. Second, *intensity* implies people have the potential to exert various levels of effort, depending on how much is needed. Third, *duration* reflects persistence of motivation over time. Motivation can thus be conceptualized along three dimensions: direction, intensity, and persistence. Each dimension has its associated issues that are relevant to both the organization and the individual.

Direction pertains to those activities on which you focus your energy. Organizations want employees who will direct themselves to their work responsibilities, and many employees want jobs that will inspire their motivation and commitment. Intensity pertains to the amount of motivation that is expended in pursuit of an activity. Organizations want employees who will exhibit high levels of energy. Such people are often referred to as *self-starters*, implying that they do not require organizational inducements to work hard. Likewise, many employees hope to find jobs that are sufficiently appealing to invite large commitments of energy. The third dimension, persistence, pertains to sustained energy over time, over the entirety of one's career.

Work motivation depends on a constellation of factors, which can often become blurred. Chief among these factors are the following:

- **Behaviour.** The overt actions from which motivation can be inferred. The behaviour in question may be typing, preparing a meal, organizing a stockroom, communicating with customers, or engaging in an endless array of other work-related activities.
- **Performance: Evaluation of behaviour.** The basic unit of observation is behaviour, but it is coupled with an assessment of the behaviour as judged against some standard. Thus, if the behaviour is typing, a judgment can be made as to whether a person's typing speed and accuracy are adequate to hold a job. The level of performance that is adequate for one job may be inadequate for another job. Most organizational theories tend to

be concerned with performance, not just behaviour. The three determinants of behaviour and performance are:

- *Ability.* Of the three determinants of behaviour and performance, ability is generally regarded as fairly stable within an individual and may be represented by a broad construct, such as intelligence, or a more specific construct, such as physical coordination.
- *Situational constraints.* The second determinant of behaviour, situational constraints are environmental factors and opportunities that facilitate or undermine performance. Examples include tools, equipment, procedures, and the like, which may enhance or hinder performance.
- *Motivation.* The third determinant of behaviour is motivation. You can think of ability as reflecting what you *can* do, motivation as what you *will* do (given your ability), and the situational constraints as what you are *allowed* to do.

Each of the three determinants is critical to the manifestation of behaviour and performance. Maximum performance is observed when a person has high ability, exhibits high motivation, and is in a supportive environment. The judgment of "poor performance" could be attributed to four factors. First, the organization in which the behaviour occurs may have high standards; in an organization with lower standards, this behaviour might result in a more positive evaluation of performance. Second, the individual may lack the ability required for the desired behaviour. Third, the individual may lack the motivation to exhibit the desired behaviour. Fourth, the individual may lack needed equipment or other crucial elements of support.

Motivation is one of the most complex concepts that I/O psychologists study (Korman, Greenhaus, & Badin, 1977; Latham & Pinder, 2005). People can be motivated by different factors, and the same person can be motivated by different factors during different stages of his or her career. Most organizations believe it is critical to their success to have a highly motivated work force.

Leadership

When you think of *leadership*, many ideas may come to mind. Your thoughts might relate to power, authority, or influence. Maybe you think of actual people, such as Pierre Trudeau, Winston Churchill, or Nelson Mandela. In short, leadership is a multidimensional concept.

I/O psychologists have tried to grapple with the multifaceted concept of leadership as it relates to behaviour in the world of work. Investigators have approached the concept from various perspectives. Recent research and theory has emphasized the role of cognitive factors in leadership, both of the leaders themselves and the cognitions of their team members about their leaders (Hodgkinson & Healey, 2008). Some research has examined what strong leaders are like as people by looking at demographic variables, personality traits, special skills, and so on. Without followers, there can be no leaders; accordingly, some research has examined leader–follower relationships. Presumably, strong leaders accomplish things that weak leaders do not.

Other research has examined the effects of leadership. An interesting question concerns how contextual factors affect leadership—for example: Is leadership of a prison more demanding than leadership of a business organization? Other areas of interest within the domain of leadership research have also been investigated. While such diversity of interest expands our understanding, it also creates ambiguity as to exactly what leadership is all about. Table C.1 identifies research topics of interest to I/O psychologists in studying leadership.

Research Topic	Unit of Analysis	Variables of Interest	Research Questions
Positional power	Organizational roles and positions	Influence tactics; use of power	Under what conditions will organizations resort to strong influence attempts?
The leader	Individual leaders	Personality characteristics; leader behaviours	What traits and behaviours differentiate effective and ineffective leaders?
The led	Work groups and subordinates	Group size; experience of subordinates	What types of subordinates desire close supervision?
Influence process	Superior–subordinate interface	Receptivity to influence; nature of influence attempts	Under what conditions are leaders most susceptible to subordinate influence attempts?
The situation	Environment or context in which leadership occurs	Situational effects on leader behaviour; factors defining favourable situations	How do various situations modify behaviour?
Leader emergence versus effectiveness	Individual and/or groups	Group dynamics and individual characteristics	How do individuals become recognized as leaders?

TABLE C.1

Research Topics and Associated Issues in Leadership Research

Source: Muchinsky, P.M. (2003). *Psychology applied to work.* Belmont, CA: Wadsworth. Reprinted by permission.

Despite the diversity of approaches used in exploring leadership, Yukl (1994) noted that there is some convergence in the empirical findings. Yukl identified three consistent themes in leadership research. First, influence is the essence of leadership. Much of the activity of leaders involves attempts to influence the attitudes and behaviours of people, including subordinates, peers, and outsiders. Motivating behaviour includes a variety of social influence techniques for developing commitment to organizational objectives and compliance with requests. Much of the influence behaviour of charismatic leaders falls into the motivating category, including inspiring commitment to new objectives and strategies, modelling exemplary behaviour for followers to imitate, and appealing to values and aspirations.

Some of the traits and skills that predict leader effectiveness relate to the use of power. Leaders with high need for power and high self-confidence make more influence attempts. Self-confidence, persuasive ability, relevant expertise, and political insight facilitate the effectiveness of influence attempts. Interpersonal skills are necessary to articulate an appealing vision and persuade people of the need for change.

Second, effective leaders establish cooperative relationships characterized by high levels of mutual trust and loyalty. Research has shown that subordinates are usually more satisfied with a leader who is friendly and helpful, shows trust and respect, and demonstrates concern for their needs, feelings, and welfare. Key here, of course, are the types of attributions that team members make for the leader's behaviour. Attributions that suggest the leader is motivated by concern for the work team's collective welfare are essential to producing acceptance of the leader's vision (Cha & Edmondson, 2006).

Several of the traits and skills predictive of leadership effectiveness appear to be important for developing favourable relationships with subordinates, peers, and superiors. Relevant interpersonal talents include tact and diplomacy, listening skills, and social sensitivity. A leader with a positive regard for others is more likely to develop friendly relationships with people. Leaders who are preoccupied with personal ambition tend to do things that jeopardize relationships with people, such as betraying a trust or reneging on a promise.

Third, much of the activity of leaders involves decision making, but leaders seldom make important decisions at a single point in time, except for problem solving in immediate crises. In dealing with day-to-day decisions, effective leaders are guided by their long-term objectives and strategies. People who effectively solve problems or develop successful strategies gain in status and power as a result. The reputation for expertise gained from successful decisions made in the past gives a person greater influence over subsequent decisions.

Several of the traits and skills predictive of leadership effectiveness are relevant for decision making. Leaders with extensive technical knowledge and cognitive skills are more likely to make high-quality decisions. These skills are important for analyzing problems, identifying causal patterns and trends, and forecasting likely outcomes of different strategies for attaining objectives. Self-confidence and tolerance for ambiguity and stress help leaders cope with the responsibility for making major decisions on the basis of incomplete information.

Putting It All Together: A Case Study

Let's take a look at a recent, very real, and extremely important problem to see how the diverse aspects of I/O psychology are relevant to the world of work. The problem involves how to improve the screening of airport passengers and their baggage. You will see how many of the topics discussed in this appendix are germane to this daunting problem.

The Problem: Improving Airport Screening

The terrorist attacks of September 11, 2001, on the World Trade Center in New York and the Pentagon in Washington, DC, focused attention on airport security personnel and their performance. These employees are entrusted with the responsibility of screening all passengers and their luggage in order to detect any objects that might be a security risk to the flight personnel or passengers. Such objects include guns and knives but also everyday objects that potentially could be used as a weapon, such as scissors, cigarette lighters, and corkscrews.

There are typically four jobs that contribute to the screening process—two devoted to passengers and two devoted to luggage. One person is responsible for ensuring that each passenger goes through the metal detector. If a passenger activates the metal detector, the passenger must step aside and be rescreened with a portable, hand-held metal detector, called a *wand*. A second employee is in charge of conducting this screening. The usual items that activate the metal detector are jewellery, metal belt buckles, and metal supports in shoes. The second employee's job is to identify the reason the metal detector was activated and to ensure that the cause is benign.

A third employee is responsible for examining the contents of passengers' luggage via an X-ray machine. As hand-carried items pass through the X-ray machine on a conveyor belt, the third employee peers at a monitor. If the employee sees an object that looks suspicious, that piece of luggage is subject to a manual search of its contents. A fourth employee is in charge of this manual search and of verifying that the contents of the luggage are harmless; this manual search may also involve "sweeping" hand luggage and electronic items for the presence of certain chemicals.

Of these four jobs, one in particular is the source of errors: visually examining the monitor of the X-ray machine. Luggage moves along the conveyor belt quickly, about six pieces per minute, 360 pieces per hour—almost 3000 pieces in an eight-hour workday. The examiner has only a few seconds to visually inspect the contents of each bag. The overwhelming majority of passengers do not pack dangerous items in their luggage. Occasionally there will be a suspicious-looking object, but it usually turns out (on manual inspection) to be harmless. If a potentially dangerous object is spotted, it is confiscated by airport security personnel.

Because passengers know that potentially dangerous objects will not be allowed on the airplane, the vast majority pack only items that are not potentially harmful to others. The consequence of this pattern of behaviour is that the X-ray machine screener is looking for a rare object. With hundreds of pieces of luggage passing through the machine every hour, it is difficult for screeners to remain vigilant and focused. Their attention begins to wander after viewing so many pieces of luggage that look alike. Hence, it is not surprising that dangerous objects sometimes make it through the screening process.

In some cases, airport authorities have intentionally "planted" knives in luggage just to see whether they would be detected. Most are, but some are not. Given the enormous importance of this screening task, even a small error rate—for example, 0.01 percent (i.e., one potentially dangerous object per 10 000 cases)—is considered unacceptable. In other words, if 99.99 percent of all luggage is screened properly, the error rate (0.01 percent) is still too high to meet desired safety standards! So, our question is: What types of solutions might an I/O psychologist propose to help improve the performance of airport security inspectors?

Possible Solutions

The topics discussed in this appendix are all potentially relevant to this problem. Let's begin with the process of recruitment. Perhaps if the airports attracted a higher quality of applicant pool from which to draw their employees, fewer errors would be made by the inspectors. If the wage level for airport security personnel was raised, perhaps more skilled individuals would be attracted to the jobs. Alternatively, it is possible that the quality of the applicant pool is satisfactory, but what is needed are better personnel selection methods to identify the best candidates. Perhaps special types of visual acuity tests could be used, or tests that measure the capacity for sustained mental alertness. Perhaps the solution lies not so much with how the employees are chosen as with how they are trained. It is possible that current training methods are insufficient or fail to capture the need for sustained vigilance over an eight-hour workday.

Finally, little is known about the degree to which airports reward security officers for effective performance. Perhaps if supervisors appraised the job performance of their security officers and acknowledged their successes, their failures would decline. There are also legal issues to consider. Passengers of certain nationalities or races cannot indiscriminately be singled out for closer scrutiny without just cause. Engaging in such a practice would be an example of "racial profiling," which is frowned on.

There is a rich organizational component to this problem that must also be considered before a

The task of improving airport screening of passengers and their baggage illustrates how problems in the workplace are often multifaceted. As the text explains, a host of strategies may be relevant to this extremely complicated and important challenge.

solution becomes evident. The organizational culture of airport security operations tells us something about the nature of flying, passengers, and safety precautions. Many airports around the world are now staffed with uniformed military personnel carrying exposed weapons. Passengers see these military figures and their weapons and realize they are entering a potentially dangerous environment. Although passengers accept the need for airport security, no one likes to be hassled and intimidated. Airport security personnel are "just doing their job," but what they do can produce stress for passengers. If passengers become sufficiently dissatisfied with the emotional experiences associated with flying, some of them will either stop flying altogether or fly far less frequently. A reduction in the number of passengers can (and has) led some airlines to lose so much money they have had to declare bankruptcy. The decline in air passenger traffic following 9/11 was one factor leading to Air Canada seeking protection from its creditors under the Bankruptcy Act.

While it is possible that different methods of recruitment, personnel selection, training, and performance appraisal may help alleviate the problem encountered in this situation, it is also true that staring into a monitor over a prolonged time period is boring. Perhaps what needs to be done is to lessen the time period of visual inspection from eight hours to two hours. Since four jobs are involved in passenger and baggage screening, perhaps the four employees could be viewed as a team, and the team members could rotate assignments every two hours to break the tedium. Such a solution would presume that all four team members are equally suited to perform each of the four jobs. This approach attempts to solve the problem of boredom and fatigue by limiting the length of time an employee is exposed to the conditions that produce them.

The psychological contract between the airport and its security personnel must also be considered. The flying passengers, our society, and governments demand a "zero-tolerance" policy for errors in screening passengers and luggage. The consequence of making errors in airport security can be extremely tragic. However, there are few jobs where a 99.99 percent success rate is judged to be not good enough. Airport security personnel are under stress from two sources. One source is the need to remain highly vigilant and attentive in what is a repetitive and boring job. The second is that they know they are responsible for the safety and welfare of the flying public.

The airport as an organization must walk a fine line between demanding very high standards of performance yet being sensitive to the conditions under which their security personnel operate. If such sensitivity and support are not shown, the security personnel would probably exhibit little loyalty to an employer that demands so much of its employees. The needed support for security personnel can come in the form of encouraging motivation and leadership. Supervisors who are present at the security area (or nearby) can provide attention, encouragement, and recognition to the security personnel. The supervisors can break the tedium of the security jobs by establishing their presence, asking questions, acknowledging the contributions of the security officers, and in general providing recognition for employees performing highly stressful work. Finally, all of these actions must be taken within yet a broader context, that of increasing security without unduly inconveniencing the flying public.

There is no reason to believe there is *one* correct solution to the problem facing airport security personnel. In reality, an I/O psychologist would probably invoke many of the possible solutions to this case, not just one. It is also possible that a solution lies in more sophisticated X-ray technology that reduces the role of human judgment in assessing potential risk. Such equipment is currently being developed, but it is extremely expensive and is therefore unlikely to be used in all airports. While such technology may reduce the human element, it will never eliminate it.

Conclusion

I/O psychologists must be prepared to use the full complement of their skills to solve increasingly complex problems in the workplace. I/O psychology is a most rewarding and useful field that endeavours to improve the quality of work life. Students interested in learning more about this field are encouraged to read P. M. Muchinsky's *Psychology Applied to Work* (2003) and to visit the Canadian Society for Industrial and Organizational Psychology's website to learn about career opportunities: http://psychology.uwo.ca/csiop.

By Vincent W. Hevern (Le Moyne College)

Toward the end of every semester in my abnormal psychology course, my students conduct a public policy forum about an important but controversial topic in psychology. To prepare for the forum, I give students a research assignment. They must gather information from various types of sources: scholarly articles in journals, professional books, popular magazines, and sites on the Internet. However, to complete the Net part of the assignment, students must hand in two types of information: Some material must come from a "good" or "excellent" website, while other material must be from a "terrible" or "poor" website. Further, students must also tell me *why* these sites are either excellent or poor. Students regularly tell me later on that they had never paid attention before to whether a Web page might be "good" or "bad." Many students actually say they appreciate learning how to recognize the difference between sites of high versus low quality.

What students tell me supports the comments that I hear from many college professors: They wish students would realize that research done with Internet-based resources can be both dangerous and misleading unless students recognize the issue of quality. Further, as psychology teachers across the California State University system noted, an important educational goal for student learning is developing the competence to "locate appropriate sources by searching electronic and traditional databases and providing evidence of the search" (Allen et al., 2000, p. 4). The important phrase is "appropriate sources." Which resources online are appropriate, and which should you avoid? Students and all other researchers need to think carefully about the quality of data and reference sources found online. Your teachers will expect it, and in the emerging Information Economy, so will many employers.

Criteria for Quality on the Net

So, what are the standards or criteria by which you can judge the quality of a Web page or resource? What can you actually *do* to increase the chances that the material you take from the Net is worth your effort? In recent years, information specialists have researched how people browsing the Internet can tell the difference. For example, University of Georgia Professor Gene Wilkinson and two doctoral students,

Kevin Oliver and Lisa Bennett, conducted an intensive study of 125 criteria by polling the webmasters of highly regarded online resource sites, while reference librarians Janet E. Alexander and Marsha Ann Tate at Widener University's Wolfgram Memorial Library consulted intensively with their colleagues around the world (Alexander & Tate, 1999).

Although these and other specialists have gathered standards in slightly different ways, they are in substantial agreement about what characteristics are associated with quality on the Web. I've summarized their findings and my own experience in Figure D.1, and I elaborate on each criterion in this appendix. Some of these standards relate to an entire website from which material may be drawn, while others relate to a specific document in which the researcher may be interested. Users of the Net must weigh both kinds of criteria. In simplest terms, the key to finding quality resources online will always be a researcher's *active exercise of judgment and critical thinking.*

Identity and Qualifications of the Authors

The Internet is a kind of worldwide democracy. Pretty much anyone can construct a Web page and put online what they want to say. With so few restrictions on Net publishing, the range and quality of online resources is bound to vary, from invaluable to completely worthless. So, researchers who turn to the Net need to ask two related questions: *Who has written this material?* and *What are their qualifications for so doing?* The answers to these questions are probably the two most important guides to quality among online resources.

Sometimes you will find no clue to the identity of the author of a particular site or resource—no name, no organizational affiliation, nothing that reveals the authorship of the material. In such cases, you should be skeptical about relying on the information. It's hard to defend the quality of a work when "Anonymous" is the author. One exception may be some "first-person" accounts dealing with sensitive personal issues such as sexuality, child abuse, and the like. Some authors understandably prefer to use pseudonyms to protect themselves. In such cases, researchers must look for other clues to quality.

Suppose one or more authors are listed by name. The next task is to discover the *qualifications* of these

Questions to Ask in Evaluating Materials on the Internet

1. Identity and qualifications of the author(s)
- Who is the author of the material? Is the author identified or anonymous?
- What is the author's academic or professional background and experience?
- Is the author writing within or outside his/her area of expertise and skill?
- If the material is the product of a group (a committee, governmental agency, or the like), what is that group's qualifications or expertise regarding this subject?

2. Publisher or sponsor of the website
- Is the material self-published by the author or is there some recognized organization (university, medical centre, government agency, nonprofit foundation, and so forth) that sponsors the website for the material?
- Does the site's sponsor or publisher have a positive reputation?

3. Balance, objectivity, and independence
- Does the material or website strive for balance and objectivity rather than use extreme, inflammatory, or highly subjective language or opinions?
- Is more than one point of view evident at the site?
- If the material takes a strong stand on one side of a controversial issue, does the author or site acknowledge there may be another side to the matter?
- Is the website sponsored by any commercial or political organization that advocates for a particular point of view?
- Does the author have any financial or commercial interest that might conflict with a fair or objective presentation of the topic?
- Is the material drawn from a site that sells a product or solicits customers for a service?

4. Quality of online presentation
- Is the site well organized or designed so that browsers can easily visit and retrieve information?
- Does the site or online material show care in its preparation, such as proper spelling and good grammar in all posted materials?
- Does the site work effectively, so that the links to subpages and external sites are accurate and helpful?
- How recently has the site been updated? Does the site show evidence that someone regularly attends to it with corrections, new materials, and so forth?

5. Other cues to quality
- Does the material contain clear and useful references to other scholarship from journals, professional books, and recognized research studies?
- Have supporting references in the material been published in recent years, or do they include mostly out-of-date, or possibly obsolete, sources?
- Have any editors or external reviewers judged the quality of the material at the site?

FIGURE D.1

Evaluating online resources.

The questions listed here, which draw heavily on the work of Alexander and Tate (1999), can help you to evaluate the quality and reliability of resource materials found on the Internet.

authors. Do they have some type of expertise to justify writing the online material or constructing the site? You should look for a statement of an author's academic credentials (such as a Ph.D. or an M.D. degree) or appropriate work experience (such as "director of personnel" at a company or "senior researcher" at a laboratory). If the data appear on a personal home page, you can discover other evidence of expertise elsewhere on the site, such as a bibliography of past writings or a résumé that demonstrates the author's competence to write about the topic under review. You should also try to determine whether the author has published on a similar topic in reputable, peer-reviewed journals or belongs to professional or scholarly organizations concerned with the subject.

There are other cautions for researchers to keep in mind. Some authors may be qualified to comment on one topic but go beyond their area of expertise into other domains of knowledge. For example, a physician may comment on economics or a biologist may pontificate on educational methods. Researchers need to be cautious about writers who move too far away from their fields of specialization. Another consideration is whether authors may also have a financial stake or commercial interest in the issue that might compromise their objectivity.

Finally, suppose the author of a Web-based publication is a corporation or an organization, such as a professional association, a government agency, or a nonprofit organization. How should qualifications be weighed in such cases? Certainly the overall reputation of the corporate author should be recognized. For example, a consensus statement on a treatment approach produced by the National Institute of Mental Health or a report on the employment characteristics of psychologists issued by the American Psychological Association would probably be an excellent reference source. Most such reports include a list of individual contributors or committee members who worked to produce the material released under the name of an organization. It is important to inquire whether these persons may also have the credentials or professional status to render their work trustworthy. Alternatively, you might look for a broad corporate board of editors or advisors associated with an institutional voice on the Net. Beware of fancy-sounding "Institutes" or "Commissions" or "Associations" that may in fact be the product of a single person or a handful of individuals and serve only to artificially embellish the opinions of their creators.

Publisher or Sponsor of the Website

Book authors traditionally use print publishers to promote and distribute their writings. In turn, publishers place their reputations on the line by issuing new books. Discerning readers rely on a publisher's overall standing when they consider whether to acquire new works. Especially in academic publishing, readers know that an editorial and review process usually precedes publication, in an effort to ensure a high level of quality for the published material. Indeed, the essence of academic scholarship lies in a willingness to submit scholarly work to the early critiques of knowledgeable colleagues. Occasionally, though, an author circumvents the editorial and peer review process and pays to have his or her book published. This practice, called "vanity publishing," is usually looked down on by other scholars.

In a practice reminiscent of vanity publishing, many Web authors post materials online directly through commercial or free Internet service providers. Because these writings have not been edited or evaluated prior to their publication, you must be cautious in judging their quality. This is not to disparage all self-published resources on the Web. Clearly, there are valuable resources that experts have laboured to bring to cyberspace. But, in the absence of a clear process of scholarly peer review, you must look for other indicators of quality. For this reason, the overall qualifications of an author as an expert may be crucial in determining whether to use a resource.

Sites sponsored by academic institutions, government agencies, and nonprofit or scholarly organizations have URLs that end with the designation *.edu, .gov,* or *.org* rather than *.com* or *.net.* For example, if you were interested in obtaining health statistics for Ontario or British Columbia, you might visit the Ontario Ministry of Health and Long-Term Care website (http://www.health.gov.on.ca) or the British Columbia website (http://www.gov.bc.ca). A particularly useful site is that of Canada's national statistical agency, Statistics Canada (http://www.statcan.gc.ca). Many of the statistics in this book are drawn from that site. Such sites would be expected to offer some assurance of higher quality for data posted there.

A particular clue to quality at corporate sites may be a copyright notice by a sponsoring organization rather than a single individual. Often located at the bottom of a Web page, this notice may signal that the organization is willing to put its reputation behind the resource. For example, online health information centres range in quality from the dismal to the superb. One excellent site, *Alice! Health Promotion Program* (http://www.alice.columbia.edu; Web Link 10.3), is maintained by Columbia University, one of the top universities in the world. The sponsor in this case is clearly identified.

Balance, Objectivity, and Independence

At the checkout line in a supermarket, shoppers often face a set of tabloid newspapers with outrageous headlines and the promise of lurid stories inside. Many people pick up a copy of their favourite tabloid as entertainment, something to be read purely for relaxation and enjoyment but not as an objective or reliable source of information about the world.

Although tabloid papers are an extreme example, other sources of information should arouse similar suspicions because of their subjective, unbalanced, and biased style of presentation. Certainly, the presence of language, graphic images, or opinions that are extreme, inflammatory, or highly subjective on a website suggests that the material should be treated with some skepticism. The more extreme, vulgar, or intemperate the manner of presentation, the less likely that the resource is reliable and trustworthy.

A more difficult case arises from material found on sites clearly advocating a particular point of view, such as those for a lobbying group, political movement, or professional advocacy or commercial trade association. Researchers should expect that resources available at these sites will support the point of view of the group. This fact does not necessarily disqualify the importance of materials found there. The sponsoring organization may provide valuable information for visitors to their sites. Greater reliance can probably be given to resources found on a site that acknowledges there is more than one side to a controversial issue. Some sites even offer links to the opposing side of a disputed topic. This openness should inspire confidence by users because it suggests fairness.

A challenge to researchers of psychological topics comes from commercial sites that stand to make money or gain new customers on the basis of what they post online. These sites may be businesses (with a *.com* Net address) or may be allied with the professional office or practice of individuals such as psychotherapists or physicians. Sometimes these sites offer a "Resource Centre" or similar area filled with articles relating to the product or service of the site's sponsor. These articles may include scientific-sounding titles, and many come from magazines, journals, or books that seem to be similarly professional. Most evaluators warn researchers to be careful when using materials from any site that has a direct financial motivation in sharing information. A close examination of the actual reference sources cited in online articles may give a clue as to how much credence a researcher should put in them. For example, are the references only for the author's own works, or do they include reputable journal articles written by a range of other scholars? Finding quality in online materials is always a judgment call, and the more you know about a topic from other sources, the better you can make that call at commercial sites.

Quality of Online Presentation

Another important index of quality is the care with which sites and materials have been organized and maintained. You should consider how easily you can use a site. Do the hypertext links within the site work, or do they point to empty or missing pages? Can browsers easily find the information they are looking for? Is there evidence that the design of the site was carefully considered and executed? Similarly, the actual text of materials retrieved from the Net should be free from any gross errors. Poor grammar and improper spelling usually indicate that something is amiss. Frankly, reputable scholars are fanatical about eliminating sloppiness or careless mistakes in what they write. They believe any such errors would suggest a parallel sloppiness in their thinking. Thus, the presence of mechanical and stylistic mistakes at a website or in a document should raise doubts about how reputable the actual content of the resource may be.

Finally, more credibility can be assigned to materials retrieved from sites that are frequently updated and carefully corrected. You should look for clear dates on pages containing important information. Ideally, one date will indicate when the page was first posted online and another when it was last changed or revised.

Other Cues to Quality

When I use the Net for research purposes, I use at least three further cues to evaluate the quality of the material or sites I find. First, in articles or papers online, I look at the references used by the author and consider whether they include scholarly materials from journals, professional books, or other recognized research sources. Second, I examine the dates of the supporting references. How recent are they? Do they include sources published in the last several years? Or do they include only older and possibly out-of-date materials? Finally, I look for evidence that the site itself has been recognized by an outside reviewer as possessing significant quality.

A Final Note of Advice

I hope the suggestions summarized here make it clear that any researcher must actively exercise judgment and critical thinking skills in evaluating online resources. Such skills are enormously enhanced when the researcher chooses a balanced overall research strategy. It is one thing to seek a quick fact or a simple definition through a website; it is another to rely on the Internet as the sole data source for a major paper or research project. Yes, for many people, the Net is an easily "surfable" medium, one that can quickly lead to information of varying levels of quality. The very ease of conducting research online often seduces student researchers to skip more difficult—but crucially important—steps offline.

The most important strategy that a student can bring to any research project is to develop an overall perspective, or a broad vantage point, regarding the topic of the project. And that means using sources of different types—scholarly books, journal and magazine articles, and printed research reports—*in addition to* materials retrieved from the Internet. It is both easy to understand, but embarrassing in the long run, when a student hands in a paper with only Internet-based sources and later discovers, in a professor's grading, that the Net provided a biased or slanted view of the topic. Without the counterbalance of non-Net sources, a student risks seriously misjudging how psychologists, medical researchers, and other scientists actually approach an issue. So, my final suggestion about research is a simple rule of thumb: The longer and more important the research project or paper, the broader the kinds of references you must use to answer the research question.

For Further Reference and Reading

To further explore the question of identifying quality in online materials and sites, consider the outstanding text by Janet Alexander and Marsha Tate: *Web Wisdom: How to Evaluate and Create Information Quality on the Web* (Mahwah, NJ: Erlbaum, 1999).

Another excellent Web-based resource on this topic is

Engle, M. (1999). *Evaluating web sites: Criteria and tools.* (Online document). Ithaca, NY: Cornell University, Olin-Kroch-Uris Libraries, Reference Division. Available at http://www.library.cornell.edu/okuref/research/webeval.html.

Many Canadian university libraries maintain website information for evaluating Web resources. For example, take a look at the guidelines suggested by the Queen's University Library website (http://library.queensu.ca/inforef/tutorials/qcat/evalint.htm).

A

Absolute refractory period The minimum length of time after an action potential during which another action potential cannot begin. (88)

Absolute threshold The minimum amount of stimulation that an organism can detect for a specific type of sensory input. (139)

Accommodation Changing existing mental structures to explain new experiences. (506)

Acculturation The degree to which a person is socially and psychologically integrated into a new culture. (359)

Achievement motive The need to master difficult challenges, to outperform others, and to meet high standards of excellence. (464)

Achievement tests Tests that gauge a person's mastery and knowledge of various subjects. (396)

Acquired immune deficiency syndrome (AIDS) A disorder in which the immune system is gradually weakened and eventually disabled by the human immunodeficiency virus (HIV). (625)

Acquisition The formation of a new conditioned response tendency. (257)

Action potential A brief change in a neuron's electrical charge. (88)

Acute stressors Threatening events that have a relatively short duration and a clear endpoint. (599)

Adaptation An inherited characteristic that increased in a population (through natural selection) because it helped solve a problem of survival or reproduction during the time it emerged. (125)

Additive colour mixing Formation of colours by superimposing lights, putting more light into the mixture than exists in any one light by itself. (154)

Adoption studies Research studies that assess hereditary influence by examining the resemblance between adopted children and both their biological and their adoptive parents. (122)

Affective forecasting Predictions of one's emotional reaction to future events. (469)

Afferent nerve fibres Axons that carry information inward to the central nervous system from the periphery of the body. (96)

Afterimage A visual image that persists after a stimulus is removed. (155)

Age of viability The age at which a baby can survive in the event of a premature birth. (493)

Aggression Any behaviour that is intended to hurt someone, either physically or verbally. (609)

Agonist A chemical that mimics the action of a neurotransmitter. (93)

Agoraphobia A fear of going out to public places. (648)

Alcohol A variety of beverages containing ethyl alcohol. (233)

Algorithm A methodical, step-by-step procedure for trying all possible alternatives in searching for a solution to a problem. (368)

Anecdotal evidence Personal stories about specific incidents and experiences. (80)

Anhedonia A diminished ability to experience pleasure. (657)

Animism The belief that all things are living. (507)

Anorexia nervosa Eating disorder characterized by intense fear of gaining weight, disturbed body image, refusal to maintain normal weight, and use of dangerous measures to lose weight. (687)

Antagonist A chemical that opposes the action of a neurotransmitter. (93)

Antecedents In behaviour modification, events that typically precede the target response. (293)

Anterograde amnesia Loss of memories for events that occur after a head injury. (332)

Antianxiety drugs Medications that relieve tension, apprehension, and nervousness. (716)

Antidepressant drugs Medications that gradually elevate mood and help bring people out of a depression. (718)

Antipsychotic drugs Medications used to gradually reduce psychotic symptoms, including hyperactivity, mental confusion, hallucinations, and delusions. (717)

Antisocial personality disorder A type of personality disorder marked by impulsive, callous, manipulative, aggressive, and irresponsible behaviour that reflects a failure to accept social norms. (677)

Anxiety disorders A class of disorders marked by feelings of excessive apprehension and anxiety. (647)

Applied psychology The branch of psychology concerned with everyday, practical problems. (15)

Approach–approach conflict A conflict situation in which a choice must be made between two attractive goals. (599)

Approach–avoidance conflict A conflict situation in which a choice must be made about whether to pursue a single goal that has both attractive and unattractive aspects. (600)

Aptitude tests Psychological tests used to assess talent for specific types of mental ability. (395)

Archetypes According to Jung, emotionally charged images and thought forms that have universal meaning. (558)

Argument One or more premises used to provide support for a conclusion. (484)

Ascending reticular activating system (ARAS) The afferent fibres running through the reticular formation that influence physiological arousal. (213)

Assimilation Interpreting new experiences in terms of existing mental structures without changing them. (506)

Assumptions Premises for which no proof or evidence is offered. (484)

Attachment A close, emotional bond of affection between infants and their caregivers. (500)

Attention Focusing awareness on a narrowed range of stimuli or events. (303)

Attitudes Positive or negative evaluations of objects of thought. (759)

Attributions Inferences that people draw about the causes of events, others' behaviour, and their own behaviour. (748)

Auditory localization Locating the source of a sound in space. (174)

Autism (autistic disorder) A developmental disorder characterized by social and emotional deficits, along with repetitive and stereotypic behaviours, interests, and activities. (681)

Autonomic nervous system (ANS) The system of nerves that connect to the heart, blood vessels, smooth muscles, and glands. (96)

Availability heuristic Basing the estimated probability of an event on the ease with which relevant instances come to mind. (377)

Aversion therapy A behaviour therapy in which an aversive stimulus is paired with a stimulus that elicits an undesirable response. (712)

Avoidance–avoidance conflict A conflict situation in which a choice must be made between two unattractive goals. (600)

Avoidance learning Learning that has occurred when an organism engages in a response that prevents aversive stimulation from occurring. (273)

Axon A long, thin fibre that transmits signals away from the neuron cell body to other neurons, or to muscles or glands. (87)

B

Basilar membrane A structure that runs the length of the cochlea in the inner ear and holds the auditory receptors, called *hair cells*. (172)

Behaviour Any overt (observable) response or activity by an organism. (7)

Behavioural contract A written agreement outlining a promise to adhere to the contingencies of a behaviour modification program. (295)

Behavioural economics A field of study that examines the effects of humans' actual (not idealized) decision-making processes on economic decisions. (379)

Behavioural genetics An interdisciplinary field that studies the influence of genetic factors on behavioural traits. (118)

Behaviourism A theoretical orientation based on the premise that scientific psychology should study only observable behaviour. (7, 561)

Behaviour modification A systematic approach to changing behaviour through the application of the principles of conditioning. (292)

Behaviour therapies Application of the principles of learning to direct efforts to change clients' maladaptive behaviours. (709)

Belief perseverance The tendency to hang on to beliefs in the face of contradictory evidence. (385)

Bilingualism The acquisition of two languages that use different speech sounds, vocabularies, and grammatical rules. (357)

Binge-eating disorder An eating disorder that involves uncontrollable eating binges that are not accompanied by the purging, fasting, and excessive exercise often seen in bulimia. (688)

Binocular depth cues Clues about distance based on the differing views of the two eyes. (163)

Biological rhythms Periodic fluctuations in physiological functioning. (205)

Biomedical therapies Physiological interventions intended to reduce symptoms associated with psychological disorders. (716)

Biopsychosocial model A model of illness that holds that physical illness is caused by a complex interaction of biological, psychological, and sociocultural factors. (596)

Bipolar disorder (formerly known as *manic-depressive disorder*) Mood disorder marked by the experience of both depressed and manic periods. (658)

Bisexuals Persons who seek emotional–sexual relationships with members of either sex. (460)

Body mass index (BMI) Weight (in kilograms) divided by height (in metres) squared (kg/m^2). (447)

Bottom-up processing In form perception, progression from individual elements to the whole. (159)

Bulimia nervosa Eating disorder characterized by habitually engaging in out-of-control overeating followed by unhealthy compensatory efforts, such as self-induced vomiting, fasting, abuse of laxatives and diuretics, and excessive exercise. (688)

Burnout Physical, mental, and emotional exhaustion that is attributable to work-related stress. (613)

Bystander effect A paradoxical social phenomenon in which people are less likely to provide needed help when they are in groups than when they are alone. (775)

C

Cannabis The hemp plant from which marijuana, hashish, and THC are derived. (233)

Case study An in-depth investigation of an individual subject. (55)

Catastrophic thinking Unrealistically pessimistic appraisals of stress that exaggerate the magnitude of one's problems. (630)

Catatonic schizophrenia A type of schizophrenia marked by striking motor disturbances, ranging from muscular rigidity to random motor activity. (670)

Catharsis The release of emotional tension. (609)

Central nervous system (CNS) The brain and the spinal cord. (97)

Centration The tendency to focus on just one feature of a problem, neglecting other important aspects. (507)

Cephalocaudal trend The head-to-foot direction of motor development. (496)

Cerebral cortex The convoluted outer layer of the cerebrum. (109)

Cerebral hemispheres The right and left halves of the cerebrum. (109)

Cerebrospinal fluid (CSF) A solution that fills the hollow cavities (ventricles) of the brain and circulates around the brain and spinal cord. (97)

Channel The medium through which a message is sent. (762)

Chromosomes Threadlike strands of DNA (deoxyribonucleic acid) molecules that carry genetic information. (118)

Chronic stressors Threatening events that have a relatively long duration and no readily apparent time limit. (599)

Chunk A group of familiar stimuli stored as a single unit. (309)

Circadian rhythms The 24-hour biological cycles found in humans and many other species. (205)

Classical conditioning A type of learning in which a neutral stimulus acquires the ability to evoke a response that was originally evoked by another stimulus. (251)

Client-centred therapy An insight therapy that emphasizes providing a supportive emotional climate for clients, who play a major role in determining the pace and direction of their therapy. (702)

Clinical psychology The branch of psychology concerned with the diagnosis and treatment of psychological problems and disorders. (15)

Clustering The tendency to remember similar or related items in groups. (313)

Cochlea The fluid-filled, coiled tunnel in the inner ear that contains the receptors for hearing. (172)

Coefficient of determination The percentage of variation in one variable that can be predicted based on the other variable. (A-11)

Cognition The mental processes involved in acquiring knowledge. (16, 349)

Cognitive-behavioural treatments Forms of therapy that emphasize in treatment the role of thinking in psychological disorders. In these treatments, therapists use varied combinations of verbal interventions and behaviour modification techniques to help clients change maladaptive patterns of thinking. (713)

Cognitive development Transitions in youngsters' patterns of thinking, including reasoning, remembering, and problem solving. (505)

Cognitive dissonance A psychological state that exists when related cognitions are inconsistent. (766)

Cognitive therapy An insight therapy that emphasizes recognizing and changing negative thoughts and maladaptive beliefs. (713)

Cohort effects Effects of differences between age groups that are due to the groups growing up in different time periods. (499)

Collective unconscious According to Jung, a storehouse of latent memory traces inherited from people's ancestral past. (558)

Collectivism Putting group goals ahead of personal goals and defining one's identity in terms of the groups one belongs to. (583)

Colour-blindness Deficiency in the ability to distinguish among colours. (155)

Commitment An intent to maintain a relationship in spite of the difficulties and costs that may arise. (754)

Comorbidity The coexistence of two or more disorders. (645, 691)

Companionate love Warm, trusting, tolerant affection for another whose life is deeply intertwined with one's own. (754)

Comparitors People, objects, events, and other standards that are used as a baseline for comparisons in making judgments. (194)

Compensation According to Adler, efforts to overcome imagined or real inferiorities by developing one's abilities. (559)

Complementary colours Pairs of colours that produce grey tones when added together. (155)

Conceptual hierarchy A multilevel classification system based on common properties among items. (313)

Concordance rate The percentage of twin pairs or other pairs of relatives that exhibit the same disorder. (651)

Conditioned reinforcers See *Secondary reinforcers*. (269)

Conditioned response (CR) A learned reaction to a conditioned stimulus that occurs because of previous conditioning. (253)

Conditioned stimulus (CS) A previously neutral stimulus that has, through conditioning, acquired the capacity to evoke a conditioned response. (253)

Conditioning Involves learning associations between events that occur in an organism's environment. (251)

Cones Specialized visual receptors that play a key role in daylight vision and colour vision. (146)

Confirmation bias The tendency to seek information that supports one's decisions and beliefs while ignoring disconfirming information. (384)

Conflict A state that occurs when two or more incompatible motivations or behavioural impulses compete for expression. (599)

Conformity The tendency for people to yield to real or imagined social pressure. (769)

Confounding of variables A condition that exists whenever two variables are linked together in a way that makes it difficult to sort out their independent effects. (51)

Conjunction fallacy An error that occurs when people estimate that the odds of two uncertain events happening together are greater than the odds of either event happening alone. (378)

Connectionist models See *Parallel distributed processing (PDP) models*. (315)

Conscious Whatever one is aware of at a particular point in time. (552)

Conservation Piaget's term for the awareness that physical quantities remain constant in spite of changes in their shape or appearance. (507)

Consolidation A hypothetical process involving the gradual conversion of information into durable memory codes stored in long-term memory. (332)

Construct validity The extent to which there is evidence that a test measures a particular hypothetical construct. (398)

Constructive coping Relatively healthful efforts that people make to deal with stressful events. (611)

Content validity The degree to which the content of a test is representative of the domain it's supposed to cover. (398)

Continuous reinforcement Reinforcing every instance of a designated response. (270)

Control group Subjects in a study who do not receive the special treatment given to the experimental group. (50)

Convergence A cue to depth that involves sensing the eyes converging toward each other as they focus on closer objects. (164)

Convergent thinking Narrowing down a list of alternatives to converge on a single correct answer. (430)

Coping Active efforts to master, reduce, or tolerate the demands created by stress. (608)

Corpus callosum The structure that connects the two cerebral hemispheres. (109)

Correlation The extent to which two variables are related to each other. (62)

Correlation coefficient A numerical index of the degree of relationship between two variables. (A-10, 397)

Couples therapy Therapy that involves the treatment of both partners in a committed, intimate relationship, in which the main focus is on relationship issues. (707)

Creativity The generation of ideas that are original, novel, and useful. (430)

Criterion-related validity Test validity that is estimated by correlating subjects' scores on a test with their scores on an independent criterion (another measure) of the trait assessed by the test. (398)

Critical period A limited time span in the development of an organism when it is optimal for certain capacities to emerge because the organism is especially responsive to certain experiences. (131)

Critical thinking The use of cognitive skills and strategies that increase the probability of a desired outcome. (38)

Cross-sectional design A research design in which investigators compare groups of subjects of differing age who are observed at a single point in time. (498)

Crystallized intelligence One's ability to apply acquired skills and knowledge in problem solving. (403)

Culture The widely shared customs, beliefs, values, norms, institutions, and other products of a community that are transmitted socially across generations. (29)

Culture-bound disorders Abnormal syndromes found in only a few cultural groups. (685)

Cumulative recorder A graphic record of reinforcement and responding in a Skinner box as a function of time. (264)

Cyclothymic disorder Exhibiting chronic but relatively mild symptoms of bipolar disturbance. (658)

D

Dark adaptation The process in which the eyes become more sensitive to light in low illumination. (147)

Data collection techniques Procedures for making empirical observations and measurements. (46)

Decay theory The idea that forgetting occurs because memory traces fade with time. (323)

Decision making The process of evaluating alternatives and making choices among them. (374)

Declarative memory system Memory for factual information. (334)

Deep brain stimulation (DBS) A surgical treatment approach in which a thin electrode is implanted in the brain and connected to an implanted pulse generator so that various electrical currents can be delivered to brain tissue adjacent to the electrode. (723)

Defence mechanisms Largely unconscious reactions that protect a person from unpleasant emotions such as anxiety and guilt. (554)

Defensive attribution The tendency to blame victims for their misfortune, so that one feels less likely to be victimized in a similar way. (750)

Deinstitutionalization Transferring the treatment of mental illness from inpatient institutions to community-based facilities that emphasize outpatient care. (730)

Delusions False beliefs that are maintained even though they are clearly out of touch with reality. (669)

Dementia An abnormal condition marked by multiple cognitive defects that include memory impairment. (529)

Dendrites Branchlike parts of a neuron that are specialized to receive information. (87)

Dependent variable In an experiment, the variable that is thought to be affected by the manipulation of the independent variable. (49)

Depth perception Interpretation of visual cues that indicate how near or far away objects are. (163)

Descriptive statistics Statistics that are used to organize and summarize data. (A-8)

Destination memory Memory that involves recalling to whom one has told what. (320)

Development The sequence of age-related changes that occur as a person progresses from conception to death. (490)

Developmental norms The average age at which individuals display various behaviours and abilities. (497)

Deviation IQ scores Scores that locate subjects precisely within the normal distribution, using the standard deviation as the unit of measurement. (404)

Diagnosis Distinguishing one illness from another. (642)

Discrimination Behaving differently, usually unfairly, toward the members of a group. (782)

Discriminative stimuli Cues that influence operant behaviour by indicating the probable consequences (reinforcement or nonreinforcement) of a response. (268)

Dishabituation An increase in the strength of a habituated response elicited by a new stimulus. (511)

Disorganized schizophrenia A type of schizophrenia in which particularly severe deterioration of adaptive behaviour is seen. (670)

Displacement Diverting emotional feelings (usually anger) from their original source to a substitute target. (554)

Display rules Cultural norms that regulate the appropriate expressions of emotions. (475)

Dissociation A splitting off of mental processes into two separate, simultaneous streams of awareness. (228)

Dissociative amnesia A sudden loss of memory of important personal information that is too extensive to be due to normal forgetting. (653)

Dissociative disorders A class of disorders in which people lose contact with portions of their consciousness or memory, resulting in disruptions in their sense of identity. (653)

Dissociative fugue A disorder in which people lose their memory of their entire lives along with their sense of personal identity. (653)

Dissociative identity disorder (DID) A type of dissociative disorder characterized by the coexistence in one person of two or more largely complete, and usually very different, personalities. Also called *multiple-personality disorder*. (654)

Distal stimuli Stimuli that lie in the distance (that is, in the world outside the body). (162)

Divergent thinking Trying to expand the range of alternatives by generating many possible solutions. (430)

Dominant gene A gene that is expressed when paired genes are heterozygous (different). (119)

Door-in-the-face technique Making a large request that is likely to be turned down as a way to increase the chances that people will agree to a smaller request later. (194)

Double-blind procedure A research strategy in which neither subjects nor experimenters know which subjects are in the experimental or control groups. (69)

Dream analysis A psychoanalytic technique in which the therapist interprets the symbolic meaning of the client's dreams. (700)

Drive An internal state of tension that motivates an organism to engage in activities that should reduce the tension. (441)

Dual-coding theory Paivio's theory that memory is enhanced by forming semantic and visual codes, since either can lead to recall. (306)

Dysthymic disorder A chronic depression that is insufficient in severity to merit diagnosis of a major depressive episode. (657)

E

Eating disorders Severe disturbances in eating behaviour characterized by preoccupation with weight concerns and unhealthy efforts to control weight. (687)

Eclecticism In psychotherapy, drawing ideas from two or more systems of therapy instead of committing to just one system. (727)

Efferent nerve fibres Axons that carry information outward from the central nervous system to the periphery of the body. (96)

Ego According to Freud, the decision-making component of personality that operates according to the reality principle. (552)

Egocentrism A limited ability to share another person's viewpoint. (507)

Elaboration Linking a stimulus to other information at the time of encoding. (305)

Electrical stimulation of the brain (ESB) Sending a weak electric current into a brain structure to stimulate (activate) it. (100)

Electroconvulsive therapy (ECT) A biomedical treatment in which electric shock is used to produce a cortical seizure accompanied by convulsions. (721)

Electroencephalograph (EEG) A device that monitors the electrical activity of the brain over time by means of recording electrodes attached to the surface of the scalp. (98, 202)

Electromyograph (EMG) A device that records muscular activity and tension. (208)

Electrooculograph (EOG) A device that records eye movements. (208)

Elicit To draw out or bring forth. (253)

Embryonic stage The second stage of prenatal development, lasting from two weeks until the end of the second month. (491)

Emit To send out. (264)

Emotion A subjective conscious experience (the cognitive component) accompanied by bodily arousal (the physiological component) and by characteristic overt expressions (the behavioural component). (468)

Emotional intelligence The ability to perceive and express emotion, assimilate emotion in thought, understand and reason with emotion, and regulate emotion. (428)

Empiricism The premise that knowledge should be acquired through observation. (28)

Encoding Forming a memory code. (302)

Encoding specificity principle The idea that the value of a retrieval cue depends on how well it corresponds to the memory code. (324)

Endocrine system A group of glands that release chemicals into the bloodstream that help control bodily functioning. (116)

Endorphins The entire family of internally produced chemicals that resemble opiates in structure and effects. (94)

Epidemiology The study of the distribution of mental or physical disorders in a population. (646)

Epigenetics The study of heritable changes in gene expression that do not involve modifications to the DNA sequence. (123)

Episodic memory system Chronological, or temporally dated, recollections of personal experiences. (335)

Escape learning A type of learning in which an organism acquires a response that decreases or ends some aversive stimulation. (273)

Ethnocentrism The tendency to view one's own group as superior to others and as the standard for judging the worth of foreign ways. (18, 784)

Etiology The apparent causation and developmental history of an illness. (642)

Evaluative conditioning Changes in the liking of a stimulus that result from pairing that stimulus with other positive or negative stimuli. (255)

Evolutionary psychology Theoretical perspective that examines behavioural processes in terms of their adaptive value for a species over the course of many generations. (20)

Excitatory PSP An electric potential that increases the likelihood that a postsynaptic neuron will fire action potentials. (90)

Experiment A research method in which the investigator manipulates a variable under carefully controlled conditions and observes whether any changes occur in a second variable as a result. (49)

Experimental group The subjects in a study who receive some special treatment in regard to the independent variable. (50)

Experimenter bias A phenomenon that occurs when a researcher's expectations or preferences about the outcome of a study influence the results obtained. (69)

Explicit attitudes Attitudes that we hold consciously and can readily describe. (760)

Explicit memory Intentional recollection of previous experiences. (334)

Exposure therapies Therapies in which clients are confronted with situations they fear so that they learn that these situations are really harmless. (711)

Expressed emotion The degree to which a relative of a schizophrenic patient displays highly critical or emotionally overinvolved attitudes toward the patient. (674)

External attributions Ascribing the causes of behaviour to situational demands and environmental constraints. (748)

Extinction The gradual weakening and disappearance of a conditioned response tendency. (258)

Extraneous variables Any variables other than the independent variable that seem likely to influence the dependent variable in a specific study. (51)

Extraverts People who tend to be interested in the external world of people and things. (558)

F

Factor analysis Statistical analysis of correlations among many variables to identify closely related clusters of variables. (548)

Family life cycle A sequence of stages that families tend to progress through. (526)

Family studies Scientific studies in which researchers assess hereditary influence by examining blood relatives to see how much they resemble each other on a specific trait. (120)

Family therapy Therapy involving the treatment of a family unit as a whole, in which the main focus is on family dynamics and communication. (707)

Farsightedness A vision deficiency in which distant objects are seen clearly but close objects appear blurry. (144)

Fast mapping The process by which children map a word onto an underlying concept after only one exposure to the word. (355)

Feature analysis The process of detecting specific elements in visual input and assembling them into a more complex form. (159)

Feature detectors Neurons that respond selectively to very specific features of more complex stimuli. (151)

Fechner's law A psychophysical law stating that larger and larger increases in stimulus intensity are required to produce perceptible increments in the magnitude of sensation. (140)

Fetal alcohol syndrome A collection of congenital (inborn) problems associated with excessive alcohol use during pregnancy. (493)

Fetal stage The third stage of prenatal development, lasting from two months through birth. (491)

Field dependence–independence Individuals' tendency to rely primarily on external versus internal frames of reference when orienting themselves in space. (372)

Fight-or-flight response A physiological reaction to threat in which the autonomic nervous system mobilizes the organism for attacking (fight) or fleeing (flight) an enemy. (606)

Fitness The reproductive success (number of descendants) of an individual organism relative to the average reproductive success of the population. (124)

Fixation According to Freud, failure to move forward from one psychosexual stage to another as expected. (556)

Fixed-interval (FI) schedule A reinforcement schedule in which the reinforcer is given for the first response that occurs after a fixed time interval has elapsed. (271)

Fixed-ratio (FR) schedule A reinforcement schedule in which the reinforcer is given after a fixed number of nonreinforced responses. (271)

Flashbulb memories Unusually vivid and detailed recollections of momentous events. (311)

Fluid intelligence One's reasoning ability, memory capacity, and speed of information processing. (403)

Foot-in-the-door technique Getting people to agree to a small request to increase the chance that they will agree to a larger request later. (787)

Forebrain The largest and most complicated region of the brain, encompassing a variety of structures, including the thalamus, hypothalamus, limbic system, and cerebrum. (107)

Forgetting curve A graph showing retention and forgetting over time. (321)

Fovea A tiny spot in the centre of the retina that contains only cones; visual acuity is greatest at this spot. (146)

Framing How issues are posed or how choices are structured. (380)

Fraternal twins Twins that result when two eggs are fertilized simultaneously by different sperm cells, forming two separate zygotes. Also called *dizygotic twins*. (121)

Free association A psychoanalytic technique in which clients spontaneously express their thoughts and feelings exactly as they occur, with as little censorship as possible. (700)

Frequency distribution An orderly arrangement of scores indicating the frequency of each score or group of scores. (A-7)

Frequency polygon A line figure used to present data from a frequency distribution. (A-8)

Frequency theory The theory that perception of pitch corresponds to the rate, or frequency, at which the entire basilar membrane vibrates. (173)

Frustration The feeling that people experience in any situation in which their pursuit of some goal is thwarted. (599)

Functional fixedness The tendency to perceive an item only in terms of its most common use. (367)

Functionalism A school of psychology based on the belief that psychology should investigate the function or purpose of consciousness, rather than its structure. (6)

Fundamental attribution error Observers' bias in favour of internal attributions in explaining others' behaviour. (749)

G

Galvanic skin response (GSR) An increase in the electrical conductivity of the skin that occurs when sweat glands increase their activity. (470)

Gambler's fallacy The belief that the odds of a chance event increase if the event hasn't occurred recently. (383)

Gate-control theory The idea that incoming pain sensations must pass through a "gate" in the spinal cord that can be closed, thus blocking pain signals. (182)

Gender Culturally constructed distinctions between masculinity and femininity. (537)

Gender differences Actual disparities between the sexes in typical behaviour or average ability. (537)

Gender roles Expectations about what is appropriate behaviour for each sex. (540)

Gender stereotypes Widely held beliefs about males' and females' abilities, personality traits, and behaviour. (537)

General adaptation syndrome Selye's model of the body's stress response, consisting of three stages: alarm, resistance, and exhaustion. (606)

Generalized anxiety disorder A psychological disorder marked by a chronic, high level of anxiety that is not tied to any specific threat. (647)

Genes DNA segments that serve as the key functional units in hereditary transmission. (118)

Genetic mapping The process of determining the location and chemical sequence of specific genes on specific chromosomes. (122)

Genotype A person's genetic makeup. (120)

Germinal stage The first phase of prenatal development, encompassing the first two weeks after conception. (491)

Glia Cells found throughout the nervous system that provide various types of support for neurons. (87)

Glucose A simple sugar that is an important source of energy. (444)

Group Two or more individuals who interact and are interdependent. (774)

Group cohesiveness The strength of the liking relationships linking group members to each other and to the group itself. (779)

Group polarization A phenomenon that occurs when group discussion strengthens a group's dominant point of view and produces a shift toward a more extreme decision in that direction. (777)

Group therapy The simultaneous treatment of several clients in a group. (706)

Groupthink A process in which members of a cohesive group emphasize concurrence at the expense of critical thinking in arriving at a decision. (778)

Gustatory system The sensory system for taste. (177)

H

Habituation A gradual reduction in the strength of a response when a stimulus event is presented repeatedly. (511)

Hallucinations Sensory perceptions that occur in the absence of a real, external stimulus, or gross distortions of perceptual input. (670)

Hallucinogens A diverse group of drugs that have powerful effects on mental and emotional functioning, marked most prominently by distortions in sensory and perceptual experience. (233)

Health psychology The subfield of psychology concerned with how psychosocial factors relate to the promotion and maintenance of health and with the causation, prevention, and treatment of illness. (596)

Hedonic adaptation An effect that occurs when the mental scale that people use to judge the pleasantness–unpleasantness of their experiences shifts so that their neutral point, or baseline for comparison, changes. (483)

Heritability ratio An estimate of the proportion of trait variability in a population that is determined by variations in genetic inheritance. (415)

Heterosexuals Persons who seek emotional–sexual relationships with members of the other sex. (460)

Heterozygous condition The situation that occurs when two genes in a specific pair are different. (119)

Heuristic A strategy, guiding principle, or rule of thumb used in solving problems or making decisions. (368)

Hierarchy of needs Maslow's systematic arrangement of needs according to priority, which assumes that basic needs must be met before less basic needs are aroused. (570)

Higher-order conditioning A type of conditioning in which a conditioned stimulus functions as if it were an unconditioned stimulus. (261)

Hindbrain The part of the brain that includes the cerebellum and two structures found in the lower part of the brainstem: the medulla and the pons. (105)

Hindsight bias The tendency to mould one's interpretation of the past to fit how events actually turned out. (344)

Histogram A bar graph that presents data from a frequency distribution. (A-7)

Homeostasis A state of physiological equilibrium or stability. (441)

Homosexuals Persons who seek emotional–sexual relationships with members of the same sex. (460)

Homozygous condition The situation that occurs when two genes in a specific pair are the same. (119)

Hormones The chemical substances released by the endocrine glands. (116)

Humanism A theoretical orientation that emphasizes the unique qualities of humans, especially their freedom and their potential for personal growth. (12, 566)

Hypnosis A systematic procedure that typically produces a heightened state of suggestibility. (225)

Hypothalamus A structure found near the base of the forebrain that is involved in the regulation of basic biological needs. (107)

Hypothesis A tentative statement about the relationship between two or more variables. (44)

I

Id According to Freud, the primitive, instinctive component of personality that operates according to the pleasure principle. (551)

Identical twins Twins that emerge from one zygote that splits for unknown reasons. Also called *monozygotic twins*. (121)

Identification Bolstering self-esteem by forming an imaginary or real alliance with some person or group. (555)

Illusory correlation A misperception that occurs when people estimate that they have encountered more confirmations of an association between social traits than they have actually seen. (747)

Immune response The body's defensive reaction to invasion by bacteria, viral agents, or other foreign substances. (619)

Immunosuppression A decrease in the production of antibodies. (256)

Implicit attitudes Covert attitudes that are expressed in subtle automatic responses over which we have little conscious control. (760)

Implicit memory Type of memory apparent when retention is exhibited on a task that does not require intentional remembering. (334)

Impossible figures Objects that can be represented in two-dimensional pictures but cannot exist in three-dimensional space. (166)

Incentive An external goal that has the capacity to motivate behaviour. (441)

Inclusive fitness The sum of an individual's own reproductive success plus the effects the organism has on the reproductive success of related others. (126)

Incongruence The degree of disparity between one's self-concept and one's actual experience. (567)

Incubation effect An effect that occurs when new solutions surface for a previously unsolved problem after a period of not consciously thinking about the problem. (372)

Independent variable In an experiment, a condition or event that an experimenter varies in order to see its impact on another variable. (49)

Individualism Putting personal goals ahead of group goals and defining one's identity in terms of personal attributes rather than group memberships. (583)

Inferential statistics Statistics that are used to interpret data and draw conclusions. (A-12)

Informational influence Type of influence that operates when people look to others for guidance about how to behave in ambiguous situations. (770)

Ingroup The group that people belong to and identify with. (747)

Inhibitory PSP An electric potential that decreases the likelihood that a postsynaptic neuron will fire action potentials. (90)

Insight In problem solving, the sudden discovery of the correct solution following incorrect attempts based primarily on trial and error. (365)

Insight therapies Psychotherapy methods characterized by verbal interactions intended to enhance clients' self-knowledge and thus promote healthful changes in personality and behaviour. (699)

Insomnia Chronic problems in getting adequate sleep. (217)

Instinctive drift The tendency for an animal's innate responses to interfere with conditioning processes. (278)

Instrumental learning. See *Operant conditioning*. (262)

Intellectual disability Subnormal general mental ability accompanied by deficiencies in everyday living skills originating prior to age 18; also called *mental retardation*. (409)

Intelligence quotient (IQ) A child's mental age divided by chronological age, multiplied by 100. (401)

Intelligence tests Psychological tests that measure general mental ability. (395)

Interference theory The idea that people forget information because of competition from other material. (323)

Intermittent reinforcement A reinforcement schedule in which a designated response is reinforced only some of the time. (271)

Internal attributions Ascribing the causes of behaviour to personal dispositions, traits, abilities, and feelings. (748)

Internet addiction Spending an inordinate amount of time on the Internet and being unable to control online use. (610)

Internet-mediated research Refers to studies in which data collection is done using the Web. (72)

Interpersonal attraction Positive feelings toward another. (753)

Interpretation In psychoanalysis, the therapist's attempts to explain the inner significance of the client's thoughts, feelings, memories, and behaviours. (700)

Intimacy Warmth, closeness, and sharing in a relationship. (754)

Introspection Careful, systematic observation of one's own conscious experience. (6)

Introverts People who tend to be preoccupied with the internal world of their own thoughts, feelings, and experiences. (558)

Irreversibility The inability to envision reversing an action. (507)

J

Journal A periodical that publishes technical and scholarly material, usually in a narrowly defined area of inquiry. (48)

Just noticeable difference (JND) The smallest difference in the amount of stimulation that a specific sense can detect. (140)

K

Keyword method A mnemonic technique in which one associates a concrete word with an abstract word and generates an image to represent the concrete word. (343)

Kinesthetic system The sensory system that monitors the positions of the various parts of one's body. (184)

L

Language A set of symbols that convey meaning, and rules for combining those symbols, that can be used to generate an infinite variety of messages. (350)

Language acquisition device (LAD) An innate mechanism or process that facilitates the learning of language. (363)

Latent learning Learning that is not apparent from behaviour when it first occurs. (281)

Lateral antagonism A process in the retina that occurs when neural activity in a cell opposes activity in surrounding cells. (148)

Law of effect The principle that if a response in the presence of a stimulus leads to satisfying effects, the association between the stimulus and the response is strengthened. (263)

Learned helplessness Passive behaviour produced by exposure to unavoidable aversive events. (608)

Learning A relatively durable change in behaviour or knowledge that is due to experience. (249)

Lens The transparent eye structure that focuses the light rays falling on the retina. (144)

Lesioning Destroying a piece of the brain. (100)

Levels-of-processing theory The theory holding that deeper levels of mental processing result in longer-lasting memory codes. (305)

Lie detector See *Polygraph*. (470)

Life changes Any noticeable alterations in one's living circumstances that require readjustment. (600)

Light adaptation The process whereby the eyes become less sensitive to light in high illumination. (147)

Limbic system A densely connected network of structures roughly located along the border between the cerebral cortex and deeper subcortical areas. (107)

Linguistic relativity The theory that one's language determines the nature of one's thought. (364)

Link method Forming a mental image of items to be remembered in a way that links them together. (342)

Long-term memory (LTM) An unlimited-capacity store that can hold information over lengthy periods of time. (311)

Long-term potentiation (LTP) A long-lasting increase in neural excitability in synapses along a specific neural pathway. (331)

Longitudinal design A research design in which investigators observe one group of subjects repeatedly over a period of time. (498)

Lowball technique Getting someone to commit to an attractive proposition before revealing the hidden costs. (787)

Lucid dreams Dreams in which people can think clearly about the circumstances of waking life and the fact that they are dreaming, yet they remain asleep in the midst of a vivid dream. (243)

M

Major depressive disorder Mood disorder characterized by persistent feelings of sadness and despair and a loss of interest in previous sources of pleasure. (656)

Manic-depressive disorder See *Bipolar disorder.* (658)

Marital therapy Therapy that involves the treatment of both partners in a committed, intimate relationship, in which the main focus is on relationship issues. (707)

Matching hypothesis The idea that males and females of approximately equal physical attractiveness are likely to select each other as partners. (753)

Maturation Development that reflects the gradual unfolding of one's genetic blueprint. (497)

MDMA A compound drug related to both amphetamines and hallucinogens, especially mescaline; commonly called *ecstasy.* (234)

Mean The arithmetic average of the scores in a distribution. (A-8)

Median The score that falls exactly in the centre of a distribution of scores. (A-8)

Medical model The view that it is useful to think of abnormal behaviour as a disease. (641)

Meditation A family of mental exercises in which a conscious attempt is made to focus attention in a nonanalytical way. (228)

Menarche The first occurrence of menstruation. (517)

Mental age In intelligence testing, a score that indicates that a child displays the mental ability typical of a child of that chronological (actual) age. (401)

Mental hospital A medical institution specializing in providing inpatient care for psychological disorders. (729)

Mental set Persisting in using problem-solving strategies that have worked in the past. (367)

Mere exposure effect The finding that repeated exposures to a stimulus promotes greater liking of the stimulus. (764)

Message The information transmitted by a source. (762)

Metalinguistic awareness The ability to reflect on the use of language. (356)

Method of loci A mnemonic device that involves taking an imaginary walk along a familiar path where images of items to be remembered are associated with certain locations. (342)

Midbrain The segment of the brain stem that lies between the hindbrain and the forebrain. (107)

Mind wandering Refers to people's experience of task-unrelated thoughts. (201)

Mirror neurons Neurons that are activated by performing an action or by seeing another animal or person perform the same action. (290)

Misinformation effect Occurs when participants' recall of an event they witnessed is altered by introducing misleading post-event information. (318)

Mnemonic devices Strategies for enhancing memory. (340)

Mode The score that occurs most frequently in a distribution. (A-8)

Model A person whose behaviour is observed by another. (564)

Monocular depth cues Clues about distance based on the image from either eye alone. (164)

Mood disorders A class of disorders marked by emotional disturbances of varied kinds that may spill over to disrupt physical, perceptual, social, and thought processes. (656)

Mood stabilizers Drugs used to control mood swings in patients with bipolar mood disorders. (720)

Morphemes The smallest units of meaning in a language. (351)

Mortality salience The degree to which subjects' mortality is prominent in their minds. (581)

Motion parallax Cue to depth that involves images of objects at different distances moving across the retina at different rates. (164)

Motivation Goal-directed behaviour. (440)

Motor development The progression of muscular coordination required for physical activities. (496)

Multiple personality disorder See *Dissociative identity disorder.* (654)

Mutation A spontaneous, heritable change in a piece of DNA that occurs in the individual organism. (125)

Myelin sheath Insulating material, derived from glial cells, that encases some axons of neurons. (87)

Myside bias The tendency to evaluate evidence in a manner slanted in favour of one's own opinions. (384)

N

Narcolepsy A disease marked by sudden and irresistible onsets of sleep during normal waking periods. (218)

Narcissism A personality trait marked by an inflated sense of importance, a need for attention and admiration, a sense of entitlement, and a tendency to exploit others. (577)

Narcotics (opiates) Drugs derived from opium that are capable of relieving pain. (232)

Natural selection Principle stating that heritable characteristics that provide a survival reproductive advantage are more likely than alternative characteristics to be passed on to subsequent generations and thus come to be "selected" over time. (6, 124)

Naturalistic observation A descriptive research method in which the researcher engages in careful, usually prolonged, observation of behaviour without intervening directly with the subjects. (54)

Nearsightedness A vision deficiency in which close objects are seen clearly but distant objects appear blurry. (144)

Need for self-actualization The need to fulfill one's potential. (570)

Negatively skewed distribution A distribution in which most scores pile up at the high end of the scale. (A-8)

Negative reinforcement The strengthening of a response because it is followed by the removal of an aversive (unpleasant) stimulus. (272)

Negative symptoms Schizophrenic symptoms that involve behavioural deficits, such as flattened emotions, social withdrawal, apathy, impaired attention, and poverty of speech. (671)

Nerves Bundles of neuron fibres (axons) that are routed together in the peripheral nervous system. (95)

Neurogenesis The formation of new neurons. (216)

Neurons Individual cells in the nervous system that receive, integrate, and transmit information. (86)

Neurotransmitters Chemicals that transmit information from one neuron to another. (89)

Nightmares Anxiety-arousing dreams that lead to awakening, usually from REM sleep. (219)

Night terrors Abrupt awakenings from NREM sleep accompanied by intense autonomic arousal and feelings of panic. (219)

Nondeclarative memory system Memory for actions, skills, and operations. (334)

Non-REM (NREM) sleep Sleep stages 1 through 4, which are marked by an absence of rapid eye movements, relatively little dreaming, and varied EEG activity. (210)

Normal distribution A symmetric, bell-shaped curve that represents the pattern in which many characteristics are dispersed in the population. (A-9)

Normative influence Type of influence that operates when people conform to social norms for fear of negative social consequences. (770)

Null hypothesis In inferential statistics, the assumption that there is no true relationship between the variables being observed. (A-13)

O

Obedience A form of compliance that occurs when people follow direct commands, usually from someone in a position of authority. (770)

Obesity The condition of being overweight. (447)

Object permanence Recognizing that objects continue to exist even when they are no longer visible. (506)

Observational learning A type of learning that occurs when an organism's responding is influenced by the observation of others, who are called *models.* (283)

Obsessive-compulsive disorder (OCD) A type of anxiety disorder marked by persistent, uncontrollable intrusions of unwanted thoughts (obsessions) and urges to engage in senseless rituals (compulsions). (648)

Oedipal complex According to Freud, children's manifestation of erotically tinged desires for their opposite-sex parent, accompanied by feelings of hostility toward their same-sex parent. (557)

Olfactory system The sensory system for smell. (177)

Operant chamber See *Skinner box.* (264)

Operant conditioning A form of learning in which voluntary responses come to be controlled by their consequences. (262)

Operational definition A definition that describes the actions or operations that will be made to measure or control a variable. (46)

Opiates See *Narcotics.* (232)

Opponent process theory The theory that colour perception depends on receptors that make antagonistic responses to three pairs of colours. (155)

Optic chiasm The point at which the optic nerves from the inside half of each eye cross over and then project to the opposite half of the brain. (149)

Optic disk A hole in the retina where the optic nerve fibres exit the eye. (146)

Optical illusion An apparently inexplicable discrepancy between the appearance of a visual stimulus and its physical reality. (165)

Optimism A general tendency to expect good outcomes. (621)

Orgasm Stage in the sexual response cycle in which arousal reaches its peak intensity; it discharges in a series of muscular contractions that pulsate through the pelvic area. (453)

Outgroup People who are not part of the ingroup. (747)

Overextension Using a word incorrectly to describe a wider set of objects or actions than it is meant to. (356)

Overlearning Continued rehearsal of material after one first appears to have mastered it. (340)

Overregularization In children, incorrect generalization of grammatical rules to irregular cases where they do not apply. (356)

Oxytocin A hormone released by the pituitary gland, which regulates reproductive behaviours. (117)

P

Panic disorder A type of anxiety disorder characterized by recurrent attacks of overwhelming anxiety that usually occur suddenly and unexpectedly. (648)

Parallel distributed processing (PDP) models Models of memory that assume cognitive processes depend on patterns of activation in highly interconnected computational networks that resemble neural networks. Also called *connectionist models*. (315)

Parallel processing Simultaneously extracting different kinds of information from the same input. (149)

Paranoid schizophrenia A type of schizophrenia that is dominated by delusions of persecution along with delusions of grandeur. (670)

Parasympathetic division The branch of the autonomic nervous system that generally conserves bodily resources. (97)

Partial reinforcement See *Intermittent reinforcement*. (271)

Participants See *Subjects*. (46)

Passionate love A complete absorption in another that includes tender sexual feelings and the agony and ecstasy of intense emotion. (754)

Pavlovian conditioning. See *Classical conditioning*. (251)

Percentile score A figure that indicates the percentage of people who score below the score one has obtained. (396, A-10)

Perception The selection, organization, and interpretation of sensory input. (138)

Perceptual asymmetries Left–right imbalances between the cerebral hemispheres in the speed of visual or auditory processing. (115)

Perceptual constancy A tendency to experience a stable perception in the face of continually changing sensory input. (165)

Perceptual hypothesis An inference about which distal stimuli could be responsible for the proximal stimuli sensed. (162)

Perceptual set A readiness to perceive a stimulus in a particular way. (158)

Peripheral nervous system All those nerves that lie outside the brain and spinal cord. (95)

Personality An individual's unique constellation of consistent behavioural traits. (548)

Personality disorders A class of psychological disorders marked by extreme, inflexible personality traits that cause subjective distress or impaired social and occupational functioning. (676)

Personality tests Psychological tests that measure various aspects of personality, including motives, interests, values, and attitudes. (396)

Personality trait A durable disposition to behave in a particular way in a variety of situations. (548)

Personal unconscious According to Jung, the level of awareness that houses material that is not within one's conscious awareness because it has been repressed or forgotten. (558)

Person perception The process of forming impressions of others. (743)

Phenomenological approach The assumption that one must appreciate individuals' personal, subjective experiences to truly understand their behaviour. (566)

Phenotype The ways in which a person's genotype is manifested in observable characteristics. (180)

Pheromones Chemical messages, typically imperceptible, that can be sent by one organism and received by another member of the same species. (180)

Phi phenomenon The illusion of movement created by presenting visual stimuli in rapid succession. (160)

Phobias Irrational fears of specific objects or situations. (250)

Phobic disorder A type of anxiety disorder marked by a persistent and irrational fear of an object or situation that presents no realistic danger. (647)

Phonemes The smallest units of sound in a spoken language. (350)

Physical dependence The condition that exists when a person must continue to take a drug to avoid withdrawal illness. (235)

Pictorial depth cues Clues about distance that can be given in a flat picture. (164)

Pituitary gland The "master gland" of the endocrine system; it releases a great variety of hormones that fan out through the body, stimulating actions in the other endocrine glands. (117)

Place theory The idea that perception of pitch corresponds to the vibration of different portions, or places, along the basilar membrane. (173)

Placebo effects The fact that subjects' expectations can lead them to experience some change even though they receive an empty, fake, or ineffectual treatment. (736)

Placenta A structure that allows oxygen and nutrients to pass into the fetus from the mother's bloodstream and bodily wastes to pass out to the mother. (491)

Pleasure principle According to Freud, the principle on which the id operates, demanding immediate gratification of its urges. (551)

Polygenic traits Characteristics that are influenced by more than one pair of genes. (120)

Polygraph A device that records autonomic fluctuations while a subject is questioned, in an effort to determine whether the subject is telling the truth. (470)

Population The larger collection of animals or people from which a sample is drawn and that researchers want to generalize about. (66)

Positively skewed distribution A distribution in which scores pile up at the low end of the scale. (A-8)

Positive psychology Uses theory and research to better understand the positive, adaptive, creative, and fulfilling aspects of human existence. (22)

Positive reinforcement Reinforcement that occurs when a response is strengthened because it is followed by the presentation of a rewarding stimulus. (272)

Positive symptoms Schizophrenic symptoms that involve behavioural excesses or peculiarities, such as hallucinations, delusions, bizarre behaviour, and wild flights of ideas. (671)

Postpartum depression A type of depression that occurs after childbirth. (659)

Postsynaptic potential (PSP) A voltage change at the receptor site on a postsynaptic cell membrane. (90)

Post-traumatic stress disorder (PTSD) Disturbed behaviour that is attributed to a major stressful event but that emerges after the stress is over. (613)

Preconscious According to Freud, the level of awareness that contains material just beneath the surface of conscious awareness that can easily be retrieved. (552)

Prejudice A negative attitude held toward members of a group. (782)

Premises The reasons presented to persuade someone that a conclusion is true or probably true. (484)

Prenatal period The period from conception to birth, usually encompassing nine months of pregnancy. (491)

Preparedness A species-specific predisposition to be conditioned in certain ways and not others. (279)

Pressure Expectations or demands that one behave in a certain way. (602)

Prevalence The percentage of a population that exhibits a disorder during a specified time period. (646)

Primary appraisal Initial evaluation of whether an event is (1) irrelevant to you, (2) relevant but not threatening, or (3) stressful. (598)

Primary reinforcers Events that are inherently reinforcing because they satisfy biological needs. (269)

Primary sex characteristics The sexual structures necessary for reproduction. (517)

Proactive interference A memory problem that occurs when previously learned information interferes with the retention of new information. (324)

Problem solving Active efforts to discover what must be done to achieve a goal that is not readily available. (365)

Problem space The set of possible pathways to a solution considered by the problem solver. (368)

Procedural memory system The repository of memories for actions, skills, and operations. (334)

Prognosis A forecast about the probable course of an illness. (642)

Projection Attributing one's own thoughts, feelings, or motives to another. (554)

Projective tests Psychological tests that ask subjects to respond to vague, ambiguous stimuli in ways that may reveal the subjects' needs, feelings, and personality traits. (588)

Prosopagnosia Inability to recognize familiar faces. (152)

Prospective memory The ability to remember to perform actions in the future. (338)

Proximal stimuli The stimulus energies that impinge directly on sensory receptors. (162)

Proximodistal trend The centre-outward direction of motor development. (497)

Psychiatrists Physicians who specialize in the diagnosis and treatment of psychological disorders. (698)

Psychiatry A branch of medicine concerned with the diagnosis and treatment of psychological problems and disorders. (26)

Psychoactive drugs Chemical substances that modify mental, emotional, or behavioural functioning. (231)

Psychoanalysis An insight therapy that emphasizes the recovery of unconscious conflicts, motives, and defences through techniques such as free association and transference. (700)

Psychoanalytic theory A theory developed by Freud that attempts to explain personality, motivation, and mental disorders by focusing on unconscious determinants of behaviour. (9)

Psychodynamic theories All the diverse theories descended from the work of Sigmund Freud that focus on unconscious mental forces. (551)

Psychological dependence The condition that exists when a person must continue to take a drug in order to satisfy intense mental and emotional craving for the drug. (236)

Psychological test A standardized measure of a sample of a person's behaviour. (395)

Psychology The science that studies behaviour and the physiological and cognitive processes that underlie it, and the profession that applies the accumulated knowledge of this science to practical problems. (23)

Psychopharmacotherapy The treatment of mental disorders with medication. (716)

Psychophysics The study of how physical stimuli are translated into psychological experience. (139)

Psychosexual stages According to Freud, developmental periods with a characteristic sexual focus that leave their mark on adult personality. (556)

Psychosomatic diseases Physical ailments with a genuine organic basis that are caused in part by psychological factors, especially emotional distress. (616)

Puberty The period of early adolescence marked by rapid physical growth and the development of sexual (reproductive) maturity. (517)

Pubescence The two-year span preceding puberty during which the changes leading to physical and sexual maturity take place. (517)

Punishment An event that follows a response that weakens or suppresses the tendency to make that response. (274)

Pupil The opening in the centre of the iris that helps regulate the amount of light passing into the rear chamber of the eye. (144)

R

Random assignment The constitution of groups in a study such that all subjects have an equal chance of being assigned to any group or condition. (51)

Rational-emotive therapy An approach to therapy that focuses on altering clients' patterns of irrational thinking to reduce maladaptive emotions and behaviour. (630)

Rationalization Creating false but plausible excuses to justify unacceptable behaviour. (554)

Reaction formation Behaving in a way that's exactly the opposite of one's true feelings. (554)

Reaction range Genetically determined limits on IQ or other traits. (417)

Reality monitoring The process of deciding whether memories are based on external sources (our perceptions of actual events) or internal sources (our thoughts and imaginations). (319)

Reality principle According to Freud, the principle on which the ego operates, which seeks to delay gratification of the id's urges until appropriate outlets and situations can be found. (551)

Recall A memory test that requires subjects to reproduce information on their own without any cues. (322)

Receiver The person to whom a message is sent. (762)

Receptive field of a visual cell The retinal area that, when stimulated, affects the firing of that cell. (148)

Recessive gene A gene whose influence is masked when paired genes are different (heterozygous). (119)

Reciprocal determinism The assumption that internal mental events, external environmental events, and overt behaviour all influence each other. (563)

Reciprocity norm The rule that people should pay back in kind what they receive from others. (787)

Recognition A memory test that requires subjects to select previously learned information from an array of options. (322)

Refractory period A time following orgasm during which males are largely unresponsive to further stimulation. (88)

Regression A reversion to immature patterns of behaviour. (555)

Regression toward the mean Effect that occurs when people who score extremely high or low on some trait are measured a second time and their new score falls closer to the mean (average). (736)

Rehearsal The process of repetitively verbalizing or thinking about information to be stored in memory. (308)

Reification Giving an abstract concept a name and then treating it as though it were a concrete, tangible object. (434)

Reinforcement An event following a response that strengthens the tendency to make that response. (264)

Reinforcement contingencies The circumstances or rules that determine whether responses lead to the presentation of reinforcers. (264)

Relearning A memory test that requires a subject to memorize information a second time to determine how much time or effort is saved by having learned it before. (322)

Reliability The measurement consistency of a test (or of other kinds of measurement techniques). (396)

REM sleep A deep stage of sleep marked by rapid eye movements, high-frequency brain waves, and dreaming. (210)

REM sleep behaviour disorder Sleep disorder marked by potentially troublesome dream enactments during REM periods. (220)

Renewal effect Phenomenon that occurs if a response is extinguished in a different environment than it was acquired; the extinguished response will reappear if the animal is returned to the original environment where acquisition took place. (259)

Replication The repetition of a study to see whether the earlier results are duplicated. (65)

Representativeness heuristic Basing the estimated probability of an event on how similar it is to the typical prototype of that event. (378)

Repression Keeping distressing thoughts and feelings buried in the unconscious. (325)

Research methods Differing approaches to the manipulation and control of variables in empirical studies. (49)

Resilience Successful adaptation to significant stress and trauma, as evidenced by a lack of serious negative outcomes. (615)

Resistance Largely unconscious defensive manoeuvres a client uses to hinder the progress of therapy. (701)

Resistance to extinction In operant conditioning, the phenomenon that occurs when an organism continues to make a response after delivery of the reinforcer for it has been terminated. (266)

Response set A tendency to respond to questions in a particular way that is unrelated to the content of the questions. (69)

Resting potential The stable, negative charge of a neuron when it is inactive. (88)

Retention The proportion of material retained (remembered). (322)

Retina The neural tissue lining the inside back surface of the eye; it absorbs light, processes images, and sends visual information to the brain. (146)

Retinal disparity A cue to depth based on the fact that objects project images to slightly different locations on the right and left retinas, so the right and left eyes see slightly different views of the object. (163)

Retrieval Recovering information from memory stores. (302)

Retroactive interference A memory problem that occurs when new information impairs the retention of previously learned information. (323)

Retrograde amnesia Loss of memories for events that occurred prior to a head injury. (331)

Retrospective memory The ability to remember events from the past or previously learned information. (338)

Reuptake A process in which neurotransmitters are sponged up from the synaptic cleft by the presynaptic membrane. (90)

Reversible figure A drawing that is compatible with two different interpretations that can shift back and forth. (158)

Risky decision making Making choices under conditions of uncertainty. (376)

Rods Specialized visual receptors that play a key role in night vision and peripheral vision. (147)

S

Saccades Eye movements made when your eyes are scanning the visual environment and making brief fixations at various parts of the stimuli. (145)

Sample The collection of subjects selected for observation in an empirical study. (66)

Sampling bias A problem that occurs when a sample is not representative of the population from which it is drawn. (67)

Scaffolding Occurs when the assistance provided to a child is adjusted as learning progresses. (511)

Scatter diagram A graph in which paired X and Y scores for each subject are plotted as single points. (A-10)

Schedule of reinforcement A specific presentation of reinforcers over time. (270)

Schema An organized cluster of knowledge about a particular object or sequence of events. (314)

Schizophrenic disorders A class of psychological disorders marked by disturbances in thought that spill over to affect perceptual, social, and emotional processes. (668)

Seasonal affective disorder A type of depression that follows a seasonal pattern. (659)

Secondary appraisal Evaluation of your coping resources and options for dealing with stress. (598)

Secondary (conditioned) reinforcers Stimulus events that acquire reinforcing qualities by being associated with primary reinforcers. (269)

Secondary sex characteristics Physical features that are associated with gender but that are not directly involved in reproduction. (517)

Sedatives Sleep-inducing drugs that tend to decrease central nervous system activation and behavioural activity. (232)

Self-actualizing persons People with exceptionally healthy personalities, marked by continued personal growth. (571)

Self-concept A collection of beliefs about one's own nature, unique qualities, and typical behaviour. (566)

Self-efficacy One's belief about one's ability to perform behaviours that should lead to expected outcomes. (564)

Self-enhancement Focusing on positive feedback from others, exaggerating one's strengths, and seeing oneself as above average. (584)

Self-referent encoding Deciding how or whether information is personally relevant. (306)

Self-report inventories Personality tests that ask individuals to answer a series of questions about their characteristic behaviour. (586)

Self-serving bias The tendency to attribute one's successes to personal factors and one's failures to situational factors. (751)

Semantic memory system General knowledge that is not tied to the time when the information was learned. (336)

Semantic network Concepts joined together by links that show how the concepts are related. (314)

Semantics The area of language concerned with understanding the meaning of words and word combinations. (351)

Sensation The stimulation of sense organs. (138)

Sensory adaptation A gradual decline in sensitivity to prolonged stimulation. (142)

Sensory memory The preservation of information in its original sensory form for a brief time, usually only a fraction of a second. (307)

Separation anxiety Emotional distress seen in many infants when they are separated from people with whom they have formed an attachment. (500)

Serial-position effect In memory tests, the fact that subjects show better recall for items at the beginning and end of a list than for items in the middle. (340)

Set-point theory The idea that the body monitors fat-cell levels to keep them (and weight) fairly stable. (450)

Settling-point theory The idea that weight tends to drift around a level at which the constellation of factors that determine food consumption and energy expenditure achieve an equilibrium. (450)

Sex The biologically based categories of male and female. (537)

Sexual orientation A person's preference for emotional and sexual relationships with individuals of the same sex, the other sex, or either sex. (460)

Shaping The reinforcement of closer and closer approximations of a desired response. (266)

Short-term memory (STM) A limited-capacity store that can maintain unrehearsed information for about 20 to 30 seconds. (308)

Signal-detection theory A psychophysiological theory proposing that the detection of stimuli involves decision processes as well as sensory processes, which are influenced by a variety of factors besides the physical intensity of a stimulus. (140)

Skinner box A small enclosure in which an animal can make a specific response that is systematically recorded while the consequences of the response are controlled. (264)

Sleep apnea A sleep disorder characterized by frequent reflexive gasping for air that awakens a person and disrupts sleep. (219)

Slow-wave sleep (SWS) Sleep stages 3 and 4, during which low-frequency delta waves become prominent in EEG recordings. (209)

Social desirability bias A tendency to give socially approved answers to questions about oneself. (68)

Socialization The acquisition of the norms, roles, and behaviours expected of people in a particular society. (540)

Social loafing A reduction in effort by individuals when they work in groups as compared to when they work by themselves. (776)

Social neuroscience An approach to research and theory in social psychology that integrates models of neuroscience and social psychology to study the mechanisms of social behaviour. (779)

Social psychology The branch of psychology concerned with the way individuals' thoughts, feelings, and behaviours are influenced by others. (742)

Social roles Widely shared expectations about how people in certain positions are supposed to behave. (768)

Social schemas Organized clusters of ideas about categories of social events and people. (744)

Social skills training A behaviour therapy designed to improve interpersonal skills that emphasizes shaping, modelling, and behavioural rehearsal. (712)

Social support Various types of aid and succour provided by members of one's social networks. (621)

Soma The cell body of a neuron; it contains the nucleus and much of the chemical machinery common to most cells. (87)

Somatic nervous system The system of nerves that connect to voluntary skeletal muscles and to sensory receptors. (96)

Somnambulism (sleepwalking) Arising and wandering about while remaining asleep. (220)

Source The person who sends a communication. (762)

Source monitoring The process of making attributions about the origins of memories. (320)

Source-monitoring error An error that occurs when a memory derived from one source is misattributed to another source. (320)

Split-brain surgery A procedure in which the bundle of fibres that connects the cerebral hemispheres (the corpus callosum) is cut to reduce the severity of epileptic seizures. (113)

Spontaneous recovery In classical conditioning, the reappearance of an extinguished response after a period of nonexposure to the conditioned stimulus. (259)

Spontaneous remission Recovery from a disorder without formal treatment. (708)

SQ3R A study system designed to promote effective reading by means of five steps: survey, question, read, recite, and review. (35)

Stage A developmental period during which characteristic patterns of behaviour are exhibited and certain capacities become established. (503)

Standard deviation An index of the amount of variability in a set of data. (A-8)

Standardization The uniform procedures used in the administration and scoring of a test. (396)

Statistical significance The condition that exists when the probability that the observed findings are due to chance is very low. (A-13)

Statistics The use of mathematics to organize, summarize, and interpret numerical data. See also *Descriptive statistics, Inferential statistics*. (A-7)

Stereotypes Widely held beliefs that people have certain characteristics because of their membership in a particular group. (745)

Stimulants Drugs that tend to increase central nervous system activation and behavioural activity. (232)

Stimulus Any detectable input from an environment. (7)

Stimulus discrimination The phenomenon that occurs when an organism that has learned a response to a specific stimulus does not respond in the same way to stimuli that are similar to the original stimulus. (260)

Stimulus generalization The phenomenon that occurs when an organism that has learned a response to a specific stimulus responds in the same way to new stimuli that are similar to the original stimulus. (259)

Storage Maintaining encoded information in memory over time. (302)

Strange situation procedure Procedure in which infants are exposed to a series of eight separation and reunion episodes to assess the quality of their attachment. (501)

Stress Any circumstances that threaten or are perceived to threaten one's well-being and that thereby tax one's coping abilities. (597)

Striving for superiority According to Adler, the universal drive to adapt, improve oneself, and master life's challenges. (559)

Structuralism A school of psychology based on the notion that the task of psychology is to analyze consciousness into its basic elements and to investigate how these elements are related. (6)

Subjective contours The perception of contours where none actually exist. (160)

Subjective well-being Individuals' perceptions of their overall happiness and life satisfaction. (480)

Subjects The persons or animals whose behaviour is systematically observed in a study. (46)

Sublimation Defence mechanism in which unconscious, unacceptable impulses are channelled into socially acceptable, perhaps even admirable, behaviours. (555)

Subliminal perception The registration of sensory input without conscious awareness. (141)

Subtractive colour mixing Formation of colours by removing some wavelengths of light, leaving less light than was originally there. (153)

Superego According to Freud, the moral component of personality that incorporates social standards about what represents right and wrong. (552)

Survey A descriptive research method in which researchers use questionnaires or interviews to gather information about specific aspects of subjects' behaviour. (56)

Sympathetic division The branch of the autonomic nervous system that mobilizes the body's resources for emergencies. (97)

Synapse A junction where information is transmitted from one neuron to the next. (87)

Synaptic cleft A microscopic gap between the terminal button of a neuron and the cell membrane of another neuron. (89)

Syntax A system of rules that specify how words can be combined into phrases and sentences. (351)

Systematic desensitization A behaviour therapy used to reduce clients' anxiety responses through counterconditioning. (710)

T

Tardive dyskinesia A neurological disorder marked by chronic tremors and involuntary spastic movements. (718)

Telegraphic speech Speech that consists mainly of content words; articles, prepositions, and other less critical words are omitted. (356)

Temperament An individual's characteristic mood, activity level, and emotional reactivity. (497)

Teratogens Any external agents, such as drugs or viruses, that can harm an embryo or fetus. (493)

Terminal buttons Small knobs at the end of axons that secrete chemicals called *neurotransmitters*. (87)

Terror management theory Concerns the psychological consequences of the "juxtaposition of a biologically rooted desire for life with the awareness of the inevitability of death." (580)

Test norms Standards that provide information about where a score on a psychological test ranks in relation to other scores on that test. (396)

Testwiseness The ability to use the characteristics and format of a cognitive test to maximize one's score. (36)

Thalamus A structure in the forebrain through which all sensory information (except smell) must pass to get to the cerebral cortex. (107)

Theory A system of interrelated ideas that is used to explain a set of observations. (28)

Theory of bounded rationality Simon's assertion that people tend to use simple strategies in decision making that focus on only a few facets of available options and often result in "irrational" decisions that are less than optimal. (380)

Threshold A dividing point between energy levels that do and do not have a detectable effect. (139)

Tip-of-the-tongue phenomenon A temporary inability to remember something, accompanied by a feeling that it's just out of reach. (316)

Token economy A system for doling out symbolic reinforcers that are exchanged later for a variety of genuine reinforcers. (294)

Tolerance A progressive decrease in a person's responsiveness to a drug. (234)

Top-down processing In form perception, a progression from the whole to the elements. (160)

Transcranial magnetic stimulation (TMS) A technique that permits scientists to temporarily enhance or depress activity in a specific area of the brain. (722)

Transfer-appropriate processing The situation that occurs when the initial processing of information is similar to the type of processing required by the subsequent measures of attention. (324)

Transference In therapy, the phenomenon that occurs when clients start relating to their therapists in ways that mimic critical relationships in their lives. (701)

Trial In classical conditioning, any presentation of a stimulus or pair of stimuli. (254)

Trial and error Trying possible solutions sequentially and discarding those that are in error until one works. (368)

Trichromatic theory The theory of colour vision holding that the human eye has three types of receptors with differing sensitivities to different wavelengths. (154)

Twin studies A research design in which hereditary influence is assessed by comparing the resemblance of identical twins and fraternal twins with respect to a trait. (121)

Type A personality Personality characterized by (1) a strong competitive orientation, (2) impatience and time urgency, and (3) anger and hostility. (616)

Type B personality Personality characterized by relatively relaxed, patient, easygoing, amicable behaviour. (616)

U

Unconditioned response (UCR) An unlearned reaction to an unconditioned stimulus that occurs without previous conditioning. (253)

Unconditioned stimulus (UCS) A stimulus that evokes an unconditioned response without previous conditioning. (253)

Unconscious According to Freud, thoughts, memories, and desires that are well below the surface of conscious awareness but that nonetheless exert great influence on behaviour. (9, 552)

Underextensions Errors that occur when a child incorrectly uses a word to describe a narrower set of objects or actions than it is meant to. (356)

Undifferentiated schizophrenia A type of schizophrenia marked by idiosyncratic mixtures of schizophrenic symptoms. (671)

V

Validity The ability of a test to measure what it was designed to measure. (397)

Variability The extent to which the scores in a data set tend to vary from each other and from the mean. (A-8)

Variable-interval (VI) schedule A reinforcement schedule in which the reinforcer is given for the first response after a variable time interval has elapsed. (271)

Variable-ratio (VR) schedule A reinforcement schedule in which the reinforcer is given after a variable number of nonreinforced responses. (271)

Variables Any measurable conditions, events, characteristics, or behaviours that are controlled or observed in a study. (44)

Vasocongestion Engorgement of blood vessels. (453)

Vestibular system The sensory system that responds to gravity and keeps people informed of their body's location in space. (184)

Visual agnosia An inability to recognize objects. (152)

W

Weber's law The theory stating that the size of a just noticeable difference is a constant proportion of the size of the initial stimulus. (140)

Working memory capacity (WMC) One's ability to hold and manipulate information in conscious attention. (311)

Working memory Limited memory storage system that temporarily maintains and stores information; provides an interface between perception, memory, and action. (310)

Z

Zone of proximal development (ZPD) The gap between what a learner can accomplish alone and what he or she can achieve with guidance from more skilled partners. (511)

Zygote A one-celled organism formed by the union of a sperm and an egg. (118)

Abbott, A. (2004). Striking back. *Nature, 429*, 338–339. Retrieved February 11, 2008, from http://www.nature.com/nature/journal/v429/n6990/full/429338a.html.

Abe, T., Komada, Y., Nishida, Y., Hayashida, K., & Inoue, Y. (2010). Short sleep duration and long spells of driving are associated with the occurrence of Japanese drivers' rear-end collisions and single-car accidents. *Journal of Sleep Research, 19*(2), 310–316.

Abel, E. L., & Kruger, M. L. (2010). Smile intensity in photographs predicts longevity. *Psychological Science, 21*(4), 542–544.

Abel, M. H. (1998). Interaction of humor and gender in moderating relationships between stress and outcomes. *Journal of Psychology, 132*, 267–276.

Abi-Dargham, A., Gil, R., Krystal, J., Baldwin, R. M., Seibyl, J. P., Bowers, M., et al. (1998). Increased striatal dopamine transmission in schizophrenia: Confirmation in a second cohort. *American Journal of Psychiatry, 155*, 761–767.

Aboud, F. E., & Amato, M. (2001). Developmental and socialization influences on intergroup bias. In R. Brown & S. L. Gaertner (Eds.), *Blackwell handbook of social psychology: Intergroup processes*. Malden, MA: Blackwell.

Abraham, C. (2002). Possessing genius: *The true account of the bizarre odyssey of Einstein's brain*. New York: St. Martin's Press.

Abraham, C. (2010, July 2). An age-old puzzle solved: Who will live to be 100. *Toronto Star*, p. A1.

Abraham, W. C. (2006). Memory maintenance. *Current Directions in Psychological Science, 15*(1), 5–8.

Abramowitz, A. J., & O'Leary, S. G. (1990). Effectiveness of delayed punishment in an applied setting. *Behavior Therapy, 21*, 231–239.

Abrams, D., & Hogg, M. A. (2010). Social identity and self-categorization. In J. F. Dovidio, M. Hewstone, P. Glick, & V. M. Esses (Eds.), *The Sage handbook of prejudice, stereotyping, and discrimination*. Los Angeles, CA: Sage.

Abrams, R. L., Klinger, M. R., & Greenwald, A. G. (2002). Subliminal words activate semantic categories (not automated motor responses). *Psychonomic Bulletin & Review, 9*(1), 100–106.

Abramson, L. Y., Alloy, L. B., & Metalsky, J. I. (1995). Hopelessness depression. In J. N. Buchanan & M. E. P. Seligman (Eds.), *Explanatory style*. Hillsdale, NJ: Erlbaum.

Abramson, L. Y., Seligman, M. E. P., & Teasdale, J. (1978). Learned helplessness in humans: Critique and reformulation. *Journal of Abnormal Psychology, 87*, 32–48.

Acker, F. (2008). New findings on unconscious versus conscious thought in decision making: Additional empirical data and meta-analysis. *Judgment and Decision Making, 3*, 292–303.

Acker, M. M., & O'Leary, S. G. (1996). Inconsistency of mothers' feedback and toddlers' misbehavior and negative affect. *Journal of Abnormal Child Psychology, 24*, 703–714.

Ackerknecht, E. H. (1968). *A short history of psychiatry*. New York: Hafner Publishing Company.

Ackerman, P. L., & Beier, M. E. (2005). Knowledge and intelligence. In O. Wilhelm & R. W. Engle (Eds.), *Handbook of understanding and measuring intelligence*. Thousand Oaks, CA: Sage.

Adair, J. G. (2001). Ethics of psychological research: New policies; continuing issues; new concerns. *Canadian Psychology, 42*, 25–35.

Adam, T. C., & Epel, E. (2007). Stress, eating and the reward system. *Physiology and Behavior, 91*, 449–458.

Adams, G. A., & Rau, B. L. (2011). Putting off tomorrow to do what you want today: Planning for retirement. *American Psychologist, 66*, 180–192.

Adams, J. L. (1980). *Conceptual blockbusting*. San Francisco: W. H. Freeman.

Adams, R. L., & Culbertson, J. L. (2005). Personality assessment: Adults and children. In B. J. Sadock & V. A. Sadock (Eds.), *Kaplan & Sadock's comprehensive textbook of psychiatry*. Philadelphia: Lippincott Williams & Wilkins.

Adams, S. J., Pitre, N. L., & Smith, A. (2001). Criminal harassment by patients with mental disorders. *Canadian Journal of Psychiatry, 46*, 173–176.

Addis, D. R., Wong, A. T., & Schacter, D. L. (2007). Remembering the past and imagining the future: Common and distinct neural substrates during event construction and elaboration. *Neuropsychologia, 45*, 1363–1377.

Addis, D. R., Wong, A. T., & Schacter, D. L. (2008). Age-related changes in the episodic simulation of future events. *Psychological Science, 19*, 33–41.

Ader, R. (2001). Psychoneuroimmunology. *Current Directions in Psychological Science, 10*(3), 94–98.

Ader, R. (2003). Conditioned immunomodulation: Research needs and directions. *Brain, Behavior, and Immunity, 17*(1), S51–S57.

Ader, R., & Cohen, N. (1984). Behavior and the immune system. In W. D. Gentry (Ed.), *Handbook of behavioral medicine*. New York: Guilford.

Ader, R., & Cohen, N. (1993). Psychoneuroimmunology: Conditioning and stress. *Annual Review of Psychology, 44*, 53–85.

Adesope, O. O., Lavin, T., Thompson, T., & Ungerleider, C. (2010). A systematic review and meta-analysis of the cognitive correlates of bilingualism. *Review of Educational Research, 80*(2), 207–245.

Adlaf, E. M., Demers, A., & Gliksman, L. (Eds.). (2005). 2004 Canadian campus survey. Toronto: Centre for Addiction and Mental Health.

Adler, A. (1917). *Study of organ inferiority and its psychical compensation*. New York: Nervous and Mental Diseases Publishing Co.

Adler, A. (1927). *Practice and theory of individual psychology*. New York: Harcourt, Brace & World.

Adler, L. L. (Ed.). (1993). *International handbook on gender roles*. Westport, CT: Greenwood.

Adolph, K. E., & Berger, S. E. (2005). Physical and motor development. In M. H. Bornstein & M. E. Lamb (Eds.), *Developmental science: An advanced textbook*. Mahwah, NJ: Erlbaum.

Adolph, K. E., & Berger, S. E. (2011). Physical and motor development. In M. H. Bornstein & M. E. Lamb (Eds.), *Developmental science: An advanced textbook* (pp. 109–198). New York, NY: Psychology Press.

Adolph, K. E., Karasik, L. B., & Tamis-Lemonda, C. S. (2010). Motor skills. In M. H. Bornstein (Ed.), *Handbook of cultural developmental science* (pp. 61–88). New York, NY: Psychology Press.

Affleck, G., Tennen, H., Urrows, S., & Higgins, P. (1994). Person and contextual features of daily stress reactivity: Individual differences in relations of undesirable daily events with mood disturbance and chronic pain intensity. *Journal of Personality and Social Psychology, 66*, 329–340.

Agarwal, P. K., Karpicke, J. D., Kang, S. K., Roediger, H., & McDermott, K. B. (2008). Examining the testing effect with open- and closed-book tests. *Applied Cognitive Psychology, 22*(7), 861–876.

Aggressive girls: Overview paper. (n.d.). Public Health Agency of Canada. Retrieved March 27, 2008, from http://www.phac-aspc.gc.ca/ncfv-cnivf/familyviolence/html/nfntsaggsr_e.html.

Agostino, A., Johnson, J., & Pascual-Leone, J. (2010). Executive functions underlying multiplicative reasoning: Problem type matters. *Journal of Experimental Child Psychology, 105*, 286–305.

Ahima, R. S., & Osei, S. Y. (2004). Leptin signaling. *Physiology & Behavior, 81*, 223–241.

Ahlgren, M., Wohlfahrt, J., Olsen, L. W., Sorensen, T. L., & Melbye, M. (2007). Birth weight and risk of cancer. *Cancer, 110*(2), 412–419.

Aiken, L. S., West, S. G., & Millsap, R. E. (2009). Improving training in methodology enriches the science of psychology. *American Psychologist, 64*, 5–56.

Aikins, D. E., & Craske, M. G. (2001). Cognitive theories of generalized anxiety disorder. *Psychiatric Clinics of North America, 24*(1), 57–74.

Ainslie, G. (2007). Foresight has to pay off in the present moment. *Behavioral and Brain Sciences, 30*, 313–314.

Ainsworth, M. D. S. (1979). Attachment as related to mother–infant interaction. In J. S. Rosenblatt, R. A. Hinde, C. Beer, & M. Busnel (Eds.), *Advances in the study of behavior* (Vol. 9). New York: Academic Press.

Ainsworth, M. D. S., Blehar, M. C., Waters, E., & Wall, S. (1978). *Patterns of attachment: A psychological study of the strange situation*. Hillsdale, NJ: Erlbaum.

Ajzen, I., & Fishbein, M. (2000). Attitudes and the attitude–behavior relation: Reasoned and automatic processes. In W. Stroebe & M. Hewstone (Eds.), *European review of social psychology* (Vol. 11). Chichester, UK: Wiley.

Ajzen, I., & Fishbein, M. (2005). The influence of attitudes on behavior. In D. Albarracin, B. T. Johnson, & M. P. Zanna (Eds.), *The handbook of attitudes*. Mahwah, NJ: Erlbaum.

Akerstedt, T., Hume, K., Minors, D., & Waterhouse, J. (1997). Good sleep—its timing and physiological sleep characteristics. *Journal of Sleep Research, 6*, 221–229.

Akgun, S., & Ciarrochi, J. (2003). Learned resourcefulness moderates the relationship between academic stress and academic performance. *Educational Psychology, 23*, 287–294.

Akimoto, S. A., & Sanbonmatsu, D. M. (1999). Differences in self-effacing behavior between European and Japanese Americans: Effect on competence evaluations. *Journal of Cross-Cultural Psychology, 30*, 159–177.

Akiskal, H. S. (2000). Mood disorders: Clinical features. In B. J. Sadock & V. A. Sadock (Eds.), *Kaplan and Sadock's comprehensive textbook of psychiatry*

(7th ed., Vol. 1, pp. 1338–1376). Philadelphia: Lippincott, Williams & Wilkins.

Akiskal, H. S. (2009). Mood disorders: Clinical features. In B. J. Sadock, V. A. Sadock, & P. Ruiz (Eds.), *Kaplan & Sadock's comprehensive textbook of psychiatry* (9th ed., pp. 1693–1733). Philadelphia, PA: Lippincott, Williams & Wilkins.

Albarracin, D., & Vargas, P. (2010). Attitudes and persuasion: From biology to social responses to persuasive intent. In S. T. Fiske, D. T. Gilbert, G. Lindzey, & S. T. Fiske (Eds.), *Handbook of social psychology,* (5th ed., Vol. 1) (pp. 353–393). Hoboken, NJ: Wiley.

Albert, M. A. (2008). Neuropsychology of the development of Alzheimer's disease. In F. I. M. Craik & T. A. Salthouse (Eds.), *Handbook of aging and cognition* (2nd ed., pp. 97–132). New York, NY: Psychology Press.

Albert, M. S., & Killiany, R. J. (2001). Age-related cognitive change and brain–behavior relationships. In J. E. Birren & K. W. Schaie (Eds.), *Handbook of the psychology of aging* (5th ed., pp. 160–184). San Diego, CA: Academic Press.

Albert, M. S., & Moss, M. B. (2002). Neuropsychological approaches to preclinical indentification of Alzheimer's disease. In L. R. Squire & D. L. Schacter (Eds.), *Neuropsychology of memory.* New York: Guilford.

Alcock, J. (1998). *Animal behavior: An evolutionary approach.* Sunderland, MA: Sinauer Associates.

Aldag, R. J., & Fuller, S. R. (1993). Beyond fiasco: A reappraisal of the groupthink phenomenon and a new model of group decision processes. *Psychological Bulletin, 113,* 533–552.

Aldington, S., Williams, M., Nowitz, M., Weatherall, M., Pritchard, A., McNaughton, A., et al. (2007). Effects of cannabis on pulmonary structure, function and symptoms. *Thorax, 62,* 1058–1063.

Aldrich, M. S. (2000). Cardinal manifestations of sleep disorders. In M. H. Kryger, T. Roth & W. C. Dement (Eds.), *Principles and practice of sleep medicine.* Philadelphia: Saunders.

Aldwin, C. M. (2007). *Stress, coping, and development: An integrative perspective* (2nd ed.). New York, NY: Guilford Press.

Aldwin, C. M., & Gilmer, D. F. (2004). Health, illness, and optimal aging: Biological and psychosocial perspectives. Thousand Oaks, CA: Sage Publications.

Alexander, C. N., Davies, J. L., Dixon, C. A., Dillbeck, M. C., Druker, S. M., Oetzel, R. M., et al. (1990). Growth of higher states of consciousness: The Vedic psychology of human development. In C. N. Alexander & E. J. Langer (Eds.), *Higher stages of human development: Perspectives on adult growth.* New York: Oxford University Press.

Alexander, C. N., Robinson, P., Orme-Johnson, D. W., Schneider, R. H., & Walton, K. G. (1994). The effects of transcendental meditation compared with other methods of relaxation and meditation in reducing risk factors, morbidity, and mortality. *Homeostasis in Health and Disease, 35,* 243–263.

Alexander, F. (1954). Psychoanalysis and psychotherapy. *Journal of the American Psychoanalytic Association, 2,* 722–733.

Alexander, F. G., & Selesnick, S. T. (1966). The history of psychiatry: An evaluation of psychiatric thought and practice from prehistoric times to the present. New York: Harper and Row.

Alexander, J., & Tate, M. (1999). Web wisdom: How to evaluate and create information quality on the web. Mahwah, NJ: Erlbaum.

Alexander, M. G., & Fisher, T. D. (2003). Truth and consequences: Using the bogus pipeline to examine sex differences in self-reported sexuality. *Journal of Sex Research, 40*(1), 27–35.

Allan, R. W. (1998). Operant–respondent interactions. In W. O'Donohue (Ed.), *Learning and behavior therapy.* Boston: Allyn & Bacon.

Allen, M. J., Noel, R., Degan, J., Halpern, D. F., & Crawford, C. (2000). Goals and objectives for the undergraduate psychology major: Recommendations from a meeting of the California State University psychology faculty. Distributed by the Office of Teaching Resources in Psychology, Society for the Teaching of Psychology, http://www.lemoyne.edu/OTRP/otrpresources/otrpoutcomes.html.

Allen, M., Emmers, T., Gebhardt, L., & Giery, M. A. (1995). Exposure to pornography and acceptance of rape myths. *Journal of Communication, 45,* 5–26.

Allgood, W. P., Risko, V. J., Alvarez, M. C., & Fairbanks, M. M. (2000). Factors that influence study. In R. F. Flippo & D. C. Caverly (Eds.), *Handbook of college reading and study strategy research.* Mahwah, NJ: Erlbaum.

Allik, J., et al. (2010). How people see others is different from how people see themselves: A replicable pattern across cultures. *Journal of Personality and Social Psychology, 99,* 870–882.

Allison, D. B., Fontaine, K. R., Manson, J. E., Stevens, J., & VanItallie, T. B. (1999). Annual deaths attributable to obesity in the United States. *Journal of the American Medical Association, 282,* 1530–1538.

Allison, D. B., Heshka, S., Neale, M. C., Lykken, D. T., & Heymsfield, S. B. (1994). A genetic analysis of relative weight among 4,020 twin pairs, with an emphasis on sex effects. *Health Psychology, 13,* 362–365.

Alloy, L. B., Abramson, L. Y., Whitehouse, W. G., Hogan, M. E., Tashman, N. A., Steinberg, D. L., et al. (1999). Depressogenic cognitive styles: Predictive validity, information processing and personality characteristics, and developmental origins. *Behavioral Research and Therapy, 37,* 503–531.

Allport, G. W. (1937). Personality: A psychological interpretation. New York: Holt.

Altman, I. (1990). Centripetal and centrifugal trends in psychology. In L. Brickman & H. Ellis (Eds.), *Preparing psychologists for the 21st century: Proceedings of the National Conference on Graduate Education in Psychology.* Hillsdale, NJ: Erlbaum.

Alvarez, P., & Squire, L. (1994). Memory consolidation and the medial temporal lobe: A simple network model. *Proceedings of the National Academy of Sciences, USA, 91,* 7041–7045.

Amabile, T. M. (1996). *Creativity in context.* Boulder, CO: Westview.

Amabile, T. M. (2001). Beyond talent: John Irving and the passionate craft of creativity. *American Psychologist, 56,* 333–336.

Amato, P. R. (2006). Marital discord, divorce, and children's well-being: Results from a 20-year longitudinal study of two generations. In A. Clarke-Stewart & J. Dunn (Eds.), *Families count: Effects on child and adolescent development* (pp. 179–202). New York, NY: Cambridge University Press.

Amato, P. R., & Dorius, C. (2010). Fathers, children, and divorce. In M. Lamb (Ed.), *The role of the father in child development* (5th ed., pp. 177–200). Hoboken, NJ: Wiley.

Ambady, N., & Rosenthal, R. (1993). Half a minute: Predicting teacher evaluations from thin slices of nonverbal behavior and physical attractiveness. *Journal of Personality and Social Psychology, 64*(3), 431–441.

Ambady, N., & Weisbuch, M. (2010). Nonverbal behavior. In S. T. Fiske, D. T. Gilbert, & G. Lindzey (Eds.), *Handbook of social psychology* (5th ed., Vol. 1) (pp. 353–393). Hoboken, NJ: Wiley.

Ambady, N., Hallahan, M., & Conner, B. (1999). Accuracy of judgments of sexual orientation from thin slices of behavior. *Journal of Personality and Social Psychology, 77*(3), 538–547.

Amedi, A., Floel, A., Knecht, S., Zohary, E., & Cohen, L. G. (2004). Transcranial magnetic stimulation of the occipital pole interferes with verbal processing in blind subjects. *Nature Neuroscience, 7,* 1266–1270.

American Association of Suicidology. (2007). *Understanding and helping the suicidal individual.* Retrieved April 12, 2007 from http://www.suicidology.org/associations/1045/files/Understanding.pdf.

American Foundation for Suicide Prevention. (2007). *When you fear someone may take their own life.* Retrieved April 12, 2007 from http://www.afsp.org/index.cfm?page_id=F2F25092-7E90-9BD4-C4658F1D2B5D19A0.

American Psychiatric Association. (1994). *Diagnostic and statistical manual of mental disorders* (4th ed.). Washington, DC: Author.

American Psychiatric Association. (2000). *Diagnostic and statistical manual of mental disorders* (4th ed. Text revision). Washington, DC: Author.

American Psychiatric Association. (2001). The practice of electroconvulsive therapy: A task force report. Retrieved May 2, 2011, from http://www.ect.org/resources/apatask.html.

American Psychological Association. (1998). Psychologists among Guggenheim winners. *APA Monitor, 29,* June 6, 1998. Retrieved May 13, 2005, from http://www.apa.org/monitor/jun98/gugg.html.

American Psychological Association. (2002). Ethical principles of psychologists and code of conduct. *American Psychologist, 57,* 1060–1073.

American Psychological Association. (2007). Guidelines for psychological practice with girls and women. *American Psychologist, 62,* 949–979.

Amir, Y. (1969). Contact hypothesis in ethnic relations. *Psychological Bulletin, 71,* 319–342.

Amodio, D. M. (2008). The social neuroscience of intergroup relations. *European Review of Social Psychology, 19,* 1–54.

Amodio, D. M., & Devine, P. G. (2006). Stereotyping and evaluation in implicit race bias: Evidence for independent constructs and unique effects on behavior. *Journal of Personality and Social Psychology, 91*(4), 652–661.

Amsterlaw, J., & Wellman, H. M. (2006). Theories of mind in transition: A microgenetic study of the development of false belief understanding. *Journal of Cognition and Development, 7*(2), 139–172.

Amyx, D., & Alford, B. L. (2005). The effects of salesperson need for achievement and sales manager leader reward behavior. *Journal of Personal Selling & Sales Management, 25*(4), 345–359

Anderson, A. E., & Yager, J. (2005). Eating disorders. In B. J. Sadock & V. A. Sadock (Eds.), *Kaplan & Sadock's comprehensive textbook of psychiatry.* Philadelphia: Lippincott Williams & Wilkins.

Anderson, B. (2003). Brain imaging and *g.* In H. Nyborg (Ed.), *The scientific study of general intelligence: Tribute to Arthur R. Jensen.* Oxford, UK: Pergamon.

Anderson, C. (2006, June 19). *Critical periods in development.* Paper presented at the annual meeting of the XVth Biannual International Conference on Infant Studies, Westin Miyako, Kyoto, Japan.

Anderson, C. A., Berkowitz, L., Donnerstein, E., Huesman, L. R., Johnson, J. D., Linz, D., et al. (2003). The influence of media violence on youth. *Psychological Science in the Public Interest, 4*(3), 81–110.

Anderson, C. A., Shibuya, A., Ihori, N., Swing, E. L., Bushman, B. J., Sakamoto, A., Rothstein, J. R., & Saleem, M. (2010) Violent video game effects on aggression: Empathy, and prosocial behavior in eastern and western countries: A meta-analytic review. *Psychological Bulletin, 136*, 151–173.

Anderson, E. A., Kohler, J. K., & Letiecq, B. L. (2002). Low-income fathers and "Responsible Fatherhood" programs: A qualitative investigation of participants' experiences. *Family Relations, 51*, 148–155.

Anderson, K. J. (1990). Arousal and the inverted-U hypothesis: A critique of Neiss's "reconceptualizing arousal." *Psychological Bulletin, 107*, 96–100.

Anderson, M. C., & Neely, J. H. (1996). Interference and inhibition in memory retrieval. In E. L. Bjork & R. A. Bjork (Eds.), *Memory*. San Diego: Academic Press.

Anderson, S. E., Dallal, G. E., & Must, A. (2003). Relative weight and race influence average age at menarche: Results from two nationally representative surveys of U.S. girls studied 25 years apart. *Pediatrics, 111*, 844–850.

Anderson-Fye, E. P., & Becker, A. E. (2004). Sociocultural aspects of eating disorders and obesity. In J. K. Thompson (Ed.), *Handbook of eating disorders and obesity*. New York: Wiley.

Andreasen, N. C. (1987). Creativity and mental illness: Prevalence rates in writers and their first-degree relatives. *American Journal of Psychiatry, 144*, 1288–1292.

Andreasen, N. C. (1990). Positive and negative symptoms: Historical and conceptual aspects. In N. C. Andreasen (Ed.), *Modern problems of pharmacopsychiatry: Positive and negative symptoms and syndromes*. Basel: Karger.

Andreasen, N. C. (1996). Creativity and mental illness: A conceptual and historical overview. In J. J. Schildkraut & A. Otero (Eds.), *Depression and the spiritual in modern art: Homage to Miro*. New York: Wiley.

Andreasen, N. C. (2005). *The creating brain: The neuroscience of genius*. New York, NY: Dana Press.

Andreasen, N. C. (2009). Schizophrenia: A conceptual history. In M. C. Gelder, N. C. Andreasen, J. J. López-Ibor, Jr., & J. R. Geddes (Eds.), *New Oxford textbook of psychiatry* (2nd ed., Vol. 1). New York, NY: Oxford University Press.

Andrews, G., Charney, D., Sirovatka, P., & Regier, D. (Eds.). (2009). *Stress-induced and fear circuitry disorders: Advancing the research agenda for DSM-V*. Arlington, VA: American Psychiatric Publishing.

Angell, M. (2000). Is academic medicine for sale? *New England Journal of Medicine, 342*, 1516–1518.

Angell, M. (2004). *The truth about the drug companies: How they deceive us and what to do about it*. New York: Random House.

Anglin, J. M. (1993). Vocabulary development: A morphological analysis. *Monographs of the Society for Research in Child Development, 58*.

Angrosino, M. V. (2007). *Naturalistic observation: Qualitative essentials*. Walnut Creek, CA: Left Coast Press.

Angst, J. (2009). Course and prognosis of mood disorders. In M. C. Gelder, N. C. Andreasen, J. J. López-Ibor, Jr., & J. R. Geddes (Eds.). *New Oxford textbook of psychiatry* (2nd ed., Vol. 1). New York, NY: Oxford University Press.

Anisman, H, & Merali, Z. (1999). Understanding stress: Characteristics and caveats. *Alcohol Research and Health, 23*, 241–249.

Ansbacher, H. (1970, February). Alfred Adler, individual psychology. *Psychology Today*, pp. 42–44, 66.

Anslem, A., Gauthier, N., Beanlands, R. S. B., & Haddad, H. (2008). Sleep apnea in chronic heart failure. *Current Opinion in Cardiology, 23*, 121–126.

Anthony, I. C., & Bell, J. E. (2008). The neuropathology of HIV/AIDS. *International Review of Psychiatry, 20*(1), 15–24.

Antonuccio, D. O., Danton, W. G., & McClanahan, T. M. (2003). Psychology in the prescription era: Building a firewall between marketing and science. *American Psychologist, 58*, 1028–1043.

Antony, M. M., & McCabe, R. E. (2003). Anxiety disorders: Social and specific phobias. In A. Tasman, J. Kay, & J. A. Lieberman (Eds.), *Psychiatry*. New York: Wiley.

Antony, M. M., & Rowa, K. (2008). Social anxiety disorder: Psychological approaches to assessment and treatment. Gottingen, Germany: Hogrefe.

Antony, M. M., & Stein, M. B. (2008). *Oxford handbook of anxiety and related disorders*. New York: Oxford University Press.

Antony, M. M., Purdon, C., & Summerfeldt, L. J. (Eds.). (2006) *Psychological treatment of OCD: Fundamentals and beyond*. Washington, DC: American Psychological Association Press.

Antrobus, J. (1993). Characteristics of dreams. In M. A. Carskadon (Ed.), *Encyclopedia of sleep and dreaming*. New York: Macmillan.

Antrobus, J. S., & Wamsley, E. J. (2009). REM/NREM differences in dream content. In R. Stickgold & M. P. Walker (Eds.), *The Neuroscience of sleep* (pp. 310–315). San Diego, CA: Academic Press.

Anwar, Y. (2007). Sleep loss linked to psychiatric disorders. *UC Berkeley News*. Retrieved from http://berkeley.edu/news/media/releases/2007/10/22_sleeploss.shtml.

Apkarian, A. V., Bushnell, M. C., Treede, R.-D., & Zubieta, J.-K. (2005). Human brain mechanisms of pain perception and regulation in health and disease. *European Journal of Pain, 9*, 463–484.

Appelbaum, P. S. (2002). Responses to the presidential debate—The systematic defunding of psychiatric care: A crisis at our doorstep. *American Journal of Psychiatry, 159*, 1638–1640.

Appelt, K. C., & Higgins, E. T. (2010). My way: How strategic preferences vary by negotiator role and regulatory focus. *Journal of Experimental Social Psychology, 46*(6), 1138–1142.

Appleby, T. (2005). Kingston police more likely to stop blacks, study finds. *Toronto Star*, May 27, p. A12.

Appleton, K. M., Gentry, R. C., & Shepherd, R. (2006). Evidence of a role for conditioning in the development of liking for flavors in humans in everyday life. *Physiology & Behavior, 87*, 478–486.

APS Observer. (2009). Memories of Robert Zajonc. Retrieved July 10, 2011, from http://www.psychologicalscience.org/observer/getArticle.cfm?id=2497.

Aquilino, W. S. (2006). Family relationships and support systems in emerging adulthood. In J. J. Arnett & J. L. Tanner (Eds.), *Emerging adults in America: Coming of age in the 21st century*. Washington, DC: American Psychological Association.

Arcelus, J., Whight, D., Langham, C., Baggott, J., McGrain, L., Meadows, L., & Meyer, C. (2009). A case series evaluation of the modified version of interpersonal psychotherapy (IPT) for the treatment of bulimic eating disorders: A pilot study. *European Eating Disorders Review, 17*(4), 260–268.

Archer, J. (1996). Sex differences in social behavior: Are the social role and evolutionary explanations compatible? *American Psychologist, 51*, 909–917.

Archer, J. (2005). Are women or men the more aggressive sex? In S. Fein, G. R. Goethals, & M. J. Sansdtrom (Eds.), *Gender and aggression: Interdisciplinary perspectives*. Mahwah, NJ: Erlbaum.

Archibald, A. B., Graber, J. A., & Brooks-Gunn, J. (2003). Pubertal processes and physiological growth in adolescence. In G. R. Adams & M. D. Berzonsky (Eds.), *Blackwell Handbook Of Adolescence*. Malden, MA: Blackwell Publishing.

Arden, R., Gottfredson, L. S., & Miller, G. (2009). Does a fitness factor contribute to the association betweenintelligence and health outcomes? Evidence from medical abnormality counts among 3654 U.S. veterans. *Intelligence, 37*(6), 581–591.

Arendt, J. (2009). Managing jet lag: Some of the problems and possible new solutions. *Sleep Medicine Reviews, 13*(4), 249–256.

Arendt, J. (2010). Shift work: Coping with the biological clock. *Occupational Medicine, 60*(1), 10–20.

Arendt, J., & Skene, D. J. (2005). Melatonin as a chronobiotic. *Sleep Medicine Review, 9*(1), 25–39.

Arendt, J., Stone, B., & Skene, D. J. (2005). Sleep disruption in jet lag and other circadian rhythm-related disorders. In M. H. Kryger, T. Roth, & W. C. Dement (Eds.). *Principles and practice of sleep medicine*. Philadelphia: Elsevier Saunders.

Argyle, M. (1987). *The psychology of happiness*. London: Metheun.

Argyle, M. (1999). Causes and correlates of happiness. In D. Kahneman, E. Diener & N. Schwarz (Eds.), *Well-being: The foundations of hedonic psychology*. New York: Russell Sage Foundation.

Argyle, M. (2001). *The psychology of happiness*. New York: Routledge.

Ariely, D. (2008). *Predictably irrational*. New York, NY: Harper Collins.

Arkes, H. R., Wortmann, R. L., Saville, P. D., & Harkness, A. R. (1981). Hindsight bias among physicians weighing the likelihood of diagnoses. *Journal of Applied Psychology, 66*, 252–254.

Arkowitz, H., & Lilienfeld, S. O. (2007). The best medicine? How drugs stack up against talk therapy for the treatment of depression. *Scientific American Mind, 18*(5), 80–83.

Armbruster, B. B. (2000). Taking notes from lectures. In R. F. Flippo & D. C. Caverly (Eds.), *Handbook of college reading and study strategy research*. Mahwah, NJ: Erlbaum.

Armstrong, J., & Makin, K. (2009). The Reena Virk murder. *Globe and Mail*, June 13.

Arndt, J., & Vess, M. (2008). Tales from existential oceans: Terror management theory and how the awareness of our mortality affects us all. *Social and Personality Psychology Compass, 2*(2), 909–928.

Arnett, J. J. (1999). Adolescent storm and stress, reconsidered. *American Psychologist, 54*, 317–326.

Arnett, J. J. (2000). Emerging adulthood: A theory of development from the late teens through the twenties. *American Psychologist, 55*, 469–480.

Arnett, J. J. (2004). Emerging adulthood: The winding road from the late teens through the twenties. New York: Oxford University Press.

Arnett, J. J. (2006). Emerging adulthood: Understanding the new way of coming of age. In J. J. Arnett & J. L. Tanner (Eds.), *Emerging adults in America: Coming of age in the 21st century* (p. 11). Washington, DC: American Psychological Association.

Arnett, J. J. (2008). The neglected 95%: why American psychology needs to become less American. *American Psychologist, 63*(7), 602–614.

Arnold, L. M. (2000). Psychocutaneous disorders. In B. J. Sadock & V. A. Sadock (Eds.), *Kaplan and Sadock's comprehensive textbook of psychiatry* (7th ed., pp. 1818–1827). Philadelphia: Lippincott/Williams & Wilkins.

Aron, A. (1970). *Relationship variables in human heterosexual attraction*. (Microfilm of typescript: Canadian theses on microfilm, No. 8501). Ottawa: National Library of Canada.

Aron, A., Fisher, H., & Mashek, D. J. (2005). Reward, motivation, and emotion systems associated with early–stage intense romantic love. *Journal of Neurophysiology, 94*(1), 327–337.

Aronson, E. (2000). *Nobody left to hate: Teaching compassion after Columbine*. New York: W. H. Freeman.

Aronson, E. (2010). *Not by chance alone: My life as a social psychologist*. New York: Basic Books.

Aronson, E., & Bridgeman, D. (1979). Jigsaw groups and the desegregated classroom: In pursuit of common goals. *Personality and Social Psychology Bulletin, 5*, 438–446.

Aronson, E., & Mills, J. (1959). The effect of severity of initiation on liking for a group. *Journal of Abnormal and Social Psychology, 59*, 177–181.

Aronson, E., Blaney, N. T., Stephan, C., Rosenfield, R., Sikes, J. (1977). Interdependence in the classroom: A field study. *Journal of Educational Psychology, 69*, 121–128.

Aronson, J., Lustina, M. J., Good, C., Keough, K., Steele, C. M., & Brown, J. (1999). When white men can't do math: Necessary and sufficient factors in stereotype threat. *Journal of Experimental Social Psychology, 35*, 29–46.

Arrigo, J. M., & Pezdek, K. (1997). Lessons from the study of psychogenic amnesia. *Current Directions in Psychological Science, 6*, 148–152.

Arsalidou, M., Pascual-Leone, J., & Johnson, J. (2010). Misleading cues improve developmental assessment of working memory capacity: The color matching task. *Cognitive Development, 25*, 262–277.

Asch, S. (1946). Forming impressions on personality. *Journal of Abnormal and Social Psychology, 41*, 258–290.

Asch, S. (1951). Effects of group pressure upon the modification and distortion of judgments. In H. Guetzkow (Ed.), *Groups, leadership and men: Research in human relations* (pp. 177–190). Oxford, England: Carnegie Press.

Asch, S. E. (1955). Opinions and social pressures. *Scientific American, 193*(5), 31–35.

Asch, S. E. (1956). Studies of independence and conformity: A minority of one against a unanimous majority. *Psychological Monographs, 70*(9, Whole No. 416).

Asendorpf, J. B., & Ostendorf, F. (1998). Is self-enhancement healthy? Conceptual, psychometric, and empirical analysis. *Journal of Personality and Social Psychology, 74*, 955–966.

Aserinsky, E., & Kleitman, N. (1953). Regularly occurring periods of eye mobility and concomitant phenomena during sleep. *Science, 118*, 273–274.

Ashton, M. C. (2007). *Individual differences and personality*. New York: Elsevier Academic Press.

Ashton, M. C., Lee, K., & Goldberg, L. R. (2004). A hierarchical analysis of 1,710 English personality-descriptive adjectives. *Journal of Personality and Social Psychology, 87*, 707–721.

Asmundson, G. J. G., & Katz, J. (2009). Understanding the co-occurrence of anxiety disorders and chronic pain: State of the art. *Depression and Anxiety, 26*, 889–901.

Aspinwall, L. G., Richter, L., & Hoffman R. R., III. (2001). Understanding how optimism works: An examination of optimists' adaptive moderation of belief and behavior. In E. C. Chang (Ed.), *Optimism and pessimism: Implications for theory, research, and practice* (pp. 217–238). Washington, DC: American Psychological Association.

Assaad, J. M., Pihl, R. O., Seguin, J., Nagin, D., Vitaro, F., & Tremblay, R. (2006). Heart rate response to alcohol and intoxicated aggressive behavior. *Alcoholism: Clinical and Experimental Research, 30*, 774–792.

Assefi, S., & Garry, M. (2003). Thinking yourself tipsy. *Psychological Science, 14*, 77–80.

Associate Press. (2010). Surgeon General: 1 Cigarette could kill you. Associated Press, December 9, 2010. Retreived May 2, 2011, from http://www.foxnews.com/health/2010/12/09/surgeon-general-cigarette-puff-kill/.

Astuti, R., & Bloch, M. (2010). Why a theory of human nature cannot be based on the distinction between universality and variability: Lessons from anthropology. *Behavioral and Brain Sciences, 33*, 83–84.

Atance, C. M., & Meltzoff, A. N. (2007). How developmental science contributes to theories of future thinking. *Behavioral and Brain Sciences, 30*, 314–315.

Atchley, R. A., & Ilardi, S. S. (2007). The promise of cognitive neuroscience for advancing depression research. *Cognitive Therapy and Research, 31*(2), 141–145.

Athens 2004 (Perdita Felicien). (2004). Retrieved May 2, 2005, from http://www.cbc.ca/story/olympics/national/2004/08/24/Sports/perdita.

Atkinson, J. W. (1974). The mainsprings of achievement-oriented activity. In J. W. Atkinson & J. O. Raynor (Eds.), *Motivation and achievement*. New York: Wiley.

Atkinson, J. W. (1981). Studying personality in the context of an advanced motivational psychology. *American Psychologist, 36*, 117–128.

Atkinson, J. W. (1992). Motivational determinants of thematic apperception. In C. P. Smith (Ed.), *Motivation and personality: Handbook of thematic content analysis*. New York: Cambridge University Press.

Atkinson, J. W., & Birch, D. (1978). *Introduction to motivation*. New York: Van Nostrand.

Atkinson, J. W., & Litwin, G. H. (1960). Achievement motive and test anxiety conceived as motive to approach success and to avoid failure. *Journal of Abnormal and Social Psychology, 60*, 52–63.

Atkinson, R. C., & Shiffrin, R. M. (1968). Human memory: A proposed system and its control processes. In K. W. Spence & J. T. Spence (Eds.), *The psychology of learning and motivation* (Vol. 2). New York: Academic Press.

Atkinson, R. C., & Shiffrin, R. M. (1971). The control of short-term memory. *Scientific American, 225*, 82–90.

Aucoin, K. J., Frick, P. J., & Bodin, S. D. (2006). Corporal punishment and child adjustment. *Journal of Applied Developmental Psychology, 27*, 527–541.

Austin, E., Saklofske, D. H., & Mastoras, S. (2010). Emotional intelligence, coping and exam-related stress in Canadian undergraduate students. *Australian Journal of Psychology, 62*(1), 42–57.

Auyeung, B., Baron-Cohen, S., Ashwin, E., Knickmeyer, R., Taylor, K., Hackett, G., & Hines, M. (2009). Fetal testosterone predicts sexually differentiated childhood behavior in girls and in boys. *Psychological Science, 20*(2), 144–148.

Aveline, M., Strauss, B., & Stiles, W. B. (2005). Psychotherapy research. In G. O. Gabbard, J. S. Beck, & J. Holmes (Eds.), *Oxford textbook of psychotherapy*. New York: Oxford University Press.

Averill, J. A. (1980). A constructivist view of emotion. In R. Plutchik & H. Kellerman (Eds.), *Emotion: Theory, research, and experience (Vol. 1): Theories of emotion*. New York: Academic Press.

Axel, R. (1995, April). The molecular logic of smell. *Scientific American, 273*, 154–159.

Ayanian, J. Z., & Cleary, P. D. (1999). Perceived risks of heart disease and cancer among cigarette smokers. *Journal of the American Medical Association, 281*, 1019–1021.

Ayotte, B. J., Margrett, J. A., & Hicks-Patrick, J. (2010). Physical activity in middle-aged and young-old adults: The roles of self-efficacy, barriers, outcome expectancies, self-regulatory behaviors and social support. *Journal of Health Psychology, 15*(2), 173–185.

Baars, B. J. (1986). *The cognitive revolution in psychology*. New York: Guilford.

Baars, B. J. (2010). Spontaneous Repetitive thoughts can be adaptive: Postscript on "Mind wandering." *Psychological Bulletin, 136*, 208–210.

Baas, M., Carsten, K. W. De Dreu, C. K., & Nijstad, B. A. (2008). A meta-analysis of 25 years of mood-creativity research: Hedonic Tone, activation, or regulatory focus. *Psychological Bulletin, 134*, 779–806.

Baccus, J. R., Baldwin, M. W., & Packer, D. J. (2004). Increasing implicit self-esteem through classical conditioning. *Psychological Science, 15*, 498–505.

Back, M. D., Schmukle, S. C., & Egloff, B. (2010). Why are narcissists so charming at first sight? Decoding the narcissism-popularity link at zero acquaintance. *Journal of Personality and Social Psychology, 98*(1), 132–145.

Bäckman, L., Small, B. J., & Wahlin, Å. (2001). Aging and memory: Cognitive and biological perspectives. In J. E. Birren & K. W. Schaie (Eds.), *Handbook of the psychology of aging* (5th ed., pp. 348–376). San Diego, CA: Academic Press.

Baddeley, A. D. (1986). *Working memory*. New York: Oxford University Press.

Baddeley, A. D. (1989). The uses of working memory. In P. R. Soloman, G. R. Goethals, C. M. Kelley, & B. R. Stephens (Eds.), *Memory: Interdisciplinary approaches*. New York: Springer-Verlag.

Baddeley, A. D. (1992). Working memory. *Science, 255*, 556–559.

Baddeley, A. D. (2001). Is working memory still working? *American Psychologist, 56*, 851–864.

Baddeley, A. D. (2003). Working memory: Looking back and looking forward. *Nature Reviews Neuroscience, 4*, 829–839.

Baddeley, A. D., & Hitch, G. (1974). Working memory. In G. H. Bower (Ed.), *The psychology of learning and motivation* (Vol. 8). New York: Academic Press.

Badlar, M. (2011). Nearly all of the world's best cities are in Canada or Australia. Retrieved May 25, 2011, from http://www.financialpost.com/Nearly+world+best+cities+Canada+Australia.

Baenninger, R. (1997). On yawning and its functions. *Psychonomic Bulletin & Review, 4,* 198–207.

Bahrick, H. P. (2000). Long-term maintenance of knowledge. In E. Tulving & F. I. M. Craik (Eds.), *The Oxford handbook of memory* (pp. 347–362). New York: Oxford University Press.

Bailey, C. H., & Kandel, E. R. (2004). Synaptic growth and the persistence of long–term memory: A molecular perspective. In M. S. Gazzaniga (Ed.), *The cognitive neurosciences*. Cambridge, MA: MIT Press.

Bailey, J. M. (2003). Biological perspectives on sexual orientation. In L. D. Garnets & D. C. Kimmel (Eds.), *Psychological perspectives on lesbian, gay, and bisexual experiences*. New York: Columbia University Press.

Bailey, J. M., & Pillard, R. C. (1991). A genetic study of male homosexual orientation. *Archives of General Psychology, 48,* 1089–1097.

Bailey, J. M., & Zucker, K. J. (1995). Childhood sex-typed behavior and sexual orientation: A conceptual analysis and quantitative review. *Developmental Psychology, 31,* 43–55.

Bailey, J. M., Pillard, R. C., Neale, M. C. I., & Agyei, Y. (1993). Heritable factors influence sexual orientation in women. *Archives of General Psychiatry, 50,* 217–223.

Baillargeon, R. (2002). The acquisition of physical knowledge in infancy: A summary in eight lessons. In U. Goswami (Ed.), *Blackwell handbook of childhood cognitive development*. Malden, MA: Blackwell Publishing.

Baillargeon, R. (2004). Infants' physical world. *Current Directions in Psychological Science, 13*(3), 89–94.

Baillargeon, R. (2008). Innate ideas revisited: For a principle of persistence in infants' physical reasoning. *Perspectives on Psychological Science, 3*(1), 2–13.

Bains, J. S., & Oliet, S. H. R. (2007). Glia: They make your memories stick! *Trends in Neuroscience, 30,* 417–424.

Bakan, P. (1971, August). The eyes have it. *Psychology Today,* pp. 64–69.

Baker, F., Ainsworth, S. R., Dye, J. T., Crammer, C., Thun, M. J., Hoffmann, M. E., et al. (2000). Health risks associated with cigar smoking. *Journal of the American Medical Association, 284,* 735–740.

Baker, G. J., Suchday, S., & Krantz, D. S. (2007). Heart disease/attack. In G. Fink (Ed.), *Encyclopedia of stress*. San Diego: Elsevier.

Baker, L. R., & McNulty, J. K. (2011). Self-compassion and relationship maintenance: The moderating roles of conscientiousness and gender. *Journal of Personality and Social Psychology, 100,* 853–873.

Balcetis, E., & Dunning, D. (2010). Wishful seeing: More desired objects are seen as closer. *Psychological Science, 21*(1), 147–152.

Balcetis, E., Dunning, D., & Miller, R. L. (2008). Do collectivists know themselves better than individualists? Cross-cultural studies of the holier than thou phenomenon. *Journal of Personality and Social Psychology, 95*(6), 1252–1267.

Baldessarini, R. J., Tondo, L., Strombom, I. M., Dominguez, S., Fawcett, J., Licinio, J., et al. (2007). Ecological studies of antidepressant treatment and suicidal risks. *Harvard Review of Psychiatry, 15,* 133–145.

Baldwin, M. W. (1992). Relational schemas and the processing of social information. *Psychological Bulletin, 112,* 461–484.

Baldwin, M. W. (2001). Does Bob Zajonc ever scowl at you from the back of your mind? In J. Bargh & D. Apsley (Eds.), *Unravelling the complexities of social life:*

A festschrift in honor of Robert B. Zajonc (pp. 55–67). Washington, DC: American Psychological Association.

Baldwin, M. W., & Main, K. J. (2001). The cued activation of relational schemas in social anxiety. *Personality and Social Psychology Bulletin, 27,* 1637–1647.

Baldwin, M. W., & Sinclair, L. (1996). Self-esteem and "if . . . then" contingencies of interpersonal acceptance. *Journal of Personality and Social Psychology, 71,* 1130–1141.

Baldwin, M. W., Baccus, J. R., & Fitzsimons, G. M. (2004). Self-esteem and the dual processing of interpersonal contingencies. *Self and Identity, 3,* 81–93.

Baldwin, M. W., Carrell, S. E., & Lopez, D. F. (1990). Priming relationship schemas: My advisor and the pope are watching me from the back of my mind. *Journal of Experimental Social Psychology, 26,* 435–454.

Baldwin, M. W., Granzberg, A., Pippus, L., & Pritchard, E. T. (2003). Cued activation of relational schemas: Self-evaluation and gender effects. *Canadian Journal of Behavioural Science, 35,* 153–163.

Baldwin, W. (2000). Information no one else knows: The value of self-report. In A. A. Stone, J. S. Turkkan, C. A. Bachrach, J. B. Jobe, H. S. Kurtzman & V. Cain (Eds.), *The science of self-report: Implications for research and practice*. Mahwah, NJ: Erlbaum.

Bale, T. L., Baram, T. Z., Brown, A. S., Goldstein, J. M., Insel, T. R., McCarthy, M. M., et al. (2010). Early life programming and neurodevelopmental disorders. *Biological Psychiatry, 68*(4), 314–319.

Ball, H. L., Hooker, E., & Kelly, P. J. (2000). Parent–infant co-sleeping: Father's roles and perspectives. *Infant and Child Development, 9*(2), 67–74.

Ball, K., Edwards, J. D., & Ross, L. A. (2007). The impact of speed of processing training on cognitive and everyday functions. *Journals of Gerontology: Series B, 62B* (Special Issue 1), 19–31.

Balsam, P. D. (1988). Selection, representation, and equivalence of controlling stimuli. In R. C. Atkinson, R. J. Herrnstein, G. Lindzey, & R. D. Luce (Eds.), *Stevens' handbook of experimental psychology*. New York: Wiley.

Balter, M. (2010). Did working memory spark creative culture? *Science, 328*(5975), 160–163.

Baltes, P. B., Staudinger, U. M., & Lindenberger, U. (1999). Lifespan psychology: Theory and application to intellectual functioning. *Annual Review of Psychology, 50,* 471–507.

Banaji, M. R., & Heiphetz, L. (2010). Attitudes. In S. T. Fiske, D. T. Gilbert, & G. Lindzey (Eds.), *Handbook of social psychology* (Vol. 1, 5th ed., pp. 353–393). Hoboken, NJ: Wiley.

Bandura, A. (1965). Influence of model's reinforcement contingencies on the acquisition of imitated responses. *Journal of Personality and Social Psychology, 1,* 589–595.

Bandura, A. (1977). *Social learning theory*. Englewood Cliffs, NJ: Prentice-Hall.

Bandura, A. (1982). The psychology of chance encounters and life paths. *American Psychologist, 37,* 747–755.

Bandura, A. (1986). *Social foundations of thought and action: A social-cognitive theory*. Englewood Cliffs, NJ: Prentice-Hall.

Bandura, A. (1990). Perceived self-efficacy in the exercise of personal agency. *Journal of Applied Sport Psychology, 2*(2), 128–163.

Bandura, A. (1993). Perceived self-efficacy in cognitive development and functioning. *Educational Psychologist, 28*(2), 117–148.

Bandura, A. (1995). Exercise of personal and collective efficacy in changing societies. In A. Bandura (Ed.), *Self-efficacy in changing societies*. New York: Cambridge University Press.

Bandura, A. (1999a). Social cognitive theory of personality. In L. A. Pervin, & O. P. John (Eds.), *Handbook of personality: Theory and research*. New York: Guilford.

Bandura, A. (1999b). A sociocognitive analysis of substance abuse: An agentic perspective. *Psychological Science, 10*(3), 214–217.

Bandura, A. (2001a). Social cognitive theory: An agentic perspective. *Annual Review of Psychology, 52,* 1–26.

Bandura, A. (2001b). The changing face of psychology at the dawning of a globalization era. *Canadian Psychology, 42,* 12–25.

Bandura, A. (2006). Toward a psychology of human agency. *Perspectives on Psychological Science, 1,* 164–180.

Bandura, A. (2008). Reconstrual of 'free will' from the agentic perspective of social cognitive theory. In J. Baer, J. C. Kaufman, & R. F. Baumeister (Eds.), *Are we free? Psychology and free will* (pp. 86–127). New York, NY: Oxford University Press.

Bandura, A., & Walters, R. H. (1959). *Adolescent aggression: A study of the influence of child-training practices and family interrelationships*. New York: The Ronald Press Company.

Bandura, A., & Walters, R. H. (1963). *Social learning and personality development*. New York: Holt, Rinehart & Winston, Inc.

Bandura, A., Ross, D., & Ross, S. A. (1961). Transmission of aggression through imitation of aggressive models. *Journal of Abnormal and Social Psychology, 63,* 575–582.

Bandura, A., Ross, D., & Ross, S. A. (1963a). Imitation of film-mediated aggressive models. *Journal of Abnormal and Social Psychology, 66*(1), 3–11.

Banich, M. T., & Heller, W. (1998). Evolving perspectives on lateralization of function. *Current Directions in Psychological Science, 7,* 1.

Banks, A., & Gartell, N. K. (1995). Hormones and sexual orientation: A questionable link. *Journal of Homosexuality, 28,* 247–268.

Banks, S., & Dinges, D. F. (2007). Behavioral and physiological consequences of sleep restriction. *Journal of Clinical Sleep Medicine, 3*(5), 519–528.

Banks, W. P., & Krajicek, D. (1991). Perception. *Annual Review of Psychology, 42,* 305–331.

Banse, R. (2007). Implicit attitudes towards romantic partners and ex-partners: A test of the reliability and validity of the IAT. *International Journal of Psychology, 42,* 149–157.

Banyard, V. L., & Williams, L. M. (1999). Memories for child sexual abuse and mental health functioning: Findings on a sample of women and implications for future research. In L. M. Williams & V. L. Banyard (Eds.), *Trauma & memory*. Thousand Oaks, CA: Sage Publications.

Banyard, V. L., Plante, E. G., Cohn, E. S., Moorhead, C., Ward, S., & Walsh, W. (2005). Revisiting unwanted sexual experiences on campus: A 12-year follow-up. *Violence Against Women, 11,* 426–446.

Bar, M. (2007). The continuum of "looking forward," and paradoxical requirements from memory. *Behavioral and Brain Sciences, 30,* 315–316.

Barak, A., & Buchanan, T. (2004). Internet-based psychological testing and assessment. In R. Krause, G. Stricker & J. Zack (Eds.), *Online counseling:*

A handbook for mental health professionals. San Diego: Elsevier Academic Press.

Baral, B. D., & Das, J. P. (2004). Intelligence: What is indigenous to India and what is shared? In R. J. Sternberg (Ed.), *International handbook of intelligence.* New York: Cambridge University Press.

Barba, G. D., Parlato, V., Jobert, A., Samson, Y., & Pappata, S. (1998). Cortical networks implicated in semantic and episodic memory: Common or unique. *Cortex, 34,* 547–561.

Barber, B. K. (1994). Cultural, family, and personal contexts of parent–adolescent conflict. *Journal of Marriage and the Family, 56,* 375–386.

Barber, L., Munz, D., Bagsby, P., & Powell, E. (2010). Sleep consistency and sufficiency: Are both necessary for less psychological strain? *Stress & Health: Journal of the International Society for the Investigation of Stress, 26*(3), 186–193.

Barber, T. X. (1979). Suggested ("hypnotic") behavior: The trance paradigm versus an alternative paradigm. In E. Fromm & R. E. Shor (Eds.), *Hypnosis: Developments in research and new perspectives.* New York: Aldine.

Barber, T. X. (1986). Realities of stage hypnosis. In B. Zilbergeld, M. G. Edelstien, & D. L. Araoz (Eds.), *Hypnosis: Questions and answers.* New York: Norton.

Barch, D. M. (2003). Cognition in schizophrenia: Does working memory work? *Current Directions in Psychological Science, 12*(4), 146–150.

Bard, P. (1934). On emotional experience after decortication with some remarks on theoretical views. *Psychological Review, 41,* 309–329.

Bargh, J. A. (1999). The cognitive monster: The case against the controllability of automatic stereotype effects. In S. Chaiken & Y. Trope (Eds.), *Dual-process theories in social psychology.* New York: Guilford.

Bargh, J. A., & McKenna, K. Y. A. (2004). The Internet and social life. *Annual Review of Psychology, 55,* 573–590.

Bargh, J. A., & Morsella, E. (2008). The unconscious mind. *Perspectives on Psychological Science, 3,* 73–79.

Bargh, J. A., Chen, M., & Burrows, L. (1996). Automaticity of social behavior: Direct effects of Trait construct and stereotype activation on action. *Journal of Personality and Social Psychology, 71,* 230–244.

Bargh, J. A., McKenna, K. Y. A., & Fitzsimons, G. M. (2002). Can you see the real me? Activation and expression of the "true self" on the Internet. *Journal of Social Issues, 58,* 33–48.

Barlow, D. H. (2010). Negative effects from psychological treatments. *American Psychologist, 65,* 13–20.

Barlow, D. H., Pincus, D. B., Heinrichs, N., & Choate, M. L. (2003). Anxiety disorders. In G. Stricker & T. A. Widiger (Eds.), *Handbook of psychology (Vol. 8): Clinical psychology.* New York: Wiley.

Barnes, V. A., Treiber, F., & Davis, H. (2001). The impact of Transcendental Meditation on cardiovascular function at rest and during acute stress in adolescents with high normal blood pressure. *Journal of Psychosomatic Research, 51,* 597–605.

Barnett, S. W. (2004). Does Head Start have lasting cognitive effects? The myth of fade-out. In E. Zigler & S. J. Styfco (Eds.), *The Head Start debates.* Baltimore: Paul H. Brooks Publishing.

Barnett, W. S. (1995). Long-term effects of early childhood programs on cognitive and school outcomes. *Future of Children, 5,* 25–50.

Barnier, A. J. (2002). Posthypnotic amnesia for autobiographical episodes: A laboratory model of functional amnesia. *Psychological Science, 13,* 232–237.

Bar-On, R., & Parker, J. D. A. (2000a). *Bar-On Emotional Quotient Inventory (Youth Version): Technical manual.* Toronto: Multi-Health Systems.

Bar-On, R., & Parker, J. D. A. (2000b). *Handbook of emotional intelligence: Theory, development, assessment, and application at home, school, and in the workplace.* San Francisco, CA: Jossey-Bass.

Barrett, L. F. (2009). Understanding the mind by measuring the brain: Lessons from measuring behavior. *Perspectives on Psychological Science, 4,* 314–318.

Barrett, D. (1988–1989). Dreams of death. *Omega, 19*(2), 95–101.

Barrett, L. F., Lindquist, K. A., & Gendron, M. (2007). Language as context for the perception of emotion. *Trends in Cognitive Science, 11,* 327–332.

Barrigón, M. L., Gurpegui, M., Ruiz-Veguilla, M., Diaz, F. J., Anguita, M., Sarramea, F., & Cervilla, J. (2010). Temporal relationship of first-episode nonaffective psychosis with cannabis use: A clinical verification of an epidemiological hypothesis. *Journal of Psychiatric Research, 44*(7), 413–420.

Barron, F. (1963). *Creativity and psychological health.* Princeton, NY: Van Nostrand.

Barry-Walsh, J. (2005). Dissociative identity disorder. *Australian & New Zealand Journal of Psychiatry, 39*(1–2), 109–110.

Barsky, A. J. (1988). The paradox of health. *New England Journal of Medicine, 318,* 414–418.

Bartlett, F. C. (1932). *Remembering: A study in experimental and social psychology.* New York: Macmillan.

Bartoshuk, L. M. (1993a). Genetic and pathological taste variation: What can we learn from animal models and human disease? In D. Chadwick, J. Marsh, & J. Goode (Eds.), *The molecular basis of smell and taste transduction.* New York: Wiley.

Bartoshuk, L. M. (1993b). The biological basis of food perception and acceptance. *Food Quality and Preference, 4,* 21–32.

Bartoshuk, L. M., Duffy, V. B., & Miller, I. J. (1994). PTC/PROP taste: Anatomy, psychophysics, and sex effects. *Physiology & Behavior, 56,* 1165–1171.

Bartz, J. A., & Hollander, E. (2006). The neuroscience of affiliation: Forging links between basic and clinical research on neuropeptides and social behavior. *Hormones and Behavior, 50*(4), 518–528.

Basbaum, A. I., & Jessell, T. M. (2000). The perception of pain. In E. R. Kandel, J. H. Schwartz, & T. M. Jessell (Eds.), *Principles of neural science.* New York: McGraw-Hill.

Bashore, T. R., Ridderinkhof, K. R., & van der Molen, M. W. (1997). The decline of cognitive processing speed in old age. *Current Directions in Psychological Science, 6,* 163–169.

Basow, S. A. (1992). *Gender: Stereotypes and roles.* Pacific Grove, CA: Brooks/Cole.

Bassiri, A. B., & Guilleminault, C. (2000). Clinical features and evaluation of obstructive sleep apnea–hypopnea syndrome. In M. H. Kryger, T. Roth & W. C. Dement (Eds.), *Principles and practice of sleep medicine.* Philadelphia: Saunders.

Bassok, M. (2003). Analogical transfer in problem solving. In J. E. Davidson & R. J. Sternberg (Eds.), *The psychology of problem solving.* New York: Cambridge University Press.

Basson, M. D., Bartoshuk, L. M., Dichello, S. Z., Panzini, L., Weiffenbach, J. M., & Duffy, V. B. (2005). Association between 6-n-propylthiouracil (PROP) bitterness and colonic neoplasms. *Digestive Diseases Sciences, 50,* 483–489.

Bassuk, E. L., Buckner, J. C., Perloff, J. N., & Bassuk, S. S. (1998). Prevalence of mental health and substance use disorders among homeless and low-income housed mothers. *American Journal of Psychiatry, 155,* 1561–1564.

Bates, E. (1999). Plasticity, localization, and language development. In S. H. Broman & J. M. Fletcher (Eds.), *The changing nervous system: Neurobehavioral consequences of early brain disorders* (pp. 214–247). New York, NY: Oxford University Press.

Bates, E., Devescovi, A., & Wulfeck, B. (2001). Psycholinguistics: A cross-language perspective. *Annual Review of Psychology, 52,* 369–396.

Bates, M. S., Edwards, W. T., & Anderson, K. O. (1993). Ethnocultural influences on variation in chronic pain perception. *Pain, 52*(1), 101–112.

Battagello, D. (2008, January 3). Dangerous ecstasy–meth pills flooding into U.S. from Canada. *National Post.* Retrieved April 1, 2008, from http://www.nationalpost.com/news/canada/story/html?id=213372.

Batterham, P. J., Christensen, H., & Mackinnon, A. J. (2009). Fluid intelligence is independently associated with all-cause mortality over 17 years in an elderly community sample: An investigation of potential mechanisms. *Intelligence, 37*(6), 551–560.

Batty, G., Deary, I., & Gottfredson, L. (2007). Premorbid (early life) IQ and later mortality risk: Systematic review. *Annals of Epidemiology, 17*(4), 278–288.

Bauby, J-D. (1997). *The diving bell and the butterfly: A memoir of life in death.* (Jeremy Leggatt, Trans.). New York: Alfred A. Knopf.

Baudry, M., & Lynch, G. (2001). Remembrance of arguments past: How well is the glutamate receptor hypothesis of LTP holding up after 20 years? *Neurobiology of Learning and Memory, 76,* 284–297.

Bauer, M. I., & Johnson-Laird, P. N. (1993). How diagrams can improve reasoning. *Psychological Science, 4,* 372–378.

Bauer, M. S. (2008). Mood disorders: Bipolar (manic-depressive) disorders. In A. J. Kay, J. A. Lieberman, M. B. First, & M. Maj (Eds.), *Psychiatry* (3rd ed.). New York, NY: Wiley-Blackwell.

Baumard, N., & Sperber, D. (2010). Weird people, yes, but also weird experiments. *Behavioral and Brain Sciences, 33,* 84–85

Baumeister, R. F. (1984). Choking under pressure: Self-consciousness and paradoxical effects of incentives on skillful performance. *Journal of Personality and Social Psychology, 46,* 610–620.

Baumeister, R. F. (1989). The optimal margin of illusion. *Journal of Social and Clinical Psychology, 8,* 176–189.

Baumeister, R. F. (1995). Disputing the effects of championship pressures and home audiences. *Journal of Personality and Social Psychology, 68,* 644–648.

Baumeister, R. F. (2000). Gender differences in erotic plasticity: The female sex drive as socially flexible and responsive. *Psychological Bulletin, 126,* 347–374.

Baumeister, R. F. (2004). Gender and erotic plasticity: Sociocultural influences on the sex drive. *Sexual and Relationship Therapy, 19,* 133–139.

Baumeister, R. F., & Leary, M. R. (1995). The need to belong: Desire for interpersonal attachments as a fundamental human motivation. *Psychological Bulletin, 117*, 497–529.

Baumeister, R. F., & Steinhilber, A. (1984). Paradoxical effects of supportive audiences on performance under pressure: The home field disadvantage in sports championships. *Journal of Personality and Social Psychology, 47*, 85–93.

Baumeister, R. F., & Twenge, J. M. (2002). Cultural suppression of female sexuality. *Review of General Psychology, 6*, 166–203.

Baumeister, R. F., Bratslavsky, E., Finkenauer, C., & Vohs, K. D. (2001a). Bad is stronger than good. *Review of General Psychology, 5*, 323–370.

Baumeister, R. F., Catanese, K. R., & Vohs, K. D. (2001b). Is there a gender difference in strength of sex drive? Theoretical views, conceptual distinctions and a review of relevant evidence. *Personality and Social Psychology Review, 5*, 242–273.

Baumeister, R. F., Masicampo, E. J., & Vohs, K. D. (2011). Do conscious thoughts cause behavior? *Annual Review of Psychology, 62*, 331–361.

Baumrind, D. (1964). Some thoughts on the ethics of reading Milgram's "Behavioral study of obedience." *American Psychologist, 19*, 421–423.

Baumrind, D. (1985). Research using intentional deception: Ethical issues revisited. *American Psychologist, 40*, 165–174.

Baumrind, D., Larzelere, R. E., & Cowan, P. A. (2002). Ordinary physical punishment: Is it harmful? Comment on Gershoff. *Psychological Bulletin, 128*, 580–589.

Bauserman, R. (1996). Sexual aggression and pornography: A review of correlational research. *Basic and Applied Social Psychology, 18*, 405–427.

Baxter, L. R., Schwartz, J. M., Bergamon, K. S., Szuba, M. P., Guze, B. H., Mazziotta, J. C., Alazraki, A., Selin, C. E., Ferng, H.-K., Munford, P., & Phelps, M. E. (1992). Caudate glucose metabolic rate changes with both drug and behavior therapy for obsessive–compulsive disorder. *Archives of General Psychiatry, 49*, 681–689.

Baylis, G. C., & Driver, J. (1995). One-sided edge assignment in vision: 1. Figure-ground segmentation and attention to objects. *Current Directions in Psychological Science, 4*, 140–146.

BBC. (2004). Why perfect is not always best. BBC News. Retrieved July 15, 2011, from http://news.bbc.co.uk/2/hi/health/3815479.stm.

Beahrs, J. O. (1983). Co-consciousness: A common denominator in hypnosis, multiple personality and normalcy. *American Journal of Clinical Hypnosis, 26*(2), 100–113.

Bearden, C. E., Jasinska, A. J., & Freimer, N. B. (2009). Methodological issues in molecular genetic studies of mental disorders. *Annual Review of Clinical Psychology, 5*, 549–569.

Beaupre, P., Turcotte, P., & Milan, A. (2006, October). Junior comes back home: Trends and predictors of returning to the parental home. Statistics Canada: *Canadian Social Trends*.

Bebko, J. M., Demark, J. L., Weiss, J. & Gomez, P. (2006). Discrimination of temporal synchrony in intermodal events by children with autism and children with developmental delays. *Journal of Child Psychology and Psychiatry, 47*, 88–98.

Beck, A. T. (1976). *Cognitive therapy and the emotional disorders.* New York: International Universities Press.

Beck, A. T. (1983). Cognitive therapy of depression: New perspectives. In P. J. Clayton & J. E. Barrett (Eds.), *Treatment of depression: Old controversies and new approaches* (pp. 265–290). New York: Raven Press.

Beck, A. T. (1987). Cognitive therapy. In J. K. Zeig (Ed.), *The evolution of psychotherapy*. New York: Brunner/Mazel.

Beck, A. T. (1997). Cognitive therapy: Reflections. In J. K. Zeig (Ed.), *The evolution of psychotherapy: The third conference*. New York: Brunner/Mazel.

Beck, A. T., & Weishaar, M. E. (2011). Cognitive therapy. In R. J. Corsini & D. Wedding (Eds.), *Current psychotherapies* (9th ed.). Belmont, CA: Brooks/Cole.

Beck, A. T., & Rector, N. A. (2004). Cognitive approaches to schizophrenia: Theory and therapy. *Annual Review of Clinical Psychology, 1*, 577–606.

Beck, C. T., & Driscoll, J. W. (2006). *Postpartum mood and anxiety disorders: A clinician's guide*. Sudbury, MA: Jones and Bartlett Publishers.

Beck, H. P., Levinson, S., & Irons, G. (2009). Finding Little Albert: A journey to John B. Watson's infant laboratory. *American Psychologist, 64*(7), 605–614.

Beck, H. P., Levinson, S., & Irons, G. (2010). The evidence supports Douglas Merritte as Little Albert. *American Psychologist, 65*, 301–303.

Becker, A. L. (2009, November 29). Science of memory: Researchers to study pieces of unique brain. *The Hartford Courant*. Retrieved from http://www.courant.com.

Becker, A., & Fay, K. (2006). Sociocultural issues and eating disorders. In S. Wonderlich, J. Mitchell, M. de Zwaan, & H. Steiger (Eds.), *Annual review of eating disorders*. Oxon, England: Radcliffe.

Becker, S., & Wojtowicz, J. M. (2007). A model of hippocampal neurogenesis in memory and mood disorders. *Trends in Cognitive Sciences, 11*(2), 70–76.

Becker-Blease, K. A., Turner, H. A., & Finkelhor, D. (2010). Disasters, victimization, and children's mental health. *Child Development, 81*, 1040–1052.

Becskei, C., Lutz, T. A., & Riediger, T. (2008). Glucose reverses fasting-induced activation in the arcuate nucleus of mice. *Neuroreport: For Rapid Communication of Neuroscience Research, 19*(1), 105–109.

Beeman, M. J., & Chiarello, C. (1998). Complementary right and left hemisphere language comprehension. *Current Directions in Psychological Science, 7*, 2–7.

Beer, J. M., Arnold, R. D., & Loehlin, J. C. (1998). Genetic and environmental influences on MMPI Factor Scales: Joint model fitting to twin and adoption data. *Journal of Personality and Social Psychology, 74*, 818–827.

Beer, J. S., Shimamura, A. P., & Knight, R. T. (2004). Frontal lobe contributions to executive control of cognitive and social behavior. In M. S. Gazzaniga (Ed.), *The cognitive neurosciences*. Cambridge, MA: MIT Press.

Behling, O. (1998). Employee selection: Will intelligence and conscientiousness do the job? *Academy of Management, 12*, 77–86.

Behrmann, M. (2010). Agnosia: Visual. In E. B. Goldstein (Ed.), *Encyclopedia of perception*. Thousand Oaks, CA: Sage.

Beidel, D. C., & Stipelman, B. (2007). Anxiety disorders. In M. Hersen, S. M. Turner, & D. C. Beidel (Eds.), *Adult psychopathology and diagnosis*. New York, NY: Wiley.

Beilin, H. (1992). Piaget's enduring contribution to developmental psychology. *Developmental Psychology, 28*, 191–204.

Beilock, S. (2010). *Choke: What the secrets of the brain reveal about getting it right when you have to*. New York: Free Press.

Beilock, S. L. (2008). Math performance in stressful situations. *Current Directions in Psychological Science, 17*(5), 339–343.

Beilock, S. L., & Gonso, S. (2008). Putting in the mind versus putting on the green: Expertise, performance time, and the linking of imagery and action. *Quarterly Journal of Experimental Psychology, 61*(6), 920–932.

Beisecker, A. E. (1990). Patient power in doctor–patient communication: What do we know? *Health Communication, 2*, 105–122.

Beiser, M. (1999). *Strangers at the gate: The "Boat People's" first ten years in Canada*. Toronto: University of Toronto Press.

Bekelman, J. E., Li, Y., & Gross, C. P. (2003). Scope and impact of financial conflicts of interest in biomedical research. *Journal of the American Medical Association, 289*, 454–465.

Békésy, G. von. (1947). The variation of phase along the basilar membrane with sinusoidal vibrations. *Journal of the Acoustical Society of America, 19*, 452–460.

Bekkouche, N. S., Holmes, S., Whittaker, K. S., & Krantz, D. S. (2011). Stress and the heart: Psychosocial stress and coronary heart disease. In R. J. Contrada & A. Baum (Eds.), *The handbook of stress science: Biology, psychology, and health* (pp. 111–121). New York, NY: Springer Publishing.

Belger, A., & Barch, D. M. (2009). Cognitive neuroscience and neuroimaging in schizophrenia. In D. S. Charney & E. J. Nestler (Eds.), *Neurobiology of mental illness* (3rd ed., pp. 303–320). New York, NY: Oxford University Press.

Belger, A., & Dichter, G. (2006). Structural and functional neuroanatomy. In J. A. Lieberman, T. S. Stroup, & D. O. Perkins (Eds.), *Textbook of schizophrenia*. Washington, DC: American Psychiatric Publishing.

Bell, A. P., Weinberg, M. S., & Hammersmith, S. K. (1981). *Sexual preference: Its development in men and women*. Bloomington: Indiana University Press.

Beller, M., & Gafni, N. (1996). The 1991 international assessment of educational progress in mathematics and sciences: The gender differences perspective. *Journal of Educational Psychology, 88*, 365–377.

Bellezza, F. S. (1996). Mnemonic methods to enhance storage and retrieval. In E. L. Bjork & R. A. Bjork (Eds.), *Memory*. San Diego: Academic Press.

Belli, R. F., Winkielman, P., Read, J. D., Schwarz, N., & Lynn, S. J. (1998). Recalling more childhood events leads to judgments of poorer memory: Implications for the recovered/false memory debate. *Psychonomic Bulletin & Review, 5*, 318–323.

Bellinger, D. C., & Adams, H. F. (2001). Environmental pollutant exposures and children's cognitive abilities. In R. J. Sternberg & E. L. Grigorenko (Eds.), *Environmental effects on cognitive abilities*. Mahwah, NJ: Erlbaum.

Belsky, J., & Pluess, M. (2009). The nature (and nurture) of plasticity in early human development. *Perspectives on Psychological Science, 4*, 345–351.

Belsky, J., & Kelly, J. (1994). *The transition to parenthood*. New York: Dell.

Belsky, J., Steinberg, L., & Draper, P. (1991). Childhood experience, interpersonal development, and reproductive strategy: An evolutionary theory of socialization. *Child Development, 62*, 647–670.

Bem, D. J. (1967). Self-perception: An alternative interpretation of cognitive dissonance phenomena. *Psychological Review, 74*, 183–200.

Bem, D. J. (2000). Exotic becomes erotic: Interpreting the biological correlates of sexual orientation. *Archives of Sexual Behavior, 29,* 531–548.

Bem, S. L. (1985). Androgyny and gender schema theory: A conceptual and empirical integration. In T. B. Sonderegger (Ed.), *Nebraska symposium on motivation, 1984: Psychology and gender* (Vol. 32). Lincoln: University of Nebraska Press.

Benca, R. M. (2001). Consequences of insomnia and its therapies. *Journal of Clinical Psychiatry, 62* (Suppl. 10), 33–38.

Bender, D. S., Skodol, A. E., Dyck, I. R., Markowitz, J. C., Shea, M. T., Yen, S., et al. (2007). Ethnicity and mental health treatment utilization by patients with personality disorders. *Journal of Consulting and Clinical Psychology, 75,* 992–999.

Bender, R., Jockel, K. H., Trautner, C., Spraul, M., & Berger, M. (1999). Effect of age on excess mortality in obesity. *Journal of the American Medical Association, 281,* 1498–1504.

Benedetti, F. (2008). *Placebo effects: Understanding the mechanisms in health and disease.* New York, NY: Oxford University Press.

Benham, G. (2010). Sleep: An important factor in stress-health models. *Stress & Health: Journal of the International Society for the Investigation of Stress, 26*(3), 204–214.

Ben-Itzchak, E. & Zachor, D. (2007). The effects of intellectual functioning and autism severity on outcome of early behavioural intervention for children with autism. *Research in Developmental Disabilities, 28,* 287–303.

Benjafield, J. G. (2008). George Kelly: Cognitive psychologist, humanistic psychologist, or something else entirely? *History of Psychology, 11,* 239–262.

Benjamin, L. T., Jr. (2000). The psychology laboratory at the turn of the 20th century. *American Psychologist, 55,* 318–321.

Benjamin, L. T., Jr. (2003). Behavioral Science and the Nobel Prize. *American Psychologist, 58,* 731–741.

Benjamin, L. T., Jr., & Simpson, J. A. (2009). The power of the situation: The impact of Milgram's obedience studies on personality and social psychology. *American Psychologist, 64,* 12–19.

Benjamin, L. T., Jr., Cavell, T. A., & Shallenberger, W. R., III. (1984). Staying with initial answers on objective tests: Is it a myth? *Teaching of Psychology, 11,* 133–141.

Ben-Porath, Y. S. (2003). Assessing personality and psychopathology with self-report inventories. In J. R. Graham & J. A. Naglieri (Eds.), *Handbook of psychology, Volume 10: Assessment psychology.* New York: Wiley.

Benson, E. (2002). Pheromones, in context. *APA Online.* Retrieved February 14, 2008, from http://www.apa.org/monitor/oct02/pheromones.html.

Benson, H. (1975). *The relaxation response.* New York: Morrow.

Benson, H., & Klipper, M. Z. (1988). *The relaxation response.* New York: Avon.

Bentall, R. P. (2009). *Doctoring the mind: Is our current treatment of mental illness really any good?* New York, NY: New York University Press.

Benton, D. (2004). Role of parents in the determination of the food preferences of children and the development of obesity. *International Journal of Obesity, 28,* 858–869.

Berenbaum, S. A., & Snyder, E. (1995). Early hormonal influences on childhood sex-typed activity and playmate preferences: Implications for the development of sexual orientation. *Developmental Psychology, 31,* 31–42.

Berenbaum, S. A., Martin, C. L., & Ruble, D. N. (2008). Gender development. In W. Damon & R. M. Lerner (Eds.), *Child and adolescent development: An advanced course* (pp. 647–681). New York, NY: Wiley.

Bergevin, T., Gupta, R., Derevensky, J., & Kaufman, F. (2006). Adolescent gambling: Understanding the role of stress and coping. *Journal of Gambling Studies, 22,* 195–208.

Bergner, S., Monk, C., & Werner, E. A. (2008). Dyadic intervention during pregnancy? Treating pregnant women and possibly reaching the future baby. *Infant Mental Health Journal, 29*(5), 399–419.

Berkowitz, L. (1989). Frustration–aggression hypothesis: Examination and reformulation. *Psychological Bulletin, 106,* 59–73.

Berkowitz, L. (1999). Evil is more than banal: Situationism and concept of evil. *Personality and Social Psychology Review, 3,* 246–253.

Berkowitz, R. I. (2003). Behavior therapies. In R. E. Hales & S. C. Yudofsky (Eds.), *Textbook of Clinical Psychiatry.* Washington, DC: American Psychiatric Publishing.

Berlin, B., & Kay, P. (1969). *Basic color terms: Their universality and evolution.* Berkeley, CA: University of California Press.

Berlin, L. J., Ispa, J. M., Fine, M. A., Brooks-Gunn, J., Brady-Smith, C., Ayoub, C., & Bai, Y. (2009). Correlates and consequences of spanking and verbal punishment for low-income White, African American, and Mexican American toddlers. *Child Development, 80*(5), 1403–1420.

Berliner, L., & Briere, J. (1999). Trauma, memory, and clinical practice. In L. M. Williams & V. L. Banyard (Eds.), *Trauma & memory.* Thousand Oaks, CA: Sage Publications.

Berman, A. L. (2009). Depression and suicide. In I. H. Gotlib & C. L. Hammen (Eds.), *Handbook of depression* (2nd ed.). New York, NY: Guilford Press.

Berman, R. F. (1991). Electrical brain stimulation used to study mechanisms and models of memory. In J. L. Martinez, Jr., & R. P. Kesner (Eds.), *Learning and memory: A biological view.* San Diego: Academic Press.

Berman, R. M., Sporn, J., Charney, D. S., & Mathew, S. J. (2009). Principles of the pharmacotherapy of depression. In D. S. Charney & E. J. Nestler (Eds.), *Neurobiology of mental illness* (pp. 491–515). New York, NY: Guilford Press.

Bernert, R. A., Merrill, K. A., Braithwaite, S. R., Van Orden, K. A., & Joiner, T. E., Jr. (2007). Family life stress and insomnia symptoms in a prospective evaluation of young adults. *Journal of Family Psychology, 21*(1), 58–66.

Bernier, R., & Gerdts, J. (2010). *Autism spectrum disorders.* Santa Barbara, CA: ABC-CLIO.

Bernstein, H. (2007). Maternal and perinatal infection-viral. In S. G. Gabbe, J. R. Niebyl, & J. L. Simpson (Eds.) *Obstetrics: Normal and problem pregnancies* (5th ed., pp. 1203–1232). Philadelphia, PA: Elsevier.

Bernstein, H. J., Beale, M. D., Burns, C., & Kellner, C. H. (1998). Patient attitudes about ECT after treatment. *Psychiatric Annuals,* 524–527.

Berridge, K. C. (2003). Comparing the emotional brains of humans and other animals. In R. J. Davidson, K. R. Scherer, & H. H. Goldsmith (Eds.), *Handbook of affective sciences.* New York: Oxford University Press.

Berridge, K. C. (2004). Motivation concepts in behavioral neuroscience. *Physiology and Behavior, 81*(2), 179–209.

Berry, D. T. R., Wetter, M. W., & Baer, R. A. (1995). Assessment of malingering. In J. N. Butcher (Ed.), *Clinical personality assessment: Practical approaches.* New York: Oxford University Press.

Berry, J. W. (1984). Towards a universal psychology of cognitive competence. In P. S. Fry (Ed.), *Changing conceptions of intelligence and intellectual functioning* (pp. 35–61). Amsterdam: Elsevier Science Publishers.

Berry, J. W. (1990). Cultural variations in cognitive style. In S. P. Wapner (Ed.), *Bio-psycho-social factors in cognitive style.* Hillsdale, NJ: Erlbaum.

Berry, J. W. (1994). Cross-cultural variations in intelligence. In R. J. Sternberg (Ed.), *Encyclopedia of human intelligence.* New York: Macmillan.

Berry, J. W., Poortinga, Y., Segall, M., & Dasen, P. (1992). *Cross-cultural psychology.* New York: Cambridge University Press.

Bersani, H. (2007). President's address 2007: The past is prologue: "MR," go gentle into that good night. *Intellectual and Developmental Disabilities, 45,* 399–404.

Berscheid, E. (1988). Some comments on love's anatomy: Or, whatever happened to old-fashioned lust. In R. J. Sternberg & M. L. Barnes (Eds.), *The psychology of love.* New Haven: Yale University Press.

Berscheid, E. (2006). Searching for the meaning of "love." In R. J. Sternberg & K. Weis (Eds.), *The new psychology of love.* New Haven, CT: Yale University Press.

Berscheid, E., & Walster, E. (1978). *Interpersonal attraction.* Reading, MA: Addison-Wesley.

Berthoud, H. R., & Morrison, C. (2008). The brain, appetite, and obesity. *Annual Review of Psychology, 59,* 55–92.

Bertram, L., & Tanzi, R. E. (2008). Thirty years of Alzheimer's disease genetics: The implications of systematic meta-analyses. *Nature Reviews Neuroscience, 9*(10), 768–778.

Bertrand, R. M., & Lachman, M. E. (2003). Personality development in adulthood and old age. In R. M. Lerner, M. A. Easterbrooks, & J. Mistry (Eds.), *Handbook of psychology, Vol. 6: Developmental psychology.* New York, NY: Wiley.

Beusterien, K. M., Davis, E. A., Flood, R., Howard, K., & Jordan, J. (2008). HIV patient insight on adhering to medication: A qualitative analysis. *AIDS Care, 20,* 251–259.

Beutler, L. E. (2002). The dodo bird is extinct. *Clinical Psychology: Science & Practice, 9*(1), 30–34.

Beutler, L. E., Bongar, B., & Shurkin, J. N. (1998). *Am I crazy, or is it my shrink?* New York: Oxford University Press.

Bhagwagar, Z., & Heninger, G. R. (2009). Antidepressants. In M. C. Gelder, N. C. Andreasen, J. J. López-Ibor, Jr., & J. R. Geddes (Eds.), *New Oxford textbook of psychiatry* (2nd ed., Vol. 1). New York, NY: Oxford University Press.

Bi, G. Q., & Poo, M.-M. (2001). Synaptic modification by correlated activity: Hebb's postulate revisited. *Annual Review of Neuroscience, 24,* 139–166.

Bialystok, E. (1991). Metalinguistic dimensions of bilingual language proficiency. In E. Bialystok (Ed.), *Language processing in bilingual children* (pp. 113–140). New York: Cambridge University Press.

Bialystok, E. (1999). Cognitive complexity and attentional control in the bilingual mind. *Child Development, 70,* 636–644.

Bialystok, E. (2001). *Bilingualism in development: Language, literacy and cognition.* Cambridge, UK: Cambridge University Press.

Bialystok, E. (2007). Cognitive effects of bilingualism: How linguistic experience leads to cognitive change. *The International Journal of Bilingual Education and Bilingualism, 10,* 210–223.

Bialystok, E. (2010a). Experience and the mind: The case of bilingualism. *Psynopsis, 32,* 17.

Bialystok, E. (2010b). Bilingulalism. Wiley Interdisciplinary reviews. *Cognitive Science, 1,* 559–572.

Bialystok, E., & Craik, F. I. M. (2010). Cognitive and linguistic processing in the bilingual mind. *Current Directions in Psychological Science, 19*(1), 19–23.

Bialystok, E., Craik, F. I. M., & Freedman, M. (2007). Bilingualism as a protection against the onset of symptoms of dementia. *Neuropsychologia, 45*(2), 459–464.

Bialystok, E., Craik, F. I. M., Klein, R., & Viswanathan, M. (2004). Bilingualism, aging, and cognitive control: Evidence from the Simon task. *Cognition and Aging, 19,* 290–303.

Bialystok, E., Majumder, S., & Martin, M. (2003). Developing phonological awareness: Is there a bilingual advantage? *Applied Psycholinguistics, 24,* 27–44.

Biblarz, T. J., & Stacey, J. (2010). How does the gender of parents matter? *Journal of Marriage and Family, 72*(1), 3–22.

Biederman, I., Hilton, H. J., & Hummel, J. E. (1991). Pattern goodness and pattern recognition. In G. R. Lockhead & J. R. Pomerantz (Eds.), *The perception of structure.* Washington, DC: American Psychological Association.

Biehl, M., Matsumoto, D., Ekman, P., Hearn, V., Heider, K., Kudoh, T., & Ton, V. (1997). Matsumoto and Ekman's Japanese and Caucasian Facial Expressions of Emotion (JACFEE): Reliability data and cross-national differences. *Journal of Nonverbal Behavior, 21,* 3–21.

Bieling, P. J., & Grant, D. A. (2008). Toward bridging the science and practice of depression prevention: What can we learn from cognitive vulnerability? *Canadian Psychology, 48,* 240–255.

Bielski, Z. (2011). Mourning a lost home. The Globe and Mail, May 25, p. L1.

Bigelow, B. J. (2006). There's an elephant in the room: The impact of early poverty and neglect on intelligence and common learning disorders in children, adolescents, and their parents. *Developmental Disabilities Bulletin, 34*(1–2), 177–215.

Bigler, E. D., Blatter, D. D., Anderson, C. V., Johnson, S. C., Gale, S. D., Hopkins, R. O., & Burnett, B. (1997). Hippocampal volume in normal aging and traumatic brain injury. *American Journal of Neuroradiology, 18,* 11–23.

Birch, L. L., & Fisher, J. A. (1996). The role of experience in the development of children's eating behavior. In E. D. Capaldi (Ed.), *Why we eat what we eat: The psychology of eating* (pp. 113–143). Washington, DC: American Psychological Association.

Birdsong, D. (1999). Introduction: Whys and why nots of the critical period hypothesis for second language acquisition. In D. Birdsong (Ed.), *Second language acquisition and the critical period hypothesis* (pp. 1–22). Mahwah, NJ: Erlbaum.

Birgegard, A., & Sohlberg, S. (2008). Persistent effects of subliminal stimulation: Sex differences and the effectiveness of debriefing. *Scandinavian Journal of Psychology, 49*(1), 19–29.

Birkeland, S. A., Manson, T. M., Kisamore, J. L., Brannick, M. T., & Smith, M. A. (2006). A meta-analytic investigation of job applicant faking on personality measures. *International Journal of Selection and Assessment, 14,* 317–335.

Birnbaum, M. H. (2004a). Base rates in Bayesian inference. In F. P. Rudiger (Ed.), *Cognitive illusions.* New York: Psychology Press.

Birnbaum, M. H. (2004b). Human research and data collection via the Internet. *Annual Review of Psychology, 55,* 803–832.

Birney, D. P., & Sternberg, R. J. (2011). The development of cognitive abilities. In M. H. Bornstein & M. E. Lamb (Eds.), *Developmental science: An advanced textbook* (pp. 353–388). New York, NY: Psychology Press.

Birney, D. P., Citron-Pousty, J. H., Lutz, D. J., & Sternberg, R. J. (2005). The development of cognitive and intellectual abilities. In M. H. Bornstein & M. E. Lamb (Eds.), *Developmental science: An advanced textbook.* Mahwah, NJ: Erlbaum.

Bischof-Köhler, D., & Bischof, N. (2007). Is mental time travel a frame-of-reference issue? *Behavioral and Brain Sciences, 30,* 316–317.

Bishop, S. I., & Primeau, I. (2002). Through the long night: Stress and group dynamics in Antarctica. International Astronautical Congress (IAC) of the International Astronautical Federation (IAF), International Academy of Astronautics (IAA), and the International Institute of Space Law (HSL), Human Factors for Long Duration Spaceflight, World Space Congress. Houston, Texas, October, 2002.

Bishop, S. R. (2002). What do we really know about mindfulness-based stress reduction? *Psychosomatic Medicine, 64*(1), 71–83.

Bjork, R. A. (1992). Interference and forgetting. In L. R. Squire (Ed.), *Encyclopedia of learning and memory.* New York: Macmillan.

Bjorklund, D. F. (1997). In search of a metatheory for cognitive development (or, Piaget is dead and I don't feel so good myself). *Child Development, 68,* 144–148.

Bjorklund, D. F. (2005). *Children's thinking: Cognitive development and individual differences.* Belmont, CA: Wadsworth.

Black, D. W. (2001). Antisocial personality disorder: The forgotten patients of psychiatry. *Primary Psychiatry, 8*(1), 30–81.

Blackburn, R. (2006). Other theoretical models of psychopathy. In C. J. Patrick (Ed.), *Handbook of Psychopathy.* New York: Guilford.

Blacker, L. (1999). The launching phase of the life cycle. In B. Carter & M. McGoldrick (Eds.), *The expanded family life cycle: Individual, family, and social perspectives* (3rd ed., pp. 287–306). Boston: Allyn & Bacon.

Blagrove, M. (1992). Dreams as a reflection of our waking concerns and abilities: A critique of the problem-solving paradigm in dream research. *Dreaming, 2,* 205–220.

Blagrove, M. (1996). Problems with the cognitive psychological modeling of dreaming. *Journal of Mind and Behavior, 17,* 99–134.

Blair, S. N., Kohl, H. W., Paffenbarger, R. S., Clark, D. G., Cooper, K. H., & Gibbons, L. W. (1989). Physical fitness and all-cause mortality: A prospective study of healthy men and women. *Journal of the American Medical Association, 262,* 2395–2401.

Blakeslee, T. R. (1980). *The right brain.* Garden City, NY: Doubleday/Anchor.

Blanchard, E. B., & Keefer, L. (2003). Irritable bowel syndrome. In A. M. Nezu, C. M. Nezu, & P. A. Geller (Eds.), *Handbook of psychology (Vol. 9): Health psychology.* New York: Wiley.

Blankenhorn, D. (1995). *Fatherless America: Confronting our most urgent social problem.* New York: Basic Books.

Blascovich, J., Wyer, N. A., Swart, L. A., & Kibler, J. L. (1997). Racisim and racial categorization. *Journal of Personality and Social Psychology, 72,* 1364–1372.

Blass, T. (1991). Understanding behavior in the Milgram obedience experiment: The role of personality, situations, and their interactions. *Journal of Personality and Social Psychology, 60,* 398–413.

Blass, T. (1999). The Milgram Paradigm after 35 years: Some things we now know about obedience to authority. *Journal of Applied Social Psychology, 29,* 955–978.

Blass, T. (2009). From New Haven to Santa Clara: A historical perspective on the Milgram obedience experiments. *American Psychologist, 64*(1), 37–45.

Blatt, S. J. (1974). Levels of object representation in anaclitic and introjective depression. *Psychoanalytic Study of the Child, 29*(10), 7–157.

Blatt, S. J. (1995). Interpersonal relatedness and self-definition: Two personality configurations and their implications for psychopathology and psychotherapy, In J. L. Singer (Ed.), *Repression and dissociation: Implications for personality theory, psychopathology, and health* (pp. 299–335). Chicago: University of Chicago Press.

Bleak, J., & Frederick, C. M. (1998). Superstitious behavior in sport: Levels of effectiveness and determinants of use in three collegiate sports. *Journal of Sport Behavior, 21,* 1–15.

Bliwise, D. L. (2005). Normal aging. In M. H. Kryger, T. Roth, & W. C. Dement (Eds.), *Principles and practice of sleep medicine.* Philadelphia: Elsevier Saunders.

Bloch, S., & Harari, E. (2009). Family therapy in the adult psychiatric setting. In M. C. Gelder, N. C. Andreasen, J. J. López-Ibor, Jr., & J. R. Geddes (Eds.), *New Oxford textbook of psychiatry* (2nd ed., Vol. 1). New York, NY: Oxford University Press.

Block, J. (1981). Some enduring and consequential structures of personality. In A. I. Rabins, J. Aronoff, A. Barclay, & R. Zucker (Eds.), *Further explorations in personality.* New York: Wiley.

Block, J. (1995). A contrarian view of the five-factor approach to personality description. *Psychological Bulletin, 117,* 187–215.

Block, J. R., & Yuker, H. E. (1992). *Can you believe your eyes?: Over 250 illusions and other visual oddities.* New York: Brunner/Mazel.

Block, L. G., & Keller, P. A. (1997). Effects of self-efficacy and vividness on the persuasiveness of health communication. *Journal of Consumer Psychology, 6,* 31–54.

Block, N. (2002). How heritability misleads us about race. In Fish (Ed.), *Race and intelligence: Separating science from myth.* Mahwah: NJ: Earlbaum.

Bloom, B. S. (Ed.). (1985). *Developing talent in young people.* New York: Ballantine.

Bloom, P. (2010). What we miss. *The New York Times,* May 27, 2010. Retrieved June 6, 2010, from http://www.nytimes.com/2010/06/06/books/review/Bloom-t.html.

Boakes, R. A. (2003). The impact of Pavlov on the psychology of learning in English-speaking countries. *The Spanish Journal of Psychology, 6*(2), 93–98.

Boase, J., & Wellman, B. (2006). Personal relationships: On and off the Internet. In A. L. Vangelisti & D. Perlman (Eds.), *The Cambridge handbook of personal relationships*. New York, NY: Cambridge University Press.

Boatswain, S., Brown, N., Fiksenbaum, L., Goldstein, L., Greenglass, E., Nadler, E., & Pyke, S. W. (2001). Canadian feminist psychology: Where are we now? *Canadian Psychology, 42*, 276–288.

Bobo, W. V., Rapoport, J. L., Abi-Dargham, A., Fatemi, H., & Meltzer, H. Y. (2008). The neurobiology of schizophrenia. In A. Tasman, J. Kay, J. A. Lieberman, M. B. First, & M. Maj (Eds.), *Psychiatry* (3rd ed.). New York, NY: Wiley-Blackwell.

Boccia, M. A., Campbell, F. A., Goldman, B. D., & Skinner, M. (2009). Differential recall of consent information and parental decisions about enrolling children in research studies. *Journal of General Psychology, 136*, 91–108.

Bodenhausen, G. V., Todd, A. R., & Richeson, J. A. (2009). Controlling prejudice and stereotyping: Antecedents, mechanisms, and contexts. In T. D. Nelson (Ed.), *Handbook of prejudice, stereotyping, and discrimination* (pp. 1–22). New York, NY: Psychology Press.

Bodenmann, G., Ledermann, T., Blattner, D., & Galluzzo, C. (2006). Associations among everyday stress, critical life events, and sexual problems. *Journal of Nervous and Mental Disease, 194*, 494–501.

Boecker, H., Sprenger, T., Spilker, M. E., Henriksen, G., Koppenhoefer, M., & Wagner, K. J., et al. (2008). The runner's high: Opioidergic mechanisms in the human brain. *Cerebral Cortex, 18*(11), 2523–2531.

Boehm, L. E. (1994). The validity effect: A search for mediating variables. *Personality and Social Psychology Bulletin, 20*, 285–293.

Bögels, S. M., & Voncken, M. (2008). Social skills training versus cognitive therapy for social anxiety disorder characterized by fear of blushing, trembling, or sweating. *International Journal of Cognitive Therapy, 1*(2), 138–150.

Bogen, J. E. (1985). The dual brain: Some historical and methodological aspects. In D. F. Benson & E. Zaidel (Eds.), *The dual brain: Hemispheric specialization in humans*. New York: Guilford.

Bogen, J. E. (1990). Partial hemispheric independence with the neocommissures intact. In C. Trevarthen (Ed.), *Brain circuits and functions of the mind. Essays in honor of Roger W. Sperry*. Cambridge, MA: Cambridge University Press.

Bogen, J. E. (2000). Split-brain basics: Relevance for the concept of one's other mind. *Journal of the American Academy of Psychoanalysis & Dynamic Psychiatry, 28*, 341–369.

Bogg, T., & Roberts, B. W. (2004). Conscientiousness and health-related behaviors: A meta-analysis of the leading behavioral contributors to mortality. *Psychological Bulletin, 130*, 887–919.

Bohannon, J. N., III, & Warren-Leubecker, A. (1989). Theoretical approaches to language acquisition. In J. Berko Gleason (Ed.), *The development of language*. Columbus, OH: Merrill.

Bohannon, J. N., III., & Bonvillian, J. D. (2009). Theoretical approaches to language acquisition. In J. B. Gleason & N. B. Ratner (Eds.), *The development of language*. Boston, MA: Pearson.

Bohner, G., & Dickel, N. (2011). Attitudes and attitude change. *Annual Review of Psychology, 62*, 391–417.

Bohner, G., & Schwarz, N. (2001). Attitudes, persuasion, and behavior. In A. Tesser & N. Schwarz (Eds.), *Blackwell handbook of social psychology: Intraindividual processes*. Malden, MA: Blackwell.

Bohner, G., Siebler, F., & Schmelcher, J. (2006). Social norms and the likelihood of raping: Perceived rape myth acceptance of others affects men's rape proclivity. *Personality and Social Psychology Bulletin, 32*, 286–297.

Boland, R. J., & Keller, M. B. (2008). Antidepressants. In A. Tasman, J. Kay, J. A. Lieberman, M. B. First, & M. Maj (Eds.), *Psychiatry* (3rd ed.). New York, NY: Wiley-Blackwell.

Boland, R. J., & Keller, M. B. (2009). Course and outcome of depression. In I. H. Gotlib & C. L. Hammen (Eds.), *Handbook of Depression* (2nd ed., pp. 23–43). New York, NY: Guilford Press.

Boldry, J. G., Gaertner, L., & Quinn, J. (2007). Measuring the measures: A meta-analytic investigation of the measures of outgroup homogeneity. *Group Processes & Intergroup Relations, 10*, 157–178.

Boles, D. B. (2005). A large-sample study of sex differences in functional cerebral lateralization. *Journal of Clinical and Experimental Neuropsychology, 27*(6), 759–768.

Bolles, R. C. (1975). *Theory of motivation*. New York: Harper & Row.

Bolling, M. Y., Terry, C. M., & Kohlenberg, R. J. (2006). Behavioral theories. In J. C. Thomas & D. L. Segal (Eds.), *Comprehensive handbook of personality and psychopathology*. New York: Wiley.

Bonanno, G. A. (2005). Resilience in the face of potential trauma. *Current Directions in Psychological Science, 14*(3), 135–138.

Bonanno, G. A., Field, N. P., Kovacevic, A., & Kaltman, S. (2002). Self-enhancement as a buffer against extreme adversity: Civil war in Bosnia and traumatic loss in the United States. *Personality and Social Psychology Bulletin, 28*, 184–196.

Bonanno, G. A., Moskowitz, J. T., Papa, A., & Folkman, S. (2005). Resilience to loss in bereaved spouses, bereaved parents, and bereaved gay men. *Journal of Personality and Social Psychology, 88*, 827–843.

Bond, R., & Smith, P. B. (1996). Culture and conformity: A meta-analysis of studies using Asch's line judgment task. *Psychological Bulletin, 119*, 111–137.

Bonnet, M. H. (2000). Sleep deprivation. In M. H. Kryger, T. Roth, & W. C. Dement (Eds.), *Principles and practice of sleep medicine*. Philadelphia: Saunders.

Bonnet, M. H. (2005). Acute sleep deprivation. In M. H. Kryger, T. Roth, & W. C. Dement (Eds.), *Principles and practice of sleep medicine*. Philadelphia: Elsevier Saunders.

Bonnet, M. H., & Arand, D. L. (2010). Hyperarousal and insomnia: State of the science. *Sleep Medicine Reviews, 14*(1), 9–15.

Bootzin, R. R., Manber, R., Loewy, D. H., Kuo, T. F., & Franzen, P. L. (2001). Sleep disorders. In P. B. Sutker & H. E. Adams (Eds.), *Comprehensive handbook of psychopathology*. New York: Kluwer Academic/Plenum.

Borbely, A. A. (1986). *Secrets of sleep*. New York: Basic Books.

Borbely, A. A., & Achermann, P. (2005). Sleep homeostasis and models of sleep regulation. In M. H. Kryger, T. Roth, & W. C. Dement (Eds.), *Principles and practice of sleep medicine*. Philadelphia: Elsevier Saunders.

Bordin, E. S. (1979). The generalizability of the psychoanalytic concept of the working alliance. *Psychotherapy: Theory, Research & Practice, 16*(3), 252–260.

Bordnick, P. S., Elkins, R. L., Orr, T. E., Walters, P., & Thyer, B. A. (2004). Evaluating the relative effectiveness of three aversion therapies designed to reduce craving among cocaine abusers. *Behavioral Interventions, 19*(1), 1–24.

Borgida, E., & Nisbett, R. E. (1977). The differential impact of abstract vs. concrete information on decisions. *Journal of Applied Social Psychology, 7*, 258–271.

Boring, E. G. (1966). A note on the origin of the word psychology. *Journal of the History of the Behavioral Sciences, 2*, 167.

Borkenau, P., Mauer, N., Riemann, R., Spinath, F. M., & Angleitner, A. (2004). Thin slices of behavior as cues of personality and intelligence. *Journal of Personality and Social Psychology, 86*(4), 599–614.

Bornstein, R. F. (1989). Exposure and affect: Overview and meta-analysis of research, 1968–1987. *Psychological Bulletin, 106*(2), 265–289.

Bornstein, R. F. (2003). Psychodynamic models of personality. In T. Millon & M. J. Lerner (Eds.), *Handbook of psychology (Vol. 5): Personality and social psychology*. New York: Wiley.

Boroditsky, L. (2001). Does language shape thought? Mandarin and English speakers' conceptions of time. *Cognitive Psychology, 43*(1), 1–22.

Bosma, H., van Boxtel, M. P. J., Ponds, R. W. H. M., Houx, P. J., Burdorf, A., & Jolles, J. (2002). Mental work demands protect against cognitive impairment: MAAS prospective cohort study. *Experimental Aging Research, 29*(1), 33–45.

Bouchard, C. (2002). Genetic influences on body weight. In C. G. Fairburn & K. D. Brownell (Eds.), *Eating disorders and obesity: A comprehensive handbook* (pp. 16–21). New York: Guilford.

Bouchard, T. J., Jr. (1997). IQ similarity in twins reared apart: Findings and responses to critics. In R. J. Sternberg, & E. L. Grigorenko (Eds.), *Intelligence, heredity, and environment*. New York: Cambridge University Press.

Bouchard, T. J., Jr. (1998). Genetic and environmental influences on adult intelligence and special mental abilities. *Human Biology, 70*, 257–279.

Bouchard, T. J., Jr. (2004). Genetic influence on human psychological traits: A survey. *Current Directions in Psychological Science, 13*(4), 148–151.

Bouchard, T. J., Jr., Lykken, D. T., McGue, M., Segal, N. L., & Tellegen, A. (1990). Sources of human psychological differences: The Minnesota study of twins reared apart. *Science, 250*, 223–228.

Boucher, J. (2009). *The autistic spectrum: Characterisitcs, causes, and practical issues*. Los Angeles, CA: Sage Publishers.

Bourgeois, J. A., Seaman, J. S., & Servis, M. E. (2003). Delirium, dementia, and amnestic disorders. In R. E. Hales & S. C. Yudofsky (Eds.), *Textbook of clinical psychiatry*. Washington, DC: American Psychiatric Publishing.

Bourgeois, J. A., Seamen, J. S., & Servis, M. E. (2008). Delirium, dementia, and amnestic and other cognitive disorders. In R. E. Hales, S. C. Yudofsky, & G. O. Gabbard (Eds.), *The American Psychiatric Publishing textbook of psychiatry*, (5th ed., pp. 30–35). Washington, DC: American Psychiatric Publishing.

Bousfield, W. A. (1953). The occurrence of clustering in the recall of randomly arranged associates. *Journal of General Psychology, 49*, 229–240.

Bouton, M. E. (2000). A learning theory perspective on lapse, relapse, and the maintenance of behavior change. *Health Psychology, 19*(1), 57–63.

Bouton, M. E. (2002). Context, ambiguity, and unlearning: Sources of relapse after behavioral extinction. *Biological Psychiatry, 52,* 976–986.

Bouton, M. E., & Woods, A. M. (2009). Extinction: Behavioral mechanisms and their implications. In J. H. Byrne (Ed.), *Concise learning and memory: The editor's selection.* San Diego, CA: Elsevier.

Bouton, M. E., Todd, T. P., Vubric, D., & Winterbauer, N. E. (2011). Renewal afte the extinction of free operant behavior. *Learning and Behavior, 39,* 57–67.

Bower, G. H. (1970). Organizational factors in memory. *Cognitive Psychology, 1,* 18–46.

Bower, G. H. (2000). A brief history of memory research. In E. Tulving & F. I. M. Craik (Eds.), *The Oxford handbook of memory* (pp. 3–32). New York: Oxford University Press.

Bower, G. H. (2008). The evolution of a cognitive psychologist: A journey from simple behaviors to complex mental acts. *Annual Review of Psychology, 59,* 1–27.

Bower, G. H., & Clark, M. C. (1969). Narrative stories as mediators of serial learning. *Psychonomic Science, 14,* 181–182.

Bower, G. H., & Springston, F. (1970). Pauses as recoding points in letter series. *Journal of Experimental Psychology, 83,* 421–430.

Bower, J. E., Moskowitz, J., & Epel, E. (2009). Is benefit finding good for your health? Pathways linking positive life changes after stress and physical health outcomes. *Current Directions in Psychological Science, 18*(6), 337–341.

Bowers, M. (2007, July/August). The making of the MFT profession: Standards, regulation. *Family Therapy Magazine,* pp. 12–18.

Bowlby, J. (1969). *Attachment and loss (Vol. 1): Attachment.* New York: Basic Books.

Bowlby, J. (1973). *Attachment and loss (Vol. 2): Separation, anxiety and anger.* New York: Basic Books.

Bowlby, J. (1980). *Attachment and loss (Vol. 3): Sadness and depression.* New York: Basic Books.

Boyce, C. J., Brown, G. D. A., & Moore, S. C. (2010). Money and happiness: Rank of income, not income, affects life satisfaction. *Psychological Science, 21,* 471–475

Boyle, G. J. (2008). Critique of the five-factor model of personality. In G. J. Boyle, G. Matthews, & D. H. Saklofske (Eds.), *The Sage handbook of personality theory and assessment: Personality theories and models* (Vol. 1, pp. 295–312). Los Angles, CA: Sage.

Boyle, M. (2007). The problem with diagnosis. *The Psychologist, 20,* 290–292.

Bradely, M., & Lang, P. J. (1999). *Affective Norms for English World (ANEW): Instruction manual and affective ratings.* Technical Report C-I, The Center for Research in Psychophysiology, University of Florida.

Bradshaw, J. L. (1981). In two minds. *Behavioral and Brain Sciences, 4,* 101–102.

Bradshaw, J. L. (1989). *Hemispheric specialization and psychological function.* New York: Wiley.

Brady, R. (2011, May 4). Dunigan to donate brain to neursurgeon's research. *The Globe and Mail,* S1, S2.

Braffman, W., & Kirsch, I. (1999). Imaginative suggestibility and hypnotizability: An empirical analysis. *Journal of Personality and Social Psychology, 77,* 578–587.

Braginsky, D. D. (1985). Psychology: Handmaiden to society. In S. Koch & D. E. Leary (Eds.), *A century of psychology as science.* New York: McGraw-Hill.

Brain Injury Association of Canada. (2009). Stopconcussions.com presents Up, Close and Personal with Keith Primeau and Friends. Retrieved from http://biac-aclc.ca/en/2011/05/02/stopconcussions-com-presents-up-close-and-personal-with-keith-primeau-and-friends/.

Brainerd, C. J. (1996). Piaget: A centennial celebration. *Psychological Science, 7,* 191–195.

Branaman, T. F., & Gallagher, S. N. (2005). Polygraph testing in sex offender treatment: A review of limitations. *American Journal of Forensic Psychology, 23*(1), 45–64.

Brannon, L., & Feist, J. (2007). Health psychology: An introduction to behavior and health. Belmont, CA: Wadsworth.

Bransford, J. D., & Stein, B. S. (1993). *The IDEAL problem solver.* New York: W. H. Freeman.

Branswell, H., & Hall, J. (2007, November 23). No time but the present. *Toronto Star,* A6.

Brase, G. L. (2006). Cues of parental investment as a factor in attractiveness. *Evolution and Human Behavior, 27,* 145–157.

Brase, G. L., Cosmides, L., & Tooby, J. (1998). Individuation, counting, and statistical inference: The role of frequency and whole-object representations in judgment under certainty. *Journal of Experimental Psychology: General, 127,* 3–21.

Braun, M., Lewin-Epstein, N., Stier, H., & Baumgärtner, M. K. (2008). Perceived equity in the gendered division of household labor. *Journal of Marriage and Family, 70*(5), 1145–1156.

Bravo, M. (2010). Context effects in perception. In E. B. Goldstein (Ed.), *Encyclopedia of perception.* Thousand Oaks, CA: Sage.

Bredt, B. M., Higuera-Alhino, D., Hebert, S. J., McCune, J. M., & Abrams, D. I. (2002). Short-term effects of cannabinoids on immune phenotype and function in HIV-1-infected patients. *Journal of Clinical Pharmacology, 42,* 90S–96S.

Breedlove, S. M. (1994). Sexual differentiation of the human nervous system. *Annual Review of Psychology, 45,* 389–418.

Breger, L. (2009). *A dream of undying fame: How Freud betrayed his mentor and invented psychoanalysis.* New York, NY: Basic Books.

Breggin, P. R. (1991). *Toxic psychiatry.* New York: St. Martin's Press.

Breggin, P. R. (2008). *Medication madness: A psychiatrist exposes the dangers of mood-altering medications.* New York, NY: St. Martin's Press.

Brehm, J. W. (1966). *A theory of psychological reactance.* New York: Academic Press.

Breland, K., & Breland, M. (1961). The misbehavior of organisms. *American Psychologist, 16,* 681–684.

Breland, K., & Breland, M. (1966). *Animal behavior.* New York: Macmillan.

Brennan, K. A., Clark, C. L., & Shaver, P. R. (1998). Self-report measurement of adult attachment: An integrative overview. In J. A. Simpson & W. S. Rholes (Eds.), *Attachment theory and close relationships.* (pp. 46–76). New York: Guilford.

Brennen, T., Vikan, A., & Dybdahl, R. (2007). Are tip-of-the-tongue states universal? Evidence from the speakers of an unwritten language. *Memory, 15,* 167–176.

Breslau, N., Kilbey, M. M., & Andreski, P. (1993). Nicotine dependence and major depression: New evidence from a prospective investigation. *Archives of General Psychiatry, 50,* 31–35.

Breslin, F. C., Zack, M., & McMain, S. (2002). An information-processing analysis of mindfulness: Implications for relapse prevention in the treatment of substance abuse. *Clinical Psychology: Science and Practice, 9,* 275–299.

Breslin, P. A. S. (2010). Taste, genetics of. In E. B. Goldstein (Ed.), *Encyclopedia of perception.* Thousand Oaks, CA: Sage.

Bretherton, I., & Munholland, K. A. (2008). Internal working models in attachment relationships: Conceptual and empirical aspects of security. In J. Cassidy & P. R. Shaver (Eds.), *Handbook of attachment: Theory, research, and clinical applications* (2nd ed., pp. 102–130). New York, NY: Guilford Press.

Breugelmans, S. M., & Poortinga, Y. H. (2006). Emotion without a word: Shame and guilt among Rarámuri Indians and rural Javanese. *Journal of Personality and Social Psychology, 91*(6), 1111–1122.

Brewer, C. L. (1991). Perspectives on John B. Watson. In G. A. Kimble, M. Wertheimer, & C. L. White (Eds.) *Portraits of pioneers in psychology* (pp. 170–186). Hillsdale, NJ: Lawrence Erlbaum Associates, Inc., Publishers.

Brewer, W. F., & Treyens, J. C. (1981). Role of schemata in memory for places. *Cognitive Psychology, 13,* 207–230.

Brewin, C. R. (2003). *Posttraumatic stress disorder: Malady or myth.* New Haven: Yale University Press.

Brewin, C. R. (2007). Autobiographical memory for trauma: Update on four controversies. *Memory, 15,* 227–248.

Brewster, K. L., & Padavic, I. (2000). Change in gender-ideology, 1977–1996: The contributions of intracohort change and population turnover. *Journal of Marriage and the Family, 62,* 477–487.

Brewster, P. W. H., Mullin, C. R., Dobrin, R. A., & Steeves, J. K. E. (2010). Sex differences in face processing are mediated by handedness and sexual orientation. *Laterality: Asymmetries of Body, Brain and Cognition, 13,* 51–70.

Brickman, P., Coates, D., & Janoff-Bulman, R. (1978). Lottery winners and accident victims: Is happiness relative? *Journal of Personality and Social Psychology, 36,* 917–927.

Bridge, J. A., Iyengar, S., Salary, C. B., Barbe, R. P., Birmaher, B., Pincus, H. A., et al. (2007). Clinical response and risk for reported suicidal ideation and suicide attempts in pediatric antidepressant treatment: A meta-analysis of randomized controlled trials. *Journal of the American Medical Association, 297,* 1683–1969.

Brien, S. E., Ronksley, P. E., Turner, B. J., Mukamal, K. J., & Ghali, W. A. (2011). Effect of alcohol consumption on biological markers associated with risk of coronary heart disease: Systematic review and meta-analysis of interventional studies. *British Medical Journal, 342*(7795), 480.

Briere, J., & Conte, J. R. (1993). Self-reported amnesia for abuse in adults molested as children. *Journal of Traumatic Stress, 6*(1), 21–31.

Bringmann, W. G., & Balk, M. M. (1992). Another look at Wilhelm Wundt's publication record. *History of Psychology Newsletter, 24*(3/4), 50–66.

Brislin, R. (1993). *Understanding culture's influence on behavior.* Fort Worth: Harcourt Brace College Publishers.

Brislin, R. (2000). *Understanding culture's influence on behavior.* Belmont, CA: Wadsworth.

Broadbent, D. E. (1958). *Perception and communication.* New York: Pergamon Press.

Brochu, P. M., Gawronski, B., & Esses, V. M. (2011). The integrative prejudice framework and different forms of weight prejudice: An analysis and expansion. *Group Processes and Intergroup Relations, 14*, 429–444.

Brock, A. C. (2006). Rediscovering the history of psychology: Interview with Kurt Danziger. *History of Psychology, 9*, 1–16.

Brock, T. C. (2008). Negligible scholarly impact of 38-witnesses parable. *American Psychologist, 63*, 561.

Bröder, A. (1998). Deception can be acceptable. *American Psychologist, 53*, 805–806.

Brody, N. (1992). *Intelligence.* San Diego: Academic Press.

Brody, N. (2000). History of theories and measurements of intelligence. In R. J. Sternberg (Ed.), *Handbook of intelligence* (pp. 16–33). New York: Cambridge University Press.

Brody, N. (2005). To *g* or not to *g*—that is the question. In O. Wilhelm & R. W. Engle (Eds.), *Handbook of understanding and measuring intelligence.* Thousand Oaks, CA: Sage Publications.

Bronstein, P., & Quina, K. (1988). Perspectives on gender balance and cultural diversity in the teaching of psychology. In P. Bronstein & K. Quina (Eds.), *Teaching a psychology of people: Resources for gender and sociocultural awareness.* Washington, DC: American Psychological Association.

Brooker, A-S., & Hyman, I. (2010). Time use. Canadian Index of Well-being. Retrieved June 30,, 2011, from http://www.ciw.ca/en/TheCanadianIndexOfWellbeing/DomainsOfWellbeing/TimeUse.aspx.

Brooks, D. (2011). Social animal. *The New Yorker,* January 17, 2011.

Brooks-Gunn, J. (1991). Maturational timing variations in adolescent girls, antecedents of. In R. M. Lerner, A. C. Petersen, & J. Brooks-Gunn (Eds.), *Encyclopedia of adolescence.* New York: Garland.

Broughton, R. (1994). Important underemphasized aspects of sleep onset. In R. D. Ogilvie & J. R. Harsh (Eds.), *Sleep onset: Normal and abnormal processes.* Washington, DC: American Psychological Association.

Broughton, R., Billings, R., Cartwright, R., Doucette, D., Edmeads, J., Edwardh, M., et al. (1994). Homicidal somnambulism: A case report. *Sleep, 17*, 253–264.

Brown, A. S., & Derkits, E. J. (2010). Prenatal infection and schizophrenia: A review of epidemiologic and translational studies. *American Journal of Psychiatry, 167*(3), 261–280.

Brown, A. S., & Susser, E. S. (2008). Prenatal nutritional deficiency and risk of adult schizophrenia. *Schizophrenia Bulletin, 34*(6), 1054–1063.

Brown, A. S., Begg, M. D., Gravenstein, S., Schaefer, C. S., Wyatt, R. J., Bresnahan, M., et al. (2004). Serologic evidence of prenatal influenza in the etiology of schizophrenia. *Archives of General Psychiatry, 61*, 774–780.

Brown, D., Scheflin, A. W., & Hammond, D. C. (1998). *Memory, trauma treatment, and the law.* New York: Norton.

Brown, E. J., Juster, H. R., Heimberg, R. G., & Winning, C. D. (1998). Stressful life events and personality styles: Relation to impairment and treatment outcome in patients with social phobia. *Journal of Anxiety Disorders, 12*, 233–251.

Brown, H. D., & Kosslyn, S. M. (1993). Cerebral lateralization. *Current Opinion in Neurobiology, 3*, 183–186.

Brown, L. (2005, February 21).,Women left unprotected by law. *Toronto Star,* p. A3.

Brown, M. (1974). Some determinants of persistence and initiation of achievement-related activities. In J. W. Atkinson & J. O. Raynor (Eds.), *Motivation and achievement.* Washington, DC: Halsted.

Brown, M. R., DeSouza, J. F., Goltz, H. C., Ford, K., Menon, R. S., Goodale, M. A., & Everling, S. (2004). Comparison of memory- and visually-guided saccades using event-related fMRI. *Journal of Neurophysiology, 91*, 873–889.

Brown, R. D., Goldstein, E., & Bjorklund, D. F. (2000). The history and zeitgeist of the repressed–false-memory debate: Scientific and sociological perspectives on suggestibility and childhood memory. In D. F. Bjorklund (Ed.), *False-memory creation in children and adults* (pp. 1–30). Mahwah, NJ: Erlbaum.

Brown, R. T. (1989). Creativity: What are we to measure? In J. A. Glover, R. R. Ronning, & C. R. Reynolds (Eds.), *Handbook of creativity.* New York: Plenum.

Brown, R., & McNeill, D. (1966). The "tip-of-the-tongue" phenomenon. *Journal of Verbal Learning and Verbal Behavior, 5*(4), 325–337.

Brown, S. C., & Craik, F. I. M. (2000). Encoding and retrieval of information. In E. Tulving & F. I. M. Craik (Eds.), *The Oxford handbook of memory* (pp. 93–108). New York: Oxford University Press.

Brown, T. T., & Dobs, A. S. (2002). Endocrine effects of marijuana. *Journal of Clinical Pharmacology, 42*, 97S–102S.

Brownell, H. H., & Gardner, H. (1981). Hemisphere specialization: Definitions not incantations. *Behavioral and Brain Sciences, 4*, 64–65.

Brownell, K. D. (2002). The environment and obesity. In C. G. Fairburn & K. D. Brownell (Eds.), *Eating disorders and obesity: A comprehensive handbook* (pp. 433–438). New York: Guilford.

Brownell, K. D., & Wadden, T. A. (2000). Obesity. In B. J. Sadock & V. A. Sadock (Eds.), *Kaplan and Sadock's comprehensive textbook of psychiatry* (7th ed., Vol. 2, pp. 1787–1796). Philadelphia: Lippincott Williams & Wilkins.

Bruch, H. (1978). *The golden cage: The enigma of anorexia nervosa.* Cambridge, MA: Harvard University Press.

Bruckner-Gordon, F., Gangi, B. K., & Wallman, G. U. (1988). *Making therapy work: Your guide to choosing, using, and ending therapy.* New York: Harper & Row.

Bruer, J. T. (2002). Avoiding the pediatricians error: How neuroscientists can help educators (and themselves). *Nature Neuroscience, 5*, 1031–1033.

Bruser, D. (2008, May 31). Stress rate soars for TTC drivers. *Toronto Star,* A12.

Bryden, M. P. (1982). *Laterality: Functional asymmetry in the intact brain.* New York: Academic Press.

Buchanan, R. W., & Carpenter, W. T. (2005). Concept of schizophrenia. In B. J. Sadock & V. A. Sadock (Eds.), *Kaplan & Sadock's comprehensive textbook of psychiatry.* Philadelphia: Lippincott, Williams & Wilkins.

Buchanan, T. (2000). Potential of the Internet for personality research. In M. H. Birnbaum (Ed.), *Psychological experiments on the Internet.* San Diego: Academic Press.

Buchanan, T. (2007). Personality testing on the Internet: What we know, and what we do not. In A. N. Joinson, K. Y. A. McKenna, T. Postmes, & U.-D. Reips (Eds.), *The Oxford handbook of Internet psychology.* New York: Oxford University Press.

Buck, L. B. (2000). Smell and taste: The chemical senses. In E. R. Kandel, J. H. Schwartz, & T. M. Jessell (Eds.), *Principles of neural science.* New York: McGraw-Hill.

Buck, L. B. (2004). Olfactory receptors and coding in mammals. *Nutrition Reviews, 62*, S184–S188.

Buck, L. B., & Axel, R. (1991). A novel multigene family may encode odorant receptors: A molecular basis for odour recognition. *Cell, 65*, 175–187.

Buckley, K. W. (1982). The selling of a psychologist: John Broadus Watson and the application of behavioral techniques to advertising. *Journal of the History of the Behavioral Sciences, 18*, 207–221.

Buckley, K. W. (1994). Misbehaviorism: The case of John B. Watson's dismissal from Johns Hopkins University. In J. T. Todd and E. K. Morris (Eds.), *Modern perspectives on John B. Watson and classical behaviorism* (pp. 37–63). Westport, CT: Greenwood Press.

Buckman, R. (2002). Communications and emotions: Skills and effort are key. *British Medical Journal, 325*, 672.

Buckner, R. L. (2007). Prospection and the brain. *Behavioral and Brain Sciences, 30*, 318–319.

Buckner, R. L. (2010). The role of the hippocampus in prediction and imagination. *Annual Review of Psychology, 61*, 27–48.

Buckner, R. L., & Carroll, D. C. (2006). Self-projection and the brain. *Trends in Cognitive Science, 11*, 49–57.

Budiansky, S. (2004). Human and animal intelligence: The gap is a chasm. *Cerebrum, 6*(2), 85–95.

Buehler, R., Messervey, D., & Griffin, D. (2005). Collaborative planning and prediction: Does group discussion affect optimistic biases in time estimation? *Organizational Behavior and Human Decision Processes, 97*, 47–63.

Bufe, B., Breslin, P. A. S., Kuhn, C., Reed, D. R., Tharp, C. D., Slack, J. P., Kim, U., Drayna, D., & Meyerhof, W. (2005). The molecular basis of individual differences in phenylthiocarbamide and propylthiouracil bitterness perception. *Current Biology, 15*, 322–327.

Buffardi, L. E., & Campbell, W. (2008). Narcissism and social networking web sites. *Personality and Social Psychology Bulletin, 34*(10), 1303–1314.

Bühler, C., & Allen, M. (1972). *Introduction to humanistic psychology.* Pacific Grove, CA: Brooks/Cole.

Bulik, C. M. (2004). Genetic and biological risk factors. In J. K. Thompson (Ed.), *Handbook of eating disorders and obesity.* New York: Wiley.

Bull, D. L. (1999). A verified case of recovered memories of sexual abuse. *American Journal of Psychotherapy, 53*, 221–224.

Buller, D. J. (2009, January 1). Four fallacies of pop evolutionary psychology. *Scientific American,* pp. 74–81.

Bullied student tickled pink by schoolmates' T-shirt campaign. (2007, September 19). *CBC News.* Retrieved Feburary 1, 2008, from http://www.cbc.ca/canada/nova-scotia/story/2007/09/18/pink-tshirts-students.html?ref=rss.

Bumpass, L., & Lu, H. (2000). Trends in cohabitation and implications for children's family contexts in the United States. *Population Studies, 54*(1), 29–41.

Bunn, G. C. (2007). Spectacular science: The lie detector's ambivalent powers. *History of Psychology, 10*, 156–178.

Burg, J., & Michalak, J. (2011). The healthy quality of mindful breathing: Associations with rumination and depression. *Cognitive Therapy and Research, 35,* 179–185.

Burger, J. M. (1999). The foot-in-the-door compliance procedure: A multiple process analysis review. *Personality and Social Psychology Review, 3,* 303–325.

Burger, J. M. (2004). *Personality.* Belmont, CA: Wadsworth.

Burger, J. M. (2009). Replicating Milgram: Would people still obey today? *American Psychologist, 64*(1), 1–11.

Burke, B. L., Martens, A., & Faucher, E. H. (2010). Two decades of terror management theory: A meta-analysis of mortality salience research. *Personality and Social Psychology Review, 14*(2), 155–195.

Burke, D. M., & Shafto, M. A. (2004). Aging and language production. *Current Directions in Psychological Science, 13*(1), 21–24.

Burkhardt, D. A. (2010). Visual processing: Retinal. In E. B. Goldstein (Ed.), *Encyclopedia of perception.* Thousand Oaks, CA: Sage.

Burlingame, G. M., & Baldwin, S. (2011). Group therapy. In J. C. Norcross, G. R. Vandenbos, & D. K. Freedheim (Eds.), *History of psychotherapy: Continuity and change* (2nd ed.). Washington, DC: American Psychological Association.

Burlingame, G. M., & McClendon, D. T. (2008). Group therapy. In J. L. Lebow (Ed.), *Twenty-first century psychotherapies: Contemporary approaches to theory and practice.* New York: Wiley.

Burns, A. B., Brown, J. S., Sachs-Ericsson, N., Plant, E. A., Curtis, J. T., Fredrickson, B. L., et al. (2008). Upward spirals of positive emotion and coping: Replication, extension, and initial exploration of neurochemical substrates. *Personality and Individual Differences, 44,* 360–370.

Burns, B. D., & Corpus, B. (2004). Randomness and inductions from streaks: "Gambler's fallacy" versus "hot hand." *Psychonomic Bulletin & Review, 11*(1), 179–184.

Burnstein, E., Crandall, C., & Kitayama, S. (1994). Some neo-Darwinian decision rules for altruism: Weighing cues for inclusive fitness as a function of the biological importance of the decision. *Journal of Personality and Social Psychology, 67,* 773–789.

Burriss, R. P., & Little, A. C. (2006). Effects of partner conception risk phase on male perception of dominance in faces. *Evolution and Human Behavior, 27,* 297–305.

Bushman, B. J. (2002). Does venting anger feed or extinguish the flame? Catharsis, rumination, distraction, anger, and aggressive responding. *Personality and Social Psychology Bulletin, 28,* 724–731.

Bushman, B. J., & Anderson, C. A. (2001). Media violence and the American public: Scientific facts versus media misinformation. *American Psychologist, 56,* 477–489.

Bushman, B. J., & Anderson, C. A. (2009). Comfortably numb: Desensitizing effects of violent media on helping others. *Psychological Science, 20*(3), 273–277.

Bushman, B. J., & Huesmann, L. R. (2001). Effects of televised violence on aggression. In D. G. Singer & J. L. Singer (Eds.), *Handbook of children and the media.* Thousand Oaks, CA: Sage.

Bushman, B. J., Rothstein H. R., & Anderson, C. A. (2010). Much ado about something: Violent video games and a school of red herring: reply to Ferguson and Kilburn (2010). *Psychological Bulletin, 136,* 182–187.

Buss, D. M. (1985). Human mate selection. *American Scientist, 73,* 47–51.

Buss, D. M. (1988). The evolution of human intrasexual competition: Tactics of mate attraction. *Journal of Personality and Social Psychology, 54,* 616–628.

Buss, D. M. (1989). Sex differences in human mate preferences: Evolutionary hypotheses tested in 37 cultures. *Behavioral and Brain Sciences, 12,* 1–49.

Buss, D. M. (1991). Evolutionary personality psychology. *Annual Review of Psychology, 42,* 459–491.

Buss, D. M. (1994a). *The evolution of desire: Strategies of human mating.* New York: Basic Books.

Buss, D. M. (1995). Evolutionary psychology: A new paradigm for psychological science. *Psychological Inquiry, 6,* 1–30.

Buss, D. M. (1996). The evolutionary psychology of human social strategies. In E. T. Higgins & A. W. Kruglanski (Eds.), *Social psychology: Handbook of basic principles.* New York: Guilford.

Buss, D. M. (1997). Evolutionary foundation of personality. In R. Hogan, J. Johnson, & S. Briggs (Eds.), *Handbook of personality psychology.* San Diego: Academic Press.

Buss, D. M. (1999). *Evolutionary psychology: The new science of the mind.* Boston: Allyn & Bacon.

Buss, D. M. (2001). Cognitive biases and emotional wisdom in the evolution of conflict between the sexes. *Current Directions in Psychological Science, 10,* 219–223.

Buss, D. M. (2009). The great struggles of life: Darwin and the emergence of evolutionary psychology. *American Psychologist, 64*(2), 140–148.

Buss, D. M., & Kenrick, D. T. (1998). Evolutionary social psychology. In D. T. Gilbert, S. T. Fiske, & G. Lindzey (Eds.), *The handbook of social psychology.* New York: McGraw-Hill.

Buss, D. M., & Reeve, H. K. (2003). Evolutionary psychology and developmental dynamics: Comment on Lickliter and Honeycutt. *Psychological Bulletin, 129,* 848–853.

Buss, D. M., & Shackelford, T. K. (2008). Attractive women want it all: Good genes, economic investment, parenting proclivities, and emotional commitment. *Evolutionary Psychology, 6*(1), 134–146.

Bussey, K., & Bandura, A. (1999). Social cognitive theory of gender development and differentiation. *Psychological Review, 106,* 676–713.

Bussey, K., & Bandura, A. (2004). Social cognitive theory of gender development and functioning. In A. H. Eagly, A. E. Beall, & R. J. Sternberg (Eds.), *The psychology of gender.* New York: Guilford.

Buster, J. E., & Carson, S. A. (2002). Endocrinology and diagnosis of pregnancy. In S. G. Gabbe, J. R. Niebyl, & J. L. Simpson (Eds.), *Obstetrics: Normal and problem pregnancies.* New York: Churchill Livingstone.

Butcher, J. N. (2005). *A beginner's guide to the MMPI-2.* Washington, DC: American Psychological Association.

Butcher, J. N. (2006). *MMPI-2: A practitioner's guide.* Washington, DC: American Psychological Association.

Butler, A. C., & Roediger, H. (2008). Feedback enhances the positive effects and reduces the negative effects of multiple-choice testing. *Memory & Cognition, 36*(3), 604–616.

Butler, E. A., Egloff, B., Wilhelm, F. H., Smith, N. C., Erickson, E. A., & Gross, J. J. (2003). The social consequences of expressive suppression. *Emotion, 3*(1), 48–67.

Butler, J. L., & Baumeister, R. F. (1998). The trouble with friendly faces: Skilled performance with a supportive audience. *Journal of Personality and Social Psychology, 75,* 1213–1230.

Button, T. M. M., Maughan, B., & McGuffin, P. (2007). The relationship of maternal smoking to psychological problems in the offspring. *Early Human Development, 83,* 727–732.

Buxton, M. N., Arkey, Y., Lagos, J., Deposito, F., Lowenthal, F., & Simring, S. (1981). Stress and platelet aggregation in hemophiliac children and their family members. *Research Communications in Psychology, Psychiatry and Behavior, 6*(1), 21–48.

Byne, W. (2007). Biology and sexual minority status. In I. H. Meyer & M. E. Northridge (Eds.). *The health of sexual minorities: Public health perspectives on lesbian, gay, bisexual, and transgender populations.* New York, NY: Springer Science & Business Media.

Byrne, J. H. (2008). Postsynaptic potentials and synapticintegration. In L. Squire, D. Berg, F. Bloom, S. Du Lac, A. Ghosh, & N. Spitzer (Eds.), *Fundamental neuroscience* (3rd ed., pp. 227–246). San Diego, CA: Elsevier.

Cabral, G. A., & Petitt, D. A. D. (1998). Drugs and immunity: Cannabinoids and their role in decreased resistance to infectious disease. *Journal of Neuroimmunology, 83,* 116–123.

Cabyoglu, M. T., Ergene, N., & Tan, U. (2006). The mechanism of acupuncture and clinical applications. *International Journal of Neuroscience, 116*(2), 115–125.

Cacioppo, J. T. (1994). Social neuroscience; Automatic, neuroendocrine, and immune responses to stress. *Psychophysiology, 31,* 113–128.

Cacioppo, J. T., & Berntson, G. G. (1999). The affect system: Architecture and operating characteristics. *Current Directions in Psychological Science, 8,* 133–137.

Cacioppo, J. T., & Berntson, G. G. (2005). *Social neuroscience.* New York: Psychology Press.

Cacioppo, J. T., Amaral, D. G., Blanchard, J. J., Cameron, J. L., Sue, C. C., Crews, D., et al. (2007). Social neuroscience: Progress and implications for mental health. *Perspectives on Psychological Science, 2,* 99–123.

Cacioppo, J. T., Berntson, G. G., & Nusbaum, H. C. (2008). Neuroimaging as a new tool in the toolbox of psychological science. *Current Directions in Psychological Science, 17,* 62–67.

Cacioppo, J. T., Klein, D. J., Berntson, G. G., & Hatfield, E. (1993). The psychophysiology of emotions. In M. Lewis & J. M. Haviland (Eds.), *Handbook of emotions.* New York: Guilford.

Cadinu, M., Maass, A., Rosabianca, A., & Kiesner, J. (2005). Why do women underperform under stereotype threat? Evidence for the role of negative thinking. *Psychological Science, 16,* 572–578.

Cahill, L. (2006). Why sex matters for neuroscience. *Nature Reviews Neuroscience, 7,* 477–484.

Cahill, L., & McGaugh, J. L. (1998). Mechanisms of emotional arousal and lasting declarative memory. *Trends in Neurosciences, 21,* 294–299.

Cahn, B. R., & Polich, J. (2006). Meditation states and traits: EEG, ERP, and neuroimaging studies. *Psychological Bulletin, 132,* 180–211.

Cai, D. J., Mednick, S. A., Harrison, E. M., Kanady, J. C., & Mednick, S. C. (2009). REM, not incubation, improves creativity by priming associative networks. *Proceedings of the National Academy of Sciences of the United States of America, 106*(25), 10130–10134.

Cain, W. S. (1988). Olfaction. In R. C. Atkinson, R. J. Herrnstein, G. Lindzey, & R. D. Luce (Eds.), *Stevens'* handbook of experimental psychology: Perception and motivation (Vol. 1). New York: Wiley.

Caine, E. D., & Lyness, J. M. (2000). Delirium, dementia, and amnestic and other cognitive disorders. In B. J. Sadock & V. A. Sadock (Eds.), *Kaplan and Sadock's comprehensive textbook of psychiatry*. Philadelphia: Lippincott, Williams & Wilkins.

Calhoun, L. G., & Tedeschi, R. G. (2006). The foundations of posttraumatic growth: An expanded framework. In L. G. Calhoun & R. G. Tedeschi (Eds.), *Handbook of posttraumatic growth: Research & practice*. Mahwah, NJ: Erlbaum.

Calhoun, L. G., & Tedeschi, R. G. (2008). The paradox of struggling with trauma: Guidelines for practice and directions for research. In S. Joseph & P. A. Linley (Eds.), *Trauma, recovery, and growth: Positive psychological perspectives on posttraumatic stress*. Hoboken, NJ: Wiley.

Callaghan, T., Rochat, P., Lillard, A., Claux, M., Odden, H., Itakura, S., et al. (2005). Synchrony in the onset of mental-state reasoning: Evidence from five cultures. *Psychological Science, 16*(5), 378–384.

Callahan, C. M. (2000). Intelligence and giftedness. In R. J. Sternberg (Ed.), *Handbook of intelligence* (pp. 159–175). New York: Cambridge University Press.

Callwood, J. (1990). *Sleepwalker*. Toronto: Lester & Orpen Dennys.

Calvert, C. (1997). Hate speech and its harms: A communication theory perspective. *Journal of Communication, 47*, 4–19.

Camaioni, L. (2001). Early language. In G. Bremner & A. Fogel (Eds.), *Blackwell handbook of infant development*. Malden, MA: Blackwell.

Camerer, C. (2005). Three cheers—psychological, theoretical, empirical—for loss aversion. *Journal of Marketing Research, 42*(2), 129–133.

Camerer, C. F., Loewenstein, G., & Rabin, M. (Eds). (2004). *Advances in behavioral economics*. Princeton, NJ: Russell Sage Foundation.

Cameron, L., Leventhal, E. A., & Leventhal, H. (1993). Symptom representations and affect as determinants of care seeking in a community-dwelling, adult sample population. *Health Psychology, 12*, 171–179.

CAMH. (2011). Drinking, cannabis use and psychological distress increase, CAMH survey finds. CAMH, retrieved June 20, 2011, from http://www.camh.net/News_events/News_releases_and_media_advisories_and_backgrounders/CAMH_monitor_2011.html

Cami, J., & Farre, M. (2003). Mechanisms of disease: Drug addiction. *New England Journal of Medicine, 349*, 975–986.

Campbell, A. (2005). Aggression. In D. M. Buss (Ed.), *The handbook of evolutionary psychology*. New York: Wiley.

Campbell, J. (1971). *Hero with a thousand faces*. New York: Harcourt Brace Jovanovich.

Campbell, K. L., Al-Aidroos, N., Fatt, R., Pratt, J., & Hasher, L. (2010). The effects of multisensory targets on saccadic trajectory deviations: Eliminating age differences. *Experimental Brain Research, 201*(3), 385–392.

Campbell, K. L., Al-Aidroos, N., Pratt, J., & Hasher, L. (2009). Repelling the young and attracting the old: Examining age-related differences in saccade trajectory deviations. *Psychology and Aging, 24*, 163–168.

Campbell, L., Simpson, J. A., Boldry, J., & Kashy, D. A. (2005). Perceptions of conflict and support in romantic relationships: The role of attachment anxiety. *Journal of Personality and Social Psychology, 88*, 510–531.

Campbell, R., & Sais, E. (1995). Accelerated metalinguistic (phonological) awareness in bilingual children. *British Journal of Developmental Psychology, 13*, 61–68.

Campbell, R., & Wasco, S. M. (2005). Understanding rape and sexual assault: 20 years of progress and future directions. *Journal of Interpersonal Violence, 20*(1), 127–131.

Campbell, W. K., & Foster, J. D. (2007). The narcissistic self: Background, an extended-agency model, and ongoing controversies. In C. Sedikides & S. J. Spencer (Eds.), *The self* (pp. 115–138). New York, NY: Psychology Press.

Campfield, L. A. (2002). Leptin and body weight regulation. In C. G. Fairburn & K. D. Brownell (Eds.), *Eating disorders and obesity: A comprehensive handbook* (pp. 32–36). New York: Guilford.

Campos, P. (2004). *The obesity myth: Why America's obsession with weight is hazardous to your health*. New York, NY: Gotham Books.

Canadian Charter of Rights and Freedoms. (1982). Department of Justice Canada: http://laws.justice.gc.ca/en/charter.

Canadian Council of Ministers of Education. (2003). Canadian Youth, Sexual Health, and HIV/AIDS study. Retrieved May 11, 2011, from http://www.cmec.ca/Publications/Lists/Publications/Attachments/180/CYSHHAS_2002_EN.pdf.

Canadian Institutes of Health Research. (2009). When I'm 65. Retrieved May 29, 2011, from http://www.cihr-irsc.gc.ca/e/39468.html.

Canadian Mental Health Association (Alberta Division). (2011). Statistics. Retrieved June 21, 2011, from http://www.cmha.ab.ca/bins/site_page.asp?cid=284-285-1258-1404&lang=1

Canadian Mental Health Association. (2005). *Physical and mental health equally important to Canadians*. Retrieved July 3, 2005, from http://www.cmha.ca/bins/content_page.asp?cid=6-20-21-386.

Canadian Mental Health Foundation. (2006). *Suicide statistics*. Retrieved November 9, 2011, from http://www.ontario.cmha.ca/fact_sheets.asp?cID=3965.

Canadian Psychological Association. (2008, June 13). *Annual report (2007–2008)*. Retrieved August 16, 2008, from http://www.cpa.ca.

Canadian Psychological Association. (n.d.). *CPA Awards*. Retrieved May 14, 2008, from http://www.cpa.ca/aboutcpa/cpaawards.

Canadian Space Agency. (n.d., c). *Role of visual cues in spatial orientation (VISO)*. Retrieved March 22, 2005, from http://www.space.gc.ca/asc/eng/missions/sts-090-neurola.

Canadian Task Force on Preventive Health Care. (2003). *Prevention of suicide*. Retrieved June 19, 2005, from http://www.canadiancrc.com/Can_Preventive_Care_suicide.htm.

Canli, T. (2008). Toward a "molecular psychology" of personality. In O. P. John, R. W. Robbins, & L. A. Pervin (Eds.), *Handbook of personality: Theory and research* (Vol. 3, pp. 311–327). New York, NY: Guilford Press.

Canli, T., Sivers, H., Whitfield, S. L., Gotlib, I. H., and Gabrieli, J. D. E. (2002). Amygdala response to happy faces as a function of extraversion. *Science, 296*, 2191.

Cannon, W. B. (1927). The James–Lange theory of emotions: A critical examination and an alternative theory. *American Journal of Psychology, 39*, 106–124.

Cannon, W. B. (1932). *The wisdom of the body*. New York: Norton.

Canter, P. H. (2003). The therapeutic effects of meditation. *British Medical Journal, 326*, 1049–1050.

Cao, Y., Vikingstad, E. M., Huttenlocher, P. R., Towle, V. L., & Levin, D. N. (1994). Functional magnetic resonance imaging studies of the reorganization of the human head sensorimotor area after unilateral brain injury. *Proceedings of the National Academy of Sciences of the United States of America, 91*, 9612–9616.

Capaldi, E. D., & VandenBos, G. R. (1991). Taste, food exposure, and eating behavior. *Hospital and Community Psychiatry, 42*(8), 787–789.

Capozza, D., & Brown, R. (2000). *Social identity processes: Trends in theory and research*. London: Sage.

Cappadocia, M., & Weiss, J. A. (2011). Review of social skills training groups for youth with Asperger syndrome and high functioning autism. *Research in Autism Spectrum Disorders, 5*(1), 70–78.

Cappuccio, F. P., Taggart, F. M., Kandala, N., Currie, A., Peile, E., Stranges, S., & Miller, M. A. (2008). Meta-analysis of short sleep duration and obesity in children and adults. *Sleep: Journal of Sleep and Sleep Disorders Research, 31*(5), 619–626.

Card, J. P., Swanson, L. W., & Moore, R. (2008). The hypothalamus: An overview of regulatory systems. In L. Squire, D. Berg, F. Bloom, S. Du Lac, A. Ghosh, & N. Spitzer (Eds.), *Fundamental neuroscience* (3rd ed., pp. 795–808). San Diego, CA: Elsevier.

Cardellini, L, & Pascual-Leone, J. (2004). On mentors, cognitive development, education, and constructivism: An interview with Juan Pascual-Leone. *Journal of Cognitive Education and Psychology, 4*, 199–219.

Cardeña, E., & Gleaves, D. H. (2007). Dissociative disorders. In M. Hersen, S. M. Turner, & D. C. Beidel (Eds.), *Adult psychopathology and diagnosis*. New York: Wiley.

Carey, B. (2008, December 4). H. M., an unforgettable amnesiac, dies at 82. *New York Times*. Retrieved December 15, 2010, from http://www.nytimes.com/2008/12/05/us/05hm.html.

Carey, B. (2009, December 21). Building a search engine of the brain, slice by slice. *The New York Times*. Retrieved from http://www.newyorktimes.com.

Carey, M. P., & Vanable, P. A. (2003). AIDS/HIV. In A. M. Nezu, C. M. Nezu, & P. A. Geller (Eds.), *Handbook of psychology (Vol. 9): Health psychology*. New York: John Wiley

Carey, S. (2010). Beyond fast mapping. *Language Learning and Development, 6*(3), 184–205.

Carli, L. L. (1999). Cognitive, reconstruction, hindsight, and reactions to victims and perpetrators. *Personality & Social Psychology Bulletin, 25*, 966–979.

Carlo, G. (2006). Care-based and altruistically based morality. In M. Killen & J. G. Smetana (Eds.), *Handbook of moral development*. Mahwah, NJ: Erlbaum.

Carlson, S. A., Fulton, J. E., Schoenborn, C. A., & Loustalot, F. (2010). Trend and prevalence estimates based on the 2008 Physical Activity Guidelines for Americans. *American Journal of Preventive Medicine, 39*(4), 305–313.

Carmichael, A. (2005). Ellard gets life sentence for role in Rena Virk's slaying. *Toronto Star*, July 8, 2005, p. A17.

Carnagey, N. L., Anderson, C. A., & Bushman, B. J. (2007). The effect of video game violence on physiological desensitization. *Journal of Experimental Social Psychology, 43*, 489–496.

Caro, R. M. (1986). The functions of stotting in Thomson's gazelles: Some tests of the predictions. *Animal Behavior, 34,* 663–684.

Carpenter, S. (2001). Sleep deprivation may be undermining teen health. *Monitor on Psychology, 32.* Retrieved March 23, 2008, from http://www.apa.org/monitor/oct01/sleepteen.html.

Carpenter, W. T. (1992). The negative symptom challenge. *Archives of General Psychiatry, 49,* 236–237.

Carpenter, W. T. (2002). From clinical trial to prescription. *Archives of General Psychology, 59,* 282–285.

Carr, E. (1972). *Fresh Seeing: Two addresses by Emily Carr.* Toronto: Clarke, Irwin & Co.

Carrillo, M., Ricci, L. A., Coppersmith, G. A., & Melloni, R. R. (2009). The effect of increased serotonergic neurotransmission on aggression: A critical meta-analytical review of preclinical studies. *Psychopharmacology, 205*(3), 349–368.

Carroll, J. B. (1993). *Human cognitive abilities: A survey of factor-analytic studies.* Cambridge: Cambridge University Press.

Carroll, J. B. (1996). A three-stratum theory of intelligence: Spearman's contribution. In I. Dennis & P. Tapsfield (Eds.), *Human abilities: Their nature and measurement.* Mahwah, NJ: Erlbaum.

Carroll, J. S., Padilla-Walker, L. M., Nelson, L. J., Olson, C. D., Barry, C. M., & Madsen, S. D. (2008). Generation XXX: Pornography acceptance and use among emerging adults. *Journal of Adolescent Research, 23*(1), 6–30.

Carroll-Ghosh, T., Victor, B. S., & Bourgeois, J. A. (2003). Suicide. In R. E. Hales & S. C. Yudofsky (Eds.), *Textbook of clinical psychiatry* (pp. 1457–1484). Washington, DC: American Psychiatric Publishing.

Carskadon, M. A., & Dement, W. C. (1994). Normal human sleep: An overview. In M. Kryger, T. Roth, and W. Dement (Eds.). *Principles and practice of sleep medicine* (pp. 3–15). Philadelphia: WB Saunders.

Carskadon, M. A., & Dement, W. C. (2005). Normal human sleep: An overview. In M. H. Kryger, T. Roth, & W. C. Dement (Eds.), *Principles and practice of sleep medicine.* Philadelphia: Elsevier Saunders.

Carskadon, M. A., & Rechtschaffen, A. (2005). Monitoring and staging human sleep. In M. H. Kryger, T. Roth, & W. C. Dement (Eds.). *Principles and practice of sleep medicine.* Philadelphia: Elsevier Saunders.

Carson, S. H. (2011). Creativity and psychopathology: A shared vulnerability model. *Canadian Journal of Psychiatry, 56,* 144–153.

Carter, B. (1999). Becoming parents: The family with young children. In B. Carter & M. McGoldrick (Eds.), *The expanded family life cycle: Individual, family, and social perspectives* (3rd ed., pp. 249–273). Boston: Allyn & Bacon.

Carter, B., & McGoldrick, M. (1999). Overview: The expanded family life cycle: Individual, family, and social perspectives. In B. Carter & M. McGoldrick (Eds.), *The expanded family life cycle: Individual, family, and social perspectives* (3rd ed., pp. 1–26). Boston: Allyn & Bacon.

Carter, E. A., & McGoldrick, M. (1988). Overview: The changing family life cycle—A framework for family therapy. In E. A. Carter & M. McGoldrick (Eds.), *The changing family cycle: A framework for family therapy* (2nd ed.). New York: Gardner Press.

Carter, P. J., & Russell, K. (2001). *Workout for a balanced brain: Exercises, puzzles & games to sharpen both sides of your brain.* Readers Digest Association.

Carter, R. (1998). *Mapping the mind.* Berkeley: University of California Press.

Cartwright, R. D. (1977). *Night life: Explorations in dreaming.* Englewood Cliffs, NJ: Prentice-Hall.

Cartwright, R. D. (1991). Dreams that work: The relation of dream incorporation to adaptation to stressful events. *Dreaming, 1,* 3–9.

Cartwright, R. D. (1994). Dreams and their meaning. In M. H. Kryger, T. Roth, & W. C. Dement (Eds.), *Principles and practice of sleep medicine* (2nd ed.). Philadelphia: Saunders.

Cartwright, R. D. (2004). The role of sleep in changing our minds: A psychologist's discussion of papers on memory reactivation and consolidation in sleep. *Learning & Memory, 11,* 660–663.

Cartwright, R. D., & Lamberg, L. (1992). *Crisis dreaming.* New York: HarperCollins.

Cartwright-Finch, U., & Lavie, N. (2007). The role of perceptual load in inattentional blindness. *Cognition, 102,* 321–340.

Carver, C. S. (2007). Stress, coping, and health. In H. S. Friedman & R. C. Silver (Eds.), *Foundations of health psychology.* New York: Oxford University Press.

Carver, C. S., & Scheier, M. F. (1994). Situational coping and coping dispositions in a stressful transaction. *Journal of Personality and Social Psychology, 66,* 184–195.

Carver, C. S., & Scheier, M. F. (1999). Optimism. In C. R. Snyder (Ed.), *Coping: The psychology of what works.* New York: Oxford University Press.

Carver, C. S., Pozo, C., Harris, S. D., Noriega, V., Scheier, M. F., Robinson, D. S., et al. (1993). How coping mediates the effect of optimism on distress: A study of women with early stage breast cancer. *Journal of Personality and Social Psychology, 65,* 375–390.

Carver, C. S., Scheier, M. F., & Weintraub, J. K. (1989). Assessing coping strategies: A theoretically based approach. *Journal of Personality and Social Psychology, 56,* 267–283.

Casanova, C., Merabet, L., Desautels, A., & Minville, K. (2001). Higher-order motion processing in the pulvinar. *Progress in Brain Research, 134,* 71–82.

Case, R. (1991a). *The mind's staircase: Exploring the conceptual underpinnings of children's thought and knowledge.* Hillsdale, NJ: Lawrence Erlbaum & Associates.

Case, R. (1991b). A neo-Piagetian approach to the issues of cognitive generality and specificity. In R. Case (Ed.), *The mind's staircase: Exploring the conceptual underpinnings of children's thought and knowledge.* Hillsdale, NJ: Lawrence Erlbaum & Associates.

Case, R. (1998). The development of conceptual structures. In W. Damon (Series Editor) D. Kuhn & R. S. Seigler (Volume Editors.), *Handbook of child psychology (Vol. 2): Cognition, perception and language* (5th ed., pp. 128–162). New York: Wiley.

Caspi, A., & Herbener, E. S. (1990). Continuity and change: Assortative marriage and the consistency of personality in adulthood. *Journal of Personality and Social Psychology, 58*(2), 250–258.

Caspi, A., & Moffitt, T. E. (2006). Gene–environment interactions in psychiatry: Joining forces with neuroscience. *Nature Reviews Neuroscience, 7,* 583–590.

Caspi, A., Roberts, B. W., & Shiner, R. L. (2005). Personality development: Stability and change. *Annual Review of Psychology, 56,* 453–484.

Caspi, O., & Burleson, K. O. (2005). Methodological challenges in meditation research. *Advances in Mind–Body Medicine, 21*(1), 4–11.

Cassel, R. N. (2000). Third force psychology and person-centered theory: From ego-status to ego-ideal. *Psychology: A Journal of Human Behavior, 37*(3), 44–48.

Cassidy, J. (2008). The nature of the child's ties. In J. Cassidy & P. R. Shaver (Eds.), *Handbook of attachment: Theory, research, and clinical applications* (2nd ed., pp. 3–22). New York, NY: Guilford Press.

Cassidy, J., & Shaver, P. R. (1999). *Handbook of attachment: Theory, research, and clinical application.* New York: Guilford Press.

Castle, D. (2008). Drawing conclusions about cannabis and psychosis. *Psychological Medicine, 38*(3), 459–460.

Castonguary, L. G., Boswell, J. F., Constantino, M. J., Goldfried, M. R., & Hill, C. E. (2010). Training implications of harmful effects of psychological treatments. *American Psychologist, 65,* 34–49.

Catania, A. C. (1992). Reinforcement. In L. R. Squire (Ed.), *Encyclopedia of learning and memory.* New York: Macmillan.

Catano, V. M., Wiesner, W. H., Hackett, R. D., & Methot, L. (2005). *Recruitment and selection in Canada* (3rd ed.). Toronto: Nelson.

Cattell, H. E. P. (2004). The Sixteen Personality Factor (16PF) Questionnaire. In M. J. Hilsenroth & D. L. Segal (Eds.), *Comprehensive handbook of psychological assessment (Vol. 2): Personality.* Hoboken, NJ: Wiley.

Cattell, H. E. P., & Mead, A. D. (2008). The sixteen personality factor questionnaire (16PF). In G. J. Boyle, G. Matthews, & D. H. Saklofske (Eds.), *The Sage handbook of personality theory and assessment: Personality measurement and testing* (Vol. 2, pp. 135–159). Los Angeles, CA: Sage.

Cattell, R. B. (1950). *Personality: A systematic, theoretical and factual study.* New York: McGraw-Hill.

Cattell, R. B. (1957). *Personality and motivation: Structure and measurement.* New York: Harcourt, Brace & World.

Cattell, R. B. (1963). Theory of fluid and crystallized intelligence: A critical experiment. *Journal of Educational Psychology, 54,* 1–22.

Cattell, R. B. (1965). *The scientific analysis of personality.* Baltimore: Penguin.

Cattell, R. B. (1966). *The scientific analysis of personality.* Chicago: Aldine.

Cattell, R. B. (1973, July). Personality pinned down. *Psychology Today,* 40–46.

Cattell, R. B. (1990). Advances in Cattellian personality theory. In L. A. Pervin (Ed.), *Handbook of personality: Theory and research.* New York: Guilford.

Cattell, R. B., Eber, H. W., & Tatsuoka, M. M. (1970). *Handbook of the Sixteen Personality Factor Questionnaire (16PF).* Champaign, IL: Institute for Personality and Ability Testing.

Cautin, R. L. (2009a). The founding of the Association for Psychological Science: Part 1. Dialectical tensions within organized psychology. *Perspectives on Psychological Science, 4,* 211–223.

Cautin, R. L. (2009b). The founding of the Association for Psychological Science: Part 2. The tipping point and early years. *Perspectives on Psychological Science, 4,* 224–235.

Cavanaugh, J. C. (1993). *Adult development and aging* (2nd ed.). Pacific Grove, CA: Brooks/Cole.

Caverly, D. C., Orlando, V. P., & Mullen, J. L. (2000). Textbook study reading. In R. F. Flippo & D. C. Caverly (Eds.), *Handbook of college reading and study strategy research.* Mahwah, NJ: Erlbaum.

CBC News. (2004). Driving and dialing. Retrieved February 27, 2011, from http://www.cbc.ca/news/background/cellphones/driving.htm.

CBC News. (2006). Dawson College: Shootings in a Montreal College. Retreived June 9, 2011, from http://www.cbc.ca/news/background/dawson-college/.

CBC News. (2008). Teens glued to screens. Retrieved February 19, 2011, from http://www.cbc.ca/consumer/story/2008.03/13/teens-obesity.html.

CBC News. (2009). Mental illness costs Canada $33B annually. Retrieved November 29, 2009, from http://www.cbc.ca/news/story/2009/11/25/canada-economy-mental-health-cost.html.

CBC News. (2009). To spank or not to spank? Retrieved Feburary 24, 2011, from http://www.cbc.ca/news/background/spanking/.

CBC News. (2010). Bear attacks Ontario woman in Montana. CBC News, July 29, 2010. Retrieved June 9, 2011, from http://www.cbc.ca/news/world/story/2010/07/29/ont-bear-mauls-woman-yellowstone-100729.html.

CBC News. (2010). Canada's astronauts. Tuesday, October 26, 2010. Retrieved June 3, 2011, from http://www.cbc.ca/news/interactives/who-cdn-astronauts/.

CBC News. (2010). Cellphone driving ban enforced in Ontario, BC. Retrieved June 27, 2011, from http://www.cbc.ca/news/canada/story/2010/02/01/phone-ban-ont-bc.html.

CBC News. (2010). Reena Virk's killer released on parole. Retrieved June 20, 2011, from http://www.cbc.ca/news/canada/british.../story/.../bc-glowatski-praole-release.html.

Ceci, S. J. (1990). *On intelligence ... more or less: A bio-ecological treatise on intellectual development.* Englewood Cliffs, NJ: Prentice-Hall.

Cedi, S. J., Williams, W. M., & Barnett, S. M. (2009). Women's underrepresentation in Science: Sociocultural and biological considerations. *Psychological Bulletin, 135,* 218–261.

Centers for Disease Control and Prevention. (2011). Diagnoses of HIV infection and AIDS in the United States and dependent areas, 2009. *HIV Surveillance Report, 21.* Retrieved from http://www.cdc.gov/hiv/surveillance/resources/reports/2009report/.

Centers for Disease Control and Prevention. (2011). Tobacco Use and Pregnancy. Retrieved May 24, 2011, from http://www.cdc.gov/reproductivehealth/tobaccousepregnancy/.

Cepeda, N. J., Pashler, H., Vul, E., Wixted, J. T., & Roher, D. (2006). Distributed practice in verbal recall tasks: A review and quantitative synthesis. *Psychological Bulletin, 132,* 354–380.

Cerletti, U., & Bini, L. (1938). Un nuevo metodo di shockterapie "L'elettro-shock." *Bull. Acad. Med. Roma, 64,* 136–138.

Cetinkaya, H., & Domjan, M. (2006). Sexual fetishism in a quail (*Coturnix japonica*) model system: Test of reproductive success. *Journal of Comparative Psychology, 120*(4), 427–432.

Cha, S. E., & Edmondson, A. C. (2006). When values backfire: Leadership, attribution, and disenchantment in a values-driven organization. *Leadership Quarterly, 17,* 57–78.

Cha, Y. (2010). Reinforcing separate spheres: The effect of spousal overwork on men's and women's employment in dual-earner households. *American Sociological Review, 75*(2), 303–329.

Chabris, C., & Simons, D. (2010). *The invisible gorilla.* New York: Crown Publishers.

Chaiken, S., & Maheswaran, D. (1994). Heuristic processing can bias systematic processing: Effects of source credibility, argument ambiguity, and task importance on attitude judgment. *Journal of Personality and Social Psychology, 66,* 460–473.

Chiao, J. Y., & Cheon, B. K. (2010). The weirdest brains in the world. *Behavioral & Brain Sciences, 33,* 28–29.

Chamber, C. G., Graham, S., & Turner, J. N. (2008). When hearsay trumps evidence: How generic language guides preschoolers' inferences about unfamiliar things. *Language and Cognitive Processes, 23*(5), 749–766.

Chambers, R., Lo, B. C. Y., & Allen, N. B. (2008). The impact of mindfulness training on attentional control, cognitive style, and affect. *Cognitive Therapy and Research, 32,* 303–322.

Chan, C. S., Paul, P. L., & Verlinde, H. (2000). A note on warped string compactification. *Nuclear Physics Bulletin, 581,* 156–164.

Chan, J. K., Thomas, A. K., & Bulevich, J. B. (2009). Recalling a witnessed event increases eyewitness suggestibility: The reversed testing effect. *Psychological Science, 20*(1), 66–73.

Chan, J. W. C., & Vernon, P. E. (1988). Individual differences among the peoples of China. In S. H. Irvine & J. W. Berry (Eds.), *Human abilities in cultural context.* New York: Cambridge University Press.

Chance, P. (1999). Thorndike's puzzle boxes and the origins of the experimental analysis of behavior. *Journal of the Experimental Analysis of Behavior, 72,* 433–440.

Chance, P. (2001, September/October). The brain goes to school: Why neuroscience research is going to the head of the class. *Psychology Today,* p. 72.

Chandler, C. C., & Fisher, R. P. (1996). Retrieval processes and witness memory. In E. L. Bjork & R. A. Bjork (Eds.), *Memory.* San Diego: Academic Press.

Chandler, M. J. & Lalonde, C. E. (2008). Cultural continuity as a protective factor against suicide in First Nations youth. *Horizons, 9*(4), 13–24.

Chandler, M. J. (2000). Surviving time: The persistence of identity in this culture and that. *Culture and Psychology, 6,* 209–231.

Chandler, M. J., & Lalonde, C. (1998). Cultural continuity as a hedge against suicide in Canada's First Nations. *Transcultural Psychiatry, 35,* 191–219.

Chandler, M. J., & Lalonde, C. E. (2004). Culture, selves, and time: Theories of personal persistence in native and non-native youth. In C. Lightfoot, C. Lalonde, & M. Chandler (Eds.), *Changing conceptions of psychological life* (pp. 207–229). Mahwah, NJ: Lawrence Erlbaum & Associates.

Chapman, B., Fiscella, K., Kawachi, I., & Duberstein, P. (2010). Personality, socioeconomic status, and all-cause mortality in the United States. *American Journal of Epidemiology, 171*(1), 83–92.

Chapman, P. D. (1988). *Schools as sorters: Lewis M. Terman, applied psychology, and the intelligence testing movement.* New York, NY: New York University Press.

Chard, J., & Badets, J. (2004). *The Ethnic Diversity Survey (EDS): Content and data availability.* (Paper presented at the 2004 Congress & RDC Symposium of the Canadian Population Society). Retrieved March 15, 2005, from http://www.canpopsoc.org/2004.secure/chardCPS.ppt.

Charrier, I., Pitcher, B. J., & Harcourt, R. G. (2009). Vocal recognition of mothers by Australian sea lion pups: Individual signature and environmental constraints. *Animal Behavior, 78*(5), 1127–1134.

Charuvastra, A., & Cloitre, M. (2008). Social bonds and posttraumatic stress disorder. *Annual Review of Psychology, 59,* 301–328.

Chase, W. G., & Simon, H. A. (1973). Perception in chess. *Cognitive Psychology, 4,* 55–81.

Chen J. K., Johnston, K. M, Petrides, M., & Ptito, A. (2008). Neural substrates of symptoms of depression following concussion in male athletes with persisting post-concussion symptoms. *Archives of General Psychiatry, 65*(1), 81–89.

Chen, A. W., Kazanjian, A., Wong, H., & Goldner, E. M. (2010). Mental health service use by Chinese immigrants with severe and persistent mental illness, *The Canadian Journal of Psychiatry, 55,* 35–42.

Chen, J. K., Johnston, K. M., Collie, A., McCrory, P., & Ptito, A. (2007). A validation of the Post Concussion Symptom Scale in the assessment of complex concussion using cognitive testing and fMRI. *Journal of Neurology, Neurosurgery and Psychiatry, 78*(11), 1231–1238.

Chen, X., & Wang, L. (2010). China. In M. H. Bornstein (Ed.), *Handbook of cultural developmental science* (pp. 424–440). New York, NY: Psychology Press.

Chen, X., Wang, L., & DeSouza, A. (2006). Temperament and socio-emotional functioning in Chinese and North American children. In X. Chen, D. French, & B. Schneider (Eds.), *Peer relationships in cultural context* (pp. 123–147). New York, NY: Cambridge University Press.

Cheney, P. (2004, May 15). Our Abu Ghraib. *The Globe and Mail,* F1, F5.

Cheng, Y., Chen, C., Lin, C., Chou, K., & Decety, J. (2010). Love hurts: An fMRI study. *NeuroImage, 51*(2), 923–929.

Chess, S., & Thomas, A. (1996). *Temperament: Theory and practice.* New York, NY: Brunner/Mazel.

Chida, Y., & Steptoe, A. (2009). The association of anger and hostility with future coronary heart disease: A meta-analytic review of prospective evidence. *Journal of the American College of Cardiology, 53*(11), 936–946.

Chien, K., Che, P., Hsu, H., Su, T., Sung, F., Chen, M., & Lee, Y. (2010). Habitual sleep duration and insomnia and the risk of cardiovascular events and all cause death: Report from a community-based cohort. *Sleep: Journal of Sleep and Sleep Disorders Research, 33*(2), 177–184.

Chiroro, P., Bohner, G., Viki, G. T., & Jarvis, C. I. (2004). Rape myth acceptance and rape proclivity: Expected dominance versus expected arousal as mediators in acquaintance–rape situations. *Journal of Interpersonal Violence, 19,* 427–441.

Chisholm, J. S. (1996). The evolutionary ecology of attachment organization. *Human Nature, 7,* 1–38.

Chisholm, N., & Gillett, G. (2005). The patient's journey: Living with lock-in syndrome. *British Medical Journal, 331,* 94–113.

Chiu, C. Y., Leung, A. K. Y., & Kwan, L. (2007). Language, cognition, and culture: Beyond the Whorfian hypothesis. In S. Kitayama & D. Cohen (Eds.), *Handbook of cultural psychology* (pp. 668–690). New York: Guilford.

Chiu, C-Y., Kim, Y-H., & Wan, W. N. (2008). Personality: Cross-cultural perspectives. In G. J. Boyle, G. Matthews, & D. H. Salofske (Eds.), *Sage handbook of personality theory and assessment* (Vol. 1, pp. 56–78). *Personality theory and testing.* London: Sage.

Cho, K., Ennaceur, A., Cole, J. C., & Kook Suh, C. (2000). Chronic jet lag produces cognitive deficits. *Journal of Neuroscience, 20*(6), RC66.

Choi, I., Nisbett, R. E., & Norenzayan, A. (1999). Causal attribution across cultures: Variation and universality. *Psychological Bulletin, 125*, 47–63.

Cholewiak, R. W., & Cholewiak, S. A. (2010). Pain: Physiological mechanisms. In E. B. Goldstein (Ed.), *Encyclopedia of perception*. Thousand Oaks, CA: Sage.

Chomsky, N. (1957). *Syntactic structures*. The Hague: Mouton.

Chomsky, N. (1959). A review of B. F. Skinner's "Verbal Behavior." *Language, 35*, 26–58.

Chomsky, N. (1965). *Aspects of theory of syntax*. Cambridge, MA: MIT Press.

Chomsky, N. (1975). *Reflections on language*. New York: Pantheon.

Chomsky, N. (1986). *Knowledge of language: Its nature, origins, and use*. New York: Praeger.

Chomsky, N. (2006). *Language and mind* (3rd ed.). New York, NY: Cambridge University Press.

Chopra, S. S. (2003). Industry funding of clinical trials: Benefit of bias? *Journal of the American Medical Association, 290*, 113–114.

Christensen, A. J., & Johnson, J. A. (2002). Patient adherence with medical treatment regimens: An interactive approach. *Current Directions in Psychological Science, 11*(3), 94–97.

Christensen, B. K., Carney, C. E., & Segal, Z. V. (2006). Cognitive processing models of depression. In D. J. Stein, D. J. Kupfer, & A. F. Schatzberg (Eds.), *Textbook of mood disorders*. Washington, DC: American Psychiatric Publishing.

Christensen, B. T., & Schunn, C. D. (2007). The relationship of analogical distance to analogical function and preinventive structure: The case of engineering design. *Memory & Cognition, 35*(1), 29–38.

Christian, L. M., Deichert, N. T., Gouin, J., Graham, J. E., & Kiecolt-Glaser, J. K. (2009). Psychological influences on neuroendocrine and immune outcomes. In G. G. Berntson & J. T. Cacioppo (Eds.), *Handbook of neuroscience for the behavioral sciences*, (Vol. 2, pp. 1260–1279). Hoboken, NJ: Wiley.

Christmas, B. (2010, May 28). Memory lapses: Why you might need a helping hand. *Globe and Mail*, B14.

Christoph, R. T., Schoenfeld, G. A., & Tansky, J. W. (1998). Overcoming barriers to training utilizing technology: The influence of self-efficacy factors on multimedia-based training receptiveness. *Human Resource Development Quarterly, 9*, 25–38.

Chrousos, G. P., & Kaltsas, G. (2007). Stress and cardiovascular disease. In G. Fink (Ed.), *Encyclopedia of stress*. San Diego: Elsevier.

Chu, J. A., Frey, L. M., Ganzel, B. L., & Matthews, J. A. (1999). Memories of childhood abuse: Dissociation, amnesia, and corroboration. *American Journal of Psychiatry, 156*, 749–755.

Chun, M. M., & Wolfe, J. M. (2001). Visual attention. In E. B. Goldstein (Ed.), *Blackwell handbook of perception*. Malden, MA: Blackwell.

Church, A. (2010). Current perspectives in the study of personality across cultures. *Perspectives on Psychological Science, 5*(4), 441–449.

Church, E., Pettifor, J. L., & Malone, J. (2006). Evolving Canadian guidelines for therapy and counselling with women. *Feminism & Psychology, 16*, 259–271.

Cialdini, R. B. (2001). *Influence: Science and practice*. Boston: Allyn & Bacon.

Cialdini, R. B. (2008). *Influence: Science and practice* (5th ed.). Boston, MA: Allyn & Bacon.

Cialdini, R. B., & Griskevicius, V. (2010). Social influence. In R. F. Baumeister & E. J. Finkel (Eds.), *Advanced social psychology: The state of the science* (pp. 385–417). New York, NY: Oxford University Press.

Cialdini, R. B., & Trost, M. R. (1998). Social influence: Social norms, conformity, and compliance. In D. T. Gilbert, S. T. Fiske, & G. Lindzey (Eds.), *The handbook of social psychology*. New York: McGraw-Hill.

Cianciolo, A. T., & Sternberg, R. J. (2004). *Intelligence: A brief history*. Malden, MA: Blackwell Publishing.

Ciborowski, T. (1997). "Superstition" in the collegiate baseball player. *Sport Psychologist, 11*, 305–317.

Cicero, T. J., Inciardi, J. A., & Munoz, A. (2005). Trends in abuse of Oxycontin and other opioid analgesics in the United States. *Journal of Pain, 6*(10), 662–672.

Clancy, B., & Finlay, B. (2001). Neural correlates of early language learning. In E. Bates & M. Tomasello (Eds.), *Language development: The essential readings*. Malden, MA: Blackwell Publishers.

Clark, D. A. (1998). Canadian perspectives on research in depression. *Canadian Journal of Behavioural Science, 30*, 2107–2212.

Clark, D. A., Steer, R. A., Beck, A. T., & Ross, L. (1995). Psychometric characteristics of revised sociotropy and autonomy scales in college students. *Behaviour Research and Therapy, 33*, 325–334.

Clark, L. A. (2007). Assessment and diagnosis of personality disorder: Perennial issues and an emerging reconceptualization. *Annual Review of Psychology, 58*, 227–257.

Clark, L. A., & Watson, D. (2003). Constructing validity: Basic issues in objective scale development. In A. E. Kazdin (Ed.), *Methodological issues & strategies in clinical research* (pp. 207–231). Washington, DC: American Psychological Association.

Clark, R. D., & Hatfield, E. (1989). Gender differences in receptivity to sexual offers. *Journal of Psychology & Human Sexuality, 2*(1), 39–55.

Clément, R. (1987). Second language proficiency and acculturation: An investigation of the effects of language status and individual characteristics. *Journal of Language and Social Psychology, 5*, 271–290.

Clements, A. M., Rimrodt, S. L., Abel, J. R., Blankner, J. G., Mostofsky, S. H., Pekar, J. J., et al. (2006). Sex differences in cerebral laterality of language and visuospatial processing. *Brain and Language, 98*(2), 150–158.

Clifasefi, S. L., Takarangi, M. K., & Bergman, J. S. (2006). Blind drunk: The effects of alcohol on inattentional blindness. *Applied Cognitive Psychology, 20*, 697–704.

Clore, G. L., & Ortony, A. (2008). Appraisal theories: How cognition shapes affect into emotion. In M. Lewis, J. M. Haviland-Jones, & L. F. Barrett, *Handbook of emotions* (3rd ed.). New York, NY: Guilford Press.

Clow, A. (2001). The physiology of stress. In F. Jones & J. Bright (Eds.), *Stress: Myth, theory, and research*. Harlow, UK: Pearson, Education.

Coates, T. J., & Collins, C. (1998). Preventing HIV infection. *Scientific American, 279*(1), 96–97.

Coelho, C., & Purkis, H. (2009). The origins of specific phobias: Influential theories and current perspectives. *Review of General Psychology, 13*(4), 335–348.

Coelho, J. S., Polivy, J., Herman, C. P., & Pliner, P. (2011). Effects of food-cue exposure on dieting-related goals: A limitation to counteractive-control theory. *Appetite, 51*, 347–349.

Coenen, A. (1998). Neuronal phenomena associated with vigilance and consciousness: From cellular mechanisms to electroencephalographic patterns. *Consciousness & Cognition: An International Journal, 7*, 42–53.

Cohan, C. L., & Kleinbaum, S. (2002). Toward a greater understanding of the cohabitation effect: Premarital cohabitation and marital communication. *Journal of Marriage and Family, 64*(1), 180–192.

Cohen, C. E. (1981). Person categories and social perception: Testing some boundaries of the processing effects of prior knowledge. *Journal of Personality and Social Psychology, 40*, 441–452.

Cohen, M. N. (2002). An anthropologist looks at "race" and IQ testing. In J. M. Fish (Ed.), *Race and intelligence: Separating science from myth* (pp. 201–224). Mahwah, NJ: Erlbaum.

Cohen, S. (2005). Pittsburgh common cold studies: Psychosocial predictors of susceptibility to respiratory infectious illness. *International Journal of Behavioral Medicine, 12*(3), 123–131.

Cohen, S., & Pressman, S. D. (2006). Positive affect and health. *Current Directions in Psychological Science, 15*(3), 122–125.

Cohen, S., Janicki-Deverts, D., & Miller, G. E. (2007). Psychological stress and disease. *Journal of the American Medical Association, 298*, 1685–1687.

Cohen, S., Kessler, R. C., & Gordon, L. U. (1995). Strategies for measuring stress in studies of psychiatric and physical disorders. In S. Cohen, R. C. Kessler, & L. U. Gordon (Eds.), *Measuring stress: A guide for health and social scientists* (pp. 3–28). New York: Oxford University Press.

Cohen, S., Lichtenstein, E., Prochaska, J. O., Rossi, J. S., Gritz, E. R., Carr, C. R., et al. (1989). Debunking myths about self-quitting: Evidence from 10 prospective studies of persons who attempt to quit smoking by themselves. *American Psychologist, 44*, 1355–1365.

Colagiuri, B., & Boakes, R. A. (2010). Perceived treatment, feedback, and placebo effects in double-blind RCTs: an experimental analsis. *Psychopharmacology, 208*, 433–41.

Colby, A., & Kohlberg, L. (1987). *The measurement of moral judgment* (Vols. 1–2). New York: Cambridge University Press.

Colmane, A. M. (2006). *Oxford dictionary of psychology* (2nd ed.). New York: Oxford University Press.

Coles, M. E., Schofield, C. A., & Pietrefesa, A. S. (2006). Behavioral inhibition and obsessive-compulsive disorder. *Journal of Anxiety Disorders, 20*, 1118–1132.

Coles, R. (1970). *Erik H. Erikson: The growth of his work*. Boston: Little, Brown.

Colflesh, G. J. H., & Conway, A. R. A. (2007). Individual differences in working memory capacity and divided attention in dichotic listening. *Psychonomic Bulletin & Review, 14*, 699–703.

Collins, A. (1988). *In the sleep room: The story of the CIA brainwashing experiments in Canada*. Toronto: Lester & Orpen Dennys.

Collins, A. M., & Loftus, E. F. (1975). A spreading activation theory of semantic processing. *Psychological Review, 82*, 407–428.

Collins, C. J., Hanges, P. J., & Locke, E. A. (2004). The relationship of achievement motivation to entrepreneurial behavior: A meta-analysis. *Human Performance, 17*(1), 95–117.

Collins, F. S., Green, E. D., Guttmacher, A. E., & Guyer, M. S. (2006). A vision for the future of genomics research: A blueprint for the genomic era. In H. T. Tavani (Ed.), *Ethics, computing, and genomics* (pp. 287–315). Boston: Jones and Bartlett.

Collins, M. A., & Zebrowitz, L. A. (1995). The contributions of appearance to occupational outcomes in civilian and military settings. *Journal of Applied Social Psychology, 25*, 129–163.

Collop, N. A. (2006). Polysomnography. In T. Lee-Chiong (Ed.), *Sleep: A comprehensive handbook*. Hoboken, NJ: Wiley-Liss.

Colom, R., Haier, R. J., Head, K., Álvarez-Linera, J., Quiroga, M., Shih, P., & Jung, R. E. (2009). Gray matter correlates of fluid, crystallized, and spatial intelligence: Testing the P-FIT model. *Intelligence, 37*(2), 124–135.

Coltrane, S. (2001). Research on household labor: Modeling and measuring the social embeddedness of routine family work. In R. M. Milardo (Ed.), *Understanding families into the new millennium: A decade in review* (pp. 427–452). Minneapolis, MN: National Council on Family Relations.

Colvin, C. R., Block, J., & Funder, D. C. (1995). Overly positive self-evaluations and personality: Negative implications for mental health. *Journal of Personality and Social Psychology, 68*, 1152–1162.

Colwill, R. M. (1993). An associative analysis of instrumental learning. *Current Directions in Psychological Science, 2*(4), 111–116.

Comas-Diaz, L. (2006). Cultural variation in the therapeutic relationship. In C. D. Goodheart, A. E. Kazdin, & R. J. Sternberg (Eds.), *Evidence-based psychotherapy: Where practice and research meet*. Washington, DC: American Psychological Association.

Combs, D. R., & Mueser, K. T. (2007). Schizophrenia. In M. Hersen, S. M. Turner, & D. C. Beidel (Eds.), *Adult psychopathology and diagnosis*. New York: Wiley.

Comer, D. R. (1995). A model of social loafing in real work groups. *Human Relations, 48*, 647–667.

Compas, B. E. (2004). Processes of risk and resilience during adolescence: Linking contexts and individuals. In R. M. Lerner & L. Steinberg (Eds.), *Handbook of adolescent psychology*. New York: Wiley.

Compton, M. T., Goulding, S. M., & Walker, E. F. (2007). Cannabis use, first-episode psychosis, and schizotypy: A summary and synthesis of recent literature. *Current Psychiatry Reviews, 3*, 161–171.

Condic. M. (2007). Unlikely stem cell therapies. *Nature Neuroscience, 10*, 803.

Confer, J. C., Easton, J. A., Fleischman, D. S., Goetz, C. D., Lewis, D. M. G., Perilloux, C., & Buss, D. M. (2010). Evolutionary psychology: Controversies, questions, prospects, and limitations. *American Psychologist, 65*(2), 110–126.

Connolly, J. A., & Johnson, A. M. (1996). Adolescents' romantic relationships and the structure and quality of their close interpersonal ties. *Personal Relationships, 3*, 185–195,

Connolly, J. F., & D'Arcy, R. C. N. (2000). Innovations in neuropsychological assessment using event-related brain potentials. *International Journal of Psychophysiology, 37*, 31–47.

Connolly, J. F., Mate-Kole, C. C., & Joyce, B. (1999). Global aphasia: An innovative assessment approach. *Archives of Physical Medicine and Rehabilitation, 80*, 1309–1315.

Connor, C. E., Pasupathy, A., Brincat, S., & Yamane, Y. (2009). Neural transformation of object information by ventral pathway visual cortex. In M. S. Gazzaniga (Ed.), *The cognitive neurosciences*. Cambridge, MA: MIT Press.

Conte, J. M., & Dean, M. A. (2006). Can emotional intelligence be measured? In K. R. Murphy (Ed.), *A critique of emotional intelligence: What are the problems and how can they be fixed?* (pp. 59–78). Mahwah, NJ: Erlbaum.

Conway, F., & Siegelman, J. (2005). *Dark hero of the information age*. New York: Basic Books.

Conway, L. C., & Schaller, M. (2002). On the verifiability of evolutionary psychological theories: An analysis of the psychology of scientific persuasion. *Personality and Social Psychology Review, 6*, 152–166.

Cook, E. H., Jr. (2001). Genetics of autism. *Child and Adolescent Psychiatric Clinics of North America, 10*, 333–350.

Cooke, L. (2007). The importance of exposure for healthy eating in childhood: A review. *Journal of Human Nutrition and Dietetics, 20*, 294–301.

Cooke, R., & Sheeran, P. (2004). Moderation of cognition-intention and cognition-behaviour relations: A meta-analysis of properties of variables from the theory of planned behaviour. *British Journal of Social Psychology, 43*, 159–186.

Cooley, C. H. (1902). *Human interaction and social order*. New York: Scribner's.

Coolidge, F. L., & Wynn, T. (2009). *The rise of homo sapiens: The evolution of modern thinking*. Malden, MA: Wiley-Blackwell.

Coon, D. J. (1994). "Not a creature of reason": The alleged impact of Watsonian behaviorism on advertising in the 1920s. In J. T. Todd and E. K. Morris (Eds.), *Modern perspectives on John B. Watson and classical behaviorism* (pp. 37–63). Westport, CT: Greenwood Press.

Coontz, S. (2000). *The way we never were: American families and the nostalgia trap*. New York: Basic Books.

Cooper, H. H., & Hedges, L. V. (Eds.). (1994). *The handbook of research synthesis*. New York, NY: Russell Sage.

Cooper, H. M. (1990). Meta-analysis and the integrative research review. In C. Hendrick & M. S. Clark (Eds.), *Research methods in personality and social psychology: Review of personality and social psychology* (Vol. 11, pp. 142–163). Thousand Oaks, CA: Sage Publications.

Cooper, H. M. (2010). *Research synthesis and metaanalysis: A step-by-step approach* (4th ed.). Thousand Oaks, CA: Sage.

Cooper, L., & Bright, J. (2001). Individual differences in reactions to stress. In F. Jones & J. Bright (Eds.), *Stress: Myth, theory and research*. Harlow, UK: Pearson Education.

Cope, M. B., Fernandez, J. R., & Allison, D. B. (2004). Genetic and biological risk factors. In J. K. Thompson (Ed.), *Handbook of eating disorders and obesity*. New York: Wiley.

Corballis, M. C. (1991). *The lopsided ape*. New York: Oxford University Press.

Corballis, M. C. (2007). The dual-brain myth. In S. Della Sala (Ed.), *Tall tales about the mind & brain: Separating fact from fiction* (pp. 291–313). New York, NY: Oxford University Press.

Corballis, M. C., Hattie, J., & Fletcher, R. (2008). Handedness and intellectual achievement: An evenhanded look. *Neuropsychologia, 46*(1), 374–378.

Corballis, P. M. (2003). Visuospatial processing and the right-hemisphere interpreter. *Brain & Cognition, 53*(2), 171–176.

Coren, S. (1992). *The left-hander syndrome: The causes and consequences of left-handedness*. New York: Free Press.

Coren, S. (1996a). Accidental death and the shift to Daylight Savings Time. *Perceptual and Motor Skills, 83*, 921–922.

Coren, S., & Aks, D. J. (1990). Moon illusion in pictures: A multimechanism approach. *Journal of Experimental Psychology: Human Perception and Performance, 16*, 365–380.

Coren, S., & Girgus, J. S. (1978). *Seeing is deceiving: The psychology of visual illusions*. Hillsdale, NJ: Erlbaum.

Corkin, S. (1984). Lasting consequences of bilateral medial temporal lobectomy: Clinical course and experimental findings in H. M. *Seminars in Neurology, 4*, 249–259.

Cornblatt, B. A., Green, M. F., Walker, E. F., & Mittal, V. A. (2009). Schizophrenia: Etiology and neurocognition. In P. H. Blaney & T. Millon (Eds.), *Oxford textbook of psychopathology* (2nd ed., pp. 298–332). New York, NY: Oxford University Press.

Cornell, D. G. (1997). Post hoc explanation is not prediction. *American Psychologist, 52*, 1380.

Cornette, M. M., Strauman, T. J., Abramson, L. Y., & Busch, A. M. (2008). Self-discrepancy and suicidal ideation. *Cognition and Emotion, 22*, 1–24.

Cornish, K., Sudhalter, V., & Turk, J. (2004). Attention and language in Fragile X. *Mental Retardation and Developmental Disabilities Research Reviews, 10*, 11–16.

Cornoldi, C., & De Beni, R. (1996). Mnemonics and metacognition. In D. J. Herrmann, C. McEvoy, C. Hertzog, P. Hertel, & M. K. Johnson (Eds.), *Basic and applied memory research: Practical applications*. Mahwah, NJ: Erlbaum.

Cornum, R., Matthews, M. D., & Seligman, M. E. P. (2011). Comprehensive soldier fitness. *American Psychologist, 66*, 4–9.

Corrigan, P. W., & Larson, J. E. (2008). Stigma. In K. T. Mueser & D. V. Jeste (Eds.), *Clinical handbook of schizophrenia* (pp. 533–540). New York, NY: Guilford Press.

Corsica, J. A., & Perri, M. G. (2003). Obesity. In A. M. Nezu, C. M. Nezu, & P. A. Geller (Eds.), *Handbook of psychology,* (Vol. 9): *Health psychology*. New York: Wiley.

Corsini, R. J. (1999). *The dictionary of psychology*. Philadelphia: Brunner/Mazel.

Cosmides, L. L., & Tooby, J. (1989). Evolutionary psychology and the generation of culture. Part II. Case study: A computational theory of social exchange. *Ethology and Sociobiology, 10*, 51–97.

Cosmides, L., & Tooby, J. (1996). Are humans good intuitive statisticians after all? Rethinking some conclusions from the literature on judgment under uncertainty. *Cognition, 58*, 1–73.

Costa, P. T., Jr., & McCrae, R. R. (1985). *NEO Personality Inventory*. Odessa, FL: Psychological Assessment Resources.

Costa, P. T., Jr., & McCrae, R. R. (1992). *Revised NEO Personality Inventory: NEO PI and NEO Five-Factor Inventory* (Professional Manual). Odessa, FL: Psychological Assessment Resources.

Costa, P. T., Jr., & McCrae, R. R. (1994). Set like plaster? Evidence for the stability of adult personality. In T. F. Heatherton & J. L. Weinberger (Eds.), *Can personality change?* Washington, DC: American Psychological Association.

Costa, P. T., Jr., & McCrae, R. R. (1997). Longitudinal stability of adult personality. In R. Hogan, J. Johnson, & S. Briggs (Eds.), *Handbook of personality psychology*. San Diego: Academic Press.

Costa, P. T., Jr., & McCrae, R. R. (2008). The revised NEO Personality Inventory (NEO-PR-R). In G. J. Boyle, G. Matthews, & D. H. Saklofske (Eds.), *The Sage handbook of personality theory and assessment: Personality measurement and testing* (Vol. 2, pp. 179–198). Los Angeles, CA: Sage.

Côté, J. E. (2006). Emerging adulthood as an institutionalized moratorium: Risks and benefits to identity formation. In J. J. Arnett & J. L. Tanner (Eds.), *Emerging adults in America: Coming of age* in the 21st century. Washington, DC: American Psychological Association.

Cotman, C. W., Berchtold, N. C., & Christie, L.-A. (2007). Exercise builds brain health: Key roles of growth factor cascades and inflammation. *Trends in Neurosciences, 30*, 464–472.

Cotter, A., & Potter, J. E. (2006). Mother to child transmission. In J. Beal, J. J. Orrick, & K. Alfonso (Eds.), *HIV/AIDS: Primary care guide* (pp. 503–515). Norwalk, CT: Crown House.

Could Zach's death have been prevented? (1999, September 14). *CBC News*. Retrieved July 31, 2008, from http://www.cbc.ca/news/story/1999/09/14/anti990914.html.

Council of Ministers of Education. (2003). *Canadian youth, sexual health and HIV/AIDS study*. Retrieved May 3, 2005, from http://www.cmec.ca/publications/aids/.

Courage, M. L., & Howe, M. L. (2002). From infant to child: The dynamics of cognitive change in the second year of life. *Psychological Bulletin, 128*(2), 250–277.

Courtney, K. E., & Polich, J. (2009). Binge drinking in young adults: Data, definitions and determinants. *Psychological Bulletin, 135*, 142–156.

Courtney, S. M. (2004). Attention and cognitive control as emergent properties of information representation in working memory. *Cognitive, Affective, and Behavioral Neuroscience, 4*, 501–516.

Coutts, A. (2000). Nutrition and the life cycle. 1: Maternal nutrition and pregnancy. *British Journal of Nursing, 9*, 1133–1138.

Cowan, N. (1988). Evolving conceptions of memory storage, selective attention, and their mutual constraints within the human information-processing system. *Psychological Bulletin, 104*, 163–191.

Cowan, N. (2010). The magical mystery four: How is working memory capacity limited, and why? *Current Directions in Psychological Science, 19*(1), 51–57.

Cowart, B. J. (2005). Taste, our body's gustatory gatekeeper. *Cerebrum, 7*(2), 7–22.

Cowart, B. J., & Rawson, N. E. (2001). Olfaction. In E. B. Goldstein (Ed.), *Blackwell handbook of perception*. Malden, MA: Blackwell.

Cox, B. J., Endler, N. S., & Swinson, R. P. (1991). Clinical and nonclinical panic attacks: An empirical test of a panic attack continuum. *Journal of Anxiety Disorders, 5*, 21–34.

Cox, B. J., Enns, M. W., Walker, J. R., Kjernisted, K., & Pidlubny, S. R. (2001). Psychological vulnerabilities in patients with major depression vs. panic disorder. *Behaviour Research and Therapy, 39*, 567–573.

Cox, B., Yu, N., Afifi, T. O., & Ladouceur, R. (2005). A national survey of gambling problems in Canada. *Canadian Journal of Psychiatry, 50*, 213–217.

Cox, D., Meyers, E., & Sinha, P. (2004). Contextually evoked object-specific responses in human visual cortex. *Science, 304*, 115–117.

Cox, M. J., Paley, B., Burchinal, M., & Payne, C. (1999). Marital perceptions and interactions across the transition to parenthood. *Journal of Marriage and the Family, 61*, 611–625.

Cox, P. D., Vinogradov, S., & Yalom, I. D. (2008). Group therapy. In R. E. Hales, S. C. Yudofsky, & G. O. Gabbard (Eds.), *The American psychiatric publishing textbook of psychiatry* (pp. 1329–1376). Washington, DC: American Psychiatric Publishing.

Coyne, J. C. (1999). Thinking interactionally about depression: A radical restatement. In T. E.

Joiner & J. C. Coyne (Eds.), *Interpersonal processes in depression* (pp. 369–392). Washington, DC: American Psychological Association.

Craig, J. C., & Rollman, G. B. (1999). Somesthesis. *Annual Review of Psychology, 50*, 305–331.

Craig, W. M., & Pepler, D. J. (1997). Observations of bullying and victimization in the schoolyard. *Canadian Journal of School Psychology, 13*, 41–60.

Craig, W., et al. (2009). A cross-national profile of bullying and victimization among adolescents in 40 countries. *International Journal of Public Health, 54*, S1–S9.

Craighead, W. E., Ritschel, L. A., Arnarson, E. O., & Gillespie, C. F. (2008). Major depressive disorder. In W. E. Craighead, D. J. Miklowitz, & L. W. Craighead (Eds.), *Psychopathology: History, diagnosis, and empirical foundations*. New York, NY: Wiley.

Craik, F. I. M. (2001). Effects of dividing attention on encoding and retrieval processes. In H. L. Roediger III, J. S. Nairne, I. Neath, & A. M. Surprenant (Eds.), *The nature of remembering: Essays in honor of Robert G. Crowder* (pp. 55–68). Washington, DC: American Psychological Association.

Craik, F. I. M. (2002). Levels of processing: Past, present … and future? *Memory, 10*(5–6), 305–318.

Craik, F. I. M., & Bialystok, E. (2005). Intelligence and executive control: Evidence from aging and bilingualism. *Cortex, 41*, 222–224.

Craik, F. I. M., & Bialystok, E. (2008). Lifespan cognitive development: The roles of representation and control. In F. I. M. Craik & T. Salthouse (Eds.), *The handbook of aging* (3rd ed., pp. 557–601). New York: Psychology Press.

Craik, F. I. M., & Bialystok, E. (2010). Bilingualism and aging: Costs and benefits. In L. Bäckman & L. Nyberg (Eds.), *Memory, aging and the brain: A Festschrift in honour of Lars-Göran Nilsson* (pp. 115–131). New York, NY: Psychology Press.

Craik, F. I. M., & Kester, J. D. (2000). Divided attention and memory: Impairment of processing or consolidation? In E. Tulving (Ed.), *Memory, consciousness, and the brain: The Tallinn conference* (pp. 38–51). Philadelphia: Psychology Press.

Craik, F. I. M., & Lockhart, R. S. (1972). Levels of processing: A framework for memory research. *Journal of Verbal Learning and Verbal Behavior, 11*, 671–684.

Craik, F. I. M., & Tulving, E. (1975). Depth of processing and the retention of words in episodic memory. *Journal of Experimental Psychology: General, 104*, 268–294.

Craik, F. I. M., Moroz, T. M., Moscovitch, M., Stuss, D. T., Winocur, G., Tulving, E., & Kapur, S. (1999). In search of the self: A positron emission tomography study. *Psychological Science, 10*, 26–34.

Cramer, P. (2000). Defense mechanisms in psychology today: Further processes for adaptation. *American Psychologist, 55*(6), 637–646.

Cramer, P. (2001). The unconscious status of defense mechanisms. *American Psychologist, 56*, 762–763.

Crane, C., et al. (2011). Suicidal imagery in a previously depressed community sample. *Clinical Psychology & Psychotherapy, 10*, 741–753.

Crane, C., Barnhofer, T., Duggan, D. S., Hepburn, S., Fennell, M. V., Williams, J. M. G. (2008). Mindfulness-based cognitive therapy and discrepancy in recovered depressed patients with a history of depression and suicidality. *Cognitive Therapy and Research, 32*, 123–137.

Craske, M. G., & Waters, A. M. (2005). Panic disorders, phobias, and generalized anxiety disorder. *Annual Review of Clinical Psychology, 1*, 197–225.

Cravens, H. (1992). A scientific project locked in time: The Terman Genetic Studies of Genius, 1920s–1950s. *American Psychologist, 47*, 183–189.

Crawford, J. D., Medendorp, W. P., & Marotta, J. J. (2004). Spatial transformations for eye–hand coordination. *Journal of Neurophysiology, 92*, 10–19.

Crawford, M., & Popp, D. (2003). Sexual double standards: A review and methodological critique of two decades of research. *Journal of Sex Research, 40*(1), 13–26.

Creed, F. (1989). Appendectomy. In G. W. Brown & T. O. Harris (Eds.), *Life events and illness*. New York: Guilford.

Creed, T. L. (1987). Subliminal deception: Pseudoscience on the college lecture circuit. *The Skeptical Inquirer, 11*, 358–366.

Creusere, M. A. (1999). Theories of adults' understanding and use of irony and sarcasm: Applications to and evidence from research with children. *Developmental Review, 19*, 213–262.

Crick, F. (1994). *The astonishing hypothesis: The scientific search for the soul*. New York: Charles Scribner's Sons.

Crick, F., & Koch, C. (2003). A Framework for consciousness. *Nature Neuroscience, 6*, 119–126.

Crits-Christoph, P. (1997). Limitations of the dodo bird verdict and the role of clinical trials in psychotherapy research: Comment on Wampold et al. *Psychological Bulletin, 122*, 216–220.

Crits-Christoph, P., & Gibbons, M. B. C. (2009). The evaluation of psychological treatment. In M. C. Gelder, N. C. Andreasen, J. J. López-Ibor, Jr., & J. R. Geddes (Eds.), *New Oxford textbook of psychiatry* (2nd ed., Vol. 1). New York, NY: Oxford University Press.

Crits-Christoph, P., Gibbons, M. B. C., Hamilton, Gallop, R., Hamilton, J., & Ring-Kurtz, S. (2011). The dependability of alliance assessments: The alliance-outcome correlation is larger than you might think. *Journal of Consulting and Clinical Psychology, 79*, 267–278.

Croizet, J., Despres, G., Gauzins, M. E., Huguet, P. Leyens, J., Meot, A. (2004). Stereotype threat undermines intellectual performance by triggering a disruptive mental load. *Personality and Social Psychology Bulletin, 30*, 721–731.

Cronbach, L. J. (1992). *Acceleration among the Terman males: Correlates in midlife and after*. Paper presented at the Symposium in Honor of Julian Stanley, San Francisco.

Cropley, A. J. (2000). Defining and measuring creativity: Are creativity tests worth using? *Roeper Review, 23*, 72–79.

Cross, S. E., & Markus, H. R. (1993). Gender in thought, belief, and action: A cognitive approach. In A. E. Beall & R. J. Sternberg (Eds.), *The psychology of gender*. New York: Guilford.

Crow, S. J., Peterson, C. B., Swanson, S. A., Raymond, N. C., Specker, S., Eckert, E. D., & Mitchell, J. E. (2009). Increased mortality in bulimia nervosa and other eating disorders. *American Journal of Psychiatry, 166*(12), 1342–1346.

Crowder, R. G., & Greene, R. L. (2000). Serial learning: Cognition and behavior. In E. Tulving & F. I. M. Craik (Eds.), *The Oxford handbook of memory* (pp. 125–136). New York: Oxford University Press.

Crowley, K., Callanan, M. A., Tenenbaum, H. R., & Allen, E. (2001). Parents explain more often to boys than to girls during shared scientific thinking. *Psychological Science, 12*, 258–261.

Croyle, R. T., & Cooper, J. (1983). Dissonance arousal: Physiological evidence. *Journal of Personality and Social Psychology, 45*, 782–791.

Cruz, C., della Rocco, P., & Hackworth, C. (2000). Effects of quick rotating schedules on the health and adjustment of air traffic controllers. *Aviation, Space, & Environmental Medicine, 71*, 400–407.

Csikszentmihalyi, M. (1994). Creativity. In R. J. Sternberg (Ed.), *Encyclopedia of human intelligence*. New York: Macmillan.

Csikszentmihalyi, M. (1999). Implications of a systems perspective for the study of creativity. In R. J. Sternberg (Ed.), *Handbook of creativity*. New York: Cambridge University Press.

Csikszentmihalyi, M. (2000). The contribution of flow to positive psychology. In J. E. Gillham (Ed.), *The science of optimism and hope: Research essays in honor of Martin E. P. Seligman*. Philadelphia: Templeton Foundation Press.

CTV News. (2010). Pink-clad students stand up against bullying. Retrieved November 22, 2010, from http://toronto.ctv.ca/servlet/an/local/CTVNews/20100414/pink_day_100414/20100414/?hub=TorontoNewHomeSchool.

CTV News. (2011, February 17). Jays lock up Bautista with five-year, US $64-million deal. Retrieved June 20, 2011, from http://www.cp24.com/servlet/an/local/CTVNews/20110217/110217_jays?hub=CP24Sports.

Cuban, L. (2004). Assessing the 20-year impact of multiple intelligences on schooling. *Teachers College Record, 106*(1), 140–146.

Cubelli, R., & Della Sala, S. (2008). Flashbulb memories: Special but not iconic. *Cortex: A Journal Devoted to the Study of the Nervous System and Behavior, 44*(7), 908–909.

Cullum, J., & Harton, H. C. (2007). Cultural evolution: Interpersonal influence, issue importance, and the development of shared attitudes in college residence halls. *Personality and Social Psychology Bulletin, 33*, 1327–1339.

Culpepper, L., Davidson, J. R. T., Dietrich, A. J., Goodman, W. K., Kroenke, K., & Schwenk, T. L. (2004). Suicidality as a possible effect of antidepressant treatment. *Journal of Clinical Psychiatry, 65*, 742–749.

Cummings, D. E. (2006). Ghrelin and the short- and long-term regulation of appetite and body weight. *Physiology & Behavior, 89*, 71–84.

Cummins, D. (2005). Dominance, status, and social hierarchies. In D. M. Buss (Ed.), *The handbook of evolutionary psychology*. New York: Wiley.

Cunningham, C. O., & Selwyn, P. A. (2005). HIV-related medical complications and treatment. In J. H. Lowinson, P. Ruiz, R. B. Millman, & J. G. Langrod (Eds.), *Substance abuse: A comprehensive textbook*. Philadelphia: Lippincott/Williams & Williams.

Cunningham, F., Leveno, K., Bloom, S., Hauth, J., Rouse, D., & Spong, C. (2010). *Williams obstetrics* (23rd ed.). New York, NY: McGraw-Hill.

Cunningham, M. (2001). The influence of parental attitudes and behaviors on children's attitudes toward gender and household labor in early adulthood. *Journal of Marriage and the Family, 63*, 111–122.

Cunningham, M. R., Druen, P. B., & Barbee, A. P. (1997). Angels, mentors, and friends: Trade-offs among evolutionary, social, and individual variables in physical appearance. In J. A. Simpson & D. T. Kenrick (Eds.), *Evolutionary social psychology*. Mahwah, NJ: Erlbaum.

Cunningham, M. R., Roberts, A. R., Barbee, A. P., Druen, P. B., & Wu, C. (1995). "Their ideas of beauty are, on the whole, the same as ours": Consistency and variability in the cross-cultural perception of female physical attractiveness. *Journal of Personality and Social Psychology, 68*, 261–279.

Cunningham, W. A., Arbuckle, N. L., Jahn, A., Mowrer, S. M., & Abduljalil, A. M. (2010). Aspects of neuroticism and the amygdala: Chronic tuning from motivational styles. *Neuropsychologia, 48*(12), 3399–3404.

Cunningham, W. A., Johnsen, I. R., & Waggoner, A. S. (in press). Orbitofrontal cortex provides cross-modal valuation of self-generated stimuli. *Social Cognitive and Affective Neuroscience.*

Cunningham, W. A., Johnson, M. K., Raye, C. L., Gatenby, C., Gore, J. C., & Banaji, M. R. (2004). Separable neural components in the processing of black and white faces. *Psychological Science, 15*, 806–813.

Cunningham, W. A., Van Bavel, J. J., & Johnsen, I. R. (2008). Affective flexibility: Evaluative processing goals shape amygdala activity. *Psychological Science, 19*, 152–160.

Curran, P. J., & Bauer, D. J. (2011). The disaggregation of within-person and between-person effects in longitudinal models of change. *Annual Review of Psychology, 62*, 583–619.

Curry, B. (2007, August 31). Mental health panel aims to stamp out discrimination. *The Globe and Mail*, A1, A8.

Curry, S. J., Mermelstein, R. J., & Sporer, A. K. (2009). Therapy for specific problems: Youth tobacco cessation. *Annual Review of Psychology, 60*, 229–255.

Curtin, S., Byers-Heinlein, K., Werker, J. F. (2011). Bilingual beginnings as a lens for theory development: PRIMIR in focus, *Journal of Phonetics, 39*, 492–504.

Cushman, P. (1992). Psychotherapy to 1992: A historically situated interpretation. In D. K. Freedheim (Ed.), *History of psychotherapy: A century of change*. Washington, DC: American Psychological Association.

Cutler, B. L., & Penrod, S. D. (1995). *Mistaken identification: The eyewitness, psychology, and the law*. New York: Cambridge University Press.

Cutting, L. P., & Docherty, N. M. (2000). Schizophrenia outpatients' perceptions of their parents: Is expressed emotion a factor? *Journal of Abnormal Psychology, 109*, 266–272.

Czeisler, C. A., Buxton, O. M., & Khalsa, S. (2005). The human circadian timing system and sleep–wake regulation. In M. H. Kryger, T. Roth, & W. C. Dement (Eds.), *Principles and practice of sleep medicine*. Philadelphia: Elsevier Saunders.

Czincz, J., & Hechanova, R. (2009). Internet addiction: debating the diagnosis. *Journal of Technology in Human Services, 27*(4), 257–272.

D'Andrade, R. G. (1961). Anthropological studies of dreams. In F. Hsu (Ed.), *Psychological anthropology: Approaches to culture and personality*. Homewood, IL: Dorsey Press.

D'Souza, D. C. (2007). Cannabinoids and psychosis. *International Review of Neurobiology, 78*, 289–326.

Dahl, R. (2003). Beyond raging hormones: The tinderbox in the teenage brain. *Cerebrum, 5*(3), 7–22.

Dallaire, R. A. (2003). *Shake hands with the devil: The failure of humanity in Rwanda*. Toronto: Random House.

Dallman, M. F., Bhatnagar, S., & Viau, V. (2007). Hypothalamic–pituitary–adrenal axis. In G. Fink (Ed.), *Encyclopedia of stress*. San Diego: Elsevier.

Daly, M., & Wilson, M. (1985). Child abuse and other risks of not living with both parents. *Ethology and Sociobiology, 6*, 197–210.

Daly, M., & Wilson, M. (1988). *Homicide*. Hawthorne, NY: Aldine.

Damish, L., Stoberrock, B., & Musswieler, T. (2010). Keep your fingers crossed! How superstition improves performance. *Psychological Science, 21*, 1014–1020.

Daniel, E. (2007). Noise and hearing loss: A review. *Journal of School Health, 77*(5), 225–231.

Daniel, L. (2009). *Gertrude Stein*. London, UK: Reakiton Books.

Daniels, H. (2005). Introduction. In H. Daniels (Ed.), *An introduction to Vygotsky*. New York, NY: Routledge.

Danks, D., & Rose, D. (2010). Diversity in representations: Uniformity in learning. *Behavioral and Brain Sciences, 33*, 90–91.

Danziger, K. (1990). *Constructing the subject: Historical origins of psychological research*. Cambridge, England: Cambridge University Press.

Dapretto, M., & Bjork, E. (2000). The development of word retrieval abilities in the second year and its relation to early vocabulary growth. *Child Development, 71*, 635–648.

Dark crystal. (2005). *CBC: The Fifth Estate*. Retrieved April 1, 2008, from http://www.cbc.ca/fifth/darkcrystal.facts.html.

Darley, J. M., & Latané, B. (1968). Bystander intervention in emergencies: Diffusion of responsibility. *Journal of Personality and Social Psychology, 8*, 377–383.

Darwin, C. (1859). *On the origin of species*. London: Murray.

Darwin, C. (1871). *Descent of man*. London: Murray.

Darwin, C. (1872). *The expression of emotions in man and animals*. New York: Philosophical Library.

Das, H. H. J., de Wit, J. B. F., & Stroebe, W. (2003). Fear appeals motivate acceptance of action recommendations: Evidence for a positive bias in the processing of persuasive messages. *Personality and Social Psychology Bulletin, 29*, 650–664.

Dasen, P. R. (1994). Culture and cognitive development from a Piagetian perspective. In W. J. Lonner & R. Malpass (Eds.), *Psychology and culture*. Boston: Allyn & Bacon.

DaSilva, A. F. M., Granziera, C., Snyder, J., & Hadjikhani, N. (2007). Thickening in the somatosensory cortex of patients with migraine. *Neurology, 69*, 190–195.

Davidoff, J. (2001). Language and perceptual categorization. *Trends in Cognitive Sciences, 5*, 382–387.

Davidoff, J. (2004). Coloured thinking. *Psychologist, 17*, 570–572.

Davidson, J. E. (2003). Insights about insightful problem solving. In J. E. Davidson & R. J. Sternberg (Eds.), *The psychology of problem solving*. New York: Cambridge University Press.

Davidson, K. W., Mostofsky, E., & Whang, W. (2010). Don't worry, be happy: Positive affect and reduced 10-year incident coronary heart disease: The Canadian Nova Scotia Health Survey. *European Heart Journal, 31*, 1065–1070.

Davidson, R. J. (2004). Well-being and affective style: Neural substrates and biobehavioural correlates. *Philosophical Transactions of the Royal Society of London, 359*, 1359–1411.

Davidson, R. J., & Sutton, S. K. (1995). Affective neuroscience: The emergence of a discipline. *Current Biology, 5*, 217–224.

Davidson, R. J., Fox, A., & Kalin, N. H. (2007). Neural bases of emotion regulation in nonhuman primates and humans. In J. J. Gross (Ed.), *Handbook of emotion regulation* (pp. 47–68). New York: Guilford.

Davidson, R. J., Jackson, D. C., & Kalin, N. H. (2000). Emotion, plasticity, context, and regulation: Perspectives from affective neuroscience. *Psychological Bulletin, 126*, 890–909.

Davidson, R. J., Kabat-Zinn, J., Schumacher, J., Rosenkranz, M., Muller, D., Santorelli, S. F., Urbanowski, F., Harrington, A., Bonus, K., & Sheridan, J. F. (2003a). Alterations in brain and immune function produced by mindfulness meditation. *Psychosomatic Medicine, 65*, 564–570.

Davidson, R. J., Pizzagalli, D. A., & Nitschke, J. B. (2009). Representation and regulation of emotion in depression: Perspectives from affective neuroscience. In I. H. Gotlib & C. L. Hammen (Eds.), *Handbook of depression* (2nd ed., pp. 218–248). New York, NY: Guilford Press.

Davidson, R. J., Pizzagalli, D., Nitschke, J. B., & Kalin, N. H. (2003b). Parsing the subcomponents of emotion and disorders of emotion: Perspectives from affective neuroscience. In R. J. Davidson, K. R. Scherer, & H. H. Goldsmith (Eds.), *Handbook of affective sciences*. New York: Oxford University Press.

Davies, I. R. L. (1998). A study of colour in three languages: A test of linguistic relativity hypothesis. *British Journal of Psychology, 89*, 433–452.

Davis, A. S., & Dean, R. S. (2005). Lateralization of cerebral functions and hemispheric specialization: Linking behavior, structure, and neuroimaging. In R. C. D'Amato, E. Fletcher-Janzen, & C. R. Reynolds (Eds.), *Handbook of school neuropsychology* (pp. 120–141). Hoboken, NJ: Wiley.

Davis, A., & Bremner, G. (2006). The experimental method in psychology. In G. M. Breakwell, S. Hammond, C. Fife-Schaw, & J. A. Smith (Eds.), *Research methods in psychology* (3rd ed.). London: Sage.

Davis, M. C., Zautra, A. J., Younger, J., Motivala, S. J., Attrep, J., & Irwin, M. R. (2008). Chronic stress and regulation of cellular markers of inflammation in rheumatoid arthritis: Implications for fatigue. *Brain, Behavior, and Immunity, 22*(1), 24–32.

Davison, G. C., Blankstein, K. R., Flett, G. L., & Neale, J. M. (2008). *Abnormal psychology* (3rd Cdn. ed.). Mississauga, ON: John Wiley & Sons.

Dawes, R. M. (2001). *Everyday irrationality: How pseudoscientists, lunatics, and the rest of us systematically fail to think rationally.* Boulder, CO: Westview Press.

Dawson, W. A. (1993). Aboriginal dreaming. In M. A. Carskadon (Ed.), *Encyclopedia of sleep and dreaming.* New York: Macmillan.

Day, R. H. (1965). Inappropriate constancy explanation of spatial distortions. *Nature, 207*, 891–893.

de Castro, J. M. (2010). The control of food intake of free-living humans: Putting the pieces back together. *Physiology & Behavior, 100*(5), 446–453.

De Cremer, D. Zeelenberg, M., & Murnighan, J. K. (2006). *Social psychology and economics.* Mahwah, NJ: Lawrence Erlbaum Associates.

De Guise, E., & Lassonde, M. (2001). Callosal contribution to procedural learning in children. *Developmental Neuropsychology, 19*, 253–272.

De Guise, E., Del Pesce, M., Foschi, N., Quattrini, A., Papo, I., & Lassonde, M. (1999). Callosal and cortical contribution to procedural learning. *Brain, 122*, 1049–1062.

de Houwer, A. (1995). Bilingual language acquisition. In P. Fletcher & B. MacWhinney (Eds.), *The handbook of child language.* Oxford, OH: Basil Blackwell.

De Houwer, J. (2001). Contingency awareness and evaluative conditioning: When will it be enough? *Consciousness & Cognition: An International Journal, 10*, 550–558.

De Houwer, J., Hendrickx, H., & Baeyens, F. (1997). Evaluative learning with "subliminally" presented stimuli. *Consciousness & Cognition: An International Journal, 6*, 87–107.

De Houwer, J., Teige-Mocigemba, S., Spruyt, A., & Moors, A. (2009a). Implicit measures: A normative analysis and review. *Psychological Bulletin, 135*, 347–368.

De Koninck, J. (1997). Sleep, the common denominator for psychological adaptation. *Canadian Psychology, 38*, 191–195.

De Koninck, J. (2000). Waking experiences and dreaming. In M. H. Kryger, T. Roth, & W. C. Dement (Eds.), *Principles and practice of sleep medicine.* Philadelphia: Saunders.

De Neys, W. (2006). Dual processing in reasoning: Two systems but one reasoner. *Psychological Science, 17*, 428–433.

De Raad, B., Barelds, D. H., Levert, E., Ostendorf, F., Mlacic, B., Blas, L., et al. (2010). Only three factors of personality description are fully replicable across languages: A comparison of 14 trait taxonomies. *Journal of Personality and Social Psychology, 98*(1), 160–173.

de St. Aubin, E., McAdams, D. P., & Kim, T. (2004). *The generative society: Caring for future generations.* Washington, DC: American Psychological Association.

de Vaus, D. A., Qu, L., & Weston, R. (2005). The disappearing link between premarital cohabitation and subsequent marital stability. *Journal of Population Research, 22*(2), 99–118.

de Vignemont, F., & Haggard, P. (2008). Action observation and execution: What is shared? *Social Neuroscience, 7*, 17–24.

De Villiers, P. (1977). Choice in concurrent schedules and a quantitative formulation of the law of effect. In W. K. Honig & J. E. R. Staddon (Eds.), *Handbook of operant behavior.* Englewood Cliffs, NJ: Prentice-Hall.

de Villiers, P. A., & de Villiers, J. G. (1992). Language development. In M. H. Bornstein & M. E. Lamb (Eds.), *Developmental psychology: An advanced textbook* (3rd ed.). Hillsdale, NJ: Erlbaum.

De Waal, F. (2001). *The ape and the sushi master: Cultural reflections of a primatologist.* New York, NY: Basic Books.

de Wijk, R. A., Schab, F. R., & Cain, W. S. (1995). Odor identification. In F. R. Schab & R. G. Crowder (Eds.), *Memory for odors.* Mahwah, NJ: Erlbaum.

De Wit, J. B. F., Das, E., & Vet, R. (2008). What works best: Objective statistics or a personal testimonial? An assessment of the persuasive effects of different types of message evidence on risk perception. *Health Psychology, 27*, 110–115.

Deal, T., & Kennedy, A. (1982). *Corporate cultures.* Reading, MA: Addison-Wesley.

DeAngelis, T. (2008). PTSD treatments grow in evidence, effectiveness. *Monitor on Psychology, 39*, 40–43.

DeAngelis, T. (2009). A new kind of delusion? *Monitor on Psychology, 40*(6). Retrieved from http://www.apa.org/monitor/2009/06/delusion.aspx.

Deary, I. J., Strand, S., Smith, P., & Fernandes, C. (2007). Intelligence and educational achievement. *Intelligence, 35*, 13–21.

Deary, I. J., Whalley, L. J., & Starr, J. M. (2009). *A lifetime of intelligence: Follow-up studies of the Scottish mental surveys of 1932 and 1947.* Washington, DC: American Psychological Association.

Deary, I. J., Whalley, L. J., Lemmon, H., Crawford, J. R., & Starr, J. M. (2000). The stability of individual differences in mental ability from childhood to old age: Follow-up of the 1932 Scottish Mental Survey. *Intelligence, 28*(1), 49–55.

Deary, I. J., Whiteman, M. C., Starr, J. M., Whalley, L. J., & Fox, H. C. (2004). The impact of childhood intelligence on later life: Following up the Scottish mental surveys of 1932 and 1947. *Journal of Personality and Social Psychology, 86*, 130–147.

Deb, S., Lyons, I., & Koutzoukis, C. (1998). Neuropsychiatric sequelae one year after a minor head injury. *Journal of Neurology, Neurosurgery, and Psychiatry, 65*, 899–902.

DeBruine, L. M., Jones, B. C., Little, A. C., & Smith, F. G. (2010). Are attractive men's faces masculine or feminine? The importance of controlling confounds in face stimuli. *Journal of Experimental Psychology, 36*, 751–758.

DeCarvalho, R. J. (1991). *The founders of humanistic psychology.* New York: Praeger.

Decety, J., & Keenan, J. P. (Eds.). (2006). Social neuroscience: A new journal. *Social Neuroscience, 1*, 1–4.

Dechêne, A., Stahl, C., Hansen, J., & Wänke, M. (2010). The truth about the truth: A meta-analytic review of the truth effect. *Personality and Social Psychology Review, 14*(2), 238–257.

DeCicco, T. L. (2002). *Skills for coping with stress and anxiety: A handbook for patients.* Toronto: James Publishing.

Décosterd, M. (2008). *Right brain/left brain leadership: Shifting style for maximum impact.* Westport, CT: Praeger Publishers/Greenwood Publishing Group.

Deecher, D., Andree, T. H., Sloan, D., & Schechter, L. E. (2008). From menarche to menopause: Exploring the underlying biology of depression in women experiencing hormonal changes. *Psychoneuroendocrinology, 33*(1), 3–17.

Deese, J. (1959). On the prediction of occurrence of particular verbal intrusions in immediate recall. *Journal of Experimental Psychology, 58*, 17–22.

Defeyter, M. A., & German, T. P. (2003). Acquiring an understanding of design: Evidence from children's insight problem solving. *Cognition, 89*(2), 133–155.

DeFrain, J., & Olson, D. H. (1999). Contemporary family patterns and relationships. In M. B. Sussman, S. K. Steinmetz, & G. W. Peterson (Eds.), *Handbook of marriage and the family* (pp. 309–326). New York: Plenum.

Degenhardt, L., Hall, W. D., Lynskey, M., McGrath, J., McLaren, J., Calabria, B., et al. (2009). Should burden of disease estimates include cannabis use as a risk factor for psychosis? *PLoS Medicine, 6*(9),1–7.

Deitmer, J. W., & Rose, C. R. (2009). Ion changes and signaling in perisynaptic glia. *Brain Research Reviews, 63*(1–2), 113–129.

Del Monte, M. M. (2000). Retrieved memories of childhood sexual abuse. *British Journal of Medical Psychology, 73*, 1–13.

Delay, J., & Deniker, P. (1952). Trente-huit cas de psychoses traitées par la cure prolongée et continue de 4560 RP. Paris: Masson et Cie.

Delgado, P. L., & Moreno, F. A. (2006). Neurochemistry of mood disorders. In D. J. Stein, D. J. Kupfer, & A. F. Schatzberg (Eds.), *Textbook of mood disorders* (pp. 101–116). Washington, DC: American Psychiatric Publishing.

Delis, D. C., & Lucas, J. A. (1996). Memory. In B. S. Fogel, R. B. Schiffer, & S. M. Rao (Eds.), *Neuropsychiatry.* Baltimore: Williams & Wilkins.

DeLisi, L. E. (2008). The effect of cannabis on the brain: Can it cause brain anomalies that lead to increased risk for schizophrenia? *Current Opinion in Psychiatry, 21,* 140–150.

DeLong, M. R. (2000). The basal ganglia. In E. R. Kandel, J. H. Schwartz, & T. M. Jessell (Eds.), *Principles of neural science* (pp. 853–872). New York: McGraw-Hill.

DeLongis, A., Folkman, S., & Lazarus, R. S. (1988). The impact of daily stress on health and mood: Psychological and social resources as mediators. *Journal of Personality and Social Psychology, 54,* 486–495.

DeLongis, A., Holtzman, S, Puterman, E., & Lam, M. (2010). Dyadic coping: Support from the spouse in times of stress. In J. Davila & K. Sullivan (Eds.), *Social support processes in intimate relationships* (pp. 151–174). New York: Oxford Press.

Delorme, M.-A., Lortie-Lussie, M., & De Koninck, J. (2002). Stress and coping in the waking and dreaming states during an examination period. *Dreaming, 12,* 171–183.

Delprato, D. J., & Midgley, B. D. (1992). Some fundamentals of B. F. Skinner's behaviorism. *American Psychologist, 47,* 1507–1520.

Dement, W. C. (1978). *Some must watch while some must sleep.* New York: Norton.

Dement, W. C. (1999). *The promise of sleep.* New York: Delacorte Press.

Dement, W. C. (2003). Knocking on Kleitman's door: The view from 50 years later. *Sleep Medicine Reviews, 7*(4), 289–292.

Dement, W. C. (2005). History of sleep psychology. In M. H. Kryger, T. Roth, & W. C. Dement (Eds.), *Principles and practice of sleep medicine.* Philadelphia: Elsevier Saunders.

Dement, W. C., & Vaughan, C. (1999). *The promise of sleep.* New York: Delacorte Press.

Dement, W. C., & Wolpert, E. (1958). The relation of eye movements, bodily motility, and external stimuli to dream content. *Journal of Experimental Psychology, 53,* 543–553.

Demo, D. H. (1992). Parent–child relations: Assessing recent changes. *Journal of Marriage and the Family, 54,* 104–117.

Demorest, S. M., Morrison, S. J., Stambaugh, L. A., Beken, M., Richards, T. L., & Johnson, C. (2010). An fMRI investigation of the cultural specificity of music memory. *Social Cognitive and Affective Neuroscience, 5,* 282–291.

Dempster, F. N. (1996). Distributing and managing the conditions of encoding and practice. In E. L. Bjork & R. A. Bjork (Eds.), *Memory.* San Diego: Academic Press.

Dennerstein, L., Dudley, E., & Guthrie, J. (2002). Empty nest or revolving door? A prospective study of women's quality of life in midlife during the phase of children leaving and re-entering the home. *Psychological Medicine, 32,* 545–550.

Dennis, W. (1966). Age and creative productivity. *Journal of Gerontology, 21*(1), 1–8.

Denys, D., Mantione, M., Figee, M., van den Munckhof, P., Koerselman, F., Westenberg, H., et al. (2010). Deep brain stimulation of the nucleus accumbens for treatment-refractory obsessive-compulsive disorder. *Archives of General Psychiatry, 67*(10), 1061–1068.

Der, G., Batty, G., & Deary, I. J. (2009). The association between IQ in adolescence and a range of health outcomes at 40 in the 1979 U.S. National Longitudinal Study of Youth. *Intelligence, 37*(6), 573–580.

Derogatis, L. R., & Coons, H. L. (1993). Self-report measures of stress. In L. Goldberger & S. Breznitz (Eds.), *Handbook of stress: Theoretical and clinical aspects* (2nd ed.). New York: Free Press.

Des Jarlais, D. C., Hagan, H., & Friedman, S. R. (2005). Epidemiology and emerging public health perspectives. In J. H. Lowinson, P. Ruiz, R. B. Millman, & J. G. Langrod (Eds.), *Substance abuse: A comprehensive textbook.* Philadelphia: Lippincott, Williams & Wilkins.

Detterman, D. K. (2010). What happened to moron, idiot, imbecile, feebleminded, and retarded? *Intelligence, 38*(5), 540–541.

Detterman, L. T., Gabriel, L. T., & Ruthsatz, J. M. (2000). Intelligence and mental retardation. In R. J. Sternberg (Ed.), *Handbook of intelligence* (pp. 141–158). New York: Cambridge University Press.

Deuchar, M. (2008). Cutting edge research in bilingualism. *The International Journal of Bilingual Review of Psychology, 59,* 255–278.

Deutch, A. Y., & Roth, R. H. (2008). Neurotransmitters. In L. Squire, D. Berg, F. Bloom, S. Du Lac, A. Ghosh, & N. Spitzer (Eds.), *Fundamental neuroscience* (3rd ed., pp. 133–156). San Diego, CA: Elsevier.

Devine, P. G., & Monteith, M. J. (1999). Automaticity and control in stereotyping. In S. Chaiken & Y. Trope (Eds.), *Dual-process theories in social psychology.* New York: Guilford.

Devine, P. G., & Sharp, L. B. (2009). Automaticity and control in stereotyping and prejudice. In T. D. Nelson (Ed.), *Handbook of prejudice, stereotyping, and discrimination* (pp. 1–22). New York, NY: Psychology Press.

Devine, P. G., Tauer, J. M., Barron, K. E., Elliot, A. J., & Vance, K. M. (1999). Moving beyond attitude change in the study of dissonance-related processes. In E. Harmon-Jones & J. Mills (Eds.), *Cognitive dissonance: Progress on a pivotal theory in social psychology.* Washington, DC: American Psychological Association.

Devlin, B., Fienberg, S. E., Resnick, D. P., & Roeder, K. (2002). Intelligence and success: Is it all in the genes? In J. M. Fish (Ed.), *Race and intelligence: Separating science from myth* (pp. 355–368). Mahwah, NJ: Erlbaum.

Devlin, M. J., Yanovski, S. Z., & Wilson, G. T. (2000). Obesity: What mental health professionals need to know. *American Journal of Psychiatry, 157,* 854–866.

Devos, T. (2008). Implicit attitudes 101: Theoretical and empirical insights. In W. D. Crano, & R. Prislin (Eds.), *Attitudes and attitude change* (pp. 61–84). New York, NY: Psychology Press.

DeVries, R. (2000). Vygotsky, Piaget, and education: A reciprocal assimilation of theories and educational practices. *New Ideas in Psychology, 18*(2–3), 187–213.

Dew, M. A., Bromet, E. J., & Switzer, G. E. (2000). Epidemiology. In M. Hersen & A. S. Bellack (Eds.), *Psychopathology in adulthood.* Boston: Allyn & Bacon.

Dewsbury, D. A. (2009). Charles Darwin and psychology at the Bicentennial and Sesquicentennial. *American Psychologist, 64,* 67–74.

Deyoub, P. L. (1984). Hypnotic stimulation of antisocial behavior: A case report. *International Journal of Clinical and Experimental Hypnosis, 32*(3), 301–306.

DeYoung, C. G., & Gray, J. R. (2009). Personality neuroscience: Explaining individual differences in affect, behaviour and cognition. In P. J. Corr & G. Matthews (Eds.), *The Cambridge handbook of personality psychology* (pp. 323–346). New York, NY: Cambridge University Press.

DeYoung, C. G., Hirsch, J. B., Shane, M. S., Papademetris, X., Rajeevan, N., & Gray, J. R. (2010). Testing predictions from personality neuroscience: Brain structure and the big five. *Psychological Science, 21*(6), 820–828.

Di Chiara, G. (1999). Drug addiction as a dopamine-dependent associative learning disorder. *European Journal of Pharmacology, 375,* 13–30.

DiForti, M., Morrison, P. D., Butt, A., & Murray, R. M. (2007). Cannabis use and psychiatric and cognitive disorders: The chicken or the egg? *Current Opinion in Psychiatry, 20,* 228–234.

Di Lorenzo, P. M., & Rosen, A. M. (2010). Taste. In E. B. Goldstein (Ed.), *Encyclopedia of perception.* Thousand Oaks, CA: Sage.

Di Lorenzo, P. M., & Youngentob, S. L. (2003). Olfaction and taste. In M. Gallagher & R. J. Nelson (Eds.), *Handbook of psychology, (Vol. 3): Biological psychology.* New York: Wiley.

Diamond, J. (2010). The benefits of multilingualism. *Science, 15,* 332–333.

Diamond, L. M. (2003). Was it a phase? Young women's relinquishment of lesbian/bisexual identities over a 5-year period. *Journal of Personality and Social Psychology, 84,* 352–364.

Diamond, L. M. (2007). The evolution of plasticity in female-female desire. *Journal of Psychology & Human Sexuality, 18,* 245–274.

Diamond, L. M. (2008). Female bisexuality from adolescence to adulthood: Results from a 10-year longitudinal study. *Developmental Psychology, 44*(1), 5–14.

Diamond, M. (2009). Pornography, public acceptance and sex related crime: A review. *International Journal of Law and Psychiatry, 32*(5), 304–314.

DiCicco-Bloom, E., & Falluel-Morel, A. (2009). Neural development & neurogenesis. In B. J. Sadock, V. A. Sadock, & P. Ruiz (Eds.), *Kaplan & Sadock's comprehensive textbook of psychiatry* (9th ed., Vol. 1, pp. 42–64). Philadelphia, PA: Lippincott, Williams & Wilkins.

Dick, D. M., & Rose, R. J. (2002). Behavior genetics: What's new? What's next? *Current Directions in Psychological Science, 11*(2), 70–74.

Dickens, W. T., & Flynn, J. R. (2001). Heritability estimates versus large environmental effects: The IQ paradox resolved. *Psychological Review, 108,* 346–369.

Dickens, W. T., & Flynn, J. R. (2006). Black Americans reduce the racial IQ gap: Evidence from standardization samples. *Psychological Science, 17,* 913–920.

Diebel, L., & Roy, C. (2004, August 27). You made me do this. *Toronto Star,* p. A1.

Diekman, A. B., & Murnen, S. K. (2004). Learning to be little women and little men: The inequitable gender equality of nonsexist children's literature. *Sex Roles, 50,* 373–385.

Diener, E., & Diener, C. (1996). Most people are happy. *Psyhological Science, 7,* 181–185.

Diener, E., & Oishi, S. (2005). The nonobvious social psychology of happiness. *Psychological Inquiry, 16*(4), 162–167.

Diener, E., & Seligman, M. E. P. (2002). Very happy people. *Psychological Science, 13,* 81–84.

Diener, E., & Seligman, M. E. P. (2004). Beyond money: Toward an economy of well-being. *Psychological Science in the Public Interest, 5*(1), 1–31.

Diener, E., Gohm, C. L., Suh, E., & Oishi, S. (2000). Similarity of the relations between marital status and subjective well-being across cultures. *Journal of Cross-Cultural Psychology, 31,* 419–436.

Diener, E., Kesebir, P., & Tov, W. (2009). Happiness. In M. Leary & R. H. Hoyle (Eds.), *Handbook of individual differences in social behavior* (pp. 147–160). New York: Guilford Press.

Diener, E., Lucas, R. E., & Scollon, C. N. (2006). Beyond the hedonic tredmill: Revising the adaptation theory of well-being. *American Psychologist, 61*, 305–314.

Diener, E., Ng, W., Harter, J., & Arora, R. (2010). Wealth and happiness across the world: Material prosperity predicts life evaluation, whereas psychosocial prosperity predicts positive feeling. *Journal of Personality and Social Psychology, 99*(1), 52–61.

Diener, E., Sandvik, E., Seidlitz, L., & Diener, M. (1993). The relationship between income and subjective well-being. Relative or absolute? *Social Indicators Research, 28*, 195–223.

Diener, E., Wolsic, B., & Fujita, F. (1995). Physical attractiveness and subjective well-being. *Journal of Personality and Social Psychology, 69*, 120–129.

Dijksterhuis, A. (2004). I like myself but I don't know why: Enhancing implicit self-esteem by subliminal evaluative conditioning. *Journal of Personality and Social Psychology, 86*, 345–355.

Dijksterhuis, A. (2004). Think different: The merits of unconscious thought in preference development and decision making. *Journal of Personality and Social Psychology, 87*, 586–598.

Dijksterhuis, A., & Aarts, H. (2009). Goals, attention, and (Un)consciousness. *Annual Review of Psychology, 61*, 470–490.

Dijksterhuis, A., & Nordgren, L. F. (2006). A theory of unconscious thought. *Perspectives on Psychological Science, 1*, 95–109.

Dijksterhuis, A., & van Knippenberg, A. (1998). The relation between perception and behavior or how to win a game of Trivial Pursuit. *Journal of Personality and Social Psychology, 74*, 865–877.

Dijksterhuis, A., Bos, M. W., Nordgren, L. F., & van Baaren, R. B. (2006). On making the right choice: The deliberation-without-attention effect. *Science, 311*, 1005–1007.

Dijksterhuis, A., Van Baaren, R. B., Bongers, Bos, M. W., Van Leeuwen, M. L., & Van der Leij, A. (in press). The rational unconscious: Conscious versus unconscious thought in complex consumer choice. In M. Wanke (Ed.), *The social psychology of consumer behaviour*. New York: Psychology Press.

Dillbeck, M. C., & Orme-Johnson, D. W. (1987). Physiological differences between transcendental meditation and rest. *American Psychologist, 42*, 879–881.

DiManno, R. (2010, February 24). Team shrinks cue word: Believe, *Toronto Star*. Retrieved May 3, 2011, from http://www.healthzone.ca/health/olympics/2010/article/770633—dimanno-team-shrink-s-cue-word-believe.

DiManno, R. (2011a, February 22). Rochette turned personal tragedy into a nation's triumph, *Toronto Star*. Retrieved May 2, 2011, from http://www.thestar.com/sports/olympics/article/943249—dimanno-rochette-turned-personal-tragedy-into-a-nation-s-triumph.

DiManno, R. (2011b, March 20). No escape valve for so much grief, *Toronto Star*. Retrieved May 2, 2011, from http://www.thestar.com/news/world/article/957069—dimanno-no-escape-valve-for-so-much-grief.

DiMatteo, M. R. (1991). *The psychology of health, illness, and medical care: An individual perspective*. Pacific Grove, CA: Brooks/Cole.

DiMatteo, M. R. (1994). Enhancing patient adherence to medical recommendations. *Journal of the American Medical Association, 271*, 79–83.

DiMatteo, M. R. (1997). Health behaviors and care decisions: An overview of professional–patient communication. In D. S. Gochman (Ed.), *Handbook of health behavior research II: Provider determinants*. New York: Plenum.

DiMatteo, M. R., & Friedman, H. S. (1982). *Social psychology and medicine*. Cambridge, MA: Oelgeschlager, Gunn & Hain.

Dimidjian, S., Hollon, S. D. (2010). How would we know if psychotherapy were harmful? *American Psychologist, 65*, 21–33.

Dimsdale, J. (2008). Psychological stress and cardiovascular disease. *Journal of the American College of Cardiology, 51*(13), 1237–1246.

Dimsdale, J., Irwin, M., Keefe, F. J., & Stein, M. B. (2005). Stress and anxiety. In B. J. Sadock & V. A. Sadock (Eds.), *Kaplan & Sadock's comprehensive textbook of psychiatry*. Philadelphia, PA: Lippincott, Williams & Wilkins.

Dinehart, M. E., Hayes, J. E., Bartoshuk, L. M., Lanier, S. L., & Duffy, V. B. (2006). Bitter taste markers explain variability in vegetable sweetness, bitterness, and intake. *Physiology & Behavior, 87*, 304–313.

Dinges, D. F. (1993). Napping. In M. A. Carskadon (Ed.), *Encyclopedia of sleep and dreaming*. New York: Macmillan.

Dingfelder, S. F. (2011). Reflecting on narcissism. *Monitor on Psychology, 42*, 65–68.

Dinsmoor, J. A. (1992). Setting the record straight: The social views of B. F. Skinner. *American Psychologist, 47*, 1454–1463.

Dinsmoor, J. A. (1998). Punishment. In W. O'Donohue (Ed.), *Learning and behavior therapy*. Boston: Allyn & Bacon.

Dion, K. (1973). Young children's stereotyping of facial attractiveness. *Developmental Psychology, 9*, 183–188.

Dion, K. K., & Dion, K. L. (1996). Cultural perspectives on romantic love. *Personal Relationships, 3*, 5–17.

Dion, K. K., Berscheid, E., & Walster, E. (1972). What is beautiful is good. *Journal of Personality and Social Psychology, 24*, 285–290.

Dion, K. L. (2003). Prejudice, racism, and discrimination. In T. Millon & M. J. Lerner (Eds.), *Handbook of Psychology (Vol. 5): Personality and social psychology*. New York: Wiley.

Dittrich, L. (2010). The brain that changed everything. *Esquire*, November, 112–119.

Dixon, M., & Laurence, J. R. (1992). Two hundred years of hypnosis research: Questions resolved? Questions unanswered! In E. Fromm & M. R. Nash (Eds.), *Contemporary hypnosis research*. New York: Guilford.

Dixon, R. A., & Cohen, A. (2003). Cognitive development in adulthood. In R. M. Lerner, M. A. Easterbrooks, & J. Mistry (Eds.), *Handbook of psychology (Vol. 6): Developmental psychology*. New York: Wiley.

Dobson, K. S. (2002). A national imperative: Public funding of psychological services. *Canadian Psychology, 43*, 65–76.

Docherty, N. M., St-Hilaire, A., Aakre, J. M., & Seghers, J. P. (2009). Life events and high-trait reactivity together predict psychotic symptom increases in schizophrenia. *Schizophrenia Bulletin, 35*(3), 638–645.

Dodds, R. A., Ward, T. B., & Smith, S. M. (2011). A review of experimental literature on incubation in problem solving and creativity. In M. A. Runco (Ed.), *Creativity Research Handbook* (Vol. 3). Cresskill, NJ: Hampton.

Dodwell, P. C., & Humphrey, G. K. (1990). A functional theory of the McCollough Effect. *Psychological Review, 97*, 78–89.

Doerr, P., Pirke, K. M., Kockott, G., & Dittmor, F. (1976). Further studies on sex hormones in male homosexuals. *Archives of General Psychiatry, 33*, 611–614.

Doghramji, P. P. (2001). Detection of insomnia in primary care. *Journal of Clinical Psychiatry, 62* (suppl 10), 18–26.

Dohrenwend, B. P. (2006). Inventorying stressful life events as risk factors for psychopathology: Toward resolution of the problem of intracategory variability. *Psychological Bulletin, 132*, 477–495.

Dolder, C. R. (2008). Side effects of antipsychotics. In K. T. Mueser & D. V. Jeste (Eds.), *Clinical handbook of schizophrenia* (pp. 168–177). New York, NY: Guilford Press.

Dollard, J., & Miller, N. E. (1950). *Personality and psychotherapy: An analysis in terms of learning, thinking and culture*. New York: McGraw-Hill.

Dollard, J., Doob, L. W., Miller, N. E., Mowrer, O. H., & Sears, R. R. (1939). *Frustration and aggression*. New Haven: Yale University Press.

Domes, G., Heinrichs, M., Michel, A., Berger, C., & Herpertz, S. C. (2007). Oxytocin improves "mindreading" in humans. *Biological Psychiatry, 61*(6), 731–733.

Domhoff, G. W. (2001). A new neurocognitive theory of dreams. *Dreaming, 11*, 13–33.

Domhoff, G. W. (2005a). The content of dreams: Methodologic and theoretical implications. In M. H. Kryger, T. Roth, & W. C. Dement (Eds.), *Principles and practice of sleep medicine*. Philadelphia: Elsevier Saunders.

Domhoff, G. W. (2005b). Refocusing the neurocognitive approach to dreams: A critique of the Hobson versus Solms debate. *Dreaming, 15*(1), 3–20.

Dominowski, R. L., & Bourne, L. E., Jr. (1994). History of research on thinking and problem solving. In R. J. Sternberg (Ed.), *Thinking and problem solving*. San Diego: Academic Press.

Domjan, M. (1992). Adult learning and mate choice: Possibilities and experimental evidence. *American Zoologist, 32*, 48–61.

Domjan, M. (1994). Formulation of a behavior system for sexual conditioning. *Psychonomic Bulletin & Review, 1*, 421–428.

Domjan, M. (2005). Pavlovian conditioning: A functional perspective. *Annual Review of Psychology, 56*, 179–206.

Domjan, M., Blesbois, E., & Williams, J. (1998). The adaptive significance of sexual conditioning: Pavlovian control of sperm release. *Psychological Science, 9*, 411–415.

Domjan, M., Cusato, B., & Krause, M. (2004). Learning with arbitrary versus ecological conditioned stimuli: Evidence from sexual conditioning. *Psychonomic Bulletin & Review, 11*, 232–246.

Donaldson, Z. R., & Young, L. J. (2008). Oxytocin, vasopressin, and the neurogenetics of sociality. *Science, 322*(5903), 900–904.

Donderi, D. C. (2006). Visual complexity: A review. *Psychological Bulletin, 132*, 73–97.

Donn, L. (1988). *Freud and Jung: Years of friendship, years of loss*. New York: Scribner's.

Donnellan, M. B., Burt, S. A., Levendosky, A. A., & Klump, K. L. (2008). Genes, personality, and attachment in adults: A multivariate behavioral genetic analysis. *Personality and Social Psychology Bulletin, 34*, 3–17.

Donnerstein, E., & Malamuth, N. (1997). Pornography: Its consequences on the observer. In L. B. Schlesinger & E. Revitch (Eds.), *Sexual dynamics of anti-social behavior*. Springfield, IL: Charles C. Thomas.

Donvan, J., & Zucker, C. (2010). Autism's first child. *The Atlantic*, October 2010. Retrieved January 20, 2011, from http://www.theatlantic.com/magazine/.../autism...s-first-child/8227/.

Dorn, L. D., Nottelmann, E. D., Susman, E. J., Inoff-Germain, G., Cutler, G. B., & Chrousos, G. P. (1999). Variability in hormone concentrations and self-reported menstrual histories in young adolescents: Menarche as an integral part of a developmental process. *Journal of Youth and Adolescence, 28*, 283–304.

Dorner, G. (1988). Neuroendocrine response to estrogen and brain differentiation. *Archives of Sexual Behavior, 17*(1), 57–75.

Doss, B. D., Rhoades, G. K., Stanley, S. M., & Markman, H. J. (2009). The effect of the transition to parenthood on relationship quality: An 8-year prospective study. *Journal of Personality and Social Psychology, 96*(3), 601–619.

Doty, R. L. (1991). Olfactory system. In T. V. Getchell, R. L. Doty, L. M. Bartoshuk, & J. B. Snow, Jr. (Eds.), *Smell and taste in health and disease*. New York: Raven.

Doty, R. L. (2010). Olfaction. In E. B. Goldstein (Ed.), *Encyclopedia of perception*. Thousand Oaks, CA: Sage.

Doty, R. L. (2010). The pheromone myth: Sniffing out the truth. *New Scientist, 2479*. Retrieved March 2, 2011, from http://www.newscientist.com/article/mg20527491.100-the-pheromone-myth-sniffing-out-the-truth.html.

Dougall, A. L., & Baum, A. (2001). Stress, health, and illness. In A. Baum, T. A. Revenson & J. E. Singer (Eds.), *Handbook of health psychology* (pp. 321–338). Mahwah, NJ: Erlbaum.

Dougherty, D. D., Baer, L., Cosgrove, G. R., Cassem, E. H., Price, B. H., Nierenberg, A. A., et al. (2002). Prospective long-term follow-up of 44 patients who received cingulotomy for treatment-refractory obsessive-compulsive disorder. *American Journal of Psychiatry, 159*, 269–275.

Douglas, A. J. (2010). Baby on board: Do responses to stress in the maternal brain mediate adverse pregnancy outcome? *Frontiers in Neuroendocrinology, 31*(3), 359–376.

Dovidio, J. F., & Gaertner, S. L. (2008). New directions in aversive racism research: Persistence and pervasiveness. In C. Willis-Esqueda (Ed.), *Motivational aspects of prejudice and racism*. New York: Springer Science + Business Media.

Dovidio, J. F., & Gaertner, S. L. (2010). Intergroup bias. In S. T. Fiske, D. T. Gilbert, & G. Lindzey (Eds.), *Handbook of social psychology* (5th ed., Vol. 1, pp. 353–393). Hoboken, NJ: Wiley.

Dovidio, J. F., Gaertner, S. L., & Kawakami, K. (2010). Racism. In J. F. Dovidio, M. Hewstone, P. Glick, & V. M. Esses (Eds.), *The Sage handbook of prejudice, stereotyping, and discrimination*. Los Angeles, CA: Sage.

Dovidio, J. F., Kawakami, K., & Gaertner, S. L. (2002). Implicit and explicit prejudice and interracial interaction. *Journal of Personality and Social Psychology, 82*, 62–82.

Downar, J., & Kapur, S. (2008). Biological theories. In K. T. Mueser & D. V. Jeste (Eds.), *Clinical handbook of schizophrenia* (pp. 25–34). New York, NY: Guilford Press.

Dozois, D. J. A. (2008). Human research participant protection in Canada: Moving ahead. *Psynopsis, 30*, 5.

Draguns, J. G. (1980). Psychological disorders of clinical severity. In H. C. Triandis & J. Draguns (Eds.), *Handbook of cross-cultural psychology* (Vol. 6). Boston: Allyn & Bacon.

Draguns, J. G. (1990). Applications of cross-cultural psychology in the field of mental health. In R. Brislin (Ed.), *Applied cross-cultural psychology*. Newbury Park, CA: Sage.

Dranovsky, A., & Hen, R. (2006). Hippocampal neurogenesis: Regulation by stress and antidepressants. *Biological Psychiatry, 59*, 1136–1143.

Draycott, S., & Dabbs, A. (1998). Cognitive dissonance 1: An overview of the literature and its integration into theory and practice of clinical psychology. *British Journal of Clinical Psychology, 37*, 341–353.

Drefus, C. (2011). The bilingual advantage. *New York Times*, May 30, 3011. Retrieved June 30, 2011, from http://www.nytimes.com/2011/05/31/science/31conversation.html.

Drevets, W. C., Gadde, K. M., & Krishnan, K. R. R. (2009). Neuroimaging studies of mood disorders. In D. S. Charney & E. J. Nestler (Eds.), *Neurobiology of mental illness* (3rd ed., pp. 461–490). New York, NY: Oxford University Press.

Drewnowski, A. (1995). Standards for the treatment of obesity. In K. D. Brownell, & C. G. Fairburn (Eds.), *Eating disorders and obesity: A comprehensive handbook*. New York: Guilford.

Drews, F. A., Pasupathi, M., & Strayer, D. L. (2008). Passenger and cell phone conversations in simulated driving. *Journal of Experimental Psychology: Applied, 14*(4), 392–400.

Drews, F. A., Yazdani, H., Godfrey, C. N., Cooper, J. M., & Strayer, D. L. (2009). Text messaging during simulated driving. *Human Factors, 51*(5), 762–770.

Driskell, J. E., Willis, R. P., & Copper, C. (1992). Effect of overlearning on retention. *Journal of Applied Psychology, 77*(5), 615–622.

Dubicka, B., Hadley, S., & Roberts, C. (2006). Suicidal behaviour in youths with depression treated with new-generation antidepressants—Meta-analysis. *British Journal of Psychiatry, 189*, 393–398.

Dubno, J. R. (2010). Aging and hearing. In E. B. Goldstein (Ed.), *Encyclopedia of perception*. Thousand Oaks, CA: Sage.

DuBois, G. E. (2010). Taste stimuli: Chemical and food. In E. B. Goldstein (Ed.), *Encyclopedia of perception*. Thousand Oaks, CA: Sage.

Dubovsky, S. (2005). Benzodiazepine receptor agonists and antagonists. In B. J. Sadock & V. A. Sadock (Eds.), *Kaplan and Sadock's comprehensive textbook of psychiatry* (pp. 2781–2790). Philadelphia: Lippincott Williams & Wilkins.

Duckworth, A. L., Steen, T. A., & Seligman, M. E. P. (2005). Positive psychology in clinical practice. *Annual Review of Clinical Psychology, 1*(1), 629–651.

Duckworth, K., & Borus, J. F. (1999). Population-based psychiatry in the public sector and managed care. In A. M. Nicholi (Ed.), *The Harvard guide to psychiatry*. Cambridge, MA: Harvard University Press.

Dudai, Y. (2004). The neurobiology of consolidation, or, how stable is the engram? *Annual Review of Psychology, 55*, 51–86.

Dudley, M., Hadzi-Pavlovic, D., Andrews, D., & Perich, T. (2008). New-generation antidepressants, suicide and depressed adolescents: How should clinicians respond to changing evidence? *Australian and New Zealand Journal of Psychiatry, 42*(6), 456–466.

Duffy, J. F., Willson, H. J., Wang, W., & Czeisler, C. A. (2009). Healthy older adults better tolerate sleep deprivation than young adults. *Journal of the American Geriatrics Society, 57*(7), 1245–1251.

Duffy, V. B. (2004). Associations between oral sensation, dietary behaviors and risk of cardiovascular disease (CVD). *Appetite, 43*(1), 5–9.

Duffy, V. B., Lucchina, L. A., & Bartoshuk, L. M. (2004). Genetic variation in taste: Potential biomarker for cardiovascular disease risk? In J. Prescott & B. J. Tepper (Eds.), *Genetic variations in taste sensitivity: Measurement, significance and implications* (pp. 195–228). New York: Dekker.

Duffy, V. B., Peterson, J. M., & Bartoshuk, L. M. (2004). Associations between taste genetics, oral sensations and alcohol intake. *Physiology & Behavior, 82*, 435–445.

Duhatschek, E. (2011, January 22). 99 turns 50. *Toronto Globe and Mail*, S4.

Dum, R. P., & Strick, P. L. (2009). Basal ganglia and cerebellar circuits with the cerebral cortex. In M. S. Gazzangia (Ed.), *The cognitive neurosciences* (4th ed., pp. 553–564). Cambridge, MA: MIT Press.

Duman, R. S., & Monteggia, L. M. (2006). A neurotrophic model for stress-related mood disorders. *Biological Psychiatry, 59*, 1116–1127.

Duman, R. S., Polan, H. J., & Schatzberg, A. (2008). Neurobiologic foundations of mood disorders. In A. Tasman, J. Kay, J. A. Lieberman, M. B. First, & M. Maj (Eds.), *Psychiatry* (3rd ed.). New York: Wiley-Blackwell.

Dunbar, K., & Blanchette, I. (2001). The in vivo/in vitro approach to cognition: The case of analogy. *Trends in Cognitive Sciences, 5*, 334–339.

Dunbar, R. (1996). *Grooming, gossip, and the evolution of language*. Cambridge, MA: Harvard University Press.

Dunbar-Jacob, J., & Schlenk, E. (2001). Patient adherence to treatment regimen. In A. Baum, T. A. Revenson, & J. E. Singer (Eds.), *Handbook of health psychology* (pp. 571–580). Mahwah, NJ: Erlbaum.

Duncan, B. L. (1976). Differential social perception and attribution of intergroup violence: Testing the lower limits of stereotyping of blacks. *Journal of Personality and Social Psychology, 34*, 590–598.

Duncan, E., Boshoven, W., Harenski, K., Fiallos, A., Tracy, H., Jovanovic, T., et al. (2007). An fMRI study of the interaction of stress and cocaine cues on cocaine craving in cocaine-dependent men. *The American Journal on Addictions, 16*(3), 174–182.

Dunfield, K. A., O'Connell, L., Kuhlmeier, V. A., & Kelley, E. A. (2011). Examining the diversity of prosocial behaviour: Helping, sharing, and comforting in infancy. *Infancy, 16*(3), 227–247

Dunham, Y., Baron, A. S., & Banaji, M. R. (2006). From American city to Japanese village: A cross-cultural investigation of implicit race attitudes. *Child Development, 77*(5), 1268–1281.

Dunkel-Schetter, C., Gurung, R. A. R., Lobel, M., & Wadhwa, P. D. (2001). Stress processes in pregnancy and birth: Psychological, biological, and sociocultural influences. In A. Baum, T. A. Revenson, & J. E. Singer (Eds.), *Handbook of health psychology* (pp. 495–518). Mahwah, NJ: Erlbaum.

Dunlop, B. W., Garlow, S. J., & Nemeroff, C. B. (2009). The neurochemistry of depressive disorders: Clinical studies. In D. S. Charney & E. J. Nestler (Eds.),

Neurobiology of mental illness (3rd ed., pp. 435–460). New York, NY: Oxford University Press.

Dunn, E. W., Buchtel, E. E., & Aknin, L. B. (2011). Consensus at the heart of division: Commentary on Norton & Ariely (2011). *Perspectives on Psychological Science, 6*, 13–14.

Dunn, D. S. (2009). *Research methods for social psychology*. New York, NY: Wiley.

Dunn, E. W. (2010). In the pursuit of happiness. *International Society for Research on Emotion, 26*, 4–5.

Dunn, E. W., Aknin, L. B., & Norton, M. I. (2008). Spending money on others promotes happiness. *Science, 319*, 1687–1688.

Dunn, E. W., Gilbert, D. T., & Wilson, T. (2011). If money doesn't make you happy then you probably aren't spending it right. *Journal of Consumer Psychology*.

Dunn, E. W., Wilson, T. D., & Gilbert, D. T. (2003). Location, location, location: The misprediction of satisfaction in housing lotteries. *Personality and Social Psychology Bulletin, 29*(11), 1421–1432.

Durlach, N. I., & Colburn, H. S. (1978). Binaural phenomenon. In E. C. Carterette & M. P. Friedman (Eds.), *Handbook of perception* (Vol. 4). New York: Academic Press.

Durlak, J. A. (2003). Basic principles of meta-analysis. In M. C. Roberts and S. S. Ilardi (Eds.), *Handbook of research methods in clinical psychology*. Malden, MA: Blackwell.

Durrant, R., & Ellis, B. J. (2003). Evolutionary psychology. In M. Gallagher & R. J. Nelson (Eds.), *Handbook of Psychology (Vol. 3): Biological psychology*. New York: Wiley.

Dutton, D. G., & Aron, A. P. (1974). Some evidence for heightened sexual attraction under conditions of high anxiety. *Journal of Personality and Social Psychology, 30*, 510–517.

Dvorak, T. (2003). Orphans used in dubious stuttering experiment remain bitter. *Chicago Sun Times*. Retrieved September 2007, from http://findarticles.com/p/articles/mi_qn4155/is/20030806/ai_n125116656.

Dweck, C. (2008). The secret to raising smart kids. *Scientific American Mind*, December 2007/January 2008, 37–43.

Dwyer, J. (1995). Popular diets. In K. D. Brownell & C. G. Fairburn (Eds.), *Eating disorders and obesity*. New York: Guilford.

Dyck, E. (2005). Flashback: Psychiatric experimentation with LSD in historical perspective. *Canadian Journal of Law and Psychiatry, 50*, 381–388.

Dyck, E. (2008). *Psychedelic psychiatry: LSD from Clinic to campus*. Baltimore, MD: Johns Hopkins University Press.

Eagly, A. H. (1992). Uneven progress: Social psychology and the study of attitudes. *Journal of Personality and Social Psychology, 63*, 693–710.

Eagly, A. H. (1995). The science and politics of comparing women and men. *American Psychologist, 50*, 145–158.

Eagly, A. H., & Chaiken, S. (1998). Attitude structure and function. In D. T. Gilbert, S. T. Fiske, & G. Lindzey (Eds.), *The handbook of social psychology*. New York: McGraw-Hill.

Eagly, A. H., & Steffen, V. J. (1986). Gender and aggressive behavior: A meta-analytic review of the social psychological literature. *Psychological Bulletin, 100*, 309–330.

Eagly, A. H., & Wood, W. (1999). The origins of sex differences in human behavior: Evolved dispositions versus social roles. *American Psychologist, 54*, 408–423.

Eagly, A. H., Ashmore, R. D., Makhijani, M. G., & Longo, L. C. (1991). What is beautiful is good, but …: A meta-analytic review of research on the physical attractiveness stereotype. *Psychological Bulletin, 110*, 109–128.

Easterlin, B. L., & Cardeña, E. (1999). Cognitive and emotional differences between short- and long-term Vipassana meditators. *Imagination, Cognition and Personality, 18*(1), 68–81.

Easton, A., & Emery, N. J. (Eds.). (2005). *The cognitive neuroscience of social behaviour*. New York: Psychology Press.

Eaton, J. (2001). Management communication: The threat of groupthink. *Corporate Communications, 6*, 183–192.

Eaton, W. W., Dryman, A., & Weissman, M. M. (1991). Panic and phobia. In L. N. Robins & D. A. Regier (Eds.), *Psychiatric disorders in America: The epidemiologic catchment area study*. New York: Free Press.

Ebbinghaus, H. (1885/1964). *Memory: A contribution to experimental psychology* (H. A. Ruger & E. R. Bussemius, Trans.). New York: Dover. (Original work published 1885).

Ebel-Lam, A. P., MacDonald, T. K., Zanna, M. P., & Fong, G. T. (2009). An experimental investigation of the interactive effects of alcohol and sexual arousal on intentions to have unprotected sex. *Basic and Applied Social Psychology, 31*, 226–233.

Ebstein, R. P. (2006). The molecular genetic architecture of human personality: Beyond self-report questionnaires. *Molecular Psychiatry, 11*(5), 427–445.

Edinger, J. D., & Krystal, A. D. (2003). Subtyping primary insomnia: Is sleep state misperception a distinct clinical entity? *Sleep Medicine Reviews, 7*(3), 203–214.

Edinger, J. D., & Means, M. K. (2005). Overview of insomnia: Definitions, epidemiology, differential diagnosis, and assessment. In M. H. Kryger, T. Roth, & W. C. Dement (Eds.), *Principles and practice of sleep medicine*. Philadelphia: Elsevier Saunders.

Edwards, D. M., Hale, K. L., Maddux, R. E., & Rapaport, M. H. (2008). Anxiolytic drugs. In A. Tasman, J. Kay, J. A. Lieberman, M. B. First, & M. Maj (Eds.), *Psychiatry* (3rd ed.). New York, NY: Wiley-Blackwell.

Edwards, S., Jedrychowski, W., Butscher, M., Camann, D., Kieltyka, A., Mroz, E., et al. (2010). Prenatal exposure to airborne polycyclic aromatic hydrocarbons and children's intelligence at 5 years of age in a prospective cohort study in Poland. *Environmental Health Perspectives, 118*(9), 1326–1331.

Efron, R. (1990). *The decline and fall of hemispheric specialization*. Hillsdale, NJ: Erlbaum.

Egan, J. P. (1975). *Signal detection theory and ROC-analysis*. New York: Academic Press.

Egan, M. F., & Hyde, T. M. (2000). Schizophrenia: Neurobiology. In B. J. Sadock & V. A. Sadock (Eds.), *Kaplan and Sadock's comprehensive textbook of psychiatry* (7th ed., Vol. 1, pp. 1129–1146). Philadelphia: Lippincott, Williams & Wilkins.

Egger, H. L., & Emde, R. N. (2011). Developmentally sensitive diagnostic criteria for mental health disorders in Early childhood: The DSM-IV, the RDC-PA, and the CD-3R. *American Psychologist, 66*, 95–106.

Eggermont, J. J. (2010). Auditory system: Damage due to overstimulation. In E. B. Goldstein (Ed.), *Encyclopedia of perception*. Thousand Oaks, CA: Sage.

Ehrenberg, O., & Ehrenberg, M. (1986). *The psychotherapy maze*. Northvale, NJ: Aronson.

Ehrenberg, O., & Ehrenberg, M. (1994). *The psychotherapy maze: A consumer's guide to getting in and out of therapy*. Northvale, NJ: Jason Aronson.

Eibl-Eibesfeldt, I. (1975). *Ethology: The biology of behavior*. New York: Holt, Rinehart & Winston.

Eich, J. E. (1980). The cue-dependent nature of state-dependent retrieval. *Memory and Cognition, 8*, 157–173.

Eich, E. (2007). Mood, memory, and the concept of context. In H. L. Roediger, Y. Dudai, & S. M. Fitzpatrick (Eds.), *Science of memory: Concepts* (pp.107–110). New York: Oxford University Press.

Eich, E., Geraerts, E., Schooler, J. W., & Forgas, J. P. (in press). Memory in and about affect. In J. Byrne (Editor in Chief), Learning and memory—A comprehensive reference. *Cognitive Psychology* (H. L. Roediger, Ed.), *4*. Oxford: Elsevier.

Eich, E., Macaulay, D., Loewenstein, R. J., & Dihle, P. H. (1997). Memory, amnesia, and dissociative identity disorder. *Psychological Science, 8*, 417–422.

Eich, J. E., & Metcalfe, J. (1989). Mood-dependent memory for internal versus external events. *Journal of Experimental Psychology: Learning, Memory and Cognition, 15*, 443–455.

Eichenbaum, H. (2003). Memory systems. In M. Gallagher & R. J. Nelson (Eds.), *Handbook of psychology (Vol. 3): Biological psychology*. New York: Wiley.

Eichenbaum, H. (2004). An information processing framework for memory representation by the hippocampus. In M. S. Gazzaniga (Ed.), *The cognitive neurosciences*. Cambridge, MA: MIT Press.

Eichenwald, E., & Stark, A. (2008). Management and outcomes of very low birth weight. *New England Journal of Medicine, 358*(16), 1700–1711.

Eid, M., & Diener, E. (2001). Norms for experiencing emotions in different cultures: Inter- and intranational differences. *Journal of Personality and Social Psychology, 81*, 869–885.

Eigsti, I., Zayas, V., Mischel, W., Shoda, Y., Ayduk, O., Dadlani, M. B., Davidson, M. C., Aber, J. L., & Casey, B. J. (2006). Predictive cognitive control from preschool to late adolescence and young adulthood. *Psychological Science, 17*, 478–484.

Einstein, G. O., & McDaniel, M. A. (2004). *Memory fitness: A guide for successful aging*. New Haven, CT: Yale University Press.

Einstein, G. O., McDaniel, M. A., Williford, C. L., Pagan, J. L., & Dismukes, R. K. (2003). Forgetting of intentions in demanding situations is rapid. *Journal of Experimental Psychology: Applied, 9*(3), 147–162.

Eippert, F., Bingel, U., Schoell, E. D., Yacubian, J., Klinger, R., Lorenz, J., & Büchel, C. (2009). Activation of the opioidergic descending pain control system underlies placebo analgesia. *Neuron, 63*(4), 533–543.

Eisenberg, N., Spinrad, T., & Sadovsky, A. (2006). Empathy-related responding in children. In M. Killen & J. G. Smetana (Eds.), *Handbook of moral development*. Mahwah, NJ: Erlbaum.

Eisner, E. W. (2004). Multiple intelligences. *Teachers College Record, 106*(1), 31–39.

Ekman, P. (1992). Facial expressions of emotion: New findings, new questions. *Psychological Science, 3*, 34–38.

Ekman, P. (1993). Facial expression and emotion. *American Psychologist, 48*, 384–392.

Ekman, P., & Friesen, W. V. (1975). *Unmasking the face*. Englewood Cliffs, NJ: Prentice-Hall.

Ekman, P., & Friesen, W. V. (1984). *Unmasking the face*. Palo Alto: Consulting Psychologists Press.

Elbert, T., Pantev, C., Weinbruch, C., Rockstroh, B., & Taub, E. (1995). Increased cortical representation of the fingers of the left hand in string players. *Science, 270,* 305–307.

Elfenbein, H. A., & Ambady, N. (2002). On the universality and cultural specificity of emotion recognition: A meta-analysis. *Psychological Bulletin, 128*(2), 203–235.

Elfenbein, H. A., & Ambady, N. (2003). Universals and cultural differences in recognizing emotions of a different cultural group. *Current Directions in Psychological Science, 12*(5), 159–164.

Elkin, J., Shea, M., Watkins, J., et al. (1989). National Insitutes of Mental Health treatment of depression collaborative research program: General effectiveness of treatments. *Archive of General Psychiatry, 46,* 971–982.

Elliot, A. J., & Maier, M. A. (2007). Color and psychological functioning. *Current Directions in Psychological Science, 16*(5), 250–254.

Elliot, A. J., & Niesta, D. (2008). Romantic red: Red enhances men's attraction to women. *Journal of Personality and Social Psychology, 95*(5), 1150–1164.

Elliot, A. J., Kayser, D. N., Greitemeyer, T., Lichtenfeld, S., Gramzow, R. H., Maier, M. A., & Liu, H. (2010). Red, rank, and romance in women viewing men. *Journal of Experimental Psychology: General, 139*(3), 399–417.

Elliot, A. J., Maier, M. A., Binser, M. J., Friedman, R., & Pekrun, R. (2009). The effect of red on avoidance behavior in achievement contexts. *Personality and Social Psychology Bulletin, 35*(3), 365–375.

Elliot, A. J., Maier, M. A., Moller, A. C., Friedman, R., & Meinhardt, J. (2007). Color and psychological functioning: The effect of red on performance attainment. *Journal of Experimental Psychology: General, 136*(1), 154–168.

Ellis, A. (1973). *Humanistic psychotherapy: The rational-emotive approach.* New York: Julian Press.

Ellis, A. (1977). *Reason and emotion in psychotherapy.* Seacaucus, NJ: Lyle Stuart.

Ellis, A. (1985). *How to live with and without anger.* New York: Citadel Press.

Ellis, A. (1987). The evolution of rational-emotive therapy (RET) and cognitive behavior therapy (CBT). In J. K. Zeig (Ed.), *The evolution of psychotherapy.* New York: Brunner/Mazel.

Ellis, A. (1996). How I learned to help clients feel better and get better. *Psychotherapy, 33,* 149–151.

Ellis, A. (2001). *Feeling better, getting better, staying better: Profound self-help therapy for your emotions.* Atascadero, CA: Impact Publishers.

Ellis, B. J., McFadyen-Ketchum, S., Dodge, K. A., Pettit, G. S., & Bates, J. E. (1999). Quality of early family relationships and individual differences in the timing of pubertal maturation in girls: A longitudinal test of an evolutionary model. *Journal of Personality and Social Psychology, 77,* 387–401.

Ellis, H. H. (1898). Autoerotism: A psychological study. *Alienist and Neurologist, 19,* 260–299.

Ellsworth, P. C., & Scherer, K. R. (2003). Appraisal processes in emotion. In R. J. Davidson, K. R. Scherer, & H. H. Goldsmith (Ed.), *Handbook of affective sciences.* New York: Oxford University Press.

Ellwood, S., Pallier, G., Snyder, A., & Gallate, J. (2009). The incubation effect: Hatching a solution? *Creativity Research Journal, 21*(1), 6–14.

Elman, J. L. (1999). The emergence of language: A conspiracy theory. In B. MacWhinney (Ed.), *The emergence of language* (pp. 1–28). Mahwah, NJ: Erlbaum.

Elmitiny, N., Yan, X., Radwan, E., Russo, C., & Nashar, D. (2010). Classification analysis of driver's stop/go decision and red-light running violation. *Accident Analysis and Prevention, 42,* 101–111.

Elms, A. C. (2009). Obedience lite. *American Psychologist, 64*(1), 32–36.

Elpers, J. R. (2000). Public psychiatry. In B. J. Sadock & V. A. Sadock (Eds.), *Kaplan and Sadock's comprehensive textbook of psychiatry* (7th ed., Vol. 2). Philadelphia, PA: Lippincott, Williams & Wilkins.

Else-Quest, N. M., Hyde, J., & Linn, M. C. (2010). Cross-national patterns of gender differences in mathematics: A meta-analysis. *Psychological Bulletin, 136*(1), 103–127.

Elton John, David Furnish celebrate after tying the knot in England. (2005, December 21). *CBC News.* Retrieved June 20, 2008, from http://www.cbc.ca/story/world/national/2005/12/21/Elton-union-051221.html.

Emavardhana, T., & Tori, C. D. (1997). Changes in self-concept, ego defense mechanisms, and religiosity following seven-day Vipassana meditation retreats. *Journal for the Scientific Study of Religion, 36,* 194–206.

Emmelkamp, P. M. G. (1994). Behavior therapy with adults. In A. E. Bergin & S. L. Garfield (Eds.), *Handbook of psychotherapy and behavior change* (4th ed.). New York: Wiley.

Emmelkamp, P. M. G. (2004). Behavior therapy with adults. In M. J. Lambert (Ed.), *Bergin and Garfield's handbook of psychotherapy and behavior change.* New York: Wiley.

Emsley, R., Rabinowitz, J., & Medori, R. (2006). Time course for antipsychotic treatment response in first-episode schizophrenia. *American Journal of Psychiatry, 163,* 743–745.

Endler, N. S. (1982). *Holiday of darkness: A psychologist's personal journey out of his depression.* New York: John Wiley and Sons.

Endler, N. S. (1997). Stress, anxiety and coping: The multidimensional interaction model. *Canadian Psychology, 38,* 136–153.

Endler, N. S. (2004). The joint effects of person and situation factors on stress in spaceflight. *Aviation, Space, and Environmental Medicine, 75,* C22–C27.

Endler, N. S., & Magnusson, D. (1976). Toward an interactional psychology of personality. *Psychological Bulletin, 83,* 956–979.

Endler, N. S., & Parker, J. D. A. (1990). *The coping inventory for stressful situations (CISS): Manual.* Toronto: Multi-Health Systems.

Engbert, R., & Kliegl, R. (2003). Microsaccades uncover the orientation of covert attention. *Vision Research, 43,* 1035–1045.

Engelmann, J. B. (2006). Personality predicts responsivity of the brain reward system. *Journal of Neuroscience, 26,* 7775–7776.

Engemann, K. M., & Owyang, M. T. (2005, April). So much for that merit raise: The link between wages and appearance. *The Regional Economist,* pp. 10–11.

Engle, R. W. (2001). What is working memory capacity? In H. L. Roediger, III, J. S. Nairne, I. Neath, & A. M. Surprenant (Eds.), *The nature of remembering: Essays in honor of Robert G. Crowder.* Washington, DC: American Psychological Association.

Engle, R. W., Tuhulski, S. W., Laughlin, J. E., & Conway, A. R. A. (1999). Working memory, short-term memory, and general fluid intelligence: A latent variable approach. *Journal of Experimental Psychology: General, 128,* 309–331.

Epley, N., & Huff, C. (1998). Suspicion, affective response, and educational benefit as a result of deception in psychology research. *Personality and Social Psychology Bulletin, 24,* 759–768.

Epstein, J., & Kinkenberg, W. D. (2001). From Eliza to Internet: A brief history of computerized assessment. *Computers in Human Behavior, 17,* 295–314.

Epstein, S., Donovan, S., & Denes-Raj, V. (1999). The missing link in the paradox of the Linda conjunction problem: Beyond knowing and thinking of the conjunction rule, the intrinsic appeal of heuristic processing. *Personality and Social Psychology Bulletin, 25,* 204–214.

Erber, M. W., Hodges, S. D., & Wilson, T. D. (1995). Attitude strength, attitude stability, and the effects of analyzing reasons. In R. E. Petty & J. A. Krosnick (Eds.), *Attitude strength: Antecedents and consequences.* Mahwah, NJ: Erlbaum.

Erdelyi, M. H. (2001). Defense processes can be conscious or unconscious. *American Psychologist, 56,* 761–762.

Erickson, R. P., DiLorenzo, P. M., & Woodbury, M. A. (1994). Classification of taste responses in brain stem: Membership in fuzzy sets. *Journal of Neurophysiology, 71,* 2139–2150.

Ericsson, K. A., & Lehman, A. C. (1996). Expert and exceptional performance: Evidence of maximal adaptation to task constraints. *Annual Review of Psychology, 47,* 273–305.

Ericsson, K. A., Roring, R. W., & Nandagopal, K. (2007). Giftedness and evidence for reproducibly superior performance: An account based on the expert performance framework. *High Ability Studies, 18*(1), 3–56.

Erickson, D. J., Toomey, T. L., Lenk, K. M., Kilian, G. R., & Fabian, L. E. A. (2011). Can we assess blood alcohol levels of attendees leaving professional sporting events? *Alcoholism: Clinical and Experimental Research, 35,* 1–6.

Erikson, E. (1963). *Childhood and society.* New York: Norton.

Erikson, E. (1968). *Identity: Youth and crisis.* New York: Norton.

Ernst, C., & Angst, J. (1983). Birth order: Its influence on personality. *Behavioral and Brain Sciences, 10*(1), 55.

Espejo, E. P., Hammen, C. L., Connolly, N. P., Brennan, P. A., Najman, J. M., & Bor, W. (2006). Stress sensitization and adolescent depressive severity as a function of childhood adversity: A link to anxiety disorders. *Journal of Abnormal Child Psychology, 35,* 287–299.

Espejo, E., Ferriter, C., Hazel, N., Keenan-Miller, D., Hoffman, L., & Hammen, C. (2011). Predictors of subjective ratings of stressor severity: The effects of current mood and neuroticism. *Stress & Health: Journal of the International Society for the Investigation of Stress, 27*(1), 23–33.

Esposito, M. J., Nielsen, T. A., & Paquette, Y. (2004). Reduced Alpha power associated with the recall of mentation from Stage 2 and Stage REM sleep. *Psychophysiology, 41,* 288–297.

Esposito's turtleneck. (n.d.). Retrieved April 27, 2005, from http://www.anecdotage.com/index.php?aid=15970.

Esser, J. K. (1998). Alive and well after twenty-five years: A review of groupthink research. *Organizational Behavior & Human Decision Processes, 73,* 116–141.

Esses, V. M., & Gardner, R. C. (1996). Multiculturalism in Canada: Context and current status. *Canadian Journal of Behavioural Science, 28,* 145–152.

Esses, V. M., Jackson, L. M., & Bennett-AbuAyyash, C. (2010). Intergroup competition. In J. F. Dovidio, M. Hewstone, P. Glick, & V. M. Esses (Eds.), *The Sage handbook of prejudice, stereotyping, and discrimination*. Los Angeles, CA: Sage.

Esterson, A. (2001). The mythologizing of psychoanalytic history: Deception and self-deception in Freud's accounts of the seduction theory episode. *History of Psychiatry, 7*, 329–352.

Estes, R. E., Coston, M. L., & Fournet, G. P. (1990). *Rankings of the most notable psychologists by department chairpersons*. Unpublished manuscript.

Estes, W. K. (1999). Models of human memory: A 30-year retrospective. In C. Izawa (Ed.), *On human memory: Evolution, progress, and reflections on the 30th anniversary of the Atkinson-Shiffrin model*. Mahwah, NJ: Erlbaum.

Evans, D. R., & Segerstrom, S. C. (in press). Why do mindful people worry less. *Cognitive Theory and Research*.

Evans, C. E., & Haynes, R. B. (1990). Patient compliance. In R. E. Rakel (Ed.), *Textbook of family practice*. Philadelphia: Saunders.

Evans, G. W. (2004). The environment of childhood poverty. *American Psychologist, 59*(2), 77–92.

Evans, J. S. B. T. (2008). Dual-processing accounts of reasoning, judgment, and social cognition. *Annual Review of Psychology, 59*, 255–278.

Evans, J. T. (2007). *Hypothetical thinking: Dual processes in reasoning and judgment*. New York: Psychology Press.

Evans, R. I. (1980). *The making of social psychology: Discussions with creative contributors*. New York: Gardner Press, Inc.

Evans, R. I. (1989). *Albert Bandura: The man and his ideas—a dialogue*. New York: Praeger.

Evers, K. E., Prochaska, J. O., Johnson, J. L., Mauriello, J. M., Padula, J. A., & Prochaska, J. M. (2006). A randomized clinical trial of a population- and transtheoretical model-based stress-management intervention. *Health Psychology, 25*, 521–529.

Ewing, L. (2005). Wheelchair racer Petitclerc wins female athlete, gymnast Shewfelt wins men's. Retrieved May 2, 2005, from http://news.h=yahoo.com/news?tmpl=story&u=cpress/20050330/ca_pr.

Eysenck, H. J. (1959). Learning theory and behaviour therapy. *Journal of Mental Science, 195*, 61–75.

Eysenck, H. J. (1967). *The biological basis of personality*. Springfield, IL: Charles C. Thomas.

Eysenck, H. J. (1976). *The biological basis of personality*. Springfield, IL: Charles C. Thomas.

Eysenck, H. J. (1982). Personality, genetics and behavior: Selected papers. New York: Praeger.

Eysenck, H. J. (1990a). Biological dimensions of personality. In L. A. Pervin (Ed.), *Handbook of personality: Theory and research*. New York: Guilford.

Eysenck, H. J. (1990b). *Decline and fall of the Freudian empire*. Washington, DC: Scott-Townsend.

Eysenck, H. J., & Kamin, L. (1981). *The intelligence controversy*. New York: Wiley.

Eysenck, M. W., Mogg, K., May, J., Richards, A., & Mathews, A. (1991). Bias in interpretation of ambiguous sentences related to threat in anxiety. *Journal of Abnormal Psychology, 100*, 144–150.

Fabrigar, L. R., & Wegener, D. T. (2010). Attitude structure. In R. F. Baumeister & E. J. Finkel (Eds.), *Advanced social psychology: The state of the science* (pp. 177–216). New York, NY: Oxford University Press.

Facts about adult gambling and problem gambling. (2008). Centre for Addiction and Mental Health. Retrieved July 24, 2008, from http://www.problemgambling.ca.

Fagan, J. F., & Holland, C. R. (2002). Equal opportunity and racial differences in IQ. *Intelligence, 30*, 361–387.

Fagan, J. F., & Holland, C. R. (2007). Racial equality in intelligence: Predictions from a theory of intelligence as processing. *Intelligence, 35*, 319–334.

Fagot, B. I., Hagan, R., Leinbach, M. D., & Kronsberg, S. (1985). Differential reactions to assertive and communicative acts of toddler boys and girls. *Child Development, 56*, 1499–1505.

Fairburn, C. G., Cooper, Z., & Murphy, R. (2009). Bulimia nervosa. In M. C. Gelder, N. C. Andreasen, J. J. López-Ibor, Jr., & J. R. Geddes (Eds.). *New Oxford textbook of psychiatry* (2nd ed., Vol. 1). New York, NY: Oxford University Press.

Fairburn, S. (2004, February 21). Teen who killed at Taber school kept in prison. *The Globe and Mail*, A7.

Fais, L., & Werker, J. F. (in press). Perceptual narrowing of linguistic sign occurs in the first year of life, *Child Development*.

Fakhoury, W., & Priebe, S. (2002). The process of deinstitutionalization: An international overview. *Current Opinion in Psychiatry, 15*(2), 187–192.

Falls, W. A. (1998). Extinction: A review of therapy and the evidence suggesting that memories are not erased with nonreinforcement. In W. O'Donohue (Ed.), *Learning and behavior therapy*. Boston: Allyn & Bacon.

Famely, P. (2004). The gift of music. (2004, June). *Hospital News*. Retrieved July 31, 2008, from http://hospitalnews/com/modules/magazines.

Fancher, R. (1979). *Pioneers of psychology*. New York: W. W. Norton and Company.

Fancher, R. E. (2000). Snapshot of Freud in America, 1899–1999. *American Psychologist, 55*, 1025–1028.

Fancher, R. E. (2005). Galton: "Hereditary talent and character." *General Psychologist, 40*(2), 13–14.

Fancher, R. E. (2009). Scientific cousins: The relationship between Charles Darwin and Francis Galton. *American Psychologist, 64*(2), 84–92.

Fanselow, M. S., & Poulos, A. M. (2005). The neuroscience of mammalian associative learning. *Annual Review of Psychology, 56*, 207–234.

Faraday, A. (1974). *The dream game*. New York: Harper & Row.

Farah, M. J. (2006). Prosopagnosia. In M. J. Farah & T. E. Feinberg (Eds.), *Patient-based approaches to cognitive neuroscience* (2nd ed., pp. 123–125). Cambridge, MA: MIT Press.

Faravelli, C., & Pallanti, S. (1989). Recent life events and panic disorders. *American Journal of Psychiatry, 146*, 622–626.

Farb, N. A. S., Segal, Z. V., Mayberg, H., et al. (2007). Attending to the present: Mindfulness meditation reveals distinct neural modes of self-reference. *Social Cognitive and Affective Neuroscience, 2*(4), 313–322.

Farrar, M. J. (1990). Discourse and the acquisition of grammatical morphemes. *Journal of Child Language, 17*, 607–624.

Farrey, T. (2007). Pathologist says Waters' brain tissue had deteriorated. ESPN. Retrieved from http://sports.espn.go.com/nfl/news/story?id=2734941.

Farrington, D. P. (2006). Family background and psychopathy. In C. J. Patrick (Ed.), *Handbook of Psychopathy*. New York: Guilford.

Fatemi, S., & Folsom, T. D. (2009). The neurodevelopmental hypothesis of schizophrenia, revisited. *Schizophrenia Bulletin, 35*(3), 528–548.

Fausto-Sterling, A. (1992). *Myths of gender*. New York: Basic Books.

Fava, G. A. (1999). Well-being therapy: Conceptual and technical issues. *Psychotherapy and Psychosomatics, 68*(4), 171–179.

Fava, G. A., Ruini, C., Rafanelli, C., Finos, L., Salmaso, L., Mangelli, L., et al. (2005). Well-being therapy of generalized anxiety disorder. *Psychotherapy and Psychosomatics, 74*(1), 26–30.

Fazio, R. (1995). Attitudes as object-evaluation associations: Determinants, consequences, and correlates of attitude accessibility. In R. Petty & J. Krosnick (Eds.), *Attitude strength: Antecedents and consequences* (pp. 247–282). Hillsdale, NJ: Erlbaum.

Fazio, R. H., & Olson, M. A. (2003). Attitudes: Foundations, functions, and consequences. In M. A. Hogg & J. Cooper (Eds.), *The Sage handbook of social psychology*. Thousand Oaks, CA: Sage.

Fearon, R., Bakermans-Kranenburg, M. J., van IJzendoorn, M. H., Lapsley, A., & Roisman, G. I. (2010). The significance of insecure attachment and disorganization in the development of children's externalizing behavior: A meta-analytic study. *Child Development, 81*(2), 435–456.

Federoff, I., Polivy, J., & Herman, C. P. (2003). The specificity of restrained versus unrestrained eaters' responses to food cues: General desire to eat, or craving for the cued food. *Appetite, 41*(1), 7–13.

Feeney, J. A. (2008). Adult romantic attachment: Developments in the study of couple relationships. In J. Cassidy & P. R. Shaver (Eds.), *Handbook of attachment: Theory, research, and clinical applications* (2nd ed., pp. 456–481). New York, NY: Guilford Press.

Fehr, B. (2001). The status of theory and research on love and commitment. In G. J. O. Fletcher & M. S. Clark (Eds.), *Blackwell handbook of social psychology: Interpersonal processes*. Malden, MA: Blackwell Publishing.

Fehr, B. (2008). Friendship formation. In S. Sprecher, A. Wenzel, & J. Harvey (Eds.), *Handbook of relationship initiation* (pp. 235–247). New York, NY: Psychology Press.

Fein, S., & Spencer, S. J. (1997). Prejudice as self-image maintenance: Affirming the self through derogating others. *Journal of Personality and Social Psychology, 73*, 31–44.

Feingold, A. (1992). Good-looking people are not what we think. *Psychological Bulletin, 111*, 304–341.

Feist, G. J. (1998). A meta-analysis of personality in scientific and artistic creativity. *Personality and Social Psychology Review, 2*, 290–309.

Feist, G. J. (2004). The evolved fluid specificity of human creativity talent. In R. J. Sternberg, E. L. Grigorenko, & J. L. Singer (Eds.), *Creativity: From potential to realization*. Washington, DC: American Psychological Association.

Feist, G. J. (2010). The function of personality in creativity: The nature and nurture of the creative personality. In J. C. Kaufman & R. J. Sternberg (Eds.), *The Cambridge handbook of creativity* (pp. 113–130). New York, NY: Cambridge University Press.

Feixas, G., & Botella, L. (2004). Psychotherapy integration: Reflections and contributions from a constructivist epistemology. *Journal of Psychotherapy Integration, 14*(2), 192–222.

Fekken, G. C. (2000). Reliability. In A. E. Kazdin (Ed.), *Encyclopedia of Psychology* (Vol. 7, pp. 30–34. Washington, DC: American Psychological Association.

Feldman, D. C., & Beehr, T. A. (2011). A three-phase model of retirement decision making. *American Psychologist, 66,* 193–203.

Feldman, D. H. (1988). Creativity: Dreams, insights, and transformations. In R. J. Sternberg (Ed.), *The nature of creativity: Contemporary psychological perspectives.* Cambridge: Cambridge University Press.

Feldman, D. H. (1999). The development of creativity. In R. J. Sternberg (Ed.), *Handbook of creativity.* New York: Cambridge University Press.

Feldman, D. H. (2003). Cognitive development in childhood. In R. M. Lerner, M. A. Easterbrooks, & J. Mistry (Eds.), *Handbook of psychology (Vol. 6): Developmental psychology.* New York: Wiley.

Feldman, P. J., Cohen, S., Doyle, W. J., Skoner, D. P., & Gwaltney, J. M., Jr. (1999). The impact of personality on the reporting of unfounded symptoms and illness. *Journal of Personality and Social Psychology, 77,* 370–378.

Feliciano, L., & Areán, S. (2007). Mood disorders: Depressive disorders. In M. Hersen, S. M. Turner, & D. C. Beidel (Eds.), *Adult psychopathology and diagnosis.* New York: Wiley.

Felker, B., & Hubbard, J. R. (1998). Influence of mental stress on the endocrine system. In J. R. Hubbard & E. A. Workman (Eds.), *Handbook of stress medicine: An organ system approach.* New York: CRC Press.

Feng, J., Spence, I., & Pratt, J. (2007). Playing an action video game reduces gender differences in spatial cognition. *Psychological Science, 18*(10), 850–855.

Fennell, C. T., Byers-Heinlein, C., & Werker, J. (2007). Using speech sounds to guide word learning: The case of bilingual infants. *Child Development, 78,* 1510–1525.

Fenwick, P. (1987). Meditation and the EEG. In M. A. West (Ed.), *The psychology of meditation.* Oxford: Clarendon Press.

Fergus, K. D., & Gray, R. E. (2009). Relationship vulnerabilities during breast cancer: Patient and partner perspectives. *Psycho-Oncology, 18,* 1311–1322.

Fergus, K. D., & Reid, D. W. (2002). Integrating constuctivist and systemic metatheory in family therapy. *Journal of Constructivist Psychology, 15,* 41–63.

Ferguson, C. J., & Hartley, R. D. (2009). The pleasure is momentary … the expense damnable? The influence of pornography on rape and sexual assault. *Aggression and Violent Behavior, 14*(5), 323–329.

Ferguson, C. J., & Kilburn, J. (2010). Much ado about nothing: The misestimation and overinterpretation of violent video game effects in eastern and western nations: Comment on Anderson et al. (2010). *Psychological Bulletin, 136,* 174–178.

Ferguson, T. (1993). Working with your doctor. In D. Goleman & J. Gurin (Eds.), *Mind–body medicine: How to use your mind for better health.* Yonkers, NY: Consumer Reports Books.

Fernald, A. (2010). Getting beyond the "convenience sample" in research on early cognitive development. *Behavioral and Brain Sciences, 33,* 91–92.

Ferster, C. S., & Skinner, B. F. (1957). *Schedules of reinforcement.* New York: Appleton-Century-Crofts.

Feshbach, S., & Tangney, J. (2008). Television viewing and aggression. *Perspectives on Psychological Science, 3,* 387–389.

Festinger, L. (1957). *A theory of cognitive dissonance.* Stanford, CA: Stanford University Press.

Festinger, L., & Carlsmith, J. M. (1959). Cognitive consequences of forced compliance. *Journal of Abnormal and Social Psychology, 58,* 203–210.

Feuerstein, G. Z., Ruffolo, R. R., Coughlin, C., Wang, J., & Miller, D. (2007). Inflammation. In G. Fink (Ed.), *Encyclopedia of stress.* San Diego: Elsevier.

Ficca, G., Axelsson, J., Mollicone, D. J., Muto, V., & Vitiello, M. V. (2010). Naps, cognition and performance. *Sleep Medicine Reviews, 14*(4), 249–258.

Fiedler, K. (2008). Language: A toolbox for sharing and influencing social reality. *Perspectives on Psychological Science, 3,* 38–47.

Fielder, K., Schmid, J., & Stahl, T. (2002). What is the current truth about polygraph lie detection? *Basic & Applied Social Psychology, 24,* 313–324.

Fields, R. D. (2004). The other half of the brain. *Scientific American, 290*(4), 54–61.

Fifer, W. P., Monk, C. E., & Grose-Fifer, J. (2001). Prenatal development and risk. In G. Bremner & A. Fogel (Eds.), *Blackwell handbook of infant development* (pp. 505–542). Malden, MA: Blackwell.

Fife-Schaw, C. (2006). Questionnaire design. In G. M. Breakwell et al. (Eds), *Research methods in psychology* (3rd ed.). London, UK: Sage Publishers.

50 Goals in 50 games. (n.d.). *CBC Archives.* Retrieved April 27, 2005, from http://archives.cbc.ca/400i.asp?IDCat=41&IDDos=1093&IDCli=6056.

Figueredo, A. J., Gladden, P., Vásquez, G., Wolf, P. S. A., & Jones, D. N. (2009). Evolutionary theories of personality. In P. J. Corr & G. Matthews (Eds.), *Cambridge handbook of personality psychology* (pp. 265–274). New York, NY: Cambridge University Press.

Figueredo, A. J., Sefcek, J. A., Vasquez, G., Brumbach, B. H., King, J. E., & Jacobs, W. J. (2005). Evolutionary personality psychology. In D. M. Buss (Ed.), *The handbook of evolutionary psychology.* New York: Wiley.

Finan, P. H., Zautra, A. J., & Wershba, R. (2011). The dynamics of emotion in adaptation to stress. In R. J. Contrada & A. Baum (Eds.), *The handbook of stress science: Biology, psychology, and health* (pp. 111–121). New York, NY: Springer.

Fine, C. (2010). From scanner to sound bite: Issues in interpreting and reporting sex differences in the brain. *Current Directions in Psychological Science, 19*(5), 280–283.

Fine, R. (1990). *The history of psychoanalysis.* New York: Continuum.

Fink, B., & Penton-Voak, I. (2002). Evolutionary psychology of facial attractiveness. *Current Directions in Psychological Science, 11*(5), 154–158.

Fink, B., Neave, N., Manning, J. T., & Grammer, K. (2006). Facial symmetry and judgments of attractiveness, health and personality. *Personality and Individual Differences, 41,* 1253–1262.

Fink, M. F. (2009). Non-pharmacological somatic treatments: Electroconvulsive therapy. In M. C. Gelder, N. C. Andreasen, J. J. López-Ibor, Jr., & J. R. Geddes (Eds.), *New Oxford textbook of psychiatry* (2nd ed., Vol. 1). New York, NY: Oxford University Press.

Finlay, B. L. (2007). Endless minds most beautiful. *Developmental Science, 10,* 30–34.

Finnegan, L. P., & Kandall, S. R. (1997). Maternal and neonatal effects of alcohol and drugs. In J. H. Lowinson, P. Ruiz, R. B. Millman, & J. G. Langrod (Eds.), *Substance abuse: A comprehensive textbook.* Baltimore: Williams & Wilkins.

First, M. B. (2008). Psychiatric classification. In A. Tasman, J. Kay, J. A. Lieberman, M. B. First, & M. Maj (Eds.), *Psychiatry* (3rd ed.). New York, NY: Wiley-Blackwell.

Fischer, K. W., & Hencke, R. W. (1996). Infants' construction of actions in context: Piaget's contribution to research on early development. *Psychological Science, 7,* 204–210.

Fischer, P., Greitemeyer, T., Pollozek, F., & Frey, D. (2006). The unresponsive bystander: Are bystanders more responsive in dangerous emergencies? *European Journal of Social Psychology, 36,* 267–278.

Fischhoff, B. (1988). Judgment and decision making. In R. J. Sternberg & E. E. Smith (Eds.), *The psychology of human thought.* Cambridge: Cambridge University Press.

Fisher, R. A. (1935a). *The design of experiments.* Edinburgh: Oliver & Boyd.

Fisher, B. S., Daigle, L. E., Cullen, F. T., & Turner, M. G. (2003). Reporting sexual victimization to the police and others: Results from a national-level study of college women. *Criminal Justice & Behavior, 30*(1), 6–38.

Fisher, S., & Greenberg, R. P. (1985). *The scientific credibility of Freud's theories and therapy.* New York: Columbia University Press.

Fisher, S., & Greenberg, R. P. (1996). Freud scientifically reappraised: Testing the theories and therapy. New York: Wiley.

Fisher, S., & Greenberg, R. P. (1997). The curse of the placebo: Fanciful pursuit of a pure biological therapy. In S. Fisher & R. P. Greenberg (Eds.), *From placebo to panacea: Putting psychiatric drugs to the test.* New York: Wiley.

Fishman, D. B., Rego, S. A., & Muller, K. L. (2011). Behavioral theories of psychotherapy. In J. C. Norcross, G. R. Vandenbos, & D. K. Freedheim (Eds.), *History of psychotherapy: Continuity and change* (2nd ed.). Washington, DC: American Psychological Association.

Fisk, J. E. (2004). Conjunction fallacy. In F. P. Rudiger (Ed.), *Cognitive illusions.* New York: Psychology Press.

Fisk, J. E., Montgomery, C., & Murphy, P. N. (2009). The association between the negative effects attributed to ecstasy use and measures of cognition and mood among users. *Experimental and Clinical Psychopharmacology, 17*(5), 326–336.

Fiske, S. T. (1998). Stereotyping, prejudice, and discrimination. In D. T. Gilbert, S. T. Fiske, & G. Lindzey (Eds.), *The handbook of social psychology.* New York: McGraw-Hill.

Fiske, S. T., & Russell, A. M. (2010). Cognitive processes. In J. F. Dovidio, M. Hewstone, P. Glick, & V. M. Esses (Eds.), *The Sage handbook of prejudice, stereotyping, and discrimination.* Los Angeles, CA: Sage.

Fiske, S. T., & Taylor, S. E. (2008). *Social cognition: From brains to culture.* New York: McGraw-Hill.

Fitness, J., Fletcher, G., & Overall, N. (2003). Interpersonal attraction and intimate relationships. In M. A. Hogg & J. Cooper (Eds.), *The Sage handbook of social psychology.* Thousand Oaks, CA: Sage.

Fitzgerald, P. B. (2009). Repetitive transcranial magnetic stimulation treatment for depression: Lots of promise but still lots of questions. *Brain Stimulation, 2*(4), 185–187.

Flavell, J. H. (1996). Piaget's legacy. *Psychological Science, 7,* 200–203.

Flavell, J. H. (1999). Cognitive development: Children's knowledge about the mind. *Annual Review of Psychology, 50,* 21–45.

Flavell, J. H. (2004). Theory-of-mind development: Retrospect and prospect. *Merrill-Palmer Quarterly, 50,* 274–290.

Flavelle, D. (2010, July 30). Bill White's 3D camera company is one of several Toronto companies pursuing the burgeoning 3D film market. *Toronto Star*, E2.

Flavelle, D. (2011, February 22). Few turn Olympic gold into dollars. *Toronto Star*, B1, B8.

Fleeson, W. (2004). Moving personality beyond the person–situation debate: The challenge and the opportunity of within-person variability. *Current Directions in Psychological Science, 13*(2), 83–87.

Fleeson, W., Malanos, A. B., & Achille, N. M. (2002). An intraindividual process approach to the relationship between extraversion and positive affect: Is acting extraverted as "good" as being extraverted? *Journal of Personality and Social Psychology, 83*, 1409–1422.

Flegal, K. M., Graubard, B. I., Williamson, D. F., & Gail, M. H. (2007). Cause-specific excess deaths associated with underweight, overweight, and obesity. *Journal of the American Medical Association, 298*, 2028–2037.

Flegal, K. M., Graubard, B. I., Williamson, D. F., & Gail, M. H. (2005). Excess deaths associated with underweight, overweight, and obesity. *Journal of the American Medical Association, 293*, 1861–1861.

Fletcher, G. J. O., & Ward, C. (1988). Attribution theory and processes: A cross-cultural perspective. In M. H. Bond (Ed.), *The cross-cultural challenge to social psychology*. Newbury Park, CA: Sage.

Flett, G. L. (2007). *Personality theory and research.* Toronto: Wiley.

Flett, G. L., & Hewitt, P. L. (2002). (Eds.). *Perfectionism: Theory, research, and treatment.* Washington, DC: American Psychological Association.

Flett, G. L., Vredenburg, K., & Krames, L. (1995). The stability of depressive symptoms in college students: An empirical demonstration of regression to the mean. *Journal of Psychopathology & Behavioral Assessment, 17*, 403–415.

Flicker, S., & Guta, A. (2008). Ethical approaches to adolescent participation in sexual health research. *Journal of Adolescent Health, 42*, 3–10.

Fliessback, K., Weber, B., Trautner, P., Dohmen, T., Sunde, U., Elger, C. E., & Falk, A. (2007). Social comparison affects reward-related brain activity in the human ventral striatum. *Science, 23*, 1305–1308.

Flippo, R. F. (2000). *Testwise: Strategies for success in taking tests.* Torrance, CA: Good Apple.

Flippo, R. F., Becker, M. J., & Wark, D. M. (2000). Preparing for and taking tests. In R. F. Flippo & D. C. Caverly (Eds.), *Handbook of college reading and study strategy research.* Mahwah, NJ: Erlbaum.

Flood, A. M., Davidson, J. R. T., & Beckham, J. C. (2008). Anxiety disorders: Traumatic stress disorders. In A. Tasman, J. Kay, J. A. Lieberman, M. B. First, & M. Maj (Eds.), *Psychiatry* (3rd ed.). New York, NY: Wiley-Blackwell.

Flora, D. B. (2008). Specifying piecewise latent trajectory models for longitudinal data. *Structural Equation Modeling, 15*, 513–533.

Florentine, M., & Heinz, M. (2010). Audition: Loudness. In E. B. Goldstein (Ed.), *Encyclopedia of perception.* Thousand Oaks, CA: Sage.

Flores, B. H., Musselman, D. L., DeBattista, C., Garlow, S. J., Schatzberg, A. F., & Nemeroff, C. B. (2004). Biology of mood disorders. In A. F. Schatzberg & C. B. Nemeroff (Eds.), *Textbook of psychopharmacology.* Washington, DC: American Psychiatric Publishing.

Flynn, E. (2006). A microgenetic investigation of stability and continuity in theory of mind development. *British Journal of Developmental Psychology, 24*(3), 631–654.

Flynn, F. J. (2005). Having an open mind: The impact of openness to experience on interracial attitudes and impression formation. *Journal of Personality and Social Psychology, 88*, 816–826.

Flynn, J. R. (1987). Massive IQ gains in 14 nations: What IQ tests really measure. *Psychological Bulletin, 101*, 171–191.

Flynn, J. R. (1994). IQ gains over time. In R. J. Sternberg (Ed.), *The encyclopedia of human intelligence.* New York: Macmillan.

Flynn, J. R. (1998). IQ gains over time: Toward finding the causes. In U. Neisser (Ed.), *The rising curve: Long-term gains in IQ and related measures.* Washington, DC: American Psychological Association.

Flynn, J. R. (1999). Searching for justice: The discovery of IQ gains over time. *American Psychologist, 54*, 5–20.

Flynn, J. R. (2000). The hidden history of IQ and special education: Can the problems be solved? *Psychology, Public Policy, & Law, 6*(1), 191–198.

Flynn, J. R. (2003). Movies about intelligence: The limitations of g. *Current Directions in Psychological Science, 12*(3), 95–99.

Flynn, J. R. (2007). *What is intelligence? Beyond the Flynn effect.* New York: Cambridge University Press.

Flynn, M. G., McFarlin, B. K., & Markofski, M. M. (2007). The anti-inflammatory actions of exercise training. *American Journal of Lifestyle Medicine, 1*, 220–235.

Fodor, E. M., & Carver, R. A. (2000). Achievement and power motives, performance feedback, and creativity. *Journal of Research in Personality, 34*, 380–396.

Foldvary-Schaefer, N. (2006). *Getting a good night's sleep.* Cleveland: Cleveland Clinic Press.

Folkman, S., & Moskowitz, J. T. (2000). Positive affect and the other side of coping. *American Psychologist, 55*, 647–654.

Folkman, S. (2008). The case for positive emotions in the stress process. *Anxiety, Stress & Coping: An International Journal, 21*(1), 3–14.

Folkman, S., & Moskowitz, J. T. (2004). Coping: Pitfalls and promise. *Annual Review of Psychology, 55*, 745–774.

Follette, W. C., & Davis, D. (2009). Clinical practice and the issue of repressed memories: Avoiding an ice patch on the slippery slope. In W. O'Donohue & S. R. Graybar (Eds.), *Handbook of contemporary psychotherapy: Toward an improved understanding of effective psychotherapy* (pp. 47–73). Thousand Oaks, CA: Sage.

Folsom, D. P., Gilmer, T., Barrio, C., Moore, D. J., Bucardo, J., Lindamer, L. A., et al. (2007). A longitudinal study of the use of mental health services by persons with serious mental illness: Do Spanish-speaking Latinos differ from English-speaking Latinos and Caucasians? *American Journal Psychiatry, 164*, 1173–1180.

Folsom, D. P., Hawthorne, W., Lindamer, L., Gilmer, T., Bailey, A., Golsham, S., Garcia, P., Unutzer, J., Hough, R., & Jeste, D. V. (2005). Prevalence and risk factors for homelessness and utilization of mental health services among 10,340 patients with serious mental illness in a large public mental health system. *American Journal Psychiatry, 162*, 370–376.

Fong, P. (2008). Forth trial in Virk killing. Retrieved from http://www.sfu.ca/criminology/newsevents/FourthtrialinVirkkilling.html.

Fontaine, J. R. J., Scherer, K. R., Roesch, E. B., & Ellsworth, P. C. (2007). The world of emotions is not two-dimensional. *Psychological Science, 18*, 1050–1057

Fontaine, K. R., Redden, D. T., Wang, C., Westfall, A. O., & Allison, D. B. (2003). Years of life lost due to obesity. *Journal of the American Medical Association, 289*, 187–193.

Foote, B., Smolin, Y., Kaplan M., Legatt, M. E., & Lipschitz, D. (2006). Prevalence of dissociative disorders in psychiatric outpatients. *American Journal of Psychiatry, 163*, 623–629.

Forbes, C. E., & Schmader, T. (2010). Retraining attitudes and stereotypes to affect motivation and cognitive capacity under stereotype threat. *Journal of Personality and Social Psychology, 99*, 740–754.

Forcier, K., Stroud, L. R., Papandonatos, G. D., Hitsman, B., Reiches, M., Krishnamoorthy, J., et al. (2006). Links between physical fitness and cardiovascular reactivity and recovery to psychological stressors: A meta-analysis. *Health Psychology, 25*, 723–739.

Forgas, J. P. (2008). Affect and cognition. *Perspectives on Psychological Science, 3*, 94–101

Forsyth, D. R. (2004). Inferences about actions performed in constraining contexts: Correspondence bias or correspondent inference? *Current Psychology: Developmental, Learning, Personality, Social, 23*(1), 41–51.

Forsyth, D. R. (2006). *Group dynamics.* Wadsworth: Belmont, CA.

Forsyth, D. R., & Strong, S. R. (1986). The scientific study of counseling and psychotherapy: A unificationist view. *American Psychologist, 41*, 113–119.

Foster, M. (2001). The motivational quality of global attributions in hypothetical and experienced situations of gender discrimination. *Psychology of Women Quarterly, 25*, 242–253.

Foster, C. (2007). Confidence man. *Stanford Magazine.* Retrieved January 24, 2007, from http://www.stanfordalumni.org/news/magazine.2006/sepoct/features.

Foster, J., Liberman, N., & Friedman, R. S. (2007). Seven principles of goal activation: A systematic approach to distinguishing goal priming from priming of non-goal constructs. *Personality and Social Psychology Review, 11*, 211–233.

Foster, M. D. (1999). Acting out against discrimination: The effects of different social identities. *Sex Roles, 40*, 167–186.

Foster, M. D. (2009a). Perceiving pervasive discrimination over time: Implications for coping. *Psychology of Women Quarterly, 33*, 172–182.

Foster, M. D. (2009b). The dynamic nature of coping with gender discrimination: Appraisals, strategies, and well-being over time. *Sex Roles, 60*, 694–707.

Foster, R. G. (2004). Are we trying to banish biological time? *Cerebrum, 6*, 7–26.

Foulkes, D. (1982). *Children's dreams.* New York: Wiley.

Foulkes, D. (1985). *Dreaming: A cognitive-psychological analysis.* Hillsdale, NJ: Erlbaum.

Foulkes, D. (1996). Dream research: 1953–1993. *Sleep, 19*, 609–624.

Foulkes, D. (1999). *Children's dreaming and the development of consciousness.* Cambridge: Harvard University Press.

Fournier, J. C., et al. (2008). Prediction of response to medication & cognitive therapy in the treatment of moderate to severe depression. *Journal of Consulting & Clinical Psychology, 77*, 775–778.

Fournier, J. C., DeRubeis, R. J., Hollon, S. D., Dimidjian, S., Amsterdam, J. D., Shelton, R. C., & Fawcett, J. (2010). Antidepressant drug effects and depression severity: A patient-level meta-analysis. *Journal of the American Medical Association, 303*(1), 47–53.

Fowers, B. J., & Davidov, B. J. (2006). The virtue of multiculturalism: Personal transformation, character, and openness to the other. *American Psychologist, 61,* 581–594.

Fox, M. J. (2002). *Lucky man: A memoir.* NY: Hyperion.

Fozard, J. L., & Gordon-Salant, S. (2001). Changes in vision and hearing with aging. In J. E. Birren & K. W. Schaie (Eds.), *Handbook of the psychology of aging* (5th ed., pp. 240–265). San Diego, CA: Academic Press.

Fraley, R. C. (2002). Attachment stability from infancy to adulthood: Meta-analysis and dynamic modeling of developmental mechanisms. *Personality and Social Psychology Review, 6,* 123–151.

Fraley, R. C., & Shaver, P. R. (2000). Adult romantic attachment: Theoretical developments, emerging controversies, and unanswered questions. *Review of General Psychology, 4,* 132–154.

Francis, M. E., & Pennebaker, J. W. (1992). Putting stress into words: The impact of writing on psychological, absentee and self-reported emotional well-being measures. *American Journal of Health Promotion, 6,* 280–287.

Frank, J. D. (1961). *Persuasion and healing.* Baltimore: Johns Hopkins University Press.

Frank, L. K. (1939). Projective methods for the study of personality. *Journal of Psychology, 8,* 343–389.

Frank, L. R. (1990). Electroshock: Death, brain damage, memory loss, and brainwashing. *The Journal of Mind and Behavior, 11*(3/4), 489–512.

Frankland, P. W., & Bontempi, B. (2005). The organization of recent and remote memories. *Nature Reviews Neuroscience, 6*(2), 119–130.

Frasure-Smith, N., & Lesperance, F. (2005). Depression and coronary heart disease: Complex synergism of mind, body, and environment. *Current Directions in Psychological Science, 14*(1), 39–43.

Fratangelo, D. (2007). Telling bullies to think pink. *MSNBC: The Daily Nightly.* Retrieved February 6, 2008, from dailynightly.msnbc.msn.com/archive/2007/10/05/399329.aspx.

Frederick, S., & Loewenstein, G. (1999). Hedonic adaptation. In D. Kahneman, E. Diener, & N. Schwarz (Eds.), *Well-being: The foundations of hedonic psychology.* New York: Russell Sage Foundation.

Fredrickson, B. L. (2001). The role of positive emotions in positive psychology: The broaden-and-build theory of positive emotions. *American Psychologist, 56,* 218–226.

Fredrickson, B. L. (2002). Positive emotions. In C. R. Snyder & S. J. Lopez (Eds.), *Handbook of positive psychology* (pp. 120–134). New York: Oxford University Press.

Fredrickson, B. L. (2005). The broaden-and-build theory of positive emotions. In F. A. Huppert, N. Baylis, & B. Keverne (Eds.), *The science of well-being* (pp. 217–238). New York: Oxford University Press.

Fredrickson, B. L. (2006). The broaden-and-build theory of positive emotions. In M. Csikszentmihalyi, & I. S. Csikszentmihalyi (Eds.), *A life worth living: Contributions to positive psychology.* New York: Oxford University Press.

Fredrickson, B. L., & Branigan, C. (2005). Positive emotions broaden the scope of attention and thought–action repertoires. *Cognition and Emotion, 19,* 313–332.

Fredrickson, B. L., & Losada, M. F. (2005). Positive affect and the complex dynamics of human flourishing. *American Psychologist, 60,* 678–686.

Fredrickson, B. L., Tugade, M. M., Waugh, C. E., & Larkin, G. R. (2003). What good are positive emotions in crises? A prospective study of resilience and emotions following the terrorist attacks on the United States on September 11, 2001. *Journal of Personality and Social Psychology, 84,* 365–376.

Fredriks, A. M., Van Buren, S., Burgmeijer, R. J. F., Muelmeester, J. F., Roelien, J., Brugman, E., et al. (2000). Continuing positive secular growth change in the Netherlands, 1955–1997. *Pediatric Research, 47,* 316–323.

Freed, D. A. (2003, September 20). Man leaps to subway tracks, saves life: Hundreds stand by and merely watch. *Toronto Star,* B5.

Freedman, J. L. (1978). *Happy people.* New York: Harcourt Brace Jovanovich.

Freedman, J. L. (2002). *Media violence and its effect on aggression.* Toronto: University of Toronto Press.

Freedman, J. L., & Fraser, S. C. (1966). Compliance without pressure: The foot-in-the-door technique. *Journal of Personality and Social Psychology, 4,* 195–202.

Freeman, N. K. (2007). Preschoolers' perceptions of gender appropriate toys and their parents' beliefs about genderized behaviors: Miscommunication, mixed messages, or hidden truths? *Early Childhood Education Journal, 34*(5), 357–366.

Freese, J., Powell, B., & Steelman, L. C. (1999). Rebel without a cause or effect: Birth order and social attitudes. *American Sociological Review, 64,* 207–231.

Freeze, C. (2005, May 14). Pensions for stress disorder skyrocket. *The Globe and Mail,* A1.

Fremouw, W. J., de Perczel, M., & Ellis, T. E. (1990). *Suicide risk: Assessment and response guidelines.* New York: Pergamon.

Freud, A. (1936). *The ego and the mechanisms of defense.* New York: International Universities Press.

Freud, S. (1900/1953). The interpretation of dreams. In J. Strachey (Ed.), *The standard edition of the complete psychological works of Sigmund Freud* (Vols. 4 and 5). London: Hogarth.

Freud, S. (1901/1960). The psychopathology of everyday life. In J. Strachey (Ed.), *The standard edition of the complete psychological works of Sigmund Freud* (Vol. 6). London: Hogarth.

Freud, S. (1905/1953). Fragment of an analysis of a case of hysteria. In J. Strachey (Ed.), *The standard edition of the complete psychological works of Sigmund Freud* (Vol. 7). London: Hogarth.

Freud, S. (1910/1957). *Leonardo da Vinci: A study in psychosexuality* (Vol. 11). London, England: Hogarth Press. (original work published 1910)

Freud, S. (1914/1953). On narcissism: An introduction. In J. Strachey (Ed., Trans.), *The standard edition of the complete psychological works of Sigmund Freud* (Vol. 1). London, England: Hogarth Press. (original work published 1914)

Freud, S. (1915/1959). Instincts and their vicissitudes. In E. Jones (Ed.), *The collected papers of Sigmund Freud* (Vol. 4). New York: Basic Books.

Freud, S. (1924). *A general introduction to psychoanalysis.* New York: Boni & Liveright.

Freud, S. (1940). An outline of psychoanalysis. *International Journal of Psychoanalysis, 21,* 27–84.

Frey, B. S., & Stutzer, A. (2002). What can economists learn from happiness research? *Journal of Economic Literature, 40,* 402–435.

Frey, B. S., & Stutzer, A. (2007). *Economics and psychology.* Cambridge, Mass: Cambridge University Press.

Freyd, J. J. (1996). *Betrayal trauma: The logic of forgetting childhood abuse.* Cambridge, MA: Harvard University Press.

Freyd, J. J. (2001). Memory and dimensions of trauma: Terror may be "all-too-well remembered" and betrayal buried. In J. R. Conte (Ed.), *Critical issues in child sexual abuse: Historical, legal, and psychological perspectives.* Thousand Oaks, CA: Sage.

Freyd, J. J., DePrince, A. P., & Gleaves, D. H. (2007). The state of betrayal trauma theory: Reply to McNally—Conceptual issues and future directions. *Memory, 15,* 295–311.

Fried, P. A., & Smith, A. M. (2001). A literature review of the consequences of prenatal marihuana exposure: An emerging theme of a deficiency in aspects of executive functioning. *Neurotoxicology and Teratology, 23,* 1–11.

Friedberg, J. M. (1983). Shock treatment II: Resistance in the 1970's. In R. F. Morgan (Ed.), *The iatrogenics handbook: A critical look at research and practice in the helping professions.* Fair Oaks, CA: Morgan Foundation Publishers.

Friedkin, N. E. (1999). Choice shift and group polarization. *American Sociological Review, 64,* 856–875.

Friedman, H. S. (2007). Personality, disease, and self-healing. In H. S. Friedman & R. C. Silver (Eds.), *Foundations of health psychology.* New York: Oxford University Press.

Friedman, H. S., & Adler, N. E. (2007). The history and background of health psychology. In H. S. Friedman & R. C. Silver (Eds.), *Foundations of health psychology.* New York: Oxford University Press.

Friedman, H. S., & Martin, L. R. (2011). *The longevity project: Surprising discoveries for health and long life from the landmark eight-decade study.* New York: Hudson Street Press.

Friedman, H. S., Tucker, J. S., Tomlinson-Keasey, C., Schwartz, J. E., Wingard, D. L., & Criqui, M. H. (1993). Does childhood personality predict longevity? *Journal of Personality and Social Psychology, 65,* 176–185.

Friedman, M., & Rosenman, R. F. (1974). *Type A behavior and your heart.* New York: Knopf.

Friedrich, J., Fetherstonhaugh, D., Casey, S., & Gallagher, D. (1996). Argument integration and attitude change: Suppression effects in the integration of one-sided arguments that vary in persuasiveness. *Personality and Social Psychology Bulletin, 22,* 179–191.

Friese, M., Wänke, M., & Plessner, H. (2006). Implicit consumer preferences and their influence on product choice. *Psychology & Marketing, 23*(9), 727–740.

Frijda, N. H. (1999). Emotions and hedonic experience. In D. Kahneman, E. Diener, & N. Schwarz (Eds.), *Well-being: The foundations of hedonic psychology.* New York: Russell Sage Foundation.

Frisco, M. L., Houle, J. N., & Martin, M. A. (2009). Adolescent weight and depressive symptoms: For whom is weight a burden? *Social Science Quarterly, 90*(4), 1019–1038.

Frishman, L. J. (2001). Basic visual processes. In E. B. Goldstein (Ed.), *Blackwell handbook of perception.* Malden, MA: Blackwell.

Friston, K. J. (2003). Characterizing functional asymmetries with brain mapping. In K. Hugdahl & R. J. Davidson (Eds.), *The asymmetrical brain* (pp. 161–186). Cambridge, MA: MIT Press

Fromm, E. (1979). The nature of hypnosis and other altered states of consciousness: An ego-psychological theory. In E. Fromm & R. E. Shor (Eds.), *Hypnosis: Developments in research and new perspectives*. New York: Aldine.

Fromm, E. (1992). An ego-psychological theory of hypnosis. In E. Fromm & M. R. Nash (Eds.), *Contemporary hypnosis research*. New York: Guilford.

Frumkes, T. E. (1990). Classical and modern psychophysical studies of dark and light adaptation and their relationship to underlying retinal function. In K. N. Leibovic (Ed.), *Science of vision*. New York: Springer-Verlag.

Fruzzetti, A. E., & Erikson, K. R. (2010). Mindfulness and acceptance interventions in cognitive behavioural therapy. In K. S. Dobson (Ed.), *Handbook of cognitive-behavioural therapies* (3rd ed., pp. 347–372). New York: Guilford Press.

Fujimori, F. (2006). Shark bites surfer's leg on North Shore. (2006, March 24). *Star Bulletin* (Honolulu). Retrieved September 21, 2008, from http://starbulletin.com/2006/03/24/news/story05.html.

Fullana, M. A., Mataix-Cols, D., Caspi, A., Harrington, H., Grisham, J. R., Moffitt, T. E., & Poulton, R. (2009). Obsessions and compulsions in the community: Prevalence, interference, helpseeking, developmental stability, and co-occurring psychiatric conditions. *American Journal of Psychiatry, 166*(3), 329–336.

Fuller, P. M., & Lu, J. (2009). Hypothalmic regulation of sleep. In R. Stickgold & M. P. Walker (Eds.), *The Neuroscience of Sleep* (pp. 91–98). San Diego, CA: Academic Press.

Funder D. C. (2009). Persons, behaviors and situations: An agenda for personality psychology in the postwar era. *Journal of Research in Personality, 43*, 120–126.

Funder, D. C. (2001). Personality. *Annual Review of Psychology, 52*, 197–221.

Fung, K. M. T., Hector, W. H. T., Corrigan, P. W., Lam, C. S., & Cheng, W-M. (2007). Measuring self-stigma of mental-illness in China and its implications for recovery. *International Journal of Social Psychiatry, 53*, 408–418.

Funk, W. (1998). *What difference does it make? The journey of a soul survivor*. Cranbrook, BC: Wild Flower Publisher.

Furnham, A., & Gunter, B. (1993). Corporate culture: Definition, diagnosis, and change. In C. L. Cooper & I. T. Robertson (Eds.), *International review of industrial and organizational psychology* (Vol. 8, pp. 234–261). London: Wiley.

Furnham, A., & Mak, T. (1999). Sex-role stereotyping in television commercials: A review and comparison of fourteen studies done on five continents over 25 years. *Sex Roles, 41*, 413–437.

Fushimi, M., Sugawara, J., & Saito, S. (2006). Comparison of completed and attempted suicide in Akita, Japan. *Psychiatry and Clinical Neurosciences, 60*, 289–295.

Fyer, A. J. (2009). Anxiety disorders: Genetics. In B. J. Sadock, V. A. Sadock, & P. Ruiz (Eds.), *Kaplan & Sadock's comprehensive textbook of psychiatry* (9th ed., pp. 1898–1905). Philadelphia, PA: Lippincott, Williams & Wilkins.

Gabbard, G. O. (1994). Reconsidering the American Psychological Association's policy on sex with former patients: Is it justifiable? *Professional Psychology: Research and Practice, 25*, 329–335.

Gabbard, G. O. (2005). Major modalities: Psychoanalytic/psychodynamic. In G. O. Gabbard, J. S. Beck, & J. Holmes (Eds.), *Oxford textbook of psychotherapy*. New York: Oxford University Press.

Gachter, S. (2010). (Dis)advantages of student subjects: What is your research question. *Behavioral and Brain Sciences, 33*, 31–43.

Gackenbach, J. I., & Sheikh, A. (Eds.). (1991). *Dream images: A call to mental arms*. New York: Baywood.

Gaddis, C. (1999, August 8). A Boggs life. *Tampa Tribune*. Retrieved from http://rays.tbo.com/rays/MGBWZ4RSL3E.html.

Gaeth, G. J., & Shanteau, J. (2000). Reducing the influence of irrelevant information on experienced decision makers. In T. Connolly, H. R. Arkes, & K. R. Hammond (Eds.), *Judgment and decision making: An interdisciplinary reader* (2nd ed., pp. 305–323). New York: Cambridge University Press.

Gage, F. H. (2002). Neurogenesis in the adult brain. *Journal of Neuroscience, 22*, 612–613.

Gais, S., & Born, J. (2004). Low acetylcholine during slow-wave sleep is critical for declarative memory consolidation. *Proceedings of the National Academy of Sciences, 101*, 2140–2144.

Galambos, N. L. (2004). Gender and gender role development in adolescence. In R. M. Lerner & L. Steinberg (Eds.), *Handbook of adolescent psychology*. New York: Wiley.

Galati, D., Scherer, K. R., & Ricci-Bitti, P. E. (1997). Voluntary facial expression of emotion: Comparing congenitally blind with normally sighted encoders. *Journal of Personality and Social Psychology, 73*, 1363–1379.

Galderisi, S., Maj, M., Mucci, A., Cassano, G. B., Invernizzi, G., Rossi, A., et al. (2002). Historical, psychopathological, neurological, and neuropsychological, aspects of deficit schizophrenia: A multicenter study. *American Journal of Psychiatry, 159*, 983–990.

Galea, S., Brewin, C. R., Gruber, M., Jones, R. T., King, D. W., King, L. A., et al. (2007). *Archives of General Psychiatry, 64*, 1427–1434.

Galloway, G. (2006, May 6). Margaret Trudeau's dark place of despair. *The Globe and Mail*, A4.

Gallup, A. C., & Gallup Jr., G. G. (2007). Yawning as a brain cooling mechanism: Nasal breathing and forehead cooling diminish the incidence of contagious yawning. *Evolutionary Psychology, 5*, 92–101.

Gallup, G. G., Jr., & Frederick, D. A. (2010). The science of sex appeal: An evolutionary perspective. *Review of General Psychology, 14*(3), 240–250.

Galton, F. (1869). *Hereditary genius: An inquiry into its laws and consequences*. New York: Appleton.

Galton, F. (1909). *Memories of my life*. New York: E. P. Dutton and Company.

Gamer, M., Verschuere, B., Crombez, G., & Vossel, G. (2008). Combining physiological measures in the detection of concealed information. *Physiology and Behavior, 95*, 333–340.

Gandhi, U. (2006, June 14). How do Canadians feel? Here's a snapshot. *The Globe and Mail*. A6.

Gangestad, S. W., Garver-Apgar, C. E., Simpson, J. A., & Cousins, A. J. (2007). Changes in women's mate preferences across the ovulatory cycle. *Journal of Personality and Social Psychology, 92*, 151–163.

Gangestad, S. W., Thornhill, R., & Garver-Apgar, C. E. (2005). Adaptations to ovulation: Implications for sexual and social behavior. *Current Directions in Psychological Science, 14*, 312–316.

Gangwisch, J. E., Heymsfield, S. B., Boden-Albala, B., et al. (2006). Short sleep duration as a risk factor for hypertension: Analyses of the first National Health and Nutrition Examination Survey. *Hypertension, 5*, 833–839.

Gantt, W. H. (1975, April 25). Unpublished lecture, Ohio State University. Cited in D. Hothersall, (1984), *History of psychology*. New York: Random House.

Garakani, A., Murrough, J. W., Charney, D. S., & Bremner, J. D. (2009). The neurobiology of anxiety disorders. In D. S. Charney & E. J. Nestler (Eds.). *Neurobiology of mental illness* (3rd ed., pp. 655–691). New York, NY: Oxford University Press.

Garb, H. N., Florio, C. M., & Grove, W. M. (1998). The validity of the Rorschach and the Minnesota Multiphasic Personality Inventory: Results form meta-analysis. *Psychological Science, 9*, 402–404.

Garcia, J. (1989). Food for Tolman: Cognition and cathexis in concert. In T. Archer & L. G. Nilsson (Eds.), *Aversion, avoidance, and anxiety: Perspectives on aversively motivated behavior*. Hillsdale, NJ: Erlbaum.

Garcia, J., & Koelling, R. A. (1966). Learning with prolonged delay of reinforcement. *Psychonomic Science, 5*, 121–122.

Garcia, J., & Rusiniak, K. W. (1980). What the nose learns from the mouth. In D. Muller-Schwarze & R. M. Silverstein (Eds.), *Chemical signals*. New York: Plenum.

Garcia, J., Clarke, J. C., & Hankins, W. G. (1973). Natural responses to scheduled rewards. In P. P. G. Bateson & P. Klopfer (Eds.), *Perspectives in ethology*. New York: Plenum.

Garcia-Rill, E. (2009). Reticular activating system. In R. Stickgold & M. P. Walker (Eds.), *The Neuroscience of sleep* (pp. 133–139). San Diego, CA: Academic Press.

Gardner, B. T., & Gardner, R. A. (1967). Teaching sign language to a chimpanzee: II. Demonstrations. *Psychonomic Bulletin, 1*(2), 36.

Gardner, E. P., & Kandel, E. R. (2000). Touch. In E. R. Kandel, J. H. Schwartz, & T. M. Jessell (Eds.), *Principles of neural science*. New York: McGraw-Hill.

Gardner, H. (1983). *Frames of mind: The theory of multiple intelligences*. New York: Basic Books.

Gardner, H. (1985). *The mind's new science: A history of the cognitive revolution*. New York: Basic Books.

Gardner, H. (1993). *Multiple intelligences: The theory in practice*. New York: Basic Books.

Gardner, H. (1998). A multiplicity of intelligences. *Scientific American Presents Exploring Intelligence, 9*, 18–23.

Gardner, H. (1999). *Intelligence reframed: Multiple intelligences for the 21st century*. New York: Basic Books Inc.

Gardner, H. (2003). Three distinct meanings of intelligence. In R. Sternberg, J. Lautrey, & T. I. Lubart (Eds.), *Models of intelligence: International perspectives* (pp. 43–54). Washington, DC: American Psychological Association.

Gardner, H. (2004). Audiences for the theory of multiple intelligences. *Teachers College Record, 106*(1), 212–220.

Gardner, H. (2006). *Multiple intelligences: New horizons*. New York: Basic Books.

Gardner, H., & Hatch, T. (1989). Multiple intelligences go to school: Educational implications of the theory of multiple intelligences. *Educational Researcher, 18*(8), 4–10.

Gardner, M., & Steinberg, L. (2005). Peer influence on risk-taking, risk preference, and risky decision-making in adolescence and adulthood: An experimental study. *Developmental Psychology, 41*, 625–635.

Gardner, R. C. (2000). Correlation, causation, motivation and second language acquisition. *Canadian Psychology, 41*, 10–22.

Gardner, R. C., & Lambert, W. E. (1959). Motivational variables in second-language acquisition. *Canadian Journal of Psychology, 13,* 266–272.

Gardos, P. S., & Mosher, D. L. (1999). Gender differences in reactions to viewing pornographic vignettes: Essential or interpretive? *Journal of Psychology & Human Sexuality, 11,* 65–83.

Garland, E. L., Gaylord, S. A., Boettiger, C. A., & Howard, M. O. (2010). Mindfulness training modifies cognitive, affective, and physiological mechanisms implicated in alcohol dependence: Results of a randomized controlled pilot trial. *Journal of Psychoactive Drugs, 42*(2), 213–235.

Garvey, C. R. (1929). List of American psychology laboratories. *Psychological Bulletin, 26,* 652–660.

Gaschler, K. (2008). Misery in motherhood. *Scientific American Mind, 19,* 66–73.

Gassmann, O., & Zeschky, M. (2008). Opening up the solution space: The role of analogical thinking for breakthrough product innovation. *Creativity & Innovation Management, 17*(2), 97–106.

Gatchel, R. J., & Maddrey, A. M. (2004). The biopsychosocial perspective of pain. In J. M. Raczynski & L. C. Leviton (Eds.), *Handbook of clinical health psychology (Vol.2): Disorders of behavior and health.* Washington, DC: American Psychological Association.

Gauthier, I., & Curby, K. M. (2005). A perceptual traffic jam on highway N170: Interference between face and car expertise. *Current Directions in Psychological Science, 14*(1), 30–33.

Gauthier, I., Tarr, M. J., Anderson, A. W., Skudlarski, P., & Gore, J. C. (1999). Activation of the middle fusiform "face area" increases with expertise in recognizing novel objects. *Nature Neuroscience, 2,* 568–573.

Gawronski, B. (2004). Theory-based bias correction in dispositional inference: The fundamental attribution error is dead, long live the correspondence bias. In W. Stroebe & M. Hewstone (Eds.), *European review*

Gawronski, B., & Bodenhausen, G. V. (2011). The associative-propositional evaluation model: Theory, evidence, and open questions. *Advances in Experimental Social Psychology, 44,* 59–127.

Gawronski, B., & Payne, B. K. (2010). *Handbook of implicit social cognition.* New York: Guilford Press.

Gawronski, B., LeBel, E. P., & Peters, K. R. (2007). What do implicit measures tell us? Scrutinizing the validity of three common assumptions. *Perspectives on Psychological Science, 2,* 181–193.

Gawronski, B., LeBel, E. P., Ranse, R., & Peters, K. R. (2009). Methodological issues in the validation of implicit measures. *Psychologial Bulletin, 135,* 369–372.

Gawryluk, J. R., D'Arcy, R. C. N., Connolly, J. F., & Weaver, D. F. (2010). Improving the clinical assessment of consciousness with advances in electrophysiological and neuroimaging techniques. *BMC Neurology, 10,* 17–26.

Gazzaniga, M. S. (1970). *The bisected brain.* New York: Appleton-Century-Crofts.

Gazzaniga, M. S. (2000). Cerebral specialization and interhemispheric communication. *Brain, 123,* 1293–1326.

Gazzaniga, M. S. (2005). Forty-five years of split-brain research and still going strong. *Nature Reviews Neuroscience, 6,* 653–659.

Gazzaniga, M. S. (2008). Spheres of influence. *Scientific American Mind, 19*(2), 32–39.

Gazzaniga, M. S., Bogen, J. E., & Sperry, R. W. (1965). Observations on visual perception after disconnection of the cerebral hemispheres in man. *Brain, 88,* 221–236.

Gazzaniga, M. S., Ivry, R. B., & Mangum, G. R. (2009). *Cognitive neuroscience: The biology of the mind* (3rd ed.). New York, NY: Norton.

Geary, D. C. (2007). An evolutionary perspective on sex difference in mathematics and the sciences. In S. J. Ceci & W. M. Williams (Eds.), *Why aren't more women in science?* (pp. 173–188). Washington, DC: American Psychological Association.

Geer, J. H., & Janssen, E. (2000). The sexual response system. In J. T. Cacioppo, L. G. Tassinary, & G. Bernston (Eds.), *Handbook of psychophysiology.* New York: Cambridge University Press.

Gegenfurtner, K. (2010). Color perception: Physiological. In E. B. Goldstein (Ed.), *Encyclopedia of perception.* Thousand Oaks, CA: Sage.

Geier, A. B., Rozin, P., & Doros, G. (2006). Unit bias: A new heuristic that helps explain the effect of portion size on food intake. *Psychological Science, 17,* 521–525.

Geiger, M. A. (1997). An examination of the relationship between answer changing, testwiseness and examination performance. *Journal of Experimental Education, 66,* 49–60.

Geller, J. L. (1992). A historical perspective on the role of state hospitals viewed from the era of the "revolving door." *American Journal of Psychiatry, 149,* 1526–1533.

Geller, J. L. (2009). The role of the hospital in the care of the mentally ill. In B. J. Sadock, V. A. Sadock, & P. Ruiz (Eds.), *Kaplan & Sadock's comprehensive textbook of psychiatry* (9th ed., pp. 4299–4314). Philadelphia, PA: Lippincott, Williams & Wilkins.

Genesee, F. (1998). French immersion in Canada. In J. Edwards (Ed.), *Language in Canada* (pp. 305–326). Cambridge, UK: Cambridge University Press.

Genesee, F. (2004). What do we know about bilingual education for majority-language students? In T. K. Bhatia & W. C. Ritchie (Eds.), *The handbook of bilingualism* (pp. 547–576). Oxford, UK: Blackwell Publishing Ltd.

Gennari, S. P., Sloman, S. A., Malt, B. C., & Fitch, W. T. (2002). Motion events in language and cognition. *Cognition, 83*(1), 49–79.

Genova, L. (2008). *Still Alice: A novel.* New York: Basic books.

Gentner, D. (1988). Metaphor as structure mapping: The relational shift. *Child Development, 59,* 47–59.

George, M. S. (2003, September). Stimulating the brain. *Scientific American, 289*(3), 66–93.

George, M. S., Bohning, D. E., Lorberbaum, J. P., Nahas, Z., Anderson, B., Borckardt, J. J., et al. (2007). Overview of transcranial magnetic stimulation: History, mechanisms, physics, and safety. In M. S. George & R. H. Belmaker (Eds.), *Transcranial magnetic stimulation in clinical psychiatry.* Washington, DC: American Psychiatric Publishing.

George, S. A. (2002). The menopause experience: A woman's perspective. *Journal of Obstetric, Gynecologic, and Neonatal Nursing, 31,* 71–85.

Geraerts, E., Raymaekers, L., & Merckelbach, H. (2008). Recovered memories of childhood sexual abuse: Current findings and their legal implications. *Legal and Criminological Psychology, 13*(2), 165–176.

Geraerts, E., Schooler, J. W., Merckelbach, H., Jelicic, M., Hauer, B. A., & Ambadar, Z. (2007). The reality of recovered memories: Corroborating continuous and discontinuous memories of childhood sexual abuse. *Psychological Science, 18*(7), 564–568.

Gergen, K. J., Gulerce, A., Lock, A., & Misra, G. (1996). Psychological science in cultural context. *American Psychologist, 51,* 496–503.

German, A. (2007). Job special: Female professors. *The Hour.* Retrieved January 31, 2008, from http://www.hour.ca.news/news.aspx?iIDArticle=11926.

Gershkoff-Stowe, L., & Hahn, E. R. (2007). Fast mapping skills in the developing lexicon. *Journal of Speech, Language, and Hearing Research, 50,* 682–696.

Gershoff, E. T. (2002). Parental corporal punishment and associated child behaviors and experiences: A meta-analytic and theoretical review. *Psychological Bulletin, 128,* 539–579.

Gershon, E. S., Berrettini, W. H., & Goldin, L. R. (1989). Mood disorders: Genetic aspects. In H. I. Kaplan & B. J. Sadock (Eds.), *Comprehensive textbook of psychiatry/V.* Baltimore: Williams & Wilkins.

Gervain, J., & Mehler, J. (2010). Speech perception and language acquisition in the first year of life. *Annual Review of Psychology, 61,* 191–218.

Gervain, J., Mehler, J., Werker, J. F., Nelson, C. A., Csibra, C., Lloyd-Fox, S., Shukla, M., & Aslin, R. N. (2011). Near-infrared spectroscopy: A report from the mcdonnell infant methodology consortium. *Developmental Cognitive Neuroscience, 1,* 22–46.

Getzel, E. E., & Wehman, P. (2005). *Going to college: Expanding opportunities with disabilities.* Baltimore: Brookes.

Gibbons, M. B. C., Crits-Christoph, P., & Hearon, B. (2008). The empirical status of psychodynamic therapies. *Annual Review of Clinical Psychology, 4,* 93–108.

Gibbs, W. W. (2005). Obesity: An overblown epidemic? *Scientific American, 292*(6), 70–77.

Gibson, C., Folley, B. S., & Park, S. (2009). Enhanced divergent thinking and creativity in musicians: A behavioral and near-infrared spectroscopy study. *Brain and Cognition, 69*(1), 162–169.

Gibson, H. B., & Heap, M. (1991). *Hypnosis in therapy.* Hillsdale, NJ: Erlbaum.

Giedd, J. N., Blumenthal, J., Jeffries, N. O., Castellanos, F. X., Liu, H., Zijdenbos, A., et al. (1999). Brain development during childhood and adolescence: A longitudinal MRI study. *Nature Neuroscience, 2,* 861–863.

Gigerenzer, G. (2000). *Adaptive thinking: Rationality in the real world.* New York: Oxford University Press.

Gigerenzer, G. (2004). Fast and frugal heuristics: The tools of bounded rationality. In D. J. Koehler & N. Harvey (Eds.), *Blackwell handbook of judgment and decision making.* Malden, MA: Blackwell Publishing.

Gigerenzer, G. (2008). Why heuristics work. *Perspective on Psychological Science, 3*(1), 20–29.

Gigerenzer, G., & Gaissmaier, W. (2011). Heuristic decision making. *Annual Review of Psychology, 62,* 451–482.

Gigerenzer, G., & Todd, P. M. (1999). Fast and frugal heuristics: The adaptive toolbox. In G. Gigerenzer, P. M. Todd, & ABC Research Group (Eds.), *Simple heuristics that make us smart* (pp. 3–36). New York: Oxford University Press.

Gigerenzer, G., Gaissmaier, W., Kurz-Milcke, E., Schwartz, L. M., & Woloshin, S. (2007). Helping doctors and patients make sense of health statistics. *Psychological Science in the Public Interest, 8*(2), 53–96.

Gilad, Y., Wiebe, V., Przeworski, M., Lancet, D., & Paabo, S. (2004). Loss of olfactory receptor genes coincides with the acquisition of full trichromatic vision in primates. *PLoS Biology, 5*(6), e148.

Gilbert, C. D. (1993). Rapid dynamic changes in adult cerebral cortex. *Current Opinion in Neurobiology, 3,* 100–103.

Gilbert, D. (2006). *Stumbling on happiness.* New York: Alfred A. Knopf.

Gilbert, D. T. (1989). Thinking lightly about others: Automatic components of the social inference process. In J. S. Uleman & J. A. Bargh (Eds.), *Unintended thought: Limits of awareness, intention, and control.* New York: Guilford.

Gilbert, D. T. (1998). Speeding with Ned: A personal view of the correspondence bias. In J. M. Darley & J. Cooper (Ed.), *Attribution and social interaction: The legacy of Edward E. Jones.* Washington, DC: American Psychological Association.

Gilbert, D. T., & Malone, P. S. (1995). The correspondence bias. *Psychological Bulletin, 117,* 21–38.

Gilbert, D. T., Driver-Linn, E., & Wilson, T. D. (2002). The trouble with Vronsky: Impact bias in the forecasting of future affective states. In L. F. Barrett & P. Salovey (Eds.), *The wisdom in feeling: Psychological processes in emotional intelligence* (pp. 114–143). New York, NY: Guilford Press.

Gilbert, D. T., Pinel, E. C., Wilson, T. D., Blumberg, S. J., & Wheatley, T. P. (1998). Immune neglect: A source of durability bias in affective forecasting. *Journal of Personality and Social Psychology, 75*(3), 617–638.

Gilgen, A. R. (1982). *American psychology since World War II: A profile of the discipline.* Westport, CT: Greenwood Press.

Gillberg, M., & Akerstedt, T. (1998). Sleep loss and performance: No "safe" duration of a monotonous task. *Physiology & Behavior, 64,* 599–604.

Gilligan, C. (1982). *In a different voice: Psychological theory and women's development.* Cambridge, MA: Harvard University Press.

Gillis, C. (2004, December 27). Chantal Petitclerc. *Macleans.*

Gilmour, H. (2008). Depression and risk of heart disease. Statistics Canada: *Health Reports, 19.* Retrieved July 17, 2008, from http://www .statcan.ca/english/freepub/82-003-XIE/2008003/ article/10649-en.htm.

Gilmour, H., & Wilkins, K. (2003). Migraine. Statistics Canada: *Health Reports, 12,* 23–40. Retrieved January 30, 2008, from http://www .statcan.ca/english/studies/82-003/feature/ hrab2000012002s4a02.htm.

Gilovich, T. D., & Griffin, D. W. (2010). Judgment and decision making. In S. T. Fiske, D. T. Gilbert, & G. Lindzey (Eds.), *Handbook of social psychology,* (5th ed., Vol. 1, pp. 542–588). Hoboken, NJ: Wiley.

Gilovich, T. D., Griffin, D., & Kahneman, D. (2002). *Heuristics and biases: The psychology of intuitive judgment.* New York, NY: Cambridge University Press.

Gim, R. H., Atkinson, D. R., & Kim, S. J. (1991). Asian-American acculturation, counselor ethnicity, and cultural sensitivity, and ratings of counselors. *Journal of Counseling Psychology, 38,* 37–62.

Gim, R. H., Atkinson, D. R., & Whitelhy, S. (1990). Asian-American acculturation, severithy of concerns, and willingness to see a counselor. *Journal of Counseling Psychology, 37,* 281–283.

Gimmig, D., Huguet, P., Caverni, J., & Cury, F. (2006). Choking under pressure and working memory capacity: When performance pressure reduces fluid intelligence. *Psychonomic Bulletin & Review, 13*(6), 1005–1010.

Giordano, G. (2005). *How testing came to dominate American schools: The history of educational assessment.* New York: Peter Lang.

Gitlin, M. J. (2009). Pharmacotherapy and other somatic treatments for depression. In I. H. Gotlib & C. L. Hammen (Eds.), *Handbook of depression* (pp. 554–585). New York, NY: Guilford Press.

Gitre, E. J. K. (2010). Importing Freud: First-wave psychoanalysis, interwar social sciences, and the interdisciplinary foundations of an American social theory. *Journal of the History of the Behavioral Sciences, 46*(3), 239–262.

Gittelman, M. (2005). The neglected disaster. *International Journal of Mental Health, 34*(2), 9–21.

Giudice, M. (2011). Sex differences in romantic attachment: A meta-analysis. *Personality and Social Psychology Bulletin, 37,* 193–314.

Gladwell, M. (2005). *Blink.* New York. Little Brown and Co.

Glaser, J., & Kahn, K. (2005). Prejudice, discrimination, and the Internet. In Y. Amichai-Hamburger (Ed.), *The social net: Understanding human behavior in cyberspace* (pp. 247–276). New York: Oxford University Press.

Glasman, L. R., & Albarracín, D. (2006). Forming attitudes that predict future behavior: A meta-analysis of the attitude–behavior relation. *Psychological Bulletin, 132,* 778–822.

Glass, R. M. (2001). Electroconvulsive therapy. *Journal of the American Medical Association, 285,* 1346–1348.

Glass, R. M. (2004). Treatment of adolescents with major depression: Contributions of a major trial. *Journal of the American Medical Association, 292,* 861–863.

Glatt, S. J. (2008). Genteics. In K. T. Mueser & D. V. Jeste (Eds.), *Clinical handbook of schizophrenia* (pp. 55–64). New York, NY: Guilford Press.

Gleaves, D. H. (1994). On "The reality of repressed memories." *American Psychologist, 49,* 440–441.

Gleaves, D. H., Smith, S. M., Butler, L. D., & Spiegel, D. (2004). False and recovered memories in the laboratory and clinic: A review of experimental and clinical evidence. *Clinical Psychology: Science & Practice, 11*(1), 3–28.

Gleaves, D. H., May, M. C., & Cardeña, E. (2007). An examination of the diagnostic validity of dissociative identity disorder. *Clinical Psychology Review, 21,* 577–608.

Gleitman, L. R., & Newport, E. (1996). *The invention of language by children.* Cambridge, MA: MIT Press.

Gleitman, L., & Papafragou, A. (2005). Language and thought. In K. J. Holyoak & R. G. Morrison (Eds.), *The Cambridge handbook of thinking and reasoning.* New York: Cambridge University Press.

Gluck, M. A., & Myers, C. E. (1997). Psychobiological models of hippocampal function in learning and memory. *Annual Review of Psychology, 48,* 481–514.

Gluck, M. E. (2006). Stress response and binge eating disorder. *Appetite, 46*(1), 26–30.

Gmelch, G. (1978). Baseball magic. *Human Nature, 1*(8), 32–39.

Gneezy, U., List, J. A., & Wu, G. (2006). The uncertainty effect: When a risky prospect is valued less than its worst possible outcome. *Quarterly Journal of Economics, 121*(4), 1283–1309.

Goddard, M. J. (2009). The impact of human intuition in psychology. *Review of General Psychology, 13,* 167–174.

Godfrey, R. (2005). *Under the bridge.* New York: Simon & Shuster.

Goetz, A. T., et al. (2010). The evolutionary psychology of violence. *Psicothema, 22,* 15–21.

Goff, D. C., & Gudeman, J. E. (1999). The person with chronic mental illness. In A. M. Nicholi (Ed.), *The Harvard guide to psychiatry.* Cambridge, MA: Harvard University Press.

Gogtay, N., Giedd, J. N., Lusk, L., Hayashi, K. M., Rapoport, J. L., Thompson, P. M., et al. (2004). Dynamic mapping of human cortical development during childhood through early adulthood. *Proceedings of the National Academy of Sciences, 101,* 8174–8179.

Goh, J. O. S., et al. (2010). Cultural differences in neural processing of faces and houses in the ventral visual cortex. *Social Cognitive and Affective Neuroscience, 5,* 227–235.

Goin, M. K. (2005). A current perspective on the psychotherapies. *Psychiatric Services, 56*(3), 255–257.

Gold, M. S., & Jacobs, W. S. (2005). Cocaine and crack: Clinical aspects. In J. H. Lowinson, P. Ruiz, R. B. Millman, & J. G. Langrod (Eds.), *Substance abuse: A comprehensive textbook.* Philadelphia, PA: Lippincott, Williams & Wilkins.

Goldberg, M. E., & Hudspeth, A. J. (2000). The vestibular system. In E. R. Kandel, J. H. Schwartz, & T. M. Jessell (Eds.), *Principles of neural science.* New York: McGraw-Hill.

Golden, C. J., Sawicki, R. F., & Franzen, M. D. (1990). Test construction. In G. Goldstein & M. Hersen (Eds.), *Handbook of psychological assessment.* New York: Pergamon Press.

Goldenberg, H. (1983). *Contemporary clinical psychology.* Pacific Grove, CA: Brooks/Cole.

Goldenberg, I., Goldenberg, H., & Pelavin, E. G. (2011). Family therapy. In R. J. Corsini & D. Wedding (Eds.), *Current psychotherapies* (9th ed.). Belmont, CA: Brooks/Cole.

Goldenberg, J. L. & Arndt, J. (2008). The implications of death for health: A terror management health model for behavioral health promotion. *Psychological Review, 115,* 1032–1053.

Goldfarb, R. (Ed.). (2006). *Ethics: A case study from fluency.* San Diego: Plural Publishing.

Goldfried, M. R., Greenberg, L. S., & Marmar, C. (1990). Individual psychotherapy: Process and outcome. *Annual Review of Psychology, 41,* 659–688.

Goldman, D. L. (1990). Dorothea Dix and her two missions of mercy in Nova Scotia. *Canadian Journal of Psychiatry, 35,* 139–142.

Goldman, G. S., Quas, J. A., & Ogle, C. M. (2009). Child maltreatment and memory. *Annual Review of Psychology, 61,* 325–351.

Goldman, R. N., Greenberg, L. A., & Pos, A. E. (2005). Depth of emotional experience and outcome. *Psychotherapy Research, 15,* 248–260.

Goldstein, D. G., & Gigerenzer, G. (2002). Models of ecological rationality: The recognition heuristic. *Psychological Review, 109,* 75–90.

Goldstein, E. B. (2001). Pictorial perception and art. In E. B. Goldstein (Ed.), *Blackwell handbook of perception.* Malden, MA: Blackwell.

Goldstein, E. B. (2010). Constancy. In E. B. Goldstein (Ed.), *Encyclopedia of perception.* Thousand Oaks, CA: Sage.

Goldstein, E., & Farmer, K. (Eds.) (1993). *True stories of false memories.* Boca Raton, FL: Sir Publishing.

Goldstein, H. W., Zedeck, S., & Goldstein, I. L. (2002). *g:* Is this your final answer? *Human Performance, 15,* 123–142.

Goldstein, W. M., & Hogarth, R. M. (1997). Judgement and decision research: Some historical context. In W. M. Goldstein, & R. M. Hogarth (Eds.),

Research on judgement and decision making. New York: Cambridge University Press.

Goldston, D. B., Molock, S. D., Whitbeck, L. B., Murakami, J. L., Zayas, L. H., Hall, G. C. (2008). *Cultural considerations in adolescent suicide prevention and psychosocial treatment. American Psychologist, 63,* 14–31.

Goldston, K., & Baillie, A. J. (2008). Depression and coronary heart disease: A review of the epidemiological evidence, explanatory mechanisms and management approaches. *Clinical Psychology Review, 28,* 288–306.

Goldstone, R. L., Roberts, M. E., & Gureckis, T. M. (2008). Emergent processes in group behaviour. *Current Directions in Psychological Science, 17,* 10–17.

Goleman, D. (1995). *Emotional intelligence.* New York: Bantam Books.

Goodale, M. A., & Humphrey, G. K. (2001). Separate visual systems for action and perception. In E. B. Goldstein (Ed.), *Blackwell handbook of perception* (pp. 309–343). Oxford UK: Blackwell Publishers Ltd.

Goodale, M. A., & Milner, A. D. (1992). Separate visual pathways for perception and action. *Trends in Neuroscience, 15,* 20–25.

Goodale, M. A., & Milner, A. D. (2004). *Sight unseen: An exploration of conscious and unconscious vision.* Oxford UK: Oxford University Press.

Goodale, M. A., & Westwood, D. A. (2004). An evolving view of duplex vision: Separate but interacting cortical pathways for perception and action. *Current Opinion in Neurobiology, 14,* 203–211.

Goodale, M. A. (2010, August 4). Transforming vision into action. *Vision Research,* epub ahead of print.

Goodall, J. (2000). *Through a window.* New York: NY. Houghton Mifflin.

Goodheart, C. D. (2006). Evidence, endeavor, and expertise in psychology practice. In C. D. Goodheart, A. E. Kazdin, & R. J. Sternberg (Eds.), *Evidence-based psychotherapy: Where practice and research meet* (pp. 37–62). Washington, DC: American Psychological Association.

Goodwin, C. J. (1991). Misportraying Pavlov's apparatus. *American Journal of Psychology, 104*(1), 135–141.

Goodwin, F. K., & Jamison, K. R. (1990). *Manic-depressive illness.* New York: Oxford University Press.

Goodwin, F. K., & Jamison, K. R. (2007). *Manic-depressive illness: Bipolar disorders and recurrent depression.* New York, NY: Oxford University Press.

Goodwin, G. (2009). Neurobiological aetiology of mood disorders. In M. C. Gelder, N. C. Andreasen, J. J. López-Ibor, Jr., & J. R. Geddes (Eds.). *New Oxford textbook of psychiatry* (2nd ed., Vol. 1). New York, NY: Oxford University Press.

Goodwin, J. C. (1999). *A history of modern psychology.* New York, NY: Wiley.

Gopie, N., & MacLeod, C. M. (2009). Destination memory: Stop me if I've told you this before. *Psychological Science, 20*(12), 1492–1499.

Gopnik, A., Meltzoff, A. N., & Kuhl, P. K. (1999). *The scientist in the crib: Minds, brains, and how children learn.* New York: Morrow.

Gorchoff, S. M., John, O. P., & Helson, R. (2008). Contextualizing change in marital satisfaction during middle age: An 18-year longitudinal study. *Psychological Science, 19*(11), 1194–1200.

Gordon, H. W. (1990). The neurobiological basis of hemisphericity. In C. Trevarthen (Ed.), *Brain circuits and functions of the mind. Essays in honor of Roger W. Sperry.* Cambridge, MA: Cambridge University Press.

Gordon, J., & Abramov, I. (2001). Color vision. In E. B. Goldstein (Ed.), *Blackwell handbook of perception.* Malden, MA: Blackwell.

Gore, A. (2008). Neuroendocrine systems. In L. Squire, D. Berg, F. Bloom, S. Du Lac, A. Ghosh, & N. Spitzer (Eds.), *Fundamental neuroscience* (3rd ed., pp. 905–930). San Diego, CA: Elsevier.

Göritz, A. S., & Wolff, H. (2007). Lotteries as incentives in longitudinal Web studies. *Social Science Computer Review, 25,* 99–110.

Göritz, A. S. (2006). Cash lotteries as incentives in online panels. *Social Science Computer Review, 24,* 445–459.

Gorman, M. E. (1989). Error, falsification and scientific inference: An experimental investigation. *Quarterly Journal of Experimental Psychology, 41*(2–A), 385–412.

Gorner, P. (2006, May 10). Daddy material? It takes just one look. *Chicago Tribune.*

Gorski, R. A. (2000). Sexual differentiation of the nervous system. In E. R. Kandel, J. H. Schwartz, & T. M. Jessell (Eds.), *Principles of Neural Science.* New York: McGraw-Hill.

Gorsuch, R. L. (1983). *Factor Analysis.* Hillsdale, NJ: Lawrence Erlbaum.

Gosden, C., Nicolaides, K., & Whitting, V. (1994). *Is my baby all right? A guide for expectant parents.* Oxford, England: Oxford University Press.

Goswami, U. (2006). Neuroscience and education: From research to practice? *Nature Reviews Neuroscience, 7*(5), 2–7.

Gotlib, I. H., & Robinson, L. A. (1982). Responses to depressed individuals: Discrepancies between self-reports and observer-rated behavior. *Journal of Abnormal Psychology, 91,* 231–240.

Gottesman, I. I. (1991). *Schizophrenia genesis: The origins of madness.* New York: W. H. Freeman.

Gottesman, I. I. (2001). Psychopathology through a life span-genetic prism. *American Psychologist, 56,* 867–878.

Gottesman, I. I., & Hanson, D. R. (2005). Human development: Biological and genetic processes. *Annual Review of Psychology, 56,* 263–286.

Gottfredson, L. S. (2002). Where and why *g* matters: Not a mystery. *Human Performance, 15,* 25–46.

Gottfredson, L. S. (2003a). Dissecting practical intelligence theory: Its claims and evidence. *Intelligence, 31,* 343–397.

Gottfredson, L. S. (2003b). G, jobs and life. In H. Nyborg (Ed.), *The scientific study of general intelligence: Tribute to Arthur R. Jensen.* Oxford, UK: Pergamon.

Gottfredson, L. S. (2009). Logical fallacies used to dismiss the evidence on intelligence testing. In R. P. Phelps (Ed.), *Correcting fallacies about educational and psychological testing* (pp. 11–65). Washington, DC: American Psychological Association.

Gottfredson, L. S., & Deary, I. J. (2004). Intelligence predicts health and longevity, but why? *Current Directions in Psychological Science, 13*(1), 1–4.

Gotto, S. G., Ando, Y., Huang, C., Yee, A., & Lewis, R. S. (2010). Cultural differences in the visual processing of meaning: Detecting incongruities between background and foreground objects using the N400. *Social Cognitive and Affective Neuroscience, 5,* 242–253.

Gould, E. (2004). Stress, deprivation, and adult neurogenesis. In M. S. Gazzaniga (Ed.), *The cognitive neurosciences* (pp. 139–148). Cambridge, MA: MIT Press.

Gould, E., & Gross, C. G. (2002). Neurogenesis in adult mammals: Some progress and problems. *Journal of Neuroscience, 22,* 619–623.

Gould, R. L. (1975, February). Adult life stages: Growth toward self-tolerance. *Psychology Today,* pp. 74–78.

Gould, S. J. (1996). *The mismeasure of man.* New York, NY: W.W. Norton & Co.

Gourevitch, M. N., & Arnsten, J. H. (2005). Medical complications of drug use. In J. H. Lowinson, P. Ruiz, R. B. Millman, & J. G. Langrod (Eds.), *Substance abuse: A comprehensive textbook.* Philadelphia: Lippincott/Williams & Wilkins.

Government of Canada. (2006). The human face of mental health and mental illness in Canada, 2006. Ottawa: Minister of Public Works and Government Services Canada.

Grabe, S., Ward, L. M., & Hyde, J. S. (2008). The role of the media in body image concerns among women: A meta-analysis of experimental and correlational studies. *Psychological Bulletin, 134,* 460–476.

Gradisar, M., Gardner, G., & Dohnt, H. (2011). Recent worldwide sleep patterns and problems during adolescence: A review and meta-analysis of age, region, and sleep. *Sleep Medicine, 12,* 110–118.

Grady, D. (2006). Management of menopausal symptoms. *New England Journal of Medicine, 355,* 2338–2347.

Graf, P., & Gallie, K. A. (1992). A transfer-appropriate processing account for memory and amnesia. In L. R. Squire & N. Butters (Eds.), *Neuropsychology of memory* (2nd ed.). New York: Guilford.

Graf, P., & Uttl, B. (2001). Prospective memory: A new focus for research. *Consciousness & Cognition: An International Journal, 10,* 437–450.

Graham, D. (2000). *Online recruiting.* Palo Alto, CA: Davies-Black.

Graham, D. (2008, January 29). Desperate for sleep. *Toronto Star.*

Graham, J. W. (2009). Missing data analysis: Making it work in the real world. *Annual Review of Psychology, 60,* 549–576.

Graham, S., & Kilbreath, C. S. (2007). It's a sign of the kind: Gestures and words guide infants' inductive inferences. *Developmental Psychology, 45,* 111–123.

Graham-Berman, S. A. (2009, May). Growing opposition to physical punishment: Empirical, human rights, and ethical arguments against an age-old practice. Paper presented at the American Psychological Association's annual convention, Toronto, Ontario.

Granberg, G., & Holmberg, S. (1991). Self-reported turnout and voter validation. *American Journal of Political Science, 35,* 448–459.

Grandner, M. A., Hale, L., Moore, M., & Patel, N. P. (2010). Mortality associated with short sleep duration: The evidence, the possible mechanisms, and the future. *Sleep Medicine Reviews, 14*(3), 191–203.

Grandner, M. A., Patel, N. P., Gehrman, P. R., Perlis, M. L., & Pack, A. I. (2010a). Problems associated with short sleep: Bridging the gap between laboratory and epidemiological studies. *Sleep Medicine Reviews, 14*(4), 239–247.

Grandner, M. A., Patel, N. P., Gehrman, P. R., Xie, D., Sha, D., Weaver, T., & Gooneratne, N. (2010b). Who gets the best sleep? Ethnic and socioeconomic factors related to sleep complaints. *Sleep Medicine, 11*(5), 470–478.

Grant, J. A., & Rainville, P. (2009). Pain sensitivity and analgesic effects of mindful states in Zen meditators: A cross-sectional study. *Psychosomatic Medicine, 71*(1), 106–114.

Grant, J. A., Courtemanche, J., Duerden, E. G., Duncan, G. H., & Rainville, P. (2010). Cortical thickness and pain sensitivity in zen meditators. *Emotion, 10*(1), 43–53.

Grantham-McGregor, S., Ani, C., & Fernald, L. (2001). The role of nutrition in intellectual development. In R. J. Sternberg & E. L. Grigorenko (Eds.), *Environmental effects on cognitive abilities* (pp. 119–156). Mahwah, NJ: Erlbaum.

Grau, R., Salanova, M., & Peiro, J. M. (2001). Moderator effects of self-efficacy on occupational stress. *Psychology in Spain, 5*(1), 63–74.

Gray, C., & Della Sala, S. (2007). The Mozart effect: It's time to face the music! In S. Della Sala (Ed.), *Tall tales about the mind & brain: Separating fact from fiction* (pp. 148–157). New York, NY: Oxford University Press.

Gray, K., & Wegner, D. M. (2008). The sting of intentional pain. *Psychological Science, 19*(12), 1260–1262.

Graziano, W. G. (1995). Evolutionary psychology: Old music, but now on CDs? *Psychological Inquiry, 6,* 41–44.

Graziano, W. G., & Tobin, R. M. (2009). Agreeableness. In M. R. Leary & R. H. Hoyle (Eds.), *Handbook of individual differences in social behavior* (pp. 46–61). New York, NY: Guilford Press.

GRE: General test overview. (2008). Educational Testing Service. Retrieved January 20, 2008, from http://www.ets.org/portal/site/ets/menuitem.1488512ecfd5b8849a77b13bc3921509/?vgnextoid=e1b42d3631df4010VgnVCM10000022f95190RCRD&vgnextchannel=5416e3b5f64f4010VgnVCM10000022f95190RCRD.

Greaves, L., & Moretti, M. M. (in press). Female perpetrated aggression. In A. Jamieson & A. Moenssens (Eds.), *Wiley encyclopedia of forensic science.*

Green, C. D. (2004). The hiring of James Mark Baldwin and James Gibson Hume at the University of Toronto in 1889. *History of Psychology, 7,* 130–153.

Green, C. D. (2009). Darwinian theory, functionalism, and the first American psychological revolution. *American Psychologist, 64*(2), 75–83.

Green, C. D., & Groff, P. R. (2003). *Early psychological thought: Ancient accounts of mind and soul.* Westport, CT: Praeger.

Green, J. P. (1999). Hypnosis, context effects, and recall of early autobiographical memories. *International Journal of Clinical & Experimental Hypnosis, 47,* 284–300.

Green, J. P. (2003). Beliefs about hypnosis: Popular beliefs, misconceptions, and the importance of experience. *International Journal of Clinical and Experimental Hypnosis, 51*(4), 369–381.

Greenberg, J., Landau, M., Kosloff, S., & Solomon, S. (2009). How our dreams of death transcendence breed prejudice, stereotyping, and conflict: Terror management theory. In T. D. Nelson (Ed.), *Handbook of prejudice, stereotyping, and discrimination* (pp. 309–332). New York, NY: Psychology Press.

Greenberg, L. S. (2002). Integrating an emotion-focused approach to treatment into psychotherapy integration. *Journal of Psychotherapy Integration, 12,* 111–125.

Greenberg, L. S. (2008). Emotion and cognition in psychotherapy: The transforming power of affect. *Canadian Psychology, 49,* 49–59.

Greenberg, L. S., & Johnson, S. M. (1988). *Emotion focussed couples therapy.* New York: Guilford Press.

Greenberg, L. S. (2011). *Emotion-focused therapy.* Washington, DC: APA Books.

Greenberg, M. A., Wortman, C. B., & Stone, A. A. (1996). Emotional expression and physical health: Revising traumatic memories or fostering self-regulation? *Journal of Personality and Social Psychology, 71,* 588–602.

Greene, B. (1999). *The elegant universe: Superstrings, hidden dimensions, and the quest for the ultimate theory.* London: Jonathan Cape.

Greene, B. (2003). A theory of everything. *PBS Online.* Retrieved July 29, 2008, from http://www.pbs.org/wgbh/nova/elegant/everything/html.

Greenfield, R. (2006). *Timothy Leary.* London: Harcourt Press.

Greenfield, S. (2008). ID: *The quest for identity in the 21st century.* London: Scepture.

Greenfield, S. A., & Collins, T. F. T. (2005). A neuroscientific approach to consciousness. *Progress in Brain Research, 150,* 11–23.

Greeno, C. G., & Wing, R. R. (1994). Stress-induced eating. *Psychological Bulletin, 115,* 444–464.

Greeno, J. G. (1978). Nature of problem-solving abilities. In W. K. Estes (Ed.), *Handbook of learning and cognitive processes* (Vol. 5). Hillsdale, NJ: Erlbaum.

Greenough, W. T. (1975). Experiential modification of the developing brain. *American Scientist, 63,* 37–46.

Greenough, W. T., & Volkmar, F. R. (1973). Pattern of dendritic branching in occipital cortex of rats reared in complex environments. *Experimental Neurology, 40,* 491–504.

Greenson, R. R. (1967). *The technique and practice of psychoanalysis* (Vol. 1). New York: International Universities Press.

Greenspan, S., & Driscoll, J. (1997). The role of intelligence in a broad model of personal competence. In D. P. Flanagan, J. L. Genshaft, & P. L. Harrison (Eds.), *Contemporary intellectual assessment: Theories, tests, and issues.* New York: Guilford.

Greenstein, T. N. (2009). National context, family satisfaction, and fairness in the division of household labor. *Journal of Marriage and Family, 71*(4), 1039–1051.

Greenwald, A. G. (1992). New look 3: Unconscious cognition reclaimed. *American Psychologist, 47,* 766–779.

Greenwald, A. G., & Banaji, M. R. (1995). Implicit social cognition: Attitudes, self-esteem, and stereotypes. *Psychological Review, 102*(1), 4–27.

Greenwald, A. G., McGhee, D. E., & Schwartz, J. K. (1998). Measuring individual differences in implicit cognition: The Implicit Association Test. *Journal of Personality and Social Psychology, 74*(6), 1464–1480.

Greenwald, A. G., Poehlman, T., Uhlmann, E., & Banaji, M. R. (2009). Understanding and using the Implicit Association Test: III. Meta-analysis of predictive validity. *Journal of Personality and Social Psychology, 97*(1), 17–41.

Gregory, R. L. (1973). *Eye and brain.* New York: McGraw-Hill.

Gregory, R. L. (1978). *Eye and brain* (2nd ed.). New York: McGraw-Hill.

Greifeneder, R., Bless, H., & Pham, M. T. (2011). When do people rely on affective and cognitive feelings in judgment. *Personality and Social Psychology Review, 15,* 107–114.

Gretzky, W., & Reilly, R. (1990). *Gretzky: An autobiography.* Toronto: HarperCollins.

Greven, C. U., Harlaar, N., Kovas, Y., Chamorro-Premuzic, T., & Plomin, R. (2009). More than just IQ: School achievement is predicted by self-perceived abilities—But for genetic rather than environmental reasons. *Psychological Science, 20*(6), 753–762.

Grigorenko, E. L. (2000). Heritability and intelligence. In R. J. Sternberg (Ed.), *Handbook of intelligence* (pp. 53–91). New York: Cambridge University Press.

Grigorenko, E. L., & Sternberg, R. J. (2001). Analytical, creative, and practical intelligence as predictors of self-reported adaptive functioning: A case study in Russia. *Intelligence, 29,* 57–73.

Grigorenko, E. L., & Sternberg, R. J. (2003). The nature–nurture issue. In A. Slater & G. Bremner (Eds.), *An introduction to development psychology.* Malden, MA: Blackwell Publishers.

Griner, D., & Smith, T. B. (2006). Culturally adapted mental health intervention: A meta-analytic review. *Psychotherapy: Theory, Research, Practice, Training, 43,* 531–548.

Grinspoon, L., Bakalar, J. B., & Russo, E. (2005). Marihuana: Clinical aspects. In J. H. Lowinson, P. Ruiz, R. B. Millman, & J. G. Langrod (Eds.), *Substance abuse: A comprehensive textbook.* Philadelphia: Lippincott/Williams & Wilkins.

Grob, C. S., & Poland, R. E. (2005). MDMA. In J. H. Lowinson, P. Ruiz, R. B. Millman, & J. G. Langrod (Eds.), *Substance abuse: A comprehensive textbook.* Philadelphia: Lippincott, Williams & Wilkins.

Grob, G. N. (1983). Disease and environment in American history. In D. Mechanic (Ed.), *Handbook of health, health care, and the health professions.* New York: Free Press.

Gross, C. G. (2000). Neurogenesis in the adult brain: Death of a dogma. *Nature Reviews Neuroscience, 1,* 67–73.

Gross, J. J. (2001). Emotion regulation in adulthood: Timing is everything. *Current Directions in Psychological Science, 10,* 214–219.

Grossman, J. B., & Ruiz, P. (2004). Shall we make a leap-of-faith to disulfiram (Antabuse)? *Addictive Disorders & Their Treatment, 3*(3), 129–132.

Grossman, R. P., & Till, B. D. (1998). The persistence of classically conditioned brand attitudes. *Journal of Advertising, 27,* 23–31.

Grossman, S. P., Dacey, D., Halaris, A. E., Collier, T., & Routtenberg, A. (1978). Aphagia and adipsia after preferential desruction of nerve cell bodies in hypothalamus. *Science, 202,* 537–539.

Grossmann, K. E., & Grossmann, K. (1990). The wider concept of attachment in cross-cultural research. *Human Development, 33,* 31–47.

Groth-Marnat, G. (1997). *Handbook of psychological assessment.* New York: Wiley.

Grubin, D., & Madsen, L. (2005). Lie detection and the polygraph: A historical review. *Journal of Forensic Psychiatry & Psychology, 16,* 357–369.

Gruenberg, A. M., & Goldstein, R. D. (2003). Mood disorders: Depression. In A. Tasman, J. Kay, & J. A. Lieberman (Eds.), *Psychiatry.* New York, NY: Wiley.

Grunberg, N. E., Berger, S. S., & Hamilton, K. R. (2011). Stress and drug use. In R. J. Contrada & A. Baum (Eds.), *The handbook of stress science: Biology, psychology, and health* (pp. 111–121). New York, NY: Springer Publishing.

Grunberg, N. E., Faraday, M. M., & Rahman, M. A. (2001). The psychobiology of nicotine self-administration. In A. Baum, T. A. Revenson, & J. E. Singer (Eds.), *Handbook of health psychology* (pp. 249–262). Mahwah, NJ: Erlbaum.

Gruneberg, M. M., Sykes, R. N., & Gillett, E. (1994). The facilitating effects of mnemonic strategies on two learning disabled adults. *Neuropsychological Rehabilitation, 4,* 241–254.

Grusec, J. E. (2006). The development of moral behavior and conscience from a socialization perspective. In M. Killen & J. G. Smetana (Eds.), *Handbook of moral development*. Mahwah, NJ: Erlbaum.

Guarda, A. S., Pinto, A. M., Coughlin, J. W., Hussain, S., Haug, N. A., & Heinberg, L. J. (2007). Perceived coercion and change in perceived need for admission in patients hospitalized for eating disorders. *American Journal of Psychiatry, 164*, 108–114.

Gudjonsson, G. H. (2001). Recovered memories: Effects upon the family and community. In G. M. Davies & T. Dalgleish (Eds.), *Recovered memories: Seeking the middle ground*. Chichester, England: Wiley.

Guenther, K. (1988). Mood and memory. In G. M. Davies & D. M. Thomson (Eds.), *Memory in context: Context in memory*. New York: Wiley.

Guerrini, I., Thomson, A. D., & Gurling, H. D. (2007). The importance of alcohol misuse, malnutrition, and genetic susceptibility on brain growth and plasticity. *Neuroscience & Biobehavioral Reviews, 31*, 212–220.

Guilbault, R. L., Bryant, F. B., Brockway, J. H., & Posavac, E. J. (2004). A meta-analysis of research on hindsight bias. *Basic & Applied Social Psychology, 26*(2–3), 103–117.

Guilford, J. P. (1959). Three faces of intellect. *American Psychologist, 14*, 469–479.

Guilford, J. P. (1985). The structure-of-intellect model. In B. B. Wolman (Ed.), *Handbook of intelligence: Theories, measurements and applications*. New York: Wiley.

Guilleminault, C., & Fromherz, S. (2005). Narcolepsy: Diagnosis and management. In M. H. Kryger, T. Roth, & W. C. Dement (Eds.). *Principles and practice of sleep medicine*. Philadelphia: Elsevier Saunders.

Gunn, D. V., Warm, J. S., Dember, W. N., & Temple, J. N. (2000). Subjective organization and the visibility of illusory contours. *American Journal of Psychology, 113*, 553–568.

Gunn, S. R., & Gunn, W. S. (2006). Are we in the dark about sleepwalking's dangers? In C. A. Read (Ed.), *Cerebrum: Emerging Ideas in brain sciences* (pp. 1–12). New York: Dana Press.

Gunter, C. (2009). Schizophrenia: missing heritability found? *Nature Reviews Neuroscience, 10*(8), 543.

Gur, R. C., & Gur, R. E. (2007). Neural substrates for sex differences in cognition. In S. J. Ceci & W. M. Williams (Eds.), *Why aren't more women in science?* (pp. 189–198). Washington, DC: American Psychological Association.

Gutchess, A. H., Hedden, T., Ketay, S., Aron, A. R., & Gabrieli, J. D. E. (2010). Neural differences in the processing of semantic relationships across cultures. *Social Cognitive and Affective Neuroscience, 5*, 254–263.

Guthrie, R. V. (1976). *Even the rat was white: A historical view of psychology*. New York: Harper & Row.

Gutierrez, P. M., & Silk, K. R. (1998). Prescription privileges for psychologists: A review of the psychological literature. *Professional Psychology: Research and Practice, 29*, 213–222.

Guyton, A. C. (1991). *Textbook of medical physiology*. Philadelphia: Saunders.

Guzman-Marin, R., Suntsova, N., Bashir, T., Nienhuis, R., Szymusiak, R., & McGinty, D. (2008). Rapid eye movement sleep deprivation contributes to reduction of neurogenesis in the hippocampal dentate gyrus of the adult rat. *Sleep: Journal of Sleep and Sleep Disorders Research, 31*(2), 167–175.

Guzzetta, F., & de Girolamo, G. (2009). Epidemiology of personality disorders. In M. C. Gelder, N. C. Andreasen, J. J. López-Ibor, Jr., & J. R. Geddes (Eds.), *New Oxford textbook of psychiatry* (2nd ed., Vol. 1). New York, NY: Oxford University Press.

Haas, L. (1999). Families and work. In M. B. Sussman, S. K. Steinmetz, & G. W. Peterson (Eds.), *Handbook of marriage and the family* (pp. 571–612). New York: Plenum.

Hackett, T. A., & Kaas, J. H. (2009). Audition. In G. G. Berntson & J. T. Cacioppo (Eds.), *Handbook of neuroscience for the behavioral sciences*. New York, NY: Wiley.

Hackman, J. R., & Katz, N. (2010). Attitudes. In S. T. Fiske, D. T. Gilbert, & G. Lindzey (Eds.), *Handbook of social psychology* (5th ed., Vol. 1, pp. 353–393). Hoboken, NJ: Wiley.

Hackney, C. M. (2010). Auditory processing: Peripheral. In E. B. Goldstein (Ed.), *Encyclopedia of perception*. Thousand Oaks, CA: Sage.

Hadjiefthyvoulou, F., Fisk, J. E., Montgomery, C., & Bridges, N. J. (2010). Everyday and prospective memory deficits in ecstasy/polydrug users. *Journal of Psychopharmacology, 25*, 453–464.

Hadjistavropoulos, H., Dash, H., Hadjistavropoulos, T., & Sullivan, T. (2007). Recurrent pain among university students: Contributions of self-efficacy and perfectionism to the pain experience. *Personality and Individual Differences, 42*, 1081–1091.

Hadjistavropoulos, T. (2005). Assessing pain in older persons with severe limitations in ability to communicate. In S. Gibson & D. Weiner (Eds), *Pain in older persons* (pp. 135–151). Seattle: IASP Press.

Hadjistavropoulous, T., Malloy, D. C., Sharpe, D., Green, S. M., & Fuchs-Lacelle, S. (2002). The relative importance of the ethical principles adopted by the American Psychological Association. *Canadian Psychology, 43*, 254–260.

Haeffel, G. J., Abramson, L. Y., Brazy, P. C., & Shah, J. Y. (2008). Hopelessness theory and the approach system: Cognitive vulnerability predicts decreases in goal-directed behavior. *Cognitive Therapy and Research, 32*, 281–290.

Hafed, Ziad M., & Clark, James J. (2002). Microsaccades as an overt measure of covert attention shifts. *Vision Research, 42*, 2533–2545.

Hafer, C. L., & Begue, L. (2005). Experimental research on just-world theory: Problems, developments, and future challenges. *Psychological Bulletin, 131*, 128–167.

Hafer, C., Bogaert, A. F., & McMullen, S.-L. (2001). Belief in a just world and condom use in a sample of gay and bisexual men. *Journal of Applied Social Psychology, 31*, 1892–1910.

Hagen, E. H. (2005). Controversial issues in evolutionary psychology. In D. M. Buss (Ed.), *The handbook of evolutionary psychology* (pp. 145–176). New York, NY: Wiley.

Hagerty, M. R. (2000). Social comparisons of income in one's community: Evidence from national surveys of income and happiness. *Journal of Personality and Social Psychology, 78*, 764–771.

Haggarty, J. M., Cernovask, Z., Husni, M., Minor, K., Kermeen, P., & Merskey, H. (2002). Seasonal affective disorder in an Arctic community. *Acta Psychiatrica Scandinavica, 105*, 378–384.

Haggbloom, S. J.,Warnick, R.,Warnick, J. E., Jones,V. K., Yarbrough, G. L., Russell,T. M. et al. (2002).The 100 most eminent psychologists of the 20th century. *Review of General Psychology, 6*, 139–152.

Hagman, M. (1999). John Clark Murray on the emancipation of women: A comparison with John Stuart Mill. *History and Philosophy of Psychology Bulletin, 11*, 11–16.

Hahn, P. Y., Olson, L. J., & Somers, V. K. (2006). Cardiovascular complications of obstructive sleep apnea. In T. Lee-Chiong (Ed.), *Sleep: A comprehensive handbook*. Hoboken, NJ: Wiley-Liss.

Haier, R. J. (2009). Neuro-intelligence, neuro-metrics and the next phase of brain imaging studies. *Intelligence, 37*(2), 121–123.

Hakuta, K. (1986). *Mirror of language*. New York: Basic Books.

Hakuta, K., Bialystok, E., & Wiley, E. (2003). Critical evidence: A test of the critical-period hypothesis for second-language acquisition. *Psychological Science, 14*, 31–38.

Hald, G., & Malamuth, N. M. (2008). Self-perceived effects of pornography consumption. *Archives of Sexual Behavior, 37*(4), 614–625.

Hald, G., Malamuth, N. M., & Yuen, C. (2010). Pornography and attitudes supporting violence against women: Revisiting the relationship in nonexperimental studies. *Aggressive Behavior, 36*(1), 14–20.

Hales, D. (1987). *How to sleep like a baby*. New York: Ballantine.

Halford, J. C. G., Gillespie, J., Brown, V., Pontin, E. E., & Dovey, T. M. (2004). Effect of television advertisements for foods on food consumption in children. *Appetite, 42*(2), 221–225.

Hall, C. B., Lipton, R. B., Sliwinski, M. M., Katz, M. J., Derby, C. A., & Verghese, J. J. (2009). Cognitive activities delay onset of memory decline in persons who develop dementia. *Neurology, 73*(5), 356–361.

Hall, C. C. I. (1997). Cultural malpractice: The growing obsolescence of psychology with the changing U.S. population. *American Psychologist, 52*, 642–651.

Hall, C. S. (1966). *The meaning of dreams*. New York: McGraw-Hill.

Hall, C. S. (1979). The meaning of dreams. In D. Goleman & R. J. Davidson (Eds.), *Consciousness: Brain, states of awareness, and mysticism*. New York: Harper & Row.

Hall, D. T., & Mirvis, P. H. (1995). Careers as lifelong learning. In A. Howard (Ed.), *The changing nature of work* (pp. 323–381). San Francisco: Jossey-Bass.

Hall, G. S. (1904). *Adolescence*. New York: Appleton.

Hall, J. & Mast, M. S. (2008). Are women always more interpersonally sensitive than men? Impact of goals and content domain. *Personality and Social Psychology Bulletin, 34*, 144–155.

Hall, J. A., Carter, J. D., & Horgan, T. G. (2000). Gender differences in the nonverbal communication of emotion. In A. Fischer (Ed.), *Gender and emotion*. Cambridge, UK: Cambridge University Press.

Halmi, K. A. (2002). Physiology of anorexia nervosa and bulimia nervosa. In C. G. Fairburn & K. D. Brownell (Eds.), *Eating disorders and obesity: A comprehensive handbook*. New York: Guilford.

Halmi, K. A. (2008). Eating disorders: Anorexia nervosa, bulimia nervosa, and obesity. In R. E. Hales, S. C. Yudofsky, & G. O. Gabbard (Eds.), *The American Psychiatric Publishing textbook of psychiatry* (5th ed., pp. 921–970). Washington, DC: American Psychiatric Publishing.

Halpern, C., Hurtig, H., Jaggi, J., Grossman, M., Won, M., & Baltuch, G. (2007). Deep brain stimulation in neurologic disorders. *Parkinsonism & Related Disorders, 13*(1), 1–16.

Halpern, D. F. (1984). *Thought and knowledge: An introduction to critical thinking*. Hillsdale, NJ: Erlbaum.

Halpern, D. F. (1996). *Thought and knowledge: An introduction to critical thinking*. Mahwah, NJ: Erlbaum.

Halpern, D. F. (1997). Sex differences in intelligence: Implications for education. *American Psychologist, 52,* 1091–1102.

Halpern, D. F. (1998). Teaching critical thinking for transfer across domains: Dispositions, skills, structure training, and metacognitive monitoring. *American Psychologist, 53,* 449–455.

Halpern, D. F. (2000). *Sex differences in cognitive abilities*. Mahwah, NJ: Erlbaum.

Halpern, D. F. (2003). *Thought and knowledge: An introduction to critical thinking*. Mahwah, NJ: Erlbaum.

Halpern, D. F. (2004). A cognitive-process taxonomy for sex differences in cognitive abilities. *Current Directions in Psychological Science, 13*(4), 135–139.

Halpern, D. F. (2007). The nature and nurture of critical thinking. In R. J. Sternberg, H. L. Roediger III, & D. F. Halpern (Eds.), *Critical thinking in psychology* (pp. 1–14). New York: Cambridge University Press.

Hambrick, D. Z., & Oswald, F. L. (2005). Does domain knowledge moderate involvement of working memory capacity in higher-level cognition? A test of three models. *Journal of Memory and Language, 52,* 377–397.

Hambrick, D. Z., & Oswald, F. L. (2005). Does domain knowledge moderate involvement of working memory capacity in higher-level cognition? A test of three models. *Journal of Memory and Language, 52,* 385–405.

Hamill, R., Wilson T. D., & Nisbett, R. E. (1980). Insensitivity to sample bias: Generalizing from atypical cases. *Journal of Personality and Social Psychology, 39,* 578–589.

Hamilton, W. D. (1964). The evolution of social behavior. *Journal of Theoretical Biology, 7,* 1–52.

Hamlin, J. K., Wynn, K., & Bloom, P. (2007). Social evaluation by preverbal infants. *Nature, 450,* 557–560.

Hammad, T. A., Laughren, T., & Racoosin, J. (2006). Suicidality in pediatric patients treated with antidepressant drugs. *Archives of General Psychiatry, 63,* 332–339.

Hammen, C. (2003). Mood disorders. In G. Stricker & T. A. Widiger (Eds.), *Handbook of psychology (Vol. 8): Clinical psychology*. New York: Wiley.

Hammen, C. (2005). Stress and depression. *Annual Review of Clinical Psychology, 1,* 293–319.

Hammer, S. M., Saag, M. S., Schechter, M., Montaner, J. S. G., Schooley, R. T., Jacobsen, D. M., et al. (2006). Treatment for adult HIV infection: 2006 recommendations of the International AIDS Society–USA panel. *Journal of the American Medical Association, 296,* 827–843.

Hampson, E., & Moffat, S. D. (2004). The psychobiology of gender: Cognitive effects of reproductive hormones in the adult nervous system. In A. H. Eagly, A. E. Beall, & R. J. Sternberg (Eds.), *The psychology of gender*. New York: Guilford.

Hampson, E., van Anders, S. M., & Mullin, L. I. (2006). A female advantage in the recognition of emotional facial expressions: Test of an evolutionary hypothesis. *Evolution and Human Behavior, 27,* 401–416.

Hampson, S. (2007, January 27). Howie Mandel: Luxuriating in the moment. *The Globe and Mail,* R3.

Hampton, T. (2004). Fetal environment may have profound long-term consequences for health. *Journal of the American Medical Association, 292,* 1285–1286.

Han, K. F. G. C. (2000). Construct validity. In A. E. Kazdin (Ed.), *Encyclopedia of psychology* (pp. 281–283). Washington, DC: American Psychological Association.

Hancock, P. A., & Ganey, H. C. N. (2003). From the inverted-U to the extended-U: The evolution of a law of psychology. *Journal of Human Performance in Extreme Environments, 7*(1), 5–14.

Haneda, K., Nomura, M., Iidaka, T., & Ohira, H. (2003). Interaction of prime and target in the subliminal affective priming effect. *Perceptual & Motor Skills, 96,* 695–702.

Haney, C., & Zimbardo, P. G. (1998). The past and future of U.S. prison policy: Twenty-five years after the Stanford Prison Experiment. *American Psychologist, 53,* 709–727.

Hannigan, J. H., & Armant, D. R. (2000). Alcohol in pregnancy and neonatal outcome. *Seminars in Neonatology, 5,* 243–254.

Hanson, K., Winward, J., Schweinsburg, A., Medina, K., Brown, S., & Tapert, S. (2010). Longitudinal study of cognition among adolescent marijuana users over three weeks of abstinence. *Addictive Behaviors, 35*(11), 970–976.

Hare, R. D. (1993). *Without conscience: The disturbing world of the psychopaths among us*. New York: Simon & Schuster.

Hare, R. D. (1991). *The Hare psychopathy checklist—revised*. Toronto: Multihealth Systems.

Hare, R. D. (1991). *Without Conscience: The disturbing world of the psychopaths among us*. New York: Guilford Press.

Hare, R. D. (1999). *Without conscience: The disturbing world of the psychopaths among us*. New York: Guilford Press.

Hare, R. D. (2006). Psychopathy: A clinical and forensic overview. *Psychiatric Clinics of North America, 29,* 709–724.

Hare, R. D., & Neumann, C. S. (2008). Psychopathy as a clinical and empirical construct. *Annual Review of Clinical Psychology, 4,* 217–246.

Harley, T. A. (2008). *The psychology of language: From data to theory*. New York: Psychology Press.

Harlow, H. F. (1958). The nature of love. *American Psychologist, 13,* 673–685.

Harlow, H. F. (1959). Love in infant monkeys. *Scientific American, 200*(6), 68–74.

Harmon-Jones, E., Gable, P. A., & Price, T. F. (2011). Toward an understanding of the influence of affective states on attentional tuning: Comment on Friedman and Förster (2010). *Psychological Bulletin, 137*(3), 508–512.

Harmon-Jones, E., & Sigelman, J. (2001). State anger and prefrontal brain activity: Evidence that insult-related relative left-prefrontal activation is associated with experienced anger and aggression. *Journal of Personality and Social Psychology, 80,* 797–803.

Harmon-Jones, E., & Winkielman, P. (Eds.). (2007). *Social neuroscience: Integrating biological and psychological explanations of social behavior*. New York: Guilford Press.

Harmsen, P., Rosengren, A., Tsipogianni, A., & Wilhelmsen, L. (1990). Risk factors for stroke in middle-aged men in Goteborg, Sweden. *Stroke, 21,* 23–29.

Haroutunian, V., & Davis, K. L. (2003). Psychiatric pathophysiology. In A. Tasman, J. Kay, & J. A. Lieberman (Eds.), *Psychiatry*. New York: Wiley.

Harrington, M. E., & Mistlberger, R. E. (2000). Anatomy and physiology of the mammalian circadian system. In M. H. Kryger, T. Roth, & W. C. Dement (Eds.), *Principles and practice of sleep medicine*. Philadelphia: Saunders.

Harris, J. E. (1984). Remembering to do things: A forgotten topic. In J. E. Harris & P. E. Morris (Eds.), *Everyday memory, actions, and absent-mindedness*. New York: Academic Press.

Harris, J. L., Bargh, J. A., & Brownell, K. D. (2009). Priming effects of television food advertising on eating behavior. *Health Psychology, 28*(4), 404–413.

Harris, J. R. (1998). *The nurture assumption: Why children turn out the way they do*. New York: Free Press.

Harris, J. R. (2000). Context-specific learning, personality, and birth order. *Current Directions in Psychological Science, 9*(5), 174–177.

Harris, L. (2000). Procedural justice and perceptions of fairness in selection practice. *International Journal of Selection and Assessment, 8,* 148–157.

Harris, L. R., Jenkin, M., Jenkin, H., Dyde, R., Zacher, J., & Allison, R. S. (2010). *Journal of Vestibular Research, 20,* 25–30.

Harris, L. R., Jenkin, M. R. M., Jenkin, H. L. M., Dyde, R. T., & Oman, C. M. (2010a). Where's the floor? *Seeing and Perceiving, 23,* 81–88.

Harris, P. L. (2006). Social cognition. In D. Kuhn, R. S. Siegler, W. Damon, & R. L. Lerner (Eds.), *Handbook of child psychology: Cognition, perception, and language* (6th ed., Vol. 2, pp. 811–858). Hoboken, NJ: Wiley.

Hart, J. W., Karau, S. J., Stasson, M. F., & Kerr, N. A. (2004). Achievement motivation, expected co-worker performance, and collective task motivation: Working hard or hardly working? *Journal of Applied Social Psychology, 34,* 984–1000.

Harte, J. L., Eifert, G. H., & Smith, R. (1995). The effects of running and meditation on beta-endorphin, corticotropin-releasing hormone and cortisol in plasma, and on mood. *Biological Psychology, 40*(3), 251–265.

Hartmann, D. P., Pelzel, K. E., & Abbott, C. B. (2011). Design, measurement, and analysis in developmental research. In M. H. Bornstein & M. E. Lamb (Eds.), *Developmental science: An advanced textbook* (pp. 109–198). New York, NY: Psychology Press.

Harvey, A. G., Talbot, L. S., & Gershon, A. (2008). Sleep disturbance in bipolar disorder across the lifespan. *Clinical Psychology: Science and Practice, 16,* 256–277.

Harvey, M. H. (1999). Memory research and clinical practice: A critique of three paradigms and a framework for psychotherapy with trauma survivors. In L. M. Williams & V. L. Banyard (Eds.), *Trauma & memory*. Thousand Oaks, CA: Sage Publications.

Harvey, P. D. (2010). Cognitive functioning and disability in schizophrenia. *Current Directions in Psychological Science, 19*(4), 249–254.

Hasher, L., & Zacks, R. (1974). Automatic processing of fundamental information: The case of frequency of occurrence. *American Psychologist, 39,* 1372–1388.

Hashimoto, K., Shimizu, E., & Iyo, M. (2005). Dysfunction of glia–neuron communication in pathophysiology of schizophrenia. *Current Psychiatry Reviews, 1,* 151–163.

Haskard, K. B., Williams, S. L., DiMatteo, M., Rosenthal, R., White, M., & Goldstein, M. G. (2008). Physician and patient communication training in primary care: Effects on participation and satisfaction. *Health Psychology, 27*(5), 513–522.

Haslam, N. (1997). Evidence that male sexual orientation is a matter of degree. *Journal of Personality and Social Psychology, 73,* 862–870.

Haslam, S. A. (2007). I think, therefore I err? *Scientific American Mind, 18*(2), 16–17.

Hassin, R. R., Ferguson, M. J., Shidlovski, D., & Gross, T. (2007). Subliminal exposure to national flags affects political thought and behavior. *Proceedings of the National Academy of Sciences, 104*(50), 19757–19761.

Hastorf, A., & Cantril, H. (1954). They saw a game: A case study. *Journal of Abnormal and Social Psychology, 49*, 129–134.

Hatfield, E., & Rapson, R. L. (1993). *Love, sex, and intimacy: Their psychology, biology, and history.* New York: HarperCollins.

Hatfield, E., Rapson, R. L., & Martel, L. D. (2007). Passionate love. In S. Kitayama & D. Cohen (Eds.), *Handbook of cultural psychology.* New York: Guilford.

Haugaard, J. J. (2008). *Child psychopathology.* New York: McGraw-Hill.

Hauri, P. J. (2000). Primary insomnia. In M. H. Kryger, T. Roth, & W. C. Dement (Eds.), *Principles and practice of sleep medicine.* Philadelphia: Saunders.

Hauri, P. J. (2002). Psychological and psychiatric issues in the etiopathogenesis of insomnia. *Journal of Clinical Psychiatry, 4*(suppl. 1), 17–20.

Hauser, M., & Carey, S. (1998). Building a cognitive creature from a set of primitives: Evolutionary and developmental insights, In D. D. Cummins & C. Allen (Eds.), *The evolution of mind.* New York: Oxford University Press.

Havermans, R. C., Siep, N., & Jansen, A. (2010). Sensory-specific satiety is impervious to the tasting of other foods with its assessment. *Appetite, 55*(2), 196–200.

Hawkins, S. A., & Hastie, R. (1990). Hindsight: Biased judgments of past events after the outcomes are known. *Psychological Bulletin, 107*, 311–327.

Haworth-Hoeppner, S. (2000). The critical shapes of body image: The role of culture and family in the production of eating disorders. *Journal of Marriage and the Family, 62*, 212–227.

Hayes, S. C. (2004). Acceptance and commitment therapy and the new behavior therapies: Mindfulness, acceptance and relationship. In S. C. Hayes, V. M. Follette, & M. Linehan (Eds.), *Mindfulness and acceptance: Expanding the cognitive behavioral tradition* (pp. 1–29). New York: Guilford.

Hayes, B. K., Heit, E., & Swendsen, H. (2010). Inductive reasoning. *Cognitive Science, 1*, 278–292.

Hayes, K. J., & Hayes, C. (1951). The intellectual development of a home-raised chimpanzee. *Proceedings of the American Philosophical Society, 95*, 105–109.

Hayes, S., Hirsch, C., & Mathews, A. (2008). Restriction of working memory capacity during worry. *Journal of Abnormal Psychology, 117*(3), 712–717.

Hayman-Abello, B. A., Hayman-Abello, S. E., & Rourke, B. P. (2003). Human neuropsychology in Canada: The 1990s (a review of research by Canadian neuropsychologists conducted over the past decade). *Canadian Psychology, 44*(2), 100–138.

Hayne, H. (2007). Verbal recall of preverbal memories: Implications for the clinic and the courtroom. In M. Garry & H. Hayne (Eds.), *Do justice and let the sky fall: Elizabeth F. Lotus and her contributions to science, law, and academic freedom.* Mahwah, NJ: Erlbaum.

Hays, K. F. (1999). *Working it out: Using exercise in psychotherapy.* Washington, DC: American Psychological Association.

Hayslip, B., Jr. (1994). Stability of intelligence. In R. J. Sternberg (Ed.), *Encyclopedia of human intelligence.* New York, NY: Macmillan.

Haywood, T. W., Kravitz, H. M., Grossman, L. S., Cavanaugh, J. L., Jr., Davis, J. M., & Lewis, D. A. (1995). Predicting the "revolving door" phenomenon among patients with schizophrenic, schizoaffective, and affective disorders. *American Journal of Psychiatry, 152*, 861–956.

Hazan, C., & Shaver, P. (1986). *Parental caregiving style questionnaire.* Unpublished questionnaire.

Hazan, C., & Shaver, P. (1987). Romantic love conceptualized as an attachment process. *Journal of Personality and Social Psychology, 52*, 511–524.

He, J., Ogden, L. G., Vupputuri, S., Bazzano, L. A., Loria, C., & Whelton, P. K. (1999). Dietary sodium intake and subsequent risk of cardiovascular disease in overweight adults. *Journal of the American Medical Association, 282*, 2027–2034.

Health Canada. (2002a). *Nutrition for a healthy pregnancy—National guidelines for the childbearing years.* Retrieved June 17, 2005, from http://www.hc-sc.gc.ca/hpfb-dgpsa/onpp-bppn/national_guidelines.

Health Canada. (2002b). *A report on mental illnesses in Canada.* Retrieved May 9, 2005, from http://www.phac-aspc.gc.ca/publicat/miic-mmac.

Health Canada. (2004a). *Canadian Tobacco Use Monitoring Survey* (CTUMS). Retrieved June 22, 2005, from http://www.hc-sc.gc.ca/hl-vs/tobac-tabac/research-recherche/stat/ctums-esutc/index_e.html.

Health Canada. (2004b). *Exclusive breastfeeding duration—2004 Health Canada recommendation.* Retrieved from http://www.hc-sc.gc.ca/hpfb-dgpsa/onpp-bppn/exclusive_breastfeeding_duration_e.html.

Health Canada. (2010). *Drug and alcohol use statistics.* Retrieved February 11, 2011, from http://www.hc-sc.ca/hc-ps/drugs-drogues/stat/index-eng.php.

Healy, D. (2004). *Let them eat Prozac: The unhealthy relationship between the pharmaceutical industry and depression.* New York: NYU Press.

Healy, D., & Whitaker, C. (2003). Antidepressants and suicide: Risk–benefit conundrums. *Journal of Psychiatry & Neuroscience, 28*(5), 28.

Hearst, E. (1988). Fundamentals of learning and conditioning. In R. C. Atkinson, R. J. Herrnstein, G. Lindzey, & R. D. Luce (Eds.), *Stevens' handbook of experimental psychology.* New York: Wiley.

Hebb, D. O. (1949). *The organization of behavior: A neuropsycholgical theory.* New York: John Wiley & Sons, Inc.

Hebb, D. O. (2002). *The organization of behavior: A neuropsychological theory.* Mahwah, NJ: Lawrence Erlbaum Associates.

Hechhausen, J., Wrosch, C., & Shulz, R. (2010). A motivational theory of life-span development. *Psychological Review, 117*, 32–60.

Hedden, T., Setay, S., Aron, A., Markus, H. R., & Gabrieli, J. D. E. (2008). Cultural influences on neural sustrates of attentional control. *Psychological Science, 19*, 12–21.

Heider, F. (1958). *The psychology of interpersonal relations.* New York: Wiley.

Heilman, M. E., & Haynes, M. C. (2005). No credit where credit is due: Attributional rationalization of women's success in male-female teams. *Journal of Applied Psychology, 90*, 905–916.

Heine, S. J., & Buchtel, E. E. (2009). Personality: The universal and culturally specific. *Annual Review of Psychology, 60*, 369–394.

Heine, S. J. (2003). Making sense of East Asian self-enhancement. *Journal of Cross-Cultural Psychology, 34*(5), 596–602.

Heine, S. J., & Hamamura, T. (2007). In search of East Asian self-enhancement. *Personality and Social Psychology Review, 11*(1), 1–24.

Heine, S. J., & Norenzayan, A. (2006). Toward a psychological science for a cultural species. *Perspectives on Psychological Sciences, 1*, 251–269.

Heine, S. J., & Renshaw, K. (2002). Interjudge agreement, self-enhancement, and liking: Cross-cultural divergences. *Personality and Social Psychology Bulletin, 28*(5), 578–587.

Heine, S. J., Kitayama, S., Lehman, D. R., Takata, T., Ide, E., Leung, C., & Matsumoto, H. (2001). Divergent consequences of success and failure in Japan and North America: An investigation of self-improving motivations and malleable selves. *Journal of Personality and Social Psychology, 81*, 599–615.

Heine, S. J., & Ruby, M. B. (2010). Cultural psychology. *Wiley Interdisciplinary Reviews: Cognitive Science, 1*, 254–266.

Heine, S., Buchtel, E. E., & Norenzayan, A. (2008). What do cross-national comparisons of personality traits tell us? *Psychological Science, 17*, 309–313.

Heinrichs, R. W. (2005). The primacy of cognition in schizophrenia. *American Psychologist, 60*, 229–242.

Heinrichs, R. W., Goldberg, J. O., Miles, A. A., & McDermid Vaz, S. (2008). Predictors of medication competence in schizophrenia patients. *Psychiatry Research, 157*(1–3), 47–52.

Heinrichs. R. W., Ammari, N., Miles, A. A., McDermid Vaz, S. (2008). Cognitive performance and functional competence as predictors of community independence in schizophrenia. *Schizophrenia Bulletin, 34*, 247.

Heisel, M. J., Duberstein, P. R., Lyness, J. M., & Feldman, M. D. (2010). Screening for suicide ideation among older primary care patients. *The Journal of the American Board of Family Medicine, 23*, 260–269.

Helgeson, V. S., Reynolds, K. A., & Tomich, P. L. (2006). A meta-analytic review of benefit finding and growth. *Journal of Consulting and Clinical Psychology, 74*, 797–816.

Hélie, S., & Sun, R. (2010). Incubation, insight, and creative problem solving: A unified theory and a connectionist model. *Psychological Review, 117*(3), 994–1024.

Heller, D., Komar, J., Lee, W. B. (2007). The dynamics of personality states, goals, and well-being. *Personality and Social Psychology Bulletin, 33*, 898–910.

Hellige, J. B. (1990). Hemispheric asymmetry. *Annual Review of Psychology, 41*, 55–80.

Hellige, J. B. (1993a). Unity of thought and action: Varieties of interaction between left and right cerebral hemispheres. *Current Directions in Psychological Science, 2*(1), 21–25.

Helmes, E. (2008). Modern applications of the MMPI/MMPI-2 in assessment. In G. J. Boyle, G. Matthews, & D. H. Saklofske (Eds.), *The Sage handbook of personality theory and assessment: Personality measurement and testing* (Vol. 2, pp. 589–607). Los Angeles, CA: Sage.

Helmholtz, H. von. (1863). *On the sensations of tone as a physiological basis for the theory of music (A. J. Ellis, Trans.).* New York: Dover.

Helms, J. E. (2006). Fairness is not validity or cultural bias in racial-group assessment: A quantitative perspective. *American Psychologist, 61*, 845–859.

Helms, J. E. (1992). Why is there no study of cultural equivalence in standard cognitive ability testing? *American Psychologist, 47*, 1083–1101.

Helson, R., Jones, C., & Kwan, V. S. Y. (2002). Personality change over 40 years of adulthood: Hierarchical linear modeling analyses of two longitudinal studies. *Journal of Personality & Social Psychology, 83,* 752–766.

Helwig, D. (1989, March 3). UWO apologizes in Rushton affair. *The Globe and Mail,* A14.

Helzer, J. E., Kraemer, H., Krueger, R., Wittchen, H., Sirovatka, P., & Regier, D. (Eds.). (2008b). *Dimensional approaches in diagnostic classification: Refining the research agenda for DSM-V.* Washington, DC: American Psychiatric Association.

Helzer, J. E., Wittchen, H.–U., Krueger, R. F., & Kraemer, H. C. (2008a). Dimensional options for DSM-V: The way forward. In J. E. Helzer, H. C. Kraemer, R. F. Krueger, H.–U, Wittchen, P. J. Sirovatka, et al. (Eds.), *Dimensional approaches in diagnostic classification: Refining the research agenda for DSM-V* (pp. 115–127). Washington, DC: American Psychiatric Association.

Hempel, S. (2005). Reliability. In J. Miles & P. Gilbert (Eds.), *A handbook of research methods for clinical and health psychology* (pp. 193–204). New York, NY: Oxford University Press.

Henderson, K. E., & Brownell, K. D. (2004). The toxic environment and obesity: Contribution and cure. In J. K. Thompson (Ed.), *Handbook of eating disorders and obesity.* New York: Wiley.

Hendrick, S. S., & Hendrick, C. (2000). Romantic love. In S. S. Hendrick & C. Hendrick (Eds.), *Close relationships.* Thousand Oaks, CA: Sage.

Heneka, M. T., O'Banion, M., Terwel, D., & Kummer, M. (2010). Neuroinflammatory processes in Alzheimer's disease. *Journal of Neural Transmission, 117*(8), 919–947.

Hennessy, D. A., & Wiesenthal, D. L. (1999). Traffic congestion, driver stress, and driver aggression. *Aggressive Behavior, 25,* 409–423.

Hennessy, D. A., & Wiesenthal, D. L. (Eds.). (2004). *Contemporary issues in road user behavior and traffic safety.* Hauppauge, NY: Nova Science Publishers.

Henrich, J., Heine, S. J., & Norenzayan, A. (2010). The weirdest people in the world. *Behavioral and Brain Sciences, 33,* 61–83.

Henriksson, M. M., Aro, H. M., Marttunen, M. J., Heikkinen, M. E., Isometsa, E. T., Kuoppasalmi, K. I., & Lonnqvist, J. K. (1993). Mental disorders and commorbidity of suicide. *American Journal of Psychiatry, 150,* 935–940.

Henry, P. J., Sternberg, R. J., & Grigorenko, E. L. (2005). Capturing successful intelligence through measures of analytic, creative, and practical skills. In O. Wilhelm & R. W. Engle (Eds.), *Handbook of understanding and measuring intelligence.* Thousand Oaks, CA: Sage.

Herbenick, D., Reece, M., Schick, V., Sanders, S. A., Dodge, B., & Fortenberry, J. (2010). An event-level analysis of the sexual characteristics and composition among adults ages 18 to 59: Results from a national probability sample in the United States. *Journal of Sexual Medicine, 7*(Suppl 5), 346–361.

Herbst, S., Pietrzak, R. H., Wagner, J., White, W. B., & Petry, N. M. (2007). Lifetime major depression is associated with coronary heart disease in older adults: Results from the national epidemiologic survey on alcohol and related conditions. *Psychosomatic Medicine, 69,* 729–734.

Herbstman, J., Sjodin, A., Kurzon, M., Lederman, S., Jones, R., Rauh, V., et al. (2010). Prenatal exposure to PBDEs and neurodevelopment. *Environmental Health Perspectives, 118*(5), 712–719.

Herek, G. M. (2000). The psychology of sexual prejudice. *Current Directions in Psychological Science, 9,* 19–22.

Herek, G. M. (2009). Sexual prejudice. In T. D. Nelson (Ed.), *Handbook of prejudice, stereotyping, and discrimination* (pp. 441–467). New York, NY: Psychology Press.

Heres, S., Davis, J., Maino, K., Jetzinger, E., Kissling, W., & Leucht, S. (2006). Why olanzapine beats risperidone, risperidone beats quetiapine, and quetiapine beats olanzapine: An exploratory analysis of head-to-head comparison studies of second-generation antipsychotics. *American Journal of Psychiatry, 163,* 185–194.

Herman, C. P., & Polivy, J. J. (2008). External cues in the control of food intake in humans: The sensory-normative distinction. *Physiology & Behavior, 94*(5), 722–728.

Herman, C. P., Ostovich, J. M., & Polivy, J. (1999). Effects of attentional focus on subjective hunger ratings. *Appetite, 33,* 181–193.

Herman, C. P., Roth, D., & Polivy, J. (2003). Effects of the presence of others on food intake: A normative interpretation. *Psychological Bulletin, 129,* 873–886.

Herman, C. P., van Strien, T., & Polivy, J. (2008). Undereating or eliminating overeating? *American Psychologist, 63,* 202–203.

Herman, L. M., Kuczaj, S. A., & Holder, M. D. (1993). Responses to anomalous gestural sequences by a language-trained dolphin: Evidence for processing of semantic relations and syntactic information. *Journal of Experimental Psychology: General, 122,* 184–194.

Hermann, R. C., Ettner, S. L., Dorwart, R. A., Hoover, C. W., & Yeung, E. (1998). Characteristics of psychiatrists who perform ECT. *American Journal of Psychiatry, 155,* 889–894.

Hermans, D., Craske, M. G., Mineks, S., & Lovibond, P. F. (2006). Extinction in human fear conditioning. *Biological Psychiatry, 60,* 361–368.

Hermans, H. J. M., & Kempen, H. J. G. (1998). Moving cultures: The perilous problems of cultural dichotomies in a globalizing society. *American Psychologist, 53,* 1111–1120.

Hernandez, D. J. (1993). *America's children: Resources from family, government, and the economy.* New York: Russell Sage Foundation.

Herr, N., Hammen, C., & Brennan, P. A. (in press). Maternal borderline personality symptoms and adolescent psychosocial functioning. *Journal of Personality Disorders.*

Herrmann, D., Raybeck, D., & Gruneberg, M. (2002). *Improving memory and study skills: Advances in theory and practice.* Ashland, OH: Hogrefe & Huber.

Herrnstein, R. J., & Murray, C. (1994). *The bell curve: Intelligence and class structure in American life.* New York: Free Press.

Hersen, M., & Gross, A. (Eds.). (2008). *Handbook of clinical psychology: Adults* (Vol. 1). Hoboken, NJ: J. Wiley & Sons.

Hertwig, R., & Gigerenzer, G. (1999). The "conjunction fallacy" revisited: How intelligent inferences look like reasoning errors. *Journal of Behavioral Decision Making, 12,* 275–306.

Hertzog, C., Kramer, A. F., Wilson, R. S., Lindenberger, U. (2009). Enrichment effects on adult cognitive development: Can the functional capacity of older adults be preserved and enhanced? *Psychological Science in the Public Interest, 9*(1), 1–65.

Hertzog, C., Kramer, A. F., Wilson, R. S., & Lindenberger, U. (2009). Enrichment effects on adult cognitive development. *Psychological Science in the Public Interest, 9,* 1–65.

Hertzsprung, E. A. M., & Dobson, K. S. (2000). Diversity training: Conceptual issues and practices for Canadian clinical psychology programs. *Canadian Psychology, 41,* 184–191.

Herzog, D. B., & Delinski, S. S. (2001). Classification of eating disorders. In R. H. Striegel-Moore & L. Smolak (Eds.), *Eating disorders* (pp. 31–50). Washington, DC: American Psychological Association.

Herzog, S. (2008). An attitudinal explanation of biases in the criminal justice system: An empirical testing of defensive attribution theory. *Crime & Delinquency, 54*(3), 457–481.

Hespos, S. J., Ferry, A. L., & Rips, L. J. (2009). Five-month-old infants have different expectations for solids and liquids. *Psychological Science, 20*(5), 603–611.

Heszen-Niejodek, I. (1997). Coping style and its role in coping with stressful encounters. *European Psychologist, 2,* 342–351.

Hetherington, E. M. (1999). Should we stay together for the sake of the children? In E. M. Hetherington (Ed.), *Coping with divorce, single parenting, and remarriage.* Mahwah, NJ: Erlbaum.

Hetherington, E. M. (2003). Intimate pathways: Changing patterns in close personal relationships across time. *Family Relations: Interdisciplinary Journal of Applied Family Studies, 52,* 318–331.

Hetherington, M. M., & Rolls, B. J. (1996). Sensory-specific satiety: Theoretical frameworks and central characteristics. In E. D. Capaldi (Ed.), *Why we eat what we eat: The psychology of eating* (267–290). Washington, DC: American Psychological Association.

Hettema, J. M., et al. (2003). A twin study of genetics of fear conditioning. *Archives of General Psychiatry, 60,* 702–708.

Hewitt, B., & de Vaus, D. (2009). Change in the association between premarital cohabitation and separation, Australia 1945–2000. *Journal of Marriage and Family, 71*(2), 353–361.

Hewitt, P. L., & Flett, G. L. (1991). Perfectionism in the self and social contexts: Conceptualization, assessment, and association with psychopathology. *Journal of Personality and Social Psychology, 60,* 456–470.

Hewitt, P. L., Flett, G. L., Ediger, E., Norton, G. R., & Flynn, C. A. (1998). Perfectionism in chronic and state symptoms of depression. *Canadian Journal of Behavioural Science, 30,* 234–242.

Hewitt, P. L., Habke, A. M., Lee-Baggley, D. L., Sherry, S. B., & Flett, G. L. (2008). The impact of perfectionistic self-presentation on the cognitive, affective, and physiological experience of a clinical interview. *Psychiatry: Interpersonal and Biological Processes, 71,* 93–122.

Hewson, C. (2003). Conducting research on the Internet. *The Psychologist, 16,* 290–293.

Hewson, C. (2007). Gathering data on the Internet: Qualitative approaches and possibilities for mixed methods and research. In A. N. Joinson, K. Y. A. McKenna, T. Postmes, & U.-D. Reips (Eds.), *The Oxford handbook of Internet psychology* (pp. 405–428). New York: Oxford University Press.

Hewstone, M. (1990). The "ultimate attribution error"? A review of the literature on intergroup causal attribution. *European Journal of Social Psychology, 20,* 311–335.

Hibben, J. G. (1926). *The problems of philosophy: An introduction to the study of philosophy.* New York: Scribner.

Higgins, E. T., & King, G. (1980). Accessibility of social constructs: Information processing consequences of individual and contextual variability. In N. Cantor & J. F. Kihlstrom (Eds.), *Personality, cognition, and social interaction* (pp. 25–46). Hillsdale, NJ: Erlbaum.

Higgins, E. T. (1987). Self-discrepancy theory. *Psychological Review, 94,* 319–340.

Higgins, E. T. (1999). Why do self-discrepancies have specific relations to emotions? The second-generation question of Tangney, Niedenthal, Covert, and Barlow (1998). *Journal of Personality and Social Psychology, 77,* 1313–1317.

Higgins, E. T. (2004). Making a theory useful: Lessons handed down. *Personality and Social Psychology Review, 8*(2), 138–145.

Higgins, E. T., Cesario, J., Hagiwara, N., Spiegel, S., & Pittman, T. S. (2010). Increasing or decreasing interest in activities: The role of regulatory fit. *Journal of Personality and Social Psychology, 98,* 559–572.

Higgins, E. T., Rholes, W. S., & Jones, C. R. (1977). Category accessibility and impression formation. *Journal of Experimental Social Psychology, 13,* 141–154.

Higgs, J. (2006). *I have America surrounded: the life of Timothy Leary.* London, UK: Friday books.

High school attack foiled: Police. (2005, March 17). *CBC News.* Retrieved June 29, 2005, from http://www.cbc.ca/cgi-bin/newsworld/viewer.cgi?FILE=NL20050318.html&TEMPLATE=newsreal_archive.ssi&SC=NL.

Highway, T. (1988). *The Rez sisters: A play in two acts.* Saskatoon: Fifth House.

Hilgard, E. R. (1965). *Hypnotic susceptibility.* New York: Harcourt, Brace & World.

Hilgard, E. R. (1986). *Divided consciousness: Multiple controls in human thought and action.* New York: Wiley.

Hilgard, E. R. (1987). *Psychology in America: A historical survey.* San Diego: Harcourt Brace Jovanovich.

Hilgard, E. R. (1992). Dissociation and theories of hypnosis. In E. Fromm & M. R. Nash (Eds.), *Contemporary hypnosis research.* New York: Guilford.

Hill, A. J. (2002). Prevalence and demographics of dieting. In C. G. Fairburn & K. D. Brownell (Eds.), *Eating disorders and obesity: A comprehensive handbook* (pp. 80–83). New York: Guilford.

Hill, J. O., & Peters, J. C. (1998). Environmental contributions to the obesity epidemic. *Science, 280,* 1371–1374.

Hilliard, A. G., III. (1984). IQ testing as the emperor's new clothes: A critique of Jensen's *Bias in Mental Testing.* In C. R. Reynolds & R. T. Brown (Eds.), *Perspectives on bias in mental testing.* New York: Plenum.

Hilton, D. J. (2008). Theory and method in economics and psychology: Levels and depth of explanation. In A. Lewis (Ed.). *Cambridge handbook of psychology and economic behavior* (pp. 9–37). Cambridge: Cambridge University Press.

Hilton, J. L., & von Hippel, W. (1996). Stereotypes. *Annual Review of Psychology, 47,* 237–271.

Hines, M. (2004). Androgen, estrogen, and gender: Contributions of the early hormone environment to gender-related behavior. In A. H. Eagly, A. E. Beall, & R. J. Sternberg (Eds.), *The psychology of gender.* New York: Guilford.

Hines, M. (2010). Sex-related variation in human behavior and the brain. *Trends in Cognitive Sciences, 14*(10), 448–456.

Hinshaw, S. P. (2007). *The mark of shame: Stigma of mental illness and an agenda for change.* New York, NY: Oxford University Press.

Hinshaw, S. P., & Stier, A. (2008). Stigma as related to mental disorders. *Annual Review of Clinical Psychology, 4,* 367–393.

Hinton, G. (2003). The ups and downs of Hebb synapses. *Canadian Psychology, 44,* 21–26.

Hirschel, M. J., & Schulenberg, S. E. (2009). Hurricane Katrina's impact on the Mississippi Gulf Coast: General self-efficacy's relationship to PTSD prevalence and severity. *Psychological Services, 6*(4), 293–303.

Hirsh, I. J., & Watson, C. S. (1996). Auditory psychophysics and perception. *Annual Review of Psychology, 47,* 461–484.

Hirshkowitz, M., Seplowitz-Hafkin, R. G., & Sharafkhaneh, A. (2009). Sleep disorders. In B. J. Sadock, V. A. Sadock, & P. Ruiz (Eds.), *Kaplan & Sadock's comprehensive textbook of psychiatry* (9th ed., Vol. 1, pp. 2150–2177). Philadelphia, PA: Lippincott, Williams & Wilkins.

Hirst, W., Phelps, E. A., Buckner, R. L., Budson, A. E., Cuc, A., Gabrieli, J. E., et al. (2009). Long-term memory for the terrorist attack of September 11: Flashbulb memories, event memories, and the factors that influence their retention. *Journal of Experimental Psychology: General, 138*(2), 161–176.

Hirt, E. R., McDonald, H. E., & Markman, K. D. (1998). Expectancy effects in reconstructive memory: When the past is just what we expected. In S. J. Lynn & K. M. McConkey (Eds.), *Truth in memory.* New York: Guilford.

Hobson, J. A. (1988). *The dreaming brain.* New York: Basic Books.

Hobson, J. A. (1989). *Sleep.* New York: Scientific American Library.

Hobson, J. A. (2002). *Dreaming: An introduction to the science of sleep.* New York: Oxford University Press.

Hobson, J. A., & McCarley, R. W. (1977). The brain as a dream state generator: An activation-synthesis hypothesis of the dream process. *American Journal of Psychiatry, 134,* 1335–1348.

Hobson, J. A., Pace-Schott, E. F., & Stickgold, R. (2000). Dreaming and the brain: Toward a cognitive neuroscience of conscious states. *Behavioral and Brain Sciences, 23,* 793–842; 904–1018; 1083–1121.

Hocevar, D., & Bachelor, P. (1989). A taxonomy and critique of measurements used in the study of creativity. In J. A. Glover, R. R. Ronning, & C. R. Reynolds (Eds.), *Handbook of creativity.* New York: Plenum.

Hochberg, J. (1988). Visual perception. In R. C. Atkinson, R. J. Herrnstein, G. Lindzey, & R. D. Luce (Eds.), *Stevens' handbook of experimental psychology* (2nd ed., Vol. 1). New York: Wiley.

Hodapp, R. M. (1994). Cultural-familial mental retardation. In R. J. Sternberg (Ed.), *Encyclopedia of human intelligence.* New York: Macmillan.

Hodges, B. H., & Geyer, A. (2006). A nonconformist account of the Asch experiments: Values, pragmatics, and moral dilemmas. *Personality and Social Psychology Review, 10*(1), 2–19.

Hodgins, D. C., Stea, J. N., & Grant, J. E. (2011). Gambling disorder. *The Lancet,* early online publication.

Hodgkin, A. L., & Huxley, A. F. (1952). Currents carried by sodium and potassium ions through the membrane of the giant axon of Loligo. *Journal of Physiology, 116,* 449–472.

Hodgkinson, G. P., & Healey, M. P. (2008). Cognition in organizations. *Annual Review of Psychology, 59,* 387–417.

Hoek, H. W. (2002). Distribution of eating disorders. In C. G. Fairburn & K. D. Brownell (Eds.), *Eating disorders and obesity: A comprehensive handbook.* New York: Guilford.

Hoerger, M., Quirk, S. W., Lucas, R. E., & Carr, T. H. (2009). Immune neglect in affective forecasting. *Journal of Research in Personality, 43*(1), 91–94.

Hofbauer, R. K., Rainville, P., Duncan, G. H., & Bushnell, M. C. (2001). Cortical representation of the sensory dimension of pain. *Journal of Neurophysiology, 86,* 402–411.

Hoff, E. (2005). *Language development.* Belmont, CA: Wadsworth.

Hoff, T. L. (1992). Psychology in Canada one hundred years ago: James Mark Baldwin at the University of Toronto. *Canadian Psychology, 33,* 683–694.

Hoffman, E. (1994). *The drive for self: Alfred Adler and the founding of individual psychology.* Reading, MA: Addison-Wesley.

Hoffstein, V. (2005). Snoring and upper airway resistance. In M. H. Kryger, T. Roth, & W. C. Dement (Eds.). *Principles and practice of sleep medicine.* Philadelphia: Elsevier Saunders.

Hofmann, W., De Houwer, J., Perugini, M., Baeyens, F., & Crombez, G. (2010). Evaluative conditioning in humans: A meta-analysis. *Psychological Bulletin, 136*(3), 390–421.

Hofstede, G. (1980). *Culture's consequences: International differences in work-related values.* Beverly Hills, CA: Sage.

Hofstede, G. (1983). Dimensions of national cultures in fifty countries and three regions. In J. Deregowski, S. Dziurawiec, & R. Annis (Eds.), *Explications in cross-cultural psychology.* Lisse: Swets and Zeitlinger.

Hofstede, G. (2001). *Culture's consequences: Comparing values, behaviors, institutions, and organizations across nations.* Thousand Oaks, CA: Sage.

Hogan, J., Barrett, P., & Hogan, R. (2007). Personality measurement, faking, and employment selection. *Journal of Applied Psychology, 92,* 1270–1285.

Hogan, M. F., & Morrison, A. K. (2008). Organization and economics of mental health treatment. In A. Tasman, J. Kay, J. A. Lieberman, M. B. First, & M. Maj (Eds.), *Psychiatry* (3rd ed.). New York, NY: Wiley-Blackwell.

Hogan, R. (2005). In defense of personality measurement: New wine for old whiners. *Human Performance, 18,* 331–341.

Hogan, R., & Stokes, L. W. (2006). Business susceptibility to consulting fads: The case of emotional intelligence. In K. R. Murphy (Ed.), *A critique of emotional intelligence: What are the problems and how can they be fixed?* (pp. 263–280). Mahwah, NJ: Erlbaum.

Hogg, M. A. (2010). Influence and leadership. In S. T. Fiske, D. T. Gilbert, & G. Lindzey (Eds.), *Handbook of social psychology* (5th ed., Vol. 1, pp. 353–393). Hoboken, NJ: Wiley.

Hogg, M. A., Turner, J. C., & Davidson, B. (1990). Polarized norms and social frames of reference: A test of the self-categorization theory of group polarization. *Basic and Applied Social Psychology, 11,* 77–100.

Høglend, P., Bøgwald, K.–P., Amlo, S., Marble, A., Ulberg, R., Sjaastad, M. C., et al. (2008). Transference interpretations in dynamic psychotherapy: Do they really yield sustained effects? *American Journal of Psychiatry, 165,* 763–771.

Hoigaard, R., & Ingvaldsen, R. P. (2006). Social loafing in interactive groups: The effects of identifiability on effort and individual performance in floorball. *Athletic Insight: Online Journal of Sport Psychology, 8*(2), 1–12.

Hoigaard, R., Säfvenbom, R., & Tonnessen, F. E. (2006). The relationship between group cohesion, group norms, and perceived social loafing in soccer teams. *Small Group Research, 37*, 217–232.

Holahan, C. J., & Moos, R. H. (1994). Life stressors and mental health: Advances in conceptualizing stress resistance. In W. R. Avison & J. H. Gotlib (Eds.), *Stress and mental health: Contemporary issues and prospects for the future.* New York, NY: Plenum.

Holahan, C. J., Moos, R. H., Holahan, C. K., Brennan, P. L., & Schutte, K. K. (2005). Stress generation, avoidance coping, and depressive symptoms: A 10-year model. *Journal of Consulting and Clinical Psychology, 73*(4), 658–666.

Holahan, C., & Sears, R. (1995). *The gifted group in later maturity.* Stanford, CA: Stanford University Press.

Holden, C. (2004). FDA weighs suicide risk in children on antidepressants. *Science, 303*, 745.

Holden, G. W. (2002). Perspectives on the effects of corporal punishment: Comment on Gershoff. *Psychological Bulletin, 128*, 590–595.

Holen, A. (2000). Posttraumatic stress disorder, delayed. In G. Fink (Ed.), *Encyclopedia of stress* (Vol. 3, pp. 179–180). San Diego: Academic Press.

Hollan, D. (1989). The personal use of dream beliefs in the Toraja Highlands. *Ethos, 17*, 166–186.

Holland, J. C., & Lewis, S. (1993). Emotions and cancer: What do we really know? In D. Goleman & J. Gurin (Eds.), *Mind/body medicine: How to use your mind for better health.* Yonkers, NY: Consumer Reports Books.

Hollander, E. & Simeon, D. (2008). Anxiety disorders. In R. E. Hales, S. C. Yudofsky, & G. O. Gabbard (Eds.), *The American Psychiatric Publishing textbook of psychiatry.* Washington, DC: American Psychiatric Publishing.

Hollis, K. L. (1997). Contemporary research on Pavlovian conditioning: A "new" functional analysis. *American Psychologist, 52*, 956–965.

Hollon, S. D., & DiGiuseppe, R. (2011). Cognitive theories of psychotherapy. In J. C. Norcross, G. R. Vandenbos, & D. K. Freedheim (Eds.), *History of psychotherapy: Continuity and change* (2nd ed.). Washington, DC: American Psychological Association.

Hollon, S. D., & Dimidjian, S. (2009). Cognitive and behavioral treatment of depression. In I. H. Gotlib & C. L. Hammen (Eds.), *Handbook of depression* (pp. 586–603). New York, NY: Guilford Press.

Hollon, S. D., Stewart, M. O., & Strunk, D. (2006). Enduring effects for cognitive behavior therapy in the treatment of depression and anxiety. *Annual Review of Psychology, 57*, 285–315.

Holmes, D. S. (1987). The influence of meditation versus rest on physiological arousal: A second examination. In M. A. West (Ed.), *The psychology of meditation.* Oxford: Clarendon Press.

Holmes, D. S. (1990). The evidence for repression: An examination of sixty years of research. In J. Singer (Ed.), *Repression and dissociation: Implications for personality, theory, psychopathology, and health.* Chicago: University of Chicago Press.

Holmes, T. H., & Rahe, R. H. (1967). The Social Readjustment Rating Scale. *Journal of Psychosomatic Research, 11*, 213–218.

Holtgraves, T. (2004). Social desirability and self-reports: Testing models of socially desirable responding. *Personality and Social Psychology Bulletin, 30*, 161–172.

Holt-Lunstad, J., Smith, T. B., & Layton, J. B. (2010). Social relationships and mortality risk: A meta-analytic review. *PLoS Medicine, 7*(7), 1–20.

Holyoak, K. J. (1995). Problem solving. In E. E. Smith & D. N. Osherson (Eds.), *Thinking* (2nd ed., pp. 267–295). Cambridge, MA: MIT Press.

Holyoak, K. J. (2005). Analogy. In K. J. Holyoak & R. G. Morrison (Eds.), *The Cambridge handbook of thinking and reasoning.* New York: Cambridge University Press.

Hong, G. K., Garcia, M., & Soriano, M. (2000). Responding to the challenge: Preparing mental health professionals for the new millennium. In I. Cuellar & F. A. Paniagua (Eds.), *Handbook of multicultural mental health: Assessment and treatment of diverse populations.* San Diego: Academic Press.

Honig, W. K., & Alsop, B. (1992). Operant behavior. In L. R. Squire (Ed.), *Encyclopedia of learning and memory.* New York: Macmillan.

Hoobler, J. M., & Brass, D. J. (2006). Abusive supervision and family undermining as displaced aggression. *Journal of Applied Psychology, 91*(5), 1125–1133.

Hooley, J. M. (2004). Do psychiatric patients do better clinically if they live with certain kinds of families? *Current Directions in Psychological Science, 13*(5), 202–205.

Hooley, J. M. (2007). Expressed emotion and relapse of psychopathology. *Annual Review of Clinical Psychology, 3*, 329–352.

Hooley, J. M. (2009). Schizophrenia: Interpersonal functioning. In P. H. Blaney & T. Millon (Eds.), *Oxford textbook of psychopathology* (2nd ed., pp. 333–360). New York, NY: Oxford University Press.

Hooper, J., & Teresi, D. (1986). *The 3-pound universe—The brain.* New York: Laurel.

Hoover, A. E., Démonet, J-F., & Steeves, J. K. E. (2010). Superior voice recognition in a patient with acquired prosopagnosia and object agnosia. *Neuropsychologia, 48*, 3725–3732.

Hopkins, W. D., & Cantalupo, C. (2008). Theoretical speculations on the evolutionary origins of hemispheric specialization. *Current Directions in Psychological Science, 17*(3), 233–237.

Hopko, D. R., Crittendon, J. A., Grant, E., & Wilson, S. A. (2005). The impact of anxiety on performance IQ. *Anxiety, Stress, & Coping: An International Journal, 18*(1), 17–35.

Hopper, K., Harrison, G., Janca, A., & Satorius, N. (2007). *Recovery from schizophrenia: An international perspective—A report from the WHO Collaborative Project, the international study of schizophrenia.* New York: Oxford University Press.

Hopper, S., Kaklauskas, F., & Greene, L. R. (2008). In M. Hersen & A. Gross. (Eds.), *Handbook of clinical psychology: Adults* (Vol. 1, pp. 647–662). Hoboken, NJ: J. Wiley & Sons.

Horn, J. L. (1985). Remodeling old models of intelligence. In B. B. Wolman (Ed.), *Handbook of intelligence.* New York: Wiley.

Horn, J. L. (2002). Selections of evidence, misleading assumptions, and oversimplifications: The political message of *The Bell Curve.* In J. M. Fish (Ed.), *Race and intelligence: Separating science from myth* (pp. 297–326). Mahwah, NJ: Erlbaum.

Horn, J. L., & Hofer, S. M. (1992). Major abilities and development in the adult period. In R. J. Sternberg & C. A. Berg (Eds.), *Intellectual development.* Cambridge: Cambridge University Press.

Hornstein, G. A. (1992). The return of the repressed: Psychology's problematic relations with psychoanalysis, 1909–1960. *American Psychologist, 47*, 254–263.

Horowitz, F. D. (1992). John B. Watson's legacy: Learning and environment. *Developmental Psychology, 28*, 360–367.

Horrey, W. J., & Wickens, C. D. (2006). Examining the impact of cell phone on driving using meta-analytic techniques. *Human Factors, 48*, 196–205.

Horvath, A. O., & Symonds, B. D. (1991) Relation between working alliance and outcome in psychotherapy: A meta-analysis. *Journal of Consulting Psychology, 38*, 139–149.

Hosseini, H. (1997). Cognitive dissonance as a means of explaining economics of irrationality and uncertainty. *Journal of Socio-Economics, 26*, 181–189.

Hothersall, D. (1995). *History of psychology.* New York, NY: McGraw-Hill

Hotz, R. L. (2011, May 8). 52 years, $750 million prove Einstein right. *The Globe and Mail*, A23.

Houben, K., & Wiers, R. W. (2008). Implicitly positive about alcohol? Implicit positive associations predict drinking behavior. *Addictive Behaviors, 33*(8), 979–986.

Hough, L. M., & Oswald, F. L. (2000). Personnel selection: Looking toward the future—remembering the past. *Annual Review of Psychology, 51*, 631–664.

Houlihan, J., Kropp, T., Wiles, R., Gray, S., & Campbell, C. (2005). *Body burden: The pollution in newborns.* Washington, DC: Environmental Working Group.

Houston, J. (2008). Inuit myth and legend. *The Canadian Encyclopedia.* Retrieved March 14, 2008, from http://www.thecanadianencyclopedia.com/index.

Howard, D. J. (1995). "Chaining" the use of influence strategies for producing compliance behavior. *Journal of Social Behavior and Personality, 10*, 169–185.

Howard, I. P., & Rogers, B. J. (1995). *Binocular vision and stereopsis.* New York: Oxford University Press.

Howard, I. P., & Templeton, W. B. (1966). *Human spatial orientation.* New York: Wiley.

Howard, I. P. (1974). Proposals for the study of anomalous perceptual schemata. *Perception, 3*, 497–513.

Howe, M. J. A. (1999). *The psychology of high abilities.* New York: New York University Press.

Howe, M. L., Gagnon, N., & Thouas, L. (2008). Development of false memories in bilingual children and adults. *Journal of Memory and Language, 58*, 669–681.

Howes, O. D., & Kapur, S. (2009). The dopamine hypothesis of schizophrenia: Version III—The final common pathway. *Schizophrenia Bulletin, 35*(3), 549–562.

Hoyer, W. J., & Verhaeghen, P. (2006). Memory aging. In J. E. Birren & K. W. Schaie (Eds.), *Handbook of the psychology of aging.* San Diego: Academic Press.

Hrdy, S. B. (1997). Raising Darwin's consciouness: Female sexuality and the prehominid origins of patriarchy. *Human Nature: An Interdisciplinary Biosocial Perspective, 8*, 1–49.

Hsee, C. K., Zhang, J., & Chen, J. (2004). Internal and substantive inconsistencies in decision making. In D. J. Koehler & N. Harvey (Eds.), *Blackwell handbook of judgment and decision making.* Malden, MA: Blackwell Publishing.

Hsu, L. K. G. (1990). *Eating disorders*. New York: Guilford.

Hsu, L. M. (1995). Regression toward the mean associated with measurement error and identification of improvement and deterioration in psychotheray. *Journal of Consulting & Clinical Psychology, 63*, 141–144.

Hu, Y., Zhang, R., & Li, W. (2005). Relationships among jealousy, self-esteem and self-efficacy. *Chinese Journal of Clinical Psychology, 13*, 165–166, 172.

Hua, J. Y., & Smith, S. J. (2004). Neural activity and the dynamics of central nervous system development. *Nature Neuroscience, 7*, 327–332.

Huang, J., Lee, T., & Lu, M. (2007). Prenatal programming of childhood overweight and obesity. *Maternal & Child Health Journal, 11*(5), 461–473.

Hubel, D. H., & Wiesel, T. N. (1962). Receptive fields, binocular interaction and functional architecture in the cat's visual cortex. *Journal of Physiology, 160*, 106–154.

Hubel, D. H., & Wiesel, T. N. (1963). Receptive fields of cells in striate cortex of very young visually inexperienced kittens. *Journal of Neurophysiology, 26*, 994–1002.

Hubel, D. H., & Wiesel, T. N. (1979). Brain mechanisms of vision. In Scientific American (Eds.), *The brain*. San Franciso: W. H. Freeman.

Hubel, D. H., & Wiesel, T. N. (1998). Early exploration of the visual cortex. *Neuron, 20*, 401–412.

Hubel, D. H., & Wiesel, T. N. (2005). *Brain and visual perception: The story of a 25–year collaboration*. New York, NY: Oxford.

Huber, R., & Tononi, G. (2009). Sleep and waking across the lifespan. In G. G. Berntson & J. T. Cacioppo (Eds.), *Handbook of neuroscience for the behavioral sciences* (Vol. 1, pp. 461–481). New York, NY: Wiley.

Hublin, C. G. M., & Partinen, M. M. (2002). The extent and impact of insomnia as a public health problem. *Journal of Clinical Psychiatry, 4*(suppl. 1), 8–12.

Hudson, J. I., Hiripi, E., Pope Jr., Harrison, G., & Kessler, R. C. (2007). The prevalence and correlates of eating disorders in the national comorbidity survey replication. *Biological Psychiatry, 61*, 348–358.

Hudson, W. (1960). Pictorial depth perception in sub-cultural groups in Africa. *Journal of Social Psychology, 52*, 183–208.

Huesmann, L. R. (1986). Psychological processes promoting the relation between exposure to media violence and aggressive behavior by the viewer. *Journal of Social Issues, 42*, 125–139.

Huesmann, L. R., & Eron, L. D. (1986). *Television and the aggressive child: A cross-national comparison*. Mahwah, NJ: Lawrence Erlbaum.

Huesmann, L. R., & Miller, L. S. (1994). Long-term effects of repeated exposure to media violence in childhood. In L. R. Huesmann (Ed.), *Aggressive behavior: Current perspectives*. New York: Plenum Press.

Huesmann, L. R., Lagerspetz, K., & Eron, L. D. (1984). Intervening variables in the television violence–aggression relation: Evidence from two countries. *Developmental Psychology, 20*, 746–775.

Huesmann, L. R., Moise-Titus, J., Podolski, C.-L., & Eron, L. (2003). Longitudinal relations between children's exposure to TV violence and their aggressive and violent behavior in young adulthood: 1977–1992. *Developmental Psychology, 39*, 201–221.

Huey, E. D., Krueger, F., & Grafman, J. (2006). Representations in the human prefrontal cortex.

Current Directions in Psychological Science, 15, 167–171.

Huey, L. Y., Cole, S., Cole, R. F., Daniels, A. S. & Katzelnick, D. J. (2009). Health care reform. In B. J. Sadock, V. A. Sadock, & P. Ruiz (Eds.), *Kaplan & Sadock's comprehensive textbook of psychiatry* (pp. 4282–4298).

Hughes, J., Smith, T. W., Kosterlitz, H. W., Fothergill, L. A., Morgan, B. A., & Morris, H. R. (1975). Identification of two related pentapeptides from the brain with the potent opiate agonist activity. *Nature, 258*, 577–579.

Huijding, J., de Jong, P. J., Wiers, R. W., & Verkooijen, K. (2005). Implicit and explicit attitudes toward smoking in a smoking and a nonsmoking setting. *Addictive Behaviors, 30*(5), 949–961.

Hull, C. L. (1943). *Principles of behavior*. New York: Appleton.

Humber, J. G., & Tononi, G. (2009). Slow wave homeostasis and synaptic plasticity. *Journal of Clinical Sleep Medicine, 5*, S16–S19.

Humphrey, G. K., & Goodale, M. A. (1998). Probing unconscious visual processing with the McCollough effect. *Consciousness and Cognition, 7*, 494–519.

Humphrey, G. K., James, T. W., Gati, J. S., Menon, R. S., & Goodale, M. A. (1999). Perception of the McCollough effect correlates with activity in extrastriate cortex: A functional magnetic resonance imaging study. *Psychological Science, 10*, 444–448.

Hung, S. P., & Mantyh, P. W. (2001). Molecular basis of pain control. *National Review of Neuroscience, 2*, 83–91.

Hunsley, J., & Johnston, C. (2000). The role of empirically supported treatments in evidence-based psychological practice: A Canadian perspective. *Clinical Psychology: Science and Practice, 7*, 269–272.

Hunsley, J., Lee, C. M., & Wood, J. M. (2003). Controversial and questionable assessment techniques. In S. O. Lilienfield, S. J. Lynn, & J. M. Lohr (Eds.), *Science and pseudoscience in clinical psychology*. New York: Guilford.

Hunt, E. (1994). Problem solving. In R. J. Sternberg (Ed.), *Thinking and problem solving*. San Diego: Academic Press.

Hunt, E. (2001). Multiple views of multiple intelligence [Review of the book Intelligence reframed: Multiple intelligence in the 21st century]. *Contemporary Psychology, 46*, 5–7.

Hunt, E., & Agnoli, F. (1991). The Whorfian hypothesis: A cognitive psychology perspective. *Psychological Review, 98*, 377–389.

Hunt, E., & Carlson, J. (2007). Considerations relating to the study of group differences in intelligence. *Perspectives on Psychological Science, 2*(2), 194–213.

Hunt, H. (1989). *The multiplicity of dreams: Memory, imagination and consciousness*. New Haven: Yale University Press.

Hunt, J. M., Smith, M. F., & Kernan, J. B. (1985). The effects of expectancy disconfirmation and argument strength on message processing level: An application to personal selling. In E. C. Hirschman & M. B. Holbrook (Eds.), *Advances in consumer research* (Vol. 12). Provo, UT: Association for Consumer Research.

Hunt, M., Schloss, H., Mooat, S., Poulous, S., & Weiland, J. (2007). Emotional processing vesus cognitive restructuring in response to a depressing life event. *Cognitive Therapy and Research, 31*, 833–851.

Hunter, J. E., & Schmidt, F. L. (2000). Racial and gender bias in ability and achievement tests:

Resolving the apparent paradox. *Psychology, Public Policy, and Law, 6*, 151–158.

Hunter, P. (2008, September 17). Petitclerc pure gold on three wheels. *Toronto Star*, S1.

Hurlemann, R., Patin, A., Onur, O. A., Cohen, M. X., Baumgartner, T., Metzler, S., et al. (2010). Oxytocin enhances amygdala-dependent, socially reinforced learning and emotional empathy in humans. *Journal of Neuroscience, 30*(14), 4999–5007.

Hurst, M. (2008). Who gets any sleep these days? Sleep patterns of Canadians. Statistics Canada. Retrieved February 9, 2011, from http://www.statcan.gc.ca/pub/11-008-x/2008001/article/10553-eng.htm.

Hurvich, L. M. (1981). *Color vision*. Sunderland, MA: Sinnauer Associates.

Hustinx, P. J., Kuyper, H., van der Werf, M. C., & Dijkstra, P. (2009). Achievement motivation revisited: New longitudinal data to demonstrate its predictive power. *Educational Psychology, 29*(5), 561–582.

Huston, A. C., & Wright, J. C. (1982). Effects of communications media on children. In C. B. Kopp & J. B. Krakow (Eds.), *The child: Development in a social context*. Reading, MA: Addison-Wesley.

Huston, A. C., Donnerstein, E., Fairchild, H., Feshbach, N. D., Katz, P. A., & Murray, J. P. (1992). *Big world, small screen: The role of television in American society*. Lincoln: University of Nebraska Press.

Hutcherson, C. A., & Gross, J. J. (2011). The moral emotions: A social-functionalist account of anger, disgust, and contempt. *Journal of Personality and Social Psychology, 100*, 719–737.

Huttenlocher, P. R. (1994). Synaptogenesis in human cerebral cortex. In G. Dawson & K. W. Fischer (Eds.), *Human behavior and the developing brain*. New York: Guilford.

Huttenlocher, P. R. (2002). *Neural plasticity: The effects of environment on the development of the cerebral cortex*. Cambridge, MA: Harvard University Press.

Huxley, A. (1954). *The doors of perception*. London: Chatto and Windus.

Huyser, B., & Parker, J. C. (1998). Stress and rheumatoid arthritis: An integrative review. *Arthritis Care and Research, 11*, 135–145.

Hwang, W. C. (2006). The psychotherapy adaptation and modification framework: Application to Asian Americans. *American Psychologist, 61*, 702–715.

Hybels, C. F., & Blazer, D. G. I. (2005). Epidemiology of psychiatric disorders. In B. J. Sadock & V. A. Sadock (Eds.), *Kaplan & Sadock's comprehensive textbook of psychiatry*. Philadelphia: Lippincott Williams & Wilkins.

Hyde, J. S. (2005a). The gender similarities hypothesis. *American Psychologist, 60*, 581–892.

Hyde, J. S. (2007). New directions in the study of gender similarities and differences. *Current Directions in Psychological Science, 16*(5), 259–263.

Hyde, J. S., & Mertz, J. E. (2009). Gender, culture, and mathematics performance. *Proceedings of the National Academy of Sciences of the United States of America, 106*(22), 8801–8807.

Hyde, M., Roehrs, T., & Roth, T. (2006). Drugs of abuse and sleep. In T. Lee–Chiong (Ed.), *Sleep: A comprehensive handbook*. Hoboken, NJ: Wiley-Liss.

Hyman, I. A. (1996). Using research to change policy: Reflections on 20 years of effort to eliminate corporal punishment in the schools. *Pediatrics, 98*, 818–821.

Hyman, I. E., Jr., & Kleinknecht, E. E. (1999). False childhood memories: Research, theory, and applications. In L. M. Williams & V. L. Banyard (Eds.), *Trauma & memory*. Thousand Oaks, CA: Sage Publications.

Hyman, I. E., Jr., Husband, T. H., & Billings, J. F. (1995). False memories of childhood experiences. *Applied Cognitive Psychology, 9*, 181–197.

Hynie, M., MacDonald, T. K., & Marques, S. (2006). Self-conscious emotions and self-regulation in the promotion of condom use. *Personality and Social Psychology Bulletin, 32*(8), 1072–1084.

Iacoboni, M. (2007). Face to face: The neural basis of social mirroring and empathy. *Psychiatric Annals, 37*(4), 236–241.

Iacoboni, M. (2009). Imitation, empathy, and mirror neurons. *Annual Review of Psychology, 60*, 653–670.

Iacoboni, M., & Dapretto, M. (2006). The mirror neuron system and the consequences of its dysfunction. *Nature Reviews Neuroscience, 7*, 942–951.

Iams, J. D., & Romero, R. (2007). Preterm birth. In S. G. Gabbe, J. R. Niebyl, & J. L. Simpson (Eds.), *Obstetrics: Normal and problem pregnancies* (5th ed., pp. 668–712). Philadelphia, PA: Elsevier.

Ickovics, J. R., Thayaparan, B., & Ethier, K. A. (2001). Women and AIDS: A contextual analysis. In A. Baum, T. A. Revenson, & J. E. Singer (Eds.), *Handbook of health psychology* (pp. 817–840). Mahwah, NJ: Erlbaum.

Idisis, Y., Ben-David, S., & Ben-Nachum, E. (2007). Attribution of blame to rape victims among therapists and non-therapists. *Behavioral Sciences & the Law, 25*(1), 103–120.

Ikier, S., Yang, L., & Hasher, L. (2008). Implicit proactive interference, age, and automatic versus controlled retrieval strategies. *Psychological Science, 19*(5), 456–461.

Ilardi, S. S., Atchley, R. A., Enloe, A., Kwasny, K., & Garratt, G. (2007). Disentangling attentional biases and attentional deficits in depression: An event-related potential P300 analysis. *Cognitive Therapy and Research, 31*(2), 175–187.

Ilgen, D. R. (1999). Teams embedded in organizations: Some implications. *American Psychologist, 54*, 129–139.

Ilgen, D. R., Hollenbeck, J. R., Johnson, M., & Jundt, D. (2005). Teams in organizations: From input–process–output models to IMIO models. *Annual Review of Psychology, 56*, 517–543.

Ilie, G., & Thompson, W. F. (2006). A comparison of acoustic cues in music and speech for three dimensions of affect. *Music Perception, 23*, 319–329.

Indiana University. 2010. *Robert J. Sternberg*. Retrieved June 20, 2011, from http://www.indiana.edu/~intell/sternberg.shtml.

Infante, J. R., Torres-Avisbal, M., Pinel, P., Vallejo, J. A., Peran, F., Gonzalez, F., et al. (2001). Catecholamine levels in practitioners of the transcendental meditation technique. *Physiology & Behavior, 72*(1–2), 141–146.

Inglehart, R. (1990). *Culture shift in advanced industrial society*. Princeton, NJ: Princeton University Press.

Ingram, J. (2005). *Theatre of the mind: Raising the curtain on consciousness*. Toronto: HarperCollins Publishers Ltd.

Ingram, R. E., Scott, W. D., & Hamill, S. (2009). Depression: Social and cognitive aspects. In P. H. Blaney & T. Millon (Eds.), *Oxford textbook of psychopathology* (2nd ed., pp. 230–252). New York, NY: Oxford University Press.

Ingram, R. E., Scott, W., & Siegle, G. (1999). Depression: Social and cognitive aspects. In T. Millon, P. H. Blaney, & R. D. Davis (Eds.), *Oxford textbook of psychopathology* (pp. 203–226). New York: Oxford University Press.

Innocenti, G. M. (1994). Some new trends in the study of the corpus callosum. *Behavioral and Brain Research, 64*, 1–8.

Insel, T. R. (2010). Psychiatrists' relationships with pharmaceutical companies: Part of the problem or part of the solution? *Journal of the American Medical Association, 303*(12), 1192–1193.

Interview with Chantal Petitclerc, Canadian wheelchair champion. (1996, September 14). *CBC Sports*. Retrieved June 10, 2008, from http://archives.cbc.ca/programs/132-8450.

Inzlicht, M., & Kang, S. K. (2010). Stereotype threat spillover: How coping with threats to social identity affects aggression, eating, decision making, and attention. *Journal of Personality and Social Psychology, 99*(3), 467–481.

Iredale, S. K., Nevill, C. H., & Lutz, C. K. (2010). The influence of observer presence on baboon (*Papio spp.*) and rhesus macaque (*Macaca mulatta*) behavior. *Applied Animal Behaviour Science, 122*(1), 53–57.

Ironson, G., Klimas, N. G., Antoni, M., Friedman, A., Simoneau, J., LaPerriere, A., et al. (1994). Distress, denial, and low adherence to behavioral interventions predict faster disease progression in gay men infected with human immunodeficiency virus. *International Journal of Behavioral Medicine, 1*, 90–98.

Irvine, S. H., & Berry, J. W. (1988). *Human abilities in cultural context*. New York: Cambridge University Press.

Isaacowitz, D. M., & Seligman, M. E. P. (2007). Learned helplessness. In G. Fink (Ed.), *Encyclopedia of stress*. San Diego: Elsevier.

Isacsson, G. G., Holmgren, A. A., Ösby, U. U., & Ahlner, J. J. (2009). Decrease in suicide among the individuals treated with antidepressants: A controlled study of antidepressants in suicide, Sweden 1995–2005. *Acta Psychiatrica Scandinavica, 120*(1), 37–44.

Ismail, M. A. (1993). Maternal-fetal infections. In C. Lin, M. S. Verp, & R. E. Sabbagha (Eds.), *The high-risk fetus: Pathophysiology, diagnosis, management*. New York: Springer-Verlag.

Isometsa, E. T., Heikkinen, M. E., Marttunen, M. J., Henriksson, M. M., Aro, H. M., & Lonnqvist, J. K. (1995). The last appointment before suicide: Is suicide intent communicated? *American Journal of Psychiatry, 152*, 919–922.

Ito, T. A., Thompson, E., & Cacioppo, J. T. (2004). Tracking the timecourse of social perception: The effects of racial cues on event-related brain potentials. *Personality and Social Psychology Bulletin, 30*, 1267–1280.

Ito, T. A., & Urland, G. R. (2003). Race and gender on the brain: Electrocortical measures of attention to the race and gender of multiply categorizable individuals. *Journal of Personality and Social Psychology, 85*, 616–626.

Iwawaki, S., & Vernon, P. E. (1988). Japanese abilities and achievements. In S. H. Irvine & J. W. Berry (Eds.), *Human abilities in cultural context*. New York: Cambridge University Press.

Izard, C. E. (1984). Emotion-cognition relationships and human development. In C. E. Izard, J. Kagan, & R. B. Zajonc (Eds.), *Emotions, cognition and behavior*. Cambridge, England: Cambridge University Press.

Izard, C. E. (1990). Facial expressions and the regulation of emotions. *Journal of Personality and Social Psychology, 58*, 487–498.

Izard, C. E. (1991). *The psychology of emotions*. New York: Plenum.

Izard, C. E. (1994). Innate and universal facial expressions: Evidence from developmental and cross-cultural research. *Psychological Bulletin, 115*, 288–299.

Izard, C. E., & Saxton, P. M. (1988). Emotions. In R. C. Atkinson, R. J. Herrnstein, G. Lindzey, & R. D. Luce (Eds.), *Stevens' handbook of experimental psychology* (Vol. 1). New York: Wiley.

Jablensky, A. (2009). Course and outcome of schizophrenia and their prediction. In M. C. Gelder, N. C. Andreasen, J. J. López-Ibor, Jr., & J. R. Geddes (Eds.). *New Oxford textbook of psychiatry* (2nd ed., Vol. 1). New York, NY: Oxford University Press.

Jackicic, J., & Gallagher, K. I. (2002). Physical activity considerations for management of body weight. In D. H. Bessesen & R. Kushner (2002), *Evaluation and management of obesity*. Philadelphia: Hanley & Belfus.

Jackson, D. N. (1968). Content and style in personality assessment. *Psychological Bulletin, 55*, 243–252.

Jackson, D. N., & Paunonen, S. V. (1980). Personality structure and assessment. *Annual Review of Psychology, 31*, 77–95.

Jackson, M. (2007). The problem of pain. *University of Toronto Magazine, 34*, 23–27.

Jackson, S. E., Joshi, A., & Erhardt, N. L. (2003). Recent research on team and organizational diversity: SWOT analysis and implications. *Journal of Management, 29*, 801–830.

Jacob, R. G., & Pelham, W. (2005). Behavior therapy. In B. J. Sadock & V. A. Sadock (Eds.), *Kaplan and Sadock's comprehensive textbook of psychiatry* (pp. 2498–2547). Philadelphia: Lippincott Williams & Wilkins.

Jacobs, B. L. (2004). Depression: The brain finally gets into the act. *Current Directions in Psychological Science, 13*(3), 103–106.

Jacobson, E. (1938). *Progressive relaxation*. Chicago: University of Chicago Press.

Jacoby, L. L. (1988). Memory observed and memory unobserved. In U. Neisser & E. Winograd (Eds.), *Remembering reconsidered: Ecological and traditional approaches to the study of memory*. Cambridge: Cambridge University Press.

Jacoby, L. L., Hessels, S., & Bopp, K. (2001). Proactive and retroactive effects in memory performance: Dissociating recollection and accessibility bias. In H. L. Roediger, J. S. Nairne, I. Neath, & A. M. Surprenant (Eds.), *The nature of remembering: Essays in honor of Robert G. Crowder* (pp. 35–54). Washington, DC: American Psychological Association.

James, W. (1884). What is emotion? *Mind, 19*, 188–205.

James, W. (1890). *The principles of psychology*. New York: Holt.

James, W. (1902). *The varieties of religious experience*. New York: Modern Library.

James, W. H. (2005). Biological and psychosocial determinants of male and female human sexual orientation. *Journal of Biosocial Science, 37*, 555–567.

Jang, K. L., Livesley, W. J., & Vernon, P. A. (1996). Heritability of the Big Five personality dimensions and their facets: A twin study. *Journal of Personality, 64*, 577–591.

Janicak, P. G., Nahas, Z., Lisanby, S. H., Solvason, H., Sampson, S. M., McDonald, W. M., et al. (2010). Durability of clinical benefit with transcranial magnetic stimulation (TMS) in the treatment of pharmacoresistant major depression: Assessment of relapse during a 6-month, multisite, open-label study. *Brain Stimulation, 3*(4), 187–199.

Janig, W. (2003). The autonomic nervous system and its coordination by the brain. In R. J. Davidson, K. R. Scherer, & H. H. Goldsmith (Eds.), *Handbook of affective sciences*. New York: Oxford University Press.

Janis, I. L. (1958). *Psychological stress*. New York: Wiley.

Janis, I. L. (1972). *Victims of groupthink*. Boston: Houghton Mifflin.

Janis, I. L. (1993). Decision making under stress. In L. Goldberger & S. Breznitz (Eds.), *Handbook of stress: Theoretical and clinical aspects* (2nd ed.). New York: Free Press.

Janssen, L., Fennis, B. M., & Pruyn, A. H. (2010). Forewarned is forearmed: Conserving self-control strength to resist social influence. *Journal of Experimental Social Psychology, 46*(6), 911–921.

Javed, N. (2009, November 19). Why can't Canada stop bullies? *Toronto Star*, A22.

Javitt, D. C., & Laruelle, M. (2006). Neurochemical theories. In J. A. Lieberman, T. S. Stroup, & D. O. Perkins (Eds.), *Textbook of schizophrenia* (pp. 85–116). Washington, DC: American Psychiatric Publishing.

Jefferson, J. W., & Greist, J. H. (2009). Lithium. In B. J. Sadock, V. A. Sadock, & P. Ruiz (Eds.), *Kaplan & Sadock's comprehensive textbook of psychiatry* (pp. 3132–3144). Philadelphia, PA: Lippincott, Williams & Wilkins.

Jenkin, H. L., Dyde, R. T., Jenkin, M. R., Howard, I. P., & Harris, L. R. (2003). Relative role of visual and non-visual cues in determining the direction of "up": Experiments in the York tilted room facility. *Journal of Vestibular Research, 13*, 287–293.

Jenkins, L. J., Yang, Y-J., Goh, J., Hong, Y-Y, & Park, E. C. (2010). Cultural differences in the lateral occipital complex while viewing incongruent scenes. *Social Cognitive and Affective Neuroscience, 5*, 236–241.

Jennings, K. (2006). *Brainiac*. New York: Villard.

Jensen, A. R. (1969). How much can we boost IQ and scholastic achievement? *Harvard Educational Review, 39*, 1–23.

Jensen, A. R. (1980). *Bias in mental testing*. New York: Free Press.

Jensen, A. R. (1998). *The g factor: The science of mental ability*. Westport, CT: Praeger.

Jensen, A. R. (2000). Testing: The dilemma of group differences. *Psychology, Public Policy, and Law, 6*, 121–127.

Jensen-Campbell, L. A., & Graziano, W. G. (2001). Agreeableness as a moderator of interpersonal conflict. *Journal of Personality, 69*, 323–362.

Jessberger, S., Aimone, J. B., & Gage, F. H. (2009). Neurogenesis. In J. H. Byrne (Ed.), *Concise learning and memory: The editor's selection*. San Diego, CA: Elsevier.

Jessell, T. M., & Kelly, D. D. (1991). Pain and analgesia. In E. R. Kandel, J. H. Schwartz & T. M. Jessell (Eds.), *Principles of neural science* (3rd ed.). New York: Elsevier.

Jessup, R. K., Veinott, E. S., Todd, P. M., & Busemeyer, J. R. (2009). Leaving the store empty-handed: Testing explanations for the too-much-choice effect using decision field theory. *Psychology & Marketing, 26*(3), 299–320.

Ji, L.-J., Peng, K., & Nisbett, R. E. (2000). Culture, control, and perception of relationships in the environment. *Journal of Personality and Social Psychology, 78*, 943–955.

Jick, H., Kaye, J. A., & Jick, S. S. (2004). Antidepressants and the risk of suicidal behaviors. *Journal of The American Medical Association, 292*, 338–343.

Jigsaw Classroom. (2011). Overview of the technique. Retrieved July 16, 2011 from http://www.jigsaw.org/overview.htm.

Joffe, R. T. (2009). Neuropsychiatric aspects of multiple sclerosis and other demyelinating disorders. In B. J. Sadock, V. A. Sadock, & P. Ruiz (Eds.), *Kaplan & Sadock's comprehensive textbook of psychiatry* (9th ed., Vol. 1, pp. 248–272). Philadelphia, PA: Lippincott, Williams & Wilkins.

John, O. P., & Gross, J. J. (2007). Individual differences in emotion regulation. In J. J. Gross (Ed.), *Handbook of emotion regulation*. New York: Guilford.

John, P. O., Naumann, L. P., & Soto, C. J. (2008). Paradigm shift to the integrative Big Five trait taxonomy: History, measurement, and conceptual issues. In O. P. John, R. W. Robbins, & L. A. Pervin (Eds.), *Handbook of personality: Theory and research* (Vol. 3, pp. 114–158). New York, NY: Guilford Press.

Johnson, A. (2003). Procedural memory and skill acquisition. In A. F. Healy & R. W. Proctor (Eds.), *Handbook of psychology, Vol. 4: Experimental psychology*. New York, NY: Wiley.

Johnson, B. A., & Ait-Daoud, N. (2005). Alcohol: Clinical aspects. In J. H. Lowinson, P. Ruiz, R. B. Millman, & J. G. Langrod (Eds.), *Substance abuse: A comprehensive textbook*. Philadelphia: Lippincott, Williams & Wilkins.

Johnson, B. T., Maio, G. R., & Smith-McLallen, A. (2005). Communication and attitude change: Causes, processes, and effects. In D. Albarracin, B. T. Johnson, & M. P. Zanna (Eds.), *The handbook of attitudes*. Mahwah, NJ: Erlbaum.

Johnson, C., & Mullen, B. (1994). Evidence for the accessibility of paired distinctiveness in distinctiveness-based illusory correlation in stereotyping. *Personality and Social Psychology Bulletin, 20*, 65–70.

Johnson, J. S., & Newport, E. L. (1989). Critical period effects in second language learning: The influence of maturational state on the acquisition of English as a second language. *Cognitive Psychology, 21*, 60–99.

Johnson, J., Im-Boulter, N., & Pascual-Leone, J. (2003). Development of mental attention in gifted and mainstream children: The role of mental capacity, inhibition, and speed of processing. *Child Development, 74*, 1594–1614.

Johnson, M. E., & Dowling-Guyer, S. (1996). Effects of inclusive vs. exclusive language on evaluations of the counselor. *Sex Roles, 34*, 407–418.

Johnson, M. H. (2005a). Sensitive periods in functional brain development: Problems and prospects. *Developmental Psychobiology, 46*, 287–292.

Johnson, M. H. (2005b). *Developmental cognitive neuroscience* (2nd ed.). Malden, MA: Blackwell Publishing.

Johnson, M. K. (1996). Fact, fantasy, and public policy. In D. J. Herrmann, C. McEvoy, C. Hertzog, P. Hertel & M. K. Johnson (Eds.), *Basic and applied memory research: Theory in context* (Vol. 1). Mahwah, NJ: Erlbaum.

Johnson, M. K. (2006). Memory and reality. *American Psychologist, 61*, 760–771.

Johnson, M. K., Kahan, T. L., & Raye, C. L. (1984). Dreams and reality monitoring. *Journal of Experimental Psychology: General, 113*, 329–344.

Johnson, S. B., & Carlson, D. N. (2004). Medical regimen adherence: Concepts assessment, and interventions. In J. M. Raczynski & L. C. Leviton (Eds.), *Handbook of clinical health psychology: Vol 2. Disorders of behavior and health*. Washington, DC: American Psychological Association.

Johnson, S. C., Dweck, C. S., & Chen, F. S. (2007). Evidence for infants' internal working models of attachment. *Psychological Science, 18*(6), 501–502.

Johnson, S. L., Joormann, J., LeMoult, & Miller, C. (2009). Mood disorders: Biological bases. In P. H. Blaney & T. Millon (Eds.), *Oxford textbook of psychopathology* (2nd ed., pp. 198–229). New York, NY: Oxford University Press.

Johnson, S. M., & Greenberg, L. S. (1995). The emotion focussed approach to problems of adult attachment. In N. S. Jacobson & A. S. Gurman (Eds.), *Clinical handbook of couples therapy* (pp. 124–144). New York: Guilford.

Johnson, W. (2010). Understanding the genetics of intelligence: Can height help? Can corn oil? *Current Directions in Psychological Science, 19*(3), 177–182.

Johnson, W., & Krueger, R. F. (2006). How money buys happiness: Genetic and environmental processes linking finances and life satisfaction. *Journal of Personality and Social Psychology, 90*, 680–691.

Johnson, W., Turkheimer, E., Gottesman, I. I., & Bouchard, T. R. (2009). Beyond heritability: Twin studies in behavioral research. *Current Directions in Psychological Science, 18*(4), 217–220.

Johnston, J. C., & McClelland, J. L. (1974). Perception of letters in words: Seek not and ye shall find. *Science, 184*, 1192–1194.

Johnstone, L. (1999). Adverse psychological effects of ECT. *Journal of Mental Health (UK), 8*, 69–85.

Joiner, T. E. (2002). Depression in its interpersonal context. In I. H. Gotlib & C. L. Hammen (Eds.), *Handbook of depression*. New York: Guilford.

Joiner, T. E., & Katz, J. (1999). Contagion of depressive symptoms and mood: Meta-analytic review and explanations from cognitive, behavioral, and interpersonal viewpoints. *Clinical Psychology: Science and Practice, 6*, 149–164.

Joiner, T. E., Jr., & Metalsky, G. I. (1995). A prospective test of an integrative interpersonal theory of depression: A naturalistic study of college students. *Journal of Personality and Social Psychology, 69*, 778–788.

Joiner, T. E., Jr., & Timmons, K. A. (2009). Depression in its interpersonal context. In I. H. Gotlib & C. L. Hammen (Eds.), *Handbook of Depression* (2nd ed., pp. 322–339). New York, NY: Guilford Press.

Joiner, T. E., Jr., Van Orden, K. A., Witte, T. K., & Rudd, M. D. (2009). *The interpersonal theory of suicide: Guidance for working with suicidal clients*. Washington: DC: American Psychological Association.

Jones, B. E. (2005). Basic mechanisms of sleep–wake states. In M. H. Kryger, T. Roth, & W. C. Dement (Eds.). *Principles and practice of sleep medicine*. Philadelphia: Elsevier Saunders.

Jones, E. E., & Davis, K. E. (1965). From acts to dispositions: The attribution process in person perception. In L. Berkowitz (Ed.), *Advances in experimental social psychology* (Vol. 2). New York: Academic Press.

Jones, E. E., & Nisbett, R. E. (1971). The actor and the observer: Divergent perceptions of the causes of behavior. In E. E. Jones, D. E. Kanouse, H. H. Kelley, R. E. Nisbett, S. Valins, & B. Weiner (Eds.), *Attribution: Perceiving the causes of behavior*. Morristown, NJ: General Learning Press.

Jonides, J., Lewis, R. L., Nee, D. E., Lustig, C. A., Berman, M. G., & Moore, K. S. (2008). The mind and brain of short-term memory. *Annual Review of Psychology, 59,* 193–224.

Jordan, B. (1983). *Birth in four cultures.* Quebec: Eden Press.

Jordan, P. J., Ashton-James, C. E., & Ashkanasy, N. M. (2006). Evaluating the claims: Emotional intelligence in the workplace. In K. R. Murphy (Ed.), *A critique of emotional intelligence: What are the problems and how can they be fixed?* (pp. 189–210). Mahwah, NJ: Erlbaum.

Jordan-Young, R. M. (2010). *Brainstorm: The flaws in the science of sex differences.* Cambridge, MA: Harvard University Press.

Jordon, C. H., & Zanna, M. P. (1999). How to read a journal article in social psychology. In R. F. Baumeister (Ed.), *The self in social psychology* (pp. 461–470). Philadelphia: Psychology Press.

Jorge, R. E., Robinson, R. G., Arndt, S. V., Starkstein, S. E., Forrester, A. W., & Geisler F. (1993). Depression following traumatic brain injury: A 1 year longitudinal study. *Journal of Affective Disorders, 27*(4), 233–243.

Jorgensen, R. S., Johnson, B. T., Kolodziej, M. E., & Schreer, G. E. (1996). Elevated blood pressure and personality: A meta-analytic review. *Psychological Bulletin, 120,* 293–320.

Joska, J. A., & Stein, D. J. (2008). Mood disorders. In R. E. Hales, S. C. Yudofsky, & G. O. Gabbard (Eds.), *The American Psychiatric Publishing textbook of psychiatry* (5th ed., pp. 457–504). Washington, DC: American Psychiatric Publishing.

Josse, G., & Tzourio-Mazoyer, N. (2004). Hemispheric specialization for language. *Brain Research Reviews, 44,* 1–12.

Judge, T. A., & Klinger, R. (2008). Job satisfaction: Subjective well-being at work. In M. Eid & R. J. Larsen (Eds.), *The science of subjective well-being* (pp. 393–413). New York: Guilford.

Judge, T. A., Hurst, C., & Simon, L. S. (2009). Does it pay to be smart, attractive, or confident (or all three)? Relationships among general mental ability, physical attractiveness, core self-evaluations, and income. *Journal of Applied Psychology, 94*(3), 742–755.

Julien, R. M., Advokat, C. D., & Comaty, J. E. (2008). A primer of drug action: A comprehensive guide to the actions, uses, and side effects of psychoactive drugs. New York: Worth.

Jung, C. G. (1917/1953). *On the psychology of the unconscious.* In H. Read, M. Fordham, & G. Adler (Eds.), *Collected works of C. G. Jung* (Vol. 7). Princeton, NJ: Princeton University Press.

Jung, C. G. (1921/1960). *Psychological types.* In H. Read, M. Fordham, & G. Adler (Eds.), *Collected works of C. G. Jung* (Vol. 6). Princeton, NJ: Princeton University Press.

Jung, C. G. (1933). *Modern man in search of a soul.* New York: Harcourt, Brace & World.

Jung, K. (1999). John Watson on authority and truth: Psychology as a moral science. *History and Philosophy of Psychology Bulletin, 11,* 17–21.

Jung, R. E., & Haier, R. J. (2007). The Parieto-Frontal Integration Theory (P-FIT) of intelligence: Converging neuroimaging evidence. *Behavioral and Brain Sciences, 30*(2), 135–154.

Jusczyk, P. W., & Klein, R. M. (1980). *The nature of thought: Essays in honour of D. O. Hebb.* Hillsdale, NJ: Erlbaum.

Kaas, J. H. (2000). The reorganization of sensory and motor maps after injury in adult mammals. In M. S. Gazzaniga (Ed.), *The new cognitive neurosciences.* Cambridge, MA: The MIT Press.

Kabat-Zinn, J. (1995). *Mindfulness meditation.* New York: Simon & Shuster.

Kagan, J. (1998, November/December). A parent's influence is peerless. *Harvard Education Letter.*

Kagan, J. (2008). Behavioral inhibition as a risk factor for psychopathology. In T. P. Beauchaine & S. P. Hinshaw (Eds.), *Child and adolescent psychopathology* (pp. 157–179). Hoboken, NJ: Wiley.

Kagan, J. (2010). Emotions and temperament. In M. H. Bornstein (Ed.), *Handbook of cultural developmental science* (pp. 175–194). New York, NY: Psychology Press.

Kagan, J. (2011). Three lessons learned. *Psychological Science, 6,* 107–113.

Kagan, J., & Fox, A. (2006). Biology, culture, and temperamental biases. In N. Eisenberg, W. Damon, & R. M. Lerner (Eds.), *Handbook of child psychology: Social, emotional, and personality development* (pp. 167–225). Hoboken, NJ: Wiley.

Kagan, J., & Snidman, N. (1991). Temperamental factors in human development. *American Psychologist, 46,* 856–862.

Kagan, J., Reznik, J. S., & Snidman, N. (1999). Biological basis of childhood shyness. In A. Slater & D. Muir (Eds.), *The Blackwell reader in developmental psychology* (pp. 65–78). Malden, MA: Blackwell.

Kagan, J., Snidman, N., & Arcus, D. M. (1992). Initial reactions to unfamiliarity. *Current Directions in Psychological Science, 1*(6), 171–174.

Kahan, T. L., & Johnson, M. K. (1992). Self-effects in memory for person information. *Social Cognition, 10*(1), 30–50.

Kahan, T. L., & LaBerge, S. (1994). Lucid dreaming as metacognition: Implications for cognitive science. *Consciousness and Cognition, 3,* 246–264.

Kahan, T. L., & LaBerge, S. (1996). Cognition and metacognition in dreaming and waking: Comparisons of first- and third-person ratings. *Dreaming, 6,* 235–249.

Kahane, H. (1992). *Logic and contemporary rhetoric: The use of reason in everyday life.* Belmont, CA: Wadsworth.

Kahn, D. (2007). Metacognition, recognition, and reflection while dreaming. In D. Barrett & P. McNamara (Eds.), *The new science of dreaming.* Westport, CT: Praeger.

Kahneman, D. (1991). Judgment and decision making: A personal view. *Psychological Science, 2,* 142–145.

Kahneman, D. (1999). Objective happiness. In D. Kahneman, E. Diener, & N. Schwarz (Eds.), *Well-being: The foundations of hedonic psychology.* New York: Russell Sage Foundation.

Kahneman, D. (2003). A perspective on judgment and choice: Mapping bounded rationality. *American Psychologist, 58,* 697–720.

Kahneman, D. (2003a). Experiences of collaborative research. *American Psychologist, 58,* 723–730.

Kahneman, D. (2003b). Maps of bounded rationality: Psychology for behavioral economics. *The American Economic Review, 93,* 1449–1475.

Kahneman, D. (2009). Behavioral economics: Commencement address to Georgetown University. Retrieved March 2, 2011, from fora.tv/2009/05/15/Nobelist_Daniel_Kahneman_on_Behavioral_economics#fullprogram.

Kahneman, D., & Deaton, A. (2010). High income improves evaluation of life but not emotional well-being. *Proceedings of the National Academy of Sciences of the United States of America, 107*(38), 16489–16493.

Kahneman, D., & Tversky, A. (1979). Prospect theory: An analysis of decision under risk. *Econometrica, 47,* 263–292.

Kahneman, D., & Tversky, A. (1982). Subjective probability: A judgment of representativeness. In D. Kahneman, P. Slovic, & A. Tversky (Eds.), *Judgment under uncertainty: Heuristics and biases.* Cambridge: Cambridge University Press.

Kahneman, D., & Tversky, A. (1984). Choices, values, and frames. *American Psychologist, 39,* 341–350.

Kahneman, D., & Tversky, A. (2000). *Choices, values, and frames.* New York: Cambridge University Press.

Kahneman, D., Krueger, A. B., Schkade, D., Schwarz, N., & Stone, A. A. (2006). Would you be happier if you were richer? A focusing illusion. *Science, 312,* 1908–1910.

Kaiser, A., Haller, S., Schmitz, S., & Nitsch, C. (2009). On sex/gender related similarities and differences in fMRI language research. *Brain Research Reviews, 61*(2), 49–59.

Kajantie, E. (2008). Physiological stress response, estrogen, and the male-female mortality gap. *Current Directions in Psychological Science, 17*(5), 348–352.

Kajantie, E., & Phillips, D. W. (2006). The effects of sex and hormonal status on the physiological response to acute psychosocial stress. *Psychoneuroendocrinology, 31*(2), 151–178.

Kako, E. (1999). Elements of syntax in the systems of three language-trained animals. *Animal Learning and Behavior, 27,* 1–14.

Kales, J. D., Kales, A., Bixler, E. O., Soldatos, C. R., Cadieux, R. J., Kashurba, G. J., & Vela-Bueno, A. (1984). Biopsychobehavioral correlates of insomnia: V. Clinical characteristics and behavioral correlates. *American Journal of Psychiatry, 141,* 1371–1376.

Kalichman, S. C. (1995). *Understanding AIDS: A guide for mental health professionals.* Washington, DC: American Psychological Association.

Kalmijn, M. (1998). Intermarriage and homogamy: Causes, patterns, trends. *Annual Review of Sociology, 24,* 395–421.

Kameda, T., Tsukasaki, T., Hastie, R., & Berg, N. (2011). Democracy under uncertainty: The wisdom of crowds and the free-rider problem in group decision-making. *Psychological Review, 118,* 76–96.

Kamin, L. J. (1974). *The science and politics of IQ.* Hillsdale, NJ: Erlbaum.

Kanai, R., Fellden, T., Firth, C., & Rees, G. (2011). Political orientations are correlated with brain structure in young adults. *Current Biology, 21,* 677–680.

Kanaya, T., Scullin, M. H., & Ceci, S. J. (2003). The Flynn effect and U. S. policies: The impact of rising IQ scores on American society via mental retardation diagnoses. *American Psychologist, 58*(10), 778–790.

Kanazawa, S. (2006). Mind the gap … in intelligence: Reexamining the relationship between inequality and health. *British Journal of Health Psychology, 11,* 623–642.

Kandel, E. R. (2000). Nerve cells and behavior. In E. R. Kandel, J. H. Schwartz, & T. M. Jessell (Eds.), *Principles of neural science* (pp. 19–35). New York: McGraw-Hill.

Kandel, E. R., & Jessell, T. M. (1991). Touch. In E. R. Kandel, J. H. Schwartz, & T. M. Jessell (Eds.), *Principles of neural science* (3rd ed.). New York: Elsevier.

Kandel, E. R., & Siegelbaum, S. A. (2000). Synaptic integration. In E. R. Kandel, J. H. Schwartz & T. M. Jessell (Eds.), *Principles of neural science* (pp. 207–228). New York: McGraw-Hill.

Kandell, J. J. (1998). Internet addiction on campus: The vulnerability of college students. *CyberPsychology and Behavior, 1*(1), 11–17.

Kandler, C., Bleidorn, W., Riemann, R., Spinath, F. M., Thiel, W., & Angleitner, A. (2010). Sources of cumulative continuity in personality: A longitudinal multiple-rater twin study. *Journal of Personality and Social Psychology, 98*(6), 995–1008.

Kane, M. J., Poole, B. J., Tuholski, S. W., & Engle, R. W. (2006). Working memory capacity and the top-down control of visual search: Exploring the boundaries of "executive attention." *Journal of Experimental Psychology: Learning, Memory, and Cognition, 32*, 749–777.

Kane, J. (1991). *Be sick well: A healthy approach to chronic illness.* Oakland, CA: New Harbinger Publications.

Kane, J. M., Stroup, T. S., & Marder, S. R. (2009). Schizophrenia: Pharmacological treatment. In B. J. Sadock, V. A. Sadock, & P. Ruiz (Eds.), *Kaplan & Sadock's comprehensive textbook of psychiatry* (pp. 1547–1555). Philadelphia, PA: Lippincott, Williams & Wilkins.

Kane, M. J., & Engle, R. W. (2002). The role of prefrontal cortex in working-memory capacity, executive attention, and general fluid intelligence: An individual-differences perspective. *Psychonomic Bulletin & Review, 9*, 637–671.

Kane, T. D., Marks, M. A., Zaccaro, S. J., & Blair, V. (1996). Self-efficacy, personal goals, and wrestlers' self-regulation. *Journal of Sport & Exercise Psychology, 18*, 36–48.

Kanner, L. (1943). Autistic disturbances of affective contact. *Nervous Child, 2*, 217–250.

Kanner, L. (1973). *Childhood psychosis: Initial studies and new insights.* New York: Wiley.

Kanwisher, N., & Yovel, G. (2009). Face perception. In G. G. Berntson & J. T. Cacioppo (Eds.), *Handbook of neuroscience for the behavioral sciences.* New York, NY: Wiley.

Kaplan, A. G. (1985). Female or male therapists for women patients: New formulations. *Psychiatry, 48*, 111–121.

Kaplan, H. I. (1989). History of psychosomatic medicine. In H. I. Kaplan & B. J. Sadock (Eds.), *Comprehensive textbook of psychiatry* (5th ed.). Baltimore: Williams & Wilkins.

Kaplan, H., & Dove, H. (1987). Infant development among the Ache of Eastern Paraguay. *Developmental Psychology, 23*, 190–198.

Kaplan, K. A., Itoi, A., & Dement, W. C. (2007). Awareness of sleepiness and ability to predict sleep onset: Can drivers avoid falling asleep at the wheel? *Sleep Medicine, 9*(1), 71–79.

Kaprio, J., Rimpela, A., Winter, T., Viken, R. J., Rimpela, M., & Rose, R. J. (1995). Common genetic influence on BMI and age at menarche. *Human Biology, 67*, 739–753.

Karasu, T. B. (2005). Psychoanalysis and psychoanalytic psychotherapy. In B. J. Sadock & V. A. Sadock (Eds.), *Kaplan and Sadock's comprehensive textbook of psychiatry* (pp. 2472–2497). Philadelphia: Lippincott Williams & Wilkins.

Karau, S. J., & Williams, K. D. (1993). Social loafing: A meta-analytic review and theoretical integration. *Journal of Personality and Social Psychology, 65*, 681–706.

Karau, S. J., & Williams, K. D. (1995). Social loafing: Research findings, implications, and future directions. *Current Directions in Psychological Science, 4*, 134–140.

Karlsgodt, K. H., Sun, D., & Cannon, T. D. (2010). Structural and functional brain abnormalities in schizophrenia. *Current Directions in Psychological Science, 19*(4), 226–231.

Karlson, P, & Luscher, M. (1959). "Pheromones": A new term for a class of biologically active substances. *Nature, 183*, 55–56.

Karon, B. P., & Widener, A. J. (1997). Repressed memories and World War II: Lest we forget! *Professional Psychology: Research & Practice, 28*, 338–340.

Karp, A., Andel, R., Parker, M. G., Wang, H., Winblad, B., & Fratiglioni, L. (2009). Mentally stimulating activities at work during midlife and dementia risk after age 75: Follow-up study from the Kungsholmen Project. *American Journal of Geriatric Psychiatry, 17*(3), 227–236.

Karpicke, J. D., & Roediger, H. (2008). The critical importance of retrieval for learning. *Science, 319*(5865), 966–968.

Karpicke, J. D., Butler, A. C., & Roediger, H. (2009). Metacognitive strategies in student learning: Do students practise retrieval when they study on their own? *Memory, 17*(4), 471–479.

Karremans, J. C., Stroebe, W., & Claus, J. (2006). Beyond Vicary's fantasies: The impact of subliminal priming and brand choice. *Journal of Experimental Psychology, 42*, 792–798.

Kass, S. J., Cole, K. S., & Stanny, C. J. (2007). Effects of distraction and experience on situation awareness and simulated driving. *Transportation Research Part F: Traffic Psychology and Behaviour, 10*, 321–329.

Kasser, T. (2002). *The high prices of materialism.* Cambridge, MA: MIT Press.

Kasser, T., & Sharma, Y. S. (1999). Reproductive freedom, educational equality, and females' preference for resource-aquisition characteristics in mates. *Psychological Science, 10*, 374–377.

Kasser, T., Ryan, R. M., Couchman, C. E., & Sheldon, K. M. (2004). Materialistic values: Their causes and consequences. In T. Kasser & A. D. Kanner (Eds.), *Psychology and consumer culture: The struggle for a good life in a materialistic world.* Washington, DC: American Psychological Association.

Kassin, S. M., Tubb, V. A., Hosch, H. M., & Memon, A. (2001). On the "general acceptance" of eyewitness testimony research: A new survey of the experts. *American Psychologist, 56*, 405–416.

Katigbak, M. S., Church, A. T., Guanzon-Lapena, M. A., Carlota, A. J., & del Pilar, G. H. (2002). Are indigenous personality dimensions culture specific? Philippine inventories and the five-factor model. *Journal of Personality and Social Psychology, 82*, 89–101.

Katz, A. N., Blasko, D. G., & Kazmerski, V. A. (2004). Saying what you don't mean: Social influences on sarcastic language processing. *Current Directions in Psychological Science, 13*(5), 186–189.

Katz, J., Asmundson, G. J. G., McRae, K., & Halket, E. (2009). Emotional numbing and pain intensity predict the development of pain disability up to one year after lateral thoracotomy. *European Journal of Pain, 13*, 870–878.

Katz, J., Buis, T., & Cohen, L. (2008). Locked out and still knocking: Predictors of excessive demands for postoperative intravenous patient-controlled analgesia. *Canadian Journal of Anesthesia, 55*, 88–99.

Kaufman, A. S. (2000). Tests of intelligence. In R. J. Sternberg (Ed.), *Handbook of intelligence* (pp. 445–476). New York: Cambridge University Press.

Kaufman, A. S. (2009). *IQ testing 101.* New York, NY: Springer.

Kaufman, J. C. (2001). The Sylvia Plath effect: Mental illness in eminent creative writers. *Journal of Creative Behavior, 35*(1), 37–50.

Kaufman, J. C. (2005). The door that leads into madness: Eastern European poets and mental illness. *Creativity Research Journal, 17*(1), 99–103.

Kaufman, J. C., & Baer, J. (2002). Could Steven Spielberg manage the Yankees? Creative thinking in different domains. *Korean Journal of Thinking & Problem Solving, 12*(2), 5–14.

Kaufman, J. C., & Baer, J. (2004). Hawking's haiku, Madonna's math: Why it is hard to be creative in every room of the house. In R. J. Sternberg, E. L. Grigorenko, & J. L. Singer (Eds.), *Creativity: From potential to realization.* Washington, DC: American Psychological Association.

Kaufman, L., Vassiliades, V., Noble, R., Alexander, R., Kaufman, J., & Edlund, S. (2007). Perceptual distance and the moon illusion. *Spatial Vision, 20*, 155–175.

Kaufman, S. B., & Sternberg, R. J. (2010). Conceptions of giftedness. In S. I. Pfeiffer (Ed.), *Handbook of giftedness in children: Psychoeducational theory, research, and best practices.* New York, NY: Springer.

Kaushanskaya, M., & Marian, V. (2009). Bilingualism reduces native-language interference during novel word learning. *Journal of Experimental Psychology: Learning, Memory, and Cognition, 35*(3), 829–835.

Kawakami, K., Steele, J. R., Cifa, C., Phills, C. E., & Dovidio, J. F. (2008). Approaching math increases math = me and math = pleasant. *Journal of Experimental Social Psychology, 44*, 818–825.

Kay, J., & Kay, R. L. (2008). Individual psychoanalytic psychotherapy. In A. Tasman, J. Kay, J. A. Lieberman, M. B. First, & M. Maj (Eds.), *Psychiatry* (3rd ed.). New York, NY: Wiley-Blackwell.

Kazdin, A. E. (2001). *Behavior modification in applied settings* (6th ed.). Belmont, CA: Wadsworth.

Kazdin, A. E. (1982). History of behavior modification. In A. S. Bellack, M. Hersen, & A. E. Kazdin (Eds.), *International handbook of behavior modification and behavior therapy.* New York: Plenum.

Kazdin, A. E. (1994). Methodology, design, and evaluation in psychotherapy research. In A. E. Bergin & S. L. Garfield (Eds.), *Handbook of psychotherapy and behavior change* (4th ed.). New York: Wiley.

Kazdin, A. E. (1998). *Research design in clinical psychology.* New York, NY: Allyn and Bacon.

Kazdin, A., & Benjet, C. (2003). Spanking children: Evidence and issues. *Current Directions in Psychological Science, 12*(3), 99–103.

Keane, T. M., Marshall, A. D., & Taft, C. T. (2006). Posttraumatic stress disorder: Etiology, epidemiology, and treatment outcome. *Annual Review of Clinical Psychology, 2*, 161–197.

Keating, D. P. (2004). Cognitive and brain development. In R. M. Lerner & L. Steinberg (Eds.), *Handbook of adolescent psychology.* New York: Wiley.

Keck, P. E., Jr., & McElroy, S. L. (2006). Lithium and mood stabilizers. In D. J. Stein, D. J. Kupfer, & A. F. Schatzberg (Eds.), *Textbook of mood disorders* (pp. 281–290). Washington, DC: American Psychiatric Publishing.

Keefauver, S. P., & Guilleminault, C. (1994). Sleep terrors and sleepwalking. In M. H. Kryger, T. Roth, & W. C. Dement (Eds.), *Principles and practice of sleep medicine* (2nd ed.). Philadelphia: Saunders.

Keefer, K., Wood, L. M., & Parker, J. D. A. (2009, June). Assessing emotional intelligence in children and adolescents: Congruence between self-report and parent ratings. Paper presented at the annual meeting of the Canadian Psychological Association, Montreal, Quebec.

Keen, R. (2011). The development of problem solving in young children: A critical cognitive skill. *Annual Review of Psychology, 62,* 1–21.

Keesey, R. E. (1993). Physiological regulation of body energy: Implications for obesity. In A. J. Stunkard & T. A. Wadden (Eds.), *Obesity theory and therapy.* New York: Raven.

Keesey, R. E. (1995). A set point model of body weight regulation. In K. D. Brownell & C. G. Fairburn (Eds.), *Eating disorders and obesity: A comprehensive handbook.* New York: Guilford.

Keesey, R. E., & Powley, T. L. (1975). Hypothalamic regulation of body weight. *American Scientist, 63,* 558–565.

Kefalov, V. J. (2010). Visual receptors and transduction. In E. B. Goldstein (Ed.), *Encyclopedia of perception.* Thousand Oaks, CA: Sage.

Kehoe, E. J., & Macrae, M. (1998). Classical conditioning. In W. O'Donohue (Ed.), *Learning and behavior therapy.* Boston: Allyn & Bacon.

Keller, P. A., & Block, L. G. (1999). The effect of affect-based dissonance versus cognition-based dissonance on motivated reasoning and health-related persuasion. *Journal of Experimental Psychology: Applied, 5,* 302–313.

Kelley, H. H. (1950). The warm–cold variable in first impressions of persons. *Journal of Personality, 18,* 431–439.

Kelley, H. H. (1967). Attributional theory in social psychology. *Nebraska Symposium on Motivation, 15,* 192–241.

Kelley, W. M., Macrae, C. N., Wyland, C. L., Caglar, S., Inati, S., & Heatherton, T. F. (2002). Finding the self? An event-related fMRI Study. *Journal of Cognitive Neuroscience, 14,* 785–794.

Kellogg, R. T., Friedman, A., Johnson, P., & Rickard, T. C. (2005). Domain-specific knowledge in intellectual skills: A symposium in honor of Lyle E. Bourne, Jr. In A. F. Healy (Ed.), *Experimental cognitive psychology and its applications* (pp. 3–15). Washington, DC: American Psychological Association.

Kellogg, S. H., & Young, J. E. (2008). Cognitive therapy. In J. L. Lebow (Ed.), *Twenty-first century psychotherapies: Contemporary approaches to theory and practice.* New York: Wiley.

Kelly, B. D., Feeney, L., O'Callaghan, E., Browne, R., Byrne, M., Mulryan, N., Scully, A., Morris, M., Kinsella, A., Takei, N., McNeil, T., Walsh, D., & Larkin, C. (2004). Obstetric adversity and age at first presentation with schizophrenia: Evidence of a dose-response relationship. *American Journal of Psychiatry, 161,* 920–922.

Kelly, G. A. (1955). *The psychology of personal constructs* (Vols. 1 & 2). New York, NY: Norton.

Kelly, J. P. (1991). The sense of balance. In E. R. Kandel, J. H. Schwartz, & T. M. Jessell (Eds.), *Principles of neural science* (3rd ed.). New York: Elsevier.

Kelly, K. M., & Schramke, C. J. (2000). Epilepsy. In G. Fink (Ed.), *Encyclopedia of stress* (pp. 66–70). San Diego: Academic Press.

Kelly, S. J., Day, N., & Streissguth, A. P. (2000). Effects of prenatal alcohol exposure on social behavior in humans and other species. *Neurotoxicology & Teratology, 22,* 143–149.

Kelman, H. C. (1967). Human use of human subjects: The problem of deception in social psychological experiments. *Psychological Bulletin, 67,* 1–11.

Kelman, H. C. (1982). Ethical issues in different social science methods. In T. L. Beauchamp, R. R. Faden, R. J. Wallace, Jr., & L. Walters (Eds.), *Ethical issues in social science research.* Baltimore: Johns Hopkins University Press.

Kelsey, J. E. (2005). Selective serotonin reuptake inhibitors. In B. J. Sadock & V. A. Sadock (Eds.), *Kaplan and Sadock's comprehensive textbook of psychiatry* (pp. 2887–2913). Philadelphia: Lippincott, Williams & Wilkins.

Kelsoe, J. R. (2004). Genomics and the human genome project: Implications for psychiatry. *International Review of Psychiatry, 16*(4), 294–300.

Kelsoe, J. R. (2009). Mood disorders: Genetics. In B. J. Sadock, V. A. Sadock, & P. Ruiz (Eds.), *Kaplan & Sadock's comprehensive textbook of psychiatry* (9th ed., pp. 1653–1663). Philadelphia, PA: Lippincott, Williams & Wilkins.

Keltner, D., Ekman, P., Gonzaga, G. C., & Beer, J. (2003). Facial expression of emotion. In R. J. Davidson, K. R. Scherer, & H. H. Goldsmith (Eds.), *Handbook of affective sciences.* New York: Oxford University Press.

Kemeny, M. E. (2007). Psychoneuroimmunology. In H. S. Friedman & R. C. Silver (Eds.), *Foundations of health psychology.* New York, NY: Oxford University Press.

Kendall, P. C., Holmbeck, G., & Verduin, T. (2004). Methodology, design, and evaluation in psychotherapy research. In M. J. Lambert (Ed.), *Bergin and Garfield's handbook of psychotherapy and behavior change.* New York: Wiley.

Kendler, K. S. (2005a). "A gene for . . .?": The nature of gene action in psychiatric disorders. *American Journal of Psychiatry, 162,* 1243–1252.

Kendler, K. S. (2005b). Psychiatric genetics: A methodologic critique. *American Journal of Psychiatry, 162,* 3–11.

Kendler, K. S., Myers, J., & Prescott, C. A. (2005). Sex differences in the relationship between social support and risk for major depression: A longitudinal study of opposite-sex twin pairs. *American Journal of Psychiatry, 162,* 250–256.

Kennedy, T. E., Hawkins, R. D., & Kandel, E. R. (1992). Molecular interrelationships between short- and long-term memory. In L. R. Squire & N. Butters (Eds.), *Neuropsychology of Memory* (2nd ed.). New York: Wiley.

Kenny, M. A., & Williams, J. M. G. (2007). Treatment-resistant depressed patients show a good response to mindfulness-based cogntive therapy. *Behaviour Research and Therapy, 45,* 616–625.

Kenrick, D. T., & Gutierres, S. E. (1980). Contrast effects and judgments of physical attractiveness: When beauty becomes a social problem. *Journal of Personality and Social Psychology, 38,* 131–140.

Kenrick, D. T., Griskevicius, V., Neuberg, S. L., & Schaller, M. (2010). Renovating the pyramid of needs: Contemporary extensions built upon ancient foundations. *Perspectives on Psychological Science, 5*(3), 292–314.

Kenrick, D. T., Trost, M. R., & Sundie, J. M. (2004). Sex roles as adaptations: An evolutionary perspective on gender differences and similarities. In A. H. Eagly, A. E. Beall, & R. J. Sternberg (Eds.), *The psychology of gender.* New York: Guilford.

Kenwood, C. (1999). The anti-sceptical psychology of George Paxton Young. *History and Philosophy of Psychology Bulletin, 11,* 4–10.

Keren, G., & Schul, U. Y. (2009). Two is not always better than one. *Perspectives on Psychological Science, 4,* 533–550.

Kermer, D. A., Driver-Linn, E., Wilson, T. D., & Gilbert, D. T. (2006). Loss aversion is an affective forecasting error. *Psychological Science, 17,* 649–653.

Kern, M. L., & Friedman, H. S. (2008). Do conscientious individuals live longer? A quantitative review. *Health Psychology, 27*(5), 505–512.

Kerns, K. A., Abraham, M. M., Schlegelmilch, A., & Morgan, T. A. (2007). Mother-child attachment in later middle-childhood: Assessment approaches and associations with mood and emotion. *Attachment & Human Development, 9*(1), 33–53.

Kesebir, P., & Diener, E. (2008). In pursuit of happiness: Empirical answers to philosophical questions. *Perspectives on Psychological Science, 3,* 117–125,

Kesebir, S., Graham, J., & Oishi, S. (2010). A theory of human needs should be human-centered, not animal-centered: Commentary on Kenrick et al. (2010). *Perspectives on Psychological Science, 5*(3), 315–319.

Kessen, W. (1996). American psychology just before Piaget. *Psychological Science, 7,* 196–199.

Kessler, R. C., & Zhao, S. (1999). The prevalence of mental illness. In A. V. Horvitz & T. L. Scheid (Eds.), *A handbook for the study of mental health: Social contexts, theories, and systems.* New York: Cambridge University Press.

Kessler, R. C., Berglund, P., Demler, O., Jin, R., Merikangas, K. R., & Walters, E. E. (2005a). Lifetime prevalence and age-of-onset distributions of DSM-IV disorders in the national comorbidity survey replication. *Archives of General Psychiatry, 62,* 593–602.

Kessler, R. C., Demier, O., Frank, R. G., Olfson, M., Pincus, H. A., Walters, E. E., et al. (2005b). Prevalence and treatment of mental disorders: 1990–2003. *New England Journal of Medicine, 352,* 2515–2523.

Kessler, R. C., McGonagle, K. A., Zhao, S., Nelson, C. B., Hughes, M., Eshleman, S., et al. (1994). Lifetime and 12–month prevalence of DSM-III-R psychiatric disorders in the United States: Results from the National Comorbidity Survey. *Archives of General Psychiatry, 51,* 8–19.

Kessler, R. C., Olfson, M., & Berglund, P. A. (1998). Patterns and predictors of treatment contact after first onset of psychiatric disorders. *American Journal of Psychiatry, 155,* 62–69.

Key, W. B. (1973). *Subliminal seduction.* Englewood Cliffs, NJ: Prentice-Hall.

Key, W. B. (1976). *Media sexploitation.* Englewood Cliffs, NJ: Prentice-Hall.

Key, W. B. (1980). *The clam-plate orgy and other subliminal techniques for manipulating your behavior.* Englewood Cliffs, NJ: Prentice-Hall.

Keys, D. J., & Schwartz, B. (2007). "Leaky" rationality: How research on behavioral decision making challenges normative standards of rationality. *Perspectives on Psychological Science, 2*(2), 162–180.

Keysers, C., & Gazzola, V. (2006). Towards a unifying theory of social cognition. In S. Aners, G. Ende, M. Junghofer, J. Kissler, & D. Wildgruber (Eds.), *Progress in Brain Research, 156,* 379–401.

Keysers, C., & Perrett, D. I. (2004). Demystifying social cognition: A Hebbian perspective. *Trends in Cognitive Science, 8,* 501–507.

Khashan, A. S., Abel, K. M., McNamee, R., Pedersen, M. G., Webb, R. T., Baker, P. N., et al. (2008). Higher risk of offspring schizophrenia following antenatal maternal exposure to severe adverse life events. *Archives of General Psychiatry, 65,* 146–152.

Kiecolt-Glaser, J. K., & Glaser, R. (1995). Measurement of immune response. In S. Cohen, R. C. Kessler, & L. U. Gordon (Eds.), *Measuring stress: A guide for health and social scientists.* New York: Oxford University Press.

Kiecolt-Glaser, J. K., Garner, W., Speicher, C., Penn, G. M., Holliday, J., & Glaser, R. (1984). Psychosocial modifiers of immunocompetence in medical students. *Psychosomatic Medicine, 46*(1), 7–14.

Kiehl, K. A., & Buckholtz, J. W. (2010). Inside the mind of a psychopath. *Scientific American Mind, 21,* 22–30.

Kielburger, C. (with Kevin Major). (1998). *Free the children: A young man's personal crusade against child labor.* New York: HarperCollins Publishers, Inc.

Kierlin, L. (2008). Sleeping without a pill: Nonpharmacologic treatments for insomnia. *Journal of Psychiatric Practice, 14*(6), 403–407.

Kieseppa, T., Partonen, T., Huakka, J., Kaprio, J., & Lonnqvist, J. (2004). High concordance of bipolar 1 disorder in a nationwide sample of twins. *American Journal of Psychiatry, 161,* 1814–1821.

Kiesler, D. J. (1999). *Beyond the disease model of mental disorders.* New York: Praeger Publishers.

Kihlstrom, J. F. (2001). Dissociative disorders. In P. B. Sutker & H. E. Adams (Eds.), *Comprehensive handbook of psychopathology* (3rd ed., pp. 259–276). New York: Kluwer Academic/Plenum Publishers.

Kihlstrom, J. F. (2004). An unbalanced balancing act: Blocked, recovered, and false memories in the laboratory and clinic. *Clinical Psychology: Science & Practice, 11*(1), 34–41.

Kihlstrom, J. F. (2005a). Dissociative disorders. *Annual Review of Clinical Psychology, 1,* 227–253.

Kihlstrom, J. F. (2005b). Is hypnosis an altered state of consciousness or what? *Contemporary Hypnosis, 22,* 34–38.

Kihlstrom, J. F. (2007). Consciousness in hypnosis. In P. D. Zelazo, M. Moscovitch, & E. Thompson (Eds.), *The Cambridge handbook of consciousness.* New York: Cambridge University Press.

Kihlstrom, J. F., Barnhardt, T. M., & Tataryn, D. J. (1992). Implicit perception. In R. F. Bornstein & T. S. Pittman (Eds.), *Perception without awareness: Cognitive, clinical, and social perspectives.* New York: Guilford.

Kihlstrom, J. F., Glisky, M. L., & Angiulo, M. J. (1994). Dissociative tendencies and dissociative disorders. *Journal of Abnormal Psychology, 103,* 117–124.

Killam Trusts. (2010). *Professor Bialkystok.* Retrieved June 20, 2011, from http://www.killamtrusts.ca/news.asp?ID=37.

Killeen, P. R. (1981). Learning as causal inference. In M. L. Commons & J. A. Nevin (Eds.), *Quantitative analyses of behavior (Vol. 1): Discriminative properties of reinforcement schedules.* Cambridge, MA: Ballinger.

Killen, M., Richardson, C. B., & Kelly, M. C. (2010). Developmental perspectives. In J. F. Dovidio, M. Hewstone, P. Glick, & V. M. Esses (Eds.), *The Sage handbook of prejudice, stereotyping, and discrimination.* Los Angeles, CA: Sage.

Kim, E.-J., & Dimsdale, J. E. (2007). The effect of psychological stress on sleep: A review of polysomnographic evidence. *Behavioral Sleep Medicine, 5,* 256–278.

Kim, H. S., Sherman, D. K., & Taylor, S. E. (2008). Culture and social support. *American Psychologist, 63*(6), 518–526.

Kim, H. S., Sherman, D. K., Ko, D., & Taylor, S. E. (2006). Pursuit of comfort and pursuit of harmony: Culture, relationships, and social support seeking. *Personality and Social Psychology Bulletin, 32*(12), 1595–1607.

Kim, H., & Markus, H. R. (1999). Deviance or uniqueness, harmony or conformity? A cultural analysis. *Journal of Personality and Social Psychology, 77,* 785–800.

Kim, K. H. (2005). Can only intelligent people be creative? *Journal of Secondary Gifted Education, 16,* 57–66.

Kim, K. H., Cramond, B., & VanTassel-Baska, J. (2010). The relationship between creativity and intelligence. In J. C. Kaufman & R. J. Sternberg (Eds.), *The Cambridge handbook of creativity* (pp. 395–412). New York, NY: Cambridge University Press.

Kimura, D. (1973). The asymmetry of the human brain. *Scientific American, 228,* 70–78.

Kimura, D. (1992, September). Sex differences in the brain. *Scientific American,* 119–125.

Kimura, D. (2004). Human sex differences in cognition: Fact not predicament. *Sexualities, Evolution and Gender, 6,* 45–53.

King, A. C., Oman, R. F., Brassington, G. S., Bliwise, D. L., & Haskell, W. L. (1997). Moderate-intensity exercise and self-rated quality of sleep in older adults: A randomized controlled trial. *Journal of the American Medical Association, 277,* 32–37.

King, B. H., Hodapp, R. M., & Dykens, E. M. (2005). Mental retardation. In B. J. Sadock & V. A. Sadock (Eds.), *Kaplan & Sadock's comprehensive textbook of psychiatry* (pp. 3076–3106). Philadelphia: Lippincott, Williams & Wilkins.

King, B. M. (2006). The rise, fall, and resurrection of the ventromedial hypothalamus in the regulation of feeding behavior and body weight. *Physiology & Behavior, 87,* 221–244.

King, C., Knutson, K., Rathouz, P., Sidney, S., Liu, K., & Lauderdale, D. (2008). Short sleep duration and incident coronary artery calcification. *Journal of the American Medical Association, 300*(24), 2859–2866.

King, G. R., & Ellinwood, E. H., Jr. (2005). Amphetamines and other stimulants. In J. H. Lowinson, P. Ruiz, R. B. Millman, & J. G. Langrod (Eds.), *Substance abuse: A comprehensive textbook.* Philadelphia: Lippincott/ Williams & Wilkins.

King, J. W., & Suzman, R. (2009). Prospects for improving cognition throughout the life course. *Psychological Science in the Public Interest, 9,* i–iii.

King, S., St-Hilaire, A., & Heidkamp, D. (2010). Prenatal factors in schizophrenia. *Current Directions in Psychological Science, 19*(4), 209–213.

Kingston, D. A., Malamuth, N. M., Fedoroff, P., & Marshall, W. L. (2009). The importance of individual differences in pornography use: Theoretical perspectives and implications for treating sexual offenders. *Journal of Sex Research, 46*(2–3), 216–232.

Kingstone, A., Smilek, D., & Eastwood, J. D. (2008). Cognitive ethology: A new approach for studying human cognition. *British Journal of Psychology, 99,* 317–340.

Kinsbourne, M. (1997). What qualifies a representation for a role in consciousness? In J. D. Cohen & J. W. Schooler (Eds.), *Scientific approaches to consciousness.* Mahwah, NJ: Erlbaum.

Kinsey, A. C., Pomeroy, W. B., & Martin, C. E. (1948). *Sexual behavior in the human male.* Philadelphia: Saunders.

Kinsey, A. C., Pomeroy, W. B., Martin, C. E., & Gebhard, P. H. (1953). *Sexual behavior in the human female.* Philadelphia: Saunders.

Kirby, S. (2007). The evolution of language. In R. I. M. Dunbar & L. Barrett (Eds.), *Oxford handbook of evolutionary psychology.* New York, NY: Oxford University Press.

Kirkpatrick, L. A. (2005). *Attachment, evolution, and the psychology of religion.* New York: Guilford.

Kirmayer, L. J. (2007). Psychotherapy and the cultural concept of the person. *Transcultural Psychiatry, 44,* 232–257.

Kirmayer, L. J., Brass, G. M., & Tait, C. L. (2000). The mental health of aboriginal peoples: Transformations of identity and community. *Canadian Journal of Psychiatry, 45,* 607–612.

Kirow, G., & Owen, M. J. (2009). Genetics of schizophrenia. In B. J. Sadock, V. A. Sadock, & P. Ruiz (Eds.), *Kaplan & Sadock's comprehensive textbook of psychiatry* (9th ed., Vol. 1, pp. 1462–1472). Philadelphia, PA: Lippincott, Williams & Wilkins.

Kirsch, I. (1997). Response expectancy theory and application: A decennial review. *Applied and Preventive Psychology, 6,* 69–79.

Kirsch, I. (2010). *The emperor's new drugs: Exploding the antidepressant myth.* New York, NY: Basic Books.

Kirsch, I., & Braffman, W. (2001). Imaginative suggestibility and hypnotizability. *Current Directions in Psychological Science, 10*(2), 57–61.

Kirsch, I., & Lynn, S. J. (1998a). Dissociation theories of hypnosis. *Psychological Bulletin, 123,* 100–115.

Kirsch, I., & Lynn, S. J. (1998b). Social-cognitive alternatives to dissociation theories of hypnotic involuntariness. *Review of General Psychology, 2,* 66–80.

Kirsch, I., Mazzoni, G., & Montgomery, G. H. (2007). Remembrance of hypnosis past. *American Journal of Clinical Hypnosis, 49,* 171–178.

Kirsh, G. A., & Kuiper, N. A. (2002). Individualism and relatedness themes in the context of depression, gender, and a self-schema model of emotion. *Canadian Psychology, 43,* 76–91.

Kitayama, S., Mesquita, B., & Karasawa, M. (2006). Cultural affordances and emotional experience: Socially engaging and disengaging emotions in Japan and the United States. *Journal of Personality and Social Psychology, 91,* 890–903.

Kitchens, A. (1991). Left brain/right brain theory: Implications for developmental math instruction. *Review of Research in Developmental Education, 8,* 20–23.

Kitner, C. (2002). Neurogenesis in embryos and adult neural stem cells. *The Journal of Neuroscience, 22,* 639–643.

Kittler, P. G., & Sucher, K. P. (2008). *Food and culture.* Belmont, CA: Wadsworth.

Klahr, D., & Chen, Z. (2011). Finding one's place in transfer space. *Child Development Perspectives.* Retrieved May 30, 2011, from http://onlinelibrary.wiley.com/doi/10.1111/j.1750-8606.2011.00171.x/full.

Klapper, D., Ebling, C., & Temme, J. (2005). Another look at loss aversion in brand choice data: Can we characterize the loss-averse consumer? *International Journal of Research in Marketing, 22,* 239–254.

Klehe, U.-C., & Anderson, N. (2007). The moderating influence of personality and culture on social loafing in typical versus maximum performance situations. *International Journal of Selection and Assessment, 15*, 250–262.

Klein, D. N. (2010). Chronic depression: Diagnosis and classification. *Current Directions in Psychological Science, 19*(2), 96–100.

Klein, M. (1948). *Contributions to psychoanalysis.* London: Hogarth.

Klein, P. D. (1997). Multiplying the problems of intelligence by eight: A critique of Gardner's theory. *Canadian Journal of Education, 22*, 377–394.

Klein, R. M. (1999). The Hebb legacy. *Canadian Journal of Behavioural Science, 53*, 1–20.

Klein, W. M. P., Geaghan, T. R., & MacDonald, T. K. (2007). Unplanned sexual activity as a consequence of alcohol use: A prospective study of risk perceptions and alcohol use among college freshmen. *Journal of American College Health, 56*, 317–323.

Kleinke, C. L. (2007). What does it mean to cope? In A. Monat, R. S. Lazarus, & G. Reevy (Eds.), *The Praeger handbook on stress and coping.* Westport, CT: Praeger.

Kleinke, C. L., Peterson, T. R., & Rutledge, T. R. (1998). Effects of self-generated facial expressions on mood. *Journal of Personality and Social Psychology, 74*, 272–279.

Kleinmuntz, B. (1980). *Essentials of abnormal psychology.* San Francisco: Harper & Row.

Kleinspehn-Ammerlahn, A., Kotter-Grühn, D., & Smith, J. (2008). Self-perceptions of aging: Do subjective age and satisfaction with aging change during old age?. *The Journals of Gerontology: Series B: Psychological Sciences and Social Sciences, 63B*(6), 377–385.

Klerman, E. B. (1993). Deprivation, selective: NREM sleep. In M. A. Carskadon (Ed.), *Encyclopedia of sleep and dreaming.* New York: Macmillan.

Klerman, E. B., & Dijk, D. J. (2008). Age-related reduction in the maximal capacity for sleep-implications for insomnia. *Current Biology, 18*, 1118–1123.

Klerman, G. L., & Weissman, M. M. E. (1993). *New applications of interpersonal therapy.* Washington, DC: American Psychiatric Press.

Kliegel, M., Zimprich, D., & Rott, C. (2004). Life-long intellectual activities mediate the predictive effect of early education on cognitive impairment in centenarians: A retrospective study. *Aging & Mental Health, 8*, 430–437.

Klimsta, T. A., Crocetti, E., Hale III, W. W., Fermani, A., & Meeus, W. H. J. (2011). Big Five personality dimensions in Italian and Dutch adolescents: A cross-cultural comparison of mean-levels, sex differences, and associations with internalizing symptoms. *Journal of Research in Personality, 45*, 285–296.

Kline, P. (1991). *Intelligence: The psychometric view.* New York: Routledge, Chapman, & Hall.

Kline, P. (1995). A critical review of the measurement of personality and intelligence. In D. H. Saklofske & M. Zeidner (Eds.), *International handbook of personality and intelligence.* New York: Plenum.

Klippenstine, J. A., Schuller, R. A., & Wall, A-M. (2007). Perceptions of sexual assault: The expression of gender differences and the impact of target alcohol consumption. *Journal of Applied Psychology, 37*, 2620–2641.

Klosch, G., & Kraft, U. (2005). Sweet dreams are made of this. *Scientific American Mind, 16*(2), 38–45.

Kluft, R. P. (1996). Dissociative identity disorder. In L. K. Michelson & W. J. Ray (Eds.), *Handbook of dissociation: Theoretical, empirical, and clinical perspectives.* New York: Plenum.

Kluft, R. P. (1999). True lies, false truths, and naturalistic raw data: Applying clinical research findings to the false memory debate. In L. M. Williams & V. L. Banyard (Eds.), *Trauma & memory.* Thousand Oaks, CA: Sage Publications.

Klump, K. L., & Culbert, K. M. (2007). Molecular genetic studies of eating disorders: Current status and future directions. *Current Directions in Psychological Science, 16*, 37–41.

Knapp, C. M., & Kornetsky, C. (2009). Neural basis of pleasure and reward. In G. G. Berntson & J. T. Cacioppo (Eds.), *Handbook of neuroscience for the behavioral sciences* (Vol. 1, pp. 781–806). New York, NY: Wiley.

Knight, J. (2004). The truth about lying. *Nature, 428*, 692–694.

Knopik, V. S. (2009). Maternal smoking during pregnancy and child outcomes: Real or spurious effect? *Developmental Neuropsychology, 34*(1), 1–36.

Knowlton, B. J., & Holyoak, K. J. (2009). Prefrontal substrate of human relational reasoning. In M. S. Gazzangia (Ed.), *The cognitive neurosciences* (4th ed., pp. 1005–1018). Cambridge, MA: The MIT Press.

Knutson, K. L., & Van Cauter, E. (2008). Associations between sleep loss and increased risk of obesity and diabetes. In D. W. Pfaff, & B. L. Kieffer (Eds.), *Annals of the New York Academy of Sciences. Molecular and biophysical mechanisms of arousal, alertness, and attention* (pp. 287–304). Malden, MA: Blackwell.

Kobak, R. (1999). The emotional dynamics of disruptions in attachment relationships: Implications for theory, research, and clinical intervention. In J. Cassidy & P. R. Shaver (Eds.), *Handbook of attachment.* New York: Guilford.

Kober, H., & Wager, T. D. (2010). Meta-analysis of neuroimaging data. *Wiley Interdisciplinary Reviews, Cognitive Science, 1*, 293–300.

Koch, C. (2004). *The quest for consciousness: A neurobiological approach.* London: Roberts & Company.

Koch, C., & Greenfield, S. (2007). How does consciousness happen? *Scientific American, 297*, 76–83.

Koch, C., & Tsuchiya, N. (2006). Attention and consciousness: Two distinct brain processes. *Trends in Cognitive Science, 11*, 16–22.

Kodama, S., Saito, K., Tanaka, S., Maki, M., Yachi, Y., Asumi, M., et al. (2009). Cardiorespiratory fitness as a quantitative predictor of all-cause mortality and cardiovascular events in healthy men and women: A meta-analysis. *Journal of the American Medical Association, 301*(19), 2024–2035.

Koehler, J. J. (1996). The base rate fallacy reconsidered: Descriptive, normative, and methodological challenges. *Behavioral Brain Sciences, 19*, 1–53.

Kogan, N. (1990). Personality and aging. In J. E. Birren & K. W. Schaie (Eds.), *Handbook of the psychology of aging.* San Diego: Academic Press.

Kohl, J. V., Atzmueller, M., Fink, B., & Grammer, K. (2003). Human pheromones: Integrating neuroendocrinology and ethology. *Neuroendrocrinology Letters, 22*, 309–321.

Kohlberg, L. (1963). The development of children's orientations toward a moral order: I. Sequence in the development of moral thought. *Vita Humana, 6*, 11–33.

Kohlberg, L. (1969). Stage and sequence: The cognitive-developmental approach to socialization. In D. A. Goslin (Ed.), *Handbook of socialization theory and research.* Chicago: Rand McNally.

Kohlberg, L. (1976). Moral stages and moralization: Cognitive-developmental approach. In T. Lickona (Ed.), *Moral development and behavior: Theory, research and social issues.* New York: Holt, Rinehart & Winston.

Kohlberg, L. (1984). *Essays on moral development (Vol. 2): The psychology of moral development.* San Francisco: Harper & Row.

Kohn, P. M., Lafreniere, K., & Gurevich, M. (1991). Hassles, health, and personality. *Journal of Personality and Social Psychology, 61*, 478–482.

Kohut, H. (1971). *Analysis of the self.* New York: International Universities Press.

Kokkinos, P., Myers, J., Kokkinos, J. P., Pittaras, A., Narayan, P., Manolis, A., et al. (2007). Exercise capacity and mortality in black and white men. *Circulation, 117*, 614–622.

Koksal, F., Domjan, M., Kurt, A., Sertel, O., Orung, S., Bowers, R., & Kumru, G. (2004). An animal model of fetishism. *Behaviour Research and Therapy, 42*(12), 1421–1434.

Kolb, B., & Gibb, B. (2007). Brain plasticity and recovery from early cortical injury. *Developmental Psychobiology, 49*, 107–118.

Kolb, B., & Whishaw, I. Q. (1998). Brain plasticity and behavior. *Annual Review of Psychology, 49*, 43–64.

Kolb, B., Gibb, R., & Robinson, T. E. (2003). Brain plasticity and behavior. *Current Directions in Psychological Science, 12*, 1–5.

Koob, G. F., & Le Moal, M. (2006). *Neurobiology of addiction.* San Diego: Academic Press.

Koob, G. F., Everitt, B. J., & Robbins, T. W. (2008). Reward, motivation, and addiction. In L. Squire, D. Berg, F. Bloom, S. Du Lac, A. Ghosh, N. Spitzer (Eds.), *Fundamental neuroscience* (3rd ed., pp. 87–111). San Diego, CA: Elsevier.

Koocher, G. P. (2007). Twenty-first-century ethical challenges for psychology. *American Psychologist, 62*, 375–384.

Koordeman, R., Anschutz, D. J., van Baaren, R. B., & Engels, R. E. (2010). Exposure to soda commercials affects sugar-sweetened soda consumption in young women. An observational experimental study. *Appetite, 54*, 619–622.

Kop, W. J., Gottdiener, J. S., & Krantz, D. S. (2001). Stress and silent ischemia. In A. Baum, T. A. Revenson & J. E. Singer (Eds.), *Handbook of health psychology* (pp. 669–682). Mahwah, NJ: Erlbaum.

Kop, W. J., Weissman, N. J., Zhu, J., Bonsall, R. W., Doyle, M., Stretch, M. R., et al. (2008). Effect of acute mental stress and exercise on inflammatory markers in patients with coronary artery disease and healthy controls. *American Journal of Cardiology, 101*, 767–773.

Koren, D., Arnon, I., & Klein, E. (1999). Acute stress response and posttraumatic stress disorder in traffic accident victims: A one-year prospective, follow-up study. *American Journal of Psychiatry, 156*, 367–373.

Koriat, A., & Bjork, R. A. (2005). Illusions of competence in monitoring one's knowledge during study. *Journal of Experimental Psychology: Learning, Memory, and Cognition, 31*(2), 187–194.

Koriat, A., & Melkman, R. (1987). Depth of processing and memory organization. *Psychological Research, 49*, 183–188.

Koriat, A., Goldsmith, M., & Pansky, A. (2000). Toward a psychology of memory accuracy. *Annual Review of Psychology, 51*, 481–537.

Koriat, A., Lichtenstein, S., & Fischhoff, B. (1980). Reasons for confidence. *Journal of Experimental Psychology, 6*, 107–118.

Korman, A. K., Greenhaus, J. H., Badin, I. J. (1977). Personnel attitudes and motivation. *Annual Review of Psychology, 28*, 175–196.

Korn, J. H. (1997). *Illusions of reality: A history of deception in social psychology*. Albany: State University of New York Press.

Korn, J. H., Davis, R., & Davis, S. F. (1991). Historians' and chairpersons' judgements of eminence among psychologists. *American Psychologist, 46*, 789–792.

Kornell, N., Castel, A. D., Eich, T. S., & Bjork, R. A. (2010). Spacing as the friend of both memory and induction in young and older adults. *Psychology and Aging, 25*(2), 498–503.

Kornell, N., Hays, M., & Bjork, R. A. (2009). Unsuccessful retrieval attempts enhance subsequent learning. *Journal of Experimental Psychology: Learning, Memory, and Cognition, 35*(4), 989–998.

Kornhaber, M. L. (2004). Multiple intelligences: From the ivory tower to the dusty classroom—But why? *Teachers College Record, 106*(1), 57–76.

Kosfeld, M., Heinrichs, M., Zak, P. J., Fischbacher, U., & Fehr, E. (2005). Oxytocin increases trust in humans. *Nature, 435*(7042), 673–676.

Koss, M. P. (1993). Rape: Scope, impact, interventions, and public policy responses. *American Psychologist, 48*, 1062–1069.

Koss, M. P., Gidycz, C. A., & Wisniewski, N. (1987). The scope of rape: Incidence and prevalence of sexual aggression and victimization in a national sample of higher education students. *Journal of Consulting and Clinical Psychology, 55*(2), 162–170.

Kostreva, M., McNelis, E., & Clemens, E. (2002). Using a circadian rhythms model to evaluate shift schedules. *Ergonomics, 45*, 739–763.

Kotovsky, K., Hayes, J. R., & Simon, H. A. (1985). Why are some problems hard? Evidence from Tower of Hanoi. *Cognitive Psychology, 17*, 248–294.

Kotter-Grühn, D., Kleinspehn-Ammerlahn, A., Gerstorf, D., & Smith, J. (2009). Self-perceptions of aging predict mortality and change with approaching death: 16-year longitudinal results from the Berlin Aging Study. *Psychology and Aging, 24*(3), 654–667.

Kotulak, R. (1996). *Inside the brain: Revolutionary discoveries of how the mind works*. Kansas City, MO: Andrews McMeel.

Koukounas, E., & McCabe, M. (1997). Sexual and emotional variables influencing sexual response to erotica. *Behaviour Research and Therpy, 35*, 221–230.

Kovelman, I., Shalinsky, M. H., Berens, M. S., & Petitto, L. A. (2008). Shining light on the brain's "bilingual signature": A functional near infrared spectroscopy investigation of semantic processing. *Neuroimage, 39*, 1457–1471.

Kozorovitskiy, Y., & Gould, E. (2007). Adult neurogenesis and regeneration in the brain. In Y. Sern (Ed.), *Cognitive reserve: Theory and applications*. Philadelphia: Taylor and Francis.

Kozulin, A. (2005). The concept of activity in Soviet psychology: Vygotsky, his disciples and critics. In H. Daniels (Ed.), *An introduction to Vygotsky*. New York, NY: Routledge.

Kracke, W. (1991). Myths in dreams, thought in images: An Amazonian contribution to the psychoanalytic theory of primary process. In B. Tedlock (Ed.), *Dreaming: Anthropological and psychological interpretations*. Santa Fe, NM: School of American Research Press.

Kraemer, H. C. (2008). DSM categories and dimensions in clinical and research contexts. In J. E. Helzer, H. C. Kraemer, R. F. Krueger, H.–U. Wittchen, P. J. Sirovatka, et al. (Eds.), *Dimensional approaches in diagnostic classification: Refining the research agenda for DSM-V* (pp. 5–17). Washington, DC: American Psychiatric Association.

Kramer, A. F., & Erickson, K. I. (2007). Capitalizing on cortical plasticity: Influence of physical activity on cognition and brain function. *Trends in Cognitive Sciences, 11*, 342–348.

Kramer, M. (1994). The scientific study of dreaming. In M. H. Kryger, T. Roth, & W. C. Dement (Eds.), *Principles and practice of sleep medicine* (2nd ed.). Philadelphia: Saunders.

Krebs, D. L., & Denton, K. (1997). Social illusions and self-deception: The evolution of biases in person perception. In J. A. Simpson & D. T. Kenrick (Eds.), *Evolutionary social psychology*. Mahwah, NJ: Erlbaum.

Kremen, W. S., Jacobsen, K. C., Xian, H., Eisen, S. A., Eaves, L. J., Tsuang, M. T., & Lyons, M. J. (2007). Genetics of verbal working memory processes: A twin study of middle-aged men. *Neuropsychology, 21*(5), 569–580.

Krendl, A. C., Macrae, C. N., Kelley, W. M., Fugelsang, J. A., & Hetherington, T. F. (2006). The good, the bad, and the ugly: An fMRI investigation of the functional anatomical correlates of stigma. *Social Neuroscience, 1*, 5–15.

Kreppner, J. M., Rutter, M., Beckett, C., Castle, J., Colvert, E., Groothues, C., et al. (2007). Normality and impairment following profound early institutional deprivation: A longitudinal follow-up into early adolescence. *Developmental Psychology, 43*, 931–946.

Kreutzer, J. S., Seel, R. T., & Gourley, E. (2001). The prevalence and symptom rates of depression after traumatic brain injury: a comprehensive examination. *Brain Injury, 15*(7), 563–576.

Kriegsfeld, L. J., & Nelson, R. J. (2009). Biological rhythms. In G. G. Berntson & J. T. Cacioppo (Eds.), *Handbook of neuroscience for the behavioral sciences* (Vol. 1, pp. 56–81). New York, NY: Wiley.

Kring, A. M. (1999). Emotion in schizophrenia: Old mystery, new understanding. *Current Directions in Psychological Science, 8*, 160–163.

Krizan, Z., Miller, J. C., & Johar, O. (2010). Wishful thinking in the 2008 U.S. presidential election. *Psychological Science, 21*(1), 140–146.

Kroger, J. (2003). Identity development during adolescence. In G. R. Adams & M. D. Berzonsky (Eds.), *Blackwell handbook of adolescence*. Malden, MA: Blackwell Publishing.

Krojgaard, P. (2005). Continuity and discontinuity in developmental psychology. *Psyke & Logos, 26*(2), 377–394.

Kroker, Kenton. (2007, July 21). The sleep of others. *New Scientist*, 2613.

Kroll, J. (2008). Juggling two languages in one mind. *APA Online Psychological Science Agenda, 22*. Retrieved January 24, 2008, from http://www.apa.org/science/psa/kroll_prnt.html.

Kroll, J., Bobb, S., & Wodniecka, Z. (2006). Language selectivity is the exception, not the rule: Arguments against a fixed locus of language selection in bilingual speech. *Bilingualism: Language and Cognition, 9*, 119–135.

Krosnick, J. A. (1999). Survey research. *Annual Review Psychology, 50*, 537–567.

Krosnick, J. A., & Fabrigar, L. R. (1998). *Designing good questionnaires: Insights from psychology*. New York: Oxford University Press.

Krosnick, J. A., & Petty, R. E. (1995). Attitude strength: An overview. In R. E. Petty & J. A. Krosnick (Eds.), *Attitude strength: Antecedents and consequences*. Mahwah, NJ: Erlbaum.

Krueger, J. (1996). Personal beliefs and cultural stereotypes about racial characteristics. *Journal of Personality and Social Psychology, 71*, 536–548.

Krueger, J., Ham, J. J., & Linford, K. M. (1996). Perceptions of behavioral consistency: Are people aware of the actor–observer effect? *Psychological Science, 7*, 259–264.

Krueger, K. R., Wilson, R. S., Kamenetsky, J. M., Barnes, L. L., Bienias, J. L., & Bennett, D. A. (2009). Social engagement and cognitive function in old age. *Experimental Aging Research, 35*(1), 45–60.

Krueger, R. F. (2005). Continuity of axes I and II: Toward a unified model of personality, personality disorders, and clinical disorders. *Journal of Personality Disorders, 19*, 233–261.

Krueger, R. F., & Johnson, W. (2008). Behavioral genetics and personality: A new look at the integration of nature and nurture. In O. P. John, R. W. Robbins, & L. A. Pervin (Eds.), *Handbook of personality: Theory and research* (Vol. 3, pp. 287–310). New York, NY: Guilford Press.

Krueger, W. C. F. (1929). The effect of overlearning on retention. *Journal of Experimental Psychology, 12*, 71–78.

Kruglanski, A. W., & Orehek, E. (2007). Partitioning the domain of social inference: Dual mode and systems. *Annual Review of Psychology, 58*, 241–316.

Kruglanski, A. W., & Stroebe, W. (2005). The influence of beliefs and goals on attitudes: Issues of structure, function, and dynamics. In D. Albarracin, B. T. Johnson, & M. P. Zanna (Eds.), *The handbook of attitudes*. Mahwah, NJ: Erlbaum.

Krull, D. S. (2001). On partitioning the fundamental attribution error: Dispositionalism and the correspondence bias. In G. B. Moskowitz (Ed.), *Cognitive social psychology: The Princeton Symposium on the legacy and future of social cognition*. Mahwah, NJ: Erlbaum.

Krull, D. S., & Erickson, D. J. (1995). Inferential hopscotch: How people draw social inferences from behavior. *Current Directions in Psychological Science, 4*, 35–38.

Kryger, M. H. (1993). Snoring. In M. A. Carskadon (Ed.), *Encyclopedia of sleep and dreaming*. New York: Macmillan.

Kryger, M. H., Roth, T., & Dement, W. C. (2005). *Principles and practice of sleep medicine*. Philadelphia: Elsevier Saunders.

Kubovy, M., Epstein, W., & Gepshtein, S. (2003). Foundations of visual perception. In A. F. Healy & R. W. Proctor (Eds.), *Handbook of psychology*. New York: Wiley.

Kudielka, B. M., & Kirschbaum, C. (2005). Sex differences in HPA axis responses to stress: A review. *Biological Pschology, 69*, 113–132.

Kuehn, B. M. (2007). Scientists probe deep brain stimulation: Some promise for brain injury, psychiatric illness. *Journal of the American Medical Association, 298*, 2249–2251.

Kuepper, R., Morrison, P. D., van Os, J., Murray, R. M., Kenis, G., & Henquet, C. (2010). Does dopamine mediate the psychosis-inducing effects of cannabis? A review and integration of findings across disciplines. *Schizophrenia Research, 121*(1–3), 107–117.

Kuepper, R., van Os, J., Lieb, R., Wittchen, H., Höfler, M., & Henquet, C. (2011). Continued cannabis use and risk of incidence and persistence of psychotic symptoms: 10 year follow-up cohort study. *British Medical Journal, 342*(7796). Retrieved from http://www.bmj.com/content/342/bmj.d738.full

Kuhl, B. A., Dudukovic, N. M., Kahn, I., & Wagner, A. D. (2007). Decreased demands on cognitive control reveal the neural processing benefits of forgetting. *Nature Neuroscience, 10,* 908–914.

Kuhl, P. K., Conboy, B. T., Coffey-Corina, S., Padden, D., Rivera-Gaxiola, M., & Nelson, T. (2008). Phonetic learning as a pathway to language: New data and native language magnet theory expanded (NLM-e). *Philosophical Transactions of the Royal Society of London, B, 363,* 979–1000.

Kuhlmeier, V. A., Bloom, P. A., & Wynn, K. (2004). Do 5-month-old infants see humans as material objects? *Cognition, 94,* 95–103.

Kuhn, D. (2006). Do cognitive changes accompany developments in the adolescent brain? *Perspectives on Psychological Science, 1*(1), 59–67.

Kuhn, H. W., & Nasar, S. (2002). *The essential John Nash*. Princeton NJ: Princeton University Press.

Kuiper, N. A., & Derry, P. (1981). The self as a cognitive prototype: An application to person perception and depression. In N. Cantor & J. F. Kihlstrom (Eds.), *Personality, cognition, and social interaction* (pp. 215–232). Hillsdale, NJ: Erlbaum.

Kuiper, N. A., & Rogers, T. B. (1979). Encoding of personal information: Self-other differences. *Journal of Personality and Social Psychology, 37,* 499–514.

Kulick, A. R., Pope, H. G., & Keck, P. E. (1990). Lycanthropy and self-identification. *Journal of Nervous & Mental Disease, 178*(2), 134–137.

Kuo, Y. T., Parkinson, J. R. C., Chaudhri, O. B., Herlihy, A. H., So, P. W., Dhillo, W. S., et al. (2007). The temporal sequence of gut peptide-CNS interactions tracked in vivo by magnetic resonance imaging. *Journal of Neuroscience, 27,* 12341–12348.

Kupfermann, I., Kandel, E. R., & Iversen, S. (2000). Motivational and addictive states. In E. R. Kandel, J. H. Schwartz, & T. M. Jessell (Eds.), *Principles of neural science*. New York: McGraw-Hill.

Kurtz, K. J., & Loewenstein, J. (2007). Converging on a new role for analogy in problem solving and retrieval: When two problems are better than one. *Memory & Cognition, 35,* 334–342.

Kurtz, M. M., & Mueser, K. T. (2008). A meta-analysis of controlled research on social skills training for schizophrenia. *Journal of Consulting and Clinical Psychology, 76*(3), 491–504.

Kutas, M., & Federmeier, K. D. (2011). Thirty years and counting: Finding meaning in the N400 component and event-related brain potential. *Annual Review of Psychology,* 621–665.

Kutchins, H., & Kirk, S. A. (1997). *Making us crazy: DSM—The psychiatric Bible and the creation of mental disorders.* New York: Free Press.

Kyle, S. D., Morgan, K., & Espie, C. A. (2010). Insomnia and health-related quality of life. *Sleep Medicine Reviews, 14*(1), 69–82.

La Bar, K. S., Gatenby, J. C., Gore, J. C., Le Doux, J. E., & Phelps, E. A. (1998). Human amygdala activation during conditioned fear acquisition and extinction: A mixed-trial fMRI study. *Neuron, 20,* 937–945.

La Cerra, P., & Kurzban, R. (1995). The structure of scientific revolutions and the nature of the adapted mind. *Psychological Inquiry, 6,* 62–65.

La Torre, M. A. (2007). Integrative perspectives. Positive psychology: Is there too much of a push? *Perspectives in Psychiatric Care, 43*(3), 151–153.

LaBerge, S. (1990). Lucid dreaming: Psychophysiological studies of consciousness during REM sleep. In R. R. Bootzin, J. F. Kihlstrom, & D. L. Schacter (Eds.), *Sleep and cognition.* Washington, DC: American Psychological Association.

LaBerge, S. (2007). Lucid dreaming. In D. Barrett & P. McNamara (Eds.), *The new science of dreaming: Content, recall, and personality correlates.* Westport, CT: Praeger.

LaBine, S. J., & LaBine, G. (1996). Determinations of negligence and the hindsight bias. *Law & Human Behavior, 20,* 501–516.

Labouvie-Vief, G. (2006). Emerging structures of adult thought. In J. J. Arnett & J. L. Tanner (Eds.), *Emerging adults in America: Coming of age in the 21st century.* Washington, DC: American Psychological Association.

Lacey, K., Zaharian, M. D., Griffiths, J., Ravindran, A. V., Merali, Z., & Anisman, H. (2000). A prospective study of neuroendocrine and immune alterations associated with the stress of an oral academic examination among graduate students. *Psychoneuroendocrinology, 25,* 339–356.

Lachman, S. J. (1996). Processes in perception: Psychological transformations of highly structured stimulus material. *Perceptual and Motor Skills, 83,* 411–418.

Lachter, J., Forster, K. I., & Ruthruff, E. (2004). Forty-five years after Broadbent (1958): Still no identification without attention. *Psychological Review, 111,* 880–913.

Lader, M. H. (2002). Managing dependence and withdrawal with newer hypnotic medications in the treatment of insomnia. *Journal of Clinical Psychiatry, 4*(suppl. 1), 33–37.

LaFee, S. (2009, November 30). H. M. recollected. *Sign On San Diego.* Retrieved December 3, 2009, from http://www.signonsandiego.com/news/2009/nov/30/hm-recollected-famous-amnesic-launches-bold-new-br/

Lagopoulos, J., Xu, J., Rasmussen, I., Vik, A., Malhi, G., Eliassen, C. F., et al. (2009). Increased theta and alpha EEG activity during nondirective meditation. *The Journal of Alternative and Complementary Medicine, 15*(11), 1187–1192.

Lahey, B. B. (2009). Public health significance of neuroticism. *American Psychologist, 64*(4), 241–256.

Laitinen, J., Ek, E., & Sovio, U. (2002). Stress-related eating and drinking behavior and body mass index and predictors of this behavior. *Preventive Medicine: An International Journal Devoted to Practice & Theory, 34,* 29–39.

Lakein, A. (1996). *How to get control of your time and your life.* New York: New American Library.

Lakey, B., & Cronin, A. (2008). Low social support and major depression: Research, theory and methodological issues. In K. S. Dobson & D. A. Dozois (Eds.), *Risk factors in depression* (pp. 385–408). San Diego, CA: Academic Press.

Lalonde, C. E. (2006). Identity formation and cultural resilience in Aboriginal communities. In Flynn, R. J., Dudding, P., & Barber, J. (Eds.), *Promoting resilience in child welfare* (pp. 52–71). Ottawa: University of Ottawa Press.

Lalonde, C. E., & Chandler, M. J. (2002). Children's understanding of interpretation. *New Ideas in Psychology: Special Issue on Folk Epistemology, 20,* 163–198.

Lalonde, C. E. (2005). *Creating an index of healthy Aboriginal communities. Developing a healthy communities index: A collection of papers,* (pp. 21–27). Report prepared for the Canadian Population Health Initiative, Canadian Institute for Health Information

Lalonde, R. N., & Gardner, R. C. (1984). Investigating a causal model of second language acquisition: Where does personality fit in? *Canadian Journal of Behavioural Science, 16,* 224–237.

Lalonde, R. N., & Gardner, R. C. (1989). An intergroup perspective on stereotype organization and processing. *British Journal of Social Psychology, 28,* 289–303.

Lalonde, R. N., & Gardner, R. C. (1993). Statistics as a second language? A model for predicting performance in psychology students. *Canadian Journal of Behavioural Science, 25,* 108–125.

Lalonde, R. N., Hynie, M., Pannu, M., & Tatla, S. (2004). The role of culture in interpersonal relationships: Do second generation South Asian Canadians want a traditional partner? *Journal of Cross-Cultural Psychology, 35,* 503–524.

Lalonde, R. N., Jones, J. M., & Stroink, M. L. (2008). Racial identity, racial attitudes, and race socialization among black Canadian parents. *Canadian Journal of Behavioural Science, 40,* 129–139.

Lamb, H. R. (1998). Deinstitutionalization at the beginning of the new millenium. *Harvard Review of Psychiatry, 6,* 1–10.

Lamb, M. E. (1998). Nonparental child care: context, quality, correlates, and consequences. In W. Damon (Ed.), *Handbook of child psychology (Vol. 4): Child psychology in practice.* New York: Wiley.

Lamb, M. E., & Lewis, C. (2011). The role of parent–child relationships in child development. In M. H. Bornstein & M. E. Lamb (Eds.), *Developmental science: An advanced textbook* (pp. 469–518). New York, NY: Psychology Press.

Lamb, M. E., Hwang, C. P., Ketterlinus, R. D., & Fracasso, M. P. (1999). Parent–child relationships: Development in the context of the family. In M. H. Bornstein & M. E. Lamb (Eds.), *Developmental psychology and advanced textbook.* Mahwah, NJ: Erlbaum.

Lambert, C. (2006). The Marof perceptions. *Harvard Magazine.* Retrieved June 20, 2011, from http://harvardmagazine.com/2006/03/the-marketplace-of-perce.html.

Lambert, M. J. (2011). Psychotherapy research and its achievements. In J. C. Norcross, G. R. Vandenbos, & D. K. Freedheim (Eds.), *History of psychotherapy: Continuity and change* (2nd ed.). Washington, DC: American Psychological Association.

Lambert, M. J., & Ogles, B. M. (2004). The efficacy and effectiveness of psychotherapy. In M. J. Lambert (Ed.), *Bergin and Garfield's handbook of psychotherapy and behavior change.* New York: Wiley.

Lambert, M. J., Bergin, A. E., & Garfield, S. L. (2004). Introduction and historical overview. In M. J. Lambert (Ed.), *Bergin and Garfield's handbook of psychotherapy and behavior change.* New York: Wiley.

Lambert, M. J., Hansen, N. B., & Finch, A. E. (2001). Patient-focused research: Using patient outcome data to enhance treatment effects. *Journal of Consulting and Clinical Psychology, 69,* 159–172.

Lambert, W. E. (1967). A social psychology of bilingualism. *Journal of Social Issues, 23,* 91–109.

Lambert, W. E. (1990). Persistent issues in bilingualism. In B. Harley, P. Allen, J. Cummins, & M. Swain (Eds.), *The development of second language proficiency.* Cambridge, England: Cambridge University Press.

Lambert, W. E., & Tucker, G. R. (1969). *Bilingual education in Canada: The St. Lambert experiment.* Rowley, MA: Newbury House.

Lampe, A., Soellner, W., Krismer, M., Rumpold, G., Kantner-Rumplmair, W., Ogon, M., & Rathner, G. (1998). The impact of stressful life events on exacerbation of chronic low-back pain. *Journal of Psychosomatic Research, 44,* 555–563.

Lampert, R., Shusterman, V., Burg, M., McPherson, C., Batsford, W., Goldberg, A., & Soufer, R. (2009). Anger-induced T-wave alternans predicts future ventricular arrhythmias in patients with implantable cardioverter-defibrillators. *Journal of the American College of Cardiology, 53*(9), 774–778.

Lampinen, J. M., Neuschatz, J. S., & Payne, D. G. (1999). Source attributions and false memories: A test of the demand characteristics account. *Psychonomic Bulletin & Review, 6,* 130–135.

Landabaso, M. A., Iraurgi, I., Sanz, J., Calle, R., Ruiz de Apodaka, J., Jimenez-Lerma, J. M., & Gutierrez-Fraile, M. (1999). Naltrexone in the treatment of alcoholism. Two-year follow up results. *European Journal of Psychiatry, 13,* 97–105.

Landel-Graham, J., Yount, S. E., & Rudnicki, S. R. (2003). Diabetes mellitus. In A. M. Nezu, C. M. Nezu, & P. A. Geller (Eds.). *Handbook of psychology (Vol. 9): Health psychology.* New York: Wiley.

Laney, C., & Loftus, E. F. (2005). Traumatic memories are not necessarily accurate memories. *Canadian Journal of Psychiatry, 50,* 823–828.

Langdon, P. E., Yagueez, L., Brown, J., & Hope, A. (2001). Who walks through the "revolving door" of a British psychiatric hospital? *Journal of Mental Health (UK), 10,* 525–533.

Lange, C. (1885). One leuds beveegelser. In K. Dunlap (Ed.), *The emotions.* Baltimore: Williams & Wilkins.

Lange, N., Froimowitz, M. P, Bigler, E. D., & Lainhart, & J. E. (2010). Associations between IQ, total and regional brain volumes, and demography in a large normative sample of healthy children and adolescents. *Developmental Neuropsychology, 35,* 296–317.

Langevin, R., & Curnoe, S. (2004). The use of pornography during the commission of sexual offenses. *International Journal of Offender Therapy & Comparative Criminology, 48,* 572–586.

Langlois, J. H., Kalakanis, L., Rubenstein, A. J., Larson, A., Hallam, M., & Smoot, M. (2000). Maxims or myths of beauty? A meta-analytic and theoretical review. *Psychological Bulletin, 126,* 390–423.

Langlois, S., & Morrison, P. (2002). Suicide deaths and suicide attempts. *Health Reports, 13*(2), 9–23. Statistics Canada, Catalogue 82-003,2 http://www.statcan.ca/english/studies/82-003/feature/hrar2002013002s0a01.pdf.

Lanyon, R. I., & Goodstein, L. D. (1997). *Personality assessment.* New York: Wiley.

LaPiere, R. T. (1934). Attitude and actions. *Social Forces, 13,* 230–237.

Lapierre, Y. D. (2003). Suicidality with selective serotonin reuptake inhibitors: Valid claim? *Journal of Psychiatry & Neuroscience, 28,* 340–347.

Lapsley, D. K. (2006). Moral stage theory. In M. Killen & J. G. Smetana (Eds.), *Handbook of moral development.* Mahwah, NJ: Erlbaum.

Larsen, D. P., Butler, A. C., & Roediger, H. L. III. (2009). Repeated testing improves long-term retention relative to repeated study: A randomised controlled trial. *Medical Education, 43*(12), 1174–1181.

Larsen, J. T., Berntson, G. G., Poehlmann, K. M., Ito, T. A., & Cacioppo, J. T. (2008). The psychophysiology of emotion. In M. Lewis, J. M. Haviland-Jones, & L. F. Barrett (Eds.), *Handbook of emotions* (3rd ed., pp. 180–195). New York, NY: Guilford Press.

Larsen, R. J., & Prizmic, Z. (2008). Regulation of emotional well-being: Overcoming the hedonic tredmill. In M. Eid & R. J. Larsen (Eds.), *The science of subjective well-being* (pp. 258–289). New York: Guilford.

Larson, R., & Wilson, S. (2004). Adolescence across place and time: Globalization and the changing pathways to adulthood. In R. M. Lerner & L. Steinberg (Eds.), *Handbook of adolescent psychology.* New York: Wiley.

Larson, R., Richards, M., Moneta, G., Holmbeck, G., & Duckett, E. (1996). Changes in adolescents' daily interactions with their families from ages 10 to 18: Disengagement and transformation. *Developmental Psychology, 32,* 744–754.

Larzelere, R. E., Schneider, W. N., Larson, D. B., & Pike, P. L. (1996). The effects of discipline responses in delaying toddler misbehavior recurrences. *Child and Family Behavior Therapy, 18,* 35–37.

Lash, T. L., & Aschengrau, A. (1999). Active and passive cigarette smoking and the occurrence of breast cancer. *American Journal of Epidemiology, 149,* 5–12.

Laska, M., Seibt, A., & Weber, A. (2000). "Microsmatic" primates revisited: Olfactory sensitivity in the squirrel monkey. *Chemical Senses, 25,* 47–53.

Lassonde, M. C., Sauerwein, H. C., & Lepore, F. (2003). A genesis of the corpus callosum. In E. Zaidel & M. Iacoboni (Eds.), *The parallel brain: The cognitive neuroscience of the corpus callosum* (pp. 357–369). Cambridge, MA: MIT Press.

Lassonde, M., & Quimet, C. (2010). The split-brain. *Cognitive Science, 1,* 191–201.

Latané, B. (1981). The psychology of social impact. *American Psychologist, 36,* 343–356.

Latané, B., & Darley, J. M. (1970). *The unresponsive bystander: Why doesn't he help?* New York: Appleton-Century-Crofts.

Latané, B., & Nida, S. A. (1981). Ten years of research on group size and helping. *Psychological Bulletin, 89,* 308–324.

Latané, B., Williams, K., & Harkins, S. (1979). Many hands make light the work: The causes and consequences of social loafing. *Journal of Personality and Social Psychology, 37,* 822–832.

Latham, G. P., & Pinder, C. C. (2005). Work motivation theory and research at the dawn of the twenty-first century. *Annual Review of Psychology, 56,* 485–516.

Lattal, K. A. (1992). B. F. Skinner and psychology [Introduction to the Special Issue]. *American Psychologist, 27,* 1269–1272.

Lattimore, P., & Caswell, N. (2004). Differential effects of active and passive stress on food intake in restrained and unrestrained eaters. *Appetite, 42,* 167–173.

Lattin, D. (2010). *The Harvard psychedelic club.* New York, NY: Harper Collins Publishers.

Latz, S., Wolf, A. W., & Lozoff, B. (1999). Cosleeping in context: Sleep practices and problems in young children in Japan and United States. *Archives of Pediatrics & Adolescent Medicine, 153,* 339–346.

Laughlin, H. (1979). *The ego and its defenses.* New York: Aronson.

Laumann, E. O., Gagnon, J. H., Michael, R. T., & Michaels, S. (1994). *The social organization of sexuality: Sexual practices in the United States.* Chicago: University of Chicago Press.

Lauriello, J., Bustillo, J. R., & Keith, J. (2005). Schizophrenia: Scope of the problem. In B. J. Sadock et al., (Eds.), *Kaplan & Sadocks comprehensive textbook of psychiatry.* Philadelphia: Lippincott, Williams & Wilkins.

Laursen, B., Coy, K. C., & Collins, W. A. (1998). Reconsidering changes in parent–child conflict across adolescence: A meta-analysis. *Child Development, 69,* 817–832.

Lavie, N. (2005). Distracted and confused? Selective attention under load. *Trends in Cognitive Sciences, 9*(2), 75–82.

Lavie, N. (2007). Attention and consciousness. In M. Velmans & S. Schneider (Eds.), *The Blackwell companion to consciousness* (pp. 489–503). Malden, MA: Blackwell Publishing.

Lavie, P. (2001). Sleep–wake as a biological rhythm. *Annual Review of Psychology, 52,* 277–303.

Lavine, H., Sweeney, D., & Wagner, S. H. (1999). Depicting women as sex objects in television advertising: Effects on body dissatisfaction. *Personality and Social Psychology Bulletin, 25,* 1049–1058.

Lavoie, K. L., & Fleet, R. P. (2002). Should psychologists be granted prescription privileges? A review of the prescription privilege debate for psychiatrists. *Canadian Journal of Psychiatry,* 443–449.

Lawless, H. T. (2001). Taste. In E. B. Goldstein (Ed.), *Blackwell handbook of perception.* Malden, MA: Blackwell.

Laws, K. R., & Kokkalis, J. (2007). Ecstasy (MDMA) and memory function: A meta-analytic update. *Human Psychopharmacology: Clinical & Experimental, 22*(6), 381–388.

Lawson, H. (2005, March 19). Dying for a drink. *The Globe and Mail,* F4.

Lazarus, A. A. (1989). Multimodal therapy. In R. J. Corsini & D. Wedding (Eds.), *Current Psychotherapies.* Itasca, IL: F. E. Peacock.

Lazarus, A. A. (1992). Multimodal therapy: Technical eclecticism with minimal integration. In J. C. Norcross & M. R. Goldfried (Eds.), *Handbook of psychotherapy integration.* New York: Basic Books.

Lazarus, A. A. (1995). Different types of eclecticism and integration: Let's be aware of the dangers. *Journal of Psychotherapy Integration, 5,* 27–39.

Lazarus, R. S. (1993). Why we should think of stress as a subset of emotion. In L. Goldberger & S. Breznitz (Eds.), *Handbook of stress: Theoretical and clinical aspects* (2nd ed.). New York: Free Press.

Lazarus, R. S. (1995). Vexing research problems inherent in cognitive-mediational theories of emotion—and some solutions. *Psychological Inquiry, 6,* 183–196.

Lazarus, R. S. (2003). Does the positive psychology movement have legs? *Psychological Inquiry, 14*(2), 93–109.

Lazarus, R., & Folkman, S. (1984). *Stress, appraisal, and coping.* New York, NY: Springer.

Le Petit, C., & Berthelot, J.-M. (2005). *Obesity: A growing issue.* Statistics Canada. Retrieved May 9, 2005, from http://www.statcan.ca/english/research/82-168-MIE/168.

Leacock, S. (1939). *Too much college; or, Education eating up life: with kindred essays in education and humour.* New York: Dodd, Mead & Company.

Leahey, T. H. (1992). The mythical revolutions of American psychology. *American Psychologist, 47*, 308–318.

Leahey, T. H. (2003). Herbert A. Simon: Nobel prize in economic sciences, 1978. *American Psychologist, 58*, 753–755.

Leary, T. (1957). *Interpersonal diagnosis of personality.* New York: Ronald Press.

Leavitt, F. (1995). *Drugs and behavior* (3rd ed.). Thousand Oaks, CA: Sage.

Leavitt, F. (2001). Iatrogenic recovered memories: Examining the empirical evidence. *American Journal of Forensic Psychology, 19*(2), 21–32.

Lebel, C., et al. (2010). Brain microstructure is related to math ability in children with fetal alcohol spectrum disorder. *Alcoholism: Clinical and Experimental Research, 34*, 354–363.

LeBoeuf, M. (1980, February). Managing time means managing yourself. *Business Horizons*, 41–46.

LeBoeuf, R. A., & Shafir, E. B. (2005). Decision making. In K. J. Holyoak & R. G. Morrison (Eds.), *The Cambridge handbook of thinking and reasoning.* New York: Cambridge University Press.

Lebow, J. L. (2008). Couple and family therapy. In J. L. Lebow (Ed.), *Twenty-first century psychotherapies: Contemporary approaches to theory and practice* (pp. 307–346). New York, NY: Wiley.

Ledbetter, A. M., Griffin, E., & Sparks, G. G. (2007). Forecasting "friends forever": A longitudinal investigation of sustained closeness between best friends. *Personal Relationships, 14*(2), 343–350.

Lederman, S. J., Klatzky, R. L., Abramowicz, A., Salsman, K., Kitada, R., & Hamilton, C. (2007). Haptic recognition of static and dynamic expressions of emotions in the live face. *Psychological Science, 18*, 158–164.

LeDoux, J. E. (1994). Emotion, memory and the brain. *Scientific American, 270*, 50–57.

LeDoux, J. E. (1995). Emotion: Clues from the brain. *Annual Review of Psychology, 46*, 209–235.

LeDoux, J. E. (1996). *The emotional brain.* New York: Simon & Schuster.

LeDoux, J. E. (2000). Emotion circuits in the brain. *Annual Review of Neuroscience, 23*, 155–184.

LeDoux, J. E., & Phelps, E. A. (2008). Emotional networks in the brain. In M. Lewis, J. M. Haviland-Jones, & L. F. Barrett, *Handbook of emotions* (3rd ed.). New York, NY: Guilford Press.

LeDoux, J. E., Cicchetti, P., Xagoraris, A., & Romanski, L. M. (1990). The lateral amydgaloid nucleus: Sensory interface of the amygdala in fear conditioning. *Journal of Neuroscience, 10*, 1062–1069.

LeDoux, J. E., Schiller, D., & Cain, C. (2009). Emotional reaction and action: From threat processing to goal-directed behavior. In M. S. Gazzangia (Ed.), *The cognitive neurosciences* (4th ed., pp. 905–924). Cambridge, MA: MIT Press.

Lee, J., Lei, A., & Sue, S. (2001). The current state of mental health research of Asian Americans. *Journal of Human Behavior in the Social Environment. 3*, 159–178.

Lee, K., & Ashton, M. C. (2008). The HEXACO personality factors in the indigenous personality lexicons of English and 11 other languages. *Journal of Personality, 76*(5), 1001–1053.

Lee, L., Loewenstein, G., Ariely, D., Hong, J., & Young, J. (2008). If I'm not hot, are you hot or not? Physical-attractiveness evaluations and dating preferences as a function of one's own attractiveness. *Psychological Science, 19*(7), 669–677.

Lee, P. J., & Brown, N. R. (2003). Delay related changes in personal memories for September 11, 2001. *Applied Cognitive Psychology, 17*, 1007–1015.

Lee, R. M., & Ramirez, M. (2000). The history, current status, and future of multicultural psychotherapy. In I. Cuellar & F. A. Paniagua (Eds.), *Handbook of multicultural mental health: Assessment and treatment of diverse populations.* San Diego: Academic Press.

Lee, R. T., & Ashforth, B. E. (1996). A meta-analytic examination of the correlates of the three dimensions of job burnout. *Journal of Applied Psychology, 81*, 123–133.

Lee, S., & Katzman, M. A. (2002). Cross-cultural perspectives on eating disorders. In C. G. Fairburn & K. D. Brownell (Eds.), *Eating disorders and obesity: A comprehensive handbook.* New York: Guilford.

Lee, T. M., Chan, C. C., Paterson, J. G., Janzen, H. L., & Blashko, C. A. (1997). Spectral properties of phototherapy for seasonal affective disorder: A meta-analysisi. *Acta Psychiatrica Scandinavia, 96*, 117–121.

Lee, Y., Gaskins, D., Anand, A., & Shekhar, A. (2007). Glia mechanisms in mood regulation: A novel model of mood disorders. *Psychopharmacology, 191*, 55–65.

Lee-Chiong, T., & Sateia, M. (2006). Pharmacologic therapy of insomnia. In T. Lee-Chiong (Ed.), *Sleep: A comprehensive handbook.* Hoboken, NJ: Wiley-Liss.

Lee-Flynn, S., Pomaki, G., DeLongis, A., Biesanz, J., & Puterman, E. (2011, February). The role of self-concept clarity in the stress process. *Personality & Social Psychology Bulletin, 37*, 255–268.

Leeper, R. W. (1935). A study of a neglected portion of the field of learning: The development of sensory organization. *Journal of Genetic Psychology, 46*, 41–75.

Lefcourt, H. M. (2001). The humor solution. In C. R. Snyder (Ed.), *Coping with stress: Effective people and processes* (pp. 68–92). New York: Oxford University Press.

Lefcourt, H. M. (2005). Humor. In C. R. Snyder & S. J. Lopez (Eds.), *Handbook of positive psychology.* New York, NY: Oxford University Press.

Lefcourt, H. M., Davidson, K., Shepherd, R., Phillips, M., Prkachin, K., & Mills, D. (1995). Perspective-taking humor: Accounting for stress moderation. *Journal of Social and Clinical Psychology, 14*, 373–391.

Leff, J., & Vaughn, C. (1981). The role of maintenance therapy and relatives' expressed emotion in relapse of schizophrenia: A two-year follow-up. *British Journal of Psychiatry, 139*, 102–104.

Leff, J., & Vaughn, C. (1985). *Expressed emotion in families.* New York: Guilford.

Leff, J., Trieman, N., & Gooch, C. (1996). Team for the Assessment of Psychiatric Services (TAPS) Project 33: Prospective follow-up study of long-stay patients discharged from two psychiatric hospitals. *American Journal of Psychiatry, 153*, 1318–1324.

Legault, E., & Laurence, J.-R. (2007). Recovered memories of childhood sexual abuse: Social worker, psychologist, and psychiatrist reports of beliefs, practices, and cases. *Australian Journal of Clinical & Experimental Hypnosis, 35*, 111–133.

Legerstee, M. (2005). *Infants' sense of people: Precursors to a theory of mind.* Cambridge: Cambridge University Press.

Legerstee, M., Haley. D., & Bornstein, M. (Eds.) (in press). *The developing infant mind: Integrating biology and experience.* New York: Guilford Press.

Lehman, A. J., Pratt, D., DeLongis, A., Collins, J. B., Shojania, K., Koehler, B., Offer, R., & Esdaile, J. M. (2011). Do spouses know how much fatigue, pain, and physical limitation their partners with rheumatoid arthritis experience? Implications for social support. *Arthritis Care & Research, 1*, 120–127.

Lehman, D. R., Chiu, C., & Schaller, M. (2004). Psychology and culture. *Annual Review of Psychology, 55*, 689–714.

Lehrer, J. (2009). Think better: Tips from a savant. *Scientific American*, April/May/June, 2009, 61–63.

Leibovic, K. N. (1990). Vertebrate photoreceptors. In K. N. Leibovic (Ed.), *Science of vision.* New York: Springer-Verlag.

Leichsenring, F. & Rabung, S. (2008). Effectiveness of long-term psychodynamic psychotherapy: A meta-analysis. *Journal of the American Medical Association, 13*, 1551–1565.

Leighton, J. P., & Sternberg, R. J. (2003). Reasoning and problem solving. In A. F. Healy & R. W. Proctor (Eds.), *Handbook of psychology (Vol. 4): Experimental psychology.* New York: Wiley.

Leiter, M. P., & Maslach, C. (2001). Burnout and health. In A. Baum, T. A. Revenson, & J. E. Singer (Eds.), *Handbook of health psychology* (pp. 415–426). Mahwah, NJ: Erlbaum.

Lemay, E. P., Jr., Clark, M. S., & Greenberg, A. (2010). What is beautiful is good because what is beautiful is desired: Physical attractiveness stereotyping as projection of interpersonal goals. *Personality and Social Psychology Bulletin, 36*(3), 339–353.

Lench, H. C. (2009). Automatic optimism: The affective basis of judgments about the likelihood of future events. *Journal of Experimental Psychology: General, 138*, 187–200.

Lenert, L., & Skoczen, S. (2002). The Internet as a research tool: Worth the price of admission? *Annals of Behavioral Medicine, 24*, 251–256.

Lenneberg, E. H. (1967). *Biological Foundations of Language.* New York: Wiley.

Leon, D. A., Lawlor, D. A., Clark, H. H., Batty, G. D., & Macintyre, S. S. (2009). The association of childhood intelligence with mortality risk from adolescence to middle age: Findings from the Aberdeen Children of the 1950s cohort study. *Intelligence, 37*(6), 520–528.

Lepine, R., Barrouillet, P., & Camos, V. (2005). What makes working memory spans so predictive of high-level cognition? *Psychonomic Bulletin & Review, 12*(1), 165–170.

Lerman, H. (1986). *A mote in Freud's eye: From psychoanalysis to the psychology of women.* New York: Springer.

Lerner, J. S., Small, D. A., & Loewenstein, G. (2004). Heart strings and purse strings: Carryover effects of emotions on economic decisions. *Psychological Science, 15*, 337–341.

Lerner, M. J. (1980). *The belief in a just world: A fundamental delusion.* New York: Plenum Press.

Lerner, M. J., & Goldberg, J. H. (1999). When do decent people blame victims? The differing effects of the explicit/rational and implicit/experiential cognitive systems. In S. Chaiken & Y. Trope (Eds.), *Dual-process theories in social psychology.* New York: Guilford.

Lesher, G. W. (1995). Illusory contours: Toward a neurally based perceptual theory. *Psychonomic Bulletin & Review, 2*, 279–321.

Lett, H. S., Blumenthal, J. A., Babyak, M. A., Sherwood, A., Strauman, T., Robbins, C., & Newman, M. F. (2004). Depression as a risk factor for coronary artery disease: Evidence, mechanisms, and treatment. *Psychosomatic Medicine, 66*, 305–315.

Leuner, B., & Gould, E. (2010). Structural plasticity and hippocampal function. *Annual Review of Psychology, 61,* 111–140.

Leuner, B., Gould, E., & Shors, T. J. (2006). Is there a link between adult neurogenesis and learning? *Hippocampus, 16,* 216–224.

LeVay, S. (1996). *Queer science: The use and abuse of research into homosexuality.* Cambridge, MA: MIT Press.

Levenson, J. L., McDaniel, J. S., Moran, M. G., & Stoudemire, A. (1999). Psychological factors affecting medical conditions. In R. E. Hales, S. C. Yudofsky & J. A. Talbott (Eds.), *Textbook of psychiatry* (3rd ed., pp. 635–662). Washington, DC: American Psychiatric Press, Inc.

Levenson, R. W. (1992). Autonomic nervous system differences among emotions. *Psychological Science, 3,* 23–27.

Leventhal, E. A., Hansell, S., Diefenbach, M., Leventhal, H., & Glass, D. C. (1996). Negative affect and self-report of physical symptoms: Two longitudinal studies of older adults. *Health Psychology, 15,* 193–199.

Leventhal, H., & Tomarken, A. J. (1986). Emotion: Today's problems. *Annual Review of Psychology, 37,* 565–610.

Leventhal, H., Weinman, J., Leventhal, E. A., & Philips, L. A. (2008). Health psychology: The search for pathways between behavior and health. *Annual Review of Psychology, 59,* 477–505.

Levesque, M. J., Nave, C. S., & Lowe, C. A. (2006). Toward an understanding of gender differences in inferring sexual interest. *Psychology of Women Quarterly, 30,* 150–158.

Levin, R., & Nielsen, T. (2009). Nightmares, bad dreams and emotion dysregulation: A review and new neurocognitive model of dreaming. *Current Directions in Psychological Science, 18,* 84–88.

Levin, S., Henry, P.J. Pratto, F., & Sidanius, J. (2003). Social dominance and social identity in Lebanon: Implications for support of violence against the West. *Group Processes and Intergroup Relations, 6,* 353–368.

Levin, M. E., & Levin, J. R. (1990). Scientific mnemonomies: Methods for maximizing more than memory. *American Educational Research Journal, 27*(2), 301–321.

Levin, R. L., Heller, W., Mohanty, A., Herrington, J. D., & Miller, G. A. (2007). Cognitive deficits in depression and functional specificity of regional brain activity. *Cognitive Therapy and Research, 31,* 211–233.

Levine, J. M., & Moreland, R. L. (1998). Small groups. In D. T. Gilbert, S. T. Fiske, & G. Lindzey (Eds.), *The handbook of social psychology.* New York: McGraw-Hill.

Levine, M., & Crowther, S. (2008). The responsive bystander: How social group membership and group size can encourage as well as inhibit bystander intervention. *Journal of Personality and Social Psychology, 95*(6), 1429–1439.

Levine, R., & Norenzayan, A. (1999). The pace of life in 31 countries. *Journal of Cross-Cultural Psychology, 30,* 178–205.

Levine, R., Sata, S., Hashimoto, T., & Verma, J. (1995). Love and marriage in eleven cultures. *Journal of Cross-Cultural Psychology, 26,* 554–571.

Levinoff, E. J., Li, K. Z. H., Murtha, S., & Chertkow, J. (2002). Selective attention impairments in Alzheimer's disease: Evidence for dissociable components. *Neuropsychology, 18,* 580–588.

Levinson, D. E. (2009). Genetics of major depression. In I. H. Gotlib & C. L. Hammen (Eds.), *Handbook of Depression* (2nd ed., pp. 165–186). New York, NY: Guilford Press.

Levinthal, C. F. (2002). *Drugs, behavior, and modern society.* Boston: Allyn & Bacon.

Levis, D. J. (1989). The case for a return to a two-factor theory of avoidance: The failure of non-fear interpretations. In S. B. Klein & R. R. Bowrer (Eds.), *Contemporary learning theories: Pavlovian conditioning and the status of traditional learning theory.* Hillsdale NJ: Erlbaum.

Levitin, D. J. (2006). *This is your brain on music: The science of a human obsession.* New York: The Penguin Group.

Levitt, A. J., Boyle, M., Joffe, R. T., & Baumal, Z. (2000). *Canadian Journal of Psychiatry, 45,* 650–654.

Levitt, J. B. (2010). Receptive fields. In E. B. Goldstein (Ed.), *Encyclopedia of perception.* Thousand Oaks, CA: Sage.

Levitt, M. J., Dane, J. D., & Levitt, J. (2005). Immigration stress, social support, and adjustment in the first post-migration year: An intergenerational analysis. *Research in Human Development, 2,* 159–177.

Levy, G. D., Taylor, M. G., & Gelman, S. A. (1995). Traditional and evaluative aspects of flexibility in gender roles, social conventions, moral rules, and physical laws. *Child Development, 66,* 515–531.

Levy, J. (1985, May). Right brain, left brain: Fact or fiction. *Psychology Today,* 38–44.

Levy, J., Trevarthen, C., & Sperry, R. W. (1972). Perception of bilateral chimeric figures following hemispheric disconnection. *Brain, 95,* 61–78.

Lewandowsky, S., Duncan, M., & Brown, G. D. A. (2004). Time does not cause forgetting in short-term serial recall. *Psychonomic Bulletin & Review, 11*(5), 771–790.

Lewin, K. (1935). *A dynamic theory of personality.* New York: McGraw-Hill.

Lewinsohn, P. M., Joiner, T. E., Jr., & Rohde, P. (2001). Evaluation of cognitive diathesis-stress models in predicting major depressive disorder in adolescents. *Journal of Abnormal Psychology, 110,* 203–215.

Lewis, A. (Ed.). (2008). *The Cambridge handbook of psychology and economic behaviour.* Cambridge, UK: Cambridge University Press.

Lewis, S., Escalona, P. R., & Keith, S. J. (2009). Phenomenology of schizophrenia. In B. J. Sadock, V. A. Sadock, & P. Ruiz (Eds.), *Kaplan & Sadock's comprehensive textbook of psychiatry* (9th ed., pp. 1433–1450). Philadelphia, PA: Lippincott, Williams & Wilkins.

Lewis, T. L., & Maurer, D. (2005). Multiple sensitive periods in human visual development: Evidence from visually deprived children. *Developmental Psychobiology, 46,* 164–183.

Lewis-Fernandez, R., Guarnaccia, P. J., & Ruiz, P. (2009). Culture-bound syndromes. In B. J. Sadock, V. A. Sadock, & P. Ruiz (Eds.), *Kaplan & Sadock's comprehensive textbook of psychiatry* (9th ed.). Philadelphia, PA: Lippincott, Williams & Wilkins.

Lewy, A. J. (1993). Seasonal mood disorders. In D. L. Dunner (Ed.), *Current psychiatric therapy* (pp. 212–234). Philadelphia, PA: Saunders Publishing Co.

Ley, P. (1997). Compliance among patients. In A. Baum, S. Newman, J. Weiman, R. West, & C. McManus (Eds.), *Cambridge handbook of psychology, health, and medicine.* Cambridge, England: Cambridge University Press.

Li, H. Z. & Browne, A. J. (2000). Defining mental illness and accessing mental health services: Perspectives of Asian Canadians. *Canadian Journal of Community Mental Health, 19,* 143–154.

Li, N. P., & Kenrick, D. T. (2006). Sex similarities and differences in preferences for short-term mates: What, whether, and why. *Journal of Personality and Social Psychology, 90,* 468–489.

Li, W., Moallem, I., Paller, K. A., & Gottfried, J. A. (2007). Subliminal smells can guide social preferences. *Psychological Science, 18,* 1044–1049.

Libby, L. K. (2008). A neural signature of the current self. *Social Cognitive and Affective Neuroscience, 3,* 192–194.

Liberman, R. P., & Kopelowicz, A. (2005). Recovery from schizophrenia: A concept in search of research. *Psychiatric Services, 56,* 735–742.

Library and Archives Canada. (2001). Statement on the introduction of the Official Languages Bill, October 17, 1968. Retrieved May 11, 2005, from http://www.collectionscanada.ca/primeministers/h4-4066-e.html.

Lichten, W., & Simon, E. W. (2007). Defining mental retardation: A matter of life or death. *Intellectual and Developmental Disabilities, 45,* 335–346.

Lichtenstein, S., Fischhoff, B., & Phillips, L. (1982). Calibration of probabilities: The state of the art to 1980. In D. Kahneman, P. Slovic, & A. Tversky (Eds.), *Judgment under uncertainty: Heuristics and biases.* Cambridge, England: Cambridge University Press.

Lichtenthal, W. G., Cruess, D. G., & Prigerson, H. G. (2004). A case for establishing complicated grief as a distinct mental disorder in DSM-V. *Clinical Psychology Review, 24,* 637–662.

Lickliter, R. (2009). The fallacy of partitioning: Epigenetics' validation of the organism-environment system. *Ecological Psychology, 21*(2), 138–146.

Lickliter, R., & Honeycutt, H. (2003). Developmental dynamics: Toward a biologically plausible evolutionary psychology. *Psychological Bulletin, 129,* 819–835.

Liddle, P. F. (2009). Descriptive clinical features of schizophrenia. In M. C. Gelder, N. C. Andreasen, J. J. López-Ibor, Jr., & J. R. Geddes (Eds.). *New Oxford textbook of psychiatry* (2nd ed., Vol. 1). New York, NY: Oxford University Press.

Liden, R. C., Wayne, S. J., Jaworski, R. A., & Bennett, N. (2004). Social loafing: A field investigation. *Journal of Management, 30,* 285–304.

Lieberman, J. A., Stoup, T. S., McEvoy, J. P., Swartz, M. S., Rosenheck, R. A., & Perkins, D. O., et al. (2005). Effectiveness of antipsychotic drugs in patients with chronic schizophrenia. *New England Journal of Medicine, 353,* 1209–1223.

Lieberman, M. D. (2007). Social cognitive neuroscience: A review of core processes. *Annual Review of Psychology, 58,* 259–289.

Lieberman, M. D. (2010). Social cognitive neuroscience. In S. Fiske, D. T. Gilbert, & G. Lindzey (Eds.)., *Handbook of social psychology* (5th ed., pp. 143–193). New York: John Wiley & Sons.

Lieberman, M. D., Ochsner, K. N., Gilbert, D. T., & Schacter, D. (2001). Do amnesics exhibit cognitive dissonance reduction? The role of explicit memory and attention in attitude change. *Psychological Science, 12,* 135–140.

Liebert, R. M., & Liebert, L. L. (1998). *Liebert & Spiegler's personality strategies and issues.* Pacific Grove: Brooks/Cole.

Liebert, R. M., & Sprafkin, J. (1988). *The early window: Effects of television on children and youth.* Oxford, England: Pergamon Press.

Liefbroer, A. C., & Dourleijn, E. (2006). Unmarried cohabitation and union stability: Testing the role of diffusion using data from 16 European countries. *Demography, 43,* 203–221.

Lien, M.-C., Ruthruff, E., & Johnston, J. C. (2006). Attentional limitations in doing two tasks at once. *Current Directions in Psychological Science, 15,* 89–93.

Life and times: Moe Norman—The king of swing. CBC. Retrieved April 21, 2005, from http://www.cbc.ca/Lifeandtimes/norman.html.

Lilienfeld, S. O. (2007). Cognitive neuroscience and depression: Legitimate versus illegitimate reductionism and five challenges. *Cognitive Therapy and Research, 31,* 263–272.

Lilienfeld, S. O., & Landfield, K. (2008). Issues in diagnosis: Categorical vs. dimensional. In W. E. Craighead, D. J. Miklowitz, & L. W. Craighead (Eds.), *Psychopathology: History, diagnosis, and empirical foundations.* New York, NY: Wiley.

Lilienfeld, S. O., & Lynn, S. J. (2003). Dissociative identity disorder: Multiple personalities, multiple controversies. In S. O. Lilienfeld, S. J. Lynn, & J. M. Lohr (Eds.), *Science and pseudoscience in clinical psychology.* New York: Guilford.

Lilienfeld, S. O., Ammirati, R., & Landfield, K. (2009). Giving debiasing away: Can psychological research on correcting cognitive errors promote human welfare? *Perspectives on Psychological Science, 4*(4), 390–398.

Lilienfeld, S. O., Lynn, S. J., Kirsch, I., Chaves, J. F., Sarbin, T. R., Ganaway, G. K., & Powell, R. A. (1999). Dissociative identity disorder and the sociocognitive model: Recalling the lessons of the past. *Psychological Bulletin, 125,* 507–523.

Lilienfeld, S. O., Lynn, S. J., Ruscio, J., & Beyerstein, B. L. (2010). *50 great myths of popular psychology: Shattering widespread misconceptions about human behavior.* Malden, MA: Wiley-Blackwell.

Lilienfeld, S. O., Wood, J. M., & Garb, H. N. (2000). The scientific status of projective tests. *Psychological Science in the Public Interest, 1*(2), 27–66.

Lilienfeld, S. O., & Arkowitz, H. (2007). What "psychopath" means. *Scientific American Mind, 18,* 80–81.

Lillard, A. (2005). *Montessori: The science behind the genius.* Oxford, UK: Oxford University Press.

Lillard, A., & Else-Quest, N. (2006). The early years: Evaluating Montessori education. *Science, 313,* 1893–1894.

Lim, M. M., & Young, L. J. (2006). Neuropeptidergic regulation of affiliative behavior and social bonding in animals. *Hormones and Behavior, 50*(4), 506–517.

Lin, S. W., & Anthenelli, R. M. (2005). Genetic factors in the risk for substance use disorders. In J. H. Lowinson, P. Ruiz, R. B. Millman, & J. G. Langrod (Eds.), *Substance abuse: A comprehensive textbook.* Philadelphia: Lippincott, Williams & Wilkins.

Lindau, S., & Gavrilova, N. (2010). Sex, health, and years of sexually active life gained due to good health: Evidence from two U.S. population based cross sectional surveys of ageing. *British Medical Journal, 340,* c810.

Lindgren, H. C. (1969). *The psychology of college success: A dynamic approach.* New York: Wiley.

Lindsay, D. S., & Read, J. D. (1994). Psychotherapy and memories of childhood sexual abuse: A cognitive perspective. *Applied Cognitive Psychology, 8,* 281–338.

Lindsay, P. H., & Norman, D. A. (1977). *Human information processing.* New York: Academic Press.

Lindsay, R. C. L., Ross, D. F., Read, J. D., & Toglia, M. (Eds.). (2007). *Handbook of eyewitness psychology: Memory for people* (Vol. 2). Philadelphia: Lawrence Erlbaum and Associates (Taylor & Francis Group, LLC).

Lindsay, S. D., Allen, B. P., Chan, J. C. K., & Dahl, L. C. (2004). Eyewitness suggestibility and source similarity: Intrusions of details from one event into memory reports of another event. *Journal of Memory & Language, 50*(1), 96–111.

Lindshield, S. M., & Rodrigues, M. A. (2009). Tool use in wild spider monkeys (*Ateles geoffroyi*). *Primates, 50*(3), 269–272.

Lipp, O. V., Oughton, N., & LeLievre, J. (2003). Evaluative learning in human Pavlovian conditioning: Extinct, but still there? *Learning and Motivation, 34,* 219–239.

Lippa, R. A. (1994). *Introduction to social psychology.* Pacific Grove, CA: Brooks/Cole.

Lippa, R. A. (2005). *Gender, nature, and nurture.* Mahwah, NJ: Erlbaum.

Lippa, R. A., Martin, L. R., & Friedman, H. S. (2000). Gender-related individual differences and mortality in the Terman longitudinal study: Is masculinity hazardous to your health? *Personality and Social Psychology Bulletin, 26,* 1560–1570.

Lipton, J. S., & Spelke, E. S. (2004). Discrimination of large and small numerosities by human infants. *Infancy, 5,* 271–290.

Liptzin, B., Gottlieb, G. L., Summergrad, P. (2007). The future of psychiatric services in general hospitals. *American Journal of Psychiatry, 164*(10), 1468–1472.

Lishner, D. A., Batson, C. D., & Huss, E. (2011). Tenderness and sympathy: distinct empathic emotions elicited by different forms of need. *Personality and Social Psychology Bulletin, 37,* 614–725.

Lissek, S., Rabin, S., Heller, R. E., Lukenbaugh, D., Geraci, M., Pine, D. S., & Grillon, C. (2010). Overgeneralization of conditioned fear as a pathogenic marker of panic disorder. *American Journal of Psychiatry, 167*(1), 47–55.

Liston, C. C., McEwen, B. S., & Casey, B. J. (2009). Psychosocial stress reversibly disrupts prefrontal processing and attentional control. *Proceedings of the National Academy of Sciences of the United States of America, 106*(3), 912–917.

Little, A. C., Jones, B. C., & Burriss, R. P. (2007). Preferences for masculinity in male bodies change across the menstrual cycle. *Hormones and Behavior, 51,* 633–639.

Liu, S., Siegel, P. Z., Brewer, R. D., Mokdad, A. H., Sleet, D. A., & Serdula, M. (1997). Prevalence of alcohol-impaired driving: Results from a national self-reported survey of health behaviors. *Journal of the American Medical Association, 277,* 122–125.

Livesley, W. J., Jang, K. L., & Vernon, P. A. (2002). The genetic basis of personality structure. In T. Million & M. J. Lerner (Eds.), *The handbook of psychology* (pp. 34–56). New York: Wiley.

Livesley, W. J., Jang, K. L., & Vernon, P. A. (2003). Genetic basis of personality structure. In T. Million & M. J. Lerner (Eds.), *Handbook of psychology (Vol. 5): Personality and social psychology.* New York: Wiley.

Lizarraga, M. L. S., & Ganuza, J. M. G. (2003). Improvement of mental rotation in girls and boys. *Sex Roles, 40,* 277–286.

Lledo, P.-M., Alonso, M., & Grubb, M. S. (2006). Adult neurogenesis and functional plasticity in neural circuits. *Nature Reviews Neuroscience, 7,* 179–193.

Lobsiger, C. S., & Cleveland, D. W. (2007). Glia cells as intrinsic components of non-cell-autonomous neurodegenerative disease. *Nature Neuroscience, 10,* 1355–1360.

Lockhart, R. S. (1992). Measurement of memory. In L. R. Squire (Ed.), *Encyclopedia of learning and memory.* New York: Macmillan.

Lockhart, R. S. (2000). Methods of memory research. In E. Tulving & F. I. M. Craik (Eds.), *The Oxford handbook of memory* (pp. 45–58). New York: Oxford University Press.

Lockhart, R. S., & Craik, F. I. (1990). Levels of processing: A retrospective commentary on a framework for memory research. *Canadian Journal of Psychology, 44*(1), 87–112.

Locurto, C. (1990). The malleability of IQ as judged from adoption studies. *Intelligence, 14,* 275–292.

Locurto, C. (1991). *Sense and nonsense about IQ: The case for uniqueness.* New York: Praeger.

Loehlin, J. C. (1992). *Genes and environment in personality development.* Newbury Park, CA: Sage.

Loehlin, J. C. (1994). Behavior genetics. In R. J. Sternberg (Ed.), *Encyclopedia of human intelligence.* New York: Macmillan.

Loehlin, J. C. (2000). Group differences in intelligence. In R. J. Sternberg (Ed.), *Handbook of intelligence* (pp. 176–195). New York: Cambridge University Press.

Loehlin, J. C., Horn, J. M., & Willerman, L. (1997). Heredity, environment, and IQ in the Texas Adoption Project. In R. J. Sternberg & E. L. Grigorenko (Eds.), *Intelligence, heredity, and environment.* New York: Cambridge University Press.

Loftus, E. F. (1979). *Eyewitness testimony.* Cambridge, MA: Harvard University Press.

Loftus, E. F. (1992). When a lie becomes memory's truth: Memory distortion after exposure to misinformation. *Current Directions in Psychological Science, 1,* 121–123.

Loftus, E. F. (1993a). Psychologist in the eyewitness world. *American Psychologist, 48,* 550–552.

Loftus, E. F. (1994). The repressed memory controversy. *American Psychologist, 49,* 443–445.

Loftus, E. F. (1997, September). Creating false memories. *Scientific American,* 71–75.

Loftus, E. F. (1998). Remembering dangerously. In R. A. Baker (Ed.), *Child sexual abuse and false memory syndrome.* Amherst, NY: Prometheus Books.

Loftus, E. F. (2000). Remembering what never happened. In E. Tulving (Ed.), *Memory, consciousness, and the brain: The Tallinn conference* (pp. 106–118). Philadelphia: Psychology Press.

Loftus, E. F. (2003). Make believe memories. *American Psychologist, 58,* 864–873.

Loftus, E. F. (2005). Planting misinformation in the human mind: A 30-year investigation of the malleability of memory. *Learning & Memory, 12,* 361–366.

Loftus, E. F., & Bernstein, D. M. (2005). Rich false memories: The royal road to success. In A. F. Healy (Ed.), *Experimental cognitive psychology and its applications* (pp. 101–113). Washington, DC: American Psychological Association.

Loftus, E. F., & Cahill, L. (2007). Memory distortion: From misinformation to rich false memory. In J. S. Nairne (Ed.), *The foundations of remembering: Essays in honor of Henry L. Roediger III.* New York: Psychology Press.

Loftus, E. F., & Mazzoni, G. A. L. (1998). Using imagination and personalized suggestion to change people. *Behavior Therapy, 29*, 691–706.

Loftus, E. F., & Palmer, J. C. (1974). Reconstruction of automobile destruction: An example of the interaction between language and memory. *Journal of Verbal Learning and Verbal Behavior, 13*, 585–589.

Loftus, E. F., Garry, M., & Feldman, J. (1998). Forgetting sexual trauma: What does it mean when 38% forget? In R. A. Baker (Ed.), *Child sexual abuse and false memory syndrome*. Amherst, NY: Prometheus Books.

Logopoulos, J., et al. (2009). Increased theta and alpha EEG activity during nondirective meditation. *Journal of Alternative and Complementary Medicine, 15*(11), 1187–1192.

Lohoff, F. W., & Berrettini, W. H. (2009). Genetics of mood disorders. In D. S. Charney & E. J. Nestler (Eds.), *Neurobiology of mental illness* (3rd ed., pp. 360–377). New York, NY: Oxford University Press.

Lohr, J. M., Olatunji, B. O., Baumeister, R. F., & Bushman, B. J. (2007). The psychology of anger venting and empirically supported alternatives that do no harm. *The Scientific Review of Mental Health Practice: Objective Investigations of Controversial and Unorthodox Claims in Clinical Psychology, Psychiatry, and Social Work, 5*(1), 53–64.

Loken, B. (2006). Consumer psychology: Categorization, inferences, affect, and persuasion. *Annual Review of Psychology, 57*, 435–485.

Longman, D. G., & Atkinson, R. H. (2002). *College learning and study skills*. Belmont, CA: Wadsworth.

Longman, R. S., Saklofske, D. H., & Fung, T. S. (2007). WAIS-III percentile scores by education and sex for U.S. and Canadian populations. *Assessment, 14*, 426–432.

Lorenz, K. (1981). *Foundations of ethology*. New York: Springer-Verlag.

Lorenzo, G. L., Biesanz, J. C., & Human, L. J. (2010). What is beautiful is good and more accurately understood: Physical attractiveness and accuracy in first impressions of personality. *Psychological Science, 21*(12), 1777–1782.

Lothane, Z. (2006). Freud's legacy—is it still with us? *Psychoanalytic Psychology, 23*(2), 285–301.

Lott, B. (1987). *Women's lives*. Pacific Grove, CA: Brooks/Cole.

Lott, B. (2002). Cognitive and behavioral distancing from the poor. *American Psychologist, 57*, 100–110.

Lovaas, O. I. (1987). Behavioral treatment and normal educational and intellectual functioning in young autistic children. *Journal of Consulting and Clinical Psychology, 55*, 3–9.

Lovinger, D. M. (2010). Neurotransmitter roles in synaptic modulation, plasticity and learning in the dorsal stratium. *Neuropharmacology, 58*(7), 951–961.

Lowden, A., Akerstedt, T., & Wibom, R. (2004). Suppression of sleepiness and melatonin by bright light exposure during breaks in night work. *Journal of Sleep Research, 12*(1), 37–43.

Lowe, M. R. (2002). Dietary restraint and overeating. In C. G. Fairburn & K. D. Brownell (Eds.), *Eating disorders and obesity: A comprehensive handbook* (pp. 88–92). New York: Guilford.

Lowinson, J. H., Ruiz, P., Millman, R. B., & Langrod, J. G. (2005). *Substance abuse: A comprehensive textbook*. Philadelphia: Lippincott/Williams & Wilkins.

Lubart, T. I. (2003). In search of creative intelligence. In R. J. Sternberg, J. Lautrey, & T. I. Lubart (Eds.), *Models of intelligence: International perspectives*. Washington, DC: American Psychological Association.

Luborsky, E. B., O'Reilly-Landry, M., & Arlow, J. A. (2011). Psychoanalysis. In R. J. Corsini & D. Wedding (Eds.), *Current psychotherapies* (9th ed.). Belmont, CA: Brooks/Cole.

Luborsky, L., & Barrett, M. S. (2006). The history and empirical status of key psychoanalytic concepts. *Annual Review Clinical Psychology, 2*, 1–19.

Luborsky, L., Diguer, L., Seligman, D. A., Rosenthal, R., Krause, E. D., Johnson, S., et al. (1999). The researcher's own therapy allegiance: A "wild card" in comparisons of treatment efficacy. *Clinical Psychology: Science & Practice, 6*(1), 95–106.

Luborsky, L., Rosenthal, R., Diguer, L., Andrusyna, T. P., Berman, J. S., Levitt, J. T., et al. (2002). The dodo bird verdict is alive and well—mostly. *Clinical Psychology: Science & Practice, 9*, 2–12.

Luborsky, L., Singer, B., & Luborsky, L. (1975). Comparative studies of psychotherapies: Is it true that everyone has won and all must have prizes? *Archives of General Psychiatry, 32*, 995–1008.

Lucas, R. E. (2007). Adaptation and the set-point model of subjective well-being: Does happiness change after major life events? *Current Directions in Psychological Science, 16*, 75–79.

Lucas, R. E. (2008). Personality and subjective well-being. In M. Eid & R. J. Larsen (Eds.), *The science of subjective well-being* (pp. 171–194). New York: Guilford.

Lucas, R. E., & Diener, E. (2008). Personality and subjective well-being. In O. P. John, R. W. Robins, & L. A. Pervin (Eds.), *Handbook of personality psychology: Theory and research* (3rd ed., pp. 795–814). New York, NY: Guilford Press.

Lucas, R. E., Clark, A. E., Georgellis, Y., & Diener, E. (2004). Unemployment alters the set point for life satisfaction. *Psychological Science, 15*(1), 8–13.

Luchins, A. S. (1942). Mechanization in problem solving. *Psychological Monographs, 54*(6, Whole No. 248).

Lucid dreaming. University of Montreal, Hôpital du Sacré-Cœur de Montréal, Centre de recherche. Retrieved March 11, 2005, from http://www.crhsc.umontreal.ca/dreams.ld.htm.

Luders, E., Narr, K. L., Thompson, P. M., & Toga, A. W. (2009a). Neuroanatomical correlates of intelligence. *Intelligence, 37*(2), 156–163.

Luders, E., Toga, A. W., Lepore, N., & Gaser, C. (2009b). The underlying anatomical correlates of long-term meditation: Larger hippocampal and frontal volumes of gray matter. *Neuroimage, 45*(3), 672–678.

Ludwig, A. M. (1994). Mental illness and creative activity in female writers. *American Journal of Psychiatry, 151*, 1650–1656.

Ludwig, A. M. (1995). *The price of greatness: Resolving the creativity and madness controversy*. New York: Guilford.

Ludwig, A. M. (1998). Method and madness in the arts and sciences. *Creativity Research Journal, 11*, 93–101.

Lugaresi, E., Cirignotta, F., Montagna, P., & Sforza, E. (1994). Snoring: Pathogenic, clinical, and therapeutic aspects. In M. H. Kryger, T. Roth, & W. C. Dement (Eds.), *Principles and practice of sleep medicine* (2nd ed.). Philadelphia: Saunders.

Luh, C. W. (1922). The conditions of retention. *Psychological Monographs, 31*.

Lui, T. C., Desai, R. A., Krishanan-Sarin, S., Cavallo, D. A., & Potenza, M. N. (2011). Problematic internet use and health in adolescents: Data from a high school survey in Connecticut. *Journal of Clinical Psychiatry, Journal of Clinical Psychiatry, 187*, 97–102.

Lund, O. C. H., Tamnes, C. K., Moestue, C., Buss, D. M., & Vollrath, M. (2007). Tactics of hierarchy negotiation. *Journal of Research in Personality, 41*, 25–44.

Lundberg, U. (2007). Catecholamines. In G. Fink (Ed.), *Encyclopedia of stress*. San Diego: Elsevier.

Luntz, B. K., & Widom, C. S. (1994). Antisocial personality disorder in abused and neglected children grown up. *Journal of Psychiatry, 151*, 670–674.

Lupart, J. L. (2004). Unravelling the mysteries of G/LD: Toward the application of cognitive theory to assessment. In T. Newman & R. Sternberg (Eds.), *Students with both gifts and learning disabilities: Identification, assessment and outcomes* (pp. 49–72). Boston, MA: Kluwer.

Lupart, J. L., & Cannon, E. (2003). SCiberMENTOR: Connecting young girls and adult mentors in science. In F. J. Monks & H. Wagner (Eds.), *Development of human potential: Investment into our future. Proceedings of the 8th conference of the European Council For High Ability (ECHA)* (pp. 230–232). Bad Honnef, Germany: K.H. Bock.

Lupart, J. L., Pyryt, M. C., Watson, S. L., & Pierce, K. (2005). Gifted education and counselling in Canada. *International Journal for the Advancement of Counselling, 27*, 173–190.

Lupien, S. J., & Maheu, F. S. (2007). Memory and stress. In G. Fink (Ed.), *Encyclopedia of stress*. San Diego: Elsevier.

Lurie, P., Almeida, C. M., Stine, N., Stine, A. R., & Wolfe, S. M. (2006). Financial conflict of interest disclosure and voting patterns at food and drug administration drug advisory committee meetings. *Journal of the American Medical Association, 295*, 1921–1928.

Lusignan, F. A., Zadra, A., Dubuc, M. J., Daoust, A. M., Mottard, J. P., Godbout, R. (2009) Dream content in chronically treated persons with schizophrenia. *Schizophrenia Research, 112*, 163–174.

Lutsky, N. (1995). When is "obedience" obedience? Conceptual and historical commentary. *Journal of Social Issues, 51*, 55–65.

Lutz, A., Dunne, J. D., & Davidson, R. J. (2007). Meditation and the neuroscience of consciousness: An introduction. In P. D. Zelazo, M. Moscovitch, & E. Thompson (Eds.), *The Cambridge handbook of consciousness* (pp. 499–551). New York: Cambridge University Press.

Lutz, C. (1987). Goals, events and understanding in Ifaluk emotion theory. In N. Quinn & D. Holland (Eds.), *Cultural models in language and thought*. Cambridge, England: Cambridge University Press.

Lutz, D. J., & Sternberg, R. J. (1999). Cognitive development. In M. H. Bornstein & M. E. Lamb (Eds.), *Developmental psychology: an advanced textbook* Mahwah, NJ: Erlbaum.

Lutz, W. (1989). *Doublespeak*. New York: Harper Perennial.

Lykken, D. T., & Tellegen, A. (1996). Happiness is a stochastic phenomenon. *Psychological Science, 7*, 186–189.

Lymburner, J. A., & Roesch, R. (1999). The insanity defense: Five years of research (1993–1997). *International Journal of Law and Psychiatry, 22*, 213–240.

Lyn, H., & Savage-Rumbaugh, E. S. (2000). Observational word learning in two bonobos (*Pan* paniscus): Ostensive and nonostensive contexts. *Language & Communication, 20,* 255–273.

Lynch, G., & Gall, C. M. (2006). Ampakines and the threefold path to cognitive enhancement. *Trends in Neurosciences, 29,* 554–562.

Lynch, M. A. (2004). Long-term potentiation and memory. *Psychological Review, 84,* 87–136.

Lynch, S. K., Turkheimer, E., D'Onofrio, B. M., Mendle, J., Emery, R. E., Slutske, W. S., et al. (2006). A genetically informed study of the association between harsh punishment and offspring behavioral problems. *Journal of Family Psychology, 20,* 190–198.

Lynn, S. J., & Nash, M. (1994). Truth in memory: Ramifications for psychotherapy and hypnotherapy. *Journal of Clinical Hypnosis, 36,* 194–208.

Lynn, S. J., Kirsch, I., & Hallquist, M. N. (2008). Social cognitive theories of hypnosis. In M. R. Nash & A. J. Barnier (Eds.), *Oxford handbook of hypnosis: Theory, research and practice* (pp. 111–140). New York, NY: Oxford University Press.

Lynn, S. J., Kirsch, I., Barabasz, A., Cardeña, E., & Patterson, D. (2000). Hypnosis as an empirically supported clinical intervention: The state of the evidence and a look to the future. *International Journal of Clinical & Experimental Hypnosis, 48,* 239–259.

Lynn, S. J., Lock, T., Loftus, E. F., Krackow, E., & Lilienfeld, S. O. (2003). The remembrance of things past: Problematic memory recovery techniques in psychotherapy. In S. O. Lilienfeld, S. J. Lynn, & J. M. Lohr (Eds.), *Science and pseudoscience in clinical psychology.* New York: Guilford.

Lynn, S. J., Neuschatz, J., & Fite, R. (2002). Hypnosis and memory: Implications for the courtroom and psychotherapy. In M. L. Eisen (Ed.), *Memory and suggestibility in the forensic interview.* Mahwah, NJ: Erlbaum.

Lynne, S. D., Graber, J. A., Nichols, T. R., & Brooks-Gunn, J., & Botwin, G. J. (2007). Links between pubertal timing, peer influences, and externalizing behaviors among urban students followed through middle school. *Journal of Adolescent Health, 40*(2), 313–342.

Lyons-Ruth, K., & Jacobvitz, D. (2008). Attachment disorganization: Genetic factors, parenting contexts, and developmental transformation from infancy to adulthood. In J. Cassidy & P. R. Shaver (Eds.), *Handbook of attachment: Theory, research, and clinical applications* (2nd ed., pp. 666–697). New York, NY: Guilford Press.

Lysaker, P. H., Davis, L., Outcalt, S. D., Gelkopf, M., & Roe, D. (2010). Therapeutic alliance in cognitive behavior therapy for schizophrenia: Association with history of sexual assault. *Cognitive Therapy and Research,* Published online.

Lytton, H. (1997). Physical punishment is a problem, whether conduct disorder is endogenous or not. *Psychological Inquiry, 8,* 211–214.

Lyubomirsky, S., & Boehm, J. K. (2010). Human motives, happiness, and the puzzle of parenthood: Commentary on Kenrick et al. (2010) *Perspectives on Psychological Science, 5*(3), 327–334.

Lyubomirsky, S., Sheldon, K. M., & Schkade, D. (2005). Pursuing happiness: The architecture of sustainable change. *Review of General Psychology, 9,* 111–131.

Lyubomirsky, S., Sousa, L., & Dickerhoff, R. (2000). The costs and benefits of writing, talking, and thinking about life's triumphs and defeats. *Journal of Personality and Social Psychology, 90,* 692–708.

Lyubomirsky, S., Tkach, C., & DiMatteo, R. M. (2006). What are the differences between happiness and self-esteem? *Social Indicators Research, 78,* 363–404.

Maas, J. B. (1998). *Power sleep.* New York: Random House.

MacCoun, R. J. (1998). Biases in the interpretation and use of research results. *Annual Review Psychology, 49,* 259–287.

MacDonald, G., Zanna, M. P., & Holmes, J. G. (2000). An experimental test of the role of alcohol in relationship conflict. *Journal of Experimental Social Psychology, 36,* 182–193.

MacDonald, K. (1998). Evolution, culture, and the five-factor model. *Journal of Cross-Cultural Psychology, 29,* 119–149.

MacDonald, T. K., & Hynie, M. (2008). Ambivalence and unprotected sex: Failing to predict sexual activity is associated with decreased condom use. *Journal of Applied Social Psychology, 38,* 1092–1107.

MacDonald, T. K., & Martineau, A. M. (2002). Self-esteem, mood, and intentions to use condoms: When does low self-esteem lead to risky health behaviors? *Journal of Experimental Social Psychology, 38,* 299–306.

MacDonald, T. K., Fong, G. T., Zanna, M. P., & Martineau, A. M. (2000). Alcohol myopia and condom use: Can alcohol intoxication be associated with more prudent behavior? *Journal of Personality and Social Psychology, 78,* 605–619.

MacGregor, J. N., Ormerod, T. C., & Chronicle, E. P. (2001). Information processing and insight: A process model of performance on the nine-dot and related problems. *Journal of Experimental Psychology: Learning, Memory and Cognition, 27,* 176–201.

Mack, A. (2003). Inattentional blindness: Looking without seeing. *Current Directions in Psychological Science, 12*(5), 180–184.

Mack, A. H., Franklin, J. E., Jr., & Frances, R. J. (2003). Substance use disorders. In R. E. Hales & S. C. Yudofsky (Eds.), *Textbook of clinical psychiatry.* Washington, DC: American Psychiatric Publishing.

MacKellar, D. A., Valleroy, L. A., Secura, G. M., Behel, S., Bingham, T., Celentano, D. D., et al. (2005). Unrecognized HIV infection, risk behaviors, and perceptions of risk among young men who have sex with men: Opportunities for advancing HIV prevention in the third decade of HIV/AIDS. *Journal of Acquired Immune Deficiency Syndromes, 38,* 603–614.

Mackie, D. M., Worth, L. T., & Asuncion, A. G. (1990). Processing of persuasive in-group messages. *Journal of Personality and Social Psychology, 58,* 812-822.

MacLean, K. (2003). The impact of institutionalization on child development. *Development and Psychopathology, 15,* 853–884.

MacLean, P. D. (1954). Studies on limbic system ("viosceal brain") and their bearing on psychosomatic problems. In E. D. Wittkower & R. A. Cleghorn (Eds.), *Recent developments in psychosomatic medicine.* Philadelphia: Lippincott.

MacLean, P. D. (1993). Cerebral evolution of emotion. In M. Lewis & J. M. Haviland (Eds.), *Handbook of emotions.* New York: Guilford.

MacLeod, R. (2011). Romero, Arencibia play game in boy's memory. *Globe and Mail.* Retrieved from http://www.theglobeandmail.com/sports/baseball/romero-arencibia-play-game-in-boys-memory/article2029334/.

MacMillan, H. L., Boyle, M. H., Wong, M. Y. Y., Duku, E. K., Fleming, J. E., & Walsh, C. A. (1999). Slapping and spanking in childhood and its association with lifetime prevalence of psychiatric disorders in a general population sample. *Canadian Medical Association Journal, 161,* 805–809.

MacMillan, H. L., Fleming, J. E., Streiner, D. L., Lin, E., Boyle, M. H., Jamieson, E., et al. (2001). Childhood abuse and lifetime psychopathology in a community sample. *American Journal of Psychiatry, 158,* 1878–1883.

MacMillan, H. L., Fleming, J. E., Trocme, N., Boyle, M. H., Wong, M., Racine, Y. A., et al. (1997). Prevalence of child physical and sexual abuse in the community: Results from the Ontario health supplement. *Journal of the American Medical Association, 278,* 131–135.

Macmillan, M. (1991). *Freud evaluated: The completed arc.* Amsterdam: North-Holland.

Macmillan, N. A., & Creelman, C. D. (2005). *Detection theory: A user's guide* (2nd ed.). Mahwah, NJ: Erlbaum.

Macpherson, F. (2010). Impossible figures. In E. B. Goldstein (Ed.), *Encyclopedia of perception.* Thousand Oaks, CA: Sage.

MacQueen, G., Marshall, J., Perdue, M., Siegel, S., & Bienenstock, J. (1989). Pavlovian conditioning of rat mucosal mast cells to secrete rat mast cell protease II. *Science, 243,* 83–86.

Macrae, C. N., & Quadflieg, S. (2010). Perceiving people. In S. T. Fiske, D. T. Gilbert, & G. Lindzey (Eds.), *Handbook of social psychology* (5th ed., Vol. 1, pp. 353–393). Hoboken, NJ: Wiley.

MacWhinney, B. (1998). Models of the emergence of language. *Annual Review of Psychology, 49,* 199–227.

MacWhinney, B. (2001). Emergentist approaches to language. In J. Bybee & P. Hooper (Eds.), *Frequency and the emergence of linguistic structure.* Amsterdam: John Benjamins Publishing.

MacWhinney, B. (2004). A multiple process solution to the logical problem of language acquisition. *Journal of Child Language, 31,* 883–914.

Madden, M., & Lenhart, A. (2006). *Online dating.* Pew Internet & American Life Project. Retrieved from http://www.pewInternet.org/pdfs/PIP_Online_Dating.pdf.

Maddux, W. W., & Galinsky, A. D. (2009). Cultural borders and mental barriers: The relationship between living abroad and creativity. *Journal of Personality and Social Psychology, 96*(5), 1047–1061.

Maddux, W. W., Adam, H., & Galinsky, A. D. (2010). When in Rome … Learn why the Romans do what they do: How multicultural learning experiences facilitate creativity. *Personality and Social Psychology Bulletin, 36*(6), 731–741.

Madsen, K. B. (1968). *Theories of motivation.* Copenhagen: Munksgaard.

Madsen, K. B. (1973). Theories of motivation. In B. B. Wolman (Ed.), *Handbook of general psychology.* Englewood Cliffs, NJ: Prentice-Hall.

Magalhaes, A. C., et al. (2010). CRF receptor 1 regulates anxiety behavior via sensitization of 5-HT2 receptor signaling. *Nature Neuroscience, 13,* 622–629.

Magnavita, J. J. (2008). Psychoanalytic psychotherapy. In J. L. Lebow (Ed.), *Twenty-first century psychotherapies: Contemporary approaches to theory and practice.* New York: Wiley.

Magno, E., & Allan, K. (2007). Self-reference during explicit memory retrieval. *Psychological Science, 18,* 672–677.

Magnusson, D., & Stattin, H. (1998). Person-context interaction theories. In W. Damon (Ed.), *Handbook of child psychology (Vol. 1): Theoretical models of human development.* New York: Wiley.

Maguire, J., & Mody, I. (2008). GABAAR plasticity during pregnancy : Relevance to postpartum depression. *Neuron, 59,* 207–213.

Maguire, W., Weisstein, N., & Klymenko, V. (1990). From visual structure to perceptual function. In K. N. Leibovic (Ed.), *Science of vision.* New York: Springer-Verlag.

Maher, B. A. (2001). Delusions. In P. B. Sutker & H. E. Adams (Eds.), *Comprehensive handbook of psychopathology* (3rd ed., pp. 309–370). New York: Kluwer Academic/Plenum Publishers.

Mahncke, H. W., Connor, B. B., Appelman, J., Ahsanuddin, O. N., Hardy, J. L., Wood, R. A., et al. (2006). Memory enhancement in healthy older adults using a brain plasticity-based training program: A randomized, controlled study. *Proceedings of the National Academy of Sciences of the United States of America, 103*(33), 12523–12528.

Mahoney, M. J. (1974). *Cognition and behavior modification.* Cambridge, MA: Ballinger.

Mahowald, M. W. (1993). Sleepwalking. In M. A. Carskadon (Ed.), *Encyclopedia of sleep and dreaming.* New York: Macmillan.

Mahowald, M. W., & Schenck, C. H. (2005a). Insights from studying human sleep disorders. *Nature, 437,* 1279–1285.

Mahowald, M. W., & Schenck, C. H. (2005b). REM sleep parasomnias. In M. H. Kryger, T. Roth, & W. C. Dement (Eds.). *Principles and practice of sleep medicine* (pp. 897–916). Philadelphia, PA: Elsevier Saunders.

Maier, M. A., Elliot, A. J., & Lichtenfeld, S. (2008). Mediation of the negative effect of red on intellectual performance. *Personality and Social Psychology Bulletin, 34*(11), 1530–1540.

Maier, N. R. F. (1931). Reasoning and learning. *Psychological Review, 38,* 332–346.

Main, M., & Solomon, J. (1986). Discovery of a new, insecure–disorganized/disoriented attachment pattern. In T. B. Brazelton & M. W. Yogman (Eds.), *Affective development in infancy.* Norwood, NJ: Ablex.

Main, M., & Solomon, J. (1990). Procedures for identifying infants as disorganized/disoriented during the Ainsworth strange situation. In M. T. Greenberg, D. Ciccehetti, & E. M. Cummings (Eds.), *Attachment in the preschool years: Theory, research, and intervention.* Chicago: University of Chicago Press.

Maio, G. R., & Esses, V. M. (2001). The need for affect: Individual differences in the motivation to approach or avoid emotions. *Journal of Personality, 69,* 883–919.

Major, B., & Townsend, S. S. M. (2010). Coping with bias. In J. F. Dovidio, M. Hewstone, P. Glick, & V. M. Esses (Eds.), *The Sage handbook of prejudice, stereotyping, and discrimination.* Los Angeles, CA: Sage.

Malamuth, N. M., Addison, T., & Koss, M. (2000). Pornography and sexual aggression: Are there reliable effects and can we understand them? *Annual Review of Sex Research, 11,* 26–91.

Maldonado, J. R., & Spiegel, D. (2008). Dissociative disorders. In R. E. Hales, S. C. Yudofsky, & G. O. Gabbard (Eds.), *The American Psychiatric Publishing textbook of psychiatry* (5th ed., pp. 665–710). Washington, DC: American Psychiatric Publishing.

Malenfant, E. C. (2004). Suicide in Canada's immigrant population. Statistics Canada: *Health Reports, 15,* 9–17.

Maletzky, B. M. (2002). The paraphilias: Research and treatment. In P. E. Nathan & J. M. Gorman (Eds.), *A guide to treatments that work.* London: Oxford University Press.

Malloy, M. H., Kao, T., & Lee, Y. J. (1992). Analyzing the effect of prenatal care on pregnancy outcome: A conditional approach. *American Journal of Public Health, 82,* 448–453.

Maltzman, I. (1994). Why alcoholism is a disease. *Journal of Psychoactive Drugs, 26,* 13–31.

Managing traumatic stress: After the hurricanes. (2005). American Psychological Association Help Centre. Retrieved July 23, 2008, from http://apahelpcenter.org/articles/article.php?id=107.

Mandel uses knuckle knock to overcome OCD. (2006). *NBC10 News.* Retrieved July 23, 2008, from http://www.nbc10.com/entertainment/9081482/detail.html.

Mandel, H. (2009). *Here's the deal: Don't touch me.* New York: Bantam Books.

Mandler, G. (1984). *Mind and body.* New York: Norton.

Mandler, G. (1989). Memory: Conscious and unconscious. In P. R. Soloman, G. R. Goethals, C. M. Kelley, & B. R. Stephens (Eds.), *Memory: Interdisciplinary approaches.* New York: Springer-Verlag.

Mandler, G. (1993). Thought, memory, and learning: Effects of emotional stress. In L. Goldberger & S. Breznitz (Eds.), *Handbook of stress: Theoretical and clinical aspects* (2nd ed.). New York: Free Press.

Mandler, G. (2002). Origins of the cognitive revolution. *Journal of the History of the Behavioral Sciences, 38,* 339–353.

Manenti, R. R., Tettamanti, M. M., Cotelli, M. M., Miniussi, C. C., & Cappa, S. F. (2010). The neural bases of word encoding and retrieval: A fMRI-guided transcranial magnetic stimulation study. *Brain Topography, 22*(4), 318–332.

Mann, J. J., & Currier, D. (2006). Understanding and preventing suicide. In D. J. Stein, D. J. Kupfer, & A. F. Schatzberg (Eds.), *Textbook of mood disorders* (pp. 485–496). Washington, DC: American Psychiatric Publishing.

Mann, T., Tomiyama, A. J., Westling, E., Lew, A. M., Samuels, B., & Chatman, J. (2007). Medicare's search for effective obesity treatments. *American Psychologist, 62,* 220–233.

Manna, A., Raffone, A., Perrucci, M., Nardo, D., Ferretti, A., Tartaro, A., et al. (2010). Neural correlates of focused attention and cognitive monitoring in meditation. *Brain Research Bulletin, 82*(1–2), 46–56.

Manning, R., Levine, M., & Collins, M. (2007). The Kitty Genovese murder and the social psychology of helping: The parable of the 38 witnesses. *American Psychologist, 62,* 555–562.

Manning, R., Levine, M., & Collins, M. (2008). The legacy of the 38 witnesses and the importance of getting history right. *American Psychologist, 63,* 562.

Mansnerus, L. (1996). Timothy Leary, pied piper of psychedilic 60's dies at 75. Obituary, *New York Times.* Retrieved February 10, 2011, from http://www.nytimes.com/learning/general/onthisday/dday/1022.html.

Manson, J. E., Skerrett, P. J., & Willett, W. C. (2002). Epidemiology of health risks associated with obesity. In C. G. Fairburn & K. D. Brownell (Eds.), *Eating disorders and obesity: A comprehensive handbook* (pp. 422–428). New York: Guilford.

Mar, R. A. (2011). The neural bases of social cognition and story comprehension. *Annual Review of Psychology, 62,* 103–134.

Mar, R. A., Tackett, J. L., & Moore, C. (2010). Exposure to media and theory-of-mind development in preschoolers. *Cognitive Development, 25,* 69–78

Marangell, L. B., Silver, J. M., & Yudofsky, S. C. (1999). Psychopharmacology and electroconvulsive therapy. In R. E. Hales, S. C. Yudofsky, & J. A. Talbott (Eds.), *American Psychiatric Press textbook of psychiatry.* Washington, DC: American Psychiatric Press.

Maratsos, M. P. (2007). Commentary. *Monographs of the Society for Research in Child Development, 72,* 121–126.

Marcelino, A. S., Adam, A. S., Couronne, T., Koester, E. P., & Sieffermann, J. M. (2001). Internal and external determinants of eating initiation in humans. *Appetite, 36,* 9–14.

Marcenes, W. G., & Sheiham, A. (1992). The relationship between work stress and oral health status. *Social Science and Medicine, 35,* 1511.

Marchel, C. & Owens, S. (2007). Qualitative research in psychology: Could William James get a job? *History of Psychology, 10,* 301–324.

Marcia, J. E. (1966). Development and validation of ego identity status. *Journal of Personality and Social Psychology, 3,* 551–558.

Marcia, J. E. (1980). Identity in adolescence. In J. Adelson (Ed.), *Handbook of adolescent psychology.* New York: Wiley.

Marcia, J. E. (1994). The empirical study of ego identity. In H. A. Bosma, T. L. G. Graafsma, H. D. Grotevant, & D. J. de Levita (Eds.), *Identity and development: An interdisciplinary approach.* Thousand Oaks, CA: Sage.

Marcus, G. F. (1996). Why do children say "breaked"? *Current Directions in Psychological Science, 5,* 81–85.

Marcus-Newhall, A., Pedersen, W. C., Carlson, M., & Miller, N. (2000). Displaced aggression is alive and well: A meta-analytic review. *Journal of Personality and Social Psychology, 78,* 670–689.

Marder, S. R., Hurford, I. M., & van Kammen, D. P. (2009). Second-generation antipsychotics. In B. J. Sadock, V. A. Sadock, & P. Ruiz (Eds.), *Kaplan & Sadock's comprehensive textbook of psychiatry* (pp. 3206–3240). Philadelphia, PA: Lippincott, Williams & Wilkins.

Marewski, J. N., Gaissmaier, W., & Gigerenzer, G. (2010). Good judgments do not require complex cognition. *Cognitive Processing, 11*(2), 103–121.

Mark, V. (1996). Conflicting communicative behavior in a split-brain patient: Support for dual consciousness. In S. R. Hameroff, A. W. Kaszniak, & A. C. Scott (Eds.), *Toward a science of consciousness. The first Tucson discussions and debates.* Cambridge, MA: MIT Press.

Markowitsch, H. J. (2000). Neuroanatomy of memory. In E. Tulving & F. I. M. Craik (Eds.), *The Oxford handbook of memory* (pp. 465–484). New York: Oxford University Press.

Marks, G. A. (2006). The neurobiology of sleep. In T. Lee-Chiong (Ed.), *Sleep: A comprehensive handbook.* Hoboken, NJ: Wiley-Liss.

Marks, I. M. (2004). The Nobel prize award in physiology to Ivan Petrovich Pavlov. *Australian and New Zealand Journal of Psychiatry, 38*(9), 674–677.

Markus, H. R., & Hamedani, M. G. (2007). Sociocultural psychology: The dynamic interdependence among self systems and social systems. In S. Kitayama & D. Cohen (Eds.), *Handbook of cultural psychology* (pp. 3–39). New York: Guilford.

Markus, H. R., & Kitayama, S. (1991). Culture and the self: Implications for cognition, emotion, and motivation. *Psychological Review, 98*, 224–253.

Markus, H. R., & Kitayama, S. (1994). The cultural construction of self and emotion: Implications for social behavior. In S. Kitayama & H. R. Markus (Eds.), *Emotions and culture: Empirical studies of mutual influence.* Washington, DC: American Psychological Association.

Markus, H. R., & Kitayama, S. (2003). Culture, self, and the reality of the social. *Psychological Inquiry, 14*(3–4), 277–283.

Markus, H. R., Kitayama, S., & Heiman, R. J. (1996). Culture and "basic" psychological principles. In E. T. Higgins, & A. W. Kruglanski (Eds.), *Social Psychology: Handbook of basic principles.* New York: Guilford.

Marschall, J. (2007). Seduced by sleep. *Scientific American, 18*, 52–57.

Marschark, M. (1992). Coding processes: Imagery. In L. R. Squire (Ed.), *Encyclopedia of learning and memory.* New York: Macmillan.

Marsella, A. J., & Yamada, A. M. (2007). Culture and psychopathology: Foundations, issues, and directions. In S. Kitayama & D. Cohen (Eds.), *Handbook of cultural psychology.* New York: Guilford.

Marsh, E. J. (2007). Retelling is not the same as recalling: Implications for memory. *Current Directions in Psychological Science, 16*(1), 16–20.

Marsh, E. J., & Tversky, B. (2004). Spinning the stories of our lives. *Applied Cognitive Psychology, 18*, 491–503.

Marshall, K. (2007, May). The busy lives of teens. Statistics Canada: *Perspectives*, 5–15.

Marshall, L., & Born, J. (2007). The contribution of sleep to hippocampus-dependent memory consolidation. *Trends in Cogntive Science, 11*, 442–450.

Marshall, P. J. (2009). Relating psychology and neuroscience: Taking up the challenges. *Perspectives on Psychological Science, 4*, 113–125.

Marteau, T. M., & Weinman, J. (2004). Communicating about health threats and treatments. In S. Sutton, A. Baum, & M. Johnston (Ed.), *The Sage handbook of health psychology.* Thousand Oaks, CA: Sage.

Martin, C. L., & Ruble, D. (2004). Children's search for gender cues: Cognitive perspectives on gender development. *Current Directions in Psychological Science, 13*(2), 67–70.

Martin, D. J., Garske, J. P., & Davis, M. K. (2000). Relation of the therapeutic alliance with outcome and other variables: A meta-analytic review. *Journal of Consulting and Clinical Psychology, 68*, 438–450.

Martin, J. H. (1991). The collective electrical behavior of cortical neurons: The electroencephalogram and the mechanisms of epilepsy. In E. R. Kandel, J. H. Schwartz, & T. M. Jessell (Eds.), *Principles of neural science* (3rd ed.). New York: Elsevier.

Martin, J. N., & Fox, N. A. (2006). Temperament. In K. McCartney & D. Phillips (Eds.), *Blackwell handbook of early childhood development* (pp. 126–146). Malden, MA: Blackwell Publishing.

Martin, L. (1986). "Eskimo words for snow": A case study in the genesis and decay of an anthropological example. *American Psychologist, 88*, 418–423.

Martin, L. R., Friedman, H. S., & Schwartz, J. E. (2007). Personality and mortality risk across the life span: The importance of conscientiousness as a biopsychosocial attribute. *Health Psychology, 26*, 428–436.

Martin, R. A. (2001). Humor, laughter, and physical health: Methodological issues and research findings. *Psychological Bulletin, 127*, 504–519.

Martin, R. A. (2007). *The psychology of humor: An integrative approach.* Burlington, MA: Elsevier Academic Press.

Martin, R. A., Puhlik-Doris, P., Larsen, G., Gray, J., & Weir, K. (2003). Individual differences in uses of humor and their relation to psychological well-being: Development of the Humor Styles Questionnaire. *Journal of Research in Personality, 37*, 48–75.

Martin, R., & Leventhal, H. (2004). Symptom perception and health care-seeking behavior. In J. M. Raczynski & L. C. Leviton (Eds.), *Handbook of clinical health psychology (Vol. 2): Disorders of behavior and health.* Washington, DC: American Psychological Association.

Martin, T., LaRowe, S. D., & Malcolm, R. (2010). Progress in cue exposure therapy for the treatment of addictive disorders: A review update. *The Open Addiction Journal, 3*, 92–101.

Martinez, M., Marangell, L. B., & Martinez, J. M. (2008). Psychopharmacology. In R. E. Hales, S. C. Yudofsky, & G. O. Gabbard (Eds.), *The American psychiatric publishing textbook of psychiatry* (pp. 1053–1132). Washington, DC: American Psychiatric Publishing.

Martinez-Conde, S. (2006). Fixational eye movements in normal and pathological vision. *Progress in Brain Research, 154*, 151–176.

Martinez-Conde, S., & Macknik, S. L. (2007). Windows on the mind. *Scientific American, 297*, 56–62.

Martocchio, J. J., & Baldwin, T. T. (1997). The evolution of strategic organizational training: New objectives and research agenda. In G. R. Ferris (Ed.), *Research in personnel and human resources management* (Vol. 11, pp. 259–329). Greenwich, CT: JAI Press.

Maslach, C., & Leiter, M. P. (1997). *The truth about burnout.* San Francisco: Jossey-Bass.

Maslach, C., & Leiter, M. P. (2000). Burnout. In G. Fink (Ed.), *Encyclopedia of stress* (Vol. 1, pp. 358–362). San Diego: Academic Press.

Maslach, C., & Leiter, M. P. (2005). Stress and burnout: The critical research. In C. L. Cooper (Ed.), *Handbook of stress medicine and health.* Boca Raton, FL: CRC Press.

Maslach, C., & Leiter, M. P. (2007). Burnout. In G. Fink (Ed.), *Encyclopedia of stress.* San Diego: Elsevier.

Maslen, R. J. C., Theakston, A. L., Lieven, E. V. M., & Tomasello, M. (2004). A dense corpus study of past tense and plural overregularization in English. *Journal of Speech, Language, & Hearing Research, 47*, 1319–1333.

Maslow, A. H. (1954). *Motivation and personality.* New York: Harper & Row.

Maslow, A. H. (1968). *Toward a psychology of being.* New York: Van Nostrand.

Maslow, A. H. (1970). *Motivation and personality.* New York: Harper & Row.

Mason, G. (2008, May 31). When do we cry? *The Globe and Mail*, F1, F4, F5.

Mason, G. F., Krystal, J. H., & Sanacora, G. (2009). Nuclear magnetic resonance imaging and spectroscopy: Basic principles and recent findings in neuropsychiatric disorder. In B. J. Sadock, V. A. Sadock, & P. Ruiz (Eds.), *Kaplan & Sadock's comprehensive textbook of psychiatry* (9th ed., Vol. 1, pp. 248–272). Philadelphia, PA: Lippincott, Williams & Wilkins.

Massar, K., & Buunk, A. P. (2009). Rivals in the mind's eye: Jealous responses after subliminal exposure to body shapes. *Personality and Individual Differences, 46*(2), 129–134.

Massaro, D. W., & Loftus, G. R. (1996). Sensory and perceptual storage: Data and theory. In E. L. Bjork & R. A. Bjork (Eds.), *Memory.* San Diego: Academic Press.

Massen, C., Vaterrodt-Plünnecke, B., Krings, L., & Hilbig, B. E. (2009). Effects of instruction on learners' ability to generate an effective pathway in the method of loci. *Memory, 17*(7), 724–731.

Master, S. L., Eisenberger, N. I., Taylor, S. E., Naliboff, B. D., Shirinyan, D., & Lieberman, M. D. (2009). A picture's worth: Partner photographs reduce experimentally induced pain. *Psychological Science, 20*(11), 1316–1318.

Masterpasqua, F. (2009). Psychology and epigenetics. *Review of General Psychology, 13*(3), 194–201.

Masters, W. H., & Johnson, V. E. (1966). *Human sexual response.* Boston: Little, Brown.

Masters, W. H., & Johnson, V. E. (1970). *Human sexual inadequacy.* Boston: Little, Brown.

Masuda, T. (2010). Cultural effects on visual perception. In E. B. Goldstein (Ed.), *Encyclopedia of perception.* Thousand Oaks, CA: Sage.

Masuda, T., & Nisbett, R. E. (2001). Attending holistically versus analytically: Comparing the context sensitivity of Japanese and Americans. *Journal of Personality and Social Psychology, 81*, 922–934.

Masuda, T., Gonzalez, R., Kwan, L., & Nisbett, R. E. (2008). Culture and aesthetic preference: Comparing the attention to context of East Asians and Americans. *Personality and Social Psychology Bulletin, 34*, 1260–1275.

Matheson, S. L., Green, M. J., Loo, C., & Carr, V. J. (2010). Quality assessment and comparison of evidence for E.C.T. and repetitive transcranial magnetic stimulation for schizophrenia. *Schizophrenia Research, 118*, 201–210.

Mathew, S. J., Hoffman, E. J., Charney, D. S. (2009). Pharmacotherapy of anxiety disorders. In D. S. Charney & E. J. Nestler (Eds.), *Neurobiology of mental illness.* New York, NY: Guilford Press.

Mathy, R. M., Schillace, M., Coleman, S. M., & Berquist, B. E. (2002). Methodological rigor with Internet samples: New ways to reach underrepresented populations. *Cyber-Psychology and Behavior, 5*, 253–266.

Matlin, M. W. (2008). *The psychology of women.* Belmont, CA: Wadsworth.

Matsumoto, D. (1994). *People: Psychology from a cultural perspective.* Pacific Grove, CA: Brooks/Cole.

Matsumoto, D. (2001). Culture and emotion. In D. Matsumoto (Ed.), *The handbook of culture and psychology* (pp. 171–194). New York: Oxford University Press.

Matsumoto, D. (2003). Cross-cultural research. In S. F. Davis (Ed.), *Handbook of research methods in experimental psychology.* Malden, MA: Blackwell Publishers.

Matsumoto, D., & Willingham, B. (2006). The thrill of victory and the agony of defeat: Spontaneous expressions of medal winners of the 2004 Athens Olympic games. *Journal of Personality and Social Psychology, 91*, 568–581.

Matsumoto, D., & Willingham, B. (2009). Spontaneous facial expressions of emotion of congenitally and noncongenitally blind individuals. *Journal of Personality and Social Psychology, 96*(1), 1–10.

Matsumoto, D., & Yoo, S. (2006). Toward a new generation of cross-cultural research. *Perspectives on Psychological Science, 1,* 234–250.

Matsumoto, D., Nezlek, J. B., & Koopmann, B. (2007). Evidence for universality in phenomenological emotion response system coherence. *Emotion, 7,* 57–67.

Matsumoto, D., Yoo, S. H., Nakagawa, S., & 37 Members of the Multinational Study of Cultural Display Rules. (2008). Culture, emotion regulation, and adjustment. *Journal of Personality and Social Psychology, 94,* 925–937.

Matthews, G., Emo, A. K., Roberts, R. D., & Zeidner, M. (2006). What is this thing called emotional intelligence? In K. R. Murphy (Ed.), *A critique of emotional intelligence: What are the problems and how can they be fixed?* (pp. 3–36). Mahwah, NJ: Erlbaum.

Matthews, R. N., Domjan, M., Ramsey, M., & Crews, D. (2007). Learning effects on sperm competition and reproductive fitness. *Psychological Science, 18,* 758–762.

Matthey, S. (1998). P < .05—But is it clinically *significant?* Practical examples for clinicians. *Behaviour Change, 15,* 140–146.

Matusov, E., & Hayes, R. (2000). Sociocultural critique of Piaget and Vygotsky. *New Ideas in Psychology, 18*(2–3), 215–239.

Matute, H., & Miller, R. R. (1998). Detecting causal relations. In W. O'Donohue (Ed.), *Learning and behavior therapy.* Boston, Allyn & Bacon.

Maugh, T. H., II. (2008, December 9). Henry M. dies at 82: Victim of brain surgery accident offered doctors key insights into memory. *Los Angeles Times.* Retrieved from http://www.latimes.com/news/science/la-me-molaison9-2008dec09,0,2820409.story

Mauk, M. D., & Thach, W. T. (2008). Cerebellum. In L. Squire, D. Berg, F. Bloom, S. Du Lac, A. Ghosh, N. Spitzer (Eds.), *Fundamental neuroscience* (3rd ed., pp. 751–774). San Diego, CA: Elsevier.

Maurer, D. (2005). Introduction to the special issue on critical periods reexamined: Evidence from human sensory development. *Developmental Psychobiology, 46,* 162.

Mauro, R., Sato, K., & Tucker, J. (1992). The role of appraisal in human emotions: A cross-cultural study. *Journal of Personality and Social Psychology, 62,* 301–317.

May, C. P., Hasher, L., & Foong, N. (2005). Implicit memory, age, and time of day. *Psychological Science, 16,* 96–100.

Mayer, J. (1955). Regulation of energy intake and the body weight: The glucostatic theory and the lipostatic hypothesis. *Annals of the New York Academy of Science, 63,* 15–43.

Mayer, J. (1968). *Overweight: Causes and control.* Englewood Cliffs, NJ: Prentice-Hall.

Mayer, J. D., Caruso, D. R., & Salovey, P. (1999). Emotional intelligence meets traditional standards for an intelligence. *Intelligence, 27,* 267–298.

Mayer, J. D., Salovey, P., & Caruso, D. R. (2008). Emotional intelligence: New ability or eclectic traits. *American Psychologist,* 503–517.

Mayer, R. E. (1995). The search for insight: Grappling with Gestalt psychology's unanswered questions. In R. J. Sternberg, & J. E. Davidson (Eds.), *The nature of insight.* Cambridge, MA: The MIT Press.

Mayer, J., Roberts, R., & Barsade, S. G. (2008). Human abilities: Emotional intelligence. *Annual Review of Psychology, 59,* 507–536.

Mayes, A. (1992). Brain damage and memory disorders. In M. M. Gruneberg, & P. E. Morris (Eds.), *Aspects of memory (Vol.1): The practical aspects* (2nd ed., pp. 86–123). Florence, KY: Taylor & Frances/Routledge.

Mayes, A. R. & Roberts, N. (2001). Theories of episodic memory. *Philosophical Transactions of the Royal Society of London, 356,* 1395–1408.

Mayo Clinic. (2011). REM sleep behavior disorder. http://www.mayoclinic.org/rem-sleep-behavior-disorder/

Mays, V. M., & Albee, G. W. (1992). Psychotherapy and ethnic minorities. In D. K. Freedheim (Ed.), *History of psychotherapy: A century of change.* Washington, DC: American Psychological Association.

Mays, V. M., Rubin, J., Sabourin, M., & Walker, L. (1996). Moving toward a global psychology: Changing theories and practice to meet the needs of a changing world. *American Psychologist, 51,* 485–487.

Mazzoni, G., & Lynn, S. J. (2007). Using hypnosis in eyewitness memory: Past and current issues. In M. P. Toglia, J. D. Read, D. F. Ross, & R. C. L. Lindsay (Eds.), *Handbook of eyewitness psychology: Volume 1. Memory for events.* Mahwah, NJ: Erlbaum.

Mazzoni, G., Heap, M., & Scoboria, A. (2010). Hypnosis and memory: Theory, laboratory research, and applications. In S. Lynn, J. W. Rhue, & I. Kirsch (Eds.), *Handbook of clinical hypnosis* (2nd ed.) (pp. 709–741). Washington, DC: American Psychological Association.

McArdle, J. J. (2009). Latent variable modeling of differences and changes with longitudinal data. *Annual Review of Psychology, 60,* 577–605

McBride-Chang, C., & Jacklin, C. N. (1993). Early play arousal, sex-typed play, and activity level as precursors to later rough-and-tumble play. *Early Education & Development, 4,* 99–108.

McBurney, D. H. (2010). Evolutionary approach: Perceptual adaptations. In E. B. Goldstein (Ed.), *Encyclopedia of perception.* Thousand Oaks, CA: Sage.

McBurney, D. H., Zapp, D. J., & Streeter. S. A. (2005). Preferred number of sexual partners: Tails of distributions and tales of mating systems. *Evolution and Human Behavior, 26,* 271–278.

McCabe, C., Rolls, E. T., & Bilderbeck, A., & McGlone, F. (2008). Cognitive influences on the affective representation of touch and the sight of touch in the human brain. *Social Cognitive and Affective Neuroscience, 3,* 97–108.

McCabe, R. E., & Antony, M. M. (2008). Anxiety disorders: Social and specific phobias. In A. Tasman, J. Kay, J. A. Lieberman, M. B. First, & M. Maj (Eds.), *Psychiatry* (3rd ed.). New York, NY: Wiley-Blackwell.

McCabe, S. B., & Toman, P. E. (2000). Stimulus exposure duration in a deployment-of-attention task: Effects on dysphoric, recently dysphoric and nondysphoric individuals. *Cognition and Emotion, 14,* 125–142.

McCabe, S. B., Gotlib, I. H., & Martin, R. A. (2000). Cognitive vulnerability for depression: Deployment of attention as a function of history of depression and current mood state. *Cognitive Therapy and Research, 24,* 427–444.

McCain, M. N., & Mustard, J. F. (1999). *Reversing the real brain drain: Early years study—Final report.* Toronto: Canadian Institute for Advanced Research.

McCann, C. D. (1990). Interpersonal factors in depression. In C. D. McCann & N. S. Endler (Eds.), *Depression: New directions in theory, research and practice* (pp. 27–47). Toronto: Wall & Emerson.

McCann, D., & Sato, T. (2000). Personality, cognition and the self. *European Journal of Personality, 14,* 449–462.

McCann, S. J. H. (2001). The precocity–longevity hypothesis: Earlier peaks in career achievement predict shorter lives. *Personality and Social Psychology Bulletin, 27,* 1429–1439.

McCann, S. J. H. (2003). Younger achievement age predicts shorter life for governors: Testing the precocity–longevity hypothesis with artifact controls. *Personality and Social Psychology Bulletin, 29,* 164–169.

McCarley, R. W. (1994). Dreams and the biology of sleep. In M. H. Kryger, T. Roth, & W. C. Dement (Eds.), *Principles and practice of sleep medicine* (2nd ed.). Philadelphia: Saunders.

McCarty, R. (2007). Fight-or-flight response. In G. Fink (Ed.), *Encyclopedia of stress.* San Diego: Elsevier.

McCauley, M. E., Eskes, G., & Moscovitch, M. (1996). The effect of imagery on explicit and implicit tests of memory in young and old people: A double dissociation. *Canadian Journal of Experimental Psychology, 50,* 34–41.

McClelland, D. C. (1975). *Power: The inner experience.* New York: Irvington.

McClelland, D. C. (1985). How motives, skills and values determine what people do. *American Psychologist, 40,* 812–825.

McClelland, D. C., & Koestner, R. (1992). The achievement motive. In C. P. Smith (Ed.), *Motivation and personality: Handbook of thematic content analysis.* New York: Cambridge University Press.

McClelland, D. C., Atkinson, J. W., Clark, R. A., & Lowell, E. L. (1953). *The achievement motive.* New York: Appleton-Century-Crofts.

McClelland, J. L. (1992). Parallel-distributed processing models of memory. In L. R. Squire (Ed.), *Encyclopedia of learning and memory.* New York: Macmillan.

McClelland, J. L. (2000). Connectionist models of memory. In E. Tulving & F. I. M. Craik (Eds.), *The Oxford handbook of memory* (pp. 583–596). New York: Oxford University Press.

McClelland, J. L., & Rogers, T. T. (2003). The parallel distributed processing approach to semantic cognition. *Nature Reviews Neuroscience, 4,* 310–322.

McClelland, J. L., & Rumelhart, D. E. (1985). Distributed memory and the representation of general and specific information. *Journal of Experimental Psychology: General, 114,* 159–188.

McClernon, F. J., & Gilbert, D. G. (2007). Smoking and stress. In G. Fink (Ed.), *Encyclopedia of stress* (2nd ed.). San Diego, CA: Academic Press.

McClintock, M. (1971). Menstrual synchrony and suppression. *Nature, 229,* 244–245.

McClure-Tone, E. B., & Pine, D. S. (2009). Clinical features of the anxiety disorders. In B. J. Sadock, V. A. Sadock, & P. Ruiz (Eds.), *Kaplan & Sadock's comprehensive textbook of psychiatry* (9th ed., pp. 1844–1855). Philadelphia, PA: Lippincott, Williams & Wilkins.

McConkey, K. M. (1992). The effects of hypnotic procedures on remembering: The experimental findings and their implications for forensic hypnosis. In E. Fromm & M. R. Nash (Eds.), *Contemporary hypnosis research.* New York: Guilford.

McConnell, J. V. (1962). Memory transfer through cannibalism in planarians. *Journal of Neuropsychiatry, 3*(Suppl. 1), 542–548.

McConnell, J. V., Cutler, R. L., & McNeil, E. B. (1958). Subliminal stimulation: An overview *American Psychologist, 13,* 229–242.

McCormick, D. A. (2008). Membrane potential and action potential. In L. Squire, D. Berg, F. Bloom, S. Du Lac, A. Ghosh, & N. Spitzer (Eds.), *Fundamental* neuroscience (3rd ed., pp. 112–132). San Diego, CA: Elsevier.

McCrae, K. (1998). Official bilingualism: From the 1960s to the 1990s. In J. Edwards (Ed.), *Language in Canada* (pp. 61–83). Cambridge, UK: Cambridge University Press.

McCrae, R. R. (1984). Situational determinants of coping responses: Loss, threat and challenge. *Journal of Personality and Social Psychology, 46,* 919–928.

McCrae, R. R. (1996). Social consequences of experimental openness. *Psychological Bulletin, 120,* 323–337.

McCrae, R. R. (2005). Personality structure. In V. A. Derlega, B. A. Winstead, & W. H. Jones (Eds.), *Personality: Contemporary theory and research.* Belmont, CA: Wadsworth.

McCrae, R. R., & Costa, P. T., Jr. (1984). *Emerging lives, enduring dispositions: Personality in adulthood.* Boston: Little, Brown.

McCrae, R. R., & Costa, P. T., Jr. (1987). Validation of the five-factor model of personality across instruments and observers. *Journal of Personality and Social Psychology, 52,* 81–90.

McCrae, R. R., & Costa, P. T., Jr. (1997). Personality trait structure as a human universal. *American Psychologist, 52,* 509–516.

McCrae, R. R., & Costa, P. T., Jr. (2003). *Personality in adulthood: A five factor theory perspective.* New York: Guilford.

McCrae, R. R., & Costa, P. T., Jr. (2004). A contemplated revision of the NEO five-factor inventory. *Personality and Individual Differences, 36,* 587–596.

McCrae, R. R., & Costa, P. T., Jr. (2007). Brief versions of the NEO-PI-3. *Journal of Individual Differences, 28,* 116–128.

McCrae, R. R., & Costa, P. T., Jr. (2008). The five-factor theory of personality. In O. P. John, R. W. Robbins, & L. A. Pervin (Eds.), *Handbook of personality: Theory and research* (Vol. 3, pp. 159–181). New York, NY: Guilford Press.

McCrae, R. R., & Costa., P. T., Jr. (1985). Updating Norman's "adequate taxonomy": Intelligence and personality dimensions in natural language and in questionnaires. *Journal of Personality and Social Psychology, 49,* 710–721.

McCrae, R. R., & Sutin, A. R. (2009). Openness to experience. In M. R. Leary & R. H. Hoyle (Eds.), *Handbook of individual differences in social behavior* (pp. 257–273). New York, NY: Guilford Press.

McCrae, R. R., & Terracciano, A. (2006). National character and personality. *Current Directions in Psychological Science, 15,* 156–161.

McCrae, R. R., Scalley, M., Abecasis, B. R., Terracciano, A., & Costa, Jr., P. T. (2010). An alternative to the search for single polymorphisms: Toward molecular personality scales for the five-factor model. *Journal of Personality Social Psychology, 99,* 1014–1024.

McCrae, R. R., Terracciano, A., & 78 Members of the Personality Profiles of Cultures Project. (2005b). Universal features of personality traits from the observer's perspective: Data from 50 cultures. *Journal of Personality and Social Psychology, 88,* 547–561.

McCrink, K., & Wynn, K. (2004). Large-number addition and subtraction by 9-month old infants. *Psychological Science, 15,* 776–81.

McCullough, M. E. (2001). Forgiving. In C. R. Snyder (Ed.), *Coping with stress: Effective people and processes* (pp. 93–113). New York: Oxford University Press.

McCullough, M. E., & Witvliet, C. V. (2002). The psychology of forgiveness. In C. R. Synder & S. J. Lopez (Eds.), *Handbook of positive psychology.* New York: Oxford University Press.

McDaniel, M. A. (2005). Big-brained people are smarter: A meta-analysis of the relationship between *in vivo* brain volume and intelligence. *Intelligence, 33,* 337–346.

McDaniel, M. A., & Einstein, G. O. (1986). Bizarre imagery as an effective memory aid: The importance of distinctiveness. *Journal of Experimental Psychology: Learning, Memory & Cognition, 12,* 54–65.

McDaniel, M. A., & Einstein, G. O. (2007). *Prospective memory: An overview and synthesis of an emerging field.* Thousand Oaks, CA: Sage.

McDaniel, M. A., Lyle, K. B., Butler, K. M., & Dornburg, C. C. (2008). Age-related deficits in reality monitoring of action memories. *Psychology and Aging, 23*(3), 646–656.

McCullough, M. E., Bellah, C. G., Kilpatrick, S. D., & Johnson, J. L. (2001). Vengefulness: Relationships with forgiveness, rumination, well-being, and the Big Five. *Personality and Social Psychology Bulletin, 27,* 601–610.

McDaniel, M. A., Roediger, H. L., & McDermott, K. B. (2007). Generalizing test-enhanced learning from the laboratory to the classroom. *Psychonomic Bulletin & Review, 14,* 200–206.

McDaniel, M. A., Waddill, P. J., & Shakesby, P. S. (1996). Study strategies, interest, and learning from text: The application of material appropriate processing. In D. J. Herrmann, C. McEvoy, C. Hertzog, P. Hertel, & M. K. Johnson (Eds.), *Basic and applied memory research: Theory in context* (Vol. 1). Mahwah, NJ: Erlbaum.

McDermott, K. B. (2007). Inducing false memories through associated lists: A window onto everyday false memories? In J. S. Nairne (Ed.), *The foundations of remembering: Essays in honor of Henry L. Roediger III.* New York, NY: Psychology Press.

McDonald, J., & Walton, R. (2007). *The Cambridge companion for Greek and Roman Theatre.* Cambridge: Cambridge University Press.

McDonald, C., & Murphy, K. C. (2003). The new genetics of schizophrenia. *Psychiatric Clinics of North America, 26*(1), 41–63.

McDonald, R. V., & Siegel, S. (2004). Intra-administration associations and withdrawal symptoms: Morphine-elicited morphine withdrawal. *Experimental and Clinical Psychopharmacology, 12,* 3–11.

McDonald, W. M., Thompson, T. R., McCall W. V., & Zormuski, C. F. (2004). Electroconvulsive therapy. In A. F. Schatzberg & C. B. Nemeroff (Eds.), *Textbook of psychopharmacology.* Washington, DC: American Psychiatric Publishing.

McEwen, B. S. (2009). Stress and coping. In G. G. Berntson & J. T. Cacioppo (Eds.), *Handbook of neuroscience for the behavioral sciences* (Vol. 2, pp. 1220–1235). Hoboken, NJ: Wiley.

McEwen, B. S., & Seeman, T. (2003). Stress and affect: Applicability of the concepts of allostasis and allostatic load. In R. J. Davidson, K. R. Scherer, & H. H. Goldsmith (Eds.), *Handbook of affective sciences.* New York: Oxford University Press, 1117–1137.

McFadden, T. J., Helmreich, R. I., Rose, R. M., & Fogg, L. F. (1994). Predicting astronauts' effectiveness: A multivariate approach. *Aviation, Space, and Environmental Medicine, 65,* 904–909.

McGaugh, J. L. (2004). The amygdala modulates the consolidation of memories of emotionally arousing experiences. *Annual Review of Neuroscience, 27,* 1–28.

McGeoch, J. A., & McDonald, W. T. (1931). Meaningful relation and retroactive inhibition. *American Journal of Psychology, 43,* 579–588.

McGlashan, T. H., & Fenton, W. S. (1992). The positive–negative distinction in schizophrenia: Review of natural history validators. *Archives of General Psychiatry, 49,* 63–72.

McGlashan, T. H., & Hoffman, R. E. (2000). Schizophrenia: Psychodynamic to neurodynamic theories. In B. J. Sadock & V. A. Sadock (Eds.), *Kaplan and Sadock's comprehensive textbook of psychiatry* (7th ed., Vol. 1, pp. 1159–1168). Philadelphia: Lippincott, Williams & Wilkins.

McGowan, P. O., Meaney, M. J., & Szyf, M. (2008). Diet and the epigenetic (re)programming of phenotypic differences in behavior. *Brain Research, 1237,* 12–24.

McGran, K. (2010, December 14). Fearless on the ice, not in the sky. *Toronto Star,* A1, A12.

McGrath, J. E., Arrow, H., & Berdahl, J. L. (2000). The study of groups: Past, present, and future. *Personality and Social Psychology Review, 4,* 95–105.

McGrath, J. J. (2007). The surprisingly rich contours of schizophrenia epidemiology. *Archives of General Psychiatry, 64*(1), 14–16.

McGrath, J., Welham, J., Scott, J., Varghese, D., Degenhardt, L., Hayatbakhsh, M., et al. (2010). Association between cannabis use and psychosis-related outcomes using sibling pair analysis in a cohort of young adults. *Archives of General Psychiatry, 67*(5), 440–447.

McGraw, K. O., Tew, M. D., & Williams, J. E. (2000). The integrity of web-delivered experiments: Can you trust the data? *Psychological Science, 11,* 502–506.

McGraw, L. A., & Walker, A. J. (2004). The more things change, the more they stay the same. In M. Coleman, & L. J. Ganong (Eds.), *Handbook of contemporary families: Considering the past, contemplating the future.* Thousand Oaks, CA: Sage.

McGrew, J. H., Wright, E. R., Pescosolido, B. A., & McDonel, E. C. (1999). The closing of Central State Hospital: Long-term outcomes for persons with severe mental illness. *Journal of Behavioral Health Services & Research, 26,* 246–261.

McGue, M., Bouchard, T. J., Jr., Iacono, W. G., & Lykken, D. T. (1993). Behavioral genetics of cognitive ability: A life-span perspective. In R. Plomin & G. E. McClearn (Eds.), *Nature, nurture and psychology.* Washington, DC: American Psychological Association.

McGuigan, F. J., & Lehrer, P. M. (2007). Progressive relaxation: Origins, principles, and clinical applications. In P. M. Lehrer, R. L. Woolfolk, & W. E. Sime (Eds.), *Principles and practice of stress management.* New York, NY: Guilford Press.

McGuire, W. J. (1985). Attitudes and attitude change. In G. Lindzey & E. Aronson (Eds.), *Handbook of social psychology* (Vol. 2). New York: Random House.

McHugh, L., Barnes-Holmes, Y., & Barnes-Holmes, D. (2004). Perspective-taking as relational responding: A developmental profile. *The Psychological Record, 54,* 115-144.

McHugh, P. R. (1995). Dissociative identity disorder as a socially constructed artifact. *Journal of Practical Psychiatry and Behavioral Health, 1,* 158–166.

McIlroy, A. (2008, August 15). Meditating through mental illness. *The Globe and Mail,* A1, A4.

McIntyre, K., Korn, J., & Matsuo, H. (2008). Sweating the small stuff: How different types of hassles result in the experience of stress. *Stress & Health: Journal of the International Society for the Investigation of Stress, 24*(5), 383–392.

McKean, K. (1985, June). Decisions, decisions. *Discover*, 22–31.

McKeefry, D. J., Burton, M. P., & Morland, A. B. (2010). The contribution of human cortical area V3A to the perception of chromatic motion: A transcranial magnetic stimulation study. *European Journal of Neuroscience, 31*(3), 575–584.

McKelvie, P., & Low, J. (2002). Listening to Mozart does not improve children's spatial ability: Final curtains for the Mozart effect. *British Journal of Development Psychology, 20*, 241–258.

McKenna, J. J. (1993). Co-sleeping. In M. A. Carskadon (Ed.), *Encyclopedia of sleep and dreaming*. New York: Macmillan.

McKenna, K. Y. A. (2008). MySpace or your place: Relationship initiation and development in the wired and wireless world. In S. Sprecher, A. Wenzel, & J. Harvey (Eds.), *Handbook of relationship initiation* (pp. 235–247). New York, NY: Psychology Press.

McKenna, K. Y. A., & Bargh, J. A. (2000). Plan 9 from cyberspace: The implications of the Internet for personality and social psychology. *Personality and Social Psychology Review, 4*, 57–75.

McKenna, K. Y. A., & Seidman, G. (2005). You, me, and we: Interpersonal processes in electronic groups. In Y. Amichai-Hamburger (Ed.), *The social net: Understanding human behavior in cyberspace* (pp. 191–218). New York: Oxford University Press.

McKenna, K. Y. A., Green, A., & Gleason, M. (2002). Relationship formation on the Internet: What's the big attraction? *Journal of Social Issues, 58*, 9–31.

McKenzie, D. (2005). Students feeling stress at exam time cope in several different ways. *Canadian Press*, April 23, 2005. Retrieved June 22, 2005, from http://www.mediresource.sympatico.ca/channel_health_news_detail.asp?channel_id=11&menu_item_id=4&news_id=6518.

McKenzie, R. B. (2010). Predictability rational? In search of defenses for rational behavior of economics. Heidelberg, Germany: Springer-Verlag

McKone, E., Crookes, K., & Kanwisher, N. (2009). The cognitive and neural development of face recognition in humans. In M. S. Gazzaniga (Ed.), *The cognitive neurosciences*. Cambridge, MA: MIT Press.

McLean, D. E., & Link, B. G. (1994). Unraveling complexity: Strategies to refine concepts, measures, and research designs in the study of life events and mental health. In W. R. Avison & I. H. Gotlib (Eds.), *Stress and mental health: Contemporary issues and prospects for the future*. New York: Plenum.

McLean, S. (2010). Why some smart people do dumb things. YFile, Wednesday, October 6, 2010. Retrieved November 2, 2010, from http://www.yorku.ca/yfile/archive/index.asp?Article=15600.

McLellan, A. T., Lewis, D. C., O'Brien, C. P., & Kleber, H. D. (2000). Drug dependence, a chronic mental illness: Implications for treatment, insurance, and outcome evaluation. *Journal of the American Medical Association, 284*, 1689–1695.

McLoyd, V. C. (1998). Socioeconomic disadvantage and child development. *American Psychologist, 53*, 185–204.

McMullin, D., & White, J. W. (2006). Long-term effects of labeling a rape experience. *Psychology of Women Quarterly, 30*(1), 96–105.

McNab, F., Varrone, A., Jucaite, A., Bystritsky, P., Forssberg, H., & Klingberg, T. (2009). Change in cortical dopamine D1 receptor binding associated with cognitive training. *Science, 323*(5915), 800–802.

McNally, R. J. (1994). Cognitive bias in panic disorder. *Current Directions in Psychological Science, 3*, 129–132.

McNally, R. J. (1996). *Panic disorder: A critical analysis*. New York: Guilford.

McNally, R. J. (2003). *Remembering trauma*. Cambridge, MA: Belknap Press/Harvard University Press.

McNally, R. J. (2007). Betrayal trauma theory: A critical appraisal. *Memory, 15*, 280–294.

McNally, R. J. (2009). Posttraumatic stress disorder. In P. H. Blaney & T. Millon (Eds.), *Oxford textbook of psychopathology* (2nd ed., pp. 176–197). New York, NY: Oxford University Press.

McNally, R. J., & Geraerts, E. (2009). A new solution to the recovered memory debate. *Perspectives on Psychological Science, 4*(2), 126–134.

McNamara, P., Nunn, C., Barton, R., Harris, E., & Capellini, I. (2007). Phylogeny of sleep and dreams. In D. Barrett & P. McNamara (Eds.), *The new science of dreaming*. Westport, CT: Praeger.

McNeil, T. F., Cantor-Graae, E., & Ismail, B. (2000). Obstetrics complications and congenital malformation in schizophrenia. *Brain Research Reviews, 31*, 166–178.

McQueen, M. B., & Blacker, D. (2008). Genetics of Alzheimer's disease. In J. W. Smoller, B. R. Sheidley, & M. T. Tsuang (Eds.), *Psychiatric genetics: Applications in clinical practice* (pp. 177–193). Arlington, VA: American Psychiatric Publishing

McShane, L. (2007, October 1). Article casts doubt on "Genovese syndrome." *The Globe and Mail*. Retrieved October 3, 2007, from http://www.theglobeandmail.com/servlet/story/RTGAM.20071001.wgenovese101.

McTeer, M. (2003). *In my own name*. Toronto: Vintage Books.

McVay, J. C., & Kane, M. J. (2010). Does mind wandering reflect executive function or executive failure? Comment on Smallwood and Schooler (2006) and Watkins (2008). *Psychological Bulletin, 136*, 188–197.

McWilliams, L. A., Becker, E. S., Margraf, J., Clara, I. P., & Vriends, N. (2007). Anxiety disorders specificity of anxiety sensitivity in a community sample of young women. *Personality and Individual Differences, 42*, 345–354.

Mead, G. H. (1934). *Mind, self and society*. Chicago: University of Chicago Press.

Mechanic, D. (1980). *Mental health and social policy*. Englewood Cliffs, NJ: Prentice-Hall.

Mechanic, D. (1999). Mental health and mental illness. In A. V. Horvitz & T. L. Scheid (Eds.), *A handbook for the study of mental health: Social contexts, theories, and systems*. New York: Cambridge University Press.

Mechelli A., Crinion J. T., Noppeney U., O'Doherty J., Ashburner J., Frackowiak R. S., Price, C. J. (2004). Structural plasticity in the bilingual brain. *Nature, 431*(7010), 757.

Medina, K., Hanson, K. L., Schweinsburg, A. D., Cohen-Zion, M., Nagel, B. J., & Tapert, S. F. (2007). Neuropsychological functioning in adolescent marijuana users: Subtle deficits detectable after a month of abstinence. *Journal of the International Neuropsychological Society, 13*(5), 807–820.

Mednick, S. A., & Mednick, M. T. (1967). The Remote Associates Test. *Journal of Creative Behavior, 2*(3), 213–214.

Mednick, S. A., Machon, R. A., Huttunen, M. O., & Bonett, D. (1988). Adult schizophrenia following prenatal exposure to an influenza epidemic. *Archives of General Psychiatry, 45*, 189–192.

Mednick, S. C., & Drummond, S. P. A. (2009). Napping. In R. Stickgold & M. P. Walker (Eds.), *The neuroscience of sleep* (pp. 254–262). San Diego, CA: Academic Press.

Mednick, S. C., Cali, D. J., Kanady, J., & Drummond, S. A. (2008). Comparing the benefits of caffeine, naps and placebo on verbal, motor and perceptual memory. *Behavioural Brain Research, 193*(1), 79–86.

Medora, N. P., Larson, J. H., Hortacsu, N., & Dave, P. (2002). Perceived attitudes towards romanticism: A cross-cultural study of American, Asian-Indian, and Turkish young adults. *Journal of Comparative Family Studies, 33*, 155–178.

Meegan, D. V., Glazebrook, C. M., Dhillon, V. P., Tremblay, L., Welsh, T. N., & Elliot, D. (2004). The Müller–Lyer illusion affects the planning and control of manual aiming movements. *Experimental Brain Research, 155*, 37–47.

Meerlo, P., Mistlberger, R. E., Jacobs, B. L., Heller, H., & McGinty, D. (2009). New neurons in the adult brain: The role of sleep and consequences of sleep loss. *Sleep Medicine Reviews, 13*(3), 187–194.

Meeus, W., van de Schoot, R., Keijsers, L., Schwartz, S. J., & Branje, S. (2010). On the progression and stability of adolescent identity formation: A five-wave longitudinal study in early-to-middle and middle-to-late adolescence. *Child Development, 81*, 1565–1581.

Mega, M. S., Cummings, J. L., Salloway, S., & Malloy, P. (1997). The limbic system: An anatomic, phylogenetic, and clinical perspective. *Journal of Neuropsychiatry & Clinical Neurosciences, 9*, 315–330.

Mehdizadeh, S. (2010). Self-presentation 2.0: Narcissism and self-esteem on Facebook. *Cyberpsychology, Behavior, and Social Networking, 13*(4), 357–364.

Mehl, M. R. (2007). Eavesdropping on health: A naturalistic observation approach for social-health research. *Social and Personality Psychology Compass, 1*, 359–380.

Mehl, M. R., Vazire, S., Holleran, S. E., & Clark, C. (2010). Eavesdropping on happiness: Well-being is related to having less small talk and more substantive conversations. *Psychological Science, 21*(4), 539–541.

Meichenbaum, D. (1977). *Cognitive-behavior modification*. New York: Plenum Press.

Meichenbaum, D. (1994). *Clinical handbook/practical therapist manual for assessing and treating adults with post-traumatic stress disorder (PTSD)*. Waterloo, ON: Institute Press.

Meichenbaum, D. (2005). 35 years of working with suicidal patients: Lessons learned. *Canadian Psychology, 46*, 64–72.

Meichenbaum, D. (2007). Cognitive–behavioral therapy with Donald Meichenbaum. *Systems of Psychotherapy Video Series*. Washington, DC: American Psychological Association.

Meinz, E. J., & Hambrick, D. Z. (2010). Deliberate practice is necessary but not sufficient to explain individual differences in piano sight-reading skill: The role of working memory capacity. *Psychological Science, 21*(7), 914–919.

Meister, B. (2007). Neurotransmitters in key neurons of the hypothalamus that regulate feeding behavior and body weight. *Physiology & Behavior, 92*, 263–271.

Meltzer, H. Y., & Bobo, W. V. (2009). Antipsychotic and anticholinergic drugs. In M. C. Gelder, N. C. Andreasen, J. J. López-Ibor, Jr., & J. R. Geddes (Eds.), *New Oxford textbook of psychiatry* (2nd ed., Vol. 1). New York, NY: Oxford University Press.

Meltzoff, A. N., & Gopnik, A. (1989). On linking nonverbal imitation, representation, and language learning in the first two years of life. In G. E. Speidel & K. E. Nelson (Eds.), *The many faces of imitation in language learning*. New York: Springer-Verlag.

Melvin, G. A., Posner, K., Standley, B. H., & Oquendo, M. A. (2008). Management of the suicidal patient. In A. Tasman, J. Kay, J. A. Lieberman, M. B. First, & M. Maj (Eds.), *Psychiatry* (3rd ed.). New York, NY: Wiley-Blackwell.

Melzack, R. (1975). The McGill pain questionnaire: Major properties and scoring methods. *Pain, 1,* 277–299.

Melzack, R. (2001). Pain and the neuromatrix in the brain. *Journal of Dental Education, 65,* 1378–1382.

Melzack, R., & Katz, J. (2004). The gate control theory: Reaching for the brain. In T. Hadjistavropoulos & K. D. Craig (Eds.), *Pain: Psychological perspectives* (pp. 13–34). Mahwah, NJ: Lawrence Erlbaum Associates, Publishers.

Melzack, R., & Wall, P. D. (1965). Pain mechanisms: A new theory. *Science, 150,* 971–979.

Melzack, R., & Wall, P. D. (1982). *The challenge of pain*. New York: Basic Books.

Memmert, D., Unkelbach, C., & Ganns, S. (2010). The impact of regulatory fit on performance in an inattentional blindness paradigm. *The Journal of General Psychology, 137,* 129–139.

Mendelson, W. B. (2005). Hypnotic medications: Mechanisms of action and pharmacologic effects. In M. H. Kryger, T. Roth, & W. C. Dement (Eds.). *Principles and practice of sleep medicine*. Philadelphia: Elsevier Saunders.

Mendoza, J. E., Elliott, D., Meegan, D. V., Lyons, J. L., & Welsh, T. N. (2006). The effect of the Müller–Lyer illusion on the planning and control of manual aiming movements. *Journal of Experimental Psychology: Human Perception and Performance, 32,* 413–422.

Mennella, J. A., & Beauchamp, G. K. (1996). The early development of human flavor preferences. In E. D. Capaldi (Ed.), *Why we eat what we eat: The psychology of eating* (pp. 83–112). Washington, DC: American Psychological Association.

Menninger, W. W. (2005). Role of the psychiatric hospital in the treatment of mental illness. In B. J. Sadock & V. A. Sadock (Eds.), *Kaplan & Sadock's comprehensive textbook of psychiatry*. Philadelphia: Lippincott Williams & Wilkins.

Mentzer, R. L. (1982). Response biases in multiple-choice test item files. *Educational and Psychological Measurement, 42,* 437–448.

Merikangas, K. R., & Kalaydjian, A. E. (2009). Epidemiology of anxiety disorders. In B. J. Sadock, V. A. Sadock, & P. Ruiz (Eds.), *Kaplan & Sadock's comprehensive textbook of psychiatry* (9th ed., pp. 1856–1863). Philadelphia, PA: Lippincott, Williams & Wilkins.

Merikangas, K. R., & Pato, M. (2009). Recent developments in the epidemiology of bipolar disorder in adults and children: Magnitude, correlates, and future directions. *Clinical Psychology: Science and Practice, 16*(2), 121–133.

Merikle, P. M. (2000). Subliminal perception. In A. E. Kazdin (Ed.), *Encyclopedia of Psychology* (pp. 497–499). New York: Oxford University Press.

Mesquita, B. (2003). Emotions as dynamic cultural phenomena. In R. J. Davidson, K. R. Scherer, & H. H. Goldsmith (Eds.), *Handbook of affective sciences*. New York: Oxford University Press.

Meston, C. M., Helman, J. R., Trapnell, P. D., & Paulus, D. L. (1998). Socially desirable responding & sexuality self-report. *Journal of Sex Research, 35,* 147–157.

Metzger, E. D. (1999). Electroconvulsive therapy. In A. M. Nicholi (Ed.), *The Harvard guide to psychiatry*. Cambridge, MA: Harvard University Press.

Meyer, D. E., & Schvaneveldt, R. W. (1976). Meaning, memory structure, and mental processes. *Science, 192,* 27–33.

Meyer, R. E. (1996). The disease called addiction: Emerging evidence in a 200-year debate. *The Lancet, 347,* 162–166.

Meyer, R. G. (1992). *Practical clinical hypnosis: Techniques and applications*. New York: Lexington Books.

Meyer-Bahlburg, H. F. L., Ehrhardt, A. A., Rosen, L. R., Gruen, R. S., Veridiano, N. P., Vann, F. H., & Neuwalder, H. F. (1995). Prenatal estrogens and the development of homosexual orientation. *Developmental Psychology, 31,* 12–21.

Meyerbröker, K., & Emmelkamp, P. G. (2010). Virtual reality exposure therapy in anxiety disorders: A systematic review of process-and-outcome studies. *Depression and Anxiety, 27*(10), 933–944.

Mezulis, A. H., Abramson, L. Y., Hyde, J. S., & Hankin, B. L. (2004). Is there a universal positivity bias in attributions? A meta-analytic review of individual, developmental and cultural differences in the self-serving attributional bias. *Psychological Bulletin, 130,* 711–747.

Mezzich, J. E., Lewis-Fernandez, R., & Ruiperez, M. A. (2003). The cultural framework of psychiatric disorders. In A. Tasman, J. Kay, & J. A. Lieberman (Eds.), *Psychiatry*. New York: Wiley.

Michaels, S. (1996). The prevelance of homosexuality in the United States. In R. P. Cabaj & T. S. Stein (Eds.), *Textbook of homosexuality and mental health*. Washington, DC: American Psychiatric Press.

Mignot, E. (2000). Pathophysiology of narcolepsy. In M. H. Kryger, T. Roth, & W. C. Dement (Eds.), *Principles and practice of sleep medicine*. Philadelphia: Saunders.

Mikami, A. Y., Szwedo, D. E., Allen, J. P., Meredyth, A. E., & Hare, A. L. (2010). Adolescent peer relationships and behavior problems predict young adults' communication on social networking websites. *Developmental Psychology, 46,* 46–56.

Mikkonen, J., & Raphael, D. (2010). Social determinants of health: The Canadian facts. Toronto: York University School of Health Policy and Management.

Mikulincer, M. (2006). Attachment, caregiving, and sex within romantic relationships: A behavioral systems perspective. In M. Mikulincer & G. S. Goodman (Eds.), *Dynamics of romantic love: Attachment, caregiving, and sex*. New York: Guilford.

Mikulincer, M., & Shaver, P. R. (2007). *Attachment in adulthood: Structure, dynamics, and change*. New York: Guilford Press.

Mikulincer, M., & Shaver, P. R. (2008). Adult attachment and affect regulation. In J. Cassidy & P. R. Shaver (Eds.), *Handbook of attachment: Theory, research, and clinical applications* (2nd ed., pp. 456–481). New York, NY: Guilford Press.

Milgram, S. (1963). Behavioral study of obedience. *Journal of Abnormal and Social Psychology, 67,* 371–378.

Milgram, S. (1964). Issues in the study of obedience. *American Psychologist, 19,* 848–852.

Milgram, S. (1968). Reply to the critics. *International Journal of Psychiatry, 6,* 294–295.

Milgram, S. (1974). *Obedience to authority*. New York: Harper & Row.

Milkman, K. L., Chugh, D., & Bazerman, M. H. (2009). How can decision making be improved? *Perspectives on Psychological Science, 4*(4), 379–383.

Miller, A. G. (1986). *The obedience experiments: A case study of controversy in social science*. New York: Praeger.

Miller, A. G. (2004). What can the Milgram obedience experiments tell us about the Holocaust?: Generalizing from the social psychology laboratory. In A. G. Miller (Ed.), *The social psychology of good and evil* (pp. 193–239). New York, NY: Guilford Press.

Miller, D. T., & Ross, M. (1975). Self-serving biases in the attribution of causality: Fact or fiction. *Psychological Bulletin, 82,* 213–225.

Miller, E. K., & Cohen, J. D. (2001). An integrative theory of prefrontal cortex function. *Annual Review of Neuroscience, 24,* 167–202.

Miller, E., & Wallis, J. (2008). The prefrontal cortex and executive brain functions. In L. Squire, D. Berg, F. Bloom, S. Du Lac, A. Ghosh, & N. Spitzer (Eds.), *Fundamental neuroscience* (3rd ed., pp. 1199–1222). San Diego, CA: Elsevier.

Miller, G. (2005). Neuroscience: Reflecting on another's mind. *Science, 308,* 945–947.

Miller, G. (2009). The Brain Collector. *Science, 324*(5935), 1634–1636.

Miller, G. A. (1956). The magical number seven, plus or minus two: Some limits on our capacity for processing information. *Psychological Review, 63,* 81–97.

Miller, G. A. (2003). The cognitive revolution: A historical perspective. *Trends in Cognitive Sciences, 7*(3), 141–144.

Miller, G. A., Galanter, E., & Pribram, K. H. (1960). *Plans and the structure of behavior*. New York: Holt, Rinehart & Winston.

Miller, G. E., & Blackwell, E. (2006). Turning up the heat: Inflammation as a mechanism linking chronic stress, depression, and heart disease. *Current Directions in Psychological Science, 15,* 269–272.

Miller, G. E., Chen, E., & Zhou, E. S. (2007). If it goes up, must it come down? Chronic stress and the hypothalamic-pituitary-adrenocortical axis in humans. *Psychological Bulletin, 133,* 25–45.

Miller, G., Tybur, J. M., & Jordan, B. D. (2007). Ovulatory cycle effects on tip earnings by lap dancers: Economic evidence for human estrus? *Evolution and Human Behavior, 28,* 375–381.

Miller, I. J., & Reedy, F. E. Jr. (1990). Variations in human taste-bud density and taste intensity perception. *Physiological Behavior, 47,* 1213–1219.

Miller, J. G. (2006). Insights into moral development from cultural psychology. In M. Killen & J. G. Smetana (Eds.), *Handbook of moral development*. Mahwah, NJ: Erlbaum.

Miller, J. M., & Peterson, D. A. M. (2004). Theoretical and empirical implications of attitude strength. *Journal of Politics, 66,* 847–867.

Miller, N. E. (1944). Experimental studies of conflict. In J. M. Hunt (Ed.), *Personality and the behavior disorders* (Vol. 1). New York: Ronald.

Miller, N. E. (1959). Liberalization of basic S-R concepts: Extension to conflict behavior, motivation, and social learning. In S. Koch (Ed.), *Psychology: A study of a science* (Vol. 2). New York: McGraw-Hill.

Miller, R. R., & Grace, R. C. (2003). Conditioning and learning. In A. F. Healy & R. W. Proctor (Eds.), *Handbook of psychology (Vol. 4): Experimental psychology*. New York: Wiley.

Milligan, E. D., & Watkins, L. R. (2009). Pathological and protective roles of glia in chronic pain. *Nature Reviews Neuroscience, 10*(1), 23–36.

Millman, J., Bishop, C. H., & Ebel, R. (1965). An analysis of test-wiseness. *Educational and Psychological Measurement, 25,* 707–726.

Millon, T. (1981). *Disorders of personality: DSM-III, Axis II.* New York: Wiley.

Millon, T. (2004). *Masters of the Mind: Exploring the story of mental illness from ancient times to the new millennium.* New York: John Wiley & Sons.

Mills, J. A. (2010). Hallucinogens as hard science: The adrenochrome hypothesis for the biogenesis of schizophrenia. *History of Psychology, 13,* 178–195.

Mills, J. S., Polivy, J., Herman, C. P., & Tiggemann, M. (2002). Effects of exposure to thin media images: Evidence of self-enhancement among restrained eaters. *Personality and Social Psychology Bulletin, 28,* 1687–1699.

Milner, A. D., & Goodale, M. A. (2008). Two visual systems re-viewed. *Neuropsychologia, 46,* 774–785.

Milner, B. (1965). Memory disturbance after bilateral hippocampal lesions. In P. Milner & S. E. Glickman (Eds.), *Cognitive processes and the brain: An enduring problem in psychology* (pp. 97–111). Princeton, NJ: D. Van Nostrand Co., Inc.

Milner, B., Corkin, S., & Teuber, H. (1968). Further analysis of the hippocampal amnesic syndrome: 14-year follow-up study of H. M. *Neuropsychologia, 6,* 215–234.

Milner, P. (2003). A brief history of the Hebbian learning rule. *Canadian Psychology, 44,* 5–9.

Mineka, S., & Öhman, A. (2002). Phobias and preparedness: The selective, automatic and encapsulated nature of fear. *Biological Psychiatry, 52,* 927–937.

Mineka, S., & Zinbarg, R. (2006). A contemporary learning theory perspective on the etiology of anxiety disorders: It's not what you thought it was. *American Psychologist, 61,* 10–26.

Minkel, J. D., & Dinges, D. F. (2009). Circadian rhythms in sleepiness, alertness, and performance. In R. Stickgold & M. P. Walker (Eds.), *The neuroscience of sleep* (pp. 183–190). San Diego, CA: Academic Press.

Minuchin, S., Rosman, B. L., & Baker, L. (1978). *Psychosomatic families: Anorexia nervosa in context.* Cambridge, MA: Harvard University Press.

Minzenberg, M. J., Yoon, J. H., & Carter, C. S. (2008). Schizophrenia. In R. E. Hales, S. C. Yudofsky, & G. O. Gabbard (Eds.), *The American Psychiatric Publishing textbook of psychiatry* (5th ed., pp. 407–456). Washington, DC: American Psychiatric Publishing.

Miranda, J., Bernal, G., Lau, A., Kohn, L., Hwang, W., & LaFromboise, T. (2005). State of the science on psychosocial interventions for ethnic minorities. *Annual Review of Clinical Psychology, 1,* 113–42.

Mirescu, C., & Gould, E. (2006). Stress and adult neurogenesis. *Hippocampus, 16,* 233–238.

Mirtle, J. (2011, April 29). Crosby suffers concussion setback. *Globe and Mail.* Retrieved from http://www.theglobeandmail.com/sports/hockey/globe-on-hockey/crosby-suffers-setback/article2004362/.

Mischel, W. (1961). Delay of gratification, need for achievement, and acquiescence in another culture. *Journal of Abnormal and Social Psychology, 62,* 543–552.

Mischel, W. (1968). *Personality and assessment.* New York: Wiley.

Mischel, W. (1973). Toward a cognitive social learning conceptualization of personality. *Psychological Review, 80,* 252–283.

Mischel, W. (1984). Convergences and challenges in the search for consistency. *American Psychologist, 39,* 351–364.

Mishra, R. C. (2001). Cognition across cultures. In D. Matsumoto (Ed.), *The handbook of culture and psychology* (pp. 119–136). New York: Oxford University Press.

Mistlberger R. E., & Rusak, B. (2005). Circadian rhythms in mammals: Formal properties and environmental influences. In *Principles and Practise of Sleep Medicine* (4th ed.). M. H. Kryger, T. Roth, and W. C. Dement (Eds.). Philadelphia: W.B. Saunders Co.

Mitchell, J. P., Macrae, C. N., & Banaji, M. R. (2004). Encoding-specific effects of social cognition on the neural correlates of subsequent memory. *Journal of Neuroscience, 26,* 4912–4917.

Mitchell, K. J., & Johnson, M. K. (2000). Source monitoring: Attributing mental experiences. In E. Tulving & F. I. M. Craik (Eds.), *The Oxford handbook of memory* (pp. 179–196). New York: Oxford University Press.

Mitsonis, C., Zervas, I., Potagas, K., Mandellos, D., Koutsis, G., & Sfagos, K. (2006). The role of stress in multiple sclerosis: Three case reports and review of the literature. *Psychiatriki, 17,* 325–342.

Miyamoto, S., Merrill, D. B., Lieberman, J. A., Fleischacker, W. W., & Marder, S. R. (2008). Antipsychotic drugs. In A. Tasman, J. Kay, J. A. Lieberman, M. B. First, & M. Maj (Eds.), *Psychiatry* (3rd ed.). New York, NY: Wiley-Blackwell.

Modestin, J. (1992). Multiple personality disorder in Switzerland. *American Journal of Psychiatry, 149,* 88–92.

Moe, A., & De Beni, R. (2004). Studying passages with the loci method: Are subject-generated more effective than experimenter-supplied loci pathways? *Journal of Mental Imagery, 28*(3–4), 75–86.

Moffitt, T. E. (2005). The new look of behavioral genetics in developmental psychopathology: Gene–environment interplay in antisocial behaviors. *Psychological Bulletin, 131,* 533–554.

Moghaddam, F. M., Taylor, D. M., & Wright, S. C. (1993). *Social psychology in cross-cultural perspective.* New York: W. H. Freeman.

Mojtabai, R., & Olfson, M. (2008). National trends in psychotherapy by office-based psychiatrists. *Archives of General Psychiatry, 65*(8), 962–970.

Mojtabai, R., & Olfson, M. (2010). National trends in psychotropic medication polypharmacy in office-based psychiatry. *Archives of General Psychiatry, 67*(1), 26–36.

Molcho, M., et al. (2009). Cross-national time trends in bullying behaviour 1994–2006. *Findings from Europe and North America,* S1–S10.

Moller, A. C., Elliot, A. J., & Maier, M. A. (2009). Basic hue-meaning associations. *Emotion, 9*(6), 898–902.

Monahan, J. (1997). Major mental disorders and violence to others. In D. M. Stoff, J. Breiling, & J. D. Maser (Eds.), *Handbook of antisocial behavior.* New York: Wiley.

Monahan, J. L., Murphy, S. T., & Zajonc, R. B. (2000). Subliminal mere exposure: Specific, general, and diffuse effects. *Psychological Science, 11,* 462–466.

Monastra, V. J. (2008). Social skills training for children and teens with ADHD: The neuroeducational life skills program. In V. J. Monastra (Ed.), *Unlocking the potential of patients with ADHD: A model for clinical practice.* Washington, DC: American Psychological Association.

Moncrieff, J. (2001). Are antidepressants overrated? A review of methodological problems in antidepressant trials. *Journal of Nervous and Mental Disorders, 189,* 288–295.

Mongrain, M., & Trambakoulos, J. (2007). A musical mood induction alleviates dysfunctional attitudes in needy and self-critical individuals. *Journal of Cognitive Psychotherapy: An International Journal, 21,* 293–304.

Mongrain, M., Chin, J. & Shapira, L. B. (2010). Practicing compassion increases happiness and self-esteem. *Journal of Happiness Studies.*

Mongrain, M., Lubbers, R., & Struthers, W. (2004). The power of love: Mediation of rejection in roommate relationships of dependents and self-critics. *Personality and Social Psychology Bulletin, 30,* 94–105.

Mongrain, M., Vettese, L. C., Shuster, B., & Kendal, N. (1998). Perceptual biases, affect, and behavior in the relationships of dependents and self-critics. *Journal of Personality and Social Psychology, 75,* 230–241.

Monk, T. H. (2005a). Aging human circadian rhythms: Conventional wisdom may not always be right. *Journal of Biological Rhythms, 20*(4), 366–374.

Monk, T. H. (2005b). Shift work: Basic principles. In M. H. Kryger, T. Roth, & W. C. Dement (Eds.). *Principles and practice of sleep medicine.* Philadelphia, PA: Elsevier Saunders.

Monk, T. H. (2006). Jet lag. In T. Lee-Chiong (Ed.), *Sleep: A comprehensive handbook.* Hoboken, NJ: Wiley-Liss.

Monroe, S. M. (2008). Modern approaches to conceptualizing and measuring human life stress. *Annual Review of Clinical Psychology, 4,* 33–52.

Monroe, S. M., & Hadjiyannakis, K. (2002). The social environment and depression: Focusing on severe life stress. In I. H. Gotlib & C. L. Hammen (Eds.), *Handbook of depression.* New York: Guilford.

Monroe, S. M., & Reid, M. W. (2009). Life stress and major depression. *Current Directions in Psychological Science, 18*(2), 68–72.

Monroe, S. M., & Slavich, G. M. (2007). Psychological stressors overview. In G. Fink (Ed.), *Encyclopedia of stress* (2nd ed.). San Diego, CA: Academic Press.

Monroe, S. M., Slavich, G. M., & Georgiades, K. (2009). The social environment and life stress in depression. In I. H. Gotlib & C. L. Hammen (Eds.), *Handbook of Depression* (2nd ed., pp. 340–360). New York, NY: Guilford Press.

Montessori, M. (1973). *The Discovery of the Child.* New York: Random House, Inc.

Montoya, R. (2008). I'm hot, so I'd say you're not: The influence of objective physical attractiveness on mate selection. *Personality and Social Psychology Bulletin, 34*(10), 1315–1331.

Mook, D. G. (1983). In defense of external invalidity. *American Psychologist, 38,* 379–387.

Moons, W. G., Mackie, D. M., & Garcia-Marques, T. (2009). The impact of repetition-induced familiarity on agreement with weak and strong arguments. *Journal of Personality and Social Psychology, 96*(1), 32–44.

Moore, B. C. J. (2010). Audition. In E. B. Goldstein (Ed.), *Encyclopedia of perception*. Thousand Oaks, CA: Sage.

Moore, D. (2007, January 8). Brainwashed "guinea pig" seeks more damages. *Toronto Star*, A4.

Moore, D. S., & Johnson, S. P. (2008). Mental rotation in human infants: A sex difference. *Psychological Science, 19*(11), 1063–1066.

Moore, K. L., & Persaud, T. V. N. (2008). *Before we are born* (7th ed.). Philadelphia, PA: Saunders.

Mora, S., Cook, N., Buring, J. E., Ridker, P. M., & Lee, I. M. (2007). Physical activity and reduced risk of cardiovascular events: Potential mediating mechanisms. *Circulation, 116*, 2110–2118.

Morahan-Martin, J. (2007). Internet use and abuse and psychological problems. In A. N. Joinson, K. Y. A. McKenna, T. Postmes, & U.-D. Reips (Eds.), *The Oxford handbook of Internet psychology*. New York: Guilford.

Moran, T. H. (2004). Gut peptides in the control of food intake: 30 years of ideas. *Physiology & Behavior, 82*, 175–180.

Morata, T. C. (2007). Young people: Their noise and music exposures and the risk of hearing loss. *International Journal of Audiology, 46*(3), 111–112.

Moretti, M. M., & Odgers, C. (2002). Aggressive and violent girls: Prevalence, profiles, and contributing factors. In R. Corrado, R. Roesch, S. Hart & J. Gierowski (Eds.), *Multi-problem and violent youth: A foundation for comparative research* (pp. 116–129). Amsterdam, Netherlands Antilles: IOS Press.

Moretti, M. M., Odgers, C., & Jackson, M. (Eds.). (2004). *Girls and aggression: Contributing factors and intervention principles*. New York: Kluwer Academic Press/Plenum Publishers.

Moretti, M. M., Odgers, C. L., & Jackson, M. (2004). *Girls and aggression: Contributing factors and intervention principles*. New York: Kluwer-Plenum.

Moretti, M. M., Rein, A. S., & Wiebe, V. J. (1998). Relational self-regulation: Gender differences in risk for dysphporia. *Canadian Journal of Behavioural Science, 30*, 243–252.

Moretti, M., Jackson, M., & Osuth, I. (in press). Translating research into intervention: Lessons learned and new directions. *Court Review: The Journal of the American Judges Association: Special Issue on Girls in the Juvenile Justice System.*

Morey, L. C. (1988). Personality disorders in DSM-III and DSM-III-R. *American Journal of Psychiatry, 145*, 573–577.

Morgan, H. (1996). An analysis of Gardner's theory of multiple intelligence. *Roeper Review, 18*, 263–269.

Morgan, M. J. (2000). Ecstacy (MDMA): A review of its possible persistent psychological effects. *Psychopharmacology, 152*, 230–248.

Morhenn, V. B., Park, J., Piper, E., & Zak, P. J. (2008). Monetary sacrifice among strangers is mediated by endogenous oxytocin release after physical contact. *Evolution and Human Behavior, 29*(6), 375–383.

Moriarity, J. L., Boatman, D., Krauss, G. L., Storm, P. B., & Lenz, F. A. (2001). Human "memories" can be evoked by stimulation of the lateral temporal cortex after ipsilateral medical temporal lobe resection. *Journal of Neurology, Neurosurgery & Psychiatry, 71*, 549–551.

Morin, C. M. (2002). Contributions of cognitive-behavioral approaches to the clinical management of insomnia. *Journal of Clinical Psychiatry, 4*(Suppl. 1), 21–26.

Morin, C. M. (2005). Psychological and behavioral treatments for primary insomnia. In M. H. Kryger, T. Roth, & W. C. Dement (Eds.), *Principles and practice of sleep medicine*. Philadelphia, PA: Elsevier Saunders.

Morin, C. M., Colecchi, C., Stone, J., Sood, R., & Brink, D. (1999). Behavioral and pharmacological therapies for late-life insomnia: A randomized controlled trial. *Journal of the American Medical Association, 281*, 991–999.

Morin, C. M., Bastien, C., & Savard, J. (2003). Current status of cognitive-behavior therapy for insomnia: Evidence for treatment effectiveness and feasibility. In M. L. Perlis & K. L. Lichstein (Eds.), *Treating sleep disorders: Principles and practice of behavioral sleep medicine* (pp. 262–285). Hoboken, NJ: John Wiley & Sons.

Morling, B., & Lamoreaux, M. (2008). Measuring culture outside the head: A meta-analysis of individualism–collectivism in cultural products. *Personality and Social Psychology Review, 12*, 199–221.

Morokoff, P. J., Quina, K., Harlow, L. L., Whitmire, L., Grimley, D. M., Gibson, P. R., & Burkholder, G. J. (1997). Sexual assertiveness scale (SAS) for women: Development and validation. *Journal of Personality and Social Psychology, 73*, 790–804.

Morris, C. D., Bransford, J. D., & Franks, J. J. (1977). Levels of processing versus transfer appropriate processing. *Journal of Verbal Learning and Verbal Behavior, 16*, 519–533.

Morris, P. E., Jones, S., & Hampson, P. (1978). An imagery mnemonic for the learning of people's names. *British Journal of Psychology, 69*, 335–336.

Morrison, C. M., & Conway, M. A. (2010). First words and first memories. *Cognition, 116*(1), 23–32.

Morry, M. M. (2007). The attraction-similarity hypothesis among cross-sex friends: Relationship satisfaction, perceived similarities, and self-serving perceptions. *Journal of Social and Personal Relationships, 24*(1), 117–138.

Morry, M. M. (2009). Similarity principle of attraction. In H. T. Reis & S. Sprecher (Eds.), *Encyclopedia of human relationships* (pp. 1500–1504). Los Angeles, CA: Sage.

Moruzzi, G. (1964). Reticular influences on the EEG. *Electroencephalography and Clinical Neurophysiology, 16*, 2–17.

Moscovitch, D. A., et al. (2011). Changes in judgment biases and use of emotion regulation strategies during cognitive behavioural therapy for social anxiety disorder: Distinguishing treatment responders from nonresponders. *Cognitive Therapy and Research*, published online.

Mosher, D., & MacIan, P. (1994). College men and women respond to X-rated videos intended for male or female audiences: Gender and sexual scripts. *Journal of Sex Research, 31*, 99–113.

Moss, P. (1994). Validity. In R. J. Sternberg (Ed.), *Encyclopedia of human intelligence*. New York: Macmillan.

Most, S. B., Scholl, B. J., Clifford, E. R., Simons, D. J. (2005). What you see is what you set: Sustained inattentional blindness and the capture of awareness. *Psychological Review, 112*(1), 217–242.

Most, S. B., Simons, D. J., Scholl, B. J., Jimenez, R., Clifford, E., & Chabris, C. F. (2001). How not to be seen: The contribution of similarity and selective ignoring to sustained inattentional blindness. *Psychological Science, 12*(1), 9–17.

Motivala, S. J., & Irwin, M. R. (2007). Sleep and immunity: Cytokine pathways linking sleep and health outcomes. *Current Directions in Psychological Science, 16*, 21–25.

Mowrer, O. H. (1947). On the dual nature of learning: A reinterpretation of "conditioning" and "problem-solving." *Harvard Educational Review, 17*, 102–150.

Mrdjenovic, G., & Levitsky, D. A. (2005). Children eat what they are served: The imprecise regulation of energy intake. *Appetite, 44*, 273–282.

Mroczek, D. K., & Almeida, D. M. (2004). The effect of daily stress, personality, and age on daily negative effect. *Journal of Personality, 72*, 355–378.

Muchinsky, P. M. (2003). *Psychology applied to work* (7th ed.). Belmont, CA: Wadsworth.

Mugitani, R., Fais, L., Kajikawa, S., Werker, J., & Amano, S. (2007). Age-related changes in sensitivity to native phonotactics in Japanese infants. *Journal of Acoustical Society of America, 122*, 1332–1335.

Mullen, B., & Copper, C. (1994). The relation between group cohesiveness and performance: An integration. *Psychological Bulletin, 115*, 210–227.

Muller, F-J., Snyder, E. Y., & Loring, J. F. (2006). Gene therapy: Can neural stem cells deliver? *Nature Reviews Neuroscience, 7*, 75–84.

Mulligan, N. W. (1998). The role of attention during encoding in implicit and explicit memory. *Journal of Experimental Psychology: Learning, Memory, & Cognition, 24*, 27–47.

Mulvaney, M. K., & Mebert, C. J. (2007). Parental corporal punishment predicts behavior problems in early childhood. *Journal of Family Psychology, 21*, 389–397.

Munafò, M. R., Yalcin, B., Willis-Owen, S. A., & Flint, J. (2008). Association of the dopamine D4 receptor (DRD4) gene and approach-related personality traits: Meta-analysis and new data. *Biological Psychiatry, 63*(2), 197–206.

Munck, A. (2007). Corticosteroids and stress. In G. Fink (Ed.), *Encyclopedia of stress*. San Diego: Elsevier.

Munk-Jorgensen, P. (1999). Has deinstitutionalization gone too far? *European Archives of Psychiatry & Clinical Neuroscience, 249*(3), 136–143.

Murdock, B. (2001). Analysis of the serial position curve. In H. L. Roediger III, J. S. Nairne, I. Neath, & A. M. Surprenant (Eds.), *The nature of remembering: Essays in honor of Robert G. Crowder* (pp. 151–170). Washington, DC: American Psychological Association.

Muris, P. (2002). Relationships between self-efficacy and symptoms of anxiety disorders and depression in a normal adolescent sample. *Personality and Individual Differences, 32*, 337–348.

Muris, P., & Merckelbach, H. (2001). The etiology of childhood specific phobia: A multifactorial model. In M. W. Vasey, & M. R. Dadds (Eds.), *The developmental psychopathology of anxiety.* (pp. 355–385). New York, NY: Oxford University Press.

Murison, R. (2001). Is there a role for psychology in ulcer disease? *Integrative Physiological and Behavioral Science, 36*(1), 75–83.

Murphy K. R., & Sideman, L. (2006a). The fadification of emotional intelligence. In K. R. Murphy (Ed.), *A critique of emotional intelligence: What are the problems and how can they be fixed?* (pp. 283–300). Mahwah, NJ: Erlbaum.

Murphy K. R., & Sideman, L. (2006b). The two EIs. In K. R. Murphy (Ed.), *A critique of emotional intelligence: What are the problems and how can they be fixed?* (pp. 37–58). Mahwah, NJ: Erlbaum.

Murphy, P. N., Wareing, M., Fisk, J. E., & Montgomery, C. (2009). Executive working memory deficits in ecstasy/MDMA users: A critical review. *Neuropsychology, 60,* 159–175.

Murphy, K. R. (2002). Can conflicting perspectives on the role of *g* in personnel selection be resolved? *Human Performance, 15,* 173–186.

Murphy, K. R. (2006). *A critique of emotional intelligence: What are the problems and how can they be fixed?* Mahwah, NJ: Erlbaum and Associates.

Murphy, K. R., & Cleveland, J. N. (1995). *Understanding performance appraisal: Social, organizational, and goal-based perspectives.* Thousand Oaks, CA: Sage.

Murray, B. (2003). The seven sins of memory. *APA Monitor, 34,* 28.

Murray, B. B., & Bramon, F. (2005). Developmental model of schizophrenia. In B. J. Sadock et al., (Eds.), *Comprehensive textbook of psychiatry* (pp. 1381–1395). Philadephia, PA: Lippincott, Williams, and Wilkins.

Murray, D., Trudeau, R., & Schaller, M. (2011). On the origins of cultural differences in conformity: Four tests of the pathogen prevalence hypothesis. *Personality and Social Psychology Bulletin, 37,* 318–329.

Murray, E. A. (2007, November). The amygdala, reward and emotion. *Trends in Cognitive Sciences, 11,* 489–497.

Murray, H. A. (1938). *Explorations in personality.* New York: Oxford University Press.

Murray, H. A. (1943). *Thematic Apperception Test—Manual.* Cambridge, MA: Harvard University Press.

Murray, R. M., & Bramon, E. (2005). Developmental model of schizophrenia. In B. J. Sadock & V. A. Sadock (Eds.), *Kaplan & Sadock's comprehensive textbook of psychiatry* (pp. 1381–1395). Philadelphia, PA: Lippincott, Williams & Wilkins.

Murstein, B. I., & Fontaine, P. A. (1993). The public's knowledge about psychologists and other mental health professionals. *American Psychologist, 48,* 839–845.

Muscatell, K. A., Addis, D. R., & Kensinger, E. A. (2010). Self-involvement modulates the effective connectivity of the autobiographical memory network. *Social Cognitive and Affective Neuroscience, 5,* 68–76.

Musson, D. M., Sandal, G. M., & Helmreich, R. L. (2004). Personality characteristics and trait clusters in final stage astronaut selection. *Aviation, Space, and Environmental Medicine, 75,* 342–349.

Mustanski, B. S., Chivers, M. L., & Bailey, J. M. (2002). A critical review of recent biological research on human sexual orientation. *Annual Review of Sex Research, 12,* 89–140.

Mutz, D. C., & Goldman, S. K. (2010). Mass media. In J. F. Dovidio, M. Hewstone, P. Glick, & V. M. Esses (Eds.), *The Sage handbook of prejudice, stereotyping, and discrimination.* Los Angeles, CA: Sage.

Muzina, D. J., Kemp, D. E., & Calabrese, J. R. (2008). Mood stabilizers. In A. Tasman, J. Kay, J. A. Lieberman, M. B. First, & M. Maj (Eds.), *Psychiatry* (3rd ed.). New York, NY: Wiley-Blackwell.

Myers, J. (2000). Qualitative research and the generalizability question: Standing firm with Proteus. *The Qualitative Report, 4*(3/4).

Myers, D. G. (1992). *The pursuit of happiness: Who is happy—and why.* New York: Morrow.

Myers, D. G. (1999). Close relationships and quality of life. In D. Kahneman, E. Diener, & N.

Schwarz (Eds.), *Well-being: The foundations of hedonic psychology.* New York: Russell Sage Foundation.

Myers, D. G. (2008). Religion and human flourishing. In M. Eid & R. J. Larsen (Eds.), *The science of subjective well-being* (pp. 323–346). New York: Guilford.

Myers, D. G. (2002). Human intuition: The brain behind the scenes. *Cerebrum, 4*(3), 100–113.

Myers, D. G., & Diener, E. (1995). Who is happy? *Psychological Science, 6,* 10–19.

Myers, D. G., & Diener, E. (1997). The pursuit of happiness. *Scientific American Special Issue, 7,* 40–43.

Myers, D. G., & Lamm, H. (1976). The group polarization phenomenon. *Psychological Bulletin, 83,* 602–627.

Myerson, J., Rank, M. R., Raines, F. Q., & Schnitzler, M. A. (1998). Race and general cognitive ability: The myth of diminishing returns to education. *Psychological Science, 9,* 139–142.

Myrtek, M. (2007). Type A behavior and hostility as independent risk factors for coronary heart disease. In J. Jordan, B. Bardé, & A. M. Zeiher (Eds.), *Contributions toward evidence-based psychocardiology: A systematic review of the literature.* Washington, DC: American Psychological Association.

N. S. town bans smoking in cars carrying children. (2007, November 18). *CBC News.* Retrieved July 25, 2008, from http://www.cbc.canada/nova-scotia/story/2007/11/19/wolfville-smoking.

Nabi, H., Singh-Manoux, A., Shipley, M., Gimeno, D., Marmot, M. G., & Kivimaki, M. (2008). Do psychological factors affect inflammation and incident coronary heart disease? The Whitehall II study. *Arteriosclerosis, Thrombosis, and Vascular Biology, 24,* 1398–1406.

Nadelson, C. C., Notman, M. T., & McCarthy, M. K. (2005). Gender issues in psychotherapy. In G. O. Gabbard, J. S. Beck, & J. Holmes (Eds.), *Oxford textbook of psychotherapy.* New York: Oxford University Press.

Nader, R., & Smith, C. (2003). A role for stage 2 sleep in memory processing. In Maquet, P., Smith, C., & Stickgold, R. (Eds.), *Sleep and brain plasticity* (pp. 87–98). Oxford, UK: Oxford University Press.

Naglieri, J. A., Drasgow, F., Schmit, M., Handler, L., Prifitera, A., Margolis, A., et al. (2004). Psychological testing on the Internet: New problems, old issues. *American Psychologist, 59,* 150–162.

Nahas, Z., Kozel, F. A., Molnar, C., Ramsey, D., Holt, R., Ricci, R., et al. (2007). Methods of administering transcranial magnetic stimulation. In M. S. George & R. H. Belmaker (Eds.), *Transcranial magnetic stimulation in clinical psychiatry* (pp. 39–58). Washington, DC: American Psychiatric Publishing.

Naidoo, J. C. (1992). The mental health of visible ethnic minorities in Canada. *Psychology and Developing Societies, 4,* 165–187

Nairne, J. S. (2002). Remembering over the short-term: The case against the standard model. *Annual Review of Psychology, 53,* 53–81.

Nairne, J. S. (2003). Sensory and working memory. In A. F. Healy & R. W. Proctor (Eds.), *Handbook of psychology (Vol. 4): Experimental psychology.* New York: Wiley.

Nairne, J. S., Pandeirada, J. N. S., & Thompson, S. R. (2008). Adaptive memory: The comparative value of survival processing. *Psychological Science, 19,* 176–180.

Narr, K. L., Woods, R. P., Thompson, P. M., Szeszko, P., Robinson, D., Dimtcheva, T., et al. (2007). Relationships between IQ and regional

cortical gray matter thickness in healthy adults. *Cerebral Cortex, 17*(9), 2163–2171.

Narrow, W. E., Regier, D. A., Rae, D. S., Manderscheid, R. W., & Locke, B. Z. (1993). Use of services by persons with mental and addictive disorders: Findings from the National Institute of Mental Health Epidemiologic Catchment Area Program. *Archives of General Psychiatry, 50,* 95–107.

NASA. (2008). *Astronaut Candidate Program.* Retrieved June 3, 2011, from http://astronauts.nasa.gov/content/broch00.htm.

Nasar, S. (1998). *A beautiful mind: A biography of John Forbes Nash, Jr., winner of the Nobel Prize in Economics.* New York: Simon & Schuster.

Näslund, E., & Hellström, P. M. (2007). Appetite signaling: From gut peptides and enteric nerves to brain. *Physiology & Behavior, 92,* 256–262.

National Defence. (2003). Statistics Canada: *CF mental health survey: A "milestone."* Retrieved June 27, 2005, from http://www.forces.gc.ca/health/information/op_health/stats_can/engraph/MH_Survey_e.asp.

National Institute on Deafness and Other Communication Disorders. (2002). Neural and behavioral aspects of early language development: Presenter: Laura-Ann Petitto. Retrieved May 10, 2005, from http://www.nidcd.nih.gov/news/meetings/02/earlylanguage/petitto.asp.

Naumann, L. P., Vazire, S., Rentfrow, P. J., & Gosling, S. D. (2009). Personality judgments based on physical appearance. *Personality and Social Psychology Bulletin, 35*(12), 1661–1671.

Navasky, M., & O'Connor, K. (2005, May 10). The new asylums. Public Broadcasting System: *Frontline.*

Nebenzahl, D. (2010, March 20). Canadians falling asleep on the job. *Toronto Star,* B8.

Needlman, R. D. (2004). Growth and development. In R. E. Behrman, R. M. Kliegman, & H. B. Jenson (Eds.), *Nelson textbook of pediatrics.* Philadelphia: Saunders.

Neisser, U. (1967). *Cognitive psychology.* New York: Appleton-Century-Crofts.

Neisser, U. (1998). Introduction: Rising test scores and what they mean. In U. Neisser (Ed.), *The rising curve: Long-term gains in IQ and related measures.* Washington, DC: American Psychological Association.

Neisser, U., & Harsch, N. (1992). Phantom flashbulbs: False recollections of hearing the news about *Challenger.* In E. Winograd & U. Neisser (Eds.), *Affect and accuracy in recall: Studies of "flashbulb" memories.* New York: Cambridge University Press.

Neisser, U., Boodoo, G., Bouchard, T. J., Jr., Boykin, A. W., Brody, N., Ceci, S. J., et al. (1996). Intelligence: Knowns and unknowns. *American Psychologist, 51,* 77–101.

Nelson, C. A., & Luciana, M. (Eds.). (2001). *Handbook of developmental cognitive neuroscience.* Boston, MA: The MIT Press.

Nelson, C. A., Bloom, F. E., Cameron, J. L., Amaral, D., Dahl, R. E., & Pine, D. (2002). An integrative, multidisciplinary approach to the study of brain–behavior relations in the context of typical and atypical development. *Development and Psychopathology, 14,* 499–520.

Nemeroff, C. B., Kalali, A., Keller, M. B., Charney, D. S., Lenderts, S. E., Cascade, E. F., et al. (2007). Impact of publicity concerning pediatric suicidality data on physician practice patterns in the United States. *Archives of General Psychiatry, 64,* 466–472.

Nemeroff, C. B. (2008). Understanding the pathophysiology of postpartum depression: Implications for the development of novel treatments. *Neuron, 59,* 185–186.

Nesse, R. M., & Ellsworth, P. C. (2009). Evolution, emotions, and emotional disorders. *American Psychologist, 64*(2), 129–139.

Nestler, E. J., & Malenka, R. C. (2004). The addicted brain. *Scientific American, 290*(3), 78–85.

Nettle, D. (2001). *Strong imagination, madness, creativity, and human nature.* New York, NY: Oxford University Press.

Nettle, D. (2006). The evolution of personality variation in humans and other animals. *American Psychologist, 61,* 622–631.

Neuberg, S. L., Kenrick, D. T., & Schaller, M. (2010). Evolutionary social psychology. In S. T. Fiske, D. T. Gilbert, & G. Lindzey (Eds.), *Handbook of social psychology,* (5th ed., Vol. 2, pp. 761–796). Hoboken, NJ: Wiley.

Neugroschl, J. A., Kolevzon, A., Samuels, S. C., & Marin, D. B. (2005). Dementia. In B. J. Sadock & V. A. Sadock (Eds.), *Kaplan & Sadock's comprehensive textbook of psychiatry* (pp. 1068–1092). Philadelphia: Lippincott Williams & Wilkins.

Neuschatz, J. S., Lampinen, J. M., Preston, E. L., Hawkins, E. R., & Toglia, M. P. (2002). The effect of memory schemata on memory and the phenomenological experience of naturalistic situations. *Applied Cognitive Psychology, 16,* 687–708.

Neuschatz, J. S., Lampinen, J. M., Toglia, M. P., Payne, D. G., & Cisneros, E. P. (2007). False memory research: History, theory, and applied implications. In M. P. Toglia, J. D. Read, D. F. Ross, & R. C. L. Lindsay (Eds.), *Handbook of eyewitness psychology: Volume 1. Memory for events.* Mahwah, NJ: Erlbaum.

New York Times. (1921). Einstein sees Boston: Fails on Edison Test. Retrieved June 20, 2011, from http://query.nytimes.com/gst/abstract.html?res=F60D15FE345B1B7A93CAA8178ED85F458285F9.

New York Times. (2009). Kim Peek, inspiration for "Rain Man" dies at 58, Obituary. Retrieved June 20, 2011, from http://www.nytimes.com/2009/12/27/us/27peek.html.

Newberg, A., Alavi, A., Baime, M., Pourdehnad, M., Santanna, J., & D'Aquili, E. (2001). The measurement of regional cerebral blood flow during the complex cognitive task of meditation: A preliminary SPECT study. *Psychiatry Research: Neuroimaging, 106*(2), 113–122.

Newborn brain cells modulate learning and memory. (2008). (Press release). Salk Institute for Biological Studies. Retrieved February 11, 2008, from http://www.salk.edu/news/news_press_details.php?ie=198.

Newcombe, N. S. (2007). Taking science seriously: Straight thinking about spatial sex differences. In S. J. Ceci & W. M. Williams (Eds.), *Why aren't more women in science?* (pp. 69–78). Washington, DC: American Psychological Association.

Newell, A., & Simon, H. A. (1972). *Human problem solving.* Englewood Cliffs, NJ: Prentice-Hall.

Newell, A., Shaw, J. C., & Simon, H. A. (1958). Elements of a theory of human problem solving. *Psychological Review, 65,* 151–166.

Newman, C. F. & Beck, A. T. (2009). Cognitive therapy. In B. J. Sadock, V. A. Sadock, & P. Ruiz (Eds.), *Kaplan & Sadock's comprehensive textbook of psychiatry* (pp. 2857–2872). Philadelphia, PA: Lippincott Williams & Wilkins.

Newman, G. E., Keil, F. C., Kuhlmeier, V. A., & Wynn, K. (2010). Early understandings of the link between agents and order. *Proceedings of the National Academy of Sciences, 107,* 17140–17145.

Newman, T. M. (2010). Assessment of giftedness in school-age children using measures of intelligence or cognitive abilities. In S. I. Pfeiffer (Ed.), *Handbook of giftedness in children: Psychoeducational theory, research, and best practices.* New York, NY: Springer.

Niccols, A. (2007). Fetal alcohol syndrome and the developing socio-emotional brain. *Brain and Cognition, 65,* 135–142.

Nickerson, C., Schwarz, N., Diener, E., & Kahneman, D. (2003). Zeroing in on the dark side of the American dream: A closer look at the negative consequences of the goal for financial success. *Psychological Science, 14,* 531–536.

Nickerson, R. S. (1998). Confirmation bias: A ubiquitous phenomenon in many guises. *Review of General Psychology, 2,* 175–220.

Nicoladis, E., & Genesee, F. (1997). Language development in preschool bilingual children. *Journal of Speech–Language Pathology & Audiology, 21,* 258–270.

Niebyl, J. R., & Simpson, J. L. (2007). Drugs and environmental agents in pregnancy and lactation: Embryology, teratology, epidemiology. In S. G. Gabbe, J. R. Niebyl, & J. L. Simpson (Eds.) *Obstetrics: Normal and problem pregnancies* (5th ed., pp. 184–214). Philadelphia, PA: Elsevier.

Niedenthal, P. M., Mermillod, M., Maringer, M. & Hess, U. (in press). The Simulation of Smiles (SIMS) Model: Embodied Simulation and the meaning of facial expression. Target article for *Behavioral and Brain Sciences.*

Niedenthal. P. M. (2007). Embodied emotion. *Science, 316,* 1002–1004.

Nielsen, T. A., & Zadra, A., et al., (2003). Typical dreams of Canadian University students. *Dreaming, 13,* 211–235.

Nielsen Media Research. (1998). *Report on television: 1998.* New York: Author.

Nielsen, T. A., & Stenstrom, P. (2005). What are the memory sources of dreaming? *Nature, 437,* 1286–1289.

Nielsen, T. A., & Zadra, A. (2000). Dreaming disorders. In M. H. Kryger, T. Roth, & W. C. Dement (Eds.), *Principles and practice of sleep medicine.* Philadelphia: Saunders.

Nielsen, T., & Levin, R. (2009). Theories and correlates of nightmares. In R. Stickgold & M. P. Walker (Eds.), *The neuroscience of sleep* (pp. 323–329). San Diego, CA: Academic Press.

Nielsen, T. A. (2000). A review of mentation in REM and NREM sleep: "Covert" REM sleep as a possible reconciliation of two opposing models. *Behavior and Brain Sciences, 23,* 793–1121.

Nieuwenhuis, S., Ridderinkhof, K. R., de Jong, R., Kok, A., & van der Molen, M. W. (2000). Inhibitory inefficiency and failures of intention activation: Age-related decline in the control of saccadic eye movements. *Psychology and Aging, 15*(4), 635–647.

Nievar, M. A., & Becker, B. J. (2008). Sensitivity as a privileged predictor of attachment: A second perspective on De Wolff and Van IJzendoorn's meta-analysis. *Social Development, 17,* 102–114.

Nikelly, A. G. (1994). Alcoholism: Social as well as psycho–medical problem—The missing "big picture." *Journal of Alcohol & Drug Education, 39,* 1–12.

Nikolic, D., Lichti, P., & Singer, W. (2007). Color opponency in synaesthetic experiences. *Psychological Science, 18,* 481–486.

Nir, Y., & Tononi, G. (2010). Dreaming and the brain: From phenomenology to neurophysiology. *Trends in Cognitive Sciences, 14*(2), 88–100.

Nisbett, R. E. (2003). *The geography of thought: How Asians and Westerners think differently … and why.* New York: Free Press.

Nisbett, R. E. (2005). Heredity, environment, and race differences in IQ: A commentary on Rushton and Jensen. *Psychology, Public Policy, and the Law, 11,* 302–310.

Nisbett, R. E. (Ed.). (1993). *Rules for reasoning.* Hillsdale, NJ: Erlbaum.

Nisbett, R. E., & Miyamoto, Y. (2005). The influence of culture: Holistic versus analytic perception. *Trends in Cognitive Sciences, 9,* 467–473.

Nisbett, R. E., & Wilson, T. D. (1977). The halo effect: Evidence for unconscious alteration of judgments. *Journal of Personality and Social Psychology, 35*(4), 250–256.

Nisbett, R. E., Peng, K., Choi, I., & Norenzayan, A. (2001). Culture and systems of thought: Holistic versus analytic cognition. *Psychological Review, 108,* 291–310.

Nist, S. L., & Holschuh, J. L. (2000). Comprehension strategies at the college level. In R. F. Flippo & D. C. Caverly (Eds.), *Handbook of college reading and study strategy research.* Mahwah, NJ: Erlbaum.

Nobel Prize. (n.d., a). David H. Hubel—Autobiography. Retrieved March 22, 2005, from http://www.nobelprize.org/medicine/laureates/1981/hubel-autob.

Nobel Prize. (n.d., b). The Nobel Prize in Physiology or Medicine 2004: Linda Buck and Richard Axel. Retrieved March 25, 2005, from http://nobelprize.org/medicine/laureates/2004.

Noble, K. G., McCandliss, B. D., & Farah, M. J. (2007). Socioeconomic gradients predict individual differences in neurocognitive abilities. *Developmental Science, 10,* 464–480.

Nobler, M. S., & Sackeim, H. A. (2006). Electroconvulsive therapy and transcranial magnetic stimulation. In D. J. Stein, D. J. Kupfer, & A. F. Schatzberg (Eds.), *Textbook of mood disorders.* Washington, DC: American Psychiatric Publishing.

Noftle, E. E., & Robins, R. W. (2007). Personality predictors of academic outcomes: Big Five correlates of GPA and SAT scores. *Journal of Personality and Social Psychology, 93,* 116–130.

Nolen, S., & Heizen, T. (2011). *Essentials of statistics for the behavioral sciences.* New York, NY: Worth Publishing Co.

Nolen-Hoeksema, S. (1991). Responses to depression and their effects on the duration of depressive episodes. *Journal of Abnormal Psychology, 100,* 569–582.

Nolen-Hoeksema, S. (2000). The role of rumination in depressive disorders and mixed anxiety/depressive symptoms. *Journal of Abnormal Psychology, 109,* 504–511.

Nolen-Hoeksema, S. (2001). Gender differences in depression. *Current Directions in Psychological Science, 10,* 173–176.

Nolen-Hoeksema, S., & Hilt, L. M. (2009). Gender differences in depression. In I. H. Gotlib & C. L. Hammen (Eds.), *Handbook of Depression* (2nd ed., pp. 386–404). New York, NY: Guilford Press.

Nolen-Hoeksema, S., Wisco, B. E., & Lyubomirsky, S. (2008). Rethinking rumination. *Perspectives on Psychological Science, 3*(5), 400–424.

Norcross, J. C. (1995). Dispelling the dodo bird verdict and the exclusivity myth in psychotherapy. *Psychotherapy, 32,* 500–504.

Norcross, J. C., & Beutler, L. E. (2011). Integrative psychotherapies. In R. J. Corsini & D. Wedding (Eds.), *Current psychotherapies* (9th ed.). Belmont, CA: Brooks/Cole.

Norcross, J. C., & Goldfried, M. R. (Eds.). (1992). *Handbook of psychotherapy integration.* New York: Basic Books.

Norcross, J. C., Hedges, M., & Castle, P. H. (2002). Psychologists conducting psychotherapy in 2001: A study of the Division 29 membership. *Psychotherapy: Theory, Research, Practice, Training, 39,* 97–102.

Norenzayan, A., & Heine, S. J. (2005). Psychological universals: What are they and how can we know? *Psychological Bulletin, 131,* 763–784.

Norman, T. R. (2009). Melatonin: Hormone of the night. *Acta Neuropsychiatrica, 21*(5), 263–265.

Norris, F. H., with Byrne, C. M., Diaz, E., & Kaniasty, K. (2001). *Risk factors for adverse outcomes in natural and human-caused disasters: A review of the empirical literature.* Retrieved November 21, 2001, from U.S. Department of Veterans Affairs National Center for PTSD Website: http://www.ncptsd.org/facts/disasters/fs_riskfactors.html.

North, C. S., Eyrich, K. M., Pollio, D. E., & Spitznagel, E. L. (2004). Are rates of psychiatric disorders in the homeless population changing? *American Journal of Public Health, 94*(1), 103–108.

Norton, G. R., Harrison, B., Haunch, J., & Rhodes, L. (1985). Characteristics of people with infrequent panic attacks. *Journal of Abnormal Psychology, 94,* 216–221.

Nosek, B. A., & Greenwald, A. G. (2009). (Part of) the case for a pragmatic approach to validity. *Psychological Bulletin, 135,* 373–376.

Nosek, B. A., Banaji, M., & Greenwald, A. G. (2002). Harvesting implicit group attitudes and beliefs from a demonstration web site. *Group Dynamics: Theory, Research, and Practice, 6*(1), 101–115.

Nosek, B. A., Greenwald, A. G., & Banaji, M. R. (2007). The Implicit Association Test at age 7: A methodological and conceptual review. In J. A. Bargh (Ed.), *Social Psychology and the Unconscious: The Automaticity of Higher Mental Processes* (pp. 265–292). London: Psychology Press.

Nova Scotia Department of Education. (2007). *Stand up against bullying day proclaimed.* Retrieved February 7, 2008, from http://www.gov.ns.ca/news/details.asp?id=20070925006.

Novemsky, N., & Kahneman, D. (2005). The boundaries of loss aversion. *Journal of Marketing Research, 42,* 119–128.

Novick, L. R., & Bassok, M. (2005). Problem solving. In K. J. Holyoak & R. G. Morrison (Eds.), *The Cambridge handbook of thinking and reasoning.* New York: Cambridge University Press.

Noyes, R., Jr., Clarkson, C., Crowe, R. R., Yates, W. R., & McChesney, C. M. (1987). A family study of generalized anxiety disorder. *American Journal of Psychiatry, 144*(8), 1019–1024.

Nucci, L. P. (2002). The development of moral reasoning. In U. Goswami (Eds.), *Blackwell handbook of childhood cognitive development.* Malden, MA: Blackwell Publishing.

Nunes, J. (2002). *Beyond Crazy: Journeys through mental illness.* Toronto: McClelland & Stewart Ltd.

Nurnberger, J. I., & Zimmerman, J. (1970). Applied analysis of human behavior: An alternative to conventional motivational inferences and unconscious determination in therapeutic programming. *Behavior Therapy, 1,* 59–69.

Nussbaum, A. D., & Steele, C. M. (2007). Situational disengagement and persistence in the face of adversity. *Journal of Experimental Social Psychology, 43,* 127–134.

O'Brien, C. P., Volkow, N., & Li, T.-K. (2006). What's in a word? Addiction versus dependence in DSM-V. *American Journal of Psychiatry, 163,* 764–765.

O'Connor, D. B., & Conner, M. (2011). Effects of stress on eating behavior. In R. J. Contrada & A. Baum (Eds.), *The handbook of stress science: Biology, psychology, and health* (pp. 111–121). New York, NY: Springer.

O'Connor, M. C., & Paunonen, S. V. (2007). Big Five personality predictors of post-secondary academic performance. *Personality and Individual Differences, 43,* 971–990.

O'Connor, T. (1995). *The feeling of greatness: The Moe Norman Story.* Toronto, ON: Evelevel Videos Inc.

O'Donnell, L. (2009). The Wechsler Intelligence Scale for Children—Fourth Edition. In J. A. Naglieri & S. Goldstein (Eds.), *Practitioner's guide to assessing intelligence and achievement* (pp. 153–190). New York, NY: Wiley.

O'Donohue, W. (1998). Conditioning and third-generation behavior therapy. In W. O'Donohue (Ed.), *Learning and behavior therapy.* Boston: Allyn & Bacon.

O'Hare, E. D., Lu, L. H., Houston, S. M., Bookheimer, S. Y., & Sowell, E. R. (2008). Neurodevelopmental changes in verbal working memory load-dependency: An fMRI investigation. *Neuroimage, 42,* 1678–1685.

O'Leary, K. D., Kent, R. N., & Kanowitz, J. (1975). Shaping data collection congruent with experimental hypotheses. *Journal of Applied Behavior Analysis, 8,* 43–51.

O'Leary, M. B., & Cummings, J. N. (2007). The spatial, temporal, and configurational characteristics of geographic dispersion in teams. *MIS Quarterly, 31,* 433–452.

O'Malley, M. (1999). Taber shooting: Questions will be answered. *CBC News Online.* Retrieved June 19, 2005, from http://www.cbc.ca/news/background/taber/omalley2.html.

O'Neill, J., Senior, T. J., Allen, K., Huxter, J. R., & Csicsvari, J. (2007). Reactivation of experience-dependent cell assembly patterns in the hippocampus. *Nature Neuroscience, 11,* 209–215.

O'Reardon, J. P., Solvason, H. B., Janicak, P. G., Sampson, S., Isenberg, K. E., Nahas, Z., et al. (2007). Efficacy and safety of transcranial magnetic stimulation in the acute treatment of major depression: A multisite randomized controlled trial. *Biological Psychiatry, 62,* 1208–1216.

O'Sullivan, D. (2006). Meta-analysis. In G. M. Breakwell, S. Hammond, C. Fife-Schaw, & J. A. Smith (Eds.), *Research methods in psychology* (3rd ed.). London: Sage.

Oakes, L. M. (2009). The "Humpty Dumpty problem" in the study of early cognitive development: Putting the infant back together again. *Perspectives on Psychological Science, 4,* 352–358.

Oakes, M. E., & Slotterback, C. S. (2000). Self-reported measures of appetite in relation to verbal cues about many foods. *Current Psychology: Developmental, Learning, Personality, Social, 19,* 137–142.

Oaten, M., Stevenson, R. J., & Case, T. I. (2009). Disgust as a disease-avoidance mechanism. *Psychological Bulletin, 135,* 303–321.

Oberauer, K., Süß, H.-M., Wilhelm, O., & Sander, N. (2007). Individual differences in working memory capacity and reasoning ability. In A. R. A. Conway, C. Jarrold, M. J. Kane, A. Miyake, & J. N. Towse (Eds.), *Variation in working memory* (pp. 49–75). New York: Oxford University Press.

Odgers, C. L., Moretti, M. M., , & Reppucci, N. D. (2010). A review of findings from the "Gender and Aggression Project" informing juvenile justice policy and practice through gender-sensitive research. *Court Review, 46,* 6–10.

Office of the Commissioner of Official Languages. (2004). *A look at bilingualism.* Retrieved May 11, 2005, from http://www.ocol-clo.gc.ca/symposium/documents/brochure/brochure_e.htm.

Ogden, J. (2010). *The psychology of eating: From healthy to disordered behavior.* Malden, MA: Wiley-Blackwell.

Ogilvie, M. (2011, April 8). Why a blow to the head is a big deal, Toronto Star. Retrieved November 16, 2011, from http://www.healthzone.ca/health/newsfeatures/article/971546-why-a-blow-to-the-head-is-a-big-deal.

Ogloff, J. R. P., & Whittemore, K. E. (2001). Fitness to stand trial and criminal responsibility in Canada. In R. A. Schuller & J. R. P. Ogloff (Eds.), *Introduction to psychology and law: Canadian perspectives* (pp. 283–313). Toronto: University of Toronto Press.

Ohayon, M. M., Carskadon, M. A., Guilleminault, C., & Vitiello, M. V. (2004). Meta-analysis of quantitative sleep parameters from childhood to old age in healthy individuals: Developing normative sleep values across the human lifespan. *Sleep: Journal of Sleep & Sleep Disorders Research, 27,* 1255–1273.

Öhman, A., & Mineka, S. (2001). Fears, phobias, and preparedness: Toward an evolved module of fear and fear learning. *Psychological Review, 108,* 483–522.

Öhman, A., & Wiens, S. (2003). On the automaticity of autonomic responses in emotion: An evolutionary perspective. In R. J. Davidson, K. R. Scherer, & H. H. Goldsmith (Eds.), *Handbook of affective sciences.* New York: Oxford University Press.

Okami, P., & Shackelford, T. K. (2001). Human sex differences in sexual psychology and behavior. *Annual Review of Sex Research, 12,* 186–241.

Olds, J. (1956). Pleasure centers in the brain. *Scientific American, 193,* 105–116.

Olds, J., & Milner, P. (1954). Positive reinforcement produced by electrical stimulation of the septal area and other regions of the rat brain. *Journal of Comparative and Physiological Psychology, 47,* 419–427.

Olds, M. E., & Fobes, J. L. (1981). The central basis of motivation: Intracranial self-stimulation studies. *Annual Review of Psychology, 32,* 523–574.

Olfson, M. & Marcus, S. C. (2009). National patterns in antidepressant medication treatment. *Archives of General Psychiatry, 66*(8), 848–856.

Olfson, M., & Marcus, S. C. (2010). National trends in outpatient psychotherapy. *The American Journal of Psychiatry, 167*(12), 1456–1463.

Olfson, M., Marcus, S. C., Druss, B., & Pincus, H. A. (2002). National trends in the use of outpatient psychotherapy. *American Journal of Psychiatry, 159,* 1914–1920.

Olio, K. (1994). Truth in memory. *American Psychologist, 49,* 442–443.

Oliveira, M. (2008, February 15). Link made between fatal crashes, fatigue. *The Globe and Mail,* A2.

Oliver, J. (2005). *Happiness: How to find it and keep it.* London, UK: Duncan Baird Publishers.

Ollendick, T. H., Öst, L.-G., Reuterskiöld, L., Costa, N., Cederlund, R., Sirbu, C., et al. (2009).

One-session treatment of specific phobias in youth: A randomized clinical trial in the United States and Sweden. *Journal of Consulting and Clinical Psychology, 77*(3), 504–516.

Oller, J. W., & Oller, S. D. (2010). *Autism: The diagnosis, treatment, & etiology of the undeniable epidemic.* Sudbury, MA: Jones and Bartlett Publishers.

Oller, K., & Pearson, B. Z. (2002). Assessing the effects of bilingualism: D. K. D. Oller & R. E. Eilers (Eds.), *Language and literacy in bilingual children.* Clevedon, UK: Multilingual Matters.

Olley, J. G., & Gutentag, S. S. (1999). Autism: Historical overview, definition, and characteristics. In D. B. Zager (Ed.), *Autism* (pp. 3–22). Hillsdale, NJ: Erlbaum and Associates.

Olson, E. J., & Park, J. G. (2006). Snoring. In T. Lee-Chiong (Ed.), *Sleep: A comprehensive handbook.* Hoboken, NJ: Wiley-Liss.

Olson, J. M., & Maio, G. R. (2003). Persuasion and attitude change. In T. Millon & M. J. Lerner (Eds.), *Handbook of psychology (Vol. 5): Personality and social psychology.* New York: Wiley.

Olson, J. M., & Roese, N. J. (1995). The perceived funniness of humorous stimuli. *Personality and Social Psychology Bulletin, 21,* 908–913.

Olson, J. M., & Stone, J. (2005). The influence of behavior on attitudes. In D. Albarracin, B. T. Johnson, & M. P. Zanna (Eds.), *The handbook of attitudes.* Mahwah, NJ: Erlbaum.

Olson, J. M., & Zanna, M. P. (1993). Attitudes and attitude change. *Annual Review of Psychology, 44,* 117–154.

Olson, J. M., Goffin, R. D., & Haynes, G. A. (2007). Relative versus absolute measures of attitudes: Implications for predicting diverse attitude-relevant criteria. *Journal of Personality and Social Psychology, 93,* 907–926.

Olson, J. M., Roese, N. J., & Zanna, M. P. (1996). Expectancies. In E. T. Higgins & A. W. Kruglanski (Eds.), *Social psychology: Handbook of basic principles.* New York: Guilford.

Olson, M. A., & Fazio, R. H. (2001). Implicit attitude formation through classical conditioning. *Psychological Science, 12,* 413–417.

Olson, M. A., & Fazio, R. H. (2002). Implicit acquisition and manifestation of classically conditioned attitudes. *Social Cognition, 20*(2), 89–104.

Olson, S. (2005). Neuroimaging: Brain scans raise privacy concerns. *Science, 307,* 1548–1550.

Olszewski-Kubilius, P. (2003). Gifted education programs and procedures. In W. M. Reynolds & G. E. Miller (Eds.), *Handbook of psychology (Vol. 7): Educational psychology.* New York: Wiley.

One in six people report being victims of racism. (2005, March 21). *The Globe and Mail,* A7.

Ones, D. S., Viswesvaran, C., & Dilchert, S. (2005). Cognitive ability in selection decisions. In O. Wilhelm & R. W. Engle (Eds.), *Handbook of understanding and measuring intelligence.* Thousand Oaks, CA: Sage.

Ong, A. D. (2010). Pathways linking positive emotion and health in later life. *Current Directions in Psychological Science, 19*(6), 358–362.

Ong, A. D., Fuller-Rowell, T., & Burrow, A. L. (2009). Racial discrimination and the stress process. *Journal of Personality and Social Psychology, 96*(6), 1259–1271.

Ono, H., & Wade, N. J. (2005). Depth and motion in historical descriptions of motion parallax. *Perception, 34,* 1263–1273.

Ono, K. (1987). Supersitious behavior in humans. *Journal of the Experimental Analysis of Behavior, 47*(3), 261–271.

Ontario Ministry of Health. (2011). *Ontario wait times.* Retrieved June 30, 2011, from http://www.health.gov.on.ca/en/public/programs/waittimes/surgery/default.aspx.

Oppliger, P. A. (2007). Effects of gender stereotyping on socialization. In R. W. Preiss, B. M. Gayle, N. Burrell, M. Allen, & J. Bryant (Eds.), *Mass media effects research: Advances through meta-analysis* (pp. 192–214). Mahwah, NJ: Erlbaum.

Ormerod, T. C., MacGregor, J. N., & Chronicle, E. P. (2002). Dynamics and constraints in insight problem solving. *Journal of Experimental Psychology: Learning, Memory and Cognition, 28,* 791–799.

Orne, M. T. (1951). The mechanisms of hypnotic age regression: An experimental study. *Journal of Abnormal and Social Psychology, 46,* 213–225.

Orne, M. T., & Dinges, D. F. (1989). Hypnosis. In H. I. Kaplan & B. J. Sadock (Eds.), *Comprehensive textbook of psychiatry* (5th ed., Vol. 2). Baltimore: Williams & Wilkins.

Orne, M. T., & Holland, C. C. (1968). On the ecological validity of laboratory deceptions. *International Journal of Psychiatry, 6,* 282–293.

Ornstein, R. E. (1997). *The right mind: Making sense of the hemispheres.* San Diego: Harcourt.

Orsillo, S. M., & Roemer, L. (2010). *The mindful way through anxiety: Break free from chronic worry and reclaim your life.* New York: The Guilford Press.

Orth, U., Trzesniewski, K. H., & Robins, R. W. (2010). Self-esteem development from young adulthood to old age: A cohort-sequential longitudinal study. *Journal of Personality and Social Psychology, 98*(4), 645–658.

Orth-Gomer, K., Wamala, S. P., Horsten, M., Schenck-Gustafsson, K., Schneiderman, N., & Mittleman, M. A. (2000). Marital stress worsens prognosis in women with coronary heart disease: The Stockholm female coronary risk study. *Journal of the American Medical Association, 284,* 3008–3014.

Ortigue, S., Bianchi-Demicheli, F., de C. Hamilton, A. F., & Grafton, S. T. (2007). The neural basis of love as a subliminal prime: An event-related functional magnetic resonance imaging study. *Journal of Cognitive Neuroscience, 19,* 1218–1230.

Ortmann, A., & Hertwig, R. (1997). Is deception acceptable? *American Psychologist, 52,* 746–747.

Oskamp, S. (1991). *Attitudes and opinions.* Englewood Cliffs, NJ: Prentice-Hall.

Ost, J. (2009). Recovered memories. In R. Bull, T. Valentine, T. Williamson & R. Bull (Eds.), *Handbook of psychology of investigative interviewing: Current developments and future directions* (pp. 181–204). Wiley-Blackwell.

Öst, L.-G. (1997). Rapid treatment of specific phobias. In G. C. L. Davey (Ed.), *Phobias: A handbook of theory, research and treatment* (pp. 227–247). Oxford, England: Wiley.

Öst, L.-G., Svensson, L., Hellström, K., & Lindwall, R. (2001). One-session treatment of specific phobias in youths: A randomized clinical trial. *Journal of Consulting and Clinical Psychology, 69,* 814–824.

Ostovich, J. M., & Sabini, J. (2004). How are socio-sexuality, sex drive, and lifetime number of sexual partners related? *Personality and Social Psychology Bulletin, 30,* 1255–1266.

Ostrom, T. M., & Sedikides, C. (1992). Outgroup homogeneity effects in natural and minimal groups. *Psychological Bulletin, 112,* 536–552.

Oswald, I., & Adam, K. (1980). The man who had not slept for ten years. *British Medical Journal, 281,* 1684–1685.

Oswald, L. M., Wong, D. F., McCaul, M., Zhou, Y., Kuwabara, H., Choi, L., et al. (2005). Relationships among ventral striatal dopamine release, cortisol secretion, and subjective responses to amphetamine. *Neuropsychopharmacology, 30,* 821–832.

Otto, M. W., Pollack, M. H., Jenike, M. A., & Rosenbaum, J. F. (1999). Anxiety disorders and their treatment. In A. M. Nicholi (Ed.), *The Harvard guide to psychiatry* (3rd ed., pp. 220–239). Cambridge, MA: Harvard University Press.

Outtz, J. L. (2002). The role of cognitive ability tests in employment selection. *Human Performance, 15,* 161–171.

Overton, S. L., & Medina, S. L. (2008). The stigma of mental illness. *Journal of Counseling & Development, 86*(2), 143–151.

Owen, A. M., Coleman, M. R., Boly, M., Davis, M. H., Laureys, S., & Pickard, J. D. (2006). Detecting awareness in the vegetative state. *Science, 313,* 1402–1406.

Oyserman, D., & Lee, S. W. S. (2008). Does culture influence what and how we think? *Psychological Bulletin, 101,* 67–99.

Ozer, D. J., & Benet-Martínez, V. (2006). Personality and the prediction of consequential outcomes. *Annual Review of Psychology, 57,* 401–421.

Ozer, E. J., Best, S. R., Lipsey, T. L., & Weiss, D. S. (2003). Predictors of posttraumatic stress disorder and symptoms in adults: A meta-analysis. *Psychological Bulletin, 129,* 52–73.

Ozgen, E. (2004). Language, learning, and color perception. *Current Directions in Psychological Science, 13*(3), 95–98.

Pace-Schott, E. F. (2005). The neurobiology of dreaming. In M. H. Kryger, T. Roth, & W. C. Dement (Eds.). *Principles and practice of sleep medicine.* Philadelphia: Elsevier Saunders.

Pace-Schott, E. F. (2009). Sleep architecture. In R. Stickgold & M. P. Walker (Eds.), *The neuroscience of sleep* (pp. 11–17). San Diego, CA: Academic Press.

Pace-Schott, E. F., Hobson, J. A., & Stickgold, R. (2008). Sleep, dreaming, and wakefulness. In L. Squire, D. Berg, F. Bloom, S. Du Lac, A. Ghosh, & N. Spitzer (Eds.), *Fundamental neuroscience* (3rd ed., pp. 959–986). San Diego, CA: Academic Press.

Pachter, W. S., Fox, R. E., Zimbardo, P., & Antonuccio, D. O. (2007). Corporate funding and conflicts of interest: A primer for psychologists. *American Psychologist, 62*(9), 1005–1015.

Packer, L. E. (2007). Tourette syndrome "plus." Retrieved July 31, 2007, from http://www.tourettesyndrome.net/index.htm.

Padgett, D. A., & Sheridan, J. F. (2000). Herpes viruses. In G. Fink (Ed.), *Encyclopedia of stress* (pp. 357–363). San Diego: Academic Press.

Pagel, J. F., Blagrove, M., Levin, R., States, B., Stickgold, B., & White, S. (2001). Definitions of dream: A paradigm for comparing field descriptive specific studies of dream. *Dreaming: Journal of the Association for the Study of Dreams, 11,* 195–202.

Paivio, A. (1969). Mental imagery in associative learning and memory. *Psychological Review, 76,* 241–263.

Paivio, A. (1986). *Mental representations: A dual coding approach.* New York: Oxford University Press.

Paivio, A. (2007). *Mind and its evolution: A dual coding theoretical approach.* Mahwah, NJ: Erlbaum.

Paivio, A., Khan, M., & Begg, I. (2000). Concreteness of relational effects on recall of adjective-noun pairs. *Canadian Journal of Experimental Psychology, 54*(3), 149–160.

Paivio, A., Smythe, P. E., & Yuille, J. C. (1968). Imagery versus meaningfulness of nouns in paired-associate learning. *Canadian Journal of Psychology, 22,* 427–441.

Paivio, S. C., Holowaty, K. A. M., & Hall, I. E. (2004). The influence of therapist adherence and competence on client reprocessing of child abuse memories. *Psychotherapy, 41,* 56–68.

Palin, J. L., Goldner, E. M., Keohoorn, M., & Hertzman, C. (2011). Primary mental health care visits in self-reported data versus provincial administrative records. Statistics Canada. Component of Statistics Canada Catalogue no. 82-003-x Health Reports.

Palladino, J. J., & Carducci, B. J. (1984). Students' knowledge of sleep and dreams. *Teaching of Psychology, 11,* 189–191.

Palmer, S. E. (2003). Visual perception of objects. In A. F. Healy & R. W. Proctor (Eds.), *Handbook of psychology (Vol. 4): Experimental psychology.* New York: Wiley.

Palmeri, T. J., & Gauthier, I. (2004). Visual object understanding. *Nature Reviews Neuroscience, 5,* 291–303.

Pan, B. A., & Uccelli, P. (2009). Semantic development: Learning the meaning of words. In J. B. Gleason & N. B. Ratner (Eds.), *The development of language.* Boston, MA: Pearson.

Panksepp, J. (1991). Affective neuroscience: A conceptual framework for the neurobiological study of emotions. In K. T. Strongman (Ed.), *International review of studies on emotion.* Chichester, England: Wiley.

Panksepp, J. (2008). The affective brain and core consciousness: How does neural activity generate emotional feelings? In M. Lewis, J. M. Haviland-Jones, & L. F. Barrett (Eds.), *Handbook of emotions* (3rd ed., pp. 47–67). New York, NY: Guilford Press.

Papp, K. V., Walsh, S. J., & Snyder, P. J. (2009). Immediate and delayed effects of cognitive interventions in healthy elderly: A review of current literature and future directions. *Alzheimer's & Dementia, 5*(1), 50–60.

Paradis, J., Crago, J., Genesee, F., & Rice, M. (2003). French–English bilingual children with SLI: How do they compare with their monolingual peers? *Journal of Speech, Language and Hearing Research, 46,* 113–127.

Paradiso, S. P., Robinson, R. G., Andreasen, N. C., Downhill, J. E., Davidson, R. J., Kirchner, P. T., et al. (1997). Emotional activation of limbic circuitry in elderly normal subjects in a PET study. *American Journal of Psychiatry, 154,* 384–389.

Paris, J. (1999). *Genetics and psychopathology: Predisposition–stress interactions.* Washington, DC: American Psychiatric Press.

Park, C. L., & Fenster, J. R. (2004). Stress-related growth: Predictors of occurrence and correlates with psychological adjustment. *Journal of Social and Clinical Psychology, 23,* 195–215.

Park, D. C., & Huang, C. (2010). Culture wires the brain: A cognitive neuroscience perspective. *Perspectives on Psychological Science, 5*(4), 391–400.

Parke, R. D. (2002). Punishment revisited—science, values, and the right question: Comment on Gershoff. *Psychological Bulletin, 128,* 596–601.

Parker, E. S., Cahill, L., & McGaugh, J. L. (2006). A case of unusual autobiographical remembering. *Neurocase, 12,* 35–49.

Parker, J. D. A., Hogan, M. J., Eastabrook, J. M., Oke, A., & Wood, L. M. (2006). Emotional intelligence and student retention: Predicting the successful transition from high school to university. *Personality and Individual Differences, 41,* 1329–1336.

Parker, J. D. A., Summerfeldt, L. J., Hogan, M. J., & Majeski, S. A. (2004). Emotional intelligence and academic success: Examining the transition from high school to university. *Personality and Individual Differences, 36,* 163–172.

Parliament of Canada. (2011). *Childhood autism in Canada: Some issues relating to behavioural intervention.* Retrieved June 20, 2011, from http://www.parl. gc.ca/Content/LOP/researchpublications/prb0593-e. htm#funding.

Parrott, A. C. (2000). Human research on MDMA (3,4-Methylene-dioxymethamphetamine) neurotoxicity: Cognitive and behavioral indices of change. *Neuropsychobiology, 42*(1), 17–24.

Partinen, M., & Hublin, C. (2005). Epidemiology of sleep disorders. In M. H. Kryger, T. Roth, & W. C. Dement (Eds.). *Principles and practice of sleep medicine.* Philadelphia: Elsevier Saunders.

Pascual-Leone, A. (2009). Characterizing and modulating neuroplasticity of the adult human brain. In M. S. Gazzangia (Ed.), *The cognitive neurosciences* (4th ed., pp. 141–152). Cambridge, MA: MIT Press.

Pascual-Leone, J. (2000). Reflections on working memory: Are the two models complementary? *Journal of Experimental Child Psychology, 77,* 138–154.

Pascual-Leone, J., & Smith, J. (1969). The encoding and decoding of symbols by children: A new experimental paradigm and a neo-Piagetian model. *Journal of Experimental Child Psychology, 8,* 328–355.

Pashler, H., & Carrier, M. (1996). Stuctures, processes, and the flow of information. In E. L. Bjork & R. A. Bjork (Eds.), *Memory.* San Diego: Academic Press.

Pashler, H., Johnston, J. C., & Ruthruff, E. (2001). Attention and performance. *Annual Review of Psychology, 52,* 629–651.

Passengers head home after icy Antarctic rescue. (2007). *CBC News.* Retrieved October 31, 2008, from http://www.cbc.ca/world/story/2007/11/23/cruise-ship-sink.html.

Pasternak, T., Bisley, J. W., & Calkins, D. (2003). Visual processing in the primate brain. In M. Gallagher & R. J. Nelson (Eds.), *Handbook of psychology: Biological psychology* (pp. 139–186). New York: Wiley.

Patel, A. D., & Iverson, J. R. (2007). The linguistic benefits of musical abilities. *Trends in Cognitive Science, 11,* 369–372.

Patel, J. K., Pinals, D. A., & Breier, A. (2008). Schizophrenia and other psychoses. In A. Tasman, J. Kay, J. A. Lieberman, M. B. First, & M. Maj (Eds.), *Psychiatry* (3rd ed.). New York, NY: Wiley-Blackwell.

Patel, S. R., Ayas, N. T., Malhotra, M. R., White, D. P., Schernhammer, E. S., Speizer, F. E., et al. (2004). A prospective study of sleep duration and mortality risk in women. *Sleep: Journal of Sleep and Sleep Disorders Research, 27,* 440–444.

Patel, S. R., Malhotra, A., Gottlieb, D. J., White, P., & Hu, F. B. (2006). Correlates of long sleep deprivation. *Sleep: Journal of Sleep and Sleep Disorders Research, 29,* 881–889.

Patel, S. R., Zhu, X., Storfer-Isser, A., Mehra, R., Jenny, N. S., Tracy, R., & Redline, S. (2009). Sleep duration and biomarkers of inflammation. *Sleep: Journal of Sleep and Sleep Disorders Research, 32*(2), 200–204.

Pato, M. T., Eisen, J. L., & Phillips, K. A. (2003). Obsessive-compulsive disorder. In A Tasman, J. Kay, & J. A. Lieberman (Eds.), *Psychiatry.* New York: Wiley.

Pato, M. T., Fanous, A., Eisen, J. L., & Phillips, K. A. (2008). Anxiety disorders: Obsessive-compulsive disorder. In A. Tasman, J. Kay, J. A. Lieberman, M. B. First, & M. Maj (Eds.), *Psychiatry* (3rd ed.). New York, NY: Wiley-Blackwell.

Patrick, C. J. (Ed.). (2007). *Handbook of psychopathy.* New York: Guilford Press.

Patrick, H., Nicklas, T. A., Hughes, S. O., & Morales, M. (2005). The benefits of authoritative feeding style: Caregiver feeding styles and children's food consumption patterns. *Appetite, 44,* 243–249.

Patriquin, M. (2005, April 30). Quebec farm segregated black workers. *The Globe and Mail,* A1, A2.

Patston, L. M., Kirk, I. J., Rolfe, M. S., Corballis, M. C., & Tippett, L. J. (2007). The unusual symmetry of musicians: Musicians have equilateral interhemispheric transfer for visual information. *Neuropsychologia, 45*(9), 2059–2065.

Pattanashetty, R., Sathiamma, S., Talakkad, S., Nityananda, P., Trichur, A., & Kutty, B. M. (2010). Practitioners of vipassana meditation exhibit enhanced slow wave sleep and REM sleep states across different age groups. *Sleep and Biological Rhythms, 8*(1), 34–41.

Patten, S., & Juby, H. (2008, February). A profile of clinical depression in Canada. Statistics Canada: *Research Data Centre Network Synthesis Series #1.* Retrieved March 1, 2008, from https://dspace. ucalgary.ca/bitstream/1880/46327/6/Patten_RSS1. pdf.

Patterson, C. J. (2003). Children of lesbian and gay parents. In L. D. Garnets & D. C. Kimmel (Eds.), *Psychological perspectives on lesbian, gay, and bisexual experiences* (2nd ed., pp. 497–548). New York, NY: Columbia University Press.

Patterson, D. R. (2004). Treating pain with hypnosis. *Current Directions in Psychological Science, 13*(6), 252–255.

Patterson, D. R., & Jensen, M. P. (2003). Hypnosis and clinical pain. *Psychological Bulletin, 129,* 495–521.

Pauk, W. (1990). *How to study in college.* Boston: Houghton Mifflin.

Paulhus, D. L. (1991). Measurement and control of response bias. In J. P. Robinson, P. Shaver, & L. S. Wrightsman (Eds.), *Measures of personality and social psychological attitudes.* San Diego: Academic Press.

Paulhus, D. L. (1998). Interpersonal and intrapsychic adaptiveness of trait self-enhancement: A mixed blessing? *Journal of Personality and Social Psychology, 74*(5), 1197–1208.

Paulhus, D. L., Fridhandler, B., & Hayes, S. (1997). Psychological defense: Contemporary theory and research. In R. Hogan, J. Johnson, & S. Briggs (Eds.), *Handbook of personality psychology.* San Diego: Academic Press.

Paulhus, D. L., Trapnell, P. D., & Chen, D. (1999). Birth order effects on personality and achievement within families. *Psychological Science, 10,* 482–488.

Paulos, J. A. (1995). *A mathematician reads the newspaper.* New York: Doubleday.

Paunonen, S. V. (2003). Big Five factors of personality and replicated predictions of behavior. *Journal of Personality and Social Psychology, 84,* 411–424.

Paunonen, S. V., & Ashton, M. C. (1998). The structured assessment of personality across cultures. *Journal of Cross-Cultural Psychology, 29,* 150–170.

Paunonen, S. V., & Jackson, D. N. (2000). What is beyond the Big Five? Plenty! *Journal of Personality, 68,*, 821–835.

Paus, T. (2005). Mapping brain maturation and cognitive development during adolescence. *Trends in Cognitive Science, 9,* 60–68.

Pavlov, I. P. (1906). The scientific investigation of psychical faculties or processes in the higher animals. *Science, 24,* 613–619.

Pavlov, I. P. (1927). *Conditioned reflexes* (G. V. Anrep, Trans.). London: Oxford University Press.

Payne, D. G., & Blackwell, J. M. (1998). Truth in memory: Caveat emptor. In S. J. Lynn & K. M. McConkey (Eds.), *Truth in memory.* New York: Guilford.

Payne, J. W., & Bettman, J. R. (2004). Walking with the scarecrow: The information-processing approach to decision research. In D. J. Koehler & N. Harvey (Ed.), *Blackwell Handbook of judgment and decision making.* Malden, MA: Blackwell Publishing.

Payne, J. W., Samper, A., Bettman, J. R., & Luce, M. (2008). Boundary conditions on unconscious thought in complex decision making. *Psychological Science, 19*(11), 1118–1123.

Peacock, E. J., & Wong, P. (1990). The stress appraisal measure (SAM): A multidimensional approach to cognitive appraisal. *Stress Medicine, 6,* 227–236.

Pearce, M. S., Deary, I. J., Young, A. H., & Parker, L. L. (2006). Childhood IQ and deaths up to middle age: The Newcastle Thousand Families Study. *Public Health, 120*(11), 1020–1026.

Pearson, S. E., & Pollack, R. H. (1997). Female response to sexually explicit films. *Journal of Psychology and Human Sexuality, 9,* 73–88.

Pedersen, A. F., Bovbjerg, D. H., & Zachariae, R. (2011). Stress and susceptibility to infectious disease. In R. J. Contrada & A. Baum (Eds.), *The handbook of stress science: Biology, psychology, and health* (pp. 111–121). New York, NY: Springer.

Pedersen, N. L., Plomin, R., Nesselroade, J. R., & McClearn, G. E. (1992). A quantitative genetic analysis of cognitive abilities during the second half of the life span. *Psychological Science, 3,* 346–353.

Pedersen, P. (1994). A culture-centered approach to counseling. In W. J. Lonner & R. Malpass (Eds.), *Psychology and culture.* Boston: Allyn & Bacon.

Peek, F. (1996). *The real Rain Man.* Salt Lake City, UT: Harkness Publishing Consultants.

Peele, S. (2000). What addiction is and is not: The impact of mistaken notions of addiction. *Addiction Research, 8,* 599–607.

Peetz, J., Wilson, A. E., & Strahan, E. J. (2009). So far away: The role of subjective temporal distance to future goals in motivation and behavior. *Social Cognition, 27,* 102–128.

Peladeau, N., Forget, J., & Gagne, F. (2003). Effect of paced and unpaced practice on skill application and retention: How much is enough? *American Educational Research Journal, 40,* 769–801.

Pellegrino, J. E., & Pellegrino, L. (2008). Fetal alcohol syndrome and related disorders. In P. J. Accardo (Eds.), *Capture and Accardo's neurodevelopment disabilities in infancy and childhood: Neurodevelopmental diagnosis and treatment* (pp. 269–284). Baltimore, MD: Paul H. Brookes Publishing.

Penfield, W. W., & Jasper, H. (1954). *Epilepsy and the functional anatomy of the human brain.* Boston, MA: Little, Brown and Company.

Penfield, W., & Perot, P. (1963). The brain's record of auditory and visual experience. *Brain, 86,* 595–696.

Penfield. W. (1977). *No man alone: A neurosurgeon's life.* Boston, MA: Little, Brown and Company.

Peng, J. H., Tao, Z. Z., & Huang, Z. W. (2007). Risk of damage to hearing from personal listening devices in young adults. *Journal of Otolaryngology, 36,* 181–185.

Pennebaker, J. W., Colder, M., & Sharp, L. K. (1990). Accelerating the coping process. *Journal of Personality and Social Psychology, 58,* 528–537.

Peplau, L. A. (2003). Human sexuality: How do men and women differ? *Current Directions in Psychological Science, 12*(2), 37–40.

Peplau, L., & Fingerhut, A. W. (2007). The close relationships of lesbian and gay men. *Annual Review of Psychology, 58,* 405–424.

Pepler, D., & Craig, W. (1995). A peek behind the fence: Naturalistic observations of aggressive children with remote audiovisual recording. *Developmental Psychology, 31,* 548–553.

Pepler, D., Craig, W., Zeigler, S., & Charach, A. (1993). A school-based antibullying intervention: Preliminary evaluation. In D. Tatum (Ed.), *Understanding and managing bullying* (pp. 70–96). New York: Heinemann Books.

Pepler, D., Jiang, D., Craig, W., & Connolly, J. (2008). Developmental trajectories of bullying and associated factors. *Child Development, 79,* 325–338.

Pepperberg, I. M. (1993). Cognition and communication in an African Grey parrot (*Psittacus erithacus*): Studies on a nonhuman, nonprimate, nonmammalian subject. In H. L. Roitblat, L. H. Herman, & P. E. Nachtigall (Eds.), *Language and communication: Comparative perspectives.* Hillsdale, NJ: Erlbaum.

Pepperberg, I. M. (2002). Cognitive and communicative abilities of grey parrots. *Current Directions in Psychological Science, 11*(3), 83–87.

Pereira, A. C., Huddleston, D. E., Brickman, A. M., Sosunov, A. A., Hen, R., McKhann, G. M., et al. (2007). An in vivo correlate of exercise-induced neurogenesis in the adult dentate gyrus. *Proceedings of the National Academy of Sciences, 104,* 5638–5643.

Peretz, I., & Zatorre, R. J. (2005). Brain organization for music processing. *Annual Review of Psychology, 56,* 89–114.

Perkins, D. O., Miller-Anderson, L., & Lieberman, J. A. (2006). Natural history and predictors of clinical course. In J. A. Lieberman, T. S. Stroup, & D. O. Perkins (Eds.), *Textbook of schizophrenia* (pp. 289–302). Washington, DC: American Psychiatric Publishing.

Perlis, R. H., Perlis, C. S., Wu, Y., Hwang, C., Joseph, M., & Nierenberg, A. A. (2005). Industry sponsorship and financial conflict of interest in the reporting of clinical trials in psychiatry. *American Journal of Psychiatry, 162,* 1957–1960.

Perone, M., Galizio, M., & Baron, A. (1988). The relevance of animal-based principles in the laboratory study of human operant conditioning. In G. Davey & C. Cullen (Eds.), *Human operant conditioning and behavior modification.* New York: Wiley.

Perreault, S., & Bourhis, R. Y. (1999). Ethnocentrism, social identification, and discrimination. *Personality and Social Psychology Bulletin, 25,* 92–103.

Perry, C., Nadon, R., & Button, J. (1992). The measurement of hypnotic ability. In E. Fromm & M. R. Nash (Eds.), *Contemporary hypnosis research.* New York: Guilford.

Perry, D. G., Kusel, S. J., & Perry, L. C. (1988). Victims of peer aggression. *Developmental Psychology, 24,* 807–814.

Perry, W., & Braff, D. L. (1994). Information-processing deficits and thought disorder in schizophrenia. *American Journal of Psychiatry, 151,* 363–367.

Person, E. S. (1990). The influence of values in psychoanalysis: The case of female psychology. In C. Zanardi (Ed.), *Essential papers in psychoanalysis.* New York: New York University Press.

Pert, C. B. (2002). The wisdom of the receptors: Neuropeptides, the emotions, and bodymind. *Advances in Mind-Body Medicine, 18*(1), 30–35.

Pert, C. B., & Snyder, S. H. (1973). Opiate receptor: Demonstration in the nervous tissue. *Science, 179,* 1011–1014.

Perugini, E. M., Kirsch, I., Allen, S. T., Coldwell, E., Meredith, J. M., Montgomery, G. H., & Sheehan, J. (1998). Surreptitious observation of response to hypnotically suggested hallucinations: A test of the compliance hypothesis. *International Journal of Clinical & Experimental Hypnosis, 46,* 191–203.

Pervin, L. A., & John, O. P. (2001). *Personality: Theory and research.* New York, NY: Wiley.

Pescosolido, B. A., Martin, J. K., Long, J., Medina, T. R., Phelan, J. C., & Link, B. G. (2010). "A disease like any other"? A decade of change in public reactions to schizophrenia, depression, and alcohol dependence. *American Journal of Psychiatry, 167*(11), 1321–1330.

Peterhans, E., & Von Der Heydt, R. (1991). Elements of form perception in monkey prestriate cortex. In A. Gorea, Y. Fregnac, Z. Kapoula, & J. Findlay (Eds.), *Representations of vision—Trends and tacit assumptions in vision research.* Cambridge, MA: Cambridge University Press.

Peters, R. (1988, February). The interagency mental health council's committee on multiculturalism and mental health: Progress update. Vancouver: Greater Vancouver Mental Health Services Society.

Petersen, A. C., Compas, B. E., Brooks-Gunn, J., Stemmler, M., Ey, S., & Grant, K. E. (1993). Depression in adolescence. *American Psychologist, 48,* 155–168.

Peterson, C. (2000). The future of optimism. *American Psychologist, 55*(1), 44–55.

Peterson, C., & Park, N. (2009). Positive psychology. In B. J. Sadock, V. A. Sadock, & P. Ruiz (Eds.), *Kaplan & Sadock's comprehensive textbook of psychiatry* (pp. 2939–2951). Philadelphia, PA: Lippincott, Williams & Wilkins.

Peterson, C., & Park, N. (2010). What happened to self-actualization? [Commentary on Kenrick et al. (2010).] *Perspectives on Psychological Science, 5*(3), 320–322.

Peterson, L. R., & Peterson, M. J. (1959). Short-term retention of individual verbal items. *Journal of Experimental Psychology, 58,* 193–198.

Petitto, L. A. (1994). Are signed languages "real" languages? Evidence from American Sign Language and Langue des Signes Québecoise. *Signpost (International Journal of the Sign Linguistics Association), 7*(3), 1–10.

Petitto, L. A. (2009). New discoveries from the bilingual brain and mind across the lifespan: Implications for education. *International Journal of Mind, Brain, and Education, 3,* 185–197.

Petitto, L. A., & Kovelman, I. (2003). The bilingual paradox: How signing-speaking bilingual children help us to resolve it and teach us about the brain's mechanisms underlying all language acquisition. *Learning Languages, 8*, 5–18.

Petitto, L. A., & Marentette, P. (1991). Babbling in the manual mode: Evidence for the ontogeny of language. *Science, 251*, 1483–1496.

Petitto, L. A., Holowka, S., Sergio, L. E., Levy, B., & Ostry, D. J. (2004). Baby hands that move to the rhythm of language: Hearing babies acquiring sign languages babble silently on the hands. *Cognition, 93*, 43–73.

Petitto, L. A., Katerelos, M., Levy, B. G., Gauna, K., Tetreault, K., & Ferraro, V. (2001). Bilingual signed and spoken language acquisition from birth: Implications for the mechanisms underlying early bilingual language acquisition. *Journal of Child Language, 28*, 453–496.

Petitto, L. A., Zatorre, R. J., Gauna, K., Nikelski, E. J., Dostie, D., & Evans, A. C. (2000). Speech-like cerebral activity in profoundly deaf people processing signed languages: Implications for the neural basis of human language. *Proceedings of the National Academy of Science USA, 97*, 13961–13966.

Petri, H. L., & Govern, J. M. (2004). *Motivation: Theory, research, and applications* (5th ed.). Toronto: Thomson/Wadsworth.

Petrie, K. J., & Pennebaker, J. W. (2004). Health-related cognitions. In S. Sutton, A. Baum, & M. Johnston (Eds.), *The Sage handbook of health psychology*. Thousand Oaks, CA: Sage.

Petrill, S. A. (2005). Behavioral genetics and intelligence. In O. Wilhelm & R. W. Engle (Eds.), *Handbook of understanding and measuring intelligence*. Thousand Oaks, CA: Sage.

Petry, N. M. (2010). Pathological gambling and the DSM-V. *International Gambling Studies, 10*(2), 113–115.

Pettit, J. W., Lewinsohn, P. M., Seeley, J. R., Roberts, R. E., & Yaroslavsky, I. (2010). Developmental relations between depressive symptoms, minor hassles, and major events from adolescence through age 30 years. *Journal of Abnormal Psychology, 119*(4), 811–824.

Pettit, M. (2008). The new woman as "tied-up dog": Amy E. Tanner's situated knowledges. *History of Psychology, 11*, 145–163.

Petty, R. E., & Brinol, P. (2008). Persuasion: From single to multiple to metacognitive processes. *Perspectives on Psychological Science, 3*, 137–147.

Petty, R. E., & Briñol, P. (2010). Attitude change. In R. F. Baumeister & E. J. Finkel (Eds.), *Advanced social psychology: The state of the science* (pp. 217–259). New York, NY: Oxford University Press.

Petty, R. E., & Cacioppo, J. T. (1986). *Communication and persuasion: Central and peripheral routes to attitude change*. New York: Springer-Verlag.

Petty, R. E., & Wegener, D. T. (1998). Attitude change: Multiple roles for persuasion variables. In D. T. Gilbert, S. T. Fiske, & G. Lindzey (Eds.), *The handbook of social psychology*. New York: McGraw-Hill.

Petty, R. E., & Wegener, D. T. (1999). The elaboration likelihood model: Current status and controversies. In S. Chaiken & Y. Trope (Eds.), *Dual-process theories in social psychology*. New York: Guilford.

Pezdek, K., & Lam, S. (2007). What research paradigms have cognitive psychologists used to study "false memory," and what are the implications of these choices? *Consciousness and Cognition: An International Journal, 16*(1), 2–17.

Pfau, M., Kenski, H. C., Nitz, M., & Sorenson, J. (1990). Efficacy of inoculation strategies in promoting resistance to political attack messages: Application to direct mail. *Communication Monographs, 57*, 25–43.

Pfaus, J. G., Kippin, T. E., & Centeno, S. (2001). Conditioning and sexual behavior: A review. *Hormones & Behavior, 40*, 291–321.

Phares, V. (1996). *Fathers and developmental psychopathology*. New York: Wiley.

Phelps, E. A. (2005). The interaction of emotion and cognition: The relation between the human amygdala and cognitive awareness. In R. R. Hassin, J. S. Uleman, & J. A. Bargh (Eds.), *The new unconcious: Oxford series in social cognition and social neuroscience* (pp. 61–76). New York: Oxford University Press.

Phelps, E. A. (2006). Emotion and cognition: Insights from studies of the human amygdala. *Annual Review of Psychology, 57*, 27–53.

Phillips, B., & Kryger, M. H. (2005). Management of obstructive sleep apnea-hypopnea syndrome. In M. H. Kryger, T. Roth, & W. C. Dement (Eds.), *Principles and practice of sleep medicine*. Philadelphia, PA: Saunders.

Phillips, W. T., Kiernan, M., & King, A. C. (2001). The effects of physical activity on physical and psychological health. In A. Baum, T. A. Revenson, & J. E. Singer (Eds.), *Handbook of health psychology* (pp. 627–660). Mahwah, NJ: Erlbaum.

Piaget, J. (1929). *The child's conception of the world*. New York: Harcourt, Brace.

Piaget, J. (1932). *The moral judgment of the child*. Glencoe, IL: Free Press.

Piaget, J. (1952). *The origins of intelligence in children*. New York: International Universities Press.

Piaget, J. (1954). *The construction of reality in the child*. New York: Basic Books.

Piaget, J. (1970). *Genetic epistemology*. New York: W.W. Norton & Company.

Piaget, J. (1983). Piaget's theory. In P. H. Mussen (Ed.), *Handbook of child psychology* (Vol. 1). New York: Wiley.

Picard, A. (2011, June 9). 17,500 Canadians hospitalized for suicide attempts and self-injury last year. *The Globe and Mail*, L6.

Picard, A. (2011, April 26). After-school exercise: A mere 14 minutes. *The Globe and Mail*, L5.

Pickering, T. G., Devereux, R. B., James, G. D., Gerin, W., Landsbergis, P., Schnall, P. L., & Schwartz, J. E. (1996). Environmental influences on blood pressure and the role of job strain. *Journal of Hypertension, 14*, S179–S185.

Pickles, J. O. (1988). *An introduction to the physiology of hearing* (2nd ed.). London: Academic Press.

Pickren, W., & Rutherford, A. (2010). *A history of modern psychology in context*. Toronto: University of Toronto Press.

Pickren, W. E. (2003). An elusive honor: Psychology, behavior, and the Nobel Prize. *American Psychologist, 58*, 721–722.

Pierce, C. M. (1992). Contemporary psychiatry: Racial perspectives on the past and future. In A. Kales, C. M. Pierce, & M. Greenblatt (Eds.), *The mosaic of contemporary psychiatry in perspective*. New York: Springer-Verlag.

Pierce, R. C., & Kumaresan, V. (2006). The mesolimbic dopamine system: The final common pathway for the reinforcing effect of drugs of abuse? *Neuroscience Biobehavioral Reviews, 30*, 215–238.

Pies, R. (2009). Should DSM-V designate "Internet addiction" a mental disorder? *Psychiatry, 6*(2), 31–37.

Pihl, R. O., Assaad, J. M., & Hoaken, P. N. S. (2003). The alcohol–aggression relationship and differential sensitivity to alcohol. *Aggressive Behavior, 29*, 302–315.

Pike, K. M., & Rodin, J. (1991). Mothers, daughters, and disordered eating. *Journal of Abnormal Psychology, 100*, 198–294.

Pilcher, J. J., & Walters, A. S. (1997). How sleep deprivation affects psychological variables related to college students' cognitive performance. *Journal of American College Health, 46*, 121–126.

Pilling, M., & Davies, I. R. L. (2004). Linguistic relativism and colour cognition. *British Journal of Psychology, 95*, 429–455.

Pincus, D. (2006). Who is Freud, and what does the new century behold? *Psychoanalytic Psychology, 23*, 367–372.

Pinder, C. C. (1998). *Work motivation in organizational behavior*. Upper Saddle River, NJ: Prentice-Hall.

Pinel, J. P. J., Assanand, S., & Lehman, D. R. (2000). Hunger, eating, and ill health. *American Psychologist, 55*, 1105–1116.

Pinker, S. (2005). So how does the mind work? *Mind and Language, 20*(1), 1–24.

Pinker, S. (1994). *Language is to us as flying is to geese*. New York, NY: Morrow.

Pinker, S. (1997). *How the mind works*. New York: W.W. Norton.

Pinker, S. (2003). Language as an adaptation to the cognitive niche. In M. Christiansen & S. Kirby (Eds.), *Language evolution: States of the Art*. New York: Oxford University Press.

Pinker, S. (2004). Language as an adaptation to the cognitive niche. In D. T. Kenrick & C. L. Luce (Eds.), *The functional mind: Readings in evolutionary psychology*. Essex, England: Pearson Education Limited.

Pinker, S. (2010, July 31). Taking the road less travelled. *Globe and Mail*, B14.

Pinker, S., & Bloom, P. (1992). Natural language and natural selection. In J. H. Barkow, L. Cosmides, & J. Tooby (Eds.), *The adapted mind: Evolutionary psychology and the generation of culture*. New York: Oxford University Press.

Pinker, S., & Jackendoff, R. (2005). The faculty of language: What's special about it? *Cognition, 95*, 201–236.

Pinquart, M., Duberstein, P. R., & Lyness, J. M. (2006). Treatments for later-life depressive conditions: A meta-analytic comparison of pharmacotherapy and psychotherapy. *American Journal of Psychiatry, 163*, 1493–1501.

Piomelli, D. (2004). The endogenous cannabinoid system and the treatment of marijuana dependence. *Neuropharmacology, 47*, 359–367.

Pi-Sunyer, F. X. (2002). Medical complications of obesity in adults. In C. G. Fairburn & K. D. Brownell (Eds.), *Eating disorders and obesity: A comprehensive handbook* (pp. 467–472). New York: Guilford.

Pittman, F., III. (1994, January/February). A buyer's guide to psychotherapy. *Psychology Today*, 50–53, 74–81.

Pittman, T. S., & Zeigler, K. R. (2007). Basic human needs. In A. W. Kruglanski & E. T. Higgins (Eds.), *Social psychology: Handbook of basic principles*. New York: Guilford Press.

Pizzagalli, D., Shackman, A. J., & Davidson, R. J. (2003). The functional neuroimaging of human emotion: Asymmetric contributions of cortical and subcortical circuitry. In K. Hugdahl & R. J. Davidson

(Eds.), *The asymmetrical brain*. Cambridge, MA: MIT Press.

Plante, T. G. (1999b). Could the perception of fitness account for many of the mental and physical health benefits of exercise? *Advances in Mind–Body Medicine, 15*, 291–295.

Plante, T. G., Caputo, D., & Chizmar, L. (2000). Perceived fitness and responses to laboratory-induced stress. *International Journal of Stress Management, 7*(1), 61–73.

Plassmann, H., O'Doherty, J., Shiv, B., & Rangel. (2008). Marketing actions can modulate neural representations of experienced pleasantness. *Proceedings of the National Academy of Science, 105*, 1050–1054.

Platek, S. M., Mohamed, F. B., & Gallup, G. G., Jr. (2005). Contagious yawning and the brain. *Cognitive Brain Research, 23*, 448–452.

Platiel, R., & Strauss, S. (1989, February 4). University chief defends professor's right to voice racial theory. *The Globe and Mail*, A6.

Plomin, R. (1993). Nature and nurture: Perspective and prospective. In R. Plomin & G. E. McClearn (Eds.), *Nature, nurture and psychology*. Washington, DC: American Psychological Association.

Plomin, R. (1994). Nature, nurture, and development. In R. J. Sternberg (Ed.), *Encyclopedia of human intelligence*. New York: Macmillan.

Plomin, R. (2003). General cognitive ability. In R. Plomin & J. C. DeFries (Eds.), *Behavioral genetics in the postgenomic era*. Washinton, DC: American Psychological Association.

Plomin, R. (2004). Genetics and developmental psychology. *Merrill-Palmer Quarterly, 50*, 341–352.

Plomin, R., & Caspi, A. (1999). Behavioral genetics and personality. In L. A. Pervin & O. P. John (Eds.), *Handbook of personality: Theory and research*. New York: Guilford.

Plomin, R., & McGuffin, P. (2003). Psychopathology in the postgenomic era. *Annual Review of Psychology, 54*, 205–228.

Plomin, R., & Spinath, F. M. (2004). Intelligence: Genetics, genes, and genomics. *Journal of Personality & Social Psychology, 86*, 112–129.

Plomin, R., DeFries, J. C., McClearn, G. E., & McGuffin, P. (2001). *Behavioral genetics*. New York: Freeman.

Plomin, R., DeFries, J. C., McClearn, G. E., & McGuffin, P. (2008). *Behavioral genetics*. New York: Worth.

Plomin, R., Kennedy, J. K. J., & Craig, I. W. (2006). The quest for quantitative, trait loci associated with intelligence. *Intelligence, 34*, 513–526.

Plotkin, H. (2004). *Evolutionary thought in psychology: A brief history*. Malden, MA: Blackwell Publishing.

Plucker, J. A., & Makel, M. C. (2010). Assessment of creativity. In J. C. Kaufman & R. J. Sternberg (Eds.), *The Cambridge handbook of creativity* (pp. 48–73). New York, NY: Cambridge University Press.

Plucker, J. A., & Renzulli, J. S. (1999). Psychometric approaches to the study of human creativity. In R. J. Sternberg (Ed.), *Handbook of creativity*. New York: Cambridge University Press.

Plumert, J. M., & Nichols-Whitehead, P. (1996). Parental scaffolding of young children's spatial communication. *Developmental Psychology, 32*, 523–532.

Plutchik, R. (1980, February). A language for the emotions. *Psychology Today*, pp. 68–78.

Plutchik, R. (1984). Emotions: A general psychoevolutionary theory. In K. R. Scherer & P.

Ekman (Eds.), *Approaches to emotion*. Hillsdale, NJ: Erlbaum.

Plutchik, R. (1993). Emotions and their vicissitudes: Emotions and psychopathology. In M. Lewis & J. M. Haviland (Eds.), *Handbook of emotions*. New York: Guilford.

Pogue-Geile, M. F., & Yokley, J. L. (2010). Current research on the genetic contributors to schizophrenia. *Current Directions in Psychological Science, 19*(4), 214–219.

Pohl, R. F. (2004). Effects of labeling. In F. P. Rudiger (Ed.), *Cognitive illusions*. New York: Psychology Press.

Poldrack, R. A., & Wagner, A. D. (2008). The interface between neuroscience and psychological science. *Current Directions between Neuroscience and Psychological Science, 17*, 61–63.

Policastro, E., & Gardner, H. (1999). From case studies to robust generalizations: An approach to the study of creativity. In R. J. Sternberg (Ed.), *Handbook of creativity*. New York: Cambridge University Press.

Polivy, J., & Herman, C. P. (1995). Dieting and its relation to eating disorders. In K. D. Brownell & C. G.Fairburn (Eds.), *Eating disorders and obesity: A comprehensive handbook*. New York: Guilford.

Polivy, J., & Herman, C. P. (2002). Causes of eating disorders. *Annual Review of Psychology, 53*, 187–213.

Polivy, J., Herman, C. P., Mills, J. S., & Wheeler, H. B. (2003). Eating disorders. In G. R. Adams & M. D. Berzonsky (Eds.), *Blackwell handbook of adolescence* (pp. 522–549). Oxford, UK: Blackwell Publishing.

Pols, H. (2002). Between the laboratory and life: Child development research in Toronto, 1919–1956. *History of Psychology, 5*, 135–162.

Pomerantz, E. M., Ng, F. F. Y., & Wang, Q. (2004). Gender socialization: A parent-child model. In A. H. Eagly, A. E. Beall, & R. J. Sternberg (Eds.), *The psychology of gender*. New York: Guilford.

Pooley, E. (2004, June 25). The road not taken. *The Globe and Mail*, A19.

Pope, H. G., Barry, S., Bodkin, A., & Hudson, J. I. (2006). Tracking scientific interest in the dissociative disorders: A study of scientific publication output 1984–2003. *Psychotherapy and Psychosomatics, 75*, 19–24.

Pope, H. G., Gruber, A. J., & Yurgelun-Todd, D. (2001). Residual neuropsychologic effects of cannabis. *Current Psychiatry Report, 3*, 507–512.

Pope, H. G., Gruber, A. J., Hudson, J. I., Huestis, M. A., & Yurgelun-Todd, D. (2001). Neuropsychological performance in long-term cannabis users. *Archives of General Psychiatry, 58*, 909–915.

Pope, H. G., Jr., & Hudson, J. I. (1998). Can memories of childhood sexual abuse be repressed? In R. A. Baker (Ed.), *Child sexual abuse and false memory syndrome*. Amherst, NY: Prometheus Books.

Pope, H. G., Oliva, P. S., Hudson, J. I., Bodkin, J. A., & Gruber, A. J. (1999). Attitudes toward DSM-IV dissociative disorders diagnoses among board-certified American psychiatrists. *American Journal of Psychiatry, 156*, 321–323.

Pope, K. S., & Brown, L. (1996). *Recovered memories of abuse: Assessment, thereapy, forensics*. Washington, DC: American Psychological Association.

Pope, K. S., Keith-Spiegel, P., & Tabachnick, B. G. (1986). Sexual attraction to clients. *American Psychologist, 41*, 147–158.

Popenoe, D. (1996). *Life without father*. New York: Pressler Press.

Popper, C. W., & Steingard, R. J. (1994). Disorders usually first diagnosed in infancy, childhood, or adolescence. In R. E. Hales, S. C. Yudofsky, & J. A.

Talbott (Eds.), *The American Psychiatric Press textbook of psychiatry*. Washington, DC: American Psychiatric Press.

Popper, C. W., Gammon, G. D., West, S. A., & Bailey, C. E. (2003). Disorders usually first diagnosed in infancy, childhood, and adolescence. In Robert E. Hales & Stuart C. Yudofsky (Eds.), *Textbook of clinical psychiatry*. Washington, DC: American Psychiatric Publishing.

Porath, A., & Fried, P. A. (2005). Effects of prenatal cigarette and marijuana exposure on drug use among offspring. *Neurotoxicology and Teratology, 27*, 267–277.

Porcerelli, J. H., Cogan, R., Kamoo, R., & Miller, K. (2010). Convergent validity of the Defense Mechanisms Manual and the Defensive Functioning Scale. *Journal of Personality Assessment, 92*(5), 432–438.

Porter, J., Craven, B., Khan, R. M., Chang, S., Kang, I., Judkewitz, B., Volpe, J., et al. (2007). Mechanisms of scent-tracking in humans. *Nature Neuroscience, 10*(1), 27–29.

Pos, A. E., Greenberg, L. S., & Warwar, S. H. (2009). Testing a model of change in the experiential treatment of depression. *Journal of Consulting and Clinical Psychology, 77*, 1055–1066.

Posada, G., Kaloustian, G., Richmond, K., & Moreno, A. J. (2007). Maternal secure base support and preschoolers' secure base behavior in natural environments. *Attachment & Human Development, 9*, 393–411.

Posner, M. I., & Rothbart, M. K. (2004). Hebb's neural networks support the integration of psychological science. *Canadian Psychology, 45*, 265–278.

Posner, M. I., & Rothbart, M. K. (2007). Research on attention networks as a model for the intergration of psychological science. *Annual Review of Psychology, 58*, 1–23.

Post, R. M., & Altshuler, L. L. (2009). Mood disorders: Treatment of bipolar disorders. In B. J. Sadock, V. A. Sadock, & P. Ruiz (Eds.), *Kaplan & Sadock's comprehensive textbook of psychiatry* (pp. 1743–1812). Philadelphia, PA: Lippincott, Williams & Wilkins.

Posthuma, D., Luciano, M., de Geus, E. J. C., Wright, M. J., Slagboom, P. E., Montgomery, G. W., et al. (2005). A genome-wide scan for intelligence identifies quantitative trait loci on 2q and 6p. *American Journal of Human Genetics, 77*, 318–326.

Postman, L. (1985). Human learning and memory. In G. A. Kimble & K. Schlesinger (Eds.), *Topics in the history of psychology*. Hillsdale, NJ: Erlbaum.

Postmes, T., Spears, R., & Cihangir, S. (2001). Quality of decision making and group norms. *Journal of Personality and Social Psychology, 80*, 918–930.

Potter, W. Z., Padich, R. A., Rudorfer, M. V., & Krishnan, K. R. R. (2006). Tricyclics, tetracyclics, and monoamine oxidase inhibitors. In D. J. Stein, D. J. Kupfer, & A. F. Schatzberg (Eds.), *Textbook of mood disorders* (pp. 251–262). Washington, DC: American Psychiatric Publishing.

Potthoff, J. G., Holahan, C. J., & Joiner, T. E., Jr. (1995). Reassurance-seeking, stress generation, and depressive symptoms: An integrative model. *Journal of Personality and Social Psychology, 68*, 664–670.

Poulin-Dubois, D., & Graham, S. A. (2007). Cognitive Processes in early word learning. In E. Hoff & M. Shatz (Eds.), *Blackwell handbook of language development* (pp. 191–212). Malden, MA: Blackwell.

Poulton, E. C. (1994). *Behavioral decision theory: A new approach.* Cambridge, England: Cambridge University Press.

Powell, L. H., & Williams, K. (2007). Hostility. In G. Fink (Ed.), *Encyclopedia of stress.* San Diego: Elsevier.

Powell, R. A. (2010). Little Albert still missing. *American Psychologist, 65,* 299–300.

Powell, R. A., & Boer, D. P. (1995). Did Freud misinterpret reported memories of sexual abuse as fantasies? *Psychological Reports, 77,* 563–570.

Powell, R. A., & Gee, T. L. (1999). The effects of hypnosis on dissociative identity disorder: A reexamination of the evidence. *Canadian Journal of Psychiatry, 44,* 914–916.

Powell, R. A., Symbaluk, D. G., & MacDonald, S. E. (2002). *Introduction to learning and behavior.* Belmont, CA: Wadsworth.

Powley, T. L. (2008). Central control of autonomic functions: Organization of the autonomic nervous system. In L. Squire, D. Berg, F. Bloom, S. Du Lac, A. Ghosh, & N. Spitzer (Eds.), *Fundamental neuroscience* (3rd ed., pp. 809–828). San Diego, CA: Elsevier.

Powley, T. L. (2009). Hunger. In G. G. Berntson & J. T. Cacioppo (Eds.), *Handbook of neuroscience for the behavioral sciences,* (Vol. 2, pp. 659–679). Hoboken, NJ: Wiley.

Pozzulo, J., Bennell, C., & Forth, A. (2006). *Forensic psychology.* Toronto: Pearson Education Inc.

Pratkanis, A. R., & Aronson, E. (2000). *Age of propaganda: The everyday use and abuse of persuasion.* New York: Freeman.

Premack, D. (1985). "Gavagai!" or the future history of the animal language controversy. *Cognition, 19,* 207–296.

Premack, D. (2010). Why humans are unique: Three theories. *Perspectives on Psychological Science, 5,* 22–32.

Prentky, R. A. (1980). *Creativity and psychopathology: A neurocognitive perspective.* New York: Praeger.

Prentky, R. A. (1989). Creativity and psychopathology: Gamboling at the seat of madness. In J. A. Glover, R. R. Ronning, & C. R. Reynolds (Eds.), *Handbook of creativity.* New York: Plenum.

Prescott, J. (2010). Taste: Supertasters. In E. B. Goldstein (Ed.), *Encyclopedia of perception.* Thousand Oaks, CA: Sage.

Pressman, S. D., & Cohen, S. (2005). Does positive affect influence health? *Psychological Bulletin, 131,* 925–971.

Pressman, S. D., Cohen, S., Miller, G. E., Barkin, A., Rabin, B. S., & Treanor, J. J. (2005). Loneliness, social network size, and immune response to influenza vaccination in college freshman. *Health Psychology, 24,* 297–306.

Price, D. D., Finniss, D. G., & Benedetti, F. (2008). A comprehensive review of the placebo effect: Recent advances and current thought. *Annual Review of Psychology, 59,* 565–590.

Price, J. (2008). *The woman who can't forget: The extraordinary story of living with the most remarkable memory known to science—A memoir* New York: Free Press.

Price, M. (2008). Div. 55's drive for RxP: The American Society for the Advancement of Pharmacotherapy pushes for prescriptive authority. *Monitor on Psychology, 39*(2).

Priester, J. R., & Petty, R. E. (1995). Source attributions and persuasion; Perceived honesty as a determinant of message scrutiny. *Personality and Social Psychology Bulletin, 21,* 637–654.

Priester, J. R., & Petty, R. E. (2001). Extending the bases of subjective attitudinal ambivalence: Interpersonal and intrapersonal antecedents of evaluative tension. *Journal of Personality and Social Psychology, 80,* 19–34.

Priester, J. R., & Petty, R. E. (2003). The influence of spokesperson trustworthiness on message elaboration, attitude strength, and advertising. *Journal of Consumer Psychology, 13,* 408–421.

Prifitera, A. (1994). Wechsler scales of intelligence. In R. J. Sternberg (Ed.), *Encyclopedia of human intelligence.* New York: Macmillan.

Prince, G. (1978). Putting the other half to work. *Training: The Magazine of Human Resources Development, 15,* 57–61.

Pringle, H. (1997). Alberta barren. *Saturday Night,* June 1997, pp. 30–74.

Prochaska, J. O. (1994). Strong and weak principles for progressing from precontemplation to action on the basis of twelve problem behaviors. *Health Psychology, 13,* 47–51.

Prochaska, J. O., Velicer, W. F., Prochaska, J. M., & Johnson, J. L. (2004). Size, consistency, and stability of stage effects for smoking cessation. *Addictive Behaviors, 29 ,* 207–213.

Proffitt, D. R., & Caudek, C. (2003). Depth perception and the perception of events. In A. F. Healy & R. W. Proctor (Eds.), *Handbook of psychology, Vol. 4: Experimental psychology.* New York, NY: Wiley.

Project Dawson. (2010). Dawson College Shooting, September 13, 2006: Report on a study conducted with students and staff of Dawson College on the psychological impact of the incident and the search for support. Retrieved May 2, 2011, from http://www.hlhl.qc.ca/documents/pdf/Recherche/publications/2a-leger-dawson-REPORT-2sept.pdf.

Prolo, P., & Chiappelli, F. (2007). Immune suppression. In G. Fink (Ed.), *Encyclopedia of stress.* San Diego: Elsevier.

Pronin, E., Gilovich, T., & Ross, L. (2004). Objectivity in the eye of the beholder: Divergent perceptions of bias in self versus others. *Psychological Review, 111,* 781–799.

Pronin, E., Lin, D. Y., & Ross, L. (2002). The bias blind spot: Perceptions of bias in self versus others. *Personality and Social Psychology Bulletin, 28,* 369–381.

Pronin, E., Wegner, D. M., McCarthy, K., & Rodriguez, S. (2006). Everyday magical powers: The role of apparent mental causation in the overestimation of personal influence. *Journal of Personality and Social Psychology, 91,* 218–231.

Proulx, C. M., Helms, H. M., & Buehler, C. (2007). Marital quality and personal well-being: A meta-analysis. *Journal of Marriage and Family, 69*(3), 576–593.

Province of Ontario. (2010). *Children's Mental Health Ontario.* Retrieved June 2, 2011, from http://www.kidsmentalhealth.ca/documents/res_cmho_final_prebudget_submission_2010_final.pdf.

Provine, R. R. (2005). Yawning. *American Scientist, 93,* 532–539.

Prudic, J. (2009). Electroconvulsive therapy. In B. J. Sadock, V. A. Sadock, & P. Ruiz (Eds.), *Kaplan & Sadock's comprehensive textbook of psychiatry* (pp. 3285–3300). Philadelphia, PA: Lippincott, Williams & Wilkins.

Prudic, J., Olfson, M., Marcus, S. C., Fuller, R. B., & Sackeim, H. A. (2004). Effectiveness of electroconvulsive therapy in community settings. *Biological Psychiatry, 55,* 301–312.

Pruitt, D. G. (1971). Choice shifts in group discussion: An introductory review. *Journal of Personality and Social Psychology, 20,* 339–360.

Psychological Corporation. (2001). *WAIS-III Canadian technical manual.* San Antonio, TX: Psychological Corporation.

Psychology Foundation of Canada. (n.d.). The struggle to juggle stress management: Stategies for you and your family. Retrieved May 20, 2011, from http://www.psychologyfoundation.org.

Psychosocial Paediatrics Committee. (2003). Impact of media use on children and youth. *Paediatric Child Health, 8,* 301–306.

Psychotherapy Networker. (2007). The top 10. The most influential therapist of the past quarter century. Retrieved June 11, 2011, from http://www.psychotherapynetworker.org/.../populartopics/219-the-top-10

Ptito, A., Chen, J. K., & Johnstone, K. M. (2007). Contributions of functional magnetic resonance imaging (fMRI) to sport concussion evaluation. *NeuroRehabilitation, 22*(3), 217–227.

Public Health Agency of Canada. (1996). Mental illness and violence: Proof or Stereotype? Retrieved May 2, 2011, from http://www.phac-aspc.gc.ca/mh-sm/pubs/mental_illness/index-eng.php.

Public Health Agency of Canada. (2002). A report on mental illnesses in Canada: Chapter 4 Anxiety Disorders. Retrieved February 17, 2011, from http://www.phac-aspc.gc.ca/publicat/miic-mmac/

Public Health Agency of Canada. (2002). *A report on mental illnesses in Canada.* Retrieved June 25, 2005, from http://www.phac-aspc.gc.ca/publicat/miic-mmac/app_b_e.html.

Public Health Agency of Canada. (2003b). *HIV/AIDS Communique.* Retrieved May 9, 2005, from http://www.phac-aspc.gc.ca/aids-sida/hiv_aids/federal_initiative/communique_sept.html.

Public Health Agency of Canada. (2006). *The human face of mental health and mental illness in Canada.* Retrieved July 31, 2008, from http://www.phac-aspc.gc.ca/publicat/human-humain06/index-eng.php.

Public Heath Agency of Canada. (n.d.). *Physical activity statistics: Canadian physical activity levels for children and youth.* Retrieved May 3, 2005, from http://www.phac-aspc.gc.ca/pau-uap/paguide/child_youth/children.

Pucetti, R. (1981). The case for mental duality: Evidence from split brain data and other considerations. *Behavioral and Brain Sciences, 4,* 93–123.

Pullum, G. K. (1991). *The Great Eskimo vocabulary hoax.* Chicago: University of Chicago Press.

Purves, D. (2009). Vision. In G. G. Berntson & J. T. Cacioppo (Eds.), *Handbook of neuroscience for the behavioral sciences.* New York, NY: Wiley.

Pusch, D., Dobson, K., Ardo, K, & Murphy, T. (1998). The relationship between sociotropic and autonomous personality styles and depressive realism in dysphoric and nondysphoric university students. *Canadian Journal of Behavioural Science, 30,* 253–265.

Pyryt, M. A. (1996). IQ: Easy to bash, hard to replace. *Roeper Review, 18,* 255–258.

Pyszczynski, T., Greenberg, J., & Solomon, S. (1999). A dual-process model of defense against conscious and unconscious death-related thoughts: An extension of terror management theory. *Psychological Review, 106,* 835–845.

Pyszczynski, T., Greenberg, J., Solomon, S., Arndt, J., & Schimel, J. (2004, May). Why do people need self-esteem? A theoretical and empirical review. *Psychological Bulletin, 130*(3), 435–468.

Pyszczynski, T., Rothschild, Z., & Abdollah, A. (2008). Terrorism, violence, and hope for peace: A terror management perspective. *Current Directions in Psychological Science, 17*, 318–322.

Pyszczynski, T., Solomon, S., & Greenberg, J. (2003). *In the wake of 9/11: The psychology of terror.* Washington, DC: American Psychological Association.

Qui, C., Xu, W., & Fratiglioni, L. (2010). Vascular and psychosocial factors in Alzheimer's disease: Epidemiological evidence toward intervention. *Journal of Alzheimer's Disease, 20*, 689–697.

Quinn, K. A., Macrae, C. N., & Bodenhausen, G. V. (2003). Stereotyping and impression formation: How categorical thinking shapes person perception. In M. A. Hogg & J. Cooper (Eds.), *The Sage handbook of social psychology.* Thousand Oaks, CA: Sage.

Quirk, G. J. (2007). Prefrontal-amygdala interactions in the regulation of fear. In J. J. Gross (Ed.), *Handbook of emotion regulation* (pp. 27–46). New York: Guilford.

Quoidbach, J., Dunn, E. W., Petrides, K. V., & Mikolajczak, M. (2010). Money giveth, money taketh away: The dual effect of wealth on happiness. *Psychological Science, 21*(6), 759–763.

Quoidbach, J., Wood, A. M., & Hansenne, M. (2009). Back to the future: The effect of daily practice of mental time travel into the future on happiness and anxiety. *Journal of Positive Psychology, 4*, 349–355.

Rachman, S. J. (1990). *Fear and courage.* New York: W. H. Freeman.

Rachman, S. J. (1992). Behavior therapy. In L. R. Squire (Ed.), *Encyclopedia of learning and memory.* New York: Macmillan.

Rachman, S. J. (2009). Psychological treatment of anxiety: The evolution of behavior therapy and cognitive behavior therapy. *Annual Review of Clinical Psychology, 5*, 97–119.

Radak, Z., Hart, N., Sarga, L., Koltai, E., Atalay, M., Ohno, H., & Boldogh, I. (2010). Exercise plays a preventive role against Alzheimer's disease. *Journal of Alzheimer's Disease, 20*(3), 777–783.

Rafal, R. (2001). Virtual neurology. *Nature Neuroscience, 4*, 862–864.

Rahe, R. H., & Arthur, R. H. (1978). Life change and illness studies. *Journal of Human Stress, 4*(1), 3–15.

Raichle, M. E. (1994). Images of the mind: Studies with modern imaging techniques. *Annual Review of Psychology, 45*, 333–356.

Raichle, M. E. (2006). Functional neuroimaging: A historical and physiological perspective. In R. Cabeza & A. Kingstone (Eds.), *Handbook of functional neuroimaging of cognition* (pp. 3–20). Cambridge, MA: MIT Press.

Raine, A. (1997). Antisocial behavior and psychophysiology: A biosocial perspective and a prefrontal dysfunction hypothesis. In D. M. Stoff, J. Breiling, & J. D. Maser (Eds.), *Handbook of antisocial behavior.* New York: Wiley.

Rains, G. D. (2002). *Principles of human neuropsychology.* New York: McGraw-Hill.

Raitt, F. E., & Zeedyk, M. S. (2003). False memory syndrome: Undermining the credibility of complainants in sexual offenses. *International Journal of Law & Psychiatry, 26*, 453–471.

Rakic, P., Bourgeois, J. P., & Goldman-Rakic, P. S. (1994). Synaptic development of the cerebral cortex: Implications for learning, memory, and mental illness. *Progress in brain research, 102*, 227–243.

Rakobowchuk, P. (2011, March 22). Senior suicides expected to rise as boomers age. *Toronto Star*, E9.

Rama, A. N., Cho, S. C., & Kushida, C. A. (2006). Normal human sleep. In T. Lee-Chiong (Ed.), *Sleep: A comprehensive handbook.* Hoboken, NJ: Wiley-Liss.

Ramachandran, V. S., & Oberman, L. M. (2006). Broken mirrors: A theory of autism. *Scientific American, 295*, 62–69.

Ramadan, N. M. (2000). Migraine. In G. Fink (Ed.), *Encyclopedia of stress* (pp. 757–770). San Diego: Academic Press.

Ramchand, R., Schell, T. L., Karney, B. R., Osilla, K., Burns, R. M., & Caldarone, L. (2010). Disparate prevalence estimates of PTSD among service members who served in Iraq and Afghanistan: Possible explanations. *Journal of Traumatic Stress, 23*(1), 59–68.

Ramey, C. T., Ramey, S. L., & Lanzi, R. G. (2001). Intelligence and experience. In R. J. Sternberg & E. L. Grigorenko (Eds.), *Environmental effects on cognitive abilities* (pp. 83–116). Mahwah, NJ: Erlbaum.

Ramey, S. L. (1999). Head Start and preschool education: Toward continued improvement. *American Psychologist, 54*, 344–346.

Ramirez-Esparza, N., Mehl, M. R., Alvarez-Bermudez, J., & Pennebaker, J. W. (2009). Are Mexicans more or less sociable than Americans? Insights from a naturalistic observation study. *Journal of Research in Personality, 43*(1), 1–7.

Ramsay, D. S., Seeley, R. J., Bolles, R. C., & Woods, S. C. (1996). Ingestive homeostasis: The primacy of learning. In E. D. Capaldi (Ed.), *Why we eat what we eat: The psychology of eating* (pp. 11–29). Washington, DC: American Psychological Association.

Rand, M. (2008). *Criminal victimization, 2007.* Washington, DC: National Crime Victimization Survey, Bureau of Justice Statistics.

Ranson, K. E., & Urichuk, L. J. (2008). The effect of parent-child attachment relationships on child biopsychosocial outcomes: A review. *Early Child Development and Care, 178*, 129–152.

Rapee, R. M., & Barlow, D. H. (2001). Generalized anxiety disorders, panic disorders, and phobias. In P. B. Sutker & H. E. Adams (Eds.), *Comprehensive handbook of psychopathology* (3rd ed., pp. 131–154). New York: Kluwer Academic/Plenum Publishers.

Rasch, B., & Born, J. (2008). Reactivation and consolidation of memory during sleep. *Current Directions in Psychological Science, 17*(3), 188–192.

Rasch, B., Buchel, C., Gais, S., & Born, J. (2007). Odor cues during slow-wave sleep prompt declarative memory. *Science, 315*, 1426–1430.

Rashid, T., & Anjum, A. (2008). Positive psychotherapy for young adults and children. In J. Z. Abela & B. L. Hankin (Eds.), *Handbook of depression in children and adolescents* (pp. 250–287). New York, NY: Guilford Press.

Raskauskas, J., & Stolz, A. D. (2007). Involvement in traditional and electronic bullying among adolescents. *Developmental Psychology, 43*, 564–575.

Raskin, N. J., Rogers, C. R., & Witty, M. C. (2011). Client-centered therapy. In R. J. Corsini & D. Wedding (Eds.), *Current psychotherapies* (9th ed.). Belmont, CA: Brooks/Cole.

Raskin, R. N., & Hall, C. S. (1979). A narcissistic personality inventory. *Psychological Reports, 45*(2), 590.

Raskin, R. N., & Hall, C. S. (1981). The Narcissistic Personality Inventory: Alternate form reliability and further evidence of construct validity. *Journal of Personality Assessment, 45*(2), 159–162.

Raskin, R. N., & Terry, H. (1988). A principal-components analysis of the Narcissistic Personality Inventory and further evidence of its construct validity. *Journal of Personality and Social Psychology, 54*(5), 890–902.

Rasmussen, C., Knapp, T. J., & Garner, L. (2000). Driving-induced stress in urban college students. *Perceptual & Motor Skills, 90*, 437–443.

Rasmussen, H. N., Scheier, M. F., & Greenhouse, J. B. (2009). Optimism and physical health: A Meta-analytic review. *Annals of Behavioral Medicine, 37*(3), 239–256.

Rasmussen, T., & Milner, B. (1977). The role of early left brain injury in determining lateralization of cerebral speech functions. *Annals of the New York Academy of Sciences, 299*, 355–369.

Ratner, N. B., Gleason, J. B., & Narasimhan, B. (1998). An introduction to psycholinguistics: What do language users know? In J. B. Gleason & N. B. Ratner (Eds.), *Psycholinguistics* (2nd ed., pp. 1–40). Fort Worth, TX: Harcourt College Publishers.

Rauscher, F. H., Shaw, G. L., & Ky, K. N. (1993). Music and spatial task performance. *Nature, 365*, 611.

Rauscher, F. H., Shaw, G. L., & Ky, K. N. (1995). Listening to Mozart enhances spatial-temporal reasoning: Towards a neurophysiological basis. *Neuroscience Letters, 185*, 44–47.

Ravindran, L. N. & Stein, M. B. (2009). Anxiety disorders: Somatic treatment. In B. J. Sadock, V. A. Sadock, & P. Ruiz (Eds.), *Kaplan & Sadock's comprehensive textbook of psychiatry* (pp. 1906–1914). Philadelphia, PA: Lippincott, Williams & Wilkins.

Rawana, J. S., Morgan, A. S., Nguyen, H., & Craig, S. G. (2010). The relation between eating- and weight-related disturbances and depression in adolescence: A review. *Clinical Child Family Psychological Review, 13*, 213–230.

Rawson, K. A., & Van Overschelde, J. P. (2008). How does knowledge promote memory? The distinctiveness theory of skilled memory. *Journal of Memory and Language, 58*, 646–688.

Ray, J. (2011). High well-being eludes the masses in most countries worldwide. Retrieved May 25, 2011, from http://www.gallup.com/poll/147167/High-Wellbeing-Eludes Masses.

Raynor, H. A., & Epstein, L. H. (2001). Dietary variety, energy regulation, and obesity. *Psychological Bulletin, 127*, 325–341.

Raynor, J. O., & Entin, E. E. (1982). Future orientation and achievement motivation. In J. O. Raynor & E. E. Entin (Eds.), *Motivation, career striving, and aging.* New York: Hemisphere.

Read, S. J., Monroe, B. M., Brownstein, A. L., Yang, Y., Chopra, G., & Miller, L. C. (2010). A neural network model of the structure and dynamics of human personality. *Psychological Review, 117*, 61–92.

Reber, R. (2004). Availability. In F. P. Rudiger (Ed.), *Cognitive illusions.* New York: Psychology Press.

Recht, L. D., Lew, R. A., & Schwartz, W. J. (1995). Baseball teams beaten by jet lag. *Nature, 377*, 583.

Rechtschaffen, A. (1994). Sleep onset: Conceptual issues. In R. D. Ogilvie & J. R. Harsh (Eds.), *Sleep onset: Normal and abnormal processes.* Washington, DC: American Psychological Association.

Rector, N. A., & Beck, A. T. (2001). Cognitive behavioral therapy for schizophrenia. An empirical review. *Journal of Nervous and Mental Disorders, 189*, 278–287.

Rector, N. A., Segal, Z., & Gemar, M. (1998). Schema research in depression: A Canadian perspective. *Canadian Journal of Behavioural Science, 30*, 213–224.

Redker, C. M., & Gibson, B. (2009). Music as an unconditioned stimulus: Positive and negative effects of country music on implicit attitudes, explicit attitudes, and brand choice. *Journal of Applied Social Psychology, 31*, 2689–2705.

Reed, J. G., & Baxter P. M. (1992). *Library use: A handbook for psychology.* Washington, DC: American Psychological Association.

Reed, J. G., & Baxter, P. M. (2003). *Library use: A handbook for psychology.* Washington, DC: American Psychological Association.

Rees, C. J., & Metcalfe, B. (2003). The faking of personality questionnaire results: Who's kidding whom? *Journal of Managerial Psychology, 18*(2), 156–165.

Reese, H. W. (2010). Regarding Little Albert. *American Psychologist, 65*, 300–301.

Reeve, C. L., & Hakel, M. D. (2002). Asking the right questions about *g. Human Performance, 15*, 47–74.

Reeves, A. J. (2010). Visual light- and dark-adaptation. In E. B. Goldstein (Ed.), *Encyclopedia of perception.* Thousand Oaks, CA: Sage.

Refinetti, R. (2006). *Circadian physiology.* Boca Raton, FL: Taylor & Francis.

Regan, P. C. (1998). What if you can't get what you want? Willingness to compromise ideal mate selection standards as a function of sex, mate value, and relationship context. *Personality and Social Psychology Bulletin, 24*, 1294–1303.

Regan, P. C. (2008). *The mating game: A primer on love, sex, and marriage* (2nd ed.). Thousand Oaks, CA: Sage.

Regehr, C., & Bober, T. (2005). *In the line of fire: Trauma in the emergency services.* New York: Oxford University Press.

Reger, G. M., Holloway, K. M., Candy, C., Rothbaum, B. O., Difede, J., Rizzo, A. A., & Gahm, G. A. (2011). Effectiveness of virtual reality exposure therapy for active duty soldiers in a military mental health clinic. *Journal of Traumatic Stress, 24*(1), 93–96.

Regier, D. A., & Burke, J. D. (2000). Epidemiology. In B. J. Sadock & V. A. Sadock (Eds.), *Kaplan and Sadock's comprehensive textbook of psychiatry.* Philadelphia: Lippincott, Williams & Wilkins.

Regier, D. A., & Kaelber, C. T. (1995). The Epidemiologic Catchment Area (ECA) program: Studying the prevalence and incidence of psychopathology. In M. T. Tsuang, M. Tohen, & G. E. P. Zahner (Eds.), *Textbook in psychiatric epidemiology.* New York: Wiley.

Regier, D. A., Narrow, W. E., & Rae, D. S. (2004). For DSM-V, It's the "disorder threshold," stupid. *Archives of General Psychiatry, 61*, 1051.

Regier, D. A., Narrow, W. E., Kuhl, E. A., & Kupfer, D. J. (2009). The conceptual development of DSM-V. *American Journal of Psychiatry, 166*(6), 645–650.

Rehm, L. P., Wagner, A., & Ivens-Tyndal, C. (2001). Mood disorders: Unipolar and bipolar. In P. B. Sutker & H. E. Adams (Eds.), *Comprehensive handbook of psychopathology.* New York: Kluwer Academic/Plenum.

Reichert, T. (2003). The prevalence of sexual imagery in ads targeted to young adults. *Journal of Consumer Affairs, 37*, 403–412.

Reichert, T., & Lambiase, J. (2003). How to get "kissably close": Examining how advertisers appeal to consumers' sexual needs and desires. *Sexuality & Culture: An Interdisciplinary Quarterly, 7*(3), 120–136.

Reid, R. C., & Usrey, W. M. (2008). Vision. In L. Squire, D. Berg, F. Bloom, S. du Lac, A. Ghosh, & N. Spitzer (Eds.), *Fundamental neuroscience.* San Diego, CA: Elsevier.

Reidy, D. E., Foster, J. D., & Zeichner, A. (2010). Narcissism and unprovoked aggression. *Aggressive Behavior, 36*(6), 414–422.

Reinharz, D., Lesage, A. D., & Contandriopoulos, A. P. (2000). Cost-effectiveness analysis of psychiatric deinstitutionalization. *Canadian Journal of Psychiatry, 45*, 533–538.

Reips, U.-D. (2007). The methodology of Internet-based experiments. In A. N. Joinson, K. Y. A. McKenna, T. Postmes, & U.-D. Reips (Eds.), *The Oxford handbook of Internet psychology* (pp. 373–390). New York: Oxford University Press.

Reis, H. T., & Aron, A. (2008). Love: What is it, why does it matter, and how does it operate? *Perspectives on Psychological Science, 3*, 80–86.

Reisner, A. D. (1998). Repressed memories: True and false. In R. A. Baker (Ed.), *Child sexual abuse and false memory syndrome.* Amherst, NY: Prometheus Books.

Reiss, S. (1991). Expectancy model of fear, anxiety and panic. *Clinical Psychology Review, 11*, 141–154.

Rennie, D., & Luft, H. S. (2000). Making them transparent, making them credible. *Journal of the American Medical Association, 283*, 2516–2521.

Renzulli, J. S. (1986). The three-ring conception of giftedness: A developmental model for creative productivity. In R. J. Sternberg & J. E. Davidson (Eds.), *Conceptions of giftedness.* Cambridge: Cambridge University Press.

Renzulli, J. S. (1999). What is this thing called giftedness, and how do we develop it? A twenty-five year perspective. *Journal for the Education of the Gifted, 23*, 3–54.

Renzulli, J. S. (2002). Emerging conceptions of giftedness: Building a bridge to the new century. *Exceptionality, 10*, 67–75.

Repetto, M., & Gold, M. S. (2005). Cocaine and crack: Neurobiology. In J. H. Lowinson, P. Ruiz, R. B. Millman, & J. G. Langrod (Eds.), *Substance abuse: A comprehensive textbook.* Philadelphia: Lippincott/Williams & Wilkins.

Repovš, G., & Baddeley, A. (2006). The multi-component model of working memory: Explorations in experimental cognitive psychology. *Neuroscience, 139*, 5–21.

Repovš, G., & Bresjanac, M. (2006). Cognitive neuroscience of working memory. A prologue. *Neuroscience, 139*, 1–3.

Rescorla, R. A. (1978). Some implications of a cognitive perspective on Pavlovian conditioning. In S. H. Hulse, H. Fowler, & W. K. Honig (Eds.), *Cognitive processes in animal behavior.* Hillsdale, NJ: Erlbaum.

Rescorla, R. A. (1980). *Pavlovian second-order conditioning.* Hillsdale, NJ: Erlbaum.

Rescorla, R. A., & Wagner, A. R. (1972). A theory of Pavlovian conditioning: Variations in the effectiveness of reinforcement and nonreinforcement. In A. H. Black & W. F. Prokasky (Eds.), *Classical conditioning: II. Current research and theory.* New York: Appleton-Century-Crofts.

Resick, P. A., Monson, C. M., & Rizvi, S. L. (2008). Posttraumatic stress disorder. In W. E. Craighead, D. J. Miklowitz, & L. W. Craighead (Eds.), *Psychopathology: History, diagnosis, and empirical foundations.* New York, NY: Wiley.

Resnick, S. M. (2006). Sex differences in regional brain structure and function. In P. W. Kapan (Ed.), *Neurologic disease in women* (2nd ed., pp. 15–26). New York, NY: Demos Medical.

Rest, J. R. (1986). *Moral development: Advances in research and theory.* New York: Praeger.

Rettner, R. (2010, July 10). Perfectionists at risk for postpartum depression. *LiveScience.* Retrieved June 18, 2011, from http://www.livescience.com/6696-perfectionists-risk-postpartum-depression.html.

Reuter-Lorenz, P. A., & Miller, A. C. (1998). The cognitive neuroscience of human laterality: Lessons from the bisected brain. *Current Directions in Psychological Science, 7*, 15–20.

Reutskaja, E., & Hogarth, R. M. (2009). Satisfaction in choice as a function of the number of alternatives: When "goods satiate." *Psychology & Marketing, 26*(3), 197–203.

Reynolds, A. G. (1991). *Bilingualism, multiculturalism, and second language learning: The McGill conference in honour of Wallace E. Lambert.* Hillsdale, NJ: Lawrence Erlbaum and Associates.

Reynolds, A. J., Temple, J. T., Robertson, D. L., & Mann, E. A. (2001). Long-term effects of an early childhood intervention on educational achievement and juvenile arrest: A 15-year follow-up of low-income children in public schools. *Journal of the American Medical Association, 285*, 2339–2346.

Reynolds, C. F., III, Kupfer, D. J., Buysse, D. J., Coble, P. A., & Yeager, A. (1991). Subtyping DSM-III-R primary insomnia: A literature review by the DSM-IV work group on sleep disorders. *American Journal of Psychiatry, 148*, 432–438.

Reynolds, C. R. (2000). Why is psychometric research on bias in mental testing so often ignored? *Psychology, Public Policy, and Law, 6*, 144–150.

Reynolds, C. R., & Ramsay, M. C. (2003). Bias in psychological assessment: An empirical review and recommendations. In J. R. Graham & J. A. Naglieri (Eds.), *Handbook of psychology (Vol. 10): Assessment psychology.* New York: Wiley.

Reynolds, E. H. (2002). Benefits and risks of folic acid to the nervous system. *Journal of Neurology, Neurosurgery & Psychiatry, 72*(5), 567–571.

Reynolds, K. J., Turner, J. C., & Haslam, S. A. (2000). When are we better than them and they worse than us? A closer look at social discrimination in positive and negative domains. *Journal of Personality and Social Psychology, 78*, 64–80.

Rhodes, G., Simmons, L. W., & Peters, M. (2005). Attractiveness and sexual behavior: Does attractiveness enhance mating success? *Evolution and Human Behavior, 26*, 186–201.

Rhodewalt, F., & Peterson, B. (2009). Narcissism. In M. R. Leary, & R. H. Hoyle (Eds.), *Handbook of individual differences in social behavior* (pp. 547–560). New York, NY: Guilford Press.

Rholes, W. S., Simpson, J. A., Kohn, J. L., Wilson, C. L., Martin, III, A. M., Tran, S., & Kashy, D. A. (2011). Attachment orientations and depression: A longitudinal study of new parents. *Journal of Personality and Social Psychology, 100*, 567–586.

Riazi, A., & Bradley, C. (2000). Diabetes, Type I. In G. Fink (Ed.), *Encyclopedia of stress* (pp. 688–693). San Diego: Academic Press.

Riba, M. B., & Miller, R. R. (2003). Combined therapies: Psychotherapy and pharmacotherapy. In A. Tasman, J. Kay, & J. A. Lieberman (Eds.), *Psychiatry.* New York: Wiley.

Rice, L. N., & Greenberg, L. S. (1992). Humanistic approaches to psychotherapy. In D. K. Freedheim (Ed.), *History of psychotherapy: A century of change*. Washington, DC: American Psychological Association.

Rice, M., & Harris, G. T. (1993). Ontario's maximum security hospital at Penetanguishene. *International Journal of Law and Psychiatry, 16*, 195–215.

Rich, J. B., Park, N. W., Dopkins, S., & Brandt, J. (2002). What do Alzheimer's disease patients know about animals? It depends on task structure and presentation format. *Journal of the International Neuropsychological Society, 8*, 83–94.

Richardson, C. R., Kriska, A. M., Lantz, P. M., & Hayword, R. A. (2004). Physical activity and mortality across cardiovascular disease risk groups. *Medicine and Science in Sports and Exercise, 36*, 1923–1929.

Richardson, F. C., & Guignon, C. B. (2008). Positive psychology and philosophy of social science. *Theory & Psychology, 18*, 605–627.

Richardson, G. S. (1993). Circadian rhythms. In M. A. Carskadon (Ed.), *Encyclopedia of sleep and dreaming*. New York: Macmillan.

Richardson, R. C. (2007). *Evolutionary psychology as maladapted psychology*. Cambridge, MA: MIT Press.

Richer, I., & Bergeron, J. (2009). Driving under the influence of cannabis: Links with dangerous driving, psychological predictors, and accident involvement. *Accident Analysis and Prevention, 41*(2), 299–307.

Richert, E. S. (1997). Excellence with equity in identification and programming. In N. Colangelo, & G. A. Davis (Eds.), *Handbook of gifted education*. Boston: Allyn & Bacon.

Rieber, R. W. (1998). The assimilation of psychoanalysis in America: From popularization to vulgarization. In R. W. Rieber & K. D. Salzinger (Eds.), *Psychology: Theoretical-historical perspectives*. Washington, DC: American Psychological Association.

Rieger, G., Linsenmeier, J. W., Gygax, L., & Bailey, J. (2008). Sexual orientation and childhood gender nonconformity: Evidence from home videos. *Developmental Psychology, 44*(1), 46–58.

Riemann, D., Spiegelhalder, K., Feige, B., Voderholzer, U., Berger, M., Perlis, M., & Nissen, C. (2010). The hyperarousal model of insomnia: A review of the concept and its evidence. *Sleep Medicine Reviews, 14*(1), 19–31.

Riemann, R., Angleitner, A., & Strelau, J. (1997). Genetic and environmental influences on personality: A study of twins reared together using the self- and peer report NEO-FFI scales. *Journal of Personality, 65*, 449–476.

Rieskamp, J., & Hoffrage, U. (1999). When do people use simple heuristics and how can we tell? In G. Gigerenzer, P. Todd, & the ABC Research Group (Eds.), *Simple heuristics that make us smart* (pp. 25–47). Oxford: Oxford University Press.

Riggio, H. R., & Halpern, D. F. (2006). Understanding human thought: Educating students as critical thinkers. In W. Buskist & S. F. Davis (Eds.), *Handbook of the teaching of psychology* (pp. 78–84). Malden, MA: Blackwell Publishing.

Righart, R., & de Gelder, B. (2008). Rapid encoding of emotional scenes on encoding of facial expressions: And ERP study. *Social Cognitive and Affective Neuroscience, 3*, 270–278.

Rihmer, Z., & Angst, J. (2009). Mood disorders: Epidemiology. In B. J. Sadock, V. A. Sadock, & P. Ruiz (Eds.), *Kaplan & Sadock's comprehensive textbook of psychiatry* (9th ed., pp. 1645–1652). Philadelphia, PA: Lippincott, Williams & Wilkins.

Riis, J., Loewenstein, G., Baron, J., Jepson, C., Fagerlin, A., & Ubel, P. A. (2005). Ignorance of hedonic adaptation to hemodialysis: A study using ecological momentary assessment. *Journal of Experimental Psychology: General, 134*(1), 3–9.

Rilling, J. K., & Sanfey, A. G. (2011). The neuroscience of social decision-making. *Annual Review of Psychology, 62*, 23–48.

Rilling, M. (1996). The mystery of the vanished citations: James McConnell's forgotten 1960s quest for planarian learning, a biochemical engram, and celebrity. *American Psychologist, 51*, 589–598.

Risen, J., & Gilovich, T. (2007). Informal logical fallacies. In R. J. Sternberg, H. L. Roediger III, & D. F. Halpern (Eds.), *Critical thinking in psychology*. New York, NY: Cambridge University Press.

Rising, K., Bacchetti, P., & Bero, L. (2008). Reporting bias in drug trials submitted to the Food and Drug Administration: Review of publication and presentation. *PLoS Medicine, 5*(11), e217.

Riskind, J. H. (2005). Cognitive mechanisms in generalized anxiety disorder: A second generation of theoretical perspectives. *Cognitive Therapy & Research, 29*(1), 1–5.

Ritter, R. C. (2004). Gastrointestinal mechanisms of satiation for food. *Physiology & Behavior, 81*, 249–273.

Ritvo, E., Glick, I. D., & Berman, E. (2008). Couples therapy. In A. Tasman, J. Kay, J. A. Lieberman, M. B. First, & M. Maj (Eds.), *Psychiatry* (3rd ed.). New York, NY: Wiley-Blackwell.

Ritvo, E., Melnick, I., & Glick, I. (2008). Couples and family therapy. In R. E. Hales (Ed.), *The American Publishing textbook of psychiatry* (pp 1303–1367). New York: American Psychiatric Publishing Co.

Rizzolatti, G., & Craighero, L. (2004). The mirror-neuron system. *Annual Review of Neuroscience, 27*, 169–192.

Rizzolatti, G., & Sinigaglia, C. (2008). *Mirrors in the brain—How our minds share actions and emotions*. Oxford, UK: Oxford University Press.

Rizzolatti, G., Fadiga, L., Gallese, V., & Fogassi, L. (1996). Premotor cortex and the recognition of motor actions. *Cognitive Brain Research, 3*, 131–141.

Rizzolatti, G., Farri-Destro, M., & Cattaneo, L. (2009). Mirror neurons and their clinical relevance. *Nature Clinical Practice, 5*, 24–34.

Roazen, P. (1976). *Erik H. Erikson: The power and limits of a vision*. New York: Free Press.

Roberson, D., Davidoff, J., Davies, I. R. L., & Shapiro, L. R. (2005). Color categories: Evidence for the cultural relativity hypothesis. *Cognitive Psychology, 50*, 378–411.

Roberson, D., Davies, I., & Davidoff, J. (2000). Color categories are not universal: Replications and new evidence from a stone-age culture. *Journal of Experimental Psychology: General, 129*, 369–398.

Roberts, B. W., & Pomerantz, E. M. (2004). On traits, situations, and their integration: A developmental perspective. *Personality and Social Psychology Review, 8*, 402–416.

Roberts, B. W., Smith J., Jackson, J. J., & Edmonds, G. (2009). Compensatory conscientiousness and health in older couples. *Psychological Science, 20*, 553–559.

Roberts, B. W., Caspi, A., & Moffitt, T. (2003). Work experiences and personality development in young adulthood. *Journal of Personality and Social Psychology, 84*, 582–593.

Roberts, B. W., Jackson, J. J., Fayard, J. V., Edmonds, G., & Meints, J. (2009). Conscientiousness. In M. R. Leary & R. H. Hoyle (Eds.), *Handbook of individual differences in social behavior* (pp. 257–273). New York, NY: Guilford Press.

Roberts, B. W., Kuncel, N. R., Shiner, R., Caspi, A., & Goldberg, L. R. (2007). The power of personality: The comparative validity of personality traits, socioeconomic status, and cognitive ability for predicting important life outcomes. *Perspectives on Psychological Science, 2*, 313–345.

Roberts, B. W., Walton, K. E., & Bogg, T. (2005). Conscientiousness and health across the life course. *Review of General Psychology, 9*(2), 156–168.

Roberts, B. W., Wood, D., & Caspi, A. (2008). The development of personality traits in adulthood. In O. P. John, R. W. Robins, & L. A. Pervin (Eds.), *Handbook of personality: Theory and research* (3rd ed., pp. 375–398). New York, NY: Guilford Press.

Roberts, M. C., Brown, K. J., & Smith-Boydston, J. M. (2003). The scientific process and publishing research. In M. C. Roberts & S. S. Ilardi (Eds.), *Handbook of research methods in clinical psychology* (pp. 31–51). London: Blackwell Publishers.

Roberts, R. D., Markham, P. M., Matthews, G., & Zeidner, M. (2005). Assessing intelligence: Past, present, and future. In O. Wilhelm & R. W. Engle (Eds.), *Handbook of understanding and measuring intelligence*. Thousand Oaks, CA: Sage.

Roberts, W. A. (2002). Are animals stuck in time? *Psychological Bulletin, 128*, 473–489.

Robins, L. N., Locke, B. Z., & Regier, D. A. (1991). An overview of psychiatric disorders in America. In L. N. Robins & D. A. Regier (Eds.), *Psychiatric disorders in America: The epidemiologic catchment area study*. New York: Free Press.

Robins, R. W., Gosling, S. D., & Craik, K. H. (1999). An empirical analysis of trends in psychology. *American Psychologist, 54*, 117–128.

Robinson, A., & Clinkenbeard, P. R. (1998). Giftedness: An exceptionality examined. *Annual Review of Psychology, 49*, 117–139.

Robinson, D. G., Woerner, M. G., McMeniman, M., Mendelowitz, A., & Bilder, R. M. (2004). Symptomatic and functional recovery from a first episode of schizophrenia or schizoaffective disorder. *American Journal of Psychiatry, 161*, 473–479.

Robinson, F. P. (1970). *Effective study* (4th ed.). New York: Harper & Row.

Robinson, N. M. (2010). The social world of gifted children and youth. In S. I. Pfeiffer (Ed.), *Handbook of giftedness in children: Psychoeducational theory, research, and best practices*. New York, NY: Springer.

Robinson, S. L., Kraatz, M. S., & Rousseau, D. M. (1994). Changing obligations and the psychological contract: A longitudinal study. *Academy of Management Journal, 37*, 137–152.

Robles, T. F., Glaser, R., & Kiecolt-Glaser, J. K. (2005). Out of balance: A new look at chronic stress, depression, and immunity. *Current Directions in Psychological Science, 14*, 111–115.

Rock, I. (1986). The description and analysis of object and event perception. In K. R. Boff, L. Kaufman, & J. P. Thomas (Eds.), *Handbook of perception and human performance* (Vol. 2). New York: Wiley.

Rodgers, J. E. (1982). The malleable memory of eyewitnesses. *Science Digest, 3*, 32–35.

Rodieck, R. W. (1998). *The first steps in seeing*. Sunderland, MA: Sinauer.

Rodin, J. (1981). Current status of the internal-external hypothesis for obesity: What went wrong? *American Psychologist, 36*(4), 361–372.

Rodin, J. (1985). Insulin levels, hunger, and food intake: An example of feedback loops in body weight regulation. *Health Psychology, 4,* 1–24.

Roediger, H. L., III, & Guynn, M. J. (1996). Retrieval processes. In E. L. Bjork & R. A. Bjork (Eds.), *Memory.* San Diego: Academic Press.

Roediger, H. L., III, & Karpicke, J. D. (2006a). Test-enhanced learning: Taking memory tests improves long-term retention. *Psychological Science, 17,* 249–255.

Roediger, H. L., III, & Karpicke, J. D. (2006b). The power of testing memory: Basic research and implications for educational practice. *Perspectives on Psychological Science, 1*(3), 181–210.

Roediger, H. L., III, & McDermott, K. B. (1995). Creating false memories: Remembering words not presented in lists. *Journal of Experimental Psychology: Learning, Memory, and Cognition, 21,* 803–814.

Roediger, H. L., III, & McDermott, K. B. (2000). Tricks of memory. *Current Directions in Psychological Science, 9,* 123–127.

Roediger, H. L., III, Agarwal, P. K., Kang, S. K., & Marsh, E. J. (2010). Benefits of testing memory: Best practices and boundary conditions. In G. M. Davies & D. B. Wright, (Eds.), *Current issues in applied memory research* (pp. 13–49). New York, NY: Psychology Press.

Roediger, H. L., III, Wheeler, M. A., & Rajaram, S. (1993). Remembering, knowing, and reconstructing the past. In D. L. Medin (Ed.), *The psychology of learning and motivation: Advances in research and theory.* San Diego: Academic Press.

Roediger, H. L., III. (1980). Memory metaphors in cognitive psychology. *Memory & Cognition, 8,* 231–246.

Roediger, H. L., III. (1990). Implicit memory: Retention without remembering. *American Psychologist, 45,* 1043–1056.

Roediger, H. L., III. (2000). Why retrieval is the key process in understanding human memory. In E. Tulving (Ed.), *Memory, consciousness, and the brain: The Tallinn conference* (pp. 52–75). Philadelphia: Psychology Press.

Roediger, H. L., III. (2008). Relativity of remembering: Why the laws of memory vanished. *Annual Review of Psychology, 59,* 225–54.

Roehrs, T., & Roth, T. (2000). Hypnotics: Efficacy and adverse effects. In M. H. Kryger, T. Roth, & W. C. Dement (Eds.), *Principles and practice of sleep medicine.* Philadelphia: Saunders.

Roehrs, T., Zorick, F. J., & Roth, T. (2000). Transient and short term insomnias. In M. H. Kryger, T. Roth, & W. C. Dement (Eds.), *Principles and practice of sleep medicine.* Philadelphia: Saunders.

Roffwarg, H. P., Muzio, J. N., & Dement, W. C. (1966). Ontogenetic development of the human sleep–dream cycle. *Science, 152,* 604–619.

Rogers, C. R. (1951). *Client-centered therapy: Its current practice, implications, and theory.* Boston: Houghton Mifflin.

Rogers, C. R. (1961). *On becoming a person: A therapist's view of psychotherapy.* Boston: Houghton Mifflin.

Rogers, C. R. (1980). *A way of being.* Boston: Houghton Mifflin.

Rogers, C. R. (1986). Client-centered therapy. In I. L. Kutash & A. Wolf (Eds.), *Psychotherapist's casebook.* San Francisco: Jossey-Bass.

Rogers, M. P., Fricchione, G., & Reich, P. (1999). Psychosomatic medicine and consultation-liaison psychiatry. In A. M. Nicholi (Ed.), *The Harvard guide to psychiatry* (3rd ed., pp. 362–389). Cambridge, MA: Harvard University Press.

Rogers, N. L., & Dinges, D. F. (2002). Shiftwork, circadian disruption, and consequences. *Primary Psychiatry, 9*(8), 50.

Rogers, T. B., Kuiper, N. A., & Kirker, W. S. (1977). Self-reference and the encoding of personal information. *Journal of Personality and Social Psychology, 35,* 677–688.

Rogers, W. T., & Yang, P. (1996). Test-wiseness: Its nature and application. *European Journal of Psychological Assessment, 12,* 247–259.

Rogoff, B. (1998). Cognition as a collaborative process. In D. Kuhn & R. S. Siegler (Eds.), *Handbook of child psychology (Vol. 2): Cognition perception, and language.* New York: Wiley.

Rogoff, B. (2003). *The cultural nature of human development.* New York, NY: Oxford University Press.

Rohner, R. P., & Veneziano, R. A. (2001). The importance of father love: History and contemporary evidence. *Review of General Psychology, 5,* 382–405.

Rohrer, D., & Taylor, K. (2006). The effects of overlearning and distributed practice on the retention of mathematics knowledge. *Applied Cognitive Psychology, 20,* 1209–1224.

Rohrer, D., Taylor, K., Pashler, H., Wixted, J. T., & Capeda, N. J. (2005). The effect of overlearning on long-term retention. *Applied Cognitive Psychology, 19,* 361–374.

Roid, G. H., & Tippin, S. M. (2009). Assessment of intellectual strengths and weaknesses with the Stanford-Binet Intelligence Scales, Fifth Edition (SB5). In J. A. Naglieri & S. Goldstein (Eds.), *Practitioner's guide to assessing intelligence and achievement* (pp. 153–190). New York, NY: Wiley.

Rojas, N. L., Sherrit, L., Harris, S., & Knight, J. R. (2008). The role of parental consent in adolescent substance use research. *Journal of Adolescent Health, 42,* 192–197.

Rollman, G. B. (1992). Cognitive effects in pain and pain judgements. In D. Algom (Ed.), *Psychophysical approaches to cognition.* Amsterdam: North Holland.

Rolls, E. T. (1990). A theory of emotion, and its application to understanding the neural basis of emotion. *Cognitive and Emotion, 4,* 161–190.

Ronksley, P. E., Brien, S. E., Turner, B. J., Mukamal, K. J., & Ghali, W. A. (2011). Association of alcohol consumption with selected cardiovascular disease outcomes: a systematic review and meta-analysis. *British Medical Journal, 342*(7795), 479.

Ronquillo, J., Denson, T. F., Lickel, B., Zhong-Lin, L., Nandy, A., & Maddox, D. B. (2007). The effect of skin tone on race-related amygdala activity: An fMRI investigation. *Social Cognitive Affective Neuroscience, 2,* 39–44.

Rorden, C., Karnath, H.-O., & Bonilha, L. (2007). Improving lesion-symptom mapping. *Journal of Cognitive Neuroscience, 19,* 1081–1088.

Rorschach, H. (1921). *Psychodiagnostik.* Berne: Birchen.

Rosa, A. (n.d.). Sir Frederick Bartlett (1886–1969). An intellectual biography. Retrieved March 14, 2011, from http://www.ppsis.cam.ac.uk/bartlett/Intellectual%Biography.htm.

Rosch, E. H. (1973). Natural categories. *Cognitive Psychology, 4,* 328–350.

Rosch, P. J. (n.d.). Reminiscences of Hans Selye, and the birth of "stress." Retrieved June 22, 2005, from http://www.stress.org/mementos.htm.

Rose, D., Wykes, T., Leese, M., Bindman, J., & Fleischmann, P. (2003). Patient's perspectives on electroconvulsive therapy: Systematic review. *British Medical Journal, 326,* 1363–1365.

Rose, H., & Rose, S. E. (2000). *Alas, poor Darwin: Arguments against evolutionary psychology.* New York: Harmony Books.

Rose, N. R. (2007). Neuroimmunomodulation. In G. Fink (Ed.), *Encyclopedia of stress.* San Diego: Elsevier.

Roseboom, T., de Rooij, S., & Painter, R. (2006). The Dutch famine and its long-term consequences for adult health. *Early Human Development, 82,* 485–491.

Rosenbaum, M., Lakin, M., & Roback, H. B. (1992). Psychotherapy in groups. In D. K. Freedheim (Ed.), *History of psychotherapy: A century of change.* Washington, DC: American Psychological Association.

Rosenbaum, R. S., Kohler, S., Schacter, D. L., Moscovitch, M., Westmacott, R., Black, S. E., et al. (2005). The case of K.C.: Contributions of a memory-impaired person to memory theory. *Neuropsychologia, 43,* 989–1021.

Rosenblum, K. (2009). Conditioned taste aversion and taste learning: Molecular mechanisms. In J. H. Byrne (Ed.), *Concise learning and memory: The editor's selection.* San Diego, CA: Elsevier.

Rosenhan, D. L. (1973). On being sane in insane places. *Science, 179,* 250–258.

Rosenthal, H. (1988). *Not with my life I don't: Preventing suicide and that of others.* Muncie, IN: Accelerated Development.

Rosenthal, L. (2006). Physiologic processes during sleep. In T. Lee-Chiong (Ed.), *Sleep: A comprehensive handbook.* Hoboken, NJ: Wiley-Liss.

Rosenthal, N. E, Sack, D. A., Gillin, J. C., Lewy, A. J., Goodwin, F. K., Davenport, Y., et al. (1984). Seasonal affective disorder: A description of the syndrome and preliminary findings with light therapy. *Archives of General Psychiatry, 41*(1), 72–80.

Rosenthal, R. (1976). *Experimenter effects in behavioral research.* New York: Halsted.

Rosenthal, R. (1991). *Meta-analytic procedures for social research* (Rev. ed.). Newbury Park, CA: Sage.

Rosenthal, R. (1994). Interpersonal expectancy effects: A 30–year perspective. *Current Directions in Psychological Science, 3,* 176–179.

Rosenthal, R. (2002). Experimenter and clinical effects in scientific inquiry and clinical practice. *Prevention & Treatment, 5*(38), 7–23.

Rosenthal, R., & Rubin, J. D. (1978). Interpersonal expectancy effects: The first 345 studies. *The Behavioral and Brain Sciences, 3,* 377–415.

Rosenzweig, M. R., & Bennett, E. L. (1996). Psychobiology of plasticity: Effects of training and experience on brain and behavior. *Behavioural Brain Research, 78*(5), 57–65.

Rosenzweig, M. R., Krech, D., & Bennett, E. L. (1961). Heredity, environment, brain biochemistry, and learning. In *Current trends in psychological theory.* Pittsburgh: University of Pittsburgh Press.

Rosenzweig, M., Krech, D., Bennett, E. L., & Diamond, M. (1962). Effects of environmental complexity and training on brain chemistry and anatomy: A replication and extension. *Journal of Comparative and Physiological Psychology, 55,* 429–437.

Rosenzweig, S. (1985). Freud and experimental psychology: The emergence of idiodynamics. In S. Koch & D. E. Leary (Eds.), *A century of psychology as a science*. New York: McGraw-Hill.

Rosler, F. (2005). From single-channel recordings to brain-mapping devices: The impact of electroencephalography on experimental psychology. *History of Psychology, 8*, 95–117.

Ross, B. (1991). William James: Spoiled child of American psychology. In G. A. Kimble, M. Wertheimer, & C. White (Eds.), *Portraits of pioneers in psychology*. Hillsdale, NJ: Erlbaum.

Ross, C. A. (1999). Dissociative disorders. In T. Millon, P. H. Blaney, & R. D. Davis (Eds.), *Oxford textbook of psychopathology* (pp. 466–484). New York: Oxford University Press.

Ross, H., & Plug, C. (2002). *The mystery of the moon illusion: Exploring the size perception*. New York, NY: Oxford.

Ross, L. D. (1988). The obedience experiments: A case study of controversy. *Contemporary Psychology, 33*, 101–104.

Ross, L. D., & Anderson, C. A. (1982). Shortcomings in the attribution process: On the origins and maintenance of erroneous social assessments. In D. Kahneman, P. Slovic, & A. Tversky (Eds.), *Judgement under uncertainty: Heuristics and biases*. Cambridge: Cambridge University Press.

Ross, L. E., Dennis, C.-L., Robertson-Blackmore, E., Stewart, D. E. (2005). *Postpartum depression: A guide for front-line health and social service providers*. Toronto: Centre for Addiction & Mental Health.

Roter, D. L., Hall, J. A., Merisca, R., Nordstrom, B., Cretin, D., & Svarstad, B. (1998). Effectiveness of interventions to promote patient compliance. *Medical Care, 36*, 1138–1161.

Roth, T., & Drake, C. (2004). Evolution of insomnia: Current status and future direction. *Sleep Medicine, 5*(Supplemental 1), S23–S30.

Rothbart, M. K., & Bates, J. E. (2008). Temperament. In W. Damon & R. M. Lerner (Eds.), *Child and adolescent development: An advanced course* (pp. 54–65). New York, NY: Wiley.

Rothenberg, A. (1990). *Creativity and madness*. Baltimore: John Hopkins University Press.

Rotter, J. B. (1982). *The development and application of social learning theory*. New York: Praeger.

Rouiller, E. M. (1997). Functional organization of the auditory pathways. In G. Ehret & R. Romand (Eds.), *The central auditory system*. Oxford, England: Oxford University Press.

Rounder, J. N., & Morey, R. D. (2009). The nature of thresholds. *Psychological Review, 116*, 655–660.

Rousseau, D. M. (1995). *Psychological contracts in organizations*. Thousand Oaks, CA: Sage.

Rousseau, D. M., & Parks, J. M. (1993). The contracts of individuals and organizations. In B. M. Staw & L. L. Cummings (Eds.), *Research in organizational behavior* (Vol. 15, pp. 1–43). Greenwich, CT: JAI Press.

Rousseau, D. M., & Schalk, R. (2000). Learning from cross-national perspectives on psychological contracts. In D. M. Rousseau & R. Schalk (Eds.), *Psychological contracts in employment: Cross-national perspectives* (pp. 283–403). Thousand Oaks, CA: Sage.

Routledge, C., Ostafin, B., Juhl, J., Sedikides, C., Cathy, C., & Lia, J. (2010). Adjusting to death: The effects of mortality salience and self-esteem on psychological well-being, growth motivation, and maladaptive behavior. *Journal of Personality and Social Psychology, 99*, 897–916.

Rowa, K., & Antony, M. M. (2008). Generalized anxiety disorders. In W. E. Craighead, D. J. Miklowitz, & L. W. Craighead (Eds.), *Psychopathology: History, diagnosis, and empirical foundations*. New York, NY: Wiley.

Rowe, D. C., & van den Oord, E. J. C. G. (2005). Genetic and environmental influences. In V. A. Derlega, B. A. Winstead, & W. H. Jones (Eds.), *Personality: Contemporary theory and research*. Belmont, CA: Wadsworth.

Rowe, S. M., & Wertsch, J. V. (2002). Vygotsky's model of cognitive development. In U. Goswami (Ed.), *Blackwell handbook of childhood cognitive development*. Malden, MA: Blackwell.

Rowny, S., & Lisanby, S. H. (2008). Brain stimulation in psychiatry. In A. Tasman, J. Kay, J. A. Lieberman, M. B. First, & M. Maj (Eds.), *Psychiatry* (3rd ed.). New York, NY: Wiley-Blackwell.

Roy, M., Piche, M., Chen, J., Peretz, I., & Rainville, P. (2009). Cerebral and spinal modulation of pain by emotions. *Proceedings of the National Academy of Sciences of the United States of America, 106*(49), 20900–20905.

Rozee, P. D., & Koss, M. P. (2001). Rape: A century of resistance. *Psychology of Women Quarterly, 25* (4), 295–311.

Rozin, P., Kabnick, K., Pete, E., Fischler, C., & Shields, C. (2003). The ecology of eating. *Psychological Science, 14*, 450–454.

Rozin, P. (1990). The importance of social factors in understanding the acquisition of food habits. In E. D. Capaldi & T. L. Powley (Eds.), *Taste, experience, and feeding*. Washington, DC: American Psychological Association.

Rozin, P. (2007). Food and eating. In S. Kitayama & D. Cohen (Eds.), *Handbook of cultural psychology* (pp. 391–416). New York: Guilford.

Rubin, D. C., Bernsten, D., & Bohni, M. K. (2008). A memory-based model of posttraumatic stress disorder: Evaluating basic assumptions underlying PTSD diagnosis. *Psychological Review, 115*, 985–1011.

Ruble, D. N., & Martin, C. L. (1998). Gender development. In W. Damon (Ed.), *Handbook of child psychology (Vol. 3): Social, emotional, and personality development*. New York: Wiley.

Rudorfer, M. V., & Goodwin, F. K. (1993). Introduction. In C. E. Coffey (Ed.), *The clinical science of electroconvulsive therapy*. Washington, DC: American Psychiatric Press.

Ruini, C., & Fava, G. A. (2004). Clinical application of well-being therapy. In P. A. Linley & S. Joseph (Eds.), *Positive psychology in practice*. Hoboken, NJ: Wiley.

Runco, M. A. (2004). Divergent thinking, creativity, and giftedness. In R. J. Sternberg (Ed.), *Definitions and conceptions of giftedness* (pp. 47–62). Thousand Oaks, CA: Corwin Press.

Runyan, J. D., & Dash, P. K. (2005). Distinct prefrontal molecular mechanisms for information storage lasting seconds versus minutes. *Learning & Memory, 12*(3), 232–238.

Rusak, B. (1990). Biological Rhythms: From Physiology to behavior. In J. Montplaisir & R. Bodbout (Eds.), *Sleep and biological rhythms: Basic mechanism and applications to psychiatry* (pp. 11–24). New York: Oxford University Press.

Rusak, B., & Zucker, I. (1979). Neural regulation of circadian rhythms. *Physiological Review, 59*, 449–526.

Ruscio, J. (2002). *Clear thinking with psychology: Separating sense from nonsense*. Belmont, CA: Wadsworth.

Rush, A. J. (1984). Cognitive therapy. In T. B. Karasu (Ed.), *The psychiatric therapies*. Washington, DC: American Psychiatric Press.

Rushowy, K. (2007, October 27). TO school will let teenagers sleep in. *Toronto Star*, A1.

Rushton, J. P. (1994). Sex and race differences in cranial capacity from International Labour Office data. *Intelligence, 19*, 281–294.

Rushton, J. P. (1995). *Race, evolution, and behavior. A life-history perspective*. New Brunswick, NJ: Transaction.

Rushton, J. P. (2003). Race differences in g and the "Jensen effect." In H. Nyborg (Ed.), *The scientific study of general intelligence: Tribute to Arthur R. Jensen*. Oxford, UK: Pergamon.

Rushton, J. P. (2008). Testing the genetic hypothesis of group mean IQ differences in South Africa: Racial admixture and cross-situational consistency. *Personality and Individual Differences, 44*, 768–776.

Rushton, J. P., & Ankney, C. D. (2007). The evolution of brain size and intelligence. In S. M. Platek, J. P. Keenan, & T. K. Shackleford (Eds.), *Evolutionary cognitive neuroscience*. Cambridge: MIT Press.

Rushton, J. P., & Irwing, P. (2011). The general factor of personality: Normal and abnormal. In T. Chamorro-Premuzic, S. von Stumm, & A. Furnham (Eds.), *The Wiley-Blackwell handbook of individual differences*. London: Blackwell.

Rushton, J. P., & Jensen, A. R. (2005). Thirty years of research on race differences in cognitive ability. *Psychology, Public Policy, and Law, 11*, 235–294.

Rushton, J. P., & Jensen, A. R. (2010). Editorial. The rise and fall of the Flynn Effect as a reason to expect a narrowing of the Black–White IQ gap. *Intelligence, 38*, 213–219.

Rushton–Suzuki debate. (1989, February 8). *CBC Digital Archives*: http://archives.cbc.ca/IDC-1-74-663-3727/people/david_suzuki/clip5.

Russell, G. F. M. (1995). Anorexia nervosa through time. In G. Szmukler, C. Dare, & J. Treasure (Eds.), *Handbook of eating disorders: Theory, treatment, and research*. New York: Wiley.

Russell, G. F. M. (2009). Anorexia nervosa. In M. C. Gelder, N. C. Andreasen, J. J. López-Ibor, Jr., & J. R. Geddes (Eds.), *New Oxford textbook of psychiatry* (2nd ed., Vol. 1). New York, NY: Oxford University Press.

Russell, J. A. (1991). Culture and the categorization of emotions. *Psychological Bulletin, 110*, 426–450.

Russell, J. A. (1994). Is there universal recognition of emotion from facial expression? A review of the cross-cultural studies. *Psychological Bulletin, 115*, 102–141.

Russell, J. A. (1995). Facial expressions of emotion: What lies beyond minimal universality? *Psychological Bulletin, 118*, 379–391.

Russell, J. A. (2007). Stress milestones. Stress: The International Journal on the Biology of Stress, 10(1), 1–2.

Rutherford, A. (2000). Radical behaviorism and psychology's public: B. F. Skinner in the popular press, 1934–1990. *History of Psychology, 3*, 371–395.

Rutherford, A. (2003). B. F. Skinner's technology of behavior in American life: From consumer culture to counterculture. *Journal of History of the Behavioral Sciences, 39*, 1–23.

Rutherford, A. (2004). A "visible scientist": B. F. Skinner writes for the popular press. *The European Journal of Behavior Analysis, 5*, 109–120.

Rutherford, A. (2005). B. F. Skinner. *Dictionary of modern American philosophers*. Bristol, England: Thoemmes Press.

Rutherford, A. (2005). *Beyond the box*. Toronto: University of Toronto Press.

Rutherford, A. (2006). Mother of behavior therapy and beyond: Mary Cover Jones and the study of the "whole child." In D. Dewsbury, L. T. Benjamin, & M. Wertheimer (Eds.), *Portraits of pioneers in psychology* (Vol. 6, pp. 189–206). Washington, DC: APA.

Rutherford, A. (2009). *Beyond the box*. Toronto: University of Toronto Press.

Rutherford, W. (1886). A new theory of hearing. *Journal of Anatomy and Physiology, 21*, 166–168.

Rutter, M. (2006). *Genes and behavior: Nature—nurture interplay explained*. Maiden, MA: Blackwell Publishing.

Rutter, M. (2007). Gene-environment interdependence. *Developmental Science, 10*(1), 12–18.

Rutter, M., & Silberg, J. (2002). Gene–environment interplay relation to emotional and behavioral disturbance. *Annual Review of Psychology, 53*, 463–490.

Ryan, C. S., Park, B., & Judd, C. M. (1996). Assessing stereotype accuracy: Implications for understanding the stereotyping process. In C. N. Macrae, C. Stangor, & M. Hewstone (Eds.), *Stereotypes and stereotyping*. New York: Guilford.

Ryckeley, R. (2005, May). Don't send in the clowns. *The Citizen*.

Ryder, A. G., et al (2008). The cultural shaping of depression: Somatic symptoms in China, psychological symptoms in North America? *Journal of Abnormal Psychology, 117*, 300–313.

Rynes, S. S. (1993). Who's selecting whom? Effects of selection practices on applicant attitudes and behavior. In N. Schmitt & W. C. Borman (Eds.), *Personnel selection in organizations* (pp. 240–274). San Francisco: Jossey-Bass.

Sabanayagam, C., & Shankar, A. (2010). Sleep duration and cardiovascular disease: Results from the National Health Interview Survey. *Sleep: Journal of Sleep and Sleep Disorders Research, 33*(8), 1037–1042.

Sack, A. T., & Linden, D. E. J. (2003). Combining transcranial magnetic stimulation and functional imaging in cognitive brain research: Possibilities and limitations. *Brain Research Reviews, 43*(1), 41–56.

Sackeim, H. A., Dillingham, E. M., Prudic, J., Cooper, T., McCall, W. V., Rosenquist, P., et al. (2009). Effect of concomitant pharmacotherapy on electroconvulsive therapy outcomes: Short-term efficacy and adverse effects. *Archives of General Psychiatry, 66*(7), 729–737.

Sackeim, H. A., Haskett, R. F., Mulsant, B. H., Thase, M. E., Mann, J. J., Pettinati, H. M., et al. (2001). Continuation pharmacotherapy in the prevention of relapse following electroconvulsive therapy: A randomized controlled trial. *Journal of the American Medical Association, 285*, 1299–1307.

Sackeim, H. A., Prudic, J., Fuller, R., Keilp, J., Lavori, P. W., & Olfson, M. (2007). The cognitive effects of electroconvulsive therapy in community settings. *Neuropsychopharmacology, 32*, 244–254.

Sackett, P. R., & Lievens, F. (2008). Personnel selection. *Annual Review of Psychology, 59*, 419–450.

Sacks, O. (2007). *Musicophilia: Tales of music and the brain*. New York: Alfred Knopf.

Sacks, O. W. (1990). *The man who mistook his wife for a hat and other clinical tales*. New York. Perennial Library.

Sadikaj, G., Moskowitz, D. S., & Zuroff, D. C. (2011). Attachment-related affective dynamics: Differential reactivity to others' interpersonal behavior. *Journal of Personality and Social Psychology, 100*, 905–917.

Sadker, M., & Sadker, D. (1994). *Failing at fairness: How America's schools cheat girls*. New York: Scribners.

Safdar, S., & Lay, C. (2003). The relations of immigrant-specific and non-specific daily hassles to distress controlling for psychological adjustment and cultural competence. *Journal of Applied Social Psychology, 33*, 299–320.

Safran, J. D., & Muran, J. C. (2000). *Negotiating the therapeutic alliance: A relational treatment guide*. New York: The Guilford Press.

Saklofske, D. H., Gorsuch, R. L., Weiss, L. G., Zhu, J., & Peterson, C. A. (2005). General ability index for the WAIS-III: Canadian norms. *Canadian Journal of Behavioural Science, 37*, 44–48.

Saks, A. M. (2006). Multiple predictions and criteria of job search success. *Journal of Vocational Behavior, 68*, 400–415.

Sala, J. B., & Courtney, S. M. (2007). Binding of what and where during working memory maintenance. *Cortex, 43*, 5–21.

Sallot, J. (2005, March 10). U.S. authorities fear influx of Canadian ecstasy. *The Globe and Mail*, A18.

Salmon, P., Sephton, S., Weissbecker, I., Hoover, K., Ulmer, C., & Studts, J. L. (2004). Mindfulness mediation in clinical practice. *Cognitive and Behavioral Practice, 11*, 434–446.

Salovey, P., & Mayer, J. D. (1990). Emotional intelligence. *Imagination, Cognition, and Personality, 9*, 185–211.

Salovey, P., Mayer, J. D., & Caruso, D. (2002). The positive psychology of emotional intelligence. In C. R. Synder & J. Lopez (Eds.), *Handbook of positive psychology*. New York: Oxford University Press.

Salsburg, D. (2001). *The lady tasting tea*. New York: W.H. Freeman Co.

Salthouse, T. A. (1991). Mediation of adult age differences in cognition by reductions in working memory and speed of processing. *Psychological Science, 2*, 179–183.

Salthouse, T. A. (1996). The processing-speed theory of adult age differences in cognition. *Psychological Review, 103*, 403–428.

Salthouse, T. A. (2000). Aging and measures of processing speed. *Biological Psychology, 54*, 35–54.

Salthouse, T. A. (2003). Memory aging from 18–80. *Alzheimer Disease & Associated Disorders, 17*(3), 162–167.

Salthouse, T. A. (2004). What and when of cognitive aging. *Current Directions in Psychological Science, 13*(4), 140–144.

Salthouse, T. A. (2006). Mental exercise and mental aging. *Perspectives on Psychological Science, 1*, 68–87.

Salvy, S., Jarrin, D., Paluch, R., Irfan, N., & Pliner, P. (2007). Effects of social influence on eating in couples, friends and strangers. *Appetite, 49*(1), 92–99.

Samelson, F. (1981). Struggle for scientific authority: The reception of Watson's behaviorism, 1913–1920. *Journal of the History of the Behavioral Sciences, 17*, 399–425.

Samelson, F. (1994). John B. Watson in 1913: Rhetoric and practice. In J. T. Todd & E. K. Morris (Eds.), *Modern perspectives on John B. Watson and classical behaviorism*. Westport, CT: Greenwood Press.

Same-sex rights Canada timeline. (2005). *CBC News Indepth*. Retrieved May 10, 2005, from http://www.cbc.ca/news/background/samesexrights/timeline.

Samet, J. M. (1992). The health benefits of smoking cessation. *Medical Clinics of North America, 76*, 399–414.

Sammons, M. T., Gorny, S. W., Zinner, E. S., & Allen, R. P. (2000). Prescriptive authority for psychologists: A consensus of support. *Professsional Psychology: Research and Practice, 31*, 604–609.

Samnaliev, M., & Clark, R. E. (2008). The economics of schizophrenia. In K. T. Mueser & D. V. Jeste (Eds.), *Clinical handbook of schizophrenia* (pp. 25–34). New York, NY: Guilford Press.

Samuelson, P. A., & Nordhaus, W. D. (2005). *Economics* (18th ed.). Boston, MA: McGraw-Hill.

Sanderson, W. C., & Barlow, D. H. (1990). A description of patients diagnosed with DSM-III-R generalized anxiety disorder. *Journal of Nervous and Mental Disease, 178*, 588–591.

Sandin, B., Chorot, P., Santed, M. A., & Valiente, R. M. (2004). Differences in negative life events between patients with anxiety disorders, depression and hypochondriasis. *Anxiety, Stress & Coping: An International Journal, 17*(1), 37–47.

Sandrini, M., & Manenti, R. (2009). Transcranial magnetic stimulation as a tool for cognitive studies. *Giornale Italiano di Psicologia, 36*(2), 347–372.

Sanger, D. J. (2004). The pharmacology and mechanisms of action of new generation, nonbenzodiazepine hypnotic agents. *CNS Drugs, 18*(Suppl1), 9–15.

Sangster, D., & Wortsman, A. (2001) Labour and business perspectives on Canada's skills challenge. *Workplace Gazette, 4*(3), 46–53.

Sanislow, C. A., & Carson, R. C. (2001). Schizophrenia: A critical examination. In P. B. Sutker & H. E. Adams (Eds.), *Comprehensive handbook of psychopathology* (3rd ed., pp. 403–444). New York: Kluwer Academic/Plenum.

Saper, C. B. (2000). Brain stem, reflexive behavior, and the cranial nerves. In E. R. Kandel, J. H. Schwartz, & T. M. Jessell (Eds.), *Principles of neural science* (pp. 873–888). New York: McGraw-Hill.

Sapolsky, R. M. (2007). Stress, stress-related disease, and emotion regulation. In J. J. Gross (Ed.), *Handbook of emotion regulation*. New York: Guilford.

Sapolsky, R. M. (1998). *Why zebras don't get ulcers*. New York: W.H. Freeman and Company.

Sareen, J., Cox, B. J., Afifi, T. O., Stein, M. B., Belik, S. L., Meadows, G., & Asmundson, G. J. G. (2007). Prevalence of mental disorders and perceived need for mental health care in a large representative sample of military personnel. *Archives of General Psychiatry, 64*, 843–852.

Sartorius, A., Kiening, K. L., Kirsch, P., von Gall, C. C., Haberkorn, U., Unterberg, A. W., et al. (2010). Remission of major depression under deep brain stimulation of the lateral habenula in a therapy-refractory patient. *Biological Psychiatry, 67*(2), e9–e11.

Sato, T. (1997). Seasonal affective disorder and phototherapy: A critical review. *Professional Psychology: Research and Practice, 28*, 164–169.

Sato, T., & McCann, D. (2002). Advances in the study of sociotropy-autonomy and depression. *Advances in Psychology Research, 15*, pp. 35–54.

Sato, T., Namiki, H., Ando, J., & Hatano, G. (2004). Japanese conception of and research on intelligence. In R. J. Sternberg (Ed.), *International handbook of intelligence* (pp. 302–324). New York: Cambridge University Press.

Savage-Rumbaugh, E. S. (1991). Language learning in the bonobo: How and why they learn. In N. A. Krasnegor, D. M. Rumbaugh, & R. L. Schiefelbusch/M. Studdert-Kennedy (Eds.), *Biological and behavioral determinants of language development*. Hillsdale, NJ: Erlbaum.

Savage-Rumbaugh, S., Rumbaugh, D. M., & Fields, W. M. (2006). Language as a window on rationality. In S. Hurley & M. Nudds (Eds.), *Rational animals?* (pp. 513–552). New York: Oxford University Press.

Savage-Rumbaugh, S., Rumbaugh, D. M., & Fields, W. M. (2009). Empirical Kanzi: The ape language controversy revisited. *Skeptic, 15*(1), 25–33.

Savage-Rumbaugh, S., Shanker, S. G., & Taylor, T. J. (1998). *Apes, language, and the human mind.* New York: Oxford University Press.

Savin-Williams, R. C. (2006). Who's gay? Does it matter? *Current Directions in Psychological Science, 15,* 40–44.

Saxe, L. (1994). Detection of deception: Polygraph and integrity tests. *Current Directions in Psychological Science, 3,* 69–73.

Sayer, L. C. (2005). Gender, time and inequality: Trends in women's and men's paid work, unpaid work and free time. *Social Forces, 84,* 285–303.

Sayette, M. A. (2007). Alcohol and stress: Social and psychological aspects. In G. Fink (Ed.), *Encyclopedia of stress.* San Diego: Elsevier.

Scarr, S. (1991). *Theoretical issues in investigating intellectual plasticity.* S. E. Brauth, W. S. Hall, & R. Dooling (Eds.), *Plasticity of development.* Cambridge, MA: MIT Press.

Scarr, S. (1997). Behavior-genetic and socialization theories of intelligence: Truce and reconciliation. In R. J. Sternberg & E. L. Grigorenko (Eds.), *Intelligence, heredity, and environment.* New York: Cambridge University Press.

Scarr, S., & Weinberg, R. A. (1977). Intellectual similarities within families of both adopted and biological children. *Intelligence, 32,* 170–190.

Scarr, S., & Weinberg, R. A. (1983). The Minnesota adoption studies: Genetic differences and malleability. *Child Development, 54,* 260–267.

Schachter, D. L., & Addis, D. R. (2007a). The optimistic brain. *Nature Neuroscience, 10,* 1345–1347.

Schachter, S. (1964). The interaction of cognitive and physiological determinants of emotional state. In L. Berkowitz (Ed.), *Advances in experimental social psychology* (Vol. 1). New York: Academic Press.

Schachter, S. (1971). *Emotion, obesity, and crime.* New York, NY: Academic Press.

Schachter, S., & Singer, J. E. (1962). Cognitive, social and physiological determinants of emotional state. *Psychological Review, 69,* 379–399.

Schachter, S., & Singer, J. E. (1979). Comments on the Maslach and Marshall–Zimbardo experiments. *Journal of Personality and Social Psychology, 37,* 989–995.

Schacter, D. (2001). *The seven sins of memory: How the mind forgets and remembers.* Boston, MA: Houghton Mifflin Company

Schacter, D. L. (1987). Implicit memory: History and current status. *Journal of Experimental Psychology: Learning, Memory and Cognition, 14,* 501–518.

Schacter, D. L. (1989). On the relation between memory and consciousness: Dissociable interactions and conscious experience. In H. L. Roediger, III, & F. I. M. Craik (Eds.), *Varieties of memory and consciousness.* Hillsdale, NJ: Erlbaum.

Schacter, D. L. (1992). Understanding implicit memory: A cognitive neuroscience approach. *American Psychologist, 47,* 559–569.

Schacter, D. L. (1994). Priming and multiple memory systems: Perceptual mechanisms of implicit memory. In D. L. Schacter & E. Tulving (Eds.), *Memory systems.* Cambridge, MA: MIT Press.

Schacter, D. L. (1996). *Searching for memory: The brain, the mind, and the past.* New York: Basic Books.

Schacter, D. L. (1999). The seven sins of memory: Insights from psychology and cognitive neuroscience. *American Psychologist, 54,* 182–203.

Schacter, D. L. (2001). The seven sins of memory: How the mind forgets and remembers. Boston, MA: Houghton Mifflin.

Schacter, D. L., & Addis, D. R. (2007b). On the constructive episodic simulation of past and future events. *Behavioral and Brain Sciences, 30,* 331–332.

Schacter, D. L., & Addis, D. R. (2007c). The ghosts of past and future. *Nature, 445,* 27.

Schacter, D. L., & Addis, D. R. (2007d). The cognitive neuroscience of constructive memory: Remembering the past and imagining the future. *Philosophical Transactions of the Royal Society, 362,* 773–786.

Schacter, D. L., Chiu, C. Y. P., & Ochsner, K. N. (1993). Implicit memory: A selective review. *Annual Review of Neuroscience, 16,* 159–182.

Schacter, D. L., Dawes, R., Jacoby, L. L., Kahneman, D., Lempert, R., Roediger, H. L., & Rosenthal, R. (2008). Policy forum: Studying eyewitness investigations in the field. *Law and Human Behavior, 21,* 3–5.

Schacter, D. L., Wagner, A. D., & Buckner, R. L. (2000). Memory systems of 1999. In E. Tulving & F. I. M. Craik (Eds.), *Oxford handbook of memory.* New York: Oxford University Press.

Schacter, D. L., & Dodson, C. S. (2001). Misattribution, false recognition and the sins of memory. *Philosophical Transactions of the Royal Society of London, 356,* 1385–1393.

Schaeffer, N. C. (2000). Asking questions about threatening topics: A selective overview. In A. A. Stone, J. S. Turkkan, C. A. Bachrach, J. B. Jobe, H. S. Kurtzman, & V. Cain (Eds.), *The science of self-report: Implications for research and practice.* Mahwah, NJ: Erlbaum.

Schafe, G. E., & Bernstein, I. E. (1996). Taste aversion learning. In E. D. Capaldi (Ed.), *Why we eat what we eat: The psychology of eating* (pp. 31–52). Washington, DC: American Psychological Association.

Schafe, G. E., Doyère, V., & LeDoux, J. E. (2005). Tracking the fear engram: The lateral amygdala is an essential locus of fear memory storage. *Journal of Neuroscience, 25,* 10010–10015.

Schaffhausen, J. (2007). The day his world stood still. *Brain Connection.* Retrieved February 28, 2007, from http://www.brainconnection.com/topics/?main=fa/hm-memory.

Schaie, K. W. (1983). The Seattle longitudinal study: A twenty-one year exploration of psychometric intelligence in adulthood. In K. W. Schaie (Ed.), *Longitudinal studies of adult psychological development.* New York: Guilford.

Schaie, K. W. (1990). Intellectual development in adulthood. In J. E. Birren & K. W. Schaie (Eds.), *Handbook of the psychology of aging* (3rd ed.). San Diego: Academic Press.

Schaie, K. W. (1993). The Seattle longitudinal studies of adult intelligence. *Current Directions, 2,* 171–175.

Schaie, K. W. (1994). The course of adult intellectual development. *American Psychologist, 49,* 304–313.

Schaie, K. W. (1996). *Adult intellectual development: The Seattle longitudinal study.* New York: Cambridge University Press.

Schaie, K. W. (2005). *Developmental influences on adult intelligence: The Seattle longitudinal study.* New York: Oxford University Press.

Schalock, R. L., Luckasson, R. A., Shogren, K. A., Borthwick-Duffy, S., Bradley, V., Buntinx, W. H. E., et al. (2007). The renaming of mental retardation: Understanding the change to the term *intellectual disability. Intellectual and Developmental Disabilities, 45,* 116–124.

Schaufeli, W. B., Leiter, M. P., & Maslach, C. (2009). Burnout: 35 years of research and practice. *The Career Development International, 14*(3), 204–220.

Schedler, J. (2010). The efficacy of psychodynamic psychotherapy. *American Psychologist, 65,* 56–68.

Scheier, M. F., & Carver, C. S. (1985). Optimism, coping and health: Assessment and implications of generalized expectancies. *Health Psychology, 4,* 219–247.

Schein, E. H. (1996). Culture: The missing concept in organizational studies. *Administrative Science Quarterly, 41,* 229–240.

Schellenberg, E. (2004). Music lessons enhance IQ. *Psychological Science, 15*(8), 511–514.

Schellenberg, E. (2005). Music and cognitive abilities. *Current Directions in Psychological Science, 14*(6), 317–320.

Schellenberg, E. (2006). Long-term positive associations between music lessons and IQ. *Journal of Educational Psychology, 98*(2), 457–468.

Scherer, K. R., & Wallbott, H. G. (1994). Evidence for universality and cultural variation of differential emotion response patterning. *Journal of Personality and Social Psychology, 66,* 310–328.

Schieber, F. (2006). Vision and aging. In J. E. Birren & K. W. Schaie (Eds.), *Handbook of the psychology of aging.* San Diego: Academic Press.

Schiff, M., & Lewontin, R. (1986). *Education and class: The irrelevance of IQ genetic studies.* Oxford: Clarendon Press.

Schiffman, J., Ekstrom, M., LaBrie, J., Schulsinger, F., Sorenson, H., & Mednick, S. (2002). Minor physical anomalies and schizophrenia spectrum disorders: A prospective investigation. *American Journal of Psychiatry, 159,* 238–243.

Schiffman, S. S., Graham, B. G., Sattely-Miller, E. A., & Warwick, Z. S. (1998). Orosensory perception of dietary fat. *Current Directions in Psychological Science, 7,* 137–143.

Schilbach, L., Eickhoff, S. B., Mojzisch, A., & Vogeley, K. (2008). What's in a smile? Neural correlates of facial embodiment in social interaction. *Social Neuroscience, 3*(1), 37–50.

Schimmack, U., & Crites, S. L. (2005). The structure of affect. In D. Albarracin, B. T. Johnson, & M. P. Zanna (Eds.), *The handbook of attitudes.* Mahwah, NJ: Erlbaum.

Schirillo, J. A. (2010). Gestalt approach. In E. B. Goldstein (Ed.), *Encyclopedia of perception.* Thousand Oaks, CA: Sage.

Schlapobersky, J., & Pines, M. (2009). Group methods in adult psychiatry. In M. C. Gelder, N. C. Andreasen, J. J. López-Ibor, Jr., & J. R. Geddes (Eds.), *New Oxford textbook of psychiatry* (2nd ed., Vol. 1). New York, NY: Oxford University Press.

Schlegel, A., & Barry, H., III. (1991). *Adolescence: An anthropological inquiry.* New York: Free Press.

Schlenger, W. E., Kulka, R. A., Fairbank, J. A., Hough, R. L., Jordan, B. K., Marmar, C. R., & Weiss, D. S. (1992). The prevalence of post-traumatic stress disorder in the Vietnam generation: A multimethod, multisource assessment of psychiatric disorder. *Journal of Traumatic Stress, 5*(3), 333–363.

Schmader, T. (2010). Stereotype threat deconstructed. *Current Directions in Psychological Science, 19*(1), 14–18.

Schmader, T., Johns, M., & Forbes, C. (2008). An integrated process model of stereotype threat effects on performance. *Psychological Review, 115*, 336–356.

Schmeichel, B. J., Gailliot, M. T., Filardo, E., McGregor, I., Gitter, S., & Baumeister, R. F. (2009). Terror management theory and self-esteem revisited: The roles of implicit and explicit self-esteem in mortality salience effects. *Journal of Personality and Social Psychology, 96*(5), 1077–1087.

Schmidt, F. L. (2002). The role of general cognitive ability and job performance: Why there cannot be a debate. *Human Performance, 15*, 187–210.

Schmidt, F. L., & Hunter, J. (2004). General mental ability in the world of work: Occupational attainment and job performance. *Journal of Personality and Social Psychology, 86*, 162–173.

Schmidt, N. B., Zvolensky, M. J., & Maner, J. K. (2006). Anxiety sensitivity: Prospective prediction of panic attacks and Axis I pathology. *Journal of Psychiatric Research, 40*, 691–699.

Schmit, D. T. (2010). The mesmerists inquire about "oriental mind powers": West meets east in the search for the universal trance. *Journal of the History of the Behavioral Sciences, 46*(1), 1–26.

Schmit, M. J. (2006). EI in the business world. In K. R. Murphy (Ed.), *A critique of emotional intelligence: What are the problems and how can they be fixed?* (pp. 211–234). Mahwah, NJ: Erlbaum.

Buss, D. M., & Schmitt, D. P. (1993). Sexual strategies theory: A evolutionary perspective on mating. *Psychological Review, 100*, 204–232.

Schmitt, D. P. (2005). Fundamentals of human mating strategies. In D. M. Buss (Ed.), *The handbook of evolutionary psychology*. New York: Wiley.

Schmitt, D. P., & 118 members of the International Sexuality Description Project. (2003). Universal sex differences in the desire for sexual variety: Tests from 52 nations, 6 continents, and 13 islands. *Journal of Personality and Social Psychology, 85*, 85–104.

Schmitt, D. P., Realo, A., Voracek, M., & Allik, J. (2008). Why can't a man be more like a woman? Sex differences in Big Five personality traits across 55 cultures. *Journal of Personality and Social Psychology, 94*(1), 168–182.

Schmitt, M. T., & Maes, J. (2002). Stereotypic ingroup bias as self-defense against relative deprivation: Evidence from a longitudinal study of the German unification process. *European Journal of Social Psychology, 32*, 309–326.

Schmitt, N., & Chan, D. (1998). *Personnel selection: A theoretical approach.* Thousand Oaks, CA: Sage.

Schmitz, J. M., & DeLaune, K. A. (2005). Nicotine. In J. H. Lowinson, P. Ruiz, R. B. Millman, & J. G. Langrod (Eds.), *Substance abuse: A comprehensive textbook.* Philadelphia: Lippincott, Williams & Williams.

Schmitz, T. W., Kawahara-Baccus, T. N., & Johnson, S. C. (2004). Metacognitive evaluation, self-relevance, and the right prefrontal cortex. *Neuroimage, 22*, 941–947.

Schmolck, H., Buffalo, E. A., & Squire, L. R. (2000). Memory distortions develop over time: Recollections of the O. J. Simpson trial verdict after 15 and 32 months. *Psychological Science, 11*, 39–45.

Schneider, B. (1987). The people make the place. *Personnel Psychology, 40*, 437–454.

Schneider, B. (1996). When individual differences aren't. In K. R. Murphy (Ed.), *Individual differences and behaviors in organizations* (pp. 548–572). San Francisco: Jossey-Bass.

Schneider, W., & Chein, J. M. (2003). Controlled and automatic processing: Behavior, theory and biological mechanisms. *Cognitive Science, 27*, 525–559.

Schneider, W., & R. M. Shiffrin. (1977). Controlled and automatic human information processing: 1. Detection, search, and attention. *Psychological Review, 84*, 1–66.

Schnittker, J. (2008). An uncertain revolution: Why the rise of a genetic model of mental illness has not increased tolerance. *Social Science & Medicine, 67*(9), 1370–1381.

Schnoll, A., et al. (2010). Effectiveness of extended duration transdermal nicotine therapy: A randomized trial. *Annals of Internal Medicine, 152*, 144–151.

Scholey, A. B., Parrott, A. C., Buchanan, T., Heffernan, T. M., Ling, J., & Rodgers, J. (2004). Increased intensity of Ecstasy and polydrug usage in the more experienced recreational Ecstasy/MDMA users: A WWW study. *Addictive Behaviors, 29*, 743–752.

Schooler, C. (2007). Use it—and keep it, longer, probably: A reply to Salthouse. *Perspectives on Psychological Science, 2*, 24–29.

Schooler, J. W. (1999). Seeking the core: The issues and evidence surrounding recovered accounts of sexual trauma. In L. M. Williams & V. L. Banyard (Eds.), *Trauma & memory*. Thousand Oaks, CA: Sage Publications.

Schooler, J. W., & Eich, E. (2000). Memory for emotional events. In E. Tulving & F. I. M. Craik, (Eds.), *The Oxford handbook of memory* (pp. 379–397). Oxford, UK: Oxford University Press.

Schrag, R. D. A., Styfco, S. J., & Zigler, E. (2004). Familiar concept, new name: Social competence. In E. Zigler & S. J. Styfco (Eds.), *The Head Start debate*. Baltimore: Paul H. Brookes Publishing.

Schramm, D. G., Marshall, J. P., Harris, V. W., & Lee, T. R. (2005). After "I do": The newlywed transition. *Marriage and Family Review, 38*, 45–67.

Schreiber, F. R. (1973). *Sybil*. New York: Warner.

Schuller, R. A., & Ogloff, J. R. P. (2001). Psychology and law. In R. A. Schuller & J. R. P. Ogloff (Eds.), *Introduction to psychology and law: Canadian perspectives* (pp. 3–28). Toronto: University of Toronto Press.

Schuller, R., Kazoleas, V., & Kawakami, K. (2009). The impact of prejudice screening procedures on racial bias in the courtroom. *Law and Human Behavior, 33*, 320–238.

Schulte, F. S., Mongrain, M., & Flora, D. B. (2008). Healthy and unhealthy dependence: Implications for major depression. *British Journal of Clinical Psychology, 47*, 341–353.

Schultz, J. H., & Luthe, W. (1959). *Autogenic training*. New York: Grune & Stratton.

Schulz-Hardt, S., Frey, D., Luethgens, C., & Moscovici, S. (2000). Biased information search in group decision making. *Journal of Personality & Social Psychology, 78*, 655–669.

Schuman, H., & Kalton, G. (1985). Survey methods. In G. Lindzey & E. Aronson (Eds.), *Handbook of social psychology* (3rd ed.). New York: Random House.

Schumann, J. (1978). The acculturation model for second language acquisition. In R. C. Gingras (Ed.), *Second-language acquisition and foreign language teaching*. Washington, DC: Center for Applied Linguistics.

Schumann, J. (1993). Some problems with falsification: An illustration from SLA research. *Applied Linguistics, 14*, 295–306.

Schusterman, R. J., & Gisiner, R. (1988). Artificial language comprehension in dolphins and sea lions: The essential cognitive skills. *Psychological Record, 38*, 311–348.

Schwartz, B. (2004). *The paradox of choice: Why more is less*. New York: Ecco.

Schwartz, B. L. (1999). Sparkling at the end of the tongue: The etiology of tip-of-the-tongue phenomenology. *Psychonomic Bulletin & Review, 6*, 379–393.

Schwartz, B., & Robbins, S. J. (1995). *Psychology of learning and behavior* (4th ed.). New York: Norton.

Schwartz, G. L., & Azzara, A. V. (2004). Sensory neurobiological analysis of neuropeptide modulation of meal size. *Physiology & Behavior, 82*, 81–87.

Schwartz, J. H. (2000). Neurotransmitters. In E. R. Kandel, J. H. Schwartz, & T. M. Jessell (Eds.), *Principles of neural science*. New York: McGraw-Hill.

Schwartz, M. W., & Seeley, R. J. (1997). The new biology of body weight regulation. *Journal of the American Dietetic Association, 97*, 54–58.

Schwartz, M. W., Peskind, E., Raskind, M., Nicolson, M., Moore, J., Morawiecki, A., et al. (1996). Cerebrospinal fluid leptin levels: Relationship to plasma levels and to adiposity in humans. *Nature Medicine, 2*, 589–593.

Schwartz, S. H. (1990). Individualism–collectivism: Critique and proposed refinements. *Journal of Cross-Cultural Psychology, 21*, 139–157.

Schwarz, A. (2008, September 23). 12 athletes leaving brains to concussion study. *New York Times*. Retrieved December 15, 2010, from http://www.nytimes.com/2008/09/24/sports/football/24concussions.html

Schwarz, N. (1999). Self-reports: How the questions shape the answers. *American Psychologist, 54*, 93–105.

Schwarz, N., & Strack, F. (1999). Reports of subjective well-being: Judgmental processes and their methodological implications. In D. Kahneman, E. Diener, & N. Schwarz (Eds.), *Well-being: The foundations of hedonic psychology*. New York: Russell Sage Foundation.

Scoboria, A., Mazzoni, G., Kirsch, I., & Milling, L. S. (2002). Immediate and persisting effects of misleading questions and hypnosis on memory reports. *Journal of Experimental Psychology: Applied, 8*(1), 26–32.

Scott, K. (2008). Chemical senses: Taste and olfaction. In L. Squire, D. Berg, F. Bloom, S. du Lac, A. Ghosh, & N. Spitzer (Eds.), *Fundamental Neuroscience*. San Diego: Elsevier.

Scott, T. R. (1990). The effect of physiological need on taste. In E. D. Capaldi & T. L. Powley (Eds.), *Taste, experience, and feeding*. Washington, DC: American Psychological Association.

Scott, V., McDade, D. M., & Luckman, S. M. (2007). Rapid changes in the sensitivity of arcuate nucleus neurons to central ghrelin in relation to feeding status. *Physiology & Behavior, 90*, 180–185.

Scoville, W. B., & Milner, B. (1957). Loss of recent memory after bilateral hippocampal lesions. *Journal of Neurology, Neurosurgery & Psychiatry, 20*, 11–21.

Scull, A. (1990). Deinstitutionalization: Cycles of despair. *The Journal of Mind and Behavior, 11*(3/4), 301–312.

Scully, J. A., Tosi, H., & Banning, K. (2000). Life event checklists: Revisiting the social readjustment rating scale after 30 years. *Educational & Psychological Measurement, 60,* 864–876.

Sealy, P., & Whitehead, P. C. (2004). Forty years of deinstitutionalization of psychiatric services in Canada: An empirical assessment. *Canadian Journal of Psychiatry, 49,* 249–257.

Searle, A., & Bennett, P. (2001). Psychological factors and inflammatory bowel disease: A review of a decade of literature. *Psychology, Health and Medicine, 6,* 121–135.

Searleman, A. (1996). Personality variables and prospective memory performance. In D. J. Herrmann, C. McEvoy, C. Hertzog, P. Hertel, & M. K. Johnson (Eds.), *Basic and applied memory research: Practical applications* (Vol. 2). Mahwah, NJ: Erlbaum.

Searleman, A., & Herrmann, D. (1994). *Memory from a broader perspective.* New York: McGraw-Hill.

Sears, D. O. (1975). Political socialization. In F. I. Greenstein & N. W. Polsby (Eds.), *Handbook of political science* (Vol. 2). Reading, MA: Addison-Wesley.

Seeley, R. J., Matson, C. A., Chavez, M., Woods, S. C., & Schwartz, M. W. (1996). Behavioral, endocrine and hypothalamic responses to involuntary overfeeding. *American Journal of Physiology, 271,* R819–R823.

Segal, Z. (1988). Appraisal of the self-schema construct in cognitive models of depression. *Psychological Bulletin, 103,* 147–161.

Segal, Z., Williams, J. M. G., & Teasdale, J. D. (Eds.) (2002). *Mindfulness-based cognitive therapy for depression.* New York: Guilford Press.

Segall, M. H., Campbell, D. T., Herskovits, M. J. (1966). *The influence of culture on visual perception.* Indianapolis: Bobbs-Merrill.

Segall, M. H., Dasen, P. R., Berry, J. W., & Poortinga, Y. H. (1990). *Human behavior in global perspective: An introduction to cross-cultural psychology.* New York: Pergamon Press.

Segall, M. H., Lonner, W. J., & Berry, J. W. (1998). Cross-cultural psychology as a scholarly discipline: On the flowering of culture in behavioral research. *American Psychologist, 53,* 1101–1110.

Segerstrom, S. C., et al. (2007). Optimism and resources: Effects on each other and on health over 10 years. *Journal of Research in Personality, 41,* 772–786.

Segerstrom, S. C., & Miller, G. E. (2004). Psychological stress and the human immune system: A meta-analytic study of 30 years of inquiry. *Psychological Bulletin, 130,* 601–630.

Segerstrom, S. C., & Roach, A. R. (2008). On the physical health benefits of self-enhancement. In E. C. Chang (Ed.), *Self-criticism and self-enhancement: Theory, research, and clinical implications* (pp. 37–54). Washington, DC: American Psychological Association.

Segerstrom, S. C., & Sephton, S. E. (2010). Optimistic expectancies and cell-mediated immunity: The role of positive affect. *Psychological Science, 21*(3), 448–455.

Seifer, R. (2001). Socioeconomic status, multiple risks, and development of intelligence. In R. J. Sternberg & E. L. Grigorenko (Eds.), *Environmental effects on cognitive abilities* (pp. 59–82). Mahwah, NJ: Erlbaum.

Sejnowski, T. J. (2003). The once and future Hebb synapse. *Canadian Psychology, 44,* 17–20.

Sekiguchi, C., Umikura, S., Sone, K., & Kume, M. (1994). Psychological evaluation of Japanese astronaut applicants. *Aviation, Space, and Environmental Medicine, 65,* 920–924.

Self, D. W. (1997). Neurobiological adaptations to drug use. *Hospital Practice, April,* 5–9.

Seligman, M. E. P. (1971). Phobias and preparedness. *Behavior Therapy, 2,* 307–321.

Seligman, M. E. P. (1974). Depression and learned helplessness. In R. J. Friedman & M. M. Katz (Eds.), *The psychology of depression: Contemporary theory and research.* New York: Wiley.

Seligman, M. E. P. (1990). *Learned optimism.* New York: Pocket Books.

Seligman, M. E. P. (1992). *Helplessness: On depression, development, and death.* New York: Freeman.

Seligman, M. E. P. (1995). The effectiveness of psychotherapy. *American Psychologist, 50,* 965–974.

Seligman, M. E. P. (2003). The past and future of positive psychology. In C. L. M. Keyes & J. Haidt (Eds.), *Flourishing: Positive psychology and the life well-lived.* Washington, DC: American Psychological Association.

Seligman, M. E. P., & Csikszentmihalyi, M. (2000). Positive psychology: An introduction. *American Psychologist, 55,* 5–14.

Seligman, M. E. P., & Hager, J. L. (1972, August). Biological boundaries of learning (The sauce béarnaise syndrome). *Psychology Today,* 59–61, 84–87.

Seligman, M. E. P., Parks, A. C., & Steen, T. (2006). A balanced psychology and a full life: In F. Huppert, B. Keverne, & N. Baylis (Eds.), *The science of well-being* (pp. 275–282). Oxford: Oxford University Press.

Seligman, M. E. P., Rashid, T., & Parks, A. C. (2006). Positive psychotherapy. *American Psychologist, 61,* 774–788.

Selye, H. (1936). A syndrome produced by diverse nocuous agents. *Nature, 138,* 32.

Selye, H. (1956). *The stress of life.* New York: McGraw-Hill.

Selye, H. (1973). The evolution of the stress concept. *American Scientist, 61*(6), 672–699.

Selye, H. (1974). *Stress without distress.* New York: Lippincott.

Selye, H. (1982). History and present status of the stress concept. In L. Goldberger & S. Breznitz (Eds.), *Handbook of stress: Theoretical and clinical aspects.* New York: Free Press.

Semmer, N. K., McGrath, J. E., & Beehr, T. A. (2005). Conceptual issues in research on stress and health. In C. L. Cooper (Ed.), *Handbook of stress medicine and health.* Boca Raton, FL: CRC Press.

Sen, S., Burmeister, M., & Ghosh, D. (2004). Meta-analysis of the association between a serotonin transporter promoter polymorphism (5-HTTLPR) and anxiety-related personality traits. *American Journal of Medical Genetics, 127B*(1), 85–89.

Senior, C., Thomson, K., Badger, J., & Butler, M. J. R. (2008). Interviewing strategies in the face of beauty: A psychophysiological investigation into the job negotiation process. *Annals of the New York Academy of Sciences, 1118,* 142–162.

Senior, J. (2010, July 4). All joy and no fun. *New York Magazine.* Retrieved July 9, 2010, from http://nymag.com/print/?/news/features67024/.

Seta, J. J., Seta, C. E., & McElroy, T. (2002). Strategies for reducing the stress of negative life experiences: An average/summation analysis. *Personality and Social Psychology Bulletin, 28,* 1574–1585.

Sewell, R., Poling, J., & Sofuoglu, M. (2009). The effect of cannabis compared with alcohol on driving. *American Journal on Addictions, 18*(3), 185–193.

Shackelford, T. K., Schmitt, D. P., & Buss, D. M. (2005). Universal dimensions of human mate preferences. *Personality & Individual Differences, 39,* 447–458.

Shadish, W. R., & Cook, T. D. (2009). The renaissance of field experimentation in evaluating interventions. *Annual Review of Psychology, 60,* 607–609.

Shafer, G., & Tversky, A. (1988). Languages and designs for probability judgement. In D. E. Bell, H. Raiffa, & A. Tversky (Eds.), *Decision making: Descriptive, normative, and prescriptive interactions.* New York: Cambridge University Press.

Shaffer, D. R. (1985). *Developmental psychology: Theory, research, and applications.* Pacific Grove, CA: Brooks/Cole.

Shafir, E., & LeBoeuf, R. A. (2002). Rationality. *Annual Review of Psychology, 53,* 491–517.

Shafir, E., & LeBoeuf, R. A. (2004). Context and conflict in multi-attribute choice. In D. J. Koehler & N. Harvey (Eds), *Blackwell handbook of judgment and decision making.* Malden, MA: Blackwell Publishing.

Shaky arguments against stem cells. (2007, April 1). *Nature Neuroscience, 10,* 393. Retrieved February 8, 2008, from http://www.nature.com/neuro/journal/v10/n4/full/nn407-393.html.

Shalinsky, M. H., Kovelman, I., Berens, J. S., & Petitto, L. A. (2009). Exploring cognitive functions in babies, children and adults with near infared spectroscopy. *Journal of Visualized Experiments, 29.*

Shanks, D. R. (2010). Learning: From association to cognition. *Annual Review of Psychology, 61,* 273–301.

Shapira, L. B., & Mongrain, M. (2010, September). The benefits of self-compassion and optimism exercises for individuals vulnerable to depression. *Journal of Positive Psychology, 5,* 377–389.

Shapiro, A. F., Gottman, J. M., & Carrère, S. (2000). The baby and marriage: Identifying factors that buffer against decline in marital satisfaction after the first baby arrives. *Journal of Family Psychology, 14,* 59–70.

Shapiro, D. H., Jr. (1984). Overview: Clinical and physiological comparison of meditation with other self-control strategies. In D. H. Shapiro, Jr., & R. N. Walsh (Eds.), *Meditation: Classic and contemporary perspectives.* New York: Aldine.

Shapiro, D. H., Jr. (1987). Implications of psychotherapy research for the study of meditation. In M. A. West (Ed.), *The psychology of meditation.* Oxford: Clarendon Press.

Shapiro, J. R., & Neuberg, S. L. (2007). From stereotype threat to stereotype threats: Implications of a multi-threat framework for causes, moderators, mediators, consequences, and interventions. *Personality & Social Psychology Review, 11,* 107–130.

Sharot, T., Riccardi, M. A., Raio, C. M., & Phelps, E. A. (2007) Neural mechanisms mediating optimism bias. *Nature, 450*(7166), 102–105.

Shatz, C. J. (1992, September). The developing brain. *Scientific American,* 60–67.

Shaver, P. R., & Mikulincer, M. (2005). Attachment theory and research: Resurrection of the psychodynamic approach to personality. *Journal of Research in Personality, 39*(1), 22–45.

Shaver, P. R., & Mikulincer, M. (2009). Attachment styles. In M. R. Leary & R. H. Hoyle (Eds.), *Handbook of individual differences in social behavior* (pp. 62–81). New York, NY: Guilford Press.

Shavitt, S., Sanbonmatsu, D. M., Smittipatana, S., & Posavac, S. S. (1999). Broadening the conditions for illusory correlation formation: Implications for judging minority groups. *Basic & Applied Social Psychology, 21*, 263–279.

Shavitt, S., Swan, S., Lowery, T. M., & Wanke, M. (1994). The interaction of endorser attractiveness and involvement in persuasion depends on the goal that guides message processing. *Journal of Consumer Psychology, 3*, 137–162.

Shaw, J. S. I., McClure, K. A., & Dykstra, J. A. (2007). Eyewitness confidence from the witnessed event through trial. In M. P. Toglia, J. D. Read, D. F. Ross, & R. C. L. Lindsay (Eds.), *Handbook of eyewitness psychology: Volume 1. Memory for events*. Mahwah, NJ: Erlbaum.

Shaw, W. S., & Dimsdale, J. E. (2007). Type A personality, type B personality. In G. Fink (Ed.), *Encyclopedia of stress*. San Diego: Elsevier.

Shea, A. K., & Steiner, M. (2008). Cigarette smoking during pregnancy. *Nicotine & Tobacco Research, 10*, 267–278.

Shearer, B. (2004). Multiple intelligences theory after 20 years. *Teachers College Record, 106*(1), 2–16.

Shedler, J. (2010). The efficacy of psychodynamic psychotherapy. *American Psychologist, 65*(2), 98–109.

Sheehan, S. (1982). *Is there no place on earth for me?* Bostom: Houghton Mifflin.

Sheilds, M., & Tremblay, M. (2008). Sedentary behaviour and obesity among Canadian adults. *Health Reports, 19*, 19–30.

Shelder, J. (2010). The efficacy of psychoanalytic psychotherapy. *American Psychologist, 65*, 98–109.

Sheldon, K. M., & Kasser, T. (2001). Goals, congruence, and positive well-being: New empirical support for humanistic theories. *Journal of Humanistic Psychology, 41*(1), 30–50.

Shelton, J. T., Elliott, E. M., Hill, B. D., Calamia, M. R., & Gouvier, W. (2009). A comparison of laboratory and clinical working memory tests and their prediction of fluid intelligence. *Intelligence, 37*(3), 283–293.

Shenton, M. E., & Kubicki, M. (2009). Structural brain imaging in schizophrenia. In B. J. Sadock, V. A. Sadock, & P. Ruiz (Eds.), *Kaplan & Sadock's comprehensive textbook of psychiatry* (9th ed., Vol. 1, pp. 1494–1506). Philadelphia, PA: Lippincott, Williams & Wilkins.

Shepard, R. N. (1990). *Mind sights*. New York: W. H. Freeman.

Shepherd, G. M. (2004). The human sense of smell: Are we better than we think? *PLoS Biology, 2*(5), 0572–0575.

Shepperd, J. A., & McNulty, J. K. (2002). The affective consequences of expected and unexpected outcomes. *Psychological Science, 13*, 85–88.

Shepperd, J., Malone, W., & Sweeny, K. (2008). Exploring causes of the self-serving bias. *Social and Personality Psychology Compass, 2*, 895–908.

Sher, L. (2003). Daily hassles, cortisol, and depression. *Australia and New Zealand Journal of Psychiatry, 37*, 383–384.

Sher, L., & Vilens, A. (Eds.). (2010). *Immigration and mental health: Stress, Psychiatric disorders and suicidal behavior among immigrants and refuges*. New York: Nova Science Publishers.

Sherif, M. (1936). *The psychology of social norms*. Oxford, England: Harper.

Sherif, M., Harvey, O., White, B., Hood, W., & Sherif, C. (1961). *Intergroup conflict and cooperation:*

The Robber's Cave experiment. Norman: University of Oklahoma, Institute of Group Behavior.

Sherman, M., & Key, C. B. (1932). The intelligence of isolated mountain children. *Child Development, 3*, 279–290.

Sherman, P. W. (1981). Reproductive competition and infanticide in Belding's ground squirrels and other animals. In R. D. Alexander & D. W. Tinkle (Eds.), *Natural selection and social behavior: Recent Research and new theory* (pp. 311–331). New York: Chiron Press.

Sherman, S. M. (2009). Thalamocortical relations. In G. G. Bernston & J. T. Cacioppo (Eds.), *Handbook of neuroscience for the behavioral sciences* (Vol. 1, pp. 201–223). New York, NY: Wiley, Inc.

Shermann, J. W., Gawronski, B., Gonsalkorale, K., Hugenberg, K., Allen, T. J., & Groom, C. J. (2008). The self-regulation of automatic associations and behavioral impulses. *Psychological Review, 115*, 314–335.

Shermer, M. (1997). *Why people believe weird things: Pseudoscience, superstition, and other confusions of our time*. New York: W. H. Freeman.

Shermer, M. (2004, March). None so blind. *Scientific American*, p. 42.

Sherry, D. F. (1992). Evolution and learning. In L. R. Squire (Ed.), *Encyclopedia of learning and memory*. New York: Macmillan.

Sherry, S. B., & Hall, P. A. (2009). The perfectionism model of binge eating: Tests of an integrative model. *Journal of Personality and Social Psychology, 96*, 690–709.

Shettleworth, S. J. (1998). *Cognition, evolution, and behavior*. New York: Oxford University Press.

Shields, M. (2008). Community belonging and self-perceived health. Statistics Canada: Health Reports, 19. Retrieved July 23, 2008, from http://www.statcan.ca/english/freepub/82-003-XIE/2008002/article/10552-en.pdf.

Shields, M., & Tremblya, M. S. (2008). Sedentary Behaviour and obesity. Statistics Canada, Retrieved May 2, 2011, from http://www.statcan.gc.ca/pub/82-003-x/2008002/article/10599-eng.pdf.

Shiffrin, R. M. (1988). Attention. In R. C. Atkinson, R. J. Herrnstein, G. Lindzey, & R. D. Luce (Eds.), *Stevens' handbook of experimental psychology* (Vol. 2). New York: Wiley.

Shimamura, A. P., Berry, J. M., Mangels, J. A., Rusting, C. L., & Jurica, P. J. (1995). Memory and cognitive abilities in university professors: Evidence for successful aging. *Psychological Science, 6*, 271–277.

Shneidman, E. S., Farberow, N. L., & Litman, R. E. (1994). *The psychology of suicide: A clinician's guide to evaluation and treatment*. Northvale, NJ: J. Aronson.

Shobe, K. K., & Schooler, J. W. (2001). Discovering fact and fiction: Case-based analyses of authentic and fabricated discovered memories of abuse. In G. M. Davies & T. Dalgleish (Eds.), *Recovered memories: Seeking the middle ground*. Chichester, England: Wiley.

Shrager, Y. & Squire, L. R. (2009). Medial temporal lobe function and human memory. In M. S. Gazzaniga (Eds.), *The cognitive neurosciences* (4th ed., pp. 675–690). Cambridge, MA: MIT Press.

Shuper, P., Sorrentino, R. M., Otsubo, Y. Hodson, G. and Walker, A. M. (2004). A theory of uncertainty orientation: Implications for the study of individual differences within and across cultures. *Journal of Cross-Cultural Psychology, 35*(4), 460–481.

Siebert, A. (1995). *Student success: How to succeed in college and still have time for your friends*. Fort Worth: Harcourt Brace Jovanovich.

Siebner, H. R., Hartwigsen, G., Kassuba, T., & Rothwell, J. C. (2009). How does transcranial magnetic stimulation modify neuronal activity in the brain? Implications for studies of cognition. *Cortex: A Journal Devoted to the Study of the Nervous System and Behavior, 45*(9), 1035–1042.

Siegel, J. M. (2005). REM sleep. In M. H. Kryger, T. Roth, & W. C. Dement (Eds.). *Principles and practice of sleep medicine*. Philadelphia: Elsevier Saunders.

Siegel, J. M. (2009). Sleep viewed as a state of adaptive inactivity. *Nature Reviews Neuroscience, 10*(10), 747–753.

Siegel, S. (1976). Morphine analgesic tolerance: Its situational specificity supports a Pavlovian conditioning model. *Science, 193*, 323–325.

Siegel, S. (2001). Pavlovian conditioning and drug overdose: When tolerance fails. *Addiction Research & Theory, 9*, 503–513.

Siegel, S. (2002). The ghost in the addict: Drug anticipation and drug addiction. *Proceedings of the Royal Society of Canada*: http://www.rsc.ca/files/publications/transactions/2002/siegel.pdfrsc.ca/files/publications/transactions/2002/siegel.pdf.

Siegel, S. (2005). Drug tolerance, drug addiction, and drug anticipation. *Current Directions in Psychological Science, 14*, 296–300.

Siegel, S., & Ramos, B. C. (2002). Applying laboratory research: Drug anticipation and the treatment of drug addiction. *Experimental and Clinical Psychopharmacology, 10*, 162–183.

Siegel, S., Baptista, M. A. S., Kim, J. A., McDonald, R. V., & Weise-Kelly, L. (2000). Pavlovian psychopharmacology: The associative basis of tolerance. *Experimental and Clinical Psychopharmacology, 8*, 276–293.

Siegler, R. S. (1992). The other Alfred Binet. *Developmental Psychology, 28*, 179–190.

Siegler, R. S. (1994). Cognitive variability: A key to understanding cognitive development. *Current Directions in Psychological Science, 3*(1), 1–5.

Siegler, R. S. (1998). *Children's thinking*. Upper Saddle River, NJ: Prentice-Hall.

Sigel, I. E. (2004). Head Start-Revisiting a historical psychoeducational intervention: A revisionist of perspective. In E. Zigler & S. J. Styfco (Eds.), *The Head Start debate*. Baltimore: Paul H. Brookes Publishing.

Sigman, M. (1994). What are the core deficits in autism. In S. H. Broman, & J. Grafman (Eds.), *Atypical cognitive deficits in developmental disorders: Implications for brain function* (pp. 139–157). Hillsdale, NJ: Erlbaum.

Signorielli, N. (2001). Television's gender role images and contribution to stereotyping: Past present future. In D. G. Singer & J. L. Singer (Eds.), *Handbook of children and the media*. Thousand Oaks, CA: Sage.

Sikh Philosophy Network. (2005, June 22). Father's parole eligibility set at 16 years in murder of daughter. Retrieved October 24, 2008, from http://www.sikhism.us/interfaith-dialogues/4441-father-get-parole-16-years-murdering.html.

Silber, L. (2004). *Organizing from the right side of the brain: A creative approach to getting organized*. New York, NY: St. Martin's Press.

Silvanto, J., & Cattaneo, Z. (2010). Transcranial magnetic stimulation reveals the content of visual short-term memory in the visual cortex. *Neuroimage, 50*(4), 1683–1689.

Silver, E., Cirincion, C., & Steadman, H. J. (1994). Demythologizing inaccurate perceptions of the insanity defense. *Law & Human Behavior, 18*, 63–70.

Silver, H., Feldman, P., Bilker, W., & Gur, R. C. (2003). Working memory deficit as a core neuropsychological dysfunction in schizophrenia. *American Journal of Psychiatry, 160,* 1809–1816.

Silverman, F. (1988). The monster study. *Journal of Fluency Disorders, 13,* 225–231.

Silverman, I., & Choi, J. (2005). Locating places. In D. M. Buss (Ed.), *The handbook of evolutionary psychology.* New York: Wiley.

Silverman, I., & Eals, M. (1992). Sex differences in spatial ability: Evolutionary theory and data. In J. Barkow, L. Cosmides, & J. Tooby (Eds.), *The adapted mind.* New York: Oxford University Press.

Silverman, I., & Phillips, K. (1998). The evolutionary psychology of spatial sex differences. In C. Crawford & D. L. Krebs (Eds.), *Handbook of evolutionary psychology: Ideas, issues, and applications.* Mahwah, NJ: Erlbaum.

Silverman, I., Choi, J., Mackewn, A., Fisher, M., Moro, J., & Olshansky, E. (2000). Evolved mechanisms underlying wayfinding: Further studies on the hunter–gatherer theory of spatial sex differences. *Evolution and Human Behavior, 21,* 201–213.

Silverstein, L. B., & Auerbach, C. F. (1999). Deconstructing the essential father. *American Psychologist, 54,* 397–407.

Silvia, P. J. (2008). Another look at creativity and intelligence: Exploring higher-order models and probable confounds. *Personality and Individual Differences, 44,* 1012–1021.

Silvia, P. J., & Kaufman, J. C. (2010). Creativity and mental illness. In J. C. Kaufman & R. J. Sternberg (Eds.), *The Cambridge handbook of creativity* (pp. 381–394). New York, NY: Cambridge University Press.

Simeon, D., Loewenstein, R. J. (2009). Dissociative disorders. In B. J. Sadock, V. A. Sadock, & P. Ruiz (Eds.), *Kaplan & Sadock's comprehensive textbook of psychiatry* (9th ed., pp. 1965–2026). Philadelphia, PA: Lippincott, Williams & Wilkins.

Simmons, H. G. (1987). Psychosurgery and the abuse of psychiatric authority in Ontario. *Journal of Health Politics, Policy, and Law, 12,* 537–550.

Simon, G. E., & Savarino, J. (2007). Suicide attempts among patients starting depression treatment with medications or psychotherapy. *American Journal of Psychiatry, 164,* 1029–1034.

Simon, G. E., Savarino, J., Operskalski, B., & Wang, P. S. (2006). Suicide risk during antidepressant treatment. *American Journal of Psychiatry, 163,* 41–47.

Simon, H. A. (1957). *Models of man.* New York: Wiley.

Simon, H. A. (1974). How big is a chunk? *Science, 183,* 482–488.

Simon, H. A., & Reed, S. K. (1976). Modeling strategy shifts in a problem-solving task. *Cognitive Psychology, 8,* 86–97.

Simon, H. A. (1991). *Models of my life.* New York: Basic Books.

Simon, R. I., & Shuman, D. W. (2008). Psychiatry and the law. In R. E. Hales, S. C. Yudofsky, & G. O. Gabbard (Eds.), *The American Psychiatric Publishing textbook of psychiatry* (5th ed. pp. 1555–1600). Washington, DC: American Psychiatric Publishing.

Simons, D. K., & Chabris, C. F. (1999). Gorillas in our midst: Sustained inattentional blindness for dynamic events. *Perception, 28,* 1059–1074.

Simonsohn, U. (2009). Direct risk aversion: Evidence from risky prospects valued below their worst outcome. *Psychological Science, 20*(6), 686–692.

Simonton, D. K. (1990). Creativity and wisdom in aging. In J. E. Birren & K. W. Schaie (Eds.), *Handbook of the psychology of aging.* San Diego: Academic Press.

Simonton, D. K. (1997). Creative productivity: A predictive and explanatory model of career trajectories and landmarks. *Psychological Review, 104,* 66–89.

Simonton, D. K. (1999a). Creativity and genius. In L. A. Pervin & O. John (Eds.), *Handbook of personality theory and research.* New York: Guilford.

Simonton, D. K. (1999b). Talent and its development: An emergenic and epigenetic model. *Psychological Review, 106,* 435–457.

Simonton, D. K. (2001). Totally made, not at all born [Review of the book *The psychology of high abilities*]. *Contemporary Psychology, 46,* 176–179.

Simonton, D. K. (2004). *Creativity in science: Chance, logic, genius, and Zeitgeist.* New York: Cambridge University Press.

Simonton, D. K. (2005). Genetics of giftedness: The implications of an emergenic-epigenetic model. In R. J. Sternberg & J. E. Davidson (Eds.), *Conceptions of giftedness.* New York, NY: Cambridge University Press.

Simonton, D. K., & Damian, R. I. (in press-a). Creativity. In D. Reisberg (Ed.), *Oxford handbook of cognitive psychology.* New York: Oxford University Press.

Simonton, D. K., & Flora, C. (2011, Winter). Spark of genius [Introduction, *Genius* Special Issue]. *Discover Magazine,* 2–3.

Simpson, J. A. (1999). Attachment theory in modern evolutionary perspective. In J. Cassidy & P. R. Shaver (Eds.), *Handbook of attachment: Theory, research, and clinical applications.* New York: Guilford.

Simpson, J. L., & Jauniaux, E. (2007). Pregnancy loss. In S. G. Gabbe, J. R. Niebyl, & J. L. Simpson (Eds.) *Obstetrics: Normal and problem pregnancies* (5th ed., pp. 628–649). Philadelphia, PA: Elsevier.

Sinclair, D. (1981). *Mechanisms of cutaneous stimulation.* Oxford, England: Oxford University Press.

Sinclair, R. C., Hoffman, C., Mark, M. M., Martin, L. L., & Pickering, T. L. (1994). Construct accessibility and the misattribution of arousal: Schachter and Singer revisited. *Psychological Science, 5,* 15–19.

Singer, L. T., Arendt, R., Minnes, S., Farkas, K., Salvator, A., Kirchner, H. L., & Kliegman, R. (2002). Cognitive and motor outcomes of cocaine-exposed infants. *Journal of the American Medical Association, 287,* 1952–1960.

Singer, L. T., Minnes, S., Short, E., Arendt, R., Farkas, K., Lewis, B., et al. (2004). Cognitive outcomes of preschool children with prenatal cocaine exposure. *Journal of the American Medical Association, 291,* 2448–2456.

Singer, W. (2007). Large-scale temporal coordination of cortical activity as a prerequisite for conscious experience. In M. Velmans & S. Schneider (Eds.), *The Blackwell companion to consciousness.* Malden, MA: Blackwell Publishing.

Singh, D., Dixson, B. J., Jessop, T. S., Morgan, B. B., & Dixson, A. F. (2010). Cross-cultural consensus for waist–hip ratio and women's attractiveness. *Evolution and Human Behavior, 31*(3), 176–181.

Sinha, D. (1983). Human assessment in the Indian context. In S. H. Irvine & J. W. Berry (Eds.), *Human assessment and cultural factors.* New York: Plenum.

Sio, U., & Ormerod, T. C. (2009). Does incubation enhance problem solving? A meta-analytic review. *Psychological Bulletin, 135*(1), 94–120.

Sivertsen, B., et al. (2006). Cognitive behavioral therapy vs Zopiclone for treatment of chronic primary insomina in older adults. *Journal of the American Medical Association, 295,* 2851–2858.

Siversten, B., et al. (2006). Cognitive behavioral therapy vs zopiclone for treatment of chronic primary insomnia in older adults. *Journal of the American Medical Association, 295,* 2851–2858.

Skilling, T. A., Harris, G. T., Rice, M. E., & Quinsey, V. L. (2002). Identifying persistently antisocial offenders using the Hare Psychopathy Checklist and the DSM antisocial personality disorder criteria. *Psychological Assessment, 14,* 27–38.

Skinner, A. E. G. (2001). Recovered memories of abuse: Effects on the individual. In G. M. Davies, & T. Dalgleish (Eds.), *Recovered memories: Seeking the middle ground.* Chichester, England: Wiley & Sons.

Skinner, B. F. (1938). *The behavior of organisms.* New York: Appleton-Century-Crofts.

Skinner, B. F. (1948a/2005). *Walden Two.* Indianapolis, IN: Hackett Publishing Company Inc.

Skinner, B. F. (1948b), "Superstition" in the pigeon. *Journal of Experimental Psychology, 38,* 168–173.

Skinner, B. F. (1953). *Science and human behavior.* New York: Macmillan.

Skinner, B. F. (1957). *Verbal behavior.* New York: Appleton-Century-Crofts.

Skinner, B. F. (1960). Pigeons in a pelican. *American Psychologist, 15,* 28–37.

Skinner, B. F. (1967). Autobiography. In E. G. Boring & G. Lindzey (Eds.), *A history of psychology in autobiography* (Vol. 5). New York: Appleton-Century-Crofts.

Skinner, B. F. (1969). *Contingencies of reinforcement.* New York: Appleton-Century-Crofts.

Skinner, B. F. (1971). *Beyond freedom and dignity.* New York: Knopf.

Skinner, B. F. (1974). *About behaviorism.* New York: Knopf.

Skinner, B. F. (1980). *Notebooks* (edited by R. Epstein). Englewood Cliffs, NJ: Prentice-Hall.

Skinner, B. F. (1984). Selection by consequences. *Behavioral and Brain Sciences, 7*(4), 477–510.

Skinner, B. F. (2003). Birth order effects in dominance: Failure to support Sulloway's view. *Psychological Reports, 92,* 387–388.

Skinner, B. F., Solomon, H. C., & Lindsley, O. R. (1953). *Studies in behavior therapy: Status report I.* Waltham, MA: Unpublished report, Metropolitan State Hospital.

Skinner, D. (2004). I was not a lab rat. *The Guardian.* Retrieved February 22, 2011, from http://www.guardian.co.uk/education/2004/mar/12/highereducation.uk.

Skitka, L., & Sargis, E. (2005). Social psychological research and the Internet: The promise and peril of a new methodological frontier. In Y. Amichai-Hamburger (Ed.), *The social net: Understanding human behavior in cyberspace* (pp. 1–26). New York: Oxford University Press.

Skitka, L., & Sargis, E. G. (2006). The Internet as psychological laboratory. *Annual Review of Psychology, 57,* 529–555.

Slamecka, N. J. (1985). Ebbinghaus: Some associations. *Journal of Experimental Psychology: Learning, Memory and Cognition, 11,* 414–435.

Slamecka, N. J. (1992). Forgetting. In L. R. Squire (Ed.), *Encyclopedia of learning and memory.* New York: Macmillan.

Slater, E., & Shields, J. (1969). Genetical aspects of anxiety. In M. H. Lader (Ed.), *Studies of anxiety*. Ashford, England: Headley Brothers.

Slater, L. (2004). *Opening Skinner's box: Great experiments of the twentieth century*. New York: W.W. Norton

Slaughter, M. (1990). The vertebrate retina. In K. N. Leibovic (Ed.), *Science of vision*. New York: Springer-Verlag.

Slavney, P. R. (1990). *Perspectives on hysteria*. Baltimore: Johns Hopkins University Press.

Slobin, D. I. (1985). *A cross-linguistic study of language acquisition*. Hillsdale, NJ: Erlbaum.

Slobin, D. I. (1992). *The cross-linguistic study of language acquisition*. Hillsdale, NJ: Erlbaum.

Slovic, P. (1990). Choice. In D. N. Osherson & E. E. Smith (Eds.), *Thinking: An invitation to cognitive science* (Vol. 3). Cambridge, MA: MIT Press.

Slovic, P., & Fischhoff, B. (1977). On the psychology of experimental surprises. *Journal of Experimental Psychology: Human Perception and Performance, 3*, 544–551.

Slovic, P., Fischhoff, B., & Lichtenstein, S. (1982). Facts versus fears: Understanding perceived risk. In D. Kahneman, P. Slovic, & A. Tversky (Eds.), *Judgment under uncertainty: Heuristics and biases*. Cambridge, England: Cambridge University Press.

Slovic, P., Lichtenstein, S., & Fischhoff, B. (1988). Decision making. In R. C. Atkinson, R. J. Herrnstein, G. Lindzey, & R. D. Luce (Eds.), *Stevens' handbook of experimental psychology* (Vol. 2). New York: Wiley.

Smallwood, J. (2010). Why the global availability of mind wandering necessitates resource competition: Reply to McVay and Kane (2010). *Psychological Bulletin, 136*, 202–207.

Smallwood, J., & Schooler, J. W. (2006). The restless mind. *Psychological Bulletin, 132*, 946–958.

Smedley, S. R., & Eisner, T. (1996). Sodium: A male moth's gift to its offspring. *Proceedings of the National Academy of Sciences, 93*, 809–813.

Smetana, J. G., Campione, B. N., & Metzger, A. (2006). Adolescent development in interpersonal and societal contexts. *Annual Review of Psychology, 57*, 255–284.

Smith, A. (1759). *The theory of moral sentiments*. London: Millar.

Smith, A. (1784). *An inquiry into the nature and causes of the wealth of nations* (3rd ed.). R. H. Campbell and A. S. Skinner (Eds.). Oxford: Clarendon Press.

Smith, C. (1996). Sleep states, memory processes and synaptic plasticity. *Behavioural Brain Research, 78*, 49–56.

Smith, C. (2003). The REM sleep window and memory processing. In Maquet, P., Smith, C., & Stickgold, R. (Eds.), *Sleep and brain plasticity* (pp. 116–133). Oxford, UK: Oxford University Press.

Smith, C. A., & Lazarus, R. S. (1993). Appraisal components, core relational themes, and the emotions. *Cognition and Emotion, 7*, 233–269.

Smith, C. P. (1992). Reliability issues. In C. P. Smith (Ed.), *Motivation and personality: Handbook of thematic content analysis*. New York: Cambridge University Press.

Smith, C., & Fazekas, A. (1997). Amounts of REM sleep and stage 2 required for efficient learning. Poster presented at the annual meeting of the Associated Professional Sleep Societies.

Smith, D. (2005, May 10). Hot Nash burns Mavs. *Toronto Star*, E1, E4.

Smith, D. A. (1999). The end of theoretical orientations? *Applied & Preventative Psychology, 8*, 269–280.

Smith, D. V., & Margolskee, R. F. (2006). Making sense of taste. *Scientific American, 16*(3), 84–92.

Smith, E. E. (2000). Neural bases of human working memory. *Current Directions in Psychological Science, 9*, 45–49.

Smith, G. T., Spillane, N. S., & Annus, A. M. (2006). Implications of an emerging integration of universal and culturally specific psychologies. *Perspectives on Psychological Science, 1*, 211–233.

Smith, G., Housen, P., Yaffe, K., Ruff, R., Kennison, R., Mahncke, H., & Zelinski, E. (2009). A cognitive training program based on principles of brain plasticity: Results from the Improvement in Memory with Plasticity-based Adaptive Cognitive Training (IMPACT) study. *Journal of the American Geriatrics Society, 57*(4), 594–603.

Smith, J. C. (1975). Meditation and psychotherapy: A review of the literature. *Psychological Bulletin, 32*, 553–564.

Smith, J. C. (2007). The psychology of relaxation. In P. M. Lehrer, R. L. Woolfolk, & W. E. Sime (Eds.), *Principles and practice of stress management*. New York, NY: Guilford Press.

Smith, M. L., & Glass, G. V. (1977). Meta-analysis of psychotherapy outcome studies. *American Psychologist, 32*, 752–760.

Smith, M. R., Fogg, L. F., & Eastman, C. I. (2009). A compromise circadian phase position for permanent night work improves mood, fatigue, and performance. *Sleep: Journal of Sleep and Sleep Disorders Research, 32*(11), 1481–1489.

Smith, M. T., Perlis, M. L., Park, A., Smith, M. S., Pennington, J., Giles, D. E., & Buysse, D. J. (2002). Comparative meta-analysis of pharmacotherapy and behavior therapy for persistent insomnia. *American Journal of Psychiatry, 159*, 5–11.

Smith, M., & Pazder, L. (1980). *Michelle remembers*. New York: Pocket Books.

Smith, N. A., & Schmuckler, M. A. (2004). The perception of tonal structure through the differentiation and organization of pitches. *Journal of Experimental Psychology: Human Perception and Performance, 30*, 268–286.

Smith, P. B. (2001). Cross-cultural studies of social influence. In D. Matsumoto (Ed.), *The handbook of culture and psychology*. New York: Oxford University Press.

Smith, P. B., & Bond, M. H. (1994). *Social psychology across cultures: Analysis and perspectives*. Boston: Allyn & Bacon.

Smith, S. (1988). Environmental context-dependent memory. In G. M. Davies & D. M. Thomson (Eds.), *Memory in context: Context in memory*. New York: Wiley.

Smith, S. M. (1995). Getting into and out of mental ruts: A theory of fixation, incubation, and insight. In R. J. Sternberg & J. E. Davidson (Eds.), *The nature of insight* (pp. 229–251). Cambridge, MA: MIT Press.

Smith, S. M., & Gleaves, D. H. (2007). Recovered memories. In M. P. Toglia, J. D. Read, D. F. Ross, & R. C. L. Lindsay (Eds.), *Handbook of eyewitness psychology: Volume 1. Memory for events*. Mahwah, NJ: Erlbaum.

Smith, S. M., McIntosh, W. D., & Bazzini, D. G. (1999). Are the beautiful good in Hollywood? An investigation of the beauty-and-goodness stereotype on film. *Basic & Applied Social Psychology, 21*, 69–80.

Smith, T. W., & Gallo, L. C. (2001). Personality traits as risk factors for physical illness. In A. Baum, T. A. Revenson, & J. E. Singer (Eds.), *Handbook of health psychology* (pp. 139–174). Mahwah, NJ: Erlbaum.

Smith, W. P., Compton, W. C., & West, W. B. (1995). Meditation as an adjunct to a happiness enhancement program. *Journal of Clinical Psychology, 51*, 269–273.

Smolak, L., & Murnen, S. K. (2001). Gender and eating problems. In R. H. Striegel-Moore & L. Smolak (Eds.), *Eating disorders: Innovative directions in research and practice* (pp. 91–110). Washington, DC: American Psychological Association.

Smolensky, P. (1995). On the proper treatment of connectionism. In C. Macdonald & G. Macdonald (Eds.), *Connectionism: Debates on psychological explanation*. Cambridge, USA: Blackwell.

Smyth, J. M., & Pennebaker, J. W. (1999). Sharing one's story: Translating emotional experiences into words as a coping tool. In C. R. Snyder (Ed.), *Coping: The psychology of what works*. New York: Oxford University Press.

Snedecor, S. M., Pomerleau, C. S., Mehringer, A. M., Ninowski, R., & Pomerleau, O. F. (2006). Differences in smoking-related variables based on phenylthiocabamide "taster" status. *Addictive Behaviors, 31*, 2309–2312.

Snodgrass, M., Bernat, E., & Shevrin, H. (2004). Unconscious perception: A model-based approach to method and evidence. *Perception & Psychophysics, 66*, 846–867.

Snow, C. E. (1998). Bilingualism and second language acquisition. In J. B. Gleason & N. B. Ratner (Eds.), *Psycholinguistics*. Fort Worth, TX: Harcourt College Publishers.

Snow, R. E. (1986). Individual differences in the design of educational programs. *American Psychologist, 41*, 1029–1039.

Snowden, L. R., & Hu, T. W. (1996). Outpatient service use in minority-serving mental health programs. *Administration and Policy in Mental Health, 24*, 149–159.

Snowden, L. R., & Yamada, A. (2005). Cultural differences in access to care. *Annual Review of Clinical Psychology, 1*, 143–166.

Snyder, A. (1989). *Relationship excellence: Right brain relationship skills for left brain personalities*. Seattle: Gresham Publishing.

Snyder, S. H. (2002). Forty years of neurotransmitters: A personal account. *Archives of General Psychiatry, 59*, 983–994.

So, K. T., & Orme-Johnson, D. W. (2001). Three randomized experiments on the longitudinal effects of the Transcendental Meditation technique on cognition. *Intelligence, 29*, 419–440.

Society for Neuroscience. (2008). *Brain briefings: Mirror neurons*. Retrieved June 20, 2011, from http://www.sfn.org/index.aspx?pagename=brainBriefings_MirrorNeurons.

Sohlberg, S., & Birgegard, A. (2003). Persistent complex subliminal activation effects: First experimental observations. *Journal of Personality and Social Psychology, 85*, 302–316.

Sokol, R. J., Janisse, J. J., Louis, J. M., Bailey, B. N., Ager, J., Jacobson, S. W., & Jacobson, J. L. (2007). Extreme prematurity: An alcohol-related birth effect. *Alcoholism: Clinical and Experimental Research, 31*, 1031–1037.

Solberg, E. C., Diener, E., Wirtz, D., Lucas, R. E., & Oishi, S. (2002). Wanting, having, and satisfaction: Examining the role of desire discrepancies in satisfaction with income. *Journal of Personality and Social Psychology, 83*, 725–734.

Solinas, M., Justinova, Z., Goldberg, S. R., & Tanda, G. (2006). Anandamide administration alone and after inhibition of fatty acid amide hydrolase (FAAH)

increases dopamine levels in the nucleus accumbens shell in rats. *Journal of Neurochemistry, 98*, 408–419.

Solinas, M., Panlilio, L. V., Antoniou, K., Pappas, L. A., & Goldberg, S. R. (2003). The cannabinoid CB1 antagonist N-piperidinyl-5-(4-chlorophenyl)-1-(2,4-dichlorophenyl)-4-methylpyrazole-3-carboxamide (SR-141716A) differentially alters the reinforcing effects of heroin under continuous reinforcement, fixed ratio, and progressive ratio schedules of drug self-administration in rats. *Journal of Pharmacology and Experimental Therapeutics, 306*, 93–102.

Soll, J. B., & Klayman, J. (2004). Overconfidence in interval estimates. *Journal of Experimental Psychology: Learning, Memory, & Cognition, 30*, 299–314.

Solms, M. (2004). Freud returns. *Scientific American, 290*(5), 83–88.

Solomon, D. A., Keller, M. B., Leon, A. C., Mueller, T. I., Lavori, P. W., Shea, M. T., et al. (2000). Multiple recurrences of major depressive disorder. *American Journal of Psychiatry, 157*, 229–233.

Solomon, S., Greenberg, J., & Pyszczynski, T. (1991). "A terror management theory of social behavior: The psychological functions of esteem and cultural worldviews." In M. P. Zanna (Ed.), *Advances in experimental social psychology* (Volume 24, pp. 93–159). New York: Academic Press.

Solomon, S., Greenberg, J., & Pyszczynski, T. (2004a). Lethal consumption: Death-denying materialism. In T. Kasser & A. D. Kanner (Eds.), *Psychology and consumer culture: The struggle for a good life in a materialistic world*. Washington, DC: American Psychological Association.

Solowij, N., Stephens, R. S., Roffman, R. A., Babor, T., Kadden, R., Miller, M., et al. (2002). Cognitive functioning of long-term heavy cannabis users seeking treatment. *Journal of the American Medical Association, 287*, 1123–1131.

Solso, R. L. (1994). *Cognition and the visual arts*. Cambridge, MA: MIT Press.

Sommer, B. (1987). *Not another diet book: A right-brain program for successful weight management*. Alameda, CA: Hunter House.

Sommer, I. E., Aleman, A., Somers, M., Boks, M. P., & Kahn, R. S. (2008). Sex differences in handedness, asymmetry of the planum temporale and functional language lateralization. *Brain Research, 1206*, 76–88.

Son Hing, L. S., Li, W., & Zanna, M. P. (2002). Inducing hypocrisy to reduce prejudicial responses among aversive racists. *Journal of Experimental Social Psychology, 38*(1), 71–78.

Song, S., Sjostrom, P. J., Reigl, M., Nelson, S., & Chklovskii, D. B. (2005). Highly nonrandom features of synaptic connectivity in local cortical circuits. *PLoS Biol, 3*(3), 1–13.

Soonhee, L., Rogge, R. D., & Reiss, H. T. (2010). Assessing the seeds of relationship decay: Using implicit evaluations to detect the early stages of disillusionment. *Psychological Science, 21*, 857–864.

Sorrentino, R. M., & Roney, C. J. R. (2000). *The uncertain mind*. Philadelphia, PA: Psychology Press.

Sotiriou, P. E. (2002). *Integrating college study skills: Reasoning in reading, listening, and writing*. Belmont, CA: Wadsworth.

Sousa, D. A. (2000). *How the brain learns: A classroom teacher's guide*. Thousand Oaks, CA: Corwin Press.

Spangler, W. D. (1992). Validity of questionnaire and TAT measures of need for achievement: Two meta-analyses. *Psychological Bulletin, 112*, 140–154.

Spanos, N. P. (1986). Hypnotic behavior: A social-psychological interpretation of amnesia, analgesia, and "trance logic." *Behavioral & Brain Sciences, 9*(3), 449–467.

Spanos, N. P. (1994). Multiple identity enactments and multiple personality disorder: A sociocognitive perspective. *Psychological Bulletin, 116*, 143–165.

Spanos, N. P. (1996). *Multiple identities and false memories*. Washington, DC: American Psychological Association.

Spanos, N. P., & Chaves, J. F. (1991). History and historiography of hypnosis. In S. J. Lynn & J. W. Rhue (Eds.), *Theories of hypnosis: Current models and perspectives* (pp. 43–78). New York: The Guilford Press.

Spanos, N. P., & Coe, W. C. (1992). A social-psychological approach to hypnosis. In E. Fromm & M. R. Nash (Eds.), *Contemporary hypnosis research*. New York: Guilford.

Sparing, R., Hesse, M. D., & Fink, G. R. (2010). Neuronavigation for transcranial magnetic stimulation (TMS): Where we are and where we are going. *Cortex: A Journal Devoted to the Study of the Nervous System and Behavior, 46*(1), 118–120.

Spear, J. H. (2007). Prominent schools or other active specialties? A fresh look at some trends in psychology. *Review of General Psychology, 11*(4), 363–380.

Spear, P. (2000). The adolescent brain and age-related behavioral manifestations. *Neuroscience and Biobehavioral Reviews, 24*, 417–463.

Spearman, C. (1904). "General intelligence" objectively determined and measured. *American Journal of Psychology, 15*, 201–293.

Spearman, C. (1927). *The abilities of man, their nature and measurement*. London: Macmillan.

Spelke, E. S. (1994). Initial knowledge: Six suggestions. *Cognition, 50*, 431–455.

Spelke, E. S., & Kinzler, K. D. (2007). Core knowledge. *Developmental Science, 10*(1), 89–96.

Spelke, E. S., & Newport, E. L. (1998). Nativism, empiricism, and the development of knowledge. In W. Damon (Ed.), *Handbook of child psychology (Vol. 1): Theoretical models of human development*. New York: Wiley.

Spence, S. A. (2005). Prefrontal white matter—The tissue of lies? *The British Journal of Psychiatry, 187*, 326–327.

Spencer, S. J., Steele, C. M., & Quinn, D. M. (1999). Stereotype threat and women's math performance. *Journal of Experimental Social Psychology, 35*, 4–28.

Sperling, G. (1960). The information available in brief visual presentations. *Psychological Monographs, 74*(11, Whole No. 498).

Sperry, R. W. (1982). Some effects of disconnecting the cerebral hemispheres. *Science, 217*, 1223–1226, 1250.

Spiegel, D. (1995). Hypnosis, dissociation, and trauma: Hidden and overt observers. In J. L. Singer (Ed.), *Repression and dissociation: Implications for personality theory, psychopathology, and health*. Chicago: University of Chicago Press.

Spiegel, D. (2003a). Hypnosis and traumatic dissociation: Therapeutic opportunities. *Journal of Trauma & Dissociation, 4*(3), 73–90.

Spiegel, D. (2003b). Negative and positive visual hypnotic hallucinations: Attending inside and out. *International Journal of Clinical & Experimental Hypnosis, 51*(2), 130–146.

Spiegel, D. (2007). Commentary: Reversing amnesia about hypnosis. *American Journal of Clinical Hypnosis, 49*(3), 181–182.

Spiegel, D., Cutcomb, S., Ren, C., & Pribram, K. (1985). Hypnotic hallucination alters evoked potentials. *Journal of Abnormal Psychology, 94*, 249–255.

Spiegel, H., Greenleaf, M., & Spiegel, D. (2000). Hypnosis. In B. J. Sadock & V. A. Sadock (Eds.), *Kaplan and Sadock's comprehensive textbook of psychiatry*. Philadelphia: Lippincott, Williams & Wilkins.

Spiegel, H., Greenleaf, M., & Spiegel, D. (2005). Hypnosis. In B. J. Sadock & V. A. Sadock (Eds.), *Kaplan & Sadock's comprehensive textbook of psychiatry*. Philadelphia: Lippincott, Williams & Wilkins.

Spiegel, K., Sheridan, J. F., & Van Cauter, E. 2002. Effect of sleep deprivation on response to immunization. *JAMA: The Journal of the American Medical Association, 288*(12), 1471–1472.

Spiegler, M. D., & Guevremont, D. C. (2010). *Contemporary behavior therapy* (5th ed.). Belmont, CA: Wadsworth.

Spinath, B., Spinath, F. M., Harlaar, N., & Plomin, R. (2006). Predicting school achievement from general cognitive ability, self-perceived ability, and intrinsic value. *Intelligence, 34*(4), 363–374.

Spironelli, C., Angrilli, A., & Stegagno, L. (2008). Failure of language lateralization in schizophrenia patients: An ERP study on early linguistic components. *Journal of Psychiatry & Neuroscience, 33*(3), 235–243.

Spitz, H. I. (2009). Group psychotherapy. In B. J. Sadock, V. A. Sadock, & P. Ruiz (Eds.), *Kaplan & Sadock's comprehensive textbook of psychiatry* (pp. 2832–2856). Philadelphia, PA: Lippincott, Williams & Wilkins.

Spitz, H. I., Spitz, S. (2009). Family and couple therapy. In B. J. Sadock, V. A. Sadock, & P. Ruiz (Eds.), *Kaplan & Sadock's comprehensive textbook of psychiatry* (pp. 2845–2856). Philadelphia, PA: Lippincott, Williams & Wilkins.

Sprecher, S., & Duck, S. (1994). Sweet talk: The importance of perceived communication for romantic and friendship attraction experienced during a get-acquainted date. *Personality and Social Psychology Bulletin, 20*, 391–400.

Sprecher, S., Schwartz, P., Harvey, J., & Hatfield, E. (2008). Thebusinessoflove.com: Relationship initiation at Internet matchmaking services. In S. Sprecher, A. Wenzel, & J. Harvey (Eds.), *Handbook of relationship initiation* (pp. 235–247). New York, NY: Psychology Press.

Sprenger, M. (2001). *Becoming a "wiz" at brain-based teaching: From translation to application*. Thousand Oaks, CA: Corwin Press.

Springer, S. P., & Deutsch, G. (1998). *Left brain, right brain*. New York: W. H. Freeman.

Squire, L. R. (1987). *Memory and brain*. New York: Oxford University Press.

Squire, L. R. (1994). Declarative and nondeclarative memory: Multiple brain systems supporting learning and memory. In D. L. Schacter & E. Tulving (Eds.), *Memory systems*. Cambridge, MA: MIT Press.

Squire, L. R. (2004). Memory systems of the brain: A brief history and current perspective. *Neurobiology of Learning & Memory, 82*(3), 171–177.

Squire, L. R. (2009). Memory and brain systems: 1969–2009. *The Journal of Neuroscience, 29*(41), 12711–12716.

Squire, L. R., & Shrager, Y. (2009). Declarative memory systems: Amnesia. In J. H. Byrne (Ed.), *Concise learning and memory: The editor's selection*. San Diego, CA: Elsevier.

Squire, L. R., Knowlton, B., & Musen, G. (1993). The structure and organization of memory. *Annual Review of Psychology, 44*, 453–495.

Sriram, T. G., & Silverman, J. J. (1998). The effects of stress on the respiratory system. In J. R. Hubbard & E. A. Workman (Eds.), *Handbook of stress medicine: An organ system approach*. New York: CRC Press.

Staats, A. W., & Staats, C. K. (1963). *Complex human behavior*. New York: Holt, Rinehart & Winston.

Staddon, J. E. R., & Simmelhag, V. L. (1971). The "superstition" experiment: A reexamination of its implications for the principles of adaptive behavior. *Psychological Review, 78*, 3–43.

Stahl, C., Unkelbach, C., & Corneile, O. (2009). On the respective contributions of awareness of unconditioned stimulus valence and unconditioned stimulus identity in attitude formation through evaluative conditioning. *Journal of Personality and Social Psychology, 97*(3), 404–420.

Staines, G. L. (2008). The relative efficacy of psychotherapy: Reassessing the methods-based paradigm. *Review of General Psychology, 12*(4), 330–343.

Stajkovic, A. D., & Luthans, F. (1998). Self-efficacy and work-related performance: A meta-analysis. *Psychological Bulletin, 124*, 240–261.

Staley, J. K., & Krystal, J. H. (2009). Radiotracer imaging and positron emission topography and single photon emission computer topography. In B. J. Sadock, V. A. Sadock, & P. Ruiz (Eds.), *Kaplan & Sadock's comprehensive textbook of psychiatry* (9th ed., Vol. 1, pp. 42–64). Philadelphia, PA: Lippincott, Williams & Wilkins.

Stalling, R. B. (1992). Mood and pain: The influence of positive and negative affect on reported body aches. *Journal of Social Behavior and Personality, 7*(2), 323–334.

Stangor, C. (2009). The study of stereotyping, prejudice, and discrimination within social psychology: A quick history of theory and research. In T. D. Nelson (Ed.), *Handbook of prejudice, stereotyping, and discrimination* (pp. 1–22). New York, NY: Psychology Press.

Stanley, M. A., & Beidel, D. C. (2009). Behavior therapy. In B. J. Sadock, V. A. Sadock, & P. Ruiz (Eds.), *Kaplan & Sadock's comprehensive textbook of psychiatry* (pp. 2781–2803). Philadelphia, PA: Lippincott, Williams & Wilkins.

Stanovich, K. E. (2009). *Decision making and rationality in the modern world*. New York: Oxford University Press.

Stanovich, K. E. (1999). *Who is rational? Studies of individual differences in reasoning*. Mahwah, NJ: Erlbaum.

Stanovich, K. E. (2003). The fundamental computational biases of human cognition: Heuristics that (sometimes) impair decision making and problem solving. In J. E. Davidson & R. J. Sternberg (Eds.), *The psychology of problem solving*. New York: Cambridge University Press.

Stanovich, K. E. (2004). *How to think straight about psychology*. Boston: Allyn & Bacon.

Stanovich, K. E. (2009). *What intelligence tests miss: The psychology of rational thought*. New Haven, CT: Yale University Press.

Stanovich, K. E., & West, R. F. (2002). Individual differences in reasoning: Implications for the rationality debate. In T. Gilovich, D. Griffin, & D. Kahneman (Eds.), *Heuristics and biases*. New York: Cambridge University Press.

Stanovich, K. E., & West, R. F. (2007). Natural myside bias is independent of cognitive ability. *Thinking & Reasoning, 13*(3), 225–247.

Stanovich, K. E., & West, R. F. (2008). On the relative independence of thinking biases and cognitive ability. *Journal of Personality and Social Psychology, 94*(4), 672–695.

Stanovich, K. E., West, R. F., & Toplak, M. E. (in press). Individual differences as essential components of heuristics and biases research. In K. Manktelow, D. Over, & S. Elqayam (Eds.), *The science of reason*. New York: Psychology Press.

Stasiewicz, P. R., Brandon, T. H., & Bradizza, C. M. (2007). Effects of extinction context and retrieval cues on renewal of alcohol cue reactivity among alcohol dependent outpatients. *Psychology of Addictive Behaviors, 21*, 244–248

Stasser, G. (1991). Pooling of unshared information during group discussion. In S. Worchel, W. Wood, & J. Simpson (Eds.), *Group process and productivity*. Beverly Hills, CA: Sage.

Stasser, G., Vaughan, S. I., & Stewart, D. D. (2000). Pooling unshared information: The benefits of knowing how access to information is distributed among group members. *Organizational Behavior and Human Decision Processes, 82*, 102–116.

Statistics Canada. (1999a). Crime statistics. *The Daily*, July 18, 1999. Retrieved May 9, 2005, from http://statcan.ca/Daily/English/000718/d000718a.htm.

Statistics Canada. (1999b). General social survey: Time use. *The Daily*, November 9, 1999. Retrieved June 21, 2005, from http://www.statcan.ca/Daily/English/991109/d991109a.htm.

Statistics Canada. (1999c). National longitudinal survey of children and youth: Transition into adolescence. *The Daily*, July 6, 1999. Retrieved June 1, 2005, from http://www.statcan.ca/Daily/English/990706/d990706a.htm.

Statistics Canada. (2001). *Disability among working-age adults (aged 15–64)*. Retrieved February 12, 2008, from http://www.statcan.ca/english/freepub/89-577-XIEE/workage.htm.

Statistics Canada. (2002a). National longitudinal survey of children and youth: Childhood obesity. *The Daily*, October 18, 2002. Retrieved April 30, 2005, from http://www.statcan.ca/Daily/English/021018/d021018b.htm.

Statistics Canada. (2002b). Participation and activity limitation survey: A profile of disability in Canada. *The Daily*, December 3, 2002. Retrieved May 17, 2005, from http://www.statcan.ca/Daily/English/021203/td021203.htm.

Statistics Canada. (2002c). Shift work and health. *The Daily*, July 25, 2002. Retrieved March 9, 2005, from http://www.statcan.ca/Daily/English/020725/d020725b.htm.

Statistics Canada. (2003a). Canadian community health survey: Mental health and well-being. *The Daily*, September 3, 2003. Retrieved June 27, 2005, from http://www.statcan.ca/Daily/English/030903/td030903.htm.

Statistics Canada. (2003b). Parent and child factors associated with youth obesity. *The Daily*, November 3, 2003. Retrieved April 30, 2005, from http://www.statcan.ca/Daily/English/031103/d031103a.htm.

Statistics Canada. (2003c). Sources of workplace stress. *The Daily*, June 25, 2003. Retrieved June 21, 2005, from http://www.statcan.ca/Daily/English/030625/d030625c.htm.

Statistics Canada. (2003d). Problem gambling. *The Daily*, December 12, 2003. Retrieved July 14, 2008, from http://www.statcan/Daily/English/031212/d031212c.htm.

Statistics Canada. (2004a). *Canadian Community Health Survey. The Daily*, June 15, 2004. Retrieved April 30, 2005, from http://www.statcan.ca/Daily/English/040615/d040615b.htm.

Statistics Canada. (2004c). Health reports: Stress and chronic conditions, excess weight and arthritis. *The Daily*, January 21, 2004. Retrieved June 21, 2005, from http://www.statcan.ca/Daily/English/040121/d040121b.htm.

Statistics Canada. (2004d). Study: Student reading performance in minority-language school. *The Daily*, March 22, 2004. Retrieved May 11, 2005, from http://www.statcan.ca/Daily/English/040322/d040322a.htm.

Statistics Canada. (2004e). Divorces. *The Daily*, May 4, 2004. Retrieved June 1, 2005, from http://www.statcan.ca/Daily/English/040504/d040504a.htm.

Statistics Canada. (2004f). French immersion 30 years later. *The Daily*, March 22, 2004. Retrieved April 27, 2008, from http://www.statcan.gc.ca/pub/81-004-x/200406/6923-eng.htm.

Statistics Canada. (2005a). *National Population Health Survey*: Obesity: A growing issue. *The Daily*, April 7, 2005. Retrieved April 11, 2005, from http://www.statcan.ca/Daily/English/050407/d050407a.htm.

Statistics Canada. (2005b). Study: Canada's visible minority population in 2017. *The Daily*, March 22, 2005. Retrieved July 7, 2005, from http://www.statcan.ca/Daily/English/050322/d050322b.htm.

Statistics Canada. (2005c). Study: Mature singles who don't expect to marry. *The Daily*, June 7, 2005. Retrieved June 7, 2005, from http://www.statcan.ca/Daily/English/050607/d050607a.htm.

Statistics Canada. (2005d). Study: The rising profile of women academics. *The Daily*, February 24, 2005. Retrieved May 12, 2010, from http://www.statcan.gc.ca/daily-quotidien/050224/dq050224c-eng.htm.

Statistics Canada. (2005f). Early sexual intercourse, condom use and sexually transmitted diseases. *The Daily*, May 3, 2005. Retrieved May 9, 2005, from http://www.statcan.ca/Daily/English/050503/d050503a.htm.

Statistics Canada. (2005g). Child care. *The Daily*, February 7, 2005. Retrieved October 4, 2005, from http://www.statcan.ca/Daily/English/050207/d050207b.htm.

Statistics Canada. (2005h). Study: Insomnia. *The Daily*, November 16, 2005. Retrieved March 1, 2008, from http://www.statcan.ca/Daily/English/051116/d051116a.htm.

Statistics Canada. (2006). General Social Survey: Commuting times. *The Daily*, July 12, 2006. Retrieved June 30, 2011, from http://www.statcan.gc.ca/daily-quotidien/060712/dq060712b-eng.htm.

Statistics Canada. (2006a). Trends in weight change among Canadian adults. *The Daily*, November 6, 2006. Retrieved June 11, 2006, from http://www.statcan.ca/english/research/82-618-MIE/82-618-MIE2006005.htm.

Statistics Canada. (2006b). Deaths. *The Daily*, December 20, 2006. Retrieved March 1, 2007, from http://www.statcan.ca/Daily/English/061220/d061220b.htm.

Statistics Canada. (2006c). Health reports: Job satisfaction, stress, and depression. *The Daily*, October 17, 2006. Retrieved October 17, 2006, from http://www.statcan.gc.ca/Daily/English/061017/d061017a.htm.

Statistics Canada. (2007a). Physically active Canadians. *The Daily*, August 22, 2007. Retrieved August 22, 2007, from http://www.statcan.ca/Daily/English/070822/d070822b.htm.

Statistics Canada. (2007b). 2006 Census: Families, marital status, households and dwelling characteristics. *The Daily,* September 12, 2007. Retrieved December 9, 2007, from http://www.statcan.ca/Daily/English/070912/d070912a.htm.

Statistics Canada. (2007c). Maternity experiences survey. *The Daily,* November 27, 2007. Retrieved November 28, 2007, from http://www.statcan.ca/Daily/English/071127/d071127d.htm.

Statistics Canada. (2007d). Returning to work after childbirth. *The Daily,* December 19, 2007. Retrieved February 1, 2008, from http://www.statcan.ca/Daily/English/071219/d071219e.htm.

Statistics Canada. (2007e). Delayed transitions of young adults. *The Daily,* September 18, 2007. Retrieved September 18, 2007, from http://www.statcan.ca/Daily/English/070918/d070918b.htm.

Statistics Canada. (2007f). Work stress and job performance. *The Daily,* December 19, 2007. Retrieved January 2, 2008, from http://www.statcan.ca/Daily/English/071219/d071219d.htm.

Statistics Canada. (2007g). Going to see the doctor. *The Daily,* February 21, 2007. Retrieved Feburary 21, 2007, from http://www.statcan.ca/Daily/English/0702.

Statistics Canada. (2007h). Depression and work impairment. *The Daily,* January 12, 2007. Retrieved January 16, 2007, from http://www.statcan.ca/Daily/English/070112/d070112a.htm.

Statistics Canada. (2008). Sexual orientation and violence. *The Daily,* February 28, 2008. Retrieved June 20, 2011, from http://www.statcan.gc.ca/daily-quotidien/080228/dq080228c-eng.htm.

Statistics Canada. (2008a). Sleep patterns of Canadians. *The Daily,* April 22, 2008. Retrieved June 30, 2011, from http://www.statcan.gc.ca/daily-quotidien/080422/dq080422b-eng.htm.

Statistics Canada. (2008a). Study: Female offenders. *The Daily,* January 24, 2008. Retrieved January 30, 2008, from http://www.statcan.ca/Daily/English/080124/d080124a.htm.

Statistics Canada. (2008b). Organized sports participation among children. *The Daily,* June 3, 2008. Retrieved June 30, 2011, from http://www.statcan.gc.ca/daily-quotidien/080603/dq080603a-eng.htm.

Statistics Canada. (2008b). University enrolment. *The Daily,* February 7, 2008. Retrieved February 8, 2008, from http://www.statcan.ca/Daily/English/080207/d080207a.htm.

Statistics Canada. (2008c). Sexual orientation and victimization. *The Daily,* February 28, 2008. Retrieved February 28, 2008, from http://www.statcan.ca/Daily/English/080228/d080228c.htm.

Statistics Canada. (2008d). Sedentary behaviour and obesity. *The Daily,* June 18, 2008. Retrieved June 23, 2008, from http://www.statcan.ca/Daily/English/080618/d080618b.htm.

Statistics Canada. (2008e). Organized sports participation among children. *The Daily,* June 3, 2008. Retrieved June 8, 2008, from http://www.statcan.ca/Daily/English/080603/d080603a.htm.

Statistics Canada. (2008f). *Hate crime in Canada: Findings.* Retrieved August 24, 2008, from http://www.statcan.ca/english/research/85F0033MIE2008017/findings.

Statistics Canada. (2009). The Internet in our daily lives. Retrieved July 10, 2011, from http://www.statcan.gc.ca/pub/56f0004m/2006013/s1-eng.htm.

Statistics Canada. (2010). Gambling. *The Daily,* August 27, 2010. Retrieved June 30, 2011, from http://www.statcan.gc.ca/daily-quotidien/100827/dq100827b-eng.htm.

Statistics Canada. (2010). Suicide rate by sex and by age group. Retrieved June 1, 2011, from http://www40.statcan.ca/l01/cst01/hlth66a-eng.htmShimizu.

Statistics Canada. (2010a). Blood pressure in adults. *The Daily,* February 17, 2010. Retrieved February 17, 2010, from http://www.statcan.gc.ca/daily-quotidien/100217/dq100217b-eng.htm.

Statistics Canada. (2010a). General social survey: victimization. *The Daily,* September 28, 2010. Retrieved September 30, 2010, from http://www.statcan.gc.ca/daily-quotien/100928/dq100928a-eng.htm.

Statistics Canada. (2010a). Police-reported hate crime. *The Daily,* June 14, 2010. Retreived July 10, 2011, from http://www.statcan.gc.ca/daily-quotidien/100614/dq100614b-eng.htm.

Statistics Canada. (2010b). A portrait of couples in mixed unions. Canadian Social Trends, no. 89. Retrieved July 15, 2011, from http://www.statcan.gc.ca/pub/11-008-x/2010001/article/11143-eng.htm.

Statistics Canada. (2010b). Deaths. *The Daily,* February 23, 2010. Retrieved Feburary 23, 2010, from http://www.statcan.gc.ca/daily-quotidien/100223/dq100223a-eng.htm.

Statistics Canada. (2010b). Survey methods and practices. *The Daily,* September 27, 2010. Retrieved September 30, 2010, from http://www.statcan.gc.ca/daily-quotien/100927/dq100927e-eng.htm.

Statistics Canada. (2010c). Canadian internet use survey. *The Daily,* May 10, 2010. Retrieved May 15, 2010, from http://www.statcan.gc.ca/daily-quotidien/100510/dq100510a-eng.htm.

Statistics Canada. (2010c). Canadian measures survey. *The Daily,* January 13, 2010. Retrieved January 14, 2010, from http://www.statcan.gc.ca/daily-quotidien/100113/dq100113a-eng.htm.

Statistics Canada. (2011). Adult obesity in Canada and the United States. Retrieved February 1, 2011, from http://www.statcan.gc.ca/pub/82-625-x/2011001/article/11411-eng.htm.

Statistics Canada. (2011). Adult obesity prevalence in Canada and the United States. Retrieved June 20, 2011, from http://www.statcan.gc.ca/pub/82-625-x/2011001/article/11411-eng.htm.

Statistics Canada. (2011). Retirement, health and employment among older Canadians. *The Daily,* January 31, 2011. Retrieved Feburary 5, 2011, from http://www.statcan.gc.ca/daily-quotidien/110131/dq110131c-eng.htm.

Steel, P., Schmidt, J., & Shultz, J. (2008). Refining the relationship between personality and subjective well-being. *Psychological Bulletin, 134,* 138–161.

Steele, C. M. (1992, April). Race and the schooling of black Americans. *The Atlantic Monthly,* pp. 68–78.

Steele, C. M. (1997). A threat in the air: How stereotypes shape intellectual identity and performance. *American Psychologist, 52,* 613–629.

Steele, C. M., & Aronson, J. (1995). Stereotype threat and the intellectual test performance of African Americans. *Journal of Personality and Social Psychology, 69,* 797–811.

Steele, C. M., Spencer, S. J., & Aronson, J. (2002). Contending with group image: The psychology of stereotype and social identity threat. In M. P. Zanna (Ed.), Advances in *Experimental Social Psychology, 34,* 379–440.

Steele, K. M. (2003). Do rats show a Mozart effect? *Music Perception, 21,* 251–265.

Steering Committee. (2002). Empirically supported therapy relationships: Conclusions and recommendations of the Division 29 Task Force. In J. C. Norcross (Ed.), *Psychotherapy relationships that work: Therapist contributions and responsiveness to patients* (pp. 441–443). New York: Oxford University Press.

Steiger, H., & Bruce, K. R. (2009). Eating disorders. In P. H. Blaney & T. Millon (Eds.), *Oxford textbook of psychopathology* (2nd ed., pp. 431–451). New York, NY: Oxford University Press.

Steiger, H., Bruce, K. R., & Israel, M. (2003). Eating disorders. In G. Stricker & T. A. Widiger (Eds.), *Handbook of psychology (Vol. 8): Clinical psychology.* New York: Wiley.

Steiger, H., Gauvin, L., Engelberg, M. J., Kin, N. M. K. N. Y., Israel, M., Wonderlich, S. A., et al. (2005). Mood- and restraint-based antecedents to binge episodes in bulimia nervosa: Possible influences of the serotonin system. *Psychological Medicine, 35,* 1553–1562.

Stein, B. E., & Meredith, M. A. (1993). *Vision, touch, and audition: Making sense of it all.* Cambridge, MA: MIT Press.

Stein, B. E., Wallace, M. T., & Stanford, T. R. (2000). Merging sensory signals in the brain: The development of multisensory integration in the superior colliculus. In M. S. Gazzaniga (Ed.), *The new cognitive neurosciences.* Cambridge, MA: The MIT Press.

Stein, B. E., Wallace, M. T., & Stanford, T. R. (2001). Brain mechanisms for synthesizing information from different sensory modalities. In E. B. Goldstein (Ed.), *Blackwell handbook of perception.* Malden, MA: Blackwell.

Stein, D. J., & Hugo, F. J. (2004). Neuropsychiatric aspects of anxiety disorders. In S. C. Yudofsky & R. E. Hales (Eds.), *Essentials of neuropsychiatry and clinical neurosciences.* Washington, DC: American Psychiatric Publishing.

Stein, G. (1898). Cultivated motor automatism: A study of character in its relation to attention. *The Psychological Review, 5,* 305, 295–306.

Stein, M. B., Forde, D. R., Anderson, G., & Walker, J. R. (1997a). Obsessive-compulsive disorder in the community: An epidemiologic survey with clinical reappraisal. *American Journal of Psychiatry, 154,* 1120–1126.

Stein, M. B., Walker, J. R., Hazen, A. L., & Forde, D. R. (1997b). Full and partial posttraumatic stress disorder: Findings from a community survey. *American Journal of Psychiatry, 154,* 1114–1119.

Steinberg, L. (2001). We know some things: Adolescent–parent relationships in retrospect and prospect. *Journal of Research on Adolescence, 11,* 1–20.

Steinberg, L. (2007). Risk taking in adolescence: New perspectives from brain and behavioral science. *Current Directions in Psychological Science, 16,* 55–59.

Steinberg, L., & Levine, A. (1997). *You and your adolescent: A parents' guide for ages 10 to 20.* New York: Harper Perennial.

Steinberg, L., & Morris, A. S. (2001). Adolescent development. *Annual Review of Psychology, 52,* 83–110.

Steinberg, L., & Steinberg, W. (1994). *Crossing paths: How your child's adolescence triggers your own crisis.* New York: Simon & Schuster.

Steinhausen, H. (2002). The outcome of anorexia nervosa in the 20th century. *American Journal of Psychiatry, 159,* 1284–1293.

Stekel, W. (1950). *Techniques of analytical psychotherapy.* New York: Liveright.

Stellar, E. (1954). The physiology of motivation. *Psychological Review, 61,* 5–22.

Stem cell basics. (2007). *Stem Cell Information.* National Institutes of Health Resource for Stem Cell Research. Retrieved Feburary 11, 2008, from http://stemcells.nih.gov./info/basics.

Stemler, S. E., Grigorenko, E. L., Jarvin, L., & Sternberg, R. J. (2006). Using the theory of successful intelligence as a basis for augmenting AP exams in psychology and statistics. *Contemporary Educational Psychology, 31,* 344–376.

Stepanski, E. J. (2000). Behavioral therapy for insomnia. In M. H. Kryger, T. Roth, & W. C. Dement (Eds.), *Principles and practice of sleep medicine.* Philadelphia: Saunders.

Stepanski, E. J. (2006). Causes of insomnia. In T. Lee-Chiong (Ed.), *Sleep: A comprehensive handbook.* Hoboken, NJ: Wiley-Liss.

Stepanski, E. J., & Wyatt, J. K. (2003). Use of sleep hygiene in the treatment of insomnia. *Sleep Medicine Reviews, 7*(3), 215–225.

Stephens, R. S. (1999). Cannabis and hallucinogens. In B. S. McCrady & E. E. Epstein (Eds.), *Addictions: A comprehensive guidebook.* New York: Oxford University Press.

Steptoe, A. (2007). Stress effects: Overview. In G. Fink (Ed.), *Encyclopedia of stress.* San Diego: Elsevier.

Steptoe, A., Gibson, E. L., Hamer, M., & Wardle, J. (2007). Neuroendocrine and cardiovascular correlates of positive affect measured by ecological momentary assessment and by questionnaire. *Psychoneuroendocrinology, 32,* 56–64.

Steriade, M. (2005). Brain electrical activity and sensory processing during waking and sleep states. In M. H. Kryger, T. Roth, & W. C. Dement (Eds.). *Principles and practice of sleep medicine.* Philadelphia, PA: Elsevier Saunders.

Stern, K., & McClintock, M. K. 1998. Regulation of ovulation by human pheromones. *Nature 392,* 177.

Stern, W. (1914). *The psychological method of testing intelligence.* Baltimore: Warwick & York.

Sternberg, R. J. (1985). *Beyond IQ: A triarchic theory of human intelligence.* New York: Cambridge University Press.

Sternberg, R. J. (1986). *Intelligence applied: Understanding and increasing your intellectual skills.* New York: Harcourt Brace Jovanovich.

Sternberg, R. J. (1988a). A three-facet model of creativity. In R. J. Sternberg (Ed.), *The nature of creativity: Contemporary psychological perspectives.* Cambridge, England: Cambridge University Press.

Sternberg, R. J. (1988b). *The triarchic mind: A new theory of human intelligence.* New York: Viking.

Sternberg, R. J. (1991). Theory-based testing of intellectual abilities: Rationale for the triarchic abilities test. In H. A. H. Rowe (Ed.), *Intelligence: Reconceptualization and measurement.* Hillsdale, NJ: Erlbaum.

Sternberg, R. J. (1995). For whom *The Bell Curve* tolls: A review of *The Bell Curve. Psychological Science, 6,* 257–261.

Sternberg, R. J. (1996). *Successful intelligence: How practical and creative intelligence determine success in life.* New York: Simon & Schuster, 1996.

Sternberg, R. J. (1998). How intelligent is intelligence testing? *Scientific American Presents Exploring Intelligence, 9,* 12–17.

Sternberg, R. J. (1999). The theory of successful intelligence. *Review of General Psychology, 3,* 292–316.

Sternberg, R. J. (2000a). Creativity is a decision. In A. L. Costa (Ed.), *Teaching for intelligence II* (pp. 85–106). Arlington Heights, IL: Skylight Training.

Sternberg, R. J. (2001). What is the common thread of creativity? Its dialectical relation to intelligence and wisdom. *American Psychologist, 56,* 360–362.

Sternberg, R. J. (2003a). Construct validity of the theory of successful intelligence. In R. J. Sternberg, J. Lautrey, & T. I. Lubart (Eds.), *Models of intelligence: International perspectives.* Washington, DC: American Psychological Association.

Sternberg, R. J. (2004). Culture and Intelligence. *American Psychologist, 59,* 325–338.

Sternberg, R. J. (2005). There are no public policy implications: A reply to Rushton and Jensen. *Psychology, Public Policy, and the Law, 11,* 295–301.

Sternberg, R. J. (2006). A duplex theory of love. In R. J. Sternberg & K. Weis (Eds.), *The new psychology of love.* New Haven, CT: Yale University Press.

Sternberg, R. J. (2007). Intelligence and culture. In S. Kitayama & D. Cohen (Eds.), *Handbook of cultural psychology* (pp. 547–568). New York: Guilford.

Sternberg, R. J. (2009). Component processes in analogical reasoning. In J. C. Kaufman & E. L. Grigorenko (Eds.), *The essential Sternberg: Essays on intelligence, psychology, and education* (pp. 145–179). New York, NY: Springer.

Sternberg, R. J. (2011). The flaw of overall rankings. Inside Higher Education, January 24, 2011. Retrieved February 28, 2011 from http://www.insidehighered.com/views/2011/01/24/sternberg.

Sternberg, R. J., & Hedlund, J. (2002). Practical intelligence, *g,* and work psychology. *Human Performance, 15,* 143–160.

Sternberg, R. J., & Jarvin, L. (2003). Alfred Binet's contributions as a paradigm for impact in psychology. In R. J. Sternberg (Ed.), *The anatomy of Impact: What makes the great works of psychology great?* (pp. 89–107). Washington, DC: American Psychological Association.

Sternberg, R. J., & O'Hara, L. A. (1999). Creativity and intelligence. In R. J. Sternberg (Ed.), *Handbook of creativity.* New York: Cambridge University Press.

Sternberg, R. J., & the Rainbow Project Collaborators. (2006). The Rainbow Project: Enhancing the SAT through assessments of analytical, practical, and creative skills. *Intelligence, 34,* 321–350.

Sternberg, R. J., & Williams, W. M. (1997). Does the Graduate Record Exam predict meaningful success in the graduate training of psychologists?: A case study. *American Psychologist, 52,* 630–641.

Sternberg, R. J., Castejon, J. L., Prieto, M. D., Hautamaeki, J., & Grigorenko, E. L. (2001). Confirmatory factor analysis of the Sternberg Triarchic Abilities Test in three international samples: An empirical test of the triarchic theory of intelligence. *European Journal of Psychological Assessment, 17,* 1–16.

Sternberg, R. J., Conway, B. E., Ketron, J. L., & Bernstein, M. (1981). People's conceptions of intelligence. *Journal of Personality and Social Psychology, 41,* 37–55.

Sternberg, R. J., Grigorenko, E. L., & Kidd, K. K. (2005). Intelligence, race, and genetics. *American Psychologist, 60,* 45–69.

Sternberg, R. J., Grigorenko, E. L., Ferrari, M., & Clinkenbeard, P. (1999). A triarchic analysis of an aptitude interaction. *European Journal of Psychological Assessment, 15,* 1–11.

Stevens, G., Raphael, B., & Dobson, M. (2007). Effects of public disasters and mass violence. In G. Fink (Ed.), *Encyclopedia of stress.* San Diego: Elsevier.

Stewart, A. J., Ostrove, J. M., & Helson, R. (2001). Middle aging in women: Patterns of personality change from the 30s to the 50s. *Journal of Adult Development, 8*(1), 23–37.

Stewart, D. E., Gagnon, A., Saucier, J.-F., Wahoush, O., & Dougherty, G. (2008). Postpartum depression symptoms in newcomers. *Canadian Journal of Psychiatry, 53,* 121–124.

Stewart, W. H., Jr., & Roth, P. L. (2007). A meta-analysis of achievement motivation differences between entrepreneurs and managers. *Journal of Small Business Management, 45,* 401–421.

Stewart-Williams, S. (2004). The placebo puzzle: Putting the pieces together. *Health Psychology, 23,* 198–206.

Stice, E. (2001). Risk factors for eating pathology: Recent advances and future directions. In R. H. Striegel-Moore & L. Smolak (Eds.), *Eating disorders: Innovative directions in research and practice* (pp. 51–74). Washington, DC: American Psychological Association.

Stich, S. P. (1990). Rationality. In D. N. Osherson & E. E. Smith (Eds.), *Thinking: An invitation to cognitive science* (Vol. 3). Cambridge, MA: MIT Press.

Stickgold, R. (2001). Toward a cognitive neuroscience of sleep. *Sleep Medicine Reviews, 5,* 417–421.

Stickgold, R. (2005). Why we dream. In M. H. Kryger, T. Roth, & W. C. Dement (Eds.). *Principles and practice of sleep medicine.* Philadelphia: Elsevier Saunders.

Stickgold, R. (2007). Of sleep, memories, and trauma. *Nature Neuroscience, 10,* 540–542.

Stickgold, R., & Walker, M. P. (2004). To sleep, perchance to gain creative insight. *Trends in Cognitive Sciences, 8*(5), 191–192.

Stickgold, R., & Walker, M. P. (2005). Memory consolidation and reconsolidation: What is the role of sleep? *Trends in Neurosciences, 28*(8), 408–415.

Stockman, A. (2010). Color mixing. In E. B. Goldstein (Ed.), *Encyclopedia of perception.* Thousand Oaks, CA: Sage.

Stoddard, G. (1943). *The meaning of intelligence.* New York: Macmillan.

Stoddard, J. J., & Miller, T. (1995). Impact of parental smoking on the prevalence of wheezing respiratory illness in children. *American Journal of Epidemiology, 141,* 96–102.

Stoicheff, B. (2002). *Gerhard Herzberg: An illustrious life in science.* Ottawa, ON: NRC Press, McGill–Queens Press.

Stone, L. (1977). *The family, sex and marriage in England, 1500–1800.* New York: Harper & Row.

Stone, W. N. (2008). Group psychotherapy. In A. Tasman, J. Kay, J. A. Lieberman, M. B. First, & M. Maj (Eds.), *Psychiatry* (3rd ed.). New York, NY: Wiley-Blackwell.

Stoner, J. A. F. (1961). *A comparison of individual and group decisions involving risk.* Unpublished master's thesis, Massachusetts Institute of Technology.

Stoohs, R. A., Blum, H. C., Haselhorst, M., Duchna, H. W., Guilleminault, C., & Dement, W. C. (1998). Normative data on snoring: A comparison between younger and older adults. *European Respiratory Journal, 11,* 451–457.

Storandt, M. (2008). Cognitive deficits in the early stages of Alzheimer's disease. *Current Directions in Psychological Science, 4,* 198–202.

Storch, M., Gaab, J., Küttel, Y., Stüssi, A.-C., & Fend, H. (2007). Psychoneuroendocrine effects of resource-activating stress management training. *Health Psychology, 26*(4), 456–463.

Storm, C., & Gurevich, M. (2001). Looking forward, looking back: Women in psychology. *Canadian Psychology*, *42*(4), 245–248.

Storr, A. (1988). *Solitude: A Return to the Self*. New York, Free Press.

Stowell, J. R. (2008). Stress and stressors. In S. F. Davis & W. Buskist (Eds.), *21st century psychology: A reference handbook*. Thousand Oaks, CA: Sage.

Strager, S. (2003). What men watch when they watch pornography. *Sexuality & Culture: An Interdisciplinary Quarterly*, *7*(1), 50–61.

Strahan, E. J., Lafrance, A., Wilson, A. E., Ethier, N., Spencer, S. J., & Zanna, M. P. (2008). Victoria's dirty secret: How sociocultural norms influence adolescent girls and women. *Personality and Social Psychology Bulletin*, *34*(2), 288–301.

Strange, D., Clifasefi, S., & Garry, M. (2007). False memories. In M. Garry & H. Hayne (Eds.), *Do justice and let the sky fall: Elizabeth F. Lotus and her contributions to science, law, and academic freedom*. Mahwah, NJ: Erlbaum.

Straus, M. A. (2000). Corporal punishment and primary prevention of physical abuse. *Child Abuse & Neglect*, *24*, 1109–1114.

Straus, M. A., & Paschall, M. J. (2009). Corporal punishment by mothers and development of children's cognitive ability: A longitudinal study of two nationally representative age cohorts. *Journal of Aggression, Maltreatment, & Trauma*, *18*(5), 459–483.

Straus, M. A., & Stewart, J. H. (1999). Corporal punishment by American parents: National data on prevalence, chronicity, severity, and duration, in relation to child family characteristics. *Clinical Child & Family Psychology Review*, *2*(2), 55–70.

Strayer, D. L., & Drews, F. A. (2007). Cell-phone-induced driver distraction. *Current Directions in Psychological Science*, *16*, 128–131.

Strayer, D. L., & Johnston, W. A. (2001). Driven to distraction: Dual-task studies of simulated driving and conversing on a cellular telephone. *Psychological Science*, *12*, 462–466.

Strayer, D. L., Drews, F. A., & Crouch, D. J. (2006). A comparison of the cell phone driver and the drunk driver. *Human Factors*, *48*, 381–391.

Streissguth, A. P. (2007). Offspring effects of prenatal alcohol exposure from birth to 25 years: The Seattle prospective longitudinal study. *Journal of Clinical Psychology in Medical Settings*, *14*, 81–101.

Streissguth, A. P., Bookstein, F. L., Barr, H. M., Sampson, P. D., O'Malley, K., & Young, J. K. (2004). Risk factors for adverse life outcomes in fetal alcohol syndrome and fetal alcohol effects. *Journal of Developmental & Behavioral Pediatrics*, *25*, 228–238.

Streit, W. J. (2005). Microglia and neuroprotection: Implications for Alzheimer's disease. *Brain Research Reviews*, *48*, 234–239.

Strenze, T. (2007). Intelligence and socioeconomic success: A meta-analytic review of longitudinal research. *Intelligence*, *35*, 401–426.

Strenzoik, M., et al. (2010). Fronto-parietal regulation of media violence exposure in adolescents: A multi-method study. *Social Cognitive and Affective Neuroscience*. Retrieved June 20, 2011, from http://scan.oxfordjournals.org/content/early/2010/10/07/scan.nsq079.full.

Strick, M., Dijksterhuis, A., & van Baaren, R. B. (2010). Unconscious-thought effects take place off-line, not on-line. *Psychological Science*, *21*, 484–488.

Strick, M., Holland, R. W., & van Knippenberg, A. (2008). Seductive eyes: Attractiveness and direct gaze increase desire for associated objects. *Cognition*, *106*, 1487–1496.

Strick, M., van Baaren, R. B., Holland, R. W., & van Knippenberg, A. (2009). Humor in advertisements enhances product liking by mere association. *Journal of Experimental Psychology: Applied*, *15*, 35–45.

Striegel-Moore, R. H., & Bulik, C. M. (2007). Risk factors for eating disorders. *American Psychologist*, *62*, 181–198.

Striegel-Moore, R. H., & Franko, D. L. (2008). Should binge eating disorder be included in the DSM-V? A critical review of the state of the evidence. *Annual Review of Clinical Psychology*, *4*, 305–324.

Stroebe, W. (2008). *Dieting, overweight, and obesity*. Washington, DC: American Psychological Association.

Strupp, H. H. (1996). The tripartite model and the *Consumer Reports* study. *American Psychologist*, *51*, 1017–1024.

Struthers, C. W., Dupuis, R., & Eaton, J. (2005). Promoting forgiveness among co-workers following a workplace transgression: The effects of social motivation training. *Canadian Journal of Behavioural Sciences* (Special Issue on Creating a Healthy Workplace) *37*(4), 299–308.

Stuart, E. W., Shimp, T. A., & Engle, R. W. (1991). A program of classical conditioning experiments testing variations in the conditioned stimulus and context. *Journal of Consumer Research*, *18*, 1–12.

Stubbe, J. H., Posthuma, D., Boomsma, D. I., & de Geus, E. J. C. (2005). Heritability of life satisfaction in adults: A twin study. *Psychological Medicine*, *35*, 1581–1588.

Stunkard, A. J., Allison, K. C., Geliebter, A., Lundgren, J. D., Gluck, M. E., & O'Reardon, J. P. (2009). Development of criteria for a diagnosis: Lessons from the night eating syndrome. *Comprehensive Psychiatry*, *50*(5), 39

Stunkard, A. J., Harris, J. R., Pederson, N. L., & McClearn, G. E. (1990). The body-mass index of twins who have been reared apart. *New England Journal of Medicine*, *322*, 1483–1487.

Stunkard, A. J., Sorensen, T., Hanis, C., Teasdale, T. W., Chakraborty, R., Schull, W. J., & Schulsinger, F. (1986). An adoption study of human obesity. *New England Journal of Medicine*, *314*, 193–198.

Sturm, V. E., Ascher, E. A., Miller, B. L., & Levenson, R. W. (2008). Diminished self-conscious emotional responding in frontotemporal lobar degeneration patients. *Emotion*, *8*, 861–869.

Stylianou-Korsnes, M., Reiner, M., Magnussen, S. J., & Feldman, M. W. (2010). Visual recognition of shapes and textures: An fMRI study. *Brain Structure & Function*, *214*(4), 355–359.

Subotnik, K. L., Nuechterlein, K. H., Ventura, J., Gitlin, M. J., Marder, S., Mintz, J., et al. (2011). Risperidone nonadherence and return of positive symptoms in the early course of schizophrenia. *American Journal of Psychiatry*, *168*(3), 286–292.

Sudak, H. S. (2005). Suicide. In B. J. Sadock & V. A. Sadock (Eds.), *Kaplan & Sadock's comprehensive textbook of psychiatry*. Philadelphia: Lippincott WIlliams & Wilkins.

Sudak, H. S. (2009). Suicide. In B. J. Sadock, V. A. Sadock, & P. Ruiz (Eds.), *Kaplan & Sadock's comprehensive textbook of psychiatry* (9th ed., pp. 2717–2731). Philadelphia, PA: Lippincott, Williams & Wilkins.

Suddendorf, T., & Corballis, M. C. (2007). The evolution of foresight: What is mental time travel, and is it unique to humans? *Behavioral and Brain Sciences*, *30*, 299–313.

Sue, D. W., & Sue, D. (1999). *Counseling the culturally different: Theory and practice*. New York: Wiley.

Sue, S. (2003). In defense of cultural competency in psychotherapy and treatment. *American Psychologist*, *58*, 964–970.

Sue, S., & Zane, N. (1987). The role of culture and cultural techniques in psychotherapy: A critique and reformulation. *American Psychologist*, *42*, 37–45.

Sue, S., Zane, N., & Young, K. (1994). Research on psychotherapy with culturally diverse populations. In A. E. Bergin & S. L. Garfield (Eds.), *Handbook of psychotherapy and behavior change* (4th ed.). New York: Wiley.

Sue, S., Zane, N., Hall, G., & Berger, L. K. (2009). The case for cultural competency in psychotherapeutic interventions. *Annual Review of Psychology*, *60*, 525–548.

Suedfeld, P. (2003). Canadian space psychology: The future may be almost here. *Canadian Psychology*, *44*, 85–92.

Suedfeld, P., & Steel, G. D. (2000). The environmental psychology of capsule inhabitants. *Annual Review of Psychology*, *51*, 227–253.

Sugarman, J. (2007). Practical rationality and the questionable promise of positive psychology. *Journal of Humanistic Psychology*, *47*, 175–197.

Sugita, Y. (2009). Innate face processing. *Current Opinion in Neurobiology*, *19*(1), 39–44.

Sulivan, H. S. (1953). *The interpersonal theory of psychiatry*. New York: Norton Press.

Sulloway, F. J. (1995). Birth order and evolutionary psychology: A meta-analytic overview. *Psychological Inquiry*, *6*, 75–80.

Sulloway, F. J. (1996). *Born to rebel: Birth order, family dynamics, and creative lives*. New York: Pantheon Books.

Suls, J. M., Luger, T., & Martin, R. (2010). The biopsychosocial model and the use of theory in health psychology. In J. M. Suls, K. W. Davidson, & R. M. Kaplan (Eds.), *Handbook of health psychology and behavioral medicine* (pp. 15–27). New York, NY: Guilford Press.

Summerfeldt, L. J. (2004). Understanding and treating incompleteness in obsessive-compulsive disorder. *Journal of Clinical Psychology*, *60*, 1155–1168.

Summerfeldt, L. J., Richter, M. A., Antony, M. M., & Swinson, R. P. (1999). Symptom structure in obsessive-compulsive disorder: A confirmatory factor-analytic study. *Behaviour Research and Therapy*, *37*, 297–311.

Summerfield, C., & Koechlin, E. (2009). Decision making and prefrontal executive function. In M. S. Gazzangia (Ed.), *The cognitive neurosciences* (4th ed., pp. 1019–1030). Cambridge, MA: MIT Press.

Sundin, J. J., Fear, N. T., Iversen, A. A., Rona, R. J., & Wessely, S. S. (2010). PTSD after deployment to Iraq: Conflicting rates, conflicting claims. *Psychological Medicine: A Journal of Research in Psychiatry and the Allied Sciences*, *40*(3), 367–382.

Super, C. M. (1976). Environmental effects on motor development: A case of African infant precocity. *Developmental Medicine and Child Neurology*, *18*, 561–567.

Supreme Court upholds spanking law. (2004, January 30). *CBC News*. Retrieved March 13, 2008, from http://www.cbc.ca/news/story/2004/01/30/spanking040130.htm.

Surra, C. A., Gray, C. R., Boettcher, T. J., Cottle, N. R., & West, A. R. (2006). From courtship to universal properties: Research on dating and mate selection, 1950 to 2003. In A. L. Vangelisti & D.

Perlman (Eds.), *The Cambridge handbook of personal relationships* (pp. 113–130). New York, NY: Cambridge University Press.

Surtees, P., & Wainwright, N. (2007). Life events and health. In G. Fink (Ed.), *Encyclopedia of stress*. San Diego: Elsevier.

Surtees, P., Wainwright, N., Luben, R., Wareham, N., Bingham, S., & Khaw, K. (2008). Depression and ischemic heart disease mortality: Evidence from the EPIC-Norfolk United Kingdom Prospective Cohort Study. *American Journal of Psychiatry, 165*(4), 515–523.

Susman, E. J., & Rogol, A. (2004). Puberty and psychological development. In R. M. Lerner & L. Steinberg (Eds.), *Handbook of adolescent psychology*. New York: Wiley.

Susman, E. J., Dorn, L. D., & Schiefelbein, V. L. (2003). Puberty, sexuality, and health. In R. M. Lerner, M. A. Easterbrooks, & J. Mistry (Eds.), *Handbook of psychology (Vol.6): Developmental psychology*. New York: Wiley.

Susser, E. B., Neugebauer, R., Hoek, H. W., Brown, A. S., Lin, S., Labovitz, D., & Gorman, J. M. (1996). Schizophrenia after prenatal famine: Further evidence. *Archives of General Psychiatry, 53*, 25–31.

Sutker, P. B., & Allain, A. N. (2001). Antisocial personality disorder. In P. B. Sutker & H. E. Adams (Eds.), *Comprehensive handbook of psychopathology*. New York: Kluwer Academic/Plenum.

Suvak, M. K., Litz, B. T., Sloan, D. M., Zanarini, M. C., & Barrett, L. F. (2011). Emotional granularity and borderline personality disorder. *Journal of Abnormal Psychology, 120*, 414–426.

Suzuki, K. (2007). The moon illusion: Kaufman and Rock's (1962) apparent-distance theory reconsidered. *Japanese Psychological Research, 49*, 57–67.

Swan, G. E., Hudmon, K. S., & Kroyan, T. V. (2003). Tobacco dependence. In A. M. Nezu, C. M. Nezu, & P. A. Geller (Eds.), *Handbook of psychology (Vol. 9): Health Psychology*. New York: Wiley.

Sweatt, J. D. (2009). Long-term potentiation: A candidate cellular mechanism for information storage in the CNS. In J. H. Byrne (Ed.), *Concise learning and memory: The editor's selection*. San Diego, CA: Elsevier.

Swim, J. K., & Hyers, L. L. (2009). Sexism. In T. D. Nelson (Ed.), *Handbook of prejudice, stereotyping, and discrimination* (pp. 1–22). New York, NY: Psychology Press.

Swim, J. K., & Sanna, L. J. (1996). He's skilled, she's lucky: A meta-analysis of observers' attributions for women's and men's successes and failures. *Personality and Social Psychology Bulletin, 22*, 507–519.

Swingley, D. (2008). The roots of the early vocabulary in infants' learning from speech. *Current Directions in Psychological Science, 17*(5), 308–312.

Symons, C. S., & Johnson, B. T. (1997). The self-reference effect in memory: A meta-analysis. *Psychological Bulletin, 121*, 371–394.

Symons, D. (2004). Mental state discourse, theory of mind, and the internalization of self-other understanding. *Developmental Review, 24*, 159–188.

Symons, D. K., Kristin-Lee, M., F., & Collins, T. B. (2006). A longitudinal study of belief and desire state discourse during mother–child play and later false belief understanding. *Social Development, 15*, 676–691.

Szasz, T. (1974). *The myth of mental illness*. New York: Harper & Row.

Szasz, T. (1990). Law and psychiatry: The problems that will not go away. *The Journal of Mind and Behavior, 11*(3/4), 557–564.

Szatmari P., & Reitzel J-A. (2004). Autism intervention: Comments on Harris and Bruinsma, Koegel and Kern Koegel. In *Encylopedia on early childhood development*. Montreal: Centre of Excellence for Early Childhood Development.

Szatmari, P. (2000). The classification of autism, Asperger's syndrome, and pervasive developmental disorder. *Canadian Journal of Psychiatry, 45*, 731–738.

Szatmari, P., Bryson, S. E., Boyle, M. H. Streiner, D. L., & Duku, E. (2003). Predictors of outcome among high functioning children with autism and Asperger syndrome. *Journal of Child Psychology and Psychiatry and Allied Disciplines, 44*, 520–528.

Szigethy, E. M. & Friedman, E. S. (2009). Combined psychotherapy and pharmacology. In B. J. Sadock, V. A. Sadock, & P. Ruiz (Eds.), *Kaplan & Sadock's comprehensive textbook of psychiatry* (pp. 2923–2931). Philadelphia, PA: Lippincott, Williams & Wilkins.

Szmukler, G. I., & Patton, G. (1995). Sociocultural models of eating disorders. In G. Szmukler, C. Dare, & J. Treasure (Eds.), *Handbook of eating disorders: Theory, treatment, and research*. New York: Wiley.

Szpunar, K. K., & McDermott, K. B. (2009). Episodic memory: An evolving concept. In J. H. Byrne (Ed.), *Concise learning and memory: The editor's selection*. San Diego, CA: Elsevier.

Szymanski, L. S., & Wilska, M. (2003). Childhood disorders: Mental retardation. In A. Tasman, J. Kay, & J. A. Lieberman (Eds.), *Psychiatry*. New York: Wiley.

Szymusiak, R. (2009). Thermoregulation during sleep and sleep deprivation. In R. Stickgold & M. P. Walker (Eds.), *The neuroscience of sleep* (pp. 218–222). San Diego, CA: Academic Press.

Tach, L., & Halpern-Meekin, S. (2009). How does premarital cohabitation affect trajectories of marital quality? *Journal of Marriage and Family, 71*(2), 298–317.

Taglialatela, J. P., Russell, J. L., Schaeffer, J. A., & Hopkins, W. D. (2008). Communicative signaling activates "Broca's" homolog in chimpanzees. *Current Biology, 18*, 1–6.

Takarangi, M. T., Polaschek, D. L., Garry, M., & Loftus, E. F. (2008). Psychological science, victim advocates, and the problem of recovered memories. *International Review of Victimology, 15*(2), 147–163.

Takeuchi, H., et al. (2010). Training of working memory impacts structural connectivity. *The Journal of Neuroscience, 30*, 3297–3303.

Talarico, J. M., & Rubin, D. C. (2003). Confidence, not consistency, characterizes flashbulb memories. *Psychological Science, 14*, 455–461.

Talarico, J. M., & Rubin, D. C. (2007). Flashbulb memories are special after all; in phenomenology, not accuracy. *Applied Cognitive Psychology, 21*, 557–578.

Talarico, J. M., & Rubin, D. C. (2009). Flashbulb memories result from ordinary memory processes and extraordinary event characteristics. In O. Luminet & A. Curci (Eds.), *Flashbulb memories: New issues and new perspectives* (pp. 79–97). New York, NY: Psychology Press.

Talbott, J. A. (2004). Deinstitutionalization: Avoiding the disasters of the past. *Psychiatric Services, 55*, 1112–1115.

Tamakoshi, A., Ohno, Y., & JACC Study Group. (2004). Self-reported sleep duration as a predictor of all-cause mortality: Results from JACC study, Japan. *Sleep: A Journal of Sleep and Sleep Disorders Research, 27*, 51–54.

Tamiji, J., & Crawford, D. A. (2010). The neurobiology of lipid metabolism in autism spectrum disorders. *NeuroSignals, 18*(2), 98–112.

Tammet, D. (2007). *Born on a blue day: Inside the extraordinary mind of an autistic savant*. New York, NY: Free Press.

Tammet, D. (2009). *Embracing the wide sky: A tour across the horizons of the mind*. New York, NY: Free Press.

Tamnes, C. K., Ostby, Y., Walhovd, K. B., Westlye, L. T., Due-Tonnessen, P., & Fjell, A. M. (2010). Neuroanatomical correlates of executive functions in children and adolescents: A magnetic resonance imaging (MRI) study of cortical thickness. *Neuropsychologia, 48*, 2496–2508.

Tanaka-Matsumi, J. (2001). Abnormal psychology and culture. In D. Matsumoto (Ed.), *The handbook of culture & psychology*. New York: Oxford University Press.

Tanapat, P., & Gould, E. (2007). Neurogenesis. In G. Fink (Ed.), *Encyclopedia of stress*. San Diego: Elsevier.

Tangney, J. P., Stuewig, J., & Mashek, D. J. (2007). Moral emotions and moral behavior. *Annual Review of Psychology, 58*, 345–372.

Tanner, J. L. (2006). Recentering during emerging adulthood: A critical turning point in life span human development. In J. J. Arnett & J. L. Tanner (Eds.), *Emerging adults in America: Coming of age in the 21st century*. Washington, DC: American Psychological Association.

Tapia, J. C., & Lichtman, J. W. (2008). Synapse elimination. In L. Squire, D. Berg, F. Bloom, S. Du Lac, A. Ghosh, & N. Spitzer (Eds.), *Fundamental neuroscience* (3rd ed., pp. 469–490). San Diego, CA: Elsevier.

Tardiff, K. (1999). Violence. In R. E. Hales, S. C. Yudofsky, & J. A. Talbott (Eds.), *American Psychiatric Press textbook of psychiatry*. Washington, DC: American Psychiatric Press.

Tart, C. T. (1988). From spontaneous event to lucidity: A review of attempts to consciously control nocturnal dreaming. In J. Gackenbach & S. LaBerge (Eds.), *Conscious mind, sleeping brain: Perspectives on lucid dreaming*. New York: Plenum.

Tashkin, D. P., Baldwin, G. C., Sarafian, T., Dubinett, S., & Roth, M. D. (2002). Respiratory and immunologic consequences of marijuana smoking. *Journal of Clinical Pharmacology, 42*, 71S–81S.

Tavris, C. (1998, September 13). Peer pressure (Review of *The Nurture Assumption*). *The New York Times Book Review, 103*, 14.

Taylor, C. A., Manganello, J. A., Lee, S. J., & Rice, J. C. (2010). Mothers' spanking of 3-year-old children and subsequent risk of children's aggressive behavior. *Pediatrics, 125*(5), 1057–1065.

Taylor, D. M., & Moghaddam, F. M. (1994). *Theories of intergroup relations: International, social psychological perspectives*. New York: Praeger Publications.

Taylor, D. M., Lydon, J. E., Bougie, E., & Johannsen, K. (2004). "Street kids": Towards an understanding of their motivational context. *Canadian Journal of Behavioural Science, 36*, 1–16.

Taylor, E. (1999). An intellectual renaissance of humanistic psychology. *Journal of Humanistic Psychology, 39*, 7–25.

Taylor, E. (2001). Positive psychology and humanistic psychology: A reply to Seligman. *Journal of Humanistic Psychology, 41*(1), 13–29.

Taylor, I., & Taylor, M. M. (1990). *Psycholinguistics: Learning and using language*. Englewood Cliffs, NJ: Prentice-Hall.

Taylor, P. (2011, January 13). Writing about fears before tests boosts student grades. *The Globe and Mail*, A9.

Taylor, S. (2004). Amnesia, folklore and folks: Recovered memories in clinical practice. *Cognitive Behaviour Therapy, 33*(2), 105–108.

Taylor, S. E. (2006). Tend and befriend: Biobehavioral bases of affiliation under stress. *Current Directions in Psychological Science, 15,* 273–277.

Taylor, S. E. (2007). Social support. In H. S. Friedman & R. C. Silver (Eds.), *Foundations of health psychology.* New York: Oxford University Press.

Taylor, S. E. (2011). *Health psychology* (8th ed.). New York: McGraw Hill.

Taylor, S. E., & Brown, J. D. (1988). Illusion and well-being: A social psychological perspective on mental health. *Psychological Bulletin, 103,* 193–210.

Taylor, S. E., & Brown, J. D. (1994). Positive illusions and well-being revisited: Separating fact from fiction. *Psychological Bulletin, 116,* 21–27.

Taylor, S. E., & Master, S. L. (2011). Social responses to stress: The tend-and-befriend model. In R. J. Contrada & A. Baum (Eds.), *The handbook of stress science: Biology, psychology, and health* (pp. 101–109). New York, NY: Springer Publishing.

Taylor, S. E., Klein, L. C., Lewis, B. P., Gruenewald, T. L., Gurung, R. A. R., & Updegraff, J. A. (2000). Biobehavioral responses to stress in females: Tend and befriend, not fight or flight. *Psychological Review, 107,* 411–429.

Taylor, S. E., Lerner, J. S., Sherman, D. K., Sage, R. M., & McDowell, N. K. (2003). Are self-enhancing cognitions associated with healthy or unhealthy biological profiles? *Journal of Personality and Social Psychology, 85,* 605–615.

Taylor, S. E., Sherman, D. K., Kim, H. S., Jarcho, J., Takagi, K., & Dunagan, M. S. (2004). Culture and social support: Who seeks it and why? *Journal of Personality and Social Psychology, 87*(3), 354–362.

Taylor, S. E., Welch, W. T., Kim, H. S., & Sherman, D. K. (2007). Cultural differences in the impact of social support on psychological and biological stress responses. *Psychological Science, 18*(9), 831–837.

Taylor, S., Cox, B. J., & Asmundson, G. J. G. (2009). Anxiety disorders: Panic and phobias. In P. H. Blaney & T. Millon (Eds.), *Oxford textbook of psychopathology* (2nd ed., pp. 119–145). New York, NY: Oxford University Press.

Tchernikov, I., & Fallah, M. (2010). A color hierarchy for automatic target selection. *PloS One, 5,* pp. 9338.

Teachman, J. (2003). Premarital sex, premarital cohabitation and the risk of subsequent marital dissolution among women. *Journal of Marriage and Family, 65*(2), 444–455.

Tearful killer granted day parole in Virk murder. (2007, June 22). *CBC News.* Retrieved January 22, 2008, from http://www.cbc.ca/canada/british-columbia/story/2007/06/22/glowatski-parole.html.

Teasdale, J. D., Segal, Z. V., Williams, J. M. G., Ridgeway, V., Soulsby, J. M., & Lau, M. A. (2000). The prevention of relapse/recurrence of major depression by mindfulness-based cognitive therapy. *Journal of Consulting and Clinical Psychology, 68,* 615–623.

Teen brain: A work in progress. (2008). National Institute of Mental Health. Retrieved June 23, 2008, from http://www.nimh.nih.gov/health/publications/teenage-brain-a-work-in-progress.shtml.

Teenage depression can be enduring, but is more often short-lived. (2005, May 27). (Press release). *Science Daily.* Retrieved January 21, 2008, from http://www.sciencedaily.com/releases/2005/05/050527235940.htm.

Tees, R. (2003). A book review of Donald O. Hebb's (1949) The Organization of behavior: A neuropsychological theory, *Canadian Psychology, 44*(1), 74–76.

Tellegen, A., Lykken, D. T., Bouchard, T. J., Jr., Wilcox, K. J., Segal, N. L., & Rich, S. (1988). Personality similarity in twins reared apart and together. *Journal of Personality and Social Psychology, 54,* 1031–1039.

Temple, J. L., Giacomelli, A. M., Roemmich, J. N., & Epstein, L. H. (2008). Dietary variety impairs habituation in children. *Health Psychology, 27,* S10–S19.

Tennen, H., & Affleck, G. (1999). Finding benefits in adversity. In C. R. Snyder (Ed.), *Coping: The psychology of what works.* New York: Oxford University Press.

Tenszen, M. (1989, February 22). Rushton ready to teach race theories: Psychology department to monitor lectures, chairman promises. *Toronto Star,* A8.

Ten-year anniversary of death of Reena Virk. (2007, November 14). Canadian Press. Retrieved January 1, 2008, from http://cnews.canoe.ca/CNEWS/Canada/2007/11/14/pf-4655263.html.

Terman, L. M. (1916). *The measurement of intelligence.* Boston: Houghton Mifflin.

Terman, L. M. (1925). *Genetic studies of genius (Vol.1): Mental and physical traits of a thousand gifted children.* Stanford, CA: Stanford University Press.

Terman, L. M., & Oden, M. H. (1959). *Genetic studies of genius (Vol. 5): The gifted group at mid-life.* Stanford, CA: Stanford University Press.

Terr, L. (1994). *Unchained memories.* New York: Basic Books.

Terracciano, A., Abdel-Khalak, A. M., Adam, N., Adamovova, L., Ahn, C. K., Ahn, H. N., et al. (2005). National character does not reflect mean personality trait levels in 49 cultures. *Science, 310,* 96–100.

Terrace, H. S. (1986). *Nim: A chimpanzee who learned sign language.* New York: Columbia University Press.

Terry, J., & Woonteiler, D. (2000). An interview with Craig Kielburger, founder of Free the Children. *Community Youth Development Journal.* Retrieved June 7, 2005, from http://www.cydjournal.org/2000Winter/kielburger.html.

Tessier-Lavigne, M. (2000). Visual processing by the retina. In E. R. Kandel, J. H. Schwartz, & T. M. Jessell (Eds.), *Principles of neural science.* New York: McGraw-Hill.

Testa, K. (1996). Church to pay $1 million in false-memory case. *San Jose Mercury News,* 8A.

Teuber, M. (1974). Sources of ambiguity in the prints of Maurits C. Escher. *Scientific American, 231,* 90–104.

Thaler, L., & Goodale, M. A. (2010). Beyond distance and direction: the brain represents target locations non-metrically. *Journal of Vision, 10,* 1–27.

Thase, M. E. (2009a). Neurobiological aspects of depression. In I. H. Gotlib & C. L. Hammen (Eds.), *Handbook of depression* (2nd ed., pp. 187–217). New York, NY: Guilford Press.

Thase, M. E. (2009b). Selective serotonin-norepinephrine reuptake inhibitors. In B. J. Sadock, V. A. Sadock, & P. Ruiz (Eds.), *Kaplan & Sadock's comprehensive textbook of psychiatry* (pp. 3184–3189). Philadelphia, PA: Lippincott, Williams & Wilkins.

Thase, M. E., & Denko, T. (2008). Pharmacotherapy of mood disorders. *Annual Review of Clinical Psychology, 4,* 53–91.

Thase, M. E., & Sloan D. M. E. (2006). Venlafaxine. In A. F. Schatzberg & C. B. Nemeroff (Eds.), *Essentials of clinical psychopharmacology.* Washington, DC: American Psychological Association.

Thatcher, P. V. (2008). University students and the "all-nighter": Correlates and patterns of students' engagement in a single night of total sleep deprivation. *Behavioral Sleep Medicine, 6,* 16–31.

Thayer, A., & Lynn, S. J. (2006). Guided imagery and recovered memory therapy: Considerations and cautions. *Journal of Forensic Psychology Practice, 6,* 63–73.

Thayer, R. E. (1996). *The origin of everyday moods.* New York: Oxford University Press.

Theeuwes, J., Belopolsky, A., & Olivers, C. N. L. (2009). Interactions between working memory, attention, and eye movements. *Acta Psychologica, 132,* 106–114.

Thelen, E. & Smith, L. B. (1994). *A dynamics systems approach to the development of cognition and action.* Cambridge, MA: Bradford Books/MIT Press.

Thelen, E. (1995). Motor development: A new synthesis. *American Psychologist, 50,* 79–95.

Thomas, A. J., Kalaria, R. N., & O'Brien, J. T. (2004). Depression and vascular disease: What is the relationship? *Journal of Affective Disorders, 79*(1–3), 81–95.

Thomas, A., & Chess, S. (1977). *Temperament and development.* New York: Brunner/Mazel.

Thomas, A., & Chess, S. (1989). Temperament and personality. In G. A. Kohnstamm, J. E. Bates, & M. K. Rothbart (Eds.), *Temperament in childhood.* New York: Wiley.

Thomas, A., Chess, S., & Birch, H. G. (1970). The origin of personality. *Scientific American, 223*(2), 102–109.

Thomas, D. R. (1992). Discrimination and generalization. In L. R. Squire (Ed.), *Encyclopedia of learning and memory.* New York: Macmillan.

Thomas, M. S. C., & Johnson, M. H. (2008). New advances in understanding sensitive periods in brain development. *Current Directions in Psychological Science, 17,* 1–5.

Thomas, R. M. (2005). *Comparing theories of child development.* Belmont, CA: Wadsworth.

Thompson, J. K., & Stice, E. (2001). Thin-ideal internalization: Mounting evidence for a new risk factor for body-image disturbance and eating pathology. *Current Directions in Psychological Science, 10*(5), 181–183.

Thompson, J. K., Roehrig, M., & Kinder, B. N. (2007). Eating disorders. In M. Hersen, S. M. Turner, & D. C. Beidel (Eds.), *Adult psychopathology and diagnosis.* New York: Wiley.

Thompson, M. M., Zanna, M. P., & Griffin, D. W. (1995). Let's not be indifferent about (attitudinal) ambivalence. In R. E. Petty & J. A. Krosnick (Eds.), *Attitude strength: Antecedents and consequences.* Mahwah, NJ: Erlbaum.

Thompson, R. A. (2008). Early attachment and later development: Familiar questions, new answers. In J. Cassidy & P. R. Shaver (Eds.), *Handbook of attachment: Theory, research, and clinical applications* (2nd ed., pp. 348–365). New York, NY: Guilford Press.

Thompson, R. A., & Nelson, C. A. (2001). Developmental science and the media: Early brain development. *American Psychologist, 56,* 5–15.

Thompson, R. A., Winer, A. C., & Goodwin, R. (2011). The individual child: Temperament, emotion, self, and personality. In M. H. Bornstein & M. E. Lamb (Eds.), *Developmental science: An advanced textbook* (pp. 427–468). New York, NY: Psychology Press.

Thompson, R. F. (1989). A model system approach to memory. In P. R. Solomon, G. R. Goethals, C. M. Kelley, & B. R. Stephens (Eds.), *Memory: Interdisciplinary approaches*. New York: Springer-Verlag.

Thompson, R. F. (1992). Memory. *Current Opinion in Neurobiology, 2,* 203–208.

Thompson, R. F. (2005). In search of memory traces. *Annual Review of Psychology, 56,* 1–23.

Thompson, R. F., & Zola, S. M. (2003). In D. K. Freedheim (Ed.), *Handbook of psychology* (Vol. 2): New York: Wiley.

Thompson, W. F. & Quinto, L. (in press). Music and emotion: Psychological considerations. In P. Goldie and E. Schellekens (Eds.), *Philosophy and Aesthetic Psychology*. New York: Oxford University Press.

Thompson, W. F. (2009). *Music, thought, and feeling: Understanding the psychology of music.* New York: Oxford University Press.

Thompson, W. F., Graham, P., & Russo, F. A. (2005). Seeing music performance: Visual influences on perception and experience. *Semiotical, 156,* 177–201.

Thompson, W. F., Schellenberg, E. G., & Husain, G. (2001). Arousal, mood and the Mozart effect. *Psychological Science, 12,* 248–251.

Thoresen, C. E., Harris, A. H. S., & Luskin, F. (1999). Forgiveness and health: An unanswered question. In M. E. McCullough, K. I. Pargament & C. E. Thoresen (Eds.), *Forgiveness: Theory, research, and practice* (pp. 254–280). New York: Guilford.

Thorndike, E. L. (1913). *Educational psychology: The psychology of learning* (Vol. 2). New York: Teachers College.

Thorndyke, P. W., & Hayes-Roth, B. (1979). The use of schemata in the acquisition and transfer of knowledge. *Cognitive Psychology, 11,* 83–106.

Thorne, B. M., & Henley, T. B. (1997). *Connections in the history and systems of psychology.* Boston: Houghton Mifflin.

Thornhill, R. (1976). Sexual selection and nuptial feeding behavior in *Bittacus apicalis* (Insecta: Mecoptera). *American Naturalist, 110,* 529–548.

Thornicroft, G. (2006). *Shunned: Discrimination against people with mental illness.* New York, NY: Oxford University Press.

Thornton, B., & Moore, S. (1993). Physical attractiveness contrast effect: Implications for self-esteem and evaluations of the social self. *Personality and Social Psychology Bulletin, 19,* 474–480.

Thornton, L. M., Mazzeo, S. E., & Bulik, C. M. (2011). The heritability of eating disorders: Methods and current findings. In R. H. Adan & W. H. Kaye (Eds.), *Behavioral neurobiology of eating disorders* (pp. 141–156). New York, NY: Springer-Verlag.

Thorpe, S. J., & Salkovskis, P. M. (1995). Phobia beliefs: Do cognitive factors play a role in specific phobias? *Behavioral Research and Therapy, 33,* 805–816.

Thorpy, M., & Yager, J. (2001). *Sleeping well: The sourcebook for sleep and sleep disorders.* New York: Checkmark Books.

3D FLIC launches into orbit at Cinespace. (2010). Yfile. Retrieved May 5, 2010, from http://www.yorku.ca/yfile/archive/index.asp?Article=14787.

Thun, M. J., Apicella, L. F., & Henley, S. J. (2000). Smoking vs. other risk factors as the cause of smoking-attributable deaths: Confounding in the courtroom. *Journal of the American Medical Association, 284,* 706–712.

Thurstone, L. L. (1931a). The measurement of social attitudes. *Journal of Abnormal and Social Psychology, 26,* 249–269.

Thurstone, L. L. (1931b). Multiple factor analysis. *Psychological Review, 38,* 406–427.

Thurstone, L. L. (1938). *Primary mental abilities* (Psychometric Monographs No. 1). Chicago: University of Chicago Press.

Thurstone, L. L. (1955). *The differential growth of mental abilities* (Psychometric Laboratory Rep. No. 14). Chapel Hill: University of North Carolina.

Tice, D. M., Bratslavsky, E., & Baumeister, R. F. (2001). Emotional distress regulation takes precedence over impulse control: If you feel bad, do it! *Journal of Personality and Social Psychology, 80,* 53–67.

Till, B. D., & Priluck, R. L. (2000). Stimulus generalization in classical conditioning: An initial investigation and extension. *Psychology and Marketing, 17,* 55–72.

Time. (1971, September 20). Behavior: A Skinnerian innovation: Baby in a box.

Tindale, R. S., Kameda, T., & Hinsz, V. B. (2003). Group decision making. In M. A. Hogg & J. Cooper (Eds.), *The Sage handbook of social psychology.* Thousand Oaks, CA: Sage.

Tippman-Peikert, M., Morgenthaler, T. I., Boeve, B. F., & Silber, M. H. (2006). REM sleep behavior disorder and REM-related parasomnias. In T. Lee- Chiong (Ed.), *Sleep: A comprehensive handbook* (pp. 435–442). Hoboken, NJ: Wiley-Liss.

Titchener, E. G. (1919). John Wallace Baird. *Science, 49,* 393–394.

Titsworth, B. S., & Kiewra, K. A. (2004). Spoken organizational lecture cues and student notetaking as facilitators of student learning. *Contemporary Educational Psychology, 29,* 447–461.

Tiwari, S. K., & Wang, J. L. (2008). Ethnic differences in mental health service use among White, Chinese, South Asian, and South East Asian populations living in Canada. *Social Psychiatry and Psychiatric Epidemiology, 43,* 866–871.

Todd, J. T., & Morris, E. K. (1992). Case histories in the great power of steady misrepresentation. *American Psychologist, 47,* 1441–1453.

Todd, M. (2003). Characteristics associated with superstitious behavior in track and field athletes: Are there NCAA divisional differences? *Journal of Sport Behavior, 26,* 168–178.

Todd, P. M., & Gigerenzer, G. (2000). Precis of simple heuristics that make us smart. *Behavioral & Brain Sciences, 23,* 727–780.

Todd, P. M., & Gigerenzer, G. (2007). Environments that make us smart: Ecological rationality. *Current Directions in Psychological Science, 16,* 167–171.

Todes, D. P. (1997). From the machine to the ghost within: Pavlov's transition from digestive physiology to conditional reflexes. *American Psychologist, 52,* 947–955.

Toga, A. W., Thompson, P. M., & Sowell, E. R. (2006). Mapping brain maturation. *Trends in Neurosciences, 29,* 148–159.

Tolman, C. (1999). Introduction. *History and Philosophy of Psychology Bulletin, 11,* 3.

Tolman, D. L., & Diamond, L. M. (2001). Desegregating sexuality research: Cultural and biological perspectives on gender and desire. *Annual Review of Sex Research, 12,* 33–74.

Tolman, E. C. (1922). A new formula for behaviorism. *Psychological Review, 29,* 44–53.

Tolman, E. C. (1932). *Purposive behavior in animals and men.* New York: Appleton-Century-Crofts.

Tolman, E. C. (1938). The determiners of behavior at a choice point. *Psychological Review, 45,* 1–41.

Tolman, E. C. (1948). Cognitive maps in rats and men. *Psychological Review, 55,* 189–208.

Tolman, E. C., & Honzik, C. H. (1930). Introduction and removal of reward, and maze performance in rats. *University of California Publications in Psychology, 4,* 257–275.

Tom, S. M., Fox, C. R., Trepel, C., & Poldrack, R. A. (2007). The neural basis of loss aversion in decision-making under risk. *Science, 315,* 515–518.

Tomkins, S. S. (1980). Affect as amplification: Some modifications in theory. In R. Plutchik & H. Kellerman (Eds.), *Emotion: Theory, research and experience* (Vol. 1). New York: Academic Press.

Tomkins, S. S. (1991). *Affect, imagery, consciousness: 3. Anger and fear.* New York: Springer-Verlag.

Tooby, J., & Cosmides, L. (1989). Evolutionary psychology and the generation of culture: Part 1. Theoretical considerations. *Ethology and Sociobiology, 10,* 29–49.

Tooby, J., & Cosmides, L. (2005). Conceptual foundations of evolutionary psychology. In D. M. Buss (Ed.), *The handbook of evolutionary psychology.* New York: Wiley.

Toplak, M. E., West, R. F., & Stanovich, K. E. (in press). The Cognitive Reflection Test as a predictor of performance on heuristics and biases tasks. *Memory & Cognition.*

Torgersen, S. (1979). The nature and origin of common phobic fears. *British Journal of Psychiatry, 119,* 343–351.

Torgersen, S. (1983). Genetic factors in anxiety disorders. *Archives of General Psychiatry, 40,* 1085–1089.

Tormala, Z. L., & Petty, R. E. (2002). What doesn't kill me makes me stronger: The effects of resisting persuasion on attitude certainty. *Journal of Personality and Social Psychology, 83,* 1298–1313.

Toronto Montessori Institute. (n.d.). *Montessori Education.* Retrieved June 22, 2008, from http://www.tmi.edu/motion.asp?menuid=4687&lgid=1&siteid=100344.

Torrance, E. P. (1962). *Guiding creative talent.* Englewood Cliffs, NJ: Prentice-Hall.

Torres, L., & Saunders, S. M. (2009). Evaluation of psychotherapy. In B. J. Sadock, V. A. Sadock, & P. Ruiz (Eds.), *Kaplan & Sadock's comprehensive textbook of psychiatry* (9th ed.). Philadelphia, PA: Lippincott, Williams & Wilkins.

Torrey, E. F. (1992). *Freudian fraud: The malignant effect of Freud's theory on American thought and culture.* New York: Harper Perennial.

Torrey, E. F. (1996). *Out of the shadows.* New York: Wiley.

Toufexis, A. (1990, December 17). Drowsy America. *Time,* pp. 78–85.

Tov, W., & Diener, E. (2007). Culture and subjective well-being. In S. Kitayama & D. Cohen (Eds.), *Handbook of cultural psychology* (pp. 691–713). New York: Guilford.

Tower, R. B., & Krasner, M. (2006). Marital closeness, autonomy, mastery, and depressive symptoms in a U.S. Internet sample. *Personal Relationships, 13,* 429–449.

Toyota, H., & Kikuchi, Y. (2004). Self-generated elaboration and spacing effects on incidental memory. *Perceptual and Motor Skills, 99*, 1193–1200.

Toyota, H., & Kikuchi, Y. (2005). Encoding richness of self-generated elaboration and spacing effects on incidental memory. *Perceptual and Motor Skills, 101*, 621–627.

Tozzi, F., Thornton, L. M., Klump, K. L., Fichter, M. M., Halmi, K. A., Kaplan, A. S., et al. (2005). Symptom fluctuation in eating disorders: Correlates of diagnostic crossover. *American Journal of Psychiatry, 162*, 732–740.

Tracy, J. L., & Robins, R. W. (2008). The automaticity of emotion recognition. *Emotion, 8*, 81–95.

Trafimow, D., & Rice, S. (2009). A test of the null hypothesis significance testing procedure correlation argument. *The Journal of General Psychology, 36*, 261–269.

Trainor, L. J. (2005). Are there critical periods for musical development? *Developmental Psychobiology, 46*, 262–278.

Travis, F. (2001). Autonomic and EEG patterns distinguish transcending from other experiences during Transcendental Meditation practice. *International Journal of Psychophysiology, 42*, 1–9.

Treffert, D. A. (2010). *Islands of genius: The bountiful mind of the autistic, acquired and sudden savant.* London: Kinglsey, Inc.

Treffert, D. A., & Christensen, D. D. (2006, June/July). Inside the mind of a savant. *Scientific American*, 50–55.

Treisman, A. (2009). Attention: Theoretical and psychological perspectives. In M. S. Gazzaniga (Ed.), *The cognitive neurosciences* (4th ed., pp. 189–204). Cambridge, MA: MIT Press.

Treisman, G. J. (1999). AIDS education for psychiatrists. *Primary Psychiatry, 6*(5), 71–73.

Trent University sleep specialist receives $48K grant. Retrieved March 9, 2005, from http://www.trentu.ca/news/pressreleases/o40318csmith2.html.

Trevino, L. (1995). Forward. In T. O'Connor, *The feeling of greatness: The Moe Norman Story.* Toronto: Evelevel Videos Inc.

Triandis, H. C., Ang, S., & Van Dyne, L. (2008). Handbook of cultural intelligence: Theory, measurement and applications. Armonk, NY: M.E. Sharpe.

Triandis, H. C. (1989). Self and social behavior in differing cultural contexts. *Psychological Review, 96*, 269–289.

Triandis, H. C. (1994). *Culture and social behavior.* New York: McGraw-Hill.

Triandis, H. C. (2001). Individualism and collectivism: Past, present, and future. In D. Matsumoto (Ed.), *The handbook of culture and psychology.* New York: Oxford University Press.

Triandis, H. C., Ang, S., & Van Dyne, L. (2008). *Handbook of cultural intelligence: Theory, measurement and applications.* Armonk, NY: M.E. Sharpe.

Triandis, H. C., & Suh, E. M. (2002). Cultural influences on personality. *Annual Review of Psychology, 53*, 133–160.

Trivers, R. L. (1971). The evolution of reciprocal altruism. *Quarterly Review of Biology, 46*, 35–57.

Trivers, R. L. (1972). Parental investment and sexual selection. In B. Campbell (Ed.), *Sexual selection and the descent of man.* Chicago: Aldine.

Tronick, E, & Beeghly, M. (2011). Infants' meaning-making and the development of Mental health problems. *American Psychologist, 66*, 107–119.

Trotter, R. J. (1986, September). The three faces of love. *Psychology Today,* pp. 46–54.

Troyer, A. K., & Rich, J. B. (2002). Psychometric properties of a new metamemory questionnaire for older adults. *The Journals of Gerontology Series B: Psychological Sciences and Social Sciences, 57*, 19–27.

Tsai , L. Y. & Ghaziuddin, M. (1992). Biomedical research in autism. In D. E. Berkell (Ed.), *Autism: Identification, education, and treatment* (pp. 53–74). Hillsdale, NJ: Erlbaum.

Tsai, J. L., Butcher, J. N., Muñoz, R. F., & Vitousek, K. (2001). Culture, ethnicity, and psychopathology. In P. B. Sutker & H. E. Adams (Eds.), *Comprehensive handbook of psychopathology.* New York: Kluwer Academic/Plenum.

Tsankova, N., Renthal, W., Kumar, A., & Nestler, E. J. (2007). Epigenetic regulation in psychiatric disorders. *Nature Reviews Neuroscience, 8*(5), 355–367.

Tseng, W. S. (2009). Culture-related specific psychiatric syndromes. In M. C. Gelder, N. C. Andreasen, J. J. López-Ibor, Jr., & J. R. Geddes (Eds.), *New Oxford textbook of psychiatry* (2nd ed., Vol. 1). New York, NY: Oxford University Press.

Tsigos, C., Kyrou, I., & Chrousos, G. P. (2005). Stress, endocrine manifestations and diseases. In C. L. Cooper (Ed.), *Handbook of stress medicine and health.* Boca Raton, FL: CRC Press.

Tucker, A. M., Dinges, D. F., & Van Dongen, H. P. A. (2007). Trait interindividual differences in the sleep physiology of healthy young adults. *Journal of Sleep Research, 16*, 170–180.

Tuckey, M. R., & Brewer, N. (2003). The influence of schemas, stimulus ambiguity, and interview schedule on eyewitness memory over time. *Journal of Experimental Psychology: Applied, 9*, 101–118.

Tugade, M. M., & Fredrickson, B. L. (2004). Resilient individuals use positive emotions to bounce back from negative emotional experiences. *Journal of Personality and Social Psychology, 86*, 320–333.

Tulving, E. (1972). Episodic and semantic memory. In E. Tulving & W. Donaldson (Eds.), *Organization of memory* (pp. 381–403). New York: Academic Press.

Tulving, E. (1983). *Elements of episodic memory.* Oxford, UK: Oxford University Press.

Tulving, E. (1986). What kind of a hypothesis is the distinction between episodic and semantic memory? *Journal of Experimental Psychology: Learning, Memory and Cognition, 12*, 307–311.

Tulving, E. (1993). What is episodic memory? *Current Directions in Psychological Science, 2*(3), 67–70.

Tulving, E. (2001). Episodic memory and common sense: How far apart? *Philosophical Transactions of the Royal Society of London, 356*, 1505–1515.

Tulving, E. (2001). Origin of autonoesis in episodic memory. In H. L. Roediger III, J. S. Nairne, I. Neath, & A. M. Surprenant (Eds.), *The nature of remembering: Essays in honor of Robert G. Crowder* (pp. 17–34). Washington, DC: American Psychological Association.

Tulving, E. (2002). Episodic memory: From mind to brain. *Annual Review of Psychology, 53*, 1–25.

Tulving, E. (2005). Episodic memory and autonoesis: Uniquely human? In H. S. Terrance & J. Metcalfe (Eds.), *The missing link in cognition: Origins of self-reflective consciousness* (pp. 3–36). Oxford, UK: Oxford University Press.

Tulving, E., & Kim, A. (2007). The medium and the message of mental time travel. *Behavior and Brain Sciences, 30*, 334–335.

Tulving, E., & Pearlstone, Z. (1966). Availability and accessibility of information in memory for words. *Journal of Verbal Learning and Verbal Behavior, 5*, 381–391.

Tulving, E., & Schacter, D. L. (1990). Priming and human memory systems. *Science, 247*, 301–306.

Tulving, E., & Thomson, D. M. (1973). Encoding specificity and retrieval processes in episodic memory. *Psychological Review, 80*, 352–373.

Tunnell, K. D. (2005). The Oxycontin epidemic and crime panic in rural Kentucky. *Contemporary Drug Problems, 32*, 225–258.

Turk, D. C. (1994). Perspectives on chronic pain: The role of psychological factors. *Current Directions in Psychological Science, 3*, 45–48.

Turk, D. C., & Okifuji, A. (2003). Pain management. In A. M. Nezu, C. M. Nezu, & P. A. Geller (Eds.), *Handbook of psychology (Vol. 9): Health psychology.* New York: Wiley.

Turkheimer, E. (1998). Heritability and biological explanation. *Psychological Review, 105*, 782–791

Turkkan, J. S. (1989). Classical conditioning: The new hegemony. *Behavioral and Brain Sciences, 12*, 121–179.

Turner, E. H., Matthews, A. M., Linardatos, E., Tell, R. A., & Rosenthal, F. (2008). Selective publication of antidepressant trials and its influence on apparent efficacy. *The New England Journal of Medicine, 358*, 252–260.

Turner, J. C., & Reynolds, K. J. (2001). The social identity perspective in intergroup relations: Theories, themes, and controversies. In R. Brown & S. L. Gaertner (Eds.), *Blackwell handbook of social psychology: Intergroup processes.* Malden, MA: Blackwell.

Turner, J. G., Hogg, M. A., Oakes, P. J., Reicher, S. D., Wetherell, M. S. (1987). *Rediscovering the social group: A self-categorization theory.* Oxford, UK: Basil Blackwell.

Turner, J. R., & Wheaton, B. (1995). Checklist measurement of stressful life events. In S. Cohen, R. C. Kessler, & L. U. Gordon (Eds.), *Measuring stress: A guide for health and social scientists.* New York: Oxford University Press.

Tversky, A. (1972). Elimination by aspects: A theory of choice. *Psychological Review, 79*, 281–299.

Tversky, A., & Kahneman, D. (1971). Belief in the law of small numbers. *Psychological Bulletin, 76*, 105–110.

Tversky, A., & Kahneman, D. (1973). Availability: A heuristic for judging frequency and probability. *Cognitive Psychology, 5*, 207–232.

Tversky, A., & Kahneman, D. (1974). Judgments under uncertainty: Heuristics and biases. *Science, 185*, 1124–1131.

Tversky, A., & Kahneman, D. (1982). Judgment under uncertainty: Heuristics and biases. In D. Kahneman, P. Slovic, & A. Tversky (Eds.), *Judgment under uncertainty: Heuristics and biases.* New York: Cambridge University Press.

Tversky, A., & Kahneman, D. (1983). Extensional versus intuitive reasoning: The conjunction fallacy in probability judgment. *Psychological Review, 90*, 283–315.

Tversky, A., & Kahneman, D. (1988). Rational choice and the framing of decisions. In D. E. Bell, H. Raiffa, & A. Tversky (Eds.), *Decision making: Descriptive, normative, and prescriptive interactions.* New York: Cambridge University Press.

Tversky, A., & Kahneman, D. (1991). Loss aversion in riskless choice: A reference-dependent model. *Quarterly Journal of Economics, 106*, 1039–1061.

Twenge, J. M., & Campbell, W. (2009). *The narcissism epidemic: Living in the age of enlightenment.* New York, NY: Free Press.

Twenge, J. M., & Foster, J. D. (2010). Birth cohort increases in narcissistic personality traits among American college students, 1982–2009. *Social Psychological and Personality Science, 1,* 99–106.

Twenge, J. M., Campbell, W. K., & Foster, C. A. (2003). Parenthood and marital satisfaction: A metaanalytic review. *Journal of Marriage and the Family, 65,* 574–583.

Twenge, J. M., Konrath, S., Foster, J. D., Campbell, W., & Bushman, B. J. (2008). Egos inflating over time: A cross-temporal meta-analysis of the Narcissistic Personality Inventory. *Journal of Personality, 76*(4), 875–902.

Tyrer, P., Coombs, N., Ibrahimi, F., Mathilakath, A., Bajaj, P., Ranger, M., Rao, B., & Din, R. (2007). Critical developments in the assessment of personality disorders. *British Journal of Psychiatry, 90,* 51–59.

U.S. Department of Health and Human Services. (1999). *Mental health: A report of the Surgeon General.* Washington, DC: U.S. Government Printing Office.

Uchida, Y., Kitayama, S., Mesquita, B., Reyes, J. A. S., & Morling, B. (2008). Is perceived emotional support beneficial? Well-being and health in independent and interdependent cultures. *Personality and Social Psychology Bulletin, 34,* 741–754.

Uchino, B. N., & Birmingham, W. (2011). Stress and support processes. In R. J. Contrada & A. Baum (Eds.), *The handbook of stress science: Biology, psychology, and health* (pp. 111–121). New York, NY: Springer Publishing.

Uchino, B. N., Uno, D., & Holt-Lunstad, J. (1999). Social support, physiological processes, and health. *Current Directions in Psychological Science, 8,* 145–148.

Uddin, L. Q., Iacoboni, M., Lange, C., & Keenan, J. P. (2007). The self and social cognition: The role of cortical midline structures and mirror neurons. *Trends in Cognitive Science, 11,* 153–157.

Uleman, J. S., Saribay, S. A., & Gonzalez, C. M. (2007). Spontaneous inferences, implicit impressions, and implicit theories. *Annual Review of Psychology, 59,* 329–360.

Ulman, S. E., et al. (2006). The role of victim–offender relationships in women's sexual assault experiences. *Journal of Interpersonal Violence, 21,* 798–817.

Umbel, V. M., Pearson, B. Z., Fernandez, S. C., & Oller, D. K. (1992). Measuring bilingual children's receptive vocabularies. *Child Development, 63,* 1012–1020.

Umberson, D., Williams, K., Powers, D. A., Chen, M. D., & Campbell, A. M. (2005). As good as it gets? A life course perspective on marital quality. *Social Forces, 84*(1), 493–511.

UNAIDS. (2006). AIDS epidemic update. Retrieved May 2, 2011, from http://data.unaids.org/pub/epireport/2006/2006_epiupdate_en.pdf.

Underwood, B. J. (1961). Ten years of massed practice on distributed practice. *Psychological Review, 68,* 229–247.

Ungerleider, L. G., & Mishkin, N. (1982). Two cortical systems. In D. J. Ingle, M. A. Goodale, & R. J. W. Mansfield (Eds.), *Analysis of visual behavior* (pp. 549–586). Cambridge MA: MIT Press.

Unsworth, N., Heitz, R. P., Schrock, J. C., & Engle, R. W. (2005). An automated version of the operation span task. *Behavior Research Methods, 37,* 498–505.

Updated guidelines for human pluripotent stem cell research. (2007, June 29). Canadian Institutes of Health Research. Retrieved February 4, 2008, from http://www.cihr-irsc.gc.ca/e/34460.html.

Urbszat, D., & Herman, C. P., & Polivy, J. (2002). Eat. Drink, and be merry for tomorrow we diet: Effects of anticipated deprivation on food intake in restrained and unrestrained eaters. *Journal of Abnormal Psychology, 111,* 396–401.

Ursano, A. M., Kartheiser, P. H., & Barnhill, L. (2008). Disorders usually first diagnosed in infancy, childhood, or adolescence. In R. E. Hales, S. C. Yudofsky, & G. O. Gabbard (Eds.), *The American Psychiatric Publishing textbook of psychiatry* (5th ed., pp. 861–920). Arlington, VA: American Psychiatric Publishing.

Ursano, R. J., Sonnenberg, S. M., & Lazar, S. G. (2008). Psychodynamic psychotherapy. In R. E. Hales, S. C. Yudofsky, & G. O. Gabbard (Eds.), *The American Psychiatric Publishing textbook of psychiatry* (pp. 1171–1190). Washington, DC: American Psychiatric Publishing.

Usborne, E., & Taylor, D. M. (in press). The role of cultural identity clarity for self-concept clarity, self-esteem and subjective well-being. *Personality and Social Psychology Bulletin.*

Usborne, E., Lydon, J. E., & Taylor, D. M. (2009). Goals and social relationships: windows into the motivation and well-being of "Street Kids." *Journal of Applied Social Psychology, 39,* 1057–1082.

Väänänen, A. (2010). Psychosocial work environment and risk of ischaemic heart disease in women. *Occupational & Environmental Medicine, 67*(5), 291–292.

Vaillancourt, T., Brittain, H., Bennett, L., Arnocky, S., McDougall, P., Hymel S., et al. (in press). Places to avoid: Populational-based study of students' reports of unsafe and high bullying areas at school. *Canadian Journal of School Psychology.*

Vaillant, G. E. (1994). Ego mechanisms of defense and personality psychopathology. *Journal of Abnormal Psychology, 103,* 44–50.

Valdez, A., Ramirez, C., & Garcia, A. (2003). Adjustment of the sleep–wake cycle to small (1–2 hour) changes in schedule. *Biological' Rhythm Research, 34,* 145–155.

Valenstein, E. S. (1973). *Brain control.* New York: Wiley.

Valli, K., & Revonsuo, A. (2009). Sleep: Dreaming data and theories. In W. P. Banks (Ed.), *Encyclopedia of Consciousness* (pp. 341–356). San Diego, CA: Academic Press.

Vallone, R. P., Griffin, D. W., Lin, S., & Ross, L. (1990). Overconfident prediction of future actions and outcomes by self and others. *Journal of Personality and Social Psychology, 58,* 582–592.

Vallortigara, G., & Rogers, L. J. (2005). Survival with an asymmetrical brain: Advantages and disadvantages of cerebral lateralization. *Behavioral and Brain Sciences, 28*(4), 575–633.

Van Boven, L. (2005). Experientialism, materialism, and the pursuit of happiness. *Review of General Psychology, 9,* 132–142.

Van de Castle, R. L. (1994). *Our dreaming mind.* New York: Ballantine Books.

van den Boom, D. C. (1994). The influence of temperament and mothering on attachment and exploration: An experimental manipulation of sensitive responsiveness among lower-class mothers and irritable infants. *Child Development, 65,* 1457–1477.

van den Bos, K., & Maas, M. (2009). On the psychology of the belief in a just world: Exploring experiential and rationalistic paths to victim blaming. *Personality and Social Psychology Bulletin, 35*(12), 1567–1578.

Van den Eynde, F., Claudino, A. M., Mogg, A., Horrell, L., Stahl, D., Ribeiro, W., et al. (2010). Repetitive transcranial magnetic stimulation reduces cue-induced food craving in bulimic disorders. *Biological Psychiatry, 67*(8), 793–795.

van der Gaag, C., Minderaa, R. B., & Keysers, C. (2007). Facial expressions: What the mirror neuron system can and cannot tell us. *Social Neuoscience, 2,* 179–222.

Van der Hart, O., & Nijenhuis, E. R. S. (2009). Dissociative disorders. In P. H. Blaney & T. Millon (Eds.), *Oxford textbook of psychopathology* (2nd ed., pp. 452–481). New York, NY: Oxford University Press.

van der Post, L. (1975). *Jung and the story of our time.* New York: Vintage Books.

Van der Stigchel, S. (2010). Recent advances in the study of saccade trajectory deviations. *Vison Research, 50,* 1619–1627.

Van Dongen, H. P. A., & Dinges, D. F. (2005). Circadian rhythms in sleepiness, alertness, and performance. In M. H. Kryger, T. Roth, & W. C. Dement (Eds.), *Principles and practice of sleep medicine.* Philadelphia: Elsevier Saunders.

van Eck, M., Nicolson, N. A., & Berkhof, J. (1998). Effects of stressful daily events on mood states: Relationship to global perceived stress. *Journal of Personality and Social Psychology, 75,* 1572–1585.

van Griensven, F., Chakkraband, M. L. S., Thienkrua, W., Pengjuntr, W., Cardozo, B. L., & Tantipiwatanaskul, P. et al. (2007). Mental health problems among adults in tsunami-affected areas in Southern Thailand. *Journal of the American Medical Association, 296,* 537–548.

Van Hoesen, G. W., Morecraft, R. J., & Semendeferi, K. (1996). Functional neuroanatomy of the limbic system and prefrontal cortex. In B. S. Fogel, R. B. Schiffer, & S. M. Rao (Eds), *Neuropsychiatry.* Baltimore: Williams & Wilkins.

van IJzendoorn, M. H., & Bakermans-Kranenburg, M. J. (2004). Maternal sensitivity and infant temperament in the formation of attachment. In G. Bremner & A. Slater (Eds.), *Theories of infant development* (pp. 233–257). Malden, MA: Blackwell Publishing.

van IJzendoorn, M. H., & Juffer, F. (2005). Adoption is a successful natural intervention enhancing adopted children's IQ and school performance. *Current Directions in Psychological Science, 14,* 326–330.

van IJzendoorn, M. H., & Kroonenberg, P. M. (1988). Cross-cultural patterns of attachment: A meta-analysis of the Strange Situation. *Child Development, 59,* 147–156.

van IJzendoorn, M. H., & Sagi-Schwartz, A. (2008). Cross-cultural patterns of attachment: Universal and contextual dimensions. In J. Cassidy & P. R. Shaver (Eds.), *Handbook of attachment: Theory, research, and clinical applications* (2nd ed., pp. 3–22). New York, NY: Guilford Press.

Van Kammen, D. P., Hurford, I., & Marder, S. R. (2009). First-generation antipsychotics. In B. J. Sadock, V. A. Sadock, & P. Ruiz (Eds.), *Kaplan & Sadock's comprehensive textbook of psychiatry* (pp. 3105–3126). Philadelphia, PA: Lippincott, Williams & Wilkins.

van Knippenberg, D., & Shippers, M. C. (2007). Work group diversity. *Annual Review of Psychology, 58,* 515–541.

van Leeuwen, M. L., & Macrae, C. N. (2004). Is beautiful always good? Implicit benefits of facial attractiveness. *Social Cognition, 22,* 637–649.

Vandenbroucke, J. P., & Psaty, B. M. (2008). Benefits and risks of drug treatments: How to combine the best evidence on benefits with the best data about adverse effects. *Journal of the American Medical Association, 300*(20), 2417–2419.

Vandereycken, W. (2002). History of anorexia nervosa and bulimia nervosa. In C. G. Fairburn, & K. D. Brownell (Eds.), *Eating disorders and obesity*. New York: Guilford.

Vanier Institute of the Family. (2005). *Family Facts*. Retrieved June 20, 2005, from http://www.vifamily.ca/library/facts/facts/html.

Varnum, M. W., Grossmann, I., Kitayama, S., & Nisbett, R. E. (2010). The origin of cultural differences in cognition: The social orientation hypothesis. *Current Directions in Psychological Science, 19*(1), 9–13.

Vartanian, L. R., Herman, C., & Wansink, B. (2008). Are we aware of the external factors that influence our food intake? *Health Psychology, 27*(5), 533–538.

Vasquez, N. A., & Buehler, R. (2007). Seeing future success: Does imagery perspective influence achievement motivation? *Personality and Social Psychology Bulletin, 33*, 1392–1405.

Vazire, S., & Funder, D. C. (2006). Impulsivity and the self-defeating behavior of narcissists. *Personality and Social Psychology Review, 10*(2), 154–165.

Veasey, S. C. (2009). Sleep apnea. In R. Stickgold & M. P. Walker (Eds.), *The neuroscience of sleep* (pp. 263–269). San Diego, CA: Academic Press.

Veenhof, B., & Timusk, P. (2009). Online activities of Canadian boomers and seniors. Canadian Social Trends (Statistics Canada), August 6, 2009. Retrieved June 20, 2011, from http://www.statcan.gc.ca/pub/11-008-x/2009002/article/10910-eng.pdf.

Veenhoven, R. (1993). *Happiness in nations*. Rotterdam, Netherlands: Risbo.

Veenhoven, R. (2008). Healthy happiness: Effects of happiness on physical health and the consequences for preventive health care. *Journal of Happiness Studies, 9*(3), 449–469.

Veer, R. van der. (2007). *Lev Vygotsky*. London: Continuum Books.

Vega, V., & Malamuth, N. M. (2007). Predicting sexual aggression: The role of pornography in the context of general and specific risk factors. *Aggressive Behavior, 33*, 104–117.

Venn, A., & Britton, J. (2007). Exposure to secondhand smoke and biomarkers of cardiovascular disease risk in never-smoking adults. *Circulation, 115*(8), 990–995.

Verhaeghen, P. (2011). Aging and executive control: Reports of a demise greatly exaggerated. *Psychological Science, 20*, 174–180.

Verhaeghen, P., & Salthouse, T. A. (1997). Meta-analyses of age-cognition relations in adulthood: Estimates of linear and nonlinear age effects and structural models. *Psychological Bulletin, 122*, 231–249.

Verheul, R. (2005). Clinical utility for dimensional models of personality pathology. *Journal of Personality Disorders, 19*, 283–302.

Vermeeren, A. (2004). Residual effects of hypnotics: Epidemiology and clinical implications. *CNS Drugs, 18*(5), 297–328.

Vernberg, E. M., La Greca, A. M., Silverman, W. K., & Prinstein, M. J. (1996). Prediction of posttraumatic stress symptoms in children after Hurricane Andrew. *Journal of Abnormal Psychology, 105*, 237–248.

Vernon, P. A., Villani, V. C., Vickers, L. C., & Harris, J. A. (2008). A behavioral genetic investigation of the Dark Triad and the Big 5. *Personality and Individual Differences, 44*, 445–452.

Vernon, P. A., Wickett, J. C., Bazana, P. G., & Stelmack, R. M. (2000). The neuropsychology and psychophysiology of human intelligence. In R. J. Sternberg (Ed.), *Handbook of intelligence* (pp. 245–266). Cambridge, MA: Cambridge University Press.

Verschuere, B., Crombez, G., Degroote, T. & Rosseel, Y. (2009). Detecting concealed information with reaction times: Validity and comparison with the polygraph. *Applied Cognitive Psychology, 23*, 1–11.

Verschuere, B., Prati, V., & De Houwer, J. (2009). Cheating the lie detector: Faking in the Autobiographical IAT. *Psychological Science, 20*, 410–413.

Vgontzas, A. N., Liao, D., Bixler, E. O., Chrousos, G. P., & Vela-Bueno, A. (2009). Insomnia with objective short sleep duration is associated with a high risk for hypertension. *Sleep: Journal of Sleep and Sleep Disorders Research, 32*, 491–497.

Victoroff, J. (2005). Central nervous system changes with normal aging. In B. J. Sadock & V. A. Sadock (Eds.), *Kaplan & Sadock's comprehensive textbook of psychiatry*. Philadelphia: Lippincott Williams & Wilkins.

Vidal, J., & Chamizo, V. D. (2009). Taste-aversion conditioning, but not immunosuppression conditioning, occurs under partial water deprivation. *The Journal of General Psychology, 36*, 71–89.

Videbech, P. (2006). Hippocampus and unipolar depression. *Directions in Psychiatry, 26*, 183–194.

Videbech, P., & Ravnkilde, B. (2004). Hippocampal volume and depression: A meta-analysis of MRI studies. *American Journal of Psychiatry, 161*, 1957–1966.

Vierck, C. (1978). Somatosensory system. In R. B. Masterston (Ed.), *Handbook of sensory neurobiology*. New York: Plenum.

Viglione, D. J., & Rivera, B. (2003). Assessing personality and psychopathology with projective methods. In J. R. Graham & J. A. Naglieri (Eds.), *Handbook of psychology (Vol. 10): Assessment psychology*. New York: Wiley.

Vihman, M. M. (1985). Language differentiation by the bilingual infant. *Journal of Child Language, 12*, 297–324.

Vineis, P. (2005). Environmental tobacco smoke and risk of respiratory cancer and chronic obstructive pulmonary disease in former smokers and never smokers in the EPIC prospective study. *British Medical Journal, 330*(7486), 277–280.

Vinogradov, S., Cox. P. D., & Yalom, I. D. (2003). Group therapy. In R. E. Hales & S. C. Yudofsky (Eds.), *Textbook of clinical psychiatry*. Washington, DC: American Psychiatric Publishing.

Virk, M. (2009). *Reena: A father's story*. Toronto, ON; Heritage House Publishing Co.

Vitiello, M. V. (2009). Recent advances in understanding sleep and sleep disturbances in older adults: Growing older does not mean sleeping poorly. *Current Directions in Psychological Science, 18*(6), 316–320.

Vogel, I., Brug, J., Hosli, E. J., van der Ploeg, C. P. B., & Raat, H. (2008). MP3 players and hearing loss: Adolescents' perceptions of loud music and hearing conservation. *Journal of Pediatrics, 152*(3), 400–404.

Vogel, I., Brug, J., van der Ploeg, C. P. B., & Raat, H. (2007). Young people's exposure to loud music: A summary of the literature. *American Journal of Preventative Medicine, 33*(2), 124–133.

Vohs, K. D., Baumeister, R. F., Schmeichel, B. J., Twenge, J. M., Nelson, N. M., & Tice, D. M. (2008). Making choices impairs subsequent self-control: A limited-resource account of decision making, self-regulation, and active initiative. *Journal of Personality and Social Psychology, 94*(5), 883–898.

Vokey, J. R., & Read, J. D. (1985). Subliminal messages: Between the devil and the media. *American Psychologist, 40*, 1231–1239.

Volkmar, F. R. & Wiesner, E. A. (2009). *A practical guide to autism: What every parent, family member, and teacher needs to know*. Hoboken, NJ: John Wiley and Sons.

Volkow, N. D., Fowler, J. S., & Wang, G. J. (2004). The addicted human brain viewed in the light of imaging studies: Brain circuits and treatment strategies. *Neuropharmacology, 47*, 3–13.

von Helmholtz, H. (1852). On the theory of compound colours. *Philosophical Magazine*, Serial 4, 4, 519–535.

von Károlyi, C., & Winner, E. (2005). Extreme giftedness. In R. J. Sternberg & J. E. Davidson (Eds.), *Conceptions of giftedness*. New York: Cambridge University Press.

Van Swol, L. M. (2009). The effects of suspicion and advisor motives on confidence and advice utilization. *Communication Research, 36*, 857–873.

Vouloumanos, A., & Werker, J. (2004). Tuned to signal: The privileged status of speech for young infants. *Developmental Science, 7*, 270–276.

Voyer, D., Bowes, A., & Soraggi, M. (2009). Response procedure and laterality effects in emotion recognition: Implications for models of dichotic listening. *Neuropsychologia, 47*, 23–29.

Voyer, D. (1996). On the magnitude of laterality effects and sex differences in functional lateralities. *Laterality, 1*, 51–83.

Voyer, D., Nolan, C., & Voyer, S. (2000). The relation between experience and spatial performance in men and women. *Sex Roles, 43*, 891–915.

Vygotsky, L. S. (1934/1962). *Thought and language*. E. Hanfmann, & G. Vakar (Trans). Cambridge, MA: MIT Press.

Vyse, S. A. (1997). *Believing in magic: The psychology of superstition*. New York, NY: Oxford University Press.

Vyse, S. A. (2000). *Believing in magic: The psychology of superstition*. New York, NY: Oxford University Press.

Vythilingam, M., Shen, J., Drevets, W. C., & Innis, R. B. (2005). Nuclear magnetic resonance imaging: Basic principles and recent findings in neuropsychiatric disorders. In B. J. Sadock & V. A. Sadock (Eds.), *Kaplan & Sadock's comprehensive textbook of psychiatry*. Philadelphia: Lippincott Williams & Wilkins.

Waage, S., Moen, B., Pallesen, S., Eriksen, H. R., Ursin, H., Åkerstedt, T., & Bjorvatn, B. (2009). Shift work disorder among oil rig workers in the North Sea. *Sleep: Journal of Sleep and Sleep Disorders Research, 32*(4), 558–565.

Wachtel, P. L. (1977). *Psychoanalysis and behavior therapy: Toward an integration*. New York: Basic Books.

Wachtel, P. L. (1991). From eclecticism to synthesis: Toward a more seamless psychotherapeutic integration. *Journal of Psychotherapy Integration, 1*, 43–54.

Wadlinger, H. A., & Isaacowitz, D. M. (2011) Fixing our focus: Training attention to regulate emotion. *Personality and Social Psychology Review, 15*, 75–102.

Wager, T. D., Hernandez, L., & Lindquist, M. A. (2009). Essentials of functional neuroimaging. In G. G. Bernston & J. T. Cacioppo (Eds.), *Handbook of neuroscience for the behavioral sciences* (Vol. 1, pp. 152–197). New York, NY: Wiley.

Wagner, H. (1989). The physiological differentiation of emotions. In H. Wagner & A. Manstead (Eds.), *Handbook of social psychophysiology*. New York: Wiley.

Wagner, U., Gais, H., Haider, H., Verleger, R., & Born, J. (2004). Sleep inspires insight. *Nature, 427,* 352–355.

Wagstaff, G. F., David, D., Kirsch, I., & Lynn, S. J. (2010). The cognitive-behavioral model of hypnotherapy. In S. J. Lynn, J. W. Rhue, & I. Kirsch (Eds.), *Handbook of clinical hypnosis* (2nd ed., pp. 179–208). Washington, DC: American Psychological Association.

Wahlsten, D. (1997a). Leilani Muir versus the Philosopher King: Eugenics on trial in Alberta. *Genetica, 20,* 185–198.

Wahlsten, D. (1997b). The malleability of intelligence is not constrained by heritability. In B. Devlin, S. E. Fienberg, D. P. Resnick, & K. Roeder (Eds.), *Intelligence, genes, and success: Scientists respond to The Bell Curve.* New York: Springer-Verlag.

Wahlsten, D. (1999). The eugenics of John M. MacEachran warrant revocation of honours. *History of Psychology and Philosophy Bulletin, 10,* 22–25.

Wai, J., Cacchio, M., Putallaz, M., & Makel, M. C. (2010). Sex differences in the right tail of cognitive abilities: A 30-year examination. *Intelligence, 38*(4), 412–423.

Wakefield, J. C. (1999b). The measurement of mental disorder. In A. V. Horvitz & T. L. Scheid (Eds.), *A handbook for the study of mental health: Social contexts, theories, and systems.* New York: Cambridge University Press.

Wakefield, J. C., & Spitzer, R. L. (2002). Lowered estimates—But of what? *Archives of General Psychiatry, 59*(2), 129–130.

Wakimoto, R. (2011). Reconstruction of the subjective temporal distance of past interpersonal experiences after mortality salience. *Personality and Social Psychology Bulletin, 37,* 687–700.

Wald, G. (1964). The receptors of human color vision. *Science, 145,* 1007–1017.

Waldman, I. D., & Rhee, S. H. (2006). Genetic and environmental influences on psychopathy and antisocial behavior. In C. J. Patrick (Ed.), *Handbook of Psychopathy.* New York: Guilford.

Waldrop, D., Lightsey, O. R., Ethington, C. A., Woemmel, C. A., & Coke, A. L. (2001). Self-efficacy, optimism, health competence, and recovery from orthopedic surgery. *Journal of Counseling Psychology, 48,* 233–238.

Walker, E., & Tessner, K. (2008). Schizophrenia. *Perspectives on Psychological Science, 3,* 30–37.

Walker, E., Kestler, L., Bollini, A., & Hochman, K. M. (2004). Schizophrenia: Etiology and course. *Annual Review of Psychology, 55,* 401–430.

Walker, E., Mittal, V., & Tessner, K. (2008). Stress and the hypothalamic pituitary adrenal axis in the developmental course of schizophrenia. *Annual Review of Clinical Psychology, 4,* 189–216.

Walker, L. J. (1988). The development of moral reasoning. In R. Vasta (Ed.), *Annals of child development* (Vol. 5). Greenwich, CT: JAI Press.

Walker, L. J. (1989). A longitudinal study of moral reasoning. *Child Development, 60,* 157–166.

Walker, L. J. (2007). Progress and prospects in the psychology of moral development. In G. W. Ladd (Ed.), *Appraising the human developmental sciences: Essays in honor of Merrill-Palmer Quarterly* (pp. 226–237). Detroit: Wayne State University Press.

Walker, L. J., & Taylor, J. H. (1991). Strange transitions in moral reasoning: A longitudinal study of developmental processes. *Developmental Psychology, 27,* 330–337.

Walker, M. P. (2009). Sleep-dependent memory processing. In R. Stickgold & M. P. Walker (Eds.), *The neuroscience of sleep* (pp. 230–240). San Diego, CA: Academic Press.

Walker, M. P., & Stickgold, R. (2004). Sleep-dependent learning and memory consolidation. *Neuron, 44,* 121–133.

Walker, M. P., Brakefield, T., Morgan, A., Hobson, J. A., & Stickgold, R. (2002). Practice with sleep makes perfect: Sleep dependent motor skill learning. *Neuron, 35,* 205–211.

Walker, M. P., & Stickgold, R. (2006). Sleep, memory, and plasticity. *Annual Review of Psychology, 57,* 139–166.

Walker, M. P., & van der Helm, E. (2009). Overnight therapy? The role of sleep in emotional brain processing. *Psychological Bulletin, 135,* 731–748.

Wallace, A. (1986). *The prodigy.* New York: E. P. Dutton.

Wallace, B., & Fisher, L. E. (1999). *Consciousness and behavior.* Boston: Allyn & Bacon.

Wallace, D. S., Paulson, R. M., Lord, C. G., & Bond, C. F., Jr. (2005). Which behaviors do attitudes predict? Meta-analyzing the effects of social pressure and perceived difficulty. *Review of General Psychology, 9,* 214–227.

Wallace, H. M., Baumeister, R. F., & Vohs, K. D. (2005). Audience support and choking under pressure: A home disadvantage? *Journal of Sports Sciences, 23,* 429–438.

Wallbott, H. G., & Scherer, K. R. (1988). How universal and specific is emotional experience? Evidence from 27 countries. In K. R. Scherer (Ed.), *Facets of emotions.* Hillsdale, NJ: Erlbaum.

Wallman, J. (1992). *Aping language.* Cambridge, England: Cambridge University Press.

Wallner, B., & Machatschke, I. H. (2009). The evolution of violence in men: The function of central cholesterol and serotonin. *Progress in Neuro-Psychopharmacology & Biological Psychiatry, 33*(3), 391–397.

Walsh, B. T., Seidman, S. N., Sysko, R., & Gould, M. (2002). Placebo response studies of major depression: Variable, substantial and growing. *Journal of the American Medical Association, 287,* 1840–1847.

Walsh, J. K., Dement, W. C., & Dinges, D. F. (2005). Sleep medicine, public policy, and public health. In M. H. Kryger, T. Roth, & W. C. Dement (Eds.). *Principles and practice of sleep medicine.* Philadelphia: Elsevier Saunders.

Walsh, M., Duffy, J., & Gallagher-Duffy, J. (2007). A more accurate approach to measuring the prevalence of sexual harassment among high school students. *Canadian Journal of Behavioural Science, 39,* 110–118.

Walsh, R., & Shapiro, S. L. (2006). The meeting of meditative disciplines and Western psychology: A mutually enriching dialogue. *American Psychologist, 61,* 227–239.

Walter, C. A. (2000). The psychological meaning of menopause: Women's experiences. *Journal of Women and Aging, 12*(3–4), 117–131.

Walter, T., & Siebert, A. (1990). *Student success: How to succeed in college and still have time for your friends.* Fort Worth: Holt, Rinehart & Winston.

Walther, E., & Grigoriadis, S. (2003). Why sad people like shoes better: The influence of mood on the evaluative conditioning of consumer attitudes. *Psychology & Marketing, 10,* 755–775.

Walther, E., & Langer, T. (2008). Attitude formation and change through association: An evaluative conditioning account. In W. D. Crano, & R. Prislin (Eds.), *Attitudes and attitude change* (pp. 61–84). New York, NY: Psychology Press.

Walther, E., Nagengast, B., & Trasselli, C. (2005). Evaluative conditioning in social psychology: Facts and speculations. *Cognition and Emotion, 19*(2), 175–196.

Walton, G. M., & Cohen, G. L. (2007). A question of belonging: Race, social fit, and achievement. *Journal of Personality and Social Psychology, 92,* 82–96.

Walton, G. M., & Spencer, S. J. (2009). Latent ability: Grades and test scores systematically underestimate the intellectual ability of negatively stereotyped students. *Psychological Science, 20*(9), 1132–1139.

Walton, K. G., Fields, J. Z., Levitsky, D. K., Harris, D. A., Pugh, N. D., & Schneider, R. H. (2004). Lowering cortisol and CVD risk in postmenopausal women: A pilot study using Transcendental Meditation program. In R. Yehuda, & B. McEwen (Eds.), *Biobehavioral stress response: Protective and damaging effects* (pp. 211–215). New York, NY: Annals of the New York Academy of Sciences.

Wampold, B. E. (2001). *The great psychotherapy debate.* Mahwah, NJ: Erlbaum.

Wang, J. T., Young, G. B., Connolly, J. F. (2004). Prognostic value of evoke responses and event-related brain potentials in coma. *Canadian Journal of Neurological Sciences, 31,* 438–450.

Wang, M., Henkens, K,. & von Solinge, H. (2011). Retirement adjustment: A review of theoretical and empirical advancements. *American Psychologist, 66,* 204–213.

Wang, P. S., Berglund, P., Olfson, M., Pincus, H. A., Wells, K. B., & Kessler, R. C. (2005). Failure and delay in initial treatment contact after first onset of mental disorders in the National Comorbidity Survey Replication. *Archives of General Psychiatry, 62,* 603–613.

Wang, P. S., Tohen, M., Bromet, E. J., Angst, J., & Kessler, R. C. (2008). Psychiatric epidemiology. In A. Tasman, J. Kay, J. A. Lieberman, M. B. First, & M. Maj (Eds.), *Psychiatry* (3rd ed.). New York, NY: Wiley-Blackwell.

Wang, S., Baillargeon, R., & Paterson, S. (2005). Detecting continuity violations in infancy: A new account and new evidence from covering and tube events. *Cognition, 95,* 129–173.

Wangensteen, O. H., & Carlson, A. J. (1931). Hunger sensation after total gastrectomy. *Proceedings of the Society for Experimental Biology, 28,* 545–547.

Wansink, B. (2010). From mindless eating to mindlessly eating better. *Physiology & Behavior, 100*(5), 454–463.

Wansink, B., & Kim, J. (2005). Bad popcorn in big buckets: Portion size can influence intake as much as taste. *Journal of Nutrition Education and Behavior, 37*(5), 242–245.

Wansink, B., Painter, J. E., & North, J. (2005). Bottomless bowls: Why visual cues of portion size may influence intake. *Obesity Research, 13*(1), 93–100.

Wardle, J., Steptoe, A., Oliver, G., & Lipsey, Z. (2000). Stress, dietary restraint and food intake. *Journal of Psychosomatic Research, 48,* 195–202.

Wargo, E. (2008). The many lives of superstition. *APS Observer, 21*(9), 18–24.

Waroquier, L., Marchiori, D., Klein, O., & Cleermans, A. (2010). Is it better to think unconsciously or to trust your first impression? A reassessment of unconscious thought theory. *Social Psychological and Personality Science, 1,* 111–118.

Warr, P. (1999). Well-being and the workplace. In D. Kahneman, E. Diener, & N. Schwarz (Eds.), *Well-being: The foundations of hedonic psychology.* New York: Russell Sage Foundation.

Warrington, E. K., & Weiskrantz, L. (1970). Amnesic syndrome: Consolidation or retrieval? *Nature, 228,* 629–630.

Washburn, M. F. (1908). *The animal mind.* New York: Macmillan.

Wasserman, J. D., & Bracken, B. A. (2003). Psychometric characteristics of assessment procedures. In J. R. Graham & J. A. Naglieri (Eds.), *Handbook of psychology (Vol. 10): Assessment psychology.* New York: Wiley.

Watanabe, M., Kikuchi, H., Tanaka, K., & Takahashi, M. (2010). Association of short sleep duration with weight gain and obesity at 1-year follow-up: A large-scale prospective study. *Sleep: Journal of Sleep and Sleep Disorders Research, 33*(2), 161–167.

Waterhouse, L. (2006). Multiple intelligences, the Mozart effect, and emotional intelligence: A critical review. *Educational Psychologist, 41,* 207–225.

Watkins, E. R. (2010). Level of construal, mind wandering, and repetitive thought: Reply to McVay and Kane (2010). *Psychological Bulletin, 136,* 198–201.

Watkins, E. R. (2010). Level of construal, mind wandering, and repetitive thought: Reply to McVay and Kane (2010). *Psychological Bulletin, 136,* 198–201.

Watkins, L. R. (2007). Immune and glial regulation of pain. *Brain, Behavior, and Immunity, 21,* 519–521.

Watkins, L. R., & Maier, S. F. (2002). Beyond neurons: Evidence that immune and glial cells contribute to pathological pain states. *Physiological Reviews, 82,* 981–1011.

Watkins, L. R., & Maier, S. F. (2003). When good pain turns bad. *Current Directions in Psychological Science, 12,* 232–236.

Watkins, L. R., Hutchinson, M. R., Ledeboer, A., Wieseler-Frank, J., Milligan, E. D., & Maier, S. F. (2007). Glia as the "bad guys": Implications for improving clinical pain control and the clinical utility of opioids. *Brain, Behavior, and Immunity, 21,* 131–146.

Watson, D. E., Heppner, P., Roos, N. D., Reid, R. J., & Katz, A. (2005). Population-based use of mental health services and patterns of delivery among family physicians. *Canadian Journal of Psychiatry, 50,* 398–406.

Watson, D. L., & Tharp, R. G. (2002). *Self-directed behavior: Self-modification for personal adjustment.* Belmont, CA: Wadsworth.

Watson, D., & Clark, L. A. (1997). Extraversion and its positive emotional core. In R. Hogan, J. Johnson, & S. Briggs (Eds.), *Handbook of personality psychology.* San Diego: Academic Press.

Watson, D., Klohen, E. C., Casillas, A., Nus Simms, E., Haig, J., & Berry, D. S. (2004). Match makers and deal breakers: Analyses of assortative mating in newlywed couples. *Journal of Personality, 72,* 1029–1068.

Watson, J. B. (1913). Psychology as the behaviorist views it. *Psychological Review, 20,* 158–177.

Watson, J. B. (1919). *Psychology from the standpoint of a behaviorist.* Philadelphia: Lippincott.

Watson, J. B. (1924). *Behaviorism.* New York: Norton.

Watson, J. B., & Rayner, R. (1920). Conditioned emotional reactions. *Journal of Experimental Psychology, 3,* 1–14.

Watson, J. C., Gordon, L. B., Stermac, L., Steckley, P., & Kalogerakos, F. (2003). Comparing the effectiveness of process-experiential with cognitive-behavioral psychotherapy in the treatment of depression. *Journal of Consulting and Clinical Psychology, 71*(4), 773–781.

Waugh, N. C., & Norman, D. A. (1965). Primary memory. *Psychological Review, 72,* 89–104.

Weatherall, A. (1992). Gender and languages: Research in progress. *Feminism & Psychology, 2,* 177–181.

Weaver, D. R., & Reppert, S. M. (2008). Circadian timekeeping. In L. Squire, D. Berg, F. Bloom, S. Du Lac, A. Ghosh, & N. Spitzer (Eds.), *Fundamental neuroscience* (3rd ed., pp. 931–958). San Diego, CA: Academic Press.

Weaver, J. (2010). Why some memories stick. *Nature,* published online.

Weaver, K., Garcia, S. M., Schwarz, N., & Miller, D. T. (2007). Inferring the popularity of an opinion from its familiarity: A repetitive voice can sound like a chorus. *Journal of Personality and Social Psychology, 92,* 821–833.

Webb, C. A., DeRubeis, R. J., Shelton, R. C., Hollon, S. J., & Dimidjian, S. (2011). Two aspects of therapeutic alliance: Differential relations with depressive symptom change. *Journal of Consulting and Clinical Psychology, 79,* 279–283.

Webb, W. B. (1992b). *Sleep: The gentle tyrant.* Bolton, MA: Anker.

Webb, W. B., & Dinges, D. F. (1989). Cultural perspectives on napping and the siesta. In D. F. Dinges & R. J. Broughton (Eds.), *Sleep and alertness: Chronobiological, behavioral, and medical aspects of napping.* New York: Raven.

Weber, E. U., & Johnson, E. J. (2009). Mindful judgment and decision making. *Annual Review of Psychology, 60,* 53–85.

Weber, L. J. (2006). *Profits before people?* Bloomington, IN: Indiana University Press.

Webster, G. D. (2009). Parental investment theory. In H. T. Reis & S. Sprecher (Eds.), *Encyclopedia of human relationships* (Vol. 3, pp. 1194–1197). Los Angeles, CA: Sage.

Webster, M. (2010). Color perception. In E. B. Goldstein (Ed.), *Encyclopedia of perception.* Thousand Oaks, CA: Sage.

Wechsler, D. (1949). *Wechsler intelligence scale for children.* New York: Psychological Corporation.

Wechsler, D. (1955). *Manual, Wechsler adult intelligence scale.* New York: Psychological Corporation.

Wechsler, D. (1967). Manual for the Wechsler preschool and primary scale of intelligence. New York: Psychological Corporation.

Wechsler, D. (1981). *Manual for the Wechsler adult intelligence scale—revised.* New York: Psychological Corporation.

Wechsler, D. (1991). *WISC-III manual.* San Antonio: Psychological Corporation.

Wechsler, D. (2003). *Wechsler Intelligence Scale for Children–Fourth Edition (WISC IV).* San Antonio, TX: Psychological Corporation.

Wechsler, H., Davenport, A., Dowdall, G., Moeykens, B., & Castillo, S. (1994). Health and behavioral consequences of binge drinking in college: A national survey of students at 140 campuses. *Journal of the American Medical Association, 272,* 1672–1677.

Wegner, D. M., & Wheatley, T. (1999). Apparent mental causation: Sources of the experience of will. *American Psychologist, 54,* 480–492.

Weikum, W. M., Vouloumanos, A., Navarra, J., Soto-Faraco, S., Sebastian-Galles, N., & Werker, J. F. (2007). Visual language discrimination in infancy. *Science, 316,* 1159–1162.

Weinberg, R. A. (1989). Intelligence and IQ: Landmark issues and great debates. *American Psychologist, 44,* 98–104.

Weinberger, J., & Westen, D. (2008). RATS, we should have used Clinton: Subliminal priming in political campaigns. *Political Psychology, 29*(5), 631–651.

Weiner, B. (1980). *Human motivation.* New York: Holt, Rinehart & Winston.

Weiner, B. (1986). *An attributional theory of motivation and emotion.* New York: Springer-Verlag.

Weiner, B. (1994). Integrating social and personal theories of achievement striving. *Review of Educational Research, 64,* 557–573.

Weiner, B. (2004). Attribution theory revisited: Transforming cultural plurality into theoretical unity. In D. M. McInerney and S. Van Etten (Eds.), *Big theories revisited* (pp. 13–29). Greenwich, CT: Information Age Publishing.

Weiner, B. (Ed.). (1974). *Achievement motivation and attribution theory.* Morristown, NJ: General Learning Press.

Weinert, F. E., & Hany, E. A. (2003). The stability of individual differences in intellectual development: Empirical evidence, theoretical problems, and new research questions. In R. J. Sternberg, J. Lautrey, & T. I. Lubart (Eds.), *Models of intelligence: International perspectives* (pp. 169–181). Washington, DC: American Psychological Association.

Weinfeld, N. S., Sroufe, L. A., Egeland, B., & Carlson, E. (2008). Individual differences in infant–caregiver attachment: Conceptual and empirical aspects of security. In J. Cassidy & P. R. Shaver (Eds.), *Handbook of attachment: Theory, research, and clinical applications* (2nd ed., pp. 78–101). New York, NY: Guilford Press.

Weinstein, A., & Lejoyeux, M. (2010). Internet addiction or excessive Internet use. *American Journal of Drug & Alcohol Abuse, 36*(5), 277–283.

Weinstein, L. N., Schwartz, D. G., & Arkin, A. M. (1991). Qualitative aspects of sleep mentation. In S. J. Ellman & J. S. Antrobus (Eds.), *The mind in sleep: Psychology and psychophysiology* (2nd ed.). New York: Wiley.

Weinstein, N. D. (1984). Why it won't happen to me: Perceptions of risk factors and susceptibility. *Health Psychology, 3,* 431–458.

Weinstein, N. D. (2003). Exploring the links between risk perceptions and preventative health behavior. In J. Suls & K. A. Wallston (Eds.), *Social psychological foundations of health and illness.* Malden, MA: Blackwell Publishing.

Weinstein, N. D., & Klein, W. M. (1995). Resistance of personal risk perceptions to debiasing interventions. *Health Psychology, 14,* 132–140.

Weinstein, N. D., & Klein, W. M. (1996). Unrealistic optimism: Present and future. *Journal of Social and Clinical Psychology, 15,* 1–8.

Weisberg, R. W. (1986). *Creativity: Genius and other myths.* New York: W. H. Freeman.

Weisberg, R. W. (1993). *Creativity: Beyond the myth of genius.* New York: W. H. Freeman.

Weisberg, R. W. (1999). Creativity and knowledge: A challenge to theories. In R. J. Sternberg (Ed.),

Handbook of creativity. New York: Cambridge University Press.

Weisberg, R. W. (2006). Creativity: Understanding innovation in problem solving, science, invention, and the arts. New York, NY: Wiley.

Weise-Kelly, L., & Siegel, S. (2001). Self-administration cues as signals: Drug self-administration and tolerance. Journal of Experimental Psychology: Animal Behavior Processes, 27, 125–136.

Weiser, D. A., & Riggio, H. R. (2010). Family background and academic achievement: Does self-efficacy mediate outcomes? Social Psychology of Education, 13(3), 367–383.

Weisler, R. H., Barbee, J. G., & Townsend, M. H. (2007). Mental health and recovery in the Gulf Coast after Hurricanes Katrina and Rita. Journal of the American Medical Association, 296, 585–588.

Weisman, R. (1995). Reflections on the Oak Ridge experiment with mentally disordered offenders, 1965–1968. International Journal of Law and Psychiatry, 18, 265–290.

Weiss, A., Bates, T. C., & Luciano, M. (2008). Happiness is a personal(ity) thing. Psychological Science, 19, 205–210.

Weiss, D., & Lalonde, R. N. (2001). Responses of female undergraduates to sexual harassment by male professors or teaching assistants. Canadian Journal of Behavioural Science, 33, 148–163.

Weiten, W. (1984). Violation of selected item-construction principles in educational measurement. Journal of Experimental Education, 51, 46–50.

Weiten, W. (1988b). Pressure as a form of stress and its relationship to psychological symptomatology. Journal of Social and Clinical Psychology, 6(1), 127–139.

Weiten, W. (1998). Pressure, major life events, and psychological symptoms. Journal of Social Behavior and Personality, 13, 51–68.

Weiten, W. (2002). Wiring the introductory psychology course: How should we harness the Internet? In S. F. Davis & B. Buskist (Eds.), The teaching of psychology: Essays in honor of Wilbert J. McKeachie and Charles L. Brewer. Mahwah, NJ: Erlbaum.

Weiten, W., & Diamond, S. S. (1979). A critical review of the jury-simulation paradigm: The case of defendant characteristics. Law and Human Behavior, 3, 71–93.

Weiten, W., & Wight, R. D. (1992). Portraits of a discipline: An examination of introductory psychology textbooks in America. In A. E. Puente, J. R. Matthews, & C. L. Brewer (Eds.), Teaching psychology in America: A history. Washington, DC: American Psychological Association.

Weizmann, F., Wiener, N. I., Weisenthal, D. L., & Ziegler, M. (1990). Differential K theory and racial hierarchies. Canadian Psychology, 31, 1–13.

Well, A. D., Pollatsek, A., & Boyce, S. J. (1990). Understanding the effects of sample size on the variability of the mean. Organizational Behavior and Human Decision Processes, 47, 289–312.

Wellman, H. M. (2002). Understanding the psychological world: Developing a theory of mind. In U. Goswami (Ed.), Blackwell Handbook of Childhood Cognitive Development (pp. 166–187). Malden, MA: Blackwell Publishing.

Wellman, H. M., & Gelman, S. A. (1998). Knowledge acquisition in foundational domians. In W. Damon (Ed.), Handbook of child psychology (Vol. 2): Cognition, perception, and language. New York: Wiley.

Wells, C. G. (1991). Right-brain sex: How to reach the heights of sensual pleasure by releasing the erotic power of your mind. New York: Avon.

Wells, G. L., & Bradfield, A. L. (1998). "Good, you identified the suspect": Feedback to eyewitnesses distorts their reports of the witnessing experience. Journal of Applied Psychology, 83, 360–376.

Wells, G. L., & Olson, E. A. (2003). Eyewitness testimony. Annual Review of Psychology, 54, 277–295.

Wells, H. G. (1895/1995). The time machine. New York: Dover Publications.

Werker, J. F. (2003). Baby steps to learning language. Journal of Pediatrics, 143 (Supplement), 62–69.

Werker, J. F., & Curtin, S. (2005). PRIMIR: A developmental framework of infant speech processing. Language and Learning Development, 1, 197–234.

Werker, J., F., & Byers-Heinlein, K. (2008). Bilingualism in infancy: First steps in perception and comprehension. Trends in Cognitive Science, 12, 144–151.

Werker, J. F., & Tees, R. C. (1999). Experiential influences on infant speech processing: toward a new synthesis. In J.T. Spence (Ed.), J.M. Darley & D.J. Foss (Associate Editors), Annual review of psychology, 50 (pp. 509–535). Palo Alto, CA: Annual Reviews.

Werker, J., F., & Tees, R. C. (2005). Speech perception as a window for understanding plasticity and commitment in language systems of the brain. Developmental Psychobiology, 46, 233–251.

Wertsch, J. V., & Tulviste, P. (2005). L. S. Vygotsky and contemporary developmental psychology. In H. Daniels (Ed.), An introduction to Vygotsky. New York, NY: Routledge.

Wertz, F. J. (1998). The role of the humanistic movement in the history of psychology. Journal of Humanistic Psychology, 38, 42–70.

Wesson, D. R., Smith, D. E., Ling, W., & Seymour, R. B. (2005). Sedative-hypnotics. In M. H. Kryger, T. Roth, & W. C. Dement (Eds.). Principles and practice of sleep medicine. Philadelphia: Elsevier Saunders.

West, R. F., & Stanovich, K. E. (1997). The domain specificity and generality of overconfidence: Individual differences in performance estimation bias. Psychonomic Bulletin & Review, 4, 387–392.

Westaby, J. D. (2006). Identifying specific factors underlying attitudes toward change: Using multiple methods to compare expectancy-value theory to reasons theory. Journal of Applied Social Psychology, 32, 1083–1106.

Westbrook, G. L. (2000). Seizures and epilepsy. In E. R. Kandel, J. H. Schwartz, & T. M. Jessell (Eds.), Principles of neural science. New York: McGraw-Hill.

Westen, D., Gabbard, G., & Ortigo, K. (2008). Psychoanalytic approaches to personality. Handbook of personality psychology: Theory and research (3rd ed.; pp. 61–113). New York: Guilford Press.

Wethington, E. (2007). Life events scale. In G. Fink (Ed.), Encyclopedia of stress. San Diego: Elsevier.

Whiffen, V. E. (1992). Is postpartum depression a distinct diagnosis? Clinical Psychology Review, 12, 485–508.

Whiffen, V. E. (2004). Myths and mates in childbearing depression. Women and therapy, 27, 151–164.

Whiffen, V. E. (2006). A secret sadness: The hidden relationship patterns that make women depressed. Toronto: New Harbinger Publications.

Whiffen, V. E., & Gotlib, I. H. (1989). Infants of postpartum depressed mothers: Temperament and cognitive status. Journal of Abnormal Psychology, 98, 274–279.

Whiffen, V. E., & Gotlib, I. H. (1993). Comparison of postpartum and nonpostpartum depression: Clinical presentation, psychiatric history, and psychosocial functioning. Journal of Counseling and Clinical Psychology, 61, 485–494.

Whincup, P., Kaye, S., Owen, C., Huxley, R., Cook, D., Anazawa, S., et al. (2008). Birth weight and risk of type 2 diabetes: A systematic review. Journal of the American Medical Association, 300(24), 2886–2897.

Whissell, C. (2006). Emotion in the sounds of pets' names. Perceptual and Motor Skills, 102, 121–124.

Whissell, C. (2008a). A comparison of two lists providing emotional norms for English words (ANEW and the DAL). Psychological Reports, 102, 597–600.

Whissell, C. (2008b). Emotional fluctuations in Bob Dylan's lyrics measured by the Dictionary of Affect accompany events and phases in his life. Psychological Reports, 102, 469–483.

Whitaker, R. (2002). Mad in America: Bad science, bad medicine, and the enduring mistreatment of the mentally ill. New York: Perseus Publishing.

Whitbourne, S. K., Sneed, J. R., & Skultety, K. M. (2002). Identity processes in adulthood: Theoretical and methodological challenges. Identity, 2, 29–45.

White, C. M., & Hoffrage, U. (2009). Testing the tyranny of too much choice against the allure of more choice. Psychology & Marketing, 26(3), 280–298.

White, S. H. (2000). Conceptual foundations of IQ testing. Psychology, Public Policy, and Law, 6, 33–43.

Whitfield, C. L. (1995). Memory and abuse: Remembering and healing the effects of trauma. Deerfield Beach, FL: Health Communications.

Whiting, J. W. M., Burbank, V. K., & Ratner, M. S. (1986). The duration of maidenhood. In J. B. Lancaster & B. A. Hamburg (Eds.), School age pregnancy and parenthood. Hawthorne, NY: Aldine de Gruyter.

Whitty, M. T. (2008). Liberating or debilitating? An examination of romantic relationships, sexual relationships and friendships on the net. Computers in Human Behavior, 24, 1837–1850.

Whorf, B. L. (1956). Science and linguistics. In J. B. Carroll (Ed.), Language, thought and reality: Selected writings of Benjamin Lee Whorf. Cambridge, MA: MIT Press.

Wichmann, C. (2005). Profile of families and children. JustResearch No. 12. Department of Justice, Canada. Retrieved June 1, 2005, from http://www.canada.justice.gc.ca/en/ps/rs/rep/jr12/jr12_005a.htm.

Wickelgren, I. (1999). Nurture helps mold able minds. Science, 283, 1832–1834.

Wickens, C. M., & Wiesenthal, D. L. (2005). State driver stress as a function of occupational stress, traffic congestion, and trait stress susceptibility. Journal of Applied Biobehavioral Research, 10, 83–97.

Wickens, T. D. (1999). Measuring the time course of retention. In C. Izawa (Ed.), On human memory: Evolution, progress, and reflections on the 30th anniversary of the Atkinson–Shiffrin model. Mahwah, NJ: Erlbaum.

Widgier, T. A. (2009). Neuroticism. In M. R. Leary & R. H. Hoyle (Eds.), Handbook of individual differences in social behavior (pp. 129–146). New York, NY: Guilford Press.

Widiger, T. A. (2007). Current controversies in nosology and diagnosis of personality disorders. Psychiatric Annals, 37, 93–99.

Widiger, T. A., & Mullins, S. (2003). Personality disorders. In A. Tasman, J. Kay, & J. A. Lieberman (Eds.), *Psychiatry*. New York: Wiley.

Widiger, T. A., & Mullins-Sweatt, S. N. (2010). Clinical utility of a dimensional model of personality disorder. *Professional Psychology: Research and Practice, 41*(6), 488–494.

Widiger, T. A., & Sankis, L. M. (2000). Adult psychopathology: Issues and controversies. *Annual Review of Psychology, 51*, 377–404.

Widiger, T. A., & Trull, T. J. (2007). Plate tectonics in the classification of personality disorder: Shifting to a dimensional model. *American Psychologist, 62*(2), 71–83.

Widiger, T. A., Livesley, W., & Clark, L. (2009). An integrative dimensional classification of personality disorder. *Psychological Assessment, 21*(3), 243–255.

Widom, C. S. (1997). Child abuse, neglect, and witnessing violence. In D. M. Stoff, J. Breiling, & J. D. Maser (Eds.), *Handbook of antisocial behavior*. New York: Wiley.

Wiener, N. (1953). *Ex-prodigy: My childhood and youth*. Cambridge: Massachusetts Institute of Technology.

Wiesel, T. N., & Hubel, D. H. (1963). Single-cell responses in striate cortex of kittens deprived of vision in one eye. *Journal of Neurophysiology, 26*, 1003–1017.

Wiggs, C. L., Weisberg, J., & Martin, A. (1999). Neural correlates of semantic and episodic memory retrieval. *Neuropsychologia, 37*, 103–118.

Wilding, J., & Valentine, E. (1996). Memory expertise. In D. J. Herrmann, C. McEvoy, C. Hertzog, P. Hertel, & M. K. Johnson (Eds.), *Basic and applied memory research: Theory in context* (Vol. 1). Mahwah, NJ: Erlbaum.

Willford, J. A., Leech, S. L., & Day, N. L. (2006). Moderate prenatal alcohol exposure and cognitive status of children at age 10. *Alcoholism: Clinical and Experimental Research, 30*, 1051–1059.

Williams, B. A. (1988). Reinforcement, choice, and response strength. In R. C. Atkinson, R. J. Herrnstein, G. Lindzey, & R. D. Luce (Eds.), *Stevens' handbook of experimental psychology*. New York: Wiley.

Williams, B. A. (1994). Conditioned reinforcement: Neglected or outmoded explanatory construct? *Psychonomic Bulletin & Review, 1*, 457–475.

Williams, C. (2001, Spring). You snooze, you lose? Sleep patterns in Canada. Statistics Canada: *Canadian Social Trends*, 10–14.

Williams, C. G., Gagne, M., Ryan, R. M., & Deci, E. L. (2002). Facilitating autonomous motivation for smoking cessation. *Health Psychology, 21*, 40–50.

Williams, G. C. (1966). *Adaptation and natural selection*. Princeton, NJ: Princeton University Press.

Williams, J. E., Paton, C. C., Siegler, I. C., Eigenbrodt, M. L., Neito, F. J., & Tyroler, H. A. (2000). Anger proneness predicts coronary heart disease risk. *Circulation, 101*, 2034–2039.

Williams, J. M. G., Watts, F. N., MacLeod, C., & Mathews, A. (1997). *Cognitive psychology and emotional disorders*. Chichester, England: Wiley.

Williams, K. D. (2007). Ostracism. *Annual Review of Psychology, 58*, 425–52.

Williams, L. M. (1994). Recall of childhood trauma: A prospective study of women's memories of child sexual abuse. *Journal of Consulting and Clinical Psychology, 62*, 1167–1176.

Williams, M. H. (1992). Exploitation and inference: Mapping the damage from therapist–patient sexual involvement. *American Psychologist, 47*, 412–421.

Williams, N. A., & Deffenbacher, J. L. (1983). Life stress and chronic yeast infections. *Journal of Human Stress, 9*(1), 26–31.

Williams, P. (2005). What is psychoanalysis? What is a psychoanalyst? In E. S. Person, A. M. Cooper, & G. O. Gabbard (Eds.), *Textbook of psychoanalysis*. Washington, DC: American Psychiatric Publishing.

Williams, J. M. G., Teasdale, J. D., Segal, Z. V., & Soulsby, J. (2000). Mindfulness-based cognitive therapy reduces overgeneral autobiographical memory in formerly depressed patients. *Journal of Abnormal Psychology, 109*, 150–155.

Williams, J. M. G., Teasdale, J., Kabat-Zinn, J., & Segal, Z. V. (2007). *The mindful way through depression: Freeing yourself from chronic unhappiness*. Oxford, UK: Oxford University Press.

Williams, R. B. (2001). Hostility (and other psychosocial risk factors): Effects on health and the potential for successful behavioral approaches to prevention and treatment. In A. Baum, T. A. Revenson, & J. E. Singer (Eds.), *Handbook of health psychology* (pp. 661–668). Mahwah, NJ: Erlbaum.

Williams, R. B., & Williams, V. P. (2001). Managing hostile thoughts, feelings, and actions: The lifeskills approach. In C. R. Snyder (Ed.), *Coping with stress: Effective people and processes* (pp. 137–153). New York: Oxford University Press.

Williams, R. E., Kaliani, L., DiBenedetti, D. B., Zhou, X., Fehnel, S. E., & Clark, R. V. (2007). Healthcare seeking and treatment for menopausal symptoms in the United States. *Maturitas, 58*, 348–358.

Williams, R. L., & Eggert, A. (2002). Notetaking predictors of test performance. *Teaching of Psychology, 29*(3), 234–237.

Williams, R., & Stockmyer, J. (1987). *Unleashing the right side of the brain: The LARC creativity program*. New York: Viking Penguin.

Williams, W. M., & Ceci, S. J. (1997). Are Americans becoming more or less alike?: Trends in race, class, and ability differences in intelligence. *American Psychologist, 52*, 1226–1235.

Williamson, D. A., Zucker, N. L., Martin, C. K., & Smeets, M. A. M. (2001). Etiology and management of eating disorders. In P. B. Sutker & H. E. Adams (Eds.), *Comprehensive handbook of psychopathology*. New York: Kluwer Academic/Plenum.

Willig, C. & Stainton-Rogers, W. (2008). *Sage handbook of qualitative research in psychology*. Los Angeles, CA: Sage Publishers.

Willig, C. (2008) *Introducing qualitative research methods in psychology* (2nd ed). Maidenhead: McGraw-Hill/Open University Press.

Willingham, D. T., & Dunn, E. W. (2003). What neuroimaging and brain localization can do, cannot do, and should not do for social psychology. *Journal of Personality and Social Psychology, 85*, 1–10.

Willis, S. L., Tennstedt, S. L., Marsiske, M., Ball, K., Elias, J., Koepke, K. M., Morris, J. N., et al. (2006). Long-term effects of cognitive training on everyday functional outcomes in older adults. *Journal of American Medical Association, 296*, 2805–2814.

Willoughby, T., Motz, M., & Wood, E. (1997). The impact of interest and strategy use on memory performance for child, adolescent, and adult learners. *Alberta Journal of Educational Research, 43*, 127–141.

Wilsnack, S. C., Wonderlich, S. A., Kristjanson, A. F., Vogeltanz-Holm, N. D., & Wilsnack, R. W. (2002). Self-reports of forgetting and remembering childhood sexual abuse in a nationally representative sample of U.S. women. *Child Abuse and Neglect, 26*(2), 139–147.

Wilson, A. E., Smith, M. D., Ross, H. S., & Ross, M. (2004). Young children's personal accounts of their sibling disputes. *Merrill-Palmer Quarterly, 50*, 39–60.

Wilson, G. T. (1982). Alcohol and anxiety: Recent evidence on the tension reduction theory of alcohol use and abuse. In K. R. Blankstein & J. Polivy (Eds.), *Self-control and self-modification of emotional behavior*. New York: Plenum.

Wilson, G. T. (2011). Behavior therapy. In R. J. Corsini & D. Wedding (Eds.), *Current psychotherapies* (9th ed.). Belmont, CA: Brooks/Cole.

Wilson, T. D., & Gilbert, D. T. (2003). Affective forecasting. In M. P. Zanna (Eds.), *Advances in experimental social psychology*, Vol. 35 (pp. 345–411). San Diego, CA: Academic Press.

Wilson, T. D., & Gilbert, D. T. (2005). Affective forecasting: Knowing what to want. *Current Directions in Psychological Science, 14*, 131–134.

Wilt, J., & Revelle, W. (2009). Extraversion. In M. R. Leary & R. H. Hoyle (Eds.), *Handbook of individual differences in social behavior* (pp. 257–273). New York, NY: Guilford Press.

Windholz, G. (1997). Ivan P. Pavlov: An overview of his life and psychological work. *American Psychologist, 52*, 941–946.

Wing, R. R., & Polley, B. A. (2001). Obesity. In A. Baum, T. A. Revenson, & J. E. Singer (Eds.), *Handbook of health psychology*. Mahwah, NJ: Erlbaum.

Wingfield, A., Tun, P. A., & McCoy, S. L. (2005). Hearing loss in older adulthood: What it is and how it interacts with cognitive performance. *Current Directions in Psychological Science, 14*, 144–148.

Winkielman, P., & Berridge, K. C. (2004). Unconscious emotion. *Current Directions in Psychological Science, 13*(3), 120–123.

Winn, P. (1995). The lateral hypothalamus and motivated behavior: An old syndrome reassessed and a new perspective gained. *Current Directions in Psychological Science, 4*, 182–187.

Winner, E. (1996). *Gifted children*. New York: Basic Books.

Winner, E. (1997). Exceptionally high intelligence and schooling. *American Psychologist, 52*, 1070–1081.

Winner, E. (1998). Uncommon talents: Gifted children, prodigies and savants. *Scientific American Presents Exploring Intelligence, 9*, 32–37.

Winner, E. (2000). The origins and ends of giftedness. *American Psychologist, 55*, 159–169.

Winner, E. (2003). Creativity and talent. In M. H. Bornstein & L. Davidson (Eds.), *Well-being: Positive development across the life course*. Mahwah, NJ: Erlbaum.

Winograd, T. (1975). Frame representations and the declarative-procedural controversy. In D. Bobrow & A. Collins (Eds.), *Representation and understanding: Studies in cognitive science*. New York: Academic Press.

Winquist, J. R., & Larson, J. R., Jr. (1998). Information pooling: When it impacts group decision making. *Journal of Personality and Social Psychology, 74*, 371–377.

Winsler, A. (2003). Introduction to special issue: Vygotskian perspectives in early childhood education. *Early Education & Development, 14*(3), 253–269.

Winter, D. G. (2010). Why achievement motivation predicts success in business but failure in politics: The importance of personal control. *Journal of Personality, 78*(6), 1637–1667.

Wintre, M. G., North, C., & Sugar, L. A. (2001). Psychologists' response to criticisms about research based on undergraduate participants:

A developmental perspective. *Canadian Psychology, 42,* 216–226.

Wintre, M. G., Sugar, L. A., Yaffe, M., & Costin, D. (2000). Generational status: A Canadian response to the editors' consortium statement with regard to race/ethnicity. *Canadian Psychology, 41,* 244–257.

Wirtz-Justice, A. (1998). Beginning to see the light. *Archives of General Psychiatry, 55,* 861–862.

Wise, J. (2011). *Extreme fear: The science of your mind in danger.* New York: Palgrave Macmillan.

Wise, M. G., Gray, K. F., & Seltzer, B. (1999). Delirium, dementia, and amnestic disorders. In R. E. Hales, S. C. Yudofsky, & J. A. Talbott (Eds.), *The American Psychiatric Press textbook of psychiatry* (3rd ed., pp. 317–362). Washington, DC: American Psychiatric Press.

Wise, R. A. (1999). Animal models of addiction. In D. S. Charney, E. J. Nestler, & B. S. Bunney (Eds.), *Neurobiology of mental illness.* New York: Oxford University Press.

Wise, R. A. (2002). Brain reward circuitry: Insights from unsensed incentives. *Neuron, 36,* 229–240.

Witelson, S. F., Kigar, D. L., & Harvey, T. (1999). The exceptional brain of Albert Einstein. *The Lancet, 353,* 2149–2153.

Witkin, H. A. (1950). Individual differences in ease of perception of embedded figures. *Journal of Personality, 19,* 1–15.

Witkin, H. A., & Goodenough, D. (1981). *Cognitive styles: Essence and origins.* New York: International Universities Press.

Witkin, H. A., Dyk, R. B., Paterson, H. F., Goodenough, D. R., & Karp, S. (1962). *Psychological differentiation.* New York: Wiley.

Witte, K., & Allen, M. (2000). A meta-analysis of fear appeals: Implications for effective public health campaigns. *Health Education & Behavior, 27,* 591–615.

Wittkower, E. D., & Warnes, H. (1984). Cultural aspects of psychotherapy. In J. E. Mezzich & C. E. Berganza (Eds.), *Culture and psychopathology.* New York: Columbia University Press.

Wolfe, D. A. (2007). Understanding anger: Key concepts from the field of domestic violence and child abuse. In T. A. Cavell & K. T. Malcolm (Eds.), *Anger, aggression, and interventions for interpersonal violence* (pp. 393–401). Mahwah, NJ: Lawrence Erlbaum Associates Publishers.

Wolfe, D. A., Jaffe, P. G., & Crooks, C. (2006). *Adolescent risk behaviours: Why teens experiment and strategies to keep them safe.* New Haven, CT: Yale University Press.

Wolfson, A. R., Spaulding, N. L., Dandrow, C., & Baroni, E. M. (2007). Middle school start times: The importance of a good night's sleep for young adolescents. *Behavioral Sleep Medicine, 5,* 194–209.

Wolitzky, D. L. (2006). Psychodynamic theories. In J. C. Thomas, & D. L. Segal (Eds.), *Comprehensive handbook of personality and psychopathology.* New York: Wiley.

Woloshin, S., Schwartz, L. M., & Welch, H. G. (2002). Risk charts: Putting cancer in context. *Journal of the National Cancer Institute, 94,* 799–804.

Wolpe, J. (1958). *Psychotherapy by reciprocal inhibition.* Stanford, CA: Stanford University Press.

Wolpe, J. (1990). *The practice of behavior therapy.* Elmsford, NY: Pergamon Press.

Won, S. (2005, March 16). At 86, a professor who is still going strong. *The Globe and Mail,* C2.

Wonder, J. (1992). *Whole brain thinking: Working both sides of the brain to achieve peak job performance.* New York: Morrow.

Wonderlich, S. A. (2002). Personality and eating disorders. In C. G. Fairburn & K. D. Brownell (Eds.), *Eating disorders and obesity: A comprehensive handbook.* New York: Guilford.

Wong, W. (2009). Retracing the steps of Willhelm Wundt: Explorations in the disciplinary frontiers of psychology and in *Völkerpsychologie. Journal of the History of Psychology, 12,* 229–265.

Wong, L. A. (2006). *Essential study skills.* Boston: Houghton Mifflin.

Wood, D. K., & Goodale, M. A. (2010). Selection of wrist posture in conditions of motor ambiguity. *Experimental Brain Research, 208,* 607–620.

Wood, E., Desmarais, S., & Gugula, S. (2002). The impact of parenting experience on gender stereotyped toy play of children. *Sex Roles, 47*(1–2), 39–49.

Wood, J. N., & Spelke, E. S. (2005). Chronometric studies of numerical cognition in five-month-old infants. *Cognition, 97,* 23–39.

Wood, J. V., Perunovic, W. Q. E., & Lee, J. W. (2009). Positive self-statements: Power for some, peril for others. *Psychological Science, 29,* 860–866.

Wood, N. L., & Cowan, N. (1995). The cocktail party phenomenon revisited: Attention and memory in the classic selective listening procedure of Cherry (1953). *Journal of Experimental Psychology: Learning, Memory, & Cognition, 21,* 255–260.

Wood, R. A., & Griffiths, M. D. (2007). A qualitative investigation of problem gambling as an escape-based coping strategy. *Psychology & Psychotherapy: Theory, Research & Practice, 80*(1), 107–125.

Wood, W., & Quinn, J. M. (2003). Forewarned and forearmed? Two meta-analytic syntheses of forewarnings of influence appeals. *Psychological Bulletin, 129,* 119–138.

Woodcock, R. W. (1994). Norms. In R. J. Sternberg (Ed.), *Encyclopedia of human intelligence.* New York: Macmillan.

Woodhead, M. (2004). "Children's rights and children's development: rethinking the paradigm" in Children's Rights Centre, *Ghent Papers on Children's Rights.* Ghent: University of Ghent.

Woods, S. C., & Stricker, E. M. (2008). Food intake and metabolism. In L. Squire, D. Berg, F. Bloom, S. du Lac, A. Ghosh, & N. Spitzer, *Fundamental neuroscience* (3rd ed.). San Diego, CA: Academic Press.

Woody, E. Z., & Sadler, P. (2008). In M. R. Nash & A. J. Barnier (Eds.). *Oxford handbook of hypnosis: Theory, research and practice* (pp. 81–110). New York, NY: Oxford University Press.

Woolfolk, R. L., & Richardson, F. C. (1978). *Stress, sanity and survival.* New York: Sovereign/Monarch.

Word, D. H., Zanna, M. P., & Cooper, J. (1974). The nonverbal mediation of self-fulfilling prophesies in interracial interaction. *Journal of Experimental Social Psychology, 10,* 109–120.

World Health Organization. (2007). *Suicide: Country reports and charts.* Retrieved August 31, 2008, from http://www.who.int/mental_health/prevention/suicide/country_reports/en/index.html.

Wormith, S. (2000). Without conscience: The disturbing world of the psychopaths among us. (Review). *Canadian Psychology, 41,* 134–137.

Worthen, J. B., & Wade, C. E. (1999). Direction of travel and visiting team athletic performance: Support for a circadian dysrhythmia hypothesis. *Journal of Sport Behavior, 22,* 279–287.

Worthington, E. L., Jr., & Scherer, M. (2004). Forgiveness is an emotion-focused coping strategy that can reduce health risks and promote health

resilience: Theory, review, and hypotheses. *Psychology and Health, 19,* 385–405.

Worthington, R. L., Soth-McNett, A. M., & Moreno, M. V. (2007). Multicultural counseling competencies research: A 20-year content analysis. *Journal of Counseling Psychology, 54,* 351–361.

Wright, J. H., Beck, A. T., & Thase, M. E. (2003). Cognitive therapy. In R. E. Hales & S. C. Yudofsky (Eds.), *Textbook of clinical psychiatry.* Washington, DC: American Psychiatric Publishing.

Wright, M. J. (1992a). The golden anniversary symposium: CPA's first 50 years. *Canadian Psychology, 33,* 695–698.

Wright, M. J. (1992b). The golden anniversary symposium: CPA's first 50 years—Introduction. *Canadian Psychology, 33,* 1–3.

Wright, M. J. (1992c). Women groundbreakers in Canadian psychology: World War II and its aftermath. *Canadian Psychology, 33,* 675–685.

Wright, M. J., & Myers, C. R. (1982). *History of academic psychology in Canada.* Toronto: C. J. Hogrefe, Inc.

Wright, S. C., & Taylor, D. M. (1995). Identity and the language of the classroom: Investigating the impact of heritage versus second language instruction on personal and collective self-esteem. *Journal of Educational Psychology, 87,* 241–252.

Wright, S. C., & Taylor, D. M. (2003). The social psychology of cultural diversity: Social stereotyping, prejudice, and discrimination. In M. A. Hogg & J. Cooper (Eds.), *The Sage handbook of social psychology.* Thousand Oaks, CA: Sage.

Wright, S. C., Taylor, D. M., & Macarthur, J. (2000). Subtractive bilingualism and the survival of the Inuit language: Heritage- versus second-language education. *Journal of Educational Psychology, 92,* 63–84.

Wu, G., Zhang, J., & Gonzalez, R. (2004). Decision under risk. In D. Koehler & N. Harvey (Eds.), The Blackwell handbook of judgment and decision making (pp. 399–423). Oxford: Oxford University Press.

Wu, Z. (1998). Recent trends in marriage patterns in Canada. *Policy Options, 3,* 3–6.

Wu-Holt, P., & Boutte, J. (1994). The relationship between daily hassles, ways of coping, and menstrual cycle symptomatology. *International Journal of Stress Management, 1,* 173–183.

Wundt, W. (1874/1904). *Principles of physiological psychology.* Leipzig: Engelmann.

Wurtz, R. H., & Kandel, E. R. (2000). Central visual pathways. In E. R. Kandel, J. H. Schwartz, & T. M. Jessell (Eds.), *Principles of neural science.* New York: McGraw-Hill.

Wynn, K. (1992). Addition and subtraction by human infants. *Nature, 358,* 749–750.

Wynn, K. (1996). Infants' individuation and enumeration of sequential actions. *Psychological Science, 7,* 164–169.

Wynn, K. (1998). An evolved capacity for number. In D. D. Cummins & C. Allen (Eds.), *The evolution of mind.* New York: Oxford University Press.

Wynn, K. (2008). Some innate foundations of social and moral cognition. In P. Carruthers, S. Laurence & S. Stich (Eds.), *The innate mind: Foundations and the future.* Oxford: Oxford University Press.

Wynne, C. D. L. (2004). *Do animals think?* Princeton, NJ: Princeton University Press.

Xu, J., & Roberts, R. E. (2010). The power of positive emotions: It's a matter of life or death—Subjective well-being and longevity over 28 years in a general population. *Health Psychology, 29*(1), 9–19.

Yaffe, K. K., Fiocco, A. J., Lindquist, K. K., Vittinghoff, E. E., Simonsick, E. M., Newman, A. B., et al. (2009). Predictors of maintaining cognitive function in older adults: The Health ABC Study. *Neurology, 72*(23), 2029–2035.

Yalom, V. (2002). Interview with Donald Meichenbaum, Ph.D. Retrieved July 4, 2005, from http://www.psychotherapy.net/totm/meichenbaum.shtml.

Yamaguchi, M., Kuhlmeier, V., Wynn, K. & van Marle, K. (2009). Continuity in social cognition from infancy to childhood. *Developmental Science, 12,* 746–752.

Yamamoto, J., Silva, J. A., Justice, L. R., Chang, C. Y., & Leong, G. B. (1993). Cross-cultural psychotherapy. In A. C. Gaw (Ed.), *Culture, ethnicity, and mental illness.* Washington, DC: American Psychiatric Press.

Yang, H., Liu, T., & Zang, D. (2000). A study of stressful life events before the onset of hypothyroidism. *Chinese Mental Health Journal, 14,* 201–202.

Yang, L., Hasher, L., & Wilson, D. E. (2007). Synchrony effects in automatic and controlled retrieval. *Psychonomic Bulletin & Review, 14,* 51–56.

Yang, L. H. (2007). Application of mental illness stigma theory to Chinese societies: Synthesis and new directions. *Singapore Medical Journal, 48,* 977–991.

Yang, Y., Raine, A., Lencz, T., Bihrle, S., Lacasse, L., & Colletti, P. (2005). Prefrontal white matter in pathological liars. *British Journal of Psychiatry, 187,* 320–325.

Yarmey, A. D. (2003). Eyewitness identification: Guidelines and recommendations for identification procedures in the United States and in Canada. *Canadian Psychology, 44*(3), 181–189.

Yates, F. A. (1966). *The art of memory.* London: Routledge & Kegan Paul.

Yeomans, M. R., Tepper, B. J., Rietzschel, J., & Prescott, J. (2007). Human hedonic responses to sweetness: Role of taste genetics and anatomy. *Physiology & Behavior, 91,* 264–273.

Yerkes, R. M., & Morgulis, S. (1909). The method of Pavlov in animal psychology. *Psychological Bulletin, 6,* 257–273.

Yeshurun, U., & Sobel, N. (2010). An odor is not worth a thousand words: From multidimensional odors to unidimensional odor objects. *Annual Review of Psychology, 61,* 219–241.

Yoo, S.-S., Gujar, N., Hu, P., Jolesz, F. A., & Walker, M. P. (2006). The human emotional brain without sleep—A prefrontal amygdala disconnect. *Current Biology, 23,* R877–R888.

Yoo, S-S., Gujar, N., Hu, P., Jolesz, F. A., & Walker, M. P. (2007). The human emotional brain without sleep—a prefrontal amygdala disconnect. *Current Biology, 17,* 877–878.

Yost, W. A. (2000). *Fundamentals of hearing: An introduction.* San Diego, CA: Academic Press.

Yost, W. A. (2001). Auditory, localization, and scene perception. In E. B. Goldstein (Ed.), *Blackwell handbook of perception.* Malden, MA: Blackwell.

Yost, W. A. (2010). Audition: Pitch perception. In E. B. Goldstein (Ed.), *Encyclopedia of perception.* Thousand Oaks, CA: Sage.

Young, D. M. (1997). Depression. In W. S. Tseng & J. Streltzer (Eds.), *Culture and psychopathology: A guide to clinical assessment.* New York: Brunner/Mazel.

Young, K. S. (1996, August). *Internet addiction: The emergence of a new clinical disorder.* Paper presented at the meeting of the American Psychological Association: Toronto, Ontario.

Young, K. S. (1998). *Caught in the net: How to recognize the signs of Internet addiction—and a winning strategy for recovery.* New York: Wiley.

Young, M. E., Mizzau, M., Mai, N. T., Sirisegaram, A., & Wilson, M. (2009). Food for thought: What you eat depends on your sex and eating companions. *Appetite, 53*(2), 268–271.

Young, T. B. (2004). Epidemiology of daytime sleepiness: Definitions, symptomatology, and prevalence. *Journal of Clinical Psychiatry, 65*(Suppl 16), 12–16.

Young, T. B., Finn, L., Peppard, P. E., Szklo-Coxe, M., Austin, D., Nieto, F., et al. (2008). Sleep-disordered breathing and mortality: Eighteen-year follow-up of the Wisconsin Sleep Cohort. *Sleep: Journal of Sleep and Sleep Disorders Research, 31*(8), 1071–1078.

Yudofsky, S. C. (1999). Parkinson's disease, depression, and electrical stimulation of the brain. *New England Journal of Medicine, 340,* 1500–1502.

Yukl, G. A. (1994). *Leadership in organizations* (3rd ed.). Englewood Cliffs, NJ: Prentice-Hall.

Zadra, A. L., & Donderi, D. C. (2000). Nightmares and Bad Dreams: Their prevalence and relationship to well-being. *Journal of Abnormal Psychology, 109,* 273–281.

Zadra, A. L., Donderi, D. C., & Pihl, R. O. (1992). Efficacy of lucid dream induction for lucid and non-lucid dreamers. *Dreaming, 2,* 85–89.

Zager, D. B. (Ed.). (1999). *Autism.* Hillsdale NJ: Erlbaum & Associates.

Zagorsky, J. L. (2007). Do you have to be smart to be rich? The impact of IQ on wealth, income and financial distress. *Intelligence, 35,* 489–501.

Zajonc, R. B. (1968). Attitudinal effects of mere exposure. *Journal of Personality and Social Psychology, 9,* 1–29.

Zajonc, R. B. (1980). Feeling and thinking: Preferences need no inferences. *American Psychologist, 35,* 151–175.

Zajonc, R. B. (1985). Emotion and facial efference: A theory reclaimed. *Science, 228,* 15–20.

Zajonc, R. B., Adelmann, P. K., Murphy, S. T, & Niedenthal, P. M. (1987). Convergence in the physical appearance of spouses. *Motivation and Emotion, 11,* 335–346.

Zak, P. J., Kurzban, R., & Matzner, W. T. (2005). Oxytocin is associated with human trustworthiness. *Hormones and Behavior, 48*(5), 522–527.

Zane, N., Hall, G. C. N., Sue, S., Young, K., & Nunez, J. (2004). Research on psychotherapy with culturally diverse populations. In M. J. Lambert (Ed.), *Bergin and Garfield's handbook of psychotherapy and behavior change.* New York: Wiley.

Zangwill, O. L. (1972). Remembering revisited. *Quarterly Journal of Experimental Psychology, 24,* 123–138.

Zanna, M. P. (1994). On the nature of prejudice. *Canadian Psychology, 35,* 11–23.

Zaragoza, M. S., Belli, R. F., & Payment, K. E. (2007). Misinformation effects and the suggestibility of eyewitness memory. In M. Garry & H. Hayne (Eds.), *Do justice and let the sky fall: Elizabeth F. Lotus and her contributions to science, law, and academic freedom.* Mahwah, NJ: Erlbaum.

Zárate, M. A. (2009). Racism in the 21st century. In T. D. Nelson (Ed.), *Handbook of prejudice, stereotyping,* *and discrimination* (pp. 1–22). New York, NY: Psychology Press.

Zarcone, V. P., Jr. (2000). Sleep hygiene. In M. H. Kryger, T. Roth, & W. C. Dement (Eds.), *Principles and practice of sleep medicine.* Philadelphia: Saunders.

Zatzick, D. F., & Dimsdale, J. E. (1990). Cultural variations in response to painful stimuli. *Psychosomatic Medicine, 52*(5), 544–557.

Zebrowitz, L. A. (1996). *Reading faces.* Boulder, CO: Westview Press.

Zebrowitz, L. A., Collins, M. A., & Dutta, R. (1998). The relationship between appearance and personality across the life span. *Personality and Social Psychology Bulletin, 24,* 736–749.

Zebrowitz, L. A., Voinescu, L., & Collins, M. A. (1996). "Wide-eyed" and "crooked-face": Determinants of perceived and real honesty across the life span. *Personality and Social Psychology Bulletin, 22,* 1258–1269.

Zechmeister, E. B., & Nyberg, S. E. (1982). *Human memory: An introduction to research and theory.* Pacific Grove, CA: Brooks/Cole.

Zeidan, F., Gordon, N. S., Merchant, J., & Goolkasian, P. (2010). The effects of brief mindfulness meditation training on experimentally induced pain. *The Journal of Pain, 11*(3), 199–209.

Zeiler, M. (1977). Schedules of reinforcement: The controlling variables. In W. K. Honig & J. E. R. Staddon (Eds.), *Handbook of operant behavior.* Englewood Cliffs, NJ: Prentice-Hall.

Zellner, D. A. (1991). How foods get to be liked: Some general mechanisms and some special cases. In R. C. Bolles (Ed.), *The hedonics of taste.* Hillsdale, NJ: Erlbaum.

Zhang, T., & Meaney, M. J. (2010). Epigenetics and the environmental regulation of the genome and its function. *Annual Review of Psychology, 61,* 439–466.

Zillmann, D., & Bryant, J. (1984). Effects of massive exposure to pornography. In N. M. Malamuth & E. Donnerstein (Eds.), *Pornography and sexual aggression.* New York: Academic Press.

Zillmer, E. A., Spiers, M. V., & Culbertson, W. C. (2008). *Principles of neuropsychology.* Belmont, CA: Wadsworth.

Zimbardo, P. G. (2007). *The Lucifer effect: Understanding how good people turn evil.* New York: Random House.

Zimiles, H. (2009). Ramifications of increased training in quantitative methodology. *American Psychologist, 64,* 51–56.

Zimmerman, B. J. (1995). Self-efficacy and educational development. In A. Bandura (Ed.), *Self-efficacy in changing societies.* New York: Cambridge University Press.

Zimmerman, I. L., & Woo-Sam, J. M. (1984). Intellectual assessment of children. In G. Goldstein & M. Hersen (Eds.), *Handbook of psychological assessment.* New York: Pergamon Press.

Zimmerman, M., & Spitzer, R. L. (2009). Psychiatric classification. In B. J. Sadock, V. A. Sadock, & P. Ruiz (Eds.), *Kaplan & Sadock's comprehensive textbook of psychiatry* (9th ed., pp. 1108–1138). Philadelphia, PA: Lippincott, Williams & Wilkins.

Zinbarg, R. E., & Griffith, J. W. (2008). Behavior therapy. In J. L. Lebow (Ed.), *Twenty-first century psychotherapies: Contemporary approaches to theory and practice.* New York: Wiley.

Zisook, S., Lesser, I., Stewart, J. W., Wisniewski, S. R., Balasubramani, G. K., Fava, M., et al. (2007). Effect of age at onset on the course of major depressive disorder. *American Journal of Psychiatry, 164*(10), 1539–1546.

Zoeller, R. F., Jr. (2007). Physical activity and fitness in the prevention of coronary heart disease and associated risk factors. *American Journal of Lifestyle Medicine, 1*, 29–33.

Zohar, J., Fostick, L., & Juven-Wetzler, E. (2009). Obsessive-compulsive disorder. In M. C. Gelder, N. C. Andreasen, J. J. López-Ibor, Jr., & J. R. Geddes (Eds.). *New Oxford textbook of psychiatry* (2nd ed., Vol. 1). New York, NY: Oxford University Press.

Zola, S. M., & Squire, L. R. (2000). The medial temporal lobe and the hippocampus. In E. Tulving & F. I. M. Craik (Eds.), *The Oxford handbook of memory* (pp. 485–500). New York: Oxford University Press.

Zorick, F. J., & Walsh, J. K. (2000). Evaluation and management of insomnia: An overview. In M. H.

Kryger, T. Roth, & W. C. Dement (Eds.), *Principles and practice of sleep medicine*. Philadelphia: Saunders.

Zorumski, C. F., Isenberg, K. E., & Mennerick, S. (2009). Cellular and synaptic electrophysiology. In B. J. Sadock, V. A. Sadock, & P. Ruiz (Eds.), *Kaplan & Sadock's comprehensive textbook of psychiatry* (9th ed., Vol. 1, pp. 129–146). Philadelphia, PA: Lippincott, Williams & Wilkins.

Zrenner, E., Abramov, I., Akita, M., Cowey, A., Livingstone, M., & Valberg, A. (1990). Color perception: Retina to cortex. In L. Spillman & J. S. Werner (Eds.), *Visual perception: The neurophysiological foundations*. San Diego: Academic Press.

Zubieta, J-K., Bueller, J. A., Jackson, L. R., Scott, D. J., Xu, Y., Koeppe, R. A., Nichols, T. E., & Stohler, C. S. (2005). Placebo effects mediated by endogenous opioid activity on µ-opioid receptors. *The Journal of Neuroscience, 25*, 7754–7762.

Zurbriggen, E. L., & Sturman, T. S. (2002). Linking motives and emotions: A test of McClelland's hypothesis. *Personality & Social Psychology Bulletin, 28*, 521–535.

Zuroff, D. C., & Mongrain, M. (1987). Dependency and self-criticism: Vulnerability factors for depressive affective states. *Journal of Abnormal Psychology, 96*, 14–22.

Zwanzger, P., Fallgatter, A. J., Zavorotnyy, M. M., & Padberg, F. F. (2009). Anxiolytic effects of transcranial magnetic stimulation—An alternative treatment option in anxiety disorders? *Journal of Neural Transmission, 116*(6), 767–775.

Name Index

Wong, L. A., 566
Wong, P., 598
Wong, W., 4
Wood, A. M., 302, 480
Wood, D., 525
Wood, E., 306, 541
Wood, J. M., 588
Wood, J. N., 511
Wood, J. V., 656
Wood, L. M., 428
Wood, N. L., 303
Wood, R. A., 609
Wood, W., 458, 539, 764
Woodbury, M. A., 177
Woodcock, R. W., 396
Woodhead, M., 434
Woods, A. M., 259
Woods, S. C., 444
Woods, T., 269, 270
Woody, E. Z., 228
Woolfolk, R. L., 604
Woonteiler, D., 490
Woo-Sam, J. M., 405
Word, D. H., 745
Wormith, S., 677
Worth, L. T., 762
Worthen, J. B., 206
Worthington, E. L., Jr., 632
Worthington, R. L., 727
Wortman, C. B., 631
Wortsman, A., A18
Wright, J. H., 713
Wright, M., 14
Wright, M. J., 13, 14
Wright, S. C., 30, 359, 782
Wrosch, C., 491
Wu, G., 375, 380
Wu, Zheng, 526
Wu-Holt, P., 619
Wulfeck, B., 355
Wundt, W., 4, 5, 12, 13, 22, 24
Wurtz, R. H., 149
Wyatt, J. K., 241
Wyland, C. L., 104
Wynn, K., 489, 500, 511, 512
Wynne, C. D. L., 361

X

Xu, W., 530

Y

Yaffe, K. K., 531
Yager, J., 240, 241, 688
Yalom, I. D., 706

Yalom, V., 713, 714
Yamada, A., 685, 727
Yamaguchi, M., 512
Yamamoto, J., 728
Yang, H., 619
Yang, L., 304
Yang, L. H., 684
Yang, P., 36
Yang, Y., 105
Yarmey, A. D., 344
Yate, F. A., 340
Yeomans, M. R., 178
Yerkes, R. M., 252
Yeshurun, U., 179
Yokley, J. L., 672
Yoo, S., 20
Yoo, S. H., 474
Yoo, S.-S., 200, 214
Yoom, J. H., 93, 670
Yost, W., 169
Yost, W. A., 174, 528
Young, D. M., 685
Young, J. E., 713
Young, K., 610, 728
Young, L. J., 117
Young, M. E., 445
Young, S., 85
Young, T., 154
Young, T. B., 212, 219
Yount, S. E., 619
Yovel, G., 151
Yudolsky, S. C., 101
Yuen, C., 459
Yuille, J. C., 306
Yuker, H. E., 158
Yukl, G. A., A24

Z

Zachariae, R., 620
Zachor, D., 682
Zacks, R., 304
Zadra, A. L., 219, 221, 222
Zager, D. B., 681
Zagorsky, J. L., 407
Zajonc, R. B., 468, 472, 764
Zak, P. J., 117
Zane, N., 727, 728
Zang, D., 619
Zangwill, O. L., 318
Zanna, M. P., 237, 745, 747, 759, 782, 784
Zapp, D. J., 455
Zaragoza, M. S., 318
Zárate, M. A., 782
Zarcone, V. P., Jr., 241

Zatorre, R., 175
Zatzick, D. F., 182
Zautra, A. J., 604
Zebrowitz, L. A., 744
Zechmeister, E. B., 33
Zedeck, S., 408
Zeedyk, M. S., 328
Zeelenberg, M., 379, 380
Zeichner, A., 580
Zeidan, F., 230
Zeiler, M., 271
Zellner, D. A., 178
Zeschky, M., 369
Zhang, J., 375, 380
Zhang, R., 564
Zhang, T., 123
Zhao, S., 646
Zhou, E. S., 608
Ziegler, M., 419
Zigler, E., 434
Zillmann, D., 459
Zillmer, E. A., 112
Zimbardo, P., 769
Zimbardo, P. G., 768, 769
Zimmerman, B. J., 564
Zimmerman, I. L., 405
Zimmerman, J., 294, 295
Zimmerman, M., 644
Zimprich, D., 531
Zinbarg, R. E., 715
Zinberg, R., 652
Zisook, S., 657
Zoeller, R. F., Jr., 624
Zohar, J., 649
Zohary, E., 111
Zola, S. M., 16, 332
Zorick, F. J., 217
Zorumski, C. F., 87, 92
Zrenner, E., 155
Zubieta, J.-K., 67, 94
Zucker, C., 681
Zucker, I., 206
Zucker, K. J., 462
Zurbriggen, E. L., 467
Zuroff, D. C., 503, 663
Zvolensky, M. J., 651
Zwanzger, P., 101

Figures and Tables are denoted with *f* and *t* following the page number.

childhood, 496–516
  attachment, 500–503
  autism, 681–682
  disorders, 680–682
  moral reasoning development, 514–516
  motor development, 496–497
  personality development, 505–514
  temperament differences, 497–500
children, giftedness, 411–412
chlorpromazine, 717
Christmas Carol, A (Dickens), 301
chromosomes, 118, 491
chronic pain, 183
chronic stressors, 599
chunk, 309–310
cingulate cortex, 471
cingulotomy, 716
circadian rhythms, 205–207
circular reasoning, 485
CISS, 608
classical conditioning, 251–262
  anxiety disorders, 651–652
  attitudes, 255
  basic processes, 257–259
  business negotiations, 296–297
  comparative overview, 288–289
  defined, 251
  drug effects, and, 257
  everyday life, 254–257
  fear/anxiety, 254–255
  higher-order conditioning, 261
  Pavlovian conditioning, 251–253
  physiological responses, 256–257
  politics, 297
  stimulus discrimination, 260
  stimulus generalization, 259–262
  terminology/procedures, 253–254
client-centred therapy, 702–704, 724
clinical psychologists, 698
clinical psychology, 15, 26
clinical social worker, 699
closure, 160, 161f
clustering, 313
CNS, 96f, 97–98
cocaine, 235, 237
cochlea, 172, 187
coefficient of determination, A11
cognition, 16, 349–350
cognitive abilities, 537–538
cognitive development, 505–514
  critical periods, 512–514
  defined, 505
  habituation-dishabituation paradigm, 511–512
  Piaget's stage theory, 505–510
  Vygotsky's sociocultural theory, 510–511
cognitive dissonance, 766–767
cognitive factors
  anxiety disorders, 652–653
  depressive disorders, 663–664
  eating disorders, 689
cognitive perspective to intelligence, 425
cognitive therapy, 713, 724
cognitive-behavioural therapy, 704, 712–715
cohort effects, 499
collective unconscious, 558, 558f
collectivism, 583, 750, 752f, 774
colour solid, 154f
colour vision, 153–157
  behaviour, and colour, 156–157
  opponent process theory, 155
  reconciling theories, 155–156

stimulus of colour, 153–154
  trichromatic theory, 154–155
colour-blindness, 155
commitment, 754
community mental health movement, 730
comorbidity, 645, 691
companionate love, 754
comparators, 194–195
compensation, 559
compensatory CRs, 257
complementary colours, 155, 155f
complex cells, 151
complexities, and decision making, 375–376
componential subtheory, 426
computerized tomography (CT) scan, 101–102
conceptual hierarchy, 313, 315
conceptual skills, 409
concordance rate, 651
concrete operational period, 506f, 507
conditional parental affection, 567
conditioned reflex, 253
conditioned reinforcers, 269
conditioned response (CR)
  acquisition/extinction/spontaneous recovery, 258f
  conditioned taste aversion, 278, 278f
  defined, 253
  Pavlov's dogs, 259
conditioned stimulus (CS)
  acquisition/extinction/spontaneous recovery, 258f
  classical conditioning apparatus, 252f
  conditioned taste aversion, 278, 278f
  defined, 253
  higher-order conditioning, 261
  immunosuppression, 256
  Pavlov's dogs, 259
  signal relations, 281–282
  stimulus discrimination, 260
conditioned taste aversion, 278–279
conditioning, 251
cones, 146, 156f
confirmation bias, 384–385
conflict, 553–554, 599–600
conformity, 769–770
confounding of variables, 51
conjunction fallacy, 378–379, 691
connectionism, 315
conscientiousness, 549, 622
conscious, 552–553
consciousness, 198–247
  altering, with drugs, 231–238. *See also* drug use
  hypnosis, 225–228. *See also* hypnosis
  meditation, 228–230
  nature of, 200–204
  sleep, 200–224. *See also* sleep
conservation, 507, 508f
consolidation, 332
construct validity, 398–399
constructive coping, 611–612
content validity, 398
contextual subtheory, 426
continuity, 160, 161f
continuous reinforcement, 270
contrast effects, 194–195
control group, 50
controlled processes, 201
conventional level, 515
convergence, 164
convergent thinking, 430
coping, 608, 611–612

Coping Inventory for Stressful Situations (CISS), 608
cornea, 145f
coronary heart disease, 616, 617f, 618
corporal punishment, 275–276
corpus callosum, 106f, 109, 109f, 539f, 540
correct rejections, 140, 140f
correlation, 62–64
correlation coefficient, 62, 397, A10
corticosteroids, 608
counselling psychologists, 698
counsellors, 699
counterarguments, 484
counterattitudinal behaviour, 766
counterconditioning, 711
couples therapy, 707–708
CPA, 13–14, 23, 74
CR. *See* conditioned response (CR)
"crack," 233
"crank," 233
creative intelligence, 426
creativity, 430–434
  correlates of, 431–433
  defined, 430
  measuring, 430–431
  nature of, 430
criterion-related validity, 398, 398f
critical period, 131, 512, 513
critical thinking, 38–39
crossing over, 118
cross-sectional research design, 498–499, 499f
crystal meth, 233
crystallized intelligence, 403
CS. *See* conditioned stimulus (CS)
CSBBCS, 15
CT scan, 101–102
cultural differences
  attachment, and, 503, 503f
  attributional tendencies, 750–753
  close relationships, and, 756–757
  cognitive style, and, 373f
  conformity/obedience, and, 773–774
  dreams, and, 222–223
  eating disorders, 689
  emotional experience, and, 473–475
  heritage, and behaviour, 30
  infant mortality, 495f
  IQ scores, 418–424
  IQ testing, Western *vs.* non-Western cultures, 408
  language/thought, and, 364–365
  motor development, 497
  personality, and, 582–584
  psychological disorders, 684
  psychology's horizons, 18–20
  psychotherapy, 727–729
  sleep, and, 212–213
  taste preferences, 178f
culture, 29
culture-bound disorders, 685
cumulative deprivation hypothesis, 416
cumulative recorder, 264, 265f
cyclothymic disorder, 658
cytokines, 620

D

DA, 92t, 234–235
DAL, 468
dark adaptation, 147, 147f
data collection techniques, 46, 46t
date rape, 460

dB, 171
DBS, 723, 723f
decay theory, 323
decentration, 507
decibel (dB), 171
decision making
  evidence-based, 81
  groups, 777–779
declarative memory system, 334–335
deep brain stimulation (DBS), 723, 723f
Deese-Roediger-McDermott (DRM)
  paradigm, 327
defence mechanism, 610, 611t
defensive attribution, 750
deinstitutionalization, 730
deliberate deception, 587
delta band, 202, 202t
delusions, 669
dementia, 529
dendrites, 87, 87f
dendritic trees, 87
dependent personality disorder, 676t
dependent variable, 49
depression, 656–658
  interpersonal factors, 666f
  positive psychotherapy, 705f
  sports concussions, and, 666–667
depressive disorders, 617, 618
depth perception, 163
descriptive statistics, 59–64, A8
descriptive/correlational research methods,
  54–58
destination memory, 320
development, 488–545. See also cognitive
  development
  adolescence, 516–524. See also adolescence
  adulthood, 525–536. See also adulthood
  childhood, 496–516. See also childhood
  defined, 490
  illustrated overview, 532–535
  prenatal, 491–496. See also prenatal
  development
developmental norms, 497
deviance, 642
deviation IQ scores, 404–405
diagnosis, 642
Diagnostic and Statistical Manual of Mental
  Disorders (DSM), 644–645, 644f
Dictionary of Affect in Language (DAL), 468
DID, 654, 655
dietary restraint, 451
Differential Aptitude Test, 395
digestive regulation, 444
dimensional approach to diagnosis, 645
disciplinary procedures, 275
discrimination
  defined, 782
  employment, A17–A18
  prejudice, and, 783f
  racial, 741
discrimination, stimulus, 268
discriminative stimuli, 268
discussion, 79
dishabituation, 511
disinhibition, 226–227
disorders. See psychological disorders
disorganized schizophrenia, 670
disorganized-disoriented attachment, 502
displacement, 554, 554f, 609
display rules, 475
dissociation, 226, 228
dissociative amnesia, 653

dissociative identity disorder (DID), 654, 655
dissonance theory, 766–767
distal stimuli, 162, 162f
distinctiveness, 548
distribution, 59–61
divergent thinking, 430
divided consciousness, 228
Diving Bell and the Butterfly, The (Bauby), 86
dizygotic twins, 121, 121f
d-lysergic acid diethylamide (LSD), 695
dominant gene, 119
door-in-the-face technique, 194, 194f
Doors of Perception, The (Huxley), 695
dopamine activity, 672, 673f
dopamine (DA), 92t, 234–235
dopamine hypothesis, 93
dorsal stream, 151, 170f
double-blind procedure, 69
Doublespeak (Lutz), 387
Down syndrome, 410
dream analysis, 700
dreams, 221–224
  common questions about, 242–243
  contents of, 221–222
  culture, and, 222–223
  lucid dreaming, 243
  theories of dreaming, 223–224
  vs. waking life, 222
drive, 441
DRM paradigm, 327
drug therapy, 716–721
drug tolerance, 256, 257
drug use, 231–238, 624–625
  cannabis, 233
  direct effects, 237
  drug action mechanisms, 234–235
  drug effects, 234
  hallucinogens, 233
  indirect effects, 237
  marijuana controversies, 237–238
  MDMA ("ecstasy"), 234, 238
  narcotics, 232
  overdose, 236–237
  physical dependence, 235–236
  during pregnancy, 493
  psychoactive drugs, 231–232
  psychological dependence, 236
  recreational, 231
  sedatives, 232
  stimulants, 232–233
DSM, 644–645, 644f
dual-coding theory, 306
duloxetine, 720
dysthymic disorder, 657

E

EAR, 54
ear
  anatomy, 173f
  external, 171, 173f
  inner, 172, 173f
  middle, 172, 173f
  sensory processing, 171–173
eardrum, 172
early childhood, 533
early intensive behavioural intervention
  (EIBI), 682
early selection, 303
eating. See hunger/eating
eating disorders, 451–452, 687–689
Ebbinghaus's forgetting curve, 321, 321f

echolia, 681
eclecticism, 727
ecstasy drug, 234, 238
ECT, 721–722
EEG. see electroencephalograph (EEG)
efferent nerve fibres, 96
Effexor, 720
ego, 552, 553
egocentrism, 507
eHarmony.com, 757
EIBI, 682
elaboration, 305–306
elaboration likelihood model, 768, 768f
Elavil, 718
Electra complex, 557
electrical stimulation of the brain (ESB),
  100–101, 108f
electroconvulsive therapy (ECT), 721–722
electroencephalograph (EEG), 99, 99f, 202
  consciousness patterns, 202t
  defined, 98
electromyograph (EMG), 208
electronically activated recorder (EAR), 54
electrooculograph (EOG), 208
elicited (drawn forth) responses, 253
elimination by aspects, 375
embryonic stage, 491
emerging adulthood, 524
EMG, 208
emitted responses, 264
emotion
  defined, 468
  pent-up, releasing, 631
  pregnancy, and, 494–495
  schizophrenic disorders, 670
emotional efference theory, 472
emotional experience, 467–479
  behavioural component, 472–473
  Cannon-Bard theory, 476–477
  cognitive component, 468–469
  culture, and, 473–475
  evolutionary theories, 477–479
  James-Lange theory, 476
  physiological component, 469–472
  Schachter's two-factor theory, 477
emotional intelligence, 428–429
emotional responses to stress, 603–605
emotion-focused couples therapy, 704
empiricism, 28
employment discrimination, A17–A18
empty nest, 528
encoding, 302
encoding specificity principle, 316, 324
endocannabinoids, 235
endocrine system, 116–118
endorphins, 92t, 94, 182–183
environmental factors
  hunger regulation, 445–447
  intelligence, 416–418
environmental tobacco smoke, 623
environmental toxins, 494
EOG, 208
epidemiology, 646
epigenetics, 123
episodic buffer, 311
episodic memory, 337–338, 530
episodic memory system, 335–336
Erikson's stage theory, 504–505, 525
ESB, 100–101, 108f
escape learning, 273
essay exams, 37
ethical considerations, 73–75

defined, 395
Galton's studies, 400
intelligence structure, 402–403
IQ scores, 403–405
reliability, 405
score stability over time, 407
Stanford-Binet Intelligence Scale, 401
validity, 406–407
vocational success, and, 407–408
Wechsler's innovations, 401–402
Western vs. non-Western cultures, 408
interactionist theories of language
    acquisition, 363
interference theory, 323
intermediate selection, 303
intermittent (partial) reinforcement, 271
internal attributions, 748
Internet
    close relationships, and, 757
    scientific research, and, 72–73
Internet addiction, 610
Internet-mediated research, 72–73
interpersonal attraction, 753
interpersonal intelligence, 427t
interpersonal psychotherapy (IPT), 56
interposition, 164
interpretation, 700–701
interpretive theory of mind, 513
intimacy, 754
intrapersonal intelligence, 427t
introduction, journal article, 78
introspection, 6
introverts, 558
inverted-U hypothesis, 605
I/O psychology, A15
IPT, 56
IQ, 401, 402
IQ scores
    cultural bias on tests, 423–424
    cultural differences, 418–420
    Flynn effect, 417
    generational increases, 417f
    mortality, and, 425f
    normal distribution, 403–405
    racial stereotypes, 422–423
    socioeconomic factors, 420–421
    stability over time, 407
    stereotype threat, 421–423
    various relationship types, compared, 415f
iris, 145f
irrational thought, 669
irrelevant information, 365–366
irrelevant reasons, 485
irreversibility, 507
It's a Girl's World, (dir. Lynn Glazier), 1

J

James-Lange theory of emotion, 476
jet lag, 206, 207f
JND, 140
job satisfaction, 482
journal, 48
journal articles, 77–79
Journal of Personality and Social Psychology, 48
Journal of Positive Psychology, The, 21
Jung's analytical psychology, 557–558
just noticeable difference (JND), 140

K

keyword method, 342–343
kinesthetic system, 184

Kinetic Art, 192
Kohlberg's stage theory, 514–515

L

language, 348–365
    animal language development, 360–361
    behaviourist theories, 362
    bilingualism, 356–360
    culture/thought, and, 364–365
    defined, 350
    development milestones, 352–356
    evolutionary context, 361–362
    interactionist theories, 363
    morphemes, 351
    nativist theories, 362–363
    semantics, 351
    structure of, 350–352
    syntax, 351–352
language acquisition device (LAD), 363
language processing, 113f
late adulthood, 525, 535
latency stage, 557
latent learning, 281
lateral antagonism, 148
lateral geniculate nucleus (LGN),
    149, 187
    late selection, 303
law, and psychological disorders, 682–684
law of effect, 262–263
law of small numbers, 383
leadership, A23–A24
learned helplessness, 608, 663
learning, 248–299, 651–652
    biological constraints on conditioning,
        277–280
    classical conditioning, 251–262. See also
        classical conditioning
    cognitive processes, 280–282
    defined, 249
    observational, 283–291. See also
        observational learning
    operant conditioning, 262–277. See also
        operant conditioning
learning theory, 764–766
left brain. See cerebral laterality
left visual field, 150f
legal considerations, and psychological
    disorders, 682–684
lens, 144, 145f
leptin, 444
lesioning, 100
Les Promenades d'Euclide (Magritte), 193f
levels-of-processing theory, 305
LGN, 149, 187
lie detector, 470, 470f
life changes, 600
lifetime prevalence, 646
light, 143–144
light adaptation, 147
likeability, 762
limbic system, 107–110
linear perspective, 164
linguistic intelligence, 427t
linguistic relativity, 364, 387
link method, 342
lithium, 720
lobotomy, 716
locked-in syndrome, 86
logical-mathematical intelligence, 427t
longitudinal research design, 498–499, 499f
long-term memory (LTM), 311–312
long-term potentiation (LTP), 331

loss aversion, 386
love, 482, 754–756
LSD, 695
LTM, 311–312
LTP, 331
lucid dreams, 222, 243
Lucky Man: A Memoir (Fox), 93
lymphocytes, 619

M

magnetic resonance imaging (MRI), 104, 104f
magnocellular channels, 149
major depressive disorder, 656–658
major disasters, 615, 650
maladaptive behaviour, 642
manic-depressive disorder. See bipolar disorder
MAO inhibitors, 718
marijuana, 237–238, 672
marital therapy, 707–708
marriage
    adjusting to, 526–527
    cultural differences, 756–757
    happiness, and, 482
Maslow's hierarchy of needs, 570–571
Maslow's theory of self-actualization, 569–572
master gland, 608
Master of the Arrest of Christ (Francesco), 188f
matching hypothesis, 753–754
mate preferences, 456–457
maturation, 497
McCollough effect, 152, 153, 153f
McGill Pain Questionnaire, 182
MDMA, 234, 238
mean, 59, A8
media
    gender-role socialization, 541
    violence controversy, 284–291
medial forebrain bundle, 109
median, 59, A8
medical advice, 628–629
medical model, 641
meditation, 228
medium tasters, 178
medulla, 105, 106f, 213f
MEIS, 428
melatonin, 206, 207
Mellaril, 717
memory, 300–347
    aging, and meta-memory, 530
    attention, 303–304
    clustering, 313
    declarative vs. procedural, 334–335
    elaboration, 305–306
    encoding, 305
    forgetting, 321–330. See also forgetting
    implicit vs. explicit, 333–334
    knowledge representation/ organization,
        312–316
    long-term memory (LTM), 311–312
    parallel distributed processing, 314–315
    physiology, 330–333
    processing levels, 304–305
    prospective vs. retrospective, 338
    retrieval, 316–320
    schemas, 313–314
    self-referent encoding, 306–307
    semantic networks, 314
    semantic vs. episodic, 335–338
    sensory, 307–308
    short-term memory (STM), 308–309
    storage capacity, 309–310
    storage durability, 309

memory (*Contd.*)
  visual imagery, 306
  working memory, 310–311
menarche, 517
menopause, 528–529
mens rea, 683
mental ability tests, 395–396
mental age, 401
mental disorders. *See* psychological disorders
mental hospital, 729
mental illness, 432–433
mental retardation. *See* intellectual disability
mental set, 367–368
mere exposure effect, 764, 764*f*
mesolimbic dopamine pathway, 235, 471
message, 762
meta-analysis, 65, 66
metalinguistic awareness, 356
meta-memory, 530
method of loci, 342
method section, 78
midbrain, 106*f*, 107, 213*f*
middle adulthood, 525, 535
middle childhood, 533
middle ear, 172, 173*f*
mindfulness meditation, 229
mindfulness-based cognitive therapy, 713–715
mind wandering, 201
Minnesota Multiphasic Personality Inventory (MMPI), 586, 587*f*
mirror neurons, 290–291, 472
misattribution, 329
misinformation effect, 318–319
misses, 140, 140*f*
mixed marriages, 757
MMPI, 586, 587*f*
M'Naghten rule, 683
mnemonic devices, 340, 341–342
mode, 59, A8
molecular geneticists, 122
monoamines, 93
monocular depth cues, 164
monozygotic twins, 121, 121*f*
mood disorders, 655–667, 678
  biological/neurochemical factors, 661–662
  bipolar disorder, 658–659
  cognitive factors, 663–664
  defined, 656
  dispositional factors, 662–663
  diversity, 659–660
  genetic vulnerability, 661
  hormonal factors, 662
  interpersonal roots, 666
  major depressive disorder, 656–658
  precipitating stress, 667
  sports concussions, and depression, 666–667
  suicide, and, 660, 661*f*
mood stabilizers, 720
moon illusion, 167, 168*f*
moral reasoning, 514–515
morphemes, 351
mortality salience, 581
motion parallax, 164
motivated forgetting, 325
motivation, 438–452
  achievement motive, 464–467. *See also* achievement motive
  defined, 440
  drive theories, 441
  evolutionary theories, 441
  hunger/eating, 443–452. *See also* hunger/eating

incentive theories, 441
range/diversity of human motives, 452
sexual. *See* sexual motivation/behaviour
motor development, 496–497, 498*f*
MRI, 104, 104*f*
Müller-Lyer illusion, 165, 165*f*, 167, 168, 168*f*
multiaxial evaluation, 645, 645*f*
Multifactor Emotional Intelligence Scale (MEIS), 428
Multifactorial Memory Questionnaire, 530
multiple personality disorder, 654
multiple sclerosis, 87
multiple-choice exams, 36–37
music, 175–176
musical intelligence, 427*t*
mutations, 118, 125
myelin sheath, 87
myside bias, 384

N

name-calling, 388–389
NAMI, 646
napping, 212
narcissism, 577–580
narcissistic personality disorder (NPD), 577, 676*t*
Narcissistic Personality Inventory (NPI), 580
narcolepsy, 199
Narcolepsy Network, 219
narcotics, 232, 232*f*, 234*t*
narrative mnemonic methods, 342, 342*f*
NASA, 137, 138*f*
National Alliance on Mental Illness (NAMI), 646
national character, 582, 583*f*
nativist theories of language acquisition, 362–363
natural disasters, 650
natural selection, 6, 124
naturalist intelligence, 427*t*
naturalistic observation, 54, 70–71
nature *versus* nurture, 400
NCRMD, 683
NE, 92*t*, 234–235
nearsightedness, 144, 146*f*
Necker cube, 163*f*
need for self-actualization, 570
negative cognitive triad, 663
negative correlation, 62, 62*f*, A10–A11
negative reinforcement
  positive reinforcement, compared, 272–274
  punishment, compared, 274, 275*f*
negatively skewed distribution, 59, 60*f*, A8
negative symptoms, schizophrenic disorders, 671
NEL intelligence, 427*t*
NEO Personality Inventory, 586
nerves, 95
nervous system, 86–98
  autonomic, 96–97, 97*f*
  brain, 98–116. *See also* brain
  central, 97–98
  nervous tissue, 86–88
  neural impulse, 88–89
  neurotransmitters, 92–97. *See also* neurotransmitters
  organization of, 95–98
  peripheral, 95–97
  somatic, 96
  spinal cord, 97–98
  synapse, 89–92

neural impulse, 88–89
neuritic plaques, 529
neurodevelopmental hypothesis of schizophrenia, 674, 674*f*
neurofibrillary tangles, 529
neurogenesis, 111, 216, 331, 608
neurons, 86–89
neuroscientists, 98
neuroticism, 549
neurotransmitters, 92–97, 651
  acetylcholine, 93–94
  defined, 89
  endorphins, 94
  GABA, 94
  glutamate, 94
  monoamines, 94–95
  neural impulse, 89*f*
NGRI. *See* not criminally responsible on account of mental disorder (NCRMD)
nightmares, 219
night terrors, 219
nominal fallacy, 245
nonclinical panic, 648
nondeclarative (procedural) memory system, 334–335
non sequitur, 485
nontasters, 178
norepinephrine (NE), 92*t*, 234–235
normal distribution, A9–A10
  defined, 61, 61*f*
  IQ scores, 403, 405*f*
normative influence, 770
not criminally responsible on account of mental disorder (NCRMD), 683
NPD, 577, 676*t*
NPI, 580
NREM) sleep, 210
Nude Descending a Staircase (Duchamp), 190, 191*f*
null hypothesis, A13
Nurture Assumption, The (Harris), 590
nutrition, 494

O

obedience, 770–773
obesity, 447–452
  BMI, 447
  defined, 447
  dietary restraint, 451
  eating disorders, 451
  excessive eating/inadequate exercise, 449–450
  external cues, 450
  genetic predisposition, 449
  set-point theory, 450–451
object permanence, 506
observational learning, 283–291, 540, 563–564
  acquisition *vs.* performance, 284
  attitudes, and, 766
  basic processes, 283–284
  brain, and, 290–291
  comparative overview, 288–289
  defined, 283
  media violence controversy, 284–290
obsessive-compulsive disorder (OCD), 648–649
obsessive-compulsive personality disorder, 676*t*
occipital lobe, 109
occupational stereotypes, 745

reinforcement. *See also* operant conditioning
  avoidance learning, 273–274
  behaviour modification, 293
  continuous, 270
  defined, 264
  escape learning, 273
  intermittent (partial), 271
  negative, 272–274, 275*f*
  positive, 272–273, 273*f*
  response strength, decreasing, 294
  schedule of, 270–272
  Skinner's demonstration, 263–264
  strengthening of a response tendency, 268–269
  superstitious behaviour, and, 269–270
reinforcement contingencies, 264
relational schemas, 314
relationships, 753–758
  attraction, evolutionary perspective, 758
  culture, and, 756–757
  Internet, and, 757–758
  love as attachment, 755–756
  passionate/companionate love, 754–755
  physical attractiveness, 753–754
  similarity effects, 754
relative refractory period, 88
relative size, 164
relativistic view of psychological disorders, 684
relaxation, 632
relaxation response, 242
relearning, 322
reliability, 396–397
religion, 482
Remote Associates Test (RAT), 430, 431*f*
REM sleep, 209–210
  dreams, 221
  selective deprivation, 214–215
REM sleep behaviour disorder (RBD), 220
Renaissance artists, 188
renewal effect, 259, 267
replication, 65–66
representation of the problem, 370–372
representativeness heuristic, 378, 690, 691
repression, 325, 554, 554*f*
research, 42–83
  behaviour, 44–49
  descriptive/correlational, 53–58
  ethical considerations, 73–75
  evaluation of, 65–69
  experimental, 49–53
  Internet, and, 72–73
  statistics, and, 58–65
research methods, 49
resilience, 615
resistance, 701
resistance to extinction, 266–267
response-outcome relations, 282
response set, 69, 588
Restaurant at the End of the Universe, The (Adams), 301
resting potential of a neuron, 88
results, journal article, 78–79
retention, 322
reticular formation, 106*f*, 213
retina, 145*f*, 146, 147*f*, 148, 150*f*, 187
retinal disparity, 163
retrieval, 302
retrieval cues, 316
retroactive interference, 323–324, 324*f*
retrograde amnesia, 331, 332*f*
retrospective memory, 338, 338*f*

reuptake, 90, 90*f*
reversibility, 507
reversible figure, 158, 162, 162*f*, 163*f*
Rez Sisters (Highway), 223
rhymes, 342
right brain. *See* cerebral laterality
right visual field, 150*f*
risk-taking, adolescence, 519*f*
risky decision making, 376–377
risky drift, 777
rods, 147
Rogers's person-centred theory, 566–569
romantic relationships. *See* relationships
RQ, 407
rumination, 664

S

saccades, 145
SAD, 659
sample, 66–67
sampling bias, 67
SAT, A7
saturation, 144*f*
savants, 411
scaffolding, 511
scatter diagram, A10–A11
Schachter's two-factor theory, 477
schedule of reinforcement, 270–272
schema, 314, 744
schizoid personality disorder, 676*t*
schizophrenic disorders, 668–675, 678
  catatonic type, 670
  disorganized type, 670
  dopamine hypothesis, 93
  etiology, 671–675
  general symptoms, 668–670
  paranoid type, 670
  stress-vulnerability model, 686*f*
  undifferentiated type, 671
schizotypal personality disorder, 676*t*
Scholastic Aptitude Test (SAT), A7
schools, 541
SCIberMENTOR, 413
scientific research. *See* research
seasonal affective disorder (SAD), 659
secondary appraisal, 598
secondary (conditioned) reinforcers, 269
secondary-process thinking, 552
secondary sex characteristics, 517
second-hand smoke, 623
secure attachment, 502, 755, 755*f*
sedatives, 232, 232*f*, 234*t*
selection, A16–A17
selective attention, 303*f*
selective breeding, 120
selective deprivation, 214–215
selective serotonin reuptake inhibitors (SSRIs), 718–720
self-actualizing persons, 571
self-concept, 566
self-discipline, 406
self-discrepancy, 569
self-efficacy, 564
self-enhancement, 584
self-indulgence, 609–610
self-instructional training, 713
self-modification program, 292–295
self-oriented perfectionism, 662
self-perception theory, 767, 767*f*
self-referent encoding, 306–307
self-report data, 68

self-report inventories, 586–588
self-serving attributional bias, 751
self-socialization, 540–541
semantic encoding, 305, 323
semantic memory system, 336, 530
semantic networks, 314, 315*f*
semantic slanting, 387–388
sensation and perception, 136–197
  auditory system, 170–176
  defined, 138
  kinesthetic system, 184
  perception *vs.* sensation, 138, 138*f*
  psychophysics, 139–143. *See also* psychophysics
  smell, 179–180
  taste, 177–179
  thresholds, 139
  touch, 180–183. *See also* touch
  vestibular system, 184
  visual system, 143–170
sensitive period, 512, 513
sensorimotor period, 506, 506*f*
sensory adaptation, 142–143
sensory distortions/ hallucinations, 226
sensory memory, 307–308
separation anxiety, 500
serial-position effect, 340, 341*f*
serotonin, 92*t*
sertraline, 718
set-point theory, 450
settling-point theory, 450–451
sex, 537, 553
sexual abuse, 326*f*
sexual arousal, 256
sexual assault, 459–460, 460*f*
sexual exploitation, 733
sexual motivation/behaviour, 452–464
  evolutionary analysis, 454–459
  excitement phase, 453
  mate preferences, gender differences, 456–457
  orgasm phase, 453–454
  plateau phase, 453
  pornography, 459–460
  resolution phase, 454
  sexual activity, gender differences, 455–456
  sexual orientation mystery, 460–464
sexual orientation, 460–464
  biological theories, 463–464
  defined, 460
  environmental theories, 462
sexual response cycle, 453, 453*f*
Shake Hands with the Devil: The Failure of Humanity in Rwanda (Dallaire), 639
shaping, 266, 267
short-term memory (STM), 308–311
short-term partner, 758
SHSS, 226
siesta cultures, 212–213
sight, 186
signal-detection theory, 140–141
similarity, 160, 161*f*
similarity effects, 754
simple cells, 151
simplicity, 160, 161*f*
16 Personality Factor (16PF) Questionnaire, 586, 587*f*
Skinner box, 264, 265*f*
Skinner's personality development theory, 561–563
skin patches, 181
Slaughterhouse-Five (Vonnegut), 301

Media Resources

PsykTrek

To view a demo: www.nelsonbrain.com/psychology/psyktrek

To order: www.nelsonbrain.com

Go to the PsykTrek website or CD-ROM for further study of the concepts in this chapter. Both online and on the CD-ROM, PsykTrek includes dozens of learning modules with videos, animations, and quizzes, as well as simulations of psychological phenomena and a multimedia glossary that includes word pronunciations.

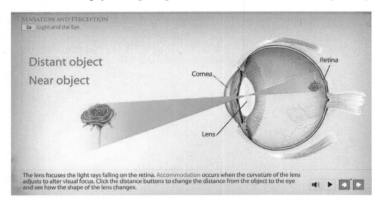

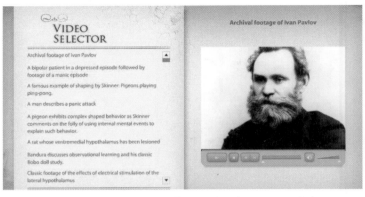

Visit the many modules mentioned throughout the textbook. Through animations and simulations you can see and hear psychological concepts and theories come to life. Here in Module 3a (Light and the Eye), accommodation is explained visually.

The Video Selector showcases many different videos featuring psychologists, various studies, and other classic footage related to the world of psychology.

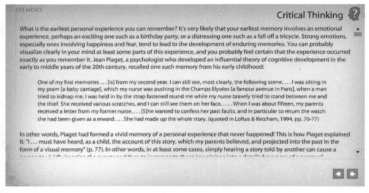

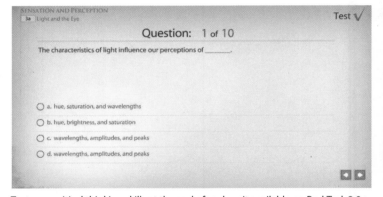

Once you work through the modules, take a multiple choice test to check your memory on the material you are learning. A longer multiple choice quiz is also available at the end of each unit available on PsykTrek 3.0.

Test your critical thinking skills at the end of each unit available on PsykTrek 3.0 in a critical thinking application.

Online Study Tools

Log in to NelsonBrain to access the resources your instructor requires. For this book, you can access the following:

CourseMate brings course concepts to life with interactive learning, study, and exam preparation tools that support the printed textbook. A textbook-specific website, Psychology CourseMate includes an integrated interactive eBook and other interactive learning tools such as quizzes, flashcards, videos, and more.

CengageNow is an easy-to-use online resource that helps you study in less time to get the grade you want—NOW. Take a pre-test for this chapter and receive a personalized study plan based on your results that will identify the topics you need to review and direct you to online resources to help you master those topics. Then take a post-test to help you determine the concepts you have mastered and what you

will need to work on. If your textbook does not include an access code cards, go to NelsonBrain.com to gain access.

Aplia. If your professor has assigned Aplia homework:
1. Sign in to your account.
2. Complete the corresponding homework exercises as required by your professor.
3. Click "Grade It Now" when you have finished, to see which areas you have mastered, which need more work, and get detailed explanations of every answer.

Visit www.nelsonbrain.com to access your account and purchase materials.

CONCEPT CHARTS

FOR STUDY AND REVIEW TO ACCOMPANY

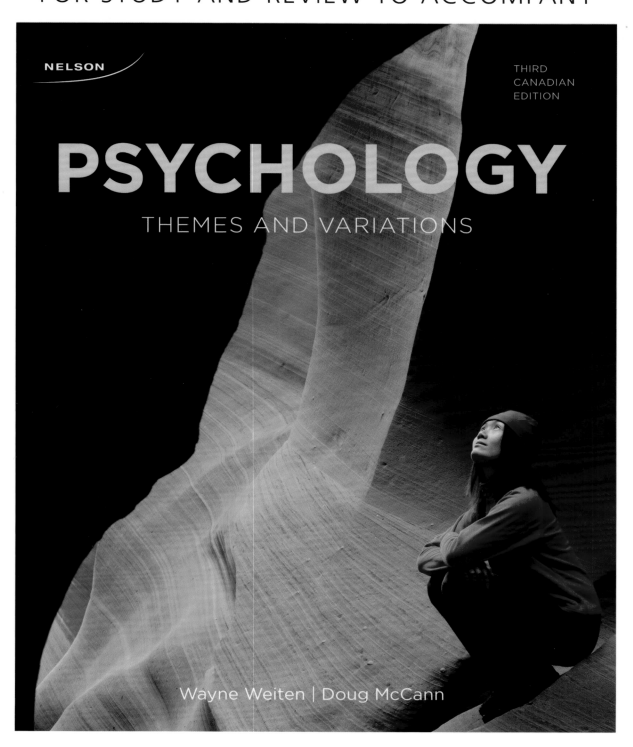

NELSON

THIRD
CANADIAN
EDITION

PSYCHOLOGY

THEMES AND VARIATIONS

Wayne Weiten | Doug McCann

Concept Charts
for Study and Review

to accompany

Psychology:
Themes and Variations

Third Canadian Edition

Concept Charts
for Study and Review

to accompany

Psychology:
Themes and Variations

Third Canadian Edition

Wayne Weiten
Doug McCann

NELSON EDUCATION

Concept Charts to accompany *Psychology: Themes and Variations,* **Third Canadian Edition**
by Wayne Weiten and Doug McCann

Vice President, Editorial Higher Education:
Anne Williams

Senior Acquisitions Editor:
Lenore Taylor-Atkins

Marketing Manager:
Ann Byford

Senior Developmental Editor:
Sandy Matos

Photo Researcher:
Jessie Coffey

Permissions Coordinator:
Jessie Coffey

Content Production Manager:
Claire Horsnell

Production Service:
MPS Limited, a Macmillan Company

Copy Editor:
Lila Campbell

Proofreader:
Lila Campbell

Senior Manufacturing Coordinator:
Joanne McNeil

Design Director:
Ken Phipps

Managing Designer:
Franca Amore

Interior Design:
David Murphy at Valid Design

Cover Design:
Martyn Schmoll

Cover Image:
© Corbis

Compositor:
MPS Limited, a Macmillan Company

COPYRIGHT © 2013, 2010
by Nelson Education Ltd.

Adapted from Concept Charts to accompany *Psychology: Themes and Variations,* Ninth Edition, by Wayne Weiten, published by Thomas Wadsworth. Copyright ©2012 by Thomas Wadsworth

Printed and bound in Canada
3 4 5 6 17 16 15 14

For more information contact Nelson Education Ltd.,
1120 Birchmount Road, Toronto, Ontario, M1K 5G4. Or you can visit our Internet site at
http://www.nelson.com

Library and Archives Canada Cataloguing in Publication

Weiten, Wayne, 1950-
Concept charts for study and review to accompany Psychology : themes and variations, third Canadian edition / Wayne Weiten, Doug McCann.

Supplement to: Psychology.

ISBN 978-0-17-664776-6

1. Psychology—Textbooks.
I. McCann, Douglas, 1951- II. Title.

BF121.W442 2012   150
C2011-908744-8

ISBN-13: 978-0-17-664776-6
ISBN-10: 0-17-664776-7

Contents

A Letter to the Student

Greetings! This booklet of Concept Charts is intended to help you organize, assimilate, and master the main ideas contained in your textbook, *Psychology: Themes & Variations,* Third Canadian Edition. In the pages that follow, you will find a two-page Concept Chart for each chapter. The Concept Charts provide you with very detailed roadmaps of the key ideas found in the main body of each chapter, including significant content created for the Canadian version of the text.

How are the Concept Charts different from the Chapter Recaps found near the end of each chapter in the book? First, they are quite a bit more detailed. Second, they are presented in an outline format. Research suggests that outlines of reading assignments can enhance students' understanding and retention of textbook material. Third, we have used colour-coded, hierarchically organized charts to create snapshots of the chapters that allow you to quickly see the relationships among ideas and sections. Seeing how it all fits together should help you to better understand each chapter. Moreover, research suggests that encoding information visually as well as verbally aids retention.

Generally, the charts are laid out to follow the order of presentation in the chapter, reading left to right and top to bottom. The colour coding shows you at a glance which ideas go together. Groups of ideas that are related all have the same background colour. Dotted lines are also used to make the connections between various groups of ideas readily apparent, including hierarchical relationships. When boxes are connected by arrows, these arrows reflect the operation of causal or time-related sequences.

How should you use the Concept Charts? Here's what we suggest:
1. Before reading each chapter, look over the relevant Concept Chart to get a quick overview of what you will be reading about. This brief preview can help you to better assimilate the chapter's information as you read.
2. After you have read a chapter, review the Concept Chart once again to make sure you have registered all the key ideas.
3. Then study the chapter as you normally would, using the Study Guide, Psyk.Trek, Web study tools, or whatever else works for you.
4. When you feel that you have mastered the chapter content reasonably well, return to the Concept Chart and make sure that you understand how it all fits together.
5. Finally, wrap up by working to memorize the key ideas outlined in the Concept Chart.

We hope these visual maps of chapter content help you to master the material in your textbook. Good luck in your studying efforts. If you have any comments about the Concept Charts that you would like to share we would love to hear from you (dmccann@yorku.ca).

Wayne Weiten
Doug McCann

Chapter 1

How Psychology Developed

The Evolution of Psychology

Psychology's intellectual parents: Philosophy and physiology

- Classical Greek philosophers, such as Socrates and Aristotle, considered issues such as mind–body and the nature of memory.
- Later philosophers, such as Descartes, Hume, and Mill, speculated on the mind and emotions.
- Physiologists, such as Gall, Broca, and Müller, demonstrated the value of an empirical approach.

A new science is born

- Psychology's founder was Wilhelm Wundt, who set up the first research lab in 1879 (in Germany).
- Wundt argued that psychology should be the scientific study of consciousness.
- G. Stanley Hall launched America's first psychology journal (in 1887) and helped establish the American Psychological Association (in 1892).

The battle of the "schools" begins

- Advocates of structuralism argued that psychology should use introspection to analyze consciousness into its basic elements.
- Advocates of functionalism argued that psychology should investigate the purposes of consciousness.
- Functionalism had a more lasting impact on psychology, as it fostered the emergence of behaviourism and applied psychology.

Evolutionary psychology gains prominence

- The 1990s saw the emergence of a major, new theoretical perspective called evolutionary psychology.
- Its crucial premise is that the patterns of behaviour seen in a species are the product of evolution, just like anatomical characteristics.
- According to evolutionary psychologists, natural selection favours behaviours that enhance organisms' reproductive success.

Psychology moves in a positive direction

- Martin Seligman, former President of APA, argued that psychology historically has focused too much on pathology and suffering. He launched the positive psychology movement in the late 1990's.
- Positive psychology uses theory and research to better understand our adaptive, creative, and fulfilling experiences and processes. It emphasizes constructs such as positive emotions, personal strength, and happiness.

Interest in cultural factors grows

- In the 1980s, Western psychologists developed increased interest in how cultural variables influence behaviour.
- This trend was stimulated by the increased cultural diversity in Western societies and by growing global interdependence.

Cognition and physiology resurface

- In its early days, psychology emphasized the study of consciousness and physiology, but these topics languished as behaviourism grew more dominant.
- During the 1950s and 1960s advances in research on mental and physiological processes led to renewed interest in cognition and the biological bases of behaviour.

Psychology becomes a profession

- In the first half of the 20th century, only a handful of psychologists were involved in the delivery of professional services to the public.
- However, stimulated by the demands of World War II, clinical psychology began rapid growth in the 1950s.
- Today, the vast majority of psychologists are involved in professional services.

Freud focuses on unconscious forces

- Although Sigmund Freud's views were controversial, they gradually became influential.
- Psychoanalytic theory emphasizes unconscious determinants of behaviour and the importance of sexuality.
- According to Freud, the unconscious consists of thoughts that one is not aware of but that still influence one's behaviour.

Specialties in Contemporary Psychology

Behaviourism debuts

- Behaviourism, founded by John B. Watson, asserted that psychology should study only observable behaviour.
- This view gradually took hold and psychology became the scientific study of behaviour (instead of consciousness).
- The behaviourists stressed the importance of environment over heredity and pioneered animal research.

Professional specialties

- Clinical psychology
- Counselling psychology
- Educational and school psychology
- Industrial and organizational psychology
- Clinical neuropsychology
- Forensic psychology

Research areas

- Developmental psychology
- Social psychology
- Experimental psychology
- Physiological psychology
- Cognitive psychology
- Personality
- Psychometrics
- Educational psychology
- Health psychology

Behaviourism flourishes with the work of Skinner

- Boosted by B. F. Skinner's research, behaviourism reached its zenith of influence in the 1950s.
- Like Watson, he emphasized animal research, a strict focus on observable behaviour, and the importance of environment.
- He generated controversy by arguing that free will is an illusion.

Key Themes

Themes related to psychology as a field of study

- **Psychology is empirical**—it is based on objective observations made through research.
- **Psychology is theoretically diverse**— a variety of perspectives are needed to enhance our understanding of behaviour.
- **Psychology evolves in a sociohistorical context**— dense connections exist between what happens in psychology and what happens in society at large.

Themes related to psychology's subject matter

- **Behaviour is determined by multiple causes**— complex causation is the rule and single-cause explanations are usually incomplete.
- **Behaviour is shaped by cultural heritage**— cultural factors exert considerable influence over some aspects of behaviour.
- **Heredity and environment jointly influence behaviour**—nature and nurture interactively shape most behavioural traits.
- **People's experience of the world is highly subjective**—people tend to see what they expect to see and what they want to see.

The humanists revolt

- Finding both behaviourism and psychoanalysis unappealing, advocates of humanism, such as Carl Rogers and Abraham Maslow, began to gain some influence in the 1950s.
- Humanism emphasizes the unique qualities of human behaviour and the irrelevance of animal research.
- The humanists also took an optimistic view of human nature, stressing humans' freedom and potential for growth.

Psychology in Canada

- The first experimental laboratory in Canada was established in 1891 at the University of Toronto by James Mark Baldwin.
- John Wallace Baird was the first Canadian President of APA (in 1918).
- The Canadian Psychological Association was formed in 1939.
- Rapid growth in Canadian psychology has been evident over the last century.

Chapter 2

The Research Enterprise in Psychology

The Scientific Approach

Goals

- Measurement and description
- Understanding and prediction
- Application and control

Steps in an investigation

1. Formulate a testable hypothesis.
2. Select the method and design the study.
3. Collect the data.
4. Analyze the data and draw conclusions.
5. Report the findings.

Advantages

Clarity and precision yield better communication.

Intolerance of error yields more reliable data.

Research approaches

1. Quantitative methods
2. Qualitative methods

Experimental Research

Elements

Independent variable (IV): Condition or event manipulated by experimenter

Dependent variable (DV): Aspect of behaviour thought to be affected by independent variable

Experimental group: Participants who receive special treatment

Control group: Similar subjects who do not receive treatment given to experimental group

Extraneous variables: Factors besides IV that might affect DV, hence they need to be controlled

Variations

- Can have one group of subjects serve as their own control group
- Can manipulate more than one independent variable in a study
- Can use multiple dependent variables in a study

Advantages and disadvantages

+ Permits conclusions about cause and effect relationships
− Manipulations and control often make experiments artificial
− Practical realities and ethical concerns make it impossible to conduct experiments on many issues

Descriptive/Correlation Research

Examples of specific methods

Naturalistic observation: Careful, systematic observation, but no intervention with subjects

Case study: In-depth investigation of single participant, typically involving data from many sources

Survey: Questionnaires and interviews are used to gather information about specific aspects of participants' behaviour

Advantages and disadvantages

+ Broadens the scope of phenomena that psychologists can study (can explore issues that could not be examined with experimental methods)
− Cannot demonstrate that two variables are causally related

Key Themes

- Psychology is empirical.
- Our experience of the world is highly subjective.

Statistics

Basic descriptive statistics

- Frequency polygons are graphs used to present data from a frequency distribution. The normal distribution, or bell-shaped curve, is one common type of distribution.

- Three measures of central tendency are the median (centre score), the mean (arithmetic average), and the mode (most frequent score).

- The mean tends to be the most useful index of central tendency, but the median may be better if the mean is inflated by a few extreme scores.

- Variability refers to how much scores vary from each other and the mean.

- The standard deviation is an index of the amount of variability in a data set.

Inferential statistics

- *Inferential statistics* are used to interpret data and draw conclusions.

- *Hypothesis testing* involves making calculations to determine whether research results are statistically significant.

- *Statistical significance* exists when the probability that observed findings are due to chance is very low.

Correlation

Correlation exists when two variables are related to each other.

Types: Positive (variables co-vary in the same direction) or negative (variables co-vary in the opposite direction)

Correlation coefficient: Numerical index of degree of relationship between two variables

Strength: The closer the correlation to either -1.00 or $+1.00$, the stronger the relationship

Prediction: The stronger the correlation, the better one can predict

Causation: Correlation is not equivalent to causation

Meta-analysis

- Combines statistical results of many studies of the same question

- Results yield an estimate of the size and consistency of a variable's effects

Common Flaws in Research

Sampling bias

Exists when a sample is not representative of the population

Placebo effects

Occur when participants' expectations lead them to experience some change even though they receive empty or fake treatment

Distortions in self-report data

Result from problems, such as social desirability bias and response sets, that happen when participants give verbal accounts of their behaviour

Experimenter bias

Occurs when a researcher's expectations or preferences about the outcome of a study influence the results obtained

Internet-Mediated Research

Issues in collecting data on the Internet

- Internet-mediated research has grown in recent years because it offers access to large and more diverse samples and to specialized samples while reducing costs and saving time

- However, Internet-mediated research raises its own concerns about sampling bias, and uncontrolled conditions during data collection

Ethical Issues

Ethical guidelines for research in psychology in Canada

- **Principle I:** Respect for the dignity of persons
- **Principle II:** Responsible caring
- **Principle III:** Integrity in relationships
- **Principle IV:** Responsibility to society

Important ethical issues

- Deception: Should researchers be permitted to mislead research participants?

- Animal research: Should researchers be permitted to subject animals to harmful or painful procedures?

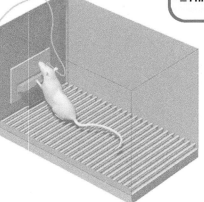

The Biological Bases of Behaviour

Communication in the Nervous System

Key parts of the neuron

Soma: Cell body

Dendrites: Branching structures that receive signals from other cells

Axon: Fibre that carries signals away from soma to other cells

Myelin sheath: Insulating material that encases some axons

Terminal buttons: Small knobs at ends of axons that release neurotransmitters at synapses

The neural impulse

Resting potential: Neuron's stable, negative charge when inactive

Action potential: Voltage spike that travels along axon

Absolute refractory period: Brief time after action potential before another action potential can begin

All-or-none law: A neuron either fires or doesn't fire

Organization of the Nervous System

Central nervous system

- **Brain**
- **Spinal cord**

Peripheral nervous system

Somatic nervous system: Nerves to voluntary muscles, sensory receptors

- **Afferent** (incoming) nerves
- **Efferent** (outgoing) nerves

Autonomic nervous system: Nerves to heart, blood vessels, smooth muscles, glands

- **Sympathetic division:** Mobilizes bodily resources
- **Parasympathet[ic] division:** Conserv[es] bodily resources

Methods for study of brain function

EEGs monitor the electrical activity of the brain over time, yielding line tracings called brain waves.

Lesioning involves destroying a piece of the brain to learn about its function.

Electrical stimulation of the brain involves sending a weak current into a brain structure to activate it.

Transcranial magnetic stimulation is a new technique that permits scientists to temporarily enhance or depress activity in a specific area of the brain.

CT scans and MRI scans can provide precise images of brain structure.

PET scans and fMRI scans can map actual activity of the brain over time.

Brain and Behaviour

Midbrain
Involved in locating things in space; dopamine synthesis

Plasticity of the bra[in]
The anatomical structure and functional organization of the b[rain] is somewhat malleable.

Forebrain

Thalamus: Relay centre for cortex; distributes incoming sensory signals, except smell

Cerebrum: Handles complex mental activities, such as sensing, learning, thinking, planning

Limbic system: Loosely connected network that contributes to emotion, memory, motivation

Hypothalamus: Regulates basic biological needs, such as hunger, thirst, sex

Frontal lobes: Primary motor cortex

Hippocampus: Contributes to memory

Amygdala: Involved in learning of fea[r] responses

Cerebellum: Coordinates fine muscle movement, balance

Hindbrain

Pons: Involved in sleep and arousal

Medulla: Regulates unconscious functions such as breathing and circulation

Prefrontal cortex: Involved in relational reasoning; working memory

Parietal lobes: Primary somatosensory cortex

Temporal lobes: Primary auditory cortex

Occipital lobes: Primary visual cortex

Neurotransmitters and behaviour

Acetylcholine: Released by neurons that control skeletal muscles

Serotonin: Involved in regulation of sleep; abnormal levels linked to depression and obsessive-compulsive disorder

Dopamine: Abnormal levels linked to schizophrenia; dopamine circuits activated by cocaine and amphetamines

Norepinephrine: Abnormal levels linked to depression; contributes to modulation of mood and arousal

GABA: Inhibitory transmitter that contributes to regulation of anxiety

Endorphins: Opiate-like chemicals involved in modulation of pain

Glutamate: Excitatory transmitter linked to memory process of long-term potentiation

Synaptic transmission

Synthesis and storage of neurotransmitters in synaptic vesicles → **Release** of neuro-transmitters into synaptic cleft → **Binding** of neuro-transmitters at receptor sites leads to excitatory and inhibitory PSPs → **Inactivation or removal** (drifting away) of neuro-transmitters

Re-uptake of neurotransmitters by presynaptic neuron

Heredity and Behaviour

Basic concepts

- *Chromosomes* are threadlike strands of DNA that carry genetic information.
- *Genes* are DNA segments that are the key functional units in hereditary transmission.
- Two genes in a specific pair may be *homozygous* (the same) or *heterozygous* (different).
- When paired genes are different, one may be *dominant* (expressed) and the other *recessive* (masked).
- *Genotype* refers to a person's genetic makeup, whereas *phenotype* refers to a person's observable characteristics.
- Most behavioural traits appear to involve polygenic *inheritance*.

Research methods

Family studies assess trait resemblance among blood relatives.

Twin studies compare trait resemblance of identical and fraternal twins.

Adoption studies compare adopted children to their adoptive parents and to their biological parents.

Genetic mapping determines the location and chemical sequence of specific genes, which can help to pinpoint links between particular genes and behavioural traits.

Epigenetics is the study of heritable changes in gene expression not involving DNA sequence modifications.

Right Brain/Left Brain

Methods for study of lateralization

Split brain surgery: Bundle of fibres (corpus callosum) that connects two emispheres is severed.

Perceptual asymmetries: Left–right imbalances in speed of processing re studied in normal subjects.

Brain imaging: fMRI scans can identify specific neural circuits in the left or ght hemisphere that appear to handle various cognitive tasks.

Left hemisphere
Usually handles verbal processing, including language, speech, reading, writing

Right hemisphere
Usually handles nonverbal processing, including spatial, musical, and visual recognition tasks

Endocrine System

- Consists of glands that secrete chemicals called hormones into the bloodstream
- Governed by the hypothalamus and pituitary gland, regulates digestion, response to stress, and sexual development
- Among other things, hormones regulate responses to stress, sexual development, insulin production, metabolic rate

Evolutionary Bases of Behaviour

Darwin's insights

1. Organisms vary in endless ways.
2. Some traits are heritable.
3. Variations in hereditary traits might affect organisms' survival and reproductive success.
4. Heritable traits that provide a survival or reproductive advantage will become more prevalent over generations (natural selection will change the gene pool of the population).

Key concepts

Fitness refers to the reproductive success of an organism relative to the population.

Adaptations are inherited characteristics sculpted through natural selection because they helped solve a problem of survival or reproduction when they emerged.

Behaviours as adaptive traits

- Species' typical patterns of behaviour often reflect evolutionary solutions to adaptive problems.
- For example, behavioural strategies that help organisms avoid predators have obvious adaptive value.
- Many behavioural adaptations improve organisms' chances of reproductive success.

Key Themes

- Psychology is empirical.
- Heredity and environment jointly shape behaviour.
- Behaviour is determined by multiple causes.

Chapter 4

Sensation and Perception

The Visual System

Light waves

vary in   which affects perceptions of

Amplitude →	**Brightness**
Wavelength →	**Colour (hue)**
Purity →	**Saturation**

Light is registered by receptors in the eye

Key eye structures

include the

Lens, which focuses light rays falling on the retina

Pupil, which regulates the amount of light passing to the rear of the eye

Retina, which is the neural tissue lining the inside back surface of the eye

Optic disk, which is a hole in the retina that corresponds to the *blind spot*

Fovea, which is a tiny spot in the centre of the retina where visual acuity is greatest

In the retina

Visual receptors

consist of *rods* and *cones,* which are organized into *receptive fields*.

Rods play a key role in night and peripheral vision and greatly outnumber cones.

Cones play a key role in day and colour vision and provide greater acuity than rods.

Receptive fields are collections of rods and cones that funnel signals to specific visual cells in the retina or the brain.

Visual signals are sent onward to the brain

Visual pathways and processing

The main visual pathway can be subdivided into the *parvocellular channel* and *magnocellular channel,* which engage in parallel processing of stimulus input.

The second visual pathway handles coordination of visual input with other sensory input.

The primary visual cortex in the occipital lobe handles the initial cortical processing of visual input.

Feature detectors are neurons in the visual cortex that respond selectively to specific features of complex stimuli.

After processing in the primary visual cortex, visual input is routed to other cortical areas along the *where pathway* (dorsal stream) and the *what pathway* (ventral stream).

Optical illusions

■ An *optical illusion* is a discrepancy between the appearance of a visual stimulus and its physical reality.

■ Optical illusions, such as the *Müller-Lyer illusion,* the *Ponzo illusion,* and the *moon illusion,* show that perceptual hypotheses can be wrong and that perception is not a simple reflection of objective reality.

Colour perception

Subtractive colour mixing works by removing some wavelengths of light, leaving less light.

Additive colour mixing works by putting more light in the mixture than any one light.

Trichromatic theory holds that the eye has three groups of receptors sensitive to wavelengths associated with red, green, and blue.

Opponent process theory holds that receptors make antagonistic responses to three pairs of colours.

Conclusion: The evidence suggests that both theories are necessary to explain colour perception.

Form perception

■ The same visual input can result in very different perceptions.

■ Form perception is selective, as the phenomenon of *inattentional blindness* demonstrates.

■ Some aspects of form perception depend on *feature analysis,* which involves detecting specific elements and assembling them into complex forms.

■ *Gestalt principles,* such as *figure and ground, proximity, closure, similarity, simplicity,* and *continuity,* help explain how scenes are organized into discrete forms.

■ Form perception often involves *perceptual hypotheses,* which are inferences about the distal stimuli that could be responsible for the proximal stimuli sensed.

Depth perception

Binocular cues are clues about distance based on the differing views of the two eyes.

Retinal disparity, for example, refers to the fact that the right and left eyes see slightly different views of objects.

Monocular cues are clues about distance based on the image in either eye alone.

Pictorial cues are monocular cues that can be given in a flat picture, such as *linear perspective, texture gradients, relative size, height in plane, interposition,* and *light and shadow.*

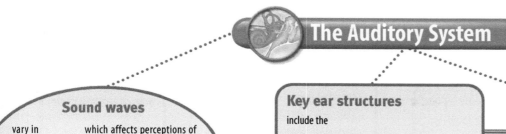

The Auditory System

Sound waves

vary in	which affects perceptions of
Amplitude	→ **Loudness**
Wavelength	→ **Pitch**
Purity	→ **Timbre**

Sound is registered by receptors in the ear

Key ear structures

include the

Pinna, which is the external ear's sound-collecting cone

Eardrum, which is a taut membrane at the end of the auditory canal that vibrates in response to sound waves

Ossicles, which are three tiny bones in the middle ear that convert the eardrum's vibrations into smaller motions

Cochlea, which is the fluid-filled, coiled tunnel that houses the inner ear's neural tissue

Basilar membrane, which holds the hair cells that serve as auditory receptors

Pitch perception

Place theory holds that perception of pitch depends on the portion of the basilar membrane vibrated.

Frequency theory holds that perception of pitch depends on the basilar membrane's rate of vibration.

Conclusion: The evidence suggests that both theories are needed to explain pitch perception.

Auditory localization

- Auditory localization involves locating the source of sounds in space.
- Critical cues include the loudness and the timing of sounds arriving at each ear.

Psychophysics

Basic concepts

Absolute thresholds are minimum detectable stimulus intensities for specific types of sensory input.

Weber's law states that the size of a just noticeable difference (JND) is a constant proportion of the size of the initial stimulus.

Fechner's law states that the magnitude of a sensory experience is proportional to the number of JNDs that the stimulus is above the absolute threshold.

Signal detection theory proposes that the detection of stimuli involves decision processes as well as sensory processes.

Subliminal perception is the registration of sensory input without conscious awareness; it is a genuine phenomenon, but the effects tend to be very weak.

Sensory adaptation is a gradual decline in sensitivity to a stimulus with prolonged stimulation.

The Chemical Senses

Taste

- Taste cells absorb chemicals in saliva and trigger neural impulses routed through the thalamus.
- Traditional views hold that our taste buds are sensitive to four basic tastes: sweet, sour, bitter, and salty.
- Recently, it has been suggested that there is a fifth basic taste sense: **umami**. Umami is a Japanese word for the savoury taste of glutamate.
- Sensitivity to these tastes is distributed somewhat unevenly across the tongue, but the variations are small.
- Taste preferences are largely learned and heavily shaped by social processes.
- Supertasters have more taste buds and are more sensitive than others to certain sweet and bitter substances.

Smell

- Olfactory cilia absorb chemicals in the nose and trigger neural impulses.
- Smell is the only sensory system that is not routed through the thalamus.
- Most olfactory receptors respond to more than one odour.
- People tend to have a hard time attaching names to odours.

The Sense of Touch

- Sensory receptors in the skin respond to pressure, temperature, and pain.
- Pain signals travel along a *fast pathway* that registers localized pain and a *slow pathway* that carries less localized pain sensations.
- Cultural variations in the experience of pain show the subjective nature of pain perception.
- *Gate-control* theory holds that incoming pain signals can be blocked in the spinal cord.
- Endorphins and a descending neural pathway appear responsible for this supression of pain.

Other Senses

The kinesthetic system

Receptors in the kinesthetic system monitor the positions of the various parts of the body.

The vestibular system

Receptors in the vestibular system provide information about the body's location in space.

Key Themes

- Psychology is characterized by theoretical diversity.
- Our experience of the world is highly subjective.
- Behaviour is shaped by one's cultural heritage.

Chapter 5

Variations in Consciousness

Consciousness

The nature of consciousness

- *Consciousness* involves varied levels of awareness.
- Mental processes continue during sleep, as some stimuli can penetrate awareness.
- Research suggests that decisions made when people do not have the chance to make conscious deliberations may sometimes be more accurate.
- The evolutionary significance of consciousness is a matter of debate.
- Changes in consciousness are correlated with changes in brain activity as measured by EEGs.

The architecture of sleep

- *Non-REM* sleep consists of stages 1–4, which are marked by an absence of rapid eye movements, relatively little dreaming, and varied EEG activity.
- *REM sleep* is a deep stage of sleep marked by rapid eye movements, high-frequency brain waves, and dreaming.
- During the course of sleep, REM periods gradually get longer and non-REM periods get shorter and shallower.
- The architecture of sleep varies somewhat from one person to the next.

Sleep deprivation

- Partial deprivation is common and can impair alertness; it appears to contribute to many accidents.
- Selective deprivation of REM and slow-wave sleep leads to increased attempts to shift into these stages of sleep and increased time spent in these stages after sleep deprivation ends.
- Recent studies suggest that REM and slow-wave sleep help firm up learning that takes place during the day—a process called "memory consolidation".
- Short sleep duration is associated with a variety of health problems, but both short and long sleepers exhibit elevated mortality rates.

Sleep

Biological Rhythms

Relations to sleep

- Circadian (24-hour) rhythms are influential in the regulation of sleep.
- Internal biological clocks are reset by exposure to light, which stimulates the SCN, which signals the pineal gland to secrete melatonin.
- The poor sleep associated with jet lag and rotating shift work is due to being out of sync with circadian rhythms.
- Administration of melatonin, and exposure to bright light appear to have some value in efforts to realign circadian rhythms that are out of sync.

Factors influencing sleep

- The REM portion of sleep declines from 50% among newborns to about 20% among adults.
- The time spent in slow-wave sleep declines during adulthood.
- Culture does not appear to have much effect on the architecture of sleep.
- Culture does influence napping practices and co-sleeping, which are normative in many societies.
- Many brain structures and neurotransmitters contribute to the regulation of sleep.

Insomnia

- Insomnia occurs in three patterns: difficulty falling asleep, difficulty remaining asleep, and persistent early morning awakenings.
- Insomnia is a fairly common sleep disorder and it has many diverse causes including the possibility that insomniacs have a higher arousal level.
- Sedative drugs are a poor long-term solution to insomnia because of the risk of overdose, escalating dependency, and carryover drowsiness.

Other sleep problems

Narcolepsy is marked by sudden and irresistible onsets of sleep during normal waking periods.

Sleep apnea involves frequent, reflexive gasping for air that disrupts sleep.

Nightmares are anxiety-arousing dreams that lead to awakening, usually from REM sleep.

Night terrors are abrupt awakenings from non-REM sleep accompanied by intense arousal and panic.

Somnambulism (sleepwalking) occurs when a person wanders about while remaining asleep.

REM sleep behaviour disorder is characterized by potentially disruptive dream enactments during REM periods.

The World of Dreams

The nature of dreams

- The concept of what constitutes a dream is being re-evaluated by scientists.
- Dreams are less exotic than widely assumed.
- Dreams may be affected by events in one's life and external stimuli.
- Cultural variations are seen in dream recall, dream content, dream interpretation, and the importance attributed to dreams.

Theories of dreaming

- Sigmund Freud asserted that the chief purpose of dreams is wish fulfillment.
- Other theorists argue that dreams provide an opportunity to think creatively about personal problems.
- The *activation–synthesis* model proposes that dreams are side effects of the neural activation that produces waking-like brain waves during REM sleep.

Hypnosis

Hypnotic induction and phenomena

- *Hypnosis* is a procedure that produces a heightened state of suggestibility.
- People vary in their susceptibility to hypnosis.
- Hypnotic susceptibility is a stable trait made up of three components: absorption, dissociation, and suggestibility.
- Hypnosis can produce a variety of effects, including anesthesia, sensory distortions, disinhibition, and posthypnotic amnesia.

Theories of hypnosis

- According to Theodore Barber, hypnosis produces a normal state of consciousness in which people act out the role of hypnotized subject.
- The role-playing view is supported by evidence that hypnotic feats can be duplicated by nonhypnotized subjects and that hypnotic subjects are often acting out a role.
- According to Ernest Hilgard, hypnosis produces an altered state of awareness characterized by dissociation.
- The altered state view is supported by evidence that divided consciousness is a common state that has continuity with everyday experience.

Meditation

Physiological correlates and long-term benefits

- Meditation refers to a family of practices that train attention to heighten awareness and bring mental processes under greater voluntary control.
- Two types of mediation are *focused attention* and *open monitoring*.
- Studies suggest that effective meditation leads to a beneficial physiological state that may be accompanied by changes in brain activity.
- Evidence suggests that meditation may reduce stress hormones, enhance self-esteem and well-being, and reduce vulnerability to a variety of diseases. Recent work highlights the efficacy of cognitive-behavioural therapy rooted in mindfulness meditation. Some critics suggest that these benefits may not be unique to meditation and are a product of relaxation.

Altering Consciousness with Drugs

Principal abused drugs

Narcotics are drugs derived from opium, such as heroin.

Sedatives are sleep-inducing drugs, such as barbiturates.

Stimulants are drugs that increase CNS activation, such as cocaine and amphetamines.

Hallucinogens, such as LSD and mescaline, produce sensory distortions and diverse mental and emotional effects.

Cannabis is the hemp plant from which marijuana, hashish, and THC are derived.

Alcohol includes a variety of beverages that contain ethyl alcohol.

MDMA (ecstasy) is a compound drug related to amphetamines and hallucinogens.

Factors influencing drug effects

- Drug effects depend on users' age, mood, personality, weight, expectations, and previous experience with drugs.
- Drug effects also depend on the potency of the drug, the method of administration, and the user's tolerance.

Mechanisms of drug action

- Psychoactive drugs exert their effects by selectively altering neurotransmitter activity.
- Increased activation in the *mesolimbic dopamine pathway* may be responsible for the reinforcing effects of many drugs.

Risks associated with drug abuse

- *Physical dependence* exists when drug use must be continued to avoid withdrawal illness.
- *Psychological dependence* exists when drug use must be continued to satisfy craving for the drug.
- Many drugs, especially CNS depressants, can produce a lethal *overdose*.
- Many drugs cause deleterious health effects by producing *direct tissue damage*.
- The negative effects of drugs on physical health are often due to *indirect behavioural effects*.

Key Themes

- Psychology is characterized by theoretical diversity.
- Our experience of the world is highly subjective.
- Behaviour is shaped by one's cultural heritage.
- Psychology evolves in a sociohistorical context.

Chapter 6

Learning

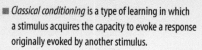
Classical Conditioning

Operant Conditioning

Description

Classical Conditioning

- *Classical conditioning* is a type of learning in which a stimulus acquires the capacity to evoke a response originally evoked by another stimulus.
- Classical conditioning was pioneered by Ivan Pavlov, who conditioned dogs to salivate when a tone was presented.
- Classical conditioning mainly regulates involuntary, reflexive responses.
- Examples include emotional responses (such as fears) and physiological responses (such as immunosuppression).

Operant Conditioning

- *Operant conditioning* is a type of learning in which responses come to be controlled by their consequences.
- E. L. Thorndike's work on instrumental learning and the *law of effect* provided the foundation for the study of operant conditioning.
- Operant conditioning was pioneered by B. F. Skinner, who showed that rats and pigeons tend to repeat responses that are followed by favourable outcomes.
- Operant conditioning mainly regulates voluntary, spontaneous responses, such as studying, going to work, telling jokes, and asking someone out.

Terminology and procedures

Classical Conditioning

- Responses controlled through classical conditioning are said to be *elicited*.
- Classical conditioning begins with an *unconditioned stimulus (UCS)* that elicits an *unconditioned response (UCR)*.
- Then a neutral stimulus is paired with the UCS until it becomes a *conditioned stimulus (CS)* that elicits a *conditioned response (CR)*.

Operant Conditioning

- Responses controlled through operant conditioning are said to be *emitted*.
- Demonstrations of operant conditioning typically occur in a *Skinner box* where an animal's reinforcement is controlled.
- The key dependent variable is the animal's response rate as monitored by a *cumulative* recorder, with results portrayed in graphs (steeper slopes are indicative of faster responding).

Basic processes

Acquisition is the formation of a conditioned response tendency.

Extinction is the gradual weakening of a conditioned response tendency.

Generalization occurs when an organism responds to new stimuli besides the original stimulus.

Discrimination occurs when an organism does not respond to other stimuli that resemble the original stimulus.

Classical Conditioning

- *Acquisition* occurs when a CS and UCS are paired, gradually resulting in a CR.
- Acquisition depends on *stimulus contiguity,* which is a temporal association between events.
- *Extinction* occurs when a CS is repeatedly presented alone until it no longer elicits a CR.
- *Spontaneous recovery* is the reappearance of an extinguished response after a period of nonexposure to the CS.
- *Generalization* occurs when a CR is elicited by a new stimulus that resembles the original CS.
- *Discrimination* occurs when a CR is not elicited by a new stimulus that resembles the original CS.
- *Higher-order conditioning* occurs when a CS functions as if it were a UCS.
- *Renewal effect* occurs when a response that has been extinguished in a context different from that in which it was acquired reappears in the original context.

Operant Conditioning

- *Acquisition* occurs when a response gradually increases due to contingent reinforcement.
- Acquisition may involve *shaping*—the reinforcement of closer and closer approximations of the desired response.
- *Extinction* occurs when responding gradually slows and stops after reinforcement is terminated.
- *Resistance to extinction* occurs when an organism continues to make a response after reinforcement for it has been terminated.
- *Generalization* occurs when responding increases in the presence of a stimulus that resembles the original discriminative stimulus.
- *Discrimination* occurs when responding does not increase in the presence of a stimulus that resembles the original discriminative stimulus.
- *Primary reinforcers* are inherently reinforcing, whereas *secondary reinforcers* develop through learning.
- *Renewal effect* occurs when a response that has been extinguished in a context different from that in which it was acquired reappears in the original context.

Intermittent reinforcement schedules

- *Reinforcement* is most effective when it is immediate; delayed reinforcement undermines response acquisition.
- *Continuous reinforcement* occurs when every instance of a designated response is reinforced.
- *Intermittent reinforcement* occurs when a response is reinforced only some of the time.
- In *ratio schedules,* the reinforcer is given after a fixed (FR) or variable (VR) number of nonreinforced responses.
- In *interval schedules,* the reinforcer is given for the first response that occurs after a fixed (FI) or variable (VI) time interval has elapsed.
- Ratio schedules (FR and VR) tend to yield higher response rates, whereas variable schedules (VR and VI) tend to yield more resistance to extinction.

Distinctions among operant outcomes

- *Positive reinforcement* occurs when a response is followed by the presentation of a rewarding stimulus.
- *Negative reinforcement* occurs when a response is followed by the removal of an aversive stimulus.
- Negative reinforcement plays a key role in *escape learning* and *avoidance learning.*
- *Punishment* occurs when an event following a response weakens the tendency to make that response.
- Punishment may result in side effects such as negative emotional responses and increased aggressive behaviour.
- When used for disciplinary reasons, punishments should be applied swiftly, just severe enough to be effective, explained, and not physical.

 New Directions in the Study of Conditioning

Recognizing biological constraints on learning

- John Garcia found that it is almost impossible to create some associations, whereas conditioned taste aversions are readily acquired in spite of long CS-UCS delays, which he attributed to evolutionary influences.
- *Preparedness,* a species-specific predisposition to be conditioned in certain ways and not others, probably explains why some phobias are particularly common.
- Differences in the adaptive challenges faced by various species have probably led to some species-specific learning tendencies.

Recognizing cognitive processes in conditioning

- Edward Tolman's research on latent learning and cognitive maps suggested many years ago that cognitive processes play a role in conditioning, but his views were ahead of their time.
- Robert Rescorla showed that the predictive value of a CS influences the process of classical conditioning.
- When a response is followed by a desirable outcome, the response is more likely to be strengthened if it appears to have caused the favourable outcome.
- Modern theories hold that conditioning is a matter of detecting the contingencies that govern events.

 Observational Learning

- *Observational learning* occurs when an organism's responding is influenced by the observation of others, called *models.*
- Observational learning was pioneered by Albert Bandura, who showed that conditioning does not have to be a product of direct experience.
- Both classical and operant conditioning can take place through observational learning.
- Observational learning depends on the processes of attention, retention, reproduction, and motivation.
- Bandura distinguishes between the *acquisition* of a learned response and the *performance* of that response, with the latter depending on reinforcement.
- Observational learning can explain why physical punishment tends to increase aggression in children even when it is intended to do the opposite, and why exposure to media violence correlates with increased aggression and desensitization to the effects of violence.
- Recent research suggests that a specific type of neuron, "mirror neurons", may partially account for some observational learning effects.

Key Themes

- Heredity and environment interactively govern behaviour.
- Psychology evolves in a sociohistorical context.

Chapter 7

Human Memory

 **Encoding**

- *Attention,* which entails a selective focus on certain input, enhances encoding.
- *Levels-of-processing theory* proposes that deeper levels of processing result in more durable memory codes.
- *Structural, phonemic,* and *semantic encoding* represent progressively deeper levels of processing.
- *Elaboration,* the use of *visual imagery, self-referent encoding,* and increasing the *motivation to remember* can enhance encoding and retention.

 **Storage**

- Information-processing theories propose that people have three memory stores: *sensory memory, short-term memory (STM),* and *long-term memory (LTM).*
- Atkinson and Shiffrin posited that incoming information passes through two temporary storage buffers before being placed into long-term memory.
- The three memory stores are not viewed as anatomical structures but as distinct types of memory.

 Retrieval

- Recall is often guided by partial information, as demonstrated by the *tip-of-the tongue phenomenon*
- Reinstating the context of an event can often enhance retrieval efforts.
- Memories are sketchy reconstructions of the past that may be distorted.
- The *misinformation effect* occurs when recall of an event is changed by misleading postevent information.
- Even the simple act of retelling a story can introduce inaccuracies into memory.
- A *source-monitoring error* occurs when a memory derived from one source is attributed to another source.
- *Reality monitoring* involves deciding whether memories are based on one's perceptions of actual events or one's thoughts and imaginations.
- *Destination memory* involves recalling to whom one has told what.

Sensory memory

- Sensory memory preserves information in its original form for a very brief time.
- Memory traces in the sensory store appear to decay in about one-quarter of a second.

Short-term memory

- Short-term memory can maintain about seven chunks of unrehearsed information for up to 20 seconds.
- Short-term memory is working memory.
- Baddeley's model of working memory consists of four components: the phonological loop, the visuospatial sketchpad, the central executive, and the episodic buffer.
- Some theorists view short-term memory as a tiny, constantly changing portion of LTM in a state of heightened activation.

Long-term memory

- Long-term memory is an unlimited capacity store that can hold information indefinitely.
- Flashbulb memories and Penfield's ESB research suggest that LTM storage may be permanent, but the data are not convincing.
- Memories can be organized in a variety of ways.

Organization in long-term memory

Conceptual hierarchies

A *conceptual hierarchy* is a multilevel classification system based on common properties among items.

Schemas

A *schema* is an organized cluster of information about an object or event.

Semantic networks

A *semantic network* consists of concepts joined by pathways linking related concepts.

Connectionist networks

PDP models assume that memories consist of patterns of activation in *connectionist networks* that resemble neural networks.

Forgetting

Types of memory failure

Daniel Schacter summarized memory failure in his seven sins of memory: transience, absent-mindedness, blocking, misattribution, suggestibility, bias, and persistence.

Measuring forgetting

- People view forgetting as a deficiency but it can be adaptive in that it can make it easier to remember important information.
- Ebbinghaus's work suggested that most forgetting occurs very rapidly, but subsequent research indicated that his *forgetting curve* was exceptionally steep.
- Retention can be assessed with a *recall* measure, a *recognition* measure, or a *relearning* measure.

Why we forget

- A great deal of forgetting, including pseudoforgetting, is due to *ineffective encoding.*
- *Decay theory* proposes that memory traces fade with time, but decay does not appear to be a factor in long-term memory.
- *Interference theory* asserts that people forget information because of competition from other material, which has proven easy to demonstrate.
- Forgetting is often due to *retrieval failure,* which may include repression.

The repressed memories controversy

- Recent years have seen a surge of reports of recovered memories of previously forgotten sexual abuse in childhood.
- While many clinicians accept these recovered memories, arguing that it is common for people to bury traumatic memories in their unconscious, many researchers point to the results of research suggesting it is easy to create inaccurate memories.

Physiology of Memory

Anatomy of memory

- *Retrograde amnesia* involves the loss of memories for events that occurred prior to the onset of amnesia. *Anterograde amnesia* involves the loss of memories for events that occur after the onset of amnesia.
- Studies of amnesia, such as the case of H.M., suggest that the *hippocampal region* and adjacent areas are critical for long-term memory.
- Theorists believe that the medial temporal lobe memory system plays a key role in the *consolidation* of long-term memories, which are then stored in widely distributed areas of the cortex.

Neural circuitry of memory

- Some theorists argue that memories may correspond to alterations in neurotransmitter activity at specific synapses.
- Some theorists believe that memories may correspond to localized *neural pathways* in the brain.
- These pathways may depend on increases in neural excitability at specific synapses, which is called *long-term potentiation.*

Key Themes

- People's experience of the world is highly subjective.
- Behaviour is determined by multiple causes.

Proposed Memory Systems

Explicit memory

- *Explicit memory* involves intentional recollection of previous experiences.
- Explicit memory is conscious, accessed directly, and best assessed with recall or recognition measures of retention.

Observed memory phenomena

Implicit memory

- *Implicit memory* is apparent when retention is exhibited on a task that does not require intentional remembering.
- Implicit memory is unconscious, accessed indirectly, and best assessed with relearning measures of retention.

Declarative memory

The *declarative memory system* handles recall of factual information, such as names, dates, events, and ideas.

Underlying memory systems

Nondeclarative memory

The *nondeclarative memory system* handles recall of actions, skills, and operations, such as riding a bike or typing.

Semantic versus episodic memory

- The *semantic memory system* contains general knowledge that is not temporally dated.
- The *episodic memory system* handles temporally dated recollections of personal experiences.

Prospective versus retrospective memory

- *Prospective memory* involves remembering to perform actions in the future.
- *Retrospective memory* involves remembering events from the past or previously learned information.

Chapter 8

Language and Thought

Language

Properties and structure

- Languages are symbolic, semantic, generative, and structured hierarchically.
- At the base of the language hierarchy are phonemes, the smallest speech units that can be distinguished.
- Morphemes are the smallest units of meaning in a language.
- Syntax is a system of rules that specify how words can be arranged into phrases and sentences.

Language development

- Starting at around 6 months, infants' babbling increasingly resembles the language spoken in the child's environment.
- Children typically utter their first words around their first birthday.
- Vocabulary growth is slow at first, but fast mapping contributes to a vocabulary spurt that often begins at around 18–24 months.
- Children begin to combine words by the end of their second year, exhibiting telegraphic speech.
- Children's mean length of utterance gradually increases, but their grammar is often marked by overregularizations.
- Youngsters continue to learn syntax during their school-age years and develop metalinguistic awareness.

Bilingualism

- There is little empirical support for the belief that bilingualism slows language development or that it has a negative effect on cognitive development.
- Evidence suggest that bilinguals have a slight handicap in language processing speed because there is no way to turn off L1 when using L2, or vice versa.
- However, bilinguals score higher than monolinguals on attentional control, working memory capacity, and other cognitive skills. Bilingualism may also afford some protection against age-related cognitive decline.

Can animals develop language?

- Scientists have taught some language skills to animals, such as the chimp Washoe, who learned American Sign Language.
- However, critics have expressed doubts about whether Washoe and other animals have really acquired the rules of language.
- Sue Savage-Rumbaugh's work with the chimp Kanzi suggests that some animals are capable of mastering the rules of language, but there is no comparison between human linguistic abilities and those of apes and other animals.

Theories of language acquisition

- According to B. F. Skinner and other *behaviourists*, children acquire language through imitation, reinforcement, and other aspects of learning and experience.
- According to Noam Chomsky and other *nativist* theorists, humans are neurologically prewired to quickly acquire the rules of language.
- According to *interactionist* theories, an innate predisposition and a supportive environment both contribute to language acquisition.

Evolution and culture

- Many theorists believe that humans' special talent for learning language is a product of natural selection.
- The linguistic relativity hypothesis asserts that one's language shapes the nature of one's thought processes.
- The research evidence suggests that thought shapes language more than vice versa.

Problem Solving

Types of problems

Greeno has distinguished between problems of inducing structure, problems of arrangement, and problems of transformation.

Barriers to problem solving

- People are often distracted by irrelevant information.
- *Functional fixedness* is the tendency to perceive an item only in terms of its most common use.
- A *mental set* exists when people persist in using strategies that have worked in the past but are no longer optimal.
- People often impose unnecessary constraints on their possible solutions.

Approaches to problem solving

- *Trial and error* is a common, albeit primitive, approach to problem solving.
- A *heuristic* is a rule of thumb or mental shortcut used in solving problems or making decisions.
- It is often useful to formulate intermediate subgoals.
- If a problem has a well-specified end point, it may help to work backward.
- If you can spot an analogy between one problem and another, a solution may become apparent.
- When progress is stalled, changing the representation of a problem or taking a break, allowing for incubation without conscious deliberation, often helps.

Culture and problem solving

- Cross-cultural disparaties have been observed in problem-solving style.
- Research suggests that Eastern cultures exhibit a more holistic cognitive style, whereas Western cultures display a more analytic cognitive style.

Decision Making

Basic strategies

- Herbert Simon's *theory of bounded rationality* asserts that people tend to use simple decision strategies that often yield seemingly irrational results because they can juggle only so much information at once. The notion that people are not always rational decision makers is also highlighted in the study of *behavioural economics*.
- An *additive decision model* is used when people rate the attributes of alternatives and select the option with the highest sum.
- *Elimination by aspects* involves gradually ruling out alternatives that fail to satisfy minimum criteria.
- When decisions involve few options and attributes, people tend to favour additive strategies, but when options get complex, people tend to favour elimination by aspects.
- When people make risky decisions, they weigh the expected value and subjective utility of various outcomes.
- In making decisions, evaluations of options fluctuate more than expected, and comparative evaluations often yield different results than separate evaluations.
- Research on deliberation-without-awareness shows that intuitive, unconscious decisions may be more satisfying than those based on conscious deliberation, especially when choices are complex.

Common heuristics and flaws

- The *availability heuristic* involves basing the estimated probability of an event on the ease with which relevant instances come to mind.
- The *representativeness heuristic* involves basing the estimated probability of an event on how similar it is to the typical prototype of that event.
- In estimating probabilities, people often ignore information on the *base rates* of events.
- The *conjunction fallacy* occurs when people estimate that the odds of two uncertain events happening together are greater than the odds of either event happening alone.
- Evolutionary psychologists assert that people perform poorly in cognitive research because it presents them with contrived, artificial problems that do not involve natural categories and have no adaptive significance.
- According to Gigerenzer, people mostly depend on *fast and frugal* heuristics that are much simpler than the complicated inferential processes studied in traditional cognitive research.

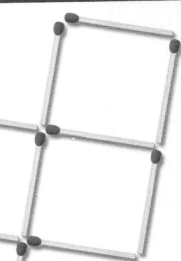

Key Themes

- Psychology is empirical.
- Heredity and environment jointly shape behaviour.
- Our experience of the world is highly subjective.
- Behaviour is shaped by one's cultural heritage.

Chapter 9

Intelligence and Psychological Testing

 Key Concepts in Testing

Standardization refers to the uniform procedures used in administering and scoring a test.

Norms indicate where a score on a test ranks in relation to other scores.

Percentile scores indicate the percentage of people who score at or below specific scores.

Types of tests

Mental ability tests measure general intelligence, aptitude for specific types of learning, or achievement in specific areas of study.

Personality tests measure various types of personality traits, as well as motives, interests, values, and attitudes.

Reliability

Refers to the measurement consistency of a test

Validity

Refers to the ability of a test to measure what it was designed to measure

Content-related validity refers to the degree to which the content of a test is representative of the domain it is supposed to cover.

Construct validity refers to the extent to which there is evidence that a test measures a specific hypothetical construct.

Criterion-related validity is estimated by correlating subjects' scores on a test with their scores on an independent measure of the trait.

 History of Intelligence Tests

- The first intelligence tests were devised by Sir Francis Galton, who sought to show that intelligence is inherited.
- Modern intelligence testing was launched in 1905 by Alfred Binet, who devised a scale to measure a child's mental age.
- Lewis Terman revised the Binet scale to produce the Stanford-Binet scales in 1916, which introduced the intelligence quotient (IQ).
- In 1939, David Wechsler published an improved measure of intelligence for adults, which introduced the *deviation IQ score* based on the normal distribution.
- Spearman argued that all cognitive tests share a core, which he called g, whereas Thurstone asserted that intelligence is made up of independent abilities.
- Both views remain influential today as researchers are primarily interested in g, but contemporary IQ tests typically subdivide g into 10–15 specific abilities.

 Essentials of Intelligence Testing

- Modern deviation IQ scores indicate where people fall in the normal distribution of intelligence for their age.
- For most modern tests, the mean score is 100 and the standard deviation is 15.
- IQ tests are intended to measure intellectual potential rather than factual knowledge, but they really reflect both.
- Individuals' IQ scores can vary across testings, but intelligence tests tend to have very high reliability and IQ scores tend to become relatively stable over time after middle childhood.
- There is ample evidence that IQ tests are valid measures of academic/verbal intelligence, but they do not tap social or practical intelligence.
- IQ scores are correlated with occupational attainment, but doubts have been raised about how well they predict performance within a specific occupation.
- IQ tests are not widely used in most non-Western cultures.

Heredity and Environment as Determinants of Intelligence

Evidence for hereditary influence

- *Twin studies* show that identical twins are more similar in intelligence than fraternal twins, suggesting that intelligence is at least partly inherited.
- Even more impressive, identical twins reared apart are more similar in intelligence than fraternal twins reared together.
- Studies also show that adopted children resemble their biological parents in intelligence.
- A *heritability ratio* is an estimate of the proportion of trait variability in a population that is determined by genetic variations.
- Estimates of the heritability of intelligence range 40% to 80%, and mostly converge around 50%, but heritability ratios have certain limitations.

Evidence for environmental influence

- *Adoption studies* find that adopted children show some IQ resemblance to their foster parents and to their adoptive siblings.
- Studies of *environmental deprivation* show that children raised in substandard circumstances tend to exhibit a gradual decline in IQ as they grow older.
- Studies of *environmental enrichment* show that children who are moved to improved environments tend to exhibit increases in IQ.
- Generational increases in measured IQ are perplexing, but they must be due to environmental changes.

Extremes of Intelligence

Intellectual disability

- Intellectual disability refers to subaverage general mental ability (IQ <70) accompanied by deficits in adaptive skills, originating before age 18.
- Intellectual disability may be mild, moderate, severe, or profound. The vast majority (85%) of individuals have mild intellectual disability.
- Many organic conditions can cause intellectual disability, but a specific organic cause can be identified in only about 50% of cases.
- Cases of unknown origin tend to involve mild disability and are believed to be mainly caused by unfavourable environmental factors.

Giftedness

- In practice, efforts to identify gifted children focus almost exclusively on IQ scores, with a score of 130 as the typical minimum.
- For the most part, gifted children tend to be above average in social and emotional maturity.
- Although gifted children tend to be successful in life, very few go on to make genius-level contributions.
- The "drudge theory" proposes that extraordinary achievement depends on intensive training and monumental effort, but critics argue that innate talent is also crucial.
- *Savant* is a term that refers to individuals who typically have below average IQ but who nonetheless show remarkable ability in very specific areas.

The interaction of heredity and environment

- The evidence clearly shows that intelligence is shaped by both heredity and environment and that these influences interact.
- The *reaction range model* posits that heredity sets limits on one's intelligence and that environmental factors determine where people fall within these limits.
- Scientists are striving to identify specific genes that influence intelligence, but progress has been slow, suggesting that intelligence may be shaped by hundreds of genes that each have tiny effects.

The debate about cultural differences in IQ scores

- Arthur Jensen and others have argued that cultural differences in IQ scores are largely due to heredity.
- Even if the heritability of IQ is high, group differences in IQ could be entirely environmental in origin.
- Socioeconomic disadvantage and cultural bias on tests may contribute to cultural differences in IQ.
- Vulnerability to negative stereotypes can undermine test performance in minority groups.

New Directions

- Recent years have brought increased interest in biological indexes of intelligence, including such things as IQ and brain size and quantity of gray and white matter in the brain.
- Recent studies have also found that IQ scores measured in childhood correlate with longevity decades later.
- Robert Sternberg's triarchic theory posits that the hallmarks of intelligence are the abilities to deal with novelty and handle familiar tasks automatically.
- According to Sternberg, successful intelligence includes three facets: analytical intelligence, creative intelligence, and practical intelligence.
- Howard Gardner has argued that there are eight largely independent types of human intelligence.
- Some theorists believe that the measurement of *emotional intelligence* can enhance the prediction of people's success, but critics question whether emotional sophistication should be viewed as a form of intelligence.

Key Themes

- Psychology evolves in a sociohistorical context.
- Heredity and environment jointly shape behaviour.
- Behaviour is shaped by one's cultural heritage.

Chapter 10

Motivation and Emotion

Motivational Theories and Concepts

- *Drive theories* emphasize how *internal* states of tension (due to disruptions of homeostasis) push organisms in certain directions.

- *Incentive theories* emphasize how *external* goals pull organisms in certain directions.

- *Evolutionary theories* assert that motives are a product of *natural selection* that have had adaptive value in terms of fostering reproductive fitness.

- Most theories of motivation distinguish between *biological motives* originating in bodily needs and *social motives* originating in social experiences.

Motivation of Hunger

Biological factors regulating hunger

- Research orginally suggested that the *lateral and ventromedial areas of the hypothalamus* were the brain's on–off switches for hunger, but the dual-centres model proved too simple.

- Today, scientists think that neural circuits passing through the *arcuate* and *paraventricular* areas of the hypothalamus play a larger role in the regulation of hunger.

- Fluctuations in blood glucose monitored by *glucostats* also influence hunger.

- In the digestive system, the stomach can send two types of satiety signals to the brain.

- Secretions of the pancreatic hormone *insulin* are associated with increased hunger.

- The recently discovered hormone *leptin* provides the hypothalamus with information about the body's fat stores.

- The hormones ghrelin and CCK carry hunger and satiety signals from the stomach to the brain.

Environmental factors regulating hunger

- Incentive-oriented theorists emphasize that the palatability, quantity, and variety of available food, and the presence of others, are key factors influencing eating behaviour.

- Hunger can be triggered by food cues in the environment, such as odours.

- Humans show some innate taste preferences, but learning is much more influential.

- Classical conditioning and observational learning shape what people prefer to eat.

- Food preferences are also governed by exposure, which is why there are huge cultural variations in eating habits.

- The external hypothesis suggests that obese individuals are extra sensitive to external cues that affect hunger.

Sexual Motivation

Controversies over pornography

- Researchers have found little evidence of an association between the availability of erotica and the incidence of sex crimes.

- Exposure to erotica may alter attitudes about sexual behaviour. In particular, aggressive pornography may contribute to sexual coercion.

Sexual orientation

- People tend to view heterosexuality and homosexuality as an all-or-none distinction, but it is more accurate to view them as endpoints on a continuum.

- Environmental explanations of sexual orientation have not been supported by research.

- Biological explanations have fared better in recent years, as twin studies have shown that genetic factors influence sexual orientation.

- Research also suggests that idiosyncrasies in prenatal hormonal secretions may influence sexual orientation.

- Females' sexual orientation appears to be characterized by more *plasticity* than that of males.

Evolutionary analyses

- According to *parental investment theory*, the sex that makes the smaller investment in offspring will compete for mating opportunities with the sex that makes the larger investment, which will be more discriminating in selecting partners.

- Human males are required to invest little in offspring, so their reproductive potential is maximized by mating with as many partners as possible.

- Human females have to invest months to years in carrying and nourishing offspring, so they maximize their reproductive potential by mating with males who are able to invest more resources in their offspring.

Cognitive component

- The cognitive component of emotion consists of subjective feelings that are often intense and difficult to control.
- Cognitive appraisals of events influence the emotions that people experience.
- Research on affective forecasting shows that people are surprisingly bad at predicting the intensity and duration of their emotional reactions to events.

Physiological component

- The physiological component of emotion is dominated by autonomic arousal.
- A *polygraph* detects emotional arousal, which is a far from perfect index of lying.
- According to Joseph LeDoux, the amygdala lies at the core of a complex set of neural circuits that process emotion.

Behavioural component

- At the behavioural level, emotions are revealed through body language.
- People can identify at least six emotions based on facial expressions.
- According to the *facial-feedback hypothesis,* facial muscles send signals to the brain that aid in the recognition of emotions.

e roots of obesity

- esity is a significant health problem that elevates one's risk for any diseases.
- search suggests that some people inherit a genetic *vulnerability* obesity.
- overweight people, energy intake from food consumption chronically ceeds energy expenditure.
- cording to *set point theory,* the body monitors fat-cell levels to keep em fairly stable, making it challenging to lose weight and keep it off.
- cording to *settling point theory,* weight tends to drift around the level which food consumption and energy expenditure tend to achieve equilibrium.
- cillations in *dietary restraint* may also contribute to obesity.

 Emotion

Cultural considerations

- Ekman and Friesen have found cross-cultural agreement in the identification of emotions based on facial expressions.
- Cross-cultural similarities have also been found in the cognitive and physiological components of emotion.
- However, there are cultural disparities in how emotions are categorized and in public displays of emotions.

Theoretical views

- The *James-Lange theory* asserted that the conscious experience of emotion results from one's perception of autonomic arousal.
- The *Cannon-Bard theory* asserted that emotions originate in subcortical areas of the brain.
- According to the *two-factor theory,* people infer emotion from autonomic arousal and then label it in accordance with their cognitive explanation for the arousal.
- *Evolutionary theories of emotion* assert that emotions are innate reactions that do not depend on cognitive processes.

 The Achievement Motive

he human sexual response

- Masters and Johnson showed that the sexual response cycle consists of four stages: excitement, plateau, orgasm, and resolution.
- Intercourse leads to orgasm in women less consistently than in men, but women are much more likely to be multiorgasmic.

ender differences

- Males think about and initiate sex more than females.
- Males are more willing to engage in casual sex and have more partners than females.
- Males around the world place more emphasis on youthfulness and attractiveness in mates than females do.
- Females around the world place more emphasis on intelligence and financial prospects in partners and pay attention to males' willingness to invest their resources in children.

- David McClelland pioneered the use of the TAT to measure individual differences in *need for achievement*.
- People who score high in the need for achievement tend to work harder and more persistently than others and are more likely to delay gratification.
- However, people high in the need for achievement tend to choose challenges of intermediate difficulty.
- The pursuit of achievement goals tends to increase when the probability of success on a task and the incentive value of success are higher.
- Achievement pursuits may be influenced by fear of failure.

Key Themes

- *Psychology is theoretically diverse.*
- *Psychology evolves in a sociohistorical context.*
- *Heredity and environment jointly influence behaviour.*
- *Behaviour is shaped by cultural heritage.*
- *Behaviour is determined by multiple causes.*

Chapter 11

Human Development Across the Life Span

Prenatal Development

Stages

- During the *germinal stage* a zygote becomes a mass of cells that implants in the uterine wall and the placenta begins to form.
- During the *embryonic stage* most vital organs and bodily systems begin to form, making it a period of great vulnerability.
- During the *fetal stage* organs continue to grow and gradually begin to function, as the fetus reaches the *age of viability* around 22–26 weeks.

Environmental influences

- Maternal malnutrition increases newborns' risk for birth complications and neurological deficits.
- Maternal consumption of alcohol, tobacco, and other drugs can have a variety of negative effects on prenatal development.
- Maternal illnesses can interfere with prenatal development, and genital herpes and AIDS can be passed to newborns at birth.

Motor development

- Motor development follows *cephalocaudal* (head-to-foot) and *proximodistal* (centre-outward) trends.
- Early progress in motor skills has traditionally been attributed to *maturation,* but recent research suggests that infants' exploration is also important.
- Cross-cultural research on motor development shows that maturation and environment are both influential.

Cognitive development

- Jean Piaget proposed that children evolve through four stages of cognitive development.
- The major achievement of the *sensorimotor period* (birth to age 2) is the development of object permanence.
- Children's thought during the *preoperational period* (ages 2–7) is marked by centration, animism, irreversibility, and egocentrism.
- In the *concrete operational period* (ages 7–11) children develop the ability to perform operations on mental representations.
- In the *formal operational period* (age 11 onward) thought becomes more systematic, abstract, and logical.
- Piaget made landmark contributions to the understanding of cognitive development, but he may have underestimated the pace of children's development and the influence of culture.
- Lev Vygotsky's sociocultural theory asserts that children's cognitive development is shaped by social interactions, language development, and cultural factors.
- According to Vygotsky, children acquire their culture's cognitive skills through collaborative dialogues with more-experienced members of their society.
- Nativists and evolutionary theorists argue that children's brains are prewired to readily understand certain concepts.
- Children's understanding, or theory, of the mind seems to turn a corner between ages 3 and 4 as they realize that people may hold false beliefs. Theory of mind refers to developments in children's understanding of the mind, how it works, and their conceptions of another's thought processes.

Approaches to research on development

- In a *longitudinal study* one group of subjects is observed repeatedly over time.
- In a *cross-sectional study* groups of subjects of varied ages are observed at a single point in time.
- Cross-sectional studies are quicker and easier, but longitudinal studies can be more sensitive.

Temperament

- *Temperament* refers to characteristic mood, activity level, and emotional reactivity.
- In a longitudinal study, Thomas and Chess found that temperament remains fairly stable as children grow up.

Attachment

- *Attachment* emerges out of a complex inte[raction] between infants and their caregivers.
- Harry Harlow's studies of infant monkeys showed that reinforcement is not the key [to] attachment.
- John Bowlby has shown that attachment [has] a biological and evolutionary basis.
- Research has shown that infant–mother attachments fall into four categories: secu[re,] anxious–ambivalent, avoidant, and disorganized–disoriented.
- Infants with a relatively secure attachmen[t tend] to become resilient, competent toddlers w[ith] high self-esteem.
- Cultural variations in child rearing influenc[e the] patterns of attachment seen in a society.

Development in Childhood

Moral development

- Lawrence Kohlberg's theory proposes that individuals progress through three levels of moral reasoning.
- *Preconventional reasoning* focuses on acts' consequences, *conventional reasoning* on the need to maintain social order, and *postconventional reasoning* on working out a personal code of ethics.
- Age-related progress in moral reasoning has been found in research, but there is a lot of overlap among stages.

Personality development

- Erik Erikson's theory proposes that individu[als] evolve through eight stages over the life s[pan.]
- *Stage theories* assume that individuals pro[gress] through stages in a particular order, that progress is strongly related to age, and tha[t] new stages bring major changes in characte[r and] behaviour.
- Erikson's four childhood stages are trust ve[rsus] mistrust, autonomy versus shame, initiative versus guilt, and industry versus inferiority.

Development in Adolescence

Physiological development

Pubescence is the 2-year span preceding puberty during which secondary sex characteristics begin to develop.

Puberty is the stage during which primary sex characteristics develop fully.

Today's adolescents tend to begin puberty at an earlier age than previous generations, perhaps because of improvements in nutrition and medical care.

Girls who mature early and boys who mature late have a greater risk for psychological and social difficulties, or subjective distress, but early sexual maturation is associated with more behavioural problems for both sexes.

Neural development

- During adolescence, neurons are becoming more myelinated and synaptic pruning continues to sculpt neural networks.

- The prefrontal cortex, which has been characterized as an executive control centre, appears to be the last area of the brain to mature fully in early adulthood.

- This reality may contribute to adolescent risk taking. However, other factors, such as peer influence, also affect risky behaviour.

The search for identity

- According to Erikson, the main challenge of adolescence is the struggle for a sense of identity.

- According to James Marcia, adolescents deal with their identity crisis in four ways: foreclosure, moratorium, identity diffusion, and identity achievement.

- Arnett argues for the existence of a new developmental stage in modern societies called "emerging adulthood," marked by feeling in between adolescence and adulthood, optimism, self-focus, and continued identity formation.

Personality development

- During adulthood, personality is marked by both stability and change, as percentile scores remain stable but mean raw scores change in predictable ways.

- The adult years tend to bring increases in agreeableness, conscientiousness, self-confidence, and emotional stability.

- According to Erikson, people evolve through three stages of development in the adult years: intimacy versus isolation, generativity versus self-absorption, and integrity versus despair.

Family transitions

- Adjusting to marriage is more likely to be difficult when spouses have different expectations about marital roles.

- Most parents are happy with their decision to have children, but the arrival of the first child represents a major transition, and the disruption of routines can be draining.

- Parent–adolescent relations are not as contentious as widely assumed, but conflicts do increase and parents tend to feel stressed.

- For many parents the transition to an empty nest seems to be less difficult than it used to be.

Physiological and neural changes

In the sensory domain, vision and hearing acuity tend to decline, but glasses and hearing aids can compensate for these losses.

Women's reactions to menopause vary and menopause is not as stressful as widely believed.

Brain tissue and weight tend to decline after age 60, but this loss does not appear to be the key to age-related dementias.

Research suggests that bilingualism and staying active cognitively may delay some changes we experience as we age.

Dementias are seen in about 15%–20% of people over age 75, but they are not part of the normal aging process.

Alzheimer's patients exhibit profound loss of brain tissue and the accumulation of characteristic neural abnormalities.

Development in Adulthood

Cognitive changes

- General intelligence is fairly stable throughout most of adulthood, with a small decline in average scores seen after age 60.

- The memory losses associated with aging are moderate and may be mostly due to declining working memory.

- Speed in cognitive processing tends to begin a gradual decline during middle adulthood.

- Some studies suggest that high levels of mental activity in late adulthood can delay the typical age-related declines in cognitive functioning.

Key Themes

- Psychology is theoretically diverse.

- Psychology evolves in a sociohistorical context.

- Heredity and environment jointly influence behaviour.

- Behaviour is shaped by cultural heritage.

- Behaviour is determined by multiple causes.

Chapter 12

Personality: Theory, Research, and Assessment

The Nature of Personality

- A *personality trait* is a durable disposition to behave in a particular way across a variety of situations.
- According to the *five-factor model,* most aspects of personality are derived from five crucial traits: neuroticism, extraversion, openness to experience, agreeableness, and conscientiousness.
- The Big Five are predictive of behaviour such as honesty, job performance, and alcohol use, as well as of important life outcomes such as grades, occupational attainment, divorce, health, and morality.

Psychodynamic Perspectives

Freud's theory

- Sigmund Freud's *psychoanalytic theory* grew out of his therapeutic work with clients and emphasized the importance of the unconscious.
- Freud divided personality structure into three components: the id, ego, and superego.
- The *id* is the instinctive component that follows the pleasure principle, the *ego* is the decision-making component that follows the reality principle, and the *superego* is the moral component.
- Freud described three levels of awareness: the *conscious* (current awareness), the *preconscious* (material just beneath the surface of awareness), and the *unconscious* (material well below the surface of awareness).
- Freud theorized that conflicts centring on sex and aggression are especially likely to lead to significant anxiety.
- According to Freud, anxiety and other unpleasant emotions are often warded off with *defence mechanisms,* which work through self-deception.
- Freud proposed that children evolve through five stages of psychosexual development: the oral, anal, phallic, latency, and genital stages.
- Certain experiences during these stages, such as the handling of the *Oedipal complex,* can shape subsequent adult personality.

Jung's theory

- Carl Jung's *analytical psychology* emphasized unconscious determinants of personality, but he divided the unconscious into the personal and collective unconscious.
- The *collective unconscious* is a storehouse of latent memory traces inherited from people's ancestral past.
- These memories consist of *archetypes,* which are emotionally charged thought forms that have universal meaning.
- Jung was the first to describe the *introverted* (inner-directed) and *extraverted* (outer-directed) personality types.

Adler's theory

- Alfred Adler's *individual psychology* emphasized how social forces shape personality development.
- Adler argued that *striving for superiority* is the foremost motivational force in people's lives.
- Adler attributed personality disturbances to excessive inferiority feelings that can pervert the normal process of striving for superiority and can result in overcompensation.
- Adler stressed the social context of personality development and did pioneering work on the effects of birth order.

Behavioural Perspectives

Skinner's theory

- B. F. Skinner's work on *operant conditioning* was not meant to be a theory of personality, but it has been applied to personality.
- Skinner's followers view personality as a collection of response tendencies that are tied to specific situations.
- Skinnerians view personality development as a lifelong process in which response tendencies are shaped by reinforcement.

Bandura's theory

- Albert Bandura's *social learning theory* emphasizes how cognitive factors shape personality.
- According to Bandura, people's response tendencies are largely acquired by *observational learning.*
- Bandura stressed the role of *self-efficacy*—one's belief about one's ability to perform behaviours that should lead to expected outcomes.
- Greater self-efficacy is associated with greater success in a variety of athletic, academic, and health pursuits.

Mischel's theory

- Walter Mischel's brand of social learning theory emphasizes how people behave differently in different situations.
- His theory has sparked debate about the relative importance of the person versus the situation in determining behaviour.

Humanistic Perspectives

Rogers's theory

- Carl Rogers's *person-centred theory* focuses on the *self-concept*—a collection of subjective beliefs about one's nature.
- *Incongruence* is the degree of disparity between one's self-concept and one's actual experiences.
- According to Rogers, unconditional love during childhood fosters congruence while conditional love fosters incongruence.
- Rogers asserts that people with highly incongruent self-concepts are prone to recurrent anxiety.

Maslow's theory

- Abraham Maslow proposed that human motives are organized into a *hierarchy of needs,* in which basic needs must be met before less basic needs are aroused.
- At the top of Maslow's hierarchy of needs is the need for *self-actualization*—the need to fulfill one's potential.
- Recently, theorists have proposed a major revision of Maslow's pyramid of needs in which the higher, growth needs are replaced by motives related to reproductive fitness.
- According to Maslow, *self-actualizing persons* are people with very healthy personalities, marked by continued personal growth.

Biological Perspectives

Eysenck's theory

- Hans Eysenck views personality structure as a hierarchy of traits in which many superficial traits are derived from a handful of fundamental traits.
- According to Eysenck, personality is largely determined by genetic inheritance.
- Eysenck theorizes that introversion and extraversion are shaped by inherited differences in arousability and ease of conditioning.

The evolutionary approach

- According to Buss, the ability to recognize and judge others' status on the Big Five traits may have contributed to reproductive fitness.
- Nettle argues that the Big Five traits themselves (rather than the ability to recognize them) are products of evolution that were adaptive in ancestral times.

Behavioural genetics research

- Identical twins reared apart tend to be more similar in personality than fraternal twins reared together, which suggests that genetics shape personality.
- *Heritability estimates* for personality tend to hover around 40–50%.
- Behavioural genetics research has revealed that differences among families have surprisingly little impact on personality.

The Neuroscience of personality

- Neuroscientists have begun to examine relations between personality and brain structure and function.
- Most current work focuses on the Big Five.

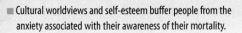

Terror Management Theory

- Cultural worldviews and self-esteem buffer people from the anxiety associated with their awareness of their mortality.
- Increasing mortality salience leads people to work harder at defending their cultural worldview and their self-esteem.
- The need to defend one's cultural worldview can fuel prejudice and can explain many aspects of behaviour, ranging from conspicuous consumption to political preferences.

Culture and Personality

- The basic trait structure of personality may be much the same across cultures as the Big Five usually emerge in cross-cultural studies.
- However, some culture variablity has been seen when researchers compare average trait scores for various cultural groups.
- Markus and Kitayama assert that American culture fosters an independant view of the self, whereas Asian cultures foster an interdependent view of the self.

Narcissism

- Narcissism is a trait marked by inflated self-importance, need for attention and tendency to exploit others.
- There is evidence to suggest that narcissism has been increasing in recent generations.

Key Themes

- Psychology is theoretically diverse.
- Psychology evolves in a sociohistorical context.
- Behaviour is shaped by cultural heritage

Chapter 13

Stress, Coping, and Health

 Stress

 Stress Response

 Stress Effec

- Stress is a common, everyday event, and even routine hassles can have harmful effects.
- People's *appraisals* of events determine what they find stressful.

Major types of stress

Frustration
- *Frustration* occurs when the pursuit of some goal is thwarted.

Conflict
- In an *approach-approach conflict*, a choice must be made between two attractive goals.
- In an *avoidance-avoidance conflict,* a choice must be made between two unattractive goals.
- In an *approach-avoidance conflict,* a choice must be made about whether to pursue a goal that has positive and negative aspects.

Change
- *Life changes* are alterations in living circumstances, including positive changes, that require adjustment.
- The Social Readjustment Rating Scale (SRRS) purports to measure change-related stress, but actually taps many types of stressful experiences.
- Many studies have shown that high scores on the SRRS are associated with increased vulnerability to physical illness and psychological problems.

Pressure
- People may be put under pressure to perform well or to conform to others' expectations.
- Pressure is a predictor of psychological symptoms.
- People under pressure may often show diminished performance.

Emotional responses
- Many emotions may be evoked by stress, but anger-rage, anxiety-fear, and sadness-grief are especially common.
- Emotional arousal may interfere with coping efforts.
- The *inverted-U hypothesis* posits that as tasks become more complex, the optimal level of arousal decreases.
- Investigators have tended to focus on negative emotions, but research shows that positive emotions also occur during periods of stress.

Physiological responses
- The *general adaptation syndrome* is Hans Selye's model of the body's response to stress, which can progress through three stages: alarm, resistance, and exhaustion.
- Stress can cause the brain to send signals to the endocrine system along two pathways.

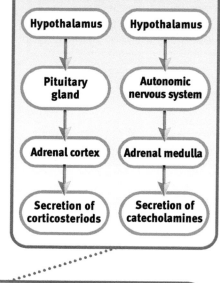

Hypothalamus	Hypothalamus
Pituitary gland	Autonomic nervous system
Adrenal cortex	Adrenal medulla
Secretion of corticosteriods	Secretion of catecholamines

Effects on psychological functioning
- Stress can lead to impaired task performa
- Chronic stress can contribute to *burnout,* involves physical and emotional exhaustic cynicism, and lowered self-efficacy.
- *Post-traumatic stress disorder,* which invol enduring disturbance attributed to a majo traumatic event, appears to be more comr than previously believed.
- High stress is associated with a diverse arr psychological disorders and everyday prob Among other things it can lead to self-indulgence in drinking and gambling.
- Research on resilience suggests that stress sometimes promote personal growth, self-improvement, and other benefits.

Effects on physical health
- Stress appears to contribute to many types of physical illness and not just psychosoma diseases.
- *Type A behaviour* has been identified as a contributing factor in coronary heart disea
- Research suggests that *hostility* may be th most toxic element of the Type A syndrome
- Recent research suggests that strong emot reactions can precipitate heart attacks and depression is a predictor of heart disease.
- The association between stress and vulnera to many diseases may reflect the negative impact of stress on immune function.
- The correlation between stress and illness modest in strength because stress is only o of many factors that influence health.

Behavioural responses
- Coping efforts may be healthy or unhealthy.
- Giving up and blaming oneself are less than optimal methods of coping with stress.
- Another unhealthy response is to strike out at others with acts of aggression.
- Indulging oneself is another common response to stress that tends to be less than optimal.
- Defensive coping protects against emotional distress, but it depends on self-deception and avoidance.
- However, several lines of research suggest that small positive illusions may be adaptive for mental health.
- Constructive coping refers to relatively healthful efforts to handle the demands of stress.

Variations in stress toleran
- There are individual differences in how mud stress people can tolerate without negative effects.
- Strong *social support* appears to buffer the impact of stress.
- *Optimism* and *conscientiousness* are two personality traits that seem to reduce the negative effects of stress.

Smoking

- Smokers have much higher mortality rates than nonsmokers because smoking elevates the risk for a wide range of diseases, including lung cancer and heart disease.
- When people quit smoking, their health risks decline fairly quickly.
- Long-term success rates for giving up smoking are only 25% or less.

Lack of exercise

- Research indicates that regular exercise is associated with increased longevity.
- Physical fitness can reduce vulnerability to deadly cardiovascular diseases, obesity-related problems, and some types of cancer.

Health-Impairing Behaviour

Alcohol and drug abuse

- Moderate drinking may offer some protection against cardiovascular disease, but heavy consumption of alcohol clearly increases one's risk for a host of diseases.
- Recreational drug use also elevates people's vulnerability to various types of illness.

Behaviour and AIDS

- Behavioural patterns influence one's risk for AIDS, which is transmitted through person-to-person contact involving the exchange of bodily fluids, primarily semen and blood.
- In the world as a whole, sexual transmission has mostly taken place through heterosexual relations.
- Many people harbour unrealistic fears that AIDS can be readily transmitted through casual contact with infected individuals.
- Many young heterosexuals foolishly downplay their risk for HIV.

Reactions to Illness

The decision to seek treatment

- Whether people view physical sensations as symptoms of illness depends on subjective interpretation.
- The biggest problem in regard to treatment seeking is the common tendency to delay the pursuit of needed treatment.
- People procrastinate because they worry about looking silly or bothering their physician, or because they are reluctant to disrupt their plans.

Communicating with health providers

- Many patients depart medical visits not understanding what they have been told.
- Barriers to effective provider–patient communication include short visits, overuse of medical jargon, and patients' reluctance to challenge physicians' authority.
- The key to improving communication is to not be a passive consumer.

Adherence to medical advice

- Nonadherence to advice from health providers is very common.
- Nonadherence is often due to the patient's failure to understand instructions.
- If a prescribed regimen is unpleasant or difficult to follow, compliance tends to decline.
- Noncompliance increases when patients have negative attitudes toward their health providers.

Key Themes

- Behaviour is determined by multiple causes.
- Our experience of the world is highly subjective.

Chapter 14

Psychological Disorders

Abnormal Behaviour

The medical model
- The medical model, which assumes that it is useful to view abnormal behaviour as a disease, led to more humane treatment for people who exhibited abnormal behaviour.
- However, the medical model has been criticized on the grounds that it converts moral and social questions into medical questions.

Criteria and prevalence of disorders
- Judgments of abnormality are based on three criteria: deviance from social norms, maladaptive behaviour, and reports of personal distress.
- Normality and abnormality exist on a continuum.
- The most common types of disorders are substance-use, anxiety, and mood disorders.

The diagnostic syste
- DSM-IV, which was released in 19 is the official psychodiagnostic classification system.
- In DSM-IV information on patien is recorded on five axes: (i) clinica syndromes, (ii) personality disorders, (iii) general medical conditions, (iv) psychosocial stressors, (v) global assessment of function
- Work is underway on DSM-5, wh may supplement the current cate gorical approach with a dimensio approach.

Anxiety Disorders

Types
- *Generalized anxiety disorder* is marked by chronic, high anxiety not tied to a specific threat.
- *Phobic disorder* is marked by a persistent, irrational fear of an object or situation that is not dangerous.
- *Panic disorder* involves recurrent, sudden anxiety attacks, and is often accompanied by agoraphobia.
- *Obsessive-compulsive disorder* is marked by uncontrollable intrusions of unwanted thoughts and urges to engage in senseless rituals.
- *Post-traumatic stress disorder* is the enduring anxiety and disturbance attributed to a major traumatic event.

Etiology
- Twin studies suggest that there is a genetic predispostion to anxiety disorders.
- Disturbances in the neural circuits using GABA and serotonin may play a role in some anxiety disorders.
- Many anxiety responses may be acquired through classical conditioning and maintained through operant conditioning.
- Cognitive theorists assert that the tendency to overinterpret harmless situations as threatening leads to anxiety disorders.
- Stress may contribute to the emergence of some anxiety disorders.

Dissociative Disorders

Types
- *Dissociative amnesia* is a sudden loss of memory for personal information that is too extensive to be due to normal forgetting.
- In *dissociative fugue*, people lose their memory for their entire lives along with their sense of identity.
- *Dissociative identity disorder* (or multiple personality disorder) involves the coexistence of two or more largely complete and usually very different personalities.

Disorders of Childhood

Types
- While children may experience many of the same disorders as adults, some disorders are specific to childhood.
- These disorders include attention-deficit/hyperactivity disorder (ADHD), separation anxiety disorder, and pervasive development disorders such as autism.

Etiology
- Children suffering from autism show three types of deficits.
- These deficits include impairment in social interaction, communication deficits, and the development of obsessions and compulsions.

Etiology
- Dissociative amnesia and fugue are usually attributed to extreme stres
- Some theorists maintain that people with dissociative identity disord are engaging in intentional role-playing to use mental illness as an excuse for their personal failings.
- Other theorists maintain that cases of dissociative identity disorder are rooted in severe emotional trauma that occurred during childhoo

Mood Disorders

Schizophrenic Disorders

...es

- ...jor depressive disorder is marked by persistent feelings of sadness and despair, loss of ...erest in previous sources of pleasure, slowed thought processes, and self-blame.

- ...olar disorder (manic-depressive disorder) is marked by the experience of depressed and ...nic episodes, with the latter involving irrational euphoria, racing thoughts, impulsive ...haviour, and increased energy.

- ...th types of mood disorders are associated with substantial elevations in suicide rates.

...logy

- ...in studies suggest that there is a genetic predispostion to mood disorders.

- ...turbances in the neural circuits using serotonin and norepinephrine appear to contribute ...mood disorders.

- ...searchers have found a correlation between depression and reduced hippocampal volume, ...ich may reflect suppressed neurogenesis due to stress.

- ...gnitive theorists assert that people who exhibit a pessimistic explanatory style are ...ecially vulnerable to depression and that rumination tends to extend and amplify ...sodes of depression.

- ...havioural theories emphasize how inadequate social skills increase vulnerability to depression.

- ...h stress is associated with increased vulnerability to mood disorders.

- ...e onset of depression has also been linked to seasonal patterns (seasonal affective disorder) ...d childbirth (postpartum depression).

General symptoms and subtypes

- The general symptoms of schizophrenia include irrational thought, delusions, deterioration of adaptive behaviour, distorted perception, hallucinations, and disturbed emotion.
- Paranoid schizophrenia is dominated by delusions of persecution and delusions of grandeur.
- Catatonic schizophrenia is marked by striking motor disturbances, ranging from muscular rigidity to random motor activity.
- Disorganized schizophrenia is marked by very severe deterioration of adaptive behaviour.
- Undifferentiated schizophrenia is marked by idiosyncratic mixtures of schizophrenic symptoms.
- Some theorists have proposed dividing schizophrenic disorders into two categories based on the dominance of negative symptoms (behavioural deficits) versus positive symptoms (behavioural excesses and peculiarities).

Etiology

- Twin studies and adoption studies suggest that there is a genetic vulnerability to schizophrenia.
- Disturbances at dopamine synapses have been implicated as a possible cause of schizophrenia.
- The neurodevelopmental hypothesis posits that vulnerability to schizophrenia is increased by disruptions of the normal maturational processes of the brain during prenatal development or at birth.
- Schizophrenic patients from families high in expressed emotion have elevated relapse rates.
- High stress is associated with increased vulnerability to schizophrenic disorders.

Personality Disorders

Culture and Pathology

- ...M-IV lists 10 personality disorders, which are marked by extreme personality traits that cause ...jective distress or impaired social or occupational funtioning.

- ...ny critics argue that the personality disorders overlap too much with Axis I disorders and with ...h other.

- ...antisocial personality disorder is marked by impulsive, callous, manipulative, aggressive, ...frequently illegal behaviour that reflects a failure to accept conventional social norms.

- ...logical factors may create a weak predisposition to antisocial behaviour, but environmental ...tors appear to be more important.

- ...isocial personalities tend to come from homes where discipline is ineffective or abusive and ...m homes in which parents model amoral, exploitative behaviour.

- The relativistic view holds that the criteria of mental illness vary considerably across cultures.
- The pancultural view holds that the criteria of mental illness are much the same around the world.
- Research indicates that serious mental disorders are identifiable in all cultures, but there are cultural variations in the recognition of less severe forms of disturbance.
- Some cultural variations are seen in symptom patterns, but the symptoms associated with the more serious disorders are largely the same across different cultures.

Pathology and the Law

- Not criminally responsible on account of mental disorder (NCRMD) is a legal status indicating that a person cannot be held responsible for his or her actions because of mental illness. In many jurisdictions this is known as the 'insanity' defense.

- Although highly publicized and controversial, the NCRMD defence is not used frequently and is rarely successful.

Key Themes

- Psychology evolves in a sociohistorical context.
- Heredity and environment jointly influence behaviour.
- Behaviour is shaped by cultural heritage.
- Behaviour is determined by multiple causes.

Chapter 15

Treatment of Psychological Disorders

Elements of Treatment

Treatment Approaches

- **Insight therapies**
- **Behaviour therapies**
- **Biomedical therapies**

Insight Therapies

Psychoanalysis

- Sigmund Freud believed that neuroses are caused by *unconscious conflicts* regarding sex and aggression left over from childhood.
- In psychoanalysis, *dream analysis* and *free association* are used to explore the unconscious.
- When an analyst's *interpretations* touch on sensitive issues, *resistance* can be expected.
- The *transference* relationship may be used to overcome resistance and promote insight.

Client-centred therapy and positive psychotherapy

- According to Carl Rogers, neurotic anxieties are due to *incongruence* between one's self-concept and reality.
- Rogers maintained that the *process* of therapy is not as crucial as the therapeutic *climate*.
- To create a healthy climate therapists must be genuine, and provide unconditional positive regard and empathy.
- The key process at work in client-centred therapy is the *clarification* of clients' feelings.
- Positive psychotherapy attempts to get clients to recognize their strengths, appreciate their blessings, savour positive experiences, and find meaning in ther lives.

Behaviour Therapies

General principles

- Behaviourists assume that even pathological behaviour is a product of learning and that what has been learned can be unlearned.
- In behaviour therapy different procedures are used for different types of clinical problems.
- Behaviour therapists emphasize the importance of measuring outcomes, and there is favourable evidence regarding the efficacy of the widely used behavioural interventions.

Systematic desensitization

- Joseph Wolpe's systematic desensitization, a treatment for phobias, involves the construction of an anxiety hierarchy, relaxation training, and movement through the hierarchy pairing relaxation with each phobic stimulus.

Group therapy and couples therapy

- Most insight therapies can be conducted on a group basis, which involves the simultaneous treatment of several clients.
- In group therapy, participants essentially function as therapists for one another as they share experiences, coping strategies, and support.
- Group therapists usually play a subtle role, staying in the background and working to promote group cohesiveness and supportive interactions.
- Couples or marital therapy includes the treatment of both partners in a committed relationship.
- Couples therapists typically help partners clarify their needs and desires and facilitate communication.

Evaluating insight therapies

- Evaluating the effectiveness of any approach to treatment is extremely complicated and subjective.
- Nonetheless, hundreds of outcome studies collectively suggest that insight theory is superior to placebo treatment and that the benefical effects of therapy are reasonably durable.
- "Common factors" may account for some of the progress that clients make in insight therapies.

Therapists

inical and counselling psychologists ecialize in the diagnosis and eatment of mental disorders and eryday problems.

Psychiatric social workers, psychiatric nurses, and *counsellors* also provide psychotherapy services.

Psychiatrists are physicians who specialize in the diagnosis and treatment of mental disorders.

Clients

People vary in their willingness to seek therapy and many who need therapy don't receive it. Some cultural groups utilize therapy services less because of stigma associated with mental illness.

Biomedical Therapies

Drug treatments

- *Antianxiety drugs,* which are used to relieve nervousness, are effective in the short term but have potential for abuse, dependence, and overdose.
- *Antipsychotic drugs* can gradually reduce psychotic symptoms, but they have many unpleasant side effects.
- *Antidepressant drugs* can gradually relieve episodes of depression, but even the newer SSRIs are not free of side effects.
- *Lithium* and other *mood stabilizers* can help to prevent future episodes of both mania and depression in bipolar patients.
- Drug therapies can lead to impressive positive effects, but critics worry that drugs produce short-lived gains, are overprescribed, and are more dangerous than widely appreciated.
- Critics also argue that conflicts of interest are a pervasive problem in research on new medications, leading to overestimates of drugs' efficacy and underestimates of their negative side effects.

Electroconvulsive therapy and new treatments

- In *electroconvulsive therapy* (ECT), electric shock is used to produce a cortical seizure and convulsions, which are believed to be useful in the treatment of depression.
- Proponents of ECT maintain that it is a very effective treatment, but critics have raised doubts, and only about 8% of psychiatrists use ECT.
- Memory losses are a short-term side effect of ECT, but there is great debate about whether ECT carries significant long-term risks.
- Transcranial magnetic stimulation may have value in the treatment of depression, and deep brain stimulation is being investigated as a treatment for depression and obsessive–compulsive disorder.

ial skills training

ial skills training is designed to improve nts' interpersonal interactions through mod- ng, behavioural rehearsal, and shaping.

rsion therapy

version therapy, a stimulus that elicits an wanted response is paired with something leasant in an effort to eliminate the mal- ptive response.

nitive-behavioural tments

nitive therapy was devised as a treatment depression, but is now used for a variety of orders.

n Beck asserts that most disorders are sed by irrational, rigid, negative thinking.

goal of cognitive therapy is to help clients n to detect and dispute their automatic ative thoughts.

dfulness CBT is one of the most recent elopments in this area.

Institutional Treatment in Transition

- Disenchantment with traditional mental hospitals led to the *community mental health movement,* which advocates local, community-based care and prevention of mental disorders.
- *Deinstitutionalization* refers to the transfer of mental health care from inpatient institutions to community-based outpatient facilities.
- Deinstitutionalization has contributed to the *revolving door problem,* which refers to the frequent readmission of patients suffering from severe disorders.
- Deinstitutionalization has also contributed to the growth of homelessness and the increased incidence of mental illness among the homeless, although homelessness is primarily an economic problem.

Current Issues in Treatment

- Insight, behavioural, and biomedical treatments can be used together, and therapists are increasingly eclectic.
- The culture-bound origins of Western therapies have raised doubts about their applicability to other cultures and even to ethnic groups in Western societies.
- Ethnic minorities underutilize mental health services because of cultural distrust, language difficulties, and institutional barriers.

Key Themes

- Psychology is theoretically diverse.
- Behaviour is shaped by cultural heritage.

Chapter 16

Social Behaviour

Person Perception

- Judgments of others can be distorted by their physical appearance, as we tend to ascribe desirable personality characteristics and competence to those who are good looking.
- Perceptions of competence based on facial appearance, which can be made in the blink of an eye, are particularly important.
- *Social schemas* and *stereotypes* can influence our perceptions of others and of our own behaviour.
- Stereotypes tend to be broad overgeneralizations that can lead us to see what we expect to see and to overestimate how often we have seen it (the *illusory correlation* effect). Stereotypes are widely held beliefs that others will have certain characteristics because of their membership in a particular group.
- Evolutionary psychologists argue that many biases in person perception, such as the tendency to quickly categorize people into *ingroups* and *outgroups,* exist because they were adaptive in humans' ancestral past.

Attribution

Basic processes

- *Attributions* are inferences that people draw about the causes of events and behaviours.
- *Internal attributions* ascribe the causes of behaviour to personal traits, abilities, and feelings, whereas *external attributions* ascribe the causes of behaviour to situational demands and environmental factors.
- According to Bernard Weiner, attributions for success and failure can be analyzed along the stable-unstable and internal-external dimensions.

Biases

- The *fundamental attribution error* refers to observers' bias in favour of internal attributions in explaining others' behaviour.
- The *actor-observer bias* refers to the fact that actors favour external attributions in explaining their own behaviour, whereas observers favour internal attributions.
- *Defensive attribution* is the tendency to blame victims for their misfortune, so that one feels less likely to be victimized in a similar manner.

Cultural influences

- Cultures vary in their emphasis on *individualism* (putting personal goals ahead of group goals) as opposed to *collectivism* (putting group goals ahead of personal goals), which influence attributional tendencies.
- People from collectivist cultures appear to be less prone to the fundamental attribution error and to the self-serving bias than people from individualist cultures.

Interpersonal Attraction

Factors in attraction

- A key determinant of romantic attraction for both sexes is physical attractiveness.
- The *matching hypothesis* asserts that males and females of roughly equal physical attractiveness are likely to select each other as partners.
- Married and dating couples tend to be similar on many traits, probably because similarity causes attraction and because attraction can foster similarity.

Cultural and evolutionary influences

- The traits that people seek in prospective mates seem to transcend culture, but societies vary in their emphasis on romantic love as a prerequisite for marriage.
- According to evolutionary psychologists, some aspects of good looks influence attraction because they have been indicators of reproductive fitness.
- Women tend to underestimate relationship commitment, whereas men tend to overestimate women's sexual interest.
- Men tend to be more interested than women in seeking youthfulness and attractiveness in mates, whereas women tend to emphasize potential mates' financial prospects.

Perspectives on love

- Some theorists distinguish between passionate love and companionate love, with the latter divisible into intimacy and commitment.
- Another approach views romantic love as an attachment process and argues that love relationships in adulthood mimic attachment patterns in infancy, which fall into three categories: secure, anxious-ambivalent, and avoidant.
- Those who are secure tend to have more satisfying romantic relationships; attachment style is related to many aspects of behaviour.

The structure of attitudes

Attitudes

Components

The *cognitive component* of an attitude is made up of the beliefs that people hold about the object of an attitude.

The *affective component* of an attitude consists of the emotional feelings stimulated by an object of thought.

The *behavioural component* of an attitude consists of predispostions to act in certain ways toward an attitudinal object.

Dimensions

Attitude strength refers to how firmly attitudes are held.

Attitude accessibility refers to how often and how quickly an attitude comes to mind.

Attitude ambivalence refers to how conflicted one feels about an attitude.

Relations to behaviour

■ Research demonstrates that attitudes are poor to mediocre predictors of people's behaviour.

■ *Explicit attitudes* are attitudes that we hold consciously and can readily describe, whereas *implicit attitudes* are covert attitudes that are expressed in subtle automatic responses. Implicit attitudes can influence behaviour.

Trying to change attitudes

Source factors

■ Persuasion tends to be more successful when a source has credibility, which may depend on expertise or trustworthiness.

■ Likability also tends to increase success in persuasion.

Message factors

■ Two-sided arguments tend to be more effective than one-sided presentations.

■ Fear appeals tend to work if they are actually successful in arousing fear.

■ Repetition of a message can be effective, perhaps because of the mere exposure effect.

Receiver factors

■ Persuasion is more difficult when the receiver is forewarned about the persuasive effort.

■ Resistance is greater when a message is incompatible with the receiver's existing attitudes and when strong attitudes are targeted.

Theories of attitude change

Learning theory

■ The affective component of an attitude can be shaped by classical conditioning.

■ Attitudes can be strengthened by reinforcement or acquired through observational learning.

Dissonance and self-perception theory

■ According to Leon Festinger, inconsistency between attitudes motivates attitude change.

■ Dissonance theory can explain attitude change after counterattitudinal behaviour or when people need to justify their great effort to attain something.

Elaboration likelihood model

■ The *central route* to persuasion depends on the logic of one's message, whereas the *peripheral route* depends on nonmessage factors, such as emotions.

■ Research indicates that the central route produces more durable attitude change.

Yielding to Others

Conformity

■ Research by Solomon Asch showed that people have a surprisingly strong tendency to conform.

■ Asch found that conformity becomes more likely as group size increases up to a size of seven.

■ However, the presence of another dissenter in a group greatly reduces the conformity observed.

■ Asch's findings have been replicated in many cultures, with even higher levels of conformity observed in collectivist societies.

Obedience

■ In Stanley Milgram's landmark study, adult men drawn from the community showed a remarkable tendency to follow orders to shock an innocent stranger, with 65% delivering the maximum shock.

■ The generalizability of Milgram's findings has stood the test of time, but his work helped stimulate stricter ethical standards for research.

■ Milgram's findings have been replicated in many modern nations and even higher rates of obedience have been seen in many places.

Behaviour in Groups

■ The bystander effect refers to the fact that people are less likely to provide help when they are in groups than when they are alone, because of diffusion of responsibility.

■ Productivity often declines in groups because of loss of coordination and social loafing, which refers to the reduced effort seen when people work in groups.

■ Group polarization occurs when discussion leads a group to shift toward a more extreme decision in the direction it was already leaning.

■ In groupthink, a cohesive group suspends critical thinking in a misguided effort to promote agreement.

Social Neuroscience

■ Social neuroscience integrates models of neuroscience and social psychology to study the mechanisms mediating behaviour in a social context.

■ Various topics including person perception, aggression, attributions, self-concept, and stereotyping have been studied from a social neuroscience perspective.

■ The amygdala has been found to be involved in cross-racial processing by racially biased individuals.

Key Themes

■ Psychology is empirical.

■ Behaviour is shaped by cultural heritage.

■ Our experience of the world is highly subjective.

33

Notes